PRAISE FOR PARALLEL COMPUTER ARCHITECTURE
A Hardware/Software Approach

Parallel computing is entering the mainstream, thanks to complementary advances in VLSI, architecture, system software, and programming support. Culler, Singh, and Gupta—outstanding researchers and outstanding educators—have helped to drive this dramatic convergence and now have brought it all together in this authoritative and readable text. Once again, Morgan Kaufmann has delivered a landmark book in computer systems.—**Edward D. Lazowska**, *Professor and Chair, Department of Computer Science & Engineering, University of Washington*

This book covers the latest machine architectures and techniques at a time when there is explosive growth in parallel machine use, but many of the older machine organizations are running out of gas. The book provides useful techniques for understanding the performance of parallel machines and gives examples of how they apply to the various architectural options. Students, researchers, and industry practitioners will find this book extremely valuable. I know I have.—**Dan Lenoski**, *SGI*

Parallel Computer Architecture offers a wealth of information about the features of actual machines, which simply cannot be found in any other book. The selection of topics strikes a good balance between research results and real life implementations. —**Michel Dubois**, *Professor, Department of Electrical Engineering-Systems, University of Southern California*

This book provides a fresh look at an important topic in computer architecture, including an in-depth examination of several of the thorny problems in parallel computing.—**David Patterson**, *Pardee Professor of Computer Science, University of California, Berkeley*

This book thoroughly presents the state of the art—delving into issues only glossed over in many research papers.—**Mark Hill**, *Professor & Romnes Fellow, Computer Sciences Department, University of Wisconsin-Madison*

Finally, the Hennessy & Patterson of parallel architectures has arrived. Written by foremost experts in the field, it is full of case studies, quantitative data, and architectural insights. Integrated hardware/software approach is the only way to understand parallel computing, and this book is an existence proof.—**Arvind**, *Charles W. & Jennifer C. Johnson Professor of Computer Science & Engineering, Massachusetts Institute of Technology*

RELATED TITLES FROM MORGAN KAUFMANN PUBLISHERS

Computer Architecture: A Quantitative Approach, Second Edition, by John L. Hennessy and David A. Patterson

Computer Organization and Design: The Hardware/Software Interface, Second Edition, by David A. Patterson and John L. Hennessy

Scalable Shared-Memory Multiprocessing, by Daniel E. Lenoski and Wolf-Dietrich Weber

The Grid: Blueprint for a New Computing Infrastructure, edited by Ian Foster and Carl Kesselman

Parallel Programming with MPI, by Peter S. Pacheco

Distributed Algorithms, by Nancy A. Lynch

Introduction to Parallel Algorithms and Architectures: Arrays, Trees, and Hypercubes, by F. Thomson Leighton

Parallel Computing Works! by Geoffrey C. Fox, Roy D. Williams, and Paul C. Messina

Parallel Processing from Applications to Systems, by Dan I. Moldovan

Synthesis of Parallel Algorithms, edited by John H. Reif

VLSI and Parallel Computation, edited by Robert Suaya and Graham Birtwistle

FORTHCOMING

Readings in Computer Architecture, edited by Mark D. Hill, Norman P. Jouppi, and Gurindar S. Sohi

Industrial Strength Parallel Computing, edited by Alice E. Koniges

Parallel Computer Architecture

A Hardware/Software Approach

About the Authors

David E. Culler, *Professor of Computer Science at University of California, Berkeley.* Dr. Culler works in the areas of computer architecture, communication, programming languages, operating systems, and performance analysis. He led the Berkeley Network of Workstations (NOW) project, which sparked the current commercial revolution in high-performance clusters. He is internationally known for his work on Active Messages for fast communication, the LogP parallel performance model, the Split-C parallel language, the TAM threaded abstract machine, and for his work on dataflow architectures. He received the Presidential Faculty Fellowship Award and the Presidential Young Investigator Award from the National Science Foundation. He received the PhD from MIT in 1989. Currently he is vice-chair of computing and networking for the Deptartment of Electrical Engineering and Computer Sciences at UC Berkeley and leads the Millennium Project, investigating campus-wide clusters.

Jaswinder Pal Singh, *Assistant Professor in the Computer Science Department at Princeton University.* Dr. Singh works at the boundary of parallel applications and multiprocessor systems, including architecture, software, and performance evaluation. He has led the development and distribution of the SPLASH and SPLASH-2 suites of parallel programs, which are very widely used in parallel systems research. While at Stanford, where he obtained his MS and PhD degrees, he participated in the DASH and FLASH multiprocessor projects, leading the applications efforts there. The technology developed in the DASH project is becoming widely available in commercial products. At Princeton, he heads PRISM, an application-driven research group that investigates supporting programming models on a variety of communication architectures and applies parallel computing to a variety of application domains. He is a recipient of the Presidential Early Career Award for Scientists and Engineers (PECASE) and a Sloan Research Fellowship.

Anoop Gupta, *Associate Professor of Computer Science and Electrical Engineering at Stanford University and Senior Researcher at Microsoft.* Dr. Gupta has worked in the areas of computer architecture, operating systems, programming languages, performance debugging tools, and parallel applications. With John Hennessy, he co-led the design and construction of the Stanford DASH machine, one of the first scalable distributed shared memory multiprocessors, and has worked on the follow-up FLASH project. The technology developed in the DASH project is now becoming widely available in commercial products. Professor Gupta has published close to 100 papers in major conferences and journals, including several award papers. Professor Gupta received the NSF Presidential Young Investigator Award and held the Robert Noyce faculty scholar chair at Stanford. He obtained the PhD from Carnegie Mellon University in 1986.

Parallel Computer Architecture

A Hardware/Software Approach

David E. Culler   Jaswinder Pal Singh

with Anoop Gupta

MORGAN KAUFMANN PUBLISHERS, INC.
San Francisco, California

Senior Editor	Denise E.M. Penrose
Director of Production and Manufacturing	Yonie Overton
Senior Production Editor	Elisabeth Beller
Editorial Coordinator	Meghan Keeffe
Cover Design	Martin Heirakuji Graphic Design
Cover Photo	Image copyright © 1998 PhotoDisc, Inc.
Text Design	Mark Ong, Side by Side Studios
Copyeditor	Jennifer McClain
Proofreaders	Jennifer McClain, Jeff Van Beuren, Ken DellaPenta, Christine Sabooni
Compositor	Nancy Logan
Illustrators	Nancy Logan, Dartmouth Publishing, Inc., Cherie Plumlee
Indexer	Steve Rath

Morgan Kaufmann Publishers, Inc.
Editorial and Sales Office
340 Pine Street, Sixth Floor
San Francisco, CA 94104-3205
USA

Telephone	415/392-2665
Facsimile	415/982-2665
Email	mkp@mkp.com
WWW	http://www.mkp.com

Order toll free 800/745-7323

Advice, Praise, and Errors: Any correspondence related to this publication or intended for the authors should be addressed to the Editorial and Sales Office of Morgan Kaufmann Publishers, Inc., Dept. PCA APE or sent electronically to *pca@mkp.com*. Please report errors by email to *pcabugs@mkp.com*. Please check the errata page at *http://www.mkp.com/pca* to see if the bug has already been reported and fixed.

03 02 01 00 99 5 4 3 2

Library of Congress Cataloging-in-Publication Data
Culler, David E.
Parallel computer architecture: a hardware/software approach / David E. Culler, Jaswinder Pal Singh, with Anoop Gupta.
p. cm.
Includes bibliographical references and index.
ISBN 1-55860-343-3
1. Parallel computers. 2. Computer architecture. I. Singh, Jaswinder Pal. II. Gupta, Anoop. III. Title.
QA76.58.C85 1999
004′.35—dc21 98-28034
CIP

To Sara, Silvia, and our families

In memory of Susanne Kreith Culler

Foreword

John L. Hennessy
Frederick Emmons Terman Dean of Engineering, Stanford University

I am delighted to be able to write the foreword for this exciting and timely new book on parallel computing. The insightful approach taken by the authors combined with a systematic and quantitative examination of different architectures distinguishes this book from all previous books on parallel architecture. The approach, which is developed in the first four chapters, has three major innovations: it builds on the recent convergence of parallel architectures, it uses applications as a driver for evaluating and analyzing architectures, and it is grounded in a solid methodology for performance evaluation.

The recent convergence among the shared memory and message-passing paradigms, which is described in Chapter 1, provides new opportunities for characterizing and analyzing architectures in a common framework. Relying on this convergence, the authors describe four fundamental design issues (communication abstraction, programming model, communication and replication, and performance) that create a framework for talking about a wide variety of architectures and implementations. Within this framework, different architectural approaches are compared and examined critically.

One cannot understand the design trade-offs or performance of multiprocessors without understanding the interaction of applications and architecture. Accordingly, Chapters 2 and 3 describe a set of parallel programs as well as how the applications are parallelized and organized for performance. These chapters illuminate both the parallel programming process and its challenges in addition to laying a foundation for quantitative evaluation of architectural approaches and implementations. These chapters are key to understanding the performance of multiprocessors, and Chapter 4 illustrates this by showing how to evaluate an architecture using a parallel workload. The authors also describe the complexities of evaluating parallel machines, including issues arising from the scaling of machine sizes and workloads. Together these three chapters form the foundation on which the remaining chapters build.

Small-to-medium-sized shared memory multiprocessors are the dominant form of parallel architecture seen today, and understanding the principles and design trade-offs of these machines is critical to anyone interested in parallel computing.

Chapter 5 describes the key concepts underlying shared memory multiprocessing: cache coherency, memory consistency, and synchronization. The authors then describe the detailed design of snoop-based shared memory multiprocessors, including two detailed case studies, in Chapter 6.

Designing multiprocessors that scale to larger numbers of processing nodes remains one of the most challenging and controversial aspects of multiprocessor architecture. Chapter 7 devotes itself to such machines, spanning the design space from message passing to shared memory. Chapter 8 extends this discussion by examining the use of directory schemes, which allow cache coherency to scale to larger numbers of processing nodes. The basics of directory-based coherence are discussed, and two detailed case studies form the core of the chapter. These case studies are the first detailed and quantitative examinations of commercial implementations of directory-based cache coherence.

Some of the most important hardware and software technologies used in multiprocessors are largely independent of the details of the architectural approach. Hence, the authors explore these key technologies in a set of three chapters. Chapter 9 describes the software implications, hardware requirements, and performance trade-offs that arise in memory systems, including both consistency issues and the extended use of caching. Chapter 10 examines interconnection technology, a key constituent of any multiprocessor. Finally, Chapter 11 examines techniques for tolerating latency, in many ways the key "universal" design problem for parallel computers.

The book concludes with an insightful discussion of future hardware and software challenges. First, the authors discuss likely evolutionary scenarios in the hardware and software domain. Then they turn to the potential hurdles in a pair of sections entitled "Hitting a wall." Finally, they examine potential breakthroughs! I found the final chapter both stimulating and thought provoking. The different backgrounds and complementary strengths of the authors help make this chapter both perspicacious and provocative.

In summary, this is an exciting and dynamic new exploration of the multiprocessor design space. The convergence in architectural approaches combined with the authors' framework has made it possible to establish a common ground on which to examine the diversity of modern parallel architectures. A few years ago, it would have been impossible to write this book because the architectural approaches were too divergent. Similarly, without the attention to quantitative measures of performance and the interaction between applications and architectures, this book would be much less distinctive. Instead, the authors have taken advantage of the convergence and the focus on an applications-driven and performance-based analysis to produce a unique and insightful exploration of parallel architectures. This approach, combined with the unique strengths and experiences of the authors, yields a treatise that is far more perceptive than any other book in parallel architecture. I congratulate the authors and commend this book to all readers interested in both the practice and concepts of parallel processing and the future of these technologies.

Contents

Preface

Parallel computing has become a critical component of the computing technology of the 1990s, and it is likely to have as much impact over the next 20 years as microprocessors have had over the past 20. Indeed, the two technologies are deeply linked, as the evolution of highly integrated microprocessors and memory chips makes multiprocessor systems increasingly attractive. Multiprocessors already represent the high-performance end of almost every segment of the computing market, from the fastest supercomputers and largest data centers to departmental servers to the individual desktop. Tightly integrated clusters of PCs, workstations, or even multiprocessors are emerging as scalable Internet servers. In the past, computer vendors employed a range of technologies and processor architectures to provide increasing performance across their product line. Today, the same state-of-the-art microprocessor is used throughout. To obtain a significant range of performance, the primary approach is to increase the number of processors, and the economies of scale make this extremely attractive. Very soon, several processors will fit on a single chip and multiprocessors will be even more widespread than they are today.

Although parallel computing has a long and rich academic history, the close coupling with commodity technology has fundamentally changed the discipline. The emphasis on radical architectures and exotic technology has given way to quantitative analysis, the realization of different programming models on the same underlying processing nodes, and careful engineering trade-offs. Our goal in writing this book is to equip designers of the emerging class of multiprocessor systems—from modestly parallel desktop computers to highly parallel information servers and supercomputers—with an understanding of the fundamental architectural and software issues and the available techniques for addressing design trade-offs. At the same time, we hope to provide designers of software systems and applications with an understanding of the likely directions of architectural evolution, the forces that will determine the specific path that hardware designs will follow, and the impact of these developments on performance-oriented programming.

The most exciting recent development in parallel computer architecture is the convergence of traditionally disparate approaches—namely, shared memory, message-passing, data parallel, and data-driven computing—on a common machine structure. This convergence is driven partly by common technological and economic forces and partly by a better understanding of parallel software. It allows us to develop a common framework in which to understand and evaluate architectural trade-offs rather than to focus on exotic designs and taxonomies. Moreover, popular parallel programming models are available on a wide range of machines, making parallel programming more portable and allowing meaningful benchmarks and evaluation methodologies to flourish. This maturing of the field makes it possible to undertake a quantitative as well as qualitative study of hardware/software interactions. In fact, it demands such an approach. The book follows a set of issues that are critical to all parallel architectures—data access, communication performance, coordination of cooperative work, and correct implementation of useful semantics—across the full range of modern designs. It describes the set of techniques available in hardware and in software to address each issue and explores how the various techniques interact. Carefully chosen, in-depth case studies provide a concrete illustration of the general principles and demonstrate specific interactions between mechanisms.

One of the motivations for writing this book is the lack of an adequate textbook for our own courses at Berkeley, Princeton, and Stanford. Several existing texts cover the material in a cursory fashion, summarizing various architectures and research results but not analyzing them in depth or providing a modern engineering framework. Others focus on specific projects but do not carry the principles over to alternative approaches. The research reports in the area provide a sizable body of ideas and empirical data, but it is not distilled into a coherent picture. By focusing on the salient issues in the context of technological and architectural convergence rather than on the rich and varied history that has brought us to this point, we hope to provide a deeper and more coherent understanding of this exciting and rapidly changing field. This was a deeply collaborative effort, reflected in the alternation of the order of our names on the book covers.

Intended Audience

The subject matter of this book is core material that is important for researchers, students, and practicing engineers in the fields of computer architecture, systems software, and applications. The relevance for computer architects is obvious, given the growing importance of multiprocessors. Chip designers must understand what constitutes a viable building block for multiprocessor systems. Bus and memory system design are dominated by issues related to parallelism. I/O system design must address fast scalable networks, clustering, and devices that are shared by multiple processors.

Systems software—including operating systems, compilers, programming languages, run-time systems, and performance debugging tools—needs to address new issues and will provide new opportunities in parallel computers. Thus, an understanding of architectural evolution and the forces guiding that evolution is critical. Research and development in compilers and programming languages have addressed aspects of parallel computing for some time. However, the new convergence with commodity technology suggests that these aspects may need to be reexamined and addressed in a more general context. The traditional boundaries between hardware, operating system, and user program are also shifting in the context of parallel computing, where programs often want more direct control over resources for better performance.

Applications areas, such as computer graphics and multimedia, scientific computing, computer-aided design, databases, decision support, and transaction processing, are all likely to see a tremendous transformation as a result of the vast computing power available at low cost through parallel computing. However, developing parallel applications that are robust and that provide good parallel speedup across current and future multiprocessors is a challenging task and requires a deep understanding of system interactions and architectural directions. The book seeks to provide this understanding but also to stimulate the exchange between the applications fields and computer architecture so that better architectures can be designed—those that make the programming task easier and performance both higher and more robust.

Organization of the Book

The book is organized into 12 chapters. Chapter 1 provides an overview of parallel architecture. It opens with a discussion of why the expanding role of multiprocessors is inevitable, given current trends in technology, architecture, and applications. It briefly introduces the diverse multiprocessor architectures that have shaped the field (shared memory, message passing, data parallel, dataflow, and systolic) and shows how the technology and architectural trends are driving a convergence in the field to a set of commodity processing nodes connected by a communication architecture. This convergence does not mean the end to innovation but, on the contrary, that we will now see a time of rapid progress, as designers start talking with each other rather than past each other. The chapter develops a layered framework (including the programming model, communication abstraction, user/system interface, and hardware/software interface) for understanding wide variety of communication architectures and implementations. Viewing the convergence of the field in this framework, the last portion of the chapter lays out the fundamental design issues that must be addressed at each of the interfaces between layers: naming, ordering, replication, and communication performance (overhead, latency, and bandwidth). These issues form an underlying theme throughout the rest of this book. The chapter ends with a set of historical references.

Chapter 2 provides an introduction to the process of parallel programming. It describes a set of motivating applications for multiprocessors that are used throughout the rest of the book. It shows what parallel programs look like in the major programming models and hence what primitives a system must support. It uses the application case studies to illustrate the steps of decomposition, assignment, orchestration, and mapping in creating a parallel program and identifies the key performance goals of these steps.

Chapter 3 describes the basic techniques that good parallel programmers use to get performance out of the underlying architecture. It provides an understanding of hardware/software trade-offs and illustrates what aspects of performance can be addressed through architectural means and what aspects must be addressed either by the compiler or the programmer. The analogy in sequential computing is that architecture cannot transform an $O(n^2)$ algorithm into an $O(n \log n)$ algorithm, but it can improve the average access time for common memory reference patterns. The chapter shows clearly the core algorithmic and programming challenges that cut across programming models as well as the model-specific orchestration issues. This material shows how architectural advance can ease the burden of effective parallel programming in addition to increasing the achievable performance. The programming techniques are a key factor in any quantitative evaluation of design trade-offs, and the chapter concludes by applying them to the motivating applications to produce high-performance versions.

Chapter 4 takes up the challenge of performing solid workload-driven evaluation of design trade-offs. Architectural evaluation is difficult even for modern uniprocessors, where we typically look at moderate design variations—such as pipeline or memory system organizations—against a fixed set of programs. In parallel architecture, we have many more degrees of freedom to explore. The interactions between aspects of the design are more profound, and the interactions between hardware and software are more significant as well as of wider scope. We are often interested in performance as the machine and the program scale, and it is impossible to scale one without affecting the other. It is easy to arrive at incomplete or even misleading conclusions if the evaluation is not methodologically sound, so the characteristics of parallel programs must be adequately understood. Chapter 4 discusses how application and architectural parameters interact and how they should be scaled together and presents benchmarks that are used throughout later chapters. It provides methodological guidelines for the evaluation of real machines and of architectural ideas through simulation. The Appendix provides additional reference material on parallel benchmarking efforts.

Chapters 5 and 6 provide a complete understanding of the bus-based, symmetric shared memory multiprocessors (SMPs) that form the bread and butter of modern commercial machines beyond the desktop. Chapter 5 presents the high-level, logical design of "snooping" bus protocols, which ensure that automatically replicated data is coherent across multiple caches. This chapter provides an important discussion of memory consistency, which brings us to terms with what shared memory really means to algorithm designers. It discusses the spectrum of design options and how machines are optimized against typical reference patterns occurring in user programs and in the operating system. Given this conceptual understanding of SMPs, the chapter reflects on the implications for parallel software, including applications and support for synchronization.

Chapter 6 examines the protocol issues in more depth as well as physical design of bus-based multiprocessors. It digs into the engineering issues that arise in supporting modern microprocessors with multilevel caches on modern buses, which are highly pipelined, as well as how the high-level protocols of the previous chapter are realized and extended on these systems. The presentation here provides a very complete understanding of the design issues in this regime. It is all the more important because these small-scale designs form a building block for large-scale designs and because many of the concepts appear later in the book on a larger scale with a broader set of concerns. The chapter also provides self-contained case studies on the SGI Challenge and Sun Enterprise servers.

Chapters 7, 8, 9, and 10 provide a complete understanding of the scalable multiprocessor architectures that represent the high end of computing and the future of the midrange as technology continues to advance.

Chapter 7 presents the hardware organization and architecture of a range of machines that are scalable to large or very large configurations. The key organizational concept is that of a network transaction, analogous to the bus transaction that is the fundamental primitive for the smaller designs in Chapters 5 and 6. However, in scalable machines the global arbitration and globally visible information is lost and a large number of transactions can be outstanding. The chapter shows how programming models are realized in terms of network transactions and studies a spectrum of important design points organized according to the level of direct hardware interpretation of the network transaction, including case studies of the nCUBE/2, Thinking Machines CM-5, Intel Paragon, Meiko CS-2, CRAY T3D, and CRAY T3E. It examines modern clusters in this framework with case studies of the Myrinet NOW and the DEC Memory Channel. A performance comparison is conducted across these designs.

Chapter 8 puts the results of the previous chapters together to demonstrate how to realize a shared physical address space with automatic hardware replication and cache coherence on scalable systems. This style of machine is increasingly popular in the industry. The chapter provides a complete treatment of directory-based cache coherence protocols and hardware design alternatives, including case studies of the SGI Origin2000 and Sequent NUMA-Q. It examines workload behavior on these machines and extends the discussions of programming implications and synchronization.

Chapter 9 examines a spectrum of alternatives for shared address space systems that push the boundaries of hardware/software trade-offs to obtain higher performance, reduce hardware cost and complexity, or both. It covers relaxed memory consistency models, cache-only memory architectures that replicate data coherently in hardware in main memory, and software-based coherent replication. Much of this material is in the transitional phase from academic research to commercial product at the time of this writing, and its role will be further shaped as cluster technology emerges. It exposes very important design concepts not treated elsewhere in the book.

Chapter 10 addresses the design of scalable high-performance communication networks, which underlies all the scalable machines discussed in previous chapters but was deferred to complete our understanding of the processor, memory system, and network interface design that drive these networks. The chapter builds a general framework for understanding where hardware costs, transfer delays, and bandwidth restrictions arise in networks. It looks at a variety of trade-offs in routing techniques, switch design, and interconnection topology with respect to these cost-performance metrics. The trade-offs are made concrete through case studies of recent designs.

Given the foundation established by the first 10 chapters, Chapter 11 examines a set of crosscutting issues involved in tolerating the significant latencies that arise in multiprocessor systems without impeding performance. The techniques exploit two basic capabilities: overlapping latency with useful work and pipelining the transfer of data. The simplest of these techniques are essentially bulk transfers, which pipeline the movement of a large regular sequence of data items and often can be offloaded from the processor. The other techniques attempt to hide the latency incurred in collections of individual loads and stores. Write latencies are hidden by exploiting weak consistency models, which recognize that ordering is conveyed by only a small set of the accesses to shared memory in a program. Read latencies are hidden by implicit or explicit prefetching of data or by lookahead techniques in modern dynamically scheduled processors. Some of the techniques extend to hiding synchronization latencies as well. The chapter provides a thorough examination of these alternatives, the impact on compilation techniques, and a quantitative evaluation of effectiveness.

Finally, Chapter 12 examines the trends in technology, architecture, software systems, and applications that are likely to shape the future evolution of the field. It looks at evolutionary scenarios, walls we may hit, and potential breakthroughs from a hardware/software perspective.

Using the Book

The book is organized to meet the needs of several potential audiences. It can serve as a graduate text, a professional reference for engineers, and as a general reference for members of the technical community who find themselves dealing ever more frequently with parallel computing. There is sufficient material, if covered in full depth, for a full-year study of parallel computing, covering the entire range of machine design and practical parallel programming experience. However, it can also be used in smaller segments.

Chapter 1 is intended to provide a stand-alone, general understanding of parallel architectures as would be appropriate for a segment of a general computer architecture course at the graduate or upper-division undergraduate level. It would also be appropriate for the engineering manager or corporate executive needing to understand the vocabulary and basic concepts of parallel computing and how the technology will impact their business. It lays out clearly where to go to learn more as your interest or need to understand parallel computing increases. The chapter can also be used as a basic background in parallel architecture for compiler, database, operating system, or programming courses. Chapters 1 and 12 together provide a well-rounded "outer skin" of parallel computer architecture.

A parallel architecture course oriented toward machine organization and design is comprised of the core material of Chapters 5, 6, 7, 8, and 10, in addition to the overview of Chapter 1. However, the chapters go into greater depth of design than has been common in traditional courses because the material was not available in any published form or put together in a design-oriented framework, and they provide detailed quantitative illustrations of trade-offs. Chapters 5 and 6 develop the key requirements of correctness in cache-coherent systems and show how to satisfy them with high performance in increasingly complex designs. Chapter 7 takes apart scalable machines in a manner not available from commercial sources or research publications and addresses emerging high-performance clusters in this framework. Chapter 8 describes the cache coherence protocols of prominent commercial distributed-memory machines in a framework and level of detail not available elsewhere. Chapter 10 provides a compact, rounded treatment of network design. The treatment is deep enough in these chapters to provide even the seasoned system designer with a new understanding and a clean design framework. A serious yet pragmatic treatment of memory consistency models is carried throughout these chapters (as well as in the first part of Chapter 9), as is a discussion of implementing synchronization operations. These chapters on machine organization and design can be supplemented with Chapter 11, which covers the increasingly important topic of latency tolerance.

The exciting opportunity presented by this text is that, with the core material packaged in a cohesive form, it becomes possible to strengthen the basic parallel architecture course along several dimensions. First, thorough coverage of Chapters 2 and 3 allows the treatment to reach across the hardware/software boundary. This gives the architecture student a much more solid grasp of the impact of architectural decisions and what parallel programming is all about. It also broadens the appeal of the course to a wider audience of operating systems, languages, and applications students who are viewing the architectural issues from a software perspective. A second dimension along which the basic course can be strengthened is quantitative performance analysis of hardware and software design decisions. Building upon a basic understanding from Chapters 2 and 3, Chapter 4, the Appendix, and the "Implications for Parallel Software" sections of the later chapters carry this thread throughout the core machine design material. They provide an informed, critical perspective with which to view published results, as well as methodological guidelines for performing evaluations. A third dimension is a sharp focus on hardware/software tradeoffs. This is the underlying issue that is framed by the quantitative analysis and explored in the synchronization and programming sections of each chapter. It comes to the fore in Chapter 9, where the division of responsibilities in providing a coherent shared address space is examined in detail, and in Chapter 11 in the discussion of latency tolerance. Each of these dimensions represents a group of professionals who have an increasing need to understand more deeply how to deal with parallel architectures.

The book also serves well as the primary text for a hands-on parallel programming course. With Chapter 1 providing a general introduction, Chapters 2 and 3 offer a strong framework for how to reason about the behavior of parallel programs. This is further solidified by the workload analysis in Chapter 4 and the "Implications for Parallel Software" sections in Chapters 5, 7, 8, and 9. This material should be supplemented with a reference on the parallel programming environment used in the course, such as MPI, parallel threads, or HPF. The case studies in Chapters 6, 7, and 8 provide thorough coverage of machines similar to what students are likely to use. Chapter 11 provides a convenient framework for an examination of how best to solve the challenges of communication in parallel programming.

We believe parallel computer architecture is an exciting core field of study and practice whose importance will continue to grow. It has reached a point of maturity at which a serious textbook based on design and engineering principles makes sense. From a rich diversity of ideas and approaches, a dramatic convergence is now occurring in the field. It is time to go beyond surveying the machine landscape to an understanding of the fundamental design principles. We have intimately participated in the convergence of the field; this text arises from our experience, and we hope it conveys some of the excitement that we feel for this dynamic and growing area. Since parallel architecture does change so rapidly, case studies, performance analyses, and workloads need to be refreshed periodically. The Web page for this book will provide a repository for such timely material, as well as for additional teaching materials, and we hope that you will help contribute to that repository through the high-quality products of your courses and commercial developments. The URL for the book is *www.mkp.com/pca*.

We also encourage readers to report any errors or bugs so that we may correct them in subsequent printings. Please email them to *pcabugs@mkp.com*. Please also check the errata page at *www.mkp.com/pca* to see if the bug has already been reported and fixed.

Acknowledgments

This book has been in gestation in various forms for quite some time, and it has benefited from the efforts of many individuals. It had its roots in notes and slides for our parallel processing courses and in our research projects. Our students and staff have been invaluable throughout. Although this is the first edition, drafts have been available on the Web as the material was being developed. In the way of the Web, we have no idea of all the institutions around the world that have used it in courses and research, but we receive suggestions from the most exotic places. Many people have made contributions to it directly, indirectly, or even anonymously, so we would like to thank all of you.

Numerous students have improved this book by their questions, ideas, solutions, and projects. We want to thank the students in CS 258 (Parallel Processors) and CS 267 (Applications of Parallel Computers) at Berkeley, CS 598 (Parallel Computer Architecture and Programming) at Princeton, and CS 315A (Parallel Computer Architecture and Programming) and CS 315B (Parallel Programming Project) at Stanford. Special thanks go to Andrea Arpaci-Dusseau, Remzi Arpaci-Dusseau, Brent Chun, Seth Goldstein, Alan Mainwaring, Rich Martin, Lok Tin Liu, Steve Lummetta, Chad Yoshikawa, and Frederick Chun Bong Wong at Berkeley; Angelos Bilas, Liviu Iftode, Dongming Jiang, Steven Kleinstein, Sanjeev Kumar, Hongzhang Shan, and Yuanyuan Zhou at Princeton; and Cheng Chen, John Heinlein, Moriyoshi Ohara, Evan Torrie, and Steven Cameron Woo at Stanford, all of whom have contributed valuable insight, data, and analysis to the book through their tireless efforts. Jiang, Kumar, Ohara, Torrie, Wong, and Woo deserve an especially hearty thanks for their contributions.

Many people in academia and industry provided invaluable assistance in reviewing drafts, explaining to us how things really worked, trying out the book, and guiding us along the path. We would especially like to thank Sarita Adve, Arvind, Russell Clapp, Michel Dubois, Mike Galles, Kourosh Gharachorloo, Jim Gray, John Hennessy, Mark Hill, Phil Krueger, James Laudon, Edward Lazowska, Dan Lenoski, W. R. Michalson, Todd Mowry, Greg Papadopoulos, Dave Patterson, Randy Rettberg, Shuichi Sakai, Klaus Schauser, Ashok Singhal, Burton Smith, Jim Smith, Mark Smotherman, Per Stenstrom, Thorsten von Eicken, Maurice Wilkes, David Wood, and Chengzhong Xu. Thanks, John and Dave, for guidance throughout. Many people assisted us by teaching from portions of the book, including our earliest adopters, Sarita Adve, Andrew Chien, Jim Demmel, Wallid Najjar, Constantine Polychronopoulos, Radhika Thekkath, and Kathy Yelick.

We also want to thank the National Science Foundation, the Defense Advanced Research Projects Agency, the Department of Energy, and numerous corporate sponsors for supporting the research that underlies the material in this book and the dramatic advance of parallel computing.

We wish to thank the impressive team at Morgan Kaufmann Publishers who managed to get this book all the way to the end. Denise Penrose picked up the reins and led the team with unbelievable energy, dedication, and enthusiasm. It was an absolute pleasure to work with her. Elisabeth Beller managed the entire production process very smoothly. Meghan Keeffe and Jane Elliott coordinated reviews and photo searches and tied up many a loose end. A crew of talented proofreaders kept all the right words in all the right places. Thanks also to Jennifer Mann, who managed the project before Denise joined up, and to Bruce Spatz, who has moved on from MKP since starting this book on its way.

We must also thank our university staff, Gabriela Aranda, Ginny Hogan, Chris Kranz, Terry Lessard-Smith, Bob Miller, Thoi Nguyen, Matt Norcross, Charlie Orgish, Jim Roberts, and Chris Tengi, for countless bits of help along the way.

Above all, our deepest thanks, appreciation, and love go to our families for their immeasurable support, patience, kindness, and wisdom throughout the entire process.

David E. Culler　　　　Jaswinder Pal Singh

1

Introduction

For over a decade, we have enjoyed explosive growth in the performance and capability of computer systems. The theme of this dramatic success story is the advance of the underlying VLSI technology, which allows clock rates to increase and larger numbers of components to fit on a chip. The plot of this story centers on computer architecture, which translates the raw potential of the technology into greater performance and expanded capability of the computer system. The story's leading character is parallelism. A larger volume of resources means that more operations can be performed at once, in parallel. Parallel computer architecture is about organizing these resources so that they work well together. Computers of all types have harnessed parallelism more and more effectively to gain performance from the raw technology, and the level at which parallelism is exploited continues to rise. Another key character is storage. The data that is operated on at an ever faster rate must be held somewhere in the machine. Thus, the story of parallel processing is deeply intertwined with data locality and communication. The computer architect must sort out these changing relationships to design the various levels of a computer system so as to maximize performance and programmability within the limits imposed by technology and cost at any particular time.

Parallelism is a fascinating perspective from which to understand computer architecture because it applies at all levels of design, it interacts with essentially all other architectural concepts, and it presents a unique dependence on the underlying technology. In particular, the basic issues of locality, bandwidth, latency, and synchronization arise at many levels of the design of parallel computer systems. The trade-offs must be resolved in the context of real application workloads.

Parallel computer architecture, like any other aspect of design, involves elements of form and function. These elements are captured nicely in the following definition (Almasi and Gottlieb 1989):

> A *parallel computer* is a "collection of processing elements that communicate and cooperate to solve large problems fast."

However, this simple definition raises many questions. How large a collection are we talking about? How powerful are the individual processing elements, and can the number be increased in a straightforward manner? How do these elements communicate and cooperate? How is data transmitted between processors, what sort of interconnection is provided, and what operations are available to sequence the actions carried out on different processors? What are the primitive abstractions that the hardware and software provide to the programmer? And finally, how does it all translate into performance? In answering these questions, we will see that small, moderate, and very large collections of processing elements each have important roles to fill in modern computing. Thus, it is important to understand parallel machine design across the scale, from the small to the very large. Some design issues apply throughout the scale of parallelism; others are most germane to a particular regime, such as within a chip, within a box, or on a very large machine. It is safe to say that parallel machines occupy a rich and diverse design space. This diversity makes the area exciting, but it also means that it is important that we develop a clear framework in which to understand the many design alternatives.

Parallel architecture is itself changing rapidly. Historically, parallel machines have demonstrated innovative organizational structures, often tied to specific programming models, as architects sought to obtain the ultimate in performance out of a given technology. In many cases, radical organizations were justified on the grounds that advances in the base technology would eventually run out of steam. These dire predictions appear to have been overstated, as logic densities and switching speeds have continued to improve and more modest parallelism has been employed at lower levels to sustain continued improvement in processor performance. Nonetheless, application demand for computational performance continues to outpace what individual processors can deliver, and multiprocessor systems occupy an increasingly important place in mainstream computing. What has changed is the novelty of these parallel architectures. Even large-scale parallel machines today are built out of the same basic components as workstations and personal computers. They are subject to the same engineering principles and cost-performance trade-offs. Moreover, to yield the utmost in performance, a parallel machine must extract the full performance potential of its individual components. Thus, an understanding of modern parallel architectures must include an in-depth treatment of engineering trade-offs, not just a descriptive taxonomy of possible machine structures.

Parallel architectures will play an increasingly central role in information processing. This view is based not so much on the assumption that individual processor performance will soon reach a plateau but rather on the estimation that the next level of system design, the multiprocessor level, will become increasingly attractive with increases in chip density. *The goal of this book is to articulate the principles of computer design at the multiprocessor level.* It examines the design issues present for each of the system components—processors, memory systems, and networks—and the relationships between these components. A key aspect is understanding the division of responsibilities between hardware and software in evolving parallel machines. Understanding this division requires familiarity with the requirements that parallel programs place on the machine and the interaction of machine design and the practice of parallel programming.

The process of learning computer architecture is frequently likened to peeling an onion, and this analogy is even more appropriate for parallel computer architecture. At each level of understanding we find a complete whole with many interacting facets, including the structure of the machine, the abstractions it presents, the technology it rests upon, the software that exercises it, and the models that describe its performance. However, if we dig deeper into any of these facets, we discover another layer of design and a new set of interactions. The holistic, multilevel nature of parallel computer architecture makes the field challenging to learn and challenging to present. Some sense of the layer-by-layer structure is unavoidable.

This introductory chapter presents the "outer skin" of parallel computer architecture. It first outlines the reasons why parallel machine design may become pervasive, from desktop machines to supercomputers. It also examines the technological, architectural, and economic trends that have led to the current state of computer architecture and that provide the basis for anticipating future parallel architectures. Section 1.1 focuses on the forces that have brought about the dramatic advance of processor performance and the restructuring of the entire computing industry around commodity microprocessors. These forces include the insatiable application demand for computing power, the continued improvements in the density and level of integration in VLSI chips, and the utilization of parallelism at higher and higher levels of the architecture.

Next is a quick look at the spectrum of important architectural styles, which give the field such a rich history and contribute to the modern understanding of parallel machines. Within this diversity of design, a common set of design principles and trade-offs arise, driven by the same advances in the underlying technology. These forces are rapidly leading to a convergence in the field, which forms the emphasis of this book. Section 1.2 surveys traditional parallel machines, including shared memory, message passing, data parallel, systolic arrays, and dataflow, and illustrates the different ways that they address common architectural issues. The discussion shows the dependence of parallel architecture on the underlying technology and, more importantly, demonstrates the convergence that has come about with the dominance of microprocessors.

Building on this convergence, Section 1.3 examines the fundamental design issues that cut across parallel machines: what can be named at the machine level as a basis for communication and coordination, what is the latency or time required to perform these operations, and what is the bandwidth or overall rate at which they can be performed? This shift from conceptual structure to performance components provides a framework for quantitative, rather than merely qualitative, study of parallel computer architecture.

With this initial broad understanding of parallel computer architecture in place, the following chapters dig deeper into its technical substance. Chapters 2 and 3 delve into the structure and requirements of parallel programs to provide a basis for understanding the interaction between parallel architecture and applications. Chapter 4 builds a framework for evaluating design decisions in terms of application requirements and performance measurements. Chapters 5 and 6 are a complete study of parallel computer architecture at the limited scale employed widely in commercial multiprocessors—from a few processors to a few tens of processors. The concepts and structures introduced here form the building blocks for more aggressive large-scale designs presented over the final five chapters.

1.1 WHY PARALLEL ARCHITECTURE

Computer architecture, technology, and applications evolve together and have very strong interactions. Parallel computer architecture is no exception. A new dimension is added to the design space—the number of processors—and the design is even more strongly driven by the demand for performance at acceptable cost. Whatever the performance of a single processor at a given time, higher performance can, in principle, be achieved by utilizing many such processors. How much additional performance is gained and at what additional cost depends on a number of factors, which we will explore throughout the book.

To better understand this interaction, let us consider the performance characteristics of the processor building blocks. Figure 1.1[1] illustrates the growth in processor performance over time for several classes of computers (Hennessy and Jouppi 1991). The dashed extensions of the trend lines represent a naive extrapolation of the trends. Although we should be careful in drawing sharp quantitative conclusions from such limited data, the figure suggests several valuable observations.

First, the performance of the highly integrated, single-chip CMOS microprocessor is steadily increasing and is surpassing the larger, more expensive alternatives. Microprocessor performance has been improving at a rate of about 50% per year. The advantages of using small, inexpensive, low-power, mass-produced processors as the building blocks for computer systems with many processors are intuitively clear. However, until recently the performance of the processor best suited to parallel architecture was far behind that of the fastest single-processor system. This is no longer true. Although parallel machines have been built at various scales since the earliest days of computing, the approach is more viable today than ever before because the basic processor building block is better suited to the job.

The second and perhaps more fundamental observation is that change, even dramatic change, is the norm in computer architecture. The continuing process of change has profound implications for the study of computer architecture because we need to understand not only how things are but how they might evolve and why. Change is one of the key challenges in writing this book—and one of the key motivations. Parallel computer architecture has matured to the point where it needs to be studied from a basis of engineering principles and quantitative evaluation of performance and cost. These are rooted in a body of facts, measurements, and designs of real machines. Unfortunately, existing data and designs are necessarily frozen in time

1. The figure is drawn from an influential paper that sought to explain the dramatic changes taking place in the computing industry (Hennessy and Jouppi 1991). The metric of performance is a bit tricky because it reaches across such a range of time and market segment. The study draws data from general-purpose benchmarks, such as the SPEC benchmark, which is widely used to assess performance on technical computing applications (Hennessy and Patterson 1996). After publication, microprocessors continued to track the prediction while mainframes and supercomputers went through tremendous crises and emerged using multiple CMOS microprocessors in their market niche.

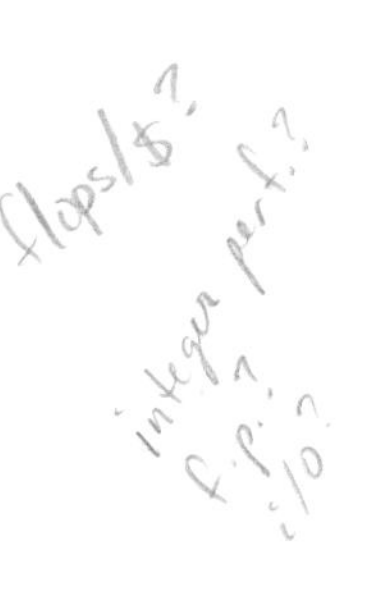

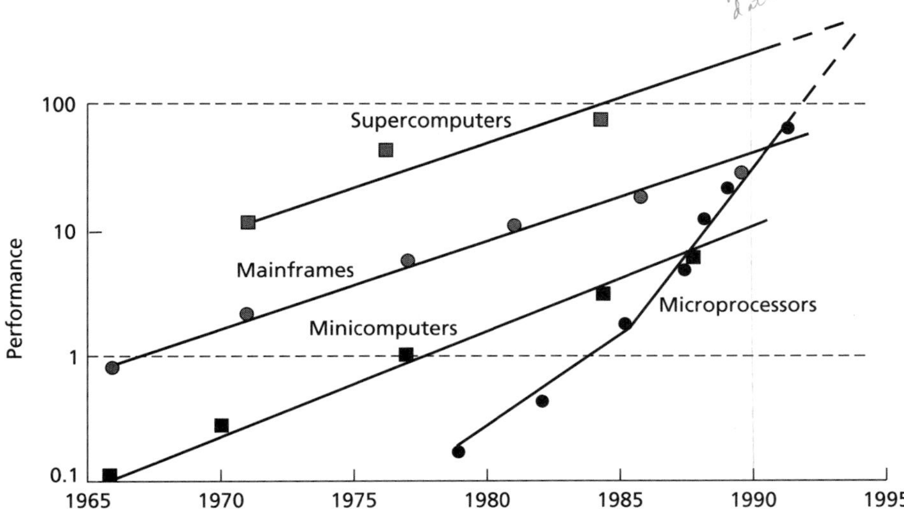

FIGURE 1.1 Performance trends over time of micros, minicomputers, mainframes, and supercomputers. Performance of microprocessors has been increasing at a rate of about 50% per year since the mid-1980s. More traditional mainframe and supercomputer performance has been increasing at a rate of roughly 25% per year. As a result, we are seeing the processor that is best suited to parallel architecture become the performance leader as well. *Source:* Hennessy and Jouppi (1991).

and will become dated as the field progresses. This book presents hard data and examines real machines in the form of a late 1990s technological snapshot in order to retain a clear grounding. However, the methods of evaluation underlying the analysis of concrete design trade-offs transcend the chronological and technological reference point of the book.

The late 1990s happens to be a particularly interesting snapshot because we are in the midst of a dramatic technological realignment as the single-chip microprocessor is poised to dominate every sector of computing and as parallel computing takes hold in many areas of mainstream computing. Of course, the prevalence of change suggests being cautious about extrapolating into the future. The remainder of this section examines more deeply the forces and trends that are giving parallel architectures an increasingly important role throughout the computing field and pushing parallel computing into the mainstream. It looks first at the application demand for increased performance and then at the underlying technological and architectural trends that strive to meet these demands. We see that parallelism is inherently attractive as computers become more highly integrated and that it is being exploited at increasingly high levels of the design. Finally, this section closes with a look at the role of parallelism in the machines at the very high end of the performance spectrum.

1.1.1 Application Trends

The demand for ever greater application performance is a familiar feature of every aspect of computing. Advances in hardware capability enable new application functionality, which grows in significance and places even greater demands on the architecture. This cycle drives the tremendous ongoing design, engineering, and manufacturing effort underlying the sustained exponential performance increase in microprocessor performance. It drives parallel architecture even harder since parallel architecture focuses on the most demanding of these applications. With a 50% annual improvement in processor performance, a parallel machine of a hundred processors can be viewed as providing to applications the computing power that will be widely available 10 years in the future, whereas a thousand processors reflects nearly a 20-year horizon.

Application demand also leads computer vendors to provide a range of models with increasing performance and capacity at progressively increasing cost. The largest volume of machines and the greatest number of users are at the low end, whereas the most demanding applications are served by the high end. One effect of this "platform pyramid" is that the pressure for increased performance is greatest at the high end and is exerted by an important minority of the applications. Prior to the microprocessor era, greater performance was obtained through exotic circuit technologies and machine organizations. Today, to obtain performance significantly greater than the state-of-the-art microprocessor, the primary option is multiple processors, and the most demanding applications are written as parallel programs. Thus, parallel architectures and parallel applications are subject to the most acute demands for greater performance.

A key reference point for both the architect and the application developer is how the use of parallelism improves the performance of the application. We may define the *speedup* on p processors as

$$\text{Speedup}(p \text{ processors}) \equiv \frac{\text{Performance}(p \text{ processors})}{\text{Performance}(1 \text{ processor})} \tag{1.1}$$

For a single, fixed problem, the performance of the machine on the problem is simply the reciprocal of the time to complete the problem, so we have the following important special case:

$$\text{Speedup}_{\textit{fixed problem}}(p \text{ processors}) = \frac{\text{Time}(1 \text{ processor})}{\text{Time}(p \text{ processors})} \tag{1.2}$$

Scientific and Engineering Computing

The direct reliance on increasing levels of performance is well established in a number of endeavors but is perhaps most apparent in the fields of computational science and engineering. Basically, in these fields computers are used to simulate physical phenomena that are impossible or very costly to observe through empirical means.

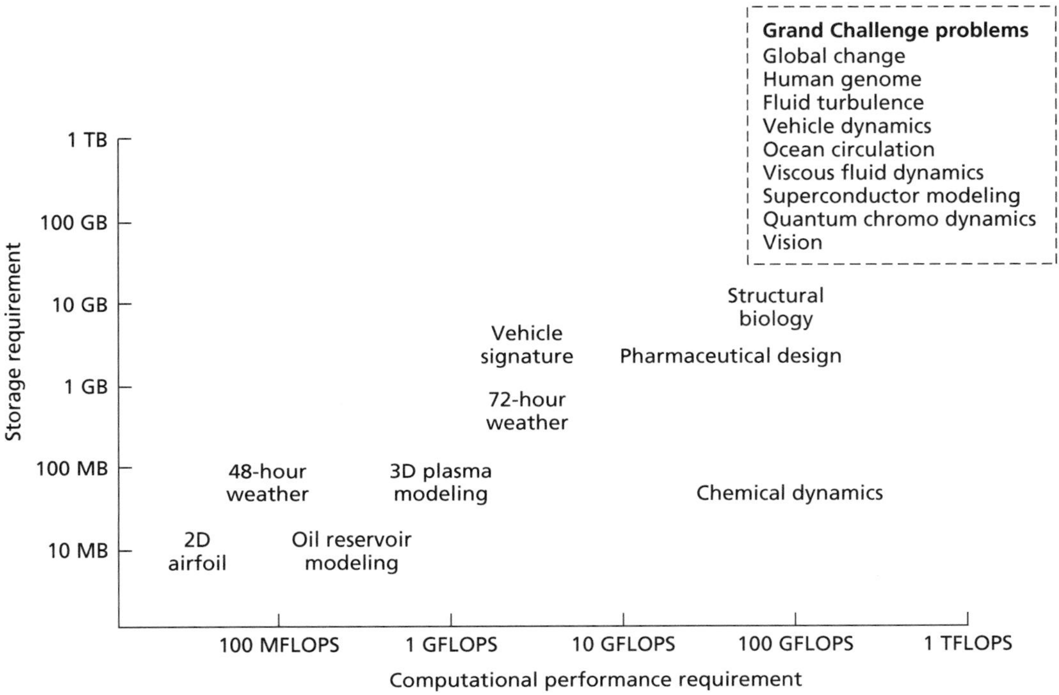

FIGURE 1.2 Grand Challenge application requirements. A collection of important scientific and engineering problems is positioned in a space defined by computational performance and storage capacity. Given the exponential growth rate of performance and capacity, both of these axes map directly to time. In the upper right corner appear some of the Grand Challenge applications identified by the U.S. High Performance Computing and Communications program.

Typical examples include modeling global climate change over long periods, the evolution of galaxies, the atomic structure of materials, the efficiency of combustion with an engine, the flow of air over surfaces of vehicles, the damage due to impacts, and the behavior of microscopic electronic devices. Computational modeling allows in-depth analyses to be performed cheaply on hypothetical designs through computer simulation. A direct correspondence can be drawn between levels of computational performance and the problems that can be studied through simulation. Figure 1.2 summarizes the 1993 findings of the Committee on Physical, Mathematical, and Engineering Sciences of the federal Office of Science and Technology Policy (1993). It indicates the computational rate and storage capacity required to tackle a number of important science and engineering problems. Even with dramatic increases in processor performance, very large parallel architectures are needed to address these problems in the near future. Some years further down the road, new grand challenges will be in view.

Parallel architectures have become the mainstay of scientific computing, including physics, chemistry, material science, biology, astronomy, earth sciences, and others. The engineering application of these tools for modeling physical phenomena is now essential to many industries, including petroleum (reservoir modeling), automotive (crash simulation, drag analysis, combustion efficiency), aeronautics (airflow analysis, engine efficiency, structural mechanics, electromagnetism), pharmaceutical (molecular modeling), and others. In almost all of these applications, there is a large demand for visualization of the results, which is itself a demanding application amenable to parallel computing.

The visualization component has brought the traditional areas of scientific and engineering computing closer to the entertainment industry. In 1995, the first full-length, computer-animated motion picture, *Toy Story,* was produced on a parallel computer system composed of hundreds of Sun workstations. This application was finally possible because the underlying technology and architecture crossed three key thresholds: the decreased cost of computing allowed the rendering to be accomplished within the budget typically associated with a feature film, and the increase in both the performance of individual processors and the scale of parallelism made it possible to complete the task in a reasonable amount of time (several months on several hundred processors). Each science and engineering application has an analogous threshold of computing capacity and cost at which it becomes viable.

Let us take an example from the Grand Challenge program to help understand the strong interaction between applications, architecture, and technology in the context of parallel machines. A 1995 study (Pfeiffer et al. 1995) examined the effectiveness of a wide range of parallel machines on a variety of applications, including a molecular dynamics package, known as AMBER (Assisted Model Building through Energy Refinement). AMBER is widely used to simulate the motion of large biological models such as proteins and DNA, which consist of sequences of residues (amino acids and nucleic acids, respectively) each composed of individual atoms. The code was developed on CRAY vector supercomputers, which employ custom processors, large and expensive SRAM memories (instead of caches), and machine instructions that perform arithmetic or data movement on a sequence, or *vector*, of data values. Figure 1.3 shows the speedup obtained on three versions of this code on a 128-processor microprocessor-based machine—the Intel Paragon, described later. The particular test problem involved the simulation of a protein solvated by water. This test consisted of 99 amino acids and 3,375 water molecules for approximately 11,000 atoms.

The initial parallelization of the code (version 8/94) resulted in good speedup for small configurations but poor speedup on larger configurations. A modest effort to improve the balance of work done by each processor, using techniques discussed in Chapter 2, improved the scaling of the application significantly (version 9/94). An additional effort to optimize communication produced a highly scalable code (version 12/94). This 128-processor version achieved a performance of 406 MFLOPS; the best previously achieved was 145 MFLOPS on a CRAY C90 vector processor. The same application on a more efficient parallel architecture, the CRAY T3D, achieved 891 MFLOPS on 128 processors. This sort of learning curve is quite typical in the

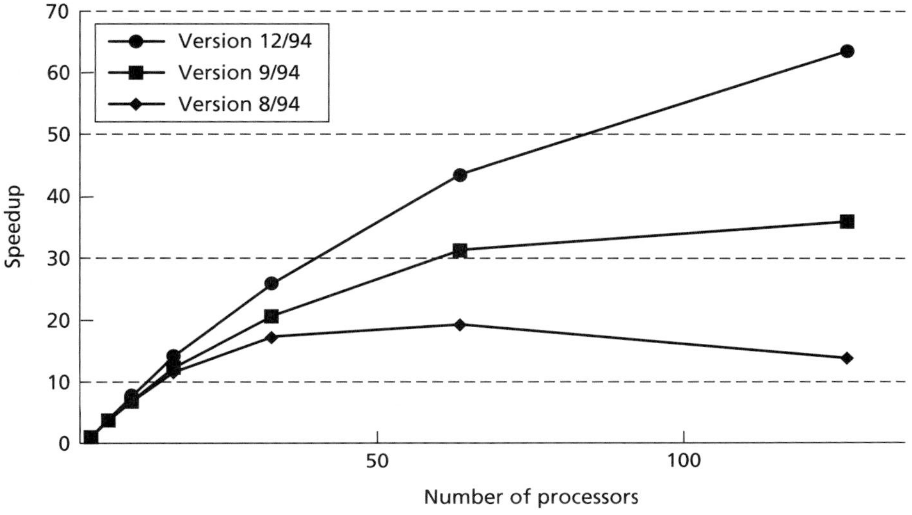

FIGURE 1.3 Speedup on three versions of a parallel program. The parallelization learning curve is illustrated by the speedup obtained on three successive versions of this molecular dynamics code on the Intel Paragon.

parallelization of important applications, as is the interaction between application and architecture. The application writer typically studies the application to understand the demands it places on the available architectures and how to improve its performance on a given set of machines. The architect may study these demands as well in order to understand how to make the machine more effective on a given set of applications. Ideally, the end user of the application enjoys the benefits of both efforts.

The demand for ever increasing performance is a natural consequence of the modeling activity. For example, in electronic CAD there is obviously more to simulate as the number of devices on the chip increases. In addition, the increasing complexity of the design requires that more test vectors be used and, because higher-level functionality is incorporated into the chip, each of these tests must run for a larger number of clock cycles. Furthermore, an increasing level of confidence is required because the cost of fabrication is so great. The cumulative effect is that the computational demand for the design verification of each new generation is increasing at an even faster rate than the performance of the microprocessors themselves.

Commercial Computing

Commercial computing has also come to rely on parallel architectures for its high end. Although the scale of parallelism is typically not as large as in scientific computing, the use of parallelism is even more widespread. Multiprocessors have provided the high end of the commercial computing market since the mid-1960s. In

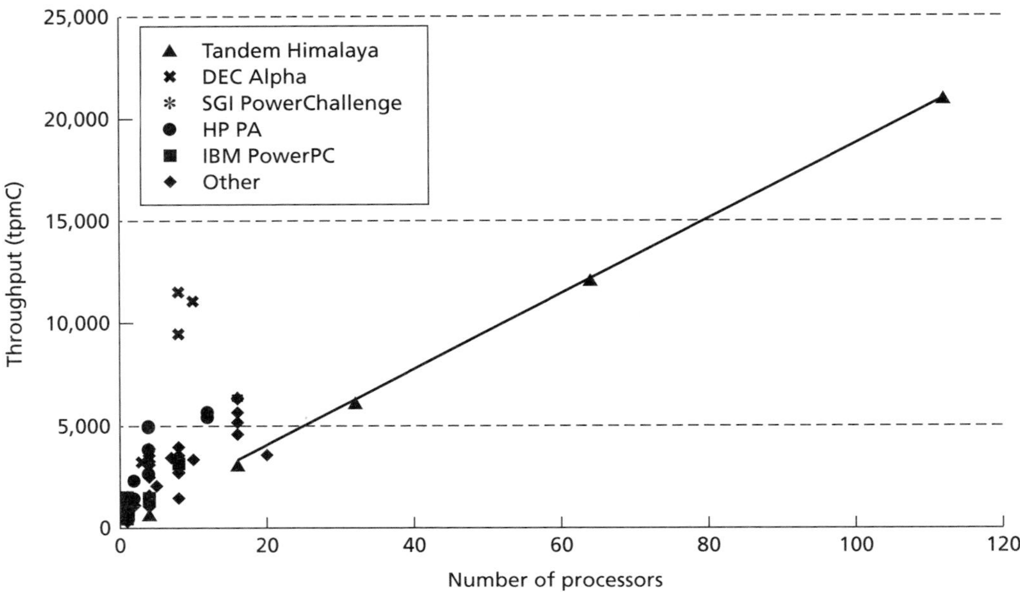

FIGURE 1.4 TPC-C throughput versus number of processors on TPC. The March 1996 TPC report documents the transaction processing performance for a wide range of systems. The figure shows the number of processors employed for all of the high-end systems, highlighting five leading vendor product lines. All of the major database vendors utilize multiple processors for their high-performance options, although the scale of parallelism varies considerably.

this arena, computer system speed and capacity translate directly into the scale of business that can be supported by the system. The relationship between performance and scale of business enterprise is clearly articulated in the on-line transaction processing (OLTP) benchmarks sponsored by the Transaction Processing Performance Council (TPC). These benchmarks rate the performance of a system in terms of its throughput in *transactions per minute* (tpm) on a typical workload. The TPC-C benchmark is an order entry application with a mix of interactive and batch transactions, including realistic features like queued transactions, aborting transactions, and elaborate presentation features (Gray 1991). The benchmark includes explicit scaling criteria to make the problem more realistic: the size of the database and the number of terminals in the system increase as the tpmC (the tpm on TPC-C) rating rises. Thus, a faster system must operate on a larger database and service a larger number of users.

Figure 1.4 shows the tpmC ratings for the collection of systems appearing in one edition of the TPC results (March 1996), with the achieved throughput on the vertical axis and the number of processors employed in the server along the horizontal axis. This data includes a wide range of systems from a variety of hardware and software vendors, a few of which are highlighted here. Since the problem solved in the benchmark run scales with system performance, we cannot simply compare times to see the effectiveness of parallelism. Instead, we use the throughput of the system as the metric of performance in Equation 1.1. The resulting speedup is illustrated in Example 1.1.

EXAMPLE 1.1 The tpmC for the Tandem Himalaya and IBM PowerPC systems are given in the following table. What is the speedup obtained on each?

tpmC		
Number of Processors	**IBM RS6000 PowerPC**	**Himalaya K10000**
1	735	
4	1,438	
8	3,119	
16		3,043
32		6,067
64		12,021
112		20,918

Answer For the IBM system, we may calculate speedup relative to the uniprocessor system; in the Tandem case, we can only calculate speedup relative to a 16-processor system. The IBM machine appears to carry a significant penalty in the parallel database implementation of moving from one to four processors; however, the scaling is very good (superlinear) from four to eight processors. The Tandem system achieves good scaling, although the speedup appears to flatten toward the 100-processor regime. ■

$\text{Speedup}_{\text{tpmC}}$		
Number of Processors	**IBM RS6000 PowerPC**	**Himalaya K10000**
1	1	
4	1.96	
8	4.24	
16		1
32		1.99
64		3.95
112		6.87

Several important observations can be drawn from the TPC data. First, the use of parallel architectures is prevalent. Essentially all of the vendors supplying database hardware or software offer multiprocessor systems that provide performance substantially beyond their uniprocessor product. Second, it is not only large-scale parallelism that is important but modest-scale multiprocessor servers with tens of processors and even small-scale multiprocessors with two or four processors.

Finally, even a set of well-documented measurements of a particular class of system at a specific point in time cannot provide a true technological snapshot. Technology evolves rapidly, systems take time to develop and deploy, and real systems have a useful lifetime. Thus, the best systems available from a collection of vendors will be at different points in their life cycle at any time. For example, the DEC Alpha and IBM PowerPC systems in the March 1996 TPC report were much newer than the Tandem Himalaya system. Furthermore, we cannot conclude, for example, that the Tandem system is inherently less efficient as a result of its scalable design. We can, however, conclude that even very large-scale systems must track the technology to retain their advantage.

The transition to parallel programming, including new algorithms or attention to communication and synchronization requirements in existing algorithms, has largely taken place in the high-performance end of computing. The transition is in progress among the much broader base of commercial engineering software. Typically, engineering and commercial applications target more modest-scale multiprocessors, which dominate the server market. In the commercial world, all of the major database vendors support parallel machines for their high-end products. Several major database vendors also offer "shared-nothing" versions for large parallel machines and collections of workstations on a fast network, often called *clusters*. In addition, multiprocessor machines are heavily used to improve throughput on multiprogramming workloads. Even the desktop demonstrates a significant number of concurrent processes, with a host of active windows and daemons. Quite often a single user will have tasks running on many machines within the local area network or will farm tasks out across the network. All of these trends provide a solid application demand for parallel architectures of a variety of scales.

1.1.2 Technology Trends

The importance of parallelism in meeting the application demand for ever greater performance can be brought into sharper focus by looking more closely at the advancements in the underlying technology and architecture. These trends suggest that it may be increasingly difficult to "wait for the single processor to get fast enough" while parallel architectures become more attractive. Moreover, the examination shows that the critical issues in parallel computer architecture are fundamentally similar to those that we wrestle with in "sequential" computers, such as how the resource budget should be divided among functional units that do the work, caches that exploit locality, and wires that provide communication bandwidth.

The primary technological advance is a steady reduction in the basic VLSI feature size. This makes transistors, gates, and circuits faster and smaller, so more fit in the same area. In addition, the useful die size is growing, so there is more area to use. Intuitively, clock rate improves in proportion to the improvement in feature size while the number of transistors grows as the square, or even faster, due to increasing overall die area. Thus, in the long run, the use of many transistors at once (i.e., parallelism) can be expected to contribute more than clock rate to the observed performance improvement of the single-chip building block.

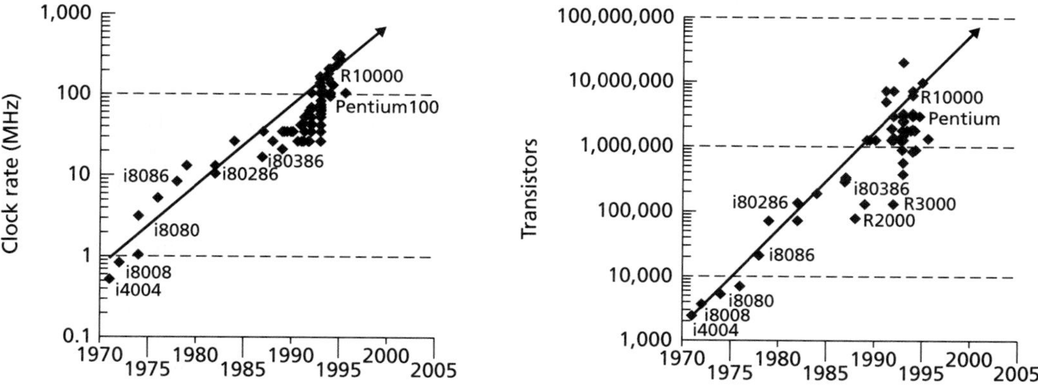

FIGURE 1.5 Improvement in logic density and clock frequency of microprocessors. Improvements in lithographic technique, process technology, circuit design, and datapath design have yielded a sustained improvement in logic density and clock rate.

This intuition is borne out by examination of commercial microprocessors. Figure 1.5 shows the increase in clock frequency and transistor count for several important microprocessor families. Clock rates for the leading microprocessors increase by about 30% per year while the number of transistors increases by about 40% per year. Thus, if we look at the raw computing power of a chip (total transistors switching per second), transistor capacity has contributed an order of magnitude more than clock rate over the past two decades.[2] The performance of microprocessors on standard benchmarks has been increasing at a much greater rate than clock frequency. The most widely used benchmark for measuring workstation performance is the SPEC suite, which includes several realistic integer programs and floating-point programs (SPEC 1995). Integer performance on SPEC has been increasing at about 55% per year and floating-point performance at 75% per year. The LINPACK benchmark (Dongarra 1994) is the most widely used metric of performance on numerical applications. LINPACK floating-point performance has been increasing at more than 80% per year. Thus, processors are getting faster in large part by making more effective use of an ever larger volume of computing resources.

The simplest analysis of these technology trends suggests that the basic single-chip building block will provide increasingly large capacity—in the vicinity of 100 million transistors by the year 2000. This raises the possibility of placing more of the computer system on the chip, including memory and I/O support, or of placing multiple processors on the chip (Gwennap 1994a). The former yields a small and

2. There are many reasons why the transistor count does not increase as the square of the clock rate. One is that much of the area of a processor is consumed by wires, serving to distribute control, data, or clock (i.e., on-chip communication). We will see that the communication issue reappears at every level of parallel computer architecture.

conveniently packaged building block for parallel architectures. The latter brings parallel architecture into the single-chip regime (Gwennap 1994b). Both possibilities are in evidence commercially, with the system-on-a-chip becoming first established in embedded systems, portables, and low-end personal computer products. The use of multiple processors on a chip is becoming established in digital signal processing (Feigel 1994).

The divergence between capacity and speed is much more pronounced in memory technology. From 1980 to 1995, the capacity of a DRAM chip increased a thousand-fold, quadrupling every three years, while the memory cycle time improved by only a factor of two. In the time frame of the 100-million-transistor microprocessor, we anticipate gigabit DRAM chips, but the gap between processor cycle time and memory cycle time will have grown substantially wider. Thus, the memory bandwidth demanded by the processor (bytes per memory cycle) is growing rapidly.

The latency of a memory operation is determined by the access time, which is smaller than the memory cycle time, but still the number of processor cycles per memory access time is large and increasing. To reduce the average latency experienced by the processor and to increase the bandwidth that can be delivered to the processor, we must make more effective use of the levels of the memory hierarchy that lie between the processor and the DRAM memory. Essentially all modern microprocessors provide one or two levels of caches on chip, and most system designs provide an additional level of external cache. A fundamental question as we move into multiprocessor designs is how to organize the collection of caches that lies between the many processors and the many memory modules. For example, one of the immediate benefits of parallel architectures is that the total size of each level of the memory hierarchy can increase with the number of processors without increasing the access time.

Extending these observations to disks, we see a similar divergence. Parallel disk storage systems, such as RAID, are becoming the norm. Large, multilevel caches for files or disk blocks are predominant.

1.1.3 Architectural Trends

Advances in technology determine what is possible; architecture translates the potential of the technology into performance and capability. Fundamentally, the two ways in which a larger volume of resources (e.g., more transistors) improves performance are parallelism and locality. Moreover, these two approaches compete for the same resources. Whenever multiple operations are performed in parallel, the number of cycles required to execute the program is reduced. However, resources are required to support each of the simultaneous activities. Whenever data references are performed close to the processor, the latency of accessing deeper levels of the storage hierarchy is avoided and the number of cycles to execute the program is reduced. However, resources are required to provide this local storage. In general, the best performance is obtained by an intermediate strategy that devotes resources to exploiting a degree of parallelism and a degree of locality. Indeed, we will see throughout the book that parallelism and locality interact in interesting ways in systems of all scales, from within a chip to across a large parallel machine. In current microprocessors, the die area is divided roughly equally between cache storage, processing, and off-chip interconnect. Larger-scale systems may exhibit a somewhat different split because of differences in cost and performance trade-offs, but the basic issues are the same.

Microprocessor Design Trends

Examining the trends in microprocessor architecture helps build intuition toward the issues we will be dealing with in parallel machines. It also illustrates how fundamental parallelism is to conventional computer architecture and how current architectural trends are leading toward multiprocessor designs. (The discussion of processor design techniques in this book is cursory since many readers are expected to be familiar with those techniques from traditional architecture texts [Hennessy and Patterson 1996] or the many discussions in the trade literature. It does provide a unique perspective on those techniques, however, and will serve to refresh your memory.)

The history of computer architecture has traditionally been divided into four generations identified by the basic logic technology: tubes, transistors, integrated circuits, and VLSI. The entire period covered by the figures in this chapter is lumped into the fourth, or VLSI, generation. Clearly, there has been tremendous architectural advance over this period, but what delineates one era from the next within this generation? The strongest delineation is the kind of parallelism that is exploited as indicated in Figure 1.6.

The period up to about 1986 is dominated by advancements in *bit-level parallelism*, with 4-bit microprocessors replaced by 8-bit, 16-bit, and so on. Doubling the width of the datapath reduces the number of cycles required to perform a full 32-bit operation. Once a 32-bit word size is reached in the mid-1980s, this trend slows, with only partial adoption of 64-bit operation obtained a decade later. Further increases in word width will be driven by demands for improved floating-point representation and a larger address space rather than performance. With address space requirements growing by less than a bit per year, the demand for 128-bit operation appears to be well in the future. The early microprocessor period was able to reap the benefits of the easiest form of parallelism: bit-level parallelism in every operation. The dramatic inflection point in the microprocessor growth curve shown in Figure 1.1 marks the arrival in 1986 of full 32-bit word operation combined with the prevalent use of caches.

The period from the mid-1980s to the mid-1990s is dominated by advancements in *instruction-level parallelism,* performing portions of several machine instructions concurrently. Full-word operation meant that the basic steps in instruction processing (instruction decode, integer arithmetic, and address calculation) could each be performed in a single cycle; with caches, the instruction fetch and data access could also be performed in a single cycle most of the time. The RISC approach demonstrated that, with care in the instruction set design, it was straightforward to pipeline the stages of instruction processing so that an instruction is executed almost every

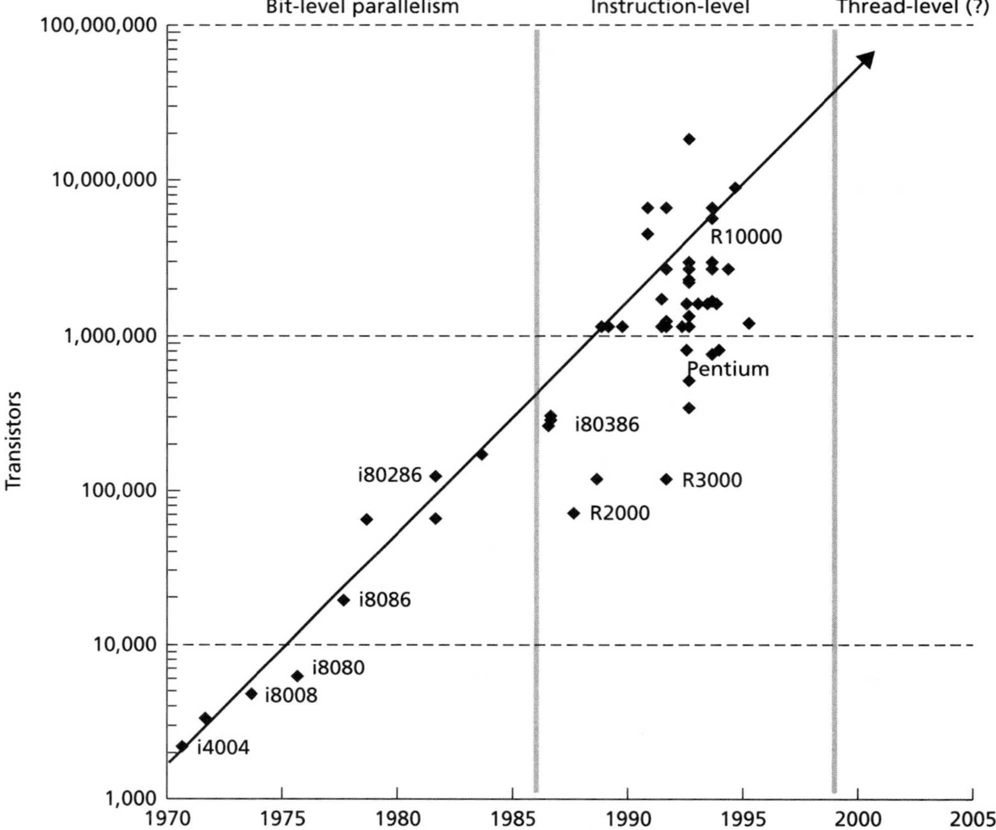

FIGURE 1.6 Number of transistors per processor chip over the last 25 years. The growth essentially follows Moore's Law, which says that the number of transistors doubles every two years. Forecasting from past trends, we can reasonably expect to be designing for a 50- to 100-million-transistor budget at the end of the decade. Also indicated are the epochs of design within the fourth, or VLSI, generation of computer architecture, reflecting the increasing level of parallelism.

cycle, on average. Thus, the parallelism inherent in the steps of instruction processing could be exploited across a small number of instructions. While pipelined instruction processing was not new, it had never before been so well suited to the underlying technology. In addition, advances in compiler technology made instruction pipelines more effective.

The mid-1980s microprocessor-based computers consisted of a small constellation of chips: an integer processing unit, a floating-point unit, a cache controller, and SRAMs for the cache data and tag storage. As chip capacity increased, these components were coalesced into a single chip, which reduced the cost of communicating among them. Thus, a single chip contained separate hardware for integer arithmetic, memory operations, branch operations, and floating-point operations. In addition to pipelining individual instructions, it became very attractive to fetch multiple instructions at a time and issue them in parallel to distinct function units whenever possible. This form of instruction-level parallelism came to be called *superscalar* execution. It provided a natural way to exploit the ever increasing number of available chip resources. More function units were added, more instructions were fetched at a time, and more instructions could be issued in each clock cycle to the function units.

However, increasing the amount of instruction-level parallelism that the processor can exploit is only worthwhile if the processor can be supplied with instructions and data fast enough to keep it busy. In order to satisfy the increasing instruction and data bandwidth requirement, larger and larger caches were placed on chip with the processor, further consuming the ever increasing number of transistors. With the processor and cache on the same chip, the path between the two could be made very wide to satisfy the bandwidth requirement of multiple instruction and data accesses per cycle. However, as more instructions are issued each cycle, the performance impact of each control transfer and each cache miss becomes more significant. A control transfer may have to wait for the depth, or *latency*, of the processor pipeline until a particular instruction reaches the end of the pipeline and determines which instruction to execute next. Similarly, instructions that use a value loaded from memory may cause the processor to wait for the latency of a cache miss.

Processor designs in the 1990s deploy a variety of complex instruction processing mechanisms in an effort to reduce the performance degradation resulting from latency in "wide-issue" superscalar processors. Sophisticated branch prediction techniques are used to avoid pipeline latency by guessing the direction of control flow before branches are actually resolved. Larger, more sophisticated caches are used to *avoid* the latency of cache misses. Instructions are scheduled dynamically and allowed to complete out of order so if one instruction encounters a miss, other instructions can proceed ahead of it as long as they do not depend on the result of the instruction. A larger window of instructions that are waiting to issue is maintained within the processor and whenever an instruction produces a new result, several waiting instructions may be issued to the function units. These complex mechanisms allow the processor to *tolerate* the latency of a cache miss or pipeline dependence when it does occur. However, each of these mechanisms places a heavy demand on chip resources and carries a very heavy design cost.

Given the expected increases in chip density, the natural question to ask is how far will instruction-level parallelism go within a single thread of control? At what point will the emphasis shift to supporting the higher levels of parallelism available as multiple processes or multiple threads of control within a process, that is, *thread-level parallelism?* Several research studies have sought to answer the first part of the question, either through simulation of aggressive machine designs (Chang et al. 1991; Horst, Harris, and Jardine 1990; Lee, Kwok, and Briggs 1991; Melvin and Patt 1991) or through analysis of the inherent properties of programs (Butler et al. 1991; Jouppi and Wall 1989; Johnson 1991; Smith, Johnson, and Horowitz 1989; Wall 1991). The most complete treatment appears in Johnson's book devoted to the topic

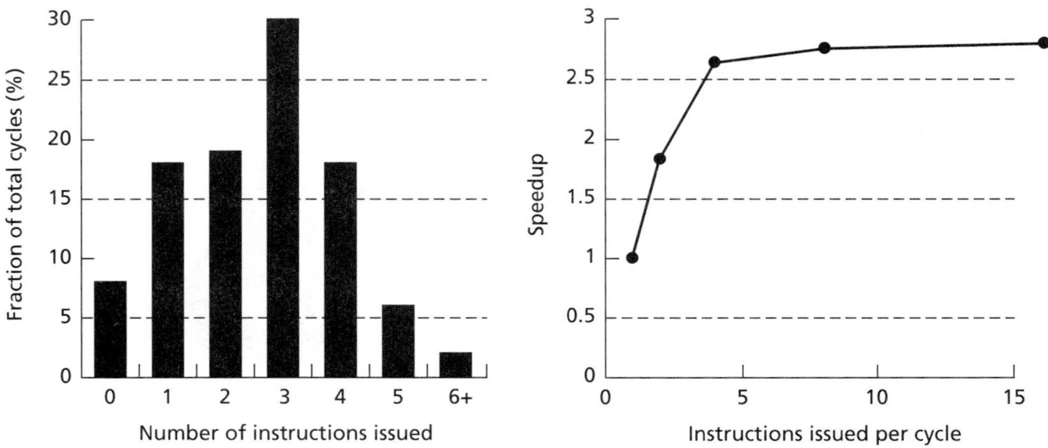

FIGURE 1.7 Distribution of potential instruction-level parallelism and estimated speedup under ideal superscalar execution. The figure shows the distribution of available instruction-level parallelism and maximum potential speedup under idealized superscalar execution, including unbounded processing resources and perfect branch prediction. Data is an average of that presented for several benchmarks by Johnson (1991).

(1991). Simulation of aggressive machine designs generally shows that two-way superscalar, that is, issuing two instructions per cycle, is very profitable and four-way offers substantial additional benefit, but wider issue widths (e.g., eight-way superscalar) provide little additional gain. The design complexity increases dramatically because control transfers occur roughly once in five instructions, on average.

To estimate the maximum potential speedup that can be obtained by issuing multiple instructions per cycle, the execution trace of a program is simulated on an ideal machine with unlimited instruction fetch bandwidth, as many function units as the program can use, and perfect branch prediction. (The latter is easy, since the trace correctly follows each branch.) These generous machine assumptions ensure that no instruction is held up because a function unit is busy or because the instruction is beyond the lookahead capability of the processor. Furthermore, to ensure that no instruction is delayed because it updates a location that is used by logically previous instructions, storage resource dependences are removed by a technique called *renaming*. Each update to a register or memory location is treated as introducing a new "name," and subsequent uses of the value in the execution trace refer to the new name. In this way, the execution order of the program is constrained only by essential data dependences; each instruction is executed as soon as its operands are available. Figure 1.7 summarizes the result of this ideal machine analysis based on data presented by Johnson (1991). The histogram on the left shows the fraction of cycles in which no instruction could issue, only one instruction could issue, and so on. Johnson's ideal machine retains realistic function unit latencies, including cache misses, which accounts for the zero-issue cycles. (Other studies ignore cache effects or ignore pipeline latencies and thereby obtain more optimistic estimates.) We see that, even with infinite machine resources, perfect branch prediction, and ideal renaming, no more than four instructions issue in a cycle 90% of the time. Based on this distribution, we can estimate the speedup obtained at various issue widths, as shown in the right portion of the figure. Recent work (Lam and Wilson 1992; Sohi, Breach, and Vijaykumar 1995) provides empirical evidence that to obtain significantly larger amounts of parallelism, multiple threads of control must be pursued simultaneously. Barring some unforeseen breakthrough in instruction-level parallelism, the leap to the next level of useful parallelism—multiple concurrent threads—is increasingly compelling as chips increase in capacity.

System Design Trends

The trend toward thread- or process-level parallelism has been strong at the computer system level for some time. Computers containing multiple state-of-the-art microprocessors sharing a common memory became prevalent in the mid-1980s, when the 32-bit microprocessor was first introduced (Bell 1985). As indicated by Figure 1.8, which shows the number of processors available in commercial multiprocessors over time, this bus-based shared memory multiprocessor approach has maintained a substantial multiplier to the increasing performance of the individual processors. Almost every commercial microprocessor introduced since the mid-1980s provides hardware support for multiprocessor configurations, as discussed in Chapter 5. Multiprocessors dominate the server and enterprise (or mainframe) markets and have migrated to the desktop.

The early multi-microprocessor systems were introduced by small companies competing for a share of the minicomputer market, including Synapse (Nestle and Inselberg 1985), Encore (Schanin 1986), Flex (Matelan 1985), Sequent (Rodgers 1985), and Myrias (Savage 1985). They combined 10 to 20 microprocessors to deliver competitive throughput on time-sharing loads. With the introduction of the 32-bit Intel i80386 as the base processor, these systems obtained substantial commercial success, especially in transaction processing. However, the rapid performance advance of RISC microprocessors, exploiting instruction-level parallelism, sapped the CISC multiprocessor momentum in the late 1980s and all but eliminated the minicomputer. Shortly thereafter, several large companies began producing RISC multiprocessor systems, especially as servers and mainframe replacements. These designs highlight the critical role of bandwidth. In most of these multiprocessor designs, all the processors plug into a common bus. Since a bus has a fixed bandwidth, as the processors become faster, a smaller number can be supported by the bus. The early 1990s brought a dramatic advance in the shared memory bus technology, including faster electrical signaling, wider datapaths, pipelined protocols, and multiple paths. Each of these provided greater bandwidth, growing with time and design experience, as indicated in Figure 1.9. This increase in bandwidth allowed the multiprocessor designs to ramp back up to the 10-to-20 range and beyond while tracking the microprocessor advances (Alexander et al. 1994; Cekleov et al. 1993;

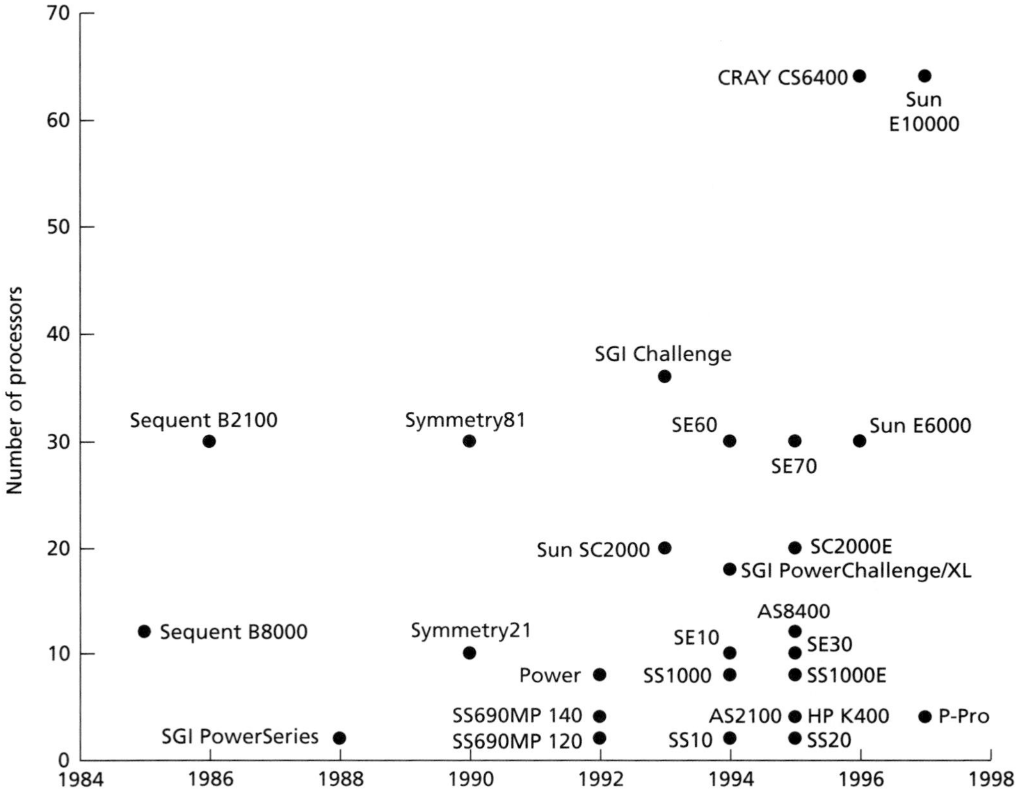

FIGURE 1.8 Number of processors in fully configured commercial bus-based shared memory multiprocessors. After an initial era of 10- to 20-way shared memory processors based on slow CISC microprocessors, companies such as Sun, HP, DEC, SGI, IBM, and CRI began producing sizable RISC-based SMPs, as did commercial vendors not shown here, including NCR/ATT, Tandem, and Pyramid.

Fenwick et al. 1995; Frank, Burkhardt, and Rothnie 1993; Galles and Williams 1993; Godiwala and Maskas 1995).

The picture in the mid-1990s is very interesting. Not only has the bus-based shared memory multiprocessor approach become ubiquitous in the industry, it is present at a wide range of scale. Desktop systems and small servers commonly support two to four processors, larger servers support tens, and large commercial systems are moving toward one hundred. Indications are that this trend will continue. As an illustration of the shift in emphasis, in 1994 Intel defined a standard approach to the design of multiprocessor PC systems around its Pentium microprocessor (Slater 1994). The follow-on Pentium Pro microprocessor allowed four-processor configurations to be constructed by wiring the chips together without even any glue logic; bus drivers, arbitration, and so on are in the microprocessor. This development is expected to make small-scale multiprocessors a true commodity. Addition-

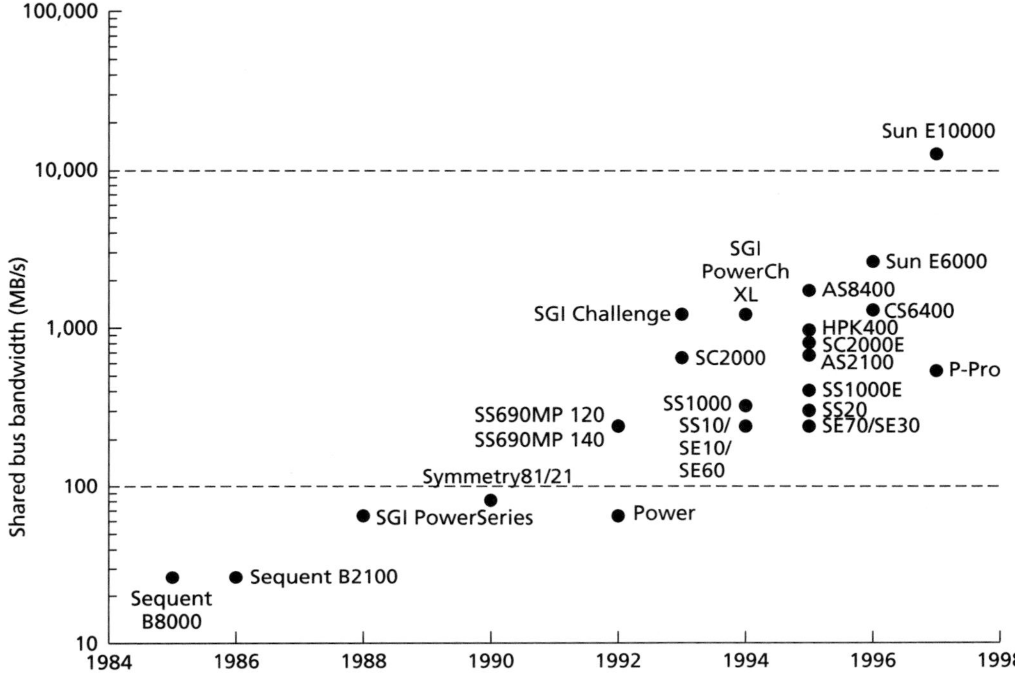

FIGURE 1.9 Bandwidth of the shared memory bus in commercial multiprocessors. After slow growth for several years, a new era of memory bus design began in 1991, which supported the use of substantial numbers of very fast microprocessors.

ally, a shift in the industry business model has been noted, where multiprocessors are being pushed by software vendors, especially database companies, rather than just by the hardware vendors. Combining these trends with the technology trends, it appears that the question is when, not if, multiple processors per chip will become prevalent.

1.1.4 Supercomputers

We have looked at the forces driving the development of parallel architecture in the general market. A second, confluent set of forces comes from the quest to achieve absolute maximum performance, known as *supercomputing*. Although commercial and information processing applications are increasingly becoming important drivers of the high end, scientific computing has historically been a kind of proving ground for innovative architecture. In the mid-1960s, this included pipelined instruction processing and dynamic instruction scheduling, which are commonplace in microprocessors today. Starting in the mid-1970s, supercomputing was dominated by *vector processors*, which perform operations on sequences of data

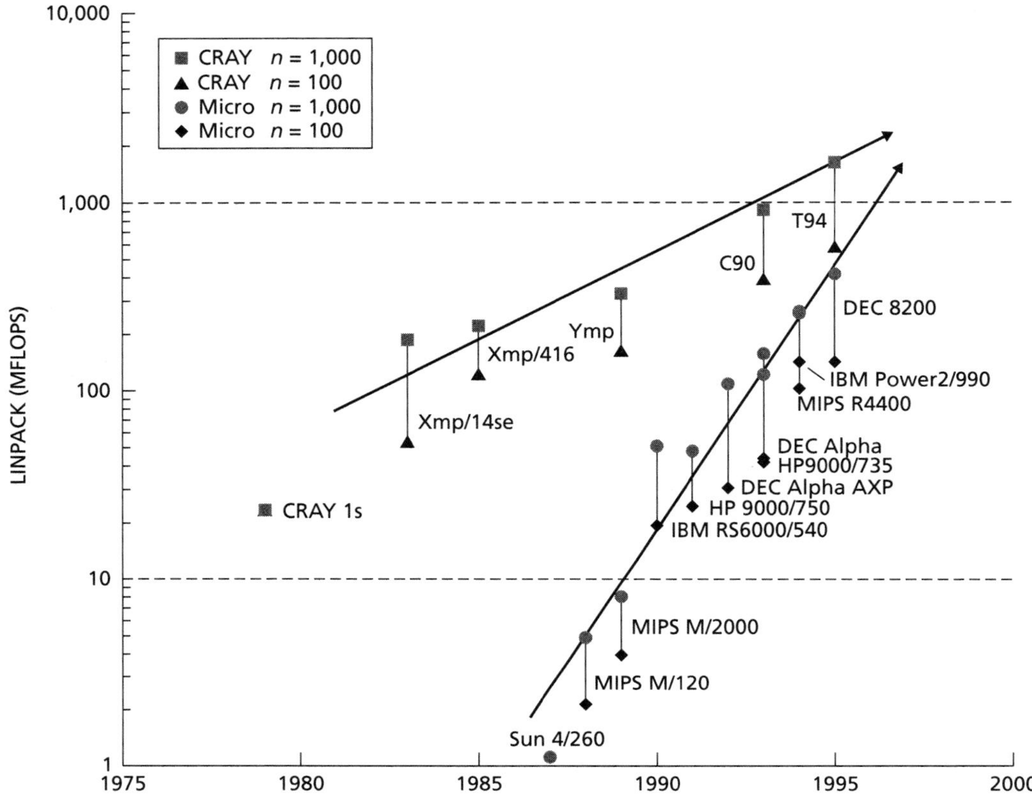

FIGURE 1.10 Uniprocessor performance of supercomputers and microprocessor-based systems on the LINPACK benchmark. Performance in MFLOPS for a single processor on solving dense linear equations is shown for the leading CRAY vector supercomputer and the fastest workstations on a 100×100 and $1,000 \times 1,000$ matrix.

elements; that is, a vector rather than individual scalar data. Vector operations permit more parallelism to be obtained within a single thread of control. In addition, these vector supercomputers were implemented in very fast, expensive, high-power circuit technologies.

Dense linear algebra is an important component of scientific computing and the specific emphasis of the LINPACK benchmark. Although this benchmark evaluates a narrow aspect of system performance, it is one of the few measurements available for a very wide class of machines over a long period of time. Figure 1.10 shows the LINPACK performance trend for one processor of the leading CRAY vector supercomputers (August et al. 1989; Russel 1978) compared with that of the fastest contemporary microprocessor-based workstations and servers. For each system two data points are provided. The lower one is the performance obtained on a 100 × 100 matrix and the higher one on a 1,000 × 1,000 matrix. Within the vector processing approach, the single-processor performance improvement is dominated by modest improvements in cycle time and more substantial increases in the vector memory bandwidth. In the microprocessor systems, we see the combined effect of increasing clock rate, using on-chip pipelined floating-point units, increasing on-chip cache size, increasing off-chip second-level cache size, and increasing use of instruction-level parallelism. The gap in uniprocessor performance is rapidly closing.

Multiprocessor architectures are adopted by both the vector processor and microprocessor designs, but the scale is quite different. The CRAY Xmp first provided two and then four processors, the Ymp eight, the C90 sixteen, and the T94 thirty-two. The microprocessor-based supercomputers initially provided about 100 processors, increasing to roughly 1,000 from 1990 on. These aggregations of processors, known as *massively parallel processors* (MPPs), have tracked the microprocessor advance, with typically a lag of one to two years behind the leading microprocessor-based workstation or personal computer. As shown in Figure 1.11, the large number of slightly slower microprocessors has proved dominant for the LINPACK benchmark. (Note the change of scale from MFLOPS in Figure 1.10 to GFLOPS here.) The performance advantage of the MPP systems over traditional vector supercomputers is less substantial on more complete applications (Bailey et al. 1994) owing to the relative immaturity of the programming languages, compilers, and algorithms; however, the trend toward MPPs is still very pronounced. The importance of this trend was apparent enough in 1993 that CRAY Research announced its T3D, based on the DEC Alpha microprocessor.

Recently, the LINPACK benchmark has been used to rank the fastest computer systems in the world. Figure 1.12 shows the number of multiprocessor parallel vector processors (PVPs), MPPs, and bus-based shared memory multiprocessors (SMPs) appearing in the list of the top 500 systems. The latter two are both microprocessor based, and the trend is clear.

1.1.5 Summary

In examining current trends from a variety of perspectives—economics, technology, architecture, and application demand—we see that parallel architecture is increasingly attractive and increasingly central. The quest for performance is so keen that parallelism is being exploited at many different levels and at various points in the computer design space. Instruction-level parallelism is exploited in all modern high-performance processors. Essentially, all machines beyond the desktop are multiprocessors, including servers, mainframes, and supercomputers. The very high end of the performance curve is dominated by massively parallel processors. The use of large-scale parallelism in applications is broadening. The focus of this book is the multiprocessor level of parallelism. We study the design principles embodied in parallel machines from the modest scale to the very large, so that we may understand the spectrum of viable parallel architectures that can be built from well-proven components.

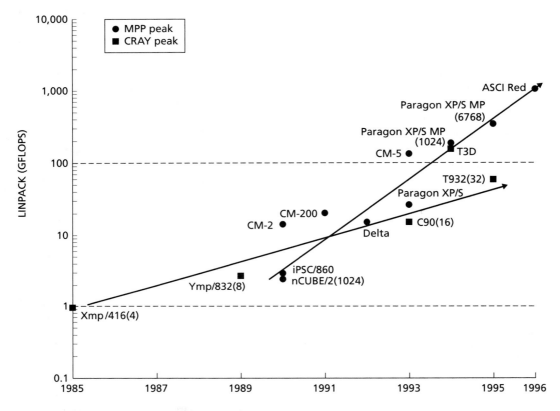

FIGURE 1.11 Performance of supercomputers and MPPs on the LINPACK peak performance benchmark. Peak performance in GFLOPS for solving dense linear equations is shown for the leading CRAY multiprocessor vector supercomputer and the fastest MPP systems. Note the change in scale from Figure 1.10 (MFLOPS to GFLOPS).

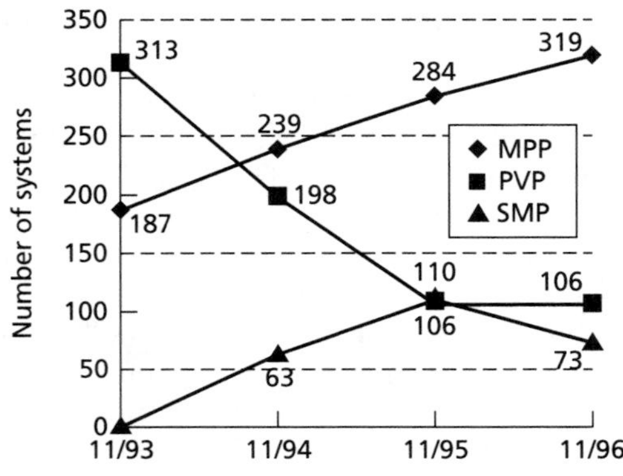

FIGURE 1.12 Types of systems used in the 500 fastest computer systems in the world. Parallel vector processors (PVPs) have given way to microprocessor-based massively parallel processors (MPPs) and bus-based symmetric shared memory multiprocessors (SMPs) at the high end of computing.

This discussion of the trends toward parallel computers has been primarily from the processor perspective, but you may arrive at the same conclusion from the memory system perspective. Consider briefly the design of a memory system to support a very large amount of data, that is, the data set of *large* problems. One of the few physical laws of computer architecture is that fast memories are small, large memories are slow. This occurrence is due to many factors, including the increased address decode time, the delays on increasingly long bit lines, the small drive of increasingly dense storage cells, and the selector delays. The result is that memory systems are constructed as a hierarchy of increasingly larger and slower memories: on average, a large hierarchical memory is fast, as long as the references exhibit good locality. The other trick we can play to cheat the laws of physics and obtain fast access on a very large data set is to use multiple processors and have the different processors access independent smaller memories. Of course, physics is not easily fooled. We pay the cost when a processor accesses nonlocal data, which we call *communication,* and when we need to orchestrate the actions of the many processors (i.e., in synchronization operations).

1.2 CONVERGENCE OF PARALLEL ARCHITECTURES

Historically, parallel machines have developed within several distinct architectural camps, and most texts on the subject are organized around a taxonomy of these designs. However, in looking at the evolution of parallel architecture, it is clear that the designs are strongly influenced by the same technological forces and similar application requirements. It is not surprising therefore that a great deal of convergence has occurred in the field. The goal of this section is to construct a framework for understanding the entire spectrum of parallel computer architectures and to build intuition as to the nature of the convergence. Along the way comes a quick overview of the evolution of parallel machines, starting from the traditional camps and moving toward the point of convergence.

1.2.1 Communication Architecture

Given that a parallel computer is "a collection of processing elements that communicate and cooperate to solve large problems fast" (Almasi and Gottlieb 1989), we may reasonably view parallel architecture as the extension of conventional computer architecture to address issues of communication and cooperation among processing elements. In essence, parallel architecture extends the usual concepts of a computer architecture with a communication architecture. Computer architecture has two distinct facets. One is the definition of critical abstractions, especially the hardware/software boundary and the user/system boundary. The architecture specifies the set of operations at the boundary and the data types that these operate on. The other facet is the organizational structure that realizes these abstractions to deliver high performance in a cost-effective manner. A *communication architecture* has these two facets as well. It defines the basic communication and synchronization operations, and it addresses the organizational structures that realize these operations.

The framework for understanding communication in a parallel machine is illustrated in Figure 1.13. The top layer is the programming model, which is the conceptualization of the machine that the programmer uses in coding applications. Each programming model specifies how parts of the program running in parallel communicate information to one another and what synchronization operations are available to coordinate their activities. Applications are written in a programming model. In the simplest case, the model consists of multiprogramming a large number of independent sequential programs; no communication or cooperation takes place at the programming level. The more interesting cases include true parallel programming models, such as shared address space, message passing, and data parallel programming. We can describe these models intuitively as follows:

- *Shared address* programming is like using a bulletin board, where you can communicate with one or many colleagues by posting information at known, shared locations. Individual activities can be orchestrated by taking note of who is doing what task.
- *Message passing* is akin to telephone calls or letters, which convey information from a specific sender to a specific receiver. There is a well-defined event when the information is sent or received, and these events are the basis for orchestrating individual activities. However, no shared location is accessible to all.
- *Data parallel* processing is a more regimented form of cooperation, where several agents perform an action on separate elements of a data set simultaneously and then exchange information globally before continuing en masse. The global reorganization of data may be accomplished through accesses to shared addresses or messages since the programming model only defines the overall effect of the parallel steps.

A more precise definition of these programming models will be developed later in the text; at this stage, it is most important to understand the layers of abstraction.

A programming model is realized in terms of the user-level communication primitives of the system, referred to here as the *communication abstraction*. Typically, the programming model is embodied in a parallel language or programming environment, so a mapping exists from the generic language constructs to the specific primitives of the system. These user-level primitives may be provided directly by the hardware, by the operating system, or by machine-specific user software that maps the communication abstractions to the actual hardware primitives. The distance between the lines in Figure 1.13 is intended to indicate that the mapping from one layer to the next may be very simple or very involved. For example, access to a shared location is realized directly by load and store instructions on a machine in which all processors use the same physical memory; however, passing a message on such a machine may involve a library or system call to write the message into a buffer area or to read it out.

The communication architecture defines the set of communication operations available to the user software, the format of these operations, and the data types they

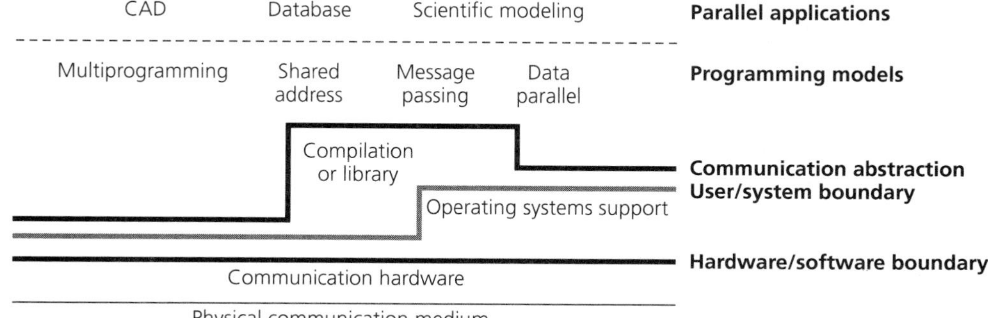

FIGURE 1.13 Layers of abstraction in parallel computer architecture. Critical layers of abstractions lie between the application program and the actual hardware. The application is written for a programming model, which dictates how pieces of the program share information and coordinate their activities. The specific operations providing communication and synchronization form the communication abstraction, which is the boundary between the user program and the system implementation. This abstraction is realized through compiler or library support using the primitives available from the hardware or from the operating system, which uses privileged hardware primitives. The communication hardware is organized to provide these operations efficiently on the physical wires connecting the machine together.

operate on, much as an instruction set architecture does for a processor. Note that even in conventional instruction sets, some operations may be realized by a combination of hardware and software, such as a load instruction that relies on operating system intervention in the case of a page fault. The communication architecture also extends the computer organization with the hardware structures that support communication.

As with conventional computer architecture, a great deal of debate has gone on over the years about what should be incorporated into each layer of abstraction in parallel architecture and how large the gap between the layers should be. This debate has been fueled by differing assumptions about the underlying technology and more qualitative assessments of "ease of programming." The hardware/software boundary in Figure 1.13 is depicted as flat to indicate that the available hardware primitives in different designs is more or less of uniform complexity. Indeed, this is becoming more the case as the field matures. In most early designs, the physical hardware organization was strongly oriented toward a particular programming model; that is, the communication abstraction supported by the hardware was essentially identical to the programming model. This "high-level" parallel architecture approach resulted in tremendous diversity in the hardware organizations. However, as the programming models have become better understood and implementation techniques have matured, compilers and run-time libraries have grown to provide an important bridge between the programming model and the underlying hardware. Simultaneously, the technological trends discussed in Section 1.1.2 have exerted a strong influence, regardless of the programming model. The result has been a convergence in the organizational structure with relatively simple, general-purpose communication primitives.

Sections 1.2.2–1.2.6 survey the most widely used programming models and the corresponding styles of machine design in past and current parallel machines. With the historical orientation to a particular programming model, it was common to lump the programming model, the communication abstraction, and the machine organization together as "the architecture," for example, shared memory architecture, message-passing architecture, and so on. This approach is less appropriate today since a large commonality exists across parallel machines and since many machines support several programming models. It is important to see how this convergence has come about, so these sections begin from the traditional perspective, looking at machine designs associated with particular programming models and explaining their intended roles and the technological opportunities that influenced their design. The goal of the survey is not to develop a taxonomy of parallel machines per se but to identify a set of core concepts that form the basis for assessing design trade-offs across the entire spectrum of potential designs today and in the future. It also demonstrates the influence that the dominant technological direction established by microprocessor and DRAM technologies has had on parallel machine design, which makes a common treatment of the fundamental design issues natural or even imperative. Specifically, shared address, message-passing, data parallel, dataflow, and systolic approaches are presented. In each case, the abstraction embodied in the programming model is explained, and the reasons for the particular style of design, as well as the intended scale and application, are presented. The technological motivations for the approach are also examined, as well as how they have changed over time. These changes are reflected in the machine organization, which determines what is fast and what is slow. The performance characteristics ripple up to influence aspects of the programming model. The outcome of this brief survey is a clear organizational convergence, which is captured in a generic parallel machine in Section 1.2.7.

1.2.2 Shared Address Space

One of the most important classes of parallel machines is *shared memory multiprocessors*. The key property of this class is that communication occurs implicitly as a result of conventional memory access instructions (i.e., loads and stores). This class has a long history, dating at least to precursors of mainframes in the early 1960s,[3] and today it has a role in almost every segment of the computer industry. Shared memory multiprocessors serve to provide better throughput on multiprogramming workloads, as well as to support parallel programs. Thus, they are naturally found across a wide range of scale, from a few processors to perhaps hundreds. This sec-

---

3. Some say that BINAC was the first multiprocessor, but it was intended to improve reliability. The two processors checked each other at every instruction. They seldom agreed, so people eventually turned one of them off.

tion examines the communication architecture of shared memory machines and the key organizational issues for small-scale designs and large configurations.

The primary programming model for these machines is essentially that of time-sharing on a single processor, except that real parallelism replaces interleaving in time. Formally, a *process* is a virtual address space and one or more threads of control. Processes can be configured so that portions of their address space are shared, that is, are mapped to a common physical location, as suggested by Figure 1.14. (Multiple threads within a process, by definition, share portions of the address space.) Cooperation and coordination among threads is accomplished by reading and writing shared variables and pointers referring to shared addresses. *Writes to a logically shared address by one thread are visible to reads of the other threads.* The communication architecture employs the conventional memory operations to provide communication through shared addresses as well as special atomic operations for synchronization. Even completely independent processes typically share the kernel portion of the address space, although this is only accessed by operating system code. Nonetheless, the shared address space model is utilized within the operating system to coordinate the execution of the processes.

Although shared memory can be used for communication among arbitrary collections of processes, most parallel programs are quite structured in their use of the virtual address space. They typically have a common code image, private segments for the stack and other private data, and shared segments that are in the same region of the virtual address space of each process or thread of the program. This simple structure implies that the private variables in the program are present in each process and that shared variables have the same address and meaning in each thread. Often, straightforward parallelization strategies are employed. For example, each process may perform a subset of the iterations of a common parallel loop or, more generally, processes may operate as a pool of workers obtaining work from a shared queue. Chapter 2 discusses the structure of parallel programs more deeply. Here we look at the basic evolution and development of this important architectural approach.

The communication hardware for shared memory multiprocessors is a natural extension of the memory system found in most computers. Essentially all computer systems allow a processor and a set of I/O controllers to access a collection of memory modules through some kind of hardware interconnect, as illustrated in Figure 1.15. The memory capacity is increased simply by adding memory modules. Additional capacity may or may not increase the available memory bandwidth, depending on the specific system organization. I/O capacity is increased by adding devices to I/O controllers or by inserting additional I/O controllers. There are two possible ways to increase the processing capacity: wait for a faster processor to become available or add more processors. On a time-sharing workload, increasing processing capacity should increase the throughput of the system. With more processors, more processes can run at once and throughput is increased. If a single application is programmed to make use of multiple threads, more processors should speed up the application. The hardware primitives are essentially one to one with the communication abstraction, and these operations are available in the programming model.

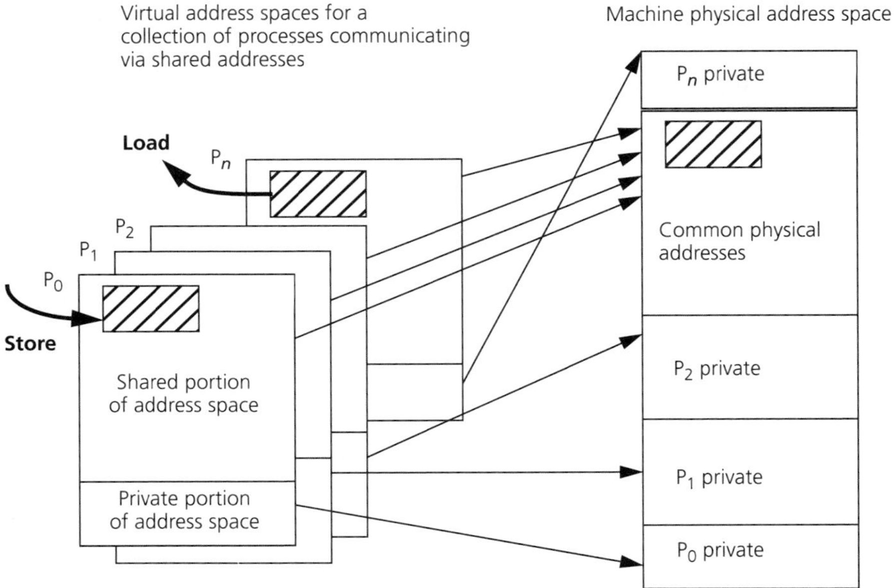

FIGURE 1.14 Typical memory model for shared memory parallel programs. Collections of processes have a common region of physical addresses mapped into their virtual address space, in addition to the private region, which typically contains the stack and private data.

Within the general framework of Figure 1.15, a great deal of evolution of shared memory machines has taken place as the underlying technology has advanced. The early machines were "high-end" mainframe configurations (Lonergan and King 1961; Padegs 1981). On the technology side, memory in early mainframes was slow compared to the processor, so it was necessary to interleave data across several memory banks to obtain adequate bandwidth for even a single processor; this required an interconnect between the processor and each of the banks. On the application side, these systems were primarily designed for throughput on a large number of jobs. Thus, to meet the I/O demands of a workload, several I/O channels and devices were attached. The I/O channels also required direct access to each of the memory banks. Therefore, these systems were typically organized with a *crossbar switch* connecting the CPU and several I/O channels to several memory banks, as indicated by Figure 1.16a. Adding processors was primarily a matter of expanding the switch; the hardware structure to access a memory location from a port on the processor and I/O side of the switch was unchanged. The size and cost of the processor limited these early systems to a small number of processors, but as the hardware density and cost improved, larger systems could be contemplated. The cost of scaling the crossbar became the limiting factor, and in many cases it was replaced by a *multistage interconnect*, suggested by Figure 1.16b, for which the cost increases more slowly with

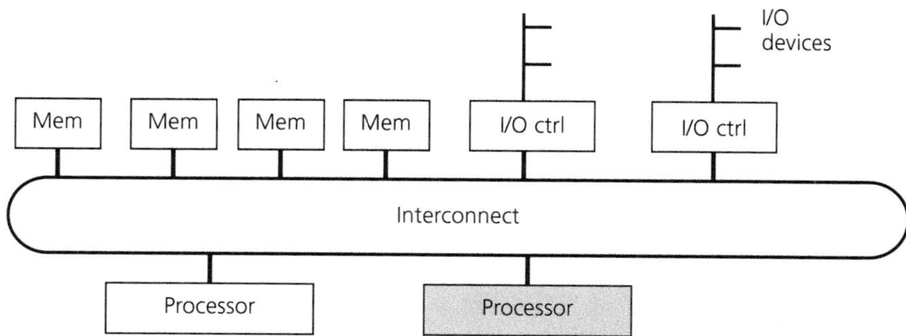

FIGURE 1.15 Extending a system into a shared memory multiprocessor by adding processor modules. Most systems consist of one or more memory modules accessible by a processor and I/O controllers through a hardware interconnect, typically a bus, crossbar, or multistage interconnect. Memory and I/O capacity are increased by attaching memory and I/O modules. Shared memory machines allow processing capacity to be increased by adding processor modules (shown as shaded).

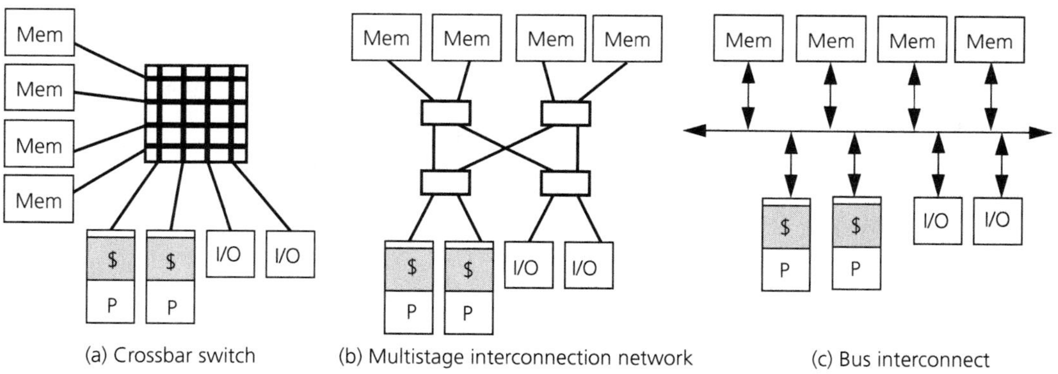

FIGURE 1.16 Typical shared memory multiprocessor interconnection schemes. The interconnection of multiple processors, with their local caches (indicated by $), and I/O controllers to multiple memory modules may be via crossbar, multistage interconnection network, or bus.

the number of ports. These savings come at the expense of increased latency and decreased bandwidth per port if all are used at once. The ability to access all memory directly from each processor has several advantages: any processor can run any process or handle any I/O event, and data structures can be shared within the operating system.

The widespread use of shared memory multiprocessor designs came about with the 32-bit microprocessor revolution in the mid-1980s because the processor, cache, floating-point, and memory management unit fit on a single board (Bell 1985) or even two to a board. Most mid-range machines, including minicomputers, servers, workstations, and personal computers, are organized around a central memory bus, as illustrated in Figure 1.16c, and the bus could be adapted to support multiple

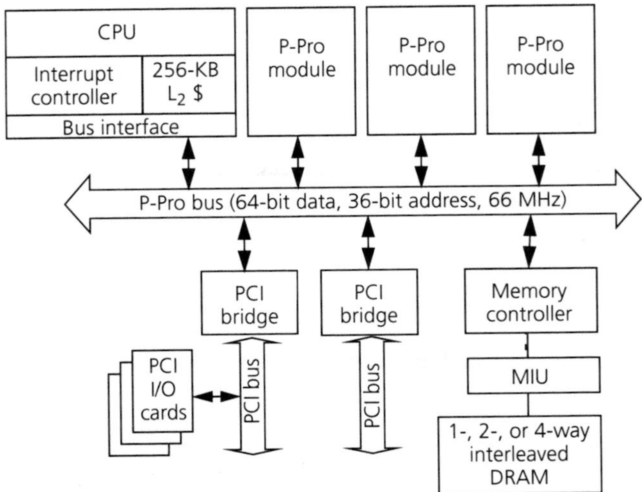

FIGURE 1.17(a) Physical and logical organization of the Intel Pentium Pro four-processor "quad pack." The Intel quad-processor Pentium Pro motherboard employed in many multiprocessor servers illustrates the major design elements of most small-scale shared memory multiprocessors. Its logical block diagram (a) shows that it can accommodate up to four processor modules, each containing a Pentium Pro processor, first-level caches, translation lookaside buffer, a 256-KB second-level cache, an interrupt controller, and a bus interface in a single chip connecting directly to a 64-bit memory bus. The bus operates at 66 MHz, and memory transactions are pipelined to give a peak bandwidth of 528 MB/s. A two-chip memory controller and four-chip memory interleave unit (MIU) connect the bus to multiple banks of DRAM. Bridges connect the memory bus to two independent PCI buses, which host display, network, SCSI, and lower-speed I/O connections. The Pentium Pro module contains all the logic necessary to support the multiprocessor communication architecture, including that required for memory and cache consistency. The structure of the Pentium Pro "quad pack" is similar to a large number of earlier SMP designs but has a much higher degree of integration and is targeted at a much larger volume. (b) shows an expanded view of a typical Pentium Pro SMP, an HP NetServer in the LX series. *Source:* Reproduced with permission of Hewlett-Packard Company.

processors. The standard bus access mechanism allows any processor to access any physical address in the system. Like the switch-based designs, all memory locations are equidistant to all processors, so all processors experience the same access time, or latency, on a memory reference. This configuration is usually called a *symmetric multiprocessor* (SMP).[4] SMPs are heavily used for execution of parallel programs as well as multiprogramming. The typical organization of the bus-based symmetric multiprocessor is illustrated in more detail by Figure 1.17, which describes the first

4. The term SMP is widely used but causes a bit of confusion. What exactly needs to be symmetric? Many designs are symmetric in some respect. The more precise description of what is intended by SMP is a shared memory multiprocessor where the cost of accessing a memory location is the same for all processors; that is, it has uniform access costs when the access actually is to memory. If the location is cached, the access will be faster, but cache access times and memory access times are the same on all processors.

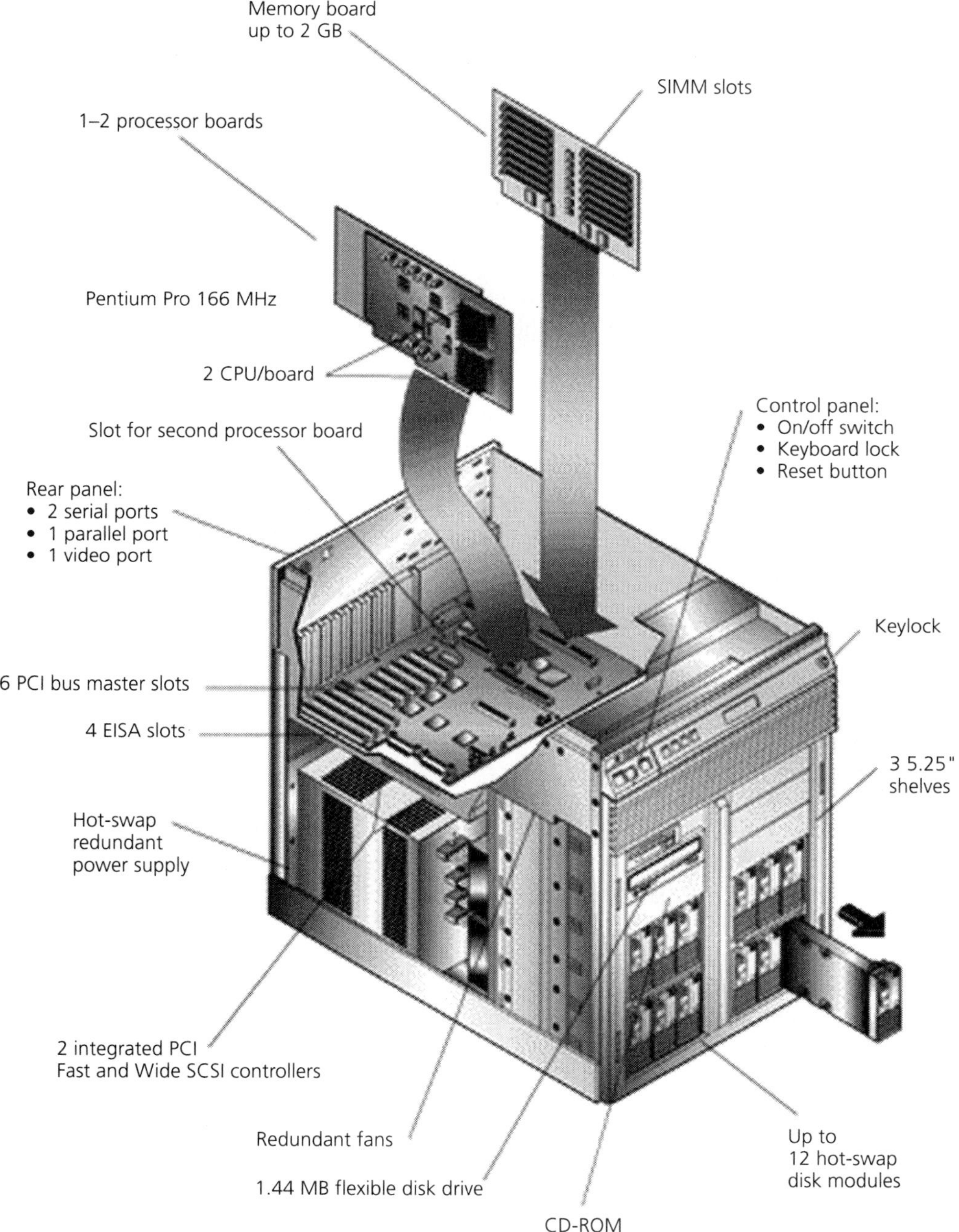

FIGURE 1.17(b) Physical organization of the Intel Pentium Pro four-processor "quad pack"

highly integrated SMP for the commodity market. Figure 1.18 illustrates a high-end server organization that distributes the physical memory over the processor modules, but retains symmetric access.

The factors limiting the number of processors that can be supported with a bus-based organization are quite different from those in the switch-based approach. Adding processors to the switch is expensive; however, the aggregate bandwidth increases with the number of ports. The cost of adding a processor to the bus is small, but the aggregate bandwidth is fixed. Dividing this fixed bandwidth among the larger number of processors limits the practical scalability of the approach. (It is this critical bus bandwidth that is depicted in Figure 1.9.) Fortunately, caches reduce the bandwidth demand of each processor since many references are satisfied by the cache rather than by the memory. However, with data replicated in local caches, there is the potentially challenging problem of keeping the caches "consistent," which will be examined in detail in Chapters 5, 6, and 8.

Starting from a baseline of small-scale shared memory machines, illustrated in Figures 1.16–1.18, we may ask what is required to scale the design to a large number of processors. The basic processor component is well suited to the task since it is small and economical, but a problem clearly exists with the interconnect. The bus does not scale because it has a fixed aggregate bandwidth. The crossbar does not scale well because the cost increases as the square of the number of ports. Many alternative scalable interconnection networks exist, such that the aggregate bandwidth increases as more processors are added, but the cost does not become excessive. We need to be careful about the resulting increase in latency because the processor may stall while a memory operation moves from the processor to the memory module and back. If the latency of access becomes too large, the processors will spend much of their time waiting, and the advantages of more processors may be offset by poor utilization.

One natural approach to building scalable shared memory machines is to maintain the uniform memory access (or "dancehall") approach of Figure 1.15 and provide a scalable interconnect between the processors and the memories. Every memory access is translated into a message transaction over the network, much as it might be translated to a bus transaction in the SMP designs. The primary disadvantage of this approach is that the round-trip network latency is experienced on every memory access and a large bandwidth must be supplied to every processor.

An alternative approach is to interconnect complete processors, each with a local memory, as illustrated in Figure 1.19. In this nonuniform memory access (NUMA) approach, the local memory controller determines whether to perform a local memory access or a message transaction with a remote memory controller. Accessing local memory is faster than accessing remote memory. (The I/O system may either be a part of every node or consolidated into special I/O nodes, not shown.) Accesses to private data, such as code and stack, can often be performed locally, as can accesses to shared data that, by accident or intent, are stored on the local node. The ability to access the local memory quickly does not increase the time to access remote data

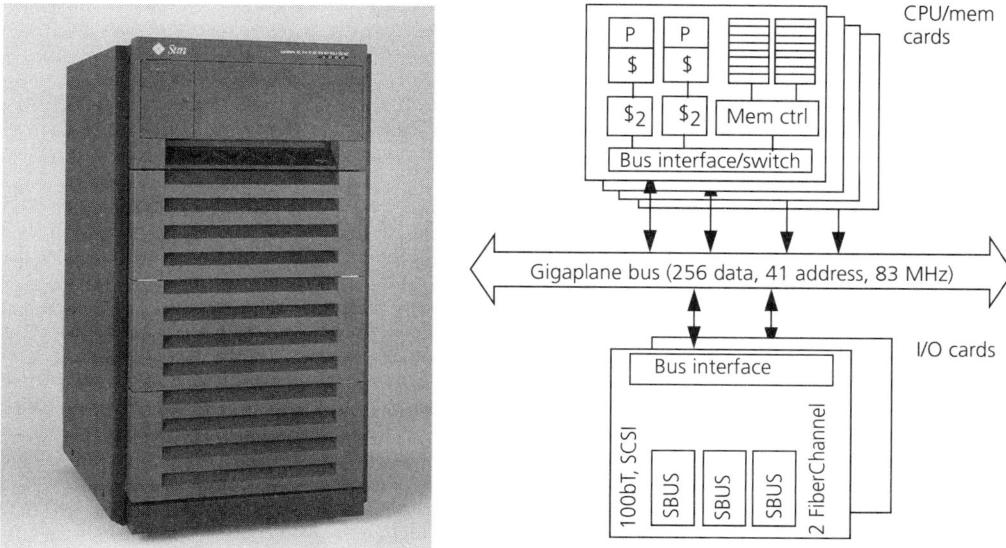

FIGURE 1.18 Physical and logical organization of the Sun Enterprise Server. A larger-scale design is illustrated by the Sun UltraSparc-based Enterprise multiprocessor server. The diagram shows its physical structure and logical organization. A wide (256-bit), highly pipelined memory bus delivers 2.5 GB/s of memory bandwidth. This design uses a hierarchical structure, where each card is either a complete dual processor with memory or a complete I/O system. The full configuration supports 16 cards of either type, with at least one of each. The CPU/mem card contains two UltraSparc processor modules, each with 16-KB level 1 and 512-KB level 2 caches, plus two 512-bit-wide memory banks and an internal switch. Thus, adding processors adds memory capacity and memory interleaving. The I/O card provides three SBUS slots for I/O extensions, a SCSI connector, a 100bT Ethernet port, and two FiberChannel interfaces. A typical complete configuration would be 24 processors and 6 I/O cards. Although memory banks are physically packaged with pairs of processors, all memory is equidistant from all processors and accessed over the common bus, preserving the SMP characteristics. Data may be placed anywhere in the machine with no performance impact. *Source:* The copyright for this photograph is owned by Sun Microsystems, Inc. and is used herein by permission.

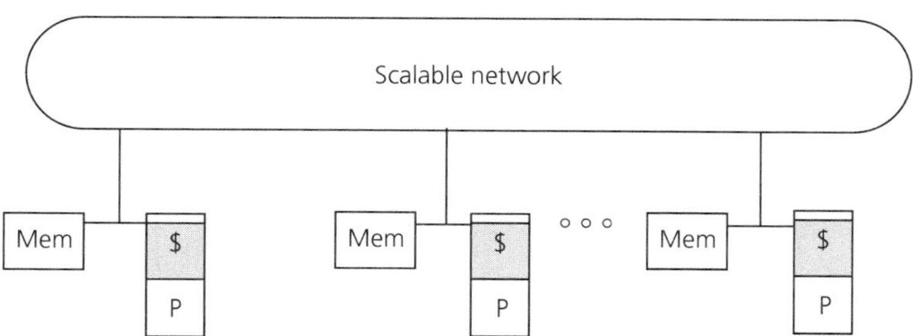

FIGURE 1.19 Nonuniform memory access (NUMA) scalable shared memory multiprocessor organization. Processor and memory modules are closely integrated such that access to local memory is faster than access to remote memories.

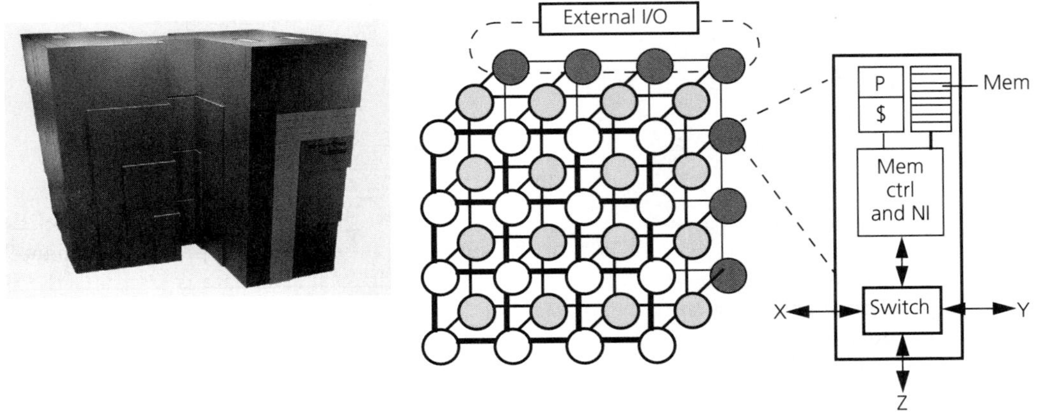

FIGURE 1.20 CRAY T3E scalable shared address space machine. The CRAY T3E is designed to scale up to a thousand processors supporting a global shared address space. Each node contains a DEC Alpha processor, local memory, a network interface integrated with the memory controller, and a network switch. The machine is organized as a three-dimensional cube, with each node connected to its six neighbors through 650-MB/s point-to-point links. Any processor can read or write any memory location; however, the NUMA characteristic of the machine is exposed in the communication architecture as well as in its performance characteristics. A short sequence of instructions is required to establish addressability to remote memory, which can then be accessed by conventional loads and stores. The memory controller captures the access to a remote memory and conducts a message transaction with the memory controller of the remote node on the local processor's behalf. The message transaction is automatically routed through intermediate nodes to the desired destination, with a small delay per "hop." The remote data is not cached since there is no hardware mechanism to keep it consistent. (We will look at other design points that allow shared data to be replicated throughout the processor caches.) The CRAY T3E I/O system is distributed over a collection of nodes on the surface of the cube, which are connected to the external world through an additional I/O network. *Source:* Photo courtesy of CRAY Research.

appreciably, so it reduces the average access time, especially when a large fraction of the accesses are to local data. The bandwidth demand placed on the network is also reduced. Although some conceptual simplicity arises from having all shared data equidistant from any processor, the NUMA approach has become far more prevalent at a large scale because of its inherent performance advantages and because it harnesses more of the mainstream processor memory system technology. One example of this style of design is the CRAY T3E, illustrated in Figure 1.20. This machine reflects the viewpoint that, although all memory is accessible to every processor, the distribution of memory across processors is exposed to the programmer. Caches are used only to hold data (and instructions) from local memory. It is the programmer's job to avoid frequent remote references. The SGI Origin is an example of a machine with a similar organizational structure, but it allows data from any memory to be replicated into any of the caches and provides hardware support to keep the caches consistent without relying on a bus connecting all the modules with a common set of wires. While this book was being written, these two designs literally converged following the merger of the two companies.

To summarize, communication and cooperation in the shared address space programming model consists of reads and writes to shared variables; these operations are mapped directly to a communication abstraction consisting of load and store instructions accessing a global, shared address space, which is supported directly in hardware through access to shared physical memory locations. The programming model and communication abstraction are very close to the actual hardware. Each processor can *name* every physical location in the machine; a process can name all data it shares with others within its virtual address space. Data is transferred either as primitive types in the instruction set (bytes, words, etc.) or as cache blocks. Each process performs memory operations on addresses in its virtual address space; the address translation process identifies a physical location, which may be local or remote to the processor and may be shared with other processes. In either case, the hardware accesses it directly, without user or operating system software intervention. The address translation realizes protection within the shared address space, just as it does for uniprocessors, since a process can only access the data in its virtual address space.

The effectiveness of the shared memory approach depends on the latency incurred on memory accesses as well as the bandwidth of data transfer that can be supported. Just as a memory storage hierarchy allows data that is bound to an address to be migrated toward the processor, expressing communication in terms of the storage address space allows shared data to be migrated toward the processor that accesses it. However, migrating and replicating data across a general-purpose interconnect presents a unique set of challenges. We will see that to achieve scalability in such a design, the entire solution, including the hardware interconnect mechanisms used for maintaining the consistent shared memory abstractions, must scale well.

1.2.3 Message Passing

A second important class of parallel machines, called *message-passing architectures*, employs complete computers as building blocks—including the microprocessor, memory, and I/O system—and provides communication between processors as explicit I/O operations. The high-level block diagram for a message-passing machine is essentially the same as the NUMA shared memory approach shown in Figure 1.19. The primary difference is that communication is integrated at the I/O level rather than into the memory system. This style of design also has much in common with networks of workstations, or *clusters,* except that the packaging of the nodes is typically much tighter, there is no monitor or keyboard per node, and the network is of much higher capability than a standard local area network. The integration between the processor and the network tends to be much tighter than in traditional I/O structures, which support connection to devices that are much slower than the processor, since message passing is fundamentally processor-to-processor communication.

In message passing, a substantial distance exists between the programming model and the actual hardware primitives, with user communication performed through operating system or library calls that perform many lower-level actions, including the actual communication operation. Thus, our discussion of message passing begins with a look at the communication abstraction and then briefly surveys the evolution of hardware organizations supporting this abstraction.

The most common user-level communication operations on message-passing systems are variants of send and receive. In its simplest form, *send* specifies a local data buffer that is to be transmitted and a receiving process (typically on a remote processor). *Receive* specifies a sending process and a local data buffer into which the transmitted data is to be placed. Together, the matching send and receive cause a data transfer from one process to another, as indicated in Figure 1.21. In most message-passing systems, the send operation also allows an identifier or *tag* to be attached to the message, and the receiving operation specifies a matching rule (such as a specific tag from a specific processor, or any tag from any processor). Thus, the user program names local addresses and entries in an abstract process-tag space. *The combination of a send and a matching receive accomplishes a pairwise synchronization event and a memory-to-memory copy, where each end specifies its local data address.* There are several possible variants of this synchronization event, depending upon whether the send completes when the receive has been executed, when the send buffer is available for reuse, or when the request has been accepted. Similarly, the receive can potentially wait until a matching send occurs or simply post the receive. Each of these variants has somewhat different semantics and different implementation requirements.

Message passing has long been used as a means of communication and synchronization among arbitrary collections of cooperating sequential processes, even on a single processor. Important examples include programming languages, such as CSP and Occam, and common operating systems functions, such as sockets. Parallel programs using message passing are typically quite structured. Most often, all nodes execute identical copies of a program, with the same code and private variables. Usually, processes can name each other using a simple linear ordering of the processes comprising a program.

Early message-passing machines provided hardware primitives that were very close to the simple send/receive user-level communication abstraction, with some additional restrictions. A node was connected to a fixed set of neighbors in a regular pattern by point-to-point links that behaved as simple FIFOs (Seitz 1985). This sort of design is illustrated in Figure 1.22 for a small 3D cube. Many early machines were *hypercubes*, where each node is connected to n other nodes differing by one bit in the binary address, for a total of 2^n nodes. Others were *meshes*, where the nodes are connected to neighbors on two or three dimensions. The network topology was especially important in the early message-passing machines because only the neighboring processors could be named in a send or receive operation. The data transfer involved the sender writing to a link and the receiver reading from the link. The FIFOs were small and so the sender would not be able to finish writing the mes-

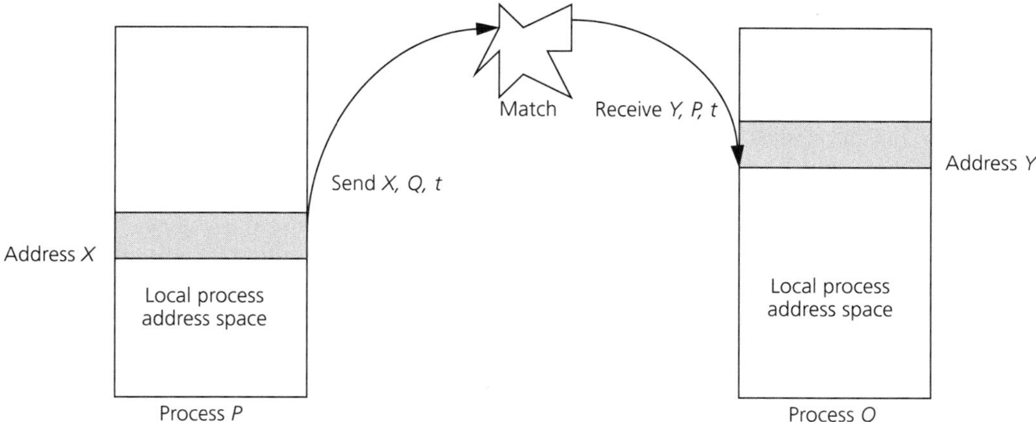

FIGURE 1.21 User-level send/receive message-passing abstraction. A data transfer from one local address space to another occurs when a send to a particular process is matched with a receive posted by that process.

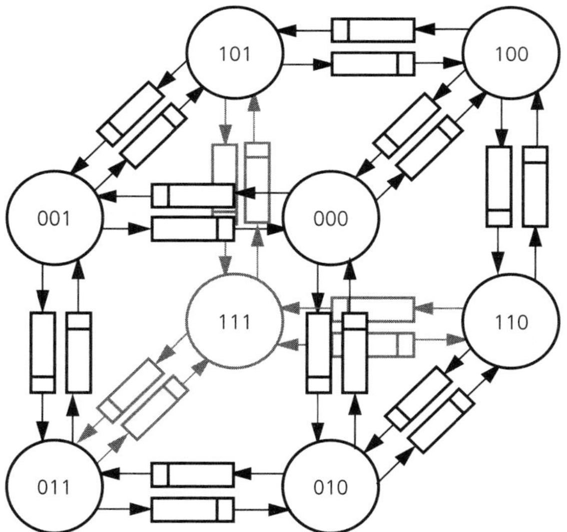

FIGURE 1.22 Typical structure of an early message-passing machine. Each node is connected to neighbors in three dimensions via FIFOs.

sage until the receiver started reading it, so the send would block until the receive occurred. (In modern terms, this is called *synchronous* message passing because the two events coincide in time.) The details of moving data were hidden from the programmer in a message-passing library, forming a layer of software between send and receive calls and the actual hardware.[5]

The direct FIFO design was soon replaced by more versatile and more robust designs that provided *direct memory access* (DMA) transfers on either end of the communication event. A DMA device is a special-purpose controller that transfers data between memory and an I/O device without engaging the processor until the transfer is complete. The use of DMA allowed *nonblocking sends*, where the sender is able to initiate a send and continue with useful computation (or even perform a receive) while the send completes. On the receiving end, the transfer is accepted via a DMA transfer by the message layer into a buffer and queued until the target process performs a matching receive, at which point the data is copying into the address space of the receiving process.

The physical topology of the communication network so dominated the programming model of these early machines that parallel algorithms were often stated in terms of a specific interconnection topology, for example, a ring, a grid, or a hypercube (Fox et al. 1988). However, to make the machines more generally useful, the designers of the message layers provided support for communication between arbitrary processors rather than only between physical neighbors. This was originally supported by forwarding the data within the message layer along links in the network. Soon this routing function was moved into the hardware (as discussed in Chapter 10), so each node consisted of a processor with memory and a switch that could forward messages. However, in this approach, known as *store-and-forward*, the time to transfer a message is proportional to the number of hops it takes through the network, so an emphasis remained on interconnection topology. (See Exercise 1.7 for a brief store-and-forward example.)

The emphasis on network topology was significantly reduced with the introduction of more general-purpose networks, which pipelined the message transfer through each of the routers forming the interconnection network (Barton, Crownie, and McLaren 1994; Bomans and Roose 1989; Dunigan 1988; Homewood and McLaren 1993; Leiserson et al. 1996; Pierce and Regnier 1994; von Eicken et al. 1992). In most modern message-passing machines, the incremental delay introduced by each hop is small enough that the transfer time is dominated by the time to simply move that data between the processor and the network, not how far it travels (Groscup 1992; Homewood and McLaren 1993; Horiw et al. 1993; Pierce and Regnier 1994). This greatly simplifies the programming model; typically, the processors are viewed as simply forming a linear sequence with uniform communication costs. In other words, the communication abstraction reflects an organizational structure much as in Figure 1.19. One important example of such a machine is the IBM SP-2, illustrated in Figure 1.23, which is constructed from RS6000 workstation nodes, a scalable network, and a network interface containing a dedicated processor. Another

5. The motivation for synchronous message passing was not just from the machine structure; it was also present in important programming languages, especially CSP (Hoare 1978), because of its clean theoretical properties. Early in the microprocessor era, the approach was captured in a single-chip building block, the Transputer, which was widely touted during its development by INMOS as a revolution in computing.

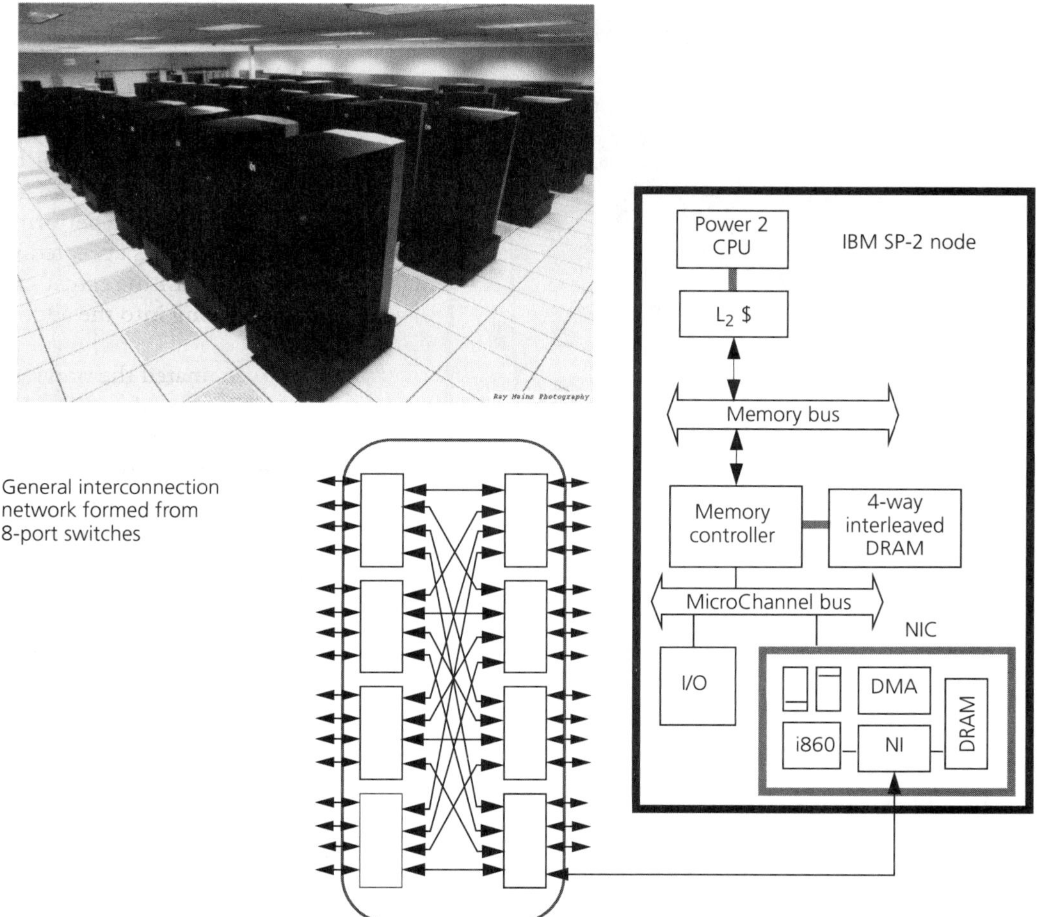

FIGURE 1.23 IBM SP-2 message-passing machine. The IBM SP-2 is a scalable parallel machine constructed essentially out of complete RS6000 workstations. Modest modifications are made to package the workstations into standing racks. A network interface card (NIC) is inserted at the MicroChannel I/O bus. The NIC contains the drivers for the actual link into the network, a substantial amount of memory to buffer message data, a direct memory access (DMA) engine, and a complete i860 microprocessor to move data between host memory and the network. The network itself is a butterfly-like structure, constructed by cascading 8 × 8 crossbar switches. The links operate at 40 MB/s in each direction, which is the full capability of the I/O bus. Several other machines employ a similar network interface design but connect directly to the memory bus rather than at the I/O bus. *Source:* Ray Mains Photography.

is the Intel Paragon, illustrated in Figure 1.24, which integrates the network interface more tightly to the processors in SMP nodes, where one of the processors is dedicated to supporting message passing.

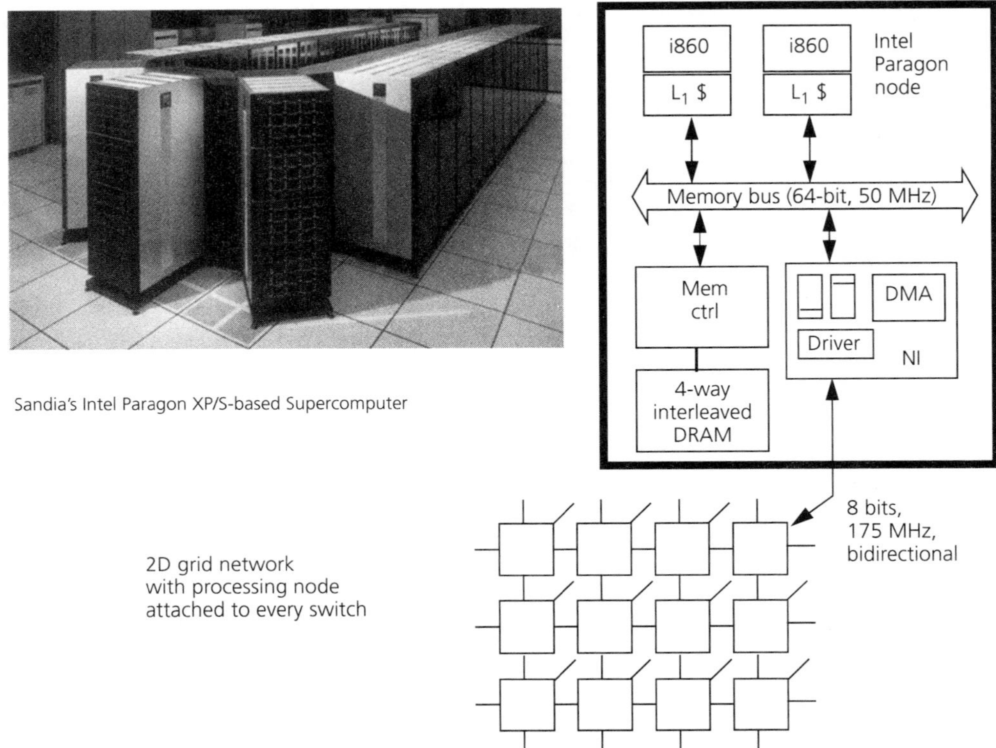

FIGURE 1.24 Intel Paragon. The Intel Paragon illustrates a much tighter packaging of nodes. Each card is an SMP with two or more i860 processors and a network interface chip connected to the cache-coherent memory bus. One of the processors is dedicated to servicing the network. In addition, the node has a DMA engine to transfer contiguous chunks of data to and from the network at a high rate. The network is a 3D grid, much like the CRAY T3E, with links operating at 175 MB/s in each direction. *Source:* Photo courtesy of Intel Corporation.

A processor in a message-passing machine can name only the locations in its local memory and each of the processors, perhaps by number or by route. A user process can only name private addresses and other processes; it can transfer data using the send/receive calls.

1.2.4 Convergence

Evolution of the hardware and software has blurred the once clear boundary between the shared memory and message-passing camps. First, consider the communication operations available to the user process.

- Traditional message-passing operations (send/receive) are supported on most shared memory machines through shared buffer storage. Send involves writing data, or a pointer to data, into the buffer; receive involves reading the data from shared storage. Flags or locks are used to control access to the buffer and to indicate events such as message arrival.
- On a message-passing machine, a user process may construct a global address space of sorts by carrying along pointers specifying the process and local virtual address in that process. Access to such a global address can be performed in software through an explicit message transaction. Most message-passing libraries allow a process to accept a message for any process, so each process can serve data requests from the others. A logical read is realized by sending a request to the process containing the object and receiving a response. The actual message transaction may be hidden from the user; it may be carried out by compiler-generated code for access to a shared variable.
- A shared virtual address space can be established on a message-passing machine at the page level. A collection of processes has a region of shared addresses but, for each process, only the pages that are local to it are accessible. Upon access to a missing (i.e., remote) page, a page fault occurs and the operating system engages the remote node in a message transaction to transfer the page and map it into the user address space.

At the level of machine organization, substantial convergence has occurred as well. Modern message-passing architectures appear essentially identical at the block diagram level to the scalable NUMA design illustrated in Figure 1.19. In the shared memory case, the network interface was integrated with the cache controller or memory controller in order for that device to observe cache misses and to conduct a message transaction to access memory in a remote node. In the message-passing approach, the network interface is essentially an I/O device. However, the trend has been to integrate this device more deeply into the memory system as well and to transfer data directly from and to the user address space. Some designs provide DMA transfers across the network, from memory on one machine to memory on the other machine, so the network interface is integrated fairly deeply with the memory system. Message passing is implemented on top of these remote memory copies (Barton, Crownie, and McLaren 1994). In some designs, a complete processor assists in communication, sharing a cache-coherent memory bus with the main processor (Groscup 1992; Pierce and Regnier 1994). Viewing the convergence from the other side, clearly all large-scale shared memory operations are ultimately implemented as message transactions at some level.

In addition to the convergence of scalable message-passing and shared memory machines, switch-based local area networks, including fast Ethernet, ATM, FiberChannel, and several proprietary designs (Boden et al. 1995; Gillett 1996) have emerged, providing scalable interconnects that are approaching what traditional parallel machines offer. These new networks are being used to connect collections of machines (which may be shared memory multiprocessors in their own right) into *clusters*, which may operate as a parallel machine on individual large problems or as many individual machines on a multiprogramming load. Essentially all SMP vendors provide some form of network clustering to obtain better reliability.

In summary, message passing and a shared address space represent two clearly distinct programming models, each providing a well-defined paradigm for sharing, communication, and synchronization. However, the underlying machine structures have converged toward a common organization, represented by a collection of complete computers, augmented by a "communication assist" connecting each node to a scalable communication network. Thus, it is natural to consider supporting aspects of both in a common framework. Integrating the communication assist more tightly into the memory system tends to reduce the latency of network transactions and improve the bandwidth that can be supplied to or accepted from the network. We will want to look much more carefully at the precise nature of this integration and understand how it interacts with cache design, address translation, protection, and other traditional aspects of computer architecture.

1.2.5 Data Parallel Processing

A third important class of parallel machines has been variously called processor arrays, single-instruction-multiple-data machines, and data parallel architectures. The changing names reflect a gradual separation of the user-level abstraction from the machine operation. *The key characteristic of the data parallel programming model is that operations can be performed in parallel on each element of a large regular data structure, such as an array or matrix.* The program is logically a single thread of control, carrying out a sequence of either sequential or parallel steps. Within this general paradigm have been many novel designs, exploiting various technological opportunities, and considerable evolution as microprocessor technology has become such a dominant force.

An influential paper in the early 1970s (Flynn 1972) developed a taxonomy of computers, known as *Flynn's taxonomy*, which characterizes designs in terms of the number of distinct instructions issued at a time and the number of data elements they operate on: conventional sequential computers being *single-instruction-single-data* (SISD) and parallel machines built from multiple conventional processors being *multiple-instruction-multiple-data* (MIMD). The revolutionary alternative was *single-instruction-multiple-data* (SIMD). Its history is rooted in the mid-1960s when an individual processor was a cabinet full of equipment and an instruction fetch cost as much in time and hardware as performing the actual instruction. The idea was that all the instruction sequencing could be consolidated in the control processor. The data processors included only the ALU, memory, and a simple connection to nearest neighbors.

In the SIMD machines, the data parallel programming model was rendered directly in the physical hardware (Ball et al. 1962; Bouknight et al. 1972; Cornell 1972; Reddaway 1973; Slotnick, Borck, and McReynolds 1962; Slotnick 1967; Vick and Cornell 1978). Typically, a control processor broadcasts each instruction to an array of data processing elements (PEs), which are connected to form a regular grid,

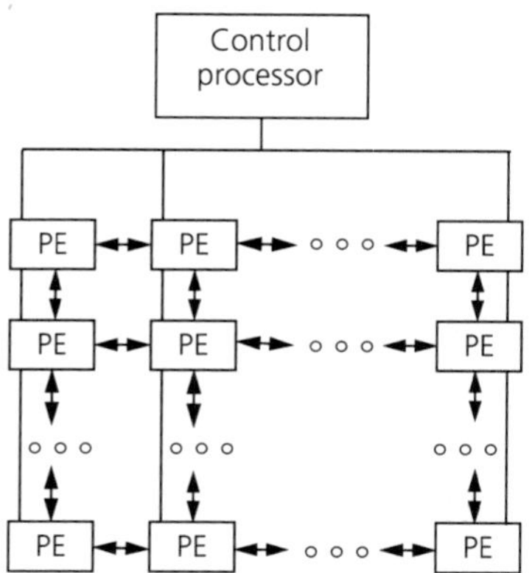

FIGURE 1.25 Typical organization of a data parallel (SIMD) machine. Individual processing elements (PEs) operate in lockstep under the direction of a single control processor. Traditionally, SIMD machines have provided a limited, regular interconnect among the PEs, although this was generalized in later machines, such as the Thinking Machines Corporation Connection Machine and the MasPar.

as suggested by Figure 1.25. It was observed that many important scientific computations involved uniform calculation on every element of an array or matrix, often involving neighboring elements in the row or column. Thus, the parallel problem data was distributed over the memories of the data processors, and scalar data was retained in the control processor's memory. The control processor instructed the data processors to each perform an operation on local data elements or to all perform a communication operation. For example, to average each element of a matrix with its four neighbors, a copy of the matrix would be shifted across the PEs in each of the four directions and a local accumulation performed in each PE. Data PEs typically included a condition flag, allowing some to abstain from an operation. In some designs, the local address could be specified with an indirect addressing mode, allowing all processors to do the same operation but with different local data addresses.

The development of arrays of processors was almost completely eclipsed in the mid-1970s with the development of vector processors. In these machines, a scalar processor is integrated with a collection of function units that operate on vectors of data out of one memory in a pipelined fashion. The ability to operate on vectors anywhere in memory eliminated the need to map application data structures onto a rigid interconnection structure and greatly simplified the problem of getting data aligned so that local operations could be performed. The first vector processor, the CDC Star-100, provided vector operations in its instruction set that combined two source vectors from memory and produced a result vector in memory. The machine only operated at full speed if the vectors were contiguous, and hence a large fraction of the execution time was spent simply transposing matrices. A dramatic change occurred in 1976 with the introduction of the CRAY-1, which extended the concept of a load-store architecture employed in the CDC 6600 and CDC 7600 (and rediscovered in modern RISC machines) to apply to vectors. Vectors in memory, of any fixed stride, were transferred to or from contiguous vector registers by vector load and store instructions. Arithmetic was performed on the vector registers. The use of a very fast scalar processor (operating at the unprecedented rate of 80 MHz), tightly integrated with the vector operations and utilizing a large semiconductor memory rather than core, took over the world of supercomputing. Over the next twenty years, CRAY Research led the supercomputing market by increasing the bandwidth for vector memory transfers, the number of processors, the number of vector pipelines, and the length of the vector registers, resulting in the performance growth indicated in Figures 1.10 and 1.11.

The SIMD data parallel machine experienced a renaissance in the mid-1980s, as VLSI advances made simple 32-bit processors just barely practical (Batcher 1974, 1980; Hillis 1985; Nickolls 1990; Tucker and Robertson 1988). The unique twist in the data parallel regime was to place 32 very simple 1-bit processing elements on each chip, along with serial connections to neighboring processors, while consolidating the instruction sequencing capability in the control processor. In this way, systems with several thousand bit-serial processing elements could be constructed at reasonable cost. In addition, it was recognized that the utility of such a system could be increased dramatically with the provision of a general interconnect allowing an arbitrary communication pattern to take place in a single, rather long step, in addition to the regular grid neighbor connections (Hillis 1985; Hillis and Steele 1986; Nickolls 1990). The sequencing mechanism that expanded conventional integer and floating-point operations into a sequence of bit-serial operations also provided a means of "virtualizing" the processing elements, so that a few thousand processing elements could give the illusion of operating in parallel on millions of data elements with one virtual PE per data element.

The technological factors that made this bit-serial design attractive also provided fast, inexpensive, single-chip floating-point units and rapidly gave way to very fast microprocessors with integrated floating point and caches. This eliminated the cost advantage of consolidating the sequencing logic and provided equal peak performance on a much smaller number of complete processors. The simple, regular calculations on large matrices that motivated the data parallel approach also have tremendous spatial and temporal locality (if the computation is properly mapped onto a smaller number of complete processors), with each processor responsible for a large number of logically contiguous data points. Caches and local memory can be brought to bear on the set of data points local to each node while communication occurs across the boundaries or as a global rearrangement of data.

Thus, while the user-level abstraction of parallel operations on large regular data structures continued to offer an attractive solution to an important class of problems, the machine organization employed with data parallel programming models evolved toward a more generic parallel architecture of multiple cooperating microprocessors, much like scalable shared memory and message-passing machines, although several designs maintain specialized network support for global synchronization. One such example of network support is for a *barrier*, which causes each process to wait at a particular point in the program until all other processes have reached that point (Horiw et al. 1993; Leiserson et al. 1996; Kumar 1992; Kessler and Schwarzmeier 1993; Koeninger, Furtney, and Walker 1994). Indeed, the SIMD approach evolved into the SPMD (single-program-multiple-data) approach, in which all processors execute copies of the same program, and has thus largely converged with the more structured forms of shared memory and message-passing programming.

Data parallel programming languages are usually implemented by viewing the local address spaces of a collection of processes, one per processor, as forming an explicit global address space. Data structures are laid out across this global address space with a simple mapping from indexes to processor and local offset. The computation is organized as a sequence of "bulk synchronous" phases of either local computation or global communication, separated by a global barrier (Valiant 1990). Because all processors perform communication together and share a global view of what is going on, either a shared address space or message passing can be employed. For example, if a phase involved every processor doing a write to an address in the processor "to the left," it could be realized by each doing a send to the left and a receive "from the right" into the destination address. Similarly, every processor doing a read can be realized by every processor sending the address and then every processor sending back the data. In fact, the code that is produced by compilers for modern data parallel languages is essentially the same as for the structured control-parallel programs that are most common in shared memory and message-passing programming models. The convergence in machine structure has been accompanied by a convergence in how the machines are actually used.

1.2.6 Other Parallel Architectures

The mid-1980s renaissance gave rise to several other architectural directions that received considerable investigation by academia and industry, but enjoyed less commercial success than the three classes just discussed and therefore experienced less use as a vehicle for parallel programming. Two approaches that were developed into complete programming systems were dataflow architectures and systolic architectures. Both represent important conceptual developments of continuing value as the field evolves.

Dataflow Architecture

Dataflow models of computation sought to make the essential aspects of a parallel computation explicit at the machine level, without imposing artificial constraints that would limit the available parallelism in the program. The idea is that the program is represented by a graph of essential data dependences, as illustrated in Figure 1.26, rather than as a fixed collection of explicitly sequenced threads of control. An instruction may execute whenever its data operands are available. The graph may be spread arbitrarily over a collection of processors. Each node specifies an operation to perform and the address of each of the nodes that need the result. In the original form, a processor in a dataflow machine operates as a simple circular pipeline. A message, or *token*, from the network consists of data and an address, or *tag*, of its destination node. The tag is compared against those in a matching store. If

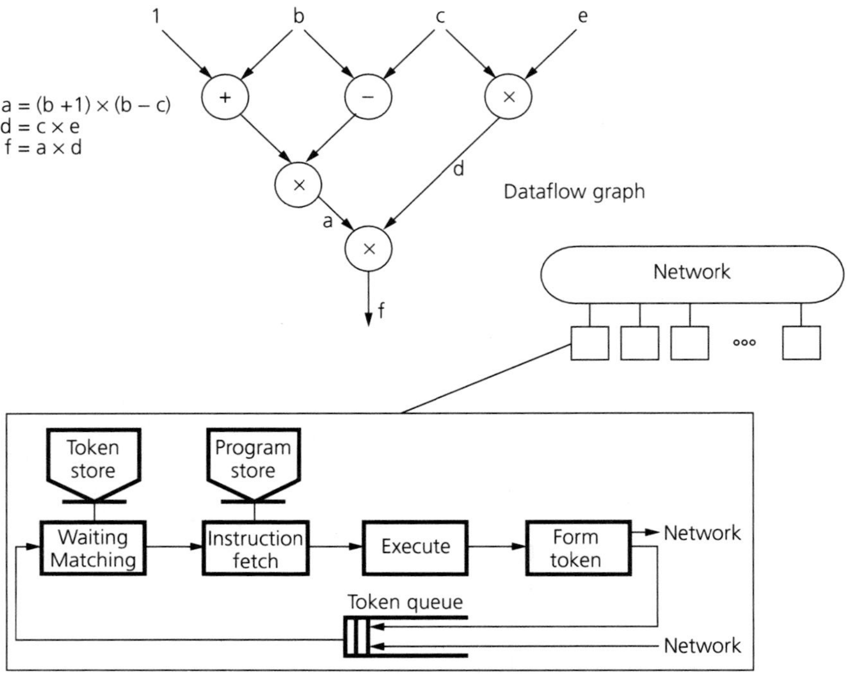

FIGURE 1.26 Dataflow graph and basic execution pipeline. A node in the graph fires when operands are present on its input. It produces results on its outputs that are delivered to adjacent nodes in the graph. The execution pipeline implements this firing rule by detecting when matching data tokens are present, fetching the corresponding instruction, performing the operation, and forming result tokens.

present, the matching token is extracted and the instruction is issued for execution. If not, the token is placed in the store to await its partner. When a result is computed, a new message or token containing the result data is sent to each of the destinations specified in the instruction. The same mechanism can be used whether the successor instructions are local or on a remote processor.

The primary division within dataflow architectures is whether the graph is *static*, with each node representing a primitive operation, or *dynamic*, in which case a node can represent the invocation of an arbitrary function, itself represented by a graph. In dynamic, or *tagged-token*, architectures, the effect of dynamically expanding the graph on function invocation is usually achieved by carrying additional context information in the tag, rather than actually modifying the program graph.

The key characteristics of dataflow architectures are the ability to name operations performed anywhere in the machine, the support for synchronization of independent operations, and dynamic scheduling at the machine level. As the dataflow machine designs matured into real systems programmed in high-level parallel languages, a more conventional structure emerged. Typically, parallelism was generated in the program as a result of parallel function calls and parallel loops, so it was attractive to allocate these larger chunks of work to processors. This led to a family of designs organized essentially like the NUMA design of Figure 1.19, the key differentiating features being direct support for a large, dynamic set of threads of control and the integration of communication with thread generation. The network is closely integrated with the processor; in many designs, the "current message" is available in special registers, and hardware support is available for dispatching to a thread identified in the message. In addition, many designs provide extra state bits on memory locations in order to provide fine-grained synchronization (i.e., synchronization on an element-by-element basis) rather than using locks to synchronize accesses to an entire data structure. In particular, each message could schedule a chunk of computation that could make use of local registers and memory.

By contrast, in shared memory machines, the generally adopted view is that a static or slowly varying set of processes operates within a shared address space, so the compiler or program maps the logical parallelism in the program to a set of processes by assigning loop iterations, maintaining a shared work queue, or the like. Similarly, message-passing programs involve a static, or nearly static, collection of processes that can name one another in order to communicate. In data parallel architectures, the compiler or sequencer maps a large set of "virtual processor" operations onto processors by assigning iterations of a regular loop nest. In the dataflow case, the machine provides the ability to name a very large and dynamic set of threads that can be mapped arbitrarily to processors. Typically, these machines provide a global address space as well. As was the case with message-passing and data parallel machines, dataflow architectures experienced a gradual separation of programming model and hardware structure as the approach matured.

Systolic Architectures

Another novel approach was *systolic architectures*, which sought to replace a single sequential processor by a regular array of simple processing elements and, by carefully orchestrating the flow of data between PEs, obtain very high throughput with modest memory bandwidth requirements. These designs differ from conventional pipelined function units in that the array structure can be nonlinear (e.g., hexagonal), the pathways between PEs may be multidirectional, and each PE may have a small amount of local instruction and data memory. They differ from SIMD in that each PE might do a different operation.

The early proposals were driven by the opportunity offered by VLSI to provide inexpensive special-purpose chips. A given algorithm could be represented directly as a collection of specialized computational units connected in a regular, space-efficient pattern. Data would move through the system at regular "heartbeats" as determined by local state. Figure 1.27 illustrates a design for computing convolutions using a simple linear array. At each beat the input data advances to the right, is multiplied by a local weight, and is accumulated into the output sequence as it also

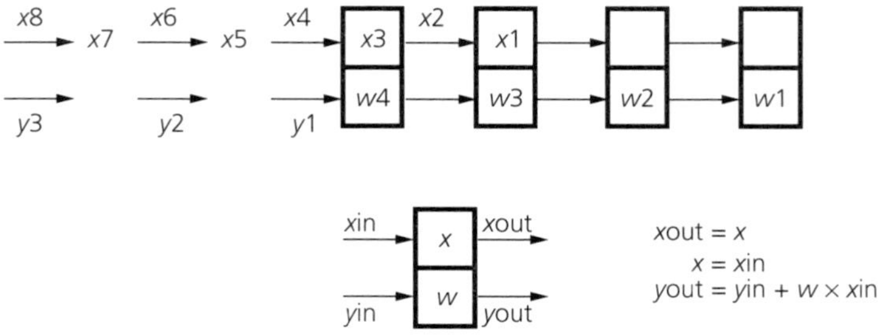

FIGURE 1.27 Systolic array computation of an inner product. Each box represents a computational unit performing a specific function. Every time the clock beats, all units accept inputs, compute results, and generate outputs. Data moves through the systolic array with each beat.

advances to the right. The systolic approach has aspects in common with message-passing, data parallel, and dataflow models but takes on a unique character for a specialized class of problems.

Practical realizations of these ideas, such as iWarp (Borkar et al. 1990), provided quite general programmability in the nodes, so that a variety of algorithms could be realized on the same hardware. The key differentiation is that the network can be configured as a collection of dedicated channels, representing the systolic communication pattern, and data can be transferred directly from processor registers to processor registers across a channel. The global knowledge of the communication pattern is exploited to reduce contention and even to avoid deadlock. The key characteristic of systolic architectures is the ability to integrate highly specialized computation under simple, regular, and highly localized communication patterns.

Systolic algorithms have also been generally amenable to solutions on generic machines, using the fast barrier to delineate coarser-grained phases. The regular, local communication pattern of these algorithms yields good locality when large portions of the logical systolic array are executed on each process, the communication bandwidth needed is low, and the synchronization requirements are simple. Thus, these algorithms have proved effective on the entire spectrum of parallel machines.

1.2.7 A Generic Parallel Architecture

In examining the evolution of the major approaches to parallel architecture, we see a clear convergence for scalable machines toward a generic parallel machine organization, illustrated in Figure 1.28. The machine comprises a collection of essentially complete computers, each with one or more processors and memory, connected through a scalable communication network via *communication assist*—a controller

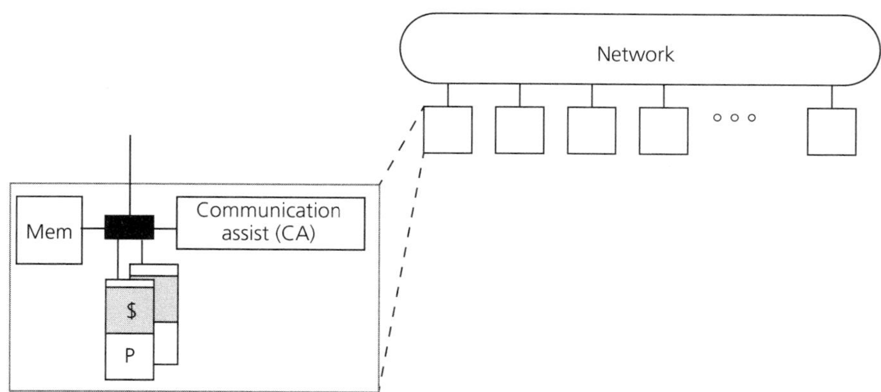

FIGURE 1.28 Generic scalable multiprocessor organization. A collection of essentially complete computers, including one or more processors and memory, communicating through a general-purpose, high-performance, scalable interconnect. Typically, each node contains a controller that assists in communication operations across the network.

or auxiliary processing unit that assists in generating outgoing messages or handling incoming messages. While the consolidation within the field may seem to narrow the design space, in fact, great diversity and debate remains, centered on what functionality should be provided within the assist and how it interfaces to the processor, memory system, and network. Recognizing that these are specific differences within a largely similar organization helps us to understand and evaluate the important organizational trade-offs.

Not surprisingly, different programming models place different requirements on the design of the communication assist and influence which operations are common and should be optimized. In the shared memory case, the assist is tightly integrated with the memory system in order to capture the memory events that may require interaction with other nodes. The assist must also accept messages and perform memory operations and state transitions on behalf of other nodes. In the message-passing case, communication is initiated by explicit actions, either at the system or user level, so it is not required that memory system events be observed. Instead, a need exists to initiate the messages quickly and to respond to incoming messages. The response may require that a tag match be performed, that buffers be allocated, that data transfer commence, or that an event be posted. The data parallel and systolic approaches place an emphasis on fast global synchronization, which may be supported directly in the network or in the assist. Dataflow places an emphasis on fast dynamic scheduling of computation based on an incoming message. Systolic algorithms present the opportunity to exploit global patterns in local scheduling. Even with these differences, it is important to observe that all of these approaches share common aspects; they need to initiate network transactions as a result of specific processor events, and they need to perform simple operations on the remote node to carry out the desired event.

We also see that a separation has emerged between programming model and machine organization as parallel programming environments have matured. For example, Fortran 90 and High Performance Fortran provide a shared address, data parallel programming model that is implemented on a wide range of machines—some supporting a shared physical address space, others with only message passing. The compilation techniques for these machines differ radically, even though the machines appear organizationally similar, because of differences in communication and synchronization operations provided in the communication abstraction and vast differences in the performance characteristics of these operations. As a second example, popular message-passing libraries, such as PVM (parallel virtual machine) and MPI (message-passing interface), are implemented on this same range of machines, but the implementation of the libraries differs dramatically from one kind of machine to another. The same observations hold for parallel operating systems.

1.3 FUNDAMENTAL DESIGN ISSUES

Given how the state of the art in parallel architecture has advanced, we need to take a fresh look at how to organize the body of material in the field. Traditional machine taxonomies, such as SIMD/MIMD, are of little help since multiple general-purpose processors are so dominant. We cannot focus entirely on programming models since in many cases widely differing machine organizations support a common programming model. We cannot just look at hardware structures either, since common elements are employed in many different ways. Instead, we should focus our attention on the architectural distinctions that make a difference to the software that is to run on the machine. In particular, we need to highlight those aspects that influence how a compiler would generate code from a high-level parallel language, how a library writer would code a well-optimized library, or how an application would be written in a low-level parallel language. We can then approach the design problem as one that is constrained from above by how programs use the machine and from below by what the basic technology can provide.

The guiding principles presented in this book for understanding modern parallel architecture are indicated by the layers of abstraction shown in Figure 1.13. Fundamentally, we must understand the operations that are provided at the user-level communication abstraction, how various programming models are mapped to these primitives, and how these primitives are mapped to the actual hardware. Excessive emphasis on the high-level programming model without attention to how it can be mapped to the machine would detract from understanding the fundamental architectural issues, as would excessive emphasis on the specific hardware mechanisms in each particular machine.

This section looks more closely at the communication abstraction and the basic requirements of a programming model. It then defines more formally the key concepts that tie the layers together: naming, ordering, and communication and replication of data. Finally, it introduces the basic performance models required to resolve design trade-offs.

1.3.1 Communication Abstraction

The communication abstraction forms the key interface between the programming model and the system implementation. It plays a role very much like the instruction set in conventional sequential computer architecture. Viewed from the software side, it must have a precise, well-defined meaning so that the same program will run correctly on many implementations. In addition, the operations provided at this layer must be simple, composable entities with clear costs, so that the software can be optimized for performance. Viewed from the hardware side, it must also have a well-defined meaning so that the machine designer can determine where performance optimizations can be performed without violating the software assumptions. While the abstraction needs to be precise, the machine designer would like it not to be overly specific, so it does not prohibit useful techniques for performance enhancement or frustrate efforts to exploit properties of newer technologies.

The communication abstraction is, in effect, a contract between the hardware and the software allowing each the flexibility to improve what it does while working correctly together. To understand the "terms" of this contract, we need to look more carefully at the basic requirements of a programming model.

1.3.2 Programming Model Requirements

A parallel program consists of one or more threads of control operating on data. A *parallel programming model* specifies what data can be *named* by the threads, what *operations* can be performed on the named data, and what *ordering* exists among these operations.

To make these issues concrete, consider the programming model for a uniprocessor. A thread can name the locations in its virtual address space and can name machine registers. In some systems, the address space is broken up into distinct code, stack, and heap segments whereas in others it is flat. Similarly, different programming languages provide access to the address space in different ways; for example, some allow pointers and dynamic storage allocation, others do not. Regardless of these variations, the instruction set provides the operations that can be performed on the named locations. For example, in RISC machines the thread can load data from or store data to memory but can perform arithmetic and comparisons only on data in registers. Older instruction sets support arithmetic on either. Compilers typically mask these differences at the hardware/software boundary, so the user's programming model is one of performing operations on variables that hold data. The hardware translates each virtual address to a physical address on every operation.

The ordering among memory operations is *sequential program order*. The programmer's view is that variables are read and modified in the top-to-bottom, left-to-right order specified in the program. More precisely, the value returned by a read to an address is the last value written to the address in the sequential execution order of the program. This ordering assumption is essential to the logic of the program. However, the reads and writes may not actually be performed in program order because the compiler performs optimizations when translating the program to the instruction set and the hardware performs optimizations when executing the instructions. Both make sure the program cannot tell that the order has been changed. The compiler and hardware preserve the *dependence order*, that is, if a variable is written and then read later in the program order, they make sure that the later operation uses the proper value, but they may avoid actually writing and reading the value to and from memory or may defer the write until later. Collections of reads with no intervening writes may be completely reordered and, generally, writes to different addresses can be reordered as long as dependences from intervening reads are preserved. This reordering occurs at the compilation level, for example, when the compiler allocates variables to registers, manipulates expressions to improve pipelining, or transforms loops to reduce overhead and improve the data access pattern. It occurs at the machine level when instruction execution is pipelined, multiple instructions are issued per cycle, or write buffers are used to hide memory latency. We depend on these optimizations for performance. They work because for the program to observe the effect of a write, it must read the variable; this creates a dependence, which is preserved. Thus, the illusion of program order is preserved while actually executing the program in the weaker dependence order.[6] We operate in a world where essentially all programming languages embody a programming model of sequential order of operations on variables in a virtual address space, and the system enforces a weaker order wherever it can do so without changing the results of the program.

Now let's return to parallel programming models. The informal discussion earlier in this chapter indicated the distinct positions adopted on naming, operation set, and ordering. Naming and operation set are what typically characterize the models; however, ordering is of key importance. A parallel program must coordinate the activity of its threads to ensure that the dependences within the program are enforced; *this requires explicit synchronization operations when the ordering implicit in the basic operations is not sufficient.* As architects (and compiler writers), we need to understand the ordering properties to see what optimization "tricks" we can play for performance. We can focus on shared address and message-passing programming models since they are the most widely used; other models, such as data parallel, are usually implemented in terms of one of them.

The shared address space programming model assumes one or more threads of control, each operating in an address space that contains a region shared between threads, and may contain a region that is private to each thread. Typically, the shared region is shared by all threads. All the operations defined on private addresses are defined on shared addresses; in particular, the program accesses and updates shared variables simply by using them in expressions and assignment statements.

Message-passing models assume a collection of processes each operating in a private address space and each able to name the other processes. The normal unipro-

6. The illusion breaks down a little bit for system programmers, say, if the variable is actually a control register on a device. Then the actual program order must be preserved. This is usually accomplished by flagging the variable as special; for example, using the volatile type modifier in C.

cessor operations are provided on the private address space, in program order. The additional operations, send and receive, operate on the local address space and the global process space. Send transfers data from the local address space to a process. Receive accepts data into the local address space from a process. Each send/receive pair is a specific point-to-point synchronization operation. Many message-passing languages offer global, or *collective*, communication operations as well, such as broadcast.

Naming

The position adopted on naming in the programming model is presented to the programmer through the programming language or programming environment. It is what the logic of the program is based upon. However, the issue of naming is critical at each level of the communication architecture. Certainly one possible strategy is to have the operations in the programming model be one to one with the operations in the communication abstraction at the user/system boundary and to have these be one to one with the hardware primitives. However, it is also possible for the compiler and libraries to provide a level of translation between the programming model and the communication abstraction, or for the operating system to intervene to handle some of the operations at the user/system boundary. These alternatives allow the architect to consider implementing the common, simple operations directly in hardware and supporting the more complex operations partly or wholly in software.

Let us consider the ramifications of naming at the layers using the two primary programming models: shared address and message passing. First, in a shared address model, accesses to shared variables in the program are usually mapped by the compiler to load and store instructions on shared virtual addresses, just like access to any other variable. This is not the only option, however. The compiler could generate special code sequences for accesses to shared variables. A machine supports a *global physical address space* if any processor is able to generate a physical address for any location in the machine and access the location in a single memory operation. It is straightforward to realize a shared virtual address space on a machine providing a global physical address space: establish the virtual-to-physical mapping so that shared virtual addresses map to the same physical location (i.e., the processes have the same entries in their page tables). However, the existence of the level of translation allows for other approaches. A machine supports *independent local physical address spaces* if each processor can only access a distinct set of locations. Even on such a machine, a shared virtual address space can be provided by mapping virtual addresses that are local to a process to the corresponding physical address. The nonlocal addresses are left unmapped so upon access to a nonlocal shared address a page fault will occur, allowing the operating system to intervene and access the remote shared data. Although this approach can provide the same naming, operations, and ordering to the program, it clearly has different hardware requirements at the hardware/software boundary. The architect's job is to resolve these design trade-offs across layers of the system implementation so that the result is efficient and cost-effective for the target application workload on available technology.

Second, message-passing operations could be realized directly in hardware, but the matching and buffering aspects of the send/receive operations are better suited to software implementation. More basic data transport primitives are well supported in hardware. Thus, in essentially all parallel machines, the message-passing programming model is realized via a software layer that is built upon a simpler communication abstraction. At the user/system boundary, one approach is to have all message operations go through the operating system as if they were I/O operations. However, the frequency of message operations is much greater than I/O operations, so it makes sense to use the operating system support to set up resources, privileges, and so on and allow the frequent, simple data transfer operations to be supported directly in hardware. On the other hand, we might consider adopting a shared virtual address space as the lower-level communication abstraction, in which case send and receive operations involve writing and reading shared buffers and posting the appropriate synchronization events.

The issue of naming arises at each level of abstraction in a parallel architecture, not just in the programming model. As architects, we need to design against the frequency and type of operations that occur at the communication abstraction, understanding that the trade-offs at this boundary involve what is supported directly in hardware and in software.

Operations

Each programming model defines a specific set of operations that can be performed on the data or objects that can be named within the model. For the case of a shared address model, these include reading and writing shared variables as well as various atomic read-modify-write operations on shared variables, which are used to synchronize the threads. For message passing, the operations are send and receive on private (local) addresses and process identifiers, as described previously. Each element of data in the program is named by a process number and a local address within the process. A message-passing model does define a global address space of sorts. However, no operations are defined on these global addresses. They can be passed around and interpreted by the program, for example, to emulate a shared address style of programming on top of message passing, but they cannot be operated on directly at the communication abstraction. As architects, we need to be aware of the operations defined at each level of abstraction. In particular, we need to be very clear on what ordering among operations is assumed to be present at each level of abstraction, where communication takes place, and how data is replicated.

Ordering

The properties of the specified order among operations have a profound effect throughout the layers of parallel architecture. Notice, for example, that the message-passing model places no assumption on the ordering of operations by distinct processes except the explicit program order associated with the send/receive operations, whereas a shared address model must specify aspects of how processes see the order of operations performed by other processes. Ordering issues are important and rather subtle. Many of the tricks that we play for performance in the uniprocessor context involve relaxing the order assumed by the programmer to gain performance, either through parallelism or improved locality or both. Exploiting parallelism and locality is even more important in the multiprocessor case. Thus, we need to understand what new tricks can be played. We also need to examine which of the old tricks are still valid. Can we perform the traditional sequential optimizations at the compiler and architecture level on each process of a parallel program? Where can the explicit synchronization operations be used to allow ordering to be relaxed on the conventional operations? To answer these questions, we need to develop a much more complete understanding of how programs use the communication abstraction, what properties they rely upon, and what machine structures we would like to exploit for performance.

A natural position to adopt on ordering is that operations in a thread are in program order. That is what the programmer would assume for the special case of one thread. However, there remains the question of what ordering can be assumed among operations performed on shared variables by different threads. The threads operate independently and, potentially, at different speeds so no clear notion of "latest" is defined. If we have in mind that the machines behave as a collection of simple processors operating on a common, centralized memory, then it is reasonable to expect the global order of memory accesses to be some arbitrary interleaving of the individual program orders. In reality we won't build the machines this way, but it establishes what operations are implicitly ordered by the basic operations in the model. This interleaving is also what we expect of a collection of threads that are time-shared, perhaps at a very fine level, on a uniprocessor.

Where the implicit ordering is not enough, explicit synchronization operations are required. Parallel programs require two types of synchronization:

- *Mutual exclusion* ensures that certain operations on certain data are performed by only one thread or process at a time. We can imagine a room that must be entered to perform such an operation, and only one process can be in the room at a time. This is accomplished by locking the door upon entry and unlocking it on exit. If several processes arrive at the door together, only one will get in and the others will wait until it leaves. The order in which the processes are allowed to enter does not matter and may vary from one execution of the program to the next; what matters is that they do so one at a time. Mutual exclusion operations tend to serialize the execution of processes.
- *Events* are used to inform other processes that some point of execution has been reached so that they can proceed knowing that certain dependences have been satisfied. These operations are like passing a baton from one runner to the next in a relay race or the starter firing a gun to indicate the start of a race. If one process writes a value that another is supposed to read, an event synchronization operation must take place to indicate that the value is ready to be read. Events may be *point-to-point*, involving a pair of processes, or they may be *global*, involving all processes or a group of processes.

1.3.3 Communication and Replication

The final issues that are closely tied to the layers of parallel architecture are communication and data replication. Communication and replication are inherently related. Consider first a message-passing operation. The effect of the send/receive pair is to copy data that is in the sender's address space into a region of the receiver's address space. This transfer is essential for the receiver to access the data. If the data is produced by the sender, it reflects a *true communication* of information from one process to the other. If the data just happens to be stored at the sender, perhaps because that was the initial configuration of the data or because the data set was simply too large to fit on any one node, then this transfer merely makes a replica of the data where it is used. In this case, the processes are not actually communicating information from one to another via the data transfer. If the data were replicated or positioned properly over the processes to begin with, there would be no need to communicate it in a message. More importantly, if the receiver uses the data over and over again, it can reuse its replica without additional data transfers. The sender can modify the region of addresses that was previously communicated with no effect on the previous receiver. If the effect of these later updates is to be communicated, an additional transfer must occur.

Consider now a conventional data access on a uniprocessor through a cache. If the cache does not contain the desired address, a miss occurs and the block is transferred from the memory that serves as a backing store. The data is implicitly replicated into the cache near the processor that accesses it. If the processor reuses the data while it resides in the cache, further transfers with the memory are avoided. In the uniprocessor case, the processor produces the data and the processor consumes it, so the "communication" with the memory occurs only because the data does not fit in the cache or is being accessed for the first time.

Interprocess communication and data transfer within the storage hierarchy become melded together in a shared physical address space. Cache misses cause a data transfer across the machine interconnect whenever the physical backing storage for an address is remote to the node accessing the address, whether the address is private or shared and whether the transfer is a result of true communication or just a data access. The natural tendency of the machine is to replicate data into the caches of the processors that access the data. If the data is reused while it is in the cache, no data transfers occur; this is a major advantage. However, when a write to shared data occurs, something must be done to ensure that later reads by other processors get the new data rather than the old data that was replicated into their caches. This will involve more than a simple data transfer.

To be clear on the relationship of communication and replication, it is important to distinguish several concepts that are frequently bundled together. When a program performs a write, it binds a data value to an address; a read obtains the data value bound to an address. The data resides in some physical storage element in the machine. A *data transfer* occurs whenever data in one storage element is transferred into another. This does not necessarily change the bindings of addresses and values. The same data may reside in multiple physical locations as it does in the uniprocessor storage hierarchy, but the one nearest to the processor is the only one that the processor can observe. If it is updated, the other hidden replicas, including the actual memory location, must eventually be updated. Copying data binds a new set of addresses to the same set of values. Generally, this will cause data transfers. Once the copy has been made, the two sets of bindings are completely independent (unlike the implicit replication that occurs within the storage hierarchy), so updates to one set of addresses do not affect the other. *Communication* between processes occurs when data written by one process is read by another. This may cause a data transfer within the machine, either on the write or the read, or the data transfer may occur for other reasons. Communication may involve establishing a new binding or not doing so, depending on the particular communication abstraction.

In general, replication avoids unnecessary communication; that is, transferring data to a consumer that was not produced since the data was previously accessed. The ability to perform replication automatically at a given level of the communication architecture depends very strongly on the naming and ordering properties of the layer. Moreover, replication is not a panacea—it too requires data transfers. It is disadvantageous to replicate data that is not going to be used. We will see that replication plays an important role throughout parallel computer architecture.

1.3.4 Performance

In defining the set of operations for communication and cooperation, the data types, and the addressing modes, the communication abstraction specifies how shared objects are named, what ordering properties are preserved, and how synchronization is performed. However, the performance characteristics of the available primitives determine how they are actually used. Programmers and compiler writers will avoid costly operations where possible. In evaluating architectural trade-offs, the decision between feasible alternatives ultimately rests upon the performance they deliver. Thus, to complete an introduction to the fundamental issues of parallel computer architecture, we need a framework for understanding performance at many levels of design.

Fundamentally, there are three important metrics: *latency*, the time taken for an operation; *bandwidth*, the rate at which operations are performed; and *cost*, the impact these operations have on the execution time of the program. In a simple world where processors do only one thing at a time, these metrics are directly related—the bandwidth (operations per second) is the reciprocal of the latency (seconds per operation), and the cost is simply the latency times the number of operations performed. However, modern computer systems do many different operations at once, and the relationship between these performance metrics is much more complex. Consider the following basic example.

EXAMPLE 1.2 Suppose a component can perform a specific operation in 100 ns. Clearly, it can support a bandwidth of 10 million operations per second. However, if the component is pipelined internally as 10 equal stages, it is able to provide a peak bandwidth of 100 million operations per second. The rate at which operations can be initiated is determined by how long the slowest stage is occupied, 10 ns, rather than by the latency of an individual operation. The bandwidth delivered on an application depends on how frequently it initiates the operations. If the application starts an operation every 200 ns, the delivered bandwidth is 5 million operations per second, regardless of how the component is pipelined. Of course, usage of resources is usually bursty, so pipelining can be advantageous even when the average initiation rate is low. If the application performed 100 million operations on this component, what is the range of cost of these operations?

Answer Taking the operation count times the operation latency would give an upper bound of 10 seconds. Taking the operation count divided by the peak rate gives a lower bound of 1 second. The former is accurate if the program waited for each operation to complete before continuing. The latter assumes that the operations are completely overlapped with other useful work, so the cost is simply the cost to initiate the operation. Suppose that on average the program can do 50 ns of useful work after each operation issued to the component before it depends on the operations result. Then the cost to the application is 50 ns per operation—the 10 ns to issue the operation and the 40 ns spent waiting for it to complete—so the total cost is 5 seconds. ■

Since the unique property of parallel computer architecture is communication, the operations that we are concerned with most often are data transfers. The performance of these operations can be understood as a generalization of our basic pipeline example.

Data Transfer Time

The time for a data transfer operation is generally described by a linear model:

$$\text{Transfer Time}(n) = T_0 + \frac{n}{B} \tag{1.3}$$

where n is the amount of data (e.g., number of bytes), B is the transfer rate of the component moving the data in compatible units (e.g., bytes per second), and the constant term, T_0, is the start-up cost. This is a very convenient model, and it is used to describe a diverse collection of operations, including messages, memory accesses, bus transactions, and vector operations. For message passing, the start-up cost can be thought of as the time for the first bit to get to the destination. For memory operations, it is essentially the access time. For bus transactions, it reflects the bus arbitration and command phases. For any sort of pipelined operation, including pipelined instruction processing or vector operations, it is the time to fill the pipeline.

Using this simple model, it is clear that the bandwidth of a data transfer operation depends on the transfer size. As the transfer size increases, it approaches the asymptotic rate of B, which is sometimes referred to as r_∞. How quickly it approaches this rate depends on the start-up cost. It is easily shown that the size at which half of the peak bandwidth is obtained, the *half-power point,* is given by

$$n_{\frac{1}{2}} = T_0 B \tag{1.4}$$

Unfortunately, this linear model does not give any indication of when the next such operation can be initiated, nor does it indicate whether other useful work can be performed during the transfer. These other factors depend on how the transfer is performed.

Overhead and Occupancy

The data transfer in which we are most interested is the one that occurs across the network in parallel machines. It is initiated by the processor through the communication assist. The essential components of this operation can be described by the following simple model:

$$\text{Communication Time}(n) = \text{Overhead} + \text{Occupancy} + \text{Network Delay} \qquad (1.5)$$

The *overhead* is the time the processor spends initiating the transfer. This may be a fixed cost, if the processor simply has to tell the communication assist to start, or it may be linear in n, if the processor has to copy the data into the assist. The key point is that this is time the processor is busy with the communication event; it cannot do other useful work or initiate other communication during this time. The remaining portion of the communication time is considered the *network latency*; it is the part that can be hidden by other processor operations.

The *occupancy* is the time it takes for the data to pass through the slowest component on the communication path. For example, each link that is traversed in the network will be occupied for time n/B, where B is the bandwidth of the link. The data will occupy other resources, including buffers, switches, and the communication assist. Often the communication assist is the bottleneck that determines the occupancy. The occupancy limits how frequently communication operations can be initiated. The next data transfer will have to wait until the critical resource is no longer occupied before it can use that same resource. If there is buffering between the processor and the bottleneck, the processor may be able to issue a burst of transfers at a frequency greater than $1/\text{Occupancy}$; however, once this buffer is full, the processor must slow to the rate set by the occupancy. A new transfer can start only when an older one finishes.

The remaining communication time is lumped into the *network delay*, which includes the time for a bit to be routed across the actual network as well as many other factors, such as the time to get through the communication assists. From the processor's viewpoint, the specific hardware components contributing to network delay are indistinguishable. What affects the processor is how long it must wait before it can use the result of a communication event, how much of this time it can use for other activities, and how frequently it can communicate data. Of course, the task of designing the network and its interfaces is very concerned with the specific components and their contribution to the aspects of performance that the processor observes.

In the simple case where the processor issues a request and waits for the response, the breakdown of the communication time into its three components is immaterial.

All that matters is the total round-trip time. However, in the case where multiple operations are issued in a pipelined fashion, each of the components has a specific influence on the delivered performance.

Indeed, every individual component along the communication path can be described by its delay and its occupancy. The network delay is simply the sum of the delays along the path. The network occupancy is the maximum of the occupancies along the path. For interconnection networks, an additional factor arises because many transfers can take place simultaneously. If two of these transfers attempt to use the same resource at once (e.g., they use the same wire at the same time), one must wait. This *contention* for resources increases the average communication time. From the processor's viewpoint, contention appears as increased occupancy. Some resource in the system is occupied for a time determined by the collection of transfers across it.

Equation 1.5 is a very general model. It can be used to describe data transfers in many places in modern, highly pipelined computer systems. As one example, consider the time to move a block between cache and memory on a miss. The cache controller spends a period of time inspecting the tag to determine that it is not a hit and then starting the transfer; this is the overhead. The occupancy is the block size divided by the bus bandwidth, unless there is some slower component in the system. The delay includes the normal time to arbitrate and gain access to the bus plus the time spent delivering data into the memory. Additional time spent waiting to gain access to the bus or waiting for the memory bank cycle to complete is due to contention. A second obvious example is the time to transfer a message from one processor to another.

Communication Cost

The bottom line is, of course, the time a program spends performing communication. A useful model connecting the program characteristics to the hardware performance is given by the following:

$$\text{Communication Cost} = \text{Frequency} \times (\text{Communication Time} - \text{Overlap}) \quad (1.6)$$

The *frequency of communication*, defined as the number of communication operations per unit of work in the program, depends on many programming factors (as we will see in Chapters 2 and 3) and many hardware design factors. In particular, hardware may limit the transfer size and thereby determine the minimum number of messages. It may automatically replicate data or migrate it to where it is used. However, a certain amount of communication is inherent to parallel execution since data must be shared and processors must coordinate their work. In general, for a machine to support programs with a high communication frequency, the other parts of the communication cost equation must be small—low overhead, low network delay, and small occupancy. The attention paid to communication costs essentially determines which programming models a machine can realize efficiently and what portion of the application space it can support. Any parallel computer with good computational performance can support programs that communicate infrequently, but as the frequency or volume of communication increase, greater stress is placed on the communication architecture.

The *overlap* is the portion of the communication operation that is performed concurrently with other useful work, including computation or other communication. This reduction of the effective cost is possible because much of the communication time involves work done by components of the system other than the processor, such as the communication assist, the bus, the network, or the remote processor or memory. Overlapping communication with other work is a form of small-scale parallelism, as is the instruction-level parallelism exploited by fast microprocessors. In effect, we may invest some of the available parallelism in a program to hide the actual cost of communication.

1.3.5 Summary

The issues of naming, operation set, and ordering apply at each level of abstraction in a parallel architecture, not just the programming model. In general, a level of translation or run-time software may intervene between the programming model and the communication abstraction, and beneath this abstraction are key hardware abstractions. At any level, communication and replication are deeply related. Whenever two processes access the same data, the data either needs to be communicated between the two or replicated so each can access a copy of it. The ability to have the same name refer to two distinct physical locations in a meaningful manner at a given level of abstraction depends on the position adopted on naming and ordering at that level. Wherever data movement is involved, we need to understand its performance characteristics in terms of latency and bandwidth and, furthermore, how these are influenced by overhead and occupancy. As architects, we need to design against the frequency and type of operations that occur at the communication abstraction, understanding that trade-offs occur across this boundary, involving what is supported directly in hardware and what is supported in software. The position adopted on naming, operation set, and ordering at each of these levels has a qualitative impact on these trade-offs, as we will see throughout the book.

1.4 CONCLUDING REMARKS

Parallel computer architecture forms an important thread in the evolution of computer architecture, rooted essentially in the beginnings of computing. For much of this history it takes on a novel, even exotic role as the avenue for advancement over and beyond what the base technology can provide. Parallel computer designs have demonstrated a rich diversity of structure, usually motivated by specific higher-level parallel programming models. However, the dominant technological forces of the VLSI generation have pushed parallelism increasingly into the mainstream, making parallel architecture almost ubiquitous. All modern microprocessors are highly parallel internally, executing several bit-parallel instructions in every cycle and even reordering instructions within the limits of inherent dependences to mitigate the costs of communication with hardware components external to the processor itself. These microprocessors have become the performance and price-performance leaders of the computer industry. From the most powerful supercomputers to departmental servers to the desktop, we see systems constructed by utilizing multiples of such processors integrated into a communications fabric. This technological focus, and increasing maturity of compiler technology, has brought about a dramatic convergence in the structural organization of modern parallel machines. The key architectural issue is how communication is integrated into the memory and I/O systems that form the remainder of the computational node. This communications architecture reveals itself functionally in terms of what can be named at the hardware level, what ordering guarantees are provided, and how synchronization operations are performed whereas, from a performance point of view, we must understand the inherent latency and bandwidth of the available communication operations. Thus, modern parallel computer architecture carries with it a strong engineering component, amenable to quantitative analysis of cost and performance trade-offs.

This book presents the conceptual foundations as well as the engineering issues of parallel computer architecture across a broad range of potential scales of design, all of which have an important role in computing today and in the future. Computer systems, whether parallel or sequential, are designed against the requirements and characteristics of intended workloads. For conventional computers, we assume that most practitioners in the field have a good understanding of what sequential programs look like, how they are compiled, and what level of optimization is reasonable to assume that the programmer has performed. Thus, we are comfortable taking popular sequential programs, compiling them for a target architecture, and drawing conclusions from running the programs or evaluating execution traces. When we attempt to improve performance through architectural enhancements, we assume that the program is reasonably good in the first place.

The situation with parallel computers is quite different. Much less general understanding exists about the process of parallel programming, and programmer and compiler optimizations have a wider scope, which can greatly affect the program characteristics exhibited at the machine level.

Chapter 2 provides an overview of parallel programs—what they look like and how they are constructed. Chapter 3 explains the issues that must be addressed by the programmer and compiler to construct a "good" parallel program, that is, one that is effective enough in using multiple processors to form a reasonable basis for architectural evaluation. Ultimately, we design parallel computers against the program characteristics at the machine level, so the goal of Chapter 3 is to draw a connection between what appears in the program text and how the machine spends its time. In effect, Chapters 2 and 3 take us from a general understanding of issues at the application level to a specific understanding of the character and frequency of operations at the communication abstraction level.

Chapter 4 establishes a framework for workload-driven evaluation of parallel computer designs. Two related scenarios are addressed. First, for a parallel machine that has already been built, we need a sound method of evaluating its performance. This proceeds by first determining the capability of individual aspects of the machine in isolation and then measuring how well they perform collectively. The understanding of application characteristics is important to ensure that the workload run on the machine stresses the various aspects of interest. Second, we need a process for evaluating hypothetical architectural advancements. New ideas for which no machine exists need to be evaluated through simulations, which imposes severe restrictions on what can reasonably be executed. Again, an understanding of application characteristics and how they scale with problem and machine size is crucial to navigating the design space.

Chapters 5 and 6 study in detail the design of symmetric multiprocessors with a shared physical address space. Going deeply into the small-scale case before examining scalable designs is important for several reasons. First, small-scale multiprocessors are the most prevalent form of parallel architecture; they are likely to be the form most students are exposed to, most software developers are targeting, and most professional designers are dealing with. Second, the issues that arise in the small scale are indicative of what is critical in the large scale, but the solutions are often simpler and easier to grasp. Thus, these chapters provide a study in the small of what the following five chapters address in the large. Third, the small-scale multiprocessor design is a fundamental building block for the larger-scale machines. The available options for interfacing a scalable interconnect with a processor-memory node are largely circumscribed by the processor, cache, and memory structure of the small-scale machines. Finally, the solutions to key design problems in the small-scale case are elegant in their own right.

The fundamental building block for the designs in Chapters 5 and 6 is the shared bus between processors and memory. The basic problem that we need to solve is to keep the contents of the caches coherent and the view of memory provided to the processors consistent. A bus is a powerful mechanism. It provides any-to-any communication through a single set of wires; moreover, it can serve as a broadcast medium, since there is only one set of wires, and even provide global status via wired-OR signals. The properties of bus transactions are exploited in designing extensions of conventional cache controllers that solve the coherence problem. Chapter 5 presents the fundamental techniques for bus-based cache coherence at the logical level and presents the basic design alternatives. These design alternatives provide an illustration of how workload-driven evaluation can be brought to bear in making design decisions. Finally, Chapter 5 examines the parallel programming issues of the earlier chapters in terms of the aspects of machine design that influence software level, especially with regard to cache effects on sharing patterns and the design of robust synchronization routines. Chapter 6 focuses on the organizational structure and machine implementation of bus-based cache coherence. It examines a variety of more advanced designs that seek to reduce latency and increase bandwidth while preserving a consistent view of memory.

Chapters 7 through 11 form a closely interlocking study of the design of scalable parallel architectures. Chapter 7 makes the conceptual step from a bus transaction as a building block for higher-level abstractions to a network transaction as a building block. To cement this understanding, the communication abstractions that we have surveyed in this introductory chapter are constructed from primitive network transactions. Then the chapter studies the design of the node-to-network interface in depth using a spectrum of case studies.

Chapters 8 and 9 go deeply into the design of scalable machines supporting a shared address space, both a shared physical address space and a shared virtual address space upon independent physical address spaces. The central issue is automatic replication of data while preserving a consistent view of memory and avoiding performance bottlenecks. The study of a global physical address space emphasizes hardware organizations that provide efficient, fine-grained sharing. The study of a global virtual address space provides an understanding of a minimal degree of hardware support required for most workloads.

Chapter 10 takes up the question of the design of the scalable network itself. As with processors, caches, and memory systems, the network design space has several dimensions, and often a design decision involves interactions along these dimensions. The chapter lays out the fundamental design issues for scalable interconnects, illustrates the common design choices, and evaluates them relative to the requirements established in Chapters 8 and 9. Chapter 11 draws together the material from the previous four chapters in the context of techniques for latency tolerance, including bulk transfer, write behind, and read ahead across the spectrum of communication abstractions. Finally, Chapter 12 looks at the overall concepts of the book in light of technological, application, and economic trends and forecasts the key ongoing developments in the field of parallel computer architecture.

1.5 HISTORICAL REFERENCES

Parallel computer architecture has a long, rich, and varied history that is deeply interwoven with advances in the underlying processor, memory, and network technologies. The first blossoming of parallel architectures occurs around 1960. This is a point where transistors have replaced tubes and other complicated and constraining logic technologies. Processors are smaller and more manageable. A relatively cheap, inexpensive storage technology exists (core memory), and computer architectures are settling down into meaningful "families."

Small-scale shared memory multiprocessors took on an important commercial role at this point with the inception of what we call mainframes today, including the Burroughs B5000 (Lonergan and King 1961) and D825 (Anderson et al. 1962) and the IBM System 360 models 65 and 67 (Padegs 1981). Support for multiprocessor configurations was one of the key extensions in the evolution of the 360 architecture to System 370. These included atomic memory operations and interprocessor interrupts. In the scientific computing area, shared memory multiprocessors were also common. The CDC 6600 provided an asymmetric shared memory organization to connect multiple peripheral processors with the central processor, and a dual CPU configuration of this machine was produced. The origins of message-passing machines come about in the RW400, introduced in 1960 (Porter 1960). Data parallel machines also emerged, with the design of the Solomon computer (Ball et al. 1962; Slotnick, Borck, and McReynolds 1962).

Through the late 1960s, tremendous innovation occurred in the use of parallelism within the processor using pipelining and replication of function units to obtain a far greater range of performance within a family than could be obtained by simply increasing the clock rate. It was argued that these efforts were reaching a point of diminishing returns, so the University of Illinois and Burroughs undertook a major research project to design and build a 64-processor SIMD machine, called Illiac IV (Bouknight et al. 1972), based on the earlier Solomon work (and in spite of Amdahl's arguments to the contrary [Amdahl 1967]). This project was very ambitious, involving research in the basic hardware technologies, architecture, I/O devices, operating systems, programming languages, and applications. By the time a scaled-down, 16-processor system was working in 1975, the computer industry had undergone massive structural change.

First, the concept of storage as a simple linear array of moderately slow physical devices had been revolutionized, beginning with the idea of virtual memory and then with the concept of caching. Work on Multics and its predecessors (e.g., Atlas and CTSS) separated the concept of the user address space from the physical memory of the machine. This required maintaining a short list of recent translations, a translation lookaside buffer (TLB), in order to obtain reasonable performance. Maurice Wilkes, the designer of EDSAC, saw this as a powerful technique for organizing the addressable storage itself, giving rise to what we now call the cache. This proved an interesting example of locality triumphing over parallelism. The introduction of caches into the 360/85 yielded higher performance than the 360/91, which had a faster clock rate, faster memory, and elaborate pipelined instruction execution with dynamic scheduling. The use of caches was commercialized in the IBM 360/185, but this raised a serious difficulty for the I/O controllers as well as the additional processors. If addresses were cached and therefore not bound to a particular memory location, how was an access from another processor or controller to locate the valid data? One solution was to maintain a directory of the location of each cache line, an idea that has regained importance in recent years.

Second, storage technology itself underwent a revolution with semiconductor memories replacing core memories. Initially, this technology was most applicable to small cache memories. Other machines, such as the CDC 7600, simply provided a separate, small, fast, explicitly addressed memory. Third, integrated circuits took hold. The combined result was that uniprocessor systems enjoyed a dramatic advance in performance, which mitigated much of the added value of parallelism in the Illiac IV system, with its inferior technological and architectural base. Pipelined vector processing in the CDC STAR-100 addressed the class of numerical computations that Illiac was intended to solve but eliminated the difficult data movement operations. The final straw was the introduction of the CRAY-1 system, with an astounding 80-MHz clock rate owing to exquisite circuit design and the use of what we now call a RISC instruction set, augmented with vector operations using vector registers and offering high peak rate with very low start-up cost. The use of simple vector processing coupled with fast, expensive ECL circuits was to dominate high-performance computing for the next 15 years.

A fourth dramatic change occurred in the early 1970s, however, with the introduction of microprocessors. Although the performance of the early microprocessors was quite low, the improvements were dramatic as bit-slice designs gave way to 4-bit, 8-bit, 16-bit, and full-word designs. The potential of this technology motivated a major research effort at Carnegie-Mellon University to design a large shared memory multiprocessor using the LSI-11 version of the popular PDP-11 minicomputer. This project went through two phases. The first, called C.mmp, connected 16 processors through a specially designed circuit-switched crossbar to a collection of memories and I/O devices, much like the dancehall design in Figure 1.15 (Wulf, Levin, and Person 1975). The second, CM*, sought to build a 100-processor system by connecting 14-node clusters with local memory through a packet-switched network in a NUMA configuration (Swan, Fuller, and Siewiorek 1977; Swan et al. 1977), as in Figure 1.19.

This trend toward systems constructed from many small microprocessors literally exploded in the early to mid-1980s, resulting in the emergence of several disparate factions. On the shared memory side, it was observed that a confluence of caches and the properties of buses made modest multiprocessors very attractive. Buses have limited bandwidth but are a broadcast medium. Caches filter bandwidth and provide an intermediary between the processor and the memory system. Research at the University of California, Berkeley and elsewhere (Goodman 1983; Hill et al. 1986) introduced extensions of the basic bus protocol that allowed the caches to maintain a consistent state. This direction was picked up by several small companies, including Synapse (Nestle and Inselberg 1985), Sequent (Rodgers 1985), Encore (Bell 1985; Schanin 1986), Flex (Matelan 1985), and others, as the 32-bit microprocessor made its debut and the vast personal computer industry took off. A decade later, this general approach dominated the server and high-end workstation market and took hold in the PC servers and the desktop. The approach experienced a temporary setback as very fast RISC microprocessors took away the performance edge of multiple slower processors. Although the RISC micros were well suited to multiprocessor design, their bandwidth demands severely limited scaling until a new generation of shared bus designs emerged in the early 1990s.

Simultaneously, the message-passing direction took off with two major research efforts. At CalTech, a project was started to construct a 64-processor system using i8086/8087 microprocessors assembled in a hypercube configuration (Seitz 1985; Athas and Seitz 1988). From this baseline, several other designs were pursued at CalTech and JPL (Fox et al. 1988), and at least two companies pushed the approach into commercialization—Intel, with the iPSC series, and Ametek. A somewhat more aggressive approach was widely promoted by the INMOS Corporation in England in the form of the Transputer, which integrated four communication channels directly onto the microprocessor. This approach was adopted by nCUBE, with a series of very large-scale message-passing machines. Intel carried the commodity processor approach forward, replacing the i80386 with the faster i860, then replacing the network with a fast grid-based interconnect in the Delta and adding dedicated message processors in the Paragon. Meiko moved away from the Transputer to the i860 in their computing surface. IBM also investigated an i860-based design in Vulcan before obtaining commercial success with the SP family, essentially a cluster of RS6000 workstations.

Data parallel systems also took off in the early 1980s, after a period of relative quiet. These included Batcher's MPP system for image processing developed by Goodyear and the Connection Machine promoted by Hillis for AI applications (Hillis 1985). The key enhancement was the provision of a general-purpose interconnect for problems demanding other than simple grid-based communication. These ideas saw commercialization with the emergence of Thinking Machines Corporation, first with the CM-1, which was close to Hillis's original conceptions, and then with the CM-2, which incorporated a large number of bit-parallel floating-point units. In addition, MasPar and Wavetracer carried the bit-serial or slightly wider organization forward in cost-effective systems.

A more formal development of highly regular parallel systems emerged in the early 1980s as systolic arrays, generally under the assumption that a large number of very simple processing elements would fit on a single chip. It was envisioned that these arrays would provide cheap, high-performance, special-purpose add-ons to conventional computer systems. To some extent, these ideas have been employed in programming data parallel machines. The iWARP project at CMU produced a more general, smaller-scale building block that has been developed further in conjunction with Intel. These ideas have also found their way into fast graphics, compression, and rendering chips.

The technological possibilities of the VLSI revolution also prompted the investigation of more radical architectural concepts, including dataflow architectures (Dennis 1980; Gurd, Kerkham, and Watson 1985; Papadopoulos and Culler 1990; Arvind and Culler 1986), which integrated the network very closely with the instruction scheduling mechanism of the processor. It was argued that very fast dynamic scheduling throughout the machine would hide the long communication latency and synchronization costs of a large machine and thereby vastly simplify programming. The evolution of these ideas tended to converge with the evolution of message-passing architectures in the form of message-driven computation (Dally, Keen, and Noakes 1993).

Large-scale shared memory designs took off as well. IBM pursued a high-profile research effort with the RP-3 (Pfister et al. 1985), which sought to connect a large number of early RISC processors (the 801) through a butterfly network. This was based on the NYU Ultracomputer work (Gottlieb et al. 1983), which was particularly novel for its use of combining operations. BBN developed two large-scale designs, the BBN Butterfly using Motorola 68000 processors and the TC2000 (Bolt Beranek and Newman 1989) using the 88100s. These efforts prompted a very broad investigation of the possibility of providing cache-coherent shared memory in a scalable setting. The DASH project at Stanford University sought to provide a fully cache-coherent distributed shared memory by maintaining a directory containing the disposition of every cache block (Lenoski et al. 1993; Lenoski et al. 1992). SCI represented an effort to standardize an interconnect and cache coherence protocol

(IEEE 1993). The Alewife project at MIT sought to minimize the hardware support for shared memory (Agarwal et al. 1995), which was pushed further by researchers at the University of Wisconsin (Wood et al. 1993). The Kendall Square Research KSR1 (Frank, Burkhardt, and Rothnie 1993; Saavedra, Gains, and Carlton 1993) went even further and allowed the home location of data in memory to migrate. Alternatively, the Denelcor HEP attempted to hide the cost of remote memory latency by interleaving many independent threads on each processor.

The 1990s have exhibited the beginnings of a dramatic convergence among these various factions. This convergence is driven by many factors. One is clearly that all of the approaches have common requirements. They all require a fast, high-quality interconnect. They all profit from avoiding latency where possible and reducing the absolute latency when it does occur. They all benefit from hiding as much of the communication cost as possible. They all must support various forms of synchronization. We have seen the shared memory work explicitly seek to better integrate message passing in Alewife (Agarwal et al. 1995) and FLASH (Kuskin et al. 1994) to obtain better performance where the regularity of the application can provide large transfers. We have seen data parallel designs incorporate complete commodity processors in the CM-5 (Leiserson et al. 1996), allowing very simple processing of messages at the user level, which provides much better efficiency for message-driven computing and shared memory (von Eicken et al. 1992; Spertus et al. 1993). There remains the additional support for fast global synchronization. We have seen fast global synchronization, message queues, and latency-hiding techniques developed in a NUMA shared memory context in the CRAY T3D (Kessler and Schwarzmeier 1993; Koeninger, Furtney, and Walker 1994), and the message-passing support in the Meiko CS-2 (Barton, Crownie, and McLaren 1994; Homewood and McLaren 1993) provides direct virtual-memory-to-virtual-memory transfers within the user address space. The new element that continues to separate the factions is the use of complete commodity workstation nodes, as in the SP-1, SP-2, and various workstation clusters using merging high-bandwidth networks (Anderson, Culler, and Patterson 1995; Kung et al. 1989; Pfister 1995). The costs of weaker integration into the memory system, imperfect network reliability, and general-purpose system requirements have tended to keep these systems more closely aligned with traditional message passing, although the future developments are far from clear.

1.6 EXERCISES

1.1 Compute the annual growth rate in number of transistors, die size, and clock rate by fitting an exponential to the technology leaders using the data in Table 1.1. Obtain more recent data from the Web, and see how well these trends have held.

1.2 Compute the annual performance growth rates for each of the benchmarks shown in Table 1.2. Comment on the differences that you observe.

Table 1.1 Basic Parameters for Several Microprocessors

Name	Year	Die (mm^2)	Total Transistors	Clock (MHz)
i4004	1971	9	2,300	0.5
i8008	1972	12.25	3,500	0.8
i8080	1974	20.25	5,000	3
M6800	1974	25	5,000	1
M68000	1979	43.56	68,000	12.5
i80286	1982	64	130,000	10
M68020	1984	84.64	180,000	25
i80386	1985	90.25	275,000	16
i80486	1988	160	1,200,000	50
MIPS R3000	1988	72	125,000	33
Motorola 68040	1989	126.4	1,200,000	25
Alpha 21064	1992	233.5	1,680,000	160
Pentium 66	1993	294	3,100,000	66.7
Alpha 21066	1994	209	1,750,000	133
MIPS R10000	1994	298	5,900,000	200
Alpha 21164	1995	298.7	9,300,000	300
UltracSparc	1995	315	3,800,000	167

Table 1.2 Performance of Leading Workstations

Machine	Year	SpecInt	SpecFP	LINPACK	n = 1,000	Peak FP
Sun 4/260	1987	9	6	1.1	1.1	3.3
MIPS M/120	1988	13	10.2	2.1	4.8	6.7
MIPS M/2000	1989	18	21	3.9	7.9	10
IBM RS6000/540	1990	24	44	19	50	60
HP 9000/750	1991	51	101	24	47	66
DEC Alpha AXP	1992	80	180	30	107	150
DEC 7000/610	1993	132.6	200.1	44	156	200
AlphaServer 2100	1994	200	291	43	129	190

1.3 Generally in evaluating performance trade-offs, we evaluate the improvement in performance, or speedup, due to some enhancement. Formally,

$$\text{Speedup due to enhancement } E = \frac{\text{Time}_{without\ E}}{\text{Time}_{with\ E}} = \frac{\text{Performance}_{with\ E}}{\text{Performance}_{without\ E}}$$

In particular, we will often refer to the speedup as a function of the machine parallel (e.g., the number of processors).

Suppose you are given a program that does a fixed amount of work, and some fraction s of that work must be done sequentially. The remaining portion of the work is perfectly parallelizable on P processors. Assuming T_1 is the time taken on one processor, derive a formula for T_p, the time taken on P processors. Use this to get a formula giving an upper bound on the potential speedup on P processors. (This is a variant of what is often called Amdahl's Law [Amdahl 1967].) Explain why it is an upper bound.

1.4 Given a histogram of available parallelism such as that shown in Figure 1.7, where f_i is the fraction of cycles on an ideal machine in which i instructions issue, derive a generalization of Amdahl's Law to estimate the potential speedup on a k-issue superscalar machine. Apply your formula to the histogram data in Figure 1.7 to produce the speedup curve shown in that figure.

1.5 Locate the current TPC performance data on the Web and compare the mix of system configurations, performance, and speedups obtained on those machines with the data presented in Figure 1.4.

1.6 In message-passing models, each process is provided with a special variable or function that gives its unique number or rank among the set of processes executing a program. Most shared memory programming systems provide a fetch&inc operation, which reads the value of a location and atomically increments the location. Write a little pseudocode to show how to use fetch&add to assign each process a unique number. Can you determine the number of processes comprising a shared memory parallel program in a similar way?

1.7 To move an n-byte message along H links in an unloaded store-and-forward network takes time $H\frac{n}{W} + (H - 1)R$, where W is the raw link bandwidth and R is the routing delay per hop. In a network with cut-through routing, this takes time $\frac{n}{W} + (H - 1)R$. Consider an 8×8 grid consisting of 40-MB/s links and routers with 250 ns of delay. What is the minimum, maximum, and average time to move a 64-byte message through the network? A 256-byte message?

1.8 Consider a simple 2D finite difference scheme where at each step every point in the matrix is updated by a weighted average of its four neighbors, $A[i, j] = A[i, j] - w(A[i-1, j] + A[i+1, j] + A[i, j-1] + A[i, j+1])$.

All the values are 64-bit floating-point numbers. Assuming one element per processor and $1{,}024 \times 1{,}024$ elements, how much data must be communicated per step? Explain how this computation could be mapped onto 64 processors so as to minimize the data traffic. Compute how much data must be communicated per step.

1.9 Consider the simple pipelined component described in Example 1.2. Suppose that the application alternates between bursts of m independent operations on the component and phases of computation lasting T ns that do not use the component. Develop an expression describing the execution time of the program based on these parameters. Graph the average message rate as a function of m for various values of T = 100 ns, 200 ns, 400 ns, 800 ns. What is the asymptote?

1.10 Show that Equation 1.4 follows from Equation 1.3.

1.11 What is the x-intercept of the line in Equation 1.3?

1.12 If we consider loading a cache line from memory, the transfer time is the time to actually transmit the data across the bus. The start-up includes the time to obtain access to the bus, convey the address, access the memory, and possibly place the data in the cache before responding to the processor. However, in a modern processor with dynamic instruction scheduling, the overhead may include only the portion spent accessing the cache to detect the miss and placing the request on the bus. The memory access portion contributes to latency, which can potentially be hidden by the overlap with execution of instructions that do not depend on the result of the load.

Suppose we have a machine with a 64-bit-wide bus running at 40 MHz. It takes two bus cycles to arbitrate for the bus and present the address. The cache line size is 32 bytes and the memory access time is 100 ns. What is the latency for a read miss? What bandwidth is obtained on this transfer?

1.13 Suppose this 32-byte line is transferred to another processor and the communication architecture imposes a start-up cost of 2 μs and a data transfer bandwidth of 20 MB/s. What is the total latency of the remote operation?

1.14 If we consider sending an n-byte message to another processor, we may use the same model as in Exercise 1.12. The start-up can be thought of as the time for a zero-length message; it includes the software overhead on the two processors, the cost of accessing the network interface, and the time to actually cross the network. The transfer time is usually determined by the point along the path with the least bandwidth, that is, the bottleneck.

Suppose we have a machine with a message start-up of 100 μs and an asymptotic peak bandwidth of 80 MB/s. At what size message is half of the peak bandwidth obtained?

1.15 In some cases, Equation 1.6 can be used for estimating data transfer performance based on design parameters. In other cases, it serves as an empirical tool for fitting measurements to a line to determine the effective start-up and peak bandwidth of a portion of a system. Assume that before transmitting a message, the data must be copied into a buffer. The basic message time is as in Exercise 1.14, but the copy is performed at a cost of 5 cycles per 32-bit word on a 100-MHz machine. Give an equation for the expected user-level message time. How does the cost of a copy compare with a typical fixed cost of entering the operating system?

1.16 Consider a machine running at 100 MIPS on some workload with the following mix: 50% ALU, 20% loads, 10% stores, and 20% branches. Suppose the instruction miss rate is 1%, the data miss rate is 5%, and the cache line size is 32 bytes. For the purpose of this calculation, treat a store miss as requiring two cache line transfers, one to load the newly updated line and one to replace the dirty line. If the machine provides a 250-MB/s bus, how many processors can it accommodate at peak bus bandwidth? What is the bandwidth demand of each processor?

1.17 Exercise 1.16 looks only at the sum of the average bandwidths. As the bus approaches saturation, however, it takes longer to obtain access for the bus, so it looks to the processor as if the memory system is slower. The effect is to slow down all of the processors in the system, thereby reducing their bandwidth demand. Let's try an analogous calculation from the other direction.

Assume the instruction mix and miss rate as in Exercise 1.16, but ignore the MIPS since that depends on the performance of the memory system. Assume instead that the processor runs at 100 MHz and has an ideal CPI (with a perfect memory system) of one. The unloaded cache miss penalty is 20 cycles. You can ignore the write back for stores. (As a starter, you might want to compute the MIPS rate for this new machine.) Assume that the memory system (i.e., the bus and the memory controller) is utilized throughout the miss. What is the utilization of the memory system U_1 with a single processor? From this result, estimate the number of processors that could be supported before the processor demand would exceed the available bus bandwidth.

1.18 Of course, no matter how many processors you place on the bus, they will never exceed the available bandwidth. Explain what happens to processor performance in response to bus contention. Can you formalize your observations?

2

Parallel Programs

To understand and evaluate design decisions in a parallel machine, we must have an idea of the software that runs on the machine. Understanding program behavior has led to some of the most important advances in uniprocessors, including memory hierarchies and instruction set design. It is all the more important in multiprocessors, both because of the increase in degrees of freedom and because of the much greater performance penalties caused by mismatches between applications and systems.

Understanding parallel software is important for algorithm designers, for programmers, and for architects. As algorithm designers, it helps us focus on designing algorithms that can be run effectively in parallel on real systems. As programmers, it helps us understand the key performance issues and obtain the best performance from a system. And as architects, it helps us understand the workloads we are designing against and their important degrees of freedom. Parallel software and its implications will be the focus of the next three chapters of this book. This chapter describes the process of creating parallel programs in the major programming models. Chapter 3 focuses on the performance issues that must be addressed in this process, exploring some of the key interactions between parallel applications and architectures. Chapter 4 relies on this understanding of hardware/software interactions to develop guidelines for using parallel workloads to evaluate architectural trade-offs. In addition to being helpful to architects, the material in these chapters is useful for users of parallel machines as well: Chapters 2 and 3 for programmers and algorithm designers, and Chapter 4 for users making decisions about what types of machines to procure. However, the major focus is on issues that architects should understand before they get into the nuts and bolts of machine design.

As architects of sequential machines, we generally take programs for granted: the field is mature, and there is a large base of programs that can (or must) be viewed as fixed. We optimize the machine design against the requirements of these programs. Although we recognize that programmers may further optimize their code—for example, as caches become larger or floating-point support is improved—we usually evaluate new designs without anticipating such software changes. Compilers may evolve along with the architecture, but the source program is still treated as fixed. In parallel architecture, there is a much stronger and more dynamic interaction between the evolution of machine designs and that of parallel software. Since parallel computing is all about performance, programming tends to be oriented toward taking advantage of what machines provide. Parallelism offers a new degree of freedom—the number of processors—and higher costs for data access and coordination, giving the programmer a wide scope for software optimizations. Even as architects, we therefore need to open the application "black box." Understanding the important aspects of the process of creating parallel software (the focus of this chapter) helps us appreciate the role and limitations of the architecture. A deeper look at performance issues in the next chapter will shed greater light on hardware/software trade-offs.

Even after a problem and a good sequential algorithm to solve it are determined, a substantial process is involved in arriving at a parallel program and the execution characteristics that it offers to a multiprocessor architecture. This chapter presents general principles of the parallelization process and illustrates them with real examples. It begins by introducing four actual problems that serve as case studies throughout the next two chapters. Then it describes the four major steps in creating a parallel program—using the case studies to illustrate—followed by examples of how a simple parallel program might be written in each of the major programming models. As discussed in Chapter 1, the dominant models from a programming perspective narrow down to three: the data parallel model, a shared address space or shared memory, and message passing between private address spaces. This chapter illustrates the primitives provided by these models and how they might be used, without much concern for performance. After the performance issues in the parallelization process are understood in Chapter 3, the four application case studies will be treated in more detail to create high-performance versions of them.

2.1 PARALLEL APPLICATION CASE STUDIES

We saw in the previous chapter that multiprocessors are used for a wide range of applications—from multiprogramming and commercial computing to so-called Grand Challenge scientific problems—and that the most demanding of these applications tend to be from scientific and engineering computing. Of the four case studies referred to throughout this chapter and the next, two are from scientific computing, one is from computer graphics, and one is from commercial computing. Besides being from different application domains, the case studies are chosen to represent a range of important behaviors found in other parallel programs as well.

The first case study simulates the motion of ocean currents by discretizing the problem on a set of regular grids and solving a system of equations on the grids. This technique is very common in scientific computing and leads to a set of very common communication patterns. The second case study represents another important form of scientific computing, in which, rather than discretizing the domain on a grid, the computational domain is represented as a large number of bodies that interact with one another and move around as a result of these interactions. These so-called n-body problems are common in many areas, such as simulating galaxies in astrophysics (our specific case study), simulating proteins and other molecules in chemistry and biology, and simulating electromagnetic interactions. As in many other areas, hierarchical algorithms for solving these problems have become very popular. Hierarchical n-body algorithms, such as the one in our case study, have also been used to solve important problems in computer graphics and some particularly difficult types of equation systems. Unlike the first case study, this one leads to irregular, long-range, and unpredictable communication.

The third case study is from computer graphics, a very important consumer of moderate-scale multiprocessors. It traverses a three-dimensional scene with highly irregular and unpredictable access patterns and renders it into a two-dimensional image for display. The first three case studies are part of a benchmark suite (Singh, Weber, and Gupta 1992) that is widely used in architectural evaluations in the literature, so a wealth of detailed information is available about them. They will be used to illustrate architectural trade-offs in this book as well.

The last case study represents an increasingly important class of commercial applications that analyze the huge volumes of data being produced by our information society to discover useful knowledge, categories, and trends. These information processing applications tend to be I/O intensive, so parallelizing the I/O activity effectively is very important.

2.1.1 Simulating Ocean Currents

To model the climate of the earth, it is important to understand how the atmosphere interacts with the oceans that occupy three-fourths of the earth's surface. This case study simulates the motion of water currents in the ocean. These currents develop and evolve under the influence of several physical forces, including atmospheric effects, wind, and friction with the ocean floor. Near the ocean walls, additional "vertical" friction is present as well, which leads to the development of eddy currents. The goal of this particular application case study is to simulate these eddy currents over time and understand their interactions with the mean ocean flow.

Good models for ocean behavior are complicated: predicting the state of the ocean at any instant requires the solution of complex systems of equations, which can only be performed numerically by computer. We are, additionally, interested in the behavior of the currents over time. The actual physical problem is continuous in both space (the ocean basin) and time, but to enable computer simulation we discretize it along both dimensions. To discretize space, we model the ocean basin as a grid of points. Every important variable—such as pressure, velocity, and various currents—has a value at each grid point in this discretization. This particular application uses not a three-dimensional grid but a set of two-dimensional, horizontal cross sections through the ocean basin, each represented by a two-dimensional grid of points (see Figure 2.1). For simplicity, the ocean is modeled as a rectangular basin and the grid points are assumed to be equally spaced. Each of the many variables is therefore represented by a separate two-dimensional array for each cross section through the ocean. For the time dimension, we discretize time into a series of finite time-steps. The equations of motion are solved at all the grid points in one time-step, the state of the variables is updated as a result, the equations of motion are solved again for the next time-step, and so on repeatedly.

Every time-step itself consists of several computational phases. Many of these are used to set up values for the different variables at all the grid points using the results

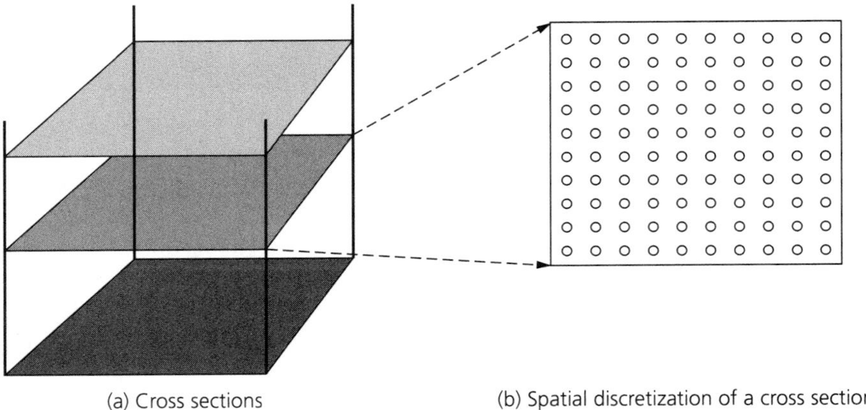

FIGURE 2.1 Horizontal cross sections through an ocean basin and their spatial discretization into regular grids

from the previous time-step. In other phases, the system of equations for a time-step is actually solved. All the phases, including the solver, involve sweeping through all points of the relevant arrays and manipulating their values. The solver phases are a little more complex, as we shall see when we discuss this case study in more detail in Chapter 3.

The more grid points we use in each dimension to represent a fixed-size ocean, the finer the spatial resolution of our discretization and the more accurate our simulation. For an ocean such as the Atlantic, with its roughly 2,000 km × 2,000 km span, using a grid of 100 × 100 points implies a distance of 20 km between points in each dimension. This is not a very fine resolution, so we would like to use many more grid points. Similarly, shorter physical intervals between time-steps lead to greater simulation accuracy. For example, to simulate 5 years of ocean movement by updating the state every 8 hours, we would need about 5,500 time-steps. The computational demands for high accuracy are large, and the need for multiprocessing is clear.

Fortunately, the application naturally affords a lot of concurrency: many of the setup phases in a time-step are independent of one another and therefore can be done in parallel, and the processing of different grid points in each phase or grid computation can itself be done in parallel. For example, we might assign different parts of each ocean cross section to different processors and have the processors perform each phase of computation on their assigned parts of the cross section grids (a data parallel formulation).

2.1.2 Simulating the Evolution of Galaxies

The second case study is also from scientific computing. It seeks to understand the evolution of stars in a system of galaxies over time. For example, we may want to study what happens when galaxies collide or how a random collection of stars folds into a defined galactic shape. This problem involves simulating the motion of a number of bodies (here stars) moving under forces exerted on each by all the others, an n-body problem. The computation is discretized in space by treating each star as a separate body or by sampling to use one body to represent many stars. Here again we discretize the computation in time and simulate the motion of the galaxies for many time-steps. In each time-step, we compute the gravitational forces exerted on each star by all the others and update the position, velocity, and other attributes of that star.

Computing the forces among stars is the most expensive part of a time-step. A simple method to compute forces is to calculate pairwise interactions among all stars. This has $O(n^2)$ computational complexity for n stars and is therefore prohibitive for the millions of stars that we would like to simulate. However, by taking advantage of insights into the force laws, smarter hierarchical algorithms are able to reduce the complexity to $O(n \log n)$. This makes it feasible to simulate problems with millions of stars in a reasonable time but only by using powerful multiprocessors. The hierarchical algorithms use the basic insight that, since the strength of the gravitational interaction falls off with distance as

$$G\frac{m_1 m_1}{r^2}$$

the influences of stars that are farther away are weaker and therefore do not need to be computed as accurately as those of stars that are close by. Thus, if a group of stars is sufficiently far from a given star, we can compute the effect of the group on the star by approximating the group as a single star at the center of the group with little loss in accuracy (see Figure 2.2). The farther away the stars are from a given star, the larger the group that can be thus approximated. In fact, the strength of many physical interactions falls off with distance, so hierarchical methods are becoming increasingly popular in many areas of computing.

The particular hierarchical force calculation algorithm used in this case study is the Barnes-Hut algorithm. (The case study is called Barnes-Hut in the literature, and this name is used here as well.) We shall see how the algorithm works in Section 3.5.2. Since galaxies are denser in some regions and sparser in others, the distribution of stars in space is highly irregular. The distribution also changes with time as the galaxy evolves. The nature of the hierarchical approach implies that stars in denser regions interact more with other stars and centers of mass—and hence have more work associated with them—than stars in sparser regions. Ample concurrency exists across stars within a time-step, but given their irregular and dynamically changing nature, the challenge is to exploit concurrency efficiently on a parallel architecture.

2.1.3 Visualizing Complex Scenes Using Ray Tracing

The third case study is the visualization of complex scenes in computer graphics. A common technique used to render such scenes into images is known as *ray tracing*.

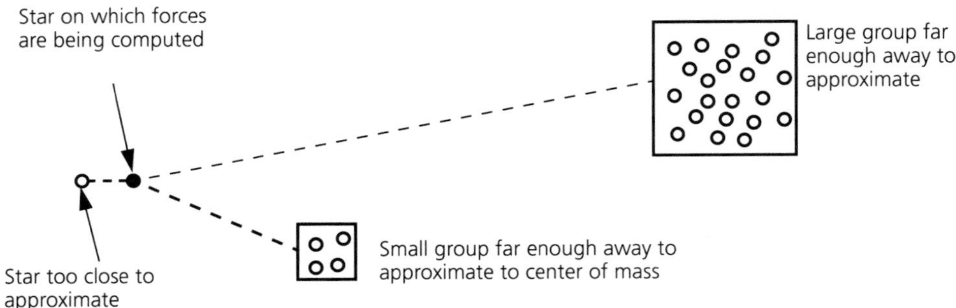

FIGURE 2.2 The insight used by hierarchical methods for *n*-body problems. A group of bodies that is far enough away from a given body may be approximated by the center of mass of the group. The farther apart the bodies, the larger the group that may be thus approximated.

The scene is represented as a set of objects in three-dimensional space, and the image being rendered is represented as a two-dimensional array of pixels (picture elements) whose color, opacity, and brightness values are to be computed. The pixels taken together represent the image, and the resolution of the image is determined by the distance between pixels in each dimension. The scene is rendered as seen from a specific viewpoint or position of the eye. Rays are shot from that viewpoint through every pixel in the image plane and into the scene. The algorithm traces the paths of these rays—computing their reflection, refraction, and lighting interactions as they strike and reflect off objects—and thus computes values for the color and brightness of the corresponding pixels. There is obvious parallelism across the rays shot through different pixels. This case study is referred to as Raytrace.

2.1.4 Mining Data for Associations

Information processing is rapidly becoming a major market for parallel systems. Businesses acquiring data about customers and products are devoting computational power to automatically extracting useful information or "knowledge" from this data. Examples from a customer database might include determining the buying patterns of demographic groups or segmenting customers according to relationships in their buying patterns. This process is called *data mining*. It differs from standard database queries in that its goal is to identify implicit trends and segmentations in data rather than simply look up the data requested by a direct, explicit query. For example, finding all customers who have bought cat food in the last week is not data mining; however, segmenting customers according to relationships in their age groups, their monthly incomes, and their preferences in cat food, in cars, and in kitchen utensils is.

A particular type of data mining is mining for associations. Here the goal is to discover relationships (associations) in the available information related to, say, different customers and their transactions and to generate rules for the inference of customer behavior. For example, the database may store for every transaction the list of items purchased in that transaction. The goal of the mining may be to determine associations between sets of commonly purchased items that tend to be purchased together—for example, the conditional probability $P(S_1/S_2)$ that a certain set of items S_1 is found in a transaction given that a different set of items S_2 is found in that transaction, where S_1 and S_2 are sets of items that occur often in customer transactions. If this probability is high, then customers who have the set S_2 in their purchase transactions may be good advertising targets of items in set S_1.

Consider the problem a little more concretely. We are given a database in which the records correspond to customer purchase transactions, as described above. Each transaction has a transaction identifier and a set of attributes, which in this case are the items purchased. The first goal in mining for associations is to examine the database and determine which sets of k items, say, are found to occur together in more than a certain threshold fraction of the transactions. A set of items (of any size) that occur together in a transaction is called an *itemset*, and an itemset that is found in more than this threshold fraction of transactions is called a *large itemset*. Once the large itemsets of size k are found, together with their frequencies of occurrence in the database, determining the association rules among them is quite easy. The problem we consider therefore focuses on discovering the large itemsets of size k and their frequencies. The database may be in main memory or more commonly on disk.

A simple way to solve the problem is to first determine the large itemsets of size one. From these, a set of candidate itemsets of size two items can be constructed—using the basic insight that an itemset can only be large if all its subsets are also large—and their frequency of occurrence in the transaction database can be counted. This results in a list of large itemsets of size two. The process is repeated until we obtain the large itemsets of size k. There is concurrency in examining large itemsets of size $k - 1$ to determine candidate itemsets of size k and in counting the number of transactions in the database that contain each of the candidate itemsets.

2.2 THE PARALLELIZATION PROCESS

The four case studies—Ocean, Barnes-Hut, Raytrace, and Data Mining—offer abundant concurrency and will help illustrate the process of creating effective parallel programs in this chapter and the next. For concreteness, we will assume that the sequential algorithm that we are to make parallel is given to us, perhaps as a description or as a sequential program. In many cases, as in these case studies, the best sequential algorithm for a problem lends itself easily to parallelization; in others, it may not afford enough parallelism, and a fundamentally different algorithm may be required. The rich field of parallel algorithm design is outside the scope of this book. However, whatever the chosen underlying sequential algorithm, a significant process of creating a good parallel program is present in all cases, and we must understand this process in order to program parallel machines effectively and evaluate architectures against parallel programs.

At a high level, the job of parallelization involves identifying the work that can be done in parallel, determining how to distribute the work and perhaps the data among the processing nodes, and managing the necessary data access, communication, and synchronization. Note that the work to be done includes computation, data access, and input/output activity. The goal is to obtain high performance while keeping programming effort and the resource requirements of the program low. In particular, we would like to obtain good speedup over the best sequential program that solves the same problem. This requires that we ensure a balanced distribution of work among processors, reduce the amount of interprocessor communication, which is expensive, and keep low the overhead of communication, synchronization, and parallelism management.

The steps in the process of creating a parallel program may be performed either by the programmer or by one of the many layers of system software that intervene between the programmer and the architecture. These layers include the compiler, the run-time system, and the operating system. In a perfect world, system software would allow users to write programs in the form they found most convenient (for example, as sequential programs in a high-level language or as an even higher-level specification of the problem) and would automatically perform the transformation into efficient parallel programs and executions. While much research is being conducted in parallelizing compiler technology and in programming languages, the goal of automatic parallelization is very ambitious and has not yet been fully achieved. In practice today, the vast majority of the process is still the responsibility of the programmer, with perhaps some help from the compiler and run-time system. Regardless of how the responsibility is divided among these parallelizing agents, the issues and trade-offs are similar, and it is important that we understand them. For concreteness, we shall assume for the most part that the programmer has to make all the decisions.

Let us now examine the parallelization process in a more structured way, by looking at the actual steps in it. Each step will address a subset of the issues needed to obtain good performance. These performance issues will be discussed in detail in Chapter 3 and only mentioned briefly here.

2.2.1 Steps in the Process

To understand the steps in creating a parallel program, let us first define three important concepts: tasks, processes, and processors. A *task* is an arbitrarily defined piece of the work done by the program. It is the smallest unit of concurrency that the parallel program can exploit; that is, an individual task is executed by only one processor, and concurrency among processors is exploited only across tasks. In the Ocean application, we can think of a single grid point in each phase of computation as being a task, or a row of grid points, or any arbitrary subset of a grid. We could even consider an entire grid computation to be a single task, in which case parallelism is exploited only across independent grid computations. In Barnes-Hut a task may be a body, in Raytrace a ray or a group of rays, and in Data Mining it may be checking a single transaction for the occurrence of a particular itemset. What exactly constitutes a task is not prescribed by the underlying sequential program; it is a choice of the parallelizing agent, though it usually matches some natural granularity of work in the sequential program structure (for example, an iteration of a loop). If the amount of work a task performs is small, it is called a *fine-grained* task; otherwise, it is called *coarse-grained.*

A *process* (referred to interchangeably as a *thread* hereafter) is an abstract entity that performs tasks.[1] A parallel program is composed of multiple cooperating processes, each of which performs a subset of the tasks in the program. Tasks are assigned to processes by some assignment mechanism. For example, if the computation for each row in a grid in Ocean is viewed as a task, then a simple assignment mechanism may be to give an equal number of adjacent rows to each process, thus dividing the ocean cross section into as many horizontal slices as there are processes. In Data Mining, the assignment may be determined both by which portions of the database are assigned to each process and by how the candidate itemsets within a list are assigned to processes to look up the database. Processes may need to communicate and synchronize with one another to perform their assigned tasks. Finally, the way processes perform their assigned tasks is by executing them on the physical *processors* in the machine.

It is important to understand the difference between processes and processors from a parallelization perspective. While processors are physical resources, processes provide a convenient way of abstracting, or *virtualizing,* a multiprocessor: we initially write parallel programs in terms of processes, not physical processors; mapping processes to processors is a subsequent step. The number of processes does not have to be the same as the number of processors available to the program in a given execution. If there are more processes, they are multiplexed onto the available processors; if there are fewer processes, then some processors will remain idle.

Given these concepts, the job of creating a parallel program from a sequential one consists of four steps, illustrated in Figure 2.3:

1. *Decomposition* of the computation into tasks
2. *Assignment* of tasks to processes
3. *Orchestration* of the necessary data access, communication, and synchronization among processes
4. *Mapping* or binding of processes to processors

Together, decomposition and assignment are called *partitioning,* since they divide the work done by the program among the cooperating processes. Let us examine the steps and their individual goals a little further.

---

1. In Chapter 1 we used the correct operating systems definition of a process: an address space and one or more threads of control that share that address space. Thus, processes and threads are distinguished in that definition. To simplify our discussion of parallel programming in this chapter, we do not make this distinction but assume that a process has only one thread of control.

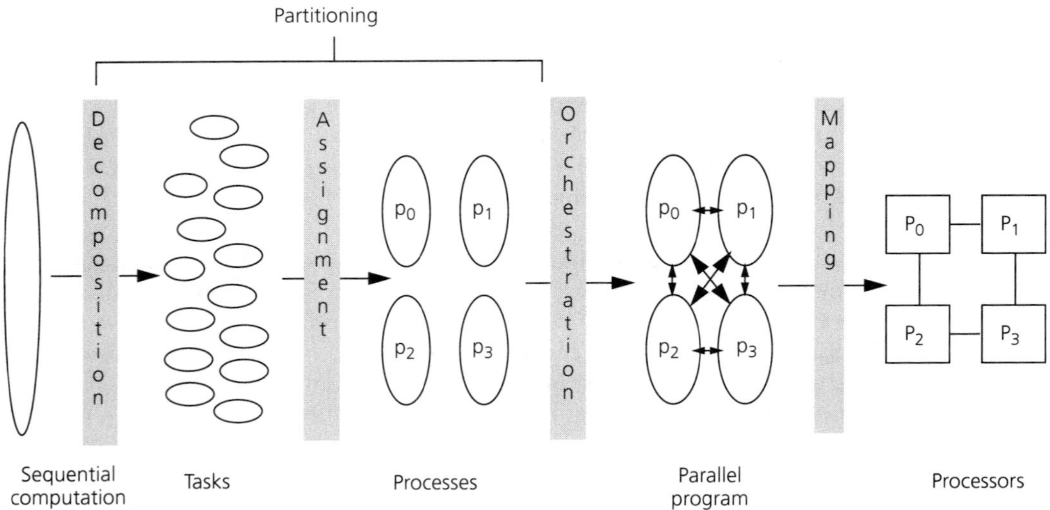

FIGURE 2.3 Steps in parallelization and the relationships among tasks, processes, and processors. The decomposition and assignment phases together are called *partitioning.* The orchestration phase coordinates data access, communication, and synchronization among processes (p), and the mapping phase maps them to physical processors (P).

Decomposition

Decomposition means breaking up the computation into a collection of tasks. In general, tasks may become available dynamically as the program executes, and the number of tasks available at a time may vary over the execution of the program. The maximum number of tasks available for execution at a time provides an upper bound on the number of processes (and hence processors) that can be used effectively at that time. Therefore, the major goal in decomposition is to expose enough concurrency to keep the processes busy at all times, yet not so much that the overhead of managing the tasks becomes substantial compared to the useful work done.

Limited concurrency is the most fundamental limitation on the speedup achievable through parallelism. It is not only the available concurrency in the underlying problem that matters but also how much of this concurrency is exposed in the decomposition. The impact of available concurrency is codified in one of the few "laws" of parallel computing, called Amdahl's Law. If some portions of a program's execution don't have as much concurrency as the number of processors used, then some processors will have to be idle for those portions and speedup will be suboptimal. To see this in its simplest form, consider what happens if a fraction s of a program's execution time on a uniprocessor is inherently sequential; that is, it cannot be parallelized. Even if the rest of the program is parallelized to run on a large number of processors in infinitesimal time, this sequential time will remain. The overall execution time of the parallel program will be at least s, normalized to a total sequential time of 1, and the speedup limited to $1/s$. For example, if $s = 0.2$ (20% of the program's execution is sequential), the maximum speedup available is 1/0.2, or 5, regardless of the number of processors used, even if we ignore all other sources of overhead. Example 2.1 provides a simple but more realistic example.

EXAMPLE 2.1 Consider an example program with two phases. In the first phase, a single operation is performed independently on all points of a two-dimensional n-by-n grid, as in Ocean. In the second phase, the sum of the n^2 grid point values is computed. If we have p processors, we can assign n^2/p points to each processor and complete the first phase in parallel in time n^2/p. In the second phase, each processor can add each of its assigned n^2/p values into a global sum variable. What is the problem with this assignment, and how can we expose more concurrency? Ignore the costs of data access and communication.

Answer The problem is that the accumulations into the global sum must be done one at a time, or *serialized*, to avoid corrupting the sum value by having two processors try to modify it simultaneously (see mutual exclusion in Section 2.3.5). Thus, the second phase is effectively serial and takes n^2 time regardless of p. The total time in parallel is $n^2/p + n^2$, compared to a sequential time of $2n^2$, so the speedup is at most

$$\frac{2n^2}{\frac{n^2}{p} + n^2}$$

or

$$\frac{2p}{p + 1}$$

which is at best 2 even if a very large number of processors is used.

We can expose more concurrency by using a little trick. Instead of summing each value directly into the global sum and serializing all the summing, we divide the second phase into two phases. In the new second phase, a process sums its assigned values independently into a private sum. Then, in the third phase, processes sum their private sums into the global sum. The second phase is now fully parallel; the third phase is serialized as before, but there are only p operations in it, not n. The total parallel time is $n^2/p + n^2/p + p$, and the speedup is at best $p \times 2n^2/(2n^2 + p^2)$. If n is large relative to p, this speedup limit is almost linear in the number of processors used. Figure 2.4 illustrates the improvement and the impact of limited concurrency. ■

More generally, given a decomposition and a problem size, we can construct a *concurrency profile,* which depicts how many operations (or tasks) are available to be performed concurrently in the application at a given time. The concurrency profile is a function of the problem, the decomposition, and the problem size. However, it is independent of the number of processors, effectively assuming that an infinite number of processors is available. It is also independent of the assignment or orchestration. These concurrency profiles may be easy to provide analytically (as in Example 2.1 and as we shall see for matrix factorization in Exercise 3.8) or they may be quite irregular. For example, Figure 2.5 shows a concurrency profile of a parallel event-driven simulation for the synthesis of digital logic systems. The x-axis is time,

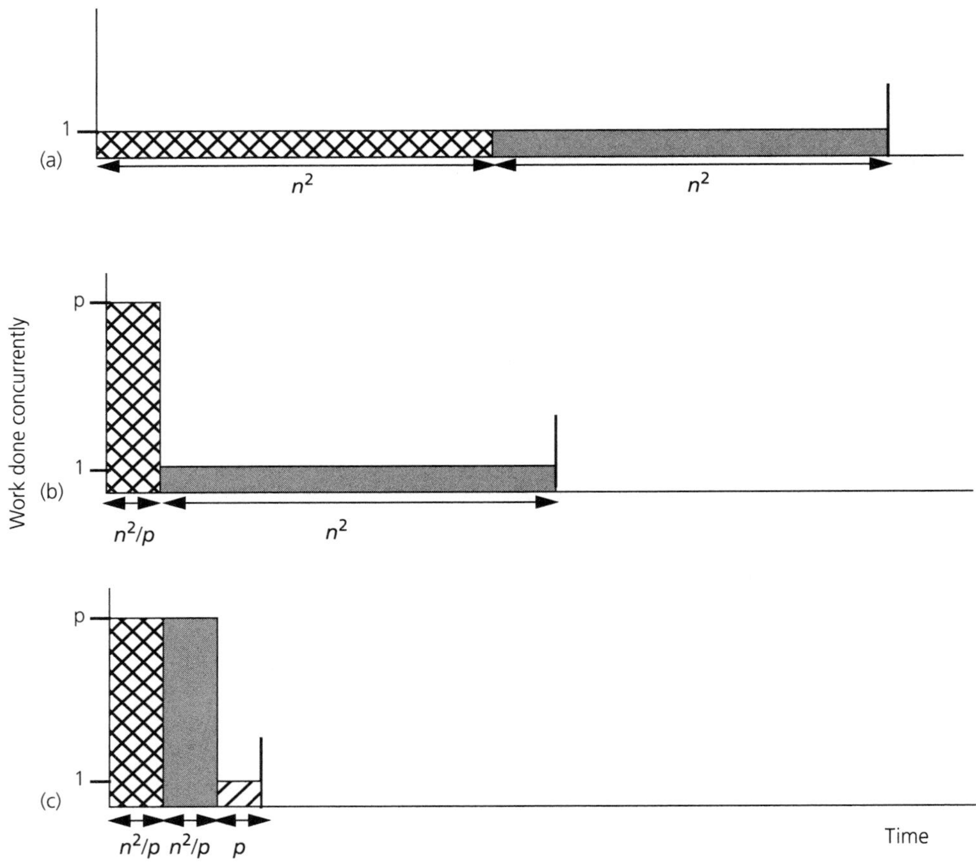

FIGURE 2.4 Illustration of the impact of limited concurrency: (a) one processor; (b) *p* processors, n^2 operations serialized; (c) *p* processors, *p* operations serialized. The *x*-axis is time, and the *y*-axis is the amount of work available (exposed by the decomposition) to be done in parallel at a given time. (a) shows the profile for a single processor. (b) shows the original case in the example, which is divided into two phases: one fully concurrent and one fully serialized. (c) shows the improved version, which is divided into three phases: the first two fully concurrent and the last fully serialized but with a lot less work in it (*O(p)* rather than *O(n)*).

measured in clock cycles of the circuit being simulated. The *y*-axis or amount of concurrency is the number of logic gates in the circuit that are ready to be evaluated at a given time, which is a function of the circuit, the values of its inputs, and time. A wide range of unpredictable concurrency exists across clock cycles, with some cycles having almost no concurrency.

The area under the curve in the concurrency profile is the total amount of work done; that is, the number of operations or tasks computed or the "time" taken on a single processor. Its horizontal extent is a lower bound on the time that it would

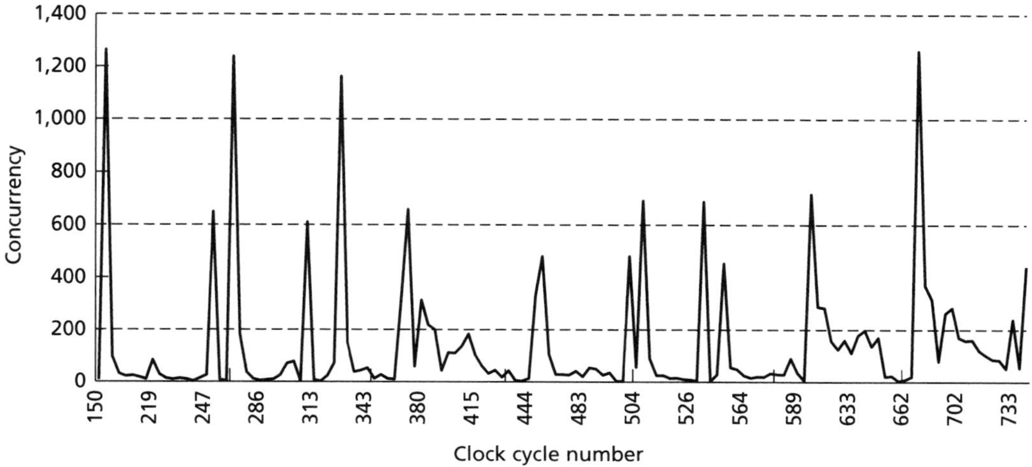

FIGURE 2.5 Concurrency profile for a distributed-time, discrete-event logic simulator. The circuit being simulated is a simple MIPS R6000 microprocessor. The *y*-axis shows the number of logic elements available for evaluation in a given simulated clock cycle.

take to run the best parallel program given that decomposition, assuming an infinitely large number of processors and that data access and communication are free. The area divided by the horizontal extent therefore gives us a limit on the achievable speedup with an unlimited number of processors, which is simply the average concurrency available in the application over time. A rewording of Amdahl's Law may therefore be

$$\text{Speedup} \leq \frac{\text{Area under Concurrency Profile}}{\text{Horizontal Extent of Concurrency Profile}}$$

For p processors, if f_k is the number of x-axis points in the concurrency profile that have concurrency k, then we can write Amdahl's Law as

$$\text{Speedup}(p) \leq \frac{\sum_{k=1}^{\infty} f_k k}{\sum_{k=1}^{\infty} f_k \left\lceil \frac{k}{p} \right\rceil} \tag{2.1}$$

It is easy to see that if the total work

$$\sum_{k=1}^{\infty} f_k k$$

is normalized to 1 and a fraction s of this is serial, then the speedup with an infinite number of processors is limited by $1/s$, and that with p processors it is limited by

$$\frac{1}{s + \frac{1-s}{p}}$$

In fact, Amdahl's Law can be applied to any overhead of parallelism (not just limited concurrency) that is not alleviated by using more processors. For now, Amdahl's Law quantifies the importance of exposing enough concurrency as a first step in creating a parallel program.

Assignment

Assignment means specifying the mechanism by which tasks will be distributed among processes. For example, which process is responsible for computing forces on which stars in Barnes-Hut? Which process will count occurrences of which itemsets, and in which parts of the database, in Data Mining?

The primary performance goals of assignment are to balance the workload among processes, to reduce the amount of interprocess communication, and to reduce the run-time overhead of managing the assignment. Balancing the workload is often referred to as *load balancing*. The workload to be balanced includes computation, input/output, and data access or communication; programs that are not balanced well among processes are said to be *load imbalanced*. Interprocess communication is expensive, especially when the processes run on different processors, and complex assignments of tasks to processes may incur overhead at run time.

Achieving these performance goals simultaneously can appear intimidating. However, most programs lend themselves to a fairly structured approach to partitioning (i.e., decomposition and assignment). For example, programs are often structured in phases, and candidate tasks for decomposition within a phase are often easily identified as seen in the case studies. The appropriate assignment of tasks is often discernible either by inspection of the code or from a higher-level understanding of the application. Where this is not so, well-known heuristic techniques are often applicable.

If the assignment is completely determined at the beginning of the program, or just after reading and analyzing the input, and does not change thereafter, it is called a *static* or *predetermined assignment*; if the assignment of work to processes is determined at run time as the program executes (perhaps to react to load imbalances), it is called a *dynamic assignment*. We shall see examples of both in Chapter 3. Note that this use of "static" is a little different from the compile-time meaning typically used in computer science. Compile-time assignment that does not change at run time would indeed be static, but the term is more general here.

Decomposition and assignment are the major algorithmic steps in parallelization. They are usually independent of the underlying architecture and programming model, although sometimes the cost and complexity of using certain primitives on a system can impact decomposition and assignment decisions. As architects, we assume that the programs that will run on our machines are reasonably partitioned. There is nothing we can do if a computation is not parallel enough or not balanced across processes and little we may be able to do if it overwhelms the machine with communication. As programmers, we usually focus on decomposition and assignment first, independent of the programming model or architecture, though in some cases the properties of the latter may cause us to revisit our partitioning strategy.

Orchestration

Orchestration is the step in which the architecture and programming model, as well as the programming language itself, play a large role. To execute their assigned tasks, processes need mechanisms to name and access data, to exchange data (communicate) with other processes, and to synchronize with one another. Orchestration uses the available mechanisms to accomplish these goals correctly and efficiently. The choices made in orchestration are much more dependent on the programming model, and on the efficiencies with which the primitives of the programming model are supported, than the choices made in the previous steps. Some questions in orchestration include how to organize data structures, how to schedule the tasks assigned to a process temporally to exploit data locality, whether to communicate implicitly or explicitly and in small or large messages, and how exactly to organize and express the interprocess communication and synchronization that resulted from assignment. The programming language is important both because this is the step in which the program is actually written and because some of the trade-offs in orchestration are influenced strongly by available language mechanisms and their costs.

The major performance goals in orchestration are reducing the cost of the communication and synchronization as seen by the processors, preserving locality of data reference, scheduling tasks so that those on which many other tasks depend are completed early, and reducing the overhead of parallelism management. The job of architects is to provide the appropriate primitives with efficiencies that simplify successful orchestration. We shall discuss the major aspects of orchestration further when we see how programs are actually written.

Mapping

The cooperating processes that result from the decomposition, assignment, and orchestration steps constitute a full-fledged parallel program on modern systems. The program may choose to control the mapping of processes to processors, but if not, the operating system will take care of it, providing a parallel execution. Mapping tends to be fairly specific to the system or programming environment.

In the simplest case, the processors in the machine are partitioned into fixed subsets, possibly the entire machine, and only a single program runs at a time in a subset. This is called *space-sharing* of the machine. The program can bind, or *pin*, processes to processors to ensure that they do not migrate during the execution; it can even control exactly which processor a process runs on so as to preserve locality of communication in the network topology. Strict space-sharing schemes, together with some simple mechanisms for time-sharing a subset among multiple applications, have so far been typical of large-scale multiprocessors. At the other extreme, the operating system may dynamically control which process runs where and when—without allowing the user any control over the mapping—to achieve better aggregate resource sharing and utilization. Each processor may employ the usual multiprogrammed scheduling criteria to manage processes from the same or different programs, and processes may be moved around among processors as the scheduler dictates. The operating system may extend the scheduling criteria to include multiprocessor-specific issues (for example, trying to have a process be scheduled on the same processor as much as possible so that the process can reuse its state in the processor cache and trying to schedule processes from the same application at the same time). In fact, most modern systems fall somewhere between these two extremes: the user may ask the system to preserve certain properties, giving the user program some control over the mapping, but the operating system is allowed to change the mapping dynamically for effective resource management.

Mapping and associated resource management issues in multiprogrammed systems are active areas of research. However, our goal here is to understand parallel programming in its basic form, so for simplicity we assume that a single parallel program has complete control over the resources of the machine. We also assume that the number of processes equals the number of processors and that neither changes during the execution of the program. By default, the operating system will place one process on every processor in no particular order. Processes are assumed not to migrate from one processor to another during execution. For this reason, the terms "process" and "processor" are used interchangeably in the rest of the chapter.

2.2.2 Parallelizing Computation versus Data

The view of the parallelization process described above has been centered on computation, or work, rather than on data. It is the computation that is decomposed and assigned. However, due to the programming model or performance considerations, we may be responsible for decomposing and assigning data to processes as well. In fact, in many important classes of problems, the decomposition of work and data are so strongly related that they are difficult or even unnecessary to distinguish. Ocean is a good example: each cross-sectional grid through the ocean is represented as an array, and we can view the parallelization as decomposing the data in each array and assigning parts of it to processes. The process that is assigned a portion of an array will then be responsible for the computation associated with that portion; this is known as an *owner computes* arrangement. A similar situation exists in Data Mining, where we can view the database as being decomposed and assigned; of course, here is also the question of assigning the itemsets to processes. Several language systems, including the high-performance Fortran standard (Koebel et al. 1994; High Performance Fortran Forum 1993), allow the programmer to specify the decomposition and assignment of data structures. The assignment of computation then follows the assignment of data in an owner computes manner. However, the distinction between computation and data is stronger in many other more irregular applications, including the Barnes-Hut and Raytrace case studies, as we shall see. Since the computation-centric view is more general, we shall retain this view and consider data management to be part of the orchestration step.

2.2.3 Goals of the Parallelization Process

As stated previously, the major goal of using a parallel machine is to improve performance by obtaining speedup over the best uniprocessor execution. Each of the steps in creating a parallel program has a role to play in achieving this overall goal, and each step has its own subset of performance goals. These are summarized in Table 2.1; the next chapter discusses them in more detail.

Creating an effective parallel program requires evaluating cost as well as performance. In addition to the dollar cost of the machine itself, we must consider the resource requirements of the program on the architecture (for example, its memory usage) and the effort it takes to develop a satisfactory program. While costs and their impact are often more difficult to quantify than performance, they are very important, and we must not lose sight of them; in fact, we often decide to compromise performance to reduce them. As algorithm designers, we should favor high-performance solutions that keep the resource requirements of the algorithm small and that don't require inordinate programming effort. As architects, we should try to design high-performance systems that facilitate resource-efficient algorithms and reduce programming effort in addition to being low cost. For example, an architecture on which performance improves gradually with increased programming effort may be preferable to one that is capable of ultimately delivering better performance but requires inordinate programming effort to even achieve acceptable performance.

Table 2.1 Steps in the Parallelization Process and Their Goals

Step	Architecture-Dependent?	Major Performance Goals
Decomposition	Mostly no	Expose enough concurrency but not too much
Assignment	Mostly no	Balance workload Reduce communication volume
Orchestration	Yes	Reduce noninherent communication via data locality Reduce communication and synchronization cost as seen by the processor Reduce serialization at shared resources Schedule tasks to satisfy dependences early
Mapping	Yes	Put related processes on the same processor if necessary Exploit locality in network topology

We can apply an understanding of the basic process and its goals to a simple but detailed example to see what the resulting parallel programs look like in the three major modern programming models introduced in Chapter 1: shared address space, message passing, and data parallel. Our focus will be on illustrating programs and programming primitives, not so much on performance, which is the subject of Chapter 3.

2.3 PARALLELIZATION OF AN EXAMPLE PROGRAM

The four case studies introduced at the beginning of the chapter all lead to parallel programs that are too complex and too long to serve as useful sample programs. Instead, this section presents a simplified version of a piece, or *kernel*, of Ocean: its equation solver. It uses the equation solver to dig deeper and to illustrate how to implement a parallel program using the three programming models. Except for the data parallel version, which necessarily uses a high-level data parallel language, the parallel programs are not written in an aesthetically pleasing language that relies on software layers to hide the orchestration and communication abstraction from the programmer. Rather, they are written in C or Pascal-like pseudocode augmented with simple extensions for parallelism, thus exposing the basic communication and synchronization primitives that a shared address space or message-passing communication abstraction must provide. Standard sequential languages augmented with primitives for parallelism also reflect the state of most real parallel programming today.

2.3.1 The Equation Solver Kernel

The equation solver kernel solves a simple partial differential equation on a grid, using what is referred to as a finite differencing method. It operates on a regular, two-dimensional grid or array of $(n + 2)$-by-$(n + 2)$ elements, such as a single horizontal cross section of the ocean basin in Ocean. The border rows and columns of the grid contain boundary values that do not change, whereas the interior n-by-n points are updated by the solver, starting from their initial values. The computation proceeds over a number of sweeps. In each sweep, it operates on all the interior n-by-n points of the grid. For each point, it replaces its value with a weighted average of itself and its four nearest-neighbor points—above, below, left, and right (see Figure 2.6). The updates are done in place in the grid, so the update computation for a point sees the new values of the points above and to the left of it and the old values of the points below and to its right. This form of update is called the Gauss-Seidel method. During each sweep, the kernel also computes the average difference of an updated element from its previous value. If this average difference over all elements is smaller than a predefined "tolerance" parameter, the solution is said to have converged and the solver exits at the end of the sweep. Otherwise, it performs another sweep and tests for convergence again. The sequential pseudocode is shown in Figure 2.7. Let us now go through the steps to convert this simple equation solver

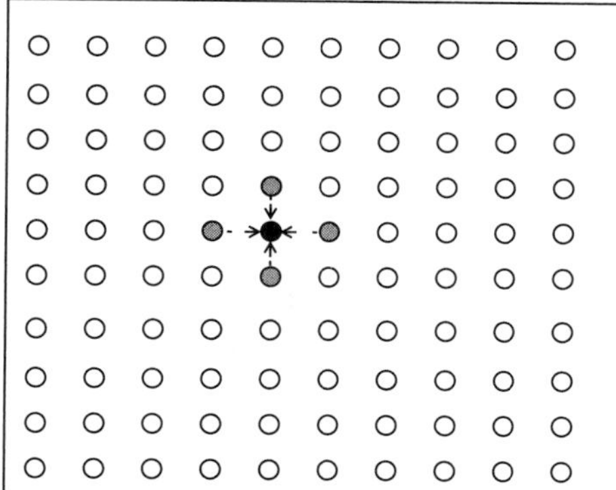

Expression for updating each interior point:

$$A[i,j] = 0.2 \times (A[i,j] + A[i,j-1] + A[i-1,j] + A[i,j+1] + A[i+1,j])$$

FIGURE 2.6 Nearest-neighbor update of a grid point in the simple equation solver. The black point is $A[i,j]$ in the two-dimensional array that represents the grid and is updated using itself and the four shaded points that are its nearest neighbors according to the equation at the right of the figure.

to a parallel program for each programming model. The decomposition and assignment steps are essentially the same for all three models, so these steps are examined in a general context. Once we enter the orchestration phase, the discussion will be organized explicitly by programming model.

2.3.2 Decomposition

For programs that are structured in successive loops or loop nests, a simple way to identify concurrency is to start from the loop structure itself. We examine the individual loops or loop nests in the program one at a time, see if their iterations can be performed in parallel, and determine whether this exposes enough concurrency. We can then look for concurrency across loops or take a different approach if necessary. Let us follow this program-structure-based approach in Figure 2.7.

Each iteration of the outermost while loop, beginning at line 15, sweeps through the entire grid. These iterations clearly are not independent since data modified in one iteration is accessed in the next. Consider the loop nest in lines 17–24, and ignore the lines containing `diff`. Look at the inner loop first (the j loop starting on line 18). Each iteration of this loop reads the grid point ($A[i,j-1]$) that was written in the previous iteration. The iterations are therefore sequentially dependent, and we call this a *sequential loop*. The outer loop of this nest is also sequential, since the elements in row $i-1$ were written in the previous ($i-1$th) iteration of this loop. So this simple analysis of existing loops and their dependences uncovers no concurrency in this example program.

In general, an alternative to relying on program structure to find concurrency is to go back to the fundamental dependences in the underlying algorithms used,

```
1.  int n;                                   /*size of matrix: (n + 2-by-n + 2) elements*/
2.  float **A, diff = 0;

3.  main()
4.  begin
5.    read(n) ;                              /*read input parameter: matrix size*/
6.    A ← malloc (a 2-d array of size n + 2 by n + 2 doubles);
7.    initialize(A);                         /*initialize the matrix A somehow*/
8.    Solve (A);                             /*call the routine to solve equation*/
9.  end main

10. procedure Solve (A)                      /*solve the equation system*/
11.   float **A;                             /*A is an (n + 2)-by-(n + 2) array*/
12. begin
13.   int i, j, done = 0;
14.   float temp;
15.   while (!done) do                       /*outermost loop over sweeps*/
16.     diff = 0;                            /*initialize maximum difference to 0*/
17.     for i ← 1 to n do                    /*sweep over nonborder points of grid*/
18.       for j ← 1 to n do
19.         temp = A[i,j];                   /*save old value of element*/
20.         A[i,j] ← 0.2 * (A[i,j] + A[i,j-1] + A[i-1,j] +
21.           A[i,j+1] + A[i+1,j]); /*compute average*/
22.         diff += abs(A[i,j] - temp);
23.       end for
24.     end for
25.     if (diff/(n*n) < TOL) then done = 1;
26.   end while
27. end procedure
```

FIGURE 2.7 Pseudocode describing the sequential equation solver kernel. The main body of work to be done in each sweep is in the nested for loop in lines 17–23. This is what we would like to parallelize. (Italics indicate keywords of the sequential programming language.)

regardless of program or loop structure. In the equation solver, we might look at the fundamental dependences in the generation and usage of data values (*data dependences*) at the granularity of individual grid points. As discussed earlier, since the computation proceeds from left to right and top to bottom in the grid, computing a particular grid point in the sequential program uses the updated values of the grid points directly above and to the left. This data dependence pattern is shown in Figure 2.8. The result is that the elements along a given anti-diagonal (southwest to northeast) have no dependences among them and can be computed in parallel, whereas the points in the next anti-diagonal depend on some points in the previous one. From this diagram, we can observe that of the $O(n^2)$ work involved in each

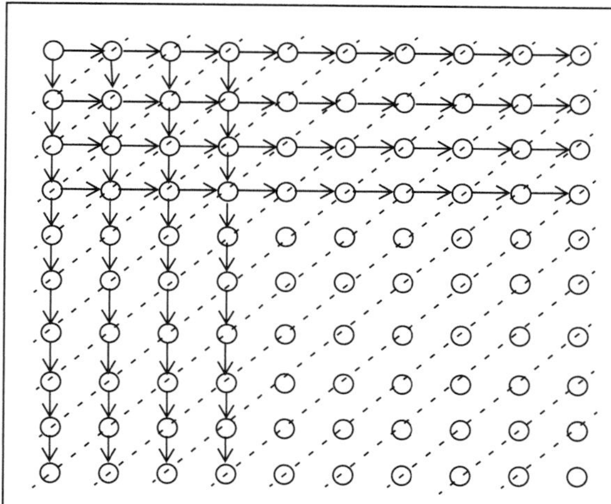

FIGURE 2.8 Dependences and concurrency in the Gauss-Seidel equation solver computation. The horizontal and vertical lines with arrows indicate dependences; the anti-diagonal, dashed lines connect points with no dependences among them that can be computed in parallel.

sweep, there is an inherent concurrency proportional to n along anti-diagonals and a sequential dependence proportional to n along the diagonal.

Suppose we decide to decompose the work into individual grid points so that updating a single grid point is a task. We can exploit the concurrency this exposes in several ways. First, we can leave the loop structure of the program as it is and insert point-to-point synchronization to ensure that the new value for a grid point has been produced in the current sweep before it is used by the points below or to its right. Thus, different loop nests (of the sequential program) and even different sweeps might be in progress simultaneously on different elements, as long as the element-level dependences are not violated. But the overhead of this synchronization at grid-point level may be too high. Second, we can change the loop structure: the first for loop (line 17) can be over anti-diagonals and the inner for loop can be over elements within an anti-diagonal. The inner loop can then be executed completely in parallel, with global synchronization between iterations of the outer for loop (to preserve dependences conservatively across anti-diagonals). Communication would be orchestrated very differently in the two cases, particularly if communication is in explicit messages. However, this approach also has problems. Global synchronization is still very frequent—once per anti-diagonal. In addition, the number of iterations in the parallel (inner) loop changes with successive outer loop iterations, as the size of the anti-diagonals changes, causing load imbalances among processes especially in the shorter anti-diagonals. Because of the frequency of synchronization, load imbalances, and programming complexity, neither of these approaches is used much on modern architectures.

The third and most common approach is based on exploiting knowledge of the problem beyond the dependences in the sequential program itself. The order in which the grid points are updated in the sequential algorithm (left to right and top to bottom) is in fact not fundamental to the Gauss-Seidel solution method; it is simply one possible ordering that is convenient to program sequentially. Since the Gauss-Seidel method is not an exact solution method (unlike Gaussian elimination, for example) but rather iterates until convergence, we can update the grid points in a different order as long as we use updated values for grid points frequently enough.[2] One such ordering that is used often for parallel versions is called *red-black* ordering. The idea here is to separate the grid points into alternating red points and black points as on a checkerboard (see Figure 2.9) so that no red point is adjacent to a black point or vice versa. Since each point reads only its four nearest neighbors, to compute a given red point, we do not need the updated value of any other red point; we need only the updated values of the black points above it and to its left (in a standard sweep) and vice versa for computing black points. We can therefore divide a grid sweep into two phases, first computing all red points and then computing all black points. Within each phase no dependences exist among grid points, so we can compute all $n^2/2$ red points in parallel, synchronize globally, and then compute all $n^2/2$ black points in parallel. Global synchronization is conservative and can be replaced by point-to-point synchronization at the level of grid points since not all black points need to wait for all red points to be computed; but global synchronization is convenient.

Since the red-black ordering is different from our original sequential ordering, it can converge in fewer or more sweeps. It can also produce different final values for the grid points (though still within the convergence tolerance). While the red-point updates do not see updated values of any black points, the black points will see the updated values of all their red neighbors from the first phase of the current sweep, not just the ones to the left and above. Whether the new order is sequentially better or worse than the old one depends on the problem. The red-black ordering also has the advantage that the produced values and the convergence properties are independent of the number of processors used since no dependences occur within a phase. If the sequential program itself uses a red-black ordering, then parallelism does not change the results or convergence properties at all, thus making the parallel program *deterministic*.

Red-black ordering itself produces a longer kernel of code than is appropriate for this illustration of parallel programming. Let us examine a simpler but still common asynchronous method that does not separate points into red and black. This method simply ignores dependences among grid points within a sweep. Global synchronization is used between grid sweeps as in the preceding approach, but the loop structure for a process within a sweep is not changed from the top-to-bottom, left-to-right order. Instead, within a sweep a process simply updates the values of all its assigned grid points, accessing its nearest neighbors whether they have been updated in the current sweep by their assigned processes or not. When only a single process is used, this defaults to the original sequential ordering of updates. When multiple processes are used, the ordering is unpredictable; it depends on the assignment of

2. Even if we don't use updated values from the current sweep (i.e., while loop iteration) for any grid points but always use the values as they were at the end of the previous sweep, the system will still converge, only much slower. This is called Jacobi, rather than Gauss-Seidel, iteration.

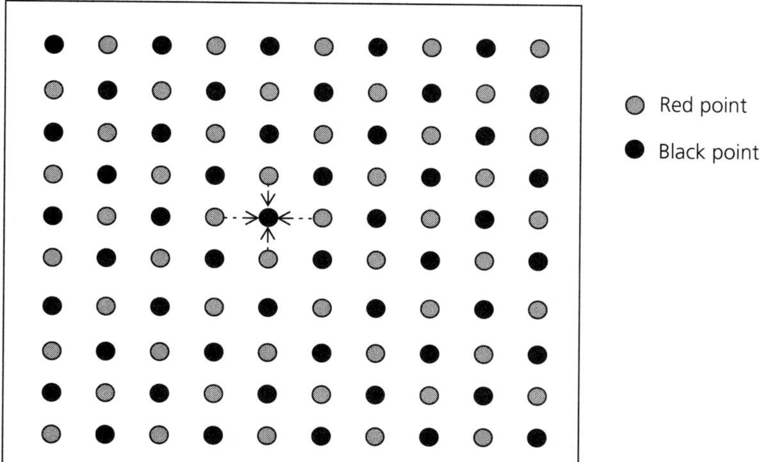

FIGURE 2.9 Red-black ordering for the equation solver. The sweep over the grid is broken up into two subsweeps: the first computes all the red points and the second all the black points. Since red points depend only on black points and vice versa, no dependences occur within a subsweep.

points to processes, the number of processes used, and how quickly different processes execute relative to one another at run time. The execution is no longer deterministic, and the number of sweeps required to converge may depend on the number of processes used; however, for most reasonable assignments the number of sweeps will not vary much.

If we choose a decomposition into individual inner loop iterations (grid points), we can express the program by revising lines 15–26 of Figure 2.7. Figure 2.10 highlights the changes to the code in boldface: all we have done is replace the keyword `for` in the parallel loops with `for_all`. A `for_all` loop simply tells the underlying hardware/software system that all iterations of the loop can be executed in parallel without worrying about dependences, but it says nothing about assignment. A loop nest with both nesting levels being `for_all` means that all iterations in the loop nest ($n*n$ or n^2 here) can be executed in parallel. The system can assign and orchestrate the parallelism in any way it chooses; the program does not take a position on this. All it assumes is an implicit global synchronization after a `for_all` loop nest.

In fact, we can decompose the computation not just into individual inner loop iterations but into any aggregated groups of iterations we desire. Notice that decomposing the computation corresponds very closely to decomposing the grid itself. Suppose we wanted to decompose into rows of grid points instead so that the work for an entire row is an indivisible task that must be assigned to the same process. We could express this by making the inner loop on line 18 a sequential loop, changing its `for_all` back to a `for`, but leaving the loop over rows on line 17 as a parallel

```
while (!done) do                                    /*a sequential loop*/
  diff = 0;
  for_all i ← 1 to n do                             /*a parallel loop nest*/
    for_all j ← 1 to n do
      temp = A[i,j];
      A[i,j] ← 0.2 * (A[i,j] + A[i,j-1] + A[i-1,j] +
        A[i,j+1] + A[i+1,j]);
      diff += abs(A[i,j] - temp);
    end for_all
  end for_all
  if (diff/(n*n) < TOL) then done = 1;
end while
```

FIGURE 2.10 Parallel equation solver kernel with decomposition into grid points and no explicit assignment. Since both for loops are made parallel by using `for_all` instead of `for`, the decomposition is into individual grid elements. Other than this change, the code is the same as the sequential code.

`for_all` loop. The parallelism, or *degree of concurrency*, exploited under this decomposition is reduced from n^2 inherent in the problem to n: instead of n^2 independent tasks of duration 1 unit each, we now have n independent tasks of duration n units each. If each task is executed on a different processor, we will have approximately $2n$ words of communication (accesses to grid points that were computed by other processors) for n points, which results in a communication-to-computation ratio of $O(1)$.

2.3.3 Assignment

Using the row-based decomposition, let us see how we might assign rows to processes explicitly. The simplest option is a static (predetermined) assignment in which each process is responsible for a contiguous block of rows, as shown in Figure 2.11. Interior row i is assigned to process

$$\left\lfloor \frac{i}{p} \right\rfloor$$

where p is the number of processes. Alternative static assignments to this so-called block assignment are also possible, such as a *cyclic* assignment in which rows are interleaved among processes (process i is assigned rows i, $i + p$, and so on). We might also consider a dynamic assignment where each process repeatedly grabs the next available (not yet computed) row after it finishes with a row task, so that it is not predetermined which process computes which rows. For now, we will work with the static block assignment. This simple partitioning of the problem exhibits good load balance across processes as long as the number of interior rows is divisible by the number of processes, since the work per row is uniform across rows. Observe

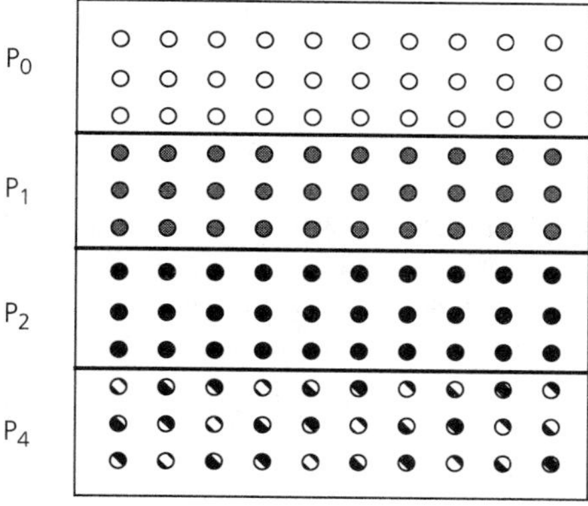

FIGURE 2.11 A simple assignment for the parallel equation solver. Each of the four processors is assigned a contiguous, equal number of rows of the grid. In each sweep, a processor will perform the work needed to update the elements of its assigned rows. Only the interior rows, which are updated in a sweep, are shown in the figure.

that the static assignments have further reduced the parallelism or degree of concurrency, from n to p, by making tasks larger, and the block assignment has reduced the communication required by assigning adjacent rows to the same processor. The communication-to-computation ratio is now only

$$O\left(\frac{p}{n}\right)$$

Having examined decomposition and assignment, we are ready to dig into the orchestration phase. This requires that we pin down the programming model. We begin with a high-level, data parallel model and then look at the two major programming models that the data parallel and other models might compile down to: shared address space and explicit message passing.

2.3.4 Orchestration under the Data Parallel Model

The data parallel model is convenient for the equation solver kernel since it is natural to view the computation as a single thread of control performing global transformations on a large array data structure (Hillis 1985; Hillis and Steele 1986). Computation and data are quite interchangeable, a simple decomposition and assignment of the data leads to good load balance across processes, and the appropriate assignments (partitions) are very regular in shape and can be described by simple expressions. Pseudocode for the data parallel equation solver is shown in Figure 2.12. We assume that global declarations (outside any procedure) describe shared data and that all other data (for example, data on a procedure's stack) is private to a process. Dynamically allocated shared data, such as the array `A`, is allocated with a `G_MALLOC` (global `malloc`) call rather than a regular `malloc`. The `G_MALLOC` allocates data in a shared region of the heap storage, which can be accessed and modified by any process. Other than this, the main differences (shown in boldface) from the sequential program are the use of `for_all` loops instead of

```
int n, nprocs;                     /*grid size (n + 2-by-n + 2) and number of processes*/
float **A, diff = 0;

main()
begin
  read(n); read(nprocs);;  /*read input grid size and number of processes*/
  A ← G_MALLOC (a 2-d array of size n+2 by n+2 doubles);
  initialize(A);                   /*initialize the matrix A somehow*/
  Solve (A);                       /*call the routine to solve equation*/
end main

procedure Solve(A)                 /*solve the equation system*/
  float **A;                       /*A is an (n + 2-by-n + 2) array*/
begin
  int i, j, done = 0;
  float mydiff = 0, temp;
  DECOMP A[BLOCK,*, nprocs];
  while (!done) do                 /*outermost loop over sweeps*/
    mydiff = 0;                    /*initialize maximum difference to 0*/
    for_all i ← 1 to n do          /*sweep over non-border points of grid*/
      for_all j ← 1 to n do
        temp = A[i,j];             /*save old value of element*/
        A[i,j] ← 0.2 * (A[i,j] + A[i,j-1] + A[i-1,j] +
          A[i,j+1] + A[i+1,j]);    /*compute average*/
        mydiff += abs(A[i,j] - temp);
      end for_all
    end for_all
    REDUCE (mydiff, diff, ADD);
    if (diff/(n*n) < TOL) then done = 1;
  end while
end procedure
```

FIGURE 2.12 Pseudocode describing the data parallel equation solver. Differences from the sequential code are shown in boldface. Italicized boldface indicates constructs designed to achieve parallelism. The decomposition is still into individual elements, as indicated by the nested `for_all` loop. The assignment, indicated by the (unfortunately) labeled `DECOMP` statement, is into blocks of contiguous rows (the first, or column, dimension is partitioned into blocks, and the second, or row, dimension is not partitioned). The `REDUCE` statement sums the locally computed `mydiffs` into a global `diff` value. The while loop is still serial.

`for` loops, the use of a `DECOMP` statement, the use of a private `mydiff` variable per process, and the use of a `REDUCE` statement.

We have already seen that `for_all` loops specify that the iterations can be performed in parallel. The parallel processes other than the one executing the main thread of control are implicit in the data parallel model and are active only during these parallel loops. The DECOMP statement has a twofold purpose. First, it specifies the assignment of the iterations to processes (DECOMP is in this sense an unfortunate word choice). Here, it is a [BLOCK, *, nprocs] assignment, which means that the first dimension (rows) is partitioned into contiguous blocks among the nprocs processes, and the second dimension is not partitioned at all. Specifying [CYCLIC, *, nprocs] would have implied a cyclic or interleaved partitioning of rows among nprocs processes, specifying [BLOCK, BLOCK, nprocs] would have implied a 2D contiguous block partitioning, and specifying [*, CYCLIC, nprocs] would have implied an interleaved partitioning of columns. The second and related purpose of DECOMP is that it also specifies how the grid data should be distributed among memories on a distributed-memory machine. (This is restricted to be the same as the assignment of computation in most current data parallel languages, following the owner computes rule, which works well in this example.) The mydiff variable is used to allow each process to first independently compute the sum of the difference values for its assigned grid points. Then, the REDUCE statement directs the system to add all the partial mydiff values together into the shared diff variable. This increases concurrency, as was discussed in Example 2.1. The REDUCE operation implements a *reduction,* which is a scenario in which many processes (all, in a global reduction) perform associative operations (such as addition, taking the maximum, etc.) on the same logically shared data. Associativity implies that the order of the operations does not matter. Floating-point operations such as the ones here are, strictly speaking, not associative since the way in which rounding errors accumulate depends on the order of operations. However, the effects are small and we usually ignore them, especially in iterative calculations that are approximate anyway. The reduction operation may be implemented in a library in a manner best suited to the underlying architecture.

While the data parallel programming model is well suited to specifying partitioning and data distribution for regular computations on large arrays of data (such as the equation solver kernel or the Ocean application), the suitability does not always hold true for more irregular applications, particularly those in which the communication pattern or the distribution of work among tasks changes unpredictably with time. (For example, think of the stars in Barnes-Hut or the rays in Raytrace, where assigning equal numbers of rays to processes would lead to severe load imbalances.) Let us look at the more flexible, lower-level programming models in which processes are explicit, have their own individual threads of control, and communicate with each other when they please.

2.3.5 Orchestration under the Shared Address Space Model

In a shared address space, we can simply declare the matrix A as a single shared array—as we did in the data parallel model—and processes can reference the parts of it they need using loads and stores with exactly the same array indices as in a sequential program. Communication is generated implicitly as necessary. With explicit parallel processes, we now need mechanisms to create the processes, coordinate them through synchronization, and control the assignment of work to

Table 2.2 Key Shared Address Space Primitives

Name	Syntax	Function
CREATE	CREATE(p,proc,args)	Create p processes that start executing at procedure proc with arguments args
G_MALLOC	G_MALLOC(size)	Allocate shared data of size bytes
LOCK	LOCK(name)	Acquire mutually exclusive access
UNLOCK	UNLOCK(name)	Release mutually exclusive access
BARRIER	BARRIER(name, number)	Global synchronization among number processes: none gets past BARRIER until number have arrived
WAIT_FOR_END	WAIT_FOR_END(number)	Wait for number processes to terminate
wait for flag	while (!flag); or WAIT(flag)	Wait for flag to be set (spin or block); used for point-to-point event synchronization
set flag	flag = 1; or SIGNAL(flag)	Set flag; wakes up process that is spinning or blocked on flag, if any

processes. The primitives we use are typical of low-level programming environments such as *parmacs* (Boyle et al. 1987) and are summarized in Table 2.2.

Pseudocode for the parallel equation solver in a shared address space is shown in Figure 2.13. The special primitives for parallelism are shown in boldface. They are typically implemented as library calls or macros, each of which expands to a number of instructions that accomplishes its goal. Although the code for the Solve procedure is remarkably similar to the sequential version, let's go through it one step at a time.

A single process is first started up by the operating system to execute the program, starting from the procedure called *main*. Let's call it the main process. It reads the input, which specifies the size of the grid *A* (recall that input n denotes an (n + 2)-by-(n + 2) grid of which n-by-n points are updated by the solver). It then allocates the grid *A* as a two-dimensional array in the shared address space using the G_MALLOC call (see Section 2.3.4) and initializes the grid. For data that is not dynamically allocated on the heap, different systems make different assumptions about what is shared and what is private to a process. Let us make the same assumptions as in the earlier data parallel example. Data declared outside any procedure, such as nprocs and n in Figure 2.13, is shared. Data on a procedure's stack (such as mymin, mymax, mydiff, temp, i, and j) is private to a process that executes the procedure, as is data allocated with a regular malloc call (and data that is explicitly declared to be private, not used in this program).

Having allocated data and initialized the grid, the program is ready to start solving the system. It creates `(nprocs - 1)` "worker" processes, which begin executing at the procedure called `Solve`. The main process then also calls the `Solve` procedure so that all `nprocs` processes enter the procedure in parallel as equal partners. All created processes execute the same code image until they exit from the program and terminate. That is, we use a structured, single-program-multiple-data (SPMD) style of programming. This does not mean that they proceed in lockstep or even execute the same instructions (as in the single-instruction-multiple-data or SIMD model) since, in general, they may follow different control paths through the code. Control over the assignment of work to processes—as well as what data they access—is maintained by a few private variables that acquire different values for different processes (e.g., `mymin` and `mymax`) and by simple manipulations of loop control variables. For example, we assume that every process upon creation automatically obtains a unique process identifier (`pid`) between 0 and `nprocs - 1` in its private address space and that it uses this `pid` (in lines 14a–b) to determine which rows are assigned to it. Processes synchronize through calls to synchronization primitives, which will be discussed shortly.

We assume for simplicity that the total number of interior rows `n` is an integer multiple of the number of processes `nprocs` so that every process is assigned the same number of rows. Each process calculates the indices of the first and last rows of its assigned block in the private variables `mymin` and `mymax`. It then proceeds to the actual solution loop.

The outermost while loop (line 15) is still over successive grid sweeps. Although the iterations of this loop proceed sequentially, each iteration or sweep is itself executed in parallel by all processes. The decision of whether to execute the next sweep is taken separately by each process or thread of control (by setting the `done` variable and computing the `while (!done)` condition) even though in this case each will make the same decision: the redundant work performed here is very small compared to the cost of communicating a completion flag or the `diff` value among the processors.

The code that performs the actual updates (lines 19–22) is essentially identical to that in the sequential program. Other than the bounds in the loop control statements, which control assignment, the only difference is that each process maintains its own private variable `mydiff`. As in the data parallel example, this private variable keeps track of the total difference between new and old values for only its assigned grid points. It is accumulated once into the shared `diff` variable at the end of the sweep, rather than adding directly into the shared variable for every grid point. In addition to the serialization and concurrency reason discussed in Section 2.2.1 (Example 2.1), all processes repeatedly modifying and reading the same shared variable cause a lot of expensive communication, so we do not want to do this once per grid point.

The interesting aspect of the rest of the program (line 25 onward) is synchronization—both mutual exclusion and event synchronization. First, the accumulations into the shared variable by different processes have to be mutually exclusive. To see why, consider the sequence of instructions that a processor executes to add its

```
    int n, nprocs;              /*matrix dimension and number of processors to be used*/
    float **A, diff;            /*A is global (shared) array representing the grid*/
                                /*diff is global (shared) maximum difference in current
                                sweep*/
    LOCKDEC(diff_lock);         /*declaration of lock to enforce mutual exclusion*/
    BARDEC (bar1);              /*barrier declaration for global synchronization between
                                sweeps*/

main()
begin
    read(n); read(nprocs);      /*read input matrix size and number of processes*/
    A ← G_MALLOC (a two-dimensional array of size n+2 by n+2 doubles);
    initialize(A);              /*initialize A in an unspecified way*/
    CREATE (nprocs-1, Solve, A);
    Solve(A);                   /*main process becomes a worker too*/
    WAIT_FOR_END (nprocs-1);    /*wait for all child processes created to terminate*/
end main

procedure Solve(A)
  float **A;                                  /*A is entire n+2-by-n+2 shared array,
                                              as in the sequential program*/
begin
  int i,j, pid, done = 0;
  float temp, mydiff = 0;                     /*private variables*/
  int mymin = 1 + (pid * n/nprocs);           /*assume that n is exactly divisible by*/
  int mymax = mymin + n/nprocs - 1            /*nprocs for simplicity here*/

  while (!done) do                  /*loop until convergence*/
    mydiff = diff = 0;              /*set global diff to 0 (okay for all to do it)*/
    BARRIER(bar1, nprocs);          /*ensure all reach here before anyone modifies diff*/
    for i ← mymin to mymax do       /*for each of my rows*/
      for j ← 1 to n do             /*for all nonborder elements in that row*/
        temp = A[i,j];
        A[i,j] = 0.2 * (A[i,j] + A[i,j-1] + A[i-1,j] +
          A[i,j+1] + A[i+1,j]);
        mydiff += abs(A[i,j] - temp);
      endfor
    endfor
    LOCK(diff_lock);                /*update global diff if necessary*/
    diff += mydiff;
    UNLOCK(diff_lock);
    BARRIER(bar1, nprocs);          /*ensure all reach here before checking if done*/
```

```
25e.      if (diff/(n*n) < TOL) then done = 1;      /*check convergence; all get
                                                      same answer*/
25f.      BARRIER(bar1, nprocs);
26.    endwhile
27.  end procedure
```

FIGURE 2.13 Pseudocode describing the parallel equation solver in a shared address space. Line numbers followed by a letter denote lines that were not present in the sequential version. The numbers are chosen to match the line or control structure in the sequential code with which the new lines are most closely related. The design of the data structures does not have to change from the sequential program. Processes are created with the `CREATE` call, and the main process waits for them to terminate at the end of the program with the `WAIT_FOR_END` call. The decomposition is into rows, since the inner loop is unmodified, and the outer loop specifies the assignment of rows to processes. Barriers are used to separate sweeps (and to separate the convergence test from further modification of the global `diff` variable), and locks are used to provide mutually exclusive access to the global `diff` variable.

`mydiff` variable (maintained, say, in register `r2`) into the shared `diff` variable (i.e., to execute the source statement `diff += mydiff`):

```
load the value of diff into register r1
add the register r2 to register r1
store the value of register r1 into diff
```

Suppose the value in the variable `diff` is 0 to begin with and the value of `mydiff` in each process is 1. After two processes have executed this code, we would expect the value in `diff` to be 2. However, it may turn out to be 1 instead if the processes happen to execute their operations interleaved in the following order (shown vertically):

P_1	P_2
`r1 ← diff` *{P_1 gets 0 in its r1}*	
	`r1 ← diff` *{P_2 also gets 0}*
`r1 ← r1 + r2` *{P_1 sets its r1 to 1}*	`r1 ← r1 + r2` *{P_2 sets its r1 to 1}*
`diff ← r1` *{P_1 stores 1 into diff}*	
	`diff ← r1` *{P_2 also stores 1 into diff}*

This is not what we intended. The problem is that a process (here P_2) may be able to read the value of the logically shared `diff` between the time that another process (P_1) reads it and writes it back. To prohibit this interleaving of operations, we would like the sets of operations from different processes to execute *atomically* (i.e., to achieve mutual exclusion) with respect to one another. The set of operations we want to execute atomically is called a *critical section*: once a process starts to execute the first of its three instructions above (its critical section), no other process can execute any of the instructions in its corresponding critical section until the former process has completed its last instruction of the critical section. The `LOCK-UNLOCK` pair around line 25b achieves mutual exclusion for the critical section composed of `diff += mydiff`.

A lock such as `diff_lock` can be viewed as a shared token that confers an exclusive right. Acquiring the lock through the `LOCK` primitive gives a process the right to execute the critical section. The process that holds the lock frees it by issuing an `UNLOCK` command when it has completed the critical section. At this point, the lock is free for another process to either acquire or be granted, depending on the implementation. The `LOCK` and `UNLOCK` primitives must be implemented in a way that guarantees mutual exclusion. Locks are expensive, and even a given lock can cause contention and serialization if multiple processes try to access it at the same time. Our `LOCK` primitive takes as its argument the name of the lock being used. Associating names with locks allows us to use different locks to protect unrelated critical sections, reducing contention and serialization.

Once a process has added its `mydiff` into the global `diff`, it waits until all processes have done so and the value contained in `diff` is indeed the total difference over all grid points. This requires global event synchronization, implemented here with a `BARRIER`. A barrier operation takes as an argument the name of the barrier and the number of processes involved in the synchronization, and it is issued by all those processes. When a process calls the barrier, it registers the fact that it has reached that point in the program. The process is not allowed to proceed past the barrier call until the specified number of processes participating in the barrier have issued the barrier operation. That is, the semantics of `BARRIER(name,p)` are as follows: wait until `p` processes get here and only then proceed. The need for the other two barriers in the program is discussed in Exercise 2.6.

Barriers are often used to separate distinct phases of computation in a program. For example, in the Barnes-Hut galaxy simulation we use a barrier between updating the positions of the stars at the end of one time-step and using them to compute forces at the beginning of the next one, and in Data Mining we may use a barrier between counting occurrences of candidate itemsets and using the resulting large itemsets to generate the next list of candidates. Since barriers implement all-to-all event synchronization, they are usually a conservative way of preserving dependences; usually, not all operations (or processes) after the barrier actually need to wait for all operations before the barrier to complete. More specific event synchronization between pairs or groups of processes would enable some processes to get past their synchronization operation earlier; however, from a programming viewpoint it is often more convenient to use a single barrier than to orchestrate the actual dependences through point-to-point synchronization among processes.

When point-to-point synchronization is needed, one way to orchestrate it in a shared address space is with wait and signal operations on semaphores, with which we are familiar from operating systems. A more common way in parallel programs is by using normal shared variables as flags for event synchronization, as shown in Figure 2.14. Since P_1 simply spins around in a tight while loop waiting for the flag variable to be set to 1, keeping the processor busy during this time, we call this *spin-waiting* or *busy-waiting*. Recall that in the case of a semaphore the waiting process

P_1	P_2
	`A = 1;`
	`b: flag = 1;`
`a: while (flag is 0) do nothing;`	
`print A;`	

FIGURE 2.14 Point-to-point event synchronization using flags. Suppose we want to ensure that a process P_1 does not get past a certain point (say, *a*) in the program until some other process P_2 has already reached another point (say, *b*). Assume that the variable flag (and *A*) was initialized to 0 before the processes arrived at this scenario. If P_1 gets to statement *a* after P_2 has already executed statement *b*, P_1 will simply pass point *a*. If, on the other hand, P_2 has not yet executed *b*, then P_1 will remain in the "idle" while loop until P_2 reaches *b* and sets flag to 1, at which point P_1 will exit the idle loop and proceed. If we assume that the writes by P_2 are seen by P_1 in the order in which P_2 issues them, then this synchronization will ensure that P_1 prints the value 1 for *A*.

does not spin and consume processor resources but rather blocks (suspends) itself and is awakened when another process signals the semaphore.

In event synchronization among subsets of processes, or *group event synchronization*, one or more processes may wait for an event and one or more processes may notify them of its occurrence. Group event synchronization can be orchestrated either using ordinary shared variables as flags or by using barriers among subsets of processes.

Returning to the equation solver in Figure 2.13, once a process is past the barrier, it reads the value of `diff` and examines whether the average difference over all grid points (`diff/(n*n)`) is less than the error tolerance used to determine convergence. If so, it sets the `done` flag to exit from the while loop; if not, it goes on to perform another sweep.

Finally, the `WAIT_FOR_END` called by the main process at the end of the program (line 8b) is a particular form of all-to-one synchronization. Through it, the main process waits for all the worker processes it created to terminate. The other processes do not call `WAIT_FOR_END` but implicitly participate in the synchronization by terminating when they exit the `Solve` procedure that was their entry point into the program.

In summary, for this simple equation solver the parallel program in a shared address space is not too different in structure from the sequential program. The major differences in the control flow are implemented by changing the bounds on some loops. Additional differences are due to creating processes, partitioning the work among them, and synchronizing through the use of simple and generic primitives. The body of the computational loop is mostly unchanged, as are the major data structures and the references to them. Given a strategy for decomposition, assignment, and synchronization, inserting the necessary primitives and making the necessary modifications to produce a correct parallel program is quite mechanical in this example. Changes to decomposition and assignment are also easy to incorporate

```
17. for i ← pid+1 to n by nprocs do        /*for my interleaved set of rows*/
18.   for j ← 1 to n do                    /*for all elements in that row*/
19.     temp = A[i,j];
20.     A[i,j] = 0.2 * (A[i,j] + A[i,j-1] + A[i-1,j] +
21.       A[i,j+1] + A[i+1,j]);
22.     mydiff += abs(A[i,j] - temp);
23.   endfor
24. endfor
```

FIGURE 2.15 Cyclic assignment of row-based solver in a shared address space. All that changes in the code from the block assignment of rows in Figure 2.13 is the first for statement in line 17. The data structures or accesses to them do not have to be changed.

as shown in Example 2.2. Although many simple programs have these properties in a shared address space, we will see later that more substantial changes are needed as we seek to obtain higher parallel performance and as we address more complex parallel programs.

EXAMPLE 2.2 How would the code for the shared address space parallel version of the equation solver (Figure 2.13) change if we retained the same decomposition into rows but changed to a cyclic (interleaved) assignment of rows to processes?

Answer Figure 2.15 shows the relevant pseudocode. All that has changed in the code is the control arithmetic in line 17. The same global data structure is used with the same indexing, and the rest of the parallel program stays exactly the same. ■

2.3.6 Orchestration under the Message-Passing Model

We now examine a possible implementation of the parallel solver using explicit message passing between private address spaces, employing the same decomposition and assignment as before. Since we no longer have a shared address space, we cannot simply declare the matrix *A* to be shared and have processes reference parts of it as they would in a sequential program. Rather, the logical data structure *A* must be represented by a collection of smaller per-process data structures, which are allocated among the private address spaces of the cooperating processes in accordance with the assignment of work. In particular, the process that is assigned a block of rows allocates those rows as an array in its private address space.

A set of simple primitives for message-passing programming are shown in Table 2.3. The message-passing program shown in Figure 2.16 uses some of these primitives and is structurally very similar to the shared address space program in Figure 2.13 (more complex programs will reveal further differences in Section 3.6). Here too a main process is started by the operating system when the program executable is invoked, and this main process creates `nprocs - 1` other processes to collaborate with it. We assume again that every created process automatically acquires a

Table 2.3 Some Basic Message-Passing Primitives

Name	Syntax	Function
CREATE	CREATE(procedure)	Create process that starts at procedure
SEND	SEND(src_addr, size, dest, tag)	Send size bytes starting at src_addr to the dest process, with tag identifier
RECEIVE	RECEIVE(buffer_addr, size, src, tag)	Receive a message with the tag identifier from the src process, and put size bytes of it into buffer starting at buffer_addr
SEND_PROBE	SEND_PROBE(tag, dest)	Check if message with identifier tag has been sent to process dest (only for asynchronous message passing, and meaning depends on semantics, as discussed in this section)
RECV_PROBE	RECV_PROBE(tag, src)	Check if message with identifier tag has been received from process src (only for asynchronous message passing, and meaning depends on semantics)
BARRIER	BARRIER(name, number)	Global synchronization among number processes: none gets past BARRIER until number have arrived
WAIT_FOR_END	WAIT_FOR_END(number)	Wait for number processes to terminate

process identifier (pid) between 0 and nprocs - 1, and that the CREATE call automatically communicates the program's input parameters (n and nprocs) to the address space of each process.[3] The outermost loop of the Solve routine (line 15) still iterates over grid sweeps until convergence, and in every iteration, a process performs the computation for its assigned rows and communicates as necessary. The major differences are in orchestration: in the data structures used to represent the logically shared matrix A and in how interprocess communication and synchronization are implemented. We shall focus on these differences.

Instead of representing the matrix to be factored as a single global (n + 2)-by-(n + 2) array A, each process in the message-passing program allocates an array called myA of size (nprocs/n + 2)-by-(n + 2) in its private address space. This array represents its assigned nprocs/n rows of the logically shared matrix A, plus two rows at the edges to hold the boundary data from its neighboring partitions (for use in the grid point updates). The boundary rows from its neighbors must be communicated to it explicitly and copied into these extra, or *ghost*, rows since their elements cannot be directly referenced otherwise as they are not in the process's

3. An alternative organization is to use what is called a "hostless" model, in which there is no single main process. The number of processes to be used is specified to the system when the program is invoked. The system then starts up that many processes and distributes the code to the relevant processing nodes. There is no need for a CREATE primitive in the program itself; every process reads the program inputs (n and nprocs) separately, though processes still acquire unique user-level pids.

```
int pid, n, nprocs;                  /*process id, matrix dimension and number of
                                     processors to be used*/
float **myA;
main()
begin
  read(n);  read(nprocs);            /*read input matrix size and number of processes*/
  CREATE (nprocs-1, Solve);
  Solve();                           /*main process becomes a worker too*/
  WAIT_FOR_END (nprocs-1);           /*wait for all child processes created to terminate*/
end main

procedure Solve()
begin
  int i,j, pid, n' = n/nprocs, done = 0;
  float temp, tempdiff, mydiff = 0;       /*private variables*/
myA ← malloc(a 2-d array of size [n/nprocs + 2] by n+2);
                                     /*my assigned rows of A*/
initialize(myA);                     /*initialize my rows of A, in an unspecified way*/

while (!done) do
  mydiff = 0;                        /*set local diff to 0*/
  if (pid != 0) then SEND(&myA[1,0],n*sizeof(float),pid-1,ROW);
  if (pid == nprocs-1) then
      SEND(&myA[n',0],n*sizeof(float),pid+1,ROW);
  if (pid != 0) then RECEIVE(&myA[0,0],n*sizeof(float),pid-1,ROW);
  if (pid != nprocs-1) then
      RECEIVE(&myA[n'+1,0],n*sizeof(float), pid+1,ROW);
                                     /*border rows of neighbors have now been copied
                                     into myA[0,*] and myA[n'+1,*]*/
  for i ← 1 to n' do                 /*for each of my (nonghost) rows*/
    for j ← 1 to n do                /*for all nonborder elements in that row*/
      temp = myA[i,j];
      myA[i,j] = 0.2 * (myA[i,j] + myA[i,j-1] + myA[i-1,j] +
        myA[i,j+1] + myA[i+1,j]);
      mydiff += abs(myA[i,j] - temp);
    endfor
  endfor
                                     /*communicate local diff values and determine if
                                     done; can be replaced by reduction and broadcast*/
```

```
25a.   if (pid != 0) then                /*process 0 holds global total diff*/
25b.     SEND(mydiff,sizeof(float),0,DIFF);
25c.     RECEIVE(done,sizeof(int),0,DONE);
25d.   else                              /*pid 0 does this*/
25e.     for i ← 1 to nprocs-1 do        /*for each other process*/
25f.       RECEIVE(tempdiff,sizeof(float),*,DIFF);
25g.       mydiff += tempdiff;           /*accumulate into total*/
25h.     endfor
25i      if (mydiff/(n*n) < TOL) then   done = 1;
25j.     for i ← 1 to nprocs-1 do        /*for each other process*/
25k.       SEND(done,sizeof(int),i,DONE);
25l.     endfor
25m.   endif
26.  endwhile
27.  end procedure
```

FIGURE 2.16 Pseudocode describing parallel equation solver with explicit message passing. Now the meaning of the data structures and the indexing of them changes in going to the parallel code. Each process has its own `myA` data structure that represents its assigned part of the grid, and `myA[i,j]` referenced by different processes refers to different parts of the logical overall grid. The communication is all contained in lines 16a–16d and 25a–25f. No locks or barriers are needed since the synchronization is implicit in the send/receive pairs. Several extra lines of code are added to orchestrate the communication with simple sends and receives.

address space. Ghost rows are used because without them the communicated data would have to be received into separate one-dimensional arrays with different names created specially for this purpose, which would complicate the referencing of the data when they are read in the inner loop (lines 20–21). Since communicated data has to be copied into the receiver's private address space anyway, programming is made easier by extending the existing data structure rather than allocating new ones.

Recall from Chapter 1 that both communication and synchronization in a message-passing program are based on two primitives: `SEND` and `RECEIVE`. The program event that initiates data transfer is the `SEND` operation, unlike in a shared address space where data transfer is usually initiated by the consumer or receiver using a read (load) instruction. When a message arrives at the destination processor, it is either kept in the network queue or temporarily stored in a system buffer until a process running on the destination processor posts a `RECEIVE` for it. With a `RECEIVE`, a process reads an incoming message from the network or system buffer into a specified portion of the private (application) address space. A `RECEIVE` does not in itself cause any data to be transferred across the network.

The simple `SEND` and `RECEIVE` primitives used in the example program assume that the data being transferred is in a contiguous region of the virtual address space. The arguments in our simple `SEND` call are: the start address of the data to be sent, which is in the sending process's private address space; the size of the message in bytes; the `pid` of the destination process, which we must be able to name explicitly now (unlike in a shared address space); and an optional tag or type associated with the message for matching at the receiver. The arguments to the `RECEIVE` call are a local address at which to place the received data, the size of the message, the sender's `pid`, and the optional message tag or type. The specified sender's `pid` and the tag, if present, are used to perform a match with the messages that have arrived and are in the system buffer, to see which one corresponds to the receive. Either or both of these fields may be wild cards, in which case they will match a message from any source process or with any tag, respectively. `SEND` and `RECEIVE` primitives are usually implemented in a library on a specific architecture, just like `BARRIER` and `LOCK` in a shared address space. A full set of message-passing primitives commonly used in real programs is part of a standard called the Message Passing Interface, or MPI (described at different levels of detail in Pacheco 1996; MPI Forum 1993; Gropp, Lusk, and Skjellum 1994). A significant extension is transfers of noncontiguous regions of memory, either with regular stride—such as every tenth word between addresses a and b, or four words every sixth word—or by using index arrays to specify unstructured addresses from which to gather data on the sending side or to which to scatter data on the receiving side. Another is a large degree of flexibility in specifying tags to match messages and in the potential complexity of a match. For example, processes may be divided into groups that communicate certain types of messages only within their group, and collective communication operations may be provided as described in the following.

Semantically, the simplest forms of `SEND` and `RECEIVE` we can use in our program are the so-called synchronous forms. A synchronous `SEND` operation returns control to the calling process only when it is clear that the corresponding `RECEIVE` has been performed. A synchronous `RECEIVE` returns control when the data has been received into the destination process's address space. With synchronous messages, our implementation of the communication in lines 16a–16d is actually deadlocked. All the processes issue their `SEND` first and stall until the corresponding receive is performed, so none will ever get to actually perform their `RECEIVE`! In general, synchronous message passing can easily deadlock on pairwise exchanges of data if we are not careful. One way to avoid this problem is to have every alternate process do its `SEND`s first followed by its `RECEIVE`s, and the others do their `RECEIVE`s first followed by their `SEND`s. The alternative is to use different semantic flavors of send and receive, as we shall see shortly.

The communication is done all at once at the beginning of each iteration, rather than grid point by grid point as needed in a shared address space. It could be done grid point by grid point, but the overhead of send and receive operations is usually too large to make this approach perform reasonably. As a result, unlike in the shared address space version, the message-passing program is deterministic. Even though one process updates its boundary rows while its neighbor is computing in the same sweep, the neighbor is guaranteed not to see the updates in the current sweep since they are not in its address space. A process therefore sees, in its neighbors' boundary rows, the values as they were at the end of the previous sweep, which may cause more sweeps to be needed for convergence as per our earlier discussion (red-black ordering would have been particularly useful here).

Once a process has received its neighbors' boundary rows into its ghost rows, it can update its assigned points using code almost exactly like that in the sequential and shared address space programs. (Although we use a different name, `myA`, for a process's local array than the `A` used in the sequential and shared address space programs, this is just to distinguish it from the logically shared entire grid `A`, which here is only conceptual; we could just as well have used the name `A`.) The loop bounds are different, extending from 1 to `nprocs/n` (substituted by `n'` in the code) for all processes rather than 0 to `n - 1` as in the sequential program or `mymin` to `mymax` as in the shared address space program. In fact, the indices used to reference `myA` are local indices, which are different than the global indices that would be used if the entire logically shared grid `A` could be referenced as a single shared array. For example, a reference, `myA[1,1]`, by different processes refers to different rows of the logically shared grid `A`. The use of local index spaces can be somewhat trickier in cases where a global index must also be used explicitly, as seen in Exercise 2.7.

Synchronization, including the accumulation of private `mydiff` variables into a logically shared `diff` variable and the evaluation of the done condition that follows, is performed very differently here than in a shared address space. Given our simple synchronous sends and receives that block the issuing process until they complete, the send/receive match encapsulates a synchronization event and no special operations (like locks and barriers) or additional variables are needed to orchestrate synchronization. Consider mutual exclusion. The logically shared `diff` variable must be allocated in some process's private address space (here process 0). The identity of this process must be known to all the others. Every process sends its `mydiff` value to process 0, which receives them all and adds them to the logically shared global `diff`. Since only process 0 can manipulate this logically shared variable, mutual exclusion and serialization occur naturally and no locks are needed. In fact, process 0 can simply use its own `mydiff` variable as the global `diff`.

Now consider the global event synchronization needed for determining the done condition. Once process 0 has received the `mydiff` values from all the other processes and accumulated them, it tests the done condition and then sends the `done` variable to all the other processes, which are waiting for it with receive calls. There is no need for a barrier because the completion of the synchronous receive implies that process 0 has sent out the `done` result and therefore that all processes' `mydiffs` have been accumulated. The processes then test the done condition locally to determine whether or not to proceed with another sweep. We could also, of course, implement lock and barrier calls using messages if that is more convenient for programming, although that may lead to request-reply communication and therefore more round-trip messages. More complex send/receive semantics than the synchronous ones we have used here may require additional synchronization beyond the messages themselves, as we shall see.

Notice that the code for the accumulation and done condition evaluation has expanded to several lines when using point-to-point sends and receives as communication operations. In practice, programming environments would provide library functions like REDUCE (accumulate values from private variables in multiple processes to a single variable in a given process) and BROADCAST (send from one process to all processes) to the programmer, which the application processes could use directly to simplify the code in these stylized situations. Using these functions, lines 25a–25m in Figure 2.16 could be replaced by the five lines in Figure 2.17. The system may provide special support to improve the performance of these and other collective communication operations (such as multicast from one-to-several or even several-to-several processes, or all-to-all communication in which every process transfers data to every other process), for example, by reducing the software overhead at the sender to that of a single message, or these operations may be built on top of the usual point-to-point send and receive in user-level libraries for programming convenience only.

Finally, it was mentioned earlier that SEND and RECEIVE operations come in different semantic flavors, which we can use to solve our deadlock problem. Let us examine this a little further. The main axis along which these flavors differ is their completion semantics—that is, when they return control to the user process that issued the send or receive. These semantics affect when the data structures or buffers they operate on can be reused without compromising correctness. The two major kinds of SEND/RECEIVE are synchronous and asynchronous; within the asynchronous class are two types: blocking and nonblocking. Let us examine these options and see how they might be used in our program.

Synchronous SENDs and RECEIVEs are what we have assumed previously because they have the simplest semantics for a programmer. A synchronous SEND returns control to the calling process only when the corresponding synchronous RECEIVE at the destination end has completed successfully and returned an acknowledgment to the sender. Until the acknowledgment is received, the sending process cannot execute any code that follows the SEND. Receipt of the acknowledgment implies that the receiver has retrieved the entire message from the system buffer into the applica-

```
     /*communicate local diff values and determine if done, using reduction and broadcast*/
25b. REDUCE(0,mydiff,sizeof(float),ADD);
25c. if (pid == 0) then
25i.   if (mydiff/(n*n) < TOL) then done = 1;
25k. endif
25m. BROADCAST(0,done,sizeof(int),DONE);
```

FIGURE 2.17 Accumulation and convergence determination in the solver using REDUCE and BROADCAST instead of SEND and RECEIVE. The first argument to the REDUCE call is the destination process. All other processes will do a send to this process in the implementation of REDUCE while this process will do a receive. The next argument is the private variable to be reduced from (in all processes other than the destination) and to (in the destination process), and the third argument is the size of this variable. The last argument is the function to be performed on the variables in the reduction. Similarly, the first argument of the BROADCAST call is the sender; this process does a send and all others do a receive. The second argument is the variable to be broadcast and received into, and the third is its size. The final argument is the optional message type.

tion space. Thus, the completion of the `SEND` guarantees (barring hardware errors) that the message has been successfully received and that all associated data structures and buffers can be reused.

A *blocking asynchronous* (or simply *blocking*) `SEND` returns control to the calling process when the message has been taken from the sending application's source data structure and is therefore in the care of the system. This means that when control is returned, the sending process can modify the source data structure without affecting that message. Compared to a synchronous `SEND`, this allows the sending process to resume much sooner, but the return of control does not guarantee that the message has been or will actually be delivered to the appropriate process. Obtaining such a guarantee would require additional handshaking between the processes. A blocking asynchronous `RECEIVE` is similar to a synchronous `RECEIVE` in that it returns control to the calling process only when the data it is receiving has been successfully removed from the system buffer and placed at the designated application address. Once it returns, the application can immediately use the data in the specified application buffer. Unlike a synchronous `RECEIVE`, however, a blocking `RECEIVE` does not send an acknowledgment to the sender.

The *nonblocking asynchronous* (or simply *nonblocking*) `SEND` and `RECEIVE` allow the greatest overlap between computation and message passing by returning control most quickly to the calling process. A nonblocking `SEND` returns control immediately. A nonblocking `RECEIVE` returns control after simply posting the intent to `RECEIVE`; the actual receipt of the message and placement into a specified application data structure is performed asynchronously at an undetermined time by the system on the basis of the posted receive. In both the nonblocking `SEND` and `RECEIVE`, however, the return of control does not imply anything about the state of the message or the application data structures it uses, so it is the user's responsibility to determine that state when necessary. Separate primitives are provided to probe (query) the state. Nonblocking messages are thus typically used in a two-phase manner: first the `SEND`/`RECEIVE` operation itself and then, when needed, the probes. The probes, which must be provided by the message-passing library, might either block until the desired state is observed or might return control immediately and simply report what state was observed.

The kind of `SEND`/`RECEIVE` semantics we choose depends on how the program uses its data structures and to what degree we wish to trade off ease of programming and portability to systems with other semantics for performance. The semantics mostly affects event synchronization, since mutual exclusion falls out naturally from having only private address spaces. In the equation solver example, using asynchronous `SEND`s and blocking asynchronous `RECEIVE`s would avoid the deadlock problem since processes would proceed past the `SEND` and to the `RECEIVE`. However, if we used nonblocking asynchronous `RECEIVE`s, we would have to use a probe before actually using the data structure specified in the `RECEIVE`. Note that a blocking `SEND/RECEIVE` is equivalent to a nonblocking `SEND`/`RECEIVE` followed immediately by a blocking probe.

To better appreciate the differences between the shared address space and message-passing programming models, it will be instructive to perform an exercise to transform the message-passing version of the equation solver to use a cyclic assignment as we did for the shared address space version in Example 2.2. The point to observe in this case is that, although the two message-passing versions will look syntactically similar, the meaning of the `myA` data structure will be completely different. In one case it is a contiguous section of the global array, and in the other it is a set of widely separated rows. Only by careful inspection of the data structures and communication patterns can you determine how a given message-passing version corresponds to the original sequential program or its shared address space counterpart.

2.4 CONCLUDING REMARKS

The process of parallelizing a sequential application is quite structured: we decompose the work into tasks; assign the tasks to processes; orchestrate data access, communication, and synchronization among processes; and optionally map processes to processors. For many applications, including the simple equation solver used in this chapter, the initial decomposition and assignment are similar or even identical regardless of whether a shared address space or message-passing programming model is used. The differences are in orchestration, particularly in the way data structures are organized and accessed and the way communication and synchronization are performed. A shared address space allows us to use the same major data structures as in a sequential program to produce a correct parallel program. Communication is implicit through data accesses, and the decomposition of data is not required at least for correctness. In the message-passing case, we must synthesize the logically shared data structure from per-process private data structures. Communication is explicit, decomposition of data explicitly among private address spaces (processes) is necessary, and processes must be able to name one another to communicate. On the other hand, whereas a shared address space program requires additional synchronization primitives separate from the reads and writes used for implicit communication, synchronization is bundled into the explicit send and receive communication in many forms of message passing. As we examine the parallelization of more complex applications, such as the four case studies introduced in this chapter, we will understand the implications of these differences for ease of programming as well as the additional considerations imposed by the desire for high performance.

The parallel versions of the simple equation solver described here were designed to illustrate programming primitives. Although these versions will not perform terribly (e.g., we reduced communication by using a block rather than cyclic assignment of rows, and we reduced both communication and synchronization dramatically by first accumulating into local `mydiffs` and only then into a global `diff`), the programs can be improved. We shall see how in the next chapter, as we turn our attention to the performance issues in parallel programming and how positions taken on these issues affect the workload presented to the architecture.

2.5 EXERCISES

2.1 Describe two examples where a good parallel algorithm must be based on a serial algorithm that is different from the best serial algorithm since the latter does not afford enough concurrency.

2.2 Which of our case study applications (Ocean, Barnes-Hut, Raytrace, and Data Mining) do you think are amenable to decomposing data rather than computation and using an owner computes rule in parallelization? What do you think the problem(s) would be with using a strict data distribution and owner computes rule in the others?

2.3 There are two dominant models for how parent and children processes relate to each other in a shared address space. In the heavyweight so-called process model, when a process creates another process, the child gets a private copy of the parent's image; that is, if the parent had allocated a variable x, then the child also finds a variable x in its address space that is initialized to the value that the parent had for x when it created the child. However, any modifications that either process makes subsequently are to its own copy of x and are not visible to the other process. In the lightweight threads model, the child process or thread gets a pointer to the parent's image, so that it and the parent now see the same storage location for x. All data that any process or thread allocates is shared in this model, except that on a procedure's stack.

   a. Consider the problem of a process having to reference its process identifier `pid` in various parts of a program, in different routines called (in a call chain) by the routine at which the process begins execution. How would you implement this in the first model? In the second? Do you need private data per process, or could you do this with all data being globally shared?

   b. A program written in the former (process) model may rely on the fact that a child process gets its own private copies of the parents' data structures. What changes would you make to port the program to the latter (threads) model for data structures that are (i) only read by processes after the creation of the child and (ii) are both read and written?

2.4 The classic bounded buffer problem provides an example of point-to-point event synchronization. Two processes communicate through a finite buffer. One process, the producer, adds data items to a buffer when it is not full; another, the consumer, reads data items from the buffer when it is not empty. If the consumer finds the buffer empty, it must wait until the producer inserts an item. When the producer is ready to insert an item, it checks to see if the buffer is full, in which case it must wait until the consumer removes something from the buffer. If the buffer is empty when the producer tries to add an item, then depending on the implementation the consumer may be waiting for notification, so the producer may need to notify the consumer. Can you implement a bounded buffer with only point-to-point event synchronization, or do you need mutual exclusion as well? Design an implementation, including pseudocode.

2.5 Would you use spinning on a flag or blocking of processes for interprocess synchronization in uniprocessor operating systems? What do you think the trade-offs are between blocking and spinning on a multiprocessor?

2.6 In the shared address space parallel equation solver (Figure 2.13), why do we need the first and third barriers in a while loop iteration (lines 16a and 25f)? Can you eliminate them without inserting any other synchronization, perhaps altering when certain operations are performed? Think about all possible scenarios.

2.7 Gaussian elimination is a well-known technique for solving simultaneous linear systems of equations. Variables are eliminated one by one until there is only one left, and then the discovered values of variables are back-substituted to obtain the values of other variables. In practice, the coefficients of the unknowns in the equation system are represented as a matrix A, and the matrix is first converted to an upper-triangular matrix (a matrix in which all elements below the main diagonal are 0). Then back-substitution is used. Let us focus on the conversion to an upper-triangular matrix by successive variable elimination. Pseudocode for sequential Gaussian elimination is shown in Figure 2.18. The diagonal element for a particular iteration of the k loop is called the *pivot element*, and its row is called the *pivot row*.

a. Draw a simple figure illustrating the dependences among matrix elements.

b. Assuming a decomposition into rows and an assignment into blocks of contiguous rows, write a shared address space parallel version using the primitives used for the equation solver in this chapter.

c. Write a message-passing version for the same decomposition and assignment, first using synchronous message passing and then any form of asynchronous message passing.

d. Can you see obvious performance problems with this partitioning? (We will discuss this further in the next chapter.)

e. Modify both the shared address space and message-passing versions to use an interleaved assignment of rows to processes.

f. Discuss the trade-offs (programming difficulty and any likely major performance differences) in programming the shared address space and message-passing versions.

2.8 Suppose that a system supporting a shared address space did not support barriers but only semaphores. Even global event synchronization would have to be constructed through semaphores or ordinary flags. The use of semaphores can be illustrated as follows. Suppose process P_2 has to indicate to process P_1 (using semaphores) that P_2 has reached a point b in the program so that P_1 can proceed past a point a (where it was waiting). P_1 performs a wait (also called P or down) operation on a semaphore when it reaches point a, and P_2 performs a signal (or V or up) operation on the same semaphore when it reaches point b. If P_1 gets to a before P_2 gets to b, P_1 suspends or blocks itself and is awakened by P_2's signal operation.

a. How might you orchestrate the synchronization in the shared address space parallel Gaussian elimination with (i) flags and (ii) semaphores replacing the

```
procedure Eliminate (A)          /*triangularize the matrix A*/
begin
for k ← 0 to n-1 do              /*loop over all diagonal (pivot) elements*/
  begin
    for j ← k+1 to n-1 do        /*for all elements in the row of, and to the right of,
                                   the pivot element*/
      A[k,j] = A[k,j] / A[k,k]);  /*divide by pivot element*/
    A[k,k] = 1;
    for i ← k+1 to n-1 do        /*for all rows below the pivot row*/
      for j ← k+1 to n-1 do      /*for all elements in the row*/
        A[i,j] = A[i,j] - A[i,k]* A[k,j];
      endfor
      A[i,k] = 0;
    endfor
  endfor
end procedure
```

FIGURE 2.18 Pseudocode describing sequential Gaussian elimination

barriers? Could you use point-to-point or group event synchronization instead of global event synchronization?

b. Answer the same for the equation solver example.

2.9 In the straightforward, loop-based approach to parallelizing Gaussian elimination discussed so far, parallelism is exploited only within an iteration of the outermost, k, loop. Since the pivot element and its row (called the *pivot row*) are effectively broadcast directly to all processes that need it, this is called the *broadcast version*. Gaussian elimination can also be parallelized in a form that is more aggressive in exploiting the available concurrency, even across outer loop iterations. During the kth iteration, the process assigned the pivot row can simply pass the pivot row on to the next process instead of broadcasting it. This process can use the pivot row to update its assigned rows immediately, as well as pass it on to the next process, and so on. As soon as this process has done its computation for the kth iteration of that loop in the sequential program, it can immediately perform its pivot row computation for the $(k + 1)$th iteration without waiting for all other processes to receive the kth row and perform their work for the kth iteration. It can then pass this $(k + 1)$th row on to the next process as well, which can use it right away instead of waiting for the entire previous k loop iteration to complete. Multiple k loop iterations are in progress at once; rows are passed down the processor pipeline as soon as they are computed and are computed as soon as the rows needed have arrived through the pipeline. We call this the *pipelined* form of parallelization.

a. Write a shared address space pseudocode, at a similar level of detail as Figure 2.13, for a version that implements pipelined parallelism at the granularity of individual elements. Show all synchronization necessary. Do you need barriers?

b. Write a message-passing pseudocode at the level of detail of Figure 2.16 for the pipelined case in part (a). Assume that the only communication primitives you have are synchronous and asynchronous (blocking and nonblocking) sends and receives. Which versions of send and receive would you use, and why wouldn't you choose the others?

c. Discuss the trade-offs in programming the loop-based versus pipelined parallelism.

2.10 Multicast (sending a message from one process to a named list of other processes) is a useful mechanism for communicating among subsets of processes.

a. How would you implement the message-passing, interleaved assignment version of Gaussian elimination with multicast rather than broadcast? Make up a multicast primitive, write pseudocode, and compare the programming ease of the two versions.

b. Which do you think will perform better and why?

c. What group communication primitives other than multicast do you think might be useful for a message-passing system to support? Give examples of computations in which they might be used.

3

Programming for Performance

The goal of using multiprocessors is to obtain high performance. With a concrete understanding of how the decomposition, assignment, and orchestration of a parallel program are incorporated in the code that runs on the machine, we are ready to examine the key factors that limit parallel performance and how they are addressed in a wide range of problems. We will see how decisions made in different steps of the programming process affect the run-time characteristics presented to the architecture, as well as how the characteristics of the architecture influence programming decisions. Understanding programming techniques and these interdependencies is important not only for parallel software designers but also for architects. Besides understanding parallel programs as workloads for the systems we build, we learn to appreciate hardware/software trade-offs. In particular, we learn which aspects of programmability and performance the architecture can positively impact and which aspects are best left to software. The interdependencies of program and system are more fluid, more complex, and more important to performance in multiprocessors than in uniprocessors; hence, this understanding is critical to our goal of designing high-performance systems that reduce cost and programming effort. We carry it with us throughout the book, starting with concrete guidelines for workload-driven architectural evaluation in Chapter 4.

The space of performance issues and techniques in parallel software is very rich: different goals trade off with one another, and techniques that further one goal may cause us to revisit the techniques used to address another. This is what makes the creation of parallel software so interesting and challenging. As in uniprocessors, most performance issues can be addressed either by algorithmic and programming techniques in software or by architectural techniques or both. The focus of this chapter is on performance issues and software techniques. Architectural techniques, sometimes hinted at here, are the subject of the rest of the book.

Although several interacting performance issues must be considered, they are not dealt with all at once. The process of creating a high-performance program is one of successive refinement. As discussed in Chapter 2, the partitioning steps—decomposition and assignment—are often largely independent of the underlying architecture or programming model and concern themselves with major algorithmic issues that depend only on the inherent properties of the problem. In particular, these steps view the multiprocessor as simply a set of processors that communicate with one another. Their goal is to resolve the tension between balancing the workload across processes, reducing the interprocess communication inherent in the program, and reducing the extra work needed to compute and manage the partitioning. We focus our attention first on addressing these partitioning issues.

Next, we open up the architecture and examine the new performance issues it raises for the orchestration and mapping steps. Opening up the architecture means recognizing two facts. The first fact is that a multiprocessor is not only a collection of processors but also a collection of memories, which an individual processor can view as an extended memory hierarchy. The management of data in these memory hierarchies can cause more data to be transferred across the network than the inherent communication mandated by the partitioning in the parallel program. The actual communication that occurs therefore depends both on the partitioning and on how the program's access patterns and locality of data reference interact with the organization and management of the extended memory hierarchy. The second fact is that the cost of communication as seen by the processor—and hence the contribution of communication to the execution time of the program—depends not only on the amount of communication but also on how it is structured to interact with the architecture. Section 3.2 discusses the relationship between communication, data locality, and the extended memory hierarchy. Then Section 3.3 examines the software techniques to address the major performance issues in orchestration and mapping: reducing the extra communication by exploiting data locality in the extended memory hierarchy and structuring communication to reduce its cost.

Of course, the architectural interactions and communication costs that we must deal with in orchestration sometimes cause us to go back and revise our partitioning methods, which is an important part of the refinement in parallel programming. Whereas interactions and trade-offs take place among all the performance issues we discuss, this chapter addresses each issue independently as far as possible and identifies trade-offs as they are encountered. Examples are drawn throughout from the four case study applications, and the impact of some individual programming techniques is illustrated through measurements on a cache-coherent machine with physically distributed memory, the Silicon Graphics Origin2000 (which is described in detail in Chapter 8). The equation solver kernel is also carried through the discussion, and performance techniques are applied to it as relevant; by the end of the discussion we will have created a high-performance parallel version of the solver.

As we examine the performance issues, we will develop simple analytical expressions for the speedup of a parallel program and illustrate how each performance issue affects the speedup equation. However, from an architectural perspective, a more concrete way of looking at performance is to examine the different components of execution time as seen by an individual processor in a machine—that is, how much time the processor spends executing instructions, accessing data in the extended memory hierarchy, and waiting for synchronization events to occur. In fact, these components of execution time can be mapped directly to the performance issues that software must address in the steps of creating a parallel program. Examining this view of performance helps us understand very concretely what a parallel execution looks like as a workload presented to the architecture, and the mapping helps us understand how programming techniques can alter this profile. These topics are discussed in Section 3.4.

Once we have studied the performance issues and techniques, we will be ready to understand how to create high-performance parallel versions of real applications—namely, the four case studies. Section 3.5 applies the parallelization process and performance techniques to each case study in turn. It illustrates how the techniques are employed together as well as the range of resulting execution characteristics that are presented to an architecture, reflected in varying profiles of execution time. We will also be ready to consider the implications of realistic applications for trade-offs between the two major lower-level programming models: a shared address space and explicit message passing. The trade-offs are in ease of programming and in performance and are discussed in Section 3.6. Let us begin with the algorithmic performance issues in the decomposition and assignment steps.

3.1 PARTITIONING FOR PERFORMANCE

For these steps, we can view the machine as simply a set of cooperating processors, largely ignoring its programming model and organization. All we need to know at this stage is that communication between processors is expensive. The three primary algorithmic issues are

- *balancing the workload* and reducing the time spent waiting at synchronization events
- *reducing communication*
- *reducing the extra work* done to determine and manage a good assignment

Unfortunately, even the three primary algorithmic goals are at odds with one another and must be traded off. A singular goal of minimizing communication would be satisfied by running the program on a single processor, as long as the necessary data fits in the local memory, but this would yield the ultimate load imbalance. On the other hand, near perfect load balance could be achieved—at a tremendous communication and task management penalty—by making each primitive operation in the program a task and assigning tasks randomly. And in many complex applications, load balance and communication could be improved by spending more time determining a good assignment, which results in extra work. The goal of decomposition and assignment is to achieve a good compromise between these conflicting demands as we see illustrated in the case studies and the equation solver kernel.

3.1.1 Load Balance and Synchronization Wait Time

In its simplest form, balancing the workload means ensuring that every processor does the same amount of work. It extends exposing enough concurrency (which we saw in Chapter 2 when discussing Amdahl's Law) with proper assignment and reduced serialization, and it gives the following simple limit on potential speedup:

$$\text{Speedup}_{problem}(p) \leq \frac{\text{Sequential Work}}{\text{max Work on Any Processor}}$$

Work in this context should be interpreted liberally because what matters is not only how many calculations are done but also the time spent doing them, which involves data accesses and communication as well.

In fact, load balancing is a little more complicated than simply equalizing work. Not only should different processors do the same amount of work, they should also be working at the same time. The extreme point would be if the work were evenly divided among processes but only one process were active at a time so there would be no speedup at all! The real goal of load balance is to minimize the time processes spend waiting at synchronization points, including an implicit one at the end of the program. This also involves minimizing the serialization of processes because of either mutual exclusion (waiting to enter critical sections) or dependences. The assignment step should ensure that low serialization is possible, and orchestration should ensure that it happens.

The process of balancing the workload and reducing synchronization wait time consists of four parts:

1. Identifying enough concurrency in decomposition and overcoming Amdahl's Law
2. Deciding how to manage the concurrency (statically or dynamically)
3. Determining the granularity at which to exploit the concurrency
4. Reducing serialization and synchronization cost

This section examines some techniques for each, using examples from the four case studies and other applications as well.

Identifying Enough Concurrency: Data and Function Parallelism

We saw in parallelizing the equation solver kernel that concurrency may be found by examining the loops of a program, by looking more deeply at the fundamental dependences, or by exploiting an understanding of its underlying problem to discover algorithms that afford more concurrency. Parallelizing loops often leads to similar (not necessarily identical) operation sequences or functions being performed on elements of a large data structure, as in the equation solver kernel. This is called *data parallelism* and is a more general form of the parallelism that inspired data parallel architectures discussed in Chapter 1. Computing forces on different particles in Barnes-Hut is another example.

In addition to data parallelism, applications often exhibit *function parallelism* as well: entirely different calculations can be performed concurrently on either the same or different data. Function parallelism is often referred to as control parallelism or task parallelism, though these are overloaded terms. For example, setting up an equation system for the solver in Ocean requires many different computations on ocean cross sections, each using a few cross-sectional grids. Analyzing dependences at the level of entire grids or arrays reveals that several of these computations are independent of one another and can be performed in parallel. Pipelining is another form of function parallelism in which different functions or stages of the pipeline are

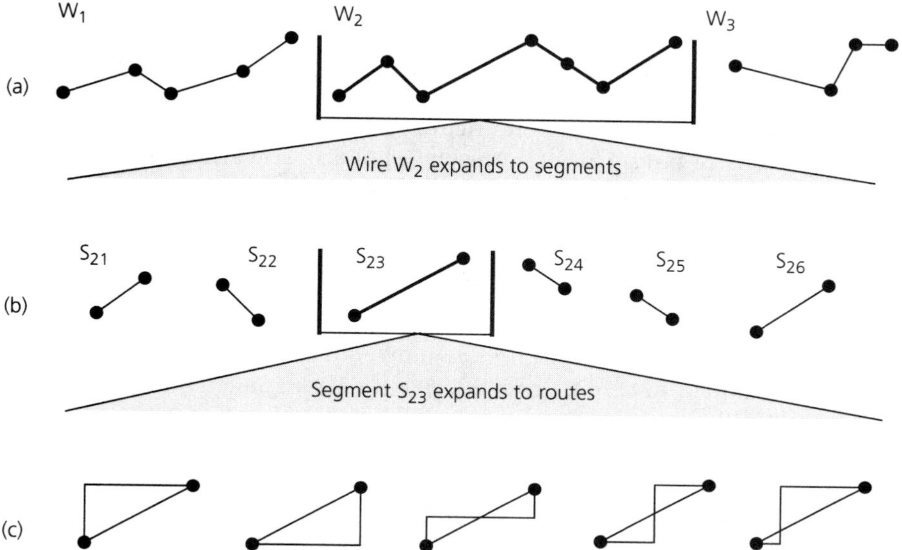

FIGURE 3.1 The three axes of parallelism in a VLSI wire-routing application: (a) wire parallelism; (b) segment parallelism; (c) route parallelism. The filled circles indicate the pins that are connected by wires.

performed concurrently on different data. For example, in encoding a sequence of video frames, each block of each frame passes through several stages: prefiltering, convolution from the time to the frequency domain, quantization, entropy coding, and so on. Pipeline parallelism is available across these stages (for example, a few processes could be assigned to each stage and operate concurrently), as is data parallelism between frames, among blocks in a frame, and within an operation on a block.

Function parallelism and data parallelism are often available together in an application and provide a hierarchy of levels of parallelism from which we must choose (e.g., function parallelism across grid computations and data parallelism within grid computations in Ocean, and the video encoding example). Orthogonal levels of data or function parallelism are found in many other applications as well; for example, applications that route wires in VLSI circuits exhibit parallelism across the wires to be routed, across the two-pin segments within a wire, and across the many routes evaluated for each segment (see Figure 3.1).

The degree of available function parallelism is usually modest and does not grow much with the size of the problem being solved. The degree of data parallelism, on the other hand, usually grows with data set size. Function parallelism is also usually more difficult to exploit in a load-balanced way, since different functions involve different amounts of work and have different scaling characteristics. Most parallel programs that run on large-scale machines are data parallel according to our loose definition of the term, and exploit function parallelism mainly to reduce the amount of global synchronization required between data parallel computations (as illustrated in Ocean in Section 3.5.1).

By identifying the different types of concurrency available in an application, we often find much more concurrency than we need for load balancing. The next step in decomposition is to restrict the available concurrency by determining the granularity of tasks. However, the choice of task size also depends on how we expect to manage the concurrency, so let us discuss this next.

Determining How to Manage Concurrency: Static versus Dynamic Assignment

A key issue in exploiting concurrency is whether a good load balance can be obtained by a static or predetermined assignment (introduced in Chapter 2) or whether more dynamic means are required. A static assignment is typically an algorithmic mapping of tasks to processes, as in the simple equation solver kernel discussed in the previous chapter. Exactly which tasks (grid points or rows) are assigned to which processes may depend on the problem size, the number of processes, and other parameters, but once it is determined, the assignment does not change again at run time. Since the assignment is predetermined, static techniques do not incur much task management overhead at run time. However, to achieve good load balance, they require that the relative amounts of work in different tasks be adequately predictable or that enough tasks exist to ensure a balanced distribution by virtue of the statistics of large numbers. In addition to the program itself, it is also important that other environmental conditions—such as interference from other applications—not perturb the relationships among processors, thus limiting the robustness of static load balancing.

Dynamic partitioning techniques adapt to load imbalances at run time. They come in two forms. In *semistatic* techniques, the assignment for a phase of computation is determined algorithmically before that phase, but assignments are recomputed periodically to restore load balance based on profiles of the actual workload distribution gathered at run time. For example, we can profile (measure) the work that each task does in one phase and use that as an estimate of the work associated with it the next time that phase is executed. This repartitioning technique is used to assign stars to processes in Barnes-Hut (Section 3.5.2) by using profiles to recompute the assignment between time-steps of the galaxy's evolution. The galaxy evolves slowly, so the workload distribution among stars does not change much between successive time-steps. Figure 3.2(a) illustrates the advantage of semistatic partitioning over a static assignment of particles to processors, for a 512-K particle execution measured on the Origin2000, despite the cost of periodic repartitioning. It is clear that the performance difference grows with the number of processors used.

The second dynamic technique, *dynamic tasking*, is used to handle cases in which either the work distribution or the system environment is too unpredictable even to

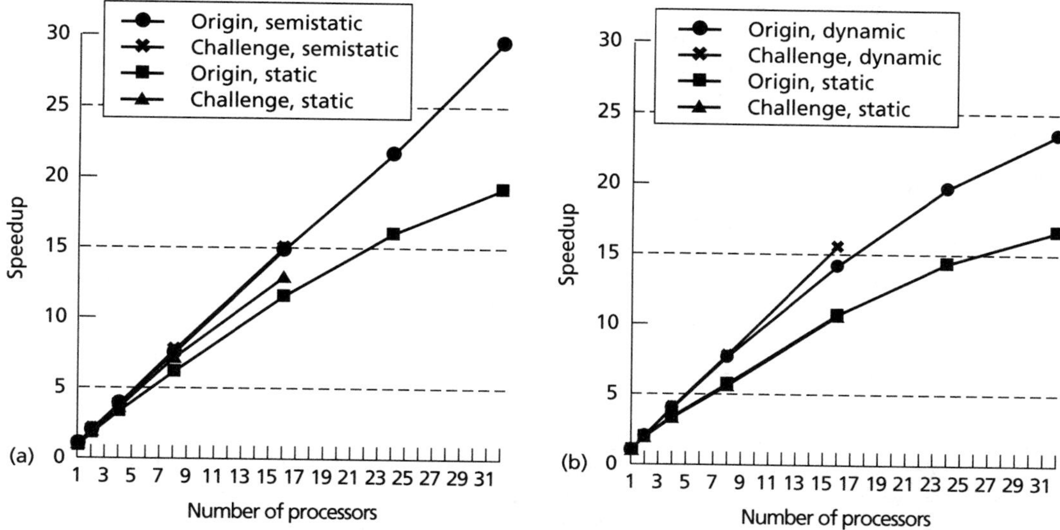

FIGURE 3.2 Illustration of the performance impact of dynamic partitioning for load balance. The graph in (a) shows the speedups of the Barnes-Hut application with and without semistatic partitioning, and the graph in (b) shows the speedups of Raytrace with and without dynamic tasking. Even in these applications that have a lot of parallelism, dynamic partitioning is important for improving load balance over static partitioning.

periodically recompute a load-balanced assignment.[1] For example, in Raytrace the work associated with each ray is impossible to predict. Even if the rendering is repeated from different viewpoints, the change in viewpoints may not be gradual. The dynamic tasking approach divides the computation into tasks and maintains a pool of available tasks (in Raytrace a task may be a ray or a set of rays). Each process repeatedly takes a task from the pool and executes it—possibly inserting new tasks into the pool—until no tasks are left. Of course, the management of the task pool must preserve the dependences among tasks—for example, by inserting a task only when it is ready for execution. Since dynamic tasking is widely used, let us look at some specific techniques to implement the task pool. Figure 3.2(b) illustrates the advantage of dynamic tasking over a static assignment of rays to processors in the

1. The applicability of static or semistatic assignment depends not only on the computational properties of the program but also on its interactions with the memory and communication systems and on the predictability of the execution environment. For example, differences in memory or communication stall time (due to cache misses, page faults, or contention) can cause imbalances observed at synchronization points even when the workload is computationally load balanced. Static assignment also may not be appropriate for time-shared or heterogeneous systems.

Raytrace application, for a data set consisting of number of balls arranged like a bunch of grapes, measured on the Origin2000.

A simple example of dynamic tasking in a shared address space is *self-scheduling* of a parallel loop. The loop counter is a shared variable accessed by all the processes that execute iterations of the loop. Processes obtain a loop iteration by incrementing the counter atomically; they repeatedly execute an iteration and access the counter again until no iterations remain. The task size can be increased by taking multiple iterations at a time, that is, adding a value larger than one to the shared loop counter. However, this can increase load imbalance. In *guided self-scheduling* (Aiken and Nikolau 1988), processes start by taking large chunks and taper down the chunk size as the loop progresses, hoping to reduce the number of accesses to the shared counter without compromising load balance.

More general dynamic task pools are usually implemented by a collection of queues into which tasks are inserted and from which tasks are removed and executed by processes. This may be a single centralized queue or a set of distributed queues, typically one per process, as shown in Figure 3.3. A *centralized queue* is simpler but has the disadvantage that every process accesses the same task queue, potentially increasing communication and causing processors to contend for queue access. Modifications to the queue (enqueuing or dequeuing tasks) must be mutually exclusive, further increasing contention and causing serialization. Unless tasks are large, and therefore queue accesses are few relative to computation, a centralized queue can quickly become a performance bottleneck as the number of processors increases.

With *distributed queues,* every process is initially assigned a set of tasks in its local queue. This initial assignment may be done intelligently to reduce interprocess communication, thus providing more control than self-scheduling and centralized queues. A process removes and executes tasks from its local queue as far as possible. If it creates tasks, it inserts them in its local queue. When no more tasks are in its local queue, it queries other processes' queues to obtain tasks from them, a mechanism known as *task stealing*. Because task stealing implies communication and can generate contention, several interesting issues arise in implementing stealing: for example, how to minimize stealing, whom to steal from, how many and which tasks to steal at a time, and so on. Stealing also introduces the important issue of *termination detection:* how do we decide when to stop searching for tasks to steal and assume that they're all done, given that tasks generate other tasks that are dynamically inserted in the queues? Simple heuristic solutions to this problem work well in practice, although a robust solution can be quite subtle and communication intensive (Dijkstra and Sholten 1968; Chandy and Misra 1988). Task queues are used both in a shared address space, where the queues are shared data structures that are manipulated using locks, and with explicit message passing, where the owners of queues service requests for them.

Although dynamic techniques generally provide good load balancing despite unpredictability or environmental conditions, they make the management of parallelism more expensive. Dynamic tasking techniques also compromise the explicit control over which tasks are executed by which processes, thus potentially increas-

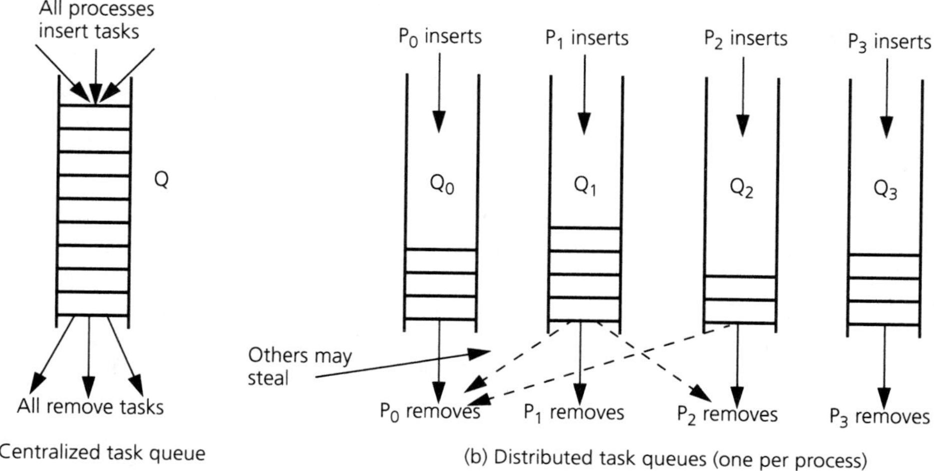

FIGURE 3.3 Implementing a dynamic task pool with a system of task queues

ing communication and compromising data locality. Static techniques are therefore usually preferable when they can provide good load balance for an application and environment.

Determining the Granularity of Tasks

If no load imbalances occur due to dependences among tasks (for example, if all tasks are ready to be executed at the beginning of a phase of computation), then the maximum load imbalance possible with a task-queue strategy is equal to the granularity of the largest task. By *task granularity,* we mean the amount of work associated with a task, which is measured by the number of instructions or, more appropriately, the execution time. The general rule for choosing a granularity at which to actually exploit concurrency is that fine-grained or small tasks have the potential for better load balance (more tasks to divide among processes and hence more concurrency), but they lead to higher task management overhead, more contention, and more interprocessor communication than coarse-grained or large tasks. Let us see why, first in the context of dynamic task queuing where the definitions and trade-offs are clearer.

Task Granularity with Dynamic Task Queuing Here, a task is explicitly defined as an entry placed on a task queue, so task granularity is the work associated with such an entry. The larger task management (queue manipulation) overhead with small tasks is clear. At least with a centralized queue, the more frequent need for queue access generally leads to greater contention as well. Finally, breaking up a task into two smaller tasks might cause the two tasks to be executed on different processors, thus increasing communication if the tasks access the same logically shared data.

Task Granularity with Static Assignment With static assignment, tasks are not explicit in the program, so it is less clear what should be called a task or a unit of concurrency. For example, in the equation solver, is a task a group of rows, a single row, or an individual element? We can define a task as the largest unit of work such that even if the assignment of tasks to processes is changed, the code that implements a task need not change. With static assignment, task size has a much smaller effect on task management overhead compared to dynamic task queuing since there are no queue accesses. Communication and contention are affected by the assignment of tasks to processors, not their size. The major impact of task size is usually on load imbalance and on exploiting data locality in processor caches.

Reducing Serialization

Finally, to reduce serialization at synchronization points, whether it is due to mutual exclusion or dependences among tasks, we must be careful about how we assign tasks as well as how we orchestrate synchronization and schedule tasks. For event synchronization, an example of excessive serialization is the use of more conservative synchronization than necessary, such as barriers instead of point-to-point or group synchronization. Even if point-to-point synchronization is used, it may preserve data dependences at a coarser grain than is required; for example, a process waits for another to produce a whole row of a matrix when the actual dependences are at the level of individual matrix elements. However, finer-grained synchronization is often more complex to program; it also implies the execution of more synchronization operations (say, one per word rather than one per larger data structure), the overhead of which may turn out to be more expensive than the savings in serialization. As usual, trade-offs abound.

For mutual exclusion, we can reduce serialization by using separate locks for separate data items and making the critical sections protected by locks smaller and less frequent if possible. Consider the former technique. In a database application, we may want to lock when we update certain fields of records that are assigned to different processes. The question is how to organize the locking. Should we use one lock per process, one per record, or one per field? The finer the granularity, the lower the contention, but the greater the space overhead and the less frequent the reuse of locks. An intermediate solution is to use a fixed number of locks and share them among records using a simple hashing function from records to locks. Another way to reduce serialization is to stagger the critical sections in time, that is, to arrange the computation so that multiple processes do not try to access the same lock at the same time.

Implementing task queues provides an interesting example of making critical sections smaller and less frequent. Suppose each process adds a task to a queue, then searches the queue for another task with a particular characteristic, and then removes this latter task from the queue. The task insertion and deletion may need to be mutually exclusive—or may not if they are done at different ends of the queue—but the searching of the queue does not. Thus, instead of using a single critical section for the whole sequence of operations, we can break it up into two critical sections (insertion and deletion) and use code that is not mutually exclusive to search the list in between.

More generally, checking (reading) the state of a protected data structure usually does not have to be done with mutual exclusion; only modifying the data structure does. If the common case is to check but not to modify, as for the tasks we search through in the task queue, we can check without locking and, only if the check returns the appropriate condition, then lock and recheck within the critical section (to ensure the state hasn't changed) before modifying. In addition, instead of using a single lock for the entire queue, we can use a lock per queue element so that elements in different parts of the queue can be inserted or deleted in parallel (without serialization). As with event synchronization, the correct trade-offs in performance and programming ease depend on the costs and benefits of the choices on a system.

We can extend our simple limit on speedup to reflect both load imbalance and time spent waiting at synchronization points as follows, where *max* in the denominator is the maximum over all processes:

$$\text{Speedup}_{problem}(p) \le \frac{\text{Sequential Work}}{\max(\text{Work} + \text{Synch Wait Time})}$$

In general, the different aspects of balancing the workload are the responsibility of software. An architecture cannot do very much about a program that does not have enough concurrency or is not load balanced. However, an architecture can help in some ways. First, it can provide efficient support for load-balancing techniques, such as task stealing, that are used widely by parallel software (applications, libraries, and operating systems). An access to a remote task queue for stealing is usually a probe or query, involving a small amount of data transfer and perhaps mutual exclusion. The more efficient the support for fine-grained communication and for low-overhead, mutually exclusive access to data, the smaller we can make our tasks and thus improve load balance. Second, the architecture can make it easy to name or access the logically shared data that a stolen task needs. Third, the architecture can provide efficient support for point-to-point synchronization, making it more attractive to use this form of synchronization instead of conservative barriers and hence allowing better load balance to be achieved.

3.1.2 Reducing Inherent Communication

Load balancing by itself is conceptually quite easy as long as the application affords enough concurrency: we can simply make tasks small and use dynamic tasking. Perhaps the most important performance goal to be traded off with load balance is reducing interprocessor communication. Decomposing a problem into multiple tasks usually means that communication will be required among tasks. If these tasks are assigned to different processes, we incur communication among processes and hence processors. The focus in this section is on reducing communication that is *inherent* to the parallel program (i.e., one process produces data values that another needs) while still preserving load balance, thus retaining the view of the machine as a set of cooperating processors. However, in a real system communication occurs for other reasons, as Section 3.2 shows.

The impact of communication is best estimated not by the absolute amount of communication but by a quantity called the *communication-to-computation ratio*. This is defined as the amount of communication (in bytes, say) divided by the computation time (or because time is influenced by many factors, by the number of instructions executed). For example, a gigabyte of communication has a much greater impact on the execution time and communication bandwidth requirements of an application if the time required for the application to execute is 1 second than if it is 1 hour! The communication-to-computation ratio may be computed as a per-process number or accumulated over all processes.

The inherent communication-to-computation ratio is primarily controlled by the assignment of tasks to processes. To reduce communication, we should try to ensure that tasks accessing the same data or requiring frequent communication with one another are assigned to the same process. For example, in a database application, communication would be reduced if queries and updates that access the same database records are assigned to the same process.

One partitioning principle that has worked very well in practice for load balancing and inherent communication is *domain decomposition*. It was initially used in data parallel scientific computations such as Ocean but has since been found applicable to many other areas. If the data set on which the application operates can be viewed as a physical domain, then it is often the case that a point in the domain requires information either directly from only a small localized region around that point or from a longer range, with the requirements falling off with increasing distance from the point. We saw an example of the latter in Barnes-Hut. For the former, consider a video application in which algorithms for motion estimation in video encoding and decoding examine only the areas of a scene that are close to the current pixel; similarly, a point in the equation solver kernel needs to access only its four nearest-neighbor points directly. The goal of partitioning in these cases is to give every process a contiguous region of the domain, while of course retaining load balance, and to shape the domain so that most of the process's information requirements are satisfied within its assigned partition. As Figure 3.4 shows, in many such cases the communication requirements for a process grow proportionally to the size of a partition's boundary, whereas computation grows proportionally to the size of its entire partition. The communication-to-computation ratio is thus a surface-area-to-volume ratio in three dimensions and a perimeter-to-area ratio in two dimensions. It can be reduced by either increasing the data set size (n^2 in the figure) or reducing the number of processors (p).

Of course, the ideal shape for partitions in a domain decomposition is application dependent, depending primarily on the information requirements of and work associated with the points in the domain. For the equation solver kernel, in Chapter 2 we

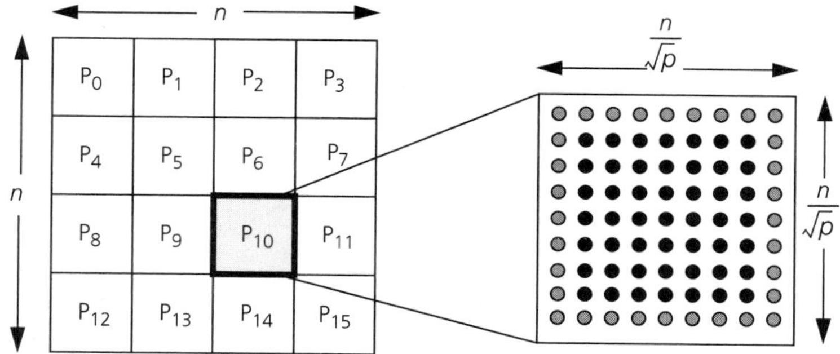

FIGURE 3.4 The perimeter-to-area relationship of communication to computation in a two-dimensional domain decomposition. The example shown is for an algorithm with localized, nearest-neighbor information exchange like the simple equation solver kernel. Every point on the grid needs information from its four nearest neighbors. Thus, the darker internal points in processor P_{10}'s partition do not need to communicate directly with any points outside the partition. Computation for processor P_{10} is thus proportional to the sum of all n^2/p points, whereas communication is proportional to the number of lighter boundary points, which is $4n/\sqrt{p}$.

chose to partition the grid into blocks of contiguous rows. Figure 3.5 shows that partitioning the grid into squarelike subgrids leads to a lower inherent communication-to-computation ratio. The impact becomes greater as the number of processors increases relative to the grid size. We shall therefore carry forward this partitioning into square subgrids (or simply "subgrids") as we continue to discuss performance. As a simple exercise, think about what the communication-to-computation ratio would be if we assigned rows to processes in an interleaved or cyclic fashion instead (row *i* assigned to process *i* mod *nprocs*).

How do we find a suitable domain decomposition that is load balanced and also keeps communication low? This can be accomplished statically or semistatically, depending on the nature and predictability of the computation:

- *Statically, by inspection*, as in the equation solver kernel and in Ocean. This requires predictability and usually leads to regularly shaped partitions, as in Figures 3.4 and 3.5.
- *Statically, by analysis.* The computation and communication characteristics may depend not only on the size of the input but also on the structure of the input presented to the program at run time, thus requiring an analysis of the input. However, the partitioning may need to be done only once after the input analysis—before the actual computation starts—so we still consider it static. Partitioning sparse matrix computations used in aerospace and automobile simulations is an example: the matrix structure is fixed but is highly irregular and requires sophisticated graph partitioning. Another example is Data Mining. Here, we may divide the database of transactions statically among processors, but a balanced assignment of itemsets to processes requires some analysis

$\frac{n}{\sqrt{p}}$

P_0	P_1	P_2	P_3
P_4	P_5	P_6	P_7
P_8	P_9	P_{10}	P_{11}
P_{12}	P_{13}	P_{14}	P_{15}

$\frac{n}{\sqrt{p}}$

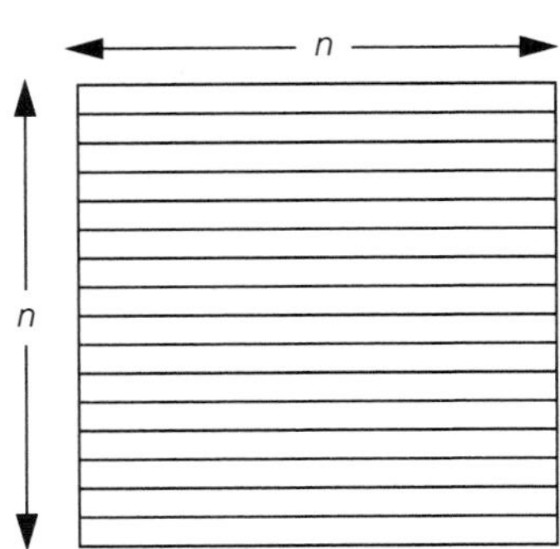

FIGURE 3.5 Choosing among domain decompositions for a simple nearest-neighbor computation on a regular two-dimensional grid. Since the work per grid point is uniform, equally sized partitions yield good load balance. But we still have choices. We might partition the elements of the grid into either strips of contiguous rows (right) or block-structured partitions that are as close to square as possible (left). The perimeter-to-area (and hence communication-to-computation) ratio in the block decomposition case is

$$\frac{4 \times n/\sqrt{p}}{n^2/p} \text{ or } \frac{4 \times \sqrt{p}}{n}$$

whereas that in strip decomposition is $\frac{2 \times n}{n^2/p}$ or $\frac{2 \times p}{n}$.

As p increases, block decomposition incurs less inherent communication for the same computation than strip decomposition.

since the work associated with different itemsets is not equal. A simple static assignment of itemsets and the database by inspection keeps communication low but does not provide load balance.

- *Semistatically, with periodic repartitioning.* This was discussed earlier for applications like Barnes-Hut whose characteristics change slowly with time. Domain decomposition is still important to reduce communication, as we see in the profiling-based Barnes-Hut case study in Section 3.5.2.
- *Statically or semistatically, with dynamic task stealing.* Even when the computation is highly unpredictable and dynamic task stealing must be used, domain decomposition may be useful in initially assigning tasks to processes. Raytrace is an example. Here there are two domains: the three-dimensional scene being rendered and the two-dimensional image plane. Since the natural tasks are rays shot through the image plane, it is much easier to manage domain decomposition of that plane than of the scene itself. We partition the image domain much like the grid in the equation solver kernel (Figure 3.4), with image pixels corresponding to grid points, and initially assign rays to the corresponding processes. This is useful because rays shot through adjacent pixels tend to access much of the same scene data. Processes then steal rays (pixels) or groups of rays dynamically for load balancing.

Of course, partitioning into a contiguous subdomain per processor is not always appropriate for high performance in all applications, as illustrated by the Gaussian elimination example in Exercise 3.9. Even Raytrace may benefit from dividing the image into more blocks than there are processors and assigning blocks to processors in an interleaved manner, trading off increased communication for better initial load balance. Different phases of the same application may also call for different partitioning. The range of techniques is very large, but common principles like domain decomposition can be found. For example, even when stealing tasks for load balancing in very dynamic applications, we can reduce communication by searching other queues in the same order every time or by preferentially stealing large tasks or several tasks at once to reduce the number of times we have to access nonlocal queues.

In addition to reducing communication volume, it is also important to keep communication (not just computation) balanced among processors. Since communication is expensive, imbalances in communication can translate directly to imbalances in execution time among processors. Overall, whether trade-offs in partitioning should be resolved in favor of load balance or communication volume depends on the cost of communication on a given system. Including communication as an explicit performance cost refines our basic speedup limit to

$$\text{Speedup}_{problem}(p) \leq \frac{\textit{Sequential Work}}{\text{max}(\textit{Work} + \textit{Synch Wait Time} + \textit{Comm Cost})}$$

Compared to the previous expression, this expression separates communication from work, which now includes instructions executed plus local data access costs.

The amount of communication in parallel programs clearly has important implications for architecture. In fact, architects examine the needs of applications to determine what communication latencies and bandwidths are worth spending extra money for (see Exercise 3.14); for example, the bandwidth provided by a machine can usually be increased by throwing hardware (and hence money) at the problem, but this is only worthwhile if applications will exercise the increased bandwidth. As architects, we assume that the programs delivered to us are reasonable in their load balance and their communication demands, and we strive to make them perform better by providing the necessary support. Let us now examine the last of the algorithmic issues that we can resolve in partitioning itself without addressing the underlying architecture.

3.1.3 Reducing the Extra Work

The preceding discussion of domain decomposition suggests that when a computation is irregular, computing a good assignment that both provides load balance and reduces communication can be quite expensive. This extra work is not required in a sequential execution and is an overhead of parallelism. Consider the sparse matrix example that was discussed previously to illustrate static partitioning by analysis. The sparse matrix can be represented as a graph, such that each node represents a row or column of the matrix and an edge exists between two nodes i and j if the matrix entry (i,j) is nonzero. The goal in partitioning is to assign each process a set of nodes such that the computation is load balanced and the number of edges that cross partition boundaries is minimized. Many clever partitioning techniques have been developed, but the ones that result in a better balance between load balance and communication require more time to partition the graph. We see this illustrated in the Barnes-Hut case study later in this chapter.

In addition to partitioning, another common source of extra work is redundant computation: multiple processes computing data values redundantly rather than having one process compute them and communicate them to the others, which may be a favorable trade-off when the cost of communication is high. Examples include all processes computing their own copy of the same shading table in computer graphics applications or of trigonometric tables in scientific computations. If the redundant computation can be performed while the processor is otherwise idle due to load imbalance, its cost can be hidden.

Finally, many aspects of orchestrating parallel programs involve extra work as well, such as creating processes, managing dynamic tasking, distributing code and data throughout the machine, executing synchronization operations and parallelism control instructions, structuring communication appropriately for a machine, and packing and unpacking data to and from communication messages. For example, the high cost of creating processes is what causes us to create them once up front and have them execute tasks until the program terminates, rather than creating and terminating processes as parallel sections of code are encountered and exited by a single main thread of computation (a *fork-join* approach, which is sometimes used with lightweight threads instead of processes). For example, in the Data Mining case study (Section 3.5.4), substantial extra work done to transform the database pays off in reducing communication, synchronization, and expensive input/output activity.

The trade-offs between extra work, load balance, and communication must be considered carefully when making partitioning decisions. The architecture can help reduce the need for extra work by making communication and task management more efficient. Based only on these algorithmic partitioning issues, the speedup limit can now be refined to

$$\text{Speedup}_{problem}(p) \leq \frac{\text{Sequential Work}}{\max\ (\text{Work} + \text{Synch Wait Time} + \text{Comm Cost} + \text{Extra Work})} \tag{3.1}$$

3.1.4 Summary

The analysis of parallel algorithm performance requires a characterization of a multiprocessor and a characterization of the parallel algorithm. Historically, the analysis of parallel algorithms has focused on algorithmic aspects like partitioning and mapping to network topologies and has not taken other architectural interactions into account. In fact, the most common model used to characterize a multiprocessor for algorithm analysis has been the Parallel Random Access Memory (PRAM) model (Fortune and Wyllie 1978). In its most basic form, the PRAM model assumes that data access is free, regardless of whether it is local or involves communication. That is, communication cost is zero in the speedup expression of Equation 3.1, and work is treated simply as instructions executed:

$$\text{Speedup-PRAM}_{problem}(p) \leq \frac{\text{Sequential Instructions}}{\max\ (\text{Instr} + \text{Synch Wait Time} + \text{Extra Instr})} \quad (3.2)$$

A natural way to think of a PRAM model is as a shared address space machine in which all data access is free. The performance factors that matter in parallel algorithm analysis using this model are load balance (including serialization) and extra work. The goal of algorithm development for PRAMs is to expose enough concurrency so the workload may be well balanced without needing too much extra work.

While the PRAM model is useful in discovering the concurrency available in an algorithm, which is the first step in parallelization, it is clearly unrealistic for modeling performance on real parallel systems. This is because communication, which it ignores, can easily dominate the cost of a parallel execution in modern systems, and imbalances in communication cost can dominate imbalances in instructions executed. In fact, analyzing algorithms while ignoring communication can easily lead to a poor choice of decomposition and assignment, to say nothing of orchestration. More recent models have been developed to include communication costs as explicit parameters that algorithm designers can use (Valiant 1990; Culler et al. 1993). We return to this issue after we have a better understanding of communication costs.

The treatment of communication costs in this section is simplified in two respects relative to real systems. First, communication inherent to the parallel program and its partitioning is not the only form of communication that is important: substantial noninherent or *artifactual* communication may occur that is caused by interactions of the program with the architecture on which it runs. Thus, we have not yet modeled the amount of communication generated by a parallel program satisfactorily. Second, the communication cost term in Equation 3.1 is determined not only by the amount of communication caused, whether inherent or artifactual, but also by the structure of the communication in the program and how it interacts with the costs of the basic communication operations in the machine. Both artifactual communication and communication structure are important performance issues that are usually addressed in the orchestration step since they are architecture dependent. To understand them we first need a deeper understanding of some critical interactions of parallel architectures with parallel software.

3.2 DATA ACCESS AND COMMUNICATION IN A MULTIMEMORY SYSTEM

In our discussion of partitioning, we have viewed a multiprocessor as a collection of cooperating processors. However, multiprocessor systems are also multimemory, multicache systems, and the role of these components is essential to performance. The role is essential regardless of programming model, though the latter may influence the nature of the specific performance trade-offs. Our discussion turns to the remaining performance issues for parallel programs, which are primarily concerned with accessing data in this multimemory system. It is useful for us to now take a different view of a multiprocessor.

3.2.1 A Multiprocessor as an Extended Memory Hierarchy

From an individual processor's perspective, we can view all the memory of the machine, including the caches of other processors, as forming levels of an extended memory hierarchy. The communication architecture glues together the parts of the hierarchy that are on different nodes. In a uniprocessor system, consider how interactions with different levels of the memory hierarchy (e.g., cache size, associativity, block size) can cause some accesses to be much faster than others and can also cause the transfer of more data between levels than is inherently necessary for the program. Similarly, in multiprocessors, interactions with the organization of the extended memory hierarchy can cause more communication (transfer of data across the network) than is inherently necessary to satisfy the processes in a parallel program. Since communication is expensive, it is particularly important that we exploit data locality in the extended hierarchy, both to improve node performance and to reduce the extra communication between nodes.

Even in uniprocessor systems, a processor's performance depends heavily on the performance of the memory hierarchy. Cache effects are so important that it hardly makes sense to talk about performance without taking caches into account. We can look at the performance of a system in terms of the time needed to complete a program, which has two components: the time the processor is busy executing instructions and the time it spends waiting for data from the memory system. (Input/output activity can be grouped with data access or treated separately.)

$$Time_{prog}(1) = Busy(1) + \text{Data Access}(1) \tag{3.3}$$

As architects, we often normalize this formula by dividing each term by the number of instructions executed and measuring time in clock cycles. We then have a convenient, machine-oriented metric of performance, cycles per instruction (CPI), which is composed of an ideal CPI plus the average number of data access stall cycles per instruction. On a modern microprocessor capable of issuing, say, four instructions per cycle, dependences within the program might limit the average issue rate to 2.5 instructions per cycle, or an ideal CPI of 0.4. If only 1% of these instructions causes a cache miss, and a cache miss causes the processor to stall for 80 cycles on average, then these stalls will account for an additional 0.8 cycles per instruction. The processor will be busy doing "useful" work only one-third of its time! Of course, the other two-thirds of the time is in fact useful: it is the time spent communicating with memory to access data. Recognizing this data access cost, we may elect to optimize either the program or the machine to perform the data access more efficiently. For example, we may change the program data layout to enhance temporal or spatial locality, or we might provide a bigger cache or mechanisms to tolerate latency.

In multiprocessors, an idealized view of this extended memory hierarchy would be local cache hierarchies connected to a single centralized memory at the next level. In reality, the picture is a bit more complex. Even on machines with centralized shared memories, beyond the local caches are a multibanked memory as well as the caches of other processors. With physically distributed memories, a part of the main memory too is local, a larger part is remote, and what is remote to one processor is local to another.

Differences in programming models reflect a difference in how certain levels of the hierarchy are managed. We take for granted that the registers in the processor are managed by the compiler. We also take for granted that the first couple of levels of caches are managed transparently by the hardware. In the shared address space model, data movement between a remote node and the local node is managed transparently to the user program as well. The message-passing model has this movement managed explicitly by the program. Regardless of the management, levels of the hierarchy that are closer to the processor provide higher bandwidth and lower latency access to data. Here too we can improve data access performance either by improving the architecture of the extended memory hierarchy or by improving the locality in the program.

Exploiting locality exposes a trade-off with parallelism similar to reducing communication. Parallelism may cause more processors to access the same data and hence move that data toward each of themselves, whereas each individual processor desires that its own data stays close to it. A high-performance parallel program needs to obtain performance from each individual processor (by exploiting locality in the extended memory hierarchy) in addition to being well parallelized.

3.2.2 Artifactual Communication in the Extended Memory Hierarchy

Data accesses that are not satisfied in the local (on-node) portion of the extended memory hierarchy generate communication. Inherent communication can be seen as part of this: the data moves from one processor through the memory hierarchy to another processor, regardless of whether it does this through explicit messages or reads and writes. However, the amount of communication that occurs in an execution of the program is usually greater than the inherent interprocess communication in the parallel algorithm. The additional communication is an *artifact* of how the program is actually implemented and how it interacts with the machine's extended memory hierarchy. There are many sources of this artifactual communication:

- *Poor allocation of data.* Data accessed by one node may happen to be allocated in the local memory of another. Accesses to remote data involve communication even if the data is not modified by other nodes. Such transfer can be eliminated by a better assignment or better distribution of data or reduced by replicating the data locally when it is accessed.
- *Unnecessary data in a transfer.* More data than needed may be communicated in a transfer. For example, a receiver may not use all the data in a message since it may have been easier for the sender to send extra data conservatively

than to determine exactly what to send. Similarly, if data is transferred implicitly in units larger than a word (e.g., cache blocks), part of the block may not be used by the requester. This artifactual communication can be eliminated with smaller transfers.

- *Unnecessary transfers due to other system granularities.* In cache-coherent machines, data is typically kept coherent at a granularity larger than a single word, which may lead to extra communication to keep data coherent, as we shall see in later chapters.
- *Redundant communication of data.* Data may be communicated multiple times (for example, every time the value of the data changes), but only the last value may actually be used. On the other hand, data may be communicated to a process that already has the latest values, again because it was too difficult to determine this.
- *Finite replication capacity.* Communicated data is usually replicated locally to avoid repeated communication when the data is accessed again by the processor. However, the capacity for replication on a node is finite—whether it be in the cache or the main memory—so data that has already been communicated from process A to process B may be replaced from B's local memory system and hence need to be transferred again even if it has not since been modified by A.

In contrast, inherent communication is what occurs given unlimited capacity for local replication, transfers as small as would be required by the program, and perfect knowledge of what logically shared data has been updated or already transferred. We will understand the sources of artifactual communication better when we get deeper into architecture. Let us look a little further at the last source of artifactual communication—finite replication capacity—which has particularly far-reaching consequences.

3.2.3 Artifactual Communication and Replication: The Working Set Perspective

The relationship between finite replication capacity and artifactual communication is quite fundamental in parallel systems, just like the relationship between cache size and memory traffic in uniprocessors; it is almost inappropriate to speak of the amount of communication without reference to replication capacity. The extended memory hierarchy perspective is useful in viewing this relationship. We may view our generic multiprocessor as a memory hierarchy with three levels: local cache is inexpensive to access, local memory is more expensive, and any remote memory is much more expensive. We can think of any level as a cache whether it is actually managed like a hardware cache or managed by system or application software. We can then classify the "misses" at any level, which generate traffic to the next level, just as we do for uniprocessors. A fraction of the traffic at any level results from *cold-start* misses, resulting from the first time data is accessed by the processor. This component, also called compulsory traffic in uniprocessors, is independent of cache size. Such cold-start misses diminish in importance as programs run longer. Then there is traffic due to *capacity* misses, which clearly decrease with increases in cache size. A third fraction of traffic may be *conflict* misses, which are reduced by greater associativity, a greater number of blocks, or changing the data access pattern. These three types of misses or traffic are called the three C's in uniprocessor architecture—cold start (or compulsory), capacity, and conflict. The new form of traffic in multiprocessors is a fourth C, a *communication* miss, caused by the inherent communication between processors or by some of the sources of artifactual communication discussed previously. Like cold-start misses, communication misses do not diminish with cache size. Each of these components of traffic may be helped or hurt by large granularities of data transfer, depending on spatial locality.

If we were to determine the traffic for a parallel program that results from each type of miss at a given level of the hierarchy as the replication capacity (i.e., the cache size) at that level is increased, we could expect to obtain a curve such as the one shown in Figure 3.6. The curve has a small number of knees, or points of inflection. These knees correspond to the *working sets* of the algorithm relevant to that level of the hierarchy.[2] For the first-level cache, they are the working sets of the algorithm itself; for others, they depend on how references have been filtered by other levels of the hierarchy and on how the levels are managed. We speak of this curve for a first-level cache (assumed fully associative with a one-word block size) as the *working set curve* for the algorithm.

Traffic resulting from any of these types of misses may cause communication across the machine's interconnection network, for example, if the backing storage happens to be in a remote node. Similarly, any type of miss may contribute to local traffic and local data access cost if the backing storage happens to be local. Thus, we might expect that many of the techniques used to reduce artifactual communication are similar to those used to exploit locality in uniprocessors. With processes running on different processors, inherent communication misses almost always generate actual communication in the machine (except if the data needed has become local in the meanwhile, as we shall see). These misses can only be reduced by changing the logical sharing patterns in the algorithm. In addition, we are strongly motivated to reduce the artifactual communication that arises either because of transfer size or limited replication capacity, which we can do by exploiting spatial and temporal locality in a process's data accesses in the extended hierarchy. Changing the assignment and orchestration can dramatically change locality characteristics, including the shape of the working set curve.

Finally, for a given amount of communication, its cost as seen by the processor is also affected by how the communication is structured. By "structure," we mean whether messages are large or small, how bursty the communication is, whether

2. The working set model of program behavior (Denning 1968) is based on the temporal locality exhibited by the data referencing patterns of programs. Under this model, a program (or a process in a parallel program) has a set of data that it reuses substantially for a period of time before moving on to other data. The shifts between one set of data and another may be abrupt or gradual. In either case, there is at most times a "working set" of data that a processor should be able to maintain in a fast level of the memory hierarchy in order to use that level effectively.

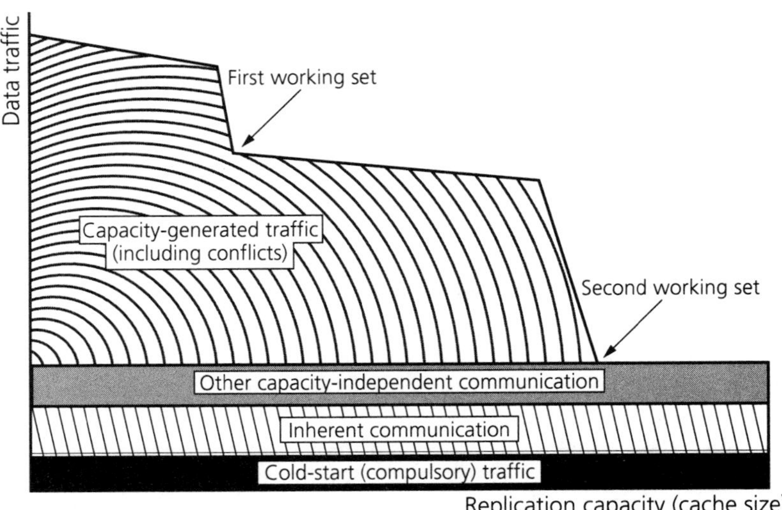

FIGURE 3.6 The data traffic between a cache (replication store) and the rest of the system and the components of the data traffic as a function of cache size. The points of inflection in the total traffic curve indicate the working sets of the program.

communication cost can be overlapped with other computation or communication (all of which are addressed in the orchestration step), and how well the communication patterns match the topology of the interconnection network, which is addressed in the mapping step. Reducing the amount of communication—inherent or artifactual—is important because it reduces the demand placed on both the system and the programmer to reduce communication cost. Now that we understand the machine as an extended hierarchy and the major issues this raises, let us see how to address these architecture-related performance issues in software—that is, how to program for performance once partitioning issues are resolved.

3.3 ORCHESTRATION FOR PERFORMANCE

We begin by discussing how we might exploit temporal and spatial locality to reduce the amount of artifactual communication and then move on to structuring communication—inherent or artifactual—to reduce its cost.

3.3.1 Reducing Artifactual Communication

In the message-passing model, both communication and replication are explicit, so even artifactual communication is explicitly coded in program messages. In a shared address space, artifactual communication is more interesting architecturally since it occurs transparently due to interactions between the program and the machine organization. Of particular interest are the finite cache size and the granularities at which data is allocated, communicated, and kept coherent. We therefore use a shared address space to illustrate issues in exploiting locality, which is done both to improve node performance and to reduce artifactual communication.

Exploiting Temporal Locality

A program is said to exhibit temporal locality if it tends to access the same memory locations repeatedly in a short time frame. Given a memory hierarchy, the goal in exploiting temporal locality is to structure an algorithm so that its working sets map well to the sizes of the different levels of the hierarchy. For a programmer, this typically means keeping working sets small, yet not so small as to lose performance for other reasons. Working sets can be reduced by several techniques. One is the same technique that reduces inherent communication—assigning tasks that tend to access the same data to the same process—which further illustrates the relationship between communication and locality. Once assignment is done, a process's assigned computation can be organized so that tasks that access the same data are scheduled close to one another in time and so that we reuse a set of data as much as possible before moving on to other data, rather than moving back and forth between sections of data.

When multiple data structures are accessed in the same phase of a computation, we must decide which are the most important candidates for exploiting temporal locality. Since communication is more expensive than local access, we might prefer to exploit temporal locality on nonlocal rather than local data. Consider a database application in which a process wants to compare all its records of a certain type with all the records of other processes. There are two choices here: (1) for each of its own records, the process can sweep through all other (nonlocal) records and compare and (2) for each nonlocal record, the process can sweep through its own records and compare. The latter exploits temporal locality on nonlocal data and is therefore likely to yield better overall performance. Example 3.1 discusses temporal locality for the equation solver kernel.

EXAMPLE 3.1 To what extent is temporal locality exploited in the equation solver kernel? How might the temporal locality be increased?

Answer The equation solver kernel traverses only a single data structure. A typical grid element in the interior of a process's partition is accessed at least five times by that process during each sweep: at least once to compute its own new value and once each to compute the new values of its four nearest neighbors. If a process sweeps through its partition of the grid in row-major order (i.e., row by row and left to right within each row, as in Figure 3.7[a]), then reuse of $A[i,j]$ is guaranteed across the updates of the three elements in the same row whose updates touch it: $A[i,j-1]$, $A[i,j]$, and $A[i,j+1]$. However, between the times that the new values for $A[i,j]$ and $A[i+1,j]$ are computed, three whole subrows of elements in that process's partition are accessed by that process. If the three subrows don't fit together in the cache, then $A[i,j]$ will no longer be in the cache when it is accessed again to compute $A[i+1,j]$.

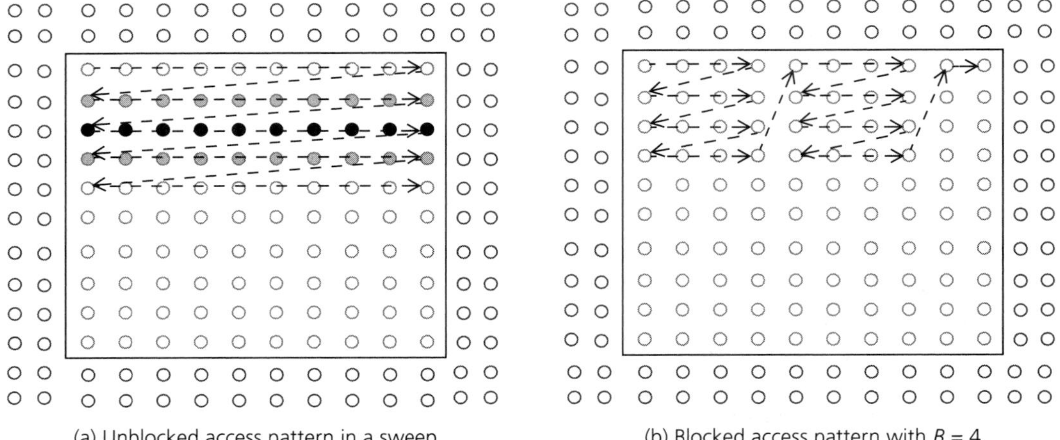

(a) Unblocked access pattern in a sweep
(b) Blocked access pattern with $B = 4$

FIGURE 3.7 Blocking to exploit temporal locality in the equation solver kernel. The figure shows the access patterns for a process traversing its partition during a sweep, with the arrow-headed lines showing the order in which grid points are updated. Updating the subrow of bold elements requires accessing that subrow as well as the two subrows of shaded elements. Updating the first element of the next (shaded) subrow requires accessing the first element of the bold subrow again, but these three whole subrows (the black and the shaded) have been accessed since the last time that first bold element was accessed. By changing the update order, the blocked access pattern improves reuse by a constant factor.

If the backing store for the data is nonlocal, artifactual communication will result. The problem can be addressed by changing the order in which elements are computed, as shown in Figure 3.7(b). Essentially, a process proceeds left to right not for the length of a whole subrow of its partition but only for a certain length B before it moves on to the corresponding portion of the next subrow. It performs its sweep in subsweeps over B-by-B blocks of its partition. The block size B is chosen so that at least three B-length rows of a partition fit in the cache. Of course, this changes the order of the updates and hence perhaps the convergence properties unless red-black ordering is used. ■

This technique, called *blocking*, structures computation so that it accesses a subset of data that fits in a level of the hierarchy, uses that data as much as possible, and then moves on to the next such set of data. In the equation solver kernel, the reduction in miss rate due to blocking is only a small constant factor (about a factor of two). The reduction is only seen when three subrows of a process's partition of a grid do not fit in the cache, so blocking is not always useful. However, blocking is used very successfully in linear algebra computations like matrix multiplication or matrix factorization, where $O(n^{k+1})$ computation is performed on a data set of size $O(n^k)$, so each data item is accessed $O(n)$ times. Using blocking effectively with B-by-B blocks in these cases can reduce the miss rate by a factor of B, which is particularly important since much of the data accessed is nonlocal. Not surprisingly, many of the same types of restructuring are used to improve temporal locality in sequential programs as well; for example, blocking is critical for high performance in sequential matrix computations, as in Exercise 3.10. Techniques for temporal locality can be used at any level of the hierarchy where data is replicated—including main memory—and for both explicit or implicit replication.

The temporal locality and data referencing patterns of applications have important implications for parallel architecture. For example, they help determine which programming model and communication abstraction a system should support, an issue we consider in Section 3.6. The sizes and scaling of working sets have obvious implications for the amounts of replication capacity needed at different levels of the memory hierarchy and for the number of levels that make sense in this hierarchy. In a cache-coherent shared address space, the sizes and compositions of working sets (i.e., whether they hold local or remote data or both) help determine whether it is useful to replicate communicated data in local main memory as well or simply to rely on caches, and if so, how this should be done. In message passing, they help us determine what data to replicate and how to manage the replication. Of course, it is not only the working sets of individual applications that matter for sizing the memory hierarchy but those of the entire workloads and the operating system that run on the machine. For hardware caches, the size of cache needed to hold a working set depends on its organization (associativity and block size) as well.

Exploiting Spatial Locality

A level of the extended memory hierarchy exchanges data with the next level at a certain *granularity of data transfer.* This granularity may be fixed (e.g., a cache block or a page of main memory) or flexible (e.g., explicit user-controlled messages or user-defined objects). It usually becomes larger as we go farther away from the processor since the latency and fixed start-up cost of each transfer become greater and should be amortized over a larger amount of data. To exploit a large granularity of communication or data transfer, we should organize our code and data structures to exploit spatial locality.[3] Not doing so can lead to artifactual communication if the transfer is to or from a remote node and is implicit (at some fixed granularity) as in a shared address space. Even if the transfer is explicit and of user-determined size, poor spatial locality can lead to more costly communication, since either smaller messages may have to be sent or the data may have to be made contiguous before it is sent. As in uniprocessors, poor spatial locality can also lead to a high frequency of TLB misses.

---

3. The principle of spatial locality states that if a given memory location is referenced now, then it is likely that memory locations close to it in the address space will be referenced in the near future. It should be clear that what is called spatial locality at the granularity of individual words can also be viewed as temporal locality at the granularity of cache blocks or larger units; that is, if a cache block is accessed now, then it (and the data on it) is likely to be accessed in the near future.

In a shared address space, artifactual communication can also result from mismatches of spatial locality with two other important granularities. One is the *granularity of allocation*, which is the granularity at which data is allocated in the local memory or replication store (e.g., a page in main memory). This determines the granularity at which the data can be distributed among physical main memories; that is, when data is allocated through the operating system at page granularity, we cannot allocate a part of a page in one node's memory and another part of the page in another node's memory. Suppose two words that are mostly accessed by two different processors fall on the same page. The page might be allocated in only one processor's local memory, in which case capacity or conflict cache misses to its word by the other processor will generate communication. The other important granularity is the *granularity of coherence*, in which case unrelated words that happen to fall on the same unit of coherence in a coherent shared address space can also cause artifactual communication. This problem, called *false sharing*, is discussed further in Chapter 5.

The techniques used for all these aspects of spatial locality in a shared address space are similar to those used on a uniprocessor, with one new aspect: we should try to keep the data accessed by a given processor close together (contiguous) in the address space and data accessed by different processors apart. Spatial locality issues in a shared address space are best examined in the context of particular architectural styles, and we do so in Chapters 5 and 8. Here, for illustration, we look at one example: how data may be restructured to interact better with the granularity of allocation in the equation solver kernel.

EXAMPLE 3.2 Consider a shared address space system in which main memory is physically distributed among the nodes and in which the granularity of allocation in main memory is a page (4 KB, say). Assume that a given page is allocated in only one node's main memory. Now consider the grid used in the equation solver kernel. What is the problem created by the granularity of allocation, and how might it be addressed?

Answer The natural data structure with which to represent a two-dimensional grid in a shared address space, as in a sequential program, is a two-dimensional array. In a typical programming language, a two-dimensional array data structure is allocated in either a row-major or column-major order.[4] The gray arrows in Figure 3.8(a) show the contiguity of virtual addresses in a row-major allocation, which is the one we assume. While a two-dimensional shared array has the programming advantage of being the same data structure used in a sequential program, it interacts poorly with the granularity of allocation on a machine with physically distributed memory.

Consider the partition of processor P_5 in Figure 3.8(a). An important working set for the processor is its entire partition, which it streams through in every sweep and reuses across sweeps. If its partition does not fit in the processor's cache hierarchy,

4. Consider the array as being a two-dimensional matrix, with the first dimension specifying the row number in the matrix and the second dimension the column number. Row-major allocation means that all elements in the first row are contiguous in the virtual address space, followed by all the elements in the second row, and so on. The C programming language, which we assume here, is a row-major language. Fortran, for example, is column-major.

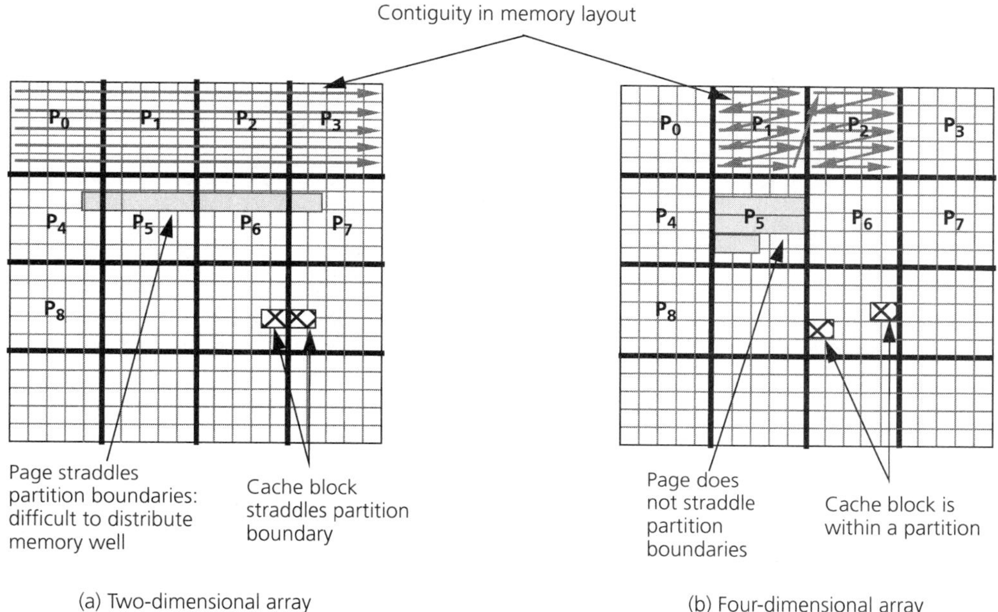

FIGURE 3.8 Two-dimensional and four-dimensional arrays used to represent a two-dimensional grid in a shared address space

we would like it to be allocated in local memory so that the misses can be satisfied locally. The problem is that consecutive subrows of this partition are not contiguous with one another in the address space but are separated by the length of an entire row of the grid (which contains subrows of other partitions). This makes it impossible to distribute data appropriately across main memories if a subrow of a partition is either smaller than a page or not a multiple of the page size or not well aligned to page boundaries. Subrows from two (or more) adjacent partitions will fall on the same page, which at best will be allocated in the local memory of one of those processors. If a processor's partition does not fit in its cache or if it incurs conflict misses, it may have to communicate every time it accesses a grid element in its own partition that happens to be allocated nonlocally.

The solution in this case is to use a higher-dimensional array to represent the two-dimensional grid. The most common example is a four-dimensional array, in which case the processes are arranged conceptually in a two-dimensional grid of partitions, as seen in Figure 3.8(b). The first two indices specify the partition or process being referred to, and the last two represent the subrow and subcolumn numbers within that partition. For example, if the size of the entire grid is 1,024 × 1,024 elements, and there are 16 processes, then each partition will be a subgrid of size

$$\frac{1{,}024}{\sqrt{16}} \times \frac{1{,}024}{\sqrt{16}}$$

or 256 × 256 elements. In the four-dimensional array representation of the grid, the array will be of size 4 × 4 × 256 × 256 elements. The key property of these higher-dimensional representations is that each process's 256 × 256 element partition is now contiguous in the address space (see the contiguity in the virtual memory layout in Figure 3.8[b]). The data distribution problem can now occur only at the endpoints of entire partitions, rather than of each subrow, and does not occur at all if the data structure is aligned to a page boundary. However, it is substantially more complicated to write code using the higher-dimensional arrays, particularly for array indexing of neighboring processes' partitions in the case of the near-neighbor computation (see Exercise 3.16). ■

More complex applications and data structures illustrate more significant trade-offs in data structure design for spatial locality, as we discuss in later chapters.

The spatial locality in processes' access patterns and how they scale with the problem size or number of processors affects the desirable sizes for various granularities in a shared address space architecture—specifically, the granularities of allocation, transfer, and coherence. It also affects the importance of providing support tailored toward small versus large messages in message-passing systems. Amortizing hardware and transfer costs pushes us toward large granularities, but granularities too large can cause performance problems, many of them specific to multiprocessors. Finally, the spatial locality of access affects the occurrence of conflict misses in a cache. Since conflict misses can generate artifactual communication when the backing store is nonlocal, multiprocessors push us toward higher associativity for caches. There are many cost, performance, and programmability trade-offs concerning support for data locality in multiprocessors, and our choices are best guided by the behavior of applications.

Finally, interesting trade-offs often emerge among algorithmic partitioning goals, implementation issues, and architectural interactions that generate artifactual communication, suggesting that careful examination of trade-offs is needed to obtain the best performance on a given architecture. Let us illustrate using the equation solver kernel in Example 3.3.

EXAMPLE 3.3 Given the performance issues discussed so far, should we choose to partition the equation solver kernel into squarelike subgrids (blocks) or into contiguous strips of rows?

Answer If we only consider inherent communication, we already know that a block domain decomposition is better than partitioning into contiguous strips of rows (see Figure 3.5). However, a strip decomposition has the advantage that it keeps a partition wholly contiguous in the address space even with the simpler, two-dimensional array representation. Hence, it does not suffer problems related to the interactions of spatial locality with machine granularities, such as the granularity of allocation mentioned previously. This particular interaction in the block case can of course be solved by using a higher-dimensional array representation. However, a more difficult interaction to solve is with the granularity of communication. In a subblock assignment, consider a neighbor element from another partition at a column-oriented partition boundary (see Figure 3.9). If the granularity of communication is large, then when a process references this element from its neighbor's partition, it will

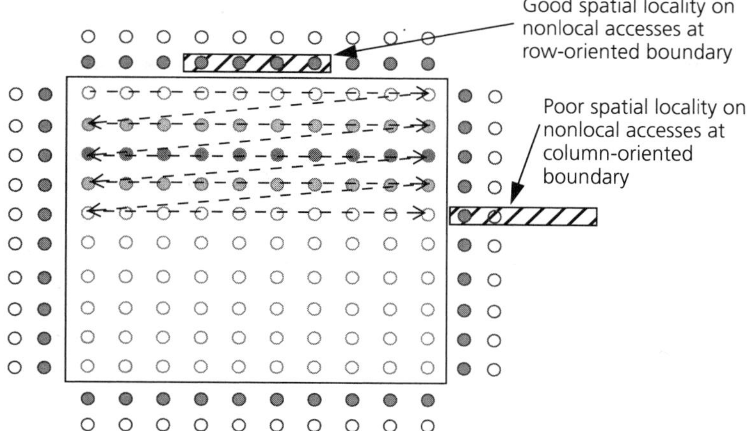

FIGURE 3.9 Spatial locality in accesses to nonlocal data in the equation solver kernel. Only one process's partition is shown, together with the area around its borders. The shaded points are the nonlocal points that the processor owning the partition accesses. The hatched rectangles are cache blocks, showing good spatial locality along the row boundary but poor locality along the column.

fetch not only that element but also a number of other elements that are on the same unit of communication. These other elements are not neighbors of the fetching process's partition regardless of whether a two-dimensional or four-dimensional representation is used, so they are useless and waste communication bandwidth. With a partitioning into strips of rows, there are no column-oriented partition boundaries; a referenced nonlocal element still causes other elements from its row to be fetched, but now these elements are indeed neighbors of the fetching process's partition. They are therefore useful, and in fact the large granularity of communication results in a valuable prefetching effect. Overall, there are many combinations of application and machine parameters for which the performance losses in block partitioning owing to artifactual communication will dominate the performance benefits from reduced inherent communication. We might imagine that strip partitioning should most often perform better when a two-dimensional array is used in the block case, but it may also do so in some cases when a four-dimensional array is used (there is no motivation to use a four-dimensional array with a strip partitioning). Thus, artifactual communication may cause us to go back and revise our partitioning method from block to strip. Figure 3.10(a) illustrates this effect for the Ocean application on the Origin2000 machine. The effect is much larger on systems that have larger granularities of communication and more expensive communication, for example, systems that support the shared address space programming model in software. Figure 3.10(b) uses the equation solver kernel with a larger grid size to illustrate the impact of data placement. Note that a strip decomposition into columns rather than rows will yield the worst of both worlds when data is laid out in memory in row-major order. ■

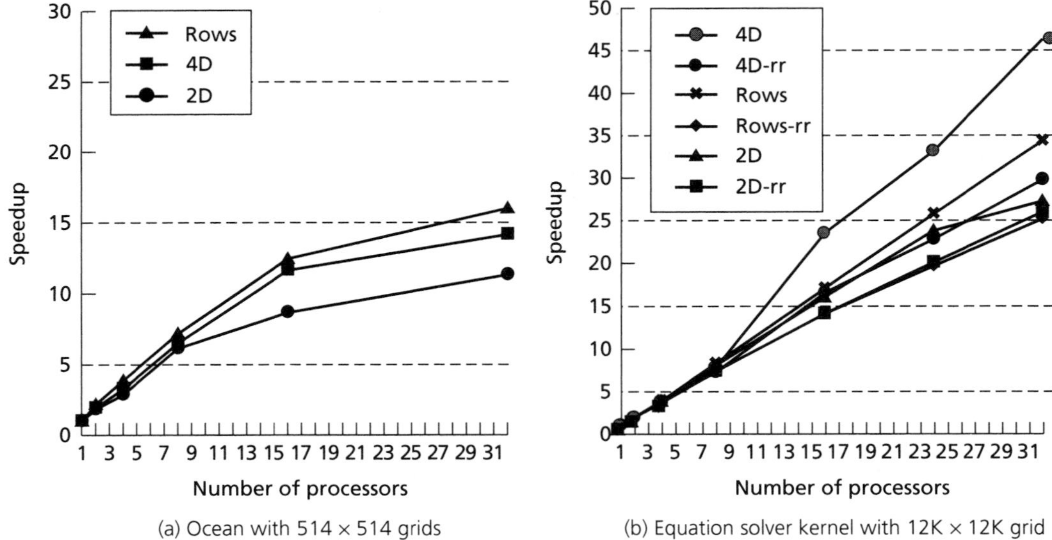

(a) Ocean with 514 × 514 grids

(b) Equation solver kernel with 12K × 12K grid

FIGURE 3.10 The impact of data structuring and spatial locality on performance. All measurements are on the SGI Origin2000. "2D" and "4D" imply two- and four-dimensional data structures, respectively, with block (squarelike) assignment. "Rows" uses the two-dimensional array with strip assignment into chunks of rows. In (b), the postfix "rr" means that pages of data are distributed round-robin among physical memories. Without "rr," it means that pages are placed in the local memory of the processor to which their data is assigned, as far as possible. We see from (a) that the strip assignment outperforms the 2D block assignment because of spatial locality interactions with long cache blocks (128 bytes on the Origin2000) and is even a little better than the 4D array block assignment due to poor spatial locality in the latter in accessing border elements at column-oriented partition boundaries. The graph in (b) shows that, despite the very aggressive communication architecture, in all partitioning schemes proper data distribution in main memory is important to performance, though least successful for the block partitions with 2D arrays. In the best case, we see superlinear speedups once enough processors are used that the size of a processor's partition of the grid (its important working set) fits into its cache. The differences are much larger on machines with less aggressive communication architectures and smaller replication stores.

3.3.2 Structuring Communication to Reduce Cost

Whether communication is inherent or artifactual, how much the communication contributes to execution time is determined by how it is organized or structured into messages. A small communication-to-computation ratio may have a much greater impact on execution time than a large ratio if the structure of the latter interacts much better with the system. This is an important issue in obtaining good performance from a real machine and is the last major performance issue we examine. Let us begin by examining more closely what the structure of communication means.

In Chapter 1, we introduced a model for the cost of communication as seen by a processor, given a frequency of program-initiated communication operations or messages (explicit messages or messages initiated implicitly by read and write operations). Combining Equations 1.5 and 1.6, that model for the cost C is

$$C = \text{Frequency} \times \left(\text{Overhead} + \textit{Delay} + \frac{\text{Length}}{\text{Bandwidth}} + \text{Contention} - \text{Overlap} \right)$$

or

$$C = F \times \left(o + l + \frac{n_c/m}{B} + t_c - \text{Overlap} \right) \tag{3.4}$$

where f is the frequency of communication messages in the program; o is the combined overhead of handling initiation and reception of a message on the sending and receiving processors, assuming no contention with other activities; l is the nonoverhead delay for the first bit of the message to reach the destination processor or memory (assuming no contention), which includes delay through the assists and network interfaces as well as the delay in the network fabric itself; n_c is the total amount of data communicated by the program; m is the number of messages (so n_c/m is the average length of a message); B is the point-to-point bandwidth of communication afforded for the transfer by the communication path, excluding the processor overhead (i.e., the rate at which the rest of the message data arrives at the destination after the first bit, assuming that the entire path through the network from source to destination acts as a single pipeline and there is no contention); t_c is the time induced by contention for resources with other activities; and *Overlap* is the amount of the communication cost that can be overlapped with computation or other communication (i.e., that is not in the critical path of a processor's execution). The bandwidth B is the inverse of the overall occupancy discussed in Chapter 1. It may be limited by the network links, the network interface, or the communication assist.

This expression for communication cost can be substituted into Equation 3.1 to yield our final expression for speedup. The portion of the cost expression inside the parentheses is our cost model for a single one-way message. If messages are round-trip, we must make the appropriate adjustments. The cost of a message, ignoring overlap, is also called its *latency.* In addition to reducing communication volume (n_c), our goals in structuring communication may include (1) reducing communication overhead ($m \times o$), (2) reducing delay ($m \times l$), (3) reducing contention ($m \times t_c$), and (4) overlapping communication with computation or other communication to hide its latency. Let us discuss programming techniques for addressing each of these issues.

Reducing Overhead

Since the overhead o associated with initiating or processing a message is usually fixed by hardware or system software, the way to reduce the cost due to communication overhead is to make messages fewer in number and hence larger—that is, to reduce the message frequency.[5] Explicitly initiated communication allows the programmer greater flexibility in specifying the sizes of messages (recall the send primitive described in Section 2.3.6). On the other hand, implicit communication through read and write operations does not afford the program direct control, and the system must take responsibility for coalescing the reads and writes into larger messages if necessary.

Making messages larger is easy in applications that have regular data access and communication patterns. For example, in the message-passing equation solver partitioned into rows, we send an entire row of data in a single message. But it can be difficult in applications that have irregular and unpredictable communication patterns, such as Barnes-Hut or Raytrace. As we shall see in Section 3.6, it may require changes to the parallel algorithm and extra work to determine which data to coalesce, resulting in a trade-off between the cost of this computation and the savings in overhead. Some computation may be needed to determine what data should be sent and to which process, and the data may have to be gathered and packed into a message at the sender and unpacked and scattered into appropriate memory locations at the receiver.

Reducing Delay

Delay through the assist and network interface can be reduced by optimizing those hardware components. There is not much a programmer can do about this delay. Consider the network transit delay—that is, the delay through the network fabric itself. In the absence of contention and assuming messages are pipelined through the network, the transit delay l of a bit through the network itself can be expressed as $h \times t_h$, where h is the number of hops between adjacent network nodes or switches that the message traverses, and t_h is the delay or latency for a single bit of data to traverse a single network hop, including the link and the router or switch. Like message overhead, t_h is determined by the system, and the program must focus on reducing the f and h components of the $f \times h \times t_h$ delay cost. (In store-and-forward rather than pipelined networks, t_h would be the time for the entire message to traverse a hop, not just a single bit.)

The number of hops h can be reduced by mapping processes to processors so that the topology of interprocess communication in the application exploits locality in the physical topology of the network. How well this can be done in general depends on the application and on the structure and richness of the network; for example, the nearest-neighbor equation solver kernel (and the Ocean application) would map very well onto a mesh-connected multiprocessor but not onto a unidirectional ring. Our other case study applications are more irregular in their communication patterns. (We examine different topologies used in real machines and discuss their trade-offs in Chapter 10.)

---

5. Some explicit message-passing systems provide different types of messages with different costs and functionalities that a program can choose from.

Research in mapping parallel algorithms to network topologies has been quite extensive since it was thought that as the number of processors p became large, poor mappings would cause the delay due to the $h \times t_h$ term to dominate the cost of messages. How important topology actually is in practice depends on several factors: how large the t_h term is relative to the overhead o of getting a message into and out of the network; the number of processing nodes on the machine, which determines the maximum number of hops h for a given topology; and whether the machine is used to run a single application at a time in "batch" mode or is multiprogrammed among applications. It turns out that network topology is not considered so important on modern machines as it once was because of the characteristics of the machines along all these three axes: overhead dominates hop latency (especially in machines that do not provide hardware support for a shared address space), the number of nodes is usually not extremely large, and the machines are often used as general-purpose, multiprogrammed servers. Topology-oriented program design might not be very useful in multiprogrammed systems since the operating system controls resource allocation dynamically and might transparently change the mapping of processes to processors at run time. For these reasons, the mapping step of parallelization receives considerably less attention than decomposition, assignment, and orchestration. However, this may change again as technology and machine architecture evolve.

Reducing Contention

The communication architectures of multiprocessors consist of many resources, including network links and switches, communication assists, memory systems, and network interfaces. All of these resources have a nonzero *occupancy*, or time for which they are occupied servicing a given transaction. Another way of saying this is that they have finite bandwidth (or rate, which is the reciprocal of occupancy) for servicing transactions. If several messages contend for a resource, some of them will have to wait while others are serviced, thus increasing message latency and reducing the bandwidth available to any single message. Resource occupancy contributes to message cost even in the absence of contention since the time taken to pass through a resource is part of the delay (or overhead, as the case may be), but it can also cause contention. The occupancy of a resource may even be greater than the delay through it.

Contention is a particularly insidious performance problem, for several reasons. First, it is easy to overlook when writing a parallel program, particularly if it is caused by artifactual communication. Second, its effect on performance can be dramatic. If p processors simultaneously contend for a resource of occupancy x, the first to obtain the resource incurs a latency of x because of that resource, whereas the last incurs a latency of at least $p \times x$. In addition to the large stall time, the differences in stall time across processors can also lead to large load imbalances and hence synchronization wait times. Thus, the contention caused by the occupancy of a resource can be much more dangerous than just the delay it contributes in uncontended cases. Third, contention for one resource can hold up other resources, thus stalling transactions that don't even need the resource that is the source of the contention. This is similar to the way contention for a single-lane exit off a multilane highway causes congestion on the entire stretch of highway. The resulting congestion also affects cars that don't need that exit but want to keep going on the highway since they may be stuck behind cars that do need that exit. The backup of cars covers up other unrelated resources (previous exits), making them inaccessible and ultimately clogging up the highway. Bad cases of contention can quickly saturate the entire communication architecture. The final reason that contention is so troublesome is related to the third: the cause of contention may be particularly difficult to identify since the effects might be felt at very different points in the program than the original cause (all the more so if communication is implicit).

Contention in a network can also be viewed as being of two types: at the links or switches within the network, called *network contention*, and at the endpoints or processing nodes, called *endpoint contention*. Network contention, like network delay, can be reduced by mapping processes and scheduling the communication appropriately in the network topology. Endpoint contention occurs when many processors need to communicate with the same processing node at the same time (or when communication transactions interfere with local memory references). When this contention becomes severe, we call that processing node or resource a *hot spot*. Let us examine a simple example of how a hot spot may be formed and how it might be alleviated in software.

Recall the case of processes that want to accumulate their partial sums into a global sum, as in our equation solver kernel. The resulting contention for the global sum can be reduced by using tree-structured communication rather than having all processes send their updates to the owning node directly. Figure 3.11 shows the structure of such many-to-one communication using a binary fan-in tree. The nodes of this tree (often called a software combining tree) are the participating processes. A leaf process sends its update to its parent, which combines its children's updates with its own and sends the combined update to its parent, and so on until the updates reach the root (the process that holds the global sum) in $\log_2 p$ steps. A similar fan-out tree can be used to send data from one to many processes. Tree-based approaches are used to design scalable synchronization primitives, such as barriers that often experience a lot of contention, as well as library routines for other communication patterns.

In general, two programming principles for alleviating contention are to avoid having too many processes communicating with the same process and to stagger messages to the same destination in time so as not to overwhelm the destination or the resources along the way. Contention is often caused when communication is bursty (i.e., the program spends some time not communicating and then suddenly goes through a burst of communication), and temporal staggering reduces burstiness. However, this must be traded off with the advantages of making messages large, which unfortunately tends to increase burstiness.

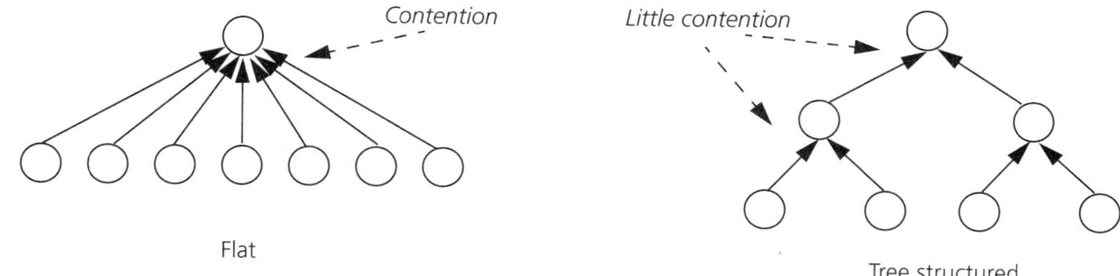

FIGURE 3.11 Two ways of structuring many-to-one communication: flat and tree structured in a binary fan-in tree. Note that the destination processor may receive up to $p - 1$ messages at a time in the flat case, whereas no processor is the destination of more than two messages in the binary tree.

Overlapping Communication with Computation or Other Communication

Despite efforts to reduce overhead and delay, the technology trends discussed in Chapter 1 suggest that the end-to-end communication latency is likely to remain very large in processor cycles. Already, it is in the hundreds of processor cycles, even on machines that provide full hardware support for a shared address space and use high-speed networks, and is at least an order of magnitude higher on message-passing machines due to the higher overhead term o caused by software management. If the processor were to remain idle (stalled) while incurring this latency for every word of data communicated, only programs with an extremely low ratio of communication to computation would yield effective parallel performance. Programs that communicate a lot must therefore find ways to hide the latency of communication from the process's critical path by overlapping it with computation or other communication as much as possible, and systems must provide the necessary support.

Techniques to hide communication latency come in different, often complementary flavors, and we shall examine them in Chapter 11. One approach is simply to make messages larger, thus incurring the latency of the first word but hiding that of subsequent words through pipelined transfer of the large message. Another approach, which we can call *precommunication,* is to initiate the communication well before the data is actually needed, so that by the time the data is needed it is likely to have already arrived. A third technique is to initiate the communication where it naturally belongs in the program but to hide its cost by finding something else for the processor to do—some computation or other communication that occurs later in the same process—while the communication is in progress. A fourth, called *multithreading,* is to switch to a different thread or process when a communication event is encountered. While the specific techniques and mechanisms depend on the communication abstraction and the approach taken, they all fundamentally require the program to have extra concurrency (also called *slackness*) beyond the number of processors used so that independent work (computation or communication) can be found to overlap with the communication latency.

Much of the focus in parallel architecture has in fact been on reducing communication cost as seen by the processor: by reducing communication overhead and delay, by increasing bandwidth and reducing occupancy, and by providing mechanisms to alleviate contention and overlap communication with computation or other communication. Many of the later chapters therefore devote a lot of attention to covering these issues—including the design of node-to-network interfaces, communication assists, and protocols that minimize both software and hardware overhead (Chapters 5 through 9); the design of network topologies, primitive operations, and routing strategies that are well suited to the communication patterns of applications (Chapter 10); and the design of mechanisms to hide communication cost from the processor (Chapter 11). Aggressive architectural methods are usually expensive, so it is important that they can be used effectively by real programs and that their performance benefits justify their costs.

3.4 PERFORMANCE FACTORS FROM THE PROCESSOR'S PERSPECTIVE

To understand the impact of the different performance factors in a parallel program on a parallel architecture, it is useful to look from an individual processor's viewpoint at the different components of time spent executing the program—that is, how much time the processor spends in different activities as it executes instructions, accesses data in the extended memory hierarchy, and coordinates its activities with other processors. These different components of time can be related quite directly to the software performance issues studied in this chapter, helping us relate software techniques to hardware performance. This view also helps us understand what a parallel execution looks like as a workload presented to the architecture and will be useful when we discuss workload-driven architectural evaluation in the next chapter.

In Equation 3.3, we described the time spent executing a sequential program on a uniprocessor as the sum of the time spent actually executing instructions (busy) and the time stalled on the memory system (data access), where the latter is a "nonideal" factor that reduces performance. Figure 3.12(a) shows a profile of a hypothetical sequential program. In this case, about 80% of the execution time is spent performing instructions, which can be reduced only by improving either the algorithm or the processor. The other 20% is spent stalled on the memory system, which can be improved by improving data locality or the memory system.

In multiprocessors, we can take a similar view, though there are more such nonideal factors. This view cuts across programming models: for example, being stalled waiting for a receive to complete is really very much like being stalled waiting for a remote read to complete or a synchronization event to occur. If the same program is parallelized and run on a four-processor machine, the execution time profile of the four processors might look like that in Figure 3.12(b). The figure assumes a global synchronization point at the end of the program so that all processes terminate at the same time. Note that the parallel execution time (55 s) is greater than one-fourth of the sequential execution time (100 s); that is, we have obtained a speedup of only

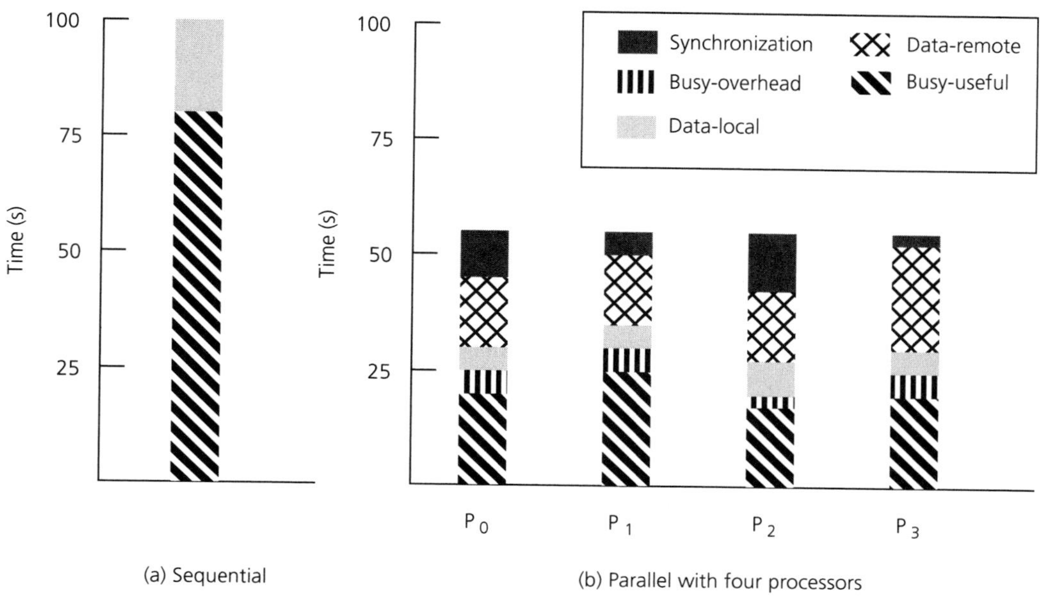

FIGURE 3.12 Components of execution time from the perspective of an individual processor

100/55, or 1.8, instead of the fourfold speedup we may have hoped for. Why this is the case and what specific software or programming factors contribute to it can be determined by examining the components of parallel execution time from the perspective of an individual processor. On our generic parallel architecture with distributed memory, there are five components of parallel execution time:

1. *Busy-useful*: the time that the processor spends executing instructions that would have been executed in the sequential program as well. Assuming a deterministic parallel program[6] that is derived directly from the sequential algorithm, the sum of the busy-useful times for all processors is equal to the busy-useful time for the sequential execution.

---

6. A parallel algorithm is deterministic if the result it yields for a given input data set is always the same independent of the number of processes used or the relative timings of events. More generally, we may consider whether all the intermediate calculations in the algorithm are deterministic. A nondeterministic algorithm is one in which the result and the work done by the algorithm to arrive at the result depend on the number of processes and relative event timing. An example is a parallel search through a graph, which stops as soon as any path taken through the graph finds a solution. Nondeterministic algorithms complicate our simple model of where time goes since the parallel program may do less useful work than the sequential program to arrive at the answer. Such situations can lead to *superlinear* speedup—that is, speedup greater than the factor by which the number of processors is increased. However, not all forms of nondeterminism have such beneficial results. Recall that the red-black equation solver described in Chapter 2 is deterministic while the asynchronous one is not.

2. *Busy-overhead*: the time that the processor spends executing instructions that are not needed in the sequential program but only in the parallel program. This corresponds directly to the extra work done in the parallel program.
3. *Data-local*: the time the processor is stalled waiting for a data reference to be satisfied by the memory system on its own processing node; that is, waiting for a reference that does not generate communication with other nodes.
4. *Data-remote*: the time the processor is stalled waiting for data to be communicated to or from another (remote) processing node, whether due to inherent or artifactual communication. This represents the cost of communication as seen by the processor.
5. *Synchronization*: the time spent waiting for another process to signal the occurrence of an event that will allow it to proceed. This includes the load imbalance and serialization in the program as well as the time spent actually executing synchronization operations and accessing synchronization variables. While it is waiting, the processor could be repeatedly polling a variable until that variable changes value—thus executing instructions—or it could be stalled, depending on how synchronization is implemented.[7]

The synchronization, busy-overhead, and data-remote components are not found in a sequential program running on a uniprocessor system and are overheads introduced by parallelism. While inherent communication is mostly included in the data-remote component, some (usually very small) part of it might show up as data-local time as well. For example, data that is assigned to the local memory of a processor P might be updated by another processor Q but asynchronously returned to P's memory (due to replacement from Q, say) before P references it. P may not see the communication cost in this case. Finally, the data-local component is interesting because it is a performance overhead in both the sequential and parallel cases. While the other overhead components tend to increase with the number of processors for a fixed problem or input data set, this component may decrease: a given processor is responsible for only a portion of the overall calculation, so it may only access a fraction of the data that the sequential program does and thus obtain better local cache and memory behavior. In fact, if the data-local overhead reduces enough, it can give rise to superlinear speedups even for deterministic parallel programs (superlinear speedup means speedup greater than the number of processors used). Figure 3.13 summarizes the correspondence between parallelization issues, the steps in which they are largely addressed, and processor-centric components of execution time.

7. Synchronization introduces components of time that overlap with other categories. For example, the time to satisfy the processor's first access to the synchronization variable for the current synchronization event, or the time spent actually communicating the occurrence of the synchronization event, may be included either in synchronization time or in the relevant data access category. Here it is included in the latter. In addition, if a processor executes instructions to poll a synchronization variable while waiting for an event to occur, that time may be defined as busy-overhead or as synchronization. This text includes it in synchronization time since it is essentially load imbalance.

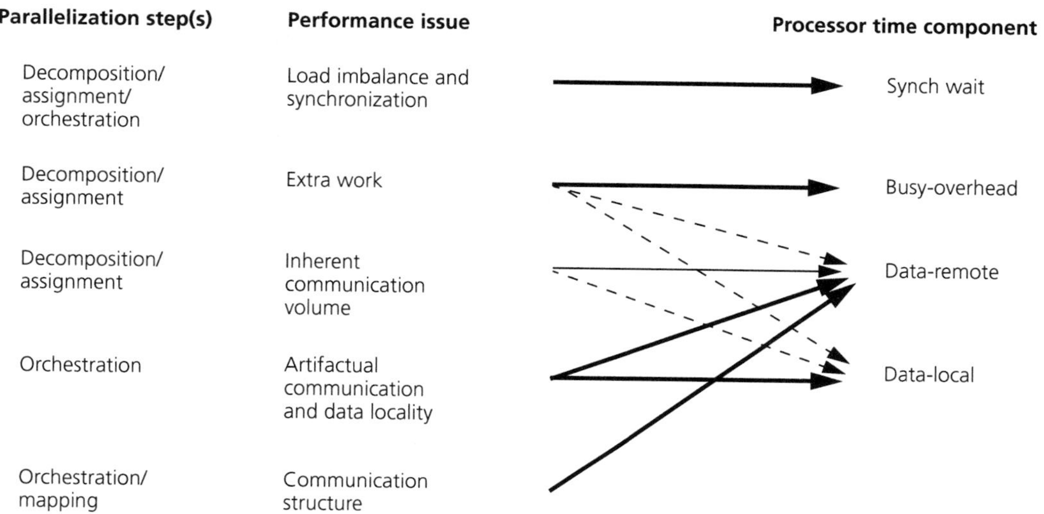

FIGURE 3.13 Mapping between parallelization issues and processor-centric components of execution time. Bold lines depict direct relationships, and dotted lines depict significant side-effect contributions. On the left is the parallelization step in which the issues are mostly addressed.

Using these components, we may further refine our model of speedup for a fixed problem as shown in Equation 3.5, once again assuming a global synchronization at the end of the execution. (Otherwise, we would take the maximum over processes in the denominator instead of taking the time profile of any single process.)

$$\text{Speedup}_{problem}(p) = \frac{\text{Busy}(1) + \text{Data}_{local}(1)}{\text{Busy}_{useful}(p) + \text{Data}_{local}(p) + \text{Synch}(p) + \text{Data}_{remote}(p) + \text{Busy}_{overhead}(p)} \quad (3.5)$$

Our goal in addressing the performance issues has been to keep the terms in the denominator low and thus minimize the parallel execution time (see Figure 3.13). As we have seen, both the programmer and the architecture have their roles to play. The architecture can do little to help if the program is poorly load balanced or if an inordinate amount of extra work exists. However, the architecture can reduce the incentive for creating such ill-behaved parallel programs by making communication and synchronization more efficient. The architecture can also reduce the artifactual communication incurred, provide convenient naming so that flexible assignment mechanisms can be easily employed, and make it possible to hide the cost of communication by overlapping it with useful work.

3.5 THE PARALLEL APPLICATION CASE STUDIES: AN IN-DEPTH LOOK

Having discussed the major performance issues for parallel programs in a general context and having applied them to the simple equation solver kernel, we are ready to examine how to achieve good parallel performance on more realistic applications on real multiprocessors. In particular, we now return to the four application case studies that motivated us to study parallel software in Chapter 2, apply the four steps of the parallelization process to each case study, and at each step address the major performance issues that arise there. In the process, we can understand and respond to the trade-offs among the different performance issues as well as between performance and ease of programming. Examining the components of execution time on a real machine will also help us see the types of workload characteristics that different applications present to a parallel architecture. Understanding the relationship between parallel applications, software techniques, and workload characteristics will be very important as we proceed through the rest of the book.

Parallel applications come in various shapes and sizes with very different characteristics and trade-offs among performance issues. Our four case studies provide an interesting though necessarily restricted cross section through the application space. In examining how to parallelize and, particularly, orchestrate the applications for good performance, we shall focus for concreteness on a specific architectural style: a cache-coherent shared address space multiprocessor with main memory physically distributed among the processing nodes.

The discussion of each application is divided into four subsections. The first describes in more detail the sequential algorithms and the major data structures used. The second describes the partitioning of the application (i.e., the decomposition of the computation and its assignment to processes), addressing the algorithmic performance issues of load balance, communication volume, and the overhead of computing the assignment. The third subsection is devoted to orchestration: it describes the spatial and temporal locality in the program as well as the synchronization used and the amount of work done between synchronization points. The fourth subsection discusses mapping to a network topology. Finally, for illustration we present the components of execution time as obtained for a real execution (using a particular problem size) on a specific machine of the chosen style: a 32-processor Silicon Graphics Origin2000. The busy-useful and busy-overhead components cannot be separated from each other in measurements on this machine, and neither can the data-local and data-remote components, so execution time is divided into three components: busy, data wait, and synchronization. While the level of detail at which we treat the case studies may appear high in some places, these details will be important in explaining the experimental results we shall obtain in later chapters using these applications.

3.5.1 Ocean

Ocean, which simulates currents in an ocean basin, resembles many important applications in computational fluid dynamics. Several of its properties are also representative of a wide range of applications, both scientific and commercial, that stream through large data structures and perform little computation at each data point. At each horizontal cross section through the ocean basin, several different variables are modeled, including the current, temperature, pressure, and friction. Each variable is discretized and represented by a regular, uniform two-dimensional grid of size $(n + 2)$-by-$(n + 2)$ points ($n + 2$ is used instead of n so that the number of internal, nonborder points that are actually updated in the equation solver is n-by-n). In all, about 25 different grid data structures are used by the application.

The Sequential Algorithm

After the currents at each cross section are initialized, the outermost loop of the application proceeds over a large, user-defined number of time-steps. Every time-step first sets up and then solves partial differential equations on the grids. A time-step consists of 33 different grid computations, each involving one or a small number of grids (variables). Typical grid computations include adding together scalar multiples of a few grids and storing the result in another grid (e.g., $A = \alpha_1 B + \alpha_2 C - \alpha_3 D$), performing a single nearest-neighbor averaging sweep over a grid and storing the result in another grid, and solving a system of partial differential equations on a grid using an iterative method.

The iterative equation solver used is the multigrid method. This is a complex but efficient variant of the simple equation solver kernel we have discussed so far. In the simple solver, each sweep traverses the entire n-by-n grid (ignoring the border columns and rows). A multigrid solver, on the other hand, performs sweeps over a hierarchy of grids. The original n-by-n grid is the finest-resolution grid in the hierarchy; the grid at each coarser level removes every alternate grid point in each dimension, resulting in grids of size $n/2$-by-$n/2$, $n/4$-by-$n/4$, and so on. The first sweep of the solver traverses the finest grid, and successive sweeps are performed on coarser or finer grids depending on the error computed in the previous sweep, terminating when the system converges within a user-defined tolerance on the finest grid. To keep the computation deterministic and make it more efficient, a red-black ordering is used (see Section 2.3.2).

Decomposition and Assignment

Ocean affords concurrency at two levels within a time-step: across grid computations (function parallelism) and within a single grid computation (data parallelism). Little concurrency is available across successive time-steps. Concurrency across grid computations can be discovered by writing down which grids each computation reads and writes and analyzing the data dependences among them at this level. The

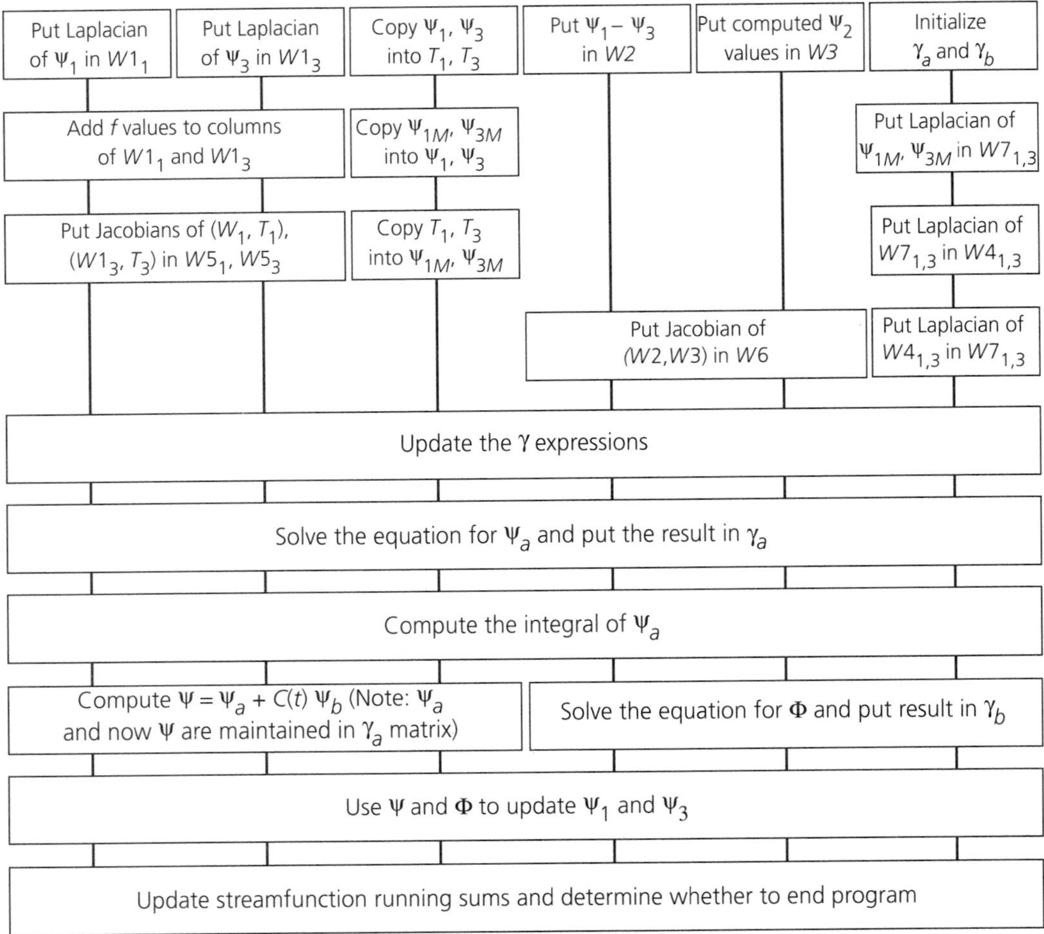

FIGURE 3.14 Ocean: The phases in a time-step and the dependences among grid computations. Each box is a grid computation (or pair of similar computations). Computations connected by vertical lines are dependent while others, such as those in the same row, are independent. The parallel program treats each horizontal row as a phase and synchronizes between phases.

resulting dependence structure and concurrency are depicted in Figure 3.14. Clearly, there is not enough concurrency across grid computations (i.e., not enough vertical sections) to occupy more than a few processors. We must therefore exploit the data parallelism within a grid computation as well, and we need to decide what combination of function and data parallelism is best.

In this case study, we choose to have all processes collaborate on each grid computation rather than to divide the processes among the available concurrent grid computations and use both levels of parallelism. Combined data and function parallelism would increase the size of each process's partition of a grid and hence reduce the communication-to-computation ratio. However, the work associated with different grid computations is quite varied and also depends on problem size in different ways, which complicates load balancing. Second, since several different computations in a time-step access the same grid, for communication and data locality reasons we would not like the same grid to be partitioned in different ways among processes in different computations. Third, all the grid computations are fully data parallel, and all grid points in a given computation do roughly the same amount of work, so we can statically assign grid points to processes. Nonetheless, knowing which grid computations are independent is useful because it allows processes to avoid synchronizing between them (see Figure 3.14).

The issues regarding inherent communication are very similar to those in the simple equation solver, so we use a block-structured (squarelike) domain decomposition of each grid. There is one complication—a trade-off between data locality and load balance related to the points at the border of the grid in some grid computations. The internal n-by-n points do similar work and are divided equally among all processes. Complete load balancing demands that border points, which often do less work, also be divided equally among processors. However, communication and data locality suggest that border points should be assigned to the processes that own the nearest internal points, which assign no border elements to several of the processes. We follow the latter strategy, incurring a slight load imbalance.

Finally, let us examine the multigrid equation solver. The grids at all levels of the multigrid hierarchy are partitioned in the same block-structured domain decomposition. However, the number of grid points per process decreases as we go to coarser levels of the hierarchy, so at the highest levels, some processes may become idle. Fortunately, relatively little (if any) time is spent at these load-imbalanced levels. The ratio of communication to computation also increases at higher levels since there are fewer points per process. This illustrates the importance of measuring speedups relative to the best sequential algorithm (here multigrid): a classical, nonhierarchical parallel iterative solver on the original (finest) grid would likely yield better *self-relative* speedups (relative to a single processor performing the same computation) than the parallel multigrid solver, but the multigrid solver is far more efficient sequentially and overall. In general, less efficient sequential algorithms often yield better self-relative speedups, but these are not useful measures for an end user.

Orchestration

Here we are mostly concerned with artifactual communication, data locality, and synchronization. Let us consider issues related to spatial locality first, then temporal locality, and finally synchronization.

Spatial Locality Within a grid computation, the issues related to spatial locality are similar to those of the simple equation solver kernel in Section 3.3.1. A four-dimensional array data structure is therefore used to represent each grid. This results in very good spatial locality, particularly on local data. Accesses to nonlocal data (the elements at the boundaries of neighboring partitions) yield good spatial locality along row-oriented partition boundaries and poor locality (hence fragmentation or waste in communication) along column-oriented boundaries. One major difference between the simple solver and the complete Ocean application is that Ocean involves 33 different grid computations in every time-step, each involving one or more out of 25 different grids, so we experience many cache conflict misses across grids. These conflict misses are reduced by ensuring that the allocated dimensions of the arrays are not powers of two (even if the program uses power-of-two grids), but it is difficult to lay out different grids relative to one another to minimize conflict misses. A second difference has to do with the multigrid solver. Since a process's partition has fewer grid points at higher levels of the grid hierarchy, spatial locality is reduced and it is more difficult to distribute data appropriately among main memories at page granularity, despite the use of four-dimensional arrays.

Working Sets and Temporal Locality Ocean has a complicated working set hierarchy, with six working sets. The first two are due to the use of near-neighbor computations within a grid and are similar to those for the simple equation solver kernel. The first working set is captured when the cache is large enough to hold a few grid points so that a point that is accessed as the right neighbor for the previous point is reused to compute itself and to serve as the left neighbor for the next point. The second working set comprises three subrows of a process's partition. When the process returns from one subrow to the beginning of the next in a near-neighbor computation, it can reuse the elements of the previous subrow.

The rest of the working sets are not well defined as single working sets and do not produce sharp knees in the working set curve. The third working set constitutes a process's entire partition of a grid used in the multigrid solver. This could be the partition at any level of the multigrid hierarchy at which the process tends to iterate, so it is not really a single working set. The fourth working set consists of the sum of a process's subgrids at several successive levels of the grid hierarchy within which it tends to iterate (in the extreme, this becomes all levels of the grid hierarchy). The fifth working set allows reuse on a grid across grid computations or even phases; thus, it is large enough to hold a process's partition of several grids. The last working set holds all the data that a process is assigned in every grid so that all the data can be reused across time-steps.

The working sets that are most important to performance are the first three or four, depending on how the multigrid solver behaves. The largest among these grows linearly with the size of the data set per process. This growth rate is common in applications that repeatedly stream through their data sets, so with large data sets, some important working sets do not fit in the local caches. Fortunately, large data sets in these streaming applications make it easy to distribute data in memory at page granularity, so the working sets for a process consist mostly of local rather than communicated data. The little reuse that nonlocal data affords is captured by the first two working sets.

Synchronization Ocean uses two types of synchronization. First, global barriers are used to synchronize all processes between computational phases (see Figure 3.14) as well as between sweeps of the multigrid equation solver. Between several of the phases, we could replace the barriers with finer-grained point-to-point synchronization at the level of grid points to obtain some overlap across phases; however, in this case the overlap is likely to be too small to justify the programming complexity and the overhead of many more synchronization operations. The second form of synchronization is the use of locks to provide mutual exclusion for global reductions, for example, to determine convergence in the solver. The work between synchronization points is large, typically proportional to the size of a process's partition of a grid.

Mapping

Given the near-neighbor communication pattern, we would like to map processes to processors such that processes whose partitions are adjacent to each other in the grid run on processors that are near each other in the network topology. Our subgrid partitioning of two-dimensional grids clearly maps very well to a two-dimensional mesh network. However, as in all our programs, mapping of processes to processors is not enforced by the program but is left to the system.

Summary

Ocean is a good representative of many applications that stream through regular arrays. The computation-to-communication ratio is proportional to $n/\sqrt{p}$ for a problem with n-by-n grids and p processors, load balance is good except when n is not large relative to p, and the parallel efficiency for a given number of processors increases with the grid size. Since a processor streams through its portion of the grid in each grid computation, since only a few instructions are executed per access to grid data during each sweep, and since significant potential exists for conflict misses across grids, data distribution in main memory can be very important on machines with physically distributed memory.

Figure 3.15 shows the breakdown of execution time into busy, waiting at synchronization points, and waiting for data accesses to complete for a particular execution of Ocean with $1{,}030 \times 1{,}030$ grids using 2D and 4D arrays on a 32-processor SGI Origin2000 machine. This machine has very large per-processor second-level caches (4 MB), so with four-dimensional array representations each processor's partition tends to fit comfortably in its cache. The problem size is large enough relative to the number of processors that the inherent communication-to-computation ratio is quite low. The major bottleneck is the time spent waiting at barriers. Smaller problems would stress communication more, whereas larger problems and proper data distribution would put more stress on the local memory system. With two-dimensional arrays, the story is clearly different. Conflict misses are frequent, and with data being difficult to distribute appropriately in main memory many of these misses are not satisfied locally, leading to long latencies, contention, and high data wait time.

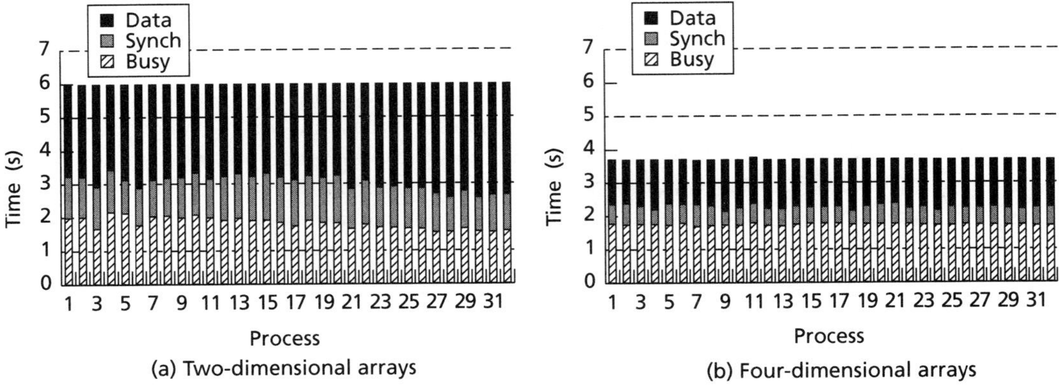

FIGURE 3.15 Execution time breakdown for Ocean on a 32-processor Origin2000. The size of each grid is 1,026 × 1,026, and the convergence tolerance is 10^{-3}. The use of four-dimensional arrays to represent the two-dimensional grids in (b) clearly reduces the time spent stalled on the memory system (including communication). This data wait time is very small because a processor's partition of the grids it uses at a given time fit very comfortably in the large 4-MB second-level caches in this machine. With smaller caches or much bigger grids, the time spent stalled waiting for (local) data would have been much larger.[8]

3.5.2 Barnes-Hut

The galaxy simulation has far more irregular and dynamically changing behavior than Ocean. Recall that it solves an *n*-body problem, in which the major computational challenge is to compute the influences that *n* bodies in a system exert on one another. The algorithm it uses for computing forces on the stars, the Barnes-Hut method, is an efficient hierarchical method for solving the *n*-body problem in $O(n \log n)$ time.

The Sequential Algorithm

The galaxy simulation proceeds over hundreds of time-steps, each step computing the net force on every body and thereby updating that body's position and other attributes. Recall the insight that the force calculation in the Barnes-Hut method is based on: if the magnitude of interaction between bodies falls off rapidly with distance (as it does in gravitation), so the effect of a large group of bodies may be approximated by a single equivalent body if that group of bodies is far enough away from the point at which the effect is being evaluated. The hierarchical application of this insight implies that the farther away the bodies, the larger the group that can be approximated by a single body.

8. In this and subsequent execution time breakdowns, there is no artificial final barrier to cause all processes to wait until the last is finished, as in Figure 3.12.

To facilitate a hierarchical approach, the Barnes-Hut algorithm represents the three-dimensional space containing the galaxies as a tree, as follows. The root of the tree represents a space cell containing all bodies in the system. The tree is built by adding bodies into the initially empty root cell and subdividing a cell into its eight equally sized children as soon as it contains more than a fixed number of bodies (here ten). The result is an oct-tree whose internal nodes are space cells and whose leaves contain the individual bodies.[9] Empty cells resulting from a cell subdivision are ignored. The tree (and the Barnes-Hut algorithm) is therefore adaptive in that it extends to more levels in regions that have high body densities. While we use a three-dimensional problem, Figure 3.16 shows a small two-dimensional example domain and the corresponding quadtree for simplicity. The positions of the bodies change across time-steps, so the tree is rebuilt every time-step. This results in the overall computational structure shown in Figure 3.17, with most of the time being spent in the force calculation phase.

The tree is traversed once per body to compute the net force acting on that body. The force calculation algorithm for a body starts at the root of the tree and conducts the following test recursively for every cell it visits. If the center of mass of the cell is far enough away from the body, the entire subtree under that cell is approximated by a single body at the center of mass of the cell, and the force this center of mass exerts on the body is computed. The rest of that subtree is not traversed. If, however, the center of mass is not far enough away, the cell must be "opened" and each of its subcells visited. A cell is determined to be far enough away if the following condition is satisfied:

$$\frac{l}{d} < \theta \tag{3.6}$$

where l is the length of a side of the cell, d is the distance of the body from the center of mass of the cell, and θ is a user-defined accuracy parameter (θ is usually between 0.5 and 1.2). In this way, a body traverses deeper into those parts of the tree representing space that is physically close to it and groups distant bodies at a hierarchy of length scales. Since the expected depth of the tree is $O(\log n)$ and the number of bodies for which the tree is traversed is n, the expected complexity of the algorithm is $O(n \log n)$. Actually it is

$$O\left(\frac{1}{\theta^2} \times n \log n\right)$$

since θ determines the number of tree cells touched at each level in a traversal (smaller θ implies greater accuracy and more tree cells touched). Bodies in denser parts of the space traverse deeper down the tree to compute the forces on themselves, so the work associated with bodies is not uniform.

9. An oct-tree is a tree in which every node has a maximum of eight children. In two dimensions, a quadtree would be used, in which the maximum number of children is four.

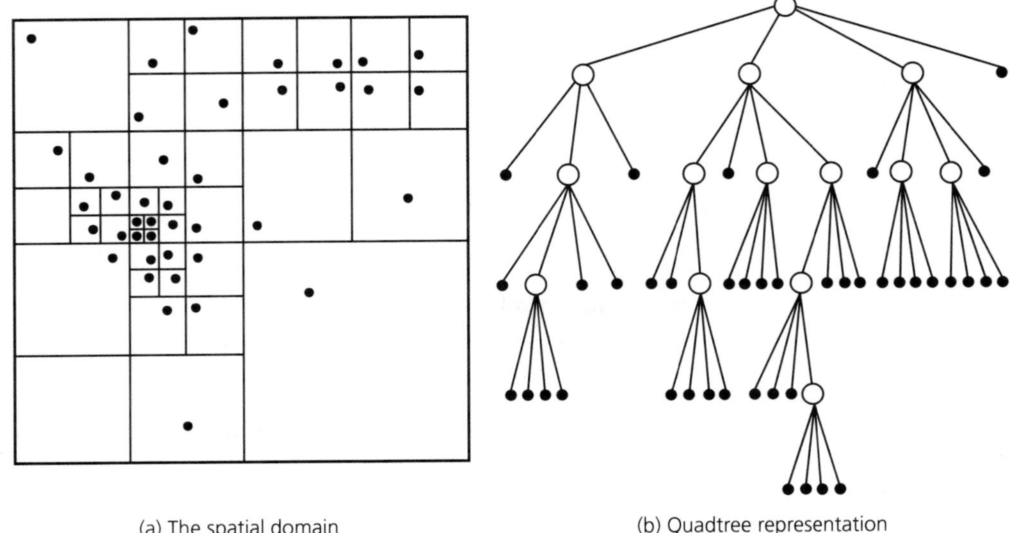

FIGURE 3.16 Barnes-Hut: A two-dimensional particle distribution and the corresponding quadtree

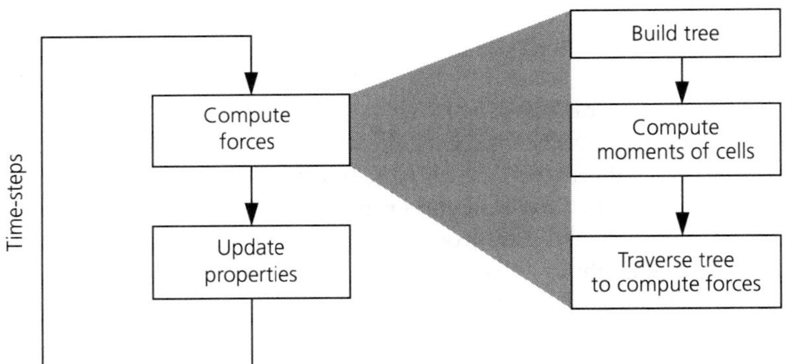

FIGURE 3.17 Flow of computation in the Barnes-Hut application. The force computation phase of an *n*-body problem expands into three phases (shown on the right) in the Barnes-Hut method.

Conceptually, the main data structure in the application is the Barnes-Hut tree. The tree is implemented in both the sequential and parallel programs with two arrays: an array of bodies and an array of tree cells. Each body and cell is represented as a structure or record. The fields for a body include its three-dimensional position, velocity, acceleration, and mass. A cell structure also has pointers to its children in the tree, and a three-dimensional center of mass. There is also a separate array of pointers to bodies and one of pointers to cells. Every process owns a contiguous chunk of pointers in these arrays, not necessarily of equal size, which in every time-step are set to point to the bodies and cells that are assigned to it in that time-step. Since the structure and partitioning of the tree changes across time-steps as the galaxy evolves, the actual bodies and cells assigned to a process are not contiguous in the body and cell arrays.

Decomposition and Assignment

Each of the phases within a time-step is executed in parallel, with global barrier synchronization between phases. The natural unit of decomposition (task) in all phases is a body, except in computing the cell centers of mass, where it is a cell.

Unlike Ocean, which has a regular and predictable structure of both computation and communication, the Barnes-Hut application presents many challenges for effective assignment. First, the nonuniformity of the galaxy implies that both the amount of work per body and the communication patterns among bodies are nonuniform, so a good assignment cannot be discovered by inspection. Second, the distribution of bodies changes across time-steps, which means that static assignment is not likely to work well. Third, since the information needs in force calculation fall off with distance equally in all directions, reducing interprocess communication demands that partitions be spatially contiguous and not biased in size toward any one direction. Fourth, the different phases in a time-step have different distributions of work among the bodies/cells, and hence different preferred partitions. For example, the work in the update phase is uniform across all bodies, whereas that in the force calculation phase clearly is not. Another challenge for good performance is that the communication needed among processes is naturally fine grained and irregular.

We focus our partitioning efforts on the force calculation phase since it is by far the most time-consuming. The partitioning is not modified for other phases in accordance with their needs since the cost of doing so, both in repartitioning and in loss of locality, outweighs the potential benefits and since similar partitions are likely to work well for tree building and moment calculation phases (although not for the update phase).

We can use profiling-based semistatic partitioning in this application, taking advantage of the fact that although the spatial distribution of bodies at the end of the simulation may be radically different from that at the beginning, it evolves slowly with time and changes little between two successive time-steps. As we perform the force calculation phase in a time-step, we record the work done by every particle in that time-step (i.e., we count the number of interactions it computes with other bodies or cells). We then use this work count as a measure of the work associated with that particle in the next time-step. Work counting is cheap since it only involves incrementing a local counter when an (expensive) interaction is performed. Now we need to combine this load-balancing method with assignment techniques that also achieve the communication goal: keeping partitions contiguous in space and not biased in size toward any one direction. We briefly discuss two techniques:

the first because it is applicable to many irregular problems and the second because it is better suited to this application and is what our program uses.

The first technique, called orthogonal recursive bisection (ORB), preserves physical locality by partitioning the domain space directly. The space is recursively subdivided into two rectangular subspaces with equal work, using the preceding load-balancing measure, until one subspace per process remains (see Figure 3.18[a]). Initially, all processes are associated with the entire domain space. Every time a space is divided, half the processes associated with it are assigned to each of the subspaces that result. The Cartesian direction in which division takes place is usually alternated with successive divisions, and a parallel median finder is used to determine where to split the current subspace. A separate binary tree of depth $\log p$ is used to keep track of the divisions and to implement ORB. (Details of using ORB for this application can be found in [Salmon 1990].)

The second technique, called costzones, recognizes that the Barnes-Hut algorithm already has a representation of the spatial distribution of bodies encoded in its tree data structure. Thus, we can partition this existing data structure itself and thereby achieve the goal of partitioning space (see Figure 3.18[b]). Every internal cell stores the total cost associated with all the bodies it contains. The total work or cost in the system is divided among processes so that every process has a contiguous, equal range or zone of work (for example, a total work of 1,000 units would be split among 10 processes so that zone 1–100 units is assigned to the first process, zone 101–200 to the second, and so on). Which costzone a body in the tree belongs to can be determined by the total cost of an in-order traversal of the tree up to that body. Processes traverse the tree in parallel, picking up the bodies that belong in their costzone. (Details can be found in [Singh et al. 1995].) The costzones method is much easier to implement than ORB. While the two result in partitions with similar load balance and inherent communication properties, the costzones method yields better overall performance in a shared address space. This is mostly because the time spent in the partitioning phase itself (i.e., computing the partitions) is much smaller, which illustrates the impact of extra work.

Orchestration

Orchestration issues in Barnes-Hut reveal many differences from Ocean, illustrating that even applications in scientific computing can have widely different behavioral characteristics of architectural interest.

Spatial Locality While the shared address space makes it easy for a process to access the parts of the shared tree that it needs in all the computational phases, distributing data to keep a process's assigned bodies and cells in its local main memory is not as easy as in Ocean. First, data would have to be redistributed dynamically as assignments change across time-steps, which can be expensive. Second, the logical granularity of data (a particle/cell) is much smaller than the physical granularity of allocation in memory (a page), and the fact that bodies/cells assigned to the same

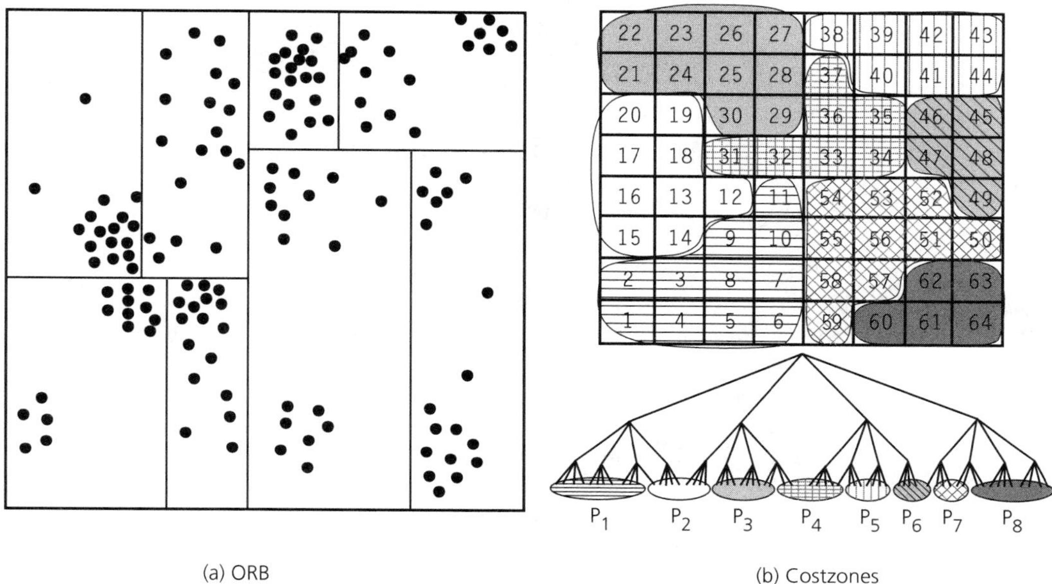

FIGURE 3.18 Partitioning schemes for Barnes-Hut: ORB and costzones. ORB partitions space directly by recursive bisection, while costzones partition the tree. (b) shows both the partitioning of the tree and how the resulting space is partitioned by costzones. ORB leads to more regular (rectangular) partitions than costzones, but their communication and load balance properties are quite similar.

process are contiguous in physical space does not mean that they are spatially contiguous in the body/cell arrays. Fixing these problems requires overhauling the data structures that store bodies and cells: using separate arrays or lists per process that are modified across time-steps as assignments change, and hence different data structures than those used in the sequential program. Fortunately, there is enough temporal locality in the application that data distribution is not so important in a shared address space (again unlike Ocean). In addition, the vast majority of the cache misses are to bodies and cells that are assigned to other processors anyway, so data distribution itself wouldn't help make the misses local. We therefore simply distribute pages of shared data in a round-robin interleaved manner among nodes, without attention to which node gets which pages.

While in Ocean large cache blocks improve local access performance, limited only by partition size, here multiword cache blocks help exploit spatial locality only to the extent that reading a particle's displacement or moment data involves reading several double-precision words of data. Very large transfer granularities might cause more fragmentation than useful prefetching to occur for the same reason that data distribution at page granularity is difficult: unlike in Ocean, locality of bodies/cells in the arrays does not match that in physical space (on which assignment is based), so fetching data from more than one body/cell in the array upon a miss may be harmful rather than beneficial. Spatial locality depends on the size of a body or cell structure and does not improve much with the number of bodies.

Working Sets and Temporal Locality The first working set in this program contains the data used to compute forces between a single body-body or body-cell pair. The interaction with the next body or cell in the traversal will reuse this data. The second working set is the most important to performance. It consists of the data encountered in the entire tree traversal to compute the force on a single body. Because of the way partitioning is done, the next body on which forces are calculated will be close to this body in space, so the tree traversal to compute the forces on that body will reuse most of this data. As we go from body to body, the composition of this working set changes slowly, but the amount of reuse is tremendous, and the resulting working set is small even though overall a process accesses a very large amount of data in irregular ways. Much of the data in this working set is from other processes' partitions, and most of this data is allocated nonlocally. Thus, it is the temporal locality exploited on shared data (both local and nonlocal) that is critical to the performance of the application, unlike in Ocean where it is data distribution.

By the same reasoning that the complexity of the algorithm is

$$O\left(\frac{1}{\theta^2} \times n \log n\right)$$

the expected size of this working set is proportional to

$$O\left(\frac{1}{\theta^2} \times \log n\right)$$

even though the overall memory requirement of the application is close to linear in n: each particle accesses about this much data from the tree to compute the force on it. The constant of proportionality is small, being the amount of data accessed from each body or cell visited during force computation. Since this working set grows slowly and fits comfortably in modern second-level caches, we do not need to replicate data in main memory. In Ocean, some important working sets grow linearly with the data set size, and we do not always expect them to fit in the cache; however, proper data distribution is easy and keeps most cache misses local, so even in Ocean we do not need replication in main memory.

Synchronization Barriers are used to maintain dependences among bodies and cells across some of the computational phases, such as between building the tree and using it to compute forces. The unpredictable nature of the dependences makes it difficult to replace the barriers by point-to-point synchronization at the granularity of bodies or cells, at least with the programming primitives we assume. The small number of barriers used in a time-step is independent of problem size or number of processors, depending only on the number of phases.

Synchronization is unnecessary within the force computation phase itself. While communication and sharing patterns in the application are irregular, they are phase structured. That is, although a process reads body and cell data from many other processes in the force calculation phase, the fields of a body structure that are written in this phase (the accelerations and velocities) are not the same as those that are read in it (the displacements and masses). The displacements are written only at the end of the update phase, and masses are not modified after initialization. However, in other phases, the program uses both mutual exclusion with locks and point-to-point event synchronization with flags in more interesting ways than Ocean. In the tree-building phase, a process that is ready to add a body to a cell must first obtain mutually exclusive access to the cell since other processes may want to read or modify the cell at the same time. This is implemented with a lock per cell. The phase that calculates cell centers of mass is essentially an upward pass through the tree from the leaves to the root, computing the moments of cells from those of their children. Point-to-point event synchronization is implemented using flags to ensure that a parent does not read the moment of its child until that child has itself been updated by all its children. This is an example of multiple-producer, single-consumer group synchronization. There is no synchronization within the update phase.

The work between synchronization points is large, particularly in the force computation and update phases, where it is

$$O\left(\frac{n \log n}{p}\right)$$

and $O(n/p)$, respectively. The need for locking cells in the tree-building and center-of-mass phases causes the work between synchronization points in those phases to be substantially smaller.

Mapping

The irregular nature makes this application more difficult to map perfectly for network locality in common networks such as meshes. The ORB partitioning scheme maps very naturally to a hypercube topology (discussed in Chapter 10) but not so well to a mesh or other less richly interconnected network. This property does not hold for costzones partitioning, which naturally maps to a one-dimensional array of processors but does not easily guarantee to keep communication local in most network topologies.

Summary

The Barnes-Hut application exhibits irregular, fine-grained, time-varying communication and data access patterns that are becoming increasingly prevalent even in scientific computing as we try to model more complex natural phenomena. Successful partitioning techniques for this application are not obvious by inspection of the code

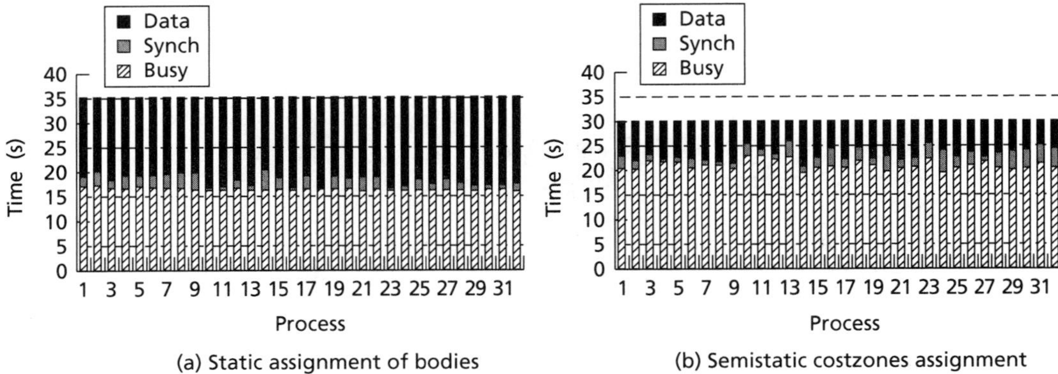

FIGURE 3.19 Execution time breakdown for Barnes-Hut with 512-K bodies on the Origin2000. The particular static assignment of bodies used is quite randomized, so given the large number of bodies relative to processors, the workload evens out due to the law of large numbers. The bigger problem with the static assignment is that because it is effectively randomized, the particles assigned to a processor are not close together in space so the communication-to-computation ratio is much larger than in the semistatic scheme. This is why data wait time is much smaller in the semistatic scheme. If we had assigned contiguous areas of space to processes statically, data wait time would be small, but load imbalance and hence synchronization wait time would be large. Even with the current static assignment, there is no guarantee that the assignment will remain load balanced as the galaxy evolves over time.

and require the use of insights from the application domain. These insights allow us to avoid using fully dynamic assignment methods, such as task queues and stealing.

Figure 3.19 shows the breakdown of execution time for this application on the 32-processor SGI Origin2000 machine. Load balance is quite good even with a static partitioning of the array of body pointers to processors precisely because there is little relationship between the locations of the bodies in the array and in physical space. However, the data access cost for a static partition is high due to a considerable amount of inherent and artifactual communication caused by the lack of contiguity in physical space. Semistatic costzone partitioning reduces this data access overhead substantially without compromising load balance.

3.5.3 Raytrace

Recall that in ray tracing rays are shot through the pixels in an image plane into a three-dimensional scene and the paths of the rays are traced as they bounce around to compute a color and opacity for the corresponding pixels. The algorithm uses a hierarchical representation of space called a Hierarchical Uniform Grid (HUG), which is similar in structure to the oct-tree used by the Barnes-Hut application. The root of the tree represents the entire space enclosing the scene, and each leaf holds a linked list of the object primitives that fall into that leaf (the maximum number of primitives per leaf is defined by the user, as are some other aspects of the tree structure). The hierarchical grid or tree makes it efficient to skip empty regions of space when tracing a ray and quickly find the next interesting cell.

The Sequential Algorithm

For a given viewpoint, the sequential algorithm fires one ray into the scene through every pixel in the image plane. These initial rays are called primary rays. At the first object that a ray encounters (found by traversing the hierarchical uniform grid), it is first reflected toward every light source to determine whether it is in shadow from that light source. If it isn't, the contribution of the light source to its color and brightness is computed. The ray is also reflected from and refracted through the object as appropriate. Each reflection and refraction spawns a new ray, which undergoes the same procedure recursively for every object that it encounters. Thus, each primary ray generates a tree of rays. Rays are terminated when they leave the volume enclosing the scene or according to some user-defined criterion (such as the maximum number of levels allowed in a ray tree). Ray tracing, and computer graphics in general, affords several trade-offs between execution time and image quality, and many algorithmic optimizations have been developed to improve performance without significantly compromising image quality.

Decomposition and Assignment

There are two natural approaches to exploiting parallelism in ray tracing. One is to divide the space and, hence, the objects in the scene among processes and have a process compute the ray interactions that occur within its space. The unit of decomposition here is a subspace. When a ray leaves a process's subspace, it will be handled by the next process whose subspace it enters. This is called a *scene-oriented* approach. The alternative *ray-oriented* approach is to divide pixels in the image plane among processes. A process is responsible for the rays that are fired through its assigned pixels, and it follows a ray in its entire path through the scene, computing the interactions of the entire ray tree that the ray generates. The unit of decomposition here is a primary ray. The decomposition unit can be made finer by allowing different processes to process rays generated by the same primary ray (i.e., from the same ray tree) if necessary. The scene-oriented approach preserves more locality in the scene data since a process only touches the scene data in its subspace and the rays that enter that subspace. However, the ray-oriented approach is much easier to program—particularly starting from a sequential program that loops over rays—and to implement with low overhead in a shared address space since rays can be processed independently without synchronization and the scene data is read-only. It is also easily used in a message-passing model with explicit replication of nonlocal scene data. This program therefore uses a ray-oriented approach. The degree of concurrency for an n-by-n plane of pixels is $O(n^2)$ and is usually ample.

Unfortunately, a static block partitioning of the image plane would not be load balanced. Rays from different parts of the image plane might encounter very different numbers of reflections and hence very different amounts of work. The distribution of work is highly unpredictable, so we use a distributed task-queuing system (one queue per processor) with task stealing for load balancing.

To determine how to initially assign rays or pixels to processes, consider communication. Since the scene data is read-only, it causes no inherent communication. If we replicated the entire scene on every node, there would be no communication at all except due to task stealing. However, this approach does not allow us to render a scene larger than what fits in a single node's memory, so the data set size cannot scale with the number of processors used. Other than task stealing, communication is generated because only $1/p$ of the scene is allocated locally on a node while a process accesses the scene widely and unpredictably. To reduce this artifactual communication, we would like processes to reuse scene data as much as possible rather than to access the entire scene randomly. For this, we can exploit spatial coherence in ray tracing: because of the way light is reflected and refracted, rays that pass through adjacent pixels from the same viewpoint are likely to traverse similar parts of the scene and to be reflected in similar ways. This suggests that we should use domain decomposition on the image plane to initially assign pixels to task queues. Since the adjacency or spatial coherence of rays works in all directions in the image plane, a block-oriented domain decomposition works well. This also reduces the communication of image pixels themselves.

Given p processors, the image plane is partitioned into p rectangular blocks of size as close to equal as possible. Every image block or partition is further subdivided into fixed-size square image *tiles*, which are the units of task granularity and stealing (see Figure 3.20 for a four-process example). These tile tasks are initially inserted into the task queue of the processor to which that block is assigned. A processor ray traces the tiles in its block in scan-line order. When it has finished with its block, it steals tile tasks from other processors that are still busy. The choice of tile size is a compromise between preserving locality through spatial coherence and reducing the number of accesses to other processors' queues, both of which reduce communication, and keeping the task size small enough to ensure good load balance. We could also initially assign tiles to processes in an interleaved manner in both dimensions (called a *scatter decomposition*) to improve load balance in the initial assignment and reduce task stealing at some cost in spatial coherence.

Orchestration

Given the preceding decomposition and assignment, let us examine spatial locality, temporal locality, and synchronization.

Spatial Locality Most of the shared data accesses are to the scene data. However, because of changing viewpoints and the fact that rays bounce about unpredictably, it is impossible to divide the scene into parts that are each accessed only (or even dominantly) by a single process. In addition, the scene data structures are naturally small

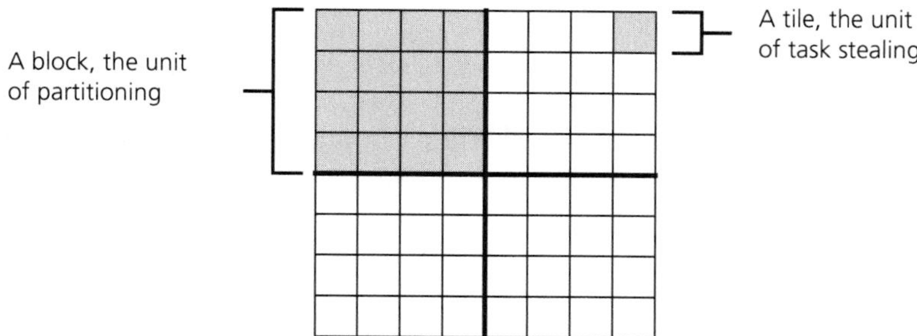

FIGURE 3.20 Image plane partitioning in Raytrace for four processors. Each tile contains several pixels. A contiguous block of tiles is assigned to every process. When a process has finished processing its assigned block, it steals available tiles from other processes.

and linked together with pointers, so it is very difficult to distribute them among memories at the granularity of pages. We therefore resort to using a round-robin layout of the pages that hold scene data to reduce hot spots and contention. Image data is small, and we try to allocate the few pages it falls on in different memories as with scene data. The block assignment described previously preserves spatial locality at cache block granularity in the image plane quite well, though it can lead to some loss of locality at tile boundaries, particularly with task stealing. A strip decomposition in rows of the image plane would be better from the viewpoint of spatial locality but would not exploit spatial coherence in the scene so well. As in Ocean, the best choices may be architecture dependent, and the assignment can be easily parameterized. Spatial locality on scene data is not very high and does not improve with larger scenes.

Temporal Locality Because of the read-only nature of the scene data, if there were unlimited capacity for replication, then only the first reference to nonlocally allocated data would cause communication. With finite replication capacity, on the other hand, data may be replaced and may have to be recommunicated. The domain decomposition and spatial coherence methods described earlier enhance temporal locality on scene data and reduce the sizes of the working sets. However, since the access patterns are so unpredictable due to the bouncing of rays, working sets are relatively large and ill defined. Note that most of the scene data accessed and hence the working sets are likely to be nonlocal. Nonetheless, this shared address space program does not replicate data in main memory: the working sets are not sharp, caches on machines are becoming larger, and replication in main memory has a cost, so it is unclear that the benefits outweigh the overhead.

Synchronization and Granularity Only a single barrier is used after an entire scene is rendered and before it is displayed. Locks are used to protect task queues and for some global variables that track statistics for the program. The work between synchronization points is the work associated with a tile of rays, which is usually quite large.

Mapping

Since Raytrace has very unpredictable access and communication patterns to its scene data, there is little scope for optimizing artifactual communication through mapping. The initial assignment partitions the image into a two-dimensional grid of blocks, making it natural to map to a two-dimensional mesh network, but the effect of mapping is not likely to be large.

Summary

This application tends to have large working sets and relatively poor spatial locality but a low communication-to-computation ratio as long as there is ample scene replication capacity. Figure 3.21 shows the breakdown of execution time on the Origin2000 machine for a standard data set consisting of a number of balls arranged in a bunch, illustrating the importance of task stealing in reducing load imbalance and hence wait time at barrier synchronization. The extra communication and synchronization incurred as a result of task stealing is well worthwhile.

3.5.4 Data Mining

A key difference in the data mining application from the previous ones is that the data being accessed and manipulated typically resides on disk rather than in memory. It is very important to reduce the number of disk accesses since their cost is very high and to reduce the contention for a disk controller by different processors. The techniques for reducing disk access cost are essentially the same as those for reducing communication and memory access cost.

Recall the basic insight used in association mining: if an itemset of size k is large (i.e., it occurs in more than a threshold fraction of the transactions), then all subsets of that itemset must also be large. For illustration, consider a database consisting of five items—A, B, C, D, and E—of which one or more may be present in a particular transaction. The items within a transaction are lexicographically sorted. Consider L_2, the list of large itemsets of size two. This list might be {AB, AC, AD, BC, BD, CD, DE}. The itemsets within L_2 are also lexicographically sorted. Given this L_2, the list of itemsets that are candidates for membership in L_3 are obtained by performing a *join* operation on the itemsets in L_2—that is, taking pairs of itemsets in L_2 that share a common first item (say, AB and AC) and combining them into a lexicographically sorted itemset of size three (here ABC). The resulting candidate list C_3 in this case is {ABC, ABD, ACD, BCD}. Of these itemsets in C_3, some may actually occur with enough frequency to be placed in L_3, and so on. In general, the join operation to obtain C_k from L_{k-1} finds pairs of itemsets in L_{k-1} whose first $k - 2$ items are the same and combines them to create a new itemset for C_k. Itemsets of size $k - 1$ that have common $(k - 2)$-sized prefixes are said to form an equivalence class (e.g., {AB, AC, AD}, {BC, BD}, {CD}, and {DE} in this example for $k = 3$). Only itemsets in the

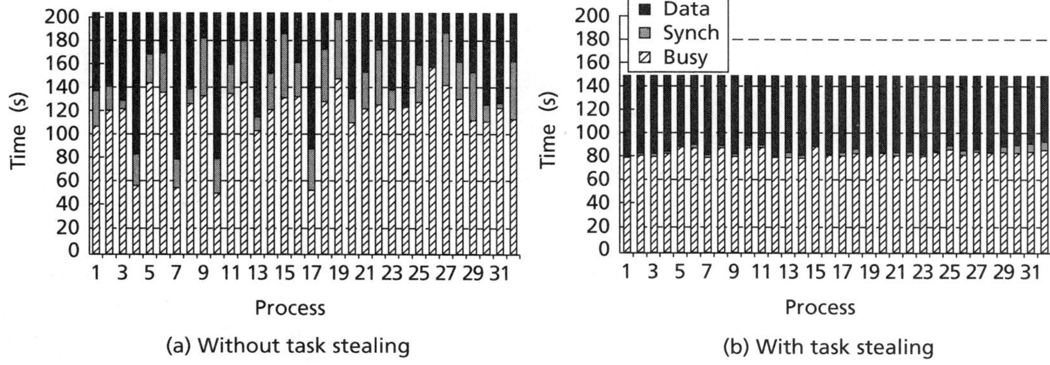

FIGURE 3.21 Execution time breakdown for Raytrace with the balls data set on the Origin2000. Task stealing is clearly very important for balancing the workload (and hence reducing synchronization wait time at barriers) in this highly unpredictable application.

same $k-2$ equivalence class need to be considered together to form C_k from L_{k-1}, which greatly reduces the number of pairwise itemset comparisons we need to do to determine C_k.

The Sequential Algorithm

A simple sequential method for association mining is to first traverse the data set and record the frequencies of all itemsets of size one, thus determining L_1. From L_1, we can construct the candidate list C_2 and then traverse the data set again to find which entries of C_2 occur frequently enough to be placed in L_2. From L_2, we can construct C_3 and then traverse the data set to determine L_3, and so on until we have found L_k. Although this method is simple, it requires reading all transactions in the database from disk k times, which is expensive.

An alternative sequential algorithm seeks to reduce the amount of work done to compute candidate lists C_k from lists of large itemsets L_{k-1} and especially to reduce the number of times data must be read from disk to determine the frequencies of the itemsets in C_k. We have seen that equivalence classes can be used to achieve the first goal. In fact, they can be used to construct a method that achieves both goals together. The idea is to transform the way in which data is stored in the database. Instead of storing transactions in the form $\{T_x, A, B, D, \ldots\}$—where T_x is the transaction identifier and A, B, D are items in the transaction—we can keep in the database records of the form $\{IS_x, T_1, T_2, T_3, \ldots\}$, where IS_x is an itemset and T_1, T_2, and so on are transactions that contain that itemset. That is, a database record is maintained per itemset rather than per transaction. If the large itemsets of size $k-1$ (i.e., the elements of L_{k-1}) that are in the same $k-2$ equivalence class are identified, then computing the candidate list C_k requires only examining all pairs of these itemsets. Since each itemset has its list of transactions attached, the size of each resulting itemset in C_k can be computed at the same time as constructing the C_k itemset itself from a pair of L_{k-1} itemsets, by simply computing the intersection of the transactions in that pair's lists.

EXAMPLE 3.4 Suppose {AB, 1, 3, 5, 8, 9} and {AC, 2, 3, 4, 8, 10} are large itemsets of size two in the same one-equivalence class (they each start with A). How will the data be accessed in disk and memory?

Answer The list of transactions that contain itemset ABC is {3, 8}, so the occurrence count of itemset ABC is two. This means that once the database is transposed and the one-equivalence classes identified, the rest of the computation for a single one-equivalence class can be done to completion (i.e., all large itemsets of size *k* found) before considering any data from other one-equivalence classes. If a one-equivalence class fits in main memory, then after the transposition of the database a given data item needs to be read from disk only once, greatly reducing the number of expensive I/O accesses. A form of blocking for temporal locality has been achieved. ■

Decomposition and Assignment

The two sequential methods also differ in their parallelization, with the latter method having advantages in this respect as well. To parallelize the first method, we could first divide the database among processors. At each step, a processor traverses only its local portion of the database to determine partial occurrence counts for the candidate itemsets, incurring no communication or nonlocal disk accesses in this phase. The partial counts are then merged into global counts to determine which of the candidates are large. Thus, in parallel this method requires not only multiple passes over the database but also interprocessor communication and synchronization at the end of every pass.

In the second method, the equivalence classes that helped the sequential method reduce disk accesses are very useful for parallelization as well. Since the computation on each one-equivalence class is independent of the computation on any other, we can simply divide the one-equivalence classes among processes that can thereafter proceed independently for the rest of the program without communication or synchronization. The itemset lists (in the transformed format) corresponding to an equivalence class can be stored on the local disk of the process to which the equivalence class is assigned, so no need for remote disk access remains after this point. As in the sequential algorithm, each process can complete the work on one of its assigned equivalence classes before proceeding to the next one, so each itemset record from the local disk should also be read only once as part of its equivalence class.

The challenge is ensuring a load-balanced assignment of equivalence classes to processes. A simple metric for load balance is to assign equivalence classes based on the number of initial entries in them. However, as the computation unfolds to compute itemsets of size k, the amount of work is determined more closely by the number of large itemsets that are generated at each step. Heuristic measures that estimate this or some other more appropriate work metric can be used as well. Otherwise, we may have to resort to dynamic tasking and task stealing, which can compromise much of the simplicity of this method (namely, that once processes are assigned their initial equivalence classes, they no longer have to communicate, synchronize, or perform remote disk access).

The first step in this approach, of course, is to compute the one-equivalence classes and the large itemsets of size two in them as a starting point for the parallel assignment. To compute these itemsets, we are better off using the original transaction-oriented form of the database rather than the transformed version, so we do not transform the database yet (see Exercise 3.18). Every process sweeps over the transactions in its local portion of the database and, for each pair of items in a transaction, increments a local counter for that item pair (the local counts can be maintained as a two-dimensional upper-triangular matrix, with the indices being items). The local counts are then merged, involving interprocess communication, and the large itemsets of size two are determined from the resulting global counts. These itemsets are then partitioned into one-equivalence classes, which are assigned to processes as described earlier.

The next step is to transform the database from the original $\{T_x$, A, B, D, . . .$\}$ organization by transaction to the $\{IS_x, T_1, T_2, T_3,$ . . .$\}$ organization by itemset, where the IS_x are initially the size two itemsets. This can be done in two steps—a local step and a communication step. In the local step, a process constructs the partial transaction lists for large itemsets of size two from its local portion of the database. In the communication step, a process (at least conceptually) "sends" the lists for those size two itemsets whose one-equivalence classes are not assigned to it to the process to which they are assigned and "receives" from other processes the lists for the equivalence classes that are assigned to it. The incoming partial lists are merged into the local lists, preserving a lexicographically sorted order, after which the process holds the transformed database for its assigned equivalence classes. It can now compute the itemsets of size k step by step for each of its equivalence classes, without any communication, synchronization, or remote disk access (if there is no task stealing). At the end of the calculation, the results for the large itemsets of size k are available from the different processes. The communication step of the transformation phase is usually the most expensive step in the algorithm and is quite like transposing a matrix, except that the sizes of the communications among different pairs of processes are different.

Orchestration

Given this decomposition and assignment, let us examine spatial locality, temporal locality, and synchronization.

Spatial Locality The organization of the computation and the lexicographic sorting of the itemsets and transactions causes most of the traversals through the data to be simple front-to-back sweeps that exhibit very good predictability and spatial locality. This is particularly important in reading from disk, since it is important to amortize the high start-up costs of a disk read over a large amount of useful data.

Temporal Locality As discussed earlier, proceeding over one equivalence class at a time is much like blocking, although how successful it is depends on whether the data for that equivalence class fits in main memory. As the computation for an equivalence class proceeds, the number of large itemsets becomes smaller, so reuse in main memory is more likely to be exploited. Note that here it is more likely that we are exploiting temporal locality in main memory rather than in the cache, although the techniques and goals are similar at any level of the extended memory hierarchy.

Synchronization The major forms of synchronization are the reductions of partial occurrence counts into global counts in the first step of the algorithm (computing the large size two itemsets) and a barrier after this to begin the transformation phase. The reduction is required only for itemsets of size two since thereafter every process continues independently to compute the large itemsets of size k in its assigned equivalence classes. Further synchronization may be needed if dynamic task management is used for load balancing.

Mapping

The communication to transform the database is all-to-all: a process may "send" different itemsets of size two and their partial transaction lists to all other processes and may "receive" or read such lists from them all. It is difficult to map all-to-all communication in a contention-free manner to network topologies (like meshes or rings) that are not very richly interconnected. Endpoint contention is reduced by communication scheduling techniques such as having each processor i at step j exchange data with processor i `xor` j so that no processor or node is overloaded.

Summary

Data mining differs from the other application case studies since disk access is a major bottleneck, and parallelization techniques aim primarily to minimize its cost. The technique we have examined treats the disk as simply another, explicitly managed level of the extended memory hierarchy. Load balance is an outstanding question that can compromise some of the local properties of the parallel program.

3.6 IMPLICATIONS FOR PROGRAMMING MODELS

We have seen throughout this and the previous chapter that while the decomposition and assignment of a parallel program are often (but not always) independent of the programming model, the orchestration step is highly dependent on it. In Chapter 1, we learned about the fundamental design issues that apply to any layer of the communication architecture, including the programming model. We learned that the two major programming models—a shared address space and explicit message passing between private address spaces—are fundamentally distinguished by functional differences, such as naming, replication, and synchronization. While either programming model can be implemented on any communication abstraction and hardware, the positions taken on these functional issues at a given layer affect (and are influenced by) performance characteristics, such as overhead, latency, and bandwidth. At that stage, we only dealt with those issues in the abstract and could not appreciate the interactions with applications and the implications regarding which programming models are preferable under what circumstances. Now that we have an in-depth understanding of several interesting parallel applications and understand the performance issues in orchestration, we can compare the programming models in light of application and performance characteristics.

We will use the application case studies to illustrate the issues, assuming a generic multiprocessor architecture with physically distributed memory. For a shared address space, we assume that read (loads) and write (stores) to shared data are the only communication mechanisms exported to the user, and we call this a read-write shared address space. Of course, in practice nothing stops a system from providing support for explicit messages as well as these primitives in a shared address space model, but we ignore this possibility for now. The shared address space model can be supported in a wide variety of ways at the communication abstraction and hardware/software interface (recall the discussion of naming models at the end of Chapter 1) with different granularities and different efficiencies for supporting communication, replication, and coherence. These affect the success of the programming model and will be discussed in detail in Chapters 8 and 9. Here we focus on the most common case in which a cache-coherent shared address space is supported efficiently at fine granularity—for example, with direct hardware support for a shared physical address space as well as for communication, replication, and coherence at the fixed granularity of cache blocks. However, contrast this common case with a hardware-supported shared address space without coherent replication, as provided by the BBN Butterfly and CRAY T3D and T3E machines. For the message-passing programming model, we will assume that it too is supported efficiently by the communication abstraction and the hardware/software interface.

As application programmers, we view the programming model as our window to the communication architecture. Differences between programming models and how they are implemented have implications for ease of programming, for the structuring of communication, for performance, and for scalability. In addition to functional aspects (like naming, replication, and synchronization), there are organizational aspects (like the granularity at which communication is performed) and performance aspects (like the endpoint overhead of a communication operation) that differ across programming models and affect programming for performance. Other performance aspects (such as latency and available bandwidth) depend largely on the network and network interface used and can be assumed to be equivalent. In addition, there are differences in the hardware overhead and complexity required to support the abstractions efficiently and in the ease with which they allow us to reason about or predict performance. Let us examine each of these aspects. The first three aspects we consider—naming, replication, and communication overhead—point to advantages of a read-write shared address space, whereas the others—message size, synchronization, hardware or design cost, and performance predictability—favor explicit message passing.

3.6.1 Naming

As seen, a shared address space makes naming logically shared data much easier for the programmer since any process can directly reference any data and the naming model is similar to that on a uniprocessor. Explicit messages are not necessary, and a process need not name other processes or know which processing node currently owns the data that it needs. In applications with regular, statically predictable communication needs, such as the equation solver kernel and Ocean, it is not difficult to determine which process's address space data resides in and to use explicit messages. However, matching ownership and use can be quite difficult, both algorithmically and for programming, in applications with irregular, unpredictable data needs. An example is Barnes-Hut, in which the parts of the tree that a process needs to traverse to compute forces on its bodies are not statically predictable and the ownership of bodies and tree cells changes with time. Determining which processes to communicate with requires extra work at run time. In Raytrace, rays shot by a process bounce unpredictably around scene data, so if data is distributed among the private address spaces of processes, then it is difficult to determine who owns the next set of data needed. These difficulties can be overcome, but this requires either altering and adding substantial complexity to the algorithm (e.g., adding an extra phase in every time-step to compute who needs what data and then transferring that data in Barnes-Hut [Salmon 1990] or using a scene-oriented rather than a ray-oriented approach in Raytrace), replicating the entire shared data structure on all nodes (not a scalable solution), or emulating an application-specific shared address space in software by hashing from bodies, cells, or scene data to processing nodes. These application-level naming solutions greatly change program appearance and are often among the greatest sources of run-time overhead. They are discussed further in (Singh, Hennessy, and Gupta 1995; Singh, Gupta, and Levoy 1994; Warren and Salmon 1993).

3.6.2 Replication

Several issues distinguish how replication of nonlocal data is managed: (1) Who is responsible for replication, that is, for making local copies of the data? (2) Where in the local memory hierarchy is the replication done? (3) At what granularity is data allocated in replication store? (4) How are the values of replicated data kept coherent? (5) And how is the replacement of replicated data managed?

With the separate, private virtual address spaces of the message-passing model, the only way to replicate communicated data is to copy the data into a process's private address space explicitly in the application program. The replicated data is explicitly renamed in the new address space, so both the virtual and physical addresses may be different for the two processes; their copies have nothing to do with each other as far as the system is concerned. Data is always replicated in main memory first (when the copies are made), and only data from the local main memory enters the processor cache. The granularity of allocation in the local memory is variable and user dependent. Ensuring that the values of replicated data are kept up-to-date (coherent) must be done by the program through explicit messages. We shall discuss replacement shortly.

Recall that in a shared address space, since nonlocal data is accessed through ordinary processor reads and writes and communication is implicit, opportunities exist for the system to replicate data transparently to the user—without copying or explicit renaming in the program—just as caches do in uniprocessors. This opens up a wide range of possibilities. For example, in a shared physical address space system, nonlocal data transparently enters the processor's cache subsystem upon access, without being replicated in main memory. Replication happens very close to the processor and at the relatively fine granularity of cache blocks, and data is kept coherent by hardware. Other systems may replicate data transparently in main memory first —either at cache block granularity through additional hardware support or at page or object granularity through system software—and may preserve coherence through a variety of methods and granularities that we discuss in Chapter 9. Still other systems may choose not to support transparent replication and/or coherence, leaving them to the user (for example, in the CRAY T3D and T3E systems).

Finally, let us examine the replacement of locally replicated data due to finite capacity. How replacement is managed has implications for the amount of communicated data that needs to be replicated at a level of the local memory hierarchy at a time. For example, hardware caches manage replacement dynamically with every reference and at a fine spatial granularity so that the cache needs to be only as large as the active working set of the workload. When replication is managed by the user program, as in message passing, a similar effect can be achieved by maintaining a cache data structure in the application in local memory and using it to emulate a hardware cache for nonlocal data. However, managing this cache complicates programming, incurs run-time overhead for software lookups and address resolution, and naturally generates fine-grained messages upon cache misses. On the other hand, the software cache can be very large and managed in an application-specific manner.

Typically, message-passing programs manage replacement less dynamically. Explicit local copies of communicated data are allowed to accumulate in local memory and are flushed out explicitly at certain points in the program, typically after a phase of computation when it can be determined that they are not needed for some time. This can require substantial extra memory for replication in some irregular applications, such as Barnes-Hut and Raytrace. For read-only data like the scene in Raytrace, many message-passing programs simply replicate the entire data set on every processing node, solving the naming problem and almost eliminating communication but also eliminating the ability to run larger problems on larger systems. In the Barnes-Hut application, in one prominent approach (Salmon 1990), a process first replicates locally all the data it needs to compute forces on all its assigned bodies and only then begins to compute forces. While this means that no communication takes place during the force calculation phase, the amount of data replicated in main memory is larger by several factors than the process's assigned partition of data and certainly much larger than the active working set, which is the data needed to compute forces on only one particle. This active working set in a shared address space typically fits in the processor cache, so there is no need for replication in main memory at all. In message passing, the large amount of replication can limit the scalability of the approach. For these reasons as well as for its generality, the approach of emulating a shared address space in software using hashing and of managing replication more dynamically using a fixed-size software cache (which is flushed at phase boundaries for coherence) is becoming increasingly popular for these irregular applications, especially as message passing becomes more efficient for small messages.

3.6.3 Overhead and Granularity of Communication

The overhead of initiating and receiving communication is greatly influenced by the extent to which the necessary tasks can be performed by hardware rather than being delegated to software, particularly to the operating system. Recall that in a shared physical address space the underlying uniprocessor hardware mechanisms suffice for address translation and protection (even when memory is physically distributed) since the shared address space is simply a large flat address space. Simply doing address translation for shared data accesses in software as opposed to hardware reduced Barnes-Hut performance by about 20% in one set of experiments (Scales and Lam 1994). The other major component of overhead is buffer management: incoming and outgoing communications need to be temporarily buffered in the network interface to allow multiple communications to be in progress simultaneously and to stage data through a communication pipeline. Communication at the fixed granularity of words or cache blocks makes it easy to manage buffers very efficiently in hardware. These factors combine to keep the overhead of communicating each cache block quite low on cache-coherent shared address space machines (a few cycles to a few tens of cycles, depending on the implementation and integration of the communication assist). On the other hand, automatic transfer of fixed-size blocks may lead to significant artifactual communication if spatial locality is poor.

In fact, the issue of communication granularity raises an important, if subtle, difference between a cache-coherent shared address space and one that provides transparent naming but not coherent replication (as in the CRAY T3D and T3E). In the former case, communication is performed transparently at a larger granularity than the word being referenced (e.g., a cache block). The cost of communication is thus amortized without the programmer having to worry about preserving the coherence of the rest of the transferred data; the system takes this responsibility. In the latter case, however, replication and coherence are the programmer's responsibility; so on a miss, the system fetches only the referenced word (otherwise, the burden on the programmer may be too large).

In message-passing systems, local references incur no more overhead than on a uniprocessor. Communication messages, however, are very flexible and therefore incur a lot of overhead. The variety of message types requires software overhead to decode the type of message and execute the corresponding handler routine at the sending or receiving end. The flexible message length, together with the use of asynchronous and nonblocking messages, complicates buffer management so that system software must often be invoked to temporarily store messages. Finally, sending explicit messages between arbitrary address spaces requires that the operating system on a node (or hardware support) intervene to provide protection. The software overhead for buffer management and protection can be substantial, particularly when the operating system must be invoked. A lot of recent design effort has focused on streamlined network interfaces and message-passing mechanisms that significantly reduce per-message overhead. These approaches can restrict flexibility and are discussed in Chapter 7. Nevertheless, the overhead per message is likely to remain several times as large as that of hardware-supported read-write shared address space interfaces, limiting the effectiveness of approaches that naturally generate fine-grained communication in irregular applications.

These three issues—naming, replication, and communication overhead—have pointed to the advantages of an efficiently supported shared address space for parallel programming. Let us now examine issues that favor message passing.

3.6.4 Block Data Transfer

Implicit communication through reads and writes in a hardware-supported cache-coherent shared address space typically causes a message to be generated for each reference, or at least for each cache block, that requires communication. The communication is usually initiated by the process that needs the data, via a cache miss, and we call it receiver-initiated communication. While the hardware support provides efficient fine-grained communication, communicating one cache block at a time is not the most efficient way to communicate a large chunk of data from one processor to another. We would rather amortize the overhead and latency by communicating the data in a single message or a group of large messages, a method called *block data transfer.*

Explicit communication, as in message passing, allows greater flexibility in choosing the sizes of messages and in choosing whether communication is receiver initiated or sender initiated, thus naturally enabling block transfer. Explicit communication can even be added to a hardware-coherent shared address space naming model, giving the programmer a choice of communication methods, and it is also possible for the system to make communication coarser grained transparently underneath a read-write programming model in some cases of predictable communication. However, the natural communication structure promoted by a shared address space is fine grained and usually receiver initiated. The advantages of block transfer in a hardware-supported shared address space are somewhat complicated by the availability of alternative latency tolerance techniques, but it clearly does have advantages.

3.6.5 Synchronization

The fact that synchronization can be contained in the (explicit) communication itself in message passing, while it is usually explicit and separate from the implicit data communication in a shared address space, tends to eliminate much of the programming concern over synchronization. Mutual exclusion is provided automatically, and few flags are used. Thus subtle race conditions and timing bugs may be less common in message passing. In addition, the difficulties of fine-grained sharing and replication tend to lead programmers to use more structured, sometimes more primitive algorithms with simpler orchestration. However, the advantage becomes less significant when asynchronous message passing is used, in which case separate event synchronization must be employed anyway to preserve correctness.

3.6.6 Hardware Cost and Design Complexity

The hardware cost and design time required to efficiently support the desirable features of a shared address space are greater than those required to support a message-passing abstraction. Since all memory transactions must be observed to determine when nonlocal cache misses occur, at least some functionality of the communication assist must be integrated quite closely into the processing node. A system with transparent replication and coherence in hardware caches requires further hardware support and the implementation of fairly complex coherence protocols. In the message-passing abstraction the assist does not need to see memory references and can be less closely integrated, for example, on the I/O bus. The actual hardware cost and complexity for supporting the different abstractions are discussed in Chapters 5, 7, and 8.

Cost and complexity, however, are more complicated issues than assist hardware cost and design time. For example, if the amount of replication needed in a message-passing program is indeed much larger than that needed in a cache-coherent shared address space (due to differences in how replacement is managed, as discussed earlier, or due to replication of the operating system), then the memory required for this replication should be compared to the hardware cost of supporting a shared address space. The same goes for the recurring cost or "design time" of developing effective programs on a machine. The design cost of protocols also diminishes with growing experience. In practice, cost and price are also determined largely by volume of sales, engineering design experience, and business rather than purely technical factors.

3.6.7 Performance Model

Finally, in designing parallel programs for an architecture we would like to have at least a rough performance model that we can use to predict whether one implementation of a program will be better than another and to guide the structure of communication. A performance model has three aspects. First, we must model the characteristics of the machine; for example, the key system granularities and the costs of primitive events, such as communication messages. Second, we must model the characteristics of the application; for example, the frequency and burstiness of the primitive events in the parallel program. And third, we must develop an analytical or numerical performance model that takes these two sets of characteristics as inputs and predicts the execution time. Modeling machine characteristics is usually not very difficult, and we have seen a simple model of communication cost in this chapter. Modeling application characteristics, however, can be quite difficult, especially when the application is complex and irregular. And developing a good analytical performance model is difficult when contention is a significant issue. It is the difficulty of modeling application characteristics that makes predicting performance in a shared address space more difficult than in message passing, since the events of interest are not explicit in the program. For a programmer, the performance guidelines in message passing are at least clear: messages are expensive; send them infrequently. In a shared address space, particularly one with coherent replication, performance modeling is complicated by the very same properties that make developing a program easier: naming, replication, and coherence are all implicit (i.e., transparent to the programmer), so it is difficult to determine how much communication occurs and when. Artifactual communication is also implicit and is particularly difficult to predict. (Consider cache mapping conflicts that generate communication!) The resulting programming guidelines are much more vague: try to exploit temporal and spatial locality and use data layout when necessary to keep communication levels low. The problem is similar to how implicit caching makes performance difficult to predict even on a uniprocessor, thus complicating the use of the simple von Neumann model of a computer, which assumes that all memory references have equal cost. However, it is of far greater magnitude here since the cost of communication is much larger than that of local memory access on a uniprocessor, and there is much greater opportunity for contention.

3.6.8 Summary

The major potential advantages of implicit communication in the shared address space model are programming ease and performance in the presence of fine-grained data sharing (at least when the model is supported in hardware). The major potential advantages of explicit communication, as in message passing, are the benefits of block data transfer, the fact that synchronization may be subsumed in message passing, better performance guidelines and prediction ability, and the ease of building machines.

Given these trade-offs, the questions that an architect has to answer are

- Is it worthwhile to provide hardware support for a shared address space (i.e., transparent naming), is software support enough, or is it easy enough for programmers to manage all communication explicitly?
- If a shared address space is worthwhile, is it also worthwhile to provide hardware support for transparent replication and coherence?
- If the answer to either of the preceding questions is yes, then is the implicit communication enough or should there also be hardware support for explicit message passing among processing nodes that can be used when desired?

The answers to these questions depend on both application characteristics and cost. Affirmative answers to any of the questions naturally lead to other questions regarding how efficiently the feature should be supported and at what granularities, which raises other sets of cost, performance, and programming trade-offs that will become clearer as we proceed through the book. Experience shows that as applications become more complex and irregular, the usefulness of transparent naming and replication increases, which argues for supporting a shared address space abstraction. However, since communication is naturally fine grained—especially in irregular applications—and since large granularities of communication and coherence cause performance problems, supporting a shared address space effectively requires an aggressive communication architecture with hardware support for most functions. Many computer companies are now building such machines as their high-end parallel systems. On the other hand, clusters of inexpensive workstations or multiprocessors are also increasingly popular. These systems are usually programmed using message passing because of its better-defined performance model, the tendency to use larger messages and amortize overhead, and the explicit control and lack of sensitivity to fixed-size machine granularities.

3.7 CONCLUDING REMARKS

The characteristics of parallel programs have important implications for the design of multiprocessor architectures. Certain key observations about program behavior led to some of the most important advances in uniprocessor computing: the recognition of temporal and spatial locality in program access patterns led to the design of caches, and an analysis of instruction usage led to streamlined instruction set design. In multiprocessors, the performance penalties for mismatches between application requirements and what the architecture provides are much larger, so it is all the more important that we understand the parallel programs and other workloads that are going to run on these machines.

Historically, many different parallel architectural genres led to many different programming styles and very little portability. Today, the architectural convergence has led to a common ground for the development of portable software environments and programming languages. The way we think about the parallelization process and many of the key performance issues is largely similar in both the shared address space and message-passing programming models, although the specific granularities, performance characteristics, and orchestration techniques are different. While we analyze the trade-offs between shared address space and message passing, both are flourishing in different portions of the architectural design space.

Another effect of architectural convergence has been a clearer articulation of the performance issues against which software must be designed. Historically, the major focus of theoretical parallel algorithm development has been the PRAM model, which ignores data access and communication cost and considers only load balance and extra work (some variants of the PRAM model capture some serialization effects when different processors try to access the same data word). The PRAM model is very useful in understanding the inherent concurrency in an application, which is the first conceptual step in developing a parallel program; however, it does not take important realities of modern systems into account, such as the fact that data access and communication costs are often the dominant components of execution time. Historically, communication has been treated separately, and the major focus in its treatment has been mapping the communication to different network topologies. With a clearer understanding of the importance of communication and the important costs in a communication transaction on modern machines, two things have happened. First, models that help analyze communication cost and hence improve the structure of communication have been developed, such as the bulk synchronous programming (BSP) model (Valiant 1990) and the LogP model (Culler et al. 1993), with the hope of replacing the PRAM as the de facto model used for parallel algorithm analysis. These models strive to expose the important costs associated with a communication event—such as latency, bandwidth, or overhead—as we have done in this chapter, allowing an algorithm designer to factor them into the comparative analysis of parallel algorithms. The BSP model also provides an elegant framework that can be used to reason about communication and parallel performance. Second, the emphasis in modeling communication cost has shifted to the cost at the nodes that are the endpoints of the communication message, so the number of messages and contention at the endpoints have become more important than mapping to network topologies. In fact, both the BSP and LogP models ignore network topology completely, modeling network delay as a constant value!

Models such as BSP and LogP are important steps toward a realistic architectural model against which to design and analyze parallel algorithms. By changing the values of the key parameters in these models, we may be able to determine how an algorithm would perform across a range of architectures and how it might be best structured for different architectures or for portable performance. However, much more difficult than modeling the architecture as a set of parameters is modeling the behavior of the parallel algorithm or application, particularly when it is not regular in structure, which is the other side of the modeling equation (Singh, Rothberg, and Gupta 1994). The key questions here include the following: What is the communication-to-computation ratio? How does it change with replication capacity? How do the access patterns interact with the granularities of the extended memory hierarchy? How bursty is the communication? And how can this be incorporated into the performance model? Modeling techniques that can capture these characteristics for realistic applications and integrate them with machine models like BSP or LogP have yet to be developed.

This chapter has discussed some of the key performance properties of parallel programs and their interactions with the basic provisions of a multiprocessor's extended memory hierarchy and communication architecture. These properties include load balance; the communication-to-computation ratio; aspects of orchestrating communication that affect communication cost; data locality and its interactions with replication capacity and with the granularities of allocation, transfer, and coherence to generate artifactual communication; and the implications for communication abstractions and the hardware/software interface that a machine may support. We have seen that the performance issues trade off with one another and that the art of producing a good parallel program lies in obtaining the right compromise between conflicting demands. Programming for performance is also a process of successive refinement; decisions made in the early steps may have to be revisited based on system or program characteristics discovered in later steps. Achieving the performance potential can take considerable effort, depending on both the application and the system. Further, the extent and manner in which different techniques are incorporated can greatly affect the characteristics of the workload presented to the architecture. We have examined in depth the four application case studies that were introduced in Chapter 2 and have seen how these issues play out in each of them. We shall encounter several of these performance issues again in more detail as we consider architectural design options, trade-offs, and evaluation in the rest of the book. However, with the knowledge of parallel programs that we have developed, we are now ready to understand how to use the programs as workloads to evaluate parallel architectures and trade-offs.

3.8 EXERCISES

3.1 For which of the applications that we have described (Ocean, Barnes-Hut, Raytrace, Data Mining) have we followed the view of decomposing data rather than computation and using an owner computes rule in our parallelization? What would be the problem(s) with using a strict data distribution and owner computes rule in the others? How would you address the problem(s)?

3.2 What are the advantages and disadvantages of using distributed task queues (as opposed to a global task queue) to implement load balancing? Do small tasks inherently increase communication, contention, and task management overhead in each case?

3.3 Draw one arc from each kind of memory system traffic (the list on the left) to the solution technique (on the right) that is the most effective way to reduce that source of traffic in a machine that supports a shared address space with physically distributed memory.

Kinds of Memory System Traffic	Solution Techniques
Cold-start traffic	Large cache sizes
Inherent communication	Data placement
Extra data communication on a miss	Algorithm reorganization
Capacity-generated communication	Larger cache block size
Capacity-generated local traffic	Data structure reorganization

3.4 Under what conditions would the sum of busy-useful time across processes (in the execution time breakdowns) not equal the busy-useful time for the sequential program, assuming both the sequential and parallel programs are deterministic? Provide examples.

3.5 As an example of hierarchical parallelism, consider an algorithm frequently used in medical diagnosis and economic forecasting. The algorithm propagates information through a network or graph such as the one in Figure 3.22. Every node represents a matrix of values. The arcs correspond to dependences between nodes and are the channels along which information must flow. The algorithm starts from the nodes at the bottom of the graph and works upward, performing matrix operations at every node encountered along the way. It affords parallelism at a minimum of two levels: nodes that do not have an ancestor-descendent relationship in the traversal can be computed in parallel, and the matrix computations within a node can be parallelized as well. How would you parallelize this algorithm, and what characteristics of the network or graph would most affect your decisions? What are the trade-offs that are most important?

3.6 To illustrate levels of parallelism, the chapter described an application that routes wires to connect pins in a VLSI chip or board. Three levels of parallelism are available: across wires, across segments within a wire that each touch only a pair of pins, and across the set of possible routes evaluated for a given segment. What are the trade-offs in determining which level to pick? What parameters of the input and of the machine affect your decision? What you would you pick for this case: 30 wires, 24 processors, 5 segments per wire, and 10 routes per segment, with each route evaluation taking the same amount of time? If you had to pick one level of parallelism and be tied to it for all cases, which would you pick? (You can make and state reasonable assumptions to guide your answer.)

3.7 If E is the set of sections of the algorithm that are enhanced through parallelism, f_k is the fraction of the sequential execution time taken up by the kth enhanced section when run on a uniprocessor, and s_k is the speedup obtained through parallelism on the kth enhanced section, derive an expression for the overall speedup obtained. Apply it to the broadcast approach for Gaussian elimination at element granularity. Draw a rough concurrency profile for the computation (a graph showing the amount of concurrency versus time where the unit of time is a logical operation, say, updating an interior active element). Assume a 100×100 element matrix. Estimate the speedup, ignoring memory referencing and communication costs.

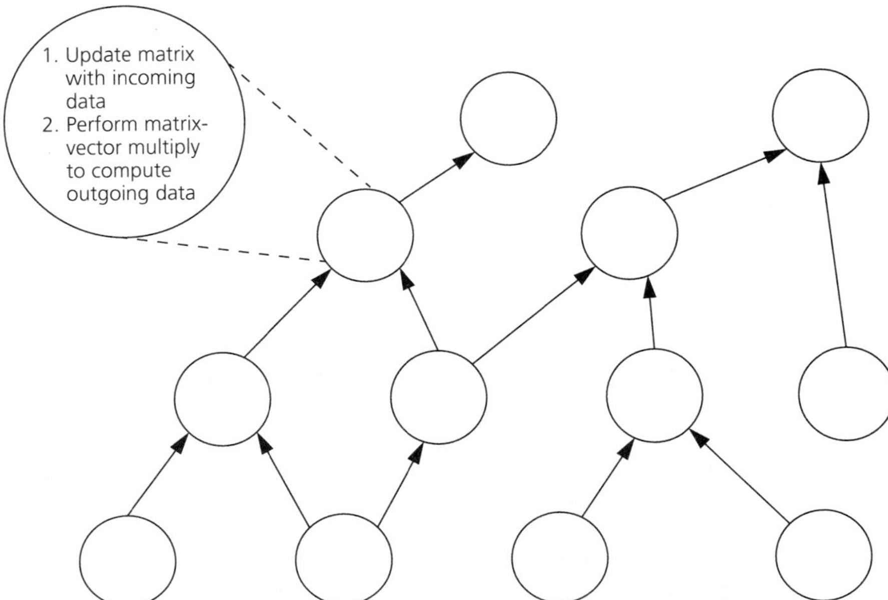

FIGURE 3.22 Levels of parallelism in a graph computation. The work within a graph node is shown in the expanded node on the left.

3.8 Consider the parallel Gaussian elimination algorithms discussed in Exercises 2.7–2.10.

a. Draw a concurrency profile showing the available concurrency versus time for the "broadcast" version. Assume that each update to a grid element is a single unit of time and of computation.

b. For an n-by-n matrix and p processes, analyze the load imbalance and communication volume assuming an assignment in contiguous chunks of rows to processes.

c. Do the same for an interleaved assignment of rows to processes.

d. Now do the same for the pipelined version where the decomposition is still in rows.

3.9 The concurrency in Gaussian elimination can also be enhanced by decomposing into individual elements rather than rows. Why is this?

a. Draw a concurrency profile for the broadcast version in this case.

b. A two-dimensional scatter (two-dimensional interleaved or cookie-cutter) assignment can be used at the granularity of individual elements instead of assignment in rows. Analyze the load imbalance and communication volume in the broadcast version in this case.

c. Analyze the load imbalance and communication volume for a pipelined version assuming a two-dimensional interleaved assignment of elements. Is there a large difference now in load imbalance and communication volume compared to a broadcast version with the same assignment?

d. Which of the versions discussed in this and the previous exercise do you think would actually perform best on a real machine and why? Can you think of a better decomposition and assignment?

3.10 We have discussed the technique of blocking that is widely used in linear algebra algorithms to exploit temporal locality (see Section 3.3.1). Consider a sequential Gaussian elimination program.

a. Write a blocked sequential version, using B-by-B blocks.

b. Provide an analytical expression for the read-miss rate for both the original (unblocked) and blocked sequential programs on a system in terms of n and B. Assume that in the unblocked version, a row of the matrix does not fit in the cache, while in the blocked version, B is chosen so that a B-by-B block is sized so that it fits in about half the cache. Ignore cache conflicts, and count only access to matrix elements. What would the read-miss rate be in the two cases with a cache size of 16 KB, a matrix size of 1,024-by-1,024 elements, and a block size of $B = 32$. Assume no reuse of blocks across block operations. If read misses cost 50 cycles, what is the performance difference between the two versions (counting each grid point update computation as one cycle and ignoring write accesses)?

c. How would you partition the blocked version for parallel execution, assuming a broadcast approach? Write pseudocode, treating the computation for a block as a single pseudo-operation.

d. Analyze the load imbalance and communication for this case, and compare with the previous partitioning approaches for the broadcast approach.

e. Considering all performance issues, not just algorithmic ones, would you use the best blocked or unblocked versions for the parallel broadcast approach on a shared address space machine? Which would you use for a message-passing machine? Why?

f. Considering pipelined approaches as well (with or without blocking), which approach would you choose overall for both a shared address space machine and a message-passing machine?

3.11 Termination detection is an interesting aspect of task stealing. Consider a task-stealing scenario in which processes produce tasks as the computation is ongoing. Design a good tasking method (where to take tasks from, how to put tasks into the pool, etc.) and think of some good termination detection heuristics. Perform worst-case complexity analysis for the number of messages needed by the termination detection methods you consider. Which one would you use in practice? Write pseudocode for one that is guaranteed to work and should yield good performance.

3.12 Consider transposing a matrix in parallel from a source matrix to a destination matrix (i.e., $B[i,j] = A[j,i]$).

a. How might you partition the two matrices among processes? Discuss some possibilities and the trade-offs. Does it matter whether you are programming a shared address space or message-passing machine?

b. Why is the interprocess communication in a matrix transpose called all-to-all personalized communication?

c. Write simple pseudocode for the parallel matrix transposition in a shared address space and in message passing (just the loops that implement the transpose). What are the major performance issues you consider in each case other than inherent communication and load balance, and how do you address them?

d. Is there any benefit to blocking the parallel matrix transpose? Under what conditions? How would you block it? (It is not necessary to write out the full code.) What, if anything, is the difference between blocking here and in Gaussian elimination?

3.13 The communication needs of applications, even expressed in terms of bytes per instruction, can help us do back-of-the-envelope calculations to determine the impact of increased bandwidth or reduced latency. For example, a Fast Fourier Transform (FFT) is an algorithm that is widely used in digital signal processing and climate modeling applications. A simple parallel FFT on n data points has a per-process computation cost of

$$O\left(\frac{n \log n}{p}\right)$$

and per-process communication volume of $O(n/p)$, where p is the number of processes. The communication-to-computation ratio is therefore $O(1/\log n)$. Suppose for simplicity that all the constants in the preceding expressions are unity and that we are performing an n = 1 M (or 2^{20}) point FFT on p = 1,024 processes. Let the average communication latency for a word of data (a point in the FFT) be 200 processor cycles, and let the communication bandwidth between any node and the network be 100 MB/s. Assume no load imbalance or synchronization cost, and ignore contention in the network.

a. With no latency hidden, for what fraction of the execution time is a process stalled due to communication latency?

b. What would be the impact on execution time of halving the communication latency?

c. What are the node-to-network bandwidth requirements without latency hiding?

d. What are the node-to-network bandwidth requirements assuming all latency is hidden, and does the machine satisfy them? If it does not, then what (qualitatively) will be the impact?

3.14 Consider the use of replication to reduce data traffic.

a. What kind of data (local, nonlocal, or both) can constitute the relevant working set in (i) main memory in a message-passing abstraction? (ii) a processor cache in a message-passing abstraction? (iii) a processor cache in a cache-coherent shared address space abstraction?

b. A proposal for cache-coherent machines has been to provide hardware support for fine-grained, coherent replication in main memory as well. Do you think this would be worthwhile? Under what conditions, and what do you think are the main drawbacks? For which of the case study applications in this chapter is it likely to be beneficial?

3.15 Write pseudocode for a reduction and a broadcast among p processes: first using a linear, $O(p)$ method and then using a tree-based, $O(\log p)$ method. Do this both for a shared address space and for message passing.

3.16 Write the equation solver kernel in a shared address space using a four-dimensional array representation for the grid in a manner such that the shape of the contiguous partitions (e.g., strips versus blocks or the number of processes along each dimension of the grid) can be specified as program input.

3.17 After the assignment of tasks to processors, the issue of scheduling the tasks that a process is assigned in some temporal order still remains. What are the major issues involved here? Which are the same as on uniprocessor programs and which are different? Construct examples that highlight the impact of poor scheduling in the different cases.

3.18 In the Data Mining case study, why are itemsets of size two computed from the original format of the database rather than from the transformed format? Analyze the computational complexity in each case.

3.19 You have been given the job of creating a word count program for a major book publisher. You will be working on a shared memory multiprocessor with 32 processors. Your only stated interface is `get_words`, which takes as its parameter an array and on return places in the array the book's next 1,000 words to be counted. The main work each processor will do should look like this:

```
while(get_words(word)) {
   for (i=0; i<1000; i++) {
      if word[i] is in list
         increment its count
      else
         add word to list
   }
}
```

*/*Once all words have been logged, the list should be printed out*/*

Using pseudocode, create a detailed description of the control flow and data structures that you will use for this parallel program. Your method should attempt to minimize space, synchronization overhead, and memory latency. This problem allows you a lot of flexibility, so state all assumptions and design decisions.

4

Workload-Driven Evaluation

The field of computer architecture is becoming increasingly quantitative. Design features are adopted only after detailed evaluations of trade-offs have been made. Once systems are built, they are evaluated and compared both by architects to understand the trade-offs and by users to make procurement decisions. In uniprocessor design, a rich base of existing machines and widely used applications supports the process of identifying and evaluating trade-offs; it is one of careful extrapolation from known quantities. Designers isolate performance characteristics of the machines by using microbenchmarks—small programs that stress a particular machine feature. Popular workloads are codified in standard benchmark suites, such as the Standard Performance Evaluation Corporation (SPEC) benchmark suite (SPEC 1995) for engineering workloads, and measurements are made on a range of existing design alternatives. Based on these measurements, assessments of emerging technology, and expected changes in the requirements of applications, designers propose new alternatives. The ones that appear promising are typically evaluated through simulation. First, a *simulator*—a program that simulates the design with and without the proposed feature of interest—is written. Then a number of programs or multiprogrammed workloads are chosen, either from the standard benchmark suites or other workloads representative of those that are likely to run on the machine. These workloads are run through the simulator and the performance impact of the feature determined. This, together with the estimated cost of the feature in hardware and design time, determines whether the feature will be included. Simulators are written to be flexible so that organizational and performance parameters can be varied to understand their impact as well.

Good workload-driven evaluation is a difficult and time-consuming process, even for uniprocessor systems. The workloads need to be renewed as technology and usage patterns change. Industry-standard benchmark suites are revised every few years. In particular, the input data sets used for the programs affect many of the key interactions with the systems and determine whether or not the important features of the system are stressed. These interactions must be understood and reflected in the use of the workloads. For example, to take into account the huge increases in processor speeds and changes in cache sizes, a major change from the SPEC92 benchmark suite to the SPEC95 suite was the use of larger input data sets to stress the memory system. Also, accurate simulators are costly to develop and verify, and the simulation runs consume huge amounts of computing time. However, these efforts are well rewarded because good evaluation yields good design.

As multiprocessor architecture has matured and greater continuity has been established from one generation of machines to the next, a similar quantitative approach has been adopted. Whereas early parallel machines were in many cases like bold works of art, relying heavily on the designer's intuition, modern design involves considerable evaluation of proposed design features. Here too, workloads are used both to evaluate real machines as well as to extrapolate to proposed designs and explore trade-offs through software simulation. For multiprocessors, the workloads of interest are either parallel programs or multiprogrammed mixes of sequential and parallel programs. Evaluation is a critical part of the new engineering approach to multiprocessor architecture; it is very important to understand the key evaluation issues before examining the core of multiprocessor architecture or the trade-offs evaluated in this book.

Unfortunately, the job of workload-driven evaluation for multiprocessor architecture is even more difficult than for uniprocessors, for several reasons:

- *Immaturity of parallel applications.* It is not easy to obtain "representative" workloads for multiprocessors, both because their use is relatively immature and because there are many new behavioral characteristics to represent.
- *Immaturity of parallel programming languages.* The software model for parallel programming has not stabilized, and programs written assuming different models can have very different behaviors.
- *Sensitivity of behavioral differences.* Different workloads, and even different decisions made in parallelizing the same sequential workload, can present vastly different execution characteristics to the architecture.
- *New degrees of freedom.* There are several new degrees of freedom in the architecture. The most obvious is the number of processors. Others include the organizational and performance parameters of the extended memory hierarchy, particularly the communication architecture. Together with the degrees of freedom of the workload (i.e., application parameters) and the underlying uniprocessor node, these parameters lead to a very large design space for experimentation, particularly when evaluating an idea or trade-off in a general context rather than evaluating a fixed machine. The high cost of communication makes performance much more sensitive to interactions among all these degrees of freedom than it is in uniprocessors, making it all the more important that we understand how to navigate the large parameter space.
- *Limitations of simulation.* Simulating multiprocessors in software to evaluate design decisions is more resource intensive than simulating uniprocessors. Multiprocessor simulations consume a lot of memory and time. Thus, although the design space we wish to explore is larger, the space that we can actually explore is often much smaller, and we must make careful trade-offs in deciding which parts of the space to simulate.

Our understanding of parallel programs from Chapters 2 and 3 will be critical in dealing with these difficulties. Throughout this chapter, we will learn that effective evaluation requires understanding the important properties of both workloads and architectures as well as how these properties interact. In particular, the relationships among application parameters and the number of processors determine fundamental program properties such as communication-to-computation ratio, load balance, and temporal and spatial locality. These properties interact with parameters of the extended memory hierarchy to influence performance in application-dependent and often dramatic ways (see Figure 4.1). Choosing workload and machine parameter values (or *sizes*) and understanding their scaling relationships is a crucial aspect of workload-driven evaluation, with far-reaching implications. It affects the experiments we design for adequate coverage of behavioral characteristics as well as the conclusions of our evaluations, and it helps us restrict the number of experiments or parameter combinations we must examine.

An important goal of this chapter is to highlight the key interactions of these properties and parameters, to illustrate their significance, and to point out the important pitfalls. Although no universal formula exists for evaluation, the chapter articulates a methodology for both evaluating real machines and assessing trade-offs through simulation. This methodology is followed in characterizing several workloads at the end of this chapter and in the illustrative evaluations that use these workloads throughout the book. It is important that we not only perform good evaluations but also understand the limitations of evaluation studies so we can keep them in perspective as we make architectural decisions.

The chapter begins by discussing the fundamental issue of scaling workload parameters as the number of processors increases and considers the implications for performance metrics and for the key inherent behavioral characteristics of parallel programs. The interactions with organizational and performance parameters of the extended memory hierarchy, and how these interactions should be incorporated into the actual design of experiments, are discussed in the next two sections, which examine the two major types of evaluations.

Section 4.2 outlines a methodology for evaluating a real machine. This involves first understanding the types of benchmark workloads we might use and their roles in such evaluation—including microbenchmarks, kernels, applications, and multiprogrammed workloads—as well as desirable criteria for choosing them. Then, given a workload, we examine how to choose its parameters to evaluate a given machine, illustrating the important considerations and pitfalls. The section ends with a discussion of various metrics that we might use to interpret and present results. Section 4.3 extends this methodological discussion to the more challenging problem of evaluating an architectural trade-off in a more general context through simulation.

Having understood how to perform workload-driven evaluation, we move on to Section 4.4, which provides the relevant characteristics of the workloads that will be used in the illustrative evaluations presented in the book. Some important publicly available workload suites for parallel computing, together with their philosophies, are described in the Appendix.

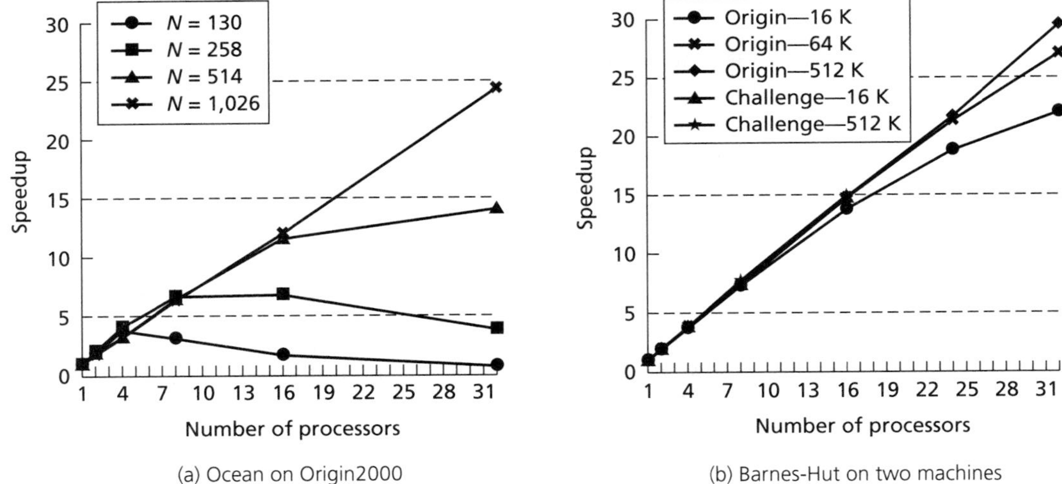

FIGURE 4.1 Impact of application parameters on parallel performance. For Ocean, the application parameter shown is the number of grid points (*N*) in each dimension, while in Barnes-Hut it is the number of bodies. These parameters determine the size of the data set used. For many applications, like Ocean in (a), the effect is dramatic, at least until the data set size becomes large enough for the number of processors. For the smallest problem, performance becomes worse rather than better in going from 4 to 8 processors and beyond; for the second smallest problem, performance drops when going from 8 to 16 processors; while for the largest problem, performance increases roughly linearly with processor count all the way to 32 processors. For other applications, like Barnes-Hut in (b), the effect of data set size is much smaller.

4.1 SCALING WORKLOADS AND MACHINES

Let us begin by discussing some basic measures of performance on a multiprocessor and using them to motivate the importance of proper scaling, before we examine scaling models and their implications.

4.1.1 Basic Measures of Multiprocessor Performance

Suppose we have chosen a parallel program as a workload and we want to use it to evaluate a machine. For a parallel machine, we can measure two performance characteristics: the *absolute performance* and the *performance improvement due to parallelism*. The latter is typically measured as the speedup, which was defined in Chapter 1 as the absolute performance achieved on p processors divided by that achieved on a single processor. Absolute performance (together with cost) is most important to the end user or buyer of a machine. However, in itself it does not tell us a great deal about how much of the performance comes from the use of parallelism and the effectiveness of the communication architecture rather than from the performance of an underlying single-processor node. Speedup tells us how much of the performance comes from the use of parallelism but with the caveat that it is easier to obtain good speedup when the individual nodes have lower performance since communication costs are less important when computation is slower. Both metrics are important, and both should be measured.

Absolute performance is best measured as work done per unit of time. Given a program, the amount of work to be done is usually defined by the input configuration on which the program operates, which is called the problem size (we shall define problem size more precisely later). This input configuration may either be available to the program up front, or it may consist of a set of continuously arriving inputs to a "server" application, such as a system that processes a bank's transactions or responds to inputs from sensors. Suppose the input configuration, and hence work, is kept fixed for a set of experiments. We can then treat the work as a fixed point of reference, measure the execution time, and define performance as the reciprocal of execution time.

In some application domains, users find it more convenient to have an explicit, domain-specific representation of work and use an explicit work-per-unit-time performance metric even when the input configuration is fixed. For example, in a transaction processing system, the metric could be the number of transactions serviced per minute; in a sorting application, the number of keys sorted per second; and in a chemistry application, the number of bonds computed per second. However, even though work is explicitly represented, performance is measured with reference to a particular input configuration or amount of work, and these performance metrics are nonetheless derived from measurements of execution time (together with the number of application events of interest). Given a fixed and known problem configuration, these domain-specific metrics present no fundamental advantage over execution time or its reciprocal. In fact, we must be careful to ensure that the explicit measure of work being used is indeed a meaningful measure from the application perspective, not something that we can cheat against. We discuss desirable properties of work metrics further as we go along and consider the more detailed issues concerning metrics in Section 4.2.5. For now, let us focus on evaluating the improvement in absolute performance due to parallelism, that is, the speedup due to using p processors instead of one.

Using execution time as our performance metric, we saw in Chapter 1 that we could simply run the program with the same input configuration on one and p processors and measure the improvement or speedup as

$$\frac{\text{Time}(1\text{proc})}{\text{Time}(p\ \text{procs})}$$

With operations per second as the performance metric, we can measure speedup as

$$\frac{\text{Operations per Second}(p\ \text{procs})}{\text{Operations per Second}(1\text{proc})}$$

A question arises about how we should measure performance on one processor; for example, is it more accurate to use the performance of the best sequential program running on one processor rather than the parallel program itself running on one processor? But this is quite easily addressed. As the number of processors is changed, we can simply run the problem on the different numbers of processors and compute speedups accordingly. Why then all the fuss about scaling?

4.1.2 Why Worry about Scaling?

Unfortunately, there are several reasons why measuring speedup with a fixed problem size is insufficient as the *only* way of evaluating the performance improvement due to parallelism across a range of machine scales.

Suppose the fixed problem size we have chosen is relatively small and is appropriate for a machine with a few processors. As we increase the number of processors for the same problem size, the overheads due to parallelism (communication, load imbalance) increase relative to useful computation. A point will come when the problem size is unrealistically small to evaluate the machine at hand. The high overheads will lead to uninterestingly small speedups, which reflect not so much the capabilities of the machine as the fact that an inappropriate problem size was used (say, one that does not have enough concurrency for the large machine). In fact, at some point using more processors may even hurt performance as the overheads begin to dominate useful work (see Figure 4.2[a]). A user would not run this problem on a machine that large, so it is not appropriate for evaluating this machine. The same is true if the problem takes a very small amount of time on the large machine.

On the other hand, if we choose a problem that is realistic for a machine with many processors, we might have the opposite problem in evaluating the performance improvement due to parallelism. This problem may be too big for a single processor because its data is too large to fit in the memory of a single node. On some machines, it may not be runnable on a single processor; on others, the uniprocessor execution will thrash severely to disk; and on still others, the overflow data will be allocated in other nodes' memories in the extended hierarchy, leading to a lot of artifactual internode communication. When enough processors are used, the data will fit in their collective memories, eliminating this artifactual communication if the data is distributed properly. The computation on each processor will be more efficient, and the result is a speedup far beyond the number of processors used. Once this has happened, further improvements in speedup will behave in a more usual way as the number of processors is increased, but the speedup over a uniprocessor is still *superlinear* in the number of processors.

This situation holds for any level of the memory hierarchy, not just main memory. For example, the aggregate cache capacity of the machine grows as each processor with its own cache hierarchy is added. If the working set per processor diminishes along with the data set, processors begin to use their caches more efficiently as the number of processors increases. An example using cache capacity is illustrated for the equation solver kernel in Figure 4.2(b). This greatly superlinear speedup due to memory system effects is not fake. Indeed, from a user's perspective the availability

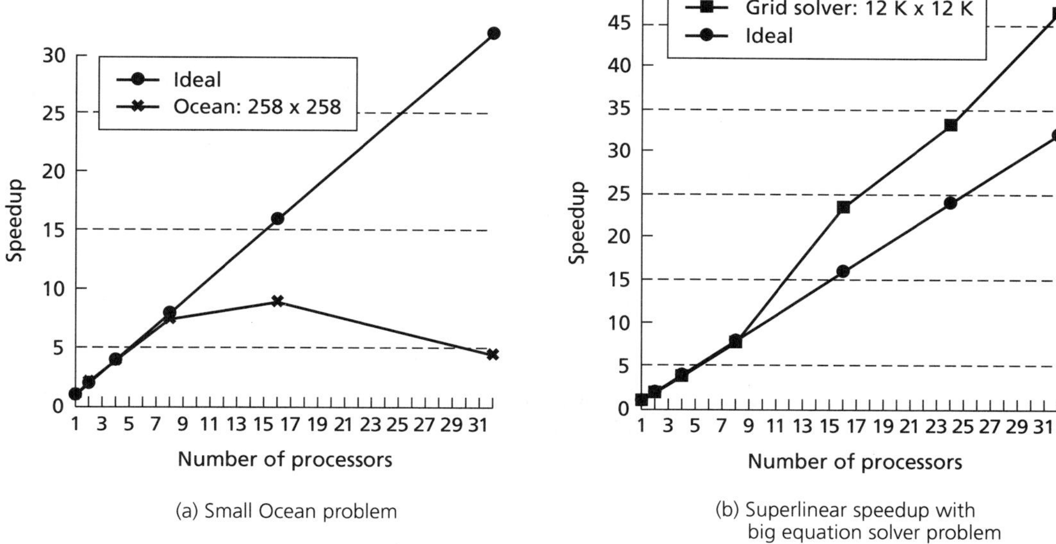

FIGURE 4.2 Speedups on the SGI Origin2000 as the number of processors increases. (a) shows the speedup for a small problem size in the Ocean application. The problem size is clearly very appropriate for a machine with about 8 processors. At a little beyond 16 processors, the speedup has saturated, and it is no longer clear that we would run this problem size on this large a machine. This is clearly the wrong problem size to run to evaluate a machine with 32 or more processors! (b) shows the speedup for the equation solver kernel, illustrating superlinear speedups when a processor's working set fits in the cache at 16 processors but does not fit when 8 or fewer processors are used.

of more, distributed memory is an important advantage of parallel systems over uniprocessor workstations since it enables them to run much larger problems and to run them much faster. However, the superlinear speedup does not allow us to separate the capacity effects from the usual improvements due to parallelism and as such does not help us evaluate the effectiveness of the machine's communication architecture.

A final limitation of maintaining the same problem size as the number of processors is increased is that this may not reflect realistic usage of the machine. Users often want to use more powerful machines to solve larger problems rather than to solve the same problem faster. In these cases, since problem size increases together with machine size in practical use of the machines, it should be scaled when evaluating the machines as well. Such scaling may overcome the problems arising from the size of mismatches just discussed, but the simplicity of comparing machine configurations on identical problems is lost.

We need well-defined scaling models for how problem size should be changed to accommodate changes in machine size so that we can evaluate machines against these models. The measure of performance is always work per unit of time, regardless of the scaling model. However, if the problem size is scaled, the work done does not stay constant, so we can no longer simply compare execution times to determine speedup. Work must be represented and measured, and the question is how. Furthermore, we want to understand how the scaling model influences program characteristics, such as the communication-to-computation ratio, load balance, and data locality in the extended memory hierarchy. For simplicity, let us focus on a single parallel application, not a multiprogrammed workload. First we need clear definitions of terms that have been used informally: scaling a machine and problem size.

Scaling a machine means making it more (or less) powerful. This can be done by making any component of the machine bigger, more sophisticated, or faster—the individual processors, the caches, the memory, the communication architecture, or the I/O system. In general, the *machine size* is a vector characterizing the per-node processing capabilities, memory hierarchy, and communication and I/O capabilities. Scaling a machine involves changing an entry or entries in the vector. Since our interest is in parallelism, we define machine size as the number of processors, and we assume that the individual node, its local cache and memory system, and the per-node communication capabilities remain the same as the machine scaled. Scaling up a machine means adding more identical nodes. For example, scaling a machine with p processors and $p \times m$ megabytes of total memory by a factor of k results in a machine with $k \times p$ processors and $k \times p \times m$ megabytes of total memory.

Problem size refers to a specific problem instance or input configuration. It is usually specified by a vector of input parameters, not just a single parameter n (e.g., an n-by-n grid in Ocean or n particles in Barnes-Hut). For example, in Ocean the problem size is specified by a vector $V = (n, \varepsilon, \Delta t, T)$, where n is the grid size in each dimension (which specifies the spatial resolution of our representation of the ocean), ε is the error tolerance used to determine convergence of the multigrid equation solver, Δt is the temporal resolution (i.e., the physical time between time-steps), and T is the number of time-steps performed. In a transaction processing system, problem size is specified by the number of terminals used, the rate at which users at the terminals issue transactions, the mix of transactions, and so on. Problem size is a major factor that determines the work done by the program.

Problem size should be distinguished from data set size. The *data set size* is the amount of storage that would be needed to run the program on a single processor. This is itself distinct from the *memory usage* of the program, which is the amount of memory used by the parallel program including replication. The data set size typically depends on a small number of program parameters. In Ocean, for example, the data set size is determined solely by the grid size n. The number of instructions and the execution time, however, depend on the other problem size parameters as well. Thus, while the problem size vector V determines many important properties of the application program—such as its data set size, the number of instructions it executes, and its execution time—it is not identical to any one of these properties.

4.1.3 Key Issues in Scaling

Given these definitions, there are two major questions to address when scaling a problem to run on a larger machine:

1. Under what constraints should the problem be scaled? To define a scaling model, some property must be kept fixed as the machine scales. These properties might include data set size, memory usage per processor, execution time, number of transactions executed per second, and number of particles or rows of a matrix assigned to each processor.
2. How should the problem be scaled? That is, how should the parameters in the problem size vector V be changed to meet the chosen constraints?

To simplify the discussion, we begin by pretending that the problem size is determined by a single parameter n and examine scaling models and their impact under this assumption. Later, in Section 4.1.6, we examine the more subtle issue of scaling workload parameters relative to one another.

4.1.4 Scaling Models and Speedup Measures

The properties used as the basis for scaling constraints can be divided into two categories: *user-oriented properties* and *resource-oriented properties*. Examples of user-oriented properties are the number of particles per processor in Barnes-Hut, the number of rows of a matrix per processor in a matrix multiplication program, the number of transactions issued to the system per processor in transaction processing, and the number of I/O operations performed per processor. Examples of resource-oriented constraints are execution time and the total amount of memory used per processor. Each of these constraints defines a distinct scaling model, since the amount of work done for a given number of processors is different when scaling is performed under different constraints. Whether user- or resource-oriented constraints are more appropriate depends on the application domain. A critical job in constructing benchmarks is to ensure that the scaling constraints are meaningful for the domain at hand.

User-oriented constraints are usually much easier to follow when performing evaluations (e.g., simply change the number of particles linearly with the number of processors). However, large-scale programs are often run under tight resource constraints, and resource constraints are more universal across application domains (time is time and memory is memory regardless of whether the program deals with particles or matrices). We will therefore use resource constraints to illustrate the effects of scaling models. Let us examine the three most popular resource-oriented models for the constraints under which an application should be scaled to run on a k times larger machine: *problem-constrained* (PC) *scaling*, *time-constrained* (TC) *scaling*, and *memory-constrained* (MC) *scaling*.

In PC scaling, the problem size is kept fixed; that is, it is not scaled at all, despite the concerns discussed earlier regarding a fixed problem size. The same input configuration is used regardless of the number of processors on the machine. In TC scaling, the wall-clock execution time needed to complete the program is held fixed. The problem is scaled so that the new problem's execution time on the large machine is the same as the old problem's execution time on the small machine (Gustafson 1988). In MC scaling, the amount of main memory used per processor is held fixed. The problem is scaled so that the new problem uses exactly k times as much main memory (including data replication) as the old problem. Thus, if the old problem just fit in the memory of the small machine, then the new problem will just fit in the memory of the large machine.

More specialized models are more appropriate in some domains. For example, in its commercial on-line transaction processing benchmark, the Transaction Processing Council (TPC) dictates a scaling rule in which the number of user terminals that generate transactions and the size of the database being accessed are scaled proportionally with the "computing power" of the system being evaluated, measured in a specified way. In this as well as in the TC and MC scaling models, scaling to meet resource constraints often requires some experimentation to find the appropriate input since resource usage may not scale in a simple way with input parameters. Memory usage is often quite predictable—especially if there is no need for replication in main memory—but it is difficult to predict the input configuration that would take the same execution time on 256 processors that another input configuration took on 16. Let us look at each of PC, TC, and MC scaling a little further and see what "work per unit of time," and hence speedup, translates to under them.

Problem-Constrained Scaling

The assumption in PC scaling is that a user wants to use the larger machine to solve the same problem faster. This is not an unusual situation. For example, if a video compression algorithm handles only one frame per second, our goal in using parallelism may not be to compress a larger image in 1 second but rather to compress 30 frames per second and hence achieve real-time compression for that frame size. As another example, if a VLSI routing tool takes a week to route a complex chip, we may be more interested in using additional parallelism to reduce the routing time rather than to route a larger chip. Since useful work in the work/time definition of performance remains fixed, the formulation of the speedup metric is simply

$$\text{Speedup}_{PC}(p \text{ processors}) = \frac{\text{Time}(1 \text{ processor})}{\text{Time}(p \text{ processors})} \tag{4.1}$$

Time-Constrained Scaling

This model assumes that users have a certain amount of time that they can wait for a program to execute, and they want to solve the largest possible problem in that fixed amount of time. (Think of a user who can afford to buy eight hours of computer time at a computer center or one who is willing to wait overnight for a run to complete but needs to have the results ready to analyze the next morning.) Whereas in PC scaling the problem size is kept fixed and the execution time varies, in TC scaling the problem size increases but the execution time is kept fixed. Since performance is work divided by time and since time stays fixed as the system is scaled, speedup can be measured as the increase in the amount of work done in that fixed execution time:

$$\text{Speedup}_{TC}(p \text{ processors}) = \frac{\text{Work}(p \text{ processors})}{\text{Work}(1 \text{ processor})} \tag{4.2}$$

The question is how to measure work. If we measure it as actual execution time for that problem configuration on a single processor, then we would have to run the larger (scaled) problem size on a single processor of the machine to obtain the numerator. Unfortunately, for interesting problems this is likely to thrash, take a long time, or be impossible to run.

Desirable properties for a work metric are that it should be easy to measure and as architecture independent as possible. Ideally, it should be easily modeled with an analytical expression based only on the application, and we should not have to perform any additional experiments to measure the work in the scaled-up problem. The measure of work should also scale linearly with sequential time complexity of the algorithm (see Example 4.1).

EXAMPLE 4.1 Why is the linear scaling property important for a work metric?

Answer The linear scaling property is important if we want the ideal speedup (ignoring memory system artifacts) to be proportional to the number of processors. To see this, suppose we use as our work metric in a matrix multiplication program the number of rows n in square matrices. Let us ignore memory system interactions completely. If the uniprocessor problem has n_0 rows, then its execution "time," or the number of multiplication operations it needs to execute, will be proportional to n_0^3. Since the problem is deterministic, the best we can hope p processors to do in the same time is $n_0^3 \times p$ operations, which corresponds to $(n_0 \times \sqrt[3]{p})$-by-$(n_0 \times \sqrt[3]{p})$ matrices. If we measure work as the number of rows, then the speedup according to Equation 4.2 even in this idealized case will be $(n_0 \times \sqrt[3]{p})/n_0$ or $\sqrt[3]{p}$ instead of p. Using the number of points in the matrix (n^2) as the work metric also does not work from this perspective, since it would result in an ideal time-constrained speedup of $p^{2/3}$. However, using n^3 (the number of multiplication operations) as the work metric leads to an ideal speedup of p, since this measure scales linearly with the $O(n^3)$ sequential time complexity of matrix multiplication. ■

The ideal work measure not only satisfies both of these properties but is also an intuitive parameter from a user's perspective. For example, in sorting integer keys using a method called radix sorting, the sequential complexity grows linearly with the number of keys to be sorted, so we can use keys as the measure of work. However, such a measure is difficult to find in real applications, particularly when multiple application parameters are scaled and affect execution time in different ways. So how should we measure work in practice?

If a single intuitive parameter that has the desirable properties cannot be found, we can try to find a measure that can be easily derived from an intuitive parameter and that scales linearly with the sequential complexity. The popular LINPACK benchmark, which performs matrix factorization, does this. It is known that the benchmark should take $2n^3/3$ floating-point operations to factorize an n-by-n matrix, and the rest of the operations are either proportional to or completely dominated by these. As with matrix multiplication in Example 4.1, this number of operations is easily computed from the input matrix dimension n and clearly satisfies the linear scaling property, so it is used as the measure of work for the benchmark.

Real applications often have multiple parameters to scale and are therefore more complex. As long as we have a well-defined rule for scaling parameters at the same time, we may be able to construct an analytical measure of work that has the desired properties. However, such work counts may no longer be simple or intuitive, and they ask a lot of the evaluator or the benchmark provider. Furthermore, analytical predictions are usually simplified in complex applications (e.g., they are the average case, or they do not reflect "implementation" activities that can be quite significant), so the actual growth rates of instructions or operations executed can be different than expected.

In such cases, a generally applicable, empirical technique is to run the sequential program and measure the work in machine operations. If a certain type of high-level operation, such as a particle-particle interaction, is known to always be directly proportional to the sequential complexity, then we can count the number of operations executed at run time. More generally, we may arrange to measure the time taken to run the problem on a uniprocessor, assuming that all memory references are cache hits and take the same amount of time (say, a single cycle), thus eliminating artifacts due to the memory system. This work measure reflects which machine instructions are actually executed when running the program, yet avoids the thrashing and superlinearity problems; we call it the *perfect-memory execution time*. (Notice that it corresponds very closely to the sequential *busy-useful* time introduced in Section 3.4.) Many computers have system utilities that allow computations to be profiled and to obtain this perfect-memory execution time. If not, we must resort to measuring how many times some high-level operation occurs.

Once we have a work measure, we can compute speedup under TC scaling as in Equation 4.2. However, determining the input configuration that yields the desired execution time and hence satisfies TC scaling may take some iterative refinement.

Memory-Constrained Scaling

This model is motivated by the assumption that the user wants to run the largest problem possible without overflowing the machine's memory, regardless of execution time. For example, it might be important for an astrophysicist to run an n-body simulation like Barnes-Hut with the largest number of bodies that the machine can accommodate in order to increase the resolution with which the bodies sample the universe. Results presented for MC scaling have often used a performance improvement metric called *scaled speedup*, which is defined as the ratio of the time that the larger (scaled) problem would take to run on a single processor to the time that it takes on the scaled machine. This metric is often attractive to vendors because such speedups tend to be high. Effectively, it measures the problem-constrained speedup on a very large problem, which tends to have a low communication-to-computation ratio and abundant concurrency and also to benefit from superlinearity effects due to memory and cache capacity. The scaled problem is not what we run on a uniprocessor anyway under MC scaling, so this is not an appropriate speedup metric.

Unlike the previous models, under MC scaling neither work nor execution time is held fixed. Using work divided by time as the performance metric as always, we can define speedup as

$$\text{Speedup}_{MC}(p \text{ processors}) = \frac{\text{Work}(p \text{ processors})}{\text{Time}(p \text{ processors})} \times \frac{\text{Time}(1 \text{ processor})}{\text{Work}(1 \text{ processor})}$$

$$= \frac{\text{Increase in Work}}{\text{Increase in Execution Time}} \tag{4.3}$$

If the increase in execution time were only due to the increase in work and not due to overheads of parallelism—and if there were no memory system artifacts, which are usually less likely under MC scaling—then the speedup would be p, which is what we want. Work is measured as discussed previously for TC scaling.

Since data set size grows faster under MC scaling than under other models, parallel overheads grow relatively slowly and speedups often tend to be better (ignoring capacity artifacts). MC scaling is indeed how many users desire to use a parallel machine. However, for many types of applications, MC scaling leads to a serious problem: the execution time (for the parallel execution) can become intolerably large. This problem can occur in any application where the work done grows more rapidly with problem size than the memory usage (see Example 4.2).

EXAMPLE 4.2 Matrix factorization is a simple example in which the serial work grows more rapidly than the memory usage. Show how MC scaling leads to a rapid increase in parallel execution time for this application.

Answer While the data set size and the memory usage for an n-by-n matrix grow as $O(n^2)$ in matrix factorization, the execution time on a uniprocessor grows as $O(n^3)$. Assume that a 10,000 × 10,000 matrix takes about 800 MB of memory and can be factorized in 1 hour on a uniprocessor. Now consider a scaled machine consisting of 1,000 processors. On this machine, under MC scaling we can factorize a 320,000 × 320,000 matrix since little or no replication is needed in main memory. However, the execution time of the parallel program (even assuming perfect, thousand-fold speedup) will now increase to about 32 hours. ■

Of the three models, time-constrained scaling is increasingly recognized as being the most generally viable. However, no model can be claimed to be the most realistic for all applications and all users. Different users have different goals, work under different constraints, and are in any case unlikely to follow a given model very strictly. Nonetheless, these three models are useful, comprehensive tools for an analysis of scaled performance as machines scale.

4.1.5 Impact of Scaling Models on the Equation Solver Kernel

Let us now examine a simple example—the equation solver kernel from Chapter 2—to see how it interacts with different scaling models and how they affect its architecturally relevant behavioral characteristics. For an n-by-n grid, the memory requirement of the simple equation solver is $O(n^2)$. Computational complexity is $O(n^2)$

times the number of iterations to convergence, which we can conservatively assume to be $O(n)$ (the number of iterations taken for values to flow from one boundary of the grid to the other). This leads to a sequential computational complexity of $O(n^3)$.

Consider the execution time and memory requirements under the three scaling models, assuming speedups due to parallelism equal to the number of processors p in all cases. With PC scaling, as the same n-by-n grid is divided among more processors p, the memory requirements per processor decrease linearly with p, as does the execution time. In TC scaling, the execution time stays the same by definition. Assuming linear speedup, this means that if the scaled grid size is k-by-k, then $k^3/p = n^3$, so $k = n \times \sqrt[3]{p}$. The amount of memory needed per processor is therefore

$$\frac{k^2}{p} = \frac{n^2}{\sqrt[3]{p}}$$

which diminishes as the cube root of the number of processors. Using MC scaling, by definition, the memory requirements per processor stay the same at $O(n^2)$ where the base grid for the single processor execution is n-by-n. This means that the overall size of the grid increases by a factor of p, so the scaled grid is now $n\sqrt{p}$-by-$n\sqrt{p}$ rather than n-by-n. Since it now takes $n\sqrt{p}$ iterations to converge, the sequential time complexity is $O((n\sqrt{p})^3)$. This means that even assuming perfect speedup due to parallelism, the execution time of the scaled problem on p processors is

$$O\left(\frac{(n\sqrt{p})^3}{p}\right)$$

or $n^3\sqrt{p}$. Thus, the parallel execution time is greater than the sequential execution time of the base problem by a factor of $\sqrt{p}$. Even under the linear speedup assumption, a problem that took 1 hour on one processor takes 32 hours on a 1,024-processor machine under MC scaling. For this simple equation solver, then, the execution time increases quickly under MC scaling, and the memory requirements per processor decrease under TC scaling.

Let us consider the effects of different scaling models on the concurrency, communication-to-computation ratio, synchronization and I/O frequency, temporal and spatial locality, and message size (in message passing).

The concurrency in this kernel is proportional to the number of grid points. It remains fixed under PC scaling, grows proportionally to p under MC scaling, and grows proportionally to $p^{0.67}$ under TC scaling.

The communication-to-computation ratio is the perimeter-to-area ratio of the grid partition assigned to each processor; that is, it is inversely proportional to the square root of the number of points per processor (n^2/p). Under PC scaling, the ratio grows as $\sqrt{p}$. Under MC scaling, the size of a partition does not change, so neither does the communication-to-computation ratio. Finally, under TC scaling, since the size of a processor's partition diminishes as the cube root of the number of processors, the ratio increases as the sixth root of p.

The equation solver synchronizes at the end of every grid sweep to determine convergence. Suppose that it also performed I/O then, for example, outputting the maximum error at the end of each sweep. Under PC scaling, the work done by each processor in a given sweep decreases linearly as the number of processors increases, so assuming linear speedup, the frequency of synchronization and I/O grows linearly with p. Under MC scaling the frequency remains fixed, and under TC scaling it increases as the cube root of p.

The size of the important working set, which indicates its temporal locality, in this equation solver is exactly the size of a processor's partition of the grid. Therefore, it and the cache requirements diminish linearly with p under PC scaling, stay constant under MC scaling, and diminish as the cube root of p under TC scaling. Thus, although the aggregate problem size grows under TC scaling, the working set size of each processor diminishes.

Spatial locality in the equation solver is best within a processor's partition and at row-oriented boundaries and worst at column-oriented boundaries. Thus, it decreases as a processor's partition becomes smaller and column-oriented boundaries become larger relative to partition area. It therefore remains constant under MC scaling, decreases quickly under PC scaling, and decreases less quickly under TC scaling.

Finally, an individual message in a message-passing model is likely to be a border row or column of a processor's partition, which is the square root of partition size. Hence, message size here scales similarly to the communication-to-computation ratio. The number of messages a process sends, however, depends only on the number of neighbor processes and is independent of n, p, or scaling model.

It is clear from the preceding discussion that as long as memory or cache capacity effects do not dominate, we should expect the lowest parallelism overhead and highest speedup under MC scaling and the next under TC scaling. We should expect speedups to degrade quite quickly under PC scaling, at least once the overheads become significant relative to useful work. It is also clear that the choice of application parameters and the scaling model greatly affect both fundamental program characteristics and architectural interactions with the extended memory hierarchy, such as spatial and temporal locality. Unless it is known that a particular scaling model is the right one for an application, or is particularly inappropriate, it is useful to evaluate a machine under all three scaling models. We examine the interactions with architectural parameters and their importance for evaluation in more detail when we discuss actual evaluations (Sections 4.2 and 4.3). First, let us take a brief look at the other important but more subtle aspect of scaling: how to scale application parameters to meet the constraints of a given scaling model.

4.1.6 Scaling Workload Parameters

In discussing the constraints under which problem size should be scaled, we made the simplifying assumption of a single application parameter n and did not examine how different application parameters that constitute the problem size vector should be scaled relative to one another to meet the chosen constraint. Let us now take away this simplifying assumption. For instance, the Ocean application has a vector of four parameters: n, ε, Δt, and T. How workload parameters should be scaled relative to one another is not an issue under PC scaling, but it is under TC or MC scaling. Different parameters are often related to one another, and it may not make sense to scale one of them without scaling others, or to scale them independently. For example, in a realistic usage of the Barnes-Hut application, the parameters θ (the force calculation accuracy) and Δt (the physical interval between time-steps) should be scaled as n (the number of bodies) changes. All of these parameters may contribute to a given execution characteristic; for example, the execution time of Barnes-Hut grows not simply as $n \log n$ but as

$$\frac{1}{\theta^2 \Delta t} n \log n$$

As a result, the increase in the number of bodies n under TC scaling is not as large as would be inferred by scaling only n.

Even the simple equation solver kernel has another parameter, ε, which is the tolerance used to determine convergence of the solver. Making this tolerance smaller—as should be done as n scales in a real application—increases the number of iterations needed for convergence and, hence, increases execution time, but it does not affect the memory requirements. Compared with scaling only n, scaling ε and n causes the per-process grid size, memory requirements, and working set size to decrease much more quickly under TC scaling, the communication-to-computation ratio to increase more quickly under TC scaling but still remain unchanged under MC scaling, and the execution time to increase even more quickly under MC scaling. As architects using workloads, it is very important that we understand the relationships among parameters from an application user's viewpoint and scale the parameters in our evaluations according to this understanding. Otherwise, we are liable to arrive at incorrect architectural conclusions.

The actual relationships among parameters and the rules for scaling them depend on the domain and the application. There are no universal rules, which makes good evaluation even more interesting. For example, in applications like Barnes-Hut and Ocean that model physical phenomena through discretization, the different application parameters usually govern different sources of error in the accuracy with which the phenomenon (such as galaxy evolution) is modeled; appropriate rules for scaling these parameters together are therefore driven by guidelines for scaling the different types of error. Ideally, benchmark suites will describe the scaling rules—and may even encode them in the application, leaving only one free parameter like n—so the architect as a user of the benchmarks does not have to worry about learning them. Exercises 4.12 and 4.13 illustrate the importance of proper application scaling by showing that scaling parameters appropriately can often lead to quantitatively and sometimes even qualitatively different architectural results than scaling only the data set size parameter n.

4.2 EVALUATING A REAL MACHINE

Now that we understand the importance of proper scaling and the effects that problem and machine size have on fundamental behavioral characteristics and architectural interactions, we are ready to develop specific guidelines for the two major types of workload-driven evaluation: evaluating a real machine and evaluating an architectural idea or trade-off in a general context. Evaluating a real machine is in many ways simpler: the organization, granularities, and performance parameters of the machine are fixed, and all we have to worry about is choosing appropriate workloads and workload parameters; also, we are not constrained by the limitations of software simulation. This section provides a prescriptive template for evaluating a real machine. We begin with the use of microbenchmarks to isolate performance characteristics. Then we look at the major issues in choosing workloads for an evaluation. This topic is followed by guidelines for evaluating a machine once a workload is chosen—first when the number of processors is fixed and then when it is allowed to be varied. The section concludes with a discussion of popular metrics for measuring the performance of a machine and for presenting the results of an evaluation. All these issues in evaluating a real machine are relevant to evaluating an architectural idea or trade-off as well.

4.2.1 Performance Isolation Using Microbenchmarks

A first step in evaluating a real machine is to understand its basic performance capabilities—that is, the performance characteristics of the primitive operations provided by the programming model, communication abstraction (user/system interface), or hardware/software interface. This is usually done with small, specially written programs called *microbenchmarks* (Saavedra, Gaines, and Carlton 1993) that are designed to isolate these performance characteristics (for example, latencies, bandwidths, overhead, etc.).

Five types of microbenchmarks are used in parallel systems; the first three are also used for uniprocessor evaluation:

1. *Processing microbenchmarks* measure the performance of the processor on operations that do not access memory, such as arithmetic operations, logical operations, and branches.
2. *Local memory microbenchmarks* determine the organization, latencies, and bandwidths of the levels of the memory hierarchy within the local node and measure the performance of local read and write operations satisfied at different levels, including those that cause TLB misses and page faults.
3. *Input-output microbenchmarks* measure the characteristics of I/O operations, such as disk reads and writes of various strides and lengths.

4. *Communication microbenchmarks* measure data communication operations, such as message sends and receives or remote reads and writes of different types.
5. *Synchronization microbenchmarks* measure the performance of different types of synchronization operations, such as locks and barriers.

The communication and synchronization microbenchmarks depend on the communication abstraction or programming model used. They may involve one or a pair of processors—for example, a single remote read miss, a send/receive pair, or the acquisition of a free lock—or they may be collective, such as broadcast, reduction, all-to-all communication, probabilistic communication patterns, many processors contending for a lock, or barriers. Different microbenchmarks may be designed to stress uncontended latency, bandwidth, overhead, and contention.

For measurement purposes, microbenchmarks are usually implemented as repeated sets of the primitive operations (e.g., 10,000 remote reads in a row). They often have simple parameters that can be varied to obtain a fuller characterization, for example, the number of participating processors in a collective communication microbenchmark or the stride between consecutive reads in a local memory microbenchmark. Figure 4.3 shows a typical profile of a machine obtained using a local memory microbenchmark. The main role of microbenchmarks is to isolate and understand the performance of basic system capabilities. A more ambitious hope, not achieved so far, is that if workloads can be characterized as weighted sums of different primitive operations, then a machine's performance on a given workload can be predicted from its performance on the corresponding microbenchmarks. We discuss some specific microbenchmarks and issues in designing them when we measure real systems in later chapters.

Having isolated the performance characteristics, the next step is to evaluate the machine on more realistic workloads. We must navigate three major axes: the workloads, their problem sizes, and the number of processors (or the machine size). Lower-level machine parameters are fixed. Let us begin with choosing workloads for an evaluation.

4.2.2 Choosing Workloads

Beyond microbenchmarks, workloads used for evaluation can be divided into three classes in increasing order of realism and complexity: kernels, complete applications, and multiprogrammed workloads. Each has its own role, advantages, and disadvantages.

Kernels are well-defined parts of real applications but are not complete applications themselves. They can range from simple kernels, such as a matrix transposition or a near-neighbor grid sweep, to more complex, substantial kernels that dominate the execution times of their applications, such as matrix factorization and iterative methods that solve partial differential equations. Examples of kernels for information processing include complex database queries used in decision support applications or sorting a set of numbers. Kernels expose higher-level interactions

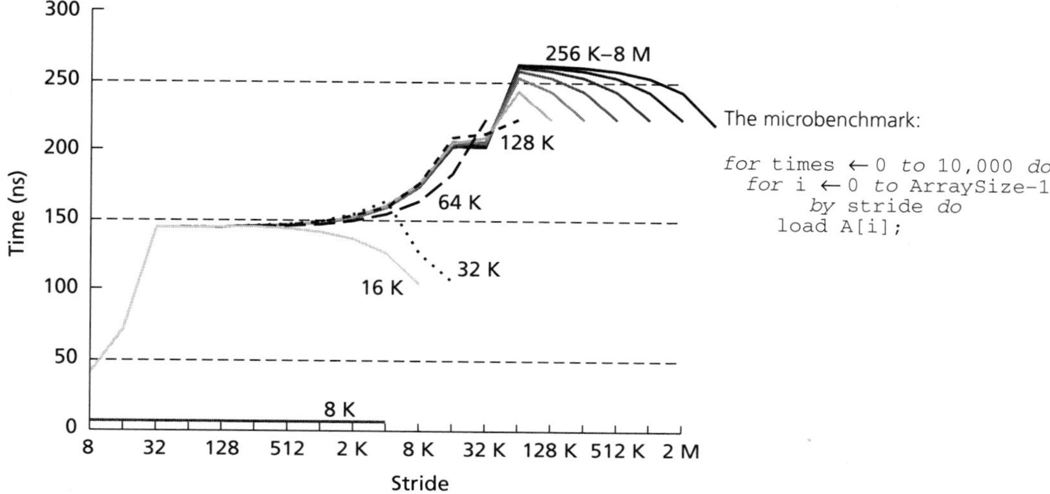

FIGURE 4.3 Results of a microbenchmark experiment on a single processing node of the CRAY T3D multiprocessor. Every processor has a small, single-level cache backed up by local main memory. The microbenchmark consists of a large number of reads from a local array. The *y*-axis shows the time per read in nanoseconds. The *x*-axis is the stride between successive reads in the loop (i.e., the difference in the addresses of the memory locations being accessed). The different curves correspond to and are labeled with the size of the array (`ArraySize`) being strided through. When `ArraySize` is less than 8 KB, the array fits in the processor cache so that all reads are hits and take 6.67 ns to complete. For larger arrays, we see the effects of cache misses. The average access time is the weighted sum of hit and miss time, until there is an inflection when the stride is longer than a cache block (32 words or 128 bytes) and every reference misses. The next rise occurs as a result of some references causing page faults, with an inflection when the stride is large enough (16 KB) that every consecutive reference causes a page fault. The final rise is due to conflicts at the memory banks in the four-bank main memory, with an inflection at 64-K stride when consecutive references always hit the same bank and the other banks remain idle.

that are not present in microbenchmarks and, as a result, lose a degree of performance isolation. Their key property is that their performance-relevant characteristics—communication-to-computation ratio, concurrency, and working sets, for example—can be easily understood and often analytically determined, so that observed performance as a result of the interactions can be explained in light of these characteristics.

Complete applications consist of multiple kernels and exhibit higher-level interactions among kernels that an individual kernel cannot reveal. Unlike kernels, complete applications are run by users to obtain an answer that they care to look at. The same large data structures may be accessed in different ways by multiple kernels in an application, and different data structures accessed by different kernels may interfere with one another in the memory hierarchy. In addition, the data structures that are optimal for a kernel in isolation may not be best in the complete application. The same holds for partitioning techniques. For example, if there are two independent kernels in an application, then we may decide not to partition each among all processes but rather to share processes among them. Different kernels that share a data structure may be partitioned in ways that strike a balance between their different access and communication patterns, leading to the maximum overall locality. The presence of multiple kernels in an application introduces many subtle interactions, and the performance-related characteristics of complete applications usually cannot be exactly determined analytically.

Multiprogrammed workloads consist of multiple sequential and parallel applications that run together on the machine. The different applications may either time-share the machine or *space-share* it (i.e., different applications run on disjoint subsets of the machine's processors) or both, depending on the operating system's multiprogramming policies. Just as whole applications are complicated by higher-level interactions among the kernels that comprise them, multiprogrammed workloads involve complex interactions among whole applications themselves.

As we move from kernels to complete applications and multiprogrammed workloads, we gain in realism, which is very important. Many critical bugs and performance problems are not revealed by microbenchmarks and even kernels but are discovered by these workloads. However, we lose in our ability to describe the workloads concisely, to explain and interpret the results unambiguously, and to isolate performance factors. In the extreme, multiprogrammed workloads are difficult not only to interpret but also to design: which applications should be included in such a workload and in what proportion? It is also difficult to obtain repeatable results from multiprogrammed workloads because of subtle timing-dependent interactions with the operating system. Each type of workload has its place. However, the higher-level interactions exposed only by complete applications and multiprogrammed workloads (and the fact that they are the workloads that will actually be run on the machine by users) make it important that we use them to ultimately determine the overall performance of a machine.

Let us examine the desirable properties in choosing such workloads (applications, multiprogrammed loads, and even complex kernels) for an evaluation. These properties include representativeness of application domains, coverage of behavioral properties, and adequate concurrency.

Representativeness of Application Domains

If we are performing an evaluation as users looking to procure a machine, and we know that the machine will be used to run only certain types of applications, then choosing a representative workload is easy. On the other hand, if the machine may be used to run a wide range of workloads, or if we are designers trying to evaluate a general-purpose machine to learn lessons for the next generation, we should choose a mix of workloads representative of a wide range of domains.

Some important domains for parallel computing today include scientific applications that model physical phenomena; engineering applications such as those in computer-aided design, digital signal processing, automobile crash simulation, and even simulations used to evaluate architectural trade-offs; graphics and visualization applications that render scenes or volumes into images; media processing applications such as image, video, and audio analysis and processing, and speech and handwriting recognition; information management applications such as databases, data mining, and transaction processing; optimization applications such as crew scheduling for an airline and transport control; artificial intelligence applications such as expert systems and robotics; multiprogrammed workloads; and a multiprocessor operating system, which is itself a complex parallel application.

Coverage of Behavioral Properties

Workloads may vary substantially along the entire range of performance-related characteristics discussed in Chapter 3. As a result, a major problem in evaluation is that it is very easy to lie with, or be misled by, workloads. For example, a study may choose workloads that stress the feature for which an architecture has an advantage (say, communication latency) but not those aspects it performs poorly (say, local access, contention, or communication bandwidth). For general-purpose evaluation, it is important that the workloads we choose, taken together, stress a range of important performance characteristics. For example, we should choose workloads with low and high communication-to-computation ratios, small and large working sets, regular and irregular access patterns, and localized and long-range or collective communication. If we are especially interested in evaluating particular architectural characteristics, such as aggregate bandwidth for all-to-all communication among processors, then we should choose at least some workloads that stress those characteristics.

Another important issue is the level of program optimization. Real parallel programs will not always be highly optimized for good performance along the lines discussed in Chapter 3, not just for the specific machine at hand but even in more general ways like reducing the communication-to-computation ratio or increasing temporal and spatial locality. This may be either because the effort involved in optimizing programs is more than the user is willing to expend or because the programs are generated with the help of automated parallelization tools. The level of optimization can greatly affect key execution characteristics and hence the degree to which architectural capabilities are stressed. In particular, four types of optimization are important to consider:

1. *Algorithmic*. The decomposition and assignment of tasks may be less than optimal—for example, strip-oriented versus block-oriented assignment for a grid computation (see Section 2.3.3)—and certain algorithmic enhancements for data locality, such as blocking, may not be implemented.
2. *Data structuring*. The data structures used may not interact optimally with the architecture, increasing artifactual communication—for example, two-dimensional versus four-dimensional arrays to represent a two-dimensional grid in a shared address space (see Section 3.3.1).

3. *Data layout, distribution, and alignment.* Even if appropriate data structures are used, they may not be distributed or aligned appropriately to pages or cache blocks, causing excess local traffic or artifactual communication.
4. *Orchestrating of communication and synchronization.* The resulting communication and synchronization may be structured in less than optimal ways—for example, sending small instead of large messages in message passing.

While optimizations can often be ad hoc, these categories impose some structure. Where appropriate, we should compare the robustness of machines or features to workloads with different levels of optimization.

Concurrency

The dominant performance bottleneck in a workload may be the computational load imbalance, either inherent to the partitioning method or due to the way synchronization is orchestrated (e.g., using barriers instead of point-to-point synchronization). If this is true, then the workload may not be appropriate for evaluating a machine's communication architecture since the architecture can do little about this bottleneck; even great improvements in communication performance may not affect overall performance much. In order to evaluate communication architectures, we should ensure that our workloads and their problem sizes exhibit adequate concurrency and load balance. A useful concept here is that of *algorithmic speedup*—the speedup that assumes that all memory references and communication operations take zero time (see the discussion of the PRAM architectural model in Chapter 3). By completely ignoring the performance impact of data access and communication, algorithmic speedup measures the computational load balance in the workload, together with the extra work done in the parallel program.

In general, we should isolate performance limitations due to workload characteristics that a machine cannot do much about from those that it can. It is also important that the workload take long enough to run to be realistic for a machine of the size being evaluated, though both this and concurrency are often more a function of the input problem size than of the workload itself.

Many efforts have been made to define standard benchmark suites of parallel applications to facilitate workload-driven architectural evaluation, taking some of the preceding criteria into account. The benchmark suites cover different application domains and have different philosophies; some of them are described in the Appendix. While the workloads used for the illustrative evaluations in the book are a very limited set, they are chosen with the preceding criteria in mind. For now, let us assume that a particular parallel program has been chosen as a workload and see how we might use it to evaluate a real machine. First the number of processors is kept fixed, which both simplifies the discussion and exposes the important interactions more cleanly. Then the number of processors is varied.

4.2.3 Evaluating a Fixed-Size Machine

Having fixed the workload and the machine size, we only have to choose the workload parameters. We have already seen that, for a fixed number of processors, changing the problem size can dramatically affect all the important execution characteristics and hence the results of an evaluation. In fact, it may even change the nature of the dominant bottleneck—that is, whether it is communication, load imbalance, or local data access. This already tells us a most significant but often ignored point: it is usually insufficient to use only a single problem size in an evaluation, even when the number of processors is fixed.

We can use our understanding of application-architecture interactions to choose problem sizes for a study. Our goal is to obtain adequate coverage of realistic inherent behaviors and architectural interactions while at the same time restricting the number of problem sizes we need. We do this in a set of structured steps, demonstrating the pitfalls of choosing only a single size in the process. The discussion will proceed one step at a time. In each step, the simple equation solver kernel will be used to illustrate the issues quantitatively. For the quantitative illustration, let us assume that we are evaluating a cache-coherent shared address space machine with 64 single-processor nodes, each with 1 MB of cache and 64 MB of main memory. The steps are as follows.

Step 1: Determine a Range of Problem Sizes

One way to choose problem sizes, applicable in some fortunate cases, is to appeal to higher powers. The high-level goals of the study may choose the problem sizes for us. For example, we may know that users of the machine are interested in only a few specified problem sizes. This simplifies our job but is uncommon and is not a general-purpose methodology. It does not apply to the equation solver kernel.

Knowledge of real usage may identify a range below which problems are unrealistically small for the machine at hand and above which the execution time is too large or users would not be interested. This too is not particularly useful for the equation solver kernel. Once we have identified a range, we can go on to the next step.

Step 2: Use Inherent Behavioral Characteristics

Inherent behavioral characteristics (such as communication-to-computation ratio and load balance) help us further restrict the range and choose problem sizes within the selected range. Since the inherent communication-to-computation ratio usually decreases with increasing data set size, large problems may not stress the communication architecture enough—at least with inherent communication—whereas small problems may stress it unrepresentatively and potentially hide other bottlenecks. Since concurrency usually increases with data set size, we would like to choose at least some problem sizes that are large enough to be load balanced but not so large that the inherent communication becomes too small (see Example 4.3). The size of the problem may also affect the fractions of execution time spent in different phases of the application, which may have very different load balance, synchronization, and communication characteristics. For example, in the Barnes-Hut application case study, smaller problems cause more of the time to be spent in the tree-building phase, which doesn't parallelize very well and has less desirable properties than the force calculation phase that usually dominates in practice. We should be careful not to choose unrepresentative scenarios in this regard.

EXAMPLE 4.3 How would you use inherent behavioral characteristics to select a range of problem sizes for the equation solver kernel?

Answer For this kernel, enough work and load balance might dictate that we have partitions that are at least 32 × 32 points. For a machine with 64 (8 × 8) processors, this means a total grid size of at least 256 × 256. This grid size requires the communication of 4 × 32, or 128, grid points per process in each iteration for a computation of 32 × 32 or 1 K points. At five floating-point operations and 8 bytes per grid point, this is an inherent communication-to-computation ratio of 1 byte every five floating-point operations. Assuming a processor that can deliver 200 MFLOPS on this calculation, this implies a bandwidth requirement of 40 MB/s. This is quite small for modern multiprocessor networks, even if it is bursty. Let us assume that below 5 MB/s communication is asymptotically small for our system. From the viewpoint of inherent properties only, there is no need to run problems larger than 256 × 256 points (only 64 K × 8 B or 512 KB of data) per processor, or 2 K × 2 K grids overall. ■

Inherent characteristics like load balance and communication vary smoothly with problem size, so to deal with them alone, we can pick a few sizes that span the interesting spectrum. If their rate of change is very slow, we may not need to choose many sizes. Experience shows that about three is a good number in most cases. For example, for the equation solver kernel we might have chosen 256 × 256, 1 K × 1 K, and 2 K × 2 K grids.

On the other hand, the interactions of temporal and spatial locality with the architecture exhibit thresholds in their performance effects, including the generation of artifactual communication as problem size changes. We may need to extend our choice of problem sizes to obtain enough coverage with respect to these thresholds. At the same time, the threshold nature can help us prune the parameter space. The next step in choosing problem sizes is to examine temporal locality and working sets.

Step 3: Use Temporal Locality and Working Sets

Working sets fitting or not fitting in a local cache or replication store can dramatically affect execution characteristics, such as local memory traffic and artifactual communication, even if the inherent communication and computational load balance do not change much. In applications like Raytrace, the important working sets are large and consist of data that is mostly assigned to remote nodes, so artifactual communication due to limited replication capacity may dominate inherent communication. This artifactual communication tends to grow rather than diminish with increasing problem size. In other applications (like Ocean), working sets not fitting in the cache can generate dramatically more local memory traffic instead of artifactual communication. We should include problem sizes that represent both sides of the threshold (fitting and not fitting) for the important working sets if such problem sizes are realistic in practice. In fact, when realistic for the application, we should also include a problem size that is very large for the machine, for example, one that almost fills the memory, even though this problem size may be uninteresting from the viewpoints of load balance and inherent communication. Large problems often exercise architectural and operating system interactions that smaller problems do not, such as TLB misses, page faults, and a large amount of traffic due to cache capacity misses. Examples 4.4 and 4.5 help illustrate how we might choose problem sizes based on working sets.

EXAMPLE 4.4 Suppose that an application has the miss rate versus cache size curve shown in Figure 4.4(a) for a fixed problem size and number of processors and for the lowest-level cache in a node of our machine (i.e., the cache that is farthest from the processor and closest to memory). If C is the cache size, how should this curve influence the choice of problem sizes used to evaluate the machine?

Answer We can see from Figure 4.4(a) that for the problem size (and number of processors) shown, the first working set fits in the cache of size C, the second fits only partially, and the third does not fit. Each of these working sets scales with problem size in its own way. This scaling determines at what problem size that working set might no longer fit in a cache of size C and therefore what problem sizes we should choose to cover the representative cases. In fact, if the curve truly consists of sharp knees, then we can draw a different type of curve, this time one for each important working set. This curve, shown in Figure 4.4(b), depicts whether or not that working set fits in our cache of size C as the problem size changes. If the problem size at which a knee in this curve occurs is within the range of problem sizes that we have determined to be realistic, then we should ensure that we include a problem size on each side of that knee. Not doing this may cause us to miss important effects related to stressing the memory or communication architecture. The fact that the curves are flat on both sides of a knee in this example means that if all we care about from the cache is the miss rate, then we need to choose only one problem size on each side of each knee for this purpose and can prune out the rest.[1] ■

EXAMPLE 4.5 How might working sets influence our choice of problem sizes for the equation solver?

Answer The most important working sets for the equation solver are encountered when two subrows of a partition fit in the cache and when a processor's entire partition fits in the cache. Both are very sharply defined in this simple kernel. Even with the largest grid we chose based on inherent communication-to-computation ratio (2 K × 2 K), the data set size per processor is only 0.5 MB, so both of these

---

1. Pruning a flat region of the miss rate curve is not necessarily appropriate if we also care about aspects of cache behavior other than miss rate that are also affected by cache size. We shall see an example when we discuss trade-offs among cache coherence protocols in Chapter 5.

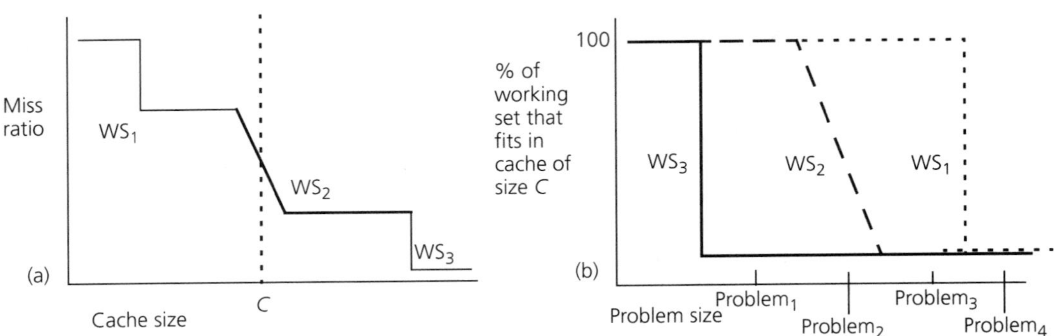

FIGURE 4.4 Choosing problem sizes based on working sets fitting in the cache. The graph in (a) shows the miss rate versus cache size curve for a fixed problem size with our chosen number of processors. C is the size of the cache or replication store under consideration. This curve identifies three knees or working sets, two very sharply defined and one less so. The graph in (b) shows, for each of the working sets, a curve depicting whether or not they fit in the cache of size C as the problem size increases. A knee in a curve represents the problem size at which that working set no longer fits. We can see that a problem of size $Problem_1$ fits WS_1 and WS_2 but not WS_3, $Problem_2$ fits WS_1 and part of WS_2 but not WS_3, $Problem_3$ fits WS_1 only, and $Problem_4$ does not fit any working set in the cache.

working sets fit comfortably in the cache (if a 4D array representation is used, there are essentially no conflict misses). Thus, we may need to choose some larger problem sizes as well. For the first working set of two subrows to exceed a 1-MB cache would imply a subrow of 64 K points, so a total grid of 64 K $\times \sqrt{64}$ or 512 K rows (or columns) for our 64-processor machine. This is a data set of 32 GB per processor, which is far too large to be realistic. However, having the other important working set—a process's whole partition—not fit in a 1-MB cache is realistic. It leads to either a lot of local memory traffic or a lot of artifactual communication (if data is not placed properly) and we would like to represent such a situation. We can do this by choosing a problem size of, say, 512×512 points (2 MB) per processor or 4 K $\times$ 4 K points overall. This does not come close to filling the machine's memory, so we might choose one more problem size for that purpose, say, 16 K $\times$ 16 K points overall or 32 MB per processor. We now have five problem sizes: 256×256, 1 K $\times$ 1 K, 2 K $\times$ 2 K, 4 K $\times$ 4 K, and 16 K $\times$ 16 K. ■

Step 4: Use Spatial Locality

Suppose that the data structure used to represent the grid in a shared address space implementation of the equation solver kernel is a two-dimensional array. A processor's partition, which is its important working set, may not remain in its cache across grid sweeps. Even if cache capacity is sufficient, cache conflicts may be quite frequent since the subrows of a processor's partition are not contiguous in the address space. In either case, if the working set does not fit, then it is important that a processor's partition be allocated in its local memory on a distributed-memory machine. The granularity of allocation in main memory is a page, which is typically 4–16 KB. If the size of a subrow is less than the page size, proper allocation becomes very dif-

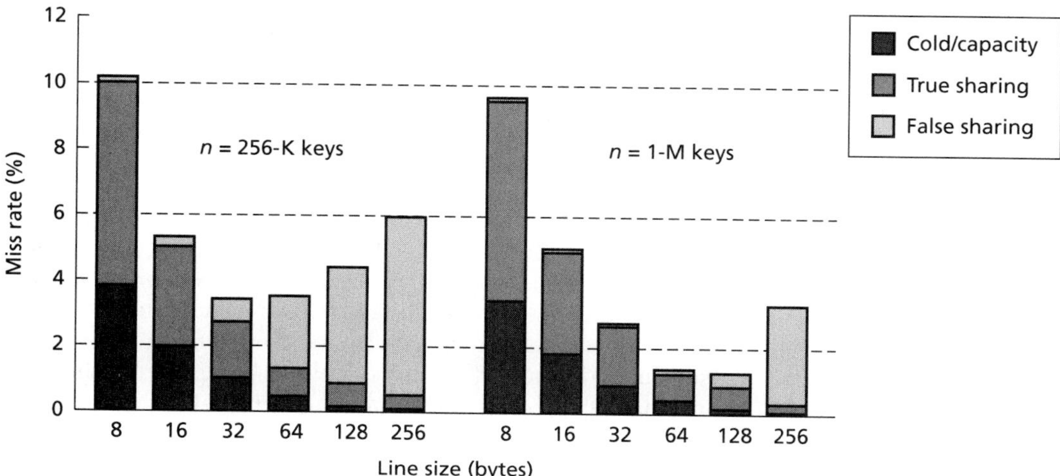

FIGURE 4.5 Impact of problem size and number of processors on the spatial locality behavior of Radix sorting. The miss rate is broken down into cold/capacity misses, true sharing (inherent communication) misses, and misses due to false sharing of data. As the block size increases for a given problem size and number of processors, there comes a point when the critical ratio discussed in the text becomes smaller than a threshold multiple of block size, and substantial false sharing is experienced. This threshold effect occurs at different block sizes for different problem sizes. A similar effect would have been observed if the problem size were kept constant and the number of processors changed.

ficult and a lot of artifactual communication may result. However, if a subrow is a multiple of the page size, allocation is not a problem and there is little artifactual communication. Both scenarios may be realistic, so we should try to represent both. If the page size is 4 KB, the first three problem sizes we have chosen so far have a subrow smaller than 4 KB, so they cannot be distributed properly; the last two have subrows greater than or equal to 4 KB, so they can be distributed well provided the grid is aligned to a page boundary. Thus, we do not need to expand our set of problem sizes for this purpose. With a 4D array representation of the grid, a process's partition of the grid is contiguous in the address space, so proper allocation is easy when partitions are large enough to make it necessary.

A more stark example of spatial locality interactions is found in a different program and architectural interaction. The program, called Radix, is a sorting program described later in this chapter, and the architectural interaction, called false sharing, was defined in Chapter 3 and is discussed further in Chapter 5. However, it is useful to look at the result here to illustrate the importance of considering spatial interactions in our choice of problem sizes. Figure 4.5 shows how the miss rate for this program running on a cache-coherent shared address space machine changes with cache block size for two different problem sizes n (sorting 256-K integers and 1-M integers) using the same number of processors p. The false sharing component of the miss rate tends to increase with cache block size. When it becomes significant, it leads to a lot of artifactual communication and can destroy the performance of this application. For the given cache block size on our machine, false sharing may or may not destroy the performance of radix sorting depending on the problem size (compare the bars for 64-byte blocks). It turns out that for a given cache block size, false sharing is large if the ratio of problem size to number of processors is smaller than a certain threshold and insignificant if it is bigger.

Many applications display these threshold effects in spatial locality interactions with problem size; in others, especially in many irregular applications, like Barnes-Hut and Raytrace, the data structures and access patterns are such that spatial locality does not increase much with problem size. Identifying the presence of such thresholds requires understanding the application's locality and its interaction with architectural parameters and illustrates some of the subtleties in evaluation.

To summarize, the simple equation solver illustrates the dependence of many execution characteristics on problem size, some exhibiting knees on threshold in interaction with architectural parameters and some not. With n-by-n grids and p processes, if the ratio n/p is large, then the communication-to-computation ratio is low, important working sets are unlikely to fit in the processor caches leading to a high-capacity miss rate, but spatial locality is good even with a two-dimensional array representation. The situation is the opposite when n/p is small: high communication-to-computation ratio, poor spatial locality and false sharing (with the 2D representation), and few local capacity misses. The dominant performance bottleneck thus changes from local access in one case to communication in the other. Figure 4.6 illustrates these effects for the Ocean application as a whole, which uses kernels similar to the equation solver.

Other applications may exhibit different specific dependences on problem size. While there are no universal formulas for choosing problem sizes to evaluate a machine, and the equation solver kernel is a trivial example, the steps presented in this chapter provide a useful methodology and should ensure that the results obtained for a machine are not due to artifacts that can be easily removed in the program. If we are to compare two machines, it is useful to choose problem sizes that exercise the preceding scenarios on both machines. Despite the variety of issues to consider, experience shows that the number of problems sizes needed to evaluate a fixed-size machine with an application is usually quite small since there are only a few important thresholds.

4.2.4 Varying Machine Size

Now suppose we want to evaluate the machine's performance as the number of processors changes. We have already seen how to scale the problem size under different scaling models and what metrics to use for performance improvement due to parallelism. The issue that remains is how to choose the problem size, at some machine size, as a starting point from which to scale. One strategy is to start from the problem sizes we chose previously for a fixed number of processors and scale each of them up or down according to the different scaling models. We may narrow down our range of base problem sizes to three—a small, a medium, and a large—which with three

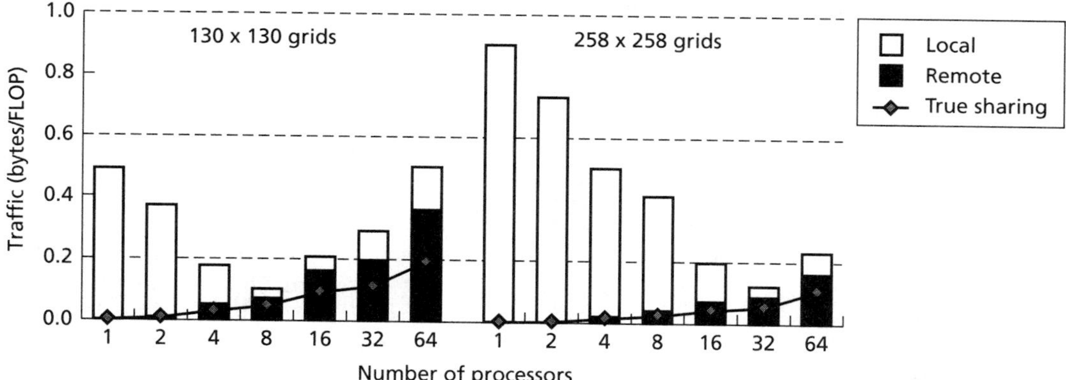

FIGURE 4.6 Effects of problem size, number of processors, and working set fitting in the cache. This figure shows the effects on the memory behavior of the Ocean application in a shared address space. The cache miss traffic (in bytes per floating-point operation or FLOP) is broken down into traffic that is local or contained in the node and traffic that is remote or traverses the network (i.e., communication). The traffic due to true sharing of data (inherent communication) is also shown separately. Remote traffic increases with the number of processors and decreases from the smaller problem to the larger. As the number of processors increases for a given problem size, the working set starts to fit in the cache, and a domination by local misses is replaced by a domination by communication. This change occurs at a larger number of processors for the larger problem since the working set is proportional to n^2/p. If we focus on the 8-processor breakdown for the two problem sizes, we see that for the small problem the traffic is dominantly remote (since the working set fits in the cache), whereas for the larger problem it is dominantly local.

scaling models will result in nine sets of performance data and speedup curves. However, it may require care to ensure that the problem sizes, when scaled down, stress the capabilities of smaller machines.

An alternative strategy is to start with a few well-chosen problem sizes on a uniprocessor and scale up under all three models. Here too, it is reasonable to choose three uniprocessor problem sizes. The small problem should be such that its working set fits in the cache on a uniprocessor. This problem will not be very useful under PC scaling on large machines but should remain fine under MC and perhaps even TC scaling. The large problem should be such that its important working set does not fit in the cache on a uniprocessor, if this is realistic for the application. Under PC scaling, the working set may fit at some point (if it shrinks with an increasing number of processors), whereas under MC scaling it is less likely to fit and is likely to keep generating capacity traffic. A reasonable choice for a large problem is one that fills most of the memory on a single node or takes a large amount of time on it. Thus, it will continue to almost fill the memory even on large systems under MC scaling. The medium-sized problem can be chosen in some judicious way in between; if possible, even it should take a substantial amount of time on the uniprocessor. The outstanding issue is how to explore PC scaling for problem sizes that don't fit in a single node's memory without experiencing superlinear speedup problems. Here the solution is to simply choose such a problem size and measure speedup not relative to a single processor but relative to a number of processors for which the problem indeed fits in memory.

4.2.5 Choosing Performance Metrics

An important question in evaluating or comparing machines is the specific metrics that should be used. Just as it is easy to mislead by not choosing workloads and parameters appropriately, it is also easy to convey the wrong impression by not measuring and presenting results in meaningful ways. In general, both cost and performance are important metrics for comparing machines or evaluating performance. And in evaluating how well a machine scales as resources (for example, processors and memory) are added, it is not only how performance increases that matters but also how cost increases. Even if speedup increases much less than linearly, if the cost of the resources needed to run the program doesn't increase much more quickly than that, then it may indeed be cost-effective to use the larger machine (Wood and Hill 1995). Overall, some measure of "cost-performance" is more appropriate than simply performance. However, cost and performance can be measured separately, and cost is very dependent on the marketplace. The focus here is therefore on metrics for measuring performance.

Absolute performance and performance improvement due to parallelism are both useful metrics. Here, we examine the subtler issues in using these metrics to evaluate and especially compare machines and consider the role of other metrics that are based on processing rate (e.g., megaflops), resource utilization, and problem size rather than directly on work and time. Some metrics are clearly important and should always be presented, whereas the utility of others depends on what we are after and the environment in which we operate.

Absolute Performance

To a user of a system the absolute performance is the performance metric that matters the most. Suppose that execution time is our metric for absolute performance. Time can be measured in different ways. First, there is a choice between user time and wall-clock time for a workload. *User time* is the time the machine spends executing the workload, excluding system activity and other programs that might be time-sharing the machine; *wall-clock time* is the total elapsed time for the workload—including all intervening activity. Second, there is the issue of whether to use the average or the maximum execution time over all processes of the program.

Since users ultimately care about wall-clock time, we must measure and present this when comparing systems. However, if other user programs—not just the operating system—interfere with a program's execution as a result of multiprogramming, then wall-clock time does not help us understand performance bottlenecks. Note that user time for that program may not be very useful in this case either, since interleaved execution with unrelated processes disrupts the memory system interactions of the program as well as its synchronization and load balance behavior. We should therefore always present wall-clock time and describe the execution environment (batch or multiprogrammed), whether or not we present more detailed information geared toward enhancing understanding. And if we want to understand performance on a particular application, we should run it in isolation with only the operating system perhaps intervening.

Similarly, since a parallel program is not finished until the last process has terminated, it is the time to this point that is important, not the average over processes. Averages tend to deemphasize imbalances. Of course, if we truly want to understand performance bottlenecks, we would like to see the execution profiles of all processes—or at least a sample—broken down into different components of time (Figure 3.12, for example). The components of execution time tell us why one system outperforms another and whether the workload is appropriate for the investigation (e.g., is not limited by load imbalance).

Performance Improvement or Speedup

A question in measuring speedup for any scaling model is what the denominator in the speedup ratio—the performance on one processor—should actually measure. We have four choices:

1. Performance of the parallel program on one processor of the parallel machine
2. Performance of a sequential implementation of the same algorithm on one processor of the parallel machine
3. Performance of the "best" sequential algorithm and program for the same problem on one processor of the parallel machine
4. Performance of the "best" sequential program on an agreed-upon standard machine

The difference between (1) and (2) is that the parallel program incurs overhead even when run on a uniprocessor, since it executes synchronization operations, parallelism management instructions, or partitioning code, or even the tests to omit these. This overhead can sometimes be significant. The distinction between (2) and (3) is that the best sequential algorithm may not be possible or easy to parallelize effectively, so the algorithm used in the parallel program may be different from the best sequential algorithm.

Using performance as defined by (3) clearly leads to a better and more accurate speedup metric than (1) and (2) from a user's perspective. From an architect's point of view, however, in many cases it may be okay to use definition (2). Definition (4) fuses the machine's uniprocessor performance back into the picture and thus results in a comparison metric that is similar to absolute performance.

Processing Rate

A metric that is often quoted to characterize the performance of machines is the number of computer operations that they execute per unit time (as opposed to operations that have meaning at the application level, such as transactions or chemical bonds). Classic examples are MFLOPS (millions of floating-point operations per second) for floating-point-intensive programs and MIPS (millions of instructions per second) for general programs. Much has been written about why these are not good general metrics for performance even though they are popular in the marketing literature of vendors. The basic reason is that, unless we use an unambiguous machine-independent measure of the number of FLOPs or instructions that are fundamentally needed to solve a problem, rather than the number actually executed, these measures can be artificially inflated: inferior, brute-force algorithms that perform many more FLOPs and take much longer may produce higher MFLOPS ratings. In fact, we can even inflate the metric by artificially inserting useless but cheap operations in the code. If the number of operations needed is unambiguously known, then using these rate-based metrics is no different from using execution time. Other problems with MFLOPS include that different floating-point operations have different costs; that even in FLOP-intensive applications, modern algorithms use smarter data structures that have many integer operations; and that these metrics are burdened with a legacy of misuse (e.g., for publishing peak hardware rates rather than rates achieved on actual applications). When used appropriately, rate-based metrics like MFLOPS and MIPS may be useful for understanding basic hardware capabilities; however, we should be very wary of using them as the main indication of a machine's performance.

Utilization

Architects sometimes measure success by how well they are able to keep their processing engines busy executing instructions rather than stalled as a result of various overheads. It should be clear by now, however, that processor utilization is not a metric of interest to a user and not a good sole performance metric. It too can be arbitrarily inflated, is biased toward slower processors, and does not say much about end performance or performance bottlenecks. However, it may be useful as a starting point to decide whether to start looking more deeply for performance problems in a program or machine. Similar arguments hold for the utilization of other resources; utilization is useful for determining whether a machine design is balanced among resources and where the bottlenecks are, but it is not useful for measuring and comparing performance.

Problem Size

Another interesting metric is the smallest problem size of a given application that obtains a specified *parallel efficiency*, which is defined as speedup divided by number of processors (under a given scaling model). Since overheads due to parallelism generally decrease with problem size, the benefit of an improved communication architecture can often be seen in the ability to run smaller problems well. Keeping parallel efficiency fixed as the number of processors increases, in a sense, introduces a new scaling model that we might call *efficiency-constrained scaling.* Of course, this metric must be used with care since capacity effects may dominate communication differences and small problems may fail to stress important aspects of the system. Parallel efficiency is useful but is not a general performance metric.

Percentage Improvement in Performance

A metric that is sometimes used to evaluate the improvement in performance due to an architectural feature is the percentage improvement in execution time or speedup delivered by the feature. Without mention of the original parallel performance (e.g., the original speedup), this metric can be misleading in parallel systems. For example, improving the speedup from 400 to 800 on a 1,024-processor system is the same percentage improvement as improving speedup from 1.1 to 2.2, but the latter is unlikely to be interesting for a 1,024-processor system. If problem size is the reason for poor speedup, then it is often the case that increasing the problem size to yield decent speedup often dramatically reduces the improvement achieved by the feature. Here too, the metric has value but must be supplemented with other metrics to avoid misleading.

In summary, both cost and performance are important to consider. From a user's viewpoint in comparing machines, the performance metric of greatest interest is wall-clock execution time. However, from the viewpoint of an architect, or of a programmer trying to understand a program's performance, or even of a user interested more generally in a machine's performance aspects, it is best to look at both execution time and speedup. Both of these metrics should be presented in the results of any study. Ideally, execution time should be broken up into its major components as discussed in Section 3.4. To understand performance bottlenecks, it is very useful to see these component breakdowns on a per-process basis or as an average and some measure of dispersion over processes (simply an average is not enough). In evaluating the impact of changes to the communication architecture, or in comparing parallel machines based on equivalent underlying nodes, size- or configuration-based metrics like the minimum problem size needed to achieve a certain goal can be useful. Metrics like MFLOPS, MIPS, and processor utilization can be used for specialized purposes, but using only them to represent performance requires a lot of assumptions about the knowledge and integrity of the presenter, and they are burdened with a legacy of misuse.

4.3 EVALUATING AN ARCHITECTURAL IDEA OR TRADE-OFF

Imagine that you are an architect at a computer company, getting ready to design the next-generation multiprocessor. You have a new architectural idea that you would like to decide whether or not to include in the machine. You may have a wealth of information about performance and bottlenecks from the previous-generation machine, which in fact may have been what prompted you to pursue this idea in the first place. However, your idea and this data are not all that is new. Technology has changed since the last machine, ranging from the level of integration to the cache sizes and organizations used by microprocessors. The processor you will use may be not only a lot faster but also a lot more sophisticated (e.g., four-way issue and dynamically scheduled versus single issue and statically scheduled), and it may have new capabilities that affect the idea at hand. The operating system has likely changed too, as has the compiler and perhaps even the workloads of interest, and these software components may change further by the time the machine is actually built and sold. The feature you are interested in has a significant cost in hardware and particularly in design time. And you have deadlines to contend with.

In this sea of change, the relevance of the data that you have for making decisions about performance and cost is questionable. At best, you could use it together with your intuition to make informed and educated guesses. But if the cost of the feature is high, you probably want to do more. What you can do is to build a simulator that models your system. You fix everything else—the compiler, the operating system, the processor, the technological and architectural parameters—to their expected configurations and simulate the system with the feature of interest absent and then present to judge its performance impact. Then perhaps you examine the sensitivity to some of the aspects that you had held fixed, but that may not be so predictable.

Building accurate simulators for parallel systems is difficult. Many complex interactions in the extended memory hierarchy are difficult to model correctly, particularly those having to do with resource occupancy and contention. Processors themselves are becoming much more complex, and accurate simulation demands that they, too, be modeled in detail. However, even if you can design a very accurate simulator that mimics your design, you still have a big problem. Simulation is expensive; it takes a lot of memory and time, especially when larger problems and machines are simulated. The implication is that you cannot simulate life-sized problem and machine sizes, and you will have to scale down your simulations somehow.

Even your technological parameters may not be fixed. You are starting with a clean slate and want to know how well the idea would work with different technological assumptions. Now, in addition to the earlier axes of workload, problem size, and machine size, the parameters of the machine are also variable. These parameters include the sizes and organizations of the levels in the local memory hierarchy; the granularities of allocation, communication, and coherence; and the performance characteristics of the communication architecture, such as latency, occupancy, and bandwidth. These parameters, together with those of the workload, lead to a vast parameter space that you must navigate. The high cost and the limitations of simulation make it all the more important that you prune this design space while not losing too much coverage. This section discusses the methodological considerations in choosing parameters and pruning the design space for simulation studies, using a particular evaluation as an example. First, let us take a quick look at multiprocessor simulation.

4.3.1 Multiprocessor Simulation

Although multiple processes and processing nodes are being simulated, the simulation itself may be run on a single processor. A *reference generator* plays the role of the processors on the parallel machine. It simulates the activities of the processors and issues memory references (together with a process identifier that tells which processor the reference is from) or commands (such as send or receive) to a simulator of the memory system and interconnection network (see Figure 4.7). If the simulation is being run on a uniprocessor, the different simulated processes time-share the uniprocessor, scheduled by the reference generator. One example of scheduling would be to deschedule a process every time it issues a reference to the memory system simulator and allow another process to run until that process issues its next reference; another example would be to reschedule processes every simulated clock cycle. The memory system simulator simulates all the caches and main memories on the different processing nodes, as well as the interconnection network itself. It can be arbitrarily complex in its simulation of datapaths, latencies, and contention.

The coupling between the reference generator (processor simulator) and the memory system simulator can be organized in various ways, depending on the accuracy needed in the simulation and the complexity of the processor model. One option is *trace-driven simulation*. In this case, a trace of the instructions executed by each process is first obtained by running the parallel program on one system, perhaps a different system than the one being evaluated. This trace takes the place of the reference generator: instructions from the trace are fed into the simulator that simulates the extended memory hierarchy of the target multiprocessor. Here, the coupling or flow of information is only in one direction: from the reference generator (here just a trace) to the memory system simulator.

The more popular form of simulation is *execution-driven simulation*, which provides coupling in both directions. In execution-driven simulation, when the memory system simulator receives a reference or command from the reference generator (which is now a program rather than a predetermined trace), it simulates the path of the reference through the extended memory hierarchy—including contention with other references—and returns to the reference generator the time that the reference took to be satisfied. This information, together with concerns about fairness and preserving the semantics of synchronization events, is used by the reference generator program to determine which simulated process to schedule next and when to issue the next instruction from that process. Thus, feedback takes place from the memory system simulator to the reference generator, influencing the activity of the latter as in a real machine and providing more accuracy than trace-driven simulation. To allow for maximum concurrency in simulating events and references, most components of the memory system and network are also modeled as separate communicating threads scheduled by the simulator. A global notion of *simulated time*—that is, the virtual time that would have been seen by the simulated machine, not real time that the simulator itself runs for—is maintained by the simulator. It is this time that we look up in determining the performance of workloads on the simulated

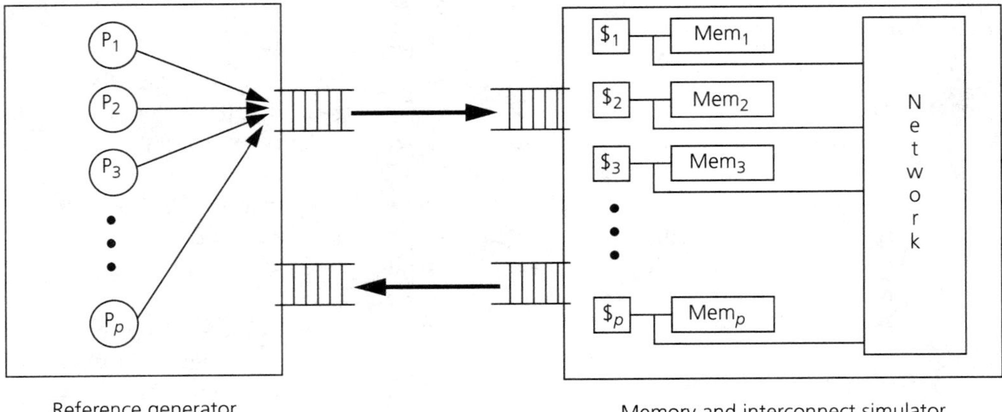

FIGURE 4.7 Execution-driven multiprocessor simulation. Simulated processors issue references to the memory system simulator, which simulates the extended memory hierarchy and feeds back timing information to the simulated processors (reference generators). $\$_1$, $\$_2$, etc. represent caches.

architecture and that is used to make scheduling decisions. In addition to time, simulators usually keep extensive statistics about the occurrence of various events of interest. This provides a wealth of detailed performance information that would be difficult, if not impossible, to obtain on a real system. However, the results may be tainted by a lack of credibility since it is, after all, a simulation. Accurate execution-driven simulation is also much more difficult when complex, dynamically scheduled, multiple-issue processors have to be modeled. Some of the trade-offs in simulation techniques are discussed in Exercise 4.9.

4.3.2 Scaling Down Problem and Machine Parameters for Simulation

Given that the simulation is done in software and involves many processes or threads that are very frequently being rescheduled (more often for more accuracy), it is not surprising that simulation is very expensive. Research is being done in simulation itself to speed it up and in using hardware emulation instead of simulation (Reinhardt et al. 1993; Goldschmidt 1993; Barroso et al. 1995), but progress has not been significant enough to change the fact that parameters must be scaled down substantially.

The tricky part about scaling down problem and machine parameters is that we want the scaled-down machine running the smaller problem to be representative of the full-scale machine running the larger problem. Unfortunately, there are no good formulas for this. Nonetheless, it is an important issue since it is the reality of most architectural trade-off evaluation. We should at least understand the limitations of such scaling, recognize which parameters can be scaled down with confidence and which cannot, and develop guidelines that help us avoid major pitfalls. Let us first examine scaling down the problem size and number of processors and then explain some further difficulties associated with lower-level machine parameters. Again, for concreteness the focus is on a cache-coherent shared address space communication abstraction.

Problem Parameters and Number of Processors

Consider problem parameters first. We should first look for those problem parameters, if any, that affect simulation time greatly but have little impact on execution characteristics related to parallel performance. An example is the number of time-steps executed in many scientific computations, like Ocean or even Barnes-Hut, or the number of iterations in the simple equation solver. The data values manipulated can change a lot across time-steps, but the behavioral characteristics don't change very much. In such cases, we can run the simulation for only a few time-steps.[2]

Unfortunately, many application parameters affect execution characteristics related to parallelism. When scaling these parameters, we must also scale down the number of processors since otherwise we may obtain highly unrepresentative behavioral characteristics. However, this is difficult to do in a representative way because we are faced with many constraints that are individually difficult to satisfy and that might be impossible to reconcile with one another. These include the following:

- *Preserving the distribution of time spent in program phases.* The relative amounts of time spent performing different types of computation—for example, in the tree-building and force calculation phases of Barnes-Hut—will most likely change with problem and machine size.
- *Preserving key behavioral characteristics.* These include the communication-to-computation ratio, load balance, and temporal and spatial locality, which may all scale in different ways!
- *Preserving scaling relationships among application parameters.*
- *Preserving contention and communication patterns.* This is particularly difficult, since burstiness, for example, is difficult to predict or control.

Rather than preserving true representativeness when scaling down, more realistic goals are to at least cover a range of realistic operating points with regard to the behavioral characteristics that matter most for a study and to avoid unrealistic scenarios. Thus, scaled-down simulations are not even claimed to be quantitatively representative but can be used to gain insight and rough estimates. With this more

---

2. Of course, we should now omit the initialization and cold-start periods of the application from the measurements since their impact is much larger in the run with reduced time-steps than it would be in practice. If we expect that the behavior over long periods of time may in fact change substantially, as is possible in Barnes-Hut or applications whose characteristics change more dynamically, then we can dump out the program state periodically from an execution on a real machine of the problem configuration we are simulating, and start a few sample simulations with these dumped-out states as their input data sets (again not measuring cold start in each sample). Other sampling techniques can also be used to reduce simulation cost.

modest goal, let us assume that we have scaled down the application parameters and the number of processors in some reasonable way and see how to scale other machine parameters.

Other Machine Parameters

Scaled-down problem and machine sizes interact differently with low-level machine parameters than the full-scale problems would. We may therefore have to scale these parameters carefully as well.

Consider the size of the cache or replication store. Suppose that the largest problem and machine configuration that we can simulate for the equation solver kernel is a 512×512 grid with 16 processors (i.e., 128 KB per processor). If we don't scale down the 1-MB cache per processor, we will never be able to represent the situation where the important working set doesn't fit in the cache. The key point with regard to scaling caches is that it should be done based on an understanding of how the relevant working sets scale as per our discussion of realistic and unrealistic operating points (Figure 4.4). Not scaling the cache size at all, or simply scaling it down proportionally with data set size or problem size, is inappropriate in general since cache size interacts most closely with working set size, not with data set or problem size. Example 4.6 and Figure 4.8 illustrate how to choose cache sizes given a problem and machine size. We should also ensure that the caches we simulate don't become extremely small since these can suffer from unrepresentative mapping and fragmentation artifacts. Similar arguments apply to replication stores other than processor caches, including those that hold only communicated data.

EXAMPLE 4.6 In the Barnes-Hut application, suppose that the size of the most important working set when running a full-scale problem with n = 1-M particles is 150 KB, that the target machine has 1-MB caches per processor, and that you can only simulate an execution with n = 16-K particles. Would it be appropriate to scale the cache size down proportionally with the data set size? How would you choose the cache size?

Answer Recall from Chapter 3 that the size of the most important working set in Barnes-Hut scales as $\log n$, where n is the number of particles and is proportional to the size of the data set. The working set of 150 KB fits comfortably in the full-scale 1-MB cache on the target machine. Given its slow growth rate, this working set is likely to always fit in the cache for realistic problems. If we scale the cache size proportionally to the data set for our simulations, we get a cache size of 1 MB × 16 K/1 M, or 16 KB. The size of the working set for the scaled-down problem is

$$150 \text{ KB} \times \frac{\log 16 \text{ K}}{\log 1 \text{ M}}$$

or 70 KB, which clearly does not fit in the scaled-down 16-KB cache. Thus, this form of cache scaling has brought us to an operating point that is not representative of reality. Since we expect the working set to fit in the cache in reality, we should rather choose a cache size large enough to always hold this working set. ■

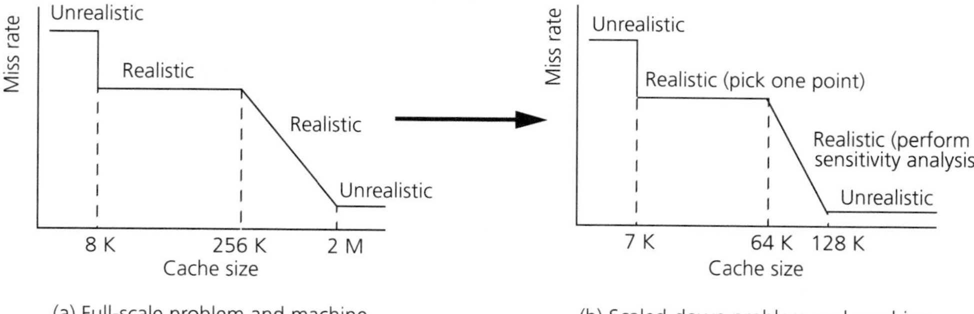

FIGURE 4.8 Choosing cache sizes for scaled-down problems and machines. (a) Based on our understanding of the sizes and scaling of working sets, we first decide what regions of the working set curve are realistic for full-scale problems running on the machine with full-scale caches. (b) We then project or measure what the working set curve looks like for the smaller problem and machine size that we are simulating, prune out the corresponding unrealistic regions in it, and pick representative operating points (cache sizes) for the realistic regions in a manner similar (but complementary) to that discussed in Example 4.4. For regions that cannot be pruned, we can perform sensitivity analysis as necessary.

As we move to still lower-level parameters of the extended memory hierarchy, scaling them representatively becomes increasingly difficult. For example, interactions with cache associativity are very difficult to predict, and usually the best we can do is leave the associativity as it is. The main danger is with retaining a direct-mapped cache when cache sizes are scaled down very low since this situation is particularly susceptible to mapping conflicts that wouldn't occur in the full-scale cache. Interactions with other organizational parameters of the memory and communication architectures—such as the granularities of data allocation, transfer, and coherence—are also complex and unpredictable unless there is near perfect spatial locality, but keeping them fixed can lead to serious, unrepresentative artifacts in many cases. We shall see some examples in the exercises. Finally, performance parameters like latency, occupancy, and bandwidth are also very difficult to scale down appropriately to preserve representativeness as the frequencies and patterns of communication change.

In summary, the best approach to simulation is to try to run realistic (if small) problem sizes to the extent possible. When scaling down is necessary, we should heed the guidelines and pitfalls we have discussed to ensure that the important types of operating points are covered, and we should extrapolate with caution. Our confidence in scaling down relies on our understanding of the application. In general, using scaled-down scenarios is okay for understanding whether certain architectural features are likely to be beneficial or not, but it is dangerous to use them to try to draw precise quantitative conclusions about full-scale situations.

4.3.3 Dealing with the Parameter Space: An Example Evaluation

Consider now the problem of the large parameter space opened up by trying to evaluate an idea in a general context. To keep the discussion concrete, let us examine an actual evaluation that we might perform using simulation. Assume again a cache-coherent shared address space machine with physically distributed memory. The default mechanism for communication is implicit communication in cache blocks through loads and stores, but we want to explore reducing the impact of endpoint communication overhead and communication delay by communicating in larger messages. We therefore wish to understand the utility of adding to such an architecture a facility to explicitly send larger messages, called a *block transfer* facility, which programs can use in addition to the standard transfer mechanisms for cache blocks (thus merging the shared address space and message-passing programming models). In the equation solver, for example, a process might send an entire border subrow or subcolumn of its partition to its neighbor process in a single block transfer.

In choosing workloads for such an evaluation, we should choose at least some with communication that is amenable to being structured in large messages, such as the equation solver. The more difficult problem is navigating the parameter space. Our goals are threefold:

1. *To avoid unrealistic execution characteristics.* We should avoid combinations of parameters (or operating points) that lead to unrealistic behavioral characteristics—that is, behavior that wouldn't be encountered in practical use of the machine.
2. *To obtain good coverage of realistic execution characteristics.* We should try to ensure that important characteristics that may arise in real usage are represented.
3. *To prune the parameter space.* Even in the realistic subspaces of parameter values, we should try to prune out points when possible based on application knowledge, in order to save time and resources without losing much coverage, and to determine when explicit sensitivity analysis is necessary.

We can prune the space based on the goals of the study, the restrictions on parameters imposed by technology (or the use of specific building blocks), and an understanding of parameter interactions.

Let us go through the process of choosing parameters, using the equation solver kernel as an example. Although we shall examine the parameters one by one, issues that arise in later stages may make us revisit decisions we made earlier. We begin with choosing the problem size and number of processors since these are limited the most by simulation resources.

Problem Size and Number of Processors

We choose the problem sizes and the numbers of processors based on the considerations of inherent program characteristics that we have discussed for evaluating a real machine and for scaling down for simulation. For example, if the problem is large enough that the communication-to-computation ratio is very small, then block transfer is not going to help overall performance much; nor will it help if the problem is small enough that load imbalance is the dominant bottleneck.

Let us now fix the problem size for the equation solver at a 514×514 grid, the number of processors at 16, and examine how to choose other parameters.

Cache/Replication Size

As usual, we choose cache sizes based on knowledge of the working set curve. Given a working set curve and knowledge of how working sets scale, the process of choosing cache sizes for a given problem size is analogous to that of choosing problem sizes for a given cache size and is illustrated in Example 4.7.

EXAMPLE 4.7 Figure 4.9 shows the well-defined working sets of the equation solver. How might you choose the cache sizes in this case?

Answer Although the sizes of important working sets often depend on application parameters and the number of processors, their nature and hence the general shape of the working set curve usually do not change with these parameters. Since we know the size of each important working set in the equation solver and how it scales with these parameters, if we know the range of cache sizes that are realistic for target machines, then we can tell whether it is (1) unrealistic to expect that working set to fit in the cache in practical situations, (2) unrealistic to expect that working set not to fit in the cache, or (3) realistic to expect it to fit for some practical combinations of parameter values and not to fit for others.[3] Thus, we can tell which of the regions between knees in the curve may be representative of realistic situations and which are not. For a given problem size and number of processors, we can use the (fixed) working set curve to choose cache sizes that avoid unrepresentative regions, cover representative ones, and prune flat regions by choosing only a single cache size from them (if all we care about from a cache is its miss rate). ■

Whether or not an important working set fits in the cache affects the benefits from block transfer greatly and in interesting ways. The effect depends on whether the working set consists of locally or nonlocally allocated data. If it consists mainly of local data—as in the equation solver when data is placed properly—but it doesn't fit in the cache, the processor spends more of its time stalled on the local memory system. As a result, communication time becomes relatively less important, and block transfer is likely to help less (block-transferred data also interferes more with the local traffic in a node, causing contention). However, if the working sets are mostly nonlocal data, we have the opposite effect: if they don't fit in the cache, then there is more communication and hence a greater opportunity for block transfer to help performance.

---

3. Whether a working set of a given size fits in the cache may depend on cache associativity and perhaps even block size in addition to cache size, but it is usually not a major issue in practice if we assume at least two-way associativity (as we shall see later). Thus, we can ignore these effects for now.

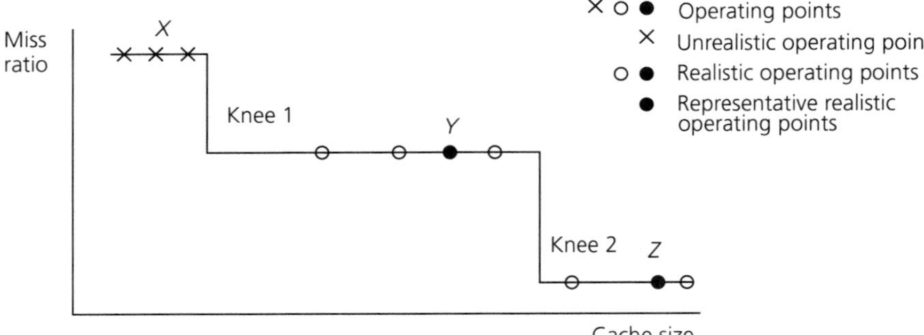

FIGURE 4.9 Picking cache sizes for an evaluation using the equation solver kernel. Knee 1 corresponds roughly to a couple of subrows of either B or $n/\sqrt{p}$ elements, depending on whether the grid traversal is blocked (with block size $B \times B$) or not. Knee 2 corresponds to a processor's partition of the matrix (i.e., data set n^2 divided by p). The latter working set may or may not fit in the cache depending on n and p, so both Y and Z are realistic operating points and should be represented. For the first working set, it is conceivable that it will not fit in the caches if the traversal is not blocked, but as we have seen in realistically large second-level caches, this is very unlikely. If the traversal is blocked, the block size B is chosen so the former working set always fits. Operating point X is therefore representative of an unrealistic region and is ignored. Blocked matrix computations are similar in this respect.

Of course, a working set curve is not always composed of relatively flat regions separated by sharply defined knees. If the curve has knees but the regions they separate are not flat (see Figure 4.10[a]), we can still prune out entire regions as before if we know they are unrealistic. However, if a region is realistic but not flat, or if there aren't any knees until the entire data set fits in the cache (as in Figure 4.10[b]), then we must resort to sensitivity analysis, picking points close to the extremes as well as perhaps some in between. Again, proper evaluation requires that we understand the key characteristics of the applications well.

The remaining question is how to determine the sizes of the knees and the shape of the working set curve between them. In simple cases, we may be able to do this analytically. However, algorithms are complex, constant factors are difficult to predict, and the effects of cache block size and associativity may be difficult to analyze. In these cases, we can obtain the curve for a given problem size and number of processors by measurement (simulation) with different cache sizes. The simulations needed are relatively inexpensive since working set sizes do not depend on detailed timing-related issues, such as latencies, bandwidths, occupancies, and contention, which therefore do not need to be simulated carefully (or at all). How the working sets change with problem size or number of processors can then be analyzed or measured again as appropriate. Fortunately, analysis of growth rates is usually easier than predicting constant factors. Also, lower-level issues like block size and associativity often don't change working sets too much for large enough caches and reasonable cache organizations (other than direct-mapped caches) (Woo et al. 1995).

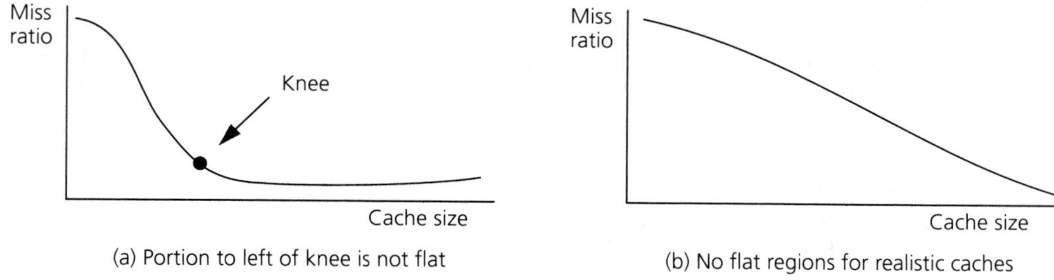

FIGURE 4.10 Miss rate versus cache size curves that do not consist of sharp knees separated by flat regions

Cache Block Size and Associativity

In addition to the problem size, the number of processors, and the cache size, the cache block size is another important parameter for determining the benefits of block transfer. The issues are a little more complicated, however. Long cache blocks themselves act like small block transfers for programs with good spatial locality, making explicit block transfer relatively less effective in these cases. On the other hand, if spatial locality is poor, then the extra traffic caused by long cache blocks (due to fragmentation or false sharing) can consume a lot more bandwidth than necessary when communicating through reads and writes. Whether poor spatial locality wastes bandwidth for block transfer as well depends on whether block transfer is implemented by pipelining whole cache blocks through the network or just the necessary words. Note that block transfer itself increases bandwidth requirements since it causes the same amount of communication to be performed (hopefully) in less time. Thus, if block transfer is implemented using pipelined cache block transfers and if spatial locality is poor, using block transfer may hurt rather than help when available bandwidth is limited since it may increase contention for the available bandwidth.

Fortunately, we are usually able to restrict the range of interesting cache block sizes either because of constraints of current technology or because of limits imposed by the set of available building blocks. For example, almost all microprocessors today support cache blocks between 32 and 128 bytes, and we may have already chosen a microprocessor that has a 64-byte cache block. When thresholds occur in the interactions of problem size and cache block size (for instance, in the radix sorting example discussed earlier), we should ensure that we cover both sides of the threshold.

While the magnitude of the impact of cache associativity is very difficult to predict, real caches are built with small associativity (usually at most four-way), so the number of choices to consider is small. If we must choose a single associativity, we are best advised to avoid direct-mapped caches (at least at the lowest level of the hierarchy, furthest from the processor) unless we know that the machines of interest will have them.

Performance Parameters of the Communication Architecture

Having discussed the organizational parameters of the extended memory hierarchy, let us consider the key performance parameters of the communication architecture—overhead, network delay or transit time, and bandwidth—and how they affect the benefits of block transfer. We should choose the base values of these parameters according to what we expect for real systems of interest, but this understanding helps us decide which parameters should be varied and how.

The higher the overhead component of a communicating cache block (on a miss, say), the more important it is to amortize it by structuring communication in larger block transfers. This is true as long as the overhead of initiating a block transfer is not so high as to drown out the benefits, since the overhead of explicitly initiating a block transfer may be larger than that of implicitly initiating the transfer of a cache block.

By the same token, the higher the network transit time between nodes, the greater the benefit of amortizing it over large block transfers (there are limits to this, which will be discussed when we examine block transfer in detail in Chapter 11). The effects of changing latency usually do not exhibit knees or thresholds, so in order to examine a range of possible latencies, we simply have to perform sensitivity analysis by choosing a few points along the range. In practice, we would usually choose latencies based on the target latencies of the machines of interest; for example, tightly coupled multiprocessors typically have much smaller latencies than workstations on a local area network.

Available bandwidth is also an important issue for our block transfer study. Bandwidth exhibits a strong knee effect as well, which is in fact a saturation effect: either enough bandwidth is available for the needs of the application, or it is not. If it is, then it may not matter too much whether the available bandwidth is four times what is needed or ten times. We can therefore pick one bandwidth that is less than that needed and one that is much more. Since the block transfer study is particularly sensitive to bandwidth, we may also choose one that is closer to the borderline. In choosing bandwidth values, we should be careful to consider the burstiness in the bandwidth demands of the application; the average bandwidth needs over the whole application may be small, but the application may still saturate a higher bandwidth during its periods of bursty communication, leading to contention.

Revisiting Choices

Finally, we may often need to revise our earlier choices for parameter values based on interactions with parameters considered later. For example, if we are forced to use small problem sizes due to lack of simulation time or resources, then we may be tempted to choose a very small cache size to represent a realistic situation where an important working set does not fit in the cache. However, choosing a very small cache may lead to severe artifacts, especially if we use a direct-mapped cache or a large cache block size (since this will lead to very few blocks in the cache and potentially a lot of fragmentation and mapping conflicts). We should therefore reconsider our choice of problem size and number of processors for which we want to represent this situation.

4.3.4 Summary

The preceding discussion shows that the results of an evaluation study can be misleading if we don't cover the space adequately: we can easily choose a combination of parameters and workloads that demonstrates good performance benefits from a feature such as block transfer (for example, a relatively small problem size, big caches, and a small cache block size), and we can just as easily choose a combination that doesn't. It is therefore very important that we incorporate sound methodological guidelines in our architectural studies and understand the relevant interactions between hardware and software.

In spite of a significant number of relevant interactions, we can fortunately identify certain parameters and properties that are at a high enough level for us to reason about, and that do not depend on lower-level timing details of the machine, upon which key behavioral characteristics of applications depend crucially. We should ensure that we cover realistic regimes of operation with regard to these parameters and properties—namely, application parameters, the number of processors, and the relationship between working sets and cache/replication size (that is, whether or not the important working sets fit in the caches). Benchmark suites should provide the basic characteristics such as concurrency, communication-to-computation ratio, and data locality for their applications, together with their dependence on these parameters, so that architects do not have to reproduce them (Woo et al. 1995).

It is also important to look for knees and flat regions in the interactions of application characteristics and architectural parameters, since these are especially useful for both coverage and pruning. Finally, the high-level goals and constraints of a study can also help us prune the parameter space.

This concludes our discussion of methodological issues in workload-driven evaluation. The remainder of this chapter introduces the rest of the parallel workloads that we shall use most often in the book. It also describes the basic methodologically relevant characteristics of all our workloads.

4.4 ILLUSTRATING WORKLOAD CHARACTERIZATION

Workloads are used extensively in this book both to quantitatively illustrate some of the architectural trade-offs we discuss and to evaluate our case study machines. Systems designed primarily to support a coherent shared address space communication abstraction are discussed in Chapters 5, 6, and 8, while message-passing and noncoherent shared address space systems are discussed in Chapter 7. Our programs for the abstractions are written in the corresponding programming models. Since programs in the two models are written very differently (as described in Chapter 2) and some of the important characteristics are different, we illustrate our characterization of workloads with the programs written for a coherent shared address space. In particular, we use six parallel applications and computational kernels that run in batch mode (i.e., one at a time) and do not include operating system activity and a multiprogrammed workload that does include operating system activity. While the number of workloads we use is small, the applications represent important classes of computation and have widely varying characteristics.

4.4.1 Workload Case Studies

All of the parallel programs we use for shared address space architectures are taken from the SPLASH-2 application suite (see Appendix). Three (Ocean, Barnes-Hut, and Raytrace) have already been described and used as case studies in previous chapters. This section briefly describes the workloads we use but haven't yet discussed: LU, Radix, Radiosity, and Multiprog. LU and Radix are computational kernels, Radiosity is a real application, and Multiprog is a multiprogrammed workload. In Section 4.4.2, we measure some methodologically relevant execution characteristics of the workloads, including the breakdown of data accesses, the communication-to-computation ratio and how it scales, and the size and scaling of the important working sets. We use this characterization to choose memory system parameters for these applications and data sets in later chapters.

LU

Dense *LU factorization* is the process of converting a dense matrix A into two matrices L, U that are lower and upper triangular, respectively, and whose product equals A (i.e., $A = LU$).[4] Its utility is in solving linear systems of equations, and it is encountered in scientific applications as well as optimization methods such as linear programming. It is a well-structured computational kernel that is nontrivial yet familiar and fairly easy to understand (Golub and Van Loan 1997).

LU factorization works like Gaussian elimination, eliminating one variable at a time by subtracting rows of the matrix from scalar multiples of other rows. The computational complexity of LU factorization is $O(n^3)$, while the size of the data set is $O(n^2)$. As we know from the discussion of temporal locality in Chapter 3, this is an ideal situation to exploit temporal locality by blocking. In fact, we use a blocked LU factorization, which is far more efficient both sequentially and in parallel than an unblocked version. The n-by-n matrix to be factored is divided into B-by-B blocks, and the idea is to reuse a block as much as possible before moving on to the next block. We now think of the matrix as consisting of n/B-by-n/B blocks rather than n-by-n elements and eliminate and update blocks one at a time just as we

4. A matrix is called *dense* if a substantial proportion of its elements are nonzero (matrices that have mostly zero entries are called sparse matrices). A *lower-triangular matrix* such as L is one whose entries are all zero above the main diagonal, whereas an *upper-triangular matrix* such as U has all zeros below the main diagonal. (The *main diagonal* is the diagonal that runs from the top left corner of the matrix to the bottom right corner.)

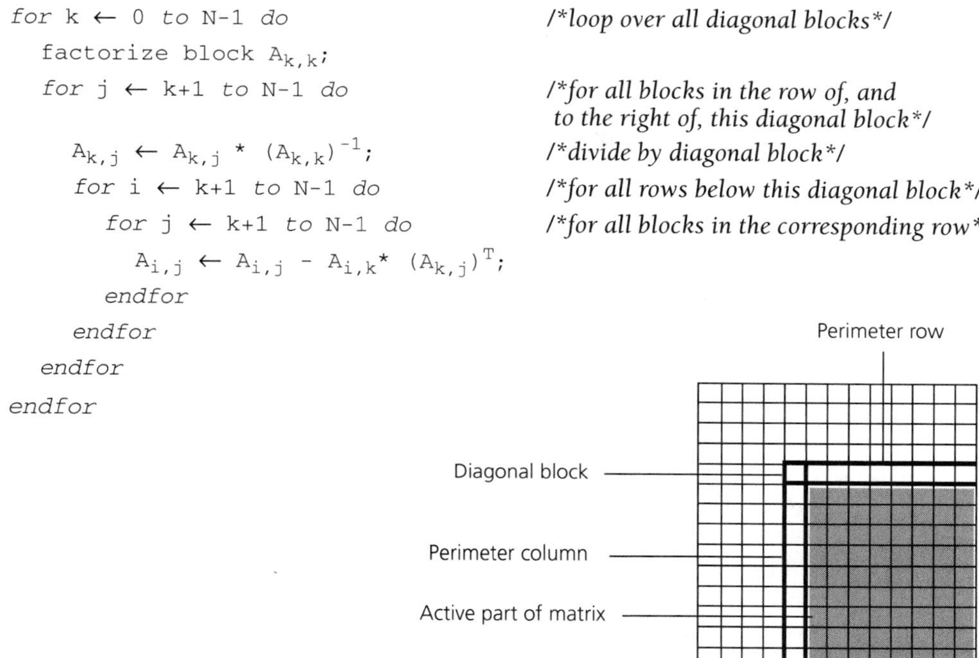

```
for k ← 0 to N-1 do                          /*loop over all diagonal blocks*/
  factorize block A_{k,k};
  for j ← k+1 to N-1 do                      /*for all blocks in the row of, and
                                               to the right of, this diagonal block*/
    A_{k,j} ← A_{k,j} * (A_{k,k})^{-1};       /*divide by diagonal block*/
    for i ← k+1 to N-1 do                    /*for all rows below this diagonal block*/
      for j ← k+1 to N-1 do                  /*for all blocks in the corresponding row*/
        A_{i,j} ← A_{i,j} - A_{i,k}* (A_{k,j})^T;
      endfor
    endfor
  endfor
endfor
```


FIGURE 4.11 Pseudocode describing sequential blocked dense LU factorization. N is the number of blocks in each dimension ($N = n/B$), and we think of the matrix as an N-by-N matrix of blocks rather than an n-by-n matrix of elements. Then, $A_{i,j}$ represents the block in the ith row and jth column of matrix A. In the kth iteration of this outermost loop, we call the block $A_{k,k}$ on the main diagonal of A the diagonal block, and the kth row and column of blocks the perimeter row and perimeter column, respectively. Note that the kth iteration does not touch any of the blocks in the first $k - 1$ rows or columns of the matrix; that is, only the shaded part of the matrix in the square region to the right of and below the diagonal block is "active" in the current outermost loop iteration. The rest of the matrix has already been computed in previous iterations and will be inactive for the rest of the factorization. In an unblocked LU factorization, we would refer similarly to a diagonal element and a perimeter row and column of elements.

would elements. Matrix operations like multiplication and inversion are used on small B-by-B blocks rather than scalar operations on elements. Sequential pseudocode for this blocked LU factorization is shown in Figure 4.11, which also defines some relevant terms.

Consider the benefits of blocking. If we did not block the computation, a processor would compute an element, then compute its next assigned element to the right, and so forth until the end of the current row, after which it would proceed to the next row. When it returned to the first active element of the next row, it would re-reference a perimeter row element (the one it used to compute the corresponding active element of the previous row). However, by this time it has streamed through data proportional to an entire row of the matrix and, given large matrices, that perimeter row element might no longer be in the cache. In the blocked version, within the block-level computations in each iteration of the innermost loop in Figure 4.11 (i.e., the computation in the line $A_{i,j} \leftarrow A_{i,j} - A_{i,k} * (A_{k,j})^T$), we proceed only B elements in a direction before returning to previously referenced data that are still in the cache and can be reused. The operations (matrix multiplications and factorizations) on the B-by-B blocks each involve $O(B^3)$ computation and data accesses, with each block element being accessed B times. If the block size B is chosen such that a block of B-by-B or B^2 elements (plus some other data) fits in the cache, then in a given block computation only the first access to an element misses in the cache. Subsequent accesses hit in the cache, resulting in B^2 misses for B^3 accesses or a miss rate of $1/B$.

In the parallel version, we can think of every computation that updates a block as a task. Figure 4.12 provides a pictorial depiction of the flow of information among blocks within an outermost loop iteration and shows how we assign blocks (and hence tasks) to processors in the parallel version. Because of the nature of the computation, blocks toward the top left of the matrix are active only in the first few outermost loop iterations of the computation, whereas blocks toward the bottom right have a lot more work associated with them. Assigning contiguous rows or squares of blocks to processes (a simple domain decomposition of the matrix) would therefore lead to poor load balance. Consequently, we interleave blocks among processes in both dimensions, leading to a partitioning called a two-dimensional *scatter decomposition* of the matrix: the processes are viewed as forming a two-dimensional $\sqrt{p}$-by-$\sqrt{p}$ grid, and this grid of processes is repeatedly stamped over the matrix of blocks like a cookie cutter. A process is responsible for computing the blocks that are assigned to it in this way, and only it writes those blocks. The interleaving alleviates—but does not eliminate load imbalance, whereas the blocking preserves locality and also allows us to use larger data transfers on message-passing systems.

The drawback of decomposing the computation into blocks rather than individual elements is that it increases task granularity and hurts load balance: concurrency is reduced since there are fewer blocks than elements, and the maximum load imbalance per iteration is the work associated with a block rather than a single element. In sequential LU factorization, the only constraint on block size is that the two or three blocks used in a block computation fit in the cache. In the parallel case, the ideal block size B is determined by a trade-off between data locality and communication overhead (particularly on a message-passing machine) pushing toward larger blocks on one hand and load balance pushing toward smaller blocks on the other. The ideal block size therefore depends on the problem size, number of processors, and other architectural parameters. In practice, block sizes of 16×16 or 32×32 elements appear to work well on large parallel machines.

Blocking provides data reuse within a block computation. Data can also be reused across different block computations. To reuse data from remote blocks, we can either copy blocks explicitly in main memory and keep them around, or on cache-coherent machines, we can perhaps rely on caches being large enough to do this automatically. However, reuse across block computations is typically not nearly as important

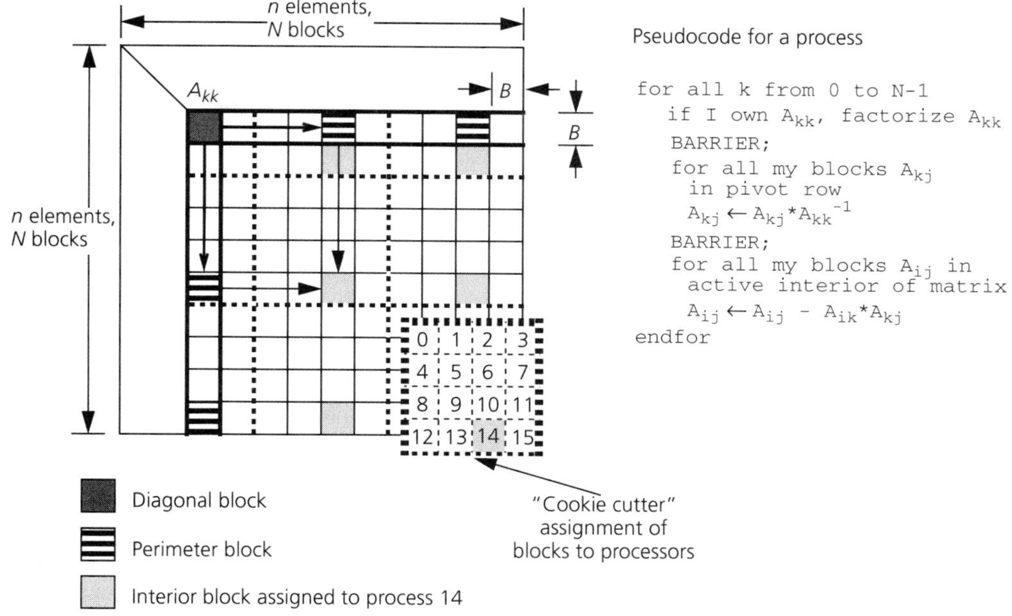

FIGURE 4.12 Parallel blocked LU factorization: flow of information, partitioning, and parallel pseudocode. The flow of information within an outer (k) loop iteration is shown by the solid arrows. Information (data) flows from the diagonal block (which is first factorized) to all blocks in the perimeter row in the first phase. In the second phase, a block in the active part of the matrix needs the corresponding elements from the perimeter row and perimeter column.

to performance as reuse within them (and explicit copying has a cost), so in our program we do not make explicit copies of blocks in main memory.

For spatial locality, since the unit of decomposition is now a two-dimensional block, the issues are quite similar to those discussed for the simple equation solver kernel in Section 3.3.1. We are therefore led to a four-dimensional array data structure to represent the matrix in a shared address space so that the data in a block is contiguous in the address space. The first two dimensions specify a block, and the next two specify an element within the block. This allows us to distribute blocks appropriately among memories at page granularity. (If blocks are smaller than a page, we can use one more array dimension to ensure that all the blocks assigned to a process are contiguous in the address space.) However, with blocking the capacity miss rate is small enough that data distribution in main memory is not a major problem in LU factorization. The more important reason to keep a block's data contiguous by using high-dimensional arrays is to reduce cache mapping conflicts across subrows of a block as well as across blocks, as we discuss in Section 5.6. Cache conflicts are very sensitive to the size of the array and number of processors, especially with direct-mapped first-level caches, and can easily negate most of the benefits of blocking.

No locks are used in parallel LU factorization. Barriers are used to separate outermost loop iterations as well as phases within an iteration (e.g., to ensure that the perimeter row is computed before the blocks in it are used). Point-to-point synchronization at the block level could have been used to exploit more concurrency, but barriers make programming much easier.

Radix

The Radix program sorts a series of integers, called *keys*, using the popular radix sorting method. Suppose there are n integers to be sorted, each of size b bits. The algorithm uses a radix of r bits, where r is chosen by the user. This means the b bits representing a key can be viewed as a set of $\lceil b/r \rceil$ groups of r bits each (see Figure 4.13). The algorithm proceeds in $\lceil b/r \rceil$ phases or iterations. Each phase, starting with the lowest-order group, sorts the keys according to their values in the corresponding group of r bits, called a *digit*.[5] The keys are completely sorted at the end of these $\lceil b/r \rceil$ phases. Two one-dimensional arrays of size n integers are used in each phase: one, called the *input array*, stores the keys as they appear in the input to a phase, and the other, called the *output array*, stores the keys as they appear in the output from the phase. The input array for one phase is the output array for the next phase, and vice versa.

Consider the parallel computation within a phase, which sorts all n keys according to their values in a particular digit. The parallel algorithm partitions the n keys in each array among the p processes so that process 0 is assigned the first n/p keys, process 1 the next n/p keys, and so on. The portion of each array assigned to a process is allocated in the corresponding processor's local memory. The n/p keys in the input array for a phase that are assigned to a process are called its *local keys* for that phase. Within a phase, a process performs the following steps:

1. Make a pass over the local n/p keys to build a local (per-process) histogram of key values. The histogram has 2^r entries, where r is the number of bits in a digit. If a key encountered has the value i in the current phase, then the ith bin of the histogram is incremented.
2. When all processes have completed step 1 (determined by barrier synchronization in this program), accumulate the local histograms into a global histogram. This is done with a parallel prefix computation, as discussed in Exercise 4.14. The global histogram keeps track of both how many keys there are of each value for the current digit and also, for each of the p process-ID values j, how many keys of a given value are owned by processes whose ID is less than j.
3. Make another pass over the local n/p keys. For each key, use the global and local histograms to determine which (sorted) position in the output array this

5. The reason for starting with the lowest-order group of r bits rather than the highest-order one is that this leads to a "stable" sort; that is, keys with the same value appear in the output in the same order relative to one another as they appeared in the input.

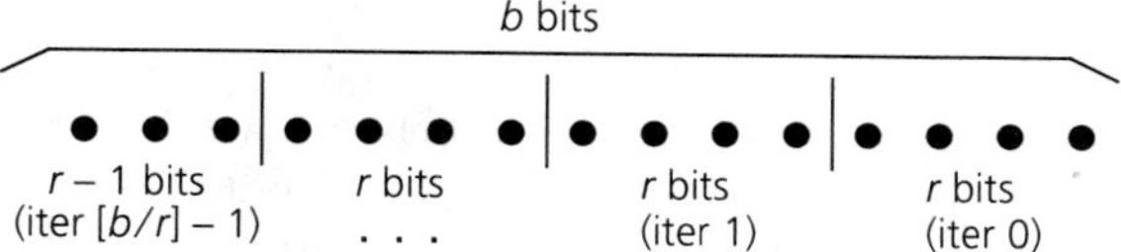

FIGURE 4.13 A *b*-bit number (key) divided into $\lceil b/r \rceil$ groups of *r* bits each. The first iteration of radix sorting uses the least significant *r* bits and so on.

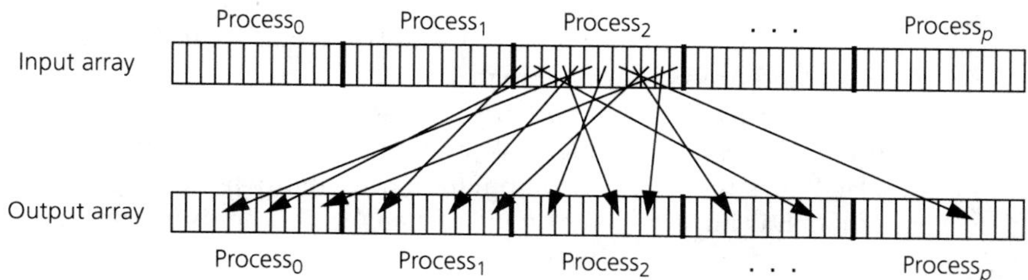

FIGURE 4.14 The permutation step of a radix sorting phase. In each of the input and output arrays (which change places in successive phases), keys (entries) assigned to a process are allocated in the corresponding processor's local memory.

key should go to, and write the key value into that entry of the output array. Note that the array element that will be written is very likely to be nonlocal, with expected likelihood $(p - 1)/p$ (see Figure 4.14). This step is called the *permutation* step.

A more detailed description of radix sorting algorithms and implementations can be found in (Blelloch et al. 1991; Culler et al. 1993). In a shared address space implementation, communication occurs when writing the keys in the permutation phase (or reading them in the histogram-generation phase of the next iteration if they stay in the writers' caches) and in constructing the global histogram from the local histograms. The permutation-related communication is all-to-all personalized (i.e., every process communicates disjoint subsets of its keys to every other) but is irregular and scattered, with the exact patterns depending on the distribution of keys. The synchronization includes global barriers between phases as well as finer-grained synchronization in the phase that builds the global histogram. The latter may take the form of either mutual exclusion or point-to-point event synchronization, depending on the implementation of this phase (see Exercise 4.14).

Radiosity

The radiosity method is used in computer graphics to compute the global illumination in a scene that contains diffusely reflecting surfaces. In the hierarchical radiosity method, a scene is initially modeled as consisting of *k* large input polygons, or *patches*. For example, the top of a table or the back of a chair may be an input patch. Light transport interactions are computed pairwise among these patches. In a simplified view of the algorithm, if the light transfer between a pair of patches is larger than a threshold, one of them (the larger one, say) is subdivided, and interactions are computed recursively between the resulting subpatches and the other patch. This process continues until the light transfer between all pairs is sufficiently low. Thus, patches are hierarchically subdivided as necessary to improve the accuracy of computing illumination. Each subdivision results in four subpatches, leading to a quadtree per patch. If the resulting final number of undivided subpatches is n, then with k original patches the complexity of this algorithm is $O(n + k^2)$. A brief description of the steps in the algorithm follows. Details can be found in (Hanrahan, Salzman, and Aupperle 1991; Singh 1993).

The input patches that comprise the scene are first inserted into a binary space partitioning (BSP) tree (Fuchs, Abram, and Grant 1983), which is a data structure that facilitates the efficient computation of visibility between pairs of patches. Every input patch is initially given an *interaction list* of other input patches that are potentially visible from it and with which it must therefore compute interactions. Then, radiosities are computed by the following iterative algorithm:

1. For every input patch, compute its radiosity due to all patches on its interaction list, subdividing it or other patches hierarchically and computing their interactions recursively as necessary (see Figure 4.15).
2. Starting from the patches at the leaves of the quadtrees, add all the patch radiosities together (weighted by their areas) to obtain the total radiosity of the scene, and compare it with that of the previous iteration to check for convergence within a fixed tolerance. If the radiosity has not converged, return to step 1. Otherwise, go to step 3.
3. Smooth the solution for display.

Most of the time in an iteration is spent in step 1, so let us examine it further. Suppose a patch i is traversing its interaction list to compute interactions with other patches (quadtree nodes). The interaction with another patch, say, j, involves computing the intervisibility of the two patches as well as the light transfer between them. (The actual light transfer is the product of the actual intervisibility and the light transfer that would have happened if there were no occlusion and hence full intervisibility.) Computing intervisibility involves traversing the BSP tree several times from one patch to the other;[6] in fact, visibility computation is a very large portion of the overall execution time. If the result of an interaction says that the "source" patch i should be subdivided, then four children are created for patch i if

6. Visibility is computed by conceptually shooting a number of rays between the two patches and seeing how many of the rays reach the destination patch without being occluded by intervening patches in the scene. For each such conceptual ray, determining whether it is occluded or not is done efficiently by traversing the BSP tree from the source to the destination patch.

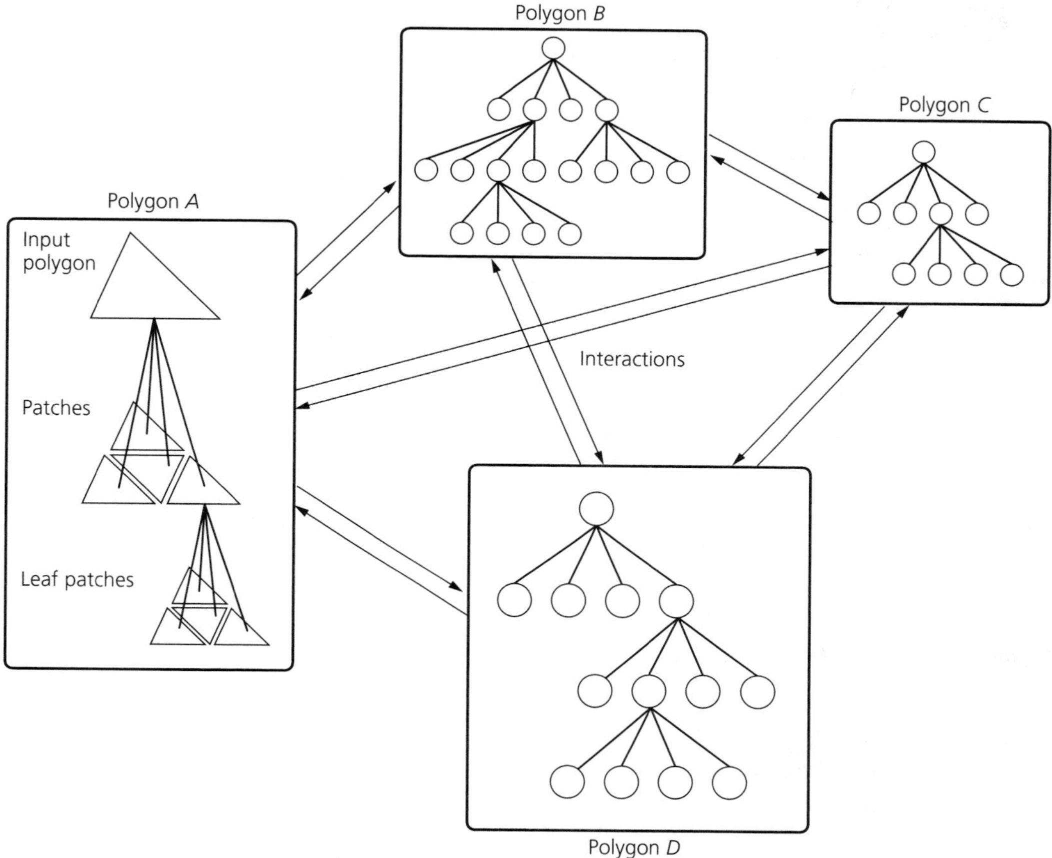

FIGURE 4.15 Hierarchical subdivision of input polygons into quadtrees as the radiosity computation progresses. Every input polygon generates a quadtree of patches that interact with patches from other quadtrees.

they don't already exist due to a previous interaction; patch *j* is removed from *i*'s interaction list and added to each of *i*'s children's interaction lists so that those interactions will be computed later. If the result is that patch *j* should be subdivided, then patch *j* is replaced by its children on patch *i*'s interaction list. This means that interactions will next be computed between patch *i* and each of patch *j*'s children. These interactions may themselves cause subdivisions, so the process continues recursively (i.e., if patch *j*'s children are further subdivided in the course of computing these interactions, patch *i* ends up computing interactions with a tree of patches below patch *j*). Since the four children patches from a subdivision replace the parent in place on *i*'s interaction list, the traversal of the tree comprising patch *j*'s descendants is depth first. Patch *i*'s interaction list is traversed fully in this way before moving on to the next patch (which may be a descendant of patch *i* or a different patch) and its interaction list. Figure 4.16 shows an example of this hierarchical refinement of interactions. After one iteration of computing all interactions and refinements is completed, the next iteration of the iterative algorithm starts with the quadtrees and interaction lists as they are at the end of the previous iteration.

Parallelism is available at three levels in this application: across the *k* input polygons, across the patches that these polygons are subdivided into (i.e., the patches in the quadtrees), and across the interactions computed for a patch. All three levels involve communication and synchronization among processors. We obtain the best performance by defining a task to be either a patch and all its interactions or a single patch-patch interaction, depending on the size of the problem, the number of processors, and the machine characteristics.

Since the computation and subdivisions are highly unpredictable, we have to use task queues and task stealing to balance the workload. The parallel implementation provides every processor with its own task queue. A processor's task queue is initialized with a subset of the initially available polygon-polygon interactions. When a patch is subdivided due to an interaction, new tasks for the subpatches are enqueued on the task queue of the processor that computed the interaction and hence did the subdivision. A processor executes tasks from its queue until no tasks are left. Then it steals tasks from other processors' queues. Locks are used to protect the task queues and to provide mutually exclusive access to patches as they are subdivided. (Note that two patches assigned to two different processes may have the same patch on their interaction list, so both processes may try to subdivide the latter patch at the same time.) Barrier synchronization is used between steps in an iteration. The parallel algorithm is nondeterministic due to task stealing and the order in which interactions and subdivisions are computed, and it has highly unstructured and unpredictable communication and data access patterns.

Multiprog

The workloads we have discussed so far include only parallel applications that run one at a time. However, a common use of multiprocessors, particularly small-scale shared address space multiprocessors, is as throughput engines for multiprogrammed workloads. The fine-grained resource sharing supported by these machines allows a single operating system image to service the multiple processors efficiently. Operating system activity is often a substantial component of such workloads, and the operating system itself constitutes an important, complex parallel application. The final workload we study is a multiprogrammed (time-shared) workload, consisting of a number of sequential applications and the operating system itself. The applications are two UNIX file `compress` jobs and two parallel compilations—or `pmakes`—in which multiple files needed to create an executable are compiled and assembled in parallel. The operating system is a version of UNIX produced by Silicon Graphics, called IRIX (version 5.2).

(1) Before refinement

(2) After the first refinement

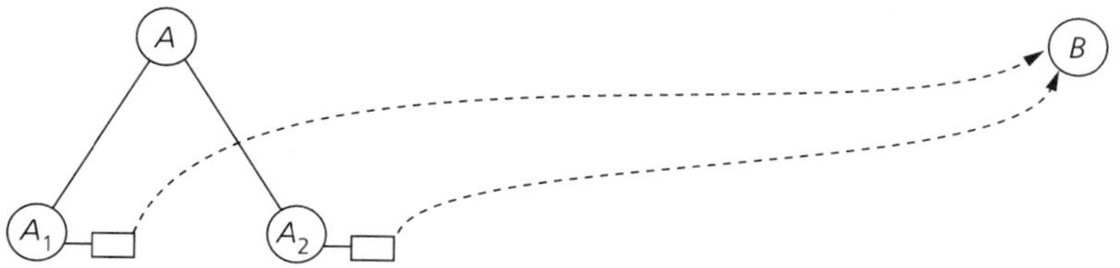

(3) After three more refinements: A_2 subdivides B; then A_2 is subdivided due to B_2; then A_{22} subdivides B_1

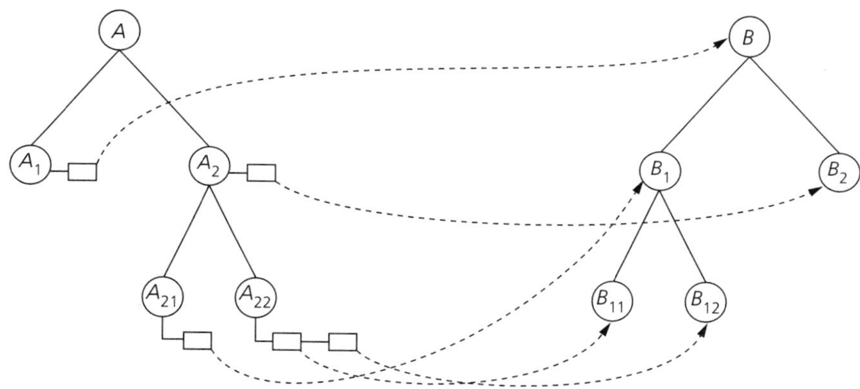

FIGURE 4.16 Hierarchical refinement of interactions and interaction lists. Binary trees are shown instead of quadtrees for clarity, and only one input polygon's interaction lists are shown.

4.4.2 Workload Characteristics

We now quantify some important basic characteristics of all our workloads, including the breakdown of data accesses into read and write or shared and private, the concurrency and inherent load balance, the inherent communication-to-computation ratio and how it scales, and the size and scaling of the important working sets. Characteristics related to spatial locality are measured in the context of specific architectural styles in later chapters. In this section, we present quantitative characterization data for 16-processor executions for our parallel applications and 8-processor executions of the multiprogrammed workload. How the characteristics of interest scale with problem size is discussed qualitatively or analytically and is sometimes measured.

Data Access and Synchronization Characteristics

Table 4.1 summarizes the basic reference counts and dynamic frequency of synchronization events (locks and global barriers) in the different workloads. The input data sets are the default problem sizes used throughout the book, unless otherwise noted. The chosen problem sizes are large enough to be of practical interest for a machine of up to about 64 processors but small enough to simulate in a reasonable time. They are therefore at the small end of the data sets we might run in practice on 64-processor machines but are quite appropriate for smaller-scale systems.

We keep track of behavioral and timing statistics only after the child processes are created by the parent. Previous references (by the main process) are simulated but are not included in the statistics. In most of the applications, measurement begins exactly after the child processes are created. The exceptions are Ocean and Barnes-Hut. In both these cases, we are able to take advantage of the opportunity to drastically reduce the number of time-steps for the purpose of simulation (as discussed in Section 4.3.2); however, we then have to ignore cold-start misses and allow the application to settle down before starting measurement. We simulate a small number of time-steps—six for Ocean and five for Barnes-Hut—and start tracking behavioral and timing statistics after the first two time-steps. For the Multiprog workload, statistics are gathered from a checkpoint taken close to the beginning of the `pmake`. While for all other applications we consider only application data references, for the Multiprog workload we also consider the impact of instruction references and furthermore partition kernel references and user application references into separate categories. The table shows that the breakdown of operations into integer and floating point, read and write, and shared and private varies substantially across workloads, indicating good coverage along these axes.

Concurrency and Load Balance

We characterize load balance by measuring the algorithmic speedups—that is, speedups on the PRAM architectural model (discussed in Chapter 3) that assumes that data accesses and communication have zero latency (they just cost the instruction it takes to issue the reference). Deviations from ideal speedup are attributable to load imbalance, serialization at critical sections, and extra work due to redundant computation and parallelism management.

Figure 4.17 shows the algorithmic speedups for the six parallel programs for up to 64 processors with the default data sets. Three of the programs (Barnes-Hut, Ocean, and to a lesser extent Raytrace) speed up very well all the way to 64 processors even with the relatively small data sets. The dominant phases in these programs are data parallel across a large data set (all the particles in Barnes-Hut, an entire grid

Table 4.1 General Statistics about Application Programs

Application	Input Data Set	Total Instructions (M)	Total FLOPS (M)	Total References (M)	Total Reads (M)	Total Writes (M)	Shared Reads (M)	Shared Writes (M)	Barriers	Locks
LU	512 × 512 matrix 16 × 16 blocks	489.52	92.20	151.07	103.09	47.99	92.79	44.74	66	0
Ocean	258 × 258 grids tolerance = 10^{-7} 4 time-steps	376.51	101.54	99.70	81.16	18.54	76.95	16.97	364	1,296
Barnes-Hut	16-K particles $\theta = 1.0$ 3 time-steps	2,002.74	239.24	720.13	406.84	313.29	225.04	93.23	7	34,516
Radix	256-K integers radix = 1,024	14.02	—	5.27	2.90	2.37	1.34	0.81	11	16
Raytrace	Car scene	833.35	—	290.35	210.03	80.31	161.10	22.35	0	94,456
Radiosity	Room scene	2,297.19	—	769.56	486.84	282.72	249.67	21.88	10	210,485
Multiprog: User	SGI IRIX 5.2, two `pmakes` + two `compress` jobs	1,296.43	—	500.22	350.42	149.80	—	—	—	—
Multiprog: Kernel		668.10	—	212.58	178.14	34.44	—	—	—	621,505

For the parallel programs, shared reads and writes simply refer to all nonstack references issued by the application processes. All such references do not necessarily point to data that is truly shared by multiple processes. The Multiprog workload is not a parallel application, so it does not access shared data. A dash in a table entry means that this measurement is not applicable to or is not measured for that application (e.g., Radix has no floating-point operations). (M) denotes that measurement in that column is in millions.

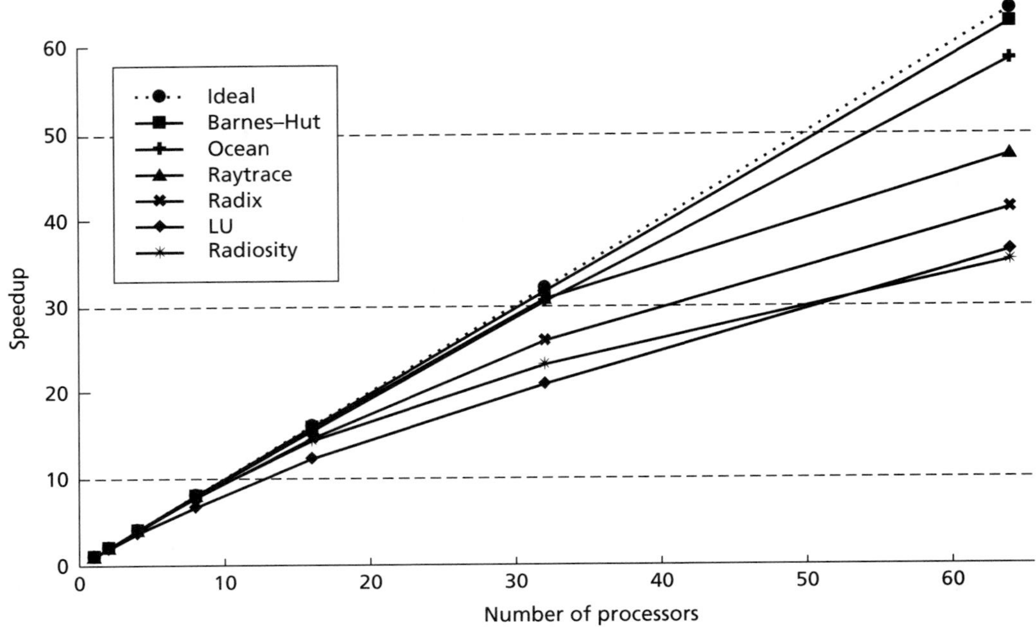

FIGURE 4.17 Algorithmic speedups for the six parallel applications. The Ideal speedup curve denotes a speedup of *p* with *p* processors.

in Ocean, and the image pixels in Raytrace). They suffer from limited parallelism and serialization only in some global reduction operations and in portions of some particular phases that are not dominant in terms of the number of instructions executed (e.g., tree building and near the root of the upward pass in Barnes, and the higher levels of the multigrid hierarchy in Ocean). Raytrace has one troublesome critical section that is heavily contended, causing serialization (in fact, this critical section is not strictly necessary for correct execution but is used to keep track of some important statistics).

All six programs display good algorithmic speedups for up to 16 or 32 processors. The programs that do not speed up very well for the higher numbers of processors with these data sets are LU, Radiosity, and Radix. In each case, this is due to the size of the input data sets rather than the inherent nature of load imbalance in the applications. In LU, the default data set results in considerable load imbalance for 64 processors, despite the block-oriented decomposition. Larger data sets (or fewer processors) reduce the imbalance by providing more blocks per processor in each step of the factorization. For Radiosity, the imbalance is also due to the use of a small data set, though it is very difficult to analyze. Finally, for Radix the poor speedup at 64 processors is due to the prefix computation when accumulating local histograms into a global histogram (see Section 4.4.1), which cannot be completely parallelized.

The time spent in this prefix computation is $O(\log p)$, while the time spent in the other phases is $O(n/p)$, so the fraction of total work in this unbalanced phase will decrease as the number of keys being sorted is increased. Thus, even these three programs can be used to evaluate larger machines, when larger data sets are chosen.

We have satisfied our criteria of not choosing parallel programs that are inherently unsuitable for the machine sizes we want to evaluate and of understanding how to choose appropriate data sets for these programs for the machine scale at hand. Let us now examine the inherent communication-to-computation ratios and working set sizes of the programs.

Communication-to-Computation Ratio

We include in the communication-to-computation ratio inherent communication as well as communication due to the first time a word is accessed by a processor, if it happens to be nonlocally allocated (i.e., cold-start misses that occur after measurement is started). Where possible, data is distributed appropriately among physically distributed memories, so we can consider this cold-start communication to be fundamental rather than artifactual. To avoid artifactual communication due to finite capacity or poor spatial locality, we simulate infinite per-processor caches and a single-word cache block. We measure communication-to-computation ratio as the number of bytes of application data communicated per instruction, averaged over all processors. For floating-point-intensive applications (LU and Ocean), we use bytes per FLOP (floating-point operation) instead of per instruction since the number of FLOPs is less sensitive to the vagaries of the compiler than the number of total instructions.

We will first look at the measured communication-to-computation ratio for the base problem size shown in Table 4.1 versus the number of processors used. This shows how the ratio increases with the number of processors under constant problem size scaling. Then, where possible, we will examine analytically how the ratio depends on the data set size and the number of processors (Table 4.2). The effects of other application parameters on the communication-to-computation ratio are discussed separately and usually qualitatively.

Figure 4.18 shows the measured results for the base problem size for our six parallel programs. The first thing we notice is that the average inherent communication-to-computation ratios are generally quite small. With processors operating at 400 million instructions per second (MIPS), a ratio of 0.1 byte per instruction is about 40 MB/s of data traffic, which is quite small for modern high-performance multiprocessor networks. Actual traffic is much higher than inherent both because of artifactual communication and because control information is sent along with data in each transfer. This indicates that it is the burstiness of communication, the other sources of communication, and the pattern of communication (e.g., all-to-all or long-range) that are likely to be the causes of communication bandwidth problems, if any. The only application for which the average ratio is quite high is Radix, so for this application, communication bandwidth is especially important to model carefully in evaluations. One reason

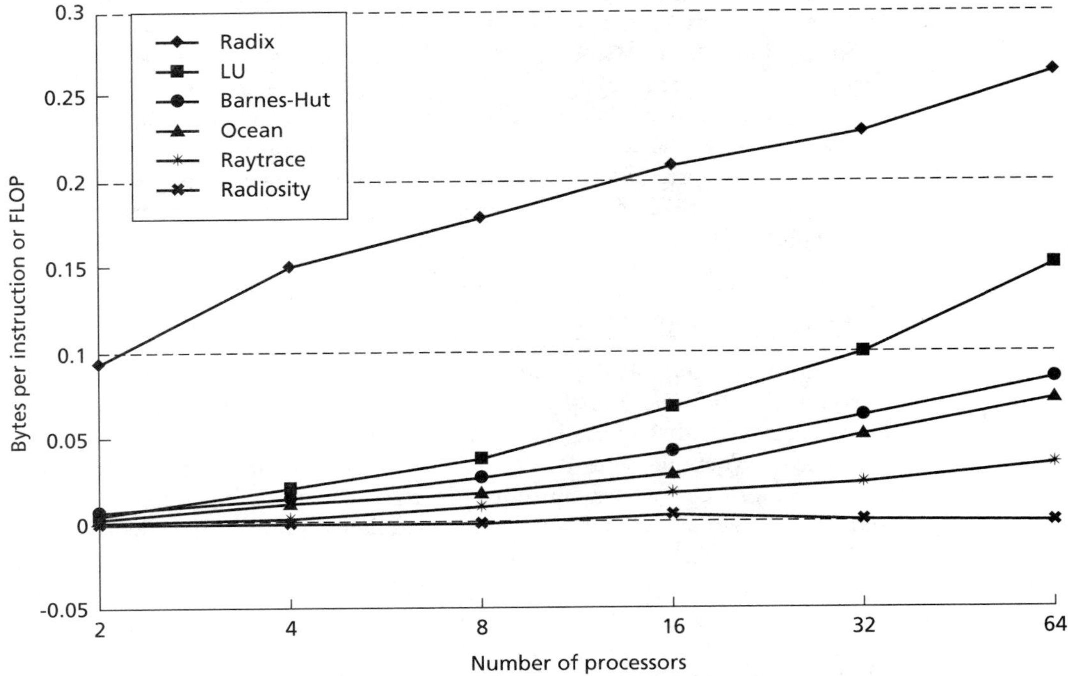

FIGURE 4.18 Communication-to-computation ratio versus processor count for the base problem size in the six parallel applications

for the low communication-to-computation ratios is that the applications we are using have been very well optimized in their assignments for parallel execution. Applications used in practice, including other versions of these applications, may exhibit higher communication-to-computation ratios.

The next observation from the figure is that the growth rates of communication-to-computation ratios are very different across applications, indicating good coverage of this behavioral property as well. These growth rates with the number of processors and with data set size (not shown in the figure) are summarized analytically in Table 4.2. The communication-to-computation ratio would change dramatically if we used a different data set size in some applications (e.g., Ocean), but at least for inherent communication it would not change much in others. Artifactual communication is a whole different story, and we shall examine communication traffic due to it in the context of different architectural types in later chapters.

While growth rates are clearly fundamental, it is important to realize that they do not reveal the constant factors in the expressions for the communication-to-computation ratio, which can be more important than asymptotic growth rates in practice. For example, if a program's ratio increases only as the logarithm of the number of processors, then asymptotically its ratio will indeed become smaller

Table 4.2 Growth Rates of Inherent Communication-to-Computation Ratio

Application	Growth Rate
LU	$\sqrt{P}/\sqrt{DS}$
Ocean	$\sqrt{P}/\sqrt{DS}$
Barnes-Hut	Approximately $\sqrt{P}/\sqrt{DS}$
Radiosity	Unpredictable
Radix	$(P-1)/P$
Raytrace	Unpredictable

DS is the data set size (in bytes, say), and *P* is the number of processes.

than that of an application whose ratio grows as the square root of the number of processors; however, it may actually be much larger for all practical machine sizes if its constant factors are much larger. The constant factors for our applications can be determined from Figure 4.18.

Working Set Sizes

The inherent working set sizes of a program are best measured using fully associative caches and a one-word cache block and simulating the program with different cache sizes to find knees in the miss rate versus cache size curve. Smaller associativity can make the size of the cache needed to hold the working set larger than the inherent working set size, as can the use of multiword cache blocks (due to fragmentation in the cache). In our measurements, we come close to measuring inherent working set sizes by using one-level fully associative caches per processor, with a least recently used (LRU) cache replacement policy and 8-byte cache blocks. We generally use cache sizes that are powers of two, but to identify knees we change cache sizes at a finer granularity in areas where the change in miss rate with cache size is substantial.

Figure 4.19 shows the resulting miss rate versus cache size curves for our six parallel applications, with the working sets labeled as level 1 working set (L_1 WS), level 2 working set (L_2 WS), and so on. An application like Ocean has several working sets, as we discussed in Chapter 3, but we focus on the two most sharply defined and important ones. In addition to these working sets, some of the applications also have tiny working sets that do not scale with problem size or the number of processors and are therefore always expected to fit even in the cache closest to the processor; we call these the level 0 working sets (L_0 WS). They typically consist of stack data that is used by the program as temporary storage for a given primitive calculation (such as a particle-cell interaction in Barnes-Hut) and reused across these calculations. These are marked on the graphs when they are visible, but we will not discuss them further.

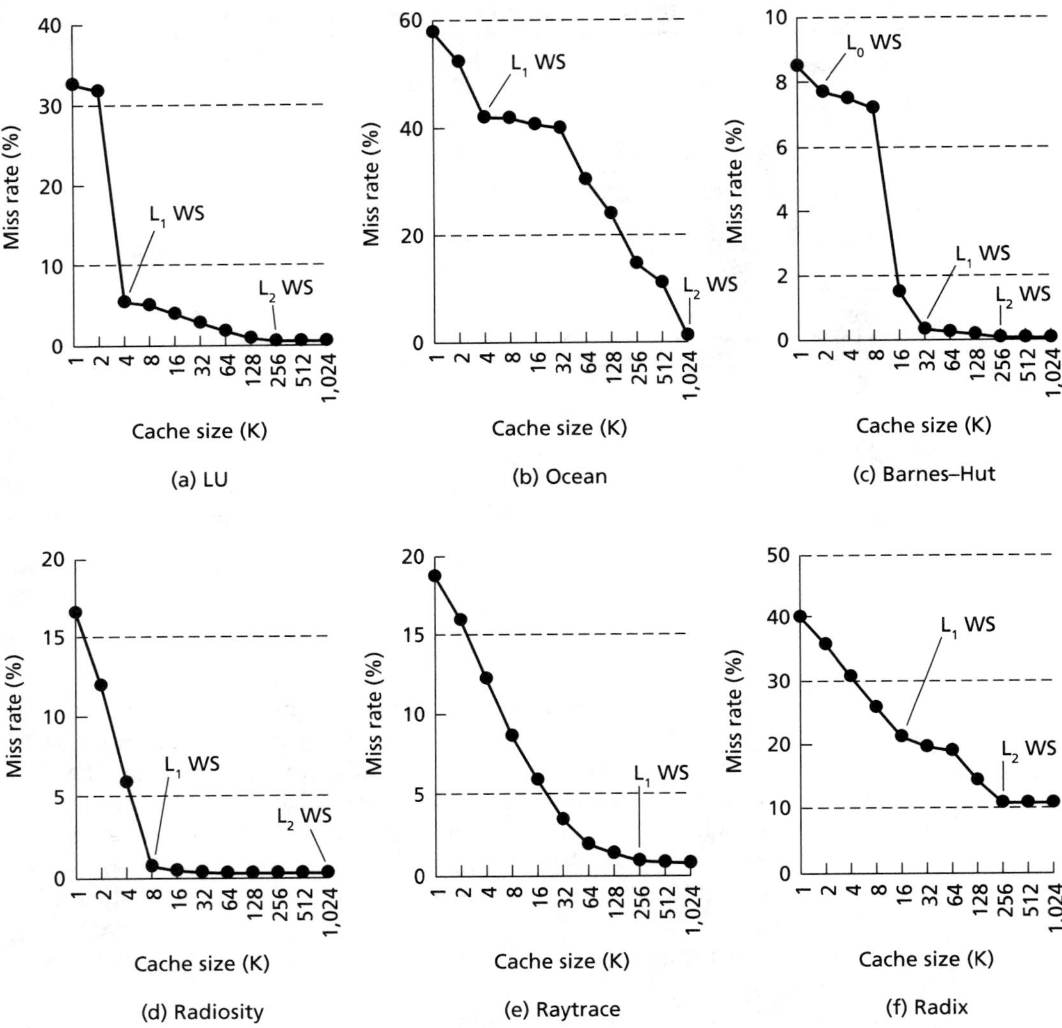

FIGURE 4.19 Working set curves for the six parallel applications in 16-processor executions. The graphs show miss rate versus cache size for fully associative first-level caches per processor and an 8-byte cache block.

We see that in most cases the working sets are very sharply defined. Table 4.3 summarizes for the different working sets how their sizes scale with application parameters and the number of processors, whether they are important to performance (at least on efficient cache-coherent machines), and whether they can be expected not to fit in a modern secondary cache for realistic problem sizes (with a

Table 4.3 Important Working Sets and Their Growth Rates for the SPLASH-2 Suite

Program	Working Set 1	Growth Rate	Important?	Realistic Not to Fit in Cache?	Working Set 2	Growth Rate	Important?	Realistic Not to Fit in Cache?
LU	One block	Fixed(*B*)	Yes	No	Partition of *DS*	*DS/P*	No	Yes
Ocean	A few subrows	$\sqrt{P}/\sqrt{DS}$	Yes	No	Partition of *DS*	*DS/P*	Yes	Yes
Barnes-Hut	Tree data for 1 body	$(\log DS)/\theta^2$	Yes	No	Partition of *DS*	*DS/P*	No	Yes
Radiosity	BSP tree	log(*polygons*)	Yes	No	Unstructured	Unstructured	No	Yes
Radix	Histogram	Radix *r*	Yes	No	Partition of *DS*	*DS/P*	Yes	Yes
Raytrace	Scene and grid data reused across rays	Unstructured	Yes	Yes	—	—	—	—

DS represents the data set size, and *P* is the number of processes.

reasonable degree of cache associativity, at least beyond direct mapped). The applications for which a working set has a "Yes" in each of the last two columns are Ocean, Radix, and Raytrace. Recall that in Ocean, all the major computations stream through a process's partition of one or more grids. The large working set consists of a process's partitions of entire grids that it might benefit from reusing. Whether or not this large working set fits in a modern secondary cache therefore depends on the grid size and the number of processors. In Radix, a process streams through all its n/p keys, at the same time heavily accessing the histogram data structure (of size proportional to the radix used). Fitting the histogram in the cache is therefore important, but this working set is not sharply defined since the keys are being streamed through at the same time. The larger working set consists of a process's entire partition of the key data set, which may or may not fit in the cache, depending on n and p. Finally, in Raytrace we have seen that the working set is diffuse and ill defined and can become quite large, depending on the characteristics of the scene being traced and the viewpoint. For the other applications, we expect the important working sets to fit in the cache for realistic problem and machine sizes. We shall take this into account according to our methodology when we evaluate architectural trade-offs in the following chapters. In particular, for Ocean, Radix, and Raytrace, we shall choose scenarios that fit and do not fit the larger working set since both situations exist in practice.

4.5 CONCLUDING REMARKS

We now have a good understanding of the major issues in workload-driven evaluation for multiprocessors: choosing workloads, scaling problems and machines, dealing with the large parameter space, and choosing metrics. For each issue, we have a set of guidelines and steps to follow, an understanding of how to avoid pitfalls, and a means to understand the limitations of investigations. We also have a basis for our own quantitative illustration of architectural trade-offs in the rest of the book. The experiments in the book illustrate important points rather than evaluate trade-offs comprehensively, since the latter would require a much wider range of workloads and parameter variations.

We've seen that workloads should be chosen to represent a wide range of applications, behavioral patterns, and levels of optimization. While complete applications and perhaps multiprogrammed workloads are indispensable, a role exists for simpler workloads, such as microbenchmarks and kernels, as well.

We have also seen that proper workload-driven evaluation requires an understanding of the relevant behavioral properties of the workloads as well as their interactions with architectural parameters. Although this problem is complex, we have examined guidelines for dealing with the large parameter space—for evaluating both real machines and architectural trade-offs—and pruning it while still obtaining coverage of realistic situations.

The importance of understanding relevant properties of workloads was underscored by the scaling issue, which affects all important characteristics and interactions. Both execution time and memory may be constraints on scaling, and applications often have more than one parameter that determines key execution properties. We should scale programs based on an understanding of these parameters, their relationships, and their impact on execution time and memory requirements. We saw that realistic scaling models driven by the needs of applications lead to very different results of architectural significance than naive models that scale only a single application parameter. In fact, scaling is important for design as well as for evaluation. Together with an appreciation for how technology scales (for example, processor speeds relative to memory and network speeds), understanding application scaling and its implications is very important for determining appropriate resource distributions for future machines (Rothberg, Singh, and Gupta 1993).

Many interesting issues also arose in our discussion of choosing metrics for evaluation and presentation. For example, we saw that execution time (preferably with a per-processor breakdown into its major components) and speedup are both very useful metrics to present, whereas rate-based metrics such as MFLOPS or MIPS or utilization metrics can be useful for specific purposes but are too susceptible to problems as general-purpose metrics.

Finally, this chapter has described the main workloads that we use in our own illustrative workload-driven evaluation of real shared address space systems and architectural trade-offs in the rest of the book and has quantified their basic characteristics. (For message-passing systems, we examine briefly the performance of a standard message-passing benchmark suite, the NAS Parallel Benchmarks II [NPB2] in Chapter 7.) We are now on a firm footing to proceed to core architecture and design.

4.6 EXERCISES

4.1 a. You are to perform a study evaluating a new feature proposed for the communication architecture of a cache-coherent machine. Your manager tells you that you may use no more than three parallel programs for the evaluation. Even though this goes against your better judgment, you have to agree. Of the seven parallel programs (excluding the multiprogrammed workload) we have examined in this chapter and in Chapter 3, which three would you choose and why?

b. Suppose you knew that the feature was designed to improve the machine's communication bandwidth. How would this affect your choice?

c. Suppose instead that the feature was designed to increase the effective replication storage for nonlocally allocated data. What programs would you choose now?

4.2 Identify a fundamental problem with TC scaling compared to MC scaling. Illustrate it with an example.

4.3 Suppose you had to evaluate the scalability of a system. One possibility is to measure the speedups under different scaling models as defined in this chapter. Another is to determine how the problem size needed to get, say, 70% parallel efficiency scales. What are the advantages and, particularly, the disadvantages or caveats for each of these? What would you actually do?

4.4 Your manager asks you to compare two types of systems based on the same uniprocessor node but with some interesting differences in their communication architectures. She tells you that she cares about only 10 particular applications. She instructs you to come up with a single numeric measure of which is better, given a fixed number of processors and a fixed problem size (of your choice) for each application, despite your arguments based on reading this chapter that averaging over parallel applications is not such a good idea. What additional questions would you ask her before choosing problem sizes? What measure of average would you report to her and why?

4.5 Often, a system may display good speedups on an application even though its communication architecture is not well suited to the application. Why might this happen? Can you design a metric alternative to speedup that measures the effectiveness of the communication architecture for the application? Discuss some of the issues and alternatives in designing such a metric.

4.6 A research paper you read proposes a communication architecture mechanism and tells you that starting from a given communication architecture on a machine with 32 processors, the mechanism improves performance by 40% on some workloads that are of interest to you. Is this enough information for you to decide to include that mechanism in the next machine you design? If not, list the major reasons why not, and say what other information you would need. Assume that the machine you are to design also has 32 processors.

4.7 Suppose you had to design experiments to compare different methods for implementing locks on a shared address space machine. What performance properties would you want to measure, and what "microbenchmark" experiments would you design? What would be your specific performance metrics? Now answer the same questions for global barriers.

4.8 You have designed a method for supporting a shared address space communication abstraction transparently in software across bus-based shared memory multiprocessors like the Intel Pentium Pro "quad" discussed in Chapter 1. Within a node or quad, coherent shared memory is supported with high efficiency in hardware; across nodes, it is supported much less efficiently and in software. Given a set of applications and the problem sizes of interest, you are about to write a research report evaluating your system. What are the interesting performance comparisons you might want to perform to understand the effectiveness of your cross-node architecture? What experiments would you design, what would each type of experiment tell you, and what metrics would you use? You have 16 bus-based multiprocessor nodes with 4 processors in each, for a total of 64 processors. Assume that you use problem-constrained scaling and that you have already chosen the problem sizes.

4.9 As discussed in this chapter, two types of simulations are often used in practice to study architectural trade-offs: trace-driven and execution-driven. What are the major trade-offs between trace-driven and execution-driven simulation? Under what conditions do you expect the results (say, a program's execution time) to be significantly different?

4.10 Consider the difficulty and accuracy of multiprocessor simulation.

a. What aspects of a system do you think are most difficult to simulate accurately and which are relatively easier—processor, memory system, network, communication assist, latency, bandwidth, or contention? What are the key difficulties in each case? Which of these do you think are most important to simulate very accurately, and which would you compromise on?

b. Consider the importance of simulating the processor pipeline appropriately when trying to evaluate the impact of trade-offs in the communication architecture. While many modern processors are superscalar and dynamically scheduled, a single-issue, statically scheduled processor is much easier to simulate. Suppose the real processor you want to model is 200 MHz with two-way issue but achieves a perfect memory CPI of 1.5. Could you model it as a single-issue 300-MHz processor for a study that wants to understand the impact of changing network transit latency on end performance? What are the major issues to consider?

4.11 Consider the familiar iterative nearest-neighbor grid computation on a two-dimensional grid, with subblock partitioning. Suppose we use a four-dimensional array representation, where the first two dimensions indicate the appropriate partition. The full-scale problem we would like to evaluate is an $8,192 \times 8,192$ grid of double-precision elements with 256 processors and 256 KB of direct-mapped cache per processor with a 128-byte cache block size. We cannot simulate this but instead simulate a 512×512 grid problem with 64 processors.

a. What cache sizes would you choose and why?

b. List some of the dangers of choosing too small a cache.

c. What cache block size and associativity would you choose, and what are the issues and caveats involved?

d. To what extent would you consider the results representative of the full-scale problem on the larger machine? Would you use this setup to evaluate the benefits of a certain communication architecture optimization? To evaluate the speedups achievable on the machine for that application?

4.12 In scientific applications like the Barnes-Hut galaxy simulation, a key issue that affects scaling is error. These applications often simulate physical phenomena that occur in nature, using several approximations to represent a continuous phenomenon by a discrete model and solving it using numerical approximation techniques. Several application parameters represent distinct sources of approximation and, hence, of error in the simulation. For example, in Barnes-Hut the number of particles n represents the accuracy with which the galaxy is sampled (spatial discretization), the time-step interval Δt represents the approximation made in discretizing time, and the force calculation accuracy parameter θ determines the approximation in that calculation. The goal of an application scientist in running larger problems is usually to reduce the overall error in the simulation and have it more accurately reflect the phenomenon being simulated. Although there are no universal rules for how scientists scale different approximations, a principle that has both intuitive appeal and widespread practical applicability for physical simulations is the following: all sources of error should be scaled so that their error contributions are about equal.

For the Barnes-Hut galaxy simulation, studies in astrophysics (Hernquist 1987; Barnes and Hut 1989) show that while some error contributions are not completely independent, the following rules emerge as being valid in interesting parameter ranges:

- n: An increase in n by a factor of s leads to a decrease in simulation error by a factor of $\sqrt{s}$.
- Δt: The method used to integrate the particle orbits over time has a global error of the order of Δt^2. Thus, reducing the error by a factor of $\sqrt{s}$ (to match that due to an s-fold increase in n) requires a decrease in Δt by a factor of $\sqrt[4]{s}$. This means $\sqrt[4]{s}$ more time-steps to simulate a fixed amount of physical time, which we assume is held constant.
- θ: The force calculation error is proportional to θ^2 in the range of practical interest. Reducing the error by a factor of $\sqrt{s}$ thus requires a decrease in θ by a factor of $\sqrt[4]{s}$.

Assume throughout this exercise that the execution time of a problem size on p processors is $1/p$ of the execution time on one processor; that is, perfect speedup is obtained for that problem size under problem-constrained scaling.

a. How would you scale the other parameters θ and Δt if n is increased by a factor of s? Call this rule *realistic* scaling, as opposed to *naive* scaling, which scales only the number of particles n.

b. In a sequential program, the data set size is proportional to n and independent of the other parameters. Do the memory requirements grow differently under realistic and naive scaling in a shared address space (assuming that the important working set fits in the cache)? In message passing?

c. The sequential execution time grows roughly as

$$\frac{1}{\Delta t} \cdot \frac{1}{\theta^2} \cdot n \log n$$

(assuming that a fixed amount of physical time is simulated). If n is scaled by a factor of s, how does the parallel execution time on p processors scale under realistic and under naive scaling, assuming perfect speedup?

d. How does the parallel execution time grow under MC scaling, both naive and realistic, when the number of processors increases by a factor of k? If the problem takes a day on the base machine (before it is scaled up), how long will it take in the scaled-up case on the bigger machine under both the naive and realistic models?

e. How does the number of particles that can be simulated in a shared address space grow under TC scaling, both realistic and naive, when the number of processors increases by a factor of k?

f. Which scaling model appears more practical for this application: MC or TC?

4.13 For the Barnes-Hut example, how do the following execution characteristics scale under realistic and naive MC, TC, and PC scaling?

a. The communication-to-computation ratio. Assume first that it depends only on n and the number of processors p, varying as $\sqrt{p}/\sqrt{n}$, and roughly plot the curves of growth rate of this ratio with the number of processors under the different models. Then comment on the likely effects of the other parameters under the different scaling models.

b. The sizes of the different working sets and, hence, the cache size you think is needed for good performance on a shared address space machine. Roughly plot the growth rate for the most important working set with number of processors under the different models. What major methodological conclusion in scaling does this reinforce? Comment on any differences between these trends and the trends for the amount of local replication needed in the locally essential trees version of message passing.

c. The frequency of synchronization (per unit computation, say), both locks and barriers. Describe qualitatively at least.

d. The average frequency and size of input/output operations, assuming that every processor prints out the positions of all its assigned bodies (i) every ten time-steps; (ii) every fixed amount of physical time simulated (e.g., every year of simulated time in the galaxy's evolution).

e. The number of processors likely to share (access) a given piece of body data during force calculation in a coherent shared address space at a time. (As we will see in Chapter 8, this information is useful in the design of cache coherence protocols for scalable shared address space machines.)

f. The frequency and size of messages in an explicit message-passing implementation. Focus on the communication needed for force calculation and assume that each processor sends only one message to every other processor, communicating the data that the latter needs from the former to compute its forces in that time-step.

4.14 The Radix sorting application requires a parallel prefix computation to compute the global histogram from local histograms. A simplified version of the computation is as follows. Suppose each of the p processes has a local value it has computed (think of this as representing the number of keys for a given digit value in the local histogram of that process). The goal is to compute an array of p entries, in which entry i is the sum of all the local values from processors 0 through $i - 1$.

a. Describe and implement the simplest linear method to compute this output array.

b. Now design a parallel method with a shorter critical path. (Hint: you can use a tree structure.) Analyze the time required for each method. Implement the two methods and compare their performance on a machine of your choice. You may use the simplified example here or the fuller example where the "local value" is in fact an array with one entry per radix digit and the output array is two-dimensional, indexed by process identifier and radix digit. That is, the fuller example does the computation for each radix digit rather than for just one.

c. Discuss the ways in which you could orchestrate synchronization in the latter method and the trade-offs among them.

5

Shared Memory Multiprocessors

The most prevalent form of parallel architecture is the multiprocessor of small to moderate scale that provides a global physical address space and symmetric access to all of main memory from any processor, often called a *symmetric multiprocessor* or SMP. Every processor has its own cache, and all the processors and memory modules attach to the same interconnect, which is usually a shared bus. SMPs dominate the server market and are becoming more common on the desktop. They are also important building blocks for larger-scale systems. The efficient sharing of resources, such as memory and processors, makes these machines attractive as "throughput engines" for multiple sequential jobs with varying memory and CPU requirements. The ability to access all shared data efficiently from any of the processors using ordinary loads and stores, together with the automatic movement and replication of shared data in the local caches, makes them attractive for parallel programming. These features are also very useful for the operating system, whose different processes share data structures and can easily run on different processors.

From the viewpoint of the layers of the communication architecture in Figure 5.1, the shared address space programming model is supported directly by hardware. User processes can read and write shared virtual addresses, and these operations are realized by individual loads and stores of shared physical addresses. In fact, the relationship between the programming model and the hardware operation is so close that they both are often referred to simply as "shared memory." A message-passing programming model can be supported by an intervening software layer—typically a run-time library—that treats large portions of the shared address space as private to each process and manages some portions explicitly as per-process message buffers. A send/receive operation pair is realized by copying data between these buffers. The operating system need not be involved since address translation and protection on the shared buffers is provided by the hardware. For portability, most message-passing programming interfaces have indeed been implemented on popular SMPs. In fact, such implementations often deliver higher message-passing performance than traditional, distributed-memory message-passing systems—as long as contention for the shared bus and memory does not become a bottleneck—largely because of the lack of operating system involvement in communication. The operating system is still used for input/output and multiprogramming support.

Since all communication and local computation generates memory accesses in a shared address space, from a system architect's perspective the key high-level design

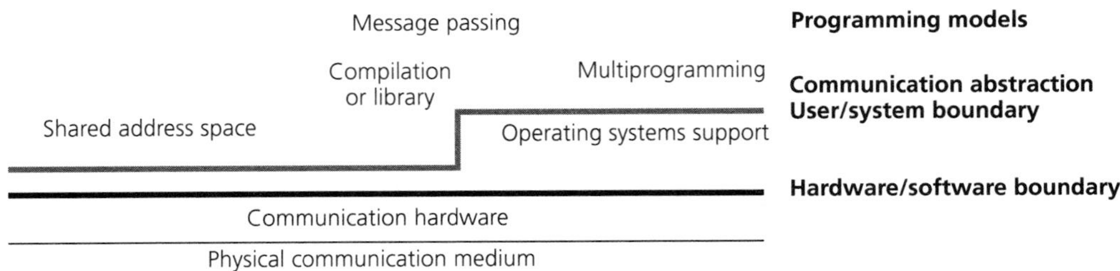

FIGURE 5.1 Layers of abstraction of the communication architecture for bus-based SMPs. A shared address space is supported directly in hardware, while message passing is supported in software.

issue is the organization of the extended memory hierarchy. In general, memory hierarchies in multiprocessors fall primarily into four categories, as shown in Figure 5.2, which correspond loosely to the scale of the multiprocessor being considered. The first three are symmetric multiprocessors (all of main memory is equally far away from all processors), while the fourth is not.

In the shared cache approach (Figure 5.2[a]), the interconnect is located between the processors and a shared first-level cache, which in turn connects to a shared main memory subsystem. Both the cache and the main memory system may be interleaved to increase available bandwidth. This approach has been used for connecting very small numbers of processors (2–8). In the mid-1980s, it was a common technique for connecting a couple of processors on a board; today, it is a possible strategy for a multiprocessor-on-a-chip, where a small number of processors on the same chip share an on-chip first-level cache. However, it applies only at a very small scale, both because the interconnect between the processors and the shared first-level cache is on the critical path that determines the latency of cache access and because the shared cache must deliver tremendous bandwidth to the multiple processors accessing it simultaneously.

In the bus-based shared memory approach (Figure 5.2[b]), the interconnect is a shared bus located between the processor's private caches (or cache hierarchies) and the shared main memory subsystem. This approach has been widely used for small- to medium-scale multiprocessors consisting of up to 20 or 30 processors. It is the dominant form of parallel machine sold today, and considerable design effort has been invested in essentially all modern microprocessors to support "cache-coherent" shared memory configurations. For example, the Intel Pentium Pro processor can attach to a coherent shared bus without any glue logic, and low-cost bus-based machines that use these processors have greatly increased the popularity of this approach. The scaling limit for these machines comes primarily due to bandwidth limitations of the shared bus and memory system.

The last two approaches are intended to be scalable to many processing nodes. The dancehall approach also places the interconnect between the caches and main memory, but the interconnect is now a scalable point-to-point network rather than a bus, and memory is divided into many logical modules that connect to logically dif-

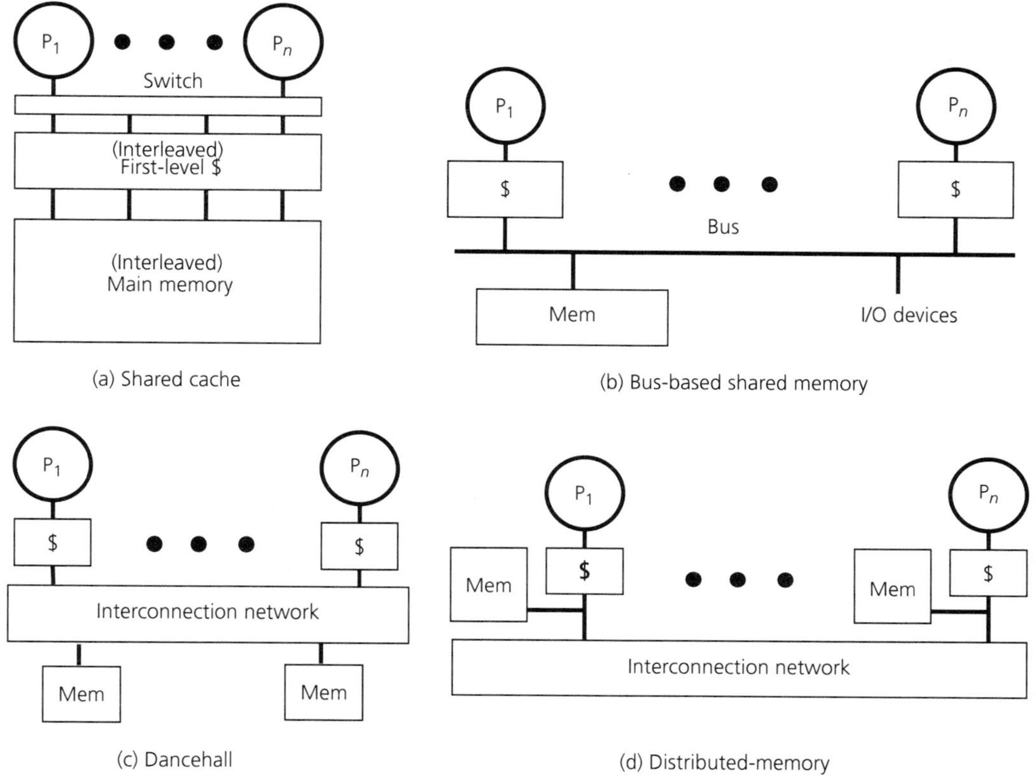

FIGURE 5.2 Common extended memory hierarchies found in multiprocessors

ferent points in the interconnect (Figure 5.2[c]). This approach is symmetric—all of main memory is uniformly far away from all processors—but its limitation is that all of memory is indeed *far* away from all processors. Especially in large systems, several "hops" or switches in the interconnect must be traversed to reach any memory module from any processor. The fourth approach, distributed-memory, is not symmetric. A scalable interconnect is located between processing nodes, but each node has its own local portion of the global main memory to which it has faster access (Figure 5.2[d]). By exploiting locality in the distribution of data, most cache misses may be satisfied in the local memory and may not have to traverse the network. This design is most attractive for scalable multiprocessors, and several chapters are devoted to the topic later in the book. Of course, it is also possible to combine multiple approaches into a single machine design—for example, a distributed-memory machine whose individual nodes are bus-based SMPs or a machine in which processors share a cache at a level of the hierarchy other than the first level.

In all cases, caches play an essential role in reducing the average data access time as seen by the processor and in reducing the bandwidth requirement each processor places on the shared interconnect and memory system. The bandwidth requirement is reduced because the data accesses issued by a processor that are satisfied in the cache do not have to appear on the interconnect. In all but the shared cache approach, each processor has at least one level of its cache hierarchy that is private. This raises a critical challenge—namely, that of *cache coherence*. The problem arises when copies of the same memory block are present in the caches of one or more processors; if a processor writes to and hence modifies that memory block, then, unless special action is taken, the other processors will continue to access the old, stale copy of the block that is in their caches.

Currently, most small-scale multiprocessors use a shared bus interconnect with per-processor caches and a centralized main memory, whereas scalable systems use physically distributed main memory. The dancehall and shared cache approaches are employed in relatively specific settings. Specific organizations may change as technology evolves. However, besides being the most popular, the bus-based and distributed-memory organizations also illustrate the two fundamental approaches to solving the cache coherence problem, depending on the nature of the interconnect: one for the case where any transaction placed on the interconnect is visible to all processors (like a bus) and the other where the interconnect is decentralized and a point-to-point transaction is visible only to the processors at its endpoints. This chapter focuses on the logical design of protocols that exploit the fundamental properties of a bus to solve the cache coherence problem. The next chapter expands on the design issues associated with realizing these cache coherence techniques in hardware. The basic design of scalable distributed-memory multiprocessors will be addressed in Chapter 7, followed by coverage of the issues specific to scalable cache coherence in Chapters 8 and 9.

Section 5.1 describes the cache coherence problem for shared memory architectures in detail and describes the simplest example of what are called *snooping* cache coherence protocols. Coherence is not only a key hardware design concept but is a necessary part of our intuitive notion of the abstraction of memory. However, parallel software often makes stronger assumptions than coherence about how memory behaves. Section 5.2 extends the discussion of ordering begun in Chapter 1 and introduces the concept of memory consistency, which defines the semantics of shared address space. This issue has become increasingly important in computer architecture and compiler design; a large fraction of the reference manuals for most recent instruction set architectures is devoted to the memory consistency model. Once the abstractions and concepts are defined, Section 5.3 presents the design space for more realistic snooping protocols and shows how they satisfy the conditions for coherence as well as for a useful consistency model. It describes the operation of commonly used protocols at the logical state transition level. The techniques used for the quantitative evaluation of several design trade-offs at this level are illustrated in Section 5.4, using aspects of the methodology for workload-driven evaluation from Chapter 4.

The latter portions of the chapter examine the implications that cache-coherent shared memory architectures have for the software that runs on them. Section 5.5 examines how the low-level synchronization operations make use of the available hardware primitives on cache-coherent multiprocessors and how algorithms for locks and barriers can be tailored to use the machine efficiently. Section 5.6 discusses the implications for parallel programming in general, and in particular, it discusses how temporal and spatial data locality may be exploited to reduce cache misses and traffic on the shared bus.

5.1 CACHE COHERENCE

Think for a moment about your intuitive model of what a memory should do. It should provide a set of locations that hold values, and when a location is read it should return the latest value written to that location. This is the fundamental property of the memory abstraction that we rely on in sequential programs, in which we use memory to communicate a value from a point in a program where it is computed to other points where it is used. We rely on the same property of a memory system when using a shared address space to communicate data between threads or processes running on one processor. A read returns the latest value written to the location regardless of which process wrote it. Caching does not interfere because all processes see the memory through the same cache hierarchy. We would like to rely on the same property when the two processes run on different processors that share a memory. That is, we would like the results of a program that uses multiple processes to be no different when the processes run on different physical processors than when they run (interleaved or multiprogrammed) on the same physical processor. However, when two processes see the shared memory through different caches, a danger exists that one may see the new value in its cache while the other still sees the old value.

5.1.1 The Cache Coherence Problem

The cache coherence problem in multiprocessors is both pervasive and performance critical. It is illustrated in Example 5.1.

EXAMPLE 5.1 Figure 5.3 shows three processors with caches connected via a bus to shared main memory. A sequence of accesses to location *u* is made by the processors. First, processor P_1 reads *u* from main memory, bringing a copy into its cache. Then processor P_3 reads *u* from main memory, bringing a copy into its cache. Then processor P_3 writes location *u*, changing its value from 5 to 7. With a write-through cache, this will cause the main memory location to be updated; however, when processor P_1 reads location *u* again (action 4), it will unfortunately read the stale value 5 from its own cache instead of the correct value 7 from main memory. This is a cache coherence problem. What happens if the caches are write back instead of write through?

Answer The situation is even worse with write-back caches. P_3's write would merely set the dirty (or modified) bit associated with the cache block holding location *u* and would not update main memory right away. Only when this cache block is subsequently replaced from P_3's cache would its contents be written back to main memory. Thus, not only will P_1 read the stale value, but when processor P_2 reads

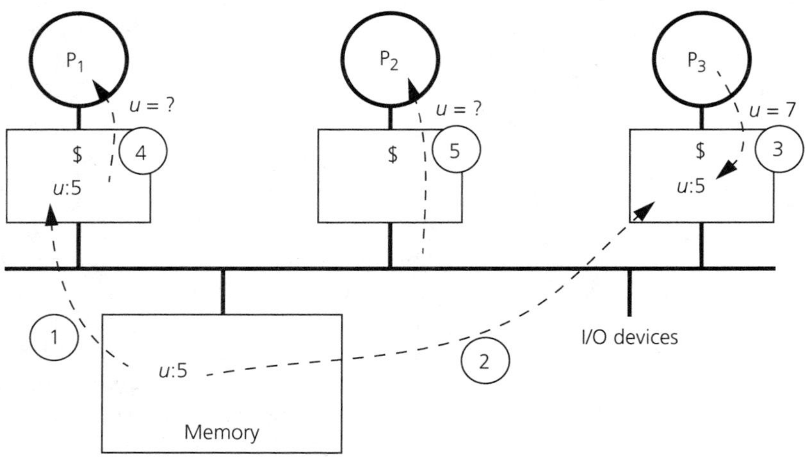

FIGURE 5.3 Example cache coherence problem. The figure shows three processors with caches connected by a bus to main memory. u is a location in memory whose contents are being read and written by the processors. The sequence in which reads and writes are done is indicated by the number listed inside the circles placed next to the arc. It is easy to see that unless special action is taken when P_3 updates the value of u to 7, P_1 will subsequently continue to read the stale value out of its cache, and P_2 will also read a stale value out of main memory.

location u (action 5), it will miss in its cache and read the stale value of 5 from main memory instead of 7. Finally, if multiple processors write distinct values to location u in their write-back caches, the final value that will reach main memory will be determined by the order in which the cache blocks containing u are replaced and will have nothing to do with the order in which the writes to u occur. ■

Clearly, the behavior described in Example 5.1 violates our intuitive notion of what a memory should do. In fact, cache coherence problems arise even in uniprocessors when I/O operations occur. Most I/O transfers are performed by direct memory access (DMA) devices that move data between memory and the peripheral component without involving the processor. When the DMA device writes to a location in main memory, unless special action is taken, the processor may continue to see the old value if that location was previously present in its cache. With write-back caches, a DMA device may read a stale value for a location from main memory because the latest value for that location is in the processor's cache. Since I/O operations are much less frequent than memory operations, several coarse solutions have been adopted in uniprocessors. For example, segments of memory space used for I/O may be marked as "uncacheable" (i.e., they do not enter the processor cache), or the processor may always use uncached load and store operations for locations used to communicate with I/O devices. For I/O devices that transfer large blocks of data at a time, such as disks, operating system support is often enlisted to ensure coherence. In many systems, the pages of memory from/to which the data is to be transferred are flushed by the operating system from the processor's cache before the I/O is allowed to proceed. In still other systems, all I/O traffic is made to flow through the processor cache hierarchy, thus maintaining coherence. This, of course, pollutes the cache hierarchy with data that may not be of immediate interest to the processor. Fortunately, the techniques and support used to solve the multiprocessor cache coherence problem also solve the I/O coherence problem. Essentially all microprocessors today provide support for multiprocessor cache coherence.

In multiprocessors, reading and writing of shared variables by different processors is expected to be a frequent event since it is the way that multiple processes belonging to a parallel application communicate with each other. Therefore, we do not want to disallow caching of shared data or to invoke the operating system on all shared references. Rather, cache coherence needs to be addressed as a basic hardware design issue; for example, stale cached copies of a shared location (like the copy of *u* in P_1's cache in Example 5.1) must be eliminated when the location is modified, either by invalidating them or updating them with the new value. In fact, the operating system itself benefits greatly from transparent, hardware-supported coherence of its data structures.

Before we explore techniques to provide coherence, it is useful to define the coherence property more precisely. Our intuitive notion that "each read should return the last value written to that location" is problematic for parallel architecture because "last" may not be well defined. Two different processors might write to the same location at the same instant, or one processor may read so soon after another writes that, due to the speed of light and other factors, there isn't time to propagate the invalidation or update to the reader. Even in the sequential case, "last" is not a chronological or physical notion but refers to latest in program order. For now, we can think of program order within a process as the order in which memory operations occur in the machine language program. The subtleties of program order are elaborated further in Section 5.2. The challenge in the parallel case is that, while program order is defined for the operations within each individual process, in order to define the semantics of a coherent memory system we need to make sense of the collection of program orders.

Let us first review the definitions of some terms in the context of uniprocessor memory systems so that we can extend the definitions for multiprocessors. By *memory operation*, we mean a single read (load), write (store), or read-modify-write access to a memory location. Instructions that perform multiple reads and writes, such as those that appear in many complex instruction sets, can be viewed as broken down into multiple memory operations, and the order in which these memory operations are executed is specified by the instruction. These memory operations within an instruction are assumed to execute atomically with respect to each other in the specified order; that is, all aspects of one appear to execute before any aspect of the next. A memory operation *issues* when it leaves the processor's internal environment and is presented to the memory system, which includes the caches, write buffers, bus, and memory modules. A very important point for ordering is that the only way the processor observes the state of the memory system is by issuing memory operations (e.g., reads); thus, for a memory operation to be *performed with respect to the*

see p. 289

processor means that it appears to have taken place, as far as the processor can tell from the memory operations it issues. In particular, a write operation is said to perform with respect to the processor when a subsequent read by the processor returns the value produced by either that write or a later write. A read operation is said to perform with respect to the processor when subsequent writes issued by the processor cannot affect the value returned by the read. Notice that in neither case do we specify that the physical location in the memory chip has been accessed or that specific bits of hardware have changed their values. Also, "subsequent" is well defined in the sequential case since reads and writes are ordered by the program order.

The same definitions for memory operations issuing and performing with respect to a processor apply in the parallel case; we can simply replace "the processor" with "a processor" in the definitions. The problem is that "subsequent" and "last" are not yet well defined since we do not have one program order; rather, we have separate program orders for every process, and these program orders interact when accessing the memory system. One way to sharpen our idea of a coherent memory system is to picture what would happen if there were a single shared memory and no caches. Every write and every read to a memory location would access the physical location at main memory. The operation would be performed with respect to all processors at this point and would therefore be said to *complete*. Thus, the memory would impose a serial order on all the read and write operations from all processors to the location. Moreover, the reads and writes to the location from any individual processor should be in program order within this overall serial order. In this case, then, the main memory location provides a natural point in the hardware to determine the order across processes of operations to that location. We have no reason to believe that the memory system should interleave accesses from different processors in a particular way, so any interleaving that preserves the individual program orders is reasonable. We do assume some basic fairness; eventually, the operations from each processor should be performed. Our intuitive notion of "last" can be viewed as most recent in a hypothetical serial order that maintains these properties, and "subsequent" can be defined similarly. Since this serial order must be consistent, it is important that all processors see the writes to a location in the same order (if they bother to look, i.e., to read the location).

The appearance of such a total, serial order on operations to a location is what we expect from any coherent memory system. Of course, the total order need not actually be constructed at any given point in the machine while executing the program. Particularly in a system with caches, we do not want main memory to see all the memory operations, and we want to avoid serialization whenever possible. We just need to make sure that the program behaves as if some serial order was enforced.

More formally, we say that a multiprocessor memory system is *coherent* if the results of any execution of a program are such that, for each location, it is possible to construct a hypothetical serial order of all operations to the location (i.e., put all reads/writes issued by all processes into a total order) that is consistent with the results of the execution and in which

1. operations issued by any particular process occur in the order in which they were issued to the memory system by that process, and

2. the value returned by each read operation is the value written by the last write to that location in the serial order.

Two properties are implicit in the definition of coherence: *write propagation* means that writes become visible to other processes; *write serialization* means that all writes to a location (from the same or different processes) are seen in the same order by all processes. For example, write serialization means that if read operations by process P_1 to a location see the value produced by write $w1$ (from P_2, say) before the value produced by write $w2$ (from P_3, say), then reads by another process P_4 (or P_2 or P_3) also should not be able to see $w2$ before $w1$. There is no need for an analogous concept of read serialization since the effects of reads are not visible to any process but the one issuing the read.

The *results* of a program can be viewed as the values returned by the read operations in it, perhaps augmented with an implicit set of reads to all locations at the end of the program. From the results, we cannot determine the order in which operations were actually executed by the machine or exactly when bits changed, only the order in which they appear to execute. Fortunately, this is all that matters since this is all that processors can detect. This concept will become even more important when we discuss memory consistency models.

5.1.2 Cache Coherence through Bus Snooping

Having defined the memory coherence property, let us examine techniques to solve the cache coherence problem. For instance, in Figure 5.3, how do we ensure that P_1 and P_2 see the value that P_3 wrote? In fact, a simple and elegant solution to cache coherence arises from the very nature of a bus. The bus is a single set of wires connecting several devices, each of which can observe every bus transaction, for example, every read or write on the shared bus. When a processor issues a request to its cache, the cache controller examines the state of the cache and takes suitable action, which may include generating bus transactions to access memory. Coherence is maintained by having all cache controllers "snoop" on the bus and monitor the transactions, as illustrated in Figure 5.4 (Goodman 1983). A snooping cache controller may take action if a bus transaction is *relevant* to it—that is, if it involves a memory block of which it has a copy in its cache. Thus, P_1 may take an action, such as invalidating or updating its copy of the location, if it sees the write from P_3. In fact, since the allocation and replacement of data in caches is managed at the granularity of a cache block (usually several words long) and cache misses fetch a block of data, most often coherence is maintained at the granularity of a cache block as well. In other words, either an entire cache block is in valid state in the cache or none of it is. Thus, a cache block is the granularity of allocation in the cache, of data transfer between caches, and of coherence.

The key properties of a bus that support coherence are the following. First, all transactions that appear on the bus are visible to all cache controllers. Second, they are visible to all controllers in the same order (the order in which they appear on the bus). A coherence protocol must guarantee that all the "necessary" transactions in

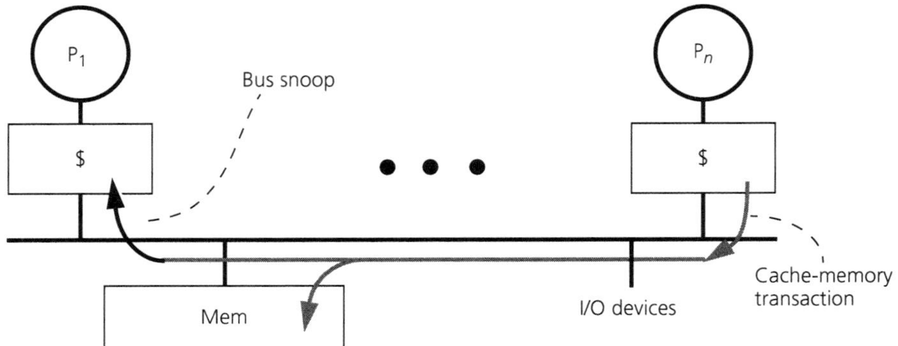

FIGURE 5.4 A snooping cache-coherent multiprocessor. Multiple processors with private caches are placed on a shared bus. Each processor's cache controller continuously "snoops" on the bus watching for relevant transaction and updates its state suitably to keep its local cache coherent. The gray arrows show the transaction being placed on the bus and accepted by main memory, as in a uniprocessor system. The black arrow indicates the snoop.

fact appear on the bus, in response to memory operations, and that the controllers take the appropriate actions when they see a relevant transaction.

The simplest illustration of maintaining coherence is a system that has single-level write-through caches. It is basically the approach followed by the first commercial bus-based SMPs in the mid-1980s. In this case, every write operation causes a write transaction to appear on the bus, so every cache controller observes every write (thus providing write propagation). If a snooping cache has a copy of the block, it either invalidates or updates its copy. Protocols that invalidate cached copies (other than the writer's copy) on a write are called *invalidation-based protocols*, whereas those that update other cached copies are called *update-based protocols*. In either case, the next time the processor with the copy accesses the block, it will see the most recent value, either through a miss or because the updated value is in its cache. Main memory always has valid data, so the cache need not take any action when it observes a read on the bus. Example 5.2 illustrates how the coherence problem in Figure 5.3 is solved with write-through caches.

EXAMPLE 5.2 Consider the scenario presented in Figure 5.3. Assuming write-through caches, show how the bus may be used to provide coherence using an invalidation-based protocol.

Answer When processor P_3 writes 7 to location *u*, P_3's cache controller generates a bus transaction to update memory. Observing this bus transaction as relevant and as a write transaction, P_1's cache controller invalidates its own copy of the block containing *u*. The main memory controller will update the value it has stored for location *u* to 7. Subsequent reads to *u* from processors P_1 and P_2 (actions 4 and 5) will both miss in their private caches and get the correct value of 7 from the main memory. ■

The check to determine if a bus transaction is relevant to a cache is essentially the same tag match that is performed for a request from the processor. The action taken may involve invalidating or updating the contents or state of that cache block and/or supplying the latest value for that block from the cache to the bus.

A snoopy cache coherence protocol ties together two basic facets of computer architecture that are also found in uniprocessors: bus transactions and the state transition diagram associated with a cache block. Recall that the first component—the bus transaction—consists of three phases: arbitration, command/address, and data. In the arbitration phase, devices that desire to initiate a transaction assert their bus request, and the bus arbiter selects one of these and responds by asserting its grant signal. Upon grant, the selected device places the command, for example, read or write, and the associated address on the bus command and address lines. All devices observe the address and, in a uniprocessor, one of them recognizes that it is responsible for the particular address. For a read transaction, the address phase is followed by data transfer. Write transactions vary from bus to bus according to whether the data is transferred during or after the address phase. For most buses, a responding device can assert a wait signal to hold off the data transfer until it is ready. This wait signal is different from the other bus signals because it is a wired-OR across all the processors; that is, it is a logical 1 if any device asserts it. The initiator does not need to know which responding device is participating in the transfer, only that there is one and whether it is ready.

The second basic facet of computer architecture leveraged by a cache coherence protocol is that each block in a uniprocessor cache has a state associated with it, along with the tag and data, which indicates the disposition of the block, (e.g., invalid, valid, dirty). The cache policy is defined by the *cache block state transition diagram*, which is a finite state machine specifying how the disposition of a block changes. Transitions for a cache block occur upon access to that block or to an address that maps to the same cache line as that block. (We refer to a cache block as the actual data, and a line as the fixed storage in the hardware cache, in exact analogy with a page and a page frame in main memory.) While only blocks that are actually in cache lines have hardware state information, logically, all blocks that are not resident in the cache can be viewed as being in either a special "not present" state or in the "invalid" state. In a uniprocessor system, for a write-through, write-no-allocate cache (Hennessy and Patterson 1996), only two states are required: valid and invalid. Initially, all the blocks are invalid. When a processor read operation misses, a bus transaction is generated to load the block from memory and the block is marked valid. Writes generate a bus transaction to update memory, and they also update the cache block if it is present in the valid state. Writes do not change the state of the block. If a block is replaced, it may be marked invalid until the memory provides the new block, whereupon it becomes valid. A write-back cache requires an additional state per cache line, indicating a "dirty" or modified block.

In a multiprocessor system, a block has a state in each cache, and these cache states change according to the state transition diagram. Thus, we can think of a block's cache state as being a vector of p states instead of a single state, where p is the number of caches. The cache state is manipulated by a set of p distributed finite state machines, implemented by the cache controllers. The state machine or state transition diagram that governs the state changes is the same for all blocks and all caches, but the current state of a block in different caches is different. As before, if a block is not present in a cache we can assume it to be in a special "not present" state or even in the invalid state.

In a snooping cache coherence scheme, each cache controller receives two sets of inputs: the processor issues memory requests, and the bus snooper informs about bus transactions from other caches. In response to either, the controller may update the state of the appropriate block in the cache according to the current state and the state transition diagram. It may also take an action. For example, it responds to the processor with the requested data, potentially generating new bus transactions to obtain the data. It responds to bus transactions by updating its state and sometimes intervenes in completing the transaction. Thus, a *snooping protocol* is a distributed algorithm represented by a collection of cooperating finite state machines. It is specified by the following components:

- the set of states associated with memory blocks in the local caches
- the state transition diagram, which takes as inputs the current state and the processor request or observed bus transaction and produces as output the next state for the cache block
- the actions associated with each state transition, which are determined in part by the set of feasible actions defined by the bus, the cache, and the processor design

The different state machines for a block are coordinated by bus transactions.

A simple invalidation-based protocol for a coherent write-through, write-no-allocate cache is described by the state transition diagram in Figure 5.5. As in the uniprocessor case, each cache block has only two states: invalid (I) and valid (V) (the "not present" state is assumed to be the same as invalid). The transitions are marked with the input that causes the transition and the output that is generated with the transition. For example, when a controller sees a read from its processor miss in the cache, a BusRd transaction is generated, and upon completion of this transaction the block transitions up to the valid state. Whenever the controller sees a processor write to a location, a bus transaction is generated that updates that location in main memory with no change of state. The key enhancement to the uniprocessor state diagram is that when the bus snooper sees a write transaction on the bus for a memory block that is cached locally, the controller sets the cache state for that block to invalid, thereby effectively discarding its copy. (Figure 5.5 shows this bus-induced transition with a dashed arc.) By extension, if any processor generates a write for a block that is cached by any of the others, all of the others will invalidate their copies. Thus, multiple simultaneous readers of a block may coexist without generating bus transactions or invalidations, but a write will eliminate all other cached copies.

To see how this simple write-through invalidation protocol provides coherence, we need to show that for any execution under the protocol a total order on the mem-

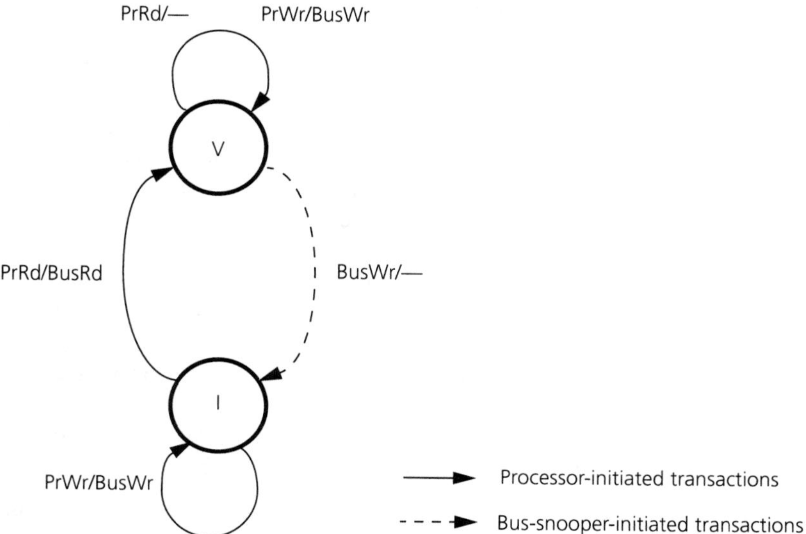

FIGURE 5.5 Snoopy coherence for a multiprocessor with write-through, write-no-allocate caches. There are two states, valid (V) and invalid (I), with intuitive semantics. The notation *A/B* (e.g., PrRd/BusRd) means if *A* is observed, then transaction *B* is generated. From the processor side, the requests can be read (PrRd) or write (PrWr). From the bus side, the cache controller may observe/generate transactions bus read (BusRd) or bus write (BusWr).

ory operations for a location can be constructed that satisfies the program order and write serialization conditions. Let us assume for the present discussion that both bus transactions and the memory operations are atomic. That is, only one transaction is in progress on the bus at a time: once a request is placed on the bus, all phases of the transaction, including the data response, complete before any other request from any processor is allowed access to the bus (such a bus with atomic transactions is called an *atomic bus*). Also, a processor waits until its previous memory operation is complete before issuing another memory operation. With single-level caches, it is also natural to assume that invalidations are applied to the caches, and hence the write completes during the bus transaction itself. (These assumptions will be continued throughout this chapter and will be relaxed when we look at protocol implementations in more detail and study high-performance designs with greater concurrency in Chapter 6.) Finally, we may assume that the memory handles writes and reads in the order in which they are presented by the bus.

In the write-through protocol, all writes appear on the bus. Since only one bus transaction is in progress at a time, in any execution all writes to a location are serialized (consistently) by the order in which they appear on the shared bus, called the *bus order*. Since each snooping cache controller performs the invalidation during the bus transaction, invalidations are performed by all cache controllers in bus order.

Processors "see" writes through read operations, so for write serialization we must ensure that reads from all processors see the writes in the serialized bus order. However, reads to a location are not completely serialized since read hits may be performed independently and concurrently in their caches without generating bus transactions. To see how reads may be inserted in the serial order of writes, consider the following scenario. A read that goes on the bus (a read miss) is serialized by the bus along with the writes; it will therefore obtain the value written by the most recent write to the location in bus order. The only memory operations that do not go on the bus are read hits. In this case, the value read was placed in the cache by either the most recent write to that location by the same processor or by its most recent read miss (in program order). Since both these sources of the value appear on the bus, read hits also see the values produced in the consistent bus order. Thus, under this protocol, bus order together with program order provide enough constraints to satisfy the demands of coherence.

More generally, we can construct a (hypothetical) total order that satisfies coherence by observing the following partial orders imposed by the protocol:

- A memory operation M_2 is subsequent to a memory operation M_1 if the operations are issued by the same processor and M_2 follows M_1 in program order.
- A read operation is subsequent to a write operation W if the read generates a bus transaction that follows that for W.
- A write operation is subsequent to a read or write operation M if M generates a bus transaction and the bus transaction for the write follows that for M.
- A write operation is subsequent to a read operation if the read does not generate a bus transaction (is a hit) and is not already separated from the write by another bus transaction.

Any serial order that preserves the resulting partial order is coherent. The "subsequent" ordering relationship is transitive. An illustration of the resulting partial order is depicted in Figure 5.6, where the bus transactions associated with writes segment the individual program orders. The partial order does not constrain the ordering of read bus transactions from different processors that occur between two write transactions, though the bus will likely establish a particular order. In fact, any interleaving of read operations in the segment between two writes is a valid serial order, as long as it obeys program order.

Of course, the problem with this simple write-through approach is that every store instruction goes to memory, which is why most modern microprocessors use write-back caches (at least at the level closest to the bus). This problem is exacerbated in the multiprocessor setting, since every store from every processor consumes precious bandwidth on the shared bus, resulting in poor scalability, as illustrated by Example 5.3.

EXAMPLE 5.3 Consider a superscalar RISC processor issuing two instructions per cycle running at 200 MHz. Suppose the average CPI (clocks per instruction) for this processor is 1, 15% of all instructions are stores, and each store writes 8 bytes of data. How many processors will a 1-GB/s bus be able to support without becoming saturated?

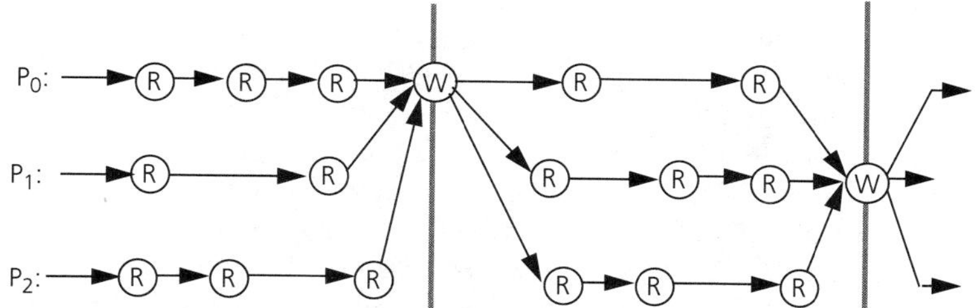

FIGURE 5.6 Partial order of memory operations for an execution with the write-through invalidation protocol. Write bus transactions define a global sequence of events between which individual processors read locations in program order. The execution is consistent with any total order obtained by interleaving the processor orders within each segment.

Answer A single processor will generate 30 million stores per second (0.15 stores per instruction × 1 instruction per cycle × 1,000,000/200 cycles per second), so the total write-through bandwidth is 240 MB of data per second per processor. Even ignoring address and other information and ignoring read misses, a 1-GB/s bus will therefore support only about four processors. ■

For most applications, a write-back cache would absorb the vast majority of the writes. However, if writes do not go to memory, they do not generate bus transactions, and it is no longer clear how the other caches will observe these modifications and ensure write propagation. Also, when writes to different caches are allowed to occur concurrently, no obvious ordering mechanism exists to sequence the writes. We will need somewhat more sophisticated cache coherence protocols to make the "critical" events visible to the other caches and to ensure write serialization.

The space of protocols for write-back caches is quite large. Before we examine it, let us step back to the more general ordering issue alluded to in the introduction to this chapter and examine the semantics of a shared address space as determined by the memory consistency model.

5.2 MEMORY CONSISTENCY

Coherence, on which we have focused so far, is essential if information is to be transferred between processors by one writing to a location that the other reads. Eventually, the value written will become visible to the reader—indeed to all readers. However, coherence says nothing about when the write will become visible. Often in writing a parallel program, we want to ensure that a read returns the value of a particular write; that is, we want to establish an order between a write and a read. Typically, we use some form of event synchronization to convey this dependence, and we use more than one memory location.

Consider, for example, the code fragments executed by processors P_1 and P_2 in Figure 5.7, which we saw when discussing point-to-point event synchronization in a shared address space in Chapter 2. It is clear that the programmer intends for process P_2 to spin idly until the value of the shared variable `flag` changes to 1 and then to print the value of variable `A` as 1, since the value of `A` was updated before that of `flag` by process P_1. In this case, we use accesses to another location (`flag`) to preserve a desired order of different processes' accesses to the same location (`A`). In particular, we assume that the write of `A` becomes visible to P_2 before the write to `flag` and that the read of `flag` by P_2 that breaks it out of its while loop completes before its read of `A` (a print operation is essentially a read). These program orders within P_1 and P_2's accesses to different locations are not implied by coherence, which, for example, only requires that the new value for `A` eventually become visible to process P_2, not necessarily before the new value of `flag` is observed.

The programmer might try to avoid this issue by using a barrier or other explicit event synchronization, as shown in Figure 5.8. We expect the value of `A` to be printed as 1 since `A` was set to 1 before the barrier. Even this approach has two potential problems, however. First, we are adding assumptions to the meaning of the barrier: not only do processes wait at the barrier until all of them have arrived, they also wait until all writes issued prior to the barrier have become visible to the other processors. Second, a barrier is often built using reads and writes to ordinary shared variables (e.g., `b1` in the figure) rather than with specialized hardware support. In this case, as far as the machine is concerned, it sees only accesses to different shared variables in the compiled code, not a special barrier operation. Coherence does not say anything at all about the order among these accesses.

Clearly, we expect more from a memory system than to "return the last value written" for each location. To establish order among accesses to the same location (say, `A`) by different processes, we sometimes expect a memory system to respect the order of reads and writes to different locations (`A` and `flag` or `A` and `b1`) issued by the same process. Coherence says nothing about the order in which writes to different locations become visible. Similarly, it says nothing about the order in which the reads issued to different locations by P_2 are performed with respect to P_1. Thus, coherence does not in itself prevent an answer of 0 from being printed by either example, which is certainly not what the programmer had in mind.

In other situations, the programmer's intention may not be so clear. Consider the example in Figure 5.9. The accesses made by process P_1 are ordinary writes, and `A` and `B` are not used as flags or synchronization variables. Should we intuitively expect that if the value printed for `B` is 2, then the value printed for `A` is 1? Whatever the answer, the two print statements read different locations and coherence says nothing about the order in which the writes by P_1 become visible to P_2. This example is in fact a fragment from Dekker's algorithm (Tanenbaum and Woodhull 1997) to determine which of two processes arrives first at a critical point as a step in ensuring mutual exclusion. The algorithm relies on writes to distinct locations by a process becoming visible to other processes in the order in which they appear in the

```
P1                                  P2
-----------------------------------------------------------------
        /*Assume initial value of A and flag is 0*/
A = 1;                      while (flag == 0); /*spin idly*/
flag = 1;                   print A;
```

FIGURE 5.7 Requirements of event synchronization through flags. The figure shows two processors concurrently executing two distinct code fragments. For programmer intuition to be maintained, it must be the case that the printed value of `A` is 1. The intuition is that because of program order, if `flag =1` is visible to process P_2, then it must also be the case that `A = 1` is visible to P_2.

```
P1                                  P2
-----------------------------------------------------------------
        /*Assume initial value of A is 0*/
A = 1;                    . . .
- - - BARRIER(b1)- - - - - - BARRIER(b1)- - - - - - -
                                print A;
```

FIGURE 5.8 Maintaining order among accesses to a location using explicit synchronization through barriers. As in Figure 5.7, the programmer expects the value printed for `A` to be 1 since passing the barrier should imply that the write of `A` by P_1 has already completed and is therefore visible to P_2.

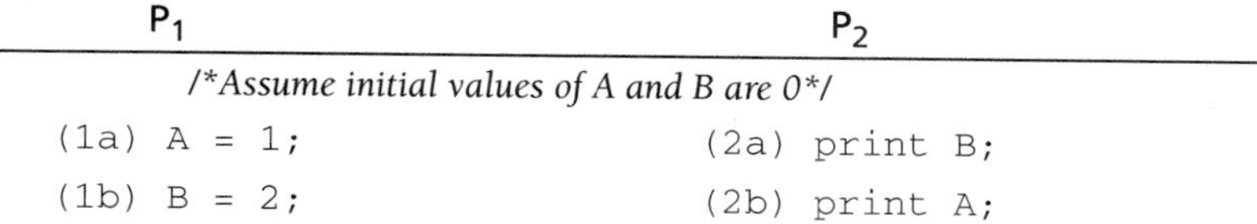

P1
P2
/*Assume initial values of A and B are 0*/
(1a) A = 1;
(2a) print B;
(1b) B = 2;
(2b) print A;

FIGURE 5.9 Order among accesses without synchronization. Here it is less clear what a programmer should expect since neither a flag nor any other explicit event synchronization is used.

program. Clearly, we need something more than coherence to give a shared address space a clear semantics, that is, an ordering model that programmers can use to reason about the possible results and hence the correctness of their programs.

A *memory consistency model* for a shared address space specifies constraints on the order in which memory operations must appear to be performed (i.e., to become visible to the processors) with respect to one another. This includes operations to the same locations or to different locations and by the same process or different processes, so in this sense memory consistency subsumes coherence.

5.2.1 Sequential Consistency

In the discussion in Chapter 1 of fundamental design issues for a communication architecture, Section 1.4 described informally a desirable ordering model for a shared address space: the reasoning that allows a multithreaded program to work under any possible interleaving on a uniprocessor should hold when some of the threads run in parallel on different processors. The ordering of data accesses within a process was therefore the program order, and that across processes was some interleaving of the program orders. That is, the multiprocessor case should not be able to cause values to become visible to processes in the shared address space in a manner that no sequential interleaving of accesses from different processes can generate. This intuitive model was formalized by Lamport as *sequential consistency* (SC), which is defined as follows (Lamport 1979):[1]

> A multiprocessor is *sequentially consistent* if the result of any execution is the same as if the operations of all the processors were executed in some sequential order, and the operations of each individual processor occur in this sequence in the order specified by its program.

Figure 5.10 depicts the abstraction of memory provided to programmers by a sequentially consistent system (Adve and Gharachorloo 1996). It is similar to the machine model we used to introduce coherence, though now it applies to multiple memory locations. Multiple processes appear to share a single logical memory, even though in the real machine main memory may be distributed across multiple processors, each with their own private caches and buffers. Every process appears to issue and complete memory operations one at a time and atomically in program order; that is, a memory operation does not appear to be issued until the previous one from that process has completed. In addition, the common memory appears to service these requests one at a time in an interleaved manner according to an arbitrary (but hopefully fair) schedule. Memory operations appear *atomic* in this interleaved order; that is, it should appear globally (to all processes) as if one operation in the consistent interleaved order executes and completes before the next one begins.

As with coherence, it is not important in what order memory operations actually issue or even complete. What matters for sequential consistency is that they appear to complete in a manner that satisfies the constraints just described. In the example in Figure 5.9, under SC the result `(0,2)` for `(A,B)` would not be allowed—preserving our intuition—since it would then appear that the writes of `A` and `B` by process P_1 executed out of program order. However, the memory operations may actually execute and complete in the order `1b`, `1a`, `2b`, `2a`. It does not matter that they actually complete out of program order since the results of the execution `(1,2)` are the same as if the operations were executed and completed in program order. On the other hand, the actual execution order `1b`, `2a`, `2b`, `1a` would not be sequentially consistent since it would produce the result `(0,2)`, which is not allowed under SC. Other examples illustrating the intuitiveness of sequential consistency can be found

1. Two closely related concepts in software systems are serializability (Papadimitriou 1979) for concurrent updates to a database and linearizability (Herlihy and Wing 1987) for concurrent objects.

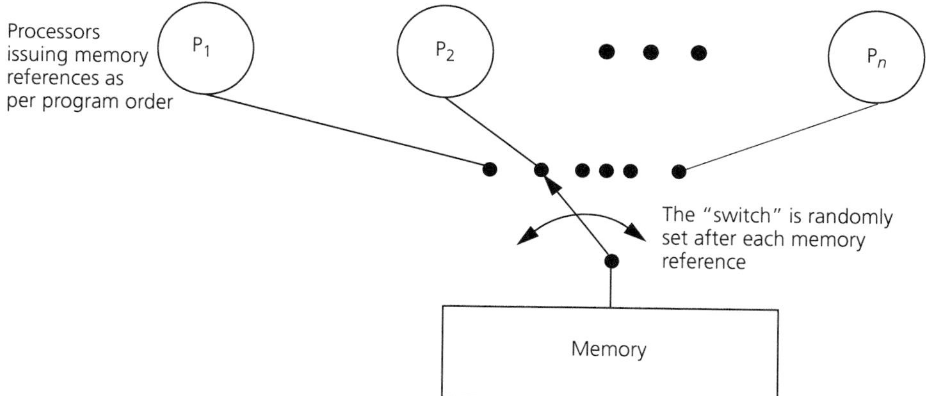

FIGURE 5.10 Programmer's abstraction of the memory subsystem under the sequential consistency model. The model completely hides the underlying concurrency in the memory system hardware (e.g., the possible existence of distributed main memory, the presence of caches and write buffers) from the programmer.

in Exercise 5.6. Note that SC does not obviate the need for synchronization. The reason is that SC allows operations from different processes to be interleaved arbitrarily and does so at the granularity of individual instructions. Synchronization is needed if we want to preserve atomicity (mutual exclusion) across multiple memory operations from a process or if we want to enforce constraints on the interleaving across processes.

The term "program order" also bears some elaboration. Intuitively, *program order* for a process is simply the order in which statements appear according to the source code that the process executes; more specifically, it is the order in which memory operations occur in the assembly code that results from a straightforward translation of source statements one by one to machine instructions. This is not necessarily the order in which an optimizing compiler presents memory operations to the hardware since the compiler may reorder memory operations (within certain constraints, such as preserving dependences to the same location). The programmer has in mind the order of statements in the source program, but the processor sees only the order of the machine instructions. In fact, there is a "program order" at each of the interfaces in the parallel computer architecture—particularly the programming model interface seen by the programmer and the hardware/software interface—and ordering models may be defined at each. Since the programmer reasons with the source program, it makes sense to use this to define program order when discussing memory consistency models; that is, we will be concerned with the consistency model presented by the language and the underlying system to the programmer.

Implementing SC requires that the system (software and hardware) preserve the intuitive constraints defined previously. There are really two constraints. The first is the program order requirement: memory operations of a process must appear to become visible—to itself and others—in program order. The second constraint guarantees that the total order or the interleaving across processes is consistent for all processes by requiring that the operations appear atomic. That is, it should appear that one operation is completed with respect to all processes before the next one in the total order is issued (regardless of which process issues it). The tricky part of this second requirement is making writes appear atomic, especially in a system with multiple copies of a memory word that need to be informed on a write. The *write atomicity* requirement, included in the preceding definition of sequential consistency, implies that the position in the total order at which a write appears to perform should be the same with respect to all processors. It ensures that nothing a processor does after it has seen the new value produced by a write (e.g., another write that it issues) becomes visible to other processes before they too have seen the new value for that write. In effect, the write atomicity required by SC extends the write serialization required by coherence: while write serialization says that writes to the same location should appear to all processors to have occurred in the same order, write atomicity says that all writes (to any location) should appear to all processors to have occurred in the same order. Example 5.4 shows why write atomicity is important.

EXAMPLE 5.4 Consider the three processes in Figure 5.11. Show how not preserving write atomicity violates sequential consistency.

Answer Since P_2 waits until `A` becomes 1 and then sets `B` to 1, and since P_3 waits until `B` becomes 1 and only then reads the value of `A`, from transitivity we would infer that P_3 should find the value of `A` to be 1. If P_2 is allowed to go on past the read of `A` and write `B` before it is guaranteed that P_3 has seen the new value of `A`, then P_3 may read the new value of `B` but read the old value of `A` (e.g., from its cache), violating our sequentially consistent intuition. ■

More formally, each process's program order imposes a partial order on the set of all operations; that is, it imposes an ordering on the subset of the operations that are issued by that process. An interleaving of the operations from different processes defines a total order on the set of all operations. Since the exact interleaving is not defined by SC, interleaving the partial (program) orders for different processes may yield a large number of possible total orders. The following definitions therefore apply:

- *Sequentially consistent execution.* An execution of a program is said to be sequentially consistent if the results it produces are the same as those produced by any one of the possible total orders (interleavings) as defined earlier. That is, a total order or interleaving of program orders from processes should exist that yields the same result as the actual execution.
- *Sequentially consistent system.* A system is sequentially consistent if any possible execution on that system is sequentially consistent.

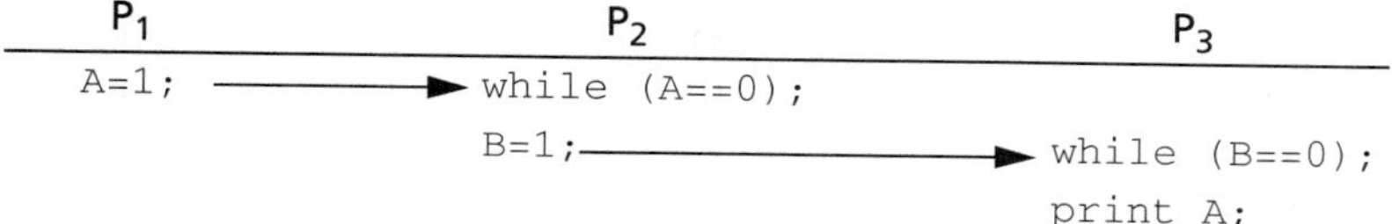

FIGURE 5.11 Example illustrating the importance of write atomicity for sequential consistency

5.2.2 Sufficient Conditions for Preserving Sequential Consistency

Having discussed the definitions and high-level requirements, let us see how a multiprocessor implementation can be made to satisfy SC. It is possible to define a set of sufficient conditions that will guarantee sequential consistency in a multiprocessor—whether bus-based or distributed, cache-coherent or not. The following set, adapted from its original form (Dubois, Scheurich, and Briggs 1986; Scheurich and Dubois 1987), is relatively simple:

1. Every process issues memory operations in program order.
2. After a write operation is issued, the issuing process waits for the write to complete before issuing its next operation.
3. After a read operation is issued, the issuing process waits for the read to complete, and for the write whose value is being returned by the read to complete, before issuing its next operation. That is, if the write whose value is being returned has performed with respect to this processor (as it must have if its value is being returned), then the processor should wait until the write has performed with respect to all processors.

The third condition is what ensures write atomicity and is quite demanding. It is not a simple local constraint because the read must wait until the logically preceding write has become globally visible. Note that these are sufficient, rather than necessary, conditions. Sequential consistency can be preserved with less serialization in many situations, as we shall see.

With program order defined in terms of the source program, it is important that the compiler should not change the order of memory operations that it presents to the hardware (processor). Otherwise, sequential consistency from the programmer's perspective may be compromised even before the hardware gets involved. Unfortunately, many of the optimizations that are commonly employed in both compilers and processors violate these sufficient conditions. For example, compilers routinely reorder accesses to different locations within a process, so a processor may in fact issue accesses out of the program order seen by the programmer. Explicitly parallel programs use uniprocessor compilers, which are concerned only about preserving dependences to the same location. Advanced compiler optimizations that greatly improve performance—such as common subexpression elimination, constant propagation, register allocation, and loop transformations like loop splitting, loop reversal, and blocking (Wolfe 1989)—can change the order in which different locations are accessed or can even eliminate memory operations.[2] In practice, to constrain these compiler optimizations, multithreaded and parallel programs annotate variables or memory references that are used to preserve orders. A particularly stringent example is the use of the `volatile` qualifier in a variable declaration, which prevents the variable from being register allocated or any memory operation on the variable from being reordered with respect to operations before or after it in program order. Example 5.5 illustrates these issues.

EXAMPLE 5.5 How would reordering the memory operations in Figure 5.7 affect semantics in a sequential program (only one of the processes running), in a parallel program running on a multiprocessor, and in a threaded program in which the two processes are interleaved on the same processor? How would you solve the problem?

Answer The compiler may reorder the writes to `A` and `flag` with no impact on a sequential program. However, this can violate our intuition for both parallel programs and concurrent (or multithreaded) uniprocessor programs. In the latter case, a context switch can happen between the two reordered writes, so the process switched in may see the update to `flag` without seeing the update to `A`. Similar violations of intuition occur if the compiler reorders the reads of `flag` and `A`. For many compilers, we can avoid these reorderings by declaring the variable `flag` to be of type `volatile integer` instead of just `integer`. Other solutions are also possible and are discussed in Chapter 9. ■

Even if the compiler preserves program order, modern processors use sophisticated mechanisms like write buffers, interleaved memory, pipelining, and out-of-order execution techniques (Hennessy and Patterson 1996). These allow memory operations from a process to issue, execute, and/or complete out of program order. Like compiler optimizations, these architectural optimizations work for sequential programs because the appearance of program order in these programs requires that dependences be preserved only among accesses to the same memory location, as shown in Figure 5.12. The problem in parallel programs is that the out-of-order processing of operations to different shared variables by a process can be detected by other processes.

Preserving the sufficient conditions for SC in multiprocessors is quite a strong requirement since it limits compiler reordering and out-of-order processing techniques. Several weaker consistency models have been proposed and techniques have been developed to satisfy SC while relaxing the sufficient conditions. We will examine these approaches in the context of scalable shared address space machines in Chapter 9. For the purposes of this chapter, we assume the compiler does not reorder memory operations, so the program order that the processor sees is the same as

---

2. Note that register allocation, performed by modern compilers to eliminate memory operations, can affect coherence itself, not just memory consistency. For the flag synchronization example in Figure 5.7, if the compiler were to register-allocate the `flag` variable for process P_2, the process could end up spinning forever: the cache coherence hardware updates or invalidates only the memory and the caches, not the registers of the machine, so the write propagation property of coherence is violated.

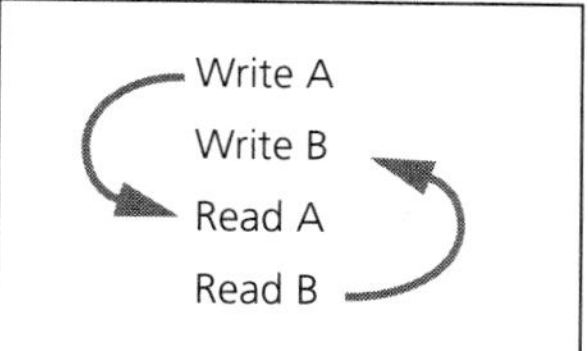

FIGURE 5.12 Preserving the orders in a sequential program running on a uniprocessor. Only the orders corresponding to the two dependence arcs must be preserved. The first two operations can be reordered without a problem, as can the last two or the middle two.

that seen by the programmer. On the hardware side, we assume that the sufficient conditions must be satisfied. To do this, we need mechanisms for a processor to detect completion of its writes so it may proceed past them (completion of reads is easy; a read completes when the data returns to the processor) and mechanisms to satisfy the condition that preserves write atomicity. For all the protocols and systems considered in this chapter, we see how they satisfy coherence (including write serialization), how they can satisfy sequential consistency (in particular, how write completion is detected and write atomicity is guaranteed), and what shortcuts can be taken while still satisfying the sufficient conditions.

For bus-based machines, the serialization imposed by transactions appearing on the shared bus is very useful in ordering memory operations. It is easy to verify that the two-state write-through invalidation protocol discussed previously actually provides sequential consistency—not just coherence—quite easily. The key observation to extend the arguments made for coherence in that system is that writes and read misses to all locations, not just to individual locations, are serialized in bus order. When a read obtains the value of a write, the write is guaranteed to have completed since it caused a previous bus transaction, thus ensuring write atomicity. When a write is performed with respect to any processor, all previous writes in bus order have completed.

5.3 DESIGN SPACE FOR SNOOPING PROTOCOLS

The beauty of snooping-based cache coherence is that the entire machinery for solving a difficult problem boils down to applying a small amount of extra interpretation to events that naturally occur in the system. The processor is completely unchanged. No explicit coherence operations must be inserted in the program. By extending the requirements on the cache controller and exploiting the properties of the bus, the reads and writes that are inherent to the program are used implicitly to keep the caches coherent, and the serialization provided by the bus maintains consistency. Each cache controller observes and interprets the bus transactions generated by others to maintain its internal state. Our initial design point with write-through caches is not very efficient, but we are now ready to study the design space for snooping protocols that make efficient use of the limited bandwidth of the shared bus. All of these use write-back caches, allowing processors to write to different blocks in their local caches concurrently without any bus transactions. Thus, extra care is required to ensure that enough information is transmitted over the bus to maintain coherence.

Recall that with a write-back cache on a uniprocessor, a processor write miss causes the cache to read the entire block from memory, update a word, and retain the block in *modified* (or *dirty*) state so it may be written back to memory on replacement. In a multiprocessor, this modified state is also used by the protocols to indicate exclusive ownership of the block by a cache. In general, a cache is said to be the *owner* of a block if it must supply the data upon a request for that block (Sweazey and Smith 1986). A cache is said to have an *exclusive* copy of a block if it is the only cache with a valid copy of the block (main memory may or may not have a valid copy). Exclusivity implies that the cache may modify the block without notifying anyone else. If a cache does not have exclusivity, then it cannot write a new value into the block before first putting a transaction on the bus to communicate with others. The writer may have the block in its cache in a valid state, but since a transaction must be generated, it is called a write miss just like a write to a block that is not present or is invalid in the cache. If a cache has the block in modified state, then clearly it is the owner and it has exclusivity. (The need to distinguish ownership from exclusivity will become clear soon.)

On a write miss in an invalidation protocol, a special form of transaction called a *read exclusive* is used to tell other caches about the impending write and to acquire a copy of the block with exclusive ownership. This places the block in the cache in modified state, where it may now be written. Multiple processors cannot write the same block concurrently since this would lead to inconsistent values. The read-exclusive bus transactions generated by their writes will be serialized by the bus, so only one of them can have exclusive ownership of the block at a time. The cache coherence actions are driven by these two types of transactions: read and read exclusive. Eventually, when a modified block is replaced from the cache, the data is written back to memory, but this event is not caused by a memory operation to that block and is almost incidental to the protocol. A block that is not in modified state need not be written back upon replacement and can simply be dropped since memory has the latest copy. Many protocols have been devised for write-back caches, and we examine the basic alternatives.

We also consider update-based protocols. Recall that in update-based protocols, whenever a shared location is written to by a processor, its value is updated in the caches of all other processors holding that memory block.[3] Thus, when these processors subsequently access that block, they can do so from their caches with low latency. The caches of all other processors are updated with a single bus transaction, thus conserving bandwidth when there are multiple sharers. In contrast, with invalidation-based protocols, on a write operation the cache state of that memory block in all other processors' caches is set to invalid, so those processors will have to obtain the block through a miss and hence a bus transaction on their next read.

3. This is a write-broadcast scenario. Read-broadcast designs have also been investigated, in which the cache containing the modified copy flushes it to the bus when it sees a read on the bus, at which point all other copies are updated too.

However, subsequent writes to that block by the same processor do not create further traffic on the bus (as they do with an update protocol) until the block is accessed by another processor. This is attractive when a single processor performs multiple writes to the same memory block before other processors access the contents of that memory block. The detailed trade-offs are more complex, and they depend on the workload offered to the machine; they will be illustrated quantitatively in Section 5.4. In general, invalidation-based strategies have been found to be more robust and are therefore provided as the default protocol by most vendors. Some vendors provide an update protocol as an option to be used for blocks corresponding to selected data structures or pages.

The choices made for the protocol (update versus invalidate) and the caching strategies directly affect the choice of states, the state transition diagram, and the associated actions. Substantial flexibility is available to the computer architect in the design task at this level. Instead of listing all possible choices, let us consider three common coherence protocols that will illustrate the design options.

5.3.1 A Three-State (MSI) Write-Back Invalidation Protocol

The first protocol we consider is a basic invalidation-based protocol for write-back caches. It is very similar to the protocol that was used in the Silicon Graphics 4D series multiprocessor machines (Baskett, Jermoluk, and Solomon 1988). The protocol uses the three states required for any write-back cache in order to distinguish valid blocks that are unmodified (clean) from those that are modified (dirty). Specifically, the states are *modified* (M), *shared* (S), and *invalid* (I). Invalid has the obvious meaning. Shared means the block is present in an unmodified state in this cache, main memory is up-to-date, and zero or more other caches may also have an up-to-date (shared) copy. Modified, also called dirty, means that only this cache has a valid copy of the block, and the copy in main memory is stale. Before a shared or invalid block can be written and placed in the modified state, all the other potential copies must be invalidated via a read-exclusive bus transaction. This transaction serves to order the write as well as cause the invalidations and hence ensure that the write becomes visible to others (write propagation).

The processor issues two types of requests: reads (PrRd) and writes (PrWr). The read or write could be to a memory block that exists in the cache or to one that does not. In the latter case, a block currently in the cache will have to be replaced by the newly requested block, and if the existing block is in the modified state, its contents will have to be written back to main memory.

We assume that the bus allows the following transactions:

- *Bus Read* (BusRd): This transaction is generated by a PrRd that misses in the cache, and the processor expects a data response as a result. The cache controller puts the address on the bus and asks for a copy that it does not intend to modify. The memory system (possibly another cache) supplies the data.
- *Bus Read Exclusive* (BusRdX): This transaction is generated by a PrWr to a block that is either not in the cache or is in the cache but not in the modified

state. The cache controller puts the address on the bus and asks for an exclusive copy that it intends to modify. The memory system (possibly another cache) supplies the data. All other caches are invalidated. Once the cache obtains the exclusive copy, the write can be performed in the cache. The processor may require an acknowledgment as a result of this transaction.

- *Bus Write Back* (BusWB): This transaction is generated by a cache controller on a write back; the processor does not know about it and does not expect a response. The cache controller puts the address and the contents for the memory block on the bus. The main memory is updated with the latest contents.

The bus read exclusive (sometimes called *read-to-own*) is the only new transaction that would not exist except for cache coherence. The new action needed to support write-back protocols is that, in addition to changing the state of cached blocks, a cache controller can intervene in an observed bus transaction and flush the contents of the referenced block from its cache onto the bus rather than allowing the memory to supply the data. Of course, the cache controller can also initiate bus transactions as described above, supply data for write backs, or pick up data supplied by the memory system.

State Transitions

The state transition diagram that governs a block in each cache in this snooping protocol is as shown in Figure 5.13. The states are organized so that the closer the state is to the top, the more tightly the block is bound to that processor. A processor read to a block that is invalid (or not present) causes a BusRd transaction to service the miss. The newly loaded block is *promoted,* moved up in the state diagram, from invalid to the shared state in the requesting cache, whether or not any other cache holds a copy. Any other caches with the block in the shared state observe the BusRd but take no special action, allowing main memory to respond with the data. However, if a cache has the block in the modified state (there can only be one) and it observes a BusRd transaction on the bus, then it must get involved in the transaction since the copy in main memory is stale. This cache flushes the data onto the bus, in lieu of memory, and *demotes* its copy of the block to the shared state (see Figure 5.13). The memory and the requesting cache both pick up the block. This can be accomplished either by a direct cache-to-cache transfer across the bus during this BusRd transaction or by signaling an error on the BusRd transaction and generating a write transaction to update memory. In the latter case, the original cache will eventually retry its request and obtain the block from memory. (It is also possible to have the flushed data picked up only by the requesting cache but not by memory, leaving memory still out-of-date, but this requires more states [Sweazey and Smith 1986].)

Writing into an invalid block is a write miss, which is serviced by first loading the entire block and then modifying the desired bytes within it. The write miss generates a read-exclusive bus transaction, which causes all other cached copies of the block to be invalidated, thereby granting the requesting cache exclusive ownership of the

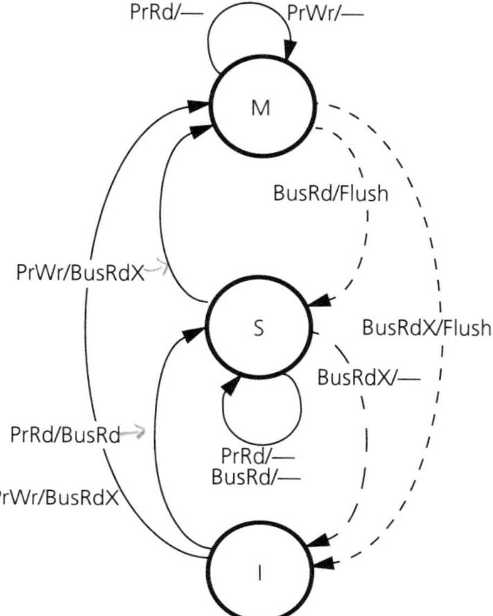

FIGURE 5.13 Basic three-state invalidation protocol. M, S, and I stand for modified, shared, and invalid states, respectively. The notation *A/B* means that if the controller observes the event *A* from the processor side or the bus side, then in addition to the state change, it generates the bus transaction or action *B.* "—" means null action. Transitions due to observed bus transactions are shown in dashed arcs, while those due to local processor actions are shown in bold arcs. If multiple *A/B* pairs are associated with an arc, it simply means that multiple inputs can cause the same state transition. For completeness, we should specify actions from each state corresponding to each observable event. If such transitions are not shown, it means that they are uninteresting and no action needs to be taken. Replacements and the write backs they may cause are not shown in the diagram for simplicity.

block. The block of data returned by the read exclusive is promoted to the modified state, and the desired bytes are then written into it. If another cache later requests exclusive access, then in response to its BusRdX transaction this block will be invalidated (demoted to the invalid state) after flushing the exclusive copy to the bus.

The most interesting transition occurs when writing into a shared block. As discussed earlier, this is treated essentially like a write miss, using a read-exclusive bus transaction to acquire exclusive ownership; we refer to it as a write miss throughout the book. The data that comes back in the read exclusive can be ignored in this case, unlike when writing to an invalid or not present block, since it is already in the cache. In fact, a common optimization to reduce data traffic in bus protocols is to introduce a new transaction, called a *bus upgrade* or BusUpgr, for this situation. A BusUpgr obtains exclusive ownership just like a BusRdX, by causing other copies to be invalidated, but it does not cause main memory or any other device to respond with the data for the block. Regardless of whether a BusUpgr or a BusRdX is used (let us continue to assume BusRdX), the block in the requesting cache transitions to the modified state. Additional writes to the block while it is in the modified state generate no additional bus transactions.

A replacement of a block from a cache logically demotes the block to invalid (not present) by removing it from the cache. A replacement therefore causes the state machines for two blocks to change states in that cache: the one being replaced changes from its current state to invalid, and the one being brought in changes from invalid (not present) to its new state. The latter state change cannot take place before the former, which requires some care in implementation. If the block being replaced was in modified state, the replacement transition from M to I generates a write-back transaction. No special action is taken by the other caches on this transaction. If the block being replaced was in shared or invalid state, then it itself does not cause any transaction on the bus. Replacements are not shown in the state diagram for simplicity.

Note that to specify the protocol completely, for each state we must have outgoing arcs with labels corresponding to all observable events (the inputs from the processor and bus sides) and must show the actions corresponding to them. Of course, the actions and state transitions can be null sometimes, and in that case we may either explicitly specify null actions (see states S and M in Figure 5.13), or we may simply omit those arcs from the diagram (see state I). Also, since we treat the not-present state as invalid, when a new block is brought into the cache on a miss, the state transitions are performed as if the previous state of the block was invalid. Example 5.6 illustrates how the state transition diagram is interpreted.

EXAMPLE 5.6 Using the MSI protocol, show the state transitions and bus transactions for the scenario depicted in Figure 5.3.

Answer The results are shown in Figure 5.14. ■

With write-back protocols, a block can be written many times before the memory is actually updated. A read may obtain data not from memory but rather from a writer's cache, and in fact it may be this read rather than a replacement that causes memory to be updated. In addition, write hits do not appear on the bus, so the concept of a write being performed with respect to other processors is a little different. In fact, to say that a write is being performed means that the write is being "made visible." A write to a shared or invalid block is made visible by the bus read-exclusive transaction it triggers. The writer will "observe" the data in its cache after this transaction. The write will be made visible to other processors by the invalidations that the read exclusive generates, and those processors will experience a cache miss before actually observing the value written. Write hits to a modified block are visible to other processors but again are observed by them only after a miss through a bus transaction. Thus, in the MSI protocol, the write to a nonmodified block is performed or made visible when the BusRdX transaction occurs, and the write to a modified block is made visible when the block is updated in the writer's cache.

Processor Action	State in P_1	State in P_2	State in P_3	Bus Action	Data Supplied By
1. P_1 reads u	S	—	—	BusRd	Memory
2. P_3 reads u	S	—	S	BusRd	Memory
3. P_3 writes u	I	—	M	BusRdX	Memory
4. P_1 reads u	S	—	S	BusRd	P_3 cache
5. P_2 reads u	S	S	S	BusRd	Memory

FIGURE 5.14 The three-state invalidation protocol in action for processor transactions shown in Figure 5.3. The figure shows the state of the relevant memory block at the end of each processor action, the bus transaction generated (if any), and the entity supplying the data.

Satisfying Coherence

Since both reads and writes can take place without generating bus transactions in a write-back protocol, it is not obvious that it satisfies the conditions for coherence, much less sequential consistency. Let's examine coherence first. Write propagation is clear from the preceding discussion, so let us focus on write serialization. The read-exclusive transaction ensures that the writing cache has the only valid copy when the block is actually written in the cache, just like a write transaction in the write-through protocol. It is followed immediately by the corresponding write being performed in the cache before any other bus transactions are handled by that cache controller, so it is ordered in the same way for all processors (including the writer) with respect to other bus transactions. The only difference from a write-through protocol, with regard to ordering operations to a location, is that not all writes generate bus transactions. However, the key here is that between two transactions for that block that do appear on the bus, only one processor can perform such write hits; this is the processor (say, P) that performed the most recent read-exclusive bus transaction w for the block. In the serialization, this sequence of write hits therefore appears (in program order) between w and the next bus transaction for that block. Reads by processor P will clearly see them in this order with respect to other writes. For a read by another processor, there is at least one bus transaction for that block that separates the completion of that read from the completion of these write hits. That bus transaction ensures that that read also sees the writes in the consistent serial order. Thus, reads by all processors see all writes in the same order.

Satisfying Sequential Consistency

To see how SC is satisfied, let us first appeal to the definition itself and see how a consistent global interleaving of all memory operations may be constructed. As with write-through caches, the serial arbitration for the bus in fact defines a total order on bus transactions for all blocks, not just those for a single block. All cache controllers observe read and read-exclusive bus transactions in the same order and perform invalidations in this order. Between consecutive bus transactions, each processor performs a sequence of memory operations (read and write hits) in program order. Thus, any execution of a program defines a natural partial order:

> A memory operation M_j is subsequent to operation M_i if (1) the operations are issued by the same processor and M_j follows M_i in program order, or (2) M_j generates a bus transaction that follows the memory operation for M_i.

This partial order looks graphically like that of Figure 5.6, except the local sequence within a segment has writes as well as reads and both read-exclusive and read bus transactions play important roles in establishing the orders. Between bus transactions, any interleaving of the sequences of local operations (hits) from different processors leads to a consistent total order. For writes that occur in the same segment between bus transactions, a processor will observe the writes by other processors ordered by bus transactions that it generates, and its own writes ordered by program order.

We can also see how SC is satisfied in terms of the sufficient conditions. Write completion is detected when the read-exclusive bus transaction occurs on the bus and the write is performed in the cache. The read completion condition, which provides write atomicity, is met because a read either (1) causes a bus transaction that follows that of the write whose value is being returned, in which case the write must have completed globally before the read; (2) follows such a read by the same processor in program order; or (3) follows in program order on the same processor that performed the write, in which case the processor has already waited for the write to complete (become visible) globally. Thus, all the sufficient conditions are easily guaranteed. We return to this topic when we discuss implementing protocols in Chapter 6.

Lower-Level Design Choices

To illustrate some of the implicit design choices that have been made in the protocol, let us examine more closely the transition from the M state when a BusRd for that block is observed. In Figure 5.13, we transition to state S and flush the contents of the memory block to the bus. Although it is imperative that the contents are placed on the bus, we could instead have transitioned to state I, thus giving up the block entirely. The choice of going to S versus I reflects the designer's assertion that the original processor is more likely to continue reading the block than the new processor is to write to the memory block. Intuitively, this assertion holds for mostly read data, which is common in many programs. However, a common case where it does not hold is for a flag or buffer that is used to transfer information back and forth between processes: one processor writes it, the other reads it and modifies it, then the first reads it and modifies it, and so on. Accumulations into a shared counter exhibit similar *migratory* behavior across multiple processors. The problem with betting on read sharing in these cases is that every write has to first generate an invalidation, thereby increasing its latency. Indeed, the coherence protocol used in the early Synapse multiprocessor made the alternate choice of going directly from M to I state on a BusRd, thus betting the migratory pattern would be more frequent.

Some machines (Sequent Symmetry model B and the MIT Alewife) attempt to adapt the protocol when such a migratory access pattern is observed (Cox and Fowler 1993; Dahlgren, Dubois, and Stenstrom 1994). These choices can affect the performance of the memory system, as we see later in the chapter.

5.3.2 A Four-State (MESI) Write-Back Invalidation Protocol

A concern arises with our MSI protocol if we consider a sequential application running on a multiprocessor. Such multiprogrammed use in fact constitutes the most common workload on small-scale multiprocessors. When the process reads in and modifies a data item, in the MSI protocol, two bus transactions are generated even though there are never any sharers. The first is a BusRd that gets the memory block in S state, and the second is a BusRdX (or BusUpgr) that converts the block from S to M state. By adding a state that indicates that the block is the only (exclusive) copy but is not modified and by loading the block in this state, we can save the latter transaction since the state indicates that no other processor is caching the block. This new state, called *exclusive-clean* or *exclusive-unowned* (or even simply "exclusive"), indicates an intermediate level of binding between shared and modified. It is exclusive, so unlike the shared state, the cache can perform a write and move to the modified state without further bus transactions; but it does not imply ownership (memory has a valid copy), so unlike the modified state, the cache need not reply upon observing a request for the block. Variants of this MESI protocol are used in many modern microprocessors, including the Intel Pentium, PowerPC 601, and the MIPS R4400 used in the Silicon Graphics Challenge multiprocessors. It was first published by researchers at the University of Illinois at Urbana-Champaign (Papamarcos and Patel 1984) and is often referred to as the Illinois protocol (Archibald and Baer 1986).

The MESI protocol thus consists of four states: modified (M) or dirty, exclusive-clean (E), shared (S), and invalid (I). M and I have the same semantics as before. E, the exclusive-clean or exclusive state, means that only one cache (this cache) has a copy of the block and it has not been modified (i.e., the main memory is up-to-date). S means that potentially two or more processors have this block in their cache in an unmodified state. The bus transactions and actions needed are very similar to those for the MSI protocol.

State Transitions

When the block is first read by a processor, if a valid copy exists in another cache, then it enters the processor's cache in the S state, as usual. However, if no other cache has a copy at the time (for example, in a sequential application), it enters the cache in the E state. When that block is written by the same processor, it can directly transition from E to M state without generating another bus transaction since no other cache has a copy. If another cache had obtained a copy in the meantime, the state of the block would have been demoted from E to S by the snooping protocol.

This protocol places a new requirement on the physical interconnect of the bus. An additional signal, called the shared signal (S), must be available to the controllers in order to determine on a BusRd if any other cache currently holds the data. During the address phase of the bus transaction, all caches determine if they contain the requested block and, if so, assert the shared signal. This signal is a wired-OR line, so the controller making the request can observe whether any other processors are caching the referenced memory block and can thereby decide whether to load a requested block in the E state or the S state.

Figure 5.15 shows a state transition diagram for a MESI protocol, still assuming that the BusUpgr transaction is not used. The notation BusRd(S) means that the bus read transaction caused the shared signal S to be asserted; BusRd($\overline{S}$) means S was unasserted. A plain BusRd means that we don't care about the value of S for that transition. A write to a block in any state will promote the block to the M state, but if it was in the E state, then no bus transaction is required. Observing a BusRd will demote a block from E to S since now another cached copy exists. As usual, observing a BusRd will demote a block from M to S state and will also cause the block to be flushed onto the bus; here too, the block may be picked up only by the requesting cache and not by main memory, but this may require additional states beyond MESI. (A fifth, *owned* state may be added, which indicates that even though other shared copies of the block may exist, this cache [instead of main memory] is responsible for supplying the data when it observes a relevant bus transaction. This leads to a five-state MOESI protocol [Sweazey and Smith 1986].) Notice that it is possible for a block to be in the S state even if no other copies exist since copies may be replaced (S $\rightarrow$ I) without notifying other caches. The arguments for satisfying coherence and sequential consistency are the same as in the MSI protocol.

Lower-Level Design Choices

An interesting question for bus-based protocols is who should supply the block for a BusRd transaction when both the memory and another cache have a copy of it. In the original (Illinois) version of the MESI protocol, the cache rather than main memory supplied the data—a technique called *cache-to-cache sharing*. The argument for this approach was that caches, being constructed out of SRAM rather than DRAM, could supply the data more quickly. However, this advantage is not necessarily present in modern bus-based machines, in which intervening in another processor's cache to obtain data may be more expensive than obtaining the data from main memory. Cache-to-cache sharing also adds complexity to a bus-based protocol: main memory must wait until it is certain that no cache will supply the data before driving the bus, and if the data resides in multiple caches, then a selection algorithm is needed to determine which one will provide the data. On the other hand, this technique is useful for multiprocessors with physically distributed memory (as we see in Chapter 8) because the latency to obtain the data from a nearby cache may be much smaller than that for a faraway memory unit. This effect can be especially important for machines constructed as a network of SMP nodes because caches

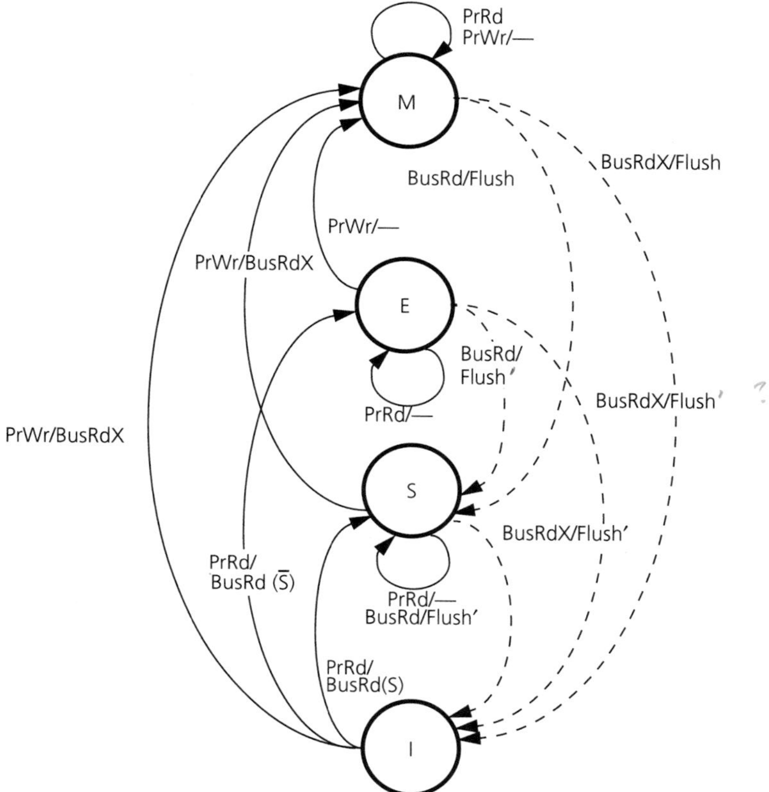

FIGURE 5.15 State transition diagram for the Illinois MESI protocol. MESI stands for the modified (dirty), exclusive, shared, and invalid states, respectively. The notation is the same as that in Figure 5.13. The E state helps reduce bus traffic for sequential programs where data is not shared. Whenever feasible, the Illinois version of the MESI protocol makes caches, rather than main memory, supply data for BusRd and BusRdX transactions. Since multiple processors may have a copy of the memory block in their cache, we need to select only one to supply the data on the bus. Flush' is true only for that processor; the remaining processors take their usual action (invalidation or no action). In general, Flush' in a state diagram indicates that the block is flushed only if cache-to-cache sharing is in use and then only by the cache that is responsible for supplying the data.

within the requestor's SMP node may supply the data. The Stanford DASH multiprocessor (Lenoski et al. 1993) used such cache-to-cache transfers for this reason.

5.3.3 A Four-State (Dragon) Write-Back Update Protocol

Let us now examine a basic update-based protocol for write-back caches. This protocol was first proposed by researchers at Xerox PARC for their Dragon multiprocessor system (McCreight 1984; Thacker, Stewart, and Satterthwaite 1988), and an enhanced version of it is used in the Sun SparcServer multiprocessors (Catanzaro 1997).

The Dragon protocol consists of four states: exclusive-clean (E), shared-clean (Sc), shared-modified (Sm), and modified (M). Exclusive-clean (or exclusive) has the same meaning and the same motivation as before: only one cache (this cache) has a copy of the block, and it has not been modified (i.e., the main memory is up-to-date). *Shared-clean* means that potentially two or more caches (including this one) have this block, and main memory may or may not be up-to-date. *Shared-modified* means that potentially two or more caches have this block, main memory is not up-to-date, and it is this cache's responsibility to update the main memory at the time this block is replaced from the cache (i.e., this cache is the owner). A block may be in Sm state in only one cache at a time. However, it is quite possible that one cache has the block in Sm state, while others have it in Sc state. Or it may be that no cache has it in Sm state, but some have it in Sc state. This is why, when a cache has the block in Sc state, memory may or may not be up-to-date; it depends on whether some other cache has it in Sm state. M signifies exclusive ownership as before: the block is modified (dirty) and present in this cache alone, main memory is stale, and it is this cache's responsibility to supply the data and to update main memory on replacement. Note that there is no explicit invalid (I) state as in the previous protocols. This is because Dragon is an update-based protocol; the protocol always keeps the blocks in the cache up-to-date, so it is always okay to use the data present in the cache if the tag match succeeds. However, if a block is not present in a cache at all, it can be imagined in a special invalid or not-present state.[4]

The processor requests, bus transactions, and actions for the Dragon protocol are similar to the Illinois MESI protocol. The processor is still assumed to issue only read (PrRd) and write (PrWr) requests. However, since we do not have an invalid state, to specify actions on a tag mismatch we add two more request types: processor read miss (PrRdMiss) and write miss (PrWrMiss). As for bus transactions, we have bus read (BusRd), bus write back (BusWB), and a new transaction called bus update (BusUpd). The BusRd and BusWB transactions have the usual semantics. The BusUpd transaction takes the specific word (or bytes) written by the processor and broadcasts it on the bus so that all other processors' caches can update themselves. By broadcasting only the contents of the specific modified word rather than the whole cache block, it is hoped that the bus bandwidth is more efficiently utilized. (See Exercise 5.4 for reasons why this may not always be the case.) As in the MESI protocol, to support the E state, a shared signal (S) is available to the cache controller. Finally, the only new capability needed is for the cache controller to update a locally cached memory block (labeled an Update action) with the contents that are being broadcast on the bus by a relevant BusUpd transaction.

4. Logically, there is another state as well, but it is rather crude and is used to bootstrap the protocol. A "miss mode" bit is provided with each cache line to force a miss when that block is accessed. Initialization software reads data into every line in the cache with the miss mode bit turned on to ensure that the processor will miss the first time it references a block that maps to that line. After this first miss, the miss mode bit is turned off and the cache operates normally.

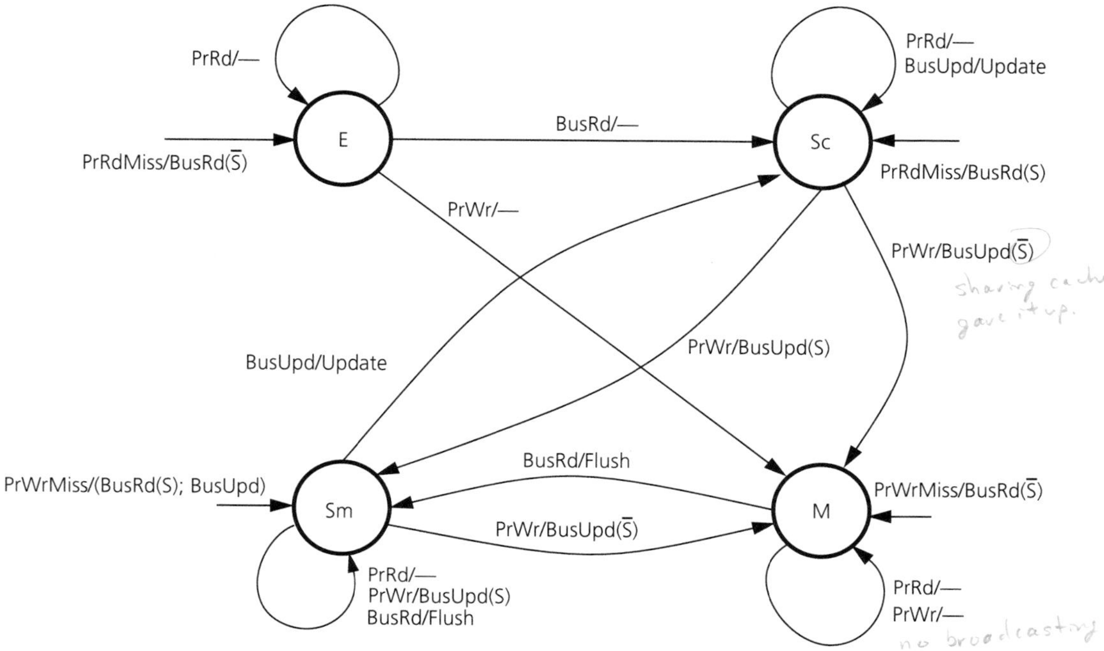

FIGURE 5.16 State transition diagram for the Dragon update protocol. The four states are exclusive (E), shared-clean (Sc), shared-modified (Sm), and modified (M). There is no invalid (I) state because the update protocol always keeps blocks in the cache up-to-date.

State Transitions

Figure 5.16 shows the state transition diagram for the Dragon update protocol. To take a processor-centric view, we can explain the diagram in terms of actions taken when a cache incurs a read miss, a write (hit or miss), or a replacement (no action is ever taken on a read hit).

- *Read miss:* A BusRd transaction is generated. Depending on the status of the shared signal (S), the block is loaded in the E or Sc state in the local cache. If the block is in M or Sm states in one of the other caches, that cache asserts the shared signal and supplies the latest data for that block on the bus, and the block is loaded in the local cache in Sc state. If the other cache had it in state M, it changes its state to Sm. If the block is in Sc state in other caches, memory supplies the data, and it is loaded in Sc state. If no other cache has a copy, then the shared line remains unasserted, the data is supplied by the main memory, and the block is loaded in the local cache in E state.
- *Write:* If the block is in the M state in the local cache, then no action needs to be taken. If the block is in the E state in the local cache, then it changes to M state and again no further action is needed. If the block is in Sc or Sm state,

however, a BusUpd transaction is generated. If any other caches have a copy of the data, they assert the shared signal, update the corresponding bytes in their cached copies, and change their state to Sc if necessary. The local cache also updates its copy of the block and changes its state to Sm if necessary. Main memory is not updated. If no other cache has a copy of the data, the shared signal remains unasserted, the local copy is updated, and the state is changed to M. Finally, if on a write the block is not present in the cache, the write is treated simply as a read-miss transaction followed by a write transaction. Thus, first a BusRd is generated. If the block is also found in other caches, a BusUpd is generated, and the block is loaded locally in the Sm state; otherwise, the block is loaded locally in the M state.

- *Replacement:* On a replacement (arcs not shown in the figure), the block is written back to memory using a bus transaction only if it is in the M or Sm state. If it is in the Sc state, then either some other cache has it in Sm state or none does, in which case it is already valid in main memory.

Example 5.7 illustrates the transitions for a familiar scenario.

EXAMPLE 5.7 Using the Dragon update protocol, show the state transitions and bus transactions for the scenario depicted in Figure 5.3.

Answer The results are shown in Figure 5.17. We can see that, whereas for processor actions 3 and 4 only one word is transferred on the bus in the update protocol, the whole memory block is transferred twice in the invalidation-based protocol. Of course, it is easy to construct scenarios in which the invalidation protocol does much better than the update protocol, and we discuss the detailed trade-offs in Section 5.4. ■

Lower-Level Design Choices

Again, many implicit design choices have been made in this protocol. For example, it is feasible to eliminate the shared-modified state. In fact, the update protocol used in the DEC Firefly multiprocessor does exactly that. The rationale is that every time the BusUpd transaction occurs, main memory can also update its contents along with the other caches holding that block; therefore, shared clean suffices, and a shared-modified state is not needed. The Dragon protocol is instead based on the assumption that the SRAM caches are much quicker to update than the DRAM main memory, so it is inappropriate to wait for main memory to be updated on all BusUpd transactions. Another subtle choice relates to the action taken on cache replacements. When a shared-clean block is replaced, should other caches be informed of that replacement via a bus transaction so that if only one cache remains with a copy of the memory block, it can change its state to exclusive or modified? The advantage of doing this would be that the bus transaction upon the replacement might not be in the critical path of a memory operation, whereas the later bus transaction that it saves might be.

Since all writes appear on the bus in an update protocol, write serialization, write completion detection, and write atomicity are all quite straightforward with a simple

Processor Action	State in P_1	State in P_2	State in P_3	Bus Action	Data Supplied By
1. P_1 reads u	E	—	—	BusRd	Memory
2. P_3 reads u	Sc	—	Sc	BusRd	Memory
3. P_3 writes u	Sc	—	Sm	BusUpd	P_3 cache
4. P_1 reads u	Sc	—	Sm	null	—
5. P_2 reads u	Sc	Sc	Sm	BusRd	P_3 cache

FIGURE 5.17 The Dragon update protocol in action for the processor actions shown in Figure 5.3. The figure shows the state of the relevant memory block at the end of each processor action, the bus transaction generated (if any), and the entity supplying the data.

atomic bus, a lot like they were in the write-through case. However, with both invalidation- and update-based protocols, we must address many subtle implementation issues and race conditions, even with an atomic bus and a single-level cache. We discuss this next level of protocol and hardware design in Chapter 6, as well as more realistic scenarios with pipelined buses, multilevel cache hierarchies, and hardware techniques that can reorder the completion of memory operations. Nonetheless, we can quantify many protocol trade-offs even at the state diagram level that we have been considering so far.

5.4 ASSESSING PROTOCOL DESIGN TRADE-OFFS

Like any other complex system, the design of a multiprocessor requires many interrelated decisions to be made. Even when a processor has been picked, we must decide on the maximum number of processors to be supported by the system, various parameters of the cache hierarchy (e.g., number of levels in the hierarchy, and for each level the cache size, associativity, block size, and whether the cache is write through or write back), the design of the bus (e.g., width of the data and address buses, the bus protocol), the design of the memory system (e.g., interleaved memory banks or not, width of memory banks, size of internal buffers), and the design of the I/O subsystem. Many of the issues are similar to those in uniprocessors (Smith 1982) but accentuated. For example, a write-through cache standing before the bus may be a poor choice for multiprocessors because the bus bandwidth is shared by many processors, and memory may need to be more greatly interleaved because it services cache misses from multiple processors. Greater cache associativity may also be useful in reducing conflict misses that generate bus traffic.

The cache coherence protocol is a crucial new design issue for a multiprocessor. It includes protocol class (invalidation or update), protocol states and actions, and lower-level implementation trade-offs. Protocol decisions interact with all the other design issues. On the one hand, the protocol influences the extent to which the latency and bandwidth characteristics of system components are stressed; on the other, the performance characteristics as well as the organization of the memory and communication architecture influence the choice of protocols. As discussed in

Chapter 4, these design decisions need to be evaluated relative to the behavior of real programs. Such evaluation was very common in the late 1980s, albeit using an immature set of parallel programs as workloads (Archibald and Baer 1986; Agarwal and Gupta 1988; Eggers and Katz 1988, 1989a, 1989b).

Making design decisions in real systems is part art and part science. The art draws on the past experience, intuition, and aesthetics of the designers, and the science is based in workload-driven evaluation. The goals are usually to meet a cost-performance target and to have a balanced system, so that no individual resource is a performance bottleneck yet each resource has only minimal excess capacity. This section illustrates some key protocol trade-offs by putting the workload-driven evaluation methodology from Chapter 4 into action.

5.4.1 Methodology

The basic strategy is as follows. The workload is executed on a simulator of a multiprocessor architecture, as described in Chapter 4. By observing the state transitions encountered in the simulator, we can determine the frequency of various events such as cache misses and bus transactions. We can then evaluate the effect of protocol choices in terms of other design parameters such as latency and bandwidth requirements.

Choosing parameters according to the methodology of Chapter 4, this section first establishes the basic state transition characteristics generated by the set of applications for the four-state Illinois MESI protocol. It then illustrates how to use these frequency measurements to obtain a preliminary quantitative analysis of the design trade-offs raised by the example protocols above, such as the use of the exclusive state in the MESI protocol and the use of BusUpgr rather than BusRdX transactions for the S → M transition. This section also illustrates more traditional design issues, such as how the cache block size—the granularity of both coherence and communication—impacts the latency and bandwidth needs of the applications. To understand this effect, we classify cache misses into categories such as cold, capacity, and sharing misses, examine the effect of block size on each category, and explain the results in light of application characteristics. Finally, this understanding of the applications is used to illustrate the trade-offs between invalidation-based and update-based protocols, again in light of latency and bandwidth implications.

The analysis in this section is based on the frequency of various important events, not on the absolute times taken or, therefore, the performance. This approach is common in studies of cache architecture because the results transcend particular system implementations and technology assumptions. However, it should be viewed as only a preliminary analysis since many detailed factors that might affect the performance trade-offs in real systems are abstracted away. For example, measuring state transitions provides a means of calculating miss rates and bus traffic, but realistic values for latency, overhead, and occupancy are needed to translate the rates into the actual bandwidth requirements imposed on the system. To obtain an estimate of bandwidth requirements, we may artificially assume that every reference takes a fixed number of cycles to complete. However, the bandwidth requirements themselves do not translate into performance directly but only indirectly by increasing the cost of misses due to contention. Contention is very difficult to estimate because it depends on the timing parameters used and on the burstiness of the traffic, which is not captured by the frequency measurements. Contention, timing, and hence performance are also affected by lower-level interactions with hardware structures (like queues and buffers) and policies.

The simulations used in this section do not model contention. Instead, they use a simple PRAM cost model: all memory operations are assumed to complete in the same amount of time (here a single cycle) regardless of whether they hit or miss in the cache. There are three main reasons for this. First, the focus is on understanding inherent protocol behavior and trade-offs in terms of event frequencies, not so much on performance. Second, since we are experimenting with different cache block sizes and organizations, we would like the interleaving of references from application processes on the simulator to be the same regardless of these choices; that is, all protocols and block sizes should see the same trace of references. With the execution-driven rather than trace-driven simulation we use, this is only possible if we make the cost of every memory operation the same in the simulations. Otherwise, if a reference misses with a small cache block but hits with a larger one, for example, then it will be delayed by different amounts in the interleaving in the two cases. It would therefore be difficult to determine which effects are inherently due to the protocol and which are due to the particular parameter values chosen. Third, realistic simulations that model contention take much more time. The disadvantage of using this simple model even to measure frequencies is that the timing model may affect some of the frequencies we observe; however, this effect is small for the applications we study.

The illustrative workloads we use are the six parallel programs (from the SPLASH-2 suite) and one multiprogrammed workload described in Chapters 3 and 4. The parallel programs run in batch mode with exclusive access to the machine and do not include operating system activity in the simulations, whereas the multiprogrammed workload includes operating system activity. The number of applications used is relatively small, but the applications are primarily for illustration as discussed in Chapter 4; the emphasis here is on choosing programs that represent important classes of computation and with widely varying characteristics. The frequencies of basic operations for the applications appear in Table 4.1. We now study them in more detail to assess design trade-offs in cache coherency protocols.

5.4.2 Bandwidth Requirement under the MESI Protocol

We begin by using the default 1-MB, single-level caches per processor, as discussed in Chapter 4. These are large enough to hold the important working sets for the default problem sizes, which is a realistic scenario for all applications. We use four-way set associativity (with LRU replacement) to reduce conflict misses and a 64-byte cache block size for realism. Driving the workloads through a cache simulator that models the Illinois MESI protocol generates the state transition frequencies shown in Table 5.1. The data is presented as the number of state transitions of a particular type per 1,000 references issued by the processors. Note in the table that a new state,

Table 5.1 State Transitions per 1,000 Data Memory References Issued by the Applications

Application	From	To: NP	I	E	S	M
Barnes-Hut	NP	0	0	0.0011	0.0362	0.0035
	I	0.0201	0	0.0001	0.1856	0.0010
	E	0.0000	0.0000	0.0153	0.0002	0.0010
	S	0.0029	0.2130	0	97.1712	0.1253
	M	0.0013	0.0010	0	0.1277	902.782
LU	NP	0	0	0.0000	0.6593	0.0011
	I	0.0000	0	0	0.0002	0.0003
	E	0.0000	0	0.4454	0.0004	0.2164
	S	0.0339	0.0001	0	302.702	0.0000
	M	0.0001	0.0007	0	0.2164	697.129
Ocean	NP	0	0	1.2484	0.9565	1.6787
	I	0.6362	0	0	1.8676	0.0015
	E	0.2040	0	14.0040	0.0240	0.9955
	S	0.4175	2.4994	0	134.716	2.2392
	M	2.6259	0.0015	0	2.2996	843.565
Radiosity	NP	0	0	0.0068	0.2581	0.0354
	I	0.0262	0	0	0.5766	0.0324
	E	0	0.0003	0.0241	0.0001	0.0060
	S	0.0092	0.7264	0	162.569	0.2768
	M	0.0219	0.0305	0	0.3125	839.507
Radix	NP	0	0	0.004746	3.524705	11.41111
	I	0.130988	0	0	1.108079	4.57868
	E	0.000759	0.002848	0.080301	0	0.00019
	S	0.029804	1.120988	0	178.1932	0.817818
	M	0.044232	11.53127	0	4.03157	802.282

continued

Table 5.1 State Transitions per 1,000 Data Memory References Issued by the Applications

Application	From	To: NP	I	E	S	M
Raytrace	NP	0	0	1.3358	1.5486	0.0026
	I	0.0242	0	0.0000	0.3403	0.0000
	E	0.8663	0	29.0187	0.3639	0.0175
	S	1.1181	0.3740	0	310.949	0.2898
	M	0.0559	0.0001	0	0.2970	661.011
Multiprog User Data References	NP	0	0	0.1675	0.5253	0.1843
	I	0.2619	0	0.0007	0.0072	0.0013
	E	0.0729	0.0008	11.6629	0.0221	0.0680
	S	0.3062	0.2787	0	214.6523	0.2570
	M	0.2134	0.1196	0	0.3732	772.7819
Multiprog User Instruction References	NP	0	0	3.2709	15.7722	0
	I	0	0	0	0	0
	E	1.3029	0	46.7898	1.8961	0
	S	16.9032	0	0	981.2618	0
	M	0	0	0	0	0
Multiprog Kernel Data References	NP	0	0	1.0241	1.7209	4.0793
	I	1.3950	0	0.0079	1.1495	0.1153
	E	0.5511	0.0063	55.7680	0.0999	0.3352
	S	1.2740	2.0514	0	393.5066	1.7800
	M	3.1827	0.3551	0	2.0732	542.4318
Multiprog Kernel Instruction References	NP	0	0	2.1799	26.5124	0
	I	0	0	0	0	0
	E	0.8829	0	5.2156	1.2223	0
	S	24.6963	0	0	1,075.2158	0
	M	0	0	0	0	0

The data assumes 16 processors (except for Multiprog, which is for 8 processors), 1-MB four-way set-associative caches, 64-byte cache blocks, and the Illinois MESI coherence protocol.

NP (not present), is introduced. This addition helps clarify transitions where, on a cache miss, one block is replaced (creating a transition from one of I, E, S, or M to NP) and a new block is brought in (creating a transition from NP to one of I, E, S, or M). The sum of state transitions can be greater than 1,000 even though we are presenting averages per 1,000 references because some references cause multiple state transitions. For example, a write miss can cause two transitions in the local processor's cache (e.g., S → NP for the old block and NP → M for the incoming block), in addition to transitions in other caches due to invalidations (I/E/S/M → I). This state transition frequency data is very useful for answering "what if" questions. Example 5.8 shows how we can determine the bandwidth requirement these workloads would place on the memory system.

EXAMPLE 5.8 Suppose that the integer-intensive applications run at a sustained 200 MIPS per processor and the floating-point-intensive applications at 200 MFLOPS per processor. Assuming that cache block transfers move 64 bytes on the data bus lines and that each bus transaction involves 6 bytes of command and address on the address lines, what is the traffic generated per processor?

Answer The first step is to calculate the amount of traffic per instruction. We determine what bus action is taken for each of the possible state transitions and therefore how much traffic is associated with each transaction. For example, an M → NP transition indicates that, due to a miss, a modified cache block needs to be written back. Similarly, an S → M transition indicates that an upgrade request must be issued on the bus. Flushing a modified block response to a bus transaction (e.g., the M → S or M → I transition) leads to a BusWB transaction as well. The bus transactions for all possible transitions are shown in Table 5.2. All transactions generate 6 bytes of address bus traffic and 64 bytes of data traffic, except BusUpgr, which only generates address traffic. We can now compute the traffic generated. Using Table 5.2, we can convert the state transitions per 1,000 memory references in Table 5.1 to bus transactions per 1,000 memory references and convert this to address and data traffic by multiplying by the traffic per transaction. Then, using the frequency of memory accesses in Table 4.1, we can convert this to traffic per instruction. Finally, multiplying by the assumed processing rate, we get the address and data bandwidth requirement for each application. The result of this calculation is shown by the leftmost bar for each application in Figure 5.18.[5] ■

5. For the Multiprog workload, to speed up the simulations, a 32-KB instruction cache is used as a filter before passing the instruction references to the 1-MB unified instruction and data cache. The state transition frequencies for the instruction references are computed based only on those references that missed in the L_1 instruction cache. This filtering does not affect how we compute data traffic, but it means that instruction traffic is computed differently. In addition, for Multiprog we present data separately for kernel instructions, kernel data references, user instructions, and user data references. A given reference may produce transitions of multiple types for user and kernel data. For example, if a kernel instruction miss causes a modified user data block to be written back, then we will have one transition for kernel instructions from NP → E/S and another transition for the user data reference category from M → NP.

Table 5.2 Bus Actions Corresponding to State Transitions in Illinois MESI Protocol

		To				
		NP	I	E	S	M
From	NP	—	—	BusRd	BusRd	BusRdX
	I	—	—	BusRd	BusRd	BusRdX
	E	—	—	—	—	—
	S	—	—	Not possible	—	BusUpgr
	M	BusWB	BusWB	Not possible	BusWB	—

The calculation in the preceding example gives the average bandwidth requirement under the assumption that the bus bandwidth is enough to allow the processors to execute at full speed. (In practice, bandwidth limitations may slow processors and events down, which in turn would lead to lower traffic per unit time.) This calculation provides a useful basis for sizing the number of processors that a system can support without saturating the bus. For example, on a machine such as the SGI Challenge with 1.2 GB/s of data bandwidth, the bus provides sufficient average bandwidth to support 16 processors on all the applications other than Radix for these problem sizes. A typical rule of thumb might be to leave 50% "headroom" to allow for burstiness of data transfers. If the Ocean and Multiprog workloads were also excluded, the bus could support up to 32 processors. If the bandwidth is not sufficient to support the application, the application will slow down. Thus, we would expect the speedup curve for Radix to flatten out quite quickly as the number of processors grows. In general, a multiprocessor is used for a variety of workloads, many with low per-processor bandwidth requirements, so the designer will choose to support configurations of a size that would overcommit the bus on the most demanding applications.

5.4.3 Impact of Protocol Optimizations

Given this base design point, we can evaluate protocol trade-offs under common machine parameter assumptions, as illustrated in Example 5.9.

EXAMPLE 5.9 We have described two invalidation protocols in this chapter—the basic three-state MSI protocol and the Illinois MESI protocol. The key difference is that the MESI protocol includes the existence of the exclusive state. How large is the bandwidth savings due to the E state?

Answer The main advantage of the E state is that no traffic need be generated when going from E → M. A three-state protocol would have to generate a BusUpgr transaction to acquire exclusive ownership for the memory block. To compute bandwidth savings, all we have to do is put a BusUpgr for the E → M transition in Table 5.2 and recompute the traffic as before. The middle bar in Figure 5.18 shows the resulting bandwidth requirements. ■

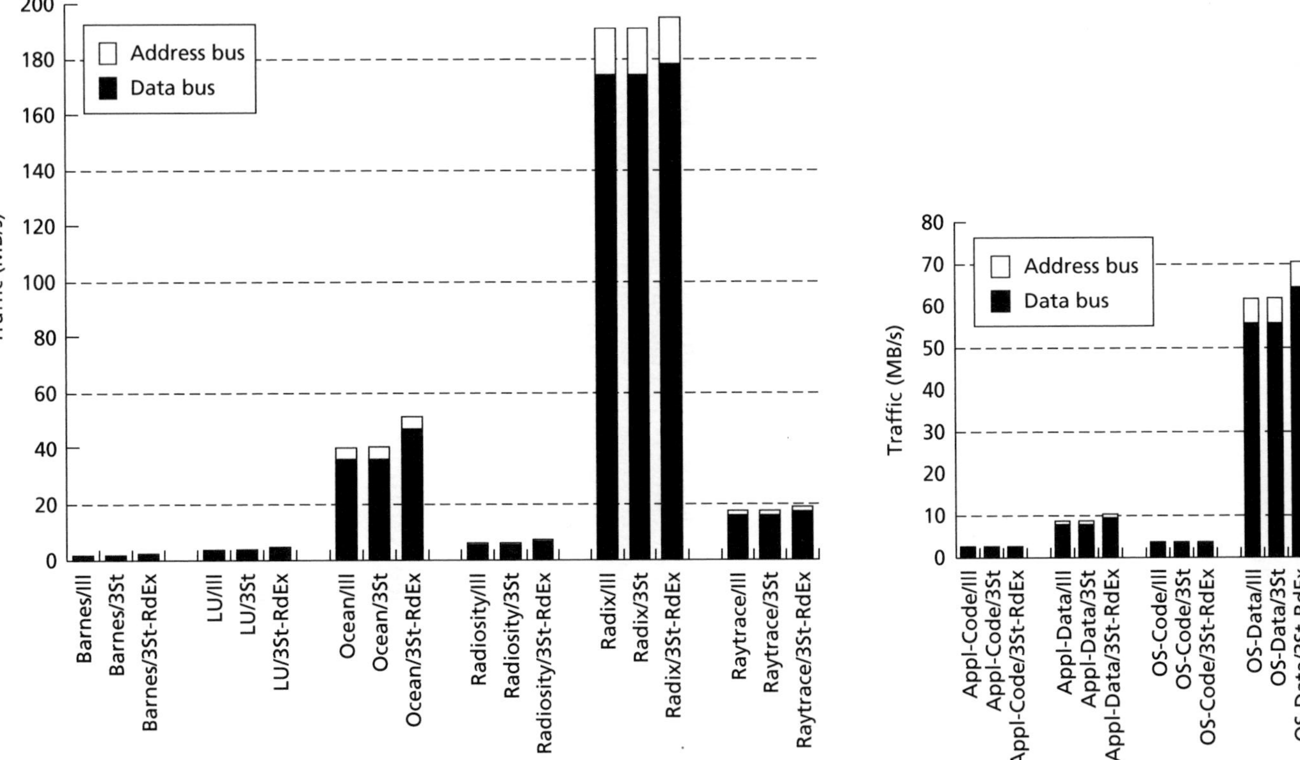

FIGURE 5.18 Per-processor bandwidth requirements for the various applications, assuming 200-MIPS/MFLOPS processors and 1-MB caches per processor. The left bar chart shows data for the parallel programs, and the right chart shows data for the Multiprog workload. The traffic is split into data traffic and address (including command) bus traffic. The leftmost bar shows traffic for the Illinois MESI protocol (Ill), the middle bar for the case where we use the basic three-state invalidation protocol without the E state (3St), and the rightmost bar for the three-state protocol when we use BusRdX instead of BusUpgr for S → M transitions (3St-RdEx).

Example 5.9 illustrates how an intuitive rationale for a more complex design may not stand up to quantitative measurement of workloads. Contrary to expectations, the E state offers negligible savings in traffic. This is true even for the Multiprog workload, which consists primarily of sequential jobs and should have benefited most. The primary reason for this negligible gain is that the fraction of E → M transitions in Table 5.1 is quite small (i.e., blocks loaded in exclusive state by a read miss are not often written while still in that state). In addition, the BusUpgr transaction that would have been needed for the S → M transition in a three-state protocol takes only 6 bytes of address traffic and no data traffic. Example 5.10 examines the advantage of the BusUpgr transaction.

EXAMPLE 5.10 Recall that even in the three-state MSI protocol, a write that finds the memory block in shared state in the cache generates a BusUpgr request on the bus rather than a BusRdX. This saves bandwidth, as no data need be transferred for a BusUpgr, but it complicates the implementation, as we shall see. The question is, how much bandwidth are we saving for taking on the extra complexity?

Answer To compute the bandwidth for the less complex implementation and a three-state protocol, all we have to do is put in BusRdX in the E → M and S → M transitions in Table 5.2 (these would all be S → M transitions in the three-state MSI protocol) and then recompute the bandwidth numbers. The results for all applications are shown in the rightmost bar in Figure 5.18. While for most applications the difference in bandwidth is small, Ocean and Multiprog kernel data references show that it can be as large as 10–20% for some applications. ■

The performance impact of these differences in bandwidth requirement depends on how the bus transactions are actually implemented. However, this high-level analysis indicates where more detailed evaluation is required.

Finally, as discussed in Chapter 4, for the input data set sizes we are using it is important that we run the Ocean, Raytrace, and Radix applications for smaller cache sizes as well, to model the situation where an important working set does not fit in the cache hierarchy. We use 64-KB caches here, which fit all but the largest working set for these problem sizes. The raw state transition data for this case is presented in Table 5.3, and the per-processor bandwidth requirements are shown in Figure 5.19. As we can see, not having one of the critical working sets fit in the processor cache can dramatically increase the bus bandwidth required due to capacity misses. A 1.2-GB/s bus can now barely support 4 processors for Ocean and Radix and 16 processors for Raytrace.

5.4.4 Trade-Offs in Cache Block Size

The cache organization is a critical performance factor in all modern computers, but it is especially so in multiprocessors. In the uniprocessor context, cache misses are typically categorized into the "three Cs": compulsory, capacity, and conflict misses (Hill and Smith 1989; Hennessy and Patterson 1996). *Compulsory misses*, or *cold misses*, occur on the first reference to a memory block by a processor. *Capacity misses* occur when all the blocks that are referenced by a processor during the execution of a program do not fit in the cache (even with full associativity), so some

Table 5.3 State Transitions per 1,000 Memory References Issued by the Applications with Smaller Caches

Application			To				
			NP	I	E	S	M
Ocean	From	NP	0	0	26.2491	2.6030	15.1459
		I	1.3305	0	0	0.3012	0.0008
		E	21.1804	0.2976	452.580	0.4489	4.3216
		S	2.4632	1.3333	0	113.257	1.1112
		M	19.0240	0.0015	0	1.5543	387.780
Radix	From	NP	0	0	9.440787	2.557865	27.36084
		I	4.354862	0	0.00057	0.157565	1.499903
		E	8.148377	0.001329	140.9295	0.012339	0.126621
		S	3.825407	0.481427	0	102.4144	0.484464
		M	23.03084	5.629429	0	2.069604	717.1426
Raytrace	From	NP	0	0	7.2642	3.9742	0.1305
		I	0.0526	0	0.0003	0.2799	0.0000
		E	6.4119	0	131.944	0.7973	0.0496
		S	4.6768	0.3329	0	205.994	0.2835
		M	0.1812	0.0001	0	0.2837	660.753

The data assumes 16 processors, 64-KB four-way set-associative caches, 64-byte cache blocks, and the Illinois MESI coherence protocol.

blocks are replaced and later accessed again. *Conflict* or *collision misses* occur in caches with less than full associativity when the collection of blocks referenced by a program that maps to a single cache set does not fit in the set. They are misses that would not have occurred in a fully associative cache. Many studies have examined how cache size, associativity, and block size affect each category of miss.

Architecturally, capacity misses are reduced by enlarging the cache. Conflict misses are reduced by increasing the associativity or increasing the number of lines to map to in the cache (by increasing cache size or reducing block size). Cold misses can be reduced only by increasing the block size so that a single cold miss will bring in more data that may be accessed thereafter as well. What makes cache design challenging in uniprocessors is that these factors trade off against one another. For example, increasing the block size for a fixed cache capacity will reduce the number of blocks, so the reduced cold misses may come at the cost of increased conflict misses. Also, variations in cache organization can affect the miss penalty or the hit time and, therefore, perhaps the processor cycle time.

Cache-coherent multiprocessors introduce a fourth category of misses: *coherence misses*. These occur when blocks of data are shared among multiple caches. There

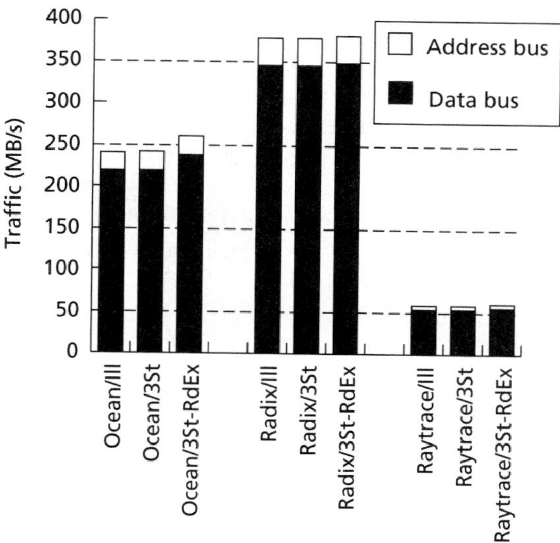

FIGURE 5.19 Per-processor bandwidth requirements for the various applications, assuming 200-MIPS/MFLOPS processors and 64-KB caches. The traffic is split into data traffic and address (including command) bus traffic. The leftmost bar shows traffic for the Illinois MESI protocol, the middle bar for the case where we use the basic three-state invalidation protocol without the E state (as described in Section 5.3.1), and the rightmost bar for the three-state protocol when we use BusRdX instead of BusUpgr for S → M transitions.

are two types: true sharing and false sharing misses. True sharing occurs when a data word produced (written) by one processor is used (read or written) by another. False sharing occurs when independent data words accessed by different processors happen to be placed in the same memory (cache) block, and at least one of the accesses is a write. The cache block size is not only the granularity (or unit) of the data fetched from the main memory, it is also typically used as the granularity of coherence. That is, on a write by a processor, the whole cache block is invalidated in other processors' caches, not just the word that is written.

More precisely, a *true sharing miss* occurs when one processor writes some words in a cache block, invalidating that block in another processor's cache, after which the second processor reads one of the modified words. It is called a "true" sharing miss because the miss truly communicates newly defined data values that are used by the second processor; such misses are essential to the correctness of the program, regardless of interactions with the machine organization or granularities. On the other hand, when one processor writes a word in a cache block and then another processor reads (or writes) a different word in the same cache block, the invalidation of the block and subsequent cache miss occurs as well, even though no useful values are being communicated between the processors. These misses are thus called *false sharing misses* (Dubois et al. 1993). As cache block size is increased, the probability of distinct variables being accessed by different processors but residing on the same cache block increases. If at least some of these variables are written, the likelihood of false sharing misses increases as well. False sharing misses would not occur with a one-word cache block size, while true sharing misses would. Technology pushes in the direction of large cache block sizes (e.g., DRAM organization and access modes and the need to obtain high-bandwidth data transfers by amortizing overhead), so it is important to understand the potential impact of false sharing misses and how they may be avoided.

True sharing misses are inherent to a given parallel decomposition and assignment, so, like cold misses, the only way to reduce them is by increasing the block size and increasing spatial locality of communicated data. False sharing misses, on the other hand, are an example of the artifactual communication discussed in Chapter 3 since they are caused by interactions with the architecture. In contrast to true sharing and cold misses, false sharing misses can be decreased by reducing the cache block size, as well as by a host of other optimizations in software (orchestration) and hardware that we shall discuss later. Thus, a fundamental tension exists in determining the best cache block size, which can only be resolved by evaluating the options against real programs.

A Classification of Cache Misses

The flowchart in Figure 5.20 gives a detailed algorithm for classifying cache misses in cache-coherent multiprocessors.[6] Understanding the details is not critical for now—it is enough for the rest of the chapter to understand only the preceding definitions—but it adds insight and is a useful exercise. In the algorithm, the *lifetime* of a block in a cache is defined as the time interval during which the block remains valid in the cache, that is, the time from the occurrence of the miss that loads the block in the cache until its invalidation, replacement, or the end of the program. We cannot classify a cache miss when it occurs but only when the fetched memory block is replaced or invalidated in the cache, because it is only then that we know whether true sharing or only false sharing occurred during that lifetime. Let us consider the simple cases first. Cases 1 and 2 are straightforward cold misses occurring on previously unwritten blocks. Cases 7 and 8 reflect false and true sharing on a block that was previously invalidated in the cache but yet replaced by another. The type of sharing is determined by whether the specific word or words modified since the invalidation are actually used during the current lifetime. Case 9 is a straightforward capacity (or conflict) miss since the block was previously replaced from the cache and the words in the block have not been modified since last accessed. All of the other cases refer to misses that occur due to a combination of factors. For example, cases 4 and 5 are cold misses because this processor has never accessed the block before; however, some other processor had written the block, so there is also

6. In this classification, we do not distinguish conflict from capacity misses since both are a result of the available resources (set or entire cache) becoming full and the difference between them does not shed additional light on multiprocessor issues.

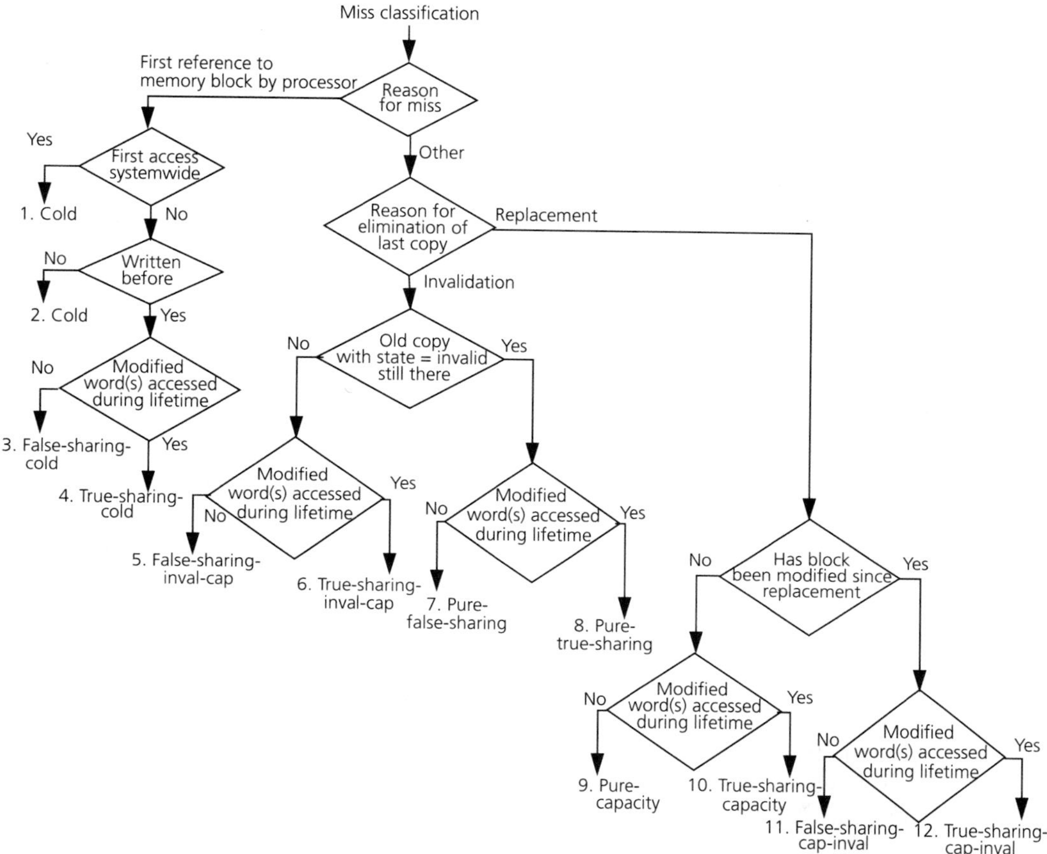

FIGURE 5.20 A classification of cache misses for shared memory multiprocessors. The four basic categories of cache misses in this classification are cold, capacity, true sharing, and false sharing misses (conflict misses are considered to be capacity misses for this purpose). Many mixed categories arise because there may be multiple causes for a miss. For example, a block may be first replaced from processor *A*'s cache, then written to by processor *B,* and then read back by processor *A,* making it a capacity-cum-invalidation false/true sharing miss. This would be labeled "false/true sharing cap-inval" in the classification since sharing takes priority and since the replacement happened before the invalidation (cases 11 and 12 in the figure). If the block were first invalidated in *A*'s cache, then the invalid block replaced, and then read again by *A,* it would be labeled "false/true sharing inval-cap" (cases 6 and 7). In terms of the four major categories, these misses all fall into true or false sharing misses, as appropriate. *Note:* the question "modified word(s) accessed during lifetime?" asks whether accesses are made by this processor in the current lifetime to word(s) within the cache block that have been modified since the last "essential coherence" miss to this block by this processor, where essential coherence misses correspond to categories 4, 6, 8, 10, and 12. This can only be determined when the current lifetime of the block ends.

sharing (false or true). Similarly, we can have false or true sharing on blocks that were previously replaced due to capacity or conflicts. Solving only one of the problems in these cases may not necessarily eliminate such misses. For example, if a miss occurs due to both false sharing and capacity problems, then eliminating the false sharing problem by reducing block size will likely not eliminate that miss. On the other hand, sharing misses are in a sense more fundamental than capacity misses since they will remain even if the size of cache is increased to infinity, so we give them priority in the classification of multiple-cause misses. All misses with true sharing in their names in the resulting classification are called *essential coherence misses*. They would occur even with infinite caches, single-word blocks, and all data preloaded into all caches (i.e., no cold misses). Example 5.11 illustrates these definitions of miss categories.

EXAMPLE 5.11 Suppose three processors, P_1, P_2, and P_3, issue the memory operations shown in the first few columns of Table 5.4 (the first column indicates virtual time or steps). Use the miss classification algorithm to classify the misses in the last column. Assume that each processor's cache consists of only a single four-word cache block and that all the caches are initially empty.

Answer The results are shown in Table 5.4. ■

Impact of Block Size on Miss Rate

Applying the classification algorithm of Figure 5.20 to simulated runs of a workload, we can determine how frequently the various kinds of misses occur in programs and how the frequencies change with variations in cache organization, such as block size. Figure 5.21 shows the decomposition of the misses for the example applications running on 16 processors, with 1-MB four-way set-associative caches each, as the cache block size is varied from 8 bytes to 256 bytes. The bars show the four basic types of misses: cold misses (cases 1 and 2), capacity—including conflict—misses (case 9), true sharing misses, (cases 4, 6, 8, 10, 12), and false sharing misses (cases 3, 5, 7, and 11). In addition, they show the frequency of *upgrades*—writes that find the block in the cache but in the shared state. Upgrades are different from the other types of misses since the cache already has the valid data and only needs exclusive ownership. While they are not included in the classification scheme of Figure 5.20, they are still usually considered to be misses since they generate traffic on the interconnect and can stall the processor.

For each individual application, the miss characteristics change with block size much as we would expect from our understanding of the program and the miss categories. Cold, capacity, and true sharing misses tend to decrease with increasing block size because the additional data brought in with each miss is accessed before the block is replaced, due to spatial locality. However, false sharing misses tend to increase with block size. In all cases, true sharing is a significant fraction of the misses, so even with ideal, infinite caches, the miss rate and bus bandwidth will not go to zero. However, the overall characteristics differ widely across programs. For example, the size of the true sharing component varies significantly. Some applica-

Table 5.4 Classifying Misses in an Example Reference Stream from Three Processors

Time	P_1	P_2	P_3	Miss Classification
1	ld w0		ld w2	P_1 and P_3 miss; but we will classify later on replace/inval
2			st w2	$P_{1.1}$: pure cold miss; $P_{3.2}$: upgrade
3		ld w1		P_2 misses, but we will classify later on replace/inval
4		ld w2	ld w7	P_2 hits; P_3 misses; $P_{3.1}$: cold miss
5	ld w5			P_1 misses
6		ld w6		P_2 misses; $P_{2.3}$: cold true sharing miss (w2 accessed)
7		st w6		$P_{1.5}$: cold miss; $P_{2.7}$: upgrade; $P_{3.4}$: pure cold miss
8	ld w5			P_1 misses
9	ld w6		ld w2	P_1 hits; P_3 misses
10	ld w2	ld w1		P_1, P_2 miss; $P_{1.8}$: pure true share miss; $P_{2.6}$: cold miss
11	st w5			P_1 misses; $P_{1.10}$: pure true sharing miss
12			st w2	$P_{2.10}$: capacity miss; $P_{3.11}$: upgrade
13			ld w7	P_3 misses; $P_{3.9}$: capacity miss
14			ld w2	P_3 misses; $P_{3.13}$: inval cap false sharing miss
15	ld w0			P_1 misses; $P_{1.11}$: capacity miss

If multiple references are listed in the same row, we assume that P_1 issues before P_2 and P_2 issues before P_3. The notation ld/st w*i* refers to load/store of word *i*. W1 through w4 are on the same cache block, and so on. The notation $P_{i.j}$ points to the memory reference issued by processor *i* at row *j*.

tions show a substantial increase in false sharing with block size, whereas others show almost none. Furthermore, the figure shows data only for the default data sets. In practice it is very important to examine the results as the input data set size and number of processors are scaled before drawing conclusions about the false sharing or spatial locality of an application (see Chapter 4). Let us investigate the properties of the applications that give rise to differences in miss characteristics observed at the machine level and that allow us to understand scaling qualitatively.

Relation to Application Structure

Multiword cache blocks exploit spatial locality by prefetching data surrounding the accessed address. Of course, beyond a point, larger cache blocks can hurt performance by (1) prefetching unneeded data, (2) causing increased conflict misses as the number of distinct blocks that can be stored in a finite cache decreases with increasing block size, and (3) causing increased false sharing misses. Spatial locality in parallel programs tends to be lower than in sequential programs because, when a

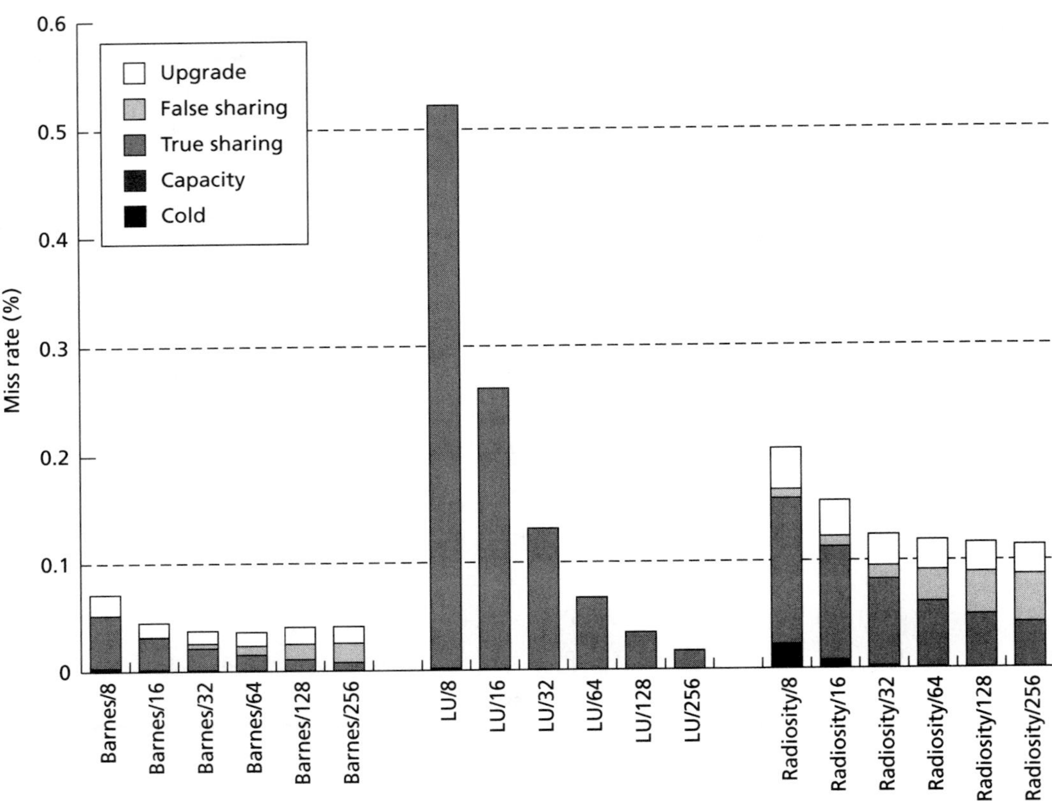

FIGURE 5.21(a) Breakdown of application miss rates as a function of cache block size for 1-MB caches per processor for Barnes-Hut, LU, and Radiosity applications. Conflict misses are included in capacity misses. The breakdown and behavior of misses vary greatly across applications, but we can observe some common trends. Cold misses and capacity misses tend to decrease quite quickly with block size as a result of spatial locality. True sharing misses also tend to decrease, whereas false sharing misses increase. While the false sharing component is usually small for small block sizes, it sometimes remains small and sometimes increases very quickly. Upgrades are shown at the top of the bars and without shading, so they can be ignored if desired.

memory block is brought into the cache, some of the data therein may belong to another processor and will not be used by the processor performing the miss. As an extreme example, some parallel programs assign adjacent elements of an array to different processors in order to ensure good load balance and in the process substantially decrease the spatial locality of the program.

The data in Figure 5.21 shows that LU and Ocean have good spatial locality and little false sharing even in the parallel case. The miss rates for many components drop proportionately to increases in cache block size, and false sharing misses are essentially nonexistent. This is in large part because these array-based codes use

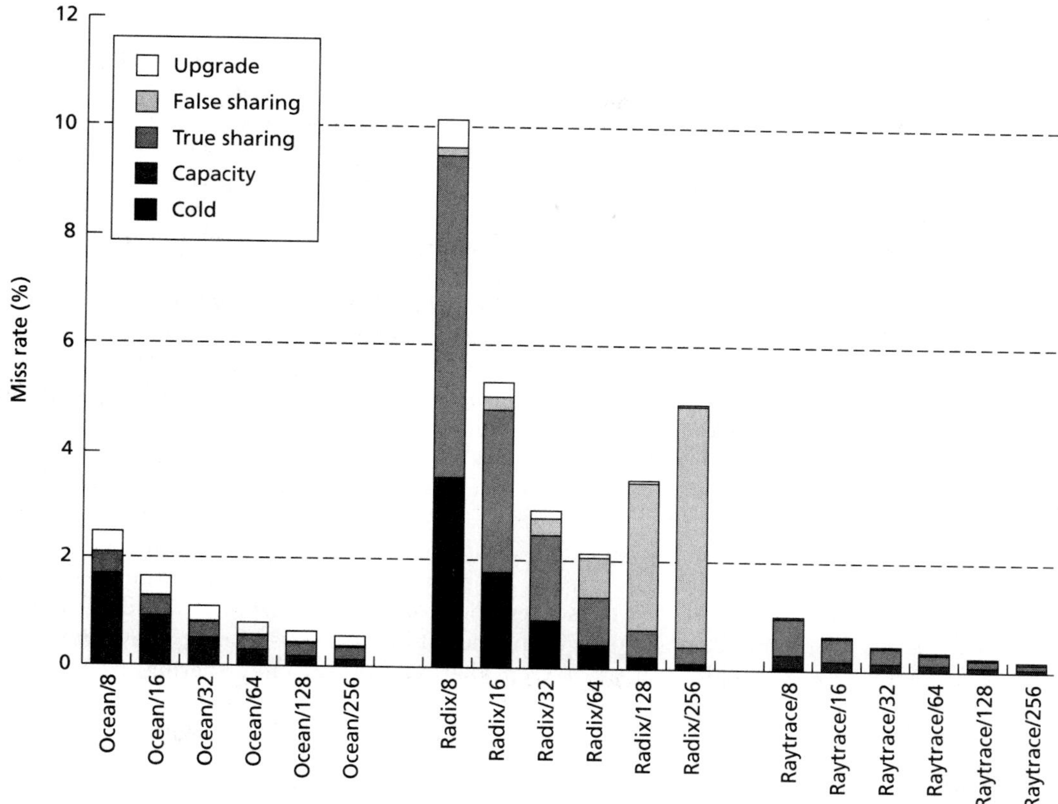

FIGURE 5.21(b) Breakdown of application miss rates as a function of cache block size for 1-MB caches per processor for Ocean, Radix, and Raytrace applications.

architecturally aware data structures, as discussed in Chapters 3 and 4. For example, a grid in Ocean is not represented as a single 2D array (which can introduce substantial false sharing at column-oriented partition boundaries) but as a 4D array: a 2D array of blocks, each of which is itself a 2D array. Such structuring, by programmers or compilers, ensures that most accesses are unit stride and over substantial, contiguous blocks of data, thus the nice behavior.

In Ocean, capacity misses are significant, but they are to the interior elements of a process's partition, so they have very good spatial locality. One difference with LU is that true sharing misses in Ocean do not exhibit such good spatial locality. Most of the true sharing misses are to elements at the borders of neighboring partitions. These exhibit good spatial locality at row-oriented borders where the data to be fetched is contiguous in the address space. However, when a processor accesses an element at a column-oriented border, it fetches an entire cache block of interior elements of its neighbor's partition, which it will not use and therefore wastes. Since capacity misses are not very large with this problem and machine configuration, overall spatial locality is limited by that of true communication. In LU, even true communication is of B-by-B contiguous blocks at a time, so spatial locality is excellent even on true sharing misses.

As for scaling, the spatial locality for these two applications is expected to remain good with no false sharing as both the problem size and the number of processors are increased (at least until partitions become unrealistically small). This should be true even for cache blocks larger than 256 bytes, at least for LU. In Ocean, how capacity versus true communication misses (and hence spatial locality) scale depends strongly on the relative scaling of data set size and processor count.

The graphics application Raytrace also shows negligible false sharing but displays somewhat worse spatial locality. False sharing is small because the main data structure (the collection of polygons constituting the scene) is read-only. The only read-write sharing happens on the image plane data structure and the task queues, but that is well controlled and small for large enough problems. This true sharing miss rate is reduced by increasing cache block size. The reason for the poor spatial locality of capacity misses (although the overall magnitude is small in this configuration) is that the access pattern to the collection of polygons is quite arbitrary since the set of objects that a ray will bounce off of is unpredictable. As for scaling, as problem size is increased (most likely in the form of more polygons), the primary effect is likely to be larger capacity miss rates; the spatial locality within individual components should not change. A larger number of processors is in many ways similar to having a smaller problem size, except that we may see more sharing in the image plane and task queue data structures.

The Barnes-Hut and Radiosity applications show moderate spatial locality and false sharing. These applications employ complex data structures, including trees encoding spatial information and arrays in which the records assigned to each processor are not contiguous in memory. For example, Barnes-Hut operates on particle records stored in an array. As the application proceeds and particles move in physical space, particle records get reassigned to different processors, with the result that after some time adjacent particles in the array most likely belong to different processors. Spatial locality is exploited well within a particle record but not very well across records. False sharing becomes a problem at large block sizes for different reasons. First, different processors may write to different records that share a cache block. Second, a particle data structure (record) contains both fields that are being modified by the owner of that particle in a phase (e.g., the current force on this particle in the force calculation phase) and fields that are read by other processors and are not being modified in this phase (e.g., the current position of the particle). Since these two fields may fall in the same cache block for large block sizes, false sharing results. It is possible to eliminate such false sharing by splitting the particle data structure according to the access patterns of the fields, but that is not done in this program since the absolute magnitude of the miss rate is small. As problem size and the number of processors are scaled, the miss rate behavior of Barnes-Hut is expected to change little. This is because the working set size changes very slowly (as the log of the number of particles, unlike Ocean and Raytrace), spatial locality is

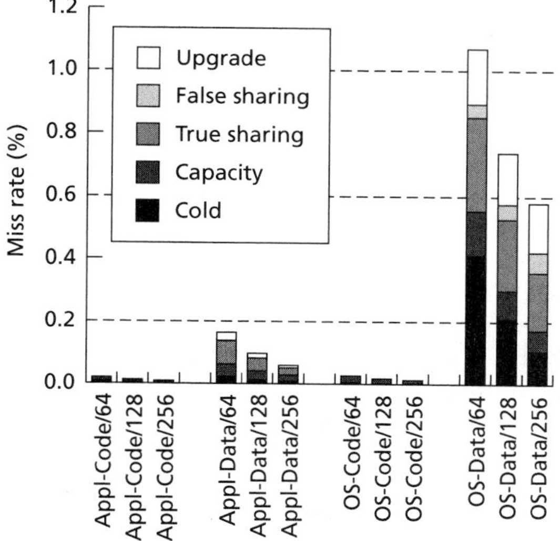

FIGURE 5.22 Breakdown of miss rates for Multiprog as a function of cache block size. The results are for 1-MB caches. Spatial locality for true sharing misses is much better for the applications than for the operating system.

determined by the size of one particle record and thus remains the same, and the sources of false sharing are not very sensitive to the number of processors. Radiosity is a much more complex application whose behavior is difficult to reason about with larger data sets or more processors; the only option is to gather empirical data showing the growth trends.

The poorest sharing behavior is exhibited by Radix, which not only has a very high miss rate even with 1-MB caches (due to cold and true sharing misses) but which gets significantly worse due to false sharing misses for block sizes of 128 bytes or more. The effect of false sharing in Radix was illustrated in Chapter 4. Let us now examine how it is governed. Consider sorting 256-K keys, using a radix of 1,024 and 16 processors. On average, this results in 16 keys per radix per processor (64 bytes of data), which are then written to a contiguous portion of a global array at an unpredictable starting point. Adjacent 64-byte chunks in this array are written by different processors. If the cache block size is larger than 64 bytes, the high potential for false sharing is clear. As the problem size is increased we will clearly see much less false sharing. The effect of increasing the number of processors is exactly the opposite. Radix illustrates quite dramatically that it is not sufficient to look at a given problem size and number of processors and, based on that, draw conclusions of whether or not false sharing or spatial locality is a problem. It is very important to understand how the results are dependent on the key parameters chosen in the experiment and how these parameters may vary in reality.

Data for the Multiprog workload for 1-MB caches is shown in Figure 5.22. The data is shown separately for user code, user data, kernel code, and kernel data. For code, there are only cold and capacity misses. Furthermore, we see that the spatial locality in operating system data references is not very good. This is true, to a somewhat lesser extent, for the application data misses as well, because `gcc` (the main application causing misses in Multiprog) uses a large number of linked lists, which do not offer good spatial locality. It is interesting that we have an observable fraction of application true sharing misses, although we are running only sequential applications. These misses arise due to process migration and are incurred when a sequential process migrates from one processor to another (a decision made by the operating system for resource management) and then references memory blocks that it wrote while it was executing on the other processor. While the spatial locality in cold and capacity misses is quite reasonable, the true sharing misses do not decrease at all for kernel data. One reason for this may be that the operating system has not been well structured as a parallel program.

Finally, let us examine the behavior of Ocean, Radix, and Raytrace for smaller 64-KB caches. The miss rate results are shown in Figure 5.23. As expected, the overall miss rates are higher, and capacity misses have increased substantially. The effects of cache block size for true sharing and false sharing misses are not significantly different from the results for 1-MB caches because these properties are quite fundamental to the assignment and orchestration used by a program and are not too sensitive to cache size. However, the behavior of capacity misses has a much larger effect on the behavior of the overall miss rate. For example, in Ocean, capacity misses now dominate sharing misses; since they have much better spatial locality, the overall miss rate decreases much more quickly with increasing block size than it did with 1-MB caches. (Very large blocks in a small cache can have the problem that blocks may be replaced from the cache due to conflicts before the processor has had a chance to reference all of the words in them.) In Raytrace, capacity misses have somewhat worse spatial locality than true sharing misses, so the overall benefits of large blocks look worse with smaller caches. Results for false sharing and spatial locality for other applications can be found in the literature (Torrellas, Lam, and Hennessy 1994; Jeremiassen and Eggers 1991; Woo et al. 1995).

While larger cache blocks reduce the miss rate for most of our applications, within the range of block sizes we consider they have two important potential disadvantages. First, they can increase the cost of each miss since more data has to be transferred across the bus (although techniques like only waiting for the referenced word to arrive before allowing the processor to proceed, called a *critical word restart* approach, can alleviate this). Second, they increase traffic, and hence contention, if the whole block is not useful.

Impact of Block Size on Bus Traffic

Let us briefly examine the impact of cache block size on bus traffic rather than miss rate. While the number of misses and total traffic generated are clearly related, their impact on observed performance can be quite different. Misses have a cost that may contribute directly to performance, even though modern microprocessors try hard to hide the latency of misses by overlapping it with other activities. Traffic, on the

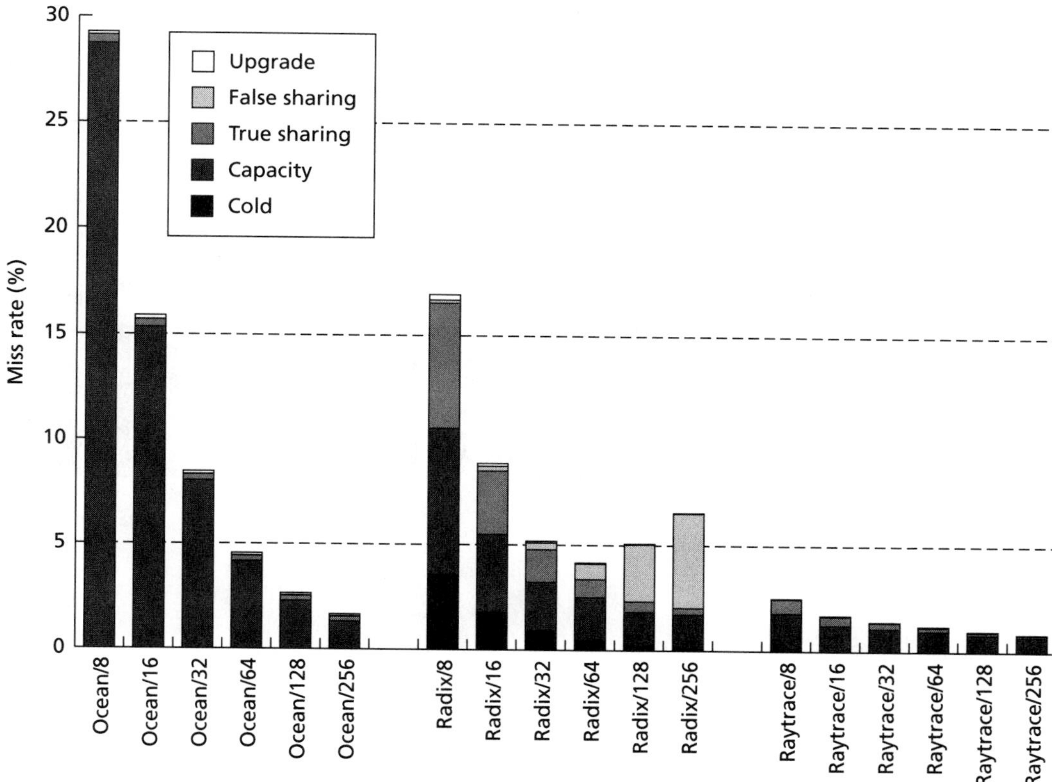

FIGURE 5.23 Breakdown of application miss rates as a function of cache block size for 64-KB caches. Capacity misses are now a much larger fraction of the overall miss rate. Capacity miss rates decrease differently with block size for different applications.

other hand, affects performance indirectly by causing contention and hence increasing the cost of other misses. For example, if an application program's misses are reduced significantly by increasing the cache block size, but the bus traffic is increased by 50%, this might be a reasonable trade-off if the application was originally using only 10% of the available bus and memory bandwidth. Increasing the bus and memory utilization to 15% is unlikely to increase the miss latencies significantly. However, if the application was originally using 75% of the bus and memory bandwidth, then increasing the block size is probably a bad idea.

Figure 5.24 shows the total bus traffic for our applications in bytes/instruction or bytes/FLOP as the cache block size is varied. Three key points can be observed from this graph. First, traffic behaves very differently than miss rate. Only LU shows monotonically decreasing total traffic for the block sizes used. Most other applications see a doubling or tripling of traffic as block size becomes large. Second, the

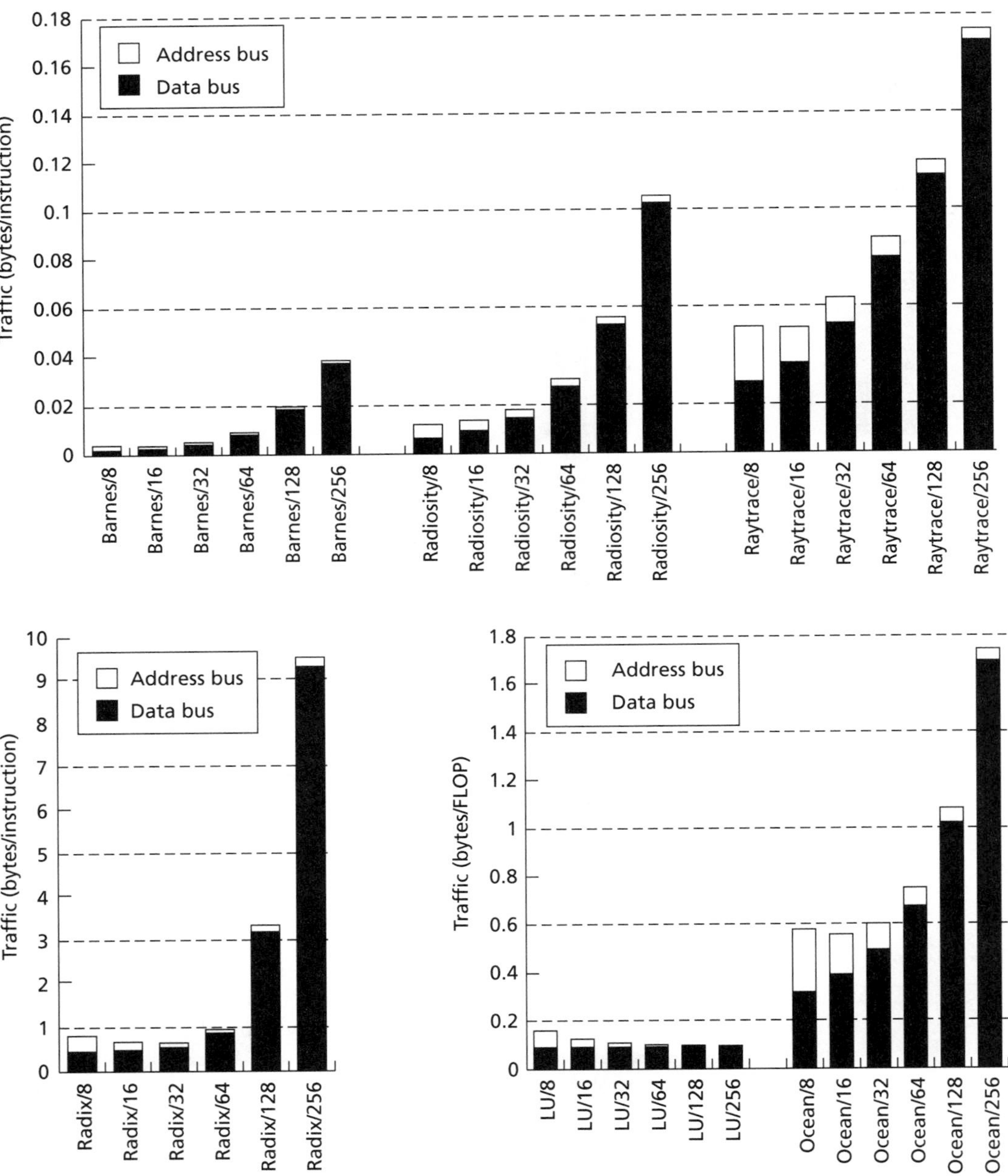

FIGURE 5.24 Traffic (in bytes/instruction or bytes/FLOP) as a function of cache block size with 1-MB caches per processor. Data traffic increases quite quickly with block size when communication misses dominate, except for applications like LU that have excellent spatial locality on all types of misses. Address (including command) bus traffic tends to decrease with block size since the miss rate and, hence, number of blocks transferred decrease.

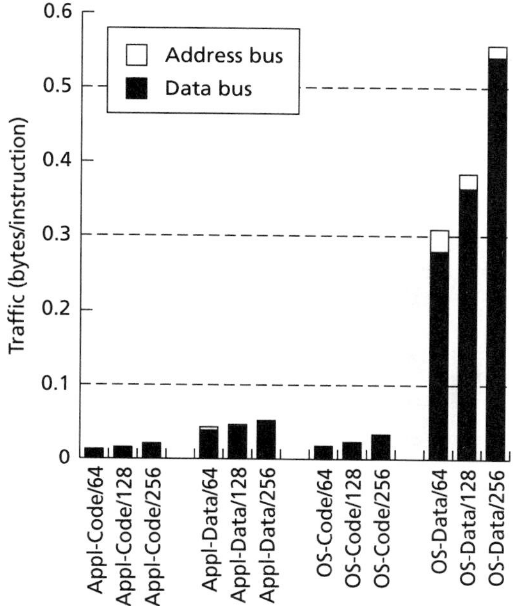

FIGURE 5.25 Traffic in bytes/instruction as a function of cache block size for Multiprog with 1-MB caches. Traffic increases quickly with block size for data references from the OS kernel.

overall traffic requirements for the applications are still small, even for 256-byte block sizes, with the exception of Radix. Radix's large bandwidth requirements (approximately 650 MB/s per processor for 128-byte cache blocks, assuming a sustained 200-MIPS processor) reflect its false sharing problems at large block sizes. Third, the constant address and command traffic overhead for each bus transaction or miss comprises a significant fraction of total traffic for small block sizes. Hence, although actual application data traffic usually increases as we increase the block size due to poor spatial locality, the total traffic is often minimized at 16–32 bytes rather than 8 bytes due to the amortization of the overhead with improved miss rates.

Figure 5.25 shows the traffic data for Multiprog. While the increase in traffic from 64-byte cache blocks to 128-byte blocks is small, the jump at 256-byte blocks is much more substantial (primarily due to kernel data references). Finally, Figure 5.26 shows the traffic results for 64-KB caches for the three relevant applications. For Ocean, even 64- and 128-byte cache blocks don't look so bad, due to the dominance of capacity misses that have good spatial locality.

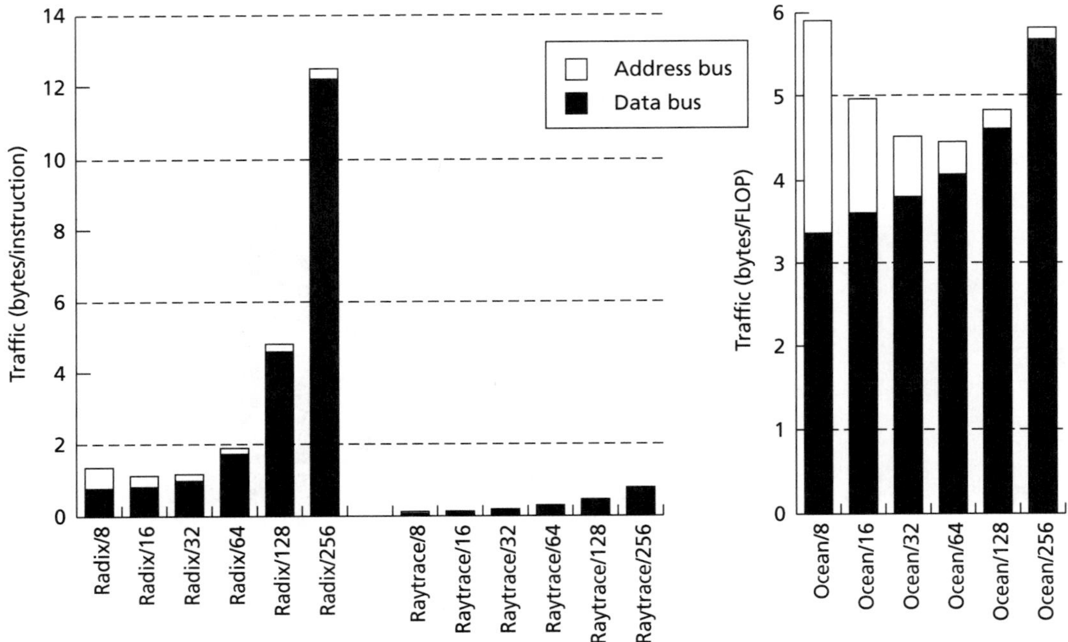

FIGURE 5.26 Traffic (in bytes/instruction or bytes/FLOP) as a function of cache block size with 64-KB caches per processor. Traffic increases more slowly now for Ocean than with 1-MB caches since the capacity misses that now dominate exhibit excellent spatial locality (traversal of a process's assigned subgrid). However, traffic in Radix increases quickly once the threshold block size that causes false sharing is exceeded.

Alleviating the Drawbacks of Large Cache Blocks

The trend toward larger cache block sizes is driven by the increasing gap between processor performance and memory access time. The larger block size amortizes the cost of the bus transaction and memory access across a greater amount of data. The increasing density of processor and memory chips makes it possible to employ large first-level and second-level caches so that the prefetching of data obtained through a larger block size dominates the small increase in conflict misses. However, this trend may bode poorly for multiprocessor designs because false sharing becomes a larger problem. Fortunately, hardware and software mechanisms can be employed to counter the effects of large block size.

Software techniques to reduce false sharing and improve locality on coherence misses are discussed in detail later in the chapter. They essentially involve organizing data structures or work assignments so that data accessed by different processes is not interleaved finely in the shared address space. One example is the use of higher-dimensional arrays so blocks or partitions are wholly contiguous. Compiler techniques have also been developed to automate some methods of laying out data to reduce false sharing (Jeremiassen and Eggers 1991).

Since false sharing is caused by a large granularity of coherence, the way to reduce it while still exploiting spatial locality is to use large blocks for data transfer but a smaller unit of coherence. A natural hardware mechanism is the use of subblocks. Each cache block has a single address tag but distinct state bits for each of several subblocks. One subblock may be valid while others are invalid or dirty. This technique is used in many uniprocessor systems to reduce the amount of data that is copied back to memory on a replacement or to reduce the memory access time on a read miss by resuming the processor when the accessed subblock is present (critical word restart). To avoid false sharing, a write by one processor may invalidate the subblock in another processor's cache while leaving the other subblocks valid. Alternatively, small cache blocks can be used, but on a miss the system can prefetch blocks beyond the accessed block. Proposals have also been made for caches with adjustable block sizes (Dubnicki and LeBlanc 1992). The disadvantage of these approaches is increased state and complexity beyond a commodity cache design.

A more subtle hardware technique is to delay propagating or applying invalidations from a processor until it has issued multiple writes. Delaying invalidations and performing them all at once reduces the occurrence of intervening read misses to those blocks. However, this sort of technique can change the memory consistency model in subtle ways, so further discussion is deferred until Chapter 9 where we consider weaker consistency models in the context of scalable machines. Another hardware technique to reduce false sharing is the use of update- rather than invalidation-based protocols.

5.4.5 Update-Based versus Invalidation-Based Protocols

Whether writes should cause other cached copies to be updated or invalidated has been the subject of considerable debate. Various vendors have taken different stands and, in fact, have changed their position from one design to the next. The controversy arises because the relative performance of update-based versus invalidation-based protocols depends strongly on the sharing patterns exhibited by the workload and on the cost of various underlying operations. Intuitively, if the processors that were using the data before it was updated (written) are likely to want to see the new values in the future, updates should perform better than invalidations. However, if the processors holding the old data are never going to use it again, the update traffic is useless and just consumes interconnect and controller resources. Invalidations would clean out the old copies and eliminate the apparent sharing. This "pack rat" phenomenon with update protocols is especially irritating under multiprogrammed use of a machine, when sequential processes migrate from processor to processor under OS control so that useless updates are performed in caches of processors that are no longer running that process. It is easy to construct cases in which either scheme does substantially better than the other, as illustrated by Example 5.12.

EXAMPLE 5.12 Consider the following two program reference patterns:

- *Pattern 1:* Repeat k times; processor 1 writes a new value into variable V and processors 2 through P read the value of V. This represents a one-producer-many-consumer scenario that may arise, for example, when processors are accessing a highly contended flag for one-to-many event synchronization.
- *Pattern 2:* Repeat k times; processor 1 writes M times to variable V and then processor 2 reads the value of V. This represents a sharing pattern that may occur between pairs of processors, where the first successfully computes and accumulates values into a variable and then when the accumulation is complete, another processor reads the value.

What is the relative cost for update- and invalidation-based protocols in terms of the number of cache misses and bus traffic? Assume that an invalidation/upgrade transaction consumes 6 bytes (5 bytes for address plus 1 byte for command), an update takes 14 bytes (6 bytes for address and command and 8 bytes of data for the updated word), and a regular cache miss takes 70 bytes (6 bytes for address and command plus 64 bytes of data corresponding to cache block size). Also assume that $P = 16$, $M = 10$, $k = 10$, and that all caches initially are empty.

Answer With an update scheme in pattern 1, the first iteration on all P processors will incur a regular cache miss (including processor 1 when it writes) plus an update due to the write. In subsequent $k - 1$ iterations, no more misses will occur and only one update per iteration will be generated. Thus, overall we will see misses = P = 16; traffic = $P \times$ RdMiss + $(k - 1) \times$ Update = $16 \times 70 + 10 \times 14$ = 1,260 bytes.

With an invalidate scheme, all P processors will incur a regular cache miss in the first iteration. In subsequent $k - 1$ iterations, processor 1 will generate an upgrade, but all others will experience a read miss. Thus, counting upgrades as misses, overall we will see misses = $P + (k - 1) \times P = 16 + 9 \times 16 = 160$, of which 151 are read misses and 9 are upgrades; traffic = read misses $\times$ RdMiss + $(k - 1) \times$ Upgrade = 151 $\times$ 70 + 9 $\times$ 6 = 10,624 bytes.

With an update scheme on pattern 2, the first iteration will incur two regular cache misses, one for processor 1 and the other for processor 2. In subsequent $k - 1$ iterations, no more misses will be generated, but M updates will be generated in each iteration. Thus, overall we will see misses = 2; traffic = $2 \times$ RdMiss + $M \times (k - 1)$ $\times$ Update = $2 \times 70 + 10 \times 9 \times 14$ = 1,400 bytes.

With an invalidate scheme, two regular cache misses will occur in the first iteration. In subsequent $k - 1$ iterations, one upgrade (for the first write only) plus one regular read miss will be generated in each iteration. Thus, counting upgrades as misses, overall we will see misses = $2 + (k - 1) \times 2 = 2 + 9 = 11$; traffic = misses $\times$ RdMiss + $(k - 1) \times$ Upgrade = $11 \times 70 + 9 \times 6$ = 824 bytes. ■

These example patterns suggest that it might be possible to design schemes that capture the advantages of both update and invalidate protocols. The success of such schemes will depend on their costs and on the sharing patterns for real parallel programs and workloads. Let us briefly explore the design options and then employ workload-driven evaluation.

Combining Update- and Invalidation-Based Protocols

One way to take advantage of both update and invalidate protocols is to support both in hardware and to decide dynamically at page granularity whether coherence for a given page is to be maintained using an update or an invalidate protocol. The decision about the choice of protocol can be indicated by making a system call. The main advantage of such schemes is that they are relatively easy to support; they utilize the TLB to indicate to the rest of the coherence subsystem which of the two protocols to use. The main disadvantage of such schemes is the burden they put on the programmer to choose protocols for pages or data structures. The decision task is also made difficult because of the coarse granularity at which control is made available; data structures that desire different protocols may fall on the same page.

An alternative is to choose the protocol at a cache block granularity, by observing the sharing behavior at run time. Ideally, for each write, we would like to be able to peer into the future references that will be made to that cache block by all processors and then decide whether to invalidate other copies or to do an update. Since this information is obviously not available, and since there are substantial perturbations due to cache replacements and false sharing, a more practical scheme is needed.

So-called competitive schemes change the protocol for a block between invalidate and update in hardware based on observed patterns at run time. The key attribute of such schemes is that if a wrong decision is made once for a cache block, the losses due to that wrong decision should be kept bounded and small (Karlin et al. 1986). For instance, if a block is currently using update mode, it should not remain in that mode if one processor is continuously writing to it but none of the other processors are reading values from it.

One class of schemes that has been proposed to bound the losses of update protocols works as follows (Grahn, Stenstrom, and Dubois 1995). Starting with the base Dragon update protocol described in Section 5.3.3, associate a countdown counter with each block. Whenever a cache block is accessed by the local processor, the counter value for that block is reset to a threshold value k. Every time an update is received for a block, the counter is decremented. If the counter goes to zero, the block is locally invalidated. The consequence of the local invalidations is that the next time an update is generated on the bus, it may find that no other cache has a valid copy; in that case, that block will switch to the modified state (as per the Dragon protocol) and will stop generating updates. If some other processor now accesses that block, the block will again switch to shared state and this mixed protocol will again start generating updates.

A related approach implemented in the Sun SparcCenter 2000 is to selectively invalidate rather than update with some probability that is a parameter set when configuring the machine (Catanzaro 1997). Other mixed approaches may also be used. For example, one approach uses an invalidation-based protocol for first-level caches and, by default, an update-based protocol for second-level caches. However, if the L_2 cache receives a second update for the block while the block in the L_1 cache is still invalid, then the block is invalidated in the L_2 cache as well. When the block is thus invalidated in all other L_2 caches, writes to the block no longer cause updates.

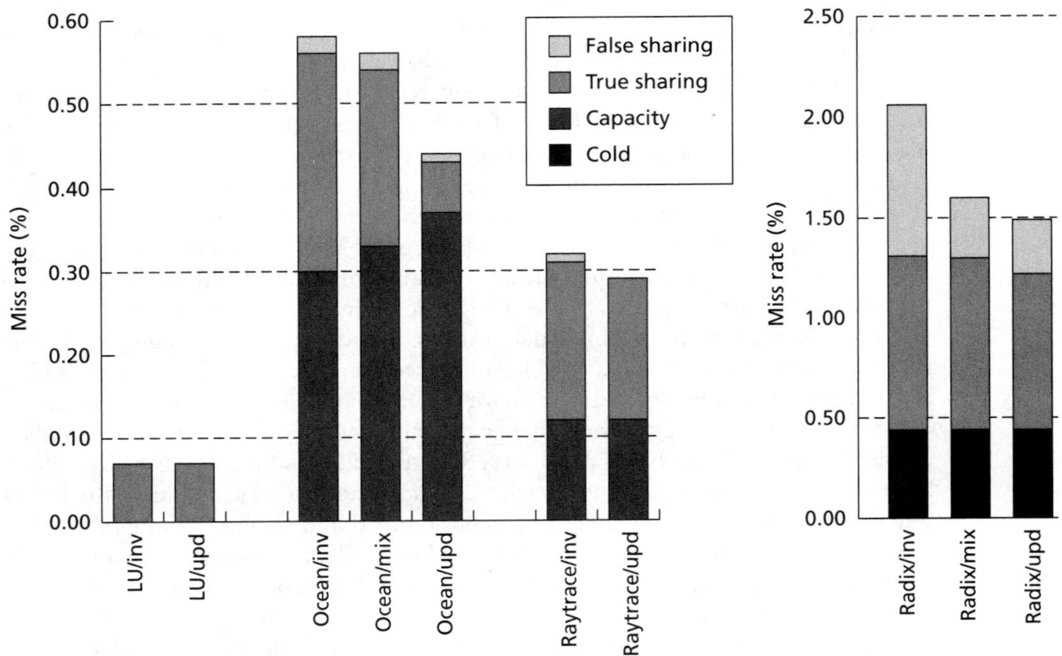

FIGURE 5.27 Miss rates and their decomposition for invalidate, update, and hybrid protocols. The data assumes 1-MB caches, 64-byte cache blocks, four-way set associativity, and threshold $k = 4$ for hybrid protocol.

Workload-Driven Evaluation

To assess the trade-offs among invalidate, update, and the mixed protocols just described, Figure 5.27 shows the miss rates by category for four applications using the default 1-MB four-way set-associative caches with a 64-byte block size. The mixed protocol used is the threshold-based scheme just described. We see that for applications with significant capacity miss rates, the misses sometimes increase with an update protocol. This makes sense because the protocol (with LRU replacement in a set) keeps data in processor caches that would have been removed by an invalidation protocol. For applications with significant true sharing or false sharing miss rates, these categories decrease with an update protocol: after a write update, the other caches holding the blocks can access them without a miss. Overall, the update protocol appears to be advantageous for the sum of these three categories and the mixed protocol falls in between. The category that is not shown in this figure, however, is the upgrade or update operations for these protocols. This data is presented in Figure 5.28. Note that the scale of the graphs has changed because update operations are roughly four times more prevalent than misses. It is useful to separate these operations from other misses because the way they are handled in the machine is

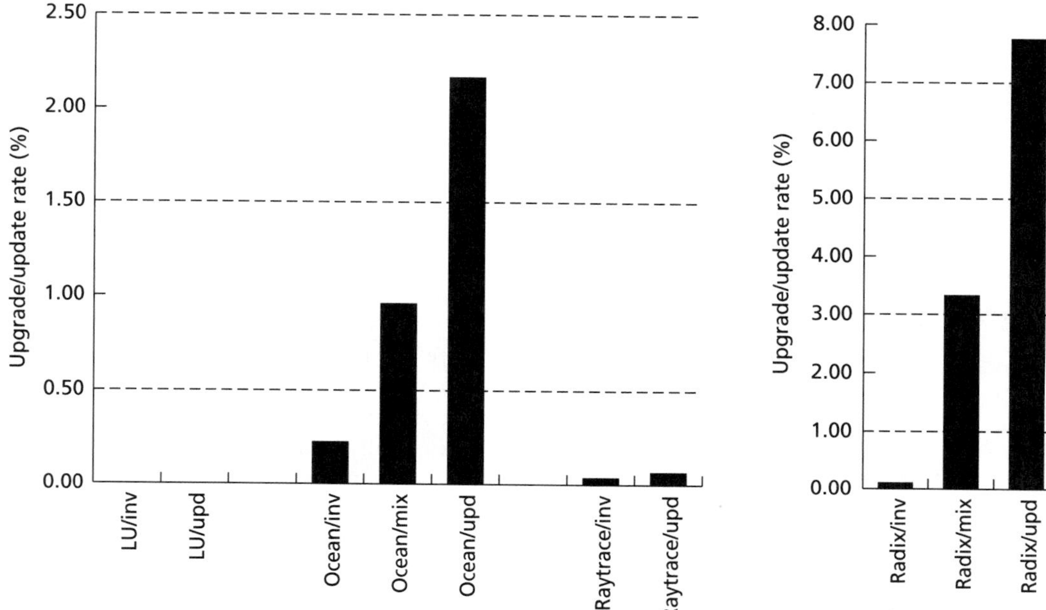

FIGURE 5.28 Upgrade and update rates for invalidate, update, and mixed protocols. The data assumes 1-MB caches, 64-byte cache blocks, four-way set associativity, and threshold $k = 4$ for hybrid protocol. Rates are measured relative to total memory references.

likely to be different. Updates are a single-word write rather than a full cache block transfer. Because the data is being pushed from where it is being produced, it may arrive at the consumer before it is needed. Even for the producer, the latency of update and upgrade operations may be less critical than that of misses since it is quite easily hidden from the processor's critical path (see Chapter 11).

Unfortunately, the traffic associated with updates is quite substantial. In large part, this occurs because multiple writes are made by a processor to the same block before a read, all generating updates. With the invalidate protocol, the first of these writes may cause an invalidation, but the rest can simply accumulate locally in the block and be transferred in one bus transaction on a flush or a write back (see Example 5.12). The increased traffic causes contention and can greatly increase the cost of misses. Sophisticated update schemes might attempt to delay the update to achieve a similar effect (by merging writes in the write buffer) or use other techniques to reduce traffic and improve performance (Dahlgren 1995). However, the increased bandwidth demand, the complexity of supporting updates, the trend toward larger cache blocks, and the pack rat phenomenon with the important case of multiprogrammed sequential workloads underlie the trend away from update-based protocols in the industry. We see in Chapter 8 that update protocols also have some other problems for scalable cache-coherent architectures, making it less attractive for microprocessors to support these protocols.

Having discussed how to keep data coherent, let us now consider how synchronization is managed in bus-based multiprocessors.

5.5 SYNCHRONIZATION

A critical interplay of hardware and software in multiprocessors arises in supporting synchronization operations: mutual exclusion, point-to-point events, and global events. There has been considerable debate over the years about how much hardware support and exactly what hardware primitives should be provided to support these synchronization operations. The conclusions have changed from time to time with changes in technology and design style. Hardware support has the advantage of speed, but moving functionality to software has the advantages of cost, flexibility, and adaptability to different situations. The classic works of Dijkstra (1965) and Knuth (1966) show that it is possible to provide mutual exclusion with only atomic read and write operations (assuming a sequentially consistent memory). However, all practical synchronization methods rely on hardware support for some sort of *atomic read-modify-write* operation, in which the value of a memory location is ensured to be read, modified, and written back atomically without intervening accesses to the location by other processors. Simple or sophisticated synchronization algorithms can be built in software using these primitives.

The history of instruction sets offers a glimpse into the evolving hardware support for synchronization. One of the key instruction set enhancements in the IBM 370 was the inclusion of a sophisticated atomic instruction, the *compare&swap* instruction, to support synchronization in concurrent programming on uniprocessor or multiprocessor systems. The compare&swap compares the value in a memory location with the value in a specified register and, if they are equal, swaps the value in the memory location with the value in a second specified register. The Intel x86 allows any instruction to be prefixed with a lock modifier to make it atomic; since the source and destination operands are memory locations, much of the instruction set can be used to implement various atomic operations involving even more than one memory location. Advocates of high-level language architecture have proposed that the user-level synchronization operations, such as locks and barriers, should be supported directly at the machine level, not just atomic read-modify-write primitives; that is, the synchronization "algorithm" itself should be implemented in hardware. This issue became very active during the reduced instruction set debates since the operations that access memory were scaled back to simple loads and stores with only one memory operand. The Sparc approach was to provide atomic operations involving a register or registers and a memory location using a simple swap (atomically swapping the contents of the specified register and memory location) and a compare&swap. MIPS left off atomic primitives in the early instruction sets, as did the IBM Power architecture used in the RS6000. The primitive that was eventually incorporated in MIPS was a novel combination of a special load and a conditional store, described later in this section, which allows a variety of higher-level read-modify-write operations to be constructed without requiring the design to implement them all. In essence, the pair of instructions can be used instead of a single instruction to implement atomic exchange or more complex atomic operations. This approach was later incorporated into the PowerPC and DEC Alpha architectures and is now quite popular. As we will see, synchronization brings to light a rich family of trade-offs across the layers of communication architecture. Not only can a spectrum of high-level operations and low-level primitives be supported by hardware, but the synchronization requirements of applications vary substantially as well.

The focus of this section is on how synchronization operations can be implemented on a bus-based cache-coherent multiprocessor through a combination of software algorithms and hardware primitives. In particular, it describes the implementation of mutual exclusion through lock-unlock pairs, point-to-point event synchronization through flags, and global event synchronization through barriers. Let us begin by considering the components of a synchronization event. This will make it clear why supporting the high-level mutual exclusion and event operations directly in hardware is difficult and is likely to make the implementation too rigid. Then, given that the hardware supports only the basic atomic operations, we can examine the role of the user software and system software in synchronization operations and then consider the hardware and software design trade-offs in greater detail.

5.5.1 Components of a Synchronization Event

There are three major components of a synchronization event:

1. *Acquire method:* a method by which a process tries to acquire the right to the synchronization (to enter the critical section or proceed past the event synchronization).
2. *Waiting algorithm:* a method by which a process waits for a synchronization to become available; for example, if a process tries to acquire a lock but the lock is not free, or to proceed past an event but the event has not yet occurred.
3. *Release method:* a method for a process to enable other processes to proceed past a synchronization event; for example, an implementation of the Unlock operation, a method for the last process arriving at a barrier to release the waiting processes, or a method for notifying a process waiting at a point-to-point event that the event has occurred.

The choice of waiting algorithm is quite independent of the type of synchronization. There are two main choices: busy-waiting and blocking. *Busy-waiting* means that the process spins in a loop that repeatedly tests for a variable to change its value. A release of the synchronization event by another processor changes the value of the variable, allowing the waiting process to proceed. Under *blocking,* the process does not spin but simply blocks (suspends) itself and releases the processor if it finds that it needs to wait. It will be awakened and made ready to run again when the release it was waiting for occurs. The trade-offs between busy-waiting and blocking are clear. Blocking has higher overhead since suspending and resuming a process involves the operating system (and suspending and resuming a thread involves the run-time system of a threads package), but it makes the processor available to other threads or processes that have useful work to do. Busy-waiting avoids the cost of suspension but consumes the processor and cache bandwidth while waiting. Blocking is strictly more powerful than busy-waiting because, if the process or thread that is being waited upon is not allowed to run, the busy-wait will never end.[7] Busy-waiting is likely to be better when the waiting period is short, whereas blocking is likely to be a better choice if the waiting period is long and if there are other processes to run. Hybrid waiting methods can be used in which the process busy-waits for a while in case the waiting period is short, and if the waiting period exceeds a certain threshold, the process blocks, allowing other processes to run (a *two-phase* waiting algorithm).

The difficulty in implementing high-level synchronization operations in hardware is not the acquire or the release component but the waiting algorithm. Thus, it makes sense to provide hardware support for the critical aspects of the acquire and release methods and allow the three components to be glued together in software. However, subtle but very important hardware/software interactions remain in how the spinning operation in the busy-wait component is realized.

5.5.2 Role of the User and System

Who should be responsible for implementing the internals of high-level synchronization operations such as locks and barriers? Typically, a programmer wants to use locks, events, or even higher-level operations without having to worry about their internal implementation. The implementation is left to the system, which must decide how much hardware support to provide and how much of the functionality to implement in software. Software synchronization algorithms using simple atomic exchange primitives have been developed that approach the speed of full hardware implementations, and the flexibility and hardware simplification they afford are very attractive. As with other aspects of system design, the utility of faster operations with more hardware support depends on the frequency of the use of those operations in the applications. So, once again, the best answer will be determined by a better understanding of application behavior.

Software implementations of synchronization constructs are usually included in system libraries. Good synchronization library design can be quite challenging. One potential complication is that the same type of synchronization (lock, barrier), and even the same synchronization variable, may be used at different times under very different run-time conditions. For example, a lock may be accessed with low contention (a small number of processors, maybe only one, trying to acquire the lock at a time) or with high contention (many processors trying to acquire the lock at the same time). The different scenarios impose different performance requirements.

7. This problem of denying resources to the critical process or thread is one that is actually made simpler with more processors. When the processes are time-shared on a single processor, strict busy-waiting without preemption is sure to be a problem. If each process or thread has its own processor, it is guaranteed not to be a problem. Multiprogramming environments on a limited set of processors may fall somewhere in between.

Under high contention, most processes will spend time waiting, and the key requirement of a lock algorithm is that it provide high lock-unlock transfer bandwidth; under low contention, the key goal is to provide low latency for lock acquisition. Different algorithms may satisfy different requirements better, so we must either find a good compromise algorithm or provide different algorithms for each type of synchronization from which a user can choose. If we are lucky, a flexible library can at run time choose the best implementation for the situation at hand. Different synchronization algorithms may also rely on different basic hardware primitives, so some may be better suited to a particular machine than others. Under multiprogramming, process scheduling and other resource interactions can change the synchronization behavior of the processes in a parallel program. A more sophisticated algorithm that addresses multiprogramming effects may provide better performance in practice than a simple algorithm that has lower latency and higher bandwidth in the dedicated case. All of these factors make synchronization a critical point of hardware/software interaction.

5.5.3 Mutual Exclusion

Mutual exclusion (lock-unlock) operations are implemented using a wide range of algorithms. The simple algorithms tend to be fast when there is little contention for the lock but inefficient under high contention, whereas sophisticated algorithms that deal well with contention have a higher cost in the low-contention case. After a brief discussion of hardware locks, this section describes the simplest software algorithms for memory-based locks using atomic exchange instructions. Following this is a discussion of how these simple algorithms can be implemented by using the special load-locked and store-conditional instruction pairs to synthesize atomic exchange, in place of atomic exchange instructions themselves, and what the trade-offs are. Next, we will look at more sophisticated algorithms that can be built using either method of implementing atomic operations.

Hardware Locks

Lock operations can be supported entirely in hardware, although this is not popular on modern bus-based machines. One option that was used on some older machines was to have a set of lock lines on the bus, each used for one lock at a time. The processor holding the lock asserts the line, and processors waiting for the lock wait for it to be released. A priority circuit determines which processor gets the lock next when there are multiple requestors. However, this approach was quite inflexible since only a limited number of locks can be in use at a time and the waiting algorithm is fixed (typically a form of busy-wait with abort after time-out). Usually, these hardware locks were used only by the operating system for specific purposes, one of which was to implement a larger set of software locks in memory. The CRAY Xmp provided an interesting variant of this approach. A set of registers was shared among the processors, including a fixed collection of lock registers. Although the architecture made it possible to assign lock registers to user processes, with only a small set of such registers it was awkward to do so in a general-purpose setting, and in practice the lock registers too were used primarily to implement higher-level locks in memory.

Simple Software Lock Algorithms

Consider a lock operation used to provide atomicity for a critical section of code. For the acquire method, a process trying to obtain a lock must check that the lock is free and, if it is, then claim ownership of the lock. The state of the lock can be stored in a binary variable, with 0 representing free and 1 representing busy. A simple way of thinking about the lock acquire operation is that a process trying to obtain the lock should check if the variable is 0 and if so set it to 1, thus marking the lock busy; if the variable is 1 (lock is busy), then it should wait for the variable to turn to 0 using the waiting algorithm. An unlock operation should simply set the variable to 0 (the release method). The following are assembly-level instructions for this attempt at a lock and unlock. (In our pseudo-assembly notation, the first operand always specifies the destination if there is one.)

```
lock:  ld   register, location /*copy location to register*/
       cmp  register, #0       /*compare with 0*/
       bnz  lock               /*if not 0, try again*/
       st   location, #1       /*store 1 into location to mark it locked*/
       ret                     /*return control to caller of lock*/
```

and

```
unlock: st location, #0        /*write 0 to location*/
        ret                    /*return control to caller*/
```

The problem with this lock, which is supposed to provide atomicity for the critical section that follows it, is that it needs (but lacks) atomicity in its own implementation. To illustrate this, suppose that the lock variable was initially set to 0 and two processes P_0 and P_1 execute the above assembly code implementations of the lock operation. Process P_0 reads the value of the lock variable as 0 and thinks it is free, so it proceeds past the branch instruction. Its next step is to set the variable to 1, marking the lock as busy, but before it can do this, process P_1 reads the variable as 0, thinks the lock is free, and passes the branch instruction too. We now have two processes simultaneously proceeding past the lock and entering the same critical section, which is exactly what the lock was meant to avoid. Putting the store instruction just after the load instruction would not help either. The two-instruction sequence—reading (testing) the lock variable to check its state and writing (setting) it to busy if it is free—is not atomic, and there is nothing to prevent these operations in different processes from being interleaved in time. What we need is a way to atomically test the value of a variable and set it to another value if the test succeeds (i.e., to atomically read and then conditionally modify a memory location) and then to return whether the atomic sequence was executed successfully or not. One way to provide this atomicity for user processes is to place the lock routine in the operating system and access it through a system call, but this is expensive and leaves the question of how the locks are supported by the operating system itself. Another option is to utilize a hardware lock around the instruction sequence for the lock routine, but this requires hardware locks and tends to be slow on modern processors.

An efficient, general-purpose solution to the lock problem is to support an atomic read-modify-write instruction in the processor's instruction set. A typical approach is to have an atomic exchange instruction: a value at a memory location specified by the instruction is read into a register, and another value is stored into the location, all in an atomic operation with no other accesses to that location allowed to intervene. Many variants of this operation exist with varying degrees of flexibility in the nature of the value that can be stored. A simple example that works for mutual exclusion is an atomic *test&set* instruction. In this case, the value in the memory location is read into a specified register, and the constant 1 is stored into the location atomically. The success of the test&set is determined by examining the value in the register. If it is 0, the test&set was successful. If it is 1, it was not successful; the value 1 written to memory by the test&set instruction is the same as was already there, so no harm is done. (1 and 0 are the values typically used, though any other constants might be used in their place.) Given such an instruction, with the mnemonic t&s, we can write a lock and unlock in pseudo-assembly language as follows:

```
lock:   t&s register, location
                             /*copy location to reg, and set location to 1*/
        bnz register, lock   /*compare old value returned with 0*/
                             /*if not 0, i.e., lock already busy, so try again*/
        ret                  /*return control to caller of lock*/
```

and

```
unlock:st location, #0       /*write 0 to location*/
        ret                  /*return control to caller*/
```

The lock implementation keeps trying to acquire the lock using test&set instructions until the test&set leaves zero in the register, indicating that the lock was free when tested (in which case the test&set has set the lock variable to 1, thus acquiring it). The unlock construct simply sets the location associated with the lock to 0, indicating that the lock is now free and enabling a subsequent lock operation by any process to succeed. A simple mutual exclusion construct has been implemented in software, relying on the fact that the architecture supports an atomic test&set instruction.

More sophisticated variants of such atomic instructions exist and, as we will see, are used by different software synchronization algorithms. One example is a *swap* instruction. Like a test&set, this reads the value from the specified memory location into the specified register, but instead of writing a fixed constant into the memory location, it writes whatever value was in the register to begin with. That is, it atomically exchanges or swaps the values in the memory location and the register. Clearly, we can implement a lock as before by replacing the test&set with a swap instruction as long as we use the values 0 and 1 and ensure that the value in the register is 1 before the swap instruction is executed; the lock has succeeded if the value left in the register by the swap instruction is 0.

Another example is the family of *fetch&op* instructions. A fetch&op instruction also specifies a location and a register. It atomically reads the current value of the location into the register and writes the value (which has been obtained by applying the operation specified by the fetch&op instruction to the current value of the location) into the location. The simplest forms of fetch&op to implement are the *fetch&increment* and *fetch&decrement* instructions, which change the current value by 1. A *fetch&add* would take another operand, which is a register or value, to add into the previous value of the location. A more complex primitive is the *compare&swap* operation. It takes two register operands and a memory location (i.e., it is a three-operand instruction, not commonly supported by RISC architectures); it compares the value in the location with the contents of the first register operand, and, if the two are equal, it swaps the contents of the memory location with the contents of the second register.

Performance of the Simple Lock

Figure 5.29 shows the performance of a simple test&set lock on the SGI Challenge.[8] Performance is measured for the following microbenchmark executed repeatedly in a loop:

```
lock(L);
critical-section(c);
unlock(L);
```

where `c` is a delay parameter that determines the size of the critical section (it is only a delay in this case, with no real work done). The benchmark is configured so that the same total number of lock calls are executed as the number of processors increases, reflecting a situation where a fixed number of tasks must be dequeued from a centralized task queue, independent of the number of processors. Performance is measured as the time per lock transfer, that is, the cumulative time taken by all processes executing the benchmark divided by the number of times the lock is obtained. The cumulative time spent in the critical section itself (i.e., `c` times the number of successful locks executed) is subtracted from the cumulative execution time so that only the time for the lock transfers themselves (or any contention caused by the lock operations) is obtained. All measurements are in microseconds.

---

8. In fact, the processor on the SGI Challenge, which is the machine for which synchronization performance is presented in this chapter, does not provide a test&set instruction. Rather, it uses alternative primitives that will be described later in this section. For these experiments, a mechanism whose behavior closely resembles that of test&set is synthesized from the available primitives. Results for real test&set-based locks on older machines like the Sequent Symmetry can be found in the literature (Granuke and Thakkar 1990; Mellor-Crummey and Scott 1991).

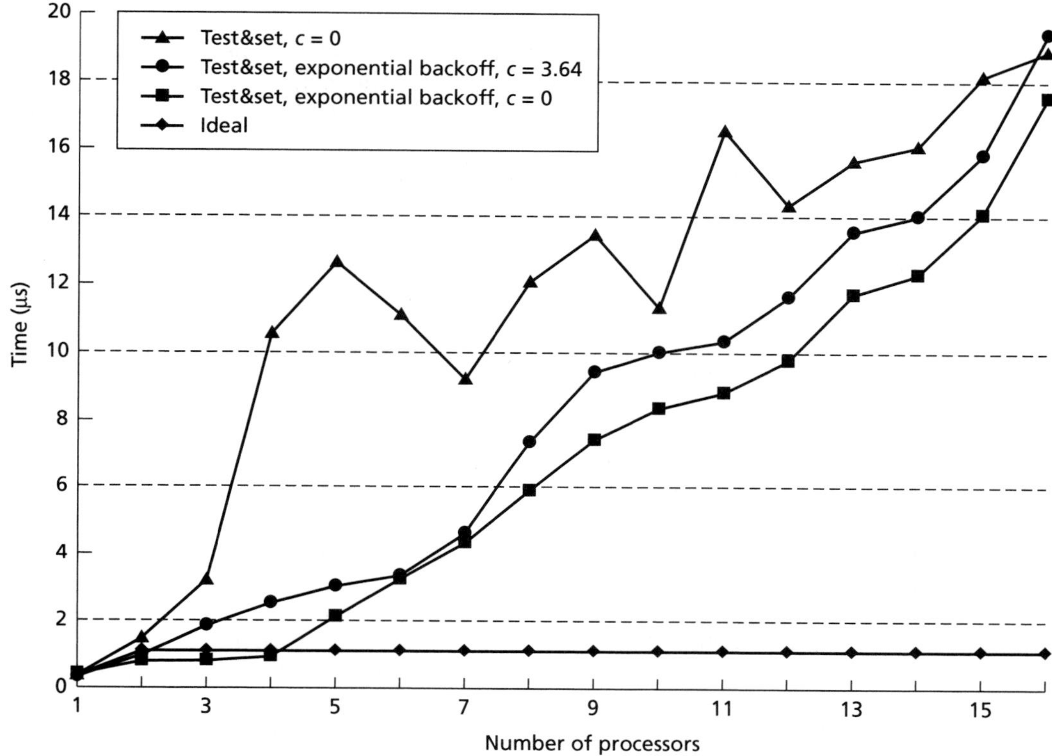

FIGURE 5.29 Performance of the synthesized test&set locks with an increasing number of competing processors on the SGI Challenge. The *y*-axis is the time per lock-unlock pair, excluding the critical section of size *c* microseconds. The irregular nature of the top curve is due to the timing dependence of the contention effects caused.

The upper curve in the figure shows the time per lock transfer with an increasing number of processors when using the test&set lock with a very small critical section (ignore the curves with "backoff" in their labels for now). Ideally, we would like the time per lock acquisition to be independent of the number of processors competing for the lock, with only one uncontended bus transaction per lock transfer, as shown in the curve labeled "ideal." However, the figure shows that performance clearly degrades with an increasing number of processors.

The problem with the test&set lock is the traffic generated during the waiting method: every attempt to check whether the lock is free to be acquired, whether successful or not, generates a write operation to the cache block that holds the lock variable (since it uses a test&set operation and writes the value to 1); since this block is currently in the cache of some other processor (which wrote it last when doing its test&set), a bus transaction is generated by each write to invalidate the previous owner of the block. Thus, all processors put transactions on the bus repeatedly and consume precious bus bandwidth even during the waiting algorithm. The resulting contention slows down the lock transfer considerably as the number of processors, and hence the frequency of test&sets and bus transactions, increases. It impedes the progress of the processor releasing the lock and of the next processor that actually acquires it. In reality, it would also impede the work done in the critical section. The high degree of contention on the bus and the resulting timing dependence of obtaining locks causes the benchmark timing to vary sharply across numbers of processors used and even across executions. The results shown are for a particular, representative set of executions with different numbers of processors.

Enhancements to the Simple Lock Algorithm

We can do two simple things to alleviate this traffic. First, we can reduce the frequency with which processes issue test&set instructions while waiting; second, we can have processes busy-wait only with read operations so they do not generate invalidations and misses until the lock is actually released. These two possibilities are called the *test&set lock with backoff* and the *test-and-test&set lock.*

Test&Set Lock with Backoff The basic idea in backoff is for a process to insert a delay after an unsuccessful attempt to acquire the lock. The delay between test&set attempts should not be too long; otherwise, processors might remain idle even when the lock becomes free. But it should be long enough that traffic is substantially reduced. A natural question is whether the delay amount should be fixed or variable. Experimental results have shown that good performance is obtained by having the delay vary "exponentially"; that is, the delay after the first attempt is a small constant k that increases geometrically, so that after the ith attempt, it is $k \times c^i$, where c is another constant. Such a lock is called a test&set lock with exponential backoff. Figure 5.29 also shows the performance for the test&set lock with backoff for two different sizes of the critical section, using the starting value k for backoff that appears to perform best. Performance improves but still does not scale very well since there is still substantial traffic interfering with the release and acquire. Performance results using backoff with a real test&set instruction on older machines can be found in the literature (Granuke and Thakkar 1990; Mellor-Crummey and Scott 1991). See also Exercise 5.14, which discusses why the performance with a nonzero critical section is worse than that with a null critical section when backoff is used.

Test-and-Test&Set Lock A more subtle change to the algorithm is to have it use instructions that do not generate as much bus traffic while busy-waiting. Processes busy-wait by repeatedly reading with a standard load, not a test&set, the value of the lock variable until it turns from 1 (locked) to 0 (unlocked). On a cache-coherent machine, the reads can be performed in-cache by all processors, without generating bus traffic, since each obtains a cached copy of the lock variable the first time it reads it. When the lock is released, the cached copies of all waiting processes are invalidated, and the next read of the variable by each process will generate a read miss. The waiting processes will then find that the lock has been made available and only then will each generate a test&set instruction to actually try to acquire the lock. One of them will succeed in this acquire attempt, while the others will fail and return to the read-based waiting method. The test-and-test&set lock substantially reduces bus traffic.

Performance Goals for Locks

Before examining more sophisticated lock algorithms and primitives, it is useful to clearly articulate some performance goals for locks and to review how the locks described here measure up. The goals include the following:

- *Low latency.* If a lock is free and no other processors are trying to acquire it at the same time, a processor should be able to acquire it with low latency.
- *Low traffic.* If many or all processors try to acquire a lock at the same time, they should be able to acquire the lock one after the other with as little generation of traffic or bus transactions as possible. As discussed earlier, contention due to high traffic can slow down lock acquisitions as well as unrelated transactions that compete for the bus (including in the critical section).
- *Scalability.* Neither latency nor traffic should scale quickly with the number of processors used. However, since the number of processors in a bus-based SMP is not likely to be large, it is not asymptotic scalability that is important but only scalability within the realistic range.
- *Low storage cost.* The information needed for a lock should be small and should not scale quickly with the number of processors.
- *Fairness.* Ideally, processors should acquire a lock in the same order as their requests are issued. At the least, starvation or substantial unfairness should be avoided. Since starvation is usually unlikely, the importance of fairness must be traded off with its impact on performance.

Consider the simple atomic exchange or test&set lock. It is very low latency if the same processor acquires the lock repeatedly without any competition, since the number of instructions executed is very small and the lock variable will stay in that processor's cache. However, we have seen that it can generate a lot of bus traffic and contention if many processors compete for the lock. The performance of the lock scales poorly as the number of competing processors increases. The storage cost is low (a single variable suffices) and does not scale with the number of processors. The lock makes no attempt to be fair, and an unlucky processor can be starved out. The test&set lock with backoff has the same uncontended latency as the simple test&set lock, generates less traffic, is somewhat more scalable, takes no more storage, and is no more fair. The test-and-test&set lock has slightly higher uncontended latency than the simple test&set lock (it does a read in addition to a test&set even when there is no competition) but generates much less bus traffic and is more scalable. It too requires negligible storage and is not fair. (Exercise 5.12 asks you to count the number of bus transactions and the time required for the test-and-test&set type of lock in different scenarios.)

In the test-and-test&set lock, since a test&set operation (and hence a bus transaction) is only issued when a processor is notified that the lock is ready, and thereafter if it fails it busy-waits (spins) on a cached block, there is no need for backoff. However, the lock does have the problem that when the lock is released, all waiting processes rush out and perform their read misses and their test&set instructions at about the same time. The bus transactions for the read misses may be combined in a smart bus protocol; however, each of the test&set instructions itself generates invalidations and subsequent misses, resulting in $O(p^2)$ bus traffic for p processors to acquire the lock once each. A random delay before issuing the test&set could help to stagger at least the test&set instructions, but it would increase the latency to acquire the lock in the uncontended case. While test-and-test&set was a major step forward at its time, better hardware primitives and better algorithms have been designed to alleviate its traffic problem.

Improved Hardware Primitives: Load-Locked, Store-Conditional

In addition to spinning with reads rather than read-modify-writes, which test-and-test&set accomplishes, we would prefer that failed attempts to complete the read-modify-write do not generate invalidations. It would also be useful to have a single primitive that allows us to implement a range of atomic read-modify-write operations—such as test&set, fetch&op, compare&swap—rather than implementing each with a separate instruction. One way to achieve both goals, increasingly supported in modern microprocessors, is to use a pair of special instructions rather than a single read-write-modify instruction to implement atomic access to a variable (let's call it a synchronization variable). The first instruction, commonly called *load-locked* or *load-linked* (LL), loads the synchronization variable into a register. It may be followed by arbitrary instructions that manipulate the value in the register—that is, the modify part of a read-modify-write. The last instruction of the sequence is the second special instruction, called a *store-conditional*. It tries to write the register back to the memory location (the synchronization variable) if and only if no other processor has written to that location (or cache block) since this processor completed its LL. Thus, if the store-conditional succeeds, it means that the load-locked, store-conditional (LL-SC) pair has read, perhaps modified in between, and written back the variable atomically. If the store-conditional detects that an intervening write has occurred to the variable or cache block, it fails and does not even try to write the value back (or generate any invalidations). This means that the atomic operation on the variable has failed and must be retried starting from the LL. Success or failure of the store-conditional is indicated by the condition codes or a return value. How the LL and store-conditional are actually implemented will be discussed later; for now, we are concerned with their semantics and performance.

Using LL-SC to implement atomic operations, the simple lock and unlock algorithms can be written as follows, where `reg1` is the register into which the current value of the memory location is loaded and `reg2` holds the value to be stored in the memory location by this atomic exchange (`reg2` could simply be the value 1 for a lock attempt, as in a test&set).

```
lock:    ll   reg1, location      /*load-locked the location to reg1*/
         bnz  reg1, lock          /*if location was locked (nonzero),
                                  try again*/
         sc   location, reg2      /*store reg2 conditionally into location*/
         beqz  lock               /*if store-conditional failed, start again*/
         ret                      /*return control to caller of lock*/
```

and

```
unlock: st location, #0           /*write 0 to location*/
        ret                       /*return control to caller*/
```

Many processors may perform the LL at the same time, but only the first one that manages to put its store-conditional on the bus will actually succeed in its store-conditional. This processor will have succeeded in acquiring the lock, whereas the others will have failed and will have to retry the LL-SC. Note that the store-conditional may fail either because it detects the occurrence of an intervening write before even attempting to access the bus or because it attempts to get the bus but some other processor's store-conditional gets there first. Of course, if the location is 1 (nonzero) when a process does its LL, it will load 1 into `reg1` and will retry the lock starting from the LL without even attempting the store-conditional.

It is worth noting that the LL itself is not a lock and the store-conditional itself is not an unlock. For one thing, the completion of the LL itself does not imply obtaining exclusive access; in fact, LL and store-conditional are used together to implement a lock operation. For another, even a successful LL-SC pair does not guarantee that the instructions between them (if any) are executed atomically with respect to those instructions on other processors, so in fact these instructions do not constitute a critical section. All that a successful LL-SC guarantees is that no conflicting writes to the synchronization variable itself intervene between the LL and store-conditional. In fact, since the instructions between the LL and store-conditional are executed unconditionally but should not be visible if the store-conditional fails, it is important that they do not modify any other important state. Typically, these instructions manipulate only the register into which the synchronization variable is loaded—for example, to perform the op part of a fetch&op—and do not modify any other program variables (modification of this register is okay since the register will be reloaded anyway by the LL in the next attempt). Microprocessor vendors that support LL-SC explicitly encourage software writers to follow this guideline and, in fact, often specify what instructions are possible to insert with a guarantee of correctness given their implementations of LL-SC. The number of instructions between the LL and store-conditional should also be kept small to reduce the probability of store-conditional failure due to an intervening write. Although the LL and store-conditional do not constitute a lock-unlock pair, they can be used directly to implement certain atomic operations on shared data structures. For example, if the desired function is a small operation on a globally shared variable (like a counter or global sum), it makes much more sense to implement it as the natural sequence (LL, register op, store-conditional, test) than to build a lock and unlock around the variable update.

Like the test-and-test&set, the spin-lock built with LL-SC does not generate bus traffic during the waiting algorithm if the LL indicates that the lock is currently held. Better than the test-and-test&set, it also does not generate invalidations on a failed attempt to obtain the lock (i.e., a failed store-conditional). However, when the lock is released, the processors spinning in a tight loop of load-locked operations will indeed miss on the location and rush out to the bus with read transactions. After this, only a single invalidation will be generated for a given lock acquisition by the processor whose store-conditional succeeds, but this will again invalidate all caches. Traffic is reduced greatly from even the test-and-test&set case and there are no read-modify-write bus transactions, but traffic still increases linearly with the number of processors (i.e., $O(p)$ bus transactions per look acquisition). Since spinning on a locked location is already done through reads (load-locked operations), no analog of a test-and-test&set exists to further improve its performance. However, backoff can be used between the LL and store-conditional to reduce bursty traffic.

The simple LL-SC lock is also low in latency and storage, but it is not a fair lock and does not reduce traffic to a minimum. More advanced lock algorithms can be used that provide both fairness and reduced traffic. They can be built using either atomic read-modify-write instructions or atomic operations of equivalent semantics synthesized with LL-SC, though of course the traffic advantages are different in the two cases. Let us consider two of these algorithms that are appropriate for bus-based machines.

Advanced Lock Algorithms

Especially when using an atomic exchange instruction like test&set, instead of LL-SC, to implement locks, it is desirable to have only one process actually attempt to obtain the lock when it is released (rather than have them all rush out to do a test&set and issue invalidations as in all the preceding algorithms). It is even more desirable to have only one process incur a read miss (even with LL-SC) when a lock is released. The *ticket lock* accomplishes the first purpose; the *array-based lock* accomplishes both goals but at a little cost in space. Unlike all the previous locks, both these locks are fair and grant the lock to processors in FIFO order.

Ticket Lock The ticket lock operates just like the ticket system in the sandwich line at a delicatessen or like the teller line at a bank. Every process wanting to acquire the lock takes a ticket number and then busy-waits on a global `now-serving` number—like the number on the LED display that we watch intently in the sandwich line—until the `now-serving` number equals the ticket number it obtained. To release the lock, a process simply increments the `now-serving` number so that the next waiting process can acquire the lock. The atomic primitive needed is a fetch&increment, which a process uses when it first reaches the lock operation to obtain its ticket number from a shared counter. No atomic operation (e.g., test&set) is needed to actually obtain the lock upon a release since only the unique process that has its ticket number equal to `now-serving` attempts to enter the critical section when it sees the release. Thus, the acquire method is the fetch&increment, the waiting algorithm is busy-waiting for `now-serving` to equal the ticket number, and the release method is to increment `now-serving`. This lock has uncontended latency about equal to the test-and-test&set lock but generates much less traffic. Although every process does a fetch&increment when it first arrives at the lock (presumably not every process at the same time), the test&set attempts upon a release of the lock are eliminated, which tend to be simultaneous and a lot more heavily contended. The ticket lock also requires constant and small storage and is fair since processes obtain the lock in the order of their fetch&increment operations.

The fetch&increment needed by the ticket lock can be implemented with LL-SC. However, since the simple LL-SC lock already avoids multiple processors issuing invalidations in trying to acquire a lock after its release, there is not a large difference in traffic between the ticket lock and the simple LL-SC lock. (The simple LL-SC lock is somewhat worse since in that case another invalidation and set of read misses occur when a processor succeeds in its store-conditional.) The key difference between these two locks is fairness.

Like the simple LL-SC lock, the ticket lock still has a read traffic problem at a release. The reason is that all processes spin on the same variable (`now-serving`). When that variable is written at a release, all processors' cached copies are invalidated, and they all incur a read miss. The read misses may be combined on some buses but can cause unnecessary traffic if the combining is unavailable or unsuccessful. One way to reduce this bursty read-miss traffic is to introduce a form of backoff. We do not want to use exponential backoff because we do not want all processors to be backing off when the lock is released so that none tries to acquire it for a while. A promising technique is to have each processor back off from trying to read the `now-serving` counter by a duration proportional to when it expects its turn to actually come—that is, by a duration proportional to the difference in its ticket number and the `now-serving` value it last read. Alternatively, the array-based lock completely eliminates this extra read traffic upon a release by having every process spin on a distinct location.

Array-Based Lock The idea here is to use a fetch&increment to obtain not a value but a unique location on which to busy-wait. If there are p processes that might possibly compete for a lock, then the lock data structure contains an array of p locations that processes can spin on, ideally each on a separate memory block to avoid false sharing. The acquire method then uses a fetch&increment operation to obtain the next available location in this array (with wraparound), the waiting method spins on this location, and the release method writes a value denoting "unlocked" to the next location in the array (after the one that the releasing processor was itself spinning on). Only the processor that was spinning on that next location has its cache block invalidated at the release; its consequent read miss tells it that it has obtained the lock. As in the ticket lock, no test&set is needed after the miss since only one process is notified when the lock is released. This lock is clearly also FIFO and hence fair. Its uncontended latency is likely to be similar to that of the test-and-test&set lock (a fetch&increment followed by a read of the assigned array location), and it is potentially more scalable than the ticket lock since only one processor incurs the read miss. For the same reason, unlike the ticket lock, it does not need any form of backoff to reduce traffic. Its only drawback for a bus-based machine is that it uses $O(p)$ space rather than $O(1)$, but with both p and the proportionality constant being small, this is usually not a very significant drawback. It has a potential drawback for machines with distributed memory, but we shall discuss this drawback and lock algorithms that overcome it in Chapter 7.

Performance

Let us briefly examine the performance of the different locks on the SGI Challenge, as shown in Figure 5.30. All locks are implemented using LL-SC since the Challenge provides only these and not atomic instructions. Results are shown for a somewhat more parameterized version of the earlier microbenchmark code, in which a process is allowed to insert a delay not only for the critical section but also between its release of the lock and its next attempt to acquire it (as will happen in a real program). That is, the code is a loop over the following body:

```
lock(L);
critical_section(c);
unlock(L);
delay(d);
```

Let us consider three cases: (1) $c = 0$, $d = 0$; (2) $c = 3.64$ μs, $d = 0$; and (3) $c = 3.64$ μs, $d = 1.29$ μs—called the *null* critical section case, the *non-null* critical section case, and the non-null critical section with *delay* case, respectively. The delays c and d are inserted in the code as round numbers of processor cycles, which translates to these microsecond numbers. Recall that in all cases, the delays c and d (multiplied by the number of lock acquisitions by each processor) are subtracted out of the total time, which is supposed to measure only the total time taken for a certain number of lock acquisitions and releases (see also Exercise 5.15).

Consider the null critical section case. The first observation, comparing Figure 5.30 with Figure 5.29, is that all the other locks are indeed better than the test&set locks, as expected.[9] The second observation is that the simple LL-SC locks actually seem to perform better than the more sophisticated ticket lock and array-based lock. For these locks, which don't encounter as much contention as the test&set lock, performance is largely determined by the number of bus transactions between a release and a successful acquire. The reason that the LL-SC locks perform so well, particularly at lower processor counts, is that they are not fair, and the unfairness is exploited by architectural interactions! In particular, when a processor that releases a lock with a write follows it immediately with the read (LL) for its next acquire, its read and the subsequent store-conditional are likely to succeed in its cache before

9. The test&set is simulated using LL-SC as follows: every time a store-conditional fails, a write is performed to another variable in the same cache block, causing invalidations as a test&set would. This method of simulating test&set with LL-SC may lead to somewhat worse performance than a true test&set primitive, but it conveys the trend.

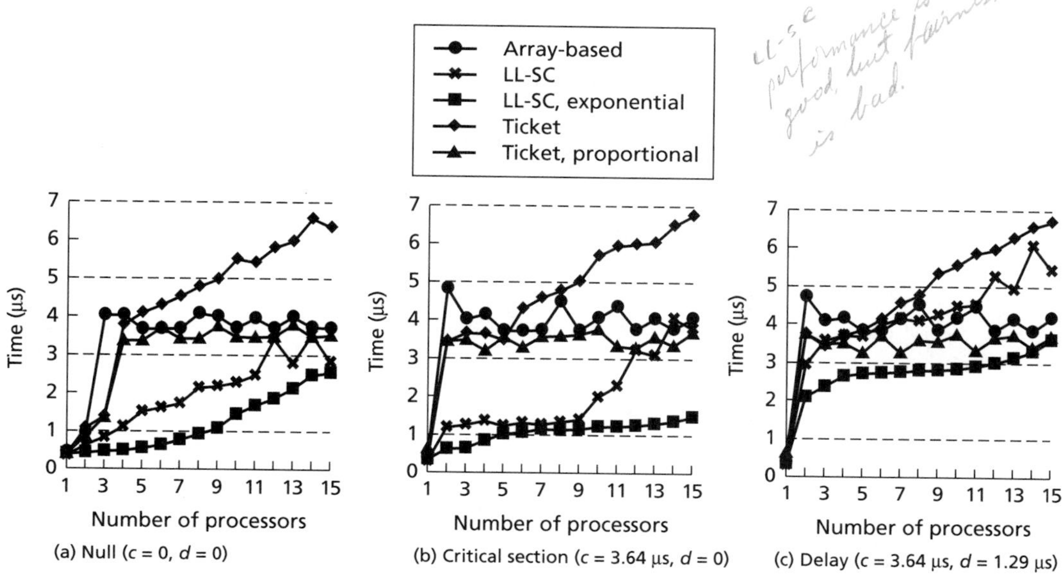

(a) Null ($c = 0$, $d = 0$) (b) Critical section ($c = 3.64$ μs, $d = 0$) (c) Delay ($c = 3.64$ μs, $d = 1.29$ μs)

FIGURE 5.30 Performance of locks on the SGI Challenge for three different scenarios

another processor can read the block across the bus. (The bias on the SGI Challenge is actually more severe, since the releasing processor can satisfy its next read from its write buffer even before the read exclusive corresponding to the releasing write gets out on the bus.) Lock transfer is very quick, and performance is good, but the same processor keeps acquiring the lock repeatedly. As the number of processors and the competition for the bus increase, the likelihood of the last releaser's store-conditional successfully obtaining the bus decreases, and hence the likelihood of self-transfers decreases. In addition, bus traffic increases due to invalidations and read misses, so the time per lock transfer increases. Exponential backoff helps reduce the burstiness of traffic and hence slows the rate of scaling, and a nonzero critical section ($c = 3.64$, $d = 0$) helps this along further.

With delays both inside and outside the critical section ($c = 3.64$, $d = 1.29$), we see the LL-SC lock not doing quite as well, even at low processor counts. This is because a processor waits after its release before trying to acquire the lock again, making it much more likely that some other waiting processor will acquire the lock before it. Self-transfers are unlikely, so lock transfers are slower even with two processors. It is interesting that performance is particularly worse for the backoff case at small processor counts when the delay d between unlock and lock is nonzero. This is because it is quite likely that while the processor that just released the lock is waiting for d to expire before doing its next acquire, all the other processors are in a backoff period and not even trying to acquire the lock. In the $d = 0$ case, the releasing processor reacquires the lock right away, especially with a small number of processors. Backoff must be used carefully for it to be successful.

Consider the other locks. These are fair, so every lock transfer is to a different processor and involves bus transactions in the critical path of the transfer. Hence, they all start off with a jump to about three bus transactions in the critical path per lock transfer even when two processors are used. Actual differences in time are due to exactly which bus transactions are generated and how much of their latency can be hidden from the processor. The ticket lock without backoff scales relatively poorly: with all processors trying to read the `now-serving` counter, the expected number of bus transactions between the release and the read by the correct processor is $p/2$, leading to the observed linear degradation in the lock transfer critical path. With successful proportional backoff, it is likely that the correct processor will be the one to issue the read first after a release, so the time per transfer is constant and does not scale with p. The array-based lock also scales well since only the correct processor issues a read.

The results illustrate the importance of detailed architectural interactions in determining the performance of locks. They also show that simple LL-SC locks perform quite well on buses that have sufficient bandwidth. On this particular machine, performance for the unfair LL-SC lock becomes as bad as or a little worse than that for the more sophisticated locks beyond 16 processors due to the higher traffic, but not by much because bus bandwidth is quite high. When exponential backoff is used to reduce traffic, the simple LL-SC lock delivers the best average lock transfer time in all cases. However, these results also illustrate the difficulty and the importance of sound experimental methodology in evaluating synchronization algorithms. Null critical sections display some interesting effects, but meaningful comparisons depend on what the synchronization patterns look like in practice—in real applications. For example, the effect of critical section and delay size on the frequency of self-transfers has a substantial impact on the comparison of unfair locks with fair locks. The nonrepresentativeness of the null case in this regard is therefore an important methodological consideration. An experiment to use LL-SC while guaranteeing round-robin acquisition among processors (fairness) by using an additional variable showed performance very similar to that of the ticket lock, confirming that unfairness and self-transfers are indeed the reason for the better performance at low processor counts. Especially if fairness is desired, the ticket lock with proportional backoff and the array-based lock perform very well on bus-based machines.

Lock-Free, Nonblocking, and Wait-Free Synchronization

An additional set of performance concerns involving synchronization arises when we consider that the machine running our parallel program is used in a multiprogramming environment. Other processes run for periods of time or, even if we have the machine to ourselves, background daemons run periodically, processes take page faults, I/O interrupts occur, and the process scheduler makes scheduling decisions with limited information about the application requirements. These events can cause the rate at which processes make progress to vary considerably. One important question is how the parallel program as a whole slows down when one process is slowed. With traditional locks, the problem can be serious: if a process holding a lock stops or slows while in its critical section, all other processes may have to wait. This problem has received a good deal of attention in work on operating system schedulers. In some cases, attempts are made to avoid preempting a process that is holding a lock. Another line of research takes the view that lock-based operations are not very robust and should be avoided; for example, if a process dies while holding a lock, other processes hang. It has been observed that most lock-unlock operations are used to support operations on a well-defined data structure or object that is shared by several processes, for example, updating a shared counter or manipulating a shared queue. These higher-level operations on the data structure can be implemented directly using atomic primitives without actually using locks, as discussed for LL-SC earlier.

A shared data structure is said to be *lock-free* if the operations defined on it do not require mutual exclusion over multiple instructions. If the operations on the data structure guarantee that some process will complete its operation in a finite amount of time, even if other processes halt, the data structure is *nonblocking*. If the operations can guarantee that every (nonfaulting) process will complete its operation in a finite amount of time, the data structure is *wait-free* (Herlihy 1993). A body of literature is available that investigates the theory and practice of such data structures, including requirements placed on the basic atomic primitives to implement them (Herlihy 1988), general-purpose techniques for translating sequential operations to nonblocking concurrent operations (Herlihy 1993), specific useful lock-free data structures (Valois 1995; Michael and Scott 1996), operating system implementations (Massalin and Pu 1991; Greenwald and Cheriton 1996), and proposals for architectural support (Herlihy and Moss 1993). The basic approach is to implement updates to a shared object by reading a portion of the object to make a copy, updating the copy, and then performing an operation to commit the change only if no conflicting updates have been made (reminiscent of LL-SC). As a simple example, consider a shared counter. The counter is read into a register, a value is added to the register copy, and the result is put in a second register. Next, a compare&swap updates the shared counter only if its value is still the same as the copy. For more sophisticated, linked-list data structures, a new element is created and then linked into the shared list if the insert is still valid. These techniques serve to limit the window in which the shared data structure is in an inconsistent state, so they improve robustness, although it can be difficult to make them efficient.

Theoretical research has identified the properties of different atomic exchange operations in terms of the time complexity of using them to implement synchronized access to variables. In particular, it has been found that simple operations like test&set and fetch&op are not powerful enough to guarantee that the time taken by a processor to access a synchronized variable is independent of the number of processors, whereas more sophisticated atomic operations like compare&swap and swapping the values of two memory locations are powerful enough to make this guarantee (Herlihy1988).

Having discussed the options for mutual exclusion on bus-based machines, let us move on to point-to-point, and then barrier, event synchronization.

5.5.4 Point-to-Point Event Synchronization

Point-to-point synchronization within a parallel program is often implemented by busy-waiting on ordinary variables, using them as flags. If we want to use blocking instead of busy-waiting, we can use semaphores, just as they are used in concurrent programming and operating systems (Tanenbaum and Woodhull 1997).

Software Algorithms

Flags are control variables, typically used to communicate the occurrence of a synchronization event rather than to transfer values. If two processes have a producer-consumer relationship on the shared variable *a*, then a flag can be used to manage the synchronization as follows:

P_1	P_2
`a = f(x);` /*set a*/	`while (flag is 0) do nothing;`
`flag = 1;`	`b = g(a);` /*use a*/

If we know that the variable *a* is initialized to a certain value (say, 0), which will be changed to a new value we are interested in by this production event, then we can use *a* itself as the synchronization flag, as follows:

P_1	P_2
`a = f(x);` /*set a*/	`while (a is 0) do nothing;`
	`b = g(a);` /*use a*/

This eliminates the need for a separate flag variable and saves the write to and read of that variable at perhaps some cost in readability and maintainability.

Hardware Support: Full-Empty Bits

This idea of special flag values has been extended in some research machines (although mostly in machines with physically distributed memory) to provide hardware support for fine-grained producer-consumer synchronization. A bit, called a *full-empty bit,* is associated with every word in memory. This bit is set when the word is "full" with newly produced data (i.e., on a write) and unset when the word is "emptied" by a processor consuming that data (i.e., on a read). Word-level producer-consumer synchronization is then accomplished as follows. When the producer process wants to write the location, it does so only if the full-empty bit is set to empty and then leaves the bit set to full. The consumer reads the location only if the bit is full and then sets it to empty. Hardware preserves the atomicity of the read or write with the manipulation of the full-empty bit. Given full-empty bits, our preceding example can be written without the spin loop as

P_1	P_2
`a = f(x);` /*set a*/	`b = g(a);` /*use a*/

Full-empty bits raise concerns about flexibility. For example, they do not lend themselves easily to single-producer-multiple-consumer synchronization or to the case where a producer updates a value multiple times before a consumer consumes it. Also, should all reads and writes use full-empty bits or only those that are compiled down to special instructions? The latter method requires support in the language and compiler, but the former is too restrictive in imposing synchronization on all accesses to a location (for example, it does not allow asynchronous relaxation in iterative equation solvers; see Chapter 2). For these reasons, and the hardware cost, full-empty bits have not found favor in most commercial machines.

Interrupts

Another important kind of event is the interrupt conveyed from an I/O device needing attention to a processor. In a uniprocessor machine, there is no question where the interrupt should go, but in an SMP any processor can potentially take the interrupt. In addition, there are times when one processor may need to issue an interrupt to another. In early SMP designs, special hardware was provided to monitor the priority of the process on each processor and to deliver the I/O interrupt to the processor running at lowest priority. Such measures proved to be of small value, and most modern machines use simple arbitration strategies. In addition, a memory-mapped interrupt control region usually exists, so at kernel level any processor can interrupt any other by writing the interrupt information at the associated address.

5.5.5 Global (Barrier) Event Synchronization

Finally, let us examine barrier synchronization on a bus-based machine. Software algorithms for barriers are typically implemented using locks, shared counters, and flags. Let us begin with a simple barrier among p processes, which is called a *centralized barrier* since it uses only a single lock, a single counter, and a single flag.

Centralized Software Barrier

A shared counter maintains the number of processes that have arrived at the barrier and is therefore incremented by every arriving process. These increments must be mutually exclusive. After incrementing the counter, a process checks to see if the counter equals p, that is, if it is the last process to have arrived. If not, it busy-waits on the flag associated with the barrier; if so, it writes the flag to release the $p - 1$ waiting processes. A simple attempt at a barrier algorithm may therefore look like

```
struct bar_type {
  int counter;
  struct lock_type lock;
  int flag = 0;
} bar_name;

BARRIER (bar_name, p)
{
  LOCK(bar_name.lock);
  if (bar_name.counter == 0)
    bar_name.flag = 0;                  /*reset flag if first to reach*/
  mycount = bar_name.counter++;         /*mycount is a private variable*/
  UNLOCK(bar_name.lock);
  if (mycount == p) {                   /*last to arrive*/
    bar_name.counter = 0;               /*reset counter for next barrier*/
    bar_name.flag = 1;                  /*release waiting processes*/
  }
  else
    while (bar_name.flag == 0) {};  /*busy-wait for release*/
}
```

Centralized Barrier with Sense Reversal

Can you see a problem with the preceding barrier? There is one. It occurs when the barrier operation is performed consecutively using the same barrier variable—for example, if each processor executes the following code:

```
some computation...
BARRIER(bar1, p);
some more computation...
BARRIER(bar1, p);
```

The first process to enter the barrier the second time reinitializes the barrier counter, so that is not a problem. The problem is the flag. To exit the first barrier, processes spin on the flag until it is set to 1. Processes that see the flag change to 1 will exit the barrier, perform the subsequent computation, and enter the barrier again. However, suppose one processor P_x does not see the flag change from the first barrier before others have reentered the barrier for the second time; for example, it gets swapped out by the operating system because it has been spinning too long. When it is swapped back in, it will continue to wait for the flag to change to 1. In the meantime, other processes may have already entered the second instance of the barrier, and the first of these will have reset the flag to 0. Now the flag can only get set to 1 again when all p processes have registered at the new instance of the barrier, which will never happen since P_x will never leave the spin loop from the first barrier.

How can we solve this problem? What we need to do is prevent a process from entering a new instance of a barrier until all processes have exited the previous instance of the same barrier. One way is to use another counter to count the processes that leave the barrier and to not let a process reset the flag in a new barrier instance until this counter has turned to p for the previous instance. However, manipulating this counter incurs further latency and contention. On the other hand, with the current setup we cannot wait for all processes to reach the barrier before resetting the flag to 0, since that is when we actually set the flag to 1 for the release. A better solution is to avoid explicitly resetting the flag value altogether and rather have processes wait for the flag to obtain a different release value in consecutive instances of the barrier. For example, processes may wait for the flag to turn to 1 in one instance and to turn to 0 in the next instance. A private variable is used per process to keep track of which value to wait for in the current barrier instance. Since by the semantics of a barrier a process cannot get more than one barrier ahead of another, we only need two values (0 and 1) that we toggle between each time. Hence we call this method *sense reversal*. Now, in the previous example, the flag need not be reset when the first process reaches the barrier; rather, the process stuck in the old barrier instance still waits for the flag to reach the old release value while processes that enter the new instance wait for the other (toggled) release value. The value of the flag is only changed once when all processes have reached the (new) barrier instance, so it will not change before processes stuck in the old instance see it. Here is the code for a simple barrier with sense reversal:

```
BARRIER (bar_name, p)
{
  local_sense = !(local_sense);          /*toggle private sense variable*/
  LOCK(bar_name.lock);
  mycount = bar_name.counter++;          /*mycount is a private variable*/
  if (bar_name.counter == p) {           /*last to arrive*/
    UNLOCK(bar_name.lock);
    bar_name.counter = 0;                /*reset counter for next barrier*/
    bar_name.flag = local_sense;         /*release waiting processes*/
  }
  else {
    UNLOCK(bar_name.lock);
    while (bar_name.flag != local_sense) {};  /*busy-wait for
                                                release*/
  }
}
```

Note that the lock is not released immediately after the increment of the counter but only after the condition is evaluated; the reason for this is revealed in an exercise (see Exercise 5.18). We now have a correct barrier that can be reused any number of times consecutively. The remaining issue is performance, which we examine next.

(Note that the `LOCK/UNLOCK` protecting the increment of the counter can be replaced more efficiently by a simple LL-SC or atomic increment operation.)

Performance

The major performance goals for a barrier are similar to those for locks. They include the following:

- *Low latency (small critical path length).* The chain of dependent operations and bus transactions needed for p processors to pass the barrier should be small.
- *Low traffic.* Since barriers are global operations, it is quite likely that many processors will try to execute a barrier at the same time. The barrier algorithm should reduce the total number of bus transactions (whether in the critical path or not) and hence the possible contention.
- *Scalability.* Latency and traffic should increase slowly with the number of processors.
- *Low storage cost.* We would, of course, like to keep the storage cost low.
- *Fairness.* We should ensure that the same processor does not always become the last one to exit the barrier (or we may want to preserve FIFO ordering).

In the centralized barrier described previously, each processor accesses the lock once, hence the critical path length is at least proportional to p. Consider the bus traffic. To complete its operation, a centralized barrier involving p processors performs $2p$ bus transactions for processors to obtain the lock and increment the counter, two bus transactions for the last processor to reset the counter and write the release flag, and another $p - 1$ bus transactions to read the flag after it has been invalidated. Note that this is better than the traffic for even a test-and-test&set lock to be acquired by p processes because, in that case, each of the p releases causes an invalidation that results in $O(p)$ processes trying to perform the test&set again, thus resulting in $O(p^2)$ bus transactions. However, the contention resulting from these competing bus transactions can be substantial if many processors arrive at the barrier simultaneously, so barriers can be expensive.

Improving Barrier Algorithms for a Bus

One part of the problem in the centralized barrier is that all processors contend for the same lock and flag variables. To address this, we can construct barriers that cause fewer processors to contend for the same variable. For example, processors can signal their arrival at the barrier through a software combining tree (see Section 3.3.2). In a binary combining tree, for example, only two processors notify each other of their arrival at each node of the tree, and only one of the two moves up to participate at the next higher level of the tree. Thus, only two processors ever access a given variable. In a distributed network with multiple parallel paths, such as those found in scalable machines, a combining tree can perform much better than a centralized barrier since different pairs of processors can communicate with each other

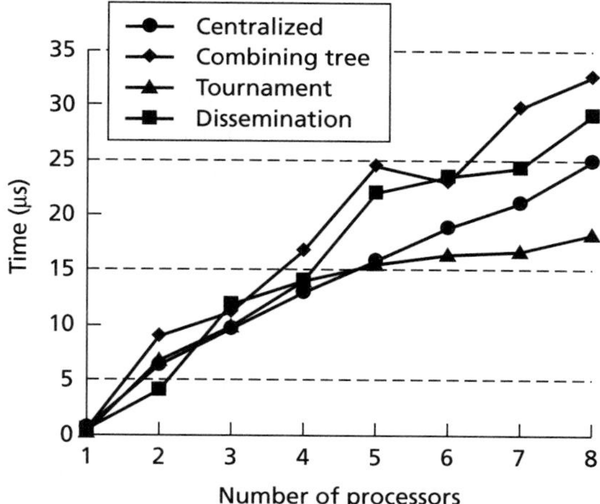

FIGURE 5.31 Performance of some barriers on the SGI Challenge. Performance is measured as average time per barrier over a loop of many consecutive barriers (with no work or delays between them). The higher critical path latency of the combining tree barrier hurts it on a bus, where it has no traffic and contention advantages.

in different parts of the network in parallel. However, with a centralized interconnect like a bus, even though pairs of processors communicate through different variables, they all generate bus transactions and hence serialization and contention on the same bus. Since a binary tree with p leaves has approximately $2p$ nodes, a combining tree requires a similar total number of bus transactions to the centralized barrier. It also has higher latency since, while it too requires $O(p)$ serialized bus transactions in all, even without bus serialization each processor must wait at least $\log p$ steps to get from the leaves to the root of the tree, each with significant work. The advantage of a combining tree for a bus is that it does not use locks but, rather, simple read and write operations, which may compensate for its larger uncontended latency if the number of processors on the bus is large. However, the simple centralized barrier performs quite well on a bus, as shown in Figure 5.31. Some of the other barriers shown in the figure for illustration will be discussed along with tree barriers in the context of scalable machines in Chapter 7.

Hardware Primitives

Since the centralized barrier uses locks and ordinary reads and writes, the hardware primitives needed depend on which lock algorithms are used. If a machine does not support atomic primitives well, combining tree barriers can be useful for bus-based machines as well.

A special bus primitive can be used to reduce the number of bus transactions for read misses in the centralized barrier (as well as for highly contended locks in which processors spin on the same variable). This optimization takes advantage of the fact that all processors issue a read miss for the same value of the flag when they are invalidated at the release. Instead of all processors issuing a separate read-miss bus transaction, a processor can monitor the bus and abort its read miss before putting it on the bus, if it sees the response to a read miss to the same location (issued by another processor that happened to get on the bus first), and simply take the return value from the bus. In the best case, this piggybacking can reduce the number of read-miss bus transactions from p to 1.

Hardware Barriers

If a separate synchronization bus is provided, as discussed for locks, it can be used to support barriers in hardware too. This takes the traffic and contention off the main system bus and can lead to higher-performance barriers. Conceptually, a single wired-AND line is enough. A processor sets its input high when it reaches the barrier and waits until the output goes high before it can proceed. (In practice, reusing barriers requires that more than a single wire be used.) Such a separate hardware mechanism for barriers can be particularly useful if the frequency of barriers is very high, as it may be in programs that are automatically parallelized by compilers at the inner loop level and that need global synchronization after every innermost loop. However, its value in practice is unclear, and it can be difficult to manage when only a portion of the processors on the machine participate in the barrier. For example, it is difficult to dynamically change the number of processors participating in the barrier or to adapt the configuration of participating processors when processes are migrated among processors by the operating system. Having multiple participating processes running on the same processor also causes complications. Current bus-based multiprocessors therefore do not tend to provide special hardware support but build barriers in software out of locks and shared variables.

5.5.6 Synchronization Summary

Some bus-based machines have provided full hardware support for synchronization operations such as locks and barriers. However, concerns about flexibility have led most contemporary designers to provide support for only simple atomic operations in hardware and to synthesize higher-level synchronization operations from them in software libraries. The application programmer generally uses the libraries and can be unaware of the low-level atomic operations supported on the machine. The atomic operations may be implemented either as single instructions or through speculative read-write instruction pairs like load-locked and store-conditional. The greater flexibility of the latter is making them increasingly popular. We have already seen some of the interplay between synchronization primitives, algorithms, and architectural details. This interplay will be much more pronounced when we discuss synchronization for scalable shared address space machines in the coming chapters.

5.6 IMPLICATIONS FOR SOFTWARE

So far, we have looked at high-level architectural issues for bus-based cache-coherent multiprocessors and at how architectural and protocol trade-offs are affected by workload characteristics. Let us now come full circle and examine how the architectural characteristics of these small-scale machines influence parallel software. That is, instead of keeping the workload fixed and improving the machine or its protocols, we keep the machine fixed and examine how to improve parallel programs. Improving synchronization algorithms to reduce traffic and latency was an example of this, but let us look at the parallel programming process more generally.

The general techniques for load balance and inherent communication discussed in Chapter 3 also apply to cache-coherent machines. In addition, one general partitioning principle that is applicable across a wide range of computations on these machines is to try to assign computation such that only one processor writes a given set of data, at least during a single computational phase. In many computations, processors read one large shared data structure and write another. In Raytrace, for example, processors read a scene and write an image. A choice is available of whether to partition the computation so the processors write disjoint pieces of the destination structure and read share the source structure, or read disjoint pieces of the source structure and write share the same memory locations in the destination. All other considerations being equal (such as load balance and programming complexity), it is usually advisable to avoid write sharing in these situations. Write sharing not only causes invalidations and, hence, cache misses and traffic, but if different processes write the same words, it is very likely that the writes must be protected by synchronization such as locks, which are even more expensive.

The structure of communication is not much of a variable: with a single centralized memory, little incentive exists to use explicit memory-to-memory data transfers, so all communication is implicit through loads and stores that lead to the transfer of cache blocks. Mapping is not an issue (other than to try to ensure that processes migrate from one processor to another as little as possible) and is invariably left to the operating system. The most interesting issues are managing data locality and artifactual communication in the orchestration step, and in particular, addressing temporal and spatial locality to reduce the number of cache misses and hence reduce latency, traffic, and contention on the shared bus.

With main memory being centralized, temporal locality is exploited in the processor caches. The specialization of the working set curve introduced in Chapter 3 for bus-based machines is shown in Figure 5.32. All capacity-related misses go to the same bus and memory and are about as expensive as coherence misses. The other three kinds of misses will occur and generate bus traffic even with an infinite cache. The major goal for temporal locality is to have working sets fit in the cache hierarchy, and the techniques are the same as those discussed in Chapter 3.

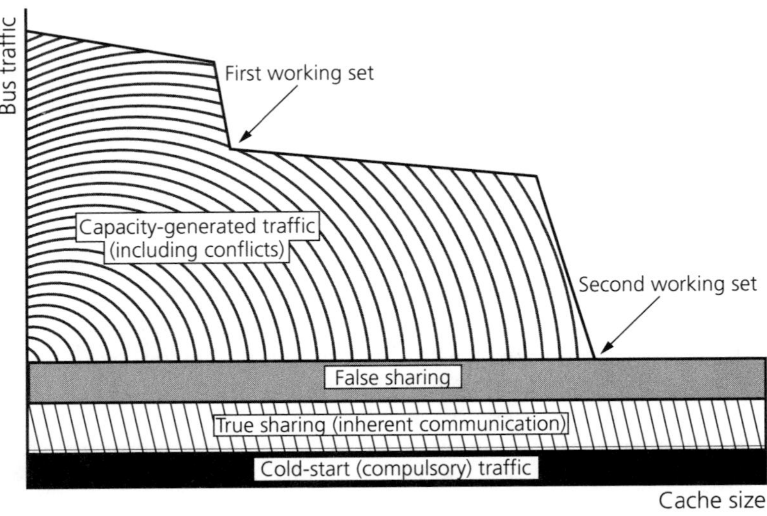

FIGURE 5.32 Data traffic on the shared bus and its components as a function of cache size. The points of inflection indicate the working sets of the program.

For spatial locality, a centralized memory makes data distribution and the granularity of allocation in main memory irrelevant (only interleaving data among memory banks to reduce contention may be an issue, just as in uniprocessors). The ill effects of poor spatial locality are *fragmentation* (i.e., fetching unnecessary data on a cache block) and false sharing. The reasons are that the granularity of communication and the granularity of coherence are both cache blocks, which are larger than a word. The former causes fragmentation, and the latter causes false sharing. (We assume here that techniques to eliminate false sharing like subblock dirty bits are not used since they are not found in most real machines.) Let us examine some techniques to alleviate these problems and effectively exploit the prefetching effects of long cache blocks, as well as techniques to alleviate cache conflicts by better spatial organization of data. Many such techniques can be found in a programmer's "bag of tricks." The following provides only a sampling of the most general ones.

- *Assign tasks to reduce spatial interleaving of access patterns.* It is desirable to assign tasks such that each processor tends to access large contiguous chunks of data. For example, if an array computation with n elements is to be divided among p processors, it is better to divide it so that each processor accesses n/p contiguous elements rather than to use a finely interleaved assignment of elements. This increases spatial locality and reduces false sharing of cache blocks. Of course, load balancing or other constraints may force us to do otherwise.
- *Structure data to reduce spatial interleaving of access patterns.* We saw an example of this in the equation solver kernel in Chapter 3, when we used higher-dimensional arrays to keep a processor's partition of an array contiguous in the

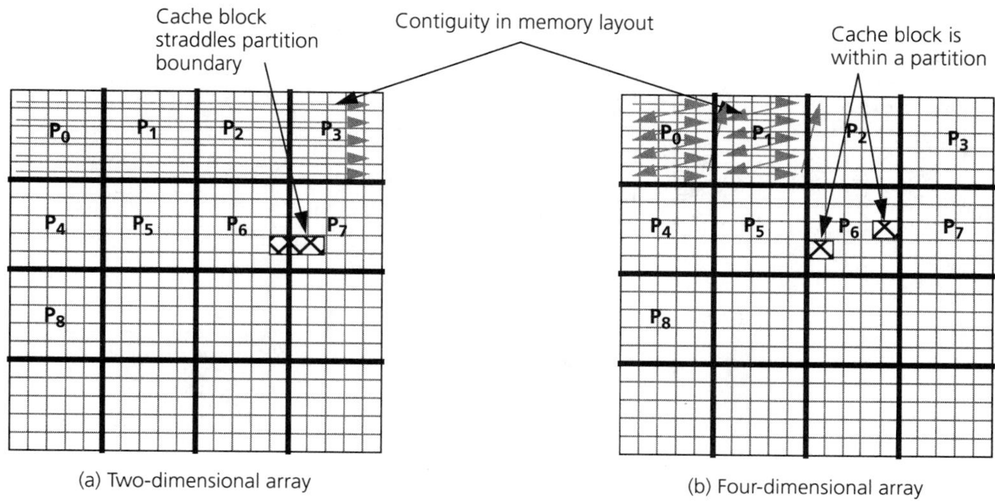

FIGURE 5.33 Reducing false sharing and fragmentation by using higher-dimensional arrays to keep partitions contiguous in the address space. In the two-dimensional array case, cache blocks straddling partition boundaries cause both fragmentation (a miss brings in useless data from the other processor's partition) as well as false sharing. The four-dimensional array representation makes partitions contiguous and alleviates these problems.

address space in order to allocate partitions locally at page granularity in physically distributed memory. This technique also helps reduce false sharing, fragmentation of data transfer, and conflict misses, as shown in Figures 5.33 and 5.34, all of which cause misses and traffic on the bus. A cache block larger than a single grid element may straddle a column-oriented partition boundary, as shown in Figure 5.33(a). If the block is larger than two grid elements, it can cause communication due to false sharing. This is easiest to see if we assume for a moment that there is no inherent communication in the algorithm; for example, suppose in each sweep a process simply adds a constant value to each of its assigned grid elements instead of performing a nearest-neighbor computation. Now, even a two-element (or larger) cache block straddling a partition boundary would be false-shared as different processors wrote different words on it. This would also cause fragmentation in communication, since a process reading its own boundary element and missing on it would also fetch other elements in the other processor's partition that are on the same cache block but that it does not need. The conflict-misses problem is explained in Figure 5.34. The issue in all these cases is noncontiguity of partitions. Thus, a single data structure transformation (as in Figure 5.33[b]) helps us solve all our spatial locality–related problems in the equation solver kernel. Figure 5.35 illustrates the performance impact of using higher-dimensional arrays to represent grids or blocked matrices in the Ocean and LU applications on the SGI

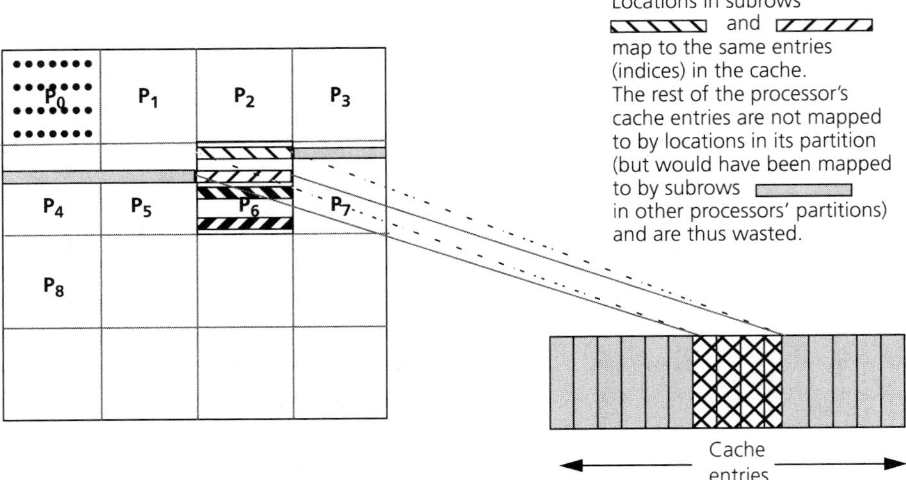

FIGURE 5.34 Cache mapping conflicts caused by a two-dimensional array representation in a direct-mapped cache. The figure shows the worst case, in which the separation between successive subrows in a process's partition (i.e., the size of a full row of the 2D array) is exactly equal to the size of the cache, so consecutive subrows map directly on top of one another in the cache. Every subrow accessed knocks the previous subrow out of the cache. In the next sweep over its partition, the processor will miss on every cache block it references, even if the cache as a whole is large enough to fit a whole partition. Many intermediately poor cases may be encountered depending on grid size, number of processors, and cache size. Since the cache size in bytes is a power of two, sizing the dimensions of allocated arrays to be powers of two is discouraged.

Challenge. The impact of conflicts and false sharing on uniprocessor and multiprocessor performance is clear.

- *Beware of conflict misses.* In illustrating conflict misses in the grid solver, Figure 5.34 shows how allocating power-of-two-sized arrays can cause pathological cache conflict problems since the cache size is also a power of two. Even if the logical size of the array that the application needs is a power of two, it is often useful to allocate a larger array that is not a power of two and then access only the amount needed. However, this strategy can interfere with allocating data at page granularity (also a power of two) in machines with physically distributed memory, so we may have to be careful. The cache mapping conflicts in this example are within a single data structure that is accessed in a predictable manner and can thus be alleviated in a structured way. Mapping conflicts are more difficult to avoid when they happen across different major data structures (e.g., across different grids used by the Ocean application), where they may have to be alleviated by ad hoc padding and alignment. However, in a shared address space they are particularly insidious when they occur on seemingly harmless shared variables or data structures that a programmer is not inclined to think about. For example, a frequently accessed pointer to an important data structure may conflict in a direct-mapped cache

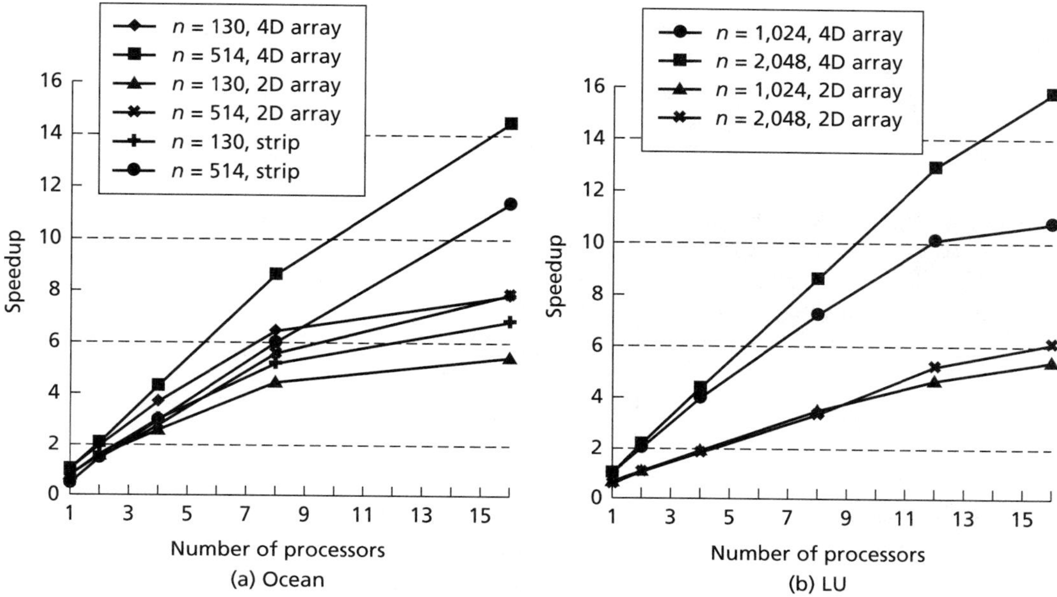

FIGURE 5.35 Performance impact of using 4D versus 2D arrays to represent two-dimensional grid or matrix data structures on the SGI Challenge. Results are shown for different problem sizes for the Ocean and LU applications. For Ocean, "strip" indicates partitioning into strips of contiguous rows (in which 2D or 4D arrays don't matter), while all other cases assume partitioning into squarelike blocks.

with a scalar variable that is also frequently accessed during the same computation, causing a lot of traffic. Fortunately, such problems tend to be infrequent in modern (large and set-associative) second-level caches. In general, efforts to exploit locality can be wasted if attention is not paid to reducing conflict misses.

- *Use per-processor heaps.* It is desirable to have separate heap regions for each processor (or process) from which it allocates data dynamically. Otherwise, if a program performs a lot of very small memory allocations, data used by different processors may fall on the same cache block.
- *Copy data to increase spatial locality.* If a processor is going to reuse a set of data that is otherwise allocated noncontiguously in the address space, it is often desirable to make a contiguous copy of the data for that period to improve spatial locality and reduce cache conflicts. Copying requires memory accesses and has a cost, and it is not useful if the data is likely to reside in the cache anyway. For example, in blocked matrix factorization or multiplication, with a 2D array representation of the matrix a block is not contiguous in the address space (just like a partition in the equation solver kernel). However, a 2D representation makes programming easier. It is therefore not uncommon to use 2D

arrays and to copy blocks used from another processor's assigned set to a contiguous temporary data structure, during the time of active use, to reduce conflict misses. The cost of copying must be traded off against the benefit of reducing conflicts. In particle-based applications, when a particle moves from one processor's partition to another, spatial locality can be improved by moving the data for that particle so that the memory for all the particles assigned to a processor remains contiguous and dense.

- *Pad arrays.* Beginning parallel programmers often build arrays that are indexed using the process identifier. For example, to keep track of load balance, an array of p integers may be maintained, each entry of which records the number of tasks completed by the corresponding processor. Since many elements of such an array fall into a single cache block, and since these elements will be updated quite often by different processors, false sharing becomes a severe problem. One solution is to pad each entry with dummy words to make its size as large as the cache block size (or, to make the code more robust, as large as the largest cache block size on anticipated machines) and then align the array to a cache block. However, padding many large arrays can result in a significant waste of memory, and it can cause fragmentation in data transfer. A better strategy is to combine all such variables for a given process into a record, pad the entire record to a cache block boundary, and create an array of such records indexed by process identifier.
- *Determine how to organize arrays of records.* Suppose we have a number of logical records to represent, such as the particles in the Barnes-Hut gravitational simulation. Should we represent them as a single array of n particles, each entry being a record with fields like position, velocity, force, mass, and so on, as in Figure 5.36(a)? Or should we represent them as separate arrays of size n, one per field, as in Figure 5.36(b)? Programs written for vector machines such as traditional CRAY computers tend to use a separate array (vector) for each property or field of an object—in fact, even one per field per physical dimension (x, y, or z). When data is accessed by field, for example, the velocity of all particles, this increases the performance of vector operations by making accesses to memory unit stride and hence reducing memory bank conflicts. In cache-coherent multiprocessors, however, new trade-offs arise, and the best way to organize data depends on the access patterns.

  An interesting tension is illustrated by the particle update and force calculation phases of the Barnes-Hut application. Consider the update phase first. A processor reads and writes only the position and velocity fields of all its assigned particles in this phase. However, its assigned particles are not contiguous in the shared particle array. Suppose there is one array of size n (number of particles) per field or property. A double-precision three-dimensional position (or velocity) is 24 bytes of data, so several of these may fit on a cache block. Since adjacent particles in the array may be read and written by different processors, false sharing can result. For this phase, it is better to have a single array of particle records, where each record holds all information about that particle; that is, to organize data by particle rather than by field.

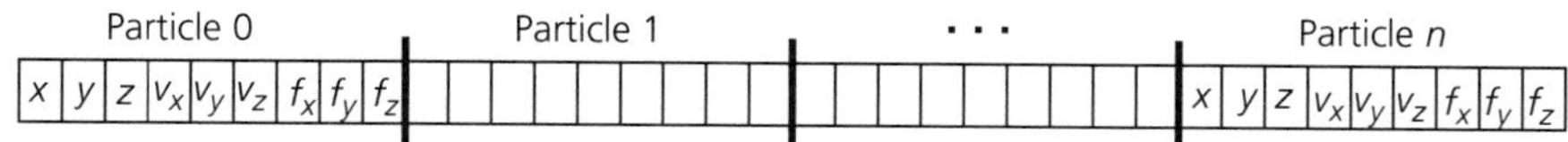

(a) Organization by particle

Position

Velocity

Force

(b) Organization of particles by property or field

FIGURE 5.36 Alternative data structure organizations for record-based data

Now consider the force calculation phase of the same application. Suppose we use an organization by particle rather than by field as above. To compute the force on a particle, a processor reads the position values of many other particles and cells; it then updates the force components of its own particle. However, the force and position components of a particle may fall on the same cache block. In updating force components, it may therefore invalidate the position values of this particle from the caches of other processors that are using and reusing them as a result of false sharing within a particle record, even though the position values themselves are not being modified in this phase of computation. In this case, it would probably be better if we were to split the single array of particle records into two arrays of size n each, one for positions (and perhaps other properties) and one for forces. The entries of the force array themselves could be padded to reduce cross-particle false sharing. In general, it is often beneficial to split arrays of records to separate fields that are used in a read-only manner in a phase from the fields whose values are updated in the same phase. Different situations or phases may dictate different organizations for a data structure, and the ultimate decision depends on which pattern or phase dominates performance.

- *Align arrays.* In conjunction with the preceding techniques, it is often necessary to align arrays to cache block boundaries to achieve the full benefits. For example, given a cache block size of 64 bytes and 8-byte fields, we may have decided to maintain a single array of particle records with *x, y, z, fx, fy,* and *fz*. To avoid cross-particle false sharing, we pad each 48-byte record with two dummy 8-byte fields to fill a cache block. However, this wouldn't help if the array started at an offset of 32 bytes from a page in the virtual address space, as this would mean that the data for each particle would now span two cache blocks, causing false sharing despite the padding. Even if a `malloc` call does not return data aligned to pages or blocks, alignment is easy to achieve by simply allocating a little extra memory through `malloc` and then suitably adjusting the starting address of the array.

As seen in the preceding list of techniques, the organization, alignment, and padding of data structures are all important for exploiting spatial locality and reducing false sharing and conflict misses. Experienced programmers and even some compilers use these techniques. As discussed in Chapter 3, these locality and artifactual communication issues can be more important to performance than inherent communication and can cause us to revisit our algorithmic partitioning decisions for an application (recall strip versus block partitioning for the simple equation solver as discussed in Section 3.1.2, and see Figure 5.35[a]).

5.7 CONCLUDING REMARKS

Symmetric shared memory multiprocessors are a natural extension of workstations and personal computers. A sequential application can run totally unchanged and yet benefit in performance by obtaining a larger fraction of a processor's time and by taking advantage of the large amount of shared main memory and I/O capacity typically available on such machines. Parallel applications are also relatively easy to bring up, as all shared data is directly accessible from all processors using ordinary loads and stores. Gradual parallelization is possible by selectively parallelizing computationally intensive portions of a sequential application, subject to the dictates of Amdahl's Law. For multiprogrammed workloads, a key advantage is the fine granularity at which resources can be shared among application processes and by the operating system, which can thus easily export a familiar, single-system image to each application. This is true both temporally, in that processors and/or main memory pages can frequently be reallocated among different application processes, and physically, in that main memory may be split among applications at the granularity of individual pages. Because of these appealing features, all major vendors of computer systems, from workstation suppliers like Sun, Silicon Graphics, Hewlett-Packard, Digital, and IBM to personal computer suppliers like Intel and Compaq, are producing and selling such machines. In fact, for some of the large workstation vendors, these multiprocessors constitute a substantial fraction of their revenue stream and a still larger fraction of their net profits because of the higher margins on these higher-end machines.

The key technical challenge in the design of symmetric multiprocessors is the organization and implementation of the shared memory system, which is used for communication between processors in addition to handling all regular memory accesses. Most small-scale parallel machines found today use the system bus as the interconnect for communication, and the challenge then becomes how to maintain coherency of the shared data in the private caches of the processors. A large variety of options are available to the system architect, including the set of states associated with cache blocks, the bus transactions and actions used, the choice of cache block size, and whether updates or invalidations are used. The key task of the system architect is to make choices that will both perform well on the data sharing patterns expected in workloads and make the task of implementation easier. Another challenge is the design and implementation of efficient synchronization techniques that are both high performance and flexible.

As processor, memory system, integrated circuit, and packaging technology continue to make rapid progress, questions arise about the future of small-scale multiprocessors and the importance of various design issues. We can expect small-scale multiprocessors to continue to be important for at least three reasons. The first is that they offer an attractive cost-performance combination. Individuals or small groups of people can easily afford them for use as a shared resource or as a compute or file server. Second, microprocessors today are designed to be multiprocessor-ready, and designers are aware of future microprocessor trends when they begin to design the next-generation multiprocessor, so there is no longer a significant time lag between the latest microprocessor and its incorporation in a multiprocessor. As we saw in Chapter 1, the Intel Pentium Pro processor line plugs "gluelessly" into a shared bus. The third reason is that the essential software technology for parallel machines (compilers, operating systems, programming languages) is maturing rapidly for small-scale shared memory machines. For example, most computer system vendors have efficient parallel versions of their operating systems ready for their bus-based multiprocessors. As levels of integration increase, multiple processors on a chip become attractive. While the optimal design points may change, the design issues that we have explored in this chapter are fundamental and will remain important with progress in technology.

This chapter has explored many of the key design aspects of bus-based multiprocessors at the "logical" level, involving cache block state transitions and complete (atomic) bus transactions. At this level, the design and implementation appears to be a rather simple extension of traditional cache controllers. However, much of the difficulty in such designs and many of the opportunities for optimization and innovation occur at the next lower level of protocol design and at the more detailed "physical" level. The next chapter goes down a level deeper into the design and organization of bus-based cache-coherent multiprocessors and some of their natural generalizations.

5.8 EXERCISES

5.1 Is the cache coherence problem an issue with processor registers? Given that registers are not kept consistent in hardware, how do current systems guarantee the desired semantics of a program?

5.2 Consider the following graph indicating the miss rate of an application as a function of cache block size on a multiprocessor. As might be expected, the curve has a U-shaped appearance. Consider the three points A, B, and C on the curve. Indicate under what circumstances, if any, each may be a sensible operating point for the machine (i.e., the machine might give better performance at that point rather than at the other two points). How would you expect the shape and placement of the curve to differ for a uniprocessor?

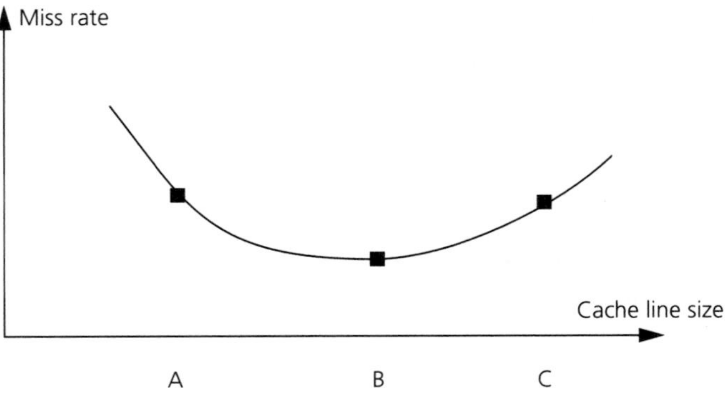

5.3 Assume the following average data memory traffic for a bus-based shared memory multiprocessor: private reads—70%; private writes—20%; shared reads—8%; shared writes—2%. Also assume that 50% of the instructions (32 bits each) are either loads or stores. With a split instruction/data cache of 32-KB total size, we get hit rates of 97% for private data, 95% for shared data, and 98.5% for instructions. The cache line size is only 16 bytes.

We want to place as many processors as possible on a bus that has 64 data lines and 32 address lines. The processor clock is twice as fast as that of the bus, and the processor CPI is 2.0 before considering memory penalties. How many processors can the bus support without saturating if we use (a) write-through caches with write-allocate strategy? (b) write-back caches? Ignore cache consistency traffic and bus contention. The probability of having to replace a dirty block in the write-back caches on a miss that fetches a new block is 0.3. For reads, memory responds with data 2 cycles after being presented the address. For writes, both address and data are presented to memory at the same time. Assume that the bus is atomic and that processor miss penalties are equal to just the number of bus cycles required for each miss.

5.4 For each of the memory reference streams given in the following, compare the cost of executing it on a bus-based machine that supports (a) the Illinois MESI protocol and (b) the Dragon protocol. Explain the observed performance differences in terms of the characteristics of the streams and the coherence protocols.

stream 1: *r*1 *w*1 *r*1 *w*1 *r*2 *w*2 *r*2 *w*2 *r*3 *w*3 *r*3 *w*3

stream 2: *r*1 *r*2 *r*3 *w*1 *w*2 *w*3 *r*1 *r*2 *r*3 *w*3 *w*1

stream 3: *r*1 *r*2 *r*3 *r*3 *w*1 *w*1 *w*1 *w*1 *w*2 *w*3

All of the references in the streams are to the same location: *r*/*w* indicates read or write, and the digit refers to the processor issuing the reference. Assume that all caches are initially empty, and use the following cost model: read/write cache hit—1 cycle; misses requiring simple transaction on bus (BusUpgr, BusUpd)—60 cycles; and misses requiring whole cache block transfer—90 cycles. Assume all caches are write allocated.

5.5 a. As miss latencies increase, does an update protocol become more or less preferable as compared to an invalidate protocol? Explain.

b. In a multilevel cache hierarchy, would you propagate updates all the way to the first-level cache or only to the second-level cache? Explain the trade-offs.

c. Why is update-based coherence not a good idea for multiprogramming workloads typically found on multiprocessor compute servers today?

d. To provide an update protocol as an alternative, some machines have given control of the type of protocol to software at the granularity of page; that is, a given page can be kept coherent either using an update scheme or an invalidate scheme. An alternative to page-based control is to provide special opcodes for writes that will cause updates rather than invalidates. Comment on the advantages and disadvantages.

5.6 Given the following code segments, say what results are possible (or not possible) under sequential consistency (SC). Assume that all variables are initialized to 0 before this code is reached.

a.

P_1	P_2	P_3
`A = 1`	`u = A`	`v = B`
	`B = 1`	`w = A`

b.

P_1	P_2	P_3	P_4
`A = 1`	`u = A`	`B = 1`	`w = B`
	`v = B`		`x = A`

c. In the following sequence, first consider the operations within a dashed box to be part of the same instruction, say, a fetch&increment. Then, suppose they are separate instructions. Answer the questions for both cases.

P_1	P_2
`u = A` `A = u + 1`	`v = A` `A = v + 1`

5.7 a. Is the reordering problem due to write buffers, mentioned in Section 5.2.2, also a problem for concurrent programs on a uniprocessor? If so, how would you prevent it? If not, why not?

b. Can a read complete before a previous write in program order issued by the same processor to the same location has completed (for example, if the write has been placed in the writer's write buffer but has not yet become visible to other processors) and still provide a coherent memory system? If so, what value should the read return? If not, why not? Can this be done and still guarantee SC?

c. If we care only about coherence and not about sequential consistency, can we declare a write to be complete as soon as the processor is able to proceed past it?

5.8 Are the sufficient conditions for SC necessary? Make them less constraining (a) as much as possible and (b) in a reasonable intermediate way, and comment on the effects on implementation complexity.

5.9 Consider the following conditions proposed as sufficient conditions for SC:

- Every process issues memory requests in the order specified by the program.
- After a read or write operation is issued, the issuing process waits for the operation to complete before issuing its next operation.
- Before a processor P_j can return a value written by another processor P_i, all operations that were performed with respect to P_i before it issued the store must also be performed with respect to P_j.

Are these conditions indeed sufficient to guarantee SC executions? If so, say why. If not, construct a counterexample, and say why the conditions that were listed in the chapter are indeed sufficient in that case. [Hint: think about in what way these conditions are different from the ones in the chapter.]

5.10 Consider a four-processor bus-based multiprocessor using the Illinois MESI protocol. Each processor executes a test&set lock to gain access to a null critical section. Assume the test&set instruction always goes on the bus and it takes the same time as a normal read transaction. The initial condition is such that processor 1 has the lock and processors 2, 3, and 4 are spinning on their caches waiting for the lock to be released. Every processor gets the lock once and then exits the program. Considering only the bus transactions related to lock-unlock operations:

a. What is the least number of transactions executed to get from the initial to the final state?

b. What is the worst-case number of transactions?

c. Repeat parts (a) and (b) assuming the Dragon protocol.

5.11 What are the main advantages and disadvantages of exponential backoff in locks? Consider the test&set lock, the test-and-test&set lock, the ticket lock, and the array-based lock. How does the situation change if LL-SC is used instead of atomic instructions?

5.12 Suppose all 16 processors in a bus-based machine try to acquire a test-and-test&set lock simultaneously (and only once each). Assume all processors are spinning on the lock in their caches and are invalidated by a release at time 0.

a. How many bus transactions will it take until all processors have acquired the lock if all the critical sections are empty (i.e., each processor simply does a LOCK and UNLOCK with nothing in between)?

b. Assuming that the bus is fair (services pending requests before new ones) and that every bus transaction takes 50 cycles, how long would it take before the first processor acquires and releases the lock? How long before the last processor to acquire the lock is able to acquire and release it?

c. What is the best you could do with an unfair bus, letting whatever processor you like win an arbitration regardless of the order of the requests?

d. Can you improve the performance by choosing a different (but fixed) bus arbitration scheme than a fair one?

e. If the variables used for implementing locks are not cached, will a test-and-test&set lock still generate less traffic than a test&set lock? Explain your answer.

5.13 For the same machine configuration as in Exercise 5.12(b) and assuming a fair bus, how many bus transactions and how much time is needed for the first and last processors to acquire and release the lock when using a ticket lock? Answer the same question for the array-based lock.

5.14 For the performance curves for the test&set lock with exponential backoff shown in Figure 5.29, why do you think the curve for the nonzero critical section is a little worse than the curve for the null critical section?

5.15 a. Why do we make the delay after an unlock d smaller than the size of the critical section c in our lock experiments? What problems might occur in measurement if we used d larger than c? [Hint: draw timelines for two processor executions.]

b. How would you expect the results comparing lock algorithms to change if we used much larger values for c and d?

5.16 a. Write pseudocode (high level plus assembly) to implement the ticket lock and array-based lock using (i) fetch&increment; (ii) LL-SC.

b. Suppose you did not have a fetch&increment primitive but only a fetch &store (a simple atomic exchange). Could you implement the array-based lock with this primitive? Describe the resulting lock algorithm.

5.17 Implement a compare&swap operation using LL-SC.

5.18 Consider the barrier algorithm with sense reversal that was described in Section 5.5.5. Would there be a problem if the UNLOCK statement were placed just after the increment of the counter rather than after each branch of the if condition? What would it be?

5.19 Suppose we have a machine that supports full-empty bits on every word in hardware. This particular machine allows for the following C code functions:

`ST_Special(loc, val)` writes `val` to data location `loc` and sets the full bit. If the full bit was already set, a trap is signaled.

`int LD_Special(loc)` waits until the data location's full bit is set, reads the data, clears the full bit, and returns the data as the result.

Write a C function swap(i,j) that uses these primitives to atomically swap the contents of two locations $A[i]$ and $A[j]$. You should allow high concurrency (if multiple processors want to swap distinct pairs of locations, they should be able to do so concurrently) and you must avoid deadlock.

5.20 The fetch&add atomic operation can be used to implement barriers, semaphores, and other synchronization mechanisms. The semantics of `fetch-and-add` is such that it adds its second argument to the memory location in its first argument and returns the value of the memory location as it was before the addition. Use the `fetch-and-add` primitive to implement a barrier operation suitable for a shared memory multiprocessor. To use the barrier, a processor must execute `BARRIER (BAR, N)`, where `BAR` is the barrier name and `N` is the number of processes that need to arrive at the barrier before any of them can proceed. Assume that `N` has the same value in each use of barrier `BAR`. The barrier should be capable of supporting the following code:

```
while (condition) {
  Compute for a while
  BARRIER(BAR, N);
    }
```

A proposed solution for implementing the barrier is the following:

```
BARRIER(Var B: BarVariable, N: integer)
{
  if (fetch-and-add(B, 1) = N-1) then
    B := 0;
  else
    while (B != 0) do {};
}
```

What is the problem with this code? Write the code for `BARRIER` in a way that avoids the problem.

5.21 Consider the following implementation of the `BARRIER` synchronization primitive, used at the end of each phase of computation of an application. Assume that `bar.releasing` and `bar.count` are initially zero and `bar.lock` is initially unlocked.

```
  struct bar_struct {
    LOCKDEC(lock);
    int count, releasing;
```

```
    } bar;
    ...
    BARRIER(N)
    {
      LOCK(bar.lock);
      bar.count++;

      if (bar.count == N) {
         bar.releasing = 1;
         bar.count--;
      } else {
         UNLOCK(bar.lock);
          while (! bar.releasing)
            ;
         LOCK(bar.lock);
         bar.count--;
         if (bar.count == 0) {
         bar.releasing = 0;
         }
      }
      UNLOCK(bar.lock);
}
```

a. This code fails to provide a correct barrier. Describe the problem with this implementation.

b. Change the code as little as possible so it provides a correct barrier implementation. Either clearly indicate your changes on the code or clearly describe the changes.

5.22 Consider migratory data: shared data objects that bounce around among processors, with each processor reading and then writing them before another processor reads them. Under the standard MESI protocol, the read miss and the write both generate bus transactions.

a. Given the data in Table 5.1, estimate the maximum bandwidth that can be saved when using upgrades (BusUpgr) instead of BusRdX.

b. It is possible to enhance the state stored with cache blocks and the state transition diagram so that such read operations that are shortly followed by writes to the same block can be recognized and so that migratory blocks can be directly brought in exclusive state into the cache on the first read miss (rather than in shared state). Suggest the extra states and the state transition diagram extensions to achieve this. Using the data in Tables 5.1, 5.2, and 5.3, compute the bandwidth savings that can be achieved. Are there any benefits other than bandwidth savings? Describe program situations where the migratory protocol may hurt performance.

5.23 The Firefly update protocol eliminates the Sm state present in the Dragon protocol by suitably updating main memory on updates. Can we further reduce the states in the Dragon and/or Firefly protocols by merging the E and M states? What are the trade-offs?

5.24 It has been observed that processors sometimes write only one word in a cache block. To optimize for this case, instead of using write-back caches in all cases, a protocol has been proposed with the following characteristics: (1) on the initial write of a block, the processor writes through to the bus and places the block in the cache in a new state called the reserved state; and (2) on a write for a block that is present in the reserved state, the line transitions to the modified state, which uses write back instead of write through.

a. Draw the state transitions for this protocol, using the `INVALID`, `SHARED`, `RESERVED`, and `MODIFIED` states. Be sure that you show an arc for each of BusRd, BusWr, ProcRd, and ProcWr for each state. Indicate the action that the processor takes after a slash (e.g., BusWr/WriteBlock). Since both word- and block-sized writes are used, indicate FlushWord or FlushBlock.

b. How does this protocol differ from the four-state Illinois protocol?

c. Describe concisely why you think this protocol is not used on a system like the SGI Challenge.

5.25 Consider the case when a processor writes a block that is shared by many processors (thus invalidating their caches). If the line is subsequently reread by the other processors, each will miss on the line. Researchers have proposed a read-broadcast scheme, in which if one processor reads the line, all other processors with invalid copies of the line read it into their second-level caches as well. Do you think this is a good protocol extension? Give at least two reasons to support your choice and at least one that argues the opposite.

5.26 Classify the misses in the following reference stream from three processors into the categories shown in Figure 5.20 (follow the format in Table 5.4). Assume that each processor's cache consists of only a single four-word cache block and that words w0 through w3 fall on the same cache block, as do words w4 through w7.

Operation Number	P_1	P_2	P_3
1	st w0		st w7
2	ld w6	ld w2	
3		ld w7	
4	ld w2	ld w0	
5		st w2	
6	ld w2		
7	st w2	ld w5	ld w5
8	st w5		

Operation Number	P_1	P_2	P_3
9		ld w3	ld w7
10		ld w6	ld w2
11		ld w2	st w7
12	ld w7		
13	ld w2		
14		ld w5	
15			ld w2

5.27 You are given a bus-based shared memory machine. Assume that the processors have a cache block size of 32 bytes and *A* is an array of four-byte integers. Now consider the following simple loop:

```
for i ← 0 to 16
  for j ← 0 to 255 {
    A[j] ← do_something(A[j]);
```

a. Under what conditions would it be better to use a dynamically scheduled loop?

b. Under what conditions would it be better to use a statically scheduled loop?

c. For a dynamically scheduled inner loop, how many iterations should a processor pick each time?

5.28 You are writing an image processing program, where the image is represented as a 2D array of pixels. The basic iteration in this computation looks like

```
for i = 1 to 1024
  for j = 1 to 1024
    newA[i,j] = (A[i,j-1]+A[i-1,j]+A[i,j+1]+A[i+1,j])/4;
```

Assume `A` is a matrix of four-byte single-precision floating-point numbers stored in row-major order (i.e., `A[i,j]` and `A[i,j+1]` are at consecutive addresses in memory). `A` starts at memory location 0. You are writing this code for a 32-processor machine. Each processor has a 32-KB direct-mapped cache, and the cache block size is 64 bytes.

a. You first try assigning 32 rows of the matrix to each processor in an interleaved assignment. What is the actual ratio of computation to bus traffic that you expect (inherent or artifactual)? Assume that each loop iteration is four units of computation, ignore all other control and assignment operations, and state any other assumptions you use.

b. Next you assign 32 contiguous rows of the matrix to each processor. Answer the question in part (a).

c. Finally, you use a contiguous assignment of columns instead of rows. Answer the same question now.

d. Suppose the matrix A started at memory location 32 rather than 0. If you use the same decomposition as in part (c), do you expect this to change the actual ratio of computation to traffic generated in the machine? If yes, will it increase or decrease, and why? If not, why not?

5.29 Consider the following simplified *n*-body code using an $O(N^2)$ algorithm (i.e., computing all pairwise interactions among bodies, here molecules). Estimate the number of misses per time-step in the steady state. Restructure the code using techniques discussed in the chapter to increase spatial locality and reduce false sharing. Try to make your restructuring robust with respect to the number of processors and cache block size. Assume 16 processors and 1-MB direct-mapped caches with a 64-byte block size. Estimate the number of misses for the restructured code. State all assumptions that you make.

```
typedef struct moltype {
  double x_pos, y_pos, z_pos;     /*position components*/
  double x_vel, y_vel, z_vel;     /*velocity components*/
  double x_f, y_f, z_f;           /*force components*/
  } molecule;

#define numMols 4096
#define numProcs 16
molecule mol[numMols]

main()
{
... declarations ...
  for (time=0; time < endTime; time++)
    for (i=myPID; i < numMols; i+=numProcs)
    {
      for (j=0; j < numMols; j++)
      {
        x_f[i] += x_fn(position of mols i & j);
        y_f[i] += y_fn(position of mols i & j);
        z_f[i] += z_fn(position of mols i & j);
      }
      barrier(numProcs);
      for (i=myPID; i < numMols; i += numProcs)
      {
        write velocity and position components
        of mol[i] based on force on mol[i];
      }
      barrier(numProcs);
    }
}
```

6

Snoop-Based Multiprocessor Design

The large differences we see in the performance, cost, and scale of symmetric multiprocessors on the market rest not so much on the choice of the cache coherence protocol but rather on the design and implementation of the organizational structure that supports the logical operation of the protocol. Protocol trade-offs are well understood, and most machines use a variant of the protocols described in the last chapter. However, the latency and bandwidth that is achieved with a protocol depend on the bus design, the cache design, and the integration with memory, as does the engineering cost of the system. This chapter examines the detailed physical design issues in snoop-based cache-coherent symmetric multiprocessors.

While the abstract state transition diagrams for coherence protocols that we saw in Chapter 5 are conceptually simple, subtle issues arise at the implementation level. An implementation must contend with at least three related goals: correctness, high performance, and minimal extra hardware. The correctness issues arise mainly because actions that are considered atomic at the abstract level are not necessarily atomic at the hardware level. The performance issues arise mainly because we want to pipeline memory operations and allow many operations to be outstanding at a time (using different components of the memory hierarchy) rather than waiting for each operation to complete before starting the next one. Unfortunately, it is in exactly these situations that correctness is likely to be compromised, due to the numerous complex interactions between these events. The product shipping dates for several commercial systems, even for microprocessors that have on-chip coherence controllers, have been delayed significantly because of subtle bugs in the coherence hardware. Overall, the design of modern communication assists (controllers) for aggressive cache-coherent multiprocessors presents a set of challenges similar in complexity and form to those of modern processor design, which also allows a large number of outstanding instructions and out-of-order execution. We need to peel off another layer in the design of snoop-based multiprocessors to understand the practical requirements embodied by state transition diagrams.

This chapter begins by enumerating the key correctness requirements for a cache-coherent memory system. A base design, using single-level caches and a one-transaction-at-a-time atomic bus, is developed in Section 6.2, and the critical events in processing individual transactions are outlined. This section assumes an invalidation protocol for concreteness, but the main issues apply directly to update protocols as well. Section 6.3 expands this design to address multilevel cache hierarchies, showing how protocol events propagate up and down the hierarchy. Section 6.4 expands the base design to utilize a split-transaction bus. In such a bus, a bus transaction is split into request and response phases that arbitrate for the bus separately, so multiple transactions can be outstanding at a time on the bus and can be handled in a pipelined fashion. The section then brings together multilevel caches and split transactions. From this design point, it is a small step to support multiple outstanding misses from each processor since all transactions are already heavily pipelined and many take place concurrently. The fundamental underlying challenge throughout is maintaining the illusion of order as required by coherence and the memory consistency model. How this is done with each increasing level of design complexity is discussed in these sections.

Once we understand the key design issues in general terms, we will be ready to study concrete designs in some detail. Section 6.5 presents two case studies, the SGI Challenge and the Sun Enterprise, and illustrates their performance with microbenchmarks and our sample applications. Finally, Section 6.6 examines a number of advanced topics that extend the design techniques in functionality and scale.

6.1 CORRECTNESS REQUIREMENTS

A cache-coherent memory system must, of course, satisfy the requirements of coherence and preserve the semantics dictated by the memory consistency model. In particular, for coherence it should ensure that stale copies are found and invalidated or updated on writes, and it should provide write serialization. If sequential consistency is to be preserved, it should provide write atomicity and the ability to detect the completion of writes. In addition, the design should have the desirable properties of any protocol implementation, which means it should be free of deadlock and livelock and should either eliminate starvation or make it very unlikely. Finally, it should cope with error conditions beyond its control (e.g., parity errors) and try to recover from them where possible.

Deadlock occurs when operations are still outstanding but all system activity has ceased. The potential for deadlock arises when multiple concurrent entities incrementally obtain shared resources and hold them in a nonpreemptible fashion, generating a cycle of resource dependences. A simple analogy is in traffic at an intersection, as shown in Figure 6.1. In the traffic example, the entities are cars and the resources are lanes. Each car needs to acquire two lane resources to proceed through the intersection, but each car is holding one and won't let it go.

In computer systems, the entities are typically controllers and the resources are buffers. For example, suppose two controllers *A* and *B* communicate with each other through buffers, as shown in Figure 6.2(a). *A*'s input buffer is full, and it refuses all incoming requests until *B* accepts a request from it (thus freeing up buffer space in *A* to accept requests from other controllers). But *B*'s input buffer is full too, and it

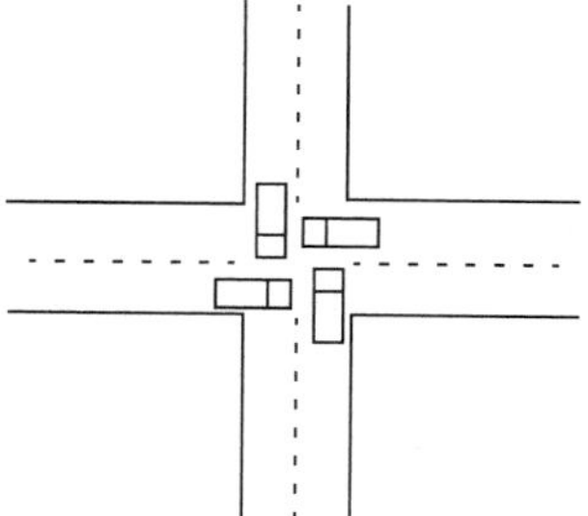

FIGURE 6.1 Deadlock at a traffic intersection. Four cars arrive at an intersection and all proceed one lane each into the intersection. They block one another since each is occupying a resource that another needs in order to make progress. Even if each decides to yield to the car on its right, the intersection is deadlocked. To break the deadlock, some cars must retreat to allow others to make progress so that they too can then make progress.

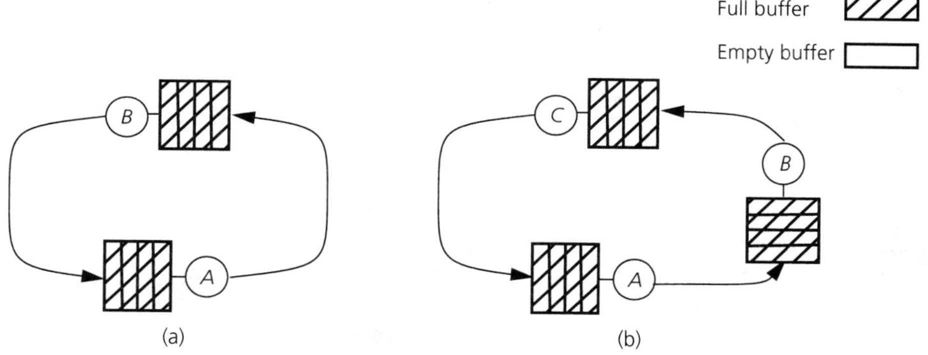

FIGURE 6.2 Deadlock in a computer system. Deadlock can easily occur in a system if independent controllers with finite buffering need to communicate with each other. If cycles are possible in the communication graph, then each controller can be stalled waiting for the one in front to free up resources. The figure illustrates cases for (a) two and (b) three controllers.

refuses all incoming requests until *A* accepts a request from it. Neither controller can accept a request, so deadlock sets in. To illustrate the problem with more than two controllers, a three-controller example is shown in Figure 6.2(b). To prevent deadlock, it is essential to either avoid such dependence cycles or break them when they occur.

A system is in *livelock* when no processor is making forward progress in its computation even though transactions are being executed in the system. Continuing the traffic analogy, each of the vehicles might elect to back up, clearing the intersection, and then try again to move forward. However, if they all repeatedly move backward and forward at the same time, there will be a lot of activity but they will end up in the same situation repeatedly with no real progress. In computer systems, livelock typically arises when independent controllers compete for a common resource, with each snatching it away from another before the other has finished with its use for the current operation.

Starvation does not stop overall progress, but is an extreme form of unfairness in which one or more processors make no progress while others continue to do so. For instance, in the traffic example, the livelock problem can be solved by a simple priority scheme. If a northbound car is given higher priority than an eastbound car, the latter must pull back and let the former through before trying to move forward again; similarly, a southbound car may have higher priority than a westbound car. Unfortunately, this does not solve starvation: in heavy traffic, an eastbound car may never pass the intersection since a new northbound car may always be ready to go through. Northbound cars make progress whereas eastbound cars are starved. A possible remedy here is to place an arbiter (e.g., a police officer or traffic light) to orchestrate the resource usage in a fair manner. The analogy extends easily to computer systems.

In general, the possibility of starvation is considered a less catastrophic problem than livelock or deadlock. Starvation does not cause the entire system to stop making progress and is usually not a permanent state. That is, just because a processor has been starved for some time in the past does not mean that it will be starved for all future time (at some point, northbound traffic will usually ease up and eastbound cars will get through). In fact, starvation is much less likely in computer systems than in this unmonitored traffic example, since it is usually timing dependent and the necessary pathological timing conditions usually do not persist. Starvation often turns out to be quite easy to eliminate in bus-based systems by having the bus arbitration be fair and using FIFO queues to access hardware resources. However, in scalable systems that we will see in later chapters, eliminating starvation completely can add substantial complexity to the protocols and can slow down common-case transactions. Many systems, therefore, do not completely eliminate starvation, though almost all try to reduce the potential for it to occur.

6.2 BASE DESIGN: SINGLE-LEVEL CACHES WITH AN ATOMIC BUS

In Chapter 5, we discussed how cache coherence protocols ensure write serialization and can satisfy the sufficient conditions for sequential consistency. We assumed that the bus was atomic, that operations from a given process were atomic with respect to one another, and that the memory operations that generate bus transactions were also atomic with respect to one another, from issue to completion even if they were from different processors. In this section, the assumptions are somewhat more physically realistic. There is still a single level of cache per processor, and transactions on the bus are atomic. The cache can stall the processor while it performs the series of steps involved in a memory operation, so operations within a process are atomic with respect to one another. However, no further assumptions are made. The section discusses the basic issues and trade-offs that arise in implementing snooping and state transitions in such a system, along with new issues that arise in providing write serialization, detecting write completion, and preserving write atomicity. Subsequent sections consider more aggressive systems, including more complex cache hierarchies and buses, as discussed earlier. In all cases, write-back caches are assumed, at least for the caches closest to the bus so they can reduce bus traffic.

Several design decisions must be made even for this simple case of single-level caches and an atomic bus. First, how should we design the cache tags and controller, given that both the processor and the snooping agent from the bus side need access to the tags? Second, the results of a snoop from the cache controllers need to be presented as part of the bus transaction; how and when should this be done? Third, even though the bus is atomic, the overall set of actions needed to satisfy a processor's memory operation uses other resources as well (such as cache controllers) and is not atomic, introducing possible race conditions. How should we design protocol state machines for the cache controllers given this lack of atomicity? What new issues arise with regard to write serialization, write completion detection, or write atomicity, as well as with regard to deadlock, livelock, and starvation? Finally, write backs from the caches can introduce interesting race conditions as well, and we must devise mechanisms to support atomic read-modify-write operations. We consider these issues one by one.

6.2.1 Cache Controller and Tag Design

Consider first a conventional uniprocessor cache. It consists of a storage array containing data blocks, tags, and state bits, as well as a comparator, a controller, and a bus interface. When the processor performs an operation against the cache, a portion of the address is used to access a cache set that potentially contains the block. The tag is compared against the remaining address bits to determine if the addressed block is indeed present. Then the appropriate operation is performed on the data and the state bits are updated. For example, a write hit to a clean cache block causes a word to be updated and the state to be set to modified. The cache controller sequences the reads and writes of the cache storage array. If the operation requires that a block be transferred from the cache to memory or vice versa, the cache controller initiates a bus operation. The bus operation requires the bus interface to perform a sequence of steps, which are typically the following: (1) assert request for bus, (2) wait for bus grant, (3) drive address and command, (4) wait for command to be accepted by the relevant device, and (5) transfer data. The sequence of actions taken by the cache controller is itself implemented as a finite state machine, as is the sequencing of steps in a bus transaction. It is important not to confuse these state machines with the state transition diagram of the protocol followed by each cache block.

To support a snooping coherence protocol, the basic uniprocessor cache controller design must be enhanced. First, since the cache controller must monitor bus operations as well as respond to processor operations, it is simplest to view the cache as having two controllers, a bus-side controller and a processor-side controller, each monitoring external events from its side. In either case, when an operation occurs the controller must access the cache tags. On every bus transaction, the bus-side controller must capture the address from the bus and use it to perform a tag check. If the check fails (a snoop miss), no action need be taken: the bus operation is irrelevant to this cache. If the snoop "hits," the controller may have to intervene in the bus transaction according to the cache coherence protocol. This may involve a read-modify-write operation on the state bits or placing a block on the bus (or both).

With only a single array of tags, it is difficult to allow the two controllers to access the array at the same time. During a bus transaction, the processor will be locked out from accessing the cache, which will degrade processor performance. If the processor is given priority, effective bus bandwidth will decrease because the snoop controller will have to delay the bus transaction until it gains access to the tags. To alleviate this problem, a coherent cache design may utilize a *dual-ported* RAM for the tags and state or it may duplicate the tag and state for every block. The data portion of the cache is not duplicated since it is not accessed so frequently. If tags are duplicated, the contents of the two sets of tags are exactly the same, except that one is used by the processor-side controller for its lookups and the other is used by the bus-side controller for its snoops (see Figure 6.3). The two controllers can read the tags and perform checks simultaneously. Of course, when the state or tag for a block is updated (e.g., when the state changes on a write or a new block is brought into the cache) both copies must ultimately be modified, so one of the controllers may have to be locked out for a time. Machine designs can play several tricks to reduce the time for which a controller is locked out, for instance, in the above case by updating the processor-side tags only when the cache data is later modified rather than immediately when the bus-side tags are updated. The frequency of tag updates is also much smaller than that of tag lookups, so bus-side tag updates are expected to have little impact on processor cache access.

Another major enhancement from a uniprocessor cache controller is that the controller now acts not only as an initiator of bus transactions but also as a responder to them. A conventional responding device, such as the controller for a memory bank, monitors the bus for transactions on the fixed subset of addresses that it contains and possibly responds to the relevant read or write operations after some number of "wait" cycles. It may even have to place data on the bus. The cache controller behaves similarly, only it is not responsible for a fixed subset of addresses but must monitor the bus and perform a tag check on every transaction to determine if the transaction is relevant. For an update-based protocol, the controller may need to snoop the new data off the bus as well. Most modern microprocessors already implement such enhanced cache controllers so that they are "multiprocessor-ready."

6.2.2 Reporting Snoop Results

Snooping introduces a new element to the bus transaction as well. In a conventional bus transaction on a uniprocessor system, one device (the initiator) places an address on the bus, all other devices monitor the address, and one device (the responder) recognizes it as being relevant. Then data is transferred between the two devices. The responder acknowledges its role by raising a wired-OR signal; if no device decides to respond within a time-out window, a bus error occurs. For snooping caches, each cache must check the address against its tags, and the collective result of the snoop from all caches must be reported on the bus before the transaction can proceed. In particular, one function of the snoop result is to inform main

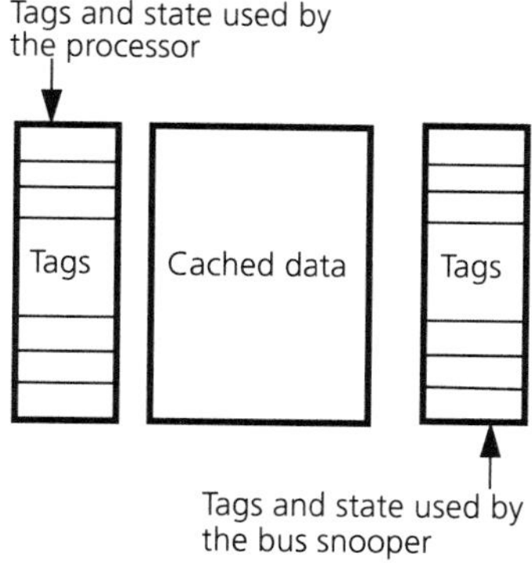

FIGURE 6.3 Organization of single-level snooping caches. For single-level caches, a duplicate set of tags and state are provided to reduce contention. One set is used exclusively by the processor while another is used by the bus snooper. Any changes to cache content or state, however, involve updating both sets of tags simultaneously.

memory whether it should respond to the request or whether some cache is holding a modified copy of the block so an alternative action is necessary. The questions are, When is the snoop result reported on the bus, and In what form?

Let us focus first on the "when" question. Obviously, it is desirable to keep the delay as small as possible so that main memory can decide quickly what to do.[1] The three major options are as follows:

1. The design could guarantee that the snoop results are available within a fixed number of clock cycles from the issue of the address on the bus. This, in general, requires the use of a dual set of tags because the processor, which usually has priority, could be accessing the tags heavily when the bus transaction appears. Even with a dual set of tags, we may need to be conservative about the fixed snoop latency because both sets of tags are made inaccessible when the processor updates the tags; for example, in the E $\rightarrow$ M state transition in the MESI protocol.[2] The advantages of this option are that the design of main memory is not affected, and the cache-to-cache handshake is very simple; the disadvantages are extra hardware and potentially longer snoop latency. The Pentium Pro quads use this approach, with the ability to extend or defer the snoop phase when necessary (see Chapter 8), as do the HP corporate business servers (Chan et al. 1993) and the Sun Enterprise.

---

1. Note that on an atomic bus there are ways to make the system less sensitive to the snoop delay. Since only one memory transaction can be outstanding at any given time, the main memory can start fetching the memory block regardless of whether it or the cache would eventually supply the data; the main memory subsystem would have to sit idle otherwise. Reducing this delay, however, is very important for a split-transaction bus, discussed later. There, multiple bus transactions can be outstanding, so the memory subsystem can be used in the meantime to service another request, for which it (and not the cache) may have to supply the data.

2. It is interesting that in the base three-state invalidation protocol we described, a cache block state is never updated unless a corresponding bus transaction is also involved. This usually gives plenty of time to update the tags.

2. The design could alternatively support a variable delay snoop. The main memory assumes that one of the caches will supply the data until all the cache controllers have snooped and have indicated otherwise. A handshake is required, but cache controllers do not have to worry about tag-access conflicts inhibiting a timely lookup, and the designer does not have to conservatively assume the worst-case delay for snoop results. The SGI Challenge multiprocessors use a slight variant of this approach, where the memory subsystem fetches the data to service the request but then stalls if the snoops have not completed by that time (Galles and Williams 1993).
3. A third alternative is for the main memory subsystem to maintain a bit per block that indicates whether this block is modified in one of the caches or not. This way, the memory subsystem does not have to rely on snooping to decide what action to take. The disadvantage here is the extra complexity added to the main memory subsystem.

In what form should snoop results be reported on the bus? For the MESI scheme, the requesting cache controller needs to know whether the requested memory block is in other processors' caches so that it can decide whether to load the block in exclusive (E) or shared (S) state. In addition, the memory system needs to know whether any cache has the block in modified state, in which case the memory need not respond. One reasonable option is to use three wired-OR signals, two for reporting these aspects of the snoop results and one indicating that the snoop result is valid. The first signal is asserted when any of the processors' caches (excluding the requesting processor) has a copy of the block. The second is asserted if any cache has the block in modified state in its cache. We don't need to know the identity of that cache since it knows what action to take itself. The third signal is an inhibit signal, asserted until all caches have completed their snoop; when it is deasserted, the requestor and memory can safely examine the other two signals. The full Illinois version of the MESI protocol is more complex because a block can be preferentially retrieved from another cache rather than from memory even if it is in shared state. If multiple caches have a copy, a priority mechanism is needed to decide which cache will supply the data. This is one reason why most commercial machines that use the MESI protocol limit cache-to-cache transfers. The Silicon Graphics Challenge and the Sun Enterprise use cache-to-cache transfers only for data that is in modified state in a cache, in which case there is a single supplier. The Challenge updates memory in the process of a cache-to-cache transfer, whereas the Enterprise does not update memory and uses the fifth, owned state of the MOESI protocol, as discussed in Chapter 5.

6.2.3 Dealing with Write Backs

Write backs complicate implementation since they involve an incoming block as well as an outgoing (modified) block that is being replaced, and hence two bus transactions. In general, to allow the processor to continue as soon as possible on a cache miss that causes a write back, we would like to delay the write back and instead first service the miss that caused it. This optimization imposes two requirements. First, it requires the machine to provide additional storage, a *write-back buffer*, where the block being replaced can be temporarily stored while the new block is brought into the cache and before the bus can be reacquired for a second transaction to complete the write back. Second, before the write back is completed, it is possible that we will see a bus transaction containing the address of the block being written back. In that case, the controller must supply the data from the write-back buffer and cancel its earlier pending request to the bus for a write back. This requires that an address comparator be added to snoop on the write-back buffer as well. We see in Chapter 8 that write backs introduce further correctness subtleties in machines with physically distributed memory.

6.2.4 Base Organization

Figure 6.4 shows a block diagram for our resulting base snooping architecture. Each processor has a single-level write-back cache. The cache is dual tagged so the bus-side controller and the processor-side controller can do tag checks in parallel. The processor-side controller initiates a transaction by placing an address and command on the bus. On a write-back transaction, data is conveyed from the write-back buffer. On a read transaction, it is captured in the data buffer. The bus-side controller snoops the write-back tag as well as the cache tags. Bus arbitration places the requests that go on the bus in a total order. For each transaction, the command and address in the request phase drive the snoop lookups in this total order. The wired-OR snoop results serve as acknowledgment to the initiator that all caches have seen the request and taken relevant action.

Using this simple design, let us examine more subtle correctness concerns that either require the state machines and protocols to be extended or require care in implementation. These include nonatomic state transitions, serialization for coherence and consistency, deadlock, livelock, and starvation.

6.2.5 Nonatomic State Transitions

In the state transition diagrams in Chapter 5, the state transitions and their associated actions were assumed to happen instantaneously or at least atomically. In fact, a request issued by a processor takes some time to complete, often including a bus transaction. While the bus transaction itself is atomic in our simple system, it is only one among the set of actions needed to satisfy a processor's request. These actions include looking up the cache tags, arbitrating for the bus, actions taken by other controllers at their caches, and the action taken by the issuing processor's controller at the end of the bus transaction (which may include actually writing data into the block). Taken as a whole, the set is not atomic. Even with an atomic bus, multiple requests from different processors may be outstanding in different parts of the system at a time, and it is possible that while a processor (or controller) P has a request outstanding—for example, waiting to obtain bus access—a request from another processor may appear on the bus and need some service from P, perhaps even for the

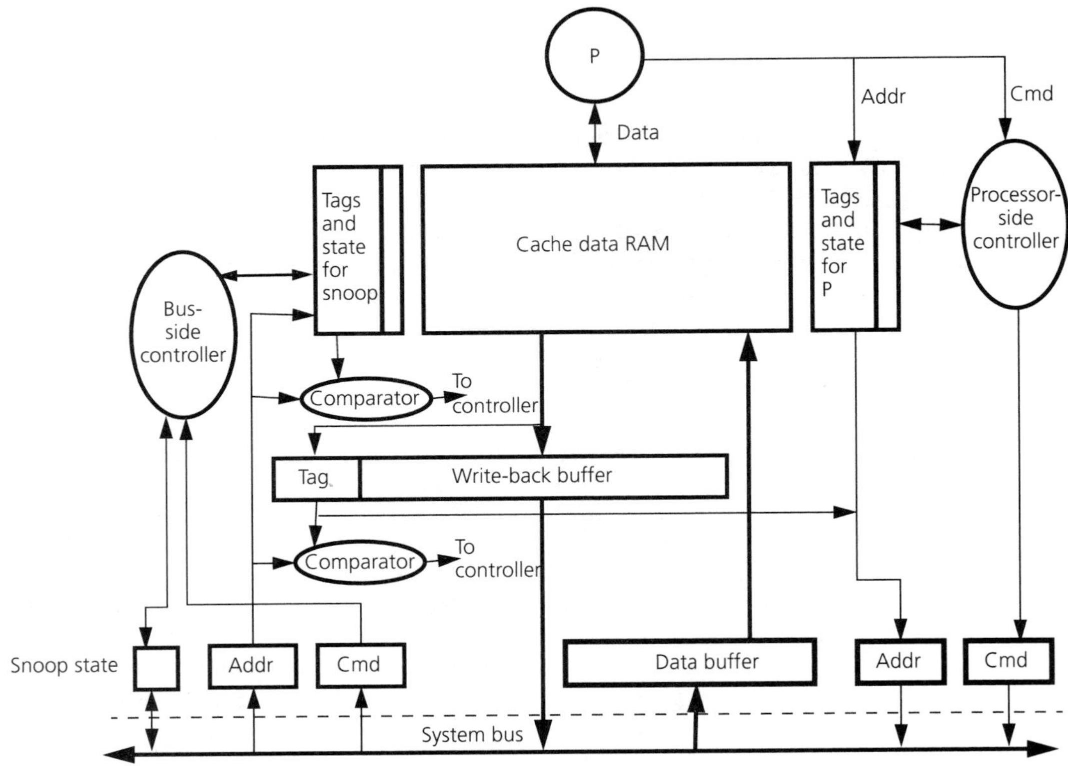

FIGURE 6.4 Design of a snooping cache for the base machine. We assume that each processor has a single-level write-back cache, an invalidation protocol is used, the processor can have only one memory request outstanding, and the system bus is atomic. To keep the figure simple, we do not show the bus arbitration logic and some of the low-level signals and buffers that are needed. We also do not show the coordination signals needed between the bus-side controller and the processor-side controller.

same memory block as P's outstanding request. The types of complications that arise are illustrated in Example 6.1.

EXAMPLE 6.1 Suppose two processors P_1 and P_2 cache the same memory block *A* in shared state, and both simultaneously issue a write to block *A*. Show how P_1 may have a request outstanding waiting for the bus while a transaction from P_2 appears on the bus and how you might solve the complication that results.

Answer Here is a possible scenario. P_1's write will check its cache, determine that it needs to promote the block's state from shared to modified before it can actually write new data into the block, and issue an upgrade bus request. In the meantime, P_2 has also issued a similar upgrade or read-exclusive transaction for *A*, and it may have won arbitration for the bus first. P_1's controller will see the bus transaction and must downgrade the state of block *A* from shared to invalid in its cache. Otherwise, when P_2's transaction is over, *A* will be in modified state in P_2's cache and in shared state in P_1's cache, which violates the protocol. But now the upgrade bus request that has P_1 outstanding is no longer appropriate and must be replaced with a read-exclusive request. Thus, a controller must also be able to check addresses snooped from the bus against its own outstanding request and modify the latter if necessary. (If there were no upgrade transactions in the protocol and read exclusives were used even on writes to blocks in shared state, the request would not have to be changed in this case even though the block state would have to be changed. These implementation requirements should therefore be considered when assessing the complexity of protocol optimizations.) ■

A convenient way to deal with the "nonatomic" nature of state transitions, and the consequent need to sometimes revise requests and actions based on observed events, is to expand the protocol state diagram with intermediate or *transient* states (the original protocol states that we have been discussing so far, such as MESI, will be referred to as *stable* states). For example, a separate state can be used to indicate that an upgrade request is outstanding. Figure 6.5 shows an expanded state diagram for a MESI protocol. In response to a processor write operation, for example, the cache controller begins arbitration for the bus by asserting a request for the bus (BusReq) and transitions to the intermediate S → M state. The transition out of this state occurs when the bus arbiter asserts a BusGrant signal for this device. At this point, the BusUpgr transaction is placed on the bus and the cache block state is updated. However, if a BusRdX or BusUpgr is observed on the bus for this block while in the S → M state, the controller treats its block as having been invalidated before this transaction and transitions to the I → M state. (We could instead retract the bus request and transition to the I state, whereupon the still pending PrWr would be handled again.) On a processor read from invalid state, the controller advances to an intermediate state (I → S, E); the next stable state to transition to is determined by the value of the shared line when the read is granted the bus. These intermediate states are not typically encoded in the cache block state bits, which are still the stable MESI states, since it would be wasteful to expend bits in every cache slot to indicate the one block in the cache that may be in a transient state. They are reflected in the combination of state bits and controller state. However, when we consider caches that allow multiple outstanding transactions, it will be necessary to have an explicit representation for the (multiple) blocks from a cache that may be in a transient state.

Expanding the number of states in the protocol increases the difficulty of proving that an implementation is correct or of testing the design. Thus, designers seek mechanisms that avoid transient states. The Sun Enterprise, for example, does not use a BusUpgr transaction in the MESI protocol but uses the result of the snoop to eliminate unnecessary data transfers in the BusRdX. Recall that on a BusRdX the caches holding the block invalidate their copy. If a cache has the block in the modified state, it raises the dirty line, thereby preventing the memory from supplying the data, and flushes the data onto the bus. No use is made of the shared line. The trick is to have the processor that issues the BusRdX snoop its own tags when the transaction actually goes on the bus. If the block is still in its cache in a valid state, it raises the shared line, which inhibits main memory. Since it already has the valid block, no cache can have it in modified state, and the data phase of the transaction is ignored.

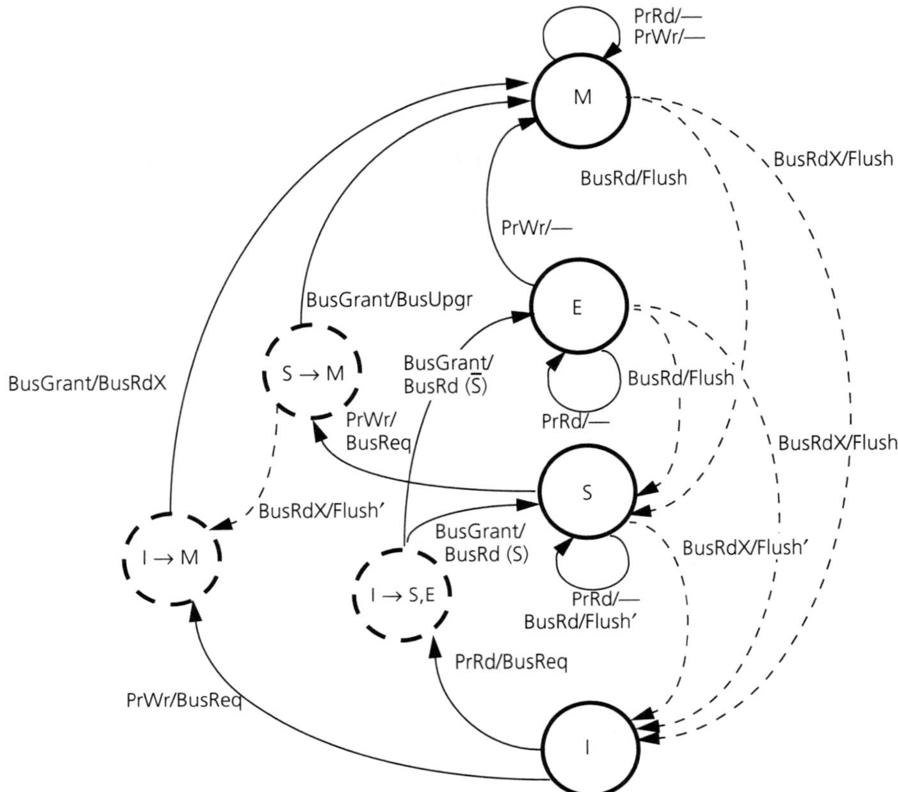

FIGURE 6.5 Expanded MESI protocol state diagram indicating transient states for bus acquisition. The cache controller monitors the bus while arbitration is ongoing for its request. A conflicting transaction may change the transition between stable states.

The cache controller does not need a transient state because, regardless of what happens, it has one action to take—place a BusRdX transaction on the bus.

6.2.6 Serialization

With the nonatomicity of memory operations issued by different processors, care must be taken in the processor-cache handshake to preserve the order determined by the serialization of bus transactions. For a read, the processor needs the result of the operation. To gain greater performance on writes, it is tempting to update the cache block and allow the processor to continue with useful instructions while the cache controller acquires exclusive ownership of the block—and possibly loads the rest of the block—via a bus transaction. The problem is that a window is open between the time the processor gives the write to the cache and the time the cache controller acquires the bus for the read-exclusive (or upgrade) transaction. As we have seen, other bus transactions (including writes) may occur in this window, which may change the state of this or other blocks in the cache. This can complicate write serialization for coherence (if the transactions are to the same block) as well as SC (if they are to other blocks). To provide write serialization or SC, these transactions must appear to the processor as occurring before the write since that is how they are serialized by the bus and appear to other processors. Conservatively, the cache controller should not allow the processor issuing the write to consider the write complete and to complete other operations past it in program order until the read-exclusive transaction occurs on the bus and makes the write visible to other processors.

In fact, the cache does not have to wait until the read-exclusive transaction is finished—that is, until other copies have actually been invalidated in their caches—before allowing the processor to continue; it can service read and write hits once the transaction is on the bus, as long as access to the block in transit is handled properly. The crux of the argument for coherence and for sequential consistency presented in Section 5.3 was that all cache controllers observe the exclusive ownership transactions (BusRdX or BusUpgr) generated by write operations in the same order and that the data is written in the cache immediately after the exclusive ownership transaction. Once the bus transaction starts, in our base design the writer knows that all other caches will invalidate their copies before another bus transaction occurs. The write is *committed*, that is, the position of the write in the serial bus order is completely determined, regardless of further actions. The writer never knows exactly where the invalidation is inserted in the local program order of the other processors; it knows only that it is before whatever operation generates the next bus transaction and that all processors insert the invalidations in the same order. Similarly, the writer's subsequent local sequence of cache hits only becomes visible at the next bus transaction. This is all that is important to maintain the necessary orderings for coherence and SC, and it allows the writer to substitute commitment for actual completion in following the sufficient conditions for SC. In fact, this basic observation is what makes it possible to implement cache coherence and sequential consistency with pipelined buses, multilevel memory hierarchies, and multiple outstanding operations per processor. Write atomicity follows the same argument as presented before in Section 5.3.

This discussion of serialization raises an important but somewhat subtle point. Write serialization and write atomicity have very little to do with when the transactions that write data back to memory occur or with when the actual location in memory is updated. Either a write or a read can cause a write back if it causes a dirty block to be replaced. The write backs are bus transactions, but they do not need to be ordered. On the other hand, a write does not necessarily cause the new value to appear on the bus, even if it misses; it causes a read exclusive. What is important to the program is when the new value is bound to the address. The write completes, in the sense that any subsequent read will return the new or later value once the BusRdX or BusUpgr transaction takes place. By invalidating the old cache blocks, it ensures that all reads that returned the old value precede the transaction. The controller issuing the transaction ensures that the new value is written in the cache after the bus transaction and that no other memory operations intervene.

6.2.7 Deadlock

A two-phase protocol, such as the request-response protocol of a memory operation, presents a form of protocol-level deadlock, sometimes called *fetch deadlock* (Leiserson et al. 1996), that is not simply a question of buffer usage. While an entity is attempting to issue its request, it needs to service incoming transactions. In an SMP with an atomic bus, this situation arises when the cache controller is awaiting the bus grant: it needs to continue performing snoops and handling requests, which may require it to flush blocks onto the bus. Otherwise, the system may deadlock if each of two controllers has an outstanding transaction that the other needs to respond to, and both are refusing to handle requests. For example, suppose a BusRd for a block *B* appears on the bus while a processor P_1 has a read-exclusive request outstanding to another block *A* and is waiting for the bus. If P_1 has a modified copy of *B*, its controller should be able to supply the data to the current bus transaction (which does not require bus arbitration with an atomic bus) and change the state from modified to shared while it is waiting to acquire the bus. Otherwise, the current bus transaction is waiting for P_1's controller while P_1's controller is waiting for the bus transaction to release the bus.

6.2.8 Livelock and Starvation

The classic potential livelock problem in an invalidation-based cache-coherent memory system is caused by all processors attempting to write to the same memory location at about the same time. Suppose that, initially, no processor has a copy of the location in its cache. A processor's write requires the following nonatomic set of events: its cache obtains exclusive ownership for the corresponding memory block (i.e., it invalidates other copies and obtains the block in modified state); a state machine in the processor realizes that the block is now present in the cache in the appropriate state; and the state machine reattempts the write. Unless the processor-cache handshake is designed carefully, it is possible that the block is brought into the cache in modified state, but before the processor is able to complete its write, the block is invalidated by a BusRdX request from another processor. The processor's write attempt misses again, and the cycle can repeat indefinitely. To avoid livelock, a write that has obtained exclusive ownership must be allowed to complete before the exclusive ownership is taken away.

With multiple processors competing for a bus, it is possible that some processors may be granted the bus repeatedly while others may not and may become starved. Starvation can be avoided by using first-come-first-served service policies at the bus arbiter and elsewhere. These usually require additional buffering, however, so sometimes heuristic techniques are used to reduce the likelihood of starvation. For example, a count can be maintained of the number of times that a request has been denied and, after a certain threshold, action is taken so that no other new request is serviced until this request is serviced, or the request's priority may be increased.

6.2.9 Implementing Atomic Operations

The last implementation aspect that we should understand for the base architecture before moving on to more realistic architectures is the implementation of atomic read-modify-write instructions, such as test&set and fetch&op, and the LL-SC primitives that can synthesize atomic operations (see Section 5.5).

Consider a simple test&set instruction. It has a read component (the test) and a write component (the set). The first question is whether the test&set (lock) variable should be cacheable so the test&set can be performed in the processor cache or uncacheable so the atomic operation is performed at main memory. The discussion of synchronization in Section 5.5 assumed cacheable lock variables. This has the advantage of allowing locality to be exploited and, hence, reducing latency and traffic when the lock is repeatedly acquired by the same processor: the lock variable remains in modified state in the cache and no invalidations or misses are generated. It also allows processors to spin in their caches, thus reducing useless bus traffic when the lock is not ready. However, performing the operations at memory can cause faster transfer of a lock from one processor to another. With cacheable locks, the processor that is busy-waiting will first be invalidated, at which point it will try to access the lock from the other processor's cache or from main memory. With uncached locks, the release goes only to memory (no invalidations are needed), and by the time it gets there the next busy-waiting read by the waiting processor is likely to be on its way to memory already, so it will obtain the lock from memory with low latency. Overall, traffic and locality considerations tend to dominate, and lock variables are usually cacheable so that processors can busy-wait without loading the bus.

A conceptually natural way to implement a cacheable test&set that is not satisfied in the cache itself is with two bus transactions: a read transaction for the test component and a write transaction for the set component. One strategy to keep this sequence atomic is to lock down the bus at the read transaction until the write completes, keeping other processors from putting accesses (especially to that variable) on the bus between the read and write components. While this can be done quite easily with an atomic bus, it is much more difficult with a split-transaction bus: not only does locking down the bus impact performance substantially but it can raise deadlock complications if one of the transactions cannot immediately be satisfied without giving up the bus.

Fortunately, better approaches are available. Consider an invalidation-based protocol with write-back caches. What a processor really needs to do is obtain exclusive ownership of the cache block (e.g., by issuing a single read-exclusive bus transaction), and then it can perform the read component and the write component in the cache as long as it does not give up exclusive ownership of the block in between; that is, even on a nonatomic bus, incoming accesses from the bus to that block would be buffered and hence delayed until the data is written in the cache. More complex atomic operations, such as fetch&op, must retain exclusive ownership until the operation is completed.

An atomic instruction that is more complex to implement is compare&swap. It requires specifying three operands in a memory instruction: the memory location, the register to compare with, and the value/register to be swapped with the memory location. RISC instruction sets are usually not equipped for this.

Implementing LL-SC requires a little special support. A typical implementation uses a hardware lock flag and a lock address register at each processor. An LL operation reads the block but also sets the lock flag and puts the address of the block in the lock address register. Incoming invalidation (or update) requests from the bus are matched against the lock address register, and a successful match (called a conflicting write) resets the lock flag. A store-conditional checks the lock flag as the indicator for whether an intervening conflicting write has occurred; if the flag has been reset, it fails, and if not, it succeeds. The lock flag is also reset (and the store-conditional will fail) if the lock variable is replaced from the cache, since then the processor may no longer see invalidations or updates to that variable. Finally, the lock flag is reset at context switches since a context switch between an LL and its store-conditional may incorrectly cause the LL of the old process to lead to the success of a store-conditional in the new process that is switched in.

Some subtle issues arise in avoiding livelock when implementing LL-SC. First, we should in fact not allow replacement of the cache block that holds the lock variable to occur between the LL and the store-conditional. Replacement would clear the lock flag and could establish a situation in which a processor keeps trying the store-conditional but never succeeds because of continual replacement of the block between repeated LL and store-conditional operations. To disallow replacements due to conflicts with instruction fetches, we can use split instruction and data caches or set-associative unified caches. For conflicts with other data references, a common solution is to simply disallow memory-referencing instructions between an LL and a store-conditional. Techniques to hide latency (e.g., out-of-order issue) can complicate matters since memory operations that are not between the LL and the store-conditional in the program code may be between LL and store-conditional in the execution. A simple solution to this problem is not to allow reorderings of memory operations across LL or store-conditional operations.

The second potential livelock situation would occur if two processes continually failed on their store-conditionals and each process's failing store-conditional invalidated or updated the other process's block, thus clearing the lock flag. Neither of the two processes would ever succeed if this pathological situation persisted. This is why it is important that a store-conditional not be treated as an ordinary write and that it not issue invalidations or updates when it fails.

Compared to implementing an atomic read-modify-write instruction, LL-SC can have a performance disadvantage since both the LL and the store-conditional can miss in the cache even when they are successful, if the LL loads the block in shared state, leading to two misses instead of one. For better performance, it may be desirable to obtain (or prefetch) the block in exclusive or modified state at the LL so that the store-conditional does not miss unless it fails. However, this reintroduces the second livelock situation: other copies are invalidated to obtain exclusive ownership, so their store-conditionals may fail without guarantee of this processor's store-conditional succeeding. If this optimization is employed, some form of backoff should be used between failed operations to minimize (though not completely eliminate) the probability of livelock.

6.3 MULTILEVEL CACHE HIERARCHIES

The simple design presented in the preceding section was illustrative, but it made two simplifying assumptions that are not valid on most modern systems: single-level caches and an atomic bus. This section relaxes the first assumption and examines the resulting design issues.

The trend in microprocessor design since the early 1990s has been to have an on-chip first-level cache and a much larger second-level cache, either on chip or off chip.[3] Many systems use on-chip secondary caches as well and an off-chip tertiary cache. Multilevel cache hierarchies would seem to complicate coherence since changes made by the processor to the first-level cache may not be visible to the lower-level cache controller responsible for bus operations, and bus transactions are not directly visible to the first-level cache. However, the basic mechanisms for cache coherence extend naturally to multilevel cache hierarchies. Let us consider a two-level hierarchy, as shown in Figure 6.6, for concreteness; the extension to the multi-level case is straightforward.

One obvious way to handle multilevel caches is to have independent bus snooping hardware for each level of the cache hierarchy. This is unattractive for several reasons. First, the L_1 cache is usually on the processor chip, and an on-chip snooper will consume precious pins to monitor the addresses on the shared bus. Second, duplicating the tags to allow concurrent access by the snooper and the processor may consume too much precious on-chip real estate. Third, duplication of effort occurs between the L_2 and L_1 snoops since, most of the time, blocks present in the L_1 cache are also present in the L_2 cache; therefore, the snoop of the L_1 cache is unnecessary.

The solution used in practice is based on this last observation. When using multi-level caches, designers ensure that they preserve the *inclusion property,* which requires the following:

1. If a memory block is in the L_1 cache, then it must also be present in the L_2cache. In other words, the contents of the L_1 cache must be a subset of the contents of the L_2 cache.
2. If the block is in an owned state (e.g., modified in MESI or MOESI, shared-modified in Dragon or owned in MOESI) in the L_1 cache, then it must also be marked modified in the L_2 cache.

3. The HP PA-RISC microprocessors are a notable exception, maintaining a large off-chip first-level cache for many years after other vendors went to small on-chip first-level caches.

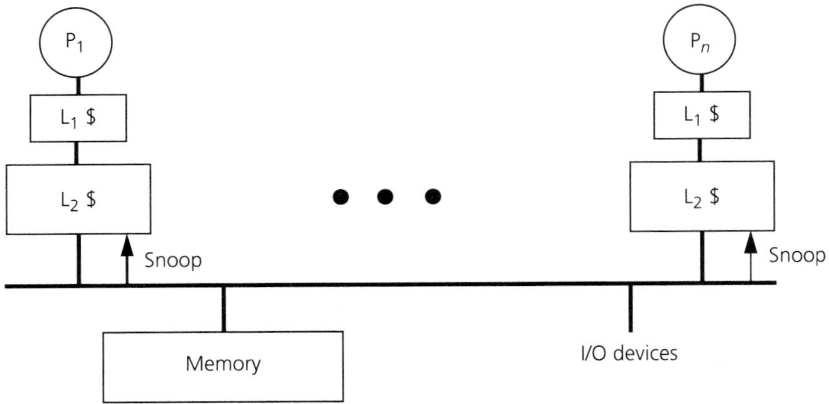

FIGURE 6.6 A bus-based machine containing processors with two-level caches

The first requirement ensures that all bus transactions that are relevant to the L_1 cache are also relevant to the L_2 cache, so having the L_2 cache controller snoop the bus is sufficient. The second ensures that if a bus transaction requests a block that is in modified state in the L_1 or L_2 cache, then the L_2 snoop can determine this fact on its own.

6.3.1 Maintaining Inclusion

The requirements for inclusion are not trivial to maintain. Three aspects need to be considered. First, processor references to the L_1 cache cause it to change state and perform replacements; these need to be handled in a manner that maintains inclusion. Second, bus transactions cause the L_2 cache to change state and flush blocks; these need to be forwarded to the first level. Finally, the modified state must be propagated out to the L_2 cache.

At first glance, it might appear that inclusion would be satisfied automatically since all L_1 cache misses go to the L_2 cache. The problem, however, is that two caches may choose different blocks or data to replace on a miss. Inclusion falls out automatically only for certain combinations of cache configuration. It is an interesting exercise to see what conditions in typical cache hierarchies can cause inclusion to be violated if no special care is taken (Baer and Wang 1988). Let us consider this before we look at how inclusion is typically maintained. For notational purposes, assume that the L_1 cache has associativity a_1, number of sets n_1, block size b_1, and thus a total capacity of $S_1 = a_1 \times b_1 \times n_1$. The corresponding parameters for the L_2 cache are a_2, n_2, b_2, and S_2. We also assume that all parameter values are powers of two.

- *Set-associative L_1 caches with history-based replacement.* The problem with replacement policies based on the history of accesses to a block, such as least recently used (LRU) replacement, is that the L_1 cache sees a different history of accesses than L_2 and other caches, since all processor references look up the L_1 cache but not all get to lower-level caches. Suppose the L_1 cache is two-way set associative with LRU replacement, both L_1 and L_2 caches have the same block size ($b_1 = b_2$), and L_2 is k times larger than L_1 ($n_2 = k \times n_1$). It is easy to show that inclusion does not hold in this simple case. Consider three distinct memory blocks m_1, m_2, and m_3 that map to the same set in the L_1 cache. Assume that m_1 and m_2 are currently in the two available slots within that set in the L_1 cache and are present in the L_2 cache as well. Now consider what happens when the processor references m_3, which happens to collide with and replace one of m_1 and m_2 in the L_2 cache as well. Since the L_2 cache is oblivious to the L_1 cache's access history, which determines whether the latter replaces m_1 or m_2, it is easy to see that the L_2 cache may replace one of m_1 and m_2 while the L_1 cache may replace the other. This is true if the L_2 cache is direct mapped or even if it is two-way set associative and m_1 and m_2 fall into the same set in it as well. In fact, we can generalize this example to see that inclusion can be violated if L_1 is not direct mapped and uses an LRU replacement policy, regardless of the associativity, block size, or cache size of the L_2 cache.

- *Multiple caches at a level.* A similar problem with replacements is observed when the first-level caches are split between instructions and data, even if they are direct mapped and are backed up by a unified second-level cache. Suppose first that the L_2 cache is direct mapped as well. An instruction block m_1 and a data block m_2 that conflict in the L_2 cache do not conflict in the L_1 caches since they go into different caches. If m_2 resides in the L_2 cache and m_1 is referenced, m_2 will be replaced from the L_2 cache but not from the L_1 data cache, violating inclusion. This can be generalized to show that if multiple independent caches are backed up by even a highly associative unified cache below them, inclusion is not guaranteed (see Exercise 6.7[b]).
- *Different cache block sizes.* Finally, caches with different block sizes can violate inclusion. Consider a miniature system with direct-mapped, unified L_1 and L_2 caches ($a_1 = a_2 = 1$), with block sizes 1 word and 2 words, respectively ($b_1 = 1$, $b_2 = 2$), and number of sets 4 and 8, respectively ($n_1 = 4$, $n_2 = 8$). Thus, the size of L_1 is 4 words, and word locations 0, 4, 8, . . . map to set 0, locations 1, 5, 9, . . . map to set 1, and so on. The size of L_2 is 16 words, and word locations 0&1, 16&17, 32&33, . . . map to set 0, locations 2&3, 18&19, 34&35, . . . map to set 1, and so on. It is now easy to see that while the L_1 cache can contain the words at both word locations 0 and 17 at the same time (they map to sets 0 and 1, respectively), the L_2 cache cannot because the words map to the same set (set 0) and they are not consecutive words (so a block size of 2 words does not help). Inclusion can be shown to be violated even if the L_2 cache is much larger or has greater associativity as long as the block size is different, and we have already seen the problems when the L_1 cache has greater associativity.

Fortunately, in one of the most commonly encountered cases, inclusion is maintained automatically. This is the situation in which the L_1 cache is direct mapped

($a_1 = 1$), L_2 can be direct mapped or set associative ($a_2 \geq 1$) with any replacement policy (e.g., LRU, FIFO, random) as long as the new block brought in is put in both L_1 and L_2 caches, the block size is the same ($b_1 = b_2$), and the number of sets in the L_1 cache is equal to or smaller than in the L_2 cache ($n_1 \leq n_2$). Using such a configuration is one popular way to get around the inclusion problem.

However, many of the cache configurations used in practice do not automatically maintain inclusion on replacements. Instead, inclusion is maintained explicitly by extending the mechanisms used for propagating coherence events in the cache hierarchy. Whenever a block in the L_2 cache is replaced, the address of that block is sent to the L_1 cache, asking it to invalidate or flush (if dirty) the corresponding blocks (there can be multiple blocks if $b_2 > b_1$).

Enhancements are also needed to handle bus transactions and processor writes. Consider bus transactions seen by the L_2 cache. Some, but not all, of the bus transactions relevant to the L_2 cache are also relevant to the L_1 cache and must be propagated to it. For example, if a block is invalidated in the L_2 cache due to an observed bus transaction (e.g., BusRdX), the invalidation must also be propagated to the L_1 cache if the data is present in it. There are several ways to do this. One is to inform the L_1 cache of all transactions that were relevant to the L_2 cache and let it ignore the ones whose addresses do not match any of its tags. This sends a large number of unnecessary interventions to the L_1 cache and can hurt performance by making cache tags unavailable for processor accesses. A more attractive solution is for the L_2 cache to keep extra state (inclusion bits) with cache blocks, which record whether the block is also present in the L_1 cache. It can then suitably filter interventions to the L_1 cache at the cost of a little extra hardware and complexity.

Finally, on an L_1 write hit, the modification needs to be communicated to the L_2 cache so it can supply the most recent data to the bus if necessary. One solution is to make the L_1 cache write through. This has the additional advantage that single-cycle writes are simple to implement (Hennessy and Patterson 1996). However, writes can consume a substantial fraction of the L_2 cache bandwidth, and a write buffer is needed between the L_1 and L_2 caches to avoid processor stalls. The requirement can also be satisfied with write-back L_1 caches since it is not necessary that the data in the L_2 cache be up-to-date but only that the L_2 cache knows when the L_1 cache has more recent data. Thus, the state information for L_2 cache blocks is augmented so that blocks can be marked "modified-but-stale." The block in the L_2 caches behaves as a modified block for the coherence protocol, but data is fetched from the L_1 cache when it needs to be flushed to the bus. (One simple approach for the modified-but-stale state is to set both the modified and invalid bits.) Both the write-through and write-back L_1 cache solutions have been used in many bus-based multiprocessors. More information on maintaining cache inclusion can be found in (Baer and Wang 1988).

6.3.2 Propagating Transactions for Coherence in the Hierarchy

Given that we have inclusion and we propagate invalidations and flush requests up to the L_1 cache as necessary, let us see how transactions percolate up and down within a processor's cache hierarchy. The intrahierarchy protocol handles processor requests by percolating them downward (away from the processor) until either they encounter a cache that has the requested block in the proper state or they reach the bus. Responses to these processor requests are sent up the cache hierarchy, updating each cache as they progress toward the processor. Read responses are loaded into each cache in the hierarchy in the shared or exclusive state whereas read-exclusive responses are loaded into all levels, except the innermost (L_1), in the modified-but-stale state. In the innermost cache, read-exclusive data is loaded in the modified state, as after the new data is written this will be the most up-to-date copy.

Requests from the bus percolate upward from the external interface (the bus), modifying the state of the cache blocks as they progress. Requests that require a block to be flushed back to the bus can be divided into flush requests that cause the block to be invalidated as well and copy-back requests that don't require invalidation. These requests percolate upward until they encounter the modified copy, at which point a response is generated for the external interface. For simple invalidations, it is not necessary for the bus transaction to be held up until all the copies are actually invalidated. The lowest-level cache controller (closest to the bus) sees the transaction when it appears on the bus, and this serves as a point of commitment to the requestor that the invalidation will be performed in the appropriate order. The response to the invalidation may be sent to the requesting processor from its own bus interface as soon as the invalidation request is placed on the bus, so no responses are generated within the destination cache hierarchies. All that is required is that certain orders be maintained between the incoming invalidations and other transactions flowing through the cache hierarchy, which we shall discuss further in the context of split-transaction buses that allow many transactions to be outstanding at a time.

Interestingly, dual tags are less critical when we have multilevel caches. The L_2 cache acts as a filter for the L_1 cache, screening out irrelevant transactions from the bus, so the tags of the L_1 cache are available almost wholly to the processor. Similarly, since the L_1 cache acts as a filter for the L_2 cache from the processor side (hopefully satisfying most of the processor's requests), the L_2 tags are almost wholly available for the bus snooper's queries (see Figure 6.7). Nonetheless, many machines retain dual tags even in multilevel cache designs.

With only one outstanding transaction on the bus at a time, the major correctness issues do not change much by using a multilevel hierarchy as long as inclusion is maintained. The necessary transactions are propagated up and down the hierarchy, and bus transactions may be held up until the necessary propagation occurs. Of course, the performance penalty for holding up the bus until a response is obtained is more onerous, so we are motivated to try to decouple these operations. Before going further down this path, let us remove the second simplifying assumption, that of an atomic bus, and examine a more aggressive, split-transaction bus. We first return to assuming a single-level processor cache for simplicity and then incorporate multilevel cache hierarchies.

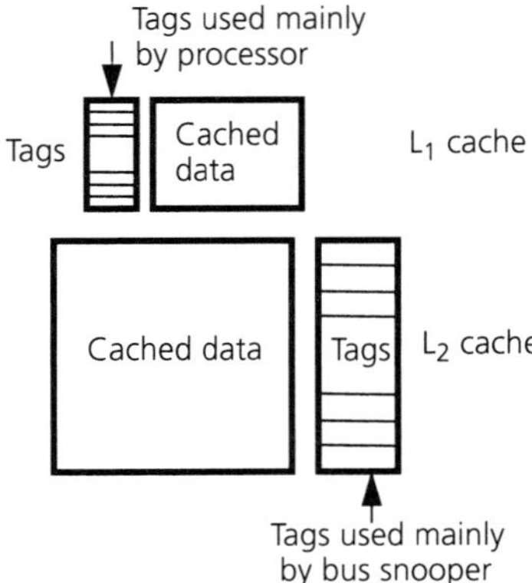

FIGURE 6.7 Organization of two-level snoopy caches. Only a single set of tags is needed for each cache.

6.4 SPLIT-TRANSACTION BUS

An atomic bus limits the achievable bus bandwidth substantially, since the bus wires are idle from the time when the address is taken off the bus until the memory system or another cache supplies the data or response. In a split-transaction bus, transactions that require a response are split into two independent subtransactions—a *request* transaction and a *response* transaction. Other transactions (or subtransactions) are allowed to intervene between them so that the bus can be used while the response to the original request is being generated. Buffering is used between the bus and the cache controllers to allow multiple transactions to be outstanding on the bus waiting for snoop and/or data responses from the controllers. The advantage, of course, is that by pipelining bus operations the bus is utilized more effectively, and hence more processors can share the same bus. The disadvantage is increased complexity.

As examples of request-response pairs, a BusRd transaction is now a request that needs a data response. A BusUpgr does not need a data response, but it does require an acknowledgment indicating that it has committed and hence been serialized. To ensure this acknowledgment does not appear on the bus as a separate transaction, it is usually sent down toward the requesting processor by its own bus controller when it is granted the bus for the BusUpgr request. A BusRdX needs a data response and an acknowledgment of commitment; typically, these are combined as part of the data response. Finally, a write back usually does not have a response.

The major new issues raised by split-transaction buses are as follows:

1. A new request can appear on the bus before the snoop and/or servicing of an earlier request are complete. In particular, *conflicting* requests (two requests to the same memory block, at least one of which is due to a write operation) may be outstanding on the bus at the same time, a case that must be handled very

carefully. Note that this is different from the earlier case of nonatomicity of overall actions despite using an atomic bus. There, a conflicting request could be observed by a cache controller before its request even obtained the bus, so the request could be suitably modified before being placed on the bus. Here, both request subtransactions have already appeared on the bus. Example 6.2 illustrates the difference.

2. The number of buffers for incoming requests and potential data responses from bus to cache controller is usually fixed and small, so we must either avoid or handle buffers filling up. This is called *flow control* since it affects the flow of transactions through the system.
3. Since requests from the bus are buffered, we need to revisit the issue of when and how snoop responses and data responses are produced on the bus. For example, are they generated in order with respect to the requests appearing on the bus or not, and are the snoop and the data part of the same response transaction?

EXAMPLE 6.2 Consider the previous example of two processors P_1 and P_2 having the block cached in shared state and deciding to write it at the same time (Example 6.1). Show how a split-transaction bus may introduce complications that would not arise with an atomic bus.

Answer With a split-transaction bus, P_1 and P_2 may generate BusUpgr requests that are granted the bus on successive cycles. For example, P_2 may get the bus before it has been able to look up the cache for P_1's request and detect it to be conflicting. If they both assume that they have acquired exclusive ownership, the protocol breaks down because both P_1 and P_2 now think they have the block in modified state. On an atomic bus, this would never happen because the first BusUpgr transaction would complete—snoops, responses, and all—before the second one got on the bus, and the latter would have been forced to change its request from BusUpgr to BusRdX. (Note that even the breakdown on the atomic bus discussed in Example 6.1 resulted in only one processor having the block in modified state and the other having it in shared state.) ■

The design space for split-transaction, cache-coherent buses is large, and a great deal of innovation is ongoing in the industry. Perhaps the most critical issue from the viewpoint of the coherence protocol is how ordering is established and when snoop results are reported. Are they part of the request phase or the response phase? The position adopted in fact influences how conflicting operations can be handled, that is, the first major issue described earlier. Decisions about flow control (as well as conflicting operations) are affected by the number of outstanding requests permitted on the bus at a time. In general, a larger number of outstanding requests allows better bus utilization but requires more buffering and design complexity. The remaining high-level design decision is whether data responses need to be returned in the same order as that in which the requests are issued. The Intel Pentium Pro and DEC Turbo Laser buses are examples of the "in order" approach whereas the SGI Challenge and Sun Enterprise buses allow responses to be out of order. The latter approach is more tolerant of variations in memory access times (memory may be able to satisfy a later request quicker than an earlier one because of memory bank conflicts or off-page DRAM access) but is more complex. Let us first examine fully how one concrete example design resolves these issues and then discuss alternatives.

6.4.1 An Example Split-Transaction Design

The example is based loosely on the Silicon Graphics Challenge bus architecture, the Powerpath-2. It takes the following positions on the three design issues. Conflicting requests are dealt with very simply, if conservatively: the design disallows multiple requests for a block from being outstanding on the bus at once. In fact, it allows only eight outstanding requests at a time on the bus, thus making the necessary conflict detection tractable. Limited buffering is provided between the bus and the cache controllers, and flow control for these buffers is implemented through *negative acknowledgment,* or *NACK,* lines on the bus. That is, if a buffer is full when a request or response transaction is observed, which can be detected as soon as the transaction appears on the bus, the transaction is rejected and NACKed; this renders the transaction invalid and asks the initiator to retry. Finally, responses are allowed to be provided in a different order than that in which the original requests appeared on the bus. It is the request phase that establishes the total (bus) order on coherence transactions; however, snoop results from the cache controllers are presented on the bus as part of the response phase, together with the data, if any.

Let us examine this example bus architecture in more detail. We begin with the high-level bus design and how responses are matched up with requests. Then we look at the flow control and snoop result issues in more depth. Finally, we examine the path of a request through the system, including how conflicting requests are kept from being simultaneously outstanding on the bus.

6.4.2 Bus Design and Request-Response Matching

The split-transaction bus design essentially consists of two separate buses, a request bus for command and address and a response bus for data. The request bus provides the type of request (e.g., BusRd, BusWB) and the target address. Since responses may arrive out of order with regard to requests, there should be a way to match returning responses with their outstanding requests. When a request (command-address pair) is granted the bus by the arbiter, it is also assigned a unique tag (3 bits since the design allows eight outstanding requests). A response consists of data on the data bus as well as the original request tag on the 3-bit-wide tag lines. The use of tags means that responses do not need to use the address lines, keeping them available for other requests. The address and the data buses can therefore be arbitrated for separately. There are separate bus lines for arbitration as well as for flow control and snoop results.

Cache blocks are 128 bytes (1,024 bits) and the data bus is 256 bits wide in this particular design, so four bus cycles plus a one-cycle turnaround time are required for the response phase. A uniform pipeline strategy is followed, so the request phase

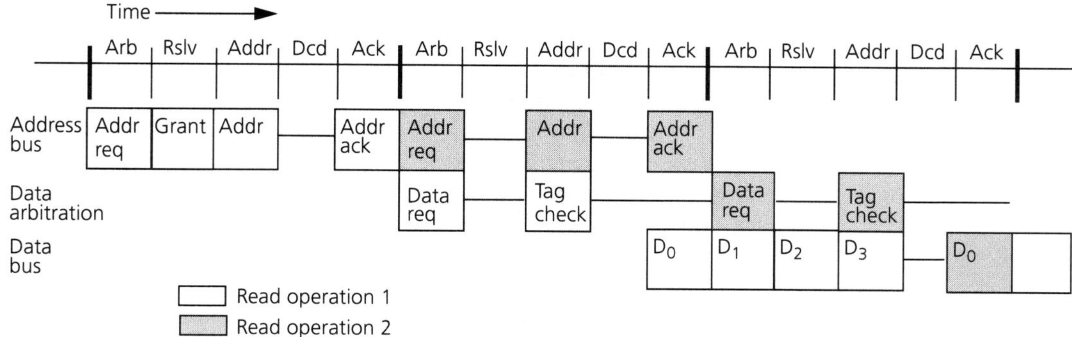

FIGURE 6.8 Complete read transaction for a split-transaction bus. A pair of consecutive read operations is performed on consecutive phases, distinguished by shaded boxes. Each phase consists of five specific cycles: arbitration, resolution, address, decode, and acknowledgment. Transactions are split into three phases: address request (which uses the address bus), data request (which uses the data bus arbitration and related logic), and data response (which uses the data bus).

is also five bus cycles: arbitration, resolution, address, decode, and acknowledgment. Overall, a complete request-response transaction takes three or more of these five-cycle phases—at the minimum an address request phase (which uses the address bus), a data request phase (which uses the data bus arbitration logic and obtains access to the data bus for the response subtransaction), and a data transfer or response phase (which uses the data bus). Three different memory operations can be in the three different phases at the same time. This basic pipelining strategy underlies several of the higher-level design decisions.

To understand this strategy, let's follow a single read operation through to completion, as shown in Figure 6.8. We begin with the address request phase. In the request arbitration cycle, a cache controller presents its request for the bus. In the request resolution cycle, all requests are considered, a single one is granted, and a tag is assigned. The winner drives the address in the following address cycle and then all controllers have a cycle to decode it and look up the cache tags to determine whether there is a snoop hit (the snoop result will be presented on the bus later). At this point, cache controllers can take the action that makes the operation visible to the processor. On a BusRd, an exclusive block is downgraded to shared; on a BusRdX or BusUpgr, blocks are invalidated. In either case, a controller owning the block as dirty knows that it will need to flush the block to the bus in the response phase. If a cache controller is not able to complete the snoop and take the necessary action during the address phase (say, if it is unable to gain access to the cache tags), it can inhibit the completion of this phase in the acknowledgment cycle until it completes the snoop. (During the acknowledgment cycle, the first data transfer cycle for the previous memory operation can take place, occupying the data lines for four cycles; see Figure 6.8.)

After the address request phase of the overall transaction, it is known which module should respond with the data: the memory or a cache. The responder may request the data bus during the arbitration cycle of the next 5-cycle phase. (Note that in this cycle a requestor also initiates a new request on the address bus.) The data bus arbitration is resolved in the next cycle, and in the address cycle the tag can be checked. If the target is ready, the data transfer starts on the acknowledgment cycle and continues for three additional cycles (i.e., into the data transfer or response phase). After a single turnaround cycle, the next data transfer (whose arbitration is proceeding in parallel) can start. The cache block sharing state (snoop result) is conveyed with the response phase, and state bits are set when the data is updated in the cache.

As discussed earlier, write backs (BusWB) consist only of a request phase. They require use of both the address and data lines together and thus must arbitrate for simultaneous use of both resources. Finally, upgrades (BusUpgr) performed to acquire exclusive ownership for a block also have only a request part since no data response is needed on the bus. The processor performing a write that generates the BusUpgr is sent a response by its own bus controller when the BusUpgr is actually placed on the bus, indicating that the write is committed and has been serialized in the bus order.

To keep track of the eight outstanding requests on the bus, each cache controller maintains an eight-entry table, called a *request table* (see Figure 6.9). Whenever a new request is issued on the bus, it is added to all request tables at the same index as part of the arbitration process. The index is the 3-bit tag assigned to that request during arbitration. (Requests are also buffered separately on their way to cache hierarchy.) A request table entry contains the address of the block associated with the request, the request type, the state of the block in the local cache (if it has already been determined), and a few other bits. The request table is fully associative, so all request table entries are examined for a match by both requests issued by the local processor and by other requests (using the address field) and responses (using the tag) observed from the bus. A request table entry is freed when a response to the request is observed on the bus. The 3-bit tag value associated with that request is reassigned by the bus arbiter only at this point, so there are no conflicts in the request tables.

6.4.3 Snoop Results and Conflicting Requests

Like the SGI Challenge, this example design uses variable delay snooping. The snoop portion of the bus consists of the three wired-OR lines discussed earlier: shared, dirty, and inhibit (which extends the duration of the current response phase). While it is determined at the end of the address request phase which module is to respond with the data, it may be many cycles before that data is ready and the responder gains access to the data bus. During this time, the snoop response is held in the request table, and other requests and responses may take place. To simplify matching snoop results with their requests, in this design the snoop results are presented on the bus by all controllers at the time they see the actual response to a

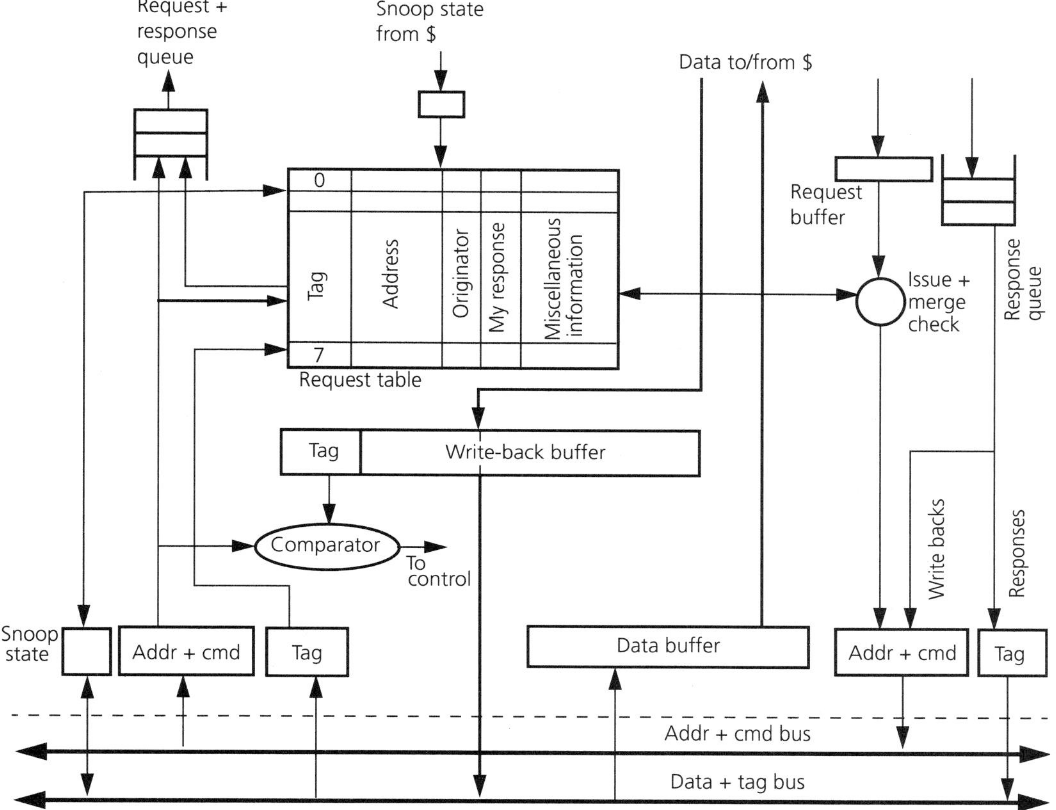

FIGURE 6.9 Extension of the bus interface logic shown in Figure 6.4 to accommodate a split-transaction bus. The key addition is an eight-entry request table that keeps track of all outstanding requests on the bus. Whenever a new request is issued on the bus, it is added at the same index in all processors' request tables. The request table serves many purposes, including request merging and ensuring that only a single request can be outstanding for any given memory block.

request being put on the bus, that is, during the response phase. Write-back and upgrade requests do not have a data response, but then they do not require a snoop response either.

Avoiding conflicting requests is easy: since every controller has a record of the pending transactions that have been issued to the bus in its request table, no request is issued for a block that has a transaction outstanding. Thus, even though the bus is pipelined, the operations for an individual location are serialized as in the atomic case. Writes are committed during the request phase, which affects the serialization.

6.4.4 Flow Control

In addition to its use for incoming requests from the bus, flow control may also be required in other parts of the system. The cache subsystem has a buffer in which responses to its requests can be stored, in addition to the write-back buffer discussed earlier. If the processor or cache allows only one outstanding request at a time, as we have been implicitly assuming, this response buffer is only one entry deep. The number of buffer entries is usually kept small anyway, since a response buffer entry contains not only an address but also a cache block of data and is therefore large. The cache controller provides flow control by limiting the number of requests it has outstanding so that buffer space is available for every response.

Flow control is also needed at main memory. Each of the (eight) pending requests can generate a write back that main memory must accept in addition to the request itself. Since write-back transactions do not require a response, they can happen in quick succession on the bus, possibly overflowing buffers in the main memory subsystem.

The SGI Challenge design provides separate NACK lines for the address and data portions of the bus since the bus allows independent arbitration for each portion. Before a request or response subtransaction has reached its acknowledgment cycle and completed, the main memory or any other processor can assert a NACK signal, for example, if it finds its buffers full. The subtransaction is then canceled everywhere and must be retried. One common option, used in the Challenge, is to have the requestor for that subtransaction retry periodically until it succeeds. Backoff and priorities can be used to reduce bandwidth consumption for failed retries and to avoid starvation. The Sun Enterprise uses an interesting alternative for data transfers that encounter a full buffer. In this case, the receiver—which could not accommodate the data on the first attempt—initiates the retry when it has enough buffer space. The original supplier simply keeps watch for the retry transaction on the bus and places the data on the data bus. The operation of the Enterprise bus ensures that the space in the destination buffer is still available when the data arrives. This guarantees that data transfers will succeed with only one retry bus transaction.

6.4.5 Path of a Cache Miss

Given this example design, we are ready to examine how various requests may be handled and what race conditions might occur. Let us first look at the case where a processor has a read miss in the cache so that the request part of a BusRd transaction should be generated. The request first checks the currently pending entries in the request table. If it finds one with a matching address, it can take two possible courses of action, depending on the nature of the pending request:

1. If the earlier request was a BusRd request for the same block, this is great news for this processor: the request needn't be put on the bus but can just obtain the data when the response to the earlier request appears on the bus. To accomplish this, we add two new bits to each entry in the request table, which say: Do I wish to obtain the data response for this request? Am I the

original generator of this request? In our situation, these bits will be set to 1 and 0, respectively. The purpose of the first bit is obvious; the purpose of the second bit is to help determine in which state (exclusive versus shared) the data response will be loaded. If a processor is not the original requestor, then it must assert the sharing line on the snoop bus when it obtains the response data from the bus so that all caches will load this block in shared state and not exclusive. If a processor is the original requestor, it does not assert the sharing line when it obtains the response from the bus, and if the sharing line is not asserted at all, then it will load the block in exclusive state.

2. If the earlier request conflicts with a BusRd (e.g., a BusRdX), the controller must hold on to the request until it sees a response to the previous request on the bus and only then attempt the request. The processor-side controller is typically responsible for this.

If the controller finds no matching entries in the request table, it can go ahead and issue the request on the bus. However, it must watch out for a race condition of the type we discussed earlier. When the controller first examines the request table, it may find no conflicting requests, so it may request arbitration for the bus. However, before it is granted the bus, a conflicting request may appear on the bus, and then it may be granted the very next use of the bus. Since this design does not allow conflicting requests on the bus, when the controller sees a conflicting request in the slot just before its own, it should (1) issue a null request (a no-action request) on the bus to occupy the slot it had been granted and (2) withdraw from further arbitration until a response to the conflicting request has been generated.

Suppose the processor does manage to issue the BusRd request on the bus. What should other cache controllers and the main memory controller do? The request is entered into the request tables of all cache controllers, including the one that issued it, as soon as it appears on the bus. The controllers start checking their caches for the requested memory block. The main memory subsystem has no idea whether this block is dirty in one of the processor's caches, so it independently starts fetching this block. Now we have three different scenarios to consider:

1. One of the caches may determine that it has the block in modified state and may acquire the bus to generate a response before main memory can respond. On seeing the response on the bus, main memory simply aborts the fetch that it had initiated, and the cache controllers that are waiting for this block load the data in a state based on the values of the snooping lines. If a cache controller has not finished snooping by the time the response appears on the bus, it will keep the inhibit line asserted and the response transaction will be extended (i.e., will stay on the bus). Main memory also receives the response since the block was dirty in a cache. If main memory does not have the buffer space needed, it asserts the NACK signal provided for flow control, and it is the responsibility of the controller holding the block dirty to retry the response transaction later.

2. Main memory may fetch the data and acquire the bus before the cache controller holding the block dirty has finished its snoop and/or acquired the bus.

The controller holding the block dirty will first assert the inhibit line until it has finished its snoop and then assert the dirty line and release the inhibit line, indicating to the memory that it has the latest copy and that memory should not actually put its data on the bus. On observing the dirty line, memory cancels its response transaction and does not actually put the data on the bus. The cache with the dirty block will acquire the bus sometime later and put the data response on it.

3. The simplest scenario is that no other cache has the block dirty. Main memory will acquire the bus and generate the response. Cache controllers that have not finished their snoop will assert the inhibit line when they see the response from memory, but once they deassert it, memory can supply the data. (Cache-to-cache sharing is not used for data in shared state in this system.)

Processor writes are handled similarly to reads. If the writing processor does not find the data in its cache in a valid state, a BusRdX is generated. As before, it checks the request table and then goes on the bus. Everything is the same as for a bus read, except that main memory will not take the data response if it comes from another cache (since it's going to be modified again by the writer) and no other processor can grab the data. If the block being written is valid but in shared state, a BusUpgr is issued. This requires no response transaction (the currently valid block is known to be in main memory as well as in the writer's cache); however, if any other processor was just about to issue a BusUpgr for the same block, it will now need to convert its request to a BusRdX as in the atomic bus.

6.4.6 Serialization and Sequential Consistency

Consider serialization to a single location. If a request subtransaction appearing on the bus is a read, no subsequent write appearing on the bus after the read should be able to change the value returned by the read. Despite multiple outstanding transactions on the bus, here this is easy since conflicting requests to the same location are not allowed simultaneously on the bus; the read response subtransaction will therefore precede the write request, and the read will complete before the write can affect the cached value. If the transaction appearing on the bus is a BusRdX or BusUpgr generated by a write operation, the requesting cache will perform the write into the cache array after the response phase and before issuing any other memory operations; subsequent (conflicting) reads to the block from any processor are allowed on the bus only after the response phase for the write, so they are guaranteed to obtain the new value. (Recall that the response phase for a write operation may be a separate action on the bus, as in a BusRdX, or may be implicitly generated once the request wins arbitration, as in a BusUpgr.)

Now consider the serialization of operations to different locations needed for sequential consistency. The logical total order on bus transactions is established by the order in which requests for the address bus are granted. Once a BusRdX or BusUpgr has obtained the bus, the associated write is committed. However, with multiple outstanding requests on the bus, the invalidations are buffered as well, and it may be a while before they are actually applied to the cache (unlike in the atomic bus where this was assumed to happen immediately). Commitment of a write does not guarantee that the value produced by the write is already visible to all other processors; only actual completion guarantees that. (Performing with respect to a processor guarantees it for that processor.) Further mechanisms are needed to ensure that the necessary orders are preserved between the bus and the processor. Example 6.3 will help make this concrete.

EXAMPLE 6.3 Consider the two code fragments shown below. What results for (A,B) are disallowed under SC? Assuming a single level of cache per processor and multiple outstanding transactions on the bus, and no special mechanisms to preserve orders between bus and cache or processor, show how the disallowed results may be obtained. Assume an invalidation-based protocol and initial values for A and B of 0 in both caches.

P_1	P_2
`A = 1`	`rd B`
`B = 1`	`rd A`

P_1	P_2
`A = 1`	`B = 1`
`rd B`	`rd A`

Answer In the first example, on the left, the result not permitted under SC is (A,B) = (0,1). However, consider the following scenario. P_1's write of A commits, so it continues with the write of B (under the revised sufficient conditions for SC). The invalidation for B is applied to the cache of P_2 before that for A because they get reordered in the buffers. P_2 incurs a read miss on B and obtains the new value of 1. However, the invalidation for A is still in the buffer and is not applied to P_2's cache even by the time P_2 issues the read of A. The read of A is a hit and completes returning the old value 0 for A from the cache.

The example on the right does not require invalidations to be reordered to violate SC. The disallowed result is (0,0). However, consider the following scenario. P_1 issues and commits its write of A and then completes the read of B, reading in the old value of 0. P_2 then writes B, which commits, so P_2 proceeds to read A. The write of B appears on the bus (commits) after the write of A, so they should be serialized in that order and P_2 should read the new value of A. However, the invalidation corresponding to the write of A by P_1 is sitting in P_2's incoming buffer and has not yet been applied to P_2's cache. P_2 sees a read hit on A and completes returning the old value of A, which is 0. ■

With commitment substituting for completion and multiple outstanding operations being buffered between bus and processor, the key property that must be preserved for sequential consistency is the following: a processor should not be allowed to actually see the new value due to a write before previous writes (in bus order, as usual) are visible to it. There are two ways to preserve this property: by not letting certain types of incoming transactions from bus to cache be reordered in the incoming queues; and by allowing these reorderings in the queues, but then ensuring that the important orders are preserved at the necessary points in the machine. Let us examine each approach briefly.

A simple way to follow the first approach is to ensure that all incoming transactions from the bus (invalidations, read-miss replies, write commitment acknowledgments, etc.) propagate to the processor in FIFO order. However, such strict ordering is not necessary. Consider preserving the desirable property just described with an invalidation-based protocol. Here, there are two ways for a new value to be brought into the cache and made available to the processor to read without it incurring another bus operation. One is through a read miss, and the other is through a write by that processor. On the other hand, writes from other processors become visible to a processor (even though the values are not yet available locally) when the corresponding invalidations are applied to its cache. For writes to be defined as previous to the operation that provides the new value, they must have appeared on the bus before the operation (or a previous bus transaction from that processor in the case of a write hit). Thus, the invalidations due to those writes are already in the incoming queue or applied to the cache when the relevant transaction appears on the bus and, hence, when its reply comes back. All we need to ensure, therefore, is that a reply (read miss or write commitment acknowledge) does not overtake an invalidation between the bus and the cache, that is, that all previous invalidations are applied before the reply is received by the cache.

Note that incoming invalidations may be reordered with regard to one another. This is because the new value corresponding to an invalidation is seen only through the corresponding read miss, and the read-miss reply is not allowed to be reordered with respect to the previous invalidation. In an update-based protocol, on the other hand, the new value due to a write can be seen as soon as the incoming update has been applied. This means not only that replies should not overtake updates but that updates should not overtake updates either.

An alternative is to allow incoming transactions from the bus to be reordered arbitrarily on their way to the cache but to ensure that all previously committed writes are applied to the cache (by servicing them from the incoming queue) before an operation from the local processor that will enable it to see a new value can be completed. After all, what really matters is not the order in which invalidations or updates are applied but the order in which the corresponding new values can be seen by the processor. There are two natural ways to accomplish this. One is to service the incoming invalidations and updates from the queue every time the processor tries to complete an operation that places a new value in the cache. In an invalidation-based protocol, this means servicing the queue before the processor is allowed to complete a read miss or a write that generates a bus transaction; in an update-based protocol, it means servicing it on every read hit as well. The other way is to service the queue when a processor is about to actually access a value (complete a read hit or miss), if a new value (i.e., a reply or an update since the last time the queue was serviced) has indeed been applied to the cache. The fact that operations are reordered from bus to cache and a new value has been applied to the cache means that invalidations or updates may be in the queue that correspond to writes that are previous to that new value; those writes should now be applied before the read can complete. Showing that these techniques disallow the undesirable results in Example 6.3 is left as an exercise that may help make the techniques concrete. As we will see soon, the extension of the techniques to multilevel cache hierarchies is quite natural.

Regardless of which approach is used, write atomicity is provided naturally by the broadcast nature of the bus. The bus implies that writes are committed in the same order with respect to all processors and that a read cannot see the value produced by a write until that write has committed with respect to all processors (recall that the writing processor ensures this locally too). With the preceding techniques, we can substitute complete for commit in this statement, thus ensuring atomicity. The other major correctness issues—deadlock, livelock, and starvation—for a split-transaction bus are discussed after we have introduced multilevel cache hierarchies in this context. First, let us look at some alternative approaches to organizing a protocol with a split-transaction bus.

6.4.7 Alternative Design Choices

Alternative positions exist for request-response ordering, dealing with conflicting requests, and flow control other than the ones taken by our example (SGI Challenge-based) split-transaction bus design. For example, ensuring that responses are generated on the bus in order with respect to requests—as cache controllers are inclined to do—would simplify the design. The fully associative request table could be replaced by a simple FIFO buffer for the purpose of request-response matching (fully associative lookups may still be needed if conflicting requests are to be disallowed). As before, a request is put into the FIFO only when it actually appears on the bus, ensuring that all entities (processors and memory system) have exactly the same view of pending requests. The cache controllers and the memory system process requests in FIFO order. At the time the response is presented (as in the earlier design), if others have not completed their snoops, they assert the inhibit line and extend the transaction duration. That is, snoops are still reported together with responses. The difference is in the case where the memory generates a response first even though a processor has that block dirty in its cache. In the previous, unordered design, the cache controller that had the block dirty released the inhibit line and asserted the dirty line and arbitrated for the bus again later when it had retrieved the data from the cache. But now to preserve the FIFO order, this response has to be placed on the bus before the response to any later request. So the controller with the dirty block does not release the inhibit line but extends the current bus transaction until it has fetched the block from its cache and supplied it on the bus. Accomplishing this does not depend on anyone else having to access the bus, so there is no deadlock problem.

Although FIFO request-response ordering is simpler, it can have performance problems. Consider a multiprocessor with an interleaved memory system. Suppose three requests *A*, *B*, and *C* are issued on the bus in that order and that *A* and *B* go to the same memory bank while *C* goes to a different one. Forcing the system to generate responses in order means that *C* will have to wait for both *A* and *B* to be processed, though data for *C* will be available well before data for *B* is available because of *B*'s bank conflict with *A*. The behavior of main memory is the major motivation for allowing out-of-order responses since caches are likely to respond to requests in order anyway.

Keeping responses in order also makes it more tractable to allow conflicting requests to the same block to be outstanding on the bus, thus eliminating the need for the fully associative request table lookup as well as increasing bandwidth. Suppose two BusRdX requests are issued on a block in rapid succession. The controller issuing the later request will invalidate its block when it sees the earlier request, as before. The tricky part with a split-transaction bus is that the controller issuing the earlier request sees the later request appear on the bus before the data response that it awaits. It cannot simply invalidate its block in reaction to the later request since the block is in flight and its own write needs to be performed before a flush or invalidate. With out-of-order responses, allowing this conflicting request may be difficult. With in-order responses, the earlier requestor knows its response will appear on the bus first, so this is actually an opportunity for a performance-enhancing optimization. The earlier requesting controller reacts to the later request by simply noting that the latter is pending. When its response block arrives, it updates the word to be written and "shortcuts" the modified block back out to the bus to serve as the response to the later request, leaving its own block invalid. This optimization reduces the latency of ping-ponging a block under write-write false sharing.

If the delay from request to snoop result is fixed, conflicting requests can be allowed even without requiring data responses to be in order. However, since conflicting requests to a block go into the same queue at memory as well, the data responses for these requests themselves usually appear in order anyway, so they can be handled using the shortcut method just described (this is done in the Sun Enterprise systems).

In fact, as long as a well-defined order can be identified among the request transactions, they do not even need to be issued sequentially on the same bus. For example, the Sun SparcCenter 2000 used two distinct split-transaction buses and the CRAY 6400 used four to improve bandwidth for large configurations. Multiple requests may thus be issued on a single cycle. However, a simple priority is established among the buses so that a logical order is defined even among the concurrent requests.

6.4.8 Split-Transaction Bus with Multilevel Caches

We are now ready to combine the two major enhancements to the basic protocol from which we started: multilevel caches and a split-transaction bus. The design we examine is a (Challenge-like) split-transaction bus and a two-level cache hierarchy. The issues and solutions generalize to deeper hierarchies. We have already seen the basic issues of request, response, and invalidation propagation up and down the hierarchy. The key new issue we need to grapple with is that it takes a considerable number of cycles for a request to propagate through the cache controllers. During this time, we must allow other transactions to propagate up and down the hierarchy as well. To maintain high bandwidth while allowing the individual units (e.g., controllers and caches) to operate at their own rates, queues are placed between levels

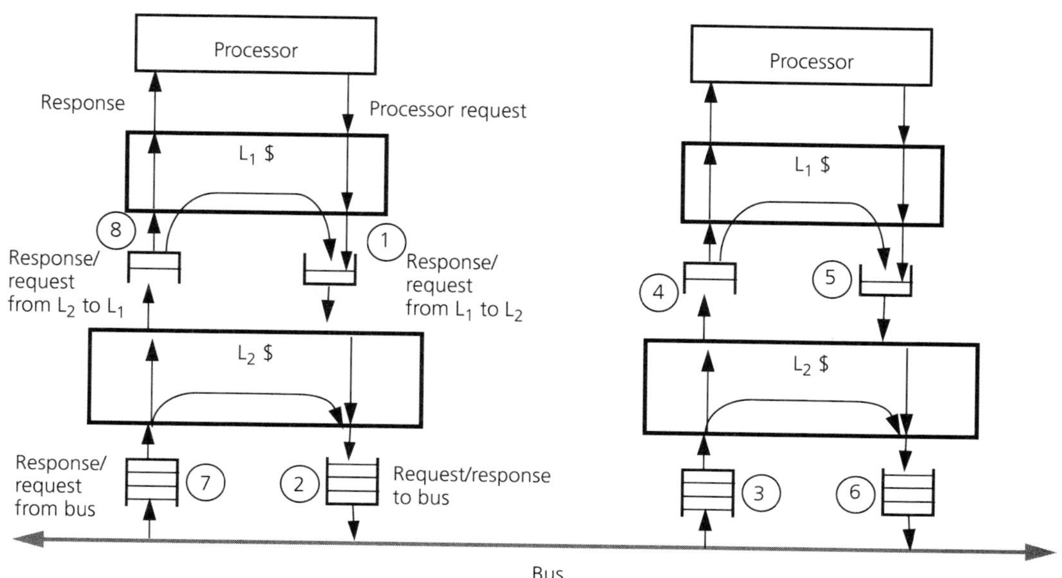

FIGURE 6.10 Internal queues that may exist inside a multilevel cache hierarchy. Each level of the hierarchy has input queues from above and below that it must service. An operation may produce a request or response to the adjacent levels. For example, a read request that misses in the L_1 cache is passed on to the L_2 cache (1). If it misses there, a request is placed on the bus (2). The read request is captured by all other cache controllers in the incoming queue (3). Assuming the block is currently in modified state in the L_1 cache of another processor, the request is queued for L_1 service (4). The L_1 demotes the block to shared and flushes it to the L_2 cache (5), which places it on the bus (6). The response is captured by the requestor (7) and passed to the L_1 (8), whereupon the word is provided to the processor.

of the hierarchy as well. However, this raises a family of questions related to deadlock and serialization.

A simple multilevel cache organization is shown in Figure 6.10. Assume that a processor can have only one request outstanding at a time, so there are no queues between the processor and first-level cache. One concern with such queue structures is deadlock. To avoid the fetch deadlock problem discussed earlier, an L_2 cache needs to be able to buffer incoming requests or responses while it has a request outstanding (as before) so that the bus may be freed up. With one outstanding request per processor, the incoming queues between the bus and the L_2 cache need to be large enough to hold the number of requests that can be outstanding on the bus from other processors plus a response to its own request. This takes care of the case where all requests are destined for a given cache while that cache has a request outstanding. If the queues are made smaller than this to conserve real estate, bus requests are NACKed when room is not available to enqueue them. This discussion applies to single-level or multilevel cache hierarchies with a split-transaction bus. One slot in the bus-to-L_2

and in the L_2-to-L_1 queues is reserved for the response to the processor's outstanding request so that each processor can always drain its outstanding responses. If NACKs are used, the bus arbitration needs to include a mechanism, such as a simple priority scheme, to ensure forward progress under heavy contention.

In addition to fetch deadlock, classical buffer deadlock can occur within the multilevel cache hierarchy as well. For example, suppose there is a queue in each direction between the L_1 and L_2 cache, both of which are write-back caches, and each queue can hold one entry. It is possible that the $L_1 \rightarrow L_2$ queue holds an outgoing read request, which can be satisfied in the L_2 cache but will generate a reply to L_1, and the $L_2 \rightarrow L_1$ queue holds an incoming read request, which can be satisfied in the L_1 cache but will generate a reply to L_2. We now have a classical circular buffer dependence, and hence deadlock. Note that this problem occurs only in hierarchies in which a higher-level cache (closer to the processor) than the one closest to the bus is a write-back cache. Otherwise, incoming requests do not generate replies from higher-level caches, so there is no circularity and no buffer deadlock problem (recall that invalidations are acknowledged implicitly from the bus itself and do not need acknowledgments from the caches).

A hardware-intensive way to deal with this buffer deadlock problem in a multilevel write-back cache hierarchy is to limit the number of outstanding requests from processors and then provide enough buffering for incoming requests and responses at each level. However, this requires a lot of real estate and is not scalable. Each request may need two outgoing buffer entries—one for the request and one for the write back it might generate. With a large number of outstanding bus transactions being allowed, the incoming buffers may need to have many entries as well. An alternative way uses a general deadlock avoidance technique for situations with limited buffering, which we discuss more fully in Chapter 7 in the context of systems with physically distributed memory, where the problem is more acute. The basic idea is to separate the operations that flow through the buffers and communication medium into requests and responses. An operation is classified as a response if it does not generate any further operations but is simply sunk by its destination. A request may generate a response, but no operation may generate another request (although in this case a request may be transferred to the next level of the hierarchy, initiating a new request-response pair and ending the first request, if it does not generate a response at the original level). With this classification, we can avoid deadlock if we provide separate queues for requests and responses in each direction and ensure that responses are always extracted (sunk) from the queues, thus allowing requests to make progress as well. After we discuss this technique in Chapter 7, we apply it to this particular situation with multilevel write-back caches in the exercises.

There are other potential deadlock considerations. For example, if the number of outstanding transactions on the bus is smaller than the number of outstanding requests allowed by the caches, it may be important for a response from a processor's cache to get to the bus before new outgoing requests from it are allowed. Otherwise, the existing requests may never be satisfied and there will be no progress. The outgoing queue or queues must be able to support responses bypassing requests when necessary.

Other than deadlock, a concern with these queue structures is maintaining sequential consistency. With multilevel caches, it is all the more important that the bus not wait for an invalidation to reach all the way up to the first-level cache and return a reply; it should instead consider the write committed when it has been placed on the bus and hence in the input queue to the lowest-level cache. The separation of commitment and completion is even greater in this case. However, the techniques discussed for single-level caches extend naturally to this case: we simply apply them at each level of the cache hierarchy. Thus, in an invalidation-based protocol, the first technique extends to ensuring at each level of the hierarchy that replies are not reordered with respect to invalidations in the incoming queues to that level (replies from a lower-level cache to a higher-level cache are treated as replies, too, for this purpose). The second technique extends to either not letting an outgoing memory operation proceed past a level of the hierarchy before the incoming invalidations to that level are applied there or draining the incoming invalidations to a level if a reply has been applied to that level since the last drain.

6.4.9 Supporting Multiple Outstanding Misses from a Processor

Although we have examined split-transaction buses, we have implicitly assumed so far that a given processor can have only one outstanding memory request at a time. This assumption is simplistic for modern processors, which permit multiple outstanding requests to tolerate the latency of cache misses even on uniprocessor systems. Whereas allowing multiple outstanding references from a processor improves performance, it can also complicate semantics since memory accesses from the same processor may complete in a different order in the memory system than that in which they were issued.

One example of multiple outstanding references is the use of a write buffer. Since we would like to let the processor proceed to other computation and even memory operations after it issues a write, we put the write in the write buffer. Until the write is serialized, it should not be made visible since, otherwise, it may violate write serialization and coherence. One possibility is to write it into the local cache but not make it available until exclusive ownership is obtained (i.e., not let the cache respond to requests for it until then). The more common approach is to keep it in the write buffer and put it in the cache (making it available to other processors through the bus) only when exclusive ownership is obtained.

Most processors use write buffers more aggressively, issuing a sequence of writes in rapid succession into the write buffer without stalling the processor. In a uniprocessor, this approach is very effective as long as reads check the write buffer to satisfy dependences. The problem in the multiprocessor case is that, in general, the processor cannot be allowed to proceed with (or at least complete) memory operations past the write until the exclusive ownership transaction for the block has been placed on the bus and hence serialized. However, there are special cases where the processor can issue a sequence of writes and consider them complete without stalling. One example is if it can be determined that the writes are to blocks that are in the local cache in modified state. Then they can be buffered between the processor and the cache as long as the cache processes the writes before servicing a request from the bus side (to the same block for coherence and to any block for SC). An important special case exists in which a sequence of writes can be buffered regardless of the cache state: the writes are all to the same block and no other memory operations from that processor are interspersed between those writes in the program order. The writes may be coalesced while the controller is obtaining the bus for the read-exclusive transaction. When that transaction occurs, it makes the entire sequence of writes visible at once. The behavior is the same as if the writes were performed locally as hits after the bus transaction but before the next one. Note that there is no problem with sequences of write backs since the protocol does not require them to be ordered.

More generally, to satisfy the sufficient conditions for sequential consistency, a processor having the ability to proceed past outstanding write, and even read, operations raises the question of which entity should wait to "issue" an operation until the previous one in program order completes. Forcing the processor itself to wait can eliminate any benefits of the sophisticated processor mechanisms (such as write buffers and out-of-order execution). Instead, since the issue is visibility, the buffers that hold the outstanding operations—such as the write buffer or the reorder buffer in dynamically scheduled out-of-order execution processors—can serve this purpose. The processor can issue the next operation right after the previous one, and the buffers take charge of making sure that write operations are not visible to the memory and interconnect systems (i.e., not issuing them to the externally visible memory system) until the appropriate time or that read operations are not allowed to complete out of program order with respect to the commitment of outstanding writes even though the processor may issue and execute them out of order. The mechanisms needed in the buffers are often already available for the purpose of providing precise interrupts in uniprocessors, and we will discuss them in later chapters. Of course, simpler processors that do not proceed past reads or writes make it easier to maintain sequential consistency. Further semantic implications of multiple outstanding references for memory consistency models are discussed when we examine consistency models in detail in Chapter 9.

From a design perspective, exploiting multiple outstanding references most effectively requires that the caches allow multiple cache misses to be outstanding at a time so that the latencies of these misses can be overlapped. This in turn requires that either the cache or some auxiliary data structure keep track of the outstanding misses, which can be quite complex since the responses may return out of order. Caches that allow multiple outstanding misses are called *lockup-free* caches (Kroft 1981), as opposed to *blocking* caches that allow only one outstanding miss. We discuss the design of lockup-free caches when we discuss latency tolerance in Chapter 11.

Finally, consider the interactions with split-transaction buses and multilevel cache hierarchies and the requirements for deadlock avoidance. Given a design that supports a split-transaction bus and a multilevel cache hierarchy, the extensions needed to support multiple outstanding operations per processor are few and are mostly for performance. We simply need to provide deeper request queues from the processor to the bus (the request queues pointing downward in Figure 6.10), so that the multiple outstanding requests can be buffered and the processor or cache does not stall. It may also be useful to have deeper response queues and more write-back and other types of buffers, since the system now affords more concurrency. As long as deadlock is handled by separating requests from replies and providing them with logically separate buffers, the exact length of any of these queues is not critical for correctness. The reason for so few changes is that the lockup-free caches themselves perform the complex task of merging requests and managing replies to the same block, so to the caches and the bus subsystem below, it simply appears that multiple requests to distinct blocks are coming from the processor. Some potential fetch deadlock scenarios might become exposed that do not arise with only one outstanding request per processor; for example, we may now see the situation where the number of requests outstanding from all processors is more than the bus can take, so we have to ensure responses can bypass requests on the way out. Nevertheless, the support discussed earlier for multiple outstanding transactions on split-transaction buses makes the rest of the system capable of handling multiple requests from a processor without deadlock.

6.5 CASE STUDIES: SGI CHALLENGE AND SUN ENTERPRISE 6000

This section places the general design and implementation issues discussed in the preceding sections into a concrete setting by describing two bus-based multiprocessor systems—the SGI Challenge and the Sun Enterprise 6000. It focuses less on logical issues and more on the organizational and engineering issues as manifested in these real systems. It illustrates how two systems take very different positions on these issues.

The SGI Challenge is designed to support up to 36 MIPS R4400 processors (peak 2.7 GFLOPS total) or up to 18 MIPS R8000 processors (peak 5.4 GFLOPS). Both systems use the same system bus, the Powerpath-2 bus, which provides a peak bandwidth of 1.2 GB/s. The Challenge supports up to 16 GB of eight-way interleaved main memory and up to four PowerChannel-2 I/O buses. Each I/O bus provides a peak bandwidth of 320 MB/s and can support multiple Ethernet connections, VME/SCSI buses, graphics cards, and other peripherals. The total disk storage on the system can be several terabytes. The operating system is a variant of SVR4 UNIX called IRIX; it is a symmetric multiprocessor kernel in that any of the operating system's tasks can be done on any of the processors in the system. Figure 6.11 presents a high-level diagram of the SGI Challenge system organization.

The Sun Enterprise 6000, introduced later than the Challenge, is designed to support up to 30 UltraSparc processors (peak 9 GFLOPs). The Gigaplane system bus provides a peak bandwidth of 2.67 GB/s, and the system can support up to 30 GB of up to 16-way interleaved memory. The 16 slots in the machine can be populated with a mix of processing boards and I/O boards, as long as at least one of each is present. Each processing board has two CPU modules and two (512-bit-wide) memory banks of up to 1 GB each, so the memory capacity and bandwidth scales with the

(a) A four-processor board

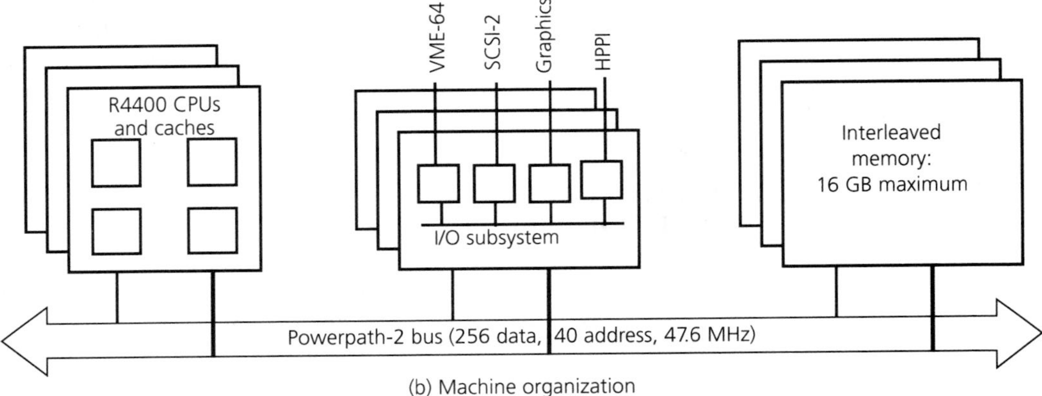

(b) Machine organization

FIGURE 6.11 The SGI Challenge multiprocessor. With 4 processors per board, the 36 processors consume nine bus slots. The Challenge can support up to 16 GB of eight-way interleaved main memory. The I/O boards each provide a separate 320-MB/s I/O bus, to which other standard buses and devices interface. The system bus has a separate 40-bit address path and a 256-bit datapath, plus command, and other signals, and supports a peak bandwidth of 1.2 GB/s. The bus is split transaction, and up to eight requests can be outstanding on the bus at any given time. *Photo:* CHALLENGE is a trademark of Silicon Graphics, Inc.

number of processors. Although some memory is physically local to a pair of processors, all of memory is accessed through the system bus and hence is of uniform access time. The board containing the memory for a particular address is called the *home board* of the address. Each I/O card provides two independent 64-bit × 25-MHz SBUS I/O buses, so the I/O bandwidth scales with the number of I/O cards. The total disk storage can be tens of terabytes. The operating system is Solaris UNIX. Figure 6.12 shows a block diagram of the Sun Enterprise system.

The next few subsections describe the SGI Challenge architecture and characterize some of its performance attributes. The following subsections do the same for the Sun Enterprise 6000.

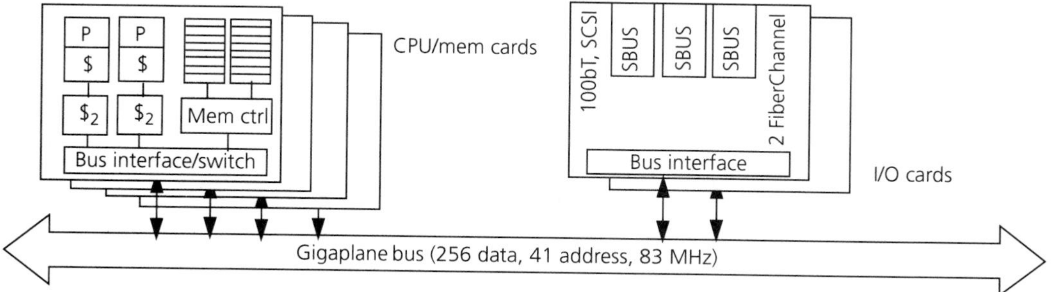

FIGURE 6.12 The Sun Enterprise 6000 multiprocessor. The system provides 16 bus slots that can be occupied by either processor or I/O boards, but there must be at least one of each. The processor board contains two processors and two banks of memory, which are uniformly accessible to all boards. The I/O board provides connectors for multiple independent peripheral buses and appears like another cache controller on the system bus. The split-transaction bus allows up to 112 outstanding transactions at a time.

6.5.1 SGI Powerpath-2 System Bus

The system bus forms the core interconnect for all components in the system. As a result, its design is affected by the requirements of all other components, and design choices made for it affect the design of other components in turn. The design choices for buses include multiplexed versus nonmultiplexed address and data buses, a wide (e.g., 256- or 128-bit) versus narrower (64-bit) data bus, clock rate of the bus (affected by signaling technology used, length of bus, and number of slots on bus), split-transaction versus atomic design, flow control strategy, and so on. The Powerpath-2 bus is nonmultiplexed, having a 256-bit-wide data portion and a separate 40-bit-wide address portion, plus command and other signals. It is clocked at 47.6 MHz, and it is a split-transaction design supporting eight outstanding read requests. While the wide datapath implies that the hardware cost of connecting to the bus is higher (it requires multiple bit-sliced chips to interface to it), the benefit is that the high bandwidth of 1.2 GB/s can be achieved at a reasonable clock rate. The bus supports sixteen slots, nine of which can be populated with 4-processor boards to obtain a 36-processor configuration. The width of the bus also affects (and is affected by) many other design issues. For example, the block size chosen for the cache closest to the bus (here the second-level cache) is 128 bytes, implying that the whole cache block can be transferred in four bus clocks; because of the dead cycle between transfers, a much smaller block size would have resulted in less effective use of the bus pipeline or a more complex design. Also, the individual board is fairly large in order to support such a large bus connector. The bus interface occupies roughly 20% of the board, in a strip along the edge, making it natural to place multiple processors on each board.

Let us look at the Powerpath-2 bus design in a little more detail. The bus consists of a total of 329 signals: 256 data, 8 data parity, 40 address, 8 command, 2 address +command parity, 8 data resource ID, and 7 miscellaneous. The types and variations

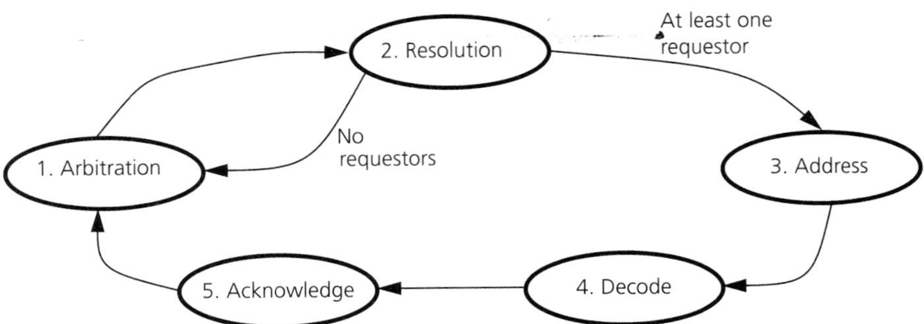

FIGURE 6.13 Powerpath-2 bus state transition diagram. The bus interfaces of all boards attached to the system bus synchronously cycle through the five states shown in the figure; this is also the duration of all address and data transactions on the bus. When the bus is idle, however, it only loops between states 1 and 2.

of transactions on the bus are small, and all transactions take exactly 5 cycles, as discussed earlier in our example design. All bus controller ASICs execute the following five-state machine synchronously: arbitration, resolution, address, decode, and acknowledge. When no transactions are occurring, each bus controller drops into a two-state idle machine. The shorter, two-state idle machine allows new requests to arbitrate immediately rather than waiting for the arbitration state to occur in the five-state machine. (Two states are required, rather than one, to prevent different requestors from driving arbitration lines on successive cycles.) Figure 6.13 shows the state machine underlying the basic bus protocol.

Since the bus is a split-transaction design, the address and data buses must be arbitrated for separately. In the arbitration cycle, the 48 address+command lines are used for arbitration. The lower 16 of these lines are used by the 16 boards (one per board) to request the data bus, and the middle 16 lines are used for address bus arbitration. For transactions that require both address and data buses together (e.g., write backs), corresponding bits for both buses can be set high. The top 16 lines are used to make *urgent*, or high-priority, requests. Urgent requests are used to avoid starvation, for example, if a processor times out waiting to get access to the bus. The availability of urgent requests allowed the designers considerable flexibility in favoring the service of some requests over others for performance reasons (e.g., reads are given preference over writes) while still being confident that no requestor will get starved.

Figure 6.14, which expands upon Figure 6.8, shows the cycles during which various bus lines are driven and their semantics. At the end of the arbitration cycle, all bus interface ASICs capture the 48-bit state of the address+command lines and thus see the bus requests from all boards. A distributed arbitration scheme is used; every controller sees all of the bus requests, and in the resolution cycle, each one independently computes the same winner. While distributed arbitration consumes more of

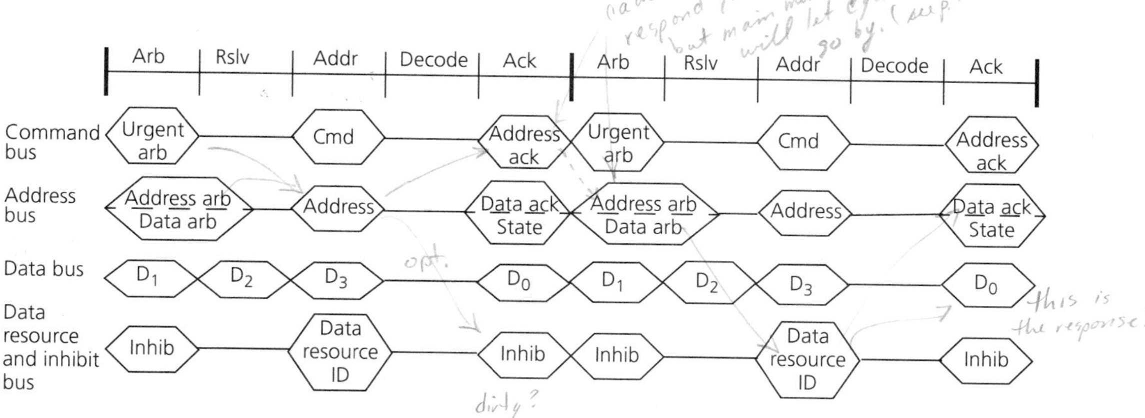

FIGURE 6.14 Powerpath-2 bus timing diagram. During the arbitration cycle, the 48 bits of the address+command bus indicate requests from the 16 bus slots for data transactions, address transactions, and urgent transactions. Each bus interface determines the results of the arbitration independently following a common algorithm. For the address request that is granted, the address+command is transferred in the address cycle, and the requests can be NACKed in the acknowledgment cycle. Similarly, for the data request that is granted, the tag associated with it (data resource ID) is transferred in the address cycle; it can be NACKed in the ack cycle, or the data is transferred in the following D_0–D_3 cycles (where D_0 is the ack cycle).

ASIC's gate resources, it saves the latency incurred by a centralized arbitrator of communicating winners to everybody via bus grant lines.

During the address cycle, the address bus winner drives the address and command buses with corresponding information. Simultaneously, the data bus winner drives the *data resource ID* line corresponding to the response. (The data resource ID is the 3-bit global tag that was assigned to the read request when it was originally issued on the bus. The use of the global tags is described in Section 6.4.2.)

During the decode cycle, no signals are driven on the address bus. Internally, each bus interface slot decides how to respond to this transaction. For example, if the transaction is a write back and the memory system currently has insufficient buffer resources to accept the data, in this cycle it will decide that it must NACK (negative acknowledge or reject) this transaction on the next cycle so that the transaction can be retried at a later time. In addition, all slots prepare to supply the proper cache coherence information.

During the acknowledge cycle, each bus interface slot responds to the data/address bus transaction. The 48 address+command lines are used as follows. The top 16 lines indicate if the device in the corresponding slot is rejecting the address bus transaction due to insufficient buffer space. Similarly, the middle 16 lines are used to possibly reject the data bus transaction. The lowest 16 lines indicate the cache state of the block (present versus not present) being transferred on the data bus. These lines help determine the state in which the data block will be loaded in the requesting processor (e.g., exclusive versus shared). Finally, in case one of the processors has not finished its snoop by this cycle, it indicates so by asserting the corresponding inhibit line. (The data resource ID lines double as inhibit lines during the acknowledgment and arbitration cycles.) It continues to assert this line until it has finished the snoop. If the snoop indicates a clean cache block, the snooping node simply drops the inhibit line and allows the requesting node to accept the memory's response. If the snoop indicates a dirty block, the node rearbitrates for the data bus, supplies the latest copy of the data, and only then drops the inhibit line.

For data bus transactions, once a slot becomes the master, the 128 bytes of cache block data are transferred in four consecutive cycles over the 256-bit-wide datapath. This four-cycle sequence begins with the acknowledgment cycle and ends at the address cycle of the following five-cycle bus phase. Since the 256-bit-wide datapath is used only for four out of five cycles, the maximum possible efficiency of these data lines is 80%. In some sense, though, this is the best that could be done; the signaling technology used in the Powerpath-2 bus requires one-cycle turnaround time between different controllers driving the lines.

6.5.2 SGI Processor and Memory Subsystems

In the Challenge architecture, each board contains multiple processors. To reduce the cost of interfacing to the bus, many of the bus interface chips are shared between the processors. Figure 6.15 shows the high-level organization of the processor board.

The processor board uses three different types of chips to interface to the bus and to support cache coherence. There is a single A-chip for all four processors that interfaces to the address bus. It contains logic for distributed arbitration, the eight-entry request tables storing currently outstanding transactions on the bus (see Section 6.4), and other control logic for deciding when transactions can be issued on the bus and how to respond to them. It passes on requests observed on the bus to the CC-chip (one for each processor), which uses a duplicate set of tags to determine the presence of that memory block in the local cache and communicates the results back to the A-chip. All requests from the processor also flow through the CC-chip to the A-chip, which then presents them on the bus. To interface to the 256-bit-wide data bus, four bit-sliced D-chips are used. The D-chips are quite simple and are shared among the processors; they provide limited buffering capability and simply pass data between the bus and the CC-chip associated with each processor (cache).

The Challenge main memory subsystem uses high-speed buffers to fan out addresses to a 576-bit-wide internal DRAM bus. The 576 bits consist of 512 bits of data and 64 bits of error correcting code (ECC), allowing for single-bit in-line correction and double-bit error detection. Fast page-mode access allows an entire 128-byte cache block to be read in two memory cycles, and data buffers pipeline the response to the 256-bit-wide system data bus. Twelve bus cycles (approximately 250 ns) after the address appears on the bus, the response data appears on the data bus. A single memory board can hold 2 GB of memory and supports a two-way interleaved memory system that is capable of saturating the 1.2-GB/s system bus.

Given the raw latency of 250 ns that the main memory subsystem takes, it is instructive to see the overall latency for a second-level cache miss experienced by

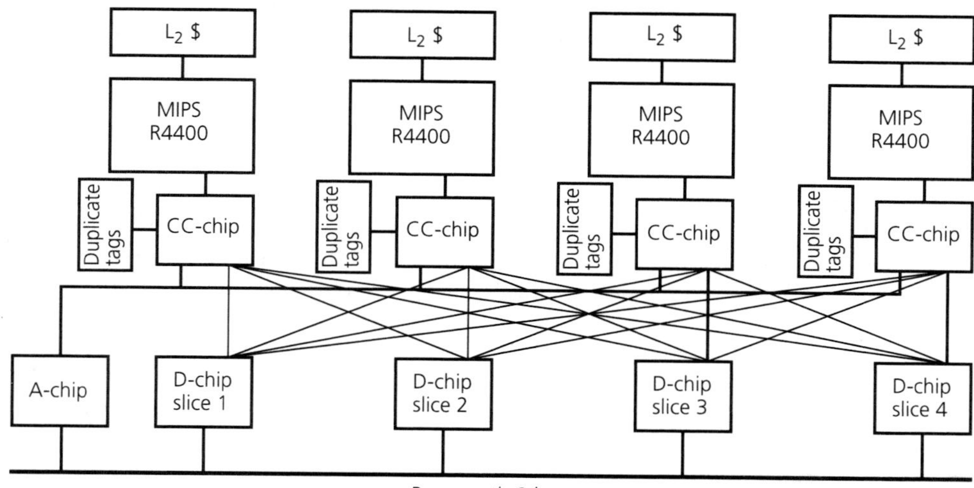

FIGURE 6.15 Organization and chip partitioning of the SGI Challenge processor board. To reduce the number of bus slots required to support 36 processors, 4 processors are put on each board. To maintain coherence and to interface to the bus, there is one cache coherence (CC) chip per processor, one shared A-chip that keeps track of requests to and from all four processors and interfaces to the address bus, and four shared bit-sliced D-chips that interface to the 256-bit-wide data bus.

the processor. On the Challenge, this number is close to 1 μs. It takes approximately 300 ns for the request to first appear on the bus; this includes time taken for the processor to realize that it has a first-level cache miss and then a second-level cache miss and then to filter through the CC-chip down to the A-chip. It takes approximately another 400 ns for the complete cache block to be delivered to the D-chips across the bus. These include the 3 bus cycles until the address stage of the request transaction, 12 bus cycles (250 ns) to access the main memory, and another 5 cycles for the data transaction to deliver the data over the bus. Finally, it takes another 300 ns for the data to flow through the D-chips, through the CC-chip, and through the 64-bit-wide interface onto the processor chip (16 cycles for the 128-byte cache block) where the data is loaded into the primary cache, and then to restart the processor pipeline.[4, 5]

4. Note that on both outgoing and return paths, the memory request passes through an asynchronous boundary. This adds a double synchronizer delay in both directions, about 30 ns on average in each direction. The benefit of decoupling is that the CPU can run at a different clock rate than the system bus, thus allowing for migration to higher-clock-rate CPUs while keeping the same bus clock rate. The cost, of course, is the extra latency.

5. The newer generation of processor, the MIPS R10000, allows the processor to restart after only the needed word has arrived, without having to wait for the complete cache block to arrive. This critical word restart mechanism reduces the miss latency.

To maintain cache coherence, the SGI Challenge uses the Illinois MESI protocol by default. It also supports update transactions. Interactions of the cache coherence protocol and the split-transaction bus are as described in Section 6.4.

6.5.3 SGI I/O Subsystem

To support the high computing power provided by multiple processors, careful attention needs to be devoted to providing matching I/O capability. The SGI Challenge provides scalable I/O performance by allowing multiple I/O cards to be placed on the system bus, each card providing a local 320-MB/s proprietary HIO I/O bus. Personality ASICs are provided to act as an interface between the I/O bus and standards-conforming (e.g., Ethernet, VME, SCSI, HPPI) and nonstandards-conforming (e.g., SGI Graphics) devices.

Figure 6.16 shows a block-level diagram of the SGI Challenge's PowerChannel-2 I/O subsystem. The bus is a 64-bit-wide multiplexed address/data bus that runs off the same clock as the system bus. It supports split read transactions, with up to four outstanding transactions per device. In contrast to the main system bus, it uses centralized arbitration, as latency is much less of a concern. However, arbitration is pipelined so that bus bandwidth is not wasted. Since the HIO bus supports several different transaction lengths (it does not require every transaction to handle a full cache block of data), transactions are required to indicate their length at time of request, and the arbiter uses this information to ensure more efficient utilization of the bus. The narrower HIO bus allows the personality ASICs to be cheaper than if they were to directly interface to the very wide system bus. In addition, common functionality needed to interface to the system bus is in this way shared by a number of personality ASICs.

HIO interface chips can request read or write DMA transfers to or from any locations in system memory using the full 40-bit system address, make a request for address translation using the mapping resource in the system interface (e.g., for 32-bit VME), request interrupting the processor, or respond to processor I/O (PIO) reads. The system bus interface provides DMA read responses and the results of address translation to the I/O devices and passes on PIO reads to them.

To the rest of the system (processor boards and main memory boards), the system bus interface on the I/O board provides a clean interface; it essentially acts like another processor board. Thus, when a DMA read request makes it through the I/O board's system bus interface onto the system bus, it becomes a Powerpath-2 read, just like one that a processor would issue. Similarly, when a full-cache-block DMA write goes out, it becomes a special block write transaction on the bus that invalidates copies of the block in all processors' caches (in addition to updating main memory). A special transaction is needed because even if a processor has the block dirty in its local cache, we do not want it to write it back in this case.

To support partial-block DMA writes, special care is needed because data must be merged coherently into main memory. To support these partial DMA writes, the system bus interface includes a fully associative, four-block cache that snoops on the Powerpath-2 system bus in the usual fashion. The cache blocks can be in one of only

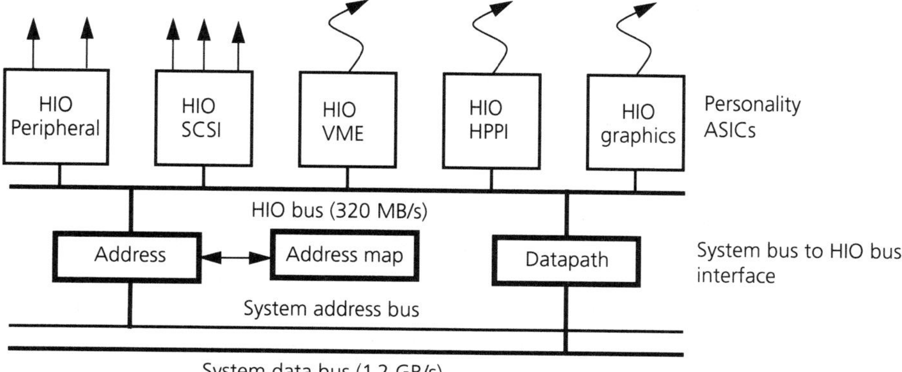

FIGURE 6.16 High-level organization of the SGI Challenge PowerChannel-2 I/O subsystem. Each I/O board provides an interface to the Powerpath-2 system bus and an internal 64-bit-wide HIO I/O bus with peak bandwidth of 320 MB/s. The narrower HIO bus lowers the cost of interfacing to it, and it supports a number of personality ASICs, which in turn support standard buses and peripherals.

two states: invalid or modified. When a partial DMA write is first issued, the block is brought into the four-block cache on the I/O board in modified state, invalidating the copies in all other processors' caches. Subsequent partial DMA writes need not go to the system bus if they hit in this cache, thus increasing the system bus efficiency. This modified block goes to the invalid state and supplies its contents on the system bus (1) on any system bus transaction that accesses this block; (2) when another partial DMA write causes the block to be replaced from the four-block cache; and (3) on any HIO bus read transaction that accesses the block. While DMA reads could have also used this four-block cache, the designers felt that partial DMA reads were rare, and the gains from such an optimization would have been minimal.

The address map RAM in the system bus interface provides general-purpose address translation for I/O devices to access main memory. For example, it may be used to map small address spaces such as VME-24 or VME-32 into the 40-bit physical address space of the Powerpath-2 bus. Two types of mapping are supported: one-level and two-level. One-level mappings simply return one of the 8-K entries in the mapping RAM, where by convention each entry maps 2 MB of physical memory. In the two-level scheme, the map entry points to the page tables in main memory. Each 4-KB page has its own entry in the second-level table, so virtual pages can be arbitrarily mapped to physical pages. Note that PIO requests (from the processors) face a similar translation problem when going down to the I/O devices. Such translation is not done using the mapping RAM but is directly handled by the personality ASIC interface chips.

The final issue that we examine for I/O is flow control. All requests proceeding from the I/O interfaces to the Powerpath-2 system bus are implicitly flow controlled;

that is, the HIO interface will not issue a read on the system bus unless it has buffer space reserved for the response. Similarly, the HIO arbiter will not grant the HIO bus to a requestor unless the system interface has room to accept the transaction. In the other direction, from the processors to the I/O devices, however, PIOs can arrive unsolicited, and they need to be explicitly flow controlled.

The explicit flow control solution used in the Challenge system is to make the PIOs appear to the HIO interface ASICs as if they were solicited. After reset, HIO interface chips (e.g., HIO-VME, HIO-HPPI) transmit their available PIO buffer space to the system bus interface using special requests called IncPIO requests. The system bus interface maintains this information in a separate counter for each HIO device. Every time a PIO is sent to a particular device, the corresponding count is decremented. Every time that device retires a PIO, it issues another IncPIO request to increment its counter. If the system bus interface receives a PIO for a device that has no buffer space available, it rejects (NACKs) that request on the system bus, and the request must be retried later.

6.5.4 SGI Challenge Memory System Performance

The access time for various levels of the SGI Challenge memory system can be determined using the simple read microbenchmark from Chapter 4. Recall that the microbenchmark measures the average access time in reading elements of an array of a given size with a certain stride. Figure 6.17 shows the read access time for a range of sizes and strides. Each curve shows the average access time for a given size as a function of the stride. Arrays smaller than 32 KB fit entirely in the first-level cache. Second-level cache accesses have an access time of roughly 75 ns, and the inflection point at 16-byte stride shows that the transfer size between the L_2 and L_1 caches is 16 bytes. The second bump shows the additional penalty of roughly 140 ns for a TLB miss and reveals that the page size is 8 KB. (Can you think why the time per miss drops back as the stride increases further?) Starting with a 2-MB array, accesses miss in the 1-MB L_2 cache, and we see that the combination of the L_2 controller, the Powerpath bus protocol, and DRAM access results in an access time of roughly 1,150 ns. The minimum bus protocol of 13 cycles from request to reply accounts for a little under 300 ns of this time, as discussed earlier. TLB misses add roughly 200 ns to this 1,150-ns figure. A simple ping-pong microbenchmark, in which a pair of nodes each spins on a flag until the flag indicates their turn and then sets the flag to signal the other, shows a round-trip time of 6.2 μs.

6.5.5 Sun Gigaplane System Bus

The Sun Gigaplane is also a nonmultiplexed, split-transaction bus with 256-bit data lines and 41-bit physical addresses but is clocked at 83.5 MHz. It is a *centerplane design*, a bus wiring and connection assembly that allows cards to plug into both sides, rather than a single-sided backplane. The total length of the bus is 18 inches, so eight boards can plug into each side with 2 inches of cooling space between boards and 1-inch spacing between connectors. In sharp contrast to the SGI Chal-

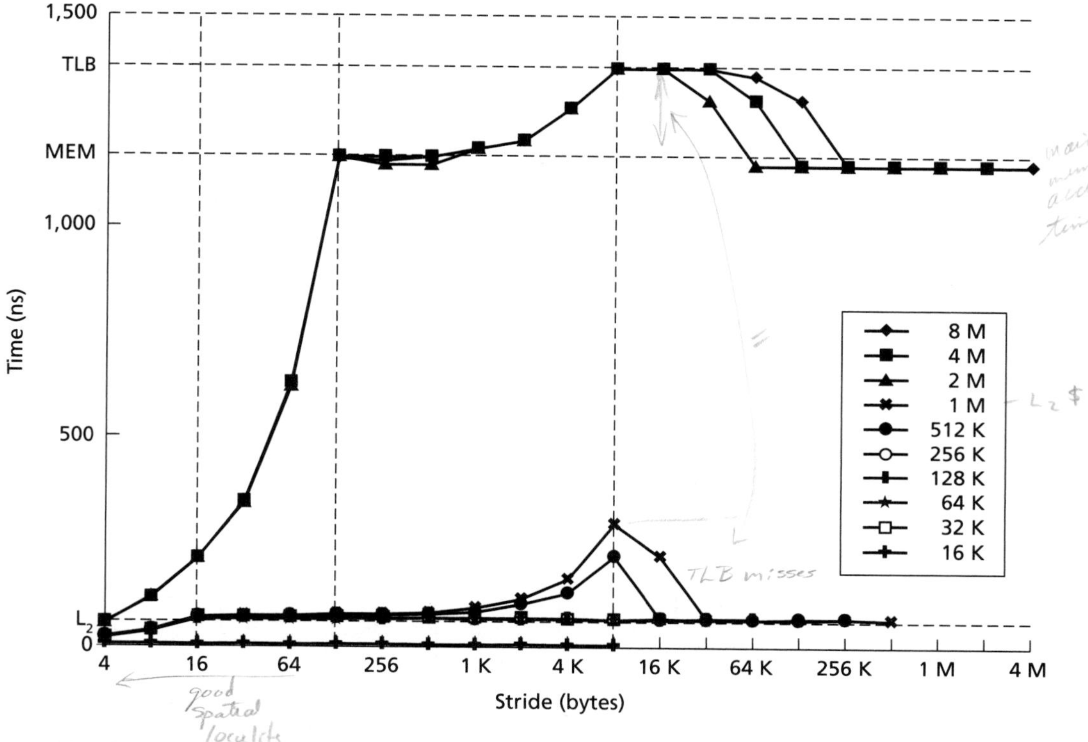

FIGURE 6.17 Read microbenchmark results for the SGI Challenge. Each curve is for an array of the size shown in the legend. The datapoints for array sizes 32 K to 256 K are so similar that they cannot be easily distinguished.

lenge Powerpath-2 bus, the bus can support up to 112 outstanding transactions, including up to 7 from each board, so it is designed for devices that can sustain multiple outstanding transactions, such as lockup-free caches. The electrical and mechanical design allows for live insertion (hot plugging) of processing and I/O modules.

The bus consists of a total of 388 signals: 256 data, 32 ECC, 43 address (with parity), 7 ID tag, 18 arbitration, and a number of configuration signals. The electrical design allows for turnaround between data transfers with no dead cycles. Emphasis is placed on minimizing the latency of operations, and the protocol (illustrated in Figure 6.18) is quite different from that on the SGI Challenge. A novel collision-based speculative arbitration technique is used to avoid the cost of bus arbitration. When a requestor arbitrates for the address bus, if the address bus is not scheduled to be in use from the previous cycle, it speculatively drives its request on the address bus in the arbitration cycle itself. If no other requestors are in that cycle, it wins arbitration and has already passed the address, so it can continue with the remainder of the transaction. If a request collision occurs, the requestor that wins

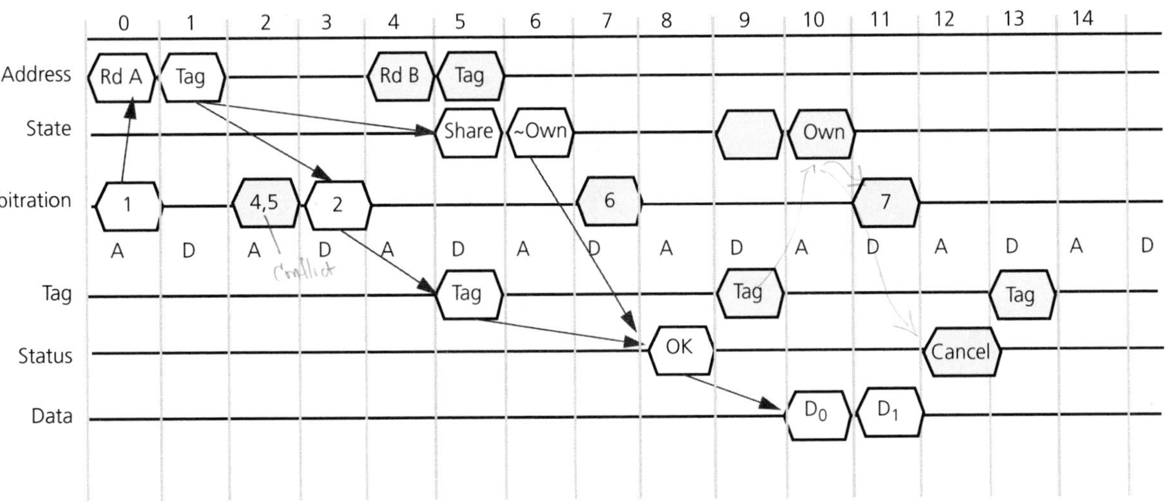

FIGURE 6.18 Sun Gigaplane signal timing for BusRd with fast address arbitration. The pipeline slots occupied by two BusRd transactions are shown, one unshaded and one shaded. The horizontal bold lines show the different components of the bus, and the vertical dotted lines delineate bus cycles. "A" and "D" under the arbitration component of the bus indicate address and data bus arbitration cycles. The arrows indicate the path of the first BusRd transaction. Board 1 initiates a read transaction with fast arbitration (so the address is successfully driven in the same cycle), which is responded to by home board 2. The snoop result indicates that no cache is the owner of the block, so the home board drives the response on the data lines. For the second BusRd transaction, boards 4 and 5 collide during address bus arbitration; board 4 wins and initiates a read transaction. Home board 6 arbitrates for the data bus and then cancels its response because the snoop result indicates ownership by a cache. Eventually the owning cache, on board 7, responds with the data. Board 5's retried transaction is not shown.

arbitration simply drives the address again in the next cycle, as it would with conventional arbitration.

The 7-bit tag associated with the request is presented on the address bus in the cycle following the address (see Figure 6.18). The snoop state is associated with the address phase, not the data phase. Five cycles after the address, all boards assert their snoop signals (shared, owned, mapped, and ignore) on the "state" bus lines. In the meantime, the board responsible for the memory address (the home board) can request the data bus three cycles after the address, before the snoop result. The DRAM access can be started speculatively as well. When the home board wins arbitration, it must assert the tag bus lines two cycles later, informing all devices of the approaching data transfer. Three cycles after driving the tag and two cycles before the data, the home board drives a status signal, which may indicate that the data transfer is canceled if some cache owns the block (as detected in the snoop state). The owner places the data on the bus by arbitrating for the data bus, driving the tag, and driving the data. Figure 6.18 shows a second (gray) read transaction, which experiences a collision in arbitration, so the address is supplied in the conventional slot. The snoop for this transaction indicates ownership by a cache, so the home board cancels its data transfer. Later, that owning cache arbitrates for the data bus and drives the data response.

Like the SGI Challenge, invalidations are ordered by the BusRdX requests appearing on the address bus and are handled in FIFO fashion by the cache subsystems; thus, no explicit acknowledgment of invalidation completion is required. To maintain sequential consistency, it is still necessary to gain arbitration for the address bus before allowing the writing processor to proceed with memory operations past the write.[6]

6.5.6 Sun Processor and Memory Subsystem

In the Sun Enterprise, each processing board has two processors, each with external L_2 caches, and two banks of memory connected through a crossbar, as shown in Figure 6.19. Data lines within the UltraSparc module are buffered to drive an internal bus, called the UPA (universal port architecture) with an internal bandwidth of 1.3 GB/s. A very wide path to memory is provided so that a full 64-byte cache block can be read in a single memory cycle, which is two bus cycles in length. The address controller adapts the UPA protocol to the Gigaplane protocol, realizes the cache coherence protocol, provides buffering, and tracks the potentially large number of outstanding transactions. It maintains a set of duplicate tags, called D-tags, for the L_2 cache. To ensure cache coherence, even accesses to the local memory module from a processor go through the address controller.

Although the UltraSparc implements a five-state MOESI protocol in the L_2 caches, the D-tags maintain an approximation using only three states: owned, shared, and invalid. They essentially combine states that are handled identically at the Gigaplane

---

6. The Sparc V9 specification weakens the consistency model in this respect to allow the processor to employ write buffers, which we discuss in more depth in Chapter 9.

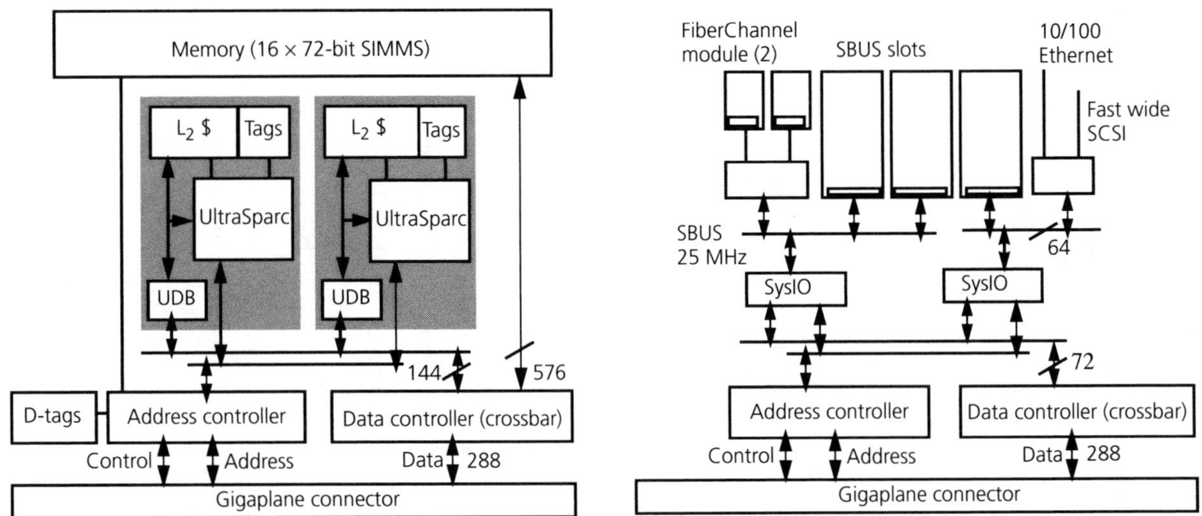

FIGURE 6.19 Organization of the Sun Enterprise processing and I/O boards. The processing board (left) contains two UltraSparc modules with L_2 caches on an internal bus and two wide memory banks interfaced to the system bus through two ASICs. The address controller adapts between the two bus protocols and implements the cache coherence protocol. The data controller is essentially a crossbar. The I/O board (right) uses the same two ASICs to interface to two I/O controllers. The SysIO ASICs appear to the bus as a one-block cache that follows the coherence protocol. On the other side, they support independent I/O buses and interfaces to FiberChannel, Ethernet, and SCSI.

level. In particular, the address controller needs to know if the L_2 cache has a copy of a block and if it is an exclusive copy. It does not need to know if that block is clean or dirty. For example, on a BusRd the block will need to be flushed onto the bus if it is in the L_2 cache in any of the following three states: modified, owned (flushed since last modified), or exclusive (not shared when read and not modified since); thus, the D-tags represent only owned. This has the advantage that the address controller need not be informed when the UltraSparc elevates a block from exclusive to modified. It will be informed of a transition from invalid, shared, or owned to modified because in these cases it needs to initiate a bus transaction.

6.5.7 Sun I/O Subsystem

An Enterprise I/O board uses the same bus interface ASICs as the processing board, but the internal bus is only half as wide and there is no memory path. Externally, the I/O boards only do cache-block-sized transactions, just like the processing boards, in order to simplify the design of the main system bus. The SysIO ASICs implement a single-block cache, which follows the coherence protocol, on behalf of the I/O devices. Internally, two independent 64-bit 25-MHz SBUSs are supported. One of these supports two dedicated FiberChannel modules providing a redundant, high-bandwidth interconnect to large disk storage arrays. The other provides dedicated Ethernet and fast wide SCSI connections. In addition, three SBUS interface cards can be plugged into the two buses to support arbitrary peripherals, including a 622-MB/s ATM interface. The I/O bandwidth, the connectivity to peripherals, and the cost of the I/O subsystem scales with the number of I/O cards.

6.5.8 Sun Enterprise Memory System Performance

The access time for various levels of the Sun Enterprise via the read microbenchmark is shown in Figure 6.20. Arrays of 16 KB or less fit entirely in the first-level cache. Level 2 cache accesses have an access time of roughly 40 ns, and the inflection point shows that the transfer size between these levels is 16 bytes. With a 1-MB array, accesses miss in the L_2 cache, and we see that the combination of the L_2 controller, bus protocol, and DRAM access result in an access time of roughly 300 ns. The minimum bus protocol of 11 cycles at 83.5 MHz accounts for 130 ns of this time. TLB misses add roughly 340 ns to the miss penalty since the machine has a software TLB handler. The simple ping-pong microbenchmark, in which a pair of nodes each spins on a flag until it indicates their turn and then sets the flag to signal the other, shows a round-trip time of 1.7 μs, roughly five memory accesses.

6.5.9 Application Performance

Now that we have an understanding of the machines and their microbenchmark performance, let us examine the performance obtained on our parallel applications. Absolute application performance for commercial machines is not presented in this book; instead, the focus is on performance improvements due to parallelism. Let us

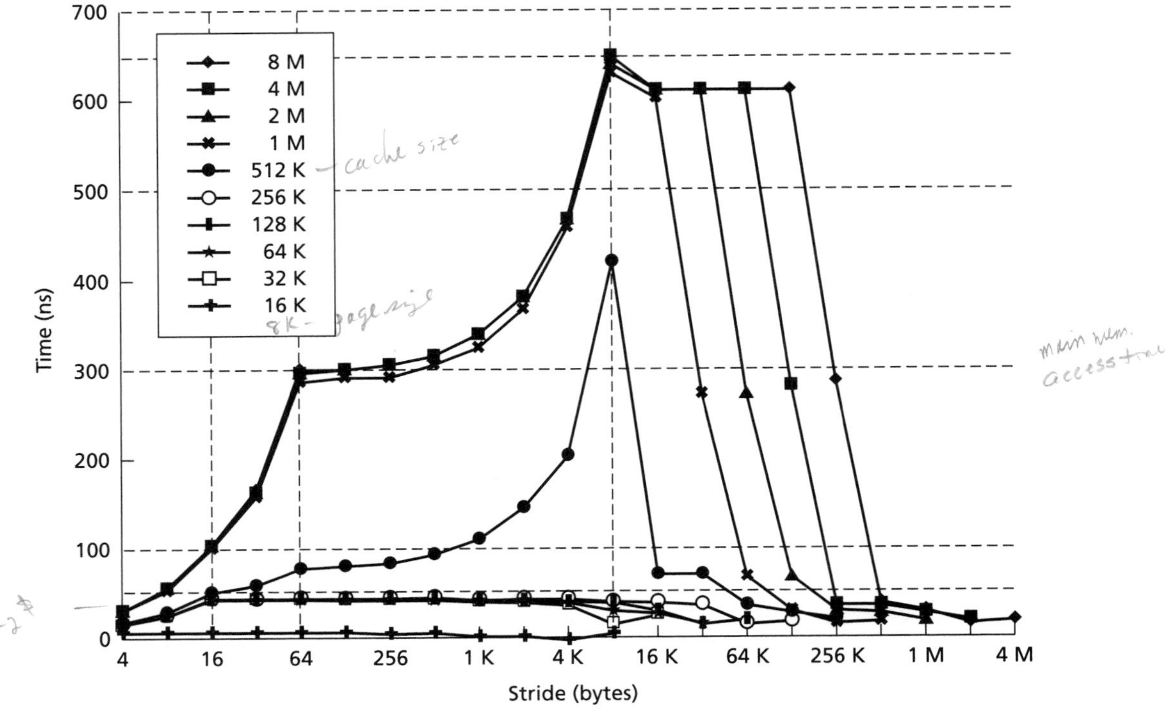

FIGURE 6.20 Read microbenchmark results for the Sun Enterprise. Each curve is for an array of the size shown in the legend.

first look at application speedups and then at scaling, using only the SGI Challenge for illustration.

Application Speedups

Figure 6.21 shows the speedups obtained on our six parallel programs for two data set sizes each. We can see that the speedups are quite good for most of the programs, with the exception of the Radix sorting kernel. Examining the breakdown of execution time for the sorting kernel shows that the vast majority of the time is spent stalled on data access. The shared bus simply gets swamped with the data and coherence traffic due to the permutation phase of the sort, and the resulting contention destroys performance. The contention also leads to severe load imbalances in data access time and, hence, time spent waiting at global barriers, even though busy time is well balanced. Contention is unfortunately not alleviated much by increasing the problem size since the communication-to-computation ratio, and hence the bandwidth demand, in the permutation phase is independent of problem size (see Section 4.4.1). The results shown are for a radix value of 256, which delivers the

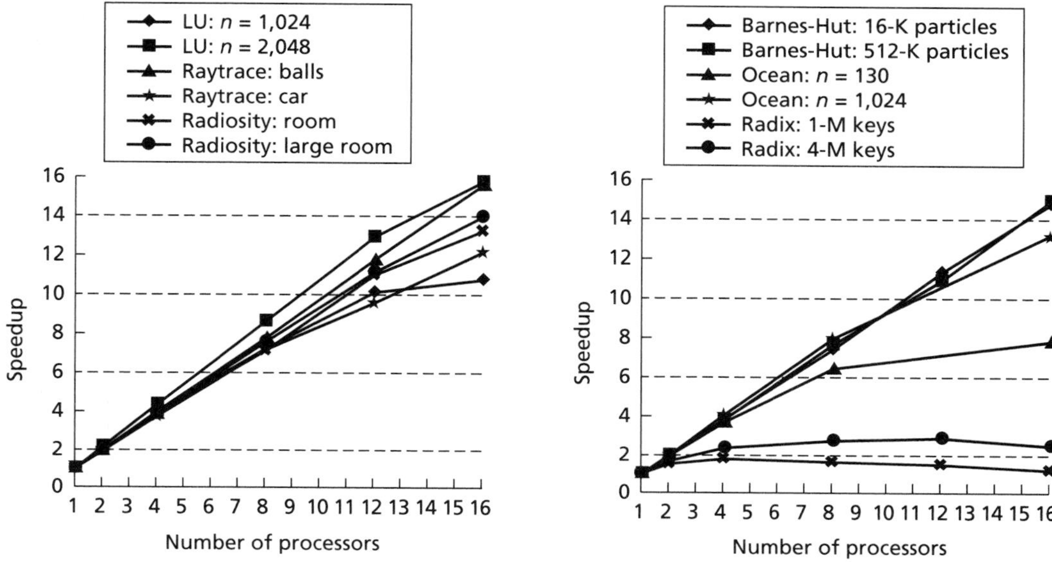

FIGURE 6.21 Speedups for the six parallel applications on the SGI Challenge. The block size for the blocked LU factorization is 32 × 32.

best performance over the range of processor counts for both problem sizes. Barnes-Hut, Raytrace, and Radiosity speed up very well even for the relatively small input problems used. LU does too, and the bottleneck for the smaller problem at 16 processors is primarily load imbalance as the factorization proceeds along the matrix. Finally, the bottleneck for the small Ocean problem size is both the high communication-to-computation ratio and the imbalance this generates since some partitions have fewer neighbors than others. Both problems are alleviated by running larger data sets.

Scaling

Let us now examine the impact of scaling for a few of the programs. According to the discussion in Chapter 4, we look at the speedups under the different scaling models as well as at how the work done and the data set size used change. Figure 6.22 shows the results for the Barnes-Hut and Ocean applications. Naive TC (time-constrained) or MC (memory-constrained) scaling refers to scaling only the parameter that chiefly governs the data set size—the number of bodies or grid points (n)—without changing the other application parameters (accuracy or the number of time-steps). It is clear that the work done under realistic MC scaling grows much faster than linearly in the number of processors in both applications, so the parallel execution time grows very quickly. The number of bodies or grid points that can be

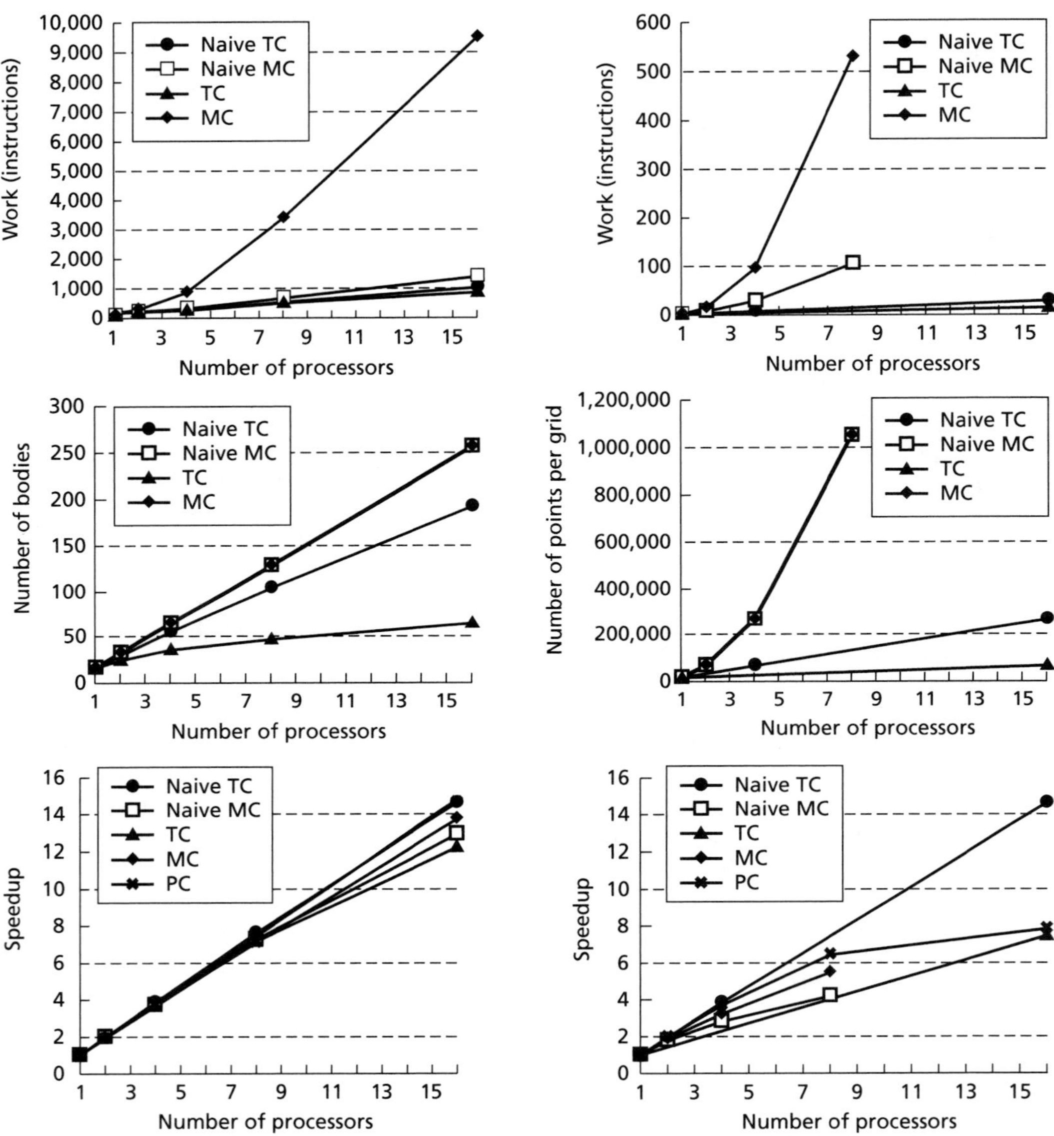

FIGURE 6.22 Scaling results for Barnes-Hut (left) and Ocean (right) on the SGI Challenge. The graphs show the scaling of work done, data set size (measured in number of bodies or grid points), and speedups under different scaling models. PC, TC, and MC refer to problem-constrained, time-constrained, and memory-constrained scaling, respectively. The baseline problem sizes are 16-K bodies for Barnes-Hut and 130 × 130 grids for Ocean. The top set of graphs shows that the work needed to solve the problem grows very quickly under realistic MC scaling for both applications. The middle set of graphs shows that the data set size that can be run grows much more quickly under MC or naive TC scaling than under realistic TC scaling. The impact of the scaling model on speedup is much larger for Ocean than for Barnes-Hut, primarily because the communication-to-computation ratio is much more strongly dependent on data set size and number of processors in Ocean.

simulated under TC scaling grows much more slowly than under MC and also much more slowly than under naive TC scaling, where it is the only application parameter scaled. Scaling the other application parameters causes the work done and execution time to increase, leaving much less room to grow n.

The speedups under different scaling models are measured as described in Chapter 4. Consider the Barnes-Hut galaxy simulation, where the speedups are quite good for this size of machine under all scaling models. The differences can be explained by examining the major performance factors. The communication-to-computation ratio in the force calculation phase depends primarily on the number of bodies. Another important factor that affects performance is the ratio of work done in the force calculation phase, which speeds up well, to that done in the tree-building phase, which does not. This ratio tends to increase with greater accuracy in force computation, that is, smaller θ. However, smaller θ (and to a lesser extent greater n) increase the working set size per processor (Singh, Hennessy, and Gupta 1993). The important working set continues to fit in the large second-level cache even under scaling, but the scaled problem that changes θ may have worse first-level cache behavior than the baseline problem does on a uniprocessor. These factors explain why naive TC scaling yields better speedups than realistic TC scaling: the working sets behave better, and the communication-to-computation ratio is more favorable since n grows more quickly when θ and Δt are not scaled.

The speedups for Ocean are quite different under different models. Here too, the major controlling factors are the communication-to-computation ratio, the working set size, and the time spent in different phases. However, all the effects are much more strongly dependent on the grid size relative to the number of processors. Under MC scaling, the communication-to-computation ratio does not change with the number of processors used, so we might expect the best speedups. However, two effects become visible as we scale. First, conflict misses across different grids increase as a processor's partitions of the grids become further apart in the address space. Second, more time is spent in the higher levels of the multigrid hierarchy in the solver, which have worse parallel performance. The latter effect turns out to be alleviated when the accuracy and time-step interval are refined as well (at least, this is beneficial for parallel speedup), so realistic MC scales a little better than naive MC. Under naive TC scaling, the growth in grid size is not fast enough to cause major conflict problems but is fast enough that the communication-to-computation ratio does not increase significantly, so speedups are very good. Realistic TC scaling causes a slower growth of grid size and hence a greater increase in the communication-to-computation ratio, resulting in lower speedups. Clearly, many effects play important roles in determining parallel performance under scaling, and which scaling model is most appropriate for an application affects the results of evaluating a machine.

6.6 EXTENDING CACHE COHERENCE

The snooping-based techniques for achieving cache coherence described in this and the previous chapter extend in many directions. This section examines a few important ones: scaling down with shared caches, scaling in functionality with virtually indexed caches and translation lookaside buffers (TLBs), and scaling up with non-bus interconnects.

6.6.1 Shared Cache Designs

Grouping processors together to share a level of the memory hierarchy (e.g., the first- or the second-level cache) is a potentially attractive option for shared memory multiprocessors, especially due to packaging considerations such as placing multiple processors on a chip. Compared with each processor having its own cache or memory at that level of the hierarchy, grouping processors together has several potential benefits. The benefits—like the drawbacks to be discussed later—are encountered when sharing at any level of the hierarchy but are most extreme when it is the first-level cache that is shared among processors. The benefits of sharing a cache among a group of processors at a level are as follows:

- It eliminates the need for a cache coherence protocol at this level. In particular, if the first-level cache is shared by all processors, then there are no multiple copies of a cache block and hence no coherence problem at all.
- It reduces the latency of communication within the group. The latency of communication between processors is closely related to the level in the memory hierarchy where they meet. When sharing the first-level cache, communication latency can be as low as 2–10 processor clock cycles. The corresponding latency when processors meet at the main memory level is usually many times larger (see the Challenge and Enterprise case studies). The reduced latency enables finer-grained sharing of data between tasks executed on the different processors.
- Once one processor misses on a piece of data and brings it into the shared cache, other processors in the group that need the data may find it already there and will not have to miss on it at that level of the hierarchy. This is called *prefetching* data across processors. With private caches, each processor would have to incur a miss separately. The reduced number of misses reduces the bandwidth requirements at the next level of the memory and interconnect hierarchy.
- It allows more effective use of long cache blocks. Spatial locality is exploited even when different words on a cache block are accessed by different processors in a group. In addition, since there is no cache coherence protocol within a group at this level, there is no false sharing either. For example, consider a situation where two processors P_1 and P_2 write every alternate word of a large array, and think about the differences when they share a first-level cache and when they have private first-level caches.
- The working sets (code or data) of the processors in a group may overlap significantly, allowing the size of the shared cache to be smaller than the combined size of the private caches if each had to hold its processor's entire working set. This reduction of cache size is especially useful for a multiprocessor on a chip, where silicon area is a significant constraint.

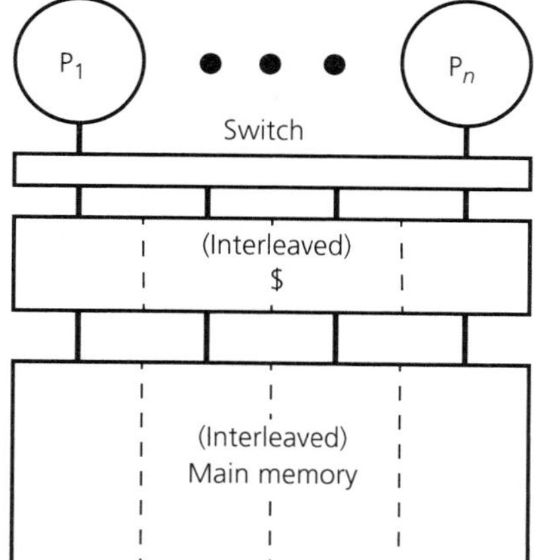

FIGURE 6.23 Generic architecture for a multiprocessor with a first-level cache shared among all processors. The interconnect is placed between the processors and the first-level cache. The shared cache is backed up directly by main memory in this design, and both the cache and the memory system may be interleaved to provide high bandwidth. Of course, such a design is appropriate only for a small number of processors due to bandwidth limitations of the shared cache or switch and the latency imposed by large switches.

- It increases the utilization of the cache hardware. The shared cache does not sit idle because one processor is stalled but, rather, services other references from other processors in the group.
- The grouping fits well with the hierarchy in packaging technologies (cabinets, boards, multichip modules, and chips) and allows us to effectively use emerging packaging technologies to achieve higher computational densities (computation power per unit area).

When sharing a first-level cache, processors are connected to the shared cache by a switch as in Figure 6.23. The switch could be a bus but is more likely a crossbar to allow cache accesses from different processors to proceed in parallel. Similarly, to support the high bandwidth demands imposed by multiple processors, both the cache and the main memory system are interleaved. An early example of such a shared cache architecture is the Alliant FX-8 machine, designed in the early 1980s. An Alliant FX-8 contained up to eight custom processors. Each processor was a pipelined implementation of the 68020 instruction set, augmented with vector instructions, and had a clock cycle of 170 ns. All eight processors were connected using a crossbar to a 512-KB four-way interleaved cache. The cache had 32-byte blocks and was write back, direct mapped, and lockup-free, allowing each processor to have two outstanding misses. The cache-to-processor bandwidth was eight 64-bit words per instruction cycle.

A somewhat different early use of the shared cache approach was exemplified by the Encore Multimax, a contemporary of the FX-8. The Multimax was a snoopy cache-coherent multiprocessor, but each cache supported two processors instead of one (with no need for coherence within a pair). The motivation for Encore at the time was to lower the cost of snooping hardware and to increase the utilization of the cache given the very slow, multiple-CPI processors.

Today, shared first-level caches are being investigated for single-chip multiprocessors, in which four to eight multiprocessors share an on-chip first-level cache. These can be used in themselves as multiprocessors or as the building blocks for larger systems that maintain coherence across the single-chip shared cache groups. As technology advances and the number of transistors on a chip reaches several tens or hundreds of millions, this approach becomes increasingly attractive. Since interprocessor communication and synchronization within a chip can be quite inexpensive, workstations using such chips will be able to offer very high performance for workloads requiring either fine-grained or coarse-grained parallelism. The question is whether this is a more effective approach or one that uses the available transistors to build more complex processors.

Unfortunately, sharing caches also has several disadvantages and challenges:

- The shared cache has to satisfy the bandwidth requirements from multiple processors, restricting the size of a group. The problem is particularly acute for shared first-level caches, which are therefore limited to very small numbers of processors. Providing the bandwidth needed is one of the biggest challenges of the single-chip multiprocessor approach.
- The hit latency to a shared cache is usually higher than to a private cache at the same level due to the interconnect in between. For shared first-level caches, the imposition of a switch between the processor and the first-level cache means that either the machine clock cycle is elongated or that additional delay slots are added for load instructions in the processor pipeline. The slowdown due to the former is obvious. While compilers have some capability to schedule independent instructions in load delay slots, the success depends on the application. Particularly for programs that don't have a lot of instruction-level parallelism, some slowdown is inevitable. The increased hit latency is aggravated by contention at the shared cache and, correspondingly, the miss latency is also increased by sharing.
- For the preceding reasons, the design complexity for building an effective shared cache is higher than for a private cache.
- Although a shared cache need not be as large as the sum of the private caches it replaces, it is still much larger and, hence, slower than each individual private cache. For first-level caches, this too will either elongate the machine clock cycle or lead to cache access times of multiple processor cycles.
- The converse of overlapping working sets (or constructive interference) is the performance of the shared cache being hurt because of cache conflicts across reference streams from different processors (destructive interference). When a shared cache multiprocessor is used to run workloads with little data sharing (e.g., a parallel compilation or a database or transaction processing workload), the interference in the cache between the data sets needed by the different processors can hurt performance substantially. In scientific computing, where performance is paramount, many programs try to manage their use of the per-processor cache very carefully so that the many arrays they access do not interfere in the cache. All this effort by the programmer or compiler can easily be undone in a shared cache system. Shared caches may require higher associativity than private caches, which may increase their access time as well.

- Finally, at the current time, shared first-level caches do not meet the trend toward using commodity microprocessor technology to build cost-effective parallel machines.

Since many microprocessors already provide snooping support for first-level caches, an attractive approach may be to have private first-level caches and a shared second-level cache among groups of processors. This approach softens both the benefits and the drawbacks of shared first-level caches but may be a good trade-off overall. The shared cache is likely to be large to reduce destructive interference. In practice, packaging considerations also have a very large impact on decisions to share caches.

6.6.2 Coherence for Virtually Indexed Caches

Recall from uniprocessor architecture the trade-offs between physically and virtually indexed caches, that is, caches that are indexed using a physical or virtual address. With physically indexed first-level caches, allowing cache indexing to proceed in parallel with address translation requires that the cache be either very small or very highly associative. This ensures that the bits that do not change under translation—$\log_2$(`page_size`) bits or a few more if page coloring is used—are sufficient to index into the cache (Hennessy and Patterson 1996). As on-chip first-level caches become larger, virtually indexed caches become more attractive. However, these have their own problems. First, different processors may use the same virtual address to refer to unrelated data in different address spaces. This can be handled by flushing the whole cache on a context switch or by associating address space identifier (ASID) tags with cache blocks in addition to virtual address tags. The more serious problem for cache coherence is synonyms: distinct virtual pages, from the same or different processes, that point to the same physical page for sharing purposes. With virtually addressed caches, the same (shared) physical memory block can be fetched into two distinct blocks at different indices in the cache. This is a problem for uniprocessors, as we know, but the problem extends to cache coherence in multiprocessors as well. If one processor writes the block using one virtual address synonym and another reads it using a different synonym, then by simply putting virtual addresses on the bus and snooping them, the write to the shared physical page will not become visible to the latter processor. Putting virtual addresses on the bus also has another drawback: it requires I/O devices and memory to do virtual-to-physical translation since they deal with physical addresses. However, putting physical addresses on the bus seems to require reverse translation to look up the virtually indexed caches during a snoop, and this does not solve the synonym coherence problem by itself anyway.

The synonym problem can be avoided in software by restricting the use of synonyms. For example, synonyms may be forced to have the same page color, that is, to be the same in the bits used to index the cache if these are more than $\log_2$(`page_size`) bits. Alternatively, processes may be required to use the same shared virtual address when referring to the same page, as in the SPUR research project (Hill et al. 1986).

Sophisticated cache designs have also been proposed to solve the synonym coherence problem in hardware (Goodman 1987). The idea is to use virtual addresses to look up the cache on processor accesses but to put physical addresses on the bus for other caches and devices to snoop. This requires mechanisms to be provided for the following: (1) to look up the cache with the physical address if a lookup with the virtual address fails (by which time the physical address is available) or if it is detected that the block was brought into the cache by a synonym access; (2) to ensure that the same physical block is never in the same cache under two different virtual addresses at the same time; and (3) to convert a snooped physical address to an effective virtual address to look up the snooping cache. One way to accomplish these goals is for caches to maintain both virtual and physical tags (and states) for their cached blocks, indexed by virtual and physical addresses, respectively, and for the two tags for a block to point to each other (i.e., to store the corresponding physical and virtual indexes, respectively; see Figure 6.24). The cache data array itself is indexed using the virtual index (or the pointer from the physical tag entry, which is the same, in the case of a snoop). Let's see at a high level how this organization provides the needed mechanisms.

A processor looks up the cache with its virtual address, and at the same time, the virtual-to-physical translation is done by the memory management unit in case it is needed. If the lookup with the virtual address succeeds, all is well. If it fails, the translated physical address is used to look up the physical tags; if this hits, the block is found through the pointer in the physical tag. This achieves the first goal as follows. A virtual miss but physical hit detects the possibility of a synonym since the physical block may have been brought in via a different virtual address. In a direct-mapped cache, it must have been brought in by a different virtual address, so let us assume a direct-mapped cache for simplicity. The pointer contained in the physical tags now points to a different block in the cache array (the synonym virtual index) than the current virtual index. We need to make the current virtual index point to this physical data and reconcile the virtual and physical tags to remove the synonym. The physical block, which is currently at the synonym virtual index, is copied over to replace the block at the current virtual index (which is written back if necessary), so references to the current virtual index will hereafter hit right away. The block at the synonym virtual index is rendered invalid or inaccessible, so the data is now accessible only through the current virtual index (or through the physical address via the pointer in the physical tag in the case of a snoop) but not through the synonym virtual index. A subsequent access to the synonym will miss on its virtual address lookup and will have to go through the same procedure. Thus, a given physical block is valid only in one (virtually indexed) location in the cache at any given time, accomplishing the second goal. Note that if both the virtual and physical address lookups fail (a true cache miss), up to two write backs may be needed. The new block brought into the cache will be placed at the index determined from the current virtual (not physical) address, and the virtual and physical tags and states will be suitably updated to point to each other.

The address put on the bus is always a physical address, whether for a write back, a read miss, or a read exclusive or upgrade. Snooping with physical addresses from

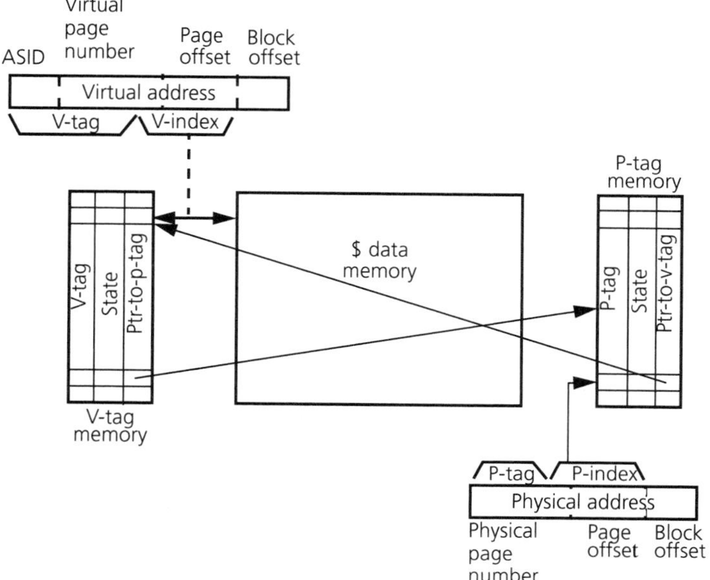

FIGURE 6.24 Organization of a dual-tagged virtually addressed cache. The v-tag memory on the left services the CPU and is indexed by virtual addresses. The p-tag memory on the right is used for bus snooping and is indexed by physical addresses. The contents of the memory block are stored based on the index of the v-tag. Corresponding p-tag and v-tag entries point to each other for handling updates to the cache.

the bus is easy. Explicit reverse translation is not required since the information needed is already there. The physical tags are looked up to check for the presence of the block, and the data is found from the pointer (corresponding virtual index) it contains. If action must be taken, the state in the virtual tag pointed to by the physical tag entry is updated as well. Further details of how such a cache system operates can be found in (Goodman 1987). This approach has also been extended to multilevel caches, where it is even more attractive: the L_1 cache is virtually tagged to speed cache access and the L_2 cache is physically tagged to facilitate snooping and avoid synonyms across processors (Wang, Baer, and Levy 1989).

6.6.3 Translation Lookaside Buffer Coherence

A processor's translation lookaside buffer (TLB) is simply a cache on the page table entries (PTEs) used for virtual-to-physical address translation. A PTE can come to reside in the TLBs of multiple processors due to either actual sharing of data or process migration. PTEs may be modified—for example, when the page is swapped out or its protection is changed—leading to direct analog of the cache coherence problem.

A variety of solutions have been used for TLB coherence. Software solutions, through the operating system, are popular since TLB coherence operations are much less frequent than cache coherence operations. The exact solutions used depend on whether PTEs are loaded into the TLB directly by hardware or under software control as well as on several other variables in how TLBs and operating systems are implemented. Hardware solutions are also used by some systems, particularly when TLB operations are not visible to software. This section provides a brief overview of four approaches to TLB coherence: virtually addressed caches, software TLB shootdown, address space identifiers (ASIDs), and hardware TLB coherence. Further details can be found in (Thompson et al. 1988; Rosenburg 1989; Teller 1990) and the papers referenced therein.

TLBs, and hence the TLB coherence problem, can be avoided entirely by using virtually addressed caches. Address translation is now needed only on cache misses, so particularly if the cache miss rate is small, we can use the page tables directly. Page table entries are brought into the regular data cache when they are accessed and are therefore kept coherent by the cache coherence mechanism. However, when a physical page is swapped out of memory or its protection changed, this is not visible to the cache coherence hardware, so the PTE must be flushed from the virtually addressed caches of all processors by the operating system. In addition, the coherence problem for virtually addressed caches must be solved. This approach was explored in the SPUR research project (Hill et al. 1986; Wood et al. 1986).

A second approach is called TLB shootdown. There are many variants that rely on different (but small) amounts of hardware support, usually including support for interprocessor interrupts and invalidation of individual TLB entries. The TLB coherence procedure is invoked by a processor, called the *initiator,* when it makes changes to PTEs that may be cached by other TLBs. Since changes to PTEs must be made by the operating system, the OS knows which PTEs are being changed and it may also know which other processors might be caching them in their TLBs (conservatively, since entries may have been replaced). The OS kernel locks the PTEs being changed (or the relevant page table sections, depending on the granularity of locking) and sends interrupts to other processors that it thinks have copies. On being interrupted, the recipients disable interrupts, look at the list of page table entries being modified (which is in shared memory), and locally invalidate those entries from their TLBs. The initiator waits for them to finish, perhaps by polling shared memory locations, and then unlocks the page table sections. A different, somewhat more complex shootdown algorithm is used in the Mach operating system (Black et al. 1989).

Some processor families, most notably the MIPS family from Silicon Graphics, use software-loaded rather than hardware-loaded TLBs, which means that the OS is involved not only in PTE modifications but also in loading a PTE into the TLB on a miss. In these cases, the coherence problem for process-private pages due to process migration can be solved using a third approach, that of ASIDs, which avoids interrupts and TLB shootdown. Every TLB entry has an ASID field associated with it to avoid flushing the entire TLB on a context switch (just as the process identifier is used in virtually addressed caches). In the case of TLBs, however, ASIDs are like tags allocated dynamically by the OS on a per-processor basis, using a free pool to which they are returned when TLB entries are replaced; they are not associated with processes for their lifetime. One way to use the ASIDs, as was done in the IRIX 5.2 operating system, follows. The OS maintains an array for each process that tracks the ASID assigned to that process on each of the processors in the system. When a process modifies a PTE, the ASID of that process for all other processors is set to zero. This ensures that when the process is migrated to another processor, it will find its ASID to be zero there; the kernel will therefore allocate it a new one, thus preventing use of stale TLB entries. TLB coherence for pages truly shared by processes is performed using TLB shootdown.

Finally, some processor families provide hardware instructions to invalidate other processors' TLBs. In the PowerPC family (Weiss and Smith 1994), the "TLB invalidate entry" instruction (`tlbie`) broadcasts the page address on the bus so that the snooping hardware on other processors can automatically invalidate the corresponding TLB entries without interrupting the processor. The algorithm for handling changes to PTEs is simple: the operating system first makes changes to the page table and then issues a `tlbie` instruction for the changed PTEs. If the TLB is hardware loaded (as it is in the PowerPC), the OS does not know which other TLBs might be caching the PTE, so the invalidation must be broadcast to all processors. Broadcast is well suited to a bus but undesirable for the more scalable systems with distributed networks that will be discussed in subsequent chapters.

6.6.4 Snoop-Based Cache Coherence on Rings

Since the scale of bus-based cache-coherent multiprocessors is limited by the bus, it is natural to ask how snoop-based coherence may be extended to other, less limited interconnects. One straightforward extension of a bus is a ring. Instead of a single set of wires onto which all modules are attached, each module is attached to two neighboring modules. A ring is an interesting interconnection network from the perspective of coherence since, like a bus, it inherently supports broadcast-based communication. A transaction from one node to another traverses link by link down the ring, and since the average distance of the destination node is half the length of the ring, it is simple and natural to let the acknowledgment simply propagate around the rest of the ring and return to the sender. In fact, a natural way to structure the communication in hardware is to have the sender place the transaction on the ring and have other nodes inspect (snoop) it as it goes by to see if it is relevant to them. Given this broadcast and snooping infrastructure, we can provide snooping cache coherence on a ring even if memory is physically distributed among the nodes on the ring. Serialization and sequential consistency on a ring are a bit more complicated than on a bus since multiple transactions may be in progress around the ring simultaneously and the modules see the transactions at different times and potentially in different order.

The potential advantage of rings over buses, other than the use of distributed memory, is that the short, point-to-point nature of the links allows them to be driven at very high clock rates. For example, the IEEE scalable coherent interface (SCI) transport standard (Gustavson 1992; IEEE 1993) is based on 500-MHz 16-bit-wide point-to-point links. The linear point-to-point nature also allows the links to be extensively pipelined, that is, new bits can be pumped onto the wire by the source before the previous bits have reached the destination. This latter feature allows the links to be made long without affecting their throughput. A disadvantage of rings is that the communication latency is high, typically higher than that of buses, and grows linearly with the number of processors in the ring (on average, $p/2$ hops need to be traversed before getting to the destination on a unidirectional ring and half that on a bidirectional ring).

Since rings are a broadcast media, snooping cache coherence protocols can be implemented quite naturally on them. An early ring-based snooping cache-coherent machine was the KSR1 sold by Kendall Square Research (Frank, Burkhardt, and Rothnie 1993). More recent commercial offerings, such as the Sequent NUMA-Q and Convex's Exemplar family (Convex 1993; Thekkath et al. 1997), use rings as the second-level interconnect to connect together multiprocessor nodes. (Both of these systems use a directory protocol rather than snooping on the ring interconnect, so we defer discussion of them until Chapter 8 when these protocols are introduced. In the NUMA-Q, the interconnect within a node is a bus; in the Exemplar, it is a richly connected low-latency crossbar.) The University of Toronto's Hector system (Vranesic et al. 1991; Farkas, Vranesic, and Stumm 1992) is a ring-based research prototype.

Figure 6.25 illustrates the organization of a ring-connected multiprocessor. Typically, rings are used with physically distributed memory, but the memory may still be logically shared. Each node consists of a processor, its private cache, a portion of the global main memory, and a ring interface. The ring interface consists of an input link from the ring, a set of latches organized as a FIFO buffer, and an output link to the ring. At each ring clock cycle, the contents of the latches are shifted forward, so the whole ring acts as a circular pipeline. The main function of the latches is to hold a passing transaction long enough so that the ring interface can decide whether to forward the message to the next node or not. A transaction may be taken out of the ring by storing the contents of the latch in local buffer memory and writing an empty-slot indicator into that latch instead. If a node wants to put something on the ring, it waits for an opportunity to fill a passing empty slot and fills it. Of course, it is desirable to minimize the number of latches in each interface to reduce the latency of transactions going around the ring.

The mechanism that determines when a node can insert a transaction on the ring, called the *ring access control mechanism,* is complicated by the fact that the datapath of the ring is usually much narrower than the size of the transactions being transferred on it. As a result, transactions need multiple consecutive slots on the ring. Furthermore, transactions (messages) on the ring can themselves have different sizes. For example, *request* messages are short and contain only the command and address whereas *data reply* messages contain the contents of the memory block and are longer. The final complicating factor is that arbitration for access to the ring must be done in a distributed manner since, unlike in a bus, there are no globally visible wires.

Three main options have been used for ring access control (i.e., arbitration): token-passing rings, register insertion rings, and slotted rings. In *token-passing rings,*

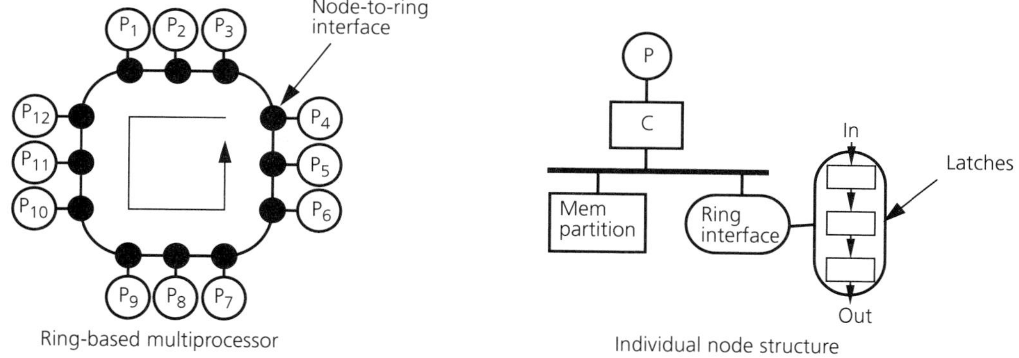

FIGURE 6.25 Organization of a single-ring multiprocessor

a special bit pattern, called a token, is passed around the ring, and only the node currently possessing the token is allowed to transmit on the ring. Arbitration is easy, but the disadvantage is that only one node may initiate a transaction at a time even though empty slots may be passing by other nodes on the ring, resulting in wasted bandwidth. *Register insertion rings* were chosen for the IEEE SCI standard. Here, a bypass FIFO between the input and output stages of the ring interface is used to buffer incoming transactions (with backward flow control to avoid overloading) while the local node is transmitting. When the local node finishes, the contents of the bypass FIFO are forwarded to the output link, and the local node is not allowed to transmit again until the bypass FIFO is empty. Multiple nodes may be transmitting at a time, and parts of the ring will stall when their bypass FIFOs are overloaded. Finally, in *slotted rings*, the ring is divided into transaction slots with labeled types (for different-sized transactions, such as requests and data replies), and these slots keep circulating around the ring. A processor ready to transmit a transaction waits until an empty slot of the required type comes by (indicated by a bit in the slot header), and then it inserts its message. A "slot" here really means a sequence of empty time slots, the length of the sequence depending on the type of message. The slotted ring can restrict the utilization of the ring bandwidth by hardwiring the mixture of available slots of different types, which may not match the actual traffic pattern for a given workload. However, for a given coherence protocol, the mix of message types is reasonably well known and little bandwidth is wasted in practice (Barroso and Dubois 1993, 1995).

While it may seem at first that broadcast and snooping waste bandwidth on a point-to-point interconnect such as a ring, in reality it is not necessarily so. A broadcast takes only twice as much bandwidth on a ring as the average random point-to-point message since the latter will, on average, traverse half the ring between two randomly chosen nodes. In addition, broadcast is needed only for request messages (read miss, write miss, upgrade requests), which are all short; data reply messages are put on the ring by the source of the data and stop at the requesting node.

Consider a cache read miss in a ring-based snooping protocol. If the main memory unit in which the block is allocated (called the *home* memory) is not on the local node, the read request is placed on the ring. If the home is local, we must determine if the block is dirty in some other node, in which case the local memory should not respond and a request should be placed on the ring. A simple solution is to place all misses on the ring as is done in the Sun Enterprise, which is a bus-based design with physically distributed memory. Alternatively, a dirty bit can be maintained for each block in home memory. This bit is turned ON if a block is cached in dirty state in some node other than the home node. If the bit is on, the request goes on the ring. The read request now circles the ring. It is snooped by all nodes, and either the home or the dirty node will respond (again, if the home were not local, the home node uses the dirty bit to decide whether or not it should respond to the request). Read-exclusive and upgrade transactions also appear on the ring, and other nodes snoop these requests and invalidate their blocks if necessary. The request and response transactions are removed from the ring when they arrive back at the requestor. The return of the request to the requesting node serves as an acknowledgment. When multiple nodes attempt to write to the same block concurrently, the winner is the one that reaches the current owner of the block first (i.e., the home node if the block is valid in main memory or the dirty node otherwise); the other nodes are implicitly or explicitly sent negative acknowledgments (NACKs), and they must retry.

From an implementation perspective, a key difficulty with snooping protocols on rings is the real-time constraint imposed: the snooper in the ring interface must examine and react to all passing messages without excessive delay or internal queuing. This can be difficult for register insertion rings since many short request messages may be adjacent to each other in the ring. With rings operating at high speeds, the requests can be too close together for the snooper to respond to in a fixed time. The problem is simplified in slotted rings, where careful choice and placement of short request messages and long data response messages (the latter are point-to-point and do not need cache lookup) can ensure that request-type messages are not too close together (Barroso and Dubois 1995). For example, slots can be grouped together in frames, and each frame can be organized to have request slots followed by response slots. Nonetheless, as with buses, bandwidth on rings is ultimately limited by snoop bandwidth at the controllers or caches rather than raw data transfer bandwidth on the interconnect.

Serialization and sequential consistency in rings are a bit trickier than on buses since the possibility exists that processors at different points on the ring will see a pair of transactions on the ring in different order (depending on where they are in the ring relative to the originators of those transactions). Using invalidation protocols simplifies this problem because writes only cause read-exclusive transactions to be placed on the ring, not the data itself, and all nodes but the home node will respond simply by invalidating their copy. The home node can determine when conflicting transactions are on the ring and take special action, but this does increase the number of transient states in the protocol substantially.

6.6.5 Scaling Data and Snoop Bandwidth in Bus-Based Systems

Several alternative methods are available to increase the bandwidth of SMP designs while preserving much of the simplicity of bus-based approaches. With split-transaction buses, we have seen that the arbitration, the address phase, and the data phase are pipelined, so each of them can go on simultaneously. Scaling data bandwidth is, in fact, the easier part; the real challenge is scaling the snoop bandwidth.

Let's consider first scaling data bandwidth. Cache blocks are large compared to the address that describes them. The most straightforward way to increase the data bandwidth is simply to make the data bus wider. We see this, for example, in the Sun Enterprise and SGI Challenge designs, both of which use 256-bit-wide data buses. In the Enterprise, a 64-byte cache block is transferred in only two cycles. The downside of this approach is cost: as the bus gets wider, it uses a larger connector, occupies more space on the board, and draws more power. It certainly pushes the limit of this style of design since an efficient, uniform pipeline demands that a snoop operation, which needs to be observed by all the caches and acknowledged, must complete in only two cycles. A more radical alternative replaces the data portion of the bus with a point-to-point crossbar, directly connecting each processor-memory module to every other one. The approach recognizes that it is only the address portion of the transaction that needs to be broadcast to all the nodes in order to determine the coherence operation and the data source (i.e., memory or cache). This approach is followed in the IBM PowerPC-based RS6000 G30 multiprocessor. A bus is used for addresses and snoop results, but a crossbar is used to move the actual data. The individual paths in the crossbar need not be extremely wide since multiple transfers can occur simultaneously.

A brute-force way to scale bandwidth in a bus-based system is simply to use multiple buses, including address buses, as mentioned in Section 6.4.7. In fact, this approach offers a fundamental contribution since it allows snoop bandwidth to be scaled as well. In order to scale the snoop bandwidth beyond one coherence result per address cycle, there must be multiple simultaneous snoop operations. Once there are multiple address buses, the data bus issues can be handled by multiple data buses, crossbars, or any other mechanism. Coherence is easy. Different portions of the address space use different buses; typically, each bus will serve specific memory banks so that a given address always uses the same bus. Multiple address buses would seem to violate the critical mechanism used to ensure sequential consistency: serialized arbitration for the address bus. Remember, however, that sequential consistency requires a logical total order, not a strict chronological order of the address events. A static ordering is logically assigned to the sequence of buses: an address operation i logically precedes j if it occurs before j in time (bus cycles) or if they happen on the same cycle but i takes place on a lower-numbered bus. This multiple bus approach is used in the Sun SparcCenter 2000, which provides two split-transaction buses, each identical to that used in the SparcStation 1000, and scales to 30 processors. The CRAY CS6400 uses four such buses and scales to 64 processors. Each cache controller snoops all of the buses separately and responds according to the cache coherence protocol. The Sun Enterprise 10000, a later machine than the Sun Enterprise 6000 discussed in this chapter, combines the use of multiple address buses and data crossbars to scale to 64 processors. Each board consists of four 250-MHz processors, four banks of memory (up to 1 GB each), and two independent SBUS I/O buses. Sixteen of these boards are connected by a 16 × 16 data crossbar with paths 144 bits wide as well as four address buses associated with the four banks on each board. Collectively, this provides 12.6 GB/s of data bandwidth and a high snoop rate of 250 MHz.

6.7 CONCLUDING REMARKS

The design issues that we have explored in this chapter are fundamental and will remain important at moderate levels of parallelism. Of course, the optimal design choices may change. For example, although not currently very popular, it is possible that sharing caches at some level of the hierarchy may become quite attractive when multichip-module packaging technology becomes cheap or when multiple processors appear on a single chip.

Although it is a powerful mechanism, a shared bus interconnect clearly has bandwidth limitations as the number of processors or the processor speed increases. Architects will surely continue to find innovative ways to squeeze more data bandwidth and more snoop bandwidth out of these designs and will continue to exploit the simplicity of a broadcast-based approach, at least at small scale. However, the general solution in building scalable cache-coherent machines is to distribute memory physically among nodes and use a scalable interconnect, together with coherence protocols that do not rely on snooping. This direction is the subject of the subsequent chapters. It is likely to find its way down to the smaller scale as processors become faster relative to bus and snoop bandwidth. It is difficult to predict what the future holds for buses and the scale at which they will be used, although they are likely to have an important role for some time to come. Regardless of that evolution, the issues discussed in this and the previous chapter in the context of buses—the placement of the interconnect within the memory hierarchy, the cache coherence problem and the various coherence protocols at the state transition level, and the key correctness and implementation issues that arise when dealing with many concurrent transactions—are all largely independent of technology and are crucial to the design of all cache-coherent shared memory architectures, regardless of the interconnect used. The specific machinery used to address the correctness and implementation issues may change, but the issues, trade-offs, and basic approaches are fundamental and can be extrapolated. Moreover, these bus-based designs provide the basic building block for larger-scale design presented in the remainder of the book.

6.8 EXERCISES

6.1 Consider two machines M_1 and M_2. M_1 is a four-processor shared L_1 cache machine whereas M_2 is a four-processor bus-based snooping cache machine. M_1 has a single shared 1-MB two-way set-associative cache with 64-byte blocks whereas each processor in M_2 has a 256-KB direct-mapped cache with 64-byte blocks. M_2 uses the Illinois MESI coherence protocol. Consider the following piece of code:

```
double A[1024,1024]; /* row-major; 8-byte elems */
double C[4096];
double B[1024,1024];

for (i=0; i<1024; i+=1) /* loop-1 */
  for (j=myPID; j<1024; j+=numPEs)
    {
     B[i,j] = (A[i+i,j] + A[i-1,j] +
          A[i,j+1] + A[i,j-1]) / 4.0;
    }
for (i=myPID; i<1024; i+=numPEs) /* loop-2 */
  for (j=0; j<1024; j+=1)
    {
     A[i,j] = (B[i+i,j] + B[i-1,j] +
          B[i,j+1] + B[i,j-1]) / 4.0;
}
```

a. Assume that the array A starts at hexadecimal address (0x) 0, array C at 0x 300,000, and array B at 0x 308,000. All caches are initially empty. Each processor executes the preceding code, and `myPID` varies from 0 to 3 for the four processors. Compute misses for M_1, separately for the two loop nests. Do the same for M_2, stating any assumptions that you make.

b. Briefly comment on how your answer to part (a) would change if array C were not present. State any other assumptions that you make.

c. What can be learned about advantages and disadvantages of shared cache architecture from this exercise?

6.2 Given your knowledge about the Barnes-Hut, Ocean, Raytrace, and Multiprog workloads from previous chapters and data in Section 5.4, comment on how each of the applications would do on a four-processor shared cache machine with a 4-MB cache versus a four-processor snoopy bus-based machine with 1-MB caches. It might be useful to verify your intuition using simulation. State any relevant assumptions.

6.3 Compared to a shared first-level cache, what are the advantages and disadvantages of having private first-level caches but a shared second-level cache? Comment on how modern microprocessors, for example, MIPS R10000 and IBM/Motorola PowerPC 620, encourage or discourage this trend. What would be the impact of packaging technology on such designs?

6.4 Using the terminology from Section 6.3 on cache inclusion, assume both L_1 and L_2 are two-way set associative, $n_2 > n_1$, $b_1 = b_2$, and the replacement policy is FIFO instead of LRU. Does inclusion hold naturally? What if replacement is random or based on a ring counter?

6.5 Give an example reference stream showing cache inclusion violation for the following situations:

a. L_1 cache is 32 bytes, two-way set associative, 8-byte cache blocks, and LRU replacement. L_2 cache is 128 bytes, four-way set associative, 8-byte cache blocks, and LRU replacement.

b. L_1 cache is 32 bytes, two-way set associative, 8-byte cache blocks, and LRU replacement. L_2 cache is 128 bytes, two-way set associative, 16-byte cache blocks, and LRU replacement.

6.6 For the following systems, state whether or not the caches provide inclusion naturally: if not, state the problem or give an example that violates inclusion.

a. L_1: 8-KB direct-mapped primary instruction cache, 32-byte line size
8-KB direct-mapped primary data cache, write through, 32-byte line size

L_2: 4-MB four-way set-associative unified secondary cache, 32-byte line size

b. L_1: 16-KB direct-mapped unified primary cache, write through, 32-byte line size

L_2: 4-MB four-way set-associative unified secondary cache, 64-byte line size

6.7 Recall the discussion of the cache inclusion property in Section 6.3.

a. The discussion stated that in a common case inclusion is satisfied quite naturally. The case is when the L_1 cache is direct mapped ($a_1 = 1$), L_2 can be direct mapped or set associative ($a_2 >= 1$) with any replacement policy (e.g., LRU, FIFO, random) as long as the new block brought in is put in both L_1 and L_2 caches, the block size is the same ($b_1 = b_2$), and the number of sets in the L_1 cache is equal to or smaller than in the L_2 cache ($n_1 =< n_2$). Show or argue why this is true.

b. The discussion claimed that the problem with multiple caches at a level being backed up by a unified cache is not solved by making the unified cache associative. Show that this is true for a simple example with direct-mapped instruction and data caches backed up by a unified, two-way set-associative cache.

6.8 Assume that each processor has separate instruction and data caches and that there are no instruction misses. Further assume that, when active, the processor issues a data cache request every 3 clock cycles, the miss rate is 1%, and miss latency is 30 cycles. Assume that tag reads take 1 clock cycle but modifications to the tag take 2 clock cycles.

a. Quantify the performance lost to cache tag contention if a single-level data cache with only one set of cache tags is used. Assume that the bus transactions requiring snoop occur every 5 clock cycles and that 10% of these invalidate a block in the cache. Further assume that snoops are given preference over processor accesses to tags. Do back-of-the-envelope calculations. Then check the accuracy of your answer by building a queuing model or writing a simple simulator.

b. What is the performance lost to tag contention if separate sets of tags for processor and snooping are used?

c. In general, would you give priority in accessing tags to processor references or bus snoops?

6.9 The designers of the SGI Challenge multiprocessor considered the following bus controller optimization to make better use of interleaved memory and bus bandwidth. If the controller finds that a request is already outstanding for a given memory bank (which can be determined from the request table), it does not issue that request until the previous one for that bank is satisfied. Discuss potential problems with this optimization and what features in the Challenge design allow this optimization.

6.10 a. Although the Challenge supports the MESI protocol states, it does not support the cache-to-cache transfer feature of the original Illinois MESI protocol.

(i) Discuss the possible reasons for this choice.

(ii) Extend the Challenge implementation to support cache-to-cache transfers. Describe the extra signals needed on the bus, if any, and keep in mind the issue of fairness.

b. Although the Challenge MESI protocol has four states, the tags stored with the cache controller chip keep track of only three states (I, S, and E+M). Explain why this is still works correctly. Why do you think they made this optimization?

c. Discuss the cost, performance, implementation, and scalability trade-offs between the multiple bus architecture of the SparcCenter and the single fast wide bus architecture of the SGI Challenge, as well as any implications for program semantics and deadlock.

6.11 a. The main memory on the Challenge speculatively initiates fetching the data for a read request even before it is determined if it is dirty in some processor's cache. Using data from Table 5.1, estimate the fraction of useless main memory accesses. Based on the data, are you in favor of the optimization? Is this data methodologically adequate? Explain.

b. The bus interfaces on the Challenge support request merging. Thus, if multiple processors are stalled waiting for the same memory block, then when the data appears on the bus, all of them can grab that data off the bus. This feature is particularly useful for implementing spin-lock-based synchronization primitives. For a test-and-test&set lock, compute the minimum traffic on the bus with and without this optimization. Assume that there are four processors, each acquiring the lock once and then doing an unlock, and that initially no processor had the memory block containing the lock variable in its cache.

6.12 The SGI Challenge bus allows for eight outstanding transactions. How did the designers arrive at that decision? Suggest a general formula to indicate how many outstanding transactions should be supported given the parameters of the bus. Use the following parameters:

P	Number of processors
M	Number of memory banks
L	Average memory latency (cycles)
B	Cache block size (bytes)
W	Data bus width (bytes)

Define any other parameters you think are essential. Keep your formula simple, clearly state any assumptions, and justify your decisions.

6.13 Consider incoming transactions (requests and responses) from the bus into the cache hierarchy in a system with two-level caches and outgoing transactions from the cache hierarchy to the bus. To ensure sequential consistency (SC) when invalidations are acknowledged early (as soon as they appear on the bus), what ordering constraints must be maintained in each direction among the ones described in the following display, and which ones can be reordered? Answer the same question for the incoming transactions at the first-level cache. Assume that each processor has only one outstanding request at a time, but the bus is split transaction.

Orderings in the upward direction (from bus toward the caches and the processor):

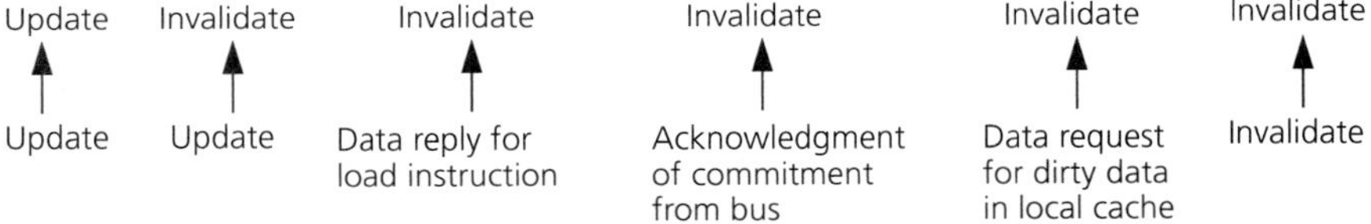

Orderings in the downward direction (from the processor and caches toward the bus):

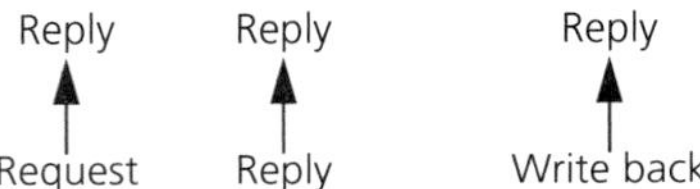

6.14 In the split-transaction solution discussed in Section 6.4, depending on the processor-to-cache interface, it is possible that an invalidation request comes immediately after the data response so that the block is invalidated before the processor has had a chance to actually access that cache block and satisfy its request. Why might this be a problem and how can you solve it?

6.15 When supporting lockup-free caches, a designer suggests that we also add more entries to the request table sitting on the bus interface of the split-transaction bus. Is this a good idea and do you expect the benefits to be large?

6.16 Apply the different techniques described in Section 6.4.6 to preserve SC with multiple outstanding bus transactions to Example 6.3 and convince yourself that they work. Under what conditions is one solution better than the other?

6.17 Assume a system bus similar to the Powerpath-2 discussed in Section 6.5. Assuming 200-MIPS/200-MFLOPS processors with 1-MB caches and 64-byte cache blocks, for each of the applications in Table 5.1, compute the bus bandwidth when using

a. the Illinois MESI protocol

b. the Dragon protocol

c. the Illinois MESI protocol, assuming 256-byte cache blocks

For each of parts, (a), (b), and (c) compute the utilization of the address+command bus separately from the utilization of the data bus. State all assumptions clearly.

d. Complete parts (a) and (b) for a single SparcCenter XDBus, which has 64-bit-wide multiplexed address and data signals. Assume that the bus runs at 100 MHz, that transmitting address information takes 2 cycles on the bus, and that 64 bytes of data take 9 cycles on the bus.

6.18 One deadlock solution proposed for multilevel caches in Section 6.4.8 is to make all queues deep enough to accommodate all incoming requests and responses. Can the queues be smaller? If so, why? Discuss why it may be beneficial to have deeper queues than the size required by deadlock considerations.

6.19 Section 6.3 presented coherence protocols assuming two-level caches. What if there are three or more levels in the cache hierarchy? Extend the Illinois MESI protocol for the middle cache in a three-level hierarchy: list any additional states or actions needed, and present the state transition diagram.

6.20 Figure 6.26 shows the details of the TLB shootdown algorithm used in the Mach operating system (Black et al. 1989). For each processor, the following basic data structures are maintained: an "active" flag, indicating whether the processor is actively using any page tables; a queue of TLB flush notices, indicating the range of virtual addresses whose mappings are to be changed; and a list indicating currently active page tables (i.e., processes whose PTEs may currently be cached in the processor's TLB). For every page table, there is a spin-lock that the processor must hold while making changes to that page table and a set of processors on which the page table is currently active. While the basic shootdown approach is simple, practical implementations require careful sequencing of steps and locking of data structures.

a. Why are page table entries modified before sending interrupts or invalidate messages to other processors in TLB coherence?

b. Why must the initiator of the shootdown in Figure 6.26 mask out interprocessor interrupts (IPIs) before acquiring the page table lock and clear its own active flag before acquiring the page table lock? Can you think of any deadlock conditions that exist in the figure, and if so, how would you solve them?

c. A problem with the Mach algorithm is that it makes all responders busy-wait while the initiator makes changes to the page table. The reason is that it was designed for use with microprocessors that autonomously wrote back the

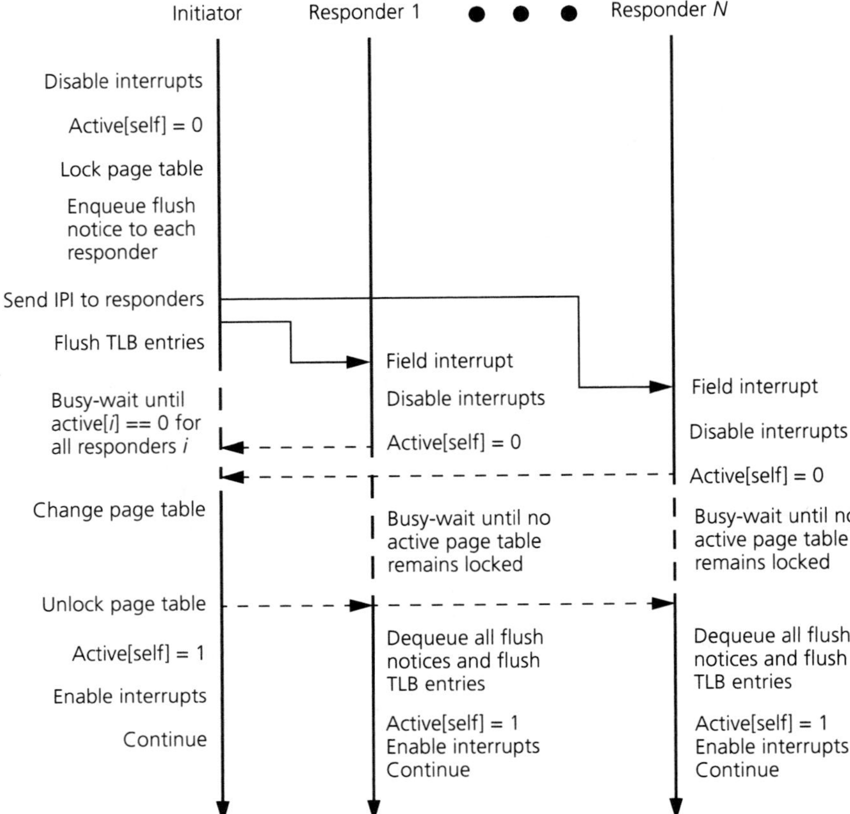

FIGURE 6.26 The Mach TLB shootdown algorithm. The initiator is the processor making changes to a page table whereas the responders are all other processors that may have entries from that page table cached in their TLBs.

entire TLB entry into the corresponding PTE whenever the dirty bit was set on a TLB replacement. Thus, for example, if other processors were allowed to use the page table while the initiator was modifying it, an autonomous write back from those processors could overwrite the new changes. How would you design the TLB hardware and/or algorithm so that responders do not have to busy-wait?

d. Under what circumstances would it be better to flush the whole TLB versus selectively trying to invalidate TLB entries?

7

Scalable Multiprocessors

In this chapter, we begin our study of the design of machines that can be scaled in a practical manner to hundreds or even thousands of processors. Scalability has profound implications at all levels of the design. For starters, it must be physically possible and technically feasible to construct a large configuration. Adding processors clearly increases the potential computational capacity of the system, but to realize this potential, all aspects of the system must scale. In particular, the memory bandwidth must scale with the number of processors. A natural solution is to distribute the memory with the processors, as in our generic multiprocessor, so that each processor has direct access to local memory. However, the communication network connecting these nodes must provide scalable bandwidth at reasonable latency. In addition, the protocols used in transferring data within the system must scale, and so must the techniques used for synchronization. With scalable protocols on a scalable network, a very large number of transactions can take place in the system simultaneously, and we cannot rely on global information to establish ordering or to arbitrate for resources. Thus, to achieve scalable application performance, scalability must be addressed as a "vertical" problem throughout each of the layers of the system design. Let us consider a couple of familiar design points to make these scalability issues more concrete.

The small-scale shared memory machines described in Chapters 5 and 6 can be viewed as one extreme point. A shared bus typically has a maximum length of a foot or two, a fixed number of slots, and a fixed maximum bandwidth, so it is fundamentally limited in scale. The interface to the communication medium is an extension of the memory interface, with additional control lines and controller states to support the coherence protocol. A global order is established by arbitration for the bus, and a limited number of transactions can be outstanding at any time. Protection is enforced on all communication operations through the standard virtual-to-physical address translation mechanism. There is total trust between processors in the system, which are viewed as under the control of a single operating system that runs on all of the processors, with common system data structures. The communication medium is contained within the physical structure of the box and is thereby completely secure. Typically, if any processor fails, the system is rebooted. Little or no software intervention takes place between the programming model and the hardware primitives. Thus, at each level of the system design, decisions are grounded in scaling limitations at layers below and assumptions of close coupling between the components. Scalable machines are fundamentally less closely coupled than bus-based shared memory multiprocessors, and we are forced to rethink how processors interact with other processors and with memories.

At the opposite extreme, we might consider conventional workstations on a local area or even a wide area network. Here, there is no clear limit to physical scaling and very little trust between processors in the system. The interface to the communication medium is typically a standard peripheral interface at the hardware level, with the operating system interposed between the user-level primitives and the network to enforce protection and control access. Each processing element is controlled by its own operating system, which treats the others with suspicion. No global order of operations is present, and consensus is difficult to achieve. The communication medium is external to the individual nodes and potentially insecure. Individual workstations can fail and restart independently, except perhaps where one is providing services to another. There is typically a substantial layer of software between the hardware primitives and any user-level communication operations, regardless of programming model, so communication latency tends to be quite high and communication bandwidth low. Since communication operations are handled in software, no clear limit is placed on the number of outstanding transactions or even the meaning of the transactions. At each level of the system design, it is assumed that communication with other nodes is slow and inherently unreliable. Thus, even when multiple processors are working together on a single problem, it is difficult to exploit the inherent coupling and trust within the application to obtain greater performance from the system.

Between these extremes is a spectrum of reasonable and interesting design alternatives, several of which are illustrated by current commercial large-scale parallel computers and emerging parallel computing clusters. Many of the *massively parallel processors* (MPPs) employ sophisticated packaging and a fast dedicated proprietary network so that a very large number of processors can be located in a confined space with high-bandwidth and low-latency communication. Other scalable machines use essentially conventional computers as nodes with more or less standard interfaces to fast networks. In either case, there is a great deal of physical security and the option of either a high degree of trust or of substantial autonomy.

The generic multiprocessor of Chapter 1 provides a useful framework for understanding scalable designs: the machine is organized as essentially complete computational nodes, each with a memory subsystem and one or more processors, connected by a scalable network. The nature of the *node-to-network interface* is one of the most critical issues in scalable system design. It allows a wide scope of possibilities, differing in how tightly coupled the processor and memory subsystems are to the network and in the processing power within the network interface itself. These issues affect the degree of trust between the nodes and the performance characteristics of the communication primitives, which in turn determine the efficiency with which various programming models can be realized on the machine.

Our goal in this chapter is to understand the design trade-offs across the spectrum of communication architectures for scalable machines. We want to understand, for example, how the decision to pursue a more specialized or a more commodity-oriented approach impacts the capabilities of the node-to-network interface, the ability to support various programming models efficiently, and the limits on scale. We begin in Section 7.1 with a general discussion of scalability, examining the requirements it places on system design in terms of bandwidth, latency, cost, and physical construction. This discussion provides a nuts-and-bolts introduction to a range of recent large-scale machines but also allows us to develop an abstract view of the scalable network on the "other side" of the node-to-network interface. We return to an in-depth study of the design of scalable networks later in Chapter 10, after having fully developed the requirements on the network in this and the following two chapters.

We focus in Section 7.2 on the question of how programming models are realized in terms of the communication primitives provided on large-scale parallel machines. The key concept is that of a *network transaction*, which is the analog for scalable networks of the bus transaction studied in the previous chapter. Working with a fairly abstract concept of a network transaction, we look at how shared address space and message-passing models are realized through protocols built out of network transactions.

The remainder of the chapter examines a series of important design points with increasing levels of direct hardware interpretation of the information in the network transaction. In a general sense, the interpretation of the network transaction is akin to the interpretation of an instruction set. Very modest interpretation suffices in principle, but more extensive interpretation is important for performance in practice. Section 7.3 investigates the case where there is essentially no interpretation of the message transaction; it is viewed as a sequence of bits and transferred blindly into memory via a physical direct memory access (DMA) operation under operating system control. This is an important design point, as it represents many early MPPs and most current local area network (LAN) interfaces.

Section 7.4 considers more aggressive designs where messages can be sent from user level to user level without operating system intervention. At the very least, this requires that the network transaction carry a user/system identifier, which is generated by the source communication assist and interpreted by the destination. This small change gives rise to the concept of a user virtual network, which, like virtual memory, must present a protection model and offer a framework for sharing the underlying physical resources. A particularly critical issue is user-level message reception since message arrival is inherently asynchronous to the user thread for which it is destined.

Section 7.5 focuses on designs that provide a global virtual address space. This requires substantial interpretation at the destination since it needs to perform the virtual-to-physical translation, carry out the desired data transfer, and provide notification. Typically, these designs use a dedicated message or communication processor (CP) so that extensive interpretation of the network transaction can be performed without the specifics of the interpretation being bound at machine design time. Section 7.6 considers more specialized support for a global physical address space. In this case, the communication assist is closely integrated with the memory subsystem and, typically, it is a specialized device supporting a limited set of network transactions. The support of a global physical address space brings us full circle to designs that are close in spirit to the small-scale shared memory machines studied in the previous chapter. However, automatic replication of shared data through coherent caches in a scalable fashion is considerably more involved than in the bus-based setting, and we devote Chapters 8 and 9 to that topic.

7.1 SCALABILITY

What does it mean for a design to "scale"? Almost all computers allow the capability of the system to be increased in some form, for example by adding memory, I/O cards, disks, or upgraded processor(s), but the increase typically has hard limits. A *scalable system* attempts to avoid inherent design limits on the extent to which resources can be added to the system. In practice, a system can be quite scalable even if it is not possible to assemble an arbitrarily large configuration because, at any point in time, crude limits are imposed by economics. If a "sufficiently large" configuration can be built, the scalability question has really to do with the incremental cost of increasing the capacity of the system and the resultant increase in performance delivered on applications. In practice, no design scales perfectly, so our goal is to understand how to design systems that scale up to a large number of processors effectively. In particular, we look at four aspects of scalability in a more or less top-down order. First, how does the bandwidth or throughput of the system increase with additional processors? Ideally, throughput should be proportional to the number of processors. Second, how does the latency or time per operation increase? Ideally, this should be constant. Third, how does the cost of the system increase, and finally, how do we actually package the systems and put them together?

It is easy to see that the bus-based multiprocessors of Chapter 6 fail to scale well in all four aspects, and the reasons are quite interrelated. In those designs, several processors and memory modules were connected via a single set of wires—the bus. When one module is driving a wire, no other module can drive it. Thus, the bandwidth of a bus does not increase as more processors are added to it; at some point, it will saturate. Even accepting this defect, we could consider constructing machines with many processors on a bus, perhaps under the belief that the bandwidth requirements per processor might decrease with added processors. Unfortunately, the clock period of the bus is determined by the time to drive a value onto the wires and have it sampled by every module on the bus, which increases with the number of modules on the bus and with wire length. Thus, a bigger bus would have longer latency and less aggregate bandwidth. In fact, the signal quality on the wire degrades with length and number of connectors, so for any bus technology there is a hard limit on the number of slots into which modules can be plugged and on the maximum wire length. Accepting this limit, it would seem that the bus-based designs have good cost scaling since processors and memory can be added at the cost of the new modules. Unfortunately, this simple analysis overlooks that even the minimum configuration is burdened by a large fixed cost for the infrastructure needed to support the maximum configuration; the bus, the cabinet, the power supplies, and other components must be sized for the full configuration. At the very least, a scalable design must overcome these limitations. The aggregate bandwidth must increase with the number of processors, the time to perform an operation should not increase substantially with the size of the machine, and a large configuration must be practical and cost-effective to build. It is also valuable if the design scales down well, so small configurations are cost-effective.

7.1.1 Bandwidth Scaling

Fundamentally, if a large number of processors are to exchange information simultaneously with many other processors or memories, a large number of independent wires must connect them. Thus, scalable machines must be organized in the manner illustrated abstractly by Figure 7.1; a large number of processor modules and memory modules connected together by *independent wires* (or links) through a large number of switches. We use the term *switch* in a very general sense to mean a device connecting a limited number of inputs to a limited number of outputs. Internally, such a switch may be realized by a bus, a crossbar, or even an ad hoc collection of multiplexers. We call the number of outputs (or inputs) the *degree* of the switch. With a bus, the physical and electrical constraints discussed previously determine its degree. Only one of the inputs can transfer information to the outputs at a time. A crossbar allows every input to be connected to a distinct output, but the degree is constrained by the cost and complexity of the internal array of cross-points. The cost of multiplexers increases rapidly with the number of ports, and latency increases as well. Thus, switches are limited in scale but may be interconnected to form large configurations, that is, *networks*. In addition to the physical interconnect between inputs and outputs, there must also be some form of controller to determine which inputs are to be connected to which outputs at each instant in time. In essence, a scalable network is like a roadway system with wires for streets, switches for intersections, and a simple way of determining which cars proceed at each intersection. If done right, a large number of vehicles may make progress to their destinations simultaneously and get there quickly.

By our definition, a basic bus-based SMP contains a single switch connecting the processors and the memories, and a simple hierarchy of bus-based switches connects these components to the peripherals. The control path in a bus is rather specialized in that the address associated with a transaction at one of the inputs is broadcast to all of the outputs and the acknowledgment determines which output is to participate. A *network switch* is a more general-purpose device, in which the information presented at the input is enough for the switch controller to determine the proper output without consulting all the nodes. Pairs of modules are connected by *routes* through network switches.

The most common structure for scalable machines is illustrated by our generic architecture of Figure 7.2, in which one or more processors are packaged together with one or more memory modules and a communication assist as an easily replicated unit, which we will call a *node*. The "intranode" switch is typically a

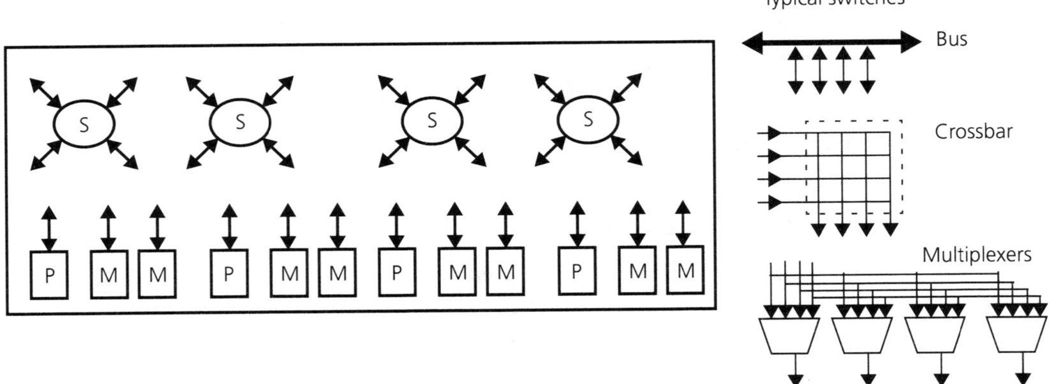

FIGURE 7.1 Abstract view of a scalable machine. A large number of processor (P) and memory (M) modules are connected by independent wires (or links) through a large number of switch modules (S), each with some limited number of degree. An individual switch may be formed by a bus, a crossbar, multiplexers, or some other controlled connection between inputs and outputs.

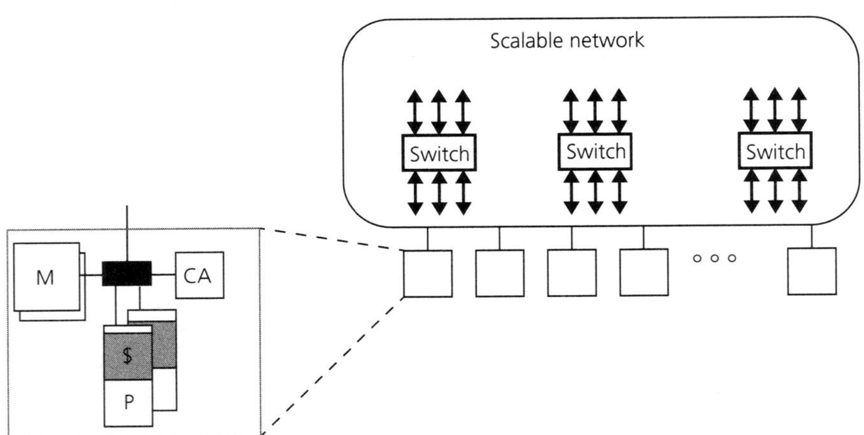

FIGURE 7.2 Generic distributed-memory multiprocessor organization. A collection of essentially complete computers, including processor and memory, that communicate through a general-purpose, high-performance, scalable interconnection network. Typically, each node contains a controller that assists in initiating and receiving communication operations.

high-performance bus. Alternatively, systems may be constructed in a dancehall configuration, in which processing nodes are separated from memory nodes by the network, as in Figure 7.3. In either case, there is a vast variety of potential switch designs, interconnection network topologies, and routing algorithms, which we will study in Chapter 10. The key property of a scalable network is that it provide a large

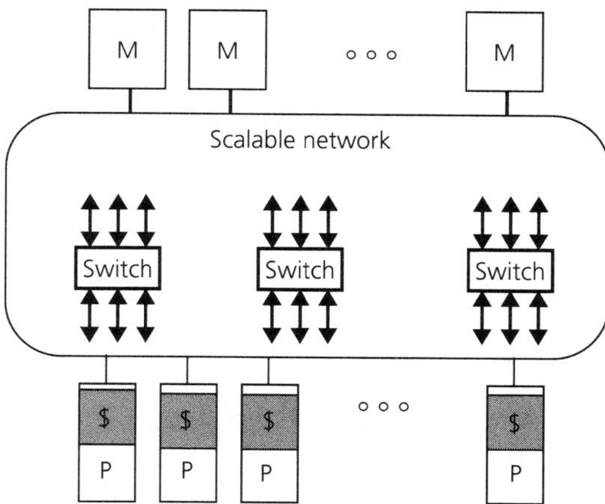

FIGURE 7.3 Dancehall multiprocessor organization. Processors access memory modules across a scalable interconnection network. Even if processes are totally independent with no communication or sharing, the bandwidth requirement on the network increases linearly with the number of processors.

number of independent communication paths between nodes such that the bandwidth increases as nodes are added. Ideally, the latency in transmitting data from one node to another should not increase with the number of nodes, nor should the cost per node, but, as we will discuss, some increase in latency and cost is unavoidable.

If the memory modules are on the opposite side of the interconnect, as in Figure 7.3, the network bandwidth requirement scales linearly with the number of processors, even when no communication occurs between processes. Providing adequate bandwidth scaling may not be enough for the computational performance to scale perfectly since the access latency increases with the number of processors. By distributing the memories across the processors, all processes can access local memory with fixed latency, independent of the number of processors; thus, the computational performance of the system can scale perfectly, at least in this simple case. The network needs to meet the demands associated with actual communication and sharing of information. How computational performance scales in the more interesting case where processes do communicate depends on how the network itself scales, how efficient the communication architecture is, and how the program communicates.

To achieve scalable bandwidth, we must abandon several key assumptions employed in bus-based designs; namely, that there are a limited number of concurrent transactions and that these are globally ordered via central arbitration and globally visible. Instead, it must be possible to have a very large number of concurrent transactions using different wires. They are initiated independently and without global arbitration. The effects of a transaction (such as changes of state) are directly visible only by the nodes involved in the transaction. (The effects may eventually become visible to other nodes as they are propagated by additional transactions.) Although it is possible to broadcast information to all the nodes, *broadcast bandwidth* (i.e., the rate at which broadcasts can be performed) does not increase with the number of nodes. Thus, in a large system broadcasts can be used only infrequently.

7.1.2 Latency Scaling

We may extend our abstract model of scalable networks to capture the primary aspects of communication latency. In general, the time to transfer *n* bytes between two nodes is given by

$$T(n) = \text{Overhead} + \text{Channel Time} + \text{Routing Delay} \quad (7.1)$$

where Overhead is the processing time in initiating or completing the transfer, Channel Time is n/B (where B is the bandwidth of the "thinnest channel"), and Routing Delay is a function $f(H,n)$ of the number of routing steps, or hops, in the transfer and possibly the number of bytes transferred.

The processing overhead may be fixed or it may increase with *n* if the processor must copy data for the transfer. For most networks used in parallel machines, there is a fixed delay per router hop, independent of the transfer size, because the message cuts through several switches.[1] In contrast, traditional data communication networks "store and forward" the data at each stage, incurring a delay per hop proportional to the transfer size.[2] Store-and-forward routing is impractical in large-scale parallel machines. Since network switches have a fixed degree, the average routing distance between nodes must increase as the number of nodes increases. Thus, communication latency increases with scale. However, the increase may be small compared to the overhead and transfer time if the switches are fast and the interconnection topology is reasonable (see Example 7.1).

EXAMPLE 7.1 Many classic networks are constructed out of fixed-degree switches in a configuration, or *topology,* such that for n nodes the distance from any network input to any network output is $\log_2 n$ and the total number of switches is $\alpha n \log n$ for some small constant α. Assuming the overhead is 1 µs per message, the link bandwidth is 64 MB/s and the router delay is 200 ns per hop. How much does the time for a 128-byte transfer increase as the machine is scaled from 64 to 1,024 nodes?

Answer At 64 nodes, six hops are required so

$$T_{64}(128) = 1.0\ \mu s + \frac{128\ B}{64\ B/\mu s} + 6 \times 0.200\ \mu s = 4.2\ \mu s$$

This increases to 5 µs on a 1,024-node configuration. Thus, the latency increases by less than 20% with a 16-fold increase in machine size. Even with this small transfer size, a store-and-forward delay would add 2 µs (the time to buffer 128 bytes) to the routing delay per hop. Thus, the latency would be

1. The message may be viewed as a train, where the locomotive makes a choice at each switch in the track and all the cars behind follow, even though some may still be crossing a previous switch when the locomotive makes a new turn.

2. The *store-and-forward* approach is like what the train does when it reaches the station. The entire train must come to a stop at a station before it can resume travel, presumably after exchanging goods or passengers. Thus, the time a given car spends in the station is linear in the length of the train.

$$T^{sf}_{64}(128) = 1.0\ \mu\text{s} + \left(\frac{128\ B}{64\ B/\mu\text{s}} + 0.200\ \mu\text{s}\right) \times 6 = 14.2\ \mu\text{s} \text{ at 64 nodes and}$$

$$T^{sf}_{1,024}(128) = 1.0\ \mu\text{s} + \left(\frac{128\ B}{64\ B/\mu\text{s}} + 0.200\ \mu\text{s}\right) \times 10 = 23\ \mu\text{s} \text{ at 1,024 nodes.} \blacksquare$$

In practice, an important connection exists between bandwidth and latency that is overlooked in Example 7.1. If two transfers involve the same node or utilize the same wires within the network, one may delay the other due to contention for the shared resource. As more of the available bandwidth is utilized, the probability of contention increases and the expected latency increases. In addition, queues may build up within the network, further increasing the expected latency. This basic saturation phenomenon occurs with any shared resource. One of the goals in designing a good network is to ensure that these load-related delays are not too large on the communication patterns that commonly occur in practice. However, if a large number of processors transfer data to the same destination node at once, there is no escaping contention. The problem must be resolved at a higher level by balancing the communication load using the techniques described in Chapter 3.

7.1.3 Cost Scaling

For large machines, scaling the cost of the system is quite important. In general, we may view this as a fixed cost for the system infrastructure plus an incremental cost of adding processors and memory to the system:

$$\text{Cost}(p,m) = \textit{Fixed Cost} + \textit{Incremental Cost}\ (p,m)$$

The fixed and incremental costs are both important. For example, the fixed cost in bus-based machines typically covers the cabinet, the power supply, and the bus supporting a full configuration. This puts small configurations at a disadvantage relative to the uniprocessor competition but encourages expansion as the incremental cost of adding processors is constant and often much less than the cost of a stand-alone processor. (Interestingly, for most commercial bus-based machines the typical configuration is about one-half of the maximum configuration. This is sufficiently large to amortize the fixed cost of the infrastructure yet leaves "headroom" on the bus and allows for expansion. Vendors who supply large SMPs, say, 20 or more processors, usually offer a smaller model providing a low-end sweet spot.) We have highlighted the incremental cost of memory in our cost equation because memory often accounts for a sizable fraction of the total system cost, and a parallel machine need not necessarily have p times the memory of a uniprocessor.

Experience has shown that scalable machines must support a wide range of configurations, not just large and extra-large sizes. Thus, the "pay-up-front" model of bus-based machines is impractical for scalable machines. Instead, the infrastructure must be modular so that, as more processors are added, more power supplies and more cabinets are added, as well as more network. For networks with good bandwidth scaling and good latency scaling, the cost of the network grows more than linearly with the number of nodes, but in practice the growth rate is not too burdensome, as illustrated in Example 7.2.

EXAMPLE 7.2 In many networks the number of network switches scales as $n \log n$ for n nodes. Assuming that at 64 nodes the cost of the system is equally balanced between processors, memory, and network, what fraction of the cost of a 1,024-node system is devoted to the network (assuming the same amount of memory per processor)?

Answer We may normalize the cost of the system to the per-processor cost of the 64-node system. The large configuration will have 10/6 as many routers per processor as the small system. Thus, assuming the cost of the network is proportional to the number of routers, the normalized cost per processor of the 1,024-node system is 1 processor $\times$ 0.33 + 1 memory $\times$ 0.33 + 10/6 routers $\times$ 0.33 = 1.22. As the system is scaled up by 16-fold, the share of cost in the network increases from 33% to 45%. (In practice, additional factors such as increased wire length may cause network cost to increase somewhat faster than the number of switches.) ■

Network designs differ in how the bandwidth increases with the number of ports, in how the cost increases, and in how the delay through the network increases, but invariably, all three do increase. There are many subtle trade-offs among these three factors, but for the most part, the greater the increase in bandwidth, the smaller the increase in latency and the greater the increase in cost. Good design involves trade-offs and compromises. Ultimately, these will be rooted in the application requirements of the target workload.

Finally, when looking at issues of cost, it is natural to ask whether a large-scale parallel machine can be cost-effective or if it is only a means of achieving greater performance. The standard definition of efficiency ($\text{Efficiency}(p) = \text{Speedup}(p)/p$) reflects the view that a parallel machine is effective only if all of its processors are effectively utilized all the time. This processor-centric view neglects to recognize that much of the cost of the system is elsewhere, especially in the memory system (Wood and Hill 1995). If we define the cost scaling of a system, *costup*, in a manner analogous to speedup ($\text{Costup}(p) = \text{cost}(p)/\text{cost}(1)$), then we can see that parallel computing is cost-effective, that is, it has a smaller cost-performance ratio, whenever $\text{Speedup}(p) > \text{Costup}(p)$. Thus, in a real application scenario, we need to consider the entire cost of the system required to run the problem of interest.

7.1.4 Physical Scaling

While it is generally agreed that modular construction is essential for large-scale machines, little consensus emerges on the specific requirements of physical scale, such as how compact the nodes need to be, how long the wires can be, the clocking strategy, and so on. In some commercial machines, the individual nodes occupy scarcely more than the microprocessor footprint whereas, in others, a node is a large fraction of a board or a complete workstation chassis. In some machines, no wire is longer than a few inches; in others, the wires are several feet long. In some machines, the links are 1 bit wide; in others, 8 or 16. Generally speaking, links tend to get slower with length, and each specific link technology has an upper limit on length due to power requirements and signal-to-noise ratio. Technologies that support very long distances, such as optical fiber, tend to have a much larger fixed cost per link for the transceivers and connectors. Thus, there are scaling advantages to a dense packing of nodes in physical space. On the other hand, a looser packing tends to reduce the engineering effort by allowing greater use of commodity components, which also reduces the time lag from availability of new microprocessor and memory technology to its availability in a large parallel machine. Thus, loose packing can have better technology scaling. The complex set of trade-offs between physical packaging strategies has given rise to a broad spectrum of designs, so it is best to look at some concrete examples. These examples also help make the other aspects of scaling more concrete.

Chip-Level Integration

A modest number of designs have integrated the communications architecture directly into the processor chip. The nCUBE/2 is a good representative of this densely packed node approach, even though the machine itself is rather old. The highly integrated node approach is also used in the MIT J-machine (Dally, Keen, and Noakes 1993) and a number of other research machines and embedded systems. The design style may gain wider popularity as chip density continues to increase.

In the nCUBE, each node had the processor, memory controller, network interface, and network router integrated in a single chip. The node chip connected directly to DRAM chips and 14 bidirectional network links on a small card occupying a few square inches, shown in actual size in Figure 7.4. The network links formed bit-serial channels connecting directly to other nodes[3] and one bidirectional channel to the I/O system. Each of the 28 wires had a dedicated DMA device on the node chip. The nodes were socketed 64 to a board, and the boards plugged into a passive wiring backplane, forming direct node-to-node wire pairs between each processor chip and log *n* other processors. The I/O links, one per processor, were brought outside the main rack to I/O nodes containing a node chip (connecting to eight processors) and an I/O device. The maximum configuration was 8,096 processors, and machines with 2,048 nodes were built in 1991. The system ran on a single 40-MHz clock in all configurations. Since some of the wires reached across the full width of the machine, dense packing was critical to limiting the maximum length.

The nCUBE/2 should be understood as a design at a point in time. The node chip contained roughly 500,000 transistors, which was large for its time. The processor was something of a reduced VAX running at 20 MHz with 64-bit integer operation

3. The nCUBE nodes were connected in a hypercube configuration. A hypercube, or *n*-cube, is a graph generalizing the cube shown in Figure 7.4, where each node connects directly to log *n* other nodes in an *n*-node configuration. Thus, 13 links could support a design of up to 8,096 nodes.

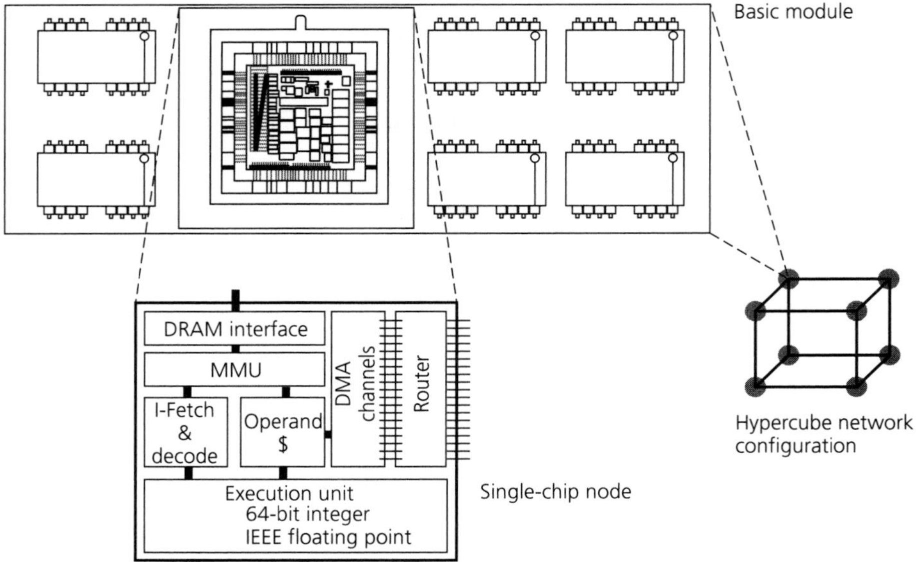

FIGURE 7.4 nCUBE/2 machine organization. The design is based on a compact module comprising a single-chip node, containing the processor, memory interface, network switch, and network interface, directly connected to DRAM chips and to other nodes.

and 64-bit IEEE floating point, with a peak of 7.5 MIPS and 2.4 MFLOPS double precision. The communication support essentially occupied the silicon area that would have been devoted to cache in a uniprocessor design of the same generation; the instruction cache was only 128 bytes, and the data cache held eight 64-bit operands. Network links were 1 bit wide, and the DMA channels operated at 2.22 MB/s each.

In terms of latency scaling, the nCUBE/2 is a little more complicated than our cut-through model. A message may be an arbitrary number of 32-bit words to an arbitrary destination, with the first word being the address of the destination node. The message is routed to the destination as a sequence of 36-bit chunks—32 data plus 4 bits of parity—with a routing delay of 44 cycles (2.2 μs) per hop and a transfer time of 36 cycles per word. The maximum number of hops with n nodes is $\log n$ and the average distance is half that amount. In contrast, the J-machine organized the nodes in a three-dimensional grid (actually a 3D torus) so that each node was connected to six neighbors with very short wires. Individual links were relatively wide (8 bits). The maximum number of hops in this organization is roughly $\frac{3}{2}\sqrt[3]{n}$, and the average is half this many.

Board-Level Integration

The most common hardware design strategy for large-scale machines obtains a moderately dense packing by using standard microprocessor components and integrating them at the board level. Representatives of this approach include the CalTech hypercube machines (Seitz 1985) and the Intel iPSC and iPSC/2, which essentially placed the core of an early personal computer on each node. The Thinking Machines CM-5 replicated the core of a Sun SparcStation 1 workstation, the CM-500 replicated the SparcStation 10, and the CRAY T3D and T3E essentially replicated the core of a DEC Alpha workstation. Most recent machines place a few processors on a board, and in some cases each board contains a bus-based multiprocessor. For example, the Intel ASCI Red machine has more than 4,000 Pentium Pro two-way multiprocessors.

The Thinking Machines CM-5 is a good representative of the board-level approach, circa 1993. The basic hardware organization of the CM-5 is shown in Figure 7.5. The node comprised essentially the components of a contemporary workstation, in this case a 33-MHz Sparc microprocessor, its external floating-point unit, and a cache controller connected to an MBUS-based memory system.[4] The network interface was an additional ASIC on the Sparc MBUS. Each node connected to two data networks, a control network, and a diagnostic network. The network was structured as a 4-ary tree with the processing nodes at the leaves. A board contained four nodes and a network switch that connected these nodes together at the first level of the tree. In order to provide scalable bandwidth, the CM-5 used a kind of multirooted tree, called a fat-tree (discussed in Chapter 10), which has the same number of network switches at each level. Each board contained one of the four network switches forming the second level of the network for 16 nodes. Higher levels of the network tree resided on additional network boards, which were cabled together. Several boards fit in a rack, but for configurations on the scale of a thousand nodes several racks were cabled together using large wiring bundles. In addition, racks of routers were used to complete the interconnection network. The links in the network were 4 bits wide, clocked at 40 MHz, delivering a peak bandwidth of about 12 MB/s. The routing delay was 10 cycles per hop, with at most $2 \log_4 n$ hops.

The CM-5 network provided a kind of scalable backplane, supporting multiple independent user partitions, as well as a collection of I/O devices. Although memory was distributed over the processors, a dancehall approach was adopted for I/O. A collection of dedicated I/O nodes were accessed uniformly across the network from the processing nodes. Other machines employing similar board-level integration, such as the Intel Paragon and the CRAY T3D and T3E, connect the boards in a grid-like fashion to keep the wires short and use wider, faster links (Dally 1990b). I/O nodes are typically on the faces of the grid or occupy internal planes of the cube.

4. The CM-5 used custom memory controllers that contained a dedicated, memory-mapped vector accelerator. This aspect of the design grew out of the CM-2 SIMD heritage of the machine and is incidental to the physical machine scaling.

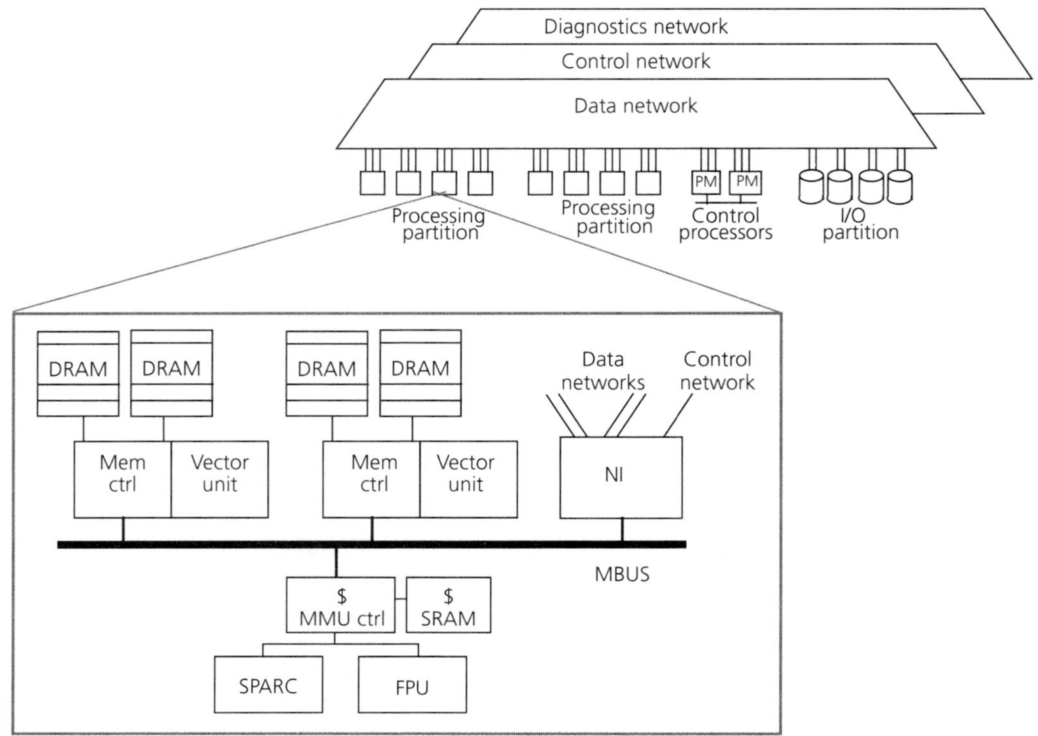

FIGURE 7.5 CM-5 machine organization. Each node is a repackaged SparcStation chip set (processor, FPU, MMU, cache, memory controller, and DRAM) with a network interface chip on the MBUS. The networks (data, control, and diagnostics) form a "scalable backplane" connecting computational partitions with I/O nodes.

System-Level Integration

Some recent large-scale machines employ less dense packaging in order to reduce the engineering time to utilize new microprocessor and operating system technology. The IBM Scalable Parallel system design (SP-1 and SP-2) is a good representative; it puts several almost complete RS6000 workstations into a rack. Since a complete, standard system is used for the node, the communication assist and network interface are part of a card that plugs into the system. For the IBM SPs, this is a Micro-Channel adapter card connecting to a switch in the base of the rack. The individual network links operate at 40 MB/s. Eight to sixteen nodes fill a rack, so large configurations are built by cabling together a number of racks, including additional switch racks. With a complete system at every node, there is the option of distributed disks and other I/O devices over the entire machine. In the SP systems, the disks on compute nodes are typically used only for swap space and temporary storage. Most of the I/O devices are concentrated on dedicated I/O nodes. This style of design allows for a degree of heterogeneity among the nodes since all that is required is that the network interface card can be inserted. For example, the SP systems support several models of workstations as nodes, including SMP nodes.

The high-speed networking technology developed for large-scale parallel machines has migrated into a number of widely used local area networks (LANs). For example, ATM (asynchronous transfer mode) is a scalable, switch-based network supporting 155-Mb/s and 622-Mb/s links. FDDI switches connecting many 100-Mb/s rings are available, along with switch-based FiberChannels and HPPI. Many vendors support switch-based 100-Mb/s Ethernet, and switch-based gigabit Ethernet is emerging. In addition, a number of higher-bandwidth, lower-latency system area networks (SANs), which operate over shorter physical distances, have been commercialized, including Myrinet, SCI, and ServerNet. These networks are very similar to traditional large-scale multiprocessor networks and allow conventional computer systems to be integrated into a "cluster" with a scalable, low-latency interconnect. In many cases, the individual machines are small scale multiprocessors. Because the nodes are complete, independent systems, this approach is widely used to provide high-availability services, such as databases, where, if one node fails, its job "fails over" to the others.

7.1.5 Scaling in a Generic Parallel Architecture

The engineering challenges of large-scale parallel machines are well understood today, with several companies routinely producing systems of several hundred to a thousand high-performance microprocessors. The tension between tighter physical integration and the engineering time to incorporate new microprocessor technology gives rise to a wide spectrum of packaging solutions, all of which have the conceptual organization of our generic parallel architecture shown in Figure 7.2. Scalable interconnection network design is an important and interesting subarea of parallel architecture that has advanced dramatically over recent years, as we will see in Chapter 10. Several good networks have been produced commercially, which offer high per-link bandwidth and reasonably low latency that increases slowly with the size of the system. Furthermore, these networks provide scalable aggregate bandwidth, allowing a very large number of transfers to occur simultaneously. They are also robust in that the hardware error rates are very low, in some cases as low as modern buses. Each of these designs has some natural scaling limit as a result of bandwidth, latency, and cost factors, but from an engineering viewpoint it is practical today to build machines on a scale that is limited primarily by financial concerns.

In practice, the target maximum scale is quite important in assessing design trade-offs. It determines the level of design and engineering effort warranted by each aspect of the system. For example, the engineering required to achieve the high packaging density and degree of modularity needed to construct very large systems may not be cost-effective at the moderate scale where less sophisticated solutions suffice. A practical design seeks a balance between computational performance, communication performance, and cost at the time the machine is produced. For example, better communication performance or better physical density might be achieved by integrating the network more closely with the processor. However, this may increase cost or compromise performance, either by increasing the latency to memory or increasing design time, and thus might not be the most effective choice. With processor performance improving rapidly over time, a more rudimentary design starting later on the technology curve might be produced at the same time with higher computational performance but perhaps lower communication performance. As with all aspects of design, it is a question of balance.

What the entire spectrum of large-scale parallel machines have in common is that a very large number of transfers can be ongoing simultaneously, there is essentially no instantaneous global information or global arbitration, and the bulk of the communication time is attributable to the node-to-network interface. These are the issues that dominate our thinking from an architectural viewpoint. It is not enough that the hardware capability scales; the entire system solution must scale, including the protocols used to realize programming models and the capabilities provided by the operating system, such as process scheduling, storage management, and I/O. Serialization due to contention for locks and shared resources within applications or even the operating system may limit the useful scaling of the system even if the hardware scales well in isolation. Given that we have met the engineering requirements to physically scale the system to the size of interest in a cost-effective manner, we must also ensure that the communication and synchronization operations required to support the target programming models scale and have a sufficiently small fixed cost to be effective.

7.2 REALIZING PROGRAMMING MODELS

In this section, we examine what is required to implement programming models on large distributed-memory machines. Historically, these machines have been most strongly associated with message-passing programming models, but shared address space programming models have become increasingly important and well represented. Chapter 1 introduced the concept of a communication abstraction, which defined the set of communication primitives provided to the user. These could be realized directly in the hardware, via system software, or through some combination of the two, as illustrated by the now familiar Figure 7.6. This perspective focuses our attention on the aspects of the node architecture that support communication. In small-scale shared memory machines, the communication abstraction is supported directly in hardware as an extension of the memory interface. The load and store operations in the coherent shared memory abstraction are implemented by a sequence of primitive bus transactions according to a specific protocol defined by a collection of state machines.

In large-scale parallel machines, the programming model is realized in a similar manner, except that the primitive events are transactions across the network, that is, network transactions rather than bus transactions. A *network transaction* is a one-way transfer of information from an output buffer at the source to an input buffer at the destination that causes some kind of action at the destination, the occurrence of which is not directly visible at the source. This is illustrated in Figure 7.7. The

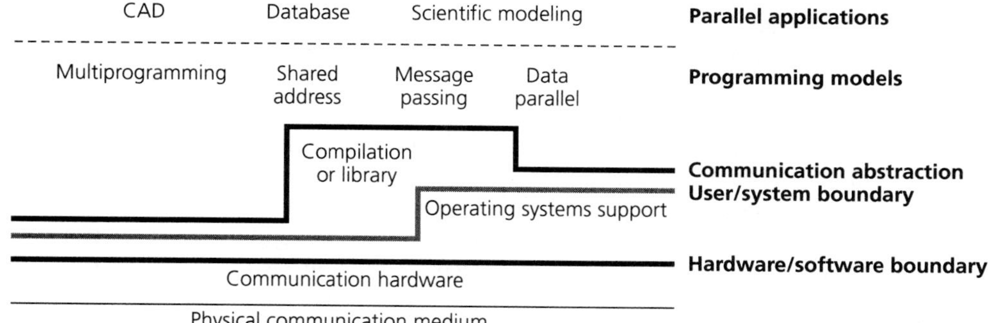

FIGURE 7.6 Layers of parallel architecture. The figure illustrates the critical layers of abstractions and the aspects of the system design that realize each of the layers.

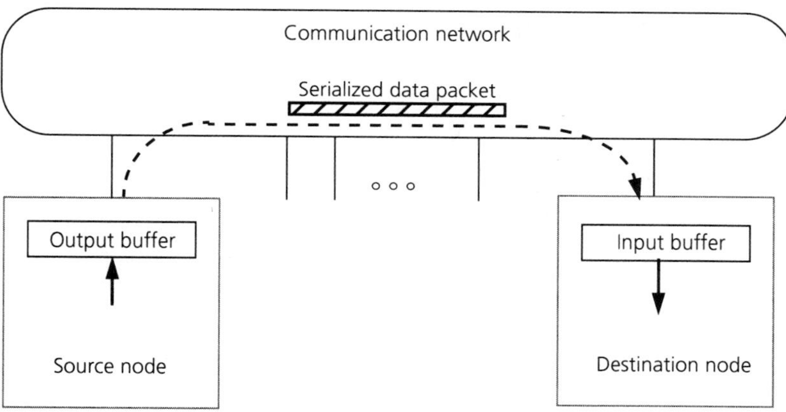

FIGURE 7.7 Network transaction primitive. A one-way transfer for information from a source output buffer to an input buffer of a designated destination, causing some action to take place at the destination.

action may be quite simple (e.g., depositing the data into an accessible location or making a transition in a finite state machine) or it can be more general (e.g., the execution of a message handler routine). The effects of a network transaction are observable only through additional transactions. Traditionally, the communication abstraction supported directly by the hardware in large-scale machines was hidden below the vendor's message-passing library, but increasingly the lower-level abstraction is accessible to user applications.

The differences between bus and network transactions have far-reaching ramifications. The potential design space is even larger than what we saw in Chapter 5, where the bus provided serialization and broadcast and the primitive events were small variations on conventional bus transactions. In large-scale machines, there is tremendous variation in the primitive network transaction itself, as well as in how these transactions are driven and interpreted at the endpoints. They may be presented to the processor as I/O operations and driven entirely by software, or they may be integrated into the memory system and driven by a dedicated hardware controller. A very wide spectrum of large-scale machines has been designed and implemented, emphasizing a range of programming models, employing a range of primitives at the hardware/software boundary, and providing widely differing degrees of direct hardware support and system software intervention.

To make sense of this great diversity, we proceed step by step. This section first defines a network transaction more precisely and contrasts it more carefully with a bus transaction. It then covers what is involved in realizing shared memory and message-passing abstractions out of this primitive without getting encumbered by the myriad of ways that a network transaction itself might be realized. In later sections, we will work systematically through the space of design options for realizing network transactions and the programming models built upon them.

7.2.1 Primitive Network Transactions

To understand what is involved in a network transaction, let us first reexamine what is involved in a bus transaction, since similar issues arise. Before starting a bus transaction, a protection check has been performed as part of the virtual-to-physical address translation. The *format* of information in a bus transaction is determined by the physical wires of the bus, that is, the data lines, address lines, and command lines. The information to be transferred onto the bus is held in special *output registers* (namely, address, command, and data registers) until it can be driven onto the bus. A bus transaction begins with *arbitration* for the medium. Most buses employ a global arbitration scheme where a processor requesting a transaction asserts a bus request line and waits for the corresponding bus grant. The *destination* of the transaction is implicit in the address. Each module on the bus is configured to respond to a set of physical addresses. All modules examine the address and one responds to the transaction. (If none responds, the bus controller detects the time-out and aborts the transaction.) Each module includes a set of *input registers*, capable of buffering any request to which it might respond. Each bus transaction involves a *request* followed by a *response*. In the case of a read, the response is the data and an associated completion signal; for a write it is just the completion acknowledgment. In either case, both the source and destination are informed of the *completion* of the transaction. In many buses, each transaction is guaranteed to complete according to a well-defined schedule. The primary variation is the length of time that it takes for the destination to turn around the response. In split-transaction buses, the response phase of the transaction may require rearbitration and may be performed in a different order than the requests.

Care is required to avoid deadlock with split transactions (and coherence protocols involving multiple bus transactions per operation) because a module on the bus may be both requesting and servicing transactions. The module must continue servicing bus requests and accept replies while it is attempting to present its own request. The bus design ensures that, for any transaction that might be placed on the bus, sufficient input buffering exists to accept the transaction at the destination. This can be accomplished in a conservative fashion by providing enough resources for the worst case or in an optimistic fashion by adding a negative acknowledgment signal (NACK). In either case, the solution is relatively straightforward because few concurrent communication operations can be in progress on a bus, and the source and destination are directly coupled by wires.

The discussion of buses raises the issues present in a network transaction as well. These issues include protection, format, output buffering, media arbitration, destination name and routing, input buffering, action, completion detection, transaction ordering, deadlock avoidance, and delivery guarantees. The fundamental difference in the network transaction as compared to the bus is that the source and destination of the transaction are *uncoupled;* that is, there may be no direct wires between them, and there is no global arbitration for the resources in the system. No global information is available to all modules at the same instant, and a huge number of transactions may be in progress simultaneously. These basic differences give the preceding issues a very different character than in a bus. Let us consider each issue in turn.

- *Protection.* As the number of components becomes larger, the coupling between components looser, and the individual components more complex, it may be worthwhile to limit how much each component trusts the others to operate correctly. Whereas in a bus-based system all protection checks are performed by the processor before placing a transaction on the bus, in a scalable system, individual components will often perform checks on the network transaction so that an errant program or faulty hardware component cannot corrupt other components of the system.
- *Format.* Most network links are narrow, so the information associated with a transaction is transferred as a serial stream. Typical links are a few (1 to 16) bits wide. The format of the transaction is dictated by how the information is serialized onto the link, unlike in a bus where it is a parallel transfer whose format is determined by the physical wires. Thus, there is a great deal of flexibility in this aspect of design. We can think of the information in a network transaction as an envelope with more information inside. The envelope includes information germane to the physical network to get the packet from its source to its destination port. This is very much like the command and address portion of a bus transaction, which tells all parties involved what to do with the transaction. Some networks are designed to deliver only fixed-size packets; others can deliver variable-size packets. Very often the envelope contains additional envelopes within it. The communication assist may wrap up the user information in an envelope germane to the remote communication assist and put this within the physical network envelope. This notion of placing information packets within larger envelopes is provides *encapsulation* as it does in traditional networking stacks. It provides a means of abstracting the layers of the communication subsystem.

- *Output buffering*. The source must provide storage to hold information that is to be serialized onto the link, either in registers, FIFOs, or memory. If the transaction is of fixed format, this may be as simple as the output buffer for a bus. Since network transactions are one-way and can potentially be pipelined, it may be desirable to provide a queue of such output registers. If the packet format is variable up to some moderate size, a similar approach may be adopted where each entry in the output buffer is of variable size. If a packet can be quite long, then typically the output controller contains a buffer of descriptors, pointing to the data in memory. It then stages portions of the packet from memory into small output buffers and onto the link, often through DMA transfer.
- *Media arbitration*. There is no global arbitration for access to the network, and many network transactions can be initiated simultaneously. (In buslike networks, such as Ethernet, there is distributed arbitration for the single or small number of transactions that can occur simultaneously.) Initiation of the network transaction places an implicit claim on resources in the communication path from the source to the destination, as well as on resources at the destination. These resources are potentially shared with other transactions. Local arbitration is performed at the source to determine whether or not to initiate the transaction. However, this usually does not imply that all necessary resources are reserved to the destination; the resources are allocated incrementally as the message moves forward.
- *Destination name and routing*. The source must be able to specify enough information to cause the transaction to be routed to the appropriate destination. This is in contrast to the bus, where the source simply places the address on the wire and the destination chooses whether it should accept the request. There are many variations in how routing is specified and performed, but basically the source performs a translation from some logical name for the destination to some form of physical address.
- *Input buffering*. At the destination, the information in the network transaction must be transferred from the physical link into some storage element. As with the output buffer, this may be simple registers or a queue, or it may be delivered directly into memory. The key difference is that transactions may arrive from many sources; in contrast, the source has complete control over how many transactions it initiates. The input buffer is in some sense a shared resource used by many remote processors; how this is managed and what happens when it fills up is a critical issue that we will examine later.
- *Action*. The action taken at the destination may be very simple, say, a memory access, or it may be complex. In either case, it may involve initiating a response.
- *Completion detection*. The source has an indication that the transaction has been delivered into the network but usually no indication that it has arrived at its destination. This completion must be inferred from a response, an acknowledgment, or some additional transaction.

- *Transaction ordering.* Whereas a bus provides strong ordering properties among transactions, in a network the ordering is quite weak. Even on a split-transaction bus with multiple outstanding transactions, we could rely on the serial arbitration for the address bus to provide a global order. Some networks ensure that a sequence of transactions from a given source to a single destination will be seen in order at the destination; others will not even provide this limited assurance. In either case, no node can perceive the global order. In realizing programming models on large-scale machines, ordering constraints must be imposed through network transactions.
- *Deadlock avoidance.* Most modern networks are deadlock-free as long as the modules on the network continue to accept transactions. Within the network, this may require restrictions on permissible routes or other special precautions, as we discuss in Chapter 10. Still, we need to be careful that our use of network transactions to realize programming models does not introduce deadlock. In particular, while we are waiting, unable to source a transaction, we usually will need to continue accepting incoming transactions. This situation is very much like that with split-transaction buses, except that the number of simultaneous transactions is much larger and there is no global arbitration or immediate feedback.
- *Delivery guarantees.* A fundamental decision in the design of a scalable network is the behavior when the destination buffer is full. This is clearly an issue on an end-to-end basis since it is nontrivial for the source to know whether the destination input buffer is available when it is attempting to initiate a transaction. It is also an issue on a link-by-link basis within the network itself. We have two basic options: discard information if the buffer is full or defer transmission until space is available. The first requires a way to detect the situation and retry; the second requires a flow control mechanism and can cause the transactions to back up. We will examine both options later in this chapter.

In summary, a network transaction is a one-way transfer for information from a source output buffer to an input buffer of a designated destination, causing some action to take place at the destination. Let us consider what is involved in realizing the communication abstractions found in common programming models in terms of this primitive.

7.2.2 Shared Address Space

Realizing the shared address space communication abstraction fundamentally requires a two-way request-response protocol, as illustrated abstractly in Figure 7.8. A global address is decomposed into a module number and a local address. For a read operation, a request is sent to the designated module requesting a load of the desired address and specifying enough information to allow the result to be returned to the requestor through a response network transaction. A write is similar, except that the data is conveyed with the address and command to the designated module

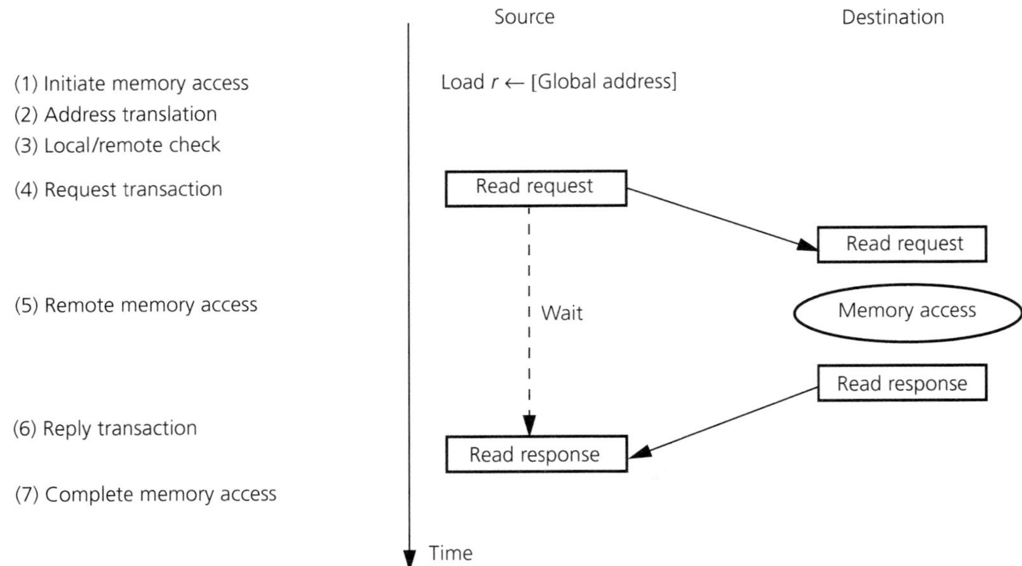

FIGURE 7.8 Shared address space communication abstraction. The figure illustrates the anatomy of a read operation in a large-scale machine in terms of primitive network transactions. (1) The source processor initiates the memory access on global address. (2) The global address is translated into a node number or route and a local address on that node. (3) A check is performed to determine if the address is local to the issuing processor. (4) If not, a read request transaction is performed to deliver the request to the designated processor, which (5) accesses the specified address, and (6) returns the value in a reply transaction to the original node, which (7) completes the memory access.

and the response is merely an acknowledgment to the requestor that the write has been performed. The response informs the source that the request has been received or serviced, depending on whether it is generated before or after the remote action. The response is essential to enforce proper ordering of transactions.

A read request typically has a simple fixed format, describing the address to read and the return information. The write acknowledgment is also simple. If only fixed-size transfers are supported (that is, a word or a cache block), then the read response and write request are also of simple fixed format. This is easily extended to support partial word transfers, say, by including byte enables; however, transfers of arbitrary length require a more general format. For fixed-format transfers, the output buffering is typically as with a bus. The address, data, and command are staged in an output register and serialized onto the link.

The destination name is generally determined as a result of the address translation process, which converts a global address to a module name (or possibly a route to the module) and an address local to that module. Succeeding with the translation usually implies authorization to access the designated destination module; however, the source must still gain access to the physical network and the input buffer at the remote end. Since a large number of nodes may issue requests to the same destination and there is no global arbitration or direct coupling between the source and destination, the combined storage requirement of the requests may exceed the input buffering at the node. The rate at which the requests can be processed is merely that of a single node, so the requests may back up through the network, perhaps even to the sources. Alternatively, the requests might be dropped in this situation, requiring some mechanism for retrying. Since the network may not be able to accept a request when the node attempts to issue it, each node must be able to accept replies and requests, even while unable to inject its own request, so that the packets in the network can move forward. This is the more general form of the fetch deadlock issue observed in the previous chapter. This input buffer problem and the fetch deadlock problem arise with many different communication abstractions, so they will be addressed in more detail after looking at the corresponding protocols for message-passing abstractions.

When supporting a shared address space abstraction, we need to ask whether it is coherent and what memory consistency model it supports. In this chapter, we consider designs that do not replicate data automatically through caches; Chapters 8 and 9 are devoted to that topic. Thus, each remote read and write goes to the node hosting the address and accesses the location, so coherence is met by the natural serialization involved in going through the network and accessing memory. One important subtlety is that the accesses from remote nodes need to be coherent with accesses from the local node. Thus, if shared data is cached locally, processing the remote reference needs to be cache coherent within the node.

Achieving sequential consistency in scalable machines is more challenging than in bus-based designs because the interconnect does not serialize memory accesses to locations on different nodes. Furthermore, since the latencies of network transactions tend to be large, we are tempted to try to hide it whenever possible. In particular, it is very tempting to issue multiple write transactions without waiting for the completion acknowledgments to come back in between. To see how this can undermine the consistency model, consider our familiar flag-based code fragment executing on a multiprocessor with physically distributed memory but no caches. The variables `A` and `flag` are allocated in two different processing nodes, as shown in Figure 7.9(a). Because of delays in the network, processor P_2 may see the stores to `A` and `flag` in the reverse of the order they are generated. Ensuring point-to-point ordering among packets between each pair of nodes does not remedy the situation because multiple pairs of nodes may be involved. A situation with a possible reordering due to the use of different paths within the network is illustrated in Figure 7.9(b). Overcoming this problem is one of the reasons why writes need to be acknowledged. A correct implementation of this construct will wait for the write of `A` to be completed before issuing the write of `flag`. By using the completion transactions for the write, and the read response, it is straightforward to meet the sufficient conditions for sequential consistency. The deeper design question is how to meet these conditions while minimizing the amount of waiting by determining that the write has been committed and appears to all processors as if it had performed.

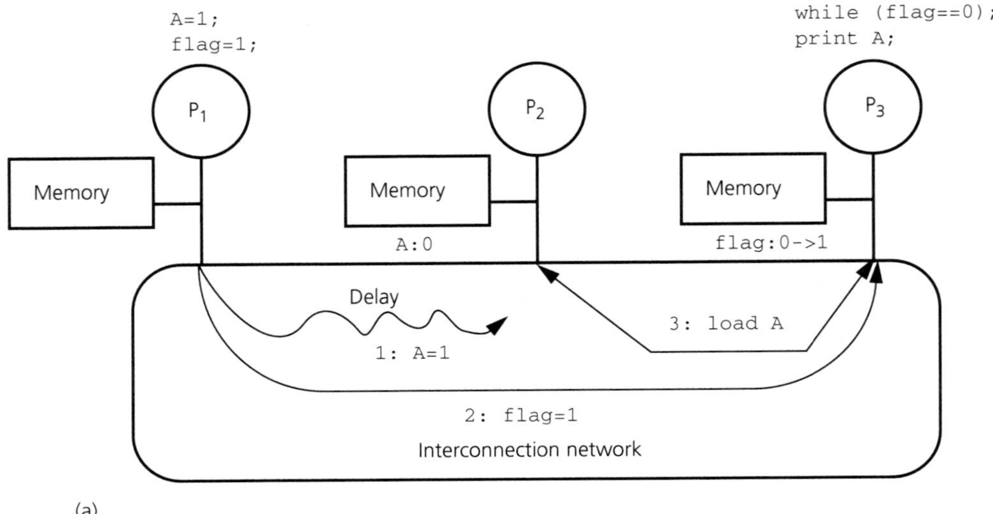

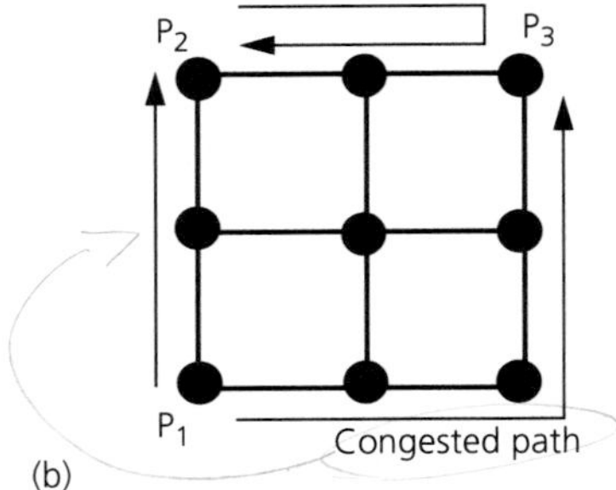

FIGURE 7.9 Possible reordering of memory references for shared flags. The network is assumed to preserve point-to-point order. The processors have no cache, as shown in part (a). The variable `A` is assumed to be allocated out of P_2's memory, whereas the variable `flag` is assumed to be allocated from P_3's memory. It is assumed that the processors do not stall on a store instruction, as is true for most uniprocessors. It is easy to see that if there is network congestion along the links from P_1 to P_2, P_3 can get the updated value of `flag` from P_1 and then read the stale value of `A (A=0)` from P_2. This situation can easily occur, as indicated in part (b), where messages are always routed first in *X*-dimension and then in *Y*-dimension of a 2D mesh.

7.2.3 Message Passing

A send/receive pair in the message-passing model is conceptually a one-way transfer from a source area specified by the source user process to a destination area specified by the destination user process. In addition, it embodies a pairwise synchronization event between the two processes. In Chapter 2, we noted the important semantic variations on the basic message-passing abstractions, such as synchronous and asynchronous message send. User-level message-passing models are implemented in terms of primitive network transactions, and the different synchronization semantics have quite different implementations (that is, different network transaction protocols). In most early large-scale machines, these protocols were buried within the vendor kernel and library software. In more modern machines, the primitive transactions are exposed to allow a wider set of programming models to be supported.

This chapter uses the concepts and terminology associated with the message-passing interface (MPI). MPI distinguishes the notion of when a call to a send or receive function returns from when a message operation completes. A *synchronous* send completes once the matching receive has executed, the source data buffer can be reused, and the data is ensured of arriving in the destination receive buffer. A *buffered* send completes as soon as the source data buffer can be reused, independent of whether the matching receive has been issued; the data may have been transmitted or it may be buffered somewhere in the system.[5] Buffered send completion is asynchronous with respect to the receiver process. A receive completes when the message data is present in the receive destination buffer. A *blocking* function, send or receive, returns only after the message operation completes. A *nonblocking* function returns immediately, regardless of message completion, and additional calls to a probe function are used to detect completion. The protocols are concerned only with message operation and completion, regardless of whether the functions are blocking.

To understand the mapping from user message-passing operations to machine network transaction primitives, let us first consider synchronous messages. The only way for the processor hosting the source process to know whether the matching receive has executed is for that information to be conveyed by an explicit transaction. Thus, the synchronous message operation can be realized with a three-phase protocol of network transactions, as shown in Figure 7.10. This protocol is for a sender-initiated transfer. The send operation causes a "ready-to-send" to be transmitted to the destination, carrying the source process and tag information. The sender then waits until a corresponding "ready-to-receive" has arrived. The remote action is to check a local table to determine if a matching receive has been performed. If not, the ready-to-send information is recorded in the table to await the matching receive. If a matching receive is found, a ready-to-receive response transaction is generated. The receive operation checks the same table. If a matching send is not recorded there, the receive is recorded, including the destination data address.

---

5. The standard MPI mode is a combination of buffered and synchronous modes that gives the implementation substantial freedom and the programmer few guarantees. The implementation is free to choose to buffer data but cannot be assumed to do so. Thus, when the send completes the send buffer can be reused, but it cannot be assumed that the receiver has reached the point of the receive call. Nor can it be assumed that send buffering will break the deadlock associated with two nodes sending to each other and then calling receive. Nonblocking sends can be used to avoid the deadlock, even with synchronous sends. The ready-mode send is a stronger variant of synchronous mode, where it is an error if the receive has not executed by the time the message arrives at the destination. Since the only way to obtain knowledge of the state of the nonlocal processes is through exchange of messages, an explicit message event would need to be used to indicate readiness. The race condition between posting the ready receive and transmitting the synchronization message is very similar to the flags example in the shared address space case.

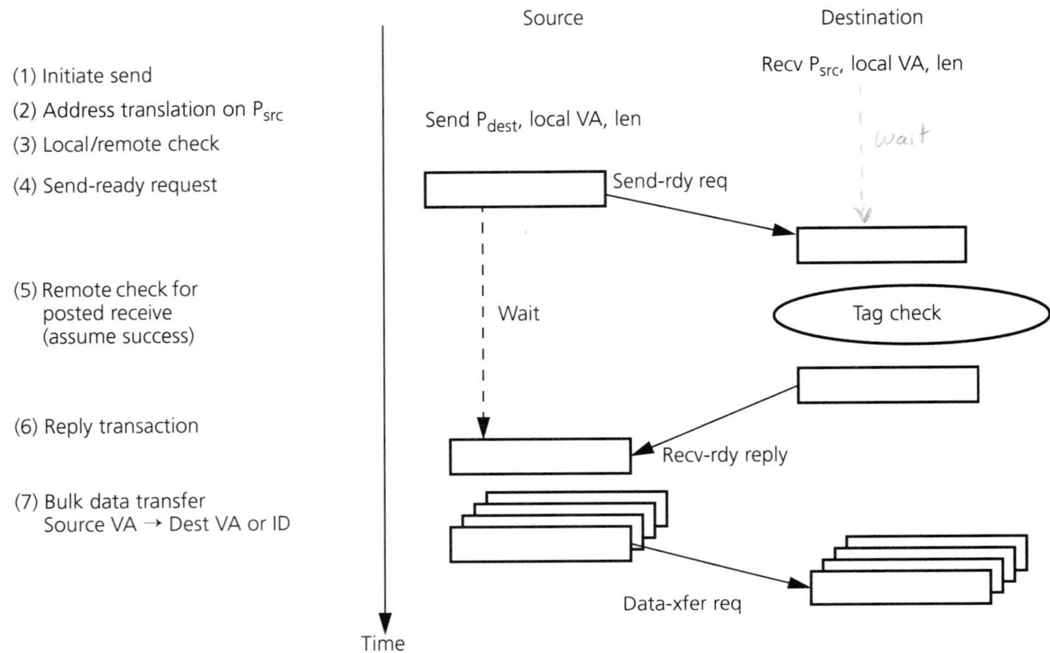

FIGURE 7.10 Synchronous message-passing protocol. The figure illustrates the three-way handshake involved in realizing a synchronous send/receive pair in terms of primitive network transactions.

If a matching send is present, the receive generates a ready-to-receive transaction. When a ready-to-receive arrives at the sender, it can initiate the data transfer. Assuming the network is reliable, the send operation can complete once all the data has been transmitted. The receive will complete once all the data arrives. Note that with this protocol both the source and destination nodes know the local addresses for the source and destination buffers at the time the actual data transfer occurs. The "ready" transactions are small, fixed-format packets whereas the data is a variable-length transfer.

In many message-passing systems, the matching rule associated with a synchronous message is quite restrictive, and the receive specifies the sending process explicitly. This allows for an alternative receiver-initiated protocol in which the match table is maintained at the sender and only two network transactions are required (receive-ready and data transfer).

The buffered send is naively implemented with an optimistic single-phase protocol, as suggested in Figure 7.11. The send operation transfers the source data in a single large transaction with an envelope containing the information used in matching (e.g., source process and tag) as well as length information. The destination strips off the envelope and examines its internal table to determine if a matching receive has been posted. If so, it can deliver the data at the specified receive address.

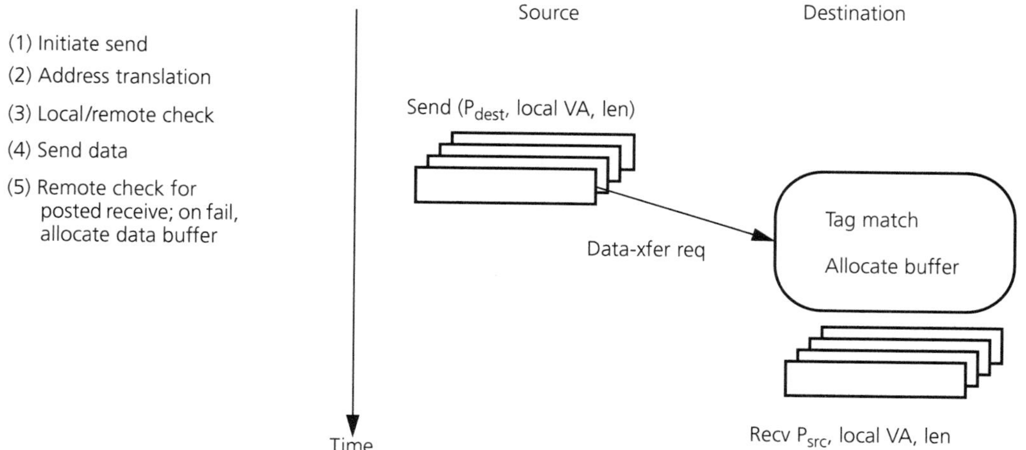

FIGURE 7.11 Asynchronous (optimistic) message-passing protocol. The figure illustrates a naive single-phase optimistic protocol for asynchronous message passing where the source simply delivers that data to the destination, without concern for whether the destination has storage to hold it.

If no matching receive has been posted, the destination allocates storage for the entire message and receives it into the temporary buffer. When the matching receive is posted later, the message is copied to the desired destination area and the buffer is freed.

This simple protocol presents a family of problems. First, the proper destination address of the message data cannot be determined until after examining the process and tag information and consulting the match table. These are fairly expensive operations, typically performed in software. Meanwhile, the message data is streaming in from the network at a high rate. One approach is to always receive the data into a temporary input buffer and then copy it to its proper destination. Of course, this introduces a store-and-forward delay and consumes a fair amount of processing resources.

The second problem with this optimistic approach is analogous to the input buffer problem discussed for a shared address space abstraction since there is no ready-to-receive handshaking before the data is transferred. In fact, the problem is amplified in several respects. First, the transfers are larger, so the total volume of storage needed at the destination is potentially quite large. Second, the amount of buffer storage depends on the program behavior; it is not just a result of the rate mismatch between multiple senders and one receiver, much less a timing mismatch where the data happens to arrive just before the receiver is ready. Several processes may choose to send many messages each to a single process, which happens not to receive them until much later. Conceptually, the asynchronous message-passing model assumes an unbounded amount of storage outside the usual program data structures. Message data is stored until the receives are posted and performed. Fur-

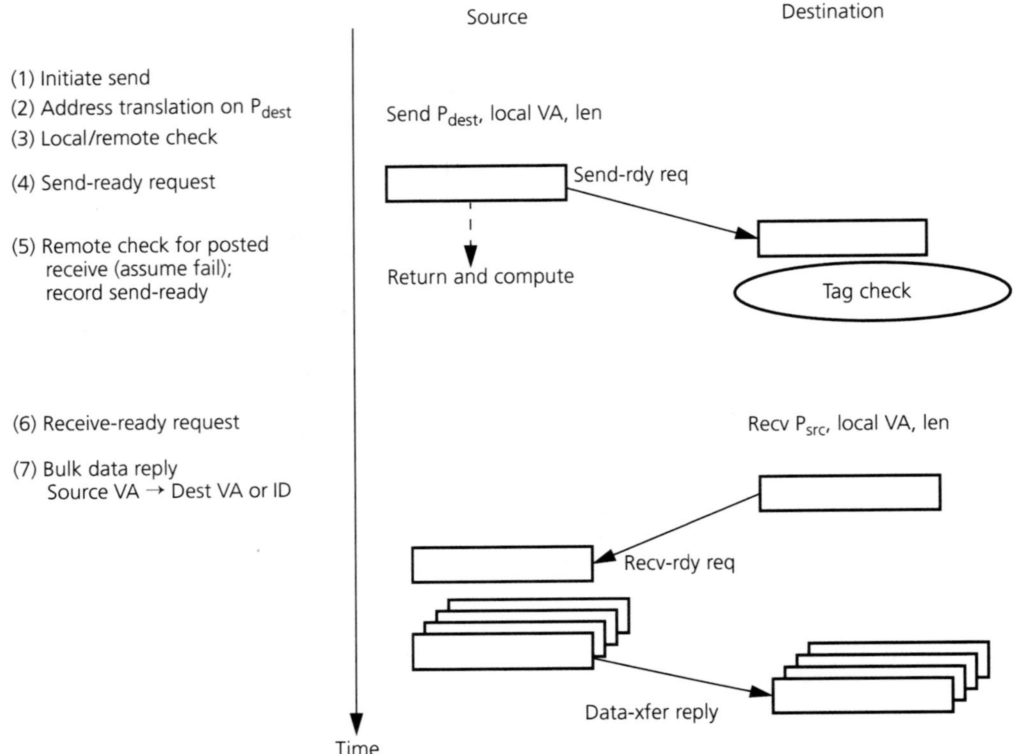

FIGURE 7.12 Asynchronous conservative message-passing protocol. The figure illustrates a one-plus-two-phase conservative protocol for asynchronous message passing. The data is held at the source until the matching receive is executed, making the destination address known before the data is delivered.

thermore, the blocking asynchronous send must be allowed to complete to avoid deadlock in simple communication patterns such as a pairwise exchange. The program needs to continue executing past the send to reach a point where a receive is posted. Our optimistic protocol does not distinguish transient receive-side buffering from the prolonged accumulation of data in the message-passing layer.

More robust message-passing systems use a three-phase protocol for long transfers, as illustrated in Figure 7.12. The send issues a ready-to-send with the envelope but keeps the data buffered at the sender until the destination can accept it. The destination issues a ready-to-receive either when it has sufficient buffer space or when a matching receive has been executed so the transfer can take place to the correct destination area. Note that in this case the source and destination addresses are known at both sides of the transfer before the actual data transfer takes place. For short messages, where the handshake would dominate the actual data transfer cost, a simple credit scheme can be used. Each process sets aside a certain amount of space for processes that might send short messages to it. When a short message is sent, the sender deducts its destination credit locally, until it receives notification that the short message has been received. In this way, a short message can usually be launched without waiting a round-trip delay for the handshake. The completion acknowledgment is used later to determine when additional short messages can be sent without the handshake.

As with the shared address space, a design issue here concerns whether the source and destination addresses are physical or virtual. The virtual-to-physical mapping at each end can be performed as part of the send and receive calls, allowing the communication assist to exchange physical addresses that can be used for the DMA transfers. Of course, the pages must stay resident during the transfer for the data to stream into memory. However, the residency is limited in time from just before the handshake until the transfer completes. In addition, very long transfers can be segmented at the source so that few resident pages are involved. Alternatively, temporary buffers can be kept resident and the processor relied upon to copy the data from and to the source and destination areas. The resolution of this issue depends heavily on the capability of the communication assist, as discussed in the following.

In summary, the send/receive message-passing abstraction is logically a one-way transfer where the source and destination addresses are specified independently by the two participating processes and an arbitrary amount of data can be sent before any is received. The realization of this class of abstractions in terms of primitive network transactions typically requires a three-phase protocol to manage the buffer space on the ends, although an optimistic single-phase protocol can be employed safely with some form of flow control.

7.2.4 Active Messages

While shared address space and message passing are the dominant programming models for modern parallel machines, it is also possible to provide a communication abstraction that is very close to the network transactions that underlie these models. The most widely used of these low-level communication abstractions is Active Messages (von Eicken et al. 1992). Active Messages constitute request and response transactions in a form that is essentially a restricted remote procedure call. Each message identifies a handler on the destination node that will be invoked upon arrival to process the transaction. A typical request consists of the destination processor address, an identifier for the message handler on that processor, and a small number of data words in the source processor registers that are passed as arguments to the handler. An optimized instruction sequence issues the message into the network via the communication assist. On the destination processor, an optimized instruction sequence extracts the message from the network and invokes the handler on the message data to perform a simple action and issue a response, which identifies a response handler on the original source processor. Higher-level programming models can then be built upon the Active Message primitives by constructing handlers that implement the appropriate protocol (Tucker and Mainwaring 1994; Shah et al. 1998).

Notification of incoming messages (i.e., invoking handlers) may be provided through interrupts or signaling a thread, but it must also be part of issuing an Active Message, in order to allow such a low-level communication operation to be deadlock-free without arbitrary buffering. When attempting to issue a request, the network may be full and the processor will need to allow handlers for incoming messages to be invoked to make progress. Thus, handler invocation can also be provided through explicitly servicing the network with a null message event, called *polling*. Unlike interrupts and threads, this allows handlers to execute synchronously with respect to the destination process.

Bulk transfers can be incorporated into the Active Messages approach either by associating a data buffer with the transaction (a pointer to a source data buffer is provided as part of the request, the buffer is copied to the destination, and a pointer to the destination buffer is provided to the handler), or a memory-to-memory copy can precede the invocation of the handler (Mainwaring and Culler 1996).

7.2.5 Common Challenges

The inherent challenges in realizing programming models in large-scale systems are that each processor has only a limited knowledge of the state of the system, a very large number of network transactions can be in progress simultaneously, and the source and destination of the transaction are decoupled. Each node must infer the relevant state of the system from its own point-to-point events. In this context, it is possible, even likely, for a collection of sources to seriously overload a destination before any of them observe the problem. Moreover, because the latencies involved are inherently large, we are tempted to use optimistic protocols and large transfers. Both of these increase the potential overcommitment of the destination. Furthermore, the protocols used to realize programming models often require multiple network transactions for an operation. All of these issues must be considered to ensure that forward progress is made in the absence of global arbitration. The issues are very similar to those encountered in bus-based designs, but the solutions cannot rely on the constraints of the bus; namely, a small number of processors, a limited number of outstanding transactions, and total global ordering.

Input Buffer Overflow

Consider the problem of contention for the input buffer on a remote node. To keep the discussion simple, assume for the moment fixed-format transfers on a completely reliable network. The management of the input buffer is simple: a queue will suffice. Each incoming transaction is placed in the next free slot in the queue. However, it is possible for a large number of processors to make a request to the same module at once. If this module has a fixed input buffer capacity, on a large system it may become overcommitted. This situation is similar to the contention for the limited buffering within the network, and it can be handled in a similar fashion. One solution is to make the input buffer large and reserve a portion of it for each source. The source must constrain its own demand when it has exhausted its allotment at the destination. The question then arises, how does the source determine that space is again available for it? There must be some flow control information transmitted back from the destination to the sender. This is a design issue that can be resolved either by acknowledging each transaction or by coupling the acknowledgment with the protocol at a higher level (for example, the reply indicates completion of processing the request).

An alternative approach, common in reliable networks, is for the destination to simply refuse to accept incoming transactions when its input buffer is full. Of course, the data has no place to go, so it remains stuck in the network for a period of time. The network switch feeding the full buffer will be in a situation where it cannot deliver packets as fast as they are arriving. Given that it also has finite buffering, it will eventually refuse to accept packets on its inputs. This phenomenon is called *back pressure*. If the overload on the destination is sustained long enough, the backlog will build in a tree all the way back to the sources. At this point, the sources feel the back pressure from the overloaded destination and are forced to slow down such that the sum of the rates from all the sources sending to the destination are no more than what the destination can receive.

We might worry that the system would fail to function in such situations. Generally, networks are built so that they are *deadlock-free*—that is, messages will make forward progress as long as messages are removed from the network at the destinations (Dally and Seitz 1987). So forward progress will occur. The problem is that with the network so backed up, messages not headed for the overloaded destination will also get stuck in traffic. Thus, the latency of all communication increases dramatically with the onset of this backlog.

Back pressure with a reliable network establishes an interesting "contract" between the processing nodes and the network. From the source point of view, if the network accepts a transaction it is guaranteed that the transaction will eventually be delivered to the destination. However, a transaction may not be accepted for an arbitrarily long period of time, and during that time the source must continue to accept incoming transactions.

Alternatively, the network may be constructed so that the destination can inform the source of the state of its input buffer. This is typically done by reserving a special acknowledgment path in the reverse direction. When the destination accepts a transaction, it explicitly acknowledges the source; if it discards the transaction, it can deliver a negative acknowledgment, informing the source to try again later. Local area networks such as Ethernet, FDDI, and ATM take more austere measures and simply drop the transaction whenever space is not available to buffer it. The source relies on time-outs to decide that it may have been dropped and tries again.

Fetch Deadlock

The input buffer problem takes on an extra twist in the context of the request-response protocols that are intrinsic to a shared address space and present in message-passing implementations. In a reliable network, when a processor attempts to initiate a request transaction, the network may refuse to accept it as a result of contention for the destination and/or contention within the network. In order to keep the network deadlock-free, the source is required to continue accepting transactions even while it cannot initiate its own. However, the incoming transaction may be a request, which will generate a response. The response cannot be initiated because the network is full.

A common solution to this *fetch deadlock* problem is to provide two logically independent communication networks for requests and responses. This may be realized as two physical networks or as separate virtual channels within a single network with separate output and input buffering. Although it is necessary to continue accepting responses while stalled on attempting to send a request, responses can be completed without initiating further transactions. Thus, response transactions will eventually make progress. This implies that incoming requests can eventually be serviced, which implies that stalled requests will eventually make progress.

An alternative solution is to ensure that input buffer space is always available at the destination when a transaction is initiated by limiting the number of outstanding transactions. In a request-response protocol it is straightforward to limit the number of requests any processor has outstanding; a counter is maintained and each response decrements the counter, allowing a new request to be issued. Standard blocking reads and writes are realized by simply waiting for the response before completing the current request. Nonetheless, with P processors and a limit of k outstanding requests per processor, it is possible for all kP requests to be directed to the same module. Space needs to be available for the $k(P-1)$ outstanding requests that might be headed for a single destination and for responses to the requests issued by the destination node. Clearly, the available input buffering ultimately limits the scalability of the system. The request transaction is guaranteed to make progress because the network can always sink transactions into available input buffer space at the destination. The fetch deadlock problem arises when a node attempts to generate a request and its outstanding credit is exhausted. It must service incoming transactions in order to receive its own responses, which enable generation of additional requests. Incoming requests can be serviced because it is guaranteed that the requestor reserved input buffer space for the response. Thus, forward progress is ensured even if the node merely queues and ignores incoming transactions while attempting to deliver a response.

Finally, we could adopt the approach we followed for split-transaction buses and NACK the transaction if the input buffer is full. Of course, the NACK may be arbitrarily delayed. Here we assume that the network reliably delivers transactions and NACKs, but the destination node may elect to drop them in order to free up input buffer space. Responses never need to be NACKed because they will be sinked at the destination node, which is the source of the corresponding request and can be assumed to have set aside input buffering for the response. While stalled attempting to initiate a request, we need to accept and sink responses and accept and NACK requests. We can assume that input buffer space is available at the destination of the NACK because it simply uses the space reserved for the intended response. As long as each node provides some input buffer space for requests, we can ensure that eventually some request succeeds and the system does not livelock. Additional precautions are required to minimize the probability of starvation.

7.2.6 Communication Architecture Design Space

In the remainder of this chapter, we will examine the spectrum of important design points for large-scale distributed-memory machines. Recall that our generic large-scale architecture consists of a fairly standard node architecture augmented with a hardware communication assist, as suggested by Figure 7.13. The key design issue is the extent to which the information in a network transaction is interpreted directly by the communication assist, without involvement of the node processor. In order to interpret the incoming information, its format must be specified, just as the format of an instruction set must be defined before we can construct an interpreter (that is, a processor) for it. The formatting of the transaction must be performed in part by the source assist, along with address translation, destination routing, and media arbitration. Thus, the processing performed by the source communication assist in generating the network transaction and that performed at the destination together realize the semantics of the lowest-level hardware communication primitives presented to the node architecture. Any additional processing required to realize the desired programming model is performed by the node processor(s), either at user or system level.

Establishing a position on the nature of the processing performed in the two communication assists involved in a network transaction has far-reaching implications

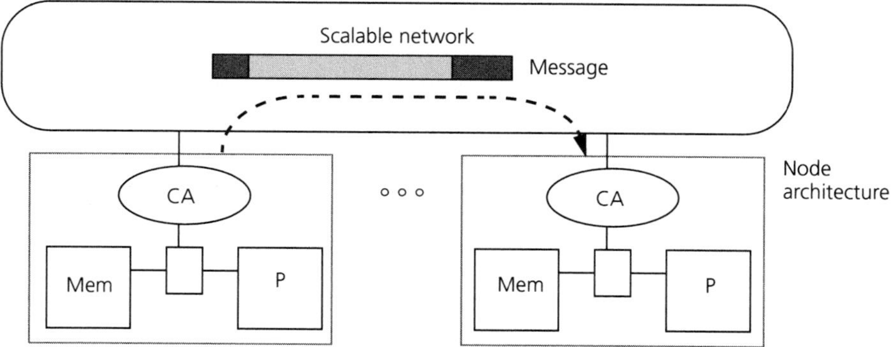

FIGURE 7.13 Processing of a network transaction in the generic large-scale architecture. A network transaction is a one-way transfer of information from an output buffer at the source to an input buffer at the destination that causes some kind of action to occur at the destination, the occurrence of which is not directly visible at the source. The source communication assist (CA) formats the transaction and causes it to be routed through the network. The destination communication assist must interpret the transaction and cause the appropriate actions to take place. The nature of this interpretation is a critical design aspect of scalable multiprocessors.

for the remainder of the design, including how input buffering is performed, how protection is enforced, how many times data is copied within the node, how addresses are translated, and so on. The minimal interpretation of the incoming transaction is not to interpret it at all. It is viewed as a raw physical bit stream and is simply deposited in memory or registers. More specific interpretation provides user-level messages, a global virtual address space, or even a global physical address space. In the following sections, we will examine each of these in turn. We look at important machines that embody the respective design points as case studies.

7.3 PHYSICAL DMA

This section considers designs where no interpretation is placed on the information within a network transaction. This approach is representative of most early message-passing machines, including the nCUBE10 and nCUBE/2, the Intel iPSC, iPSC/2, iPSC860, the Delta, the Ametek, and the IBM SP-1. In addition, most LAN interfaces follow this approach. The hardware can be very simple and the user communication abstraction can be very general, but typical processing overheads are large.

7.3.1 Node-to-Network Interface

The hardware essentially consists of support for physical DMA, as suggested by Figure 7.14. A DMA device or channel typically has associated with it address and length registers, status (e.g., transmit ready, receive ready), and interrupt enables. Either the device is memory mapped or privileged instructions are provided to access the registers. Addresses are physical,[6] so the network transaction is transferred from a contiguous region of memory. Sending typically requires a trap to the operating system. Privileged software can then provide the source address translation, translate the logical destination node to a physical route, arbitrate for the physical media, and access the physical device. Typically, the data will be copied into a kernel area so that the envelope, including the route and other information, can be constructed. Portions of the envelope, such as the error detection bits, may be generated by the communication assist. The kernel selects the appropriate outgoing channel, sets the channel address to the physical address of the message, and sets the count. (Alternatively, it may build a descriptor containing this information and post it on the transmit queue.) The DMA engine will push the message into the network. When transmission completes, the output channel ready flag is set, and an interrupt is generated, unless it is masked. The message will work its way through the network to the destination, at which point the DMA at the input channel of the destination node must be started to allow the message to continue moving through the network and into the node. (If a delay occurs in starting the input channel or if the message collides in the network with another using the same link, typically the mes-

6. One exception to this is the SBUS used in Sun workstations and servers. It provides virtual DMA, allowing I/O devices to operate on virtual, rather than physical, addresses.

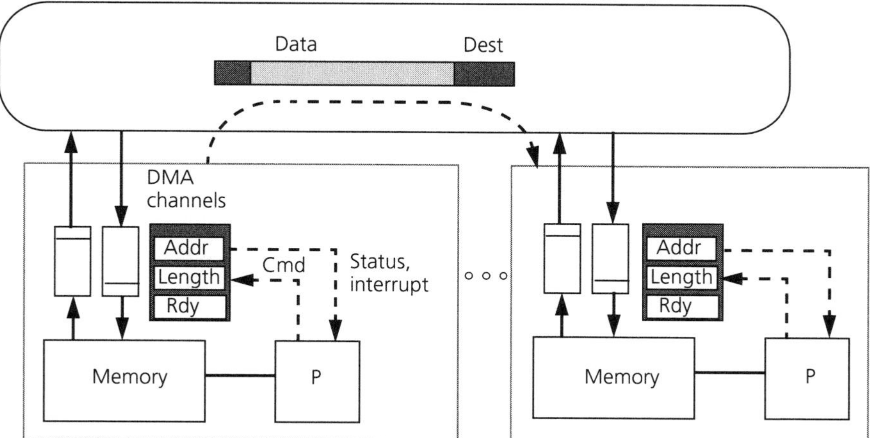

FIGURE 7.14 Hardware support in the communication assist for blind physical DMA. The minimal interpretation is blind physical DMA, which allows the destination communication assist merely to deposit the transaction data into storage, whereupon it will be interpreted by the processor. Since the type of transaction is not determined in advance, kernel buffer storage is used, and processing the transaction will usually involve a context switch and one or more copies.

sage just sits in the network.) Generally, the input channel address register is loaded in advance with the base address where the data is to be deposited. The DMA will transfer words from the network into memory as they arrive. The end-of-message causes the input ready status bit to be set and an interrupt to be generated, unless masked. In order to avoid deadlock, the input channels must be activated to receive messages and drain the network, even if there are output messages that need to be sent on busy output channels.

The key property of this approach is that the destination processor initiates a DMA transfer from the network into a region of memory and the next incoming network transaction is blindly deposited in the specified region of memory. When the system sets up the inbound DMA on the destination side, it cannot determine whether the next message will be a user message or a system message. It will be transferred blindly into the predefined physical region. Message arrival will typically cause an interrupt, so privileged software can inspect the message and either process it or deliver it to the appropriate user process. System software on the node processor interprets the network transaction and (hopefully) provides a clean abstraction to the user.

One potential way to reduce the communication overhead is to allow user-level access to the DMA device. If the DMA device is memory mapped, as most are, this is a matter of setting up the user virtual address space to include the region of the I/O space containing the device control registers. However, with this approach, the protection domain and the level of resource sharing is quite crude. The current user gets the whole machine. If the user misuses the network, the operating system may not be able to intervene other than to reboot the machine. This approach has certainly been employed in an experimental setting but is not very robust and tends to make the parallel machine into a very expensive personal computer.

7.3.2 Implementing Communication Abstractions

Since the hardware assist in these machines is relatively primitive, the key question becomes how to deliver the newly received network transaction to the user process in a robust, protected fashion. This is where the linkage between programming model and communication primitives occurs. The most common approach is to support the message-passing abstraction directly in the kernel. An interrupt is taken on arrival of a network transaction. The process identifier and tag in the network transaction is parsed, and a protocol action is taken along the lines specified by Figure 7.10 or Figure 7.12. For example, if a matching receive has been posted, the data can be copied directly into the user memory space. If not, the kernel provides buffering or allocates storage in the destination user process to buffer the message until a matching receive is performed. Alternatively, the user process can preallocate communication buffer space and inform the kernel where it wants to receive messages. Some message-passing layers allow the receiver to operate directly out of the buffer rather than receiving the data into its address space.

It is also possible for the kernel software to provide the user-level abstraction of a global virtual address space. In this case, read and write requests are issued either directly through a system call or by trapping on a load or store to a logically remote page. The kernel on the source issues the request and handles the response. The kernel on the destination extracts the user process, command, and destination virtual address from the network transaction and performs the read or write operation (along the lines of Figure 7.8), issuing a response. Of course, the overhead associated with such an implementation of the shared address abstraction is quite large, especially for word-at-a-time operation. Greater efficiency can be gained through bulk data transfers, which make the approach competitive with message passing. Many software shared virtual memory systems have been built along these lines, mostly on clusters of workstations, but the thrust of these efforts is on automatic replication to reduce the amount of communication. They are described in Chapter 9.

Other linkages between the kernel and user are possible. For example, the kernel could provide the abstraction of a user-level input queue and simply append the message to the appropriate queue, following some well-defined policy on queue overflow (Brewer et al. 1995).

7.3.3 A Case Study: nCUBE/2

A representative example of the physical DMA style of machine is the nCUBE/2. The network interface is organized as illustrated in Figure 7.15, where each of the DMA output channels drives an output port and each input DMA channel is associated

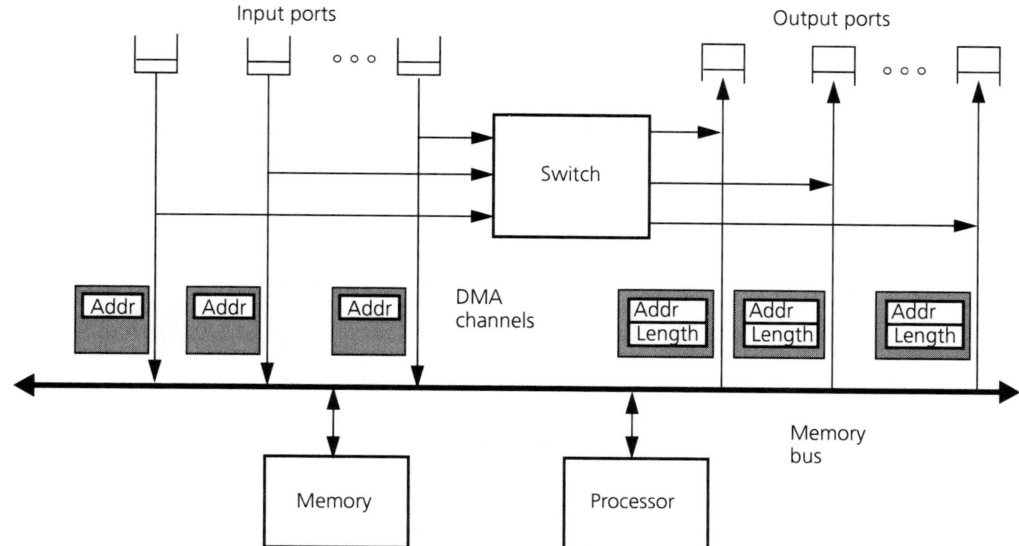

FIGURE 7.15 Network interface organization of the nCUBE/2. Multiple DMA channels drive network transactions directly from memory into the network or from the network into memory. The inbound channels deposit data into memory at a location determined by the processor, independent of the contents. To avoid copying, the machine allows multiple message segments to be transferred as a single unit through the network. A more typical approach is for the processor to provide the communication assist with a queue of inbound DMA descriptors, each containing the address and length of a memory buffer. When a network transaction arrives, a descriptor is popped from the queue and the data is deposited in the associated memory buffer.

with an input port. This machine is an example of a *direct network*, in which data is forwarded from its source to its destination through intermediate nodes. The switch forwards network transactions from input ports to output ports. The network interface inspects the envelope of messages arriving on each input port and determines whether the message is destined for the local node. If so, the input DMA is activated to drain the message into memory. Otherwise, it is forwarded to the proper output port.[7] Link-by-link flow control ensures that delivery is reliable. User programs are assigned to contiguous subcubes, and the routing is such that the links of the subcube are only used for traffic among the nodes within that subcube; so with space-shared use of the machine, user programs cannot interfere with one another. A peculiarity of the nCUBE/2 is that no count register is associated with the input channels, so the kernels on the source and destination nodes must ensure that incoming messages never overrun the input buffers in memory.

---

7. This routing step is the primary point where the interconnection network topology, an *n*-cube, is bound into the design of the node. As we will discuss in Chapter 10, the output port is given by the position of the first bit that differs in the local node address and the message destination address.

To assist in interpreting network transactions and delivering the user data into the desired region of memory without copies, in the nCUBE it is possible to send a series of message segments as a single, contiguous transfer. At the destination, the input DMA will stop at each logical segment. Thus, the destination can take the interrupt and inspect the first segment in order to determine where to direct the remainder, for example, by performing the lookup in the receive table. However, this facility is costly since a start-DMA and interrupt (or busy-wait) is required for each segment.

The best strategy at the kernel level is to keep an input buffer associated with every incoming channel while output buffers are being injected into the output ports (von Eiken et al. 1992). Typically, each message will contain a header, allowing the kernel to dispatch on the message type and take appropriate action to handle it, such as performing the tag match and copying the message into the user data area.

The most efficient and most carefully documented communication abstraction on this platform Active Messages (von Eiken et al. 1992). The first word of the user message contains the address of the user routine that will handle the message. The message arrival causes an interrupt, so the kernel performs a return-from-interrupt to the message handler, with the interrupted user address on the stack. With this approach, a message can be delivered into the network in 13 μs (16 instructions, including 18 memory references, costing 260 cycles) and extracted from the network in 15 μs (18 instructions, including 26 memory references, costing 300 cycles). Comparing this with the 150-μs start-up of the vendor message-passing library reflects the gap between the hardware primitives and the user-level operations in the message-passing programming model. The vendor's message-passing layer uses an optimistic one-way protocol, but matching and buffer management is required.

7.3.4 Typical LAN Interfaces

The simple DMA controllers of the nCUBE/2 are typical of parallel machines and qualitatively different from what is usually found in DMA controllers for peripheral devices and local area networks. Notice that each DMA channel is capable of a single, contiguous transfer. A short instruction sequence sets the channel address and channel limit for the next input or output operation. Traditional DMA controllers provide the ability to chain together a large number of transfers. To initiate an output DMA, a DMA descriptor is chained onto the output DMA queue. The peripheral controller polls this queue, issuing DMA operations and informing the processor as they complete.

Most LAN controllers, including Ethernet LANCE, Sun ATM adapters, and many others, provide a queue of transmit descriptors and a queue of receive descriptors. (There is also a free list of each kind of descriptor. Typically, the queue and its free list are combined into a single ring.) The kernel builds the output message in memory and sets up a transmit descriptor with its address and length, as well as some control information. In some controllers, a single message can be described by a sequence of descriptors, so the controller can gather the envelope and the data from separate regions of memory. Typically, the controller has a single port into the network, so it pushes the message onto the wire. For Ethernets and rings, each of the controllers inspects the message as it comes by, so a destination address is specified on the transaction rather than a route.

The inbound side is more interesting. Each receive descriptor has a destination buffer address. When a message arrives, a buffer descriptor is popped off the queue, and a DMA transfer is initiated to load the message data into the associated region of memory. If no receive descriptor is available, the message is dropped, and higher-level protocols must retry (just as if the message was garbled in transit). Most devices have configurable interrupt logic, so an interrupt can be generated on every arrival after so many bytes or after a message has waited for too long. The operating system driver manages these input and output queues. The number of instructions required to set up even a small transfer is quite large with such devices, partly because of the formatting of the descriptors and the handshaking with the controller.

7.4 USER-LEVEL ACCESS

The most basic level of hardware interpretation of the incoming network transaction distinguishes user messages from system messages and delivers user messages to the user program without operating system intervention. Each network transaction carries a user/system flag that is examined by the communication assist as the message arrives. In addition, it should be possible to inject a user message into the network at the user level; the communication assist automatically inserts the user flag as it generates the transaction. In effect, this design point provides a *user-level network port*, an access path to the network that can be written and read without system intervention.

7.4.1 Node-to-Network Interface

A typical organization for a parallel machine supporting user-level network access is shown in Figure 7.16. A region of the address space is mapped to the network input and output ports as well as the status register, as indicated in Figure 7.17. The processor can generate a network transaction by writing the destination node number and the data into the output port. The communication assist performs protection check, translates the logical destination node number into a physical address or route, and arbitrates for the medium. It also inserts the message type and any error checking information. Upon arrival, a system message will cause an interrupt so the system can extract it from the network, whereas a user message can sit in the input queue until the user process reads it from the network, popping the queue. If the network backs up, attempts to write messages into the network will fail, and the user process will need to continue to extract messages from the network to make forward progress. Since current microprocessors do not support user-level interrupts, an interrupting user message is treated by the communication assist as a system message, and the system rapidly transfers control to a user-level handler.

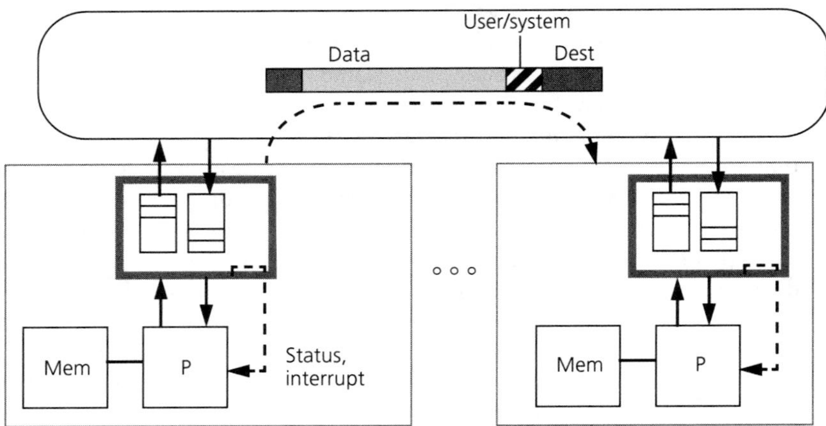

FIGURE 7.16 Hardware support in the communication assist for user-level network ports. The network transaction is distinguished as either system or user. The communication assist provides network input and output FIFOs accessible to the user or system. It marks user messages as they are sent and checks the transaction type as they are received. User messages may be retained in the user input FIFO until extracted by the user application. System transactions cause an interrupt so that they may be handled in a privileged manner by the system. In the absence of user-level interrupt support, interrupting user transactions are treated as special system transactions.

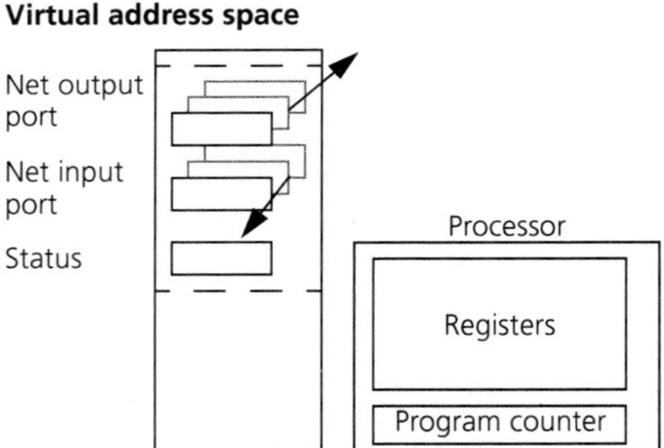

FIGURE 7.17 Typical user-level architecture with network ports. In addition to the storage presented by the instruction set architecture and memory space, a region of the user's virtual address space provides access to the network output port, input port, and status register. Network transactions are initiated and received by writing and reading the ports, plus checking the status register.

One implication of this design point is that the communication primitives allow a portion of the process state to be in the network, having left the source but not arrived at the destination. Thus, if the collection of user processes forming a parallel program is time-sliced out, the collection of in-flight messages for the program needs to be swapped as well. They will be reinserted into the network or the destination input queues when the program is resumed.

7.4.2 Case Study: Thinking Machines CM-5

The first commercial machine to seriously support a user-level network was the CM-5, introduced in late 1991 by Thinking Machines Corporation. The communication assist is contained in a network interface (NI) chip attached at the memory bus as if it were an additional memory controller, as illustrated in Figure 7.5. The NI provides an input and output FIFO for each of two data networks and a "control network," which is specialized for global operations such as barrier, broadcast, reduce, and scan. The functionality of the communication assist is made available to the processor by mapping the network input and output ports as well as certain status registers into the address space, as shown in Figure 7.17. The kernel can access all of the FIFOs and registers whereas a user process can only access the user FIFO and status. In either case, communication operations are initiated and completed by reading and writing the communication assist registers using conventional loads and stores. In addition, the communication assist can raise an interrupt. In the CM-5, each network transaction contains a small tag, and the communication assist maintains a table to indicate which tags should raise an interrupt. (All system tags raise an interrupt.)

In the CM-5, it is possible to write a five-word message into the network in 1.5 μs (50 cycles) and read one out in 1.6 μs. In addition, the latency across an unloaded network varies from 3 μs for neighboring nodes to 5 μs across a 1,024-node machine. An interrupt vectored to user level costs roughly 10 μs. The user-level handler may process several messages if they arrive in rapid succession. The time to transfer a message into or out of the network interface is dominated by the time spent on the memory bus since these operations are performed as uncached writes and reads. If the message data starts out in registers, it can be written to the network interface as a sequence of buffered stores. However, this must be followed by a load to check if the message was accepted, at which point the write latency is experienced as the write buffer is retired to the NI.

If the message data originates in memory and is to be deposited in memory rather than registers, it is interesting to evaluate whether DMA should be used to transfer data to and from the NI. The critical resource is the memory bus. When using conventional memory operations to access the user-level network port, each word of message data is first loaded into a register and then stored into the NI or memory. If the data is uncachable, each data word in the network transaction involves four bus transactions. If the memory data is cachable, the transfers between the processor and memory are performed as cache block transfers or are avoided if the data is in the cache. However, the NI stores and loads remain. With DMA transfers, the data is moved only once across the memory bus on each end of the network transaction, using burst mode transfers. However, the DMA descriptor must still be written to the NI. The performance advantages of DMA are lost altogether if the message data cannot be in cachable regions of memory, so the DMA transfer performed by the NI must be coherent with respect to the processor cache. Thus, it is critical that the node memory architecture support coherent caching. On the receiving side, the DMA must be initiated by the NI based on information in the network transaction and state internal to the NI; otherwise, we are again faced with the problems associated with blind physical DMA. This leads us to place additional interpretation on the network transaction in order to have the communication assist extract address fields. We will consider this approach further in Section 7.5.

The two data networks in the CM-5 provide a simple solution to the fetch deadlock problem: one network can be used for requests and one for responses (Leiserson et al. 1996). When blocking on a request, the node continues to accept incoming replies and requests, which may generate outgoing replies. When blocked on sending a reply, only incoming replies are accepted from the network. Eventually the reply will succeed, allowing the request to proceed. Alternatively, buffering can be provided at each node, with some additional end-to-end flow control to ensure that the buffers do not overflow. Should a user program be interrupted when it is partway through popping a message from the input queue, the system will extract the remainder of the message and push it back into the front of the input queue before resuming the program.

7.4.3 User-Level Handlers

Several experimental architectures have investigated a tighter integration of the user-level network port with the processor, including the Manchester Dataflow Machine (Gurd, Kerkham, and Watson 1985), Sigma-1 (Shimada, Hiraki, and Nishida 1984), iWARP (Borkar et al. 1990), Monsoon (Papadopoulos and Culler 1990), EM-4 (Sakai, Kodama, and Yamaguchi 1991), and the J-machine (Dally, Keen, and Noakes 1993). The key difference is that the network input and output ports are processor registers, as suggested by Figure 7.18, rather than special regions of memory. This substantially changes the engineering of the node since the communication assist is essentially a function unit in the processor. The latency of each of the operations is reduced substantially since data is moved in and out of the network with register-to-register instructions. The bandwidth demands on the memory bus are reduced, and the design of the communication support is divorced from the design of the memory system. However, the processor is involved in every network transaction. Large data transfers consume processor cycles and are likely to pollute the processor cache.

Interestingly, the experimental machines have arrived at a similar design point from vastly different approaches. The iWARP machine (Borkar et al. 1990), developed jointly by CMU and Intel, binds two registers in the main register file to the head of the network input and output ports. The processor may access the message on a word-by-word basis as it streams in from the network. Alternatively, a message can be spooled into memory by a DMA controller. The processor specifies which message it desires to access via the port registers by specifying the message tag, much as in a traditional receive call. Other messages are spooled into memory by the

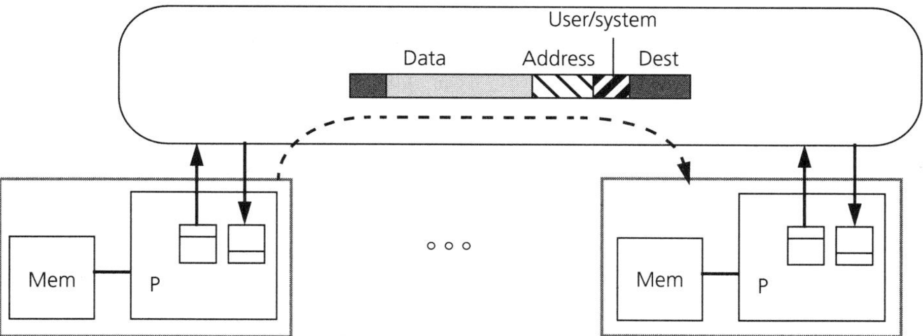

FIGURE 7.18 Hardware support in the communication assist for user-level handlers. The basic level of support required for user-level handlers is that the communication assist can determine that the network transaction is destined for a user process and make it directly available to that process. This either means that each process has a logical set of FIFOs, or a single set of FIFOs is time-shared among user processes.

DMA controller using an input buffer queue to specify the destination address. The extra hardware mechanism to direct one incoming and one outgoing message through the register file was motivated by systolic algorithms where a stream of data is pumped through processors in a highly regular pipeline, doing a small amount of computation as the stream flows through. By interpreting the tag, or virtual channel in iWARP terms, in the network interface, the memory-based message flows are not hindered by the register-based message flow. By contrast, in a CM-5 style of design, all messages are interleaved through a single input buffer.

The *T machine (Nikhil, Papadopoulos, and Arvind 1993), proposed by MIT and Motorola, offered a more general-purpose architecture for user-level message handling. It extended the Motorola 88110 RISC microprocessor to include a network function unit containing a set of registers much like the floating-point unit. In this design, a multiword outgoing message is composed in a set of output registers, and a special instruction causes the network function unit to send it out. There are several output register sets forming a queue and the send advances the queue, exposing the next available set to the user. Function unit status bits indicate whether an output set is available; these can be used directly in branch instructions. There are also several input message register sets, so when a message arrives, it is loaded into an input register set and a status bit is set or an interrupt is generated. Additional hardware support is provided to allow the processor to dispatch rapidly to the address specified by the first word of the message.

The *T design drew heavily on previous efforts supporting message-driven execution and dataflow architectures, especially the J-machine (Dally, Keen, and Noakes 1993), Monsoon (Papadopoulos and Culler 1990), and EM-4 (Sakai, Kodama, and Yamaguchi 1991). These earlier designs employ rather unusual processor architectures, so the communication assist is not clearly articulated. The J-machine design provides two execution contexts, each with a program counter and small register set.

The "system" execution context has priority over the "user" context. The instruction set includes a segmented memory model, with one segment being a special on-chip message input queue. There is also a message output port for each context. The first word of the network transaction is specified as being the address of the handler for the message. Whenever the user context is idle and a message is present in the input queue, the head of the message is automatically loaded into the program counter and an address register is set up to reference the rest of the message. The handler must extract the message from the input buffer before suspending or completing. Arrival of a system-level message preempts the user context and initiates a system handler.

In the Monsoon design, a network transaction is of fixed format and specified to contain a handler address, data frame address, and a 64-bit data value. The processor supports a large queue of such small messages. The basic instruction scheduling mechanism and the message handling mechanism are deeply integrated. In each instruction fetch cycle, a message is popped from the queue, and the instruction specified by the first word of the message is executed. Instructions are in a $1 + x$ address format and specify an offset relative to the frame address where a second operand is located. Each frame location contains *presence bits*, which indicate if the location is full or empty. If the location is empty the data word of the message is stored in the specified location (like a store accumulator instruction). If the location is not empty, its value is fetched, an operation is performed on the two operands, and one or more messages carrying the result are generated, either for the local queue or a queue across the network. In earlier, more traditional dataflow machines, the network transaction carries an instruction address and a tag, which is used in an associative match to locate the second operand, rather than simple frame relative addressing. Later hybrid machines (Nikhil and Arvind 1989; Grafe and Hoch 1990; Culler et al. 1991; Sakai, Kodama, and Yamaguchi 1991) execute a sequence of instructions for each message dequeue-and-match operation.

7.5 DEDICATED MESSAGE PROCESSING

A third important design style for large-scale distributed-memory machines seeks to allow sophisticated processing of the network transaction using dedicated hardware resources but without binding the interpretation in the hardware design. The interpretation is performed by software on a dedicated communication (or message) processor (CP) that operates directly on the network interface. With this capability, it is natural to consider off-loading the protocol processing associated with the message-passing abstraction to the CP. It can perform the buffering, matching, copying, and acknowledgment operations. It is also reasonable to support a global address space where the CP performs the remote read operation on behalf of the requesting node. The CPs can cooperate to provide a general capability to move data from one region of the global address space to another. The CP can provide synchronization operations and even combinations of data movement and synchronization, such as writing data and setting a flag or enqueuing data. This section looks at the basic organizational properties of machines of this class to understand the key design issues. We will examine in detail two machines as case studies, the Intel Paragon and the Meiko CS-2.

A generic organization for this style of design is shown in Figure 7.19, where the compute processor (P) and communication processor (CP) are symmetric and both reside on the memory bus. This essentially starts with a bus-based SMP as the node (as outlined in Chapter 5), extended with a primitive network interface similar to that described in the previous two sections. One of the processors in the SMP node is specialized in software to function as a dedicated CP. An alternative organization is to have the CP embedded into the network interface, as shown in Figure 7.20. These two organizations have different latency, bandwidth, and cost trade-offs, which we will examine a little later. Conceptually, they are very similar. The CP typically executes at the system privilege level, relieving the machine designer of the issues associated with a user-level network interface discussed previously. The two processors communicate via shared memory, which typically takes the form of a command queue and response area, so the change in privilege level comes essentially for free as part of the hand-off. Since the design assumes that a system-level processor is responsible for managing network transactions, these designs generally allow word-by-word access to the NI FIFOs as well as DMA. The CP can inspect portions of the message and decide what actions to take. The CP can poll the network and the command queues to move the communication process along.

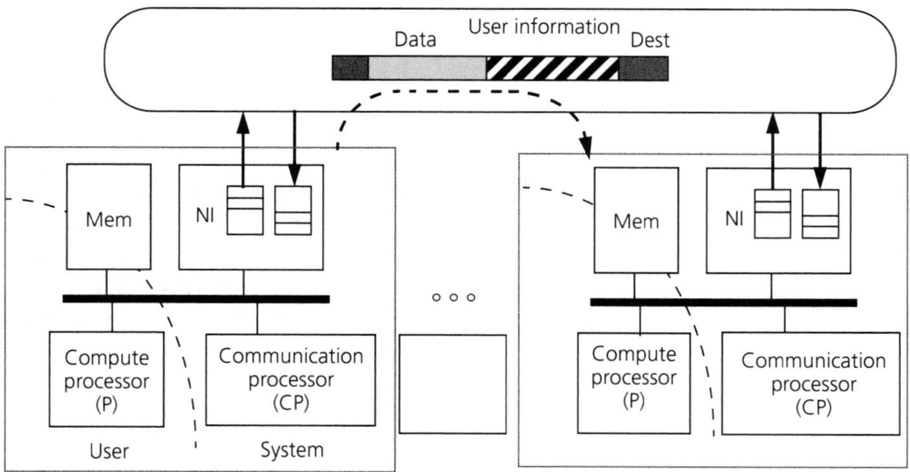

FIGURE 7.19 Machine organization for dedicated message processing with a symmetric processor. Each node has a processor, symmetric with the main processor on a shared memory bus, that is dedicated to initiating and handling network transactions. Being dedicated, it can always run in system mode, so transferring data through memory implicitly crosses the protection boundary. The CP can provide any additional protection checks of the contents of the transactions.

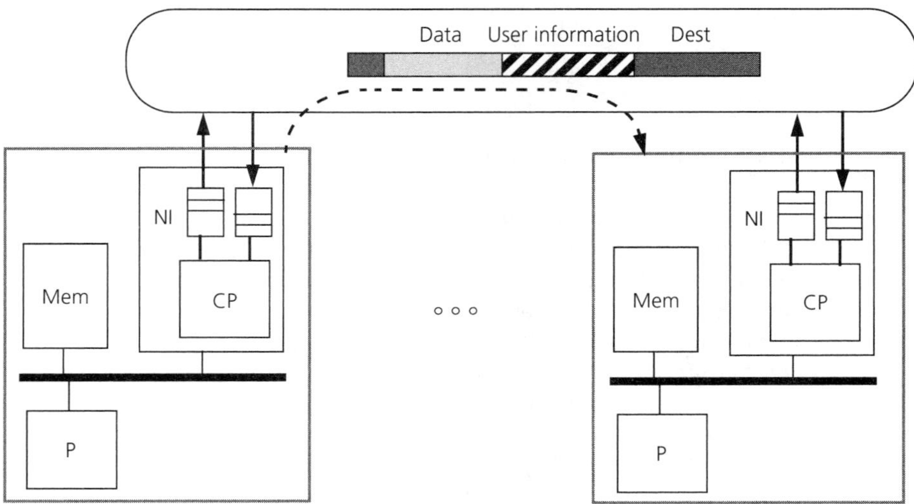

FIGURE 7.20 Machine organization for dedicated message processing with an embedded processor. The communication assist consists of a dedicated, programmable CP embedded in the network interface. It has a direct path to the network that does not utilize the memory bus shared by the main processor.

The CP provides the compute processor with a very clean abstraction of the network interface. All the details of the physical network operation are hidden, such as the hardware input/output buffers, the status registers, and the representation of routes. A message can be sent by simply writing it, or a pointer to it, into shared memory. Control information is exchanged between the processors using familiar shared memory synchronization primitives, such as flags and locks. Incoming messages can be delivered directly into memory by the CP, along with notification to the compute processor via shared variables. With a well-designed user-level abstraction, the data can be deposited directly into the user address space. A simple low-level abstraction provides each user process in a parallel program with a logical input queue and output queue. In this case, the flow of information in a network transaction is as shown in Figure 7.21.

These benefits are not without costs. Since communication between the compute processor and CP is via shared memory within the node, communication performance is strongly influenced by the efficiency of the cache coherency protocol. A review of Chapter 5 reveals that these protocols are primarily designed to avoid unnecessary communication when two processors are operating on mostly distinct portions of a shared data structure. The shared communication queues are a very different situation. The producer writes an entry and sets a flag. The consumer must see the flag update, read the data, and clear the flag. Eventually, the producer will see the cleared flag and rewrite the entry. All the data must be moved from the producer to the consumer with minimal latency. We will see shortly that inefficiencies in tra-

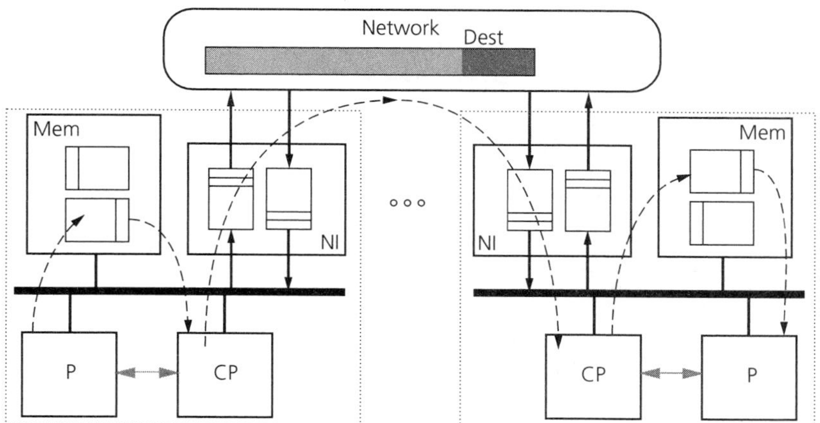

FIGURE 7.21 Flow of a network transaction with a symmetric communication processor. Each network transaction flows through memory or at least across the memory bus in a cache-to-cache transfer between the main processor and the memory processor. It crosses the memory bus again between the CP and the network interface.

ditional coherency protocols make this latency significant. For example, before the producer can write a new entry, the copy of the old one in the consumer's cache must be invalidated. One might imagine that an update protocol or even uncached writes might avoid this situation, but then a bus transaction will occur for every word rather than every cache block.

A second problem is that the function performed by the CP is concurrency intensive. It handles requests from the compute processor, messages arriving from the network, and messages going out and into the network all at once. By folding all these events into a single sequential dispatch loop, they can only be handled one at a time. This can seriously impair the message processing rate of the hardware.

Finally, the ability of the CP to deliver messages directly into memory does not completely eliminate the possibility of fetch deadlock at the user level, although it can ensure that the physical resources are not stalled when an application deadlocks. A user application may need to provide some additional level of flow control.

7.5.1 Case Study: Intel Paragon

To make these general issues concrete, let us examine how they arise in an important machine of this ilk—the Intel Paragon, first shipped in 1992. Each node is a shared memory multiprocessor with two or more 50-MHz i860XP processors, a network interface (NI) chip, and 16 or 32 MB of memory, connected by a 64-bit, 400-MB/s, cache-coherent memory bus, as shown in Figure 7.22. In addition, two DMA engines (one for sending and the other for receiving) are provided to burst data

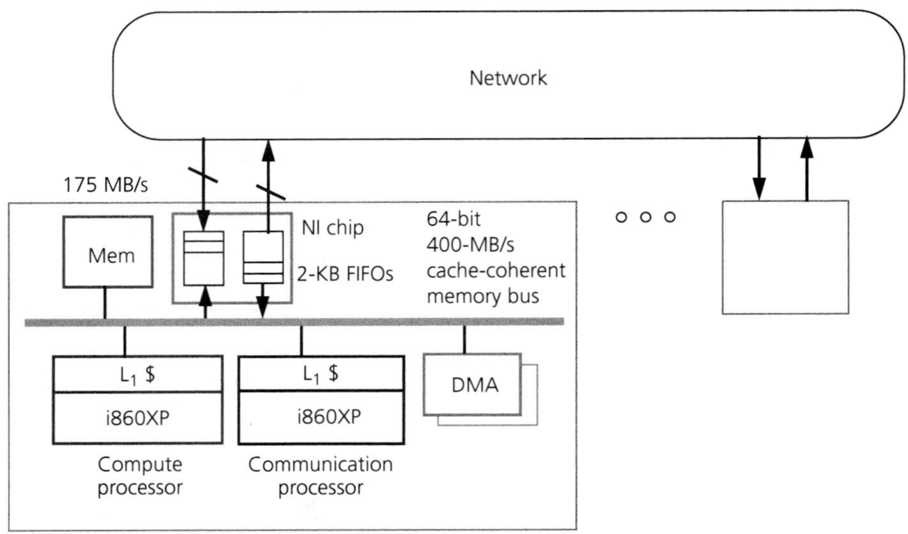

FIGURE 7.22 Intel Paragon machine organization. Each node of the machine includes a dedicated CP, identical to the compute processor on a cache-coherent memory bus, which has a simple, system-level interface to a fast, reliable network and two cache-coherent DMA engines that respect the flow control of the NIC.

between memory and the network. DMA transfers operate within the cache coherency protocol and are throttled by the network interface before buffers are over- or underrun. One of the processors is designated as a CP to handle network transactions and message-passing protocols while the other is used as a compute processor for general computing. "I/O nodes" are formed by adding I/O daughter cards for SCSI, Ethernet, and HPPI connections.

The i860XP uses write-back caching normally, but it can also be configured to use write-through and write-once policies under software or hardware control. The write buffers can hold two successive stores to prevent stalling on write misses. The cache controllers of the i860XP implement a variant of the MESI (modified, exclusive, shared, invalid) cache consistency protocol discussed in Chapter 5. The external bus interface also supports a three-stage address pipeline (i.e., 3 outstanding bus cycles) and burst mode with transfer length of 2 or 4 at 400 MB/s.

The NI chip connects the 64-bit synchronous memory bus to 16-bit asynchronous (self-timed) network links. A 2-KB transmit FIFO (tx) and a 2-KB receive FIFO (rx) are used to provide rate matching between the node and a full-duplex 175-MB/s network link. The head of the rx FIFO and the tail of the tx FIFO are accessible to the node as a memory-mapped NI chip I/O register. In addition, a status register contains flags that are set when the FIFO is full, empty, almost full, or almost empty and when an end-of-packet marker is present. The NI chip can optionally generate an interrupt when each flag is set. Reads and writes to the NI chip FIFOs are uncached and must be done one double word (64 bits) at a time. The first word of a message must contain the route (X-Y displacements in a 2D mesh), but the hardware does not impose any other restriction on the message format. In particular, it does not distinguish between system and user messages. In addition, the NI chip also performs parity and CRC checks to maintain end-to-end data integrity.

Two DMA engines, one for sending and the other for receiving, can transfer a contiguous block of data between main memory and the NI chip at 400MB/s. The memory region is specified as a physical address, aligned on a 32-byte boundary, with a length between 64 bytes and 16 KB (one DRAM page) in multiples of 32 bytes (a cache block). During DMA transfer, the DMA engine snoops on the processor caches to ensure consistency. Hardware flow control prevents the DMA from overflowing or underflowing the NI chip FIFOs. If the output buffer is full, the send-DMA will pause and free the bus. Similarly, the receive-DMA pauses when the input buffer is empty. The bus arbitrator gives priority to the DMA engine over the processors. A DMA transfer is started by storing an address-length pair to a memory-mapped DMA register using the `stio` instruction. Upon completion, the DMA engine sets a flag in a status register and optionally generates an interrupt.

With this hardware configuration, a small message of just less than two cache blocks (seven words) can be transferred from registers in one compute processor to registers waiting on the transfer in another compute processor in just over 10 μs (500 cycles). This time breaks down almost equally between the three processor-to-processor transfers: compute processor to CP across the bus, CP to CP across the network, and CP to compute processor across the bus on the remote node. It may seem surprising that transfers between two processors on a cache-coherent memory bus would have the same latency as transfers between two CPs through the network, especially since the transfers between the processor and the network interface involve a transfer across the same bus.

Let's look at this situation in a little more detail. An i860 processor can write a cache block from registers using two quad-word store instructions. Suppose that part of the block is used as a full-empty flag. In the typical case, the last operation on the block was a store by the consumer to clear the flag; with the Paragon MESI protocol, this writes through to memory, invalidates the producer block, and leaves the consumer in the exclusive state. The producer's load on the flag that finds the flag clear misses in the producer cache, reads the block from memory, and downgrades the consumer block to shared state. The first store writes through and invalidates the consumer block, but it leaves the producer block in shared state since sharing was detected when the write was performed. The second store also writes through, but since there is no sharer it leaves the producer in the exclusive state. The consumer eventually reads the flag, misses, and brings in the entire line. Thus, four bus transactions are required for a single cache block transfer. (By having an additional flag that allows the producer to check that several blocks are empty, this can be reduced to three bus transactions. This is left as an exercise.) Data is written to the network interface as a sequence of uncached double-word stores. These are all pipelined through the write buffer; however, they do involve multiple bus transfers. Before writing the data, the CP needs to check that room is available in the output buffer to hold it. Rather than pay the cost of an uncached read, it checks a bit in the processor status word corresponding to a masked "output buffer empty" interrupt. On the receiving end, the CP reads a similar "input nonempty" status bit and then reads the message data as a series of uncached loads. The actual NI-to-NI transfer takes only about 250 ns plus 40 ns per hop in an unloaded network.

For a bulk memory-to-memory transfer, there is additional work for the CP to start the send-DMA from the user source region. This requires about 2 μs (100 cycles). The DMA transfer bursts at 400 MB/s into the network output buffer of 2,048 bytes. When the output buffer is full, the DMA engine backs off until a number of cache blocks are drained into the network. On the receiving end, the CP detects the presence of an incoming message, reads the first few words containing the destination memory address, and starts the receive-DMA to drain the remainder of the message into memory. For a large transfer, the send-DMA engine will still be moving data out of memory when the receive-DMA engine is moving data into memory, and a portion of the transfer occupies the buffers and network links in between. At this point, the message moves forward at the 175 MB/s of the network links. The send- and receive-DMA engines periodically kick in and move data to or from network buffers in 400-MB/s bursts.

A review of the requirements on the CP shows that it is responding to a large number of independent events on which it must take action. These include the current user program writing a message into the shared queue, the kernel on the compute processor writing a message into a similar "system queue," the network delivering a message into the NI input buffer, the NI output buffer going empty as a result of the network accepting a message, the send-DMA engine completing, and the receive-DMA engine completing. The bandwidth of the CP is determined by the time it takes to detect and dispatch on these various events. While handling any one of the events, all the others are effectively locked out. Additional hardware, such as the DMA engines, is introduced to minimize the work in handling any particular event and to allow data to flow from the source storage area (registers or memory) to the destination storage area in a fully pipelined fashion. However, the communication rate (messages per second) is still limited by the sequential dispatch loop in the CP. In addition, the software on the CP, which keeps data flowing, avoids deadlock, and avoids starving the network, is rather tricky. Logically, it involves a number of independent cooperating threads, but these are folded into a single sequential dispatch loop that keeps track of the state of each of the partial operations. This concurrency problem is addressed by our next case study.

The basic architecture of the Paragon is employed in the ASCI Red machine, which is the first machine to sustain a TFLOPS (one trillion floating-point operations per second). This machine will contain 4,536 nodes with dual 200-MHz Pentium Pro processors and 64 MB of memory. It uses an upgraded version of the Paragon network with 400-MB/s links, still in a grid topology. The machine is spread over 85 cabinets, occupying about 1,600 square feet and drawing 800 kW of power. Forty of the nodes provide I/O access to large RAID storage systems, an additional 32 nodes provide operating system services to a lightweight kernel operating on the individual nodes, and 16 nodes provide "hot" spares.

Many cluster designs employ SMP nodes as the basic building block, with a scalable high-performance LAN or SAN. This approach admits the option of dedicating a processor to message processing or of having that responsibility taken on by processors as demanded by message traffic. One key difference is that networks such as that used in the Paragon will back up and stop all communication progress, including system messages, unless the inbound transactions are serviced by the nodes. Thus, dedicating a processor to message handling provides a more robust design. (In special cases, such as attempting to set the record on the LINPACK benchmark, even the Paragon and ASCI Red are run with both processors doing user computation.) Clusters usually rely on other mechanisms to keep communication flowing, such as dedicated processing within the network interface card, as we will discuss in Section 7.7.

7.5.2 Case Study: Meiko CS-2

The Meiko CS-2 provides a representative concrete design with an asymmetric CP that is closely integrated with the network interface and has a dedicated path to the network. The node architecture is essentially that of a Sun SparcStation 10, with two standard superscalar Sparc modules on the MBUS, each with an L_1 cache on chip and an L_2 cache on the module. Ethernet, SBUS, and SCSI connections are also accessible over the MBUS through a bus adapter to provide I/O. (A high-performance variant of the node architecture includes two Fujitsu μVP vector units sharing a three-ported memory system. The third port is the MBUS, which hosts the two compute processors and the communications module, as in the basic node.) The communications module functions as either another processor module or a memory module on the MBUS, depending on its operation. The network links provide 50-MB/s bandwidth in each direction. This machine takes a unique position on how the network transaction is interpreted and on how concurrency is supported in communication processing.

A network transaction on the Meiko CS-2 is a code sequence transferred across the network and executed directly by the remote CP. The network is *circuit switched*, which means that a channel is established and held open for the duration of the network transaction execution. The channel closes with an acknowledgment if the channel was established and the transaction executed to completion successfully. A NACK is returned if connection is not established, a CRC error occurs, the remote execution times out, or a conditional operation fails. The control flow for network transactions is straight-line code with conditional abort but no branching. A typical cause of time-out is a page fault at the remote end. The kinds of operations that can be included in a network transaction include read, write, or read-modify-write of remote memory; setting events; simple tests; DMA transfers; and simple reply transactions. Thus, the format of the information in a network transaction is fairly extensive. It consists of a context identifier, a start symbol, a sequence of operations in a concrete format, and an end symbol. A transaction is between 40 and 320 bytes long. We will return to the operations supported by network transactions in more detail after looking at the machine organization.

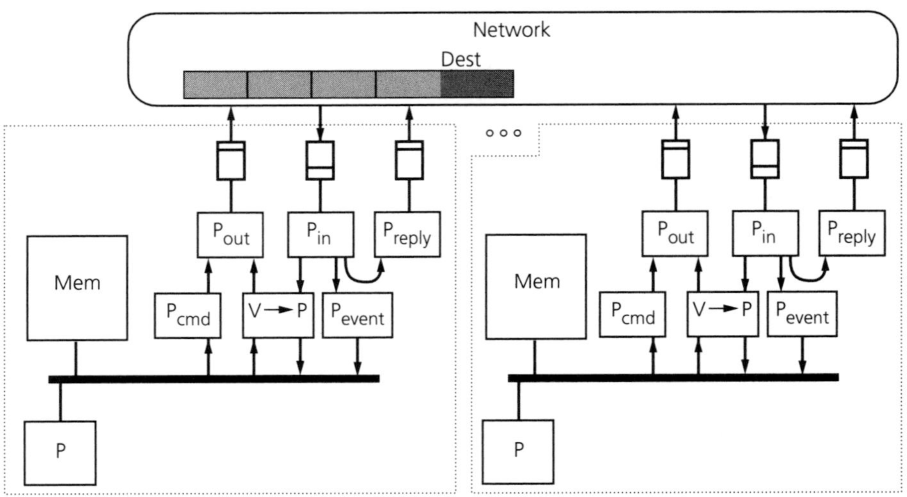

FIGURE 7.23 Meiko CS-2 conceptual structure with multiple specialized communication processors. Each of the individual aspects of generating and processing network transactions is associated in independently operating hardware function units.

Based on the preceding discussion, it makes sense to consider decomposing the CP into several independent processors, as indicated by Figure 7.23. A command processor (P_{cmd}) waits for communication commands to be issued on behalf of the user or system and carries them out. Since it resides as a device on the memory bus, it can respond directly to reads and writes of addresses for which it is responsible, rather than polling a shared memory location as would a conventional processor. It carries out its work by pushing route information and data into the output processor (P_{out}) or by moving data from memory to the output processor. It may require assistance of a device responsible for virtual-to-physical (V→P) address translation. It also provides whatever protection checks are required for user-to-user communication. The output processor P_{out} monitors the status of the network output FIFO and delivers network transactions into the network. An input processor (P_{in}) waits for the arrival of a network transaction and executes it. This may involve delivering data into memory, posting a command to an event processor (P_{event}) to signal completion of the transaction, or posting a reply operation to a reply processor (P_{reply}), which operates very much like the output processor.

The Meiko CS-2 essentially provides these independent functions, although they operate as time-multiplexed threads on a single microprogrammed processor called the *elan* (Homewood and McLaren 1993). This makes the communication between the logical processors very simple and provides a clean conceptual structure, but it does not actually keep all the information flows progressing smoothly. The actual functional organization of the elan is depicted in Figure 7.24. A command is issued by the compute processor to the command processor via an exchange instruction, which swaps the value of a register and a memory location. The memory location is

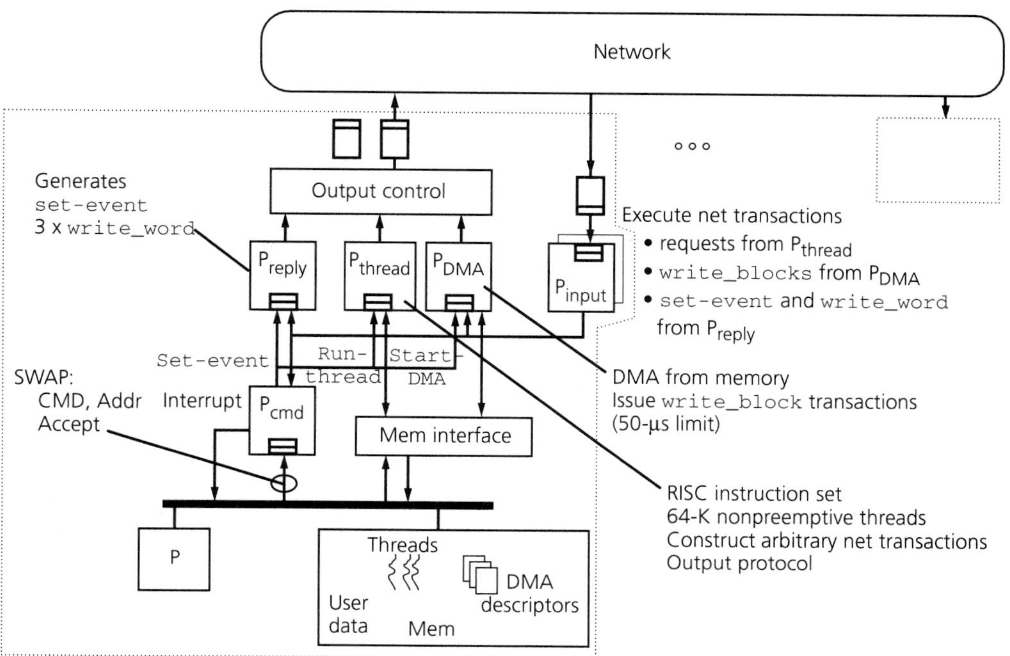

FIGURE 7.24 Meiko CS-2 machine organization. The communication assist provides five simple processors as time slices on a single microcoded processor. Four of them are dedicated to specific functions: receiving commands from the host, accepting transactions from the network, performing DMA transfers, and issuing replies. One, the thread processor, executes user-level code to generate network transactions and issue requests to the other processors.

mapped to the head of the command processor input queue. The value returned to the processor indicates whether the enqueue command was successful or whether the queue was already full. The value given to the command processor contains a command type and a virtual address. The command processor basically supports three commands: `start-DMA`, in which case the address points to a DMA descriptor; `set-event`, in which case the address refers to a simple event data structure; or `start-thread`, in which case the address specifies the first instruction in the thread. The DMA processor reads data from memory and generates a sequence of network transactions to cause data to be stored into the remote node. The command processor also performs event operations, which involve updating a small event data structure and possibly raising an interrupt for the main processor in order to wake a sleeping thread. The start-thread command is conveyed to a simple RISC thread processor, which executes an arbitrary code sequence to construct and issue network transactions. Network transactions are interpreted by the input processor, which may cause threads to execute, DMA to start, replies to be issued, or events to be set. The reply is simply a set-event operation with an optional write of three words of data.

To make the machine operation more concrete, let us consider a few simple operations. Suppose a user process wants to write data into the address space of another process of the same parallel program. Protection is provided by a capability for a communication context that both processes share. The source compute processor builds a DMA descriptor and issues a start-DMA command. Its DMA processor reads the descriptor and transfers the data as a sequence of blocks, each of which involves loading up to 32 bytes from memory and forming a `write_block` network transaction. The input processor on the remote node will receive and execute a series of `write_block` transactions, each containing a user virtual memory address and the data to be written at that address. Reading a block of data from a remote address space is somewhat more involved. A thread is started on the local CP, which issues a start-DMA transaction. The input processor on the remote node passes the start-DMA and its descriptor to the DMA processor on the remote node, which reads data from memory and returns it as a sequence of `write_block` transactions. To detect completion, these can be augmented with set-event operations.

In order to support direct user-to-user transfers, the communications processor on the Meiko CS-2 contains its own page table. The operating system on the main processor keeps this consistent with the normal page tables. If the CP experiences a page fault, an interrupt is generated at the processor so that the operating system there can fault in the page and update the page tables.

The major shortcoming with this design is that the thread processor is quite slow and is nonpreemptively scheduled. This makes it very difficult to off-load any but the most trivial processing to the thread processor. In addition, the set of operations provided by network transactions is not powerful enough to construct an effective remote enqueue operation with a single network transaction (Schauser and Scheiman 1995).

7.6 SHARED PHYSICAL ADDRESS SPACE

This section examines a fourth major design style for the communication architecture of scalable multiprocessors—a shared physical address space. This builds directly upon the modest-scale shared memory machines and provides the same communication primitives: loads, stores, and atomic operations on shared memory locations. Many machines have been developed to extend this approach to large-scale systems, including CM*, C.mmp, NYU Ultracomputer, BBN Butterfly, IBM RP3, Denelcor HEP-1, BBN TC2000, and the CRAY T3D (Scott 1996). Most of the early designs employed a dancehall organization, with the interconnect between the memory and the processors, whereas most of the later designs use distributed-memory organization. The communication assist translates bus transactions into network transactions. The network transactions are very specific, since they describe only a predefined set of memory operations, and are interpreted directly by the communication assist at the remote node.

A generic machine organization for a large-scale distributed shared physical address machine is shown in Figure 7.25. The communication assist is best viewed as forming a *pseudo-memory module* and a *pseudo-processor*, integrated into the

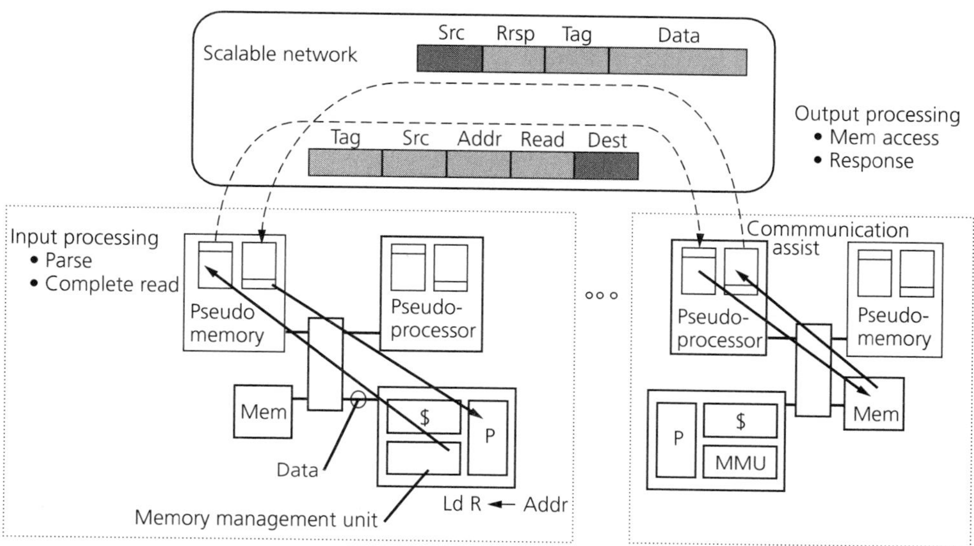

FIGURE 7.25 Shared physical address space machine organization. In scalable shared physical address machines, network transactions are initiated as a result of conventional memory instructions. They have a fixed set of formats, interpreted directly in the communication assist hardware. The operations are request-response, and most systems provide two distinct networks to avoid fetch deadlock. The communication architecture must assume the role of pseudo-memory unit on the issuing node and pseudo-processor on the servicing node. The remote memory operation is accepted by the pseudo-memory unit on the issuing node, which carries out request-response transactions with the remote node. The source bus transaction is held open for the duration of the request network transaction, the remote memory access, and the response network transaction. Thus, the communication assist must be able to access the local memory on the remote node even while the processor on that node is stalled in the middle of its own memory operation.

processor-memory connection. Consider, for example, a load instruction executed by the processor on one node. The on-chip memory management unit (MMU) translates the virtual address into a global physical address that is presented to the memory system. If this physical address is local to the issuing node, the memory simply responds with the contents of the desired location. If not, the communication assist must act like a memory module while it accesses the remote location. The pseudo-memory controller accepts the read transaction on the memory bus, extracts the node number from the global physical address, and issues a network transaction to the remote node to access the desired location. Note that at this point the load instruction is stalled between the address phase and the data phase of the memory operation. The remote communication assist receives the network transaction, reads the desired location, and issues a response transaction to the original node. The remote communication assist appears as a pseudo-processor to the memory system on its node when it issues the proxy read to the memory system. An important point to note is that when the pseudo-processor attempts to access memory on behalf of a remote node, the main processor there may be stalled in the middle of its own remote load instruction. A simple memory bus supporting one outstanding operation is inadequate for the task. Either there must be two independent paths into memory or the bus must support a split-phase operation with unordered completion. Eventually, the response transaction will arrive at the originating pseudo-memory controller. It will complete the memory read operation just as if it were a (slow) memory module.

A key issue, which we will examine deeply in the next chapter, is the cachability of the shared memory locations. In most modern microprocessors, the cachability of an address is determined by a field in the page table entry for the containing page, which is extracted from the TLB when the location is accessed. In this discussion, it is important to distinguish two orthogonal concepts. An address may be either private to a process or shared among processes, and it may be either physically local to a processor or physically remote. Clearly, addresses that are private to a process and physically local to the processor on which that process executes should be cached. This requires no special hardware support. Private data that is physically remote can also be cached, although this requires that the communication assists support cache block transactions rather than just single words. No processor change is required to cache remote blocks since remote memory accesses appear identical to local memory accesses, only slower; however, coherence is not an issue as long as the process stays put since no other process accesses the private data. If physically local and logically shared data is cached locally, then accesses on behalf of remote nodes performed by the pseudo-processor must be cache coherent. If local shared data is cached only in write-through mode, this only requires that the pseudo-processor invalidate cached data when it performs writes to memory on behalf of remote nodes. To cache shared data as write back, the pseudo-processor needs to be able to cause data to be flushed out of the cache. The most natural solution is to integrate the pseudo-processor on a cache-coherent memory bus, but the bus must also be split phase, with some number of outstanding transactions reserved for the pseudo-processor. The final option is to cache shared, remote data. The hardware support for accessing, transferring, and placing a remote block in the local cache is completely covered by the preceding options. The new issue is keeping the possibly numerous copies of the block in various caches coherent. We must also deal with the consistency model for such a distributed shared memory with replication. These issues require substantially greater design consideration, and we devote the next two chapters to addressing them. It is clearly attractive from a performance viewpoint to cache shared, remote data that is for the most part accessed locally.

7.6.1 Case Study: CRAY T3D

The CRAY T3D provides a concrete example of a shared global physical address design. The design follows the basic outline of Figure 7.13, with a pseudo-memory controller and pseudo-processor providing remote memory access via a scalable network supporting independent delivery of request and response transactions. There

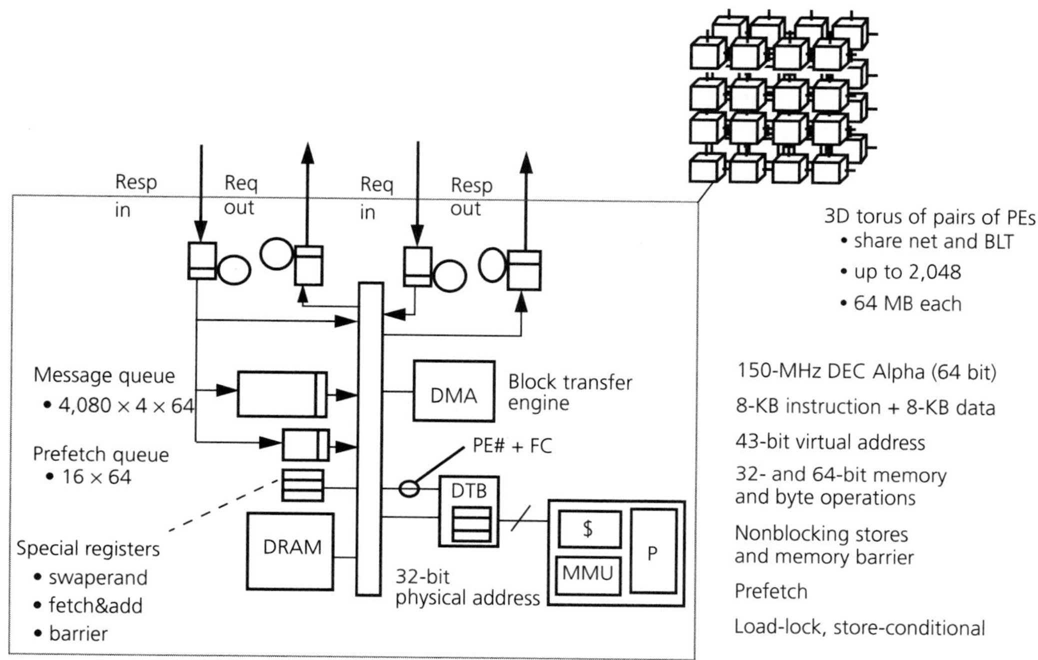

FIGURE 7.26 CRAY T3D machine organization. Each node contains an elaborate communication assist, which includes the pseudo-memory and pseudo-processor functions required for a shared physical address space. In addition, a set of external segment registers (the DTB) is provided to extend the machine's limited physical address space. A prefetch queue supports latency hiding through explicit read ahead. A message queue supports events associated with message-passing models. A DMA unit provides block transfer capability, and special pointwise and global synchronization operations are supported. The machine is organized as a 3D torus, as the name might suggest.

are seven specific network transaction formats, which are interpreted directly in hardware. However, the design extends the basic shared physical address approach in several significant ways. The T3D system is intended to scale to 2,048 nodes, each with a 150-MHz dual-issue DEC Alpha 21064 microprocessor and up to 64 MB of memory, as illustrated in Figure 7.26. The DEC Alpha architecture is intended to be used as a building block for parallel architectures (Digital Equipment Corporation 1992), and several aspects of the 21064 strongly influenced the T3D design. In this case study, we first look at salient aspects of the microprocessor itself and the local memory system. Then we will discuss the assists constructed around the basic processor to provide a shared physical address space, latency tolerance, block transfer, synchronization, and fast message passing. The CRAY designers sometimes refer to this as the "shell" of support circuitry around a conventional microprocessor that embodies the parallel processing capability.

The Alpha 21064 has 8-KB on-chip instruction and data caches as well as support for an external L_2 cache. In the T3D design, the L_2 cache is eliminated in order to reduce the time to access main memory. The processor stalls for the duration of a cache miss, so reducing the miss latency directly increases the delivered bandwidth. The CRAY design is biased toward access patterns typical of vector codes, which scan through large regions of memory. The measured access time of a load that misses to memory is 155 ns (23 cycles) on the T3D, compared to 300 ns (45 cycles) on a DEC Alpha workstation at the same clock rate with a 512-KB L_2 cache (Arpaci et al. 1995). (The CRAY T3D access time increases to 255 ns if the access is off page within the DRAM.) These measurements are very useful in calibrating the performance of the global memory accesses.

The Alpha 21064 provides a 43-bit virtual address space in accordance with the Alpha architecture; however, the physical address space is only 32 bits in size. Since the virtual-to-physical translation occurs on chip, only the physical address is presented to the memory system and communication assist. A fully populated system of 2,048 nodes with 64 MB each would require 37 bits of global physical address space. To enlarge the physical address space of each node, the T3D provides an external register set, called the DTB Annex, which uses 5 bits of the physical address to select a register containing a 21-bit node number; this is concatenated with a 27-bit local physical address to form a full global physical address.[8] The annex registers also contain an additional field specifying the type of access, for example, cached or uncached. Annex register 0 always refers to the local node. The Alpha load-lock and store-conditional instructions are used in the T3D to read and write the annex registers. Updating an annex register takes 23 cycles, just like an off-chip memory access, and can be followed immediately by a load or store instruction that uses the annex register.

A read or write of a location in the global address space is accomplished by a short sequence of instructions. First, the processor number part of the global virtual address is extracted and stored into an annex register. Then, a temporary virtual address is constructed so that the upper bits specify this annex register and the lower bits specify the address on that node. Finally, a load or store instruction is issued on this temporary virtual address. The load operation takes 610 ns (91 cycles), not including the annex setup and address manipulation. (This number increases by 100 ns [15 cycles] if the remote DRAM access is off page. In addition, if a cache block is brought over, it increases to 785–885 ns.)

Remember, the virtual-to-physical translation occurs in the processor issuing the load. The page tables are set up so that the annex register number is simply carried through from the virtual address to the physical address. So that the resulting physical address will make sense on the remote node, the physical placement of all processes in a parallel program is identical (paging is not supported). In addition, care is exercised to ensure that all processes in a parallel program have extended their heap to the same length.

8. This situation is not altogether unusual. The C.mmp employed a similar trick to overcome the limited addressing capability of the LSI-11 building block. The problems that arose from this led to a famous quote, attributed variously to Gordon Bell or Bill Wulf, that the only flaw in an architecture that is hard to overcome is too small an address space.

The Alpha 21064 provides only nonblocking stores. Execution is allowed to proceed after a store instruction without waiting for the store to complete. Writes are buffered by a write buffer, which is four deep, and in each entry up to 32 bytes of write data can be merged. Several store instructions can be outstanding. A "memory barrier" instruction is provided to ensure that writes have completed before further execution commences. The Alpha nonblocking store allows remote stores to be overlapped so that high bandwidth can be achieved in writes to remote memory locations. Remote writes of up to a full cache block can issue from the write buffer every 250 ns, providing up to 120 MB/s of transfer bandwidth from the local cache to remote memory. A single blocking remote write involves a sequence to issue the store, push the store out of the write buffer with a memory barrier operation, and then wait on a completion flag provided by the network interface. This requires 900 ns, plus the annex setup and address arithmetic.

The Alpha provides a special prefetch instruction, intended to encourage the memory system to move important data closer to the processor. This is used in the T3D to hide the remote read latency. An off-chip prefetch queue of 16 words is provided. A prefetch causes a word to be read from memory and deposited into the queue. Reading from the queue pops the word at its head. The prefetch issue instruction is treated like a store and takes only a few cycles. The pop operation takes the 23 cycles typical of an off-chip access. If eight words are prefetched and then popped, the network latency is completely hidden, and the effective latency of each word is less than 300 ns.

The T3D also provides a bulk transfer engine, which can move blocks or regular strided data between the local node and a remote node in either direction. Reading from a remote node, the block transfer bandwidth peaks at 140 MB/s; writing to a remote node, it peaks at 90 MB/s. However, use of the block transfer engine requires a kernel trap to provide the virtual-to-physical translation. Thus, the prefetch queue provides better performance for transfers of up to 64 KB of data, and nonblocking stores are faster for any length. The primary advantage of the bulk transfer engine is the ability to overlap communication and computation. This capability is limited to some extent since the processor and the bulk transfer engine compete for the same memory bandwidth.

The T3D communication assist also provides special support for synchronization. First, there is a dedicated network to support global-or and global-and operations, used primarily for barriers. This allows processors to raise a flag indicating that they have reached the barrier, to continue executing, and then to wait for all to enter before leaving. Each node also has a set of external synchronization registers to support atomic swap and fetch&inc. There is also a user-level message queue, which will either cause a message to be enqueued or a thread to be invoked on a remote node. Unfortunately, either of these actions involves a remote kernel trap, so the two operations take 25 μs and 70 μs, respectively. In comparison, building a queue in memory using the fetch&inc operation allows a four-word message to be enqueued in 3 μs and dequeued in 1.5 μs.

7.6.2 Case Study: CRAY T3E

The CRAY T3E (Scott 1996) follow-on to the CRAY T3D provides an illuminating snapshot of the trade-offs in large-scale system design. The two driving forces in the design were the need to provide a more powerful, more contemporary processor in the node and to simplify the shell. The CRAY T3D has many complicated mechanisms for supporting similar functions, each with unique advantages and disadvantages. The T3E uses the 300-MHz, quad-issue Alpha 21164 processor with a sizable (96 KB) second-level on-chip cache. Since the L_2 cache is on chip, eliminating it is not an option as on the T3D. However, the T3E forgoes the board-level tertiary cache typically found in Alpha 21164-based workstations. The various remote access mechanisms are unified into a single external register concept. In addition, remote memory accesses are performed using virtual addresses that are translated to physical addresses by the remote communication assist.

A user process has access to a set of 512 E-registers of 64 bits each. The processor can read and write contents of the E-registers using conventional load and store instructions to a special region of the memory space. Operations are also provided to get data from global memory into an E-register, to put data from an E-register into global memory, and to perform atomic read-modify-writes between E-registers and global memory. Loading remote data into an E-register involves three steps. First, the processor portion of the global virtual address is constructed in an E-address register. Second, the get command is issued via a store to a special region of memory. A field of the address used in the command store specifies the get operation, and another field specifies the destination data E-register. The command-store data specifies an offset to be used relative to the address E-register. The command store has the side effect of causing the remote read to be performed and the destination E-register to be loaded with the data. Finally, the data is read into the processor via a load to the data E-register. The process for a remote put is similar, except that the store data is placed in the data E-register, which is specified in the put command store. This approach of causing loads and stores to data registers as a side effect of operations on address registers goes all the way back to the CDC-6600 (Thornton 1964), although it seems to have been largely forgotten in the meanwhile.

The utility of the prefetch queue is provided in E-registers by associating a full-empty bit with each E-register. A series of gets can be issued, and each one sets the associated destination E-register to empty. When a get completes, the register is set to full. If the processor attempts to load from an empty E-register, the memory operation is stalled until the get completes. The utility of the block transfer engine is provided by allowing vectors of four or eight words to be transferred through E-registers in a single operation. This has the added advantage of providing a means of efficient gather operations.

The improvements in the T3E greatly simplify code generation for the machine and offer several performance advantages; however, these are not at all uniform. The computational performance is significantly higher on the T3D due to the faster processor and larger on-chip cache. On the other hand, the remote read latency is more than twice that of the T3D, increasing from 600 ns to roughly 1500 ns. The increase is due to the L_2 cache miss penalty and the remote address translation. The remote write latency is essentially the same in the two machines. The prefetch cost is improved by roughly a factor of two, obtaining a rate of one word read every 130 ns. Each of the memory modules can service a read every 67 ns. Nonblocking writes have essentially the same performance on the two machines. The block transfer capability of the T3E is far superior to the T3D. A bandwidth of greater than 300 MB/s is obtained without the large start-up cost of the block transfer engine. The bulk write bandwidth is greater than 300 MB/s, three times the T3D.

7.6.3 Summary

Wide variation exists in the degree of hardware interpretation of network transactions in modern large-scale parallel machines. These variations result in a wide range in the overhead experienced by the compute processor in performing communication operations as well as in the latency added to that of the actual network by the communication assist. By restricting the set of transactions, specializing the communication assist to the task of interpreting these transactions, and tightly integrating the communication assist with the memory system of the node, the overhead and latency can be reduced substantially. Hardware specialization can also provide the concurrency needed within the assist to handle several simultaneous streams of events with high bandwidth.

7.7 CLUSTERS AND NETWORKS OF WORKSTATIONS

Along with the use of commodity microprocessors, memory devices, and even workstation operating systems in modern large-scale parallel machines, scalable communication networks similar to those used in parallel machines have become available for use in a limited local area network setting. This naturally raises the question, To what extent are networks of workstations (NOWs) and parallel machines converging? Before entertaining this question, a little background is in order.

Traditionally, collections of complete computers with dedicated interconnects, often called *clusters*, have been used to serve multiprogramming workloads and to provide improved availability (Kronenberg, Levy, and Strecker 1986; Pfister et al. 1985). In multiprogramming clusters, a single front-end machine usually acts as an intermediary between a collection of compute servers and a large number of users at terminals or remote machines. The front end tracks the load on the cluster nodes and schedules tasks onto the most lightly loaded nodes. Typically, all the machines in the cluster are set up to function identically; they have the same instruction set, the same operating systems, and the same file system access. In older systems, such as the Vax VMS cluster (Kronenberg, Levy, and Strecker 1986), this was achieved by connecting each of the machines to a common set of disks. More recently, this *single-system image* is usually achieved by mounting common file systems over the network. By sharing a pool of functionally equivalent machines, better utilization can be achieved on a large number of independent jobs.

Availability clusters seek to minimize downtime of large critical systems, such as important on-line databases and transaction processing systems. Structurally, they have much in common with multiprogramming clusters. A very common scenario is to use a pair of SMPs running identical copies of a database system with a shared set of disks. Should the primary system fail due to a hardware or software problem, operation rapidly "fails over" to the secondary system. The actual interconnect that provides the shared disk capability can be dual access to the disks or some kind of dedicated network.

Increasingly, clusters are being used as parallel machines, often called *networks of workstations* (NOWs). A major influence on clusters has been the rise of popular public domain software, such as Condor (Litzkow, Livny, and Mutka 1988) and PVM (Geist et al. 1994), that allows users to farm jobs over a collection of machines or to run a parallel program on a number of machines connected by an arbitrary local area or even wide area network. Although the communication performance capability is quite small, typical latencies are a millisecond or more for even small transfers, and the aggregate bandwidth is often less than 1 MB/s, these tools provide an inexpensive vehicle for a class of problems with a very high ratio of computation to communication.

The technology breakthrough that presents the potential of clusters taking on an important role in large-scale parallel computing is a scalable, low-latency interconnect, similar in quality to that available in parallel machines but deployed like a local area network. Several potential candidate networks have evolved from three basic directions. Local area networks have traditionally been either a shared bus (e.g., Ethernet) or a ring (e.g., token ring and FDDI) with fixed aggregate bandwidth, or a dedicated point-to-point connection (e.g., HPPI). In order to provide scalable bandwidth to support a large number of fast machines, there has been a strong push toward switch-based local area networks (e.g., HPPI switches, FDDI switches [Lukowsky and Polit 1997], and FiberChannels). A significant development is the widespread adoption of the ATM (asynchronous transfer mode) standard, developed by the telecommunications industry, as a switched LAN. Several companies offer ATM switches with up to 16 ports at 155-Mb/s (19.4-MB/s) link bandwidth. These can be cascaded to form a larger network. Under ATM, a variable-length message is transferred on a preassigned route, called "virtual circuit," as a sequence of 53-byte cells (48 bytes of data and 5 bytes of routing information). We will look at these networking technologies in more detail in Chapter 10. In terms of the model developed in Section 7.1, current ATM switches typically have a routing delay of about 10 µs in an unloaded network, although some are much higher. A second major standardization effort is represented by SCI (scalable coherent interconnect), which includes a physical layer standard and a particular distributed cache coherency strategy. A third is the widespread use of switching for fast Ethernet and the standardization of gigabit Ethernet.

A strong trend has also emerged to evolve the proprietary networks used within MPP systems into a form that can be used to connect a large number of independent workstations or PCs over a sizable area. Examples of this include ServerNet from Tandem Corporation (Horst 1995) and Myrinet (Boden et al. 1995). The Myrinet switch provides eight ports at 160 MB/s each, which can be cascaded in regular or irregular topologies to form a large network. It transfers variable-length packets with a routing delay of about 350 ns per hop. Link-level flow control is used to avoid dropping packets in the presence of contention.

As with more tightly integrated parallel machines, the hardware primitives in emerging NOWs and clusters remain an open issue and subject to much debate. Conventional TCP/IP communication abstractions over these advanced networks exhibit large overhead (a millisecond or more) (Keeton, Anderson, and Patterson 1995), in many cases larger than that of common Ethernet. A very fast processor is required to move even 20 MB/s using TCP/IP. However, the bandwidth does scale with the number of processors, at least if there is little contention. Several more efficient communication abstractions have been proposed, including Active Messages (Anderson, Culler, and Patterson 1995; von Eicken et al. 1992; von Eicken, Basu, and Buch 1995) and reflective memory (Gillett 1996; Gillett and Kaufmann 1997). Active Messages provide user-level network transactions, as discussed previously. *Reflective memory* allows writes to special regions of memory to appear as writes into regions on remote processors; there is no ability to read remote data, however. Supporting a true shared physical address space in the presence of potential unreliability (i.e., node failures and network failures) remains an open question. An intermediate strategy is to view the logical network connecting a collection of communicating processes as a fully connected group of queues. Each process has a communication endpoint consisting of a send queue, a receive queue, and a certain amount of state information, such as whether notifications should be delivered on message arrival. Each process can deliver a message to any of the receive queues by depositing it in its send queue with an appropriate destination identifier. This approach is being standardized by an industry consortium—led by Intel, Microsoft, and Compaq—as the Virtual Interface Architecture (Dunning et al. 1998), based on several research efforts including Berkeley NOW, Cornell UNET, Illinois FM, and Princeton SHRIMP.

The hardware support for the communication assists and the interpretation of the network transactions within clusters and NOWs span most of the range of design points discussed in the preceding sections. However, since the network plugs into existing machines rather than being integrated into the system at the board or chip level, typically it must interface at an I/O bus rather than at the memory bus or closer to the processor. In this area too, there is considerable innovation. Several relatively fast I/O buses have been developed that maintain cache coherency, the most notable being PCI. Experimental efforts have integrated the network through the graphics bus (Martin 1994; Banks and Prudence 1993) or the SIMM attachment (Minnich, Burns, and Hady 1995).

An important technological force further driving the advancement of clusters is the availability of relatively inexpensive SMP building blocks. For example, clustering a few tens of Pentium Pro "quad pack" commodity servers yields a fairly large parallel machine with very little effort. At the high end, most of the very large machines are being constructed as highly optimized clusters of the vendor's largest commercially available SMP node. For example, in the 1997–1998 window of machines purchased by the Department of Energy as part of the Accelerated Strategic Computing Initiative, the Intel machine is built as 4,536 dual-processor Pentium Pros. The IBM machine is to be 512 four-way PowerPC 604s, upgraded to eight-way PowerPC 630s. The SGI/CRAY machine is initially sixteen 32-way Origins interconnected with many HPPI 6400 links, eventually to be integrated into larger cache-coherent units, as described in Chapter 8.

7.7.1 Case Study: Myrinet SBUS Lanai

A representative example of an emerging NOW is illustrated in Figure 7.27. A collection of UltraSparc workstations is integrated using Myricom's Myrinet scalable network via an intelligent network interface card (NIC). Let us start with the basic hardware operation and work upward. The network illustrates what is becoming known as a *system area network* (SAN) as opposed to a tightly packaged parallel machine network or a widely dispersed local area network (LAN). The links are parallel copper twisted pairs (18 bits wide) and can be a few tens of feet long, depending on link speed and cable type. The communication assist follows the dedicated communication processor approach similar to the Meiko CS-2 and the IBM SP-2. The NIC contains a small embedded "Lanai" processor to control message flow between the host and the network. A key difference in the cluster design is that the NIC contains a sizable amount of SRAM storage. All message data is staged through NIC memory between the host and the network. This memory is also used for Lanai instruction and data storage. There are three DMA engines on the NIC, one for network input, one for network output, and one for transfers between the host and the NIC memory. The host processor can read and write NIC memory using conventional loads and stores to proper regions of the address space, that is, through programmed I/O. The NIC processor uses DMA operations to access host memory. The kernel establishes regions of host memory that are accessible to the NIC. For short transfers, it is most efficient for the host to move the data directly into and out of the NIC, whereas for long transfers it is better for the host to write addresses into the NIC memory and have the NIC pick up these addresses and use them to set up DMA transfers. The Lanai processor can read and write the network FIFOs, or it can drive them by DMA operations from or to NIC memory.

The firmware program executing on the Lanai primarily manages the flow of data by orchestrating DMA transfers in response to commands written to it by the host and packet arrivals from the network. Typically, a command is written into NIC memory, where it is picked up by the NIC processor. The NIC transfers data, as required, from the host and pushes it into the network. The Myricom network uses source-based routing, so the header of the packet includes a simple routing directive for each network switch along the path to the destination. The destination NIC receives the packet into NIC memory. It can then inspect the information in the transaction and process it as desired to support the communication abstraction.

The NIC is implemented as four basic components: a bus interface; a link interface; SRAM; and the Lanai chip, which contains the processor, DMA engines, and link FIFOs. The link interface converts from on-board CMOS signals to long-line

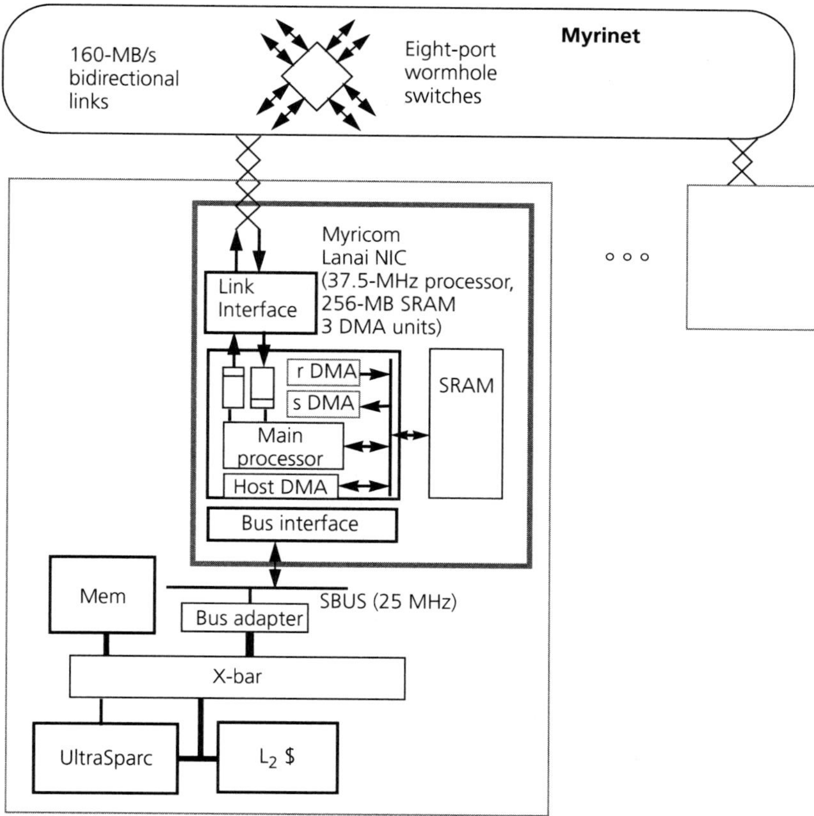

FIGURE 7.27 NOW organization using Myrinet and dedicated message processing with an embedded processor. Although the nodes of a cluster are complete conventional computers, a sophisticated communication assist can be provided within the interface to a scalable, low-latency network. Typically, the network interface is attached to a conventional I/O bus, but increasingly vendors are providing means of tighter integration with the node architecture. In many cases, the communication assist provides dedicated processing of network transactions.

differential signaling over twisted pairs. A critical aspect of the design is the bandwidth to the NIC memory. The three DMA engines and the processor share an internal bus, implemented within the Lanai chip. The network DMA engines can demand 320 MB/s, whereas the host DMA can demand short bursts of 100 MB/s on an SBUS or long bursts of 133 MB/s on a PCI bus. The design goal for the firmware is to keep all three DMA engines active simultaneously; however, this is a little tricky because once it starts the DMA engines, its available bandwidth and hence its execution rate are reduced considerably by competition of the SRAM.

Typically, the NIC memory is logically divided into a collection of functionally distinct regions, including instruction storage, internal data structures, message queues, and data transfer buffers. Each page of the NIC memory space is independently mapped by the host virtual memory system. Thus, the NIC processor code and data space can be made accessible only to the kernel. The remaining communication space can be partitioned into several disjoint communication regions. By controlling the mapping of these communication regions, several user processes can have *communication endpoints* that are resident on the NIC, each containing message queues and associated data transfer areas (Chun, Mainwaring, and Culler 1998). In addition, a collection of host memory frames can be mapped into the I/O space accessible from the NIC. Thus, several user processes can have the ability to write messages into the NIC and read messages directly from the NIC, or to write message descriptors containing pointers to data that is to be DMA transferred through the card. These communication endpoints can be managed much like conventional virtual memory so that writing into an endpoint causes it to be made resident on the NIC. The NIC firmware is responsible for multiplexing messages from the collection of resident endpoints onto the actual network link. It detects when a message has been written into a send queue and forms a packet by translating the user's destination address into a route through the network to the destination node and an identifier of the destination endpoint on that node. In addition, it can place a source identifier in the header, which can be checked at the destination. The NIC firmware inspects the header for each incoming packet. If it is destined for a resident endpoint, then it can be deposited directly in the associated receive buffer; optionally, for a bulk data transfer, if the destination region is mapped, the data can be DMA transferred into host memory. If these conditions are not met, or if the message is corrupted or the protection check violated, the packet can be NACKed to the source. The driver that manages the mapping of endpoints and data buffer spaces is notified to cause the situation to be remedied before the message is successfully retried.

7.7.2 Case Study: PCI Memory Channel

A second important representative cluster communication assist design is the Memory Channel (Gillett 1996) developed by Digital Equipment Corporation, based on the Encore reflective memory and on research efforts in virtual memory–mapped communication (Blumrich et al. 1994; Dubnicki et al. 1996). This approach seeks to provide a limited form of a shared physical address space without fully integrating the pseudo-memory device and pseudo-processor into the memory system of the node. It also preserves some of the autonomy and independent failure characteristics of clusters. As with other clusters, the communication assist is contained in a network interface card that is inserted into a conventional node on an extension bus, in this case the PCI bus.

The basic idea behind reflective memory is to establish a connection between a region of the address space of one process—a transmit region—and a receive region in another, as indicated by Figure 7.28. Data written to a transmit region by the source is "reflected" into the receive region of the destination. Usually, a collection of processes will have a fully connected set of transmit-receive region pairs. The transmit regions on a node are allocated from a portion of the physical address space that

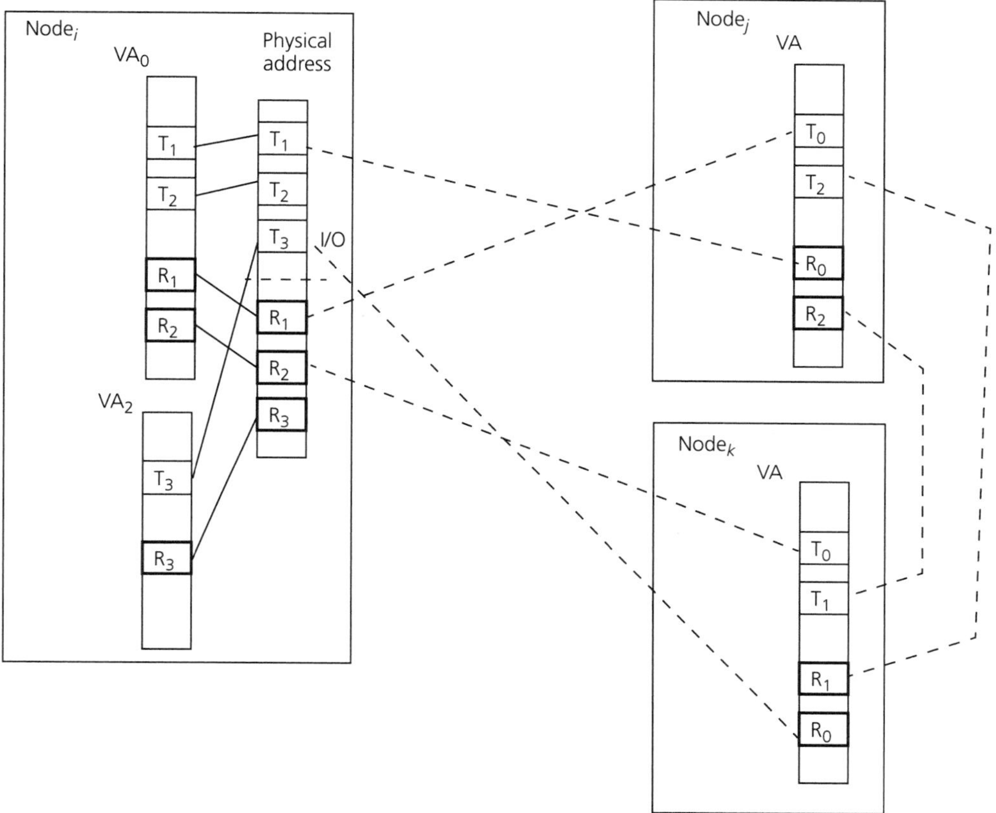

FIGURE 7.28 Typical reflective memory address space organization. Transmit regions of the virtual address space of the processes on a node (VA) are mapped to regions in the physical address space associated with the NIC. Receive regions are pinned in memory, and mappings within the NIC are established so that it can DMA-transfer the associated data to host memory. Here, Node$_i$ has two communicating processes, one of which has established reflective memory connections with processes on two other nodes. Writes to a transmit region generate memory transactions against the NIC. It accepts the write data, builds a packet with a header identifying the receive page and offset, and routes the packet to the destination node. The NIC, upon accepting a packet from the network, inspects the header and DMA-transfers the data into the corresponding receive page. Optionally, packet arrival may generate an interrupt. In general, the user process scans receive regions for relevant updates. To support message passing, the receive pages contain message queues.

is mapped to the NIC. The receive regions are locked down in memory via special kernel calls, and the NIC is configured so that it can DMA-transfer data into them. In addition, the source and destination processes must establish a connection between the source transmit region and the destination receive region. Typically, this is done by associating a key with the connection and binding each region to the key. The regions are an integral number of pages.

The DEC Memory Channel is a PCI-based NIC, typically placed in an Alpha-based SMP, described by Figure 7.29 (Gillett 1996). In addition to the usual transmit and receive FIFOs, it contains a page control table (PCT), a receive-DMA engine, and transmit and receive controllers. A block of data is written to the transmit region with a sequence of stores. The Alpha write buffer will attempt to merge updates to a cache block, so the transmit controller will typically see a cache block write operation. The upper portion of the address given to the controller is the frame number, which is used to index into the PCT to obtain a descriptor for the associated receive region (i.e., the destination node or route to the node, the receive frame number, and the associated control bits). This information, along with the source information, is placed into the header of the packet that is delivered to the destination node through the network. The receive controller extracts the receive frame number and uses it to index into the PCT. After checking the packet integrity and verifying the source, the data is DMA-transferred into memory. The receive regions can be cachable host memory since the transfers across the memory bus are cache coherent. If required, an interrupt is raised upon write completion.

As with a shared physical address space, this approach allows data to be transferred between nodes by simply storing the data from the source and loading it at the destination. However, the use of the address space is much more restrictive since data that is to be transferred to a particular node must be placed in a specific transmit page and receive page. This is quite different from the scenario where any process can write to any shared address and any process can read that address. Typically, shared data structures are not placed in the communication regions. Instead, the regions are used as dedicated message buffers. Data is read from a logically shared data structure and transmitted to a process that requires it through a logical memory channel. Thus, the communication abstraction is really one of memory-based message passing. There is no mechanism to read a remote location; a process can only read the data that has been written to it. To better support the "write by one, read by any" aspect of shared memory, the DEC Memory Channel allows transmit regions to multicast to a group of receive regions, including a loopback region on the source node. To ease construction of distributed data structures—in particular, a distributed lock manager—the FIFO order is preserved across operations from a transmit region. Since reflective memory builds upon, rather than extends, the node memory system, the write to a transmit region finishes as soon as the NIC accepts the data. To determine that the write has actually occurred, the host checks a status register in the NIC.

The raw Memory Channel interface obtains a one-way communication latency of 2.9 μs and a transfer bandwidth of 64 MB/s between two 300-MHz DEC AlphaServers (Lawton et al. 1996). The one-way latency for a small MPI message over Memory Channel is about 7 μs, and a maximum bandwidth of 61 MB/s is achieved on long messages. Using the TruCluster Memory Channel software (Cardoza, Glover, and Snaman 1996), acquiring and releasing an uncontended spin-lock takes approximately 130 μs and 120 μs, respectively.

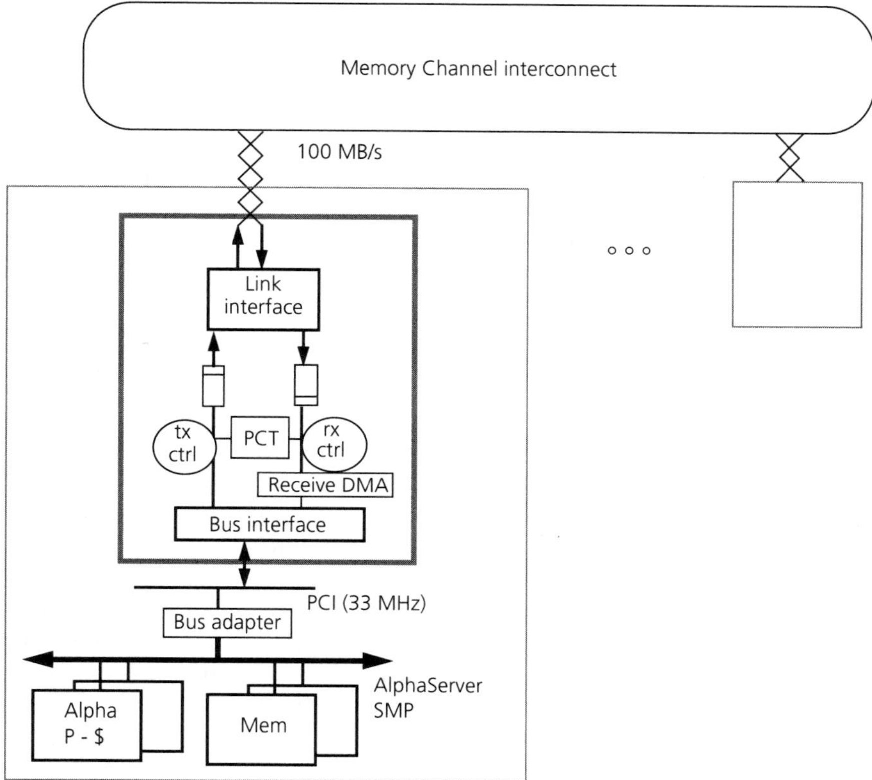

FIGURE 7.29 DEC Memory Channel hardware organization. A Memory Channel cluster consists of a collection of AlphaServer SMPs with PCI Memory Channel adapters. The adapter contains a page control table, which maps local transmit regions to remote receive regions and local receive regions to locked-down physical page frames. The transmit controller (tx ctrl) accepts PCI write transactions, constructs a packet header using the store address and PCT entry contents, and deposits a packet containing the write data into the transmit FIFO. The receive controller (rx ctrl) checks the CRC and parses the header of an incoming packet before initiating a DMA transfer of the packet data into host memory. Optionally, an interrupt may be generated. In the initial offering, the Memory Channel interconnect is a shared 100-MB/s bus, but this is intended to be replaced by a switch. Each of the nodes is typically a sizable SMP AlphaServer.

The Princeton SHRIMP designs (Blumrich et al. 1994; Dubnicki et al. 1996) extend the reflective memory model to better support message passing. They allow the receive offset to be determined by a register at the destination so that successive packets will be queued into the receive region. In addition, a collection of writes can be performed to a transmit region, and then a segment of the region can be transmitted to the receive region.

7.8 IMPLICATIONS FOR PARALLEL SOFTWARE

Now that we have seen the design spectrum of modern scalable distributed-memory machines, we can solidify our understanding of the impact of these design trade-offs in terms of the communication performance that is delivered to applications. In this section, we will examine communication performance through microbenchmarks at three levels. The first set of microbenchmarks uses a communication abstraction that closely approximates the basic network transaction on a user-to-user basis. The second uses a shared address space and the third the standard MPI message-passing abstraction. In making this comparison, we can see the effects of the different organizations and of the protocols used to realize the communication abstractions.

7.8.1 Network Transaction Performance

Many factors interact to determine the end-to-end latency of the individual network transaction as well as the abstractions built on top of it. When we measure the time per communication operation, we observe the cumulative effect of these interactions. In general, the measured time will be larger than what we would obtain by adding up the time through each of the individual hardware components. As architects, we may want to know how each of the components impacts performance; however, what matters to programs is the cumulative effect, including the subtle interactions that inevitably slow things down.

We will take an empirical approach to determining the communication performance of several of our case study machines. A simple user-level communication abstraction, Active Messages, is used as a basis for this study. We want to measure not only the total message time but the portion of this time that is overhead in our data transfer equation (Equation 1.5) and the portion that is due to occupancy and delay.

The microbenchmark that uses Active Messages is a simple echo test, where the remote processor is continually servicing the network and issuing replies. This eliminates the timing variations that would be observed if the processor was busy doing other work when the request arrived. In addition, since our focus is on the node-to-network interface, we pick processors that are adjacent in the physical network. All measurements are performed by the source processor since many of these machines do not have a global synchronous clock and the "time skew" between processors can easily exceed the scale of an individual message time. To obtain the end-to-end message time, the round-trip time for a request-response transaction is divided by two. However, this one-way message time has three distinct portions, as illustrated by Figure 7.30. When a processor injects a message, it is occupied for a number of cycles as it interfaces with the communication assist. We call this the *send overhead*, as it is time spent that cannot be used for useful computation. Similarly, the destination processor spends a number of cycles extracting or otherwise dealing with the message, called the *receive overhead*. The portion of the total message cost that is not covered by overhead is the *communication latency*. In terms of the communication cost expression developed in Chapter 3, this includes the portions of the transit

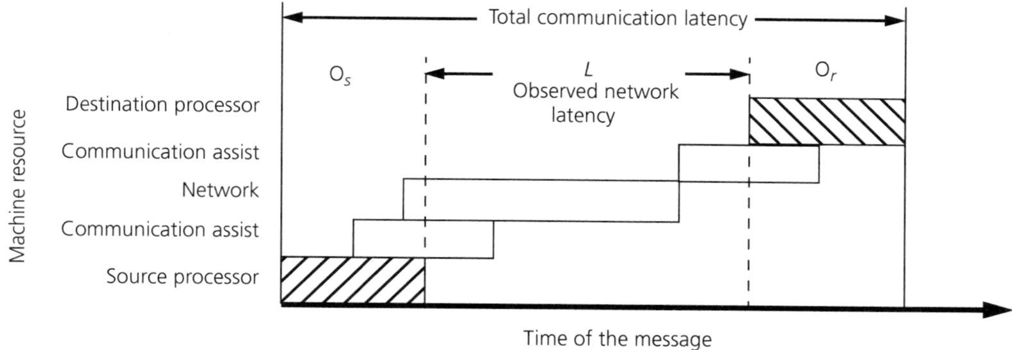

FIGURE 7.30 Breakdown of message time into send overhead, network latency, and receive overhead. This depicts the machine operation associated with our basic data transfer model for communication operations. The source processor spends O_S cycles injecting the message into the communication assist, during which time it can perform no other useful work, and similarly the destination experiences O_r overhead in extracting the message. To actually transfer the information involves the communication assists and network interfaces as well as the links and switches of the network. As seen from the processor, these subcomponents are indistinguishable. It experiences the portion of the transfer time that is not covered by its own overhead as latency that can be overlapped with other useful work. The processor also experiences the maximum message rate, which is specified in terms of the minimum average time between messages, or gap.

delay and occupancy components that are not overlapped with send or receive overhead. It can potentially be masked by other useful work or by processing additional messages, as we will discuss in detail in Chapter 11.

In our microbenchmark, we seek to determine the length of these three portions. The processor cannot distinguish time spent in the communication assists from that spent in the actual links and switches of the interconnect. In fact, the communication assist may begin pushing the message into the network while the source processor is still checking status, but this work will be masked by the overhead.

The left portion of the graph in Figure 7.31 shows a comparison of one-way Active Message time for the Thinking Machines CM-5 (Section 7.4.2), the Intel Paragon (Section 7.5.1), the Meiko CS-2 (Section 7.5.2), a cluster of workstations called the NOW Ultra (Section 7.7.1), and the CRAY T3D (Section 7.6.1). The bars show the total one-way latency of a small (five-word) message divided into three segments, indicating the processing overhead on the sending side (O_S), the processing overhead on the receiving side (O_r), and the remaining communication latency (L). The bars on the right (g) show the time per message for a pipelined sequence of request-response operations. For example, on the Paragon, an individual message has an end-to-end latency of about 10 µs, but a burst of messages can go at about 7.5 µs per message, or a rate of 1/7.5 µs = 133,000 messages per second. Let us examine each of these components in more detail.

The send overhead is nearly uniform over the five designs; however, the factors determining this component are different on each system. On the CM-5, this time is

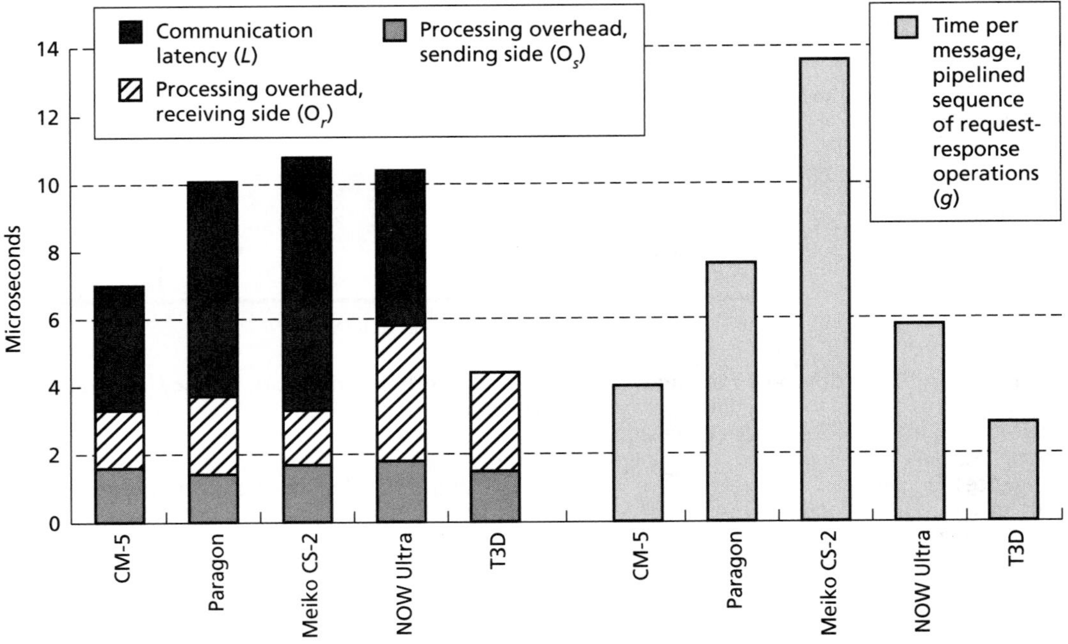

FIGURE 7.31 Performance comparison at the network transaction level via Active Messages. The bars on the left show the overall latency for five machines described in this chapter divided into components of send overhead, receive overhead, and network latency. The latter component is dominated by the communication assist occupancy but includes the network delay. The bars on the right show the time per message, called the gap, for these machines when transferring a series of small messages. This is determined primarily by the communication assist occupancy.

dominated by uncached writes of the data plus the uncached read of the NI status to determine if the message was accepted. The status also indicates whether an incoming message has arrived, which is convenient since the node must receive messages even while it is unable to send. Unfortunately, two status reads are required for the two networks. (A later model of the machine, the CM-500, provided more effective status information and substantially reduced the overhead.) On the Paragon, the send overhead is determined by the time to write the message into the memory buffer shared by the compute processor and communication (or message) processor (CP). The compute processor is able to write the message and set the "message present" flag in the buffer entry with two quad-word stores, unique to the i860, so it is surprising that the overhead is so high. The reason has to do with the inefficiency of the bus-based cache coherence protocol within the node for such a producer-consumer situation discussed earlier. The compute processor has to pull the cache blocks away from the CP before refilling them. In the Meiko CS-2, the message is built in cached memory, and then a pointer to the message (and command) is enqueued in the NI with a single swap instruction. This instruction is provided in the Sparc instruction set to support synchronization operations. In this context, it provides a way of passing information to the NI and getting status back indicating whether the operation was successful. Unfortunately, the exchange operation is considerably slower than the basic uncached memory operations. In the NOW system, the send overhead is due to a sequence of uncached double-word stores and an uncached load across the I/O bus to NI memory. Surprisingly, these have the same effective cost as the more tightly integrated designs.

An important point revealed by this comparison is that the cost of uncached operations, misses, and synchronization instructions, generally considered to be infrequent events and therefore a low priority for architectural optimization, is critical to communication performance. The time spent in the cache controllers before they allow the transaction to be delivered to the next level of the storage hierarchy dominates even the bus protocol. The comparison of the receive overhead for these designs shows that cache-to-cache transfer from the network processor to the compute processor is more costly than uncached reads from the NI on the memory bus of the CM-5 and CS-2. However, the NOW system is subject to the greater cost of uncached reads over the I/O bus.

Several facets of the machine contribute to the latency component, including the processing time on the communication assist or in the network interface, the time to channel the message onto a link, and the delay through the network. Different facets are dominant in our case study machines. The CM-5 links operate at 20 MB/s (4 bits wide at 40 MHz). Thus, the occupancy of a single wire to transfer a message with 40 bytes of data (the payload), plus an envelope containing route information, CRC, and message type, is nearly 2.5 μs. Each router adds a delay of roughly 200 ns, and there are at most $2 \log_4 N$ hops. The network interface occupancy is essentially the same as the wire occupancy, as it is a very simple device that spools the packet on or off the wire.

In the Paragon, the latency is dominated by processing in the CP at the source and destination. With 175-MB/s links, the occupancy of a link is only about 300 ns. The routing delay per hop is also quite small; however, in a large machine the total delay may be substantially larger than the link occupancy, as the number of hops can be $2\sqrt{N}$. The dominant factor is the assist (CP) occupancy in writing the message across the memory bus into the NI at the source and reading the message from the destination. These steps account for 4 μs of the latency. Eliminating the CPs in the communication path on the Paragon decreases the latency substantially (Krishnamurthy et al. 1996). Surprisingly, it does not increase the overhead much; writing and reading the message to and from the NI have essentially the same cost as the cache-to-cache transfers. However, since the NI does not provide sufficient interpretation to enforce protection and to ensure that messages move forward through the network adequately, avoiding the CPs is not a viable option in practice.

The Meiko has a very large latency component. The network accounts for a small fraction of this, as it provides 40-MB/s links and topology similar to the CM-5. The CP is closely coupled with the network on a single chip. The latency is almost entirely due to accessing system memory from the CP. Recall that the compute processor provides the CP with a pointer to the message. The CP performs DMA operations to pull the message out of memory. At the destination, it writes the message into a shared queue. An unusual property of this machine is that a circuit through the network is held open through the network transaction and an acknowledgment is provided to the source. This mechanism is used to convey to the source CP whether it successfully obtained a lock on the destination incoming message queue. Thus, even though the latency component is large, it is difficult to hide through pipelining communication operations since source and destination CPs are occupied for the duration.

The latency in the NOW system is distributed fairly evenly over the facets of the communication system. The link occupancy is small with 160-MB/s links, and the routing delay is modest with 350 ns per hop. The data is deposited into the NI by the host and accessed directly from the NI. Time is spent on both ends of the transaction to manipulate message queues and to perform DMA operations between NI memory and the network. Thus, the two NIs and the network each contribute about one-third of the 4-μs latency.

The CRAY T3D provides hardware support for user-level messaging in the form of a per-processor message queue. The capability in the DEC Alpha to extend the instruction set with privileged subroutines, called PAL code, is used. A four-word message is composed in registers, and a PAL call is issued to send the message. It is placed in a user-level message queue at the destination processor; the destination processor is interrupted, and control is returned either to the user application thread, which can poll the queue, or to a specific message handler thread. The send overhead to inject the message is only 0.8 μs; however, the interrupt has an overhead of 25 μs and the switch to the message handler has a cost of 33 μs (Arpaci et al. 1995). A packet can be inserted in the message queue, without interrupts or thread switch, using the fetch&increment registers provided for atomic operations. The fetch&increment to advance the queue pointer and the writing of the message takes 1.5 μs, whereas dispatching on the message and reading the data via uncached reads takes 2.9 μs.

The Paragon, Meiko, and NOW machines employ a complete operating system on each node. The systems cooperate using messages to provide a single-system image and to run parallel programs on collections of nodes. The CP is instrumental in multiplexing communication from many user processes onto a shared network and demultiplexing incoming network transactions to the correct destination processes. It also provides flow control and error detection. The MPP systems rely on the physical integrity of a single box to provide highly reliable operation. When a user process fails, the other processes in its parallel program are aborted. When a node crashes, its partition of the machine is rebooted. The more loosely integrated NOW must contend with individual node failures that are a result of hardware errors, software errors, or physical disconnection. As in the MPPs, the operating systems cooperate to control the processes that form a parallel program. When a node fails, the system reconfigures to continue without it.

7.8.2 Shared Address Space Operations

It is useful to compare the communication architectures of the case study machines for shared address space operations: read and write. These operations can easily be built on top of the user-level message abstraction, but this does not exploit the opportunity to optimize for these simple, frequently occurring operations. In addition, on machines where the assist does not provide enough interpretation, the remote processor is involved whenever its memory is accessed. In machines with a dedicated CP, it can potentially service memory requests on behalf of remote nodes without involving the compute processor. On machines supporting a shared physical address, this memory request service is provided directly in hardware.

Figure 7.32 shows the performance of a read of a remote location for the case study machines (Krishnamurthy et al. 1996). The bars on the left show the total read time, broken down into the overhead associated with issuing the read and the latency of the remaining communication and remote processing. The bars on the right show the minimum time between reads in the steady state. For the CM-5, there is no opportunity for optimization since the remote processor must handle the network transaction. In the Paragon, the remote CP performs the read request and replies. The remote processing time is significant because the CP must read the message from the NI, service it, and write a response to the NI. Moreover, the CP must

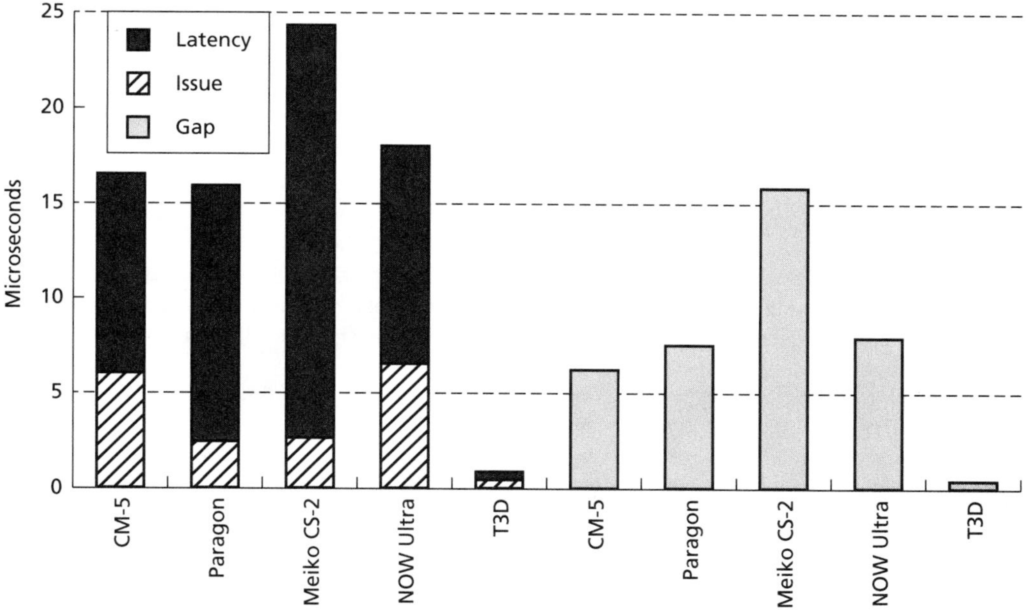

FIGURE 7.32 Performance comparison on shared address read. For the five case study platforms, the bars on the left show the total time to perform a remote read operation and isolate the portion of that time that involves the processor issuing and completing the read. The remainder can be overlapped with useful work, as is discussed in depth in Chapter 11. The bars on the right show the minimum time between successive reads, which is the reciprocal of the maximum rate.

perform a protection check and the virtual-to-physical translation. On the Paragon with the OSF1/AD operating system, the CP runs in kernel mode and operates on physical addresses; thus, it performs the page table lookup for the requested address (which may not be for the currently running process) in software. The Meiko CS-2 provides read and write network transactions, where the source-to-destination circuit in the network is held open until the read response or write acknowledgment is returned. The remote processing is dedicated and uses a hardware page table to perform the virtual-to-physical transaction on the remote node. Thus, the read latency is considerably less than a pair of messages but still substantial. If the remote CP performs the read operation, the latency increases by an additional 8 μs. The NOW system achieves a small performance advantage by avoiding the use of the remote processor. As in the Paragon, the message processor must perform the protection check and address translation, which are quite slow in the embedded CP. In addition, accessing remote memory from the network interface involves a DMA operation and is costly. The major advantage of dedicated processing of remote memory operations in all of these systems is that the performance of the operation does not depend on the remote compute processor servicing incoming requests from the network.

The T3D shows an order-of-magnitude improvement available through dedicated hardware support for a shared address space. Given that the remote reads and writes are implemented through add-on hardware, there is a cost of 400 ns to issue the operation. The transmission of the request, the remote service, and the transmission of the reply take an additional 450 ns. For a sequence of reads, performance can be improved further by utilizing the hardware prefetch queue. Issuing the prefetch instruction and the pop from the queue takes about 200 ns. The latency is amortized over a sequence of such prefetches and is almost completely hidden if eight or more are issued.

7.8.3 Message-Passing Operations

Let us also take a look at the measured message-passing performance of several large-scale machines. As discussed earlier, the most common performance model for message-passing operations is a linear model for the overall time to send n bytes, given by

$$T(n) = T_0 + \frac{n}{B} \tag{7.2}$$

The start-up cost, T_0, is logically the time to send zero bytes, and B is the asymptotic bandwidth. The delivered data bandwidth is simply $BW(n) = n/T(n)$. Equivalently, the transfer time can be characterized by two parameters, r_∞ and $n_{1/2}$, which are the asymptotic bandwidth and the transfer size at which half of this bandwidth is obtained (i.e., the half-power point).

The start-up cost reflects the time to carry out the protocol as well as whatever buffer management and matching is required to set up the data transfer. The asymptotic bandwidth reflects the rate at which data can be pumped through the system from end to end.

Table 7.1 Message-Passing Start-Up Costs and Asymptotic Bandwidths

Machine	Year	T_0 (μs)	Maximum Bandwidth (MB/s)	Cycles per T_0	MFLOPS per Processor	Floating-Point Operations per T_0	$n_{1/2}$
iPSC/2	1988	700	2.7	5,600	1	700	1,400
nCUBE/2	1990	160	2	3,000	2	300	300
iPSC/860	1991	160	2	6,400	40	6,400	320
CM-5	1992	95	8	3,135	20	1,900	760
SP-1	1993	50	25	2,500	100	5,000	1,250
Meiko CS-2*	1993	83	43	7,470	24	1,992	3,560
Paragon	1994	30	175	1,500	50	1,500	7,240
SP-2	1994	35	40	3,960	200	7,000	2,400
CRAY T3D (PVM)	1994	21	27	3,150	94	1,974	1,502
NOW	1996	16	38	2,672	180	2,880	4,200
SGI Power-Challenge	1995	10	64	900	308	3,080	800
Sun E6000	1996	11	160	1,760	180	1,980	2,100

Although this model is easy to understand and useful as a programming guide, it presents a couple of methodological difficulties for architectural evaluation. As with network transactions, the total message time is difficult to measure unless a global clock is available since the send is performed on one processor and the receive on another. This problem is commonly avoided by measuring the time for an echo test—one processor sends the data and then waits until it receives a message. However, this approach only yields a reliable measurement if the receive is posted before the message arrives; otherwise, it is measuring the time for the remote node to get around to issuing the receive. If the receive is preposted, then the test does not measure the full time of the receive and does not reflect the costs of buffering data since the match succeeds. Finally, the measured times are not linear in the message size, so fitting a line to the data yields a T_0 parameter that has little to do with the actual start-up cost. Usually, there is a flat region for small values of n, so the start-up cost obtained through the fit will be smaller than the time for a 0-byte message, perhaps even negative. These methodological concerns are not a problem for older machines, which had very large start-up costs and simple, software-based message-passing implementations.

Table 7.1 shows the start-up cost and asymptotic bandwidth reported for commercial message-passing libraries on several important large parallel machines over a period of time. (Also shown in the table are two small-scale SMPs, discussed in Chapter 6.) The start-up cost T_0 has dropped by an order of magnitude in less than a

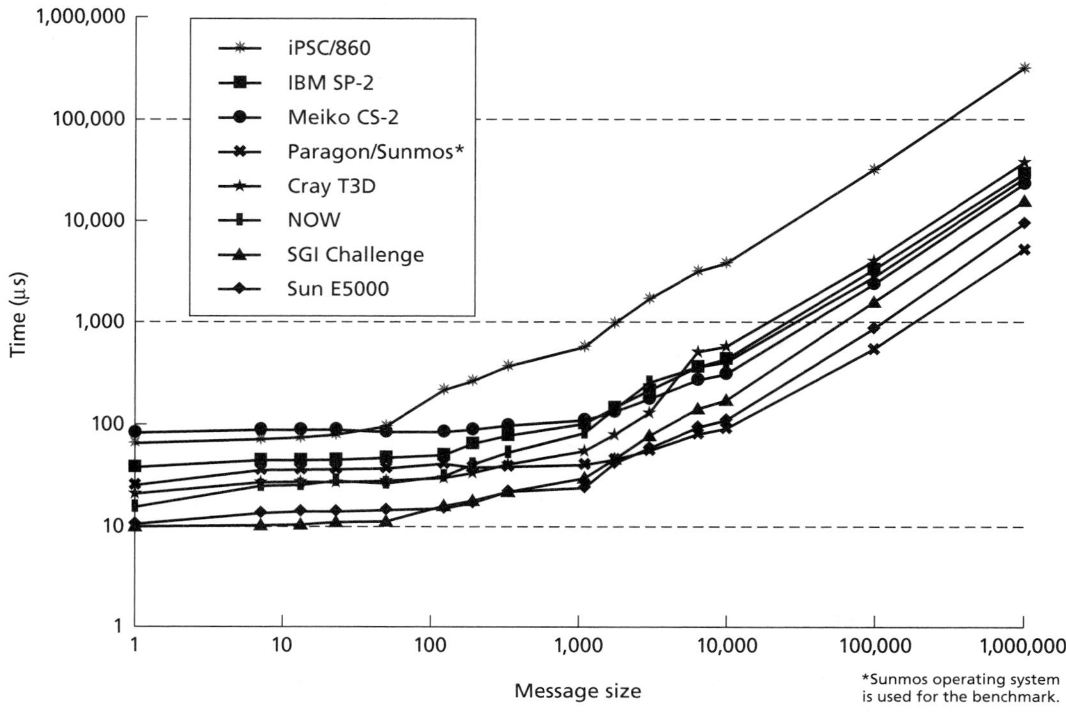

FIGURE 7.33 Time for message-passing operation versus message size. Message-passing implementations exhibit nearly an order-of-magnitude spread in start-up cost, and the cost is constant for a range of small message sizes, introducing a substantial nonlinearity in the time per message. The time is nearly linear for a range of large messages, where the slope of the curve gives the bandwidth.

decade; this improvement essentially tracks improvements in cycle time, as indicated by the middle column of the table. As illustrated by the columns on the right, improvements in start-up cost have failed to keep pace with improvements in either floating-point performance or in bandwidth. Notice that the start-up costs are on an entirely different scale from the hardware latency of the communication network, which is typically a few microseconds to a fraction of a microsecond. It is dominated by processing overhead on each message transaction, the protocol, and the processing required to provide the synchronization semantics of the message-passing abstraction.

Figure 7.33 shows the measured one-way communication time on the echo test for several machines as a function of message size. In this log-log plot, the difference in start-up costs is apparent, as is the nonlinearity for small messages. The bandwidth is given by the slope of the lines. This is more clearly seen from plotting the equivalent $BW(n)$ in Figure 7.34. A caveat must be made in interpreting the bandwidth data for message passing, since the pairwise bandwidth only reflects the data rate on a point-to-point basis. We know, for example, that for the bus-based

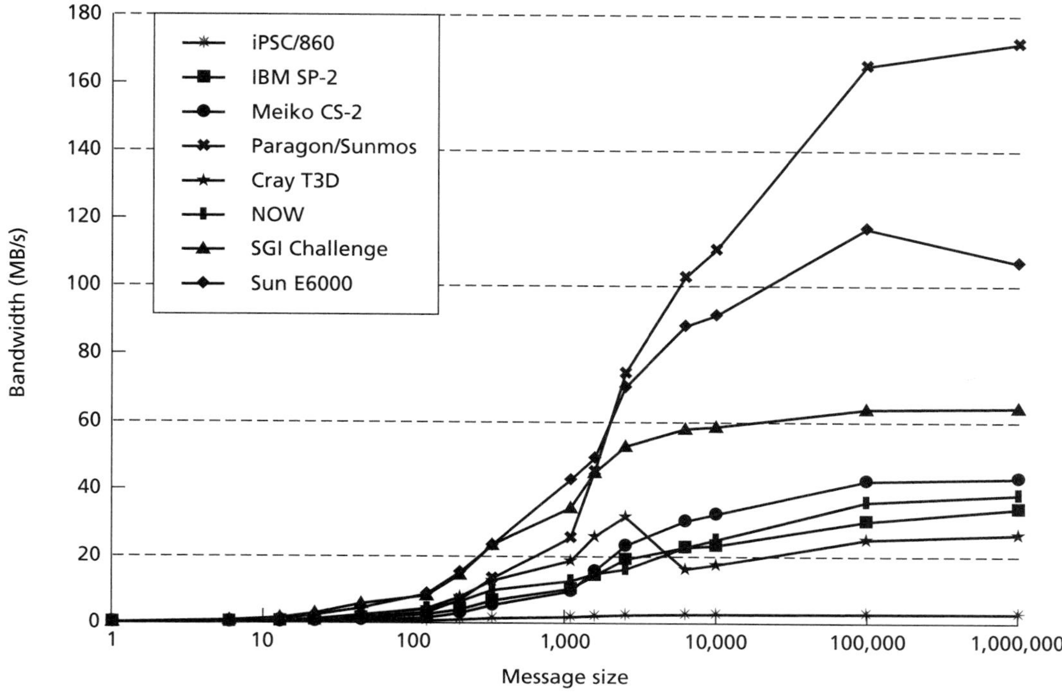

FIGURE 7.34 Bandwidth versus message size. Scalable machines generally provide a few tens of MB/s per node on large message transfers, although the Paragon design shows that this can be pushed into the hundreds of MB/s. The bandwidth is limited primarily by the ability of the DMA support to move data through the memory system, including the internal buses. Small-scale shared memory designs exhibit a point-to-point bandwidth dictated by out-of-cache memory copies when few simultaneous transfers are ongoing.

machines this is not likely to be sustained if many pairs of nodes are communicating. We will see in Chapter 10 that some networks can sustain much higher aggregate bandwidths than others. In particular, the Paragon data is optimistic for many communication patterns involving multiple pairs of nodes, whereas the other large-scale systems can sustain the pairwise bandwidth for most patterns.

7.8.4 Application-Level Performance

The end-to-end effects of all aspects of the computer system come together to determine the performance obtained at the application level. This level of analysis is most useful to the end user and is usually the basis for procurement decisions. It is also the ultimate basis for evaluating architectural trade-offs, but this requires mapping cumulative performance effects down to root causes in the machine and in the program. Typically, this mapping involves profiling the application to isolate the portions where most time is spent and extracting the usage characteristics of the application to determine its requirements. This section briefly compares performance on our case study machines for two of the NAS parallel benchmarks in the NPB2 suite (NAS Parallel Benchmarks 1998).

The *LU benchmark* solves a finite difference discretization of the 3D compressible Navier-Stokes equations used for modeling fluid dynamics through a block-lower-triangular, block-upper-triangular approximate factorization of the difference scheme. The LU factored form is cast as a relaxation and is solved by symmetric successive overrelaxation (SSOR). The LU benchmark is based on the NAS reference implementation from 1991 using the Intel message-passing library, NX (Barszcz et al. 1993). It requires a power-of-two number of processors. A 2D partitioning of the 3D data grid onto processors is obtained by halving the grid repeatedly in the first two dimensions, alternating between x and y, until all processors are assigned, resulting in vertical pencil-like grid partitions. Each pencil can be thought of as a stack of horizontal tiles. The ordering of point-based operations constituting the SSOR procedure proceeds on diagonals that progressively sweep from one corner on a given z plane to the opposite corner of the same z plane, thereupon proceeding to the next z plane. This constitutes a diagonal pipelining method and is called a "wavefront" method by its authors (Barszcz et al. 1993). The software pipeline spends relatively little time filling and emptying and is well load balanced. Communication of partition boundary data occurs after completion of computation on all diagonals that contact an adjacent partition. The result is a relatively large number of small communications. Still, the total communication volume is small compared to computation expense, making this parallel LU scheme relatively efficient. Cache block reuse in the relaxation sections is high.

Figure 7.35 shows the speedups obtained on sparse LU with the Class A input (200 iterations on a $64 \times 64 \times 64$ grid) for the IBM SP-2 (wide nodes), the CRAY T3D, and the UltraSparc cluster (NOW). The speedup is normalized to the performance on four processors, shown in the right portion of the figure, because this is the smallest number of nodes for which the problem can be run on the T3D. We see that scalability is generally good to beyond 100 processors, but both the T3D and NOW scale considerably better than the SP-2. This is consistent with the ratio of the processor performance to the performance of small message transfers.

The *BT algorithm* solves three sets of uncoupled systems of equations—first in the x, then in the y, and finally in the z direction. These systems are block tridiagonal with 5×5 blocks and are solved using a multipartition scheme (Bruno and Cappello 1988). The multipartition approach provides good load balance and uses coarse-grained communication. Each processor is responsible for several disjoint subblocks of points (cells) of the grid. The cells are arranged such that for each direction of the line-solve phase, the cells belonging to a certain processor will be evenly distributed along the direction of the solution. This allows each processor to perform useful work throughout a line solve, instead of being forced to wait for the partial solution to a line from another processor before beginning work. Additionally, the information from a cell is not sent to the next processor until all sections of linear equation systems handled in this cell have been solved. Therefore, the granularity of commu-

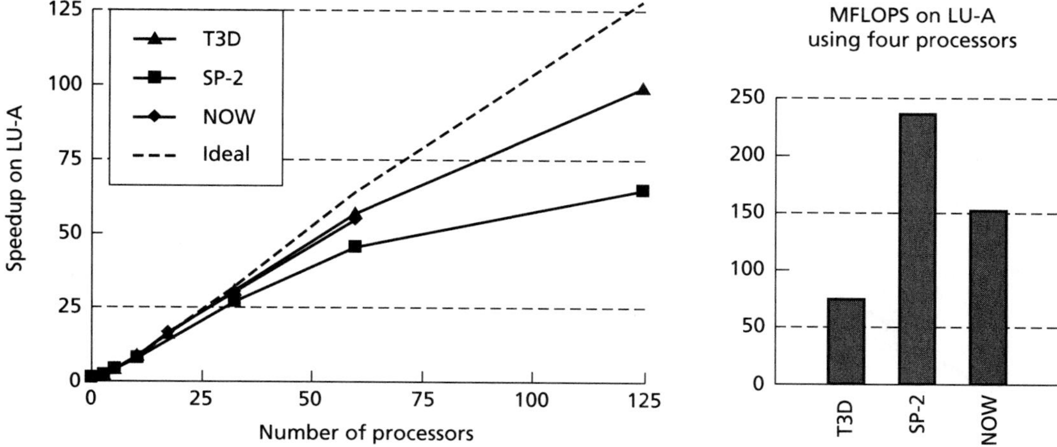

FIGURE 7.35 Application performance on sparse LU NAS parallel benchmark. Scalability of the IBM SP-2, the CRAY T3D, and the NOW UltraSparc cluster on the sparse LU benchmark is shown (left) normalized to the performance obtained on four processors. The base performance of the three systems is shown on the right.

nication is kept large and fewer messages are sent. The BT codes require a square number of processors. These codes have been written so that if a given parallel platform permits only a power-of-two number of processors to be assigned to a job, then unneeded processors are deemed inactive and are ignored during computation but are counted when determining MFLOPS rates.

Figure 7.36 shows the scalability of the IBM SP-2, the CRAY T3D, and the UltraSparc NOW on the Class A problem of the BT benchmark. Here the speedup is normalized to the performance on 25 processors, shown in the right portion of the figure, because that is the smallest T3D configuration for which performance data is available. The scalability of all three platforms is good, with the SP-2 still lagging somewhat but having much higher per-node performance

To understand why the scalability is less than perfect, we need to look more closely at the characteristics of the application, in particular at the communication characteristics. To focus our attention on the dominant portion of the application, we will study one iteration of the main outermost loop. Typically, the application performs a few hundred of these iterations after an initialization phase. Rather than employ the simulation methodology of the previous chapters to examine communication characteristics, we collect this information by running the program using an instrumented version of the MPI message-passing library. One useful characterization is the histogram of messages by size. For each message that is sent, a counter associated with its size bin is incremented. The result, summed over all processors, is shown in the top portion of Table 7.2 for a fixed problem size and processors scaled from 4 to 64. For each configuration, the nonzero bins are indicated along with the number of messages of that size and an estimate of the total amount of data

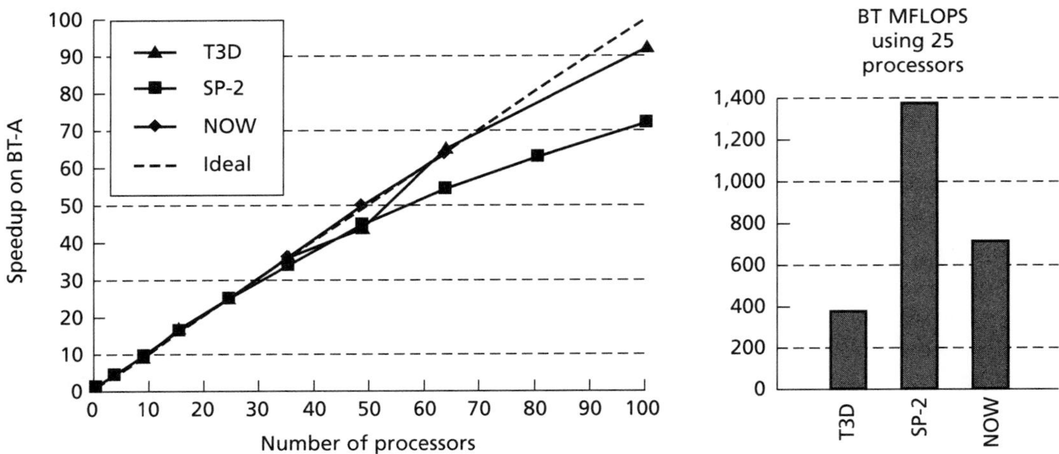

FIGURE 7.36 Application performance on BT NAS parallel benchmark. Scalability of the IBM SP-2, the CRAY T3D, and an UltraSparc cluster on the BT benchmark is shown (left) normalized to the performance obtained on 25 processors. The base performance of the three systems is shown on the right.

transferred in those messages. We see that this application essentially sends three sizes of messages, but these sizes and frequencies vary strongly with the number of processors. Both of these properties are typical of message-passing programs. Well-tuned programs tend to be highly structured and use communication sparingly. In addition, since the problem size is held fixed, as the number of processors increases, the portion of the problem that each processor is responsible for decreases. Since the data transfer size is determined by how the program is coded, rather than by machine parameters, it can change dramatically with configuration. Whereas on small configurations the program sends a few very large messages, on a large configuration it sends many relatively small messages. The total volume of communication increases by almost a factor of eight when the number of processors increases by 16. This increase is certainly one factor affecting the speedup curve. In addition, the machine with higher start-up cost is affected more strongly by the decrease in message size.

It is important to observe that with a fixed problem size scaling rule, the workload on each processor changes with scale. Here we see it for communication, but it also changes cache behavior and other factors. The bottom portion of Table 7.2 gives an indication of the average communication requirement for this application. Taking the total communication volume and dividing by the time per iteration[9] on the UltraSparc cluster, we get the average delivered message data bandwidth. Indeed, the

9. The execution time is the only data in the table that is a property of the specific platform. All of the other communication characteristics are a property of the program and are the same when measured on any platform.

Table 7.2 Communication Characteristics for One Iteration of BT on the Class A Problem over a Range of Processor Counts

	4 Processors			16 Processors			36 Processors			64 Processors		
	Message Size (KB)	Messages	Total Data Transfer (KB)	Message Size (KB)	Messages	Total Data Transfer (KB)	Message Size (KB)	Messages	Total Data Transfer (KB)	Message Size (KB)	Messages	Total Data Transfer (KB)
	43.5+	12	513	11.5+	144	1,652	4.5+	540	2,505	3+	1,344	4,266
	81.5+	24	1,916	61+	96	5,742	29+	540	15,425	19+	1,344	25,266
	261+	12	3,062	69+	144	9,738	45+	216	9,545	35.5+	384	13,406
Total Communication Volume (KB)			5,491			17,132			27,475			42,938
Time per Iteration (s)			5.43			1.46			0.67			0.38
Average Bandwidth (MB/s)			1.0			11.5			40.0			110.3
Average Bandwidth per Processor (MB/s)			0.25			0.72			1.11			1.72

communication rate scales substantially, increasing by a factor of more than 100 over an increase in machine size of 16. Dividing further by the number of processors, we see that the average per-processor bandwidth is significant but not extremely large. It is in the same general ballpark as the rates we observed for shared address space applications on simulations of SMPs in Section 5.4. However, we must be extremely careful about making design decisions based on average communication requirements because communication tends to be very bursty. Often, substantial periods of computation are punctuated by intense communication. For the BT application, we can get an idea of the temporal communication behavior by taking snapshots of the message histogram at regular intervals. The result is shown in Figure 7.37 for several iterations on one of the 64 processors executing the program. For each sample interval, the bar shows the size of the largest message sent in that interval. For this application, the communication profile is similar on all processors because it follows a bulk synchronous style with all processors alternating between local computation and phases of communication. The three sizes of messages are

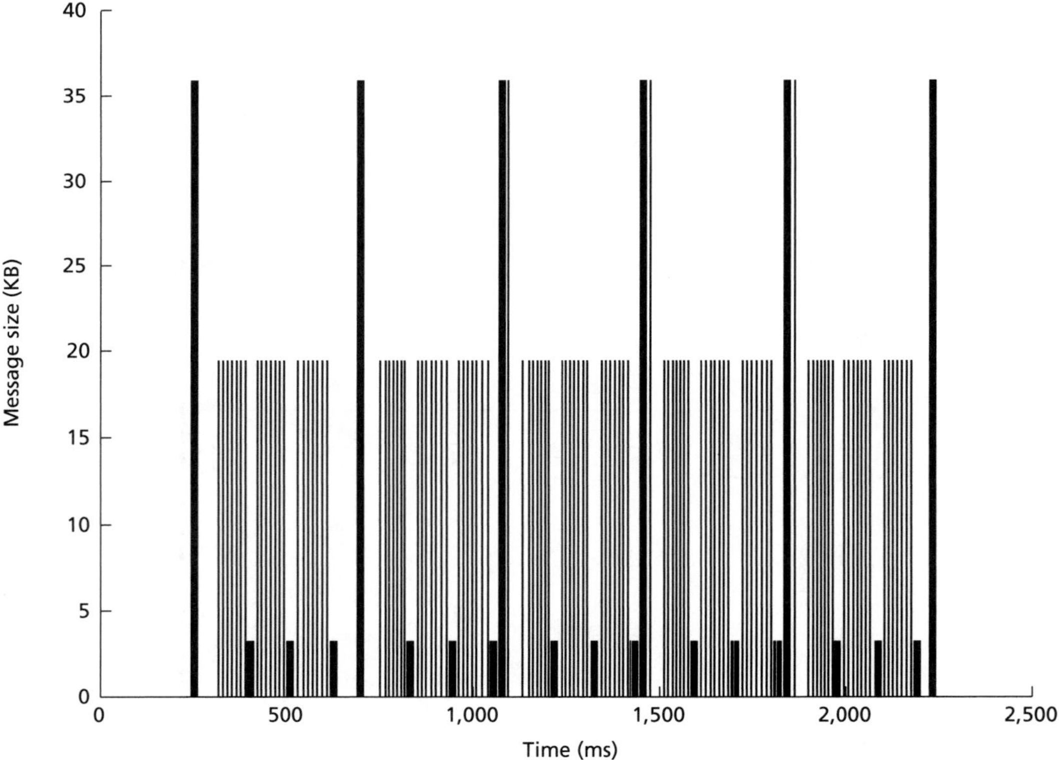

FIGURE 7.37 Message profile over time for BT-A on 64 processors. The program is executed with an instrumented MPI library that samples the communication histogram at regular intervals. The graph shows the largest message sent from one particular processor during each sample interval. It is clear that communication is regular and bursty.

clearly visible, repeating in a regular pattern with the two smaller sizes more common than the larger one. Overall, there is substantially more white space than dark, so the average communication bandwidth is more of an indication of the ratio of communication to computation than it is of the rate of communication during a communication phase.

If we apply the framework provided by Equation 3.1 to the speedup measurements on the NAS parallel benchmarks, we find that all of the parallelism costs increase with the number of processors. The extra work increases, the amount of communication increases, the cost of that communication increases, and the wait time increases. Nonetheless, several of these benchmarks obtain perfect speedup on a sizable number of processors. The reason is that the computational work becomes more efficient as the same size problem is spread over a larger number of processors. In particular, the working set behavior illustrated in Figure 3.6 has a very significant impact, even though the programs are in a message-passing programming model. The impact of this effect can be seen in Figure 7.38 for LU. Each curve in the figure shows the cache miss rate on a typical node executing the parallel program as a function of the cache size. This is obtained by running the program in parallel, collecting a cache trace on each node, and feeding the trace through a cache simulator that models fully associative caches with 64-byte blocks of various sizes. The key point to observe is that each machine size has a different working set profile. On four processors, the knee occurs at 512 KB, whereas on 32 processors it occurs at

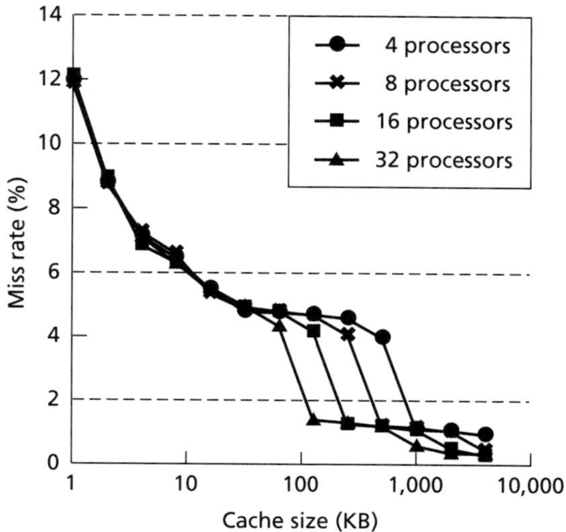

FIGURE 7.38 Working set curves for the NAS Parallel Benchmark LU on a range of machine sizes. With the CPS scaling, the curve changes for each machine size since the data set is spread over a different number of nodes. The separation of the curves for large cache sizes improves the observed speedup by reducing the time spent in computation. This effect does not occur, indeed the opposite often appears, for small cache configurations common in the mid-1980s.

64 KB. Thus, on a machine with 256-KB caches, the miss rate drops from 5% to 1% as the configuration scales from four to sixteen or more processors. Indeed, the sum of the computational time over all the processors drops as the configuration scales, so perfect speedup is obtained even though the time spent communicating increases. This effect is less pronounced on the SP-2 because the basic node is optimized for operation on data that does not fit in the cache.

7.9 SYNCHRONIZATION

Scalability is a primary concern in the combination of software and hardware that implements synchronization operations in large-scale distributed-memory machines. With a message-passing programming model, mutual exclusion is a given since each process has exclusive access to its local address space. Point-to-point events are implicit in every message operation. The more interesting case is orchestrating global or group synchronization from point-to-point messages. An important issue here is balance: it is important that the communication pattern used to achieve the synchronization be balanced among nodes, in which case high message rates and efficient synchronization can be realized. In the extreme, we should avoid having all processes communicate with or wait for one process at a given time. Machine designers and implementers of message-passing layers attempt to maximize the message rate in such circumstances, but only the program can relieve the load imbalance. Other issues for global synchronization are similar to those for a shared address space.

In a shared address space, the issues for mutual exclusion and point-to-point events are essentially the same as those discussed in Chapter 5. As in small-scale shared memory machines, the trend in scalable machines is to build user-level synchronization operations (like locks and barriers) in software on top of basic atomic exchange primitives. Two major differences, however, may affect the choice of algorithms. First, the interconnection network is not centralized but has many parallel paths. On one hand, this means that disjoint sets of processors can coordinate with one another in parallel on entirely disjoint paths; on the other hand, it can complicate the implementation of synchronization primitives. Second, physically distributed memory may make it important to allocate synchronization variables appropriately among memories. The importance of this depends on whether the machine caches nonlocal shared data or not and is clearly greater for machines that do not, such as the ones described in this chapter. This section covers new algorithms for locks and barriers appropriate for machines with physically distributed memory and interconnect, starting from the algorithms discussed for shared memory machines. We will return to this comparison once we have studied scalable cache-coherent systems in the next chapter. Let us begin with algorithms for locks.

7.9.1 Algorithms for Locks

Section 5.5 presents the basic test&set lock, the test&set lock with backoff, the test-and-test&set lock, the ticket lock, and the array-based lock. Each successive step went further in reducing bus traffic and fairness but often at a cost in overhead. For example, the ticket lock allowed only one process to issue a test&set when a lock was released, but all processors were notified of the release through an invalidation and a subsequent read miss to determine who should issue the test&set. The array-based lock fixed this problem by having each process wait on a different location and the releasing process notify only one process of the release by writing the corresponding location.

However, the array-based lock has two potential problems for scalable machines with physically distributed memory. First, each lock requires space proportional to the number of processors. Second, and more important for machines that do not cache remote data, there is no way to know ahead of time which location a process will spin on since this is determined at run time through a fetch&increment operation. This makes it impossible to allocate the synchronization variables in such a way that the variable a process spins on is always in its local memory (in fact, all of the locks in Chapter 5 have this problem). On a distributed-memory machine without coherent caches, such as the CRAY T3D and T3E, this is a big problem since processes will spin on remote locations, causing inordinate amounts of traffic and contention. Fortunately, a software lock algorithm is available that both reduces the space requirements and ensures all spinning will be on locally allocated variables. This lock, known as a *software queuing lock*, is a software implementation of a lock originally proposed for an all-hardware implementation by the Wisconsin Multicube project (Goodman, Vernon, and Woest 1989). The idea is to have a distributed linked list or a queue of waiters on the lock. The head node in the list represents the process that holds the lock. Every other node is a process that is waiting on the lock and is allocated in that process's local memory. A node points to the process (node) that tried to acquire the lock just after it. There is also a tail pointer that points to the last node in the queue, that is, the last node to have tried to acquire the lock. Let us look pictorially at how the queue changes as processes acquire and release the lock; then we will examine the code for the acquire and release methods.

Assume that the lock in Figure 7.39 is initially free. When process A tries to acquire the lock, it gets it, and the queue looks as shown in Figure 7.39(a). In step (b), process B tries to acquire the lock, so it is put on the queue and the tail pointer now points to it. Process C is treated similarly when it tries to acquire the lock in step (c). B and C are now spinning on local flags associated with their queue nodes while A holds the lock. In step (d), process A releases the lock. It then "wakes up" the next process, B, in the queue by writing the flag associated with B's node, and leaves the queue. B now holds the lock and is at the head of the queue. The tail pointer does not change. In step (e), B releases the lock similarly, passing it on to C. There are no other waiting processes, so C is at both the head and tail of the queue. If C releases the lock before another process tries to acquire it, then the lock pointer will be NULL and the lock will be free again. In this way, processes are granted the lock in FIFO order with regard to the order in which they tried to acquire it. The latter order will be defined next.

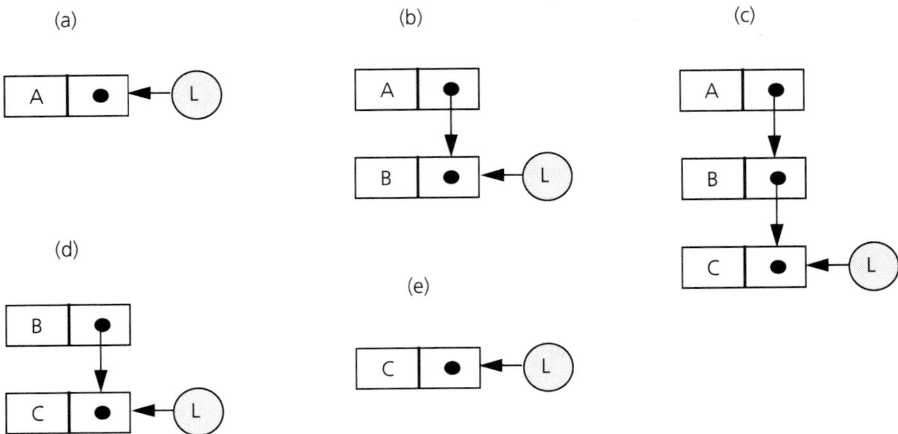

FIGURE 7.39 States of the queue for a lock as processes try to acquire and as processes release. The queue grows as new waiters are added to the tail. When the lock is released, the next waiter at the head is notified. Waiters always spin on local locations.

The code for the acquire and release methods is shown in Figure 7.40. In terms of primitives needed, the key is to ensure that changes to the tail pointer are atomic. In the acquire method, the acquiring process wants to change the lock pointer to point to its node. It does this using an atomic *fetch&store* operation, which takes two operands: it returns the current value of the first operand (here the current tail pointer) and then sets it to the value of the second operand, returning only when it succeeds. The order in which the atomic fetch&store operations of different processes succeed defines the order in which they acquire the lock.

In the release method, we want to atomically check if the process doing the release is the last one in the queue, and if so, set the lock pointer to `NULL`. We can do this using an atomic *compare&swap* operation, which takes three operands: it compares the first two (here the tail pointer and the node pointer of the releasing process), and if they are equal, it sets the first (the tail pointer) to the third operand (here `NULL`) and returns `TRUE`; if they are not equal, it does nothing and returns `FALSE`. The setting of the lock pointer to `NULL` must be atomic with the comparison since otherwise another process could slip in between and add itself to the queue, in which case setting the lock pointer to `NULL` would be the wrong thing to do. Recall from Chapter 5 that a compare&swap is difficult to implement as a single machine instruction since it requires three operands in a memory instruction (the functionality can, however, be implemented using load-locked and store-conditional instructions). It is possible to implement this queuing lock without a compare&swap—using only a fetch&store—but the implementation is more complicated (it allows the queue to be broken and then repairs it), and it loses the FIFO property of lock granting (Michael and Scott 1996).

```
struct node {
   struct node *next;
   int locked;
} *mynode, *prev_node;
shared struct node *Lock;

lock (Lock, mynode) {
   mynode->next = NULL;                /*make me last on queue*/
   prev_node = fetch&store(Lock, mynode);
                                       /*Lock currently points to the previous tail of
                                       the queue; atomically set prev_node to the
                                       Lock pointer and set Lock to point to my node
                                       so I am last in the queue*/
   if (prev_node != NULL) {            /*if by the time I get on the queue I am not the
                                       only one, i.e., some other process on queue
                                       still holds the lock*/
      mynode->locked = TRUE;           /*Lock is locked by other process*/
      prev_node->next = mynode;        /*connect me to queue*/
      while (mynode->locked) {};       /*busy-wait till I am granted the lock*/
   }
}

unlock (Lock, mynode) {
   if (mynode->next == NULL) {         /*no one to release, it seems*/
      if compare&swap(Lock,mynode,NULL)/*really no one to release*/
         return;                       /*i.e., Lock points to me, then set Lock to
                                       NULL and return*/
      while (mynode->next == NULL);    /*if I get here, someone just got on the
                                       queue and made my c&s fail, so I should wait
                                       till they set my next pointer to point to
                                       them before I grant them the lock*/
   }
   mynode->next->locked = FALSE;       /*someone to release; release them*/
}
```

FIGURE 7.40 Algorithm for the software queuing lock. The data for the lock is a list of length equal to the number of waiters. A node requests the lock by atomically adding an item to the tail of the list and spinning on the local item until an unlock by a previous requestor provides notification.

It should be clear that the software queuing lock needs only as much space per lock as the number of processes waiting on or participating in the lock, not space proportional to the number of processes in the program. It is the lock of choice for machines that support a shared address space with distributed memory but without coherent caching (Kägi, Burger, and Goodman 1997).

7.9.2 Algorithms for Barriers

In both message-passing and shared address space models, global events like barriers are a key concern. A question of considerable debate is whether special hardware support is needed for global operations or whether sophisticated software algorithms upon point-to-point operations are sufficient. The CM-5 represented one end of the spectrum, with a special "control" network providing barriers, reductions, broadcasts, and other global operations over a subtree of the machine. The CRAY T3D provided hardware support for barriers also. Since it is easy to construct barriers that spin only on local variables or use only point-to-point messages, many scalable machines provide no special support for barriers at all but build them in software libraries.

In the centralized barrier used on bus-based machines, all processors used the same lock to increment the same counter when they signaled their arrival, and all waited on the same flag variable until they were released. On a large machine, the allowing for all processors to access the same lock and to read and write the same variables can lead to a lot of traffic and contention. Again, this is particularly true of machines that are not cache coherent, where the variable quickly becomes a hot spot as several processors spin on it without caching it.

It is possible to implement the arrival and departure in a more distributed way, in which not all processes have to access the same variable or lock. The coordination of arrival or release can be performed in phases or rounds with subsets of processes coordinating with one another in each round, such that after a few rounds all processes are synchronized. The coordination of different subsets can proceed in parallel with no serialization needed across them. In a bus-based machine, distributing the necessary coordination actions wouldn't matter much since the bus serializes all actions that require communication anyway; however, it can be very important in machines with distributed memory and interconnect where different subsets can coordinate in different parts of the network. The techniques used in a shared address space closely reflect natural message-passing approaches. Let us examine a few such distributed-barrier algorithms.

Software Combining Trees

A simple distributed way to coordinate the arrival or release of processes is through a tree structure (see Figure 7.41), just as was suggested for avoiding hot spots in Chapter 3. An arrival tree is a tree that processors use to signal their arrival at a barrier. It replaces the single lock and counter of the centralized barrier by a tree of counters. The tree may be of any chosen degree or branching factor, say, k. In the simplest case, each leaf of the tree is a process that participates in the barrier. When a process arrives at the barrier, it signals its arrival by performing a fetch&increment on the counter associated with its parent (or by sending a message to the parent). It then checks the value returned by the fetch&increment to see if it was the last of its siblings to arrive. If not, its work for the arrival is done and it simply waits for the release. If so, it considers itself chosen to represent its siblings at the next level of the

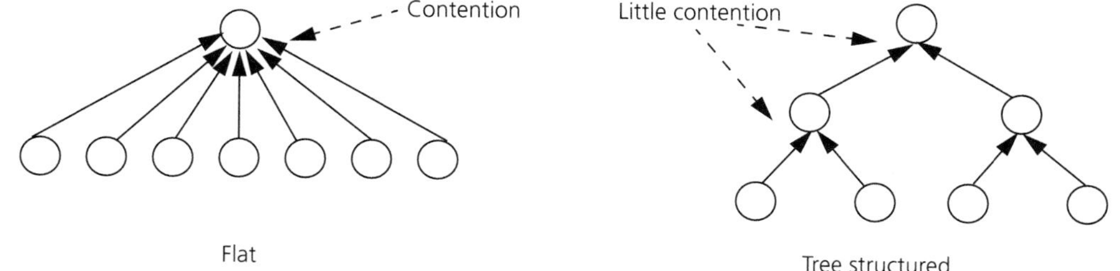

FIGURE 7.41 Replacing a flat arrival structure for a barrier by an arrival tree (here of degree 2). A deeper tree with smaller branching utilizes the many paths through the network of a large-scale machine to avoid serialization.

tree and so does a fetch&increment on the counter at that level. In this way, each tree node sends only a single representative process up to the next higher level in the tree when all the processes represented by that node's children have arrived. For a tree of degree k, it takes $\log_k p$ levels and hence that many steps to complete the arrival notification of p processes. If subtrees of processes are placed in different parts of the network and if the counter variables at the tree nodes are distributed appropriately across memories, fetch&increment operations on nodes that do not have an ancestor-descendent relationship need not be serialized at all.

A similar tree structure can be used for the release as well, so all processors don't busy-wait on the same flag. That is, the last process to arrive at the barrier sets the release flag associated with the root of the tree, on which only $k - 1$ processes are busy-waiting. Each of the k processes then sets a release flag at the next level of the tree, on which $k - 1$ other processes are waiting, and so on down the tree until all processes are released. (Similarly, messages can be passed down the tree.) The critical path length of the barrier in terms of the number of dependent or serialized operations (e.g., network transactions) is thus $O(\log_k p)$ as opposed to $O(p)$ for the centralized barrier or $O(p)$ for any barrier on a centralized bus. The code for a simple combining tree barrier with sense reversal is shown in Figure 7.42.

Although this tree barrier distributes traffic in the interconnect, it has the same problem as the simple lock for machines that do not cache remote shared data: the variables that processors spin on are not necessarily allocated in their local memory. Multiple processors spin on the same variable, and which processors reach the higher levels of the tree and spin on the variables there depends on the order in which processors reach the barrier and perform their fetch&increment instructions, which is impossible to predict. This leads to a lot of network traffic while spinning.

Tree Barriers with Local Spinning

There are two ways to ensure that a processor spins on a local variable. One is to predetermine which processor moves up from a node to its parent in the tree, based on the process identifier and the number of processes participating in the barrier. In this

```
struct tree_node {
   int count = 0;                        /*counter initialized to 0*/
   int local_sense;                      /*release flag implementing sense reversal*/
   struct tree_node *parent;
}

struct tree_node tree[P];                /*each element (node) allocated in a different
                                           memory*/

private int sense = 1;
private struct tree_node *myleaf;        /*pointer to this process's leaf in the tree*/

barrier () {
   barrier_helper(myleaf);
   sense = !(sense);                     /*reverse sense for next barrier call*/
}

barrier_helper(struct tree_node *mynode) {
   if (fetch&increment (mynode->count) == k-1){      /*last to reach node*/
     if (mynode->parent != NULL)
       barrier_helper(mynode->parent);                /*go up to parent node*/
     mynode->count = 0;                               /*set up for next time*/
     mynode->local_sense = !(mynode->local_sense);    /*release*/
   endif
   while (sense != mynode->local_sense) [];           /*busy-wait*/
```

FIGURE 7.42 A software combining barrier algorithm with sense reversal. Each time the barrier is used, the sense of the flag is reversed, so the flag does not need to be reset.

case, a binary tree makes local spinning easy since the flag to spin on can be allocated in the local memory of the spinning processor rather than the one that goes up to the parent level. In fact, in this case, it is possible to perform the barrier without any atomic operations like fetch&increment but with only simple reads and writes as follows. For arrival, one process arriving at each node simply spins on an arrival flag associated with that node. The other process associated with that node simply writes the flag when it arrives. The process whose role was to spin now simply spins on the release flag associated with that node while the other process now proceeds up to the parent node. Such a static binary tree barrier has been called a "tournament barrier" in the literature, since one process can be thought of as dropping out of the tournament at each step in the arrival tree. (As an exercise, think about how you might modify this scheme to handle the case where the number of participating processes is not a power of two and to use a nonbinary tree.)

The other way to ensure local spinning is to use p-node trees to implement a barrier among p processes, where each tree node (leaf or internal) is assigned to a unique process. The arrival and wake-up trees can be the same, or they can be main-

```
struct tree_node {
  struct tree_node *parent;
  int parent_sense = 0;
  int wkup_child_flags[2]; /*flags for children in wake-up tree*/
  int child_ready[4];      /*flags for children in arrival tree*/
  int child_exists[4];
}
                           /*nodes are numbered from 0 to P – 1 level-by-level starting
                           from the root*/
struct tree_node tree[P];  /*each element (node) allocated in a different memory*/
private int sense = 1, myid;
private me = tree[myid];

barrier() {
  while (me.child_ready is not all TRUE) {}; /*busy-wait*/
  set me.child_ready to me.child_exists; /*reinitialize for next barrier call*/
  if (myid !=0) {             /*set parent's child_ready flag, and wait for release*/

    tree[⌊(myid – 1)/4⌋].child_ready[(myid-1) mod 4] = true;

    while (me.parent_sense != sense) {};
  }
  me.child_pointers[0] = me.child_pointers[1] = sense;
  sense = !sense;
```

FIGURE 7.43 A combining tree barrier that spins on local variables only. Each tree node is assigned to a unique process and allocated in the memory that is local to the process.

tained as different trees with different branching factors. Each internal node (process) in the tree maintains an array of arrival flags, with one entry per child, allocated in that node's local memory. When a process arrives at the barrier, if its tree node is not a leaf, then it first checks its arrival flag array and waits until all its children have signaled their arrival by setting the corresponding array entries. Then it sets its entry in its parent's (remote) arrival flag array and busy-waits on the release flag associated with its tree node in the wake-up tree. When the root process arrives and when all its arrival flag array entries are set, this means that all processes have arrived. The root then sets the (remote) release flags of all its children in the wake-up tree; these processes break out of their busy-wait loop and set the release flags of their children, and so on until all processes are released. The code for this barrier is shown in Figure 7.43, assuming an arrival tree of branching factor 4 and a wake-up tree of branching factor 2. In general, choosing branching factors in tree-based barriers is largely a trade-off between contention and critical path length counted in network transactions. Either of these types of barriers may work well for scalable machines without coherent caching.

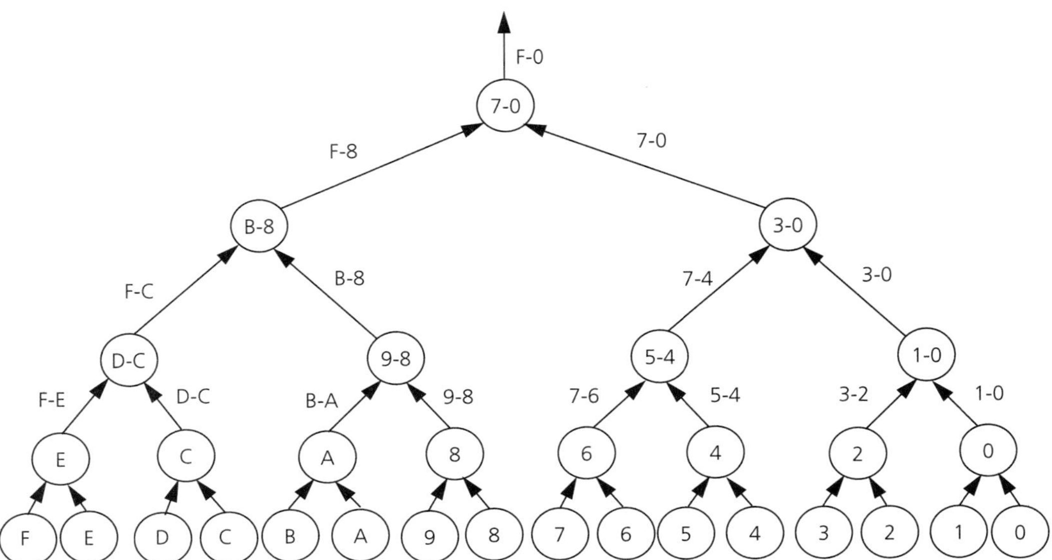

FIGURE 7.44 Upward sweep of the parallel prefix operation. Each node receives two elements from its children, combines them and passes the result to its parent, and holds the element from the least significant (right) child.

Parallel Prefix

In many parallel applications, a point of global synchronization is associated with combining information that has been computed by many processors and distributing a result based on the combination. Parallel prefix operations are an important, widely applicable generalization of reductions and broadcasts (Blelloch 1993). Given some associative binary operator $\oplus$, we want to compute $S_i = x_i \oplus x_{i-1} \ldots \oplus x_0$ for $i = 0, \ldots, P$. A canonical example is a running sum, but several other operators are useful. The carry-lookahead operator from adder design is actually a special case of a parallel prefix circuit. The surprising fact about parallel prefix operations is that they can be performed as quickly as a reduction followed by a broadcast, with a simple pass up a binary tree and back down. Figure 7.44 shows the upward sweep, in which each node applies the operator to the pair of values it receives from its children and passes the result to its parent, just as with a binary reduction. (The value that is transmitted is indicated by the range of indices next to each arc; this is the subsequence over which the operator is applied to get that value.) In addition, each node holds onto the value it received from its least significant child (rightmost in the figure). Figure 7.45 shows the downward sweep. Each node waits until it receives a value from its parent. It passes this value along unchanged to its rightmost child. It combines this value with the value that was held over from the upward pass and passes the result to its left child. The nodes along the right edge of the tree are

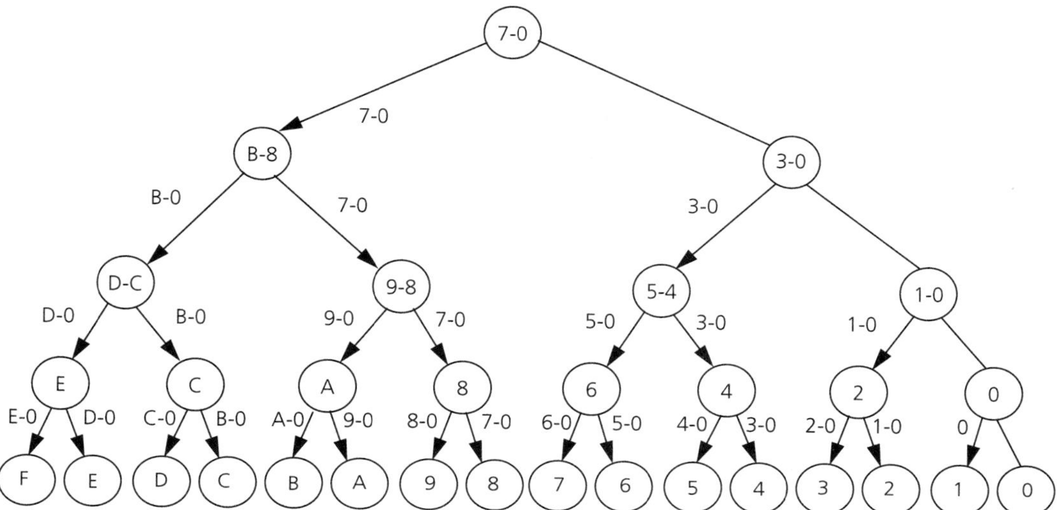

FIGURE 7.45 Downward sweep of the parallel prefix operation. When a node receives an element from above, it passes the data down to its right child, combines it with its stored element, and passes the result to its left child. Nodes along the rightmost branch need nothing from above.

special because they do not need to receive anything from their parent. This parallel prefix tree can be implemented either in hardware or in software.

All-to-All Personalized Communication

All-to-all personalized communication occurs when each process has a distinct set of data to transmit to every other process. The canonical example of this is a transpose operation, say, where each process owns a set of rows of a matrix and needs to access data in a set of columns. Another important example is remapping a data structure between blocked and cyclic layouts. Many other permutations of this form are widely used in practice. Quite a bit of work has been done in implementing all-to-all personalized communication operations efficiently on specific network topologies (i.e., with no contention internal to the network). If the network is highly scalable, the internal communication flows within the network become secondary, but contention at the endpoints of the network is critical, regardless of the quality of the network. A simple, widely used scheme is to schedule the sequence of communication events so that P rounds of disjoint pairwise exchanges are performed. In round i, process p transmits the data it has for process $q = p \oplus i$ obtained as the exclusive-or of the binary number for p and the binary representation of i. Since exclusive-or is commutative, $p = q \oplus i$, and the round is indeed an exchange.

7.10 CONCLUDING REMARKS

We have seen in this chapter that most modern large-scale machines are constructed from general-purpose nodes with a complete local memory hierarchy augmented by a communication assist interfacing to a scalable network. However, a wide range of design options is available for the communication assist. The design is influenced very strongly by where the communication assist interfaces to the node architecture: at the processor, at the cache controller, at the memory bus, or at the I/O bus. It is also strongly influenced by the target communication architecture and programming model. Programming models are implemented on large-scale machines using protocols constructed out of primitive network transactions. The challenges in implementing such a protocol are that a large number of transactions can be outstanding simultaneously and that global arbitration is unavailable. Essentially, any programming model can be implemented on any of the available primitives at the hardware/software boundary, and many of the correctness and scalability issues are the same; however, the performance characteristics are quite different. The performance ultimately influences how the machine is viewed by programmers.

Modern large-scale parallel machine designs are rooted heavily in the technological revolution of the mid-1980s—the single-chip microprocessor—which was coined the "killer micro" as the MPP machines began to take over the high-performance market from traditional vector supercomputers. However, these machines pioneered a technological revolution of their own—the single-chip scalable network switch. Like the microprocessor, this technology has grown beyond its original intended use, and a wide class of scalable system area networks are emerging, including switched gigabit (perhaps multigigabit) Ethernets. As a result, large-scale parallel machine design has split somewhat into two branches. Machines oriented largely around message-passing concepts and explicit get/put access to remote memory are being overtaken by clusters because of their extreme low cost, ease of engineering, and ability to track technology. The other branch is made up of machines that deeply integrate the network into the memory system to provide cache-coherent access to a global physical address space with automatic replication—in other words, machines that look to the programmer, like those of the previous chapter, but that are built like the machines in this chapter. Of course, the challenge is advancing the cache coherence mechanisms in a manner that provides scalable bandwidth and low latency. This is the subject of Chapter 8.

7.11 EXERCISES

7.1 A radix-2 FFT over n complex numbers is implemented as a sequence of $\log n$ completely parallel steps, requiring $5n \log n$ floating-point operations while reading and writing each element of data $\log n$ times. Calculate the communication-to-computation ratio on a dancehall design where all processors access memory through the network, as in Figure 7.3. What communication bandwidth would the network need to sustain for the machine to deliver $250p$ MFLOPS on p processors?

7.2 If the data in Exercise 7.1 is spread over the memories in a NUMA design using either a cycle or block distribution, the $\log n/p$ of the steps will access data in the local memory, assuming both n and p are powers of two, and in the remaining $\log p$ steps half of the reads and half of the writes will be local. (The choice of layout determines which steps are local and which are remote, but the ratio stays the same.) Calculate the communication-to-computation ratio on a distributed-memory design where each processor has a local memory, as in Figure 7.2. What communication bandwidth would the network need to sustain for the machine to deliver $250p$ MFLOPS on p processors? How does this compare with Exercise 7.1?

7.3 If the programmer pays attention to the layout, the FFT can be implemented so that a single, global transpose operation is required where $n - n/p$ data elements are transmitted across the network. All of the $\log n$ steps are performed on local memory. Calculate the communication-to-computation ratio on a distributed-memory design. What communication bandwidth would the network need to sustain for the machine to deliver $250p$ MFLOPS on p processors? How does this compare with Exercise 7.2?

7.4 Reconsider Example 7.1 where the number of hops for an n-node configuration is $\sqrt{n}$. How does the average transfer time increase with the number of nodes? What about $\sqrt[3]{n}$?

7.5 Formalize the cost scaling for the designs in Exercise 7.4.

7.6 Consider a machine as described in Example 7.1, where the number of links occupied by each transfer is $\log n$. In the absence of contention for individual links, how many transfers can occur simultaneously?

7.7 Reconsider Example 7.1 where the network is a simple ring. The average distance between two nodes on a ring of n nodes is $n/2$. How does the average transfer time increase with the number of nodes? Assuming each link can be occupied by at most one transfer at a time, how many such transfers can take place simultaneously?

7.8 For a machine as described in Example 7.1, suppose that a broadcast from a node to all the other nodes uses n links. How would you expect the number of simultaneous broadcasts to scale with the number of nodes?

7.9 Suppose a 16-way SMP lists at \$10,000 plus \$2,000 per node, where each node contains a fast processor and 128 MB of memory. How much does the cost increase when doubling the capacity of the system from 4 to 8 processors? From 8 to 16 processors?

7.10 Prove the statement from Section 7.1.3 that parallel computing is more cost-effective whenever $\text{Speedup}(p) > \text{Costup}(p)$.

7.11 Assume a bus transaction with n bytes of payload occupies the bus for

$$4 + \left\lceil \frac{n}{8} \right\rceil$$

cycles, up to a limit of 64 bytes. Draw a graph comparing the bus utilization for programmed I/O and DMA for sending various-sized messages where the message data is in memory, not in registers. For DMA, include the extra work to inform the communication assist of the DMA address and length. Consider both the case where the data is in cache and where it is not. What assumptions do you need to make about reading the status registers?

7.12 The Intel Paragon has an output buffer of size 2 KB, which can be filled from memory at a rate of 400 MB/s and drained into the network at a rate of 175 MB/s. The buffer is drained into the network while it is being filled, but if the buffer gets full, the DMA device will stall. In designing your message layer you decide to fragment long messages into DMA bursts that are as long as possible without stalling behind the output buffer. Clearly, these can be at least 2 KB in size, but in fact they can be longer. Calculate the apparent size of the output buffer driving a burst into an empty network, given these rates of flow.

7.13 Based on a rough estimate from Figure 7.33, which of the machines will have a negative T_0 if a linear model is fit to the communication time data?

7.14 Use the message frequency data presented in Table 7.2 to estimate the time each processor would spend in communication on an iteration of BT for the machines described in Table 7.1.

7.15 Table 7.3 describes the communication characteristics of sparse LU.

a. How do the message size characteristics differ from that of BT? What does this say about the application?

b. How does the message frequency differ?

c. Estimate the time each processor would spend in communication on an iteration of LU for the machines described in Table 7.1.

Table 7.3 Communication Characteristics for One Iteration of LU on the Class A Problem over a Range of Processor Counts

	4 Processors			16 Processors			32 Processors			64 Processors		
	Message Size (KB)	Messages	Total Data Transfer (KB)	Message Size (KB)	Messages	Total Data Transfer (KB)	Bins (KB)	Messages	Total Data TRans-fer (KB)	Bins (KB)	Messages	Total Data Transfer (KB)
	1+	496	605	0.5–1	2,976	2,180	0–0.5	2,976	727	0–0.5	13,888	3,391
	163.5+	8	1,279	81.5+	48	3,382	0.5–1	3,472	2,543	81.5	224	8,914
							40.5+	48	1,910			
							81.5+	56	4,471			
Total Communication Volume (KB)			1,884			5,562			9,651			12,305
Time per Iteration (s)			2.4			0.58			0.34			0.19
Average Bandwidth (MB/s)			0.77			10.1			27.7			63.2
Average Bandwidth per Processor (MB/s)			0.19			0.63			0.87			0.99

8

Directory-Based Cache Coherence

This chapter examines an important part of the development of parallel architectures: putting together cache coherence and a scalable, distributed-memory machine organization. We have studied cache coherence for bus-based machines with centralized memory. We have also seen that in order to scale up machines, memory is distributed, a scalable point-to-point interconnection network is introduced, and a communication assist provides varying degrees of interpretation of network transactions to support programming models. Regardless of the sophistication of that assist, all of the scalable machines we have studied have the generic structure depicted in Figure 8.1.

At the final point in our design spectrum so far, the communication assist provides a shared address space in hardware. However, while the natural inclination of caches is to replicate referenced data in a shared address space, we have not yet examined how cache coherence may be provided. In fact, to avoid the coherence problem and simplify memory consistency, the machines in that final design point disable the hardware caching of logically shared but physically remote data, restricting the programming model.

This chapter takes on the important issue of how implicit caching and coherence may be provided in hardware on a machine with physically distributed memory, without the benefits of a globally snoopable interconnect such as a bus. Not only must the hardware latency and bandwidth scale well, as we have seen, but so must the protocols used for coherence, at least up to the scales of practical interest. We focus on full hardware support for cache coherence and particularly on the most common approach called directory-based cache coherence. In terms of the layers of abstraction, the shared address space programming model with coherent replication is supported directly at the hardware/software interface, as shown in Figure 8.2. Other programming models, such as message passing, can be implemented in software. The next chapter describes some alternative approaches that take different positions on hardware/software trade-offs, such as coherent replication in main memory rather than in the caches, coherence under software control, and alternative memory consistency models.

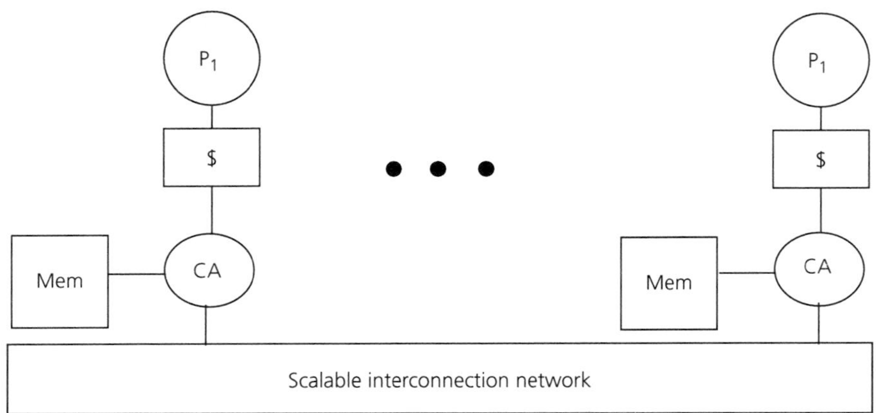

FIGURE 8.1 A generic scalable multiprocessor. This diagram represents the generic structure of the machines discussed in Chapter 7: processing nodes with physically distributed memory and a scalable interconnect. The processing nodes may be uniprocessors (as shown) or multiprocessors.

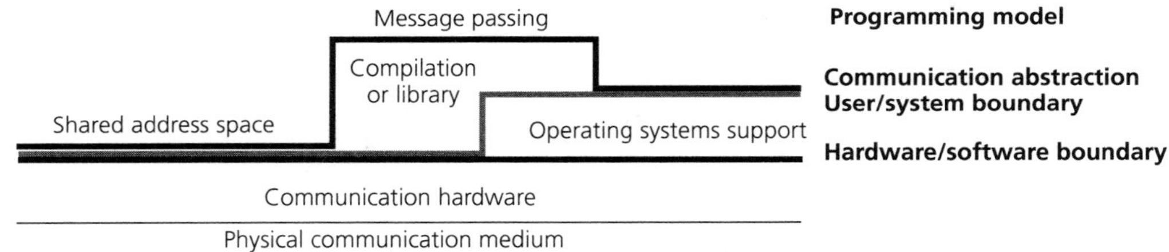

FIGURE 8.2 Layers of abstraction for systems discussed in this chapter. A coherent, shared physical address space is supported directly in hardware and message passing through software layers.

Scalable cache coherence is typically based on the concept of a directory. Since the state of a block in the caches can no longer be determined implicitly by placing a request on a shared bus and having it snooped by the cache controllers, the idea is to maintain this state explicitly in a place—called a *directory*—where requests can go and look it up. Consider a simple example. Imagine that each cache-line-sized block of main memory has associated with it a record of the caches that currently contain a copy of the block and the state of the block in those caches. This record is called the *directory entry* for that block (see Figure 8.3). As in bus-based systems, there may be many caches with a clean, readable block, but if the block is writable (possibly modified) in one cache, then only that cache may have a valid copy. When a node incurs a cache miss, it first communicates with the directory entry for the block using point-to-point network transactions. Since the directory entry is colocated with the

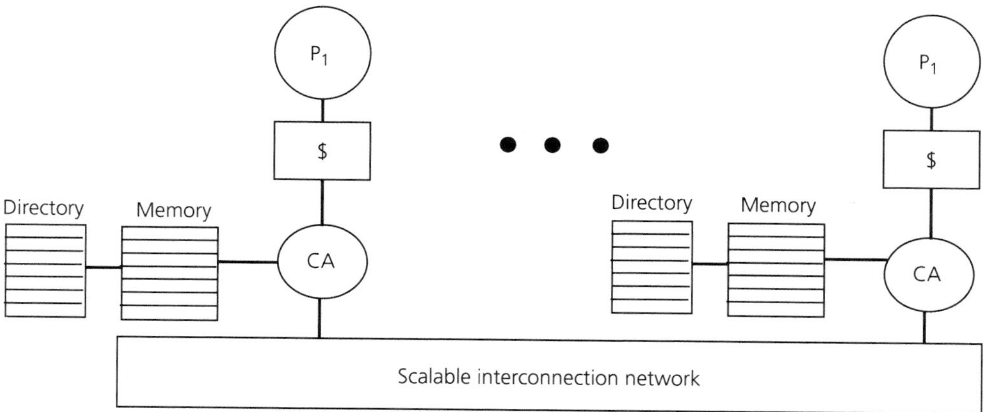

FIGURE 8.3 A scalable multiprocessor with directories. Every block of main memory, the size of a cache block, has a directory entry that keeps track of its cached copies and their state.

main memory for the block, its location can be determined from the address of the block. From the directory, the node determines where the valid cached copies (if any) are and what further actions to take. It then communicates with the cached copies as necessary using additional network transactions. For example, it may obtain a modified block from another node or, on a write operation, send invalidations to other nodes and receive acknowledgments from them. The resulting changes to the states of cached blocks are also communicated to the directory entry through network transactions, so the directory stays up-to-date.

In a directory protocol, requests, replies, invalidations, updates, and acknowledgments across nodes are all network transactions like those of the previous chapter, only here the endpoint processing at the destination of the transaction (invalidating blocks, retrieving and replying with data) is typically done by the communication assist rather than the main processor. (As in previous chapters, we will call response transactions that carry data "replies" and all others simply "responses.") Since directory schemes rely on point-to-point network transactions, they can be used with any interconnection network. Important questions for directories include the form in which the directory information is stored and how correct, efficient protocols may be designed using these representations.

While directories constitute the dominant approach to scalable cache coherence, other approaches can be contemplated. One approach that has been tried is to extend the broadcast and snooping mechanism, using a hierarchy of broadcast media like buses or rings. This is conceptually attractive because it builds larger systems hierarchically out of existing small-scale mechanisms. However, it does not apply to general network topologies such as meshes and cubes, and we will see that it has problems with latency and bandwidth, so it has not become very popular. An approach that is popular is a limited, two-level protocol hierarchy. Each node of the machine is itself a multiprocessor. The caches within a node are kept coherent by one coherence protocol called the *inner protocol*. Coherence across nodes is maintained by another, possibly different protocol called the *outer protocol*. To the outer protocol, each multiprocessor node looks like a single cache, and coherence within the node is the responsibility of the inner protocol. Usually, an adapter or a shared tertiary cache is used to represent a node to the outer protocol. A common organization is for the outer protocol to be a directory protocol and the inner one to be a snooping protocol (Lovett and Clapp 1996; Lenoski et al. 1993; Clark and Alnes 1996; Weber et al. 1997). However, other combinations such as snooping-snooping (Frank, Burkhardt, and Rothnie 1993), directory-directory (Convex Computer Corporation 1993), and even snooping-directory may be used (see Figure 8.4).

Putting together smaller-scale machines to build larger machines in a two-level organization is an attractive engineering option: it amortizes fixed per-node costs over the processors in a node, may take advantage of packaging hierarchies, and may satisfy much of the interprocessor communication less expensively within a node. The main focus of this chapter will be on directory protocols across nodes, regardless of whether the node is a uni- or multiprocessor or what coherence method it uses. The interactions among two-level protocols are also discussed. While we focus on directory protocols because they have been most successful and are likely to remain the most popular, we will briefly examine the less popular hierarchical approaches as well. As we examine the organizational structure of the directory, the protocols used to support coherence and consistency, and the requirements placed on the communication assist, we will find another rich and interesting design space.

The first section of this chapter presents a framework for understanding the different approaches to providing coherent replication in a shared address space, including snooping, directories, and hierarchical snooping. Section 8.2 introduces the basic operation of a directory protocol using a simple directory representation and then provides an overview of alternative directory organizations and protocols. This is followed by a quantitative assessment of some high-level issues and architectural trade-offs for directory protocols in Section 8.3.

The next few sections cover the issues and techniques involved in actually designing correct, efficient protocols. Section 8.4 discusses the major new challenges introduced by the presence of multiple copies of data without a serializing interconnect. The next two sections delve deeply into the two most popular types of directory-based protocols, discussing various design alternatives and using two commercial architectures as case studies: the Origin2000 from Silicon Graphics, Inc. and the NUMA-Q from Sequent Computer Systems, Inc. Section 8.7 examines the impact of key performance parameters of the communication architecture on the end performance of parallel programs under directory protocols.

Synchronization for directory-based multiprocessors is discussed in Section 8.8 and the implications for parallel software in Section 8.9. Section 8.10 covers some advanced topics, including the approaches of hierarchically extending snooping and directory protocols for scalable coherence.

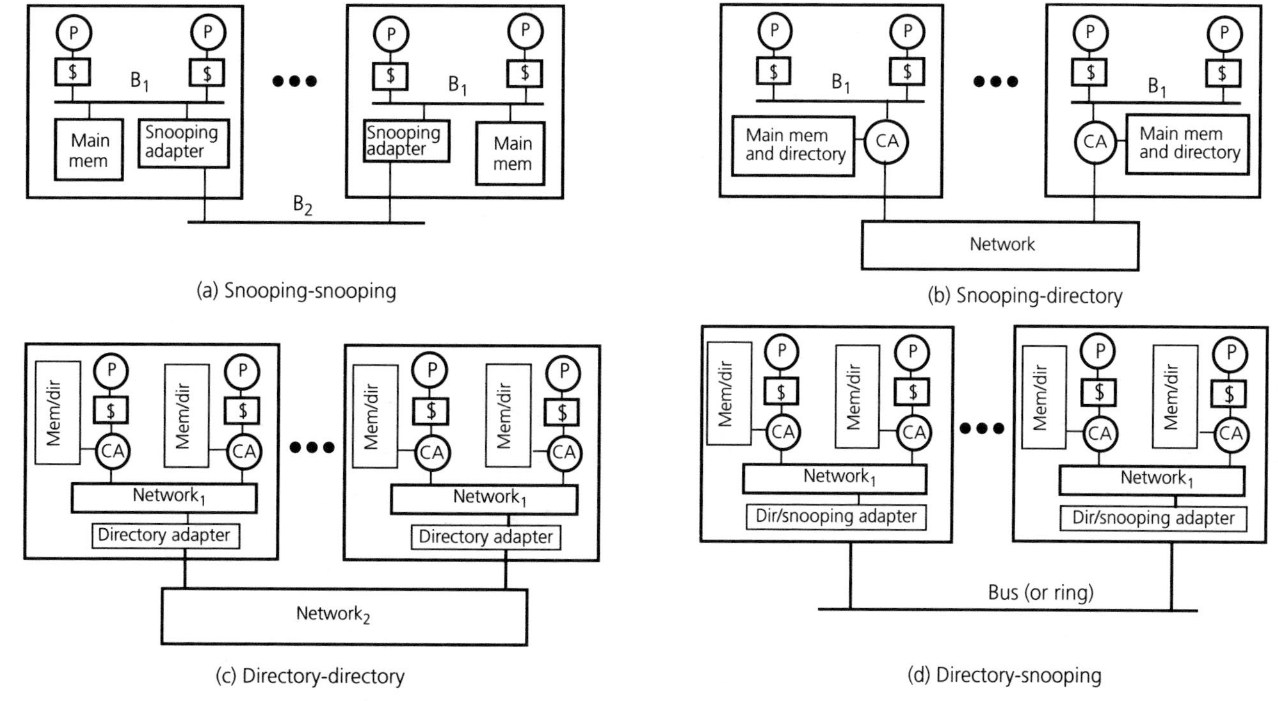

(a) Snooping-snooping

(b) Snooping-directory

(c) Directory-directory

(d) Directory-snooping

FIGURE 8.4 Some possible organizations for two-level cache-coherent systems. Each node visible at the outer level is itself a multiprocessor. B_1 is a first-level bus, and B_2 is a second-level bus. CA is the communication assist. The label snooping-directory, for example, means that a snooping protocol is used to maintain coherence within a multiprocessor node, and a directory protocol is used to maintain coherence across nodes.

8.1 SCALABLE CACHE COHERENCE

This section briefly lays out the major organizational alternatives for providing coherent replication in a multiprocessor's extended memory hierarchy and introduces the basic mechanisms that any approach to coherence must provide.

On a machine with physically distributed memory, nonlocal data may be replicated either only in the processors' caches or in the local main memory. If coherent replication is provided in main memory, additional support for keeping caches coherent may not be necessary since only data that is already coherent in the local main memory may enter the cache. This chapter assumes that data is automatically replicated only in the caches, not in main memory, and that it is kept coherent in hardware at the granularity of cache blocks, just as in bus-based machines. Since main memory is physically distributed and has nonuniform access costs to a processor, architectures of this type are often called *cache-coherent, nonuniform memory access* or CC-NUMA architectures. More generally, systems that provide a shared address space programming model with physically distributed memory and coherent replication (either in caches or main memory) are called *distributed shared memory* (DSM) systems.

Any approach to coherence, including the snooping coherence discussed in Chapters 5 and 6, must provide certain critical mechanisms. First, a block can be in each cache (or local replication store) in one of a number of states, potentially in different states in different caches. The protocol must provide these cache states as well as the state transition diagram, according to which blocks in different caches independently change states, and the set of actions associated with the state transition diagram. Directory-based protocols also have a *directory state* for each block, which is the state of the block as known to the directory. The protocol may be invalidation based, update based, or hybrid, and the stable cache states themselves are very often the same (e.g., MESI), regardless of whether the system is based on snooping or directories. The trade-offs in the choices of stable cache states are very similar to those discussed in Chapter 5 and are not revisited in this chapter. Conceptually, for any protocol, the cache state of a memory block is a vector containing its state in every cache in the system. The same state transition diagram governs the copies in different caches, though the current state of the block at any given time may be different in different caches. The state changes for a block in different caches are coordinated through transactions on the interconnect, whether bus transactions or more general network transactions.

Given a protocol at the cache state transition level, a coherent system must provide mechanisms for managing the protocol. First, a mechanism is needed to determine when (i.e., on which operations) to invoke the protocol. This is done in the same way on most systems: through an *access fault* (cache miss) detection mechanism. The protocol is invoked if the processor makes an access that its cache cannot satisfy by itself, for example, an access to a block that is not in the cache or a write access to a block that is present but in shared state. However, even when they use the same set of cache states, transitions, and access fault mechanisms, approaches to cache coherence differ substantially in the mechanisms they provide for three important functions that may need to be performed when an access fault occurs:

1. Finding out enough information about the state of the location (cache block) in other caches to determine what action to take
2. Locating those other copies, if needed (e.g., to invalidate them)
3. Communicating with the other copies (e.g., obtaining data from them or invalidating or updating them)

In snooping protocols, all three functions are performed by the broadcast and snooping mechanism. The processor puts a "search" request on the bus, containing the address of the block, and other cache controllers snoop and respond. It is possible to use a broadcast and "snooping" method in distributed machines as well; the assist at the node incurring the miss can broadcast messages to all nodes, and their assists can examine the incoming request and respond as appropriate. However, broadcast does not scale since it generates a large amount of traffic (at least p network transactions on every miss on a p-node machine). Scalable approaches include hierarchical snooping and directory-based approaches.

In a hierarchical snooping approach, the interconnection network is not a single broadcast bus (or ring) but a tree of buses. The processors are in the bus-based snooping multiprocessors at the leaves of the tree. Parent buses are connected to children by interfaces that snoop the buses on both sides and propagate relevant transactions upward or downward in the hierarchy. Main memory may be centralized at the root or distributed among the leaves. In this case, all of the preceding functions are performed by the hierarchical extension of the broadcast and snooping mechanism: a processor puts a search request on its bus as before, and it is propagated up and down the hierarchy as necessary based on snoop results. The hope is that most of the time a request will not have to be propagated very far. Hierarchical snooping systems are discussed further in Section 8.10.2.

In the simple directory approach introduced earlier in the chapter, information about the state of blocks in other caches is found by looking up the directory through network transactions. The location of the copies is also found from the directory, and the copies are communicated with using point-to-point network transactions in an arbitrary interconnection network, without resorting to broadcast. How the directory information is actually organized influences how protocols might be structured around this organization using network transactions and, hence, how the protocol addresses the three key functions required for coherence.

8.2 OVERVIEW OF DIRECTORY-BASED APPROACHES

This section begins by more fully describing a simple directory scheme and how it might operate using cache states, directory states, and network transactions. It then discusses the organizational issues in scaling directories to large numbers of nodes, provides a classification of scalable directory organizations, and discusses the basics of protocols associated with these organizations.

The following definitions are useful for our discussion of directory protocols. For a given cache or memory block:

- The *home node* is the node in whose main memory the block is allocated.
- The *dirty node* is the node that has a copy of the block in its cache in modified (dirty) state. Note that the home node and the dirty node for a block may be the same.
- The *owner node* is the node that currently holds the valid copy of a block and must supply the data when needed; in directory protocols, this is either the home node (when the block is not in dirty state in a cache) or the dirty node.
- The *exclusive node* is the node that has a copy of the block in its cache in an exclusive state, either dirty or (clean) exclusive as the case may be. (Recall from Chapter 5 that the cache state called exclusive means this is the only valid cached copy and that the block in main memory is up-to-date.) Thus, the dirty node is also the exclusive node.
- The *local node*, or *requesting node*, is the node containing the processor that issues a request for the block.
- Blocks whose home is local to the issuing processor are called *locally allocated* or simply *local blocks*, whereas all others are called *remotely allocated* or *remote blocks*.

Let us begin with the basic operation of directory-based protocols, using a very simple directory organization.

8.2.1 Operation of a Simple Directory Scheme

When a cache miss (access control fault) is incurred, the local node sends a request network transaction to the home node where the directory information for the block is located. On a read miss, the directory indicates from which node the data may be obtained, as shown in Figure 8.5(a). On a write miss, the directory identifies the copies of the block, and invalidation or update network transactions may be sent to these copies (Figure 8.5[b]). (Recall that a write to a block in shared state is also considered a write miss.) Since invalidations or updates are sent to multiple copies through potentially disjoint paths in the network, determining the completion or commitment of a write now requires that all copies reply to invalidations with explicit acknowledgment transactions; we cannot assume completion or commitment when the read-exclusive or update request obtains access to the interconnect as we did on a shared bus since we cannot guarantee ordering with respect to other transactions within the interconnect.

A natural way to organize a directory is to maintain the directory information for a block together with the block in main memory, that is, at the home node for the block. A simple organization for the directory information for a block is as a bit vector of p *presence bits*—which indicate for each of the p nodes (uniprocessor or multiprocessor) whether that node has a cached copy of the block—together with one or more state bits (see Figure 8.6). Let us assume for simplicity that there is only one state bit, called the *dirty* bit, which indicates if the block is dirty in one of the node

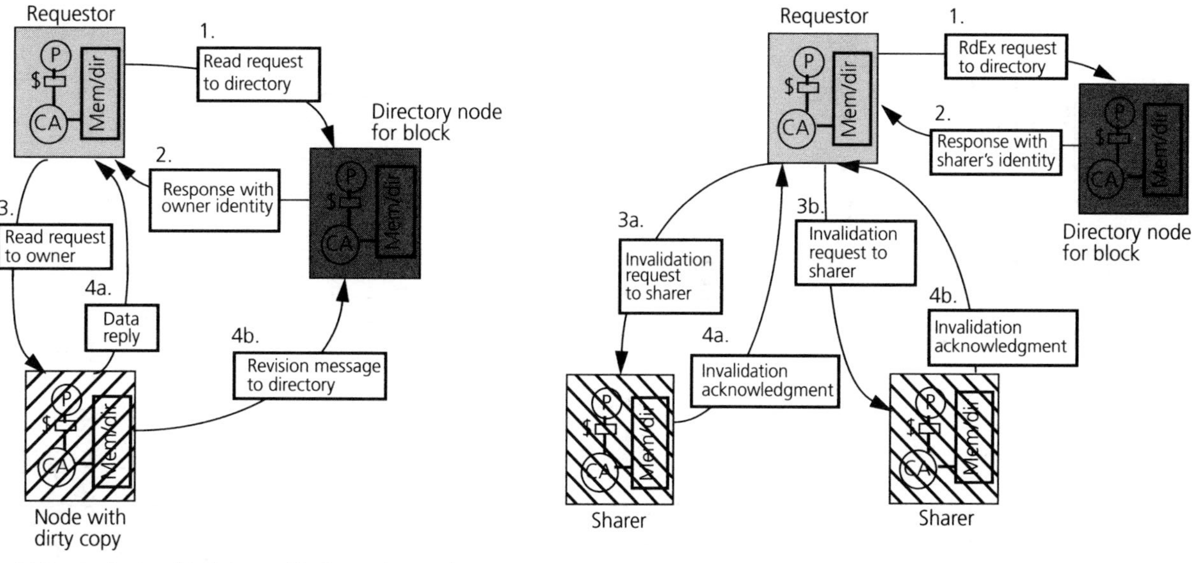

(a) Read miss to a block in modified state in a cache

(b) Write miss to a block with two sharers

FIGURE 8.5 Basic operation of a simple directory. Two example operations are shown. On the left is a read miss to a block that is currently held in modified (dirty) state by a node that is not the requestor or the node that holds the directory information. A read miss to a block that is clean in main memory (i.e., at the directory node) is simpler: the main memory simply replies to the requestor with the data, and the miss is satisfied in a single request-response pair of transactions. On the right is a write miss to a block that is currently in shared state in two other nodes' caches (the two sharers). The big rectangles are the nodes, and the arcs (with boxed labels) are network transactions. The numbers 1, 2, and so on next to a transaction show the serialization of transactions. Different letters next to the same number indicate that the transactions can be performed in parallel and hence overlapped.

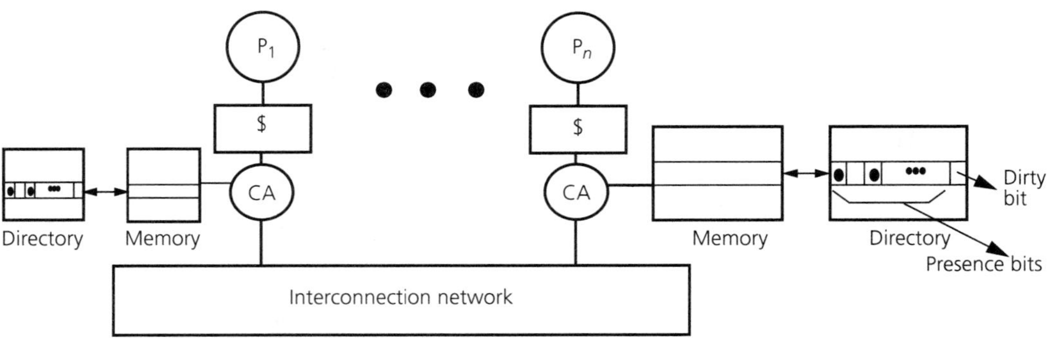

FIGURE 8.6 Directory information for a distributed-memory multiprocessor. In simple organization, the directory entry for a block is a vector of *p* presence bits, one for each node, and a dirty bit indicating whether any node has the block in modified state.

caches. Of course, if the dirty bit is ON, then only one node (the dirty node) should be caching that block and only that node's presence bit should be ON. With this structure, a read miss can easily determine from looking up the directory which node, if any, has a dirty copy of the block or if the block is valid in main memory at the home, and a write miss can determine which nodes are the sharers that must be invalidated.

The directory information for a block is simply main memory's view of the cache state of that block in different caches. The directory does not necessarily need to know the exact state (e.g., MESI) in each cache but only enough information to determine what actions to take. The number of states at the directory is therefore typically smaller than the number of cache states. In fact, since the directory and the caches communicate through a distributed interconnect, there will be periods when a directory's knowledge of a cache state is incorrect since the cache state has been modified but notice of the modification has not reached the directory. During this time, the directory may send a message to the cache based on its old (no longer valid) knowledge. The race conditions caused by this distribution of state make directory protocols interesting, and we see how they are handled using transient states or other means in Sections 8.4 through 8.6.

To see in greater detail how a read miss and write miss might interact with this bit vector directory organization, consider a protocol with three stable cache states (MSI), a single level of cache per processor, and a single processor per node. The protocol is orchestrated by the assists, which are also referred to as *coherence controllers* or *directory controllers*. On a read miss or a write miss at node *i* (including an upgrade from shared state), the local communication assist or controller looks up the address of the memory block to determine if the home is local or remote. If it is remote, a network transaction is sent to the home node for the block. There, the directory entry for the block is looked up, and the assist at the home may treat the miss as follows, using network transactions similar to those that were shown in Figure 8.5 (other, more optimized treatments are discussed later in the chapter):

- If the dirty bit is OFF, then the assist obtains the block from main memory, supplies it to the requestor in a reply network transaction, and turns the ith presence bit, *presence[i]*, ON.
- If the dirty bit is ON, then the assist responds to the requestor with the identity of the node whose presence bit is ON (i.e., the owner or dirty node). The requestor then sends a request network transaction to that owner node. At the owner, the cache changes its state to shared and supplies the block to both the requesting node, which stores the block in its cache in shared state, as well as to main memory at the home node. At memory, the dirty bit is turned OFF, and *presence[i]* is turned ON.

A write miss by processor i goes to memory and is handled as follows:

- If the dirty bit is OFF, then main memory has a clean copy of the data. Invalidation request transactions must be sent to all nodes j for which *presence[j]* is ON. Assuming a strict request-response scenario, as in Figure 8.5, the home node supplies the block to the requesting node i together with the presence bit vector. The directory entry is cleared, leaving only *presence[i]* and the dirty bit ON. (If the request is an upgrade instead of a read exclusive, an acknowledgment containing the bit vector is returned to the requestor instead of the data itself.) The assist at the requestor sends invalidation requests to the required nodes and waits for invalidation acknowledgment transactions from the nodes, indicating that the write has completed with respect to them. Finally, the requestor places the block in its cache in dirty state.
- If the dirty bit is ON, then the block is first recalled from the dirty node (whose presence bit is ON), using network transactions with the home and the dirty node. That cache changes its state to invalid, and then the block is supplied to the requesting processor, which places the block in its cache in dirty state. The directory entry is cleared, leaving only *presence[i]* and the dirty bit ON.

On a replacement of a dirty block by node i, the dirty data being replaced is written back to main memory, and the directory is updated to turn off the dirty bit and *presence[i]*. (As in bus-based machines, write backs cause interesting race conditions that are discussed later in the context of real protocols.) Finally, if a block in shared state is replaced from a cache, a message may or may not be sent to the directory to turn off the corresponding presence bit so an invalidation is not sent to this node the next time the block is written. This message is called a *replacement hint*; whether it is sent or not does not affect the correctness of the protocol or the execution.

A directory scheme similar to this one was introduced as early as 1978 (Censier and Feautrier 1978). It was designed for use in systems with a few processors and a centralized main memory and was used in the S-1 multiprocessor project at Lawrence Livermore National Laboratories (Widdoes and Correll 1980). However, directory schemes in one form or another were in use even before this. The earliest scheme was used in IBM mainframes, which had a few processors connected to a centralized memory through a high-bandwidth switch rather than a bus. With no broadcast medium to snoop on, a duplicate copy of the cache tags for each processor was maintained at the main memory, and it served as the directory. Requests coming to the memory looked up all the tags to determine the states of the block in the different caches (Tang 1976; Tucker 1986). Of course, the tag copies at main memory had to be kept up-to-date. Since the directory was centralized in these early schemes, they are called *centralized directory schemes*.

The value of directories is that they keep track of which nodes have copies of a block, eliminating the need for broadcast. This is clearly very valuable on read misses since a request for a block will either be satisfied at the main memory or the directory will tell it exactly where to go to retrieve the exclusive copy. On write misses, the value of directories over the simpler broadcast approach is greatest if the number of sharers of the block (to which invalidations or updates must be sent) is usually small and does not scale up quickly with the number of processing nodes.

We might already expect the typical number of sharers to be small from our understanding of parallel applications. For example, in a near-neighbor grid computation, usually two, and at most four, processes should share a block at a partition boundary, regardless of the grid size or the number of processors. Even when a location is actively read and written by all processes in an application, the number of sharers to be invalidated at a write depends upon the temporal interleaving of reads and writes by processors. A common example is *migratory* data, which is read and written by one processor, then read and written by another processor, and so on (for example, a global sum into which processes accumulate their values). Although all processors read and write the location, only one other processor on a write—the previous writer—has a valid copy and must be invalidated since all others were invalidated before the previous write.

Empirical measurements of program behavior show that the number of valid copies on most writes to shared data is indeed very small the vast majority of the time, that this number does not grow quickly with the number of processors used, and that the frequency of writes that generate many invalidations is very low. Such data for our parallel applications will be presented and analyzed in light of application characteristics in Section 8.3.1. (Note that even if all processors running the application have to be invalidated on most writes, directories are still valuable for writes if the application does not run on all nodes of the multiprocessor.) These facts are also promising for the scalability of directory-based approaches and help us understand how to organize directories cost-effectively.

8.2.2 Scaling

The main goal of using directory protocols is to allow cache coherence to scale beyond the number of processors that may be sustained by a bus. It is important to understand the scalability of directory protocols in terms of both performance and the storage overhead for directory information. A system with distributed memory and interconnect already provides good scalability of raw latency and bandwidth under well-behaved loads. The major performance scaling issues for a protocol are how the latency and bandwidth demands it presents to the system scale with the number of processors used. The bandwidth demands are governed by the number of network transactions generated per miss (multiplied by the frequency of misses) and latency by the number of these transactions that are in the critical path of the miss. In turn, these quantities are affected both by the directory organization and by how well the flow of network transactions is optimized in the protocol (given a directory organization). Storage, however, is affected only by how the directory information is organized. For the simple bit vector organization, the number of presence bits needed scales linearly with both the number of processing nodes (*p* bits per memory block) and the amount of main memory (1 bit vector per memory block), leading to a potentially large storage overhead for the directory. With a 64-byte block size and 64 processors, the directory storage overhead as a fraction of nondirectory (i.e., data) memory is 64 bits (plus state bits) divided by 64 bytes, or 12.5%, which is not so bad. With 256 processors and the same block size, the overhead is 50%, and with 1,024 processors it is 200%! The directory overhead does not scale well, though it may be acceptable if the number of nodes visible to the directory at the target machine scale is not very large.

Fortunately, there are many other ways to organize directory information that improve the scalability of directory storage. The different organizations naturally lead to different high-level protocols with different ways of addressing the three protocol functions presented in Section 8.1 and different performance characteristics. The rest of this section lays out the space of directory organizations and briefly describes how individual read and write misses might be handled in straightforward protocols that use these organizations. The discussion assumes that no other cache misses are in progress at the time, hence no race conditions, so the directory and the caches are always encountered as being in stable states. Deeper protocol issues are discussed in Sections 8.4 through 8.6.

8.2.3 Alternatives for Organizing Directories

Since communication with cached copies is always done through network transactions, the real differentiation among approaches is in the first two functions of coherence protocols: finding the source of the directory information upon a miss and determining the locations of the relevant copies.

The two major classes of alternatives for finding the source of the directory information for a block are known as *flat directory schemes* and *hierarchical directory schemes*.

The simple directory scheme described earlier is a flat scheme. Flat schemes are so named because the source of the directory information for a block is in a fixed place, usually at the home that is determined from the address of the block; on a miss, a single request network transaction is sent directly to the home node to look up the directory (if the home is remote) regardless of how far away the home is.

In hierarchical schemes, the source of directory information is not known a priori. Memory is again distributed with the processors, but the directory information for each block is logically organized as a hierarchical data structure (a tree). The processing nodes, each with its portion of memory, are at the leaves of the tree. The internal nodes of the tree are simply hierarchically maintained directory information for the block: a node keeps track of whether each of its children has a copy of a block. Upon a miss, the directory information for the block is found by traversing up the hierarchy level by level through network transactions until a directory node is reached that indicates its subtree has the block in the appropriate state. Thus, a processor that misses simply sends a search message up to its parent, and so on, rather than directly to the home node for the block with a single network transaction. The directory tree for a block is logical, not necessarily physical, and can be embedded in any general interconnection network. Every block has its own logical directory tree. In fact, in practice, every processing node in the system not only serves as a leaf node for the blocks it contains but also stores directory information as an internal tree node for other blocks.

In the hierarchical case, the information about locations of copies is also maintained through the hierarchy itself; copies are found and communicated with by traversing up and down the hierarchy guided by directory information. For example, a directory entry at a node may indicate not only whether its subtree has valid copies of the block but also if copies of blocks allocated within its subtree may exist beyond its subtree. In flat schemes, how this information about copies is stored varies considerably. At the highest level, flat schemes can be divided into two classes: memory-based schemes and cache-based schemes. *Memory-based schemes* store the directory information about all cached copies at the home node of the block. The basic bit vector scheme described earlier is memory based: the locations of all copies are discovered at the home, and they can be communicated with directly through point-to-point messages. In *cache-based schemes,* the information about cached copies is not all contained at the home but is distributed among the copies themselves. The home simply contains a pointer to one cached copy of the block. Each cached copy then contains a pointer to (or the identity of) the node that has the next cached copy of the block, in a distributed linked-list organization. The locations of copies are therefore determined by traversing this list via network transactions.

Figure 8.7 summarizes the taxonomy. Hierarchical directories have some potential advantages. For example, a read miss to a block whose home is far away in the interconnection network topology might be satisfied closer to the issuing processor if another copy is found nearby as the request traverses up and down the hierarchy, instead of going all the way to the home. In addition, requests from different nodes can potentially be combined at a common ancestor in the hierarchy, with only one request sent on from there. These advantages depend on how well the logical hierarchy matches the underlying physical network topology. However, instead of only a few point-to-point network transactions needed to satisfy a miss in many flat schemes, the number of network transactions needed to traverse up and down the hierarchy can be much larger, which tends to have much greater impact on performance than distance traversed in the network (since the endpoint cost of initiating and handling network transactions dominates the per-hop cost). Each transaction along the way needs to look up (and perhaps modify) the directory information at its destination node, making transactions more expensive. As a result, the latency and bandwidth characteristics of hierarchical directory schemes tend to be much worse than for flat schemes, and these organizations are not popular on modern systems. Hierarchical directories are not, therefore, discussed much in this chapter but

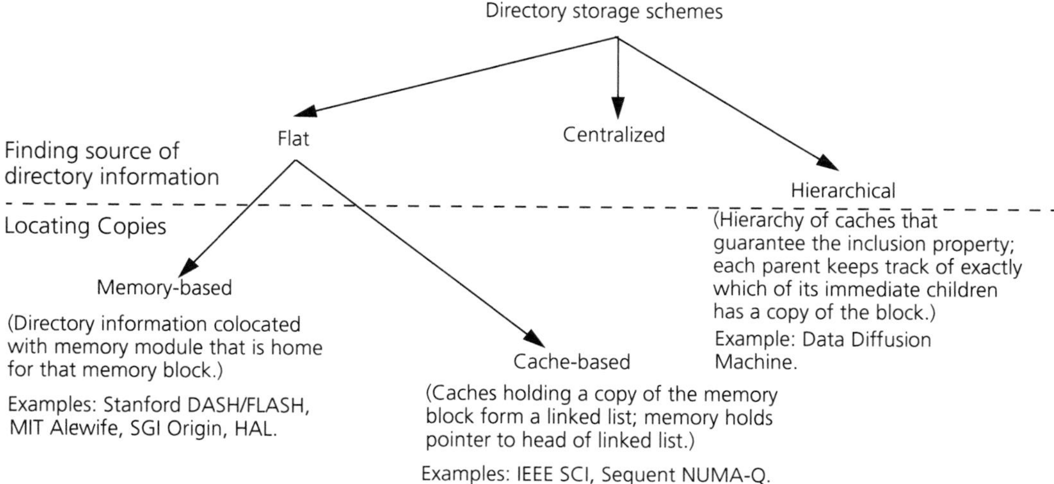

FIGURE 8.7 Alternatives for storing directory information. The two-level taxonomy is based on how the source of directory information and the copies themselves are located. In the hierarchical case, the same mechanism performs both functions.

are described briefly together with hierarchical snooping approaches in Section 8.10.2. The rest of this section examines flat directory schemes, both memory based and cache based, looking at directory organizations, storage overhead, the structure of protocols, and the impact on performance characteristics.

Flat, Memory-Based Directory Schemes

The bit vector organization described earlier, called a *full bit vector* organization, is the most straightforward way to store directory information in a flat, memory-based scheme. The style of protocol that results has already been discussed. Consider its basic performance characteristics on writes. Since it preserves information about sharers precisely and at the home, the number of network transactions per invalidating write grows only with the number of actual sharers. Because the identity of all sharers is available at the home, invalidations sent to them can be overlapped or even sent in parallel; the number of fully serialized network transactions in the critical path is thus not proportional to the number of sharers, reducing latency.

The main disadvantage of full bit vector schemes, as discussed earlier, is storage overhead. There are two ways to reduce this overhead for a given number of processors while still using full bit vectors. The first is to increase the cache block size. The second is to put multiple processors, rather than just one, in a node that is visible to the directory protocol; that is, to use a two-level protocol. For example, the Stanford DASH machine uses a full bit vector scheme, and its nodes are four-processor bus-based multiprocessors. These two methods actually make full bit vector directories quite attractive for even fairly large machines: using four-processor nodes and 128-byte cache blocks, the directory memory overhead for a 256-processor machine is only 6.25%. As small-scale multiprocessors become increasingly attractive building blocks, this storage problem may not be severe.

However, these methods reduce the overhead by only a small constant factor each. The total directory storage is still proportional to $P*M$, where P is the number of processing nodes and M is the number of total memory blocks in the machine ($M = P*m$, where m is the number of blocks per local memory), and would become intolerable in very large machines. The overhead can be reduced further by addressing each of the factors in the $P*M$ expression. We can reduce the number of bits per directory entry, or *directory width*, by not letting it grow proportionally to P. Or we can reduce the total number of directory entries, or *directory height*, by not having an entry per memory block.

Directory width is reduced by using what are called *limited pointer directories*, which are motivated by the earlier observation that most of the time only a few caches have a copy of a block when the block is written. Limited pointer schemes therefore do not store yes or no information for all nodes but simply maintain a fixed number of pointers (say, i), each pointing to a node that currently caches a copy of the block (Agarwal et al. 1988). Each pointer takes $\log P$ bits of storage for P nodes, but the number of pointers used is small. For example, for a machine with 1,024 nodes, each pointer needs 10 bits, so even having 100 pointers uses less storage than a full bit vector scheme. In practice, five or less pointers seem to suffice. Of course, these schemes need some kind of backup or overflow strategy for the situation when more than i readable copies are cached since they can keep track of only i copies precisely. One strategy is to resort to broadcasting invalidations to all nodes when there are more than i copies. Many other strategies have been developed to avoid broadcast even in these cases. Different limited pointer schemes differ primarily in their overflow strategies and in the number of pointers they use.

Directory height can be reduced by organizing the directory itself as a cache, taking advantage of the fact that since the total amount of cache in the machine is much smaller than the total amount of memory, only a very small fraction of the memory blocks will actually be present in caches at a given time, so most of the directory entries will be unused anyway (Gupta, Weber, and Mowry 1990; O'Krafka and Newton 1990). Section 8.10 discusses techniques reducing directory width and height in more detail.

Regardless of these storage-reducing optimizations, the basic approach to finding copies and communicating with them (protocol functions [2] and [3]) remains the same for the different flat, memory-based schemes. The identities of the sharers are maintained at the home and (at least when there is no overflow) the copies are communicated with by sending point-to-point transactions to each.

Flat, Cache-Based Directory Schemes

In flat, cache-based schemes, there is still a home main memory for the block; however, the directory entry at the home node does not contain the identities of all

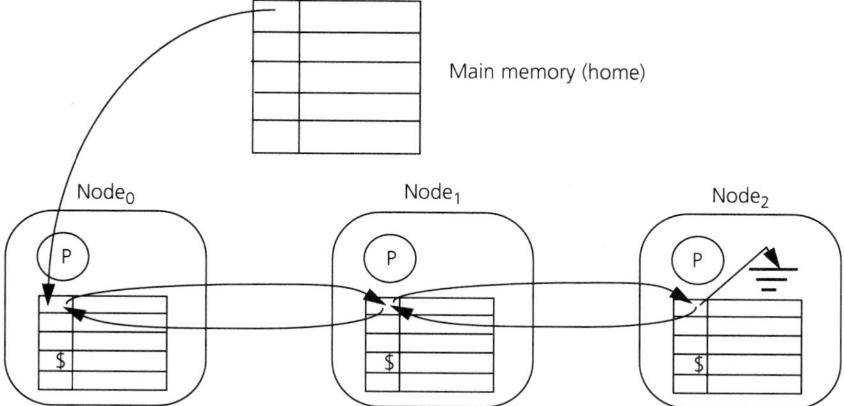

FIGURE 8.8 A doubly linked-list distributed directory organization. A cache line contains not only data and state for the block but also forward and backward pointers for the distributed linked list.

sharers but only a pointer to the first sharer in the list plus a few state bits. This pointer is called the *head pointer* for the block. The remaining nodes caching that block are joined together (using additional pointers that are associated with each cache line in a node) in a *distributed, doubly linked list*—that is, a cache that contains a copy of the block also contains pointers to the next and previous caches that have a copy, called the *forward* and *backward* pointers, respectively (see Figure 8.8).

On a read miss, the requesting node sends a network transaction to the home memory to find out the identity of the head node of the linked list, if any, for that block. If the head pointer is null (no current sharers), the home replies with the data. If the head pointer is not null, then the requestor must be added to the list of sharers. The home responds to the requestor with the head pointer. The requestor then sends a message to the head node, asking to be inserted at the head of the list and hence to become the new head node. The net effect is that the head pointer at the home now points to the requestor, the forward pointer of the requestor's own cache entry points to the old head node (which is now the second node in the linked list), and the backward pointer of the old head node points to the requestor. The data for the block is provided by the home if it has the latest copy or by the head node, which always has the latest copy (is the owner) otherwise.

On a write miss, the writer again obtains the identity of the head node, if any, from the home. It then inserts itself into the list as the head node as before (if the writer was already in the list as a sharer and is now performing an upgrade, it is deleted from its current position in the list and inserted as the new head). Following this, the rest of the distributed linked list is traversed node by node via network transactions to find and invalidate successive copies of the block. If a block that is written is shared by three nodes A, B, and C, the home only knows about A so the writer sends an invalidation message to it; the identity of the next sharer B can only be known once A is reached, and so on. Acknowledgments for these invalidations are sent to the writer. Once again, if the data for the block is needed by the writer, it is provided by either the home or the head node as appropriate. The number of messages per invalidating write—the bandwidth demand—is proportional to the number of sharers as in the memory-based schemes, but now so is the number of messages in the critical path, that is, the latency. Each of these serialized messages invokes the communication assist at its destination, increasing latency and overall assist occupancy further. In fact, even a read miss to a clean block involves the assists of three nodes to insert the node in the linked list.

Write backs or other replacements from the cache also require that the node delete itself from the sharing list, which means communicating with the nodes that are before and after it in the list. This is necessary because the new block that replaces the old one in the cache will need the forward and backward pointer slots of the cache entry for its own sharing list. Synchronization is required to avoid simultaneous replacement of adjacent nodes in the list, and the involvement of multiple nodes increases overall assist occupancy. An example cache-based protocol is described in more depth in Section 8.6.

To counter the latency and occupancy disadvantages, cache-based schemes have some important advantages over memory-based schemes. First, the directory overhead is small. Every block in main memory has only a single head pointer. The number of forward and backward pointers is proportional to the number of cache blocks in the machine, which is much smaller than the number of memory blocks. The second advantage is that a linked list records the order in which accesses were made to memory for the block, thus making it easier to provide fairness and to avoid livelock in a protocol (most memory-based schemes do not keep track of request order, as we will see). Third, the work to be done by assists in sending invalidations is not centralized at the home but rather distributed among sharers, thus perhaps spreading out assist occupancy and reducing the corresponding bandwidth demands placed on a particularly busy home assist.

Manipulating insertion in and deletion from distributed linked lists can lead to complex protocol implementations. For example, deleting a node from a sharing list requires careful coordination and mutual exclusion with processors ahead of and behind it in the linked list since those processors may also be trying to replace the same block concurrently. These complexity issues have been greatly alleviated by the formalization and publication of a standard for a cache-based directory organization and protocol: the IEEE 1596-1992 Scalable Coherent Interface (SCI) standard (Gustavson 1992). The standard includes a full specification and C code for the protocol. Several commercial machines use this protocol (e.g., Sequent NUMA-Q [Lovett and Clapp 1996], Convex Exemplar [Convex Computer Corporation 1993; Thekkath et al. 1997], and Data General [Clark and Alnes 1996]), and variants that use alternative list representations (singly linked lists instead of the doubly linked lists in SCI) have also been explored (Thapar and Delagi 1990). We shall examine the SCI protocol itself in more detail in Section 8.6 and so defer detailed discussion of advantages and disadvantages.

Summary of Directory Organization Alternatives

To summarize, there are many different ways to organize how directories store the cache state of memory blocks. Simple bit vector representations work well for machines that have a moderate number of nodes visible to the directory protocol. For larger machines, many alternatives are available to reduce the memory overhead. The organization chosen does, however, affect the complexity of the coherence protocol and the performance of the directory scheme against various sharing patterns. Hierarchical directories have not been popular on real machines, whereas machines with flat memory-based and cache-based (linked-list) directories have been built and used for some years now.

The next section quantitatively assesses the behavior of parallel programs and the implications for directory-based approaches as well as some important protocol and architectural trade-offs at this basic level.

8.3 ASSESSING DIRECTORY PROTOCOLS AND TRADE-OFFS

As in Chapter 5, this section uses a simulator to examine some relevant characteristics of applications that can inform architectural trade-offs but that cannot be measured on real machines. Issues such as three-state versus four-state or invalidation-based versus update protocols that were discussed in Chapter 5 are not revisited here. The focus is on invalidation-based protocols, since update protocols have an additional disadvantage in scalable machines: useless updates incur a separate network transaction for each destination rather than a single bus transaction that is snooped by all caches. In addition, update-based protocols make it much more difficult to preserve the desired memory consistency model in directory-based systems. This section quantifies the distribution of invalidation patterns in directory protocols, examines how the distribution of traffic between local and remote changes as the number of processors is increased for a fixed problem size, and revisits the impact of cache block size on traffic. In all cases, the experiments assume a memory-based flat directory protocol. Two changes are made from the experiments in Chapter 5. Since Radix sorting would exhibit a lot of false sharing at larger processor counts (our default here is 32 rather than 16 processors), we use a problem size of 1M rather than 256K keys. And we use 8-KB rather than 64-KB caches in all our smaller cache size experiments, to see the effect of even fewer working sets fitting in the cache.

8.3.1 Data Sharing Patterns for Directory Schemes

It was claimed earlier that the number of invalidations that need to be sent out on a write is usually small, which makes directories especially valuable and can reduce directory storage overhead without hurting performance. This subsection quantifies that claim for our parallel application case studies. It also develops a framework for categorizing data structures in terms of sharing patterns and understanding how the invalidation patterns scale, and explains the behavior of the application case studies in light of this framework. The simulated protocol assumes only the three basic cache states (MSI) for simplicity.

Sharing Patterns for Application Case Studies

For invalidation-based directory protocols, it is important to understand two aspects of an application's data sharing patterns: (1) the frequency with which processors issue writes that may require invalidating other copies (i.e., writes to data that is not in modified state in the writer's cache in an MSI protocol, or *invalidating writes*), called the *invalidation frequency*; and (2) the distribution of the number of invalidations (sharers) needed upon these writes, called the *invalidation size distribution*. Directory schemes are particularly advantageous if the average invalidation size is small and the frequency is significant enough that using broadcast all the time would indeed be a performance problem. Figure 8.9 shows the invalidation size distributions for our parallel application case studies running on 64-node systems (one processor per node) for the default problem sizes presented in Chapter 4. Infinite per-processor caches are used in these simulations to capture inherent sharing patterns. With finite caches, replacement hints sent to the directory may turn off presence bits and reduce the number of invalidations sent on writes in some cases (though traffic will not be reduced since the replacement hints have to be sent). A write may send zero invalidations in an MSI protocol if the block was loaded in shared state but there are currently no other sharers. This would not happen with infinite caches in a MESI protocol. With infinite caches, invalidation frequency is proportional to the communication-to-computation ratio.

It is clear that the invalidation sizes are usually small, indicating both that directories are indeed likely to be very useful in containing traffic and that it is not necessary for the directory to maintain a presence bit per processor in a flat memory-based scheme. The nonzero frequencies of very large invalidation sizes are usually due to synchronization variables, where many processors spin on a variable and one processor writes it, invalidating them all. We are interested not just in the results for a given problem size and number of processors but also in how they scale. The communication-to-computation ratios discussed in Chapter 4 give us a good idea about how the frequency of invalidating writes should scale. For the size distributions, we can appeal to our understanding of applications and their usage of data structures (and validate with experiments), which can also help explain the basic results observed in Figure 8.9.

A Framework for Sharing Patterns

Data access patterns in applications can be categorized in many ways: predictable versus unpredictable, regular versus irregular, coarse-grained versus fine-grained (or contiguous versus noncontiguous in the address space), near-neighbor versus long-range in an interconnection topology, and so on. For understanding invalidation patterns, the relevant categories are read-only, producer-consumer, migratory, and irregular read-write. (A similar categorization can be found in [Gupta and Weber 1992].)

- *Read-only.* Read-only data structures are never written once they have been initialized. There are no invalidating writes, so data in this category is not an issue for directories. Examples include program code and the scene data in the Raytrace application.

- *Producer-consumer.* A processor produces (writes) a data item, then one or more processors consume (read) it, then a processor produces it again, and so on. Flag-based synchronization is an example, as is the near-neighbor sharing in an iterative grid computation. The producer may be the same process every time or it may change; for example, in a branch-and-bound algorithm, the bound variable may be written by different processes as they find improved bounds. The invalidation size for this category is determined by how many consumers there have been each time the producer writes the value. We can have situations with one consumer, all processes being consumers, or a few processes being consumers. These situations may have different frequencies and scaling properties, although for most applications either the size does not scale quickly with the number of processors or the frequency has been found to be low.[1]
- *Migratory.* Migratory data bounces around, or migrates, from one processor to another, being written (and usually read) by each processor to which it bounces. An example is a global sum, into which different processes add their partial sums. Each time a processor writes the variable, only the previous writer has a copy (since it invalidated the previous "owner" when it did its write); so only a single invalidation is generated upon a write, regardless of the number of processors used.
- *Irregular read-write.* This corresponds to irregular or unpredictable read and write access patterns to data by different processes. A simple example is a distributed task-queue system. Processes will probe (read) the head pointer of a task queue when they are looking for work to steal, and this head pointer will be written when a task is added at the head. These and other irregular patterns usually lead to wide-ranging invalidation size distributions, but in most observed applications the frequency concentration tends to be very much toward the small end of the spectrum (see the Radiosity example in Figure 8.9).

---

1. Examples of the producer-consumer size distribution not scaling up are the noncorner border elements in a near-neighbor regular grid partition and the key permutations in Radix. They lead to an invalidation size of one, which does not increase with the number of processors or the problem size. Examples of all processes being consumers (invalidation size $p - 1$) are a global energy variable that is read by all processes during a time-step of a physical simulation and then written by one at the end or a synchronization variable on which all processes spin. While the invalidation size here is large, such writes fortunately tend to happen very infrequently in real applications. Finally, examples of a few processes being consumers are the corner elements of a grid partition or the flags used for tree-based synchronization. This leads to an invalidation size of a few, which may or may not scale with the number of processors (it doesn't in these two examples).

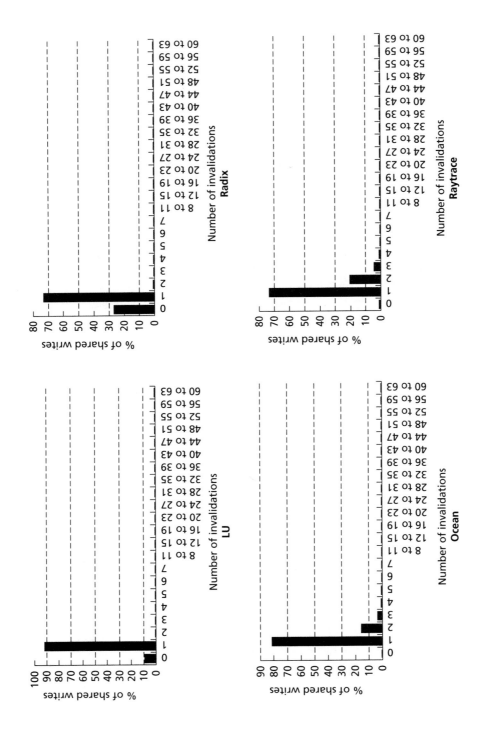

FIGURE 8.9 Invalidation patterns with default data sets and 64 processors

(continued)

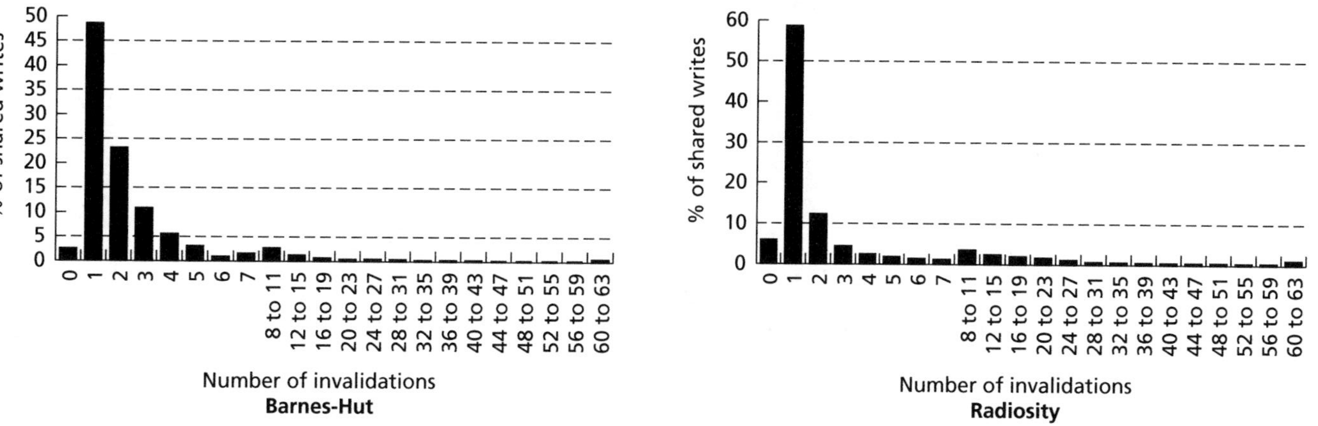

FIGURE 8.9 Invalidation patterns with default data sets and 64 processors. The *x*-axis shows the invalidation size (number of active sharers) upon an invalidating write, and the *y*-axis shows the percentage of invalidating writes whose size takes that *x*-axis value. The invalidation size distribution was measured by simulating a full bit vector directory representation and recording for every invalidating write how many presence bits (other than the writer's) are set when the write occurs. The data is averaged over all the 64 processors used.

Applying the Framework to the Application Case Studies

Let us now look briefly at each of the applications in Figure 8.9 to interpret the results in light of these four sharing patterns and to understand how the size distributions might scale.

In the LU factorization program, when a block is written it has previously been read only by the same processor that is doing the writing (the process to which it is assigned). This means that no other processor should have a cached copy, and zero invalidations should be sent. Once it is written, it is read by several other processes and no longer written further. The reason that we see one invalidation being sent in the figure is that the matrix is initialized by a single process; particularly with the infinite caches we use, that process has a copy of the entire matrix in its cache and will be invalidated the first time another processor does a write to a block. An insignificant number of invalidating writes invalidates all processes, which is due to some global variables and not the main matrix data structure. Scaling the problem size or the number of processors does not change the invalidation size distribution for the matrix but only for the global variables. Of course, the invalidation frequencies do change with scaling, just like the communication-to-computation ratio.

In the Radix sorting kernel, invalidations are sent in two producer-consumer situations. In the permutation phase, the word or block written has been read since the last write only by the process to which that key is assigned, so at most a single invalidation is sent out. The same key position in the destination array may be written by different processes in different outer loop iterations of the sort; however, in each iteration there is only one reader of a key, so even this infrequent case generates only two invalidations (one to the reader and one to the previous writer). If there is false sharing, all sharers are writing the block, so there is only one invalidation each time. The other situation that generates invalidations is the histogram accumulation, which is done in a tree-structured fashion and usually leads to a small number of invalidations at a time. These invalidations to multiple sharers are clearly very infrequent. In Radix too, increasing the problem size does not change the invalidation size in either phase (though it may change the relative invalidation frequencies in the two phases), whereas increasing the number of processors increases the sizes but only in some infrequent parts of the histogram accumulation phase. The dominant pattern by far remains 0 or 1 invalidations.

The nearest-neighbor, producer-consumer communication pattern on a regular grid in Ocean leads to most of the invalidations being sent to 0 or 1 processes (at the borders of a partition). At partition corners, more frequently encountered in the multigrid equation solver, two or three sharers may need to be invalidated. This does not grow with problem size or number of processors. At the highest levels of the multigrid hierarchy, the border elements of a few processors' partitions might fall on the same cache block, causing four or five sharers to be invalidated. There are also some global accumulator variables, which display a migratory sharing pattern (1 invalidation), and a couple of very infrequently used one-producer, all-consumer global variables (other than synchronization variables).

In Raytrace the dominant data structure is the scene data, which is read-only. The major read-write data consists of the image and the task queues. Each word in the image is written only once by one processor per frame. This leads to either 0 invalidations if the same processor writes a given image pixel in consecutive frames (as is usually the case) or 1 invalidation if different processors do, as might be the case when tasks are stolen or if there is write-write false sharing. The task queues themselves lead to the irregular read-write access patterns discussed earlier, with a wide-ranging distribution that is dominated in frequency by the low end (hence the very small nonzeros all along the *x*-axis in this case). Here too we find some infrequently written one-producer, all-consumer global variables.

In the Barnes-Hut application, the important data is the body and cell positions, the pointers used to link up the tree, and some global variables used as energy values. The position data is of the producer-consumer type. A given body's position is usually read by one or a few processors during the force calculation (tree traversal) phase. The positions (centers of mass) of the cells are read by many processes, the number increasing toward the root, which is read by all. This data thus causes a fairly wide range of invalidation sizes when it is written by its assigned processor in the update and tree construction phases that follow force calculation. The root and upper-level cells are responsible for invalidations being sent to all processors, but their frequency is quite small. The tree pointers are similar in their behavior to the cell centers of mass. The first write to a pointer in the tree-building phase invalidates the caches of the processors that read it in the previous force calculation phase; subsequent writes invalidate those processors that have read the pointer during the current tree-building phase, which is an irregularly sized but mostly small set of processors. As the number of processors is increased, the invalidation size distribution tends to shift to the right as more processors tend to read a given item, but the shift is slow and the dominant invalidations are still to a small number of processors. The reverse effect (also slow) is observed when the number of bodies is increased.

Finally, the Radiosity application has very irregular access patterns to many different types of data, including data that describes the scene (patches and elements) and the task queues. The resulting invalidation patterns show a wide distribution; however, even here the greatest frequency by far is concentrated toward 0 to 2 invalidations. Many of the accesses to the scene data behave in a migratory way, as do a few counters, and a couple of global variables are one-producer, all-consumer.

The empirical data and categorization framework indicate that in most cases the invalidation size distribution is dominated by small numbers of invalidations. The common use of parallel machines as multiprogrammed compute servers for sequential or small-way parallel applications further limits the number of sharers (process migration usually leads to invalidations of size 1). Sharing patterns that cause large numbers of invalidations are empirically found to be very infrequent at run time. A possible exception is highly contended synchronization variables, which are usually handled specially by software or hardware, as we shall see. In addition to validating the directory-based approach and suggesting its potential for performance scalability, these results suggest that limited-pointer directory representations should be successful since the frequency of overflows will be small.

8.3.2 Local versus Remote Traffic

A key property for systems with distributed memory is how much of the traffic due to cache misses or protocol activity is kept within a node (local) rather than going on the interconnect (remote). For a given number of processors and machine organization, the fraction of traffic that is local depends on the problem size. However, it is instructive to examine how the traffic and its distribution change with the number of processors even when the problem size is held fixed (i.e., under PC scaling). Figure 8.10 shows the results for the default problem sizes, breaking down the remote traffic into various categories such as sharing (true or false), capacity, cold start, write back, and overhead. A MESI rather than MSI protocol is used in this and the next subsection. Overhead includes the fixed header sent across the network with each cache block of data as well as the traffic associated with protocol transactions like invalidations and acknowledgments that do not carry any data. This protocol traffic component is different from that on a bus-based machine: each individual point-to-point invalidation consumes traffic, and acknowledgments place traffic on the interconnect too. Traffic is shown in bytes per FLOP or bytes per instruction for different applications.

We can see that both local traffic and capacity-related remote traffic tend to decrease when the number of processors increases, due to both decrease in per-processor working sets and decrease in cold misses that are satisfied locally instead of remotely. However, sharing-related traffic increases as expected. In applications with small working sets, like Barnes-Hut, LU, and Radiosity, the fraction of capacity-related traffic is very small, at least beyond a couple of processors. In irregular applications like Barnes-Hut and Raytrace, most of the capacity-related traffic is remote, all the more so as the number of processors increases, since data cannot be distributed easily at page granularity for capacity misses to be satisfied locally. In cases like Ocean, the capacity-related traffic is substantial even with the large cache and is almost entirely local when pages are placed properly (which can be done quite easily with 4D array data structures). With round-robin placement of shared pages, we would have seen most of the local capacity misses in Ocean turn to remote ones.

When we use smaller caches to capture the realistic scenario of working sets not fitting in the cache in Ocean and Raytrace, capacity traffic becomes much larger. In Ocean, most of this traffic is still local due to good data distribution, and the trend for remote traffic versus number of processors doesn't change. Poor distribution of pages would have swamped the network with traffic, but with proper distribution, remote traffic is quite low. In Raytrace, however, the capacity-related traffic is mostly remote, and the fact that it now dominates changes the slope of the curve of total remote traffic compared to that with large caches, where sharing traffic dominates. Remote traffic still increases with the number of processors but much more slowly since the working set size and, hence, capacity miss rate does not depend as much on the number of processors as the sharing miss rate.

When a miss is satisfied remotely, whether it is satisfied at the home or it needs another message to obtain the data from a dirty node depends not only on whether it is a sharing miss or a capacity/conflict/cold miss but also on the size of the cache. In a small cache, dirty data may be replaced and written back, so a sharing miss by another processor may be satisfied at the home node rather than at the previously dirty node. For applications like Ocean that allow data to be placed easily in the memory of the node to which they are assigned (i.e., to be appropriately distributed for locality), it is often the case that only that node writes the data, so even if the data is found dirty, it is found so in a cache at the home node itself. The extent to which this is true depends on the data access patterns of the application, the granularity of data allocation in memory, and whether the data is indeed distributed properly by the program.

8.3.3 Cache Block Size Effects

The effects of block size on cache miss rates and bus traffic were assessed in Chapter 5, at least up to 16 processors. For miss rates, the trends beyond 16 processors extend quite naturally, except for threshold effects in the interaction of problem size, number of processors, and block size, as discussed in Chapter 4. This section examines the impact of block size on the components of local and remote traffic in machines with distributed memory.

Figure 8.11 shows how traffic scales with block size for 32-processor executions of the applications with 1-MB caches per processor. In Barnes-Hut, the overall traffic increases slowly until about a 64-byte block size and more rapidly thereafter primarily due to false sharing. However, the amount of traffic is small. Since the overhead per block moved through the network is fixed (as is the cost of invalidations and acknowledgments), the overhead component tends to shrink with increasing block size to the extent that there is spatial locality (i.e., if larger blocks reduce the number of blocks transferred). LU has perfect spatial locality, so the data traffic remains fixed as block size increases. Overhead is reduced, so overall traffic in fact shrinks with increasing block size. In Raytrace, the remote capacity traffic has poor spatial locality, so it grows quickly with block size. In both Barnes-Hut and Raytrace, the true sharing traffic has poor spatial locality too, as is the case in Ocean at column-oriented partition borders (spatial locality even on remote data is good at row-oriented borders). Finally, the graph for Radix clearly shows the impact of false sharing on remote traffic when it occurs past the threshold block size (here about 128 or 256 bytes). Results with smaller caches show the behavior of capacity misses playing a dominant role, as expected.

8.4 DESIGN CHALLENGES FOR DIRECTORY PROTOCOLS

Designing a correct, efficient directory protocol involves issues that are more complex and subtle than the simple organizational choices we have discussed so far, just as designing a bus-based protocol was more complex than choosing the number of states and drawing the state transition diagram for stable states. We had to deal with the nonatomicity of state transitions, split-transaction buses, serialization and ordering issues, deadlock, livelock, and starvation. Now that we understand the basics of

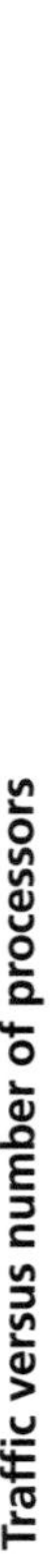

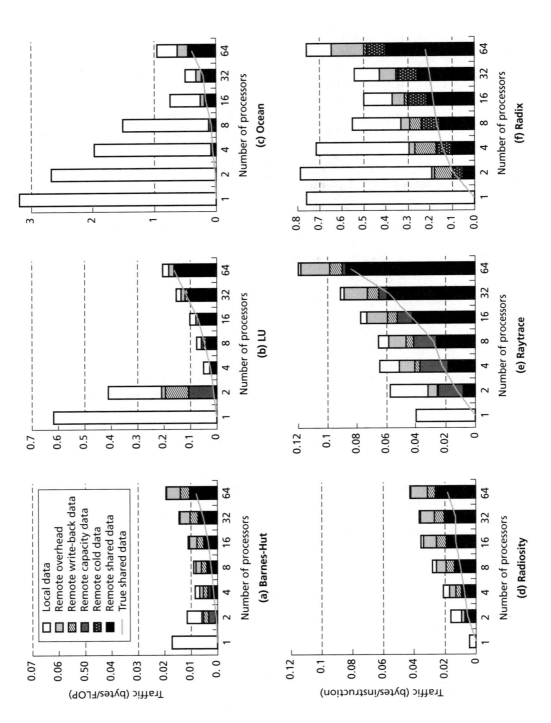

FIGURE 8.10 Traffic versus number of processors

(continued)

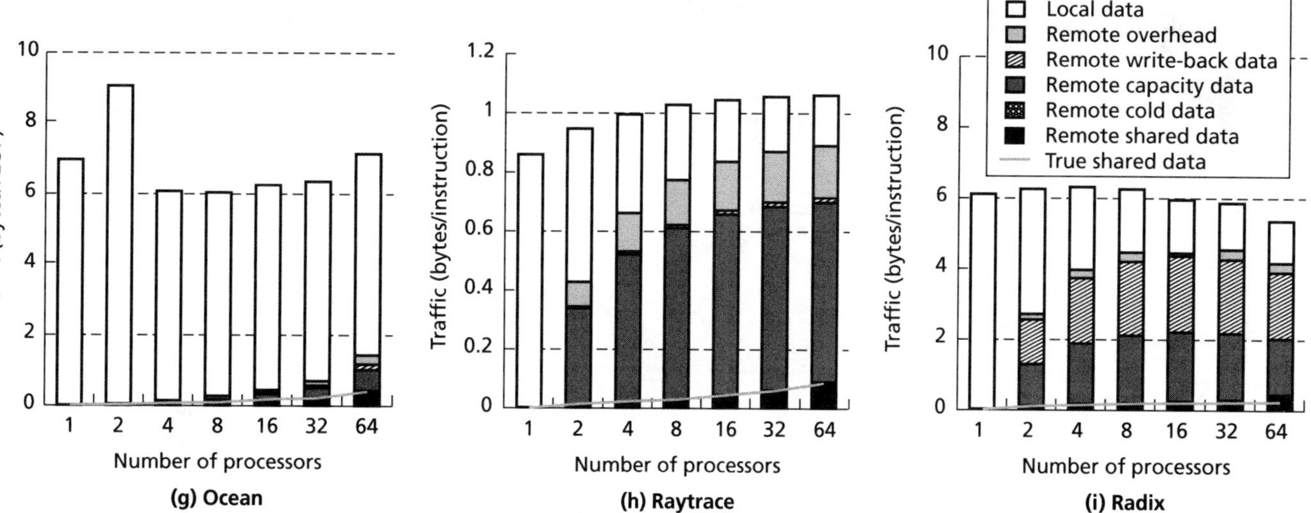

FIGURE 8.10 Traffic versus number of processors. The overhead per block transferred across the network is 8 bytes. No overhead is considered for local accesses. Graphs (a)–(f) assume 1-MB caches per processor and graphs (g)–(i), 8 KB. The caches have a 64-byte block size and are four-way set associative.

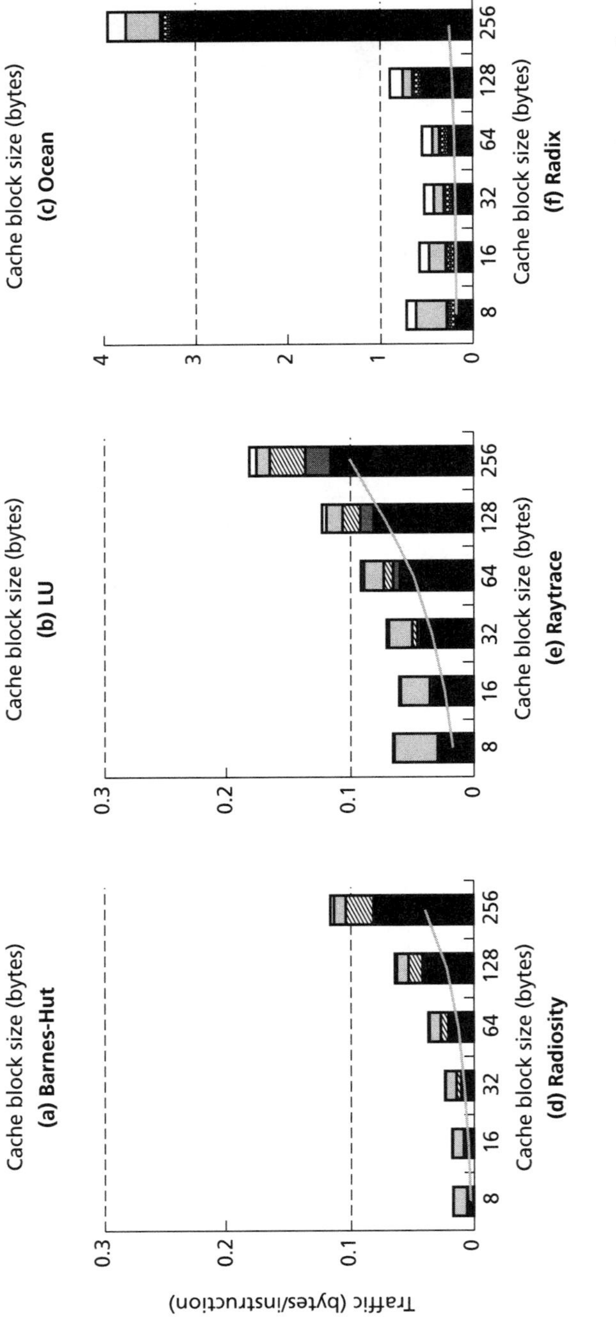

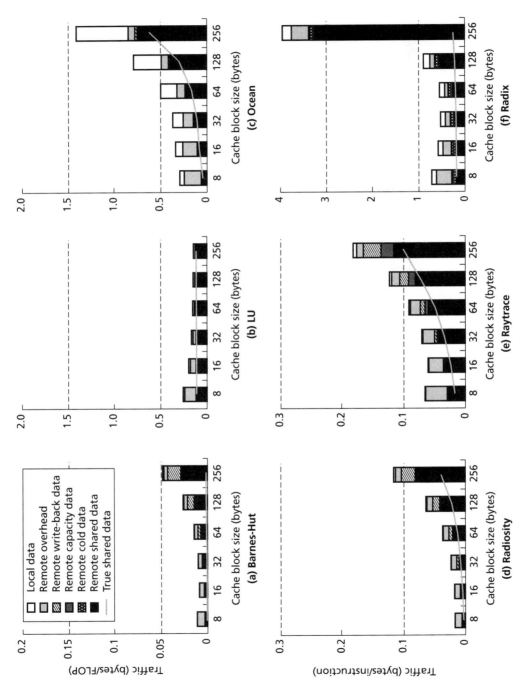

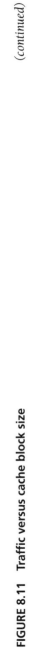

FIGURE 8.11 Traffic versus cache block size

(continued)

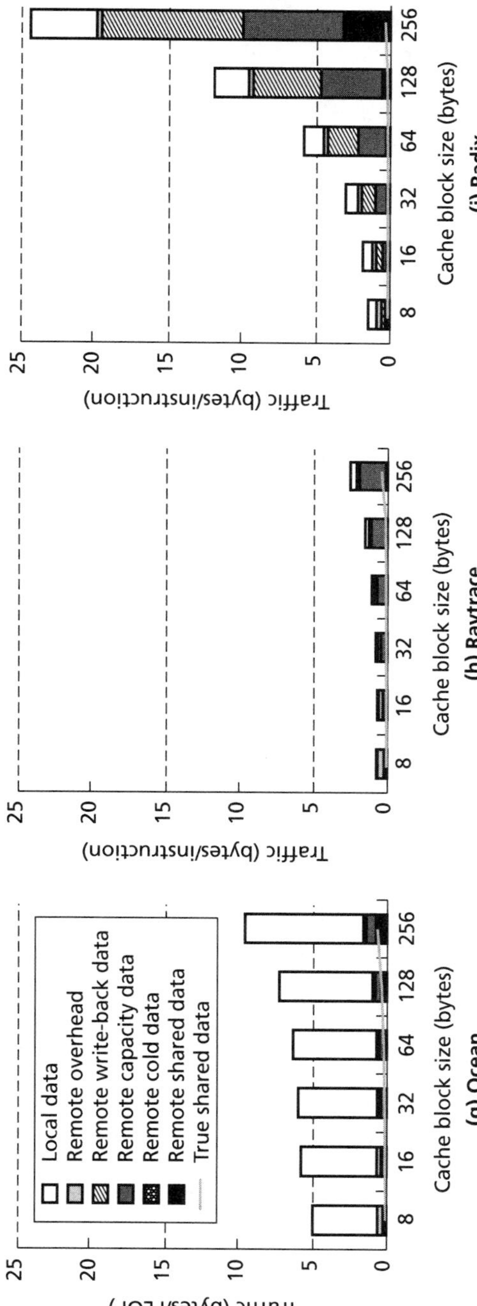

FIGURE 8.11 Traffic versus cache block size. Data are shown for 32-processor executions. The overhead per block transferred over the network is 8 bytes. No overhead is considered for local access. Graphs (a)–(f) show the data for 1-MB caches per processor and (g)–(i) for 8-KB caches. All caches are four-way set associative.

directories, we are ready to dive into these issues for them as well. This section discusses the new protocol-level design challenges that arise in correctly implementing directory protocols for high performance and identifies general techniques for addressing these challenges. In the next two sections, the techniques are specialized in the case studies of memory-based and cache-based directory protocols.

As always, the design challenges for scalable coherence protocols are to provide high performance while preserving correctness and to contain the complexity that results. Let us look at performance and correctness in turn, focusing on issues that were not already addressed for bus-based or noncaching systems. Since performance optimizations tend to increase concurrency and complicate correctness, let us examine them first.

8.4.1 Performance

The network transactions on which cache coherence protocols are built differ from those used in explicit message passing in two ways. First, they are automatically generated by the system—in particular, by the communication assists or controllers—in accordance with the protocol. Second, they are individually small, each carrying either a request, an acknowledgment, or a cache block of data plus some control bits. However, the basic performance model for network transactions developed in earlier chapters applies here as well. A typical network transaction incurs some overhead on the processor at its source (traversing the cache hierarchy on the way out and back in); some work or occupancy on the communication assists at its endpoints (typically looking up state, generating requests, or intervening in the cache); and some delay in the network due to transit latency, network bandwidth, and contention. Typically, the processor itself is not directly involved at the home, the dirty node, or the sharers but only at the requestor (although it may suffer at the other nodes as well due to contention).

It is useful to understand performance in terms of the layers of a multiprocessor system introduced earlier (Figure 8.2). The protocol layer of a system implements the programming model, using the network transactions provided by the communication abstraction. Thus, the protocol layer does not have much leverage on the basic communication costs of a single network transaction—transit latency, network bandwidth, assist occupancy, and processor overhead—but it can determine the number and structure of the network transactions needed to realize memory operations like reads and writes under different circumstances. In general, there are three classes of techniques for improving performance: (1) protocol optimizations, (2) high-level machine organization, and (3) hardware specialization to improve the basic communication parameters. The first two assume a fixed set of performance parameters for the communication architecture and are discussed in this section. The impact of varying the basic performance parameters will be examined in Section 8.7.

Protocol Optimizations

The two major performance goals at the protocol level are to reduce the number of network transactions generated per memory operation, which reduces the bandwidth demands placed on the network and the communication assists; and to reduce the number of actions, especially network transactions, that are on the critical path of the processor, thus reducing uncontended latency. The latter can be done by overlapping the transactions needed for a memory operation as much as possible. To some extent, protocol design can also help reduce the endpoint assist occupancy per transaction—especially when the assists are programmable—which reduces both uncontended latency as well as endpoint contention. The traffic, latency, and occupancy characteristics should not scale up quickly with the number of processing nodes used and should perform gracefully under pathological conditions like hot spots.

As we have seen, the manner in which directory information is stored determines the number of network transactions in the critical path of a memory operation. For example, a memory-based protocol can issue invalidations in an overlapped manner from the home whereas, in a cache-based protocol, the distributed list must be walked by network transactions to learn the identities of the sharers. However, even within a class of protocols, there are many ways to improve performance.

Consider a read miss to a remotely allocated block that is dirty in a third node in a flat, memory-based protocol. The strict request-response option described earlier is shown in Figure 8.12(a). The home responds to the requestor with a message containing the identity of the owner node. The requestor then sends a request to the owner, which replies to it with the data (the owner also sends a "revision" message to the home, which updates memory with the data and sets the directory state to be shared).

There are four network transactions in the critical path for the read operation and five transactions in all. One way to reduce these numbers is *intervention forwarding*. In this case, the home does not respond to the requestor but simply forwards the request as an intervention transaction to the owner, asking it to retrieve the block from its cache. An intervention is just like a request but is issued in reaction to a request and is directed at a cache rather than memory (it is similar to an invalidation in this sense but also seeks data from the cache). The owner then replies to the home with the data or an acknowledgment (if the block is in exclusive rather than modified state), at which time the home updates its directory state and replies to the requestor with the data (Figure 8.12[b]). Intervention forwarding reduces the total number of transactions needed to four, reducing bandwidth needs, but all four are still in the critical path. A more aggressive method is *reply forwarding* (Figure 8.12[c]). Here too, the home forwards the intervention message to the owner node, but the intervention contains the identity of the requestor and the owner replies directly to the requestor itself. The owner also sends a revision message to the home so that the memory and directory can be updated, but this message is not in the critical path of the read miss. This keeps the number of transactions at four but reduces

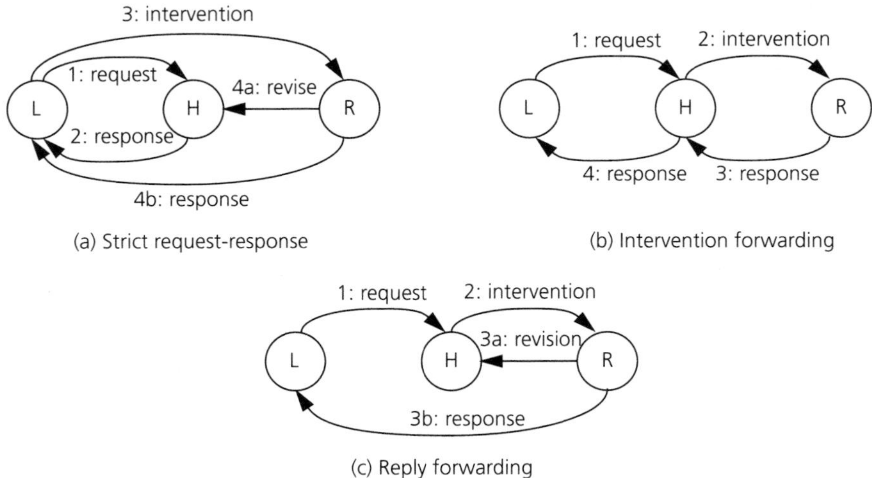

FIGURE 8.12 Reducing latency in a flat, memory-based protocol through forwarding. The case shown is of a read request to a block in exclusive state. L represents the local or requesting node, H is the home for the block, and R is the remote owner node that has the exclusive copy of the block.

the number in the critical path to three (request → intervention → reply-to-requestor); it is, therefore, called a *three-message miss*. Notice that with either of intervention forwarding or reply forwarding the protocol is no longer strictly request-response since a request to the home generates another request (to the owner node, which in turn generates a response). This can complicate deadlock avoidance, as we shall see later.

Besides being only intermediate in its latency and traffic characteristics, intervention forwarding has the disadvantage that outstanding intervention requests are kept track of at the home rather than at the requestor, since responses to the interventions are sent to the home. Because requests that cause interventions may come from any of the nodes, the home node must keep track of up to $k*P$ interventions at a time, where k is the number of outstanding requests allowed per node. A requestor, on the other hand, would only have to keep track of at most k outstanding interventions. Reply forwarding does not require the home to keep track of outstanding requests and also has better performance characteristics, so systems prefer to use it. Similar forwarding techniques can be used to reduce latency in cache-based schemes at the cost of strict request-response simplicity, as shown in Figure 8.13.

In addition to forwarding, other protocol optimizations to reduce latency include overlapping transactions and activities by performing them speculatively. For example, when a request arrives at the home, the assist can read the data from memory in parallel with the directory lookup, in the hope that in most cases the block will indeed be clean at the home. If the directory lookup indicates that the block is dirty in some cache, then the memory access is wasted and must be ignored. Finally, pro-

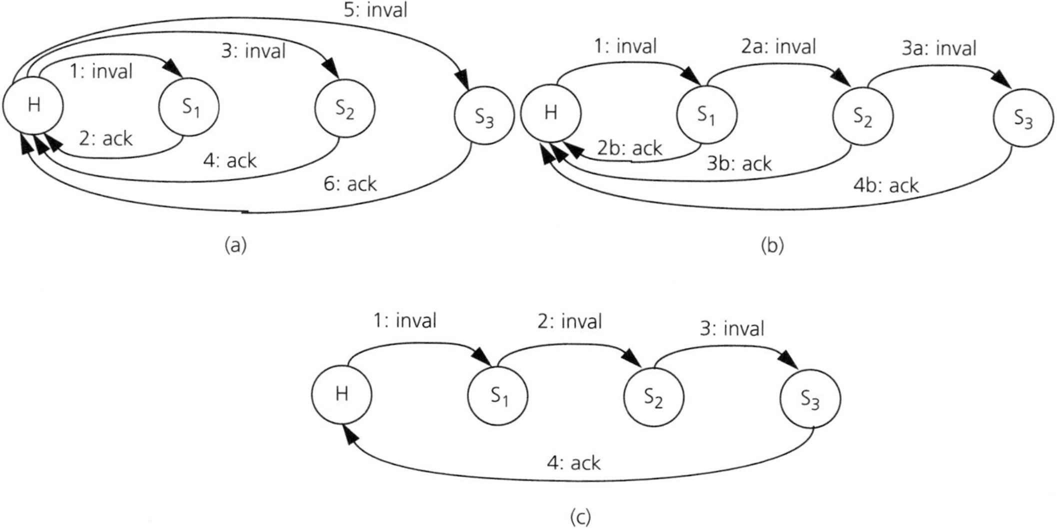

FIGURE 8.13 Reducing latency in a flat, cache-based protocol. In this scenario, invalidations are sent from the home H to the sharers S_i on a write operation. In the strict request-response case (a), every node includes in its acknowledgment (response) the identity of the next sharer on the list, and the home then sends that sharer an invalidation. The total number of transactions in the invalidation sequence is $2s$, where s is the number of sharers and all are in the critical path. In (b), each invalidated node forwards the invalidation to the next sharer and in parallel sends an acknowledgment to the home. The total number of transactions is still $2s$, but only $s + 1$ are in the critical path. In (c), only the last sharer on the list sends a single acknowledgment telling the home that the sequence is done. The total number of transactions is $s + 1$. (b) and (c) are not strict request-response cases.

tocols may also automatically detect common sharing patterns to which the standard invalidation-based protocol is not ideally suited and adjust themselves at run time to interact better with these patterns (see Exercises 8.9 and 8.10).

High-Level Machine Organization

Machine organization can interact with the protocol to help improve performance as well. For example, the use of large tertiary caches within a node can reduce the number of protocol transactions generated by artifactual communication. For a fixed total number of processors, using multiprocessor rather than uniprocessor nodes in a two-level organization may be useful as well.

The potential advantages of a two-level organization are in both cost and performance. On the cost side, certain fixed per-node costs may be amortized among the processors within a node, and it is possible to use existing SMPs that may themselves be commodity parts. On the performance side, advantages may arise from sharing characteristics that reduce the number of accesses that involve the directory protocol and generate network transactions across nodes. If one processor brings a block of data into its cache, another processor in the same node may be able to satisfy its miss to that block (for the same or a different word) more quickly through the local protocol using cache-to-cache sharing, especially if the block is allocated remotely. Requests may also be combined: if one processor has a request outstanding to the directory protocol for a block, another processor's request within the same SMP can be combined with, and obtain the data from, the first processor's response, reducing latency, network traffic, and potential hot spot contention. These advantages are similar to those of full hierarchical approaches and of shared caches. In fact, within an SMP, processors may even share a cache at some level of the hierarchy, in which case all the trade-offs for shared caches discussed in Chapter 6 apply. With fewer nodes, more of the main memory is local as well. Finally, cost and performance characteristics may be improved by using a hierarchy of packaging technologies appropriately.

Of course, the extent to which the two-level sharing hierarchy can be exploited depends on the locality in the sharing and data access patterns of applications, how well processes are mapped to processors in the hierarchy, and the cost difference between communicating within a node and across nodes. For example, applications that have wide but physically localized read-only sharing in a phase of computation, like the Barnes-Hut galaxy simulation, can benefit significantly from cache-to-cache sharing if the miss rates are high to begin with. Applications that exhibit nearest-neighbor sharing (like Ocean) can also have most of their accesses satisfied within a multiprocessor node if processes are mapped properly to nodes. However, although some processes may have all their accesses satisfied within their node, others will have accesses along at least one border satisfied remotely, so load imbalances will result and the benefits of the hierarchy will be diminished (performance will be limited by that of the most penalized processor). In all-to-all communication patterns, the savings in inherent communication is more modest. Instead of communicating with $p - 1$ remote processors in a p-processor system, a processor now communicates with $k - 1$ local processors and $p - k$ remote ones (where k is the number of processors within a node), a savings of at most $(p - k)/(p - 1)$ in internode communication. Finally, with several processes sharing a main memory unit, it may also be easier to distribute data appropriately among processors at page granularity. Some of these trade-offs and application characteristics are explored quantitatively in (Weber 1993; Erlichson et al. 1995). Of our two case study machines, the Sequent NUMA-Q uses four-processor, bus-based, cache-coherent SMPs as the nodes. The SGI Origin takes an interesting position: two processors share a bus and memory (and a board) to amortize cost, but they are not kept coherent by a snoopy protocol on the bus; rather, a single directory protocol keeps all caches in the machine coherent.

Compared to using uniprocessor nodes, the major potential disadvantage of using multiprocessor nodes is the sharing of communication resources by processors within a node. When processors share a bus, an assist, or a network interface, they amortize its cost but compete for its bandwidth. If their bandwidth demands are not reduced much by locality in sharing patterns, the resulting contention can hurt performance. The solution is to increase the throughput of these resources as well when processors are added to the node, but this compromises the cost advantages. Sharing a bus within a node has some particular disadvantages. First, if the bus has to accommodate several processors, it becomes longer and is not likely to be contained in a single board or other packaging unit. These effects slow the bus down, increasing the latency to both local and remote data. Second, if the bus supports snooping coherence within the node, a request that must be satisfied remotely typically has to wait for local snoop results to be reported before it is sent out to the network, causing unnecessary delays. Third, with a snooping bus at the remote node too, many references that do go remote will require snoops and data transfers on the local bus as well as the remote bus, increasing latency and reducing effective data access bandwidth. Finally, snooping accesses second-level cache tags, which may cause unnecessary contention with processor accesses if the snoops are not often successful in achieving cache-to-cache sharing. Nonetheless, several directory-based systems use snoop-based coherent multiprocessors as their individual nodes (Lenoski et al. 1993; Lovett and Clapp 1996; Clark and Alnes 1996; Weber et al. 1997).

The final approach to improving protocol performance—improving the performance parameters of the communication architecture—is discussed in Section 8.7.

8.4.2 Correctness

As with snoop-based systems, correctness considerations can be divided into three classes. First, the protocol must ensure that the relevant blocks are invalidated/updated and retrieved as needed and that the necessary state transitions occur. We can assume this happens in all cases and not consider it much further. Second, the serialization and ordering relationships defined by coherence and the consistency model must be preserved. Third, the protocol and implementation must be free from deadlock, livelock, and, ideally, starvation. Several aspects of scalable protocols and systems complicate the latter two sets of issues beyond what we have seen for bus-based cache-coherent machines or scalable noncoherent machines. There are two basic problems. First, we now have multiple cached copies of a block but no single agent that can see all relevant transactions and serialize them. Second, with many processors, a large number of requests may be directed toward a single node, accentuating the input buffer problem discussed in Chapter 7. These problems are aggravated by the high latencies in the system, which push us to exploit protocol optimizations of the sort discussed previously; these optimizations allow more transactions to be in progress simultaneously and do not preserve a strict request-response nature, further complicating correctness. This subsection describes the major new issues and types of solutions that are commonly employed in each area of correctness. Some specific solutions used in the case study protocols are discussed in more detail in subsequent sections.

Serialization to a Location for Coherence

Recall the write serialization clause of coherence. Not only must a given processor be able to construct a serial order out of all the operations to a given location—at least out of all write operations and its own read operations—but all processors must see the writes to a given location as having happened in the same order.

One mechanism we need for serialization is an entity that sees the necessary memory operations to a given location from different processors (the operations that are not contained entirely within a processing node) and determines their serialization. In a bus-based system, operations from different processors are serialized by the order in which their requests appear on the bus. In a distributed system that does not cache shared data, the consistent serializer for a location is the main memory that is the home of a location. For example, the order in which writes become visible to all processors is the order in which they reach the memory, and which write's value a read sees is determined by when that read reaches the memory. In a distributed system with coherent caching, the home memory is again a likely candidate for the entity that determines serialization to a given location, at least in a flat directory scheme, since all relevant operations first come to the home. If the home could satisfy all requests itself, then it could simply process them one by one in FIFO order of arrival and determine serialization. However, with multiple copies, visibility of an operation to the home does not imply visibility to all processors. It is easy to construct scenarios where processors may see operations to a location appear to be serialized in different orders than that in which the requests reached the home, as well as where different processors see operations complete in different orders.

As a simple example, consider an update-based protocol and a network that does not preserve point-to-point order of transactions between the same endpoints. If two write requests for shared data arrive at the home in one order, the updates they generate may arrive at the copies in different orders. As another example, suppose a block is in modified state in a dirty node and two nodes issue read-exclusive requests for it in an invalidation-based protocol. In a strict request-response protocol, the home will provide the requestors with the identity of the dirty node, and they will send requests to it. However, with different requestors, even in a network that preserves point-to-point order there is no guarantee that the requests will reach the dirty node in the same order as they reached the home. Which entity provides the globally consistent serialization in this case, and how is this orchestrated when multiple operations for this block may be simultaneously in flight and potentially needing service from different nodes?

Several types of solutions can be used to ensure serialization to a location. Most of them use additional directory states called *busy states* or *pending states*. A block being in busy state at the directory indicates that a previous request that came to the home for that block is still in progress and has not been completed. When a new request comes to the home and finds the directory state to be busy, serialization may be provided by one of the following mechanisms.

- *Buffer at the home.* The request may be buffered at the home as a pending request until the previous request that is in progress for the block has completed, regardless of whether the previous request was forwarded to a dirty node or whether a strict request-response protocol was used (the home should, of course, process requests for other blocks in the meantime). This method ensures that requests will be serviced everywhere in FIFO order of their arrival at the home, but it reduces concurrency. It also requires that the home be notified when a write has completed or, more commonly, when the home's involvement with the write is over. Finally, it increases the danger of the input buffer at the home overflowing since this buffer holds pending requests for all blocks for which it is the home. One strategy in this case is to let the input buffer overflow into main memory, thus providing effectively infinite buffering as long as there is enough main memory and avoiding potential deadlock problems. This scheme is used in the MIT Alewife prototype (Agarwal et al. 1995).

- *Buffer at the requestors.* Pending requests may be buffered not at the home but at the requestors themselves, by constructing a distributed linked list of pending requests. This is a natural extension of a cache-based approach, which already has the support for distributed linked lists. It is used in the SCI protocol (Gustavson 1992; IEEE Computer Society 1993). Now the number of pending requests that a node may need to keep track of is small and determined only by the node itself.
- *NACK and retry.* An incoming request may be NACKed by the home (i.e., a negative acknowledgment sent to the requestor) rather than buffered when the directory state is busy. The request will be retried later by the requestor's assist and will be serialized in the order in which it is actually accepted by the directory (attempts that are NACKed do not enter in the serialization order). This is the approach used in the Origin2000 (Laudon and Lenoski 1997).
- *Forward to the dirty node.* If the directory state is busy because a request has been forwarded to a dirty node, subsequent requests for that block are not buffered at the home or NACKed. Rather, they too are forwarded to the dirty node, which determines their serialization. The order of serialization is thus determined by the home node when the block is clean at the home and by the order in which requests reach the dirty node when the block is dirty. If the block in the dirty node leaves the dirty state before a forwarded request reaches it (for example, due to a write back or a previous forwarded request), the request may be NACKed by the dirty node and retried. It will be serialized at the home or a dirty node when the retry is successful. This approach was used in the Stanford DASH protocol (Lenoski et al. 1990; Lenoski et al. 1993).

Unfortunately, with multiple copies in a distributed network, simply identifying a serializing entity is not enough. The problem is that the home or serializing agent may know (or be informed) when its involvement with a request is done, but this does not mean that the request has completed with respect to other nodes. Some transactions for the next request to that block may reach other nodes and perform with respect to them before some remaining transactions for the previous request. We see concrete examples and solutions in our case study protocols in Sections 8.5 and 8.6. Essentially, these show that, in addition to the system providing a global serializing entity for a block, individual nodes (e.g., requestors) should also preserve a local serialization with respect to each block; for example, they should not apply an incoming transaction to a block while they still have a transaction outstanding for that block.

Serialization across Locations for Sequential Consistency

Recall the two most interesting components of preserving the sufficient conditions for satisfying sequential consistency (SC): detecting write completion (needed to preserve program order) and ensuring write atomicity. In a bus-based machine, we saw that the restricted nature of the interconnect allows the requestor to detect write completion early; the write commits and can be acknowledged to the processor as soon as it obtains access to the bus, without waiting for it to actually invalidate or update other caches (Chapter 6). By providing a centralized path through which all transactions pass and ensuring FIFO ordering in the visibility of new data values beyond that path, a bus-based system also makes write atomicity quite natural to ensure.

In a machine that has a distributed network but does not cache shared data, detecting the completion of a write requires an explicit acknowledgment from the memory that holds the location (Chapter 7). In fact, the acknowledgment can be generated early, once we know the write has reached that node and been inserted in a FIFO queue to memory; at this point, the write has committed since it is clear that all subsequent reads that enter the queue will no longer see the old value, and we can use commitment as a substitute for completion to preserve program order. Write atomicity falls out naturally: a write is visible only when it reaches main memory, and at that point it is visible to all processors.

With both multiple copies and a distributed network, it is difficult to assume write completion before the invalidations or updates have actually reached all the nodes. A write cannot be acknowledged to the requestor once it has reached the home and be assumed to have effectively completed. The reason is that a subsequent write *Y* in program order may be issued by the same requestor after receiving such an acknowledgment for a previous write *X*, but *Y* may become visible to another processor before *X*, thus violating SC. This may happen because the invalidation or update transactions corresponding to *Y* take a different path through the network or because the network does not provide point-to-point order. Completion, or commitment, can only be assumed once explicit acknowledgments are received from all copies. Of course, a node with a copy can generate the acknowledgment as soon as it receives the invalidation—before it is actually applied to the caches—as long as it guarantees the appropriate ordering within its cache hierarchy (just as commitment is used instead of completion in Chapter 6). To satisfy the sufficient conditions for SC, a processor may wait after issuing a write until all acknowledgments for that write have been received and only then proceed past the write to a subsequent memory operation.

Write atomicity is similarly difficult when there are multiple copies and a distributed interconnect. To see this, Figure 8.14 shows how the semantics assumed by an example code fragment from Chapter 5 (Figure 5.11) that relies on write atomicity can be violated. The constraints of sequential consistency have to be satisfied by orchestrating network transactions appropriately. A common solution for write atomicity in an invalidation-based scheme is for the current owner of a block (the main

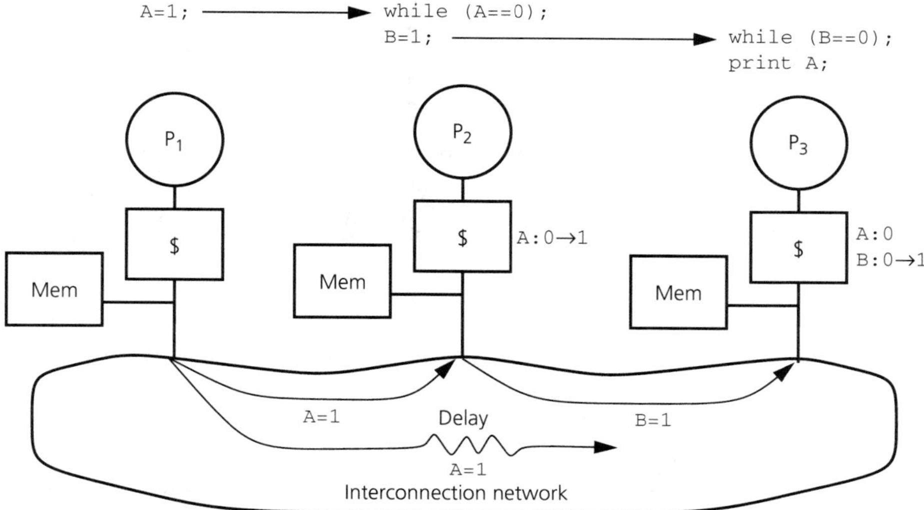

FIGURE 8.14 Violation of write atomicity in a scalable system with caches. The figure shows three processors and the code fragments that they execute. Assume that the network preserves point-to-point order and every cache starts out with copies of A and B initialized to 0. Transactions to look up directories and to satisfy read misses are ignored for simplicity. Under SC, we expect P_3 to print 1 as the value of A. However, P_2 sees the new value of A and jumps out of its while loop to write B even before it knows whether the previous write of A by P_1 has become visible to P_3. This write of B becomes visible to P_3 before the write of A by P_1, because the invalidation or update corresponding to the latter was delayed in a congested part of the network (that the other transactions did not have to go through at all). Thus, P_3 reads the new value of B but the old value of A, yielding a nonintuitive result.

memory module or the processor holding the dirty copy in its cache) to provide the appearance of atomicity by not allowing access to the new value by any process until all invalidation acknowledgments for the write that generated that value have returned. Thus, no processor can see the new value until it is visible to all processors. Maintaining the appearance of atomicity is much more difficult for update-based protocols since the data is sent to the sharers and, hence, is accessible immediately. Ensuring that no sharer reads the value until it is visible to all sharers requires a two-phase interaction. In the first phase, the copies of that memory block are updated in all relevant processors' caches, but those processors are prohibited from accessing the new value. In the second phase, after the first phase is known to have completed through acknowledgments as above, those processors are sent messages that allow them to use the new value. This difficulty and its performance implications help to make update protocols less attractive for scalable directory-based machines than for bus-based machines.

Deadlock

In Chapter 7, we discussed an important source of potential deadlock in request-response protocols such as those of a shared address space: the filling up of a finite input buffer. Three solutions were proposed for buffer deadlock:

1. Provide enough buffer space, either by buffering requests at the requestors using distributed linked lists or by providing enough input buffer space (in hardware or main memory) for the maximum number of possible incoming transactions.
2. Use NACKs.
3. Provide separate request and response networks, whether physically separate or multiplexed with separate buffers, to prevent backups in the potentially poorly behaved request network from blocking the progress of well-behaved response transactions.

Two separate networks would suffice in a protocol that is strictly request-response; that is, in which all transactions can be separated into requests and responses such that a request transaction generates only a response (or nothing) and a response generates no further transactions (and is, in this sense, better behaved since it does not generate further dependences). However, we have seen that in the interest of performance many practical coherence protocols use forwarding and are not always strictly request-response, breaking the deadlock avoidance assumption. In general, we need as many networks (physical or virtual) as the longest chain of different transaction types needed to complete a given operation so that the transaction at the end of a chain (that does not generate further transactions) is always guaranteed to make progress. However, using multiple networks is expensive and many of them will be underutilized. In addition to the approaches that provide enough buffering (as in the HAL S1 and MIT Alewife) or use NACKs throughout, two different approaches deal with deadlock in protocols that are not strict request-response. Both initially pretend that the protocol is strict request-response and provide two real or virtual networks, then rely on detecting situations when deadlock appears possible and resort to a different mechanism to avoid deadlock in these cases. That mechanism may be NACKs or reverting to a strict request-response protocol.

The detection of potential deadlock situations may be done in many ways. In the Stanford DASH machine, a node conservatively assumes that deadlock may be about to happen when both its input request and output request buffers fill up beyond a threshold and the request at the head of the input request buffer is one that may need to generate further requests like interventions or invalidations (i.e., that request is a violator of strict request-response operation and hence capable of causing deadlock). An alternative strategy is to assume the potential for deadlock when the output request buffer is full and has not had a transaction removed from it for T cycles. When potential deadlock is detected, the DASH system takes the first, NACK-based approach to avoiding deadlock: the node takes such requests off from the head of the input queue one by one and sends NACK messages back for them to the requestors. It does this until the request at the head is no longer one that can generate further requests or until it finds that the output request queue is no longer full. The NACKed requestors will retry their requests later.

A different deadlock avoidance approach is taken by the Origin2000. When potential deadlock is detected, instead of sending a NACK to the requestor, the node sends it a response asking it to send the intervention or invalidation requests directly to the sharers; that is, the system dynamically backs off from a forwarding protocol to a strict request-response protocol, compromising performance temporarily but not allowing deadlock cycles. The advantage of this approach is that NACKing is a statistical rather than robust solution to such congestion-related problems: requests may have to be retried several times in bad situations, leading to increased network traffic and increased latency to the time the operation completes. Dynamic backoff also has advantages related to livelock, as we shall see next.

Livelock

In protocols that avoid deadlock by providing enough buffering of requests, whether centralized or through distributed linked lists, livelock and starvation are taken care of automatically as long as the buffers are FIFO. The other cases do not, in themselves, address livelock and starvation. In these cases, the classic livelock problem due to the race condition of multiple processors trying to write a block at the same time is often taken care of by letting the first request to get to the home go through but NACKing all the others.

NACKs are useful mechanisms for resolving race conditions like the preceding without livelock. However, when used to avoid deadlock in the face of input buffering limitations, as in the DASH solution outlined previously, they have, in fact, the potential to cause livelock. For example, when the node that detects a possible deadlock situation NACKs some requests, it is possible that all those requests are retried at the same time. With extreme pathology, the same situation could repeat itself continually and livelock could result.[2] The alternative solution to deadlock, of switching to a strict request-response protocol in potential deadlock situations, does not cause this livelock problem. It guarantees forward progress and removes the request-request dependence at the home once and for all.

Starvation

The occurrence of starvation is unlikely in well-designed protocols; however, it is not ruled out as a possibility. The fairest solution to starvation is to buffer all requests in FIFO order, which also solves deadlock and livelock. However, this can

2. While the DASH architecture is designed to use NACKs, the actual prototype implementation steps around this problem by using a large enough request input buffer since both the number of nodes and the number of possible outstanding requests per node are small. However, this is not a robust solution for larger, more aggressive machines that cannot provide enough buffer space.

have performance disadvantages, and for protocols that do not do this, avoiding starvation can be difficult to guarantee. Deadlock or livelock solutions that use NACKs and retries are often more susceptible to starvation, which is most likely when many processors repeatedly compete for a resource. Some may keep succeeding while one or more may be very unlucky in their timing and may always get NACKed.

A protocol could decide to do nothing about starvation and rely on the variability of delays in the system not to allow such an indefinitely repeating pathological situation to occur. The DASH machine uses this solution and times out with a bus error if the situation persists beyond a threshold time. Alternatively, a random delay can be inserted between retries to further reduce the small probability of starvation. Finally, requests may be assigned priorities based on the number of times they have already been NACKed, a technique that is used in the Origin2000 protocol.

Having an understanding of the basic directory organizations and high-level protocols as well as the key performance and correctness issues in a general context, we are now ready to dive into actual case studies of memory-based and cache-based protocols. We will see what protocol states and activities look like in actual realizations, how directory protocols interact with and are influenced by the underlying processing nodes, what scalable cache-coherent machines look like, and how actual protocols trade off performance with the complexity of maintaining correctness and of debugging or validating the protocol.

8.5 MEMORY-BASED DIRECTORY PROTOCOLS: THE SGI ORIGIN SYSTEM

Our discussion begins with flat, memory-based directory protocols, using the SGI Origin architecture as a case study. At least for moderate-scale systems, this machine uses essentially a full bit vector directory representation. A similar directory representation but slightly different protocol was also used in the Stanford DASH research prototype (Lenoski et al. 1990), which was the first distributed-memory machine to incorporate directory-based coherence. We follow a similar discussion template for both this and the next case study (the SCI protocol as used in the Sequent NUMA-Q). We begin with the basic coherence protocol, including the directory structure, the directory and cache states, how operations such as reads, writes, and write backs are handled, and the performance enhancements used. Then we will briefly discuss the position taken on the major correctness issues, followed by some prominent protocol extensions for extra functionality. Next, we will examine the rest of the machine as a multiprocessor and how the coherence machinery fits into it. This includes the processing node, the interconnection network, the input/output system, and any interesting interactions between the directory protocol and the underlying node. The case study ends with some important implementation issues (illustrating how it all works and the important data and control pathways), the basic performance characteristics (latency, occupancy, bandwidth) of the protocol, and the resulting application performance for our sample applications.

8.5.1 Cache Coherence Protocol

The Origin system is composed of a number of processing nodes connected by a switch-based interconnection network (see Figure 8.15). Every processing node contains two MIPS R10000 processors, each with first- and second-level caches, a fraction of the total main memory on the machine, an I/O interface, and a single-chip communication assist or coherence controller, called the Hub, that implements the coherence protocol. The Hub is integrated into the memory system. It sees all (second-level) cache misses issued by the processors in that node, whether they are to be satisfied locally or remotely; it receives transactions coming in from the network (in fact, the Hub implements the network interface); and it is capable of retrieving data from the local processor caches.

In terms of the performance issues discussed in Section 8.4.1, at the protocol level, the Origin2000 uses reply forwarding as well as speculative memory operations in parallel with directory lookup at the home. At the machine organization level, the decision in Origin to have two processors per node is driven mostly by cost: several other components on a node (the Hub, the system bus, and so on) are shared between the processors, thus amortizing their cost while hopefully still providing substantial bandwidth per processor. The Origin designers believed that the latency and bandwidth disadvantages of interacting with a snooping bus within a node outweighed its advantages and chose not to maintain snooping coherence between the two processors within a node. Rather, the SysAD (system address and data) bus is simply a shared physical link that is multiplexed between the two processors in a node. This sacrifices the potential advantage of cache-to-cache sharing within the node but eliminates the latency, occupancy, and cache tag contention added by snooping. In particular, with only two processors per node, the likelihood of successful cache-to-cache sharing is small, so the disadvantages may dominate. With a Hub shared between two processors, the combining of requests to the network (not to the directory protocol) could nonetheless have been supported, but it is not, due to the additional implementation cost. When discussing the protocol in this section, let us assume for simplicity that each node contains only one processor, together with its cache hierarchy, a Hub, and main memory. We consider the impact of using two processors per node on the directory structure and protocol later in this section.

Other than reply forwarding, the most interesting aspects of the Origin protocol are its use of busy states and NACKs to resolve race conditions and provide serialization to a location, its deadlock and livelock solution, the way in which it handles race conditions caused by write backs, and its nonreliance on any order preservation among transactions in the network (not even point-to-point order among transactions between the same endpoint nodes). To show how a complete protocol works in the presence of races as well as to illustrate the performance enhancement techniques used in different cases, we will look at how the Origin puts the techniques together to process read and write operations.

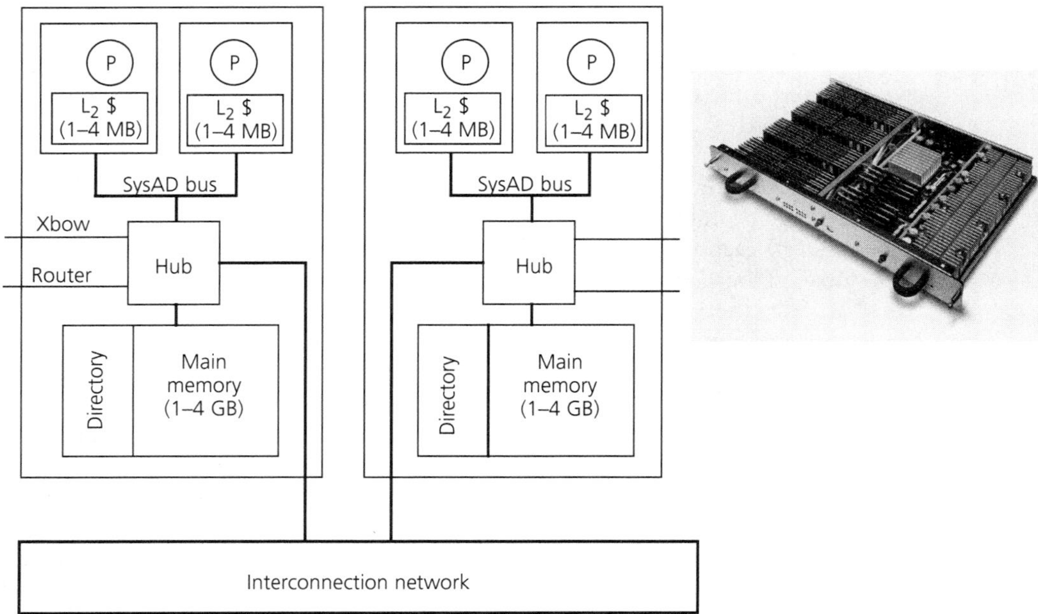

FIGURE 8.15 Block diagram of the Silicon Graphics Origin2000 multiprocessor. Each node contains two processors, a communication assist or controller called the Hub, and main memory with the associated directory. The photograph shows a single node board. *Source:* Photo courtesy of Silicon Graphics, Inc.

Directory Structure and Protocol States

The directory information for a memory block is maintained at the home node for that block. We assume a full bit vector approach for now and examine how the directory organization changes with machine size later.

In the caches, the protocol uses the same MESI states as used in Chapter 5. At the directory, a block may be in one of seven states. Three of these are stable states: *unowned*, or no cached copies in the system; *shared*, that is, zero or more read-only cached copies whose whereabouts are indicated by the presence vector; and *exclusive*, or one read-write cached copy in the system, indicated by the presence vector. An exclusive directory state means the block may be in either dirty or (clean) exclusive state in the cache (i.e., either the M or E states of the MESI protocol). Three other states are *busy* states. As discussed earlier, these imply that the home has received a previous request for that block but was not able to complete that operation itself (e.g., the block may have been dirty in a cache in another node); transactions to complete the request are still in progress in the system, so the directory at the home is not yet ready to handle a new request for that block. The three busy states correspond to three different types of requests that might still be in progress: a read, a read exclusive or upgrade, and an uncached read (a read whose result does not enter the processor caches and is not kept coherent thereafter). Busy states and NACKs (rather than large amounts of buffering) are used by this protocol to avoid race conditions and provide serialization to a location. The seventh state is a *poison* state, which is used to implement a lazy TLB shootdown method for migrating pages among memories. (Protocol extensions like uncached operations and page migration are discussed in Section 8.5.4.) Given these states, let us see how the coherence protocol handles read, write, and write-back requests from a node.

Handling Read Requests

Suppose a processor issues a read that misses in its cache hierarchy. The address of the miss is examined by the local Hub to determine the home node, and a read request transaction is sent to the home node to look up the directory entry. If the home is local, the directory is looked up by the local Hub itself. At the home, the data for the block is accessed speculatively in parallel with looking up the directory entry. The directory entry lookup, which completes a cycle earlier than the speculative data access, may indicate that the memory block is in one of several different states—and different actions are taken in each case.

- *Shared* or *unowned*. This means that main memory at the home has the latest copy of the data (so the speculative access was successful). If the state is shared, the bit corresponding to the requestor is set in the directory presence vector; if it is unowned, the directory state is set to exclusive (achieving the functionality provided by the shared signal in snooping systems). The home then sends the data for the block back to the requestor in a reply transaction. These cases satisfy a strict request-response protocol. Of course, if the home node is the same as the requesting node, then no network transactions or messages are generated and it is a locally satisfied miss.
- *Busy*. This means that the home should not handle the request at this time since a previous request for the block is still in progress. The requestor is sent a negative acknowledge (NACK) message, asking it to try again later. A NACK is categorized as a response, but like an acknowledgment it does not carry data.
- *Exclusive*. This is the most interesting case. If the home is not the owner of the block, the valid data for the block must be obtained from the owner and must find its way to the requestor as well as to the home (since the state will change to shared). The Origin protocol uses reply forwarding; the request is forwarded to the owner, which replies directly to the requestor, sending a revision message to the home. If the home itself is the owner, then the home can simply reply to the requestor, change the directory state to shared, and set the requestor's bit in the presence vector. In fact, in general the directory treats a cache at the home just like any other cache; the only difference is that a "message" between the home directory and a cache at the home does not translate to a network transaction.

Let us look in a little more detail at what really happens when a read request arrives at the home and finds the state exclusive. (This and several other cases we discuss are illustrated in Figure 8.16.) The main memory block is accessed speculatively in parallel with the directory as usual. When the directory state is discovered to be exclusive, it is set to the busy-exclusive state to deal with subsequent requests, and the request is forwarded to the exclusive node. We cannot set the directory state to shared yet since memory does not yet have an up-to-date copy, and we do not want to leave it as exclusive since then a subsequent request might chase the same exclusive copy of the block as the current request does, requiring that serialization be determined by the current owner node rather than by the home.

Having set the directory entry to a busy state, the presence vector is changed to set the requestor's bit and unset the current owner's. Why this is done at this time becomes clear when we examine write-back requests. Now we see an interesting aspect of the protocol: even though the directory state is exclusive, the home optimistically assumes that the block will be in the (clean) exclusive rather than dirty state in the owner's cache and sends the speculatively accessed memory block at the home as a *speculative reply* (i.e., a reply with data that may or may not be useful) to the requestor. At the same time, the home forwards the intervention request to the owner. The owner checks the state in its cache and performs one of the following actions. If the block is in dirty state, it sends a reply with the data directly to the requestor and a revision message containing the data to the home. At the requestor, the response overwrites the stale speculative reply that was sent by the home. The revision message with data sent to the home is called a *sharing write back* since it writes the data back from the owning cache to main memory and tells it to set the block to shared state. If the block is in exclusive state, the reply to the requestor and the revision message to the home do not contain data since both already have the latest copy (the requestor has it via the speculative reply from the home). The response to the requestor is simply a completion acknowledgment, and the revision message is called a *downgrade* since it asks the home to downgrade the state of the block from (busy) exclusive to shared. In either case, when the home receives the revision message, it changes the state from busy to shared.

You may have noticed that the use of speculative replies does not have any significant performance advantage in this case since the requestor has to wait to know the real state at the exclusive node anyway before it can use the data. In fact, a simpler alternative to this scheme would be to simply assume that the block is dirty at the owner, not send a speculative reply, and always have the owner send back a reply with the data regardless of whether it has the block in dirty or (clean) exclusive state. Why then does the Origin protocol use speculative replies? There are two reasons, which illustrate how a protocol is influenced by the quirks of existing processors and how different protocol optimizations influence each other. First, the cache controller of the R10000 processor that the Origin uses happens not to return data when it receives an intervention to an exclusive (rather than dirty) cached block since memory is assumed to have a valid copy. Second, speculative replies enable a different optimization in the protocol, which is to allow a processor to simply drop a (clean) exclusive block when it is replaced from the cache, rather than notify main

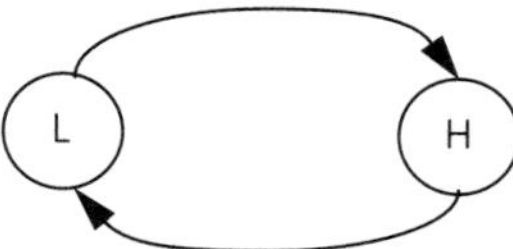

(a) A read or read-exclusive request to a block in unowned state at the directory or a read request to a block in shared state. An exclusive response is sent even in the read case if the block is in unowned state at the directory so that it may be loaded in E rather than S state in the cache.

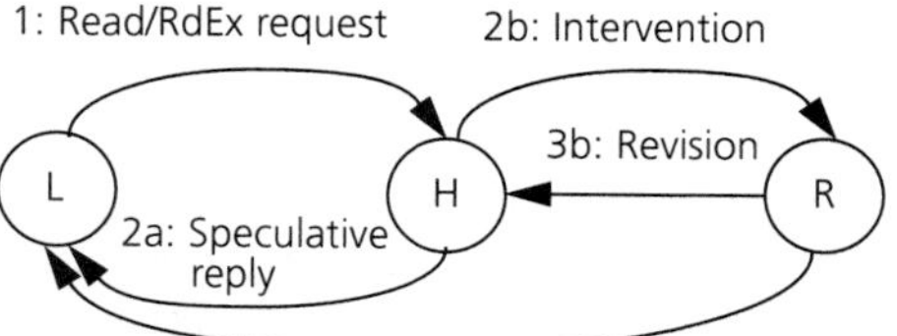

(b) Read or RdEx to a block in the directory in exclusive state. The intervention may be of type shared or exclusive, respectively, with the latter causing invalidation as well. The revision message is a sharing write back or an ownership transfer.

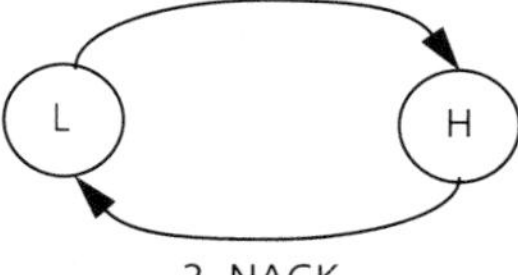

(c) Read/RdEx request to directory in busy state or upgrade request to directory in busy, unowned, or exclusive states.

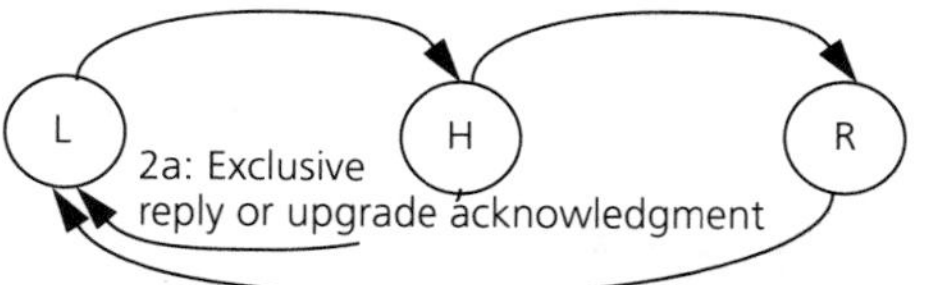

(d) RdEx or upgrade request to directory in shared state.

(e) Write-back request to directory in exclusive state.

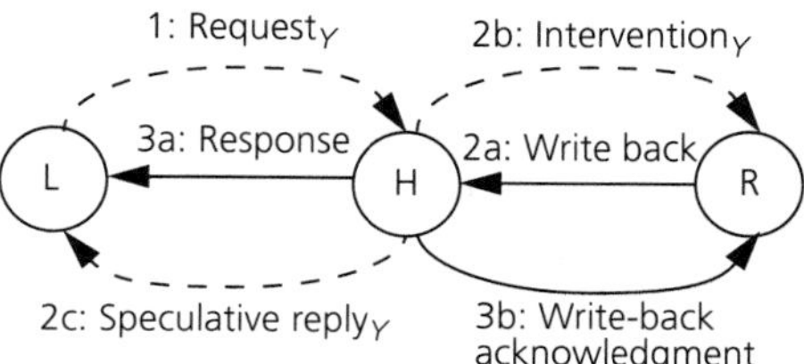

(f) Write-back request to directory in busy state (the *Y*-subscripted transactions and dashed arcs are those for the other request that made the directory busy).

FIGURE 8.16 Protocol actions in response to requests in the Origin multiprocessor. The case or cases under consideration appear below the diagram, indicating the type of request and the state of the directory entry when the request arrives at the home. The messages or types of transactions are listed next to each arc. Since the same diagram represents different combinations of request type and directory state, different message types are listed on each arc.

memory that it now has the only copy and should reply to subsequent requests since main memory will in any case send a speculative reply when needed.

Handling Write Requests

As we saw in Chapter 5, write misses that invoke the protocol may generate either read-exclusive requests, which request both data and ownership, or upgrade requests that request only ownership since the requestor's data is valid. In either case, the request goes to the home where the directory state is looked up to determine what actions to take. If the state at the directory is anything but unowned (or busy, which NACKs the request), the copies in other caches must be invalidated. To preserve the ordering model, invalidations must be explicitly acknowledged.

As in the read case, a strict request-response protocol, intervention forwarding, or reply forwarding can be used (see Exercise 8.4). Origin chooses reply forwarding to reduce latency: the home updates the directory state and sends the invalidations directly; it also includes the identity of the requestor in the invalidations so that they are acknowledged directly back to the requestor itself. The actual handling of the read-exclusive and upgrade requests depends on the state of the directory entry when the request arrives; that is, whether it is unowned, shared, exclusive, or busy.

- *Unowned.* If the request is an upgrade, the state at the directory is expected to be shared. The state being unowned means that the block has been replaced from the requestor's cache and the directory notified since it sent the upgrade request (this is possible since the Origin protocol does not assume point-to-point network order). An upgrade is no longer the appropriate request, so it is NACKed. The write operation will be retried, presumably as a read exclusive. If the request is a read exclusive, the directory state is changed to exclusive and the requestor's presence bit is set. The home replies with the data from memory.
- *Shared.* The block must be invalidated in the caches that have copies. The Hub at the home first makes a list of sharers that are to be sent invalidations, using the presence vector. It then sets the directory state to exclusive and sets the presence bit for the requestor. This ensures that the next request for the block will be forwarded to the requestor. If the request was a read exclusive, the home next sends a response to the requestor (called an "exclusive reply with invalidations pending") that also contains the number of sharers from whom to expect invalidation acknowledgments. If the request was an upgrade, the home sends an "upgrade acknowledgment with invalidations pending" to the requestor, which is similar but does not carry the data for the block. In either case, the home next sends invalidation requests to all the sharers, which in turn send acknowledgments to the requestor (not the home). The requestor waits for all acknowledgments to come in before it "closes" or completes the operation. If a new request for the block comes to the home in the meantime, it will see the directory state as exclusive and will be forwarded as an intervention to the current requestor. This current requestor will not handle the intervention immediately but will buffer it until it has received all acknowledgments for its own request and closed that operation. (Further, requests coming to the home in the meantime will find the block in busy-exclusive state, as discussed earlier.)
- *Exclusive.* If the request is an upgrade, then an exclusive directory state means another write has beaten this request to the home. An upgrade is no longer the appropriate request and is NACKed. For a read-exclusive request, the following actions are taken. As with reads, the home sets the directory to a busy

state, sets the presence bit of the requestor, and sends a speculative reply to it. An invalidation request is sent to the owner, containing the identity of the write requestor (if the home is the owner, this is just an invalidation to the local cache and not a network transaction). If the owner has the block in dirty state, it sends a "transfer of ownership" revision message to the home (no data) and a reply with the data to the requestor. This reply overrides the speculative reply that the requestor receives from the home. If the owner has the block in (clean) exclusive state, it relies on the speculative reply from the home and simply sends an acknowledgment to the requestor and a "transfer of ownership" revision message to the home.

- *Busy.* The request is NACKed as in the read case and must try again.

Handling Write-Back Requests and Replacements

When a node replaces a block that is dirty in its cache, it generates a write-back request. This request carries data and is replied to with an acknowledgment by the home. The directory cannot be in unowned or shared state when a write-back request arrives because the write-back requestor has a dirty copy. (A read request cannot change the directory state to shared in between the generation of the write back and its arrival at the home since such a request would have been forwarded to the very node that is requesting the write back and the directory state would have been set to busy.) Let us see what happens when the write-back request reaches the home for the two possible directory states: exclusive and busy.

- *Exclusive.* The directory state transitions from exclusive to unowned (since the only cached copy has been replaced from its cache), and an acknowledgment is returned.
- *Busy.* This indicates an interesting race condition. The directory state can only be busy because an intervention for the block (due to a request from another node *Y*, say) has been forwarded to the very node *X* that is doing the write back. The intervention and write back have crossed each other in the interconnect. Now we are in a funny situation. The other operation from *Y* is already in progress and cannot be undone. We cannot let the write back be dropped, or we would lose the only valid copy of the block. Nor can we NACK the write back and retry it after the operation from *Y* completes, since then *Y*'s cache will have a valid copy while a different dirty copy is being written back to memory from *X*'s cache! This protocol solves the problem by essentially combining the two operations, using the write back as the response to *Y*'s request (see Figure 8.16[f]). The write back that finds the directory state busy changes the state to either shared (if the state was busy-shared, i.e., the request from *Y* was for a read copy) or exclusive (if it was busy-exclusive). The data returned in the write back is then forwarded by the home to the requestor *Y*. This serves as the response to *Y* instead of the response it would have received directly from *X* if there were no write back. When *X* receives an intervention for the block due to *Y*'s request, it simply ignores it (see Exercise 8.13). The directory also

sends a write-back acknowledgment to *X*. Node *Y*'s operation is complete when it receives the response, and the write back is complete when *X* receives the write-back acknowledgment. We will see an exception to this treatment in a more complex case when we discuss the serialization of operations. In general, write backs introduce many subtle situations into directory-based coherence protocols.

If the block being replaced from a cache is in shared state, the node may or may not choose to send a replacement hint message back to the home, asking the home to clear its presence bit in the directory. Replacement hints avoid the next useless invalidation to that block and can reduce the occurrence in limited-pointer directory representations, but they incur assist occupancy and do not reduce traffic. In fact, if the block is not written again by another node, then the replacement hint is a waste. The Origin protocol does not use a limited-pointer representation and does not use replacement hints.

In all, the number of transaction types for coherent memory operations in the Origin protocol is 9 requests, 6 invalidations and interventions, and 39 responses. For noncoherent operations such as uncached memory operations, I/O operations, and special synchronization support, the number of transactions is 19 requests and 14 replies (no invalidations or interventions since there is no coherent caching).

8.5.2 Dealing with Correctness Issues

So far, we have seen what happens at different nodes upon read and write misses and how some important race conditions are resolved. Let us now take a different cut through the Origin protocol, examining the specific solutions it adopts for the correctness issues discussed in Section 8.4.2 and the features that the machine provides to deal with errors that may occur.

Serialization to a Location for Coherence

The entity designated to serialize cache misses from different processors is the home. As we have seen, serialization is provided not by buffering requests at the home until previous ones have completed or forwarding them to the owner node even when the directory is in a busy state but by NACKing requests from the home when the state is busy and causing them to be retried. Requests are forwarded only from stable directory states. Serialization is determined by the order in which the home *accepts* the requests—that is, satisfies them itself or forwards them—not the order in which they first arrive at the home.

The general discussion of serialization techniques in Section 8.4.2 suggested that more was needed for serialization to a given location than simply a global serializing entity since the serializing entity does not have full knowledge of when transactions related to a given operation are completed at all the relevant nodes. With a sufficiently in-depth understanding of a protocol, we now examine some concrete examples of this problem (Lenoski 1992) and see how it might be addressed (see Examples 8.1 and 8.2).

EXAMPLE 8.1 Consider the following simple piece of code.

P_1	P_2
`rd A (i)`	`wr A`
`BARRIER`	`BARRIER`
`rd A (ii)`	

The write of `A` may happen either before the first read of `A` or after it, but it should be serializable with respect to that first read. The second read of `A` should in any case return the value written by P_2. However, it is quite possible for the effect of the write to get lost if we are not careful. Show how this might happen in a protocol like the Origin's, and discuss possible solutions.

Answer Figure 8.17 shows how the problem can occur, with the text in the figure explaining the transactions, the sequence of events, and the problem. There are two possible solutions. An unattractive one is to have read replies themselves be acknowledged explicitly and let the home go on to process the next request only after it receives this acknowledgment. This further violates the request-response nature of the protocol, causes buffering and potential deadlock problems, and leads to long delays. The more likely solution is to ensure that a node that has a request outstanding for a block, such as P_1, does not allow access by another request, such as the invalidation, to be applied to that block in its cache until its outstanding request completes. P_1 may buffer the incoming invalidation request and apply it only after the read reply is received and completed. Or P_1 can apply the invalidation even before the read reply is received and then consider the reply invalid (a NACK) when it returns and retry the read. Origin uses the former solution whereas the latter is used in DASH. The order of P_1's (first) read with respect to P_2's write is different in the two machines, but both orders are valid. The buffering needed is small and does not cause deadlock problems. ■

EXAMPLE 8.2 In addition to the requestor, the home too may have to disallow new operations from actually being applied to a block (or its directory state) before previous ones have completed as far as it is concerned. Otherwise, directory information may be corrupted. Show an example illustrating this need and discuss solutions.

Answer This example is more subtle and is shown in Figure 8.18. The node issuing the write request detects completion of the write (as far as its involvement is concerned) through acknowledgments before processing another request for the block. The problem is that the home does not wait for its involvement in the write operation—which includes waiting for the revision message and directory update—to complete before it allows another access (here the write back) to be applied to the block. The Origin protocol prevents this from happening by using its busy state: the directory will be in busy-exclusive state when the write back arrives before the revision message. When the directory detects that the write back is coming from the same node whose request put the directory into busy-exclusive state, the write back is NACKed and must be retried. (Recall from the discussion of handling write backs that the write back was treated differently if the request that set the state to busy came from a different node than from the one doing the write back; in that case, the write back was not NACKed but was sent on as the response to the requestor.) ■

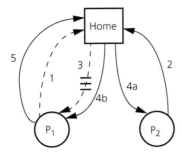

1. P_1 sends read request to home node for `A`.
2. P_2 sends read-exclusive request to home (for the write of `A`). Home (serializer) won't process it until it is done with read from P_1, which it receives first.
3. In response to (1), home sends reply to P_1 (and sets directory presence bit). Home now thinks read is complete (there are no acknowledgments for a read reply). Unfortunately, the reply does not get to P_1 right away.

4a. In response to (2), home sends data reply to P_2 corresponding to request 2.

4b. In response to (2), home sends invalidation to P_1; it reaches P_1 before transaction 3 (no point-to-point order is assumed in Origin, and in general the invalidation is a request and 3 is a response, so they may travel on different networks).

5. P_1 receives and applies invalidation, sends acknowledgment to home.

Finally, the read reply (3) reaches P_1 and overwrites the invalidated block. When P_1 reads `A` after the barrier, it reads this old value rather than seeing an invalid block and fetching the new value. The effect of the write by P_2 is lost as far as P_1 is concerned.

FIGURE 8.17 Example illustrating the need for local serialization of operations at a requestor. The example shows how a write can be lost even though home thinks it is doing things in order. Transactions associated with the first read operation are shown with dotted lines, and those associated with the write operation are shown in solid lines. The three solid bars through a transaction indicate that it is delayed in the network.

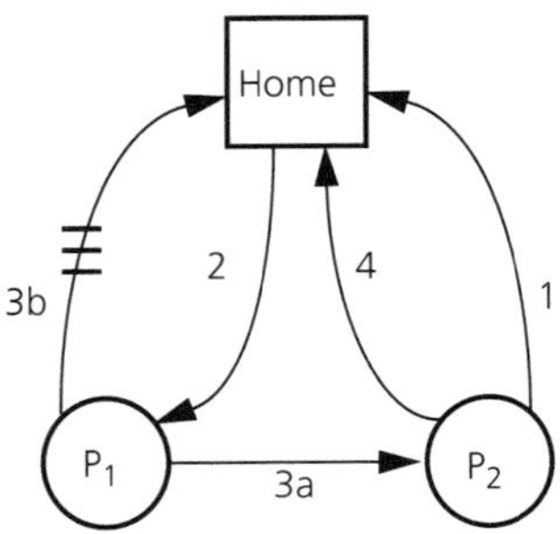

Initial condition: block is in dirty state in P_1's cache.

1. P_2 sends read-exclusive request to home.
2. Home forwards request to P_1 (dirty node).
3. P_1 sends data reply to P_2 (3a) and "ownership transfer" revision message to home to change owner to P_2 (3b).
4. P_2, having received its reply, considers write complete. Proceeds, but incurs a replacement of the just dirtied block, causing it to be written back in transaction 4.

This write back is received by the home before the ownership transfer revision message from P_1 (even point-to-point network order wouldn't help), and the block is written into memory. Then when the revision message arrives at the home, the directory is made to point to P_2 as having the dirty copy. But this is untrue, and our protocol is corrupted.

FIGURE 8.18 Example illustrating the need for local serialization of operations at a home node. The example shows how directory information can be corrupted if a home node does not wait for its involvement with a previous request to be over (e.g., a revision message to be received from the owner node) before it allows a new access to the same block.

These examples illustrate the importance of another general requirement that nodes must locally fulfill for proper serialization, beyond the existence of a global serializing entity for a block: any node, not just the serializing entity, should not apply a transaction corresponding to a new memory operation to a block until a previously outstanding memory operation on that block (that the node has begun to handle) is complete as far as that node's involvement is concerned.

Preserving the Memory Consistency Model

The dynamically scheduled R10000 processor allows independent memory operations to issue out of program order, allowing multiple operations to be outstanding at a time and achieving some overlap among them. However, it ensures that operations complete in program order and, in fact, that writes leave the processor environment and become visible to the memory system in program order with respect to other operations, thus preserving sequential consistency (Chapter 11 discusses the necessary processor mechanisms further). The processor does not satisfy the sufficient conditions for sequential consistency spelled out in Chapter 5 in that it does not wait to issue the next operation until the previous one completes, but a system that uses this processor and provides atomicity satisfies the model itself.[3]

Since the processor guarantees visibility and completion in program order, the extended memory hierarchy can perform any reorderings to different locations that it desires without violating this property. The Origin protocol provides write atomicity as discussed earlier: a node does not allow any incoming accesses to a block for which invalidations are outstanding until the acknowledgments for those invalidations have returned (i.e., the write is committed). Nonetheless, one implementation consideration is important in maintaining SC that is due to the Origin protocol's interactions with the processor. Recall from Figure 8.16(d) what happens on a write request (read exclusive or upgrade) to a block that is in shared state at the directory. The requestor receives two types of responses: an *exclusive reply* from the home, discussed earlier, whose role is to indicate that the write has been serialized at memory with respect to other operations for the block and perhaps to return data; and *invalidation acknowledgments*, indicating that the other copies have been invalidated and the write has completed. The microprocessor, however, expects only a single response to its write request, as in a uniprocessor system, so these different responses have to be dealt with by the requesting Hub. To ensure sequential consistency, the Hub must pass the response on to the processor—allowing it to declare completion of the write—only when both the exclusive reply and the invalidation acknowledgments have been received. It must not pass on the response simply when the exclusive reply has been received since that would allow the processor to complete later accesses to other locations even before all invalidations for this one have been

3. This is true for accesses that are under the control of the coherence protocol. The processor also supports memory operations that are not visible to the coherence protocol, called noncoherent memory operations, for which the system does not guarantee any ordering: it is the user's responsibility to insert synchronization to preserve a desired ordering in these cases.

acknowledged, violating sequential consistency. We see in Section 9.1 that such violations are useful when more relaxed memory consistency models than SC are used.

Deadlock, Livelock, and Starvation

The Origin uses finite input buffers and a protocol that is not strict request-response. As discussed in Section 8.4.2, to avoid deadlock, it uses the technique of reverting to a strict request-response protocol when it detects a high-contention situation that may cause deadlock. Since NACKs are not used to alleviate the contention, livelock is avoided in these situations too. The classic livelock problem due to multiple processors trying to write a block at the same time is avoided by using busy states and NACKs (recall that NACKs avoid rather than cause livelock in this case). The first of these requests to get to the home sets the state to busy and makes forward progress while others are NACKed and must retry.

In general, the philosophy of the Origin protocol is twofold: (1) to be "memory-less," that is, every node reacts to incoming events using only current local state and no history of previous events; and (2) not to allow an operation to hold globally shared resources while it is requesting other resources. The latter leads to the choices of NACKing rather than buffering for a busy resource and helps prevent deadlock. These decisions greatly simplify the hardware yet provide high performance in most cases. However, since NACKs are used rather than FIFO ordering, the problem of starvation still exists. This is addressed by associating a priority with a request, which is a function of the number of times the request has been NACKed.[4]

Error Handling

Despite a correct protocol, hardware and software errors can occur at run time. These can corrupt memory or write data to different locations than expected (e.g., if the address on which to perform a write becomes corrupted). The Origin system provides many standard mechanisms to handle hardware errors on components. All caches and memories are protected by error correction codes (ECCs), and all router and I/O links are protected by cyclic redundancy checks (CRCs) and a hardware link-level protocol that automatically detects and retries failures. In addition, the system provides mechanisms to contain failures within the part of the machine in which the program that caused the failure is running. Access protection rights are

4. The priority mechanism works as follows. The directory entry for a block has a "current" priority associated with it. Incoming transactions that will not cause the directory state to become busy are always serviced. Other transactions will potentially be serviced only if their priority is greater than or equal to the current directory priority. If such a transaction is NACKed (e.g., because the directory is in busy state when it arrives), the current priority of the directory is set to be equal to that of the NACKed request. This ensures that the directory will no longer service another request of lower priority until this one is serviced upon retry. To prevent a monotonic increase and "topping out" of the directory entry priority, it is reset to zero whenever a request of priority greater than or equal to it is serviced.

provided on both memory and I/O devices, preventing unauthorized nodes from making modifications. These access rights allow the operating system to be structured into cells or partitions, an organization called a *cellular operating system*. A cell is a number of nodes, configured at boot time. If an application runs within a cell, it may be disallowed from writing memory or I/O outside that cell. If the application fails and corrupts memory or I/O, it can only affect other applications or the system running within that cell and cannot harm code running in other cells. Thus, a cell is the unit of fault containment in the system.

8.5.3 Details of Directory Structure

While we have assumed a full bit vector directory organization so far for simplicity, the actual structure of the Origin directory entry is a little more complex for two reasons: first, to deal with the two processors per node and, second, to allow the directory structure to scale to more than 64 nodes with a 64-bit entry. There are, in fact, three possible formats or interpretations of the directory bits. If a block is in an exclusive state (i.e., modified or exclusive) in a processor cache, then the rest of the directory entry is not a bit vector with one bit turned on but rather contains an explicit pointer to that specific processor (not node). This means that interventions forwarded from the home are targeted to a specific processor. Otherwise, for example, if the directory state is shared, the directory entry is interpreted as a bit vector. Bits in the bit vector correspond to nodes, so even though the two processor caches within a node are not kept coherent by the bus, the unit of visibility to the directory in this format is a node or Hub, not a processor. If an invalidation is sent to a Hub, unlike an intervention, it is broadcast to both processors in the node over the SysAD bus that connects the two processors and the Hub. There are two sizes for presence bit vectors: 16 bit and 64 bit (in the 16-bit case, the directory entry is stored in the same DRAM as the main memory whereas in the 64-bit case the rest of the bits are in an extended directory memory module that is looked up in parallel). The 16-bit vector therefore supports up to 32 processors, and the 64-bit vector supports up to 128 processors.

For larger systems, the interpretation of the bits changes to the third format. In a p-node system, each bit now corresponds to a fixed set of $p/64$ nodes. The bit is set when any one (or more) of the nodes in the corresponding set has a copy of the block. If a bit is set when a write happens, then invalidations are sent to all the $p/64$ nodes represented by that bit (and are then broadcast to both processors in each of those nodes). For example, with the maximum supported size of 1,024 processors (512 nodes), each bit corresponds to 8 nodes. This is called a *coarse vector* representation, and we see it again when we discuss overflow strategies for directory representations as an advanced topic in Section 8.10. In fact, the system dynamically chooses between the bit vector and coarse vector representation on a large machine: if all the nodes sharing the block are within the same 64-node octant of the machine, a bit vector representation is used; otherwise, a coarse vector is used.

8.5.4 Protocol Extensions

In addition to the protocol optimizations discussed earlier, the Origin protocol provides some extensions to support special operations and activities that interact with the protocol. These include input/output and DMA operations, page migration, and synchronization.

Support for Input/Output and DMA Operations

To support memory reads by a DMA device, the protocol provides "uncached read-shared" requests. Such a request returns to the DMA device a snapshot of a coherent copy of the data, but that copy is then no longer kept coherent by the protocol. The request is used primarily by the I/O system and the block transfer engine provided in the Hub and as such is intended for use by the operating system. For writes to memory from a DMA device, the protocol provides "write invalidate" requests. A write invalidate simply blasts the new value of a word into memory, overwriting the previous value. It also invalidates all existing cached copies of the block in the system, thus returning the directory entry to unowned state. From a protocol perspective, it behaves much like a read-exclusive request, except that it modifies the block in memory and leaves the directory in unowned state.

Support for Automatic Page Migration

As we discussed in Chapter 3, on a machine with physically distributed memory it is often important to allocate data appropriately across physical memories so that most capacity, conflict, and cold misses are satisfied locally. On CC-NUMA machines like the Origin, data is allocated in memory at the granularity of a page (16 KB, in this case). Despite the very aggressive communication architecture in the Origin, the latency of an access satisfied by remote memory is at least 2–3 times that of a local access even without contention. The appropriate distribution of pages among memories might change dynamically at run time, either because a parallel program's access patterns change or because the operating system decides to migrate an application process from one processor to another for better resource management across multiprogrammed applications. It is therefore useful for the system to detect the need for moving pages at run time and migrate them automatically to where they are needed.

For every page in main memory, Origin provides an array of miss counters, one per node, to help determine when most of the misses to a page are coming from a nonlocal processor so that the page should be migrated. The miss counters are stored in directory memory at the home. When a request comes in for a page, the miss counter for that node is incremented and compared with the miss counter for the home node. If it exceeds the latter by more than a threshold, then the page can be migrated to that remote node. (Sixty-four counters are provided per page, and in a system with more than 64 nodes, 8 nodes share a counter.) Page migration is typically very expensive, which often annuls the advantage of doing the migration. The major reason for the high cost is not so much moving the page (which with the block transfer engine in the Hub takes about 25–30 μs for a 16-KB page) as changing the virtual-to-physical mappings in the TLBs of all processors that have referenced the page. Migrating a page keeps the virtual address the same but changes the physical address, so the old mappings in the page tables of processes are now invalid. As page table entries are changed, it is important that the cached versions of those entries in the TLBs of processors be invalidated (much like TLB shootdown discussed in Chapter 6). In fact, all processors must be sent a TLB invalidation message since we don't know which ones have a mapping for the page cached in their TLB. The processors are interrupted, and the invalidating processor has to wait for the last among them to respond before it can update the page table entry and continue. This process typically takes over 100 μs, in addition to the cost to move the page itself.

To reduce this cost, Origin uses a distributed, lazy TLB invalidation mechanism supported by its seventh directory state, the poisoned state. The idea is not to invalidate TLB entries when the page is moved but rather to invalidate a processor's TLB entry only when that processor next references the page. Not only is the time to invalidate all TLBs removed from the critical path of the processor that manages the migration, but TLB entries end up being invalidated for only those processors that subsequently reference the page. Let's see how this works. To migrate a page, a block transfer engine reads all cache blocks from the source page location using special "uncached read-exclusive" requests. This request type returns the latest coherent copy of the data and invalidates any existing cached copies (like a regular read-exclusive request), but it also causes the destination main memory to be updated with the latest version of the block and puts the directory in the poisoned state. The migration itself takes only the time to do this block transfer. When a processor next tries to access a block from the old physical page, using its stale TLB entry, it will miss in the cache and will find the block in poisoned state at the directory. At that time, the poisoned state will cause the requesting processor to see a bus error. The special OS handler for this bus error invalidates the processor's TLB entry so that it will obtain the new mapping from the page table when it retries the access. Of course, the old physical page must be reclaimed by the system at some point to avoid wasting storage. Once the block transfer has completed, the OS invalidates one TLB entry per time quantum of the OS scheduler so that after some fixed amount of time the old page can be moved on to the free list.

Support for Synchronization

Origin provides two types of support for synchronization. First, the load-locked store-conditional (LL-SC) instructions of the R10000 processor are available to compose synchronization operations, as we saw in the previous chapters. Second, for situations in which many processors contend to update a location, such as a global counter or a barrier, uncached fetch&op primitives are provided. These fetch&op operations are performed at the main memory; the block is not replicated in the caches, so successive nodes trying to update the location do not have to retrieve it from the previous writer's cache. The cacheable LL-SC is better when the same node tends to repeatedly access the shared (synchronization) variable, and the uncached fetch&op is better when different nodes tend to update in an interleaved or contended way. Producer-consumer communication of event synchronization can also be aided by uncached write and read operations since at most two network transactions are needed instead of four and since the producer and consumer transactions may even overlap on their way to the home node. However, spinning on a remote uncached location may cause a lot of traffic.

8.5.5 Overview of the Origin2000 Hardware

The preceding protocol discussion has provided us with a fairly complete picture of how a flat, memory-based directory protocol is implemented out of network transactions and state transitions, just as a bus-based protocol was implemented out of bus transactions and state transitions. Let us now turn our attention to the actual hardware of the Origin2000 machine that implements this protocol. This subsection provides an overview of the system hardware organization and is followed by a deeper examination of how the Hub controller is actually implemented (in Section 8.5.6). Finally, the performance of the machine is discussed in Section 8.5.7. (Readers interested in only the protocol can skip the rest of this section without loss of continuity.)

In addition to the two MIPS R10000 processors connected by a system bus, each node of the Origin2000 contains a fraction of the main memory on the machine (1–4 GB per node), the Hub (which is the combined communication/coherence controller and network interface), and an I/O interface called the Xbow. All components but the Xbow are on a single 16" × 11" printed circuit board. Each processor in a node has its own separate L_1 and L_2 caches, with the L_2 cache configurable from 1 to 4 MB with a cache block size of 128 bytes and two-way set associativity. There is one directory entry per main memory block. Memory is interleaved from 4 ways to 32 ways, depending on the number of modules plugged in (4-way interleaving at 4-KB granularity within a module and up to 32-way at 512-MB granularity across modules). The system has up to 512 such nodes, that is, up to 1,024 processors. With a 195-MHz R10000 processor, the peak performance per processor is 390 MFLOPS or 780 MIPS (four instructions per cycle), leading to an aggregate peak performance of almost 500 GFLOPS in a maximally sized machine. The peak bandwidth of the SysAD bus that connects the two processors is 780 MB/s, as is that of the Hub's connection to memory. Memory bandwidth itself for data is about 670 MB/s. The Hub connections to the off-board network router chip and Xbow I/O interface are 1.56 GB/s each, using the same link technology. A detailed picture of the node board is shown in Figure 8.19.

The Hub chip is the heart of the machine. It sits on the system bus of the node and connects the processors, local memory, network, and Xbow, which communicate with one another through it. All cache misses, whether to local or remote memory, go through the Hub (which implements the coherence protocol), as do all

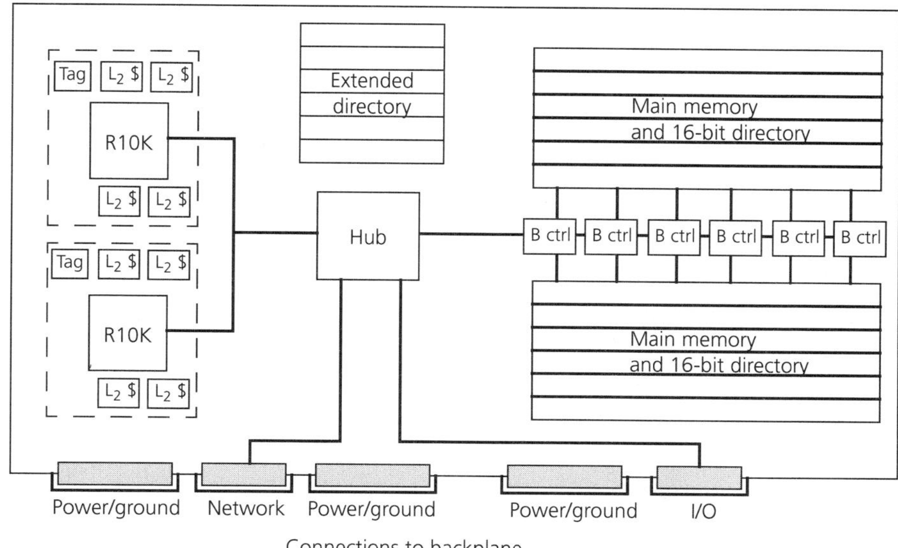

FIGURE 8.19 A node board on the Origin multiprocessor. "L_2 $" stands for secondary cache chips and "B ctrl" for memory bank controller.

uncached operations. It is a highly integrated, 500-K gate standard-cell design in 0.5-μ CMOS technology. It contains outstanding transaction buffers for each of its two processors (each processor itself allows four outstanding requests), a pair of block transfer engines that support block memory copy and fill operations at full system bus bandwidth, and interfaces for the network, the SysAD bus, the memory/directory, and the I/O subsystem. The Hub also implements the at-memory, uncached fetch&op instructions and page migration support discussed earlier.

The interconnection network has a hypercube topology for machines with up to 64 processors but a different topology, called a *fat cube,* beyond that. (This topology is discussed in Chapter 10.) Each router supports six links. The network links have high bandwidth (1.56 GB/s total per link in the two directions) and low latency (41 ns pin-to-pin through a router) and can use flexible cabling up to three feet long for the links. Each link supports four *virtual channels*. Virtual channels are described in Chapter 10; for now, we can think of the machine as having four distinct networks such that each has about one-fourth of the physical link bandwidth. One of these virtual channels is reserved for request network transactions, one for responses. Two can be used for congestion relief and high-priority transactions, thereby violating point-to-point order, or can be reserved for I/O as is usually done.

The Xbow chip connects the Hub to other I/O interfaces. It is itself implemented as a crossbar with eight ports. Typically, two nodes (Hubs) might be connected to one Xbow and, through it, to six external I/O cards as shown in Figure 8.20. The Xbow is quite similar to the router chip (called SPIDER) but with simpler buffering

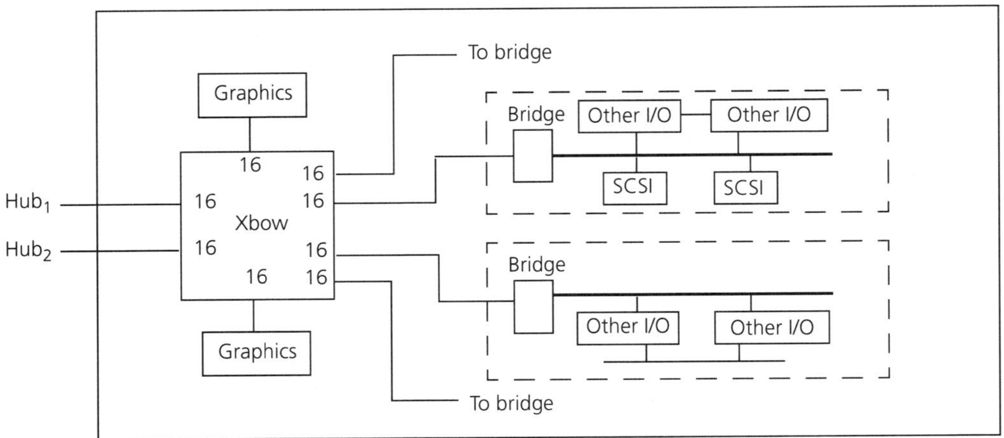

FIGURE 8.20 Typical Origin I/O configuration shared by two nodes. High-performance graphics devices connect directly to the Xbow, while other I/O devices connect to I/O buses that are linked to the Xbow through bridges.

and arbitration that allow eight ports to fit on the chip rather than six. The arbiter also supports the reservation of bandwidth for certain devices to support real-time needs like video I/O. High-performance I/O cards like graphics connect directly to the Xbow ports, but most other ports are connected through a bridge and an I/O bus that allows multiple cards to plug into it. Any processor can reference any physical I/O device in the machine, either through uncached references to a special I/O address space or through coherent DMA operations. An I/O device, too, can transfer data to and from any memory in the system, not just the memory on the node to which it is directly connected through the Xbow, thus taking advantage of the shared address space. Communication between the processor and the appropriate Xbow is handled transparently by the Hubs and network routers. Thus, like memory, I/O is physically distributed but globally accessible, so locality in I/O distribution is also a performance rather than correctness issue.

8.5.6 Hub Implementation

The communication assist—the Hub—must have certain basic abilities to implement the coherence protocol. It must be able to observe all cache misses, synchronization events, and uncached operations; keep track of outgoing requests while moving on to handle other outgoing and incoming transactions; guarantee the sinking of responses coming in from the network; invalidate cache blocks; and intervene in the caches to retrieve data. It must also coordinate the activities and dependences of all the different types of transactions that flow through it from different components and implement the necessary pathways and control. The design of such controllers is, therefore, challenging. This subsection briefly describes the major components of the Hub controller used in the Origin2000 and points out some of its salient features used to implement the coherence protocol. Further details of the actual data and control pathways through the Hub, as well as the mechanisms used to actually control the interactions among messages, are also useful for understanding how scalable cache coherence is implemented and can be read elsewhere (Singh 1997).

The Hub is divided into four major interfaces, one for each type of external entity that it connects together: the processor interface or PI, the memory/directory interface or MI, the network interface or NI, and the I/O interface or II (see Figure 8.21). These interfaces communicate with one another through an on-chip crossbar switch. Each interface is divided into a few major structures, including FIFO queues to buffer messages to/from other interfaces and to/from external entities. A key property of the design is for each interface to shield its external entity from the details of other interfaces and entities (and vice versa). For example, the PI hides the processors from the rest of the world, so any other interface must only know the behavior of the PI and not of the processors and SysAD bus themselves. Let us discuss the structures of the PI, MI, and NI briefly, as well as some examples of the shielding provided by the interfaces.

The Processor Interface (PI)

The PI has the most complex control mechanisms among the interfaces since it keeps track of outstanding protocol requests and responses and must match them. The PI interfaces with the memory (SysAD) buses of the two R10000 processors on one side and with incoming and outgoing FIFO queues connecting it to each of the other Hub interfaces on the other side (Figure 8.21). Each physical FIFO is logically separated into independent request and response "virtual FIFOs" by providing separate logic and staging buffers. In addition, the PI itself contains three pairs of coherence control buffers that keep track of outstanding transactions, control the flow of messages through the PI, and implement the interactions among messages dictated by the protocol. These buffers do not, however, hold the messages themselves. There are two read request buffers (RRBs) that track outstanding read requests from each processor, two write request buffers (WRBs) that track outstanding write requests, and two intervention request buffers (IRBs) that track incoming invalidation and intervention requests. Access to the three sets of buffers is through a single bus, so all messages contend for access to them.

A message that is recorded in one type of buffer may also need to look up another type to check for conflicting accesses or interventions to the same address from the processor. For example, an outgoing read request performs an associative lookup in the WRB to see if a write back to the same address is pending as well. If there is a conflicting WRB entry, a read request is not placed in the PI's outgoing request FIFO; rather, a bit is set in the RRB entry to indicate that when the WRB entry is freed, the read request should be reissued (i.e., when the write back is acknowledged or is canceled by an incoming invalidation as per the protocol). Buffers are also looked up to close an outstanding PI transaction in them when a completion response comes in

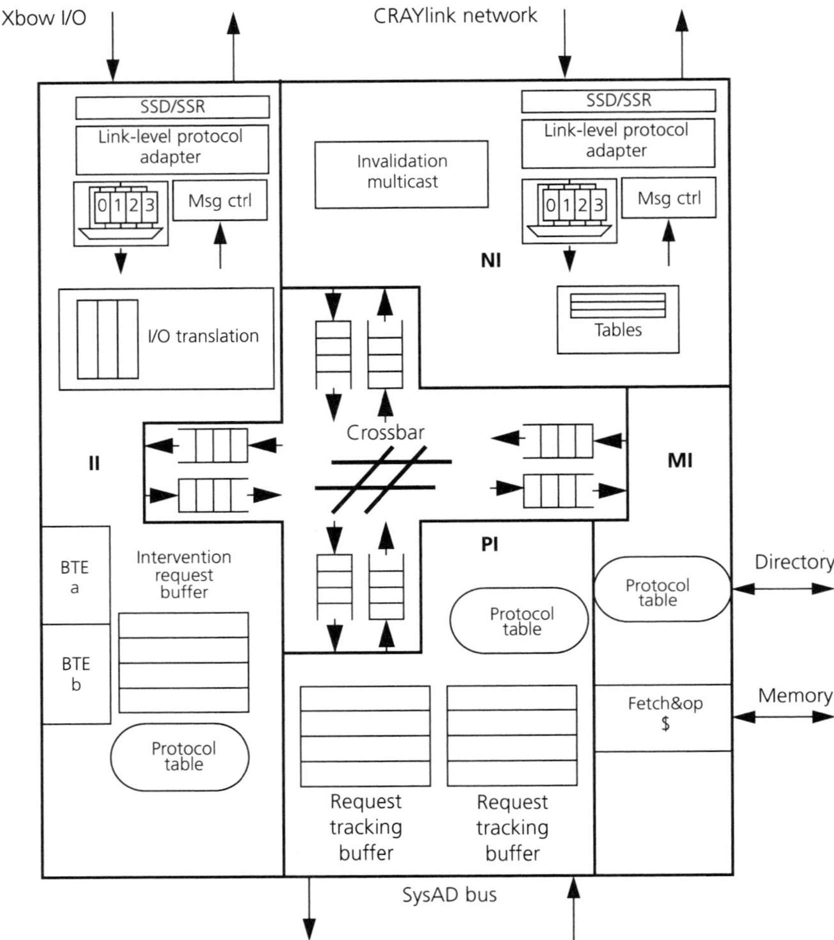

FIGURE 8.21 Layout of the Hub chip. The crossbar at the center connects the buffers of the four different interfaces. Clockwise from the bottom left, the BTEs are the block transfer engines. The top left corner is the I/O interface or II (the SSD and SSR translate signals to and from the I/O ports). Next is the network interface (NI), including the routing tables. The bottom right is the memory/directory interface (MI), and at the bottom is the processor interface (PI) with its request tracking buffers.

from either the processors in the node or from another interface. Since the order of transactions closing is not deterministic, a new transaction must go into any available slot, so these tracking buffers are implemented as fully associative rather than FIFO buffers (the queues that hold the actual messages are FIFO). The buffer lookups determine whether the PI should issue a request to either a processor or the other interfaces.

The PI is a good example of the shielding provided by interfaces. If the processor (or cache) provides data as a reply to an incoming intervention, it is the logic in the PI's outgoing FIFO that expands the reply into the two responses required by the protocol, one to the home as a sharing write-back revision message and one to the requestor. The processor itself does not have to be modified to generate two replies. Another example is in the mechanisms used to keep track of and match incoming and outgoing requests and responses. All requests passing through the PI in either direction are given request numbers, and responses carry these request numbers as well. However, the processor itself does not know about request numbers, and it is the PI's job to ensure that when it passes on incoming requests (interventions or invalidations) to the processor, it can match the processor's responses to the outstanding interventions/invalidations without the processor having to deal with request numbers.

The Memory/Directory Interface (MI)

The MI also has FIFOs between it and the Hub crossbar. The FIFO from the Hub crossbar to the MI separates headers from data so that the header of the next message can be examined by the directory while the current one is being serviced; this allows writes to be pipelined and performed at peak memory bandwidth. The MI also contains a directory interface, a memory interface, and a controller. The directory interface contains the logic and tables that determine what protocol actions to take and hence implement the coherence protocol. It also contains the logic that generates outgoing message headers, while the memory interface contains the logic that generates outgoing message data. Both the memory and directory RAMS have their own address and data buses. Some messages, like revision messages coming to the home, may not access the memory but only the directory.

On a read request, the read is issued to memory at the home speculatively, simultaneously with starting the directory operation. The directory state is available a cycle before the memory data, and the controller uses this (plus the message type and initiator) to look up the directory protocol table. This hardwired table directs the controller to the action to be taken and the message to send. The directory block sends the latter information to the memory interface, where the message headers are assembled and inserted into the outgoing FIFO together with the data returning from memory. The directory lookup itself is a read-modify-write operation. For this, the MI provides support for partial writes of memory blocks and a one-entry merge buffer to hold the bytes from the time they are read from memory to the time they are written back. Finally, to speed up the at-memory fetch&op accesses provided for synchronization, the MI contains a four-entry LRU fetch&op cache to hold the data for recent fetch&op variables and, hence, to avoid a memory or directory access. This reduces the best-case serialization time at memory for a fetch&op to 41 ns, about four 100-MHz Hub cycles.

The Network Interface (NI)

The NI interfaces the Hub crossbar to the network router for that node. The router and the Hub internals use different data transport formats, protocols, and speeds (100 MHz in the Hub versus 400 MHz in the router), so one major function of the NI is to translate between the two. Toward the router side, the NI implements a flow control mechanism to avoid network congestion (Singh 1997). The FIFOs between the NI and the network also implement separate virtual FIFOs for requests and responses, thus implementing separate virtual networks. The outgoing FIFO also has an invalidation destination generator that takes the bit vector of nodes to be invalidated and generates individual messages for them, a routing table that predetermines the routing decisions based on source and destination nodes, and virtual channel selection logic.

8.5.7 Performance Characteristics

The peak hardware bandwidths of the Origin2000 system were stated earlier: 780-MB/s SysAD bus, 670-MB/s local memory, and 780-MB/s node-to-network each way. The occupancy of the Hub at the home for a transaction on a cache block is about 20 Hub cycles (about 40 processor cycles), though it varies between 18 and 30 Hub cycles depending on whether successive directory pages accessed are in the same bank of the directory RAM and on the exact pattern of successive transactions. The latencies of memory operations depend on many factors, such as the type of operation, whether the home is local or not, where and in what state the data is currently cached, and how much contention there is for resources along the way. The latencies can be measured using microbenchmarks. Let us examine microbenchmark results for latency and bandwidth first, followed by the performance and scaling of our six parallel applications.

Characterization with Microbenchmarks

Unlike the MIPS R4400 processor used in the SGI Challenge, the Origin's MIPS R10000 processor is dynamically scheduled and does not stall on a read miss. This makes it more difficult to measure read latency, raising an interesting methodological issue. We cannot, for example, measure the unloaded latency of a read miss by simply executing the microbenchmark from Chapter 4 that reads the elements of an array with stride greater than the cache block size. Since the misses are to different locations, subsequent misses will simply be overlapped with one another and the processor will not see their full latency. Instead, this microbenchmark will give us a measure of the throughput that the system can provide on successive read misses issued from a processor. The throughput is the inverse of the latency remaining after overlap, which we can call the *pipelined latency*.

To measure the full latency, we need to ensure that subsequent operations are dependent on each other. To do this, we can use a microbenchmark that chases pointers down a linked list: the address for the next read is not available to the pro-

Table 8.1 Back-to-Back and True Unloaded Latencies for Different System Sizes

Where Miss is Satisfied	Network Routers Traversed	Back-to-Back Latency (ns)	True Unloaded Latency (ns)
L_1 cache	0	5.5	5.5
L_2 cache	0	56.9	56.9
Local memory	0	472	329
4P remote memory	1	582	449
8P remote memory	2	775	621
16P remote memory	3	826	702

The first column shows where in the extended memory hierarchy the misses are satisfied. For the 8P case, for example, the misses are satisfied in the node furthest away from the requestor in a system of 8 processors. Given the Origin2000 topology, this means traversing through two network routers in this case.

cessor until the previous read (of the pointer) completes, so the reads cannot be overlapped. However, it turns out this is a little pessimistic in determining the unloaded read latency. The reason is that the processor implements critical word restart; that is, it can use the value returned by a read as soon as that word is returned to the processor, without waiting for the rest of the cache block to be loaded in the caches. With the pointer-chasing microbenchmark, the next read will be issued before the previous block has been loaded and will contend for cache access with the loading of the rest of that block. The latency obtained from this microbenchmark, which includes this contention, can be called *back-to-back latency* (one read miss issued just as the previous one completes). Avoiding this contention between successive accesses requires that we put some computation between the read misses; the computation should depend on the data being read, so it cannot execute in parallel with the read miss, but should not access the cache between two misses. The goal is to have this computation overlap the time it takes for the rest of the cache block to load into the caches after a read miss so that the next read miss will not have to stall on cache access. The time for this overlap computation must, of course, be subtracted from the elapsed time of the microbenchmark to measure the true unloaded read-miss latency, assuming critical word restart. We can call this the *true unloaded latency.* Table 8.1 shows the back-to-back and true unloaded latencies measured on the Origin2000. Only one processor executes the microbenchmark, but the data that is accessed is distributed among the memories of different numbers of processors. The back-to-back latency is usually about 13 SysAD bus cycles (133 ns) longer because the L_2 cache block size (128 B) is 12 double words longer than the L_1 cache block size (32 B) and there is one cycle for bus turnaround.

Table 8.2 lists the back-to-back latencies for different initial states of the block being referenced (Hristea, Lenoski, and Keen 1997). Recall that the owner node is the home node when the block is in unowned or shared state at the directory and is the node that has a cached copy when the block is in exclusive state. The true unloaded latency for the case where both the home and the owner are the local node

Table 8.2 Back-to-Back Latencies (in ns) for Different Initial States of the Block

		State of Block		
Home	Owner	Unowned	Clean-Exclusive	Modified
Local	Local	472	707	1,036
Remote	Local	704	930	1,272
Local	Remote	472	930	1,159
Remote	Remote	704	917	1,097

The first column indicates whether the home of the block is local or not, the second indicates whether the current owner is local or not, and the last three columns give the latencies for the block being in different states. Of course, the owner node should be ignored for the unowned state.

(i.e., if the block is owned by main memory, the other processor in the same node) is 338 ns for the unowned state, 656 ns for the clean-exclusive state, and 892 ns for the modified state. Note that no contention is encountered with operations from other processors in this microbenchmark; latencies under real workloads will be larger.

Application Speedups

Figure 8.22 shows the speedups for the six parallel applications on a 32-processor Origin2000, using two problem sizes for each application. We see that most of the applications speed up well, especially once the problem size is large enough. The dependence on problem size is particularly stark in applications like Ocean and Raytrace. The exceptions to good speedup at this scale are Radiosity and, to an extent, Radix. In the case of Radiosity, even the larger problem is relatively small for a machine of this size and power. We can expect to see better speedups for larger scenes. For Radix, the problem is the highly scattered, bursty pattern of writes in the permutation phase. These writes are mostly to locations that are allocated remotely, and the flood of requests to and from the directories, invalidations, acknowledgments, and replies that they generate causes tremendous contention and hot spotting at Hubs and memories. Running larger problems alleviates only false sharing, since there is no other computation than the data permutation during this phase so the communication-to-computation ratio is essentially independent of problem size; in fact, the situation worsens once a processor's partition of the keys does not fit in its cache, at which point frequent write-back transactions are also thrown into the mix. For applications like Radix (and an FFT, not shown) that exhibit all-to-all bursty communication, the fact that two processors share a Hub and two Hubs share a router also causes contention at these resources, despite their high peak bandwidths (Jiang and Singh 1998). For these applications, the machine would perform better if it had only a single processor per Hub and per router. However, the sharing of resources does reduce cost and does not get in the way of the other applications.

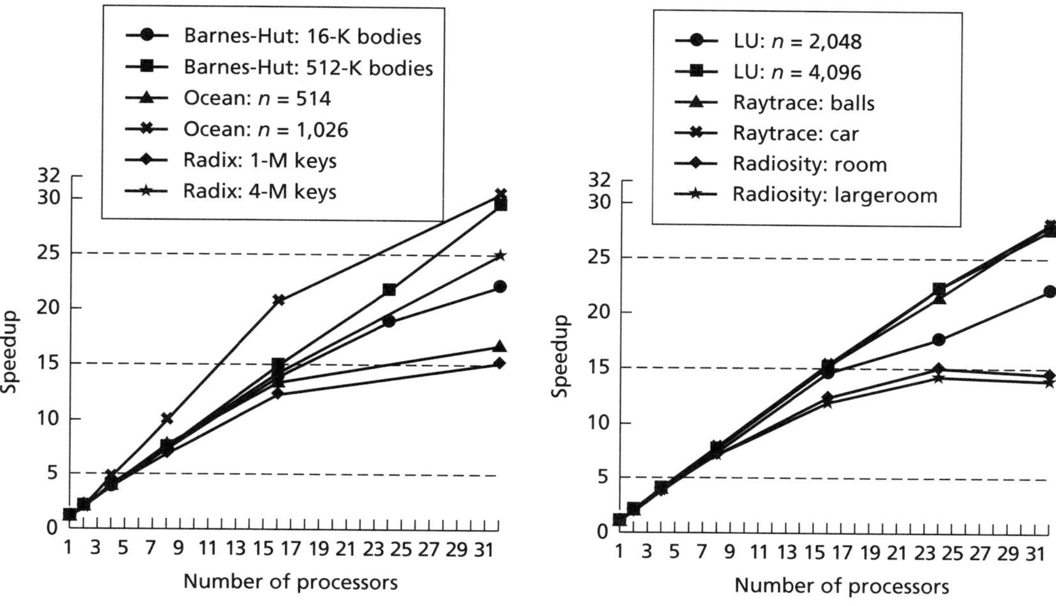

FIGURE 8.22 Speedups for the parallel applications on the Origin2000. Two problem sizes are shown for each application. The Radix sorting program does not scale well, and the Radiosity application is limited by the available input problem sizes. The other applications speed up quite well when reasonably large problem sizes are used.

Breakdowns of execution time into components on a per-processor basis on this machine were shown in Chapters 3 and 4, giving us a good idea of where time is spent.

Scaling

Figure 8.23 shows the speedups under different scaling models for the Barnes-Hut galaxy simulation on the Origin2000. The results are quite similar to those on the SGI Challenge in Chapter 6—although extended to more processors—and the analysis there largely applies. For applications like Ocean (not shown), in which an important working set is proportional to the data set size per processor, machines like the Origin2000 display an interesting effect in comparing scaling models when we start from a problem size where the working set does not fit in the cache on a uniprocessor. Under PC and TC scaling, the data set size per processor diminishes with an increasing number of processors. Thus, although the communication-to-computation ratio increases, we observe superlinear speedups once the working set starts to fit in the cache (since the performance within each node becomes much

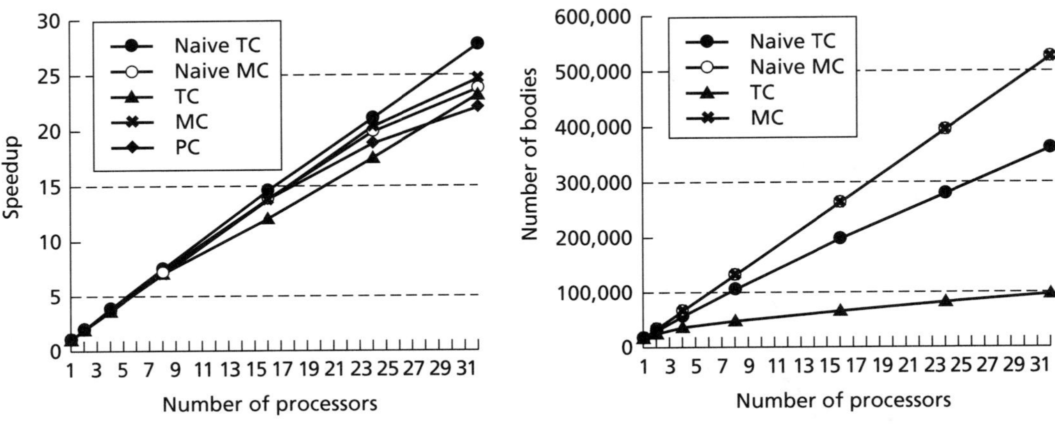

FIGURE 8.23 Scaling of speedups and number of bodies simulated under different scaling models for the Barnes-Hut galaxy simulation on the Origin2000. As with the results for bus-based machines in Chapter 6, the speedups are very good under all scaling models, and the number of bodies that can be simulated grows much more slowly under realistic TC scaling than under MC or naive TC scaling.

better when the working set fits in the cache). Under MC scaling, the communication-to-computation ratio does not change, but neither does the working set size per processor. As a result, although the demands on the communication architecture scale more favorably under MC scaling than under TC or PC scaling (the capacity misses due to the working sets are almost entirely local), speedups are not so good because the beneficial effect on node performance of the working set suddenly fitting in the cache is no longer observed. Also, even local capacity misses occupy the Hub and memory, contributing to contention.

8.6 CACHE-BASED DIRECTORY PROTOCOLS: THE SEQUENT NUMA-Q

The flat, cache-based directory protocol described in our second case study is the IEEE standard Scalable Coherent Interface (SCI) protocol (Gustavson 1992). As a case study of this protocol, we examine the NUMA-Q machine from Sequent Computer Systems, Inc., a machine targeted toward commercial workloads such as databases and transaction processing (Lovett and Clapp 1996). This machine relies heavily on third-party commodity hardware, using stock Intel SMPs as the processing nodes, stock I/O links, and the DataPump network interface from Vitesse Semiconductor Corporation to move data between the node and the network. The only customization is in the IQ-Link board used to implement the SCI directory protocol. A similar directory protocol is also used (with much more customization) in the Convex Exemplar series of machines (Convex Computer Corporation 1993; Thekkath et al. 1997), which, like the SGI Origin, is targeted more toward scientific computing.

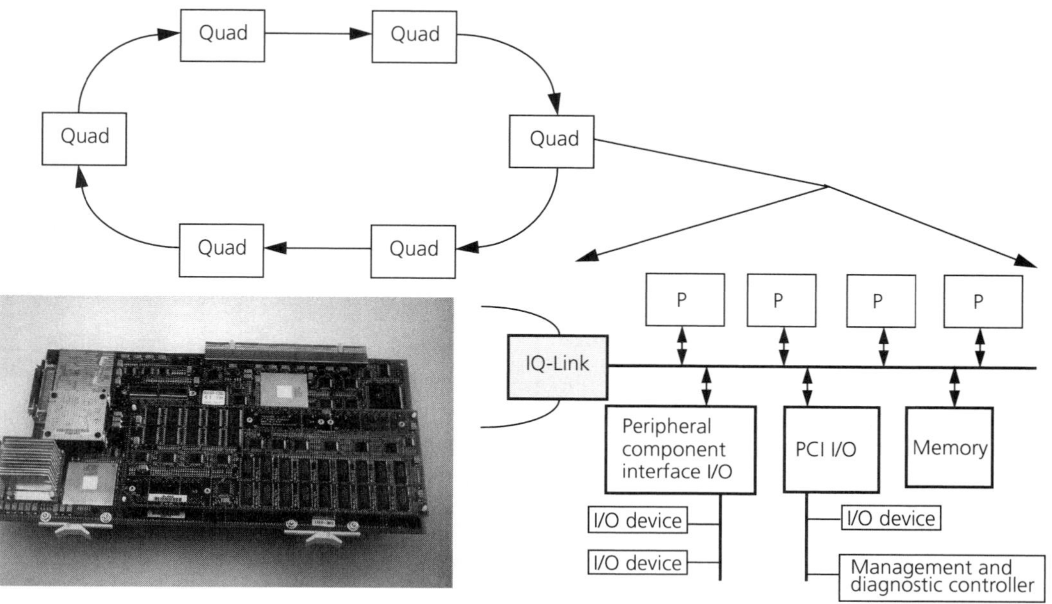

FIGURE 8.24 Block diagram of the Sequent NUMA-Q multiprocessor. The diagram shows the high-level organization of the machine, both across nodes and within a node. The photograph shows an IQ-Link board. *Source:* Photo courtesy of Sequent Computer Systems, Inc.

NUMA-Q is a collection of homogeneous processing nodes interconnected by high-speed links in a ring configuration (Figure 8.24). Each processing node is an inexpensive Intel quad bus-based multiprocessor with four Intel Pentium Pro microprocessors, which illustrates the use of high-volume SMPs as building blocks for larger systems. Systems from Data General (Clark and Alnes 1996) and from HAL Computer Systems (Weber et al. 1997) also use Pentium Pro quads as their processing nodes, the former also using an SCI protocol similar to NUMA-Q across quads and the latter using a memory-based protocol inspired by the Stanford DASH protocol. (In the Convex Exemplar series, the individual nodes connected by the SCI protocol are not bus based but are small directory-based multiprocessors kept internally coherent by a different directory protocol.) We described the quad SMP node in Chapter 1 (see Figure 1.17) and so do not discuss it further.

The IQ-Link board in each quad plugs into the quad memory bus and takes the place of the Hub in the SGI Origin. In addition to the directory logic and storage and the datapath between the quad bus and the network, it also contains a large (expandable) 32-MB, four-way set-associative remote access cache for blocks that are fetched to the node from remote memory. This *remote access cache,* hereafter called the *remote cache,* represents the quad to the cross-node SCI directory protocol. It is the only cache in the quad that is visible to that protocol; the individual processor caches are kept coherent with the remote cache through the snooping bus protocol within the quad. The directory protocol is for the most part oblivious to how many processors there are within a node and even to the bus protocol itself. Inclusion is preserved between the remote cache and the processor caches within the node, so if a block is replaced from the remote cache it is invalidated in the processor caches, and if a block is placed in modified state in a processor cache then the state in the remote cache reflects this. The cache block size of the remote cache is 64 bytes, which is therefore the granularity of both communication and coherence across quads.

8.6.1 Cache Coherence Protocol

While two interacting coherence protocols are used in the Sequent NUMA-Q machine, this section focuses on the SCI directory protocol across remote caches and ignores the multiprocessor nature of the quad nodes. Interactions with the snooping MESI protocol within the quads are discussed in Section 8.6.5.

Directory Structure

The directory structure of SCI is the flat, cache-based distributed doubly linked-list scheme that was described in Section 8.2.3 and illustrated in Figure 8.8. There is a linked list of sharers per block, and the pointer to the head of this list is stored with the main memory that is the home of the corresponding memory block. An entry in the list corresponds to a remote cache in a quad. The remote cache is stored in synchronous DRAM memory in the IQ-Link board of that quad, together with the forward and backward pointers for the list. Figure 8.25 shows a simplified representation of a list. The first element (node) is called the head of the list and the last node the tail. The head node has both read and write permission on its cached block whereas the other nodes have only read permission (except in a special-case extension, called pairwise sharing, that we discuss briefly in Section 8.6.3). The pointer in a node that points to its neighbor in the direction toward the tail of the list is called the forward or downstream pointer, and the other is called the backward or upstream pointer. Let us see how the cross-node SCI coherence protocol uses this directory representation.

States

Since processor caches are not visible to the directory protocol, and since a block never enters the remote cache at its home node, unlike in the Origin, the directory protocol in the NUMA-Q does not keep track of cached copies at the home. Keeping the copy in the home memory coherent with these cached copies is the job of the bus protocol. A block in main memory can be in one of three directory states whose names are defined by the SCI protocol as follows. The states are similar to but not the same as the directory states in the Origin protocol.

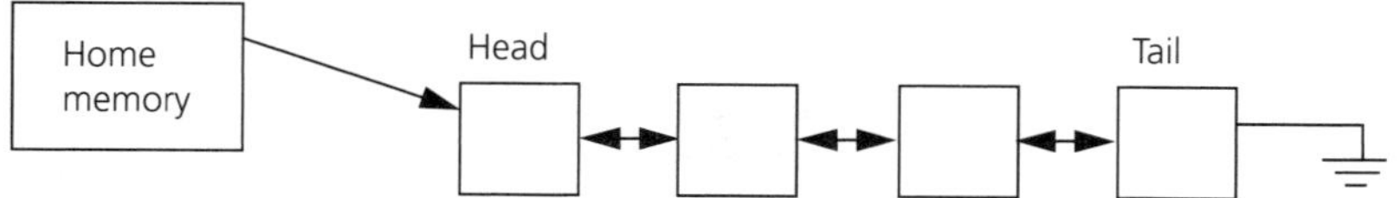

FIGURE 8.25 An SCI sharing list. Each element of the list in NUMA-Q is a multiprocessor node, represented by its remote cache.

- *Home*: No remote cache (quad) in the system contains a copy of the block (of course, a processor cache in the home quad itself may have a copy since this is not visible to the SCI coherence protocol but is managed by the bus protocol within the quad). This is like the unowned directory state in the Origin.
- *Fresh*: One or more remote caches may have a read-only copy, and the copy in memory is valid.This is like the shared state in the Origin.
- *Gone*: Another remote cache contains a writable (exclusive or dirty) copy. No valid copy exists on the local node. This is like the exclusive directory state in the Origin.

Consider the cache states for blocks in a remote cache. While the processor caches within a quad use the standard MESI stable states, the SCI scheme that governs the remote caches has a large number of possible cache states. In fact, 7 bits are used to represent the state of a block in a remote cache, and the standard describes 29 stable states and many pending (busy) or transient states. Each stable state can be thought of as having two parts, which is reflected in the naming structure of the states. The first part describes where that cache entry is located in the sharing list for that block. This may be ONLY (for a single-node list), HEAD, TAIL, or MID (which means neither the head nor the tail of a multiple-node list). The second part describes the actual state of the cached block. This includes states like dirty (modified and writable); clean (unmodified, same contents as memory, but writable, like the exclusive state in MESI); fresh (data may be read but may not be written until memory is informed); copy (unmodified and readable); and several others. A full description can be found in the SCI standards document (IEEE Computer Society 1993). We shall encounter some of these states (such as HEAD-DIRTY, TAIL-CLEAN, etc.) as we go along.

The SCI standard defines three primitive operations that can be performed on a distributed sharing list. Memory operations such as read misses, write misses, write backs, and replacements are implemented using these three primitive operations:

1. *List construction*: adding a new node (sharer) to the head of a sharing list.
2. *Rollout*: removing a node from a list, which requires that a node communicate with its upstream and downstream neighbors, informing them of their new neighbors so they can update their pointers.
3. *Purging (invalidation)*: the node at the head may purge or invalidate all other nodes, thus resulting in a single-element list. Only the head node of a list can issue a purge.

The SCI standard also describes three levels of increasingly sophisticated SCI protocols. The *minimal* protocol does not permit even read sharing; that is, only one node at a time can have a cached copy of a block. The *typical* protocol is what most systems are expected to implement. It has provisions for read sharing (multiple copies), efficient access to data that is in FRESH state in memory, as well as options for efficient DMA transfers and robust recovery from errors. Finally, the *full* protocol implements all of the options defined by the standard, including optimizations for pairwise sharing between only two nodes and queue-on-lock-bit (QOLB) synchronization (to be discussed later). The NUMA-Q system implements the typical protocol, and this is the one we discuss. Let us see how different types of memory operations—read misses, write misses, and replacements (including write backs)—are handled. In each case, the identity of the home node is first determined from the address of the block.

Handling Read Requests

Suppose the read request needs to be propagated off quad. We can think of this node's remote cache as the requesting cache as far as the SCI protocol is concerned. The requesting cache first allocates an entry for the block if necessary and sets the cache state of the block to a pending (busy) state; in this state, it will not process other requests for that block that come to it. (The SCI protocol often puts cached blocks in busy states at requestors in this way, to keep transactions for a block atomic and to facilitate serialization, much like the Origin protocol did with its busy states at the directory. However, it does not use NACKs, as we shall see.) It then begins a list construction operation to add itself to the head of the sharing list by sending a request to the home node. When the home receives the request, its block may be in one of the three directory states identified earlier: HOME, FRESH, or GONE.

If the directory state is HOME, there are no cached copies and the copy in memory is valid. On receiving the read request, the home updates its state for the block to FRESH and sets its head pointer to point to the requesting node. The home then replies to the requestor with the data, which upon receipt updates its state from PENDING to ONLY_FRESH. All actions at a node in response to a given transaction are atomic (the processing for one is completed before the next one is handled), and a strict request-response protocol is followed in all cases (unlike in Origin).

If the directory state is FRESH, there is already a sharing list, but the copy at the home is also valid. The home changes its head pointer to point to the requesting cache instead of the previous head of the list. It then sends back a transaction to the requestor containing the data as well as a pointer to the previous head. On receipt, the requestor moves to a different pending state and sends a transaction to that previous head asking to be attached as the new head of the list (the list construction operation). The previous head reacts to this message by changing its state from HEAD_FRESH to MID_VALID or from ONLY_FRESH to TAIL_VALID as the case may be, updating its backward pointer to point to the requestor and sending an acknowledgment to the requestor. When the requestor receives this acknowledgment, it sets its forward pointer to point to the previous head and changes its state

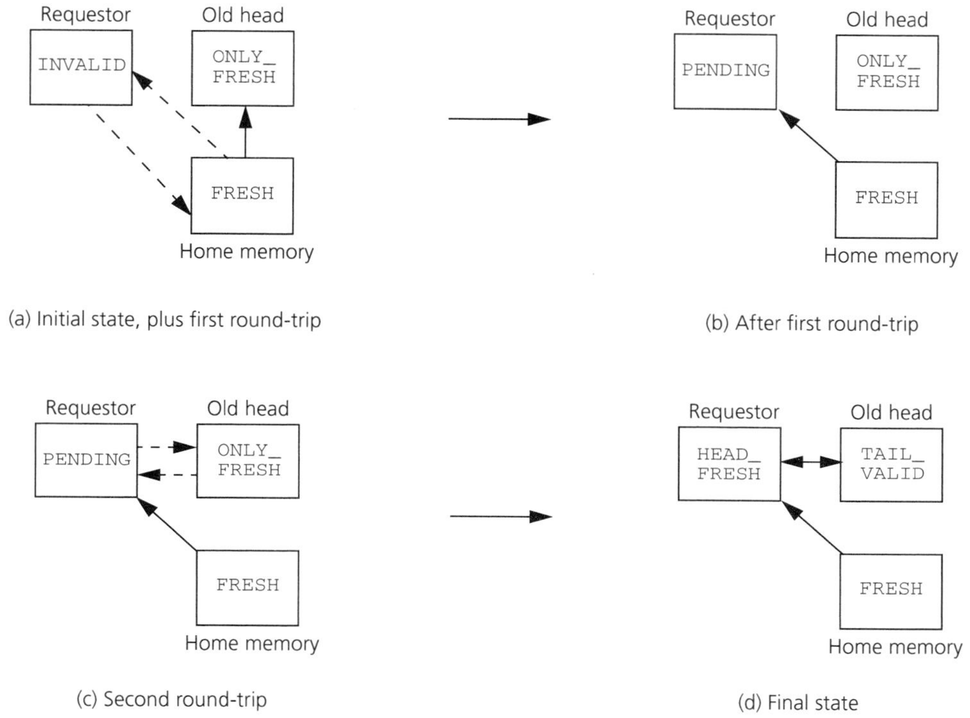

FIGURE 8.26 An example of a read miss in the SCI protocol. The figure shows the messages and state transitions for a read miss to a block that is initially in the FRESH state at home, with one node on the sharing list. Solid lines are the pointers in the sharing list, whereas dotted lines represent network transactions. Null pointers are not shown.

from the pending state to HEAD_FRESH. The sequence of transactions and actions is shown in Figure 8.26 for the case where the previous head is in state HEAD_FRESH when the request comes to it.

If the directory state is GONE, the cache at the head of the sharing list has an exclusive (clean or modified) copy of the block. Now, the memory does not reply with the data but simply stays in the GONE state and sends a pointer to the previous head back to the requestor. The requestor goes to a new pending state and sends a request to the previous head, asking both for the data and to attach to the head of the list (list construction). The previous head changes its state from HEAD_DIRTY to MID_VALID or from ONLY_DIRTY to TAIL_VALID (or whatever is appropriate), sets its backward pointer to point to the requestor, and returns the data to the requestor. (The data may have to be retrieved from a processor cache in the previous head node.) The requestor then updates its copy, sets its state to HEAD_DIRTY, and sets its forward pointer to point to the new head, all in a single atomic action as always. Note that even though the reference was a read, the head of the sharing list is left in HEAD_DIRTY state. This does not have the standard meaning of dirty that we are familiar with; that is, that the head node can write that data without having to invalidate any other caches. It means that it can indeed write the data into the cache without communicating with the home (and even before sending out the invalidations), but it must invalidate the other nodes in the sharing list since they are in valid state.

It is possible to fetch a block in HEAD_DIRTY state even when the directory state is not GONE, for example, when the requesting node is expected to write that block soon afterward. In this case, if the directory state is FRESH the memory returns the data to the requestor, together with a pointer to the old head of the sharing list, and then puts itself in GONE state. The requestor then prepends itself to the sharing list by sending a request to the old head and puts itself in the HEAD_DIRTY state. The old head changes its state from HEAD_FRESH to MID_VALID or from ONLY_FRESH to TAIL_VALID as appropriate, and other nodes on the sharing list remain unchanged.

In the preceding cases, a requestor is always directed by the home to the old head. It is possible that the old head (let's call it *A*) is in a pending state when the request from the new requestor (*B*) reaches it since it may itself have a memory operation outstanding on that block. This is dealt with not by buffering the request at the old head or NACKing it but by extending the sharing list backward into a (still distributed) *pending list*. That is, node *B* will indeed be physically attached to the head of the list but in a pending state waiting to truly become the head. If another node *C* now makes a request to the home, it will be forwarded to node *B* and will also attach itself to the pending list (the home will now point to *C*, so subsequent requests will be directed there, and so on). At any time, we call the "true head" (here *A*) simply the *head* of the sharing list, we call the part of the list before the true head the *pending list,* and we call the latest element to have joined the pending list (here *C*) the *pending head* (see Figure 8.27). When *A* leaves the pending state and completes its operation, it will pass on the "true head" status to *B,* which will in turn pass it on to *C* when its request is completed. Note also that, unlike in the Origin, no pending or busy state exists at the directory, which always simply takes atomic actions to change its state and head pointer and returns the previous state/pointer information to the requestor, a point we will revisit when discussing how correctness issues are addressed.

Handling Write Requests

The head node of a sharing list is assumed to always have the latest copy of the block (unless the head node is in a pending state). Thus, only the head node is allowed to write a block and issue invalidations. When a node incurs a write miss, three cases are possible. In the first case, the writer is already at the head of the list, but it does not have the sole modified copy (e.g., there may be other sharers). It first ensures that it is in the appropriate state for this case, by communicating with the home if necessary (and in the process ensuring that the home block is already in or transitions to the GONE state). It then modifies the data locally and invalidates the rest of the nodes in the sharing list. (This case is elaborated on in the next two para-

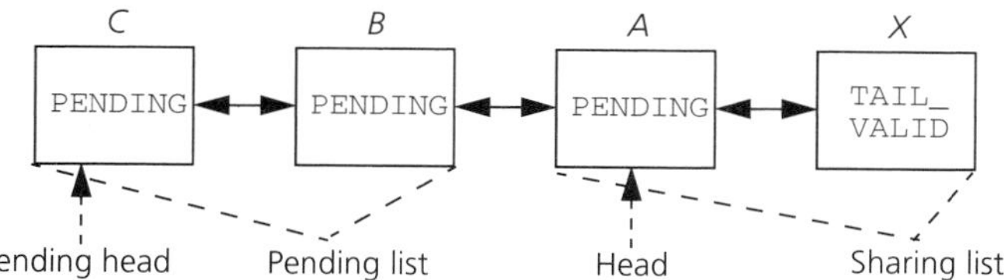

FIGURE 8.27 Pending lists in the SCI protocol. The pending list is a continuation (in the reverse direction) of the regular sharing list. The true head (called the head) and the nodes in the pending list are in pending states.

graphs.) In the second case, the writer is not in the sharing list at all. The writer must first allocate space for and obtain a copy of the block, then add itself to the head of the list using the list construction operation, and then perform the preceding steps to complete the write. The third case is when the writer is in the sharing list but not at the head. In this case, it must remove itself from the list (rollout), then add itself to the head (list construction), and finally perform the preceding steps. We discuss rollout further in the context of replacement, where it is also needed, and we have already seen list construction. Let us focus now on the case where the writing node is already at the head of the list.

If the block is in the HEAD_DIRTY state in the writer's cache, it is modified right away (since the directory must already be in GONE state) and then the writing node purges the rest of the sharing list. The purge operation is done in a serialized request-response manner: an invalidation request is sent to the next node in the sharing list, which rolls itself out from the list and sends back to the head a pointer to the next node in the list. The head then sends this node a similar request, and so on until all entries are purged (i.e., until the response to the head contains a null pointer; see also Figure 8.28). The writer, or head node, stays in a pending state while the purging is in progress. During this time, new attempts to add to the sharing list are delayed in a pending list as usual. The latency of purging a sharing list is a few serialized round-trips (invalidation request, acknowledgment, and the rollout transactions) plus the associated actions per sharing list entry, so it is important that long sharing lists are not encountered often on writes. It is possible to reduce the number of network transactions in the critical path by having each node pass on an invalidation request to the next node and perhaps acknowledge the previous node rather than return the identity to the writer. This is not part of the SCI standard since it distributes the state of the invalidation progress and hence complicates protocol-level recovery from errors; however, practical systems may be tempted to take advantage of this shortcut, especially if sharing lists are long.

If the writer is the head of the sharing list but has the block in HEAD_FRESH state, then it must be changed to HEAD_DIRTY before the block can be modified and the rest of the entries purged. The writer goes into a pending state and sends a request to the home, the home changes from FRESH to GONE state and replies to the message, and then the writer goes into a different pending state and purges the rest

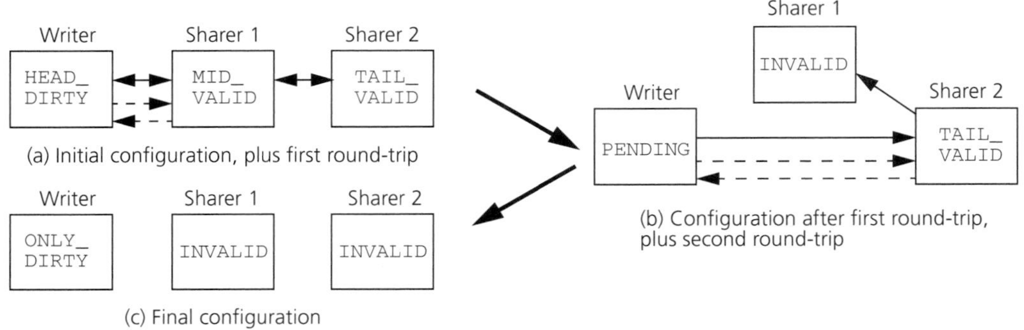

FIGURE 8.28 Purging a sharing list from a HEAD_DIRTY node in SCI. Solid arrows connecting list nodes are list pointers, while dashed arrows indicate network transactions that implement the transition to the next configuration.

of the blocks as was just described. It may be that when the request reaches the home the home is no longer in FRESH state, but it points to a newly queued node that got there in the meantime and has been directed to the writer. When the home looks up its state, it detects this situation and sends the writer a corresponding response that is like a NACK. When the writer receives this response, based on its local pending state it deletes itself from the sharing list (how it does this, given that a request is coming at it, is discussed in the next subsection) and tries to reattach as the head in HEAD_DIRTY or ONLY_DIRTY state by sending the appropriate new request to the home. This is not a retry, in the sense that the writer does not try the same request again, but is a suitably modified request to reflect the new state of itself and the home (similar to modifying an upgrade to a read exclusive in the race condition due to nonatomic state transitions discussed in Chapter 6). The last case for a write by a head node is if the writer has the block in ONLY_DIRTY state, in which case it can modify the block without generating any network transactions.

Handling Write-Back and Replacement Requests

A node that is in a sharing list for a block may need to delete itself, either because it must become the head in order to perform a write operation, or because it must be replaced in its remote cache for capacity or conflict reasons, or because it is being invalidated. In the case of a replacement, even if the block is in shared state and does not have to write data back, the space in the cache (and the pointers) will now be used for another block and its list pointers, so to preserve a correct representation the block being replaced must be removed from its sharing list. These replacements and list removals use the rollout operation.

Consider the general case of a node trying to roll out from the middle of a sharing list. The node first sets itself to a pending state, then sends a request each to its upstream and downstream neighbors asking them to update their forward and backward pointers, respectively, to skip that node. The pending state is needed since there is nothing to prevent two adjacent nodes in a sharing list from trying to roll themselves out at the same time, which can lead to a race condition in the updating of pointers. Even with the pending state, if two adjacent nodes indeed try to roll out at the same time, they may set themselves to pending state simultaneously and send messages to each other. This can cause deadlock since neither will respond while it is in pending state. A simple priority system is used to avoid such deadlock: by convention, the node closer to the tail of the list has priority and is rolled out first. The roll-out operation is completed by setting the state of the rolled-out cache entry to invalid when both the neighbors have replied. The neighbors of the node that is rolling out do not have to change their state except when the node being rolled out is the second in a two-node list; in that case, the head of the list may change its state from HEAD_DIRTY or HEAD_FRESH to ONLY_DIRTY or ONLY_FRESH as appropriate.

If the entry to be rolled out is the head of the list, then the entry may be in dirty state (a write back) or in fresh state (a replacement). The same set of transactions is used in either case. The head puts itself in a pending state and first sends a transaction to its downstream neighbor. This causes the latter to set its backward pointer to the home memory and change its state appropriately (e.g., from TAIL_VALID or MID_VALID to HEAD_DIRTY or from MID_FRESH to HEAD_FRESH). When the replacing (head) node receives a response, it sends a transaction to the home, which updates its pointer to point to the new head but need not change its state. The home sends a response to the replacer, which is now out of the list and sets its state to INVALID. Of course, if the replacer is the only node in the list, then it needs to communicate only with memory, which will set its state to HOME.

This scenario of a head node rolling out provides another example of the state at the recipient of a request not being compatible with that request when it arrives. By the time the message from the replacer gets to the home, the home may have set its head pointer to point to a different node *X* from which it has received a request for the block in the interim. In general, whenever a transaction comes in, the recipient looks up its local state and the incoming request type; if it detects a mismatch, the general strategy adopted by the protocol is as we saw earlier in the example of a write to a block in HEAD_FRESH state: the recipient does not perform the operation that the request solicits but issues a response that is a lot like a NACK. The requestor will then check its local state again and take an appropriate action. In this specific case, the home detects that the incoming transaction type requires that the requestor be the current head; this is not true, so it NACKs the request. The replacer keeps retrying the request to the home and keeps being NACKed. At some point, the request from node *X* that was redirected to the replacer will reach the replacer, asking to be prepended to the list. The replacer will look up its (pending) state and send a response to that requestor, telling it to instead go to the downstream neighbor (the real head since the replacer is rolling out of the list). The replacer is now off the list and in a different pending state; it is waiting to go to INVALID state, which it will do when the next NACK from the home reaches it. Thus, the SCI protocol does include NACKs, but not in the traditional sense of asking requests to retry when a node or resource is busy. NACKs are used just to indicate inappropriate requests and facilitate changes of state at the requestor; the difference is that in this case a request that is NACKed will never succeed in its original form but may cause a new type of request to be generated, which may succeed.

Finally, when a block needs to be written back upon a miss, an important performance question is whether the miss should be satisfied first or the block should be written back first. In discussing bus-based protocols, we saw that most often the miss is serviced first and the block to be written back is put in a write-back buffer. In NUMA-Q, the simplifying decision is made to service the write back (rollout) first and only then satisfy the miss. Although this slows down the miss, the complexity of the buffering solution is greater here than in bus-based systems (where the write-back buffer can simply be snooped). Also, the replacements and hence write backs we are concerned with here are from the remote cache, which is large enough (tens of megabytes) that replacements are likely to be very infrequent.

8.6.2 Dealing with Correctness Issues

A major emphasis in the SCI standard is providing well-defined, uniform mechanisms for preserving serialization, resolving race conditions, and avoiding deadlock, livelock, and starvation. The standard takes a stronger position on starvation and fairness than many other coherence protocols. It was mentioned earlier that most of the correctness considerations are satisfied by the use of distributed lists of sharers as well as pending requests, but let us look at how this works in more detail.

Serialization of Operations to a Given Location

In the SCI protocol, the home node is the entity that determines the order in which cache misses to a block are serialized. However, unlike in the Origin protocol, here the order is that in which the requests first arrive at the home, and the mechanism used for ensuring this order is very different. There is no busy state at the home. Generally (except for some race conditions described earlier), the home accepts every request that comes to it, either satisfying it wholly by itself or directing it to the node that it sees as the current head of the sharing list (the pending head if there is a pending list). Before it directs the request to another node, it first updates its head pointer to point to the current requestor. The next request for the block from any node will see the updated state and pointer (i.e., to the current requestor) even though the operation corresponding to the current request is not globally complete. This ensures that the home does not direct two conflicting requests for a block to the same node at the same time, avoiding race conditions. As we have seen, if a request cannot be satisfied at the head node to which it was directed—that is, if that node is in pending state—the requestor will attach itself to the distributed pending list for that block and await its turn as long as necessary (see Figure 8.27). Nodes in the pending list obtain access to the block in FIFO order, ensuring that the order in which they complete is indeed the same as that in which they first reached the home.

While the home may NACK requests when some race conditions are encountered, those requests will never succeed in their current form, so they do not count in the serialization. They may be modified to new, different requests that will succeed, and in that case those new requests will be serialized in the order in which they first reach the home.

Memory Consistency Model

The SCI standard defines both a coherence protocol and a transport layer, including a network interface design. However, it does not specify many other aspects, like details of the physical implementation or even the memory consistency model. Such matters are left to the system implementor. NUMA-Q does not satisfy sequential consistency but uses a more relaxed memory consistency model called *processor consistency* that we shall discuss in Section 9.1. Interestingly, as in Origin, the consistency model chosen for the system is the one supported by the underlying microprocessor.

Deadlock, Livelock, and Starvation

The fact that a distributed pending list is used to hold waiting requests at the requestors themselves, rather than a hardware queue shared at the home node by all blocks allocated in it, implies that there is no danger of input buffers filling up and, hence, no deadlock problem at the protocol level. A strict request-response protocol is used as well. Since requests are not NACKed from the home to alleviate blockages or contention (only under certain race conditions when they must be altered) but will simply join the pending list and always make progress, livelock does not occur. The list mechanism also ensures that the requests are handled in FIFO order as they first come to the home, thus preventing starvation.

The total number of pending lists that a node can be a part of is the number of requests it can have outstanding, and the storage for the pending lists is already available in the cache entries, so there is little need for extra buffering at the protocol level. (Replacement of a pending entry is not allowed; the memory operation that causes the replacement stalls until the entry is no longer pending.) While the SCI standard does not take a position on queuing and buffering issues at the lower transport level, most implementations, including NUMA-Q, use separate request and response queues on each of the incoming and outgoing paths.

Error Handling

The SCI standard provides some options in the typical protocol to recover from errors at the hardware link level. NUMA-Q does not implement these but, rather, assumes that the hardware links are reliable. Standard ECC and CRC checks are provided to detect and recover from hardware errors in the memory and network links. Robustness to errors at the protocol level often comes at the cost of performance.

For example, SCI's decision to have the writer send all the invalidations one by one, serialized by responses, simplifies error recovery since the writer knows how many invalidations have been completed when an error occurs; however, it but compromises performance. While NUMA-Q retains this feature, other systems may choose not to.

8.6.3 Protocol Extensions

While the SCI protocol is fair and quite robust to errors, many types of operations can generate several serialized network transactions and therefore become quite expensive. A read miss requires two network transactions with the home, at least two with the head node if there is one, and perhaps more with the head node if it is in pending state. A replacement requires a rollout, which requires communication with both neighbors. But, potentially, the most troublesome operation from a scalability viewpoint is invalidation on a write since the cost of the invalidation scales linearly with the number of nodes on the sharing list with a fairly large constant (more than a round-trip time). The use of distributed pending lists can increase latency too, and, in general, the latency of misses tends to be larger than in memory-based protocols. Extensions have been proposed to SCI to deal with widely shared data through a combination of hardware organization and protocol. For example, instead of a single large ring interconnect, the SCI standard envisions building large systems by connecting many smaller rings together in a hierarchy using bridges and switches; the protocol can exploit combining transactions in this hierarchy. Some extensions require changes to the basic protocol and hardware structures whereas others are compatible with the basic SCI protocol and only require new implementations of the bridges. The complexity of the extensions may reduce performance for low degrees of sharing. They are not finalized in the standard and are beyond the scope of this discussion. More information can be found in (IEEE Computer Society 1995; Kaxiras and Goodman 1996; Kaxiras 1996). One extension that is included in the standard specializes the protocol for the case in which only two nodes share a cache block and they ping-pong ownership of it back and forth between themselves by both writing it repeatedly. This is described in the SCI protocol document (IEEE Computer Society 1993). NUMA-Q includes another protocol extension that is a special protocol operation that enables a processor to obtain a copy of a block even while it is invalidating the (nonhome) source of the block.

Unlike Origin, NUMA-Q does not provide hardware or OS support for dynamic page migration. With the very large remote caches, capacity misses in the processor caches to remotely allocated data are almost always satisfied in the remote cache in the local node. However, proper page placement can still be useful when a processor writes and has to obtain ownership for data. If nobody else has a copy (e.g., in the interior portion of a processor's partition in the equation solver kernel or in Ocean), then if the home is local, obtaining ownership does not generate network traffic; however, if home is remote, a round-trip to the home is needed to look up directory state. The NUMA-Q position is that data migration in main memory is the responsibility of user-level software. The exception is when a process migrates, in which case the OS uses a heuristic to possibly migrate that process's active pages as well, making them local at the new location. The designers considered this to be the important context for page migration. Similarly, little hardware support is provided for synchronization beyond simple atomic exchange primitives like test&set.

8.6.4 Overview of NUMA-Q Hardware

Within a quad multiprocessor node, the second-level caches per processor currently shipped in NUMA-Q systems are 512 KB or 1 MB large and four-way set associative with a 32-byte block size. The quad bus is a 532-MB/s split-transaction in-order bus, with limited facilities for out-of-order responses that are needed by a two-level coherence scheme. (Even if the bus within an SMP node provides in-order responses, when a request must go to a remote node it is infeasible to have its response be in-order with respect to responses generated within the local node.) A quad also contains up to 4 GB of globally addressable main memory; two 32-bit-wide 133-MB/s peripheral component interface (PCI) buses connected to the quad bus by PCI bridges and to which I/O devices and a memory and diagnostic controller can attach; and the IQ-Link board that plugs into the memory bus and includes the communication assist and the network interface.

In addition to the directory information for locally allocated data and the tags for remotely allocated but locally cached data (which it keeps on both the bus side and the directory side), the IQ-Link board consists of four major functional blocks as shown in Figure 8.29: the bus interface controller, the DataPump, the SCI link interface controller, and the RAM arrays. The *Orion bus interface controller* (OBIC) provides the interface to the shared quad bus, managing the remote cache data arrays and the bus snooping and requesting logic. It acts as both a pseudo memory controller that snoops and translates accesses to nonlocal data as well as a pseudo-processor that puts incoming transactions from the network onto the bus. The *DataPump*, a gallium arsenide chip built by Vitesse Semiconductor Corporation, provides the link and packet-level transport protocol of the SCI standard. It provides an interface to a ring interconnect, pulling off packets that are destined for its quad node and letting other packets go by. The *SCI link interface controller* (SCLIC) interfaces to the DataPump and the OBIC as well as to the interrupt controller and the directory tags. Its main function is to manage the SCI coherence protocol, using one or more programmable protocol engines. The *RAM arrays* implement the data and the different tags needed for the remote cache. These components are described further when we discuss the implementation of the IQ-Link in Section 8.6.6.

For the interconnection across quads, the SCI standard defines both a transport layer and a cache coherence protocol. The transport layer defines a functional specification for a node-to-network interface and a network topology that consists of rings made of point-to-point links. In particular, it defines a 1-GB/s ring interconnect and the transactions that can be generated on it. The NUMA-Q system is initially a single-ring topology of up to eight quads as shown in Figure 8.24. Cables from the quads connect to the ports of a ring that is contained in a single box called the IQ-Plus. Larger systems will include multiple eight-quad systems connected

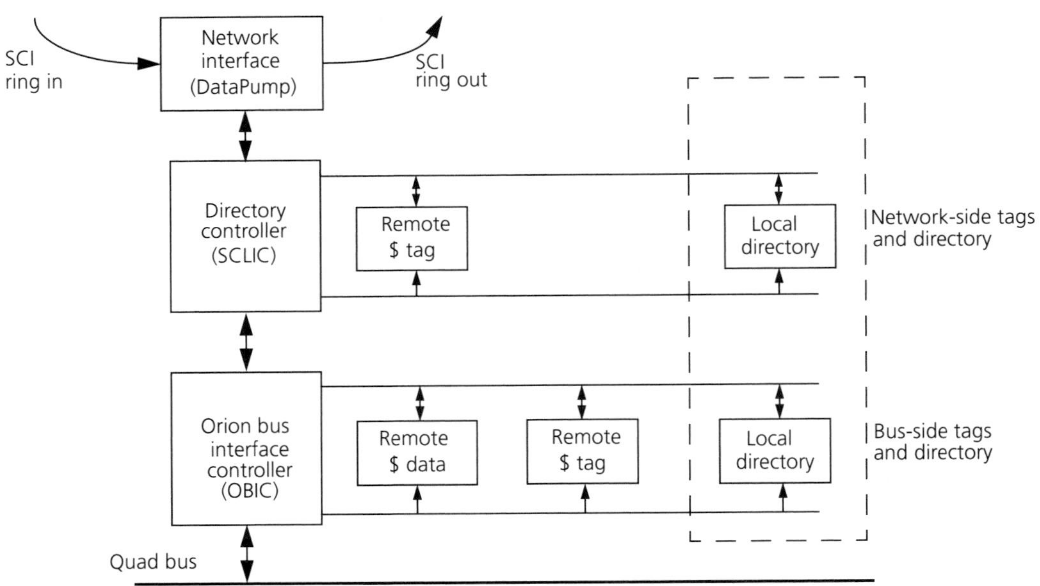

FIGURE 8.29 Functional block diagram of the NUMA-Q IQ-Link board. The remote cache data is implemented in synchronous DRAM (SDRAM). The bus-side tags and directory are implemented in Static RAM (SRAM) whereas the network-side tags and directory can afford to be slower and are therefore implemented in SDRAM.

with local area networks. As mentioned earlier, the SCI standard envisions that, because of the high latency of long rings, larger systems will generally be built out of multiple rings interconnected by switches. With a small number of outstanding requests per node, the latency of a long ring severely limits the node-to-network bandwidth that a node can achieve (see Chapter 11). The transport layer of SCI will be discussed further in Chapter 10.

Since the machine is targeted toward database and transaction processing workloads, I/O is an important focus of the NUMA-Q design. As in Origin, I/O is globally addressable, so any processor can directly write to or read from any I/O device, not just those attached to the local quad. A nonlocal processor does not have to send an explicit message to the quad to which the device is attached and have a processor on that quad issue the access. This is very convenient for commercial applications, which are not often structured so that a processor need only access its local disks. I/O devices are connected to the two PCI buses that attach through PCI bridges to the quad bus. Each PCI bus is clocked at half the speed of the memory bus and is half as wide, yielding roughly one-quarter the bandwidth. Physically, there are two ways for a processor to access I/O devices on other quads. One is through the SCI rings, whether through the cache coherence protocol or through uncached writes, just as Origin does through its Hubs and network. However, bandwidth is a precious resource on a

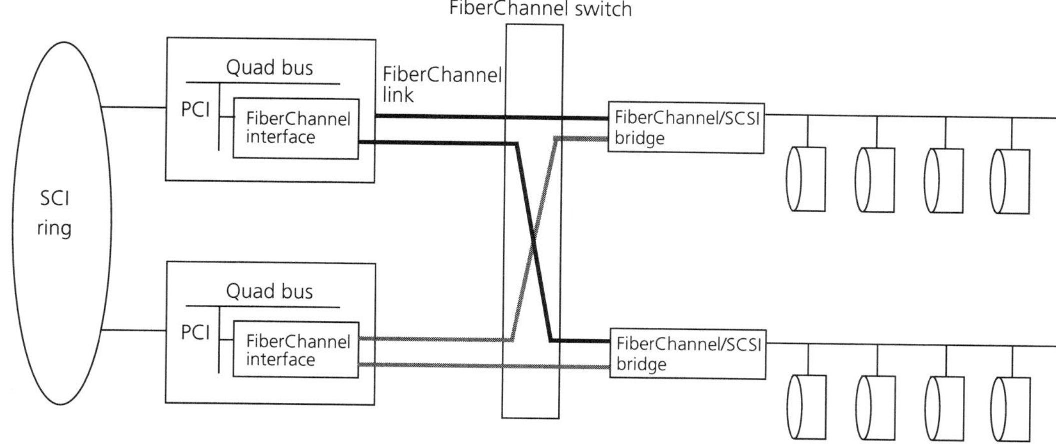

FIGURE 8.30 I/O subsystem of the Sequent NUMA-Q. I/O is globally addressable, and I/O data transfers among nodes can travel through FiberChannel via PCI buses or through the SCI ring used for memory operations.

ring network. I/O transfers can occupy substantial bandwidth, interfering with memory accesses. NUMA-Q therefore provides a separate communication substrate through the PCI buses for interquad I/O transfers, which is the default I/O path. A "FiberChannel" link connects to a PCI bus on each node. These links are connected to all the shared disks in the system through either point-to-point connections, an arbitrated FiberChannel loop, or a FiberChannel switch, depending on the scale of the processing and I/O systems (Figure 8.30).

FiberChannel talks to the disks at over 50 MB/s sustained through a bridge that converts the FiberChannel data format to the SCSI format that the disks accept. I/O to any disk in the system usually takes a path through the local PCI bus and the FiberChannel switch; however, if this path fails for some reason, the operating system causes I/O transfers to go through the SCI ring to another quad and through its PCI bus and FiberChannel link to the disk. FiberChannel may also be used to connect multiple NUMA-Q systems in a loosely coupled fashion and to have multiple systems share disks. Finally, a management and diagnostic controller connects to a PCI bus on each quad; these controllers are linked with one another and to a system console through a private local area network like Ethernet for system maintenance and diagnosis.

8.6.5 Protocol Interactions with SMP Node

The earlier discussion of the SCI protocol ignored the multiprocessor nature of the quad node and the bus-based protocol within it. Now that we understand the hardware structure of the node and the IQ-Link, let us examine the interactions of the two protocols, the requirements that the interacting protocols place upon the quad and IQ-Link, and some particular problems raised by the use of an off-the-shelf SMP as a node.

A read request illustrates some of the interactions. A read miss in a processor's second-level cache first appears on the quad bus. In addition to being snooped by the other processor caches, it is snooped by the OBIC bus controller on the IQ-Link board. The OBIC looks up the remote cache as well as the directory state bits for locally allocated blocks to see if the read can be satisfied within the quad or if it must be propagated off node. In the former case, main memory or one of the other caches satisfies the read, and the appropriate MESI state changes occur. (Snoop results are reported, in order, after a fixed number of bus cycles [four]; if a controller cannot finish its snoop within this time, it asserts a stall signal for another two bus cycles, after which memory checks for the snoop result again. This continues until all snoop results are available.) The quad bus implements in-order data responses to requests. However, if the OBIC detects that the request must be propagated off node, then it must intervene. It does this by asserting a *deferred response* signal, telling the bus to violate its in-order response property and proceed with other transactions and that the OBIC will take responsibility for responding to this request. This would not have been necessary if the quad bus implemented out-of-order responses. The OBIC then passes on the request to the SCLIC to engage the directory protocol. When the response comes back, it is passed from the SCLIC back to the OBIC, which places it on the bus and completes the deferred transaction. Note that when extending any bus-based system to be the node of a larger cache-coherent machine, it is essential that the bus be split transaction, not only for performance but also to simplify correctness. Otherwise, the bus will be held up for the entire duration of a remote transaction, not allowing even local misses to complete and not allowing incoming network transactions to be serviced by processor caches (potentially causing deadlock).

Writes take a similar path out of and back into a quad. The state of the block in the remote cache, snooped by the OBIC, indicates whether the block is owned by the local quad or a request must be propagated to the home through the SCLIC. Putting the node at the head of the sharing list and invalidating other nodes, if necessary, is taken care of by the SCLIC. When the SCLIC is done, it places a response on the quad bus (via the OBIC), which completes the operation. An interesting situation arises due to a limitation of the quad itself. Consider a read miss or write miss to a locally allocated block that is cached remotely in a modified state. When the response returns and is placed on the bus as a deferred response, it should update the main memory. However, the quad memory was not implemented to deal with deferred requests and responses and does not update itself on seeing a deferred response. Thus, when a deferred response is passed down to the bus through the OBIC, the OBIC must also ensure that it updates the memory through a special action before it gives up the bus. Another limitation arises from how the OBIC uses the quad bus protocol. If two processors in a quad issue read-exclusive requests back to back, and the first one propagates to the SCLIC, we would like the second one to be buffered and accept the response from the first in the appropriate state. However, the implementation NACKs the second request, which will then have to retry until the first one returns and it succeeds.

Finally, consider serialization. Since serialization at the SCI protocol level is done at the home, incoming transactions at the home have to be serialized not only with respect to one another but also with respect to accesses by the processors in the home quad. For example, suppose a block is in the HOME state at the home. At the SCI protocol level, this means that no remote cache in the system (which must be on some other node) has a valid copy of the block. However, unlike the unowned state in the Origin protocol, this does not mean that no processor cache in the home node has a copy of the block. In fact, the directory will be in HOME state even if one of the processor caches at the home has a dirty copy of the block. Even to obtain the right value, a request coming in for a locally allocated block at a home node must therefore be broadcast on the quad bus as well and cannot be handled entirely by the SCLIC and OBIC. Similarly, an incoming request that makes the directory state change from HOME or FRESH to GONE must be put on the quad bus so that the copies in the processor caches can be invalidated. Since both incoming requests and local misses to data at the home appear on the quad bus, it is natural to let this bus be the actual serializing agent at the home.

Similarly, serialization issues need to be addressed in a requesting quad for accesses to remotely allocated blocks. Activities within a quad relating to remotely allocated blocks are serialized at the local SCLIC rather than the local bus. Thus, requests from local processors for a block in the remote cache and incoming requests from the SCI interconnect for the same block are serialized at the local SCLIC. Similarly, the SCLIC takes care of the local serialization between outstanding invalidations at a requestor and incoming requests. Other interactions with the node protocol are discussed once we have considered the implementation of the IQ-Link board components.

8.6.6 IQ-Link Implementation

Unlike the single-chip Hub in Origin, the SCLIC directory controller, the OBIC bus interface controller, and the DataPump are separate chips on the IQ-Link board, which also contains some SRAM and SDRAM chips for tags, state, and remote cache data (see Figure 8.29).

The data in the remote cache is directly accessible by the OBIC. Two sets of tags are used to reduce communication between the SCLIC and the OBIC: the network-side tags for access by the SCLIC and the bus-side tags for access by the OBIC. The same is true for the directory state for locally allocated blocks. The bus-side tags and directory state contain only the information that is needed for the bus snooping and are implemented in SRAM so they can be looked up at bus speed. The network-side tags and state need more information and can be slower, so they are implemented in synchronous DRAM (SDRAM). The bus-side local directory SRAM contains only the 2 bits of directory state per 64-byte block (to distinguish the HOME, FRESH, and GONE states) whereas the network-side directory contains the 6-bit SCI head pointer as well. The bus-side remote cache tags also have only 4 bits of state and do not contain the SCI forward and backward list pointers. They keep track of 14 states, some of which are transient states that ensure forward progress within the quad (e.g., that keep track of blocks that are being rolled out or of the particular bus agent that has an outstanding retry on the bus and so must get priority for that block). The network-side remote cache tags, which are part of the directory protocol, contain 7 bits to represent all protocol states plus two 6-bit pointers per block (as well as the 13-bit cache tags themselves).

Unlike the hardwired protocol tables in Origin, the SCLIC coherence controller in NUMA-Q is programmable. This means the protocol can be written in software or firmware rather than hardwired into a finite state machine. Every protocol-invoking operation from a local processor, as well as every incoming transaction from the network, invokes a software "handler" or task that runs on the protocol engine. These software handlers, written in microcode, may manipulate directory state, put interventions on the quad bus, generate network transactions, and so on. The SCLIC engine has multiple register sets to support 12 read/write/invalidate transactions and 1 interrupt transaction concurrently. To allow the standard intraquad interrupt interface to be used across quads, the SCLIC provides a bridge for routing standard intraquad interrupts between quads and provides some extra bits to include the destination quad number when generating such interrupts.

A programmable protocol engine has several potential advantages. It allows the protocol to be debugged in software and corrected by simply downloading new protocol code. It provides the flexibility to experiment with or change protocols even after the machine is built and bottlenecks are discovered, and allows multiple protocols to be supported by the machine. And it enables code to be inserted into the handlers to monitor chosen events for performance debugging, which is especially valuable given the implicit nature of communication and the potential impact of artifactual communication in a shared address space. The disadvantage is that a programmable protocol engine has higher occupancy per transaction than a hardwired one, so a performance cost is associated with this decision. Attempts are made to reduce this performance impact in the NUMA-Q SCLIC. The protocol processor has a three-stage pipeline and issues up to two instructions (a branch and another instruction) every cycle. It uses a cache to hold recently used directory state and tag information rather than accessing the directory RAMs every time. Finally, it is specialized to support the kinds of bit-field manipulation operations that are commonly needed in directory protocols as well as useful instructions that speed up handler dispatch and management, like "queue on buffer full" and "branch on queue space available" instructions. A somewhat different programmable protocol engine is used in the Stanford FLASH multiprocessor (Kuskin et al. 1994), the successor to the hardwired Stanford DASH machine.

Each Pentium Pro processor can have up to four requests outstanding. The quad bus can have eight requests outstanding at a time and ensures that snoop and data responses come in order (except when deferred responses are used, as discussed earlier). The OBIC can have four external requests outstanding to the SCLIC and can buffer two incoming transactions to the quad bus at a time. If a fifth request from the

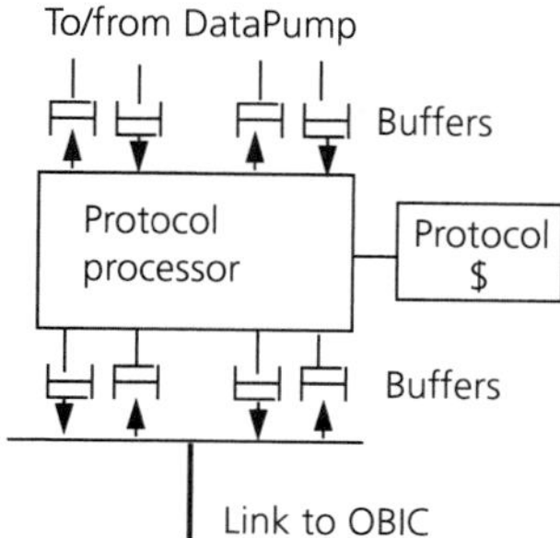

FIGURE 8.31 Simplified block diagram of the SCLIC chip. It contains a programmable protocol processor, a cache for directory information, and buffers to interface with the OBIC (bus) and DataPump (network).

quad bus needs to go off quad, the OBIC will NACK it until a buffer entry is free but will not cause the quad bus to stall for local operations. The SCLIC can have up to eight requests outstanding and can buffer four incoming requests at a time. A simplified illustration of the SCLIC is shown in Figure 8.31. Finally, the DataPump request and response buffers are each two entries deep outgoing to the network and four entries deep incoming. All request and response buffers, whether incoming or outgoing, are physically separate in this implementation.

In addition to the ability to instrument protocol handlers in software, all three components of the IQ-Link board also provide performance counters to enable nonintrusive measurement of various events and statistics. There are three 40-bit memory-mapped counters in the SCLIC and four in the OBIC. Each can be set in software to count any of a large number of events, such as protocol engine utilization, memory and bus utilization, queue occupancies, the occurrence of SCI command types, and the occurrence of transaction types on the quad bus. The counters can be read by software on the main processors at any time or can be programmed to generate interrupts when they cross a predefined threshold value. The Pentium Pro processor module itself provides a number of performance counters to count first- and second-level cache misses as well as the frequencies of request types and the occupancies of internal resources, among other properties. Together with the programmable handlers, these counters can provide a wealth of information about the behavior of the machine when running workloads.

8.6.7 Performance Characteristics

The quad bus has a peak bandwidth of 532 MB/s, and the SCI ring interconnect can transfer 500 MB/s in each direction across the node-to-network interface. The IQ-Link board can transfer data between these two interconnects at about 30 MB/s in each direction (note that only a small fraction of the transactions appearing on the quad bus or on the SCI ring are expected to be relevant to the other interconnect). The latency for a local read miss satisfied in main memory (or the remote cache) is expected to average about 250 ns under ideal conditions. The latency for a read satisfied in remote memory in a two-quad system is expected to be about 2.5 μs, a ratio

Table 8.3 Characteristics of Microbenchmarks and Workloads Running on an Eight-Quad NUMA-Q

Workload	Latency of L_2 Misses		SCLIC Utilization	Percentage of L_2 Misses Satisfied in			
	All	Remotely Satisfied		Local Memory	Other Local Cache	Local "Remote Cache"	Remote Node
Remote Read Misses	8,020 ns	8,300 ns	95%	1.5%	0%	2%	96.5%
Remote Write Misses	9,350 ns	9,625 ns	95%	1%	0%	2%	97%
TPC-B–like	630 ns	4,300 ns	54%	80%	2%	11.5%	6.5%
TPC-D (Q9)	580 ns	3,950 ns	40%	85%	5.5%	4%	5.5%

of about 10 to 1. However, the inclusion of a remote access cache keeps the frequency of artifactual communication very low. The latency through the DataPump network interface for the first 18 bits of a transaction is 16 ns and then 2 ns for every 18 bits thereafter. In the network itself, it takes about 26 ns for the first bit to get from the DataPump output of a quad into the IQ-Plus box that implements the ring and back out to the DataPump of the next quad along the ring.

The designers of the NUMA-Q have performed several experiments on the machine with microbenchmarks and with database and transaction processing workloads. To obtain a flavor for the microbenchmark performance capabilities of the machine, how latencies vary under load, and the characteristics of such workloads, let us take a brief look at the results. For a single-quad system with all four processors simultaneously generating cache misses as quickly as they can, back-to-back read misses are found to take 600 ns each and obtain a combined transfer bandwidth to the processors of 290 MB/s. Under similar conditions, back-to-back write misses, which cause a read followed by a write back, take 585 ns, and sustain 195 MB/s. For a single-quad system with multiple I/O controllers on each PCI I/O bus generating inbound writes from the I/O devices to the local memory as quickly as possible, each cache block transfer takes 360 ns at 111 MB/s sustained bandwidth.

Table 8.3 shows the latencies and characteristics under load as seen in various workloads running on multiple-quad systems. The first two rows are for microbenchmarks designed to have all quads simultaneously issuing read misses that are satisfied in remote memory. The third row is for the Transaction Processing Council's on-line transaction processing benchmark TPC-B (see Appendix). The last row is for Query 9 of the TPC-D benchmark suite, which represents decision support applications. The latencies are measured using the performance counters embedded in the OBIC and SCLIC and are measured not from the processor but from the bus request to the first data response. All workloads are run with four quads (16 processors), except the decision support workload, which is run with eight. Write misses to locally allocated

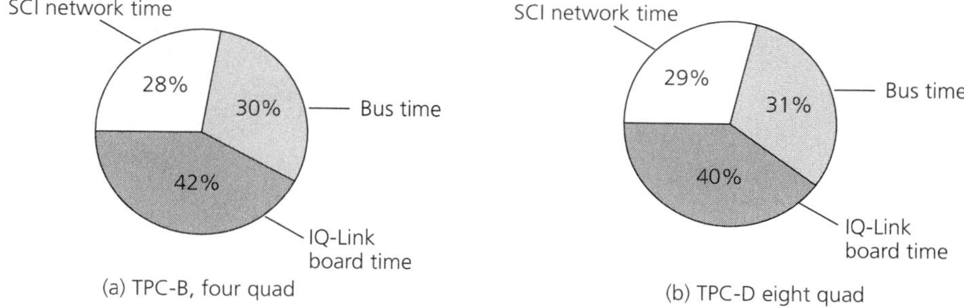

FIGURE 8.32 Components of average remote miss latency in two workloads on an eight-quad NUMA-Q. In both cases, most of the time is spent in the IQ-Link board, which includes data transfers between the SCLIC and the DataPump or the OBIC. Time in the OBIC chip itself is included in bus time in this figure.

data that cause invalidations to be sent remotely are very few and are included in the last column.

Remote data access latencies are clearly significantly higher than the unloaded latencies. In general, the SCI ring and protocol have higher latencies than those of more distributed networks and memory-based protocols, as discussed earlier. However, at least in these transaction processing and decision support workloads, much of the time in a remote access is spent passing through the IQ-Link board itself and not in the bus or ring. Figure 8.32 shows the breakdowns of average remote latency into three components for two workloads on four- and eight-quad systems. The path to improved remote access performance, both under load and not under load, is to make the IQ-Link board more efficient. The designers are considering a number of opportunities, including redesigning the SCLIC, perhaps using two instruction sequencers instead of one in the programmable SCLIC, and optimizing the OBIC, with the hope of reducing the remote access latency to about 2 μs under heavy load in the next generation. The remote cache is found to be very useful in keeping capacity misses local. The TPC-D (Q9) workload has lower SCLIC utilization than the TPC-B workload because it generates fewer invalidations.

8.6.8 Comparison Case Study: The HAL S1 Multiprocessor

The S1 multiprocessor from HAL Computer Systems is an interesting combination of some features of the NUMA-Q and the Origin2000. Like the NUMA-Q, the S1 also uses Pentium Pro quads as the processing nodes; however, it uses a memory-based directory protocol like that of the Origin2000 across quads rather than the cache-based SCI protocol. In addition, to reduce latency and assist occupancy, it integrates the coherence machinery more tightly with the node than the NUMA-Q does, coming closer to the Origin in this regard. Instead of using separate chips for the directory protocol controller (SCLIC), bus interface controller (OBIC), and network interface (DataPump), the S1 integrates the entire communication assist and the network interface into a single chip called the mesh coherence unit (MCU), with separate chips used for storage. On the other hand, the cache-coherent design scales to only four quads, does not have the flexibility of a programmable controller, and does not include a remote access cache to reduce remote capacity misses.

Since the memory-based protocol does not require the use of forward and backward pointers with each cache entry, there is no need for a quad-level remote data cache to provide this functionality (which processor caches do not provide); in memory-based protocols, remote caches are useful only to reduce capacity misses, and the S1 does not use them. The directory information is maintained in separate SRAM chips, but the directory storage needed is greatly reduced by maintaining directory information not for all memory blocks but only for those blocks that are in fact cached remotely, organizing the directory itself as a cache (as discussed in Section 8.10.1). The MCU also contains a DMA engine to support explicit message passing as well as block data transfers in a cache-coherent shared address space (see Chapter 11). Message passing or explicit data transfers can be implemented either through the DMA engine (preferred for large messages) or through the transfer mechanism used for cache blocks (preferred for small messages). The MCU is hardwired instead of programmable, which reduces its occupancy for protocol processing and hence improves its performance under contention. The MCU also has substantial hardware support for performance monitoring. Other than the MCU, the only custom chip used is the network router, which is a six-ported crossbar with 1.9 million transistors, optimized for speed. The network is clocked at 200 MHz. The latency through a single router is 42 ns, and the usable per-link bandwidth is 1.6 GB/s in each direction—both similar to that of the Origin2000 network. The initial S1 interconnect implementation scales to 32 nodes (128 processors).

A major goal of integrating all the assist functionality into a single chip in S1 was to reduce remote access latency and increase remote bandwidth. From the designers' simulated measurements, the best-case unloaded latency for a read miss that is satisfied in local memory is 240 ns, for a read miss to a block that is clean at a nearby remote home is 1,065 ns, and for a read miss to a block that is dirty in a (nearby) third node is 1,365 ns. The remote-to-local latency ratio ranges from 4 to 5 (including contention), which is a little worse than on the SGI Origin2000 but better than on the NUMA-Q. However, microbenchmark comparisons of latencies are not very meaningful as predictors of overall performance on workloads since they ignore important considerations like remote caches and flexibility that can greatly affect the frequency of communication.

The bandwidths achieved by the HAL S1 in copying a single 4-KB page are instructive. The achieved bandwidth is 105 MB/s from local memory to local memory through processor reads and writes (limited primarily by the quad memory controller that has to handle both the reads and writes of memory), about 70 MB/s between local memory and a remote memory (in either direction) when accomplished through processor reads and writes, and about 270 MB/s in either direction between local and remote memory when performed through the DMA engines in the

MCUs. The case of remote transfers through processor reads and writes is limited primarily by the limit on the number of outstanding memory operations from a processor, which is not an issue for the DMA case. The DMA case has the additional advantage that it requires only one bus transaction at the initiating end for each memory block rather than two split-transaction pairs in the case of processor reads and writes (once for the read and once for the write). At least in the absence of contention across transfers, the local quad bus becomes a bandwidth bottleneck long before the interconnection network does.

Now that we understand the protocol layer that implements the coherent shared address space programming model in some depth for both memory-based and cache-based protocols, let us briefly examine some key interactions of protocols with the basic performance parameters of the communication architecture in determining the performance of applications.

8.7 PERFORMANCE PARAMETERS AND PROTOCOL PERFORMANCE

Recall that there are four major performance parameters in a communication architecture: overhead on the main processor, occupancy of the communication assist, network transit delay, and network bandwidth. Processor overhead is usually quite small on cache-coherent machines (unlike on message-passing systems, where it often dominates) and is determined entirely by the underlying node. In the best case, the portion that we can call processor overhead, and which cannot be hidden from the processor through overlap, is the cost of issuing the memory operation. In the worst case, it is the cost of traversing the processor's cache hierarchy and reaching the assist (which can be quite significant). All other protocol processing actions are off-loaded to the communication assist (e.g., the Hub or the IQ-Link). Network link bandwidth, too, is usually adequate for most applications in high-performance multiprocessor networks (Holt et al. 1995). The more critical issues under the control of the communication architecture are, therefore, network delay and assist occupancy.

As we have seen, the communication assist has many roles in protocol processing, including generating a request, looking up the directory state, accessing the data for a response, and sending out and receiving invalidations and acknowledgments. The occupancy of the assist for processing a transaction not only contributes to the uncontended latency of that transaction but can also cause contention at the assist and hence increase the cost of other transactions. This is especially true in cache-coherent machines because of the large number of small transactions—both data-carrying transactions and others like requests, invalidations, and acknowledgments—which implies that the occupancy is incurred very frequently and not amortized very well. The situation is better than in shared address space machines that are not cache coherent, where a transaction transfers only the referenced word rather than a whole cache block because replication and coherence must be managed by the programmer (see the discussion in Section 3.6), but the amortization is still small. In fact, assist occupancy very often dominates the data transfer bandwidth of the node-to-network interface as the key bottleneck to throughput at the endpoints (Holt et al. 1995). It is therefore very important to keep assist occupancy small. At the protocol level, it is important both to ensure that the assist is not tied up by an outstanding transaction while other unrelated transactions are available for it to process and to reduce the amount of processing needed from the assist per transaction. For example, if the home forwards a request to a dirty node, the home assist should not be held up until the dirty node returns a response—which would dramatically increase its effective occupancy—but should go on to service the next transaction and deal with the response later when it comes. At the hardware design level, it is important to specialize the assist enough and integrate it tightly with the node's memory system so that its effective occupancy per transaction is low. The tighter the integration and the greater the specialization, the less commodity oriented the design but the lower the occupancy.

Impact of Network Delay and Assist Occupancy

Figure 8.33 shows the impact of assist occupancy and network latency on performance, assuming an efficient memory-based directory protocol similar to that of the SGI Origin2000. In the absence of contention, assist occupancy behaves just like network transit delay or any other component of the latency in a transaction's path: increasing occupancy by d cycles would have the same impact as keeping occupancy constant but increasing network delay by d cycles. Since the x-axis is total uncontended round-trip latency for a remote read miss (including the cost of network delay and assist occupancies incurred along the way), if no contention is induced by increasing occupancy, then all the curves for different values of occupancy will be identical. In fact, they are not, and the separation of the curves indicates the impact of the contention induced by increasing assist occupancy.

The smallest value of occupancy (o) in the graphs is intended to represent that of an aggressive hardwired assist that is tightly integrated with the cache or memory controller, such as the one used in the Origin2000. The least aggressive one represents placing a slow general-purpose processor on the memory bus to play the role of communication assist. The most aggressive network delays used represent modern high-end multiprocessor interconnects whereas the least aggressive ones are closer to using commodity system area networks like asynchronous transfer mode (ATM). We can see that for an aggressive occupancy, the latency curves take the expected $1/l$ shape. The contention induced by assist occupancy has a major impact on performance for applications that stress communication throughput (especially those in which communication is bursty), particularly for the low-delay networks used in multiprocessors. Thus the curves for higher occupancies are far apart from one another toward their left ends. For reasonable occupancies, the curves become closer to one another at larger network delays, since the greater time spent by transactions in the network keeps the assist less busy and hence keeps contention at the assist smaller. For higher occupancies, the curve almost flattens, at least with lower network delays, indicating that the assist is saturated. The problem is especially

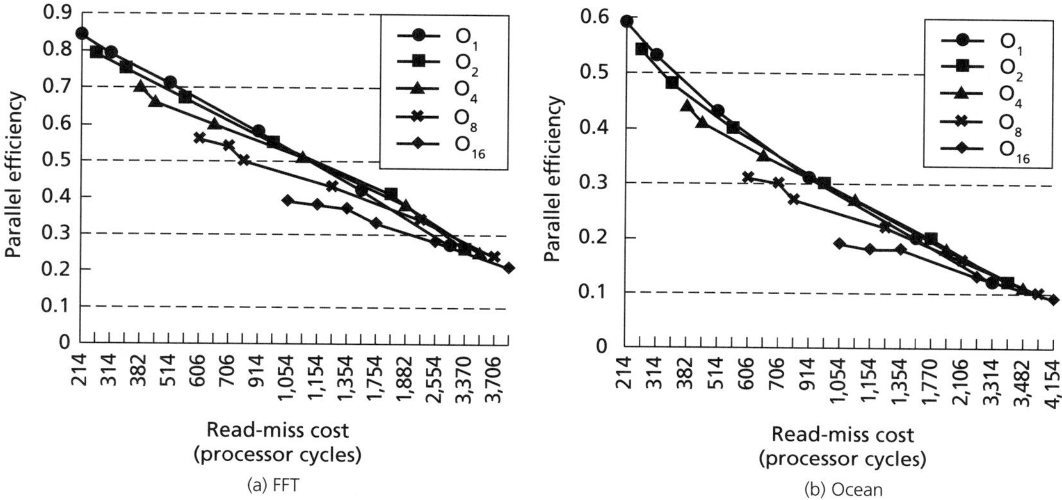

FIGURE 8.33 Impact of assist occupancy and network latency on the performance of memory-based cache coherence protocols. The *y*-axis is the parallel efficiency, which is the speedup over a sequential execution divided by the number of processors used (1 is ideal speedup). The *x*-axis is the uncontended round-trip latency of a read miss that is satisfied in main memory at the home, including all components of cost (occupancy, transit latency, time in buffers, and network bandwidth). Each curve is for a different value of assist occupancy (*o*), while along a curve the only parameter that varies is the network transit delay (*l*). The lowest occupancy assumed is 7 processor cycles, which is labeled O_1. O_2 corresponds to twice that occupancy (14 processor cycles) and so on. All other costs, such as the time to propagate through the cache hierarchy and through buffers and the node-to-network bandwidth, are held constant. The graphs are for simulated 64-processor executions. The main conclusion is that the contention induced by assist occupancy is very important to performance, especially in low-latency networks.

severe for applications with bursty communication, such as sorting and FFTs, since there the rate of communication relative to computation during the communication phase does not change much with problem size, so larger problem sizes do not help alleviate the contention during that phase. Assist occupancy is a less severe problem for applications in which communication events are separated by significant computation and whose communication bandwidth demands are small (e.g., Barnes-Hut). When latency tolerance techniques are used (discussed in Chapter 11), bandwidth is stressed even further, so the impact of assist occupancy is much greater even at higher transit latencies, and the curves at the highest occupancies are almost completely flat for FFT and sorting (Holt et al. 1995). This data shows that it is very important to keep assist occupancy low in machines that communicate and maintain coherence at a fine granularity such as that of cache blocks. The impact of contention due to assist occupancy tends to increase with the number of processors used to solve a given problem since the communication-to-computation ratio tends to increase.

Effects of Assist Occupancy on Protocol Trade-Offs

The occupancy of the assist has an impact not only on the performance of a given protocol but also on the trade-offs among protocols. We have seen that cache-based protocols can have higher latency on write operations than memory-based protocols since the transactions needed to invalidate sharers are serialized. The SCI cache-based protocol also tends to have more protocol processing to do on a given memory operation than a memory-based protocol, so the effective occupancy of the assist tends to be significantly higher, especially when assists are programmable rather than hardwired. Combined with the higher latency on writes, this would tend to cause memory-based protocols to perform better. This difference between the performance of the protocols will become greater as assist occupancy and its performance impact increase. On the other hand, the protocol processing occupancy for a given memory operation (e.g., a write) in SCI is distributed over more nodes and assists, so, depending on the communication patterns of the application, it may experience less contention at a given assist. For example, when hot spotting becomes a problem due to bursty irregular communication in memory-based protocols (as in radix sorting), it may be somewhat alleviated in SCI. How these trade-offs play out in practice will depend on the characteristics of real programs and machines, although overall we might expect memory-based protocols to perform better in optimized implementations.

Improving Performance Parameters in Hardware

There are many ways to use more aggressive, specialized hardware to improve performance characteristics such as delay, occupancy, and bandwidth. Some notable techniques include the following. First, an SRAM directory cache may be placed close to the assist to reduce directory lookup cost, as is done in NUMA-Q and in the Stanford FLASH multiprocessor (Kuskin et al. 1994). Second, a single bit of SRAM can be maintained per memory block at the home to keep track of whether or not the block is in clean state in the local memory. If it is, then on a read miss to a locally allocated block, there is no need to invoke the communication assist any further. Third, if the assist occupancy is high, it can be pipelined into stages of protocol processing, as is also done in the NUMA-Q and Stanford FLASH (e.g., decoding a request, looking up the directory, generating a response), or its occupancy can be overlapped with other actions. Pipelining the assist reduces contention but not the uncontended latency of individual memory operations; the opposite (and complementary) result can be achieved by having the assist generate and send out a response or a forwarded request even before all the cleanup it needs to do is done.

8.8 SYNCHRONIZATION

Software algorithms for synchronization on scalable non-cache-coherent shared address space systems using atomic exchange instructions or LL-SC are discussed in Section 7.9. Recall that the major focus of these algorithms compared to those for bus-based machines is to exploit the parallelism of independent paths in the interconnect and to ensure that processors will spin on local rather than nonlocal variables. The same algorithms are applicable to scalable cache-coherent machines. However, there are two differences. First, the performance implications of spinning on remotely allocated variables are likely to be much less significant since a processor caches the variable and then spins on it locally until it is invalidated. Having processors spin on different variables rather than the same one is of course useful in preventing all processors from rushing out to the same home memory when the variable is written and invalidated, thereby reducing contention. And good placement of synchronization variables has the benefit of converting the misses that occur after invalidation into two-hop misses from three-hop misses. However, there is only one (very unlikely) situation when it may actually be very important to performance that the variable a processor spins on be allocated locally: if all levels of the cache hierarchy are unified and direct mapped and the instructions for the spin loop conflict with the variable itself, in which case conflict misses will be satisfied locally. Second, while these performance aspects of synchronization algorithms are less critical, implementing atomic primitives and LL-SC is more interesting when it interacts with a coherence protocol. This section examines the performance and implementation aspects, first comparing the performance of the different synchronization algorithms for the locks described in Chapters 5 and 7 on the SGI Origin2000 and then discussing some new implementation issues for atomic primitives beyond the issues already encountered in Chapter 6 for bus-based machines.

8.8.1 Performance of Synchronization Algorithms

The experiments used here to illustrate synchronization performance are the same as those used on the bus-based SGI Challenge in Section 5.5, again using LL-SC as the primitive to construct atomic operations. The delays used are the same in processor cycles and therefore different in actual microseconds. The results for the lock algorithms described in Chapters 5 and 7 are shown in Figure 8.34 for 16-processor executions. Here again, three different sets of values are used for the delays within and after the critical section for which processors repeatedly contend.

Here too, until we use delays between critical sections, the simple locks behave unfairly and yield higher throughput. Exponential backoff often helps the simple LL-SC lock in the event of a null critical section since this is the case where significant contention needs to be alleviated. The ticket lock scales quite poorly in this case, as it did on a bus, but scales very well when proportional backoff is used. The array-based lock also scales very well. With coherent caches, the better placement of lock variables in main memory afforded by the software queuing lock is not particularly useful. If we force the simple locks to behave fairly, they behave much like the ticket lock without proportional backoff.

If we use a non-null critical section and a delay between lock accesses (Figure 8.34[c]), all locks behave fairly. Now the simple LL-SC locks don't have

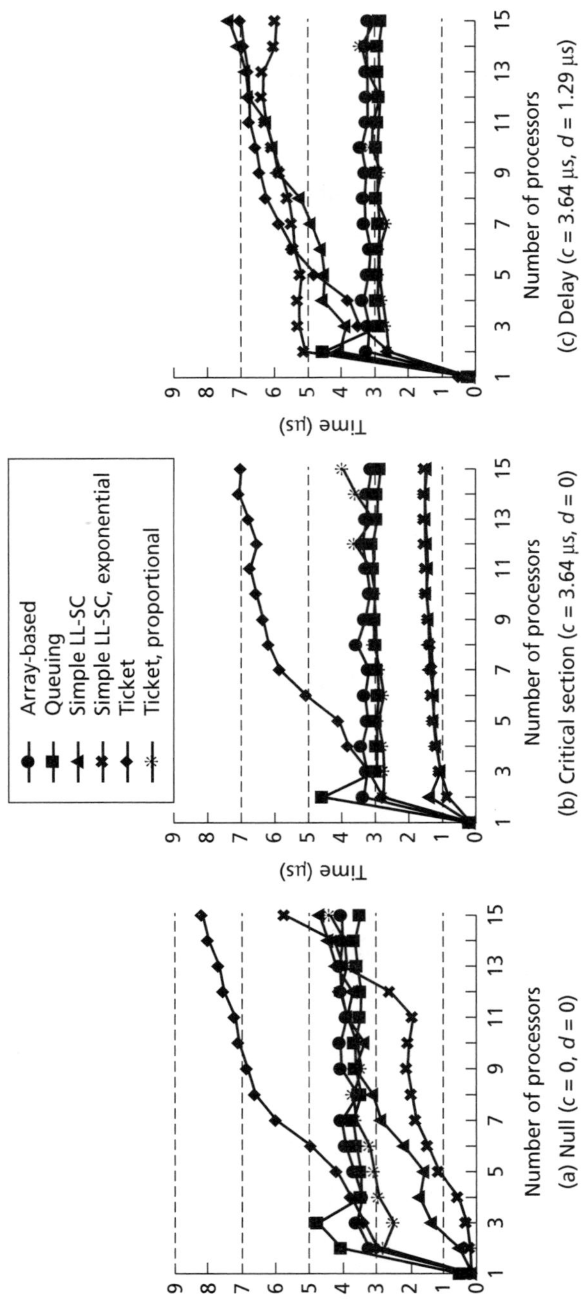

FIGURE 8.34 Performance of locks on the SGI Origin2000 for three different scenarios

their advantage, and their scaling disadvantage shows through. The array-based lock, the queuing lock, and the ticket lock with proportional backoff all scale well (at least to this small number of processors). The better data placement of the queuing lock does not matter, but neither is the contention any worse for it. The bad performance of the queuing lock at two processors is due to a specific interaction in constructing the software queue (Mellor-Crummey and Scott 1991). While experiments with larger-scale machines are warranted, the flattening of the curves indicates that, overall, the array-based lock and the ticket lock perform quite well and robustly for scalable cache-coherent machines, at least when implemented with LL-SC. The simple LL-SC lock with exponential backoff performs best when no delay occurs between an unlock and the next lock due to repeated unfair successful access by a processor in its own cache. The sophisticated queuing lock is unnecessary but also performs well with delays between unlock and lock.

More aggressive hardware support for locks has been proposed. The most prominent example is a hardware version of the queuing lock called QOLB (queue on lock bit). A distributed linked list of nodes waiting on a lock is maintained in hardware, and a releaser grants the lock to the first waiting node without affecting the others (Kägi, Burger, and Goodman 1997). Since the SCI protocol already has hardware support for a distributed list of waiting nodes (namely, the pending list), QOLB locks fit very well with SCI. This aggressive hardware support may reduce the lock transfer time as well as the interference of lock traffic with data access and coherence traffic; however, it is unlikely to change the scaling trends of the lock microbenchmarks, and, as with all system features, its true value to performance is best evaluated with real applications and workloads.

Algorithms and hardware support for barriers are discussed in Section 7.9. Since barriers reached simultaneously by multiple nodes cause contention for read-modify-write access to a shared counter, a number of interesting questions arise: Should this counter variable be a cacheable location or an uncached location accessed at main memory? Or can mechanisms be developed to allow processors to spin in their caches and either be updated at the release or read the release value from main memory rather than from the releaser's cache? Or is the hardware support for at-memory fetch&op operations particularly valuable as provided by machines like the Origin2000?

8.8.2 Implementing Atomic Primitives

Consider implementing atomic exchange (read-modify-write) primitives like test&set performed on a memory location. What matters for atomicity is that a conflicting write to that location by another processor occur either before the read component of the read-modify-write operation or after its write component. As we discussed for bus-based machines in Section 5.5.3, the read component may be allowed to complete as soon as the write component is serialized with respect to other writes and as long as we ensure that no incoming invalidations are applied to the block until the read has completed. If the read-modify-write is implemented at the processor (using cacheable primitives), this means that the read can complete once the write has obtained ownership and even before invalidation acknowledgments have returned. Atomic operations can also be implemented at the memory, but it is easier to do this if we disallow the block from being cached in dirty state by any processor. Then all writes go to memory, and the read-modify-write can be serialized with respect to other writes as soon as it gets to memory. Memory can send a response to the read component in parallel with sending out invalidations corresponding to the write component.

Implementing LL-SC requires all the same consideration to avoid livelock as it did for bus-based machines, with one further complication. Recall that a store-conditional should not send out invalidations or updates if it fails since, otherwise, two processors may keep invalidating or updating each other and failing, causing livelock. To detect failure of a store-conditional, the requesting processor needs to determine if some other processor's write to the block has been serialized before the store-conditional. In a bus-based system, the cache controller can do this by checking upon a store-conditional whether the cache no longer has a valid copy of the block or whether there are incoming invalidations or updates for the block that have already appeared on the bus. The latter detection of serialization order cannot be done locally by the cache controller with a distributed interconnect, so a different mechanism is necessary. In an invalidation-based protocol, if the block is still in valid state in the cache, then the read-exclusive request corresponding to the store-conditional goes to the directory at the home. There it checks to see if the requestor is still on the sharing list. If it isn't, then the directory knows that another conflicting write has been serialized before the store-conditional, so it does not send out invalidations corresponding to the store-conditional and the store-conditional fails. Otherwise, it succeeds. In an update protocol, this is more difficult since, even if another write has been serialized before the store-conditional, the store-conditional requestor will still be on the sharing list. One solution (Gharachorloo 1995) is to again use a two-phase protocol as was used to provide write atomicity for updates. When the store-conditional reaches the directory, it locks down the entry for that block so that no other requests can access it. Then, the directory sends a message back to the store-conditional requestor, which upon receipt checks to see if the lock flag for the LL-SC has been cleared (by an update that arrived between the current time and the time the store-conditional request was sent out). If so, the store-conditional has failed and a message is sent back to the directory to this effect (and to unlock the directory entry). If not, then as long as point-to-point order is guaranteed in the network, we can conclude that no conflicting write beat the store-conditional to the directory, so the store-conditional should succeed. The requestor sends an acknowledgment back to the directory, which unlocks the directory entry and sends out the updates corresponding to the store-conditional, and the store-conditional succeeds.

8.9 IMPLICATIONS FOR PARALLEL SOFTWARE

Let us now consider the implications for parallel software more generally than for synchronization. What distinguishes the coherent shared address space systems described in this chapter from those described in Chapters 5 and 6 is that they have physically distributed rather than centralized main memory. Distributed memory is at once an opportunity to improve performance and scalability through data locality and a burden on software to exploit this locality. As we saw in Chapter 3, on cache-coherent architectures with physically distributed memory (or CC-NUMA machines), such as those discussed in this chapter, parallel programs may need to be aware of physically distributed memory, particularly when their important working sets don't fit in the cache. Artifactual communication occurs when data is not allocated in the memory of a node that incurs capacity, conflict, or cold misses on that data. This situation can lead to some artifactual communication even when data does fit in the cache since looking up the directory on write misses (including upgrades) will generate network traffic and contention. Finally, consider a multiprogrammed workload in which application processes are migrated among processing nodes for load balancing. Migrating a process will turn what should be local misses into remote misses unless the system moves all the migrated process's data to the new node's main memory as well. For all these reasons, it may be important that data be allocated appropriately across the distributed memories.

In the CC-NUMA machines discussed in this chapter, the management of main memory is typically done at the fairly large granularity of pages. The large granularity can make it difficult to distribute shared data structures appropriately since data that should be allocated on two different nodes may fall on the same unit of allocation. The operating system may transparently migrate pages to the nodes that incur cache misses on them most often, using information obtained from hardware counters; or the run-time system of a programming language may migrate pages based on user-supplied hints or compiler analysis. (We saw that the Origin2000 provides protocol support for efficient migration.) More commonly today, the programmer may direct the operating system to place pages in the memories closest to particular processes. This may be as simple as providing these directives to the system—such as, "Place the pages in this range of virtual addresses in this process *X*'s local memory"—or it may additionally involve padding and aligning data structures to page boundaries so they can be placed properly, or it may even require that data structures be organized differently to allow such placement at page granularity. We saw examples of the need for all three in using four-dimensional instead of two-dimensional arrays in the equation solver kernel and in Ocean. Simple, regular cases like these may also be handled by sophisticated compilers. In Barnes-Hut, on the other hand, proper placement would require a significant reorganization of data structures as well as code. Instead of having a single linear array for all particles (or cells), each process would have an array or list of its own assigned particles that it could allocate in its local memory; between time-steps, particles that were reassigned would be moved from one array or list to another. However, as we have seen, data placement is not very useful for this application due to the small working sets and low capacity miss rate and may even hurt performance due to its high costs. It is important that we understand the costs and potential benefits of data migration before using it. Similar issues hold for software-controlled replication of data instead of migration, and the next chapter discusses alternative approaches to coherent replication and migration in main memory.

One of the most difficult problems for a programmer to deal with in a coherent shared address space is contention. Contention can be caused not only by data traffic that is implicit and often unpredictable but also by "invisible" protocol transactions, such as ownership requests, invalidations, and acknowledgments that a programmer is not inclined to think about at all and that are now point-to-point rather than amortized by a broadcast medium. All of these types of transactions occupy the protocol processing portion of the communication assist, reinforcing the importance of keeping the occupancy of the assist per transaction very low to contain endpoint contention. Invisible protocol messages and contention make performance problems like false sharing all the more important for a programmer to avoid, particularly when they cause a lot of protocol transactions to be directed toward the same node. Thus, while the software techniques for inherent communication and for spatial locality and false sharing at cache block granularity are the same as on bus-based machines, the potential impact on performance is different. For example, we are often tempted to structure some kinds of data as an array with one entry per process. If the entries are smaller than a page, several of them will fall on the same page. If these array entries are not padded to avoid false sharing or if they incur conflict misses in the cache, all the misses and traffic will be directed at the home of that page, causing considerable contention. In a distributed-memory machine it is advantageous not only to structure such data as an array of records rather than multiple arrays of scalars (as we do in Chapter 5 to avoid false sharing) but also to pad and align the records to a page and place the pages in the appropriate local memories.

An interesting example of how contention can cause different orchestration strategies to be used in message-passing and shared address space systems is illustrated by a high-performance parallel FFT. Conceptually, the computation is structured in phases. Phases of local computation are separated by phases of communication, which involve the transposition of a matrix. A process reads columns from a source matrix and writes them into its assigned rows of a destination matrix and then performs local computation on its assigned rows of the destination matrix. In a message-passing system, it is important to coalesce data into large messages, so it is necessary for performance to structure the communication this way (as a phase separate from computation). However, in a cache-coherent shared address space there are two differences. First, transfers are always done at cache block granularity. Second, each fine-grained transfer involves invalidations and acknowledgments (each local block that a process writes is likely to be in shared state in the cache of another processor from a previous phase and so must be invalidated), which cause contention at the coherence controllers. It may therefore be preferable to perform the communication on demand at fine grain while the computation is in progress, rather than all at once in a separate transpose phase, thus staggering the communication and easing the contention on the controller: a process that otherwise computes using a row of the destination matrix after the transpose can read the words of the corresponding source matrix column from a remote node on demand while it is computing, performing the transpose in the process. Which method is better may depend on the architecture.

Finally, synchronization can be expensive in scalable systems, so programs should make a special effort to reduce the frequency of high-contention locks or global barrier synchronization.

8.10 ADVANCED TOPICS

Before concluding the chapter, we cover two additional topics. The first deals with the actual techniques used to reduce directory storage overhead in flat, memory-based schemes. The second addresses techniques for hierarchical coherence, both snooping and directory based.

8.10.1 Reducing Directory Storage Overhead

The discussion of flat, memory-based directories in Section 8.2.3 stated that the size or width of a directory entry can be reduced by using a limited number of pointers rather than a full bit vector and that doing so requires some overflow mechanism when the number of copies of the block exceeds the number of available pointers. Based on the empirical data about sharing patterns, the number of hardware pointers likely to be provided in limited pointer directories is very small, so it is important that the overflow mechanism be efficient. This section first discusses some possible overflow methods. It then examines techniques to reduce the number of directory entries, or directory "height," by organizing the directory as a cache rather than having an entry for every memory block in the system. The limited pointer schemes with i pointers are named Dir_i followed by an abbreviation of their overflow methods, which include broadcast, no broadcast, coarse vector, software overflow, and dynamic pointers.

Overflow Methods for Reduced Directory Width

The overflow strategy in the *broadcast* or *Dir_iB scheme* (Agarwal et al. 1988) is to set a broadcast bit in the directory entry when the number of available pointers i is exceeded. When that block is written again, invalidation messages are sent to all nodes in the system, regardless of whether or not they were caching the block. It is not semantically incorrect to send an invalidation message to a processor not caching the block; however, network bandwidth may be wasted and latency stalls may be increased if the processor performing the write must wait for acknowledgments before proceeding. The advantage of the method is its simplicity.

The *no broadcast* or *Dir_iNB scheme* (Agarwal et al. 1988) avoids broadcast by never allowing the number of valid copies of a block to exceed i. Whenever the number of sharers is i and another node requests a shared copy of the block, the protocol invalidates the copy in one of the existing sharers and frees up that pointer in the directory entry for the new requestor. A major drawback of this scheme is that it

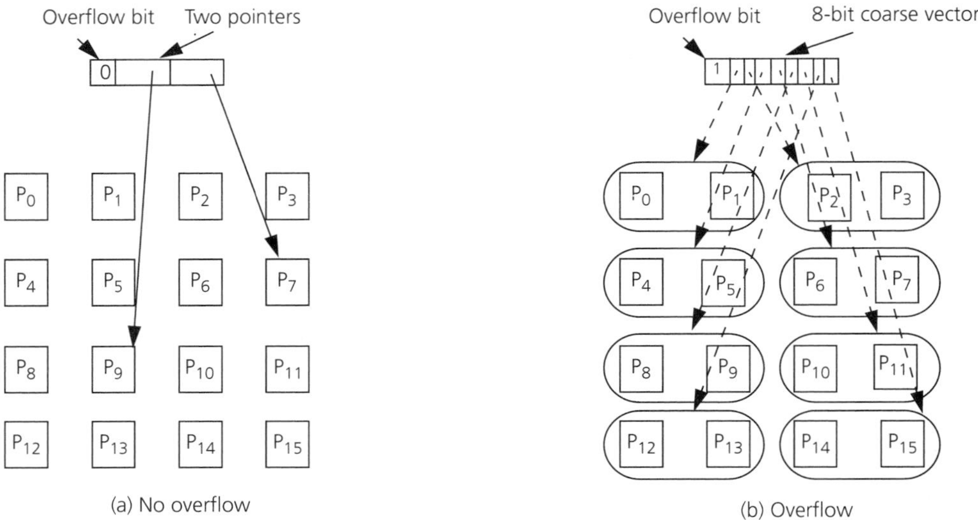

FIGURE 8.35 The change in representation in going from limited pointer representation to coarse vector representation on overflow. Upon overflow, the two 4-bit pointers (for a 16-node system) are viewed as an 8-bit coarse vector, each bit corresponding to a group of two nodes. The overflow bit is also set, so the nature of the representation can be easily determined. The dotted lines in (b) indicate the correspondence between bits and node groups.

does not deal well with data that is actively read by many processors during a period (e.g., tables of precomputed values or even program code), since copies will unnecessarily be invalidated and a continual stream of misses generated. Although special provisions can be made for blocks containing code (e.g., their consistency may be managed by software instead of hardware), it is not clear how to handle widely shared read-mostly data well in this scheme.

The *coarse vector* or *Dir_iCV_r scheme* (Gupta, Weber, and Mowry 1990) also uses *i* pointers in its initial representation, but on overflow the representation changes to a coarse bit vector like the one used by the Origin2000 for large machines. In this representation, each bit of the directory entry indicates not a node but a unique group of the nodes in the machine (the subscript *r* in Dir_iCV_r indicates the size of the group), and that bit is turned ON whenever any node in that partition is caching that block (see Figure 8.35). When a processor writes that block, all nodes in the groups whose bits are turned ON are sent an invalidation message, regardless of whether they have actually accessed or are caching the block. As an example, consider a 256-node machine for which we store eight pointers in the directory entry. Since each pointer needs to be 8 bits wide, 64 bits are available for the coarse vector on overflow. Thus, we can implement a Dir_8CV_4 scheme, with each coarse vector bit pointing to a group of 256/64 or four nodes. An additional single bit per entry keeps track of whether the current representation is that of the normal limited pointer or the coarse vector. As shown in Figure 8.36, an advantage of a scheme like Dir_iCV_r (and,

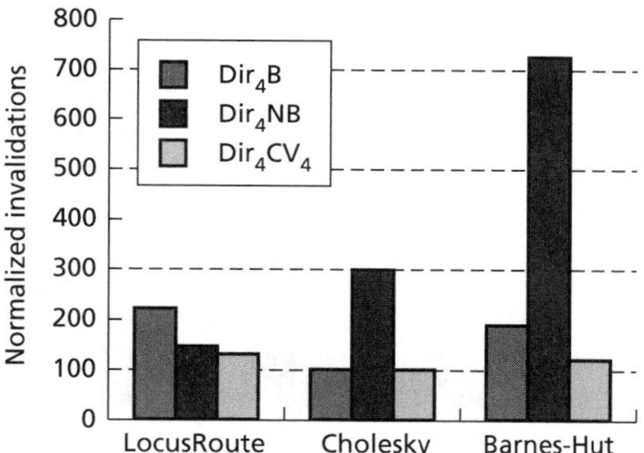

FIGURE 8.36 Robustness of the coarse vector overflow method relative to broadcast and no broadcast. The figure shows a comparison of invalidation traffic generated by Dir_4B, Dir_4NB, and Dir_4CV_4 schemes normalized to that generated by the full bit vector scheme (represented as 100 invalidations). The results are taken from (Weber 1993), so the simulation parameters are different from those used in this book. The number of processors (1 per node) is 64. The data for the LocusRoute wire-routing application, which has data that is written quite frequently and read by many nodes, shows the potential pitfalls of the Dir_iB scheme. Cholesky and Barnes-Hut, which have data that is read shared by large numbers of processors (e.g., nodes close to the root of the tree in Barnes-Hut) show the potential pitfalls of the Dir_iNB scheme. The Dir_iCV_r scheme is found to be reasonably robust.

even more so, of the following schemes) over Dir_iB and Dir_iNB is that its behavior is more robust to different sharing patterns.

The *software overflow* or *Dir_iSW scheme* is different from the previous ones in that it does not throw away the precise caching status of a block when overflow occurs. Rather, the current i pointers and a pointer to the new sharer are saved into a special portion of the node's local main memory by software. This frees up space for new pointers, so i new sharers can be handled by hardware before software must be invoked to store pointers away into memory again. The overflow also causes an overflow bit to be set in hardware. This bit ensures that when a subsequent write is encountered the pointers that were stored away in memory will be read out, and invalidation messages will be sent to those nodes as well. In the absence of a very sophisticated (programmable) communication assist, the overflow situations (both when pointers must be stored into memory and when they must be read out and invalidations sent) are handled by software running on the main processor, so the processor must be interrupted or a trap generated upon these events. The advantages of this scheme are that precise information is kept about sharers even upon overflow, so there is no extra invalidation traffic generated compared to a full bit vector (or unlimited pointer) representation, and that the complexity of overflow handling is managed by software. The major overhead is the cost of the interrupts and software processing. This disadvantage takes three forms: (1) the processor at the home of the block spends time handling the interrupt instead of performing the user's computation; (2) the overhead of interrupts and of handling these requests is large, thus potentially becoming a bottleneck for contention and slowing down other requests; and (3) the requesting processor may stall longer because of the higher latency of the requests that can cause interrupts as well as increased contention.[5]

Software overflow for limited pointer directories was used in the MIT Alewife research prototype (Agarwal et al. 1995) and was called the LimitLESS scheme (Agarwal et al. 1991). The Alewife machine is designed to scale to 512 processors with one processor per node. Each directory entry is 64 bits wide. It contains five 9-bit pointers to record remote nodes caching the block and 1 dedicated bit to indicate whether the local node is also caching the block (thus saving 8 bits when this is true). Overflow pointers are stored in a hash table in the main memory. The main processor in Alewife has hardware support for multithreading (see Chapter 11), with support for fast handling of traps upon overflow. Nonetheless, although the latency of a request that causes five invalidations and can be handled in hardware is only 84 cycles on a 16-processor system, a request requiring six invalidations and, hence, software intervention takes 707 cycles.

The *dynamic pointers* or *Dir$_i$DP scheme* (Simoni and Horowitz 1991) is a variation of the Dir$_i$SW scheme. In addition to the i hardware pointers, each directory entry in this scheme contains a hardware pointer into a special portion of the local node's main memory. This special memory has a free list associated with it, from which pointer structures can be dynamically allocated to processors as needed. The key difference from Dir$_i$SW is that all linked-list manipulation is done in hardware by a special-purpose protocol processor rather than by the general-purpose processor of the local node. As a result, interrupts are not needed and the overhead of manipulating the linked lists is small. Because it also contains a hardware pointer to memory, the number of hardware pointers i used in this scheme is typically very small. The Dir$_i$DP scheme is the default directory organization for the Stanford FLASH multiprocessor (Kuskin et al. 1994). Because the pool of dynamic pointers is limited and because lists are traversed on invalidations, the use of replacement hints usually accompanies this approach.

Among these many alternative schemes for maintaining directory information in a memory-based protocol, it is quite clear that the Dir$_i$B and Dir$_i$NB schemes are not very robust to different sharing patterns. However, the actual performance (and cost-performance) trade-offs among the schemes are not very well understood for real applications on large-scale machines. The general consensus seems to be that full bit vectors are appropriate for machines that have a moderate number of processing nodes that are visible to the directory protocol. The most likely candidates for hardware overflow schemes are coarse vector and dynamic pointer: the former may suffer from lack of accuracy on overflow, while the latter has greater processing cost due to hardware list manipulation and free list management.

5. It is actually possible to respond to a requestor before the trap is handled and thus not affect the latency seen by it. However, that simply means that the next processor's request to that node is delayed and that processor may experience a stall.

Reducing Directory Height

In addition to reducing directory entry width, an orthogonal way to reduce directory memory overhead is to reduce the total number of directory entries used by not using one per memory block (Gupta, Weber, and Mowry 1990; O'Krafka and Newton 1990); that is, to go after the *M* term in the *P***M* expression for directory memory overhead. Since the two methods of reducing overhead are orthogonal, they can be traded off against each other: reducing the number of entries allows us to make entries wider (use more hardware pointers) without increasing cost and vice versa.

The observation that motivates the use of fewer directory entries is that the total amount of cache memory is much less than the total main memory in the machine. This means that only a very small fraction of the memory blocks will be cached at a given time. For example, each processing node may have a 1-MB cache and 64 MB of main memory associated with it. If there were one directory entry per memory block, then across the whole machine 63/64 or 98.5% of the directory entries will correspond to memory blocks that are not cached anywhere in the machine. That is a tremendous number of directory entries lying idle with no bits turned ON (especially when replacement hints are used). This waste of memory can be avoided by organizing the directory as a cache and dynamically allocating the entries in it to directory entries, just as cache lines are allocated to memory blocks containing program data. In fact, if the number of entries in this directory cache is small enough, it may enable us to use fast SRAMs instead of slower DRAMs for directories, thus reducing the access time to directory information. As we know, this access time is in the critical path that determines the latency seen by the processor for many types of memory references. Such a directory organization is called a *sparse directory*, for obvious reasons. (The HAL S1 system, described in Section 8.6.8, uses this approach.)

While a sparse directory operates quite like a regular processor cache, there are some significant differences. First, this cache has no need for a backing store: when an entry is replaced from it, if any node's bits (or pointers) in it are turned on then we can simply send invalidations or flush messages to those nodes. Second, there is only one directory entry per block in this cache, so spatial locality is not an issue. Third, a sparse directory handles references from potentially all processors, whereas a processor cache is only accessed by the processor(s) attached to it. And finally, the references stream that the sparse directory sees is heavily filtered, consisting of only those references that were not satisfied in the processor caches. For a sparse directory not to become a bottleneck, it is essential that it be large enough and have enough associativity that it does not incur too many replacements of actively accessed blocks. Some experiments and analysis studying the sizing of the sparse directory can be found in (Weber 1993).

8.10.2 Hierarchical Coherence

The introduction to this chapter mentions that one way to build scalable coherent machines is to hierarchically extend the snoopy coherence protocols based on the buses and rings that are discussed in Chapters 5 and 6. We have also been introduced to hierarchical directory schemes in this chapter. This section describes these hierarchical approaches to coherence further. Although hierarchical ring-based snooping has been used in commercial systems (e.g., in the Kendall Square Research KSR1 [Frank, Burkhardt, and Rothnie 1993]) as well as research prototypes (e.g., in the University of Toronto's Hector system [Vranesic et al. 1991; Farkas, Vranesic, and Stumm 1992]), and hierarchical directories have been studied in academic research, these approaches have not gained much favor. Nonetheless, building large systems hierarchically out of smaller ones is an attractive abstraction, and it is useful to understand the basic techniques.

Hierarchical Snooping

The issues in hierarchical snooping are similar for buses and rings, so we study them mainly through the former. A bus hierarchy is a tree of buses. The leaves are bus-based multiprocessors that contain the processors. The buses that constitute the internal nodes of the tree don't contain processors but are used for interconnection and coherence control: they allow transactions to be snooped and propagated up and down the hierarchy as necessary. Hierarchical machines can be built with main memory either centralized at the root or distributed among the leaf multiprocessors (see Figure 8.37). While a centralized main memory may simplify programming, distributed memory has advantages in bandwidth and performance if locality is exploited. (Note, however, that if data is not distributed such that most cache misses are satisfied locally, remote data may actually be further away than the root of the hierarchy in the worst case, potentially leading to worse performance.) In addition, with distributed memory, a leaf in the hierarchy is a complete bus-based multiprocessor, which is already a commodity product with cost advantages. Let us focus on hierarchies with distributed memory, leaving centralized memory hierarchies to be explored in the exercises.

The processor caches within a leaf node (multiprocessor) are kept coherent by any of the snooping protocols discussed in Chapter 5. In a simple, two-level hierarchy, we connect several of these bus-based systems together using another bus (B_2). (The extension to multilevel hierarchies is straightforward.) What we need is a coherence monitor associated with each B_1 bus that monitors (snoops) the transactions on both buses and decides which transactions on its B_1 bus should be forwarded to the B_2 bus and which ones that appear on the B_2 bus should be forwarded to its B_1 bus. This device acts as a filter, forwarding only the necessary transactions in both directions, and thus reduces the bandwidth demands on the buses.

In a system with distributed memory, the coherence monitor for a node has to worry about two types of data for which transactions may appear on either the B_1 or B_2 bus: data that is allocated remotely but cached by some processor in the local node and data that is allocated locally but cached remotely. To watch for the former data, a *remote access cache* or *remote cache* per node can be used as in the Sequent NUMA-Q. This cache maintains inclusion (see Section 6.3.1) with regard to remote data cached in any of the processor caches on that node, including a dirty-but-stale

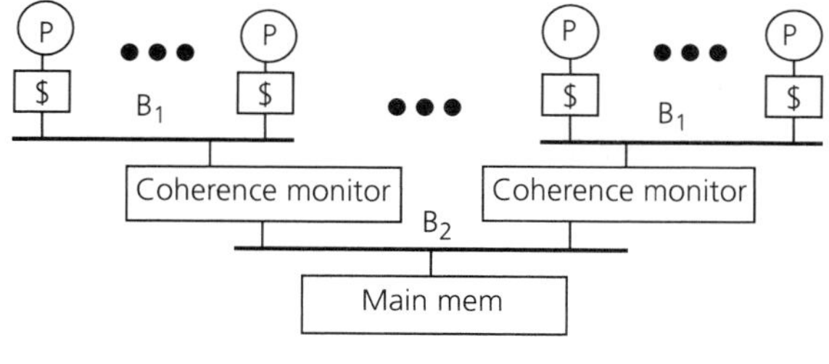

(a) Centralized memory

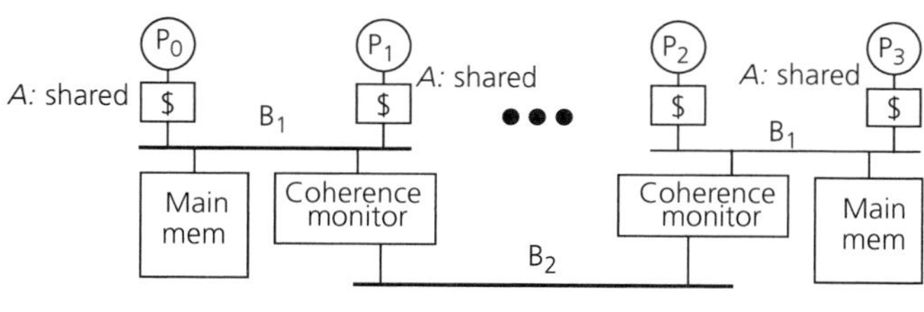

(b) Distributed memory

FIGURE 8.37 Hierarchical bus-based multiprocessors, shown with a two-level hierarchy. Main memory may be centralized at the root or physically distributed, and coherence monitors connect parent and child buses.

bit per block indicating when a processor cache in the node has the block dirty (data allocated in local memory does not enter the remote cache). This gives it enough information to determine which transactions are relevant in each direction and pass them along.

For locally allocated data, bus transactions can be handled entirely by the local memory or caches, except when the data is cached by processors in other (remote) nodes. For the latter data, there is no need to keep the data itself in the coherence monitor since the valid data is either already available locally or is in modified state remotely; in fact, we would not want to keep it there since the amount of data may be as large as the local memory. However, the monitor keeps state information for this data and snoops the local B_1 bus so that relevant transactions for this data can be forwarded to the B_2 bus if necessary. Let's call this part of the coherence monitor the *local state monitor*. Finally, the coherence monitor also watches the B_2 bus for transactions to its local addresses and passes them onto the local B_1 bus unless the local state monitor says they are cached remotely in a modified state. Both the remote cache and the local state monitor are looked up on B_1 and B_2 bus transactions.

Consider the three coherence protocol functions outlined in Section 8.1: (1) enough information about the state in other nodes of the hierarchy is implicitly available in the local node's coherence monitor (remote cache and local state monitor) to determine what action to take; (2) if this information indicates a need to find other copies beyond the local node, the request or search is broadcast on the next bus (and so on hierarchically in deeper hierarchies), and other relevant monitors will respond; and (3) communication with the other copies is performed simultaneously as part of finding them through the hierarchical broadcasts on buses.

Let us examine the path of a read miss more closely, assuming a shared physical address space. A BusRd request appears on the local B_1 bus. If the remote access cache, the local memory, or another local processor cache has a valid copy of the block, they will supply the data. Otherwise, either the remote cache or the local state monitor will know to pass the request onto the B_2 bus. When the request appears on B_2, the coherence monitors of other nodes will snoop it. If a node's local state monitor determines that a valid copy of the data exists in that node, it will pass the request onto its B_1 bus, wait for the response, and put it back on the B_2 bus. If a node's remote cache contains the data and has it in shared state, it may simply place a reply on the B_2 bus; if in dirty state, it will reply and broadcast a read request on its B_1 bus to have the dirty processor cache downgrade the block to shared; and if dirty-but-stale, it will simply broadcast the read request on its B_1 bus and reply with the result obtained. In the last case, the processor cache that has the data dirty will change its state from dirty to shared and put the data on the B_1 bus. The remote cache will accept the data reply from the B_1 bus, change its state from dirty-but-stale to shared, and pass the reply onto the B_2 bus. When the data reply appears on B_2, the requestor's coherence monitor picks it up, installs it and changes state in its remote cache if appropriate, and places it on its local B_1 bus. (If the block has to be installed in the remote cache, it may replace some other block, which will trigger a flush/invalidation request on that B_1 bus to ensure the inclusion property.) Finally, the requesting cache picks up the response to its BusRd request from the B_1 bus and stores it in shared state.

For writes, consider the specific situation shown in Figure 8.37(b), with P_0 in the left node issuing a write to location *A*, which is allocated in the memory of a third node (not shown). Since P_0's own cache has the data only in shared state, an ownership request (BusUpgr) is issued on the local B_1 bus. As a result, the copy of *A* in P_1's cache is invalidated. Since the block is not available in the remote cache in dirty-but-stale state (which would have been incorrect since P_1 had it in shared state), the monitor passes the BusUpgr request to bus B_2, to invalidate any other copies in the system, and at the same time updates the state for the block in the remote cache to dirty-but-stale. In another node, P_2 and P_3 have the block in their caches in shared state. Because of the inclusion property, their associated remote cache is also guaranteed to have the block in shared state. This remote cache therefore passes the BusUpgr request from B_2 onto its local B_1 bus and invalidates its own copy. When the request appears on the B_1 bus, the copies of *A* in P_2 and P_3's caches are invalidated. If there is a node on the B_2 bus whose processors are not caching the block containing *A*, the upgrade request will not pass onto its B_1 bus. Now suppose another processor P_4 in the left node issues a store to location *B*. This request will be satisfied within the local node, with P_0's cache supplying the data and the remote cache retaining the data in dirty-but-stale state, and no transaction will be passed onto the B_2 bus.

The implementation requirements on the processor caches and cache controllers remain unchanged from those discussed in Chapter 6. However, some constraints do apply to the remote access cache. It should be larger than the sum of the processor caches and quite associative to maintain inclusion without excessive replacements. It should also be *lockup-free;* that is, able to handle multiple requests at a time from processors in the local node while some requests are still outstanding (more on this in Chapter 11). Finally, whenever a block is replaced from the remote cache, an invalidation or flush request must be issued on the B_1 bus, depending on the state of the replaced block (shared or dirty-but-stale, respectively). Minimizing the access time for the remote cache is less critical than increasing its hit rate since it is not in the critical path that affects the clock rate of the processor. Remote caches are therefore more likely to be built out of DRAM than SRAM. The remote cache controller must also deal with the nonatomicity issues in requesting and acquiring the buses that were discussed in Chapter 6.

Finally, consider write serialization and determining store completion. From our earlier discussion of how these work on a single bus in Chapter 6, it should be clear that serialization between two requests will be determined by the order in which those requests appear on the closest bus to the root on which they both appear. For writes that are satisfied entirely within the same leaf node, the order in which they may be seen by other processors—within or without that leaf—is their serialization order provided by the local B_1 bus. Likewise, for writes that are satisfied entirely within the same subtree, the order in which they are seen by other processors—within or without that subtree—is the serialization order determined by the root bus of that subtree. It is easy to see this if we view each bus hanging off a common bus as a processor and recursively use the same reasoning applied to a single bus in Chapters 5 and 6. Similarly, for the store completion detection needed for sequential consistency, a processor cannot assume its store has committed until it appears on the closest bus to the root on which it will appear. An acknowledgment (which now may have to be an explicit bus transaction) cannot be generated until that time, and even then the appropriate orders must be preserved between this acknowledgment and other transactions on the way back to the requesting processor (see Exercise 8.26). Once this acknowledgment is sent back from a bus, the invalidations themselves no longer need to be acknowledged as they make their way down toward the processor caches, as long as the appropriate orders are maintained along this path (just as with multilevel cache hierarchies in Chapter 6).

One of the earliest machines that used the approach of hierarchical snooping buses with distributed memory was the Gigamax (Wilson 1987; Woodbury et al. 1989) from Encore Corporation. The system consisted of up to eight Encore Multimax machines (each a regular snooping bus-based multiprocessor) connected together by fiber-optic links to a ninth global bus, forming a two-level hierarchy. Figure 8.38 shows a block diagram. Each node is augmented with a uniform interconnection card (UIC) and a uniform cluster (node) cache (UCC) card. The UCC is the remote access cache, and the UIC is the local state monitor. The monitoring of the global bus is done differently in the Gigamax due to its particular organization. Nodes are connected to the global bus through a fiber-optic link, so while a node's

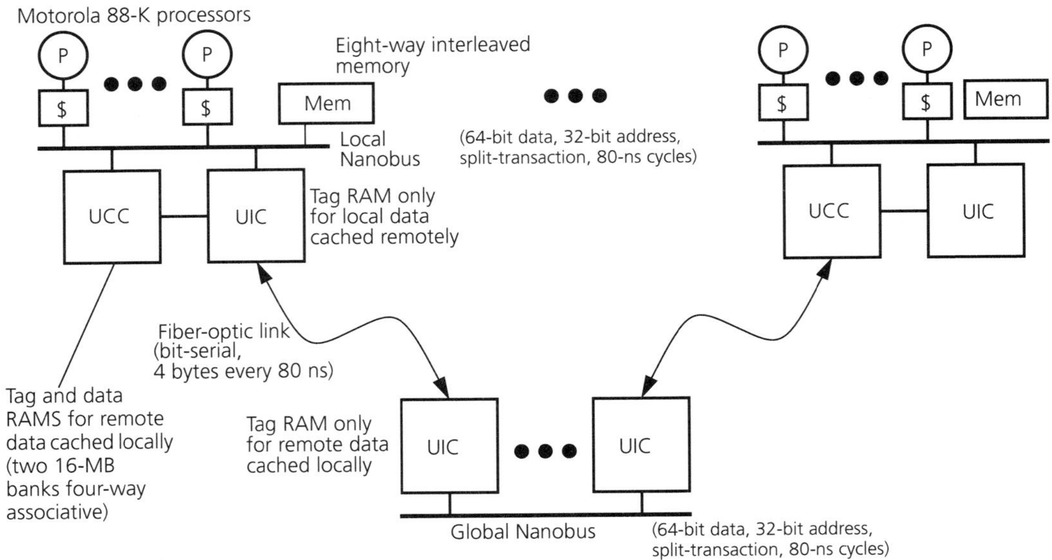

FIGURE 8.38 Block diagram for the Encore Gigamax multiprocessor. A two-level hierarchy of buses is used with memory distributed among the leaf nodes.

remote access cache (the UCC) caches remote data, it does not snoop the global bus directly. Rather, every node also has a second UIC on the global bus, which monitors global bus transactions for remote memory blocks that are cached in this local node. It then passes on the relevant requests to the local bus. If the UCC indeed sat directly on the global bus as well, the UIC on the global bus would not be necessary. The reason the Gigamax uses fiber-optic links and not a single UIC per node that sits on both buses is that high-speed buses are usually short: the Nanobus used in the Encore Multimax and Gigamax is 1 foot long (light travels 1 foot in a nanosecond, hence the name Nanobus). Since each node is at least 1 foot wide and the global bus is also 1 foot wide, flexible cabling is needed to hook these together. With fiber, links can be made quite long without affecting their transmission capabilities.

The extension of snooping cache coherence to hierarchies of rings is much like the extension to hierarchies of buses with distributed memory. Figure 8.39 shows a block diagram. The local rings and the associated processors constitute nodes, and these are connected by one or more global rings. The coherence monitor takes the form of an inter-ring interface, serving the same roles as the coherence monitor in a bus hierarchy.

Hierarchical Directory Schemes

Hierarchical directory schemes use point-to-point network transactions rather than snooping. However, as discussed earlier, unlike in flat directory schemes, the source

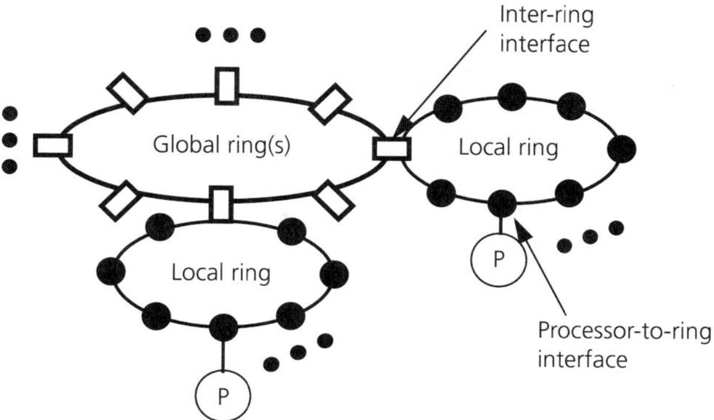

FIGURE 8.39 Block diagram for a hierarchical ring-based multiprocessor. In the two-level hierarchy shown, each local ring is a node as viewed by the global ring, and an inter-ring interface propagates relevant transactions between the two.

of the directory information in hierarchical directories is not found by going to a fixed node. The locations of copies are found neither at a fixed home node nor by traversing a distributed list pointed to by that home. Invalidation messages are not sent directly to the nodes with copies. Rather, all these activities are performed by sending messages up and down a hierarchy (tree) built upon the nodes, with the only direct communication being between parents and children in the tree.

At first blush, the organization of hierarchical directories is much like hierarchical snooping. Consider the example shown in Figure 8.40. The processing nodes are at the leaves of the tree and main memory is distributed along with the processing nodes. Every block has a home memory (leaf) in which it is allocated, but this does not mean that the directory information is maintained or rooted there. The internal nodes of the tree are not processing nodes but only hold directory information. Each such directory node keeps track of all memory blocks that are being cached or recorded by its subtrees. It uses a presence vector per block to tell which of its subtrees have copies of the block and a bit to tell whether one of them has it dirty. It also records information about local memory blocks (i.e., blocks allocated in the local memory of one of its descendants) that are being cached by processing nodes outside its subtree. As with hierarchical snooping, this information is used to decide when requests originating within the subtree should be propagated further up the hierarchy. Since the amount of directory information to be maintained by a directory node that is close to the root can become very large, the directory information is usually organized as a cache to reduce its size and maintains the inclusion property with respect to its children's caches or directories. This requires that on a replacement from a directory cache at a certain level of the tree, the replaced block must be flushed out of all of its descendent directories in the tree as well. Similarly, replacement of the information about a block allocated within that subtree requires that copies of the block in nodes outside the subtree be invalidated or flushed. These operations can be quite expensive.

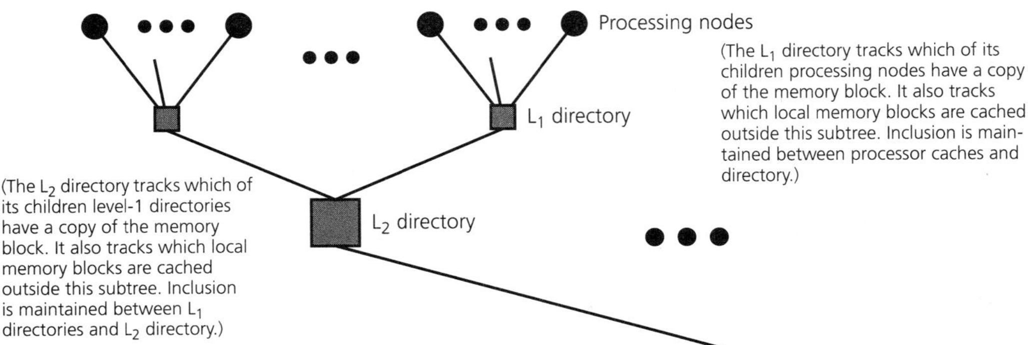

FIGURE 8.40 Organization of hierarchical directories. The processing nodes are at the leaves of the logical tree, and the internal nodes contain only directory information. There is one logical tree for each cached memory block. Logical trees may be embedded in any physical hierarchy.

A read miss from a node flows up the hierarchy either until a directory indicates that its subtree has a copy (clean or dirty) of the memory block being requested or until the request reaches the directory that is the first common ancestor of the requesting node and the home node for that block, and that directory indicates the block is not dirty outside that subtree. The request then flows down the hierarchy to the appropriate processing node to pick up the data. The data reply follows the same path back, updating the directories on its way. If the block was dirty, a copy of the block also finds its way to the home node.

A write miss in the cache flows up the hierarchy until it reaches a directory whose subtree contains the current owner of the requested memory block. The owner is either the home node, if the block is clean, or a dirty cache. The request travels down to the owner to pick up the data, and the requesting node becomes the new owner. If the block was previously in clean state, invalidations are also propagated through the hierarchy to all nodes caching that memory block. Finally, all directories involved in the preceding memory operation are updated to reflect the new owner and the invalidated copies.

In hierarchical snoopy schemes, the interconnection network is physically hierarchical to permit the snooping. With point-to-point communication, hierarchical directories do not need to rely on physically hierarchical interconnects. The hierarchy discussed here is a logical hierarchy, or a hierarchical data structure. It can be implemented either on a network that is physically hierarchical (that is, an actual tree network with directory caches at the internal nodes and processing nodes at the leaves) or on a general, nonhierarchical network such as a mesh with the hierarchical directory embedded in this general network. In fact, there is a separate hierarchical directory structure for every block that is cached. Thus, the same physical node in a general network can be a leaf (processing) node for some blocks and an internal (directory) node for others (see Figure 8.41).

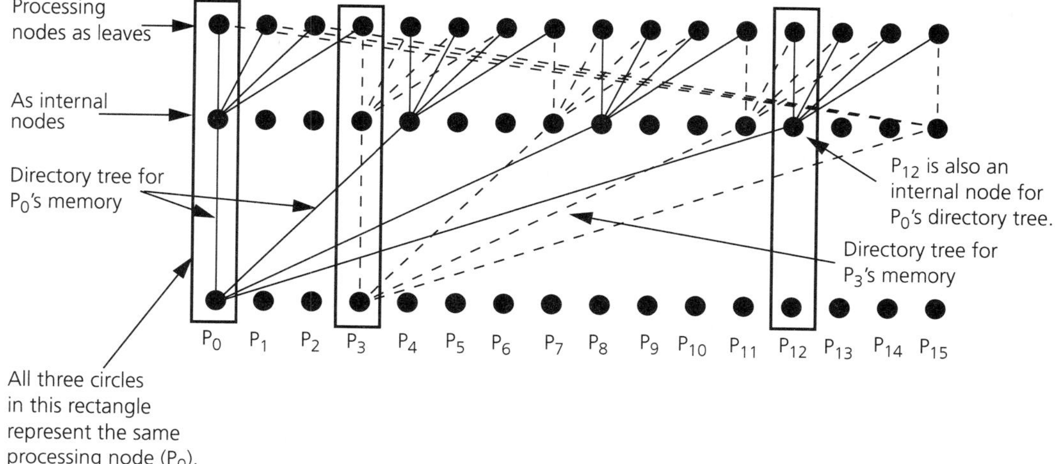

FIGURE 8.41 A multirooted hierarchical directory embedded in an arbitrary network. A 16-node hierarchy is shown. For the blocks in the portion of main memory that is located at a processing node, that node itself is the root of the (logical) directory tree. Thus, for *P* processing nodes, there are *P* directory trees. The figure shows only two of these. In addition to being the root for its local memory's directory tree, a processing node is also an internal node in the directory trees for the other processing nodes. The address of a memory block implicitly specifies a particular directory tree and guides the physical traversals to get from parents to children and vice versa in this directory tree.

Finally, the storage overhead of the hierarchical directory has attractive scaling properties. It is the cost of the directory caches at each level. The number of entries in the directory goes up as we go further up the hierarchy toward the root (to maintain inclusion without excessive replacements), but the number of directories becomes smaller. As a result, the total directory memory needed for all directories at any given level of the hierarchy is typically about the same. The directory storage needed is not proportional to the size of main memory but rather to that of the caches in the processing nodes, which is attractive. The overall directory memory overhead relative to main memory is proportional to

$$\frac{C \times \log_b P}{M \times B}$$

where C is the cache size per processing node at the leaf, M is the main memory per node, B is the memory block size in bits, b is the branching factor of the hierarchy, and P is the number of processing nodes at the leaves (so $\log_b P$ is the number of levels in the tree). More information about hierarchical directory schemes can be found in the literature (Scott 1991; Wallach 1992; Hagersten 1992; Joe 1995).

Performance Implications of Hierarchical Coherence

Hierarchical protocols, whether snoopy or directory, have some potential performance advantages that are extensions of the advantages of the two-level protocols discussed earlier. One is the combining of requests for a block as they go up and down the hierarchy. If a processing node is waiting for a memory block to arrive, another processing node that requests the same block can observe at their common ancestor directory that the block has already been requested. It can then wait at the intermediate directory and accept the response when it comes back rather than send a duplicate request. This combining of transactions can reduce traffic and, hence, contention. The sending of invalidations and gathering of invalidation acknowledgments can also be done hierarchically through the tree structure. Another advantage is that upon a miss, if a nearby node in the hierarchy has a cached copy of the block, then the block can be obtained from that nearby node (cache-to-cache sharing) rather than having to go to the home, which may be much further away in the network topology. This can reduce transit latency as well as contention at the home. Of course, this second advantage depends on how well locality in the hierarchy maps to locality in the underlying physical network as well as how well the sharing patterns of the application match the hierarchy.

While locality in the tree network can reduce transit delay on links, particularly for very large machines, the overall latency and bandwidth characteristics are usually not advantageous for hierarchical schemes. Consider hierarchical snooping schemes first. With buses, there is a bus transaction and snooping latency at every bus along the way. With rings, traversing rings at every level of the hierarchy further increases latency to potentially very high levels. For example, the uncontended latency to access a location on a remote ring in a fully populated Kendall Square Research KSR1 machine (Frank, Burkhardt, and Rothnie 1993) was higher than 25 microseconds (Saavedra, Gaines, and Carlton 1993), so other architectural techniques (discussed in Chapter 9) were used to reduce ring remote capacity misses. The commercial systems that have used hierarchical snooping have tended to use quite shallow hierarchies (the largest KSR machine was a two-level ring hierarchy with up to 32 nodes per ring). The fact that there are several processors per node also implies that the bandwidth between a node and its parent or child must be large enough to sustain their combined demands. The processors within a node will compete not only for bus or link bandwidth but also for snoop bandwidth and for the occupancy, buffers, and request tracking mechanisms of the node-to-network interface. To alleviate link bandwidth limitations near the root of the hierarchy, multiple buses or rings can be used closer to the root; however, bandwidth scalability in practical hierarchical systems remains quite limited.

For hierarchical directories, the latency problem is that the number of network transactions sent up and down the hierarchy to satisfy a request tends to be larger than in a flat, memory-based scheme. Even though these transactions may be more localized in the network, each one is a full-fledged network transaction that also requires either looking up or modifying the directory at its (intermediate) destination node. This increased endpoint overhead at the nodes along the critical path tends to far outweigh any reduction in the total number of network hops traversed and hence network delay, especially given the characteristics of modern networks. Although some pipelining can be used—for example, the data reply can be forwarded toward the requesting node while a directory node is being updated—in practice, the latencies can still become quite large compared to machines with no hierarchy (Hagersten 1992; Joe 1995). Hierarchies with large branching factors can alleviate the latency problem but they increase contention. As with hierarchical snooping, the root of the directory hierarchy can become a bandwidth bottleneck, for both link bandwidth and directory lookup bandwidth. Multiple links may be used closer to the root (particularly appropriate for physically hierarchical networks [Leiserson et al. 1996]), and the directory cache may be interleaved among them. Alternatively, since each block has a separate logical hierarchy, a multirooted directory hierarchy may be embedded in a nonhierarchical, scalable point-to-point interconnect (Scott 1991; Wallach 1992; Scott and Goodman 1993). Figure 8.41 shows a possible organization. Like hierarchical directory schemes themselves, however, these techniques have only been in the realm of research so far.

8.11 CONCLUDING REMARKS

Scalable systems that support a coherent shared address space are an increasingly important part of the multiprocessing landscape since they combine the ease of programming of a coherent shared address space programming model with the scaling advantages of a distributed memory and interconnect. Hardware support for cache coherence is becoming increasingly popular in commercial multiprocessors designed for both technical and commercial workloads. Most of these systems use directory-based protocols, whether memory based or cache based. They are found to perform well, at least at the moderate scales at which they have been built so far, and to afford significant ease of programming compared to explicit message passing for many applications.

Directory-based cache coherence protocols are quite complex, with many transient states and "corner cases" to deal with. Figure 8.42 conveys a sense of the complexity by showing the almost complete state transition diagrams of the Origin2000 and NUMA-Q protocols.

While supporting cache coherence in hardware has a significant design cost, it is alleviated by increased experience, the appearance of standards, and the fact that microprocessors themselves provide support for cache coherence. Once the microprocessor coherence protocol is available designers can develop the multiprocessor protocol and communication architecture even before the microprocessor is ready so that not so much of a lag occurs between the two. Commercial multiprocessors today typically use the latest microprocessors available at the time they ship, alleviating the fear that multiprogrammers would have to play catch-up with the processor technology curve.

Some interesting open questions for hardware-coherent shared address space systems include whether their performance on real applications will indeed scale to

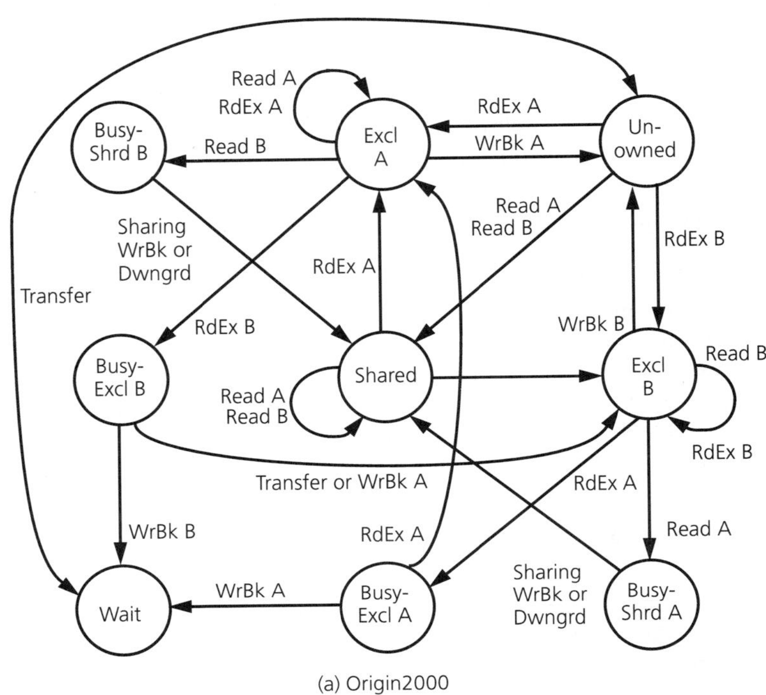

(a) Origin2000

FIGURE 8.42 Expanded directory state diagrams for the case study multiprocessors of this chapter. The state diagram for the SGI Origin2000 in (a) is quite simplified: it shows the busy states at the directory but leaves out I/O operations, the poisoned state, and several race conditions. To show the use of busy states, accesses from two nodes A and B are shown. For example, a state labeled "Excl A" means that the directory thinks the block is in exclusive state in node A, and an arc labeled "RdEx B" indicates a read-exclusive operation from node B. The transfer operation and the wait state are used to handle write backs, as described in the text. The state diagram for the Sequent NUMA-Q in (b) is much more complete, though it also excludes a few corner cases. The arcs are not labeled in this diagram and several of the state labels are not explained; the purpose of this diagram is not to convey the complete protocol but simply to show that full-blown state transition diagrams can become quite complex in real systems.

large processor counts (and whether significant changes to current protocols will be needed for this), whether the appropriate node for a scalable system will be a small-scale multiprocessor or a uniprocessor, the extent to which commodity communication architectures will be successful in supporting this abstraction efficiently, and the success with which a communication assist can be designed that supports the most appropriate mechanisms for both cache coherence and explicit message passing. Some critical hardware/software trade-offs for coherent shared address space systems are discussed in the next chapter.

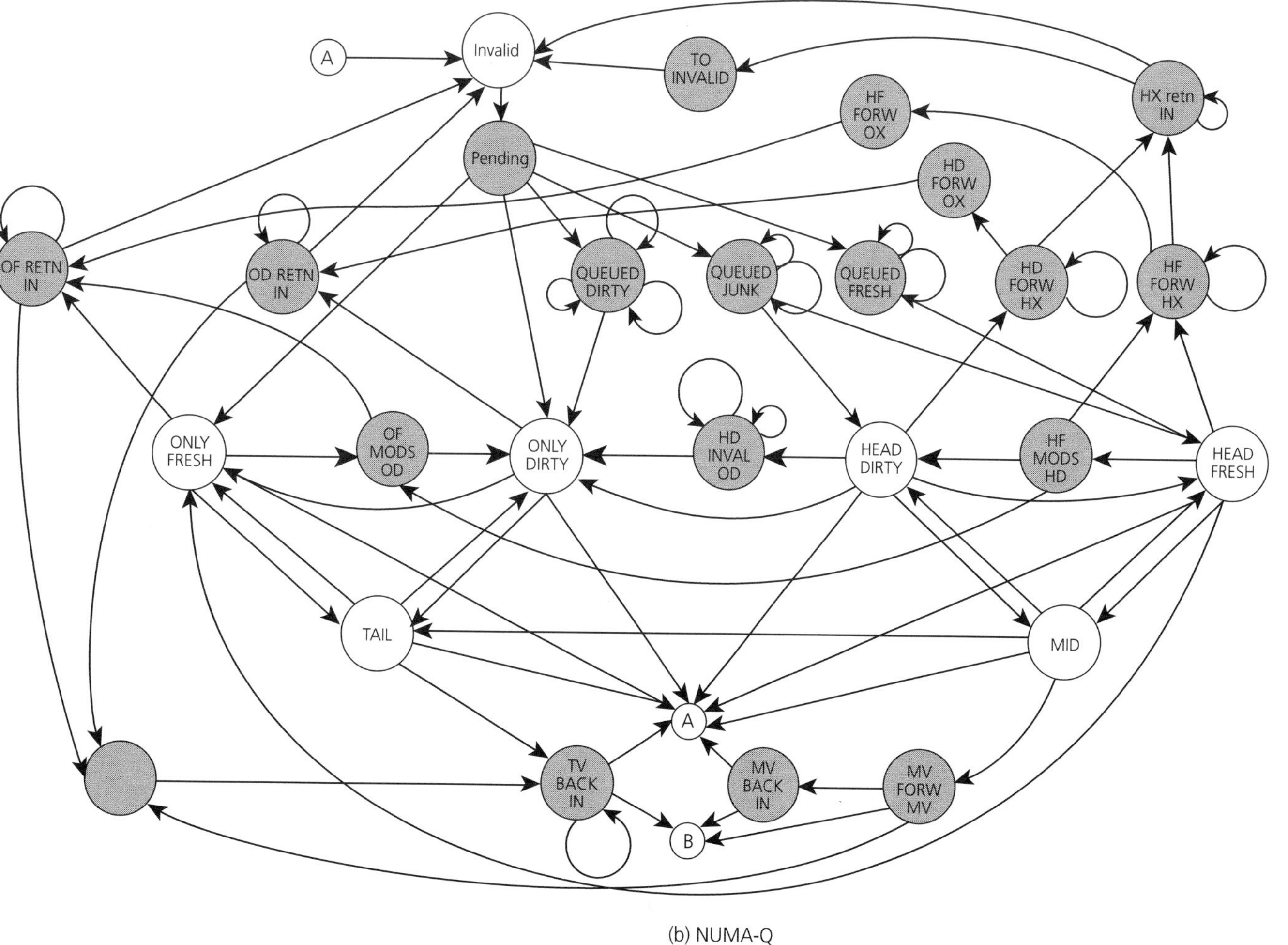

FIGURE 8.42 Expanded directory state diagrams for the case study multiprocessors of this chapter

8.12 EXERCISES

8.1 What are the inefficiencies and efficiencies in emulating message passing on a cache-coherent machine compared to the kinds of machines discussed in Chapter 7?

8.2
a. For which of the case study parallel applications used in this book do you expect a substantial advantage in using multiprocessor rather than uniprocessor nodes (assuming the same total number of processors)? For which do you think there might be disadvantages, and under what circumstances?

b. How might your answer to the previous question differ with increasing scale of the machine? That is, how do you expect the performance benefits of using fixed-size multiprocessor nodes to change as the machine size is increased to hundreds of processors?

c. Are there any special benefits that the Illinois MESI coherence scheme offers for organizations with multiprocessor nodes?

8.3 Given a 512-processor system in which each node visible to the directory has 8 processors and 1 GB of main memory and a cache block size of 64 bytes, what is the directory memory overhead for (a) a full bit vector scheme, and (b) Dir_iB with $i = 3$?

8.4 The chapter provided diagrams showing the network transactions for strict request-response, intervention forwarding, and reply forwarding for read operations in a flat, memory-based protocol like that of the SGI Origin (see Figure 8.12). Do the same for write operations.

8.5 The Origin protocol assumed that acknowledgments for invalidations are gathered at the requestor. An alternative is to have the acknowledgments sent back to the home (from where the invalidation requests come) and have the home send a single acknowledgment back to the requestor. This solution is used in the Stanford FLASH multiprocessor. What are the main performance and complexity trade-offs between these two choices?

8.6 Draw the network transaction diagrams (like those in Figure 8.16) for an uncached read-shared request, an uncached read-exclusive request, and a write-invalidate request in the Origin protocol. State one example of a use of each.

8.7 Instead of the doubly linked list used in the SCI protocol, it is possible to use a singly linked list. What is the advantage? Describe what modifications would need to be made to the following operations if a singly linked list were used:

a. Replacement of a cache block that is in a sharing list.

b. Write to a cache block that is in a sharing list.

Qualitatively discuss the effects this might have on large-scale multiprocessor performance.

8.8 How might you reduce the latency of writes that cause invalidations in the SCI protocol? Draw the network transactions. What are the major trade-offs?

8.9 When a variable exhibits migratory sharing, a processor that reads the variable will be the next one to write it. What kinds of protocol optimizations could you use to reduce traffic and latency in this case, and how would you detect the situation dynamically? Describe a scheme or two in some detail.

8.10 Another pattern that might be detected dynamically is a producer-consumer pattern, in which one processor repeatedly writes (produces) a variable and another processor repeatedly reads (consumes) it. Is the standard MESI invalidation-based protocol well suited to this? Why or why not? What enhancements or protocol might be better, and what are the savings in latency or traffic? How would you dynamically detect and employ the changes?

8.11 Why is write atomicity more difficult to provide with update protocols than with invalidation-based protocols in directory-based systems? How would you solve the problem? Does the same difficulty exist in a bus-based system?

8.12 Consider the following program fragment running on a cache-coherent multiprocessor, assuming all values to be 0 initially.

P_1	P_2	P_3	P_4
`A = 1`	`u = A`	`w = A`	`A = 2`
	`v = A`	`x = A`	

There is only one shared variable (`A`). Suppose that a writer magically knows where the cached copies are and sends updates to them directly without consulting a directory node. Construct a situation in which write atomicity may be violated, assuming an update-based protocol.

a. Show the violation of sequential consistency that occurs in the results.

b. Can you produce a case where coherence is violated as well? How would you solve these problems?

c. Can you construct the same problems for an invalidation-based protocol?

d. Can you construct them for update protocols on a bus?

8.13 In handling write backs in the Origin protocol, we said that when the node doing the write back receives an intervention, it ignores it. Given a network that does not preserve point-to-point order, of what situations do we have to be careful in deciding to ignore the intervention? How do we detect that this intervention should be dropped? Would there be a problem with a network that preserved point-to-point order?

8.14 Can the serialization problems discussed for Origin in Section 8.5.2 arise even with a strict request-response protocol, and do the same guidelines apply? Show example situations, including the examples discussed in that section.

8.15 Consider the serialization of writes in NUMA-Q, given the two-level hierarchical coherence protocol. If a node has the block dirty in its remote cache, how might writes from other nodes that come to it get serialized with respect to writes from processors in this node? What transactions would have to be generated to ensure the serialization?

8.16 In the Origin implementation, incoming request messages to the memory/directory interface are given priority over incoming responses unless there is a danger of responses being starved. Why do you think this choice of giving priorities to requests was made? Describe some methods for how you might detect when to invert the priority. What would be the danger with responses being starved?

8.17 a. Why is it necessary to flush TLBs when doing migration or replication of pages?

b. For a CC-NUMA multiprocessor with software-reloaded TLBs, suppose a page needs to be migrated. Which one of the following TLB flushing schemes would you pick and why: (i) only TLBs that currently have an entry for a page, (ii) only TLBs that have loaded an entry for a page since the last flush, or (iii) all TLBs in the system. [Hint: the selection should be based on the following two criteria: the cost of doing the actual TLB flush and the difficulty of tracking necessary information to implement the scheme.]

8.18 For a simple two-processor CC-NUMA system, the traces of cache misses for three virtual pages *X*, *Y*, *Z* from the two processors P_0 and P_1 are shown. Time goes from left to right. "R" is a read miss and "W" is a write miss. There are two memories M_0 and M_1, local to P_0 and P_1 respectively. A local miss costs 1 time unit and a remote miss costs 4 units. Assume that read misses and write misses cost the same.

Page *X*:
P_0: RRRR R R RRRRR   RRR
P_1: R   R R R R   RRRR   RR
Page *Y*:
P_0: no accesses
P_1: RR WW RRRR RWRWRW WWWR
Page *Z*:
P_0: R   W   RW   R R RRWRWRWRW
P_1: WR RW   RW W W   R

a. In which local memories would you place pages *X*, *Y*, and *Z*, assuming complete knowledge of the entire trace?

b. Assume that all three pages were initially placed in M_0. You have prior knowledge of the entire trace. You can do one migration, or one replication, or nothing for each page at the beginning of the trace at zero cost. What action would be appropriate for each of the pages?

c. Answer part (b) where a page migration or replication costs 10 units. In addition, give the final memory access cost for each page.

d. Answer part (c) where a migration or replication costs 60 units.

e. Answer part (d) where the cache miss trace for each page is the shown trace repeated 10 times. (You still can only do one migration or replication at the beginning of the entire trace.)

8.19 Full-empty bits, introduced in Section 5.5, provide hardware support for fine-grained synchronization and have been proposed for CC-NUMA machines. What are the advantages and disadvantages of full-empty bits, and why do you think they are not used in modern systems?

8.20 With an invalidation-based protocol, lock transfers take more network transactions than necessary. An alternative to cached locks is to use uncached locks, where the lock variable stays in main memory and is always accessed at the memory itself.

a. Write pseudocode for a simple lock and a ticket lock using uncached operations.

b. What are the advantages and disadvantages relative to using cached locks? Which would you deploy in a production system?

c. Can you describe a scheme that uses both cached and uncached read and write operations to improve the performance of locks? What specific operations would your scheme require?

8.21 Since high-contention and low-contention situations are best served by different lock algorithms, one strategy that has been proposed is to have a library of synchronization algorithms and provide hardware support to switch between them "reactively" at run time based on observed access patterns to the synchronization variable.

a. Which locks would you provide in your library?

b. Assuming a memory-based directory protocol, design simple hardware support and a policy for switching between locks at run time.

c. Describe an example where this support might be particularly useful.

d. What are the potential disadvantages?

8.22 You are performing an architectural study using four applications: Ocean, blocked LU factorization, an FFT that performs local calculations on rows separated by a matrix transposition, and Barnes-Hut. For each application, answer the following questions, assuming a CC-NUMA system:

a. What modifications or enhancements in data structuring or layout would you use to ensure good interactions with the extended memory hierarchy?

b. What are the interactions with cache size and granularities of allocation, coherence, and communication that you would be particularly careful to represent or not represent?

8.23 Consider the example of transposing a matrix of data in parallel, as is used in computations such as high-performance FFTs. Figure 8.43 shows the transpose pictorially. Every process transposes one "patch" of its assigned rows to every other processor, including one to itself. Before the transpose, a process has read and written its assigned rows of the source matrix of the transpose, and after the transpose it reads and writes its assigned rows of the destination matrix. The rows assigned to a process in both the source and destination matrix are allocated in its local memory. There are two ways to perform the transpose: a process can read the local elements from its rows of the source matrix and write them to the appropriate elements of the

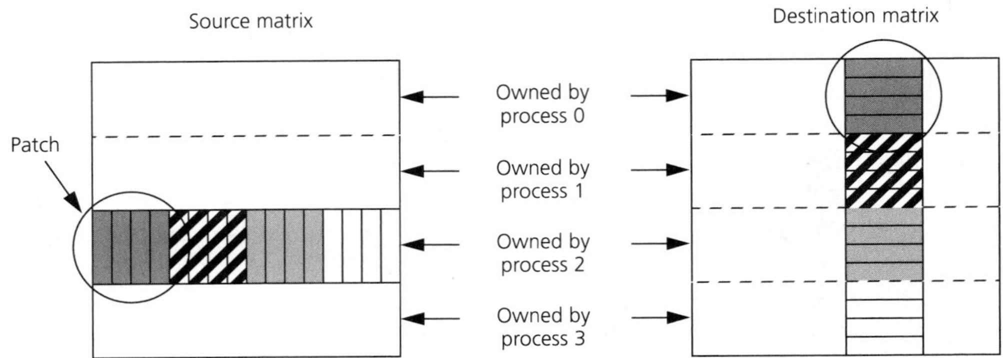

FIGURE 8.43 Sender-initiated matrix transposition. The source and destination matrices are partitioning among processes in groups of contiguous rows. Each process divides its set of n/p rows into p patches of size $(n/p)*(n/p)$. Consider process 2 as a representative example: one patch assigned to it ends up in the assigned set of rows of every other process, and it transposes one patch (third from left, in this case) locally.

destination matrix, whether they are local or remote, as shown in the figure (called a sender-initiated transpose); or a process can write the local rows of the destination matrix and read the appropriate elements of the source matrix, whether they are local or remote (called a receiver-initiated transpose).

a. Given an invalidation-based directory protocol, which method do you think will perform better and why?

b. How do you expect the answer to (a) to change if you assume an update-based directory protocol?

c. Consider the following implementation of a matrix transpose, which you plan to run on eight processors. Each processor has one level of cache, which is fully associative, 8 KB, with 128 byte lines. (*Note:* `AT` and `A` are not the same matrix.)

```
Transpose(double **A, double **AT)
{
    int i,j,mynum;

    GETPID(mynum);

    for (i=mynum*nrows/p; i<((mynum+1)*(nrows/p)); i++) {
        for (j=0; j<1024; j++) {
            AT[i][j] = A[j][i];
        }
    }
}
```

The input data set is a $1,024 \times 1,024$ matrix of double-precision floating-point numbers (i.e., `nrows` in 1,024), decomposed so that each processor is responsible for generating a contiguous block of rows in the transposed matrix `AT` (i.e., a receiver-initiated transpose). Ignoring the contention problem caused by all processors first going to processor 0, what is the major performance problem with this code? What technique would you use to solve it? Restructure the code to alleviate all performance problems as much as possible. Write the entire restructured loop.

8.24 Consider a hierarchical bus-based system with a centralized memory at the root of the hierarchy rather than distributed memory as discussed in the chapter. What would be the main differences in how reads and writes are satisfied? Briefly describe the path taken by reads and writes.

8.25 Could you construct a hierarchical bus-based system with centralized memory (say) without pursuing the inclusion property between the remote access cache and the L_1 caches in a node? If so, what complications would it cause?

8.26 To ensure sequential consistency in a two-level hierarchical bus design, is it okay to return an acknowledgment when the invalidation request reaches the B_2 bus? If so, what constraints are imposed on the design and implementation of the caches and the orders preserved among transactions? If not, why not? Would it be okay if the hierarchy had more than two levels?

8.27 Suppose two processors in two different nodes of a hierarchical bus-based machine issue an upgrade for a block at the same time. Trace their paths through the system, discussing all state changes and when they must happen as well as what precautions prevent deadlock and prevent both processors from gaining ownership.

8.28 An optimization in distributed-memory bus-based hierarchies is cache-to-cache sharing: if another processor's cache on the local bus can supply the data, we do not have to go to the global bus and remote node. What are the trade-offs of supporting this optimization in ring-based hierarchies?

8.29 What branching factor would you choose in a machine with a hierarchical directory? Highlight the major trade-offs. What techniques might you use to alleviate the performance trade-offs? Be as specific in your description as possible.

8.30 Is it possible to implement hierarchical directories without maintaining inclusion in the directory caches? Design a protocol that does that and discuss the advantages and disadvantages.

9

Hardware/Software Trade-Offs

This chapter addresses the potential limitations of the directory-based, cache-coherent systems discussed in Chapter 8 and the hardware/software trade-offs that arise in overcoming these limitations. The primary limitations of those systems are the following:

- *High waiting time at memory operations.* Sequential consistency (SC) is the memory consistency model of choice for the programmer and, so far, has been assumed for both snooping and directory-based systems. To satisfy the sufficient conditions for SC, a processor would have to wait for its previous memory operation to complete before issuing the next one. This has an even greater impact on performance in scalable systems than in bus-based systems since communication latencies are longer and more network transactions are in the critical path. Worse still, it is very limiting for compilers, which potentially cannot reorder memory operations to shared data at all if the programmer assumes sequential consistency.
- *Limited capacity for replication.* Communicated data is automatically replicated only in the processor cache, not in local main memory. This can lead to capacity misses and artifactual communication when working sets are large and include nonlocal data or when conflict misses are numerous.
- *High design and implementation cost.* The communication assist contains hardware that is specialized for supporting cache coherence and is tightly integrated into the processing node. Protocols are complex, and getting them right in hardware takes substantial design time. (By cost, here we mean the cost of hardware and of system design time. However, recall from Chapter 3 that a programming cost is also associated with achieving good performance, and approaches that reduce system cost can often increase this cost dramatically.)

This chapter focuses on these three limitations. The approaches that have been developed to address them are still controversial to varying degrees, but aspects of them are being adopted by designers of commercial parallel machines. Other limitations are often encountered as well, including the addressability limitations of a shared physical address space—as discussed for the CRAY T3D in Chapter 7—and the fact that a single protocol is hardwired into the machine. However, solutions to these problems are often incorporated in solutions to the primary problems, and they are discussed as advanced topics.

The problem of waiting too long at memory operations can be addressed in two ways in hardware. First, the implementation can be designed not to satisfy the sufficient conditions for SC, which modern nonblocking processors are not inclined to do anyway, but to satisfy the SC model itself. That is, a processor need not wait for the previous operation to complete before issuing the next one; however, the system ensures that operations do not complete or become visible out of program order. This method is used in the SGI Origin2000 system discussed in Chapter 8. Second, the memory consistency model can itself be relaxed so program order does not have to be maintained so strictly. Relaxing the consistency model changes the semantics of the shared address space and has implications for both hardware and software. It requires more care from the programmer in writing correct programs but enables the hardware to overlap and reorder operations to a greater extent. Importantly, it also allows the compiler to reorder memory operations within a process before they are even presented to hardware, as optimizing compilers are wont to do. Relaxed memory consistency models are discussed in Section 9.1.

The problem of limited capacity for replication can be addressed by automatically caching data in main memory, not just in the processor caches, and keeping this data coherent. Unlike in hardware caches, replication and coherence in main memory can be performed at a variety of granularities—for example, a cache block, a page, or a user-defined object—and can be managed either directly by hardware or through software. This provides a very rich space of protocols, hardware/software implementations, and cost-performance trade-offs. An approach directed primarily at improving performance is to manage the local main memory as a hardware cache, providing replication and coherence at cache block granularity there as well. This approach is called cache-only memory architecture, or COMA, and is discussed in Section 9.2. It relieves software from worrying about capacity misses and the initial distribution of data across main memories while still providing coherence at fine granularity and hence avoiding false sharing. However, it is hardware intensive and requires per-block tags and state to be maintained in main memory as well.

Finally, there are many approaches to addressing the problem of hardware cost. One approach is to integrate the communication assist and network less tightly into the processing node, at the cost of increasing communication latency and assist occupancy. Another is to provide automatic replication and coherence in software rather than hardware, leading to a range of possible system implementations, as illustrated in Figure 9.1. The software approaches provide replication and coherence in main memory and can operate at a variety of granularities. They enable the use of off-the-shelf commodity parts for the nodes and interconnect, reducing hardware cost but pushing much more of the (now much greater) burden of achieving good performance onto the programmer. These approaches to reduce hardware cost are discussed in Section 9.3.

The three issues are closely related. For example, cost is strongly related to the manner in which replication and coherence are managed in main memory: at what granularities and whether directly in hardware or through a run-time or operating

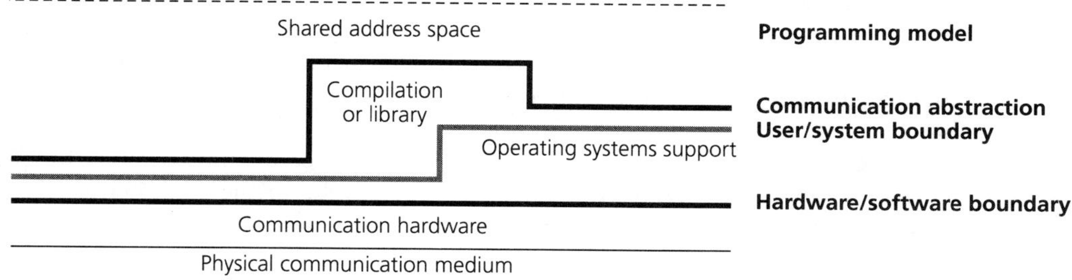

FIGURE 9.1 Layers of the communication architecture for systems discussed in this chapter. The diagram represents the degrees to which software intervention is used to support a coherent shared address space.

system. Cost and granularity are also related to the memory consistency model: lower-cost, lower-performance solutions and larger granularities benefit more from relaxing the memory consistency model, and implementing the protocol in software makes it easier to fully exploit the relaxation of the semantics. A useful framework to understand the space of alternatives is based on the granularities at which data is allocated in the local replication store, kept coherent, and communicated. Section 9.4 constructs such a framework to summarize and relate the alternatives. This framework leads naturally to an approach that strives to achieve a good compromise between the high-cost COMA approach and the low-cost all-software approach. This approach, called Simple COMA, is discussed in Section 9.4 as well.

The implications for parallel software of the systems discussed in this chapter are explored in Section 9.5. Finally, Section 9.6 covers some advanced topics, including the techniques to address the potential limitations of a shared physical address space and a fixed coherence protocol.

9.1 RELAXED MEMORY CONSISTENCY MODELS

Recall from Chapter 5 that the memory consistency model for a shared address space specifies the constraints on the order in which memory operations (to the same or different locations) can appear to execute with respect to one another, enabling programmers to reason about the behavior and correctness of their programs. In fact, any system layer that supports a shared address space naming model has a memory consistency model: the programming model or programmer's interface, the user/system interface, and the hardware/software interface. Software that interacts with a layer must be aware of its memory consistency model. We focus mainly on the consistency model as seen by the programmer—that is, at the interface between the programmer and the rest of the system composed of the compiler, operating system, and hardware—since that is the one with which programmers reason.[1] For example, a processor may preserve all program orders presented to it among memory operations, but if the compiler has already reordered operations then programmers can no longer reason with the simple model exported by the hardware.

The consistency model at the programmer's interface has implications for programming languages, compilers, and hardware as well. To the compiler and hardware, it indicates the constraints within which they can reorder accesses from a process and the orders that they cannot appear to violate, thus telling them what performance optimizations they can use. Programming languages must provide mechanisms to introduce such constraints if necessary, as we shall see. In general, the fewer the reorderings of memory accesses from a process that we allow the system to perform, the more intuitive the programming model we provide to the programmer but the more we constrain performance optimizations. The goal of a memory consistency model is to impose ordering constraints that strike a good balance between programming complexity and performance. The model should also be portable; that is, the specification should be implementable on many platforms so that the same program can run on all these platforms and preserve the same semantics.

The sequential consistency model that we have assumed so far provides an intuitive semantics to the programmer—program order within each process and a consistent interleaving across processes—and can be quite easily implemented by satisfying its sufficient conditions. However, its drawback is that, by preserving a strict order among accesses, it restricts many of the performance optimizations that modern uniprocessor compilers and microprocessors employ. With the high cost of memory access, computer systems achieve higher performance by reordering or overlapping the servicing of multiple memory or communication operations from a processor. Preserving the sufficient conditions for SC clearly does not allow for much reordering or overlap in hardware, and approaches that preserve SC without preserving the sufficient conditions also have limitations. With SC at the programmer's interface, the compiler cannot reorder memory accesses even if they are to different locations, thus disallowing critical performance optimizations such as code motion, common-subexpression elimination, software pipelining, and even register allocation as illustrated in Example 9.1.

EXAMPLE 9.1 Show how register allocation can lead to a violation of SC even if the hardware satisfies SC.

Answer Consider the code fragment shown in Figure 9.2(a). After register allocation, the code produced by the compiler and seen by hardware might look like that in Figure 9.2(b). The result $(u,v) = (0,0)$ is disallowed under SC hardware in (a) but not

1. The term "programmer" here refers to the entity that is responsible for generating the parallel program. For example, if a human programmer writes a sequential program that is automatically parallelized by system software, then it is the system software that has to deal with the memory consistency model; the programmer simply assumes sequential semantics as on a uniprocessor.

P_1	P_2
`B = 0`	`A = 0`
`A = 1`	`B = 1`
`u = B`	`v = A`

(a) Before register allocation

P_1	P_2
`r1 = 0`	`r2 = 0`
`A = 1`	`B = 1`
`u = r1`	`v = r2`
`B = r1`	`A = r2`

(b) After register allocation

FIGURE 9.2 Example showing how register allocation by the compiler can violate SC. The code in (a) is the original code with which the programmer reasons. `r1`, `r2` are registers, and the code in (b) is as it might appear after register allocation performed by the compiler.

only can but will be produced by SC hardware in (b). In effect, register allocation reorders the write of `A` and the read of `B` on P_1 and reorders the write of `B` and the read of `A` on P_2. A uniprocessor compiler might easily perform these optimizations in each process: they are valid for sequential programs since the reordered accesses are to different locations. ■

Providing SC at the programmer's interface implies supporting SC at lower-level interfaces, including the hardware/software interface. If the sufficient conditions for SC are met, a processor waits for an access to complete or at least commit before issuing the next one, so most of the latency suffered by memory references is directly seen by processors as stall time. Although a processor may continue executing non-memory instructions while a single outstanding memory reference is being serviced, the expected benefit from such overlap is tiny, since even without instruction-level parallelism, on average every third instruction is a memory reference (Hennessy and Patterson 1996). We need to do something about this performance problem.

One approach we can take is to preserve sequential consistency at the programmer's interface but find ways to hide the long latency stalls from the processor. This can be done in several ways, which fall into two categories (Gharachorloo, Gupta, and Hennessy 1991). The techniques and their performance implications are discussed further in Chapter 11; here, we simply provide an intuition about them. In the first category, the system still preserves the sufficient conditions for SC and the compiler does not reorder memory operations. Latency tolerance techniques such as prefetching of data or multithreading are used to overlap data transfers with one another or with computation—thus hiding much of their latency from the processor—but the actual read and write operations are not issued before previous ones complete in program order.

In the second category, the system preserves SC but not the sufficient conditions at the programmer's interface. The compiler can reorder operations as long as it can guarantee that sequential consistency will not be violated in the results. Compiler algorithms have been developed for this (Shasha and Snir 1988; Krishnamurthy and Yelick 1994, 1995), but they are expensive and their analysis is currently quite conservative. At the hardware level, memory operations are issued and executed out of program order but are guaranteed to become visible to other processors in program order. This approach is well suited to dynamically scheduled processors that use an instruction lookahead buffer to find independent instructions to issue; for example, the R10000 processor in the SGI Origin2000. The instructions are inserted in the lookahead buffer in program order; they are chosen from the instruction lookahead buffer and executed out of order, but they are guaranteed to retire from the lookahead buffer in program order. Operations may even issue and execute out of order past an unresolved branch in the lookahead buffer based on branch prediction—called *speculative execution*—but since the branch will be resolved and retire before them, they will not become visible to the register file or external memory system before the branch is resolved. If the branch was mispredicted, the effects of those operations will never become visible. The technique called *speculative reads* goes a little further. Here, the values returned by reads are used even before they are known to be correct; later checks determine if they were incorrect, and if so, the computation is rolled back to reissue the read. Note that it is not possible to speculate with stores in this manner because once a store is made visible to other processors, it is extremely difficult to roll back and recover: a store's value should not be made visible to other processors or the external memory system environment until all previous references have correctly completed.

Some or all of these techniques are supported by many modern microprocessors, such as the MIPS R10000, the HP PA-8000, and the Intel Pentium Pro. However, while they are increasingly popular, they require substantial hardware resources and complexity, their success at hiding multiprocessor latencies is not yet clear (see Chapter 11), and not all processors support them. Perhaps most critically, these techniques work for processors, but they do not help compilers perform the reorderings of memory operations that are critical for their optimizations.

A completely different way to overcome the performance limitations imposed by SC is to change the memory consistency model itself; that is, not to guarantee such strong ordering constraints to the programmer but still retain semantics that are intuitive enough to be useful. By relaxing the ordering constraints, these *relaxed consistency models* allow the compiler to reorder accesses before presenting them to the hardware, at least to some extent. At the hardware level, they allow multiple memory accesses from the same process not only to be outstanding at a time but even to complete or become visible out of order, thus allowing much of the latency to be overlapped and hidden from the processor. The intuition behind relaxed models is that SC is usually too conservative; many of the orders it preserves are not really needed to satisfy a programmer's intuition in most situations. Detailed treatments of relaxed memory consistency models can be found in (Adve 1993; Gharachorloo 1995; Adve and Gharachorloo 1996).

Consider the simple example shown in Figure 9.3. On the left are the orderings that will be maintained by an SC implementation. On the right are the orderings that are necessary for intuitively correct program semantics. The latter are far fewer. For example, writes to variables `A` and `B` by P_1 can be reordered in this case without affecting the results observed by the program; all we must ensure is that both of them complete before the variable `flag` is set to 1. Similarly, reads to variables `A` and

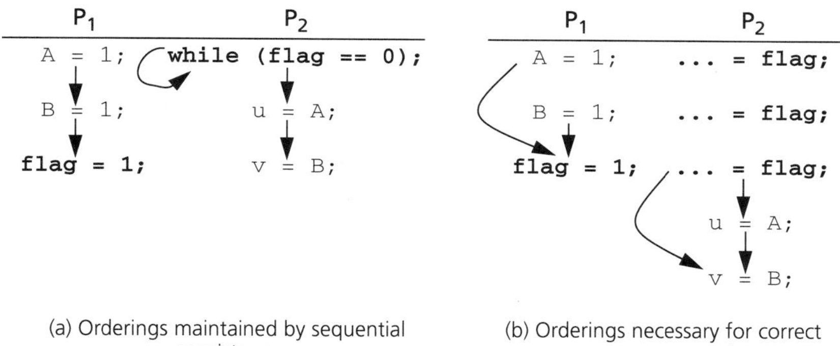

(a) Orderings maintained by sequential consistency

(b) Orderings necessary for correct program semantics

FIGURE 9.3 Intuition behind relaxed memory consistency models. The arrows in the figure indicate the orderings maintained. Part (a) shows the orderings maintained by the sequential consistency model. Part (b) shows the orderings that are necessary for "correct" or "intuitive" semantics. Bold font indicates that the accesses to the `flag` variable are the important ones for ordering and are in fact being used to orchestrate event synchronization.

`B` can be reordered at P_2 once `flag` has been observed to change to value 1.[2] Even with these reorderings, the results look just like those of an SC execution. On the other hand, although the accesses to `flag` are also simple variable accesses, a model that allowed them to be reordered with respect to `A` and `B` at either process would compromise the intuitive semantics and SC results. It would be wonderful if system software or hardware could automatically detect which program orders are critical to maintaining SC semantics and allow the others to be violated for higher performance (Shasha and Snir 1998). However, the problem is intractable (in fact, undecidable) for general programs, and inexact solutions are often too conservative to be very useful.

A complete solution for a relaxed consistency model consists of three parts:

1. *The system specification.* This is a clear specification of two things: first, what program orders among memory operations are guaranteed to be preserved, in an observable sense, by the system, including whether write atomicity will be maintained; and second, if not all program orders are guaranteed to be preserved by default, then what mechanisms the system provides for a programmer to enforce order explicitly when desired. As should be clear by now, the compiler and the hardware have their own system specifications, but we focus on the specification that the two together or the system as a whole presents to

2. Actually, it is possible to further weaken the requirements for correct execution. For example, it is not necessary for writes to `A` and `B` to complete before the write to `flag` is done; it is only necessary that they be complete by the time processor P_2 observes that the value of `flag` has changed to 1. It turns out that such relaxed models are difficult to implement in hardware. In software, some of these more relaxed models make sense, and we discuss them in Section 9.2.

the programmer. For a processor architecture, the specification it exports governs the reorderings that it allows and the order-preserving primitives it provides and is often called the *processor's memory model.*

2. *The programmer's interface.* The system specification is itself a consistency model. A programmer may use it to reason about correctness and insert the appropriate order-preserving mechanisms. However, this is a very low-level interface for a programmer: parallel programming is challenging enough without having to think about reorderings and write atomicity! The specific reorderings and order-enforcing mechanisms supported are different across system specifications, compromising portability. What a programmer therefore wants is a methodology for writing "safe" programs. This is a contract such that if the program follows certain high-level rules or provides enough program annotations—such as telling the system that `flag` in Figure 9.3 is in fact used as a synchronization variable—then any system on which the program runs will always guarantee a sequentially consistent execution, regardless of the default reorderings permitted by the system specifications it supports. The programmer's responsibility is to follow the rules and provide the annotations, which hopefully does not involve reasoning at the level of potential reorderings. The system's responsibility is to use the rules and annotations as constraints to maintain the illusion of sequential consistency. The implication for programming languages is that they should support the necessary annotations and provide an intuitive programming interface.
3. *The translation mechanism.* This translates the programmer's annotations to the interface (specifically, the order-preserving mechanisms) exported by the system specification, so that the system may do its job.

In the following discussion of relaxed consistency models, we first examine different low-level specifications exported by systems and particularly by microprocessors. Then Section 9.1.2 discusses the programmer's interface or contract and how the programmer might provide the necessary annotations.Section 9.1.3 briefly discusses translation mechanisms. Section 9.1.4 discusses current practice with regard to memory consistency models. A detailed treatment of implementation complexity and performance benefits is postponed until we discuss latency tolerance mechanisms in Chapter 11.

9.1.1 The System Specification

Several different reordering specifications have been proposed by microprocessor vendors and by researchers, each with its own mechanisms for enforcing orders. These include *total store ordering* (TSO) (Sindhu, Frailong, and Cekleov 1991; Sun Microsystems 1991), *partial store ordering* (PSO) (Sindhu, Frailong, and Cekleov 1991; Sun Microsystems 1991), and *relaxed memory ordering* (RMO) (Weaver and Germond 1994) from the Sun Sparc V8 and V9 specifications; *processor consistency* (PC) described in (Goodman 1989; Gharachorloo 1990) and used in the Intel Pentium processors; *weak ordering* (WO) (Dubois, Scheurich, and Briggs 1986; Dubois and Scheurich 1990); *release consistency* (RC) (Gharachorloo 1990); and the Digital Alpha (Sites 1992) and IBM/Motorola PowerPC (May et al. 1994) models. Of course, a particular implementation of a processor may not support all the reorderings that its system specification allows. The system specification defines the semantic interface for that architecture, that is, what reorderings the programmer must assume might happen; the implementation determines what reorderings actually happen and how much performance can actually be gained.

Let us discuss some of the specifications or consistency models, using the relaxations in program order that they allow as our primary axis for grouping models together (Gharachorloo 1995). The first set of models, which includes TSO and PC, only allows a read to bypass (complete before) an earlier incomplete write in program order (i.e., allows the write → read order to be reordered). The next set, which includes PSO, also allows writes to bypass previous writes (i.e., write → write reordering). The final set, which includes WO, RC, RMO, Alpha, and PowerPC, allows reads or writes to bypass previous reads as well (i.e., allows all reorderings among read and write accesses). A read-modify-write operation is treated as being both a read and a write, so it is reordered with respect to another operation only if both a read and a write can be reordered with respect to that operation. In all cases, we assume basic cache coherence—write propagation and write serialization—and that uniprocessor data and control dependences are maintained within each process. The specifications discussed have in most cases been motivated by and defined for the processor architectures themselves, that is, the hardware interface. All are applicable to compilers as well; however, since sophisticated compiler optimizations require the ability to reorder all types of accesses, most compilers have not supported as wide a variety of ordering models. In fact, at the programmer's interface, all but the last set of models have limited utility because they do not allow many important compiler optimizations.

Relaxing the Write-to-Read Program Order

The main motivation for this class of models is to allow the hardware to hide the latency of write operations. While the write miss is still in the write buffer and not yet visible to other processors, the processor can issue and complete reads that hit in its cache or even a single read that misses in its cache. The benefits of hiding write latency can be substantial, as we see in Chapter 11, and most processors can take advantage of this relaxation.

The models in this class (like TSO and PC) preserve the programmer's intuition quite well, for the most part, even without any special operations. For example, the common idiom of spinning on a flag for event synchronization works without modification (Figure 9.4[a]). This is because TSO and PC models preserve the ordering of writes so that the write of the flag is not visible until all previous writes in program order have completed in the system. For this reason, most early multiprocessors supported one of these two models, including the Sequent Balance, Encore Multimax, Vax-8800, SparcCenter 1000/2000, SGI 4D/240, SGI Challenge, and even

P_1	P_2
`A = 1;`	`while (Flag==0);`
`Flag = 1;`	`print A;`

(a)

P_1	P_2
`A = 1;`	`print B;`
`B = 1;`	`print A;`

(b)

P_1	P_2	P_3
`A = 1;`	`while (A==0);`	`while (B==0);`
	`B = 1;`	`print A;`

(c)

P_1	P_2
`A = 1;` (i)	`B = 1;` (iii)
`print B;` (ii)	`print A;` (iv)

(d)

FIGURE 9.4 Example code sequences repeated to compare TSO, PC, and SC. Both TSO and PC provide the same results as SC for code segments (a) and (b), PC can violate SC semantics for segment (c) (TSO still provides SC semantics), and both TSO and PC violate SC semantics for segment (d).

the Pentium Pro quad, and it has been relatively easy to port even complex programs, such as the operating systems, to these machines.

Of course, the semantics of these models is not SC, so there are situations in which the differences show through. Figure 9.4 shows four code examples, three of which we have seen earlier, in which we assume that all variables start out having the value 0. Code fragment (a) is the example of spinning on a flag. In fragment (b), SC guarantees that if `B` is printed as 1 then `A` too will be printed as 1, since the writes of `A` and `B` by P_1 cannot be reordered. For the same reason, TSO and PC also have the same semantics in this fragment as well. For fragment (c), only TSO offers SC semantics and prevents `A` from being printed as 0, not PC. The reason is that PC does not guarantee write atomicity. Finally, for fragment (d), no interleaving of the operations under SC can result in 0 being printed for both `A` and `B`. To see why, consider that program order implies the precedence relationships (i) → (ii) and (iii) → (iv) in the interleaved total order. If `B = 0` is observed, it implies (ii) → (iii), which therefore implies (i) → (iv). But (i) → (iv) implies `A` will be printed as 1. Similarly, a result of `A = 0` implies `B = 1`. A popular software-only mutual exclusion algorithm called Dekker's algorithm—used in the absence of hardware support for atomic read-modify-write operations (Tanenbaum and Woodhull 1997)—relies on the property that both `A` and `B` will not be read as 0 in this case. SC provides this property, further contributing to its view as an intuitive consistency model. Neither TSO nor PC guarantees it since they both allow the read operation corresponding to the print to complete before previous writes are visible.

To ensure SC semantics when desired (e.g., to port a program written under SC assumptions to a TSO or PC system), we need mechanisms to enforce two types of extra orderings: (1) to ensure that a read does not complete before an earlier write in program order (applies to both TSO and PC) and (2) to ensure write atomicity for a read operation (applies only to PC). For the former, different processor architectures provide somewhat different solutions. For example, the Sun Sparc V9 specification (Weaver and Germond 1994) provides *memory barrier* (MEMBAR) or *fence* instructions of different flavors that can ensure any desired ordering. Here, we would insert a write-to-read ordering flavored MEMBAR before the read. This MEMBAR prevents any read that follows it in program order from issuing before all writes that precede it have completed. On architectures that do not provide memory barrier instructions, it is possible to achieve this effect by substituting an atomic read-modify-write operation or sequence for the original read. A read-modify-write is treated as being both a read and a write, so it cannot be reordered with respect to previous writes in these models. Of course, the value written in the read-modify-write must be the same as the value read to preserve correctness. Replacing a read with a read-modify-write also guarantees write atomicity at that read on machines supporting the PC model. The details of why this works are subtle, and the interested reader can find them in the literature (Adve et al. 1993).

Relaxing the Write-to-Read and Write-to-Write Program Orders

Allowing writes as well to bypass earlier writes (to different locations) allows the write buffer to merge and even retire writes before previous writes in program order complete. Thus, it enables multiple write misses to be fully overlapped and to become visible out of program order. The motivation is to further reduce the impact of write latency on processor stall time and to improve communication efficiency between processors by making new data values visible to other processors sooner. Sun Sparc's PSO model (Sindhu, Frailong, and Cekleov 1991; Sun Microsystems 1991) is the only model in this category. Like TSO, it guarantees write atomicity.

Unfortunately, reordering of writes can violate our intuitive SC semantics quite a bit. Even the use of ordinary variables as flags for event synchronization (Figure 9.4[a]) is no longer guaranteed to work since the write of `flag` may become visible to other processors before the write of `A`. This model must therefore demonstrate a substantial performance benefit to be attractive.

The only additional instruction we need over TSO is one that enforces write-to-write ordering in a process's program order. In Sun Sparc V9, this can be achieved by using a MEMBAR instruction with the write-to-write flavor turned on (the earlier Sparc V8 specification provided a special instruction called store barrier or STBAR to achieve this effect). For example, to achieve the intuitive semantics, we would insert such an instruction between the writes of `A` and `flag`.

Relaxing All Program Orders: Weak Ordering and Release Consistency

In this final class of specifications, no program orders are guaranteed by default (other than data and control dependences within a process, of course). The benefit is that multiple read requests can also be outstanding at the same time, can be bypassed by later writes in program order, and can themselves complete out of order, thus allowing us to hide read latency. These models are particularly well matched to dynamically scheduled processors whose implementation indeed allows them to proceed past read misses to other memory references. They are also the only models that allow many of the key reorderings and elimination of accesses as done by compiler optimizations. Given the importance of these compiler optimizations for node performance, as well as their transparency to the programmer, these may in fact be the only reasonable high-performance memory models for multiprocessors (unless compiler analysis of potential violations of consistency makes dramatic advances). Prominent models in this group are weak ordering (WO) (Dubois, Scheurich, and Briggs 1986; Dubois and Scheurich 1990), release consistency (RC) (Gharachorloo 1990), Digital Alpha (Sites 1992), Sparc V9 relaxed memory ordering (RMO) (Weaver and Germond 1994), and IBM PowerPC (May et al. 1994; Corella, Stone, and Barton 1993). WO is the seminal model, RC is an extension of WO supported by the Stanford DASH prototype (Lenoski et al. 1993), and the last three are supported in commercial architectures. Let us discuss these models individually and see how they deal with the problem of providing intuitive semantics despite all the reordering; for instance, how they deal with the flag synchronization example.

Weak Ordering The motivation behind the weak ordering model (also known as the *weak consistency model*) is quite simple. Most parallel programs use synchronization operations to coordinate accesses to data when this is necessary. Between synchronization operations, they do not rely on the order of accesses being preserved. Two examples are shown in Figure 9.5. The left fragment (a) uses a lock-unlock pair to delineate a critical section inside which the head of a linked list is updated (Adve and Gharachorloo 1996). The right fragment (b) uses flags to control access to variables participating in a producer-consumer interaction (e.g., `A` and `D` are produced by P_1 and consumed by P_2). The key in the flag example is to think of the accesses to the flag variables as synchronization operations since that is indeed the purpose they are serving. If we do this, then in both situations the intuitive semantics are not violated by any program reorderings that happen between synchronization operations or accesses (i.e., in the critical section in segment [a] and in the four statements after the while loop in segment [b]) as long as synchronization operations are not reordered with respect to data accesses or one another. Based on these observations, weak ordering relaxes all program orders for nonsynchronization memory operations by default and guarantees that orderings will be maintained only at synchronization operations that can be identified by the system as such. Further orderings can be enforced by adding synchronization operations or labeling some memory operations as synchronization. How appropriate operations are identified as synchronization operations is discussed in Section 9.1.2.

The left side of Figure 9.6 illustrates the reorderings of memory operations allowed by weak ordering. Each block with a set of reads/writes represents a contiguous run of nonsynchronization memory operations from a processor. Synchronization operations are shown separately. Sufficient conditions to ensure a WO system are as follows. Before a synchronization operation is issued, the processor waits for all previous operations in program order (both reads and writes) to have completed. Similarly, memory accesses that follow the synchronization operation are not issued until the synchronization operation completes. Read, write, and read-modify-write operations that are not labeled as synchronization can be arbitrarily reordered

$P_1, P_2, \ldots, P_n$

```
. . .
Lock(TaskQ)
newTask→next = Head;
if (Head != NULL)
   Head→prev = newTask;
Head = newTask;
UnLock(TaskQ)
. . .
```

(a)

P_1	P_2
`TOP: while(flag2==0);`	`TOP: while(flag1==0);`
`A = 1;`	`x = A;`
`u = B;`	`y = D;`
`v = C;`	`B = 3;`
`D = B * C;`	`C = D / B;`
`flag2 = 0;`	`flag1 = 0;`
`flag1 = 1;`	`flag2 = 1;`
`goto TOP;`	`goto TOP;`

(b)

FIGURE 9.5 Use of synchronization operations to coordinate access to ordinary shared data variables. The synchronization may be through the use of explicit lock, unlock, and barrier operations or through the use of flag variables for point-to-point events.

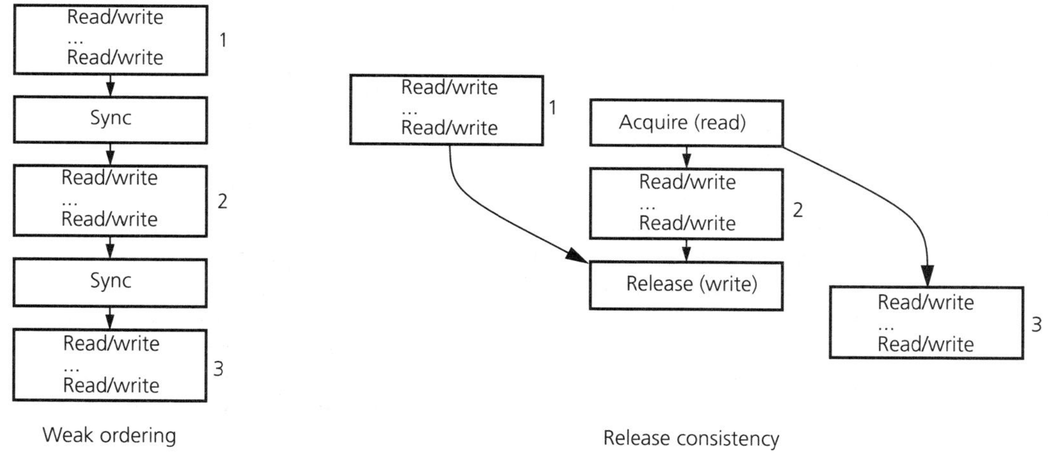

FIGURE 9.6 Comparison of the weak ordering and release consistency models. The operations in block 1 precede the first synchronization operation, which is an acquire, in program order. Block 2 occurs between the two synchronization operations, and block 3 follows the second synchronization operation, which is a release.

between synchronization operations. Especially when synchronization operations are infrequent, as in many parallel programs, WO typically provides considerable reordering freedom to the hardware and compiler.

Release Consistency Release consistency observes that weak ordering does not go far enough. It extends the weak ordering model by distinguishing among types of synchronization operations and exploiting their semantics. In particular, it divides synchronization operations into acquires and releases. An *acquire* is a read operation (it can also be a read-modify-write) that is performed to gain access to a set of operations or variables. Examples include the `Lock(TaskQ)` operation in part (a) of Figure 9.5, and the accesses to `flag` variables within the while conditions in part (b). A *release* is a write operation (or a read-modify-write) that grants permission to another processor to gain access to some operations or variables. Examples include the `UnLock(TaskQ)` operation in part (a) of Figure 9.5, and the statements setting the `flag` variables to 1 in part (b).

The separation into acquire and release operations can be used to further relax ordering constraints, as shown in Figure 9.6. The purpose of an acquire is to delay memory accesses that follow the acquire operation until the acquire completes. It has nothing to do with accesses that precede it in program order (accesses in block 1), so there is no reason to wait for those accesses to complete before the acquire can be issued or completed. That is, the acquire itself can be reordered with respect to previous accesses. Similarly, the purpose of a release operation is to grant access to the new values of data that are modified before it in program order. It has nothing to do with accesses that follow it in program order (accesses in block 3), so these need not be delayed until the release has completed. However, we must wait for accesses in block 1 to complete as well before the release is visible to other processors (since they precede the release too, and we do not know exactly which variables are associated with the release or are "protected" by the release[3]), and similarly we must wait for the acquire to complete before the operations in block 3 can be performed. Besides these constraints, the memory operations in blocks 1, 2, and 3 can be overlapped and reordered. Thus, the sufficient conditions for providing an RC interface are as follows: before an operation labeled as a release is issued, the processor waits until all previous operations in program order have completed; operations that follow an acquire operation in program order are not issued until that acquire operation completes. These are sufficient conditions, and we examine more aggressive implementations when we discuss alternative approaches to a shared address space that rely on relaxed consistency models for good performance. Note that the write propagation clause of coherence, as defined in Chapter 5, is not guaranteed unless enough synchronization is present, nor is write serialization, a point we return to in Section 9.3.3.

Digital Alpha, Sparc V9 RMO, and IBM PowerPC memory models While the WO and RC models are specified in terms of using labeled synchronization operations to enforce orders, they do not take a position on the exact operations (instructions) that must be used. The memory models of some commercial microprocessors provide no ordering guarantees by default (for memory or synchronization operations) but provide specific hardware instructions called *memory barriers* or *fences* that can

---

3. It is possible that the release is intended to also grant access to the results of operations outside of (before) the operations controlled by the preceding acquire. The exact association of variables with synchronization accesses is very difficult to exploit at the hardware level. Software implementations of relaxed models, however, do exploit such optimizations, as we shall see in Section 9.3.

be used to enforce orderings. To implement WO or RC with these microprocessors, operations that the WO or RC program labels as synchronizations (or acquires or releases) cause the compiler to insert the appropriate special instructions, or the programmer can insert these instructions directly.

The Alpha architecture (Sites 1992), for example, supports two kinds of fence instructions: the memory barrier (MB) and the write memory barrier (WMB). The MB fence is like a synchronization operation in WO: it waits for all previously issued memory accesses to complete before issuing any new accesses. It does not have flavors like the Sparc MEMBAR instructions. The WMB fence imposes program order only between writes (it is like the STBAR in PSO). Thus, a read issued after a WMB can still bypass (complete before) a write access issued before the WMB, but a write access issued after the WMB cannot. The Sparc V9 relaxed memory order (RMO) (Weaver and Germond 1994) provides a fence or MEMBAR instruction with four flavor bits associated with it, as discussed earlier. Each bit indicates a particular type of ordering to be enforced between previous and following load-store operations (the four possibilities are read-to-read, read-to-write, write-to-read, and write-to-write orderings). Any combinations of these bits can be set, offering a variety of ordering choices. Finally, the IBM PowerPC model (May et al. 1994; Corella, Stone, and Barton 1993) provides only a single fence instruction, called SYNC, that is equivalent to Alpha's MB fence. It differs from the Alpha and RMO models in that the writes are not atomic, as in the processor consistency (PC) model. The model envisioned by PowerPC is WO, to be synthesized by putting SYNC instructions before and after every synchronization operation. We see how different models can be synthesized with these primitives in Exercise 9.13.

The prominent specifications just discussed are summarized in Table 9.1 (Adve and Gharachorloo 1996).[4] They have different performance implications and require different kinds of annotations to ensure orderings. It is worth noting again that if program order is defined as seen by the programmer, then only the models that allow both read and write operations to be reordered within sections of code (WO, RC, Alpha, RMO, and PowerPC) allow the flexibility needed by many important compiler optimizations. This may change if substantial improvements are made in compiler analysis to determine what reorderings are possible given a consistency model. The difficulty of reasoning with allowable reorderings and inserting order-enforcing instructions should be clear, as should the portability problem of the specifications. For example, a program with enough memory barriers to work "correctly" (produce intuitive or sequentially consistent executions) on a TSO system will not necessarily work "correctly" when run on an RMO system: it will need more special

4. The relaxation "read own write early" in the table is relevant to both program order and write atomicity. The processor is allowed to read its own previous write before the write is serialized with respect to other writes to the same location (i.e., before the write completes). A common hardware optimization that relies on this relaxation is the processor reading the value of a variable from its own write buffer. This relaxation can be used with almost all models without violating their semantics. It can even be used with SC as long as other program order and atomicity requirements are maintained.

Table 9.1 Characteristics of Various System Specifications

Model	Write-to-Read Reorder	Write-to-Write Reorder	Read-to-Read / Write Reorder	Read Other's Write Early	Read Own Write Early	Operations for Ordering
SC					yes	
TSO	yes				yes	MEMBAR, RMW
PC	yes			yes	yes	MEMBAR, RMW
PSO	yes	yes			yes	STBAR, RMW
WO	yes	yes	yes		yes	SYNC
RC	yes	yes	yes	yes	yes	REL, ACQ, RMW
RMO	yes	yes	yes		yes	various MEMBARs
Alpha	yes	yes	yes		yes	MB, WMB
PowerPC	yes	yes	yes	yes	yes	SYNC

A "yes" in the appropriate column indicates that those orders can be violated by that system-centric model. "Read other's write early" means that a processor is allowed to see the result of a write operation before that write operation has completed globally.

operations. Let us therefore examine higher-level interfaces that are more convenient for programmers and portable to the different systems, safely exploiting the performance benefits and reorderings that each system affords.

9.1.2 The Programmer's Interface

The programming interfaces are inspired by the WO and RC models, in that they assume that program orders do not have to be maintained at all between synchronization operations. The idea is for the program to ensure that all synchronization operations, including point-to-point event synchronization using flags, are explicitly labeled or identified as such. This is the programmer's part of the contract. The compiler or run-time library translates these synchronization operations into the appropriate order-preserving operations (memory barriers or fences) called for by the system specification. Then the system (compiler plus hardware) guarantees sequentially consistent executions even though it may reorder operations between synchronization operations in any way it desires (without violating dependences to a location within a process). This is the system's part of the contract. This contract allows the compiler sufficient flexibility between synchronization points for the reorderings it desires. It also allows the processor to perform as many reorderings as permitted by its memory model or implementation and is therefore portable: if SC executions are guaranteed even with the weaker models that allow all reorderings, they surely will be guaranteed on systems that allow fewer reorderings. The consistency model presented at the programmer's interface should be at least as weak (relaxed) as that at the hardware interface but need not be the same.

Programs that label all synchronization events are called *synchronized programs.* Formal models for specifying synchronized programs have been developed, namely, the *data-race-free* models influenced by weak ordering (Adve and Hill 1990a) and the *properly labeled* model (Gharachorloo et al. 1992) influenced by release consistency (Gharachorloo et al. 1990). Interested readers can obtain more details from these references (the differences between the models are minor). The basic question the programmer must address is which operations to label as synchronization operations. This is, of course, already done in the majority of cases when explicit, system-specified programming primitives such as locks and barriers are used. These are usually also easy to distinguish as acquire or release, for memory models such as RC that can take advantage of this distinction; for example, a lock is an acquire and an unlock is a release, and a barrier contains both since arrival at a barrier is a release (indicating completion of previous accesses) whereas leaving it is an acquire (obtaining permission for the new set of accesses). The real question is how to determine which memory operations on ordinary variables (such as our flag variables) should be labeled as synchronization operations. Often, programmers can identify these easily since they know when they are using this event synchronization idiom. The following definitions describe a more general method for identifying synchronization events when all else fails.

- *Conflicting operations:* Two memory operations from different processes are said to *conflict* if they access the same memory location and at least one of them is a write.
- *Competing operations:* These are a subset of the conflicting operations. Two conflicting memory operations (from different processes) are said to be *competing* if it is possible for them to appear next to each other in a sequentially consistent total order (execution), that is, to appear one immediately following the other in such an order with no intervening memory operations on shared data between them.
- *Synchronized program:* A parallel program is *synchronized* if all competing memory operations have been labeled as synchronization operations (perhaps differentiated into acquire and release by labeling the read operations as acquires and the write operations as releases).

The fact that "competing" means competing under any possible SC interleaving is an important aspect of the programming interface. Even though a system uses a relaxed consistency model, the reasoning about where annotations are needed can itself be done while assuming an intuitive, SC execution model, shielding the programmer from reasoning directly in terms of reorderings. Of course, the programmer's task would be a lot simpler if the compiler could automatically determine what operations are conflicting or competing. However, this problem is similar to that of determining what reorderings are possible under a consistency model, and since the known analysis techniques are expensive and/or conservative (Shasha and Snir 1988; Krishnamurthy and Yelik 1994, 1995), the job is almost always left to the programmer.

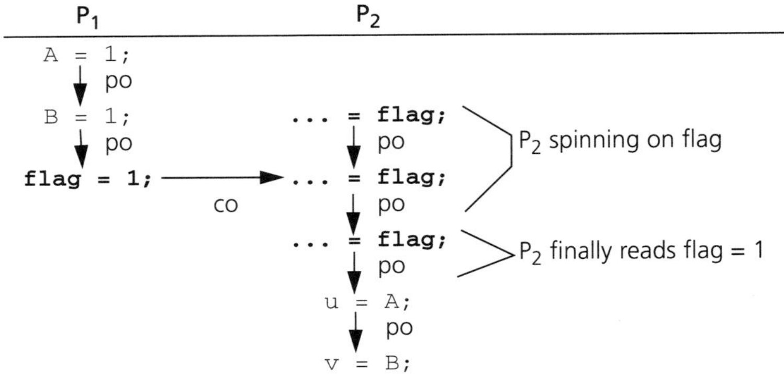

FIGURE 9.7 An example code sequence illustrating program and conflict orders. The arcs labeled "po" show program order, and the one labeled "co" shows conflict order. Notice that between the write to `A` by P_1 and the read to `A` by P_2 is a chain of accesses formed by program order and conflict order arcs. This will be true in all SC executions of the program. Such chains that have at least one program order arc imply that the accesses are noncompeting; they will not be present for accesses to the variable `flag` between which there is only a conflict order arc. Boldface indicates that the accesses to the `flag` variable are the important ones for ordering and are in fact being used to orchestrate event synchronization.

Consider the example in Figure 9.7, repeated from Figure 9.3. The accesses to the variable `flag` are competing operations by the preceding definition. What this really means is that on a multiprocessor they may execute simultaneously on their respective processors, unordered with respect to each other, so we have no guarantee about which executes or appears to complete first. Thus, they are also said to constitute *data races*. In contrast, the accesses to variable `A` (and to `B`) by P_1 and P_2 are conflicting operations, but they are necessarily separated in any SC interleaving and hence ordered by an intervening write to the variable `flag` by P_1 and a corresponding read of `flag` by P_2. Thus, they are not competing accesses and do not have to be labeled as synchronization operations.

To be a little more formal, given a particular SC execution order, the *conflict order* is the order in which the conflicting operations to a location occur (from any process). In addition, we have the *program order* for each process. Figure 9.7 shows arcs corresponding to the program orders and conflict order for a sample execution of our code fragment. Two accesses are noncompeting if under all possible SC executions (interleavings) a chain of other references always exists between them, such that at least one link in the chain is formed by a program order rather than conflict order arc. Otherwise, they are competing. The complete formalism can be found in (Gharachorloo 1995).

Of course, the definition of synchronized programs allows a programmer to conservatively label more operations than necessary as synchronization operations without compromising correctness. In the extreme, labeling all memory operations as synchronization operations always yields a synchronized program. This extreme case will, of course, deny us the performance benefits that the system might otherwise provide by reordering nonsynchronization operations and will, on most systems, yield much worse performance than straightforward SC implementations due to the overhead of the order-preserving instructions that will be inserted. The goal is to label only competing operations as synchronization operations.

In specific circumstances, we may want to allow data races in the program and may, therefore, decide not to label some competing accesses as synchronization operations. Now we are no longer guaranteed SC semantics, but we may know through application knowledge that the competing operations are not being used as synchronization operations and that we do not need such strong ordering guarantees in certain sections of code. An example in Chapter 2 is the use of the asynchronous equation solver rather than red-black ordering. There is no synchronization between barriers or grid sweeps, so within a sweep the read and write accesses to the border elements of a partition are competing accesses. If they are not labeled, the program will not satisfy SC semantics on a system that allows access reorderings, but this is okay since the solver repeats the sweeps until convergence: even if the processes sometimes read old values in a sweep and sometimes new in an unpredictable manner, they will read updated values in the next sweep (after the barrier) and make progress toward convergence. If we had labeled the competing accesses, we would have compromised access reordering and performance. The number of sweeps to convergence might have been a little smaller, but the cost of each sweep would have been larger.

The last issue related to the programming interface is how the labels for competing accesses are to be specified by the programmer. In many cases, this is quite stylized and already present in the programming language. Some parallel programming languages, for example, High Performance Fortran (High Performance Fortran Forum 1993), allow parallelism to be expressed in only stylized ways from which it is trivial to extract the relevant information. For example, in `FORALL` loops (loops in which all iterations are independent) only the implicit barrier at the end of the loop needs to be labeled as synchronization: the `FORALL` specifies that there are no data races within the loop body that the system should worry about. In more general programming models, if programmers use a library of synchronization primitives such as `LOCK`, `UNLOCK`, and `BARRIER`, then, even if these primitives are implemented using ordinary memory operations, the code that implements them can be labeled by the designer of the library; the programmer needn't do anything special. Finally, if the application programmer wants to add further labels at memory operations—for example, at flag variable accesses or to preserve some other orders, as in the examples of Figure 9.4—we need support from a programming language or library. A programming language could provide an attribute for variable declarations that indicates that all references to a variable are synchronization accesses; or there could be annotations at the statement level, indicating that a particular access is to be labeled as a synchronization operation. This tells the compiler to constrain its reordering across those points, and the compiler in turn translates these references to the appropriate order-preserving mechanisms for the processor.

9.1.3 The Translation Mechanism

For most microprocessors, translating labels to order-preserving mechanisms amounts to inserting a suitable memory barrier or fence instruction before and/or after each operation that is labeled as a synchronization (or acquire or release). It would save instructions if we could have flavor bits associated with individual loads and stores themselves, indicating what orderings to enforce and thus avoiding extra instructions; but since the operations are usually infrequent, making such core changes to the instruction set is not the direction that most microprocessors have taken so far.

9.1.4 Consistency Models in Real Multiprocessor Systems

With the large growth in sales of multiprocessors, modern microprocessors are designed so that they can be seamlessly integrated into these machines. As a result, microprocessor vendors expend substantial effort defining and precisely specifying the memory model presented at the hardware/software interface. While sequential consistency remains the best model for programmers to reason with, many vendors allow orders to be relaxed for performance reasons. Some vendors like Silicon Graphics (in the MIPS R10000 processor) continue to support SC even in multiple-issue, dynamically scheduled processors by allowing out-of-order issue and execution of operations but not out-of-order completion or visibility. This allows substantial overlapping of memory operations by the dynamically scheduled processor and does not satisfy the sufficient conditions for SC, but it forces operations to complete in program order. The Intel Pentium family supports a processor consistency model, so reads can complete before previous writes in program order, and many microprocessors from Sun Microsystems support TSO, which allows the same reorderings. Many other vendors have moved to models that allow all orders to be relaxed (e.g., Digital Alpha and IBM PowerPC) and that provide memory barriers to enforce orderings where necessary.

At the hardware interface, multiprocessors usually follow the consistency model exported by the microprocessors they use since this is the easiest thing to do. For example, we saw that the NUMA-Q hardware exports the processor consistency model of its Pentium Pro processors. In particular, on a write, the ownership and perhaps data is obtained before the invalidations begin; the processor is allowed to complete its write and go on as soon as the ownership is received, and the SCLIC communication assist takes care of the sequence of invalidations and acknowledgments. It is also possible for the communication assist to alter the model, within limits. We have seen an example in the Origin2000, where preserving the processor's SC model requires that the assist (Hub) only reply to the processor on a write once the exclusive reply and all invalidation acknowledgments have been received (called *delayed-exclusive* replies). The dynamically scheduled processor can then retire its write from the instruction lookahead buffer and allow subsequent operations to retire and complete as well. If the Hub replies as soon as the exclusive reply is received and before invalidation acknowledgments are received (called *eager-*

exclusive replies), then the write will retire and subsequent operations (including writes) may become visible and complete before the write is actually completed, so the consistency model is more relaxed. Essentially, the Hub fools the processor about the completion of the write.

Having the assist fool the processor can enhance performance but increase design complexity, as in the case of eager-exclusive replies. The handling of invalidation acknowledgments must now be done asynchronously by the assist through tracking buffers in its processor interface even after the reply has been passed to the processor, in accordance with the desired relaxed consistency model. There are also questions about whether subsequent accesses to a block from other nodes, forwarded to this processor from the home, should be serviced while invalidations for a write on that block are still outstanding (see Exercise 9.3) and about what happens if the processor has to write that block back to memory due to replacement while invalidations are still outstanding in the assist. In the latter case, either the write back has to be buffered by the assist and delayed until all invalidations have been acknowledged, or the protocol must be extended so a later access to the written-back block is not satisfied by the home until the acknowledgments are received by the requestor. The extra complexity and the limited performance improvement perceived by the Origin2000 designers led them to persist with a sequential consistency model and delayed-exclusive replies.

On the compiler side, the picture for memory consistency models is currently not so well defined, complicating matters for programmers. It does not do a programmer much good for the processor to support sequential consistency or processor consistency if the compiler reorders accesses as it pleases before they even get to the processor (as uniprocessor compilers do). Microprocessor memory models are defined at the hardware interface; they tend to be concerned with program order as presented to the processor and assume that a separate arrangement will be made with the compiler. As we have discussed, exporting intermediate models such as TSO, PC, and PSO up to the programmer's interface does not allow the compiler enough flexibility for reordering. Programmers might assume that in practice the compiler will not reorder or eliminate operations in a manner that would violate the consistency model, for example, since most compiler reorderings of memory operations tend to focus on loops; but this is a very dangerous assumption, and sometimes the orders we rely upon indeed occur in loops. To really use these models at the programmer's interface, uniprocessor compilers would have to be modified to follow their restriction on reordering, compromising performance significantly. These intermediate models are supported at the hardware interface but are not very appropriate for the programmer's interface. (Of course, the point would be moot if the compiler could detect competing operations, in which case it could export the strongest SC model to the programmer and yet itself perform the reorderings of the most relaxed models we discuss.)

More relaxed models like Alpha, RMO, PowerPC, WO, RC, and synchronized programs can be used even at the programmer's interface because they allow the compiler the flexibility it needs. The mechanisms used to communicate ordering constraints at the programmer's interface must be heeded not only by the processor but also by the compiler, and compilers for multiprocessors are beginning to do so (see Section 9.5). Beneath a relaxed model at the programmer's interface, the hardware interface can use the same or stronger ordering model, as we saw in the context of synchronized programs. However, significant motivation exists to use relaxed models even at the processor interface in this case to realize the performance potential. As we move now to discussing alternative approaches to supporting a shared address space with coherent replication of data, we see that relaxed consistency models can be critical to performance when we want to support coherence at larger granularities than cache blocks. We also see that the consistency model can be relaxed even beyond release consistency. (Can you think how?)

9.2 OVERCOMING CAPACITY LIMITATIONS

In a CC-NUMA system like the SGI Origin2000, a processor cache replicates remotely allocated data directly upon reference, without it being replicated in the local main memory first. On a cache miss, the assist determines from the physical address whether to look up local memory and directory state or to send the request directly to a remote home node. The granularity of communication, of coherence, and of allocation in the replication store (cache) is a cache block. As discussed earlier, a problem with these systems is that the capacity for local replication is limited to the hardware cache. If a remotely installed block is replaced from the cache, it must be fetched from remote memory if it is needed again, incurring artifactual communication. The goal of the systems discussed in this section is to overcome the replication capacity problem while still providing coherence in hardware at the granularity of cache blocks.

9.2.1 Tertiary Caches

One way to achieve this goal is to use a large but slower remote access cache, as in the Sequent NUMA-Q and Convex Exemplar (Convex Computer Corporation 1993; Thekkath et al. 1997). This may be needed for functionality anyway if the nodes of the machine are themselves small-scale multiprocessors, in order to present a single per-node cache to the protocol across nodes. This remote access cache keeps track of remotely allocated blocks that are currently in the local processor caches and can simply be made larger for performance. Then it will also hold replicated remote blocks that have been replaced from local processor caches. In NUMA-Q, this DRAM remote cache is at least 32 MB whereas the sum of the four lowest-level processor caches in a node is only 2–4 MB. A similar method, which is sometimes called the *tertiary cache* approach, is to take a fixed portion of the local main memory and manage it like a remote cache, requiring additional hardware for per-block tags and state.

These approaches replicate data in main memory at fine grain, but they do not automatically *migrate* or change the home of a block to the node that incurs cache misses most often on that block. Space is always allocated for the block in main memory at the original home. Thus, if data were not distributed appropriately in main memory by the application, then in the tertiary cache approach, even if only one processor ever accesses a given memory block (no need for multiple copies or replication), the system may end up wasting half of its available main memory: there are two copies of each block in main memory, one at the home and one in the tertiary cache, but only one is ever used. In addition, a statically established tertiary cache is wasteful if its replication capacity is not needed for performance. The cache-only memory architecture or COMA approach to increasing replication capacity is to treat all of local memory as a hardware-controlled cache. This approach, which achieves both replication and migration, does not have these problems and is discussed in more depth next. In all these cases, replication and coherence are managed at a fine granularity, though this does not necessarily have to be the same as the block size in the processor caches. Only data that is already in the local memory, remote cache, or tertiary cache is brought into the processor cache hierarchy; since the data is kept coherent across nodes at the outer level, processor caches themselves do not have to be kept coherent across nodes through a separate internode protocol but must only be kept coherent with the local memory or remote/tertiary cache.

9.2.2 Cache-Only Memory Architectures (COMA)

In COMA machines, every fine-grained memory block in the entire main memory has a hardware tag associated with it. There is no fixed node where space is always guaranteed to be allocated for a memory block. Rather, data dynamically moves to and is replicated in the main memories of the nodes that access and hence "attract" it; these main memories, organized as caches, are therefore called *attraction memories*. When a remote block is accessed, it is replicated in attraction memory as well as being brought into the processor cache and is kept coherent by hardware. Migration of a block is achieved through replacement or invalidation in the attraction memory: if block *x* originally resides in node *A*'s main (attraction) memory, then when node *B* reads it, *B* will obtain a copy (replication); if the copy in *A*'s memory is later invalidated or replaced by another block that *A* references, then the only copy of that block left is now in *B*'s attraction memory. Thus, we do not have the problem of wasted original copies that we potentially had with the tertiary cache approach, and both data migration and space management are demand driven. Since a data block may reside in any attraction memory and move transparently from one to the other, the location of data is decoupled from its physical address. Automatic data migration also has substantial advantages for multiprogrammed workloads in which the operating system may decide to migrate processes among nodes at any time, although in this case software migration of pages may be successful too.

Hardware/Software Trade-Offs

Like the other approaches, the COMA approach introduces clear hardware/software trade-offs. By overcoming the cache capacity limitations of the pure CC-NUMA approach, the goal is to free parallel software from worrying about data distribution in main memory. The programmer can view the machine as if it had a centralized main memory and worry only about inherent communication and false sharing (of course, cold misses may still be satisfied remotely if data is not distributed well). Although this makes the task of software writers much easier, COMA machines require a lot more hardware support than pure CC-NUMA machines since they implement main memory as a hardware cache. This includes per-block tags and state in main memory as well as the necessary comparators. There is also the extra memory overhead needed for replication in the attraction memories, which we discuss later in this section. Finally, the coherence protocol for attraction memories is more complicated than what we saw for processor caches. There are two reasons for this, both having to do with the fact that data moves dynamically to where it is referenced and does not have a fixed "home" to back it up. First, the location of the data must be determined upon an attraction memory miss, since it is no longer bound to the physical address. Second, with no space necessarily reserved for the block at the home, it is important to ensure that the last or only copy of a block is not lost from the system by being replaced from its attraction memory. This extra complexity is not a problem in the tertiary cache approach.

Performance Trade-Offs

Performance has its own interesting set of trade-offs. Although the number of remote accesses due to artifactual communication is reduced, COMA machines tend to increase the latency of accesses that do need to be satisfied remotely, including cold, true sharing, and false sharing misses. The reason is that even a cache miss that will not be satisfied in the local attraction memory needs to first look up that memory to see if it has a local copy of the block. Also, the attraction memory access itself is a little more expensive than a standard DRAM access because the attraction memory is usually implemented to be set associative, so a tag selection may be in the critical path.

In terms of performance, then, COMA is most likely to be beneficial for applications that have high capacity miss rates in the processor cache (large working sets) to data that is not allocated locally to begin with and most harmful to applications where performance is dominated by coherence misses. The advantages are also greatest when access patterns are unpredictable or when accesses from different processes are spatially interleaved at fine grain, so data placement, replication, or migration at page granularity in software would be difficult on CC-NUMA machines. For example, COMA machines are likely to be more advantageous when a two-dimensional array representation is used for a near-neighbor grid computation than when a four-dimensional array representation is used because, in the latter case, appropriate data distribution at page granularity through the OS is not difficult in software; in fact, the higher cost of communication may make COMA machines perform worse than pure CC-NUMA when four-dimensional arrays are used with proper data distribution. Figure 9.8 summarizes the trade-offs in terms of application characteristics. Let us briefly look at some design options for COMA protocols

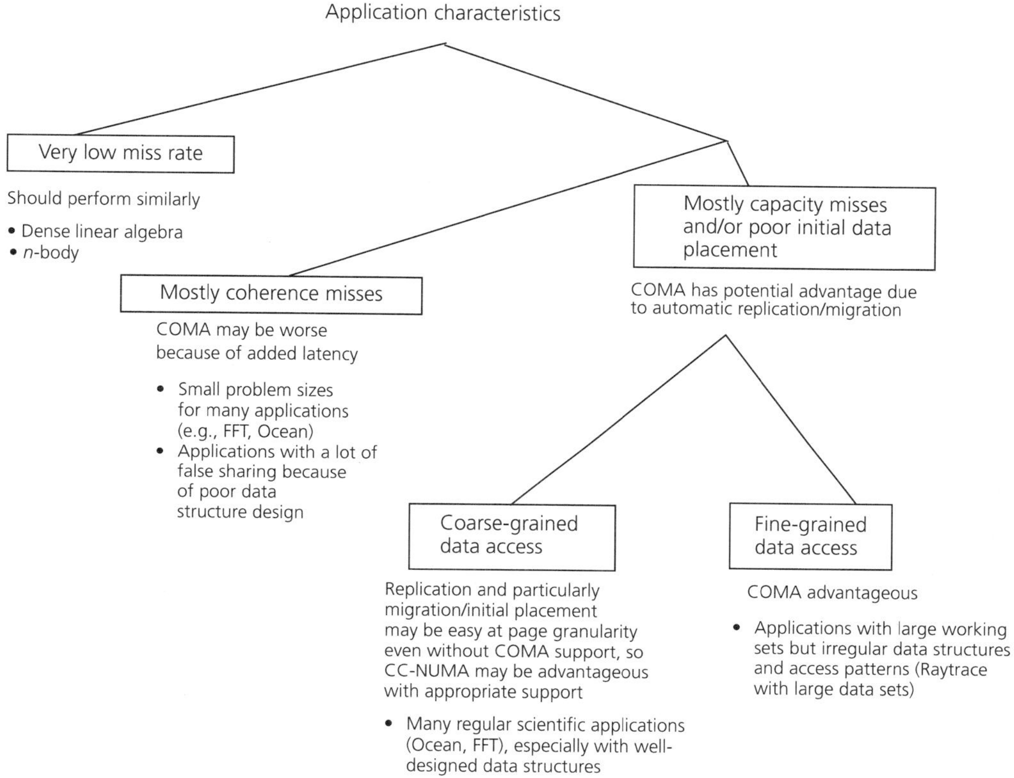

FIGURE 9.8 Performance trade-offs between COMA and CC-NUMA architectures. The application characteristics are in boxes. Below each box is the expected performance comparison of COMA and CC-NUMA systems built with similar technology for that set of characteristics followed by a list of example application areas.

and how they might solve the protocol problems of finding the data on a miss and not losing the last copy of a block.

Design Options: Flat versus Hierarchical Approaches

COMA machines can be built with hierarchical or with flat directory schemes or even with hierarchical snooping (see Section 8.10.2). Hierarchical directory-based COMA was used in the Data Diffusion Machine prototype (Hagersten, Landin, and Haridi 1992; Hagersten 1992), and hierarchical-snooping COMA was used in commercial systems from Kendall Square Research (Frank, Burkhardt, and Rothnie 1993). In these *hierarchical COMA* schemes, data is found on a miss by traversing the hierarchy, just as in non-COMA hierarchical protocols discussed in Chapter 8. The difference is that whereas in non-COMA machines there is a fixed home node for a memory block in a processing node, here there is not. When a reference misses in the local attraction memory, it proceeds up the hierarchy until a node is found that indicates the presence of the block in its subtree in the appropriate state. The request then proceeds down the hierarchy to the appropriate processing node (which is at a leaf), guided by directory lookups or snooping at each node along the way.

In *flat COMA* schemes, there is still no home for a memory block in the sense of a reserved location for the data; however, there is a fixed home where just the directory information can be found (Stenstrom, Joe, and Gupta 1992; Joe 1995). This fixed home is determined from either the physical address (as in CC-NUMA) or a global identifier obtained from the physical address. The (static) location of the directory information is also decoupled from the (dynamically changing) location of the actual data. A miss in the local attraction memory goes to the home to look up the directory information, and the directory keeps track of where copies actually are in either a memory-based or cache-based way. The trade-offs for hierarchical directories versus flat directories are very similar to those without COMA (see Section 8.10.2).

Let us see how hierarchical and flat schemes can solve the last copy replacement problem. If the block being replaced from an attraction memory is in shared state, then if we are certain that there is another copy of the block in the system, we can safely discard the replaced block. But for a block that is in an exclusive state or is the last copy in the system, we must ensure that it finds a place in some other attraction memory and is not thrown away. In the hierarchical case, for a block in shared state we simply have to go up the hierarchy until we find a node that indicates that a copy of the block exists somewhere in its subtree. Then we can discard the replaced block as long as we have updated the state information on the path along the way. For a replaced block in an exclusive state, we go up the hierarchy until we find a node that has a block in invalid or shared state somewhere in its subtree, which this block can replace. If the replaceable block is in shared rather than invalid state, then its replacement will require the same procedure to be followed; an invalid block is the easier case.

In a flat COMA, more machinery is required for the last copy problem since there is no built-in mechanism to search for available space. One mechanism is to label one copy of a memory block as the *master* copy and to ensure that the master copy is not dropped upon replacement. A new cache state called *master* is added in the attraction memory. When data is initially allocated, every block is a master copy. Later, a master copy is either an exclusive copy or one of the shared copies. When a shared copy of a block that is not the master copy is replaced, it can be safely dropped (we may, if we like, send a replacement hint to the directory entry at the home). If a master copy is replaced, a replacement message must be sent to the home. The home then chooses another node to send this master copy to in the hope of finding room and sets that node to be the master. If all available blocks in that set of the attraction memory at this new destination are also masters, then the request is sent back to the home, which tries another node and so on. Otherwise, one of the replaceable blocks in the set is replaced and discarded (some optimizations are discussed in [Joe and Hennessy 1994]).

Regardless of whether a hierarchical or flat COMA protocol is used, the initial data set of the application should not fill the entire main or attraction memory, in order to ensure that enough space is available in the system for a replaced last (master) copy to find a new residence. To help find replaceable blocks, the attraction memories should be quite highly associative as well. Not having enough extra (initially unallocated) memory available for replication can cause performance problems for several reasons. First, it makes the COMA nature of the machine less effective in satisfying cache capacity misses locally. Second, it implies that useful replicated blocks are more likely to be replaced to make room for replaced master copies. And third, the traffic generated by replaced last copies can become substantial, which can cause a lot of contention in the system. How much memory should be set aside for replication and how much associativity is needed can be determined empirically (Joe and Hennessy 1994).

Summary: Path of a Read Operation

Consider a flat COMA scheme. A virtual address is first translated to a physical address by the memory management unit. This may cause a page fault and a new mapping to be established, as in a uniprocessor, though in the COMA case the actual data for the page is not loaded into memory. The physical address is used to look up the cache hierarchy. If it hits, the reference is satisfied. If not, then it must look up the local attraction memory. Some bits from the physical address are used to find the relevant set in the attraction memory, and the tag store maintained by the hardware is used to check for a tag match. If the block is found in an appropriate state, the reference is satisfied. If not, then a remote request must be generated, and the request is sent to the home determined from the physical address. The directory at the home determines where to forward the request and whether the data is in shared or exclusive state, and the owner node uses the physical address as an index into its own attraction memory to find and return the data. The directory protocol ensures that states are maintained correctly, as usual.

9.3 REDUCING HARDWARE COST

The last of the major issues discussed in this chapter is hardware cost. Reducing cost often implies moving some functionality from specialized hardware to software that runs on existing or commodity hardware. In this case, the functionality in question is managing replication and coherence. Since it is much easier for software to control these functions in main memory than in the hardware cache, the low-cost approaches tend to provide replication and coherence in main memory, like COMA or tertiary cache systems do. The differences from COMA or tertiary caches are the higher overhead or assist occupancy for communication and, often, the granularity at which replication and coherence are managed.

Consider the hardware cost of a pure CC-NUMA approach. The portion of the communication architecture that is on a node can be divided into four parts: the part of the assist that checks for access control violations, the per-block tags and state that it uses for this purpose, the part that does the actual protocol processing (including intervening in the processor cache), and the network interface itself. To keep data coherent at cache block granularity in hardware, the access control part needs to see every load or store to shared data that misses in the cache so that it can take the necessary protocol action. Thus, the assist must be able to snoop on the local memory system (as well as issue requests to the local memory system, including the cache, in response to incoming requests from the network).

For coherence to be managed efficiently, each of the other functional components of the assist can benefit greatly from hardware specialization and integration. Determining access faults quickly requires that the tags per block of main memory be located close to the access control part of the assist. The speed with which protocol actions can be invoked and the assist can intervene in the processor cache increases as the assist is integrated closer to the cache. Performing protocol operations quickly demands that the assist be either hardwired or, if programmable (as in the Sequent NUMA-Q), specialized for the types of operations that protocols perform most often (e.g., bit-field extractions and manipulations). Finally, moving small pieces of data quickly between the assist and network interface asks that the network interface be tightly integrated with the assist. Thus, for highest performance, we would like the four parts of the communication assist to be tightly integrated, with as few bus crossings as possible to communicate among them, and the whole assist to be specialized and tightly integrated into the node's memory system.

Early cache-coherent machines accomplished this by integrating a hardwired assist into the cache controller and integrating the network interface tightly into the assist. However, modern processors tend to have even their second-level cache controllers on the processor chip, so it is difficult to integrate the assist into this controller once the processor is built. The SGI Origin therefore integrates its hardwired Hub into the memory controller, the Stanford FLASH integrates its specialized programmable protocol engine into the memory controller, and the Sequent NUMA-Q and Hal S1 attach specialized controllers to the memory bus. By using such specialized, tightly integrated hardware support for cache coherence, these approaches do not leverage inexpensive commodity parts for the communication architecture. They are therefore expensive, more so in design and implementation time than in the amount of actual hardware needed.

Research efforts are attempting to lower this cost with several different approaches. One approach is to perform access control in specialized hardware but delegate much of the other activity to software and commodity hardware. Other approaches perform access control in software as well, thus providing a coherent shared address space abstraction on commodity nodes and networks with no specialized hardware support. Access control is provided either at fine granularity by instrumenting the program code, at page granularity by leveraging the existing virtual memory support, or at the granularity of user-defined objects by using a run-time layer that exports an object-based programming interface.

Let us discuss each of these approaches, which are all currently at the research stage. We cover the page-based approach more thoroughly because it changes the granularity at which data is allocated, communicated, and kept coherent while still preserving the same transparent programming interface as hardware-coherent systems, because it requires substantially different protocols than we have seen so far, and because it illustrates the mechanisms needed to fully exploit the relaxations afforded by relaxed memory consistency models.

9.3.1 Hardware Access Control with a Decoupled Assist

While specialized hardware support is used for fine-grained access control in this approach, some or all of the other aspects (protocol processing, tags, and network interface) can be decoupled from this specialized hardware and from one another. They can then either use commodity hardware attached to less intrusive parts of the node like the I/O bus or use no extra hardware beyond that on the uniprocessor node. For example, the per-block tags and state can be kept in special fast memory or in regular DRAM, and protocol processing can be done in software either on a separate, inexpensive general-purpose processor or even on the main processor itself. The network interface usually has some specialized support for fine-grained communication to reduce the endpoint overheads. Some possible combinations of how the various functions might be integrated are shown in Figure 9.9.

The problem with the decoupled hardware approach, of course, is that it increases the latency of protocol invocation, protocol processing, and communication since the interaction of the different components with each other and with the node is slower (e.g., it may involve several bus crossings). More critically, the effective occupancy of the decoupled communication assist is much larger than that of a specialized, integrated assist, which can hurt performance substantially for many applications as described in Section 8.7.

9.3.2 Access Control through Code Instrumentation

It is possible to use no additional hardware support over a standard uniprocessor node but perform all the functions needed for fine-grained replication and coherence in main memory in software. The trickiest part of this is fine-grained access control in main memory, for which a standard uniprocessor does not provide support. To accomplish this, individual read and write operations can be instrumented in software by adding instructions to look up per-block tag and state data structures maintained in main memory (Schoinas et al. 1994; Scales, Gharachorloo, and Thekkath 1996). To the extent that cache misses can be predicted, only the reads and writes that miss in the processor cache hierarchy need to be thus instrumented. The necessary protocol processing can be performed on the main processor or on whatever form of communication assist is provided. In fact, such software instrumentation allows us to provide access control and coherence at any granularity, even different granularities for different data structures.

Software instrumentation incurs a run-time cost since it inserts extra instructions into the code to perform the necessary checks. The approaches that have been developed use several tricks to reduce the number of checks and lookups needed (Scales,

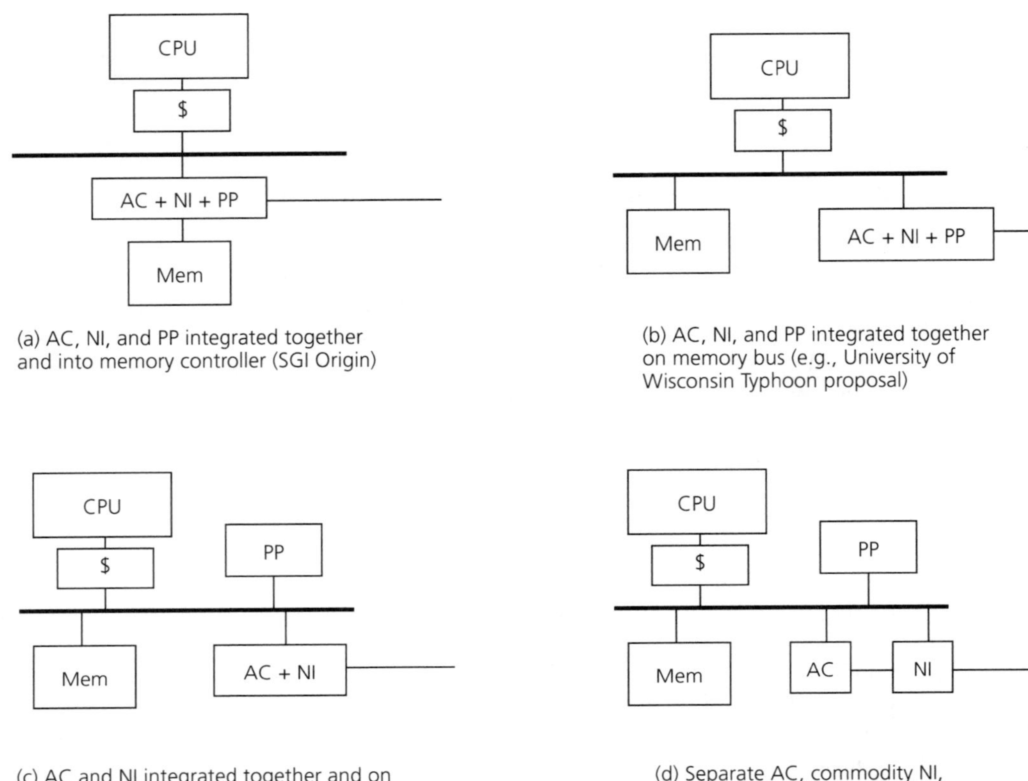

FIGURE 9.9 Some alternatives for reducing cost over a highly integrated and specialized assist. AC is the access control facility, NI is the network interface, and PP is the protocol processing facility (whether hardwired finite state machine or programmable). The highly integrated solution is shown in (a) with alternative, less integrated solutions shown in (b), (c), and (d). As the distance between parts increases, so does the number of expensive bus crossings required for the parts to communicate with one another to process a transaction. In these designs, the commodity PP in (c) and (d) is a complete processor like the main CPU, with its own cache system.

Gharachorloo, and Thekkath 1996), so the cost of access control and protocol invocation may well be competitive with that in the decoupled hardware approach. Protocol processing in software on the main processor also has a significant cost, and while the network interface and interconnects used by such systems usually provide support for fine-grained communication, they are usually commodity based and, hence, less efficient than in tightly coupled multiprocessors.

9.3.3 Page-Based Access Control: Shared Virtual Memory

Another approach to providing access control and coherence with no additional hardware support is to leverage the virtual memory support provided by the memory management units of microprocessors and by the operating system. Memory management units already perform access control in main memory at the granularity of pages (e.g., to detect page faults) and manage main memory as a fully associative cache on the virtual address space. By embedding a coherence protocol in the page fault handlers, we can provide replication and coherence at page granularity and manage the main memories of the nodes as coherent, fully associative caches on a shared virtual address space (Li and Hudak 1989). Access control now requires no special tags, and the assist needn't even see every cache miss. Data enters the local cache only when the corresponding page is already present in local memory. As in the previous two approaches, the processor caches themselves do not have to be kept coherent across nodes by hardware since when a page is invalidated the TLB will not let the processor access its blocks in the cache (care must, of course, be taken to keep processor caches coherent with the local memory and vice versa).

This approach is called *page-based shared virtual memory* or SVM for short. Since the costs can be amortized over a whole page of data, protocol processing is often done on the main processor itself, and we can more easily do without special hardware support for fine-grained communication in the network interface. Thus, there is less need for hardware assistance beyond that available on a standard uniprocessor system.

A very simple form of shared virtual memory coherence is illustrated in Figure 9.10, following an invalidation protocol very similar to those in pure CC-NUMA. A few aspects are worthy of note. First, since the memory management units of different processors manage their main memories independently, the physical address of the page in P_1's local memory may be completely different from that of the copy in P_0's local memory, even though the pages have the same (shared) virtual address. There is a shared virtual address space but private physical address spaces. Second, a page fault handler that implements the protocol must be able to perform the three protocol functions discussed in Chapter 8 (finding the source of state information, finding the appropriate copy or copies, and communicating with the copies) before it can set the page's access rights as appropriate and return control to the application process. A directory mechanism can be used for this—every page may have a home, determined by its virtual address, and a directory entry maintained at the home—though high-performance SVM protocols tend to be more complex, as we shall see.

The problems with page-based shared virtual memory are the high overheads of protocol invocation and processing and the large granularity of coherence and communication. The former is expensive because most of the work is done in software on a general-purpose uniprocessor. Page faults take time to cause an interrupt or trap and to switch into the operating system and invoke a handler; the protocol processing itself is done in software, and the messages sent to other processors use the underlying message-passing mechanisms that are expensive, especially with commodity nodes and interconnects. On a representative SVM system in 1998, the

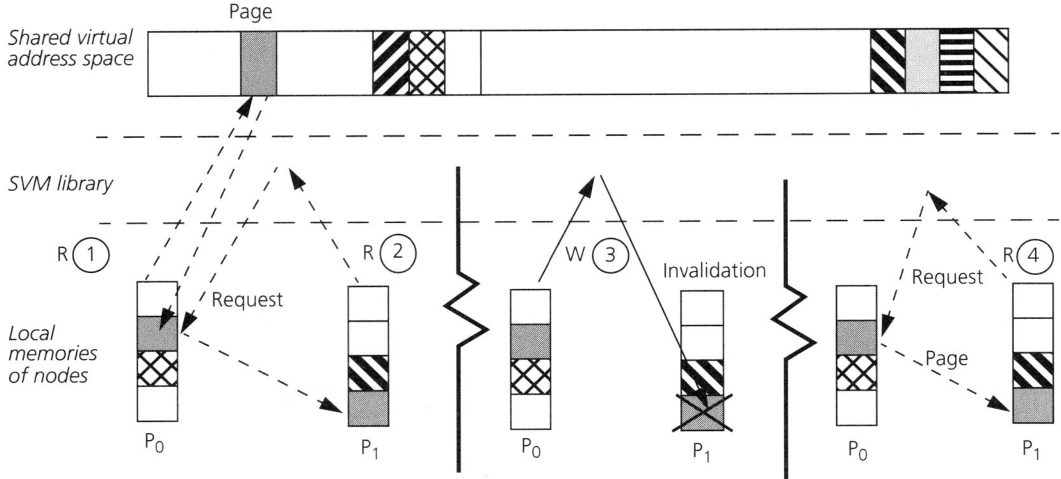

FIGURE 9.10 Illustration of simple shared virtual memory. At the beginning, no node has a copy of the stippled shared virtual page with which we are concerned. Events occur in the order 1, 2, 3, 4. Read 1 incurs a page fault during address translation and fetches a copy of the page to P_0 (presumably from disk). Read 2, shown in the same frame, incurs a page fault and fetches a read-only copy to P_1 (from P_0). This is the same virtual page but is at two different physical addresses in the two memories. Write 3 incurs a page fault (write to a read-only page), and the SVM library, implemented in the page fault handlers, determines that P_1 has a copy and causes it to be invalidated. P_0 now obtains read-write access to the page, which is like the modified or dirty state. When Read 4 by P_1 tries to read a location on the invalid page, it incurs a page fault and fetches a new copy from P_0 through the SVM library.

round-trip cost of satisfying a remote page fault ranges from a few hundred microseconds with aggressive system software support to over a millisecond. This should be compared with less than a microsecond needed for a read miss on aggressive hardware-coherent systems. In addition, since protocol processing is typically done on the main processor (to avoid additional hardware support), even incoming requests interrupt the processor, pollute the cache, and slow down the currently running application thread (which may have nothing to do with that request).

The large granularity of communication and coherence is problematic for two reasons. First, if spatial locality is not very good, it causes a lot of fragmentation in communication and hence useless data transfer (only a word is needed but a whole page is fetched). Second, it can easily lead to false sharing, which causes expensive protocol operations and communication to be invoked frequently. Under a sequential consistency model, invalidations are propagated and performed as soon as a write is detected, so pages may be frequently ping-ponged back and forth among processors due to either true or false sharing. (Figure 9.11 shows an example.) The high cost and high frequency of the operations are an unfortunate combination, so it is very important that the effects of false sharing and the frequency of communication in general be alleviated. This leads to very different protocols and approaches

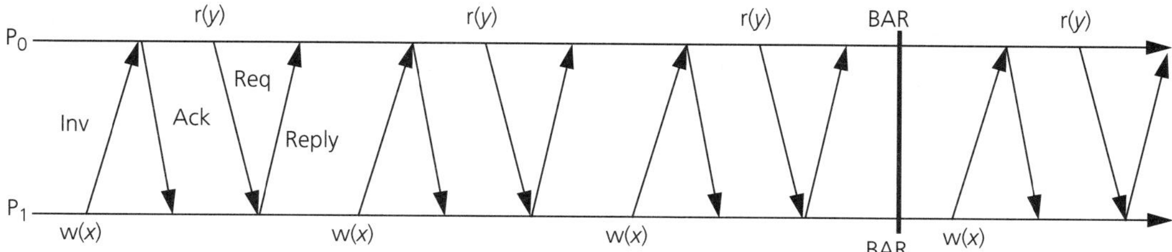

FIGURE 9.11 Problem with sequential consistency for SVM. Time proceeds from left to right in the figure. The operations that a process performs are shown above or below the horizontal timeline for that process. Process P_0 repeatedly reads variable *y* while process P_1 repeatedly writes variable *x*, which happens to fall on the same page as *y*. Since P_1 cannot proceed under SC until invalidations are propagated and acknowledged, the invalidations are propagated immediately, and substantial (and very expensive) communication ensues repeatedly due to this false sharing.

than those used for fine-grained coherence, where false sharing is much less significant, so let us examine them in some depth.

Using Relaxed Memory Consistency

The frequency of communication is reduced by exploiting a relaxed memory consistency model such as release consistency. This allows coherence actions such as invalidations or updates, collectively called *write notices* in SVM systems, to be postponed until the next synchronization point (writes do not have to become visible until then). Let us continue to assume an invalidation-based protocol. Figure 9.12 shows the same example as Figure 9.11: the writes to *x* by processor P_1 will not generate invalidations to the copy of the page at P_0 until the barrier is reached, so the effects of false sharing will be greatly mitigated and none of the reads of *y* by P_0 before the barrier will incur page faults. Of course, when P_0 accesses *y* after the barrier, it will incur a page fault due to false sharing since the page has now been invalidated. Similar communication reduction would be observed for true sharing as well, since the protocol does not distinguish between the two: even true sharing modifications would not be observed until the next synchronization point, which is okay according to the consistency model.

There is a significant difference here from how relaxed consistency is typically used in hardware-coherent machines or writes. There, it is used to avoid stalling the processor to wait for acknowledgments (completion), but the invalidations are usually propagated and applied as soon as possible since this is the natural thing for hardware to do. Although release consistency does not guarantee that the effects of the writes will be seen until the synchronization, in fact they usually will be. The amount of false sharing of cache blocks is therefore not reduced much, even within a period with no synchronization, nor is the number of network transactions or messages; the goal is mostly to hide latency from the processor. In the SVM case, the system takes the contract literally: invalidations are actually not propagated until the

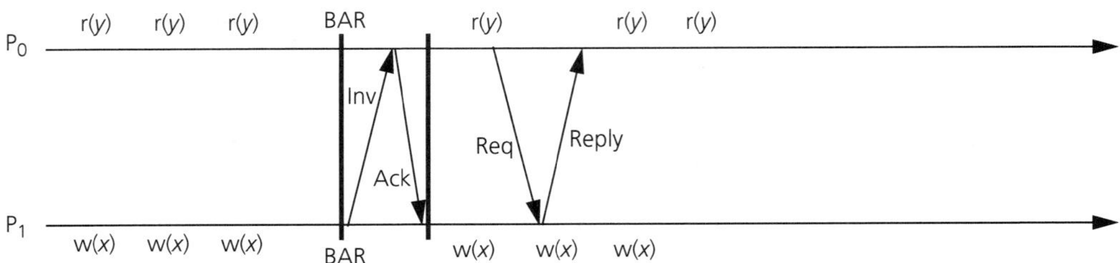

FIGURE 9.12 Reducing SVM communication due to false sharing by using a relaxed consistency model. No communication occurs at reads and writes until a synchronization event, at which point invalidations are propagated to make pages coherent. Only the first access to an invalidated page after a synchronization point generates a page fault and hence a request.

synchronization points. Of course, this makes it critical for correctness that all synchronization points be clearly labeled and communicated to the system.[5]

When exactly should invalidations (or write notices) be propagated from the writer to other copies, and when should they be applied? One possibility is to propagate them when the writer issues a release operation. At a release, invalidations for each page that the process wrote since its previous release are propagated to all processes that have copies of the page. If we wait for the invalidations to complete before proceeding past the release, this satisfies the sufficient conditions for RC that were presented earlier. However, even this propagation is sooner than necessary: under release consistency, a given process does not really need to see the write notice until it does an acquire. Propagating and applying write notices to all copies at release points, called *eager release consistency* or ERC (Carter, Bennett, and Zwaenepoel 1991, 1995), is conservative because the system does not know when the next acquire by another processor will occur or whether a given process will even perform an acquire and need to see those write notices. As shown in Figure 9.13(a), it can send expensive invalidation messages to more processes than necessary (P_2 need not have been invalidated by P_0); it requires separate messages for invalidations and lock acquisitions; and it may invalidate processes earlier than necessary, thus causing false sharing (see the false sharing between variables *x* and *y*, as a result of which the page is fetched twice by P_1 and P_2—once at the read of *y* and once at the write of *x*). The extra messages problem is even more significant when an update-based protocol is used and repeated writes to a page generate repeated updates. These issues and alternatives are discussed further in Exercises 9.23–9.25.

5. In fact, a similar approach can be used to reduce the effects of false sharing in hardware as well. Invalidations may be buffered in hardware at the requestor and sent out only at a release or a synchronization (depending on whether release consistency or weak ordering is being followed) or when the buffer becomes full. Or they may be buffered at the destination and only applied at the next acquire point by that destination. This approach has been called *delayed consistency* (Dubois et al. 1991) since it delays the propagation of invalidations. As long as processors do not see the invalidations, they continue to use their copies without any coherence actions, alleviating false sharing effects.

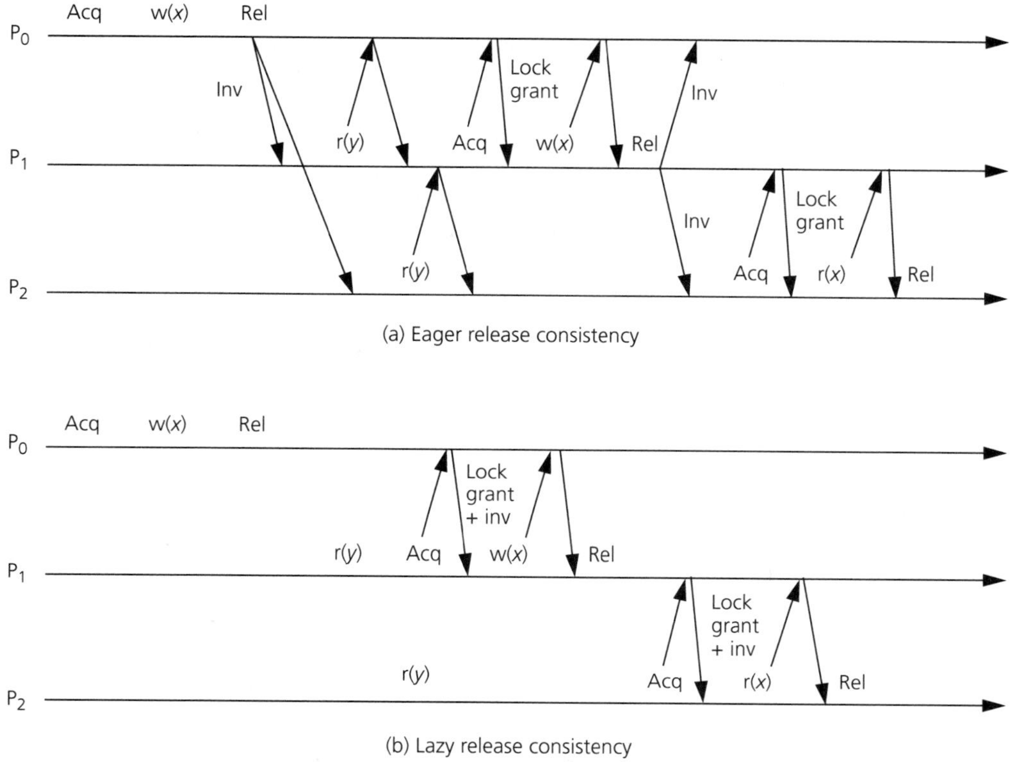

FIGURE 9.13 Eager versus lazy implementations of release consistency. Eager release consistency performs consistency actions (invalidation) at a release point, whereas lazy release consistency performs them at an acquire. Variables *x* and *y* are on the same page. The reduction in communication can be substantial, particularly for SVM systems with their large granularity of coherence.

The best-known SVM systems tend to use a form of release consistency, called *lazy release consistency* or LRC. As shown in Figure 9.13(b), LRC propagates and applies invalidations to a given process not at the release that follows the writes but only at the next acquire by that process (Keleher, Cox, and Zwaenepoel 1992). On an acquire, the process obtains the write notices corresponding to all previous release operations that occurred between its previous acquire operation and its current acquire operation and applies them to the relevant pages. Identifying which are the release operations that occurred before a given acquire is an interesting question. They can be defined as all releases that would have to appear before this acquire in any sequentially consistent ordering of the synchronization operations (that preserves dependences among them as well).[6] Another way of putting this is that two

6. The ordering could even be processor consistent since RC allows acquires (reads) to bypass previous releases (writes) in program order.

types of partial orders are imposed on synchronization operations: program order within each process and a dynamically determined dependence order among acquires and releases to the same synchronization variable (by all processes). Accesses to a synchronization variable form a chain of successful acquires and releases in the dependence order. When an acquire request comes to a releasing process P, the synchronization operations that have occurred before that release are those that precede it in the intersection of these program orders and dependence orders. These synchronization operations are said to have occurred before the release in a *causal* sense. The operations before the acquire are the union of these operations with the operations that precede the acquire in program order. Figure 9.14 clarifies this concept of causal order among synchronization operations.

By further postponing coherence actions to acquires, LRC alleviates the three problems associated with ERC; for example, if memory operations that exhibit false

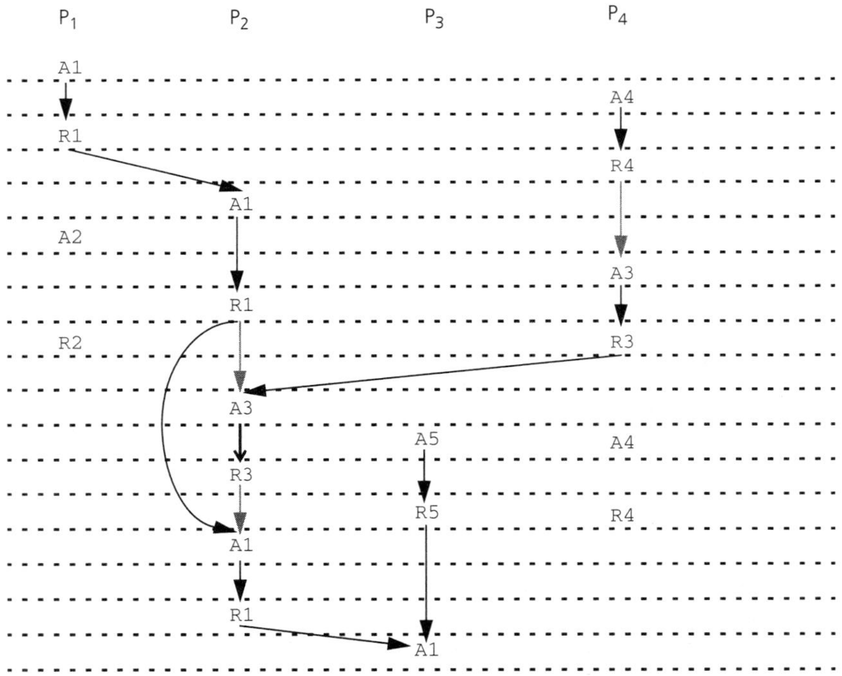

FIGURE 9.14 The causal order among synchronization operations and hence the groups of data accesses between them. The figure shows what the synchronization operations are before the acquire A1 (by process P_3) and the release R1 (by process P_2) that enables it. The dotted horizontal lines are time increments, increasing downward, indicating a possible interleaving in time. The bold arrows show dependence orders along an acquire-release chain, whereas the gray arrows show the program orders that are part of the causal order. The A2, R2 and A4, R4 pairs that are untouched by arrows do not happen before the acquire of interest in causal order, so the data accesses after the acquire are not guaranteed to see the accesses between those pairs.

sharing on a page occur before the acquire but not after it, their ill effects will not be seen (there is no page fault on the read of y in Figure 9.13[b]). On the other hand, some of the work and communication to be done is shifted from release point to acquire point, and LRC is significantly more complex to implement than ERC, as we shall see. Intermediate approaches are possible, such as propagating write notices at a release but applying them only at an acquire, thus saving not on write traffic but on page faults. However, LRC is currently the method of choice.

The relationship between these page-based software protocols and the consistency models developed for hardware-coherent systems is also interesting. The software protocols do not satisfy the requirements of coherence discussed in Chapter 5 since writes are not automatically guaranteed to be propagated unless the appropriate synchronization is present. Making writes visible only through synchronization operations also makes write serialization more difficult to guarantee. Different processes may see the same writes through different synchronization chains and hence in different orders, so most software systems do not guarantee write serialization. In fact, synchronization-based relaxed consistency specifications like release consistency do not guarantee coherence according to the definitions of Chapter 5. Finally, the only difference between hardware implementations of release consistency and software ERC lies in when writes are propagated. However, by propagating write notices only at acquires, LRC implementations may differ from release consistency even in whether writes are propagated and hence may allow results that are not permitted under release consistency. LRC is therefore a different consistency model than release consistency and requires greater programming care (see Example 9.2), whereas ERC is simply a different implementation of release consistency. However, if a program is properly labeled, in the sense of labeling all synchronization operations as discussed in Section 9.1.2, then it is guaranteed to run "correctly" under both RC and LRC, and both coherence and sequential consistency will appear to be satisfied.

EXAMPLE 9.2 Design an example in which LRC produces a different result than RC. How would you avoid the problem?

Answer Consider the code fragment below, assuming the pointer `ptr` is initialized to NULL.

P_1	P_2
lock L1;	
`ptr = non_null_ptr_val;`	
unlock L1;	`while (ptr == null) {};`
	lock L1;
	`a = ptr;`
	unlock L1;

Under RC and ERC, the new non-null pointer value is guaranteed to propagate to P_2 before the unlock (release) by P_1 is complete, so P_2 will see the new value and jump out of the loop as expected. Under LRC, P_2 will not see the write by P_1 until it performs its lock (acquire operation); it will therefore enter the while loop, never see the write by P_1, and hence never exit the while loop. The solution is to put the appropriate acquire synchronization before the reads in the while loop or to label the accesses to `ptr` appropriately as synchronizations to create a properly labeled program. ■

The fact that coherence information is propagated only at synchronization operations that are recognized by the software SVM layer has an interesting, related implication. It may be difficult to run existing application binaries "as is" on SVM systems that use relaxed consistency models, even if those binaries were compiled for systems that support a very relaxed consistency model and they are properly labeled. The reason is that the labels have already been compiled down to the specific fence instructions used by the commercial microprocessor, and those fence instructions may not be visible to the software SVM layer. Of course, if the source code or assembly code with the labels is available, then the labels can be translated to primitives recognized by the SVM layer; and if only the binary is available then it can be edited, using available tools, and instrumented to make the labels visible to the SVM runtime system.

Multiple Writer Protocols

Delaying write notices works very well in mitigating the effects of false sharing when only one of the sharers writes the page in the interval between two synchronization points, as in our previous examples (the others may read the page). However, it does not in itself solve the multiple writer problem. Consider the revised example in Figure 9.15. Now P_0 and P_1 both modify the same page between the same two barriers. If we follow a protocol in which only a single writer is allowed at a time, then each of the writers must obtain ownership of the page before writing it, leading to ping-ponging communication even between the synchronization points and compromising the potential benefits of the relaxed consistency model (which allows multiple writers to coexist). To truly exploit the benefits of relaxed consistency, we need a *multiple writer* protocol. This is a protocol that allows each processor writing a page between synchronization points to modify its own copy locally, letting the copies become inconsistent, and makes the copies consistent only at the next synchronization point as needed by the consistency model. Let us look briefly at some multiple writer mechanisms that can be used with either eager or lazy release consistency.

The first method is used in the TreadMarks SVM system from Rice University (Keleher et al. 1994). The idea is quite simple. To capture the modifications to a shared page, it is initially write protected. At the first write after a synchronization point, a protection violation occurs. At this point, the system makes a copy of the page (called a *twin*) in software and then unprotects the actual page so further writes can happen without protection violations. Later, at the next release or incoming acquire at that process (for ERC or LRC, respectively), the twin and the current copy are compared to create a "diff," which is simply a compact encoded representation of

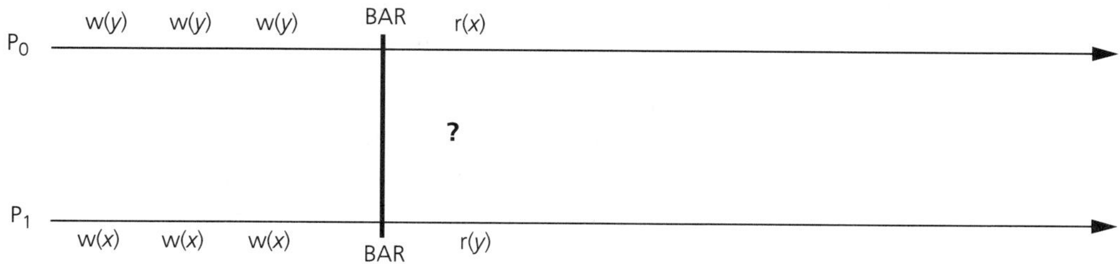

FIGURE 9.15 The multiple writer problem. At the barrier, two different processors have written the same page independently, and their modifications need to be merged.

the differences between the two. The diff therefore captures the modifications that processor has made to the page in that synchronization interval. When a processor incurs a page fault, it must obtain the diffs for that page from other processors that have created them and merge them into its copy of the page. As with write notices, several alternatives are available for when we might compute the diffs and when we might propagate them to other processors with copies of the page (see Exercise 9.23). If diffs are propagated eagerly at a release, they and the corresponding write notices can be freed immediately and the storage reused. In a lazy implementation, diffs and write notices may be kept at the creator until they are requested. In that case, they must be retained until it is clear that no other processor needs them. Since the amount of storage needed by these diffs and write notices can become very large, garbage collection becomes necessary (by forcibly propagating diffs and write notices, for example). This garbage collection algorithm is quite complex and expensive since when it is invoked each page may have uncollected diffs distributed among many nodes (Keleher et al. 1994).

An alternative software multiple writer method gets around the garbage collection problem for diffs while still implementing LRC and makes a different set of performance trade-offs (Iftode, Singh, and Li 1996b; Zhou, Iftode, and Li 1996). The idea here is to not maintain the diffs at the writer until they are requested nor to propagate them to all the copies at a release, but rather to do something in between. Every page has a home node, just like in flat hardware cache coherence schemes, and the diffs are propagated to the home at a release. The releasing processor can then free the storage for the diffs as soon as it has sent them to the home. The arriving diffs are merged into the home copy of the page (and the diff storage freed there too), which is therefore kept up-to-date. A processor performing an acquire obtains write notices for pages from the previous releaser just as before. However, when it has a subsequent page fault on one of those pages, it does not obtain diffs from all previous writers but rather fetches the whole page from the home. This is called a *home-based protocol.* In addition to much lower storage overhead and better storage scalability, it has the performance advantage that on a page fault only one round-trip message is required to fetch the data whereas, in the previous scheme, diffs had to be obtained from all the previous ("multiple") writers. Also, a processor never incurs a page fault for a page for which it is the home. The disadvantages are that whole pages are fetched rather than diffs (though this can be traded off with storage and protocol processing overhead by storing the diffs at the home and not applying them there and then fetching diffs from the home) and that the distribution of pages among homes becomes important for performance despite replication in main memory. Which scheme performs better will depend on how the application sharing patterns manifest themselves at page granularity and on the performance characteristics of the communication architecture.

Alternative Methods for Propagating Writes

Diff processing—twin creation, diff computation, and diff application—incurs significant overhead, requires substantial additional storage, and can also pollute the first-level processor cache, replacing useful application data. Some recent systems provide hardware support for fine-grained communication in the network interface, particularly fine-grained propagation of writes to remote memories, that can be used to accelerate these home-based, multiple writer SVM protocols and avoid diffs altogether. The idea of hardware propagation of writes originated in the PRAM (Lipton and Sandberg 1988) and PLUS (Bisiani and Ravishankar 1990) systems; modern examples include the network interface of the SHRIMP multicomputer prototype at Princeton University (Blumrich et al. 1994) and the Memory Channel from Digital Equipment Corporation (Gillett, Collins, and Pimm 1996).

These network interfaces allow mappings to be established between a pair of pages on different nodes so that the writes performed to the source page are propagated in hardware to the destination page. The writes can be detected by snooping the memory bus (as in the SHRIMP case, called an *automatic update mechanism*) or by software instrumention of write operations to generate special writes to a different address space (as in the Memory Channel, called a *write doubling mechanism*). The detected writes are then propagated according to the mappings by the network interface, which may even reside on the I/O bus. The snooping approach may require that caches be write through, while the latter approach experiences extra instruction overhead and requires instrumentation. By establishing such mappings from the copies of a page to the home copy (when those copies are first made), writes will be propagated to the home, which can be kept up-to-date according to the consistency model (see Figure 9.16). Consistency actions like propagating and applying write notices are managed at synchronization points exactly as before, and the entire page is fetched from the home on a page fault. Home-based protocols have been developed using these features (Iftode et al. 1996; Iftode, Singh, and Li 1996a; Kontothanassis and Scott 1996), and in fact they inspired the all-software home-based protocols. These fine-grained write propagation approaches avoid diffs entirely; however, they require hardware support and they increase data traffic by propagating all writes rather than only the final new values produced by the end of a synchronization interval.

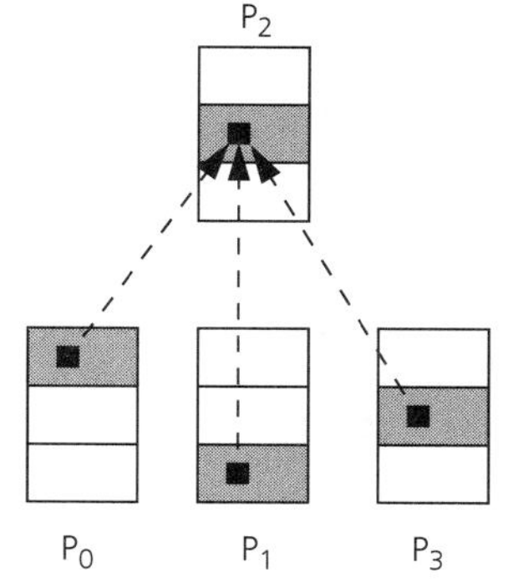

(a) The automatic update mechanism

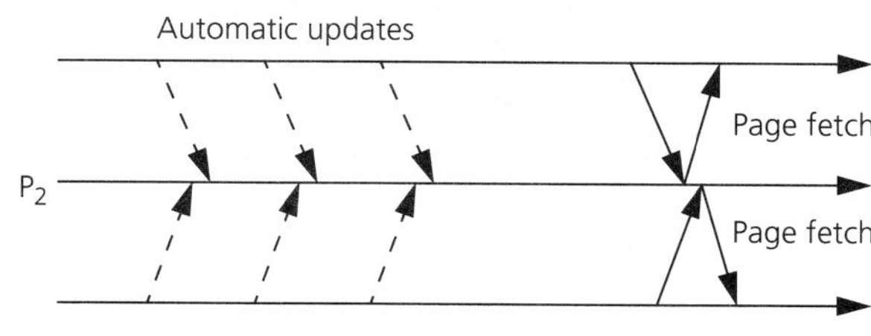

(b) Supporting multiple writers using automatic update

FIGURE 9.16 Using an automatic update mechanism to solve the multiple writer problem. The variables *x* and *y* fall on the same page, which has node P_2 as its home. If P_0 (or P_1) were the home, it would not need to propagate automatic updates and would not incur page faults on that page (only the other node would).

An all-software alternative to computing diffs is to maintain dirty bits per word or per block in main memory in software (Zekauskas, Sawdon, and Bershad 1994). A *dirty bit* for a word keeps track of whether that word has been written by the local node since the dirty bit was last cleared. Dirty bits are cleared at synchronization points, and the dirty bits that are found to be set in a page upon reaching a synchronization point indicate the equivalent of a diff for that page. While determining diffs does not require pages to be compared with their twins, the setting and unsetting of dirty bits requires extra instructions and instrumentation, similar to that needed by the write propagation in the Memory Channel interface. Software analysis can be used to reduce the overhead, but it remains significant.

The discussion so far has focused on the functionality of different degrees of laziness but has not addressed implementation. How do we ensure that the necessary write notices to satisfy the partial orders of causality get to the right places at the right time, and how do we reduce the number of write notices transferred? A range of methods and mechanisms is available for implementing release consistency protocols of different forms (single versus multiple writer, acquire- versus release-based, degree of laziness actually implemented). The mechanisms, the forms of laziness each can support, and their trade-offs are interesting and are discussed in Section 9.6.2.

Summary: Path of a Read Operation

To summarize the behavior of an SVM system, let us look at the path of a read. We examine the behavior of a home-based system since it is simpler. A read reference first undergoes address translation from a virtual to a physical address in the processor's memory management unit. If a local page mapping is found, the cache hierarchy is looked up and it behaves just like a regular uniprocessor operation. If a local page mapping is not found, a page fault occurs and then the page is mapped in, providing a physical address. If the operating system indicates that the page is not currently mapped on any other node, then it is mapped in from disk with read-write permission, otherwise it is obtained from another node with read-only permission. Now the cache is looked up. If inclusion is preserved between the local memory and the cache hierarchy, as it normally will be to keep the caches coherent with local memory, the reference will miss and the block is loaded into the cache from local main memory where the page is now mapped. Note that inclusion means that a page must be flushed from the cache (or the state of the cache blocks changed) when it is invalidated in the local main memory, downgraded from read-write to read-only mode, or replaced. If a write reference is made to a read-only page, then a page fault is also incurred and ownership of the page obtained before the reference can be satisfied by the cache hierarchy.

Performance Implications

Lazy release consistency and multiple writer protocols improve the performance of SVM systems dramatically compared to sequentially consistent implementations. However, there are still many performance problems compared with machines that manage coherence in hardware at cache block granularity. The problems of false sharing and either extra communication or protocol processing overhead do not disappear with relaxed models, and the page faults and fetches that remain are still expensive to satisfy. The high cost of communication and the contention induced by higher endpoint processing overhead often greatly magnifies imbalances in communication volume and, hence, execution time among processors. Another problem in SVM systems is that synchronization is performed in software through explicit software messages and is very expensive. This is exacerbated by the fact that expensive page misses often occur within critical sections, artificially dilating them and hence greatly increasing the serialization at critical sections. The result is that while applications with coarse-grained data access patterns (little false sharing or communication fragmentation) and synchronization perform quite well on SVM systems, applications with finer-grained access patterns (i.e., accesses from different processes being interleaved finely in the shared virtual address space) and especially synchronization do not migrate well from hardware cache-coherent systems to SVM systems unless they are manufactured (Jiang, Shan, and Singh 1997). The scalability of SVM systems is also undetermined, both in performance and in the ability to run large problems since the storage overhead of auxiliary data structures grows with the number of processors.

Overall, it is still unclear whether fine-grained applications that run well on hardware-coherent machines can be restructured to run efficiently on SVM systems as well and whether or not such systems are viable for a wide range of applications. Research is being done to understand the performance issues and bottlenecks

(Dwarkadas et al. 1993; Iftode, Singh, and Li 1996a; Kontothanassis et al. 1997; Jiang, Shan, and Singh 1997) as well as the value of adding some hardware support for fine-grained communication while still maintaining coherence in software at page granularity (Kontothanassis and Scott 1996; Iftode, Singh, and Li 1996a; Bilas, Iftode, and Singh 1998). With the dramatically increasing popularity of low-cost SMPs, there is also a lot of research in extending SVM protocols to build coherent shared address space machines as a two-level hierarchy: hardware coherence within the SMP nodes and software SVM coherence across SMP nodes (Erlichson et al. 1996; Stets et al. 1997; Samanta et al. 1998). The goal is for the outer SVM protocol to be invoked as infrequently as possible and only when cross-node coherence is needed, while still preserving laziness within the node as well. The extension to cache-coherent distributed-memory nodes rather than SMP nodes is natural to contemplate. In fact, instead of an inexpensive but low-performance substitute for hardware coherence across uniprocessor nodes, software shared memory approaches like SVM can be seen as a way of extending the coherent shared address space programming model from available hardware-coherent multiprocessor nodes to clusters of such nodes and thus constructing large-scale systems. Let us examine some other software approaches.

9.3.4 Access Control through Language and Compiler Support

Language and compiler support can also be enlisted to support coherent replication. One approach is to program in terms of data objects or "regions" of data and have the run-time system that manages these objects provide access control and coherent replication at the granularity of objects. By explicitly using objects, this approach does not view memory as a flat address space. This "shared object space" programming model motivates the use of even more relaxed memory consistency models, as we shall see next. We shall also briefly discuss compiler-based coherence and approaches that provide a shared address space in software but do not provide automatic replication and coherence.

Object-Based Coherence

The release consistency model takes advantage of the "when" dimension of memory consistency—it tells us when it is necessary for writes by one process to be performed with respect to another process. This allows successively lazy implementations to be developed, as we have discussed, which delay the performing of writes as long as possible. However, even with release consistency, if the synchronization in the program requires that process P_1's writes be performed or become visible at process P_2 by a certain point, this means that all of P_1's writes to all the data it wrote become visible even if P_2 does not need to see all the data (see Figure 9.17). More relaxed consistency models take into account the "what" dimension, by propagating invalidations or updates only for that data that the process acquiring the synchronization may

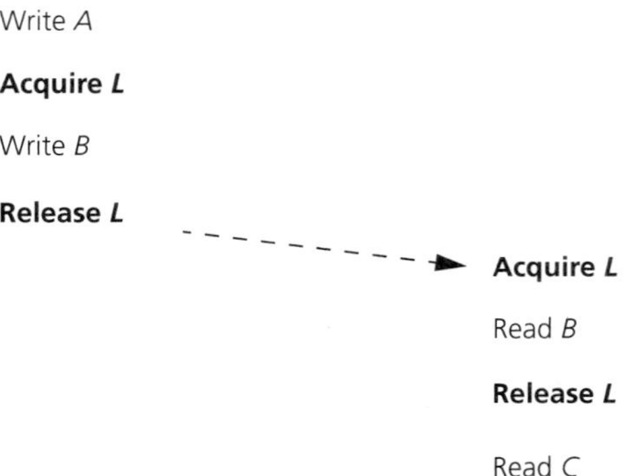

FIGURE 9.17 Why release consistency is conservative. Suppose *A* and *B* are on different pages. Since P_1 wrote *A* and *B* before releasing *L* (even though *A* was not written inside the critical section), invalidations for both *A* and *B* will be propagated to P_2 and applied to the copies of *A* and *B* there. However, P_2 does not need to see the write to *A* but only that to *B*. Suppose now P_2 reads another variable *C* that resides on the same page as *A*. Since the page containing *A* has been invalidated, P_2 will incur a page miss on its access to *C* due to false sharing. If we could somehow associate the page containing *B* with the lock *L*, then only the invalidation of *B* could be propagated on the acquire of *L* by P_2, and the false sharing miss would be saved.

actually need to see according to the causal synchronization relationships. The when dimension in release consistency is specified by the programmer through the synchronization inserted in the program. The question is how to specify the what dimension. It is possible to associate with a synchronization event (or variable) the set of pages that must be made consistent with respect to that event. However, this is very awkward for a programmer to do.

Region- or object-based approaches provide a better solution. The programmer breaks up the data into logical objects or regions (regions are arbitrary, user-specified ranges of virtual addresses that are treated like objects but do not require object-oriented programming). A run-time library then maintains consistency at the granularity of these regions or objects rather than leaving it entirely to the operating system to do at the granularity of pages. The disadvantages of this approach are the additional programming burden of specifying and using regions or objects appropriately and the need for a sophisticated run-time system between the application and the OS. The major advantages are (1) the use of logical objects (rather than fixed machine granularities as coherence units) by itself can help reduce false sharing and fragmentation to begin with, and (2) they provide a handle on specifying data logically and can be used to relax the consistency using the what dimension.

For example, in the *entry consistency* model (Bershad, Zekauskas, and Sawdon 1993), the programmer associates a set of data (regions or objects) with every synchronization variable such as a lock or barrier or with every synchronization event in the program (these associations or bindings can be changed at run time, with some cost). At synchronization events, only those objects or regions that are associated with that synchronization variable are guaranteed to be made consistent. Write notices for other modified data do not have to be propagated or applied. If no bindings are specified for a synchronization variable, the default release consistency model is used for it. However, the bindings are not hints: if they are specified, they must be complete and correct or the program will obtain the wrong answer. The need for explicit, correct bindings imposes a substantial burden on the programmer, and sufficient performance benefits have not yet been demonstrated to make this worthwhile. The Jade programming language achieves a similar effect, although by specifying data usage in a different way (Rinard, Scales, and Lam 1993). Finally, attempts have been made to exploit the association between synchronization and data implicitly even in a page-based shared virtual memory approach, using a model called *scope consistency* (Iftode, Singh, and Li 1996b).

Compiler-Based Coherence

Research has focused on having the compiler keep caches coherent in a shared address space, by using additional hardware support in the processor system. These approaches rely on the compiler (or programmer) to identify parallel loops. A simple approach to coherence is to insert a barrier at the end of every parallel loop and flush the caches between loops. However, this does not allow any data locality to be exploited in caches across loops. Even if only shared data is flushed, data that is declared in the shared address space but is not actively shared will also be unnecessarily flushed. More sophisticated approaches have been proposed that require support for selective invalidations and fairly sophisticated hardware support to keep track of which blocks to invalidate (Cheong and Viedenbaum 1990). Other than nonstandard hardware and compiler support for coherence, the major problem with these approaches is that they rely on the automatic parallelization of sequential programs by the compiler, which is not very successful yet for realistic programs.

Shared Address Space without Coherent Replication

Systems in this category support a shared address space abstraction through the language and compiler but without automatic replication and coherence, just like the CRAY T3D and T3E did in hardware. One type of example is a data parallel language like High Performance Fortran (see Chapter 2). The distributions of data specified by the user, together with the owner computes rule, are used by the compiler or runtime system to translate off-node memory references to explicit messages, to make messages larger, to align data for better spatial locality, and so on. Replication and coherence are usually left up to the user, which compromises ease of programming; alternatively, system software may try to manage coherent replication in main memory automatically. Efforts similar to HPF are being made with languages based on C and C++ as well (Bodin et al. 1993; Larus, Richards, and Viswanathan 1996).

A more flexible language- and compiler-based approach is taken by the Split-C language (Culler et al. 1993). Here, the user explicitly specifies arrays as being local or global (shared) and for global arrays specifies how they should be laid out among physical memories. Computation may be assigned independently of the data layout, and references to global arrays are converted into messages by the compiler or run-time system based on the layout. The decoupling of computation assignment from data distribution makes the language much more flexible than an owner computes rule for load-balancing irregular programs, but it still does not provide automatic support for replication and coherence, which can be difficult for the programmer to manage. Of course, all these software systems can be easily ported to hardware-coherent shared address space machines, in which case the shared address space, replication, and coherence are implicitly provided. In this case, the run-time system may be used to manage replication and coherence in main memory and to transfer data in larger chunks than cache blocks, but these capabilities may not be necessary.

9.4 PUTTING IT ALL TOGETHER: A TAXONOMY AND SIMPLE COMA

The approaches to managing replication and coherence in the extended memory hierarchy discussed in this chapter have a range of goals: improving performance by replicating in main memory in the case of COMA and reducing cost in the case of SVM and the other systems of the previous section. Examining the management of replication and coherence in a unified framework leads to the design of alternative systems that can pick and choose aspects of existing ones. A useful framework is one that distinguishes the approaches along two closely related axes:

1. the granularities at which they allocate data in the lowest-level replication store, keep data coherent, and communicate data between nodes
2. the degree to which they utilize additional hardware support in the communication assist beyond that available in uniprocessor systems

The two axes are related because some functions are either not possible at fine granularity without additional hardware support (e.g., allocation of data in main memory) or not possible with high performance. The framework applies whether replication is done only in the cache (as in CC-NUMA) or in main memory.

Figure 9.18 depicts the overall framework and places different types of systems in it. We divide granularities into "page" and "block" (cache block) since these are the most common in transparent shared address space systems that do not require a stylized programming model such as objects. Other fine granularities such as individual words and coarse granularities such as objects or regions of memory can also be included in this framework. The granularities of allocation, coherence (access control), and communication influence one another, as we shall see.

On the left side of the figure are COMA systems, with allocation in main memory at the granularity of cache blocks using additional hardware support. CC-NUMA

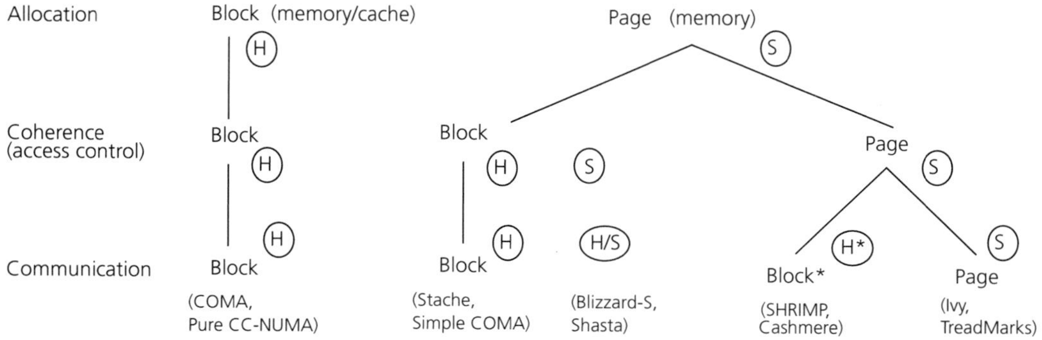

FIGURE 9.18 Granularities of allocation, coherence, and communication in coherent shared address space systems. The granularities specified are for the replication store in which data is first replicated automatically when it is brought into a node. This level is main memory in all the systems, except for pure CC-NUMA where it is the cache. Below each leaf in the taxonomy are listed some representative systems, protocols, or system families of that type, and next to each node is a letter indicating whether the support for that function is usually provided in hardware (H) or software (S). The asterisk next to "block" and "H" in one case means that not all communication is performed at fine granularity. Citations for these systems or system families include COMA (Hagersten, Landin, and Haridi 1992; Stenstrom, Joe, and Gupta 1992; Frank, Burkhardt, and Rothnie 1993), pure CC-NUMA (Laudon and Lenoski 1997), Stache (Reinhardt, Larus, and Wood 1994), Simple COMA (Saulsbury et al. 1995), Blizzard-S (Schoinas et al. 1994), Shasta (Scales, Gharachorloo, and Thekkath 1996), SHRIMP (Blumrich et al. 1994; Iftode et al. 1996), Cashmere (Kontothanassis and Scott 1996), Ivy (Li and Hudak 1989), and TreadMarks (Keleher et al. 1994).

systems that replicate data only in the cache, called pure CC-NUMA systems, also fall in this category. Given allocation at cache block granularity, it makes sense to keep data coherent at a granularity at least this fine as well and to communicate at fine granularity.[7]

On the right side of the figure are systems that allocate and manage space in main memory at page granularity, with no extra hardware needed for this function. These systems may provide access control and hence coherence at page granularity as well, as in SVM, in which case they may or may not provide support for fine-grained communication. Or they may provide access control and coherence at a finer, block granularity, using either software instrumentation or hardware support. Systems that support coherence at fine granularity typically provide some form of hardware support for efficient fine-grained communication as well.

7. This does not mean that fine-grained allocation necessarily implies fine-grained coherence or communication. For example, it is possible to exploit communication at coarse grain even when allocation and coherence are at fine grain to gain the benefits of large data transfers. However, the situations discussed are indeed the common case, and we shall focus on these.

9.4.1 Putting It All Together: Simple COMA and Stache

While COMA and SVM both replicate in main memory, and each addresses some but not all of the limitations of pure CC-NUMA, they are at two ends of the spectrum in the preceding taxonomy. COMA is a hardware-intensive solution and maintains fine granularities, but some issues that it raises in managing main memory (such as the last copy problem) are challenging for hardware. SVM leaves these complex memory management problems to system software—which simplifies hardware and enables main memory to be managed as a fully associative cache through the OS virtual-to-physical mappings—but its performance may suffer due to the large granularities and software overhead of coherence. The framework in Figure 9.18 leads to interesting ways to combine the low cost and hardware simplicity of SVM with the performance advantages and ease of programming of COMA; namely, the Simple COMA (Saulsbury et al. 1995) and Stache (Reinhardt, Larus, and Wood 1994) approaches shown in the middle of the figure. These approaches divide the task of coherent replication in main memory into two parts: memory management (address translation, allocation, and replacement) and coherence (including replication and communication). Like COMA, these approaches provide coherence at fine granularity with specialized hardware support for high performance, but like SVM (and unlike COMA), they leave memory management to the operating system at page granularity. Let us begin with Simple COMA.

The major appeal of Simple COMA relative to COMA is design simplicity. Performing memory management through the virtual memory system simplifies the hardware protocol and also allows fully associative management of the attraction memory with arbitrary replacement policies. To provide coherence or access control at fine grain in hardware, each page in a node's main memory is divided into coherence blocks of any chosen size (say, a cache block), and state information is maintained in hardware for each of these blocks. Unlike in COMA, there is no need for tags since the presence check is done at page level. The page permission is checked, as usual, before the block is accessed. The state of the block is checked in parallel with the memory access when a miss occurs in the processor cache. Thus, there are two levels of access control: for the page, under operating system control, and if that succeeds, then for the block, under hardware control.

Consider the performance trade-offs relative to COMA. Simple COMA reduces the latency for accesses satisfied in the local attraction memory (which is hopefully the frequent case among cache misses). There is no need for the hardware tag comparison and selection used in COMA or in fact for the local/remote address check that is needed in pure CC-NUMA machines to determine whether to look up the local memory. On the other hand, every cache miss looks up the local attraction memory, so like in COMA the path of a nonlocal access is longer. Since a shared page can reside in different physical addresses in different memories, controlled independently by the node operating systems, unlike in COMA we cannot simply send a block's physical address across the network on a miss and use it at the other end. This means that we must support a shared virtual, rather than physical, address space. However, the virtual address issued by the processor is no longer available by the time the attraction memory miss is detected. The physical address, which is available, must be "reverse translated" to a virtual address or other globally consistent identifier; this identifier is sent across the network and is translated back to a (potentially different) physical address by the other node. This process incurs some added latency and is discussed further in Section 9.6.

Another drawback of Simple COMA compared to COMA is that, although communication and coherence are at fine granularity, allocation is at page granularity. This can lead to fragmentation in main memory when the access patterns of an application do not match page granularity well. If a processor accesses only one word of a remote page, only that coherence block will be communicated, but space will be allocated in the local main memory for the whole page. Similarly, if only one block is brought in for an unallocated page, it may have to replace an entire page of useful data (fortunately, the replacement is fully associative and under the control of software, which can make sophisticated choices). In contrast, COMA systems typically allocate space for only that coherence block in the attraction memory. Simple COMA is therefore more sensitive to spatial locality than COMA.

An approach similar to Simple COMA is taken in the Stache design proposed for the Typhoon system (Reinhardt, Larus, and Wood 1994) and implemented in the Typhoon-0 research prototype (Reinhardt, Pfile, and Wood 1996). Unlike Simple COMA, Stache does not manage all of memory as a cache but uses the tertiary cache approach discussed earlier for replication in main memory; however, like Simple COMA it manages allocation at page level in software and coherence at fine grain in hardware. The assist in the Typhoon systems is programmable, and physical addresses are reverse translated to virtual addresses rather than other global identifiers to enable protocol handlers to be written in user-level software (see Section 9.6). Designs have also been proposed to combine the benefits of CC-NUMA and Simple COMA (Falsafi and Wood 1997).

Summary: Path of a Read Reference

Consider the path of a read in Simple COMA. The virtual address is first translated to a physical address by the processor's memory management unit. If a page fault occurs, space must be allocated for a new page, though data for the page is not loaded in. The virtual memory system decides which page to replace, if any, and establishes the new mapping. To preserve inclusion, data for the replaced page must be flushed or invalidated from the cache. All blocks on the newly mapped page are set to invalid. The physical address is then used to look up the cache hierarchy. If it hits (it will not if a page fault occurred), the reference is satisfied. If not, then it looks up the local attraction memory, where by now the locations are guaranteed to correspond to that page. If the block of interest is in a valid state, the reference completes. If not, the physical address is reverse translated to a global identifier that plays the role of a virtual address, which is sent across the network guided by the directory coherence protocol. The remote node translates this global identifier to a local physical address, uses this physical address to find the block in its memory hierarchy, and sends the block back to the requestor. The block is then loaded into the local attraction memory and cache and the data is delivered to the processor.

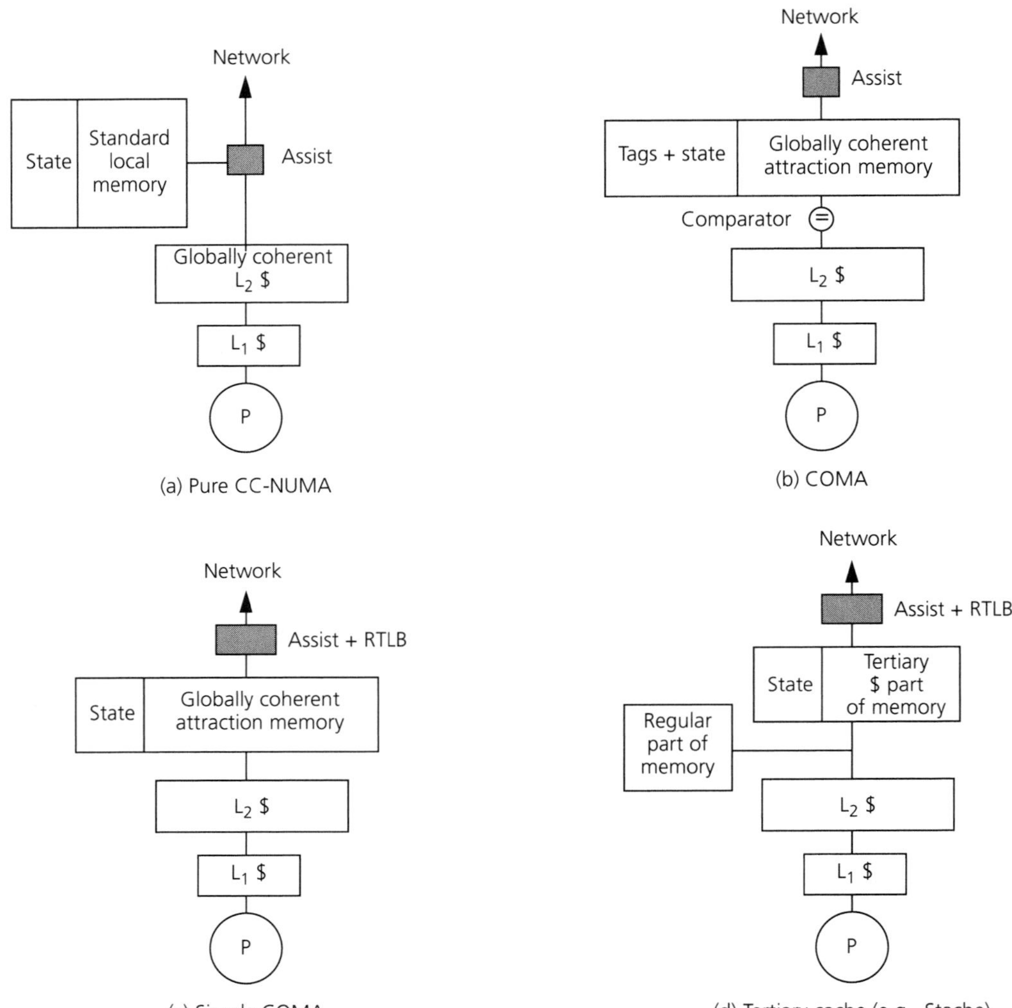

FIGURE 9.19 Logical structure of a typical node in four approaches to a coherent shared address space. The common property of the approaches is that they maintain coherence at fine granularity in hardware. A vertical path through the node in the figures traces the path of a read miss that must be satisfied remotely (going through main memory means that main memory must be looked up, though this may be done in parallel with issuing the remote request if speculative lookups are used). RTLB stands for reverse translation lookaside buffer, and is a structure that provides reverse translation of addresses from physical to virtual (or to a global identifier).

Figure 9.19 summarizes the node structure of the approaches that use hardware support to preserve coherence at fine granularity.

9.5 IMPLICATIONS FOR PARALLEL SOFTWARE

Let us examine the implications for parallel software of all the approaches discussed in this chapter, beyond the parallel programming issues already discussed in earlier chapters.

Relaxed memory consistency models require that parallel programs label the desired conflicting accesses as synchronization operations. The insertion points are usually quite stylized, for example, looking for variables that a process spins on in a while loop before proceeding; but sometimes orders must be preserved even without spin-waiting, as in some of the examples in Figure 9.4. A programming language may provide support to label some variables or accesses as synchronization, which will then be translated by the compiler to the appropriate order-preserving instructions. Current programming languages do not provide integrated support for such labeling but rely on the programmer inserting special instructions or calls to a synchronization library. Labels can also be used by the compiler itself to restrict its own reorderings of accesses to shared memory. One mechanism is to declare some (or all) shared variables to be of a "volatile" type, which means that those variables will not be allocated in registers and will not be reordered with respect to the accesses around them. Recall that register allocation of shared variables can cause coherence to be violated as well, so key shared variables like flags are often declared to be volatile for coherence itself, even under sequential consistency. Some new compilers also recognize explicit synchronization calls and don't reorder memory operations across them (perhaps distinguishing between acquire and release calls) or obey orders with respect to special order-preserving instructions that the program may insert.

The automatic, fine-grained replication and migration provided by COMA machines is designed to allow the programmer to ignore the distributed nature of main memory. It is very useful when capacity or conflict misses dominate and data accesses are fine-grained. Experience with parallel applications indicates that because of the nature of working sets and the sizes of caches in modern systems, the migration feature may be more broadly useful than replication and coherence; that is, the benefits arise less frequently from having copies of a block present in multiple main (attraction) memories and more frequently from bringing the single copy of the data to the right attraction memory for a phase of computation. Of course, systems with small caches or applications with large, unstructured working sets can benefit from replication in main memory as well. Fine-grained, automatic migration is particularly useful when the data structures in the program cannot easily be distributed appropriately at page granularity, so page migration techniques such as those provided by the Origin2000 or even explicit page migration or placement may not be so successful; for example, when data that should be allocated on two different nodes falls on the same page (see Section 8.9). Data migration is also very useful in conjunction with process migration, although this case is likely to be handled quite well by data migration at page granularity.

In general, although COMA systems suffer from higher communication latencies than CC-NUMA systems, they may allow a wider set of workloads to perform well with less programming effort. Interestingly, in flat COMA systems, explicit migration and proper data (home) placement can still be moderately useful despite the COMA nature. This is because ownership requests on writes still go to the directory, which may be remote and does not migrate with the data, and thus can cause extra traffic and contention even if only a single processor ever writes a page.

Commodity-oriented systems put more pressure on software not only to reduce communication volume but also to orchestrate data access and communication carefully since the costs and/or granularities of communication are much larger. Consider shared virtual memory, which performs communication and coherence at page granularity. The actual data access and sharing patterns interact with this granularity to produce an induced sharing pattern at page granularity, which is the pattern relevant to the system (Iftode, Singh, and Li 1996a). Other than by a high communication-to-computation ratio, performance is adversely affected when the induced pattern involves write sharing (and hence multiple writers of the same page) or fragmentation in communication. This makes it important to try to structure programs so that accesses from different processes tend not to be interleaved at a fine granularity in the address space. The high cost of synchronization and the dilation of critical sections due to page faults within them makes it especially important to reduce the use of synchronization in programming for SVM systems. Finally, the high cost of communication and synchronization may make it more difficult to use task stealing successfully for dynamic load balancing in SVM systems. The remote accesses and synchronization needed for stealing may be so expensive that little work is left to steal by the time stealing is successful. It is therefore much more important to have a well-balanced initial assignment of tasks for a task-stealing-based computation in an SVM system than in a hardware-coherent system (Jiang, Shan, and Singh 1997). In general, the importance of different programming and algorithmic optimizations depend on the communication costs and granularities of the system at hand.

9.6 ADVANCED TOPICS

Before we conclude this chapter, let us discuss two other topics: other limitations of the traditional CC-NUMA approach and the mechanisms and techniques that enable software to take advantage of relaxed memory consistency models, for example, in shared virtual memory protocols.

9.6.1 Flexibility and Address Constraints in CC-NUMA Systems

Two other limitations of traditional, pure CC-NUMA systems are the fact that a single coherence protocol is hardwired into the machine and the potential limitations of addressability in a shared physical address space. Let us discuss each in turn.

Providing Flexibility

One size never really fits all. It is always possible to find workloads that would be better served by a different protocol than the one hardwired into a given machine.

For example, while we have seen that invalidation-based protocols overall have advantages over update-based protocols for cache-coherent systems, update-based protocols are advantageous for purely producer-consumer sharing patterns. For a one-word producer-consumer interaction, in an invalidation-based protocol the producer will generate an invalidation that will be acknowledged, and then the consumer will issue a read miss that the producer will satisfy, leading to four network transactions; an update-based protocol will need only one transaction in this case. As another example, if large amounts of predeterminable data are to be communicated from one node to another, then it may be useful to transfer them in a single large explicit message instead of one cache block at a time through load and store misses. A single protocol may not even best fit all phases or all data structures of a single application, or even the same data structure in different phases of the application. If the performance advantages of using different protocols in different situations are substantial, it may be useful to support multiple protocols in the communication architecture. This is particularly likely when the performance penalty for mismatched protocols is very high, as in commodity-based systems with less efficient communication architectures.

Protocols can be altered—or mixed and matched—by making the protocol processing part of the communication assist programmable rather than hardwired, thus implementing the protocol in software rather than hardware. This is clearly quite natural in software implementations of coherence protocols where the protocol is in programmable software handlers. For hardware-supported, fine-grained coherence, it turns out that the requirements placed on a programmable assist by different protocols are usually very similar. On the control side, they all need quick dispatch to a protocol handler, based on a transaction type, and support for efficient bit-field manipulation in tags. On the data side, they need high-bandwidth, low-overhead pipelined movement of data through the controller and network interface. The Sequent NUMA-Q discussed in Chapter 8 provides a pipelined, specialized programmable coherence controller, as does the Stanford FLASH design (Kuskin et al. 1994; Heinrich et al. 1994). Note that the controller being programmable doesn't alter the need for specialized hardware support for coherence; those issues remain the same as with a fixed protocol.

The protocol code that runs on the controllers in these fine-grained coherent machines operates in privileged mode so that it can communicate and use the physical addresses that it sees on the bus directly. Some researchers also advocate that users be allowed to write their own protocol handlers in user-level software so they can customize protocols to match the needs of individual applications much better than a predetermined library of system protocols can (Falsafi et al. 1994). While this can be advantageous, particularly on machines with less efficient communication architectures, it introduces several complications. For example, since the address translation is already done by the processor's memory management unit by the time a cache miss is detected, the assist sees only physical addresses on the bus. However, to maintain protection, user-level protocol software cannot be allowed access to these physical addresses. So if protocol software is to run on the assist at the other end at the user level, the physical addresses must be reverse translated back to virtual addresses before this software can use them. Such reverse translation (which was also needed for Simple COMA systems for a different reason) requires further hardware support, increases latency, and is complicated to implement. In addition, since protocols have many subtle complexities related to correctness and deadlock and are difficult to debug, it is not clear how desirable it is to allow users to write protocols that may deadlock a shared machine.

Overcoming Physical Address Space Limitations

In a shared physical address space, the assist making a request sends the physical address of the location (or cache block) across the network, to be interpreted by the assist at the other end. While this has the advantage that the assist at the other end does not have to reverse translate addresses before accessing physical memory, a problem arises when the physical addresses generated by the processor may not have enough bits to serve as global addresses for the entire shared physical address space, as we saw for the CRAY T3D in Chapter 7 (the Alpha 21064 processor emitted only 32 bits of physical address, insufficient to address the 128 GB or 37 bits of physical memory in a 2,048-processor machine). In the T3D, segmentation through the annex registers was used to extend the address space, potentially introducing delays into the critical paths of memory accesses. The alternative is not to have a shared physical address space but to send virtual addresses across the network that will be retranslated to (potentially different) physical addresses at the other end. As we have seen, SVM and Simple COMA systems use this approach of implementing a shared virtual rather than physical address space, as do user-level programmable protocols.

One advantage of this approach is that now only the virtual addresses need to be large enough to index the entire shared (virtual) address space; physical addresses need only be large enough to address a given processor's main memory. A second advantage, seen earlier, is that each node manages its own address space and virtual-to-physical translations, so more flexible allocation and replacement policies can be used in main memory. However, this approach does require address translation at both ends of each communication.

9.6.2 Implementing Relaxed Memory Consistency in Software

The discussion of shared virtual memory schemes that exploit release consistency showed that such schemes can be either single writer or multiple writer and can propagate coherence information at either release or acquire operations. A range of techniques can be used to implement these schemes, successively adding complexity, enabling new schemes, and making the propagation of write notices and data lazier. The techniques are too complex and require too many structures to implement in hardware, and the problems they alleviate are much less severe in that case. However, they are quite well suited to software implementation. Although SVM is not currently a mainstream commercial technology, the techniques are valuable for understanding what is necessary for preserving different degrees of the laziness afforded by a relaxed consistency model. This section examines the techniques and their trade-offs.

The three basic functions for coherence protocols that were raised in Section 8.1 are answered somewhat differently in SVM schemes. To begin with, the protocol is invoked not only at data access faults as in the hardware cache coherence schemes but both at access faults (to find the necessary data) and at synchronization points (to communicate coherence information in write notices). The first two important functions—finding the source of coherence information and determining with which processors to communicate—depend on whether release-based or acquire-based coherence is used. In the former, we need to send write notices to all valid copies at a release, so we need a mechanism to keep track of the copies. In the latter, the acquirer communicates with only the last releaser of the synchronization variable and pulls all the necessary write notices from there to only itself, so there is no need to explicitly keep track of all copies. The last function is communication with the necessary nodes (or copies), which is typically done with point-to-point messages.

Since coherence information is not propagated at individual write faults but only at synchronization events, a new question arises: how do we determine for which pages write notices should be sent? In release-based schemes, since write notices are sent at every release to all currently valid copies, a node has only to send out write notices for writes that it performed since its previous release. All previous write notices in a causal sense (see Section 9.3.3) have already been sent to all relevant copies, either directly at the corresponding previous releases or indirectly through other processes. In acquire-based methods, we must ensure that causally necessary write notices, which may have been produced by many different nodes, will be seen even though the acquirer goes only to the previous releaser to obtain them. The releaser cannot simply send the acquirer the write notices it has produced since its last release or even the write notices it has ever produced, but must also send the causally related write notices that it has received from other nodes at its own previous acquires. In both release- and acquire-based cases, several mechanisms are available to reduce the number of write notices communicated and applied. These include version numbers and time stamps, and we shall see them as we go along. Protocols also vary in when they propagate write notices (and data) and when they apply, implementing different degrees of laziness within an acquire- or release-based approach, as we will see.

To understand the issues more clearly, let us first examine how we might implement single writer release consistency using both release-based and acquire-based approaches. Then we will do the same thing for multiple writer protocols.

Single Writer with Consistency at Release

The simplest way to maintain consistency is to send write notices at every release to all sharers of the pages that the releasing processor has written since its last release. In a single writer protocol, the copies can be kept track of by making the current owner of a page (the one with write permission) maintain the current sharing list and by transferring the list at ownership changes (when another node writes the page). At a release, a node sends write notices for all pages it has written to the nodes indicated on its sharing lists (see Exercise 9.31).

There are two performance problems with this scheme. First, since ownership transfer does not cause copies to be invalidated (read-only copies may coexist with one writable copy, unlike in hardware coherence schemes), a previous owner and the new owner may very well have the same nodes on their sharing lists. When both of them reach release points (whether of the same synchronization variable or different ones), they will both send invalidations to some of the same pages, so a page may receive multiple (unnecessary) invalidations. This problem can be solved by using a single designated place to keep track of which copies of a page have already been invalidated, for example, by using memory-based directories to keep track of sharing lists instead of maintaining them at the dynamically changing owners. The directory is looked up before write notices are sent, and invalidated copies are recorded at the directory so that multiple invalidations won't be sent to the same copy.

The second problem is that a release may invalidate a more recent copy of the page than the one that was written, which it needn't have done, as illustrated in Figure 9.20. (It won't invalidate the most recent copy at the current owner, so this is not a correctness problem.) This can be solved by associating a *version number* with each copy of a page. A node increments its version number for a page whenever it obtains ownership of that page from another node. Without directories, a processor will send write notices to all sharers at a release (since it doesn't know their version numbers) together with its version number for that page, but only the receivers that have smaller version numbers will actually invalidate their pages. With directories, the write notice traffic can be reduced as well, not just the number of invalidations applied and page faults experienced, by maintaining the version numbers of copies at the directory entry for the page and only sending write notices to copies that have lower version numbers than the releaser. Both ownership and write notice requests come to the directory, so this is easy to manage. Thus, using directories together with version numbers solves both of the preceding problems. However, this is still a release-based scheme, so invalidations may be sent out and applied earlier than necessary, causing unnecessary page faults.

Single Writer with Consistency at Acquire

Here is a simple way to use the fact that coherence activity is not needed until an acquire: the releaser still sends out write notices to all copies but does this only when the next acquire request from any process comes in, not at the release. This delays the sending of write notices. However, the incoming acquire must wait until the releaser has sent out the write notices and acknowledgments have been received, which is now in the critical path of the acquire operation. The best bet for such fundamentally release-based approaches would be to send write notices out eagerly at the release but wait for acknowledgments only before responding to the next incoming acquire request. This allows the propagation of write notices and acknowledgments to be overlapped with the computation done between the release and the next incoming acquire. Regardless of when write notices are propagated (which affects traffic), a receiving process may choose to apply them to pages as soon as they are

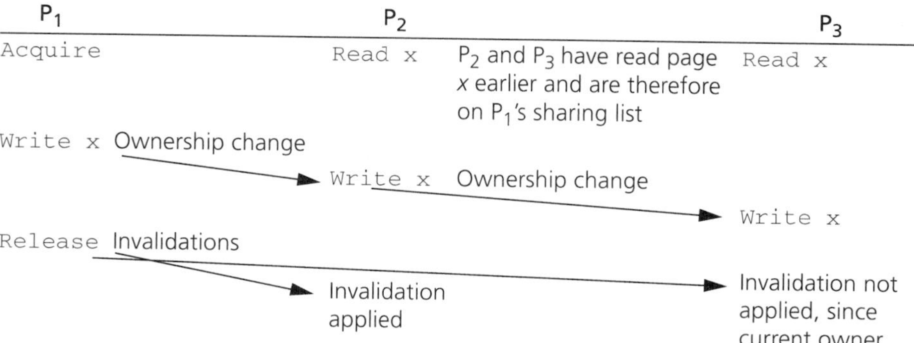

FIGURE 9.20 Invalidation of a more recent copy in a simple single writer protocol. Processor P_2 takes ownership from P_1 and then P_3 from P_2. But P_1's release happens after all this. At the release, P_1 sends invalidations to both P_2 and P_3. P_2 applies the invalidation even though its copy is more recent than P_1's (since it doesn't know) while P_3 does not apply the invalidation since it is the current owner.

received or at the next acquire that it performs, thus implementing different degrees of laziness.

Consider now the lazier, pull-based method of propagating consistency information only at an acquire, from the releaser to only that acquirer. The acquirer sends a request to the last releaser (the current holder) of the synchronization variable, whose identity it can obtain from a designated manager node for that variable. This is the only place from which the acquirer is obtaining information, yet it must see all writes that have happened before it in the causal order. With no additional support, the releaser must send to the acquirer all write notices that the releaser has either produced so far or received from others (at least since the last time it sent this acquirer write notices, if it keeps track of that). It cannot send only those that it has produced since the last release since it has no idea how many of the other necessary write notices the acquirer has already seen through previous acquires from other processes. The acquirer, too, must retain those write notices to pass on to the next acquirer.

Carrying around an entire history of write notices is obviously not a good idea. Version numbers, incremented at changes of ownership as before, can help reduce the number of invalidations applied (and hence access faults) if they are communicated along with the write notices, but they do not help reduce the number of write notices sent. The acquirer cannot communicate version numbers to the releaser to reduce traffic since it has no idea for which pages the releaser wants to send it write notices. And directories with version numbers don't help reduce the traffic either since the releaser would have to send the directory the history of write notices. In fact, what the acquirer wants is the write notices corresponding to all releases that precede it causally and that it hasn't already obtained through its previous acquires.

Keeping information at page level doesn't help to achieve this, since neither acquirer nor releaser knows which pages the other has seen write notices for and neither wants to send the information it knows for all pages. The solution is to establish a system of per-process or per-node virtual time, in which time-steps are demarcated by synchronization events. Conceptually, every node keeps track of the virtual time period up to which it has seen write notices from each other node. An acquire sends the previous releaser only this time vector; the releaser compares it with its own and sends the acquirer write notices corresponding to time periods that the releaser has seen but the acquirer hasn't. Since the partial orders to be satisfied for causality are based on synchronization events, associating time increments with synchronization events lets us represent these partial orders explicitly.

More precisely, the execution of every process is divided into a number of *intervals*, a new one beginning (and a local interval counter for that process incrementing) whenever the process successfully executes a release or an acquire. The intervals of different processes are partially ordered by the desired precedence relationships of causality discussed in Section 9.3.3: (1) intervals on a single process are totally ordered by the program order, and (2) an interval on process P precedes an interval on process Q if its release precedes Q's acquire for that interval in a chain of release-acquire operations on the same variable. That is, intervals are also ordered by dependence order, which may not be statically determined. Since interval numbers are maintained and incremented locally per process, the partial order described in (2) does not mean that the acquiring process's interval number will necessarily be larger than the releasing process's interval number. What it does mean, and what we must ensure, is that if a releaser has seen write notices for interval 8 from process X, then the next (dynamic) acquirer of that synchronization variable should also have seen at least interval 8 from process X before it is allowed to complete its acquire. To keep track of what intervals a process has seen from other processes and hence preserve the partial orders, every process maintains a *vector time stamp* for each of its intervals (Keleher et al. 1994). Let V^P_i be the vector time stamp for interval i on process P. The number of elements in the vector V^P_i equals the number of processes. The entry for process P itself in V^P_i is equal to i. For any other process Q, the entry denotes the most recent interval of process Q that precedes interval i on process P in the partial orders. Thus, the vector time stamp indicates the most recent interval from every other process for which this process should have already received and applied write notices (through a previous acquire) by the time it enters interval i.

On an acquire, a process P needs to obtain from the last releaser R write notices pertaining to intervals (from any process) that R has seen before its release but the acquirer has not yet seen through a previous acquire. This is enough to ensure causality: any other intervals that P should have seen from other processes, it would have seen through previous acquires in its program order. P therefore sends its current vector time stamp (for its interval $i - 1$) to R, thus telling it which are the latest intervals from other processes it has seen before this acquire. R compares P's incoming vector time stamp with its own, entry by entry, and piggybacks on its reply to P write notices for all intervals that are included as having been seen in R's current time stamp but not in P's (this is conservative since R's current time stamp may have seen more than R had at the time of the relevant release). Since P has now received these write notices, it sets its new vector time stamp (for the interval i that starts with the current acquire) to the pairwise maximum of R's vector time stamp and its own previous one. P is now up-to-date in the partial orders. This means that a process must retain the write notices that it has either produced or received from other processes until it is certain that no later acquirer will need them. This is unlike a release-based protocol in which write notices could be discarded by the releaser once they had been sent to all copies. It can lead to significant storage overhead and may require garbage collection techniques to keep the storage in check.

Multiple Writer with Release-Based Consistency

With multiple writers, the key new issue is the management and merging of data (e.g., diffs) from multiple writers. The type of protocol we use for write notices and consistency depends on how the propagation of data is managed; that is, whether diffs are maintained at the multiple writers or propagated at a release to a fixed home. In either case, with release-based schemes a process need only send write notices for the writes it has done since its previous release to all copies and wait for acknowledgments for them at the next incoming acquire, as in the single writer case. However, since there is no single owner (writer) of a page at a given time, we cannot rely on an owner having an up-to-date copy of the sharing list. We must either broadcast write notices or use a mechanism like a directory to keep track of copies.

The next question is, how does a process find the necessary data (diffs) when it incurs a page fault after an invalidation? If a home-based protocol is used to manage multiple writers, then this is easy: the page or diffs can be found at the home (a release must wait until the diffs reach the home before it completes so that a page fault following a dependent acquire is guaranteed to see the corresponding writes). If diffs are maintained at the writers (i.e., in a distributed form), the faulting process must know not only from where to obtain the diffs but also in what order they should be applied. This is because diffs for the same data may have been produced either in different intervals in the same process or in intervals on different processes but in the same causal chain of acquires and releases; when they arrive at a processor, they must be applied in accordance with the partial orders needed for causality. The locations of the diffs may be determined from the incoming write notices, but the order of application is difficult to determine without vector time stamps. However, vector time stamps obtain their full use only in acquire-based protocols, as we have seen. This is why, when homes are not used for data, simple directory and release-based (eager) multiple writer coherence schemes use updates rather than invalidations as the write notices: the diffs themselves are sent to the sharers at the release. Thus, the protocol and mechanisms used for consistency are changed from the single writer release-based case. Since a release waits for acknowledgments before completing, there is no ordering problem in applying diffs even though vector time stamps are not used. The diffs are guaranteed to reach processors exactly according to the desired partial order. This type of update-based, eager, multiple writer protocol was used in the Munin system (Carter, Bennett, and Zwaenepoel 1991).

Consider the use of more sophisticated tracking mechanisms for consistency. Version numbers are not useful with multiple writer schemes. We can no longer update version numbers at ownership changes (since there are none) but only at release points. And, in that case, version numbers don't help us save write notices: since the releaser has just obtained the latest version number for the page at the release itself, there is no question of another node having a more recent version number for that page. In addition, because a releaser has to send only the write notices (or diffs) it has produced since its previous release, there is no need for vector time stamps with an update-based eager protocol. (Time stamps would have been needed to ensure that diffs were applied in the correct order if diffs were not sent out at a release but retained at the releaser in an invalidation-based protocol, as discussed previously.)

Multiple Writer with Acquire-Based Consistency

The issues and mechanisms for a multiple writer acquire-based protocol are very similar to the single writer acquire-based schemes—the main difference is in how the data is managed. With no special support, the acquirer must obtain from the last releaser all write notices that the releaser has produced or received since their last interaction, so large histories must be maintained and communicated. As in the single writer case, version numbers can help reduce the number of invalidations applied but not the number transferred. (With home-based schemes, the version number can be incremented every time a diff gets to the home, but the releaser must wait to receive this number before it satisfies the next incoming acquire; without homes, a separate version manager must be designated anyway for a page, which causes complications.) The best method is to use vector time stamps as described earlier. The vector time stamps manage the transfers of write notices (coherence information) for home-based schemes; for nonhome-based schemes, they also manage the obtaining and application of diffs (i.e., data) in the right order (the order dictated by the time stamps that came with the write notices).

To implement acquire-based LRC, then, a processor has to maintain many auxiliary data structures. These include the following:

- An array, indexed by process, for every page in its local memory, each entry of which is a list of write notices or diffs received from that process for that page.
- A separate single array, indexed by process, each entry of which is a pointer to a list of interval records. The entry for a process represents the intervals of that process for which the current process has already received write notices. An interval record points to the corresponding list of write notices, and each write notice points to its interval record.
- A free pool for creating diffs.

Since these data structures, especially diffs, may have to be kept around for a period that is determined by the partial precedence orders established at run time, they can limit the sizes of problems that can be run and the scalability of the approach. Home-based approaches help reduce diff storage: diffs do not have to be retained at the releaser past the release, and the first array listed previously does not have to maintain lists of diffs received. Details of these mechanisms can be found in (Keleher et al. 1994; Zhou, Iftode, and Li 1996).

9.7 CONCLUDING REMARKS

The alternative approaches to supporting coherent replication in a shared address space discussed in this chapter raise many interesting sets of hardware/software trade-offs. Relaxed memory models increase the burden on application software to label programs correctly but allow compilers to perform their optimizations and hardware to exploit more low-level concurrency. COMA and related systems require greater hardware complexity but simplify the job of the programmer by reducing the importance of data placement. Their effect on performance depends greatly on the characteristics of the application (i.e., whether sharing misses or capacity misses dominate internode communication) and on the extent to which remote access latency and assist occupancy are increased. Finally, commodity-based approaches reduce system cost and provide a better incremental procurement model for users, but they often require substantially greater programming care to achieve good performance.

These alternative approaches are still controversial, and the trade-offs have not shaken out. While relaxed memory models are very useful for compilers, we will see in Chapter 11 that some modern processors are electing to implement sequential consistency at the hardware/software interface (or processor consistency in the case of the Intel Pentium Pro) with increasingly sophisticated alternative techniques to obtain overlap and hide latency. Contracts between the programmer and the system have also not been very well integrated into current programming languages and compilers. As for replication in main memory, full hardware support for COMA was implemented in the KSR1 (Frank, Burkhardt, and Rothnie 1993) but is not very popular in systems being built today because of its cost. However, approaches similar to Simple COMA are beginning to find acceptance in commercial products.

All-software approaches like page-grained SVM and fine-grained software access control have been demonstrated to achieve good performance at a relatively small scale for some classes of applications. Because they are very easy to build and deploy, they will likely be used on clusters of workstations and SMPs in several environments. However, the gap between these and the all-hardware systems is still quite large in programmability as well as in performance on a wide range of applications, more so than for message passing, and their scalability has not yet been demonstrated. The commodity-based approaches are still in the research stages, and it remains to be seen if they will become viable competitors to hardware cache-coherent machines for a large enough set of applications. It may be that the commoditization of hardware coherence assists and the methods to integrate them into memory systems will make these all-software approaches more marginal, for use largely in those environments that do not wish to purchase parallel machines but rather to use clusters of existing machines as shared address space multiprocessors when they are otherwise idle (or to develop early versions of parallel applications). At least in the short term, economic reasons might nonetheless provide all-software solutions with another role. Since vendors are likely to build tightly coupled systems with only a few tens or a hundred nodes, connecting these hardware-coherent systems together with a software coherence layer may be the most viable way to construct very large machines that still support the coherent shared address space programming model. While supporting this programming model on scalable systems with physically distributed memory is well established as a desirable way to build systems, only time will tell how these alternative approaches will play out.

9.8 EXERCISES

9.1 Why are update-based coherence schemes relatively incompatible with the sequential consistency memory model in a directory-based machine?

9.2 The Intel Paragon machine discussed in Chapter 7 has two processing elements per node, one of which always executes in kernel mode to support communication. Could this processor be used effectively as a programmable communication assist to support cache coherence at cache block granularity in hardware, like the programmable assist of the Stanford FLASH or the Sequent NUMA-Q?

9.3 In the Origin protocol discussed in Chapter 8, it would be possible for other read and write requests to come to the requestor that has outstanding invalidations before the acknowledgments for those invalidations come in.

a. Is this possible or a problem with delayed-exclusive replies? With eager-exclusive replies? If it is a problem, what is the simplest way to solve it?

b. Suppose you did indeed want to allow the requestor with invalidations outstanding to process incoming read and write requests. Consider write requests first, and construct an example where this can lead to problems. (Hint: consider the case where P_1 writes to a location A, P_2 writes to location B and then writes a flag, and P_3 spins on the flag and then reads the value of location B.) How would you allow the incoming write to be handled but still maintain correctness? Is it easier if invalidation acknowledgments are collected at the home (as in the Stanford FLASH machine) or at the requestor (as in the Origin)?

c. Now answer the questions in part (b) for incoming read requests.

d. What if you were using an update-based protocol? What complexities arise in allowing an incoming request to be processed for a block that has updates outstanding from a previous write, and how might you solve them?

e. Overall, would you choose to allow incoming requests to be processed while invalidations or updates are outstanding, or deny them?

9.4 Suppose a block needs to be written back while invalidations are pending for it. Can this lead to problems, or is it safe? If it is problematic, how might you address the problem?

9.5 Are eager-exclusive replies useful with an underlying SC model? Are they at all useful if the processor itself allows out-of-order completion of memory operations, unlike the MIPS R10000?

9.6 Do the trade-offs between collecting acknowledgments at the home and at the requestor change if eager-exclusive replies are used instead of delayed-exclusive replies?

9.7 If the compiler reorders accesses according to WO and the processor's memory model is SC, what is the consistency model at the programmer's interface? What if the compiler is SC and does not reorder memory operations but the processor implements RMO?

9.8 In addition to reordering memory operations (reads and writes) as discussed in Example 9.1 in this chapter, register allocation by a compiler can also eliminate memory accesses entirely. Consider the following example code fragment. Show how register allocation can violate SC. Can a uniprocessor compiler do this? How would you prevent it in the compiler you normally use?

P_1	P_2
`A = 1`	`while (flag == 0);`
`flag = 1`	`u = A`

9.9 Consider all the system specifications discussed in this chapter. Arrange them in order of weakness; that is, draw arcs between models such that an arc from model *A* to model *B* indicates that *A* is stronger than *B* (i.e., any execution that is correct under *A* is also correct under *B* but not necessarily vice versa).

9.10 Which of PC and TSO is better suited to update-based directory protocols, and why?

9.11 Can you describe a more relaxed system specification than release consistency without explicitly associating data with synchronization, as in entry consistency? Does it require additional programming care beyond RC?

9.12 Can you describe a looser set of sufficient conditions for WO? For RC?

9.13 Using the fence operations provided by the DEC Alpha and Sparc RMO consistency specifications, describe how you would need to insert these operations to ensure that a program obeys each of the following models: RC, WO, PSO, TSO, and SC? Which ones do you expect to be implemented efficiently in this way and which ones not, and why?

9.14 A *write-fence* operation (like the write-memory barrier in the Alpha architecture) stalls subsequent write operations until all of the processor's previous write operations have completed. A *full fence* stalls the processor until all of its previous memory operations have completed.

a. Insert the minimum number of fence instructions into the following code to make it sequentially consistent, assuming that otherwise the system does not preserve any program orders. Don't use a full fence when a write fence will suffice.

```
ACQUIRE LOCK1
LOAD A
STORE A
RELEASE LOCK1
LOAD B
STORE B
ACQUIRE LOCK1
LOAD C
STORE C
RELEASE LOCK1
```

b. Repeat part (a) to guarantee release consistency.

9.15 Given the following code segments, what combination of values for (*u*,*v*,*w*,*x*) are not allowed by SC? In each case, do the IBM 370, TSO, PSO, PC, RC, and WO models preserve SC semantics without any ordering instructions or labels, or do they not? (The IBM 370 consistency model is much like TSO, except that it does not allow a read to return the value written by a previous write in program order until that write has completed.) If not, insert the necessary fence operations to make them conform to SC. Assume that all variables had the value 0 before this code fragment was reached.

a.

P_1	P_2
A = 1	B = 1
u = A	v = B
w = B	x = A

b.

P_1	P_2
A = 1	B = 1
C = 1	C = 2
u = C	v = C
w = B	x = A

9.16 Consider a two-level coherence protocol with snooping-based SMPs connected by a memory-based directory protocol, using release consistency. While invalidation acknowledgments are still pending for a write to a memory block, is it okay to supply the data to another processor in (a) the same SMP node, or (b) a different SMP node? Justify your answers and state any assumptions.

9.17 Can a program that is not properly labeled run correctly on a system that supports release consistency? If so, how, and if not, why not?

9.18 Why are there four flavor bits for memory barriers in the Sun Sparc V9 specification? Why not just two bits, one to wait for all previous writes to complete and another for previous reads to complete?

9.19 To communicate labeling information to the hardware (i.e., that a memory operation is labeled as an acquire or a release), there are two options: one is to associate the label with the address of the location; the other is to associate the label with the specific operation in the code. What are the trade-offs between the two?

9.20 Two processors P_1 and P_2 are executing the following code fragments under the sequential consistency (SC) and release consistency (RC) models.

P_1	P_2
`LOCK (L1)`	`LOCK (L1)`
`A = 1`	`x = A`
`B = 2`	`y = B`
`UNLOCK (L1)`	`x1 = A`
	`UNLOCK (L1)`
	`x2 = B`

Assume an architecture where both read and write misses take 100 cycles to complete. However, you can assume that accesses that are allowed to be overlapped under the consistency model are indeed fully overlapped. Acquiring a free lock from another processor or unlocking a lock takes 100 cycles, and no overlap is possible with lock-unlock operations from the same processor. Assume all the variables and locks are initially uncached and all locks are unlocked, that all memory locations are initialized to 0, and that all memory locations are distinct and map to different indices in the caches (i.e., different cache lines).

a. What are the possible outcomes for `x` and `y` under SC? Under RC?

b. Assume P_1 gets the lock first. After how much time from the start of P_1's lock operation will P_2 complete all its operations while satisfying the sufficient conditions for SC described in Chapter 5? What if it satisfies the sufficient conditions for RC described in this chapter?

9.21 Given the following code fragment, we want to compute its execution time under various memory consistency models. Assume a processor architecture with an arbitrarily deep write buffer. All instructions take 1 cycle, ignoring memory system effects. Both read and write misses take 100 cycles to complete (i.e., to perform globally). Locks are cacheable and loads are nonblocking. Assume all the variables and locks are initially uncached and all locks are unlocked. Further assume that once a line is brought into the cache it does not get invalidated for the duration of the code's execution. All memory locations referenced here are distinct; furthermore, they all map to different cache lines.

```
LOAD A
STORE B
LOCK (L1)
STORE C
LOAD D
UNLOCK (L1)
LOAD E
STORE F
```

a. If the sufficient conditions for sequential consistency are maintained, how many cycles will it take to execute this code?

b. Repeat part (a) for weak ordering.

c. Repeat part (a) for release consistency.

9.22 The following code is executed on an aggressive dynamically scheduled but single-issue processor. The processor can have multiple outstanding operations, the cache allows for multiple outstanding misses, and the write buffer can hide store latencies (of course, these features may only be used if allowed by the memory consistency model).

```
Processor 1:
sendSpecial(int value) {
  A = 1
  LOCK(L);
  C = D*3;
  E = F*10
  G = value;
  READY = 1;
  UNLOCK(L);
}
```

```
Processor 2:
receiveSpecial() {
  LOCK(L);
  if (READY) {
    D = C+1;
    F = E*G;
  }
  UNLOCK (L);
}
```

Assume that locks are noncacheable and are acquired either 50 cycles from an issued request or 20 cycles from the time a release completes (whichever is later). A release takes 50 cycles to complete. Read hits take 1 cycle to complete and writes take 1 cycle to put into the write buffer. Read misses to shared variables take 50 cycles to complete. Writes take 50 cycles to complete. The write buffer on the processors is sufficiently large that it never fills completely. Only count the latencies of reads and writes to shared variables (those listed in capitals) and the locks. All shared variables are initially uncached with a value of 0. Assume that processor 1 obtains the lock first.

a. Under SC, how many cycles will it take from the time processor 1 enters the `sendSpecial()` routine to the time that processor 2 leaves `receive`

`Special()`? Make sure that you justify your answer. Also make sure to note the issue and completion time of each synchronization event.

b. How many cycles will it take to return from `receiveSpecial()` under release consistency?

9.23 In eager release consistency, diffs, like write notices, are created and also propagated at release time, whereas in one form of lazy release consistency they are created at release time but propagated only at acquire time (that is, when the acquire synchronization request comes to the processor). In general, data may be propagated with varying degrees of laziness just like write notices.

a. Describe some other possibilities for when diffs might be created, propagated, and applied in all-software lazy release consistency (think of release time, acquire time, or access fault time). What is the laziest scheme you can design?

b. What complications does each lazier scheme cause in implementation? Which scheme would you choose to implement and why?

9.24 Delaying the propagation of invalidations until a release point or even until the next acquire point (as in lazy release consistency) can be done in hardware-coherent systems as well. Why is LRC not used in hardware-coherent systems? Would delaying invalidations until a release (not an acquire) be advantageous?

9.25 Suppose you had a co-processor to perform the creation and application of diffs in an all-software SVM system and therefore did not have to perform this activity on the main processor. Considering eager release consistency and the lazy variants you designed in Exercise 9.23, comment on the extent to which protocol processing activity can be overlapped with computation on the main processor. Draw timelines to show what can be done on the main processor and on the co-processor. Do you expect the savings in performance to be substantial? What do you think would be the major benefit and major implementation complexity of having all protocol processing and management performed on the co-processor?

9.26 Why is garbage collection more important and more complex in TreadMarks-style lazy release consistency than in eager release consistency? What about in home-based lazy release consistency? Design a scheme for periodic garbage collection (discussing both when and how), and discuss the complications.

9.27 In systems like Blizzard-S or Shasta that instrument read and write operations in software to provide fine-grained access control, a key performance goal is to reduce the overhead of instrumentation. Describe some techniques that you might use to do this. To what extent do you think the techniques can be automated in a compiler or a tool for executable instrumentation?

9.28 When messages (e.g., page requests or lock requests) arrive at a node in a software shared memory system, whether fine grained or coarse grained, there are two major ways to handle them in the absence of a programmable communication assist. One is to interrupt the main processor, and the other is to have the main processor poll for messages.

a. What are the major trade-offs between the two methods?

b. How would you manage the polling by the main processor; in particular, when would you poll?

c. Which do you expect to perform better for page-based shared virtual memory and why? For fine-grained software shared memory? What application characteristics would most influence your decision?

d. What new issues arise and how might the trade-offs change if each node is an SMP rather than a uniprocessor?

e. How do you think you would organize message handling with SMP nodes? That is, where would incoming messages be handled, and how would message notification be managed?

9.29 List all the trade-offs you can think of between LRC based on diffs (not home based) versus based on automatic update (home based). Which do you think would perform better? What about home-based LRC based on diffs versus based on automatic update?

9.30 Is a properly labeled program guaranteed to run correctly under LRC? Under ERC? Under RC? Is a program that runs correctly under ERC guaranteed to run correctly under LRC? Is it guaranteed to be properly labeled (i.e., can a program that is not properly labeled run correctly under ERC? Is a program that runs correctly under LRC guaranteed to run correctly under ERC?

9.31 Consider a single writer release-based protocol. On a release, does a node need to obtain the up-to-date sharing list for each page it has modified since the last release from the current owner or just send write notices to nodes on its version of the sharing list for each such page? Explain why.

9.32 Consider page version numbers without directories. Does this avoid the problem of sending multiple invalidates to the same copy in a single writer release-based protocol? Explain why, or give a counterexample.

9.33 Trace the path of a write reference in (a) a pure CC-NUMA, (b) a flat COMA, (c) an SVM with automatic update, (d) an SVM protocol without automatic update, and (e) a simple COMA. (Hint: see how it was done for read references in the chapter.)

9.34 You are performing an architectural study using four applications: Ocean, LU, an FFT that uses a matrix transposition between local calculations on rows (see Exercise 8.23), and Barnes-Hut. For each application, answer the following questions, assuming a page-grained SVM system (these questions were asked for a CC-NUMA system in Chapter 8):

a. What modifications or enhancements in data structuring or layout would you use to ensure good interactions with the extended memory hierarchy?

b. Methodologically, what are the interactions with cache size and with granularities of allocation, coherence, and communication that you would be particularly careful to represent or not represent? What new ones become important in SVM systems that were not so important in CC-NUMA, and which ones become less important relative to others?

c. Are the interactions with cache size as important in SVM as they are in CC-NUMA? If they are of different importance, say why.

9.35 Consider the FFT calculation with a matrix transpose described in Exercise 8.23. Suppose you are running this program on a page-based SVM system using an all-software, home-based multiple writer protocol.

a. Would you rather use the method in which a processor reads locally allocated data and writes remotely allocated data to implement the transpose or the one in which the processor reads remote data and writes local data?

b. Now suppose you have hardware support for automatic update propagation to further speed up your home-based protocol. How does this change the trade-off, if at all?

c. What protocol artifacts limit performance, and what protocol optimizations can you think of that would substantially increase the performance of one scheme or the other?

10

Interconnection Network Design

We have seen throughout this book that scalable high-performance interconnection networks lie at the core of parallel computer architecture. Our generic parallel machine has three basic components: the processor-memory nodes, the node-to-network interface, and the network that holds it all together. The previous chapters have given a general understanding of the requirements placed on the interconnection network of a parallel machine; this chapter examines in depth the design of high-performance interconnection networks for parallel computers. These networks share basic concepts and terminology with local area networks (LANs) and wide area networks (WANs), which may be familiar to many readers, but the design trade-offs are quite different because of the dramatic difference of time scale.

Parallel computer networks are a rich and interesting topic because they have so many facets, but this richness also makes the topic difficult to understand in an overall sense. For example, parallel computer networks are generally wired together in a regular pattern. The topological structure of these networks has elegant mathematical properties, and there are deep relationships between these topologies and the fundamental communication patterns of important parallel algorithms. However, pseudo-random wiring patterns have a different set of nice mathematical properties and tend to have more uniform performance without really good or really bad communication patterns. There is a wide range of interesting trade-offs to examine at this abstract level, and a huge volume of research papers focus completely on this aspect of network design. On the other hand, passing information between two independent asynchronous devices across an electrical or optical link presents a host of subtle engineering issues. These are the kinds of issues that give rise to major standardization efforts. From yet a third point of view, the interactions between multiple flows of information competing for communications resources have subtle performance effects that are influenced by a host of factors. The performance modeling of networks is another huge area of theoretical and practical research. Real network designs address issues at each of these levels. The goal of this chapter is to provide a holistic understanding of the many facets of parallel computer networks so that the reader may see the diverse network design space within the larger problem of parallel machine design as driven by application demands.

As with all other aspects of design, network design involves understanding trade-offs and making compromises so that the solution is near optimal in a global sense rather than optimized for a particular component of interest. The performance impact of the many interacting facets can be quite subtle. Moreover, no clear consensus exists in the field on the appropriate cost model for networks since trade-offs can be made between very different technologies; for example, bandwidth of the links may be traded against complexity of the switches. It is also very difficult to establish a well-defined workload against which to assess network designs since program requirements are influenced by every other level of the system design before being presented to the network. This is the kind of situation that commonly gives rise to distinct "design camps" and rather heated debates, which often neglect to bring out the differences in base assumptions. In the course of developing the concepts of computer networks, this chapter points out how the choice of cost model and of workload lead to various important design points, which reflect key technological assumptions.

Previous chapters have illuminated the factors that drive network design. The communication-to-computation ratio of the program places a requirement on the data bandwidth the network must deliver if the processors are to sustain a given computational rate. However, this load varies considerably between programs; the flow of information may be physically localized or dispersed, and it may be bursty in time or fairly uniform. In addition, the waiting time of the program is strongly affected by the latency of the network, and the time spent waiting affects the bandwidth requirement. We have seen that different programming model implementations tend to communicate at different granularities (which impacts the size of data transfers seen by the network) and that they use different protocols at the network transaction level to realize the higher-level programming model.

This chapter begins with a set of basic definitions and concepts that underlie all networks. Simple models of communication latency and bandwidth are developed in Section 10.2 to reveal the core differences in network design styles. The key components that are assembled to form networks are described concretely in Section 10.3. Section 10.4 explains the rich space of interconnection topologies in a common framework, and Section 10.5 ties the design trade-offs back to cost, latency, and bandwidth under basic workload assumptions. Section 10.6 explains the various ways that messages are routed within the topology of the network in a manner that avoids deadlock and describes the further impact of routing on communication performance. Section 10.7 dives deeper into the hardware organization of the switches that form the basic building block of networks in order to provide a more precise understanding of the engineering trade-offs of various options and the mechanics underlying the more abstract network concepts. Then Section 10.8 explores the alternative approaches to flow control within a network. With this grounding in place, Section 10.9 brings together the entire range of issues in a collection of case studies and examines the transition of parallel computer network technology into other network regimes, including the emerging system area networks (SANs).

10.1 BASIC DEFINITIONS

The job of an interconnection network in a parallel machine is to transfer information from any source node to any desired destination node, in support of the net-

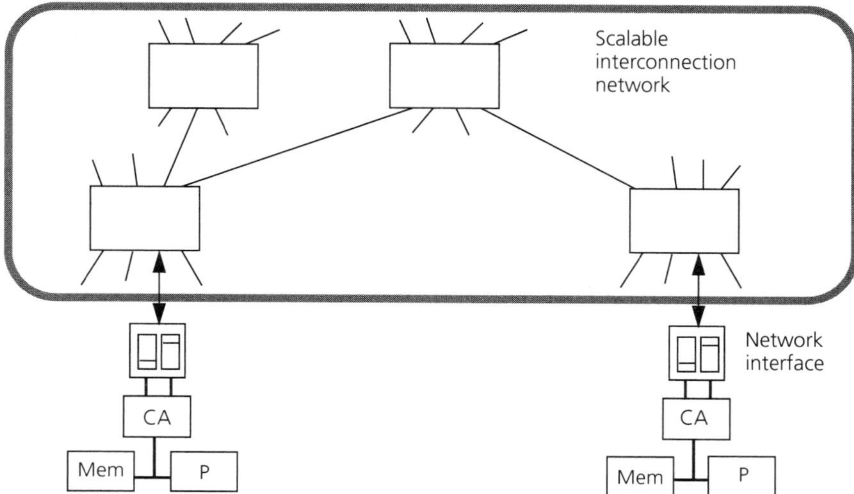

FIGURE 10.1 Generic parallel machine interconnection network. The communication assist initiates network transactions on behalf of the processor or memory controller through a network interface that causes information to be transmitted across a sequence of links and switches to a remote node where the network transaction takes place.

work transactions that are used to realize the programming model. It should accomplish this task with as small a latency as possible, and it should allow a large number of such transfers to take place concurrently. In addition, it should be inexpensive relative to the cost of the rest of the machine.

The expanded diagram for our generic large-scale parallel architecture in Figure 10.1 illustrates the structure of an interconnection network in a parallel machine. The communication assist on the source node initiates network transactions by pushing information through the network interface (NI). These transactions are handled by the communication assist, processor, or memory controller on the destination node, depending on the communication abstraction that is supported.

The network is composed of links and switches that provide a means to route the information from the source node to the destination node. A *link* is essentially a bundle of wires or fibers that carries an analog signal. For information to flow along a link, a transmitter converts digital information at one end into an analog signal that is driven down the link and converted back into digital symbols by the receiver at the other end. The *physical protocol* for converting between streams of digital symbols and an analog signal forms the lowest layer of the network design. The transmitter, link, and receiver collectively form a *channel* for digital information flow between switches (or NIs) attached to the link. The *link-level protocol* segments the stream of symbols crossing a channel into larger logical units, called *packets* or *messages*, that are interpreted by the switches in order to steer each unit arriving on an input channel to the appropriate output channel. Processing nodes communicate across a sequence of links and switches. The *node-level protocol* embeds commands for the remote communication assist within the packets or messages exchanged between the nodes to accomplish network transactions.

Formally, a parallel machine interconnection network is a graph, where the vertices V are processing hosts or switch elements connected by communication channels $C \subseteq V \times V$. A *channel* is a physical link between host or switch elements, including a buffer to hold data as it is being transferred. It has a width w and a signaling rate $f = 1/\tau$ (for cycle time τ), which together determine the *channel bandwidth* $b = wf$. The amount of data transferred across a link in a cycle is called a physical unit, or *phit*.[1] Switches connect a fixed number of input channels to a fixed number of output channels; this number is called the switch *degree*. Hosts typically connect to a single switch but can be multiply connected with separate channels. Messages are transferred through the network from a source host node to a destination host along a path, or *route*, comprised of a sequence of channels and switches.

A useful analogy to keep in mind is a roadway system composed of streets and intersections. Each street has a speed limit and a number of lanes, determining its peak bandwidth. It may be either unidirectional (one-way) or bidirectional. Intersections allow travelers to switch among a fixed number of streets. In each trip, a collection of people travel from a source location along a route to a destination. They may use any of many potential routes, many modes of transportation, and many different ways of dealing with traffic encountered en route. A very large number of such trips may be in progress in a city concurrently, and their respective paths may cross or share segments of the route.

A network is characterized by its topology, routing algorithm, switching strategy, and flow control mechanism.

- The *topology* is the physical interconnection structure of the network graph; this may be regular, as with a two-dimensional grid (typical of many metropolitan centers), or it may be irregular. Most parallel machines employ highly regular networks. A distinction is often made between direct and indirect networks; *direct* networks have a host node connected to each switch whereas *indirect* networks have hosts connected only to a specific subset of the switches, which form the edges of the network. Many machines employ mixed strategies, so the more critical distinction is between the two types of nodes: hosts generate and remove traffic whereas switches only move traffic along.
- The *routing algorithm* determines which routes messages may follow through the network graph. The routing algorithm restricts the set of possible paths to a smaller set of legal paths. There are many different routing algorithms, providing different guarantees and offering different performance trade-offs. For example, continuing the traffic analogy, a city might eliminate gridlock by leg-

1. Since many networks operate asynchronously rather than being controlled by a single global clock, the notion of a network "cycle" is not as widely used as in dealing with processors. We could equivalently define the network cycle time as the time to transmit the smallest physical unit of information, a phit. For parallel architectures, it is convenient to think about the processor cycle time and the network cycle time in common terms. Indeed, the two technological regimes are becoming increasingly similar.

islating that cars must travel east-west before making a single turn north or south toward their destination rather than being allowed to zigzag across town. We will see that this does indeed eliminate deadlock, but it limits a driver's ability to avoid traffic en route. In a parallel machine, we are only concerned with routes from a host to a host.

- The *switching strategy* determines how the data in a message traverses its route. There are basically two switching strategies. In *circuit switching*, the path from the source to the destination is established and reserved until the message is transferred over the circuit. (This strategy is like reserving a parade route; it is good for moving a lot of people through, but advanced planning is required and it tends to be unpleasant for any traffic that might cross or share a portion of the reserved route, even when the parade is not in sight. It is also the strategy used in phone systems, which establish a circuit through possibly many switches for each call.) The alternative is *packet switching*, in which the message is broken into a sequence of packets. A packet contains routing and sequencing information as well as data. Packets are individually routed from the source to the destination. (The analogy to traveling as small groups in individual cars is obvious.) Packet switching typically allows better utilization of network resources because links and buffers are only occupied while a packet is traversing them.
- The *flow control mechanism* determines when the message, or portions of it, moves along its route. In particular, flow control is necessary whenever two or more messages attempt to use the same network resource (e.g., a channel) at the same time. One of the traffic flows could be stalled in place, shunted into buffers, detoured to an alternate route, or simply discarded. Each of these options places specific requirements on the design of the switch and influences other aspects of the communication subsystem. (Discarding traffic is clearly unacceptable in our traffic analogy.) The minimum unit of information that can be transferred across a link and either accepted or rejected is called a flow control unit, or *flit*. It may be as small as a phit or as large as a packet or message.

To illustrate the difference between a phit and a flit, consider the nCUBE case study in Section 7.1.4. The links are a single bit wide, so a phit is 1 bit. However, a switch accepts incoming messages in chunks of 36 bits (32 bits of data plus 4 parity bits). It only allows the next 36 bits to come in when it has a buffer to hold it, so the flit is 36 bits. In many more recent machines, such as the T3D, the phit and flit are the same.

An important property of a topology is the *diameter* of a network, which is the length of the maximum shortest path between any two nodes. The *routing distance* between a pair of nodes is the number of links traversed en route; this is at least as large as the shortest path between the nodes and may be larger. The *average distance* is simply the average of the routing distance over all pairs of nodes; this is also the expected distance between a random pair of nodes. In a direct network, routes must be provided between every pair of switches, whereas in an indirect network, it is

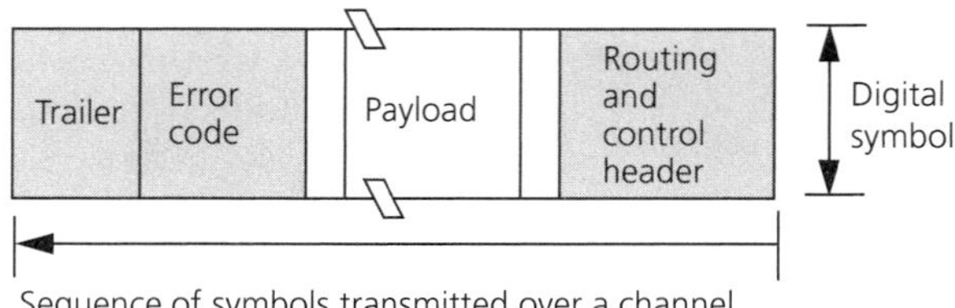

FIGURE 10.2 Typical packet format. A packet forms the logical unit of information that is steered along a route by switches. It is comprised of three parts: a header, a data payload, and a trailer. The header and trailer are interpreted by the switches as the packet progresses along the route, but the payload is not. The node-level protocol is carried in the payload.

only required that routes are provided between hosts. A network is *partitioned* if a set of links or switches are removed such that some hosts are no longer connected by routes.

Most of the discussion in this chapter centers on packets because packet switching is used in most modern parallel machine networks. Where specific important properties of circuit switching arise, they are pointed out. A *packet* is a self-delimiting sequence of digital symbols and logically consists of three parts, illustrated in Figure 10.2: a header, a payload, and a trailer. The *header* is the front of the packet and usually contains the routing and control information so that the switches and network interface can determine what to do with the packet as it arrives. The *payload* is the part of the packet containing data transmitted across the network. The *trailer* is the end of the packet and typically contains the error-checking code so that it can be generated as the message spools out onto the link. The header may also have a separate error-checking code.

The two basic mechanisms for building abstractions in the context of networks are encapsulation and fragmentation. *Encapsulation* involves carrying higher-level protocol information in an uninterpreted form within the message format of a given level. *Fragmentation* involves splitting the higher-level protocol information into a sequence of messages at a given level. Although these basic mechanisms are present in any network, the layers of abstraction in parallel computer networks tend to be much shallower than in, say, the Internet and are designed to fit together very efficiently. To make these notions concrete, observe that the header and trailer of a packet form an envelope that is interpreted by the switches and encapsulates the data payload. Information associated with the node-level protocol is contained within this payload. For example, a read request is typically conveyed to a remote memory controller in a single packet, and the cache line response is a single packet. The memory controllers are not concerned with the actual route followed by the packet or with the format of the header and trailer. At the same time, the network is not concerned with the format of the remote read request within the packet payload. A large bulk data transfer would not typically be carried out as a single packet; instead, it would be fragmented into several packets. Each would need to contain information to indicate where its data should be deposited or which fragment in the overall data sequence it represents. Dropping down a layer, an individual packet is fragmented at the link level into a series of symbols that are transmitted in order across the link, so there is no need for sequencing information. This situation in which higher-level information is carried within an envelope, or multiple such envelopes, that is interpreted by the lower-level protocol occurs at every level (or layer) of network design.

10.2 BASIC COMMUNICATION PERFORMANCE

There is much to understand on each of the four major aspects of network design, but before going into these aspects in detail it is useful to have a general understanding of how they interact to determine the performance and functionality of the overall communication subsystem. Building on the brief discussion of networks in Chapter 7, let us look at performance from the latency and bandwidth perspectives.

10.2.1 Latency

To establish a basic performance model for understanding networks, we may expand the model for the communication time that we have used since Chapter 1. The time to transfer *n* bytes of information from its source to its destination has four components, as follows.

$$Time(n)_{S-D} = Overhead + Routing\ Delay + Channel\ Occupancy + Contention\ Delay \tag{10.1}$$

The *overhead* associated with getting the message into and out of the network on the ends of the actual transmission has been discussed extensively in dealing with the node-to-network interface in previous chapters. We have seen machines that are designed to move cache-line-sized chunks and others that are optimized for large-message DMA transfers. As to the remaining components, the routing delay and channel occupancy are effectively lumped together in previous chapters as the *unloaded latency* of the network for typical message sizes, and contention has been largely ignored. These other components are the focus of this chapter.

The *channel occupancy* provides a convenient lower bound on the communication latency, independent of where the message is going or what else is happening in the network. As we look at network design in more depth, we see below that the occupancy of each link is influenced by the channel width, the signaling rate, and the amount of control information, which is in turn influenced by the topology and routing algorithm. Whereas previous chapters were concerned with the channel occupancy seen from "outside" the network—the time to transfer the message across the bottleneck channel in the route—the view from within the network is that a channel occupancy is associated with each step along the route. The communication assist is occupied for a period of time accepting the communication request from the processor or memory controller and spooling a packet into the network.

Each channel the packet crosses en route is occupied for a period of time by the packet, as is the destination communication assist.

For example, an issue that we need to be aware of is the efficiency of the packet encoding. The packet envelope increases the occupancy because header and trailer symbols are added by the source and stripped off by the destination. Thus, for a payload of size n the occupancy of a channel is

$$\frac{n + n_E}{b}$$

where n_E is the size of the envelope and b is the raw bandwidth of the channel. This issue is addressed in the "outside view" by specifying the *effective bandwidth* of the link, derated from the raw bandwidth by

$$\frac{n}{n + n_E}$$

at least for fixed-size packets. However, within the network, packet efficiency remains a design issue. The effect is more pronounced with small packets, but it also depends on how routing is performed.

The *routing delay* is seen from outside the network as the time to move a given symbol, say, the first bit of the message, from the source to the destination. Viewed from within the network, each step along the route incurs a routing delay that accumulates into the delay observed from the outside. The routing delay is a function of the number of channels on the route, called the *routing distance*, h, and the delay Δ incurred at each switch as part of selecting the correct output port. (It is convenient to view the node-to-network interface as contributing to the routing delay like a switch.) The routing distance depends on the network topology, the routing algorithm, and the particular pair of source and destination nodes. The overall delay is strongly affected by switching and routing strategies.

With packet-switched, *store-and-forward* routing, the entire packet is received by a switch before it is forwarded on the next link, as illustrated in Figure 10.3(a). This strategy is used in most wide area networks and was used in several early parallel computers. The unloaded network latency for an n-byte packet, including envelope, with store-and-forward routing is

$$T_{sf}(n, h) = h\left(\frac{n}{b} + \Delta\right) \tag{10.2}$$

where Δ is the additional routing delay per hop.

Equation 10.2 would suggest that the network topology is paramount in determining network latency since the topology fundamentally determines the routing distance, h. In fact, the story is more complicated.

First, consider the switching strategy. With circuit switching, we expect a delay proportional to h to establish the circuit, configure each of the switches along the route, and inform the source that the route is established. After this time, the data should move along the circuit in time n/b plus an additional small delay propor-

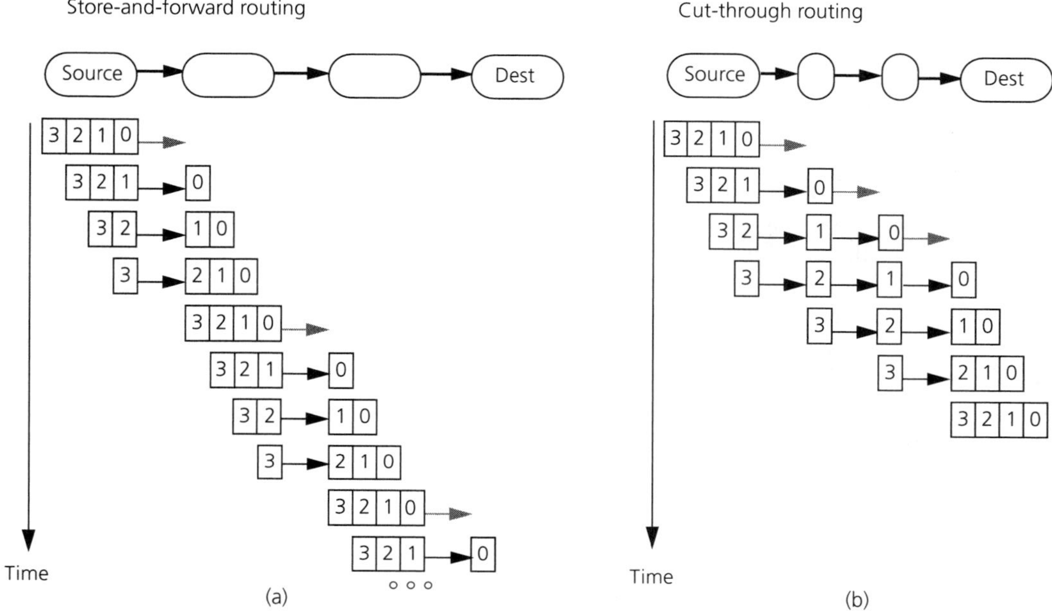

FIGURE 10.3 Store-and-forward versus cut-through routing for packet-switched networks. A four-flit packet traverses three hops from source to destination under store-and-forward and cut-through routing. Cut-through achieves lower latency by making the routing decision (gray arrow) on the first flit and pipelining the packet through a sequence of switches. Store-and-forward accumulates the entire packet before routing it toward the destination.

tional to h. Thus, the unloaded latency in units of the network cycle time, τ, for an n-byte message traveling distance h in a circuit-switched network is

$$T_{cs}(n, h) = \frac{n}{b} + h\Delta \tag{10.3}$$

In Equation 10.3, the setup and routing delay is an additive term, independent of the size of the message. Thus, as the message length increases, the routing distance, and hence the topology, becomes an insignificant fraction of the unloaded communication latency. Circuit switching is traditionally used in telecommunications networks since the call setup is short compared to the duration of the call. It is used in a minority of parallel computer networks, including the Meiko CS-2 and the BBN Butterfly. One important difference is that in parallel machines the circuit is established by routing the message through the network and holding open the route as a circuit. The more traditional approach is to compute the route on the side, configure the switches, and then transmit information on the circuit.

It is also possible to retain packet switching and yet reduce the unloaded latency from that of naive store-and-forward routing. The key concern with Equation 10.2 is that the delay is the product of the routing distance and the occupancy for the full message. However, a long message can be fragmented into several small packets, which flow through the network in a pipelined fashion. In this case, the unloaded latency is

$$T_{sf}(n, h, n_p) = \frac{n - n_p}{b} + h\left(\frac{n_p}{b} + \Delta\right) \tag{10.4}$$

where n_p is the size of the fragments. The effective routing delay is proportional to the packet size rather than the message size. This is basically the approach adopted (in software) for traditional data communication networks such as the Internet.

In parallel computer networks, the idea of pipelining the routing and communication is carried much further. Most parallel machines use packet switching with *cut-through* routing, in which the switch makes its routing decision after inspecting only the first few phits of the header and allows the remainder of the packet to "cut through" from the input channel to the output channel, as indicated by Figure 10.3(b), so the transmission of even a single packet is pipelined. (If we may return to our vehicle analogy, cut-through routing is like what happens when a train encounters a switch in the track. The first car is directed to the proper output track and the remainder follow along behind. By contrast, store-and-forward routing is like what happens at the station, where all the cars in the train arrive and stop before the first proceeds toward the next station.) For cut-through routing, the unloaded latency has a form similar to the circuit switch case

$$T_{ct}(n, h) = \frac{n}{b} + h\Delta \tag{10.5}$$

although the routing coefficient, Δ, may differ since the mechanics of the process are rather different. Observe that with cut-through routing a single message may occupy the entire route from the source to the destination, much like circuit switching. The head of the message establishes the route as it moves toward its destination, and the route clears as the tail moves through.

The preceding discussion of communication latency addresses a message flowing from source to destination without running into traffic along the way. In this unloaded case, the network can be viewed simply as a pipeline, with a start-up cost, pipeline depth, and time per stage. The different switching and routing strategies change the effective structure of the pipeline whereas the topology, link bandwidth, and fragmentation determine the depth and time per stage. Of course, the reason that networks are so interesting is that they are not a simple pipeline but rather an interwoven fabric of portions of many pipelines. The whole motivation for using a network rather than a bus is to allow multiple data transfers to occur simultaneously. This means that one message flow may collide with others and contend for resources. Fundamentally, the network must provide a mechanism for dealing with contention. The behavior under contention depends on several facets of the network design—the topology, the switching strategy, and the routing algorithm—but the bottom line is that at any given time a channel can only be occupied by one message. If two messages attempt to use the same channel at once, one must be deferred. Typically, each switch provides some means of arbitration for the output channels. Thus, a switch will select one of the incoming packets contending for each output and the others will be deferred in some manner.

An overarching design issue for networks is how contention is handled. This issue recurs throughout the chapter, so let's first just consider what it means for latency. Clearly, contention increases the communication latency experienced by the nodes. Exactly how it increases latency depends on the mechanisms used for dealing with contention within the network, which in turn differ depending on the basic network design strategy. For example, with packet switching, contention may be experienced at each switch. Using store-and-forward routing, if multiple packets that are buffered in the switch need to use the same output channel, one will be selected and the others are blocked in buffers until they are selected. Thus, contention adds queuing delays to the basic routing delay. With circuit switching, the effect of contention arises when trying to establish a circuit; typically, a routing probe is extended toward the destination, and if it encounters a reserved channel it is retracted. The network interface retries establishing the circuit after some delay. Thus, the start-up cost in gaining access to the network increases under contention, but once the circuit is established the transmission proceeds at full speed for the entire message.

With cut-through packet switching, two packet blocking options are available. The *virtual cut-through* approach is to spool the blocked incoming packet into a buffer so that the behavior under contention degrades to that of store-and-forward routing. The *wormhole* approach buffers only a few flits in the switch and leaves the tail of the message in place along the route. The blocked portion of the message is very much like a circuit held open through a portion of the network.

Switches have limited buffering for packets, so under sustained contention the buffers in a switch may fill up. What happens to incoming packets if there is no buffer space to hold them in the switch? In traditional data communication networks, the links are long and little feedback occurs between the two ends of the channel, so the typical approach is to discard the packet. Thus, under contention the network becomes highly unreliable, and sophisticated protocols (e.g., TCP/IP slow-start) are used at the nodes to adapt the requested communication load to what the network can deliver without a high loss rate. Discarding on buffer overrun is also used with most ATM switches, even if they are employed to build closely integrated clusters. Like the wide area case, the source receives no indication that its packet was dropped, so it must rely on some kind of time-out mechanism to deduce that a problem has occurred.

In parallel computer networks, a packet headed for a full buffer is typically blocked in place, rather than discarded; this requires a handshake between the output port and input port across the link, that is, link-level flow control. Under sustained congestion, traffic "backs up" from the point in the network where contention for resources occurs toward the sources that are driving traffic into that point. Eventually, the sources experience back pressure from the network (when it refuses to accept packets), which causes the flow of data into the network to slow down to a rate that can move through the bottleneck.[2] Increasing the amount of buffering within the network allows contention to persist longer without causing back pressure at the source, but it also increases the potential queuing delays within the network when contention does occur.

One of the concerns that arises in networks with message blocking is that the backup can impact traffic that is not headed for the highly contended output. Suppose that the network traffic favors one of the destinations, say, because it holds an important global variable that is widely used. This is often called a "hot spot." If the total amount of traffic destined for that output exceeds the bandwidth of the output, this traffic will back up within the network. If this condition persists, the backlog will propagate backward through the tree of channels directed at this destination, which is called *tree saturation* (Pfister and Norton 1985). Any traffic that crosses the tree will also be delayed. In a wormhole-routed network, an interesting alternative to blocking the message is to discard it but to inform the source of the collision. For example, in the BBN Butterfly machine the source held onto the tail of the message until the head reached the destination (i.e., formed the circuit) and if a collision occurred en route, the worm was retracted all the way back to the source (Rettberg and Thomas 1986). This greatly reduces the impact of tree saturation.

We can see from this brief discussion that all aspects of network design—link bandwidth, topology, switching strategy, routing algorithm, and flow control—combine to determine the latency per message. It should also be clear that a relationship exists between latency and bandwidth. If the communication bandwidth demanded by the program is low compared to the available network bandwidth, collisions will be few, buffers will tend to be empty, and latency will stay low, especially with cut-through routing. As the bandwidth demand increases, latency will increase due to contention.

An important and often overlooked point is that parallel computer networks are effectively a *closed system* with feedback from the network to its traffic sources. The load placed on the network depends on the rate at which processing nodes request communication, which in turn depends on how fast the network delivers this communication. Program performance is affected most strongly by latency when some kind of dependence is involved: the program must wait until a read completes or until a message is received to continue; while it waits, the load placed on the network drops and the latency decreases. This situation is very different from that of file transfers across the country contending with unrelated traffic. In a parallel machine, a program largely contends with itself for communication resources. If the machine is used in a multiprogrammed fashion, parallel programs may also contend with one another, but the request rate of each will be reduced as the service rate of the network is reduced due to the contention. Since low-latency communication is critical

2. This situation is exactly like multiple lanes of traffic converging on a narrow tunnel or bridge. When the traffic flow is less than the flow rate of the tunnel, almost no delay occurs, but when the inbound flow exceeds the tunnel bandwidth, traffic backs up. When the traffic jam fills the available storage capacity of the roadway, the aggregate traffic moves forward slowly enough that the aggregate bandwidth is equal to that of the tunnel.

to parallel program performance, the emphasis in this chapter is on cut-through packet-switched networks.

10.2.2 Bandwidth

Network bandwidth is critical to parallel program performance, in part because higher bandwidth decreases occupancy, in part because higher bandwidth reduces the likelihood of contention, and in part because phases of a program may push a large volume of data around without waiting for transmission of individual data items to be completed. Since networks behave like pipelines, it is possible to deliver high bandwidth even when the latency is large.

It is useful to look at bandwidth from two points of view: the "global" aggregate bandwidth available to all the nodes through the network and the "local" individual bandwidth available to a node. If the total communication volume of a program is M bytes and the aggregate communication bandwidth of the network is B bytes per second, then clearly the communication time is at least M/B seconds. On the other hand, if all of the communication is to or from a single node, this estimate is far too optimistic; the communication time would be determined by the bandwidth through that single node.

Let us look first at the bandwidth available to a single node and see how it may be influenced by network design choices. We have seen that the effective local bandwidth is reduced from the raw link bandwidth by the density of the packet

$$b\frac{n}{n + n_E}$$

Furthermore, if the switch blocks the packet for the routing delay of Δ cycles while it makes its routing decision, then the effective local bandwidth is further derated to

$$b\left(\frac{n}{n + n_E + w\Delta}\right)$$

since $w\Delta$ is the opportunity to transmit data that is lost while the link is blocked. Thus, network design issues such as the packet format and the routing algorithm will influence the bandwidth seen by even a single node. If multiple nodes are communicating at once and contention arises, the perceived local bandwidth will drop further (and the latency will rise). Contention at the endpoints happens in any network if multiple nodes send messages to the same node, but it may occur within the interior of the network as well. The choice of network topology and routing algorithm affects the likelihood of contention within the network.

If many of the nodes are communicating at once, it is useful to focus on the global bandwidth that the network can support rather than only the bandwidth available to each individual node. First, we should sharpen the concept of the aggregate communication bandwidth of a network. The most common notion of aggregate bandwidth is the *bisection bandwidth* of the network, which is the sum of the bandwidths of the minimum set of channels that, if removed, partition the network into two equal unconnected sets of nodes. This is a valuable concept because, if the communication pattern is completely uniform, half of the messages are expected to cross the bisection in each direction. We will see in the following that the bisection bandwidth per node varies dramatically in different network topologies. However, bisection bandwidth is not entirely satisfactory as a metric of aggregate network bandwidth because communication is not necessarily distributed uniformly over the entire machine. If communication is localized rather than uniform, bisection bandwidth will give a pessimistic estimate of communication time. An alternative notion of global bandwidth that caters to localized communication patterns would be the sum of the bandwidth of the links from the nodes to the network. The concern with this notion of global bandwidth is that the internal structure of the network may not support it. Clearly, the available aggregate bandwidth of the network depends on the communication pattern; in particular, it depends on how far the packets travel, so we should look at this relationship more closely.

The total bandwidth of all the channels (or links) in the network is the number of channels, C, times the bandwidth per channel, that is, Cb bytes per second, Cw bits per cycle, or C phits per cycle. If each of N hosts issues a packet every M cycles with an average routing distance of h, then each packet occupies, on average, h channels for $l = n/w$ cycles, and the total load on the network is Nhl/M phits per cycle. The average link utilization is at least

$$\rho = M\frac{C}{Nhl} \tag{10.6}$$

and this obviously must be less than one. One way of looking at this is that the number of links per node, C/N, reflects the communication bandwidth (phits per cycle per node) available, on average, to each node. This bandwidth is consumed in direct proportion to the routing distance and the message size. The number of links per node is a static property of the topology. The average routing distance is determined by the topology, the routing algorithm, the program communication pattern, and the mapping of the program onto the machine. Good communication locality may yield a small h, whereas random communication will travel the average distance and really bad patterns may traverse the full diameter. The message size is determined by the program behavior and the communication abstraction. In general, the aggregate communication requirement in Equation 10.6 says that as the machine is scaled up, the channels per node must scale with the increase in expected latency.

In practice, several factors limit the channel utilization, ρ, well below unity. The load may not be perfectly balanced over all the links. Even if it is balanced, the routing algorithm may prevent all the links from being used for the particular communication pattern employed in the program. And even if all the links are usable and the load is balanced over the duration, stochastic variations in the load and contention for low-level resources may arise. All these factors affect the network's *saturation point*, which represents the total channel bandwidth it can usefully deliver. As illustrated in Figure 10.4, if the bandwidth demand placed on the network by the processors (called the *offered bandwidth*) is moderate, the latency remains low, and the delivered bandwidth increases with the offered bandwidth. However, at some point, demanding more bandwidth only increases the contention for resources and the

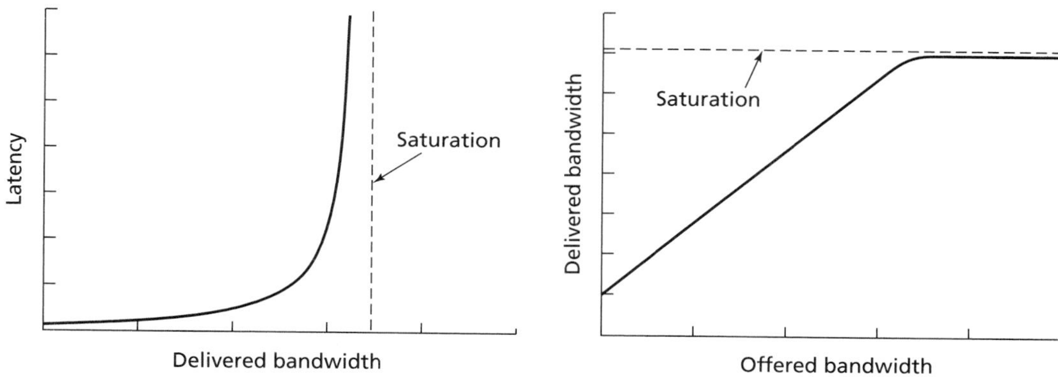

FIGURE 10.4 Typical network saturation behavior. Networks can provide low latency when the requested bandwidth is well below that which can be delivered. In this regime, the delivered bandwidth scales linearly with that requested. However, at some point, the network saturates and additional load causes the latency to increase sharply without yielding additional delivered bandwidth.

latency increases dramatically. The network is essentially moving as much traffic as it can, so additional requests just get queued up in the buffers. Increasing offered bandwidth does not increase what is delivered. We attempt to design parallel machines so that the network stays out of saturation, either by providing ample communication bandwidth or by limiting the demands placed by the processors.

A word of caution is in order regarding the dramatic increase in latency illustrated in Figure 10.4 as the network load approaches saturation. The behavior illustrated in the figure is typical of all queuing systems (and networks) under the assumption that the load placed on the system is independent of the response time. The sources keep pushing messages into the system faster than it can service them, so a queue of arbitrary length builds up somewhere and the latency grows with the length of this queue. In other words, this simple analysis assumes an *open system*, whereas in reality, parallel machines are closed systems. There is only a limited amount of buffering in the network and, usually, only a limited amount of communication buffering in the network interfaces. Thus, if these "queues" fill up, the sources will slow down, reducing their demand to the service rate since there is no place to put the next packet until one is removed. The flow control mechanisms affect this coupling between source and sink. Moreover, dependences within the parallel programs inherently embed some degree of end-to-end flow control because a processor must receive remote information before it can do additional work that depends on the information and generate additional communication traffic. Nonetheless, it is important to recognize that a shared resource, such as a network link, is not expected to be 100% utilized even in the best of circumstances.

This brief performance modeling of parallel machine networks shows that the latency and bandwidth of real networks depends on all aspects of the network design, which we will examine in some detail in the remainder of the chapter. Performance modeling of networks is itself a rich area with a voluminous literature base, and the interested reader should consult the following references as a starting point: Agarwal (1991), Dally (1990b), Karol et al. (1987), Kermani and Kleinrock (1979), Kruskal and Snir (1983), and Peterson and Davie (1996). In addition, it is important to note that performance is not the only driving factor in network designs. Cost and fault tolerance are two other critical criteria. For example, the wiring complexity of the network is a critical issue in several large-scale machines. As these issues depend quite strongly on specifics of the design and the technology employed, we will discuss them along with examining the design alternatives.

10.3 ORGANIZATIONAL STRUCTURE

This section outlines the basic organizational structure of a parallel computer network. It is useful to think of this issue in the more familiar terms of the processor organization and the applicable engineering constraints. We normally think of the processor as being composed of datapath, control logic, and memory interface, including perhaps the on-chip portions of the memory hierarchy. The datapath is further broken down into ALU, register file, pipeline latches, and so forth. The control logic is built up from examining the data transfers that take place in the datapath. Local connections within the datapath are short and scale well with improvements in VLSI technology whereas control wires and buses are long and become slower relative to gates as chip density increases. A very similar notion of decomposition and assembly applies to the network. Scalable interconnection networks are composed of three basic components: links, switches, and network interfaces. A basic understanding of these components, their performance characteristics, and their inherent costs is essential for evaluating network design alternatives. The set of operations the components perform is quite limited, fundamentally moving packets toward their intended destination.

10.3.1 Links

A link is a cable of one or more electrical wires or optical fibers with a connector at each end that is attached to a switch or network interface port. It allows an analog signal to be transmitted from one end, received at the other, and sampled to obtain the original digital information stream. In practice, there is tremendous variation in the electrical and physical engineering of links; however, their essential logical properties can be characterized along three independent dimensions: length, width, and clocking.

1. A *short link* is one in which only a single logical value can be on the link at any time; a *long link* is viewed as a transmission line where a series of logical values propagate along the link simultaneously at a fraction of the speed of light (1–2 feet per ns, depending on the specific medium).
2. A *narrow link* is one in which data, control, and timing information are multiplexed onto each wire, such as on a single serial link; a *wide link* is one that can simultaneously transmit data and control information. In either case, net-

work links are typically narrower than to internal processor datapaths, say, 4 to 16 data bits.

3. Clocking may be synchronous or asynchronous. In the *synchronous* case, the source and destination operate on the same global clock, so data is sampled at the receiving end according to the common clock; in the *asynchronous* case, the source encodes its clock in some manner within the analog signal that is transmitted, and the destination recovers the source clock from the signal and transfers the information into its own clock domain.

A short electrical link behaves like a conventional connection between digital components. The signaling rate is essentially determined by the time to charge the wire until it represents a logical value on both ends. This time increases only logarithmically with length if enough power can be used to drive the link.[3] In addition, the wire must be terminated properly to avoid reflections, which is why it is important that the link be point to point, as opposed to multipoint, like a bus.

The CRAY T3D is a good example of a wide, short, synchronous link design. Each bidirectional link contains 24 bits in each direction: 16 for data, 4 for control, and 4 providing flow control for the link in the reverse direction so that a switch will not try to deliver flits into a full buffer. The entire machine operates under a single 150-MHz clock. A flit is a single phit of 16 bits. Two of the control bits identify the phit type (00 no info, 01 routing tag, 10 packet, 11 end of packet).

In a long wire or optical fiber, the signal propagates along the link from source to destination. For a long link, the delay is clearly linear in the length of the wire. The signaling rate is determined by the time to correctly sample the signal at the receiver, so the length is limited by the signal decay along the link. If more than one wire is in the link, the signaling rate and wire length are also limited by the signal skew across the wires.

A correctly sampled analog signal can be viewed as a stream of digital symbols (phits) delivered from source to destination over time. Logical values on each wire may be conveyed by voltage levels or voltage transitions. Typically, the encoding of digital symbols is chosen so that it is easy to identify common failures (such as stuck-at faults and open connections) and easy to maintain clocking. Within the stream of symbols, individual packets must be identified. Thus, part of the signaling convention of a link is its *framing*, which identifies the start and end of each packet. In a wide link, distinct control lines may identify the head and tail phits. For example, a packet line goes high with the first header phit and stays high until the last tail phit. In the T3D, the routing tag phit and end-of-packet phit provide packet framing. In a narrow link, special control symbols are inserted in the stream to provide framing. In an asynchronous serial link, the clock must be extracted from the

3. The RC delay of a wire increases with the square of the length, so for a fixed amount of signal drive, the network cycle time is strongly affected by length. However, if the driver strength is increased using a driver tree, the time to drive the load of a longer wire only increases logarithmically. (If τ_{inv} is the propagation delay of a basic gate, then the effective propagation delay of a short wire of length l grows as $t_s = K\tau_{inv}\log l$.)

incoming analog signal as well; this is typically done with a unique synchronization burst in the sequence of binary values (Peterson and Davie 1996).

The CRAY T3E network provides a convenient contrast to the T3D. It uses a long, wide, asynchronous link design. The link is 14 bits wide in each direction, operating at 375 MHz. Each "bit" is conveyed by a low-voltage differential signal (LVDS) with a nominal swing of 600 mV on a pair of wires; that is, the receiver senses the difference in the two wires rather than the voltage relative to ground. The clock is sent along with the data. The maximum transmission distance is approximately 1 meter, but even at this length multiple bits will be on the wire at a time. A flit contains five phits, so the switches operate at 75 MHz on 70-bit quantities containing one 64-bit word plus control information. Flow control information is carried on data packets and idle symbols over the link in the reverse direction. The sequence of flits is framed into single-word and eight-word read and write request packets, message packets, and other special packets. The maximum data bandwidth of a link is 500 MB/s.

In general, the encoding of the packet within the frame is interpreted by the nodes attached to the link. Typically, the envelope is interpreted by the switch to do routing and error checking. The payload is delivered uninterpreted to the destination host, at which point further layers or internal envelopes are interpreted and peeled away. However, the destination node may need to inform the source whether it was able to hold the data. This requires some kind of node-to-node information that is distinct from the actual communication, for example, an acknowledgment in the reverse direction. With wide links, control lines may run in both directions to provide this information. Narrow links are almost always bidirectional so that special flow control signals can be inserted into the stream in the reverse direction as in the T3E.[4]

The Scalable Coherent Interface (SCI) defines both a long, wide copper link and a long, narrow fiber link. The links are unidirectional and nodes are always organized into rings. The copper link comprises 18 pairs of wires using differential signaling on both edges of a 250-MHz clock. It carries 16 bits of data, the clock, and a flag bit. The fiber link is serial and operates at 1.25 Gb/s. Packets are a sequence of 16-bit phits, with the header consisting of a destination node number phit and a command phit. The trailer consists of a 32-bit CRC (cyclic redundancy check) word. The flag bit provides packet framing by distinguishing idle symbols from packet phits. At least one idle phit occurs between successive packets.

Many evaluations of networks treat links as having a fixed cost. Common sense would suggest that the cost increases with the length of the link and its width. This is actually a point of considerable debate within the field because the relative quality of different networks depends on the cost model that is used in the evaluation. Much of the cost is in the connectors and the labor involved in attaching them, so the fixed cost is substantial. The connector cost increases with width whereas the wire cost increases with width and length. In many cases, the key constraint is the

4. This view of flow control as inherent to the link is quite different from the view in more traditional networking applications, where flow control is realized on top of the link-level protocol by special packets.

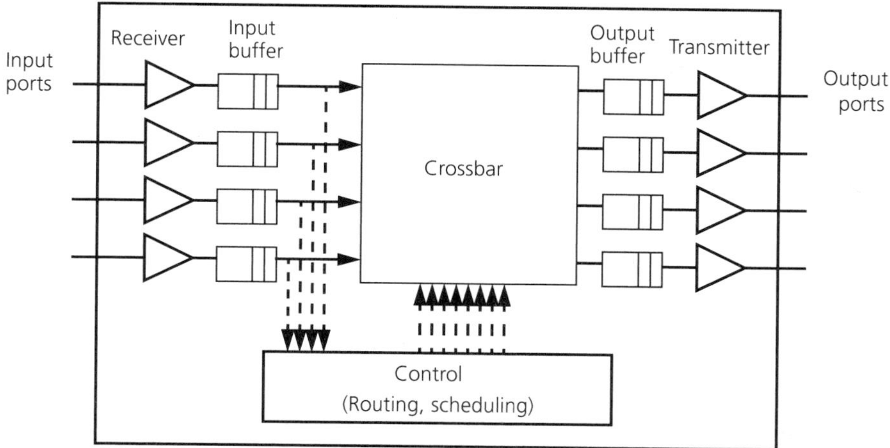

FIGURE 10.5 Basic switch organization. A set of input ports is connected to a set of output ports through a crossbar. The control logic affects the input/output connection at each point in time.

cross-sectional area of a bundle of links, say, at the bisection; this increases with width.

10.3.2 Switches

A switch consists of a set of input ports, a set of output ports, an internal "crossbar" connecting each input to every output, internal buffering, and control logic to effect the input/output connection at each point in time, as illustrated in Figure 10.5. Usually, the number of input ports is equal to the number of output ports, which is called the *degree* of the switch.[5] Each output port includes a transmitter to drive the link. Each input port includes a matching receiver. The input port has a synchronizer in most designs to align the incoming data with the local clock domain of the switch. This is essentially a FIFO, so it is natural to provide some degree of buffering with each input port. There may also be buffering associated with the outputs or shared buffering for the switch as a whole. The complexity of the control logic depends on the routing and scheduling algorithm, as we will discuss. At the very least, it must be possible to determine the output port required by each incoming packet and to arbitrate among input ports that need to connect to the same output port.

5. As with most rules, there are exceptions. For example, in the BBN Monarch design, two distinct kinds of switches were used that had an unequal number of input and output ports (Rettberg et al. 1990). Switches that routed packets to output ports based on routing information in the header could have more outputs than inputs. An alternative device, called a *concentrator*, routed packets to any output port, which were fewer than the number of input ports and all went to the same node.

Many evaluations of networks treat the switch degree as its cost. This is clearly a major factor, but again there is room for debate. The cost of some parts of the switch is linear in the degree, for example, the transmitters, receivers, and port buffers. However, the internal interconnect cost may increase with the square of the degree. The amount of internal buffering and the complexity of the routing logic also increase more than linearly with the degree. With recent VLSI switches, the dominant constraint tends to be the number of pins, which is proportional to the number of ports times the width of each port.

10.3.3 Network Interfaces

The network interface (NI) contains one or more input/output ports to source packets to and sink packets from the network under the direction of the communication assist, which connects it to the processing node as we have seen in previous chapters. The network interface, or host nodes, behave quite differently than switch nodes and may be connected via special links. The NI formats the packets and constructs the routing and control information. It may have substantial input and output buffering compared to a switch. It may perform end-to-end error checking and flow control. Clearly, its cost is influenced by its storage capacity, processing complexity, and number of ports.

10.4 INTERCONNECTION TOPOLOGIES

Now that we understand the basic factors determining the performance and the cost of networks, we can examine each of the major dimensions of the design space in relation to these factors. This section covers the set of important interconnection topologies. Each topology is really a class of networks scaling with the number of host nodes N, so we want to understand the key characteristics of each class as a function of N. In practice, the topological properties, such as distance, are not entirely independent of the physical properties, such as length and width, because some topologies fundamentally require longer wires when packed into a physical volume, so it is important to understand both aspects.

10.4.1 Fully Connected Network

A fully connected network is essentially a single switch, which connects all inputs to all outputs. The diameter is 1 link. The degree is N. The loss of the switch wipes out the whole network; however, the loss of a link removes only one node. One such network is simply a bus, and this provides a useful reference point to describe the basic characteristics. It has the nice property that the cost scales as $O(N)$. Unfortunately, only one data transmission can occur on a bus at once, so the total bandwidth is $O(1)$, as is the bisection. In fact, the bandwidth scaling is worse than $O(1)$ because the clock rate of a bus decreases with the number of ports due to RC delays. (An Ethernet is really a bit-serial, distributed bus; it just operates at a low enough frequency that a large number of physical connections are possible.) Another fully connected network is a crossbar. It provides $O(N)$ bandwidth, but the cost of the interconnect is proportional to the number of cross-points, or $O(N^2)$. In either case, a fully connected network is not scalable in practice. This is not to say they are not important. Individual switches are often fully connected internally and provide the basic building block for larger networks. A key metric of technological advance in networks is the degree of a cost-effective switch. With increasing VLSI chip density, the number of nodes that can be fully connected by a cost-effective switch is increasing.

10.4.2 Linear Arrays and Rings

The simplest network is a linear array of nodes numbered consecutively $0, \ldots, N-1$ and connected by bidirectional links. The diameter is $N-1$, the average distance is roughly $2/3\ N$, and removal of a single link partitions the network, so the bisection width is 1 link. Routing in such a network is trivial since there is exactly one route between any pair of nodes. To describe the route from node A to node B, let us define $R = B - A$ to be the *relative address* of B from A. This signed $\log N$ bit number is the number of links to cross to get from A to B with the positive direction being away from node 0. Since there is a unique route between a pair of nodes, clearly the network provides no fault tolerance. The network consists of $N-1$ links and can easily be laid out in $O(N)$ space using only short wires. Any contiguous segment of nodes provides a subnetwork of the same topology as the full network.

A *ring* or *torus* of N nodes can be formed by simply connecting the two ends of an array. With unidirectional links, the diameter is $N-1$, the average distance is $N/2$, the bisection width is 1 link, and there is one route between any pair of nodes. The relative address of B from A is $(B - A) \bmod N$. With bidirectional links, the diameter is $N/2$, the average distance is $N/3$, the degree of the node is 2, and the bisection is 2. There are two routes (two relative addresses) between pairs of nodes, so the network can function with degraded performance in the presence of a single faulty link. The network is easily laid out with $O(N)$ space using only short wires, as indicated by Figure 10.6, by simply folding the ring. The network can be partitioned into smaller subnetworks; however, the subnetworks are linear arrays rather than rings.

Although these one-dimensional networks are not scalable in any practical sense, they are an important building block conceptually and in practice. The simple routing and low hardware complexity of rings has made them very popular for local area interconnects, including FDDI, FiberChannel Arbitrated Loop, and Scalable Coherent Interface (SCI). Since they can be laid out with very short wires, it is possible to make the links very wide. For example, the KSR1 used a 32-node ring that was 128 bits wide as a building block. SCI obtains its bandwidth by using 16-bit links.

10.4.3 Multidimensional Meshes and Tori

Rings and arrays generalize naturally to higher dimensions, including 2D *grids* and 3D *cubes*, with or without end-around connections. A d-dimensional array consists

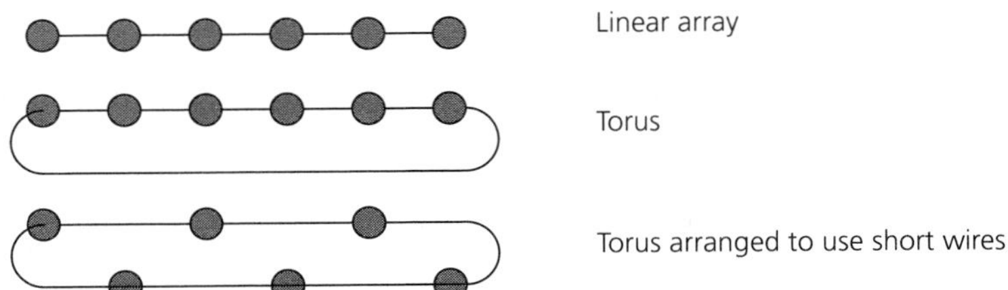

FIGURE 10.6 Linear and ring topologies. The linear array and torus are easily laid out to use uniformly short wires. The distance and cost grow as $O(N)$ whereas the aggregate bandwidth is only $O(1)$.

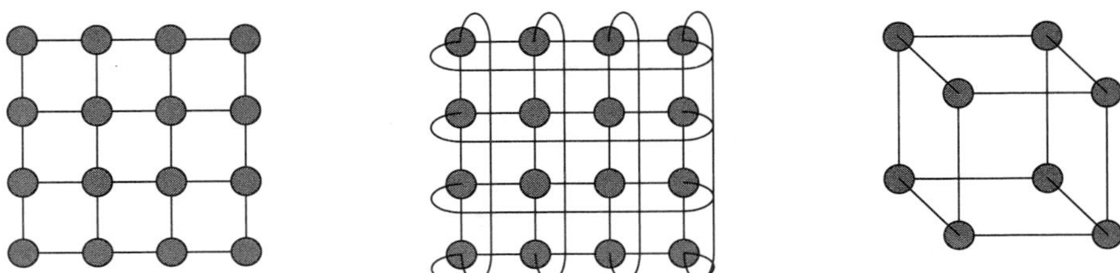

FIGURE 10.7 Grid, torus, and cube topologies. Grids, tori, and cubes are special cases of k-ary d-cube networks, which are constructed with k nodes in each of d dimensions. Low-dimensional networks pack well in physical space with short wires.

of $N = k_{d-1} \times \ldots \times k_0$ nodes, each identified by its d-vector of coordinates $(i_{d-1}, \ldots, i_0)$, where $0 \le i_j \le k_j - 1$ for $0 \le j \le d - 1$. Figure 10.7 shows the common cases of two and three dimensions. For simplicity, we will assume the length along each dimension is the same, so $N = k^d$ ($k = \sqrt[d]{N}$, $r = \log_d N$). This is called a d-dimensional k-ary mesh. (In practice, engineering constraints often result in nonuniform dimensions, but the theory is easily extended to handle that case.) Each node is a switch addressed by a d-vector of radix k coordinates and is connected to the nodes that differ by one in precisely one coordinate. The node degree varies between d and $2d$, inclusive, with nodes in the middle having full degree and the corners having minimal degree.

For a d-dimensional k-ary torus, the edges wrap around from each face, so every node has degree $2d$ (in the bidirectional case) and is connected to nodes differing by one (mod k) in each dimension. We will refer to arrays and tori collectively as meshes. The d-dimensional k-ary unidirectional torus is a very important class of networks, often called a k-ary d-cube, employed widely in modern parallel machines. These networks are usually configured as direct networks, so an additional switch degree is required to support the bidirectional host connection from each switch. They are generally viewed as having low degree, 2 or 3, so the network scales by increasing k along some or all of the dimensions.

To define the routes from node A to node B in a d-dimensional array, let $R = (b_{d-1} - a_{d-1}, \ldots, b_0 - a_0)$ be the relative address of B from A. A route must cross $r_i = b_i - a_i$ links in each dimension i, where the sign specifies the appropriate direction. The simplest approach is to traverse the dimensions in order, so for $i = 0 \ldots d - 1$, travel r_i hops in the ith dimension. This corresponds to traveling between two locations in a metropolitan grid by driving in, say, the east-west direction, turning once, and driving in the north-south direction. Of course, we can reach the same destination by first traveling north-south and then east-west or by zigzagging anywhere between these routes. In general, we may view the source and destination points as corners of a subarray and follow any path between the corners that reduces the relative address from the destination at each hop.

The diameter of the network is $d(k - 1)$. The average distance is simply the average distance in each dimension, roughly

$$d\frac{2}{3}k$$

If k is even, the bisection of a d-dimensional k-ary array is k^{d-1} bidirectional links. This is obtained by simply cutting the array in the middle by a (hyper)plane perpendicular to one of the dimensions. (If k is odd, the bisection may be a little bit larger.) For a unidirectional torus, the relative address and routing generalizes along each dimension just as for a ring. All nodes have degree d (plus the host degree), and k^{d-1} links cross the middle in each direction.

It is clear that a two-dimensional mesh can be laid out with $O(N)$ space in a plane with short wires and three-dimensional mesh in $O(N)$ volume in free space. In practice, engineering factors come into play. It is not really practical to build a huge 2D structure, and mechanical issues arise in how 3D is utilized, as illustrated by Example 10.1.

EXAMPLE 10.1 Using a direct 2D mesh topology, such as in the Intel Paragon, where a single cabinet holds 64 processors forming a 4-wide by 16-high array of nodes (each node containing a message processor and one to four compute processors), how might you configure cabinets to construct a large machine with only short wires?

Answer Although there are many possible approaches, the one used by Intel is illustrated in Figure 1.24 of Chapter 1. The cabinets stand on the floor, and large configurations are formed by attaching these cabinets side by side, forming a $16 \times k$ array. The largest configuration was a 1,824-node machine at Sandia National Laboratory configured as a 16×114 array. The bisection bandwidth is determined by the 16 links that cross between cabinets. ■

Other machines have found alternative strategies for dealing with real-world packaging restrictions. The MIT J-machine is a 3D torus where each board comprises an 8×16 torus in the first two dimensions. Larger machines are constructed by stacking these boards next to one another, with board-to-board connections providing the links in the third dimension. The Intel ASCI Red machine with 4,536 compute nodes is constructed as 85 cabinets. It allows long wires to run between

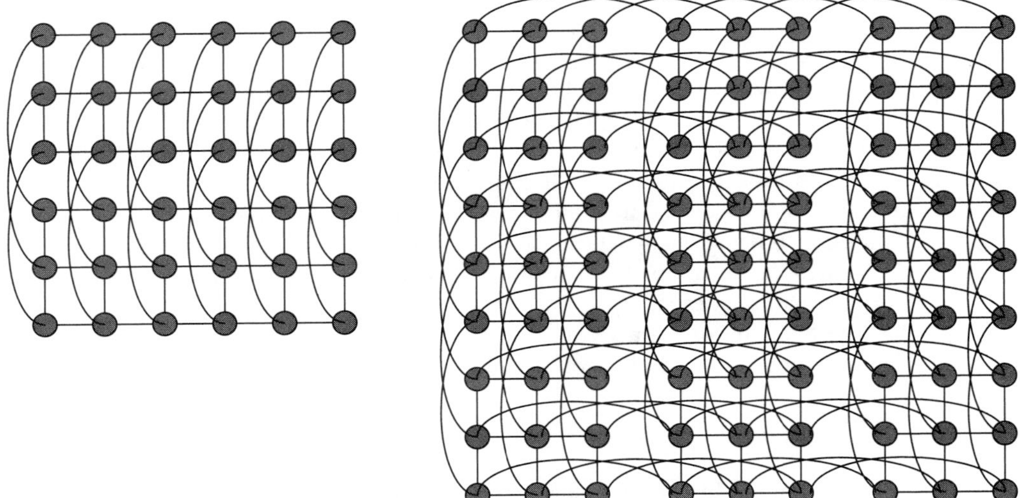

FIGURE 10.8 Embeddings of many logical dimensions in two physical dimensions. A higher-dimensional *k*-ary *d*-cube can be laid out in 2D by replicating a 2D slice and then connecting slices across the remaining dimensions. The wiring complexity of these higher-dimensional networks can be easily seen in the figure.

cabinets in each dimension. In general, with higher-dimensional meshes, several logical dimensions are embedded in each physical dimension using longer wires. Figure 10.8 shows a $6 \times 3 \times 2$ array and a four-dimensional 3-ary array embedded in a plane. It is clear that, for a given physical dimension, the average wire length and the number of wires increases with the number of logical dimensions.

10.4.4 Trees

In meshes, the diameter and average distance increases with the dth root of N. Many other topologies exist where the routing distance grows only logarithmically. The simplest of these is a tree. A binary tree has degree 3. Typically, trees are employed as indirect networks with hosts as the leaves, so for N leaves the diameter is $2 \log N$. (Such a topology could be used as a direct network of $N = k \log k$ nodes.) In the indirect case, we may treat the binary address of each node as a $d = \log N$ bit vector specifying a path from the root of the tree—the high-order bit indicates whether the node is below the left or right child of the root and so on down the levels of the tree. The levels of the tree correspond directly to the "dimension" of the network. One way to route from node A to node B would be to go all the way up to the root and then follow the path down specified by the address of B. Of course, we really only need to go up to the first common parent of the two nodes before heading down. Let $R = B \oplus A$, the bitwise *xor* of the node addresses, be the relative address of A and B

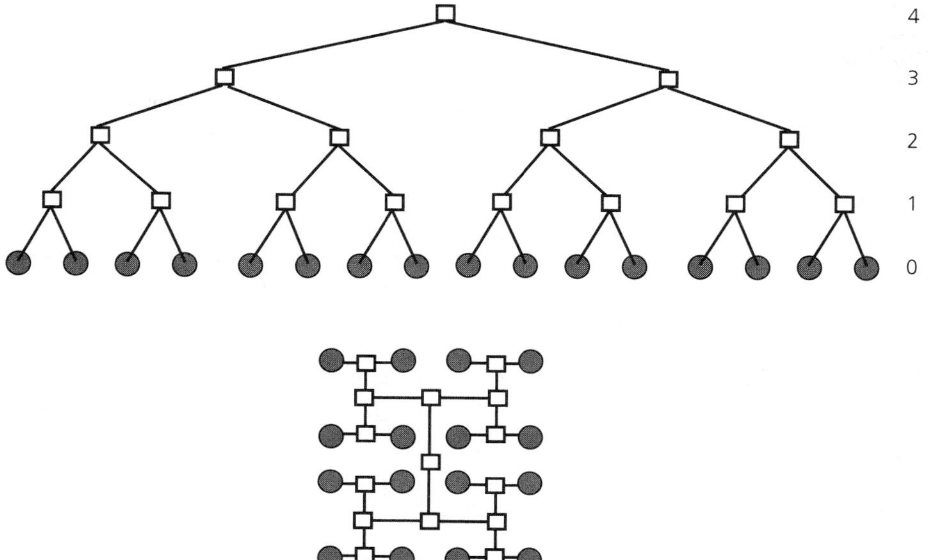

FIGURE 10.9 Binary trees. Trees are a simple network with logarithmic depth that can be laid out efficiently in 2D by using an H-tree configuration. Routing is simple, and they contain trees as subnetworks. However, the bisection bandwidth is only $O(1)$.

and i be the position of the most significant 1 in R. The route from node A to node B is simply $i + 1$ hops up followed by $i + 1$ hops down, with the direction at each branch specified by the low-order $i + 1$ bits of B.

Formally, a complete indirect binary tree is a network of $2N - 1$ nodes organized as $d + 1 = \log_2 N + 1$ levels. Host nodes occupy level 0 and are identified by a d-bit address $A = a_{d-1}, \ldots, a_0$. A switch node is identified by its level i and its $d - i$ bit address $A^{(i)} = a_{d-1}, \ldots, a_i$. A switch node $[i, A^{(i)}]$ is connected to a parent $[i + 1, A^{(i+1)}]$ and two children $[i - 1, A^{(i)} || 0]$ and $[i - 1, A^{(i)} || 1]$ where the vertical bars indicate bitwise concatenation. There is a unique route between any pair of nodes by going up to the least common ancestor, so no fault tolerance is present. The average distance is almost as large as the diameter and the tree partitions into subtrees. One virtue of the tree is the ease of supporting broadcast or multicast operations from one node to many.

Clearly, by increasing the branching factor of the tree the routing distance is reduced. In a k-ary tree, each node has k children, the height of the tree is $d = \log_k N$, and the address of a host is specified by a d-vector of radix k coordinates describing the path down from the root.

One potential problem with trees is that they seem to require long wires. After all, when we draw a tree in a plane, the lines near the root usually grow exponentially in length with the number of levels, as illustrated in the top portion of Figure 10.9, resulting in an $O(N \log N)$ layout with $O(N)$ long wires. This is really a matter of how you look at it. The same 16-node tree is laid out compactly in two dimensions using a recursive "H-tree" pattern, which allows an $O(N)$ layout with only $O\sqrt{N}$ long wires (Bhatt and Leiserson 1982). We can imagine using the H-tree pattern with multiple nodes on a chip, among nodes (or subtrees) on a board, or between cabinets on a floor, but the linear layout might be used between boards.

The more serious problem with the tree is its bisection. Removing a single link near the root bisects the network. It has been observed that computer scientists have a funny notion of trees; real trees get thicker toward the trunk. An even better analogy is the human circulatory system where the heart forms the root and the cells the leaves. Blood cells are routed up the veins to the root and down the arteries to the cells. Bandwidth is essentially constant across each level so that blood flows evenly. This idea has been addressed in an interesting variant of tree networks, called *fat-trees,* where the upward link to the parent has twice the bandwidth of the child links. Of course, packets don't behave quite like blood cells, so some issues need to be sorted out on exactly how to wire this up. These will fall out easily from butterflies.

10.4.5 Butterflies

The constriction at the root of the tree can be avoided if there are "lots of roots." This is provided by an important logarithmic network called a butterfly. (The butterfly topology arises in many settings in the literature. It is the inherent communication pattern on an element-by-element level of the FFT, the Batcher odd-even merge sort, and other important parallel algorithms. It is isomorphic to topologies in the networking literature, including the Omega and SW-Banyan networks, and is closely related to the shuffle-exchange network and the hypercube, which we will discuss later.) Given 2×2 switches, the basic building block of the butterfly is obtained by simply crossing one of each pair of edges, as illustrated in the top of Figure 10.10. This is a tool for correcting one bit of the relative address—going straight leaves the bit the same, crossing flips the bit. These 2×2 butterflies are composed into a network of $N = 2^d$ nodes in $\log_2 N$ levels of switches by systematically changing the cross edges as shown by the 16-node butterfly illustrated in the bottom portion of Figure 10.10. This configuration shows an indirect network with unidirectional links going upward so that hosts deliver packets into level 0 and receive packets from level d. Each level corrects one additional bit of the relative address. Each node at level d forms the root of a tree with all the hosts as leaves, and from each host is a tree of routes reaching every node at level d.

A d-dimensional indirect butterfly has $N = 2^d$ host nodes and $d2^{d-1}$ switch nodes of degree 2 organized as d levels of $N/2$ nodes each. A switch node at level i, $[i, A]$ has its outputs connected to nodes $[i + 1, A]$ and $[i + 1, A \oplus 2^i]$. To route from A to B, compute the relative address $R = A \oplus B$ and at level i use the "straight edge" if r_i is 0 and the cross edge otherwise. The diameter is $\log N$. In fact, all routes are $\log N$ long. The bisection is $N/2$. (A slightly different formulation with only one host connected to each edge switch has bisection N but twice as many switches at each level and one additional level.)

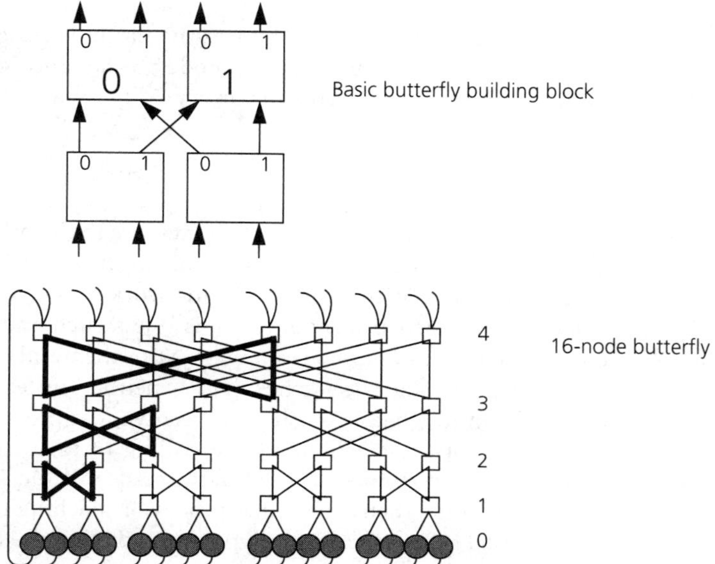

FIGURE 10.10 Butterfly. The butterfly is a logarithmic depth network constructed by composing 2 × 2 blocks that correct one bit in the relative address. It can be viewed as a tree with multiple roots.

A d-dimensional k-ary butterfly is obtained using switches of degree k, a power of two. The address of a node is then viewed as a d-vector of radix k coordinates, so each level corrects $\log k$ bits in the relative address. In this case, there are $\log_k N$ levels. In effect, this fuses adjacent levels into a higher radix butterfly.

There is exactly one route from each host output to each host input, so no inherent fault tolerance is present in the basic topology. However, unlike the 1D mesh or the tree where a broken link partitions the network, there is the potential for fault tolerance in the butterfly. For example, the route from A to B may be broken, but there is a path from A to another node C and from C to B. There are many proposals for making the butterfly fault tolerant by just adding a few extra links. One simple approach is to add an extra level to the butterfly so there are two routes to every destination from every source. This approach was used in the BBN T2000.

The butterfly appears to be a qualitatively more scalable network than meshes and trees because each packet crosses $\log N$ links and there are $N \log N$ links in the network, so on average it should be possible for all the nodes to send messages anywhere all at once. By contrast, a 2D torus or tree has only two links per node, so nodes can only send messages a long distance infrequently and very few nodes are close. A similar argument can be made in terms of bisection. For a random permutation of data among the N nodes, $N/2$ messages are expected to cross the bisection in each direction. The butterfly has $N/2$ links across the bisection whereas the d-dimensional mesh has only

$$N^{\frac{d-1}{d}}$$

links and the tree only one. Thus, as the machine scales, a given node in a butterfly can send every other message to a node on the other side of the machine whereas a node in a 2D mesh can send only every

$$\sqrt[d]{\frac{N}{2}}\text{th}$$

message and the tree only every Nth message to the other side.

This analysis has two potential problems, however. The first is cost. In a tree or d-dimensional mesh, the cost of the network is a fixed fraction of the cost of the machine. For each host node there is one switch and d links. In the butterfly, the cost of the network per node increases with the number of nodes since for each host node there are log N switches. Thus, neither scales perfectly. The real question comes down to what a switch costs relative to a processor and what fraction of the overall cost of the machine we are willing to invest in the network to be able to deliver a certain communication performance. If the switch and link is 10% of the cost of the node, then on a 1,024-processor machine the network will be only one-half the total cost with a butterfly. On the other hand, if the switch is equal in cost to a node, we are unlikely to consider more than a low-dimensional network. Conversely, if we reduce the dimension of the network, we may be able to invest more in each switch.

The second problem is that even though the butterfly has enough links to support the bandwidth × distance product of a random permutation, the topology of the butterfly will not allow an arbitrary permutation of N messages among the N nodes to be routed without conflict. A path from an input to an output blocks the paths of many other input/output pairs because there are shared edges. In fact, even when allowed to go through the butterfly twice, permutations exist that cannot be routed without conflicts. However, if two butterflies are laid back to back so that a message goes forward through one and in the reverse direction through the other, then for any permutation there exists a choice of intermediate positions that allows a conflict-free routing of the permutation. This back-to-back butterfly is called a Benes network (Benes 1965; Leighton 1992), and it has been extensively studied because of its elegant theoretical properties. It is often seen as having little practical significance because it is costly to compute the intermediate positions and the permutation has to be known in advance. On the other hand, there is another interesting theoretical result that says that on a butterfly any permutation can be routed with very few conflicts (with high probability) by first sending every message to a random intermediate node and then routing the messages to the desired destination (Leighton 1992). These two results come together in a very nice practical way in the fat-tree network, as follows.

A d-dimensional k-ary fat-tree is formed by taking a d-dimensional k-ary Benes network and folding it back on itself at the high-order dimension, as illustrated in Figure 10.11. The collection of $N/2$ switches at level i is viewed as N^{d-i} "fat nodes"

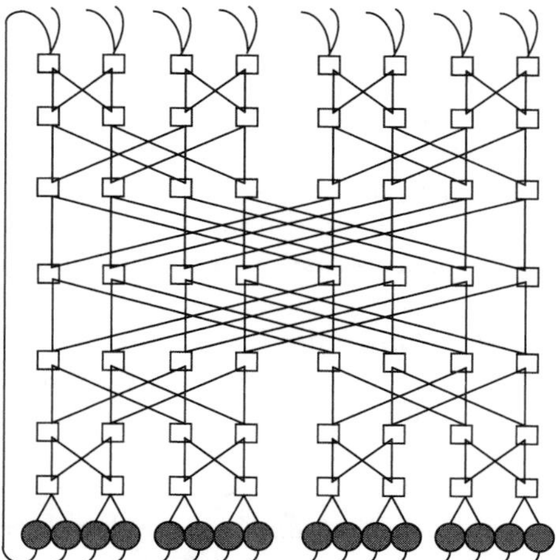

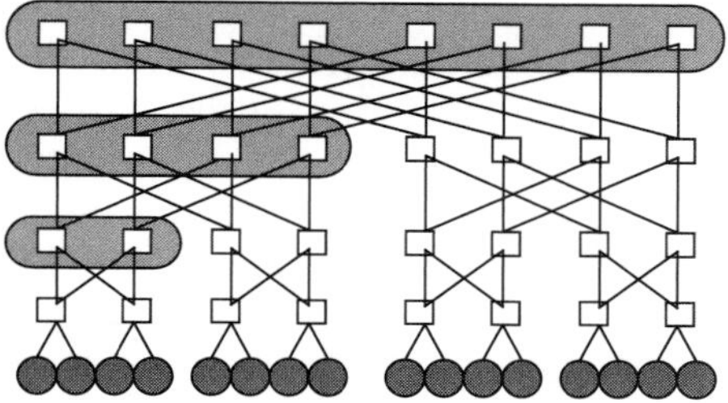

FIGURE 10.11 Benes network and fat-tree. A Benes network is constructed essentially by connecting two butterflies back to back. It has the interesting property that it can route any permutation in a conflict-free fashion, given the opportunity to compute the route off-line. Two forward-going butterflies do not have this property. The fat-tree is obtained by folding the second half of the Benes network back on itself and fusing the two directions so that it is possible to turn around at each level. Collections of switches serve as fat nodes.

of 2^{i-1} switches. The edges of the forward-going butterfly go up the tree toward the roots and the edges of the reverse butterfly go down toward the leaves. To route from *A* to *B*, pick a random node *C* in the least common ancestor fat node of *A* and *B* and take the unique tree route from *A* to *C* and the unique tree route back down from *C* to *B*. Let *i* be the highest dimension of difference in *A* and *B;* then there are 2^i root nodes to choose from, so the longer the routing distance the more the traffic can be distributed. This topology clearly has a great deal of fault tolerance—it has the bisection of the butterfly, the partitioning properties of the tree, and allows essentially all permutations to be routed with very little contention. It is used in the Connection Machine CM-5 and the Meiko CS-2. In the CM-5, the randomization on the upward path is done dynamically by the switches; in the CS-2, the source node chooses the ancestor. A particularly important practical property of butterflies and fat-trees is that the nodes have a fixed degree independent of the size of the network. This allows networks of any size to be constructed with the same switches. As is indicated in Figure 10.11, the physical wiring complexity of the higher levels of a fat-tree or any butterfly-like network becomes critical, since a large number of long wires connect to different places.

10.4.6 Hypercubes

It may seem that the straight edges in the butterfly are a target for potential optimization since they take a packet forward to the next level in the same column. Consider what happens if we collapse all the switches in a column into a single log N degree switch. This has brought us full circle; it is a d-dimensional 2-ary torus! Actually, we need to split the switches in a column in half and associate them with the two adjacent nodes. It is called a *hypercube* or *binary n*-cube. Each of the $N = 2^d$ nodes is connected to the d nodes that differ by exactly one bit in address. The relative address $R(A, B) = A \oplus B$ specifies the dimensions that must be crossed to go from A to B. Clearly, the length of the route is equal to the number of ones in the relative address. The dimensions can be corrected in any order (corresponding to the different ways of getting between opposite corners of the subcube), and the butterfly routing corresponds exactly to dimension order routing, called *e-cube routing* in the hypercube literature. Fat-tree routing corresponds to picking a random node in the subcube defined by the high-order bit in the relative address, sending the packet "up" to the random node and back "down" to the destination. Observe that the fat-tree uses distinct sets of links for the two directions, so to get the same properties we need a pair of bidirectional links between nodes in the hypercube.

The hypercube is an important topology that has received tremendous attention in the theoretical literature. For example, lower-dimensional meshes can be embedded one to one in the hypercube by choosing an appropriate labeling of the nodes. Recall from digital design that a graycode sequence orders the numbers from 0 to $2^d - 1$ so that adjacent numbers differ by 1 bit. This shows how to embed a 1D mesh into a d-cube, and it can be extended to any number of dimensions (see Exercise 10.7). Clearly, butterflies, shuffle-exchange networks, and the like embed easily. (Interestingly, a d-cube does not quite embed a $d - 1$ level tree because one extra node is in the d-cube.)

Practically speaking, the hypercube was used by many of the early large-scale parallel machines, including the Cal Tech research prototypes (Seitz 1985), the first three Intel iPSC generations (Ratner 1985), and three generations of nCUBE machines. Later large-scale machines, including the Intel Delta, the Intel Paragon, and the CRAY T3D, use low-dimensional meshes. One of the reasons for the shift is that in practice the hypercube topology forces the designer to use switches of a degree that supports the largest possible configuration. Ports are wasted in smaller configurations. The k-ary d-cube approach provides the practical scalability of allowing arbitrarily sized configurations to be constructed with a given set of components, that is, with switches of fixed degree. Nonetheless, this begs the question, what should the degree be?

The general trend in network design in parallel machines is toward switches that can be wired in an arbitrary topology. We see this, for example, in the IBM SP-2, SGI Origin, Myricom network, and most ATM switches. The designer may choose to adopt a particular regular topology or may wire together configurations of different sizes differently. At any point in time, technology factors such as pin-out and chip area limit the largest potential degree.

10.5 EVALUATING DESIGN TRADE-OFFS IN NETWORK TOPOLOGY

The k-ary d-cube provides a convenient framework for evaluating design alternatives for direct networks. The design question can be posed in two ways. Given a choice of dimension, the design of the switch is determined and we can ask how the machine scales. Alternatively, for the machine scale of interest, that is, $N = k^d$, we may ask what the best dimensionality is under salient cost constraints. We have the 2D torus at one extreme, the hypercube at the other, and a spectrum of networks between. As with most aspects of architecture, the key to evaluating trade-offs is to define the cost model and performance model and then to optimize the design accordingly. Network topology has been a point of lively debate over the history of parallel architectures. To a large extent, this is because different positions make sense under different cost models and the technology keeps changing. Once the dimensionality (or degree) of the switch is determined, the space of candidate networks is relatively constrained, so the question is how large a degree is worth working toward.

Let's collect what we know about this class of networks in one place. The total number of switches is N, regardless of degree; however, the switch degree is d, so the total number of links is $C = Nd$ and there are $2wd$ pins per node. The average routing distance is

$$d\left(\frac{k-1}{2}\right),$$

the diameter is $d(k - 1)$, and $k^{d-1} = N/k$ links cross the bisection in each direction (for even k). Thus, there are $2Nw/k$ wires crossing the middle of the network.

If our primary concern is the routing distance, then we are inclined to maximize the dimension and build a hypercube. This would be the case with store-and-forward routing, assuming that the degree of the switch and the number of links were not a significant cost factor. In addition, we get to enjoy its elegant mathematical properties. Accordingly, this was the topology of choice for most of the first-generation large-scale parallel machines. However, with cut-through routing and a more realistic hardware cost model, the choice is much less clear. If the number of links or the switch degree is the dominant cost, we are inclined to minimize the dimension and build a mesh. For the evaluation to make sense, we want to compare the performance of design alternatives with roughly equal cost. Different assumptions about what aspects of the system are costly lead to very different conclusions.

The assumed communication pattern influences the decision too. If we look at the worst-case traffic pattern for each network, we will prefer high-dimensional networks where essentially all the paths are short. If we look at patterns where each node is communicating with only one or two near neighbors, we will prefer low-dimensional networks since only a few of the dimensions are actually used.

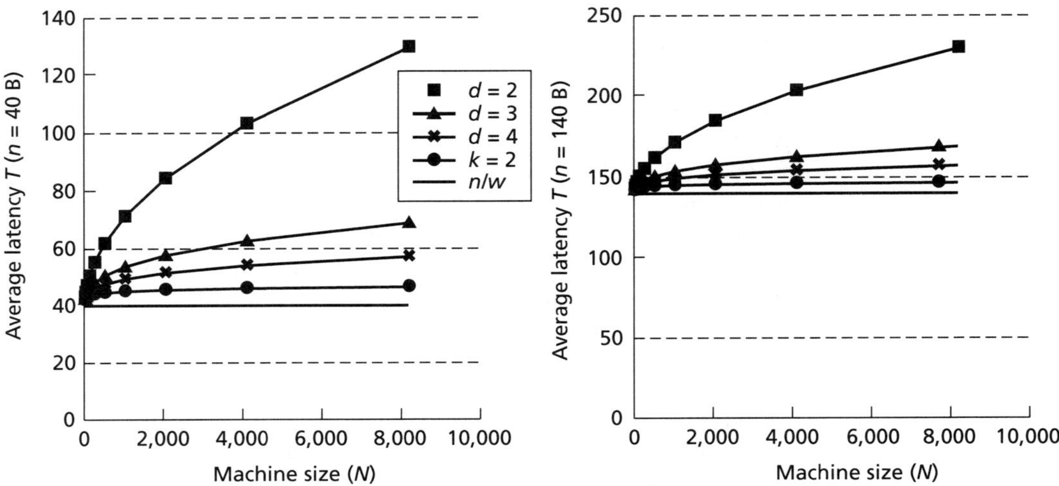

FIGURE 10.12 Unloaded latency scaling of networks for various dimensions with fixed link width. The *n*/*w* line shows the channel occupancy component of message transmission, that is, the time for the bits to cross a single channel, which is independent of network topology. The curves show the additional latency due to routing.

10.5.1 Unloaded Latency

Figure 10.12 shows the increase in average unloaded latency under our model of cut-through routing for 2-, 3-, and 4-cubes, as well as binary *d*-cubes ($k = 2$), as the machine size is scaled up. It assumes unit routing delay per stage ($\Delta = 1$) and shows message sizes of 40 and 140 bytes, with $w = 1$ byte. The bottom line shows the portion of the latency resulting from channel occupancy. As we should expect, for smaller messages (or larger routing delay per stage) the scaling of the low-dimension networks is worse because a message experiences more routing steps, on average. However, in making comparisons across the curves in this figure, we are tacitly assuming that the difference in degree is not a significant component of the system cost. In addition, 1 cycle routing is very aggressive; more typical values for high-performance switches are 4–8 network cycles (see Table 10.1). On the other hand, larger message sizes are also common.

To focus our attention on the dimensionality of the network as a design issue, we can fix the cost model and the number of nodes that reflects our design point and examine the performance characteristics of networks with fixed costs for a range of *d*. Figure 10.13 shows the unloaded latency for short messages as a function of the dimensionality for four machine sizes. For large machines, the routing delays in low-dimensionality networks dominate. For higher dimensionality, the latency approaches the channel time. This "equal number of nodes" cost model has been widely used to support the view that low-dimensional networks do not scale well.

Table 10.1 Link Width and Routing Delay for Various Parallel Machine Networks

Machine	Topology	Cycle Time (ns)	Channel Width (bits)	Routing Delay (cycles)	Flit (data bits)
nCUBE/2	Hypercube	25	1	40	32
TMC CM-5	Fat-Tree	25	4	10	4
IBM SP-2	Banyan	25	8	5	16
Intel Paragon	2D Mesh	11.5	16	2	16
Meiko CS-2	Fat-Tree	20	8	7	8
CRAY T3D	3D Torus	6.67	16	2	16
DASH	Torus	30	16	2	16
J-Machine	3D Mesh	31	8	2	8
Monsoon	Butterfly	20	16	2	16
SGI Origin	Hypercube	2.5	20	16	160
Myricom	Arbitrary	6.25	16	50	16

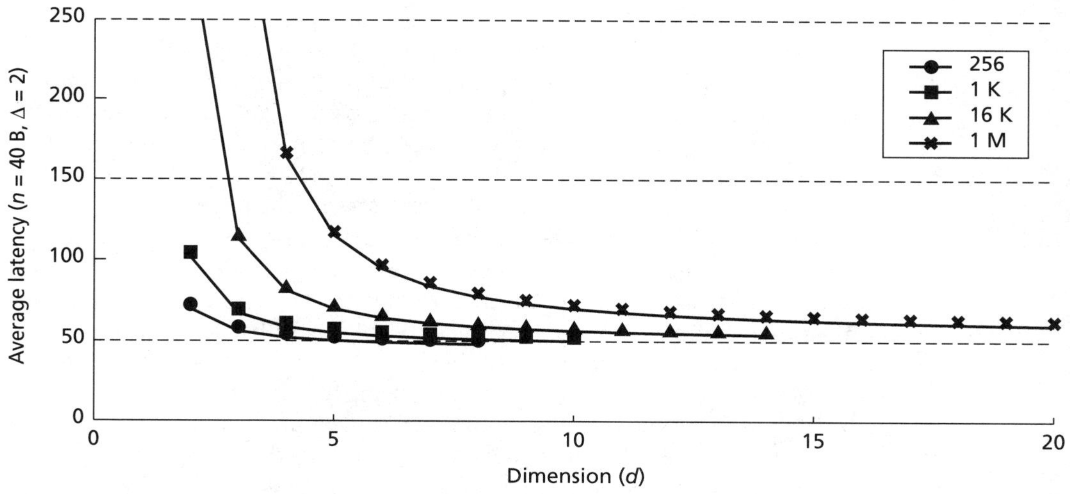

FIGURE 10.13 Unloaded latency for k-ary d-cubes with equal node count (n = 40 B, Δ = 2) as a function of degree. With the link width and routing delay fixed, the unloaded latency for large networks rises sharply at low dimensions due to routing distance.

It is not surprising that higher-dimensional networks are superior under the cost model of Figure 10.13 since the added switch degree, number of channels, and channel length come essentially for free. The high-dimension networks have a much larger number of wires and pins and bigger switches than the low-dimension networks. For the rightmost end of the graph in Figure 10.13, the network design is quite impractical. The cost of the network is a significant fraction of the cost of the large-scale parallel machine, so it makes sense to compare equal cost designs under appropriate technological assumptions. As chip size and density improve, the switch internals tend to become a less significant cost factor whereas pins and wires remain critical. In the extreme, the physical volume of the wires presents a fundamental limit on the amount of interconnection that is possible. So let's compare these networks under assumptions of equal wiring complexity.

One sensible comparison is to keep the total number of wires per node constant, that is, fix the number of pins, $2dw$. Let's take as our baseline a 2-cube with channel width $w = 32$, so there are a total of 128 wires per node. With more dimensions, there are more channels and they must each be thinner. In particular, $w_d = \lfloor 64/d \rfloor$. So in an 8-cube, the links are only 8 bits wide. Assuming 40- and 140-byte messages, a uniform routing delay of 2 cycles per hop, and uniform cycle time, the unloaded latency under equal pin scaling is shown in Figure 10.14. This figure shows a very different story. As a result of narrower channels, the channel time becomes greater with increasing dimension; this mitigates the reduction in routing delay stemming from the smaller routing distance. The very large configurations still experience large routing delays for low dimensions, regardless of the channel width, but all the configurations have an optimum unloaded latency at modest dimension.

If the design is not limited by pin count, the critical aspect of the wiring complexity is likely to be the number of wires that cross through the middle of the machine. If the machine is viewed as laid out in a plane, the physical bisection width grows only with the square root of the area, and in three-space it only grows as the two-thirds power of the volume. Even if the network has a high logical dimension, it must be embedded in a small number of physical dimensions, so the designer must contend with the cross-sectional area of the wires crossing the midplane.

We can focus on this aspect of the cost by comparing designs with an equal number of wires crossing the bisection. At one extreme, the hypercube has N such links. Let us assume these have unit size. A 2D torus has only $2\sqrt{N}$ links crossing the bisection, so each link could be $\sqrt{N}/2$ times the width of that used in the hypercube. By the equal bisection criteria, we should compare a 1,024-node hypercube with bit-serial links with a torus of the same size using 32-bit links. In general, the d-dimensional mesh with the same bisection width as the N-node hypercube has links of width $w_d = \sqrt[d]{N}/2 = k/2$. Assuming cut-through routing, the average latency of an n-byte packet to a random destination on an unloaded network is as follows.

$$
\begin{aligned}
T(n, N, d) &= \frac{n}{w_d} + \Delta \cdot d\left(\frac{k-1}{2}\right) \\
&= \frac{n}{k/2} + \Delta \cdot d\left(\frac{k-1}{2}\right) = \frac{n}{\sqrt[d]{N}/2} + \Delta \cdot d\left(\frac{\sqrt[d]{N}-1}{2}\right) \qquad (10.7)
\end{aligned}
$$

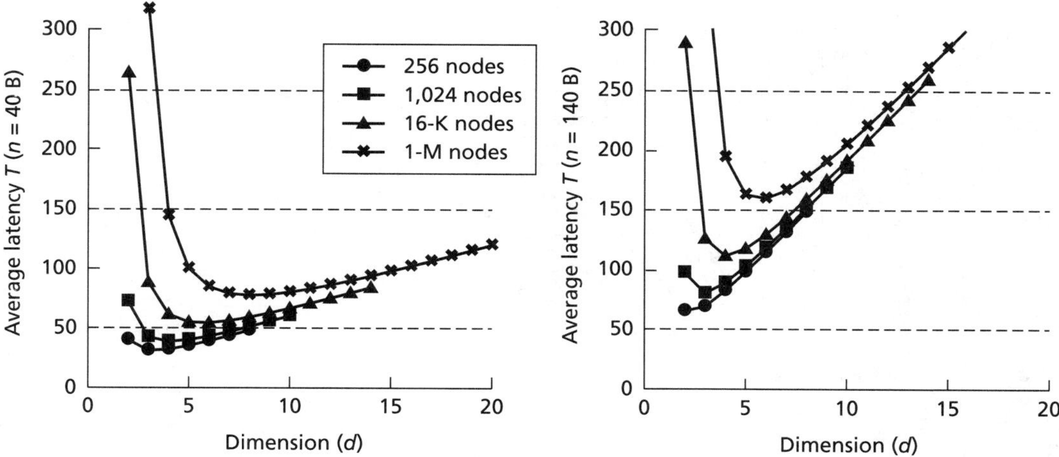

FIGURE 10.14 Unloaded latency for *k*-ary *d*-cubes with equal pin count (*n* = 40 B and *n* = 140 B, Δ = 2). With equal pin count, higher dimensions imply narrower channels, so the optimal design point balances the routing delay (which increases with lower dimension) against channel time (which increases with higher dimension).

Thus, increasing the dimension tends to decrease the routing delay but increase the channel time, as with equal pin count scaling. (The reader can verify that the minimum latency is achieved when the two terms are essentially equal.)

Figure 10.15 shows the average latency for 40-byte messages, assuming $\Delta = 2$, as a function of the dimension for a range of machine sizes. As the dimension increases from $d = 2$, the routing delay drops rapidly, whereas the channel time increases steadily throughout as the links get thinner. (The $d = 2$ point is not shown for $N = 1M$ nodes because it is rather ridiculous; the links are 512 bits wide and the average number of hops is 1,023.) For machines up to a few thousand nodes, $\sqrt[3]{N}/2$ and $\log N$ are very close, so the impact of the additional channels on channel width becomes the dominant effect. If large messages are considered, the routing component becomes even less significant. For large machines, the low-dimensional meshes under this scaling rule become impractical because the links become very wide.

Thus far, we have concerned ourselves with the wiring cross-sectional area, but we have not worried about the wire length. If a d-cube is embedded in a plane, that is, if $d/2$ dimensions are embedded in each physical dimension such that the distance between the centers of the nodes is fixed, then each additional dimension increases the length of the longest wire by a $\sqrt{k}$ factor. Thus, the length of the longest wire in a d-cube is $k^{n/2 - 1}$ times that in the 2-cube. Accounting for increased wire length further strengthens the argument for a modest number of dimensions. This accounting might be done in three ways. If we assume that multiple bits are pipelined on the wire, then the increased length effectively increases the routing delay. If

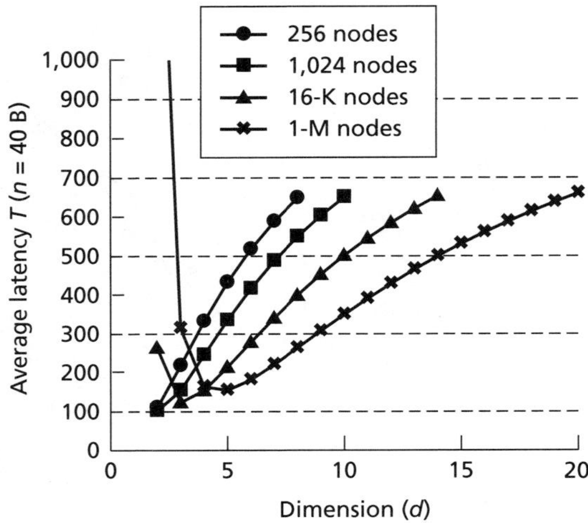

FIGURE 10.15 Unloaded latency for *k*-ary *d*-cubes with equal bisection width (n = 40 B, Δ = 2). The balance between routing delay and channel time shifts even more in favor of low-degree networks with an equal bisection width scaling rule.

the wires are not pipelined, then the cycle time of the network is increased as a result of the time to drive the wire, which is logarithmic in the wire length.

The embedding of the d-dimensional network into few physical dimensions introduces second-order effects that may enhance the benefit of low dimensions. If a high-dimension network is embedded systematically into a plane, the wire density tends to be highest near the bisection and low near the perimeter. A 2D mesh has uniform wire density throughout, so it makes better use of the area that it occupies.

We should also look at the trade-offs in network design from a bandwidth viewpoint. The key factor influencing latency with equal wire complexity scaling is the increased channel bandwidth at low dimension. Wider channels are beneficial if most of the traffic arises from or is delivered to one or a few nodes. If traffic is localized so that each node communicates with just a few neighbors, only a few of the dimensions are utilized, and again the higher-link bandwidth dominates. If a large number of nodes are communicating throughout the machine, then we need to model the effects of contention on the observed latency and see where the network saturates.

Before leaving the examination of trade-offs for latency in the unloaded case, we should note that the evaluation is rather sensitive to the relative time to cross a wire and to cross a switch. If the routing delay per switch is 20 times that of the wire, the picture is very different, as shown in Figure 10.16. This is the reason for using a higher-dimensionality network in the SGI Origin.

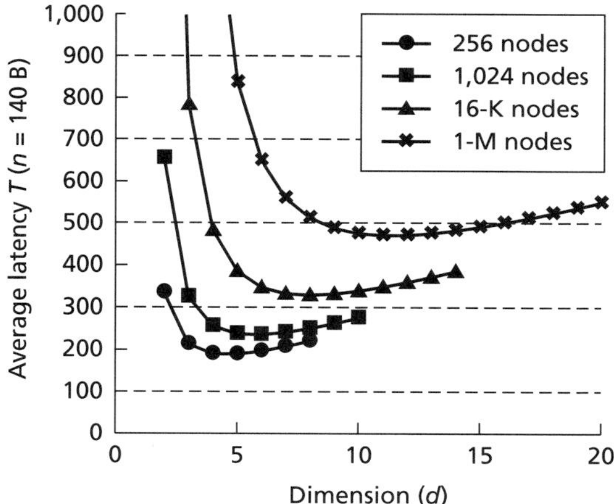

FIGURE 10.16 Unloaded latency for *k*-ary *d*-cubes with equal pin count and larger routing delays (n = 140 B, Δ = 20). When the time to cross a switch is significantly larger than the time to cross a wire, as is common in practice, higher-degree switches become much more attractive.

10.5.2 Latency under Load

In order to analyze the behavior of a network under load, we need to capture the effects of traffic congestion on all the other traffic that is moving through the network. These effects can be subtle and far reaching. Returning to the traffic analogy, notice when you are next driving down a loaded freeway, for example, that where a pair of freeways merge and then split, the traffic congestion is even worse than a series of on-ramps merging into a single freeway. There is far more driver-to-driver interaction in the interchange, and at some level of traffic load the whole thing just seems to stop. Networks behave in a similar fashion, but there are many more interchanges. In order to evaluate these effects in a family of topologies, we must take a position on the traffic pattern, the routing algorithm, the flow control strategy, and a number of detailed aspects of the internal design of the switch. We can then either develop a queuing model for the system or build a simulator for the proposed set of designs. The trick, as in most other aspects of computer design, is to develop models that are simple enough to provide intuition at the appropriate level of design yet accurate enough to offer useful guidance as the design refinement progresses.

We will use a closed-form model of contention delays developed in Agarwal (1991) for random traffic k-ary d-cubes using dimension-order cut-through routing and unbounded internal buffers, so flow control and deadlock issues do not arise. The model predictions correlate well with simulation results for networks meeting the same assumptions. This model is based on earlier work by Kruskal and Snir (1983) modeling the performance of indirect (Banyan) networks. Without going through the derivation, the main result is that we can model the latency for random communication of messages of size n on a k-ary d-cube with channel width w at a load corresponding to an aggregate channel utilization of ρ by

$$T(n, k, d, w, \rho) = \frac{n}{w} + h_{ave}(\Delta + W(n, k, d, w, \rho)), \text{ where}$$

$$W(n, k, d, w, \rho) = \frac{n}{w} \cdot \frac{\rho}{1 - \rho} \cdot \frac{h_{ave} - 1}{h_{ave}^2} \cdot \left(1 + \frac{1}{d}\right), \text{ and where} \tag{10.8}$$

$$h_{ave} = d\left(\frac{k-1}{2}\right)$$

Using this model, we can compare the latency under load for networks of low or high dimension of various sizes, as we did for unloaded latency. Figure 10.17 shows the predicted latency on a 1,024-node 32-ary 2-cube and a 1,000-node 10-ary 3-cube as a function of the requested aggregate channel utilization, assuming equal channel width, for relatively small message sizes of 4, 8, 16, and 40 phits. We can see from the right end of the curves that the two networks saturate at roughly the same channel utilization; however, this saturation point decreases rapidly with the message size. The left end of the curves indicates the unloaded latency. The higher-degree switch enjoys a lower base routing delay with the same channel time since there are fewer hops and equal channel widths. As the load increases, this difference becomes less significant. Notice how large the contended latency is compared to the unloaded latency. Clearly, in order to deliver low-latency communication to the user program, it is important that the machine is designed so that the network does not go into saturation easily, either by providing excess network bandwidth or by conditioning the processor load.

The data in Figure 10.17 raises a basic trade-off in network design. How large a packet should the network be designed for? The data shows clearly that networks move small packets more efficiently than large ones. However, smaller packets have worse packet efficiency due to the routing and control information contained in each one and require more network interface events for the same amount of data transfer. For any given technology and detailed design, there is an optimal point.

We must be a bit careful about the conclusions we draw from Figure 10.17 regarding the choice of network dimension. The curves in the figure show how efficiently each network utilizes the set of channels it has available to it. The figure suggests that both use their channels with roughly equal effectiveness. However, the higher-dimensional network has a much greater available bandwidth per node; it has 1.5 times as many channels per node and each message uses fewer channels. In a k-ary d-cube, the available phits per cycle under random communication are

$$\frac{Nd}{d\frac{(k-1)}{2}}$$

or $2/(k - 1)$ phits per cycle per node ($2w/k - 1$ bits per cycle). The 3-cube in our example has almost four times as much available bandwidth at the same channel uti-

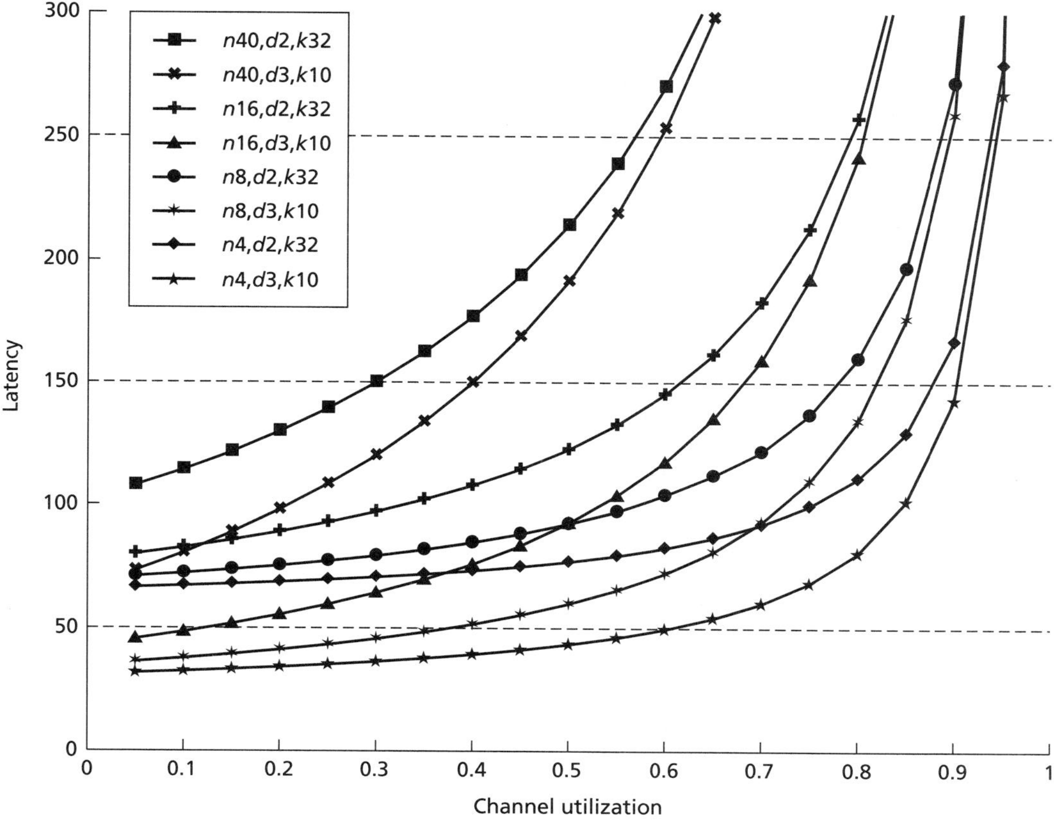

FIGURE 10.17 Latency with contention versus load for 32-ary 2-cube and 10-ary 3-cube with routing delay 2. At low channel utilization, the higher-dimensional network has significantly low latency with equal channel width, but as the utilization increases they converge toward the same saturation point.

lization, assuming equal channel width. Thus, if we look at latency against delivered bandwidth, the picture looks rather different, as shown in Figure 10.18. The 2-cube starts out with a higher base latency and saturates before the 3-cube begins to feel the load.

This comparison brings us back to the question of appropriate equal cost comparison. As an exercise, you can investigate the curves for equal pin-out and equal bisection comparison. Widening the channels shifts the base latency down by reducing channel time, increases the total available bandwidth, and reduces the waiting time at each switch since each packet is serviced faster. Thus, the results are quite sensitive to the cost model.

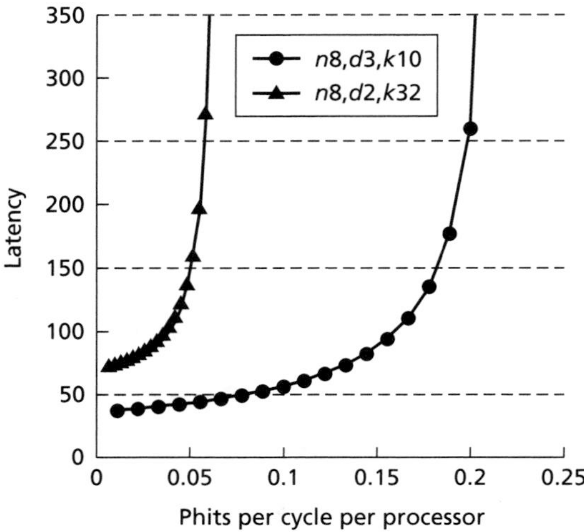

FIGURE 10.18 Latency versus phits per cycle with contention. Comparing the 32-ary 2-cube and 10-ary 3-cube with routing delay 2 at equal average traffic per link shows that the higher-degree networks handle greater load before saturating.

Some interesting observations arise when the width is scaled against dimension. For example, using the equal bisection rule, the capacity per node is

$$C(N,d) = W_d \cdot \frac{2}{k-1} \approx 1$$

The aggregate capacity for random traffic is essentially independent of dimension! Each host can expect to drive, on average, a fraction of a bit per network clock period. This observation yields a new perspective on low-dimension networks. Generally, the concern is that each of several nodes must route messages a considerable distance along one dimension. Thus, each node must send packets infrequently. Under the fixed bisection width assumption, with low dimension the channel becomes a shared resource pool for several nodes whereas high-dimension networks partition the bandwidth resource for traffic in each of several dimensions. When a node uses a channel in the low-dimension case, it uses it for a shorter amount of time. In most systems, pooling results in better utilization than partitioning.

In current machines, the area occupied by a node is much larger than the cross section of the wires, and the scale is generally limited to a few thousand nodes. In this regime, the bisection of the machine is often realized by bundles of cables. This represents a significant engineering challenge, but it is not a fundamental limit on the machine design. The tendency is to use wider links and faster signaling in topologies with short wires, as illustrated by Table 10.1, but it is not as dramatic as the equal bisection scaling rule would suggest.

10.6 ROUTING

Recall that the routing algorithm of a network determines which of the possible paths from source to destination are used as routes and how the route followed by each particular packet is determined. We have seen, for example, that in a k-ary d-cube the set of shortest routes is completely described by the relative address of the source and destination, which specifies the number of links that need to be crossed in each dimension. Dimension order routing restricts the set of legal paths so that there is exactly one route from each source to each destination—the one obtained by first traveling the correct distance in the low-order dimension, then the next dimension, and so on. This section describes the different classes of routing algorithms that are used in modern machines and the key properties of good routing algorithms, such as producing a set of deadlock-free routes, maintaining low latency, spreading load evenly, and tolerating faults.

10.6.1 Routing Mechanisms

Let's start with the nuts and bolts. Recall that the basic operation of a switch is to monitor the packets arriving at its inputs and for each input packet to select an output port on which to send it out. Thus, a routing algorithm is a function $R : N \times N \rightarrow C$, which at each switch maps the destination node n_d to the next channel on the route. High-speed switches basically use three mechanisms to determine the output channel from information in the packet header: arithmetic, source-based port select, and table lookup. In parallel computer networks, the switch needs to be able to make the routing decision for all its inputs every few cycles, so the mechanism needs to be simple and fast.

Simple arithmetic operations are sufficient to select the output port in most regular topologies. For example, in a 2D mesh, each packet can carry the signed distance to travel in each dimension $[\Delta x, \Delta y]$ in the packet header. The routing operation at switch ij is given by the following:

Direction	Condition
West $(-x)$	$\Delta x < 0$
East $(+x)$	$\Delta x > 0$
South $(-y)$	$\Delta x = 0, \Delta y < 0$
North $(+y)$	$\Delta x = 0, \Delta y > 0$
Processor	$\Delta x = 0, \Delta y = 0$

To accomplish this kind of routing, the switch needs to test the address in the header and decrement or increment one routing field. Typically, routes in a grid are determined by first moving in the Δx direction and then in the Δy. More generally, in a k-ary d-cube, the routes are determined by moving in each dimension from lowest numbered to highest, called *dimension order* routing. For a binary cube, the switch computes the position of the first bit that differs between the destination and the local node address (or the first nonzero bit if the packet carries the relative address of the destination) and traverses the link in this dimension, called *e-cube* routing. This kind of mechanism is used in Intel and nCUBE hypercubes, the Paragon, the Cal Tech Torus Routing Chip (Seitz and Su 1993), and the J-machine, among others.

A more general approach is *source-based routing*, in which the source builds a header consisting of the output port number for each switch along the route, $p_0, p_1, \ldots, p_{h-1}$. Each switch simply strips off the port number from the front of the message and sends the message out on the specified channel. This allows a very simple switch with little control state and without even arithmetic units to support sophisticated routing functions on arbitrary topologies. All of the intelligence is in the host nodes. It has the disadvantage that the header tends to be large and usually of variable size. If the switch degree is d and routes of length h are permitted, the header may need to carry $h \log d$ routing bits. This approach is used in MIT Parc and Arctic routers, Meiko CS-2, and Myrinet.

A third approach, which is general purpose and allows for a small fixed-size header, is *table-driven routing*, in which each switch contains a routing table R and the packet header contains a routing field i so that the output port is determined by indexing into the table by the routing field, $o = R[i]$. This is used, for example, in HPPI and ATM switches. Generally, the table entry also gives the routing field for the next step in the route, $o, i' = R[i]$, to allow more flexibility in the table configuration. The disadvantage of this approach is that the switch must contain a sizable amount of routing state, and it requires additional switch-specific messages or some other mechanism for establishing the contents of the routing table. Fairly large tables are required to simulate even simple routing algorithms. This approach is better suited to LAN and WAN traffic where only a few of the possible routes among the collection of nodes are used at a time, most of which are long-lasting connections. By contrast, in a parallel machine there is often traffic among all the nodes.

Traditional networking routers contain a full processor that can inspect the incoming message, perform an arbitrary calculation to select the output port, and build a packet containing the message data for that output. This kind of approach is employed in routers and (sometimes) bridges that connect completely different networks (e.g., those that route between Ethernet, FDDI, ATM) or at least different data link layers; it really does not make sense at the time scale of the communication within a high-performance parallel machine.

10.6.2 Deterministic Routing

A routing algorithm is *deterministic* (or *nonadaptive*) if the route taken by a message is determined solely by its source and destination regardless of other traffic in the network. For example, dimension order routing is deterministic; the packet will follow its path regardless of whether a link along the way is blocked. Dimension order and *e*-cube routing are examples of deterministic algorithms. *Adaptive* routing algorithms allow the route for a packet to be influenced by traffic it meets along the way. For example, in a mesh, the route could zigzag toward its destination if links along the dimension order path were blocked or faulty. In a fat-tree, the upward path toward the common ancestor could steer away from blocked links rather than following a specific path determined when the message was injected into the network. If a routing algorithm only selects shortest paths toward the destination, it is *minimal*; otherwise it is *nonminimal*. Allowing multiple routes between each source and destination is clearly required for adaptation (and fault tolerance), and it also provides a way to spread load over more links. These virtues are enjoyed by source-based and table-driven routing, but the choice is made when the packet is injected. Adaptive routing delays the choice until the packet is actually moving through the network, which clearly makes the switch more complex but has the potential of obtaining better link utilization.

We will concentrate first on deterministic routing algorithms and develop an understanding of some of the most popular routing algorithms and the techniques for proving them deadlock-free before investigating adaptive routing.

10.6.3 Deadlock Freedom

In our discussions of network latency and bandwidth, we have tacitly assumed that messages make forward progress, so it is meaningful to talk about performance. This section shows how to go about proving that a network is deadlock-free. Recall that *deadlock* occurs when a packet waits for an event that cannot occur, for example, when no message can advance toward its destination because the queues of the message system are full and each is waiting for another to make resources available. This can be distinguished from *indefinite postponement*, which occurs when a packet waits for an event that can occur but never does, and from *livelock,* which occurs when the routing of a packet never leads to its destination. Indefinite postponement is primarily a question of fairness, and livelock can only occur with adaptive nonminimal routing. Being free from deadlock is a basic property of well-designed networks that must be addressed from the very beginning.

Deadlock can occur in a variety of situations. A "head-on" deadlock may occur when two nodes attempt to send to each other and each begins sending before either receives. It is clear that if they both attempt to complete sending before receiving, neither will make forward progress. We saw this situation at the user message-passing layer using synchronous send and receive, and we saw it at the node-to-network interface layer. Within the network, it could potentially occur with half-duplex channels or if the switch controller were not able to transmit and receive simultaneously on a bidirectional channel. We should think of the channel as a shared resource that is acquired incrementally, first at the sending end and then at the receiver. In each case, the solution is to ensure that nodes can continue to receive while being unable to send. A reliable network can only be deadlock-free if the nodes are able to remove packets from the network even when they are unable to send packets. (Alternatively, we might recover from the deadlock by eventually detecting a time-out and aborting one or more of the packets, effectively preempting the claim on the shared resource. This does raise the possibility of indefinite postponement, which we will address later.) In this head-on situation there is no routing involved; instead, the problem is due to constraints imposed by the switch design.

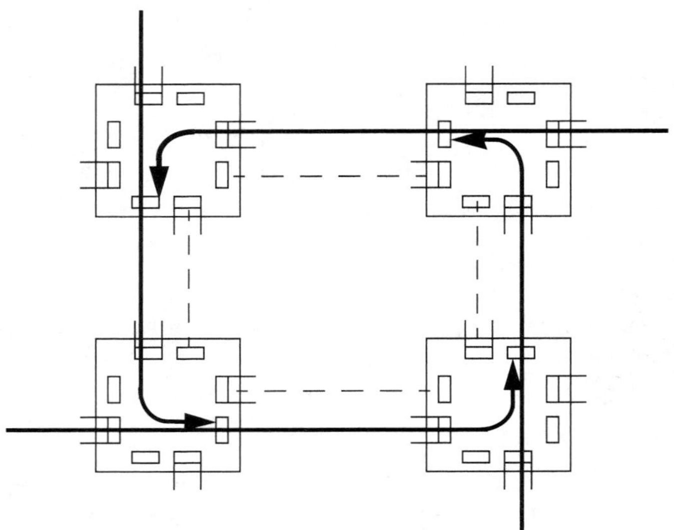

FIGURE 10.19 Examples of network routing deadlock. Each of four switches has four input and output ports. Four packets have each acquired an input port, an output buffer, and an input port, and all are attempting to acquire the next output buffer as they turn left. None will relinquish their output buffer until it moves forward, so none can progress.

A more interesting case of deadlock occurs when multiple messages are competing for resources within the network, as in the routing deadlock illustrated in Figure 10.19. Here we have several messages moving through the network where each message consists of several flits. We should view each channel in the network as having associated with it a certain amount of buffer resources; these may be input buffers at the channel destination, output buffers at the channel source, or both. In our example, each message is attempting to turn to the left, and all of the packet buffers associated with the four channels are full. No message will release a packet buffer until after it has acquired a new packet buffer into which it can move. One could make this example more elaborate by separating the switches with additional switches and channels, but it is clear that the channel resources are allocated incrementally within the network on a distributed basis as a result of messages being routed through, and the resources are nonpreemptible, at least without packet loss. Hence, there is a potential for deadlock.

This routing deadlock can occur with store-and-forward or with cut-through routing, although with cut-through there are greater opportunities for deadlock since each packet stretches over several flit buffers. Only the header flits of a packet carry routing information, so once the head of a message is spooled forward on a channel, all of the remaining flits of the message must spool along on the same channel. Thus, a single packet may hold onto channel resources across several switches. The essential point in these examples is that resources are logically associated with channels and that messages introduce dependences between these resources as they move through the network.

The basic technique for proving a network deadlock-free is to articulate the dependences that can arise between channels as a result of messages moving through the network and to show that there are no cycles in the resulting channel dependence graph; this implies that no traffic patterns can lead to deadlock. The most common way of doing this is to number the channel resources such that each legal route follows a monotonically increasing (or decreasing) sequence; therefore, no dependence cycles can arise. For a butterfly, this is trivial because the network itself is acyclic. It is also simple for trees and fat-trees as long as the upward and downward channels are independent. For networks with cycles in the channel graph, the situation is more interesting.

To illustrate the basic technique for showing a routing algorithm to be deadlock-free, let us show that Δx, Δy routing on a k-ary 2D array is deadlock-free. To prove this, view each bidirectional channel as a pair of unidirectional channels numbered independently. Assign each positive-x channel $\langle i, y \rangle \rightarrow \langle i+1, y \rangle$ the number i, and similarly number the negative-x channels starting from 0 at the most positive edge. Number the positive-y channel $\langle x, j \rangle \rightarrow \langle x, j+1 \rangle$ the number $N + j$, and similarly number the negative-y edges from the most positive edge. This numbering is illustrated in Figure 10.20. Any route consisting of a sequence of consecutive edges in one x direction, a 90-degree turn, and a sequence of consecutive edges in one y direction is strictly increasing. The channel dependence graph has a node for every unidirectional link in the network, and there is an edge from node A to node B if it is possible for a packet to traverse channel A and then channel B. All edges in the channel dependence graph go from lower-numbered nodes to higher-numbered ones, so there are no cycles in the channel dependence graph (even though there are many cycles in the network).

This proof easily generalizes to any number of dimensions and, since a binary d-cube consists of a pair of unidirectional channels in each dimension, to show that e-cube routing is deadlock-free on a hypercube. Observe, however, that the proof does not apply to k-ary d-cubes in general because the channel number decreases at the wraparound edges. Indeed, it is not hard to show that for $k > 4$, dimension order routing will even introduce a dependence cycle on a unidirectional torus ($d = 1$).

Notice that the deadlock-free routing proof applies even if only a single flit of buffering is on each channel and that the potential for deadlock exists in a k-ary d-cube even with multiple packet buffers and store-and-forward routing since a single message may fill up all the packet buffers along its route. However, if the use of channel resources is restricted, it is possible to break the deadlock. For example, consider the case of a unidirectional torus with multiple packet buffers per channel and store-and-forward routing. Suppose that one of the packet buffers associated with each channel is reserved for messages destined for nodes with a larger number than their source, that is, packets that do not use wraparound channels. This means that it will always be possible for positive-going messages to make progress. Although wraparound messages may be postponed, the network does not deadlock. This solution is typical of the family of techniques for making store-and-forward

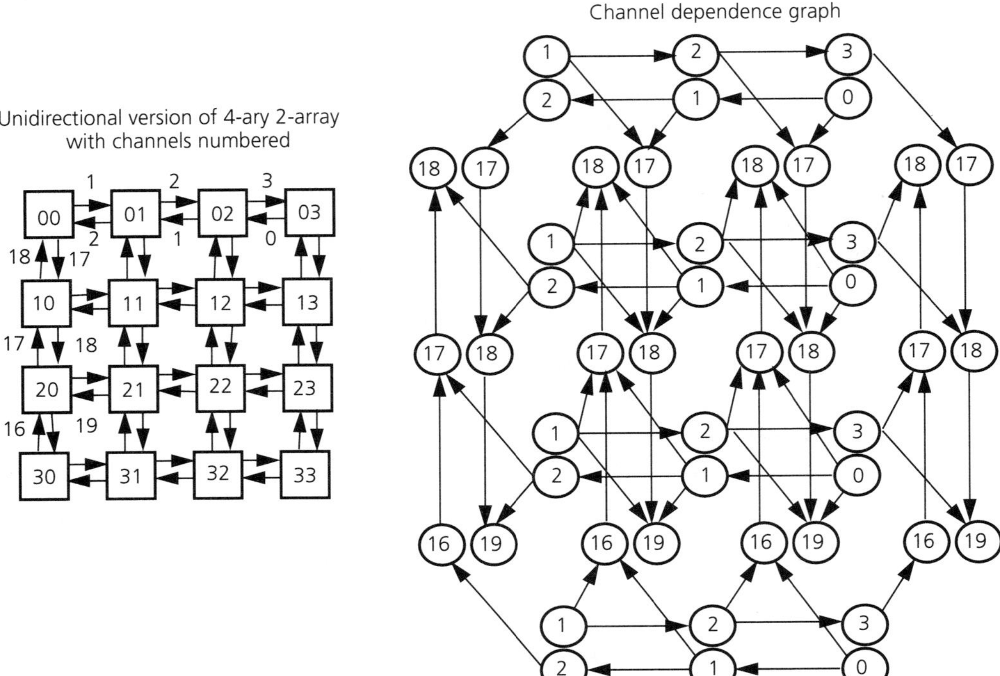

FIGURE 10.20 Channel ordering in the network graph and corresponding channel dependence graph. To show that the routing algorithm is deadlock-free, it is sufficient to demonstrate that the channel dependence graph has no cycles.

packet-switched networks deadlock-free; there is a concept of a *structured buffer pool* (in which certain buffers have specific functions) and the routing algorithm restricts the assignment of buffers to packets to break dependence cycles. This solution is not sufficient for wormhole routing since it tacitly assumes that packets of different messages can be interleaved as they move forward.

Observe that deadlock-free routing does not mean the system is deadlock-free. The network is deadlock-free only as long as it is drained into the NIs, even when the NIs are unable to send. If two-phase protocols are employed, we need to ensure that fetch deadlock is avoided. This means either providing two logically independent networks or ensuring that the two phases are decoupled through NI buffers as discussed in Chapter 7. Of course, the program may still have deadlocks, such as circular waits on locks or head-on collision using synchronous message passing. We have worked our way down from the top, showing how to make each of these layers deadlock-free as long as the next layer below is deadlock-free.

Given a network topology and a set of resources per channel, there are two basic approaches for constructing a deadlock-free routing algorithm: restrict the paths that packets may follow or restrict how resources are allocated. This observation

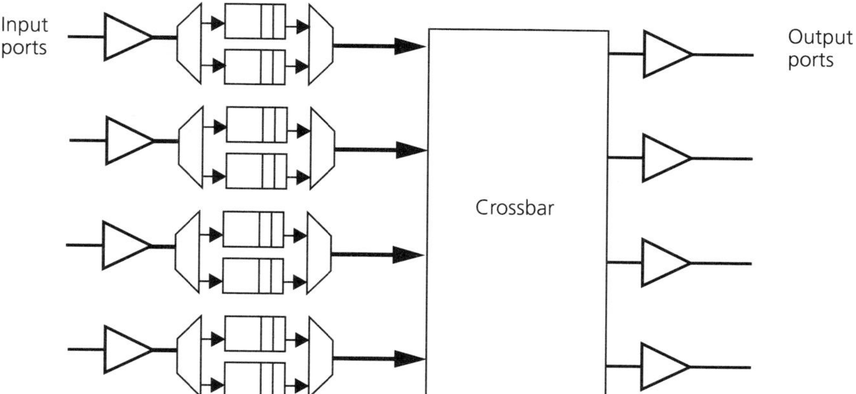

FIGURE 10.21 Multiple virtual channels in a basic switch. Each physical channel is shared by multiple virtual channels. The input ports of the switch split the incoming virtual channels into separate buffers; however, these are multiplexed through the switch to avoid expanding the crossbar.

raises a number of interesting questions. Is there a general technique for producing deadlock-free routes with wormhole routing on an arbitrary topology? Can such routes be adaptive? Is some minimum amount of channel resources required?

10.6.4 Virtual Channels

The basic technique for making networks with wormhole routing deadlock-free is to provide multiple buffers with each physical channel and to split these buffers into a group of *virtual channels*. Going back to our basic cost model for networks, this does not increase the number of links in the network nor the number of switches. In fact, it does not even increase the size of the crossbar internal to each switch since only one flit at a time moves through the switch for each output channel. As indicated in Figure 10.21, it does require additional selectors and multiplexers within the switch to allow the links and the crossbar to be shared among multiple virtual channels per physical channel.

Virtual channels are used to avoid deadlock by systematically breaking cycles in the channel dependence graph. Consider, for example, the four-way routing deadlock cycle of Figure 10.19. Suppose we have two virtual channels per physical channel, and messages at a node numbered higher than their destination are routed on the high channels while messages at a node numbered less than their destinations are routed on the low channels. As illustrated in Figure 10.22, the dependence cycle is broken. Applying this approach to the k-ary d-cube, treat the channel labeling as a radix $d + 1 + k$ number of the form ivx, where i is the dimension, x is the coordinate of the source node of the channel in dimension i, and v is the virtual channel number. In each dimension, if the destination node has a smaller coordinate than the source node in that dimension (i.e., if the message must use a wraparound edge),

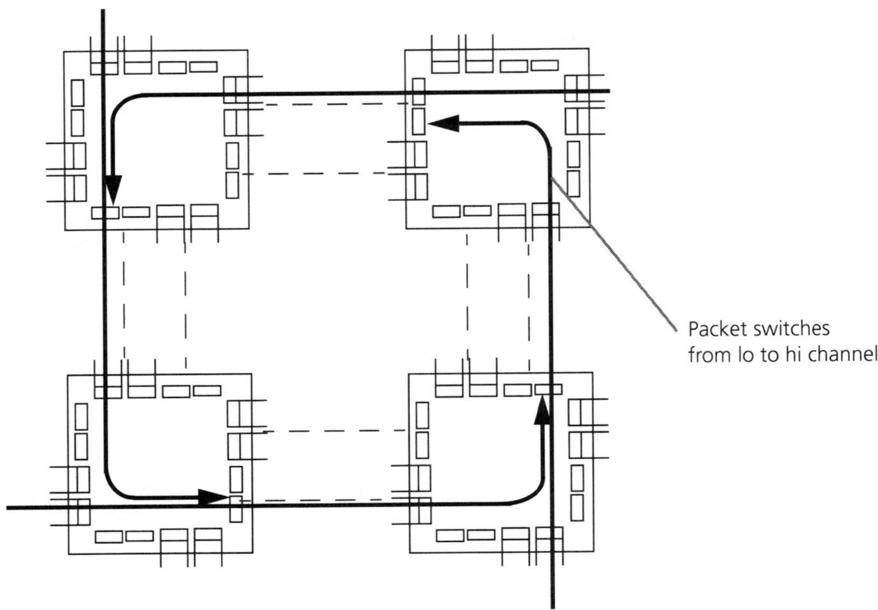

FIGURE 10.22 Breaking deadlock cycles with virtual channels. Each physical channel is broken into two virtual channels; call them lo and hi. The virtual channel "parity" of the input port is used for the output except on turns north to west, which make a transition from lo to hi.

use the $v = 1$ virtual channel in that dimension. Otherwise, use the $v = 0$ channel. You can verify that dimension order routing is deadlock-free with this assignment of virtual channels. Similar techniques can be employed with other popular topologies (Dally and Seitz 1987). Notice that with virtual channels we need to view the routing algorithm as a function $R : C \times N \rightarrow C$ because the virtual channel selected for the output depends on which channel it came in on.

10.6.5 Up*-Down* Routing

Are virtual channels required for deadlock-free wormhole routing on an arbitrary topology? No. If we assume that all the channels are bidirectional, there is a simple algorithm for deriving deadlock-free routes for an arbitrary topology. Not surprisingly, it restricts the set of legal routes. The general strategy is similar to routing in a tree, where routes go up the tree away from the source and then down to the destination. We assume the network consists of a collection of switches, some of which have one or more hosts attached to them. Given the network graph, we want to number the switches so that the numbers increase as we get farther away from the hosts. One approach is to construct a spanning tree of the graph with hosts at the leaves and numbers increasing toward the root. It is clear that for any source host, any destination host can be reached by an *up*-down** path consisting of a sequence of zero or more up channels (toward higher-numbered nodes), a single turn, and a series of zero or more down channels. Moreover, the set of routes following such paths are deadlock-free. The network graph may have cycles, but the channel dependence graph under up*-down* routing does not. The up channels form a directed acyclic graph (DAG) and the down channels form a DAG. The up channels depend only on lower-numbered up channels, and the down channels depend only on up channels and higher-numbered down channels.

This style of routing was developed for Autonet (Anderson et al. 1992), which was intended to be self-configuring. Each of the switches contained a processor that could run a distributed algorithm to determine the topology of the network and find a unique spanning tree. Each of the hosts would compute up*-down* routes as a restricted shortest-paths problem. Then routing tables in the switches could be established. A breadth-first search variant is used by Atomic (Felderman et al. 1994) and Myrinet (Boden et al. 1995), where the switches are passive and the hosts determine the topology by probing the network. Each host runs an algorithm that partitions the network into levels with host nodes at level zero and each switch at the level corresponding to its maximum distance from a host. The numbering is given by a breadth-first search from the highest numbered switch and the algorithm determines the set of source-based routes from the host to the other nodes. A key challenge in automatic mapping of networks, especially with simple switches that only move messages through without any special processing, is determining when two distinct routes through the network lead to the same switch (Mainwaring et al. 1997). One solution is to try returning to the source by reversing routes from previously known switches; another is detecting when identical paths exist from two supposedly distinct switches to the same host.

10.6.6 Turn-Model Routing

We have seen that a deadlock-free routing algorithm can be constructed by restricting the set of routes within a network or by providing buffering with each channel that is used in a structured fashion. How much do we need to restrict the routes? Is there a minimal set of restrictions or a minimal combination of routing restrictions and buffers? An important development in this direction is turn-model routing (Glass and Ni 1992). Consider, for example, a 2D array. There are eight possible turns, which form two simple cycles, as shown in Figure 10.23. (The figure is illustrating cycles appearing in the network involving multiple messages. There is a corresponding cycle in the channel dependence graph.) Dimension order routing prevents the use of four of the eight turns—when traveling in $\mp x$ it is legal to turn in $\mp y$, but once a packet is traveling in $\mp y$ it can make no further turns. The illegal turns are indicated by gray lines in the figure. Intuitively, it seems possible to prevent cycles by eliminating only one turn in each cycle.

Of the 16 different ways to prohibit two turns in a 2D array, 12 prevent deadlock. These consist of the three unique algorithms shown in Figure 10.24 and rotations of these. The west-first algorithm is so named because no turn is allowed into the $-x$

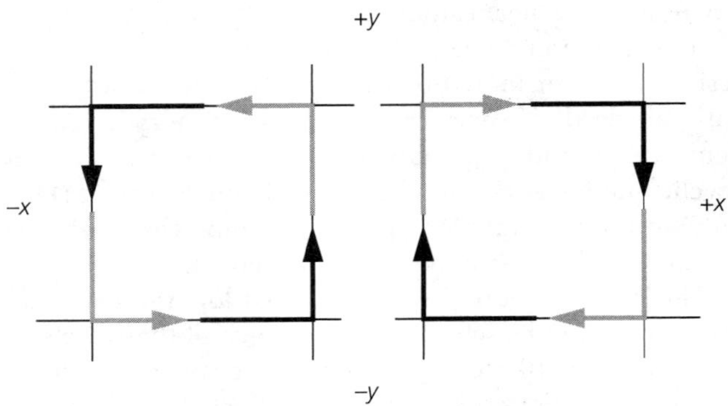

FIGURE 10.23 Turn restrictions of Δx, Δy routing. Dimension order routing on a 2D array prohibits the use of four of the eight possible turns, thereby breaking both of the simple dependence cycles. A deadlock-free routing algorithm can be obtained by prohibiting only two turns.

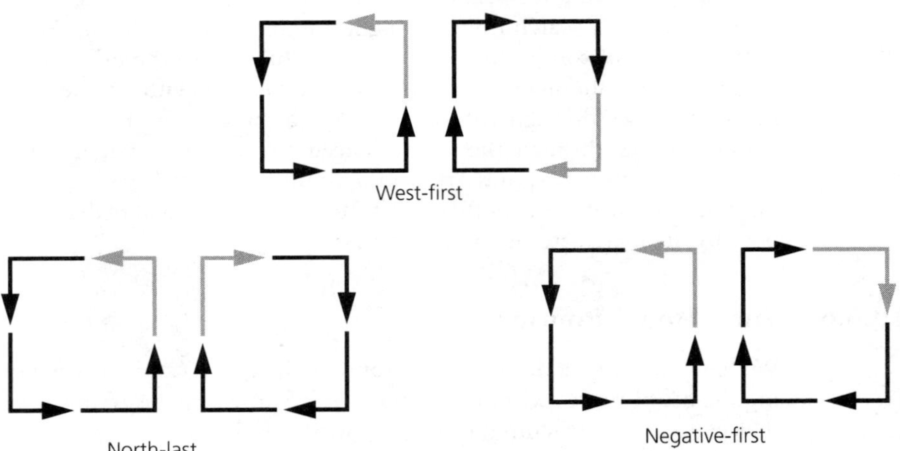

FIGURE 10.24 Minimal turn-model routing in 2D. Only two of the eight possible turns need be prohibited in order to obtain a deadlock-free routing algorithm. Legal turns are shown for three such algorithms.

direction; therefore, if a packet needs to travel in this direction, it must do so before making any turns. Similarly, in north-last there is no way to turn out of the $+y$ direction, so the route must make all its other adjustments before heading in this direction. Finally, negative-first prohibits turns from a positive direction into a negative direction, so the route must go as negative as its needs to before heading in either positive direction.

Each of these turn-model algorithms allows complex, even nonminimal routes. For example, Figure 10.25 shows some of the routes that might be taken under

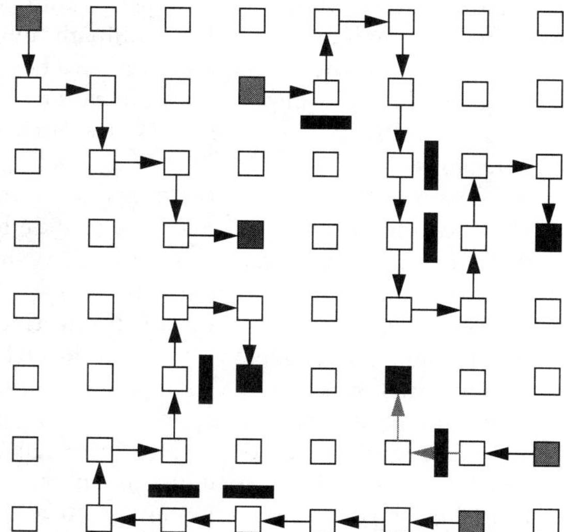

FIGURE 10.25 Examples of legal west-first routes in an 8 × 8 array. Substantial routing adaptation is obtained with turn-model routing, thus providing the ability to route around faults in a deadlock-free manner.

west-first routing. The elongated rectangles indicate blockages or broken links that might cause such a set of routes to be used. It should be clear that minimal turn models allow a great deal of flexibility in route selection. There are many legal paths between pairs of nodes.

The turn-model approach can be combined with virtual channels, and it can be applied in any topology. (In some networks, such as unidirectional *d*-cubes, virtual channels are still required.) The basic method is as follows: (1) partition the channels into sets according to the direction they route packets (excluding wraparound edges); (2) identify the potential cycles formed by "turns" between directions; and (3) prohibit one turn in each abstract cycle, being careful to break all the complex cycles as well. Finally, wraparound edges can be incorporated as long as they do not introduce cycles. If virtual channels are present, treat each set of channels as a distinct virtual direction.

Up* down* is essentially a turn-model algorithm with the assumption of bidirectional channels, using only two directions. Indeed, in reviewing the up*-down* algorithm, many shortest paths may conform to the up*-down* restriction, and certainly many nonminimal up*-down* routes are in most networks. Virtual channels allow the routing restrictions to be loosened even further.

10.6.7 Adaptive Routing

The fundamental advantage of loosening the routing restrictions is that it allows multiple legal paths between pairs of nodes. This is essential for fault tolerance. If the routing algorithm allows only one path, failure of a single link will effectively leave the network disconnected. With multipath routing, it may be possible to steer around the fault. In addition, it allows traffic to be spread more broadly over available channels and thereby improves the utilization of the network. When a vehicle is parked in the middle of the street, it is often nice to have the option of driving around the block.

Simple deterministic routing algorithms can introduce tremendous contention within the network, even when the communication load is spread evenly over independent destinations. For example, Figure 10.26 shows a simple case where four packets are traveling to distinct destinations from distinct sources in a 2D mesh; under dimension order routing they are all forced to travel through the same link. The communication is completely serialized through the bottleneck while links for other shortest paths are unused. A multipath routing algorithm could use alternative channels, as indicated in the right portion of the figure. For any network topology there exist bad permutations (Gottlieb and Kruskal 1984), but simple deterministic routing makes these bad permutations much easier to run across. The particular example in Figure 10.26 has important practical significance. A common global communication pattern is a transpose. On a 2D mesh with dimension order routing, all the packets in a row must go through a single switch before filling in the column.

Multipath routing can be incorporated as an extension of any of the basic switch mechanisms. With source-based routing, the source simply chooses among the legal routes and builds the header accordingly. No change to the switch is required. With table-driven routing, this can be accomplished by setting up table entries for multiple paths. For arithmetic routing, additional control information would need to be incorporated in the header and interpreted by the switch.

Adaptive routing is a form of multipath routing where the choice of routes is made dynamically by the switch in response to traffic encountered en route. Formally, an adaptive routing function is a mapping of the form $R_A : C \times N \times \Sigma \rightarrow C$, where Σ represents the switch state. In particular, if one of the desired outputs is blocked or failed, the switch may choose to send the packet on an alternative channel. Minimal adaptive routing will only route packets along shortest paths to their destination, that is, every hop must reduce the distance to the destination. An adaptive algorithm that allows all shortest paths to be used is *fully adaptive*, otherwise it is *partially adaptive*. An interesting extreme case of nonminimal adaptive routing is what is called "hot potato" routing. In this scheme the switch never buffers packets. If more than one packet is destined for the same output channel, the switch sends one toward its destination and "misroutes" the rest onto other channels.

Adaptive routing is not widely used in current parallel machines, although it has been studied extensively in the literature (Ngai and Seitz 1989; Linder and Harden 1991), especially through the Chaos router (Kostantantindou and Snyder 1991). The CRAY T3E provides minimal adaptive routing in a cube. The nCUBE/3 is to provide minimal adaptive routing in a hypercube. The network proposed for the Tera machine (Alverson et al. 1990) is to use hot potato routing, with 128-bit packets delivered in one 3-ns cycle.

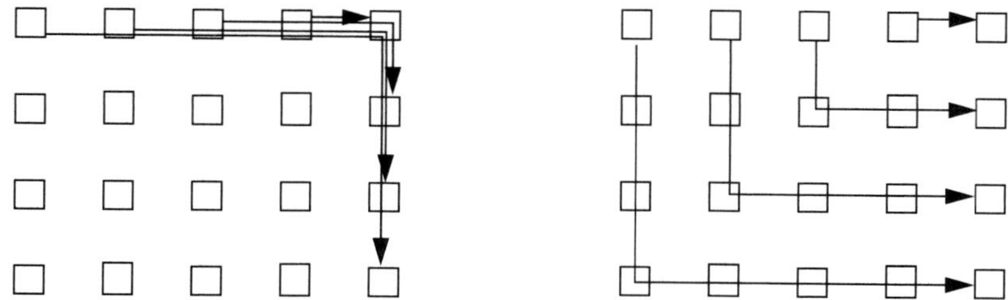

FIGURE 10.26 Routing path conflicts under deterministic dimension order routing. Several messages from distinct source to distinct destination contend for resources under dimension order routing, whereas an adaptive routing scheme may be able to use disjoint paths.

Although adaptive routing has clear advantages, it is not without its disadvantages. Clearly, it adds to the complexity of the switch, which can only make the switch slower. The reduction in bandwidth can outweigh the gains of the more sophisticated routing—a simple deterministic network in its linear operating regime is likely to outperform a clever adaptive network in saturation. In nonuniform networks, such as a *d*-dimensional array, adaptivity hurts performance on uniform random traffic. Stochastic variations in the load introduce temporary blocking in any network. For switches at the boundary of the array, this will tend to propel packets toward the center. As a result, contention forms in the middle of the array that is not present under deterministic routing. Adaptive routing can cause problems with certain kinds of nonuniform traffic as well, as we will see in Section 10.8.3.

Nonminimal adaptive routing tends to perform poorly as the network reaches saturation because packets traverse extra links and hence consume more bandwidth. The throughput of the network tends to drop off as load is increased rather than flattening at the saturation point, as illustrated in Figure 10.17.

Recently, there have been a number of proposals for low-cost partially and fully adaptive routing that use a combination of a limited number of virtual channels and restrictions on the set of turns (Chien and Kim 1992; Schwiebert and Jayasimha 1995). It appears that most of the advantages of adaptive routing, including fault tolerance and channel utilization, can be obtained with a very limited degree of adaptability.

10.7 SWITCH DESIGN

Ultimately, the design of a network boils down to the design of the switch and how the switches are wired together. The degree of the switch, its internal routing mechanisms, and its internal buffering determine what topologies can be supported and what routing algorithms can be implemented. Now that we understand the higher-level network design issues, let us return to switch design in more detail. Like any other hardware component of a computer system, a network switch comprises datapath, control, and storage. This basic structure was illustrated at the beginning of the chapter in Figure 10.5. Throughout the early history of parallel computing, switches were built from a large number of low-integration components occupying a board or a rack. Since the mid-1980s, most parallel computer networks are built around single-chip VLSI switches—exactly the same technology as the microprocessor. (This transition began in LANs a decade later.) Thus, switch design is tied to the same technological trends discussed in Chapter 1: decreasing feature size, increasing area, and increasing pin count. We should view modern switch design from a VLSI perspective.

10.7.1 Ports

The total number of pins is essentially the total number of input and output ports times the channel width. Since the perimeter of the chip grows slowly compared to area, switches tend to be pin limited. This pushes designers toward narrow, high-frequency channels. Very high-speed serial links are especially attractive because they use the least pins and eliminate problems with skew across the bit lines in a channel. However, with serial links the clock and all control signals must be encoded within the framing of the serial bit stream. With parallel links, one of the wires is essentially a clock for the data on the others. Flow control is realized using an additional wire, providing a ready/acknowledge handshake.

10.7.2 Internal Datapath

The datapath is the connectivity between each of a set of input ports (i.e., input latches, buffers, or FIFO) and every output port. This is generally referred to as the internal crossbar, although it can be realized in many different ways. A *nonblocking crossbar* is one in which each input port can be connected to a distinct output in any permutation simultaneously. Logically, for an $n \times n$ switch the nonblocking crossbar is nothing more than an n-way multiplexer associated with each destination, as shown in Figure 10.27(a). The multiplexer may be implemented in a variety of different ways, depending on the underlying technology. For example, in VLSI it is typically realized as a single bus with n tristate drivers, shown in Figure 10.27(b). In this case, the control path provides n enable points per output. A technique that is becoming increasingly common is to use a memory as a crossbar by writing for each input port and reading for each output port; see Figure 10.27(c).

It is clear that the hardware complexity of the crossbar is determined by the wires. There are nw data wires in each direction, requiring $(nw)^2$ area. There are also n^2 control wires, which add to this significantly. How do we expect switches to track improvements in VLSI technology? Assume that the area of the crossbar stays constant, but the feature size decreases. The ideal VLSI scaling law says that if the feature size is reduced by a factor of s (including the gate thickness) and the voltage level is reduced by the same factor, then the speed of the transistors improves by a factor of $1/s$, the propagation delay of wires connecting neighboring transistors

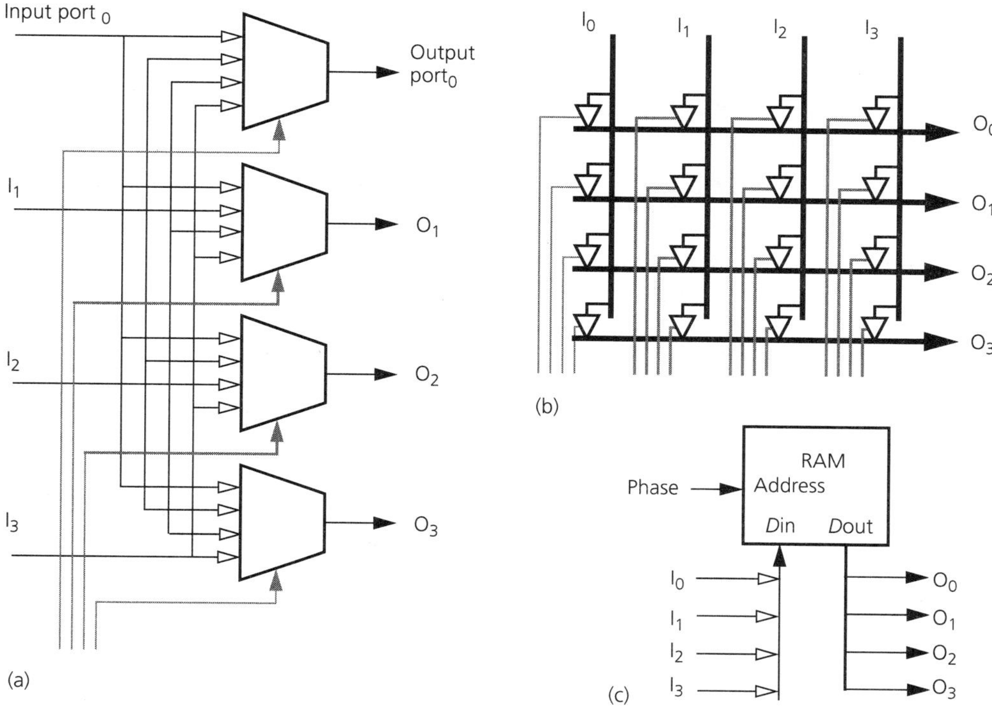

FIGURE 10.27 Crossbar implementations. The crossbar internal to a switch can be implemented as (a) a collection of multiplexers, (b) a grid of tristate drivers, or (c) via a contentional static RAM that time-multiplexes across the ports.

improves by a factor of $1/s$, and the total number of transistors per unit area increases by $1/s^2$ with the same power density. For switches, this means that the wires get thinner and closer together, so the degree of the switch can increase by a factor of $1/s$. Notice that the switch degree improves as only the square root of the improvement in logic density. The bad news is that these wires run the entire length of the crossbar, hence the length of the wires stays constant. The wires get thinner, so they have more resistance. The capacitance is reduced and the net effect is that the propagation delay is unchanged (Bakoglu 1990). In other words, ideal scaling gives us an improvement in switch degree for the same area but no improvement in speed. The speed does improve by a factor of $1/s$ if the voltage level is held constant, but then the power increases with $1/s^2$. Increases in chip area will allow larger degree, but the wire lengths increase and the propagation delays will increase.

Some degree of confusion exists over the term "crossbar." In the traditional switching literature, multistage interconnection networks that have a single controller are sometimes called crossbars, even though the datapath through the switch is organized as an interconnection of small crossbars. In many cases these are connected in a manner similar to a butterfly topology, called a Banyan network. A

Banyan network is nonblocking if its inputs are sorted, so some nonblocking crossbars are built as batcher sorting networks in front of a Banyan network (Peterson and Davie 1996). An approach that has many aspects in common with Benes networks is to employ a variant of the butterfly, called a delta network, and use two of these networks in series. The first serves to randomize a packet's position relative to the input ports and the second routes to the output port. This is used, for example, in some commercial ATM switches (Turner 1988). In VLSI switches, it is usually more effective to actually build a nonblocking crossbar since it is simple, fast, and regular. The key limit is pins anyway.

It is clear that VLSI switches will continue to advance with the underlying technology, although the growth rate is likely to be slower than the rate of improvement in storage and logic. The hardware complexity of the crossbar can be reduced if we give up the nonblocking property and limit the number of inputs that can be connected to outputs at once. In the extreme, this reduces to a bus with n drivers and n output selects. However, the most serious issue in practice turns out to be the length of the wires and the number of pins, so reducing the internal bandwidth of the individual switches provides little savings and a significant loss in network performance.

10.7.3 Channel Buffers

The organization of the buffer storage within the switch has a significant impact on the switch performance. Traditional routers and switches tend to have large SRAM or DRAM buffers external to the switch fabric whereas, in VLSI switches, the buffering is internal to the switch and comes out of the same silicon budget as the datapath and the control section. There are four basic options: no buffering (just input and output latches), buffers on the inputs, buffers on the outputs, or a centralized shared buffer pool. A few flits of buffering on input and output channels decouples the switches on either end of the link and tends to provide a significant improvement in performance. As chip size and density increase, more buffering is available and the network designer has more options, but still the buffer real estate comes at a premium and its organization is important. Like so many other aspects in network design, the issue is not just how effectively the buffer resources are utilized but how the buffering affects the utilization of other components of the network.

Intuitively, we might expect sharing of the switch storage resources to be harder to implement but to allow better utilization of these resources than partitioning the storage among ports. All of the communication ports need to access the shared pool simultaneously, requiring a very high-bandwidth memory. More surprisingly, sharing the buffer pool on demand can hurt the network utilization in some cases because a single congested output port can hog most of the buffer pool and thereby prevent other traffic from moving through the switch.

Input Buffering

One attractive approach is to provide independent FIFO buffers with each input port, as illustrated in Figure 10.28. Each buffer needs to be able to accept a phit

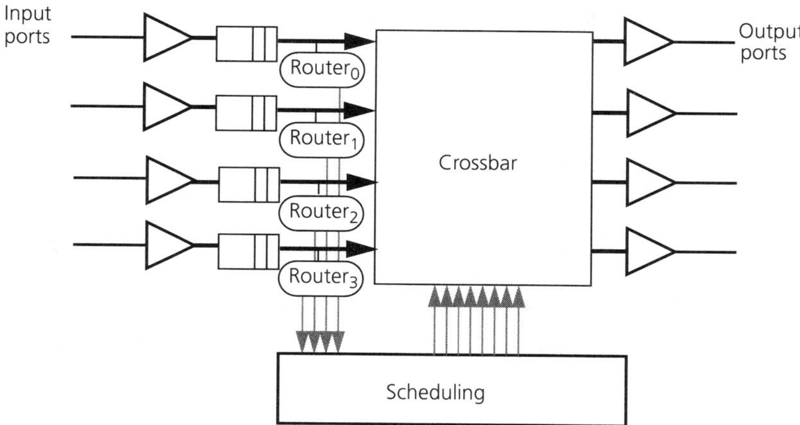

FIGURE 10.28 Input buffered switch. A FIFO is provided at each of the input ports, but the controller can only inspect and service the packets at the heads of the input FIFOs.

every cycle and deliver one phit to an output, so the internal bandwidth of the switch is easily matched to the flow of data coming in. The operation of the switch is relatively simple; it monitors the head of each input FIFO, computes the desired output port of each, and schedules packets to move through the crossbar accordingly. Typically, routing logic is associated with each input port to determine the desired output. This is trivial for source-based routing; it requires an arithmetic unit per input for algorithmic routing and, typically, a routing table per input with table-driven routing. With cut-through routing, the decision logic does not make an independent choice every cycle but only every packet. Thus, the routing logic is essentially a finite state machine, which spools all the flits of a packet to the same output channel before making a new routing decision at the packet boundary (Seitz and Su 1993).

One problem with the simple input buffered approach is the occurrence of "head-of-line" blocking. Suppose that two ports have packets destined for the same output port. One of them will be scheduled onto the output and the other will be blocked. The packet just behind the blocked packet may be destined for one of the unused outputs (there are guaranteed to be unused outputs), but it will not be able to move forward. This head-of-line blocking problem is familiar in our vehicular traffic analogy; it corresponds to having only one lane approaching an intersection. If the car ahead is blocked in attempting to turn, there is no way to proceed down the empty street ahead.

We can easily estimate the effect of head-of-line blocking on channel utilization. If we have two input ports and randomly pick an output for each, the first succeeds and the second has a 50/50 chance of picking the unused output. Thus, the expected number of packets per cycle moving through the switch is 1.5 and, hence, the expected utilization of each output is 75%. Generalizing this, if $E(n, k)$ is the expected number of output ports covered by k random inputs to an n-port switch, then

$$E(n, k+1) = E(n, k) + \frac{n - E(n, k)}{n}$$

Computing this recurrence up to $k = n$ for various switch sizes reveals that the expected output channel utilization for a single cycle of a fully loaded switch quickly drops to about 65%. Queuing theory analysis shows that the expected utilization in steady state with input queuing is 59% (Karol, Hluchyj, and Morgan 1987).

The impact of head-of-line blocking can be more significant than this simple probabilistic analysis indicates. Within a switch, there may be bursts of traffic for one output followed by bursts for another, and so on. Even though the traffic is evenly distributed, given a large enough window, each burst results in blocking on all inputs (Li 1988). Even if there is no contention for an output within a switch, the packet at the head of an input buffer may be destined for an output that is blocked due to congestion elsewhere in the network. Still, the packets behind it cannot move forward. In a wormhole routed network, the entire worm will be stuck in place, effectively consuming link bandwidth without going anywhere. A more flexible organization of buffer resources might allow packets to slide ahead of packets that are blocked.

Output Buffering

The basic enhancement we need to make to the switch is to provide a way for it to consider multiple packets at each input as candidates for advancement to the output port. A natural option is to expand the input FIFOs to provide an independent buffer for each output port so that packets sort themselves by destination upon arrival, as indicated by Figure 10.29. (This is the kind of switch assumed by the conventional delay analysis in Section 10.5; the analysis is simplified because the switch does not introduce additional contention effects internally.) With a steady stream of traffic on the inputs, the outputs can be driven at essentially 100%. However, the advantages of such a design are not without a cost; additional buffer storage and internal interconnect are required.[6] Along with the sorting stage and the wider multiplexers, this may increase the switch cycle time or increase its routing delay.

It is a matter of perspective whether the buffers in Figure 10.29 are associated with the input or the output ports. If viewed as output port buffers, the key property is that each output port has enough internal bandwidth to receive a packet from every input port in one cycle. This could be obtained with a single output FIFO, but it would have to run at an internal clock rate of n times that of the input ports.

6. It is possible to provide the capability of the output buffered switch but avoid the storage and interconnect penalty (Joerg 1994). The set of buffers at each input forms a pool and each output has a list of pointers to packets destined for it. The timing requirement in this design is the ability to push n pointers per cycle into the output port buffer rather than n packets per cycle.

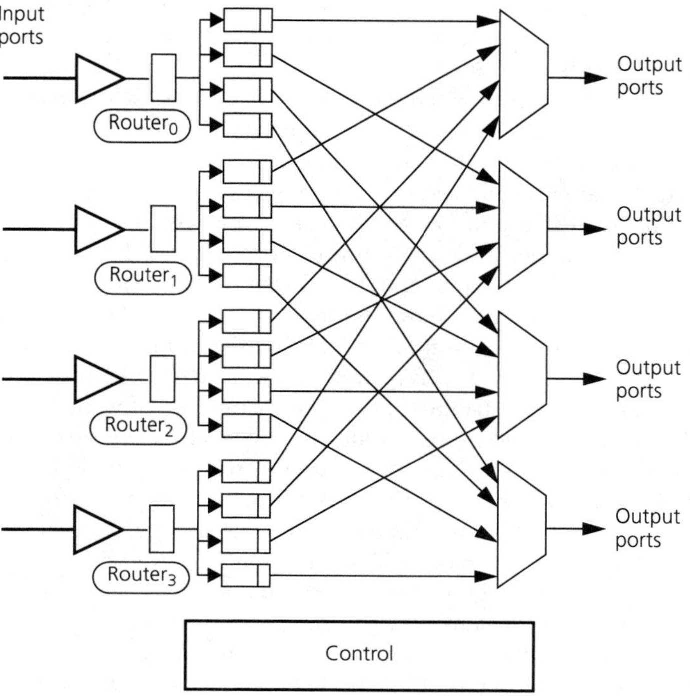

FIGURE 10.29 Switch design to avoid head-of-line blocking. Packets are sorted by output port at each input port so that the controller can schedule a packet for an output port if any input has a packet destined for that output.

Shared Pool

With a shared pool, each of the input ports deposits data into a central memory, and each of the output buffers reads from it. Head-of-line blocking is avoided because input ports can write to the pool regardless of output port, assuming space is available. The challenge is to match the bandwidth of the n-input and n-output ports. A common trick is to make the internal datapath to the pool $2n$ times as wide as the links. Each input port buffers $2n$ phits before writing it to the pool, and each output port gets $2n$ phits at a time. Often these shared pools are built from the SRAM technology used for caches.

Virtual Channels Buffering

Virtual channels suggest an alternative way of organizing the internal buffers of the switch. Recall that a set of virtual channels provides transmission of multiple independent packets across a single physical link. As illustrated in Figure 10.21, to support virtual channels the flow across the link is split upon arrival at an input port into distinct channel buffers. These are multiplexed together again, either before or after the crossbar, onto the output ports. If one of the virtual channel buffers is blocked, it is natural to consider advancing the other virtual channels toward the outputs. Again, the switch has the opportunity to select among multiple packets at each input for advance to the output ports; however, in this case the choice is among different virtual channels rather than different output ports. It is possible that all the virtual channels will need to route to the same output port, but expected coverage of the outputs is much better. In a probabilistic analysis, we can ask: what is the expected number of distinct output ports covered by choosing among vn requests for n ports, where v is the number of virtual channels?

Simulation studies show that large (256- to 1,024-node) 2-ary butterflies using wormhole routing with moderate buffering (16 flits per channel) saturate at a channel utilization of about 25% under random traffic. If the same 16 flits of buffering per channel are distributed over a larger number of virtual channels, the saturation bandwidth increases substantially. It exceeds 40% with just two virtual channels (8-flit buffers) and is nearly 80% at 16 channels with single-flit buffers (Dally 1990a). While this study keeps the total buffering per channel fixed, it does not really keep the cost constant. Notice that a routing decision needs to be computed for each virtual channel rather than each physical channel, if packets from any of the channels are to be considered for advancement to output ports.

By now you are probably jumping a step ahead to additional cost-performance trade-offs that might be considered. For example, if the crossbar has an input per virtual channel, then multiple packets can advance from a single input at once. This increases the probability of each packet advancing and, hence, the channel utilization. The crossbar increases in size in only one dimension, and the multiplexers are eliminated since each output port is logically a vn-way multiplexer. Switch design allows a great deal of room for innovation.

10.7.4 Output Scheduling

We have seen routing mechanisms that determine the desired output port for each input packet, datapaths that provide a connection from the input ports to the outputs, and buffering strategies that allow multiple packets per input port to be considered as candidates for advancement to the output port. A key missing component in the switch design is the *scheduling algorithm,* which selects the packets to advance in each cycle. Given a selection, the remainder of the switch control asserts the control points in the crossbars or multiplexers and the buffers or latches to effect the register transfer from each selected input to the associated output. As with the other aspects of switch design, there is a spectrum of solutions varying from simple to complex.

A simple approach is to view the scheduling problem as n independent arbitration problems, one for each output port. Each candidate input buffer has a request line to each output port and a grant line from each port, as indicated by Figure 10.30. (The figure shows four candidate input buffers driving three output ports to indicate that routing logic and arbitration input is on a per-input-buffer

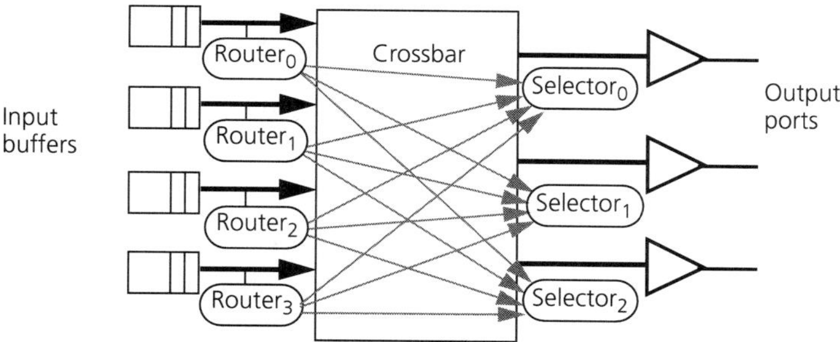

FIGURE 10.30 Control structure for output scheduling. Associated with each input buffer is routing logic to determine the output port, a request line, and a grant line per output. Each output has selection logic to arbitrate among asserted requests and to assert one grant, causing a flit to advance from the input buffer to the output port.

basis rather than per input port.) The routing logic computes the desired output port and asserts the request line for the selected output port. The output port scheduling logic arbitrates among the requests, selects one, and asserts the corresponding grant signal. Specifically, with the crossbar using tristate drivers in Figure 10.27(b), output port j enables input buffer i by asserting control enable e_{ij}. The input buffer logic advances its FIFO as a result of one of the grant lines being asserted.

An additional design question is the arbitration algorithm used for scheduling flits onto the output. Options include static priority, random, round-robin, and oldest-first scheduling. Each of these have different performance characteristics and implementation complexity. Clearly, static priority is the simplest; it is simply a priority encoder. However, in a large network it can cause indefinite postponement. In general, scheduling algorithms that provide fair service to the inputs perform better. Round-robin requires extra state to change the order of priority in each cycle. Oldest-first tends to have the same average latency as random assignment but significantly reduces the variance in latencies (Dally 1990a). One way to implement oldest-first scheduling is to use a control FIFO of input port numbers at each output port. When an input buffer requests an output, the request is enqueued. The oldest request at the head of the FIFO is granted.

It is useful to consider the implementation of various routing algorithms and topologies in terms of Figure 10.30. For example, in a direct d-cube there are $d + 1$ inputs (let's number them $i_0, \ldots, i_d$) and $d + 1$ outputs (numbered $o_1, \ldots, o_{d+1}$) with the host connected to input i_0 and output o_{d+1}. The straight path $i_j \rightarrow o_j$ corresponds to routing in the same dimension; other paths are a change in dimension. With dimension order routing, packets can only increase in dimension as they cross the switch. Thus, the full complement of request/grant logic is not required. Input j need only request outputs $j, \ldots, d + 1$ and output j need only grant inputs $0, \ldots, j$. Obvious static priority schemes assign priority in increasing or decreasing numerical order.

What are the implementation requirements of adaptive routing? First, the routing logic for an input must compute multiple candidate outputs according to the specific rules of the algorithm, for example, turn restrictions or plane restrictions. For partially adaptive routing, this may be only a couple of candidates. Each output receives several requests and can grant one. (Or if the output is blocked, it may not grant any.) The tricky point is that an input may be selected by more than one output. It will need to choose one, but what happens to the other outputs? Should it iterate on its arbitration and select another input or go idle? This problem can be formalized as one of *on-line bipartite matching* (Karp, Vazirani, and Vazirani 1990). The requests define a bipartite graph with inputs on one side and outputs on the other. The grants (one per output) define a matching of input/output pairs within the request graph. The maximum matching would allow the largest number of inputs to advance in a cycle, which ought to give the highest channel utilization. Viewing the problem in this way, the switch scheduling logic should approximate a fast parallel matching algorithm (Anderson et al. 1992). The basic idea is to form a tentative matching using a simple greedy algorithm, such as random selection among requests at each output followed by selection of grants at each input; then, for each unselected output, try to make an improvement to the tentative matching. In practice, the improvement diminishes after a couple of iterations. Clearly, this is another case of sophistication versus speed. If the scheduling algorithm increases the switch cycle time or routing delay, it may be better to accept a little extra blocking and get the job done faster.

This maximum matching problem applies to the case where multiple virtual channels are multiplexed through each input of the crossbar, even with deterministic routing. (Indeed, the technique was proposed for the AN2 ATM switch to address the situation of scheduling cells from several "virtual circuits."[7]) Each input port has multiple buffers that it can schedule onto its crossbar input, and these may be destined for different outputs. The selection of the outputs determines which virtual channel to advance. If the crossbar is widened, rather than multiplexing the inputs, the matching problem vanishes and each output can make a simple independent arbitration.

10.7.5 Stacked Dimension Switches

Many aspects of switch design are simplified if there are only two inputs and two outputs, including the control, arbitration, and datapaths. Several designs, including the torus routing chip (Seitz and Su 1993), the J-machine, and the CRAY T3D, have used a simple 2×2 building block and stacked these to construct switches of higher dimension, as illustrated in Figure 10.31. If we have in mind a d-cube, traffic continuing in a given dimension passes straight through the switch in that dimension, whereas if it needs to turn into another dimension it is routed vertically through the

7. Virtual circuits should not be confused with virtual channels. The former is a technique for associating routing of resources along an entire source-to-destination route. The latter is a strategy for structuring the buffering associated with each link.

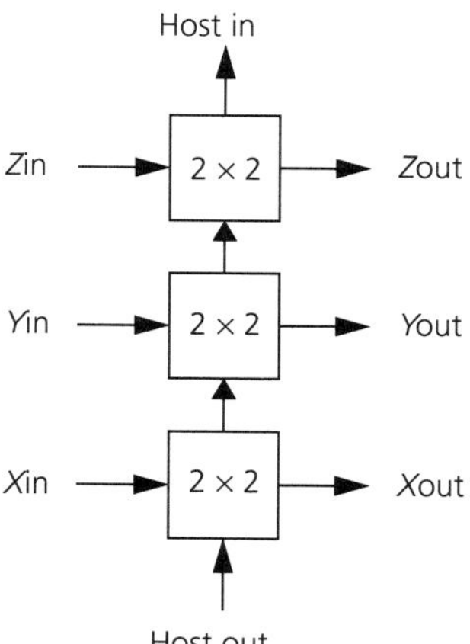

FIGURE 10.31 Stacked dimension switch. Traffic continuing in a dimension passes straight through one 2 × 2 switch, whereas when it turns to route in another dimension it is routed vertically up the stack.

switch. Notice that this adds a hop for all but the lowest dimension. This same technique yields a topology called *cube-connected cycles* when applied to a hypercube. Each $n \times n$ node of the hypercube is replaced by a ring of n 2 × 2 nodes.

10.8 FLOW CONTROL

In this section, we consider in detail what happens when multiple flows of data in the network attempt to use the same shared network resources at the same time. Some action must be taken to control these flows. If no data is to be lost, some of the flows must be blocked while others proceed. The problem of flow control arises in all networks and at many levels, but it is qualitatively different in parallel computer networks from that in local and wide area networks. In parallel computers, network traffic needs to be delivered about as reliably as traffic across a bus, and a very large number of concurrent flows occur on very small time scales. No other networking regime has such stringent demands. We will look briefly at some of these differences and then examine in detail how flow control is addressed at the link level and end to end in parallel machines.

10.8.1 Parallel Computer Networks versus LANs and WANs

To build intuition for the unique flow control requirements of the parallel machine networks, let us take a little digression and examine the role of flow control in the networks we deal with every day for file transfer and the like. We will look at three examples: Ethernet-style collision-based arbitration, FDDI-style global arbitration, and unarbitrated wide area networks.

In an Ethernet, the entire network is effectively a single shared wire, like a bus, only longer. (The aggregate bandwidth is equal to the link bandwidth.) However, unlike a bus, there is no explicit arbitration unit. A host attempts to send a packet by first checking that the network appears to be quiet and then (optimistically) driving its packet onto the wire. All nodes watch the wire, including the hosts attempting to send. If only one packet is on the wire, every host will "see" it, and the host specified as the destination will pick it up. If there is a collision, every host will detect the garbled signal, including the multiple senders. The minimum that a host may drive a packet (i.e., the minimum channel time) is about 50 μs; this is to allow time for all hosts to detect collisions.

The flow control aspect is how the retry is handled. On a collision, each sender backs off for a random amount of time and then retries. With each repeated collision, the retry interval from which the random delay is chosen is increased. The collision detection is performed within the network interface hardware, and the retry is handled by the lowest level of the Ethernet driver. If there is no success after a large number of tries, the Ethernet driver gives up and drops the packet. However, the message operation originated from some higher-level communication software layer that has its own delivery contract. For example, the TCP/IP layer will detect the delivery failure via a time-out and engage its own adaptive retry mechanism, just as it does for wide area connection, which we will look at next. The UDP layer will ignore the delivery failure, leaving it to the user application to detect the event and retry. The basic concept of the Ethernet rests on the assumption that the wire is very fast compared to the communication capability of the hosts. (This assumption was reasonable in the mid-1970s when Ethernet was developed.) A great deal of study has been given to the properties of collision-based media access control, but basically as the network reaches saturation, the delivered bandwidth drops precipitously.

Ring-based LANs, such as token ring and FDDI, use a distributed form of global arbitration to control access to the shared medium. A special arbitration token circulates the ring when there is an empty slot. A host that desires to send a packet waits until the token comes around, grabs it, and drives the packet onto the ring. After the packet is sent, the arbitration token is returned to the ring. In effect, flow control is performed at the hosts on every packet as part of gaining access to the ring. Even if the ring is idle, a host must wait for the token to traverse half the ring, on average. (This is why the unloaded latency for FDDI is generally higher than that of Ethernet.) However, under high load, the full link capacity can be used. Again, the basic assumption underlying this global arbitration scheme is that the network operates on a much smaller timescale than the communication operations of the hosts.

In the wide area case, each TCP connection (and each UDP packet) follows a path through a series of switches, bridges, and routers across media of varying speeds between source and destination. Since the Internet is a graph rather than a simple linear structure, at any point a set of incoming flows may have a collective bandwidth greater than the outgoing link. Traffic will back up as a result. Wide area routers provide a substantial amount of buffering to absorb stochastic variations in the flows, but if the contention persists, these buffers will eventually fill up. In this case, most routers will just drop the packets. Wide area links may be stretches of fibers many miles long, so when the packet is driven onto a link it is hard to know if it will find buffer space available when it arrives at the other end. Furthermore, the flows of data through a switch are usually unrelated transfers. They are not, in general, a collection of flows from within a single parallel program, which imposes a degree of inherent end-to-end flow control by waiting for data it needs before continuing. The TCP layer provides end-to-end flow control and adapts dynamically to the perceived characteristics of the route occupied by a connection. It assumes that packet loss (detected via time-out) is a result of contention at some intermediate point, so when it experiences a loss, it sharply decreases the send rate (by reducing the size of its burst window). It slowly increases this rate (i.e., the window size) as data is transferred successfully (detected via acknowledgments from destination to source) until it once again experiences a loss. Thus, each flow is controlled at the source governed by the occurrence of time-outs and acknowledgments.

Of course, the wide area case operates on a timescale of fractions of a second whereas parallel machine networks operate on a scale of nanoseconds. Thus, one should not expect the techniques to carry over directly. Interestingly, the TCP flow control mechanisms do work well in the context of collision-based arbitration such as Ethernet (partly because the software overhead time tends to give a chance for the network to clear). However, with the emergence of high-speed, switched local and wide area networks, especially ATM, the flow control problem has taken on many more of the characteristics of the parallel machine case. Most commercial ATM switches provide a sizable amount of buffering per link (typically 64 to 128 cells per link) but drop cells when this is exceeded. Each cell is 53 bytes, so at the 155-Mb/s OC-3 rate, a cell transfer time is 2.7 μs. Buffers fill very rapidly compared to typical LAN/WAN end-to-end times. The TCP mechanisms can be ineffective in the ATM settings when contending with more aggressive protocols, such as UDP, prompting the ATM standardization efforts to include link-level flow and rate control measures.

10.8.2 Link-Level Flow Control

Essentially all parallel machine interconnection networks provide link-level flow control. The basic problem is illustrated in Figure 10.32. Data is to be transferred from an output port of one node across a link to an input port of a node operating autonomously. The storage may be a simple latch, a FIFO, or buffer memory. The link may be short or long, wide or narrow, synchronous or asynchronous. The key point is that, as a result of circumstances at the destination node, storage at the input port may not be available to accept the transfer, so the data must be retained at the source until the destination is ready. This may cause the buffers at the source to fill, and it in turn may exert pressure back on its sources.

The implementation of link-level flow control differs depending on the design of the link, but the main idea is the same. The destination node provides feedback to the source, indicating whether it is able to receive additional data on the link. The source holds onto the data until the destination indicates that it is able. Before we examine how this feedback is incorporated into the switch operation, let us look at how the flow control is implemented on different kinds of links.

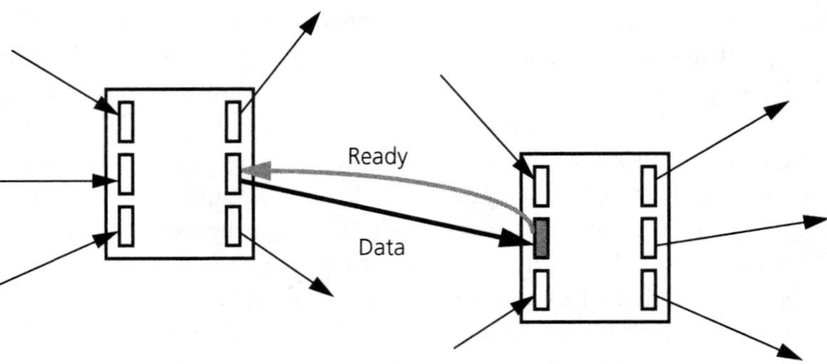

FIGURE 10.32 Link-level flow control. As a result of circumstances at the destination node, the storage at the input port may not be available to accept the data transfer, so the data must be retained at the source until the destination is ready.

With short-wide links, the transfer across the link is essentially like a register transfer within a machine, extended with a couple of control signals. We may view the source and destination registers as being extended with a full-empty bit, as illustrated in Figure 10.33. If the source is full and the destination is empty, the transfer occurs, the destination becomes full, and the source becomes empty (unless it is refilled from its source). With synchronous operation (e.g., in the CRAY T3D, IBM SP-2, TMC CM-5, and MIT J-machine), the flow control determines whether a transfer occurs for the clock cycle. It is easy to see how this is realized with edge-triggered or multiphase level-sensitive designs. If the switches operate asynchronously, the behavior is much like a register transfer in a self-timed design. The source asserts the request (req) signal when it is full and ready to transfer; the destination uses this signal to accept the value (when the input port is available) and asserts an acknowledgment (ack) when it has accepted the data. With short-narrow links, the behavior is similar, except that a series of phits is transferred for each req/ack handshake.

The req/ack handshake can be viewed as the transfer of a single token or credit between the source and the destination. When the destination frees the input buffer, it passes the token to the source (i.e., increases its credit). The source uses this credit when it sends the next flit and must wait until its account is refilled. For long links, this credit scheme is expanded so that the entire pipeline associated with the link propagation delay can be filled. Suppose that the link is sufficiently long that several flits are in transit simultaneously. As indicated by Figure 10.34, it will also take several cycles for acks to propagate in the reverse direction, so a number of acks (credits) may be in transit as well. The obvious credit-based flow control is for the source to keep account of the available slots in the destination input buffer. The counter is initialized to the buffer size. It is decremented when a flit is sent, and the output is blocked if the counter reaches zero. When the destination removes a flit from the input buffer, it returns a credit to the source, which increments the counter. The input buffer will never overflow; there is always room to drain the link into the buffer. This approach is most attractive with wide links, which have dedicated control lines

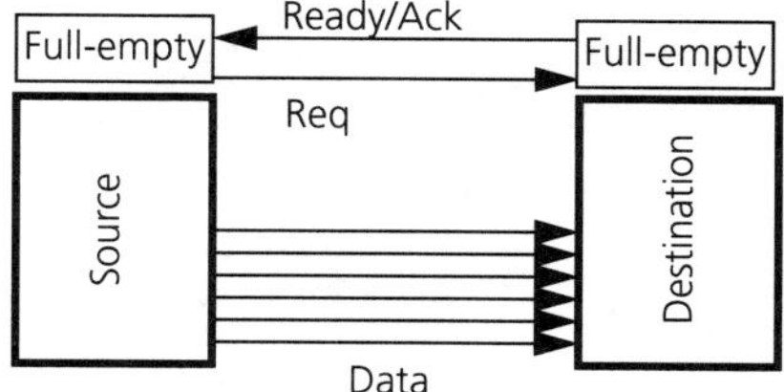

FIGURE 10.33 Simple link-level handshake. The source asserts its request when it has a flit to transmit; the destination acknowledges the receipt of a flit when it is ready to accept the next one. Until that time, the source repeatedly transmits the flit.

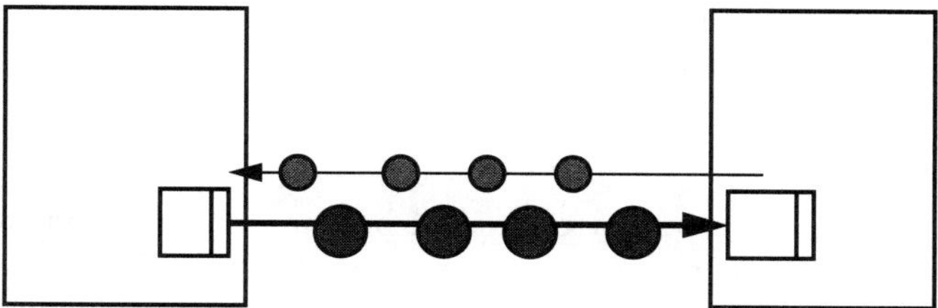

FIGURE 10.34 Transient flits and acks with long links. With longer links, the flow control scheme needs to allow more slack in order to keep the link full. Several flits can be driven onto the wire before waiting for acks to come back.

for the reverse ack. For narrow links that multiplex ack symbols onto the opposite-going channel, the ack per flit can be reduced by transferring bigger chunks of credit. However, the problem remains that the approach is not very robust to the loss of credit tokens.

Ideally, when the flows are moving forward smoothly there is no need for flow control. The flow control mechanism should be a governor that gently nudges the input rate to match the output rate. The propagation delays on the links give the system momentum. An alternative approach to link-level credits is to view the destination input buffer as a staging tank with a low-water mark and a high-water mark, as in Figure 10.35. When the fill level drops below the low mark, a GO symbol is sent to the source, and when it goes over the high mark, a STOP symbol is generated. There must be enough room below the low mark to withstand a full round-trip delay (the GO propagating to the source, being processed, and the first of a stream of flits propagating to the destination). In addition, there must be enough headroom above the high mark to absorb the round-trip's worth of flits that may be in flight. A nice property of this approach is that redundant GO symbols may be sent anywhere below the high mark and STOP symbols may be sent anywhere above the low mark with no harmful effect, so they are simply sent periodically in the two regimes. The fraction of the link bandwidth used by flow control symbols can be reduced by

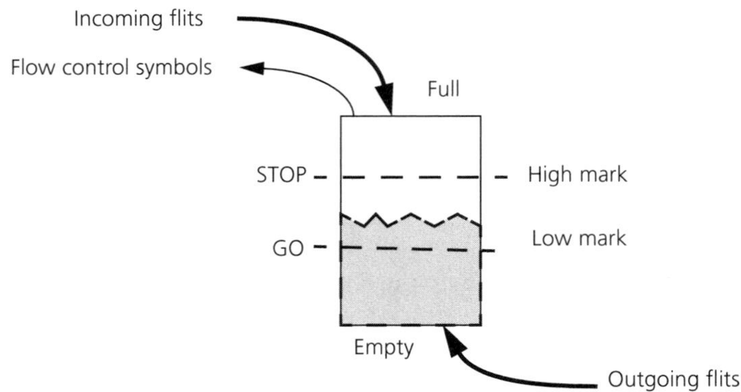

FIGURE 10.35 Slack buffer operation. When the fill level drops below the low mark, a GO symbol is sent to the source, and when it goes over the high mark, a STOP symbol is generated.

increasing the amount of storage between the low and high marks in the input buffer. This approach is used, for example, in Cal Tech routers (Seitz and Su 1993) and the Myrinet commercial follow-on (Boden et al. 1995). Similar techniques are used in modems.

It is worth noting that the link-level flow control is used on host-switch links as well as switch-switch links. In fact, it is generally carried over to the processor-NI interface as well. However, the techniques may vary for these different kinds of interfaces. For example, in the Intel Paragon the 175-MB/s network links are all short with very small flit buffers. However, the NIs have large input and output FIFOs. The communication assist includes a pair of DMA engines that can burst at 300 MB/s between memory and the network FIFOs. It is essential that the output (input) buffer not hit full (empty) in the middle of a burst because holding the bus transaction would hurt performance and potentially lead to deadlock. Thus, the burst is matched to the size of the middle region of the buffer and the high/low marks to the control turnaround between the NI and the DMA controller.

10.8.3 End-to-End Flow Control

Link-level flow control exerts a certain amount of end-to-end control because if congestion persists, buffers will fill up and the flow will be controlled all the way back to the source host nodes, called *back pressure*. For example, if k nodes are sending data to a single destination, they must eventually all slow to an average bandwidth of $1/k$th the output bandwidth. If the switch scheduling is fair and all the routes through the network are symmetric, back pressure will be enough to affect this. The problem is that by the time the sources feel the back pressure and regulate their output flow, all the buffers in the tree from the hot spot to the sources are full.

Hot Spots

The hot spot problem received quite a bit of attention as the technology reached a point where machines of several hundred to a thousand processors became reasonable (Pfister and Norton 1985). If a thousand processors deliver on average any more than 0.1% of their traffic to any one destination, that destination becomes saturated. If this situation persists, as it might if frequent accesses are made to an important shared variable, a saturation tree forms in front of this destination that will eventually reach all the way to the sources. At this point, all the remaining traffic in the system is severely impeded. The problem is particularly pernicious in butterflies since there is only one route to each destination and a great deal of sharing takes place among routes from one destination. Adaptive routing proves to make the hot spot problem even worse because traffic destined for the hot spot is sure to run into contention and to be directed to alternate routes. Eventually, the entire network clogs up. Large network buffers do not solve the problem; they just delay the onset. The time for the hot spot to clear is proportional to the total amount of hot spot traffic buffered in the network, so adaptivity and large buffers increase the time required for the hot spot to clear after the load is removed.

Various mechanisms have been developed to mitigate the causes of hot spots, such as having all nodes that need to increment a shared variable perform a parallel scan operation, as discussed in Chapter 7, or to implement combining fetch&add operations within the network (Pfister et al. 1985; Gottlieb, Lubachevsky, and Rudolph 1983). However, these only address situations where the problematic traffic is logically related. The more fundamental problem is that link-level flow control is like stopping on the freeway. Once the traffic jam forms, you are stuck. The better solution is not to get on the freeway at such times. With fewer packets inside the network, the normal mechanisms can do a better job of getting traffic to its destinations. This is one of the reasons that the BBN butterfly retracts the circuit established by a message upon collision.

Global Communication Operations

Problems with simple back pressure have been observed with completely balanced communication patterns, such as each node sending k packets to every other node. This occurs in many situations, including transposing a global matrix, converting between blocked and cyclic layouts, or the decimation step of an FFT (Brewer and Kuszmaul 1994; Dusseau et al. 1996). Even if the topology is robust enough to avoid serious internal bottlenecks on these operations, which is true of a fat-tree but not a low-degree dimension order mesh (Leighton 1992), a temporary backlog can have a cascading effect. When one destination falls behind in receiving packets from the network, a backlog begins to form. If priority is given to draining the network, this node will fall behind in sending to the other nodes. They, in turn, will send more than they receive and the backlog will tend to grow.

Simple end-to-end protocols in the global communication routines have been shown to mitigate this problem in practice. For example, a node may wait after sending a certain amount of data until it has also received this amount, or it may wait for chunks of its data to be acknowledged. These precautions keep the processors more closely in step and introduce small gaps in the traffic flow, which decouples the processor-to-processor interaction through the network. (Interestingly, this technique is employed with the metering lights on heavily used bridges. Periodically, a wavefront of cars is injected into the bridge, separated by small gaps. This reduces the stochastic temporary blocking and avoids cascading blockage.)

Admission Control

With shallow, cut-through networks, the latency is low below saturation. Indeed, in most modern parallel machine networks, a single small message (or perhaps a few messages) will occupy an entire path from source to destination. If the remote network interface is not ready to accept the message, it is better to keep it within the source NI rather than blocking traffic within the network. One approach to achieving this is to perform NI-to-NI credit-based flow control. One study examining such techniques for a range of networks (Callahan and Goldstein 1995) indicates that allowing a single outstanding message per pair of NIs gives good throughput and maintains low latency.

10.9 CASE STUDIES

Networks are a fascinating area of study from a practical design and engineering viewpoint because they do one simple operation—move information from one place to another—and yet there is a huge space of design alternatives. Although the most apparent characteristics of a network are its topology, link bandwidth, switching strategy, and routing algorithm, several more characteristics must be specified to completely describe the design. These include the cycle time, link width, switch buffer capacity and allocation strategy, routing mechanism, switch output selection algorithm, and flow control mechanism. Each component of the design can be understood and optimized in isolation, but they all interact in interesting ways to determine the network performance on any particular traffic pattern in the context of the node architecture and the dependences embedded in the programs running on the platform.

This section summarizes a set of concrete network design points in important commercial and research parallel architectures. Using the framework established in this chapter, it systematically outlines the key design parameters.

10.9.1 CRAY T3D Network

The CRAY T3D network consists of a three-dimensional bidirectional torus of up to 1,024 switch nodes, each connected directly to a pair of processors,[8] with a data rate

8. Special I/O gateway nodes attached to the boundary of the cube include two processors each attached to a two-dimensional switch node connected into the x and z dimensions.

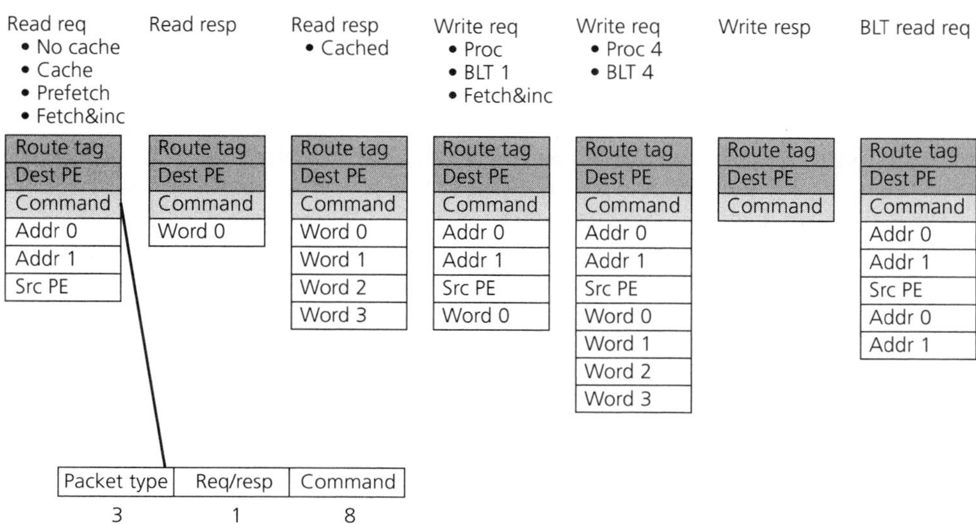

FIGURE 10.36 CRAY T3D packet formats. All packets consist of a series of 16-bit phits, with the first three being the route and tag, the destination processor number, and the command. Parsing and processing of the rest of the packet is determined by the tag and command.

of 300 MB/s per channel. Each node is on a single board, along with two processors and memory. There are up to 128 nodes (256 processors) per cabinet; larger configurations are constructed by cabling together cabinets. Dimension order, cut-through, packet-switched routing is used. The design of the network is very strongly influenced by the higher-level design of the system. Logically independent request and response networks are supported, with two virtual channels each to avoid deadlock, over a single set of physical links. Packets are variable length in multiples of 16 bits, as illustrated by Figure 10.36, and network transactions include various reads and writes plus the ability to start a remote block transfer engine (BLT), which is basically a DMA device. The first phit always contains the route, followed by the destination address, and the packet type or command code. The remainder of the payload depends on the packet type, consisting of relative addresses and data. All of the packet is parity protected, except the routing phit. If the route is corrupted, it will be misrouted, and the error will be detected at the destination because the destination address will not match the value in the packet.[9]

T3D links are short, wide, and synchronous. Each unidirectional link is 16 data and 8 control bits wide, operating under a single 150-MHz clock. Flits and phits are 16 bits. Two of the control bits identify the phit type (00 no info, 01 routing tag, 10

9. This approach to error detection reveals a subtle aspect of networks. If the route is corrupted, there is a very small probability that it will take a wrong turn at just the wrong time and collide with another packet in a manner that causes deadlock within the network; in this unlikely case the end node error detection will not be engaged.

packet, 11 last). The routing tag phit and the last-packet phit provide packet framing. Two additional control bits identify the virtual channel (req-hi, req-lo, resp-hi, resp-lo). The remaining four control lines are acknowledgments in the opposite direction, one per virtual channel. Thus, flow control per virtual channel and phits can be interleaved between virtual channels on a cycle-by-cycle basis.

The switch is constructed as three independent dimension routers, in six 10-K gate arrays. There is a modest amount of buffering in each switch (eight 16-bit parcels for each of four virtual channels in each of three dimensions), so packets compress into the switches when blocked. There is enough buffering in a switch to store small packets. The input port determines the desired output port by a simple arithmetic operation. The routing distance is decremented, and if the result is nonzero the packet continues in its current direction on the current dimension; otherwise, it is routed into the next dimension. Each output port uses a rotating priority among input ports requesting that output. For each input port, there is a rotating priority for virtual channels requesting that output.

The network interface contains eight packet buffers, two per virtual channel. The entire packet is buffered in the source NI before being transmitted into the network. It is buffered in the destination NI before being delivered to the processor or memory system. This store-and-forward delay effectively decouples the network and node operations. In addition to the main data communication network, separate treelike networks for logical-AND (Barrier) and logical-OR (Eureka) are provided.

The presence of bidirectional links provides two possible options in each dimension. A table lookup is performed in the source network interface to select the (deterministic) route consisting of the direction and distance in each of the three dimensions. An individual program occupies a partition of the machine consisting of a logically contiguous subarray of arbitrary shape (under operating system configuration). Shift and mask logic within the communication assist maps the partition-relative virtual node address into a machinewide logical <*X,Y,Z*> coordinate address. The machine can be configured with spare nodes, which can be brought in to replace a failed node. The <*X,Y,Z*> is used as an index for the route lookup, so the NI routing tables provide the final level of translation, identifying the physical node by its <$\pm\Delta x$, $\pm\Delta y$, $\pm\Delta z$> route from the source. This routing lookup also identifies which of the four virtual channels is used. To avoid deadlock within either the request or response (virtual) network, the high channel is used for packets that cross the wrap-around links and the low channel otherwise.

10.9.2 IBM SP-1, SP-2 Network

The network used in the IBM SP-1 and SP-2 parallel machines (Abali and Aykanat 1994; Stunkel et al. 1994) is in some ways more versatile than that in the CRAY T3D but of lower performance and without support for two-phase, request-response operations. It is packet switched, with cut-through, source-based routing and no virtual channels. The switch has eight bidirectional 40-MB/s ports and can support a wide variety of topologies. However, in the SP machines, a collection of switches are

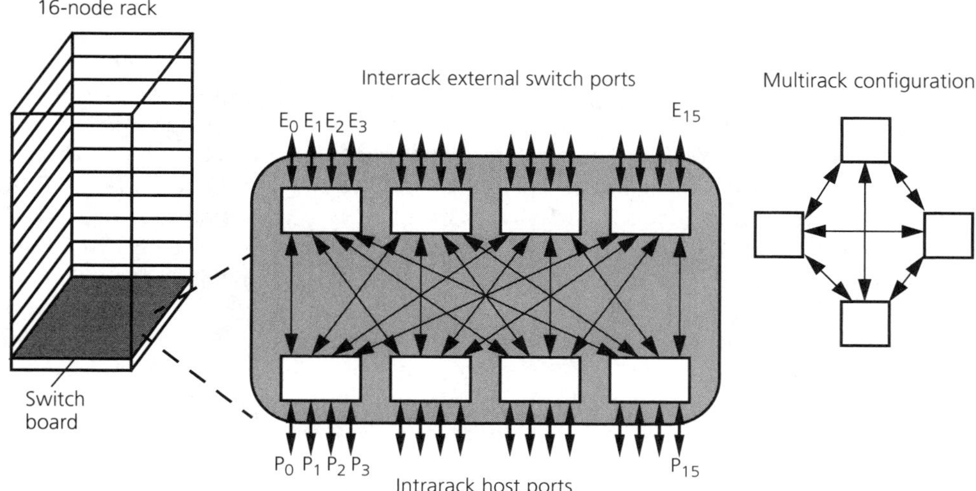

FIGURE 10.37 SP switch packaging. The collection of switches within a rack provides the bidirectional connection between 16 internal ports and 16 external ports.

packaged on a board as a 4-ary 2-dimensional butterfly with 16 internal connections to hosts in the same rack as the switch board and 16 external connections to other racks, as illustrated in Figure 10.37. The rack-level topology varies from machine to machine but is typically a variant of a butterfly. Figure 1.23 in Chapter 1 shows the large IBM SP-2 configuration at the Maui High-Performance Computing Center. Individual cabinets have the first level of routing at the bottom connecting the 16 internal nodes to 16 external links. Additional cabinets provide connectivity between collections of cabinets. The wiring for these additional levels is located beneath the machine room floor. Since the physical topology is not fixed in hardware, the network interface inserts the route for each outgoing message via a table lookup.

Packets consist of a sequence of up to 255 bytes; the first byte is the packet length, followed by one or more routing bytes and then the data bytes. Each routing byte contains two 3-bit output specifiers with an additional selector bit. The links are synchronous, wide, and long. A single 40-MHz clock is distributed to all the switches, with each link tuned so that its delay is an integral number of cycles. (Interboard signals are 100-K ECL differential pairs. Onboard clock trees are also 100-K ECL.) The links consist of 10 wires: 8 data bits, a framing "tag" control bit, and a reverse flow control bit. Thus, the phit is 1 byte. The tag bit identifies the length and routing phits. The flit is 2 bytes; two cycles are used to signal the availability of 2 bytes of storage in the receiver buffer. At any time, a stream of data/tag flits can be propagating down the link while a stream of credit tokens propagate in the other direction.

The switch provides 31 bytes of FIFO buffering on each input port, allowing links to be 16 phits long. In addition, there are 7 bytes of FIFO buffering on each output and a shared central queue holding 128 8-byte chunks. As illustrated in Figure 10.38, the switch contains both an unbuffered byte-serial crossbar and a 128- × 64-bit dual port RAM as the interconnect between the input and output ports. After 2 bytes of the packet have arrived in the input port, the input port control logic can request the desired output. If this output is available, the packet cuts through via the crossbar to the output port, with a minimum routing delay of 5 cycles per switch. If the output port is not available, the packet fills into the input FIFO. If the output port remains blocked, the packet is spooled into the central queue in 8-byte "chunks." Since the central queue accepts one 8-byte input and one 8-byte output per cycle, its bandwidth matches that of the 8-byte serial input and output ports of the switch. Internally, the central queue is organized as eight FIFO linked lists, one per output port, using an auxiliary 128- × 7-bit RAM for the links. One 8-byte chunk is reserved for each output port. Thus, the switch operates in byte-serial mode when the load is low, but when contention forms, it time-multiplexes 8-byte chunks through the central queue, with the inputs acting as a deserializer and the outputs as a serializer.

Each output port arbitrates among requests on an LRU basis, with chunks in the central queue having priority over bytes in input FIFOs. Output ports are served by the central queue in LRU order. The central queue gives priority to inputs with chunks destined for unblocked output ports.

The SP network has three unusual aspects. First, since the operation is globally synchronous, instead of including CRC information in the envelope of each packet, time is divided into 64-cycle "frames." The last two phits of each frame carry the CRC. The input port checks the CRC and the output port generates it (after stripping it of used routing phits). Second, the switch is a single chip, and every switch chip is shadowed by an identical switch. The pins are bidirectional I/O pins, so one of the chips merely checks the operation of the other. (This will detect switch errors but not link errors.) Finally, the switch supports a circuit-switched "service mode" for various diagnostic purposes. The network is drained free of packets before changing modes.

10.9.3 Scalable Coherent Interface

The Scalable Coherent Interface provides a well-specified case study in high-performance interconnects because it emerged through a standards process rather than as a proprietary design or academic proposal. It was a standard long time in coming but has gained popularity as implementations have gotten under way. It has been adopted by several vendors, although in many cases only a portion of the specification is followed. Essentially, the full SCI specification is used in the interconnect of the HP/Convex Exemplar and in the Sequent NUMA-Q. The CRAY SCX I/O network is based heavily on SCI.

A key element of the SCI design is that it builds around the concept of unidirectional rings, called *ringlets,* rather than bidirectional links. Ringlets are connected by switches to form large networks. The specification defines three layers: a physical

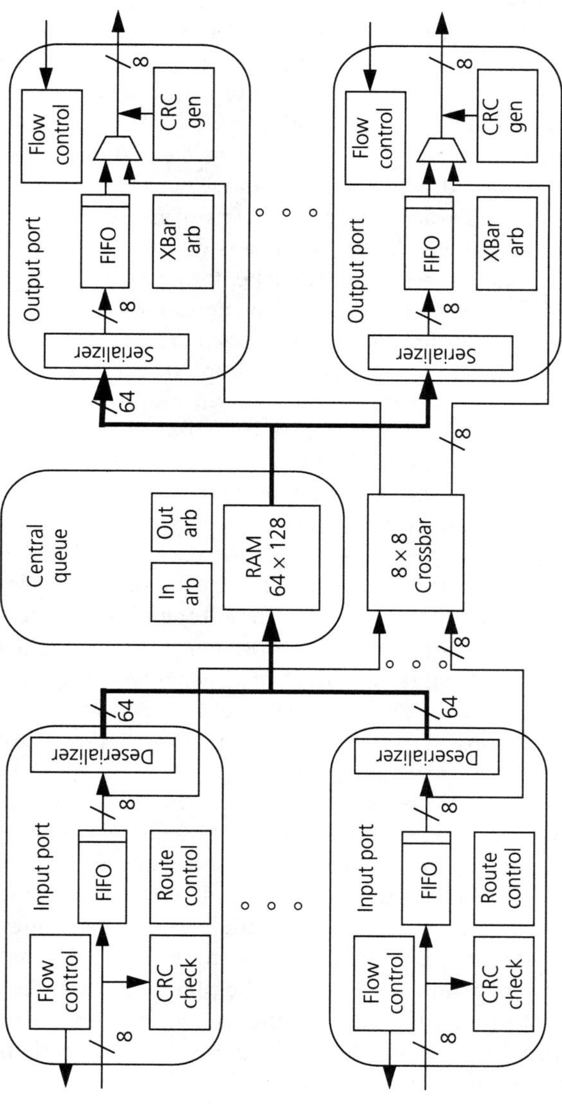

FIGURE 10.38 IBM SP (Vulcan) switch design. The IBM SP switch uses a crossbar for unbuffered packets passed directly from input port to output port, but all buffered packets are shunted into a common memory pool. Arbitration logic schedules flits into and out of the central queue RAM.

layer, a packet layer, and a transaction layer. The physical layer is specified in two 1-GB/s forms. Packets consist of a sequence of 16-bit units, much like the CRAY T3D packets. As illustrated in Figure 10.39, all packets consist of a TargetID, Command, and SourceID, followed by zero or more command-specific units and finally a 32-bit CRC. One unusual aspect is that source and target IDs are arbitrary 16-bit node addresses. The packet does not contain a route. In this sense, the design is like a bus: the source puts the target address on the interconnect, and the interconnect determines how to get the information to the right place. Within a ring, this is simple because the packet circulates the ring and the target extracts the packet. In the general case, switches use table-driven routing to move packets from ring to ring.

An SCI transaction, such as read or write, consists of two network transactions (request and response), each of which has two phases on each ringlet. Let's take this step by step. The source node issues a request packet for a target. The request packet circulates on the source ringlet. If the target is on the same ring as the source, the target extracts the request from the ring and replaces it with an echo packet, which continues around the ring back to the source whereupon it is removed from the ring. The echo packet serves to inform the source that the original packet was either accepted by the target, or rejected, in which case the echo contains a NACK. It may be rejected either because of a buffer-full condition or because the packet was corrupted. The source maintains a timer on outstanding packets so it can detect if the echo gets lost or corrupted. If the target is not on the source ring, a switch node on the ring serves as a proxy for the target. It accepts the packet and provides the echo once it has successfully buffered the packet. Thus, the echo only tells the source that the packet successfully left the ringlet. The switch will then initiate the packet onto another ring along the route to the target. Upon receiving a request, the target node will initiate a response transaction. It too will have a packet phase and an echo phase on each ringlet on the route back to the original source. The request echo packet informs the source of the Transaction ID assigned to the target; this is used to match the eventual response, much as on a split-phase bus.

Rather than have a clean envelope for each of the layers, in SCI they blur together a bit in the packet format where several fields control queue management and retry mechanisms. The control tpr (transaction priority), command mpr (maximum ring priority), and command spr (send priority) together determine one of four priority levels for the packet. The transaction priority is initially set by the requestor, but the actual send priority is established by nodes along the route based on what other blocked transactions they have in their queues. The phase and busy fields are used as part of the flow control negotiation between the source and target nodes.

In the Sequent NUMA-Q, the 18-bit-wide SCI ring is driven directly by the DataPump in a quad at 1-GB/s node-to-network bandwidth. The transport layer follows a strict request-reply protocol. When the DataPump puts a packet on the ring, it keeps a copy of the packet in its outgoing buffer until an *echo* is returned. When a DataPump removes an incoming packet from the ring, it replaces it by a *positive echo*. If a DataPump detects a packet destined for it but does not have space to remove that packet from the ring, it sends a *negative echo*, which causes the sender to retry its transmission (still holding the space in its outgoing buffer).

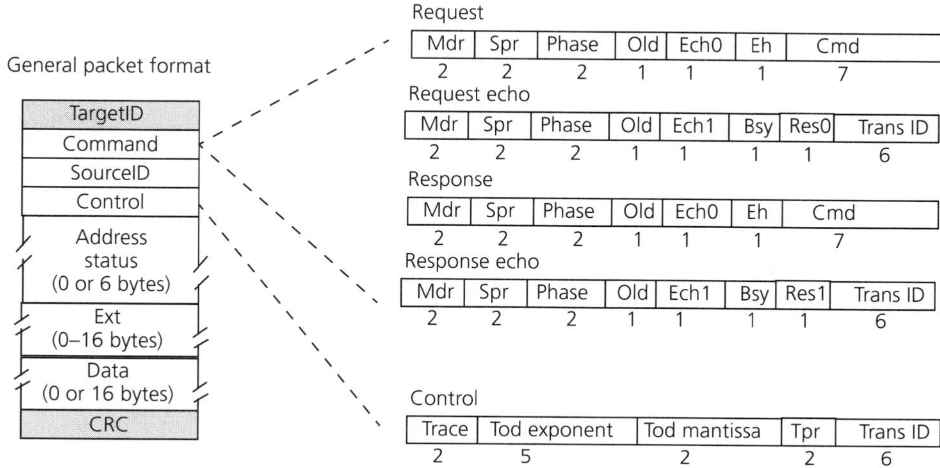

FIGURE 10.39 SCI packet formats. SCI operations involve a pair of transactions: a request and a response. Owing to its ring-based underpinnings, each transaction involves conveying a packet from the source to the target and an echo (going the rest of the way around the ring) from the target back to the source. All packets are a sequence of 16-bit units, with the first three being the destination node, command, and source node, and the final being the CRC. Requests contain a 6-byte address, optional extension, and optional data. Responses have a similar format, but the address bytes carry status information. Both kinds of echo packets contain only the minimal four units. The command unit identifies the packet type through the phase and ech fields. It also describes the operation to be performed (request cmd) or matched (trans id). The remaining fields and the control unit address lower-level issues of how packet queuing and retry are handled at the packet layer.

Since the latency of communication on a ring increases linearly with the number of nodes on it, large high-performance SCI systems are expected to be built out of smaller rings interconnected in arbitrary network topologies. For example, a performance study indicates that a single ring can effectively support four to eight high-performance processing nodes (Scott, Vernon, and Goodman 1992).

10.9.4 SGI Origin Network

The SGI Origin network is based on a flexible switch, called SPIDER, that supports six pairs of unidirectional links, each pair providing over 1.56 GB/s of total bandwidth in the two directions. Two nodes (four processors) are connected to each switch so there are four pairs of links to connect to other switches. This building block is configured in a family of topologies related to hypercubes, as illustrated in Figure 10.40. The links are flexible (long, wide) cables that can be up to 3 meters long. Messages are pipelined through the network, and the latency through the router itself is 41 ns from pin to pin. Routing is table driven, so as part of the network initialization the routing tables are set up in each switch. This allows routing to be programmable so that it is possible to support a range of configurations, to

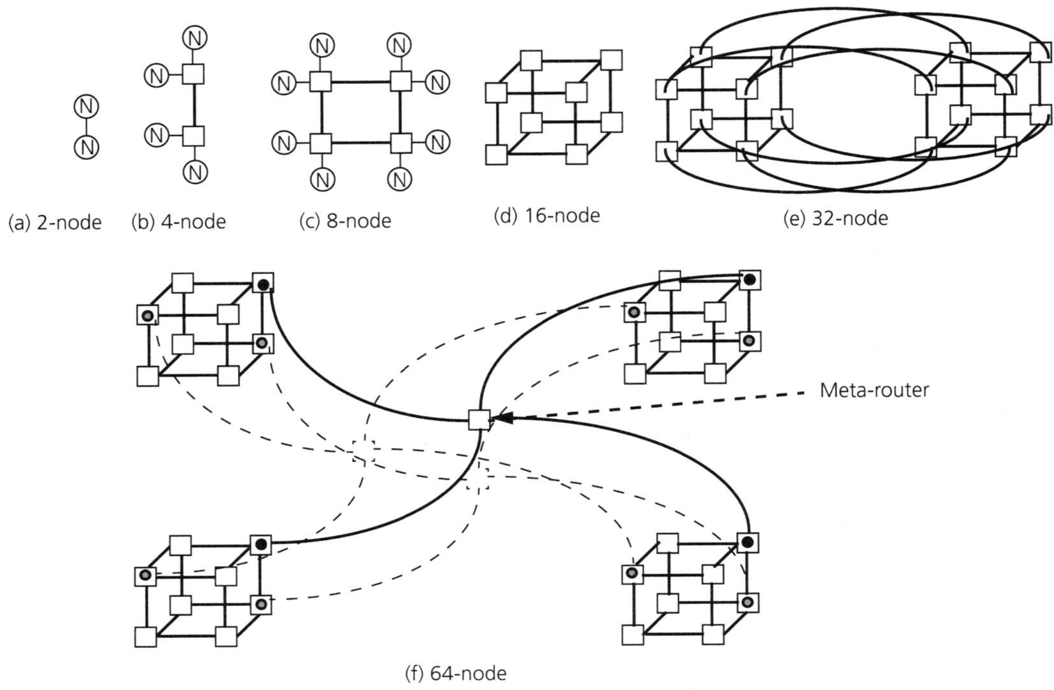

FIGURE 10.40 Network topology and router connections in the SGI Origin multiprocessor. Hypercube topologies are used for up to 32 nodes, as in (a)–(e), and beyond that a fat-tree variant is employed. Configurations (d)–(f) show only the routers and omit the two nodes connected to each for simplicity. Configuration (f) also shows only a few of the fat-cube connections across hypercubes; the routers that connect 16-node subcubes are called meta-routers. For a 512-node (1,024-processor) configuration, each meta-router itself would be replaced by a 5-*d* router hypercube.

have a partially populated network (i.e., not all ports are used), and to route around faulty components. Availability is also aided by the fact that the routers are separately powered and provide per-link error protection with hardware retry upon error. The switch provides separate virtual channels for requests and replies and supports 256 levels of message priority, with packet aging.

10.9.5 Myricom Network

As a final case study, we briefly examine the Myricom network (Boden et al. 1995) used in several cluster systems. The communication assist within the network interface card was described in Section 7.7. Here we are concerned with the switch that is used to construct a scalable interconnection network. Perhaps the most interesting aspect of its design is its simplicity. The basic building block is a switch with eight bidirectional ports of 160 MB/s each. The physical link is a 9-bit-wide long wire. It can be up to 25 m, and 23 phits can be in transit simultaneously. The encoding allows control flow, framing symbols, and "gap" (or idle) symbols to be interleaved with data symbols. Symbols are constantly transmitted between switches across the links so that the switch can determine which of its ports are connected. A packet is simply a sequence of routing bytes followed by a sequence of payload bytes and a CRC byte. The end of a packet is delimited by the presence of a gap symbol. The start of a packet is indicated by the presence of a nongap symbol.

The operation of the switch is extremely simple: it removes the first byte from an incoming packet, computes the output port by adding the contents of the route byte to the input port number, and spools the rest of the packet to that port. The switch uses wormhole routing with a small amount of buffering for each input and each output. The routing delay through a switch is less than 500 ns. The switches can be wired together in an arbitrary topology. It is the responsibility of the host communication software to construct routes that are valid for the physical interconnection of the network. If a packet attempts to exit a switch on an invalid or unconnected port, it is discarded. When all the routing bytes are used up, the packet should have arrived at an NIC. The first byte of the message has a bit to indicate that it is not a routing byte, and the remaining bits indicate the packet type. All higher-level packet formatting and transactions are realized by the NIC and the host; the interconnection network only moves the bits.

10.10 CONCLUDING REMARKS

Parallel computer networks present a rich and diverse design space that brings together several levels of design. The physical link-level issues represent some of the most interesting electrical engineering aspects of computer design. In a constant effort to keep pace with the increasing rate of processors, link rates are ever improving. Currently, we are seeing multigigabit rates on copper pairs, and parallel fiber technologies offer the possibility of multigigabyte rates per link in the near future. One of the major issues at these rates is dealing with errors. If bit error rates of the physical medium are in the order of 10^{-19} per bit and data is being transmitted at a rate of 10^9 bytes per second, then an error is likely to occur on a link roughly every 10 minutes. With thousands of links in the machine, errors occur every second. These must be detected and corrected rapidly.

The switch-to-switch layer of design also offers a rich set of trade-offs, including how aspects of the problem are pushed down into the physical layer and how they are pushed up into the packet layer. For example, flow control can be built into the exchange of digital symbols across a link, or it can be addressed at the next layer in terms of packets that cross the link or even one layer higher, in terms of messages sent from end to end. There is a huge space of alternatives for the design of the switch itself, and these are again driven by engineering constraints from below and design requirements from above.

Even the basic topology, switching strategy, and routing algorithm reflect a compromise of engineering requirements and design requirements from below and above. We have seen, for example, how a basic question like the degree of the switch depends heavily on the cost model associated with the target technology and the characteristics of the communication pattern in the target workload. Finally, as with many other aspects of architecture, there is significant room for debate as to how much of the higher-level semantics of the node-to-node communication abstraction should be embedded in the hardware design of the network itself. The entire area of network design for parallel computers is bound to be exciting for many years to come. In particular, there is a strong flow of ideas and technology between parallel computer networks and advancing, scalable networks for local area and system area communication.

10.11 EXERCISES

10.1 Consider a packet format with 10 bytes of routing and control information and 6 bytes of CRC and other trailer information. The payload contains a 64-byte cache block, along with 8 bytes of command and address information. If the raw link bandwidth is 500 MB/s, what is the effective data bandwidth on cache block transfers using this format? How would this change with 32-byte cache blocks? 128-byte blocks? 4-KB page transfers?

10.2 Suppose the links are 1 byte wide and operating at 300 MHz in a network where the average routing distance between nodes is $\log_4 P$ for P nodes. Compare the unloaded latency for 80-byte packets under store-and-forward and cut-through routing, assuming 4 cycles of delay per hop to make the routing decision and P ranging from 16 to 1,024 nodes.

10.3 Perform the comparison in Exercise 10.2 for 32-KB transfers fragmented into 1-KB packets.

10.4 Find an optimal fragmentation strategy for an 8-KB message, as is common for page-sized transfers under the following assumptions. There is a fixed overhead of o cycles per fragment, there is a store-and-forward delay through the source and the destination NI, packets cut through the network with a routing delay of R cycles, and the limiting data transfer rate is b bytes per cycle.

10.5 Suppose an $n \times n$ matrix of double-precision numbers is laid out over P nodes by rows. In order to compute on the columns you desire to transpose it to have a column layout. How much data will cross the bisection during this operation?

10.6 Consider a 2D torus direct network of N nodes with a link bandwidth of b bytes per second. Calculate the bisection bandwidth and the average routing distance. Compare the estimate of aggregate communication bandwidth using Equation 10.6 with the estimate based on bisection. In addition, suppose that every node communicates only with nodes 2 hops away. Then what bandwidth is available? What if each node communicates only with nodes in its row?

10.7 Show how an N-node torus is embedded in an N-node hypercube such that neighbors in the torus (i.e., nodes of distance one) are neighbors in the hypercube. [Hint: observe what happens when the addresses are ordered in a graycode sequence.] Generalize this embedding for higher-dimensional meshes.

10.8 Perform the analysis of Equation 10.6 for a hypercube network. In the last step, treat the row as being defined by the graycode mapping of the grid into the hypercube.

10.9 Calculate the average distance for a linear array of N nodes (assume N is even) and for a 2D mesh and 2D torus of N nodes.

10.10 A more accurate estimate of the communication time can be obtained by determining the average number of channels traversed per packet, h_{ave}, for the workload of interest and the particular network topology. The effective aggregate bandwidth is at most

$$\frac{\|C\|}{h_{ave}}B$$

Suppose the orchestration of a program treats the processors as a $\sqrt{p} \times \sqrt{p}$ logical mesh where each node communicates n bytes of data with its eight neighbors in the four directions and on the diagonal. Give an estimate of the communication time on a grid and a hypercube.

10.11 Show how an N-node tree can be embedded in an N-node hypercube by stretching one of the tree edges across two hypercube edges.

10.12 Use a spreadsheet to construct a comparison of Figure 10.12 with a design point of 10 cycle routing delays and 16-bit-wide links. Extend this comparision for 1,024-byte messages. What conclusions can you draw?

10.13 Verify that the minimum latency is achieved under equal pin scaling in Figure 10.14 when the routing delay is equal to the channel time.

10.14 Derive a formula for dimension that achieves the minimum latency under equal bisection scaling based on Equation 10.7.

10.15 Under the equal bisection scaling rule, how wide are the links of a 2D mesh with 1 million nodes?

10.16 Compare the behavior under load of 2D and 3D cubes of roughly equal size, as in Figure 10.17, for equal pin and equal bisection scaling.

10.17 Specify the Boolean logic used to compute the routing function in the switch with Δx, Δy routing on a 2D mesh.

10.18 If Δx, Δy routing is used, what effect does decrementing the count in the header have on the CRC in the trailer? How can this issue be addressed in the switch design?

10.19 Specify the Boolean logic used to compute the routing function in the switch dimension order routing on a hypercube.

10.20 Prove that the e-cube routing in a hypercube is deadlock-free.

10.21 Construct the table-based equivalent of Δx, Δy routing in a 2D mesh.

10.22 Show that permitting the pair of turns not allowed in Figure 10.24 leaves complex cycles. [Hint: they look like a figure eight.]

10.23 Show that with two virtual channels, arbitrary routing in a bidirectional network can be made deadlock-free.

10.24 Pick any flow control scheme in the chapter and compute the fraction of bandwidth used by flow control symbols.

10.25 Revise latency estimates of Figure 10.14 for stacked dimension switches.

10.26 Table 10.1 provides the topologies and an estimate of the basic communication performance characteristics for several important designs. For each, calculate the network latency for 40-byte and 160-byte messages on 16- and 1,024-node configurations. What fraction of this is routing delay and what fraction is occupancy?

11

Latency Tolerance

In Chapter 1, we saw that while the speed of microprocessors increases by more than a factor of ten per decade, the access time of commodity memories (DRAMs) is only halved. Thus, the latency of memory access in terms of processor clock cycles grows by more than a factor of five in ten years! Multiprocessors greatly exacerbate the problem. In bus-based systems, latency is increased by snooping. In distributed-memory systems, the latency of the network, network interface, and endpoint processing is added to that of accessing the local memory on the node. Caches help reduce the frequency of high-latency accesses, but they are not a panacea: they do not reduce inherent communication, and programs have significant miss rates from other sources as well. Latency usually grows with the size of the machine since more nodes implies more communication relative to computation, more hops in the network for general communication, and likely more contention.

The goal of the protocols developed in the previous chapters has been to reduce the frequency of long-latency events and the bandwidth demands imposed on the communication media while providing a convenient programming model. The goal of the underlying hardware design has been to reduce the latency of data access while maintaining high, scalable bandwidth. Usually, we can improve bandwidth by throwing hardware at the problem (for example, using wider links or richer topologies), but latency is a more fundamental limitation.

So far, we have seen three ways to reduce the effective latency of data access in a multiprocessor system—the first two the responsibility of the system and the third the responsibility of the application.

1. *Reduce the access time to each level of the extended memory hierarchy.* This requires careful attention to detail in making each step in the access path efficient. The processor-to-cache interface can be made very tight. The cache controller needs to act quickly on a miss to reduce the penalty in going to the next level. The network interface can be closely coupled with the node and designed to format, deliver, and handle network transactions quickly. The network itself can be designed to reduce routing delays, transfer time, and congestion delays. With careful design, we can try not to exceed the inherent latency of the technology too much. Nonetheless, the costs add up, and data access takes time.

2. *Structure the system to reduce the frequency of high-latency accesses.* This is the basic job of automatic replication, such as in caches that take advantage of spatial and temporal locality in the program access pattern to keep the most important data close to the processor that accesses it. We can make replication more effective by tailoring the machine structure; for example, by providing a substantial amount of storage in each node.
3. *Structure the application to reduce the frequency of high-latency accesses.* This involves decomposing and assigning computation to processors to reduce inherent communication and structuring access patterns to increase spatial and temporal locality.

In addition to data access and communication, there are other potentially high-latency events, such as synchronization, for which similar efforts can be made. These system and application efforts to reduce latency help greatly, but often they do not suffice. This chapter discusses another approach to dealing with the latency that remains. This approach is to *tolerate the remaining latency;* that is, hide the latency from the processor's critical path by overlapping it with computation or other high-latency events. The processor is allowed to perform other useful work or even data access and communication while the high-latency event is in progress. The key to latency tolerance is in fact parallelism since the overlapped activities must be independent of one another. The basic idea is very simple, and we use it all the time in our daily lives. If you are waiting for one thing (e.g., a load of clothes to finish in the washing machine), you do something else (e.g., run an errand) while you wait.

Latency tolerance cuts across all of the issues discussed in the book and has implications for hardware as well as software, so it serves a useful role in "putting it all together." As we shall see, the success of latency tolerance techniques depends on both the characteristics of the application as well as on the efficiency of the mechanisms provided by the machine.

Latency tolerance is familiar to us from multiprogramming in uniprocessors. On a disk access, which is a truly long-latency event, the processor does not stall waiting for the access to complete. Rather, the operating system blocks the process that made the disk access and switches in another one, typically from another application, thus overlapping the latency of the access with useful work. The blocked process is resumed later, hopefully after the disk access completes. This is latency tolerance: although the disk access itself does not complete any more quickly, the underlying resource (e.g., the processor) is not stalled and accomplishes other useful work in the meantime. Switching from one process to another via the operating system takes many instructions, but the latency of disk access is high enough that this is worthwhile. In this multiprogramming example, we do not succeed in reducing the execution time of any one process—in fact, we might increase it—but we improve the system's throughput and utilization. More overall work gets done and more processes complete per unit time.

The latency tolerance in this chapter is different from the preceding example in two important ways. First, we focus primarily on trying to overlap the latency with work from the same application; that is, our goal is to use latency tolerance to reduce the execution time of a given application. Second, we are trying to tolerate the latencies of the memory and communication systems, not disks. These latencies are much smaller, and the events that cause them are usually not visible to the operating system. Thus, the time-consuming switching of applications or processes via the operating system is not a viable solution.

Before we go further, it may be useful to define a few terms that will be used throughout the chapter. The *latency* of a memory access or communication operation includes all components of the time that elapses from issue by the processor until completion. For communication, this includes the processor overhead, assist occupancy, transit delay, bandwidth-related costs, and contention. The latency may be for one-way transfer of communication or round-trip transfers, which will usually be clear from the context, and it may include the cost of protocol transactions like invalidations and acknowledgments in addition to the cost of data transfer. *Synchronization latency* is the duration that begins when a processor issues a synchronization operation (e.g., lock or barrier) and continues until it gets past that operation; this includes accessing the synchronization variable as well as the time spent waiting for an event that it depends on to occur. *Instruction latency* is the duration that begins when an instruction is issued and ends when it completes in the processor pipeline, assuming no memory, communication, or synchronization latency. Much of instruction latency is already hidden from the processor by pipelining, but some may remain due to long instructions (e.g., floating-point divides) or bubbles in the pipeline. Different techniques are capable of tolerating some subset of these different types of latencies. Our primary focus will be on tolerating communication latencies, whether for explicit or implicit communication, but some of the techniques discussed are applicable to local memory, synchronization, and instruction latencies and hence to uniprocessors as well.

Communication from one node to another that is triggered by a single user operation is called a *message*, regardless of its size. For example, a `send` in the explicit message-passing abstraction constitutes a message, as does each network transaction triggered by a cache miss that is not satisfied locally in a shared address space (if the miss is satisfied locally, its latency is called *local memory latency* or simply *memory latency*; if satisfied remotely, it is called *communication latency*). Finally, an important aspect of communication is whether it is initiated by the sender (source) or receiver (destination) of the data. Communication is said to be *sender initiated* if the operation that causes the data to be transferred is initiated by the process that has produced or currently holds the data without solicitation from the receiver, for example, an unsolicited send operation in message passing. It is said to be *receiver initiated* if the data transfer is caused or solicited by an operation issued by the process that obtains the data, for example, a read miss to nonlocal data in a shared address space. Sender- and receiver-initiated communication is discussed in more detail later in the context of specific programming models.

The discussion of latency tolerance in this chapter proceeds as follows. Section 11.1 examines the problems that result from memory and communication latency and introduces four approaches to latency tolerance: block data transfer, precommunication, proceeding past an outstanding communication event in the same thread, and multithreading or finding independent work to overlap in other threads of execution. It also discusses the basic system and application requirements that apply to any latency tolerance technique and the potential benefits and fundamental limitations of exploiting latency tolerance in real systems.

The rest of the chapter examines how the four approaches are applied in the two major communication abstractions. Section 11.2 discusses how the approaches may be used with explicit message passing. The discussion for a shared address space follows and is more detailed since latency is likely to be a more significant bottleneck when communication is performed through individual loads and stores than through flexibly sized transfers. In addition, latency tolerance exposes interesting interactions with the architectural support already provided for a shared address space, and many of the techniques used in this abstraction are applicable to uniprocessors as well. Section 11.3 provides an overview of latency tolerance in a shared address space, and each of the next four sections focuses on one of the approaches, describing the implementation requirements, the performance benefits, the trade-offs and synergies among techniques, and the implications for hardware and software. One of the requirements across all the techniques is that caches be nonblocking or lockup-free, so Section 11.8 discusses techniques for implementing lockup-free caches.

11.1 OVERVIEW OF LATENCY TOLERANCE

To begin our discussion of tolerating communication latency, let us look at a very simple producer-consumer example that will be used throughout the chapter.

A process P_A computes and writes n elements of an array A, and another process P_B reads them. Each process performs some unrelated computation during the loop in which it writes or reads the data in A, and A is allocated in the local memory of the processor on which P_A runs. With no latency tolerance, the process generating the communication would simply perform it a word at a time—explicitly or implicitly as per the communication abstraction—and would wait until each word-length message completes before doing anything else. This will be referred to as the *baseline communication structure*. Figure 11.1(a) shows how the computation might look with explicit message passing, and Figure 11.1(b) shows how it might look with implicit, read-write communication in a shared address space. In the former, it is typically the send operation issued by process P_A that generates the actual communication of the data whereas in the latter it is typically the read of `A[i]` by P_B.[1] We assume that the read stalls the processor until it completes and that a synchronous send is used (as was described in Section 2.3.6). The resulting timelines for the processes that initiate the communication are shown in Figure 11.2. A process spends most of its time stalled waiting for communication.

1. The examples are in fact not exactly symmetric in their baseline communication structure since in the message-passing version the communication of data happens after each array entry is produced whereas in the shared address space version it happens after the entire array has been produced. However, implementing the fine-grained synchronization necessary for the exactly analogous shared address space version would require synchronization for each array entry, and the communication needed for this synchronization would complicate the discussion. The asymmetry does not affect the discussion of latency tolerance.

(a) Message passing

```
PA:
for i←0 to n-1 do
    compute A[i];
    write A[i];
    send (A[i] to PB);
    compute f(C[i]);
        /*unrelated*/
end for

PB:
for i←1 to n-1 do
    receive (myA[i]);
    use myA[i];
    compute g(B[i]);
        /*unrelated*/
end for
```

(b) Shared address space

```
PA:
for i←0 to n-1 do
    compute A[i];
    write A[i];
    compute f(C[i]);
end for
flag ← 1;

PB:
while flag = 0{};
    for i←1 to n-1 do
    read A[i];
    use A[i];
    compute g(B[i]);
end for
```

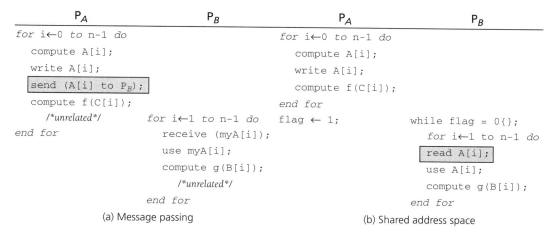

FIGURE 11.1 Pseudocode for the example computation. Pseudocode is shown for explicit message passing (a) and for implicit read-write communication in a shared address space (b), with no latency hiding in either case. The boxes highlight the operations that generate the data transfer.

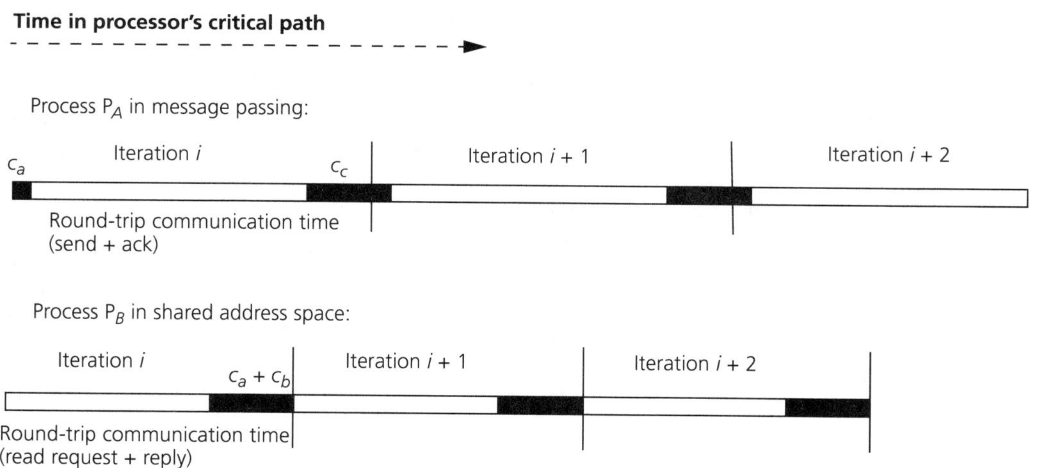

FIGURE 11.2 Timelines for the processes that initiate communication, with no latency hiding. The black segments of the timeline are local processing time (which in fact includes the time spent stalled to access local data), and the white segments are time spent stalled on communication. c_a, c_b, c_c are the durations to compute an array entry `A[i]` and to perform the unrelated computations `f(B[i])` and `g(C[i])`, respectively.

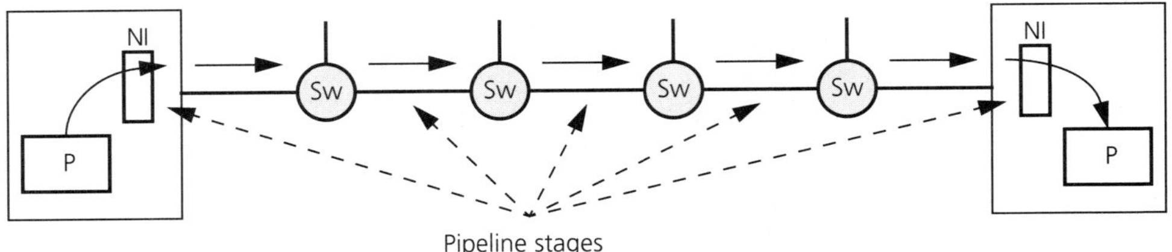

FIGURE 11.3 The network viewed as a pipeline for a communication sent from one processor to another. The stages of the pipeline include the network interfaces (NI) and the hops between successive switches (Sw) on the route between the two processors (P).

11.1.1 Latency Tolerance and the Communication Pipeline

Approaches to latency tolerance are best understood by looking at how the resources in the machine are utilized. From the viewpoint of a processor, the communication architecture from one node to another can be viewed as a pipeline. The stages of the pipeline clearly include the network interfaces at the source and destination, as well as the network links and switches along the way (see Figure 11.3). There may also be stages in the communication assist, the local memory/cache system, and even the main processor, depending on how the architecture manages communication. It is important to recall that the endpoint overhead of instructions incurred on the processor (not necessarily memory accesses) itself cannot be hidden from the processor, though all the other components potentially can. Systems with high endpoint overhead per message therefore have a difficult time tolerating latency. Unless otherwise mentioned, this overview ignores the processor overhead; we assume that most of the endpoint processing of messages is performed on the communication assist and focus on assist occupancy at the endpoints since this has a chance of being hidden too. We also assume that this message initiation and reception cost is incurred as a fixed cost once per message (i.e., it is not proportional to message size).

Not tolerating latency leads to poor utilization of the pipeline and other resources. Figure 11.4 shows the utilization problem for the baseline communication structure described earlier: either the processor or the communication architecture is busy at a given time, and, if the latter, then only one stage of the communication is busy at a time.[2] The goal in latency tolerance is to overlap the use of these resources as much as possible. From a processor's perspective, there are three major types of overlap that can be exploited. The first is within the *communication pipeline* between two nodes, which allows us to transmit multiple words at a time through the network resources, just like instruction pipelining overlaps the use of different resources in the processor (instruction fetch unit, register files, execute unit, etc.). These words may be from the same message, if messages are larger than a single word, or

2. For simplicity, we ignore the fact that the width of the network link is often less than a word, so even a single word may occupy multiple stages of the network part of the pipeline.

Time in processor's critical path

Process P_A in message passing:

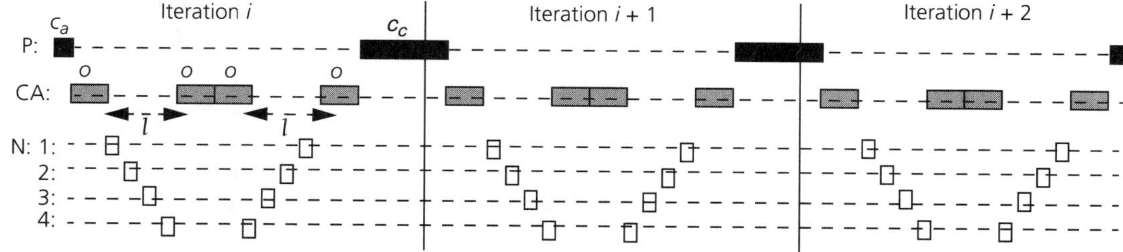

Process P_B in shared address space:

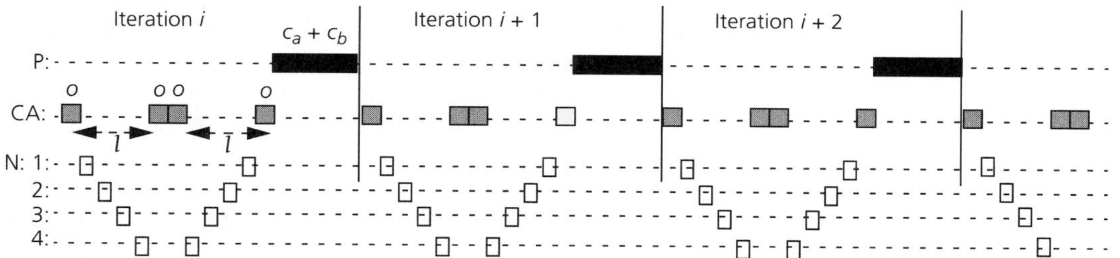

FIGURE 11.4 Timelines for the message-passing and shared address space programs with no latency hiding. Time for a process is divided into that spent on the processor (P) (including the local memory system), on the communication assist (CA), and in the network (N). The numbers under the network category indicate different hops or links in the network on the path of the message. The endpoint overhead o in the message-passing case is shown to be larger than in the shared address space, which we assume to be hardware supported. l is the network latency, which is the time spent that does not involve the processing node itself.

from different messages. The second exploits the overlap across different point-to-point communication pipelines, in different portions of the network, by having communication outstanding with different nodes at once. In both cases, from a processor's perspective the communication of one word is overlapped with that of other words, so we call this overlapping *communication with communication*. The third type of overlap is that of *computation with communication*; that is, a processor continues to do useful local work while a communication operation it has initiated is in progress.

11.1.2 Approaches

There are four key approaches to exploiting this overlap of hardware resources and thus tolerating latency. The first, which is called *block data transfer*, is to make individual messages larger so they communicate more than a word and can be pipelined through the network. The other three overlap a message with computation or with other messages and are thus complementary to block data transfer. They are *precommunication*, *proceeding past communication in the same thread*, and *multithreading*. Each approach can be used in both the shared address space and message-passing abstractions, although the specific techniques and the support required are different in the two cases. A brief introduction to each of the approaches follows.

Block Data Transfer

Making messages larger has several advantages. First, it exploits the communication pipeline between the two nodes to overlap communication with communication. The processor sees the latency of the first word in the message, but subsequent words arrive every network cycle or so, limited only by the rate or bandwidth of the pipeline. Second, it amortizes the per-message endpoint overhead over the large amount of data being sent. Third, depending on how packets are structured, it may also amortize the per-packet routing and header information. Finally, a large message may require only a single acknowledgment rather than one per word, which can reduce latency as well as traffic and contention. These advantages are similar but on a different scale to those obtained by using long cache blocks to transfer data from memory to cache in a uniprocessor. Figure 11.5 shows the effect of employing a single large message in the explicit message-passing case while still using synchronous messages and without overlapping computation. For simplicity of illustration, the network stages have been collapsed into one (pipelined) stage.

Although making messages larger helps keep the pipeline between two nodes busy, it does not in itself keep the processor or communication assist busy while a message is in progress or keep other paths through the network busy. The other approaches address these opportunities as well. They are complementary to block data transfer in that they are applicable whether messages are large or small. Let us examine them one by one.

Precommunication

Generating the communication before the point where the operation naturally appears in the program so that it is partially or entirely completed before data is actually needed can be done either in software, by inserting a precommunication operation earlier in the code, or in hardware, by detecting the opportunity and issuing the communication operation early.[3] The operations that actually use the data typically remain where they are in the program. Of course, the precommunication transaction itself should not stall the processor until it completes, or overlap will not

3. Recall that several of the techniques, including this one, are applicable to hiding local memory access latency as well, even though we are speaking in terms of communication since we can think of local access as communication with the local memory system.

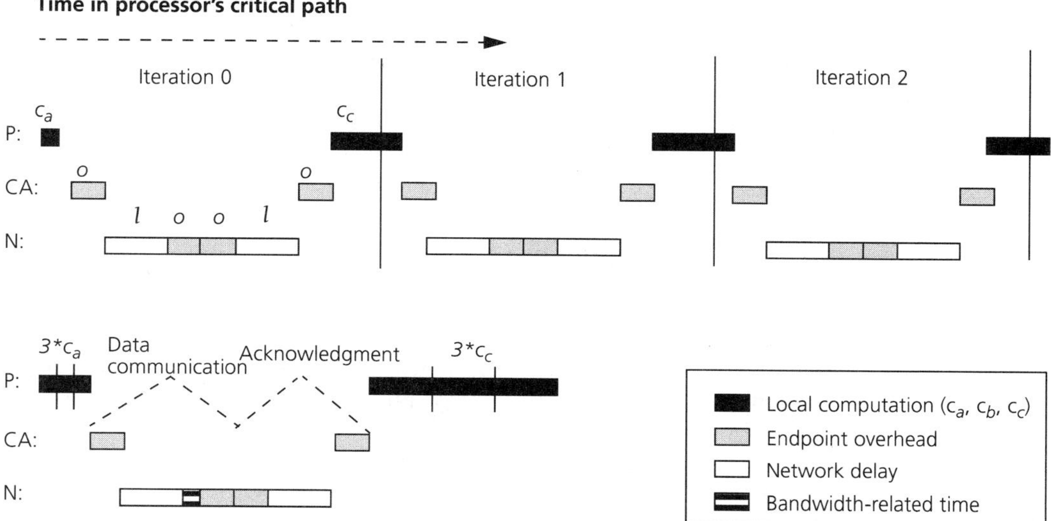

FIGURE 11.5 Effect of making messages larger on the timeline for the example message-passing program. The figure assumes that three iterations of the loop are executed. The sender process (P_A) first computes the three values `A[0..2]` to be sent (the computation c_a), then sends them in one message, and then performs all three pieces of unrelated computation `f(C[0..2])`, that is, the computation c_c. The overhead of the data communication is amortized, and only a single acknowledgment is needed. A bandwidth-related cost is added to the data communication for the time taken to get the remaining words into the destination node after the first word arrives, but this is tiny compared to the savings in latency and overhead. This additional bandwidth cost is not required for the acknowledgment, which is also small.

be achieved. Many forms of precommunication require that long-latency events be predictable so that hardware or software can anticipate them and issue them early.

Sender-initiated communication is naturally initiated soon after the sender produces the data, so the data may reach the receiver before it is actually needed, resulting in a form of precommunication for free for the receiver. On the other hand, it may be difficult for the sender to move the communication any earlier to hide the latency that the sender sees. Actual precommunication, by generating the communication operation early, is therefore more common in receiver-initiated communication where communication is naturally initiated when the data is needed, which may be long after it has been produced.

Proceeding Past Communication in the Same Thread

The communication operation may be generated where it naturally occurs in the program, but the processor is allowed to proceed past it and find other independent computation or communication that would come later in the same process or thread of execution. Thus, while precommunication causes the communication to be overlapped with other instructions from that thread that are before the point where the communication-generating operation appears in the original program, this technique causes communication to be overlapped with instructions from later in the thread. These instructions may themselves cause communication or memory accesses, or there may be overlap with those activities as well. As we might imagine, this latency tolerance method is generally easier to use effectively with sender-initiated communication since the instructions that immediately follow the communication operation on the sender do not depend on that communication operation and can therefore be easily overlapped. In receiver-initiated communication, a receiver naturally tries to access data only just before it is actually needed, so there is not much independent work to be found in between the communication and the use. It is, of course, possible to delay the actual use of the data by trying to push it further down in the instruction stream, or equivalently to find independent work even beyond the use, and compilers and processor hardware can exploit some overlap in this way. In either case, either hardware or software must check that the data transfer has completed before executing an instruction that depends on it.

Multithreading

This approach is similar to the previous case, except that the independent work is found by switching to another thread that has been mapped to run on the same processor. This makes the latency of receiver-initiated communication easier to hide than the previous case, and so this method lends itself easily to hiding latency from either a sender or a receiver. In fact, since the overlap here is with other threads, multithreading is the approach that is least concerned with the type and structure of the latency to be tolerated and is in this sense the most general technique. However, multithreading implies that a given processor must have multiple threads that are concurrently executable so that it can switch from one thread to another when a long-latency event is encountered. The multiple threads may be from the same parallel program or from completely different programs, as in our earlier multiprogramming example. A multithreaded program is usually no different from an ordinary parallel program; it is simply decomposed and assigned among P processes, where P is larger than the actual number of physical processors p, and P/p threads are mapped to the same physical processor. Thus, multithreading requires that the additional parallelism needed for latency tolerance be explicit in the form of additional threads.

11.1.3 Fundamental Requirements, Benefits, and Limitations

Before we apply these approaches to specific programming models and systems, it is useful to understand the fundamental requirements, benefits, and limitations of latency tolerance, regardless of the technique used. This basic analysis bounds the extent of the performance improvement we can expect. It is based solely on overlap in the use of resources and on the occupancies of these resources.

Requirements

Tolerating latency requires extra parallelism, increased bandwidth, and, in many cases, more sophisticated hardware and protocols.

- *Extra parallelism*, or *slackness*. Since the overlapped activities (computation or communication) must be independent of one another, the parallelism in the application must be greater than the number of processors used. The additional parallelism may be explicit in the form of additional threads, as in multithreading, or it may exist within a thread. Even communicating two words from the same process in parallel implies a lack of total serialization between them and hence extra parallelism.
- *Increased bandwidth*. Whereas tolerating latency may reduce the execution time, it does not reduce the amount of communication performed. The same communication performed in less time means a higher rate of communication per unit time and hence a larger bandwidth requirement imposed on the communication architecture. In fact, if the bandwidth requirements increase much beyond the bandwidth afforded by the machine, the resulting resource contention may slow down other unrelated transactions, and latency tolerance may hurt performance rather than help it.
- *More sophisticated hardware and protocols*. Except for the case of making messages larger, the processor must be allowed to proceed past a long-latency operation before the operation completes, and it must be allowed to have multiple outstanding long-latency operations if they are to be overlapped with one another and not just with computation.

These requirements imply that all latency tolerance techniques have significant costs. We should therefore try to use algorithmic techniques to reduce the frequency of high-latency events before relying on techniques to tolerate latency. The fewer the long-latency events, the less aggressively we need to hide latency.

Potential Benefits

A simple analysis can give us bounds on the performance benefits we might expect from latency tolerance, thus establishing realistic expectations. Let us focus on tolerating the latency of communication and assume that the latency of local memory references is not hidden. Suppose the execution time as seen by a processor has the following profile when no latency tolerance is used: T_c cycles are spent computing locally, T_{ov} cycles processing message overhead on the processor, T_{occ} (occupancy) cycles on the communication assist, and T_l cycles waiting for message transmission in the network. If we can assume that other resources can be perfectly overlapped with the activity on the main processor, then the potential speedup can be determined by a simple application of Amdahl's Law. The processor must be occupied for $T_c + T_{ov}$ cycles; the maximum latency that we can hide from the processor is $T_l + T_{occ}$, so the maximum speedup due to latency hiding is

$$\frac{T_c + T_{ov} + T_{occ} + T_l}{T_c + T_{ov}}$$

or

$$\left(1 + \frac{T_{occ} + T_l}{T_c + T_{ov}}\right).$$

This limit is an upper bound since it assumes perfect overlap of resources and no extra cost imposed by latency tolerance. However, it gives us a useful perspective. For example, if the process originally spends at least as much time computing locally or in processor overhead as stalled on the communication system, then the maximum speedup that can be obtained from tolerating communication latency is a factor of two. If the original communication stall time is overlapped only with processor activity, not with other communication, then the maximum speedup is a factor of two, regardless of how much communication latency there is to hide. This is illustrated in Figure 11.6.

How much latency can actually be hidden depends on many factors involving the application and the architecture. Relevant application characteristics include the structure of the communication and how much other work can be overlapped with it. Architectural issues are: how much of the endpoint processing is performed on the main processor versus on the assist; can communication be overlapped with computation, other communication, or both; how many messages involving a given processor may be outstanding at a time; to what extent can endpoint overhead processing be overlapped with data transmission in the network for the same message; and what are the occupancies of the assist and the stages of the network pipeline.

Figure 11.7 illustrates the effects on the timeline for a few different kinds of message structuring and overlap. The figure is merely illustrative. For example, it assumes that overhead per message is quite high relative to transit latency and does not consider contention anywhere. Under these assumptions, larger messages are often more attractive than many small overlapped messages because they amortize overhead. Further, with small messages the pipeline rate might be limited by the endpoint processing of each message (which determines the gap between messages) rather than by the network link speed. Other assumptions may lead to different results. Exercise 11.2 looks more quantitatively at an example of communication that only overlaps with other communication.

Clearly, some components of communication latency are easier to hide than others. For example, instruction overhead incurred on the processor cannot be hidden from that processor, and latency incurred off node—either in the network or in the other node being communicated with—is generally easier to hide by overlapping with other messages than occupancy incurred on the assist or elsewhere within the node. Let us examine some of the key limitations that may prevent us from achieving the upper bounds on latency tolerance.

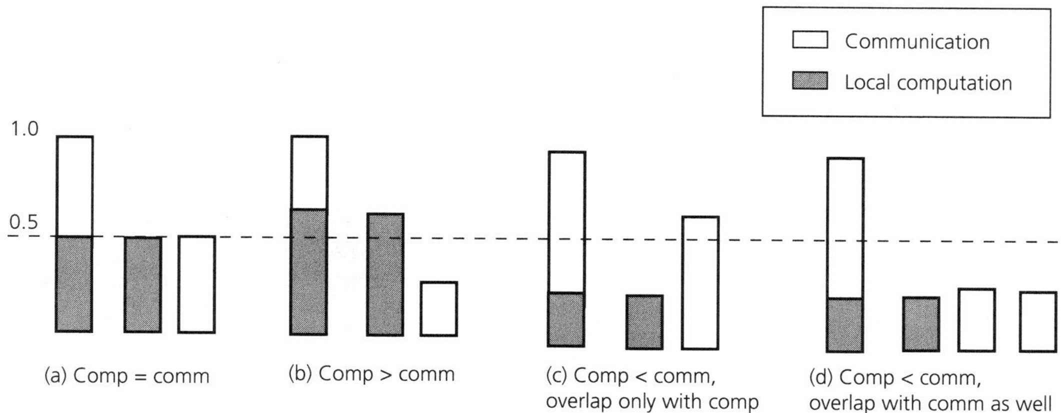

FIGURE 11.6 Bounds on the benefits from latency tolerance. Each figure shows a different scenario. Gray identifies computation time, and white identifies communication time in each case. The bar on the left shows the time breakdown without latency hiding, normalized to 1.0 units, whereas the bars on the right show the situation with latency hiding. When computation time (Comp) equals communication time (Comm), shown in (a), the upper bound on speedup is 2. When computation exceeds communication, the upper bound is less than 2 since we are limited by computation time (b). The same is true of the case in which communication exceeds computation but can be overlapped only with computation (c). The way to obtain a better speedup than a factor of two is to have communication time originally exceed computation time but to let communication be overlapped with communication as well (d).

Limitations

The major limitations can be divided into three classes: application limitations, limitations of the communication architecture, and processor limitations.

Application Limitations The amount of independent computation time that is available to overlap with the latency may be limited, so all the latency may not be hidden and the processor will have to stall for some of the time. Even if the program has enough work and extra parallelism, the structure of the program may make it difficult for the system or programmer to identify the concurrent operations and orchestrate the overlap, as we shall see when we discuss specific latency tolerance mechanisms.

Communication Architecture Limitations The communication architecture may restrict the number of messages or the number of words that can be outstanding from a node at a time, and the performance parameters of the communication architecture may limit the latency that can be hidden (Culler 1994).

With only one message outstanding, independent computation can be overlapped with both assist processing and network transmission. However, assist processing

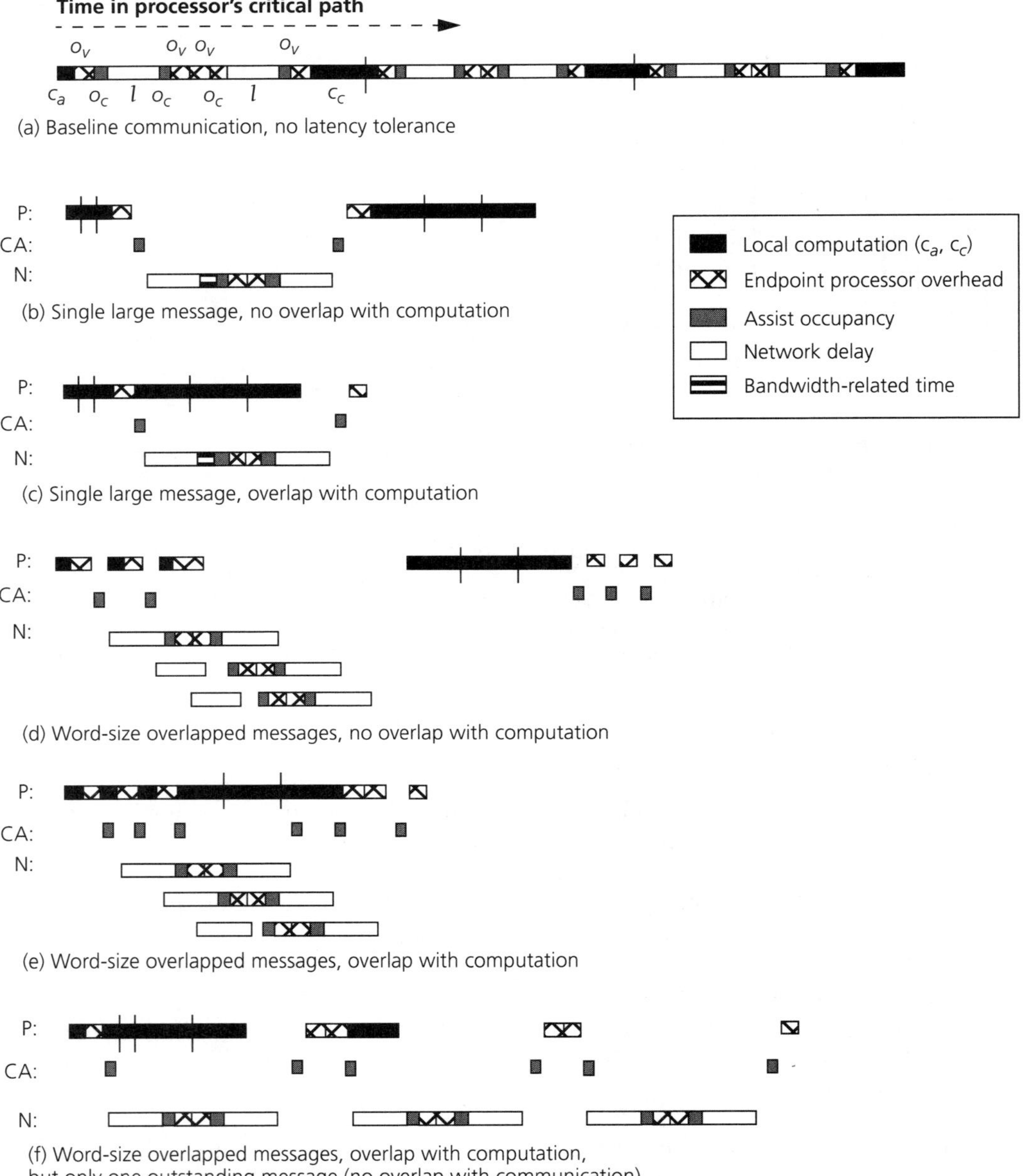

FIGURE 11.7 Timelines for different forms of latency tolerance. P indicates time spent on the main processor, CA on the local communication assist, and N nonlocal (in the network or on other nodes). The timelines are shown from the perspective of process P_A in the message-passing example in Figure 11.1.

may or may not be overlapped with network transmission for that message, and the network pipeline itself can be kept busy only if the message is large. With multiple messages outstanding, processor time, assist occupancy, and network transmission can all be overlapped. The network pipeline itself can be kept well utilized even when messages are very small since several may be in progress simultaneously. Thus, for messages of a given size, more latency can be tolerated if each node allows multiple messages to be outstanding at a time. If L is the latency per message we can possibly hide, and r cycles of independent computation are available to be overlapped with each message, we need $\lceil L/r \rceil$ messages to be outstanding for maximal latency hiding. More outstanding messages do not help since whatever latency could be hidden already has been. Similarly, the number of words outstanding is important. If k words can be outstanding from a processor at a time, from one or multiple messages, then in the best case the network delay as seen by the processor can be reduced by almost a factor of k. More precisely, for one-way messages to the same destination, it is reduced from $k*l$ cycles to $l + k/B$, where l is the network transit time for a bit and B is the bandwidth or rate of the communication pipeline (network and perhaps assist) in words per cycle.

Assuming that enough messages and words are allowed to be outstanding, the performance parameters of the communication architecture can become limitations as well. Let us examine some of these parameters, assuming that the message sizes are predetermined and the per-message latency of communication we want to hide is L cycles. For simplicity, we shall consider one-way data messages without acknowledgments.

- *Overhead.* The message-processing overhead incurred on the processor cannot be hidden.
- *Assist occupancy.* The occupancy of the assist can be hidden by overlapping with computation. Whether it can be overlapped with other communication (in the same message or in different messages) depends on whether the assist is internally pipelined and whether assist processing for a message can be overlapped with transmission of the message data through the network.

  An endpoint message processing time (overhead or occupancy) of o cycles per message establishes an upper bound on the frequency with which we can issue messages to the network (at best, every o cycles). If we assume that on average a processor receives as many messages as it sends and that the overhead of sending and receiving is the same, then the time spent in endpoint processing per message sent is $2o$; so the largest number of messages that we can have outstanding from a processor in a period of L cycles is $L/2o$. If $2o$ is greater than the r cycles of computation we can overlap with each message, then we cannot have the L/r messages outstanding that we would need to hide all the latency. The impact of per-message overhead and occupancy limitations is especially severe when messages are small.
- *Point-to-point bandwidth.* Even if overhead is not an issue, for example, if messages are large, the rate of injecting words into the network may be limited by the slowest link in the entire network pipeline from source to destination; that is, the stages of the network itself, the node-to-network interface, or even any

assist occupancy or processor overhead incurred per word. Just as an endpoint overhead of o cycles between messages limits the number of outstanding messages in an L cycle period to L/o (ignoring incoming messages), a pipeline stage time of s cycles per word in the network limits the number of outstanding words to L/s.

- *Network capacity.* The number of messages a processor can have outstanding is also limited by the total bandwidth or data carrying capacity of the network since different processors compete for this finite capacity. If each link is one word wide, a message of M words traveling h hops in the network may require the equivalent of up to $M*h$ links in the network at a given time. If each processor has k such messages outstanding, then each processor may require up to $M*h*k$ links at a given time. However, if there are D links in the network in all, and all processors are transmitting in this way, then each processor on average can only occupy D/p links at a given time. Thus, the number of outstanding messages per processor k is limited by the relation

$$M \times h \times k < D/p, \text{ or } k < \frac{D}{p \times M \times h}$$

Processor Limitations In a cache-coherent shared address space, spatial locality through long cache blocks already allows more than one word of communication to be outstanding at a time. To hide latency beyond this, a processor and its cache subsystem must allow multiple cache misses to be outstanding simultaneously. This is costly, as we shall see, so processor-cache systems have relatively small limits on this number of outstanding misses (and these include local misses that don't cause communication). Explicit communication requires less hardware tracking and has more flexibility in this regard, though the system may limit the number of messages that can be outstanding at a time.

It is clear from the preceding discussion that making the communication architecture efficient (high bandwidth, low endpoint overhead or occupancy) is very important for tolerating latency effectively. We have seen the properties of some real machines in terms of network bandwidth, node-to-network bandwidth, and endpoint overhead, as well as where the endpoint overhead is incurred, in the last few chapters. From the data for overhead, communication latency, and gap between messages, we can compute two useful numbers in understanding the potential for latency hiding. The first is the ratio L/o for the limit imposed by communication performance on the number of messages that can be outstanding at a time in a period of L cycles, assuming that other processors are not sending messages to this one at the same time. The second is the inverse of the gap, which is the rate at which messages can be pipelined into the network and is also influenced by o. If there is not enough computation to overlap with the latency of L/o overlapped messages, then the only way to hide the remaining latency is to make messages larger. The values of L/o for remote reads in a shared address space and for explicit message passing using message-passing libraries can be computed from Figures 7.31 and 7.32 and from the microbenchmark data for the Origin2000 in Chapter 8, as shown in Table 11.1.

Table 11.1 Number of One-Word Microbenchmark Messages Outstanding at a Time as Limited by *L/o* Ratio and Rate at Which Messages Can Be Issued to the Network

Machine	One-Way Network Transaction		Remote Read		Machine	One-Way Network Transaction		Remote Read	
	L/2*o*	Msgs/ms	*L/o*	Msgs/ms		*L*/2*o*	Msgs/ms	*L/o*	Msgs/ms
TMC CM-5	2.12	250	1.75	161	*NOW-Ultra*	1.79	172	1.77	127
Intel Paragon	2.72	131	5.63	133	*CRAY T3D*	1.00	345	1.13	2,500
Meiko CS-2	3.28	74	8.35	63.3	*SGI Origin*				5,000

L here is the total latency of a message, including overhead. Two types of operations are considered: a one-word, round-trip remote read in a shared address space, and a one-way network transaction including both send and receive operations. For a remote read, *o* is the overhead on the initiating processor, which cannot be hidden. For one-way message-passing network transactions, we assume symmetry in messages and therefore count 2*o* to be the sum of the send and receive overhead. For machines with full hardware support for a shared address space, the gap and hence rate of message injection is limited not by processor overhead but by assist occupancy, which is small. The main limitation in these cases is the number of outstanding misses allowed by the processor or assist, but these are ignored in the table.

For the message-passing systems (CM-5, Paragon, CS-2, NOW-Ultra), it is clear that the number of messages that can be outstanding at a time is quite small and that hiding latency with small messages is clearly limited by the endpoint processing overheads. Making messages larger is therefore likely to be more successful at hiding latency than trying to overlap multiple small messages. The hardware-supported shared address space machines (T3D and Origin) are limited much less by performance parameters of the communication architecture in their ability to hide the latency of small messages. Here, the major limitations tend to be the number of outstanding requests supported by the processor or cache system and the fact that a given memory operation may generate several protocol transactions (messages), which stress assist occupancy.

With an understanding of the basics, we are now ready to look at individual techniques in the context of the two major communication abstractions. Since the treatment of latency tolerance for explicit message-passing communication is simpler, the next section discusses all four general techniques in its context.

11.2 LATENCY TOLERANCE IN EXPLICIT MESSAGE PASSING

To understand which latency tolerance techniques are most effective and how they might be employed, it is useful to consider the structure of communication in an abstraction; in particular, how sender- and receiver-initiated communication is orchestrated and whether messages are of fixed or variable size.

11.2.1 Structure of Communication

The actual transfer of data in explicit message passing is typically sender initiated; a receive operation does not in itself cause data to be communicated across the network but rather copies data from an incoming buffer into the application address space. Receiver-initiated communication is performed by sending a request message to the process that is the source of the data, which, in turn, sends the data back.[4] The baseline communication structure in the example in Figure 11.1 uses synchronous sends and receives, with sender-initiated communication. A synchronous send operation has a communication latency equal to the time it takes to communicate all the data in the message to the destination, plus the time for receive processing, plus the time to return an acknowledgment. The latency of a synchronous receive operation is its processing overhead, including copying the data into the application, plus the additional wait time if the data has not yet arrived. We would like to hide these latencies at both ends. Let us continue to assume that the overhead at each end is incurred on a communication assist and not on the main processor, so that it can be hidden, and see how the four classes of latency tolerance techniques might be applied in classical sender-initiated message passing.

11.2.2 Block Data Transfer

Making messages large is important for amortizing overhead and for ensuring that the rate of the communication pipeline is not limited by the endpoint overhead of message processing. These benefits can be obtained even with synchronous messages. However, if we also want to overlap the communication with computation or with other messages, then we must use one or more of the other three approaches to latency tolerance. Although they can be used with either small or large (block transfer) messages and are in this sense complementary to block transfer, we shall illustrate them with the small messages that are in our baseline communication structure.

11.2.3 Precommunication

Figure 11.8 shows a precommunicating version of the message-passing program introduced in Figure 11.1. The loop on the sender, P_A, is split in two. All the sends are pulled up before the computations of the function `f(B[])`, which are postponed to a separate loop. The sends are made asynchronous, so the process does not stall waiting for them to complete before proceeding.

Is this a good idea? The advantage is that messages are sent to the receiver as early as possible; the disadvantages are that less work is overlapped on the sender between messages, and the pressure on the buffers at the receiver is higher since

4. In other abstractions built on message-passing machines and discussed in Chapter 7, like remote procedure call or active messages, the receiver sends a request message, and a handler that processes the request at the data source sends the data back without involving the application process there. However, we shall focus on classical send/receive message passing, which dominates at the programming model layer.

P_A	P_B
for i←0 *to* n-1 *do*	a_receive (myA[0] from P_A);
compute A[i];	*for* i←0 *to* n-2 *do*
write A[i];	a_receive (myA[i+1] from P_A);
a_send (A[i] to proc.P_B);	while (!recv_probe(myA[i]) {};
end for	use myA[i];
for i←0 *to* n-1 *do*	compute g(B[i]);
compute f(C[i]);	*end for*
	while (!received(myA[n-1]) {};
	use myA[n-1];
	compute g(B[n-1])

FIGURE 11.8 Hiding latency through precommunication in the message-passing example. In the pseudocode, `a_send` and `a_receive` are asynchronous send and receive operations, respectively.

messages may arrive well before they are needed. Whether the net result is beneficial depends on the overhead incurred per message, the number of messages that a process is allowed to have outstanding at a time, and how much later the receives would have occurred than the sends anyway. For example, if only one or two messages may be outstanding, then we are better off interspersing computation (of `f(B[])`) between asynchronous sends, thus building a *software pipeline* of communication and computation instead of waiting for those two messages to complete before doing anything else. The same is true if the overhead incurred on the assist is high so that we can keep the processor busy while the assist is incurring this high per-message overhead. The ideal case would be to build a balanced software pipeline in which we pull sends up but do just the right amount of computation between message sends.

Now consider the receiver P_B in Figure 11.8. To hide the latency of the receives through precommunication, we try to pull them up earlier in the code and we use asynchronous receives. The `a_receive` call simply posts the specification of the receive to the message layer and allows the processor to proceed. When the data comes in, the assist is notified and it moves the data to the application data structures, transparently to the processor. The application must check that the data has arrived (using the `recv_probe` call) before it can use the data reliably. If the data has already arrived when the `a_receive` is posted (preissued), then what we can hope to hide by preissuing is the cost of the receive processing incurred on the assist; otherwise, we might hide both transit time and receive processing.

Receive overhead is usually larger than send overhead, as discussed in Chapter 7, so if many asynchronous receives are to be issued (or preissued), it is usually beneficial to intersperse computation between them rather than issue them back to back. Otherwise, the assist cannot process them as fast as the processor issues them, so the processor will stall when the buffer between it and the assist fills. One way to do this is to build a software pipeline of communication and computation, as shown in Figure 11.8. Each iteration of the loop issues an `a_receive` for the data needed for the next iteration and then does the processing for the current iteration. Hopefully, by the time the next iteration is reached, the message for which the `a_receive` was posted in the current iteration will have arrived and will have been processed, and the data will be ready to use. If the receive overhead is much higher than the computation per iteration, the `a_receive` can be issued several iterations ahead instead of just one iteration ahead.

The software pipeline has three parts. In addition to the *steady-state* loop just described, some work must be done to start the pipeline and some to wind it down. In this example, the prologue must post a receive for the data needed in the first iteration of the steady-state loop, and the epilogue must process the code for the last iteration of the original loop (this is left out of the steady-state loop since we do not want to post an asynchronous receive for a nonexistent next iteration). A similar software pipeline strategy could be used if communication were truly receiver initiated, for example, if an `a_receive` or `get` operation sent a request to the node running P_A, and a handler there reacted to the request by supplying the data without needing an explicit send operation in the program. The precommunication strategy is known as *prefetching* the data since the receive (or get) truly causes the data to be fetched across the network. We see prefetching in more detail in the context of a shared address space in Section 11.6 since there the communication is frequently truly receiver initiated.

11.2.4 Proceeding Past Communication in the Same Thread

Now suppose we do not want to pull communication operations up in the code but leave them where they are. One way to hide latency in this case is to simply make the communication messages asynchronous and proceed past them to either computation or other asynchronous communication messages in the same thread. We can continue doing this until we come to a point where we depend on a communication message completing or run into a limit on the number of messages we may have outstanding at a time. Of course, as with prefetching, the use of asynchronous receives means that we must add probes or synchronization to ensure that the data is available before we try to use it (and, on the sender side, that the source data has been copied or sent out before we reuse the corresponding storage).

11.2.5 Multithreading

To exploit multithreading, when a process issues a send or receive operation, it may suspend itself and allow another ready-to-run process or thread from the application to run. If this thread issues a send or receive, then it too is suspended and another thread is switched in. The hope is that by the time we run out of threads and the first thread is rescheduled, the communication operation that thread issued will have completed. The switching and management of threads can be managed by the message-passing library, rather than the application, using calls to the operating system to change the program counter and perform other protected thread management functions. For example, the implementation of the send primitive might automatically cause a thread switch after initiating the send (of course, if there is no other ready thread on that processing node, then the same thread will be switched back in). Multithreading allows latency tolerance even with a synchronous message-passing programming model. This approach was the basis of the Occam language on the Transputer.

Switching a thread requires that we save the processor state needed to restart it, including the processor registers, the program counter, the stack pointer, and various processor status words. The state must be restored when the thread is switched back in. Saving and restoring state in software is expensive and can undermine the benefits obtained from multithreading. Some message-passing architectures have therefore provided hardware support for multithreading, for example, by providing multiple sets of registers and program counters in hardware. Note that systems that support asynchronous message handlers that are separate from the application process but that run on the main processor, are essentially multithreaded between the application process and the handler, even if applications themselves do not use multithreading. This form of multithreading has also been supported in hardware by some research architectures (e.g., the message-driven processor of the J-machine [Dally et al. 1992; Noakes, Wallach, and Dally 1993]). We discuss these hardware support issues in more detail in Section 11.7 where we examine multithreading in a shared address space.

11.3 LATENCY TOLERANCE IN A SHARED ADDRESS SPACE

The rest of this chapter focuses on latency tolerance in the context of a hardware-supported shared address space. This discussion is more detailed than the message-passing discussion for several reasons. First, the existing hardware support for communication brings the techniques and requirements much closer to the architecture and the hardware/software interface. Second, the implicit nature of long-latency events (such as communication) makes it more likely that much of the latency tolerance will be addressed by the system rather than by the user program. Third, the granularity of communication and efficiency of the underlying communication mechanisms require that the latency tolerance techniques be hardware supported to be effective. And finally, since much of the latency is that of reads, writes, and perhaps instructions—not explicit communication operations like sends and receives—most of the techniques are applicable to uniprocessors as well. In fact, since we don't know ahead of time which read and write operations will generate communication, latency hiding is treated in much the same way for local accesses as for communication in shared address space multiprocessors. The difference is in the magnitude of the latencies and, in cache-coherent systems, in the interactions with the cache coherence protocol.

Much of our discussion of latency tolerance in a shared address space applies to cache-coherent systems as well as those that do not cache shared data. For the most part, we assume that the shared address space (and cache coherence) is supported in hardware and that the default communication and coherence are at the granularity of individual words or cache blocks. The experimental results presented in the following sections are taken from the literature. These results use several of the same applications that we have used in previous chapters, but they typically use different versions with somewhat different communication-to-computation ratios and other behavioral characteristics, and they do not always follow the methodology outlined in Chapter 4. The system parameters used also vary across studies, so the results cannot be compared across techniques and are presented purely for illustrative purposes. As with message passing, let us begin by briefly examining the structure of communication in this abstraction.

11.3.1 Structure of Communication

The baseline communication in a shared address space is through reads and writes and is called *read-write communication* for convenience. Receiver-initiated communication is typically performed with memory operations that result in data from another processor's memory or cache being accessed. It is thus a natural extension of data access in the uniprocessor programming model: accessing words of memory when you need to use them.

If there is no caching of shared data, sender-initiated communication may be performed through writes to data that are allocated in remote memories.[5] With cache coherence, the effect of writes is more complex. Whether writes lead to sender- or receiver-initiated communication depends on the cache coherence protocol. For example, suppose processor P_A writes a word that is allocated in P_B's memory. In the most common case of an invalidation-based cache coherence protocol with write-back caches, the write will only generate a read-exclusive or upgrade request and perhaps some invalidations, and it may bring data to itself. It will not actually cause the newly written data to be transferred to P_B. While requests and invalidations involve network transactions too, and it is important to hide their latency, the actual communication of the new value from P_A to P_B will be generated by the later read or write of the data by P_B. In this sense, it is receiver initiated. Alternatively, the data transfer may be caused by an asynchronous replacement of the data from P_A's cache, which will cause it to go back to its home in P_B's memory. In an update protocol, on the other hand, the write itself will communicate the data from P_A to P_B if P_B had a cached copy.

Whether receiver initiated or sender initiated, the communication in a hardware-supported read-write shared address space is naturally fine grained, which makes latency tolerance particularly important. The different approaches to latency tolerance are better suited to different types and magnitudes of latency and have achieved different levels of acceptance in commercial products. We examine these approaches in some detail in the next sections.

---

5. An interesting case is the one in which a processor writes a word that is allocated in a different processor's memory and a third processor reads the word. In this case, we have two data communication events to transfer data from producer to consumer—one "sender initiated" and one "receiver initiated."

P_A	P_B
for i←0 *to* n-1 *do*	
A[i]←...;	
end for	
put (A[0..n-1] to tmp[0..n-1]);	
flag ← 1;	while (!flag) {}; /*spin-wait*/
for i←0 *to* n-1 *do*	*for* i←1 *to* n-1 *do*
compute f(C[i]);	use tmp[i];
end for	compute g(B[i]);
	end for

FIGURE 11.9 Using block transfer in a shared address space for the example of Figure 11.1. The array *A* is allocated in processor P_A's local memory and the array `tmp` in processor P_B's local memory.

11.4 BLOCK DATA TRANSFER IN A SHARED ADDRESS SPACE

In a shared address space, coalescing data to make messages larger (called block data transfer) and initiating the block transfers can be done either explicitly in the user program or transparently by the system. For example, the prevalent use of long cache blocks on modern machines is a means of transparent block transfers in cache-block-sized messages. Relaxed memory consistency models further allow us to buffer words or cache blocks and send them in coalesced messages only at synchronization points, a fact utilized particularly by software shared address space systems, noted in Chapter 9. However, let us focus here on explicit initiation of block transfers.

11.4.1 Techniques and Mechanisms

Explicit block transfers are initiated by explicitly issuing a put command, similar to a `send` but with both source and destination addresses specified by the sender, in the user program, as shown in the simple example in Figure 11.9. The put command is interpreted by the communication assist, which transfers the data in a pipelined manner from the source node to a destination node. At the destination, the communication assist transfers data from the network and into the specified locations. The path is shown in Figure 11.10. The major differences with send/receive message passing arise from the ability of the sending process to directly specify the program data structures (virtual addresses) where the data is to be placed at the destination, since these locations are in the shared address space. Receive operations are not needed in the programming model since the incoming message specifies where the data should be put in the program address space. System buffering or copying is also

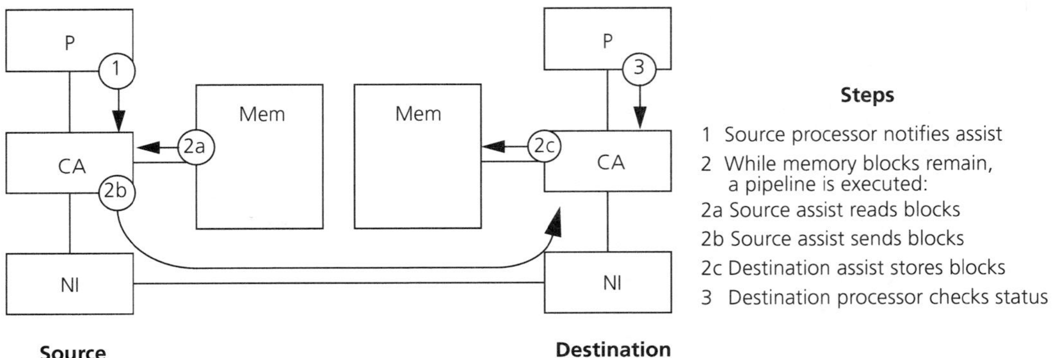

FIGURE 11.10 Path of a block transfer from a source node to a destination node in a shared address space machine. The transfer is done in terms of cache blocks since that is the granularity of communication for which the machine is optimized.

not needed in main memory at the destination, if the destination assist is available to put the data directly from the network interface into the user data structures in memory. However, some form of synchronization (like spinning on a flag or blocking) must be used to determine that the data has arrived before it is used by the destination process as well as to ensure that the destination region is ready to be overwritten before the data arrives. It is also possible to use receiver-initiated block transfer, in which case the request to transfer the data is issued by the receiver and handled by the source communication assist.

The communication assist on a node that performs the block transfer could be the same one that processes coherence protocol transactions or a separate DMA engine dedicated to block transfer. It can be designed with varying degrees of aggressiveness in its functionality; for example, it may allow contiguous data transfers only, uniform strides, or more general scatter-gather operations. The block transfer may leverage the support provided for efficient transfer of cache blocks, or it may be a completely separate mechanism. Since block transfers may need to interact with the coherence protocol in a coherent shared address space, we shall assume that the block transfer is built on top of pipelined transfers of entire cache blocks; that is, the block transfer engine is a part of the source assist that reads cache blocks out of memory and transfers them into the network in a pipelined manner. Figure 11.10 shows the steps in a possible implementation of block transfer in a cache-coherent shared address space.

11.4.2 Policy Issues and Trade-Offs

Two policy issues are of particular interest in block transfer: how interactions with the underlying shared address space and cache coherence protocol are handled, and where the block-transferred data is placed in the destination node.

Interactions with the Cache-Coherent Shared Address Space

The first interesting interaction is with the shared address space itself, regardless of whether it includes automatic coherent caching or not. The data that a processor "puts" in a block transfer may not be allocated in its local memory but in another processing node's memory or may even be scattered among other node's memories. The options here are to disallow such transfers, have the initiating node retrieve the data from the other memories and forward it in a pipelined manner, or have the initiating node send messages to the owning nodes' assists asking them to perform the relevant transfers.

The second interaction is specific to a cache-coherent shared address space since now the same data structures may be communicated using two different protocols: block transfer and cache coherence. Regardless of which main memory the data is allocated in, it may be cached in the sender's cache in dirty state, the receiver's cache in shared state, or another processor's cache (including the receiver's) in dirty state. The first two cases create what is called the *local coherence* problem; that is, ensuring that the data sent constitutes the most up-to-date values on the sending node and that copies of that data on the receiving node are left in coherent state after the transfer. The third case is called the *global coherence* problem; that is, ensuring that the values transferred are the latest values for those addresses anywhere in the system (according to the consistency model) and that the data involved in the transfer is left in coherent state in the whole system. Once again, the options are to provide no guarantees in any of these three cases, to provide only local but not global coherence, or to provide full global coherence. Each successive case makes the programmer's job easier but imposes more requirements on the communication assist. To provide coherence, the assist must check the state of every block being transferred, retrieve data from the appropriate caches, and invalidate data in the appropriate caches. The data being transferred may not be properly aligned with cache blocks, which makes interactions with the block-level coherence protocol even more complicated, as does the possibility that the directory information for the blocks being transferred may not be present at the sending node. The explicit message-passing programming model is simpler in this regard: it requires local coherence but not global coherence since any data that a process can access—and hence transfer—is allocated in its private address space and cannot be cached by any other processors.

For block transfer to maintain even local coherence, the assist has some work to do for every cache block and becomes an integral part of the transfer pipeline. It can therefore easily become the bottleneck in transfer bandwidth, affecting even those blocks for which no interaction with caches is required. Global coherence may require the assist to send network transactions around before sending each block, reducing bandwidth dramatically. It is therefore important that a block transfer system have a "pay for use" property; that is, providing coherent transfers should not significantly hurt the performance of transfers that do not need coherence, particularly if the latter are a common case. For example, if block transfer is used in the system only to support explicit message-passing programs, and not to accelerate coarse-grained communication in an otherwise read-write shared address space program, then it may make sense to provide only local coherence but not global coherence. However, as shown in Example 11.1, global coherence is essential if we want to provide true integration of block transfer with a coherent read-write shared address space and not make the programming model restrictive.

EXAMPLE 11.1 Give a simple example of a situation where global coherence may be needed for block transfer in a cache-coherent shared address space.

Answer Consider false sharing. The data that a processor P_1 wants to send P_2 may be allocated in P_1's local memory and produced by P_1, but another processor P_3 may have written other words on those cache blocks more recently. The cache blocks will be in invalid state in P_1's cache, and the latest copies must be retrieved from P_3 in order to be sent to P_2. False sharing is only an example: it is not difficult to see that in a true shared address space program the words that P_1 sends to P_2 might themselves have been written most recently by another processor. ■

More details on implementing block transfer in cache-coherent machines can be found in the literature (Kubiatowicz and Agarwal 1993; Heinlein et al. 1994; Woo, Singh, and Hennessy 1994; Heinlein et al. 1997).

Where to Place the Transferred Data

The other interesting policy issue is whether the data that is block transferred should be placed in the main memory of the destination, in the cache, or in both. Since the destination processor will read the data, having the data come into its cache is useful. However, it has some disadvantages as well. First, it requires intervening in the processor cache, which is expensive on modern systems and may prevent the processor from accessing the cache at the same time. Second, unless the block-transferred data is used soon it may be replaced before it is used, so we should transfer data into main memory as well to keep the resulting cache misses local. And third and most dangerous, the transferred data might replace other useful data from the cache, perhaps even data that is currently in the processor's active working set. For these reasons, large block transfers into a small first-level cache are not likely to be a good idea, whereas transfers into a large or second-level cache may be more useful.

11.4.3 Performance Benefits

Using large explicit transfers in a shared address space has several advantages compared to communicating implicitly in cache-block-sized messages. However, some of the advantages discussed earlier for message passing are compromised and there are disadvantages as well. Let us discuss the trade-offs qualitatively and then look at some performance data.

Potential Advantages and Disadvantages

The following are the major performance advantages of using block transfer. (The first two items were discussed in the context of message passing, so we only point out the differences here.)

- *Amortized per-message overhead.* This advantage may be less important in a hardware-supported shared address space since the endpoint overhead for cache block communication is already quite small. In fact, explicit, flexibly sized transfers tend to have higher endpoint overhead than small, fixed-size transfers, since buffering for the latter can easily be done in hardware while the former may require software management and copying. As a result, the per-communication overhead is likely to be substantially larger for block transfer than for read-write communication. Block transfer engines on many systems are like DMA devices, operating on physical addresses, so they run in kernel mode and require a system call, greatly increasing overhead. This increase turns out to be a major stumbling block for several commercial hardware-coherent machines, which currently use the facility more for operating system operations like page migration than for application activity. However, in less efficient communication architectures, such as those that use commodity parts, the overhead per message can be large even for cache block communication and the amortization due to block transfer can be very important.
- *Pipelined transfer of large chunks of data.*
- *Less wasted bandwidth.* In general, the larger the message, the less the relative overhead of headers and routing information compared to the payload (the data transferred that is useful to the end application). This advantage may be lost when the block transfer is built on top of the existing cache line transfer mechanism, in which the header information is sent once per cache block anyway. When used properly, block transfer can reduce the number of protocol messages (e.g., invalidations, acknowledgments) as well.
- *Replication of transferred data in the destination main memory.* Since block transfer is usually done into main memory, subsequent capacity misses at the destination node will be satisfied locally. This reduces the number of capacity misses at the destination that have to be satisfied remotely, as in COMA machines. However, without a COMA architecture, it implies that the user must manage the coherence and replacement of the replicated data in main memory.
- *Bundling of synchronization with data transfer.* Synchronization notifications can be piggybacked on the same message that transfers data rather than having to communicate separately for data and synchronization. This reduces the number of messages needed, though the absence of an explicit blocking receive operation implies that, functionally, synchronization still has to be managed separately from data transfer at the endpoints, just as in asynchronous message passing.

The potential performance disadvantages of using block transfer are

- *Higher overhead per transfer.*
- *Increased contention.* Long messages tend to incur higher contention, both at the endpoints and in the network, because they occupy more resources in the network at a time: the latency tolerance they provide places greater bandwidth demands on the communication architecture. On the other hand, bandwidth demand due to protocol messages is reduced compared to a cache coherence protocol, as discussed earlier.
- *Extra work.* Programs may have to do extra work to organize themselves so communication can be performed in large transfers (if this can be done effectively at all). This extra work may turn out to have a higher cost than the benefits achieved from block transfer (see the discussion of the Barnes-Hut application in Section 3.6).

Example 11.2 illustrates the performance improvements that can be obtained by using block transfers rather than reads and writes, particularly from amortized overhead and pipelined data transfer.

EXAMPLE 11.2 Suppose we want to communicate 4 KB of data from a source node to a destination node in a cache-coherent shared address space machine with a cache block size of 64 bytes. Assume that the data is contiguous in memory so that spatial locality is exploited perfectly (Exercise 11.6 discusses the issues that arise when spatial locality is not good). Suppose it takes the source assist 40 processor cycles to read a cache block out of memory, 50 cycles to push a cache block out through the network interface, and the same numbers of cycles for the complementary operations at the receiver. Assume that the local read-miss latency is 60 cycles, the remote read-miss latency is 180 cycles, and the time to start up a block transfer is 200 cycles. What is the potential performance advantage of using block transfer rather than communication through cache misses, assuming that the processor blocks on memory operations until they complete?

Answer The cost of getting the data through read misses, as seen by the processor, is 180*(4,096/64) = 11,520 cycles. With block transfer, the rate of the transfer pipeline is limited by max(40,50,50,40) or 50 cycles per block. This brings the data to the local memory at the destination, from where it will be read by the processor through local misses, each of which costs 60 cycles. Thus, the cost of getting the data to the destination processor with block transfer is 200 + (4,096/64)*(50 + 60) or 7,240 cycles. Using block transfer therefore gives us a speedup of 11,520/7,240, or 1.6. ■

Another way to achieve block transfers is with vector operations, for example, a vector read from remote memory. In this case, a single instruction causes the data to appear in the (vector) registers; individual load and store instructions are not required even locally, and a savings in instruction bandwidth and perhaps local cache misses results. Vector registers are typically managed by software, which has the disadvantages of aliasing and tying up register names but the advantage of not suffering from cache conflicts. However, many high-performance systems today do not include vector operations, so we shall focus on block transfers that still need individual local read and write operations to access and use the data.

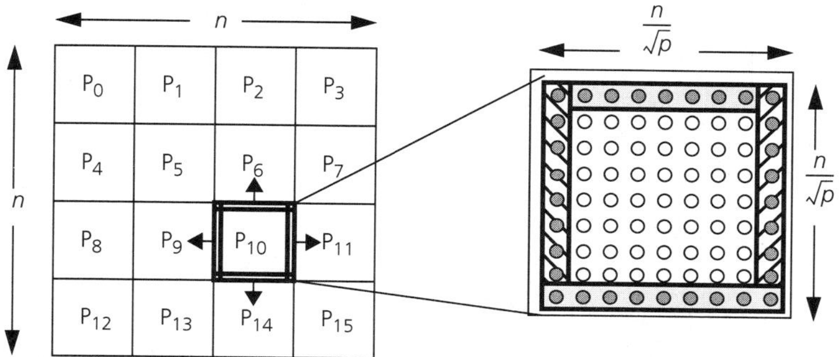

FIGURE 11.11 The use of block transfer in a near-neighbor equation solver. A process can send an entire boundary subrow or subcolumn of its partition to the process that owns the neighboring partition in a single message. The size of each message is $n/\sqrt{p}$ elements.

Performance Benefits and Limitations in Real Programs

Whether block transfer can be used effectively in real programs depends on both program and system characteristics. Consider a simple example amenable to block transfer, a near-neighbor equation solver on a grid, to see how the performance issues play out. Let us ignore the coherence complications discussed previously by assuming that the transfers are done from the source main memory to the destination main memory and that the data is not cached anywhere. We assume a four-dimensional array representation of the two-dimensional grid and a processor's partition of the grid allocated in its local memory.

Instead of communicating elements at partition boundaries through individual cache blocks, a process can simply send a single message containing all the appropriate boundary elements to its neighbor, as shown in Figure 11.11. The communication-to-computation ratio is proportional to $\sqrt{p}/n$. Since block transfer is intended to improve communication performance, this ratio in itself would tend to increase the relative effectiveness of block transfer as the number of processors increases. However, the size of an individual block transfer is $n/\sqrt{p}$ elements and therefore decreases with p. Smaller transfers make the additional overhead of initiating a block transfer relatively more significant. The trade-offs between these two factors combine to yield a sweet spot in the number of processors for which block transfer is most effective for a given grid size, as suggested by Figure 11.12. The sweet spot moves to larger numbers of processors as the grid size increases.

Figure 11.13 illustrates this sweet spot effect for a Fast Fourier Transform (FFT) on a simulated architecture that models the Stanford FLASH multiprocessor and is quite close to the SGI Origin2000 (though much more aggressive in its block transfer capabilities and performance). We can see that the relative benefit of block transfer over ordinary cache-coherent communication diminishes with increasing cache block size since the excellent spatial locality in this program causes long cache

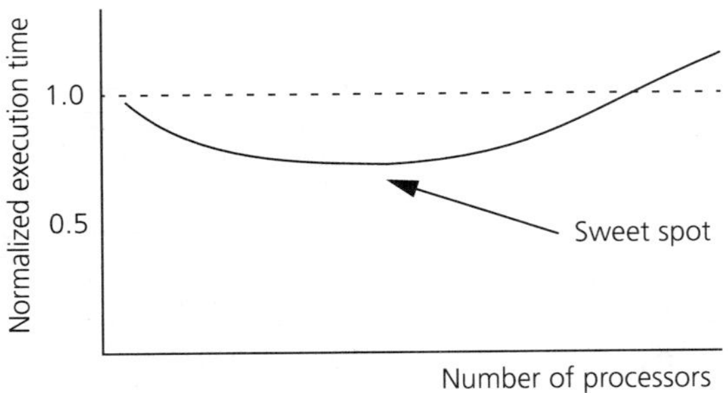

FIGURE 11.12 Relative performance improvement with block transfer. The figure illustrates the execution time using block transfer normalized to that using loads and stores. The sweet spot occurs when communication is high enough that block transfer matters, and the transfers are also large enough that overhead doesn't dominate.

blocks to themselves behave like small block transfers. For the largest cache block size of 128 bytes (the actual block size of the SGI Origin2000), the benefits of using block transfer are small, even with a very efficient block transfer engine. Figure 11.14 shows results for Ocean, a more complete, regular application whose communication is a variant of the nearest-neighbor communication in Figure 11.11. Block transfers at row-oriented partition boundaries transfer contiguous data, but this communication also has very good spatial locality; at column-oriented partition boundaries, spatial locality in communicated data is poor, but it is also difficult to exploit block transfer well. When block transfer is implemented using pipelined transfers of whole cache blocks (as assumed here), each word at a column boundary will be transferred on a separate cache block unless the boundary column is first copied to a contiguous data structure, so the lack of spatial locality hurts block transfer as well. Overall, the communication-to-computation ratio in Ocean is much smaller than in FFT. Although the ratio increases at higher levels of the grid hierarchy in the multigrid solver—as processor partitions become smaller—block transfers also become smaller at these levels and are less effective at amortizing overhead. The result is that block transfer is a lot less helpful for this application, and the relative benefits of block transfer do not depend so greatly on cache block size. Quantitative data for other applications can be found in (Woo, Singh, and Hennessy 1994).

Block transfer may be useful for some aspects of parallelism management. For example, in a task-stealing scenario, if the task descriptors for a stolen task are large, they can be sent using a block transfer, as can the data associated with the task, and the necessary synchronization for task queues can be piggybacked on these transfers as well.

One situation in which block transfer is clearly beneficial is when the overhead to initiate remote read-write accesses is very high; for example, when the shared address space is implemented in software. To see the effects of other parameters of the communication architecture, such as network delay and point-to-point bandwidth, let us look at the benefits of block transfer more analytically. Let us continue

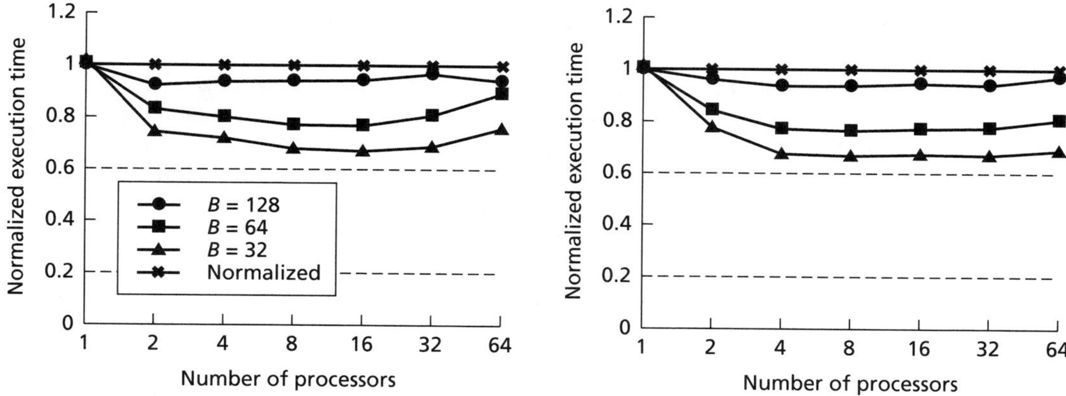

FIGURE 11.13 The benefits of block data transfer in a Fast Fourier Transform program. The two graphs are for two problem sizes. The architectural model and parameters used resemble those of the Stanford FLASH multiprocessor (Kuskin et al. 1994) and are similar to those of the SGI Origin2000. Each curve is for a different cache block size (*B*) in the second-level cache. For each curve, the *y*-axis shows the execution time normalized to that of an execution without block transfer using the same cache block size. Thus, the different curves are normalized differently (self-normalized) and different points for the same *x*-axis value are not normalized to the same number. The greater the *y*-axis value of a point, the less the improvement obtained by using block transfer over regular read-write communication for that case.

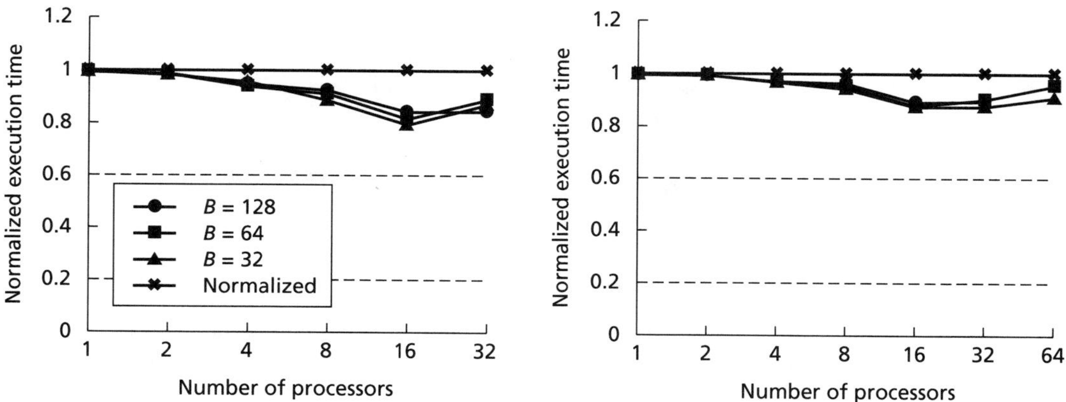

FIGURE 11.14 The benefits of block transfer in the Ocean application. The platform and data interpretation are exactly the same as in Figure 11.13. *B* is the second-level cache block size of the machine. The benefits and their dependence on cache block size are not as great as in the Fast Fourier Transform program.

to assume that read misses stall the processor and do not have their latency hidden. In general, the time to communicate a large block of data through remote read misses is (*# of read misses*remote read-miss time*), and the time to get the data to the destination processor through block transfer is (*start-up overhead + # of cache blocks transferred*pipeline stage time per cache block + # of read misses*local read-miss time*). The simplest case to analyze is a very large contiguous chunk of data for which we can ignore the start-up cost and assume perfect spatial locality. In this case, the speedup due to block transfer is limited by the ratio

$$\frac{\text{Remote Read-Miss Time}}{\text{Block Transfer Pipeline Stage Time} + \text{Local Read-Miss Time}} \tag{11.1}$$

where the block transfer pipeline stage time is the maximum of the time spent in any stage of the pipeline that was shown in Figure 11.10.

A longer network delay implies that the remote read-miss time is increased. If the point-to-point network bandwidth does not decrease with increased network delay, then the other terms are unaffected and longer delays favor block transfer. Alternatively, network bandwidth may decrease proportionally to the increase in delay, for example, if delay is increased by decreasing the clock speed of the network. In this case, as delay increases, at some point the rate at which data can be pushed into the network becomes smaller than the rate at which the assist can move the data to or from main memory. Up to this point, the memory access time dominates the block transfer pipeline stage time, so increases in network delay do not change block transfer performance and hence favor block transfer. After this point, the numerator and denominator in the ratio increase at the same rate with network delay, so the relative advantage of block transfer is unchanged.

Finally, suppose delay and overhead stay fixed but bandwidth changes (e.g., more wires are added to each network link). We might think that communication based on stalling remote reads is latency bound whereas block transfer is bandwidth bound, so increasing bandwidth should favor block transfer. This is true up to the point where network bandwidth limits the block transfer pipeline stage time. However, increasing network bandwidth past that point means that the memory access time may become the bottleneck, so increasing bandwidth further does not improve the performance of block transfer. Reducing bandwidth has the inverse effect. Thus, if the other variables are kept constant in each case, block transfer is more effective with increased per-message overhead, increased network delay, and increased bandwidth, up to a point.

In summary, the performance improvement obtained from block transfer over read-write cache-coherent communication depends on the following factors:

- the fraction of the execution time spent in communication that is amenable to block transfer
- the extra work that must be done to structure this communication as block transfers
- the problem size and number of processors, which affect the communication-to-computation ratio as well as the sizes of the transfers

- the overheads, delays, and bandwidths in the system
- the spatial locality in the program and how it interacts with the granularity of data transfer

If we can really make all messages large enough, then the delay components of communication may not be the problem; bandwidth becomes a more significant constraint. But if not, we still need to hide the latency of data accesses by overlapping them with computation or with other accesses. The other three latency tolerance approaches do this; however, to be successful at cache block granularity, they require support in the microprocessor as well. Instead of precommunication, let us begin with techniques to move past long-latency accesses in the same thread of computation.

11.5 PROCEEDING PAST LONG-LATENCY EVENTS

A processor can proceed past a memory operation to other instructions if the memory operation is made nonblocking. For writes, this is usually straightforward: the write is put in a write buffer, and the processor goes on while the buffer takes care of issuing the write to the memory system and tracking its completion as necessary. Many processors also support nonblocking reads in which the processor performs instructions while the read is outstanding. Without additional support, the processor stalls when it encounters an instruction that attempt to use the results of the read. The problem is that in most programs such a dependent instruction is likely to follow soon after the read. If the read misses in the cache, very little of its miss latency is likely to be hidden in this manner. Hiding read latency effectively requires that we look ahead in the instruction stream past the dependent instruction to find other instructions that are independent of the read. This requires support in the compiler instruction scheduling, the hardware, or both. Hiding write latency does not usually require instruction lookahead: we can allow the processor to stall when it encounters a dependent instruction since it is not likely to encounter one soon.

Proceeding past operations before they complete can benefit from both buffering and pipelining. Buffering of memory operations allows the processor to proceed with other activity, to delay the propagation and application of requests like invalidations, and to merge operations to the same word or cache block in the buffer. (The page-based, all-software, shared virtual memory protocols discussed in Chapter 9 are an extreme example of buffering, delaying propagation until synchronization points.) Pipelining multiple memory operations into the memory hierarchy allows their latencies to be overlapped. These advantages hold for uniprocessors as well as multiprocessors.

In multiprocessors, proceeding past memory operations before they complete or commit violates the sufficient conditions for sequential consistency stated in Chapter 5. Whether or not it actually violates SC itself depends on whether the operations are allowed to become visible out of program order. By requiring that memory operations from the same thread should not appear to perform out of program order with respect to other processors, SC restricts—but by no means eliminates—the amount of buffering and overlap that can be exploited. Relaxed consistency models allow greater overlap, including by allowing some types of memory operations to complete out of order. The extent of overlap possible is thus determined by both the machine mechanisms and the consistency model: relaxed models may not be useful if the mechanisms needed to support their reorderings (e.g., write buffers, compiler support, or dynamic scheduling) are not provided, and the success of some types of aggressive implementations for overlap may be restricted by the consistency model.

Our discussion of proceeding past operations is organized around increasingly aggressive mechanisms needed for overlapping the latency of read and write operations. Each of these mechanisms is naturally associated with a particular class of consistency models—the class that allows those operations to complete out of order—but can also be exploited in more limited ways with stricter consistency models by allowing overlap but not out-of-order completion. In each case, we examine the performance gains and the implementation complexity, assuming the most aggressive consistency model needed to fully exploit that overlap, as well as the extent to which sequential consistency can exploit the overlap mechanisms. The focus is on hardware cache-coherent systems, though many of the issues apply quite naturally to systems that don't cache shared data or are software coherent. To simplify the discussion, let us begin by examining mechanisms to hide only write latency since hiding read latency requires more elaborate support (albeit provided in many modern microprocessors). Reads are initially assumed to be blocking, so the processor cannot proceed past them; later, hiding read latency is examined as well.

11.5.1 Proceeding Past Writes

Let us start with a simple, statically scheduled processor with blocking reads. To proceed past write misses, the only support we need in the processor is a write buffer. Writes that miss in the first-level cache are simply placed in the buffer, and the processor proceeds to other work in the same thread. The processor (or the first-level cache) stalls upon a write only if the write buffer is full. The write buffer may also be placed before the first-level cache, in which case all writes are placed in it.

The write buffer is responsible for controlling the visibility of writes to the rest of the extended memory hierarchy, and hence to other processors, and for the completion of writes relative to other operations from that processor. This frees the processor's internal execution unit and the extended memory hierarchy from worrying about these orders. Consider overlap with reads. For correct uniprocessor operation, a read may be allowed to bypass the write buffer and may be issued to the memory system as long as a write to the same location is not pending in the write buffer. If it is, the value from the write buffer may be forwarded to the read even before the write completes, or the write buffer may be flushed and the read issued to the memory system thereafter. Forwarding allows reads to complete out of order with respect to earlier writes in program order, thus violating SC in multiprocessors, while flushing does not. Reads bypassing the write buffer will also violate SC unless the read is not allowed to complete (bind its value) before those writes. Thus, SC can take advantage of write buffers, but the benefits are limited. We know from Chapter 9 that processor consistency (PC) and total store ordering (TSO) are the consistency models that allow only reads to complete before previous writes.

Now consider the overlap among writes themselves. Multiple writes may be placed in the write buffer, which determines the order in which they are made visible or in which they complete. If writes are allowed to complete out of order, a great deal of flexibility and overlap among writes can be exploited by the buffer. First, a write to a location or cache block that is currently in the buffer can be merged (coalesced) into that cache block and only a single ownership request sent out for the block by the buffer, thus reducing traffic as well. Especially if the merging is not into the last entry of the buffer, this leads to writes becoming visible out of program order. Second, buffered writes can be retired from the buffer when they issue to the memory system, making it possible for other writes behind them to get through before they complete. This allows the ownership requests of the writes to be pipelined through the extended memory hierarchy, but it can make the writes visible to other processors out of program order and can violate write atomicity.

Partial store order (PSO) or more relaxed consistency models allow writes to complete out of program order. Stricter models like SC, TSO, and PC essentially restrict merging into the write buffer to the last block in the buffer, and even then in restricted circumstances since other processors must not be able to see the writes to different words in the block in a different order. Retiring writes early to let others pass through is possible under the stricter models only if the order of visibility and completion among these writes is preserved in the extended memory hierarchy. This is relatively easy in a bus-based machine but very difficult in a distributed-memory machine with different home memories and independent network paths. On the latter systems, guaranteeing program order among writes, as needed for SC, TSO, and PC, essentially requires that a write not be retired from the head of the FIFO buffer until it has committed with respect to all processors.

Overall, a strict model like SC can utilize write buffers to overlap write latency with reads and other writes but to a limited extent. Greater latency tolerance requires relaxing the consistency model. Under relaxed models, exactly when write operations are sent out to the extended memory hierarchy and made visible to other processors depends on implementation and performance considerations as well. For example, invalidations may be sent out as soon as the writes are able to get through the write buffer, or they may be delayed in the buffer until the next synchronization point. The latter option allows greater merging of writes as well as reduction of invalidations and misses due to false sharing. However, it also implies that invalidation-related traffic will be bursty at synchronization points rather than pipelined throughout the computation.

Performance Impact

Simulation studies have shown the benefits of allowing the processor to proceed past writes on the parallel applications in the original SPLASH application suite (Singh, Weber, and Gupta 1992), assuming blocking reads but without maintaining SC (Gharachorloo, Gupta, and Hennessy 1991a; Gharachorloo 1995). The resulting techniques are separated into those that allow the program order between a write and a following read (write → read order) to be violated, satisfying TSO or PC, and those that also allow the order between two writes (write → write order) to be violated, satisfying PSO. The latter is essentially the best that more relaxed models like relaxed memory order (RMO), weak ordering (WO), or release consistency (RC) can accomplish given that reads are blocking.

Figure 11.15 shows with single-issue, statically scheduled processors the reduction in execution time, divided into different components, for two representative parallel programs when the write → read and write → write orders are allowed to be violated. The programs are older versions of the Ocean and Barnes-Hut applications, running with small problem sizes on 16-processor, simulated, directory-based cache-coherent systems that are considerably less aggressive in instruction scheduling than current microprocessors. The baseline for comparison is the straightforward implementation of sequential consistency that satisfies the sufficient conditions: the processor issuing a read or write stalls until that reference completes. (Using the write buffer but preserving SC by stalling a read until the write buffer is empty shows only a very small performance improvement over stalling the processor on all writes themselves.)

The second bars in the figure show that, with a deep write buffer and these system assumptions, simply allowing write → read reordering is usually enough to hide most of the write latency from the processor. It is less successful in Ocean, where there is a greater frequency of write misses. The full study also showed some interesting secondary effects. In some cases, the read stall time increases slightly from the base SC case. This is because the additional bandwidth demands of hiding write latency contend with read misses, making them more costly. This is a relatively small effect with simple processors, though it may be more significant with modern, dynamically scheduled processors that also hide read latency. Another beneficial effect is that synchronization wait time is also sometimes reduced. As memory stall time is reduced, imbalances in memory stall time across processors are reduced, and hence load imbalance is diminished. Also, if the latency write performed inside a critical section is hidden, then the critical section completes more quickly. The lock protecting it can be passed more quickly to another processor, which therefore incurs less wait time for that lock.

The third bars in the figure show the results for the case in which the write → write order is allowed to be violated as well. Write merging is now enabled to any block in the same 16-entry write buffer and a write is allowed to retire from the write buffer as soon as it reaches the head, even before it is committed. Thus, pipelining of writes through the memory and interconnect is given priority over buffering them for more time (which would enable merging and delayed invalidations)876. Of course, having multiple writes outstanding in the memory system requires that the caches allow multiple outstanding misses.

The write-write overlap hides whatever write latency remained with write-read overlap, even in Ocean. Since writes retire from the write buffer at a faster rate, the write buffer does not fill up and stall the processor as easily. Synchronization wait time is reduced further in some cases since a sequence of writes before a release

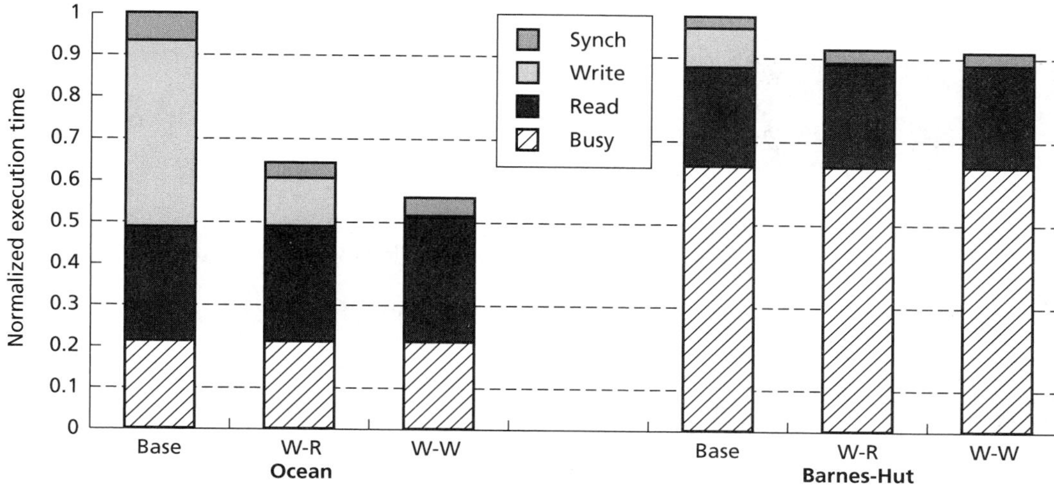

FIGURE 11.15 Performance benefits from proceeding past writes by taking advantage of relaxed consistency models. The results assume a statically scheduled processor model. For each application, Base is the case with no latency hiding, W-R indicates that reads can bypass writes (i.e., the write → read order can be violated), and W-W indicates that both writes and reads can bypass writes. The execution time for the Base case is normalized to 100 units. The system simulated is a cache-coherent multiprocessor using a flat, memory-based directory protocol much like that of the Stanford DASH multiprocessor (Lenoski et al. 1993). The simulator assumes write-through first-level and write-back second-level caches, with deep, 16-entry write buffers between the two. The processor is single issue and statically scheduled, with no special scheduling in the compiler targeted toward latency tolerance. The write buffer is aggressive, with read bypassing of it and read forwarding from it enabled. To preserve the write → write order (in the case where this reordering is not permitted), writes are not merged in the write buffer and the write at the head of the FIFO write buffer is not retired until it has completed. The data access parameters assumed for a read miss are 1 cycle for an L_1 hit, 15 cycles for an L_2 hit, 29 cycles if a miss is satisfied in local memory, 101 cycles for a two-message remote miss, and 132 cycles for a three-message remote miss. Write latencies are a little smaller in each case. The system thus assumes a much slower processor relative to a memory system than modern systems.

completes more quickly. In most applications, however, write-write overlap provides little benefit since most of the write latency is already hidden by allowing reads to bypass previous writes. Another factor limiting the effectiveness of write-write overlap is that the processor model assumes that reads are blocking, so write-write overlap cannot be exploited past read operations. The differences between models like weak ordering and release consistency as well as subtle differences among models (such as TSO, which preserves write atomicity, and PC, which does not) do not seem to affect performance substantially.

Since performance is highly dependent on implementation and on problem and cache sizes, it is useful to examine less aggressive write buffers and second-level cache architectures as well as cache sizes where an important working set does not fit in the cache. A lockup-free L_2 cache is very important for obtaining good performance improvements, as we might expect. Bypassable write buffers are very important for a system that allows write → read reordering, particularly when the L_2 cache is lockup-free, but less important for the system that allows write → write reordering as well. The reason is that in the former case writes retire from the buffer only after completion, so it is quite likely that when a read misses in the first-level cache it will find a write still in the write buffer, and stalling the read until the write buffer empties will hurt performance. In the latter case, writes retire much faster, so the likelihood of finding a write in the buffer to bypass is smaller. For the same reason, write buffer size is less critical when write → write reordering is allowed. Without lockup-free caches, the ability for reads to bypass writes in the buffer is much less advantageous whether or not write → write reordering is allowed, since the stalling of the L_2 cache becomes the bottleneck. All parts of the system must be appropriately designed to obtain the benefits of overlap.

Results from the study with smaller L_1 and L_2 caches are shown in Figure 11.16, as are results for varying the cache block size. Consider cache size first. With smaller caches, write latency is still hidden effectively by allowing write → read and write → write reordering. (As discussed in Chapter 4, for Barnes-Hut the smallest caches do not represent a realistic scenario.) Interestingly, the impact of hiding write latency on overall performance is often larger with larger caches even though the total write latency to be hidden is smaller. This is because larger caches are more effective in reducing read latency than write latency, so the latter becomes relatively more important to hide. All of these results assume a cache block size of only 16 bytes, which is quite unrealistic today. Larger cache blocks tend to reduce the miss rates for these applications and hence somewhat reduce the impact of these reorderings on execution time, as seen for Ocean in Figure 11.16(b).

11.5.2 Proceeding Past Reads

To hide read latency effectively, we need both nonblocking reads and a mechanism to look ahead beyond dependent instructions. Both compiler and hardware mechanisms are complicated by the fact that the dependent instructions may be followed soon after by branches. Predicting future paths through the code to find independent instructions requires effective branch prediction as well as speculative execution past predicted branches. Speculatively executed instructions in turn demand hardware support to cancel their effects upon detecting misprediction.

The trend in the microprocessor industry today is toward increasingly sophisticated processors that provide all these features in hardware. For example, they are included by processor families such as the Intel Pentium Pro (Intel Corporation 1996), the Silicon Graphics R10000 (MIPS Technologies 1996), the Sun UltraSparc (Lee, Kwok, and Briggs 1991), and the Hewlett-Packard PA8000 (Hunt 1996) because latency hiding and overlapped operation of the memory system and functional units are very important even in uniprocessors. The mechanisms have a high design and hardware cost, but since they are already present in the microprocessors they can be used to hide latency in multiprocessors as well. Once present, they can hide write latency as well, so a separate write buffer may not be needed.

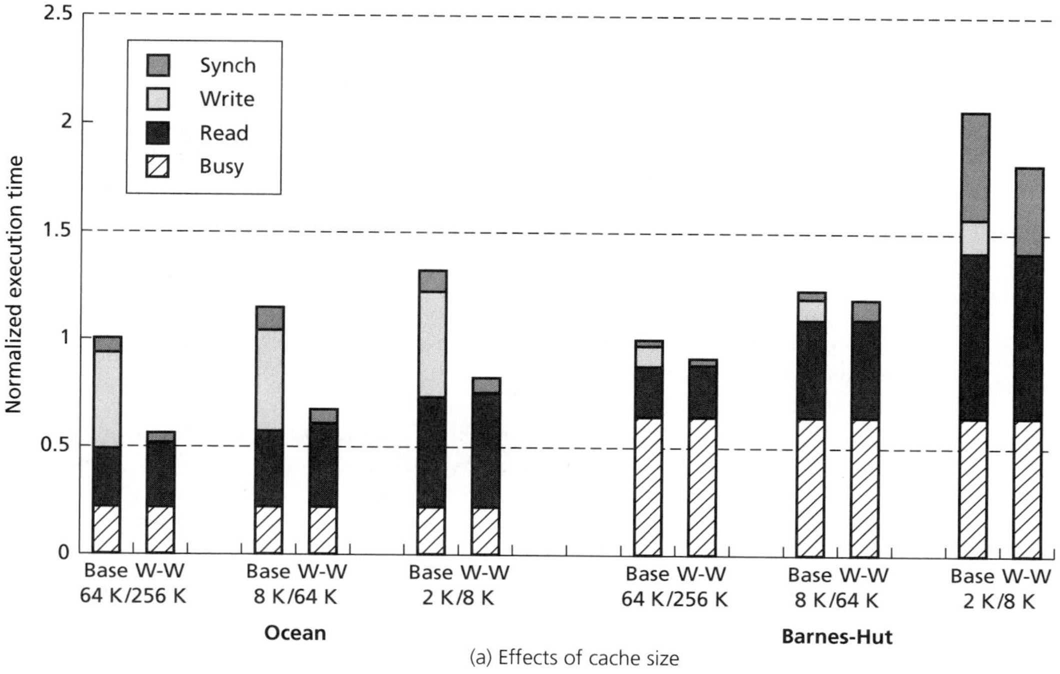

(a) Effects of cache size

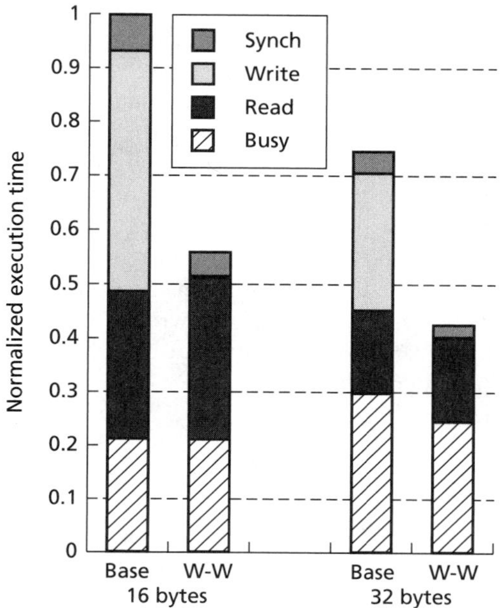

(b) Effects of cache block size for Ocean

FIGURE 11.16 Effects of cache size and cache block size on the benefits of proceeding past writes. In (a), which varies cache size, the cache block size assumed is the (small) 16-byte default size used in the study. The cache sizes specified on the *x*-axis are the L_1 and L_2 cache sizes, separated by a slash. In (b), which varies cache block size, the cache sizes are assumed to be the default 64-KB L_1 cache and 256-KB L_2 cache used in the study. The *y*-axis is the normalized execution time so that the leftmost bar in each graph is one unit.

Dynamic Scheduling and Speculative Execution

To understand how to hide memory latency by using dynamic scheduling and speculative execution and especially how the techniques interact with memory consistency models, let us briefly recall from uniprocessor architecture how the methods work. More details can be found in texts, such as (Hennessy and Patterson 1996). *Dynamic scheduling* means that instructions are fetched and decoded in program order as presented by the compiler, but they are executed by the functional units in the order in which their operands become available at run time. One way to orchestrate this out-of-order execution is through reservation stations and Tomasulo's algorithm (Hennessy and Patterson 1996). Dynamic scheduling does not necessarily imply that memory operations will become visible or complete out of program order, as we will see. *Speculative execution* means allowing the processor to look at and schedule for execution instructions that are not necessarily going to be useful to the program's execution, for example, instructions past a future branch instruction. The functional units can execute these instructions, assuming that they will indeed be useful, but the results are not committed to registers or made visible to the rest of the system until the validity of the speculation has been determined (e.g., the branch has been resolved).

The key mechanism used for speculative execution is an instruction *lookahead* or *reorder* buffer. As instructions are decoded by the decode unit, whether in-line or speculatively past predicted branches, they are placed in the reorder buffer. The reorder buffer therefore holds instructions in program order. Among these, instructions that are not dependent on an incomplete instruction can be chosen from the reorder buffer for execution. It is quite possible that independent long-latency instructions (e.g., reads) further ahead in the buffer have not yet been executed or completed, so in this way the processor proceeds past incomplete memory operations and other instructions. Instructions in the reorder buffer become ready for execution as soon as their operands are produced by other instructions, not necessarily waiting until the operands are available in the register file. An instruction keeps its results with it in the reorder buffer without committing them to the register file and is retired from the buffer only when it reaches the head, that is, in program order. It is only at this retirement point that the result of a read or other instruction may be put in the destination register and that the value produced by a write is free to be made visible to the memory system. Thus, even with aggressive out-of-order execution, memory operations can complete in program order.

Retiring instructions in program order simplifies speculation: if a branch is found to be mispredicted, which is determined before the branch retires from the reorder buffer, then no instruction after it (in program order) could have retired from the reorder buffer and committed its effects. No read has updated a register, and no write has become visible to the memory system. Upon detecting misprediction, all instructions after the branch are invalidated in the reorder buffer and the reservations stations, and decoding is resumed from the correct branch target. In-order retirement also makes it easy to implement precise exceptions. However, in-order retirement does mean that if a read miss reaches the head of the buffer before its data value has come back, the reorder buffer (not the processor) stalls and later instructions cannot be retired. This FIFO nature and stalling implies that the extent of latency tolerance may be limited by the size of the reorder buffer.

Hiding Latency under Sequential and Release Consistency

The difference between an operation retiring from the reorder buffer and completing is important. A read completes when its value is bound, which may be before it reaches the head of the reorder buffer and can retire (modifying the processor register). On the other hand, a write is not complete even when it reaches the head of the buffer and retires to the memory system; it completes only when it has actually become visible to all processors. Understanding this difference helps us understand how out-of-order, speculative processors can hide latency under both SC and more relaxed models like release consistency (RC).

Under RC, a write may indeed be retired from the buffer before it completes, allowing operations behind it to retire more quickly. Under SC, a write is retired from the buffer only when it has completed (or at least committed with respect to all processors), so it may hold up the reorder buffer longer once it reaches the head and is sent out to the memory system. Under RC, a read may be issued to the memory system and complete anytime after it is inserted in the reorder buffer, unless an acquire operation before it has not completed. Under SC, although a read may still be issued to the memory system and complete before it reaches the head of the buffer, it is not issued to the memory system before all previous memory operations in the reorder buffer have completed (not necessarily retired). Thus, SC exploits less overlap than RC, but the difference is not as great as with in-order execution.

Additional Techniques to Enhance Latency Tolerance

Additional techniques—including a form of hardware prefetching, speculative reads, and write buffers—can be used with dynamically scheduled, speculative processors to hide latency further under SC as well as RC (Gharachorloo, Gupta, and Hennessy 1991b). The hardware may issue prefetch operations for memory operations that are in the reorder buffer but are not yet permitted by the consistency model to actually issue to the memory system. For example, the processor might prefetch a read that is preceded in the buffer by another incomplete memory operation in SC or by an incomplete acquire operation in RC, thus overlapping them. For writes, prefetching allows the data and ownership to be brought to the cache before the write actually gets to the head of the buffer and can be issued to the memory system. Basically, the read-exclusive transaction is issued early. These prefetches are *nonbinding*, which means that the data is brought into the cache, but not into a register or the reorder buffer, and is still visible to the coherence protocol so the prefetches do not violate the consistency model. If the block is invalidated before the read commits, the only harm is a little extra memory traffic. (Prefetching in a more general context will be discussed in Section 11.6.)

Hardware prefetching is ineffective when the address to be prefetched is not known and determining the address itself requires the completion of a long-latency operation. For example, if a read miss to an array entry $A[I]$ is preceded by a read miss to the array index I, then the two operations cannot be overlapped because the processor does not know the address of $A[I]$ until the read of I completes. It can prefetch I, but to obtain the address of $A[I]$ requires that the read of I complete. To increase the overlap, a processor can use speculative read operations. A *speculative read* is a read that completes speculatively even before its completion is permitted by the consistency model, that is, before it reaches the head of the reorder buffer, in the case of SC. Its value can then be used as an address for future memory operations, but the use will be guarded as for instructions after a predicted branch. Essentially, the processor speculates that the (prefetched) value will not be changed between the time of the speculative read and the time that the real read is allowed to be performed according to the memory consistency model. If the value is indeed changed during this time, then the effects of the speculative read and all operations that have been issued after it must be undone.

In the current example, I is not only prefetched but also speculatively read before it has reached the head of the buffer, so the read of $A[I]$ can be prefetched early as well. We need to be sure that we use the correct value for I and hence read the correct location for $A[I]$. For this reason, speculative reads are loaded not into the registers themselves but into a buffer called the speculative read buffer where they stay until the read retires from the reorder buffer. The speculative read buffer "watches" the cache and is apprised of cache actions to those blocks. If an invalidation, update, or even cache replacement occurs on a block whose address is in the speculative read buffer, then the speculative read and all instructions following it in the reorder buffer must be cancelled and the execution rolled back, just as on a mispredicted branch. Such hardware prefetching and speculative read support are present in processors like the Pentium Pro (Intel Corporation 1996), the MIPS R10000 (MIPS Technologies 1996), and the HP PA-8000 (Hunt 1996). Note that under SC every read issued before previous memory operations have completed is a speculative read and goes into the speculative read buffer, whereas under RC reads are speculative (and have to watch the cache) only if they are issued before a previous acquire has completed.

A final optimization used to increase overlap, even in a dynamically scheduled processor, is a separate write buffer. Instead of writes waiting at the head of the reorder buffer until they complete, holding up the reorder buffer, they are removed from the reorder buffer and placed in the write buffer when they reach the head. The write buffer allows them to become visible to the extended memory hierarchy and keeps track of their completion as required by the consistency model. Write buffers are clearly useful with relaxed models like RC and PC in which reads are allowed to bypass writes. The reads will now reach the head of the reorder buffer and retire more quickly. Under SC, we can put writes in the write buffer, but a read stalls when it reaches the head of the reorder buffer anyway until the write completes. Thus, much of the latency that the write would have seen may instead be seen by the next read to reach the head of the reorder buffer.

Performance Impact

Simulation studies have examined the extent to which hardware prefetching, speculative read, and write buffering techniques can hide latency under different consistency models. One study assuming an RC model finds that a substantial portion of read latency can indeed be hidden using a dynamically scheduled processor with speculative execution and that the amount of read latency that can be hidden increases with the size of the reorder buffer even up to buffers as large as 64 to 128 entries (Gharachorloo, Gupta, and Hennessy 1992). A detailed study compares the performance of the SC and RC consistency models with aggressive, multiple-issue, dynamically scheduled processors (Pai et al. 1996). It also examines the benefits obtained individually from hardware prefetching and speculative reads with each model. Because a write takes longer to complete even on an L_1 hit when the L_1 cache is write through rather than write back, the study examines both types of L_1 caches, always assuming a write-back L_2 cache. The studies are preliminary since they use very small problem sizes and scaled-down caches. They also do not use sophisticated compiler technology to schedule instructions in a way that can obtain increased benefits from dynamic scheduling and speculative execution. (For example, placing more independent instructions close after a memory operation or miss may allow smaller reorder buffers to suffice.) However, the results shed light on the interactions between mechanisms and models.

The most interesting question is whether, with aggressive, dynamically scheduled processors, RC still buys substantial performance gains over SC at the hardware/software interface. If not, the programming burden of relaxed consistency models may not be justified with these processors. (Relaxed models may still be important at the programmer's interface to allow compiler optimizations, but the programming burden may be lighter if it is only the compiler that may reorder operations.) The results of the second study, shown for two programs in Figures 11.17 and 11.18, indicate that RC is still beneficial, even though the gap has closed substantially compared to the case of processors with blocking reads. The figures show the results for SC without any of the more sophisticated optimizations (hardware prefetching, speculative reads, and write buffering) and then with those optimizations applied cumulatively one after the other. Results are also shown for processor consistency (PC) and for RC. The PC and RC cases always assume write buffering and are shown first without the other two optimizations and then with those applied cumulatively.

When hardware prefetching and speculative reads are not used, RC has substantial advantages over SC even with a dynamically scheduled processor. This is primarily because RC is able to hide write latency more successfully than SC, as was the case with simple processors. It allows writes to be retired faster and allows later accesses to be issued to the memory system and to complete before previous writes. The improvement due to RC is even greater with write-through caches since under SC a write that reaches the head of the buffer issues to the memory system but has to wait until the write performs in the second-level cache even if it hits in the first-level cache. While read latency is hidden with some success even under SC, RC allows for much earlier issue, completion, and hence retirement of reads.

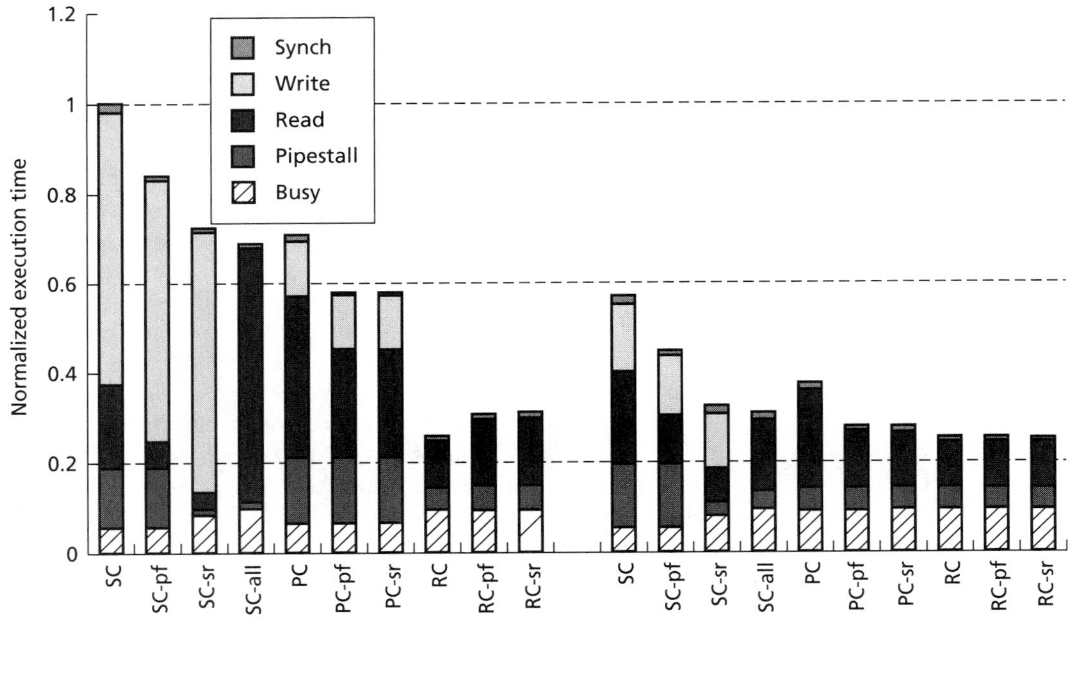

FIGURE 11.17 Performance of an FFT kernel with different consistency models, assuming a dynamically scheduled processor with speculative execution. The set of ten bars on the left assumes write-through first-level caches, while the ten bars on the right assume write-back first-level caches. Second-level caches are always write back. SC, PC, and RC are sequential, processor, and release consistency, respectively. For SC there are four bars. The first bar excludes hardware prefetching, speculative reads, and write buffers; the second bar (pf) includes the use of hardware prefetching, the third bar (sr) includes the use of speculative reads as well, and the fourth bar (all) includes all three optimizations. For PC and RC, the use of write buffers is always assumed, so there are only three sets of bars each (pf now means hardware prefetching and write buffering, and sr includes all three optimizations). The processor model assumed resembles the MIPS R10000 (MIPS Technologies 1996). The processor is clocked at 300 MHz and is capable of issuing 4 instructions per cycle. It uses a reorder buffer of size 64 entries, a merging write buffer with 8 entries, a 4-KB direct-mapped first-level cache, and a 64-KB, 4-way set-associative second-level cache. Small caches are chosen since the data sets are small, but they may exaggerate the effect of latency hiding. More detailed parameters can be found in (Pai et al. 1996).

The effects of hardware prefetching and speculative reads are much greater for SC than for RC since in RC, memory operations are allowed to issue and complete out of order anyway. However, even with these optimizations a significant gap still remains compared to RC, especially in write latency. Write buffering is not very useful under SC for the reason discussed earlier.

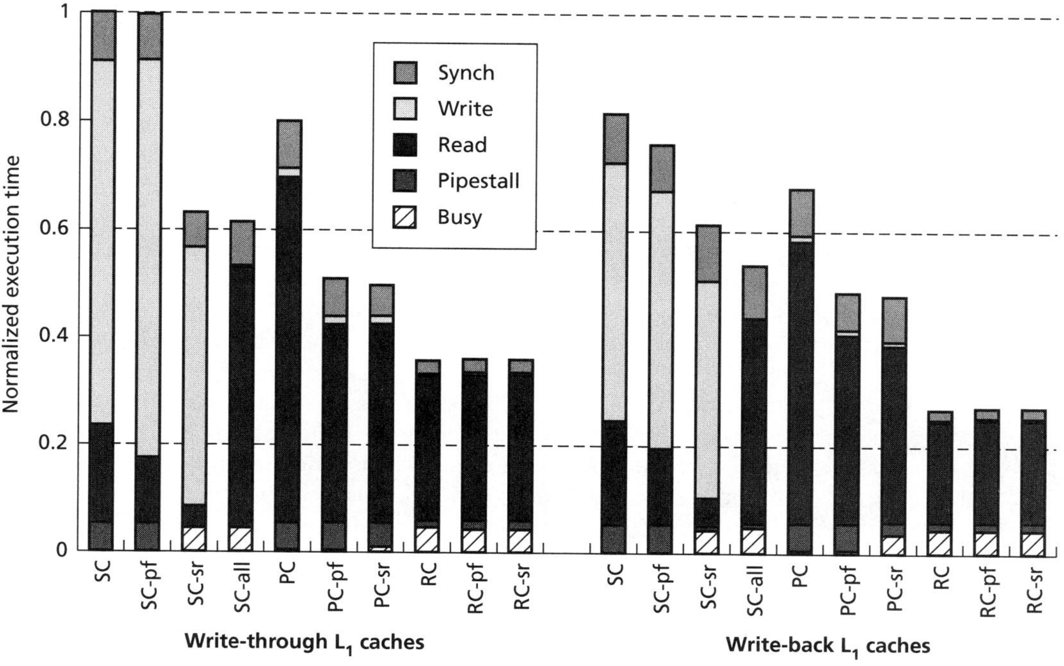

FIGURE 11.18 Performance of Radix with different consistency models, assuming a dynamically scheduled processor with speculative execution. The system assumptions and the organization of the figure are the same as in Figure 11.17.

The figures also confirm that write latency is a more significant problem with write-through first-level caches under SC than with write-back caches but is hidden equally well under RC with both types of caches. The difference in write latency between write-through and write-back caches under SC is larger for FFT than for Radix because in FFT the writes are to locally allocated data and hit in the write-back cache for this problem size whereas in Radix they are to nonlocal data and miss in both cases. Overall, PC rates between SC and RC, with hardware prefetching helping but speculative reads not helping as much as in SC.

Finally, the graphs appear to reveal an anomaly: the processor busy time is different in different schemes, even for the same application, problem size, and memory system configuration. The reason is an interesting methodological point for superscalar processors. Since several instructions can be issued every cycle, how do we decide whether to attribute a cycle to busy time or to a particular type of stall time?

There isn't a very good answer. The decision made in most studies in the literature, and in these results, is to attribute a cycle to busy time only if all instruction slots issue in that cycle. If not, then the cycle is attributed to whatever form of stall is seen by the first instruction (starting from the head of the reorder buffer) that should have issued in that cycle but didn't. Since this pattern changes with consistency models and implementations, the busy time is not the same across schemes.

It is interesting to examine the interactions with hardware prefetching and speculative reads in a little more detail, particularly in how they interact with application characteristics. Prefetching for operations that are in the reorder buffer works most successfully when a number of operations that will otherwise miss are close together in the code so that they will appear together in the reorder buffer. This happens in the matrix transposition phase of an FFT, so the gains from prefetching in Figure 11.17 are substantial. It can be aided in other programs by appropriate scheduling of operations by the compiler. The situation that motivated speculative reads in the first place—the address to be prefetched is not known until a read completes—is encountered in the Radix sorting application, shown in Figure 11.18. Here, the relevant misses are to array entries indexed by histogram values that have to be read as well. An interesting effect in both programs is that the processor busy time is reduced as well by speculative reads. This is because the ability to consume the values of reads speculatively makes many more otherwise dependent instructions available to execute, greatly increasing the utilization of a superscalar processor. Interestingly, speculative reads help reduce read latency in FFT even though it does not have indirect array accesses. This is because conflict misses in the L_2 cache are reduced due to greater combining of accesses to an outstanding cache block: accesses that would otherwise have caused conflict misses in the L_2 cache are overlapped by using speculative reads and are therefore combined by the mechanism used to keep track of outstanding L_2 misses. This illustrates that important observed effects sometimes are not directly due to the feature being studied. Although speculative reads, and speculative execution in general, are hurt by misspeculation and consequent rollbacks, this occurs rarely in the programs studied, which take quite predictable and straightforward paths through the code. The results may be different for programs with highly unpredictable control flow and access patterns.

11.5.3 Summary

The extent to which latency can be tolerated by proceeding past reads and writes in a multiprocessor depends on both the aggressiveness of the implementation and the memory consistency model. Tolerating write latency is relatively easy in cache-coherent multiprocessors, even with simple blocking-read processors, when the memory consistency model is relaxed. Modern dynamically scheduled processors can hide both read and write latency, but only partially. The instruction lookahead window (reorder buffer) size needed to hide read latency can be substantial and grows with the latency to be hidden. Fortunately, latency is hidden increasingly as window size increases rather than needing a very large threshold size before any significant latency hiding takes place. In fact, with the mechanisms that are widely available in modern processors, read latency can be hidden reasonably well even under sequential consistency, at least on moderate-scale systems. Compiler scheduling of instructions can help processors hide latency even better.

In general, conservative design choices—such as blocking reads or blocking caches—make preserving orders easier, but at the cost of performance. For example, in dynamically scheduled processors, delaying the retirement of writes from the reorder buffer until all previous instructions are complete to avoid rolling back on writes (e.g., for precise exceptions) makes it easier to preserve SC, but it makes write latency more difficult to hide under SC. Both read and especially write latency are hidden better by using relaxed consistency models. The implementation requirements for relaxed consistency models in hardware-coherent systems are not very demanding beyond what is provided to hide write and read latency in modern uniprocessors and what is needed even for sequential consistency (see Exercise 11.9). Most of the support for preserving a given consistency model is in the buffers and caches close to the processor; the rest of the memory hierarchy can then reorder transactions as it pleases.

The approach of hiding latency by proceeding past operations has two significant drawbacks. The first is that it may very well require relaxing the consistency model to be very effective, especially with simple statically scheduled processors but also with dynamically scheduled ones. This places a greater burden on the programmer to label synchronization (competing) operations or insert memory barriers, although relaxing the consistency model is to a large extent needed to allow compilers to perform many of their optimizations anyway. The second drawback is the diffculty of hiding read latency effectively with processors that are not dynamically scheduled and the resource requirements of hiding multiprocessor read latencies even with processors that are dynamically scheduled, especially as latencies become larger. In these situations, other methods like precommunication and multithreading might be more successful at hiding read latency and other forms of latency and may be used in conjunction with proceeding past memory operations in the same thread.

11.6 PRECOMMUNICATION IN A SHARED ADDRESS SPACE

Precommunication support, especially prefetching, has also been widely adopted in commercial microprocessors, and its importance is likely to increase in the future. To understand the techniques for precommunication, let us first consider a shared address space with no caching of shared data, whereby all data accesses go to the relevant main memory. After the introduction of some basic concepts, we examine prefetching in a cache-coherent shared address space, including performance benefits and implementation issues.

11.6.1 Shared Address Space without Caching of Shared Data

In a shared address space without caching of shared data, receiver-initiated communication is triggered by reads of nonlocally allocated data, and sender-initiated communication is triggered by writes to nonlocally allocated data. In the baseline communication structure of our example code (Figure 11.1), the communication is sender initiated if we assume that the array *A* is allocated in the local memory of process P_B, not P_A. As with the sends in the message-passing case, the most precommunication we can do is to perform all the writes to *A* before we compute any of the `f(B[])` by splitting into two loops (see the first column of Figure 11.19). Making the writes nonblocking allows some of the write latency to be overlapped with the `f(B[])` computations; however, this would have happened anyway if writes were made nonblocking and left where they were. The more important effect of the precommunication is to have the writes on P_A complete earlier, hence allowing the reader P_B to emerge from its while loop more quickly.

If the array *A* is allocated in the local memory of P_A, the communication is receiver initiated. The writes by the producer P_A are now local, and the reads by the consumer P_B are remote. Precommunication in this case means *prefetching* the elements of *A* before they are actually needed, just as we issued `a_receive`s before they were needed in the message-passing case. The difference is that the prefetch is not just posted locally, like the receive, but rather causes data transfer across the network: a prefetch request is sent across the network to the remote node (P_A) where the communication assist responds to the request by actually transferring the data back. In the meantime, P_B proceeds with other work. There are many ways to implement prefetching, as we shall see. One is to issue a special *prefetch* instruction and build a software pipeline as in the message-passing case. The shared address space code with prefetching is shown in Figure 11.19. The software pipeline has a prologue that issues a prefetch for the first iteration, a steady-state period of $n-1$ iterations in which a prefetch is issued for the next iteration and the current iteration is executed, and an epilogue consisting of the work for the last iteration. Note that a prefetch instruction does not replace the actual read of the data item (the load instruction), which happens in its original place in the program. Further, the prefetch instruction itself must be nonblocking (must not stall the processor) if it is to achieve its goal of hiding latency through overlap.

Since shared data is not cached in this case, the prefetched data is brought into a special hardware structure called a prefetch buffer. When the word is actually loaded into a register in the next iteration, it is read from the head of the prefetch buffer rather than from memory. If the latency to hide were much larger than the time to compute a single loop iteration, we would prefetch several iterations ahead and the prefetch buffer would potentially hold several words at a time. The CRAY T3D multiprocessor provides such a prefetch buffer and ensures that data becomes available in the buffer in the order that the prefetches issue, so the processor can read from it in the same order. The CRAY T3E uses a set of external registers as a prefetch buffer.

Even if data cannot be prefetched early enough to have arrived by the time the actual reference is made, prefetching is beneficial. If the actual reference finds that the address it is accessing has an outstanding prefetch associated with it, then it can simply wait for the remaining time until the prefetched data returns, thus hiding part of the latency. In addition, depending on the number of prefetches allowed to be outstanding at a time, prefetches can be issued back to back to overlap their laten-

P_A	P_B

for i←0 *to* n-1 *do*
  compute A[i];
  write A[i];
end for
flag ← 1;
for i←0 *to* n-1 *do*
  compute f(B[i]);
	while flag = 0 {};
	prefetch(A[0]);
	for i←0 *to* n-2 *do*
	  prefetch (A[i+1]);
	  read A[i] from prefetch_buffer;
	  use A[i];
	  compute g(C[i]);
	end for
	read A[n-1] from prefetch_buffer;
	use A[n-1];
	compute g(C[n-1])

FIGURE 11.19 Prefetching in the shared address space example. The example assumes that shared data is not cached, so prefetched data is read from the prefetch buffer rather than the cache.

cies. This provides pipelined data movement, although the pipeline rate may be limited by the overhead of issuing prefetches.

11.6.2 Cache-Coherent Shared Address Space

Precommunication is much more interesting in a cache-coherent shared address space since shared nonlocal data may be precommunicated directly into a processor's cache rather than a special buffer and since precommunication interacts with the cache coherence protocol. We therefore discuss the techniques in more detail in this context.

Consider an invalidation-based coherence protocol. A read miss fetches the data from wherever it is. A write that generates a read exclusive fetches both data and ownership (by informing the home, perhaps invalidating other caches, and receiving acknowledgments), and a write that generates an upgrade fetches only ownership. All of these "fetches" have latency associated with them, so all are candidates for prefetching. We can prefetch data or ownership or both.

Update-based coherence protocols generate sender-initiated communication, and like other sender-initiated communication techniques they provide a form of precommunication from the viewpoint of the destinations of the updates. Although update protocols are not very prevalent, techniques to selectively update copies can be used for sender-initiated precommunication even with an underlying invalidation-based protocol. One possibility is to selectively insert software instructions that generate updates; another is to use hybrid update-invalidate methods. Some of these techniques are discussed later in this section.

Prefetching Concepts

Two broad categories of prefetching are applicable to multiprocessors and uniprocessors: hardware-controlled and software-controlled prefetching. In hardware-controlled prefetching, no special instructions are added to the code; rather, special hardware is used to predict future accesses from observed behavior and to prefetch data based on these predictions. In software-controlled prefetching, the decisions of what and when to prefetch are made by the programmer or compiler (hopefully the compiler!) by analyzing the code, and appropriate prefetch instructions are inserted in the code. Trade-offs between hardware- and software-controlled prefetching are discussed later in this section. Prefetching can also be combined with block data transfer in *block prefetch* (receiver-initiated prefetch of a large block of data) and *block put* (sender-initiated) techniques.

In a multiprocessor, a key issue that dictates how early a prefetch can be issued in both software- and hardware-controlled prefetching is whether prefetches are binding or nonbinding. A *binding* prefetch means that the value of the prefetched data is bound at the time of the prefetch; that is, when the process later reads the variable through a regular read (load instruction), it will see the value that the variable had when it was prefetched even if the value has been modified by another processor and the new value has become visible to the reader's cache in between the prefetch and the actual read. The prefetch we discussed in the non-cache-coherent case (prefetching into a prefetch buffer, see Figure 11.19) is typically a binding prefetch, as is prefetching directly into processor registers. A *nonbinding* prefetch means that the value brought by a prefetch instruction remains subject to modification or invalidation until the actual operation that needs the data is executed, as discussed in Section 11.5.2. For example, in a cache-coherent system with nonbinding prefetch, the prefetched data is brought into the cache rather than into a register or prefetch buffer (neither of which is typically under control of the coherence protocol), and a modification by another processor that occurs between the time of the prefetch and the time of the use will update or invalidate the prefetched block according to the protocol. This means that nonbinding prefetches can be issued at any time without affecting the semantics of a parallel program or the results it may produce. Binding prefetches, on the other hand, affect program semantics, so we have to be careful about issuing them too early. For example, if processes increment a shared counter in a critical section, it is unsafe to issue a binding prefetch for the counter before (outside) the critical section since another process may obtain the lock and modify the counter between the prefetch and the lock acquisition; however, issuing a nonbinding prefetch before the critical section is safe. Since nonbinding prefetches can be generated as early as desired, they have performance advantages as well.

The other important issues concern determining what data to prefetch (*analysis*) and when to initiate prefetches (*scheduling*). Prefetching a given reference is considered *possible* only if the address of the reference can be determined ahead of time. For example, if the address can be computed only just before the word is referenced, then it may not be possible to prefetch. This is an important consideration for applications with irregular and dynamic data structures implemented using pointers, such as linked lists and trees.

The *coverage* of a prefetching technique is the percentage of the original cache misses (without any prefetching) that the technique is able to prefetch earlier than just before the actual reference. Achieving high coverage is not the only goal, however. We should not issue prefetches for data that will not be accessed by the processor or for data that is already in the cache that is the target of a prefetch. These prefetches will consume overhead and precious cache access bandwidth, interfering with regular accesses without doing anything useful. More is not necessarily better for prefetching. These are called *unnecessary* prefetches. Avoiding them requires that we analyze the data locality in the application's access patterns and how it interacts with the cache size and organization so that prefetches are issued only for data that is not likely to be present in the cache.

Finally, timing and luck play important roles in prefetching. A prefetch may be possible and not unnecessary, but it may be initiated too late to hide most of the latency from the actual reference. Or it may be initiated too early, so it arrives in the cache but is then either replaced or invalidated before the actual reference. Thus, a prefetch should be *effective*: early enough to hide the latency and late enough so the chances of replacement or invalidation are small.

The goal of prefetching analysis is to maximize coverage while minimizing unnecessary prefetches, and the goal of scheduling is to maximize effectiveness. Let us now consider hardware-controlled and software-controlled prefetching in some detail and see how successfully they address these important aspects.

Hardware-Controlled Prefetching

The goal in hardware-controlled prefetching is to provide hardware that can detect patterns in data accesses at run time. Hardware-controlled prefetching assumes that accesses in the near future will follow past patterns. Under this assumption, the cache blocks containing this data can be prefetched and brought into the processor cache so the later accesses may hit in the cache. The following discussion assumes nonbinding prefetches.

Both analysis and scheduling are the responsibility of hardware, with no special software support, and both are performed dynamically as the program executes. Analysis and scheduling are very closely coupled since the prefetch for a cache block is initiated as soon as it is determined that the block should be prefetched: it is difficult for hardware to make separate decisions about these issues.

The hardware should be simple and inexpensive, and it should not be in the critical path of the processor cycle time.

Many simple hardware prefetching schemes have been proposed. At the most basic level, the use of long cache blocks itself is a form of hardware prefetching, exploited well by programs with good spatial locality. No analysis is used to restrict unnecessary prefetches, the coverage depends on the degree of spatial locality in the program, and the effectiveness depends on how much time elapses between when the processor accesses the first word and when it accesses the other words on the block. For example, if a process simply traverses a large array with unit stride, the coverage of the prefetching with long cache blocks will be quite good (75% for a cache block of four words) and there will be no unnecessary prefetches—but the effectiveness is not likely to be great since the prefetches are issued too late. Extending the idea of long cache blocks are *one-block lookahead* (OBL) schemes, in which a reference to cache block i may trigger a prefetch of block $i + 1$. Several variants for analysis and scheduling may be used in this technique; for example, block $i + 1$ can be prefetched whenever a reference to block i is detected, or only if a cache miss to i is detected, or when i is referenced for the first time after it is prefetched. Extensions may include prefetching several blocks ahead (e.g., blocks $i + 1$, $i + 2$, and $i + 3$) instead of just one (Dahlgren, Dubois, and Stenstrom 1995), an adaptation of the idea of *stream buffers* in uniprocessors where several subsequent blocks are prefetched into a separate buffer, rather than the cache, when a miss occurs (Jouppi 1990). Such techniques are useful when accesses are mostly unit stride.

A simple way to detect and prefetch accesses with nonunit or large stride is to keep the address of the previously accessed data item for a given instruction (i.e, for a given program counter value) in a history table indexed by program counter (PC). When the same instruction is issued again (e.g., in the next iteration of a loop), if the PC is found in the table, the stride is computed as the difference between the current data address and the one in the history table for that instruction or PC. A prefetch is issued for the data address computed as the current data address plus the stride (Fu and Patel 1991; Fu, Patel, and Janssens 1992). The history table, managed much like a branch history table, essentially detects regular strides in data accesses by an instruction and predicts that future accesses by that instruction will follow the same stride. This scheme is likely to work well when the stride is constant; however, most other prefetching schemes that we shall discuss, hardware or software, are likely to work well in this case too.

While the schemes so far find ways to detect simple regular patterns, they do not guard against unnecessary prefetches when references do not follow these patterns. For example, if the same stride is not maintained between three successive accesses by the same instruction, then the previous scheme will prefetch useless data. The traffic generated by these unnecessary prefetches can be detrimental to performance by competing for resources with useful regular accesses.

In more sophisticated hardware prefetching schemes, the history table stores not only the data address accessed the last time by an instruction but also the stride between the previous two addresses accessed by it (Baer and Chen 1991; Chen and Baer 1992). If the current data address accessed by that instruction is separated from the previous address by the same stride, then a regular stride pattern is detected and a prefetch may be issued. If not, then a break in the pattern is detected and a prefetch is not issued, thus reducing unnecessary prefetches. In addition to the address and stride, the table entry also contains some state bits that keep track of whether the accesses by this instruction have recently been in a regular stride pattern, have been in an irregular pattern, or appear to be transitioning into or out of a regular stride pattern. A set of simple rules is used to determine, based on the stride match and the current state, whether to potentially issue a prefetch or not. If the result is to potentially prefetch, the cache is looked up to see if the block is already there, and if not the prefetch is issued.

While this scheme improves the analysis, it does not yet do a great job of scheduling prefetches. In particular, in a loop it will prefetch only one loop iteration ahead. If the amount of work to do in a loop iteration is small compared to the latency that needs to be hidden, this will not be sufficient to tolerate the latency. The goal of scheduling is to achieve just-in-time prefetching, that is, to have a prefetch issued about l cycles before the instruction that needs the data, where l is the latency we want to hide, so that prefetched data arrives just before the actual instruction that needs it is executed and the prefetch is likely to be effective. This means that the prefetch should be issued $\lceil l/b \rceil$ loop iterations ahead of the instruction that needs the data, where b is the predicted execution time of an iteration of the loop body.

One way to implement such scheduling in hardware is to use a *lookahead program counter* (LA-PC) that tries to remain l cycles ahead of the actual current PC. The LA-PC is used to access the history table and generate prefetches instead of (but in conjunction with) the actual PC. The LA-PC starts out a single instruction ahead of the regular PC but is incremented every cycle even when the processor (and PC) stalls on a cache miss, thus letting it get ahead of the PC. The LA-PC also looks up the branch history table, just like the PC, so the branch prediction mechanism can be used to modify it when necessary and to try to keep it on the right track. When a mispredicted branch for the LA-PC is detected, the LA-PC is set back to being equal to PC + 1. A limit register controls how far the LA-PC can get ahead of the PC. The LA-PC stalls when this limit is exceeded or when the buffer of outstanding references is full (i.e., it cannot issue any prefetches).

Both the LA-PC and the PC look up the prefetch history table every cycle (of course, they are likely to access different entries). The lookup by the PC updates the "previous address" and the state fields for the entry that it hits, in accordance with the rules, but does not generate prefetches. A new "times" field is added to each history table entry, which keeps track of the number of iterations (encounters of that instruction) that the LA-PC is ahead of the PC. The lookup by the LA-PC increments this field for the entry that it hits (if any) and generates an address for potential prefetching according to the rules. The address generated is the times field multiplied by the stride stored in the entry, plus the previous address field. The times field is decremented when the PC encounters that instruction in its lookup of the prefetch history table. More details can be found in (Chen and Baer 1992).

Prefetches in these hardware schemes are treated as hints since they are nonbinding, so actual cache misses get priority over them in the extended hierarchy. If a prefetch raises an exception (for example, a page fault or other violation), the prefetch is simply dropped rather than handling the exception. More elaborate hardware-controlled prefetching schemes have been proposed to try to prefetch references with irregular stride (Zhang and Torrellas 1995). However, even the simpler techniques have not found their way into microprocessors for multiprocessors. Instead, the trend is to provide prefetch instructions for use by software-controlled prefetching schemes. Let us examine software-controlled prefetching before we discuss its relative advantages and disadvantages with respect to hardware-controlled schemes.

Software-Controlled Prefetching

In software-controlled prefetching, the analysis of what to prefetch and the scheduling of when to issue prefetches are typically done statically, by software. The compiler (or programmer) inserts special prefetch instructions into the code at points that it deems appropriate. As we saw in Figure 11.19, this may require restructuring the loops in the program to some extent as well. The hardware support needed is the provision of these nonblocking instructions, a cache that allows multiple outstanding accesses, and some mechanism for keeping track of outstanding accesses. The latter two mechanisms are in fact required for all forms of latency tolerance in a system based on reads and writes.

Let us first consider software-controlled prefetching from the viewpoint of a processor trying to hide latency in its reference stream without complications due to interactions with other processors. This problem is equivalent to prefetching in uniprocessors, except with a wider range of latencies. Then we discuss the complications introduced by multiprocessing.

Prefetching with a Single Processor

Consider a simple loop, such as our example from Figure 11.1. A naive approach would be to always issue a prefetch instruction one iteration ahead on array references within loops. This would lead to a software pipeline like the one in Figure 11.19, with two differences: the data is brought into the cache rather than into a prefetch buffer, and the later load of the data will be from the address of the data rather than from the prefetch buffer (i.e., `read(A[i])` and `use(A[i])`). This can easily be extended to approximate just-in-time prefetching by issuing prefetches multiple iterations ahead as discussed earlier (see Exercise 11.15).

To minimize unnecessary prefetches, it is important to analyze and predict the temporal and spatial locality in the program as well as the addresses of future references. For example, blocked matrix factorization reuses the data in the current block many times in the cache, so it does not make sense to prefetch all references to the block. In the software case, unnecessary prefetches have an additional disadvantage beyond cache lookup bandwidth and potentially useless traffic: they introduce useless prefetch instructions in the code, which add execution overhead. The prefetch instructions are often placed within conditional expressions, and with irregular data structures extra instructions are often needed to compute the address to be prefetched, both of which further increase the instruction overhead.

How easy is it to identify which references to prefetch in software? In particular, can a compiler do it, or must it be left to the programmer? The answer depends on the program's reference patterns. References are most predictable when they traverse an array in some regular way. For example, a simple case to predict is when the elements of an array are referenced inside a loop nest, and the array index is an affine function of the loop indices in the loop nest (i.e., a linear combination of loop index values). The following code shows an example:

```
for i ← 1 to n
  for j ← 1 to n
    sum = sum + A[3i+5j+7];
  end for
end for
```

Given the amount of latency we wish to hide, we can try to issue the prefetch that many iterations ahead in the relevant loop. The amount of array data accessed and the spatial locality in the traversal are easy to predict in this example, which makes locality analysis for minimizing unnecessary prefetches easy. The major complication in analyzing data locality is predicting cache misses due to mapping conflicts.

A more difficult class of references to analyze is indirect array references; for example,

```
for i ← 1 to n
  sum = sum + A[index[i]];
end for
```

Whereas we can easily predict the values of `i` and hence the elements of the `index` array that will be accessed, we cannot predict the value in `index[i]` and hence the elements of `A` that we shall access. To predict the accesses to `A` we must first prefetch `index [i]` well enough in advance and then use the prefetched value to determine the element of array `A` to prefetch. The latter requires additional instructions to be inserted. For scheduling, if the number of iterations that we would normally prefetch ahead is k, we should prefetch `index [i]` $2k$ iterations ahead so it returns k iterations before we need `A[index [i]]`, at which point we can use the value of `index[i]` to prefetch `A[index [i]]`. Analyzing temporal and spatial locality in these cases is more difficult than predicting addresses. It is impossible to perform accurate analysis statically since we do not know ahead of time what the spatial relationships among the references to `A` are nor even how many different locations of `A` will be accessed (different entries in the index array may have the same value). Our choices are therefore to prefetch all references to `A[index [i]]`, to prefetch none at all, to obtain profile information about access patterns gathered at run time and use it to make decisions, or to use higher-level programmer knowledge.

Compiler technology has advanced to the point where it can handle the preceding types of array references in loops quite well, within the constraints described. Locality analysis (Wolf and Lam 1991) is used first to predict when array references are expected to miss in a given cache (typically the first-level cache). This results in a prefetch predicate, which can be thought of as a conditional expression inside which a prefetch should be issued for a given iteration. Scheduling based on latency is then used to decide how many iterations ahead to issue the prefetches. Since the compiler may not be able to determine which level of the extended memory hierarchy the miss will be satisfied in, it may be conservative and assume the worst-case latency.

Predicting conflict misses is particularly difficult. Locality analysis, based on fully associative caches, may tell us that a block should still be in the cache so a prefetch should not be issued, but the block may have been replaced because of conflict misses and therefore would benefit from a prefetch. A possible approach is to assume that a small associativity cache of C bytes effectively behaves like a fully associative cache that is smaller by some factor, but this is not reliable. Multiprogramming also throws off the predictability of misses across process switches since one process might pollute the cache state of another, although the time scales are such that locality analysis often doesn't assume blocks to stay in the cache that long anyway. Despite these problems, limited experiments have shown potential for success with compiler-generated prefetching when most of the cache misses are to affine or indirect array references in loops (Mowry 1994). These include programs on regular grids or dense matrices as well as sparse matrix computations (in which indirect array references are used, but most of the data is often stored in a packed, dense form anyway for efficiency). These experiments are performed through simulation since real machines are only just beginning to provide the underlying hardware support needed for effective software-controlled prefetching.

Accesses that are truly difficult for a compiler to predict are those that involve pointers or linked data structures (such as linked lists and trees). Unlike array indexing, traversing these data structures requires dereferencing pointers along the way; the address contained in the pointer within a list or tree element is not known until that element is reached in the traversal, so it cannot be easily prefetched. Predicting locality for such data structures is also very difficult. Currently, prefetching in these cases must be done by the programmer, exploiting higher-level semantic knowledge of the program and its data structures, as shown in Example 11.3. Compiler analysis for prefetching pointer-based, linked data structures is the subject of research (Luk and Mowry 1996) and will be helped by progress in alias analysis for pointers. In general, limitations of a compiler in other areas (e.g., interprocedural analysis) may limit the effectiveness of its prefetching analysis.

EXAMPLE 11.3 Consider the tree traversal to compute the force on a particle in the Barnes-Hut application described in Chapter 3. The traversal is repeated for each particle assigned to the process, and consecutive particles reuse much of the tree data, which is likely to stay in the cache across particles. How should prefetches be inserted in this tree traversal code? Discuss some possibilities and their trade-offs.

Answer The traversal of the oct-tree proceeds in depth-first manner. However, if it is determined that a tree cell needs to be opened, then all its eight children will be examined as long they are present in the tree. Thus, we can insert prefetches for all the children of a cell as soon as we determine that the cell will be opened (or we can speculatively issue prefetches as soon as we touch a cell and are hence able to dereference the pointers to its children). Since we expect the working set to at least fit in the L_2 cache (which a compiler is highly unlikely to be able to determine), we should prefetch a cell only the first time that we access it (i.e., for the first particle that accesses it), not for subsequent particles. Cache conflicts may occur, which cause unpredictable misses, but there is likely little we can do about that statically. Note that we need to do some work to generate prefetches (determine if this is the first time we are visiting the cell, access and dereference the child pointers, etc.), so the overhead of a prefetch is likely to be several instructions. If the overhead is incurred a lot more often than successful prefetches are generated, it may overcome the benefits of prefetching. Another problem with this scheme is that we may not be prefetching early enough when memory latencies are high. Since we prefetch all the children at one time, in most cases the depth-first work done for the first child (or two) should be enough to hide the latency of the rest of the children, but this may not be the case. The only way to improve this is to speculatively prefetch multiple levels down the tree when we encounter a cell, dereferencing speculatively prefetched pointers to determine prefetch addresses, hoping that we will indeed touch all the cells we prefetch and they will still be in the cache when we reach them. Since prefetches are nonbinding, correctness is not violated. Other applications that use linked lists in unstructured ways may be even more difficult for a compiler or even a programmer to prefetch successfully. ■

Interactions with a Multiprocessor Coherence Protocol

Two additional issues we must consider when prefetching in parallel programs are prefetching communication misses and prefetching with ownership. Both arise from the fact that other processors might also be accessing and modifying the data that a process references.

In an invalidation-based cache-coherent multiprocessor, data may be removed from a processor's cache—and misses therefore incurred—not only because of replacements but also because of sharing. We should not prefetch data so early that it might be invalidated in the cache before it is used, and we should ideally recognize when data might have been invalidated so that we can prefetch it again before actually using it. Fortunately, nonbinding prefetching makes these performance issues rather than correctness issues.

It is difficult for a compiler to predict incoming invalidations and perform the necessary analysis because the communication in the application cannot be easily deduced from an explicitly parallel program in a shared address space. The one case where the compiler has a good chance is when the compiler itself parallelizes the program. But even then, dynamic task assignment and false sharing of data compromise the success of the analysis.

A programmer has the semantic information about interprocess communication, so it is easier for the programmer to insert and schedule prefetches as necessary in the presence of invalidations. The one kind of information that a compiler does have is that conveyed by explicit synchronization statements in the parallel program. Since synchronization usually implies that data is being shared (for example, in a "properly labeled" program, the modification of data by one process and its use by another process is separated by a labeled synchronization operation), the compiler analysis can assume that communication is taking place and that all the shared data in the cache has been invalidated whenever it sees a synchronization event. Of course, this is conservative and it may lead to unnecessary prefetches, especially when synchronization is frequent and little data is actually invalidated between synchronization events. It would be nice if a synchronization event conveyed some information about which data might be modified, or if this could be efficiently determined, but this is usually not the case (Wood et al. 1993).

As a second enhancement, since a processor often wants to fetch a cache block with exclusive ownership (or simply fetch ownership) in preparation for a write, it makes sense to prefetch in exclusive mode before a write. This can have two benefits

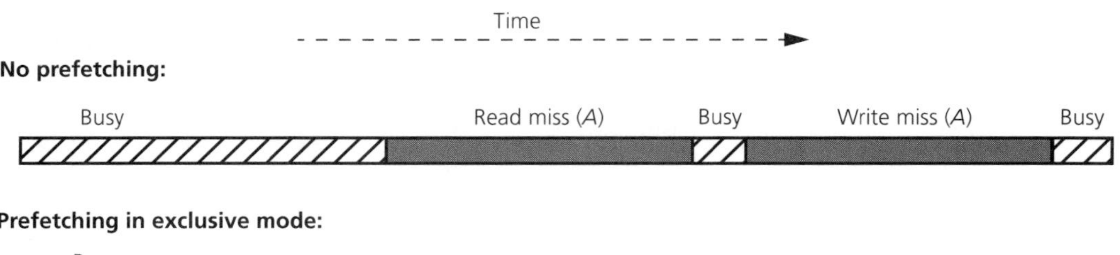

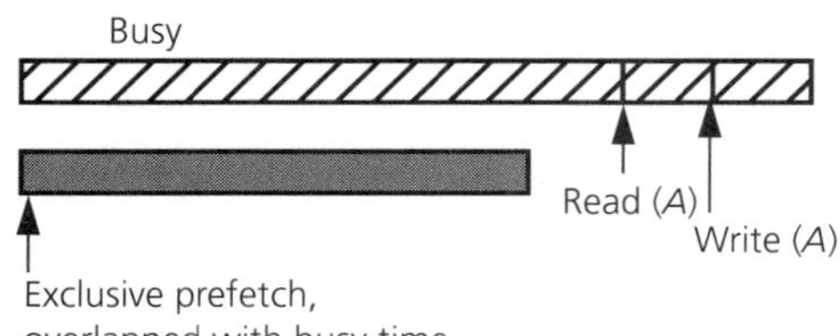

FIGURE 11.20 Benefits from prefetching with ownership. Suppose the latest copy of *A* is not available locally to begin with but is present in other caches and that a read and then a write are performed. Normal hardware cache coherence would fetch the corresponding block in shared state for the read and then communicate again to obtain ownership upon the write. With prefetching, if we recognize this read-write pattern, we can issue a single prefetch with exclusivity before the read itself and not have to incur any further communication at the write. By the time the write occurs, the block is already present in exclusive state. Prefetching in shared mode before the read hides the read latency but not the write latency since the write will still miss.

when used judiciously. First, it reduces the latency of the actual write operations that follow since the write does not have to invalidate other blocks and wait to obtain exclusive ownership (that was already done by the prefetch). Whether or not this has an impact on performance depends on whether write latency is already hidden by other methods such as by using a relaxed consistency model. The second advantage is in the common case where a process first reads a variable and then shortly thereafter writes it. A single prefetch with ownership even before the read in this case hides both read and write latency. It also halves the traffic, as seen in Figure 11.20, and hence improves the performance of other references as well by reducing contention and bandwidth needs. The quantitative benefits of prefetching in exclusive mode are discussed in (Mowry 1994).

Hardware-Controlled versus Software-Controlled Prefetching

Having seen how hardware-controlled and software-controlled prefetching work, let us consider their relative advantages. The most important advantages of hardware-controlled prefetching are: it does not require any software support from the programmer or compiler; it does not require recompiling code (which may be very important in practice when the source code is not available); and it does not incur instruction overhead or code expansion. On the other hand, its most obvious disadvantages are that it requires substantial hardware support and the prefetching algorithms are hardwired into the machine. However, there are many other trade-offs having to do with coverage, minimizing unnecessary prefetches, and maximizing effectiveness. Let us summarize these trade-offs, focusing on compiler-generated rather than programmer-generated prefetches in the software case.

- *Coverage.* The hardware and software schemes take very different approaches to analyzing what to prefetch. Software schemes can examine all the data accesses in the code but have only static information, whereas hardware observes a window of dynamic access patterns and predicts future references based on current patterns. Software schemes have greater potential for achieving coverage of complex access patterns but are limited by the analysis, whereas hardware may be limited by the cost of maintaining sophisticated history and the accuracy of necessary techniques like branch prediction. Unlike hardware, the compiler (or even programmer) cannot react to some forms of dynamic information, such as the occurrence of replacements due to unpredicted cache conflicts. Progress is being made in improving the coverage of both approaches in prefetching more types of access patterns (Zhang and Torrellas 1995; Luk and Mowry 1996), but the costs in the hardware case appear high. It is possible to use run-time feedback to improve software prefetching coverage, but there has not been much progress in this direction.
- *Reducing unnecessary prefetches.* Hardware prefetching is driven by increasing coverage and does not perform locality analysis to reduce unnecessary prefetches. It may therefore waste cache access bandwidth, and even interconnect bandwidth, and may replace useful data from the cache. Especially on a bus-based machine, wasting too much interconnect bandwidth on prefetches has at least the potential to saturate the bus and to reduce rather than enhance performance (Tullsen and Eggers 1993).
- *Maximizing effectiveness.* In software prefetching, scheduling is based on prediction. However, it is often difficult to predict how long a prefetch will take to complete, for example, where in the extended memory hierarchy it will be satisfied, and how much contention it will encounter. Hardware can in theory adapt its scheduling at run time since it lets the lookahead PC get only as far ahead as it needs to. However, hiding long latencies becomes difficult because of branch prediction, and every mispredicted branch causes the lookahead PC to be reset, leading to ineffective prefetches until it gets far enough ahead of the PC again. Thus, both the software and hardware schemes have potential problems with effectiveness or just-in-time prefetching.

Hardware prefetching is used in dynamically scheduled microprocessors to prefetch data for operations that are waiting in the reorder buffer but cannot yet be issued. However, in that case, hardware does not have to detect patterns and analyze what to prefetch. While this restricted form of hardware prefetching is becoming popular in microprocessors, so far the on-chip support needed for more general hardware analysis and prefetching of nonunit stride accesses has not been considered worthwhile. On the other hand, microprocessors are increasingly providing prefetching instructions to be used by software (even in uniprocessor systems). Compiler technology for prefetching is progressing as well. Usually, software prefetching brings data into the first-level cache rather than into a prefetch buffer. This and some other policy issues for prefetching are discussed in Exercise 11.19.

Sender-Initiated Precommunication

In addition to update-based protocols, support for explicit, software-controlled "update," "deliver," or "producer prefetch" instructions has been explored. An example is the "poststore" instruction in the KSR1 multiprocessor from Kendall Square Research, which pushes the contents of the whole cache block into the caches that currently contain a (presumably old) copy of the block. A reasonable place to insert these update instructions is at the last write to a shared cache block before a release synchronization operation since it is that data that is likely to be needed by consumers. The destination nodes of the updates are the sharers in the directory entry, just as with update protocols, under the usual assumption that past sharing patterns are a good predictor of future behavior. (Alternatively, the destinations may be specified in software by the instruction itself, or the data may be pushed only to the home main memory rather than other caches, i.e., a write through rather than an update, which hides some but not all of the latency from the destination processors.) These software-based update techniques have some of the same problems as hardware update protocols but to a lesser extent since not every write generates a bus transaction. As with update protocols, competitive hybrid schemes are also possible (Ohara 1996; Grahn and Stenstrom 1996).

Compared to prefetching, the software-controlled sender-initiated communication has the advantage that communication happens just when the data is produced. Also, it reduces traffic for repeating producer-consumer patterns compared to an invalidation-based scheme. However, it has several disadvantages. For one, the data may be communicated too early and may be replaced from the consumer's cache before use, particularly if it is placed in the primary cache. For another, this scheme precommunicates only communication (coherence) misses, not capacity or conflict misses. In addition, whereas a consumer knows what data it will reference and can issue prefetches for that data, a producer may deliver unnecessary data into processor caches if past sharing patterns are not a perfect predictor of future patterns or may even deliver the same data value multiple times. Further, a prefetch checks the cache and is dropped if the data is found in the cache, reducing unnecessary network traffic; the software update or deliver performs no such checks and can increase traffic and contention, though it reduces traffic when it is successful since it deposits the data in the right places without requiring multiple protocol transactions. Finally, the receiver no longer controls how many precommunicated messages it receives, so buffer overflow may occur. The wisdom gleaned from simulation results so far is that prefetching schemes work better than deliver or update schemes for most applications (Ohara 1996), though the two can complement each other if both are provided (Abdel-Shafi et al. 1997).

Both prefetch and software update schemes can be extended with the capability to transfer larger blocks of data (e.g., multiple cache blocks, a whole object, or an arbitrarily defined region of addresses) rather than a single cache block. These are called block prefetch and block put mechanisms (block put differs from the block transfer discussed in Section 11.5 in that the data is deposited in the cache and not in main memory). The issues here are similar to those encountered by prefetch and software update instructions, except for differences due to their size. For example, it may not be a good idea to prefetch or deliver a large block to the primary cache.

11.6.3 Performance Benefits

Performance results from prefetching so far have mostly been examined through simulation. To illustrate the potential, let us examine results from programmer-inserted software prefetches in some of the example applications used in this book (Woo, Singh, and Hennessy 1994). Programmer-inserted prefetches are used since they can be more aggressive than the best available compiler algorithms. We also consider results from state-of-the-art compiler algorithms.

Benefits with Single-Issue, Statically Scheduled Processors

Let us first look at how prefetching performs for the programs and platform presented in Section 11.4.3. To facilitate comparison with block transfer, this experiment focuses on prefetching only remote accesses (cache misses that cause communication). Figure 11.21(a) shows that for a program with predictable access patterns and very good spatial locality like FFT, prefetching remote data helps performance substantially. As with block transfer, the benefits are less for large cache blocks than for small ones since large cache blocks already achieve significant prefetching in themselves. Figure 11.21(b) directly compares the performance of block transfer with that of the prefetched version and shows that the results are quite similar for this program. Prefetching is able to deliver most of the benefits of even the very aggressive block transfer that we assume as long as enough prefetches are allowed to be outstanding at a time. Figure 11.22 shows the same results for the Ocean application. Like block transfer, prefetching helps little here since less time is spent in communication and since not all of the prefetched data is useful (due to poor spatial locality on communicated data along column-oriented partition boundaries).

Prefetching is often much more successful on local accesses. For example, in the iterative nearest-neighbor grid computations in the Ocean application, with barriers between sweeps it is difficult to issue prefetches for boundary elements from a neighbor partition far enough in advance: the new values are produced only a short while before they are needed. However, a process can very easily issue prefetches early enough for grid points within its assigned partition, which are not touched by any other process. Results from a state-of-the-art compiler algorithm show that the compiler can be quite successful in prefetching regular computations on dense arrays, where the access patterns are very predictable (Mowry 1994). These results, shown for two applications in Figure 11.23, include both local and remote accesses for 16-processor executions. Typically, the only problems in these cases are in the

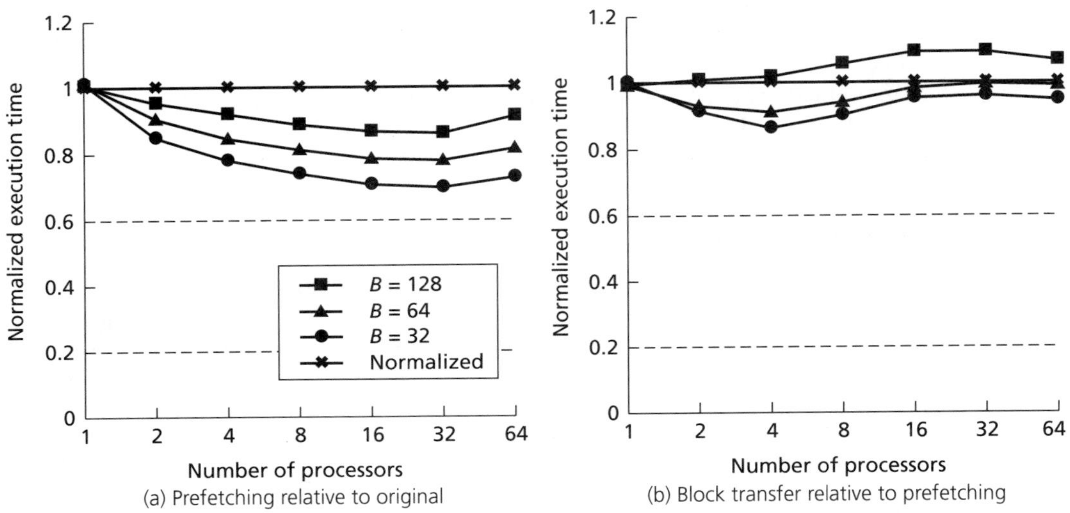

(a) Prefetching relative to original

(b) Block transfer relative to prefetching

FIGURE 11.21 Performance benefits of prefetching remote data in a Fast Fourier Transform. (a) shows the performance of the prefetched version relative to that of the original version. The graph can be interpreted just as described in Figure 11.13: each curve shows the execution time of the prefetched version relative to that of the nonprefetched version for the same cache block size (*B*) for each number of processors. (b) shows the performance of the version with block transfer (but no prefetching), described earlier, relative to the version with prefetching (but no block transfer) rather than relative to the original version. It enables us to compare the benefits from block transfer with those from prefetching remote data. The prefetching experiments allow a total of 16 simultaneous outstanding memory operations, including prefetches, from a processor.

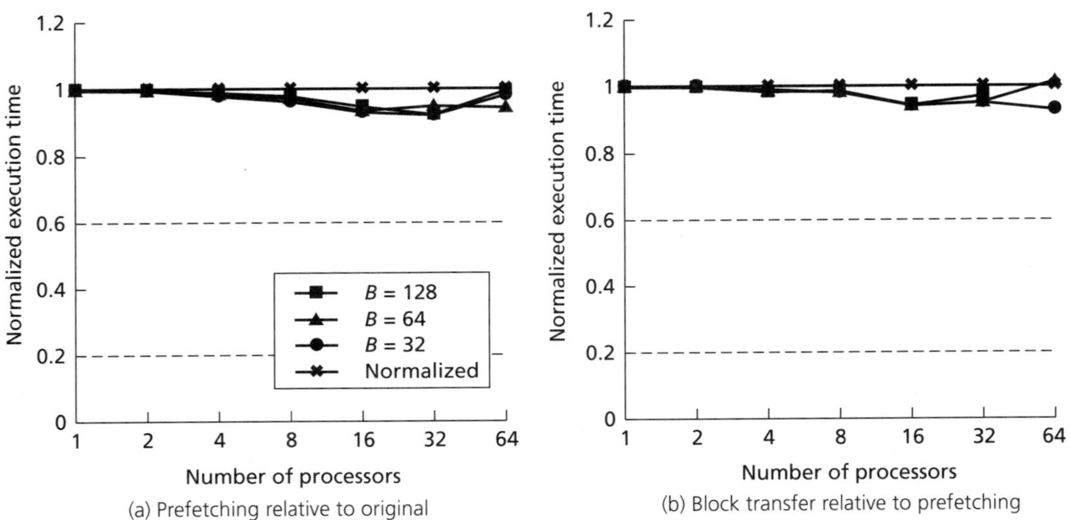

(a) Prefetching relative to original

(b) Block transfer relative to prefetching

FIGURE 11.22 Performance benefits of prefetching remote data in Ocean

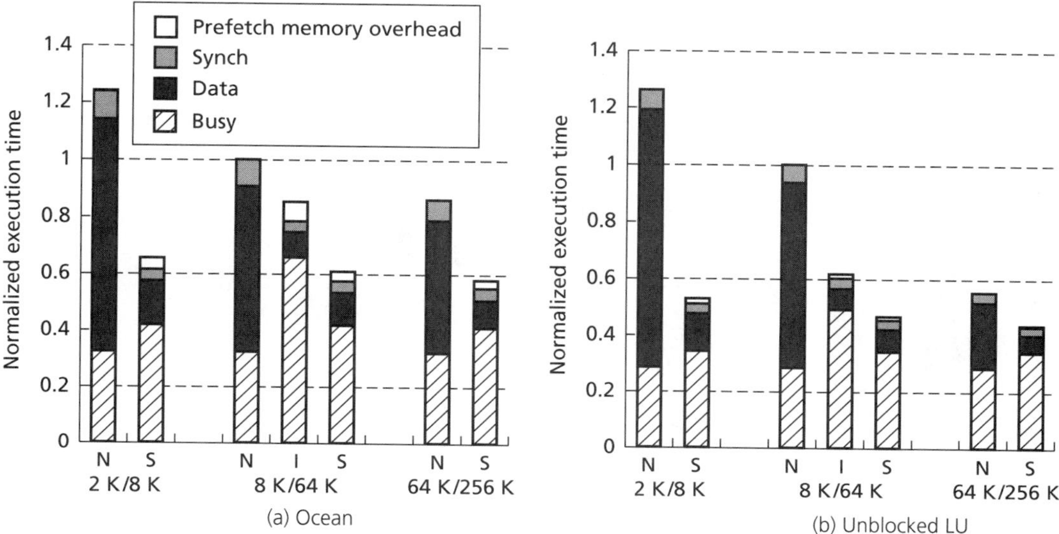

FIGURE 11.23 Performance benefits from compiler-generated prefetching. Results are shown for two parallel programs running on 16-processor simulated machines. The first is an older version of the Ocean simulation program, which partitions in chunks of complete rows and hence both has a higher inherent communication-to-computation ratio and does not have the problem of poor spatial locality at column-oriented boundaries. The second is an unblocked and, hence, lower-performance dense LU factorization. Both local and remote accesses are prefetched, unlike in Figures 11.21 and 11.22. There are three sets of bars for different combinations of L_1/L_2 cache sizes. The bars for each combination are the execution times for no prefetching (N) and selective prefetching (S). For the intermediate combination (8-K L_1 cache and 64-K L_2 cache), results are also shown for the case where prefetches are issued indiscriminately (I), without locality analysis. All execution times are normalized to the time without prefetching for the 8-K/64-K cache size combination. The processor, memory, and communication architecture parameters are chosen to approximate those of the relatively old Stanford DASH multiprocessor and can be found in (Mowry 1994). Latencies on modern systems are much larger relative to processor speed than on DASH. We can see that prefetching helps performance and that the choice of cache sizes makes a substantial difference to the impact of prefetching. The increase in "busy" time with prefetching (especially indiscriminate prefetching) is due to the fact that prefetch instruction overhead is included in busy time. Note that the benefits of prefetching would be much smaller for blocked LU factorization since there would be much less data wait time to hide; since blocked LU factorization is much more popular in practice than unblocked, this raises an important methodological point.

ability to prefetch far enough in advance (e.g., when the misses occur at the beginning of a loop nest or just after a synchronization point) and in the ability to analyze and predict conflict misses.

Some success has also been achieved on sparse array or matrix computations that use indirect addressing, but more irregular, pointer-based applications have not seen much success through compiler-generated prefetching. For example, the compiler algorithm is not successful for the tree traversals in the Barnes-Hut application for the reasons discussed in Example 11.3. Programmers can often do a better job in

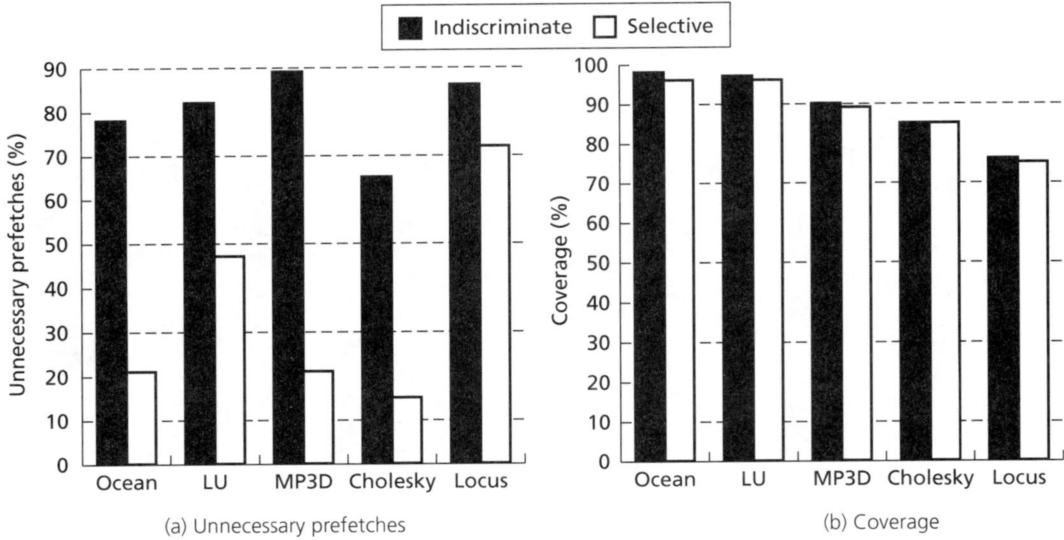

FIGURE 11.24 The benefits of selective prefetching through locality analysis. The fraction of prefetches that are unnecessary is reduced substantially while the coverage is not compromised. MP3D is an application for simulating rarefied hydrodynamics, Cholesky is a sparse matrix factorization kernel, and LocusRoute (abbreviated here as "Locus") is a wire-routing application from VLSI CAD. MP3D and Cholesky use indirect array accesses, while LocusRoute uses pointers to implement linked lists and therefore makes it more difficult to achieve good coverage.

these cases, as discussed earlier, and profile data gathered at run time may be useful to identify the data accesses that generate the most misses.

For the cases where prefetching is successful overall, locality analysis has been found to substantially reduce the number of prefetches issued without losing much in coverage and hence to perform much better than indiscriminate prefetching of all predictable accesses without locality analysis (see Figure 11.24). Prefetching with exclusive ownership is found to hide write latency substantially in an architecture in which the processor implements sequential consistency by stalling on writes, but it is less important when write latency is already being hidden through a relaxed memory consistency model. It does reduce traffic considerably in any case.

Finally, quantitative evaluations show that as long as caches are reasonably large, cache interference effects due to prefetching are negligible (Mowry 1994; Chen and Baer 1994). They also illustrate that by being more selective, software prefetching indeed tends to induce less unnecessary traffic and fewer cache conflict misses than hardware prefetching. However, the overhead due to extra instructions and associated address calculations can sometimes be substantial in software schemes, especially for applications with irregular access patterns.

Benefits with Multiple-Issue, Dynamically Scheduled Processors

The effectiveness of software-controlled prefetching has been measured (through simulation) on multiple-issue, dynamically scheduled processors (Luk and Mowry 1996; Bennett and Flynn 1996a, 1996b) and compared with its effectiveness on simple, statically scheduled processors (Ranganathan et al. 1997). Despite the latency tolerance already provided by dynamically scheduled processors (including hardware prefetching of operations in the reorder buffer), software-controlled prefetching is found to be effective in further reducing execution time. The percentage reduction in data wait time is somewhat smaller than in statically scheduled processors. However, since data wait time is a greater fraction of execution time (dynamically scheduled superscalar processors reduce instruction processing time much more effectively than they can reduce memory stall time), the percentage improvement in overall execution time due to prefetching is often comparable in the two cases.

Prefetching is less effective in reducing data wait time with dynamically scheduled superscalar processors for two reasons. The increased instruction processing rate means there is less computation time to overlap with prefetches and prefetches often end up being late. Also, dynamically scheduled processors tend to cause more contention for resources that are encountered by a memory operation even before it reaches the L_1 cache (e.g., outstanding request tables, functional units, tracking buffers, etc.). This is because they allow more memory operations to be outstanding at the same time and they do not block on read misses. Prefetching tends to further increase the contention for these resources, thus increasing the latency of non-prefetch accesses. Since this latency occurs before the L_1 cache, it is not hidden effectively by prefetching. Resource contention of this sort is also the reason that simply issuing prefetches earlier does not always solve the late prefetches problem: not only are early prefetches often wasted but they also tie up these processor resources for an even longer time since they tend to keep more prefetches outstanding at a time. The study in (Ranganathan et al. 1997) was unable to improve performance significantly by varying how early prefetches are issued. One advantage of dynamically scheduled superscalar processors compared to single-issue statically scheduled processors from the viewpoint of prefetching is that the instruction overhead of prefetching is usually much smaller since the prefetch instructions can occupy empty slots in the superscalar processor and are hence overlapped with other instructions.

Comparison with Relaxed Memory Consistency

Studies that compare prefetching with relaxed consistency models have found that the two techniques are quite complementary on statically scheduled processors with blocking reads (Gupta et al. 1991). Relaxed models tend to reduce write stall time but do not do much for read stall time, whereas prefetching helps to reduce read stall time. A substantial difference in performance remains between sequential and relaxed consistency even after adding prefetching to both, however, since prefetching is not able to hide write latency as effectively as relaxed consistency can. On dynamically scheduled processors with nonblocking reads, relaxed models are helpful in reducing read stall time as well as write stall time. Prefetching also helps reduce both, so it is interesting to examine whether starting from sequential consistency performance is helped more by prefetching only or by using only a relaxed consistency model. Even when all optimizations to improve the performance of sequential consistency are applied (like hardware prefetching, speculative reads, and write buffering), it is found to be more advantageous to use a relaxed model without software prefetching than to use a sequentially consistent model with software prefetching on dynamically scheduled processors (Ranganathan et al. 1997). The reason, again, is that although prefetching can help reduce read stall time somewhat better than relaxed consistency, it does not help to hide write latency nearly as well as can be done with relaxed consistency.

11.6.4 Summary

To summarize our discussion of precommunication in a cache-coherent shared address space, the most popular method to date is for microprocessors to provide support for prefetch instructions to be used by software-controlled prefetches, whether inserted by a compiler or a programmer. The same mechanisms are used for either uniprocessor or multiprocessor systems. Prefetching has been found to be quite successful in hiding latency in predictable applications with relatively regular data access patterns, and successful compiler algorithms have been developed for this case. On hardware-coherent, prefetching turns out to be quite successful in competing with block data transfer even in cases where the latter technique works well, even though prefetching involves the processor on every cache block access. (Block transfer is likely to be relatively more successful in systems in which the end-point overhead per communication is much larger, for example, in software implementations of a shared address space.) However, prefetching irregular computations, particularly those that use pointers heavily, has a long way to go. Programmer-inserted prefetching still tends to outperform compiler-generated prefetching since the programmer has knowledge of access patterns across computations that enable earlier or better scheduling of prefetches. Hardware prefetching is popular only in very limited forms, as in prefetching operations that are in the reorder buffer in dynamically scheduled processors. While hardware prefetching has important advantages in not requiring that programs be recompiled, it is not used for analysis and scheduling in general-purpose prefetching and its future in microprocessors is not clear. Support for sender-initiated precommunication instructions is also not as popular as support for prefetching. Some implementation issues for prefetching are discussed in Exercise 11.18.

11.7 MULTITHREADING IN A SHARED ADDRESS SPACE

Hardware-supported multithreading is perhaps the most versatile technique for hiding latency. It has the following conceptual advantages over other approaches:

- It requires no special software analysis or support (other than having more explicit threads or processes in the parallel program than the number of processors).
- Because it is invoked dynamically, it can handle unpredictable situations, like cache conflicts and communication misses, just as well as predictable ones.
- Whereas the previous techniques are targeted at hiding memory access latency, it can potentially tolerate any long-latency event just as easily, as long as the event can be detected at run time. This includes synchronization and instruction latency.
- Like prefetching, it does not change the memory consistency model since it does not reorder the actual memory operations within a thread.

Despite these potential advantages, multithreading is currently the least popular latency tolerating technique in commercial systems, for two reasons. First, it requires substantial changes to the microprocessor architecture. Second, its utility has so far not been adequately proven for uniprocessor or desktop systems, which constitute the vast majority of the marketplace. We shall see why in the course of this discussion. However, with latencies becoming increasingly longer relative to processor speeds, with more sophisticated microprocessors that already provide mechanisms that can be extended for multithreading, and with new multithreading techniques being developed to combine multithreading with instruction-level parallelism, this trend may change in the future.

Let us begin with the simple form of multithreading that we considered in the context of message passing, in which instructions are executed from one thread until that thread encounters a long-latency event, at which point it is switched out and another thread switched in. The state of a thread is called the *context* of that thread, so multithreading is also called *multiple-context processing*. The state, which must be saved and restored across context switches, includes the processor registers, the program counter, the stack pointer, and some per-process parts of the processor status word (e.g., the condition codes). The cost of a context switch may also involve flushing or squashing instructions already in the processor pipeline, as we shall see. If the latency that we are trying to tolerate is large enough, then we can save the context to memory in software when the thread is switched out and load it back when the thread is switched back in. This is how multithreading is typically orchestrated on message-passing machines, so a standard single-threaded microprocessor can be used in that case. In a hardware-supported shared address space, and even more so on a uniprocessor, the latencies we are trying to tolerate are not that high. The overhead of saving and restoring state in software may be too high to be worthwhile, and we are likely to require hardware support. Let us examine this relationship between switch overhead and latency a little more quantitatively.

Consider processor utilization, that is, the fraction of time that a processor spends executing useful instructions rather than being stalled or incurring overhead. The time a thread spends executing before it encounters a long-latency event is called the *busy* time. The total amount of time spent switching among threads is called the *switching* time. If no other thread is ready, the processor is stalled until one becomes ready or until the long-latency event it stalled on completes. The total amount of time spent stalled for any reason is called the *idle* time. The utilization of the processor can then be expressed as

$$Utilization = \frac{Busy}{Busy + Switching + Idle} \tag{11.2}$$

It is clearly important to keep the switching cost low. Even if we are able to tolerate all the latency through multithreading, thus removing idle time completely, utilization and hence performance are limited by the time spent context switching.

11.7.1 Techniques and Mechanisms

For current microprocessors that issue instructions from only a single thread in a given cycle, hardware-supported multithreading falls broadly into two categories, determined by the decision about *when to switch threads*. The approach assumed so far—in message passing, in multiprogramming to tolerate disk latency, and in this section—has been to let a thread run until it encounters a long-latency event (e.g., a cache miss, a synchronization event, or a high-latency instruction such as a divide) and then switch to another ready thread. This is called the *blocked* approach since a context switch happens only when a thread is blocked or stalled for some reason. Among shared address space systems, this approach is used in the MIT Alewife research prototype (Agarwal et al. 1995). The other major hardware-supported approach is to simply switch threads every processor cycle if possible, whether a long-latency event occurs or not, effectively interleaving the processor resource among a pool of ready threads at a single-cycle granularity. When a thread encounters a long-latency event, it is marked as not being ready and is not available to run until that event completes and the thread joins the ready pool again. This is called the *interleaved* approach. Let us examine both approaches in some detail, looking at their qualitative features and trade-offs as well as their quantitative evaluation and implementation details. After covering both approaches for processors that issue instructions from only a single thread in a cycle, we will examine the integration of multithreading with instruction-level (superscalar) parallelism, which has the potential to overcome the limitations of the traditional approaches (see Section 11.7.5).

Blocked Multithreading

The hardware support for blocked multithreading usually involves maintaining multiple hardware register files and program counters for use by different threads. An *active thread*, or a context, is a thread that is currently assigned one of these hardware copies. The number of active threads may be smaller than the number of *ready threads* (threads that are not stalled but are ready to run) and is limited by the number of hardware copies of the resources. Let us first take a high-level look at the relationship among the latency to be tolerated, the thread-switching overhead, and the

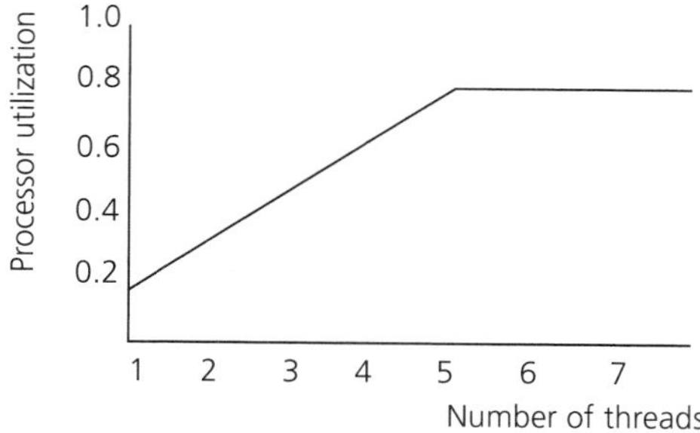

FIGURE 11.25 Processor utilization versus number of threads in blocked multithreading. The figure shows the two regimes of operation: the linear regime and saturation. It assumes $R = 40$, $L = 200$, and $C = 10$ cycles.

number of active threads by using the same type of analysis we used earlier for processor utilization (Culler 1994).

Suppose a processor provides support for N active threads at a time (N-way multithreading). And suppose that each thread operates by repeating the following sequence: execute useful instructions without stalling for R cycles (R, the busy time between stalls, is called the *run length*); encounter a high-latency event and switch to another thread. Now suppose that the latency we are trying to tolerate each time is L cycles and the overhead of a thread or context switch is C cycles. Given a fixed set of values for R, L, and C, a graph of processor utilization versus the number of threads N will look like that shown in Figure 11.25. There are two distinct regimes of operation: the utilization increases linearly with the number of threads up to a threshold, at which point it saturates. Let us see why.

Initially, increasing the number of threads allows more useful work to be done by other threads in the interval L that a thread is stalled, and latency continues to be hidden. Once N is sufficiently large, by the time we cycle through all the other threads—each with its run length of R cycles and switch cost of C cycles—and return to the original thread, we may have tolerated all L cycles of latency. Beyond this, there is no benefit to having more threads since the latency is already hidden. The value of N for which this saturation occurs is given by $(N - 1)\, R + NC = L$, or

$$N_{sat} = \frac{R + L}{R + C}$$

Beyond this point, the processor is always either busy executing a run from a thread or incurring switch overhead, so the utilization according to Equation 11.2 is

$$u_{sat} = \frac{R}{R + C} = \frac{1}{1 + \frac{C}{R}} \qquad (11.3)$$

If N is not large enough relative to L, then the runs of all $N - 1$ other threads will complete before the latency L passes. A processor therefore does useful work for $R + (N - 1) {*} R$ or NR cycles out of every $R + L$ and is either idle or switching for the rest of the time, leading to a utilization in this linear regime of

$$u_{lin} = \frac{NR}{R+L} = N \cdot \frac{1}{1+\frac{L}{R}} \tag{11.4}$$

This analysis is clearly simplistic since it uses a fixed average run length of R cycles and ignores the burstiness of misses and other long-latency events. Average-case analysis may lead us to assume that less threads suffice than are actually necessary to handle the bursty situations where latency tolerance may be most crucial. (A more accurate queuing model is given by [Culler 1994].) However, the analysis suffices to make the key points. Since the best utilization we can get with any number of threads, u_{sat}, decreases with increasing switch cost C, it is very important that we keep switch cost low. Switch cost also affects the types of latency that we can hide; for example, pipeline latencies or the latencies of misses that are satisfied in the second-level cache may be difficult to hide unless the switch cost is very low.

Switch cost can be kept low if we provide hardware support for several active threads, including separate register files, PCs, and so on. We can simply switch from one hardware state to another upon a context switch without saving and restoring state in software, which is the approach taken in most hardware multithreading proposals. Typically, a large register file is either statically divided into as many equally sized register frames as the active threads support (called a *segmented register file*), or the register file is dynamically managed as a cache that holds the registers of active contexts.

Although replicating context state in hardware can bring the cost of this aspect of switching among active threads down to a single cycle (it's like changing a pointer instead of copying a large data structure), there is another time cost for context switching that we have not discussed so far. This cost arises from the use of pipelining in instruction execution.

When a long-latency event occurs, we want to switch out the current thread. Suppose the long-latency event is a cache miss. The cache access is made only in the data fetch stage of the instruction pipeline, which is quite late in the pipeline. Typically, the hit/miss result is only known in the write-back stage, which is at the end of the pipeline. This means that by the time we know that a cache miss has occurred and the thread should be switched out, several other instructions from that thread (potentially k instructions, where k is the pipeline depth) have already been fetched and are in the pipeline (see Figure 11.26). We are faced with three possibilities: (1) allow these subsequent instructions to complete, but start to fetch instructions from the new thread at the same time; (2) allow the instructions to complete before starting to fetch instructions from the new thread; or (3) squash the instructions from the pipeline and then start fetching from the new thread.

The first case is complex to implement for two reasons. First, since instructions from different threads will be in the pipeline at the same time, the standard uniprocessor pipeline registers and dependence resolution mechanisms (interlocks) must be modified. Every instruction must be tagged with its context as it proceeds through the pipeline, and/or multiple sets of pipeline registers may be used to distinguish results from different contexts. In addition to the increase in area, the use of multiple pipeline registers at each pipeline stage means that the registers must be

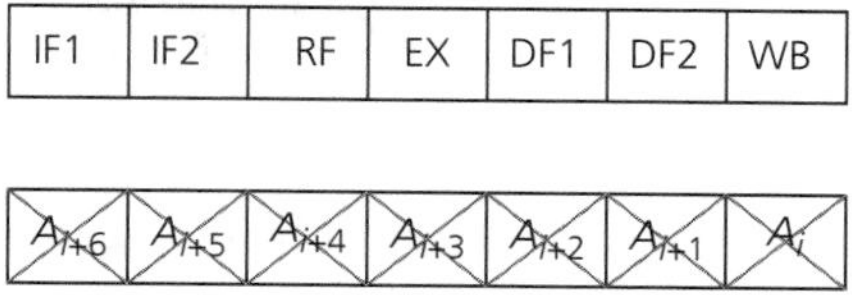

FIGURE 11.26 Impact of late miss detection in a pipeline. Thread A is the current thread running on the processor. A cache miss occurring on instruction A_i from this thread is only detected after the second data fetch stage (DF2) of the pipeline (i.e., in the write-back [WB] cycle of A_i's traversal through the pipeline). At this point, the following six instructions from thread A (A_{i+1} through A_{i+6}) are already in the different stages of the assumed seven-stage pipeline (two cycles of instruction fetch [IF], one cycle of register fetch [RF], one cycle of execute [EX], followed by two cycles of data fetch and the write back). If all the instructions are squashed when the miss is detected (the crossed-out slots in the lower drawing), we lose at least seven cycles of work.

multiplexed onto the latches for the next stage, which may increase the processor cycle time. Since part of the motivation for the blocked scheme is its design simplicity and its ability to use commodity processors with as little design effort and modification as possible, this may not be a very appropriate choice. The second problem with this choice is that the instructions already in the pipeline from the thread that incurred the cache miss may stall the pipeline because they may depend on the data returned by the miss.

The second choice avoids having instructions from multiple threads simultaneously in the pipeline but still must contend with stalls due to dependent instruction. The third choice avoids both problems and is simple to implement since the standard uniprocessor pipeline suffices and already has the ability to squash instructions. It is the favored choice for the blocked scheme, even though it does cause a number of cycles equal to the pipeline depth to be wasted on a switch.

How does a context switch get triggered in the blocked approach to hide the different kinds of latency? On a cache miss, the switch can be triggered by the detection of the miss in hardware. For synchronization latency, we can simply ensure that an explicit context switch instruction follows every synchronization event that is expected to incur latency (or even all synchronization events). Since the synchronization event may need to be satisfied by another thread that runs on the same processor, an explicit switch is necessary to avoid deadlock without waiting for timeouts. Long pipeline stalls can also be handled by inserting a switch instruction following a long-latency instruction such as a divide. Finally, short pipeline stalls like data hazards are likely to be very difficult to hide with the blocked approach.

To summarize, the blocked approach has a relatively low implementation cost (as we shall see in more detail later) and good single-thread performance (if only a single thread runs on a processor, there are no context switches and this scheme performs just like a standard uniprocessor would). The disadvantage is that the context switch overhead is high: approximately the depth of the pipeline, even when registers and other processor state do not have to be saved to or restored from memory.

This overhead limits the types of latencies that can be hidden as well as the effectiveness. Example 11.4, taken from (Laudon, Gupta, and Horowitz 1994), examines the performance impact.

EXAMPLE 11.4 Suppose four threads, *A, B, C,* and *D,* run on a processor. The threads have the following activity:

A issues two instructions, with the second instruction incurring a cache miss, then issues four more.

B issues one instruction, followed by a two-cycle pipeline dependence, followed by two more instructions, the last of which incurs a cache miss, followed by two more.

C issues four instructions, with the fourth instruction incurring a cache miss, followed by three more.

D issues six instructions, with the sixth instruction causing a cache miss, followed by one more.

Show how successive pipeline slots are either occupied by threads or wasted in a blocked multithreaded execution. Assume a simple four-stage pipeline, and hence a four-cycle context switch time, and a cache miss latency of 10 cycles (small numbers are used here for ease of illustration).

Answer The solution is shown in Figure 11.27, assuming that threads are chosen round-robin starting from thread *A*. We can see that while most of the memory latency is hidden, this is at the cost of context switch overhead. Assuming the pipeline is in steady state at the beginning of this sequence, we can count cycles starting from the time the first instruction reaches the WB stage (i.e., the first cycle shown for the multithreaded execution in the bottom part of the figure). Of the 51 cycles taken in the multithreaded execution, 21 are useful busy cycles, 2 are pipeline stalls, no idle cycles are stalled on memory, and 28 are context switch cycles, leading to a processor utilization of (21/51)*100, or only 41%, despite the extremely low cache miss penalty assumed. ■

Interleaved Multithreading

In the interleaved approach, in every processor clock cycle a new instruction is chosen from a different thread that is ready and active (i.e., assigned a hardware context) so that threads are switched every cycle rather than only on long-latency events. When a thread incurs a long-latency event, it is simply disabled or removed from the pool of ready threads until that event completes and the thread is labeled ready again (it is still active in that it retains its hardware state resources). Segmented or replicated register files are used here as well to avoid the need to save and restore registers. The key advantage of the interleaved scheme is that there is no context switch overhead. No event needs to be detected in order to trigger a context switch since this is done every cycle, and with enough threads, instructions from the same thread will not be in the pipeline at the same time, so there is no need to squash instructions. Thus, if there are enough concurrent threads, in the best case all latency will be hidden without any switch cost, and the processor will perform useful work in every cycle. An example of this ideal scenario is shown in Figure 11.28, where we assume six active threads for illustration. The typical disadvantage

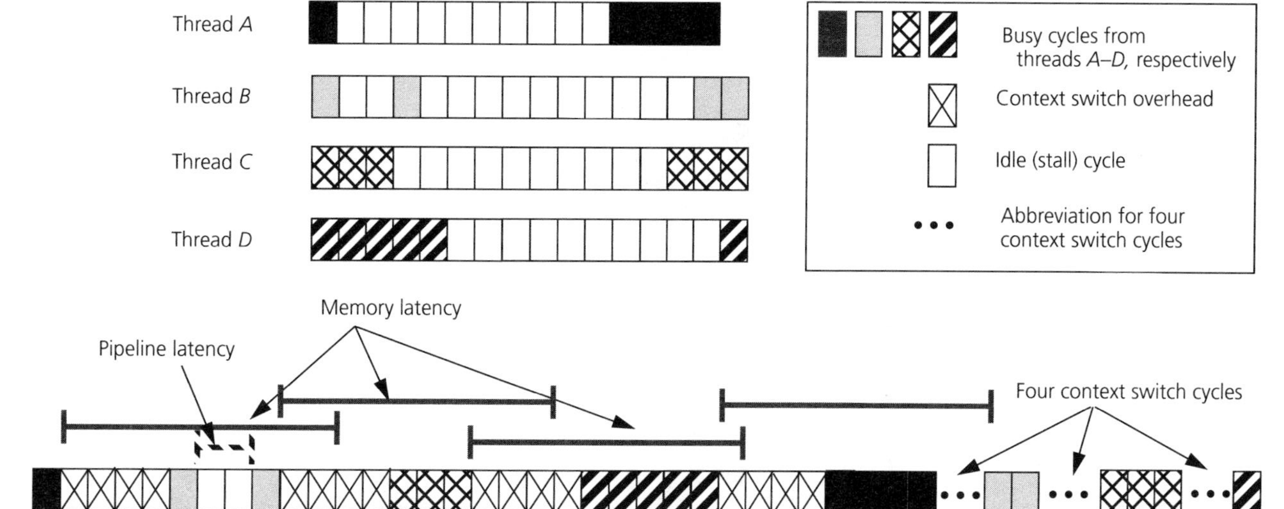

FIGURE 11.27 Latency tolerance in the blocked multithreading approach. The instruction shown in each slot is the one that is (or would be) in the last (WB) stage of the pipeline in that cycle. The top part of the figure shows how the four active threads on a processor would behave if each was the only thread running on the processor. For example, the first thread issues one instruction (whose WB cycle is the first cycle shown for thread *A* at the top of the figure), then issues a second one that incurs a cache miss (so the second cycle shown for thread *A*, which would have been the WB cycle of that instruction, is empty, as are several following), then issues some more. The bottom part shows how the processor switches among threads when they incur a cache miss. If the second instruction from thread *A* had not missed, it would have been in the WB state in the second cycle shown at the bottom. However, since it misses, that cycle is wasted and the three other instructions from thread *A* that have already been fetched into the four-deep pipeline have to be squashed in order to switch contexts. Note that the two-cycle pipeline latency does not generate a thread switch since the switch overhead of four cycles is larger than this latency.

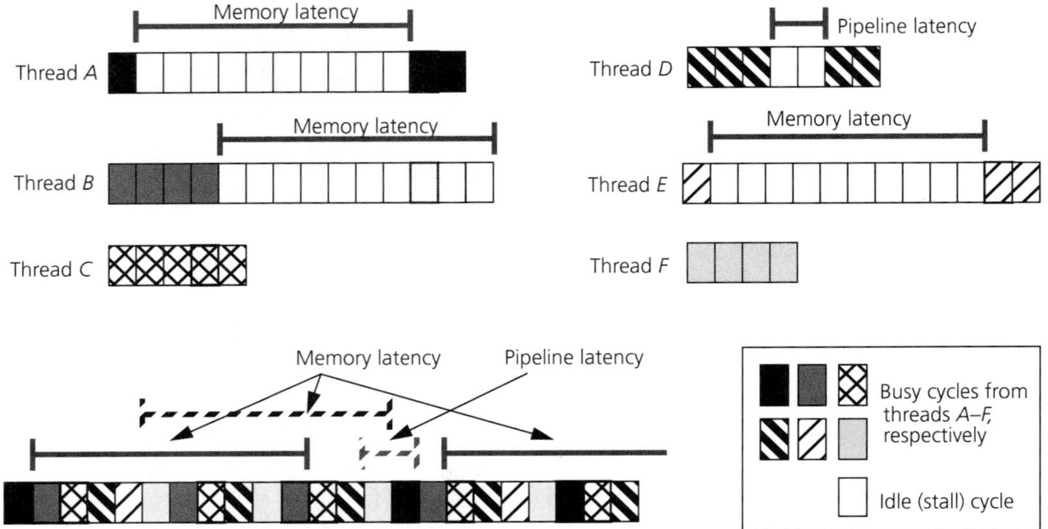

FIGURE 11.28 Latency tolerance in an ideal setting in the interleaved multithreading approach. The top part of the figure shows how the six active threads on a processor would behave if each was the only thread running on the processor. The bottom part shows how the processor switches among ready threads round-robin every cycle, leaving out those threads whose last instruction caused a stall that has not been satisfied yet. For example, thread *A* (solid) is not chosen again until its high-latency memory reference is satisfied and its turn comes again in the round-robin scheme.

of the interleaved approach is the higher hardware cost and complexity, though the specifics of this and other potential disadvantages depend on the particular type of interleaved approach used.

Interleaved schemes have undergone a fair amount of evolution. The early schemes severely restricted the number and type of instructions from a given thread that could be in the processor's pipeline at a time. This reduced the need for hardware interlocks and squashing instructions. It simplified processor design but had severe implications for the performance of single-threaded programs. More recent interleaved schemes greatly reduce these restrictions, as we shall see. In practice, another distinguishing feature among interleaved schemes is whether they use caches to reduce latency before trying to hide it. Machines built so far using the interleaved technique do not use caches at all but rely completely on latency tolerance through multithreading (Smith 1981; Alverson et al. 1990). More recent research proposals advocate the use of interleaved techniques and full pipeline interlocks with caches. (Laudon, Gupta, and Horowitz 1994). (Recall that blocked multithreaded systems use caching since they want to keep a thread running efficiently for as long as possible.) Let us look at some interesting stages in the development of interleaved schemes.

The Basic Interleaved Scheme

The first interleaved multithreading scheme was used in the Denelcor HEP (heterogeneous element processor) multiprocessor, developed between 1978 and 1985 (Smith 1981). Each processor had up to 128 active contexts, 64 user-level and 64 privileged, though only about 50 were actually available to the user. The large number of active contexts was needed even though the memory latency was small—about 20–40 cycles without contention—since the machine had no caches, and the memory latency was incurred on every memory reference. (Memory modules were all on the other side of a multistage interconnection network, but the processor had an additional direct connection to one of these modules that it could consider its "local" module). The 128 active contexts were supported by replicating the register file and other critical state 128 times. The pipeline on the HEP was 8 cycles deep. It supported interlocks among nonmemory instructions but did not allow more than one memory, branch, or divide operation to be in the pipeline at a given time. This meant that several threads had to be active on each processor at a time to utilize the pipeline effectively, even without any memory or other stalls. The absence of caches and the need to hide memory latency further increased the number of threads needed.This meant that the degree of explicit concurrency in a program had to be much larger than the number of processors, restricting the range of applications that would perform well..

Better Use of the Pipeline

The drawbacks of allowing only a single memory operation from a thread in the pipeline at a time are poor single-thread performance and the very large number of threads needed. Systems descended from the HEP have therefore alleviated this restriction. These systems include the Horizon (Kuehn and Smith 1988) and the more recent Tera (Alverson et al. 1990) multiprocessors. They still do not use caches to reduce latency, relying completely on latency tolerance for all memory references.

The first of these designs, the Horizon, was never actually built. Unlike HEP, the design allows multiple memory operations from a thread to be in the pipeline simultaneously. Yet it does not provide hardware pipeline interlocks even for nonmemory instructions. Rather, the analysis of dependences is left to the compiler. The idea is quite simple. Based on compiler analysis, every instruction is tagged with a three-bit "lookahead" field, which specifies the number of immediately following instructions in that thread that are sure to be independent of that instruction. Suppose the lookahead field for an instruction has the value five. This means that the next five instructions (memory or otherwise) are independent of the current instruction, and so can be in the pipeline with the current instruction even though there are no hardware interlocks to resolve dependences. Thus, if a long-latency event is encountered by that instruction, the thread does not immediately become unready but can issue five more instructions before it becomes unready. The maximum value of the lookahead field is seven: the machine will prohibit more than seven instructions from the current thread from entering the pipeline until the current one leaves. The small number of lookahead bits provided is influenced by the high premium on bits in the instruction word, by the ability of the compiler to utilize more lookahead, and particularly by the register pressure introduced by having three results per instruction times the number of lookahead instructions; more lookahead and greater register pressure might have been counterproductive for instruction scheduling.

Each "instruction" or cycle in Horizon can include up to three operations, one of which may be a memory operation. This means that 21 independent operations must be found to achieve the maximum lookahead, so sophisticated instruction scheduling by the compiler is clearly very important. For a typical program it is likely that a memory operation is issued every instruction or two. Since the maximum lookahead size is larger than the average distance between memory operations, it is very useful to allow multiple memory operations at a time in the pipeline. However, with the absence of caches every memory operation is a long-latency event, so a large number of ready threads is still needed to hide latency. In particular, single-thread performance—the performance of programs that are not multithreaded—is not helped much by a small amount of lookahead without caches and may still be quite limited.

The Tera architecture, built by Tera Computer Company, is the latest in the series of interleaved multithreaded architectures that do not use caches. Tera manages instruction dependences differently than Horizon and HEP, using a combination of the approaches. It provides hardware interlocks for instructions that do not access memory (like HEP) and Horizon-like lookahead for memory instructions.

The Tera machine separates operations into memory operations, arithmetic (or logical) operations, and control operations (e.g., branches). The unusual, custom-designed processor can issue three operations per instruction, much like Horizon, either one from each category or two arithmetic operations and one memory operation. Arithmetic and control operations go into one pipeline, which has hardware interlocks to allow multiple operations from the same thread. The pipeline is very deep, and there is a sizable minimum issue delay between consecutive instructions from a thread even if there are no dependences between them (about 16 cycles, with the pipeline being deeper than this). Thus, while more than one instruction from a thread can be in this pipeline at the same time, several interleaved threads (about 16) are required to hide even the instruction latency. Even without memory references, a single thread would at best complete one instruction every 16 cycles.

Memory operations pose a bigger problem. Although Tera uses very aggressive memory and network technology, the average latency of a memory reference without contention is about 70 cycles (a processor cycle is 2.8 ns). Tera therefore uses compiler-generated lookahead fields for memory operations, with a slightly different semantics than in Horizon. Every instruction that includes a memory operation (called a memory instruction) has a 3-bit lookahead field that tells how many immediately following instructions (memory or otherwise) are independent of that memory operation. Those following instructions do not have to be independent of one another, just of that memory operation. The thread can then issue that many instructions past the memory instruction before it has to render itself unready. This change in the use of lookahead makes it easier for the compiler to schedule instructions to have larger lookahead values and eases register pressure as well. Example 11.5 makes this concrete.

EXAMPLE 11.5 Suppose that the minimum issue delay between consecutive instructions from a thread in Tera is 16 and the average memory latency to hide is 70 cycles. What is the smallest number of threads that would be needed to hide latency completely in the best case, and how much lookahead would we need per memory instruction in this case?

Answer A minimum issue delay of 16 means that we need about 16 threads to keep the pipeline full without considering memory. Since memory operations are almost one per instruction in each thread, 16 threads can suffice to hide 70 cycles of memory latency if each thread issues about four independent instructions before it is made unready after a memory operation, that is, if a lookahead of about 4 can be sustained. Since latencies are in fact often larger than the average uncontended 70 cycles, a higher lookahead of at most 7 (3 bits) is provided. Even longer latencies would ask for larger lookahead values and sophisticated compilers (or more threads). So would a desire for fewer threads, though this would require reducing the minimum issue delay in the nonmemory pipeline as well. ■

While it may seem from the above that supporting a few tens of active threads should be enough, Tera, like HEP, supports 128 active threads in hardware. For this, it replicates all processor state (program counter, processor status word, and registers) 128 times, resulting in a total of 4,096 64-bit general registers (32 per thread) and 1,024 branch target registers (8 per thread) in the processor. The large number of threads is supported for several reasons and reflects the fundamental reliance of the machine on latency tolerance rather than reduction. First, some instructions may not have much lookahead at all, particularly read instructions; with three operations per instruction, a lookahead value of four instructions implies that there must be 12 independent operations between the read and the dependent use. Second, with most memory references going into the network, they may incur contention, in which case the latency to be tolerated may be much longer than 70 cycles. Third, the goal is not only to hide instruction and memory latency but also to tolerate synchronization wait time, which is caused by load imbalance or contention for critical resources and is usually much larger than data access latency.

The designers of the Tera system and its predecessors take a much more radical view to the redesign of the multiprocessor building block than advocated by the other latency-tolerating techniques. Unlike the approach we have followed so far—reduce latency first, then hide the rest—this approach does not pay much attention to reducing latency at all; the processor is redesigned with a primary focus on tolerating the latency of fine-grained accesses through interleaved multithreading. The argument is that the commodity microprocessor building block, with its reliance on caches and support for only one or a small number of hardware contexts, is inappropriate for general-purpose multiprocessing. Because of the high latencies and physically distributed memory in modern convergence architectures, the use of relatively "latency-intolerant" commodity microprocessors as the building block implies that much attention must be paid to data locality in both the caches and in data distribution at the main memory level. This makes the task of programming for performance too complicated, especially since compilers have not yet succeeded in managing locality automatically, in any but the simplest cases, and their potential is unclear. The Tera approach argues that the only way to make multiprocessing truly general purpose is to take this burden of locality management off software and place it on the architecture in the form of much greater latency tolerance support in the processor. If enough extra threads can be found and this technique is successful, the programmer's view of the machine can indeed be a PRAM (i.e., the cost of data access can be ignored), and the programmer can concentrate on concurrency rather than latency management. Of course, this approach sacrifices the tremendous leverage obtained by using commodity microprocessors and caches and faces head-on the challenge of the enormous effort that must be invested in the design of a nonstandard high-performance processor and the associated system software. It is also likely to result in poor single-thread performance, which means that even uniprocessor applications must be heavily multithreaded (or the system very heavily multiprogrammed) to achieve good performance.

Full Single-Thread Pipeline Support and Caching

While the interleaved approach described so far is very different than the blocked multithreading approach, both have several limitations. The Tera interleaved approach improves the basic HEP approach, but still requires many concurrent threads for good utilization. Not using caches implies that every memory operation is a long-latency operation. In addition to increasing the number of threads needed and the difficulty of hiding the latency, this means that every memory reference consumes memory and perhaps communication bandwidth, so the machine must provide tremendous bandwidth as well.

The blocked multithreading approach, on the other hand, requires less modification to a commodity microprocessor. It utilizes caches and does not switch threads on cache hits, thus providing good single-thread performance and requiring a smaller number of threads. However, it has high context switch overhead and cannot hide short latencies. The high switch overhead also makes it less suited to tolerating the not-so-large latencies on uniprocessors. It is therefore difficult to justify either of these schemes for uniprocessors and hence for the high-volume marketplace.

It is possible to use an interleaved approach with both caching and full single-thread pipeline support, thus requiring a smaller number of threads to hide memory latency, incurring lower context switch overhead than a blocked scheme and providing better support for uniprocessors. One such proposal has been studied in detail (Laudon, Gupta, and Horowitz 1994). From the HEP and Tera approaches, this interleaved approach takes the idea of maintaining a set of active threads, each with its own set of registers and status words, and having the processor select an instruction from one of the ready threads every cycle. The selection may be simple, such as round-robin among the ready threads. A thread that incurs a long-latency event makes itself unready until the event completes, as before. A key difference is that the pipeline is a standard microprocessor pipeline and has full bypassing and forwarding support so that instructions from the same thread can be issued in consecutive cycles (as in a blocked scheme); there is no minimum issue delay as in Tera. In the best case, a k-deep pipeline may contain k instructions from the same thread. In addition, the use of caches to reduce latency implies that most memory operations are not long-latency events; a given thread is therefore ready a larger fraction of the time, and the number of threads needed to hide latency is kept small. For example, if each thread incurs a cache miss every 30 cycles, and a miss takes 120 cycles to complete, then only five threads (the one that misses and four others) are needed to achieve full processor utilization.

The overhead in this interleaved scheme arises from the same source as in the blocked scheme. A cache miss, which renders a thread unready, is detected late in the pipeline; if there are only a few interleaved threads, then the thread that incurs the miss may have fetched other instructions into the pipeline by this time. Unlike in the Tera, where the compiler guarantees through lookahead that such subsequent instructions in the pipeline are independent of the memory instruction, here we must do something about these instructions. For the same reason as in the blocked scheme, the proposed approach chooses to squash these instructions, that is, to mark them as not being allowed to modify any processor state. The key difference with the blocked scheme is that, because instructions from other threads are interleaved cycle by cycle in the pipeline, not all instructions need to be squashed—only those from the thread that incurred the miss. The cost of making a thread unready is therefore typically much smaller than that of a context switch in the blocked scheme, where all instructions in the pipeline must be squashed. In fact, if enough ready and active threads are available, which requires a larger degree of hardware state replication than is advocated by this approach, other instructions from the thread that misses may not be in the pipeline at all, and no instructions will need to be squashed (as in the HEP/Tera approaches). The comparison with the blocked approach is shown in Figure 11.29.

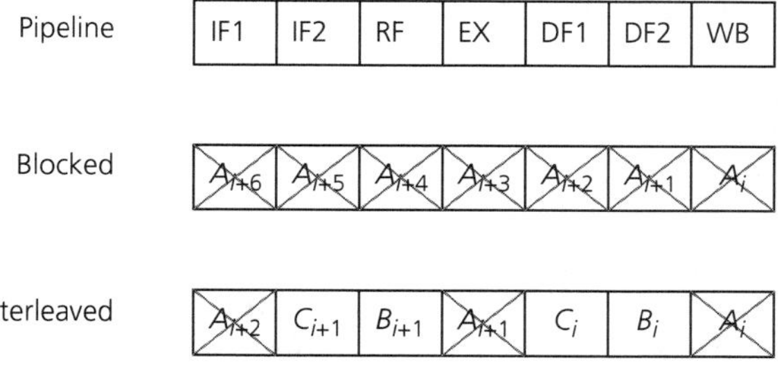

FIGURE 11.29 The cost of making a thread unready in the interleaved scheme with full single-thread support compared with the context switch cost in the blocked scheme. The figure first shows the assumed seven-stage pipeline, followed by the impact of late miss detection in the blocked scheme in which all instructions in the pipeline are from thread A and have to be squashed, followed by the situation for the interleaved scheme. In the interleaved scheme, instructions from three different threads are in the pipeline, and only those from thread A need to be squashed. The switch cost, or overhead incurred on a miss, is three cycles rather than seven in this case.

The result of the lower cost of making a thread unready is that shorter latencies, such as local memory access or long instruction latencies, can be tolerated more easily than in the blocked case, making this interleaved scheme more appropriate for multithreading on uniprocessors as well. Very short latencies that cannot be hidden by the blocked scheme, such as those of short pipeline hazards, are usually hidden naturally by the cycle-by-cycle interleaving of threads without even needing to make a thread unready. The effect of the differences on the simple four-thread, four-deep pipeline example used for the blocked scheme in Figure 11.27 is illustrated in Figure 11.30. In this simple example, assuming the pipeline is in steady state at the beginning of this sequence, the processor utilization is 21 cycles out of the 30 cycles taken in all, or 70% (compared to 21 out of 51 cycles or 41% for the blocked scheme example in Figure 11.27). While this example is contrived and uses unrealistic parameters for ease of graphical illustration, the fact remains that on modern superscalar processors that issue a memory operation in almost every cycle, the context switch overhead of switching on every cache miss in a blocked scheme may become quite expensive. The disadvantage of this scheme compared to the blocked scheme is greater implementation complexity.

The blocked scheme and this last interleaved scheme (henceforth called "the interleaved scheme") start with simple, commodity processors with full pipeline interlocks and caches and modify them to make them multithreaded. As stated earlier, even if they are used with superscalar processors, they only issue instructions from within a single thread in a given cycle. A more sophisticated multithreading approach exists for superscalar processors, but for simplicity let us first examine the performance and implementation issues for these two more directly comparable approaches.

11.7.2 Performance Benefits

Simulation studies have shown that both the blocked scheme and the interleaved scheme (with full pipeline interlocks and caching) can hide read and write latency quite effectively (Laudon, Gupta, and Horowitz 1994; Kurihara, Chaiken, and Agarwal 1991). The number of active contexts needed is found to be quite small, usually in the vicinity of four to eight, although this may change as the latencies become longer relative to processor cycle time.

Let us examine some of the simulation results for parallel programs (Laudon 1994). The architectural model is again a cache-coherent multiprocessor with 16 processors using a flat, memory-based directory protocol. The processor model is single issue and modeled after the MIPS R4000 for the integer pipeline and the DEC Alpha 21064 for the floating-point pipeline. The cache hierarchy used is a small (64-KB) single-level cache, and the latencies for different types of accesses are modeled after the Stanford DASH multiprocessor prototype (Lenoski et al. 1992). Overall, both the blocked and interleaved schemes were found to improve performance substantially. Of the seven applications studied, the speedup from multithreading ranged from 2.0 to nearly 3.5 for three applications, from 1.2 to 1.6 for three others, and was negligible for the last application because it had very little extra parallelism

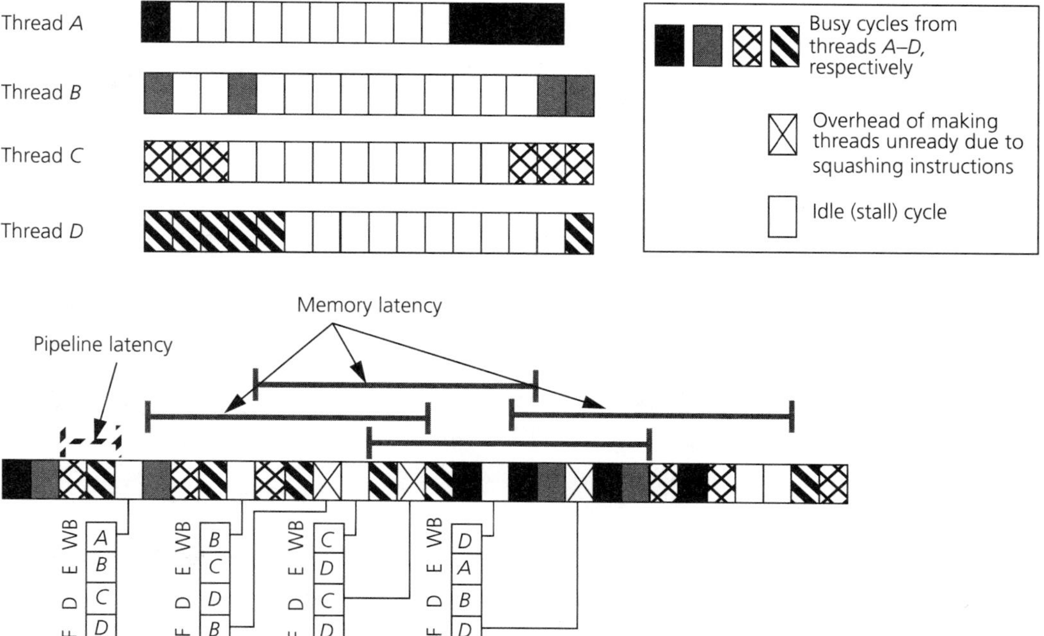

FIGURE 11.30 Latency tolerance in the interleaved scheme. A four-stage pipeline is assumed, the stages being instruction fetch (IF), decode (D), execute (E), and write back (WB). The top part of the figure shows how the four active threads on a processor would behave if each was the only thread running on the processor. The bottom part shows how the processor switches among threads. As in Figure 11.27, the instruction in a slot (cycle) is the one that retires (or would retire) from the pipeline in that cycle. In the first four cycles shown, an instruction from each thread retires. In the fifth cycle, *A* would have retired its second instruction but discovers that it has missed and needs to become unready, so that slot is an idle slot. The three other instructions in the pipeline at that time (shown below the idle slot) are from the three other threads, so there is no switch cost except for the one cycle due to the instruction that missed. When *B*'s next instruction reaches the WB stage (the ninth cycle), it detects a miss and has to become unready. At this time, since *A* is already unready, an instruction each from *C* and *D* have entered the pipeline, as has one more from *B* (this one is now in its IF stage, as shown, and would have retired in the twelfth cycle). Thus, the instruction from *B* that misses wastes a cycle, and one instruction from *B* has to be squashed. Similarly, *C*'s instruction that would have retired in the thirteenth cycle misses and causes another instruction from *C* to be squashed, and so on.

to begin with (see Figure 11.31). The interleaved scheme was found to always outperform the blocked scheme, as expected from the preceding discussion, with a geometric mean speedup over all applications of 2.75 compared to 1.9.

The advantages of the interleaved scheme are found to be greatest for applications that incur a lot of latency due to short pipeline stalls (such as those for result dependences in floating-point add, subtract, and multiply instructions) since this latency cannot be hidden by the blocked scheme and is hidden with no overhead by the interleaved scheme. Longer pipeline latencies, such as the tens of cycle latencies of

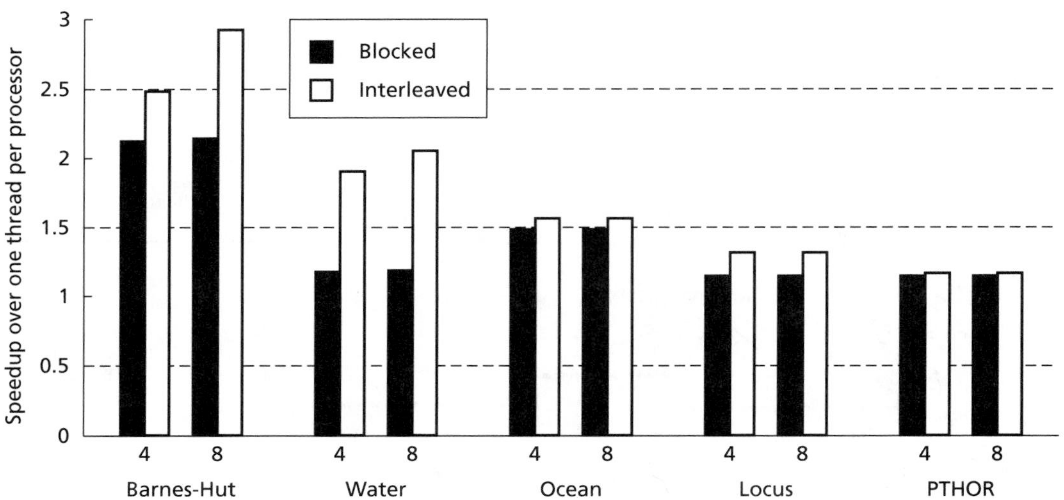

FIGURE 11.31 Speedups for blocked and interleaved multithreading. The bars show speedups for different numbers of contexts (4 and 8) relative to a single-context-per-processor execution for seven applications. All results are for 16 processor executions. The Locus application was introduced in Figure 11.24. Water is a molecular dynamics simulation of water molecules in liquid state. PTHOR is a parallel event-driven simulator of logic circuits whose concurrency profile was shown in Figure 2.5. The multiprocessor simulation model assumes a single-level, 64-KB, direct-mapped write-back cache per processor. The memory system latencies assumed are 1 cycle for a hit in the cache, 24–45 cycles with a uniform distribution for a miss satisfied in local memory, 75–135 cycles for a miss satisfied at a remote home, and 96–156 cycles for a miss satisfied in a dirty node that is not the home. These latencies are clearly low by modern standards. The MIPS R4000-like integer unit has a 7-cycle pipeline, and the floating-point unit has a 9-stage pipeline (5 execute stages). The divide instruction has a 61-cycle latency, and unlike other functional units the divide unit is not pipelined. Both schemes switch threads (or make the thread unready) on a divide instruction. The blocked scheme uses an explicit switch instruction on synchronization events and divides, which has a cost of 3 cycles (less than a full 7-cycle context switch because the decision to switch is known after the decode stage rather than at the write-back stage). The interleaved scheme uses a backoff instruction (discussed in Section 11.7.4) in these cases, which has a cost of 1–3 cycles depending on how many instructions need to be squashed as a result.

divide operations, can be tolerated quite well by both schemes, though the interleaved scheme still performs better because of its lower switch cost. The advantages of the interleaved scheme are found to be retained even when the organizational and performance parameters of the extended memory hierarchy are changed (for example, longer latencies and multilevel caches). They are, likely to be even greater with modern processors that issue multiple operations per cycle since the frequency of cache misses and, hence, context switches is likely to increase. A potential disadvantage of both types of multithreading is that multiple threads of execution share the same cache, TLB, and branch prediction unit, raising the possibility of negative interference between them (e.g., mapping conflicts across threads in a low-associativity cache); however, these negative effects have been found to be quite small in published studies.

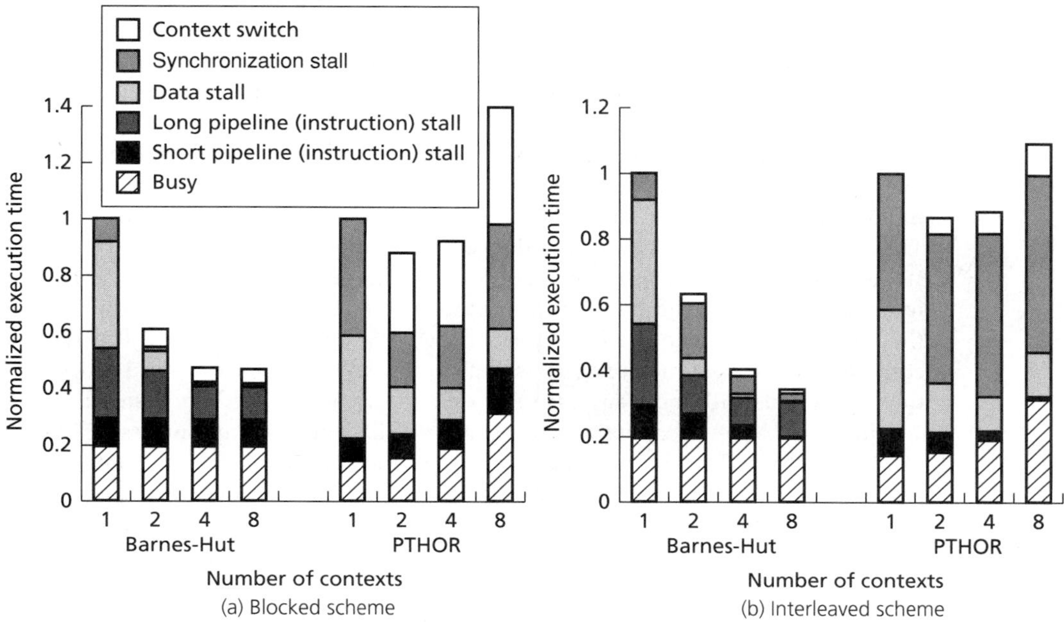

FIGURE 11.32 Execution time breakdowns for two applications under multithreading. Busy time is the time spent executing application instructions; the pipeline stall time is the time spent stalled due to pipeline or instruction dependences; data stall time and synchronization stall time are the time spent stalled on the memory system and at synchronization events, respectively. Finally, context switch time is the time spent in context switch overhead.

Figure 11.32 shows more detailed breakdowns of execution time, averaged over all processors, for two applications that illustrate interesting effects. With a single context, Barnes-Hut shows significant memory stall time due to the small single-level direct-mapped cache used (as well as the small problem size of only 4-K bodies). The use of more contexts per processor is able to hide most of the data access latency, and the lower switch cost of the interleaved scheme is clear from the figure. The other major form of latency in Barnes-Hut (and in Water) is pipeline stalls due to long-latency floating-point instructions, particularly divides. The interleaved scheme is able to hide this latency more effectively than the blocked scheme. However, both start to taper off in their ability to hide divide latency at more than four contexts. This is because the simulated divide unit is not pipelined, so it quickly becomes a resource bottleneck when divides from different contexts compete for it. PTHOR is an example of an application in which the use of more contexts does not help very much and even hurts as more contexts are used. Memory latency is hidden quite well as soon as we go to two contexts, but the major bottleneck is synchronization latency. The application simply does not have enough extra parallelism (slackness) to exploit multiple contexts effectively: even though multiple threads are used, they spend most of their time serialized at synchronization points. Note that busy time increases with the number of contexts in PTHOR. This is because the application uses a set of distributed task queues, and more time is spent maintaining these queues as the number of threads increases. These extra instructions cause more cache misses as well.

Multithreading hides the same types of data access latency as prefetching, and one may be better than the other in certain circumstances (recall that multithreading also hides synchronization and instruction latency, which prefetching doesn't directly). The performance benefits of using the two techniques together are not well understood. For example, the use of multithreading may cause constructive or destructive interference in the cache among threads; this is very difficult to predict, which makes the analysis of what to prefetch more difficult. Like prefetching, multithreading complements relaxed memory consistency quite well with blocking-read processors; the interactions with more aggressive processors are not yet well understood.

The next two subsections discuss some detailed implementation issues for the blocked and interleaved schemes, focusing on the additional implementation complexity needed to implement each scheme beyond that needed for a commodity microprocessor. Readers can skip to Section 11.7.5 to see the more sophisticated multithreading scheme for superscalar processors without loss of context.

11.7.3 Implementation Issues for the Blocked Scheme

Both the blocked and interleaved schemes have three kinds of requirements: *state replication, program counter (PC) unit enhancements,* and *control enhancements*. State replication essentially involves replicating the registers, program counter, and relevant portions of the processor status word once per active context, as discussed earlier. The PC of the processor requires significant changes for multithreading control. For control enhancements, logic and registers are needed to manage switching between contexts, making contexts ready and unready, and so on. We treat each of these requirements in turn.

State Replication

Let us look at the register file and the processor status word separately. Giving every active context its own register file or piece of a larger, statically segmented register file allows registers to be accessed quickly, though this may not use the silicon area efficiently (see Figure 11.33). For example, since only one context runs at a time until it encounters a long-latency event in the blocked scheme, only one register file is actively being used for some time while the others are idle. At the very least, we would like to share the read and write ports across register files since these ports often take up a substantial portion of the silicon area of the files. In addition, some contexts might require more or fewer registers than others, and the relative needs may change dynamically. Thus, allowing the contexts to share a large register file dynamically according to need may provide better register utilization than dividing

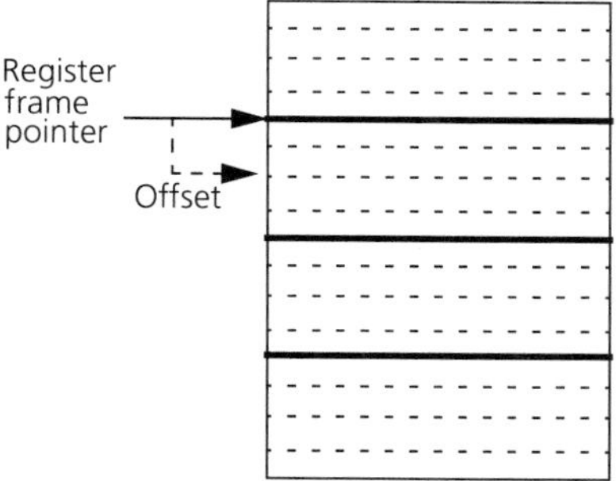

FIGURE 11.33 A segmented register file for a multithreaded processor. The file is divided into four frames, assuming that four contexts can be active at a given time. The register values for each active context remain in that context's register frame across context switches, and each context's frame is managed by the compiler as if it were itself a complete register file. A register in a frame is accessed through the current (hardware) register frame pointer, by specifying an offset within the frame, so the compiler need not be aware of which particular frame a context is using (which is determined at run time). Switching to a different active context requires only that the current frame pointer be changed.

the registers statically. This results in a cachelike structure, indexed by context identifier and register offset, with the potential disadvantage that the register file is larger and so has a higher access time. Several proposals have been made to improve register file efficiency (Nuth and Dally 1995; Laudon 1994; Omondi 1994; Smith 1985), but substantial replication is needed in all cases. The MIT Alewife machine uses the register windows mechanism of a modified Sun Sparc processor to provide a replicated register file.

A modern "processor status word" is actually several registers; only some parts of it (such as floating-point status/control, etc.) contain process-specific state rather than global machine state, so only these parts need to be replicated. In addition, multithreading introduces a new global status word called the *context status word* (CSW). This contains an identifier that specifies which context is currently running, a bit that says whether context switching is enabled (we shall see that it may be disabled while exceptions are handled), and a bit vector that tells us which of the currently active contexts are ready to execute. Finally, TLB control registers need to be modified to support different address space identifiers from the different contexts and to allow a single TLB entry to be used for a page that is shared among contexts.

Program Counter Unit

Different active contexts must also have their PCs available in hardware. Processors that support exceptions efficiently provide a mechanism to do this with minimal hardware replication since in many ways exceptions behave like context switches. In addition to the PC chain, which holds the PCs for the instructions that are in the different stages of the pipeline, a register called the *exception program counter* (EPC) is provided in such processors. The EPC is fed by the PC chain, so it always contains the address of the last instruction retired from the pipeline. When an exception occurs, the loading of the EPC is stopped with the faulting instruction, all the incomplete instructions in the pipeline are squashed, and the exception handler address is put in the PC. When the exception handler returns, the EPC is loaded into the PC so that the faulting instruction is reexecuted. This is exactly the functionality we need for multiple contexts. We simply need to replicate the EPC register, providing one per active context. The EPC for a context serves to handle both exceptions as well as context switches for that thread. When a given context is operating, the PC chain feeds into its EPC while the EPCs of other contexts simply retain their values. On an exception, the current context's EPC behaves exactly as just described for the single-threaded case. On a context switch, the current context's EPC stops being loaded at the faulting (long-latency) instruction, and the incomplete instructions in the pipeline are squashed (as for an exception). The PC is loaded from the EPC of the next selected context, which therefore starts executing from its first unexecuted instruction, and so on. The only drawback of using the EPCs for these dual purposes is that now an exception handler cannot take a context switch (since the address of the next unexecuted instruction loaded into its EPC by the context that incurred the exception will be lost), so context switches may have to be disabled when an exception occurs and reenabled when the exception handler returns. However, the PCs can still be managed through software saving and restoring even in this case.

Control

The key functions of the control logic in a blocked implementation are to detect when to switch contexts, to choose the context to switch to, and to orchestrate and perform the switch. Let us discuss each briefly.

A context switch in the blocked scheme may be triggered by three events: a cache miss; an explicit context switch instruction, used for synchronization events and very long-latency instructions; and a time-out. The time-out is used to ensure that a single context does not run too long or spin waiting on a flag to be set by another thread running on the same processor. The decision to switch on a cache miss is based on three signals: the cache miss notification, the bit that says that context switching is enabled, and a signal that states that another context is ready to run. A simple way to implement an explicit context switch instruction is to have it behave as if the following instruction generated a cache miss (i.e., to raise the cache miss signal or generate another signal that has the same effect on the context switch logic); this will cause the context to switch and to be restarted later from that following instruction. Finally, the time-out signal can be generated via a resettable threshold counter.

While many policies can be used to select the next context upon a switch, in practice simply switching to the next active and ready context in a round-robin fashion—without concern for special relationships among contexts or the history of the contexts' executions—seems to work quite well. The signals this requires are the current context identifier, the vector of ready and active contexts, and the signal that detects the need to switch.

Finally, orchestrating a context switch in the blocked scheme requires the following actions. They are required to complete by different stages in the processor pipeline, so the control logic must enable the corresponding signals in the appropriate time windows.

- Save the address of the first uncompleted instruction from the current thread (in that context's EPC, say).
- Squash all incomplete instructions in the pipeline.
- Start executing from the (saved) PC of the selected context, obtained from its EPC.
- Load the appropriate address space identifier in the TLB's bound registers.
- Load the relevant control/status registers from the (saved) processor status words of the new context, including the floating-point control/status register and the context identifier.
- Switch the register file control to the register file for the new context, if applicable.

In summary, the major costs of implementing blocked context switching come from replicating and managing the register file, which increases both area and perhaps register file access time. If the latter is in the critical path of the processor cycle time, it may require the pipeline depth to be increased to maintain a high clock rate, which can increase the penalty for branch mispredictions. All these factors must be considered in evaluating performance benefits. The other hardware costs are very small.

11.7.4 Implementation Issues for the Interleaved Scheme

A key reason that the blocked scheme is relatively easy to implement is that most of the time the processor behaves like a single-threaded processor, invoking additional complexity and processor state changes only at context switches. The interleaved scheme needs a little more support since it switches among threads every cycle. The processor state may have to be changed every cycle and the instruction issue unit must be capable of issuing from multiple active streams in consecutive cycles. A mechanism is also needed to make contexts active and inactive and to feed the active/inactive status into the instruction unit every cycle. Let us again look at the state replication, PC unit, and control needs separately.

State Replication

The register file must be replicated or managed dynamically as for the blocked scheme, but the pressure on fast access to different parts of the entire register file is greater since successive cycles may access the registers of different contexts. We cannot rely on the more gradually changing access patterns of the blocked scheme. (Thus, the Tera processor uses a banked or interleaved register file, and a thread may be rendered unready because of a busy register bank as well.) The parts of the process status word that must be replicated are similar to those in the blocked scheme, though again the processor must be able to switch status words every cycle.

Program Counter Unit

The greatest difference in changes is to the PC unit. Instructions from different threads are in the pipeline at the same time, and the processor must be able to issue instructions from a different thread every cycle, avoiding unready threads. The processor pipeline is also impacted since, to implement bypassing and forwarding correctly, the processor's PC chain must now carry a context identifier for each pipeline stage. In the PC unit itself, new mechanisms are needed for handling context availability and for squashing instructions, for keeping track of the next instruction to issue, for handling branches, and for handling exceptions. Let us examine some of these issues briefly. A fuller treatment can be found in the literature (Laudon 1994).

Consider context availability. Contexts become unavailable because of either cache misses or explicit backoff instructions that make the context unavailable for a specified number of cycles. The backoff instructions are issued, for example, at synchronization events (if the synchronization event has not been satisfied by the time the specified backoff period expires and the thread is made available again, the cycles for that thread may be wasted until the synchronization event is satisfied, or another backoff may be issued). The issuing of further instructions from that context is stopped by clearing a "context available" signal. To squash the instructions already in the pipeline from that context, we must broadcast a squash signal as well as the context identifier to all stages since we don't know which stages contain instructions from that context. In the case of a cache miss, the address of the instruction that caused the miss is loaded into the EPC. Once the cache miss is satisfied and the context becomes available again, the PC bus is loaded from the EPC when that context is selected next. Explicit backoff instructions are handled similarly to cache misses, except that we do not want the context to resume from the backoff instruction itself but rather from the instruction that follows it. A bit called the *next bit* can be included in the EPC to orchestrate resumption from either the faulting instruction or the next one.

Even in a standard, single-context uniprocessor, three sources can determine the next instruction to be issued from a given thread: the next sequential instruction, the predicted branch from the branch target buffer (BTB), and the computed branch if the prediction is detected to be wrong. When only a single context is in the pipeline at a time, the appropriate next instruction address can be driven onto the PC bus from the "next PC" (NPC) register as soon as it is determined. In an interleaved processor, however, in the cycle when the next instruction address for a given context is determined and ready to be put on the PC bus, it may not be the context scheduled for that cycle. Further, since the NPC for a context may be determined in different pipeline stages for different instructions—for example, it is determined much later for a mispredicted branch than for a correctly predicted branch or a nonbranch instruction—different contexts could produce their NPC value during the

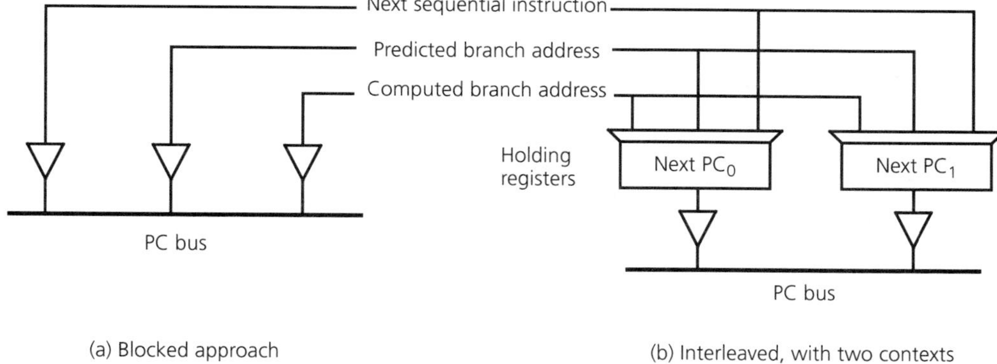

FIGURE 11.34 Driving the PC bus in the blocked and interleaved multithreading approaches, with two contexts. If more contexts were used, the interleaved scheme would require more replication whereas the blocked scheme would not.

same cycle. Thus, the NPC value for each context must be held in a holding register until it is time to execute the next instruction from that context, at which point it will be driven onto the PC bus (see Figure 11.34).

Branches too require some additional mechanisms. The context identifier must be broadcast to the pipeline stages when squashing instructions due to a mispredicted branch, but this is the same functionality needed when making contexts unavailable. By the time the actual branch target is computed, the predicted instruction that was fetched speculatively could be anywhere in the pipeline or may not even have been issued yet (since other contexts will be interleaved unpredictably). To find this predicted instruction address to determine the correctness of the prediction, it may be necessary for branch instructions to carry along with them their predicted address as they proceed along the pipeline stages. For example, a *predicted PC* register chain can run along parallel to the PC chain and be loaded and checked as the branch reaches the appropriate pipeline stages.

Finally, consider what happens when an exception occurs in one context. One choice is to have that context be rendered unready to make way for the exception handler and let the exception handler be interleaved with the other user contexts (the Tera takes an approach similar to this). In this case, another user thread may also take an exception while the first exception handler is running, so the exception handlers must be able to cope with multiple concurrent handler executions. Another option is to render all the contexts unready when an exception occurs in any context, squash all the instructions in the pipeline, and reenable all contexts when the exception handler returns. This can cause a loss of performance if exceptions are frequent. It also means that, when an exception occurs, the exception PCs (EPCs) of all active contexts must be loaded with the address of the first uncompleted instruction from their respective threads. This is more complicated than in the blocked case, where only the single EPC of the currently running (excepting) context needs to be saved.

Control

Two interesting issues related to control outside of the PC unit are tracking context availability information and feeding it to the PC unit, and choosing and switching to the next context every cycle. The "context available" signal is modified on a cache miss, when the miss returns, and on backoff instructions and their expiration. Availability status due to cache misses can be tracked by maintaining pending miss registers per context, which are loaded upon a miss and checked upon miss return to reenable the appropriate context. For explicit backoff instructions, we can maintain a counter per context, initialized to the backoff value when the backoff instruction is encountered (the context availability signal is also cleared at this time). The counter is decremented every cycle until it reaches zero, at which point the availability signal for that context is set again.

Backoff instructions can be used to tolerate instruction latency as well, but with the interleaving of contexts it may be difficult to choose a good number of backoff cycles. This is further complicated by the fact that the compiler may rearrange instructions transparently. Backoff values are implementation specific and may have to be changed for subsequent generations of processors. Fortunately, short instruction latencies are often handled naturally by the interleaving of other contexts without any backoff instructions, as we saw in Figure 11.30. Robust solutions for long instruction latencies may require more complex hardware support such as scoreboarding.

As for choosing the next context, a reasonable approach once again is to select contexts round-robin qualified by context availability.

11.7.5 Integrating Multithreading with Multiple-Issue Processors

So far, our discussion of multithreading has been orthogonal to the number of operations issued per cycle. While the Tera system issues three operations per cycle, the packing of operations from a thread into wider instructions is done by the compiler, and the hardware simply chooses a three-operation instruction from a single thread in every cycle. A single thread usually does not have enough instruction-level parallelism to fill all the available slots in every cycle, as is already being found in modern multiple-issue processors and is likely to become worse if support for issuing more operations per cycle is provided. With many threads available, a natural alternative is to let available operations from different threads be scheduled in the same cycle, thus filling the issue slots more effectively. This approach has been called *simultaneous multithreading*, and there have been many proposals for it (Hirata et al. 1992; Tullsen, Eggers, and Levy 1995). It is like interleaved multithreading, but operations from the different available threads compete for the issue slots and functional units in every cycle.

Put another way, traditional multiple-issue processors suffer from two inefficiencies. First, not all slots in a given cycle are filled due to limited ability to find instruction-level parallelism within a thread. Second, many cycles have nothing scheduled because of long-latency instructions. Simple multithreading addresses the

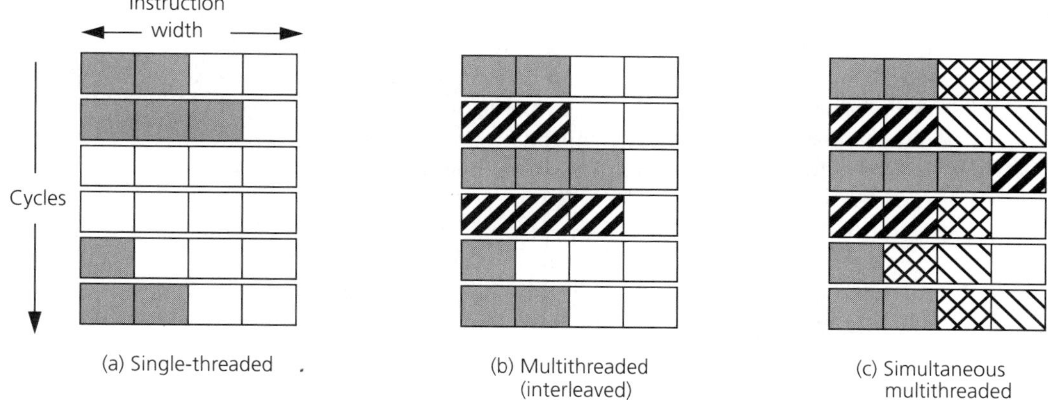

FIGURE 11.35 Simultaneous multithreading. The potential improvements are illustrated for both simple interleaved multithreading and simultaneous multithreading for a four-issue processor. Shaded and patterned boxes distinguish operations from different threads, while blank boxes indicate empty slots in instructions.

second problem but not the first whereas simultaneous multithreading tries to address both (see Figure 11.35).

Choosing operations from different threads to schedule in the same cycle may be difficult for a compiler, but many of the mechanisms for it are already present in dynamically scheduled microprocessors. The instruction fetch unit must be extended to fetch operations from different hardware contexts in a cycle, but once operations from the different contexts are fetched and placed in the reorder buffer, the issue logic can choose operations from this buffer regardless of which context they are from. Studies of single-threaded, multiple-issue dynamically scheduled processors have shown that the causes of empty cycles and empty slots are quite well distributed among instruction latencies, cache misses, TLB misses, and load delay slots (with the first two often being particularly important). The variety of the sources of wasted time and of their latencies indicates that fine-grained multithreading may be a good solution.

In addition to the issues we discussed for interleaved multiprocessors, several new issues arise in implementing simultaneously multithreaded processors (Tullsen et al. 1996). First, how flexible should instruction fetching from different threads be? The greater the flexibility allowed—compared to fetching from only one context in a cycle or fetching at most two operations from each thread in a cycle—the greater the complexity in the fetching logic and instruction cache design. However, more flexibility reduces the frequency of empty fetch slots. Second, how should we choose which context or contexts to fetch instructions from in the next cycle? We could choose contexts in a fixed order of priority (say, try to fill from context 0 first, then fill the rest from context 1, and so on) or we could choose based on execution characteristics of the contexts (for example, give priority to the context that has the fewest instructions currently in the fetch unit or the reorder buffer or to the context that currently has the fewest outstanding cache misses). Finally, which operations should we choose from the reorder buffer among the ones that are ready in each cycle? The standard practice in dynamically scheduled processors is to choose the oldest operation that is ready, but other choices, based on which threads the operations are from and how the threads are behaving, may be more appropriate in this case.

Little or no performance data exists on simultaneous multithreading in the context of multiprocessors. For uniprocessors, a performance study examining the potential benefits as well as the impact of some of the trade-offs just discussed finds that the technique is promising and that support for speculative execution is less important with simultaneous multithreading than with single-threaded dynamically scheduled processors because there are more available threads and, hence, nonspeculative instructions to choose from (Tullsen et al. 1996).

Overall, as data access and synchronization latencies become larger relative to processor speed, and as the data access patterns of multiprocessor applications become more complex and unpredictable (as multiprocessing continues to mature and expand), multithreading promises to become increasingly successful in hiding latency. Whether it will actually be incorporated in microprocessors depends on a host of factors, such as what other latency tolerance techniques are employed (e.g., prefetching, dynamic scheduling, and relaxed consistency models) and how multithreading interacts with them. Since multithreading already requires extra explicit threads and significant complexity and replication of state, an interesting alternative is to place multiple simpler processors on a chip with the multiple threads running on different processors. While the qualitative trade-offs are quite clear, how this organization compares with multithreading in cost and performance is not yet well understood, either for desktop systems or as a node for a larger multiprocessor.

Table 11.2 summarizes and compares some key features of the four major techniques for hiding latency in a shared address space, as presented in Sections 11.4–11.7. The techniques can be and often are combined. For example, processors with blocking reads can use relaxed consistency models to hide write latency and prefetching or multithreading to hide read latency. And we have seen that dynamically scheduled processors can benefit from all of prefetching, relaxed consistency models, and multithreading individually. How these different techniques interact in dynamically scheduled processors, how well prefetching might complement multithreading even in blocking read processors, and how these techniques succeed in hiding latency as the gap between processor speed and data access latency widens is likely to be better understood in the future.

11.8 LOCKUP-FREE CACHE DESIGN

Throughout this chapter, we have seen that in addition to the support needed in the processor—and the additional bandwidth and low occupancies needed in the memory and communication systems—several latency tolerance techniques in a shared

Table 11.2 Key Properties of the Four Latency Tolerance Techniques in a Shared Address Space

Property	Relaxed Models	Prefetching	Multithreading	Block Data Transfer
Types of Latency Tolerated	Write (blocking read processors) Read and write (dynamically scheduled processors)	Write Read	Write Read Synchronization Instruction	Write Read
Requirements of Software	Labeling synchronization operations	Predictability	Explicit extra concurrency	Identifying and orchestrating block transfers
Extra Hardware Support	Little	Little	Substantial	Not in processor but block transfer engine in memory system
Support in Commercial Micros?	Yes	Yes	Currently no	Not needed

address space require that the cache allow multiple outstanding misses at a time if the techniques are to be effective. Before we conclude the chapter, let us examine the design of such a lockup-free cache.

There are several key design questions for a cache subsystem that allows multiple outstanding misses:

- How many and what kinds of misses can be outstanding at the same time? Like the processor, it is easier for the cache to support multiple outstanding writes than reads. Two distinct points in design complexity are (1) a single read and multiple writes and (2) multiple reads and writes.
- How do we keep track of the outstanding misses? For reads, we need to track: the address of the word requested; the type of read request (i.e., read, read exclusive, or prefetch and single-word or double-word read); the place to return data when it comes into the cache (e.g., to which register within a processor or to which processor if multiple processors are sharing a cache); and the current status of the outstanding request. For writes, we do not need to track where to return the data, but the new data being written must be merged with the data block (if any) returned by the next level of the memory hierarchy. A key issue here is whether to store most of this information within the cache blocks themselves or to have a separate set of transaction buffers for outstanding misses. Of course, while fulfilling these requirements, we need to ensure that the design is free of deadlock and livelock.
- How do we deal with conflicts among multiple outstanding references to the same memory block? What kinds of conflicting misses to a block should we disallow (e.g., by stalling the processor)? For example, should we allow writes to words within a block to which a read miss is outstanding?

- How do we deal with conflicts between multiple outstanding requests that map to the same line in the cache, even though they refer to different memory blocks?

To illustrate the options, let us examine two different designs. They differ primarily in where they store the information that keeps track of outstanding misses. The first design uses a separate set of transaction buffers for tracking requests. The second design, to the extent possible, keeps track of outstanding requests in the cache blocks themselves.

The first design is a simplified version of that used in Control Data Corporation's Cyber 835 mainframe, introduced in 1979 (Kroft 1981). It adds a number of miss state holding registers (MSHRs) to the cache, together with some associated logic. Each MSHR handles one or more outstanding misses to a single memory block. This design allows considerable flexibility in the kinds of requests that can be simultaneously outstanding to a block, so a significant amount of state is stored in each MSHR as shown in Table 11.3.

The MSHRs are accessed in parallel to the regular cache. If the access hits in the cache, the normal cache hit actions take place. If the access misses in the cache, the actions depend on the contents of the MSHRs:

- If no MSHR is allocated for that block, a new one is allocated and initialized (if no MSHR is free, or if all cache lines within that set in the cache have pending requests, then the processor stalls). If the cache line on which the miss occurs currently contains dirty data, a write back is initiated. Then, if the processor request is a write, the data is written at the proper offset into the block in the cache, and the corresponding partial write code bits are set in the MSHR. A request to fetch the block from the main memory subsystem (e.g., BusRd, BusRdX) is also initiated.
- If an MSHR is already allocated for the block, the new request is merged with the previously pending requests for the same block. For example, a new write request can be merged by writing the data into the allocated cache block and by setting the corresponding partial write bits in the MSHR. A read request to a word that has been written completely in the cache (by earlier writes) can simply read the data from the cache already. A read request to a word that has not been requested is handled by setting the proper unit identification tags. If it is to a word that has already been requested, then either a new MSHR must be allocated (since there is only one unit identification tag per word) or the processor must be stalled. Since a write does not need a unit identification tag, a write request for a word to which a request is already pending is handled easily: the data returned by main memory can simply be forwarded to the processor. Of course, the first such write to a block will have to generate a request that asks for exclusive ownership.

Finally, when the data for the block returns to the cache, the cache block pointer in the MSHR indicates where to put the contents. The partial write codes are used to avoid overwriting more recently written data in the cache, and the send-to-CPU bits and unit identification tags are used to forward replies to waiting functional units.

Table 11.3 MSHR State Entries and Their Roles

State	Description	Purpose
Cache Block Pointer	Pointer to cache block allocated to this request	Specifies cache line within a set in a set-associative cache
Request Address	Address of pending request	Allows merging of requests
Unit Identification Tags (one per word)	Identifies requesting unit in processor	Where to return this word
Send-to-CPU status (one per word)	Valid bits for unit identification tags	Is unit ID tag valid?
Partial Write Codes (one per word)	Bit vector for tracking partial writes to a word	Which words returning from memory to overwrite
Valid Indicator	Valid MSHR contents	Are contents valid?

This design requires an associative lookup of MSHRs but allows the cache to have all kinds of memory references outstanding at the same time. Fortunately, since the MSHRs do the complex task of merging requests and tearing apart replies for a given block, to the extended memory hierarchy below it appears simply as if there are requests to distinct blocks coming from the processor. The coherence protocols we have discussed in the previous chapters are already designed to handle these multiple outstanding requests to different blocks without deadlock.

The alternative to this design is to store most of the relevant state for outstanding write requests in the cache lines themselves and not use separate MSHRs. In addition to the standard MESI states for a write-back cache, we add three transient or pending states: *invalid pending* (IP), *shared pending* (SP), and *exclusive pending* (EP), which indicate what the state of the block was when a currently outstanding write miss was issued. In each of these three states, the cache tag is valid and the cache block is awaiting data from the memory system. Each cache block also has a bit vector of *subblock write bits* (SWBs), with 1 bit per word. In both the EP and SP states, the bits that are turned ON indicate the words in the block that have been written by the processor since the block was requested from memory and that the data returned from memory should not overwrite. However, words for which the bits are OFF are considered invalid in the EP state but valid (not stale) in the SP state. Finally, there is a set of separate pending read registers; these contain the address and type of pending read requests.

The key benefit of keeping this extra state information with each cache block is that no additional storage is needed to keep track of pending write requests. On a write that does not find the block in modified state, the block simply goes into the appropriate pending state, initiates the appropriate transaction, and sets the SWB bits to indicate which words the current write has modified so the subsequent merge will happen correctly. Writes that find the block already in pending state only require that the word is written into the line and the corresponding SWB is set. Reads may use the pending read registers. If a read finds the desired word in a valid state in the block (including a pending state with the SWB on), then it simply returns it. Otherwise, it is placed in a pending read register that keeps track of it.

If the block accessed on a read or write is not in the cache (no tag match), then a write back may be generated. The block is set to the invalid pending state, all SWBs are turned off (except for the word being written if it is a write), and the appropriate transaction is placed on the bus. If the tag does not match and the existing block is already in pending state, then the processor stalls. Finally, when a response to an outstanding request arrives, the corresponding cache block is updated except for the words that have their SWBs on. The cache block moves out of the pending state. All pending read registers are checked to see if any are waiting for this cache block; if so, data is returned for those requests and those pending read registers are freed. Details of the actual state changes, actions, and race conditions can be found in (Laudon 1994). One key observation that makes race conditions relatively easy to deal with is that, even though words are written into cache blocks before ownership is obtained for the block, those words are not visible to requests from other processors until ownership is obtained.

Overall, these two lockup-free cache designs are not that different conceptually. The latter solution keeps the state for writes in the cache blocks and reduces the number of pending registers needed and the complexity of the associative lookups; however, it is more memory intensive than MSHRs since extra state is stored with all lines in the cache, even though very few of them will have an outstanding request at a time. The correctness interactions with the rest of the protocol are similar and modest in the two cases.

11.9 CONCLUDING REMARKS

With the increasing gap between processor speeds and memory access and communication times, latency tolerance will be increasingly critical in future multiprocessors (and uniprocessors as well). Many latency tolerance techniques have been developed, and each has its relative advantages and disadvantages. They all rely on excess concurrency in the application program beyond the number of processors used, and they all tend to increase the bandwidth demands placed on the communication architecture. This greater stress makes it all the more important that the other performance aspects of the communication architecture (the processor overhead, the assist occupancy, and the network bandwidth) be efficient and well balanced. For example, since the overhead incurred on the main processor cannot be hidden from that processor, if overhead is a dominant component of data access latency, then latency tolerance techniques other than making messages larger might not be very effective.

For cache-coherent multiprocessors, latency tolerance techniques are supported in hardware by both the processor and the cache memory system, leading to a rich space of design alternatives. Most of these hardware-supported latency tolerance techniques are also applicable to uniprocessors; in fact, their commercial success depends on their viability in the high-volume uniprocessor market where the latencies to be hidden are smaller. Techniques like dynamic scheduling, relaxed memory consistency models, and prefetching are commonly encountered in microprocessor architectures today. The most general latency hiding technique—multithreading—is not yet popular commercially, largely because it is unproven for uniprocessors. Recent directions in integrating multithreading with dynamically scheduled superscalar processors appear promising, but they bear comparison with multiple simpler processors on a chip. An interesting general question is how well the provisions made for hiding uniprocessor latencies will succeed in hiding multiprocessor latencies.

Despite the rich space of issues and alternatives in hardware support, much of the latency tolerance problem today is also a software problem. To what extent can a compiler automate prefetching so a user does not have to worry about it? And if automation to a desirable extent is not possible, how can the user naturally convey information about what and when to prefetch to the compiler? If block transfer is indeed useful on cache-coherent machines, how will users program to this mixed model of both implicit communication through reads and writes as well as explicit transfers? Relaxed consistency models carry with them the software problem of specifying the appropriate constraints on reordering (i.e., of labeling conflicting operations as necessary). Finally, will programs be decomposed and assigned with enough extra explicit parallelism (extra threads) that multithreading will be successful? Automating and simplifying the software support required for latency tolerance is a task that is far from fully accomplished. In fact, how latency tolerance techniques will play out in the future and what software support they will use remain interesting open questions in parallel architecture.

11.10 EXERCISES

11.1 Why is latency reduction generally a better idea than latency tolerance?

11.2 Suppose a processor communicates k words in m messages of equal size, the assist occupancy for processing a message is o, and there is no overhead on the processor. What is the best-case latency as seen by the processor if only communication, not computation, can be overlapped with communication? First, assume that acknowledgments are free (i.e., are propagated instantaneously and don't incur overhead); then include acknowledgments. Draw timelines and state any important assumptions.

11.3 You have learned about a variety of different techniques to tolerate and hide latency in shared memory multiprocessors. These techniques include blocking, prefetching, multiple context processors, and relaxed consistency models. For each of the following scenarios, discuss why each technique will or will not be an effective means of reducing/hiding latency. Assume a processor with blocking reads and list any other assumptions that you make.

a. A complex graph algorithm with abundant concurrency using linked pointer structures.

b. A parallel sorting algorithm where communication is producer initiated and is achieved through long-latency write operations. Receiver-initiated communication is not possible.

c. An iterative equation solver in which the inner loop consists of a matrix-matrix multiply. Assume both matrices are huge and don't fit into the cache.

11.4 You are charged with implementing message passing on a new parallel supercomputer. The architecture of the machine is still unsettled, and your boss says the decision of whether to provide hardware cache coherence will depend on the message-passing performance of the two systems under consideration since you want to be able to run message-passing applications that ran on the previous-generation architecture.

In the system without cache coherence (the "NCC" system), the engineers on your team tell you that message passing should be implemented as successive transfers of 1 KB. To avoid problems with buffering at the receiver side, you're required to acknowledge each individual 1-KB transfer before the transmission of the next one can begin (so only one block can be in flight at a time). Each 1-KB transfer requires 200 cycles of setup time, after which it begins flowing into the network. This overhead accounts for time to determine where to read the buffer from in memory and to set up the DMA engine, which performs the transfer. Assume that from the time that the 1-KB chunk reaches the destination it takes 20 cycles for the destination node to generate a response, and it takes 50 cycles on the sending node to accept the ACK and proceed to the next 1-KB transfer.

In the system with cache coherence (the "CC" system), messages are sent as a series of 128-byte cache line transfers. In this case, however, acknowledgments only need to be sent at the end of every 4-KB page. Here, each transfer requires 50 cycles of setup time, during which time the line can be extracted from the cache, if necessary, to maintain cache coherence. This line is then injected into the network, and only when the line is completely injected into the network can processing on the next line begin.

The following are the system parameters: clock rate = 10 ns (100 MHz), network latency = 30 cycles, network bandwidth = 400 MB/s. State any other assumptions that you make.

a. What is the latency (until the last byte of the message is received at the destination) and achieved bandwidth for a 4-KB message in the NCC system?

b. What is the corresponding latency and bandwidth in the CC system?

c. A designer on the team shows you that you can easily change the CC system so that the processing for the next line occurs while the previous one is being injected into the network. Calculate the 4-KB message latency for the CC system with this modification.

11.5 Consider the example of transposing a matrix of data in parallel, as is used in computations such as high-performance Fast Fourier Transforms. Figure 11.36 shows the transpose pictorially. Every processor transposes one "patch" of its assigned rows to every other processor, including one to itself. Performing the transpose through reads and writes was discussed in the Chapter 8 Exercises. Since it is completely predictable which data a processor has to send to which other processors, a processor can send an entire patch at a time in a single message rather than communicate the patches through individual read or write cache misses.

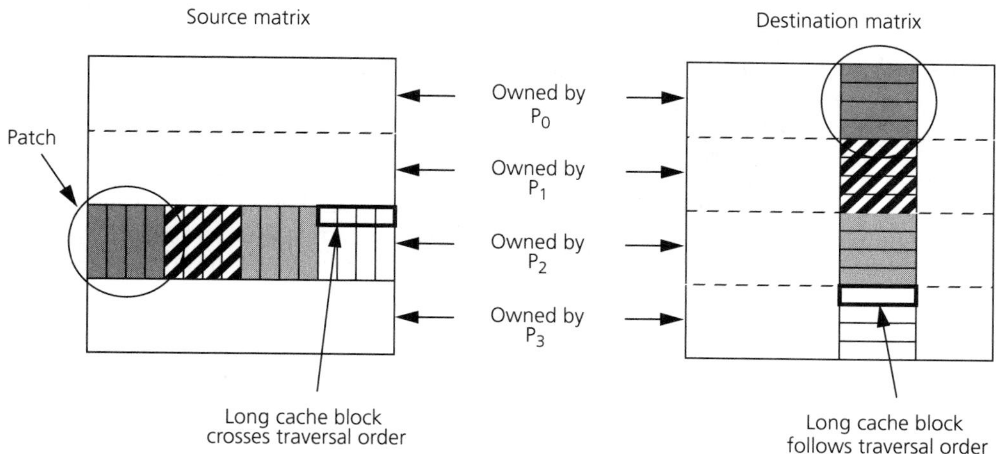

FIGURE 11.36 Sender-initiated matrix transposition. The source and destination $n \times n$ matrices are partitioning among processes in groups of contiguous rows. Each process divides its set of n/p rows into p patches of size $n/p*n/p$. Consider process P_2 as a representative example: it sends one patch to every other process and transposes one patch (third from left in this case) locally. Every patch may be transferred as a single block transfer message rather than through individual remote writes or remote reads (if receiver initiated).

a. What would you expect the curve of block transfer performance relative to read-write performance to look like?

b. What special features would the block transfer engine benefit most from?

c. Write pseudocode for the block transfer version of the code.

d. Suppose you want to use block data transfer in the Raytrace application. For what purposes would you use it and how? Do you think you would gain significant performance benefits?

11.6 An interesting performance issue in block data transfer in a cache-coherent shared address space has to do with the impact of long cache blocks and spatial locality. Assume that the data movement in the block transfer leverages the cache coherence mechanisms. Consider the simple equation solver on a regular grid, with its near-neighbor communication. Suppose the n-by-n grid is partitioned into square subblocks among p processors.

a. Compared to the results shown for FFT in this chapter, how would you expect the curves for this application to differ when each boundary row or column is sent directly in a single block transfer, and why?

b. How might you structure the block transfer to send only useful data, and how would you expect performance in this case to compare with the previous one?

c. What parameters of the architecture would most affect the trade-offs in part (b)?

d. If you indeed wanted to use a block cache transfer, what deeper changes might you make to the parallel program?

11.7 If the second-level cache is a blocking cache in the performance study of proceeding past writes with blocking reads, is there any advantage to allowing write → write reordering over not allowing it? If so, under what conditions?

11.8 a. Write buffers can allow several optimizations, such as buffering itself, merging writes to the same cache line that is in the buffer, and forwarding values from the buffer to read operations that find a match in the buffer. What constraints must be imposed on these optimizations to maintain program order under SC? Is there a danger with the merging optimizations for the processor consistency model?

b. To maintain all program orders as in SC, we can optimize in the following way. In our baseline implementation, the processor stalls immediately upon a write until the write completes. The alternative is to place the write in the write buffer without stalling the processor. To preserve the program order among writes, the write buffer retires a write (i.e., passes it further along the memory hierarchy and potentially makes it visible to other processors) only after the write is complete. The order from writes to reads is maintained by flushing the write buffer upon a read miss.

(i) What overlap does this optimization provide?

(ii) Would you expect it to yield a large performance improvement? Why or why not?

11.9 Consider the implementation requirements for proceeding past memory operations in a cache-coherent shared address space. To proceed past writes, we need a write buffer and nonblocking writes. To proceed past reads effectively, we need nonblocking reads as well as instruction lookahead and speculative execution. At the memory system level, we need lockup-free caches with multiple outstanding misses. These structures close to the processor take care of preserving the consistency model, and the rest of the extended memory hierarchy can reorder operations as it pleases. Consider now the mechanisms needed to preserve a consistency model, given this support.

a. Most of the mechanisms we need have to do with determining completion of an operation or operations. In a processor with blocking reads, what new mechanisms are needed for preserving release consistency compared to sequential consistency, and what additional structures, if any, would you use to implement them?

b. Suppose a write→write MEMBAR is encountered in a processor whose write buffer otherwise allows writes to be reordered. Does the processor have to stall, or can it proceed past the MEMBAR? Explain how the write→write ordering dictated by the MEMBAR will be provided and when the write buffer and processor must stall.

c. A key mechanism needed for any consistency model is to count incoming acknowledgments for writes that generate invalidations. The machinery needed to do this can be located near the processor or near the memory controller. What are the main trade-offs, and what empirical information would help you decide what to do?

11.10 a. How early can you issue a binding prefetch in a cache-coherent system?

b. We have talked about the advantages of nonbinding prefetches in multiprocessors. Do nonbinding prefetches have any advantages in uniprocessors over binding prefetches that prefetch into the register file?

11.11 Sometimes a predicate must be evaluated to determine whether or not to issue a prefetch. This introduces a conditional (if) expression around the prefetch inside the loop containing the prefetches. Construct a simple example, with pseudocode, and describe the performance problem. How would you fix the problem?

11.12 Describe situations in which a producer-initiated deliver operation might be more appropriate than prefetching or an update protocol. Would you implement a deliver instruction if you were designing a machine?

11.13 Consider the loop

```
for i ←1 to 200
  sum = sum + A[index[i]];
end for
```

Write a version of the code with nonbinding software-controlled prefetches inserted. Include the prologue, the steady state of the software pipeline, and the epilogue. Assume the memory latency is such that it takes five iterations of the loop for a data item to return and that data is prefetched into the primary cache.

a. When prefetching indirect references as in this example, extra instructions are needed for address generation. One possibility is to save the computed address in a register at the time of the prefetch and then reuse it later for the load. Are there any problems with or disadvantages to this?

b. What if an exception occurs when prefetching down multiple levels of indirection in accesses? What complications are caused and how might they be addressed?

11.14 Describe some hardware mechanisms (at a high level) that might be able to prefetch irregular accesses, such as records or lists.

11.15 Show how the following loop would be rewritten with prefetching so as to hide latency on a uniprocessor:

```
for i=0 to 128 {
  for j=1 to 32
    A[i,j] = B[i] * C[j]
}
```

Try to reduce overhead by prefetching only those references that you expect to miss in the cache. Assume that a read prefetch is expressed as `PREFETCH(&variable)` and it fetches the entire cache line in which `variable` resides in shared mode. A read-exclusive prefetch operation, which is expressed as `RE_PREFETCH`

`(&variable)`, fetches the line in exclusive mode. The machine has a cache miss latency of 32 cycles. Explicitly prefetch each needed variable (don't take into account the cache block size). Assume that the cache is large (so you don't have to worry about conflict misses) but not so large that you can prefetch everything at the start. In other words, we are looking for just-in-time prefetching. The matrix `A[i,j]` is stored in memory with `A[i,j]` and `A[i,j+1]` contiguous. Assume that the computation in the loop takes 8 cycles to complete.

11.16 Describe two examples in which a prefetching compiler's decision to assume that everything in the cache is invalidated when it sees a synchronization operation is very conservative, and show how a programmer can do better. It might be useful to think of the case study applications used in the book.

11.17 One alternative to prefetching is to use nonblocking load operations and to issue these operations significantly before the data is needed for computation. What are the trade-offs between prefetching and using nonblocking loads in this way?

11.18 Implementation issues for software-controlled prefetching can be divided into two categories: instruction set enhancements and keeping track of outstanding prefetches.

a. In what ways are prefetch instructions different from ordinary instructions?

b. There are many options for the format that a prefetch instruction can take. For example, some architectures allow a load instruction to have multiple flavors, one of which can be reserved for a prefetch. Or in architectures that reserve a particular register to always have the value zero (e.g., the MIPS and Sparc architectures), a load with that register as the destination can be interpreted as a prefetch since such a load does not change the contents of the register. A third option is to have a separate prefetch instruction in the instruction set, with a different opcode than a load.

(i) Which do you think is the best alternative and why?

(ii) What addressing mode would you use for a prefetch instruction and why?

c. Is it necessary to maintain state in the processor itself for outstanding prefetches? Does it improve performance? Why or why not? Would you merge this support with that for keeping track of outstanding writes or use separate structures? Discuss the trade-offs.

11.19 Consider some policy issues for software-controlled prefetching.

a. Suppose we issue prefetches when we expect the corresponding references to miss in the primary (first-level) cache. A question that arises is, which levels of the memory hierarchy beyond the first-level cache should we probe to see if the prefetch can be satisfied there? Since the compiler algorithm usually schedules prefetches by conservatively assuming that the latency to be hidden is the largest latency (uncontended, say) in the machine, one possibility is not to even check intermediate levels of the cache hierarchy but to always get the data from main memory or from another processor's cache (if the block is dirty). What are the problems with this method, and which one do you think is most important?

b. Since prefetches are hints, they can be dropped by the hardware without affecting correctness. Would you drop a prefetch (i) when it incurs a TLB miss, and (ii) when the buffer that keeps track of outstanding memory operations (including prefetches) is full? What are the key issues that inform your choices in the two cases?

11.20 Consider the trade-offs between prefetching into the primary cache and prefetching only into the second-level cache.

a. What are the qualitative trade-offs and issues that inform a choice? What would you do?

b. Using only the following parameters, construct an analytical expression for the circumstances under which prefetching into the primary cache is beneficial. p_t is the number of prefetches that bring data into the primary cache early enough, p_d is the number of cases in which the prefetched data is displaced from the cache before it is used, p_c is the number of cache conflicts in which prefetches replace useful data, p_f is the number of prefetch fills (i.e., the number of times a prefetch tries to put data into the primary cache), l_s is the access latency to the second-level cache (beyond that to the primary cache), and l_f is the average number of cycles that a prefetch fill stalls the processor. After generating the full-blown general expression, your goal is to find a condition on l_f that makes prefetching into the first-level cache worthwhile. To do this, you can make the following simplifying assumptions: $p_s = p_t - p_d$, and $p_c = p_d$. What about the analysis, or what it leaves out, strikes you as making it most difficult to rely on it in practice?

11.21 Consider a "blocked" context-switching processor (i.e., a processor that switches contexts only on long-latency events). Assume that arbitrarily many threads and contexts are available and clearly state any other assumptions that you make in answering the following questions. The threads of a given application have been analyzed to show the following execution profile:

- 40% of cycles spent on instruction execution (busy cycles)
- 30% of cycles spent stalled on L_1 cache misses but L_2 hits (10-cycle miss penalty)
- 30% of cycles spent stalled on L_2 cache misses (30-cycle miss penalty)

a. What will be the busy time if the context switch latency (cost) is 5 cycles?

b. What is the maximum context switch latency that will ensure that busy time is greater than or equal to 50%?

11.22 In blocked, multiple-context processors with caches, a context switch occurs whenever a reference misses in the cache. The blocking context at this point goes into "stalled" state, and it remains there until the requested data arrives back at the cache. At that point, it returns to "ready" state, and it will be allowed to run when the active contexts ahead of it block. When an active context first starts to run, it reissues the reference it had blocked on. In the scheme just described, can the interaction between the multiple contexts potentially lead to deadlock? If so, concretely describe an example where none of the contexts make forward progress. How might you prevent the problem? If not, say why not.

11.23 What do you think would happen to the idealized curve for processor utilization versus degree of multithreading in Figure 11.25 if cache misses were taken into account? Draw this more realistic curve on the same figure as the idealized curve.

11.24 Write the logic equation that decides whether to generate a context switch in the blocked scheme, given the following input signals: CacheMiss or CM, MissSwitch-Enable or MSE (enable switching on a cache miss), CE (signal that allows processor to enable context switching), OneCount(CValid) (number of ready contexts), ES (explicit context switch instruction), and TO (time-out). Write another equation to decide when the processor should stall rather than switch.

11.25 In discussing the implementation of the PC unit for the blocked multithreading approach, we said that the use of the exception PC for exceptions as well as context switches meant that context switching must be disabled upon an exception. Does this indicate that the kernel cannot use the hardware-provided multithreading at all? If so, why? If not, how would you arrange for the kernel to use the multiple hardware contexts?

11.26 Why is exception handling more complex in the interleaved scheme than in the blocked scheme? How would you handle the issues that arise?

11.27 How do you think the Tera processor might do lookahead across branches? The processor provides `JUMP_OFTEN` and `JUMP_SELDOM` branch operations. Why do you think it does this?

11.28 Consider a simple, HEP-like multithreaded machine with no caches. Assume that the average memory latency is 100 clock cycles. Each context has blocking loads and the machine enforces sequential consistency.

a. Given that 20% of a typical workload's instructions are loads and 10% are stores, how many active contexts are needed to hide the latency of the memory operations?

b. How many contexts would be required if the machine supported release consistency (still with blocking loads)? State any assumptions that you make.

c. How many contexts would be needed for parts (a) and (b) if we assumed a blocked multiple-context processor instead of the cycle-by-cycle interleaved HEP processor? Assume cache hit rates of 90% for both loads and stores.

d. For part (c), what is the peak processor utilization, assuming a context switch overhead of 10 cycles?

11.29 Studies of applications have shown that combining release consistency and prefetching always results in better performance than when either technique is used alone. This is not the case when multiple contexts and prefetching techniques are combined; the combined performance can sometimes be worse. Explain the latter observation, using an example situation to illustrate.

12

Future Directions

In the course of writing this book, the single factor that stood out most among the many interesting facets of parallel computer architecture was the tremendous pace of change. Critically important designs became "old news" as they were replaced by newer designs. Major open questions were answered while new ones took their place. Start-up companies left the marketplace as established companies made bold strides into parallel computing and powerful competitors joined forces. The first teraflops performance was achieved, and workshops had already been formed to understand how to accelerate progress toward petaflops. The movie industry produced its first full-length computer-animated motion picture on a large cluster, and for the first time a parallel chess program defeated a grand master. Meanwhile, multiprocessors emerged in huge volume with the Intel Pentium Pro and its glueless cache coherence memory bus. Parallel algorithms were put to work to improve uniprocessor performance by better utilizing the storage hierarchy. Networking technology, memory technology, and even processor design were all thrown up for grabs as we began looking seriously at what to do with a billion transistors on a chip.

Looking forward to the future of parallel computer architecture, the one prediction that can be made with certainty is continued change. The incredible pace of change makes parallel computer architecture an exciting field to study and in which to conduct research. We need to continually revisit basic questions, such as, What are the proper building blocks for parallel machines? What are the essential requirements on the processor design, the communication assist and how it integrates with the processor, and the memory and the interconnect? Will these continue to utilize commodity desktop components, or will a new divergence take place as parallel computing matures and the great volume of computers shifts into everyday appliances? The pace of change makes for rich opportunities in the industry but also for great challenges.

Although it is impossible to precisely predict where the field will go, this final chapter seeks to outline some of the key areas of development in parallel computer architecture and the related technologies. Whatever directions the market takes and whatever technological breakthroughs occur, the fundamental issues addressed throughout this book will still apply. The realization of parallel programming models will still rest upon the support for naming, ordering, and synchronization. Designers will still battle with overhead, latency, bandwidth, and cost. The core techniques for addressing these issues will remain valid; however, the way that they are employed will surely change as the critical coefficients of performance, cost, capacity, and scale continue to change. New algorithms will be invented, changing the fundamental application workload requirements, but the basic analysis techniques will remain.

Given the approach taken throughout the book, it only makes sense to structure the discussion of potential future directions around hardware and software. For each, we need to ask which trends are likely to continue, thus providing a basis for evolutionary development, and which are likely to stop abruptly, either because a fundamental limit is struck or because a breakthrough changes the direction. Section 12.1 examines trends in technology and architecture; Section 12.2 looks at how changing software requirements may influence the direction of system design and considers how the application base is likely to broaden and change.

12.1 TECHNOLOGY AND ARCHITECTURE

Technological forces shaping the future of parallel computer architecture can be placed into three categories: evolutionary forces, as indicated by past and current trends, fundamental limits that wall off further progress along a trend, and breakthroughs that create a discontinuity and establish new trends. Of course, only time will tell how these actually play out. This section examines all three scenarios and the architectural changes that might arise.

To help sharpen the discussion, let us consider two questions. At the high end, how will the next factor-of-1,000 increase in performance be achieved? At the more moderate scale, how will cost-effective parallel systems evolve? In 1998, computer systems form a parallelism pyramid roughly as in Figure 12.1. Overall shipments of uniprocessor PCs, workstations, and servers is on the order of tens to hundreds of millions. The 2–4 processor end of the parallel computer market, which makes up the second level, is on the scale of 100,000 to a few million. These are almost exclusively servers, with some growth toward the desktop. This segment of the market grew at a moderate pace throughout the 1980s and early 1990s and then shot up with the introduction of low-cost SMPs manufactured by leading PC vendors, as well as the traditional workstation and server vendors pushing costs down to expand volume. The next level is occupied by machines of 5 to 30 processors. These are exclusively high-end servers. The volume is in the tens of thousands of units and has been growing steadily; this segment dominates the high-end server market, including the enterprise market, which used to be the mainframe market. At the scale of several tens to a hundred processors, the volume is on the order of a few thousand systems. These tend to be dedicated engines supporting massive databases, large scientific applications, or major engineering investigations, such as oil exploration, structural modeling, or fluid dynamics. Volume shrinks rapidly beyond a hundred processors, with the order of tens of systems at the thousand-processor scale. Machines at the very top end have been on the scale of 1,000 to 2,000 processors since 1990. In 1996–1997, this figure stepped up toward 10,000 processors. The most visible machines at the very top end are dedicated to advanced scientific com-

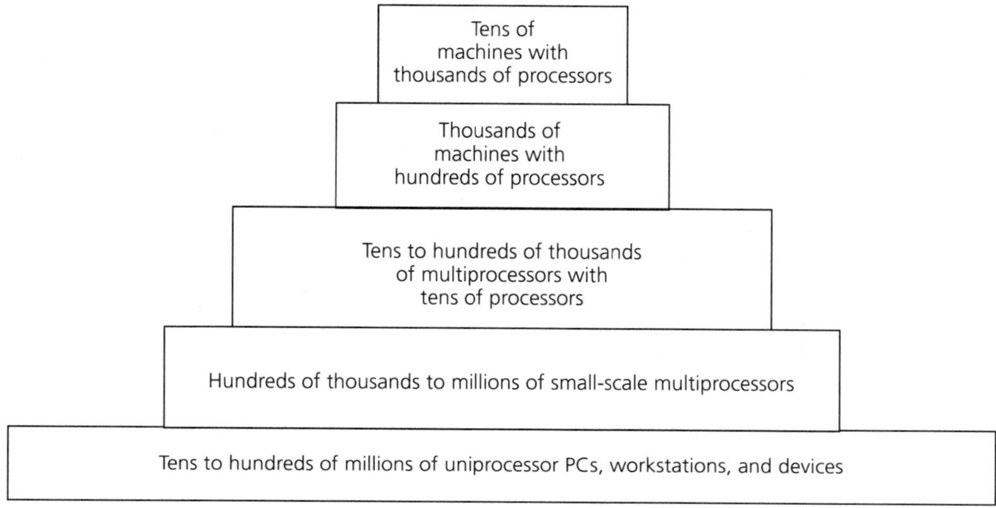

FIGURE 12.1 Market pyramid for parallel computers. The most powerful machines—parallel computers—at the tip of the market pyramid are focused on the requirements of the most demanding applications and must harness the latest advances in technology.

puting, including the U.S. Department of Energy "ASCI" teraflops machines and the Hitachi SR2201 funded by the Japanese Ministry of Technology and Industry.

12.1.1 Evolutionary Scenario

If current technology trends hold, parallel computer architecture can be expected to follow an evolutionary path in which economic and market forces play a crucial role. Let's expand this evolutionary forecast so that we can consider how the advance of the field may diverge from this path. Currently, we see processor performance increasing by about a factor of 100 per decade (or 200 per decade if the basis is LINPACK or SpecFP). DRAM capacity also increases by about a factor of 100 per decade (quadrupling every three years). Thus, current trends would suggest that the basic balance of computing performance to storage capacity (MFLOPS/MB) of the nodes in parallel machines could remain roughly constant. This ratio varies considerably in current machines, depending on application target and cost point, but under the evolutionary scenario the family of options would be expected to continue into the future with large increases in both capacity and performance. Simply riding the commodity growth curve, we could look toward achieving petaflops-scale performance by the year 2010, or perhaps a couple of years earlier if the scale of parallelism is increased, but such systems would be in excess of $100 million to construct. It is less clear what level of communication performance these machines will provide, for reasons that are discussed in the following. To achieve this scale of performance a lot earlier in a general-purpose system would involve an investment and a scale of engineering that is probably not practical, although special-purpose designs may advance the time frame for a limited set of applications.

To understand what architectural directions may be adopted, the VLSI technology trends underlying the performance and capacity trends of the components are important. Microprocessor clock rates are increasing by a factor of 10–15 per decade while transistors per microprocessor increase by more than a factor of 30 per decade. DRAM cycle times, on the other hand, improve much more slowly—roughly a factor of two per decade. Thus, the gap between processor speed and memory speed is likely to continue to widen. In order to stay on the processor performance growth trend, the increase in the ratio of memory access time to processor cycle time will require that processors employ better latency avoidance and latency tolerance techniques. In addition, the increase in processor instruction rates, due to the combination of cycle time and parallelism, will demand that the bandwidth delivered by the memory increase.[1]

Both of these factors—the need for latency avoidance and for high memory bandwidth—as well as the increase in on-chip storage capacity will cause the storage hierarchy to continue to become deeper and more complex. These two factors will cause the degree of dynamic scheduling of instruction-level parallelism to increase. Latency tolerance fundamentally involves allowing a large number of instructions, including several memory operations, to be in progress concurrently. Providing the memory system with multiple operations to work on at a time allows pipelining and interleaving to be used to increase bandwidth. Thus, the VLSI technology trends are likely to encourage the design of processors that are both more insulated from the memory system and more flexible so that they can adapt to the behavior of the memory system. This bodes well for parallel computer architecture because the processor component is likely to become increasingly robust to infrequent long-latency operations.

Unfortunately, neither caches nor dynamic instruction scheduling reduces the actual latency on an operation that crosses the processor chip boundary. Historically, each level of cache added to the storage hierarchy increases the cost of access to memory. (For example, we saw that the CRAY T3D and T3E designers eliminated a level of cache in the workstation design to decrease the memory latency, and the presence of a second-level on-chip cache in the T3E increased the communication latency.) This phenomenon of increasing latency with hierarchy depth is natural because designers rely on the hit being the frequent case; increasing the hit rate and reducing the hit time do more for processor performance than decreasing the miss penalty. The trend toward deeper hierarchies presents a problem for parallel architecture since communication, by its very nature, involves crossing out of the lowest level of the memory hierarchy on the node. The miss penalty contributes to the communication overhead, regardless of whether the communication abstraction is

1. Often, in observing the widening processor-memory speed gap, comparisons are made between processor rates with memory access times by taking the reciprocal of the access time. Comparing throughput and latency in this way makes the gap appear artificially wider.

shared address access or messages. Good architecture and clever programming can reduce the unnecessary communication to a minimum, but still each algorithm has some level of inherent communication. It is an open question whether designers will be able to achieve the low miss penalties required for efficient communication while attempting to maximize processor performance through deep hierarchies. There are, however, some positive indications in this direction. Many scientific applications have relatively poor cache behavior because they sweep through large data sets. Beginning with the IBM Power2 architecture and continuing in the SGI Power-Challenge and Sun UltraSparc, attention has been paid to improving the out-of-cache memory bandwidth, at least for sequential access. These efforts have proved very valuable for database applications. So we may be able to look forward to node memory structures that can sustain high bandwidth, even in the evolutionary scenario.

Indications are strong that multithreading will be utilized in future processor generations to hide the latency of local memory access. By introducing thread-level parallelism on a single processor, this direction further reduces the cost of the transition from one processor to multiple processors, thus making small-scale SMPs even more attractive on a broad extent. It also establishes an architectural direction that may yield much greater latency tolerance in the long term.

Link and switch bandwidths are increasing, although this phenomenon does not have the smooth evolution of CMOS under improving lithography and fabrication techniques. Links tend to advance through discrete technological changes. For example, copper links have transitioned through a series of driver circuits: unterminated lines carrying a single bit at a time were replaced by terminated lines with multiple bits pipelined on the wire; these may be replaced by active equalization techniques (Horowitz 1997). At the same time, links have gotten wider as connector technology has improved, allowing finer-pitched, better-matched connections, and cable manufacturing has advanced, providing better control over signal skew. For several years, it has seemed that fiber would soon take over as the technology of choice for high-speed links. However, the cost of transceivers and connectors has impeded its progress. This may change in the future, as the efficient LED arrays that have been available in gallium arsinide (GaAs) technologies become effective in CMOS. The real driver of cost reduction, of course, is volume. The arrival of gigabit Ethernet, which uses the FiberChannel physical link, may finally drive the volume of fiber transceivers up enough to cause a dramatic cost reduction. In addition, high-quality parallel fiber has been demonstrated. Thus, flexible high-performance fiber with a small physical cross section may provide an excellent link technology for some time to come.

The bandwidths that are required even for a uniprocessor design, and the number of simultaneous outstanding memory transactions needed to obtain this bandwidth, are stretching the limits of what can be achieved on a shared bus. Many system designs have already streamlined the bus design by requiring all components to transfer entire cache lines. Adapters for I/O devices are constructed with one-block caches that support the cache coherency protocol. Thus, essentially all systems will be constructed as SMPs, even if only one processor is attached. Increasingly, the bus is being replaced by a switch and the snooping protocols are being replaced by directories. For example, the HP/Convex Exemplar uses a crossbar, rather than a bus, with the PA-8000 processor, and the Sun UltraSparc UPA has a switched interconnect within the 2–4 processor node, although these nodes are connected by a packet-switched bus in the Enterprise 6000. The IBM PowerPC-based G30 uses a switch for the datapath but still uses a shared bus for address and snoop. The SGI Origin and Sun Enterprise 10000 have gone entirely to switches. Where buses are still used, they are packet switched (split phase). Thus, even in the evolutionary scenario, we can expect to see high-performance networks integrated ever more deeply into high-volume designs. This trend makes the transition from high-volume, moderate-scale parallel systems to large-scale, moderate-volume parallel systems more attractive because less new technology is required.

Higher-speed networks are a dominant concern for current I/O subsystems as well. A great deal of attention has been paid to improved I/O support, with PCI replacing traditional vendor I/O buses. There is a very strong desire to support faster local area networks, such as gigabit Ethernet, OC-12 ATM (622 Mb/s), SCI, Fiber-Channels, and P1394.2. A standard PCI bus can provide roughly 1 Gb/s of bandwidth. Extended PCI with 64-bit, 66-MHz operation exists and promises to become more widespread in the future, offering multigigabit performance on commodity machines. Several vendors are looking at ways of providing direct memory bus access for high-performance interconnects or distributed shared memory extensions.

These trends ensure that small-scale SMPs will continue to be very attractive and that clusters and more tightly packaged collections of commodity nodes will remain a viable option for the large scale. It is very likely that these designs will continue to improve as high-speed network interfaces become more mature. We are already seeing a trend toward better integration of network interfaces with the cache coherence protocols so that control registers can be cached and DMA can be performed directly on user-level data structures (Mukherjee and Hill 1997). For many reasons, large-scale designs are likely to use SMP nodes, so clusters of SMPs are likely to be a very important vehicle for parallel computing. With the recent introduction of the CC-NUMA-based designs, such as the HP/Convex SPP, the SGI Origin, and especially the Pentium Pro–based machines, large-scale cache-coherent designs look increasingly attractive. The core question is whether a truly composable SMP-based node will emerge so that large clusters of SMPs can essentially be snapped together as easily as adding memory or I/O devices to a single node.

12.1.2 Hitting a Wall

So, if current trends hold, the evolution of parallel computer architecture looks bright. Why might this not happen? Might we hit a wall instead? There are three basic possibilities: a latency wall, an overhead wall, and a cost or power wall.

The latency wall fundamentally is the speed of light or, rather, of the propagation of electrical signals. We will soon see processors operating at clock rates in excess of 1 GHz or a clock period of less than 1 ns. Signals travel about a foot per ns. In the evolutionary view, the physical size of the node does not get much smaller; it gets faster with more storage, but it is still several chips with connectors and PC board traces. Indeed, from 1987 to 1997, the footprint of a basic processor and memory module did not shrink much. There was an improvement from two nodes per board to about four when first-level caches moved on chip and DRAM chips were turned on their side as SIMMs, but most designs maintained one level of cache off chip. Even if the off-chip caches are eliminated (as in the CRAY T3D and T3E), the processor chip consumes more power with each generation, and a substantial amount of surface area is needed to dissipate the heat. Thus, 1,000-processor machines will still be meters across, not inches.

Although the latency wall is real, there are several reasons why it probably will not impede the practical evolution of parallel architectures in the foreseeable future. One reason is that latency tolerance techniques at the processor level are quite effective on the scale of tens of cycles. Some studies have suggested that caches are losing their effectiveness even on uniprocessors because of memory access latency (Burger, Goodman, and Kagi 1996). However, these studies assume memory operations that are not pipelined and a processor typical of mid-1990s designs. Other studies suggest that if memory operations are pipelined and if the processor is allowed to issue several instructions from a large instruction window, then branch prediction accuracy is a far more significant limit on performance than latency (Jouppi and Ranganathan 1997). With perfect prediction, such an aggressive design can tolerate memory access times in the neighborhood of 100 cycles for many applications. Multithreading techniques provide an alternative source of instruction-level parallelism that can be used to hide latency, even with imperfect branch prediction. But such latency tolerance techniques fundamentally demand bandwidth, and bandwidth comes at a cost. The cost arises either through higher signaling rates, more wires, more pins, more real estate, or some combination of these. In addition, the degree of pipelining that a component can support is limited by its occupancy. To hide latency requires careful attention to the occupancy of every stage along the path of access or communication. Where the occupancy cannot be reduced, interleaving techniques must be used to reduce the effective occupancy.

Following the evolutionary path, speed-of-light effects are likely to be dominated by bandwidth effects on latency. Currently, a single cache-line-sized transfer is several hundred bits in length, and since links are relatively narrow, a single network transaction reaches entirely across the machine with fast cut-through routing. As links get wider, the effective length of a network transaction (i.e., the number of phits) will shrink, but quite a bit of room for growth remains before it takes more than a couple of concurrent transactions per processor to cover the physical latency. Moreover, cache block sizes are increasing just to amortize the cost of a DRAM access, so the length of a network transaction and, hence, the number of outstanding transactions required to hide latency may be nearly constant as machines evolve. Explicit message sizes are likely to follow a similar trend since processors tend to be inefficient in manipulating objects smaller than a cache block.

Much of the communication latency today is in the network interface (in particular, in the store-and-forward delay at the source and at the destination) rather than in the network itself. The network interface latency is likely to be reduced as designs mature and as it becomes a larger fraction of the network latency. Consider, for example, what would be required to cut through one or both of the network interfaces. On the source side, there is no difficulty in translating the destination to a route and spooling the message onto the wire as it becomes available from the processor. However, the processor may not be able to provide the data into the NI as fast as the NI spools data into the network; so as part of the link protocol, it may be necessary to hold back the message (transferring idle phits on the wire). This machinery is already built into most switches. Machines such as the Intel Paragon, Meiko CS-2, and CRAY T3D provide flow control all the way through the NI and back to the memory system in order to perform large block transfers without a store-and-forward delay. Alternatively, it may be possible to design the communication assist such that once a small message starts onto the wire (e.g., a cache line) it is completely transferred without delay.

Avoiding the store-and-forward delay on the destination is a bit more challenging because, in general, it is not possible to determine that the data in the message is good until the data has been received and checked. If it is spooled directly into memory, junk may be deposited. The key observation is that it is much more important that the address be correct than that the data contents be correct because we do not want to spool data into the wrong place in memory. A separate checksum can be provided on the header. The header is checked before the message is spooled into the destination node. A large transfer typically involves a completion event so that data can be spooled into memory and checked before being marked as "arrived." Note that this means that the communication abstraction should not allow applications to poll data values within the bulk transfer to detect completion. For small transfers, a variety of tricks can be played to move the data into the cache speculatively. Basically, a line is allocated in the cache and the data is transferred, but if it does not checksum correctly, the valid bit on the line is never set. Thus, greater attention will need to be paid to communication events in the design of the communication assist and memory system, but it is possible to streamline network transactions much more than the current state of the art to reduce latency.

The primary reason that parallel computers will not hit a fundamental latency wall is that overall communication latency will continue to be dominated by overhead. The latency will be there, but it will still be a modest fraction of the actual communication time. The reason for this lies deep in the current industrial design process. Where there are one or more levels of cache on the processor chip, an off-chip cache, and then the memory system, in designing a cache controller for a given level of the memory hierarchy, the designer is given a problem that has a fast side toward the processor and a slow side toward the memory. The design goal is to minimize the expression

$$\text{Average Memory Access}\ (S) = \text{Hit Time} \times \text{Hit Rate}_S + (1 - \text{Hit Rate}_S) \times \text{Miss Time} \tag{12.1}$$

for a typical address stream, S, delivered to the cache on the processor side.

This design goal presents an inherent trade-off because improvements in any one component generally come at the cost of worsening the others. Thus, along each direction in the design space, the optimal design point is a compromise between extremes. The *H*it Time is generally fixed by the target rate of the fast component. This establishes a limit against which the rest of the design is optimized; that is, the designer will do whatever is required to keep the *H*it Time within this limit. We can consider cache organizational improvements, such as higher associativity, to improve the *H*it Rate, but only as long as it can be accomplished in the desired *H*it Time (Przbylski, Horowitz, and Hennessy 1988). The critical aspect for parallel architecture concerns the *M*iss Time. How hard is the designer likely to work to drive down the *M*iss Time? The usual rule of thumb is to make the two additive components roughly equal. This guarantees that the design is within a factor of two of optimal and tends to be good in practice. The key point is that since *M*iss Rates are small for a uniprocessor, the *M*iss Time can be a large multiple of the *H*it Time. For first-level caches with greater than 95% hit rates, it may be 20 times the *H*it Time and for lower-level caches it will still be an order of magnitude. A substantial fraction of the *M*iss Time is occupied by the transfer to the lower level of the storage hierarchy, and small additions to this have only a modest effect on uniprocessor performance. The cache designer will utilize this small degree of freedom in many useful ways. For example, cache line sizes can be increased to improve the *H*it Rate, at the cost of a longer *M*iss Time.

In addition, each level of the storage hierarchy adds to the cost of the data transfer because another interface must be crossed. In order to modularize the design, interfaces tend to decouple the operations on either side. There is some cost to the handshake between caches on chip; there is a larger cost in the interface between an on-chip cache and an off-chip cache and a much larger cost to the more elaborate protocol required across the memory bus. In addition, for communication, there is the protocol associated with the network itself. The accumulation of these effects is why the actual communication latency tends to be many times the lower bound imposed by the speed of light. The natural response of the designer responsible for dealing with communication aspects of a design is invariably to increase the minimum data transfer size, for example, increasing the cache line size or the smallest message fragment. This shifts the critical time from latency to occupancy. If each transfer is large enough to amortize the overhead, the additional speed-of-light latency is again a modest addition.

Wherever the design is partitioned into multiple levels of storage hierarchy with the emphasis placed on maximizing a level relative to the processor-side reference stream, the natural tendency of the designers will result in a multiplication of overhead with each level between the processor and the communication assist. In order to get close to the speed-of-light latency limit, a very different design methodology will need to be established for processor design, cache design, and memory design. One of the architectural trends that may bring about this change is the use of extensive out-of-order execution or multithreading to hide latency, even in uniprocessor systems. These techniques change the cache designer's goal. Instead of minimizing the sum of the two components in Equation 12.1, the goal is essentially to minimize each component.

When a miss occurs, the processor does not wait for it to be serviced; it continues executing and issues more requests, many of which hit. In the meantime, the cache is busy servicing the miss. Hopefully, the miss will be complete by the time another miss is generated or the processor runs out of things it can do without the miss completing. The miss needs to be detected and dispatched for service without many cycles of processor overhead, even though it will take some time to process it. In effect, the miss needs to be handed off for processing essentially within the *Hit* Time budget.

Moreover, it may be necessary to sustain multiple outstanding requests to keep the processor busy, as fully explained in Chapter 11. The *Miss* Time may be too large for a one-to-one balance in the components of Equation 12.1 to be met, either because of latency or occupancy effects. Misses and communication events tend to cluster, so the interval between operations that need servicing is frequently much less than the average.

Little's Law suggests the existence of another potential wall—a cost wall. It says that if the total latency that needs to be hidden is L and the rate of long-latency requests is ρ, then the number of outstanding requests per processor when the latency is hidden is ρL, or greater when clustering is considered. With this number of communication events in flight, the total bandwidth delivered by the network with P processors needs to be $P\rho L(P)$, where $L(P)$ reflects the increase in latency with machine size. This requirement establishes a lower bound on the cost of the network. To deliver this bandwidth, the aggregate bandwidth of the network itself will need to be much higher, as discussed in Chapter 10, since there will be bursts, collisions, and so on. Thus, to stay on the evolutionary path, latency tolerance will need to be considered in many aspects of the system design, and network technology will need to improve in bandwidth and in cost.

12.1.3 Potential Breakthroughs

We have seen so far a rosy evolutionary path for the advancement of parallel architecture, with some dark clouds that might hinder this advance. Is there also a silver lining? Are there aspects of the technological trends that may create new possibilities for parallel computer design? The answer is certainly in the affirmative, but the specific directions are not certain. Whereas it is possible that dramatic technological changes, such as quantum devices, free space optical interconnects, molecular computing, or nanomechanical devices, are around the corner, there appears to be substantial room left in the advance of conventional CMOS VLSI devices (Patterson 1995). The simple fact of the continued increase in the level of integration is likely to bring about a revolution in parallel computer design.

From an academic viewpoint, it is easy to underestimate the importance of packaging thresholds in the process of continued integration, but history shows that these factors are dramatic indeed. The general effect of the thresholds of integration is illustrated in Figure 12.2, which shows two qualitative trends. The straight line

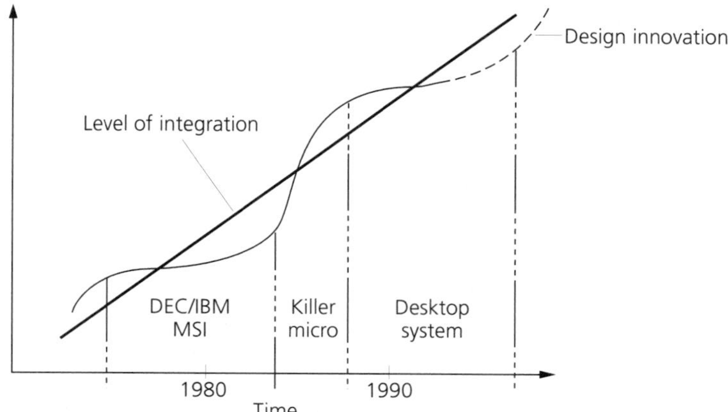

FIGURE 12.2 Tides of change. The history of computing oscillates between periods of stable development and rapid innovation. Enabling technology generally does not hit all of a sudden; it arrives and evolves. The "revolutions" occur when technology crosses a key threshold. One example is the arrival of the 32-bit microprocessor in the mid-1980s, which broke the stable hold of the less integrated minicomputers and mainframes and enabled a renaissance in computer design, including low-level parallelism on chip and high-level parallelism through multiprocessor designs. In the late1990s, this transition is fully mature, and microprocessor-based desktop and server technology dominate all segments of the market. There is tremendous convergence in parallel machine design. However, the level of integration continues to rise, and soon the single-chip computer will be as natural as the single-board computer of the 1980s. The question is what new renaissance of design this will enable.

reflects the steady increase in the level of systems integration with time. Overlaid on this is a curve depicting the amount of innovation in system design. A given design regime tends to be stable for a considerable period in spite of technological advance, but when the level of integration crosses a critical threshold, many new design options are enabled and a design renaissance takes place. The figure shows two of the epochs in the history of computer architecture.

Recall that during the late 1970s and early 1980s computer system design followed a stable evolutionary path with clear segments: minicomputers, dominated by the DEC Vax in engineering and academic markets; mainframes, dominated by IBM in the commercial markets; and vector supercomputers, dominated by CRAY Research in the scientific market. The minicomputer had burst on the scene as a result of an earlier technology threshold where MSI and LSI components, especially semiconductor memories, permitted the design of complex systems with relatively little engineering effort. In particular, this level of integration permitted the use of microprogramming techniques to support a large virtual address space and complex instruction set. The mainframes had persisted from an earlier epoch. The vector supercomputer niche reflected the end of a transition. Its exquisite ECL circuit design, coupled with semiconductor memory in a clean load-store architecture wiped out the earlier, more exotic parallel machine designs. These three major segments evolved in a predictable, evolutionary fashion, each with their market segment, while the microprocessor marched forward from 4 bits to 8 bits to 16 bits, bringing with it the personal computer and the graphics workstation.

In the mid-1980s, the microprocessor reached a critical threshold where a full 32-bit processor fit on a chip. Suddenly, the entire picture changed. A complete computer of significant performance and capacity fit on a board. Several such boards could be put in a system. Bus-based cache-coherent SMPs appeared from many small companies, including Synapse, Encore, Flex, and Sequent. Relatively large message-passing systems appeared from Intel, nCUBE, Ametek, Inmos, and Thinking Machines Corporation. At the same time, several minisupercomputer vendors appeared, including Multiflow, FPS, Culler Scientific, Convex, Scientific Computing System, and Cydrome. Several of these companies failed as the new plateau was established. The workstation and later the personal computer absorbed the technical computing aspect of the minicomputer market. SMP servers took over the larger-scale data centers, transaction processing, and engineering analysis, eliminating the minisuper. The vector supercomputers gave way to massively parallel microprocessor-based systems. Since that time, the evolution of designs has again stabilized. The understanding of cache coherence techniques has advanced, allowing shared address support at an increasingly large scale. The transition of scalable, low-latency networks from MPPs to conventional LAN or computer room environments has allowed casually engineered clusters of PCs, workstations, or SMPs to deliver substantial performance at very low cost, essentially as a personal supercomputer. Several very large machines are constructed as clusters of shared memory machines of various sizes. The convergence observed throughout this book is clearly in progress, and the basic design question facing parallel machine designers is how the commodity components will be integrated, not what components will be used.

Meanwhile, the level of integration in microprocessors and memories is fast approaching a new critical threshold where a complete computer fits on a chip, not a board. Microprocessors are on the way to 100 million transistors by the turn of the century. Soon after the turn of the century, the gigabit DRAM chip will arrive. This new threshold is likely to bring about a new design renaissance as profound as that of the 32-bit microprocessor of the mid-1980s, the semiconductor memory of the mid-1970s, and the integrated circuit of the 1960s. Basically, the strong differentiation between processor chips and memory chips will break down, and most chips will have processing logic and memory.

It is easy to enumerate reasons why the processor-and-memory level of integration will take place and is likely to enable dramatic change in computer design, especially parallel computer design. Several research projects are investigating aspects of this new design space, under a variety of acronyms (PIM, IRAM, C-RAM, etc.). To avoid confusion with these acronyms, let us give the processor-and-memory concept yet another acronym—PAM. Only history will reveal which old architectural ideas will gain new life and which completely new ideas will arrive. Let's look at some of the technological factors leading toward new design options.

Table 12.1 Fraction of Microprocessor Chips Devoted to Memory

Year	Microprocessor	On-Chip Cache Size	Total Transistors	Fraction Devoted to Memory	Die Area (mm^2)	Fraction Devoted to Memory
1993	Intel Pentium	I: 8 KB D: 8 KB	3.1 M	32%	~300	32%
1995	Intel Pentium Pro	I: 8 KB D: 8 KB L_2: 512 KB	P: 5.5 M +L_2: 31 M	P: 18% +L_2: 100% (Total: 88%)	P: 242 +L_2: 282	P: 23% +L_2: 100% (Total: 64%)
1994	Digital Alpha 21164	I: 8 KB D: 8 KB L_2: 96 KB	9.3 M	77%	298	37%
1996	Digital Strong-Arm SA-110	I: 16 KB D: 16 KB	2.1 M	95%	50	61%

I: instruction; D: data; P: processor die; L_2: level 2

One clear factor is that microprocessor chips are mostly memory. It is SRAM memory used for caches, but memory nonetheless. Table 12.1 shows the fraction of the transistors and die area used for caches and memory interface, including store buffers and so on, for four recent microprocessors from two vendors (Patterson et al. 1997). The actual processor is a small and diminishing component of the microprocessor chip, even though processors are getting quite complicated. This trend is made even more clear by Figure 12.3, which shows the fraction of the transistors devoted to caches in several microprocessors over the past decade (Burger 1997).

The vast majority of the real estate and an even larger fraction of the transistors are used for data storage and organized as multiple levels of on-chip caches. This investment in on-chip storage is necessary because of the time to access off-chip memory, that is, the latency of chip interface, off-chip caches, memory bus, memory controller, and the actual DRAM. For many applications, the best way to improve performance is to increase the amount of on-chip storage.

One clear opportunity this technological trend presents is putting multiple processors on chip. Since the processor is only a small fraction of the chip real estate, the potential peak performance can be increased dramatically at a small incremental cost. The argument for this approach is further strengthened by the diminishing returns in performance for processor complexity; for example, the real estate devoted to register ports, the instruction prefetch window, and hazard detection, and bypassing each increase more than linearly with the number of instructions issued per cycle while performance improves little beyond four-way issue superscalar. Thus, for the same area, multiple processors of a less aggressive design can be employed (Olukotun et al. 1996). This motivates reexamination of sharing issues

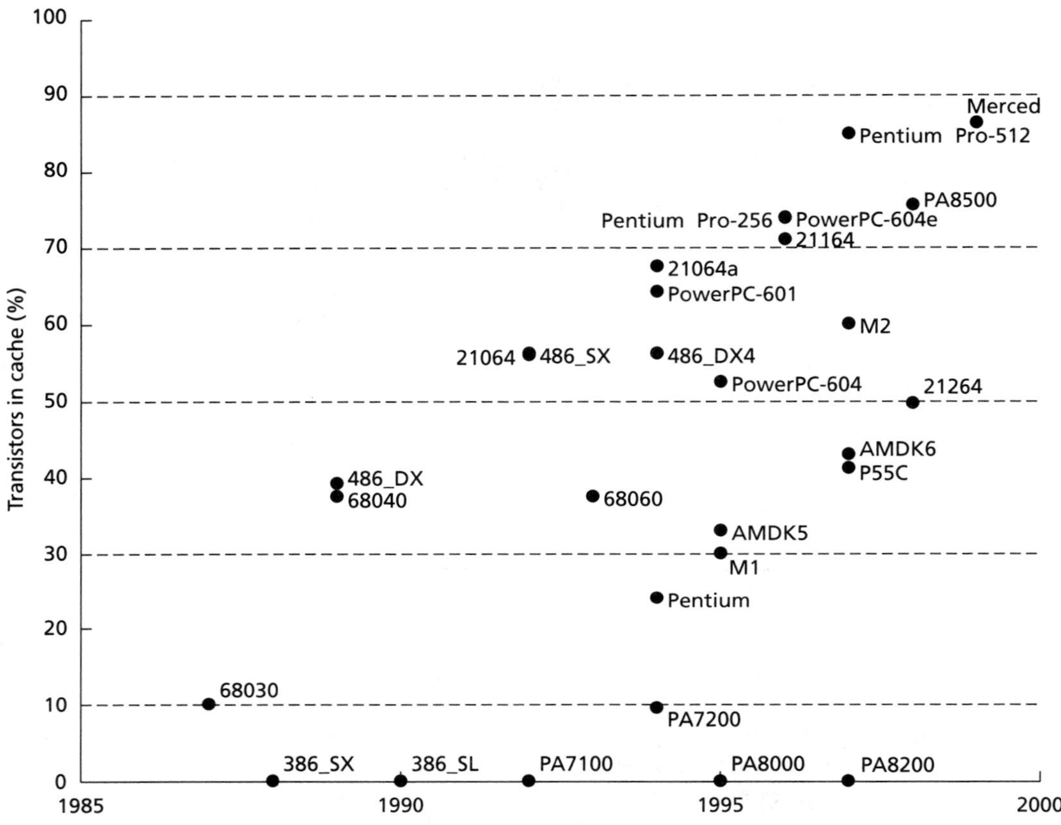

FIGURE 12.3 Fraction of transistors on microprocessor chips devoted to caches. Since caches migrated on chip in the mid-1980s, the fraction of the transistors on commercial microprocessors that are devoted to caches has risen steadily. Although the processors are complex and exploit substantial instruction-level parallelism, only by providing a great deal of local storage and exploiting locality can their bandwidth requirements be satisfied at reasonable latency.

that have evolved along with technology on SMPs since the mid-1980s. Most of the early machines shared an off-chip first-level cache, then there was room for separate caches, then L_1 caches moved on chip, and L_2 caches were sometimes shared and sometimes not. Many of the basic trade-offs remain the same in the board-level and chip-level multiprocessors: sharing caches closer to the processor allows for finer-grained data sharing and eliminates further levels of coherence support but increases access time due to the interconnect on the fast side of the shared cache. Sharing at any level presents the possibility of positive or negative interference, depending on the application usage pattern. However, the board-level designs were largely determined by the particular properties of the available components. With multiple processors on chip, all the design options can be considered within the same homogeneous medium. In addition, the specific trade-offs are different because of the different costs and performance characteristics. Given the broad emergence of inexpensive SMPs, especially with glueless cache coherence support, multiple processors on a chip is a natural path of evolution for multiprocessors.

A somewhat more radical change is suggested by the observation that the large volume of storage next to the processor could be DRAM, rather than SRAM, storage. Traditionally, SRAM uses the same manufacturing techniques as processors, and DRAM uses quite different techniques. The engineering requirements for microprocessors and DRAMs are traditionally very different. Microprocessor fabrication is intended to provide high clock rates and ample connectivity for datapaths and control using multiple layers of metal, whereas DRAM fabrication focuses on density and yield at minimal cost. The packages are very different. Microprocessors use expensive packages with many pins for bandwidth and materials designed to dissipate large amounts of heat. DRAM packages have few pins, low cost, and are suited to the low-power characteristics of DRAM circuits. However, these differences are diminishing. DRAM fabrication processes have become better suited for processor implementations, with two or three levels of metal and better logic speed (Saulsbury, Pong, and Nowatzyk 1996).

The drive toward integrating logic into the DRAM is driven partly by necessity and partly by opportunity. The immense increase in capacity (factor of four every three years) has required that the internal organization of the DRAM and its interface change. Early designs consisted of a single, square array of bits. The address was presented in two pieces, so a row could be read from the array and then a column selected. As the capacity increased, it was necessary to place several smaller arrays on the chip and to provide an interconnect between the many arrays and the pins. In addition, with limited pins and a need to increase the bandwidth, part of the DRAM chip needs to run at a higher rate. Many modern DRAM designs, including synchronous DRAM, enhanced DRAM, and RAMBUS, make effective use of the row buffers within the DRAM chip and provide high bandwidth transfers between the row buffers and the pins. These approaches require that DRAM processes be capable of supporting logic as well. At the same time, there were many opportunities to incorporate new logic functions into the DRAM, especially for graphics support in video RAMs. For example, 3D-RAM places logic for z-buffer operations directly in the video RAM chip that provides the frame buffer.

The attractiveness of integrating processor and memory is very much a threshold phenomenon. Although processor design was constrained by chip area, there was certainly no motivation to use fabrication techniques other than those specialized for fast processors; and although memory chips were small, so many were used in a system that there was no justification for the added cost of incorporating a processor. However, the capacity of DRAMs has been increasing more rapidly than the transistor count or, more importantly, the area used for processors. At the gigabit DRAM or perhaps the following generation, the incremental cost of the processor is modest, perhaps 20%. From the processor designer's viewpoint, the advantage of DRAM over SRAM is that it has better density by more than an order of magnitude.

However, access time is greater, access is more restrictive, and refresh is required (Saulsbury, Pong, and Nowatzyk 1996).

Somewhat more subtle threshold phenomena further increase the attractiveness of PAM. The capacity of DRAM has been growing faster than the demand for storage in most applications. The rapid increase in capacity has been beneficial at the high end because it became possible to run very large problems, which tends to reduce the communication-to-computation ratio and make parallel processing more effective. At the low end, it has had the effect of reducing the number of memory chips sold per system. When there are only a few memory chips, traditional DRAM interfaces with few pins do not work well, so new DRAM interfaces with high-speed logic are essential. When there is only one memory chip in a typical system, a huge cost savings results by bringing the processor on chip and eliminating everything in between. However, this raises a question of what the memory organization should be for larger systems.

Augmenting the impact of critical thresholds of evolving technology are new technological factors and market changes. One is high-speed CMOS serial links. Standard cells are available that will drive in excess of 1 Gb/s on a serial link, and substantially higher rates have been demonstrated in laboratory experiments. Previously, these rates were only available with expensive ECL circuits or GaAs technology. High-speed links using a few pins provide a cost-effective means of integrating PAM chips into a large system and can form the basis for the parallel machine interconnection network. A second factor is the advancement and widespread use of configurable logic technology. This makes it possible to fabricate a single building block with processor, memory, and unconfigured logic, which can then be configured to suit a variety of applications. The final factor is the development of low-power microprocessors for the rapidly growing market of network appliances, sometimes called WebPCs or Java stations, palmtop computers, and other sophisticated electronic devices. For many of these applications, modest single-chip PAMs provide ample processing and storage capacity. The huge volume of these markets may indeed make PAM the commodity building block rather than the desktop system.

The question presented by these technological opportunities is how the organizational structure of the computer node should change. The basic starting point is indicated by Figure 12.4, which shows that each of the subsystems between the processor and the DRAM bit array presents a narrow interface because pins and wires are expensive, even though they are relatively wide internally, and add latency. Within the DRAM chips, the datapath is extremely wide. The bit array itself is a collection of incredibly tightly packed trench capacitors, so little can be done there. However, the data buffers between the bit array and the external interface are still wide, less dense, and essentially SRAM and logic. Recall that when a DRAM is read, a portion of the address is used to select a row, which is read into the data buffer, and then another portion of the address is used to select a few bits from the data buffer. The buffer is written back to the row since the read is destructive. On a write, the row is read, a portion is modified in the buffer, and eventually it is written back.

Current research investigates three basic restructuring possibilities, each of which has substantial history and can be understood, explored, and evaluated in terms of

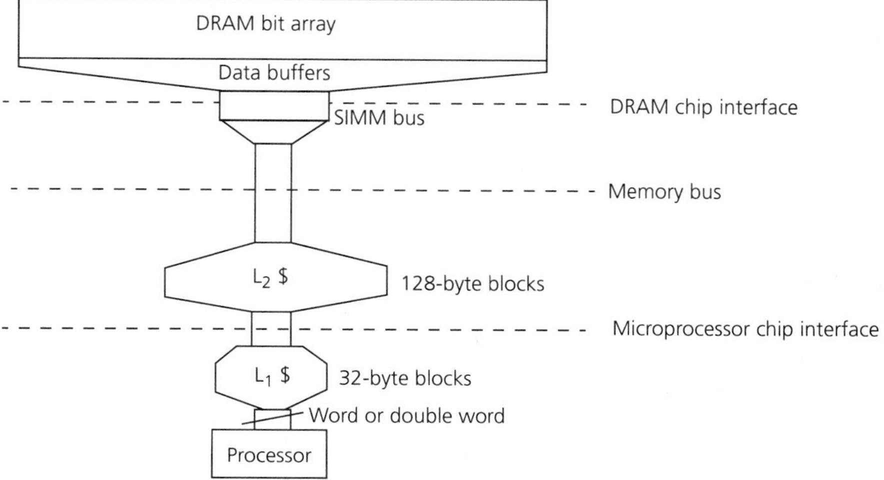

FIGURE 12.4 Bandwidths across a computer system. The processor datapath is several words wide but typically has a couple word-wide interface to its L_1 cache. The L_1 cache blocks are 32 or 64 bytes wide, but they are constrained between the processor word-at-a-time operation and the microprocessor chip interface. The L_2 cache blocks are even wider, but they are constrained between the microprocessor chip interface and the memory bus interface, both width critical. The SIMMS that form a bank of memory may have an interface that is wider and slower than the memory bus. Internally, this is a small section of a very wide data buffer, which is transferred directly to and from the actual bit arrays.

the fundamental design principles put forward in this book. They are surveyed briefly here, but the reader will surely want to consult the most recent literature and the Web.

The first option is to place simple, dedicated processing elements into the logic associated with the data buffers of more or less conventional DRAM chips, indicated in Figure 12.5. This approach has been called *processor-in-memory* (PIM) (Gokhale, Holmes, and Iobst 1995) and *Computational RAM* (Kogge 1994; Elliot, Snelgrove, and Stumm 1992). It is fundamentally SIMD processing of a restricted class of data parallel operations. Typically, these will be small bit-serial processors providing basic logic operations, but they could operate on multiple bits or even a word at a time. As we saw in Chapter 1, the approach has appeared several times in the history of parallel computer architecture. Usually it appears at the beginning of a technological transition when a general-purpose operation is not quite feasible, so the specialized operation enjoys a generous performance advantage. Each time it has proved applicable for a limited class of operations, usually image processing, signal processing, or dense linear algebra, and each time it has given way to more general-purpose solutions as the underlying technology evolves.

For example, in the early 1960s, there were numerous SIMD machines proposed that would allow construction of a high-performance machine by replicating only the function units and sharing a single-instruction sequencer, including Staran,

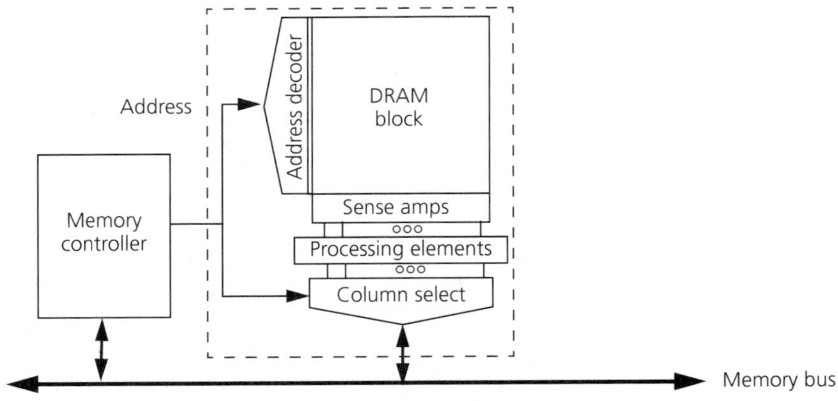

FIGURE 12.5 Processor-in-memory organization. Simple function units (processing elements) are incorporated into the data buffers of fairly conventional DRAM chips.

PEPE, and Illiac. The early effort culminated in the development of the Illiac IV at the University of Illinois, which took many years and became operational only months before the CRAY-1. In the early 1980s, the approach appeared again with the ICL DAP, which provided an array of compact processors and got a big boost in the mid-1980s when processor chips got large enough to support 32-bit serial processors but not a full 32-bit processor. The Goodyear MPP, Thinking Machines CM-1, and MasPar grew out of this window of opportunity. The key recognition that made the latter two machines much more successful than any previous SIMD approach was the need to provide a general-purpose interconnect between the processing elements, not just a low-dimensional grid, which is clearly cheap to build. Thinking Machines also was able to capture the arrival of the single-chip floating-point unit and to modify the design in the CM-2 to provide operations on 2-K 32-bit PEs rather than 64-K 1-bit PEs. However, these designs were fundamentally challenged by Amdahl's Law since the high-performance mode could only be applied on the fraction of the problem that fits the specialized operations. Within a few years, they yielded to MPP designs with a few thousand general-purpose microprocessors, which could perform SIMD operations and more general operations so that the parallelism could be utilized more of the time. The PIM approach was deployed in the CRAY 3/SSS (before the company filed Chapter 11) to provide special support for the National Security Agency. It has also been demonstrated for more conventional technology (Aimoto et al. 1996; Shimuzu et al. 1996).

A second restructuring option is to enhance the data buffers associated with banks of DRAM so they can be used as vector registers, as in Figure 12.6 (Patterson et al. 1997). There can be high-bandwidth transfers between DRAM rows and vector registers using the width of the bit arrays, but arithmetic is performed on vector registers by streaming the data through a small collection of conventional function

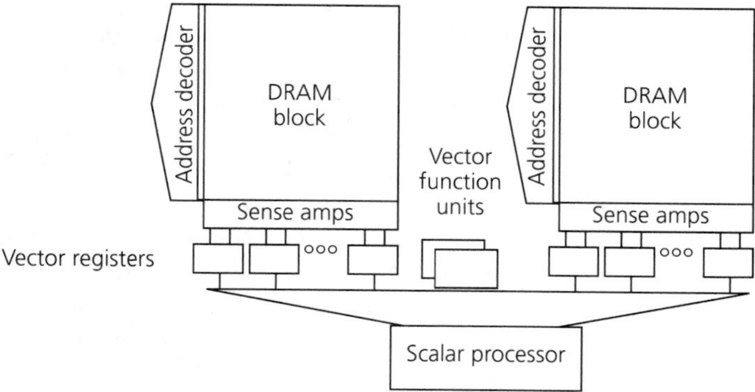

FIGURE 12.6 Vector DRAM organization. DRAM data buffers are enhanced to provide vector registers, which can be streamed through pipelined function units. On-chip memory system and vector support is interfaced to a scalar processor, possibly with its own caches.

units. This approach also rests on a good deal of history, including the very successful CRAY machines as well as several unsuccessful attempts. The CRAY-1 success was startling in part because of the contrast with the unsuccessful CDC Star-100 vector processor a year earlier. The Star-100 internally operated on short segments of data that were streamed out of memory into temporary registers. However, it provided vector operations only on contiguous (stride 1) vectors, and the core memory it employed had long latency. The success of the CRAY-1 was not just a matter of exposing the vector registers but a combination of its use of fast semiconductor memory, providing a general interconnect between the vector registers and many banks of memory so that nonunit stride and (later) gather/scatter operations could be performed, and a very efficient coupling of the scalar and vector operations. In other words, it provided low latency and high bandwidth for general access patterns and efficient synchronization. Several later attempts at this style of design in newer technologies failed to appreciate these lessons completely, including the FPS-DMAX, which provided linear combinations of vectors in memory; the Stellar, Ardent, and Stardent vector workstations; the Star-100 vector extension to the SparcStation; the vector units in the memory controllers of the CM-5; and the vector function units on the Meiko CS-2. It is easy to become enamored with the peak performance and low cost of the special case, but if the start-up costs are large, addressing capability is limited, or interaction with scalar access is awkward, the fraction of time that the extension is actually used drops quickly and the approach is vulnerable to the general-purpose solution.

The third option pursues a general-purpose design but removes the layers of abstraction that have been associated with the distinct packaging of processors, off-chip caches, and memory systems. Basically, the data buffers associated with the DRAMs are utilized as the final layer of caches. This is quite attractive since advanced DRAM designs have essentially been using the data buffers as caches for several years. However, in the past, they were constrained by the narrow interface out of the DRAM chips and the limited protocols of the memory bus. In the more integrated design, the DRAM buffer caches can interface directly to the higher-level caches of one or more on-chip processors. This approach changes the basic cache design trade-offs somewhat, but conventional analysis techniques apply. The cost of long lines is reduced since the transfer between the data buffer and the bit array is performed in parallel. The current high cost of logic near the DRAM tends to place a higher cost on associativity. Thus, many approaches use direct-mapped DRAM buffer caches and employ victim buffers or analogous techniques to reduce the rate of conflict misses (Saulsbury, Pong, and Nowatzyk 1996). When these integrated designs are used as a building block for parallel machines, the expected effects are observed of long cache blocks causing increased false sharing along with improved data prefetching when spatial locality is present (Nayfeh, Hammond, and Olukotun 1996).

When the PAM approach moves from the stage of academic, simulation-based study to active commercial development, we can expect to see an even more profound effect arising from the change in the design process. No longer is a cache designer in a position of optimizing one step in the path, constrained by a fast interface on one side and a slow interface on the other. The boundaries will have been removed, and the design can be optimized as an end-to-end problem. All of the possibilities we have seen for integrating the communication assist are present: at the processor, into the cache controller, or into the memory controller; but in PAM they can be addressed in a uniform framework rather than within the particular constraint of each component of the system.

However the detailed design of integrated processor and memory components shakes out, these components are likely to provide a new, universal building block for larger-scale parallel machines. Clearly, collections of them can be connected together to form distributed-memory machines, and the communication assist is likely to be much better integrated with the rest of the design since it is all on one chip. In addition, the interconnect pins are likely to be the only external interface, so communication efficiency will be even more critical. It will clearly be possible to build parallel machines on a scale far beyond what has been possible. A practical limit that has stayed roughly constant since the earliest computers is that large-scale systems are limited to about 10,000 components. Larger systems have been built but tend to be difficult to maintain. In the early days, it was 10,000 vacuum tubes, then 10,000 gates, then 10,000 chips. Recently, large machines have had about 1,000 processors and each processor required about 10 components, either chips or memory SIMMS. The first teraflops machine has almost 10,000 processors, each with multiple chips, so we will see if the pattern has changed. The complete system on a chip may well be the commodity building block of the future, used in all sorts of intelligent appliances at a volume much greater than the desktop and hence at a much lower cost. In any case, we can look forward to much larger-scale parallelism as the processors per chip continue to rise.

A very interesting question is what happens when programs need access to more data than fits on the PAM. One approach is to provide a conventional memory interface for expansion. A more interesting alternative is to simply provide cache-coherent access to other PAM chips. The techniques are now very well understood, as is the minimal amount of hardware support required to provide this functionality. If the processor component of the PAM is indeed small, then even if only one process in the system is ever used, the additional cost of the other processors sitting near the memories is small. Since parallel software is becoming more and more widespread, the extra processing power is there when applications demand it.

12.2 APPLICATIONS AND SYSTEM SOFTWARE

Clearly, the future of parallel computer architecture will increasingly be a story of parallel software and of hardware/software interactions. We can view parallel software as falling into five different classes: applications, compilers, languages, operating systems, and tools. In parallel software too, the same basic categories of change apply: evolution, hitting walls, and breakthroughs.

12.2.1 Evolutionary Scenario

Whereas data management and information processing are likely to be the dominant applications that exploit multiprocessors, applications in science and engineering have always been the proving ground for high-end computing. Early parallel scientific computing focused largely on models of physical phenomena that result in fairly regular computational and communication characteristics. This allowed simple partitionings of the problems to be successful in harnessing the power of multiprocessors, just as it led earlier to effective exploitation of vector architectures. As the understanding of both the application domains and parallel computing grew, early adopters began to model the more complex, dynamic, and adaptive aspects that are integral to most physical phenomena, leading to applications with irregular, unpredictable characteristics. This trend is expected to continue, bringing with it the attendant complexity for effective parallelization.

As multiprocessing becomes more and more widespread, the domains of its application will evolve, as will the applications whose characteristics are most relevant to computer manufacturers. Large optimization problems encountered in finance and logistics—for example, determining good crew schedules for commercial airlines—are very expensive to solve, have high payoff for corporations, and are amenable to scalable parallelism. Methods developed under the fabric of artificial intelligence, including searching techniques and expert systems, are finding practical use in several domains and can benefit greatly from increased computational power and storage. In the area of information management, an important direction is toward increased use of extracting trends and inferences from large volumes of data, using data mining and decision support techniques (in the latter, complex queries are made to determine trends that will provide the basis for important decisions). These applications are often computationally intensive as well as database intensive and mark an interesting marriage of computation and data storage/retrieval to build computation-and-information servers. Such problems are increasingly encountered in scientific research areas as well, for example, in manipulating and analyzing the tremendous volumes of biological sequence information that is rapidly becoming available through the sciences of genomics and sequencing and in computing on the discovered data to produce estimates of three-dimensional structure. The rise of wide-scale distributed computing—enabled by the Internet and the World Wide Web—and the abundance of information in modern society make this marriage of computing and information management all the more inevitable as a direction of rapid growth. Multiprocessors have already become servers for Internet search engines and World Wide Web queries. The nature of the queries coming to an information server may also span a broader range, from a few, very complex mining and decision support queries at a time to a staggeringly large number of simultaneous queries in the case where the clients are home computers or handheld information appliances.

As the communication characteristics of networks improve and the need for parallelism with varying degrees of coupling becomes stronger, we are likely to see a strong convergence of parallel and distributed computing. Techniques from distributed computing will be applied to parallel computing to build a greater variety of information servers that can benefit from the better performance characteristics "within the box," and parallel computing techniques will be employed in the other direction to use distributed systems as platforms for solving a single problem in parallel. Multiprocessors will continue to play the role of servers—database and transaction servers, compute servers, and storage servers—though the data types manipulated by these servers are becoming much richer and more varied. From information records containing text, we are moving to an era where images, three-dimensional models of physical objects, and segments of audio and video are increasingly stored, indexed, queried, and served out as well. Matches in queries to these data types are often approximate, and serving them out often uses advanced compression techniques to conserve bandwidth, both of which require computation as well.

Finally, the increasing importance of graphics, media, and real-time data from sensors—for military, civilian, and entertainment applications—will lead to increasing significance of real-time computing on data as it streams in and out of a multiprocessor. Instead of reading data from a storage medium, operating on it, and storing it back, this may require operating on data on its way through the machine between input and output data ports. How processors, memory, and networks integrate with one another, as well as the role of caches, may have to be revisited in this scenario. As the application space evolves, we will learn what kinds of applications can truly utilize large-scale parallel computing and what scales of parallelism are most appropriate for others. We will also learn whether scaled-up general-purpose architectures are appropriate for the highest end of computing or whether the characteristics of these applications are so differentiated that they require substantially different resource requirements and integration to be cost-effective.

As parallel computing is embraced in more domains, we begin to see portable, prepackaged parallel applications that can be used in multiple application domains. A good example of this is an application called Dyna3D that solves systems of partial differential equations on highly irregular domains, using a technique called the finite element method. Dyna3D was initially developed at government research laboratories for use in modeling weapons systems on exotic, multimillion-dollar supercomputers. After the cold war ended, the technology transitioned into the commercial sector, and it became the mainstay of crash modeling in the automotive industry and elsewhere on widely available parallel machines. By the time this book was written, the code was widely used on cost-effective parallel servers for performing simulations on everyday appliances, such as what happens to a cellular phone when it is dropped.

A major enabling factor in the widespread use of parallel applications has been the availability of portable libraries that implement programming models on a wide range of machines. With the advent of the message-passing interface (MPI), this has become a reality for message passing, which is used in Dyna3D: the application of Dyna3D to different problems is usually done on very different platforms, from machines designed for message passing (like the Intel Paragon) to machines that support a shared address space in hardware (like the CRAY T3D) to networks of workstations. Similar portability across a wide range of communication architecture performance characteristics has not yet been achieved for a shared address space programming model but is likely soon.

As more applications are coded in both the shared address space and message-passing models, we find a greater separation of the algorithmic aspects of creating a parallel program (decomposition and assignment) from the more mechanical and architecture-dependent aspects (orchestration and mapping), with the former being relatively independent of the programming model and architecture. Galaxy simulations and other hierarchical *n*-body computations, like Barnes-Hut, provide an example. The early message-passing parallel programs used an orthogonal recursive bisection method to partition the computational domain across processors and did not maintain a global tree data structure. Shared address space implementations, on the other hand, used a global tree and a different partitioning method that led to a very different domain decomposition. With time and with the improvement in message-passing communication architectures, the message-passing versions also evolved to use similar partitioning techniques to the shared address space version, including building and maintaining a logically global tree using hashing techniques. Similar developments have occurred in ray tracing, where parallelizations that assumed no logical sharing of data structures gave way to logically shared data structures that were implemented in the message-passing model using hashing. A continuation of this trend will also contribute to the portability of applications between systems that preferentially support one of the two models.

Like parallel applications, parallel programming languages are also evolving apace. The most popular languages for parallel computing continue to be based on the most popular sequential programming languages (C, C++, and Fortran), with extensions for parallelism. The nature of these extensions is now increasingly driven by the needs observed in real applications. In fact, it is not uncommon for languages to incorporate features that arise from experience with a particular class of applications and then are found to generalize to some other classes of applications as well. In a similar vein, portable libraries of commonly occurring data structures and algorithms for parallel computing are being developed, and templates for these are being defined for programmers to customize according to the needs of their specific applications.

Several styles of parallel languages have been developed. The least common denominator is MPI for message-passing programming, which has been adopted across a wide range of platforms, and a sequential language enhanced with primitives like the ones we discussed in Chapter 2 for a shared address space. Many of the other language systems try to provide the programmer with a natural programming model, often based on a shared address space, and hide the properties of the machine's communication abstraction through software layers. One major direction has been explicitly parallel object-oriented languages, with emphasis on appropriate mechanisms to express concurrency and synchronization in a manner integrated with the underlying support for data abstraction. Another has been the development of data parallel languages with directives for partitioning, such as high-performance Fortran, that are currently being extended to handle irregular applications. A third direction has been the development of implicitly parallel languages. Here, the programmer is not responsible for specifying the assignment, orchestration, or mapping, but only for the decomposition into tasks and for specifying the data that each task accesses. Based on these specifications, the run-time system of the language determines the dependences among tasks and assigns and orchestrates them appropriately for parallel execution on a platform. The burden on the programmer is decreased, or at least localized, but the burden on the system is increased. With the increasing importance of data access for performance, several of these languages have proposed language mechanisms and run-time techniques to divide the burden of achieving data locality and reducing communication between the progammer and the system in a reasonable way.

Finally, the increasing complexity of the applications being written and the phenomena being modeled by parallel applications has led to the development of languages to support composability of bigger applications from smaller parts. We can expect much continued evolution in all these directions—appropriate abstractions for concurrency, data abstraction, synchronization, and data management; libraries and templates; explicit and implicit parallel programming languages—with the goal of achieving a good balance between ease of programming, performance, and portability across a wide range of platforms (in both functionality and performance).

The development of compilers that can automatically parallelize programs has also been evolving over the last decade or two. With significant developments in the analysis of dependences among data accesses, compilers are now able to automatically parallelize simple array-based Fortran programs and achieve respectable performance on small-scale multiprocessors. Advances have also been made in compiler algorithms for managing data locality in caches and main memory and in optimizing the orchestration of communication given the performance characteristics of an architecture (for example, making communication messages larger for message-passing machines). However, compilers are still not able to parallelize more complex programs effectively, especially those that make substantial use of pointers. Since the address stored in a pointer is not known at compile time, it is very difficult to determine whether a memory operation made through a pointer is to the same or a different address than another memory operation. In acknowledging this difficulty, one approach that is increasingly being taken is that of interactive parallelizing compilers. Here, the compiler discovers the parallelism that it can and then gives intelligent feedback to the user about the places where it failed and asks the user questions about choices it might make in decomposition, assignment, and orchestration. Given the directed questions and information, a user familiar with the program may have or may discover the higher-level knowledge of the application that the compiler did not have. Another approach in a similar vein is integrated compile-time and run-time parallelization tools, in which information gathered at run time may be used to help the compiler—and perhaps the user—parallelize the application successfully. Compiler technology will continue to evolve in these areas as well as in the simpler area of providing support to deal with relaxed memory consistency models.

Operating systems are making the transition from uniprocessors to multiprocessors and from multiprocessors used as batch-oriented compute engines to multiprogrammed servers of computational and storage resources. In the former category, the evolution has included making operating systems more scalable by reducing the serialization within the operating system and making the scheduling and resource management policies of operating systems take spatial and temporal locality into account (for example, not moving processes around too much in the machine; having them scheduled close to the data they access; and having them scheduled, as far as possible, on the same processor every time). In the latter category, a major challenge is managing resources and process scheduling in a way that strikes a good balance between fairness and performance, just as was done in uniprocessor operating systems. Attention is paid to data locality in scheduling application processes in a multiprogrammed workload as well as to parallel performance in determining resource allocation. For example, the relative parallel performance of applications in a multiprogrammed workload may be used to determine how many processors and other resources to allocate to it at the cost of other programs. Operating systems for parallel machines are also increasingly incorporating the characteristics of multiprogrammed mainframe machines that were the mainstay servers of the past. One challenge in this area is exporting to the user the image of a single operating system (called single-system image) while still providing the reliability and fault tolerance of a distributed system. Other challenges include containing faults so that only the faulting application or the resources that the faulting application uses are affected by a fault and providing the reliability and availability that people expect from mainframes. This evolution is necessary if scalable microprocessor-based multiprocessors are to truly replace mainframes as "enterprise" servers for large organizations, running multiple applications at a time.

With the increasing complexity of application-system interactions and the increasing importance of the memory and communication systems for performance, it is very important to have good tools for diagnosing performance problems. This is particularly true of a shared address space programming model since communication there is implicit, and artifactual communication can often dominate other performance effects. Contention is a particularly prevalent and difficult performance effect for a programmer to diagnose, especially because the point in the program (or machine) where the effects of contention are felt can be quite different from the point that causes the contention. Performance tools continue to evolve, providing feedback about where the largest overhead components of execution time are in the program, what data structures might be causing the data access overheads, and so on. We are likely to see progress in techniques to increase the visibility of performance monitoring tools, which will be helped by the recent increasing willingness of machine designers to add a few registers or counters at key points in a machine solely for the purpose of performance monitoring. We are also likely to see progress in the quality of the feedback that is provided to the user, ranging from where in the program code a lot of time is being spent stalled on data access (available today) to which data structures are responsible for the majority of this time to what the cause of the problem is (communication overhead, capacity misses, conflict misses with another data structure, or contention). The more detailed the information and the better it is cast in terms of the concepts the programmer deals with rather than in machine terms, the more likely that a programmer can respond to the information and improve performance. Evolution along this path will hopefully bring us to a good balance between software and hardware support for performance diagnosis.

A final aspect of the evolution will be the continued integration of the system software pieces described in the preceding. Languages will be designed to make the compiler's job easier in discovering and managing parallelism and to allow more information to be conveyed to the operating system to make its scheduling and resource allocation decisions.

12.2.2 Hitting a Wall

On the software side, there is a wall that we have been hitting up against for many years now, which is the wall of programmability. While programming models are becoming more portable, architectures are converging, and good evolutionary progress is being made in many areas, it is still the case that parallel programming is much more difficult than sequential programming. Programming for good performance takes a lot of work, sometimes in determining a good parallelization and other times in implementing and orchestrating it. Even debugging parallel programs for correctness is an art or at best a primitive science. The parallel debugging task is difficult because of the interactions among multiple processes with their own program orders and because of sensitivity to timing. Depending on when events in one process happen to occur relative to events in another process, a bug in the program may or may not manifest itself at run time in a particular execution. And if it does, instrumenting the code to monitor certain events can cause the timing to be perturbed in such a way that the bug no longer appears.

Although evolutionary progress has greatly increased the adoption of parallel computing, overcoming the wall will take a breakthrough that will truly allow parallel computing to realize the potential afforded to it by technology and architectural trends. It is unclear whether this breakthrough will be in languages per se, or in programming methodology, or whether it will simply be evolutionary improvements crossing a critical threshold.

12.2.3 Potential Breakthroughs

Other than breakthroughs in parallel programming languages or methodology and parallel debugging, we may hope for a breakthrough in performance models for reasoning about parallel programs. Although many models have been quite successful at exposing the essential performance characteristics of a parallel system (Valiant 1990; Culler et al. 1996) and some have even provided a methodology for using these parameters, the more challenging aspect is modeling the properties of complex parallel applications and their interactions with the system parameters. There is not yet a well-defined methodology for programmers or algorithm designers to use for this purpose in order to determine how well an algorithm will perform in parallel on a system or which among competing partitioning or orchestration approaches will perform better. Another breakthrough may come from architecture if we can somehow design machines in a cost-effective way that makes it much less important for a programmer to worry about data locality and communication; that is, to truly design a machine that can look to the programmer like a PRAM. An example of this would be if all latency incurred by the program could be tolerated by the architecture. However, this is likely to require tremendous bandwidth, which has a high cost, and it is not clear how best to invest the application concurrency for a mix of parallel execution and latency tolerance.

The ultimate breakthrough, of course, will be the complete success of parallelizing compilers in taking a wide range of sequential programs and converting them into efficient parallel executions on a given platform, achieving good performance at a scale close to that inherently afforded by the application (i.e., close to the best you could do by hand). Besides the problems discussed, parallelizing compilers tend to look for and utilize low-level, localized information in the program and are not currently good at performing high-level, global analysis transformations. Compilers also lack semantic information about the application; for example, if a particular sequential algorithm for a phase of a problem does not parallelize well, there is nothing the compiler can do to choose another one. And for a compiler to take data locality and artifactual communication into consideration and manage the extended memory hierarchy of a multiprocessor is very difficult. However, even effective programmer-assisted compiler parallelization, keeping the programmer involvement to a minimum, would be perhaps the most significant software breakthrough in making parallel computing truly mainstream.

Whatever the future holds, it is certain that the continuing evolutionary advance will cross critical thresholds; significant walls will be encountered, but there are likely to be ways around them and unexpected breakthroughs will occur. Parallel computing will remain the place where exciting changes in computer technology and applications are first encountered in an ever evolving cycle of hardware/software interactions.

Appendix: Parallel Benchmark Suites

Despite the difficulty of identifying "representative" parallel applications and the immaturity of parallel software (languages and programming environments), the quantitative workload-driven evaluation of machines and architectural ideas must go on. To this end, several suites of parallel "benchmarks" have been developed and distributed. The term *benchmarks* is in quotations because of the difficulty of relying on a single suite of programs to make definitive performance claims in parallel computing. Benchmark suites for multiprocessors vary in the kinds of application domains and run-time characteristics they cover; whether they include toy programs, kernels, or real applications; the communication abstractions they are targeted for; and their philosophy toward benchmarking or architectural evaluation. What follows is a discussion of some of the most widely used, publicly available benchmark/application suites for parallel processing. Table A.1 shows how these suites can currently be obtained.

A.1 SCALAPACK

The ScaLapack suite (Dongarra and Walker 1995; Choi et al. 1992) consists of parallel, message-passing implementations of the LAPACK linear algebra kernels. The LAPACK suite includes routines to solve linear systems of equations, eigenvalue problems, singular value problems, matrix multiplications, matrix factorizations, and eigenvalue solvers. Information about the ScaLapack suite and the suite itself can be obtained from the Netlib repository maintained at the Oak Ridge National Laboratories (see Table A.1).

A.2 TPC

The Transaction Processing Performance Council (TPC), founded in 1988, has created a set of publicly available benchmarks, called TPC-A, TPC-B, TPC-C, and TPC-D that are representative of different kinds of inputs and queries to transaction processing and database system programs (Transaction Processing Council 1998). While database and transaction processing workloads are very important in actual usage of parallel machines, source codes for these programs are almost impossible to obtain because of their competitive value to their developers.

Table A.1 Obtaining Public Benchmark and Application Suites

Benchmark Suite	Communication Abstraction	Domain of Application	How to Obtain Code or Information
ScaLapack	Message passing	Scientific	*http://www.netlib.org*
TPC	Either (not provided parallel)	Database/transaction processing	*http://www.tpc.org*
SPLASH-2	Shared address space (CC)	Scientific/engineering/ graphics	*http://www-flash.stanford.edu/ apps/SPLASH*
SPLASH-3	Shared address space (CC)	Varied	*http://www.cs.princeton.edu/ prism/splash-3*
NAS	Either (paper and pencil)	Scientific	*http://www.nas.nasa.gov*
NPB2	Message passing	Scientific	*http://science.nas.nasa.gov/ Software/NPB*
PARKBENCH	Message passing	Scientific	*netlib@ornl.gov*

TPC has a rigorous policy for reporting results. They use two metrics: (1) throughput in transactions per second, subject to a constraint that over 90% of the transactions have a response time less than a specified threshold; and (2) cost-performance in price per transaction per second, where price is the total system price and maintenance cost for five years. The benchmarks scale with the power of the system in order to measure it realistically.

The first TPC benchmark was TPC-A, consisting of a single, simple, update-intensive transaction. It was intended to provide a simple, repeatable unit of work designed to exercise the key features of an on-line transaction processing (OLTP) system, such as that of a bank's customer records or an airline reservation system. The chosen banking transaction consisted of reading 100 bytes from a terminal, updating the account, branch, and teller records, writing a history record, and finally writing 200 bytes to a terminal. TPC-A is no longer used.

TPC-B is a more centralized database (not OLTP) benchmark designed to exercise the system components necessary for update-intensive database transactions. It therefore has significant disk I/O but moderate system and application execution time, and it requires transaction integrity. Unlike OLTP, it does not require terminals or networking. These first two benchmarks were declared obsolete in 1995 and have been wholly replaced by TPC-C and now TPC-D.

TPC-C was approved in 1992. It is designed to be more realistic than TPC-A but to carry over many of its characteristics. TPC-C is a multiuser benchmark and requires a remote terminal emulator to emulate a population of users with their terminals. It models the activity of a wholesale supplier with a number of geographically distributed sales districts and supply warehouses, including customers placing orders, making payments, or making inquiries, as well as deliveries and inventory checks. The database size scales with the throughput of the system. TPC-C has a more complex database structure compared to TPC-A, multiple transaction types of varying complexity, on-line and deferred execution modes, higher levels of contention on data access and update, patterns that simulate hot spots, access by primary as well as nonprimary keys, realistic requirements for full-screen terminal I/O and formatting, requirements for full transparency of data partitioning, and transaction rollbacks.

TPC-D is a decision support benchmark. According to the TPC, decision support describes a system's capability to support the formulation of business decisions through complex queries against a database. The queries access large portions of the database, not individual records only (as in OLTP) and include operations like multitable joins, extensive sorting, grouping and aggregations, and sequential scans. While OLTP (TPC-C) consists of small, mostly update transactions, decision support queries are large, individually time consuming, and read-only on the database. Decision support databases are updated only infrequently, either by periodic batch runs or by background "trickle" update activity. These update activities are also included in TPC-D. TPC-D models ad hoc queries like determining sales trends, as opposed to regular business operations in TPC-C, and has only a few concurrent users.

TPC plans to add more benchmarks, including an enterprise server benchmark, which provides concurrent OLTP and batch transactions as well as heavyweight read-only OLTP transactions with tighter response time constraints. A client-server benchmark is also under consideration. Information about all these benchmarks can be obtained by contacting the Transaction Processing Performance Council (see Table A.1).

A.3 SPLASH

The SPLASH (Stanford ParalleL Applications for Shared Memory) suite (Singh, Weber, and Gupta 1992) was originally developed at Stanford University to facilitate the evaluation of architectures that support a shared address space with coherent replication. It was replaced by the SPLASH-2 suite (Woo et al. 1995), which enhanced some applications and added several more, broadening the coverage of domains and characteristics substantially. The SPLASH-2 suite currently contains seven complete applications and five computational kernels. Some of the applications and kernels are provided in different versions, with different levels of optimization in the way data structures are designed and used (see the discussion of levels of optimization in Section 4.2.2). The programs represent various computational domains, mostly scientific and engineering applications and computer graphics. They are all written in C and use the Parmacs macro package from Argonne National Laboratories (Boyle et al. 1987) for parallelism constructs. Their characteristics together with methodological guidelines for using them can be found in (Woo et al. 1995). All of the parallel programs used for workload-driven evaluation of shared address space machines in this book come from the SPLASH-2 suite. The suite and its documentation can be obtained as described in Table A.1. The designers of the

SPLASH suites plan to add new shared address space programs from a variety of application domains in a new release called SPLASH-3.

A.4 NAS PARALLEL BENCHMARKS

The NAS benchmarks (Bailey et al. 1991, 1995) were developed by the Numerical Aerodynamic Simulation group at the National Aeronautic and Space Administration (NASA). They are a set of eight computations—five kernels and three pseudo-applications (not complete applications but more representative than the kernels of the kinds of data structures, data movement, and computation required in real aerophysics applications). The computations are each intended to focus on some important aspect of the types of highly parallel computations encountered in aerophysics applications. The kernels include an embarrassingly parallel computation, a multigrid equation solver, a conjugate gradient equation solver, a three-dimensional FFT equation solver, and an integer sorting program. Two different data sets, one small and one large, are provided for each benchmark. The benchmarks are intended to evaluate and compare real machines against one another, and an elaborate reporting and validation policy is in place.

The original NAS benchmarks take a different approach to benchmarking than the other suites described here. Those suites provide programs that are already written in a high-level language (such as Fortran or C, with constructs for parallelism). The NAS benchmarks, on the other hand, originally did not provide parallel implementations but were so-called paper-and-pencil benchmarks. They specified the problem to be solved in complete detail (the equation system and constraints, for example) and the high-level method to be used (multigrid or conjugate gradient method, for example) but did not provide the parallel program to be used. Instead, they left it up to the user to use the best parallel implementation for the machine at hand. The user is free to choose any language constructs for parallelism (though the language must be an extension of Fortran or C), data structures, communication abstractions and mechanisms, processor mapping, memory allocation and usage, and low-level optimizations (with some restrictions on the use of assembly language). The motivations for this approach to benchmarking are that since parallel architectures are diverse in their performance characteristics and the programming model toward which they are biased, and since no established dominant programming language or communication abstraction is most efficient on all architectures, a parallel program implementation that is best suited to one machine may not be appropriate for another. If we want to compare two machines using a given computation or benchmark, we should use the most appropriate implementation for each machine. This approach puts a greater burden on the user of the benchmarks but is more appropriate for comparing widely disparate machines. Providing the codes themselves, on the other hand, makes the user's task easier and may be a better approach for exploring architectural trade-offs among a well-defined class of similar architectures. While this philosophy remains, the NAS group provides message-passing implementations of the programs that can be used as starting points.

Because the NAS benchmarks, particularly the kernels, are relatively easy to implement and represent an interesting range of computations for scientific computing, they have been widely embraced by multiprocessor vendors. With the portability provided by the Message Passing Interface (MPI) standard, a recent follow-on effort called NPB2 utilizes fixed applications written in MPI rather than pencil-and-paper benchmarks, just like traditional benchmark suites. The benchmarks and their documentation can be obtained from NAS, as described in Table A.1.

A.5 PARKBENCH

The PARKBENCH (PARallel Kernels and BENCHmarks) effort (PARKBENCH Committee 1994) is a large-scale effort to develop a suite of microbenchmarks, kernels, and applications for benchmarking parallel machines, with at least an initial focus on explicit message-passing programs written in Fortran77. Versions of the programs in the High Performance Fortran (HPF) language (High Performance Fortran Forum 1993) are also furnished in order to provide portability across message-passing and shared address space platforms. The programs are taken from scientific computing.

PARKBENCH provides the different types of benchmarks we have discussed: low-level benchmarks or microbenchmarks, kernels, compact applications, and compiler benchmarks (the last two categories yet to be fully provided). The lowest-level microbenchmarks measure per-node performance. The purpose of these uniprocessor microbenchmarks is to characterize the performance of various aspects of the architecture and compiler system and to obtain some parameters that can be used to understand the performance of the kernels and compact applications. The uniprocessor microbenchmarks include timer calls, arithmetic operations, and memory bandwidth and latency stressing routines. There are also multiprocessor microbenchmarks that test communication latency and bandwidth—both point-to-point and all-to-all—as well as global barrier synchronization. Several of these multiprocessor microbenchmarks are taken from the earlier Genesis benchmark suite (Hey 1991).

The kernel benchmarks are divided into matrix kernels (multiplication, factorization, transposition, and tridiagonalization), Fourier transform kernels (a large 1D FFT and a large 3D FFT), partial differential equation kernels (a 3D successive-over-relaxation iterative solver and the multigrid kernel from the NAS suite), and others including the conjugate gradient, integer sort, and embarrassingly parallel kernels from the NAS suite and a paper-and-pencil I/O benchmark.

Compact applications (full but perhaps simplified applications) are intended in the areas of climate and meteorological modeling, computational fluid dynamics, financial modeling and portfolio optimization, molecular dynamics, plasma physics, quantum chemistry, quantum chromodynamics, and reservoir modeling, among others. Finally, the compiler benchmarks are intended for people developing High Performance Fortran compilers to test their compiler optimizations, not so much to evaluate architectures. The available PARKBENCH benchmarks can be obtained from the Netlib repository at Oak Ridge National Laboratories, as described in Table A.1.

A.6 OTHER ONGOING EFFORTS

SPEC/HPCG: The developers of the widely used SPEC (Standard Performance Evaluation Corporation) suite for uniprocessor benchmarking (SPEC 1995) have teamed up with the developers of the Perfect (PERFormance Evaluation for Cost-effective Transformations) Club benchmarks for traditional vector supercomputers (Berry et al. 1989) to form the SPEC/HPG (High Performance Group) to develop a suite of benchmarks (Eigenmann and Hassanzadeh 1996) measuring the performance of systems that "push the limits of computational technology," notably multiprocessor systems. These, too, are focused on scientific computing.

Many other benchmarking efforts exist. As we can see, most of the suites so far are for message-passing computing, though some of these may be beginning to provide versions in High Performance Fortran that can be run on any of the major communication abstractions with the appropriate compiler support. We can expect the development of more shared address space benchmarks, such as in the SPLASH and SPLASH-2 suites, in the future. Many of the existing suites are also targeted toward scientific computing (the PARKBENCH and NAS efforts being the most large scale among these), though there is increasing interest in producing benchmarks for other classes of workloads (including commercial and general-purpose server workloads) for parallel machines. Almost all the benchmarks are designed to be a single application running on the machine at a time. Good benchmarks for multiprogrammed and other workloads that exercise the operating system do not yet exist (except for TPC); nor do we have well-established I/O-intensive benchmarks for parallel machines. In general, developing benchmarks and workloads that are representative of real-world parallel computing and are also effectively portable to real machines is a very difficult but very important problem (since the conclusions we draw about architectural trade-offs depend on the benchmarks used), and the preceding are all steps in the right direction.

References

Abali, B., and C. Aykanat. 1994. Routing Algorithms for IBM SP1. *Lecture Notes in Computer Science, Vol. 853*. New York: Springer-Verlag, 161–175.

Abdel-Shafi, H. A., J. Hall, S. V. Adve, and V. S. Adve. 1997. An Evaluation of Fine-Grain Producer-Initiated Communication in Cache-Coherent Multiprocessors. *Proc. Third Symposium on High Performance Computer Architecture* (February).

Adve, S. V. 1993. *Designing Memory Consistency Models for Shared-Memory Multiprocessors.* Ph.D. diss., University of Wisconsin-Madison. Available as Tech. Report #1198, University of Wisconsin-Madison, Computer Science (December).

Adve, S. V., and K. Gharachorloo. 1996. Shared Memory Consistency Models: A Tutorial. *IEEE Computer* 29(12):66–76.

Adve, S. V., K. Gharachorloo, A. Gupta, J. L. Hennessy, and M. Hill. 1993. Sufficient Systems *Requirements for Supporting the PLpc Memory Model.* Tech. Report #1200, University of Wisconsin-Madison, Computer Science (December). Also available as Tech. Report #CSL-TR-93-595, Stanford University.

Adve, S. V., and M. Hill. 1990a. Weak Ordering: A New Definition. 1990. *Proc. 17th Int'l Symposium on Computer Architecture* (May):2–14.

———. 1990b. Implementing Sequential Consistency in Cache-Based Systems. *Proc. 1990 Int'l Conference on Parallel Processing* (August):47–50.

———. 1993. A Unified Formalization of Four Shared-Memory Models. *IEEE Transactions on Parallel and Distributed Systems* 4(6):613–624.

Agarwal, A. 1991. Limit on Interconnection Performance. *IEEE Transactions on Parallel and Distributed Systems* 2(4):398–412.

Agarwal, A., R. Bianchini, D. Chaiken, K. L. Johnson, D. Kranz, J. Kubiatowicz, B.-H. Lim, K. Mackenzie, and D. Yeung. 1995. The MIT Alewife Machine: Architecture and Performance. *Proc. 22nd Int'l Symposium on Computer Architecture* (May/June):2–13.

Agarwal, A., and A. Gupta. 1988. Memory-Reference Characteristics of Multiprocessor Applications Under MACH. *Proc. ACM SIGMETRICS Conference on Measurement and Modeling of Computer Systems* (May):215–225.

Agarwal, A., B.-H. Lim, D. Kranz, and J. Kubiatowicz. 1990. (April): A Processor Architecture for Multiprocessing. *Proc. 17th Annual Int'l Symposium on Computer Architecture* (June):104–114.

———. 1991. LimitLESS Directories: A Scalable Cache Coherence Scheme. *Proc. Fourth Int'l Conference on Architectural Support for Programming Languages and Operating Systems* (April):224–234.

Agarwal, A., R. Simoni, J. Hennessy, and M. Horowitz. 1988. An Evaluation of Directory Schemes for Cache Coherence. *Proc. 15th Int'l Symposium on Computer Architecture* (June):280–289.

Aiken, A., and A. Nicolau. 1988. Optimal Loop Parallelization. *Proc. SIGPLAN Conference on Programming Language Design and Implementation* (June):308–317. Also published in SIGPLAN Notices 23(7).

Aimoto, Y., T. Kimura, Y. Yabe, H. Heiuchi, et al. 1996. A 7.68GIPS 3.84GB/s 1W Parallel Image-Processing RAM Integrating a 16Mb DRAM and 128 Processors. *International Solid-State Circuits Conference*, San Francisco (February):372–373.

Alexander, T. B., K. G. Robertson, D. T. Lindsay, D. L. Rogers, J. R. Obermeyer, J. R. Keller, K. Y. Oka, and M. M. Jones II. 1994. Corporate Business Servers: An Alternative to Mainframes for Business Computing (HP K-Class). *Hewlett-Packard Journal* (June):8–33.

Almasi, G. S., and A. Gottlieb. 1989. *Highly Parallel Computing*. Redwood City, CA: Benjamin/Cummings.

Alverson, R., D. Callahan, D. Cummings, B. Koblenz, A. Porterfield, and B. Smith. 1990. The Tera Computer System. *Proc. 1990 Int'l Conference on Supercomputing* (June): 1–6.

Amdahl, G. M. 1967. Validity of the Single Processor Approach to Achieving Large Scale Computing Capabilities. *AFIPS 1967 Spring Joint Computer Conference* 40:483–485.

Anderson, J. P., S. A. Hoffman, J. Shifman, and R. Williams. 1962. D825-A Multiple-Computer System for Command and Control. *AFIP Proc. FJCC* 22:86–96.

Anderson, J., and M. Lam. 1993. Global Optimizations for Parallelism and Locality on Scalable Parallel Machines. *Proc. SIGPLAN'93 ConferenceConference on Programming Language Design and Implementation* (June).

Anderson, T. E., D. E. Culler, D. Patterson. 1995. A Case for NOW (Networks of Workstations). *IEEE Micro* 15(1):54–6

Anderson, T. E., S. S. Owicki, J. P. Saxe, and C. P. Thacker. 1992. High Speed Switch Scheduling for Local Area Networks. *Proc. ASPLOS V* (October):98–110

Archibald, J., and J.-L. Baer. 1986. Cache Coherence Protocols: Evaluation Using a Multiprocessor Simulation Model. *ACM Transactions on Computer Systems* 4(4):273–298.

Arnould, E. A., F. J. Bitz, E. C. Cooper, H. T. Kung, R. D. Sansom, and P. A. Steenkiste. 1989. The Design of Nectar: A Network Backplane for Heterogeneous Multicomputers. *Proc. ASPLOS III* (April):205–216.

Arpaci, R. H., D. E. Culler, A. Krishnamurthy, S. G. Steinberg, and K. Yelick. 1995. Empirical Evaluation of the Cray-T3D: A Compiler Perspective. *Proc. 22nd Int'l Symposium on Computer Architecture* (June):320–331.

Arvind, and D. E. Culler. 1986. Dataflow Architectures. *Annual Reviews in Computer Science* 1:225–253. Palo Alto, CA: Annual Reviews. Reprinted in *Dataflow and Reduction Architectures*. Edited by S. S. Thakkar. Los Alamitos, CA: IEEE Computer Society Press, 1987.

Athas, W. C., and C. L. Seitz. 1988. Multicomputers: Message-Passing Concurrent Computers. *IEEE Computer* 21(8):9–24.

August, M. C., G. M. Brost, C. C. Hsiung, and A. J. Schiffleger. 1989. Cray X-MP: The Birth of a Supercomputer. *Computer* 22(1):45–52.

Baer, J.-L., and T.-F. Chen. 1991. An Efficient On-Chip Preloading Scheme to Reduce Data Access Penalty. *Proc. Supercomputing '91* (November):176–186.

Baer, J.-L., and W.-H. Wang. 1988. On the Inclusion Properties for Multi-Level Cache Hierarchies. *Proc. 15th Annual Int'l Symposium on Computer Architecture* (May):73–80.

Bailey, D. H. 1990. FFTs in External or Hierarchical Memory. *Journal of Supercomputing* 4(1):23–35. Also published in *Proc. Supercomputing '89* (November):234–242.

———. 1991. Twelve Ways to Fool the Masses When Giving Performance Results on Parallel Computers. *Supercomputing Review* (August):54–55.

———. 1993. Misleading Performance Reporting in the Supercomputing Field. *Scientific Programming* 1(2):141–151. Also published in *Proc. Supercomputing '93.*

Bailey, D. H., E. Barszcz, J. Barton, D. Browning, R. Carter, L. Dagum, R. Fatoohi, S. Fineberg, P. Frederickson, T. Lasinski, R. Schreiber, H. Simon, V. Venkatakrishnan, and S. Weeratunga. 1991. The NAS Parallel Benchmarks. *Intl. Journal of Supercomputer Applications* 5(3):66–73. Also published as Tech. Report RNR-94-007, Numerical Aerodynamic Simulation Facility, NASA Ames Research Center (March 1994).

Bailey, D. H., E. Barszcz, L. Dagum, and H. D. Simon. 1994. NAS Parallel Benchmark Results 3–94. *Proc. Scalable High-Performance Computing Conference,* Knoxville, TN (May):111–120.

Bailey, D., T. Harris, W. Saphir, R. van der Wijngaart, A. Woo, and M. Yarrow. 1995. *The NAS Parallel Benchmarks 2. 0.* Report NAS-95-020, Numerical Aerodynamic Simulation Facility. NASA Ames Research Center (December).

Baker, W. E., R. W. Horst, D. P. Sonnier, and W. J. Watson. 1995. A Flexible ServerNet-Based Fault-Tolerant Architecture. Proc. *25th Int'l Symposium on Fault-Tolerant Computing* (June). Los Alamitos, CA: IEEE Computer Society Press, 2–11.

Bakoglu, H. B. 1990. *Circuits, Interconnection, and Packaging for VLSI.* Reading, MA: Addison-Wesley.

Ball, J. R., R. C. Bollinger, T. A. Jeeves, R. C. McReynolds, D. H. Shaffer. 1962. On the Use of the Solomon Parallel-Processing Computer. *Proc. AFIPS Fall Joint Computer Conference* 22:137–146.

Banks, D., and M. Prudence. 1993. A High Performance Network Architecture for a PA-RISC Workstation. *IEEE Journal on Selected Areas in Communication* 11(2):191–202.

Barnes, J. E., and P. Hut. 1989. Error Analysis of a Tree Code. *Astrophysics Journal Supplement* 70(June):389–417.

Barosso, L., and M. Dubois. 1993. The Performance of Cache-Coherent Ring-Based Multiprocessors. *Proc. 20th Annual Int'l Symposium on Computer Architectures (ISCA)* (May):268–277.

———. 1995. Performance Evaluation of the Slotted Ring Multiprocessors. *IEEE Transactions on Computers* 44(7):878–890.

Barroso, L. A., S. Iman, J. Jeong, K. Oner, K. Ramamurthy, and M. Dubois. 1995. RPM: A Rapid Prototyping Engine for Multiprocessor Systems. *IEEE Computer* 28(2):26–34.

Barszcz, E., Fatoohi, R., Venkatakrishnan, V., and Weeratunga, S. 1993. *Solution of Regular, Sparse Triangular Linear Systems on Vector and Distributed-Memory Multiprocessors.* Tech. Report NAS RNR-93-007, NASA Ames Research Center, Moffett Field, CA (April).

Barton, E., J. Crownie, and M. McLaren. 1994. Message Passing on the Meiko CS-2. *Parallel Computing* 20(4):497–507.

Baskett, F., T. Jermoluk, and D. Solomon. 1988. The 4D-MP Graphics Superworkstation: Computing + Graphics = 40 MIPS + 40 MFLOPS and 100,000 Lighted Polygons per Second. *Proc. 33rd IEEE Computer Society Int'l Conference—COMPCON '88* (February):468–471.

Batcher, K. E. 1974. Staran Parallel Processor System Hardware. *Proc. AFIPS National Computer Conference,* 405–410.

———. 1980. Design of a Massively Parallel Processor. *IEEE Transactions on Computers* C-29(9):836–840.

Bell, C. G. 1985. Multis: A New Class of Multiprocessor Computers. *Science* 228:462–467.

Benes, V. 1965. *Mathematical Theory of Connecting Networks and Telephone Traffic.* San Diego, CA: Academic Press.

Bennett, J. E., and M. J. Flynn. 1996a. *Latency Tolerance for Dynamic Processors*. Tech. Report #CSL-TR-96-687, Computer Systems Laboratory, Stanford University.

———. 1996b. *Reducing Cache Miss Rates Using Prediction Caches*. Tech. Report #CSL-TR-96–707, Computer Systems Laboratory, Stanford University.

Berry, M., D. Chen, P. Koss, et al. 1989. The PERFECT Club Benchmarks: Effective Performance Evaluation of Computers. *Int'l Journal of Supercomputer Applications* 3(3):5–40.

Bershad, B. N., M. J. Zekauskas, and W. A. Sawdon. 1993. The Midway Distributed Shared Memory System. *Proc. COMPCON '93* (February).

Bhatt, S. M. and C. E. Leiserson. 1983. How to Assemble Tree Machines. *ACM Symposium on Theory of Computing (STOC '82)*. New York: ACM Press.

Biagioni, E., E. Cooper, and R. Sansom. 1993. Designing a Practical ATM LAN. *IEEE Network* (March).

Bilas, A., L. Iftode, and J. P. Singh. 1998. Evaluation of Hardware Support for Next-Generation Shared Virtual Memory Clusters. *Proc. Int'l Conference on Supercomputing* (July)

Bisiani, R., and M. Ravishankar. 1990. PLUS: A Distributed Shared-Memory System. *Proc. 17th Int'l Symposium on Computer Architecture* (May):115–124.

Black, D., R. Rashid, D. Golub, C. Hill, R. Baron. 1989. Translation Lookaside Buffer Consistency: A Software Approach. *Proc. Third Int'l Conference on Architectural Support for Programming Languages and Operating Systems,* Boston (April):113–122.

Blackford, L. S., J. Choi, A. Cleary, E. D'Azevedo, J. Demmel, I. Dhillon, J. Dongarra, S. Hammarling, G. Henry, A. Petitet, K. Stanley, D. Walker, and R. C. Whaley. 1997. *ScaLAPACK Users' Guide*. Philadelphia, PA: Society for Industrial and Applied Mathematics (SIAM).

Blelloch, G. 1993. Prefix Sums and Their Applications. In *Synthesis of Parallel Algorithms*. Edited by J. Reif. San Francisco: Morgan Kaufmann, 35–60.

Blelloch, G. E., C. E. Leiserson, B. M. Maggs, C. G. Plaxton, S. J. Smith, and M. A. Zagha. 1991. Comparison of Sorting Algorithms for the Connection Machine CM-2. *Proc. Symposium on Parallel Algorithms and Architectures* (July):3–16.

Blumrich, M. A., C. Dubnicki, E. W. Felten, K. Li, M.R. Mesarina. 1994. Two Virtual Memory Mapped Network Interface Designs. *Proc. Hot Interconnects II Symposium* (August).

Blumrich, M., K. Li, R. Alpert, C. Dubnicki, E. Felten, and J. Sandberg. 1994. A Virtual Memory Mapped Network Interface for the Shrimp Multicomputer. *Proc. 21st Int'l Symposium on Computer Architecture* (April):142–153.

Boden, N., D. Cohen, R. Felderman, A. Kulawik, C. Seitz, J. Seizovic, and W. Su. 1995. Myrinet: A Gigabit-per-Second Local Area Network. *IEEE Micro* 15(1):29–38.

Bodin, F., P. Beckman, D. Gannon, S. Yang, S. Kesavan, A. Malony, and B. Mohr. 1993. Implementing a Parallel C++ Runtime System for Scalable Parallel Systems. *Proc. Supercomputing '93* (November):588–597. Also in *Scientific Programming* 2(3).

Bolt Beranek and Newman Advanced Computers. 1989. *TC2000 Technical Product Summary*. Cambridge, MA: Bolt Beranek and Newman.

Bomans, L., and D. Roose. 1989. Benchmarking the iPSC/2 Hypercube Multiprocessor. *Concurrency: Practice and Experience*, 1(1):3–18.

Borkar, S., R. Cohn, G. Cox, T. Gross, H. T. Kung, M. Lam, M. Levine, B. Moore, W. Moore, C. Peterson, J. Susman, J. Sutton, J. Urbanski, and J. Webb. 1990. Supporting Systolic and Memory Communication in iWarp. *Proc. 17th Annual Int'l Symposium on Computer Architecture*, Seattle, WA (May):70–81. Revised version appears as Tech. Report #CMU-CS-90–197, Carnegie Mellon University.

Bouknight, W. J., S. A Denenberg, D. E. McIntyre, J. M. Randall, A. H. Sameh, and D. L. Slotnick. 1972. The Illiac IV System. *Proc. IEEE* 60(4):369–388.

Boyle, J., R. Butler, T. Disz, B. Glickfield, E. Lusk, W. R. Overbeek, J. Patterson, and R. Stevens. 1987. *Portable Programs for Parallel Processors.* New York: Holt, Rinehart and Winston.

Brewer, E. A., F. T. Chong, F. T. Leighton. 1994. Scalable Expanders: Exploiting Hierarchical Random Wiring. *Proc. 1994 Symposium on the Theory of Computing,* Montreal, Canada (May):144–152.

Brewer, E. A., F. T. Chong, L. T. Liu, J. Kubiatowicz, S. D. Sharma. 1995. Remote Queues: Exposing Network Queues for Atomicity and Optimization. *Proc. Seventh Annual Symposium on Parallel Algorithms and Architectures* (July):42–53.

Brewer, E. A., and B. C. Kuszmaul. 1994. How to Get Good Performance from the CM-5 Data Network. *Proc. 1994 Int'l Parallel Processing Symposium,* Cancun, Mexico (April):858–867.

Bruno, J., P. R. Cappello. 1988. Implementing the Beam and Warming Method on the Hypercube. *Proc. Third Conference on Hypercube Concurrent Computers and Applications,* Pasadena, CA, Jan 19–20.

Burger, D. 1997. *System-Level Implications of Processor-Memory Integration.* Workshop on Mixing Logic and DRAM: Chips that Compute and Remember. Presented at the Int'l Symposium on Computer Architecture (ISCA) '97 (June).

Burger, D., J. Goodman, and A. Kagi. 1996. Memory Bandwidth Limitations in Future Microprocessors. *Proc. 23rd Annual Symposium on Computer Architecture* (May):78–89.

Burkhardt, H., et al. 1992. *Overview of the KSR-1 Computer System.* Tech. Report KSR-TR-9202001, Kendall Square Research, Boston (February).

Butler, M., T-Y. Yeh, Y. Patt, M. Alsup, H. Scales, and M. Shebanow. 1991. Single Instruction Stream Parallelism Is Greater Than Two. *Proc. Annual Int'l Symposium on Computer Architecture (ISCA),* 276–86

Callahan, T., and S. C. Goldstein. 1995. NIFDY: A Low Overhead, High Throughput Network Interface. *Proc. 22nd Annual Symposium on Computer Architecture* (June):230–241.

Cardoza, W., F. Glover, and W. Snaman Jr. 1996. Design of a TruCluster Multicomputer System for the Digital UNIX Environment. *Digital Technical Journal* 8(1):5–17.

Carter, J. B., J. K. Bennett, and W. Zwaenepoel. 1991. Implementation and Performance of Munin. *Proc. 13th Symposium on Operating Systems Principles* (October):152–164.

———. 1995. Techniques for Reducing Consistency-Related Communication in Distributed Shared-Memory Systems. *ACM Transactions of Computer Systems* 13(3):205–244.

Catanzaro, B. 1997. *Multiprocessor System Architectures: A Technical Survery of Multiprocessor/Multithreaded Systems Using SPARC, Multi-level Bus Architectures and Solaris (SunOS).* Mountain View, CA: Sun Microsystems.

Cekleov, M., D. Yen, P. Sindhu, J.-M. Frailong, et al. 1993. SPARCcenter 2000: Multiprocessing for the 90s, Digest of Papers. *Proc. COMPCON Spring '93.* Los Alamitos, CA: IEEE Computer Society Press, 345–353.

Censier, L., and P. Feautrier. 1978. A New Solution to Cache Coherence Problems in Multiprocessor Systems. *IEEE Transaction on Computer Systems* C-27(12):1112–1118.

Chan, K., et al. 1993. Multiprocessor Features of the HP Corporate Business Servers. *Proc. COMPCON* (Spring):330–337.

Chandy, K. M., and J. Misra. 1988. *Parallel Program Design: A Foundation.* Reading, MA: Addison Wesley.

Chang, P. P., S. A. Mahlke, W. Y. Chen, N. J. Warter, and W. W. Hwu. 1991. IMPACT: An Architectural Framework for Multiple-Instruction Issue Processors. *Proc. 18th Int'l Symposium on Computer Architecture (ISCA)* 19(3):266–275.

Chen, T.-F., and J.-L. Baer. 1992. Reducing Memory Latency via Non-Blocking and Prefetching Caches. *Proc. Fifth Int'l Conference on Architectural Support for Programming Languages and Operating Systems* (October):51–61.

———. 1994. A Performance Study of Software and Hardware Data Prefetching Schemes. *Proc. 21st Annual Symposium on Computer Architecture* (April):223–232.

Cheong, H., and A. Viedenbaum. 1990. Compiler-directed Cache Management in Multiprocessors. *IEEE Computer* 23(6):39–47.

Chien, A. A., and J. H. Kim. 1992. Planar-Adaptive Routing: Low-Cost Adaptive Networks for Multiprocessors. *Proc. 19th Annual International Symposium on Computer Architecture (ISCA),* Gold Coast, Australia (May):268–277.

Choi, J., J. J. Dongarra, R. Pozo, and D. W. Walker. 1992. ScaLAPACK: A Scalable Linear Algebra Library for Distributed Memory Concurrent Computers. *Proc. Fourth Symposium on the Frontiers of Massively Parallel Computation*, McLean, VA. Los Alamitos, CA: IEEE Computer Society Press, 120–127.

Chun, B. N., A. M. Mainwaring, and D. E. Culler. 1998. Virtual Network Transport Protocols for Myrinet. *IEEE Micro* (January):53–63

Clark, R., and K. Alnes. 1996. An SCI Chipset and Adapter. *Symposium Record, Hot Interconnects IV* (August):221–235.

Cohen, D., G. Finn, R. Felderman, and A. DeSchon. 1993. ATOMIC: A Low-Cost, Very High-Speed, Local Communication Architecture. *Proc. 1993 Int. Conference on Parallel Processing.*

Convex Computer Corporation. 1993. *Exemplar Architecture*. Richardson, TX: Convex Computer Corp.

Corella, F., J. Stone, C. Barton. 1993. *A Formal Specification of the PowerPC Shared Memory Architecture.* Tech. Report Computer Science RC 18638 (81566), IBM Research Division, T.J. Watson Research Center (January).

Cornell, J. A. 1972. Parallel Processing of Ballistic Missile Defense Radar Data with PEPE. *COMPCON 72*, 69–72.

Cox, A., and R. Fowler. 1993. Adaptive Cache Coherency for Detecting Migratory Shared Data. *Proc. 20th Int'l Symposium on Computer Architecture* (May):98–108.

Crowther, W., J. Goodhue, R. Gurwitz, R. Rettberg, and R. Thomas. 1985. The Butterfly Parallel Processor. *IEEE Computer Architecture Technical Newsletter,* 18–46.

Culler, D. E. 1994. Multithreading: Fundamental Limits, Potential Gains, and Alternatives. In *Multithreaded Computer Architecture: A Summary of the State of the Art.* Edited by R. Iannucci. Dordrecht, Germany; Norwell, MA: Kluwer Academic Publishers, 97–138.

Culler, D. E., A. C. Dusseau, S. C. Goldstein, A. Krishnamurthy, S. Lumetta, T. von Eicken, and K. Yelick. 1993. Parallel Programming in Split-C. *Proc. Supercomputing '93* (November):262–273.

Culler, D. E., A. C. Dusseau, R. P. Martin, and K. E. Schauser. 1993. Fast Parallel Sorting under LogP: From Theory to Practice. In *Portability and Performance for Parallel Processing,* Chapter 4. New York: John Wiley & Sons, 71–98.

Culler, D. E., R. M. Karp, D. A., Patterson, A. Sahay, K. E. Schauser, E. Santos, R. Subramonian, and T. von Eicken. 1993. LogP: Toward A Realistic Model of Parallel Computation. *ACM SIGPLAN Symposium on Principles and Practice of Parallel Programming* (May):1–12.

———. 1996. LogP: A Practical Model of Parallel Computation. *CACM* 39(11):78–85.

Culler, D. E., A. Sah, K. E. Schauser, T. von Eicken, and J. Wawrzynek. 1991. Fine-Grain Parallelism with Minimal Hardware Support. *Proc. Fourth Int'l Symposium on Arch. Support for Programming Languages and Systems* (ASPLOS) (April):164–175.

Culler, D. E., K. E. Schauser, and T. von Eicken. 1993. Two Fundamental Limits on Dataflow Multithreading. *Proc. IFIP WG 10.3 Working Conference on Architectures and Compilation Techniques for Fine and Medium Grain Parallelism,* Orlando, FL.

Dahlgren, F. 1995. Boosting the Performance of Hybrid Snooping Cache Protocols. *Proc. 22nd Int'l Symposium on Computer Architecture* (June):60–69.

Dahlgren, F., M. Dubois, and P. Stenstrom. 1994. Combined Performance Gains of Simple Cache Protocol Extensions. *Proc. 21st Int'l Symposium on Computer Architecture* (April):187–197.

———. 1995. Sequential Hardware Prefetching in Shared-Memory Multiprocessors. *IEEE Transactions on Parallel and Distributed Systems* 6(7).

Dally, W. J. 1990a. Virtual-Channel Flow Control. *Proc. 17th Annual Int'l Symposium on Computer Architecture (ISCA)*, Seattle, WA, (May):60–68.

Dally, W. J. 1990b. Performance Analysis of *k*-ary *n*-cube Interconnection Networks. *IEEE-TOC* 39(6):775–85.

Dally, W. J., A. Chien, S. Fiske, W. Horwat, J. Keen, J. Larivee, R. Lethin, P. Nuth, S. Willis. 1989. The J-Machine: A Fine-Grained Concurrent Computer. *Proc. IFIP 11th World Computer Congress, Information Processing '89*, 1147–1153.

Dally, W. J., J. A. S. Fiske, J. S. Keen, R. A. Lethin, M. D. Noakes, and P. R. Nuth. 1992. The Message Driven Processor: A Multicomputer Processing Node with Efficient Mechanisms. *IEEE Micro* (April):23–39.

Dally, W. J., J. S. Keen, M. D. Noakes. 1993. The J-Machine Architecture and Evaluation. *Digest of Papers. COMPCON Spring '93*, San Francisco, CA (February):183–188.

Dally, W. J., and C. Seitz. 1987. Deadlock-Free Message Routing in Multiprocessor Interconnections Networks. *IEEE-TOC* C-36(5):547–553.

Denning, P. J. 1968. The Working Set Model for Program Behavior. *Communications of the ACM* 11(5):323–333.

Dennis, J. B. 1980. Dataflow Supercomputers. *IEEE Computer* 13(11):93–100.

Digital Equipment Corporation. 1992. *Alpha Architecture Handbook.* Maynard, MA: Digital Equipment Corp.

Dijkstra, E. W. 1965. Solution of a Problem in Concurrent Programming Control. *Communications of the ACM* 8(9):569.

Dijkstra, E. W., and C. S. Sholten. 1968. Termination Detection for Diffusing Computations. *Information Processing Letters* 1:1–4.

Dongarra, J. J. 1990. *Performance of Various Computers Using Standard Linear Equations Software in a Fortran Environment.* Tech. Report CS-89-85, University of Tennessee, Computer Science Dept. (March).

———. 1994. *Performance of Various Computers Using Standard Linear Equation Software.* Tech. Report CS-89-85, University of Tennessee, Computer Science Dept. (November); current report available from *netlib@ornl.gov*

Dongarra, J. J., J. Martin, and J. Worlton. 1987. Computer Benchmarking: Paths and Pitfalls. *IEEE Spectrum* (July):38.

Dongarra, J. J., and D. W. Walker. 1995. Software Libraries for Linear Algebra Computations on High performance Computers. *SIAM Review* 37:151–180.

Dongarra, J. J., and W. Gentzsch, eds. 1993. *Computer Benchmarks.* Amsterdam: Elsevier Science B. V., North-Holland.

Dubnicki, C., L. Iftode, E. W. Felten, K. Li. 1996. Software Support for Virtual Memory-Mapped Communication. *Tenth Int'l Parallel Processing Symposium* (April).

Dubnicki, C., and T. LeBlanc. 1992. Adjustable Block Size Coherent Caches. *Proc. 19th Annual Int'l Symposium on Computer Architecture* (May):170–180.

Dubois, M., and C. Scheurich. 1990. Memory Access Dependencies in Shared-Memory Multiprocessors. *IEEE Transactions on Software Engineering*16(6):660–673.

Dubois, M., C. Scheurich, and F. Briggs. 1986. Memory Access Buffering in Multiprocessors. *Proc. 13th Int'l Symposium on Computer Architecture* (June):434–442.

Dubois, M., J. Skeppstedt, L. Ricciulli, K. Ramamurthy, and P. Stenstrom. 1993. The Detection and Elimination of Useless Misses in Multiprocessors. *Proc. 20th Int'l Symposium on Computer Architecture* (May):88–97.

Dubois, M., J.-C. Wang, L. A. Barroso, K. Chen and Y.-S. Chen. 1991. Delayed Consistency and Its Effects on the Miss Rate of Parallel Programs. *Proc. Supercomputing '91* (November):197–206.

Dunigan, T. H. 1988. *Performance of a Second Generation Hypercube* Tech. Report ORNL/TM-10881, Oak Ridge National Lab. (November).

Dunning, D., G. Regnier, G. McAlpine, D. Camaron, B. Shubert, F. Berry, A. M. Merritt, E. Gronke, and C. Dodd. 1998. The Virtual Interface Architecture. *IEEE Micro* 18(2).

Dusseau, A. C., D. E. Culler, K. E. Schauser, and R. P. Martin. 1996. Fast Parallel Sorting under LogP: Experience with the CM-5. *IEEE Transactions on Parallel and Distributed Systems* 7(8):791–805.

Dwarkadas, S., P. Keleher, A. L. Cox, and W. Zwaenepoel. 1993. Evaluation of Release Consistent Software Distributed Shared Memory on Emerging Network Technology. *Proc. 20th Int'l Symposium on Computer Architecture* (May):144–155.

Eggers, S., and R. Katz. 1988. A Characterization of Sharing in Parallel Programs and Its Application to Coherency Protocol Evaluation. *Proc. 15th Annual Int'l Symposium on Computer Architecture* (May):373–382.

———. 1989a. The Effect of Sharing on the Cache and Bus Performance of Parallel Programs. *Proc. Third Int'l Conference on Architectural Support for Programming Languages and Operating Systems* (May):257–270.

———. 1989b. Evaluating the Performance of Four Snooping Cache Coherency Protocols. *Proc. 16th Annual Int'l Symposium on Computer Architecture* (May):2–15.

Eigenmann, R., and S. Hassanzadeh. 1996. Benchmarking with Real Industrial Applications: The SPEC High Performance Group. *IEEE Computational Science and Engineering* (spring).

Elliott, D. G., W. M. Snelgrove, and M. Stumm. 1992. Computational RAM: A Memory-SIMD Hybrid and Its Application to DSP. *Custom Integrated Circuits Conference*, Boston, MA (May):30.6.1–30.6.4.

Elliott, D. G., M. Stumm, and W. M. Snelgrove. 1997. *Computational RAM: The Case for SIMD Computing in Memory.* Workshop on Mixing Logic and DRAM: Chips that Compute and Remember. Presented at Annual International Symposium on Computer Architecture (ISCA) '97 (June).

Erlichson, A., B. Nayfeh, J. P. Singh and Oyekunle Olukotun. 1995. The Benefits of Clustering in Cache-Coherent Multiprocessors: An Application-Driven Investigation. *Proc. Supercomputing* '95 (November).

Erlichson, A., N. Nuckolls, G. Chesson, and J. L. Hennessy. 1996. SoftFLASH: Analyzing the Performance of Clustered Distributed Virtual Shared Memory. *Proc. Seventh Int'l Conference on Architectural Support for Programming Languages and Operating Systems* (October):210–220.

Falsafi, B., A. R. Lebeck, S. K. Reinhardt, I. Schoinas, M. D. Hill, J. R. Larus, A. Rogers, and D. A. Wood. 1994. Application-Specific Protocols for User-Level Shared Memory. *Proc. Supercomputing '94* (November):380–389.

Falsafi, B. and D. A. Wood. 1997. Reactive NUMA: A Design for Unifying S-COMA and CC-NUMA. *Proc. 24th Int'l Symposium on Computer Architecture* (June):229–240.

Farkas, K., Z. Vranesic, and M. Stumm. 1992. Cache Consistency in Hierarchical Ring-Based Multiprocessors. *Proc. Supercomputing '92* (November).

Feigel, C. P. 1994. TI Introduces Four-Processor DSP Chip. *Microprocessor Report* (March):28.

Felderman, R., et al. 1994. Atomic: A High Speed Local Communication Architecture. *Journal of High Speed Networks* 3(1):1–29.

Fenwick, D. M., D. J. Foley, W. B. Gist, S. R. VanDoren, and D. Wissell. 1995. The AlphaServer 8000 Series: High-End Server Platform Development. *Digital Technical Journal* 7(1):43–65.

Flanagan, J. L. 1994. Technologies for Multimedia Communications. *IEEE Proceedings* 82(4):590–603.

Flynn, M. J. 1972. Some Computer Organizations and Their Effectiveness. *IEEE Transactions on Computing* C-21(September):948–960.

Fortune, S., and J. Wyllie. 1978. Parallelism in Random Access Machines. *Proc. 10th ACM Symposium on Theory of Computing* (May).

Fox, G., M. Johnson, G. Lyzenga, S. Otto, J. Salmon, and D. Walker. 1988. *Solving Problems on Concurrent Processors, vol 1.* Englewood Cliffs, NJ: Prentice Hall.

Frailong, J.-L., et al. 1993. The Next Generation SPARC Multiprocessing System Architecture. *Proc. COMPCON* (spring):475–480.

Frank, S., H. Burkhardt III, and J. Rothnie. 1993. The KSR1: Bridging the Gap between Shared Memory and MPPs. *Proc. COMPCON, Digest of Papers* (spring):285–294.

Fu, J. W. C., and J. H. Patel. 1991. Data Prefetching in Multiprocessor Vector Cache Memories. *Proc. 18th Annual Symposium on Computer Architecture* (May):54–63.

Fu, J. W. C., J. H. Patel., and B. L. Janssens. 1992. Stride Directed Prefetching in Scalar Processors. *Proc. 25th Annual Int'l Symposium on Microarchitecture* (December):102–110.

Fuchs, H., G. Abram, and E. Grant. 1983. Near Real-Time Shaded Display of Rigid Objects. *Proc. SIGGRAPH.*

Galles, M., and E. Williams. 1993. Performance Optimizations, Implementation, and Verification of the SGI Challenge Multiprocessor. *Proc. 27th Hawaii Int'l Conference on System Sciences Vol. I: Architecture* (January). Also in *SGI Challenge.* Edited by T. N. Mudge and B. D. Shriver. Los Alamitos, CA: IEEE Computer Society Press, 1994, 134–143.

Geist, A., A. Beguelin, and J. Dongarra, W. Jiang, R. Manchek, and V. Sunderam. 1994. *PVM 3.0 Users' Guide and Reference Manual.* Tech. Report ORNL/TM-12187, Oak Ridge, TN: Oak Ridge National Laboratory (February). *http://www.eece.ksu.edu/pvm3/ug.ps.*

Geist, A., A. Beguelin, J. Dongarra, R. Manchek, W. Jiang, and V. Sunderam. 1994. *PVM: A Users' Guide and Tutorial for Networked Parallel Computing.* Cambridge, MA: MIT Press.

Geist, G. A., and V. S. Sunderam. 1992. Network Based Concurrent Computing on the PVM System. *Journal of Concurrency: Practice and Experience* 4(4):293–311.

Gharachorloo, K. 1995. *Memory Consistency Models for Shared-Memory Multiprocessors.* Ph.D. diss., Computer Systems Laboratory, Stanford University (December). Also published as Tech. Report #CSL-TR-95-685.

Gharachorloo, K., S. Adve, A. Gupta, M. Hill, and J. L. Hennessy. 1992. Programming for Different Memory Consistency Models. *Journal of Parallel and Distributed Computing* 15(4):399–407.

Gharachorloo, K., A. Gupta, and J. L. Hennessy. 1991a. Performance Evaluation of Memory Consistency Models for Shared-Memory Multiprocessors. *Proc. 4th Int'l Conference on Architectural Support for Programming Languages and Operating Systems* (April):245–257.

———. 1991b.Two Techniques to Enhance the Performance of Memory Consistency Models. *Proc. Int'l Conference on Parallel Processing* (August): I355–I364.

———. 1992. Hiding Memory Latency Using Dynamic Scheduling in Shared Memory Multiprocessors. *Proc. 19th Int'l Symposium on Computer Architecture* (May):22–33.

Gharachorloo, K., D. Lenoski, J. Laudon, P. Gibbons, A. Gupta, and J. L. Hennessy. 1990. Memory Consistency and Event Ordering in Scalable Shared-Memory Multiprocessors. *Proc. 17th Int'l Symposium on Computer Architecture* (May):15–26.

Gillett, R. 1996. Memory Channel Network for PCI. *IEEE Micro* 16(1):12–18.

Gillett, R., M. Collins, and D. Pimm. 1996. Overview of Network Memory Channel for PCI. *Proc. IEEE Spring COMPCON '96* (February).

Gillett, R., and R. Kaufmann. 1997. Using Memory Channel Network. *IEEE Micro* 17(1):19–25.

Glass, C. J., and L. M. Ni. 1992. The Turn Model for Adaptive Routing. *Proc. Annual International Symposium on Computer Architecture (ISCA)* (May): 278–287.

Godiwala, N. D., and B. A. Maskas. 1995. The Second-Generation Processor Module for AlphaServer 2100 Systems. *Digital Technical Journal* 7(1).

Gokhale, M., B. Holmes, and K. Iobst. 1995. Processing in Memory: The Terasys Massively Parallel PIM Array. *IEEE Computer* 28(3):23–31.

Goldschmidt, S. R. 1993. *Simulation of Multiprocessors: Speed and Accuracy.* Ph.D. diss., Stanford University (June).

Golub, G., and C. Van Loan. 1997. *Matrix Computations 3e.* Baltimore, MD: Johns Hopkins University Press.

Goodman, J. R. 1983. Using Cache Memory to Reduce Processor-Memory Traffic. *Proc. 10th Annual Int'l Symposium on Computer Architecture* (June):124–131.

———. 1987. Coherency for Multiprocessor Virtual Address Caches. *Proc. Second Int'l Conference on Architectural Support for Programming Languages and Operating Systems*, Palo Alto, CA (October):72–81.

———. 1989. *Cache Consistency and Sequential Consistency.* Tech. Report #1006, University of Wisconsin-Madison, Computer Science Dept. (February).

Goodman, J. R., M. K. Vernon, P J. Woest. 1989. Set of Efficient Synchronization Primitives for a Large-Scale Shared-Memory Multiprocessor. *Proc. Third Int'l Conference on Architectural Support for Programming Languages and Operating Systems* (April):64–75.

Gottlieb, A., R. Grishman, C. P. Kruskal, K. P. McAuliffe, L. Rudolph, and M. Snir. 1983. The NYU Ultracomputer—Designing an MIMD Shared Memory Parallel Computer. *IEEE Transactions on Computers* C-32(2):175–189.

Gottlieb, A., and C. P. Kruskal. 1984. Complexity Results for Permuting Data and Other Computations on Parallel Processors. *Journal of the ACM* 31(April):193–209.

Gottlieb, A., B. Lubachevsky, and L. Rudolph. 1983. Basic Techniques for the Efficient Coordination of Large Numbers of Cooperating Sequental Processes. *ACM Transactions on Programming Languages and Systems* 5(2).

Grafe, V. G., and J. E. Hoch. 1990. The Epsilon-2 Hybrid Dataflow Architecture. *Proc. COMPCON Spring '90*, San Francisco, CA (March):88–93.

Grahn, H., and P. Stenstrom. 1996. Evaluation of a Competitive-Update Cache Coherence Protocol with Migratory Data Detection. *Journal of Parallel and Distributed Computing* 39(2):168–180.

Grahn, H., P. Stenstrom, and M. Dubois. 1995. Implementation and Evaluation of Update-Based Protocols under Relaxed Memory Consistency Models. *Future Generation Computer Systems* 11(3):247–271.

Granuke, G., and S. Thakkar. 1990. Synchronization Algorithms for Shared Memory Multiprocessors. *IEEE Computer* 23(6):60–69.

Gray, J. 1991. *The Benchmark Handbook for Database and Transaction Processing Systems.* San Francisco: Morgan Kaufmann.

Green, S. A., and D. J. Paddon. 1990. A Highly Flexible Multiprocessor Solution for Ray Tracing. *The Visual Computer* 6:62–73.

Greenberg, R. I. and C. E. Leiserson. 1989. Randomized Routing on Fat-Trees. *Advances in Computing Research* 5:345–374.

Greenwald, M., and D. R. Cheriton. 1996. The Synergy between Non-Blocking Synchronization and Operating System Structure. *Proc. Second Symposium on Operating System Design and Implementation, USENIX*, Seattle (October):123–136.

Gropp, W., E. Lusk, and A. Skjellum. 1994. *Using MPI: Portable Parallel Programming with the Message-Passing Interface.* Cambridge, MA: MIT Press.

Groscup, W. 1992. The Intel Paragon XP/S Supercomputer. *Proc. Fifth ECMWF Workshop on the Use of Parallel Processors in Meteorology* (November):262–273.

Gunther, K. D. 1981. Prevention of Deadlocks in Packet-Switched Data Transport Systems. *IEEE Transactions on Communication* C-29(4):512–24.

Gupta, A., J. L. Hennessy, K. Gharachorloo, T. Mowry, and W.-D. Weber. 1991. Comparative Evaluation of Latency Reducing and Tolerating Techniques. *Proc. 18th Int'l Symposium on Computer Architecture* (May):254–263.

Gupta, A., and W.-D. Weber. 1992. Cache Invalidation Patterns in Shared-Memory Multiprocessors. *IEEE Transactions on Computers* 41(7):794–810.

Gupta, A., W.-D. Weber, and T. Mowry. 1990. Reducing Memory and Traffic Requirements for Scalable Directory-Based Cache-Coherence Schemes. *Proc. Int'l Conference on Parallel Processing* I(August):312–321.

Gurd, J. R., C. C. Kerkham, and I. Watson. 1985. The Manchester Prototype Dataflow Computer. *Communications of the ACM* 28(1):34–52.

Gustafson, J. L. 1988. Reevaluating Amdahl's Law. *Communications of the ACM* 31(5):532–533.

Gustafson, J. L., and Q. O. Snell. 1994. *HINT: A New Way to Measure Computer Performance.* Tech. Report, Ames Laboratory, U.S. Dept. of Energy, Ames, IA.

Gustavson, D. 1992. The Scalable Coherence Interface and Related Standards Projects. *IEEE Micro* 12(1):10–22.

Gwennap, L. 1994a. Microprocessors Head Toward MP on a Chip. *Microprocessor Report* (May).

———. 1994b. PA-7200 Enables Inexpensive MP Systems. *Microprocessor Report* (March).

Hagersten, E. 1992. *Toward Scalable Cache Only Memory Architectures.* Ph.D. diss., Swedish Institute of Computer Science (October).

Hagersten, E., A. Landin, and S. Haridi. 1992. DDM—A Cache Only Memory Architecture. *IEEE Computer* 25(9):44–54.

Hanrahan, P., D. Salzman, and L. A. Aupperle. 1991. A Rapid Hierarchical Radiosity Algorithm. *Proc. SIGGRAPH* (July).

Hayashi, K., T. Doi, T. Horie, Y. Koyanagi, O. Shiraki, N. Imamura, T. Shimizu, H. Ishihata, and T. Shindo. 1994. AP1000+: Architectural Support of PUT/GET Interface for Parallelizing Compiler. *ACM SIGPLAN Notices* 29(11):196.

Heinlein, J., R. P. Bosch, Jr., K. Gharachorloo, M. Rosenblum, and A. Gupta. 1997. Coherent Block Data Transfer in the FLASH Multiprocessor. *Proc. 11th Int'l Parallel Processing Symposium* (April).

Heinlein, J., K. Gharachorloo, S. Dresser, and A. Gupta. 1994. Integration of Message Passing and Shared Memory in the Stanford FLASH Multiprocessor. *Proc. 6th Int'l Conference on Architectural Support for Programming Languages and Operating Systems* (October):38–50.

Heinrich, M., J. Kuskin, D. Ofelt, J. Heinlein, J. Baxter, J. P. Singh, R. Simoni, K. Gharachorloo, D. Nakahira, M. Horowitz, A. Gupta, M. Rosenblum, and J. L. Hennessy. 1994. The Performance Impact of Flexibility on the Stanford FLASH Multiprocessor. *Proc. 6th Int'l Conference on Architectural Support for Programming Languages and Operating Systems* (October):274–285.

Hennessy, J. L., and N. Jouppi. 1991. Computer Technology and Architecture: An Evolving Interaction. *IEEE Computer* 24(9):18–29.

Hennessy, J. L., and D. A. Patterson. 1996. *Computer Architecture: A Quantitative Approach.* 2nd ed. San Francisco: Morgan Kaufmann.

Herlihy, M. P. 1988. Impossibility and Universality Results for Wait-Free Synchronization. *Seventh ACM SIGACTS-SIGOPS Symposium on Principles of Distributed Computing* (August):276–290.

———. 1991. Wait-Free Synchronization. *ACM Transactions on Programming Languages and Systems* 13(1):124–149.

———. 1993. A Methodology for Implementing Highly Concurrent Data Objects. *ACM Transactions on Programming Languages and Systems* 15(5):745–770.

Herlihy, M. P., and J. E. B. Moss. 1993. Transactional Memory: Architectural Support for Lock-Free Data Structures. *Proc. 20th Annual Symposium on Computer Architecture*, San Diego, CA (May):289–301.

Herlihy, M. P., and J. Wing. 1987. Axioms for Concurrent Objects. *Proc. 14th ACM Symposium on Principles of Programming Languages* (January):13–26.

Hernquist, L. 1987. Performance Characteristics of Tree Codes. *Astrophysics Journal Supplement* 64(August):715–734.

Hey, A. J. G. 1991. The Genesis Distributed Memory Benchmarks. *Parallel Computing* 17:1111–1130.

High Performance Fortran Forum. 1993. High Performance Fortran Language Specification. *Scientific Programming* 2(1):1–270.

Hill, M. D., S. J. Eggers, J. R. Larus, G. S. Taylor, G. Adams, B. K. Bose, G. A. Gibson, P. M. Hansen, J. Keller, S. I. Kong, C. G. Lee, D. Lee, J. M. Pendleton, S. A. Ritchie, D. A. Wood, B. G. Zorn, P. N. Hilfinger, D. A Hodges, R. H. Katz, J. Ousterhut, and D. A. Patterson. 1986. Design Decisions in SPUR. *IEEE Computer* 19(10):8–22. Also in *Computers for Artificial Intelligence Processing.* Edited by B. W. Wah and C. V. Ramamoorthy. New York: John Wiley and Sons, 273–299

Hill, M. D., and A. J. Smith. 1989. Evaluating Associativity in CPU Caches. *IEEE Transactions on Computers* C-38(12):1612–1630.

Hillis, W. D. 1985. *The Connection Machine.* Cambridge, MA: MIT Press.

Hillis, W. D., and G. L. Steele. 1986. Data Parallel Algorithms. *Communications of the ACM* 29(12):1170–1183.

Hillis, W. D., and L. W. Tucker. 1993. The CM-5 Connection Machine: A Scalable Supercomputer. *Communications of the ACM* 36(11):31–40.

Hirata, H., K. Kimura, S. Nagamine, Y. Mochizuki, A. Nishimura, Y. Nakase, and T. Nishizawa. 1992. An Elementary Processor Architecture with Simultaneous Instruction Issuing from Multiple Threads. *Proc. 19th Int'l Symposium on Computer Architecture* (May):136–145.

Hoare, C. A. R. 1978. Communicating Sequential Processes. *Communications of the ACM* 21(8):666–667.

Hockney, R. W., and C. R. Jesshope. 1988. *Parallel Computers 2*. London: Adam Hilger.

Holt, C., M. Heinrich, J. P. Singh, E. Rothberg and J. L. Hennessy. 1995. *The Effects of Latency, Occupancy, and Bandwidth in Distributed Shared Memory Multiprocessors*. Tech. Report #CSL-TR-95-660, Computer Systems Laboratory, Stanford University (January).

Homewood M., and M. McLaren. 1993. Meiko CS-2 Interconnect Elan—Elite Design. *Hot Interconnects* (August).

Horiw, T., K. Hayashi, T. Shimizu, and H. Ishihata. 1993. Improving the AP1000 Parallel Computer Performance with Message Passing. *Proc. 20th Annual Int'l Symposium on Computer Architecture* (May):314–325

Horowitz, M. 1997. Limits of Electrical Signalling. *Hot Interconnects Keynote* (August)

Horst, R. 1995. TNet: A Reliable System Area Network. *IEEE Micro* 15(1):37–45.

Horst, R. W., and T. C. K. Chou. 1985. An Architecture for High Volume Transaction Processing. *Proc. 12th Annual Int'l Symposium on Computer Architecture* (June):240–245, Boston MA. (Tandem NonStop II)

Horst, R. W., R. L. Harris, and R. L. Jardine. 1990. Multiple Instruction Issue in the NonStop Cyclone Processor. *Proc. Annual International Symposium on Computer Architecture (ISCA)*, 216–226.

Hristea, C., D. Lenoski, and J. Keen. 1997. Measuring Memory Hierarchy Performance of Cache Coherent Multiprocessors Using Micro Benchmarks. *Proc. SC97* (November; all-Web conference proceeding).

Hunt, D. 1996. *Advanced Features of the 64-Bit PA-8000*. Palo Alto, CA: Hewlett Packard Corp.

IEEE Computer Society. 1993. *IEEE Standard for Scalable Coherent Interface (SCI)*. IEEE Standard 1596–1992. Washington, DC: IEEE Computer Society.

———. 1995. *IEEE Standard for Cache Optimization for Large Numbers of Processors Using the Scalable Coherent Interface (SCI)* Draft 0.35 (September). Washington, DC: IEEE Computer Society.

Iftode, L., C. Dubnicki, E. W. Felten, and K. Li. 1996. Improving Release-Consistent Shared Virtual Memory Using Automatic Update. *Proc. Second Symposium on High Performance Computer Architecture* (February):14–25.

Iftode, L., J. P. Singh, and K. Li. 1996a. Understanding Application Performance on Shared Virtual Memory Systems. *Proc. 23rd Int'l Symposium on Computer Architecture* (April):122–133.

———. 1996b. Scope Consistency: A Bridge between Release Consistency and Entry Consistency. *Proc. Symposium on Parallel Algorithms and Architectures* (June).

Intel Corporation. 1994. *I750, I860, I960 Processors and Related Products*. Santa Clara, CA: Intel Corp.

———. 1996. *Pentium® Pro Family Developer's Manual*. Santa Clara, CA: Intel Corp.

Jeremiassen, T. E., and S. J. Eggers. Eliminating False Sharing. *Proc. 1991 Int'l Conference on Parallel Processing* (August):377–381.

Jiang, D., H. Shan, and J. P. Singh. 1997. Application Restructuring and Performance Portability on Shared Virtual Memory and Hardware-Coherent Multiprocessors. *Proc. Sixth ACM SIGPLAN Symposium on Principles and Practice of Parallel Programming* (June):217–229.

Jiang, D., and J. P. Singh. 1998. A Methodology and an Evaluation of the SGI Origin2000. *Proc. SIGMETRICS Conference on Measurement and Modeling of Computer Systems* (June).

Joe, T. 1995. *COMA-F: A Non-Hierarchical Cache Only Memory Architecture.* Ph.D. diss., Computer Systems Laboratory, Stanford University (March).

Joe, T., and J. L. Hennessy. 1994. Evaluating the Memory Overhead Required for COMA Architectures. *Proc. 21st Int'l Symposium on Computer Architecture* (April):82–93.

Joerg, C. F. 1994. *Design and Implementation of a Packet Switched Routing Chip.* Tech. Report MIT/LCS/TR-482, MIT Laboratory for Computer Science (August).

Joerg, C. F., and A. Boughton. 1991. The Monsoon Interconnection Network. *Proc. ICCD* (October).

Johnson, M. 1991. *Superscalar Microprocessor Design.* Englewood Cliffs, NJ: Prentice Hall.

Jordan, H. F. 1985. HEP Architecture, Programming, and Performance. In *Parallel MIMD Computation: The HEP Supercomputer and Its Applications.* Edited by J S. Kowalik. Cambridge, MA: MIT Press, 8.

Jouppi, N. P. 1990. Improving Direct-Mapped Cache Performance by the Addition of a Small Fully-Associative Cache and Prefetch Buffers. *Proc. 17th Annual Symposium on Computer Architecture* (June):364–373.

Jouppi, N. P., and P. Ranganathan. 1997. *The Relative Importance of Memory Latency, Bandwidth, and Branch Limits to Performance.* Workshop on Mixing Logic and DRAM: Chips that Compute and Remember. Presented at the Annual Int'l Symposium on Computer Architecture (ISCA) '97 (June).

Jouppi, N. P., and D. Wall. 1989. Available Instruction-Level Parallelism for Superscalar and Superpipelined Machines. *ASPLOS III,* 272–282.

Kägi, A., D. Burger, and J. R. Goodman. 1997. Efficient Synchronization: Let Them Eat QOLB. *Proc. 24th Int'l Symposium on Computer Architecture (ISCA)* (June):170–180.

Karlin, A. R., M. S. Manasse, L. Rudolph and D. D. Sleator. 1986. Competitive Snoopy Caching. *Proc. 27th Annual IEEE Symposium on Foundations of Computer Science.*

Karol, M., M. Hluchyj, and S. Morgan. 1987. Input versus Output Queueing on a Space Division Packet Switch. *IEEE Transactions on Communications* 35(12):1347–1356.

Karp, R., U. Vazirani, and V. Vazirani. 1990. An Optimal Algorithm for On-Line Bipartite Matching. *Proc. 22nd ACM Symposium on the Theory of Computing* (May):352–358.

Kaxiras, S. 1996. Kiloprocessor Extensions to SCI. *Proc. 10th Int'l Parallel Processing Symposium*

Kaxiras, S., and J. Goodman. The GLOW Cache Coherence Protocol Extensions for Widely Shared Data. *Proc. Int'l Conference on Supercomputing* (May):35–43.

Keeton, K. K., T. E. Anderson, and D. A. Patterson. 1995. LogP Quantified: The Case for Low-Overhead Local Area Networks. *Hot Interconnects III: Symposium on High Performance Interconnects* (August).

Keleher, P., A. L. Cox, S. Dwarkadas, and W. Zwaenepoel. 1994. TreadMarks: Distributed Shared Memory on Standard Workstations and Operating Systems. *Proc. Winter USENIX Conference* (January):15–132.

Keleher, P., A. L. Cox, and W. Zwaenepoel. 1992. Lazy Consistency for Software Distributed Shared Memory. *Proc. 19th Int'l Symposium on Computer Architecture* (May):13–21.

Kermani, P., and L. Kleinrock. 1979. Virtual Cut-Through: A New Computer Communication Switching Technique. *Computer Networks* 3(September):267–286.

Kessler, R. E., and J. L. Schwarzmeier. 1993. Cray T3D: A New Dimension for Cray Research. *Proc. Papers, COMPCON Spring'93*, San Francisco (February):176–182.

Knuth, D. E. 1966. Additional Comments on a Problem in Concurrent Programming Control. *Communications of the ACM* 9(5):321–322.

Koebel, C., D. Loveman, R. Schreiber, G. Steele, and M. Zosel. 1994. *The High Performance Fortran Handbook*. Cambridge, MA: MIT Press.

Koeninger, R. K., M. Furtney, and M. Walker. 1994. A Shared Memory MPP from Cray Research. *Digital Technical Journal* 6(2):8–21.

Kogge, P. M. 1994. EXECUBE—A New Architecture for Scalable MPPs. *1994 Int'l Conference on Parallel Processing* (August):177–184.

Kontothanassis, L. I., G. Hunt, R. Stets, N. Hardavellas, M. Cierniak, S. Parthasarathy, W. Meira, S. Dwarkadas, and M. Scott. 1997. VM-Based Shared Memory on Low-Latency, Remote-Memory-Access Networks. *Proc. 24th Int'l Symposium on Computer Architecture* (June).

Kontothanassis, L. I., and M. L. Scott. 1996. Using Memory-Mapped Network Interfaces to Improve the Performance of Distributed Shared Memory. *Proc. Second Symposium on High Performance Computer Architecture* (February):166–177.

Kostantantindou, S., and L. Snyder. 1991. Chaos Router: Architecture and Performance. *Proc. 18th Annual Symposium on Computer Architecture* (May):212–221.

Krishnamurthy, A., K. E. Schauser, C. J. Scheiman, R. Y. Wang, D. E. Culler, and K. Yelick. 1996. Evaluation of Architectural Support for Global Address-Based Communication in Large-Scale Parallel Machines. *ACM SIGPLAN Notices* 31(9):37–48.

Krishnamurthy, A., and K. A. Yelick. 1994. Optimizing Parallel SPMD Programs. *Seventh Annual Workshop on Languages and Compilers for Parallel Computing*. Ithaca, NY (August).

———. 1995. Optimizing Parallel Programs with Explicit Sychronization. *Programming Language Design and Implementation,* 196–204.

———. 1996. Analyses and Optimizations for Shared Address Space Programs. *JPDC* 38(2):130–144.

Kroft, D. 1981. Lockup-Free Instruction Fetch/Prefetch Cache Organization. *Proc. Eighth Int'l Symposium on Computer Architecture* (May):81–87.

Kronenberg, N. P., H. Levy, and W. D. Strecker. 1986. Vax Clusters: A Closely-Coupled Distributed System. *ACM Transactions on Computer Systems* 4(2):130–146.

Kruskal, C. P., and M. Snir. 1983. The Performance of Multistage Interconnection Networks for Multiprocessors. *IEEE Transactions on Computers* C-32(12):1091–1098.

Kubiatowicz, J., and A. Agarwal. 1993. The Anatomy of a Message in the Alewife Multiprocessor. *Proc. Int'l Conference on Supercomputing* (July):195–206.

Kuehn, J. T, and B. J. Smith. 1988. The Horizon Supercomputing System: Architecture and Software. *Proc. Supercomputing '88* (November):28–34.

Kumar, M. 1992. Unique Design Concepts in GF11 and Their Impact on Performance. *IBM Journal of Research and Development* 36(6):990–1000.

Kumar, V., A. Grama, A. Gupta, and G. Karypis. 1994. *Introduction to Parallel Computing: Design and Analysis of Algorithms*. Redwood City, CA: Benjamin/Cummings Publishing Company.

Kumar, V., and A. Gupta. 1991. Analysis of Scalability of Parallel Algorithms and Architectures: A Survey. *Proc. Int'l Conference on Supercomputing* (June):396–405.

Kung, H. T., R. Sansom, S. Schlick, P. A. Steenkiste, M. Arnould, F. J. Bitz, F. Christianson, E. C. Cooper, O. Menzilcioglu, D. Ombres, and B. Zill. 1989. Network-Based Multicomputers: An Emerging Parallel Architecture. *Proc. Supercomputing '91 Conference* (November):664–673.

Kurihara, K., D. Chaiken, and A. Agarwal. 1991. Latency Tolerance through Multithreading in Large-Scale Multiprocessors. *Proc. Int'l Symposium on Shared Memory Multiprocessing* (April):91–101.

Kuskin, J., D. Ofelt, M. Heinrich, J. Heinlein, R. Simoni, K. Gharachorloo, J. Chapin, D. Nakahira, J. Baxter, M. Horowitz, A. Gupta, M. Rosenblum, and J. Hennessy. 1994. The Stanford FLASH Multiprocessor. *Proc. 21st Int'l Symposium on Computer Architecture* (April): 302–313.

Lam, M S., and R P. Wilson. 1992. Limits on Control Flow on Parallelism. *Proc. 19th Annual Int'l Symposium on Computer Architecture* (May):46–57.

Lamport, L. 1979. How to Make a Multiprocessor Computer that Correctly Executes Multiprocess Programs. *IEEE Transactions on Computers* C-28(9):690–691.

Larus, J. R., B. Richards, and G. Viswanathan. 1996. Parallel Programming in C**: A Large-Grain Data-Parallel Programming Language. In *Parallel Programming Using C++*. Edited by G. V. Wilson and P. Lu. Cambridge, MA: MIT Press.

Laudon, J. P. 1994. *Architectural and Implementation Tradeoffs in Multiple-Context Processors.* Ph.D. diss., Stanford University, Stanford, California. Also published as Tech. Report #CSL-TR-94-634, Computer Systems Laboratory, Stanford University (May).

Laudon, J., A. Gupta, and M. Horowitz. 1994. *Architectural and Implementation Tradeoffs in the Design of Multiple-Context Processors.* In *Multithreaded Computer Architecture: A Summary of the State of the Art.* Edited by R. A. Iannucci. Dordrecht, Germany; Norwell, MA: Kluwer Academic Publishers, 167–200.

Laudon, J. P., and D. Lenoski. 1997. The SGI Origin: A ccNUMA Highly Scalable Server. *Proc. 24th Int'l Symposium on Computer Architecture.*

Lawton, J. V., J. J. Brosnan, M. P. Doyle, S.D. O'Riodain, and T. G. Reddin. 1996. Building a High-Performance Message-Passing System for MEMORY CHANNEL Clusters. *Digital Technical Journal* 8(2):96–116.

Lee, C. G. 1989. Multi-Step Gradual Rounding. *IEEE Transactions on Computers* 38(4):595–600.

Lee, R. L., A. Y. Kwok, and F. A. Briggs. 1991. The Floating Point Performance of a Superscalar SPARC Processor. *Proc. 4th Symposium on Architectural Support for Programming Languages and Operating Systems* (April):28–37.

Leighton, F. T. 1992. *Introduction to Parallel Algorithms and Architectures.* San Francisco: Morgan Kaufmann.

Leiserson, C. E. 1985. Fat-Trees: Universal Networks for Hardware-Efficient Supercomputing. *IEEE Transactions on Computers* C-34(10):892–901.

Leiserson, C. E., Z. S. Abuhamdeh, D. C. Douglas, C. R. Feynman, M. N. Ganmukhi, J. V. Hill, W. D. Hillis, B. C. Kuszmaul, M. A. St. Pierre, D. S. Wells, M. C. Wong, S. Yang, and R. Zak. 1996. The Network Architecture of the Connection Machine CM-5. *Journal of Parallel and Distributed Computing* 33(2):145–158. Also in *Proc. Fourth Symposium on Parallel Algorithms and Architectures '92* (June):272–285.

Lenoski, D. 1992. *The Stanford DASH Multiprocessor.* Ph.D. diss., Computer Systems Laboratory, Stanford University.

Lenoski, D., J. Laudon, K. Gharachorloo, A. Gupta, and J. L. Hennessy. 1990. The Directory-Based Cache Coherence Protocol for the DASH Multiprocessor. *Proc. 17th Int'l Symposium on Computer Architecture* (May):148–159.

Lenoski, D., J. Laudon, T. Joe, D. Nakahira, L. Stevens, A. Gupta, and J. L. Hennessy. 1992. The DASH Prototype: Implementation and Performance. *Proc. 19th Int'l Symposium on Computer Architecture,* Gold Coast, Australia (May):92–103.

———. 1993. The DASH Prototype: Logic Overhead and Performance. *IEEE Transactions on Parallel and Distributed Systems* 4(1):41–61.

Li, K., and P. Hudak. 1989. Memory Coherence in Shared Virtual Memory Systems. *ACM Transactions on Computer Systems* 7(4):321–359.

Li, S.-Y. 1988. Theory of Periodic Contention and Its Application to Packet Switching. *Proc. INFOCOM '88* (March):320–325.

Lim, B.-H., and A. Agarwal. 1994. Reactive Syncronization Algorithms for Multiprocessors. *Proc. Sixth Int'l Conference on Architectural Support for Programming Languages and Operating Systems,* 25–35.

Linder, D., and J. Harden. 1991. An Adaptive Fault Tolerant Wormhole Strategy for k-ary n-cubes. *IEEE Transactions on Computer* C-40(1):2–12.

Lipton, R., and J. Sandberg. 1988. *PRAM: A Scalable Shared Memory.* Tech. Report #CS-TR-180–88, Computer Science Dept., Princeton University (September).

Litzkow, M., M. Livny, and M. W. Mutka. 1988. Condor—A Hunter of Idle Workstations. *Proc. Eighth Int'l Conference of Distributed Computing Systems* (June):104–111.

Lo, J. L., S. J. Eggers, J. S. Emer, H. M. Levy, R. L. Stamm, and D. M. Tullsen. 1997. Converting Thread-Level Parallelism into Instruction-Level Parallelism via Simultaneous Multithreading. *ACM Transactions on Computer Systems* (August).

Lonergan, W., and P. King. 1961. Design of the B 5000 System. *Datamation* 7(5):28–32

Lovett, T., and R. Clapp. 1996. STiNG: A CC-NUMA Computer System for the Commercial Marketplace. *Proc. 23rd Int'l Symposium on Computer Architecture* (May):308–317.

Luk, C.-K., and T. C. Mowry. 1996. Compiler-Based Prefetching for Recursive Data Structures. *Proc. Seventh Symposium on Architectural Support for Programming Languages and Operating Systems (ASPLOS-VII)* (October):222–233.

Lukowsky, J., and S. Polit. 1997 (date accessed). IP Packet Switching on the GIGAswitch/FDDI System. *http://www.networks.digital.com:80/dr/techart/gsfip-mn.html.*

Mainwaring, A., B. Chun, S. Schleimer, and D. Wilkerson. 1997. System Area Network Mapping. *Proc. Ninth Annual ACM Symposium on Parallel Algorithms and Architecture,* Newport, RI (June):116–126.

Mainwaring, A., and D. E. Culler. 1996. *Active Message Applications Programming Interface and Communication Subsystem Organization.* Tech. Report CSD-96-918, University of California at Berkeley.

Martin, R. 1994. HPAM: An Active Message Layer of a Network of Workstations. Presented at *Hot Interconnects II* (August).

Massalin, H., and C. Pu. 1991. *A Lock-Free Multiprocessor OS Kernel.* Tech. Report CUCS-005-01, Columbia University, Computer Science Dept. (October).

Matelan, N. 1985. The FLEX/32 Multicomputer. *Proc. 12th Annual Int'l Symposium on Computer Architecture,* Boston, MA. (Flex) (June):209–213

May, C., E. Silha, R. Simpson, and H. Warren, eds. 1994. *The PowerPC Architecture: A Specification for a New Family of RISC Processors.* San Francisco: Morgan Kaufmann.

McCreight, E. 1984. *The Dragon Computer System: An Early Overview.* Tech. Report, Xerox Corp. (September).

Mellor-Crummey, J. and M. Scott. 1991. Algorithms for Scalable Synchronization on Shared Memory Mutiprocessors. *ACM Transactions on Computer Systems* 9(1):21–65.

Melvin, S., and Y. Patt. 1991. Exploiting Fine-Grained Parallelism through a Combination of Hardware and Software Techniques. *Proc. Annual Int'l Symposium on Computer Architecture (ISCA)*, 287–296.

Michael, M., and M. Scott. 1996. Simple, Fast, and Practical Non-Blocking and Blocking Concurrent Queue Algorithms. *Proc. 15th Annual ACM Symposium on Principles of Distributed Computing*, Philadelphia, PA (May): 267–276.

Minnich, R., D. Burns, and F. Hady. 1995. The Memory-Integrated Network Interface. *IEEE Micro* 15(1):11–20.

MIPS Technologies. 1991. *MIPS R4000 User's Manual*. Mountain View, CA: MIPS Technologies.

———. 1996. *R10000 Microprocessor User's Manual, Version 1.1* (January). Mountain View, CA: MIPS Technologies.

Miyoshi, H.; M. Fukuda, T. Iwamiya, T. Nakamura, M. Tuchiya, M. Yoshida, K. Yamamoto, Y. Yamamoto, S. Ogawa, Y. Matsuo, T. Yamane, M. Takamura, M. Ikeda, S. Okada, Y. Sakamoto, T. Kitamura, H. Hatama, M. Kishimoto, M. Arnould, F. J. Bitz, E. C. Cooper, H. T. Kung, R. Sansom, S. Schlick, P. A. Steenkiste, and B. Zill. 1994. Development and Achievement of NAL Numerical Wind Tunnel (NWT) for CFD Computations. *Proc. Supercomputing '94*, Washington, DC (November):685–692.

Mowry, T. C. 1994. *Tolerating Latency through Software-Controlled Data Prefetching*. Ph.D. diss., Computer Systems Laboratory, Stanford University. Also published as Tech. Report #CSL-TR-94-628, Computer Systems Laboratory, Stanford University (June).

MPI Forum. 1993. *Document for a Standard Message-Passing Interface*. Tech. Report CS-93-214, University of Tennessee, Knoxville, Computer Science Dept. (November).

———. 1994. MPI: A Message Passing Interface. *Int'l Journal of Supercomputing Applications* 8(3/4). Special Issue on MPI. (updated 5/95). Also published in *Proc. Supercomputing '93 Conference* (May). Los Alamitos, CA: IEEE Computer Society Press, 878–883. Updated spec at *http://www.mcs.anl.gov/mpi/*.

Mukherjee, S., and M. Hill. 1997. A Case for Making Network Interfaces Less Peripheral. *Hot Interconnects* (August).

NAS Parallel Benchmarks. 1998 (date accessed). *http://science.nas.nasa.gov/Software/NPB/*.

Nayfeh, B. A., L. Hammond, K. Olukoton. 1996. Evaluation of Design Alternatives for a Multiprocessor Microprocessor. *Proc. 23rd Annual Int'l Symposium on Computer Architecture* (May). New York: ACM Press, 67–77.

Nestle, E., and A. Inselberg. 1985. The Synapse N+1 System: Architectural Characteristics and Performance Data of a Tightly-Coupled Multiprocessor System. *Proc. 12th Annual Int'l Symposium on Computer Architecture*, Boston, MA (Synapse) (June):233–239.

Ngai, J., and C. Seitz. 1989. A Framework for Adaptive Routing in Multicomputer Networks. *Proc. 1989 Symposium on Parallel Algorithms and Architectures* (June):2–10.

Nickolls, J. R. 1990. The Design of the MasPar MP-1: A Cost Effective Massively Parallel Computer. *COMPCON Spring '90, Digest of Papers*, San Francisco, CA (February/March):25–28.

Nikhil, R. S., and Arvind. 1989. Can Dataflow Subsume von Neumann Computing? *Proc. 16th Annual Int'l Symposium on Computer Architecture* (May):262–72.

Nikhil, R., G. Papadopoulos, and Arvind. 1993. *T: A Multithreaded Massively Parallel Architecture. *Proc. Annual Int'l Symposium on Computer Architecture (ISCA) '93* (May):156–167.

Noakes, M. D, D. A. Wallach, and W. J. Dally. 1993. The J-Machine Multicomputer: An Architectural Evaluation. *Proc. 20th Int'l Symposium on Computer Architecture* (May):224–235.

Nuth, P., and W. J. Dally. 1992. The J-Machine Network. *Proc. Int'l Conference on Computer Design: VLSI in Computers and Processors* (October).

———. 1995. The Named-State Register File: Implementation and Performance. *Proc. First Int'l Symposium on High-Performance Computer Architecture* (January):4–13.

O'Krafka, B., and A. Newton. 1990. An Empirical Evaluation of Two Memory-Efficient Directory Methods. *Proc. 17th Int'l Symposium on Computer Architecture* (May):138–147.

Office of Science and Technology Policy. 1993. *Grand Challenges 1993: High Performance Computing and Communications, A Report by the Committee on Physical, Mathematical, and Engineering Sciences.* Washington, DC: Office of Science and Technology Policy.

Ohara, M. 1996. *Producer-Oriented versus Consumer-Oriented Prefetching: A Comparison and Analysis of Parallel Application Programs.* Ph.D. diss., Computer Systems Laboratory, Stanford University. Available as Tech. Report #CSL-TR-96-695, Stanford University (June).

Olukotun, K., B. A. Nayfeh, L. Hammond, K.Wilson and K. Chang. 1996. The Case for a Single-Chip Multiprocessor. *Proc. ASPLOS* (October):2–11.

Omondi, A. R. 1994. Ideas for the Design of Multithreaded Pipelines. In *Multithreaded Computer Architecture: A Summary of the State of the Art.* Edited by R. Iannucci. Dordrecht, Germany; Norwell, MA: Kluwer Academic Publishers, 1994. See also A. R. Omondi, Design of a High Performance Instruction Pipeline. *Computer Systems Science and Engineering* 6(1):13–29 (1991).

Pacheco, P. 1996. *Parallel Programming with MPI.* San Francisco: Morgan Kaufmann.

Padegs, A. 1981. System/360 and Beyond. *IBM Journal of Research and Development* 25(5):377–390.

Pai, V. S., P. Ranganathan, S. V. Adve, and T. Harton. 1996. An Evaluation of Memory Consistency Models for Shared-Memory Systems with ILP Processors. *Proc. Seventh Symposium on Architectural Support for Programming Languages and Operating Systems (ASPLOS-VII)* (October):12–23.

Papadimitriou, C. H. 1979. The Serializability of Concurrent Database Updates. *Journal of the ACM* 26(4):631–653.

Papadopoulos, G. M., and D. E. Culler. 1990. Monsoon: An Explicit Token-Store Architecture. *Proc. 17th Annual Int'l Symposium on Computer Architecture,* Seattle, WA (May):82–91.

Papamarcos, M., and J. Patel. 1984. A Low Overhead Coherence Solution for Multiprocessors with Private Cache Memories. *Proc. 11th Annual Int'l Symposium on Computer Architecture* (June):348–354.

PARKBENCH Committee. 1994. Public International Benchmarks for Parallel Computers. *Scientific Programming* 3(2). Also published as Tech. Report CS93-213, University of Tennessee, Knoxville, Dept. of Computer Science (November).

Patterson, D. A. 1995. Microprocessors in 2020. *Scientific American* (September).

Patterson, D. A., T. Anderson, N. Cardwell, R. Fromm, K. Keeton, C. Kozyrakis, R. Thomas, and K.Yelick. 1997. A Case for Intelligent RAM. *IEEE Micro* 17(2):34–44.

Peterson, L., and B. Davie. 1996. *Computer Networks.* San Francisco: Morgan Kaufmann.

Pfeiffer, W., S. Hotovy, N. Nystrom, D. Rudy, T. Sterling, M. Straka. 1995 (date accessed). JNNIE: The Joint NSF-NASA Initiative on Evaluation. *http://www.tc.cornell.edu/JNNIE/finrep/jnnie.html.*

Pfister, G. F. 1995. *In Search of Clusters—The Coming Battle for Lowly Parallel Computing.* Englewood Cliffs, NJ: Prentice Hall.

Pfister, G. F., W. C. Brantley, D. A. George, S. L. Harvey, W. J. Kleinfelder, K. P. McAuliff, E. A. Melton, V. A. Norton, and J. Weiss. 1985. The IBM Research Parallel Processor Prototype (RP3): Introduction and Architecture. *Proc. Int'l Conference on Parallel Processing* (August):264–771.

Pfister, G. F., and V. A. Norton. 1985. Hot Spot Contention and Combining Multistage Interconnection Networks. *IEEE Transactions on Computers* C-34(10).

Pierce, P. 1988. The NX/2 Operating System. *Proc. Third Conference on Hypercube Concurrent Computers and Applications* (January):384-390.

Pierce, P., and G. Regnier. 1994. The Paragon Implementation of the NX Message Passing Interface. *Proc. Scalable High-Performance Computing Conference* (May):184–90.

Porter, R. E. 1960. *Datamation* 6(1):8–14.

Przybylski, S., M. Horowitz, J. L. Hennessy. 1988. Performance Tradeoffs in Cache Design. *Proc. 15th Annual Symposium on Computer Architecture* (May):290–298.

Ranganathan, P., V. S. Pai, H. Abdel-Shafi, and S. V. Adve. 1997. The Interaction of Software Prefetching with ILP Processors in Shared-Memory Systems. *Proc. 24th Int'l Symposium on Computer Architecture* (June).

Ratner, J. 1985. Concurrent Processing: A New Direction in Scientific Computing. *Proc. 1985 National Computing Conference,* 835.

Reddaway, S. F. 1973. DAP—A Distributed Array Processor. *First Annual Int'l Symposium on Computer Architecture* (December):61–65.

Reinhardt, S. K., M. D. Hill, J. R. Larus, A. R. Lebeck, J. C. Lewis, and D. A. Wood. 1993. The Wisconsin Wind Tunnel: Virtual Prototyping of Parallel Computers. *Proc. ACM SIGMETRICS Conference on Measurement and Modeling of Computer Systems* (May):48–60.

Reinhardt, S. K., J. R. Larus, and D. A. Wood. 1994. Tempest and Typhoon: User-Level Shared Memory. *Proc. 21st Int'l Symposium on Computer Architecture* (April):325–337.

Reinhardt, S. K., R. W. Pfile, and D. A. Wood. 1996. Decoupled Hardware Support for Distributed Shared Memory. *Proc. 23rd Int'l Symposium on Computer Architecture* (May):34–43.

Rettberg, R., W. Crowther, P. Carvey, and R. Tomlinson. 1990. The Monarch Parallel Processor Hardware Design. *IEEE Computer* (April):18–30.

Rettberg, R., and R. Thomas. 1986. Contention is No Obstacle to Shared-Memory Multiprocessing. *Communications of the ACM* 29(12):1202–1212.

Rinard, M. C., D. J. Scales, and M. S. Lam. 1993. Jade: A High-Level, Machine-Independent Language for Parallel Programming. *IEEE Computer* 26(6).

Rodgers, D. 1985. Improvements on Multiprocessor System Design. *Proc. 12th Annual Int'l Symposium on Computer Architecture,* Boston, MA (Sequent B8000) (June):225–231,

Rosenblum, M., S. A. Herrod, E. Witchel, and A. Gupta. 1995. Complete Computer Simulation: The SimOS Approach. *IEEE Parallel and Distributed Technology* 3(4).

Rosenburg, B. 1989. Low-Synchronization Translation Lookaside Buffer Consistency in Large-Scale Shared-Memory Multiprocessors. *Proc. Symposium on Operating Systems Principles* (December).

Rothberg, E., J. P. Singh, and A. Gupta. 1993. Working Sets, Cache Sizes, and Node Granularity Issues for Large-Scale Multiprocessors. *Proc. 20th Int'l Symposium on Computer Architecture* (May):14–25.

Russel, R. M. 1978. The CRAY-1 Computer System. *Communications of the ACM* 21(1):63–72.

Saavedra-Barrera, R. H., D. E. Culler, T. von Eicken. 1990. Analysis of Multithreaded Architectures for Parallel Computing. *Second Annual ACM Symposium on Parallel Algorithms and Architectures* (July):169–178.

Saavedra, R. H., R. S. Gaines, and M. J. Carlton. 1993. Micro Benchmark Analysis of the KSR1. *Proc. Supercomputing '93,* Portland, OR (November):202–213.

Saavedra, R. H., and A. J. Smith. 1996. Analysis of Benchmark Characteristics and Benchmark Perforemance Prediction. *ACM Transactions on Computer Systems* 14(4):344–384.

Sakai, S., Y. Kodama, and Y. Yamaguchi. 1991. Prototype Implementation of a Highly Parallel Dataflow Machine EM4. *Proc. Fifth Int'l Parallel Processing Symposium*, Anaheim, CA (April/May):278–286.

Salmon, J. 1990. *Parallel Hierarchical N-body Methods.* Ph.D. diss., California Institute of Technology.

Salmon, J. K., M. S. Warren, and G. S. Winckelmans. 1994. Fast Parallel Treecodes for Gravitational and Fluid Dynamical N-body Problems. *Intl. Journal of Supercomputer Applications* 8:129–142.

Samanta, R., A. Bilas, L. Iftode, and J. P. Singh. 1998. Home-Based SVM Protocols for SMP Clusters: Design, Simulations, Implementation, and Performance. *Proc. 23rd Annual Int'l Symposium on Computer Architecture* (February).

Saulsbury, A., F. Pong, and A. Nowatzyk. 1996. Missing the Memory Wall: The Case for Processor/Memory Integration. *Proc. 23rd Annual Int'l Symposium on Computer Architecture* (May):90–101.

Saulsbury, A., T. Wilkinson, J. Carter, and A. Landin. 1995. An Argument For Simple COMA. *Proc. First IEEE Symposium on High Performance Computer Architecture* (January):276–285.

Savage, J. 1985. Parallel Processing as a Language Design Problem. *Proc. 12th Annual Int'l Symposium on Computer Architecture,* Boston, MA (Myrias 4000) (June):221–224.

Scales, D. J., K. Gharachorloo, and C. A. Thekkath. 1996. Shasta: A Low Overhead, Software-Only Approach for Supporting Fine-Grain Shared Memory. *Proc. Seventh Int'l Conference on Architectural Support for Programming Languages and Operating Systems* (October):174–185.

Scales, D. J., and M. S. Lam. 1994. The Design and Evaluation of a Shared Object System for Distributed Memory Machines. *Proc. First Symposium on Operating System Design and Implementation* (November):101–114.

Schanin, D.J. 1986. The Design and Development of a Very High Speed System Bus—The Encore Multimax Nanobus. In *Proc. Fall Joint Computer Conference (Encore),* Dallas, TX (November). Edited by H. S. Stone. Los Alamitos: IEEE Computer Society Press, 410–418.

Schauser, K. E., and C. J. Scheiman. 1995. Experience with Active Messages on the Meiko CS-2. *Proc. Ninth Int'l Symposium on Parallel Processing* (IPPS'95) (April):140–149,

Scheurich, C. and M. Dubois. 1987. Correct Memory Operation of Cache-Based Multiprocessors. *Proc. 14th Int'l Symposium on Computer Architecture* (June):234–243.

Schoinas, I., B. Falsafi, A. R. Lebeck, S. K. Reinhardt, J. R. Larus, and D. A. Wood. 1994. Fine-Grain Access Control for Distributed Shared Memory. *Proc. 6th Int'l Conference on Architectural Support for Programming Languages and Operating Systems* (October):297–306.

Schroeder, M. D., A. D. Birrell, M. Burrows, H. Murray, R. M. Needham, T. L. Rodeheffer, E. H. Satterthwaite, and C. P. Thacker. 1991. Autonet: A High-Speed, Self-Configuring Local Area Network Using Point-to-Point Links. *IEEE Journal on Selected Areas in Communications* 9(8):1318–1335.

Schwiebert, L., and D. N. Jayasimha. 1995. A Universal Proof Technique for Deadlock-Free Routing in Interconnection Networks. *Symposium on Parallel Algorithms and Architecture* (July):175–184.

Scott, S. 1991. A Cache-Coherence Mechanism for Scalable Shared-Memory Multiprocessors. *Proc. Int'l Symposium on Shared Memory Multiprocessing* (April):49–59.

———. 1996. Synchronization and Communication in the T3E Multiprocessor. *Proc. Seventh Int'l Conference on Architectural Support for Programming Languages and Operating Systems* (October):26–36, Cambridge, MA,.

Scott, S., and J. R. Goodman. 1993. Performance of Pruning Cache Directories for Large-Scale Multiprocessors. *IEEE Transactions on Parallel and Distributed Systems* 4(5):520–534.

———. 1994. The Impact of Pipelined Channels on k-ary n-Cube Networks. *IEEE Transactions on Parallel and Distributed Systems* 5(1):2–16.

Scott, S., M. Vernon, and J. R. Goodman. 1992. Performance of the SCI Ring. *Proc. 19th Int'l Symposium on Computer Architecture* (May):403–414.

Seitz, C. L. 1984. Concurrent VLSI Architectures. *IEEE Transactions on Computers* 33(12):1247–1265.

———. 1985. The Cosmic Cube. *Communications of the ACM* 28(1):22–33.

Seitz, C. L., and W.-K. Su. 1993. A Family of Routing and Communication Chips Based on Mosaic. *Proc. of Univ. of Washington Symposium on Integrated Systems.* Cambridge, MA: MIT Press, 320–337.

Shah, G., J. Nieplocha, J. Mirza, C. Kim, R. Harrison, R. K. Govindaraju, K. Gildea, P. DiNicola, and C. Bender. 1998. Performance and Experience with LAPI—A New High-Performance Communication Library for the IBM RS/6000 SP. *Twelfth Int'l Parallel Processing Symposium* (March):260–266

Shasha, D., and M. Snir. 1988. Efficient and Correct Execution of Parallel Programs that Share Memory. *ACM Transactions on Programming Languages and Operating Systems* 10(2):282–312.

Shimada, T., K. Hiraki, and K. Nishida. 1984. An Architecture of a Data Flow Machine and Its Evaluation. *Proc. COMPCON* '84, 486–90.

Simoni, R., and M. Horowitz. 1991. Dynamic Pointer Allocation for Scalable Cache Coherence Directories. *Proc. Int'l Symposium on Shared Memory Multiprocessing* (April): 72–81.

Sindhu, P., J.-M. Frailong, and M. Cekleov. 1991. *Formal Specification of Memory Models.* Tech. Report (PARC) CSL-91-11. Xerox Corp., Palo Alto Research Center, Palo Alto, CA.

Sindhu, P., et al. 1993. XDBus: A High-Performance, Consistent, Packet Switched VLSI Bus. *Proc. COMPCON* (Spring): 338–344.

Singh, J. P. 1993. *Parallel Hierarchical N-body Methods and Their Implications for Multiprocessors.* Ph.D. diss., Tech. Report #CSL-TR-93-565, Stanford University (March).

———. 1998. *Some Aspects of Controlling Scheduling in Hardware Control Prefetching.* To be published as Tech. Report, Princeton University, Computer Science Dept.

Singh, J. P., A. Gupta, and M. Levoy. 1994. Parallel Visualization Algorithms: Performance and Architectural Implications. *IEEE Computer* 27(6).

Singh, J. P., J. L. Hennessy, and A. Gupta. 1993. Scaling Parallel Programs for Multiprocessors: Methodology and Examples. *IEEE Computer* 26(7):42–50.

———. 1995. Implications of Parallel Hierarchical N-body Applications for Multiprocessors. *ACM Transactions on Computer Systems* (May).

Singh, J. P., C. Holt, T. Totsuka, A. Gupta, and J. L. Hennessy. 1995. Load Balancing and Data Locality in Hierarchial N-body Methods: Barnes-Hut, Fast Multipole and Radiosity. *Journal of Parallel and Distributed Computing* (June).

Singh, J. P., T. Joe, A. Gupta, and J. L. Hennessy. 1993. An Empirical Comparison of the KSR-1 and DASH Multiprocessors. Proc. *Supercomputing '93* (November).

Singh, J. P., E. Rothberg, and A. Gupta. 1994. Modeling Communication in Parallel Algorithms: A Fruitful Interaction between Theory and Systems? *Proc. 10th Annual ACM Symposium on Parallel Algorithms and Architectures.*

Singh, J. P., W.-D. Weber, and A. Gupta. 1992. SPLASH: The Stanford ParalleL Applications for SHared Memory. *Computer Architecture News* 20(1):5–44.

Sites, R. L., ed. 1992. *Alpha Architecture Reference Manual.* Hudson, MA: Digital Press, Digital Equipment Corp.

Slater, M. 1994. Intel Unveils Multiprocessor System Specification. *Microprocessor Report* (May):12–14.

Slotnick, D. L. 1967. Unconventional Systems. *Proc. AFIPS Spring Joint Computer Conference* 30: 477–481.

Slotnick, D. L., W. C. Borck, and R. C. McReynolds. 1962. The Solomon Computer. *Proc. AFIPS Fall Joint Computer Conference* 22: 97–107.

Smith, A. J. 1982. Cache Memories. *ACM Computing Surveys* 14(3):473–530.

Smith, B. J. 1981. Architecture and Applications of the HEP Multiprocessor Computer System. *Proc. SPIE: Real-Time Signal Processing IV* 298(August):241–248.

———. 1985. The Architecture of HEP. In *Parallel MIMD Computation: The HEP Supercomputer and Its Applications.* Edited by J.S. Kowalik. Cambridge, MA: MIT Press, 41–55.

Smith, M. D., M. Johnson, and M. A. Horowitz. 1989. Limits on Multiple Instruction Issue. *Proc. Third Int'l Conference on Architectural Support for Programming Languages and Operating Systems,* 290–302, Apr.

Snir, M., S. Otto, S. H. Lederman, D. Walker, and J. Dongarra. 1995. *MPI: The Complete Reference.* Cambridge, MA: MIT Press.

Sohi, G., S. Breach, and T. N. Vijaykumar. 1995. Multiscalar Processors. *Proc. 22nd Annual Int'l Symposium on Computer Architecture* (June):414–425.

SPEC (Standard Performance Evaluation Corporation). 1995 (date accessed). *http://www.specbench.org/.* (SPEC Benchmark Suite Release 1.0., 1989)

Spertus, E., S. C. Goldstein, K. E. Schauser, T. von Eicken, D. E. Culler, W. J. Dally. 1993. Evaluation of Mechanisms for Fine-Grained Parallel Programs in the J-Machine and the CM-5. *Proc. 20th Annual Symposium on Computer Architecture* (May):302–313

Stenstrom, P., T. Joe, and A. Gupta. 1992. Comparative Performance Evaluation of Cache-Coherent NUMA and COMA Architectures. *Proc. 19th Int'l Symposium on Computer Architecture* (May):80–91.

Stets, R., S. Dwarkadas, N. Hardavellas, G. Hunt, L. Kontothanassis, S. Parthasarathy, and M. Scott. 1997. Cashmere-2L: Software Coherent Shared Memory on a Clustered Remote-Write Network. *Proc. 16th ACM Symposium on Operating Systems Principles* (October).

Stone, H. S. 1970. A Logic-in-Memory Computer. *IEEE Transactions on Computers* C-19(1):73–78.

Stunkel, C. B., D. G. Shea, D. G. Grice, P. H. Hochschild, and M. Tsao. 1994. The SP-1 High Performance Switch. *Proc. Scalable High Performance Computing Conference* (May):150–157 Knoxville, TN.

Stunkel, C. B., et al. 1998 (date accessed). *The SP2 Communication Subsystem. http://ibm.tc.cornell.edu/ibm/pps/doc/css/css.ps.*

SUN Microsystems. 1991. *The SPARC Architecture Manual.* #800-199-12, Version 8 (January). Mountain View, CA: SUN Microsystems.

Sunderam, V. S. 1990. PVM: A Framework for Parallel Distributed Computing. *Concurrency: Practice and Experience* 2(4):315–339.

Sunderam, V. S., J. Dongarra, A. Geist, and R Manchek. 1994. The PVM Concurrent Computing System: Evolution, Experiences, and Trends. *Parallel Computing* 20(4):531–547.

Swan, R. J., A. Bechtolsheim, K.-W. Lai, and J. K. Ousterhout. 1977. The Implementation of the CM* Multi-Microprocessor. *Proc. AFIPS Conference/National Computer Conference* (46):645–655.

Swan, R. J., S. H. Fuller, and D. P. Siewiorek. 1977. CM*—A Modular, Multi-Microprocessor. *Proc. AFIPS Conference/National Computer Conference* (46):637–44.

Sweazey, P., and A. J. Smith. 1986. A Class of Compatible Cache Consistency Protocols and Their Support by the IEEE Futurebus. *Proc. 13th Int'l Symposium on Computer Architecture* (May):414–423.

Tamir, Y., and G. L. Frazier. 1988. High-Performance Multi-Queue Buffers for VLSI Communication Switches. *Proc. 15th Annual Int'l Symposium on Computer Architecture,* 343–354.

Tanenbaum, A. S., and A. S. Woodhull. 1997. *Operating System Design and Implementation 2nd ed.* Englewood Cliffs, NJ: Prentice Hall.

Tang, C. 1976. Cache Design in a Tightly Coupled Multiprocessor System. *Proc. AFIPS Conference* (June):749–753.

Teller, P. 1990. Translation-Lookaside Buffer Consistency. *IEEE Computer* 23(6):26–36.

Thacker, C., L. Stewart, and E. Satterthwaite, Jr. 1988. Firefly: A Multiprocessor Workstation. *IEEE Transactions on Computers* 37(8):909–20.

Thapar, M., and B. Delagi. 1990. Stanford Distributed-Directory Protocol. *IEEE Computer* 23(6):78–80.

Thekkath, R., A. P. Singh, J. P. Singh, J. Hennessy, and S. John. 1997. An Application-Driven Evaluation of the Convex Exemplar SP-1200. *Proc. Int'l Parallel Processing Symposium* (June).

Thompson, M., J. Barton, T. Jermoluk, and J. Wagner. 1988. Translation Lookaside Buffer Synchronization in a Multiprocessor System. *Proc. USENIX Technical Conference* (February).

Thornton, J. E. 1964. Parallel Operation in the Control Data 6600. *AFIPS Proc. Fall Joint Computer Conference,* Part 2 26:33–40. Reprinted in Siework, Bell, and Newell. 1982. *Computer Structures: Principles and Examples.* New York: McGraw-Hill.

Tomasulo, R. M. 1967. An Efficient Algorithm for Exploiting Multiple Arithmetic Units. *IBM Journal of Research and Development* 11(1):25–33.

Torrellas, J., M. S. Lam, and J. L. Hennessy. 1994. False Sharing and Spatial Locality in Multiprocessor Caches. *IEEE Transactions on Computers* 43(6):651–663.

Transaction Processing Council. 1998. *http://www.tpc.org*

Traw, C., and J. Smith. 1991. A High-Performance Host Interface for ATM Networks. *Proc. ACM SIGCOMM Conference* (September):317–325.

Traylor, R., and D. Dunning. 1992. Routing Chip Set for Intel Paragon Parallel Supercomputer. *Proc. Hot Chips '92 Symposium* (August).

Tucker, L. W., and A. Mainwaring. 1994. CMMD: Active Messages on the CM-5. *Parallel Computing* 20(4):481–496.

Tucker, L. W., and G. G. Robertson. 1988. Architecture and Applications of the Connection Machine. *IEEE Computer* 21(8):26–38

Tucker, S. 1986. The IBM 3090 System: An Overview. *IBM Systems Journal* 25(1):4–19.

Tullsen, D. M., and S. J. Eggers. 1993. Limitations of Cache Prefetching on a Bus-Based Multiprocessor. *Proc. 20th Annual Symposium on Computer Architecture* (May):278–288.

Tullsen, D. M., S. J. Eggers, J. S. Emer, H. M. Levy, J. L. Lo, and R. L. Stamm. 1996. Exploiting Choice: Instruction Fetch and Issue on an Implementable Simultaneous Multithreading Processor. *Proc. 23rd Int'l Symposium on Computer Architecture* (May):191–202.

Tullsen, D. M., S. J. Eggers, and H. M. Levy. 1995. Simultaneous Multithreading: Maximizing On-Chip Parallelism. *Proc. 20th Annual Symposium on Computer Architecture* (June):278–288.

Turner, J. S. 1988. Design of a Broadcast Packet Switching Network. *IEEE Transactions on Communication* 36(6):734–743.

Valiant, L. G. 1990. A Bridging Model for Parallel Computation. *Communications of the ACM* 33(8): 103–111.

Valois, J. 1995. Lock-Free Linked Lists Using Compare-and-Swap. *Proc. 14th Annual ACM Symposium on Principles of Distributed Computing,* Ottawa, Canada (August):214–222.

Vick, C. R., and J. A. Cornell. 1978. PEPE Architecture—Present and Future. *Proc. AFIPS Conference* 47:981–1002.

von Eicken, T., A. Basu, and V. Buch. 1995. Low-Latency Communication Over ATM Using Active Messages. *IEEE Micro* 15(1):46–53.

von Eicken, T., D. E. Culler, S. C. Goldstein, and K. E. Schauser. 1992. Active Messages: A Mechanism for Integrated Communication and Computation. *Proc. 19th Annual Int'l Symposium on Computer Architecture,* Gold Coast, Australia (May):256–266

Vranesic, Z., M. Stumm, D. Lewis, and R. White. 1991. Hector: A Hierarchically Structured Shared Memory Multiprocessor. *IEEE Computer* 24(1):72–78.

Wall, D. W. 1991. Limits of Instruction-Level Parallelism. *ASPLOS IV* (April):176–188.

Wallach, D. A. 1992. *PHD: A Hierarchical Cache Coherence Protocol.* S.M. thesis, Massachusetts Institute of Technology. Also available as Tech. Report #1389, Artificial Intelligence Laboratory, Massachusetts Institute of Technology, Boston, MA (August).

Wang, W.-H., J.-L. Baer and H. M. Levy. 1989. Organization and Performance of a Two-Level Virtual-Real Cache Hierarchy. *Proc. 16th Annual Int'l Symposium on Computer Architecture* (June):140–148.

Warren, M. S., and J. K. Salmon. 1993. A Parallel Hashed Oct-Tree N-body Algorithm. *Proc. Supercomputing '93.* Washington, DC: IEEE Computer Society, 12–21.

Weaver, D., and T. Germond, eds. 1994. *The SPARC Architecture Manual.* SPARC International, Version 9. Englewood Cliffs, NJ: Prentice Hall.

Weber, W.-D. 1993. *Scalable Directories for Cache-Coherent Shared-Memory Multiprocessors.* Ph.D. diss., Computer Systems Laboratory, Stanford University (January). Also available as Tech. Report #CSL-TR-93-557, Stanford University.

Weber, W.-D., S. Gold, P. Helland, T. Shimizu, T. Wicki, and W. Wilcke. 1997. The Mercury Interconnect Architecture: A Cost-Effective Infrastructure for High-Performance Servers. *Proc. 24th Int'l Symposium on Computer Architecture* (June):98–107.

Weiss, S. and J. Smith. 1994. *Power and PowerPC.* San Francisco: Morgan Kaufmann.

Widdoes, L., Jr., and S. Correll. 1980. The S-1 Project: Developing High Performance Computers. *Proc. COMPCON* (Spring):282–291.

Wilson, A., Jr. 1987. Hierarchical Cache / Bus Architecture for Shared Memory Multiprocessors. *Proc. 14th Int'l Symposium on Computer Architecture* (June):244–252.

Wolf, M. E., and M. S. Lam. 1991. A Data Locality Optimizing Algorithm. *Proc. ACM SIGPLAN'91 Conference on Programming Language Design and Implementation* (June):30–44.

Wolfe, M. 1989. *Optimizing Supercompilers for Supercomputers.* Cambridge, MA. MIT Press.

Woo, S. C., J. P. Singh, and J. L. Hennessy. 1994. The Performance Advantages of Integrating Block Data Transfer in Cache-Coherent Multiprocessors. *Proc. 6th Int'l Conference on Architectural Support for Programming Languages and Operating Systems* (October):219–229, San Jose, CA,

Woo, S. C., M. Ohara, E. J. Torrie, J. P. Singh, and A. Gupta. 1995. The SPLASH-2 Programs: Characterization and Methodological Considerations. *Proc. 22nd Annual Int'l Symposium on Computer Architecture* (June):24–36

Wood, D. A., S. Chandra, B. Falsafi, M. D. Hill, J. R. Larus, A. R. Lebeck, J. C. Lewis, S. S. Mukherjee, S. Palacharla, and S. K. Reinhardt. 1993. Mechanisms for Cooperative Shared Memory. *Proc. 20th Annual Symposium on Computer Architecture* (May):156–167.

Wood, D. A., S. J. Eggers, G. Gibson, M. D. Hill, J. M. Pendleton, S. A. Ritchie, G. S. Taylor, R. H. Katz, and D. A. Patterson. 1986. An In-Cache Address Translation Mechanism. *Proc. 13th Annual Symposium on Computer Architecture* (June):358–365.

Wood, D. A., and M. D. Hill. 1995. Cost-Effective Parallel Computing. *IEEE Computer* 28(2):69–72.

Woodbury, P., A. Wilson, B. Shein, I. Gertner, P.Y. Chen, J. Bartlett, and Z. Aral. 1989. Shared Memory Multiprocessors: The Right Approach to Parallel Processing. *Proc. COMPCON* (Spring):72–80.

Wulf, W., R. Levin, and C. Person. 1975. Overview of the Hydra Operating System Development. *Proc. 5th Symposium on Operating Systems Principles* (November):122–131.

Yamashita, N., T. Kimura, Y. Fujita, Y. Aimoto, T. Manaba, S. Okazaki, K. Nakamura, and M. Yamashina. 1994. A 3.84GIPS Integrated Memory Array Processor LSI with 64 Processing Elements and 2Mb SRAM. *Int'l Solid-State Circuits Conference,* San Francisco (February):260–261.

Zekauskas, M. J., W. A. Sawdon, and B. N. Bershad. 1994. Software Write Detection for a Distributed Shared Memory. *Proc. Operating Systems Design and Implementation Symposium* (November):87–100

Zhang, Z., and J. Torrellas. 1995. Speeding Up Irregular Applications in Shared-Memory Multiprocessors: Memory Binding and Group Prefetching. *Proc. 22nd Annual Symposium on Computer Architecture* (May):188–199.

Zhou, Y., L. Iftode, and K. Li. 1996. Performance Evaluation of Two Home-Based Lazy Release Consistency Protocols for Shared Virtual Memory Systems. *Proc. Operating Systems Design and Implementation Symposium* (October).

Index

E

M

N

O

S

T

X–Z

Amsterdam A.D. 166
de Passeerder
de Rose
Rokin
Beurs.
Dam
Stadhuis
Westerkerk
Nieuwe Kerk
Damrak
Oude Kerk
Het Y.

R.v.R.

The Life & Times of
Rembrandt van Rijn

REMBRANDT

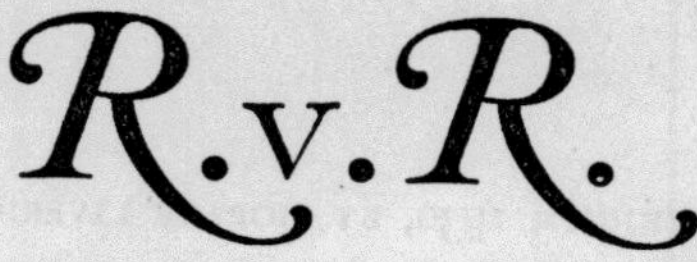

R.v.R.

BEING AN ACCOUNT OF THE LAST YEARS AND THE DEATH
OF ONE

Rembrandt Harmenszoon van Rijn

A PAINTER AND ETCHER OF SOME RENOWN
WHO LIVED AND WORKED (WHICH IN HIS CASE WAS THE SAME)
IN THE TOWN OF *Amsterdam*
(WHICH IS IN *Holland*)
AND DIED OF GENERAL NEGLECT AND DIVERSE OTHER UNFORTUNATE
CIRCUMSTANCES
ON THE FOURTH OF OCTOBER OF THE YEAR OF GRACE 1669
(GOD HAVE MERCY UPON HIS SOUL)
AND WHO WAS ATTENDED IN HIS AFFLICTIONS
BY ONE

Joannis van Loon

DOCTOR MEDICINAE AND CHIRURGEON IN EXTRAORDINARY
TO A VAST NUMBER OF HUMBLE CITIZENS
WHOSE ENDURING GRATITUDE HAS ERECTED HIM
A MONUMENT
LESS PERISHABLE THAN GRANITE AND MORE ENDURING THAN PORPHYRY
AND WHO
DURING A MOST BUSY LIFE
YET FOUND TIME TO WRITE DOWN THESE PERSONAL RECOLLECTIONS
OF THE GREATEST OF HIS FELLOW-CITIZENS
AND WHICH ARE NOW
FOR THE FIRST TIME PRESENTED
(PROVIDED WITH AS FEW NOTES, EMENDATIONS
AND CRITICAL OBSERVATIONS AS POSSIBLE)
BY HIS GREAT-GREAT-GRANDSON, NINE TIMES REMOVED

Hendrik Willem van Loon

IN THE YEAR OF GRACE 1930
AND IN THE TOWN OF *Veere*
WHICH IS IN *Zeeland*
AND PRINTED BY

The Literary Guild

NEW YORK
1930

PRINTED IN U. S. A.

BY THE QUINN & BODEN CO., INC., RAHWAY, N. J.

To

Dr. Alice R. Bernheim

List of Chapters

List of Illustrations

Foreword

EXPLAINING HOW I CAME TO WRITE THIS BOOK

Amsterdam, October 9th, 1669
In the house called De Houttuyn

We buried him yesterday and I shall never forget that terrible morning. The rain, which had been pouring down ever since the beginning of the month, had ceased. A cold and gloomy fog had thrown a dark and chilling pall over the whole city. The empty streets seemed filled with a vague sense of futile uselessness. The small group of mourners stood silently by the side of the church-door, waiting for the coffin to arrive.

Last Friday, a few hours before he died and during a moment of semi-consciousness, he had whispered to me that he wanted to rest next to Saskia. He must have forgotten that he had sold her grave long ago, when Hendrickje passed away and when he was caught without a penny and had been forced to sell the family lot in the Old Church to buy a grave for his second wife. I promised him that I would do my best, but of course the thing was out of the question. I am glad I told him this lie, for he went to his last sleep fully convinced that soon all would be well and that his dust would mingle with that of the woman he had loved in the days of his youth.

And then three days ago Magdalena van Loo called. I had never cared for her. I had found her mean and jealous and apt to whine, but I had tried to like her on account of her father-in-law and of the poor boy she had married.

She told me a long rambling story about some gold pieces which apparently had belonged to Cornelia and to her. Over and over again she repeated the same sentences: "I am sure father took some of that money before he died. And now what shall we do? We can't even buy milk for the baby. I am sure father took it," and so on and so forth.

Then followed a long and circumstantial account of her being sick and being unable to nurse the baby herself. I tried to reassure her. The money undoubtedly would be found. Had she looked for it carefully? No, she had not, but she felt convinced that the old man had appropriated some of it. For weeks and weeks he had sold nothing. He had just sat and stared or he had scratched meaningless lines on the back of some old copper plates. He had been without a cent when Titus died, for uncle Uylenburgh had paid for the funeral. That she knew for a fact. All the same, the old man had been able to buy himself food and drink, especially drink. He must have stolen some of Cornelia's gold, and "half of it was to come to me!" It was impossible to get her mind off the subject and so I asked her whether the sexton had been around to see her about the funeral.

Then she broke into tears once more. She felt so ashamed that she could not possibly hope to survive this last humiliation. The sexton had not come himself. He had merely sent one of the grave-diggers. The man had been drunk and quite rude. He has asked her how much she could pay and she had answered that she wanted things done very simply and could not afford more than five guilders. He had laughed out loud. People from the poor-house were given a better burial than that, but then, of course, what could one expect of those fine gentlemen who never did a stroke of work, who merely sat before an easel all day long and gave themselves airs! Finally he had got her into such a state of vapors that she had cried out for the shoe-maker who lived on the ground floor to come and help her. He had taken the unruly ruffian by the scruff of the neck and had thrown him out into the street and that, at least, had made her happy.

I then asked her whether that was where matters stood and she answered yes and at once went off on another tirade, telling me that no woman had ever been treated as she had been treated ever since she had married into that irresponsible family of painter people, and much more to the same effect, until in sheer despair I had ordered a hackney-coach and had driven her to the Roozengracht to see the sexton of the West Church (a man I cordially detested, but what will you? The corpse could not remain above ground for ever) and had asked him what he meant by such conduct. At once the miserable creature became most obsequious. He apologized for the behavior of his grave-digger, and then annoyed me with his confidences. "If only you knew, Doctor," he said, "how hard it is to get good workmen these days! The job does no longer pay so very well and what is found in the old graves nowadays is not worth the digging. Ever since it has become the custom to bury people merely in their shrouds, the money has gone out of the grave-digging business."

I bade him hold his tongue and after some preliminaries we settled on a "full funeral"—that is to say, sixteen men to carry the coffin and the usual length of broadcloth to cover the remains. I paid him fifteen guilders and gave him some extra stivers for beer-money for the men, and he promised in advance that everything would be done in a first-class manner, very quietly and with great dignity.

But when I got to the church yesterday morning, the men were there, but they gave every evidence of having visited the alehouse before they went to work and I felt so strongly upon the subject that I mentioned it to Abraham Francen, one of the master's old friends, who was leaning against a tree in the yard.

"This is an outrage," I said.

But one drunken scoundrel heard me and scowled at me and gave me an evil look and—

"And why not?" he leered. "Our friend here didn't mind a drop himself at the right time, did he?"

When I called the sexton to task, he merely repeated what he had told me the day before—that it was terribly difficult to get respectable men for his sort of work. For now that the war with England had come to an end, everybody had plenty of money and nobody wanted to be a gravedigger any more.

Finally we came to the spot that had been chosen and without any further ceremony the coffin was lowered into the grave. I had meant to say a few words to bid my old friend a last farewell, but I was not given the chance, for as soon as the ropes had been pulled out from underneath the coffin the sexton said quite loudly: "Come now, my men, don't stand there doing nothing and just looking sheepish. Get busy! We have four other customers this morning." Whereupon we all turned around (there were, as I said, only a handful of us) and I walked to the part of the church reserved for divine service and I knelt down (something I had not done a single time these last five and thirty years) and I prayed whatever God might hear my supplication that he might deal mercifully with the soul of this poor, suffering mortal, who had given so much to this world and had received so little in return.

Then I slowly walked home, but while crossing the Dam, I ran across old Vondel, the poet. He had changed so greatly since I last saw him that I hardly recognized him. He seemed sick and he was shivering beneath his shabby, threadbare coat. It hurt me to see such a person in such a condition. The town these last few months has been full of a strange new affliction of the lungs, and those who were weakest were of course the first to be attacked. I asked him whether he had breakfasted and he said "No," but then he rarely took anything before noon. I suggested that we have a cup of coffee in one of those new taverns that make a specialty of this beverage, and he accepted my offer with pathetic eagerness. He even mentioned that there was a new coffee shop a few doors away where the coffee was very good and the prices were not exorbitant. I must have looked surprised, for he added, "You see, these places are often patronized by sailors and there is always a chance that one of them may bring me news of my son."

The human heart is a strange thing. Small loss when young Vondel was packed off to the Indies, these many years ago. The boy was an utter misfit. He drank. He gambled. He ran after women, and what sort of women! He was directly responsible for his father's financial failure. And here the old man was wasting his few hard-earned pennies, drinking coffee in mean taverns because some day one of the sailors might perhaps bring him some news of "his darling child."

We sat down and I pretended to be hungry and ordered some bread and cheese. "You might keep me company," I suggested to Vondel, and he consented. But a moment later he jumped to his feet. "Pardon me," he said, "but there is Captain Jan Floriszoon of the *Dolphin.* He got in yesterday from Malacca. He may have news for me from my boy."

"Bring him over here," I called out, and a moment later the captain appeared. He was a sailor of the old school, hard as nails and thrifty as the Bank, but not unkind. Yes, he would take something. He would take something with much pleasure. It was a cold and wet day. A gin and bitters would not be amiss. He had had a most prosperous voyage, only a year and a half for the round trip and less than forty percent of his crew had died. Ever hear of a certain Jan van den Vondel? No, never! Could not remember that he had ever run across him. But that of course meant nothing. There were so many ships and India was a big country, hundreds and thousands of islands. Some day the boy would undoubtedly show up and come back.

The captain was more considerate than I had expected a man of his caliber to be and I asked the poet how he himself was getting along. Vondel, with an eager face, hastened to inform me that things could not be better. Poor devil! He reminded me of a patient I had visited the day before in the poor-house and who had asked me not to let him die because he had been allowed to raise a crocus in his little room and he was afraid that the poor little plant would not be able to survive if he were not there to take care of it.

Here I was, sitting face to face with the greatest genius that ever handled our language—a shabby, broken-down clerk—and he was explaining that he really had every reason to feel deeply grateful for the way in which fate had treated him.

"Their Lordships have been most kind to me," he explained. "Of course, the pawn-shop can't afford to pay me very much, but my needs are small and besides, I have a lot of time for myself. With the exception of Saturdays, when we stay open till midnight, I rarely work more than ten hours a day and quite often they allow me to come a little later in the morning, that I may make the rounds of the harbor and ask for news of my son. Within another year I hope to get my pension. I want to finish my last play, 'Noah,' and I must get at it before I am too old to handle a pen."

And so on and so forth. Until the honest captain interrupted him and turned to me and remarked with a polite bow that he was pleased to have made my acquaintance, for he had often heard of me from his sister, Anneke Floriszoon, the wife of Antony Blauw, whom I remembered as one of my patients a number of years ago, and then he ordered another gin at my expense and drank to my health and said that he was glad to see that the Amsterdam chirurgeons took their work seriously and were going about at such an early hour of the morning. But I told him that I rarely visited this part of Amsterdam at that hour, but that I had happened to cross the Dam on my way home from the funeral of a friend.

"And who might that be?" the old poet asked, "for I am not aware that any one of importance has died."

"No," I answered, "I suppose not. He died quite suddenly. Yet you knew the man. It was Rembrandt van Rijn."

He looked at me with slight embarrassment.

"Of course I knew him," he said. "A very great artist. Of course, I could not always follow him and he thought very differently from me upon many subjects. For one thing, I don't believe that he was ever truly a Christian. But a great painter, nevertheless. Only tell me, Doctor, are you sure it was not an impostor? For Rembrandt, if I recollect rightly, died five years ago, yes, more than five years ago. He died in Hull in England. He had gone there to escape from his creditors. That is, if I remember correctly."

"Hull?" interrupted the captain. "Hull nothing! I know all about that fellow. He did a piece once of Joris de Caullery with whom I served as second mate in the battle of Dover in '52 when we licked Blake. Yes, I know all about him. It was he who had that quarrel with the dominies about his servant girl. But he went to Sweden some six or seven years ago. I have a friend who sails to Danzig, and he took him to Gothenburg in '61 or '62. He told me so himself and so I know it to be true."

"Nevertheless, my good friends," I answered, "Rembrandt died last Friday and we buried him this morning."

"Strange, very strange!" Vondel murmured. "Died right here in this town, and I did not even know he was still alive!"

"Well," said the good-natured captain, willing to make all the world feel as merry as he did himself and signaling to the waiter to bring him a third gin and bitters, "well, that is too bad. But we all have to die sooner or later and I am sure there are plenty of painters left. So here is to you, gentlemen! Happy years and many of them!"

. . . .

Hofwyck, Voorburg, October 23, 1669.

Two weeks have gone by and a great many things have happened.

The evening of the funeral I dropped in at the house on the Roozengracht to prescribe a sedative for poor Magdalena who was still worrying about that little bag of gold that had belonged to Cornelia and her and that had disappeared. A few days later, Cornelia was to find it behind a pile of clean sheets, but just then Rembrandt was still suspected of having stolen his daughter's money and so Magdalena wept and whined until at last she dropped off to sleep and I went back to the hospital and composed a letter to My Lord Constantin Huygens, who had had some dealings with the dead painter in the days of the late Prince Henry and who had been ever full of admiration for his genius, and late that same night I carried it to the skipper of the boat to The Hague, who promised me as a personal favor that he would deliver it to His Lordship the next morning together with some official-looking documents which had been entrusted to him by the Burgomasters and had to do with a vacancy in the Board of Aldermen.

Three days later I received an answer from the famous old diplomat, who by this time must have been well past seventy.

> "I have to thank you, my dear Doctor," so he wrote in his precise Latin (for he never got over the feeling that a letter in the vernacular was a breach of good form, almost as inexcusable as paying an official call without a ruff or finishing a dinner without wiping off one's mouth), "I have to thank you for your favor of October the ninth and I was deeply shocked to hear your most unfortunate news. I knew him well, this extraordinary miller's son, upon whom the gods had bestowed such exceeding gifts. What a sad—a most sad ending! But such seems to be the fate of those among us who dare to storm the tops of high Olympus. In any other country he would have been deemed worthy of a national funeral; kings would have felt honored to march behind his bier. But did not the Athenians banish Pheidias? And what reward but a sentence of death did Florence ever bestow upon the greatest of her many gifted sons?
>
> "I am an old man now, my learned friend, and I live far away from the vapid noise of the turbulent world. I have had another (and serious) attack of the gout and writing does not come easily to me these days. You must be in need of a change of scene after these most distressing events. Why not visit me here in my quiet retreat for a few days? I have little to offer you but a most cordial welcome and some of that noble vintage from the ancient city of Avignon, which almost persuades an old heretic like myself that there must have been some good in the institution of a Supreme Pontiff. For truly, the men who grew that wine must have been past-masters in the art of living.
>
> "Farewell for the nonce and send me your reply by messenger. Tell me the hour of your arrival and a carriage will await you at Veur and it is only a short ride to the humble roof of your most faithful and obedient servant,
>
> "C. H."

I had no reason to refuse. Young Willem was away at his studies in Leyden. The excellent Jantje could look after the household and my cousin Fijbo (one of the Frisian van Loons, come to settle in Amsterdam three years ago) could take care of my practice. I answered that I would accept with pleasure and three days later I took the boat for the south.

An uneventful trip, except for an acrimonious debate between a short, fat man who looked like a clergyman (and proved to be a shoe-maker) and a tall, lean fellow who looked like a shoe-maker (and proved to be a clergyman) who for some obscure reason revived the ancient quarrel about "homoousian" and "homoiousian" and got so excited about the "unbegotten begotten son" as opposed to the "ever begotten son" that they would surely have come to blows if the skipper had not threatened to throw them both overboard unless they moderate their language.

Except for this unfortunate incident, unavoidable in a country like ours where everybody is certain that he alone possesses a key to the right kind of Truth, the voyage was pleasant and dull (as a pleasant voyage should be) and at Veur I found Pieter, the old coachman, waiting for me and an hour later I was sitting in front of a bright open fire in that corner room that I knew so well and that looked across the fields all the way to the leaning tower of Delft.

I can't say that I ever enjoyed a holiday quite so much. For a holiday it has been so far, in the best and truest sense of the word. A holiday enlivened by good talk, good fare and the constant consideration of a courteous host. Indeed, if this strange new land of ours had done naught but produce this one man, I would not consider the experiment to have been a failure. He has been everywhere. He has known every one. Yet he has remained as simple as the gardener who delighted him yesterday with a few fresh radishes. He writes Latin like his native tongue, but handles our obstinate language as if it were the pliable vernacular of Ariosto. He is well versed in music and has fair skill in the art of drawing and painting. His mathematical ability has come to glorious fruition in his son Christiaan, who is now in Paris making further experiments with his pendulum clock. He seems to have suffered some financial reverses during the recent war with England, but the simplicity of the household is so perfect in all its details that life at the court of the Grand Monarch himself could be no more agreeable than existence here at Hofwyck.

I spend the morning in my own room which overlooks the old marshes of Schieland, now turned into fertile pastures. There is an excellent library on the ground floor and I am urged to take as many books to my own quarters as suits my fancy.

Old Pieter, who has been with his master for almost forty years, brings me my breakfast and informs me about the state of the weather which has been fairly good since I arrived last Thursday.

At one o'clock I take a short walk in the garden which has been laid out according to the French taste (and which the French for some unaccountable reason call a "Dutch garden"). At two o'clock we take a short drive and the afternoon and evening we spend together. And of course the conversation almost invariably turns to the loss of our friend of the Roozengracht.

I am a physician and familiar with death. I am not much of a churchman and cannot for the life of me understand the gruesome delight with which Christians, ever since the days of the Catacombs, have been pleased to enlarge upon the horrors of the charnel-house. The people of ancient times were much more rational in their attitude toward that sublime sleep that is bestowed upon us as a pleasant sample of eternity. They knew that the world only exists through contrasts. That there is no light, unless there be darkness, no joy unless there be sorrow, no life unless there be death. I accept their wisdom and it is not so much the fact that Rembrandt has ceased to exist that worries me (God knows, life held little of pleasure for him) as the realization of the utter futility of all effort.

I sometimes am afraid of the conclusions to which this sort of reasoning may lead us and yesterday My Lord Huygens read me a serious lecture upon the dangers of this sort of speculation.

"Have a care," he said, "or I shall have to send your doubts to my neighbor, the learned Jew, and he will wash them in a mixture of Cartesian and Baconian philosophies and then he will bleach them in the light of his own merciless logic and when they are returned to you, they will have shrunk to the three letters Q.E.D. neatly embroidered on the remnants of something that only a short while before was still a fairly useful garment that might have kept people from freezing in the realm of doubt."

"No," I answered, "that would not solve the difficulty. I have little love for that strange celestial potentate whom our Calvinists call their righteous Jehovah, but neither do I want the Almighty to be reduced to a mathematical formula. And my worries are not of the theological variety.

"I knew Spinoza in the old days, before his own people so kindly tried to murder him. A charming man. A learned man. An honest man. But I am a little wary of those philosophers who try to weave their spiritual garments out of their own inner consciousness. I am not enough of a mystic and prefer the 'Praise of Folly' to all the metaphysical cogitations in the world. No, what worries me is not the fate of poor old Rembrandt. He is either entirely out of it or he is trying so hard to solve the problem of reducing the Light Everlasting to a few smears of chrome-yellow and flake-white that he will forget everything else. No, it is something else that is on my mind."

"The living, rather than the dead?"

"Exactly. Here we are. Since we got our freedom, our land has been blessed beyond anything that has ever been seen before. Our dominies, with their usual sense of modesty, take all the credit upon themselves and see in these riches an expression of approval of the Lord Almighty and an endorsement of the policies of the House of Orange. They may be right, but it seems to me that our fortunate geographic location may have as much to do with our favorable rate of exchange as the approbation of an ancient Jewish deity who had tantrums and liked the smell of burning entrails. I hope I am not offending you?"

My Lord Constantin shook his head. "These are hardly the expressions I would have used when I dined with King James (of blessed memory) and dozed my way through the endless sessions of the Great Synod. But here we are alone and old Pieter is deaf and, to tell you the truth, I too prefer one page of Erasmus to all the homilies of the sour-faced doctor from Geneva. So go ahead and tell me your troubles."

"Well, as I was saying, here we are part of a strange new experiment in state-craft. We have turned a swamp into another Rome. We rule black people and yellow people and red people—millions of them in every part of the world. Until a short time ago we kept a larger standing army than any one had ever dreamed possible and we paid for it and it did not ruin us. We probably have a larger navy than any other country and, somehow or other, we seem to have enough funds to keep the ships going without an unusual number of riots.

"We juggle with slices of territory larger than the Holy Roman Empire as if we were children playing with marbles, and one day we take a few hundred thousand square miles of forests in North America and say that they belong to us and half a century later, we trade them off for a couple of hundred thousand square miles of sugar lands in South America and nobody knows and nobody cares and it really makes no difference either one way or another.

"We supply the whole world with grain and with fish and whalebone and linen and hides and our store-houses fairly burst with the bales of nutmeg and pepper that are dumped into them twice or three times a year and in between we fight a couple of wars and the people at home go to church and pray for victory and then go back to business and make a little more money and speculate in Indian shares and in tulips and in Spitzbergen sperm-oil and in Amsterdam real estate and lose fortunes and gain fortunes as if they never had been doing anything else all their lives and as if we had not known their fathers and grandfathers when they were perfectly respectable bakers and butchers and candle-stick makers who had to work devilishly hard for every stiver they made and were contented if once every fifteen years they could afford a new suit of Sunday clothes.

"But that is not so much what fills me with such anxiety for the future. We have all of us got to begin sometime. When the Emperor of Austria tried to raise funds on the Amsterdam exchange to develop his mercury mines, he had a prospectus printed to prove that he was descended in a straight line from Julius Caesar, but in the days of my grandfather, whenever old Charles of Habsburg got full on Louvain beer and French cognac, and was told by my grandpapa that no human stomach on earth could stand such atrocious mixtures, he used to weep and ask him what one could expect of a fellow who was half Spanish peasant and half Flemish bastard and whose earliest ancestor had driven a Swiss ox-cart as a sutler in the army of Charlemagne.

"Perhaps he exaggerated a bit, but when the great French Queen visited Amsterdam and the Burgomasters forced her to listen to endless speeches about 'Your Majesty's illustrious forebears, the enlightened rulers of Tuscany,' or wherever it was, I remember that when it was my turn to be presented and she was told that I was the consultant physician of the Hospital of St. Catherine, and silly old Witsen, who knew my aversion to drugs, said, 'Yes, Your Majesty, and he has prescribed more pills in his day than any other man now alive,' the old Queen smiled rather sourly and said, 'Monseigneur, I know all about pills. I have got three of them in my coat-of-arms.'

"No, it isn't that we are rich that worries me. It is rather pleasant to see every one well fed and decently clothed and it never did any harm to a man's self-respect to have an extra change of linen. But what are we going to do with all our wealth? The envoy of His late Majesty James of England (the tactful one who is said to have given a party the day they killed old John of Barneveldt) in his usual charming way wrote to his royal master and asked what one could expect of a country that was merely 'a counting-house defended by a navy?'

"But that Puritan boor was right. At least in part. As long as our merchants are able to make one hundred percent on their money, by buying something for a guilder and selling it for two, and as long as the common people are fairly obedient to Their Lordships, and go to church three times on Sunday, we ask no questions and we are contented to be rich and smug and not any too finicky in our pastimes, but when it comes to something not of this earth earthy, we let our greatest poet handle a goose-quill in a dirty pawn-shop ten hours a day to keep himself from starving; we drag the greatest painter of our time through every court in the whole bailiwick and a couple of rice-peddlers who have just spent thousands of guilders for an escutcheon with sixteen quarterings swindle him out of his last pennies and even your fine old Prince has to be dunned eight or nine times before he will pay him.

"And what happens to Rembrandt and Vondel has happened to all the others. The King of Spain and the King of Denmark and the Emperor and the King of England and even that wild potentate of Muscovy (wherever that is) keep agents in Amsterdam to supply them with the work of our great men. And we quietly let them die in the poor-house as if they were so many tramps."

I talked along that vein most of the afternoon and My Lord Constantin listened with great patience, but I do not think that he answered me very fully. Perhaps he did, but I am a bit hazy about it.

• • • • • •

I am tired and have a pain at the back of my head. I shall go to bed and finish this to-morrow.

Hofwyck, December 20, 1669.

For a while, it looked as if there were to be no "to-morrow" at all.

I must have caught a cold on the day of Rembrandt's funeral, for I remember that I had one or two chills on board the canal-boat when I traveled to Voorburg, and that my teeth were chattering when I reached Hofwyck. I hear that my kind old host consulted with no less than three doctors from The Hague and when they were unable to break the fever, he had sent to Leyden for a young professor who was experimenting with the cinchona bark and who gave me of his tincture with apparent success, for from that day on I am told that I began to improve.

And whether my affliction was "march poison," as the ague fits and the dry heat seemed to indicate, or an attack of the "English sweat" which had been so common during the last century, or some entirely new disease come to us from America or Asia, upon that point my learned professional brethren do not seem to have been able to make a decision. But the cinchona bark was apparently quite effective (I shall try it on my own patients as soon as I return to practice) or perhaps it was the excellent care which I received at the hands of my good host which kept me from joining the Great Majority.

Most important of all, I do not appear to be suffering from anemia or any of the other after effects which are so common and so disastrous in cases of this sort. But as soon as I was allowed to sit up and as soon as I once more began to take an interest in my surroundings, I noticed (what had so often worried me with my own patients) that I seemed mentally exhausted and could not rid myself of a few simple thoughts which kept repeating themselves in my mind and kept repeating and repeating themselves until I was ready to shriek and had to be restrained from doing myself bodily harm.

After a few days there was a slight improvement, but then it began to look as if something in my mind had congealed at the moment I was taken ill and that it refused, no matter how hard I tried, to let itself be thawed out. The death of Rembrandt, I am willing to confess it, had made more of an impression upon me than almost anything else that had ever happened to me. I had come to Hofwyck full of his sad fate and until I was taken ill, I had thought and talked of practically nothing else.

All during the fever, whenever I wandered in my delirium (so My Lord Constantin told me last week) I had been fighting Rembrandt's battles. No doubt he had deserved a better fate and no doubt most of our people are hopelessly indifferent about the really great men who bring honor to our nation. But I used to be possessed of a certain philosophic calm and I used to accept the iniquities of this world with great and satisfying equanimity of soul.

Whenever as children we got greatly excited about some particularly stupid piece of business on the part of our neighbors, our grandfather used to warn us to remember the safe advice of our famous cousin Erasmus that "Since the world loved to be swindled, we might just as well let it be swindled." He admonished us to keep strictly to honest practices in our own dealings with mankind, but not let ourselves be upset every time we came in contact with some particular phase of human folly.

"For once you begin to take the human race too seriously," he warned us, "you will either lose your sense of humor or turn pious, and in either case, you had much better be dead."

In a general way I had always been able to stick to this wise and tolerant rule of conduct. I had never wasted much time pitying my fellowmen nor had I indulged in too great expressions of merriment when for the millionth time in history I watched how they hoisted themselves with the petard of their own willful ignorance. I had simply accepted them as I found them and had not tried to improve too much upon God's unfortunate handiwork.

But now something had happened. Try however I might, I could not rid myself of the obsession that in one way or another I was responsible for the death of my friend and no matter how hard my host and my doctor friend from Leyden tried (he knew something beyond mere powders and pills, which I can't say for most of my colleagues) I could not purge my poor, tired brain of the vision of that last terrible morning in the West Church, with the grinning pall-bearers and the drinking, cursing grave-diggers who handled that sacred coffin as if it had held the carcase of some indifferent lout, killed in a drunken street-brawl.

And yet, if life, if my life at least, had to go on, I must first of all purge my mind of these all-too-persistent depressions and I knew it and at the same time I could not do it and then the consciousness that I knew it and could not do it added itself to my other tribulations, and thereupon Hell itself held no such terrors as I experienced during those weeks I was trying to regain my physical health and to establish some sort of mental equilibrium.

And I know not what the end would have been, had not My Lord Constantin, trying to divert me and so get me away from my own depressing thoughts, one day called on me in the company of the learned Jew of whom we had been talking a short time before I was taken ill.

I had met Spinoza several times before in the olden days in Amsterdam and I had once visited him in Rijnsburg, but so many things had happened since then, that I had almost forgotten what a charming and simple-minded fellow he was. Of his ideas, as I have said before, I have never understood a great deal and anyway, theological and philosophical speculations have never been very much to my taste. But Spinoza proved a veritable godsend to a man recovering from a long illness and I bade him (with my host's gracious permission) to come again and to come as often as he could.

He was living in very modest quarters in the village of Voorburg, which was only a few minutes away, and quite frequently, after he got through with his day's work, he used to drop in for a short talk. I admired the liberality of mind of my host, for soon the people of The Hague must have heard that Hofwyck was being patronized by the most dangerous heretic then alive and five days after his first visit (which took place on a Tuesday) not fewer than three clergymen in that gossipy village (God forbid that it should ever acquire the dignity of a town) made veiled allusions in their sermons to "the influence which certain people of libertine principles were said to be gaining once more upon those in close connection with the House of Orange."

But as My Lord Constantin merely shrugged his shoulders when he heard of it, I did not let it worry me and continued to enjoy the visits of this keen-eyed young Jew with the soft Portuguese accent, who actually seemed to believe that all the eternal verities could be reduced to mathematical equations.

Now whether my host had mentioned my strange mental affliction to this amiable and kindly prophet (great Heavens! what an improvement that boy was upon the average ranting and maundering rabbi of his quarrelsome tribe!) but in the most tactful way he one day brought the conversation upon the subject of Rembrandt and how shocked he had been to hear of his untimely death and how much he had admired his work—especially his etchings which were more in keeping with his own mathematical turn of mind, and then he asked me to tell him about the last days of the great master and about his funeral and of course, I was only too delighted and he repeated this performance three days in succession, and then quite suddenly one day he said:

"You know, Doctor, you are bound for the lunatic asylum, and they tell me it is not pleasant in there."

To which, with unusual calm and clearness of vision, I answered: "Yes, my friend, I know that, but what can I do about it?"

To which he gave me the totally unexpected answer: "Write it all down and get rid of it that way, before you go insane. That is what I am doing myself."

Amsterdam, April 3, 1670.

The cure has worked.

And I, in my old age, discover that I have most unexpectedly become the father of a book.

I did not mean to write one, for I am a physician and not an author, but what of it? These pages will be carefully packed away among my other belongings. They have no literary value. My son is not interested in such things and they will never be published, no matter what happens.

And Rembrandt, if he knows, will understand.

My task is finished. And now I must go back to the business of living, for I have loafed long enough and there is work to be done, a great deal of work.

Two weeks from next Monday I shall be seventy years old. That is not as old as my good host of Hofwyck, who is well in the seventies, but neither is it an age to take lightly. Ten more good years at the very most. After that—whatever follows.

And so I bid farewell to this labor of love which has well served me during my days of reconvalescence.

From now on, my hand shall only touch the scalpel. May it be as true and honest in all things as the brush that lies on my desk, the only tangible memory of the dearest of my friends and the greatest of my race.

JAN VAN LOON.

R.v.R.

The Life & Times of Rembrandt van Rijn

Chapter 1

HOW I HAPPEN TO REMEMBER THAT IT RAINED ON A CERTAIN DAY IN NOVEMBER OF THE YEAR 1641

It was late in the evening of one of the last days of November of the year '41 and it was raining very hard.

Let me tell how I happen to be so sure about this. I have a very bad memory for dates and for names, but a curiously strong gift of recollection for all sorts of completely irrelevant details which most people find it only too easy to forget.

Now in the spring of '41, my uncle Gerard, from whom I have inherited my present house on the Houtmarkt in Amsterdam, died. It took all summer to settle his estate, but early in October (I have forgotten the exact date) I received word from Veere that everything was ready and would I please come and sign the necessary papers. I was very busy at the time and asked whether these legal affairs could not be attended to by correspondence. But notaries are notaries, all the world over. It was money in their pocket to make the affair drag as long as possible and they informed me that I had to come myself.

And so I bade farewell to my patients and after four fairly uncomfortable days in draughty boats and damp beds (our village inns are as bad now as they were a hundred years ago) I reached the little town where I had spent the only happy days of my entire childhood. I had not been in the place for almost ten years and at once noticed a difference. The harbor seemed less full of ships. There were fewer people in the streets and one rarely heard a word of English, whereas in former days, English and Scotch had been as common as Dutch and every child had been able to swear almost as readily in one language as in the other.

I stayed at the inn and it was very dull. In former days there always had been at least a dozen guests. Now there were only a decrepit-looking Scotchman and a German. The Scotchman had come to wind up his affairs, and the German (a dull citizen from Danzig with a pock-marked face and such extraordinary ideas of cleanliness that at first I thought him to be a Pole) was apparently trying to get hold of a good piece of business for very little money. Neither of these worthies was very pleasant company, and please remember that it rained steadily, day and night, all the time I was in Veere and that I was forced to share the tap-room with these fossils for two solid weeks, before the lawyers and the notaries were ready to submit the last of their dockets, affidavits, quit-claims, transfers and licenses.

Rather than listen to the shorter English catechism (as composed privately by the Scotchman's grandfather and as recited by the grandson with touching regularity after the sixth or seventh hot toddy), or playing chess with the spurious Teuton (who had to be watched like a hawk lest he make queens and knights do certain things which nature and the rules of the game had never intended them to do), I used to withdraw to my room and rather than spend my evenings perusing those bales of official documents (without which no decent citizen of our republic can either hope to enter or leave this world) I would read such trash as had been left behind by former visitors and which the proprietor of the establishment kept behind lock and key and to which he invariably referred as his Temple of Solomon. It was pretty terrible stuff but the endless rain storms had so thoroughly spoiled the road to Middelburg that it was impossible to send to that city for fresh literary supplies and in consequence I was bored beyond words.

Then I made a great discovery which filled my heart with sudden and unexpected visions of a happy fortnight. My good uncle in his younger days had been one of the suitors of a young lady whose fame since then has spread far and wide and who will be remembered as one of the most resourceful women our country has ever produced. But she was after bigger game than a mere ship-builder and she had given herself in marriage to a youthful lawyer of French descent but Dutch parentage, who had started his career as a sort of literary infant prodigy; who ere he was ten years of age had recited his own-made Greek hexameters before half of the crowned heads of Europe; and who at the tender age of twelve had commenced to edit and revise a dozen of the most ponderous and erudite among the minor prophets of Latin literature. A most facile juggler of easy-flowing verse, who one day would compose him a drama on Adam in exile, the next week would turn out a history of the rebellion of the Netherlands and in between these manifold activities, would find time to devote himself in a most thorough-going fashion to the pursuit of the law and the costly pastime of practical politics.

When this incredible young man presented himself as a candidate for the hand and the favor of my uncle's inamorata, when this wandering encyclopedia of classical and legal information began to bombard the simple Veere girl with endless love letters, couched in terms of truly Ciceronian eloquence, her other swains (of whom there were many, for in those days she had not yet fallen a victim to those fits of temper which afterwards were to turn the Grotius household into such a merry hell) had felt that their cause was lost and had tactfully withdrawn. But of course they had been very curious to see what manner of man had so ignominiously defeated them and when the happy pair descended from the boat that had brought them from Holland to spend their honeymoon with Maria's parents, they had all been present at the dock and in a spirit of good feeling had presented the new Mrs. Grotius with an enormous bouquet of roses, an unexpected attention which the delighted young bride had rewarded with kisses for the entire assembled multitude.

A few of the boys had been curious to see what effect this outburst of osculatory generosity might have upon the happy groom, but he apparently had taken no notice of the incident, being too much occupied with the unloading of two vast trunks, filled with books, and upon which he bestowed so much attention that he had neither eyes nor ears for his beautiful wife.

This strange honeymoon had given rise to many rather ribald jokes, for the lovely Reigersberg child was an entirely normal product of that fertile Zeeland clay which raises the most powerful horses, the richest grain and the bluest of all blue grapes, and it was generally conceded that in matters of the heart, the young lady had no need of a printed edition of Ovid's "Amatory Art."

In her despair Maria had turned to my uncle (who was a little older than her other childhood friends) and had favored him with her confidence.

"Hugh is a fine fellow," she had told him, "and I am very fond of him. He is very devoted to me and I like being the wife of so important a man, but I hate to go to bed with Martianus Capella, and Cicero, although no doubt a most talented orator, is a dull companion in the morning when the sun is shining and the wind is blowing and the birds are singing and all those ancient worthies seem a hundred million years dead and buried."

In consequence of this interview my uncle, who was the incarnation of commercial honesty, had committed the only crime of his life. While the Reigersberg family was away on a state visit to their relatives in Middelburg, he had broken into their house and had removed the contents of the two fatal trunks to his own attic where he had carefully hidden them behind a worm-eaten chest that had stood there ever since the days of his great-grandmother.

Of course the affair had leaked out (small cities are proverbially leaky when it comes to the domestic affairs of their inhabitants) and my uncle had acquired a reputation for unselfish loyalty which stuck to him (as a mild and amiable joke) until the end of his days.

Now in my despair I remembered the existence of this long lost treasure. I sent the old housekeeper to investigate the attic. She reported that it contained nothing but two moldy chests of drawers, a trunk filled with discarded clothes, and a pile of books in various stages of neglect and decomposition and all of them fit for the rubbish pile.

I, however, knowing the contempt mixed with fear and suspicion which the illiterate feel toward the printed word, told the old lady to take a bucket of water and a sponge and set to work to remove the ravages of almost fifty years of neglect as best she could. She murmured a few vague words about "No good ever coming of all this book-learning," but I encouraged her by telling her that she might keep whatever books of sermons might be found among my uncle's hidden relics, and two days later, neatly packed into three large clothes-baskets, this extraordinary collection was delivered at my door.

I approached those books with a feeling of shyness and respect. I seemed to be committing a sacrilege. There, on the fly-leaf of each book, stood a name that had carried the fame of our country into every corner of the civilized world. But because the erstwhile owner of these imposing-looking quartos had steadfastly defended the principles of mutual forbearance upon which our commonwealth was based, he had been driven into ignominious exile by those selfsame bigots and Pharisees who had been responsible for the violent death of my dear Lord John of Barneveldt.

It is said that when the great King Gustavus Adolphus was killed at the battle of Lutzen, a copy of Grotius' work on international relations was the only volume found in his tent except his Bible and that His Majesty never went to sleep without reading one or two chapters from the New Testament and from this treatise on the laws that should regulate the behavior of nations, whether at war or in peace.

And yet even while I was sitting there, aimlessly handling these parchment bindings, that marvelous man who had ever been received by emperors and kings as their equal could not return to the land of his birth because an ill-tempered French theologian with a bad liver and the hallucinations of a village Messiah had decreed that tolerance was an invention of the Devil, that there was only one way of salvation to which he and only he and his disciples held the key and which was therefore closed to all those whose charity and kindliness of spirit forbade them from sharing the arrogant conceits of the two-penny dictator of a mean Swiss town.

And these reflections, together with the apparent hopelessness of our age-old struggle against human stupidity and ignorance, filled my heart with such despair that soon I sent the books back to the attic whence they had come, and braving the endless dampness, set forth to find a somewhat more energetic form of diversion of the spirit than the patient perusal of Aratus, Arienus, and the commentaries of the late and unlamented Scaliger.

Of course all this is only indirectly connected with the fact that it rained very hard and very continually during the fall of the year 1641. And if this manuscript should ever fall into the hands of some one else (which God forbid!) he might well remark, "The poor old fellow is wandering all over the place."

But I would answer him: "Dear friend, isn't all of life a matter of jibing and tacking and sailing all over the place? Has any one ever undertaken to navigate the high seas of experience without continually being driven hither and yon by the storms of adversity and the currents of ill-fate?" And I shall peacefully continue my literary peregrinations as the spirit moves me, for that is the way I have lived and that is the way I hope to die. I shall be immobile and stationary for many years to come, but that will happen when my craft is safely anchored near the consoling shores of some convenient cemetery.

And now let me return to that dreary and rain-soaked fortnight in the fall of the year 1641 when I sat shivering in a village inn, signed legal documents all day long and passed through one of the weirdest adventures of a career that has been rather full of extraordinary incidents.

Because I was restless and bored, I used to take long solitary walks. One evening I was struck by a most extraordinary noise that issued forth from two rather poor-looking houses, not far from the ancient church of Our Lady in a part of the town occupied by fishermen, many of whom hailed from the near-by village of Arnemuiden, where the people were experiencing difficulties with their harbor.

After a little study, I vaguely recognized a few of the better known tunes of Petrus Dathenus and I thought: "Oh, well, here are some of the children of Zion come together for a little private worship," and I forgot all about it until one night (it must have been between six and seven o'clock of the evening, for I had just finished my supper, but it was already quite dark) just when I passed the bigger of the two houses, the door opened and four men appeared carrying an enormous wooden box from which there issued such a cackling, gobbling and guggling as I had never heard before in all my livelong days.

And the next evening at precisely the same hour I beheld (this time, however, coming from the other house) a small procession of women and children, heavily loaded with cages and crates which seemed to contain a miniature menagerie of all the better known household pets and which (though in a different manner) produced almost as many cacophonic sounds as the wooden contraption which had attracted my attention the night before.

My curiosity was now thoroughly aroused. It did not seem a matter of very great importance, but I was bored and when one is thoroughly bored in a small town, even the clandestine transportation of a humble hencoop means a most welcome diversion. I made it a point to walk past these two houses every evening after dinner. It used to get dark shortly after four o'clock, and what with the rain and the absolute lack of any sort of street illumination, there was little chance of detection.

I was familiar with the religious tendencies of the simple fisherfolk who inhabit these southern islands and the singing and shouting alone would hardly have attracted my attention. I would have thought that some new Elijah had arisen or that some obscure John the Baptist was busy trying to impress his neighbors with that consciousness of sin which ever since the beginning of history has allowed the prophets of Heaven to lead a comfortable and dignified existence at the expense of their neighbors—and the next moment I would have forgotten all about it.

But the large bundles and boxes did not quite seem to fit into the general order of things and in a casual way I mentioned these to my notary friend during one of our interminable sessions at his office. This office, by the way, was situated in the same house in which the excellent Valerius, his predecessor in office, had made his interesting collection of contemporary war songs. All music, however, had long since departed from the premises and life had become dreadfully serious.

The good man was terribly upset by what I told him. He was so startled that he dropped his pen into the lime-pot instead of the ink-stand and then in trying to salvage the pen (for he was a careful book-keeper), dribbled lime all over the papers which meant that each and every one of them had to be copied again and that business—for that day at least—had come to a standstill. And when I tried to quiet him down, with such simple speeches as: "Why get excited about so small an occurrence?" and: "Just a few pious brethren holding a little private meeting—no use bothering about them," or words to that effect, he flew into a veritable rage.

"Simple indeed!" he bellowed. "Simple indeed! and singing psalms while they are betraying their country!" and he burst forth out of the office and to my horror I saw him pass by, a few minutes later, followed by the sheriff and two deputies, all of them armed with swords and halberds.

Now in order to understand this remark, you ought to know that during the early forties, the people were in a terrible state of both suspicion and suspense. Don't ask me why, for I could not possibly tell you. Such attacks of unrest are very much like the epidemics of a mysterious disease. One day everybody is well and happy, and the men sit in the taverns and drink their ale and tobacco and talk business and the women swap stories across the doorsteps and little boys and girls play in the gutter and every one is sure that all is well with the world, or at least as well as ever it can be. And the next day, those same men are dead, and terror-stricken women are desperately clutching at their whimpering children, lest the green-eyed monster get hold of them and drag them to an untimely grave.

Yet nothing has happened. The evil winds that carry disease have not blown from east or west, or south or north. None of the dreaded comets that influence our lives have appeared upon the horizon. No vapors (as far as any one could notice) have arisen from either river or sea to cause this blight. The affliction is there and those who believe that everything has been predicted since the beginning of time say: "This pestilence comes to us as the vengeance of a just God to punish us because we loved Satan too much" and those who hold that Evil is all-powerful in this world stammer: "It is Satan who wants to chastise us because we loved God too much," and those who are convinced (upon very slender evidence, I must confess) that our universe is based upon reason and understanding, confess: "We don't know. We may know in the fullness of time, but at present, we are still too deeply steeped in ignorance and prejudice either to know or to find out."

And all this holds good with equal truth of those strange spiritual maladies that have afflicted the nations of our globe as long ago as the days of Genesis and Deuteronomy. The sun is shining and the harvests stand ready and peace reigneth on earth. The swords have been hammered into plow-shares and kings and potentates call each other "Brother." Ships sail across the seven seas and merchants trade far and wide without the slightest fear of molestation. It looks as if the dream of the great King Henry of France was about to come true and that henceforth a Parliament of Nations shall settle the difficulties that arise between the different countries without the usual idiotic appeal to violence and bloodshed.

And then, almost overnight, something happens and Paradise is turned into Hell, that same English merchant who has been dealing with his Dutch rival in peace and harmony for twenty or thirty years, has become an untrustworthy scoundrel and must be watched from the moment he sets foot on our soil, until he leaves it again. Otherwise he might poison the wells or set fire to hospitals and orphan asylums and in a hundred other ways show what a fiend he really is and has been all the time he was being received as a welcome guest.

Substitute, if you wish, Frenchmen for Englishmen or Russians or Turks and substitute Danish for Dutch or German or Spanish, but the result will be the same. The moment this "dementia maxima" descends upon earth, human reason ceases to function and no matter what those, who are able to think a little clearer than the majority of their fellow-citizens, will say or suggest or do or write, the illness must take its natural course, until having slain its thousands or tens of thousands, it departs once more as mysteriously and as suddenly as the plague or the black death or that strange sweating sickness of which nearly one tenth of the people of Amsterdam died only three years ago.

Well, during the early forties we were once again threatened by an outbreak of this unpleasant international delirium. Nominally we were still in rebellion against our lawful sovereign, the King of Spain. But I doubt whether more than a dozen people among all my vast acquaintance knew the name of the King whom they were supposed to be defying. To the younger generation, even such names as Leyden or Haarlem, that had filled my heart with horror when I was a child, meant practically nothing. They probably remembered that those cities had suffered a succession of sieges and that their people had eaten rats and mice and the bodies of dead men and women rather than open their gates to Alva's hirelings. But I doubt whether they took those yarns about starvation and heroism very seriously.

They would listen to grandpa with polite patience, but when it came to his stories of Spanish tyranny and cruelty, they were apt to shrug their shoulders. It was almost forty years since the last of the Spanish garrisons had been driven from the northern parts of the Republic and the capture of Breda had shown that the enemy could no longer hold his own even in the South, where the populace had remained staunchly faithful to the old religion and where the names of Calvin and Luther were identified with the Beast of the Book of Revelation.

In the Far East, the capture of Ceylon and Malacca had filled the last gap in the road to the Indies and ships bound for Java could now travel as safely and comfortably as the daily canal-boat between Amsterdam and Haarlem. The opening up of Japan had proved a most lucrative business and the merchant who sent a ship to Hirado or Deshima and did not make a full five hundred percent on his investment thought himself cheated out of his legitimate profits and was apt to petition the government to get himself reimbursed for his trouble.

The whales of Spitzbergen continued as plentiful as in the days of Barendszoon and Hudson and the town of Smeerenberg had three saloons for every try-house.

In Brazil, Count John Maurice of Nassau was busy laying the foundations for a new empire that was to offer greater opportunities for speculation and investment than anything we had ever undertaken before. The West India Company was growing rich on the slave trade to Spanish America. The Baltic grain trade was still entirely in the hands of our own people and by smuggling flour to the starving people of Spain (what did a war mean to these poor hungry wretches?) and by making them pay through the nose for every sack of wheat, our merchants were gathering in enough money to pay almost half the costs of our admiralties.

As for the industries at home, the mills were working overtime, for all this rich plunder from all over the world had to be prepared for the market—the wood had to be sawed, the rice had to be husked, the wheat had to be ground, the tobacco had to be cut, the spices had to be cleaned, the fish had to be dried and in order to keep the vast fleets of merchantmen continuously on the high seas, ships had to be built and ships had to be repaired and sails had to be made and the rope-yards had to be kept busy and everywhere there was such terrific activity that those who went hungry did so solely because they were either too incompetent or too lazy to grab their share of the golden manna which poured down upon us from a kindly disposed Heaven.

I know that I am talking like that famous master of rhetoric who at the opening of the University of Utrecht tried to prove that the inhabitants of the Low Countries were no other than the two lost tribes of Israel, at last come into their own. But I want to give an adequate picture of the background against which those regrettable events took place, which I am now about to relate.

I am not sufficiently familiar with the people of the South to know whether they perhaps are incapable of enjoying themselves without a consciousness of imminent danger. But those of us who descend from the race of the Batavians seem to have an infinite capacity for needless suffering, both of the body and the soul. I remember how once as a boy I was invited to go sailing on the Zuyder Zee and a very persistent wind from the south-west carried us to the shores of Friesland. It was the first (and last) time I visited this distant province and I was struck by the immense richness of its meadows and fields. "Surely," I said to myself, "these peasants ought to be happy and contented." But wherever we went we saw none but dejected faces and heard naught but talk of great despondency and discouragement, until an honest yeoman from the neighborhood of Franeker, liberally supplied with vast quantities of that excellent gin which is a specialty of the city of Leeuwarden, could at last be induced to tell us the cause for so profound a feeling of dejection among the Frisian husbandmen. "It is the potatoes," he explained, "the damn potatoes! The crop is marvelous this year—never had a crop like it before—not a bad one among them—and we are up against it—what shall we now give to our hogs?"

Well, in the year '41 the whole of the Republic was enjoying such prosperity that every one was more or less worrying about "feeding the hogs." And since no fault could be found with the government, the conduct of the war, the management of the various trading companies or even with the wages that were being paid to the artisans, the people eagerly began to look for some other cause for discontent.

In no other way can I explain the strange feeling of hostility and suspicion that then arose against the kingdom of England with which so far we had lived on a footing of a most complete and cordial unity. Wherever I went I heard stories about British perfidy and British malice and British knavery and people who had never seen a Britisher in all their lives, who would not have known one had they seen one, would tell me hair-raising stories about the personal characteristics and habits of a race with which they were as familiar as they were with Eskimos or Tartars.

What struck me as even more amazing was the sudden personal hatred against the person of His Majesty the King. This poor sovereign was now held to blame for all the sins of his fathers and even more for those of his cousin, the late Elizabeth of Tudor. That red-haired fury had undoubtedly used us badly and it is true that the English episode in the Low Countries had ended most unfortunately for all concerned. But I never could see that it made very much difference under such circumstances whether the Queen had actually slept with the man who afterwards was to become the leader of the expedition to Holland (as many pious people stoutly maintained, though God knows they had never been able to peep into Her Majesty's bedroom) or whether she had led a chaste life and had died a virgin (as all of her subjects so firmly believe). That particular "Sweet Robin" had not been the sort of man that ought to have been sent upon that sort of an errand and the Queen, like many another woman in a humbler position, had merely mistaken a neatly turned leg for a neatly turned brain, and that was all.

But no, the old virago must now be dug out of her grave and be held responsible for everything from the unpaid bills of her dear friend Leicester to the treason of Stanley and York, though there was hardly a man alive to tell what sort of treason these two Englishmen had committed. As for poor King James, he was called a true son of his mother, for genealogical details rarely interest the multitude, and when once upon a time, in the cabin of the *Rotterdam,* I tried to prove that he was not the son of Elizabeth of England but of Mary of Scotland, whose head had been cut off by her British cousin, I was immediately pounced upon from all sides and a very excited apothecary, who knew for certain that I was an agent in the pay of the English minister, was all for throwing me overboard and he might have succeeded in making things very uncomfortable for me, hadn't the skipper (an old friend of my grandfather's) descended into the cockpit and offered to brain the first person who laid hands on his beloved doctor.

Indeed, I could never see what reason we had to hate this unfortunate monarch, who had allowed himself to be cheated out of the greater part of the indemnity which we still owed him for the English expedition of 1596. I love my pipe, and I shall always think that a man who is capable of writing a treatise against tobacco shows a regrettable lack of the common decencies of civilized existence. But all this outcry against the shuffling old Scotchman seemed very silly to me and what can I say about the deluge of abuse that was now being heaped upon his son, who, if we were to believe the news-sheets, had more than enough troubles of his own.

Of course as so often happens in similar outbreaks of national fury, the person who was suspected and accused of any number of crimes had really nothing to do with the case. He was merely a convenient dummy, and as England was one of our closest neighbors, the British rulers usually had to play the rôle of scape-goat when the real offending parties lived behind the Pyrenees or on the other side of the Danube and were therefore out of reach of the public wrath. And it was clear to any one who had paid any attention to the political development of that day that fear of the Church rather than fear of the English was at the bottom of the panic that was sweeping across the country.

The fact that the Queen of England had recently appointed a diplomatic representative of her own in Rome had somehow or other become public property. Brussels in those days was the center of all European intrigues and our spies, well supplied with money, had first choice of all the scandals and gossip of at least half a hundred foreign courts. The comings and goings of Father Carr, who acted as Her Majesty's intermediary between the English court and the Bishop of Rome, were closely watched by Their Lordships at the Hague and when Her Majesty used the uprising among the so-called Puritans (a sect of very strict Calvinists who were in very close relations with our own people) to collect vast sums of money from those of her subjects who had secretly remained faithful to the Papist cause, the fat was in the fire and from a hundred pulpits one heard the dreaded word "Jesuit" followed by the even more terrible threat of a "return of the Inquisition."

In how far there was any truth in the widely spread story of a Jesuit plot to murder the Estates General and overthrow the Republic, I do not know. But of course ever since the murder of good Prince William by a poor, bigoted Frenchman who had been encouraged to commit this crime by an enthusiastic Jesuit from Treves, and ever since the murder of Henry III by a Dominican friar and the attempt upon the life of his successor by a pupil of the Jesuits and the final murder of this good king by a poor maniac who was known to have tried to become a member of that terrible society, the people of our country had been convinced that Rome was preparing for a counter-offensive and meant to reconquer the lost provinces as soon as an opportunity should offer itself.

The plot to blow up the members of the House of Parliament, who had voted for the expulsion of all Catholic priests from England, had caused a tremendous sensation in our country and ever since (and it must have happened more than thirty-five years ago) it had been rumored that the Scarlet Woman would stop short at no act, however vile or repugnant, to reëstablish her dominion over the people of our own country.

Of course, all these stories were greatly embellished during their rounds of the taverns and ale-houses. Acquaviva, the General of the Jesuit Company, was closely identified with Antichrist and hundreds of thousands of otherwise intelligent burghers fondly believed that he breakfasted every morning on a couple of stolen Protestant babies. Every ship arriving from a Mediterranean port was carefully searched, lest a cargo of figs and dates might prove to be really a cargo of Jesuit friars, and even in far distant Brazil and Java, everything that went awry was the fault of one of the disciples of Loyola.

Let the King of Jacatra object to the price he received for his coffee, and at once it was known: "A Spanish Jesuit from Manila has had access to the princely ear and is trying to start trouble between the company and the natives." Let a cacique of the Recife refuse to supply a sufficient number of Indians to work on the fortifications of Macão and of course he has taken a bribe offered him by a Portuguese Jesuit from Rio.

Meanwhile at home, even in the most remote parts of the country provinces, the mysterious influence of the Jesuits was ever a subject of daily discussion. It was enough for a boy who had played hookey to explain his absence from school by a "dark-faced, dark-haired man who spoke with a foreign accent and promised me some candy if I would follow him, and who frightened me so terribly that I ran away and did not dare come home until after dark," to set an entire village in motion and make peasants, heavily armed with blunderbusses and scythes, search the highways and byways for the traitor who had threatened their child.

Upon some rare occasions such bands of crazy yokels actually caught a Papist, but invariably he proved to be some perfectly harmless priest who had ventured back into the country, notwithstanding the drastic laws against the Papish idolatry, or some kind-hearted soul bent upon an errand of mercy at some isolated farm-house where people of his faith were dying and had asked for his assistance. For though I am quite convinced that men like Acquaviva or Vitelleschi would have sacrificed hundreds of their enemies without the slightest pang of conscience, if by so doing they could have brought a single erring soul back into the fold, and would have burned thousands of my neighbors with utter equanimity of soul if they had thought that it would further the cause of their beloved Church, neither the Neapolitan nor his Roman successor were fools and they knew that the time had not yet come for a concentrated action in our particular part of the northern world. But they rather approved of the mental terrorism which the mere mentioning of their name was able to call forth and they encouraged the myth of their omnipresence and omniscience in every possible way. That the terror-stricken people, looking for somebody to hate and unable to lay their hands upon any bona fide Jesuits, had then fastened their anger upon the King of England, who was at war with his Calvinistic subjects, and whose wife was known to be a friend of the Pope, why, that was just a bit of great good luck which they meant to turn to their own advantage as soon as the opportunity should offer itself.

This is rather a long-winded explanation of a very simple situation, but I had to tell all this if I were to make quite clear how an innocent evening perambulation (the result of a man's boredom in a rain-soaked little town) could lead to such absolutely unforeseen complications and could become the cause of great misery to a large group of perfectly harmless religious fanatics.

I have already written down that I had last seen my notary friend when accompanied by the arm of the law he was hurrying in the general direction of the church near which the houses were located about which I had spoken to him. I am by nature averse to all forms of public disorder and excitement and whenever I see a crowd in the distance, I usually take the nearest side street, rather than be brought face to face with some drunken brawl or a quarrel between husband and wife. From the agitated behavior of the old legal dignitary and the presence of the sheriff, I understood that my perfectly harmless remark must have created some sort of excitement. I felt sincerely sorry that I should have been the cause of this upheaval. I had mentioned the matter from sheer lack of suitable topics for conversation and not to start an inquiry which might end God only knew where and how.

And so, rather than await further developments, I returned to my room and ordered my dinner which consisted of a fresh shrimp salad, but when I asked for the meat, the girl who waited on me came rushing back from the kitchen, all pale and trembling, and explained to me that the cook was gone.

"Why so?" I asked her. "Is there a fire or a flood?"

"Oh, no, Sir," the poor creature replied. "Much worse! They have discovered a plot to murder all of us in our beds to-night!"

Really, this was getting to be too silly for words. A chance remark to a decrepit old scribe and a whole town thrown into the madness of a panic. I took my hat and rushed to the house of the notary. He had just returned from the Town Hall. He welcomed me with outstretched arms. His hands were shaking as if he had just lifted a weight too great for his strength.

"Magnificent!" he shouted. "Magnificent! We shall never forget what you have done for us."

At this I grew angry.

"Listen," I objected, "please listen to me for one moment. I am sorry I ever opened my mouth about those poor devils. I thought it would make for conversation and you know I have a hard time keeping my mind on your damned legal paraphernalia. But these poor fellows probably belonged to some new sect of religious lunatics, and now what have you done to them?"

"Done to them?" the old fellow interrupted me. "We have done to them what they deserved. They are locked up, all of them, eight men and eight women and seventeen children, locked up in the cellars of the Town Hall. To-morrow they will send troops from Middelburg and take them to the Abbey where they will be safer. We are too near the coast here."

"But for Heaven's sake," and I tried to stop his flow of words, "for Heaven's sake, man, be reasonable! The whole town has been turned topsy-turvy because I was bored and went walking in the rain and heard a few fishermen singing their hideous songs and because I made a casual remark about . . ." But I got no further, for Mr. Notary arose from his seat with great dignity and with a voice quivering with emotion he proclaimed:

"There is nothing ever 'casual' in the sight of God. I know your indifference in religious matters. But let me tell you that you were the instrument in God's hand, through which we may yet save our dear country."

"Save it from what?"

"From Antichrist!"

For such was the state of apprehension and uncertainty which dominated the minds of vast numbers of people of that day that a single careless remark of an inconsequential visitor could in less than ten seconds change an amiable and easy-going old conveyancer into an eager young Torquemada and could turn a well-balanced little town of peaceful citizens into a seething mass of open-mouthed lunatics for no better reason than that some one somewhere had whispered the word "Jesuits" and "British spies."

Of course, what happened afterwards has become common knowledge. The news-sheets and year-books have seen to that.

The day after I had indulged in this disastrous conversation (thank God, it taught me a lesson never to be facetious with those who take themselves seriously) a detachment of soldiers appeared from Middelburg and amidst the cat-calls of the assembled populace of Veere and amidst threats of the gallows and the block marched the poor victims to the capital of the Province. It was pouring, for the rain never seemed to cease during the latter half of that year. The sight of the small children wading through the mud of the ill-paved road, shivering and dazed and anxiously clutching the skirts of their mothers, was quite painful. And the burghers of Veere, being by nature rather kindly, had already begun to repent of their fury of the day before. And so suddenly a few peasant carts appeared from nowhere in particular and first the bedraggled infants were loaded on board and then the women and finally even the men were permitted to ride, so that they did not reach Middelburg in too exhausted a condition.

As I, entirely against my will, had been the cause of all this commotion, I took a horse and rode to Middelburg very early the next morning and I went to see the law officers and explained just exactly how all this had come about and tried to convince them that in all likelihood the prisoners were neither British spies nor Jesuit agents, but belonged to some obscure religious sect which had invented a new religion of its own and was practicing a strange ritual, like the Baptists who believe in total immersion or the Collegiates who have no ministers to address them and who consider every human being a potential prophet to whom the others should listen whenever the Spirit moves him.

In the end even these suspicious magistrates understood that I had been right and in less than a week's time the prisoners were discharged and were sent home with a small gift of money to compensate them for their suffering. And then it all came out, and an absurd story it was!

In a near-by village on one of the other islands a certain Reverend Jodocus Poot had started a new sect. The Reverend Jodocus was not a regularly ordained minister of the gospel. He had begun life as a tailor. Then he had married a girl from his native town of Ierseke with some money. He had taken a few lessons in Latin from the local minister, had bought himself a few inspiring-looking books, and quite by chance had got hold of Reuchlin's "De Arte Cabbalistica" which had so impressed him that thereafter he had completely discarded the New Testament, which he declared to be a Pauline heresy (don't ask me how he came to this conclusion, for I would not be able to tell you!) and had set up shop as a sort of Protestant rabbi, ready to explain and interpret the more obscure passages of the books of the Pentateuch.

During his studies he had come to some very queer conclusions and as a result his disciples would wear no clothes beyond those absolutely necessary for the sake of Christian decency, for any protection (in the form of an overcoat or gloves) against the blasts of winter would have been open defiance of the will of God who had divided the year into a cold season and a warm one and whose will must be obeyed at all costs. Neither, if they were farmers, would they fertilize their fields, for if God had intended them (the fields) to be covered with manure, He would undoubtedly have attended to that matter at the day of creation. Nor, if they were sailors, would they learn to swim, for if God meant them to be drowned, it was not within their humble human province to frustrate His designs by keeping afloat until they were saved.

This noble orator (he could out-distance and out-shout every dominie within the whole province of Zeeland) had made a good thing out of his peculiar form of theology. Like a second John the Baptist he refused to accept any remuneration for his exhortations, but once a year his followers were allowed to bring an offering to Jehovah through his most unworthy servant, the Reverend Jodocus Pedesius, for although the good man was a sworn enemy of all book-learning, he had Latinized his name as soon as he had given up the tailor's bench for the pulpit.

He therefore was able to live a happy and carefree existence, but in order to maintain his hold upon his disciples, he was continuously obliged to increase the strength of the spiritual potions which he offered his audiences three times on Sundays and once on Wednesday evening.

Indeed, he reminded me (through what I heard of him, for I never saw him in the flesh) of those musicians who are so addicted to playing fortissimo that in the end, when they really wish to accentuate a passage, they cease to produce music and merely make a noise. The terrible rainstorms of the last four months had given him a new and bright idea. One day he publicly announced that a careful study of Genesis VI-IX had convinced him that the end of the world was near at hand, not through fire, as had so often been predicted, but through another deluge. The Lord was in despair about the wickedness of his recalcitrant children (like all the half educated, the Reverend Jodocus loved big words) and the fastnesses of the great ocean were about to be broken up and the windows of Heaven were about to be opened.

"Prepare, all ye sinners, for the Day of Judgment is at hand, when those who have worshiped the Beast and the Image shall drink of the wine of the wrath of God and shall be tormented with fire and brimstone in the presence of the holy angels and in the presence of the Lamb!"

By this time a number of lay-preachers had fallen under the spell of Pedesius' eloquence and throughout the Island of Walcheren quite a number of shoe-makers and tailors (cobblers and habit-makers lead a sedentary life and have much time for solitary meditation) were busily engaged spreading the Pedesian doctrines. The most violent among these was a cordwainer in the near-by town of Arnemuiden which ever since the Reformation had been a stronghold of the "precise" doctrine, as the stricter sort of Calvinists used to call their own brand of theology. This honest man, who was slightly lame and besides suffered from the "morbus demoniacus" (he was never so inspired as when he had a "fit," his parishioners used to say with pride), welcomed the idea of a second deluge with such vehemence that he soon out-rivaled all other Pedesians by the vividness and lucidity of his descriptions of the rapidly approaching aquatic catastrophe.

He even could give the exact date. It was to take place on Friday, the fourth of November, of the year 1641, at thirteen minutes past eight in the morning.

It appeared during the trial that two families of Veere fishermen had belonged to the congregation of this strange prophet, that for more than five years they had regularly walked from Veere to Arnemuiden (a distance of some three hours) to hear the messages of this limping herald of doom, and that in the end they themselves had begun to have hallucinations.

One small girl of seven especially had been pursued by strange dreams and during one of these an angel by the name of Ameshaspentas had appeared at the foot of her bed (the angel, according to description, had been a very beautiful woman dressed all in gold and with silver wings) and had commanded her to tell her parents and her uncle that they and their families alone among all the creatures of this earth had found favor in the eyes of the Lord; that they, and they alone, would be spared during the coming flood; and that they must hasten and build themselves an Ark in which to save themselves and a couple of all the birds, the insects and the mammals which then inhabited the surface of the planet. Nothing was said about the fishes. It was supposed that they would take care of themselves.

Now it happened that the fishermen unto whom this message came were dreadfully poor. Their vessels were old and leaky and there was not a soul in the whole town who would offer to give them a stiver's worth of credit. Furthermore, they had seen pictures of elephants and dromedaries and all sorts of strange animals which lived in far-off countries and how were they to get hold of these and how were they to capture the birds? And in trying to catch a couple of wasps, the youngest child had been badly stung and both his hands had been so swollen that they had to send him to the leech.

There indeed was a problem. But it was settled by the little girl, who most conveniently had another dream, during which the angels Abdiel and Zadriel had told her not to worry about this detail. Not only was the Lord incensed about the behavior of the human race, but the majority of the animals, too, had been guilty of grave wickedness and it would suffice therefore if the future Noahs took only such beasties as lived on the Island of Walcheren.

The big boxes, therefore, which originally had attracted my attention, contained nothing more ferocious than a few rabbits and a few chickens and a couple of hares and pheasants and two small pigs. These poor dumb creatures had been completely forgotten while the trial lasted. Neither had any one dared to approach the fatal ships, for during the first few days there issued from their respective holds such a weird agglomeration of doleful sounds that every one supposed the crafts to be haunted and when the rightful owners finally returned to their vessels to release their live-stock, they found that all of the poor prisoners had died of starvation, except one small weasel, who had broken out of his cage and had grown fat upon the remains of his neighbors.

Thus ended this strange episode which was entirely due to my own lack of discretion in trying to pass small-talk with people who recognized no coin but the Eternal Verities and which would never have occurred had not the fall of the year '41 been such a period of such incessant and relentless rainstorms.

Incidentally just before I left Veere to return to Amsterdam, the notary handed me a small package which my uncle had entrusted to him, with instructions not to give it to me until I should have obeyed the different stipulations of his somewhat complicated and rather elaborate testament. As I had now signed all the necessary papers, had paid over (without a murmur, I am happy to say) the various sums that he had willed to a number of local charities and in a general way had tried to behave like a decent heir (as I had every reason to be, since I had held the old gentleman in a very sincere and grateful affection) I was allowed to open this mysterious message which came to me from the other side of the grave.

It contained a letter, dated Veere, May 1st, of the year of Grace 1623, which read:

"My Beloved Nephew:

"You have chosen the one profession which I myself would have followed, had I not been forced by outward circumstances to enter a business career.

"Now there are several sorts of doctors, in this world—those who regard themselves as messengers of our dear Lord, sent to this earth to minister to the needs of the poor and the miserable and those who exercise their trade as if they were selling draperies or cheese, instead of dispensing the mercy of God. I have watched you very carefully these last twenty years and believe that I know your character as well as my dear sister would have known it had she been spared to see you grow up. I have often wished that you had been more thoroughly imbued with the seriousness of life or had understood a little more clearly that the whole of our existence on this earth is merely the prelude to the vastly greater joys of Heaven. But perhaps our dear Lord in His wisdom does not yet think that the time has come to incline your heart towards Him to whom the highest of our mountains are but a grain of sand and who holds the oceans in the hollow of His hands as if they were drops of water.

"Meanwhile, although you confess yourself a disciple of the old Pagan philosophers, I have never discovered in you that pride of wisdom and that contempt for the humble in spirit which so often mars the usefulness of those who call themselves the true followers of Plato and Aristotle.

"I think that you will go far in your chosen field of work and I remember that you have quite frequently told me of the efforts that are being made by some of the most eminent of our chirurgeons to alleviate the pains of those who must undergo surgical treatment. I do not in any way wish to influence you in your career, but if you would devote yourself to the study of such artificial catalepsy (you will have to forgive an old wood-merchant if he is not entirely up to the nomenclature of medicine) I for one shall most certainly not be displeased and I can think of no other pursuit of human happiness that would have been more in accordance with the wishes of your sainted mother.

"Therefore, and in order that you shall not be obliged to spend all your time upon an ordinary practice, but shall have full liberty to experiment with different narcotics, I have this day invested the sum derived from the sale of my branch office in Flushing in ten securities of the recently re-chartered United East-Indian Companies. They are Common Stock, entirely safe and not apt to be greatly influenced by the fluctuations of the stock-market and they represented a capital of about 30,000 guilders. If they should bear an average interest of eight percent (as it seems not unreasonable to expect) they will assure you an income of 2,400 guilders a year. This is not a great deal of money, but we are simple folk and it ought to be sufficient for your needs if you will remain faithful to the mode of living to which you have been accustomed since the days of your childhood.

"You will of course understand that this is not an outright gift to you as my nephew, but a sacred trust which I bestow upon you as an instrument which in God's hand and through the mercy of our Saviour, Jesus Christ, and through the industry and application of your own unworthy brain may lead to the mitigation of some of that misery and pain which have been our share ever since that terrible day when Adam in his willful disobedience defied the wrath of a righteous Jehovah.

"Farewell, and think in kindness of

"Your devoted Uncle,

"GERARD VAN LOON."

I walked home that night through the pouring rain with the envelope carefully tucked away in the inside pocket of my coat. I was so moved by this letter that I did not examine the further contents of the small package until I was back in Amsterdam. I was totally ignorant of financial affairs, having thus far lived entirely by my practice, except during the years of preparation when my uncle allowed me a small stipend and I therefore took these shares to my good friend, Lodewijk Schraiber, who was a merchant with connections both in Paris and London and whose knowledge of such things was only surpassed by the respect he enjoyed in commercial circles.

He slowly loosened the thin red ribbon with which the small bundle of securities had been fastened together, spread them out upon his table. Then he put his hand across his bald head, as he was wont to do whenever pleased, and said:

"Your uncle has done pretty well by you, eh?"

I agreed that the old gentleman had always been most kind and lenient to me.

"And now he made a loafer of you!"

This puzzled me and I answered that Amsterdam being one of the most expensive cities of the whole world (as was well known to all those who came there from other towns to transact business), I could hardly expect to go and live on my income, since it would average me only 2,400 guilders a year.

"Then you don't know," and he looked at me in a puzzled way, "what these shares are worth?"

"Yes," I said, "ten times three thousand guilders, or thirty thousand guilders in all."

"And you never heard that they have increased just a little in value?"

"No," I replied, "have they?"

"A mere trifle. Only six hundred percent!"

"Great Heavens! Then now they are worth more than 30,000 guilders?"

"Haven't you ever learned to do simple sums in arithmetic?"

"I have, but that was long ago."

"Well, to-day they are worth exactly 180,000 guilders."

. . . .

And that was another reason why I remembered that the fall of the year '41 was very rainy, for not only did it pour in the streets, but through the thoughtfulness of this kindly old gentleman, I was quite unexpectedly placed in a position where all my future cares of a material nature were washed away as if by magic, and where I could now give all my time and strength to the work of my choice—the study of those drugs which eventually (so I hoped) would elevate the chirurgeon from a mere butcher (which he now only too often was) to a merciful prophet of new health and a new hope of life.

Chapter 2

I MEET SASKIA FOR THE FIRST TIME AND FIND HER A VERY SICK WOMAN

The fall of the year '41, therefore (as I hope to have proved beyond a shadow of doubt), was a period of endless rainstorms and the month of November was by far the worst. There were floods, and a great many head of cattle were drowned and the cities lay drenched by the endless dampness and the walls were covered with mildew, for as it had begun to rain before the peat had been shipped to town, the available fuel was all water-logged and either refused to burn at all, or filled the room with such vast clouds of smoke that most people preferred to shiver rather than choke.

There was a great deal of sickness and when Jantje, the second-maid (for I could afford two servants by now and have ever held that the highest form of thinking goes best with the most comfortable mode of living, and I firmly believe that Thomas à Kempis would have been a more enjoyable and more useful philosopher if he had spent his days in the pleasant tower of the Sieur de Montaigne rather than among the sandy hills of Overijsel)—when Jantje entered and told me that there was a girl who had come to ask me to visit a sick woman, I thought: "Oh, well, another case of a bad cold! I wish that they would leave me in peace."

For by this time I had practically discontinued my general practice. I still went to the hospital every day because I wanted to learn as much of surgery as I possibly could, but I took no further private patients and spent all my days in a small workshop or laboratory which I had fixed up in the basement of my house where I had a large fire-place (which I heated with coal) and could experiment without the danger of setting the house on fire.

I went into the hall and found not a girl but a middle-aged woman, whose face did not in the least appeal to me, and I was about to send her away and bid her go and find some one else, when she interrupted me in a scolding tone of voice and said: "If it were not a matter of great urgency, my master would have sent for some well-known physician, but my mistress seems to be dying and they told me to get the nearest leech I could find—any one would do."

Somehow or other, the utter lack of graciousness, the painful directness of this person who had come to ask a favor and found the opportunity to offer an insult, appealed to my sense of humor. The good Doctor François Rabelais, who cured more people by his laughter than by his pills and poultices, would have been delighted with this sharp-tongued shrew. He probably would have given her in marriage to Pantagruel and his life thereafter would have been about as merry as that of Socrates during his more domestic periods. And so I did not answer her as I should have done, but took my cloak and followed her.

We did not have far to go. We went down the Houtkoopers Gracht and turned to the left past the Anthonie Sluys and into the Anthonie Breestraat, where we stopped before a two-story brick house which looked as if it were the house of some well-to-do merchant.

The door was opened almost before we had knocked and an anxious voice asked, "Is that the doctor?" To which my unpleasant companion sharply answered, "Well, it is some sort of a leech. He was the nearest one I could find. I hope he will do." To which the voice replied, "Keep a civil tongue in your head, my good woman, and ask the Master to step in while I get a candle."

For indeed the hall was very dark and it was filled with the sharp odor of some acid which made me think for a moment that I had come to the house of a person who occupied himself in his spare time with experiments in alchemy. But when the candle was lit, I saw at once that this was not a laboratory, for the small table in the center and the chairs were all of them covered with drawings and sketches, and against the walls (though I could only see them dimly) there stood a number of canvases, but they were painted in such somber colors that I could not make out the subjects they represented.

Nor could I place the man who had apparently made them. He was a stockily built fellow with the shoulders and arms of a mason or carpenter. Indeed, the first impression I got when he opened the door was that of some better-class working-man, some one accustomed to heavy physical exercise but at the same time trained to read charts and architectural plans—perhaps the foreman of a building company. Such a fellow, however, would hardly have lived in a house of his own on one of the best streets in town, but in that strange city of ours, with new blocks of houses going up like mushrooms and new fortunes being made overnight (especially by those who were in some way connected with the board of aldermen) all things were possible and some of the best houses on the Heerengracht belonged to people who only a few years before had never seen a fork or known the use of a napkin. And so I quietly accepted the situation and asked: "Where is the patient?"

"In the Big Room," he answered, and his voice struck me, for it was very gentle and not in the least in keeping with his somewhat rough and plebeian exterior. Wherefore, while I removed my coat (which was wet, for of course outside the rain was pouring) and now suspecting that I had to deal with a member of my own class, I introduced myself and said: "I am Doctor van Loon."

And he extended his hand (he had put the candle down on a chair to help me with my cloak) and gave me a slight bow and said: "I am glad you came, Doctor. My name is van Rijn and it is my wife who needs your services," and he picked up the candle once more and led me across the hall into the room situated in the rear part of the house. Here a small oil lamp was burning and there was a fire and as a result it was not quite dark and I got a general impression of the apartment, and it increased the feeling of discomfort which had come over me when I first entered the house.

It is always very difficult to define such emotions and a doctor is at a disadvantage, for he lives so closely with his patients that he often loses track of the sequence of events, and because this particular patient eventually died, it would be easy to argue that those presentiments of doom which had struck me so forcibly when I first entered that house had been invented by me long after the final disaster; indeed, that my unconscious self had invented them as a consolation for the complete failure of my ministrations.

But in this instance at least that was not true. As I have already taken the opportunity to explain, I am not a religious man in the usual, conventional sense of the word. I am, alas, a true descendant of my gloriously blasphemous grandfather, who having had his ears cut off by one brand of religion and his livelihood destroyed by another variety, decided that he would compose himself a new faith of his own which he did by rejecting everything except that famous law of Christ which bids us be pleasantly spoken and amiable to our neighbors—that rule of Kung-fu-Tze, the great Chinese philosopher, which states that the truly wise man minds his own business, and one single line borrowed from a famous Latin poet, who fifteen hundred years before had discovered that there really was no reason in the world why we should not speak the truth with a smile.

To this mixture compositum I had added a liberal supply of the writings of a Frenchman by the name of Michel de Montaigne, who was just then beginning to be known in our country and who (in my opinion) gave us the most honest book that has ever been written by the pen of mortal man.

In this home-made system of theology (which my grandfather bestowed upon me much as my grandmother revealed unto me with profound injunctions of secrecy the family recipe for the making of a perfect omelette, an art almost as simple yet as complicated as that of saving souls)—in this concise but exceedingly handy "Guide to Every Day Happiness" there was no room for spooks, miracles and ectoplastic manifestations of a premonitory nature. It was then the habit in our city (a habit not restricted by any means to the more ignorant classes) never to undertake a single action without first consulting a sooth-sayer. Some patronized crystal-gazers and others went to the descendants of the ancient Haruspices who explained the future from the bowels of some unfortunate cat who was slaughtered for the occasion. Many took great stock in the stars and not a few tried to read the divine mysteries by a study of names or numbers or a handful of grass, plucked at random from some near-by churchyard.

I never fell a victim to any of these absurd superstitions. Sometimes I wished that I had been able to become a confirmed pyromancist or rhabdomancist or psephomancist (or whatever these strange cults call themselves), for if once I could have convinced myself that red-hot irons or fountains or pebbles were able to reveal the intentions of the Almighty, I might have been able to believe (as the vast majority of my neighbors did) that all the wisdom of the ages lay buried between the covers of a single book, writ two or three thousand years before by a tribe of wandering shepherds and peddlers whose ignorance was only surpassed by their love for bloodthirsty detail and their conviction that they and they alone held the true key to salvation.

And so, with the possible exception of a slight leaning towards predicting the weather by means of a game of lansquenet (a harmless enough trick which I had learned from the captain of a Swiss regiment of foot, and which failed as often as it came true), I never took any interest in the supernatural and let myself be guided exclusively by the dictates of my conscience as revealed unto me by the wisdom of Socrates, and by the sum total of those scientific conclusions which had been left unto us by the great sages of the ancient world.

Therefore when I speak of certain chill premonitions which gripped me when I entered this house, I do not refer to anything supernatural. But I hold with Pythagoras of Samos that there is neither life nor death—that all creation is but the tangible expression of one Primeval Force, just as all clouds and rivers and glaciers and snowstorms, yea, even wells and subterranean sources, are manifestations in somewhat different forms and shapes of one vast body of water which encircles and covers the greater part of our globe.

I further believe with him that nothing can ever be added to this original mass of what the Greeks called Energy nor that anything can ever be taken away from it. As a result of this profound conviction, I am able to anticipate Death (that hideous bugaboo of all my Christian friends) without the slightest qualm of fear. For I know that there is neither beginning nor end, but that all life is merely the visible manifestation of that Eternal Continuity which is the one and only mystery we shall never be able to fathom or understand.

But when the time has come to surrender that spark of Energy which one has been allowed (for a shorter or a longer period) to borrow from the great store-house of the Eternal Force, there are certain unmistakable evidences of the impending change, such as occur in nature just before a thunderstorm or just before the eruption of a volcano. What these consist of, I could not possibly tell. I have never been able to classify them as I am able to classify the flowers in my garden or to describe them as I can describe the symptoms of an affliction of the throat. But I have met people in the street or in some merry company and suddenly I have known that "that man" or "that woman" would not live much longer and very shortly afterwards I have heard that he or she had died before the end of a month or a week. And I have had the same experience with animals and even with plants. Once I remember a young couple who had but one child (and could never have another) and who concentrated every thought upon their small offspring. The boy was guarded day and night by two maids who had been carefully trained never to let him out of their sight. He was not allowed to go to school lest he breathe the air contaminated by the breath of the other pupils, but he was taught by private tutors. He never even was taken for a walk, but was made to play in the garden, a very large garden, by the way, so that he had plenty of room for exercise. I knew the father slightly (he had studied law at the University of Leyden while I was taking my course in anatomy there) and he had shown me the boy and had proudly boasted that this son of his some day was going to be one of the greatest people our country had ever produced and that he was going to take no chances with his safety or his health. I knew that he was going to be disappointed and that the poor infant would not live very much longer, but of course I said nothing. A few weeks later the boy, while playing in his garden, was stung by a wasp. It hurt him and of course he scratched, as any one will do under the circumstances. And three days afterwards, he was dead from blood poisoning.

Millions of little children are stung every year by millions of wasps and nothing happens. But this particular boy was doomed and if it had not been a wasp it would have been a bee or a stroke of lightning or a falling beam, but something somewhere would have arisen across his path to bring about this unexpected result. I have never seen it to fail and the moment I entered this house on the Anthonie Breestraat, I knew: "Here the eternal process of change is about to take place and there will be crape on the door before the passing of another year."

And then I ceased to think any further upon the subject (this whole meditation which fills so many pages of script had flashed through my mind in less than two seconds) and I assumed that air of grave concern which sick people expect in their physicians and which often proves itself much more beneficial than barrels of powders and hogsheads of pills.

The patient was lying in a big bed that had been built within the wall, for only the very rich have thus far taken to the French custom of sleeping in those four-postered affairs that stand in the middle of the room and are exposed to all the draughts of the night. By her side there was a cradle and I had to move it before I could come near enough to examine her. I asked the husband to let me have his candle and whispered to him to ask if his wife were asleep. But ere he could answer, the woman had opened her eyes and in a very low and listless tone of voice, she said, "No. I am not asleep. But I am so tired—so dreadfully tired."

And then I sat down by the side of the bed and went through the examination which is customary upon such occasions and asked a number of questions, but these seemed to exhaust the patient so terribly that I made the ordeal as short as possible, felt her pulse, which was very weak and very irregular but much too high, put my hand on her forehead and found it to be cold and moist and then covered her up with her blue counterpane (I had noticed that everything in the room was blue, the walls were covered with a bluish tapestry and all the chairs had blue seats) and told her to try and sleep and that I would soon send her a potion which would make her rest. Then I turned to her husband (and where had I seen that man before? While I was sitting by the side of the bed, it had suddenly come over me that I had seen him somewhere before—but where?) and beckoned to him that I wanted to speak to him alone and he once more picked up his candle, went to the door and said to the nurse (the woman who had called for me and who had waited all this time in the hall and who now acted in a somewhat guilty way, as if she had been listening at the keyhole):

"Geertje, you watch over your mistress and take care of the child, while I go upstairs a moment with the doctor."

And together we climbed the stairs and went into a big room in the front of the house which was so full of vases and plates and pewter tankards and old globes and bits of statuary and strange, outlandish-looking swords and helmets and pictures . . . pictures everywhere . . . pictures on the walls and pictures leaning against the chairs and leaning against the table and leaning against each other, that for an instant the thought struck me, "This man is a dealer in antiquities, and not an artist at all."

But a moment later he bade me be seated (on a chair from which he had first removed a heavy book bound in parchment, a dozen or so etchings or sketches, and on top of it all a small Roman bust of some ancient emperor or general), and he did this with so much grace and ease of manners that I came back to my first impression of a painter or an engraver, only I could not quite remember ever having heard his name before, and yet all the while I felt that I ought to know who he was and furthermore, I knew positively that this was not our first meeting.

He then carefully picked up a large lacquered box and a small cup and saucer which together with two small porcelain figures had been balancing perilously on the seat of another chair, placed them on a table crowned with the grinning head of a blackamoor, and sat down, folded his hands, threw back his head with a curious gesture (which is so common among short-sighted people) and said in an even tone of voice:

"You need not lie to me. Her illness is very dangerous, isn't it?"

To which at first I made no reply, and then in order to gain time, I said, "It may be dangerous or not. But before I draw any definite conclusions, you had better answer me a few questions," and I asked him about his wife's previous history with considerable detail and what I heard, confirmed the worst of my fears and suspicions. They had been married seven years. No, his wife was not an Amsterdam girl. She came from Friesland, across the Zuyder Zee. He himself was born in Leyden. His father had been a miller and had died eleven years before at the age of sixty-two and his mother had died only a year ago at the age of fifty-one and there had been six children, two girls and three other boys besides himself. They had all of them been well enough as far as he knew. "Of course," he said, "that had really nothing at all to do with the case of poor Saskia, but I am thinking of my Titus, for the baby does not look very strong to me and I want you to know that from my side at least he comes of fairly healthy stock."

But from his wife's side the report was not quite so favorable. "You see," he explained to me, "she is really of much better family than I and I have noticed that somehow or other, such children don't seem to get along as well in the world as we who slept three in a bed when we were very young and who were left to shift for ourselves."

I might have heard her father's name. He was that Rombertus van Uylenburgh who had been lunching with the Prince of Orange when Gerard murdered him. He had been Burgomaster of Leeuwarden and had been sent to the Prince to talk about the political situation in the North. He, van Rijn, had never known his father-in-law, for the old man had died in '24 when Saskia was just twelve. There had been eight other children in the family but after the death of the parents (the mother had died a year or so before the husband) the home had been broken up and Saskia had come to Amsterdam with her cousin Hendrick who had a curiosity shop and occasionally dealt in pictures and there he had met her and then she had sat for him for her portrait a couple of times. "In the beginning, the Uylenburghs had been a little aloof," the painter told me, "but Hendrick, who was not much of a business man, borrowed some money from me and he probably felt that I would not dun him quite so easily if his young relative posed for me and, besides, the poor girl knew very few people in Amsterdam and was rather bored and liked a little excitement and coming to my studio with her sister was quite an adventure, for you know what the respectable world thinks about us painters." The end had been that they had become engaged and then they had been married. "And now," he continued, "I am afraid that I shall lose her, for ten months ago, a short time before our boy was born, she had a hemorrhage and she hardly lived through the confinement and this evening, just before we sent for you, she had another one, not quite as bad as the first, but it showed that there still is something the matter with her and the surgeon who usually tends her has himself fallen sick of some malady of the lungs and until he recovers, I wish that you would look after her, for you live near by and she often has such terrible attacks of suffocation that I think she will die and I would like to have a doctor who is not too far away."

This did not seem the most fortunate of grounds for the choice of a physician, but the man interested me (where had I seen that face before?) and he was such a strange mixture of a rather arrogant grand seigneur and a helpless child and the whole house with its jumbled masses of pictures and furniture and china and Roman senators struck me as so utterly incongruous in our respectable city of Amsterdam, that I agreed to accept the case and told him so.

And he said, "Thank you," though without any great show of gratitude, and apparently wanted to go back downstairs, but I bade him to be seated again, for what he had told me was all very interesting, but there were a few other questions I wanted to ask him before I could express any opinion upon the chances of recovery.

"Have there been any other children besides the boy downstairs?"

"Yes, several. A boy who was born a year after our marriage and who died while quite small, and two girls who also died soon after they were born."

"What did they die of?"

"Nothing in particular. They just did not seem to have strength enough to live. Their mother was too weak to nurse them and that may have made some difference, but even after we had found an excellent wet-nurse, they did not gain. They never cried. They just lay very still and then they died."

"And the present child was strong when it was born?"

"No! Not very. For several hours after he was born, the boy looked as if he too were going to die right away." Then the midwife had given him a cold bath and he began to cry and that apparently had saved him. But his mother had never been able to nurse him. They had a nurse now, the woman who had been sent to fetch me, and who was now taking care of the sick woman downstairs. But the child did not gain and it cried a good deal and it looked terribly pale.

Then I asked him a question: "Have you another room in the house, except the big one downstairs, where you could put the child up for the time being?"

"Yes, several. There is one downstairs and there is this room and my studio and the room with the etching-press."

"Which one has most sun and air?"

"The one in which my wife is."

"Is there no other?"

"A small one where my press stands."

"Let the child sleep there."

"But then it will be impossible to work there. I have four boys who do my printing for me. They have just started on a new plate of Dominie Anslo. Yesterday I pulled the first three proofs and changed the plate a little. But to-morrow they are going to begin work on it. I have had orders for twenty-five copies. It will be a great nuisance if I have to turn that room into a nursery."

"Nevertheless, the child had better not be in the same room with the mother for some time."

"Then you know what she has?"

"No, I don't. I am not certain. I may know within a day or two. Meanwhile, the nurse had better take the little boy to your printing room. She can probably fix herself some sort of a bed in there."

"We have an extra cot."

"Very well."

"And you will come again to-morrow?"

"I certainly will."

"And there is nothing you can do now?"

"Nothing. She will probably be very tired. She ought to sleep as much as possible. I will pass by the apothecary on my way home and will order him to make her a sleeping potion. If she is restless you can give her two small spoonfuls in some water every other hour. But don't give it to her more than three times. I don't want to tax her heart too much. And now I had better be going."

The painter got up from his chair and opened the door for me. Once more I noticed the powerful shoulders underneath the blue linen smock and the broad forehead and the sad, troubled eyes, together with the common nose and the broad chin that was almost a challenge to the world to come and be damned. A strange mixture of the gentleman and the hod-carrier and where had I seen it before?

On my way out I passed through the sick room but the poor woman seemed to be asleep. I put my hand upon her forehead, which was cold and clammy. She had apparently no longer any fever, but her color had grown worse. When I had first seen her, she had been very pale with a brilliant red spot on both cheeks. Now the red spots were gone and the color of her skin was an unhealthy gray. Her pulse had grown so weak that I could hardly notice it. I put my hand upon her heart. It was beating, but very faintly. She was a very sick woman indeed and seemed to have reached that point of exhaustion when the slightest shock might be fatal. If she could sleep through the night, we had a fine chance to bring her back to life in the morning, but I was not very hopeful.

Just then I heard the angry voice of the woman who had come to fetch me and who was now talking to the painter in the hall.

"I won't do it! I just won't do it!"

And when he answered, "Sh-sh! Not so loud. My wife will wake up," she continued even more sharply, "Sh-sh yourself! I just won't do it."

"But the doctor says you must."

"Bah! Doctors don't know anything. The idea! I have taken care of children all my life. I never heard such nonsense. It is just a little cold your wife has caught. All this fuss about a little cold! But of course, doctors must give you their fool advice so that they can ask you for more money."

At that moment, the sick woman woke up and softly whimpered. I tiptoed to the door and spoke sharply to the nurse. "You will do what I say," I told her, "or to-morrow I shall report you to the medical guild. You may not care for my opinion, but you will care if you never get another case."

She looked at me with great arrogance.

"All right, Doctor," she said sweetly. "I shall do what you tell me," and she went into the room to get the child.

Van Rijn saw me out to the front step.

"I am sorry," he apologized, "but it is so terribly hard to get a good nurse just now."

"Yes," I answered, "but if I were you, I would get rid of this woman as soon as I could. I don't like her eyes. She looks as if she might go crazy any moment."

"I will try and find another one to-morrow," he promised me, and then I bade him farewell and turned to the left to go to the Oude Singel where I knew that there was an apothecary who kept late hours, as he was an amateur musician and had once sold me a viola da gamba of his own making.

I found him still at work in a little room at the back of the house. He had a theory that the tone of fiddles depended upon the sort of varnish that was used and had for years been experimenting with different sorts of oil and resin. He had just obtained a new sort of resin called "copalene" or some such thing—a funny-looking yellow mess which he had ordered from England. He wanted to tell me all about it and how now his fiddles would sound like those of the great Nicolo Amati of Cremona. But it was late and I was tired and I bade him wash his hands and go to his dispensary and mix me the dose which I meant to prescribe for my new patient. While he was busy with his bottles, I asked him whether he had a boy who could run an errand and deliver the bottle.

"Is it far?" he asked.

"About ten minutes. That big house in the Breestraat. The second one from the Saint Anthonie Lock."

"You mean the new house of Rembrandt?"

"I thought his name was van Rijn?"

"So it is. I think he comes from Leyden and his father owns a malt-mill on the old Rhine. But he is usually known by his first name."

"Then he is well known?"

The apothecary looked at me in wonder. "They say he is painting quite a number of pictures for the Prince of Orange. He must be pretty good."

"Yes," I answered. And then I went home and when I passed by the Breestraat, I noticed that there still was a light in the upstairs room.

"A strange man," I said to myself. "And soon he will be a very unhappy man. But where did I ever see that face before?"

Chapter 3

CONCERNING THE PEOPLE WHO WERE MY FRIENDS DURING THE DAYS OF MY YOUTH

I was soaking wet when I came home and so I took my clothes off and put them to dry in front of the fire in my bedroom. The only luxury that came into my life when I inherited that small fortune was an open fire in my bedroom and though it was regarded as a sacrilege by my friends who called me a "weakling" and a "Sybarite" and predicted every sort of disease as a result of this self-coddling process, I was never so happy as when I woke up and saw those cheerful flames enacting all the plays of the famous Mr. William Shakespeare upon the beams of the ceiling, and as for my friends—well, they may have disapproved of this "voluptuous incandescence" as one of them addicted to the "Metamorphoses" of Ovid called it, but I noticed that they were apt to gather together in my bedroom upon every possible occasion and that they lingered there long after the time had come to return to their own frozen closets. This evening while a blast of hail (for now that winter was approaching, we were getting a mixed diet of rain, snow and hail) was threatening to smash my costly window panes, the little bits of smoldering peat looked more inviting than ever. I took the kettle that hung over the fire, made myself a hot rum-punch, opened the doors of the bedstead and crept between the sheets.

I slept soundly for a couple of hours.

Then my cat Cocaine (I had called the animal after a new American plant which seemed to bear pain-killing qualities and which had recently been brought to Europe by a Spanish friar) wanted to get in (I had closed all the windows on account of the rain) and I had to get up to let the leisurely creature get into the house and then she insisted upon having some milk, and she took her time about drinking it (or eating it or whatever cats do with milk, for they seem to eat and even chew it) and by the time she got through, and of course wanted to get out again, I was so thoroughly awake that I could not go back to sleep, but lay rolling over in bed and thinking of a million things—as one will do under such circumstances and then suddenly and for no apparent reason it struck me where I had seen that man's face before and I remembered the whole episode which for a few days had threatened to throw our entire city into a state of turmoil and revolution and which had completely passed out of my mind, what with my recent adventures at Veere and the rain and everything.

It must have been in the year 1628. I am not absolutely certain, but I think that it was a few months before the capture of the Spanish treasure fleet by Admiral Piet Hein, an event which also ended in a riot, as the sailors wanted a bonus of seventeen months' wages and only got sixteen and in their fury pulled down several of the buildings of the West India Company, where the golden millions were said to lie hidden.

Yes, it must have been the year '28 and I had been in Amsterdam a little over a year and I had just opened my first office on the Bloemgracht, which was not as famous then as a couple of years later when Jan Blaeu moved there from the Damrak and began to print his tremendous atlas there on those nine presses which were called after the nine muses and which gained almost as great a reputation as their Greek sisters.

The Bloemgracht then was in a comparatively new part of the town and for a young physician it seemed to offer better opportunities than one of the older neighborhoods, where the rents were so much higher.

I passed by the house the other day after the funeral of Rembrandt, for the Bloemgracht ran parallel to the Roozengracht, and it was a melancholy trip, for the days I spent in that little house were the happiest days of my life. It is true that I was very poor, but my God! what glorious friends I had!

And where are they now? Two of them are dead, and the third one has gone back to his native country. At first he used to write to me. Then came a letter saying: "The sun is setting over the waters of the Golden Horn. The cypresses of my garden are throwing long shadows upon the walls of Shah Zadeh. Soon the time will come when I shall receive an answer to those questions which used to puzzle us so many, many years ago. Farewell, dear friend. Life has been good." And after that, silence.

I asked an acquaintance, whose ships ply between here and the Levant, to try and get me some news about old Selim. After eight months, one of the captains who knew a little Turkish, sent me a report. Selim was still alive, but no one had seen him for almost six years. He had inherited his father's wealth and was considered one of the richest men of Constantinople. As soon as he had come into his fortune, he had closed his harem, had liberally endowed all of his wives, and had sent them back to their villages, thanking them for their charming company of the last twenty years and wishing them that peace and quiet which he himself now expected to enjoy. He had then ordered a small house to be built in the middle of his vast gardens and had surrounded it with a high wall. His old palace, which had been completely rebuilt a decade before, he had given to the city as a home for orphans on condition that any dog or cat who strayed into the premises must be fed and lodged for as long as he or she cared to stay. He had then sent for his children (there were fifteen sons and eleven girls) and against all precedent he had offered to divide his fortune among them equally and give it to them right away instead of letting them wait until he died, on condition that they would accept a settlement and sign some sort of quit-claim which relieved him and his executors of all further worry about family jealousies and family quarrels.

When that had been done, he and one old and trusted servant had retired to the little house in the garden—the single door that gave access to this small paradise (for it was filled with the choicest of flowers and shrubs) had been barricaded—and once a day a cart came with provisions which the old servant pulled up in a basket which he had previously let down from the top of the wall. The grocer and the baker and the butcher were paid by a French banking house in Stamboul to which Selim had entrusted a small fund for that purpose on condition that he would never be bothered with an accounting. He received no visitors. He refused to receive letters and sent none except once, when to the astonishment of his neighbors (who never grew tired of watching these strange proceedings) he had asked that a letter of his be transmitted to an address in Amsterdam and had given the baker-boy who took charge of the transaction an order for ten Turkish pounds on his French banker. No one knew whether he was dead or alive, but the basket of food was delivered regularly every day and so it was presumed that he and his servant were still alive. That was all the honest skipper had been able to find out, but it was enough.

Selim had done exactly what he had always threatened to do and rather than live in a world he despised, and too much of a gentleman to leave it until his appointed hour, he had retired to the contemplation of beautiful flowers and little humming-birds and bumble-bees. A strange ending for a man who could have ruled an empire! But how very sensible!

Jean-Louys de la Tremouille, the famous skeptic, the man who professed to be subject to no ordinary human emotion, got so homesick for his own people after he had finished his last great work on mathematics that together with his man-of-all-work, a poor devil of a former galley-slave who had been condemned to the bagno for having been kind to a Huguenot minister, he set sail for France in a tiny boat and was probably lost at sea, for we never heard of him again after that day.

And as for Bernardo Mendoza Soeyro, that strangely romantic creature with his tender body and his brave soul, one of the few people who had ever been in a prison of the Inquisition and had lived to tell the tale, died full of years and glory (but far away from his friends) as an Indian chieftain in a small village of the Mohegans.

I have every reason to be grateful that I was born in a time so active, so full of color, so rich as the present. But most of all do I give thanks that I was able to start my career in a city which in more than one sense of the word happened to be the center of the whole civilized world. For where else on this planet would it have been possible to bring together such a strange group of human beings as right here in this incredible town of ours? The son of a French duke, a young man who through ancient precedent was allowed to remain covered and seated in the presence of his sovereign and now a quiet student of mathematics and philosophy, living unobtrusively in a couple of rooms of an old tower; a Sephardic Jew, descendant of kings of Israel, a wanderer, no parents, no relatives, no wife, no children, no home, poor as a church-mouse and proud as a peacock, at one time one of the richest students of the University of Salamanca, now contented to make a bare living as the bookkeeper for old Isaac Ashalem, who lived in the Lazarus Street and dealt in dried Norwegian fish and Greek currants; and then Selim, whose real name we never were able to discover (it was too complicated, he told us, and anyway it could not be spelled out in Dutch), whose father had been grand-vizier to Murad IV, the conquerer of Bagdad, who at the age of ten had had forty servants of his own and who had quarreled with his father, a most devout Moslem and passionately devoted to his brilliant son, because he had once dared to serve him with a new sauce containing a few drops of Malaga, who had then been obliged to leave the country and was living in Amsterdam in amiable splendor and explained his presence in these northern climes by his desire to translate Homer into Arabic, "In order," as he used to say, "that my compatriots may learn of the glorious deeds of their ancestors, for what after all were the Trojans but the earliest keepers of the holy road to Stamboul and what were the Greeks but the predecessors of those predatory Christians who have ever since the beginning of history tried to deprive the people of Asia of their legitimate possessions?

Remains the question—how did four such utterly different characters ever happen to meet each other and in so simple a house as mine?

Well, that I could not tell you.

It was one of those mysteries which one accepts but does not question. I think that I first met Selim, who dressed in European clothes but looked for all the world like the pictures of Solomon which were to be found in the Bibles of my childhood. I ran across him, if I am not mistaken, in the "Cave of Despair"—an inn which for a time was a close rival of the "King of Bohemia" and where a few of us used to gather on Friday evenings to play draughts and chess. He was a brilliant but most inconsequential chess player, who would overpower his opponents with his openings and then, when the game seemed to be his for the taking, would lose interest and of course would lose the game.

As for Bernardo (who was so very particular about that "o" at the end of his name) I happened to see him one cold winter morning on the Ververs Gracht. He was going to his place of business (the fish shop of old Ashalem) and a mob of little boys had chosen him as the target for their snow-balls. That in itself was harmless enough, but as the victim refused to pay any attention, neither grew angry nor accelerated his pace, the urchins decided to mix their snow with certain other ingredients

THE CHURCH

which are forever present in a busy commercial city where all the hauling is done by horses. When this failed to bring forth the desired results, they started to abuse him.

"Ah, the dirty Yiddisher! Kill the Yiddisher!" and other expressions even less flattering but equally obnoxious. Then one of the boys fished a piece of ice out of the canal and was about to heave that at the poor Jewman when I lost my temper (something I am very apt to do upon such occasions) and gave him a sound whack across the ears.

For some strange reason, there seems to be a superstition in our community that children must not be interfered with during their more playful moments on the highways and byways of our good town. At school for seven or eight hours of every day they are cuffed and spanked and are forced to suffer all sorts of indignities to both their courage and self-respect. They are made to recite endless verses from the less intelligible chapters of the Old Testament and are forced to learn a vast number of things which can never be of the slightest possible practical value to any human being. In short, while they are in the class-room, they must behave like little angels. But the moment they are back in the fresh air, they are cheerfully permitted to behave like little demons and no good Dutchman of my time would have dreamed of interfering with the sweet darlings while they were destroying flowers or cutting down shrubs or making life miserable for the stray cats and dogs of our alley-ways.

When that young man therefore discovered that a grown-up person had dared to deprive him of the pleasure of throwing a miniature ice-floe at a perfectly harmless stranger, he was so surprised that he dropped his missile and abruptly turned around to see who it was that had undertaken to play the rôle of God. But in so doing, he slipped and fell and hit his head against a tree and although he had got no more than a scratch, he set up such a terrific yell that soon from all the houses there appeared irate fathers and even more irate mothers asking in no uncertain tone of voice who it was that had dared to chastise their little darling. Of course, the wounded brat made the best of his opportunities, hastily smeared the few drops of blood all over his face until it looked as if he had just escaped from the massacre of Saint Bartholomew's night and then shrieked, "He tried to kill me. He is a dirty Papist. He tried to kill me!"

Well, to make a long and not very interesting story as short as it can possibly be, ere five minutes had gone by I was the center of a mob of wild Indians who were all for pitching me into the canal. And they might have succeeded, for a short time before I had sprained my left arm and I was therefore fairly helpless. But suddenly (how it was done, I do not know, although it happened right before my eyes) half a dozen of the loudest-shouting ruffians were sprawling on the snow and the rest were running for dear life and I heard a voice with a strange guttural accent say: "You had better come with me right away before they discover that I am alone," and here was that mild-looking Jew, who only a few minutes before had seemed to be too meek to fight back the children that were tormenting him, wiping five very bloody knuckles on the edge of his very shabby coat as if he had just taken part in a duello and was ready to accept the apologies of his former opponent.

So much for our first meeting with Bernardo.

Jean-Louys joined us a little later and he too entered our circle completely by accident. He had come to Amsterdam in the early thirties (for he was a little older than the rest of us) and for years he had not spoken to a soul (finding his neighbors little to his liking) until he felt obliged to buy himself a dog—"from fear," as he explained to me once in a rare moment of confidence, "that I would lose the use of my vocal cords."

He belonged to that class of apparently open-hearted people who are really much more secretive about their own affairs than the close-lipped brethren who pride themselves on the fact that no one will ever be able to read their emotions. He talked easily, yea, fluently, about his past, but in the end one knew exactly as much as one had known in the beginning, which was nothing at all.

Now by nature, I am not a gossiping sort of person. Most of my life I have gone my own way and I have done a large number of things which were perfectly clear to me but not in the least clear to my fellow-countrymen. It may be different in big countries like France or England, but in the small cities of a small republic like ours, everybody considers himself his brother's keeper and as a result, I have for years been an interesting topic of conversation for most of my neighbors, and the more they were puzzled by my behavior, the less flattering they were in their comment. I knew of course that a really high-minded man should be completely indifferent to the remarks his friends make about him behind his back, but it so happens that I am not sufficiently aloof not to care. It took me years before I could accustom myself to the sneering looks and the whispered remarks of the honest bakers and butchers among whom I spent my days and, what was infinitely worse, among whom I was obliged to make a living. The tortures I suffered during that period taught me to be exceedingly lenient and careful in my judgment about the acts of others and not to condemn my fellow-men even when all the appearances were against them.

And when I now confess that I made a careful study of the antecedents of our delightful French friend, I do not want to appear in the light of the usual small-town busy-body. I happen to be a scientist and scientists are people who prefer a world of law and order to a universe of chance and guess. When they run across a brilliantly intelligent human being who quietly defies all the laws and regulations of the community in which he lives—who plays the profligate grand seigneur in a commonwealth of penny-saving shopkeepers—who openly proclaims his disbelief in

Heaven or Hell in a community where ninety-nine percent of his neighbors are upset by the fear of doing or saying something that in some way might be contrary to the will of God—and yet succeeds in gaining great happiness out of existence and in achieving a most perfect equanimity of soul, they of course want to know how this could possibly have come about and they will study the strange phenomenon until they have come to understand it as closely as one human being can ever hope to understand another.

In the case of Jean-Louys it took me several years and this is the story of his life, as I finally came to know it.

His real name I saw but once. He had asked me to witness a deed of gift of certain farms and houses to his wife, and I went with him to my notary whose mother was a Huguenot and who therefore spoke French as fluently as he spoke Dutch and I listened while the endless document was being read. There were seven or eight Christian names, Jean-Louys, François, Antoine, Henri and a few others which I have forgotten. Then followed an enumeration of titles, a page and a half long: Baron de la Tremouille, Baron de Seignerolle and Peletier-Desorts, Knight of the order of Saint Lazarus of Jerusalem, Knight of the order of Malta, Knight of the order of Our Lady of Mount Carmel, Hereditary Keeper of the Falcons of His Majesty the King, and a vast variety of dignities which meant as much to me as the enumeration of the ninety-nine holy attributes of the Moslem God with which Selim loved to delight us after he had partaken of his third glass of forbidden gin and water.

But these honors which (if I am rightly informed) meant more to the average Frenchman than his wife and children and his property, sat lightly upon the shoulders of this tall, slow-moving young man with the high forehead and the aquiline nose, who at first called himself Vicomte de Legre, after a small river near Bordeaux, upon which most of his property was situated. When he grew tired of the mute admiration with which the plain citizens of our republic stared at a live vicomte, he threw the "de" overboard, let go of the "Legre," and henceforth was known simply as Monsieur Jean-Louys.

For the first forty years of his life he had been an only son. And as his mother had died at his birth, it looked as if he would be the sole heir to his father's estates and his father was deemed one of the richest men in the whole of Gascony. But at the age of sixty-five the old gentleman (who was of a vigorous nature) married a girl of eighteen from Bilbao, just across the Spanish frontier, and exactly nine months later, Jean-Louys had a little brother. He had never seen the child, having left his native country before the child was born, but when his father died, he had treated him most generously and to the best of his knowledge the young man had used the greater part of his inheritance to buy himself a captaincy in a regiment of Royal Musketeers of which some day he hoped to be the commander-in-chief.

There had been no sisters and poor Jean-Louys, left alone with his father in the enormous castle on the banks of the Legre, had spent a lonely but most extraordinary youth. For the old Baron de la Tremouille like so many people of his age (he was born in 1570) was a fanatic upon the subject of education.

Of course, a nobleman of his rank could not attend a university like any ordinary commoner. Therefore Monsieur de la Tremouille, père, as soon as he had succeeded his father (the boon companion and minister of King Henry IV, who could be of an exceedingly liberal nature towards those who served him well) had surrounded himself with a veritable court of learned and eloquent humanists. A refugee Byzantine, by the name of Simon Hagiadopoulos (there still were a few Byzantine refugees peddling their learning, although it was more than a century since the fall of their city), and the learned Theofrastus Molestus, the famous editor of the speech of Appius Claudius Caecus (a ten-page pamphlet upon the study of which Molestus had spent the greater part of thirty years), taught him the rudiments of Latin and Greek syntax until the restless baron, bored by so much erudition, got the old scholars appointed as professors of rhetoric and ancient history to the University of Grenoble and imported a young Italian by the name of Paolo Parentese who paid less attention to grammar, but who with the help of an unexpurgated copy of "The Golden Ass" of Apuleius taught his pupil a fair amount of Latin in less than a year and then remained for an extra twelve months to explain the mysteries of the "Decameron" in the original tongue of Giovanni Boccaccio.

In the meantime, a fourth teacher had appeared in the person of Rabbi Sholem ben Yehiel, who was to give instruction in Hebrew. For although this tongue was pre-classical rather than classical, the Gascon country-gentleman, in abject awe before everything even remotely connected with the Rebirth of Civilization, decided to follow the full program as laid down by the immortal John Reuchlin. All the great humanists had taken lessons in Hebrew, therefore the Baron de la Tremouille, who meant to be considered their humble disciple, meant to take lessons in Hebrew as well. But the experiment was not a success. Forty years spent in reading and explaining the less intelligible parts of the Talmud to the over-eager and under-nourished children of the Viennese Ghetto had not exactly fitted poor Sholem ben Yehiel for the task of teaching the delicate mysteries of his holy hieroglyphics to an old French country squire who rode ten miles every morning before breakfast and ate five hearty meals a day except on fast-days, when he made it six, because he held that fish was less nourishing than meat or venison. Nothing could come of such an arrangement.

Before they had even reached the fifth letter of the alphabet, the student and his professor had engaged in such a terrific battle of words that that same afternoon, the Rabbi together with his books and manuscripts had been packed off to Arcachon with the injunction never to set foot again on the premises. The departure of the pious Talmudist in a dense cloud of dust, followed by the jeers of all the villagers (who had greatly, though secretly, objected to his presence and had even gone to their priest to ask him to lay the matter before the authorities at Bordeaux) and the outbreak of fury on the part of M. le Baron which extended over a period of several months, had attracted a great deal of attention and this attention had changed into admiration when the Bishop of La Rochelle preached a sermon upon the subject in which he commended the Gascon nobleman for his loyalty to the faith, for although the world was most sadly afflicted by the tendencies of an age which boldly dared to proclaim the wisdom of the pagan philosophers superior to that of the Fathers of the Church, this noble knight took his stand with the saints when he defended his Saviour against the ill-conditioned attacks of an unbelieving Jew.

This story was ever the delight of Jean-Louys, who had heard it a thousand times from his different nurses, his gardeners, his stablemen and all the other retainers of Château Tremouille, who had promoted the hapless Rabbi to the rank of Satan and who loved to depict their master fighting with his bare hands against the claws and hoofs of the Evil One.

When he reached the years of discretion, Jean-Louys had one day asked his father about the truth of the matter. The old man had burst out laughing. "Devil be damned!" he said, pounding the table with his fist, so that at least one decanter of wine fell upon the floor, "Devil be damned! That fool Jew wanted to tell me that trout tastes best when fried in butter and would not agree with me that it ought to be done in olive-oil, and so I chased him away."

But after this unfortunate occurrence, the Baron had decided that perhaps he had been a little too old to devote himself to classical studies with that patience and devotion which such studies demanded. He did not intend, however, to let this experience go entirely to waste. What he now needed was a brand new son who should be taken in hand while a suckling babe and should be turned into a combination of Lorenzo de' Medici, William the Conqueror and Dante, by a new educational method which had just been explained to him by a friend who lived in the neighboring province of Guyenne.

To find the prospective mother for this infant prodigy was the work of a few days. Her rank and riches did not matter, the husband had enough of those for two people. She must have health and beauty. A candidate richly provided with both was detected in a near-by village. Her father was a day-laborer and the girl could neither read nor write. But she had the finest set of teeth in ten counties and she could carry a small calf as easily as if it had been a kitten. Incidentally she had been engaged for three years to a poor sheep-farmer of the Lake of Caran, but that of course was a negligible detail.

She was duly washed and garbed by the old women of her hamlet and the marriage took place with as much solemnity as if she had been a princess of the blood. Exactly nine months after her nuptials, she had given birth to a sickly child, had lived long enough to whisper, "I hate it!" had turned over on her side and had died.

The infant, however, with the help of a devoted aunt, had managed to live until the age of four when his father took him in hand and exposed him to that famous system which was to change a puny Gascony baby into a superman. What had ever put these strange pedagogical notions into the old Baron's head, Jean-Louys did not know. He had once asked his father whether it was not the same system as that which had been followed by M. Pierre de Montaigne in educating his son Michel. Whereupon the father had soundly boxed his ears and had asked him: "Since when have the la Tremouilles been obliged to get their inspiration from a family of fish-dealers and Jews?" and had sent his son to bed without supper.

The details of this extraordinary pedagogic experiment were related unto me in great detail, for Jean-Louys never tired of enumerating the glorious absurdities of the scheme.

"You know," he used to say, "every town is filled with inventors who spend half of their lives devising elaborate methods by which they can drive smoke down the wrong side of the chimney and by which they can make their ships sail the wrong way. My father belonged to that class of enthusiasts. At the end of twelve years of training, I knew exactly as much as the average child that has been to an ordinary school for half the time. I had learned enough Latin to be able to translate the inscriptions in the village cemetery. I could spell my way through a Greek sentence, but I did not know what it meant. I could hum a song, but could not carry a tune. And whenever I mounted a horse on one side, I fell off on the other. Clearly my father knew that he had made a mistake. But he was an obstinate old fellow. The son had failed him. Very well, he would try a grandson. And so they set forth to find a wife for me.

"They could not find one in all Paris, but reports came from Pampeluna on the other side of the Spanish frontier that there was a virgin in that town of such exceeding pulchritude that even a king might wish her for his consort, though I have never noticed that sovereigns were very particular about the looks of their females. Anyway, Papa crossed the mountains, severely criticized the strategic methods displayed by Roland at Roncesvalles, and a week later he returned with my fiancée.

"She did not speak a word of French, but my God! how lovely she was, and I considered myself a lucky devil. A day after our marriage, I knew the truth. She was dumb, and she used a perfume that smelled like sandal-wood and reminded me of my dead ancestors in the family crypt. Also she was very pious, but she became pregnant almost at once and the eager grandfather was contented.

"The child was born in January and at the age of one, my father took it in hand. He had come to the conclusion that he had begun too late in life with me to accomplish anything. This time he meant there to be no mistake. And little Jean-Louys II moved from the nursery to the school-room before he was twelve months old. I sat alone with my wife.

"The poor woman! She was terrible. It had been the pride of her family that they lived in the same house in which Inigo de Loyola (you remember the converted rake who turned saint?) had been nursed after part of his leg had been blown away by a French cannon-ball. That had been in the days of her great-grandmother, but it seemed that the family had never talked of anything else ever since. They had been presented with part of the bone that had been cut out of the leg of the holy man and she had brought it with her when she came to Tremouille, 'to insure her happiness in marriage.'

"Well, that was the beginning of her affliction. She got what our doctors called 'the malady of the reliquaries.' She began to collect souvenirs of sanctity. I was a good Catholic in those days and still may be, for all I know, but too much is too much, even in the matter of saints.

"In the beginning, while I was quite crazy about her (she was so incredibly lovely, though she was rapidly growing stout and was developing a slight mustache) I did not mind how much she spent, but when she used the entire revenue of our estates for a period of three years to build a shrine for the splintered fibula of a defunct Spanish warrior, who had fallen fighting the blackamoors, I became slightly agitated. I tried to talk to her, but she told me I was wicked and devoid of all piety, that her confessor had told her before she left her native land that all Frenchmen were mockers of God and that now she knew it to be true, but that she meant to save the soul of the father of her child, no matter how much it might cost me and that she had sent to Meaux for a tooth of Saint Fiacre, from whose intervention she expected great results for our vineyards and an added revenue which she hoped to spend upon further objects of sanctity.

"Of course, the good Lord, who dearly loves his little joke, provided southern France with such a marvelous summer that that year we derived about twice as much money from the sale of our wines as ever before. And of course the tooth of Saint Fiacre was responsible.

"The extra revenue was invested in a piece of the elbow of Saint Faro. That may have been accident, or good salesmanship on the part of the dealer in Meaux who had sold her her first purchase.

"After that in quick succession she acquired a lock of hair of Sainte Dorothea to improve the quality of our apple cider (but Dorothea's hair proved less successful than Fiacre's bicuspid, for myriads of caterpillars descended upon our apple orchard and we did not have a decent apple to sell for four whole years) and a piece of the thumb of Saint Fridolin, to give us good weather for our harvest (but we had a plague of locusts which ate all our grain), and next a pearl of the crown of Sainte Gertrude, which failed, however, to kill the mice (as it should have done, according to the written guarantee by the Prior of the Cloister of Nivelles who arranged the transaction), and then (without further reference to our agricultural needs) a bit of the skull of Saint Athanasius; the original sword of Saint Pancratius; the original ax of Saint Boniface; a piece of hail which had lain in the hand of Saint Barnabas and had become so miraculously petrified that it looked for all the world like a common pebble; a feather from the wing of the dove of Saint Basilius; a link from the chain of Saint Paulinus of Nola, the original goose-quill with which Saint Jerome had written the Vulgate; a bottle containing some ashes from the pyre of Saint Polycarp, the martyr; the other half of the coat of Saint Martin of Tours, a shoe of Saint Hedwig of Silesia, and a leaf of the castor-oil plant of Jonah, although I never quite understood by what right this unsuccessful prophet of woe, who had lived and died eight hundred years before the birth of our Saviour, happened to be included among the Christian martyrs.

"All this represented a considerable outlay of money, but the upkeep was even worse. For each and every one of those relics had to be encased in a golden receptacle, richly adorned with the pearls and emeralds which were one of the proudest heirlooms of our family. And then she began to build little chapels all over the place, each one dedicated to his own little saint, until our estate began to look like a vast cemetery. Next, each one of these chapels was entrusted to the care of one or two guardians, who of course had to be paid for their services and of course I was supposed to do the paying. From far and wide, people began to flock to our estates to visit the shrines and as was quite inevitable, the relics began to perform miracles. Saint Pancratius specialized in toothache while Saint Cyprian made the lame walk and Saint Faro cured the seven-day itch. It was a lucrative business, not for me but for the holy men who administered these clinics. And soon there was bitter rivalry between the different shoulder-blades and finger-joints and molars, and pitched battles were in almost daily occurrence.

"As for me, I had not only become entirely superfluous, but even a little ludicrous. Of course, I tried to bring my wife to reason. But it was no use. She went about dressed up as a nun and declared that she had had a vision of Saint Clara who had told her that in time our place would become a second St. Damascus in which she (my wife) would play the rôle of Saint Francis' former lady-friend.

"I had stood for a good deal, but this began to look a little too much like spiritual adultery to me and I decided to leave. My father, who notwithstanding his extraordinary educational notions was an excellent man of business, had greatly increased the revenue of our estates. I asked him for a yearly allowance. He asked me what I wanted to do and I answered that I wanted to go abroad.

"'To do what?'

"'To study.'

"'To study what?'

"'Everything. Nothing in particular.'

"'That will exactly suit your taste.'

"And he bade me farewell as cheerfully and happily as if I had informed him that I was going to Bordeaux for a few days to order some new clothes.

"A week later I left. I really don't know whether I was happy or unhappy. My wife had long since left me for her weird collection of celestial remains. My child had been estranged from me and a Greek grammar and a Latin dictionary formed an unpassable barrier between father and son. I suppose that I ought to have asserted myself long before then, but for one reason or another I had allowed things to drift and of course I had lost out and so I wandered and having always had an interest in military tactics and being somewhat of an amateur mathematician, I finally drifted towards the Low Countries, because there at that moment past masters of that game were playing each other for the highest stakes and I thought that there I would be able to learn more than anywhere else. I went first of all to Brussels and then to Cologne, for I could not very well tell the Spanish authorities that I was on my way to join their enemies and from Cologne I went by boat to Rotterdam and there I took the shilling and enlisted in a regiment of infantry with the promise that I would be allowed to enter a company of artillery as soon as an obliging bullet should have caused a convenient vacancy.

"But in those days the art of siege and counter-siege had been carried to such a pitch of perfection that there were very few casualties and so I did my turn of duty in a regiment of the line and it was dull work, though the hours were easy and I was able to read a great deal.

"And now a strange thing happened. Those same classics that had driven me to desperation when I was able to read them sitting comfortably in an armchair at home, became a positive source of delight when I read them by the flickering light of a candle in a leaky tent surrounded by a dozen snoring ruffians and sick unto death from the terrible food which a stealing commissary-sergeant had thought good enough for the shivering cannon-fodder entrusted to his care. And of course that strangely indifferent luck that had without any apparent reason turned me, the heir to vast estates, into a homeless wanderer (a solvent wanderer with money in his pocket, but a wanderer, nevertheless) followed me even here.

"The Dutch and Spanish concluded a truce that was to last twelve years and contrary to the general expectations, they remained faithful to the terms of the agreement. Military life became garrison life, a dull succession of totally useless duties, marching to no place in particular—standing guard over nothing in particular—polishing guns and swords that were never to be put to any practical use. It was pretty terrible, but in a first moment of enthusiasm, I had enlisted for five years, and there I was.

"Then one night we were garrisoned in some God-forsaken little village in Brabant amidst a sullen population which hated us because we had taken away their churches, had removed all the pictures and statuary, had covered the walls with three inches of white-wash and had turned them into hideous Calvinistic meeting-houses. And there was nothing to do, absolutely nothing but drink and gamble and read and then do some more drinking and gambling and reading with an occasional turn of duty! Well, one night I was standing guard and it was raining cats and dogs and the roads were lakes and I heard a soldier from another regiment come wallowing through the mud. When he was quite near me, he slipped and almost fell, but instead of the string of oaths which I was expecting, I heard the well-known lines of Horace: 'Desiderantem quod satis est, neque tumultuosum . . .' Whereupon I continued: '. . . Sollicitat mare . . .' and so on and so forth and then of course, we spoke to each other and I discovered him to be a fellow-Frenchman, a fellow by the name of Descartes, a commoner, but an exceedingly intelligent person who seemed to have made almost as much of a failure of his education as I.

"Well, we came to be good friends and in the year '19, when our enlistments ran out, we decided that life in the Low Countries was too dull for a couple of honest philosophers and as there was chance of trouble in Germany (I have forgotten now what it was all about. I think it had something to do with the election of a new king of Bohemia) we went east and took service with the Habsburgs and we fought or rather we stood and waited and finally we ran at the battle of Weisserberg and then the war petered out and we were once more out of a job.

"I soon became convinced that the Descartes man had a much better brain than I and being trained by the Jesuits and not by a father with a theory, he knew how to study. But through my association with him I found that I was not quite as much of a blockhead as my dear father had always tried to make me believe. I discovered that I had a brain and that brain was beginning to demand that it be satisfied, just as my stomach would demand that it be satisfied after a long and tiring march.

"But unlike my stomach (which would digest anything except pork, cucumbers and radishes) my brain was very particular in the choice of its food. Philology did not interest it very much and theology it would utterly reject. I tried a mixed diet of philosophy and history, but it remained indifferent. I talked it over with Descartes. He, lucky dog, had no such troubles. For this quiet-spoken Tourainian was somewhat of a mystic and although one of the most brilliant scientists I have ever met, he also believed in dreams.

"Yes, he was a regular Saint Paul and one night he had a vision. We were in Neuburg in Bavaria and we had been rolling dice (for Descartes was a great gambler and would risk his last penny on a pair of sixes) and we had drunk a quantity of a very sour wine which they grew along the banks of the Danube and whether it was the wine or the fact that he had lost about forty thalers to me, I don't of course know, but that night he dreamed that he was to be the prophet and founder of a new science and that idea got hold of him so firmly that soon afterwards he resigned from the army and began to prepare for what he called his 'mission.'

"He was a restless person, forever on the move. I heard that for a while he drifted back into the army and that he was present at the siege of La Rochelle, when the Protestants and the English were driven out. And of course he has spent a great deal of his time right here in Amsterdam, as you probably know.

"Well, anyway, there I was all alone, bored to death by life among the dull and bigoted peasants of Bavaria and try as I might, I could not dream dreams, and whenever I had visions, I knew that it was the sour Suabian wine and not a message from High Heaven. And then one day, while looking aimlessly through some volumes at a bookstore in Munich (where we had gone into winter quarters) the bookseller came up to me and asked me whether I had not been a friend of Herr René Descartes, and that this Herr Descartes was a swindler and a scoundrel for he had ordered a work of mathematics to be sent to him all the way from Edinburgh in Scotland and the book had arrived and it cost three thalers, but Herr Descartes had never appeared to claim it and as no one else wanted it and it could not be returned (Scotch publishers never allowed you to return books) it was a total loss and therefore Herr Descartes was a swindler and a scoundrel and a great deal more to the same effect.

"To stop the garrulous Teuton from any further abuse of my friend, I paid him his three thalers, put the little volume (it was no more than a paper-bound pamphlet of about 150 pages) into my knapsack and departed. But three thalers were three thalers. I could easily do without them, but like all good Frenchmen, I was careful of my money and driven by the instinct that I must always get my money's worth, I one day picked it up and read it. God knows, the title was forbidding enough. 'Mirifici Logarithorum Canonis descriptio, ejusque usus, in utraque trigonometria' and a lot more which I cannot quote from memory.

"But that little book proved my Damascus. Suddenly my eyes were opened to my true mission in life. The author, a young Scotchman and some sort of a mathematical infant prodigy, had like myself started out with an interest in the problems of modern artillery and was the inventor of a gun that could fire ten times as fast as any of the cannon we had used heretofore. But as his fellow-countrymen used their pieces of ordnance merely to kill each other on account of their eternal theological squabbles, he had turned his mind to more peaceful pursuits and had invented a new method of computation by which one could substitute addition and subtraction for multiplication. I shall not try and explain his idea to you, for your practical medical mind would not be able to grasp something so beautifully abstract. But this was the fodder for which my mind had been waiting all those many years. I got out of the service as quickly as I could and went down the Rhine once more to find a ship to take me to Edinburgh and visit this young genius. But in Rotterdam I heard that he had died from the gout or something. He was still quite young when he returned to the ultimate zero, and how he had had time to do all the work he did and think all the thoughts he thought, I don't know and neither does it matter very much. As far as I personally was concerned, he had served his purpose. I was quite ready to devote the rest of my days to those calculations which he, in his own words, was willing to leave 'to others less afflicted by the ailments of the body.'

"I moved to Amsterdam, took those rooms in the old mill of the Rijzenhoofd which you know and have never again left the town nor do I ever mean to leave it until I shall be quite through with my tables of logarithms, and that, according to the best of my knowledge, will take me between two and three hundred years."

. . . . .

So much for the story which Jean-Louys told me about his past and the reasons which had brought him to our city. There remains the story of how we first met.

Jean-Louys was the perfect type of the French gentleman, ever courteous, ever willing to be agreeable, ever ready to laugh at himself or at Fate, a brilliant mind and inexhaustible curiosity about everything and everybody and totally incapable of learning a single word of a foreign language. He had spent almost six years of his life in the service of the Habsburgs, and did not know a word of German. He lived in Holland for more than forty years and never got beyond "ja" and "neen" and even those two words he managed with such a strange intonation that half of the time people understood him to say "yes" when he meant "no" and "no" when he meant "yes." Furthermore, like the vast majority of his fellow-countrymen, he could never accustom himself to any food except French food. The way our roasts were done reminded him of a cannibal feast "where savages swallow large slabs of raw meat." Our marvelous vegetables were spoiled for him because "we drown them in water." He tried a succession of cooks, Dutch, French, Polish, even a

Tartar who claimed that he had been chef at the court of the Grand Duke of Muscovy, but all to no avail. He was slowly dying of starvation until he decided to do his own housekeeping. He led a most regular existence, got up at six, lit his candle and worked at his logarithms, took a cup of bouillon and a slice of bread at nine, worked at his tables until twelve, ate his dinner, read for an hour in Xenophon (of whom for some strange reason he was inordinately fond), worked at his mathematical tables until six, ate his supper, puttered around his rooms and went to bed at eight with the exception of Saturdays, when he called on me after supper and when we played chess, and of the Sunday afternoon, which we usually spent with the Turk and the Jew.

But after a few years of this sedentary life, he began to suffer certain internal discomforts and a leech to whom he went (for like all Frenchmen he had implicit faith in the curative power of a good bleeding) told him that there was nothing the matter with him but a lack of exercise. Unfortunately, like most brain workers, he detested exercise and so he compromised by going forth every day to buy his own provisions and in order that the walk should do him some good, he selected a vegetable store and a meat shop near the Kloveniersdoelen on the Amstel River, fully twenty minutes away from his own place of residence. He could not speak Dutch but he could pay and he always paid cash and so he was a welcome customer, and furthermore he smiled so pleasantly that the fat old vegetable woman took quite a liking to him and let him roam through her fruit stalls at will and often when she was in the rear of the house, taking care of her brood of chickens, the Frenchman would simply take whatever he needed and would deposit as much money as he thought was necessary on the window-sill and would depart.

Now it happened during this period that the whole country had gone crazy about tulips. We had been raising tulips for quite a number of years, but no one had thought much of them. Indeed, a number of florists regarded them as a rather objectionable foreign weed which never ought to have been imported into a respectable Christian country. And then quite suddenly, and for no reason known to either God or man, all the world began to buy tulips and raise tulips and sell tulips and speculate in tulips and hyacinths, and even the humble crocus was worth its weight in gold. Overnight, a single bulb which in the olden days had sold for a couple of stivers might bring a thousand or two thousand or even three thousand guilders and in one instance, in the town of Alkmaar, a new variety called the "Admiral of Enkhuizen" sold for not less than 5200 guilders.

Now when a whole nation goes mad, no matter for what cause, it is useless to try and reason about it. In God's own good time, order will be reëstablished, a few people will have made a lot of money, many more will have lost all they had and everything will be as it was before until the next outbreak of wholesale lunacy.

And I would not have paid any attention to this unfortunate business if it had not been for a most absurd incident which occurred during the spring of the year 1637.

I was returning from my morning's duty at the hospital and I was just about to cross the bridge which led to the city's quarry-works, when I heard a terrific noise issuing from a small vegetable store on the corner of the old Singel. A woman was letting loose such a flow of profanity in such a marvelous mixture of different low-class dialects that I could not help but listen with that rapture which one feels before a perfect work of art. Whenever she gasped for breath (which occurred every two or three minutes) a man's voice would try to answer her in the most polished of French phrases. A delighted crowd of loafers stood in front of the store, eagerly awaiting the moment when hostilities should begin that they might take the side of their poor abused fellow-citizen and pitch into the dirty little Frenchman who undoubtedly had been up to one of the usual tricks of his untrustworthy race. I had not the slightest desire to get mixed up in this business, but the Frenchman, seeing some one who looked as if he might speak a few words of his tongue, suddenly rushed out of the store, grabbed me by the arm and said, "Monsieur, for God's sake, play the good Samaritan and tell me what this is all about!"

The fury of the vegetable female having meanwhile spent itself somewhat, she also accepted my offer that I should act as interpreter and the story which then slowly unraveled itself would have delighted the heart of Boccaccio or one of those other famous tellers of tales.

As I have said before, Jean-Louys for quite a long time had been in the habit of coming into the store and helping himself to whatever he wanted if the greengrocer happened to be occupied with her domestic duties. One day he would take spinach and the next day it would be a cabbage or a cauliflower or whatever happened to be in season. Of course, Jean-Louys, like all people from southern climes, was very fond of onions.

Well, the previous day, while rummaging through the shop, he had come upon something that for all the world looked to him like some new and slightly larger variety of onions. He had put them into his basket, had left two stivers, the usual price for a couple of onions, had taken them home, had mixed them into his salad and had found them to be absolutely without taste. This morning he had gone forth upon his customary errands a little earlier than before, intending to complain about those savorless onions ("for what is the use of an onion unless it be really an onion?" he asked me with true Gallic logic) but no sooner had he made his appearance than Madame had heaved a cabbage at him, followed by a couple of rich, ripe cucumbers and a very unripe and hard-skinned melon. He had tried to argue, had pointed to the onion basket and had shaken his head in token of disgust, but then the fat had really been in the fire and the ensuing quarrel might have ended in a general massacre when I happened to make my appearance and was so unceremoniously invited to act as intermediary.

What had happened was really absurd beyond words. The good vegetable woman, like everybody else, had been speculating in tulips. She had taken her life's savings out of the stocking in which they lay hidden among her extra woolen towels and had invested every penny she owned in two bulbs, a "semper Argentus" and a "Paragon of Delft." At eleven o'clock in the morning of the day before they had been delivered by the skipper of the Haarlem boat, just when the third youngest child had stung itself on a wasp and set up such howls that the mother had been obliged to go to its assistance.

Well, with one thing and another, she had forgotten all about her precious treasures and not until she had come back to the store in the afternoon had she realized what had happened. The two stivers lying patiently by the side of the regular onion basket had told the tale.

Jean-Louys never winked an eye. He had eaten the tulips and he meant to pay for them. The greengrocer's wife vowed that the French Baron was a perfect gentleman and he, from his side, proclaimed that now he was a greater personage than the King of France. "For His Majesty," so he reasoned, "spends a thousand florins a day on all his meals. While I, all alone, consumed a salad worth two thousand."

And then he accepted my invitation to a less elaborate and costly meal and that is how our friendship started.

Chapter 4

HOW WE AMUSED OURSELVES WHEN THE WORLD WAS SIMPLER THAN IT IS TO-DAY

During the winter we only saw each other on Saturday evening, but when spring came, the four of us often used to meet on Sundays for a walk into the country and afterwards we had dinner either at a tavern in town or in the rooms of Jean-Louys' tower or on the Rijzenhoofd.

For of course we had rather placed ourselves outside the pale of polite society. A Jew was pretty bad. A Turk was a little worse. But a Papist was beyond the limit. A combination of the three, plus a Dutchman who was suspected of being a Libertine (the word in my youth did not mean a "rake" as it does to-day but merely a "liberal" in questions of theology) was something which the good town of Amsterdam had never seen before and hoped never to see again.

The reverend clergy, of course, was greatly upset by this conspicuous friendship among four people who by every rule of the game as played in their church (this metaphor would make them shudder, could they read it) ought to be each other's mortal enemies and ought to hate each other with venomous fury. But when a young man, recently graduated from the University of Utrecht and full of zeal for the True Doctrine as taught exclusively in his own academy of learning (which had been founded only a short time ago to counteract the dangerous influence of Leyden, where science was now being taught and which therefore had acquired a terrible reputation for "radicalism")—when this misguided young orator delivered himself of a learned allocution in which he suggested that those four mysterious friends whose comings and goings so much interested the good people of Amsterdam would have made ideal citizens for the late and unlamented city of Sodom and that the authorities ought to take a hand in the matter, the Burgomaster did take a hand in the matter and warned this brilliant exponent of Christian charity that a repetition of this oratorical masterpiece would lead to a sentence of expulsion and confiscation of his household goods, whereupon he hastily changed his attitude and by way of apology preached a sermon extolling the virtues of Hagar, as the mother of the Moslem religion, and giving great praise to Mahomet, whom he placed among the major prophets, right between Elijah and John the Baptist.

This put him once more into the good graces of Their Lordships of the Town Hall, who were contemplating a little private treaty of commerce and friendship between themselves and the Sultan of Turkey and who did not want to see their plans come to grief because a half-literate peasant from a village in some muddy polder did not approve of the private conduct of a young foreigner of distinction, who was the son of a famous padisha and who recently had been appointed Ottoman consul to the city of Amsterdam.

Exactly what this consulship amounted to, we were never able to find out, for all commerce between the Levantine harbors and Holland was carried on by Dutch vessels and although there were quite a number of Armenians in our country, they would hardly appeal to a Turk in case of help or need. But Selim liked the distinction which his new title bestowed upon him and he made use of his official position to send his distinguished father a large number of complicated mechanical devices, clocks from Switzerland that said "cookoo" when the hour struck and watches from Nuremberg with little ships painted on their dials, and a bronze hen that walked and a cock that crowed and flapped its wings, and other similar toys which seem to delight the hearts of children and foreign potentates.

To gain the good will of the skippers to whom he entrusted these treasures, Selim always gave them imposing-looking letters of introduction. The first captain to deliver such a message afterwards confessed that he had done so in great fear and trepidation. He had run all over Amsterdam, trying to find some one who could translate it for him, but his search had been in vain. And when he finally presented himself and his letter at the palace gate of Selim Senior, he did not know whether he was carrying his death-warrant or a note on the imperial treasury. When five minutes after his arrival he suddenly saw himself surrounded by a hundred long-bearded savages with red breeches, yellow coats and green turbans, he felt that his last hour had come and that he was about to be taken to the drowning-pool. When these ferocious-looking creatures took all his clothes from his back and garbed him in a long silken dressing gown (at least so it looked) and removed his shoes, he began to hope that he might be decapitated rather than suffocated between silken pillows. But as soon as this ceremony had been performed, the hundred dancing dervishes, with one accord, fell upon their knees, threw their hands up to high Heaven, and shouted "Ka-wa-wah! Ka-wa-wah!" which the skipper afterwards learned meant "welcome." And from that moment, until a week later, when he was allowed to return to his vessel, the poor sailor had lived a life of such luxury as he had never been able to imagine, even in the most licentious of his dreams. For the old Padisha dearly loved his son, and though he would never be able to forgive him the indiscretion of that alcoholized gravy, he wished him well and would stop at no trouble or expense if in that way he could further his boy's career. Such stories, greatly embellished during the course of many repetitions, had elevated Selim to the rank of a Prince of the Realm and the city fathers of Amsterdam expected great things of him during the forthcoming negotiations.

From that side, therefore, he had nothing to fear. As for Bernardo, the fact that he had spent three years in solitary confinement in a dungeon of the Inquisition gave him a peculiar position in a community which still sent its children to bed with the threat that the Spaniards would get them if they were not good. Indeed, he enjoyed that distinction which a fishing-village bestows upon the sole survivor of a famous shipwreck. He was a man to be pointed at with awe and to be treated with consideration, no matter what he did.

Finally as for Jean-Louys, he was one of those fortunate people who carried their passport upon their face and who had a "laissez passer" for all countries and for all classes of society in the charm of their manners.

Such types as he are very rare in our Republic. Once upon a time we had had an aristocracy but it had been killed off during the bloody years of the Reformation and during the first decade of the rebellion. But we never had a court, in the French or English sense of the word. William of Orange, had he lived a few years longer, might have made himself the center of such a court, in the truest and noblest sense of the word. But his sons missed all talent for the higher graces of life. I have, in my humble professional quality, attended them both, upon one or two occasions when they needed the services of a surgeon. They were Germans and remained Germans all their lives long. Marvelous fighters, great masters of strategy, equipped with excellent, mathematical brains. But they always smelled slightly of horses and frequently of that bad perfumery which is so beloved of ladies of certain professional qualities. Frederick Henry was better than his older brother Maurice, but even he would have made a sad figure at the palace of St. James or in gardens of the Tuileries. And as for Their Lordships, who are our actual rulers, with their coats of arms and their liveries and their armorial carvings upon their solemn church-pews and their stout wives in satins and pearls, why, they are merely tradespeople disguised as dukes. They know it and we know it and they know that we know that they know that we know it and as a result, they are never at their ease, but always must endeavor to play a rôle for which they are fitted neither by nature nor inclination.

One of the few exceptions to this rule was my dear friend and protector, Constantin Huygens. I remember once, shortly after my recovery from that illness which overtook me in his house in Voorburg that he decided to give me a few days relaxation by a boating-party. We were bound for the city of Gouda but when only a few hours out, near the village of Bleiswijk a sudden gust of wind broke our mainmast and the little yacht had to come to a standstill until the damage should have been repaired.

It was Saturday afternoon. On Sunday, of course, no one would do a stroke of work, there were no masts to be had there anyway, and we found ourselves doomed to spend three days in as God-forsaken a little hamlet as I had ever visited. There were six of us and if we had been left to ourselves, we would have hated each other after the first day and would have cut each other's throats the second. What we would have done on the third, I do not know, but it would have been pretty terrible. Then My Lord Constantin came to the fore and made so wonderful a display of that tact and good sense which he had learned during his youth in France and England and Italy that those three days of exile from the civilized world will ever remain in my memory as one of the most agreeable incidents in my life.

Before we had been in that dreary village an hour, he had discovered that the grouchy landlord was a great fisherman and he talked to him of trouts and sturgeons (which the poor fellow had never seen) and of salmon and for good measure he threw in a couple of whales, until that mean sutler went into his cellar and produced the only good bottle of wine that had ever been served in his place. Next he got leave to visit the kitchen and he got that slovenly maid interested in a story about a visit he had paid as a young man to the Doge of Venice and how the Italians could make the most wonderful dishes with the help of a little brazier of charcoal and she worked her head off before her stove, until we had a meal fit for Master Dandolo himself. Then after the meal, when he heard that there was an old peasant living near by who could play the old-fashioned theorbo, but who had been snubbed once by a singing teacher from the city and now refused to perform before the gentry, he walked all the way to the man's house, told him how as a boy he had played the lute before James I, until that happy rustic carted his homemade theorbo all the way to our inn and amused us all night long with his songs and would not take a penny for his trouble, but thanked us humbly when he took his leave for the great honor we had bestowed upon him.

For three whole days this sort of thing continued. From somewhere or other an old copy of Horace was produced and we spent many amusing hours trying to translate some of his less difficult odes into a semblance of Dutch. And there was fishing and there were walks and there were a couple of stray pups we had picked up on our walks and a kitten which was a terrible drunkard and used to lick the wine out of our glasses until it was so tipsy it could not keep its eyes open, and the last evenings we gave a performance of the Frogs of Aristophanes as serious-minded Vondel would have written it and Spinoza in an enormous wig made out of rope played Dionysus and put so much pathos into the rôle, filling in long spaces with the Hebrew prayers he had learned as a child (and which we pretended was the original Greek) that the peasants whom we had invited to attend this noble production roared with laughter and stamped their feet so violently that he had to give an encore.

Well, this same rare quality of mind which was so characteristic of My Lord Constantin, and which invariably made him say the right thing at the right moment in the right tone of voice and which allowed him to project himself into the tastes and preferences and prejudices and superstitions of others, the gods in their wisdom had also bestowed upon the heir of the house of Tremouille. He had been taught to go through life with a minimum of social friction and as a result, no matter in what situation he suddenly found himself, he could remain superior to it and dominate it. For without the slightest sacrifice to his own principles, or dignity, he was able to placate those who at first felt inclined to oppose him until he had gained their good will and respect. And after that of course the rest was easy.

During the first year of his voluntary exile, he had plenty of chances to exercise this wonderful faculty. He was a mysterious person and mysterious people are not welcome in small communities that are on all sides beset by enemies. But this opposition soon passed away and when his knowledge of mathematics enabled him to suggest several changes in the handling of heavy siege-guns (for like Napier, his teacher, he was keenly interested in the science of ballistics) and his recommendations were accepted by the Prince, who not only favored him with a personal letter but sent for him to visit him in his camp, his place in the community was so firmly established that never thereafter and until the day of his departure was he subjected to the slightest annoyance. Even the clergy left him alone, though he made no secret of his opinion that the change from a man-made religion to a book-made religion had caused more harm than good and that nature was a matter of organized common-sense, rather than the haphazard product of some deity who had wanted a week's entertainment.

Chapter 5

UNDER WHAT CIRCUMSTANCES I FIRST HAD MET REMBRANDT

Thank God, I am not trying to write a book, for here I have wasted a dozen goose-quills writing about my dear friends, while I ought to have been busy with my patient. But poor Saskia was such a colorless person that she could not make herself interesting even on her death-bed while her husband came to play such a rôle in my life that every detail connected with our first meeting had become important to me. When I left his house that rainy evening, I was worried by a vague recollection of having seen the man before. I will now tell under what circumstances this happened and then it will be seen that my strangely assorted companions had something to do with it. Besides, they were such wonderful people, it does me good to write about them. And in a private diary that is not meant for publication, such little excursions ought to be allowed.

And so I continue my story once more by going a few years back (which is the way most stories in life are told) and it is April of the year 1626 and this time it does not rain, but the sun is shining and it is Easter morning and the good people of Amsterdam have all gone to church, but the bad people, Selim and Jean-Louys and Bernardo and myself, have decided to start forth upon a new venture this day and hire ourselves a small yacht and sail to the island of Marken. This was quite an undertaking, for the people of that isolated sandbank were of a savage nature and enjoyed a reputation as amateur pirates and highway robbers which made most travelers keep far away from their shores unless they were itinerant ministers of the Gospel, when they could count upon a most cordial welcome.

But Selim declared that he had had great experience along that line from a trip which he had once taken as captain of a Turkish man-of-war to the northern shores of the Black Sea, a desolate and swampy region inhabitated by wandering tribes of a strange race, called the Slavs. How Selim had ever got himself appointed commander of a war vessel, when he managed to be seasick while crossing the harbor on a ferry-boat had always been a puzzle to me. But by that time I had learned not to wonder at anything pertaining to the morals, the habits or the customs of the wily follower of the Prophet. Furthermore we were accompanied by Jean-Louys and his ability to win the good will of almost any creature on either two or four legs was such that I thought him capable of taming even those wild men of the Zuyder Zee.

Anyway, we had arranged that we should meet at ten o'clock near the Montelbaans Tower, the old tower near the harbor which twice a month was the scene of great gayety and great misery, when the soldiers and sailors who had signed up for service in the Indies embarked from there for Batavia amidst the beating of many drums, the singing and shouting of a thousand tipsy women and the general jubilation of the crimps who felt that they had done their duty as soon as they had delivered this latest batch of human cattle into the hands of their new master and were now entitled to a few days of drunken relaxation. The rest of the time, however, the tower stood in dignified silence and it seemed an ideal meeting place for four respectable citizens bound upon a peaceful picnic.

I was a little earlier than the others, not having to come quite so far, but as soon as I had reached the Oude Schans, I had felt that there was something unusual in the air. Excited men and women were standing in small groups along the side of the canal, and all of them had their eyes fixed on a single house (a perfectly commonplace, respectable house such as you might find in any street in Amsterdam) and occasionally some one would shout, "I saw one of them!" or "The whole place is full of them!" or again, "There is one now! He is trying to get across the roof!" followed by a cry of "Look out! They are going to shoot!" Whereupon every one would run as fast as possible to find safety behind a tree or the bales of merchandise that were lying beneath tarpaulin covers awaiting the return of the stevedores on Tuesday morning.

The whole thing seemed too absurd for words. Our town was famous for its orderliness. The militia was a heavy-fisted organization and Their Lordships, who could under certain circumstances be persuaded to overlook ordinary misdemeanors of a private nature, knew no mercy when it came to rioting. If one rioted and one was caught, one was hung from one of the windows of the Town Hall and that was all there was to it. "Go as far as you like," the Burgomaster seemed to say. "Rob each other occasionally and even kill each other occasionally, but keep the peace of the community and do not upset the system of law and order as laid down by our wise decrees."

The idea therefore of a riot and of all things, on Easter morning, seemed little short of preposterous and I turned to a tight-lipped individual with mean yellow eyes, who was standing by my side and who was apparently drawing great personal satisfaction from this unusual proceeding.

"Pray tell me," I asked him, "what is this all about?"

He at once grew suspicious.

"Oh, don't you know? Why, that is curious, that you shouldn't know!"

I assured him that since I had only come a few minutes before, I had hardly had time to know.

"Well," he said, "the house is full of Arminians. They are holding a service there and they just tried to kill a child and use its blood for their ceremonies."

Of course, if I had been sensible, I would not have continued this conversation. But in those days, I suffered from a dreadful spiritual complaint. I simply could not get over the notion that since all men had been created after God's image, they also must be endowed with certain primitive faculties for logical reasoning. Of course I knew that some people were not quite as bright as others, but I always told myself that that was merely the result of different backgrounds and different opportunities for development. "Give them a chance," I would tell my friends when they informed me that I was a silly-minded old fool. "Give them a chance. They have never had one. No one has ever appealed to their higher instincts. Talk to them! Reason it out with them and sooner or later you will find their vulnerable point and they will be forever grateful to you for having shown the right way towards the Truth."

I was so thoroughly convinced of the correctness of this point of view that almost every week I would waste endless valuable hours in utterly futile discussions with people to whom even the proposition of $2 \times 2 = 4$ was an unfathomable mystery and something to be regarded with profound suspicion, as it did not occur within the pages of Holy Writ. And no one short of a perfect lunatic would have undertaken to start an argument with that type of religious zealot and under such circumstances. But I was not very bright in those days and still believed in the efficacy of orderly argumentation and I answered:

"But surely, my dear sir, the people have not revived that silly old lie about the Jews for the benefit of the Arminians?"

Good Lord! how the fellow bristled! But he was the typical coward. He turned to a group of men and boys who had stationed themselves carefully behind a dozen big wooden boxes.

"Hey, boys!" he shouted. "I have caught one of them. This fellow here is a black Arminian. Come and get him."

Wherefore the crowd left its shelter and swooped down upon me and no doubt would have attacked me, when suddenly the door of the house opened and a dozen men and women, like frightened rabbits, made a dash for life and liberty towards the left of the street, which did not seem to be so well guarded. With a howl of joy, the mob rushed after its victims and I was left standing alone, looking as sheepish as one does when one is conscious of having done something very foolish.

But a pleasant voice behind me said: "Trying to solve the problems of this world by the usual appeal to reason, or just merely a friendly little argument?" And there were Jean-Louys and Bernardo and they said: "Selim was here a moment ago but he left, as he said it always hurt his tender Moslem heart to see Christians murder each other and he is waiting for us in the Ridder Straat and you had better leave before these brutes come back."

But ere we could turn into the next side street, we heard the beating of drums and from the north a company of militia was coming marching along, and so we found ourselves caught between the rioters and the soldiers and not contemplating our position with any pleasure (for the mob looked as if it wanted to fight) we stood aimlessly still for a moment and then when Bernardo said, "There! Look, there is a tavern!" we made for the door of the inn just as some one from the other side was trying to lock it.

Indeed, our attempt to force our way in almost led to another violent encounter, when suddenly and by a stroke of great good luck, I recognized the inn-keeper as an old patient of the city hospital and he recognized me too, for he said: "Come in as fast as you can, for there is going to be trouble and I don't want them to plunder my house."

For the moment at least we were safe and having nothing better to do we sat down and ordered three glasses of gin and asked our host what had caused all the trouble and he said that he was not quite sure either but apparently one of the houses further down the street belonged to a member of the Arminian community. Since the followers of Jacobus Arminius had been read out of the Church by act of the General Synod half a dozen years before, they had been in the habit of meeting at this house on the Oude Schans to listen to one of their ministers and fortify each other in their misfortunes by common prayer and an avowal of faith. These clandestine meetings were of course against the law and the clergy of Amsterdam had protested violently, but the Arminians or Remonstrants or by whatever name they were called, were industrious and respectable citizens and Their Lordships of the Town Hall refused to proceed against them, even if those black-souled sinners publicly confessed that they had serious doubts upon the subject of predestination and infant damnation. As long as they paid their taxes and were discreet about their weekly gatherings, they could sing and pray and preach as they liked and Their Lordships would most certainly not interfere.

Well, this morning some boys who had stayed away from Sunday-school had used the stoop of this house for a game of knuckle-bones and they had been very noisy about it and some one had come out of the house and had told them to go and play somewhere else. But of course, no other stoop would do and half a dozen times they had been told to go away and half a dozen times they had used vile language until the poor Arminian, forgetting all the precepts of his creed, had lost his temper and had boxed the ears of a young lout who had called him a name which I shall not here repeat. The youthful mucker, instead of taking his medicine, had shrieked that he had been murdered. A few passers-by had taken his side as is the habit of our common people who, regardless of the merits of the case, will always support one of their own class. Some one else then had raised the cry of "The Arminians and the Papists are in that house!" and the fat had been in the fire. For by this time the angry horde had been augmented by those who were returning from early service and they were in no mood to obey the orders of the officer of the guard who marched up to them all alone and bade them disperse.

I was looking through a little peephole in one of the blinds which had been hastily pulled across the windows, for the rattle of breaking glass told us what was happening a few doors away. I saw the officer parley and then hesitate. Evidently he did not want to use force, but that one short moment of trepidation was enough to decide the fate of the besieged worshipers. The crowd set up a terrific yell and a fresh volley of stones and sticks and mud was directed against the offending house. But one of the stones, either intentionally or accidentally, hit one of the soldiers who were waiting at some distance. He was perfectly willing to see the dirty Arminians get their just rewards, but he would be damned if he would stand there and have his nose broken by a brick and just stand there and do nothing about it. I saw him level his musket. At the same moment, one of the leaders of the rabble, an evil-looking ruffian with a cobble stone in each hand and a long knife held between his lips, in a sudden outburst of fury turned on his heels and made for the officer who still alone, and with his sword undrawn, was absolutely unable to defend himself, and undoubtedly he would have killed him, had not the soldier fired his gun and caught the assailant right between the eyes. The man dropped his knife, threw up his arms, stones and all, jumped about four feet in the air and fell down dead.

This was the sign for a general mêlée and during the next half hour there was a great deal of desultory fighting and several of the crowd were taken prisoner and since the danger of a bombardment was now considerably less, we persuaded our host to let us open the blind, for such outbreaks of popular fury are very interesting to people with a philosophical turn of mind and we did not want to let the opportunity go by of studying our neighbors in the act of breaking skulls and windows for the greater glory of their mysterious God.

And then suddenly I saw something that struck me as most extraordinary. Leaning against a tree and standing there as unconcernedly as if he were all alone in the park drawing a bird or a squirrel, a young man was making a sketch of one of the inevitable beggars who had hastened to be present when the plundering should begin (our beggars have a very sensitive nose for that sort of thing) and who now with some of his colleagues was debating whether they had better go on or whether they should retreat as the game had been spoiled anyway by the arrival of the guards. A few evidently were in favor of seeing the thing out, but others of a more cautious nature seemed to be in favor of flight.

While they were still debating this point, the battle between the rioters and the soldiers suddenly took a fresh impetus from the arrival of a number of sailors from some near-by East Indiamen, who armed with cutlasses were all for showing the damned heretics that they could not preach their stinking doctrines in their city and hope to get away with it. It was a bitter fight and many heads were broken and many fingers were split and stones flew to and fro, but through it all that strange young man kept working away at his sketches and appeared totally unconscious of the fact that at any moment he too might be killed. All three of us were fascinated by the sight of him. He was very simply dressed, like a student or a better class artisan and he wore his hair long as was then the fashion. But he had eyes, and all three of us remarked on those eyes.

"We must speak to him," Jean-Louys cried out, delighted with so much sang-froid, "and we must invite him to accompany us on our trip. He will be very useful in our negotiations with the natives."

But finally, when the soldiers had swept away the rabble and we could open the door and go out on the street, the young man was gone. We looked for him everywhere, but could not find him. And so we gave up the search and thanked our host and gave him a handsome tip (for maybe he had saved our lives) and went to the Ridder Straat and at the appointed tavern found Selim busily engaged in explaining the mysteries of a ring he wore to the serving girl, who was so fascinated that she had let him put an arm around her—"So that she should be closer to the subject"—as he explained to us when we entered.

Of course, our picnic and our sailing party had been spoiled for that whole part of the town remained smoldering with anger for several days and it was not safe to get too close to a pleasure yacht. The people felt full of righteous indignation. They had tried to protect their homes, their families, their children, against the pollution of a terrible heresy and as a reward for their devotion to the cause of True Religion they had been shot down like dogs. The idea that any one under such circumstances could be so utterly indifferent to the interests of the community as to go sailing for pleasure might have caused a new outbreak and at the suggestion of Jean-Louys we went to his tower and he made us an omelette in the true French style (they don't use flour in France for their omelettes as we do and get something much lighter and much more digestible than our own domestic pancakes) and Selim made us a strange dish of little bits of meat and rather pasty-looking flour which he called Ish-kebab, which he informed us was the favorite dish of His Majesty Murad IV and Bernardo mixed us a salad after the true Portuguese style which was not unpleasant although a little too oily and garlicky and I sat wondering who this strange young man might have been who could lose himself so completely in his task that he kept on drawing pictures while all around him, people were killing each other.

For a long time his face continued to haunt me. But I never saw him again. Until that rainy evening in the month of November of the year 1641 when suddenly it dawned upon me, as I lay tossing in my bed. The strange young man of the riot of fifteen years before was none other than the husband of my new patient. It was Rembrandt van Rijn.

Chapter 6

A DISAGREEABLE WOMAN IS AS A RULE A VERY DISAGREEABLE WOMAN

When I called again at the house in the Breestraat, I mentioned the riot of fifteen years before as we sat in the studio after I had visited my patient. I had been right. Rembrandt had been there. Just by chance. For at that time he was not living in Amsterdam. He had been there for a short time in '23, studying with Lastman, but in '26 he had been back in Leyden, and he had only been in Amsterdam for a fortnight to try and sell some of his pictures. The trip had not been very successful. The pictures were bad, but not quite bad enough to find a customer and he had returned to Leyden, as he explained, "because the meals at home cost nothing and because I could send my laundry to the family wash."

As for the incident of the riot, yes, he remembered vaguely that there had been a lot of shouting while he was drawing, "but I really have forgotten," he added. "All I remember is that I found myself face to face with one of the most picturesque hoodlums I had ever seen. I have always had a secret liking for those wandering vagabonds, who obey neither God nor man. They neither spin nor weave or whatever it is that they are supposed to do. They lie and steal and cheat and loaf and gamble and get hung or die miserably by the side of the road, but they make no pretense to be anything else and when they are dirty, they are dirty, and when they are drunk, they are drunk, and one knows what one is painting. I will show you the one I saw that day. I have done him in an etching. Some other time—when I have not got this worry—then I will look it up for you—some other time—when Saskia is better."

"Better!" I thought. "You poor devil, I ought to tell you right now. But why should I? She won't live a day longer for my telling you. No! You might as well have hope until the final end." And so we talked of this and that and the other thing, but mostly of this and that, as the "other thing" (taking it to mean the events of the big world) did not interest my new friend in the least.

I sometimes tried to bring up the sort of subjects that were of importance to the average run of my patients, the trouble the King of England seemed to have with his people and how it would affect our own trade if there should be war between the King and his Parliament, and the difficulties that never seemed to come to an end between Sweden and Denmark about the tolls in the Sund, and how it would mean a great loss to our own grain-trade if there were an open outbreak of hostilities and how it might force us to take sides just when our navy was needed for a final attack upon Spain, and what a lot all that would cost and how some one had written a book to prove that somewhere between Asia and America, in the southern part of the Pacific there must be a large piece of land and how certain merchants in our town were interested in the idea and wanted to send out an expedition to discover this mysterious land and take possession of it and exploit it, which would mean a wonderful new source of revenue, but to all these problems he nodded a polite "yes" without ever offering a suggestion of his own.

And then I talked of art, of which (with the exception of music) I am entirely ignorant, and I told him of two pictures by an Italian, whose name I had forgotten but they represented the Colosseum by moonlight and the ruins of the Forum early in the morning and I said what an inspiration it must be to any young man to be able to go to that wonderful country for a short while and study the ancient masters, and he said, yes, perhaps it was a good thing for a few of them. If they were born to be bad painters, they had better be bad painters on the other side of the Alps than on this side, and of course, the old masters had been wonderful, the greatest painters that had ever lived, but the story they had to tell was best told by their pictures and these one could see in Holland just as well as anywhere else.

For it really did not matter much where one painted, but it all depended upon how one painted and all these hundreds of young men, ruining their families because they had to learn their art abroad, had better stay home and join the bakers-guild or become tailors or longshoremen, for if they had talent, it would show itself even if they never left their own little alleyway or their own room and if they had not, all the Italian sunsets and French sunrises and Spanish saints and German devils would not turn them into real artists.

And when he was still quite young and had only painted a few pictures—it must have been in 1630 or '31—My Lord Constantin Huygens, who had seen his work and that of his friend Jan Lievens had told them that what they were doing was very nice and really very promising, but they were an arrogant couple of brats who thought that they were so smart that no one could teach them anything, and if only they would go to Italy for a while and study Raphael and Michelangelo, they might really amount to something. But they had answered that they could not afford to waste their time on such a long voyage and they had stayed right where they were and after all they had learned their trade just as well as the others and they had never lost the habit of working, which was one of the worst sides of the life 'neath the pleasant Italian skies, with all the women in the world at one's disposal and even more wine.

So that was that, and invariably after a couple of minutes our minds went back to the sick woman in the Big Room downstairs and the baby in the Small Room upstairs and what the chances were for the mother's speedy recovery and whether the child had inherited her weak constitution or whether he would pull through. As for the child, I really knew nothing about it. It looked strong enough but it was restless and wept a great deal and this annoyed the mother and tired her. For of course, as soon as I was out of the house, the nurse would find a pretext to move the child from the etching room upstairs back to the living room downstairs.

If I happened to come in upon such an occasion, there always was a vague excuse. The Master had to use his press that morning, or the room smelled so badly of ink that it had to be aired and they were afraid that the child would catch cold or she had to tend to the baby's laundry and could not leave the child alone while she was in the garden. And so on and so forth.

The reason for this opposition was not hard to find. The old-fashioned dry-nurse holds a curious position in our community. She is usually a woman of very simple origin, but because she spends her days in the houses of the rich, she has acquired a certain dignity of manner which deceives a great many people. There are undoubtedly a number of members of that profession who are faithful and efficient and competent and who render exceedingly useful services. But there are all too many who are lazy and indifferent and who do more harm than good with their superstitions and their methods which go back straight to those Middle Ages when men knew sometimes how to die but rarely how to live.

These women are really a menace to the community. They come into people's houses when everything is topsy-turvy and when the husband is half crazy with fright. They quickly succeed in surrounding themselves with a nimbus of indispensability. "If it were not for them, of course everything would have gone wrong, but they saved the mother and they also saved the child," and more of the same sort, until the poor male parent believes that a fat, complacent woman with the mind of a cow is the savior of his domestic happiness, and bows to the creature as if she were a goddess. And the relatives too fall a victim to this nonsense and the dry-nurse shows them the beautiful new infant and pockets her tips and allows everybody to wait on her as if it were she and not the mother who had gone through the ordeal of child-bearing.

Whenever she sees that she is in danger of losing her exalted position, she draws upon her large stock of so-called "nurse's tales" and frightens the poor parents with stories about children who suddenly grew an extra couple of hands or who died of mysterious diseases or who were eaten up by werewolves because the dry-nurse was not there to drive away the devils and spooks and the bogeymen which cause those afflictions with one of those mysterious but efficacious abracadabras of which they alone possess the secret.

Yes, I have known of cases when the dry-nurse, who felt that she was being neglected, deliberately doped the child with a weak solution of gin and milk so as to "save it from a horrible death" and thereby gain the everlasting gratitude of the entire household, which did not know that the "cure" consisted in substituting milk for gin and allowing the child to sleep off the effects of its youthful debauch.

The nurse in the painter's family belonged to this latter category. She was an unpleasant-looking person with large, coarse features and an arrogant voice with a whine in it. Such a combination may seem impossible but she really was possessed of it and reminded me of certain curs which are able to yelp and bark at the same time. She was (as I afterwards discovered) the widow of an army-trumpeter and often talked of the days when she had had her own place and had not been obliged to eat other people's bread. Her game was so simple that any other man would have looked through it right away. She knew enough about sick people to understand that the man for whom she worked would soon be a widower. She meant to fill the empty place. She probably felt that I, as an outsider, might not be so easily deceived and would try to warn the husband, for the whole thing was so transparent that it could not well remain hidden from the patient to whom any sort of excitement might prove fatal. Hence she had a double reason to hate me. In the first place, because as a doctor I was bound to disapprove of a great many things which to her were part of an ancient ritual and an easy way of getting some extra money, and in the second place because I might upset her plan of becoming the second Mrs. van Rijn.

It may seem that I pay more attention to this woman than she deserves, for the world is full of hysterical and scheming females and they are rarely very interesting. But soon after the death of Saskia it appeared that I had been right in my diagnosis of Geertje's hidden intentions and for years, the poor painter's life was made miserable by this former servant and her lamentations and complaints.

From all this Rembrandt might have saved himself if he had done what I bade him do and had sent her packing. But this man, who was without mercy for himself when it came to his work, who would actually live and sleep and sit and paint and walk in his clothes for weeks at a time if he got interested in a problem of light and dark, who would content himself with a slice of bread and a couple of herrings as his only meal for months at a time because he was too busy with an etching to think of anything else, this slave-driver who kept his mind and body going full tilt until he pitched himself headlong into an early grave, was weak as butter when it came to women.

He did not understand them and in his heart of hearts, I think he rather disliked them. He was a vigorous fellow with the strength of a bull and other qualifications which are usually associated with that useful animal. And therefore he was sometimes in dire need of a woman, just a woman, any woman would do. He was by nature exceedingly kind-hearted and, of course, the other sex was quick to recognize this defect in his armor and to use his vulnerability to its own advantage. As a result Rembrandt was forever in some sort of trouble about his domestic relations.

The truth of course was that a man like him should never have been married at all. For no matter what sort of union he contracted, the moment he promised that he would love and cherish a certain female for the rest of his days, he was uttering a lie. He had already given his word to some one else, years and years ago, and she was a most jealous mistress and would never let go of him.

Once shortly after Saskia's death I tried to explain this to one of her relatives, a respectable Frisian dominie. He was horrified.

"Then you mean to say," he stammered, "that my poor niece was married to an adulterer?"

"Yes," I answered, "just as much as any other woman who undertakes to become the life-companion of a man who is more in love with his work than with anything else."

For that, alas, was the truth. And it caused a vast amount of misery to a few human beings and brought inconceivable beauty into the lives of millions of others.

This balance sheet will please a few and others will throw it away in disgust.

But nature ofttimes chooses strange ways her miracles to perform. And who shall say that she is wrong?

Chapter 7

SASKIA'S ILLNESS

Yes, Saskia was a very sick woman but like so many sufferers from phthisis, she was totally unaware of the seriousness of her condition. She felt weak, of course, desperately weak at times, and the fever slowly burned up her strength. She was losing weight at a terrible rate of speed, but she felt no pain, no discomfort, and except for an occasional fit of coughing, she would hardly have known that there was anything the matter with her at all.

Perhaps the Gods, who are not renowned for their mercy in dealing with the ailments of the human race, recognized that this affliction was just a little more than most people would be able to bear unless mitigated by some spiritual anesthetic, consisting in this instance of an irrepressible form of gayety and a steadfast optimism which makes it impossible for them to believe that there is no hope and that death is merely a question of weeks or months, or at the best, a few years.

Every time I visited the house on the Breestraat, Saskia was doing "just a little better than the last time you saw me, dear Doctor." She was so lovely and so pathetic and so patient and so totally ineffectual that my heart was full of pity for her and sometimes I bought a few flowers for her from the flower-woman just around the corner of the Anthonie Sluys, a strange old creature who was said to be the widow of a ship's captain, who had been eaten up by the savages of some mysterious Indian island, but who as I found out one day was the relict of a plain sailor hung for insubordination and who had invented the story of her romantically consumed spouse in order to attract more customers.

Upon such occasions, Saskia was as happy as a child and one day I remember I had brought her a bunch of country violets and she made a little wreath and put it on the head of the baby, for of course, no matter what I might say the child continued to live in the big downstairs room where the mother lay dying. She even tried to make little Titus dance on her knees while she was sitting propped up in her chair in front of the fire. But the effort was too much for her and she had a coughing spell and when I tried to make her lie down, she refused and said she would be all right as soon as she had taken some of her medicine.

This puzzled me, for I had given her no medicine except a sleeping potion, knowing only too well that in the whole of the pharmacopoeia no drug was to be found that could prevail against the onslaughts of this dreadful disease. And then I discovered to my horror that that unspeakable nurse had prevailed upon her to try the mixture of a well-

PORTRAIT OF SASKIA

(1633)

lead pencil

known mountebank who had come to Amsterdam a few years before and pretended that he was a Babylonian prince who had discovered the secret formula of King Solomon's elixir of life, hidden among the ruins of the temple of Jerusalem. He was an absolute fraud. But he wore a long bright red cloak and a green turban and he was a very clever scoundrel who had had an enormous amount of experience in almost every city of Europe and had worked his way out of at least a dozen jails and he played upon the emotions of his patients with as much agility and virtuosity as if he had been the late Jan Sweelinck trying out the organ of some humble village church, and his waiting room was always filled with eager crowds of suffering mortals who listened to him with great awe and declared themselves cured before they had even left his house.

He advertised that since he had been sent by God he was not allowed to charge for his services and indeed, the consultation itself was entirely free of charge. But in order to prevent a relapse, he persuaded most of his customers to buy a couple of bottles of his famous "Elixir Vitae" which he sold at a florin apiece. I now had a chance to examine this mixture for as soon as we had put Saskia back to bed and she was resting quietly, I took my departure, but was careful to remove the bottle. At home I examined the contents as well as I could and found that it consisted of licorice, camomile and water with a dash of sugar to make it a little more palatable. No wonder this quack could afford a handsomer carriage than any of the regular members of our Surgeons' Guild.

I spoke to the husband the next day about this incident and told him what I had discovered, that this licorice water might not be directly harmful to his wife, but neither would it do her any good, as she needed plenty of milk and eggs, but that she must avoid all things that would tend to upset her stomach or spoil her appetite. He was very angry and promised to dismiss the nurse at once. When I returned the next day, I found her gone. I expressed my joy and asked where the child was.

"Oh," the painter answered with a somewhat sheepish look, "the nurse is taking the child out for a little walk. She said that she thought it needed some air and it was such a lovely day!"

A lovely day indeed! A sharp eastern wind was making the blinds rattle. The streets were full of dust. When I came into the sick room I found it filled with smoke. And the mother lay gasping in her bed.

"The nurse said it would be all right," she whispered to me hoarsely, "but there is such a storm and it is blowing down the chimney and I could not get up and I called, but no one heard me." And she wept bitterly for this was one of the rare days when her customary cheerfulness had left her and she felt very sorry for herself.

I was thoroughly angry with van Rijn and I made no attempt to disguise or hide my feelings. He had remained upstairs in his studio as I knew he would, for he felt so utterly helpless in the midst of these domestic upheavals that most of the time he tried to persuade himself that they did not exist by locking himself up in his studio and keeping his mind engaged upon his work. I now told him in no uncertain tones that something had to be done or I would no longer be responsible.

Then I suddenly realized that he had never yet understood the seriousness of his wife's illness. His thoughts had been so completely concentrated upon his paintings that nothing short of a brutal and point-blank announcement of imminent disaster could break through the man's "unawareness" of his physical surroundings. Now he went to the other extreme. He accused himself bitterly of his neglect, called himself his wife's murderer, carefully washed his brushes in a jar of turpentine, carefully wiped them upon a rag, took off his painter's blouse, turned his easel away from the light, went out of the door, locked the door behind him, went downstairs, sat himself down by the side of his wife's bed, took her hand and said: "Saskia sweet, now I shall be thy nurse." And as far as I know, he never left her room again until she died.

For he loved this woman very deeply and very tenderly. Indeed, he loved her as much as he was ever able to love anything made of flesh and blood, and not of canvas and paint or the gold-gleaming copper of the etcher's plate.

Chapter 8

I BEGIN TO LEARN SOMETHING NEW ABOUT ART WHEN REMBRANDT INVITES ME INTO HIS STUDIO

After this there was some sort of order in the big house on the Breestraat. Van Rijn had put a cot up in a corner of the Big Room. A cleaning woman had been called in and the bottles of acid and the pans with rosin had been removed to a small cabinet to the left of the front door. One or two paintings which smelled too strongly of fresh varnish had been temporarily relegated to the studio upstairs and the peat-fire had been changed for one of wood. It cost a good deal more, but as the man seemed to be making plenty of money, there was no reason why he should worry over a little extra expense. The nurse Geertje was still on the premises, but she carefully kept out of my sight. Three times a day she was permitted to bring the child to see its mother and on those occasions, if mere looks could have killed, I would have died as miserably as Saint Sebastian, for her eyes were as powerful as a whole regiment of Roman archers. But as long as she obeyed my instructions I did not care how little she loved me or how much she hated me. It was my duty to try and prolong the life of my patient for as long as it could be done. She needed rest and regular hours and she now had both, for van Rijn guarded her day and night with a patience and care which were as touching as ineffectual.

For once in his life he had escaped from the dreadful mistress who heretofore had never given him a moment's respite. He did not touch a brush and although I had heard that he had been ordered to do a large piece for the new clubhouse of the Town Guards, I never saw him busy with any sketches. I asked him whether it had been finished and he said no, it had been begun, but it could wait and that people would like it anyway and that he did not care a tinker's dam whether it was ever finished or not if only he could keep his wife alive and get her better. And he used to sit by her side for hours and speak to her softly, which seemed to be the best way to make her go to sleep, for after ten or fifteen minutes she would close her eyes and lie very still with a smile upon her lovely face and she looked so young, not a day older than twenty, that it seemed incredible that she was going to die very soon; but our art has never yet found a way to combat this affliction and so the winter passed and the new year came and I knew that it would be Saskia's last one and I was quite miserable about it when something happened in my own life that made me completely forget the difficulties of the van Rijn household. For we human beings are so complicated that the miseries of our neighbors mean nothing to us the moment we ourselves get into trouble. And it was during this winter that an event occurred which for a time threatened to upset the whole of my existence and which made me an exile from my country for almost a dozen years.

Now it was customary in those days for each of the members of the Surgeons' Guild in town to give a course in anatomy for the benefit of the students of medicine and those leeches and barbers who wanted to prepare themselves a little more thoroughly for their daily tasks. The last time I had given this course of lectures and demonstrations had been in the summer of the year 1636, and now I was told by the Dean of our Guild to prepare myself to teach elementary anatomy once more during the months of March, April and May of the coming year. As I had devoted myself almost entirely to the study of drugs during the last decade, I was a bit rusty and felt the need of refreshing my memory and so I went to Anatomical Hall of the Surgeons' Guild, situated these last eight years on the second floor of the Saint Anthonie Gate, right above the local meat-market, a somewhat unfortunate location as it gave the ribald minded a chance to make rather pointed remarks about this close proximity between butchers and doctors.

I must confess that I had not been near the place since my last lectureship and I was surprised to find one side of the wall entirely filled with a large picture, showing Doctor Nicolaes Pieterszoon in the midst of his students. Pieterszoon had gone far since the day he posed for this portrait, for he had been High Sheriff of our town and had been elected Burgomaster two or three times. Also he had taken the name of Tulp after a large tulip that stood carved in the façade of his house on the Keizersgracht.

The picture struck me very forcibly for in it I found something which I had rarely discovered in any other painting—though I must confess at once that this form of art had never been my strong point. As a child I had always wanted to draw, but my father, with his narrow religious ideas, felt convinced that young people should be trained to do that which was most distasteful to them, rather than be allowed to follow their natural bent. Therefore when it became apparent (from my eternal scribbling on slates and walls and rarer pieces of paper) that I had not only some gift for drawing but an absolute urge to express myself in lines and curves, representing a large variety of subjects from our old maid Jacoba to Jonah being spewed out by the whale, my father then and there decided that I must become a musician.

He did not ask whether I had a good ear, whether I had the sort of fingers one needs to become an experienced player of the violin. He "decided," and in my youth when a father "decided" a child obeyed and that was all there was to it. And so from the age of six until I was fourteen I went twice a week to the room of Signor Tomasso Staccato, player-in-extraordinary and virtuoso of the Chamber to his Grace, the late Marquis Ercole II of Este.

The little Italian, if he spoke the truth, must have been about a hundred years old, for Ercole, as I happened to discover one day in a history of architecture, lived during the first half of the sixteenth century. But such small lies, due to the vanity of simple-minded and otherwise loveable people, are easily pardoned and Signor Staccato was one of the most charming men I have ever met. He played the violin, the viola da gamba and viola da basso with equal dexterity and was besides no mean performer on the clavecin, an instrument of great charm and much more dependable than the viols which in our wet and damp climate are apt to be as moody as the spoiled wives of indulgent husbands.

There was a tradition, when I was a child, that all music teachers were fair game for naughty little boys and that it was the holy duty of the pupils to make the lives of these poor creatures as miserable as they possibly could. And of course music-teachers were supposed to be artists and artists could not handle the birch like ordinary school-masters, for it would have been beneath their dignity to spank any one. Signor Staccato carefully stuck to this rule, that there must be no physical violence mixed with his teaching. But at one time in his career he had acquired a bow made out of steel. Good God! I still shiver when I think of that long, thin steel bow which used to descend upon my fingers with unexpected violence whenever I did not pay sufficient attention. "B flat," he would say in his falsetto voice, "and you played B sharp," and both B sharp and B flat were accompanied by a short, sharp whack across the knuckles with that fatal bow. If that seemed too mild a form of punishment he would discover that the left hand was not in the right position and then it would be hammered into the correct place with a quick succession of rapid blows. "There!—a little further back if you please, my child—a little further back—still a leetle more!" Bang! Bang! Bang!

It was a strange system to make one learn to play the violin. But somehow or other, it worked, and although I had very little talent, I learned to render some of the simpler pieces of Orlando di Lasso and Arcadelt with a certain degree of accuracy. But my playing was something I had learned out of a book. It was not something that came out of the heart, and whereas if I had been allowed to follow my natural inclination, I might have developed into a fair draughtsman, I had now reached the age of forty, an indifferent performer on the viol and hopelessly ignorant of that form of graphic self-expression towards which I had always felt so strongly inclined.

I had in the meantime seen a great many paintings. Our city was full of them. It sometimes seemed to me that our town would burst from sheer riches, like a sack too heavily loaded with grain. Our harbors were more crowded than ever. The streets near the Exchange gave one the impression of a continual county-fair. During the morning hours, when the musicians played on the Dam, one saw as many Turks and Germans and Blackamoors and Frenchmen and Britishers and Swedes, and even people from far-away India, as one did Dutchmen. All roads appeared to be leading to Amsterdam and the great rivers of the world flowed no longer towards the North Pole, but carried their ships right to our port—ships bulging with spices and with silks and with grain and with whale-oil and every product from the shores of the Seven Great Seas.

There were those who believed that these wonderful blessings were being poured into our laps because as a nation we had found special favor in the eyes of God. How or by what means, I failed to understand, for it never struck me that we were much kinder or more generous or more humble than many of our neighbors and those surely were the virtues which ought to have appealed most directly to the Almighty Ruler of Heaven. And as far as I could reason things out (though I was careful to keep this opinion to myself) we owed this prosperity to the fortunate circumstance that we had been obliged to fight so long and so bitterly for our mere existence. The weaker ones among our people had died long ago. They had not been able to survive the endless sieges, the hunger, the anxiety for parents or children who at any moment might be hanged or burned or broken on the wheel. The strong ones had survived. And when the enemy was driven off our territory, those strong ones were so full of energy and enthusiasm, that they had to find some new outlet for their surplus of high spirits. The sight of a map would drive them crazy with excitement. Our small country could no longer hold them. They had forced the King of Spain to his knees. Old Charles of England had his hands full with that psalm-singing rebel called Cromwell. Louis of France was just nobody at all, and his mother and her dear friend the Cardinal, who ruled France between their quarrels and their bickerings, did not count except as agreeable topics for scandal and rather ribald tavern songs. The Swedes and Danes might be bothersome with their silly quarrels, but somehow or other, the straits that led to the Baltic grain fields would be kept open and a curse upon both of them if they tried to interfere with our honest trade. Finally there were the minor potentates of Germany and the Mediterranean, but they were just funny without being bothersome.

And so, for no other reason than that they must ever and again prove to themselves what fine fellows they were, my neighbors must go forth and pull the pigtail of the Emperor of China and singe the beard of the Sultan of Turkey and pull the tails of the polar bears in Spitzbergen and make love to the daughters of the Cacique of Virginia and drink beer in the pagodas of India and light their pipes with the eternal lamp of some holy shrine in Calicut and do any number of scandalous, dangerous and altogether outrageous things which ought to have cost them their lives, but which on the contrary filled their pockets with ducats and made them twice as foolhardy and brave and devil-may-care as they had ever been before. But of course after ten or twenty years of this sort of life, they would grow a little too old for this sort of pastime and then they would retire from the business of storming the gates of Heaven and Hell and would turn respectable and they would buy themselves large and uncomfortable houses in one of the newly laid out parts of the town (and how they were robbed by our good burgomasters who speculated in this sort of real estate as if the whole city were their private property and they were responsible to no one no matter how much they stole from the community) and of course they must show their neighbors how rich they were (what is the fun of having bags and bags and bags of money if no one knows it?) and so they filled their houses with elegant French chairs that weighed a ton and with Spanish chests that only a mule could move and with pictures—rows and rows and still more rows of pictures.

I don't suppose that most of them knew what those pictures were about or cared a straw for them either one way or the other. But they knew that in the older days the abbots of the churches and the princes of Italy and Spain and the barons of England and the nobles of France had adorned their houses with paintings and so of course they must have paintings too. As a result, wherever I went, whether my patient happened to be a simple butcher from the Voldersstraat or a rich Indian merchant living on the fashionable side of the Heerengracht, I found myself surrounded by miles and miles of colored canvases. Some of them were probably very good and a few of them were undoubtedly very bad, but most of them were of a very decent quality, as the Guild of St. Luke maintained the highest possible standards and no one could hope to qualify as a master until he had spent years and years in a very exacting and very difficult apprenticeship.

But for one reason or another, I had never known much about this form of art until I met Rembrandt.

Of course there always had been certain pictures I liked and others I did not like quite so well. I had taken them more or less for granted. A portrait of a man or a woman was that same man or woman made of linseed-oil and diverse pigments instead of flesh and blood. A landscape in a golden frame was not in any way different from that same landscape as I could see it from my own front windows. A lamb-chop or a dead fish in color was still a lamb-chop or a dead fish. It was all very fine and very clever, but it was dead.

And now I suddenly made the discovery that such things could have a soul.

I don't like that word "soul." It smacks too much of those theological discussions I have heard going on around me ever since I was a child, but just now I can't think of any other expression that describes equally well what I mean and so I shall let it go at that and repeat that I suddenly came face to face with the animate quality of supposedly inanimate substances (for what else is a picture but a bit of hemp covered with a messy layer of vegetable matter?) and I was forced to realize that the terms "dead" and "alive" were a little less definite than I had always presumed them to be.

This dawned upon me not slowly and gradually through my conversations with Rembrandt (who however could rarely be induced to talk about his work) or through the contemplation of those paintings by different famous masters with which the walls of his house were covered. The first revelation came to me quite suddenly that morning I went to the rooms of the Surgeons' Guild and stood in front of the portrait of Nicolaes Tulp and half a dozen of my colleagues, busy with some anatomical demonstration. I had known Claes Tulp ever since I had come to Amsterdam and was on pleasant speaking-terms with most of the other men whose faces appeared on the picture. During my student days I had attended hundreds of dissections. I understood that it had become fashionable among the better-known among my colleagues to have themselves painted carving up some unfortunate victim of the gallows or the poor ward. Together with the whole town I had laughed when one rather vain old physician, who had engaged in a bitter professional quarrel with one of the young men, had ordered a portrait of this sort and had bribed the artist to make one of the "students" look like his hated rival, thereby drawing attention to his own superior position in life. And together with the whole country I had roared when the younger man, not to be outdone in civilities of this sort, had favored the Surgeons' Guild with a large canvas (not particularly well done, I am sorry to say) in which he himself was shown "demonstrating" the entrails of a very unappetizing corpse, which bore a striking if somewhat greenish resemblance to the learned Professor who had humiliated him in picture No. 1.

But all of those popular "anatomical lessons" were mere records of past events. They told the spectator that "on such and such a day, in such and such a room, Doctor A., surrounded by Doctors B., C., D. and E., had dissected the mortal remains of the late F. and had found that the praecentral gyrus was still situated between the postcentral gyrus and the superior frontal gyrus (as it ought to be) or had opened up the abdomen and had decided that the patient had died of a distemper of the liver, brought about by years and years of assiduous toping."

Well, I don't know how to explain it, but Rembrandt's picture of Nicolaes Tulp was different, quite different. It did not merely tell a story. It gave tangible expression of an abstract idea—an idea so all-preponderant that the story connected with it dwindled down to insignificant proportions, like the piece of inconsequential parchment upon which the original of the Sermon on the Mount was first written by those who heard the great prophet lay down the law of human forbearance.

Nicolaes Tulp ceased to be a distinguished and fashionable practitioner in the most opulent town of that period—the brilliant son of a rich father—a clever politician who four times in succession got himself appointed to the highest office in his community—a distinguished anatomist and an executive of no mean talent who had reorganized the entire pharmaceutical system of his own time. Instead, he became the living symbol of that divine curiosity which prying into the secrets of nature may some day set the human race free from most of its manifold ills and miseries.

And the faces of the men around him were no longer those of humdrum hard-working leeches, come hither to learn a few things and perhaps improve their standing in the medical world and charge a little higher fees than before and buy their wives new silken dresses for going-to-meeting. Those eyes looked beyond the corpse stretched out before them. Those eyes saw more than the tendons of a single arm. They were gazing into the mystery that underlies all existence—the one hopeless and eternal mystery: "What was it that made those muscles move?"

I am trying to make my own impression clear to myself and I am afraid that I am not succeeding very well. Nor did I derive much support in my speculations from Rembrandt when we were sitting together one night in the etching room. (Saskia had had a bad attack of coughing but at last she had fallen asleep.) I told him what had happened to me and I grew rather rhetorical and used big words and spoke of art and the mission of art, the way I had heard certain painters and sculptors speak when they spent an evening together at a tavern and some one paid for their drinks.

He was interested, but not particularly interested or surprised.

"You always impressed me as an intelligent person, Doctor," he said, "and those little sketches which you have shown me are quite nice. You may not have learned as much as some of the boys who went to art-school, but the Lord was good to you at birth and you started out with a whole lot more than any of those poor devils will ever get, no matter how hard they work. And yet, here you are, forty years old, or even more, and you have never yet discovered what all truly intelligent people have known since the beginning of time."

"And that is?" I asked him.

"That nothing counts in this world except the inner spirit of things."

"Meaning the immortal soul of man?"

"Meaning the immortal soul of everything that was ever created."

"The immortal soul of tables and chairs and cats and dogs and houses and ships?"

"Just so."

"And the immortal soul of books and scissors and flowers and clouds?"

"Exactly."

I was silent for a while. Then I looked at this strange man with the tired eyes and the tired droop of the strong unwieldy shoulders.

"How many people in all the world will be able to understand that?"

He smiled and lifted up both hands in a gesture of resignation. Then he answered me slowly: "Well, perhaps three or four in every hundred. At the most, four. In very exceptional cases, five."

"And the others?"

"They will never know what we are talking about, but they will have their revenge."

"In what way?"

"They will let us starve to death."

The conversation was rapidly getting beyond my depth.

"Good night," I said, and held out my hand. He took it.

"Good night, Doctor, and thank you and if you have a few moments after dinner to-morrow, say at three or two-thirty, I wish you would come here. There is something I want to show you." And with that he showed me through the hall and bade me good night.

It was a dark night and it was raining. In the house of the Rabbi, a few doors further down, a light was still burning. Menasseh ben Israel was busy with his presses. He was always busy with those presses and people said he printed his books from golden letters. He was a clever man of great learning, a simple and loveable character. For a moment I thought that I would drop in and see what he was doing. But just then the tower of the South Church struck twelve. Bang—bang—bang—bang—

One could write a book about that, I thought. The spirit of the hour-glass, the spirit of the clock. Bang—bang—bang—bang—birth, life and death—happiness, sickness and health—hope and despair—bang—bang—bang—bang.

It was a good mood in which to go to sleep. I pulled my cloak around me a little closer and I turned the corner.

The door of a tavern opened and closed. Drunken voices filled the street.

"Lemme tell you," a man was drooling into the ear of another. "Now, what I am talking about, when a thing is so, it is so, and not otherwise, see? and when a man is so, he is so and that is all there is to him, see?"

"Sure, Jan, I see," the other answered.

"That's good," the tipsy philosopher volunteered, "for if you didn't agree with me that what is so, is so, I'd have knocked your damn head between your shoulders, see?"

The other one said that he did.

I left them to their discussion and I went home.

It was still raining when I lifted the latch.

Chapter 9

REMBRANDT PAINTS A VERY LARGE PICTURE WHICH HE EXPECTS TO MAKE HIM FAMOUS

The next morning I spent at the hospital. Then I went home for dinner and a little after three I called at the Breestraat. The patient was having one of her bad days. Nevertheless she had insisted upon leaving her bed and was sitting in a chair, propped up with many pillows. The child was on her lap. The nurse was busy hanging some clothes to dry near the fire. I had told her not to do the washing in the same room with the sick woman, but of course she had not obeyed my instructions. She grumbled something when I entered, picked up the baby's things, threw them into a wicker basket, slammed the door behind her and left.

"She has one of her terrible days, when I can do nothing with her," Saskia complained. "Sometimes I almost think she is mad."

"I am sorry," I replied, "your husband ought to have discharged her long ago."

"I know it. But he hates to be bothered with such things. He is a good man and he tries to interest himself in the household. But his heart is in his work. And she is very devoted to the baby and you know how little I can do. But soon I shall be better. I feel ever so much stronger than I did a few weeks ago. I looked at myself in the mirror to-day. My cheeks were as red as before I had this attack of a bad cold. Don't you think I look well?"

I assured her that I had never seen her look so beautiful. Nor was it necessary for me to lie. The poor woman had a raging fever and her cheeks were flushed a deep, dark crimson. What she had taken for a sign of new health was merely the harbinger of death. Four months from that day, or at least five or six, she would be resting beneath a slab of granite in the Old Church. It was our duty to make her last few days on earth as happy as possible. I said something nice about the child, who was a very fine boy, but like all children, had an instinctive dislike of sick people and was trying hard to get away.

"Isn't he lovely?" she asked, trying to lift him up but finding him too much for her slender arms. "Oh, he is such a darling! And we are going to make a sailor of him."

"Not a great painter, like his father?"

She slowly shook her head. "No," she said, "I want him to be happy and carefree, and I don't believe artists ever are."

"But surely you cannot doubt that Rembrandt is happy! He has his work. He has you"—I noticed my mistake and hastily tried to correct myself.—"He has you and the baby and . . ." But here she interrupted me. "You were right the first time," she said. "He has his work and in his spare time, he has me and then he dresses me up to look like a princess (which I am not) or like a fairy-queen (which I am even less) and I become part of his work!"

"The most beautiful part," I suggested with a smile.

"Oh, well, it is very kind of you to say that but all the same, I am only part of his work, and never part of his life."

"You became part of his life when you gave him this lovely child."

She looked at me with a puzzled expression. All her cheerfulness left her and her high spirits made way for a sudden fit of melancholia. "Do you really believe that?" she asked me with a puzzled look. "For if I didn't think so myself, I would want to die to-morrow. Now I am contented to wait until the day comes, and I am afraid it will come soon enough."

I tried to contradict her with the usual foolish stories which are the stock-in-trade of our profession, but just then Rembrandt entered the room. He was in great anger and was swearing most heartily.

"The idiot!" he shouted. "The perfectly hopeless, clumsy idiot! I thought that I had at last shown him how to use that press. The last time he soaked the paper until it turned to pulp as soon as one touched it. And now he has put the plate underneath the roller without using any felt. The copper is bent like a hoop. I shall have to do the whole thing over again. I might easily have sold a hundred copies. Old Dominie Anslo is always good for a hundred copies, and the Mennonites don't mind what they spend when it comes to pictures of their preachers."

Saskia held out her hand, a very white and very thin hand, but lovely of shape. "Come and sit down here for a moment, my dear," she asked him. "Why don't you tell the boy to go home? If he is just a common nuisance, you surely don't want him around in your place."

At once her husband's anger vanished. "I had thought of it," he answered, "but the next one would probably be just as bad or even worse. And this one pays me a hundred florins a year for the privilege of being one of my pupils. But I will tell you what I will do. Don't we need some kindling for the fire?"

"We always do."

"Very well. I shall turn him out into the yard to cut wood. I shall tell him that the exercise is good for his biceps and that a painter needs strong muscles. A brilliant idea. And I owe it to you. If I had been left to my own devices for another two minutes, I would have fired him, and now, my good doctor, you and I will take a little walk and I will show you something and perhaps I will tell you something—that is to say, if my wife will let you go for a few minutes?"

Poor Saskia made a faint effort to smile, but it was not a very successful one. The color had once more left her cheeks. She looked wasted and coughed terribly while we carried her back to bed.

"She ought not to be doing so much," I warned when we were out on the street.

Rembrandt shook his head. "I know it," he said, "but how can I keep her in bed when she insists upon getting up? Besides, if I didn't help her, she would call for the nurse."

"I thought you would get rid of the woman?"

"I wanted to. And I tried to. Really, I tried very hard. But it was rather difficult. You see, I am very busy and it would have taken a great deal of time . . ."

I understood. This man knew only one thing in the world and that was his work. He had acquired a household. Sooner or later, we all do, and most of us manage to muddle through. But this poor devil, who was a giant when it came to his own particular form of art, was a miserable little dwarf as soon as he found himself face to face with the silly troubles of daily life. He was willing to try and solve problems of light and dark which no one before him had ever dared to tackle. But when he was called upon to read the riot act to a shrew of a nurse who was a menace to the health of his wife and child, he got frightened and ran away.

Well, we all are as we are and what we are and there is no use trying to change the human race from one thing to another, for it just can't be done. And with this wise reflection I followed my host into the street when he stopped and asked me:

"Do you mind, if before we go to the Amstel we take a short walk through the Jewish quarter? You will see some rare sights." And I answered, "Of course not," and so instead of turning to the left we turned to the right and soon we found ourselves in a world that was as different from the rest of the city as the moon from the sun.

The reason for this strange development in our city was a very simple one. Forty years ago this suburb had been a swamp. Later on it had been drained after a fashion but the houses were still very damp and so they could be rented to no one but the poorest among the poor. Of these there were vast quantities, for ever since we had declared ourselves independent from Spain, our town had been a haven of refuge to tens of thousands of people from every part of the world. Some of them had come because they had heard that we were rich beyond the wildest dreams of avarice and that therefore it was much easier to make a living in Holland than anywhere else. Others belonged to one of the innumerable sects that had sprung up immediately after the Reformation. These had hastened to the great and free Republic because they either hoped to escape persecution at the hands of their enemies or (as happened quite as frequently) because they thought that in a country where the magistrates were reported to be very lenient, they might be able to do a little persecuting of their own.

Then during the eighties of the last century, Portugal had been annexed by Spain and of course the first thing King Philip had done was to pass an edict by which he had deprived his newly acquired territory of the only people who ever thought it worth their while to do a little work.

My grandmother used to tell me how in the nineties, when the first of the Portuguese immigrants began to arrive, people used to flock to the shores of the Y whenever it was reported that a ship with fugitives was about to enter the harbor. And she described the terrible conditions on board those vessels, men and women and children all huddled together with their few belongings (they never were given more than twenty-four hours' warning before they were expelled and were obliged to sell their houses and real estate and their merchandise during those hours besides doing their packing) and how quite often when the hatches were opened it was found that half of them had died or were on the point of passing away from lack of food and drink and fresh air and how the survivors would be taken on shore and given milk and bread and were taken to the houses of private citizens to recuperate, among great manifestations of horror and pity.

And my grandfather, with a noble oath, was apt to interrupt her recital at this point to fulminate against the Reverend Clergy who denounced that sort of public charity because the Jews, some fifteen hundred years before, had killed one of their own prophets. "As if," so the old man tried to defend the Sanhedrin, "there has ever been a people that has not murdered its great men!" And then the old lady would bid him remember that he was a Christian and must not say such things and he would roar with laughter and would say, "A Christian? Me? I am a rebel, a good, honest rebel, and I have fought all my life and I have cursed all my life, and I never let a chance go by to get hold of an honest drink or a dishonest woman, and I have killed my enemies and I have loved my friends and I have hated the Pope of Rome and that bastard Pope of Geneva. Long live the Prince! and when I die, I shall go straight up to God and I shall tell him just what I think of him, and everything he has done to all those I loved and then undoubtedly I shall go to hell and I shall be a rebel there as I have been on earth, but thank the Lord, it won't be as cold there as among the harp-strumming little angels with their freshly laundered petticoats!"

And then these two charming old people would look at each other with great and sincere affection and being very ancient and rather feeble, they would smile a pleasant smile and before you could count three, they would be fast asleep, holding each other's hand as if they had been married only day before yesterday.

They have been dead now for a good many years and the former immigrants have grown rich and have moved to a more fashionable neighborhood. But every year some new recruits arrive from foreign lands and in the part of the town through which Rembrandt took me, one still hears more Spanish and Portuguese and Yiddish and German than Dutch; the shops still look like bazaars and the food continues to smell like the devil. And as for the women who live there, for reasons unknown to the astonished Gentiles, they still persist in shaving their heads and bedecking themselves with wigs that are as silly as they are unbecoming.

I had rarely visited this Little Jerusalem, for these people have their own doctors (very good ones, too, though they favor some extraordinary remedies) and whenever I had time for a little fresh air, I preferred to go to the harbor and watch the ships come in. But Rembrandt seemed to know this part of the town by heart and was apparently on speaking terms with half the population, for wherever we went, he was greeted with great obsequiousness and caps were taken off to "der Meister" as if he had been a burgomaster or some great official instead of being merely a painter.

But he explained it to me at once. "Don't think for a moment that they are so civil because they have the slightest understanding for my work. I am a good customer. I pay cash whenever I can and I don't bargain more than is necessary. That is all." And then he told me that this ghetto was a veritable treasure-house and contained more color than all the rest of Amsterdam put together.

"You know how it is," he said, stepping aside to avoid the contents of an unmentionable piece of domestic furniture which was being emptied from a second-story window, "our civilization is drab and gray. We seem to regard color as an expression of the sinful flesh. Our men are dressed in black, our women are dressed in black, our children are dressed in black, our churches look like white-washed sepulchers. When we give a party, we all sit around with sour faces until we get very drunk, and then we behave as Jan Steen shows us in his pictures, and a clever boy he is, too, even if he came from Leyden, the same as I do. I wish that I knew something more about my own family. I don't mean my brothers and sisters. They are good people, but they don't interest me, and to tell you the truth, they are pretty common-place. My grandparents, too, were dull, small trades-people from a village near Leyden. They had never been anywhere. They had never seen anything. But how about my great-grandparents or still further back? Was there ever an Italian in our family or even a Fleming? For they tell me that the Flemings are much more lively than we are. I bought a picture of Rubens once and it was wonderful! Then again, our religion may have something to do with it. It is hard to tell. I have known a few old people who could remember back to the days before Amsterdam and Leyden had gone reformed. They say that life was much gayer then than now. It was not very pleasant to have quite so many priests and deacons and monks wandering aimlessly through the streets, but if you left them alone, they left you alone and provided you went to mass once in a long while, no questions were asked. To-day, every time you smile, some one comes around to read you a couple of chapters from Job, just as a warning. Of course, in the end, the Church had to go. We are a slow-moving people and we don't think very fast but at least we think. All that had to disappear, but I sometimes wonder whether I would not have been happier if I had been born in Italy."

"Did you ever think of going there?"

"Of course I did. Every youngster who paints thinks of going to Italy at some time in his career."

"But you never went?"

"No. I thought of it seriously in '31. I even talked it over with Jan Lievens when we were studying together in Leyden. We could have got the money too. That malt-mill of my father was not doing badly at all and there were some rich people who were taking an interest in us. But it seemed a waste of time. I was very unhappy in those days and did not think that I would live long. I wanted to use every hour of daylight and could not afford to waste a couple of months trying to get to a place where the daylight probably was not so very different from what it is here. Of course there have been some great masters in Italy. But I can see their work just as well in Amsterdam as in Rome. They bring it to us by the ship loads. I have copied quite a number of them. They are being sold as genuine, but, then, our art dealers would sell pictures by St. Luke himself if they saw a chance to make a profit. Funny that the only apostle who was not a Jew should have done so much to make the Jews rich, with all due respect to my dear cousin Uylenburgh, for he is in the art business too. And so am I, in a way, for a few days ago I let him have another thousand guilders. What he has done with it, I don't know, but I will sell you my claim for half of what I paid!"

While this conversation was going on, we had almost reached the outskirts of the Jewish quarter and I asked Rembrandt whether he hadn't forgotten that he was bound upon some errand.

"I know," he answered, "but that is in still another part of the town. I just instinctively turn to this warren whenever I go out. But I am after something better to-day than I can find here. I think that I have got hold of a genuine bit by Michelangelo. I have only seen it once. Then they asked too much for it. It is a small thing, the head of a child. If they will let me have it for fifteen hundred guilders, I shall take it."

He mentioned the sum as casually as if it had been a couple of shillings. I had heard that he got a great deal more for his portraits than any one else and of course everybody knew that he had married a rich wife, but I was not quite prepared for such nonchalance. The habits of my very simple childhood stuck to me pretty closely and I asked whether that was not a great deal of money for one picture. He seemed a bit surprised at the question but answered that he did not think so.

"I suppose, when you look at it from one point of view, it is a good deal of money. But Michelanglo was a very wonderful painter. No, I don't think fifteen hundred guilders is too much. I am getting more than that myself."

"For a single picture?"

"Yes, and if you will have patience with me for a few minutes longer, I will show it to you. But first I must go down the cellar for a little light."

The "cellar" to which he referred when we came to it proved to be the basement of the old archery-house on the Singel. The archers had long since been blown out of existence by the musketeers and their club-house was now merely a sort of better class tavern, where one was allowed to look at the pictures of famous old warriors in exchange for a bottle of wine or a few glasses of beer. The top floor of the building was rented to a glove merchant who used the attics to dry his skins and in the basement (as I now saw for the first time) there was an antique shop, run by a Jew whose name was mentioned on a sign outside the door, but it was so covered with dirt which obliging children had smeared upon it that I could not read it. This worthy man was garbed in a long cloak that reached to the floor and beyond, so that he was continually tripping over his own garment. It looked like a relic from the flood and had seen very little water since that day Mount Ararat once more raised its summit from among the waves. As the rooms were very dark and the owner of the premises hid his face behind very black and very bushy whiskers, one was continually bumping up against him and he was forever begging one's pardon in a jargon compounded of two thirds Portuguese, one sixth German and one sixth Dutch with a liberal sprinkling of what I took to be the original language of King David's psalms.

I discovered to my great amazement that Rembrandt not only understood this home-made dialect, but actually spoke it with great fluency for once the product of Michelangelo's brush had been produced from a corner where the darkness was not only visible but also tangible, he addressed himself to the hirsute dealer in such an eloquent mixture of all the less current vituperations of the different tongues just enumerated, that I was quite sure the two men must come to blows at any moment, in which case I decided that I would not take sides, but would make for the exit with all possible speed. But nothing happened. On the contrary, after half an hour's animated conversation, during which (as far as I was able to comprehend) frequent references were made to the immediate ancestors of the contending parties, they separated in the best of spirits. Rembrandt had succeeded in forcing the price down by one hundred florins. But the art-dealer from his side had persuaded him to buy the frame, which he swore was worth two hundred guilders, but which he would let him have for half the amount. The whole transaction therefore, as far as I could see, remained in the statu quo ante. Each party to the deal, however, seemed profoundly convinced that he had got the better of his opponent. Wherefore everybody was happy and we parted with mutual expressions of esteem and a promise to return as soon as there was another bargain to be had.

The fresh air was pleasant after this entrance to purgatory. I awaited some explanation of the mysterious proceedings that had taken place in the catacombs of art, and I got one.

"I wanted that picture," Rembrandt confessed, "and I wanted it badly. The old Jew asked too much. I got it for a hundred guilders less."

"But the frame! How about that frame? He charged you a hundred guilders for it."

The poor painter looked puzzled, like a child that has been caught in some foolish expenditure of a hard-earned stiver. But he quickly recovered. "After all," he asked in a somewhat querulous tone, as if I had unjustly accused him of wasting his son's patrimony, "what is the money for in this world of ours except to spend it? Fifteen hundred guilders is rather a large sum. But next week, next month, at the very least, I shall have eighteen hundred florins coming in for some work I have just finished. And I did want that painting and I wanted it badly!"

With which irrefutable piece of logic we retraced our steps whence we had come, crossed the Rokin and then turned to the right until we reached the Amstel. In the olden days, before the great expansion that followed in the wake of our declaration of independence, this had been the outer limit of the city's territory. There had been only a few scattered houses along the banks of the stream (it really was a canal, but our poets loved to compare it to the Tiber or the Seine or the Thames) and the gardens and open spaces had been much in demand by the archers of the old militia companies who used to come together here on Sunday afternoons for target practice.

During the latter half of the fifteenth century, when all the little cities of our country fought each other (just as the nations nowadays are forever making war upon their neighbors) a heavy bulwark had been erected at this point. The name of one enormous stone tower which still stood intact and was called "Swijght-Utrecht" or "Keep-Quiet-Utrecht," showed only too clearly from what side danger had threatened our forefathers. The Bishop of Utrecht was no longer a menace for he had ceased to exist shortly after the construction of this dungeon and the walls now extended far beyond the other side of the Amstel. But the brick monster continued to stand where it had been built in the year 1482. But it was now a perfectly peaceful part of the famous Kloveniersdoelen, the meeting-place and club-house of the culverin-carrying town companies which had succeeded the archers of medieval fame as soon as gunpowder had been invented.

During the great war of independence, those town companies had rendered the most signal services. Without them we never would have been able to gain our freedom, for the German and the Swiss and English mercenaries whom we hired to fight for us from time to time were professionals who had nothing much to gain and everything to lose and in nine cases out of ten they disappeared when the fighting began and did not return until the signal had been given to begin looting.

Of course twenty years ago, when all those things I am here writing down happened, there was no longer a single enemy within a hundred miles of Amsterdam, except an occasional prisoner-of-war, brought in by the fleet. But every self-respecting young man thought it his duty to join one of the town companies and devote some of his spare time to the practice of arms. That many of those militia regiments were rapidly degenerating into mere social organizations, without the slightest military ambition or strategic value, was becoming more evident almost every day. But such a development seems inevitable (if the history I have read means anything at all, which I sometimes doubt) and in order to be perfectly fair, I ought to state that several crack companies took their duties just as seriously as their fathers and grandfathers had done before them and certainly in the year 1650 when William II made his dastardly attack upon our beloved city, they proved that they were fully able to handle the situation and forced the foolish princeling to return whence he had come with no other glory than a pair of wet feet. And during the early forties (and please remember that I am telling you about certain events that happened in the year 1642 and therefore a very long time ago) there was a sudden return of interest in the noble profession of arms.

The different companies were trying hard to attract desirable recruits and all the social and economic advantages of associating one's self with this or that or the other captain were carefully enumerated and made a subject of conversation in all of the better-class taverns. (The more notorious dram-shops were equally interested, but from a somewhat different angle, as the town-militia was also the town-police and the sworn enemy of all lawbreakers and rioters.)

Now since the beginning of time, it has been the proud privilege of the children of Mars to be more resplendent in their outer raiment than ordinary citizens, who follow a peaceful if more lucrative and useful profession. Nature, when she began her interesting task, bestowed her gifts of beauty and attractiveness almost exclusively upon the male members of the different sorts of animals. I do not claim that I have an inner knowledge of her secret intentions, but she probably thought that it would be better for the future development of her menagerie if the males should be more attractive than the females and if the competition for favors should not come too exclusively from one side. But when she finally came to the human race, she had either grown tired or had become discouraged, for she changed her policy completely and arranged things in such a way that among us mortals the woman should be the attractive member of society, while the man might look like anything or nothing at all. The women of course have made the best of their advantage while we poor men are still trying (though mostly in vain) to find some compromise by which we would be able to make ourselves a little less painfully plain than we were apparently meant to be. Scholars and other learned doctors put on beautiful silken garments whenever they can find an excuse for doing so. Judges affect scarlet and ermine. I have never seen a priest of the old church in his official garments, for they are not allowed in our city, but from the stories of my grandmother, I judge that the multi-colored coat of Joseph was as nothing compared to an archbishop or a cardinal in full canonicals. That old church, by the way, was very wise in more ways than one and it recognized the need of the average human being to revel in color once in a while by providing a special season when every clodhopper and lout was allowed to dress up like a royal duke and strut about like a lovesick peacock.

But the soldiers have understood the value of a gaudy appearance better than any one else. With them, it probably was a matter of necessity. Their profession, except in times of peace, offered few advantages. Endless marches along hot and dusty roads, bad sleeping-quarters, poor food and the danger every moment of losing an arm or a leg or getting a ball through one's brain. There had to be some compensation to attract the unwary and beguile the simple minded into taking the king's shilling.

Of course this could have been accomplished by raising the men's wages, but then the officers no longer would have been able to regard their regiments as profitable sources of revenue and they would have asked for better pay for themselves and all the royal treasuries of Europe would have gone bankrupt. Also as an inducement to enlistening discipline might have been slightly relaxed and there might have been a little less flogging and hanging, but this would have been impossible in view of the sort of people who took most readily to the business of organized murder. The easiest way out was to allow these honorable jail-birds and paupers (and when I call them that I surely offer no insult to the average members of a regiment of mercenaries) to garb themselves as if they were really fine fellows, instead of being mere deplorable cannon-fodder. This gave them a feeling of superiority and the average man will go through almost any hardships and will suffer every form of indignity and degradation if in the end he is allowed to feel himself (if only for a moment) superior to his fellow-beings.

This incidentally accounts for the noble behavior of so many criminals on the scaffold. By assuming an attitude of noble resignation, they place themselves hand and foot above the mob of jeering hoodlums who surround the gallows and they jump off the ladder, saying to themselves, "Ah, what a fine fellow I am, compared to this rabble!" It also accounts for the readiness of hundreds of thousands of poor yokels who leave their plows and the simple pleasures of an humble rustic life to prance about dressed in plumes and gold braid for one hour each day, though they are forced to obey the whims of a drunken and bullying drill-sergeant for the other twenty-three.

I hope that all my medical diagnoses may be as correct as this estimate of the motives that inspired the brave heroes who used to strut down our streets whenever we were obliged to hire extra troops for our operations against the Spaniards. It will be understood that I am not now talking of the ordinary citizen who, exasperated by the endless hangings and quarterings of our dear Liege Lord finally rose in open rebellion.

They fought because they had to, just as they would go and work on the dikes whenever their city was threatened by floods. It was a matter of live or die and quite naturally they preferred to take a chance at living, even if they had to expose themselves to a little occasional dying in order to accomplish this very sensible purpose. But there was very little outer glory connected with their martial careers. I am too young to have known many of these men myself, but I have seen their pictures, honest, simple citizens, butchers and bakers and shipowners with honest, plain faces and great big hands that could cleave an ox or pull a sail as well as the best of them. Their officers would perhaps wear an orange scarf to set them apart from the rest of their men, but that would be the only bit of color in the whole picture.

But to-day, whenever a company sallies forth to guard a gate that really needs no guarding, or patrol a wall that is as safe as my own back yard, both the common soldiers and the lieutenants and captains resemble warships on parade. They have plumes on their hats and gold braid on their coats and they wrap themselves up in yards and yards of colored scarfs and every sixth man waves a flag that is as big as a house and the servant girls and the scullery maids leave their kitchens to stare at these gallant heroes and to admire them and to giggle at them and the poor fools feel flattered by these basement attentions and spend a night shivering in a guard-house (instead of snoring comfortably by the side of their spouses) and they will repeat the performance next week and week after and week after merely for this short period of popular glory. And when they get themselves painted, they pose around a table that looks as if great King Louis of France were entertaining the Ambassador from the Republic of Venice, and they are all of them dressed up as if they were the keepers of the harem of the Grand Padisha of Turkey and they dine on dishes that our grandfathers would have regarded as the last word in useless luxury and altogether they disport themselves as if they were the sort of young British lords who once in a while honor our city with their visit and they tell me that the artists have to send to Paris to get some of the gilt that has to be laid on the swords and arquebuses.

All of which many and varied meditations passed rapidly through my brain as we were walking in the general direction of the Kloveniersdoelen, for I knew that it was used as a meeting place by some of the smartest regiments and that the captains' rooms were filled with pictures by van der Helst and Govaert Slinck and Claes Elias and I feared that Rembrandt, having started the day bright and early by buying himself a genuine Michelangelo, might wind up the afternoon by dragging me through one of those things I dread most of all—a picture gallery.

And when he stood in front of the entrance-gate and he said: "Let us go in here a moment," the worst of my fears was about to be realized. These buildings had been added to so often and they were by now composed of so many remnants of walls and towers, bits of old walls and decapitated pieces of even older private houses, that one almost needed a guide to find one's way. But Rembrandt opened the door of the taproom (no military club-house has ever been perfect without a well-provided bar) and said: "It has been quite a walk. You will like a glass of beer. I am not a member of this honorable guild, but I have worked here on and off for quite a long time and they let me use their common-room. Come in."

We sat down and Rembrandt ordered two mugs of beer. Then he said: "You must be hungry! You are not? Do you mind if I eat something? The meals at home have become a little sketchy since Saskia was taken sick and I have had nothing all day and so if you will pardon me . . ." and he asked that they bring him a plate of fried eggs and one of fresh herring and some bread and he went after the food with a most excellent appetite and between the beer and the fish he told me why he had brought me there.

"I don't want to talk about myself," he said, "but these last four years have been rather lonely and I have had a pretty hard struggle, what with an ailing wife, a pretty difficult family-in-law, a new house which is really much too big and expensive for me, and a few other little items with which I shan't bother you, as you probably have troubles enough of your own. But I shall tell you something and then you will know what is going to happen. It is always pleasant to be on the inside of things. It makes one feel that one really is somebody. And something very interesting is going to happen here soon. Are you sure you don't want any of this herring? It is exceedingly good. But never mind, and here is my story.

"You know that I come from very simple folk. And you know how they look upon such things in our Republic. In Flanders, they think so much of Rubens that they make him an ambassador. They tell me there is a man in Spain by the name of Velasquez who is said to be the greatest painter that ever lived. I have never seen anything he did, but I have heard that he can make an empty room look really like an empty room and that is the hardest thing of all. I may learn to do that too, but it will take me another twenty years of practice. But I hear that this Don Diego Velasquez is held in such great esteem that he is allowed to sit in the presence of the King, when all other courtiers, even the highest nobles in the land, must stand and do homage. And when he is in Rome, the Pope is happy to receive him and invite him to live in the private villa of the Medici family.

"Well, we can't all be the same in this world and every country handles such matters according to its own notions of what is right and suitable and what is not. Here people look upon an artist as a better-class laboring man. Some of us make money. None of us are rich, but some of us get fairly good wages, not any better than those which a dike-worker or a book-keeper or a baker's assistant makes with much less trouble. And so our parents don't mind and are rather proud of their little boy who is sometimes allowed to associate with gentlemen, that is, when he is allowed to paint their portraits, though of course they always fear that in the end he will share the fate of Roghman or old Hercules Seghers and die in the alms-house or break his neck in a grog-shop.

"That these poor fellows came to such an end because their neighbors were too dull to appreciate them, that never seems to dawn upon them. They think it a good joke that Hercules finally had to paint his pictures on his old shirts and the back of his old breeches and had to sell his etchings to the butchers of the Rokin for wrapping-paper. 'My steak came this morning, packed in Tobias and the Angel,' says one, and his friend roared with laughter and answers: 'I bought a landscape the other day, paid five guilders for it—it was on a piece of the old man's pants. Ha! ha! ha!' And they go and put a thousand or ten thousand guilders in a 'sure' investment that some one sells them on the say-so of his grandfather who knew a man who had met a Spaniard or a Pole who had told him that he had heard from some one, whose name he could not remember, that it was a good thing.

"You know this to be so and I know it to be so and all of us know it to be so, but I for one had seen enough of poverty not to want any more of it than I had to have. Some people can stand misery better than others. I loved old Seghers. He was a great man. Hercules has forgotten more about painting and etching than most of us will ever know. I was a youngster and he was quite an old man when I first came to Amsterdam and I did not see him often. But one night I went to his place with a few friends. A bare room with a horrible-looking woman in one corner doing something to a large stone jar filled with vegetables. She seemed to be his wife. Half a dozen dirty children on the floor and the old man with a pleasant bun on, completely oblivious of the mess around him, working at a storm, as fine a piece of painting as I have ever seen. He had fastened it against the wall with two nails and he stood in front of it. The wife wanted to know what we had come for and asked me whether we were sheriffs?

"That afternoon, the Jew with whom he did business had brought him back his last etching, the finest piece of work he had ever done. Sorry, but he could not sell it. And Hercules had taken a copper file and had cut the plate into four pieces because he could not afford a new one and must work. He was crazy with work. He worked morning, noon and night. They say he was a drunkard. Well, drunken people don't paint the sort of pictures he did. But sometimes it got to be too much for him and then he would take a glass or two, just enough not to hear the bawling wife and the howling infants.

"That afternoon, it seemed, while she had gone out to pawn his easel, he had stolen the last sheet out of the children's bed and had cut it up to be used as canvas. I shall spare you the rest. I was not very rich then and, anyway, he had nothing for sale as everything had been either pawned or had been bartered away for butter and eggs and milk for the children. Afterwards, with a great deal of trouble, I got hold of six of his pictures. You may have seen them in my house. One of them is hanging in the front hall and one in the side room and a few others in the little alcove behind the side room. I keep them all over the house, in the first place because I like them immensely and in the second place because they are a constant reminder. They take me back to the day when I stood in Seghers' stable (it really wasn't a house he was living in) and said to myself: 'Rembrandt, my boy, you are a good deal of a dreamer and you are apt to do foolish things. Well, do all the foolish things you want, but see that you get paid well in the meantime. A plumber and a coppersmith get paid for what they do. See to it that you get paid too.'

"Besides, I need a lot of money. I like color around me. I need it. I would have died in a place like that of Hercules in less than a week. I want to buy things. I hate haggling. I hate to beat old Jacob down for a couple of guilders. And when I go to an auction and see something I would like for my collection, I go ahead and let them push up the price and I know that in the end I will probably pay more than the thing is worth, but I have to have it, and that is all, for when I want something, I want it then and there and not next week or a year later. I must be able to make experiments if I am to do good work. Saskia is a lovely woman. You ought to have seen her a couple of years ago when she was still a girl and before she got so sick. But I must try her out, test her, so to speak, see what is in her, dress her up in silks and satins and hang pearls on her and rubies, paint her a hundred different ways. Poor child, I don't think she always enjoyed it. But she was very good-natured about it. I needed that sort of foolishness to find out what I could do and she said yes. She is really very sweet. She always says yes and I suppose at times, I am very unreasonable. All that is, however, beside the point and I will tell you what I am going to do. Want to smoke?"

The herring was gone and the fried eggs were gone and the beer was gone and I said: "Yes, I would enjoy a pipe." And so Rembrandt ordered two fresh mugs and two pipes of tobacco and then he leaned his elbows on the table and leaned over to me and went on:

"You know that I have been doing a great deal of portrait work. I could give you names, but they are neither here nor there. People came to me to sit for their portraits. I painted them and they paid me four or five and sometimes even six hundred guilders. I don't know why. Even van der Helst never got more than that amount for a picture as big as a house with a dozen or twenty figures and that meant a lot more work than I had to do, for each one of those twenty fools would think that he was the handsomest of the crowd and would insist upon being done in great detail. So you see I was about the only one who had no kick coming. I was even asked to do some pictures for the Prince. I don't think he liked them any too well for I believe that His Highness is more interested in the pretty ladies of Jake Jordaens than in religious subjects and I hear that he is going to build himself a new palace in the woods and that he is going to use no one but Flemish painters. But that may be just studio gossip. You know how much there is of that nowadays and I finally got paid, though I had the devil's own time collecting and I would never have got a penny if it had not been that My Lord Huygens, who thinks all the world of my work, had got the bills approved.

"But what I mean is this: everybody had heard of me and it became the fashion for rich people to have themselves painted by me.

"'Very well,' I used to say to myself, 'I shall paint you and sometimes I shall even paint you as you want to be painted.'

"For I needed the money. Our first child was coming. There was the new house into which I wanted to move (I had to mortgage it rather heavily) and there were all the other things I wanted. People used to say that I was a lucky devil because I had married a rich wife. But Saskia was not rich. There were nine children and old Uylenburgh had been too busy with politics to pay much attention to his estate. I have never seen him, for he died some eight years before I met my wife.

"The old fellow was quite a famous character. You must have heard of him. He was dining with Prince William the day he was called away from the table and was shot by what's-his-name, that friend of the Jesuits whom King Philip hired to murder him. Then he was burgomaster of Leeuwarden and sheriff but he was so busy with public affairs he had very little time to look after his own interests.

"When he died, each of the children was supposed to get about forty thousand guilders. Quite a sum, I grant you, and my neighbors of course added an extra couple of zero's and made it four hundred thousand. They might have made it forty million florins, for all the actual cash we ever saw. For everything was invested in farms and houses and as soon as we wanted to divide the estate, the farms could not be rented and the houses could not be sold. And of course I am living here in Amsterdam and the other heirs are living in Friesland, a couple of days away.

"Did you ever have anything to do with Frisians? A strange race. The most obstinate and pig-headed people there are in the world. And stingy! My God! Only a couple of years ago I had to go to law to get a few thousand guilders that an aunt had left her in '34. Six whole years of waiting. When we finally got it, the other heirs tried to cheat us out of the interest—out of six years' accumulated interest—and I had to hire a lawyer and spend two hundred guilders on fees before my wife could pry a penny loose from those dear relatives of hers.

"They are a nice tribe! They kiss every stiver a dozen times before they spend it and when I made a lot of money painting portraits and bought a few pictures and statues and things (just because I liked them, and after all, it was my money I spent and not theirs, so why should they worry?) they must jabber to all the neighbors about the 'scandalous way in which I was squandering Saskia's patrimony' and I had to go to law once more and sue them for libel and then they perjured themselves all over the place and the judge said that he could not do anything and threw the case out of court.

"Did that stop them? Of course not. They went right on and I had to bring suit once more in Friesland before I heard the last of this famous 'squandering of my wife's patrimony.' Squandering, indeed! When I need thirteen thousand guilders cash to buy the house in the Breestraat, I have to give notes that will keep me busy for the rest of my days. Do you think I would have done that if I could have laid my hands on a little cash? No, that story of the poor painter and the rich wife is so much moonshine. We are not poor, and I have enough to keep living the way I want to live, but I intend to be careful.

"Only you know how it is! I get interested in a subject. I see or rather I feel a lot of things others don't see or don't feel. I put them into my picture and the man who sat for his portrait and considered himself a fine fellow gets angry, says the likeness is not there or I have given him a look in his eyes that will prove to his neighbors that he is a miser or mean to his wife, and in the end he either refuses the picture or he will offer to pay me half of what he promised.

"This won't do, for just now I am not only painting for the sake of my 'art'—whatever that may mean—though you will hear a lot about it if to-night you will go to the Dirty Towel or the Dark Cellar and will listen to the brethren of the brush who come together there every evening to drink their beer and talk of their plans. No, just now I want to make all the money I can. I have got to pay for that house and Saskia will probably be sick for quite a long time and the boy will have to go to a good school and to the University afterwards.

"Besides you know how it is; there exists a fashion in portrait-painters as well as a fashion in women's clothes. I have been the fashion now for several years and I know what many people are hoping to say soon: 'Oh, yes, that man van Rijn! He was quite good a little while ago, but he has lost something of his old—well, what shall we call it?—of his old pep and stamina.' And what they mean of course is that I am beginning to paint them as they are and no longer as they want to think that they are and now I will show you— Hey there, Hendrick, bring me the bill for what we have had. Thank you!—I shall now take you upstairs, and I shall show you."

Hendrick dutifully brought the bill, observed that it was remarkably good weather for the time of year (since it had not rained for almost three entire days) pocketed the change without Rembrandt paying the slightest attention to him, and bowed us out of the door. We then turned towards the left, walked up two flights of broad and comfortable stairs and came into a large room which was used as an assembly hall whenever some important matter made it necessary to call the entire company together. It was quite dark when we entered. The high windows were covered with green baize curtains. On the walls I vaguely noticed one or two pictures—large pictures—the usual company-portraits that one would expect to find in such places. Then, when my eyes got accustomed to the dim light I saw that at the other end of the hall there was a vast wooden structure, supporting an enormous canvas, the most gigantic picture I had ever seen, but what it was meant to represent I could not make out.

Suddenly Rembrandt pulled the curtains aside and the room was flooded with brilliant sunlight and I suffered a physical shock, as if I had been struck in the face by a palette full of the richest colors ever devised by the hand of man. Homer, who undoubtedly was the greatest master of the word that ever lived, might have been able to revaluate an impression like that into terms of words. Dante would have mumbled something divine but obscure. Montaigne would have smiled and kept silent, but I, being only a humble leech, and a simple Hollander could only say one word: "Damnation!"

Whereupon Rembrandt, who was not given much to outward manifestations of affection, threw both his arms around me and shouted: "Splendid! For now at least I know that one person has understood what I meant to do."

And then he pulled a heavy bench in front of the picture, once more closed the curtains that were furthest away from the picture (thereby fairly forcing the figure in white in the center of the painting to march right out of the frame), made me sit down, himself sat down with his elbows on his knees, rested his chin in the palms of his hands (a favorite position of his whenever he was thinking very hard) and said:

"Now you know why I dragged you up here. This is my chance! My great chance! It came to me by accident. The company of Captain Banning Cocq was going to have its portrait done. First they talked of van der Helst doing it and then some one wanted Flinck and some others wanted some one else again but one day My Lord of Purmerend came to me and said he had seen the portrait I had done of the mother of Jan Six and the one of Dominie Anslo and his wife and he liked the way in which I had arranged the good dominie and his wife, with the books on the table and the man talking to the woman—not two people just sitting, but a husband and wife really talking to each other and being interested too in what was being said—and he had had an idea. His company wanted to have its picture painted. Most of the men wanted the usual thing—soldiers and officers all grouped around a table with a couple of pewter plates filled with dead oysters and a lot of wine bottles—everybody looking very proud and very brave and slightly the worse for having eaten so much. What he wanted to know—hadn't this sort of thing been done a little too often? Wasn't there some other way in which such a picture could be painted?

"Well, at first I was a little frightened by the idea. For I had never tried my hand at large groups of people. But then I said that I would try if he gave me a few days to think it over. He answered that he would be delighted and would I come and see him when I was ready.

"So I set to work, but most of the sketches I did not like at all and I threw them away. And then suddenly it came to me, as I told you coming up here, that those regiments of volunteers don't mean so very much in our day. As a rule they are just an excuse for pleasant social gatherings. But that is because we are living in times of peace. Probably if there were another war (of course I know we are still at war with Spain, but who cares? The Spaniards are broke and we are rich and we can hire all the men in the whole wide world and let them do our fighting for us.) If there were another war they would once more amount to something. And there is a very definite ideal hidden somewhere in the idea of an 'armed citizenry.'

"It is easy to poke fun at those pompous house-painters and gin-distillers and fish-mongers marching forth in plumes and feathers, toting heavy swords and lances and carrying gigantic arquebuses and powder-horns as if they were going to drive the Turks out of Europe when all of us know that they are going to spend the greater part of the night throwing dice in the guard-house and drinking small beer for no more serious purpose than to prevent the peasant women from Buiksloot and the Beemster from smuggling their butter and eggs and chickens past the revenue officer at the city gate.

"But that is only part of the story and by no means the most interesting part. Those men are the sons and the grandchildren of just such house-painters and gin-distillers and fish-dealers who got hanged and burned and broken on the wheel, fighting for something that was on their conscience, something that had nothing at all to do with selling gin or codfish or printing-houses, for God knows, they could have done that just as well while they were being ruled by a king as while they were being ruled by Their Lordships of the Town Hall. There was something in them somewhere, that made them rather fine and noble. Well, if it was there, I was going to find it and paint it.

"And so I went to see My Lord of Purmerend one evening in his house on the Singel (you know the big one with the dolphin which de Keyser built originally for his father-in-law, the old burgomaster) and he was most kind to me and even introduced me to his family and then we sat in his office and I took some paper (I can't talk without drawing at the same time) and I explained to him what I wanted to do—paint him and his men just as they were leaving the arsenal for a turn of duty—everything still in great disorder, one old fellow beating the alarm and some of the soldiers taking down their pikes and others getting their guns ready and little boys and little girls getting out from underneath the feet of the men (there are always a couple of kids running around on such occasions) and the inevitable dog that is present at every parade and always in the midst of it and one Man who is The Leader—one man who has himself in hand and who knows what he is doing, who is quietly going ahead because he realizes that the others will follow no matter what he does.

"I am not quite sure that I am making myself clear. But you told me that you had liked my picture of Nicolaes Tulp. Well, in that case I did not paint a learned doctor giving a lesson in anatomy. I tried to make it mean something a little more general—a little more abstract, if you allow me to use one of the big words of your French friend, the Count. I tried to paint science, rather than a group of scientists. Just as here I have done my best to give one an impression of 'civic duty' rather than merely show them a number of inconsequential citizens doing their own little particular duties. Do you follow me?"

I did follow him. I followed him so well that for a moment I could say nothing in reply. It is strange that anything that is really "perfect" affects me that way. Most people when they see a perfect sunset or hear a perfect song or see a perfectly beautiful woman, grow eloquent—shout—wave their arms—climb on chairs—feel that they must do something, anything at all, to let the world know how deeply they have been impressed.

With me, it works the other way.

I grow absolutely dumb and can't say a word.

If anybody interrupts my gloomy meditation, I will curse him as if I were the stevedore of some Indiaman who had slipped on the gang-plank and had dropped a bale of rice on his own feet. Then I fall back into that utter silence of desperation which overtakes me whenever I happen to find myself face to face with something really beautiful and only after hours of silent wandering along the back streets or sitting alone in a darkened room, am I able to regain my normal composure.

But Rembrandt, who was not always the most tactful of men and apt to be rather brusque and short-tempered, seemed to understand what had happened to me, for he found an excuse to bid me farewell.

"It is getting late," he said. "I just heard the chimes play and I think the clock struck six. I shall run back home and see how poor Saskia is faring. I am sorry that I have taken so much of your time, but now you will understand why I brought you here. I had to do something really big, something tremendous, to make the people see what I can accomplish when they give me free rein. And this picture will do it. The world will hear about the trick. I shall have more customers than ever. I shall be able to make experiments. I shall have greater freedom than ever before and all through this picture, for, mark my words, it will make people talk."

Chapter 10

AND AS A RESULT OF THIS PICTURE REMBRANDT BECOMES THE JOKE OF AMSTERDAM

Rembrandt was right.

People talked about his picture.

As a matter of fact, they have not stopped talking yet.

The first result of this "new departure in artistic arrangement," of this attempt "to put an idea into colors" and "translate an emotion into lights and shades" was a gigantic roar of laughter. The members of Captain Cocq's company started it. Their wives and children laughed next. Then their sweethearts laughed. Soon the whole town laughed and then quite suddenly the victims of this "unseemly hoax" ceased to be quite as hilarious as they had been in the beginning. For a joke could be carried too far and they were the ones who would have to pay, weren't they? And pay for what? That is what they asked each other and asked all those willing to listen.

Pay a hundred or two hundred guilders apiece for the privilege of having the back of their heads shown or their feet or one hand or one shoulder?

Pay a hundred or two hundred guilders for the honor of being a dim, unrecognizable figure, amidst a number of dim, unrecognizable figures in the dark recesses of an enormous gate, "a piece of animated shade," as one funny observer remarked, while others who had not paid a penny more had been placed right in the center of the stage and in the full light of day?

What had that poor fool tried to do, anyhow?

What had he been thinking of while he was painting this picture?

Surely one man's money was as good as the next!

And when one had paid one's share, one was entitled to as good treatment as one's neighbor. This business of showing favors would never do. Not if they, the soldiers, knew anything about it. They were not such simpletons as this stranger seemed to think. There had been pictures of boards of regents and military companies in Amsterdam long before this smart young man had left his native mill in the distant town of Leyden to come and tell the benighted people of the metropolis how (in his opinion) the thing ought to be done. All he had to do, if he really cared to find out (but he probably thought that he knew better than any one else) was to pay a visit to the Town Hall or to the orphan asylums or to any of the guild houses. He would then see what the customers who paid him their hard-earned guilders had a right to expect from the artist they employed, and so on and so forth, with a great deal of talk of "going to law about it" and downright refusals to pay money for value not received.

But it was not only the rabble in the street who talked that way. Men and women who surely ought to have known better joined in the chorus of abuse. Vondel, our great poet, driven to despair by those bright peasant lads who disguised as ministers of the Gospel and shepherds of the human soul were every whit as narrow-minded and intolerant as the worst of the ancient Inquisitors, had bade farewell to the Calvinist community a year or so before and had boldly proclaimed his return to the church of his fathers. I can't exactly say that his friends were pleased. My Lord Hooft of Muiden bade him never darken his door again. That seemed rather superfluous and I made bold to tell him so one day when he had asked Jean-Louys and myself to visit him at his charming old castle where he kept open house over the week-end and with a rare gift for the social amenities of life entertained poets and painters and musicians without ever letting them fly at each other's throats.

"How happens it," I asked him, "that you, My Lord, a true liberal in mind and thought and act, now take the side of those who think a man's conduct should be judged by the religious company he keeps?"

"Stuff and nonsense!" he replied. "I got irritated because that foolish old poet made such a great to-do about his so-called conversion. Calvinism is a curse. I agree with him fully. It is a curse which eventually will destroy us. But the Roman creed that went before was just as bad. Neither of them ever seemed to have heard of a certain Jesus of Nazareth who bade us love each other and be of good will to our neighbors. Now I can understand a man who comes to me and says: 'Sir, I have the measles. I don't like them. And so I want to go ahead and be cured.' But I can't follow him when he whines: 'I have got the measles, I don't like them and therefore I think that I will exchange them for the small-pox.'"

That being more or less the attitude of most of his former friends, the poor fellow, who besides had just lost his wife and had found himself all alone in the world with a good-for-nothing scoundrel of a son, began to growl and snarl at everybody and everything, as an outlet for his own misery and self-reproach. Besides, like so many of his kind, the poor poet was of a very jealous disposition, and being some twenty years older than Rembrandt, he had never forgiven him that he, the upstart, had gained fame and riches, lived in a noble mansion and had married a beautiful woman, while he, the modern rejuvenated Homer, the divinely inspired bard, acclaimed by all the world as the greatest word-painter of modern times, was obliged to sell stockings for a living. He now saw his chance and composed a ditty in which Rembrandt's work was compared with that of his rival, Govaert Flinck (a perfectly competent manufacturer of "official" pictures, but without the slightest touch of originality) and was of course found wanting on account of its "artificial

REMBRANDT IN HIS WORKING DRESS

gloom and its pedantic use of shadows and half lights" and he wound up by dubbing the former "the Prince of Darkness," a witticism that stuck to Rembrandt for all the rest of his days.

The other painters, also dearly loving a colleague who had done pretty well in a worldly sense, were not slow to catch up with the general chorus of disapproval. They talked of their poor, misguided friend, who seemed to have shot his bolt in this latest picture and let it be known that they had of course always thought him a great man, but that it was a pity he had reached the limits of his art at such a comparatively tender age. Still others, especially the art-dealers with whom Rembrandt had refused to do business, were even more to the point.

"The temporary infatuation of the public, which had made this eccentric young man the fashionable painter of the hour, has now probably reached its end," was one of their more good-natured comments. While in their less guarded moments, they simply shouted: "Another bubble that has burst!" and rubbed their hands in anticipatory glee.

Why go on with this sad recital of human stupidity?

My wise doctor-friend, who three thousand years or so ago wrote that very wise book which we call "Ecclesiastes" summed it all up in the words: "Vanity of vanities, and all is vanity."

Here was a man who had dared to think a new thought and tell a new truth. Proudly he had turned to his fellow-men saying these noble words: "Behold! a little yellow and a little black and a little green and ocher and red and presto! I change them into an Idea." And the Philistines had loudly guffawed, had poked each other in the ribs and had shouted: "The clown! The mountebank! He wants to show us! Teach us! Tell us! As if we were not bright enough to know what we want for ourselves!"

And from that moment on, Rembrandt was doomed.

He might have returned to fame at some royal court, and indeed, it would have been better if right then and there he had moved to England or France. But in a Republic, such a thing was impossible. He had set himself up to be better than his neighbors. There was only one answer—death and oblivion.

The only question was: How long would it take the pack to get and devour him?

Chapter 11

WE TAKE A WALK AND TALK ART WITH AN HONEST MILLER

Of course there were exceptions to the general chorus of disapproval. There were a few people who "suspected" that something very fine and extraordinary had been added to the sum total of the world's beauty. There were others who went beyond "suspecting" and who felt convinced that this was one of the most beautiful things ever wrought by the hand of man.

I frequently discussed the matter with my friends during our Sunday walks which continued as in the older days. It was interesting to get the reactions of those three men, so utterly different, yet bound to each other by the ties of a common understanding.

Selim was the least interested of them. "Why," he used to ask, "all this fuss about something quite as useless and immaterial as a bit of canvas, covered with white lead and zinc and old extracts from dead vegetables and dead animals? No, the Prophet was right. The human race ought not to care for such trifles. There are more important things in this world than men and women made of linseed-oil and madder."

"Such as?" he was asked.

"Men and women of flesh and blood, especially the latter," he replied, and refused to devote any more of his energy and strength to a discussion that seemed so far removed from his charming and simple little universe.

Bernardo took it all very calmly. A man who has stood tied up against the wooden pole that was to be his own funeral pyre and who has lived to tell the tale can look upon the affairs of everyday life from such a high and such an immeasurably detached point-of-vantage that little items like frustrated careers and ruined reputations mean nothing to him, or less than nothing.

We had walked out to a mill not far from the plague house (about half an hour beyond that part of the city's bulwarks called "de Passeerder") and the miller, glad to have some one to amuse him on a rather dreary Sabbath, had invited us to come in and drink a glass of beer. Even here in this remote spot the story had become known, for it seemed that Rembrandt had often sketched the mill and had even promised the people that he would some day make an etching of it and they all liked him, for he always had a pleasant word for the children and often brought them a bit of candy and once even a toy house which he had carried all the way from town. The miller therefore was a heavy partisan of the painter and cursed the soldiers, who, he said, were no good anyway and much more proficient at the business of drinking than that of fighting.

"And what is more," he said, and his eyes shone with honest indignation, "if they make it impossible for this man with all their foolish talk to gain his livelihood in the city, all he needs to do is to come out here, for we like him and we will see to it that he does not starve. If he can paint animals too I have got a job for him right away. We have a pet hog. We are so fond of it, we have never been able to kill it. If he will paint it for us, I will gladly give him five brand new guilders."

We reassured him and told him that Rembrandt still had a few friends and was in no immediate danger of starvation, whereupon the excellent fellow said, "That is good," breathed deeply three or four times, and dozed off, to spend the Sabbath afternoon in his usual fashion by taking a nap and getting rested up from the excitement and the worry of the previous week.

This left us to ourselves and it was then that Bernardo delivered the only commentary I ever heard him make upon the case. "I may seem to be lacking in enthusiasm," he remarked slowly, "but you must not forget that I am reasonably well versed in the history of my own country. I suppose the histories of other countries would be very much the same, but perhaps we started writing our adventures down a few years earlier than our neighbors and so we know a little better what happened than some other countries.

"Well, what did happen? We produced great spiritual leaders who were able to reason things out for themselves and show us the way out of the wilderness of ignorance through which we had been wandering for a much longer period than the proverbial forty years. Did the people appreciate them and joyfully acclaim them as their kings? I never heard of it. Upon a few rare occasions, they cried Hosanna because it flattered their national pride to think that the Jewish race had been bright enough to give birth to such wonderful prophets. But they soon grew tired of giving praise to one whom they must (whether they liked to or not) consider superior to themselves and then they stoned him or threw him before the wild animals. Why should you expect your own people to be different?"

Jean-Louys, too, assumed an attitude of aloofness, though he knew a good picture from a bad one and had expressed the greatest admiration for one or two small sketches which Rembrandt had given me and which I had had framed and which were hanging on the walls of my dining-room. But he liked to play at being a sort of philosophic St. Simeon Stylites.

"My dear children," he announced solemnly, "why get all het up about some new folly of the human race? There is only one friend in this world upon whom you can always depend, who will never betray you, no matter under what circumstances, who will always be true, who will not humiliate you before your circle of intimate acquaintances by some signal act of public idiocy."

"And who might that be?" Bernardo interrupted him. "Perhaps the tables of stone of my great-uncle Moses?"

"By no means," the Frenchman answered quietly, "but the tables of logarithms of my great teacher, Napier. But if this ancient medico here will do something for the good of our souls, I suggest that he invite us all to his house some time and let us meet this painting prodigy from the town of Leyden. Imagine a great man coming from a town full of professors! But bring him in some fine day and we will tell you what we think of him."

Whereupon we made our adieux to the good miller, who had returned to consciousness and was now standing in front of his window to inform us that if it did not rain it would probably stay good weather, and we walked back to town and went to Jean-Louys' tower, and he cooked us a chicken in the French style (that is to say, in a large earthen pot together with all sorts of vegetables and a noble brown sauce) and we remained until all hours of the night and we were genuinely happy and we spoke of a thousand and one different things, but what we said I no longer know, for whenever friends talk among themselves, they add so much of mutual respect and good will to the mere spoken word that no human being, be he ever so well-versed in the art of writing, could ever hope to do justice to such a conversation.

"Faithful friends are the medicine of life," said Ecclesiasticus.

God be praised, that old Israelite knew whereof he was talking.

Chapter 12

REMBRANDT MEETS MY FRIENDS AND SASKIA GROWS WEAKER

The meeting between Rembrandt and my friends took place much sooner than I had expected and this is the way it came about.

A couple of times a week I would go to the painter's house and we would spend the evening playing back-gammon. I don't know whether anybody still takes an interest in this game, but thirty years ago it was quite popular.

Saskia had now reached the stage where she could no longer leave her bed and Rembrandt used to sit by her side and read to her from the Bible. For she no longer expected to get better. The optimism of the first four months had been replaced by a profound and very pathetic form of melancholia. She did not complain. She did not rage against her fate, as so many of her fellow-sufferers do. She had resigned herself to the idea that she must die young and must leave her child to the care of strangers. She was almost too weak to care very much, but she sometimes complained that it lasted so long. She was tired. She was most dreadfully tired and she wanted to go to sleep, but she was too tired to come to rest and she used to beg me to give her something that would make her forget, at least for a short while, and I sometimes let her have a little theriaca, but that compound seemed to have little effect upon her and the poor girl would lie tossing in her bed all day and all night long, her cheeks flushed and her lovely eyes wide open—a picture of abject misery and yet there was nothing that we could do for her except sometimes read to her from those chapters in the New Testament which she remembered from her childhood and which brought back the days of her youth when she had been as strong and well as the best of them.

After an hour or so, however, even listening to the quiet voice of her husband would exhaust her and she would whisper to him and ask him to cease. But at the same time she would beg not to be left alone.

"I shall be alone so long," she once said to me with a little smile. "I shall be alone so long before either Rembrandt or the boy joins me. I want their company every minute of both day and night as long as I can still have it."

And so every evening the baby's cradle was carried to one corner of the room (I insisted that the child be placed as far away from the mother as possible on account of the danger of contagion) and Rembrandt would light the candles on the table that had been pushed against the wall, so that the light would not disturb the patient and he would read to her for an hour or so, until she showed signs of exhaustion and then he would occupy himself quietly with his own business. He would sharpen a steel needle for his dry-points or he would examine a plate and correct some corner that had not come out as he wished or he would sign the pictures his pupils had printed that day in the little alcove upstairs. But his eyes were not very strong, he had suffered slightly from near-sightedness since early childhood and drawing or etching by candle-light would give him a stinging pain right behind his eye-balls, and so whenever I could join him for a game of back-gammon, he would be most grateful to me and he would go down into his cellar and return with a bottle of a very wonderful Rhenish wine which was called "The Milk of Our Lady" and which most certainly was worthy of that name.

But after a short time, the clicking of the dice as we threw them upon the boards got to be too exhausting for Saskia. We then threw them upon a heavy wad of fine muslin, the muslin he used to wipe his plates with, but even then sometimes one dice would slightly touch another and the patient invariably complained that the noise sent shivers all through her and as we could not talk either, and neither of us had the slightest liking for cards, we were hard put to it to find some way of passing the evening without just sitting and staring at each other.

Then one day I happened to mention to Rembrandt that I had just learned a new game from Jean-Louys which was very interesting and took a considerable amount of thought and foresight and which was called "chess" and which was so old that some people said it had been played by the heroes outside of Troy and which originally had been a war game, devised for the amusement of the Shahs of Persia, who used to be great potentates and who had ruled Asia until great Alexander had come and had deprived them of their power and had taken away their land to give it to his own generals.

The very name, calling forth visions of Oriental tyrants with beautiful diamond-studded turbans, lying in tapestried tents in the heart of some wind-swept desert, surrounded by dashing knights and armor-covered elephants bearing turreted castles on their ponderous backs, appealed to his imagination and he at once asked me to introduce him to my friend and let him learn the game too.

I waited until Saskia was feeling a little better and then one evening I invited both men to my house for supper. They took to each other at once and became fast friends. And this was rather curious, as they represented two entirely different classes of society and as Jean-Louys treated even the most distinguished among the Dutch patricians with that mixture of civil aloofness and amused condescension which the rich Amsterdam merchant would bestow upon a former butler who had gone to the Indies, had done rather well by himself and had now returned to the city of his former activities with a couple of million rupees and who had become a personage whom one must treat with a certain amount of economic respect, while at the same time keeping him at a respectable social distance, never for a moment allowing him to forget that the gap between inherited and recently acquired wealth was a divinely ordained institution across which no earthly wealth could ever hope to build a means of escape.

The Count de la Tremouille was the incarnation of what is commonly called "good breeding." Never during all the many years we spent together have I heard him give offense unintentionally, which surely is the highest tribute one can pay to a man's standard of courtesy. Like all wise people, he moved through life vertically rather than horizontally, but no matter in what company he found himself, I have never known the occasion upon which this unpretentious exile was not sitting "at the head of the table" or when anybody felt inclined to offer the man with the funny accent the slightest familiarity.

How and in what way he had acquired this gift of dominating his surroundings without in any way trying to dominate his audience, I do not know. But he had it and as a result, while he himself never seemed to remember that he had been born the Baron de la Tremouille, his surroundings were never quite able to forget it and even his fishdealer would insist upon selling him six pence worth of shrimps as if he had been a foreign potentate, come to negotiate a great international loan. Upon very rare occasions, however, the invisible courtiers who seemed to watch every one of his thoughts and actions were given a day off and silently departed for a quiet evening in town. Then his brain resembled a munificent, royal palace, from which all the guards had fled. The doors and windows stood wide open and one could enter at will, to wander through the vast halls and admire the accumulated treasures of recollection and observation, or to find a quiet nook in the formal gardens at the back of the edifice and there meditate upon the strange vicissitudes of the great adventure commonly known as life.

But in order to enjoy this privilege, one had to be recognized as a blood brother of the mind. Mere physical relationship counted for nothing, affinity of feeling for everything. I have seen a first cousin of M. le Baron come all the way from Gascony in connection with some question of an inheritance, sit for hours in the little kitchen that lay just off the study, cooling his heels and swearing impatiently because Jean-Louys was talking to the first-mate of a whaler who could neither read nor write but who had observed curious irregularities of behavior on the part of his compass while passing those extreme northern shores of Lapland where it is said that there are a number of vast iron deposits.

And it is a well-known fact that the Baron de la Tremouille forgot to attend the dinner which the Burgomasters of Amsterdam were giving in honor of a cousin of the King of Denmark (in the vain hope of obtaining a slight reduction of the Sund tolls by getting His Royal Highness disgracefully drunk on Dutch gin) because he had promised to sit up with his sick shoe-maker, an amateur philosopher of a singularly amusing trend of thought, who had made a careful study of the anagrams by means of which the Reverend Jacobus Bruinesteek had proved that the Psalms of David had really been written by King Solomon, who had applied these to the Revelations of St. John, and the Gospel of St. Luke, and had come to the somewhat startling conclusions that Judas Iscariot had written the former, while the latter was the work of Pontius Pilate.

One never knew therefore what reaction to expect from a meeting between one's ordinary friends and this strange product of French feudal practices and neo-mathematical theories except that his outward manner would always be in inverse ratio to the respect he inwardly felt for his new acquaintance. When he was sublimely polite, the case was hopeless. When he was just every-day polite, there was hope and one might give the candidate another chance. When he dropped all reserve, the victory had been won. During the first five minutes after I had introduced Rembrandt to him, I was in great fear that the encounter would be a failure. For the painter, conscious of his own low birth (his Uylenburgh in-laws had seen to that) was awkward and surly and ready to take offense at the slightest provocation, or even provide a little of the provocation himself.

The dinner was to be at my house, but Jean-Louys had promised to do the cooking. He held that cooking, after mathematics, was the greatest contribution towards human progress. "After all," he often asked, when his sleeves rolled up to his elbows, he walked between his study and the kitchen beating his eggs and his oil and quoting profusely from Ennius and from Simonides of Ceos, "after all, in what consists the difference between man and beast except in the possibilities of the former to learn the art of dining, while the latter is forever doomed to feed? I grant you that most men still are in the state of savagery when they take food for the mere pleasure of filling their bellies. I grant you that the vast majority of our fellow-citizens still handle their forks and spoons as if they were a farmer loading a wagon of hay. But a few have at last seen the light. A few of them 'dine.' Whereas my dog Nouille, the noblest beast that ever pulled a fox out of a hole, a creature of such intellect and refinement that if he could only have worn a wig and cassock they would have made him Cardinal-Archbishop of Paris, had the table manners of a hog and unless he were very closely watched, would regale himself with delicacies which were more fit for a starving hyena than for an over-fed turn-spit."

And unless he were interfered with at this spot, he would proceed to explain that a man's table manners were the safest index to his general character, that one could measure the degree of a friend's greed or honesty by watching the way in which he moved his fork or knife to his mouth. If the progress of the food from the plate to lips were even and uninterrupted, one could trust that guest for any amount up to a hundred thousand francs. If, on the other hand, the moment the food approached the mouth, there was a snatching movement on the part of the teeth and a hurrying on the part of the fingers, then that person had still a few hundred thousand years to go before he was fit to associate with civilized people.

All of which was very amusing, but a little dangerous in view of the "catch as catch can" method of eating which was still being practiced by the majority of our neighbors. And alas! Rembrandt was no exception. When he was hard at work upon some new picture or when he was struggling with a new idea for an etching, he could be terribly absent-minded. Upon such occasions he seemed to be completely oblivious of his surroundings. As I have already written down in a former part of my diary I have known him to go without either food or drink for as long as two days and two nights at a time. Then when he finally broke his fast, his table manners were rather painfully reminiscent of the days in the Weddesteeg, when the six van Rijn infants were all of them standing around the paternal table, dipping their spoons into the common bowl of pap and fishing out the few chunks of meat left behind by their father and mother. Now he not only had his work to worry him (I knew that he was finishing a portrait of the Widow Swartenhout and the old lady, who had a will of her own, despite her seventy-five years, was not the easiest of sitters) but also had a very sick wife on his hands and a rather sickly child (not to mention a hellishly ill-tempered nurse), I had good reason to fear that he might be in one of his vague and irritable moods and then one never could foretell just exactly what he would do or say or how he would react to the simplest remark, if by some miraculous stretch of the imagination it could be construed as a reflection upon his personal behavior.

And when Jean-Louys appeared from the kitchen in his shirt-sleeves, wearing an apron over his silk ruffles (for though he affected no colors in his outer garments, he remained scrupulously faithful to the reigning fashions until the day of his death), carrying a large blue Delft bowl full of batter and loudly quoting Seneca's "Convivae certe tui dicant, Bibamus!" suddenly I had the feeling: this party is going to be the wreck of an old friendship. For Rembrandt, who knew a very little Latin but no French whatsoever, looked as if he were going to say: "Well, my fine young man, and what about it, and have you lived here all this time without learning enough of our language to wish me at least a civil good morning in my own tongue?" But Jean-Louys, without paying the slightest attention, greeted him with a very deep and ceremonial bow and said in the nearest approach to Dutch I ever heard issue from the mouth of a Frenchman, "Mijn Heer, I welcome the successor of Pheidias, who did not think an old woman making pancakes a subject beneath his august dignity. Wherefore with your kind permission, I shall now make you an alemette the recipe of which I got straight from the chief cook of the Abbot of Thelème."

Whether Rembrandt got the allusion to the greatest of all the past masters of ancient France, I had reason to doubt, for as he often told me, he lived for the day and not for day before yesterday. And I am afraid that not half a dozen people in the whole town of Amsterdam knew (or cared) what sort of friars had inhabited the delectable abbaye of old Doctor Rabelais' invention. But the reference to the pancake woman, a rather mediocre etching of his early days which hardly any one knew, greatly flattered his pride. And he at once dropped the bristling attitude with which he had watched the advent of our amateur cook, bowed low and answered with a courtly wave of the hand:

"And if the product of your art, Monsieur, comes up to what certain reports of your culinary powers make me anticipate, then even great Jupiter would consider himself fortunate to be invited to this feast."

Which so surprised and delighted de la Tremouille that he almost dropped his bowl of batter on my instrument case, bowed even lower than before, pronounced himself Monsieur van Rijn's most humble servitor and ever after treated him with such marks of esteem and good will that the French commercial agent (who was supposed to collect business information for his royal master, but filled most of his letters with social gossip of what he supposed to be the better sort of Amsterdam society) filled three entire letters with the details of this famous meeting and hinted in no uncertain terms that M. de la Tremouille was rapidly approaching that stage of democratic debasement where a hint to the judicial authorities of Amsterdam and a Lettre de Cachet held ready at the nearest frontier town might not be out of place—a fine piece of diplomatic reasoning which in the course of its peregrinations towards Paris was duly copied by the post-master of The Hague, was forwarded by him to My Lord Huygens, and so reached my humble home in Amsterdam with a request for the recipe of that famous alemette, which he spelled wrong and called an "omelette."

But to return to our dinner-party, we really had a very pleasant evening. Selim at first held himself slightly aloof. "The graphic arts," he offered as an excuse, "are not quite in my line. The Koran does not allow me to take an interest in them."

"And in which chapter, my friend, does the Koran mention the graphic arts?" came the voice of Bernardo, who knew that this excellent follower of the Prophet (not unlike a good many Christians) never gave a thought to these holy works except upon those frequent occasions when he needed their authority to talk himself out of doing something which he really did not want to do. For example, whenever he went to the house of friends and was offered beer, which he detested, Selim would solemly lift his eyes toward Heaven and in a sepulchral voice he would declaim: "Alas and alack! does not the Angel Gabriel in the fifth verse of the second Sura declare unto the faithful: 'In the name of Allah, the compassionate compassioner, abstain, ye lovers of righteousness, from all those things that benumb the spirit.'"

But should his host take the hint and dive into his cellar for a bottle of Burgundy (which the young Moslem dearly loved) then Selim would proceed: "But what does the Prophet himself in the twenty-third verse of the eighteenth Sura have to say upon the duties of those who wander abroad in foreign lands? 'Listen, all ye faithful, and act ye so in all ways that he who offereth ye food and drink shall never feel himself slighted, for true hospitality is the founding-stone of friendship, the bulwark of goodwill.'" And he would continue to misquote these highfalutin passages until either the supply of wine had been completely consumed or the rest of the guests had passed underneath the table.

He would, however, be a little more careful with his texts whenever Bernardo was present, for the Jew, having spent several years of his life in a Portuguese prison in the company of a holy man from Fez had used the endless hours of this interminable bondage to learn the greater part of the Koran by heart, in return for which he had taught the poor blackamoor the Psalms of David, the book of Judges and the Canticle of Solomon. He had long since thrown this useless intellectual ballast overboard, but enough remained to allow him to control the more phantastic statements of our amateur Moollah and the quarrels of these two Semites about the relative merits of their ancestral creeds (for neither of which either one of them felt the slightest respect) added a great deal to the gayety of our small society.

It caused considerable scandal among our Christian neighbors (who were never invited to our parties, yet knew everything we had said and done as accurately as if they had been present in person) but they were as a rule too busy fighting among themselves to pay very much attention to our hilarious heresies. And this evening, Selim, true to his custom, had no sooner relieved himself of his noble sentiment about the Koran and the art of painting, than he asked for a pencil and paper and spent the rest of the evening entertaining my small son with accounts of the glorious deeds of Harun al-Raschid, illuminating his talk with very amusing little pictures in which that great warrior was depicted in the act of decapitating rows and rows of Crusaders with such bloodthirsty realism that the poor infant could not sleep for five nights in succession.

As for the rest of us, immediately after dinner we went to my workroom and spent the evening playing chess. Jean-Louys, who claimed that this game was the best remedy for gout and nagging wives (the two evils he most dreaded) had recently taken a very serious interest in it and had made it a subject of careful study.

"What will you?" he used to ask. "I can work at my tables for only eight or nine hours a day. After that the figures put their hats and coats on and begin to dance minuets all over the page. I have got to do something to keep myself from going woozy and I can't live without mathematics, just as others can't live without gin or rum or theology or women.

There is music. But that is no longer what it used to be. Too much sentiment in it nowadays. And so let us have the board."

We got the board (a home-made affair, for in the whole of Amsterdam I had not been able to get one and in most shops I had been told that such a thing did not exist) and Jean-Louys got out his copy of Ruy Lopez (a little book which he had ordered all the way from Sevilla in Spain) and he turned to page nineteen and carefully followed all the instructions from opening to attack and in eighteen moves, he had been checkmated by Bernardo, who had learned the game only the week before and who had no more idea about "gambits" and "end plays" than I had of raising pheasants, but who beat us all with a regularity that was as much of a surprise to us as it was to himself.

But what interested me most of all was Rembrandt's reaction to this game. I had already taught him the moves, king—one square at a time, forward, backward, sideways—castles up and down the whole line as may be desirable—knights one square forwards, two squares sideways—etc., etc., and much to my surprise he had learned it in an astoundingly short time. One or two evenings had been enough to give him a general idea of the game. But he played chess as he painted.

I have said before that he would rarely talk about the theory of his art and used to say that one hour of practice was better than a week of discussion and I do not believe that he ever put a single thought upon the subject on paper, although he had quite a gift for expressing himself in writing. But a few nights after our dinner party he approached the subject himself and what he said was quite interesting.

"I like your Frenchman," he said in connection with some remark of mine upon the excellence of Jean-Louys' virtuosity as a cook. "I grant you that he makes a most excellent pancake, but these fancy dishes are not very much to my taste. I am accustomed to simpler fare. But I like him for the line he follows in playing that strange new game and it is upon 'line' that everything in this world depends.

"You know that I have a number of pupils. Some of them have been rather successful. Flinck has already made his mark and you will hear of Bol and Douw, for they are sound craftsmen and know their trade. Of course I did not really teach them very much. In their own way they are just as good as I am. It just happens that I am a little older and have had time to learn a few tricks which I can hand down to them.

"But of course, people see that Flinck has got a new commission from the Prince or they hear that Bol is painting a dozen portraits a year and they say to themselves: Here is our little Willem or our little Jantje and he is making wonderful pictures with that box of colors grandpa gave him for Saint Nicholas. We must send him to this man van Rijn and let him grow up to be as great an artist as Eeckhout or perhaps as the master himself and make a lot of money and go about all dressed up in silks and plumes, for you know what foolish ideas there are abroad about a profession which counts so many of its most honored members among the inmates of the poor-house.

"But what can I do? I can't make a living merely painting portraits. I need pupils. None of those boys are very easy to handle. They are young and models are willing. I have not got the slightest inclination to play the school-master, but I can at least be careful that I don't waste my time upon material that is too absolutely hopeless. And so I have made it a rule that they must bring me their drawings.

"Their drawings, mind you, not their paintings. For almost anybody, if he is not absolutely color-blind and has had a good teacher, can learn to paint some sort of a picture. But a line never lies. Give me a scrap of a man's drawings, anything at all, and in five seconds I will tell you whether he has any talent or whether he had better become a brewer.

"Besides, painting is not merely a question of technique. There has got to be temperament, character, personality. Without those, there is no life and the world is dull enough as it is. No need to clutter it up with miles of dead canvas. Yes, a painter should learn his trade and be able to finish a picture, attend to all the details just as a tailor should be able to finish a suit of clothes or a carpenter to finish a cupboard.

"Perhaps I don't make myself quite clear. There are others who could tell you much better what is in my mind than I can tell you myself. But mark my words, a man has a 'line' or he has not. And that Frenchman has a line. He has got it in his manner. He has got it in his manners. He has got it in his pancakes. He has got it in his chess. He has got it in everything. While I . . ."

I looked at him in surprise, for this was a new note I had never heard before.

"While you?"

"While I have got too much of it in my drawing and too little in my life. But I am still young. Give me a few more years of experience, and I too may learn."

Chapter 13

SASKIA QUIETLY GOES TO SLEEP FOR ALL TIME

Rembrandt did learn certain things about life and he learned them much sooner than he had expected. It was a fortnight after our dinner-party and the painter and I were spending an evening as usual, watching over Saskia.

I had long since given up all hope of ever being able to do something for her. I had brought in two of my colleagues who had studied her disease in Grenoble and in London. As with patients of this sort a great deal depends upon their own state of mind and they must be encouraged in their strange belief that they will soon be cured (their occasional attacks of melancholia are the worst thing that can happen to them) my learned rivals had been introduced to her as art-dealers from Antwerp who wanted to inspect Rembrandt's etchings and she felt quite flattered that two such distinguished-looking gentlemen should have come all the way from Flanders to pay homage to her husband's genius and had asked a good many questions about Rubens, whether he really had been paid a hundred guilders a day while he was painting a picture for some one and whether his wife had really been as handsome and well-dressed as she had heard and whether she had ever posed for him in the nude, because that was something she herself never could have done, however much she might love her husband.

To which they had answered to the best of their ability and being experienced physicians and therefore accustomed to the telling of many innocent lies, they had so well acquitted themselves of the task that Saskia was quite satisfied and had dozed off, firmly convinced that she was a much better-looking woman than Helen Fourment and also, to a certain extent, a much more respectable one, since she had sometimes appeared in her man's pictures as Flora but never as Venus.

Then we had bade Rembrandt leave us and the three of us had examined the sleeping woman, for the short interview had already exhausted her waning strength, and I had shown them my record of the case and they both had looked solemn and they both had shaken their heads and the first one had whispered, "mors," and the second one had whispered, "mors," and then we had waited a few minutes to make the husband believe that we were discussing the matter in detail and that there still might be some hope and the elder of the two doctors had said: "One month more, at the very most." And the younger had answered, after the fashion of young physicians who try to show their superior experience before an elder confrère: "It seems to me that she might live another six weeks."

But I had said nothing, for I had seen her lose weight steadily for the last two months and I knew that it was a question of days rather than weeks and I took them upstairs and we all uttered some platitudes to Rembrandt, who had used that half hour to pull two proofs of a little etching of the three Magi, on which he had been working for quite a long time and which he now offered with a few complimentary words to my two doctor friends who were rather touched, for there was something very pathetic and almost naïve about this man who kept on laboring as unconcernedly as if his little household were not, at that very moment, on the brink of collapse and extinction.

Then they bade him farewell, declining his offer that he show them some further hospitality in token of his gratitude for their services and we went downstairs to the big hall and made ready for our evening's game.

Saskia was still asleep. Her right hand, very white and dreadfully thin, was resting on the counterpane. She had always been very fond of flowers and now that summer had come at last, Rembrandt brought her some fresh roses every morning. One of these she had stuck in her hair to give herself a more festive appearance, before the arrival of the "Antwerp art-dealers." It lay on her pillow. It was a very red rose and her cheeks by contrast looked even more pallid than usual. But she was breathing easily and regularly and there was a smile on her lips. I softly pulled the curtains of the bed together and tiptoed back to the table.

"She seems to be doing very well," I said. "What will you play, backgammon or chess?"

"Chess," Rembrandt answered. "I think that I can beat you to-night. The last time we played, I lost my queen almost at the very beginning. I will do better to-night."

I took two pawns and let him choose.

He pointed to my left hand and got red.

We began in the usual way, king's pawn, queen's pawn, king's bishop, queen's rook and whatever followed. I have forgotten how the game ran, but I remember that after only five or six moves, he had brought his queen out and was using her to force me into a defensive position. I warned him. What he was doing had a certain quality of brilliancy. It might make him win the game in about ten or fifteen moves, but only on condition that I overlooked a counter-attack which I could make with my knights, in which case his lack of reserves would put him into a fatal position. I watched him closely. He was so engrossed in his own calculations that he seemed completely unaware of the danger that threatened him from the side of my knights. I warned him once more. "This is all very fine," I told him, "but you are playing this to win."

"But this is so amusing," he answered. "I know that I am running a few risks but I have the position well in hand. I shall beat you the next move if I can extricate my queen."

"But can you?" I asked him, taking his bishop's pawn and thereby opening an avenue of attack for my bishop.

"I think I can— Why, it would be absurd if I couldn't! I had the game in hand only a moment ago and now—"

"And now," I answered, "I have your queen and you are mate in three moves."

He pushed back his chair.

"Too bad," he consoled himself. "Too bad. I thought that I had you this time. Let me try again. Just a moment till I make sure that Saskia is all right."

He picked up one of the two candles, went to the bed and pushed aside the curtains. Then he turned to me and whispered: "Look how quiet she is to-night! I never saw her sleep so soundly. She must be really getting better."

I stood by his side and put my hand upon her heart.

Saskia was dead.

Chapter 14

SASKIA IS BURIED AND REMBRANDT GOES BACK TO WORK

I am writing this in the year 1669 and Saskia died in '42. That is twenty-seven years ago and twenty-seven years are a long time in a man's life. I can't complain about my memory. It is causing me very little trouble, and as I shall be seventy next year, I have no right to expect too much. The greater part of my contemporaries are either dead or rapidly becoming senile and the former are better off than the latter.

What Fate holds in store for me, I do not know. But when the end comes, I hope that it will be sudden and swift and that I shall never have to pass through those periods of slow mental decay which seem to be the inevitable concomitant of old age.

But I have noticed something curious whenever I try to reconstruct the events of my own past. I can recollect the most unimportant details of my early childhood. I still know with absolute assurance what presents I received on Saint Nicholas day when I was seven and eight and nine and ten. I could tell you what we had to eat on the few occasions when we entertained guests. Could I handle a pencil, I would be able to draw you the absolute likeness of all my school-teachers and most of my friends.

The same holds good for the two years I spent studying anatomy and surgery at the University of Leyden. Every detail of every day, almost every detail of every hour of every day, is firmly fixed in my mind. But suddenly after my twentieth birthday, the picture becomes hazy. I still know in a general way what occurred during the years that I practiced medicine in Amsterdam, but I often lose track of the sequence of events. For example, I will remember with perfect clarity that such and such a person fell ill of such and such a disease and I could give you a fairly accurate account of the development of his case. But should you ask me to name the year, I would be hopelessly at a loss. I would be obliged to answer that I did not know. It might have been '46 or '56 and then again, it might have been '49 or '59. I just simply would not know. I could tell you whether the patient had a temperature on the third or on the fourth day of his affliction, but I might be off on the date all the way from five to ten years.

I have often speculated upon the true nature of this curious mental trick and I think that it is due to the increase in speed of both the months and the years as we grow older. When I was ten years of age, a single day resembled eternity, only on a somewhat smaller scale. It was composed of twenty-four hours, each one of which bore a distinct character of its own and offered countless possibilities for new adventures and fresh experiences.

Gradually human existence became more commonplace. One got up, did one's work, ate a few meals, talked to a few friends, worried a bit, laughed a bit, read a few chapters in a book and went to bed again.

The humdrum became the normal. One commenced to accept whatever Fate had in store without murmuring, for what was the use of trying to fight God? At first, of course, there still were the seasons. The spring, when the trees and the plants were in flower, the summer when it was hot, the fall when the grain was harvested, the winter when it was cold and one was obliged to wear heavy woolen coats and mufflers.

But after one's fiftieth birthday, even those natural divisions of the year seemed to lose their importance. One no longer grumbled about the frost or the heat or the rain or the snow. They were there! Impossible to do anything about them, anyway. That was the last great surrender. From that moment on, time ceased to have a personal entity. It became a smudge. Some gigantic joker had wiped his dirty thumb across the vault of Heaven and that was called life. Then the last final sleep and grateful oblivion for the rest of eternity.

Those thoughts have been continually in my mind during the last twenty years. Hence dates and hours mean very little to me and as I have never been in the habit of keeping a diary until now, as I never saved a single letter or a single scrap of paper that was in any way connected with my own existence (it seemed such a silly thing to do, as if my own funny little adventures were really of the slightest general importance), as, in short, I am writing this entirely from memory, I find it rather difficult to state when exactly Saskia departed this life or even when she was buried.

She died (I am quite sure about that) some time during the summer of 1642, for I remember that it was during the same year in which Tasman discovered that mysterious island in the Pacific Ocean which was called Nieuw Zeeland, after my beloved Zeeland, and sailed around the great south land about which we had had so many strange reports during the last forty years.

As always I was interested in any reports he might bring home about the narcotics in use among the natives. Everywhere in the world the inhabitants seem to have some favorite way of bringing about temporary forgetfulness. In most instances they were only interested in their miserable hasheesh as a momentary means of escape from lives that were none too happy. But I am convinced that some day we shall find a plant which will enable us to do something infinitely more important to perform surgical operations without that dreadful agony which now turns the operating-room into a torture chamber and makes people avoid the hospital as if it were the lepers' house. And there always is a chance that one of those explorers, coming back from distant parts of Asia or Africa or

America, shall bring us the answer to this age-old question. I had therefore made it a rule to keep track of all new voyages and when I heard that this new big island, called van Diemen's Land (after My Lord Anthony van Diemen, the governor-general of the Indies, who also conquered Formosa and who had equipped this most recent expedition)—when I heard that it was inhabited by woolly-haired aborigines who could make battle-axes return to their hands after they had thrown them at their enemies, I decided that people clever enough to invent such a curious device (the true nature of which I never heard explained) might also have discovered some new methods of bringing about a state of artificial oblivion. But the reports that were printed about these new explorations remained exceedingly brief and far from satisfactory. Finally I addressed a letter to the directors of the India Company and was informed that Their Lordships were conducting a business enterprise and were not managing a museum of natural curiosities and had no information to give me upon the subject in which I seemed interested.

Well, that famous voyage happened in 1642 (though I only heard about it two years later) but the date stuck in my memory, for the very silly reason that I had had a dispute with one of Rembrandt's brothers-in-law whether Lutjegast in which Tasman was born was situated in Friesland or in Groningen and finally I had bet him a rijksdaalder that it was in Groningen and not in Friesland and he had taken me up and I had been right and he had never paid me that rijksdaalder, claiming that by rights the hamlet ought to have been a part of his native province. (A pretty feeble excuse, it seemed to me.) And ever since, when some one said, "Sixteen-hundred and forty-two," I instinctively added, "Tasman from Lutjegast and Saskia, too." It was a foolish little jingle and not a very dignified one, but as long as the particular compartment of our brain occupied by our memory resembles a pawnshop the morning after a fire, with everything helter-skelter and in hopeless disorder, I suppose that such absurd combinations are inevitable.

Anyway that terrible rime allows me to remember that the poor girl died in the year 1642 and that is enough for the present purpose. She died in the summer of '42 and if I am not mistaken, it was during the middle of June, for the push-cart vendors were selling their first cherries and there were flowers everywhere, and the trees along the Burchtwal looked fresh and green as we slowly carried Saskia to her last resting place.

When we came to the Old Church, we found that the officials had not expected us so early and that the building was still locked. The coffin was put down while some one went to get the sexton and we all stood around in a small group and we wanted to say something and we did not know quite what to say and the noise of the traffic in the near-by Warmoesstraat served as a background for our silence and then all of a sudden, there was the grating sound of heavy bolts that were being pushed aside and the doors opened slowly as if pushed aside by invisible hands, and inside everything was very quiet, but in the distance some one was hammering at a bench that needed repair and I looked at Rembrandt and I saw that he had turned pale, as if they were hammering nails into his wife's coffin.

We buried her right underneath the small organ, not far away from the monument erected to Admiral van Heemskerk who had died off Gibraltar and who had been the first man to try and reach the Indies by way of the North Pole.

The ceremony took only a few minutes. The heavy black cloth which had completely covered the casket was carefully folded up by two of the professional pall-bearers who performed this office with such absurd dignity that they reminded me of my grandmother and her maid Rika, doing the sheets when the half-yearly laundry came home. Then the coffin was placed upon two heavy ropes. Eight men, four on each side, took hold of the ropes. The minister stepped forward with an enormous Bible which he opened and placed on a small wooden stand which had been placed there for the occasion and while he read the one hundred and third psalm, Saskia was slowly and silently lowered into the cavernous darkness of her open grave.

I have gone to many funerals in my day and every time I have been struck by the inability of the creed of Calvin and Luther to express its emotions in anything beyond mere words. The music in our churches is hideous. The singing is atrocious. We cover the walls with a dozen coats of whitewash, we paint the ceiling gray, and we varnish the benches until they are stained a dark brown and then we ask the congregation to come and sit still on incredibly uncomfortable seats while some one talks to them.

In our churches, some one is forever telling somebody else what he ought to think or do. Instead of agreement there is argument. Instead of being urged to lose our souls in quiet contemplation, we are exhorted to follow the intricate subtleties of violent controversies and to take sides in never-ending disputes. Heaven knows, I do not wish a return of those good old days of which our Catholic neighbors are secretly talking. Deprived of their ancient shrines and obliged to worship their own Lord in the attic of some innocent-looking warehouse, they must of course look back to the period before our town went Protestant as a sort of Paradise Lost. But their church had to go. It was too foreign to the nature of our people and we shall have to continue our present way until we shall be rid of it for all time.

No, it is not that I want. But I can't for the life of me see why we had to go so far in the other direction and why everything we do must be ugly and devoid of symbolic meaning. Most people are starving for a little color in their lives. They hunger for some variety of mysterious emotion that shall (for the moment at least) allow them to forget the all too brutal facts of human existence.

We fortunate ones who are not forever beset by the necessities of finding enough to eat and to drink and maintaining a roof over our children's heads, don't know what the poorer classes suffer. We go in for music or for painting or we write sonnets or study mathematics or lose ourselves in the works of the ancient philosophers. But all those roads of escape are closed to them. The Church alone can give them relief. And I never enter one of these sepulchral places of worship without wondering why our churches are so hopelessly one-sided and always appeal to the brain but never to the emotions.

Take that funeral of Saskia. Surely if there was a tragedy it was the death of this lovely creature. She was young and until a few months before her death, very lovely. She was married to one of the most remarkable men of her day and age, who was devoted to her and could have given her a life full of beauty and interest. She had a child. She had many friends. She was not very bright, perhaps, but no one asked of her that she be able to translate Auveer into Latin hexameters.

And then she died. Died before she was fully thirty years old. Died and left everything she loved behind, to become a mere number in a row of hideous graves and molder away in a threadbare shroud until her poor bones should be evicted to make room for some new candidate.

A ghastly tragedy, the negation of everything that men and women are supposed to live for. But a marvelous opportunity for the Church to stand forth as the prophet of hope, to maintain boldly and in the face of all this incriminating evidence, that life is good and that death is but another form of living, to surround these assertions with beautiful gestures and honest music, with symbols that should speak uncontrovertibly of the Eternal Verities.

Instead of which a young farmhand, speaking an accent that betrayed no breeding whatsoever, read some very fine verses, the meaning of which, however, he did not seem to understand in the least. Then sixteen men, who during the rest of the day were drivers of beer-wagons and eel-fishers, their working clothes badly hidden by long black cassocks and still smelling of the ale-house, took the large wooden box containing all this loveliness and with an ill-concealed "one, two, three!" they hurriedly lowered it into its stone cage. Then they turned away to carry the stretcher to the store-room in the back of the church where such paraphernalia were kept whenever there was no demand for their services, and hastened to the door to gather in the tips of the mourners.

I suppose there were those among us who wanted to linger a moment longer—to say something for the last time to the shadow that lay at our feet. But we were given no time. The minister left. The sexton was rattling his keys. There was nothing for us to do but to go.

And so we returned to the house in the Anthonie Breestraat and the nurse with the help of some of the neighbors had prepared a meal and the table was set in the same room from which they had carried the corpse away only an hour before (a dreadful and barbarous custom which we have undoubtedly inherited from our savage ancestors) and we were all of us bade to enter and regale ourselves.

I remained a few minutes, for not to have done so would have attracted too much attention. Then I looked for Rembrandt. He was not there. Driven by some sort of premonition, I softly tiptoed upstairs to the studio. Rembrandt, still in his mourning clothes, a long veil of black crape hanging down from his hat and black gloves on his hands, but completely oblivious of the world around him, was busy painting. I went up to him and put my hand on his shoulder, but he never turned his head and I don't think he noticed me.

For he was working once more at a portrait of Saskia, a portrait of Saskia as she had looked the day he had married her.

Chapter 15

REMBRANDT UNEXPECTEDLY CALLS AND BORROWS FIFTY GUILDERS

I left the studio without saying a word, talked to a few people downstairs, uttered the usual platitudes which belong to such an occasion, went home, changed my clothes and walked to the hospital where I spent the rest of the day. But to my great surprise, just after I had finished my supper, the maid told me that Mr. van Rijn had come to see me, and of course I bade him come in and asked why this formality of having himself announced, to which he replied vaguely that he did not know, and took a chair and sat down. Then I noticed that he was still in the same black clothes he had worn at the funeral and that there was something wild about the way in which he stared around the room.

In the case of any one else, I would have thought: "This man has been drinking." But he was dead sober and indeed it was not until much later, when anxiety about losing his eyesight was added to all his other worries, that he occasionally tried to find a few moments of oblivion by means of that false friend who dwelleth at the bottom of a brown jar of Schiedam gin.

There was but one other explanation for his disheveled looks; he was utterly exhausted.

I asked him whether he had had anything to eat that day, when he had last dined? He tried to remember, but could not. "Two or three days ago," he answered. And so I went into the kitchen and with my own hands prepared a meal of soft-boiled eggs and toasted bread and I sent the maid out for some milk, which I slightly heated, and he ate everything and then said: "I am dreadfully tired," and I took him upstairs and practically had to undress him (for he could hardly lift a finger) and I put him into my own bed and went downstairs again and made myself some sort of a couch out of chairs and cushions and the family Bible, which I used as a pillow, and blew out the candle and it seemed to me that I had hardly slept an hour when I was awakened by a loud banging on the front door, and of course I thought it was a patient and I went to the front door and to my great surprise, noticed that the sun was shining brightly and that it must be between eight or nine o'clock in the morning, and then I opened the door and there stood the nurse of little Titus, her hair hanging down her forehead and her bare feet in leather slippers.

"This is a fine thing to happen!" she began, but I shushed her and bade her come in and said sharply: "Keep a civil tongue in your head, woman. What is it you want?"

"Is he here?" she asked.

"He? What do you mean by 'he'?"

"Rembrandt."

"And since when do you call your master by his first name, or refer to him as 'he'?"

"Oh, well, he isn't so much, and for a widower to spend the night after his wife's funeral outside of the house! It is disgraceful! The neighbors will talk about it. They are already talking more than is good. It is disgraceful. And here I am, slaving myself to death to keep everything going nicely, and I cooked the finest meal ever served in our street after a funeral, and he does not even come down to say 'how do you do?' to a single one of the guests. And he forgets to give me money to buy beer and I have to pay for it out of my own pocket and then he does not come down to the meal and everybody will be talking about it!" and so on and so forth, an hysterical woman feeling very sorry for herself.

As there was no use arguing the case, I told her that she was a very badly used woman, that her master had been sadly negligent in his duties and that I would speak to him as soon as he had rested from the terrible exhaustion of the last few days, and having in this way quieted her somewhat, I prevailed upon her to go back home and take care of the baby and I would return with the master just as soon as I could.

The harpy actually left me and I returned to the dining-room to dress and to make up my mind what to say to Rembrandt, for although his household no longer needed my professional assistance, I felt that it was in even greater need of my services as a fairly sober-minded and not entirely unpractical human being. And when Rembrandt finally came downstairs, a little after eleven, and after he had eaten three ordinary breakfasts, I pushed my chair back (why can't one think with one's feet underneath the table?) and I said: "Listen, my good friend, but this will never do! If I have told you once I have told you ten dozen times, that woman ought to go. She is no good. She is irresponsible. I don't quite want to say that she is crazy but she isn't far away from it. Pay her her wages and let her go, but let her go right away, for unless I am much mistaken, she is rapidly losing her mind and she may end by murdering you or your child."

This startled him considerably and he asked: "Do you really think so, or do you say that because you do not like her?" To which I answered, not without some heat, that my personal likes or dislikes had nothing to do with the case, that in such matters I firmly believed in keeping professional and private opinions strictly separate, but that as a doctor who had done his best to save his wife and was now doing his best to save his son, I felt it my duty to warn him against so dangerous a companion, and I ended once more with the admonition: "Pay her and let her go."

But he answered that that was not as easy as it seemed and I asked him why? For the position between servants and master was clearly defined and regulated by the laws of Amsterdam. One might have to pay a servant or a nurse a few weeks extra wages, but that was all, and as long as the financial obligations were fulfilled, the magistrate took no notice when irate scullions stormed their council-chamber with their complaints and grievances. He might be obliged to give her a full month's wages, but then he would be able to ask her to leave his house at once, and good riddance.

All those arguments, however, seemed to make very little impression upon him. He kept repeating that it would not be so easy as I thought and finally took his leave, but just as I opened the door to show him out, he made a remark which puzzled me a great deal. "You are right," he said, "and I will do what you tell me. I will try to raise the money to-day."

"Raise the money to-day . . ."—a question of twenty or thirty guilders at the very most. "Raise the money"—when one lived in the biggest house on the Jodenbreestraat, bought pictures by Rubens and Raphael as if they had been ten-cent prints and was known to have married one of the richest girls of Friesland!

"I will try to raise the money to-day!" Thus far we had had tragedy. Now mystery had been added. And I decided to have a serious talk with him as soon as he should have recovered from the emotions of the last few days.

A man who any day could lay his hands on fifty thousand guilders in cash (every one knew that Saskia had not had a penny less) telling me that he would try and raise a servant's wages—no, something was wrong there.

But one can't very well ask questions of that sort and so I waited and went the usual rounds of my professional duties, for I knew that when people have something on their mind, they sooner or later must relieve themselves or go mad.

In the olden days, so I am told, one could go to a priest and tell him all about everything. Then came the new dispensation and people were admonished to address themselves directly to God.

And God lives so very far away and a doctor is conveniently near by, right around the corner. And so the doctor often gets the confidences that were really meant for the Almighty. I therefore made up my mind that I would not call at the Breestraat, and would wait, for the patient would appear soon enough.

Rembrandt, however, appeared to be struggling hard to keep his trouble to himself. The days grew into weeks and he never came near the Houtgracht.

And then suddenly one day when I returned from the hospital late in the afternoon I found him in my working-room. He must have been waiting quite a long time, for he had amused himself copying a bust of

Hippocrates that stood on my book-case, and the drawing was almost finished.

"I have come to speak to you about something," he said, without offering me the usual salutation. "I am in a rather difficult position. Can you let me have fifty guilders?" And then he told me his story, and it was a strange one, as you shall see for yourself.

Chapter 16

I LEARN A FEW THINGS ABOUT SASKIA'S FAMILY

"I am just back from the Old Church," he began. "I have bought the grave in which Saskia is buried. It is mine now and she will never have to lie there with strangers. I had to sell two of my pictures to raise the amount. I don't know what has happened. I had thought that they would bring me six hundred florins. I only got half. But the grave is mine. I went to the notary this morning. The papers have been signed and are in my pocket. Now could you let me have fifty guilders? I owe the nurse thirty for past wages and twenty for letting her go without the usual notice. Can I have the money?"

I told him that of course he could have the money, but why did he need it? It was a difficult subject. I decided not to try and be too delicate. Such mental operations are very much like physical ones, and the tender-hearted surgeons, who try to save the feelings of their patients, are the ones who do the most harm. And so I said: "Of course your affairs are none of my business and I would gladly give you a thousand guilders if you really needed them. But there is the house. You once told me that you had paid thirteen thousand guilders for it. You will grant me that I have never pried into your affairs, but one day when you were pulling a proof and I was talking to you in the little room upstairs, you remarked that you made between two thousand and three thousand florins a year from your etchings alone. Then there are your pupils. I don't know how much they pay you, but it ought to be a fairly decent sum. Then there are your portraits. There is the picture of Banning Cocq's company. The other day (it was at the funeral of Saskia, to be exact) young Uylenburgh, her cousin, told me that you had got five thousand florins for it. And then there is Saskia's inheritance. She must have had quite a good deal. Her father was a man of importance. I don't know what became of it, but I suppose you got some of it."

"I got everything."

"Well, you ought to be able to realize on it." (I hated to talk like a damn school-master, but in many ways the man to whom I was speaking was still a child.)

"I can," he answered. "It is merely a question of time. You see, Saskia had made a will about two weeks before she died. We did not tell you, because you had given orders that she must not be disturbed, and as a matter of fact, I did not know about it until it was all finished. But the thing had been on her mind for quite a long time and one afternoon, when I had gone out to talk about a new portrait, she sent the nurse to get her a notary. He came to see her and drew up everything in true legal form. She signed the documents nine days before she died and she left everything to me. It is understood that I will look after the boy and see that he gets a first-rate education and if I ever marry again, which I doubt, all the money goes to Titus. And some other details which are neither here nor there. But the most wonderful thing of all—and I never thought that the poor girl had cared quite so much for me—came at the end. She stipulated that I should never be asked to give any sort of an accounting. It is all mine to do with as I please. Of course, I shall merely regard it as a trust-fund for the benefit of little Titus. I may use some of it to pay for the house. Half of it has been paid already but I still owe some seven thousand florins on it and a few years' interest. In the end it will go to Titus anyway and so that means nothing.

"I am really much better fixed than ever before. But I have no head for business and I would rather paint three pictures than add one single sum of figures. And things have been sort of slow coming in these last six months. I know that people say that I got five thousand guilders for that big militia piece. Well, sixteen hundred is a little nearer to the truth, and even of that, I am not quite sure, for they now tell me that it is too large for the hall and they want to cut a piece off at both sides, and some of the soldiers who stood pretty near the edge of the picture threaten that they won't give me a cent unless they show up as well as the rest of the company. And then there are four or five of that crowd who claim that I have not done them justice. They don't want to be painted with their backs to the public. They say that they had agreed to pay an equal sum, all of them, and that therefore they have a right to as much canvas as their neighbors. One of them stopped me the other day on the Ververs Gracht and caused quite a scandal, and he was a sergeant, too. What did I mean by hiding his face behind the arm of another fellow, who was only a corporal and a man he did not care for to boot?

"Well, I did not lose my temper, though I was sorely tempted to do so. Instead I bought him a beer and took him to the Kloveniersdoelen and I spent an hour trying to show that beetlehead that I had tried to do something more than paint a nice, polite picture of himself and his companions, that I had not tried to paint one particular company of soldiers, but all the soldiers of all the ages, going forth to defend their homesteads. I made quite a speech. Did I convince him? Of course not! All my fine words did not make the slightest impression upon the creature's dumb brain. Whenever I thought that I had made my point clear, he would look at me and shake his head and say: 'I paid as much as the rest of them and I want to be shown as big as the rest of them, or I shan't give you a cent.' And in the end he got quite abusive and asked me whether the little girl in the center had paid her share and what she was doing there anyway, and then I gave up in despair, and I shall count myself lucky if I get half of what they promised me.

"You are right, I used to have quite a number of pupils, but you know how it is. Those who have talent are usually too poor to pay me anything and those who can pay have not got the talent and they are just a common nuisance. They might at least have given me some rest when Saskia died. Well, a few had the decency to go home. But half a dozen came from too far away to go home and they stayed. And one evening I heard a lot of noise in the attic (you know that is where they have their rooms) and I went upstairs to investigate and I heard two people snickering behind a door and then I heard the high giggle of one of the models, who had no business to be there at all, and then the boy said: 'And now we are in good company, for we are like Adam and Eve in Paradise.' So I told them that I would make that wish come true and would play the Angel with the Flaming Sword and would drive them out, and I threw them out of the house then and there, because I have got to have discipline in my own home, but of course people talked about it and as a result three of the other boys have left me.

"And so you see how it goes. I have several thousand guilders still coming to me for portraits I have done. But it seems that it is harder to collect nowadays than formerly. Some people claim that we may conclude peace with Spain almost any day now and that there will be quite a terrible crisis then, but why war should be more profitable than peace is something I don't quite understand. If I had ever kept books I would be able to tell you where all the money has gone, for I must have made quite a great deal these last ten years. And anyway, it does not matter. It is only a question of a few months—as soon as the formalities connected with the inheritance shall have been completed. You know how slow our courts are about such things. There must be a guardian for little Titus and the Chamber of Orphans must be consulted. I hate all such legal complications. I don't understand them. They worry me and keep me from working and so I just try to forget them. But everything will be all right in a couple of months.

"Meanwhile, it will be much better for everybody concerned if that damned nurse goes before the end of another day. I could sell something out of my collection, but then the whole town would say that those Frisian relations who said that I was a spendthrift and was wasting my wife's money had been right. I need fifty guilders and I need them right away and I need them very quietly. I can pay you back in September or October and I shall give you six percent, which seems fair. Can I have them?"

I said yes, he could have them, and went to the little safe in my bedroom in which I kept the East Indian shares I had inherited from my grand-uncle and I took out five golden riders and I gave them to Rembrandt and I bade him forget about the interest—it was just a small loan between friends, and that evening I wrote a long letter to a friend of mine in Leeuwarden, a young man with whom I had studied in Leyden, but who had given up medicine and had gone in for the law. He belonged to an excellent family which had remained faithful to the King of Spain after the outbreak of the revolution and had therefore been deprived of all its possessions. He often declared that while poverty might be no disgrace, it had very little else to recommend it to a sensible person, and he had made no secret of it then that he meant to marry money—a great deal of money—just as soon as he had the opportunity. He had been as good as his word. Almost immediately upon graduation he had married the daughter of a very rich cattle-owner from the neighborhood of Franeker. A former acquaintance who had gone to Franeker to finish his studies (finding Leyden a little too diverting for that constant application to his work which his father deemed necessary) had been present at the wedding. I ran across him one day when he was passing through Amsterdam and he told me all about it.

"The bride squinted and she was slightly lame," he informed me, "but she was an orphan and had two hundred thousand guilders in cash. The groom looked very meek and dignified and kept awake all during the service. He has bought out one of the best notary offices in the capital—specializes in farmers' cases, has become the financial adviser of every honest plowman in all of the sixteen counties—coins in the money almost as fast as the Mint can turn it out—is a very decent husband to the unsightly wife and is just as amusing and honest a companion as in the days before he got rich."

I wrote to this provincial Croesus and asked him to find out for me whether Saskia van Uylenburgh had really been as rich as people said and to give me all the particulars he could lay hands on—that I was not acting in an indiscreet fashion, but that I had a friend who was greatly interested, etc., etc., and would he please let me know by return mail.

Three weeks later I had his answer and his letter showed that he had not changed a bit from the days when we used to walk to Noordwijk on a fine Sunday afternoon to eat a supper of bread and cheese in the Golden Hyacinth and felt that this world was by far the best sort of a world anybody could wish to live in.

This is what he wrote:

"Ornatissime!

"Magno cum gaudio accepi letteras tuas atque maximo cum—now what in thunder was 'haste' in Latin? But anyway, I got your letter and the question you ask can refer to only one person, the great Maestro Rembrandtus van Rijn, painter-in-extraordinary to the Rabbis of Amsterdam and who not long ago, if I am to believe my correspondents, has given up the use of colors altogether and now distills himself a new sort of picture out of a mixture of soot, lamp-black and coal-ashes.

"For who else could be interested in the affairs of that poor Uylenburgh girl, who left here so long ago that few of her contemporaries remember her? Be reassured, however. I have done a little quiet investigating and here is my general impression of the case.

"I don't think that there is very much money in that particular quarter, or if there be any, that it will ever be of great use to him, as most of the renowned Uylenburgh millions exist only on paper, or wherever they exist 'in naturalia,' are so hopelessly mortgaged, hypothesized or hypothecated (take your choice) debentured and generally tied-up, that in case of a sudden sale, I doubt whether they would realize one twentieth of their normal value. I am on agreeable terms of professional cordiality with the notary who has handled the affairs of the family ever since the old man was elected sheriff for the first time and that must have been shortly after the flood. He threw up his hands in despair and said: 'Don't talk to me about that case! It will be my death yet. For now, so I understand, that the youngest daughter has died, the one who married that miller or painter or whatever he is in Holland, the widower will probably write us a letter and ask for a settlement but Solomon in all his wisdom could not unravel that estate.' And then he gave me many details, all in a perfectly professorial manner, and I shall not even try to explain his speech in plain Dutch, but I shall merely give you the gist of his observations.

"Old Rombertus van Uylenburgh, the father, had been quite a famous man in local Frisian politics. A big frog in a small puddle. During the critical years of the rebellion, he had several times been Burgomaster of Leeuwarden and he it was who conducted the negotiations between the Estates of Friesland and the Prince of Orange about choosing the latter to be sovereign ruler of the new commonwealth. But William was murdered before they had been able to reach an agreement. As you undoubtedly know old Rombertus was lunching with William the day the latter was shot and held him in his arms when he died. All this had brought a great deal of honor, but he had been away from home so much that he had little time to look after his own affairs.

"The mother had brought up the children, of whom there had been nine at the time of her death in '21 or '22. In '24 Rombertus himself had gone to join the angels. At that moment, two of the sons were engaged in the law and a third one had become an officer in a regiment of the line. Of the daughters, the eldest, Antje, is married to a certain Maccovius, a professor of theology in the University of Franeker, a rather unpleasant person of very violent convictions, but very popular among his neighbors whose views are about as broad as that of a birdseed. The second one, Hiskia, is married to Gerrit van Loo, who holds a political office in a little village north of Franeker. The third one, Titia, is married to a certain Frans Copal, who is engaged in business and who is said to spend much of his time in Holland. The fourth one is the wife of a Frisian gentleman of good family and some fortune, one Doede van Ockema, and the fifth one is the spouse of an artist by the name of Wybrand de Geest, a native of her own beloved town of Leeuwarden, who enjoys an excellent reputation as a portrait painter in this remote part of the world and who has done portraits of practically all of the members of the House of Orange who have ever visited Friesland.

"That, as our friends the French would say, is the 'tableau' of the immediate Uylenburgh family. There also are a vast number of uncles and aunts and cousins and second cousins and third cousins and some of them have remained at home, but others have boldly crossed the Zuyder Zee to try their luck in Amsterdam and of these you probably know more in Amsterdam than we do in Leeuwarden.

"Now as to the financial status of this Gens Uylenburghiensis. It is a most intricate matter, for as far as my informant knew, there never had been a division of the funds, and although the father had now been dead for almost twenty years, the estate had not yet been settled and it was doubtful whether a settlement would be possible at the present time, when the general fear that the war would come to an end has made money so tight that one is glad to pay twenty or even twenty-five percent for a loan of a few thousand guilders. In short, once upon a time there was a considerable fortune which belonged to the Uylenburgh children and of which they received so much per annum in the form of rents. But if any one of them should ever get into trouble and would ask for an immediate accounting, I am very doubtful whether the matter could be arranged without a dreadful sacrifice on the part of all concerned.

"Wherefore [so the letter ended], if your friend should be hard up for ready cash, I would advise him to go to the Jews and the money-lenders. They will give him better terms and they will prove to be more charitable than his beloved relations on this side of the Zuyder Zee. From all I have been able to gather, they are none too friendly towards this 'foreign' connection (any one not born within spitting distance of our beloved tower of Oldehove is considered a 'foreigner' in these parts) whose father ran a mill, whose brother is a shoemaker or some such terrible thing, who paints rabbis and associates openly with Turks and Frenchmen and other immoral races and who (something they will never forgive him) once paid 424 guilders for a picture by a certain Rubens who not only was an out-and-out Papist but who furthermore chose his subjects by preference from some heathenish story book, making it impossible for decent Christians to contemplate the same without a feeling of utter shame and mortification."

Then followed some very intimate and rather ribald remarks about the pleasant habits and manners of the populace among whom my old friend had cast his fortunes and the usual salutations in execrable Latin.

"Vale ornatissime atque eruditissime doctor medicinarum artium atque me miserum in hac urbe taediossissima visitare atque consolare festina.

"P.S.—You might send me some dried sprats as soon as the season opens. I confess to a liking for the lowly, petrified fish. In return for which I

Mijn heer

Soo ist dan dat ick met sijn excellensij verders 2 stucken
toe sende die ick meen dat soodanich sullen
bevonden worden dat sijn Hoocheijt mij nu selfs voor ider
mij niet niet min als duijsent gulden toe leggen
sal doch soo sijn Hoocheijt dunckt dat sijt niet
en meerijteert sal naer sijn eijgen believen
minder geven mij verlaetende op sijn Hoocheijts
kennis en discresij. sals mij danckbaerlick
daer met laeten contenteeren ende blijvende
nevens mijne groetenisse sijne

U onderdanige dienaer

Rembrandt

Het geene ick aende lijsten
ende kas verschooten hebbe is 44 gulden
in alles

FACSIMILE OF A LETTER TO HUYGENS

promise to keep you faithfully informed about anything that happens here in the matter of the U. family. But my general advice would be not to count on a penny. The money is there without a doubt. But how to get it away from the dear brethren and sistern—ah, my friend—there is the rub!

"P.P.S.—My wife wants to be remembered to you, ignota ignoto. She wonders whether you can find her a good cook in Amsterdam. Such a thing no longer exists in this part of the world. We have grown too prosperous. The wenches, all of them marry sailors, become ladies, and go about dressed up in silks and satins.

"P.P.P.S.—I meant bloaters, and not sprats. We can get sprats here by the ton, but the bloater is a delicacy. Ad nunc, vale definitissime atque favere mihi perge. . . ."

I put the document aside and did some fast thinking. Between the lines of his crazy letter, my old friend had told me everything I wanted to know and my heart was filled with sad forebodings. For by this time I had come to know Rembrandt quite well. He lived in a world of his own making and thus far life had been fairly easy to him. Now he had undoubtedly reached a crisis. His wife was dead. He had a small boy to bring up. It would cost a great deal to maintain the house in the Breestraat and public taste was rapidly changing and no longer looked with favor upon what people had begun to call his "phantastic experiments." The fact that he had asked me (still a comparative stranger) for a loan of fifty guilders, showed that he was very hard up for ready cash. Now if he had only been made to understand that he was poor and would have to begin all over again to provide for himself and his son, all might have been well, for he was a hard worker and never spent a penny upon his own comforts. But there was this strange streak of the grand seigneur in him. He must play fairy-godfather to his poor colleagues and whenever he went to an auction, he must outbid all the professional art dealers, just to show them that he was Rembrandt, the great Rembrandt, who need not bother about trifles.

If only he had been put face to face with the fact that he did not have a cent in the whole wide world! But he had fallen heir to Saskia's fortune! There was that pathetic will, leaving everything to her "beloved man" and leaving it without any restrictions or reservations whatsoever. If only she had insisted upon a guardian for her son, then there would have been a public appraisal and Rembrandt might have discovered what I now knew and what I could not very well tell him without running the risk of being called a busybody—a man who poked his nose into affairs that were none of his business.

My hands were tied and I was forced to stand by and see the poor fellow play the millionaire on the strength of a paper promise which was not worth its weight in lead.

Nevertheless, I might have done something, but just then an incident occurred that upset my own life so completely that it was years before I saw Rembrandt again.

And when I returned from my foreign travels, it was too late.

The bubble had burst, the house had been sold, and the painter was peddling his pictures from one pawnshop to the next, to buy bread for his children.

Chapter 17

I RELATE A FEW INTERESTING STORIES ABOUT MY GRANDFATHER

And now I come to that strange period in my life to which I have already alluded a few pages ago, when through circumstances over which I had no control whatsoever, I was an exile for almost eight years.

I have always been exceedingly sorry that this happened. I can never quite get over the feeling that things might have gone differently with Rembrandt if I had been there.

I am not thinking in the first place of the financial end of things. Since the death of my grand-uncle I really had more than I needed for my very simple needs and I might have been able to help him out of a few of his difficulties. But it would not have been an easy task. For Rembrandt (as I have said so often before) was absolutely blind on the subject of money. He was indeed blind upon most subjects related directly or indirectly with the business of living a quiet and respectable existence, as those terms were understood by the vast majority of his neighbors. He was a man possessed of a single idea. Within the realm of color and form, he felt himself like unto God. His ambition along that line sometimes assumed almost divine proportions. He wanted to capture the entire existing world around him and hold it his prisoner on canvas or paper. Life, alas, was so short and there was so much to be done. He had to work and work and work. He was sick. Never mind, he must work. His wife (one of the few persons who ever assumed the shape of a definite human being in his preoccupied mind) died. He must rush through the funeral and go back to work. He was acclaimed the fashionable painter of the hour and made twenty or thirty thousand guilders a year. Put them away in that cupboard over there or go to the Jew around the corner and buy out his whole stock of curiosities or give them to some poor devil of a fellow-painter who lies starving in a garret. Do anything you want with the money, as long as you don't bother him by talking about it. For he must work and life was short and there was a great deal to be done. A letter has just arrived from the sheriff saying that a number of outstanding notes are long overdue and should be paid right then and there or there would be difficulties. Visits from the Honorable Masters in Bankruptcy. Forced sales—fines—imprisonment, even. Fiddlesticks! it is winter and at three o'clock in the afternoon it is too dark to paint. One has to be economical and save every minute in times like these. The sheriff is a fool. Tell him so. Bid him come or stay away, for it is all the same as long as one can only work and work and work. No, a man like that could not be helped with an occasional check—with the loan of a few thousand guilders. They would have meant just as much to him as to a beaver busily engaged upon building a dam, or a bird constructing its nest.

All one could do for an unfortunate fellow like this, mad with the beauty of the outer world, crazy with joy at the myriad manifestations of the mysterious inner spirit, was to give him some understanding and then some more understanding and still more understanding and ask for nothing in return. Amen.

For the lonely pioneers who do the work that the rest of us shirk ask for very little. They are willing to go hungry and to slave for mean wages and to be humiliated by those who in God's own good time, in a thousand different ways, won't be allowed to hold the stirrup of their horses.

But they die unless at least once in a long while some one comes their way who stops in his tracks and bids them a cheery good-morning and casually remarks: "That is a pretty fine piece of work you are doing there."

For such is their nature.

And it is part of the penalty they pay for the greatest of their manifold blessings—the weregild they must contribute for never having grown up.

Here I must call a halt.

I had intended to write about a very dear friend, now dead and gone, and from the very beginning I had meant to keep myself and my own affairs as much as possible out of these recollections.

But when two lives are as absolutely entwined and interwoven as those of Rembrandt and my own, it is very difficult to accomplish this as completely as I meant to do it.

The next few pages therefore will be mainly about myself. But I shall be very short and above all things, I shall try to be honest.

My grandfather was an almost mythological figure to me. I knew him well, for he did not die until I was almost thirty. But when I was young, the men who had taken part in the great struggle for liberty were fast dying out and the few survivors were regarded with that awed respect which the Greeks would have bestowed upon the Titans, had one of them managed to escape from Tartarus to find his way to Athens.

As a young man, while serving as first-mate on a ship that plied between Rotterdam and Antwerp, he had once been caught with a copy of a Dutch New Testament which in the kindness of his heart he had promised to bring to a Lutheran minister awaiting a sentence of death in one of the Flemish prisons. He himself (as far as I was ever able to find out) took very little interest in theological questions. Whenever a dispute of that sort arose (and in our Republic, next to the making of money, people seem to have very few other interests) he would leave the room and whistle for his dog and go out for a walk, if it were daytime, or if it were night, go to bed and read the colloquies of Erasmus, which were an everlasting source of entertainment to him and which he could enjoy in the original, as shortly after the siege of Haarlem he had spent a year in a Spanish prison and had shared his cell with an Anabaptist preacher who happened to be quite a scholar and had whiled away the tedious hours of their common confinement by teaching his room-mate the rudiments of the Latin grammar.

No, he belonged to that vast group of men and women who had happened to be born just about the time Luther and Calvin had started their reformatory activities and who had been so thoroughly exasperated by the cruelty, the intolerance and the bigotry of both Catholics and Protestants that they had been obliged to seek a refuge among the philosophers of ancient days.

Nominally, my grandfather called himself a Christian.

In his heart, he was a contemporary of Socrates. Jesus, if he ever thought of him at all, he regarded as a well-meaning but rather futile and slightly bewildered young Jewish prophet, who in the aloofness of his primitive mountain village and totally ignorant of whatever lay beyond his own poverty-stricken hillsides (peasants always despise what they do not understand), had done more to arrest the normal development of the civilized world than any other agency, either human or divine.

He often talked to me of these matters during the last years of his life, but asked me not to mention it to any one else.

"What would be the use?" he would say. "Our wily old cousin was right. The average man is too weak to stand firmly upon his own feet. He needs some outward support, some pleasant fairy-story that shall make him forget the horrors, the boredom, the dull disappointment of his daily routine. Let him have his tales of giants and gods, his heroes and paladins.

"When you were a boy and believed in Santa Claus, Dominie Slatterius came to your father and said that this old saint was a relic of heathenism and you ought to be told and your father, being a fool, was ready to do so. I took the reverend gentleman by the scruff of the neck and threw him down the stoop and I told your father he would go the same way if he ever tried to substitute one of his dreadful Jewish fishermen or tentmakers for that amiable holy man who has made more children happy than all the church fathers and apostles together. That was not a very tolerant thing to do but look what has happened right here in our own country?

"Who started the great rebellion? A handful of men. What did they have to gain? Very little except the chance of being hung on the nearest tree. Of course, once the thing was under way, there were a lot of ardent patriots who knew that it was good fishing in troubled waters and who came over to our side. But who were the men who planned everything and took the risks and pawned their plate and their wives' diamonds and took extra mortgages on their houses to hire troops and buy guns and powder and ships and everything that was needed? A mere handful of honest fellows who hated to see poor devils of weavers and fishermen and carpenters being hacked to pieces and boiled alive and drowned like kittens merely because they happened to think differently from their neighbors upon subjects of which the neighbors couldn't possibly know more than they did themselves.

"I don't want to claim that we were saints. We were nothing of the sort. We drank and we cursed and we knew the difference between a handsome young wench and a homely old hag. And I don't swear that we would ever have moved a finger if it had not been for those endless processions of men and women, trudging patiently from the jail to the gallows, perfectly respectable citizens, hard-working little artisans with mumbling lips and staring eyes, going to be tied to a ladder and thrown into a slow-burning coal fire because they disagreed upon some utterly idiotic point of divine law with a fat old Italian who lived a thousand miles away, and who needed some money to give his daughter a suitable dowry.

"That is what started me. That and nothing else. And then, when it was all over, what did one see? The same men whom we had dragged away from the gallows by main force—those same men and women for whom we had ruined ourselves that they might think as they pleased—started murdering those who only a short while before had murdered them. The victim turned executioner, and the former executioners were now merrily dangling from a hundred trees. Could anything have been more absurd? We got rid of those hordes of mendicants and begging friars, because they were an obscene nuisance. And then, as soon as they were gone and we thought, 'Now we shall have peace,' our cities and our villages and our cross-roads and our homes were invaded by platoons of even more unpleasant brethren with long brown coats and long black faces, but every whit as stupid, as narrow minded, as objectionable, as their pestiferous predecessors.

"What is it all about, anyway?

"I am an old man. I have spent most of my life fighting for an absurd ideal of tolerance. And as soon as we had kicked the enemy out of the front door, he came in again by the back entrance.

"Bring me a pipe of tobacco and let me sit and smoke. It is the only sensible thing beside raising strawberries, and for that I am no longer young enough."

These conversations (and we had many of them, and they were all of them more or less alike) were typical of the old skipper and it will give you an idea of the sort of man he was. He must have been a terrific fighter in his day. He stood six feet three in his stockings and weighed well over two hundred pounds. He once figured out that he had passed through six formal sieges and taken part in eighteen naval engagements, not to mention skirmishes and three pitched battles upon those not infrequent occasions when the sailors waded ashore and joined the infantry. Several times he had been badly wounded, but he had the constitution of a young ox and even recovered from the blood-lettings with which in those early days my colleagues tried to cure everything from a broken leg to a case of anemia.

At one time or another of his career he must have accumulated considerable wealth. He once told me that during the expedition against Cadiz, when he commanded the second squadron, his share of the plunder alone amounted to fifty thousand ducats, and that was only one occasion among many when he had a plentiful chance to line his pockets with Spanish doubloons. What had become of all this money, I don't know. Nobody seemed to know. But he was the incarnation of generosity. He was so absolutely open-handed that in the middle of a battle he would have given his sword to his enemy, had the latter asked him for it, and would have continued to fight with his bare hands rather than say "no" to a courteous request.

Not that he was exactly poor when I came to know him a little better. He lived in a very decent house on the river front near Rotterdam and after the death of my grandmother he kept but one single servant, an old sailor whom he had once saved from being hung for an act of insubordination—a most excusable case of insubordination, as he explained to me, for the fellow had merely gone on shore to kill a landlubber who had stolen his girl from him. The old sailor was not only his devoted servant but also a perfect cook.

To return to my grandfather, he spent very little money upon his personal adornment, but a great deal upon books, and until the last years of his life he kept a small sailing-boat with which he used to putter around from morning till night and which at last was the cause of his death, for one day, leaving the harbor of Brielle, he saw how a small boy, who had been bombarding his craft with chunks of dried mud, lost his balance and fell into the water and was on the point of being carried away by the tide. He jumped overboard, saved the brat, gave him a most terrific walloping and continued his voyage without bothering to change his clothes. That night he had a chill and three days later he was dead from pneumonia, a fitting end for one who had spent his life doing the sort of things he had done.

When his last will and testament was opened, it was found that he had left every cent he possessed to an old sailors' home on condition that once a year a rousing feast be given to all the inmates upon which occasion they were to be allowed to get as drunk and hilarious as they pleased.

On the last day of his life he was visited by a minister. Rumor had gone about that the old skipper was on the point of dying and it seemed inconceivable that any one should go to his final rest without a word of commendation on the part of a duly ordained clergyman. The Reverend Doctor who made his appearance was a genial soul, the only one among the fourteen local shepherds who had sometimes been suspected of certain worldly inclinations. In the language of that day he was a "libertine," a man who took liberties with Holy Script and who was more interested in the spiritual message of Jesus than in the color of the cloak he had worn while delivering it. Upon this occasion his brethren had probably delegated him to call upon the dying sinner, as the one least likely to be shown the door. And the good dominie acquitted himself of his task with great dexterity, being neither too cordial nor too distant and aloof. He casually remarked that most people when they found themselves on the point of reporting for duty to the Great Commander of us all (a bit of joviality which was not appreciated by the patient) liked to have the opportunity to discuss their past record with some one who devoted all his time to matters of the soul.

"Dominie," the old man answered, "I know who you are and I have heard a good deal about you that I like. For one thing, most of your colleagues wish that you would slip on an apple skin and fall in a canal and drown. In this house, that is a recommendation. But what could you possibly hope to do for me?"

"Well," the reverend gentleman replied, "we might have a little talk about your chances of salvation. What for example has been your attitude towards the Lord's most holy covenants?"

"Yes," said my grandfather, "that is rather a leading question, but I like your courage and I will answer you. I think your Ten Commandments are a waste of time."

"But isn't that a dangerous remark for a man who is on the brink of the grave?"

"I don't see why. I am perfectly willing to have this out with the Lord himself. The best proof that he does not believe in them himself is the fact that he has never kept them."

"That is pure blasphemy!"

"Not in the least. But short of keeping the Sabbath, he has broken every one of them."

"I am afraid that I have nothing to say to you."

"Now there you go again, like a good Christian! Have a moment's patience with a dying man and I will explain. How about that idea of not killing your fellow-men? My dear friend, the whole Old Testament is full of killing. Your Jehovah is a mean and vindictive creature and suffers from tantrums like any badly brought up child. When he has one of his attacks (and almost anything may bring them on) he hits and strikes and thumps and prances like a drunken sailor in a bar-room brawl. Villages, towns, whole nations are wiped off the face of the earth—and what have they done? Often nothing for which an ordinary magistrate would dare to fine them.

"Take that business in Egypt. It has always struck me that the Egyptians were completely in the right. After all, it was their country. After all, the Jews had come to them to keep from starving to death and they had been pretty decently treated too. And according to what I have heard of them, they were a fine people—much nicer than their guests who were like the cuckoo and always put their eggs into another bird's nest. But they must be visited with all sorts of plagues and lose their children and suffer hunger and pestilence because your absurd Jehovah had another attack of anger and wanted to do a little smiting."

The minister looked perplexed. "I never heard it explained quite that way," he remarked.

"I am sure you never did and I am sorry if I should hurt your feelings. But that happens to be the way I look upon it."

"Anyway," in a feeble effort to spar for time, "that happened before he gave us his precious Law."

"Precious Law indeed! But afterwards it was just as bad. I know He kept the Sabbath, but that is about all. It was easy for him to tell us to honor our parents, as he did not have any himself to exasperate him with their everlasting complaints about being an 'undutiful child.' And as for the seventh commandment, have you ever thought of the way Joseph must have looked upon this divine command about respecting the integrity of another man's wife?"

The minister made ready to go, but the sick man held him back. "Don't go, Dominie," he said. "If this hurts your feelings, we will talk of something else."

"It does not hurt my feelings," the minister replied, "but it fills my heart with grief that any one who has spent his whole life among Christians should speak and think the way you do."

"That is just it! I have spent my whole life among Christians. When I was forty, I made a vow. I said to myself that if I met three Christians who really and truly lived up to the lessons of their master—three men or women who were truly humble and kind and tolerant and forgiving—yet professed themselves to belong to your creed, I would join the Church."

"And now you are how old?"

"Eighty-two, though I shall never see eighty-three."

"And you are still a pagan."

"No, Dominie, I am not that either."

"Then what do you call yourself?"

"Exactly what I am. Look here," and with great effort he pulled his night-gown from his left shoulder, for he was in terrible pain and very weak. "Look at this. Can you still see it after these sixty years? A big red letter H. The Inquisition burned it on my back so that if they ever caught me again, they would know me as a heretic and could treat me accordingly. When I come to the Gates of Heaven, I will show Saint Peter this and I am sure he will let me in, for what was he himself but a heretic when he turned his back upon the law of his fathers? And I will come to the throne of God and I will show him this and I will say: 'Holy Father, I fought sixty years for what I believed to be right and that red H is all I got to show for my labors. They gave it to me because I felt, like a very wonderful sage of olden times, that the still small voice from within was the best guide to follow in dealing with one's fellow-man.

"'They burned it into my quivering flesh because they said I was a heretic—a person who did not hold with the established opinions. They meant it as a disgrace, but I have worn it as a badge of honor ever since. I don't know, God, what your intentions were with us poor mortals. Perhaps you ought to have devoted another week or fortnight to the business of getting our world started, for although I mean no offense, it is a pretty sad mess at the present moment and if all the history I have read means anything, it has been a muddle ever since you turned your back upon it and left us to the mercies of old Adam. Now I may be all wrong, but the only way in which I can see that anything will ever be accomplished is for some of us now and then to take an unpopular stand. The aye-sayers never get anywhere. But the no-sayers irritate the rest of their neighbors occasionally into doing the right thing. And I am a no-sayer, a heretic, a man who does not hold with the majority. As long as you turned me loose into this world with a mind of my own, I took it for granted that you meant me to do something with it.

"'But that meant that I had to have doubts, to ask questions, to take every problem apart and see what I could make of it. Blame me and punish me, God, if I have done wrong, but I would have disgraced your Holy Name had I done differently and not used that brain you put into my skull to the best of my ability to show my fellow-men the way to a more reasonable world.'"

The old man exhausted himself by this supreme effort and lay panting for breath. The minister, who was really a very kindly person, tried to change the subject.

"Our Heavenly Father no doubt will know how to answer that question better than I can hope to do. But how about this world? You were a mariner. You depended upon a compass to set your course. And yet you lived without a single rule by which to guide your conduct."

The old man opened his eyes and smiled, though very feebly. "I am sorry, Dominie, but once more you are mistaken. I was quite young when I learned that my fellow-men had to be loved in spite of themselves, not to speak of trusting them. The only creature that I could depend upon, besides my wife (but she was an exception), was a dog. And I have never been without one since I was a boy of fifteen.

"I know you don't think very much of dogs. You won't even let them have a soul or go to Heaven. Think of golden streets with nothing but holy people and not a single dog! No, I have never spent either a day or a night without one of those four-footed companions. They cost me a lot of time, but they amply repaid me for my trouble. For dogs are very wise. Much wiser than men. People say they can't speak. Perhaps they know how but refuse to use their voice to save themselves an endless amount of bother and vague discussion. But they know all sorts of things we don't know, and they have a finer feeling for the difference between right and wrong than we do. And when I came home at night, or back to my ship, after the day's work (and pretty rough work it was at times) I would look my dog in the face and if he still wagged his tail at me, I knew that everything was all right, but if he didn't, I knew that something, somewhere, had gone wrong. It may sound a bit simple, but it is true, and best of all, it worked."

"And our system does not work?"

"Your system does not work. It merely talks and now if you will pardon me, I will go to sleep. I am not very strong any more and to-morrow, if you are right, I will have to engage in another conversation of this sort, and I still have to prepare my little speech."

"And if I am wrong?"

"If you are wrong, I shall be able to rest—rest for ever and ever."

"Then you are very tired?"

"Incredibly tired."

"Of living?"

"No, just of having been alive," and with this the sick man pulled the blankets around his shoulders and never spoke again.

The next morning the sailor-servant came to open the curtains and ask after his master's wishes.

But the skipper had received an answer to all his questions.

He was dead.

Chapter 18

UNDER WHAT PECULIAR CIRCUMSTANCES MY GRANDMOTHER HAPPENED TO MARRY MY GRANDFATHER

So much for my grandfather and now a few words about that even more extraordinary person who became my grandmother.

She died ten years before her husband, but I still knew her quite well and as she disliked her only son (my own father) as cordially as her husband detested him, she had concentrated all her love upon her two grandchildren. She was a tiny woman and she had never had the smallpox and her bright little eyes shone out from a face that had retained the complexion of a small girl, although it was well provided with wrinkles, for life as the wife of this extraordinary man had not been exactly easy.

"But it has always been interesting," she used to say when people tried to tell her how sorry they were for her that she, the daughter of an Antwerp burgomaster, had not been able to do better for herself and for the greater part of her life had been obliged to do her own housework and her own washing.

"It has never been dull for a moment, and what else counts except the few moments when we realize that we are something better than cabbages or cucumbers?"

But there was something else that set her apart from all other people in the minds of those who knew her. She had a smile. She rarely laughed and I have never known her to grin or to give a too exuberant manifestation of joy. But she was endowed with a most wondrous smile. I find it difficult to describe that smile. Rembrandt once showed me the reproduction (a very bad one) of a portrait painted by an Italian called Leonardo. It was the portrait of a woman, the wife, I believe of a Florentine merchant. That woman had the same smile, and it made her look as if she were the sole possessor of a terribly amusing secret which she could not impart to anybody in the whole wide world, but which kept her interested all the time and allowed her to rise sublimely superior to the common ills of mortal men.

I don't know anything about the private life of the Italian who was responsible for that painting. I think I have read somewhere that the lady in question was the third or fourth wife of a rich and old man and the anticipation of getting rid of him at an early date and becoming the mistress of a vast fortune may have kindled that inner glow of happiness which played around her eyes.

In the case of my grandmother the reason was more apparent and a great deal more creditable. Once upon a time and while she was still quite young, she had not only defied the power of Church and State, but had cheerfully thumbed her nose at all the established authorities and had so completely beaten them at their own game that for a moment at least she had been the most popular woman of western Europe.

She rarely talked about it and never mentioned it to us children, but I got the story from my uncle and this is what had happened.

My grandfather used to be mate on a vessel that plied between Rotterdam and Antwerp, while his brother attended to the family wood-yards in Veere. In those days no one was safe against the activities of thousands of spies—literally thousands of them. They were everywhere, and apparently never slept. A few of them were regular passengers on board my grandfather's boat, but he kept to his own business and was never much bothered by them. Besides, he needed all his time on the deck, for the King's Majesty being practically bankrupt, beacons and buoys and lighthouses had been deserted by their rightful keepers and navigation had become a matter of ability and of luck.

But that was not all. The inhabitants of the coastal regions, being deprived of the greater part of their revenue by the fact that no one any longer bothered about the old fast-days, but ate meat seven times a week, instead of fish (as they should have done), were turning more and more to piracy for a living. After all, they had wives and large broods of children to support and hunger has never been known to improve people's tempers nor increase their patience.

As the mariners of His Majesty's Navy (whose pay was three years overdue) took only a very luke-warm interest in protecting His Majesty's ports against freebooters, the honest fishermen sailed forth as buccaneers and soon were robbing friend and enemy with a sublime disregard for the rules of war or common decency. My grandfather's ship was twice attacked by them. Both times he got away without great damage but on the second occasion he was rather badly hurt by a bullet in his left arm. He had been warned to be extra cautious because among the passengers there was one of the Burgomasters of Antwerp and his daughter and they would have brought a handsome ransom had they been captured. He had not paid much attention to the old man. He had remarked to himself that the girl was a very handsome little creature, but though a cat may look at a king, the mate of a small trading-vessel had better not cast a too-longing eye upon the daughter of so great a magistrate as an Antwerp burgomaster. And he had forgotten all about her, except that when she went down the gangplank when he was standing waiting for the arrival of a doctor to bandage his arm and remove the bullet which was still imbedded in the muscles, the girl had suddenly turned to him, had whispered, "I think you are a wonderful man," and had thereupon departed.

Well, it was nice that she had noticed him, but life was full of a number of things that either had to be done or were agreeable in the doing, and he had promptly forgotten all about her.

Six weeks later on his third round trip he was arrested, denounced by a Dominican who had been on board and who had taken the trouble to go through the mate's luggage while the latter was attending to his business on deck. A copy of a Dutch translation of the New Testament, addressed to a citizen of Antwerp was found among his clothes. My grandfather was arrested and locked up in the Steen. He offered as his defense that he had carried that package with him in perfect good faith without bothering to open it or see what it contained. Yes, he believed that his friend had told him that it was a Bible, but he was a sailor, not a theologian. They showed him a passage (I think it was the gospel of St. John) where the apostle says: "And as we are saved through Christ Jesus" and where the translator had added the words: "And through him alone," as if it were possible to find salvation without the intermediary of a duly ordained priest and they asked him what he thought of that? He answered that he had really never thought of it at all, but that it seemed sensible.

They asked him whether he knew what had become of the man who had dared to print such violent heresies. He said no, and they told him that he had been burned at the stake. He answered that that seemed a bit severe for a mere four words and the chief Inquisitor, bidding him hold his tongue, told him that one word, yea, one single letter of one single word, was often enough in the sight of God to condemn a man to eternal punishment and he had answered that he supposed God was too busy with more important affairs to count the exact number of words in every book that was being printed, whereupon the president of the court lost all patience, called the young sailor a blasphemous fiend from Hell and a few other names which I have forgotten and after a moment's consultation with his colleagues, declared that the prisoner was hopeless, that it was not even necessary to torture him, as he had already confessed to everything the judges had suspected, and that they condemned him to be surrendered to the civil court which would know how to handle such a case and see that justice be done.

Up to that moment, it seems that my grandfather never even suspected the serious plight in which he so suddenly found himself. He expected that he would be fined or perhaps kept in jail for a couple of weeks. It was too absurd to punish a man more severely for a crime which he had really never committed. Besides, the book had not reached its destination and so he asked himself, in his simple way, "What harm has been done?" But the fact that he was removed from the common room in which all suspects were herded together and placed in solitary confinement in an evil-smelling dark hole, right underneath the watch-tower, gave him his first inkling that all was not right! He sat there in that smelly dungeon for three days without food or drink, was then heavily manacled and taken before the special court that dealt with cases of rebellion and within fifteen minutes he found himself condemned to be burned alive.

Of what thereafter happened, he only retained some very hazy recollections. All day and all night long he sat in his dark hole, sharing his loneliness with a small army of rats, as hungry as himself. Fortunately hunger and thirst tortured him so severely that he did not have much strength left to ponder upon his terrible fate. The whole affair continued to appear to him in the light of a very ill-timed joke. He just could not take it seriously. Tie a man to a stout iron post and pile fagots up all around him and set fire to those fagots and burn a living human being for no other possible reason than that he had been found in the possession of a book to which some poor fanatic had added four words of his own? It was preposterous and it could not possibly be true.

Nevertheless, on the fifth day of his confinement, the executioner appeared in his dungeon, removed his irons and bade him change his clothes for a loose-fitting yellow cloak, richly ornamented with black devils chasing lost souls with long pitchforks (he remembered those little long-tailed devils dancing furiously up and down by the light of the flickering candle which the hangman had put on the floor). When the cloak had been neatly adjusted he told him that within another hour he would be visited by a priest who would hear his confession. The execution was to take place that same afternoon and there were seventeen other candidates for glory.

With these cheerful words, his evil-looking visitor had bade him godspeed and he had been left with his own thoughts until from sheer exhaustion he had fallen asleep, and had slept for what seemed to him at least a whole day and a whole night. Curiously enough, he had been right, but sailors often have a feeling for time which ordinary people lack. When he came back to life, he found quite a number of people in his cell and there were torches and the rumor of many voices and he knew that his hour had come.

He tried to get up, but he could not stand, and then to his surprise the chains were removed from his hands and his feet and he was asked whether he was strong enough to understand what was being said to him and he answered yes, that he thought he was and some one who looked like the clerk of some legal office read him a long paper, from which after an endless number of whereas's and wherefore's it appeared that ever since the memory of man, there had been a law in the land of Flanders according to which a man, condemned to death, would have his life spared if there were a virgin willing to marry him as he was being taken to the scaffold, ready to be executed; that there was a woman in Antwerp who had offered to take him as husband; that the counselors of the Inquisition had objected that this law did not hold in cases of "an offense against God," but that the highest authorities in the city had been consulted and had declared that the law held good, even in cases of "an offense against God"; that therefore the prisoner had to be approached and had to be given the choice between being burned alive or contracting matrimony with a totally unknown person, after which he would be exiled from the territory of Antwerp and the province of Flanders for all time.

My grandfather quite naturally chose the latter course. He imagined that some old hag had decided to use him as her means of escape from spinsterhood, but he was still young and life, even by the side of a homely female, with a hunchback and no teeth, was better than being slowly roasted to death in the public square of Antwerp. And he had answered yes, that he was ready to accept the lady's kind offer, though he must apologize for not appearing at his wedding in more fitting garments. Whereupon the clerk of the court (for that is who he was) said that the clothes did not matter, as there still was some other detail to be attended to, that the authorities could not run the risk of having so dangerous a person return to their province without means of recognizing him, and that as a perpetual souvenir of this memorable occasion, they had condemned him to be branded before they would surrender him to his lawful bride.

He was at once taken to the torture chamber, where everything was ready for his reception, and in less than five minutes the stench of burning human flesh told him that justice in the true Spanish fashion had been done and that one more person had been marked in indelible form with that letter H, which was reserved exclusively for heretics and prostitutes.

The pain and the anger at finding himself helpless and in the hands of a foul-smelling and slightly drunken butcher's boy, who was learning the executioner's trade in his leisure hours and who bungled the job and hurt him much more than was necessary, made my grandfather faint. When he came to he found himself in the Chapel of the Steen, and a monk was throwing water into his face.

"He is coming to," he said. "You can bring in the bride."

My grandfather prepared for the worst.

The door opened and in came the daughter of the Antwerp burgomaster who had been on board his ship that time they had been attacked by a band of hungry fishermen.

"I am sorry," she said, "that I am doing this to you. But you are too handsome a thing to die so young, and besides, I want you."

An hour later, the couple was on board a vessel bound for Flushing.

And that is the way my grandmother married my grandfather.

Chapter 19

A HONEYMOON IN THE YEAR 1572

This strange wedding led to a companionship so beautiful and so lasting that I have never seen the like of it. Those two people understood each other even when they were a thousand miles apart. And when they were together in a room they seemed to be one person. Yet neither of them seemed to be obliged to sacrifice his or her own personality in order to be the absolute counterpart of the other. For in all minor details, they stuck closely to their own individuality. My grandfather was a confirmed freethinker but one of the true sort who could be pleasant and tolerant to his neighbors even when he felt them to be hopelessly and completely in the wrong. My grandmother on the other hand remained faithful to the faith of her youth until the day of her death.

"There is not very much faith in it of the sort of faith you learn in your catechism," she used to explain to us when we were still very young children whenever we looked with fear and delight upon the Holy Family of beautifully colored earthenware that stood in the corner of her room, "and you precious darlings should not take it too seriously. But your grandmother is a simple soul and can't live without the fairy stories she used to believe as a child."

And she would tell us wonderful tales of saints who were boiled in oil and cut into little pieces or flayed alive, but who went on doing good to the poor just as unconcernedly as if nothing had happened to them, and she made the adventures of these holy men so natural and so real to us that my brother and I believed them all to be true and even began to write an illustrated history of the lives of the Saints—a literary enterprise which lasted exactly four weeks and carried us only from Adalbert of Prague to Afra of Augsburg.

For then our father, having been tipped off by the minister to whom we went for our religious training, discovered the manuscript, gave us both a sound thrashing and slowly burned our beloved pictures and our somewhat clumsy text over a small peat fire which had been lit especially for the occasion.

He then (as we afterwards heard) went to see his mother to complain of her action in telling us children a pack of lies, whereupon the old lady got so furious that she boxed his ears (boxed the ears of an Elder of the Dutch Reformed Church) and bade him be gone and leave the house forever. This does not sound like a happy family life, and as a matter of fact, the relations between my father and my grandmother were little short of grotesque.

How it was ever possible that such a man and such a woman, the incarnation of all that was good and true and brave and cheerful, should have given birth to the sad-eyed, morose and prejudiced creature who was the author of my being, is something I shall never be able to understand. I know that the old philosophers proclaimed that "nature makes no jumps." I am afraid that they were wrong, and that nature at times is the greatest "jumper" of them all. For, during my thirty-five years of practice I have seen her perform the strangest hops and bounds and capers. It may be that she acts according to certain definite though hidden laws of growth and development and that everything is for the best, which in her case means, "the inevitable." But I would have been a great deal happier if she had not chosen our particular family to demonstrate to what extents she could go when she was on one of her merry gambols.

According to those who hold that children born out of a great passion are the most gifted and the most brilliant, my father ought to have been one of the most remarkable men of his day and age. But circumstances interfered and whatever original impulses there may have been to give the child every possible advantage, they came to naught when the mother, just before the time of her confinement, was almost starved to death and for the greater part of three months had to subsist on a diet of boiled leaves and horse-meat.

That had happened in the year 1574. My grandparents had been married in the month of March, 1572. They had first gone to Flushing and when they found that they were no further molested by the Inquisition, they had gone to Veere to decide upon plans for the future. My grandfather had lost his job. Every respectable ship-owner was afraid to employ a man who had been branded like a common criminal. As for his wife, her noble act of self-sacrifice (for God knows, it took a great deal of courage on her part to take such a step) had completely estranged her from all her relatives. Her father had publicly cursed her. Her mother had died soon afterwards. My grandmother had written to her just before her death, but her letter had been returned to her unopened. In her pride, she had then completely broken with her own past, and to this very day I don't know her maiden name. I once asked her, for I was rather curious to know what blood might be flowing in my veins. She said: "Dear boy, I have never told any one and never shall tell any one. My life began the day I married your grandfather. Let that be enough."

She had been an only daughter and since according to Flemish law, a father could not disinherit his children, she ought to have come into a considerable inheritance. But this time the attorneys were prepared, and a clause was found in some ancient code (though to tell you the truth, it was no more superannuated than the law which had made it possible for her to marry my grandfather and save his life) by which all the money had been deviated to religious purposes before the death of her father and she had been unwilling to fight the case, as she wanted to be forgotten by all those among whom she had spent her childhood.

Anyway, the couple immediately after the great adventure were not only without funds but without the slightest prospect of making a living. Then one day early in April, when their last guilder was about to be spent, news reached Veere that a small squadron of freebooters, flying the flag of the Prince of Orange, had attacked the town of Brielle, a few miles to the north, and instead of plundering it (as had been their habit thus far) had decided to make it the center of operations against Spain.

The next morning, as captain of an eighteen-foot fishing-smack with eleven sailors and six arquebuses, my grandfather had left the harbor of Veere, bound for Brielle. He had been in luck. During the night a Spanish trading vessel carrying olive-oil from Cadiz to Amsterdam had run aground on the Onrust, a bank just off the mouth of the Scheldt. The dozen eager patriots, seeing the chance of a little extra profit, decided to attack the Spaniard, who measured at least three hundred tons. They waited till low tide and then five of them ran for the ship, which towered high above the yellow sand, leaning slightly over to one side, so that its guns either pointed to high heaven or were useless (on the leaning side) because the balls would not stay in them. The Spaniards tried to fire at their enemies with muskets, but they safely reached the vessel and crawling close to the bottom of the monster, they started making a fire out of some dried pieces of sail which they had carried with them.

The fire was not a success, but the rotten sail made a lot of smoke and the Spaniards, unaccustomed to this sort of warfare, surrendered for fear that they might be burned alive. Meanwhile a heavy breeze had sprung up from the west, the tide rose higher than usual, and grandfather not only succeeded in salvaging the vessel but brought it safely to Brielle where it was sold for 90,000 guilders, which after all the deductions for taxes and legal fees, gave each one of them the neat little sum of five thousand ducats.

It also drew the attention of the rebel commander to the young skipper of the Veere fishing-smack. He offered him a position on board his own vessel and in this way, grandfather drifted, entirely by chance, into the work for which he was most fit.

The next year he took part in the battle of the Zuyder Zee in which the Dutch for the first time captured a Spanish admiral and then he returned to Zeeland and took an active part in the operations which forced Middelburg, the capital of the province, to take the side of the rebellion.

Meanwhile in anticipation of difficulties in Zeeland (which, however, never occurred), my grandfather had sent his wife to Leyden where he had some distant relatives from his mother's side. As the Spaniards had tried to take the town but had retreated after a short while from fear of being drowned out of their trenches, this seemed as safe a place as any. But suddenly in the month of May they reappeared and cut the town so completely off from the rest of the country that during the first two months of the siege, only six people succeeded in breaking through the lines and reaching the headquarters of the Prince, who now lived in Delft, which was then considered the strongest fortress of the province of Holland.

The siege lasted six months and all that time my grandfather had only twice heard from his wife. Both times she wrote, "Doing well." But the last message, brought by carrier pigeon, carried the words: "Please hurry. I am getting terribly hungry." As indeed she was, together with the other inhabitants of the town, for the cows and pigs and sheep had all of them been eaten up—the horses were fast going, and the regular diet of the long-suffering people consisted of soup made from the leaves of trees and a hideous stew made out of grass and cabbages. Six thousand people had died of hunger or disease and the garrison was so weak from lack of food that there were hardly soldiers enough to man the guns. Nevertheless the town held out as the example of Haarlem, where the people had surrendered meekly to the mercy of the King's Majesty (and had been drowned wholesale by being bound back to back and then thrown into the lake), had taught them a lesson. And the local magistrates decided that everything should be done to save Leyden from a similar fate.

Early in August, the dikes near Rotterdam were cut and two weeks later a fleet of rafts and flat-bottomed ships stormed the first line of dams that was held by the Spaniards. Cursing and swearing and hacking and tearing, the exasperated crews swam and waded through the mud and through the hidden ditches and took these natural fortifications with their bare hands. What had once been a rebellion, had now developed into a war of extermination and all prisoners were drowned on the spot.

Even so, almost six seeks went by before the vessels came within the sight of Leyden. First, the wind was wrong, and next there was not enough water. Then the farmers of the region, in fear of losing their crops (they would have let their next door neighbor starve to death if in this way they could have saved their own crops), interfered and filled the holes in the dikes just as soon as they had been cut. Then the Rhine and the Maas turned traitor and carried less water to the sea than they had done for a hundred years and of course, this meant that the artificial lake to the north of Rotterdam ran practically dry. But late in September the wind changed. It grew into a storm. A spring tide on the night between the 29th and 30th of September did the rest. On the 3d of October the fleet appeared before the gates of Leyden and among the first to enter the town was my grandfather.

He did not find his wife at the home of her relatives. A neighbor, a pale shadow of a woman, told him that his relatives had all of them died but the strange lady who lived with them had been taken away to the house of My Lord Jan van der Does, one of the magistrates who seemed to have interested himself in her case. He actually found his wife at the given address, very cheerful, very brave, and very weak and on the point of giving birth to her first child. The midwife expected it within two or three days.

Conditions in the town were terrible. The plague had returned as a result of the terrible things the people had been forced to eat. The chances that the child would survive any such conditions were small. My grandfather consulted his host, the courteous and genial van der Does. He said: "This town will mean death for all women and children for a good long time to come. Get out of it."

"But where shall we go? Everything within miles has been plundered by the Spaniards."

But van der Does could help them. He owned some property in Noordwijk, that seemed to have escaped the attention of the invaders. If they could get a boat as far as Rijnsburg they could go the rest of the way on foot.

They got their boat and safely reached Rijnsburg, but when they came to Noordwijk, they found that the farm to which van der Does had sent them had been burned five months before. The tenants were living in the pig-sty out of which they had chased the usual inhabitants and were none too eager to take in any unexpected guests. But they knew that My Lord Jan owned a mill, a mill not far from Noordwijk. It had still been standing a few days before and probably would be intact as the Spaniards had already left a fortnight ago. It was another hour before they reached that mill. The door was locked. The miller had fled. By this time, the first pains of labor had commenced, and it was impossible to leave the poor woman any longer out there in the cold. My grandfather smashed a window and climbed inside and opened the door. From the near-by stable he brought in straw, a bed was made on the floor, a trough served as cradle. Empty grain bags were used as covers and a little after midnight on the seventh of October of the year 1574 my father was born.

Years afterwards I told this story to Rembrandt and he said, "Yes, I know that mill. I once visited it with my brother Willem. He was more interested in our family's history than I. He told me that that mill had been sold a year after the siege to my grandmother, whose second husband also had been a miller but why she had decided to sell it again, he did not know. Maybe because it was a grain-mill and it had become more profitable to go in for malt, now that the breweries were working overtime and everybody had money again and was drinking beer. And maybe because Noordwijk was too far away from Leyden. And maybe because, with a brood of children, they could not attend to two mills at once. Anyway, it no longer belonged to our people when I was born.

I saw it that once and a few months later, lightning struck it and it burned down to the ground. So that one monument to your father's glory is gone."

A monument to my father's glory!

Little did he know of what he was talking.

Chapter 20

EVEN AS A VERY YOUNG CHILD I HAD STRANGE DOUBTS ABOUT THE FIFTH COMMANDMENT

What then, exactly, was the matter with my father?

From the point of view of his children, everything.

He was quite a good-looking man, having inherited my grandfather's physical strength and a great deal of the personal charm of my grandmother. He was a man of many abilities. When he was young he used to play the lute with great dexterity, and during a visit to his uncle in Veere he copied most of the revolutionary tunes which the town notary, the famous Valerius, had collected during the early part of the rebellion, and he sung these with great success to his own accompaniment. At least, so I heard from some of his old friends, for when we were children, he never touched the instrument and declared all music to be an invention of the Devil. He also seemed to have had a great natural gift for drawing from nature. But nothing remained to show that he had ever taken an interest in such a worldly pastime.

When my brother and I were about fifteen years old, we called one day on a friend whose father possessed one of those famous "Libri Amicorums" which were so popular during the last century. It was a Sunday afternoon and as a great privilege we were allowed to see the pictures in this mysterious and delightful book instead of having to look at images of the deluge and the plagues of Egypt in the family Bible. And to our great delight, we found a picture drawn some twenty years before by our father and representing a young goddess and a young god telling each other something amidst a bower of vines. What they were telling each other was written underneath in a couple of verses, but neither of us was well enough skilled in the art of the penmanship of that day (a very flowery and curlycuey sort of writing) to be able to read them. But of course, as children will do, when we came home we proudly told of our discovery and how our father was a great painter and just as good, we felt convinced, as the wonderful men who had illustrated our Bible.

Our father said nothing to this, but quite contrary to his custom, which made him spend the Sabbath evening at home reading to us from the Old Testament (as far as I can remember, he never mentioned the New Testament to us), he left us immediately after supper and did not come home until at a very late hour. But when we called on the same friend a month or so later, and begged to see the wonder book, the young god and goddess were no longer there and we were too scared to ask what had become of them.

Of course, children never really "know" anything about their parents. They can merely "guess." But in our case, we were denied even that consoling luxury. All we could do was to suffer in silence, and suffer we did.

As soon as we were old enough to ask an occasional question, it was made clear to us that we had no will of our own. We were sinful, misbegotten creatures, hideous and loathsome in the sight of Jehovah (God was rarely mentioned to us), a stench in the nostrils of the Truly Righteous. These Truly Righteous, so we were gradually able to discover, were my father and those who agreed with him upon every comma and semi-colon of the Old Testament, but only in a very small and badly printed edition which had appeared in Amsterdam in the year 1569. All other translations were discarded as anathema, and the work of Satan, and if my father had had his way, they would have been gathered together and burned in the market square, right underneath the wooden nose of our great fellow-townsman, Erasmus, whom my father and his friends held in particular abhorrence on account of a little book which he had written in praise of that glorious Goddess of Folly, which ever since the beginning of time has ruled the world with much greater success than either Wisdom or Pity.

I find it difficult to reconstruct those years of mute suffering. My mother probably loved us, but the spirit inside of her had been killed by years and years of a most meticulous form of abuse of which my father seemed to hold the secret.

Were we ever really badly treated, in the ordinary sense of the word?

No, I can't say that we were.

We had decent clothes. We ate decent food and never went hungry. We slept in comfortable rooms. We were sent to quite good schools and rarely were beaten more than any other children of that day and age, when it was considered necessary to spank the average boy at least once a day in order to remind him of his duty to love and honor his parents.

Then what made our existence such hell and cast such a blight upon all the rest of our lives and eventually brought such terrible disaster upon the heads of my brother and myself?

I hardly think that I can put the case into so many words. But here is a little incident I remember from the days when I received my first lessons in religious instruction. The dominie talked about our Father in Heaven and how God is so good to us that we must always call him Father and must approach him as if he were our real father, and I suddenly burst into tears and shrieked that I would then be obliged to hate God, that the word "father" was the most terrible word in the language, that I hated my father and would always hate him.

As I was taken sick the next day with the pox (of which on that occasion three of my other brothers and two of my sisters died) and probably was sick and feverish at the time of this occurrence, there probably was a special reason for this most unseemly outburst of honesty on the part of a child of nine. But all this is rather hazy in my mind. I recollect that the reverend doctor gave me a terrible beating and that I returned home more dead than alive, but too miserable to mind much what had happened.

That, however, was exactly the way I felt about that dreadful man whose very memory, after the lapse of fifty years or more, makes me shiver whenever I think of him.

The man was the walking incarnation of a spiritual spoil-sport. He loved righteousness (his own sort of righteousness, as I have already remarked) and hated everything else. He hated laughter and he hated tears. He hated the sun and he hated the moon. He hated the summer and he hated the winter. He radiated hate and gloom as other people radiate joy and contentment. His capacity for execration was unlimited and his ability to give concrete expression to his feeling of detestation surpassed even that of his deeply revered master, the tenebrous tyrant of the Sinaitic mountain tops.

If, as a child, we made ourselves a little boat out of a piece of cork and an old rag and a mast cut out of an old broom-stick (as every child brought up along the water-front was sure to do), he would wait until we had finished our craft and then he would smash it underneath the heel of his boot. If we painted a picture on an old China plate or a piece of parchment, he would slowly and deliberately hold it underneath the pump in our back yard until the colors were washed off. If we had a particularly favorite toy (and our grandparents were most lavish in providing us with houses and soldiers and little carts with real barrels and boxes on them) he would, as soon as he discovered that we had attached ourselves a little too seriously to one of those "worldly baubles," deprive us of our playthings and burn them on the peat fire that was supposed to keep our back room warm. If we showed a special liking for one of the boys with whom we went to school, he would allow us to invite him to our house, and then, when we all stood around the table, eating our dinner, he would find a way to humiliate the poor child until it could bear it no longer and broke out in tears or fled from this chamber of horrors, never to darken our door again.

He once urged us to invite all our little friends for a boat ride and hired a boat and made my mother spend days preparing food, and then, when we all, in our Sunday best, stood ready to embark, he told us that the party was off and that we had better go home to meditate upon "the benefits of disappointment."

In consequence of these occurrences, we gradually lost caste among all the other boys of our age and our will was so completely broken on the anvil of parental ill-will and bitterness that we became mere puppets in the hands of Fate, rudderless ships on the ocean of inexperience and doubt.

As a result, the terrible events took place which so completely changed the even tenor of my life and for almost eight years made me an exile from my own land and drove me away from Rembrandt at a time when he was perhaps most in need of such friendship as I was able to give him.

During my recent illness, when I was searching my mind for the causes of that strange melancholia which had so completely got hold of me, I discussed these matters with Spinoza, the man who more than any other has been able to dissect and understand the inner motives of the human heart. And while giving him an account of my father and of our childhood, I mentioned the episode of the Armada, that strange incident in my father's early years which quite by chance I had heard my grandfather tell one day.

It seems that during the early eighties of the last century, the King of Spain decided to eradicate all heresies from this world by destroying both England and Holland with one blow. For this purpose he ordered a fleet to be built of hundreds and hundreds of ships and an army to be equipped that was to embark on board those ships and conquer London and Amsterdam and then do whatever was to be done to bring all the people back into the folds of Mother Church. The men-of-war were to be built in Spain, but the soldiers were to be gathered in Dunkirk. For this special purpose His Majesty, who was practically bankrupt, had raised seven million ducats and the Pope had chipped in with an extra million. Naturally enough an expedition on such a large scale could not be kept a secret and as early as the fall of '86 the people in Holland knew what was going to happen.

Ambassadors were sent to London to discuss a general plan of defense with the English, but as usual, their Queen, who always insisted upon doing everything herself, could not quite make up her mind. One day she was all for fighting and the next she would send a letter to the King of Spain and remind him of the ancient friendship between their two respective countries and so on and so forth. And very likely nothing at all would have been accomplished if the Pope had not seen fit at that moment to issue a bull in which he called Her Majesty a bastard and a tyrant and graciously bestowed her realm upon her dear cousin of Spain, who was at the same time given the exalted title of "Defender of the Christian Faith." After that slur upon her birth, the old lady was all for fighting, and she began her operations with a raid upon peaceful Dutch merchantmen, and for a moment it looked as if the heretics (after the manner of heretics) were going to tear each other to pieces, but in the end the two nations came to terms and the Hollanders and Zeelanders undertook to watch and guard the harbor of Dunkirk, so that no troops should be able to reach the ships while the ships should be prevented from reaching the port and calling for the soldiers.

While Howard and Drake kept up a running fight with the great clumsy vessels which were at such a terrific disadvantage among the shallow waters of the Channel, a Zeeland squadron together with a number of ships from the admiralty of Holland, lay off the Flemish coast. My grandfather had been put in command of a fast sailing sloop of eighteen pieces, called in a spirit of fun *The Cardinal's Hat*. It was to act as a sort of guide for a squadron of fire-ships and was to try and pilot a few of these into the harbor of Dunkirk. As a rule, those fire-ships, well provided with grappling irons, had only a crew of about six men who started the pitch barrels burning as soon as their craft was safely headed for one of the enemy's galleons and then made for the little boat and rowed for safety while the rest of the cargo caught fire. Of course, my grandfather had taken his son along. A boy of fifteen in those days was supposed to take a man's share in the battles of his country and the son of an old freebooter was sure of a place of honor in an undertaking of this sort.

Furthermore, according to the story grandfather told me, my father in those days was a regular fire-eater. He was a good-looking devil, he was full of life and fun, he had been brought up on the stories of the glorious episodes of the early days of the rebellion. He knew all about sieges and pitched battles and hand-to-hand encounters on the slippery slopes of some muddy dike. He had seen the people whose ears had been cut off and whose noses had been slit by the Inquisition and his uncles and aunts had told him of the diet of mice and rats upon which they had subsisted when grain and meat had given out when the Spaniards had laid siege to their town. And as he was a bright and eager lad, full of imagination, he had vowed that some day he would do his best to avenge those hideous wrongs.

This was his first opportunity and he was going to show the stuff he was made of. He begged and implored everybody to give him a chance, until finally he was offered the command of the second of the fireships that were to be let loose against the Spanish vessels anchored peacefully in Dunkirk harbor that same evening.

A fire-boat, commanded by Hendrick van Cadzand, an old pilot who knew that part of the Belgian coast by heart, was to show the way, but everything depended upon quick work, for the instant these ships were detected, the expedition was at the mercy of the batteries on shore.

As soon as it was dark, the vessels made for Dunkirk and my father, holding the rudder, waved a cheerful good-by to his comrades and all went well until they were near the breakwater. At that moment, one of the Spanish sentinels on the pier fired his gun. It probably was an accidental shot and had nothing to do with the approaching vessels.

But then and there, something terrible happened to my father. He fainted. He fell into a dead faint. They threw pails of water over him and he came to, but every time a shot was fired, he would shriek and try as he might he could not keep from weeping or crouching behind the nearest bit of shelter. Through his clumsy maneuvering, the fire-vessels had got into disorder and the attack failed miserably. Of course, his behavior caused a terrible scandal. If he had not been the son of a father, known for his bravery, he would have been hanged immediately for cowardice. Under the circumstances, it was reported that he had suddenly been taken ill and had been sent home for treatment.

That was the story as I was told it and as I repeated it to Spinoza, and used it as an argument to prove that my father had always been an unreasonable and contemptible being. But he looked at me a long time out of his sad, black eyes, and then he said: "But don't you see?" And I answered "No," and he continued: "But it is all so very simple. Can't you really understand? You are supposed to take care of men's bodies and what have you learned about their minds, which so strongly affect those bodies? Nothing, I fear me. Now really, can't you understand what happened and how it all came about?"

I said no, that perhaps the recollection of the things I had suffered made me unfair, but that this seemed entirely in keeping with all I had ever known about my father. He ended life as a gloomy tyrant, who hated everybody and everything and whose chief aim during his waking hours seemed to be to make everybody miserable.

"And you don't know why?" Spinoza interrupted me.

"I can't say that I do. I suppose that he was born that way."

"But how about your grandfather's story which you just told me, of early years, of his courage, his fun, his good looks?"

"Nevertheless, he showed himself a coward."

"And that is just it. Some day we shall perhaps understand what cowardice is. Very likely we shall then be obliged to change our opinion about heroes too."

"You mean to say, in his case, that his fear of getting killed was stronger than his will to live and distinguish himself?"

"Of course it was. He probably had all the ambition and energy of your grandfather, who was then in the hey-day of his power. But he was born at the moment your grandmother had passed through a terrible experience. These two antecedents, these two personalities, clashed and were at war with each other right there within his soul. The stronger of the two won. He had a tremendous desire to distinguish himself. But something within himself defeated that impulse and defeated it quite ignominiously. As a result, he came to hate the world. . . ."

"Because he so thoroughly hated himself!"

"And he took his revenge upon his children."

"Because they were part of him—because in torturing them, he was really torturing himself."

Perhaps (as in so many other instances) Spinoza was right, though it was difficult for me to follow him quite so far.

He looked upon the problem from the pleasant and detached point of view of a professional philosopher. My father to him was merely an unknown quantity, an interesting x or y in the great mysterious equation of life.

Whereas to my brother and to myself, he was a fact, a fact that even at this late date makes me wake up sometimes in the middle of the night and shriek. For I hear silent foot-steps. Father is making his rounds, trying to discover something for which he can punish us to-morrow morning. Honor thy father and thy mother.

It is an ancient law. Perhaps it is a good law.

But methinks it is a little too one-sided.

Chapter 21

OF THE BROTHER WHOM I HAD AND LOST

My brother Willem was three years older than myself. He and I were the only children who had survived the pox when it attacked our family during the frightful epidemic of 1616.

Three years difference means a great deal when one is five or six, and even more when the age of ten has been reached. But from the very beginning we had been forced to make common cause. Otherwise our spirits would have been entirely crushed in that terrible and gloomy house which we were supposed to call our home. Of course, there was our mother who loved us very sincerely in her own way. But although she went through the gesture of being alive, got up in the morning, dressed herself, attended to the needs of the household, repaired our clothes, went to bed again at night, she had long since given up hope that anything would ever happen to set her free from the drudgery of waiting upon the will of a tyrant who found an excuse for every one of his selfish acts in the chapters of that dreadful Jewish history, the mere thought of which makes me shudder, now after a lapse of more than forty years.

Why had she married him? Well, he had been a "good party" in the usual sense of the word. He belonged to a respectable family, he had a good business, he would be able to provide for her and in those days, in our class of society, that was about all that mattered. His mania for fault-finding and his almost incredible capacity for making himself obnoxious had not yet assumed those outrageous proportions that were to make him a marked man in after life. He was moody and rather difficult. He also was reported to be rich and had fine prospects of growing richer as time went on. What more could one want?

And so my mother was married to him amidst the eager plaudits of her delighted family and never knew a happy day until that morning when she went forth to do her marketing, fell down in the street right in front of our door, and died then and there without so much as a sigh of relief that the end had come.

My brother and I were at school at the time this happened, but we were sent for immediately and when we came home, we were taken right into the room where mother lay dead. Her face was as white as wax, her hands were folded. She seemed to be asleep and in her sleep she smiled as if she understood why she had lived and why she had suffered and what it had been all about. But something gave me a terrible fright, a shock from which I never quite recovered—the firm expression of her lovely mouth told me that she had taken her secret with her and that I would never know it—that I was never going to find out the riddle of existence until I too should have passed beyond those portals from which there is no return.

I probably was too young to have reasoned it out in detail that way and these thoughts may have come to me much later. I am not sure, either one way or the other. I am growing to be an old man and my memory often plays me queer pranks. But ever since, when in the course of my professional duties, I have attended a death-bed, I have been struck by that same strange, other-worldly expression upon the faces of those who have just died.

They smile at us with infinite pity.

For they "know" and we poor mortals, who must go on bearing the burdens of existence, we can only "guess."

And the advantage is all with the still, white faces that now, after years of struggle and pain, have gained the greatest of all blessings, "peace and certainty."

My father, of course, took his loss in his usual selfish way. Somehow or other, he counted the sudden death of her who according to him was as yet "unprepared to meet her Creator" as a reflection upon his own piety. For a moment he ceased his studies of the Old Testament to search among the pages of the Book of Revelation for an answer to the question: "What have I done that I, poor sinner, should be afflicted in this manner?"

I doubt whether it ever dawned upon him that in dying my mother might have suffered certain inconveniences. She had been his wife, his hand-maiden, his cook, his seamstress, a convenient possession of which he had been proud on account of her beauty and her competent way of managing his household. Her loss meant an interruption of a pleasant routine and he sometimes seemed to feel that she had died merely to be disagreeable to him and put him to extra expense. And as the Apocalypse failed to give him an answer to his doubts, and he once more suffered a sense of utter defeat and futility, he grew even more morose than ever before and from that time on until we were old enough to leave the parental roof, our lives were one uninterrupted series of humiliations and sufferings.

It was then that my brother, with noble unselfishness, stepped forward to defend me against the tantrums and the unjust punishment of our mutual tormentor. And I from my side, hardly understanding what was happening, came to be bound to him by certain ties of gratitude and affection which were far stronger than the mere physical fact of sharing the same flesh and blood.

My dear brother was both father and mother to me in the truest sense of the word. He took care of me when I was sick (and I was never very strong as a child) and consoled me when I was punished for some imaginary infringement of the endless rules of conduct that were forced upon us to make us realize the seriousness of salvation. My father was dreadfully jealous of his son's influence upon me and more than once tried to break our intimacy by a threat of separating us and sending my brother to London under the pretext of having him serve his apprenticeship with an English goldsmith. But in the end he had to give in to the pressure that came from the side of our relatives who knew the miseries we suffered but were unable to interfere on our behalf, as the law was entirely on the side of the parents in those early days shortly after the Reformation and as children (in exchange for having been given the privilege of being born) were supposed to have many duties but not a single right.

Of course all the time we were growing older and bigger and finally the point was reached at which it was no longer possible to rule us with a cane. The day my father tried to whip me because I had smiled in church when the minister, reading the names of the ancestors of King David, had got his consonants mixed and had been forced to begin all over again, and had taken a heavy birch rod and then, after the first blow, had had it jerked out of his hand by my brother, who vowed that he would kill him if he ever touched me again, that day was probably the happiest day in his life, for now he had a grievance which made him akin to several of his favorite heroes of old Judean history—his own flesh and blood had turned against him.

He used that incident in a thousand different ways to make us feel his own spiritual superiority and we both thanked our stars when at last we were able to escape, my brother to take service with a well-known silver-smith in Leyden and I to visit the academy of that same town. But even then, although we were now free from daily, yes, almost hourly, interference with our own will, and the constant frustration of our most reasonable desires, we never quite succeeded in getting rid of that feeling of utter submission which came over us whenever my father spoke to us in his rôle as the Creator of our Being.

And when it was time for us to marry (and we were sufficiently well off through the death of our mother to marry quite young) we found ourselves supplied with wives with the choice of whom we had had nothing to do, but who had been selected for us by my father, because they were good Christian women and suitable mothers for such children as it might please Almighty Heaven to bestow upon us after our lawful union.

It happened that neither my brother nor I cared a whit for the women with whom we were thus unceremoniously thrown together. But we obeyed out of the sheer habit of obeying and we suffered the martyrdom of boredom because we did not know any better and because it never dawned upon us that love might mean something more than spending one's days and nights by the side of a female creature whom one detested at those rare moments when one did not merely bear their presence.

My wife (poor wretch, she was surely quite as unhappy as I, for she

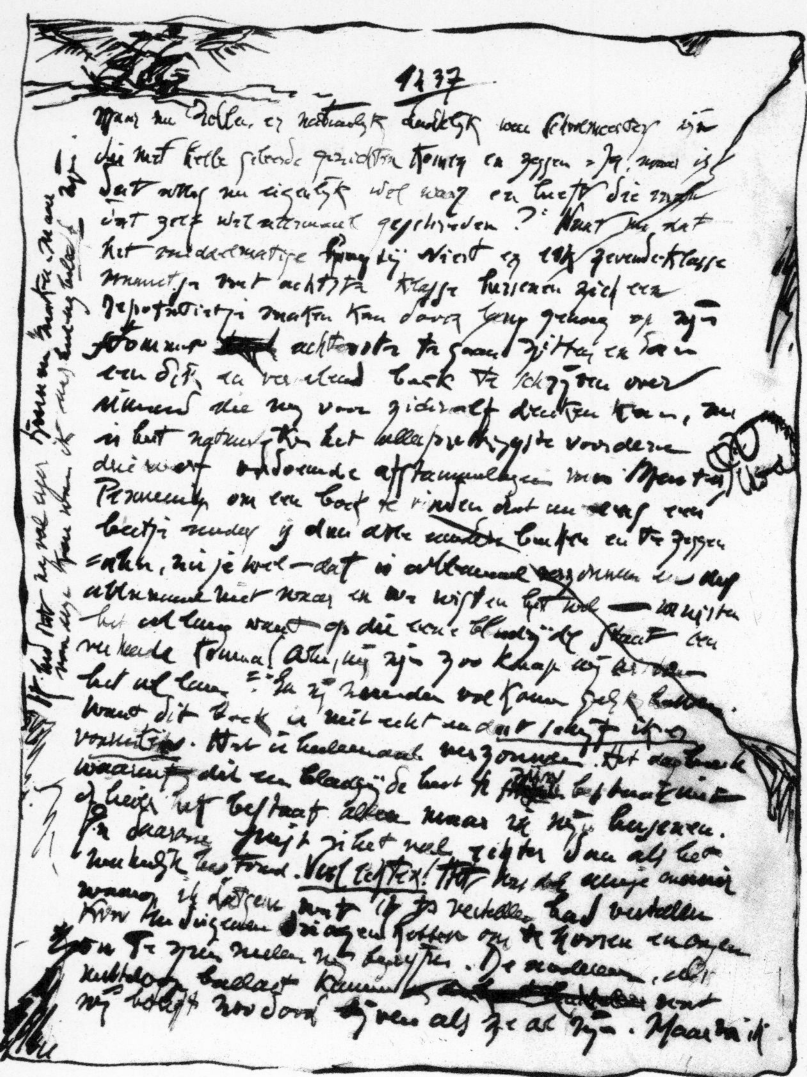

AN EXPLANATORY PAGE FROM THE DIARY

had wanted to marry a draper's clerk and hated everything connected with poor people and their ailments)—well, my wife, fortunately for both of us, died shortly after she had given birth to a son. I buried her decently and lost myself in my studies, which soon meant infinitely more to me than all the women in the whole world. But my brother, who was a clever craftsman, but had no interest whatsoever beyond his profession and therefore had no means of escape, was thoroughly miserable and to make matters worse, the woman he had married proved to be both a shrew and absolutely averse to any sexual connection with the man whose name she bore but whose bed she steadfastly refused to share, except for the immediate purpose of having children, an arrangement which so thoroughly disgusted her husband that he never touched her again as long as he lived.

In the end, of course, such an unnatural way of living was to avenge itself in a most dreadful fashion. Early in the year 1650, my father died. He had tried to deprive us of our inheritance by giving all his money to an old men's home, but the courts quickly decided that such a thing was contrary to the law of the land and both my brother and I received several thousand florins besides a share in a number of houses on the Rotterdam water-front. I used my little capital to take a trip through the universities of northern Italy where medicine was then being taught much more successfully than at home. But my brother had been so terribly repressed for such a number of years that this stroke of good luck proved his undoing.

He had never known what it was to be a child or a boy. He meant to make up for lost time and at forty, he set out to recapture the joys of youth, of which he had heard a great deal but which he had never experienced at first hand. The thing was impossible and the poor fellow only succeeded in making himself slightly ridiculous without in any way getting repaid for his outlay in time and money and energy.

We had always been a very sober family and he therefore now felt it to be his duty to drink large quantities both of gin and beer. The gin made him sick and the beer made him sleepy. He greatly disliked the taste of both those beverages, but he had heard all his life of "Divine old Bacchus, to thee we lift, etc." and about the "good cheer of a group of jolly fellows with a pint of ale," and whatever other nonsense the poets have been pleased to compose upon this silly subject and now he was going to experience these joys or die in the attempt. Upon one occasion he almost had his wish and it took me weeks of hard work to bring him back to health. And during his period of reconvalescence, I used to remonstrate with him. An anomalous position. There I sat by the side of my hero and guardian-angel, trying to prevent him from making a fool of himself. It was all terribly humiliating and worst of all, the poor fellow could offer so many plausible excuses for his extraordinary conduct.

"I know that all this is absurd, especially at my age," he used to say, "but I will go crazy unless I have some sort of a fling now. I have never been allowed to do the things I wanted to do and all my life long I have been forced to do the things I did not want to do. I think that our father used to call that 'educating' us. I am forty-five now and there are whole pages in the record of my past existence that are a blank. I intend to write something upon them before I die. That is my good right and you should not try and interfere."

"But listen," I would argue, "there is a time and a place for everything. It is all right for you to drink milk out of a bottle when you are one. But it is a little silly when you are thirty. You can play with dolls until you are five. After that, the other boys will call you a sissy."

He shook his head sadly. "I know that you are right," he answered, "but I just can't help myself. I am angry with Fate. I am so damnably angry! I could go out and kill some one just because I am so angry. I have been cheated. We both have been cheated of everything that is most worth while.

"After all, what is our youth for? To gather such a rich stock of pleasant recollections that we can live upon them for the rest of our days. And what can you and I remember? Misery and tears and horribly dull hours and horribly dull days and even more horribly dull years. That terrible 'No' that stood at the beginning of every sentence our father ever uttered! Such a life isn't fit for human beings.

"You are lucky. You can escape among your pots and pans and all those books full of hieroglyphics. But look at me. I have got a job I hate. I wanted to be a sailor like grandfather, and I am forced to make ornamental salt-cellars for rich cattle-dealers who come in from the countryside and don't know how to use them once they have got them. I wanted to ride the sea in a great big ship and I sit all day long in a stuffy workshop. I wanted a woman of my own, children, I suppose. Look what I got! an animated edition of Holy Writ, not even nicely bound but in a dreadful linen cover."

Then I began all over again trying to convince him that while all he said was perfectly true, he did not make it any better by adding self-injury to the insults he had suffered at the hands of others, but all to no avail. He never went so far as to neglect his business. Somehow or other he managed to stick with great faithfulness to that bench and table he so thoroughly detested. But for the rest, he followed a course that could only lead to disaster. And then in an ill-fated moment, he joined a dramatic club.

These "rhetorical associations" or "master-singer societies" or "poets' unions" or whatever they were pleased to call themselves, had greatly flourished during the twelfth and thirteenth and fourteenth centuries, and every town and village had had a dramatic company of its own, enacting plays written by one of its members. Those plays, as a rule, had been pretty terrible, but they had served as an emotional outlet for a large number of people who otherwise would have spent their time singing bawdy songs in an ale-house. But during a period when everything was tinged with theology, even the theater could not escape.

First of all, the Lutherans captured the stage and used it to popularize their own doctrines. The Spanish authorities, not quite knowing what to do about that sort of propaganda, had quickly put an end to their performances. But not for long, as the Reformation was successful and the Catholics were sent about their business. But after a very short while, the Lutherans, who were too tame for our people, were replaced by the followers of Calvin and as soon as they noticed that people went to these performances not merely to be instructed but also to amuse themselves, they proclaimed theater-going a mortal sin and ordered all rhetorical clubs to be closed.

But the urge to rime and strut about on the stage and make a public exhibition of one's self was much too strong to be entirely suppressed and a way out was found when the amateur actors promised not to play for profit but to hand over all their revenues to the local hospitals and orphan asylums.

Those institutions had been in a state of painful bankruptcy ever since the days of the Reformation when the so-called "good works" had become highly suspicious as an invention of either the Devil or the Pope of Rome. As long as it was sufficient for a man's salvation if he "believed" the right thing, it did not matter so much what he "did." As a result of which the orphans went hungry and the sick remained untended, and a few extra guilders, even though they were derived from "play-acting," were more than welcome. It had seemed a very sensible arrangement, but in no time the Reverend Clergy was back on the job, bombarding Their Lordships of the Town Hall with complaints about this and that and the other piece of acting. One play was much too popish, the next was too full of liberal ideas, a third one showed a lack of respect for the cloth, a fourth one made sin too attractive, a fifth one failed to make vice unattractive enough, and so on and so forth, until the unfortunate day when old man Vondel, already seriously suspected of Papist leanings and an open and avowed enemy of the clerical zealots who had killed his political hero, John of Barneveldt, decided to write him a play in which it should be clearly proved and demonstrated that that unfortunate statesman had been the innocent victim of a great Calvinistic conspiracy.

Heaven knows he ought to have known better, after the authorities had almost clapped him in jail for making Mary Stuart, a sweet and innocent young thing, cruelly persecuted by an old and jealous hag called Elizabeth of England and showing all the virtues of this world to be on the side of Catholic Mary and none on the side of Protestant Bess.

No sooner had this storm in the theatrical tea-pot subsided when behold! there cometh the hurricane of a famous judicial assassination perpetrated well within the memory of the average man. There was a terrific outbreak of popular anger and of course my poor brother, all eager for what he called the "new emotions" and the "novel sensations," must take an active part in it. He had inherited his grandfather's liberal outlook upon life and being by nature a very humble man (most unhappy people are humble) he was the last person on earth to claim that one set of opinions was right and another was wrong. But when the clergy attacked poor old Vondel for his "secret Papist leanings" my brother must needs set up as one of the staunchest defenders of that unfortunate and misguided poet and make himself a mouthpiece of those who for one reason or another (mostly another) were known as the open and avowed enemies of the party then in power.

Their Lordships of the Town Hall were too clever to let themselves be dragged into a public debate, the outcome of which seemed very uncertain. They had other ways at their disposal to rid themselves of an uncomfortable opponent. They boycotted my brother's business and as he was dependent for his living upon the good will of the rich, he soon found himself without a single customer. Next the collectors of internal revenue paid an official visit to his premises and discovered that his merchandise had been assessed at much too low a value. An extra-assessment, and a fine for having sent in a false declaration, were the results of this investigation.

My brother, the soul of honesty, went to law about this and won his case, but the fees and the expense connected with all court pleadings in the Republic used up all his ready cash. At the same time his wife's relatives started proceedings before the magistrates, asking that their brother-in-law be forced to give an accounting of all his business relations during the last six years and hand over the greater part of his revenue to his "dutiful and pious wife, who had suffered grievously both in body and soul through the grave neglect on the part of her husband, who far from following his trade in a peaceful manner as behooved a good Christian and citizen, has wasted his time in the company of pamphleteers, play-actors, painters and other reprehensible characters, etc., etc." A whole catalogue of the most terrible grievances, mortifications, worries and annoyances, duly enumerated to show the eager populace just what sort of a person their highly respected neighbor really was.

Meanwhile rumor of this uproar had traveled abroad and the managers in England and France had not been slow to recognize its importance. Where there was smoke, there undoubtedly was fire and where there was so much discussion of theatrical affairs, there must be a vast number of people anxious to see a good play. The company from the "Théâtre du Pont Neuf" in Paris hastened to the Low Countries with Cyrano de Bergerac's "Le Pédant joué," dreaming of showers of well-rounded Dutch florins, and the Blackfriars Theater in London despatched a dozen of its worst performers directly to Amsterdam to entertain the natives of that distant city with the works of a certain William Shakespeare who seems to have been an actor in the days of Queen Elizabeth and who also on occasions wrote plays.

The interest, however, of the populace in the drama proved to be entirely theoretical, or rather theological. People delighted in discussing the problematical attitude of Jehovah towards the stage. But as for attending a single performance to see what the stage was really like, why, our good Calvinist neighbors would much rather have been broken on the wheel than consent to setting foot within the "Temple of Satan."

The French company therefore beat a hasty retreat, providing itself with sufficient money for the home voyage by selling all its costumes and stage-properties. The English troopers fared almost as badly. They opened their season with "Shylock, or the Merchant of Venice," a piece which proved to be highly distasteful to the Jews in our town. The day after the performance, the Dam in front of the Town Hall was one seething mass of excited Hebrews in long kaftans, wildly gesticulating and calling down violent curses upon the head of the poor scribe (dead, God knows how many years) who had so cruelly and unjustly called attention to one of their supposed racial weaknesses.

The magistrates, who just then were contemplating a rather important loan to finance the city's extension in the direction of the old Plague House, did not wish to start a financial panic and promised immediate redress. The Blackfriars people thereupon switched over to a play by a certain Ford, called "It's a Pity She's a Whore" which roused such a terrific storm of protest among the clergy that it had to be taken off after a single performance, when in their despair they chose a perfectly harmless piece by a certain John Fletcher called "The Faithful Shepherdess" which did not seem to have done very well in London at the time of its first performance, but which was quite a success in Amsterdam where people had not been spoiled in matters theatrical.

Now in the years of which I am writing, it was not customary for women to appear upon the scene. The female parts were taken by young boys who had been specially trained for this sort of work. But as a great innovation, the Blackfriars announced that the rôle of the Shepherdess would be played by a real woman.

Of the storm that thereupon broke loose, it would be difficult to give one who had not lived through these turbulent days an adequate idea.

Solemn processions proceeded to the Town Hall to offer petitions which ran all the way from humble and pious supplications for redress to open and avowed threats of rebellion. But the magistrates, being in an angry mood on account of a sermon preached a few weeks before in which a zealous young candidate for holy orders had publicly accused the Town Fathers of all sorts of improper speculations in connection with the city's extension (of which I wrote a moment ago), those magistrates were in no mood to listen to further remonstrances. They declared that they saw no reason to forbid the play in question and bade the petitioners be gone. When these honest citizens, undaunted by the failure of the day before, reappeared on the Dam the next morning, they saw that a number of gallows had been erected in front of the Town Hall and being able to take a hint, they dispersed and returned to their various professions.

But two nights later, the poor woman who played the rôle of the Shepherdess, at the beginning of the second act, was suddenly pelted with volley after volley of rotten eggs and bricks carefully packed in sheets of paper that afterwards proved to be parts of the petitions which the Burgomasters had refused to consider. She was hurt quite badly. The town guards were hastily summoned. A number of arrests were made and it was discovered that the gallery had been filled with people, none of whom had ever before graced a theater with his presence. But as every man, woman and child among them swore that they had not seen their neighbors lift a finger, let alone throw eggs or broken bottles in the direction of the stage, nothing could be done and the company, thoroughly defeated by the triumphant dominies, hastily left for London.

The unfortunate shepherdess, however, remained behind. Her arms and her face had been terribly cut and after trying to doctor herself for a few days, she was brought to the hospital where I cleaned her wounds and bandaged her and discovering that she was quite feverish, ordered her to be taken to a cot.

Even then she was not left in peace. On the day after she had been admitted to the God's House, a bottle of wine was received for her with a card which read: "From an admirer." This bottle was stolen by a boy in the porter's lodge. Immediately afterwards, he was taken ill with dreadful pains and convulsions. I happened to be on duty and was called for immediately, but before I could do anything, the poor fellow was dead. The bottle was discovered in his pocket, and suspecting foul play, I examined the contents. I found that the wine had been poisoned, though I never was able to determine the exact nature of the poison nor could I ever find out whence it had been sent. But when it is considered that this particular crime was still being punished by the rack and the wheel, and that the chances of detection in cases of that sort were very serious, then it will become plain how terribly excited some people had got about such a very simple affair as a woman playing the part of a woman in a theatrical play.

I mentioned this matter quite casually to my brother who happened to be staying with me for a few weeks in the hope that the silly agitation against him in his native town would meanwhile die down. I wish I had never broached the woman's name to him, for right off he flew into a terrible passion about those devils who would not even stop short at murder to further their own ends and who tried to make all people subject to their own prejudices, and as soon as the lacerated shepherdess had sufficiently recovered to leave the hospital, he hastened to pay her his respects and that was the beginning of the end, as far as he was concerned.

I don't want to be too hard on the poor female. I only saw her three times in all my life and as I had good reason to dislike her most cordially, my judgment about her would be hardly fair. This much I will say. She was exceedingly fair, but her beauty was like a bonfire on ice—it spread a wondrous light but gave absolutely no heat. And the same was true of her art.

She was, so I heard afterwards, the daughter of a man who had learned his trade with no one less than the famous William Shakespeare himself and who had been trained in the best traditions of what then was undoubtedly the best school of acting in the whole of Europe. And he in turn had taught her all he knew, which made it very difficult to find out exactly how much natural talent she actually had.

For "talent" and "training" are two very different things, as one comes to understand very soon when one has to deal with people in my profession. The possession of what we commonly call talent (the "well-balanced mind" of the ancient Greeks) allows the happy owner of this unusual quality to get along in this world without a great deal of training. While a great deal of sound training will make it possible for those, not endowed with too much talent, to find their way quite nicely and keep out of the poorhouse. Meanwhile there is a tremendous difference between the two, almost as much as there is between a rose grown by the good Lord and one painted by Melchior d'Hondecoeter, though the latter probably has no rival when it comes to rendering flowers on wood or canvas.

That same girl who was a most fascinating person when she went through her paces in the rôle of the Shepherdess, every line and every word carefully rehearsed by her father, became a dull and vain and highly irritating person the moment she was off the stage. My brother probably would have seen this for himself if she had not been made the object of such a bitter attack on the part of the dominies. The unreasonable hatred of the yellow-faced mob that had pelted her with stones on that fatal evening threw everything into a different light. She was Andromeda on the point of being sacrificed to the hydra-headed monster of religious bigotry while he was Perseus rushing forth to save her from her terrible fate. All this was pure nonsense. But it suited his starved power of imagination. All his life he had waited for a chance to play a noble and heroic rôle. In his heart of hearts he had wanted to be like our great-grandfather, but Fate had condemned him to spend his days by the side of a narrow-minded shrew sitting in a dingy room, hammering mythological figures on ornamental salt-cellars and chiseling phantastic coats-of-arms on those golden goblets with which our successful merchants celebrated the arrival of a son and heir to their recently acquired riches.

It really was not quite fair. The cards were stacked too heavily against this poor soul, starved so pitiably for a little color and a few emotions. Yes, my brother might have escaped if— But the word "if" has no place in the dictionary of human relationships and from the moment he first lay eyes on that woman, he was doomed though no one could have guessed how terrible his end would be.

I am an old man now and generally speaking I accept life as I find it. No use my trying to improve upon the handiwork of God. But if ever he contemplates a reorganization of his universe, I wish that he would rid us of one thing—the good woman who has the instincts of the courtesan. I have seen some of my younger (and older) friends do strange things when they fell into the clutches of the sort of females we are accustomed to call "bad." But their suffering and their humiliations could never bear comparison to the agonies that are suffered by the victims of the professionally "good" women. When it comes to despoiling a man of all those qualities which we associate with self-respect and common decency and pride of achievement, the "good" women can give aces and spades to their less fortunate sisters. For in everything they do, however mean and selfish and calculating their real motive, they will always fall back upon the one consolation, that they have still retained their virginity, though why our world should set so much store by something that is at best a mere biological detail, I, as a medicine man, am utterly unable to perceive.

The ancients, as far as I remember from reading a not inconsiderable number of classical authors, treated this subject much more intelligently than we do, as something beyond good and evil, a "brutum factum," an unavoidable and therefore "neutral" fact, that one had to accept together with life, like the necessity for eating or breathing or sleeping. But those unfortunate slaves who during the first four hundred years of our era crept to power by way of the altar and the confession-booth must hate this wonderous gift of Heaven as they must hate everything else that reminded them a little too closely of their former masters and of a system of civilization that had showered its benefits upon the Few at the expense and to the everlasting humiliation of the Many.

I sometimes wonder what would have happened to this continent of ours if we had received the message of Christ directly from Him without the discourteous intermediaryship of that loquacious tent-maker from Tarsus. For Paul, notwithstanding all his loud protestations to the contrary, was a Jew of the Jews and a Pharisee of the Pharisees. The nastiest and dirtiest and most degrading thing that has ever been said about love—that it is better to marry than to burn—could only have come up in the mind of some one who from father to son had been reared to regard women as a necessary evil, a piece of personal property, created solely for man's convenience and relief.

I know of course that to many honest Christians such a conception of things is most repellent. And the lovely edifices built all over our land to the glory of the Blessed Virgin bear witness to man's irrepressible desire to sanctify that greatest of all mysteries and make it an integral part of the divine law of our being.

But the Reformation (in our part of the world at least) was not a return to an older and nobler form of Christianity. It was the final triumph of Paul. It was a return to Judaism. And woman once more was pulled down from her pedestal to become a household drudge, a breeding-mare and part of her husband's less cherished possessions. Under those circumstances she had only one thing that was really her own until her lord and master claimed it for himself. And I suppose that was at the base of that strange belief that "purity" was something physical rather than something spiritual.

Needless to say I hated the woman who destroyed my brother and I repeat that I may be unfair when I try to make her the center of a religious and philosophic discussion, of which she would not have understood a single iota, and which at best, would have struck her as something that was merely nasty and altogether unworthy of the consideration of what she was pleased to call a lady. I therefore hasten to add that my sympathy at first was entirely on her side, when my brother, having fallen deeply in love with the object of his chivalrous devotion, decided that she must return his sentiments and run away with him to foreign lands, there to begin a new and glorious existence, etc., etc. I bluntly told him that he was crazy, that he was a married man and had no right to talk or think the way he did. And I called on the subject of his affection, then recovering in a small hostelry near the Damrak from her late inconveniences, to offer her my sympathy and suggest that she allow me to find accommodations for her safe return home.

But I was not accorded the reception I had expected. She gave me to understand in no uncertain terms that she was fully able to mind her own affairs and that she would depart when, how and in such manner as she might deem suitable and necessary. And so I took my hat and cane and departed fully expecting to hear that she had taken the next boat from Hellevoetsluis. But to my surprise she was still in Amsterdam a month later, still "recovering" and still protesting to my brother that she was a "good" woman and expected him to treat her as such, although at the same time allowing him to spend the greater part of his days in her company and depending upon him for everything from buying a new pair of stays to getting her the necessary papers to leave the territory of the Republic and providing her with funds for her current expenses, which my brother (having neglected his business beyond all hope of repair) was unable to meet and which he was forced to obtain from me, by giving me all sorts of feeble excuses for being "temporarily slightly embarrassed."

At last, thank God! I heard that she was leaving us. The wounds on her hands and face had fully recovered and there was no excuse for staying any longer in the inhospitable city on the Amstel River. She was to have gone early on a Friday in November and in the afternoon, I called at the house where my brother had taken lodgings when he first began to devote himself to the cause of the oppressed, or in plain language, ever since his imagination and his power of phantasy had got the better of his sense of reality and he had started out in quest of those problematic joys of early youth which had never been his share. His rooms were empty. There was a note on the table, addressed to me. It read: "Bless you, my dear boy. I have followed her. She needs me."

How she needed him I heard almost a year afterwards from a ship's captain who came to the hospital for the amputation of one of his thumbs, caught in a coil of rope. He noticed my name and asked me whether I had any relations in London. I told him yes, that I thought my brother had gone to live there.

"Strange," he said when he recovered slightly from the bottle of brandy which we had given him to bear the ordeal of cutting and sewing. "Strange that I should have met him in that rabbit-warren of humanity."

And he went on to tell me how one evening, walking down London Bridge to look at the shops, he had come across a man turning the leaves of a Dutch volume that was offered for sale among some old second-hand books, how he jokingly had remarked, "Well, Mr. Englishman, you won't be able to make much of that," and how the man had answered him, "But it is my own language."

How he had thereupon invited him to a near-by tavern and how his newly found friend had taken him to his rooms, very simple but very decent rooms, one of which was used for living quarters, while the other one served as a silver-smith's work-shop.

"That is how I make my living," the stranger had told him. "I have quite a trade. I make these so-called Dutch salt-cellars for the jewelers in the city. They pay me well. But then, I have to make quite a lot of money, for I have others to support besides myself."

"A wife and children?" the honest captain had asked with a sly nod. But the other, quite seriously, had answered, "No, I am not married, but I have obligations," and then they had talked of other things and soon afterwards the sailor had bade his adieux and had left to return to his vessel.

I asked my patient to take a letter for me the next time he went to London and four months later I had an answer. In a most affectionate way my brother thanked me for my eager interest in his well-being and happiness. "But don't worry about me," he begged. "Don't worry. I am perfectly contented with my fate. I have at last found something to worship. And angels themselves could ask nothing more or better of life than that."

The captain who brought me this message, however, was not quite so cheerful. He had taken some information about this strange, dignified man who seemed so absolutely out of place in a dingy house in a small alley just off Threadneedle Street and he had discovered that the former Shepherdess had bade farewell to the stage to become the lawful wife of a very doubtful young man who made a living as a juggler and sleight-of-hand artist, giving performances for the benefit of the nobility and having (according to a handbill which he presented to his rich patrons) been privileged upon several occasions to show his "art" to no one less than King Charles and Queen Henrietta Maria. In reality (as the captain discovered without very great difficulty) the young man was a card-sharp who operated in several of the less favorably known gambling houses that were maintained for the special benefit of the landed gentry on their annual pilgrimage to the national capital. But of late he had not been seen in his usual haunts and it seemed that he had retired completely from his somewhat dangerous profession. "I have married a rich wife," he was in the habit of boasting to his drinking companions, "so why should I work?"

"Rich wife?" I asked in surprise. "When the woman was here, she had nothing but the clothes on her back. What does he mean by rich wife?"

"It is your brother," the captain explained. "I am sorry to say it, but he supports not only the woman but also her husband."

"And in return?"

"In return he gets nothing. Absolutely and completely nothing. She is a most virtuous wife. She loves the young scoundrel she has married. He beats her and two or three times your brother had threatened to thrash him if he ever laid hands on her again. Meanwhile he sits in his little room and works, hammers and hammers and hammers all day long at his silver disks, making the most lovely figures and getting good pay (the highest paid craftsman in London he is, so I was told) and carrying it all to this miserable woman, who treats him as if he were her lackey and does not even say thank you."

"And he gets nothing in return for all his trouble?"

"Absolutely nothing, but a fair amount of abuse."

"Nor for his devotion?"

"Absolutely nothing."

And then I knew that the good captain was surely talking of my brother.

For no other man on this planet of ours would have been such a sublime fool.

Chapter 22

I ASK MY BROTHER TO RETURN TO ME

The last time I heard of my brother was in the fall of the year 1641, some eight or nine months before Saskia died.

One evening, when I was sitting by the fire (for it was raining hard and the room was cold and damp) a visitor was announced, and behold, it was my old friend the captain, whom I had not seen for almost two whole years.

"I have news for you," he said, "but you won't like it much. It is not very good news." And he told me how during his last visit to London he had been curious to see what had become of his friend the silversmith. He had found him in his old rooms, hammering away as usual. He had asked him for dinner on board his ship, but he said no, he could not come. He was too busy. He was busier than ever before. He had to make even more money than last year. And finally he had told the reason why. I asked my informant whether he could repeat it to me and he answered that he could.

"Fancy," he said, "that woman's husband now protests that he is of high and noble lineage. He lets it be whispered about that he is some vague connection of the House of Stuart and hints at certain indiscretions of the late Queen Mary. He is a dark-faced villain and talks a great deal about the southern blood of the Rizzios. But he is far from Italian in his love for that virulent usquebaugh, which his compatriots hail as their most important contribution to the happiness of nations. He is drunk every night and when he is in his cups, he becomes abusive of all the world and more especially of his wife, who waits upon him with dog-like devotion and publicly prides herself upon her steadfast loyalty, as one of the main duties of a good woman towards the man whom she has promised to love, honor and obey.

"But in the morning she goes to your brother to ask for the 'loan' of one or five or even ten guineas to tide herself and her husband over until he shall have received a remittance (ever overdue) from his estate in the Scottish highlands. And believe me or not, but the poor fellow accepts all this as the gospel truth. And he hurries to Threadneedle Street and borrows from the jewelers for whom he works until he can give her the sum for which she asks. And she takes the money without so much as saying 'by your leave' or 'thank you' and all day long he is beamingly happy, because he had been allowed—'privileged' he calls it—to be of some slight service to that incomparable creature.

"But that is not all. The husband, when he gets in his cups, is as rude as the captain of a Swiss regiment of lansquenets. He will abuse anybody and everybody in sight and I need not tell you that often leads to fights, for although the English are a peaceful people, they will only take so much insult and then they will hit back. Well, you will probably call me a liar when I tell you that your brother then takes his side, and steps forward to defend this miserable sot against the people who threaten to throw him out into the street. On one occasion he got hurt quite badly. An equally drunken Irishman, a descendant of the kings of Connemara (all Irishmen I ever bossed in my fo'c'sle are descendants of kings when they get a pint of our Geneva in them) began to brag about the glories of the court of Kilmacduagh or some such place as compared to those of the court of Scone or something to that effect and in a moment they had their rapiers out and your brother, in trying to separate them, got badly cut across the knuckles and could not do any work for almost two months.

"But the harpy and her husband did not leave him a moment's peace. What sort of a man was he anyway to leave them in the lurch at this important moment in their career when they might realize a fortune by selling one of their estates and investing the money in a new Muscovy company? And didn't he have very rich relatives in the Low Countries who could help him out until he could go back to work? How about the brother of his who was said to be one of the best-known surgeons in the richest town on the Continent? Surely he would do something for him if he explained the circumstances that had led to his unfortunate adventure. But your brother refused. He refused point-blank. His own humiliation was bad enough. No use letting his relatives at home know what had happened to him. I talked to him like a grandfather. I told him that now was the time to escape, now or never. He said yes, that he knew that I was right but how could he help himself?

"I said, 'Go back to Amsterdam. Your brother loves you. He will be only too delighted to see you again. He will give you his house. He will give you anything he has. I know, for he has told me so, time and again. He wants you back. Go home and be happy.'

"But he answered that he must have time to think. 'She would never let me go alone,' he finally said. 'She would follow me and she would bring her husband with her. That would lead to all sorts of scandals, for the fellow is utterly irrepressible when he gets a few drops of spirits in him. No, I must think this over very carefully. I want to see my brother, I want to see him most terribly. But I must not drag him down with me.'

"And so I left him, for the wind was blowing from the west and I had a cargo of some sort of funny striped English cows on board, and I was in a hurry."

"And that was the last you saw of him?" I asked.

"The very last. The next time I came to London, his rooms were closed. I asked his landlady but she did not know where he had gone."

"That was how long ago?"

"About six weeks."

And that was the last I heard from my brother.

I was to see him again once more, but not to speak to him.

Chapter 23

MY BROTHER COMES HOME

In the fall of the fatal year 1642, it was (as I have already written down) my turn to conduct the anatomical experiments which were held at the College of Surgeons for the benefit of the students who walked our hospitals.

Three years before we had moved into new quarters on the second floor of the St. Anthonie weigh-house and we were very proud of our institution. The clergy of course did not wholly approve of our efforts, but the fact that our laboratories were situated in rooms that had previously belonged to one of those amateur theatrical clubs which had caused so much scandal to the pious citizens of the town made them regard us, their successors, a little more leniently than they might have done otherwise. Furthermore, our institution enjoyed the cordial and avowed approval of Their Lordships of the Town Hall. As good merchants they appreciated the value of health in terms of guilders and quarters. A sick sailor or book-keeper was a dead loss, even if eventually he recovered. And not only did they protect us against those who thought it a sacrilege to pry too closely into the secrets of the human body, but they also gave us a liberal annual subsidy and they even passed a law that the remains of all those who died a violent death in the streets of the city should be surrendered to us for our investigations. We also drew for our daily supply upon the public wards of our hospitals but only when the patient had died without leaving behind any one who could lay claim to his body.

As Amsterdam, with its strict laws and its excellent system of town-guards, was a fairly peaceful town, the great majority of our customers came to us from the God's House, or hospital, but now and then some other unfortunate fellow would slip through after a drunken brawl in a tavern or as a result of one of those short-lived but violent popular upheavals which are very apt to occur in cities that are visited every day by thousands of sailors from every port of the inhabitable and from most parts of the uninhabitable globe.

We had two assistants who prepared the bodies for us. All we doctors had to do was to make an appearance at the appointed hour (usually late in the afternoon after we got through with our practice) and demonstrate some particular problem for the benefit of the students and the younger medical men, who flocked around the operating table. We followed a regular plan by which we tried to cover the whole field in a course of lectures and demonstrations covering the greater part of two years. But that fall I had been asked to deviate from the regular program and discuss certain problems of physiology which at that moment held the center of all our medical attention.

When I was quite a young student I remember how one day the lecturer who explained Galen to us had made a few sneering remarks about a certain Englishman called Harvey or some such name who had undertaken to prove that the blood in the human body was in a state of constant flux and not stationary as we had always held so far. The learned professor had grown very funny about the famous "circulator" who seemed to have discovered certain peculiarities of the human body which had remained a secret to all the famous medical investigators of ancient times. Young people are apt to be very conservative. They have been obliged to take such terrible pains to learn the few things they know, that they regard the man who tries to convince them of the opposite as their natural enemy. And all of us had loudly applauded our dear teacher when he continued to be witty at the expense of his British colleague.

But once mentioned, the idea would not die down. Some claimed that Aristotle had already drawn attention to this fact and others said that the eminent Doctor Servetus, burned at the stake by orders of John Calvin almost a century before (on account of some difference of opinion about the Holy Trinity), had also been of this opinion, though I was never able to get hold of the books in which he had tried to prove his point. But in the year 1628 this fellow Harvey had finally published his new theory in a book devoted exclusively to this subject and every medical man had read it or at least parts of it and for the last fifteen years our profession had been openly divided into "circulators" and "anti-circulators." Truth to tell, there were very few of the latter left at the time of which I am now speaking and the new theory had been so completely incorporated into the sum total of our observations and hypotheses which we sometimes erroneously call our "science of medicine" that it was decided to explain the subject in a special course of lectures and I was asked to give the first one of these.

I still remember the day. It was a Thursday and it was raining. It was so dark in the low-ceilinged rooms in which we met that it was necessary to light a number of candles. Furthermore, as word had gone about that we were going to discuss something comparatively new, a large number of idle people had flocked to our meeting place. For our so-called fashionable people are apt to be so exasperated by the emptiness of their existence that any novelty, however gruesome or extraordinary, is welcome provided it promises them a few minutes' respite from their own boredom. And for lack of a regular stage performance, they were more than willing to brave the horrors of the dissecting theater that they might boast to their friends, "Oh, you know . . . that new theory . . . I have forgotten which one . . . by that man . . . well, I just don't seem able to recollect his name . . . but you ought to have been there . . . it was just too fascinating for words. . . ."

All the same, since our institution was maintained by public funds, we were supposed to allow everybody who cared to come to make himself at home, though fortunately the greater part of that sort of an audience never stayed very long. After the first incision, they turned pale. After the second one, they turned green. After the third one they made for the nearest door.

That afternoon while going upstairs, I met one of our assistants. "Quite a crowd to-day," I remarked.

"Doctor," he said, "there is an awful mob up there. But they won't stay long."

Then I made some inquiries about the body upon which I was to demonstrate. "Is it a man or a woman?" I asked.

"A man," he answered. "They brought him here yesterday morning. They had found him just outside 'The Empty Wine-Barrel' on the Achterburgwal. A pretty low dive, that infamous 'Wine-Barrel.' The poor fellow must have been killed during a quarrel inside and they seem to have thrown him out for fear of the police. His face is in a terrible condition. I have covered it up. At least half a dozen slashes with a broken bottle or a very sharp knife. They don't know who he is, but then, this town is full of foreign scum, though this fellow's clothes looked quite respectable. Anything else I can do, Doctor?"

I said no and went upstairs and with a few words I explained the ideas of Doctor Harvey, that the blood circulates all through our body like the tides that at regular intervals sweep around the globe and how this theory had completely revolutionized the practice of medicine, especially in the field of surgery. And then I took up my scalpel and saw and opened up the chest and laid bare the heart and I took it into my hands to remove it and just then one of the students who stood on my right reached for his note-book which was in his left pocket and his hand brushed against the towel that had been placed across the head of the corpse and the small square of white linen fell on the floor and I recognized the face of my brother.

That is how he came home, and how I welcomed him, holding his dead heart in my hand.

Chapter 24

REMBRANDT ASKS ME TO CALL

A sinner in our town was a sinner. He had offended the majesty of God and must bear the punishment, no matter how undeservedly.

That same evening, after I had made my terrible discovery, I called on one of the Burgomasters who was under some slight obligation to me, as I had once taken care of his oldest boy and had pulled him through a very dangerous attack of croup. I explained to him what had happened and he sent his maid out (very few of our rich people dared to employ male servants, as this smacked too much of foreign manners) with a note for the High Sheriff, asking him to call for a few moments. The Sheriff came and promised that he would do his best to get some information upon the unfortunate incident. Meanwhile, the corpse of my brother remained in the dissecting room, for he was supposed to have come to his end as the result of "being the participant in an act of violence with one or more persons whose identity remained unknown." And according to the laws of Amsterdam, such a person could not be given proper burial but was either handed over to the medical profession or hanged from the gibbet outside the gate until his body rotted away or was devoured by the birds.

Fortunately the Sheriff was a very active man. In less than twenty-four hours, he came to my house with his news.

Two of his assistants had made a round of the different taverns and the first one reported as follows:

Three people, two men and a woman, apparently English, though one of them spoke fluent Dutch, had come to Amsterdam last Monday and had taken rooms in the inn run by an old woman known as Mother Joosten. They had stayed indoors most of the time, claiming that they still felt indisposed from the voyage which had been exceptionally rough and they had had their meals sent up to their rooms. One of the men drank a great deal and seemed to quarrel with the woman, who was apparently his wife. On Tuesday at about five they had gone out. Mother Joosten had asked them whether they needed anything for the night and they had said no, but the smaller of the two men had turned to her and had shown her a piece of paper on which he had written the word Houtgracht, indicating by gestures that he wanted to know where that street was. She had told him as best she could and they had departed.

Late that same evening the husband and wife had returned and had asked that their bill be prepared as they were obliged to leave early the next morning. Then they had told their landlady that they wanted to take another stroll and had gone out in the darkness.

In the morning when Mother Joosten knocked on their door, there had been no answer. The man and the woman were gone. They had left their baggage behind. It consisted of one very shabby leather trunk, containing a few odds and ends of personal apparel, without any value. The bill of nineteen florins and eighty cents (most of this had gone for gin) remained unpaid. (Bill annexed to the report.)

The second constable had followed their track after they had left the place of Mother Joosten. They apparently had started out to find me, for in the "King of Bohemia" where they had eaten and where one of the two men had drunk a great deal of French wine, they had once more asked the shortest road to the Houtgracht. When they left, the smaller of the two men was apparently very much under the influence of liquor and had stumbled across the door-step. He would have fallen if the woman had not caught him, but instead of being grateful to her for this assistance, he had cursed her and the other man had intervened and had suggested that they had better go home. But the smaller of the two men had said no, and had added something to the effect that that night would serve them as well as any other. Thereupon they had departed and it had been impossible to retrace their track.

They apparently had visited several other taverns but the inn-keepers, fearing that they might be implicated in a scandal and a scandal connected with murder and highway robbery (for my brother's pockets were absolutely empty when the body was found) had all of them lied like troopers. Yes, they had seen three people who answered the description given of them, but they had only entered their place of business for a moment and then had gone away, apparently in the best of spirits and that was all they knew, until the moment some highly respectable citizens, returning from a wedding, had stumbled across the dead body and had warned the police.

Under the circumstances and since it was becoming fairly evident that the victim had not been killed in a fight but had been deliberately murdered when he refused to show his companions the way to my house, Their Lordships felt that they might make an exception. They could not very well give me permission to bury my brother in one of the churches, but they had no objection if I could find room for him in one of the yards surrounding those places of worship where occasionally some of the poorer people were interred. I followed him to his grave one drab and rainy morning. But when I reached the cemetery, I found my three friends waiting for me. How they knew or how they had ever found out, I am unable to tell. But they were there and when the coffin had been silently lowered into the grave, Bernardo took a small book from his pocket and opened it.

"This poor man has suffered much," he said. "We will therefore bid him farewell with one short chapter of consolation." And he read the one hundred and thirtieth psalm. Then the sexton and his helpers quickly filled the grave and we went home.

At the bridge of the St. Anthonie locks, I bade them farewell, but Jean-Louys followed me.

"Friends," he said, "are the only dependable refuge in time of sorrow." And he came and stayed with me and said very little, but whenever I went out or whenever I returned home, he was there with a pleasant smile and a cheerful word of welcome. God knows how I would otherwise have pulled through those dreadful weeks.

And one evening, a few days later, a small flat package was brought to the house. Inside of it was a copy of an etching of "The Return of the Prodigal," and underneath it, in pencil, the words: "In Memoriam. Come and see me and let me share your sorrow. Rembrandt."

Chapter 25

I HAVE THE HONOR TO DINE WITH ONE OF THE BURGOMASTERS

When I was a small boy I was taught that all of life was tragedy, and when I grew a little older I sometimes tried to convince myself that all of life was comedy, but now, when I am fast approaching the traditional "three score and ten" I know that both those definitions were wrong.

Life is neither tragedy nor comedy, it is melodrama and melodrama of such a primitive sort that should any playwright dare to put it on the stage, his work would be hooted off the boards and he himself would be publicly derided as an impostor.

Here was my brother, the most peaceful and loveable of men—a hard-working and intelligent craftsman—just the sort of person to be the father of a cheerful family, spending the greater part of his days in quest of the unfindable and left for dead on the door-step of a mean ale-house. And there I was myself—a person with just one interest in life—to sit quietly in my study and try to find some way to alleviate the suffering of sick humanity—at best a very timid creature—rather afraid of life and perfectly willing to spend all my days in the same house on the same street in the same city with the same faithful friends—suddenly condemned to go to the other end of the earth and to spend eight long and lonely years in a wilderness which no white man had ever visited before.

It was all very strange and yet it seemed so hopelessly unavoidable. The hand of Fate was clearly discernible in everything that happened. I struggled as all of mankind has struggled since the beginning of time. I objected. I fought back. I cursed. I insisted upon an answer. And the gods whispered "Inevitable" and again withdrew behind the high clouds in indifferent aloofness.

Plainly it was impossible for me to continue much longer in a town where every stick and stone reminded me of the calamity that had overtaken me. My friends recognized this. They urged me to take a trip, to visit some of the universities of Italy where I would be able to see and hear much that would be of interest to my own investigations. But I lacked the courage and the energy.

I did my work and went to the hospital at the usual hours and made my rounds and saw my patients, but I resembled one of those automatic machines they make in Nuremberg—one that had been wound up long ago and the key of which had been mislaid by a careless servant.

Every day I felt myself grow a little weaker. Like most people of these northern climes, I had a very decided tendency towards melancholia. Thus far I had always rather despised the infamous "black humor" as a confession of moral weakness. And now, so help me God, I too was fast becoming one of its victims.

A few more weeks or months and I would begin to feel sorry for myself. That, as I well knew, was the beginning of the end. The next step would be a slow trip to the cemetery. Not from any wish to die so long before my time, but from a sheer lack of interest in keeping alive.

And then, just when I was beginning to tell everybody that the music had gone out of existence (I rather fancied that expression) and that the sky had lost its color and the flowers had lost their fragrance, in short, when I was beginning to be a terrible nuisance both to myself and to those who were patient enough to bear up with me, the "unexpected inevitable" or the "inevitable unexpected" that always stands hidden in the wings of the magnificent theater devoted to Human Folly, suddenly jumped to the center of the stage, whacked me gayly on the head with the jawbone of Balaam's ass, picked me up, threw me bodily across a couple of seas and oceans and left me stranded high and dry amidst such strange surroundings that I was soon forced to forget all about my own woes or suffer the indignity of being eaten up by a wolf or a bear. And the beginning of these strange adventures came to me in the form of a note which was delivered to me early one morning and in which My Lord Andries Bicker requested the pleasure of my company at his house on such and such a date for dinner and a private talk afterwards.

And this in itself was rather mysterious, for the Burgomasters of our good city did not as a rule extend their hospitality to private citizens like myself. It is true that I had visited his house once or twice in my professional capacity, but that was hardly a social introduction. And most of my neighbors still regarded me as a better-class barber. To-day the study of medicine is beginning to be elevated to the dignity of a science, and a few of us actually rank a little higher than mere leeches or pill-purveyors. But thirty years ago no mayor of the sovereign city of Amsterdam would break bread with a humble disciple of Aesculapius unless there was something he wanted to get from him and wanted very much indeed.

My Lord Andries Bicker was one of four brothers, who on the death of their father had inherited his vast fortune and then quietly divided the entire world among themselves as if it had been a parcel of real estate in one of the suburbs. There were those who said that the Republic ought not to be called the United Seven Netherlands but the United Four Bickerlands, and they were right. I have never been much interested in financial affairs. Perhaps that is not quite correct. I am interested in them, but in a vague sort of a way. Figures and statistics mean nothing to me at all. Tell me to-day that last year we imported eight hundred thousand lemons and four million pounds of rice and five hundred thousand pounds of almonds or that ten years ago the East India Company paid 22½ percent dividend and last year only 18 percent and I shall answer you very politely, "Yes, indeed, and how very interesting!" But an hour later, I shall have forgotten all about it. But tell me that Jansen's father died of such and such a disease and his grandfather of such and such an affliction and if I am called in to see this same Jansen, fifty years hence, I shall have half my diagnosis ready before I have even entered the sick-room.

My grandfather, who was what you call a "practical man," more than once had held the Bicker family up for my youthful admiration. "The backbone of our country," he used to say. "Honest, hard-working people. There is no foolishness about them. In any other country they would be dukes and grandees and live in fine castles, and give themselves airs." (Grandfather could play the plain, simple democrat with great effect on such occasion.) "Just look at them! They must have two hundred ships between them and more shares in the big companies than any one else. Their income is a hundred times larger than that of many a German princeling who goes about boasting of his titles and his ancestors. And yet they continue to live right here in the midst of their wharves and breweries and store-houses and they tell me that they eat meat only once a week, like any ordinary citizen."

But these breweries and wharves and store-houses and those shares in East and West India companies and North Pole companies and South Pole companies meant nothing to me. But I had known both the father and the mother of these remarkable brothers and I was a good friend of the physician who had taken care of them for a number of years and I could have told any one of them offhand what he should eat and drink and what he should avoid and (had he been interested) I could have foretold him with a very fair degree of accuracy what illness would eventually take him to his grave. But as body and soul are not two different entities, as the church fathers of the Middle Ages told us, but are different expressions of one and the same mysterious occurrence, which we call life, I felt that I did not go too hopelessly unprepared to this strange meeting and that I would be able to hold my own in the conversation that was to follow, for I would understand the probable trend of thought of my host much better than he could possibly comprehend mine. Not that I expected anything very unusual. His Lordship probably contemplated some change in the conduct of the city's hospitals and wanted to consult a physician before he introduced the subject in the meeting of Their Lordships the Burgomasters.

But it came quite different, as I was soon to experience.

Our dinner too was more elaborate than I had anticipated. The whole family was present and I was introduced to the ladies of the household which was a signal honor to a member of my humble profession.

I was even taken aside to accept the solemn salutation of a very pretty little girl of six or seven, with a rich abundance of auburn curls. She made me a very pretty curtsey and said, "Good afternoon, Doctor," and I bowed low and kissed her hand with great formality. (For people are mistaken when they think that children don't observe our manners just as closely as we do theirs.) And I said, "Good afternoon, my dear, and what might your name be?" And she answered, "Wendela, sir, and I am staying with Uncle Andries because my sister has got the mumps," and then made me another curtsey and shyly ran back to her aunt who kissed her and said, "And now good night, little Mamselle, it is time you were in your coach with the white horses," whereupon she asked, "May I have just one pear?" and proudly marched off with her possession tightly clutched in her small right hand, the left one holding her long silken petticoats for fear that she might trip on the stairs.

I was not to see her again for a good many years and then under very different circumstances. For she afterwards married My Lord de Witt, whom many esteem the greatest statesman of our age, and she had a number of children, but after her last confinement in '65 she never quite recovered and I was called in on consultation and I had to tell her that as far as she was concerned, the Book of Life was closed and that another birth would mean the death both of herself and of her child, an announcement which seemed to fill her heart with great grief, "For," said she, "my husband is away so much of the time on business of state, and what shall I do to pass away the lonely hours, when the nursery is empty?"

But to return to our dinner. It was excellent and it was short, the highest praise one can give to that sort of function. It consisted of oysters and soup and a large roasted capon. "We ought to have sacrificed a cock to Aesculapius to-night," My Lord Andries explained while carving the fowl, "but seeing that it is not Aesculapius himself, but merely his trusted disciple, we thought that a capon would do just as well. Besides, these beasts are infinitely more tender than their less incomplete brethren." And he offered me the drum-stick, which was another token of honor for which I was not in the least prepared.

"These good people want something from me," I said to myself, and I soon found out that I was right. For immediately the feast had been served, the women bade us good day and my host and his brother Cornelis suggested that I follow them upstairs and they took me to a large room in the front of the house, the walls of which were entirely covered with book-cases and maps and bade me sit down in a low chair by the side of a large globe, and then the maid came in with a tray containing bottles of French wines and of Malaga and Madeira and glasses, and My Lord Andries filled me a glass and said, "Try this wine. It comes from Burgundy. It grew on the estate of a man who for fifty years faithfully served the King of France. Then he committed an act, most honorable in itself, but which went contrary to the personal interests of his Sovereign. He died in the Bastille and my brother and I, who had had business dealings with him, bought his vineyard to keep his wife from going to the poorhouse. Here is your good health."

And my Lord Cornelis took a large copper box, filled with tobacco, out of his pocket and handing me a fresh clay pipe he said, "Try this noble weed. It is of the same quality as that smoked by Sir Walter Raleigh on his way to the scaffold. He also had wasted fifty years of his life waiting upon a queen who called him an atheist for all his troubles and threw him over to please a silly boy who was her lover and serving a king who cut off his head as soon as he failed to find him that gold mine which everybody knew did not exist."

And then both brothers, lifting their glasses, said, "Here is to ourselves. God knows, we are coming on hard times."

And when my looks showed that I was slightly bewildered by this strange performance, they bade me light my pipe again (I always forget to keep those clay contraptions going and wish that some one would invent us a more agreeable way of inhaling the pleasant fumes of nicotine) and Cornelis said, "Fear not, dear Doctor, we have not lost our reason," and Andries added, "This is just our little joke, and now let us come to business," and he delivered quite a speech, which seemed so important to me that as soon as I returned home that evening, I wrote down everything I remembered of it and here are my notes of that evening.

"Doctor," he began, "we want your help. Perhaps you will think that we are slightly crazy but I can assure you that neither of us ever was in better health. Only one thing I must beg of you. All this must remain strictly between ourselves. Nothing is ever accomplished in an open meeting. God himself could not rule this world if he had to discuss everything he did with a dozen committees of arch-angels and was surrounded all the time by a mob of common little angels who more than half of the time would not know what he was talking about. What we are about to propose to you can only serve the weal of our own fatherland. But if our plans are to succeed, we must keep them a secret. At least for quite a number of years."

And when I had nodded my assent, he continued. "I don't want to give you a lecture on current politics, but you are no fool. Otherwise I need not assure you we would never have sent for you, which I mean as a compliment though perhaps I am a little too direct, but you have a good pair of eyes and an excellent pair of ears and you know just as well as I what is actually happening and more important still, what is going to happen in a couple of years.

"Of course you have heard what they say about us. That we run the Republic as if it were our own property. Well, what of it? We are business men. It is our duty to show profits. Is there any one who dares to claim that we don't make money? We make it for ourselves, but by making it for ourselves, we make it for every one else. Has this town ever been as rich as it has since the day our father joined the government? Has the Republic ever been as mighty as in these days when I and my brothers tell them how things ought to be done? There are a lot of lazy loafers who spend their waking hours in the taverns drinking mean gin and telling each other that we are tyrants, that we ought to be assassinated, that in ancient Greece and in ancient Rome the people ruled the state. Perhaps they are right, but this isn't ancient Rome nor ancient Greece. This is the Republic of the United Seven Netherlands and we now write the year of our Lord 1642.

"No, that 'vox populi' business and all that nonsense about democracy and Brutus and Caesar won't get us anywhere. Nor, to tell the truth, will it do us much harm. We are in power and we feel that we exercise this power for the common good. We therefore mean to keep it firmly in our own hands and we can do it, as the rabble will discover the moment it tries to start something. We are peaceful burghers. I and my brother would not harm a fly. But we must have law and order and prosperity! Let any one dare to interfere with us and he will swing outside the Town Hall windows and no mistake about it!

"But there is one little item that worries us a good deal. Some day, very soon, the war with Spain will come to an end. We are practically independent now, but when peace is signed, the whole world will have to recognize us as a sovereign commonwealth. What is going to happen then? And what will the House of Orange try to do? We have always been on good terms with those Germans. Old William was a great man. I have heard our grandfather speak about him. He knew him well. And so did our father. A very great man, wise and shrewd and very liberal. Not much of a soldier, but then, the world is full of soldiers and statesmen are as rare as roses in January. A terrible pity he was murdered just when we needed him so badly. A great many things would have come differently had he lived just a couple of years longer. But that is the way it goes in this world, and no use crying over spilt milk.

"His sons too have been very useful. But in a different way. Old William was a man of learning, a man of taste. He had vision and knew what was what. He would have made a good business executive. He knew how to row with the oars that were at his disposal. If he needed the support of the church party to further the interests of the land, he would go and associate with the ministers of the Gospel. If he thought that they were going too far and were trying to dominate the situation (and give that sort of people one finger and they will try to take the whole hand) he tactfully but sternly reminded them of their proper place and they went back into Clio's box until they were needed again. When there was fighting to be done, he not only found an army (and mind you, most of the time his treasury was completely empty, and did you ever hear of a professional soldier who fought for the love of the thing?) but he accomplished the impossible by enlisting the good will of all the different elements that under the leadership of a less clever man would have cut each other's throats long before they had seen a single enemy. But once the fighting was done, back they went again into their little wooden box, and that was that. He played on men and their emotions as old Sweelinck plays on his organ and as a result we had a decently balanced form of government. The Republic, as he saw it in his mind's eye, could have lived and might have lasted longer even than Venice or Genoa. But then he was murdered, and we got his sons.

"Excellent fighting men. Old Maurice never had a thought in his head except that it had to do with guns or horses or regiments of foot or ordnance. In the summer he laid siege to cities and in the winter he laid siege to women and I never heard of him to fail in getting whatever he wanted.

"But he was a German. His father had been a German too, but somehow or other, one never thought of him that way. He belonged to the world at large, but Maurice, for all his fine palaces and his courts and his gentlemen-in-waiting, always reminded me of an ordinary landjunker. He always smelled of horses and of stale beer, and when he dined at our house, we had to keep the windows open for a week afterwards.

"I am telling you now a few of our professional secrets. The crowd believe that the Stadholders of the Republic and the Burgomasters of Amsterdam are bosom friends, all coöperating most heartily for the ultimate benefit of our common country. Let them believe what they will. As long as we remain safely seated on those comfortable cushions of the Town Hall, we can afford a few amiable fairy-tales of that sort.

"But how long will we be able to hide the fact that we are really at cross-purposes? How soon before the man in the street discovers that all is not well? It has already happened once, upon one memorable occasion of which I need not remind you. Undoubtedly you are old enough to remember that terrible Monday the thirteenth. The greatest man our country had produced so far was murdered that day and murdered by the people for whom he had slaved for more than fifty years of his life. He had understood what few people before him suspected, that we were fast drifting towards a monarchy, and that the Republic would become another little German principality as soon as the Prince was allowed to forget that we, the people who make this commonwealth what it is, are his employers and pay him his salary as we pay that of any of our other servants.

"But of course Maurice would have been helpless without some political organization to back him up in his plans. I don't know who the bright man was who suggested that he make common-cause with the church party, but he did. And ever since, none of us have been quite safe. What happened to Oldenbarneveldt may happen to any of us almost any day. The present Stadholder is not a very strong man. He suffers from violent outbursts of temper and such people are always easily managed. Besides, he is too busy with his army. A marvelous fellow in his own field! Bois-le-Duc. Maastricht, Breda, Roermond, Wezel, he captured them all as neatly and as easily as a good chess player takes the pawns of his opponent. And not a single false move. But he is wasting himself physically. By the time he gets the last Spaniard out of our last city, he will be dead. He has a weak chest. Mark my words, we will sign our peace over his coffin.

"And then, what will become of all those German junkers who are now making a fine living as officers in our armies? We shall let our troops go the moment the war is over. Those captains and colonels and quarter-master-generals will all be out of a job and they won't like it. They have grown accustomed to three or four square meals a day, and plenty of wine. Do you think they will ever content themselves with the watery gruel of their beloved homeland, the beer-soup of Pomerania? I doubt it, and if all we hear of the way in which the Emperor's troops and the Swedes are chasing each other across the German lands is true, there won't be much even of that.

"Well, you can draw your own conclusions. They will want to remain right here where it is nice and comfortable and warm and where even the beggars won't touch their charity porridge unless it has about half a pound of sugar in it. And how will they accomplish this? By making themselves indispensable. And to whom? To the only man who has any need of their services, to the Prince.

"It is all very well to be the highest paid official in the Republic. But it would be a great deal more agreeable to step out of the salaried class and become an independent little potentate. I am not saying anything against the young prince. He is only a child. But at sixteen, a boy in his position is old enough to give us some inkling about his character and I don't trust that infant. I don't trust him for a moment! If he merely aspired to his father's place, why was he in such a hurry to marry the daughter of King Charles? Charles is hard up for money. He is having troubles with his people. I can't blame the people much, for their beloved sovereign seems a pretty slippery customer and he is costing them the devil of a lot of money. But of course he needs all the help he can get and so our young princeling was able to marry himself a princess of the blood at the moment the dear lady was going cheap.

"Well, what will he do next? He has the army, for as I have just pointed out to you, the officers know on what side their bread is buttered and a pleasant and solvent miniature court right here in Amsterdam or perhaps in The Hague would suit them remarkably well.

"But the army alone is not enough. We still have credit with the banks. We could send to Switzerland for a dozen regiments of infantry or we could buy half a dozen army corps from the Emperor, with cavalry and horses and all, enough to make an end to all this foolishness. And the navy is on our side and if the worst came to the worst, we could bring the men on shore and they are rough customers. But there are still a number of other people in this land of ours who have mighty little love for us and who would rally to anybody who promised them a chance to get even with their betters. That is the church party.

"I am a good Christian myself, as my father has been before me, and my mother too, and as I hope that my children will be after me. But those [and here His Lordship used a number of terms which I had never expected to hear from his lips and which I deem it wiser not to repeat] —but those stupid, narrow-minded, vain-glorious plow-boys, who have spent four years in some theological seminary and then come to town and frighten the rabble with their cock and bull stories about punishment and Hell and try to tell us—us!—how we should run the government of our own city and our own country! No, thank you, I'd rather flood the land again as they did when old Prince William was still alive and die in the last ditch than give in to these fellows one tenth of an inch.

"And that, I think, is the way all of us feel in the Town Hall. Well, of course the dominies know it and the Prince knows it and all his uncles and nephews and bastard little cousins know it. And there you have the lay of the land. As soon as the war with Spain is over, the war at home will begin. On the one hand, we the merchants who have made this country what it is, and on the other hand the Prince who wants to become a king and the rabble that believe everything he promises them and that see in him their savior who will lead them out of what they are pleased to call the wilderness of paganism into the promised land of that terrible man, Calvin."

Now when my Lord Andries got to this point, I thought it was time to rise respectfully to a few points of doubt. In the first place, had the House of Orange really ever had such ambitions as he had just implied? Surely, if they had wanted to make themselves the absolute rulers of the country, they could have done so repeatedly ere now. And in the second place, was he quite fair to the humble men and women who had fought and starved and died like flies during the first years of the great struggle for freedom and who had silently and contentedly borne such sufferings as would have broken the spirit of almost any other nation? But the Burgomaster was right there with his answer:

"I follow your objections," he said, "but don't you see that all this has changed completely since we practically gained our freedom? I will say this much for the doctrines of the learned Doctor Calvin, they absolutely suited the circumstances of the time. They were an excellent code of behavior for a town that was in a state of siege. They made men hard and women invincible. They put iron into the souls even of small children. It was a system that even the veterans of that old cut-throat Alva could not break. When he took Haarlem and drowned a couple of hundred of our people, they would grasp at the executioners with their dying fingers and would try to drag them down with them.

"But that sort of religion is of no earthly use to any one in times of peace. It is like the hammer of a smith that needs an anvil in order to function properly. Take the anvil away and it is just a useless tool that smashes people's toes when it is handed about and gets in everybody's way. Our ministers knew this and they still know it to-day. They must be forever standing on the ramparts of some beleaguered town. They must go snooping through the streets looking for hidden traitors. They must exhort and expostulate and urge and incite their poor disciples as if the enemy were still at the gate, ready to plunder and rape as did the soldiers of His Most Catholic Majesty. They must keep the people in a white hot rage against some threatening iniquity in their midst or go out of business altogether. And so for ever they are keeping the country in unrest and are forever setting the crowd off on a wild goose chase after a bugaboo that in reality does not exist.

"One day they clamor for the head of Oldenbarneveldt and keep the people happy with the lurid details of his execution. Then they must appoint a commission to examine the old man's affairs and show the world what a scoundrel he has been and behold! the commission reports that never in their lives have they come across so much honesty. That ends the search in that particular direction. But they are right away on the scent of a group of other miscreants and this time it is the members of some unfortunate sect that does not see fit to think of the Trinity as the old man in Geneva did.

"The Trinity is far removed from human affairs and it will be a long time before we shall really find out who is right in the matter. But that is a detail about which they don't bother. Those people don't think the way we do. Therefore they are in the pay of Satan. To the gallows with them! They made poor Hoogerbeets hang himself. De Groot is an exile somewhere in Sweden or France. And a couple of hundred of perfectly harmless preachers, some of the best and kindliest of men who ever trod this earth, are deprived of their livelihood, are making a living as bakers' assistants, have turned cobblers, have fled to one of those dreadful towns in northern Germany where they have to send their children begging in order to keep alive. All that is the work of the men of the great Synod.

"They are ideal shepherds for those who believe that they have seen the Devil sliding down our chimney on a long black broomstick and that we are making ready to massacre the children of Zion just as soon as the necessary formalities shall have been fulfilled with the King of Darkness.

"You think that I exaggerate? Well, think of what happened when you were young and the fights we had to fight right here in this city before we put an end to the tyranny of these clerical upstarts. What happened then taught us a lesson. This commonwealth was built upon the principle of live and let live, believe and let believe. That was the creed of Father William, and it is our creed to-day. We intend to maintain ourselves upon that basis. If we cannot do it, we shall fight. Meanwhile, like good merchants, we should provide for the future and that is why we asked you to come here. We are delighted to see you as our guest.

But we also want to make you a business proposition. I shall light another couple of candles, to show you something. Meanwhile, have another glass of wine and fill yourself another pipe."

My Lord Andries went to a cupboard and took two candles which he fastened into a brass candle-stick and those he put in front of one of the large maps that hung on one side of the walls. He beckoned me to come nearer and I got up and I recognized one of Mercator's charts of the world, one of those new geographic maps that are said to have done so much to further the art of navigation.

"It is quite an old map," My Lord Andries remarked, "but it will do until the Blaeus give us a new one, which they have promised us very soon. Now look for a moment," and he showed me different parts of Asia and Africa and America, "all this belongs to us. Here all these islands," and he pointed to the Malayan Archipelago, "are possessions of the East India Company. Here, Ceylon has been ours for the last four years. Formosa old Carpentier has conquered. We have an open door that leads into Japan by way of Deshima. It is not very much of a door but a mighty profitable one. Here along the coast of Coromandel and Malabar we hold at least two dozen ports, we have a trading station at Mascate and control the trade in the Persian Gulf. Then down to Mauritius, and they say that Governor van Diemen is going to send Tasman to see what there is in this old story of several vast continents somewhere between Java and the South Pole.

"Sorry to bother you with these details. I sound like a schoolmaster, teaching a class of little boys their geography. In a moment you will see what I am driving at. Here on the west coast of Africa we possess a couple of harbors where our ships can get fresh provisions, then way up north here, Spitzbergen, where our whaling companies have built themselves a town where the money flows like sperm-oil, and down here in Brazil where we have a chance to build ourselves a vast empire of coffee and tea and tobacco, though unfortunately all this territory belongs to the West India Company and God knows how beautifully they mismanage it! And then here are all these islands in the West Indies. Old man Columbus surely was off the track when he mistook these bits of rock for part of the realm of the Great Mogul, but we are beginning to grow things on them and in due time they will pay their way. And then here in the north, the land we got from the discovery of Hudson. That is the spot to which we want to draw your attention for the moment, right here at the mouth of the Mauritius River, that one and this other bit of land at the tip of the African continent, right here where it says the Cape of Good Hope.

"I told you that we are afraid of what may happen to us as soon as we conclude peace with Spain and the soldiers join the great army of the unemployed, the people who are now working in our arsenals and navy-yards and powder-mills and who will have quite a hard time finding new jobs. Well we intend to be prepared. That is why we asked you to come here to-night. You can help us and I will tell you in what way, but first of all sit down again and have some more of this wine and another pipe of tobacco. The pipe will remind you of the fate that awaits those who put their faith in princes. But then, we are only burgomasters."

The glasses were filled and My Lord Andries took a sheet of paper and cut himself a new pen.

"I can think better when I have a piece of paper and a pen in my hands," he said. "You first had a lesson in practical politics and then one in geography. Allow me to add a little mathematics, the only science that should be of any real interest to the members of our merchants guild. Come over here near my desk and I will show you the conclusions we have drawn from many years of careful study."

With a few rough strokes he drew a picture that looked like a see-saw and two small soup-plates connected with pieces of string.

"What is this?" he asked.

"A pair of scales," I guessed, and I was right.

"That pair of scales represents the Republic," he continued. "That is the situation at the present time. The scales are well balanced," and he drew a small square in each of them and wrote in one of them "The Prince" and in the other, "The Merchants."

"In order that we may continue to be prosperous, this balance should be maintained. We merchants have no objection whatsoever to a strong central government. We are too busy with our own affairs to look after a lot of executive details, that can be much better attended to by the Stadholder, who is trained for that sort of work and whose family has made a specialty of it for God knows how many centuries. We need such a man in the Republic and we really don't care very much whether he wants to call himself a Stadholder or a King or anything else, as long as he does not interfere with our affairs and lets us free to make the money without which the commonwealth would be as helpless as a ship without sails. I am afraid that I am beginning to mix my different figures of speech. I am not a literary man, but I hope that I have made myself clear."

I told His Lordship that he had made himself entirely clear.

"Very well," he went on, and he drew another square in the soup-plate that had already been honored with the princely cargo. Then he wrote "The Church" inside the square and once more showed it to me.

"Suppose I add this extra load to one side of my scales, then what will happen?"

This mathematical catechism was beginning to amuse me.

"Then the balance would be disturbed," I answered.

"And in order to reëstablish that balance?"

"You would be obliged to find a counter-weight."

"Just so, Doctor! You ought to have been a mathematician instead of

THE WINDMILL

making pills. And what sort of a counter-weight would you suggest?"

I thought a moment and not wanting the conversation to become too serious, I said, "You might try moral persuasion."

The two Bicker brothers looked at each other and then lifted their glasses. "We must drink to that. 'Moral persuasion' to balance the dominies! A fine idea. But you know what became of the first man who tried to outweigh the power of a monarch by moral persuasion?"

I said yes, that I thought I remembered only too well.

"And of all the others?"

Again I nodded my assent.

"Very well, Doctor. Now be very bright for once and give us another guess."

"Money," I hinted.

"You are getting there. And how much money?"

"A great deal of it."

"An awful lot of it," My Lord observed.

"And even more," his brother added, and then he went on with his lecture.

"How is money made?" he asked me.

"By industry and perseverance."

"Yes, in the copy-books from which you learned your reading and writing when you were a little boy. But how is it really made?"

I told him that I had never thought of it. I was interested in only one problem, how sick people could be made well again. How was money made?

"Well," he observed in the tone of a school-master who is trying to be patient with a very dull pupil, "in a variety of ways. I don't want to go back all the way to the days of Moses and Julius Caesar or even those of those noble barons and knights who are now trying to marry our daughters if we are willing to give them enough of a dowry. I know the Greeks and the Phoenicians or whatever their names used to peddle their wares around the Mediterranean, and in the Middle Ages the Jews did a lot of buying and selling and had their teeth pulled out as often as some twopenny potentate was in need of a small loan. But generally speaking, before Venice and Genoa and Nuremberg and Antwerp and now our city taught them better, people made money by catching a few boatloads of their fellow-citizens by fastening dog-collars around their necks and forcing them to work for their own benefit as if they had been horses or dogs, which undoubtedly they were except that the man who killed a first-class stallion was punished a little more severely than the fellow who merely murdered a serf.

"But all that belongs to the past, at least in the civilized part of the world—which of course means our own part of the world. What the rest of our blessed continent does, hardly interests me. Perhaps from a business point of view, it is just as well that they remain a little backward. Meanwhile we will try and make 'profits.' Now what are profits? I have something that costs me ninety-nine cents and I sell it for a florin and I grow rich. I have something that costs me a florin and I sell it for ninety-nine cents, and I go to the poor-house. Business is really very simple. It merely consists in buying cheaply and selling dearly. All the rest is stuff and nonsense and belongs in one of those pamphlets about the 'rights of stockholders,' etc., that certain clever lawyers write in taverns when they have had a couple of drinks. Buying cheaply and selling dearly is the whole secret, and how can you do that best of all?"

Again I confessed my ignorance.

"You don't know? You really don't know? And yet it is so terribly simple. All you have to do is to get hold of some convenient little monopoly. Once you have got it, your troubles have come to an end. You can sit peacefully in your office and hire some one else to count your profits. Soon you will need a dozen people just to keep track of the figures."

I interrupted him with some irritation. "And that is where you need me? You want me to give up the practice of surgery and become a book-keeper?"

His Lordship jumped to his feet. "God forbid," and he waved his hands in despair. "The world is full of good book-keepers, honest, intelligent, obliging fellows who will work all their lives for five florins a week and will never have a thought or a desire as long as they live. Book-keeper, fiddlesticks! Whenever we let it be known that the house of Bicker needs a new book-keeper, there is a line outside our door from here to Zaandam. No, we don't want you to turn book-keeper."

I looked at him in surprise. "Then, My Lord, how in Heaven's name do I come to figure in your plans and calculations?"

"Very simply. We want you to go and find that little monopoly for us," and once more His Lordship picked up his pen and began to do some figuring.

"In order to hold our own against the political combination we anticipate and fear," he said without looking up from his pothooks, "we need a great deal of added revenue. For this we need the exclusive hold upon one of the necessities of life. Most of these are already in other hands. The East India Company has got all the spices. They are out. The West India Company has got the slave trade. That is out. Besides, it is a nasty sort of business and I am not enough of a theologian to be able to drug my soul with those passages from Holy Script which elevate slave-raiding to the dignity of a semi-religious duty. Then in the North, there is whale oil and whale bone. But all this is in the hands of a single company and they won't allow any outsider to look in on their fishery preserves. Besides, I hear that they have gone after those poor dumb whales with such murderous violence that soon there won't be a whale left within a thousand miles of Spitzbergen. And suppose the French dressmakers decree that women shall not wear corsets any longer, what then would become of the whale-bone industry? It would lie flat on its back in less than a month.

"That does not seem to leave very much for us, does it? Of course, my brother and I are stockholders in all those companies and directors, and we get our share of the dividends. But the people on the other side of the fence, the partisans of the Prince are stockholders too and occasionally they are able to outvote us. And that is just what we don't want to happen. We want a monopoly of our own that shall be entirely in the hands of our own family and a few of our relatives, a water-tight and air-tight monopoly that is ours, to use as we shall see fit. And we think that we have found one.

"Let me give you a few more figures. Man has to eat in order to live. Granted! The staple article of daily consumption in most households is bread. Also granted! Bread is made out of a substance called grain. On that point there probably won't be any dispute. Where does that grain come from? Most assuredly not from the territory of the Republic. We have had two of our brightest book-keepers study this problem for three years. They have examined all the reports of the harbor-master and they have carefully gone through the tax returns of the commissioners of internal revenue. Here they are" (and he opened a drawer of his writing table and took out a blue cover which held a number of papers)—"here you are. Last year our city alone needed about forty-two thousand tons of grain, but one third of that went to the breweries and as you know, we make the beer for practically the whole of the country. The rest of the Republic used up another forty thousand tons. The total import was 160,000 tons so that almost eighty thousand tons were exported again and at an excellent profit I can assure you. For even under the present circumstances, our country has practically a monopoly of the carrying trade of all grain. Our agents in Copenhagen report that of the 793 ships that crossed the sound on their way from the Baltic to the North Sea, 702 flew the red, white and blue of the Republic. That is not a bad showing, is it? Of those 702, not less than 590 were bound for our city and more than half of those were loaded with grain. That grain is grown in Poland and Curland and Esthland, the old possessions of the German Order, and in Ukrania, which is part Polish and part Russian.

"In the olden days, this trade was easy enough. Of course the Danes with their infernal tolls made our lives miserable, but as long as we paid (although often enough we paid through the nose), we got our ships. But the political situation around the Baltic Sea is beginning to fill our hearts with fear. Poland is getting more disorderly every day. A republican monarchy, in which one foolish knight (be he drunk or sober, but as a rule he is drunk) has the power to upset any law that all the others want, such a country is bound to go to pieces sooner or later. The Swedes have conquered Esthland and Livland, but Gustavus Adolphus is dead, his daughter Christina (even if she had had sense enough to send for Grotius to act as one of her advisers) is—well, let us say rather 'unbalanced.' I hear that she has begun to see spooks and wants to travel to Rome to tell the Pope how to rule the world and then go into a monastery. That country, therefore, is out of our calculations for the present at least. All the Wasas have been a little bit crazy—very brilliant many of them—but always just a trifle unreliable.

"And then there is the famous Grand Duke of Muscovy, who now calls himself 'Caesar' and prattles sweetly of being heir to all the rights and prerogatives of the old Emperors of Byzantium. What all that will eventually lead to, God only knows. We have an agent in Moscow and he tells us that ever since Czar Ivan (you remember? The one who beat his son to death) the Russians have been talking of their 'ancestral rights' to the whole of the east coast of the Baltic. What those ancestral rights are I don't know. But I do know that there are a terrible lot of these wild people and once they are on the war-path, neither Swede nor Pole nor Prussian will be able to stop them.

"A nice little war in those parts that lasted let us say two or three years would make all of us starve. We need grain and Spain needs grain and Italy needs grain. We need it because there is more water than land in this country and no one so far has invented a method of growing grain in a swamp like rice. Spain and Italy need grain because they are so full of monasteries that there isn't room enough left to sow a few acres of wheat of their own. But think what it would mean to our carrying trade if we should be cut off from our base of supply in the Baltic! More than half of our ships would lie idle. And the greater part of the other half would be forced out of business because we would not have gold enough with which to buy the things we need from abroad. Now, Doctor, what is the answer?"

I confessed that I did not know.

"The answer is very simple. We must no longer content ourselves merely with transporting and selling other people's grain. We must grow it ourselves. And there are only two places where we can do that. One is on the Cape of Good Hope. But the East India Company would never allow us to settle there. Until now they have not taken possession of it themselves, but I hear that they may do so almost any moment and their charter gives them the right to claim the whole of southern Africa, as part of their dominions and then we would have done all our work in vain. I have no desire to be another LeMaire. That poor devil was no doubt well within his rights when he claimed that he had not infringed upon the charter of the company when he sailed to the Indies via Cape Horn. But old Coen took his ship away from him just the same and young LeMaire died from sheer disappointment and the father took the case to the supreme court and won it, but by the time the last judge had signed the last decree, the old fellow was a bankrupt and that is what would happen to us too if we were ever foolish enough to try it. No, there is but one way out. Come over here a moment," and His Lordship picked up a candle and went back to the map on the wall and pointed to the central part of the North American continent and he said:

"Right here and now we will tell you what you can do for us. All this of course belongs to the West India Company. It was given to them by the charter of 1621. But that company has never done well. I don't exactly know why. I suppose the East India Company has absorbed all our available surplus capital. In the Indies, almost everything will grow and the natives are patient little brown men who all work for you if you treat them badly enough. In America the natives will die rather than work for some one else. And the climate is annoying. No pepper, no cinnamon, no nutmeg. A few beaver-skins and a little dried fish and even for these you have to barter with a naked red man with feathers in his hair and a large battle-ax in his strong right hand.

"And they have been terribly unfortunate with the people they have sent out. They began wrong. That man Hudson may have been a fine navigator (I suppose he was) but he was about as loyal to his employers as those other Englishmen we hired to fight for us, and who sold Zutphen and Deventer to the Spaniards. I will say that he did a fine piece of work in sailing up the Mauritius River, but if Adriaan Block had not lost his ship off Manhattan Island (a strange accident that fire was too, but in this case a very fortunate one) and if Block had not been the man he was we would know no more about America to-day than we did when Hudson first invited the natives on board his *Half Moon,* and got them so beautifully drunk on Dutch gin. That was a pretty terrible performance and that bad beginning seems to have put a special hoodoo on everything we have ever tried to do in that part of the world. We have had a fine lot of men as governors of the Moluccas and Java, but there on the banks of the Mauritius, one terrible person has succeeded the other. Pieter Minuit was an honorable man. But the others, great Heavens, what a sad collection of incompetent scoundrels! May was a common clerk and not even an honest one. No one knows why he was ever appointed except that he happened to be on the spot when they needed some one in a hurry. Krol was a run-away dominie and absolutely untrustworthy. Van Twiller was a fool who thought that his good connections would keep him out of jail when he engaged in a little private speculation, as they afterwards did. Kieft, who is supposed to rule that colony to-day, is an undischarged bankrupt. You can still see his picture fastened to the gallows.

"He seems to belong to that unfortunate race of 'energetic' people who always must be 'doing' something, especially when they would serve their purpose much better by doing nothing at all. He got the company into a nice war with the natives. I have forgotten their names, Algonquins or something like that.

"The good ship *Fortune* came in port last week with a cargo of beaver-skins and I had a long talk with her captain. He used to work for us years ago when we had more breweries than we do now and needed more grain. He married a wife with some money and he put it into West India shares and then he went into the service of the company because, as he said, that was the only way to discover what they were doing with his funds. He has traded all over America from the Trask River to Cape Hinloopen. We are old friends and he knew that he could trust me. I learned more from him in five minutes' talk than from all the endless written reports of these half literate but long winded governors.

"The trouble with the Indians, so he told us, has been absolutely uncalled for. Anybody with half a grain of common sense (uncommon sense is more to my liking but it is so terribly hard to find)—any one with half a grain of uncommon sense would have been able to avoid those difficulties. The savages in that part of the world seem to be harmless enough, a bit dirty and a bit lazy from our own point of view, but rather like children, good natured until they discover that you have tried to cheat them when they suddenly lose all control of themselves and slash and burn and kill until their anger is spent and they smile once more as if nothing had happened.

"Our friend had dealt with them for a dozen years or more. He had visited their villages and spent nights in their tents, absolutely unarmed and the only white man within a hundred miles. But nothing had ever happened to him. If it had not been for the slightly embarrassing and not entirely unodorous expressions of affection on the part of the wives and daughters of these poor heathen, he told me that he would rather settle down in almost any Indian village than in the place of his birth, which lies somewhere in the darkest interior of Friesland.

"You therefore need have no fear on that score. You won't be eaten up or burned at the stake or thrown to the dogs. I know that that has happened to a few of the Jesuit missionaries who operate in the neighborhood of Fort Orange. I am sorry for them, but why didn't they stay at home? Can you imagine a couple of priests and sorcerers of those Algonquins, or whatever the name, right here on the Dam near the fish-market, let us say, telling the dear public that is busy buying and selling shrimps and mussels, that they ought to stop buying and selling shrimps and ought to listen to the words of the Great White Spirit from the hills, who bids men and women paint their faces a bright red and stick a feather in their hair and say 'Walla, walla, walla' forty times in succession to escape the disfavor of the Great Black Spirit? Can you imagine such an episode and can you imagine what would happen to the poor heathen? Well, I can and I suppose you can too.

"No, the natives will be the least of your worries. You are a man of tact and we shall give you a shipload of these gimcracks and little mirrors and beads and bangles that seem to delight the hearts of those simple children of nature. And then, at your leisure, we want you to sail across the ocean and go to Nieuw Amsterdam. We have collected a great deal of information about you before we asked you to come here. We know that you are deeply interested in the problem of reducing the pain connected with those surgical operations that take place in our hospitals. Mind you, I don't say that they are not necessary, but I was a victim myself once. It was not much of an affair as such things go, but I still turn green and cold whenever I think of what they did to me. Very well, you let it be known that you are going to take a trip to America because you want to investigate those stories that are coming to us continuously about certain plants which the natives of the New World use to alleviate pain."

I interrupted His Lordship. "I am sorry," I said, "but why lie about it?"

But this rather downright question did not worry the speaker for a moment.

"In the first place," he continued, "it would not be quite a lie. My book-seller sends me every account of American exploration that appears. He has standing offers for such books in London and Sevilla and Lisbon. I can't read those printed in Portuguese, but I have those translated by a bright young Jew, a curious fellow who seems to be the only man who ever got away from the Inquisition and lived to tell the tale."

"I know him," I said. "He is one of my best friends."

"Really? Well, he is a bright fellow and ought to have a better job than he has now. We have offered to employ him ourselves, but he seems to be content to jog along. Well, as I was saying, I read every word that is being printed about those mysterious aborigines and what strikes me most is that they seem to know a great many things of which we, with all our learning, have not the faintest idea. They do seem to be able to deaden their bodies against pain. It may be just a funny story, like that one connected with the famous gold of Sir Walter Raleigh which proved to be some sort of copper or the Fountain of Youth of that old Spaniard whom they buried in the Mississippi (you see, I know my American geography) and so you won't be wasting your time if you consent to spend a few years collecting shrubs and weeds and interviewing medicine-men with rings through their noses."

I agreed that it would be a wonderful opportunity, but why not tell the truth?

"Because," my Lord Andries answered, "it would be one of those occasions where telling the truth would be fatal. What we really want to do, and now I am coming to the kernel of the business, is to get hold of vast tracts of land where grain can be grown at a very small cost. According to the best of our information, the coastal regions are too rocky and too densely covered with woods to be suitable for that purpose. But a few hundred miles inland, as I have found stated in any number of books, there are enormous plains where grain will grow almost over night.

All the land from the Atlantic to the next ocean (most likely it is the Pacific, but we are not sure yet. Hudson, so I hear, claimed to have found another sea much higher up in the north, a small ocean that may reach as far as Mexico) for all we know. All the land between the Fresh River and the South River belongs to the West India Company however. That organization is terribly hard up for money and the directors would listen with both ears if we offered to buy a few hundred thousand square miles and pay cash.

"That is what we want to do as soon as you come back and tell us that the soil is suitable for our purpose. We have the money and we mean to keep this a strictly family affair. No one outside of our own city will be allowed to invest a penny. No committees of Seventeen or Gentlemen Nineteen for us, if we can help it. This time the enterprise is going to be well managed. That is why we shall depend so greatly upon your report. If you tell us that the land will grow grain, we shall buy vast tracts. We are already at work upon a system of colonization. There are thousands of people in the Republic who would go abroad and settle in Java or Brazil or even in the New Netherlands if they were not obliged to go there in a state of semi-serfdom. If we find that we cannot work our farms without slave labor, we shall import a sufficient number of them from Africa. I don't approve of it much myself, but if that is the only way to make money, well then, we shall do as the others do.

"But what we have in mind will bear very little resemblance to those trading-posts which are the eternal stand-by of all our Indian companies. We want permanency. We want to turn our possessions over there (if ever we get them) really and truly into some sort of a New Netherlands. So that if things go wrong over here in the old Netherlands, we have another home in another world upon which we can fall back.

"Maybe I am a little too pessimistic. Maybe that young Orange prince is not bright enough or has not got courage enough to try and do all those things of which we suspect him. In that case, if we are successful, we shall have another source of income and a little extra pin-money is always acceptable even to the best of us. On the other hand, if things go badly we shall have a new fatherland. And new hope and courage for thousands of people."

He stopped abruptly and turned to his brother. "All this seems clear to you?" he asked.

"Perfectly," my Lord Cornelis answered.

"Then," turning to me, "have you any questions to ask?"

"Yes," I replied. "The one at which I hinted a moment ago. Why all this secrecy? Why not let everybody know what the purpose of my voyage is?"

"For a variety of reasons. In the first place, if the Prince and the Church people are conspiring to deprive us of our power and turn the Republic into a monarchy, they will of course take measures to prevent you from going, if they know what your mission is, and they will do their best to spoil our ideas, and as yet we are not powerful enough to hold our own against such a combination of forces. In the second place, if the direction was to hear of this, they would ask such extortionate prices for their land that the whole plan would come to nothing. In the third place . . ."

But I did not care to hear any further reasons. I already knew enough. My personal sympathies were entirely on the side of those two men who saw the ideals for which our fathers had fought so valiantly, go to ruin on the cliffs of selfishness, partisanship and religious bigotry. Of course they were business-men and figured things out in terms of florins and daalders, more than I would have done who lived vaguely in that realm of science where money is rarely discussed because it is so seldom seen in sufficient quantities to attract people's attention. But on the whole, I did not doubt the integrity of their motives. Only I would need a little time to think things over. I told them so and they agreed most readily.

"Take as long as you like, Doctor," they urged me most cordially. "We have expressed ourselves quite openly to you and have placed ourselves in your hands. Go home now, for you must be tired after listening to this lecture and let us know what you intend to do just as soon as you have made up your mind."

I bade my adieux and slowly walked home. When I crossed the bridge of the Saint Anthonie locks, I noticed that there was still light burning in the upstairs windows of Rembrandt's house. I had not seen anything of him since the funeral of my brother and thought that I would drop in for a minute. I needed some one with whom to talk things over before I went to bed, for I was much too excited to be able to go to sleep right off.

I knocked on the door but got no answer.

I knocked again and a little louder.

I heard people stumbling about in the back part of the house.

Finally the door was opened a few inches. The nurse of little Titus was standing there. She was holding a candle in her hand and looked at me as if she were ready to kill me.

"The master has gone to bed and can't be disturbed," she snapped. "Please go away." And she locked the door in my face.

I went home.

I didn't quite like what I had just seen.

Chapter 26

WE TAKE ANOTHER TRIP INTO THE COUNTRY AND DISCUSS DIVERSE METHODS OF NAVIGATION

The next Sunday was one of those incredibly fine days which we sometimes get in our part of the world as a compensation for all the rain and fog and slush and mud of the rest of the year. And so, although the regular season for our Sabbatical wanderings had already come to an end, we decided to take a walk and shortly after breakfast we left the Saint Anthonie Gate and walked to the Diemermeer.

I still remember the old "meer" as it was until a dozen years ago, a deep and malignant pool inhabited by wild ducks and wild geese and made unsafe by very ferocious poachers who liked to bring a little variety into their otherwise monotonous lives by robbing the occasional visitor and who were reported to have as little consideration for human life as some of my colleagues whose names, however, I prefer not to reveal to posterity.

But now that the lake has been converted into a polder and that some of our richest and even some of our most respectable citizens have chosen that spot for the erection of their country houses, the place is as safe as the inside of the bank and sitting peacefully in the tap-room of the Arms of Abcoude, one would hardly believe it possible that only a few years before, this selfsame spot lay covered underneath sixteen feet of water. After we had finished our meal, I told my friends of my future plans.

Perhaps this is not stating the case quite fairly. Way down deep in my mind I had decided already that I would accept the offer of the Bicker family. It was too fine a chance for me to escape for a while from a city where everything reminded me of the tragedy that had befallen our family, and furthermore I would be given the opportunity to make some very serious experiments in a field of science that seemed to me more worth while than anything else in the world.

Of course I would to a certain extent sail under false colors. My real mission would have to be kept a secret. But why not? When the late King Henry of France had to choose between his Protestant faith and the crown of France, he is said to have remarked that after all, the privilege of living in Paris as its sovereign master was worth an occasional visit to Holy Mass. I think that in due time I shall be able to pacify my conscience with that very shrewd observation of the man who gave us half a dozen witty words and one very fine sauce. But I have never been one of those strong and determined characters that could come to a decision one, two, three! and then close the door upon all further considerations because "they have made up their minds." In my case, the door of possible regrets almost always remains ajar, just a tiny little bit. And in order to be quite comfortable I need the reassurance of friends that I am really doing the right thing.

In this case they appeared to be unanimously agreed that this was the best thing I could possibly hope to do. They were sorry to lose me, for so long a time, but it was a rare chance. I absolutely must accept. They would write me about all that happened of any importance and would call on my small son to see that he fared well. (Good God! I had completely forgotten the child, but I supposed that I could safely leave him with the old nurse who took care of him anyway whether I was there or not.) And they would do anything for me they could, but I must say yes.

And so on and so forth, to the great secret joy of my "Demon," for though I am by no means another Socrates, the "still inner voice" that dwelleth within my breast can upon occasions shout louder than the most experienced of our town-criers, announcing the arrival of a fresh load of peat. And so we remained together until a very late hour, drinking a moderate amount and talking an immoderate amount and I, or rather the country of my future residence, became the center of an animated and learned geographical discussion during which Selim drew upon his vast knowledge of Moslem devils and monsters to populate the new world with a choice collection of satyrs and Calibans and ghouls, all of them anthropophagous and living by preference on the blood of surgeons and leeches, until he had completely exhausted the field of demonology when he switched from America to his own beloved Asia and depicted the charms of the gazelle-eyed houris and the black-haired peris in such colorful terms that a most respectable couple of Dutch people who sat at a neighboring table hastily bundled their daughters into their most respectable woolen shawls and dragged them to safety before this strange-looking "foreigner" should begin to put his seductive theories into practice.

In the meantime Jean-Louys (to the intense disgust of the landlord who, however, did not quite dare to remonstrate with a person of such palpable dignity) had poured some wine into a cup and by using his finger as his brush, had covered the freshly scoured wooden table with its beautiful white top with a variety of lines and curves which were supposed to represent a map of the countries bordering upon the Atlantic Ocean. And then calling for pen and paper, he set forth to figure out the distance between the roads of Texel and the mouth of the Mauritius River and he did this by means of a new method of nautical calculation which he had found the week before in a handbook on navigation written by a German professor of theology, who in his introduction had boasted that he would some day be recognized as one of the greatest of all marine experts as he had never seen either a sea nor a ship and therefore could not possibly be distracted from his "theoretical conclusions" by some of those so-called "practical observations" with which ship's captains were apt to disfigure their works.

In how far Jean-Louys had misunderstood or was now misinterpreting the "theory" of the learned man, I do not know, but when he came to the "theoretical conclusion" that the Atlantic Ocean was only half as wide as the Zuyder Zee, we decided that an occasional trip on board a fishing-smack might have done the erudite Teuton more good than the fifty years he seemed to have spent in his library in the genial company of those Babylonian and Ninevehian and Egyptian sources upon which he had based his contentions to the exclusion of everything and every one else.

"A fine system of navigation," Jean-Louys finally confessed, wiping the winish map of the Atlantic off the table with the help of his useless notes. "A splendid piece of work, as thorough a piece of investigation as half of the stuff that comes out of that mysterious land. A pity it was not published a couple of years before. It would have been of immense value to Jonah when he sailed his whale from Joppa to Tarsus. But I am afraid that you had better stick to Cunningham and Davis. That is to say, if you care to get there and if we, my friends, care to get back to Amsterdam before they close the gate on us, we had better be starting right now."

Thereupon he called for the landlord, still smarting under the damage done to his freshly cleaned table, made that sour-looking citizen the subject of an impromptu speech in which he not only praised the food and wine but also dwelled so impressively upon the charm of the man's taproom, the beauty of his wife and daughters and the virtues of his cook (and all of this in broad Gascon French of which the innkeeper did not understand a word) that the poor fellow almost trembled with excitement and gratitude and would not let us go before we had all drunk his health in a special sort of French brandy which he had suddenly produced from a mysterious hiding-place and which, according to his story, had been brought him directly from the cellar of His Majesty, King Louis of France.

"No doubt a special gift which it has pleased His Majesty, my most august sovereign, to bestow upon you for just such a meal as the one with which you have just favored us?" Jean-Louys asked, using me as an interpreter.

"No, Your Worship, but I have a brother who is a cook . . ."

"On board a ship which plies between Amsterdam and Rouen."

The landlord stopped in surprise. "How did Your Worship know?"

"Because people who can afford to drink cognac like that, usually have brothers, who are . . ."

"Cooks on ships to Rouen!"

"Exactly."

And thereupon these two men who had suddenly discovered a common ground of philosophic interest by way of a brother who was a cook on a vessel from Amsterdam to Rouen, solemnly shook hands. Then all of us most solemnly shook hands and we walked back to Amsterdam through the light haze of the dying day and said little and thought much and were happy in each other's company.

But the gate was locked when we arrived.

And we had to pay two stivers each to get in and we had to listen to a short sermon on the part of the sergeant who was on guard and who in daily life exercised the profession of a shoemaker and who did not believe in "all this walking on the Sabbath just for the sake of pleasure."

"But, Sergeant," Jean-Louys stopped him, "we are not idle people. We are pilgrims returning from a long voyage."

"Long voyage!" the sergeant sneered. "I have been here all day long. I saw you go out this morning."

"But since then much has happened. We have made a great and profound discovery."

"I'd like to know what that was?"

"That even an humble cook on board a ship to Rouen may have his uses."

And then we bade the sergeant good night with great politeness and went to our respective homes.

But the next morning on my way to the Hospital I met My Lord Banning Cocq, who stopped me and asked me whether I and my friends had taken a walk to the Diemermeer the day before and I said yes, we had. And he answered, "I thought so," and I asked him, "Why, My Lord?" and he laughed and said, "Because my sergeant, poor devil, came to me in a state of great perturbation this morning and told me that he felt greatly worried, as he had let four lunatics into the town the night before, and then of course I knew it must have been you and your friends."

I thanked him sincerely for the compliment, for I knew that he was a genial man and would have dearly liked to join us on our walks if his position in society had permitted him to associate with a leech and a bookkeeper and a nondescript French nobleman, not to forget a Turk who made an open profession of his heathenish faith. But he shook his head rather sadly.

"My good Doctor," he remarked, "you are an older man than I. But I have been obliged to spend a whole morning keeping a half-witted trooper from running to the Burgomasters with a tale of four crazy men running wild in Amsterdam. Do you mind if I give you a bit of advice?"

I answered that of course I would be delighted.

"Then never try to be funny with common people. It does not make them happy and it will get you yourself into trouble. Good-by and by the way, I hear you are going to America on some sort of scientific expedition. . . ."

Chapter 27

I DECIDE TO BECOME A VOLUNTARY EXILE FROM MY OWN COUNTRY

"And by the way, I hear you are going to America?"

If I heard that once during the next six days, I heard it a thousand times. I had only told my friends and they were very discreet people. Besides they lived very solitary lives and hardly spoke to a soul from one week-end to the next.

The Bickers knew, too, but they would probably not think it to their advantage to let the fact be known before all their many preparations had been finished.

Then how had the news traveled abroad so fast?

To this day it has remained a mystery to me. But the experience strengthened me in my belief that there exists something closely akin to what I would like to call a "communal soul." And this communal soul is not restricted to densely populated countries. It functions just as effectively in the desert or in the wilderness or in the midst of a trackless forest as it does in the heart of Amsterdam or London. It travels with the rapidity of light which according to that learned friar, Roger Bacon, has a velocity that is even faster than that of a falling star. But whereas a stone cast from a height moves only in one direction, a bit of news that is of real importance to a vast number of people goes in all directions at once and recognizes neither east nor west nor south nor north nor up nor down, but seems to obey that same mysterious law which claims that nature abhors a vacuum, while it defies our mathematical maxim that no given body can be in two different places at one and the same time.

When I got up in the morning and had a cup of hot milk, my housekeeper said, "And so I hear, Master, that you are going to America, and what will become of me? and the child when I am gone?" And when I went to the Hospital, the old man who acts as a gate-keeper said, "Good morning, Doctor, and so I hear you are going to America." And when I left at noon and visited the barber, who is a member of the same guild as I and treats me with colleagual familiarity, he said, "Ah, my sly friend, I hear that you are going to leave us and are going to America." And so it went all day and in the evening after I returned home I found a note waiting for me from Rembrandt. It really was not a note, but an old sketch, underneath which he had scribbled a few words as follows:

"I hear that you are going to America and I want to ask you and your friends to drop in next Thursday evening, for I have finished a picture I want to show you."

This message I received with a certain amount of irritation. My reception at his house a few days before had hardly been of a sort to make me want to call again. Indeed, I was so annoyed by the recollection of what had happened on that occasion that I threw the letter into the fire, but it happened to land upside down and I saw that there was some writing on the back of the sheet and hastily fished it out of the flames (and burned my fingers in doing so) and I read:

"I am terribly sorry I missed you the other night. I was pulling a few proofs of a new landscape I had just started (most unsatisfactorily, so far) and the miserable woman never even let me know it was you who had called. I want to see you badly." And then three times underlined, "The woman is hopeless. I hope to God I shall be able to get rid of her positively before the end of next week."

I understood. The terrible nurse had had one of her attacks of ill-temper. "I hope to God I shall be able to get rid of her positively by the end of next week." A pious wish, to which I could say Amen with all my heart.

When the appointed evening came (the intervening days I had listened with such patience as was still at my command to one thousand three hundred and ninety-seven people telling me, "Oh, by the way, I hear that you are going to America!") I was detained at the Hospital by a boy who had been hit by the wings of one of the mills on the Blauwbrug bulwark and whose shoulder-blade had been horribly mutilated, and it was past nine o'clock before I reached the house on the Anthonie Breestraat. My friends were there and a middle-aged man of the Jewish race whom I recognized at once as a Rabbi of whom Rembrandt had made an etching a couple of years before and which had had a very favorable sale among the members of his congregation. I was now introduced to him and learned his name. He was the famous Samuel Menasseh ben Israel and Bernardo had often spoken to me about him for they were compatriots, they had both been born in Lisbon and had fled to the Republic when Portugal had been occupied by the Habsburgs and the Inquisition had been reëstablished in that unfortunate country.

His family, if I remembered rightly, had first gone to La Rochelle, but the eternal wrangling between the Protestants and the Catholics in that city had been very bad for business and the family had moved further away from home and had come to live in Amsterdam. The boy had been apprenticed to a painter, but he had wanted to study theology, until his father, old Joseph ben Israel, a well-known character about town and a practical man of great common sense, suggested that he practice both professions at the same time.

Of course as soon as there had been more than a dozen Jews in our town, there had been three dozen quarrels. What these quarrels were about, the rest of us were never able to discover, but a people that has spent two thousand years in endless and angry disputes about the relative value of inverted commas and semi-colons in a number of books which no sensible person takes the trouble to read, such maniacs of the written word can always find something to disagree about. And when in 1619 the government had granted them full religious liberty, they had celebrated the occasion by establishing three synagogues where there had only been one before. Menasseh fortunately did not belong to the extreme radicals and he was so broad-minded and so learned and so full of the true spirit of tolerant brotherhood that many Christians, exasperated by the sectorial hair-splitting of their own clergy, had fallen into the habit of going to his synagogue rather than attending divine service in one of their own churches. And even Catholic visitors of distinction had gone to Beth-Israel to hear this pleasant-voiced man hold forth upon the affairs of the day with such irrepressible good humor and in such fine temper of spirit that all the difficulties of this world seemed to solve themselves like the early fogs that are dispelled by the rays of the summer's sun.

All this I had heard long before I ever met him but I was to hear a great deal more that evening. For when I entered, the guests were sitting around the table examining a heavy volume bound beautifully in leather and Rembrandt, drawing me into the general conversation, said, "Look at this—I wish that I could draw the way our friend here paints." And he showed me a page of something which I could not read but which seemed to me to be a Hebrew edition of the Psalms, as it was printed in very short sentences and as the chapter was much briefer than those of the rest of the Old Testament.

I had guessed right, it was a Hebrew edition of the Psalms printed in the basement of the house diagonally across from that of Rembrandt where Menasseh lived and had also his workshop. Quite naturally the talk then drifted to the difficulty of getting foreign type in a city like Amsterdam and I learned to my surprise that there were not only two printing establishments that could handle Hebrew type, and that not only French and German and English and Spanish and Portuguese books were manufactured wholesale in our town, but that a great many Arabic and Persian and Armenian texts went forth into the world bearing the "cum privilegio" of the magistrates of Amsterdam, and when I expressed my surprise and asked the Rabbi how this had happened to come about, he answered, "Your rulers are very wise people. They are out after profit. Why shouldn't they be? They are business men and this is a business country. Did you ever hear of an innkeeper who could afford to ask too closely into the religious preferences of his guests and at the same time keep his trade? Well, I never did. And so they leave us alone as long as we don't say anything that is too disagreeable about themselves. And why should we? Imagine living in a country where there isn't any censorship!"

"But surely," I interrupted, "there is some sort of a censorship. You can't say just anything you want?"

"Almost anything you want. It is all in the saying. And as long as you don't print that Their Lordships of the Town Hall eat little children for breakfast or that they make a specialty of seducing little girls, you can go ahead and write whatever you want and the censors won't bother you any more than they do me," and then he continued (how nice to hear that once again!), "They tell me that you are going to America soon."

I said yes. I had heard something about it myself and I was beginning to feel that there might be some truth in the statement and I added in a spirit of fun, "Wouldn't your reverence care to come with me?"

But the good man suddenly became very serious and answered, "Yes. There is nothing I would like to do better than that. But the time has not yet come for God's people to come out of the wilderness," and when I showed, I am afraid, some surprise at this remark, he continued, "Most honored Doctor, you are a man of culture and breeding and do you mean to tell me that you don't know what has become of the Lost Tribes of the people of Israel? Why, they moved across the Pacific Ocean when it was still dry land and to-day they dwell in the land of America." And he made this extraordinary announcement so solemnly that all of us suddenly kept quiet and looked at each other in mute astonishment as if the door had opened and one of the ancient prophets had suddenly walked in upon us.

Upon such occasions it is almost inevitable that some one should make an utterly commonplace remark. I don't remember who was guilty, but of course some one said, "That is an interesting notion, but how about the Indians? Wouldn't they have killed them off long ago?"

But Menasseh, without showing the slightest sign of impatience, had his answer ready. "They undoubtedly would have done so if they could. But it would have meant suicide. For the Indians of America are the lost tribes of Zion." And he delivered us quite a lecture and told us how ten of the long-suffering tribes (I have forgotten their names and anyway, that is a detail), after the destruction of Jerusalem had wandered across Turkestan and China, how they had made converts on the way which still dwelled in Cathay, and had finally crossed over into that enormous tract of land that stretched its vast and uninhabited confines from the North Pole to the South Pole and that had been given unto them as their eternal heritage.

It was a very interesting story, but it did not sound very convincing to me. For one thing, remembering the trouble that small patch of land on the Mediterranean had caused to the world, the endless wars and quarrels with all the endless neighbors, I thought with horror of what would happen to us if we were to be faced by an entire continent filled with this peculiar race of men who had never been able to agree among themselves and who had never been able to agree with any one else either, and who seemed to have spent their entire time, ever since Abraham had set forth from the land of Ur, insisting that the whole world was out of step with the exception of themselves. But I held my tongue and did not say so, and as the nurse just then entered and in her usual surly way announced that supper was ready, the subject was allowed to drop and fortunately did not return to life amidst the excellent dishes of herring salad and boiled barley with sugar which awaited us in the front room.

And after supper Rembrandt took us up to his studio and showed us several sketches he had made of a landscape, an imaginary landscape with a couple of trees in the foreground, and told us that recently he had come into the possession of a number of sketches by a certain Altdorfer, a German architect who was apparently enamored of trees.

"That man seemed to regard trees as if they were human beings," he said. "Look at this and at this and at this. Those things aren't trees. They are wise old philosophers, who have spent a thousand years contemplating the follies of human existence. Look at this one with the blue background and the little man sitting all by himself at the foot of that grandfather among trees. That little man is so forlorn, so lonely, he would almost make you weep. And the tree stands in the foreground so fine and wise. Strange people, those Germans. I don't care to own any of their pictures, they don't seem to have a feeling for color. They think in lines, but they think more clearly and more distinctly than any of the rest of us. But when I asked Dirck Bleecker (the one who painted that terrible Venus for which the Prince paid him seventeen hundred florins cash, whereas I had to write seven or eight begging letters and wait God knows how many years to get a paltry six hundred for a Resurrection that was a hundred times better)—when I asked Bleecker, who had been in Regensburg on his way to Italy, whether there was any work of Altdorfer left in that town he answered me, 'Sure! a fine slaughter house and a couple of bulwarks outside the city gates.' Can you imagine it? Would it be possible in any other country? This blue tree and a fine slaughter-house! But I suppose he had to make a living. We all do."

Meanwhile in another corner of the room the good Rabbi was endeavoring to prove his point by a weird mixture of geographic and philologic and messianic information and was trying to make his hearers believe that the existence of such places as Dankhar and Dango and Dano showed the probable route taken by the tribe of Dan on its way from Palestine to the East. The argument sounded rather far-fetched to me. If Dankhar and Dango were to be accepted as evidence of the Israelites having been in Asia, how about Danzig and Danemark and the Danube as living testimony to their presence in Europe on their way from the old promised land to the new one?

For one short moment I thought of saying what was in my mind, but what was the use? Every one of us is entitled to at least one pet delusion. The most intelligent of men must be crazy on some one point to be really well-balanced and a useful member of society.

Menasseh was a delightful person, wise, witty and in everything he did inspired by a most good-natured tolerance towards all humanity. Why deprive him of the happy illusion that those tribes, so lamentably lost during one of the endless mishaps that were forever overtaking his people, had finally reached the shores of a better and happier land than that from which they had been forced to flee?

Why indeed?

I took another helping of herring salad.

Maybe at that very moment somewhere in the deepest abyss of the North Sea some ancient and learned herring patriarch was telling his great-great-great-great-grandchildren how some of their ancestors had swum away to parts unknown and had given birth to a race of gigantic whales that dominated the whole of the Pacific Ocean.

And meanwhile, mixed with potatoes and gherkins, I was eating them and thinking that they made really a very fine dish.

Chapter 28

OF THE DIFFICULTIES OF BEING A "SURGEON" AND NOT A "DOCTOR MEDICINAE" IN THE YEAR I SAILED FOR AMERICA

My Lord Andries proved a man of his word. No sooner had I let him know that I was willing to accept his offer than wheels within wheels began to move with that silence and efficiency one expects from a competent engine and within less than a week I was informed that the Amsterdam Chamber of the West India Company had appointed me one of its doctors with orders to proceed at once to the New Netherlands.

But then a strange difficulty presented itself, the sort of difficulty that could only arise in our Republic and that no one would have been able to anticipate.

My position in the medical world of Amsterdam had always been slightly anomalous. Everybody in the country belonged to one of the guilds as a matter of plain, everyday fact. When I was young and first went to Leyden to receive my training, I soon discovered that I had chosen a rather difficult career. The tremendous physical and intellectual energy which I had inherited from that glorious old man who had elevated our family from being "just people" to something just a little different had manifested itself in my case in the form of an insatiable curiosity about everybody and everything and an almost fanatical hatred of what I in my youthful arrogance used to deride as "human stupidity" and what, since then, I have learned to pity as merely another manifestation of that universal mental inertia which is born out of ignorance and fear. All around me I saw people suffering woefully and as a rule helplessly from a large variety of causes, most of which (please remember that I was only eighteen years old at that time) were entirely preventable.

I never was a very good Christian and I am quite sure I was not inspired by motives of a spiritual nature when I decided to devote my life to the study of medicine. I had never felt a particular urge to "love my neighbor" in the truly Biblical sense of the word. Loving some one at somebody else's command, even if that somebody else be God himself, has always been just a little too difficult for most people. But there was no earthly reason why we should not learn to "respect" our fellow-men. That meditation led me to a fresh difficulty. How could I respect a man when he was guilty of an error of judgment which had made him sick? There was only one way out of this puzzle. If I were to be true to myself, I must devote myself to the task of showing my neighbors just what sort of mistakes against the laws of nature and common sense they had committed to be as sadly afflicted as most of them were.

I am now more than sixty years old and during the last thirty years I have lived a very full life. I shudder when I think of the sublime self-assurance with which I approached the most perplexing puzzle of human life long before I had even begun to shave myself. But in a way I still hold that I was right though perhaps I might have expressed my opinions with a little less vehemence, and the other day, when I found an old anatomical note-book of mine on the title page of which I had written: "Mankind has only one enemy, its own ignorance. Let us destroy that ignorance," I felt a sudden happy pang of recognition and not entirely of regret.

The sentiment, after all these many years, sounded a bit hollow not to say platitudinous. But the boy who had composed it or had vaguely remembered it from one of Erasmus' colloquies and had transcribed it with many fine flourishes of the pen, had on the whole remained faithful to the promise of his youth. He hated "ignorance" when he was sixteen. He still hated it when he was sixty. The only difference was this, that now, having more or less reached the age of discretion and insight, he was beginning to realize that he was fighting against hopeless odds. The Good Book (this was the way my grandfather had reasoned) tells us that God created the world in six days and then took a vacation for the rest of eternity. If only He had spent one single extra day on His task and had devoted the Sabbath to giving men "reason," what a different world this would have been. But God did not and that is all there is to it and it is up to us to make the best of our bad bargain.

But if we try hard enough, we may be able to find a "compromise" and as that seems to be the only possible and definite answer to all the manifold problems of our existence, I feel that I have reason to consider myself a very lucky man. For all during my entire lifetime I have been able to do the things in which I was most vitally interested. Now I am approaching the end. Soon my time shall come to bid farewell to this curious planet. But if my heirs can put that on my grave as my one and only epitaph, I shall be contented, for I shall know that I have not wasted my time.

Meanwhile, when I was sixteen and still believed that there were such colors as "absolute white" and "absolute black" and "absolute red" and "absolute green" (Rembrandt has taught me differently since then), the question of my future career caused me considerable difficulties.

During the last fifty years there has been such enormous improvement in the field of medicine that it is almost impossible for the people of the present generation to understand the quandary in which those of us who aspired to be something more than mere barbers found themselves as soon as we had learned enough bad Latin and Greek to understand the hodge-podge of the so-called "learned" treatises of that day.

I think it was one of the great Arab physicians of ancient Spain who had drawn the maxim that "there are no sicknesses in this world, but that there are only sick people." By which of course he did not mean to deny the existence of certain definite afflictions, which almost any one with an ounce of intelligence can come to understand and diagnose (and sometimes even cure) but which was his way of saying that the individual is the basis of everything human and that we ought to judge each separate case upon its own merits.

But when I was young, the science of medicine was only slowly recovering from the complete intellectual apathy of the Middle Ages. The Church, with her eyes lifted upon an imaginary Heaven, was not sufficiently interested in the affairs of this world to pay much attention to the immediate physical needs of her children. As long as the immortal soul was saved, the perishable body was cheerfully surrendered to the million and one forces that work for decay and destruction. As soon as the tyranny of that unyielding institution was beginning to weaken, there had been a tremendous rebirth of that divine curiosity which is the cornerstone upon which we must base our sole hope for a better future.

But we, in our distant swamp along the banks of the North Sea, never felt the influence of such a movement until a century or more later. The universities of Palermo and Naples and Montpellier had been teaching anatomy hundreds of years before we ever suspected that such a thing was possible without invoking the immediate wrath of a vengeful God. In our cities there were a few people, often foreigners, who called themselves "doctors" and made a great to-do about their academic bulls (which not infrequently they had bought from a public scribe in a French or Italian market-place) but the great majority of the people, both in the towns and in the country districts, had been forced to content themselves with the simple services of the local barber. It sometimes happened that those barbers were intelligent men and could pull teeth and apply a poultice without killing their patients. But in most cases they were poor devils forced into their jobs because their father before them had belonged to the barbers' guild and because that was the only way in which they could make a living.

No wonder the general populace held them in light esteem. No wonder that both they and the so-called "doctors of medicine" were invariably mentioned in one breath with the quacks and mountebanks and other impostors who made our kermesses unsafe with their "infallible remedies" and their "unfailing cures" for everything from dandruff and corns to heart-failure and malignant tumors.

Then came the Reformation early during the last century, but that great spiritual upheaval affected the brain of the average man much less than people at this distance are apt to think. The spiritual world changed masters, that was all. Instead of taking our orders from a man whom no one ever saw because he lived behind the high walls of a Roman fortress, we were now supposed to obey a book that had been written so long ago that no one knew for sure who was responsible for its contents. In short, people fought valiantly to escape from one sort of tyranny to fall immediately into the clutches of a new despot who was almost as exacting as the old one and a great deal less human. What previously had been called green was now called yellow and what formerly had been called yellow was now called green, and that was about all the change there was.

And it was the same within my own field of work. The monks and nuns, of whom there were by far too many, were sent about their business. Hordes of holy mendicants now became plain, ordinary, everyday beggars. Formerly one had been obliged to receive them in one's house and feed them and lodge them and listen to their ill-mannered hiccoughing. Now one could surrender them to the police and have them flogged out of the city gate. That undoubtedly was a great step forward. But the decent and respectable men and women who had taken the words of Christ seriously (and of such there always were a few even during the worst days of the Church's downfall) they also were forced to give up their former profession and as most of these had devoted themselves to the care of the poor and the sick, our hospitals and almshouses suddenly found themselves deprived not only of their former revenue but also of the nurses and doctors who had thus far tended the lame, the halt and the blind.

The new creed loudly proclaimed its disbelief in the efficacy of good works as against the value of a correct spiritual attitude towards God. The old clergy with the wisdom acquired during centuries of a very close observation of human nature had never inquired too closely into the motives that made powerful princes and rich merchants suddenly disgorge a few hundred thousand guilders for the benefit of their hospitals or orphan asylums. "The orphans," so they reasoned, "have got to be fed and clothed and the poor have to be fed, and all that costs money. Let us gratefully accept the money and leave it to God to ask questions."

The new masters, inspired no doubt by the noblest of motives but without much practical experience along those lines, insisted that the gift in itself amounted to nothing. It was only the spirit behind it that mattered. And their parishioners were made to understand that all the good works in the world would not save them from one moment in Hell if their heart were not in the right place, and in many instances they were directly encouraged to stop giving their hard-earned pennies for public purposes.

Habit, however, was too strong or humanity was too decent, but this much I know, that the poor and the afflicted (in our cities at least) were never for a moment allowed to suffer through the hard-hearted righteousness of the new rulers. The saints were removed from their ancient niches and the chapels were turned into store-rooms and the fast days were no longer celebrated with an extra supply of wine or beer, but for the rest, everything remained pretty much as it had been during the last thousand years. The hospitals continued to be known as "God's Houses." Charitable old men and women continued to act as Boards of Regents and to administer the funds with scrupulous honesty. Pious girls continued to devote their lives to the care of their unfortunate fellow-citizens and continued to perform the most menial and disgusting tasks with that cheerful optimism that had been so characteristic of the old nuns.

And all of them were just as convinced as their fathers and grandfathers and great-grandfathers had been that existence on this planet was merely a preparatory experience, a gift of small account, and without any value except in so far as it led to the blessed happiness of Heaven or the dreadful punishments of Hell.

It was just as difficult to convince people of this sort of the necessity of taking proper care of the human body as it had been to persuade their predecessors that patients needed an occasional bath if they were not to die of infection, and hospitals remained, what they had always been before, almshouses and places of refuge for those too old or too sick to take care of themselves, quiet sanctuaries where they could be sure of a bed and a plate of porridge until merciful Death paid his final visit, but not (as many of us felt that they ought to be) temples of light and good cheer where the temporarily unfit were shown how to get themselves back to health and profitable employment.

Of course, whenever a sailor tumbled out of a mast and broke a leg or whenever a mason fell down from a scaffold and smashed his arms, some barber with a knack for surgery was called in to repair the damage. But those who suffered from an internal and not absolutely mechanical ailment were put on a diet of sermons and texts and for the rest were allowed to live or die as God and their own constitutions seemed to think best.

The "doctors," as differentiated from the mere "barbers" and "surgeons" who dwelled on a very much lower social plane, were supposed to occupy themselves with the problems affecting the behavior of all the invisible organs. And the doctors were few and far between, for there were practically no schools to train them and only a few of them could afford to visit one of those Mediterranean countries where the Moors held sway for a number of centuries. But here in the North, where we are centuries behind in the art of living, they could not learn very much of any importance to either themselves or to their future patients. I don't mean to imply that we lacked the necessary brains. The man who has done most during the last two thousand years to further our knowledge of the inner secrets of the human body was a Fleming. But he had to go to Italy to practice his art. As Professor Vesalius of Padua he could make a career. As plain Master Andries van Wesel he would have spent his days bleeding the good citizens of Brussels on week days and on Saturday he would have shaved their week's accumulation of whiskers and he would have counted himself happy if he had died as chairman of the barbers' guild.

Take the conditions in Leyden in the year 1617 when I made my appearance in that somewhat unsober seat of learning. The entire medical faculty consisted of only three professors, one who taught botany (for the benefit of future apothecaries), one who gave instruction in anatomy for the future chirurgeons and one who was supposed to hold clinical demonstrations to supplement the theoretical knowledge which the future doctors were supposed to gather from their text-books on medicine. Unfortunately at the time I registered, the plague had just visited Leyden and had killed more than one fifth of the total number of inhabitants, among them the professor of therapeutics and the professor of anatomy, the learned Petrus Pava, and the regents, for reasons of economy, had not yet decided upon their successors. But as it was felt that we should not be left in complete idleness, the dean of the theological faculty was asked to lecture to us upon the medicine of the ancient Hebrews. He was a ponderous and dull old patriarch with a long white beard and devoid of all eloquence. Besides we wanted to know how the art of healing had been taught in Athens, not in Jerusalem. But the plague had been followed by an even more serious epidemic of religious frenzy. The whole country was divided into sublapsarians and superlapsarians, people were thrown into jail and sometimes killed because they denied that children were already doomed to everlasting perdition while still in their mothers' wombs, and honorable clergymen with a record of fifty years of faithful service were deprived of their livelihood for no other reason than that they believed, or failed to believe, something which the majority of their neighbors held to be the gospel truth or an invention of Satan.

Leyden itself, where the quarrel had started, was of course seething with excitement. The University had always been suspected of "libertine" tendencies and the true believers had already founded a rival academy of their own in distant Groningen to keep the faith pure and free from the insiduous heresies of the learned and amiable Jacob Arminius. They were now contemplating a second university in Utrecht and perhaps from their point of view they were quite right. For our Alma Mater was the spiritual child of that small group of brilliant humanists who had been the intellectual body-guard and chief advisers of Prince William. The Great Silent One (more shrewd than silent, if we are to believe all the stories about him) had been that rare thing among mortals, a statesman with a concrete ideal. He had seen enough burning and hanging and quartering during the first twenty years of his life to satisfy him for the rest of his days, and he meant, should he ever acquire enough power, to establish a commonwealth in which all men should be allowed to seek salvation in their own way. The casual remark of one of the first rectors of the university he founded that "men could be led but never driven" had become the motto upon which our school had based its educational policy at least during the first half century of its existence.

In some ways this had been a dangerous experiment. The great majority of our students came from very humble homes. A few were very poor and a few were very rich. But all of them were far removed from the ordinary ties of parents and friends, and without any special preparation they found themselves flung into a community that was as little suited for a contemplative life as any place could possibly have been. The siege had left its stamp upon the manners of the town. The garrison that had occupied it for years afterwards had done likewise. The owners of the linen factories who paid their workmen miserable wages and filled the streets and alleys with a hungry and miserable set of men and women (not to speak of the children) had done likewise. And the climate had done the rest.

Left to their own devices, living in cheap quarters (for the town was dreadfully over populated and in bad need of a few thousand more houses), eating indifferent food in cheap inns, spending their evenings in cold and uncomfortable rooms without any other place to go, most of the students tried to find solace at the bottom of a bottle of wine or a jar of gin. And in most cases, five or six months of this sort of existence seemed sufficient to kill every vestige of intellectual curiosity and turn the eager young boy, who had left his native village prepared to do great things in the world outside, into a disappointed lad trying to get a degree with the least possible exertion and quite contented if the prestige of his official diploma helped him to get a safe and comfortable berth in the village or city of his birth, where such a document was still regarded as a guarantee of superior qualities and often proved a very handy key to place and preferment.

I am proud to say that there was a small minority which notwithstanding the many physical disadvantages of life and the disappointment of discovering that the royal road to learning led through the dismal swamps of boredom and pedantry, refused to surrender to the general atmosphere of the place and remained faithful to the enthusiasms of his undergraduate days. And curious to relate, they were the boys who most often got into conflict with the authorities. For whereas the faculty, during the period of clerical domination of which I am now speaking and which had begun shortly before I first matriculated in the year 1617, was willing to overlook a great many of the misdemeanors of the more rowdy elements among the students with a shrug of the shoulders and a jovial, "Oh, well, you know, boys will be boys," they were forever on their guard against what they called the "libertine tendencies" of the more independent-minded scholars.

It was a long cry from the days of the great teacher who laid down the maxim that it was better to try and lead men than drive them. It was the era during which Calvinism Triumphant was endeavoring to systemize and classify and standardize every manifestation of life and faith. To the average professor, independence of mind on the part of one of his pupils was anathema. And a tendency to inquire by personal investigation into the truth or error of the grandiloquent verities which the teacher had propounded from a hoary text-book, was a thing accursed in the sight of God.

The student body as a mass was ready to take the hint and asked no questions. And in return, when time came for examination, the professor from his side asked easy questions, and in this way everybody was happy.

But there were about a hundred of us who refused to submit to this new spiritual autocracy and we had to suffer in consequence. Most of us were the sons or grandsons of men who had taken an active part in the Rebellion. We seemed to have inherited something of the spirit of freedom that had inspired our fathers and grandfathers when they foreswore their legitimate sovereign on the ground that a monarch should be a father to his subjects and that they did not care for the sort of father King Philip happened to make.

Besides, the vast majority of the boys who came from such families had been brought up in an atmosphere of amiable skepticism. They had been taught to study the Scriptures from behind a pair of Erasmian spectacles, and from childhood on had been urged to take life with a pinch of that divine salt which is called "humor."

Such a point of view was, however, most abhorrent to the new sort of instructors. And although the "libertines" of my time were famous for their sobriety and their industry and without making a manifestation of their virtues, tried to lead reasonable and well-balanced lives, they were forever in trouble with the learned men who were supposed to rule this commonwealth of erudition. Let our friends, the "Regulars," stage a pitched battle with the denizens of the tenement districts, let them set fire to the house of a peaceful citizen on the ground that his daughter would make such a charming picture in her night-gown, let them engage in fights with harmless burghers returning from a picnic and make off with their wives and nothing would happen beyond a formal declaration of official investigation. But let one of the "libertines" so much as whisper a doubt about the erstwhile tendency of snakes to engage in conversation and he would find himself immediately ordered to appear before a board of inquiry and he would be obliged to eat humble pie of a very unpalatable sort lest he be prevented from taking his degree. Or let him merely "look" his doubts when the professor of exegesis expounded one of those eternal verities that are half as young as the Pyramids and are already showing much greater signs of wear and tear, and the faculty would be after him with the speed of the Amsterdam bucket-brigade, chasing a fire in the city's wood-yard.

We who were supposed to be studying the sciences secretly enjoyed this curious intellectual warfare and acquired great skill in lying in ambush while keeping clear from the traps that were placed in our own path. But the incident that brought about my expulsion was not of our making. It was the work of two cheerful roisterers, of two boys who were possessed both of brains and of money, but who long since had given up all hope of ever accomplishing anything at all in an academic way. They stayed on in Leyden because they were happy there and sometimes during their moments of semi-lucidity they could be very funny.

I have already noted that in the year 1617 in consequence of the plague the chairs of anatomy and therapeutics happened to be vacant and how the professor of theology had volunteered to fill the gap by lecturing to the future surgeons and doctors on the medicine of the ancient Hebrews. As a rule this good man gave his classes in his own home in a large room at the back of the house. But nobody ever came. This hurt his pride and he let it be known that on such and such a day he would demonstrate the seven deadly sins and the seven cardinal virtues in the anatomical theater of the University. This was an unusual thing to do. As a rule professors did not advertise their coming engagements as if they were quacks peddling nostrums. But that was not the end of the story. The day before this famous demonstration of the seven deadly sins and the seven cardinal virtues a little slip of paper on the bulletin board outside the rector's office let the people know that the lecture would be thrown open to the public and furthermore, "In order to make his points entirely clear, the distinguished speaker will avail himself of the corpse of a lying Arminian, hanged this morning for theft and false testimony."

Evidently he was going to have what in the parlance of the students was called a "circus."

On the morning of the day for this extraordinary occurrence, the anatomical lecture-hall was chock full of people. Half the student body was present. For it had been whispered about that our Light of Learning would improve the occasion by a scathing denunciation of all and sundry enemies of the true faith. In consequence whereof all the supralapsarians (or sublapsarians, I have forgotten which, but I mean the adherents of the late John Calvin) were present en masse, ready to give evidence of their principles by entering this much feared chamber of horrors which under ordinary circumstances they avoided as if it had been the lepers' hospital. But I also noticed a large number of young men who were famous for their devotion to the less studious sides of life and who were reputed to have sworn an oath that they would never attend a lecture until just seven weeks prior to their examinations. What they were doing there and why they had come at this unearthly hour, I didn't know. Probably for the same reason that had brought me, plain, ordinary curiosity.

Ten o'clock came. Five minutes past ten. The professor entered from the rear. There was terrific applause, also a very unusual thing. The professor sat down and beckoned to the assistants of the anatomical laboratory. They left the room but immediately returned bringing in a large wooden table on which there lay a corpse. But oh, my God! what a corpse! I have seen a great many dead people in my life. And some of them did not look so pretty. But this one was terrible, monstrous, incredible. The face was a bright green, the hair hanging down in long, disorderly streaks, was a nondescript yellow. A brilliant red piece of cloth had been thrown across the chest.

The professor began. But instead of sticking to his subject, he launched into a violent denunciation of all those who opposed his own views. Every point he made was loudly applauded by his adherents. The other party said nothing. Encouraged by his success, the foolish old man grew more and more bold. He jerked away the red cloth, exposing the corpse in all its gruesome nakedness.

"Ah, my beloved friends," he said in his best ministerial tone, "my poor, beloved brethren, to-day I shall speak unto you upon the subject of sin and virtue, the seven deadly sins and the seven cardinal virtues; the seven cardinal virtues as exemplified by the life of the blessed and spotless Lamb, the seven deadly sins all gathered together in the putrid breast of this miscreant, this devil in human form, who unwilling to listen to Heavenly council, followed false prophets, worshiped before false altars, thinking in his pride and folly, 'I, poor human mortal, can defy the laws of Heaven as laid down in God's own catechism as edited by his beloved disciples Zacharias Ursinus and Kaspar Olevianus in the year of our Lord, 1563, Amen.' Oh, my friends, what wickedness! what vicious greed! what dissolute contempt stand graven upon that brow, what salacious, misbegotten vileness!"

He stopped, his mouth wide open, for at that moment the dead man sat straight up on his table, gave a terrific sneeze, said, "Pardon me, Professor. But pray continue!" and laid himself down once more in the expectant position of a corpse momentarily awaiting the anatomist's scalpel.

For just the fraction of a second, every one stood still. No one dared to breathe.

Then pandemonium broke loose and the laughter that shook the windows came straight from the belly and went straight to the heart.

The whole thing was glorious. But not for very long, for a sallow-faced young theologian, dressed in sacrimonial brown and with an enormous white collar (all in the best orthodox fashion) walked up to the dead man and feebly hit him with a shaking fist, saying, "How dare you!" Whereupon the corpse gave him such a terrific whack on top of his wide-brimmed hat that that piece of wearing apparel would have come down upon his neck if it had not been stopped by his ears.

That was the sign for a free-for-all fight in which, I regret to say, the forces of Satan completely and quickly defeated the cohorts of righteousness, drove them out into the street and would have thrown them into the canal if the young divines had not shown a very definite aptitude for at least one pagan virtue by proving themselves quite as fleet-footed as Mercury and Achilles.

With the enemy gone, the others decided to make a day of it. From a near-by tavern they suddenly produced two bag-pipe artists and a drummer who opened the procession. Then followed eight bright young men carrying the table on which the corpse was reclining in a becoming but slightly indecent posture, throwing kisses to all the servant girls who at that hour in the morning (it being Friday, the traditional cleaning-day) were scrubbing the façades of their masters' houses. Then followed the men who had taken part in this strange resurrection, marching four abreast and chanting an inspired and a not very proper song to the tune of a bag-pipes. I followed them for a short distance as one will, caught against his will in such an affair, but not desirous of showing himself either aloof or superior to the pastime of rather amiable people who were making fools of themselves out of sheer good animal spirits. But as soon as I could conveniently do so, I slipped into a side street and went home.

Of course in less than half an hour the whole community had heard about it and thousands of town people joined the parade until the University authorities in their panic asked the magistrates to ring the riot bells. The garrison was called out and there was some fighting, but it suddenly began to pour, as it always does in Leyden whenever there is a celebration of some sort, and everybody rushed for home to get himself some dry clothes and a great deal of wet gin.

The next day it was announced that the lectures on anatomy and therapeutics were "discontinued for the season," and that, it seemed to me, was the end of the affair.

But a week later, I was unexpectedly invited to appear before the Rector and when I arrived at his office, I found about a dozen other students there, who without exception belonged to the group that was suspected of libertine tendencies. Without further ado we were ushered into the presence of the Rector, whom we found surrounded by his staff, including the unfortunate theologian who by his sheer eloquence had raised the dead.

Our names were read. We were asked whether we had een present that morning. I spoke up for the others, being somewhat older than the rest, and said yes, we had indeed been present as a matter of routine. We were supposed to follow certain lectures. The lecture had been given. We had been there.

Next question: Had we laughed at this unseemly incident?

Answer: Yes. How could we help ourselves?

Question: Had we taken part in the parade?

Answer: Only so far as the parade had followed the route we were obliged to follow in order to get home.

Question: Then we had been present at the parade?

Answer: In the same way that everybody who happened to be on the street at that moment had taken part in it.

Question: Please answer yes or no.

Answer: Yes and no.

Question: Do you think arrogance and defiance will help you?

Answer: I am merely telling the truth.

Question: That will do. Please step outside.

By what process of reasoning the learned doctors came to the conclusion that I had been the instigator of the whole absurd comedy, merely because I had laughed when it occurred, had afterwards stood around on the street with the others and had acted as spokesman for those cited before their august tribunal, I do not know. But I was expelled, together with half a dozen other students who had taken no more active part in arranging and executing this episode than I. The erstwhile corpse, whose father was one of the Burgomasters of Utrecht, was suspended for six months, and that was all.

But it had been a great victory for the orthodox party. All over the country, the dominies delivered fulminating speeches against those "rebellious spirits" who "in sheer defiance of Holy Writ had tried to bring ridicule upon the head of one of the humble servants of God." And naturally, whatever they said was accepted as gospel truth by their hearers and of course the hearers added a few embellishments to the story and of course my father was so shocked and angered by the occurrence that he threatened to send me to the Indies as a cabin-boy and of course my grandfather laughed so heartily that he almost had a stroke and then remarked, "Now you don't have to go back to this New Zion and you can learn your trade decently in some foreign city where they are all Papists anyway and don't worry about their convictions more than twice a year," and when I asked, "But where shall I go?" he answered, "Montpellier. Rabelais learned medicine there from the Jews and became a first-rate author and that is the place for a bad Dutch boy who won't take his dominie seriously."

Well, that is the way I happened to go to Montpellier, where I found that very much less difference was made between doctors and surgeons than at home. Even at that early age, I was most of all interested in experiments with narcotic drugs and the professor of clinical medicine happened to share my enthusiasm and urged me to qualify as a physician and not as a surgeon. Therefore when I returned to Holland, I was a full-fledged doctor who also had had considerable experience as a surgeon.

But then the difficulty arose that I had to make a living (all this happened many years before I came into my uncle's inheritance) and there were much better chances for surgeons than for doctors. I therefore joined the surgeons' guild, or rather, because there were not enough surgeons in our town to allow them to establish a guild of their own, I joined the wooden-shoe-makers' guild, of which they formed part. I never opened a barber-shop, which made the majority of my colleagues regard me as a silly upstart who believed himself too good for his trade. But I was not interested in scraping people's beards and stuck to surgery work. At times people also used to call me in as a doctor, but I never joined the guild of the physicians (they belonged officially to the peddlers' guild) and I was known as Master Jan, though many people, out of courtesy or in order to flatter my pride, called me Doctor van Loon.

But when My Lord Bicker applied to the Board of Direction of the West India Company for a berth for me as doctor in their colony of the New Netherlands, there was at once a tremendous outcry among the other medicine-men. I was a surgeon and not a doctor . . . I had never joined the physicians' guild . . . I had no right to call myself a doctor as I had only graduated in a foreign university . . . all the doctors in Amsterdam would in the future refuse to lend their professional services to the West India Company if I were allowed to sail as a doctor instead of as a plain surgeon . . . and so on and so forth . . . until I assured His Lordship that the matter was entirely immaterial to me, that I would just as soon go to America as a surgeon or even a leech (I drew the line at barbering) as in the quality of a full-fledged doctor. This satisfied my esteemed colleagues and on the seventh of February of the year 1643 I received my patent as ship's surgeon of the West India Company, with destination of New Amsterdam.

I was to sail in April.

A week before I left, Bernardo called on me. One could never tell whether he was sad or happy, but this time the animation of his voice told me that something extraordinary had occurred. I asked him what the good news was?

"I am going with you," he answered.

"Coming with me? Why—how—what are you going to do over there? Keep books for a fish-dealer? It is bad enough as it is here. What will the job be like over there?"

"I don't know," he replied, "and I don't care. I am through with fish and through with book-keeping. I am an explorer now. An explorer and an investigator."

"Investigator of what?"

"Of the lost tribes of Israel." And then he told me that Rabbi Menasseh ben Israel had been to see him, had told him that there were a number of Jews in Amsterdam who believed like himself that the copper-colored but black-haired natives of the New World were the direct descendants of the black-haired and yellow-skinned inhabitants of ancient Palestine. They were so convinced of the truth of this hypothesis that they had subscribed a certain sum of money to send some one across the ocean to investigate the matter.

"And you know," Bernardo remarked dryly, "ever since my little trouble with the Inquisition, I have been regarded by my fellow-countrymen as some strange physical phenomenon, a survivor from some great natural cataclysm of Sodom, a relic of the Flood. I am deemed the ideal messenger to send to the other end of the world and report upon the present status of my little nephews across the ocean. I hate my present job.

JOHANNES LUTMA

I know I was offered other work, but it would have merely meant that I moved from one set of ledgers to the next. I have done enough figuring in my life to last me for all eternity. I have sold enough fish to stock a dozen planets. And so I accepted almost humbly. You never guessed it, but I was born to be the hero of strange adventures. If you care to have me, I shall be your faithful traveling companion. But watch out for the adventures. Wherever I go, they follow me about. Probably because I look so little like the part!"

I answered him (and with absolute sincerity) that no one could have been more welcome to share my cabin and my loneliness.

And on the eighth of April of the year of Grace 1643 we left Amsterdam. Four days later we were on board the good ship *Dubbele Arend* bound from Texel to the mouth of the Mauritius River.

It was a brave little vessel of 320 tons and it was raining so hard when we lifted anchor that we could not see the buoys and ran on a bank. But the next high tide set us free. When I got up in the morning, the sun was shining brightly and the coast of Holland was no longer in sight.

Chapter 29

I DEPART FOR A NEW WORLD

I was to have spent two years in America. I stayed seven. And although I had many interesting adventures and many strange experiences, I feel that I am not entitled to enumerate them in a diary which after all might fall into the wrong hands.

For although I went across the ocean in the capacity of a surgeon of the West India Company, I was really in the service of My Lord Andries and his brother Cornelis. They suggested that I go and they paid for the trip. When I returned, I drew them up a detailed report containing all my observations and a few suggestions. They thanked me cordially and assured me that they were entirely satisfied, had no regret at the expense and hoped that from my side too the voyage had not been a disappointment. Then they asked me to keep the whole matter a secret until they had studied my records and had decided what to do. They would let me know within a few months.

But all sorts of things intervened. The Prince of Orange made his attack upon Amsterdam and the political party to which the Bickers belonged was forced to withdraw temporarily from the city's government. Soon afterwards, My Lord Andries and his brother Cornelis died and what became of my report I was never able to find out.

The younger generation of the Bickers, reëstablished in all their ancient dignities as soon as their brother-in-law and cousin, John de Witt, had deprived the House of Orange of its power (which he did shortly after my return to Holland), were very different people from their fathers and grandfathers. The new generation was beginning to lose contact with those business enterprises that had brought their ancestors fame and fortune. The Republic no longer had an established aristocracy. There were a few titled personages left, but they had lost all influence except in some of the more backward provinces of the east where those country squires had been able to maintain themselves in dreary glory in their lonely castles and where they continued to rule the peasants in a haphazard patriarchal way as they had done since the year one.

But by the middle of the seventeenth century the sons and grandsons of the men who had made the country what it was were beginning to regret that they must spend all their days as plain citizens with no other rank than the "My Lord" and "Your most Honorable, Well and Highborn Excellency," titles which they had bestowed upon themselves and which meant about as much as the high-sounding dignity of "Archbishop of Trebizond," held by an amiable little man who during the week professed to be a simple book-seller and who on Sundays in the attic of a house on the Oude-Zijds Voorburgwal read mass for the benefit of his Catholic parishioners.

In order to escape from this (to them) most humiliating position, these younger sons were trying to withdraw their money from business enterprises and were investing their inherited wealth in landed estates which had formerly belonged to the true nobility and which gave them a chance to write the names of a few villages behind the simple patronymic which they had received from their ancestors. During the next ten or twenty years, the old names would then be discreetly dropped and marriage with the daughters of impoverished domestic and foreign noblemen would do the rest. It was a bad day for the country when these young men, who ought to have spent their time on the Exchange, hastened every afternoon to the dancing schools of the Kalverstraat to let some former French waiter teach them the latest "elegances" of the court of King Louis. It is small consolation to remember that such a thing has happened in practically every other country that has grown rich through trade. For every one of those nations has either come to grief, or like Venice and Genoa is rapidly going to ruin to-day. Eventually we shall probably follow their example. I have only one consolation. I shall not be alive when that happens.

Of course, many things happen during eight years, and that is perhaps the reason I saw the change so clearly when I returned. The old Bickers had been so sure of their position in the community that they could associate with me, a simple surgeon, on terms of intimacy and friendship. The sons were polite but distant. They were afraid of what their friends would say. Suppose one of them had remarked, "Oh, I saw you with that leech to-day. Is that a new crony of yours?" My Lord Andries would have answered, "Yes, and what of it?" And the next day would have dealt that curious young man such a terrific blow on the Exchange that it would have taken him a couple of years to recover. The new generation was of a different mettle. They were much more polished and infinitely more suave than their fathers. They were not as ferocious in their hatreds. Neither were they as loyal in their affections. They were lukewarm and that, I fear, is a quality which one should only tolerate in certain kinds of vegetables.

About a dozen years after my return from America I heard that there were plans for a new and independent colony that was to be established in some part of the New Netherlands and was to be managed by the city of Amsterdam without the interference of the West India Company. It was an open secret that the latter was really in a state of bankruptcy and it would have been the right moment to acquire some of her property at a very low price. As soon as I had gathered a few of the details and had been told that the Bicker family was interested in the matter, I went to pay my respects and to offer my services if the directors of the new organization should desire some first-hand information upon a subject with which I was thoroughly familiar.

I was politely enough received but made to understand that I had better stick to my work in the hospital. I was somewhat taken aback by this attitude and guardedly referred to my report and to my willingness to elaborate it by word of mouth, should such a course be deemed advisable. There was a vaguely mumbled answer: "Report? Oh, yes, we know all about it. And now, if you will excuse us, there is a great deal of important business awaiting us. Yes, the man at the door will give you your cloak and hat."

The new company was actually founded, but in quite a different part of the New Netherlands from the spot I had suggested. It would be uncharitable on my part to say that I was actually pleased when it failed less than a dozen years later. But neither did I lose any sleep when I thought of the 600,000 florins the investors had wasted. After all, I had done my duty. And if the others refused to listen to my advice that was their affair and not mine. My own conscience was clear and as far as I was concerned, there the matter ended.

As for my observations in that distant land, since I had been sworn to secrecy before I left, I have never felt at liberty to speak of them to any one nor shall I mention them here. The results of my investigations about the so-called "narcotics" used by the natives of the New World in their practice of medicine have all been set down in my little book, "De Herbis Medicis Indorum," which was published in Leyden in the year 1652. And so there remain only a few personal details of the long voyage and since I am trying to put some order into the chaos of my personal recollections, it may serve a good purpose if I mention them.

First of all, the incredible six days while we were trying to make the English Channel in the face of a terrific southern gale. The *Dubbele Arend* was a staunch ship and the captain knew his business. Nevertheless we lost both our anchors, the fore-mast and half our sails and I suffered an amount of physical discomfort which I shall not forget as long as I live.

But it was not only the agony of aching bones and stomach that made those endless hours so miserable. None of the passengers were of course allowed out on deck, but even if I had been given permission to go out into the fresh air, I could not have done so as I was by far too weak to move my eye-lashes, let alone my hands and feet. I therefore lay flat on my back for almost seven solid days and nights, cooped up in a small, dark cupboard (we were not allowed to light even a candle, the ship rocked so terribly), and I had plenty of opportunity to think.

Now, even if my thoughts had been at all pleasant, this enforced residence in a tumbling, pitching, rolling tomb would have been bad enough. But just before I left, something else had occurred that had hurt me very badly and that was still causing me great distress.

I had bade farewell to all my other friends but I had kept Rembrandt for the last moment. I had grown very fond of this lonely soul and vaguely sensed a disaster in the household on the Breestraat. The Dircx woman was still staying with him. Under the pretext that little Titus had developed a cold and needed her care more than ever lest he die of the same disease as his mother, she was making herself more and more indispensable every day. She was undoubtedly very fond of the child, but in a strange and violent fashion, not pleasant to behold and decidedly dangerous for the object of her affection. One moment she would be kissing and petting the poor infant and the next she would scold it or cuff it for some trifling mistake which an ordinary, sensible person would have wisely overlooked.

As I had already told Rembrandt at least a dozen times, the woman was really not responsible for her actions. She suffered from "hysteria," a mysterious affliction of the womb already mentioned by Galen and not uncommon in females of her age. For days at a time she would be perfectly normal and then suddenly, without the slightest provocation, she would break into a fit of frenzied anger, would smash plates and dishes, would pull the clothes off her back and in other ways would make herself thoroughly detestable, while Rembrandt stood hopelessly by and tried to pacify her by the most extravagant of promises.

When these brought no relief he would appeal to her on behalf of "poor little Titus who needed her so badly," and she would burst forth into tears and that, for the moment at least, would be the last of the seizure. Twenty-four hours of sleep would completely restore her and she would be quite all right for another fortnight or so.

Once or twice, when the attacks were very severe, Rembrandt had sent for me, though there was nothing I could do. But every time I would warn him once again that he ought to get rid of the woman. She was too dangerous. People who suffer from the complaint of the "hysteria" are not only absolutely untrustworthy but they are very malicious and are very clever liars, and as they are absolutely unaccountable for their acts, they cannot be held responsible for what they either say or do.

In every possible way I tried to make the painter see the sort of trouble the woman might cause him. In a small religious community like ours, every artist was held to be a rake and a spendthrift. He might live the most strait-laced life possible, love, yea, even support his wife and children in decent comfort, and all the same his neighbors would say, "Oh, yes, a member of the guild of St. Luke. You know what *they* are! Better be careful and not see too much of him." When such a man was reported to be living all alone in one and the same house with the widow of a soldier, every one of these good Christians would be absolutely convinced that she was his mistress and they would shun this House of Sin as they would avoid doing a kind deed for some one who belonged to a different creed.

I told Rembrandt so, time and again, but it did absolutely no good. He would only get irritated. "Nonsense," he would reply. "Stuff and nonsense! The woman is a little difficult at times but no one could be more devoted to little Titus than she. She even thinks of making a will in the child's favor so that if she should suddenly die during one of her attacks— She has not done so yet, but she often speaks of it and that shows the way she feels about the boy—just as if he were her own son. Of course, I shall let her go eventually, but not just now. It would be unfair, after all she has done for the child."

But of course that was not the real reason why he was so slow in sending her packing. It was the old, old story. He knew of no life outside his work. He wanted to paint or etch, morning, noon and night. Nothing must interfere with the daily routine of the studio and the printing-room. A new housekeeper or a new nurse would mean a slight loss of time. He would be obliged to break her in, show her what was needed in that happy-go-lucky household of his. Out of devotion to his palette and his brushes, he neglected his own interests and those of Titus. Geertje Dircx, with all her failings, her tantrums, her everlasting whining and complaining, at least allowed him to work in peace, and that was all he asked of her or anybody else.

"But listen," I continued in a final attempt, "you are a portrait painter. A landscape painter does not come in personal contact with his public. He can be a drunkard and a scoundrel, but those who buy his pictures won't see him personally and so they won't care. But you draw portraits. People have to come to your studio. The general public is a terrible coward. The moment they hear some talk about Geertje and you, you are lost."

He could not see it. He just could not see it that way.

"If people care so little for my work that they won't come to my house because they think I sleep with the nurse, they had better stay away," was his only reply. And when I tried to reopen the subject, he impatiently interrupted me. "I know the woman is a fool," he said, "and I shall get rid of her just as soon as I can. But not just now. It would not be practical and it wouldn't be quite fair either. She will go soon enough, but give me time."

It was my last evening with him and there were a great many points I had wanted to discuss. But something had come between us. It was this miserable woman, and try as we might, we could not remove her from our consciousness. In the end, I made a fatal mistake. Rembrandt was a great painter, probably the greatest we ever had, but he was also of very simple origin and more than once some of his rich patrons had made him feel what they thought of the social status of an artist whose father had been a miller and whose brother was known to be a cobbler. Rembrandt was exceedingly sensitive about such slights (foolishly sensitive I thought), and because he was so sensitive and furthermore because at heart he was exceedingly shy, he could on occasions be one of the most abrupt and ill-mannered persons I have ever met.

On this particular evening he was at his worst. He was fond of me, as I was fond of him, and he hated to see me go. I too was unhappy and therefore terribly ill at ease. Otherwise I would never have been so foolish as to say what I did.

It was about eleven o'clock and I still had a great many things to do at home. I got up and lightly remarked, "Au revoir, and if ever you are in need of anything, write me and I will come right back."

He jumped from his chair. "I am not in need of anything," he almost snarled. "I am not in need of you or anybody else. It is very kind of you to offer your services, but I can take perfectly good care of myself, thank you."

I held out my hand. "Good-by then," I said.

"Good-by," he answered, but he did not take the hand I offered him, and he (on other occasions the most punctiliously polite of all my friends) let me find my way to the door alone.

All day long, the next twenty-four hours, I tried to find an excuse to call on him again. But my house was filled with people who wanted this or that and I had no opportunity to rush to the Jodenbreestraat and tell my poor friend that I was sorry, that everything was all right between us, and to show him in what friendship and affection I still held him. Then they came for the trunks and I had to go.

Such had been the manner of our farewell. The recollection of that terribly unhappy moment was almost worse than the sickness of which I suffered. And I thanked the good Lord when at last we reached Dover and I could once more place both feet firmly on dry land. I would have at least one whole week of decent sleep and decent food. And renewed vigor would give me strength to get rid of those recollections that had made me so unhappy the last nine days.

As I was soon to discover, our repairs would take much longer than any of us (the captain included) had thought, and we were in England for over a month. It was not a very pleasant month, either. The country seemed to be on the brink of a civil war and outsiders were as welcome as a falcon in a chicken-coop. Everybody suspected everybody else but all of them suspected a foreigner.

The first day I was on shore, I walked along the harbor and out of sheer boredom watched a gloomy-looking citizen who was fishing. Immediately he pulled up his net and barked at me, "You are a foreigner, eh? What are you doing here?"

I told him that I was a passenger on board a ship that had suffered from the recent storm and had been driven into port for repairs.

"Where from?" he asked.

"From Holland," I replied.

"Oh, Holland, eh?" he sneered. "Holland where the people call themselves Christians and then support the wicked enemies of God who would make this nation another Babylon."

I assured him that I had no idea of what he was talking—that as far as I knew, Babylon had been destroyed by Alexander the Great at least two thousand years before, and that the only reason for my standing there at that particular moment was my sincere desire to see him catch a fish.

But the man was in no mood for humor.

"You had better be gone," he threatened, "before I call the Sheriff. You are probably a spy. You are probably in the pay of your Queen."

"But listen, my friend," I interrupted him, "I have no queen. There is no Queen of Holland. There never has been one."

"Then what is the Stuart woman doing in your country?"

"Stuart woman? You mean the daughter of your own King Charles?"

"I do!"

"Well, she is the wife of one of our officials."

"So she is, and she is conspiring with her father to bring him back to London and kill all those who truly love God. Even now she may be sailing up the Thames with the navy of your dastardly country. Christians indeed! You are worse than Judas who betrayed our Lord for money."

I decided that I had to do with a madman and went my way, leaving the poor demented fellow to his illusory fish and his equally illusory "Queen of Holland."

I saw an inn and I went to the tap-room where I ordered a gin and water, as I had heard all my friends who had been in England tell that that was the national beverage of the British people. A few minutes later a fine-looking young cavalier with a noble lace collar and carrying a rapier at least eight feet long entered and sat at the table next to mine.

"Landlord," he called, "bring me a bottle of claret. I want to drink to the everlasting curse of that thrice-damned nation, the Dutch. Here goes!" and he emptied a bumper of what to me seemed an excellent vintage which should be sipped at leisure but never, under any circumstances, should be washed down one's throat as if it were beer.

The landlord, anticipating a profitable evening, bent over his patriotic customer. "And what, My Lord, might the Dutch have been doing now," he inquired, "that they should have incurred Your Lordship's displeasure?"

"What have they done now? *Now,* you say? What have they ever not ceased doing? Was there ever a more perfidious, contemptible and disreputable race on this planet of ours? What have they done now? Come here, all of you!" And here he addressed himself to a dozen pleasant-looking loafers who were standing in front of the bar and who, on the chance of a few free drinks, hastened to His Lordship's table.

"Sit down, all of you, and have a glass of this poison which our landlord calls claret. What have the Dutch done? Do you remember, my friends, how our gracious Sovereign most graciously allowed their Stadholder—some sort of high-sheriff, for all I know—to marry his royal daughter? A Dutch square-head marrying a Stuart! Very well. The deed was done. A royal princess," and here he lowered his voice, "dwelleth in The Hague—a genuine, honest-to-goodness royal princess dwelling in a Dutch hamlet. But what do you think? Were those fishmongers and cheese-merchants grateful? Not a thought of it! When Our Majesty got into trouble with those psalm-singing bastards of Hampden and What-do-you-call-him Cromwell, His Majesty sent his august consort to the Holland city to ask for their support in chastising his traitorous subjects. What I really mean, is to allow them to put their money for once into a cause that was wholly just and wholly righteous. What did they do?" Here he stopped for emphasis. "Nothing! absolutely nothing! Gave her a few thousand ducats and their good wishes! A few thousand, where they ought to have given millions. I know it for a fact. My brother is just back from Oxford. The Queen was there. A brave woman, a fine woman, one of God's noblest women! Had spent ten days at sea. Had braved death and seasickness without a flicker. And all that to be insulted by the damned Dutch with a present of a waiter's tip!"

I decided that it was apparently not a lucky day for the Dutch and I paid for my gin and water and went to my bed. But the next morning I thought I had better find out why we were quite so unpopular with everybody and I asked my landlady who the best surgeon in town was and I paid him a visit.

As a rule our colleagues in other cities are happy to see us for we often have heard of some new method of cutting the stone or applying the irons from those with which they are familiar and they are apt to learn something, just as we are ourselves. I found a crabbed old man, in a very cold room, with a woolen muffler around his neck, reading out of an enormous volume which proved to be the Book of Revelation, edited with myriads of notes by some English divine whose name I have forgotten.

No sooner had I told him that I was a member of the Amsterdam surgeons' guild, bound for the New Netherlands and driven into the harbor of Dover by inadvertent winds and that I wanted to pay my respects to one whose name was so generally and so honorably known (flattery is the oil of all social machinery) than he closed the book before him with a loud bang, pushed back his chair and delivered himself of one of the bitterest denunciations to which I have ever been obliged to listen.

"Bound from the Old Netherlands to the New Netherlands, eh?" he asked. "The New Netherlands indeed! And who told you, you house-breaking robbers and pirates, that you could take a piece of land that belonged to the Children of Zion? The Children of Zion, I say and I mean it! When God meant to chastise us by giving us a Stuart to rule over us as our king, we who truly love Him and His service could only save His holy cause by carrying it to the other side of the ocean and founding a new and happier England amidst these savages, that were infinitely less cruel and blood-thirsty than our own Staffords and Lauds. God in His infinite wisdom had prepared this sanctuary for His own people when He sent Cabot across the ocean to take possession of all this part of America in our name, which is also His name. Then you came with your intrusions. You built yourselves castles within the realm of Israel. You raised armies to keep the Chosen People from their just reward. Now the hour of Judgment is at hand. The Evil One has arisen again. His name is Charles Stuart."

Here I interrupted him. "My very dear sir," I said, "I only came here out of colleagual politeness. The people in my country are greatly interested in the work of one of your physicians. I for one would like to talk of the ideas of Doctor Harvey."

I thought that the old man would attack me. "Harvey!" he shouted. "A vile and contemptible traitor. Harvey! a son of honest yeomen, who prefers to serve a popish king. Harvey, who this very moment is at Oxford to cure his royal master from the result of his youthful debaucheries!"

Once more I interrupted him, for the interview was getting to be very painful. I said that no doubt it was very sad that Doctor Harvey should have chosen to side with the wrong party (what did I know or care about his stupid parties? I had enough of them at home). And I argued that I had come to exchange some ideas upon science, not upon irrelevant religious quarrels. Those words, "irrelevant religious quarrels," brought about the explosion.

"Irrelevant!" the man hissed (if it be possible to hiss a word with so many r's) "irrelevant, sir! Just as 'irrelevant' as Pilate washing his hands of the ultimate fate of our Saviour. Here we have spent years building the New Zion, the New England, that at the great hour of our crisis we might have a weapon with which to strike at our enemy and save the old England. And here you, a member of the race that has steadily opposed us, that has almost ruined our plans, dares penetrate into my house and home and use the word 'irrelevant'! Out of my sight, sir! Out of my house!"

So that ended that third interview and I decided to go back to the ship and invite the captain for dinner and ask him what my pleasant-tempered British colleague had meant with his New Zion and how and why we poor Hollanders were accused of having interfered with the plans of Jehovah.

Captain Bontekoe, an honest sailor from Franeker and in contrast with most of his fellow Frisians a good Erasmian, had made nine previous trips to the West Indies and when I told him what had happened to me that afternoon, he was not in the least surprised.

"The same old story," he smiled pleasantly. "The same old story, or the same old fable, or the same old lie or whatever you want to call it. Look here, Doctor, I shall tell you the story in a nut-shell. The English take their souls seriously. They don't care much for the arts. They have to have some sort of an outlet for their emotions and so they quarrel about hymn-books and snakes that have talked or not talked, and infant damnation and other pleasant subjects like that and they burn each other and hang each other and draw and quarter each other with absolute good humor, but in the most murderous spirit imaginable. Until a couple of dozen years ago they were at least ruled by one of their own people. That made the hanging and burning a little less painful. It is much pleasanter to be sent to the scaffold by one of your own people than by an outsider. But red-haired old Bess, the wily old scoundrel, she died and they got the Stuarts to be their masters. They are no good, these Stuarts. They never have been. Besides, they are foreigners from a distant land; Scotchmen from Edinburgh, twice as far from London as Paris, four times as far as Amsterdam. The Stuarts have never understood their English subjects and the dear subjects have never understood their Scottish masters. And besides, personally they were no earthly good, very weak with women and even more so with their given word. A fine kettle of fish! And of course, sooner or later, it had to boil over. It seems to be boiling over right now. Parliament is in London, the King is in Oxford, and the armies of the two are somewhere between. We shall be lucky if we get away from here before they fight a pitched battle."

"Yes," I said, "that is undoubtedly interesting, but what in God's name has New Amsterdam got to do with that?"

"Nothing in the world of ordinary, normal people, but this afternoon, from what I can make up from what you tell me, you were not dealing with an ordinary, normal person. Don't forget that just now they are having the same kind of trouble in this country that we had thirty years ago. You know how that ended. We killed the only really great man we had ever had so far. In the end over here they will probably cut off the King's head. Mark my words! If Charles is not very careful, they will cut his head off. For these people (just as we were when you and I were still younger than we are to-day) have got themselves in a fine state of religious delirium tremens. They won't wake up and be cured until they have had the shock of their lives—some enormous sensation—a war—or a first-rate murder—or a trial, of the whole nation against one single statesman or even against the King. Can't you see it? All these sad-faced brethren sitting in some large hall behind an enormous Bible, turning the leaves and finding passages urging 'God's People' to commit tyrannicide or whatever the professors call it?"

"Yes," I interrupted him once more, "yes, Captain, I know and all this is tremendously interesting, but what does it have to do with New England and . . ."

"Pardon me," the skipper replied, "I am sorry, but I have been coming to this country on and off for the last thirty years. It used to be a damn amusing country, and now look at it! But you were asking a question.

You were asking me why this poor old leech was so angry with you to-day when you said you were a Hollander. Well, it is this way. He probably was one of the leading local lights in the camp of what they call here the 'noncomformists.' Thirty years ago you never heard of them. They may have existed, but they kept to themselves. Nowadays they are everywhere. Had one on board yesterday with some sort of city ordinance, that the crews of vessels, even foreign vessels, temporarily in the harbor of Dover, are expected to attend divine service on Sunday. Can you beat that? As if we came here for the fun of it!

"Well, where was I? Oh, yes, about New England. Yes, I have been there. Trip before last. Caught in a gale off Newfoundland, lost one of my masts, had to drop into Charleston harbor to get a new one. A convenient enough harbor, but, my God, what a people! I had to stay there four weeks. Never been so bored in all my life.

"There was another village nearby. It was called Boston. Same name as that place on the Bristol Channel. Everybody I met, when he or she heard I came from Holland, wanted to know all about the big synod of '18. The one the dominies held in Dordrecht when they held 180 meetings and spent 300,000 guilders to decide that a minister should dress in black and not in brown. That was not very important and it always seemed to me that they could have saved themselves a great deal of trouble and the taxpayers a lot of money by dressing them in black right at the beginning. But the first time I said so I got into serious difficulties. Afterwards, I just answered that I had been too young when this holy gathering was held to remember anything about it. And somehow or other, I got by with that reply, though many people suspected me of all sorts of terrible doctrines, in which, God knows, they were right.

"But, your question, why did they hate us down there where we are, near the South River or the Mauritius River or the Hudson (everybody calls it by a different name)?

"Well, don't you see, those poor deluded people are so thoroughly convinced that present-day England is going to perdition that they want to move to America, man, woman and child, bag and baggage and everything. That is what the grouchy old pill referred to this afternoon when he said that we were working against the forces of righteousness. They want a strong, independent state over there, run by the clergy (their clergy, of course, all the others are chased into the wilderness where the Injuns get them).

"But it is the devil of a place to start a new state. Rocky soil—a winter that lasts fourteen months of seven weeks each—no rivers—no ways of getting into the interior. Of course they never really wanted to go there.

"You studied in Leyden, didn't you? Ever walk through the Kloksteeg on a Sunday? Remember some terrific psalm-singing that went on there? Those were the people who first had the notion of that New Zion on the shores of America. They could, of course, have stayed right where they were. But they were peasants, cobblers, as simple a lot as I ever saw. I brought part of them from Delfshaven back to England in the summer of '20. As ungrateful a lot of people as I ever came across. Nothing had suited them in our country. Most of them had lived there a dozen years, but they didn't speak a word of our language. They complained about everything. They hadn't liked our food and it had always rained and our houses were too low and our boys had made love to their girls and that was wrong, for of course, they would never have dreamed of marrying their offspring to foreigners. Do you get that, Doctor? Foreigners! We were 'foreigners,' in our own country! Can you beat that? And then the war was beginning again, you know, after the Spanish truce, and they might have to serve in the army to defend a 'foreign' country—a 'foreign' country in which they had been given hospitality for a dozen years! And things at home were not going so well ('home' of course was Scrooby or whatever hole they came from) and they must go to Virginia and start a new country of their own.

"Of course the poor devils had no idea where Virginia was or how far away it was. For that matter, even to-day Virginia is just a name on the map. But they had heard about Virginia and that it was a good land and that one could grow tobacco there, thousands of pounds a year, and grow rich. They also told me that the colony was ruled by a godly man of their own persuasion who had passed a law that all people who did not believe every word in the Bible or did not go to church twice on the Sabbath day or who had doubts about the exact composition of the Trinity should be executed. Should be executed, if you please, for not going to church twice every Sunday! This fellow had been recalled a year or so before, but they did not know that, being the sort of fortunate people who can always just miss knowing what does not entirely fit in with their own plans or ideas.

"Very well! They got permission from the Virginia Company to settle within the jurisdiction of that august body, and they sailed from Plymouth or from Southampton, I forget which, but from somewhere in the south of England. Their captain did not know his business. If you compare his course with that of Hudson, fourteen years before, or even old man Smith who was what we call a 'fancy navigator,' it was pretty sad work. He landed his passengers, or whatever there was left of them—for they didn't seem to have known how to take care of themselves at all—he finally dumped the whole outfit on a piece of rock a couple of thousand miles north from the place for which they were bound, in the most miserable part of that God-forsaken wilderness of rocks and reefs that lies just south of the Saint Lawrence.

"He had the decency to offer to take them back on board his ship and try once more whether he could find the coast of Virginia. But they would not hear of it. They had had enough to last them for a dozen life-times. Better stay where they were and freeze than go back on that leaky scow and be seasick and drift about helplessly for another couple of months. Besides, now that they were on dry land they could eventually walk to Virginia. On the map it did not look very far. And then (and that is where we come in) they found a large chunk of that map covered with the startling legend, 'This belongs to the Dutch West India Company.'

"That made things different again. There were those same miserable 'foreigners' from whom they had just escaped after enjoying their hospitality for a dozen years. And they had got hold of the biggest river and they had built forts all along its borders and villages and cities. It was enough to make even a latter-day saint very mad. They wrote about it to London. The 'foreigners' by now had become 'intruders.' London looked through the archives. Old Cabot had first visited that part of the world (or rather had first seen it, for he never set foot on ground), in 1498. He had been sent out by Henry VII. Henry was King of England. Therefore everything Cabot had seen belonged to England. Could anything be simpler? On the basis that 'seeing is possessing,' the English government had most generously handed that whole part of the world over to a couple of English trading companies. Most of these had been failures and now that one of them at last was doing a little better we were found to be comfortably established right in the middle of all this 'exclusive' piece of English territory.

"No wonder they are annoyed. And no wonder the disappointed brethren who thought that they were going to erect the New Jerusalem on the spot where we have built our own town of New Amsterdam don't like it a bit. If you will follow my advice, don't enter into any further conversations with the people here. I shall hurry the repairs as much as I can for I don't like this country any better than you do. If possible I like it less. But sit quiet and don't talk with the natives. They aren't in a talky mood just now. Play checkers with that nice Jew friend of yours. Or back-gammon or whatever you like. But don't talk. Just pretend that you are dumb or that you can only speak Dutch. That is very much the same in the end and it will save us all a terrible lot of trouble."

And with these words the captain bade me a good night and I went to bed and read for a while in the "Praise of Folly" and thought how very little the world had changed during the last hundred years.

It was not a very brilliant thought, but it was late and I was sleepy.

Chapter 30

THE TOWN OF NIEUW AMSTERDAM PROVES SOMEWHAT OF A DISAPPOINTMENT, BUT WHAT A MARVELOUS COUNTRY!

The captain was as good as his word. In less than three weeks the repairs had been finished. Before the middle of May we had passed Land's End. The next day a heavy gale from the south almost blew us upon one of the rocks that surround the Scilly Islands. The wind changed. Then it died down. Then it veered around to the east and for the rest of the voyage we had splendid weather with a steady, stiff breeze which made us do the trip in less than a month.

To be perfectly sincere with myself, I did not in the least care for life on the ocean. I had heard the charms and the graces of this turbulent expanse of blue-green water chanted until I had come to believe that a sailor's life was the merriest of all. But those odes of praise must have been composed by Roman poets whose knowledge of nautical matters must have been derived from rowing across the Umbrian Lakes or wading across the Tiber. As for me, notwithstanding the discomfort of coaches, the stupidity of horses that are forever running you into a ditch or down a bridge, the terrible roads that are either mud-flats or dust-bins, and the wet blankets of most inns, as for me I shall travel on land every time I get a chance and let the sea be the sea for those who like to be uncomfortable on principle.

One day I picked up a little hand-book on navigation that was lying in the skipper's cabin. It informed me that seven-eighths of the planet was covered with water. Another one of God's little mistakes. At the end of this volume there was a short treatise on the rules of conduct of a captain towards his crew and vice versa. There were some charming items in it. But they struck me as a little too one-sided, for if I remember correctly, the captain could do about everything to the crew from flogging them several times in a single day to hanging them from the yard-arm or leaving them behind on an uninhabited island while the men from their side, if the treatment they had suffered had been sufficiently mild to allow them to recover from the after effects, had the right to complain to the ship's owners but only (and that was the interesting part) after they had first submitted to their punishment.

One day I saw how the system worked. As far as I could make out from talking to a large number of the sailors, Captain Bontekoe was conceded to be one of the kindest and most humane of commanders then in the service of the company. What some one a little less "good-natured" would have done under the circumstances, the Lord only knows. But this is what happened.

There was a nasty-looking young devil among the sailors who was said to be from Dublin. No one knew how he got on board, but at the last moment three men had been missing, the mate had sent to the gin-shops near the Montelbaans Tower for three extra men, "drunk or sober." He had found them, but in what state I need not tell. The crimp who had brought them on board had got his money and the ship was far out at sea before the poor devils discovered what had happened to them. Two of them took it good-naturedly. One ship after all was very much like another. The third one, however, seemed to have a girl in Amsterdam and he was wild with rage. His anger turned especially against one of his comrades in misery whom he held responsible for his fate. And one night he waited for him at the door of the fo'c'sle and mauled him terribly with his knife. I was called forward to bandage the victim. His face was in threads but he was a tough customer and recovered, although he had to go through life with only part of his nose left.

The next morning, with a glorious sun shining placidly upon a sea of shimmering silver, all the men were called aft by three short blasts of the bugler's trumpet. The young Irishman, his hands tightly fastened behind his back, was brought up from below. He had spent the night in the brig. The captain asked him whether he were guilty of having attacked one of his comrades. He nodded yes, he had done it, he was glad he had done it and would do it again if he had a chance. The captain disregarded the latter part of this speech.

"Fasten him to the mast," he said, "and be sure it is the same knife, for that is the rule of the sea."

The young fellow's arms were loosened and he was taken to the mast by the ship's carpenter. Then the knife with which the crime had been committed and which was now in the possession of the mate, was handed to the carpenter. With one quick blow and using the knife as a nail, he hammered the man's right hand to the mast, a little higher than his head, so that he would not lose too much blood. Then the bugler blew "dismissed" and everybody went about his business as if nothing had happened, leaving the poor devil standing there until he should have pulled the knife out of his lacerated hand by his own effort. But he remained obstinate. He had lost his girl and he no longer cared what happened. In the evening, the ship was pitching quite badly, but the knife held, and the prisoner still stood nailed to the mast. I went to the skipper and asked whether the time had not come to set the youngster free. Bontekoe shook his head. It just could not be done. The other men would take this as a sign of weakness and it was absolutely necessary for the safety of both the officers and the passengers (we carried two dozen emigrants between deck) that discipline be enforced in the old way, which as far as he, the captain, could tell, was the only possible way.

I went on deck late that evening. The man was still standing there. I felt such pity for him that contrary to all rules, I offered him a drink of gin. He refused. He refused it with an oath and kicked at me savagely with one of his heavy sea-boots. There was nothing to be done and I went to bed. In the morning, earlier than usual, I returned on deck. A little puddle of blood at the foot of the mast told of the tragedy.

I asked the mate who was on watch whether the boy had suffered any bad after effects from this long exposure and the loss of blood. He shook his head. "I don't know," he said. "He is gone. He was there at twelve. When we made the rounds at one, he was gone. The knife was lying on the deck."

"And the man?"

The mate made a gesture and I understood.

"Drowned himself?"

"Most likely. Those Irish people are very emotional."

And that, as far as I could discover, was the last time anybody gave the matter a thought. Whether it was due to this incident or whether we had an exceptionally well-mannered crew, I don't know, but we had no other adventures until we reached the mouth of the North River, the Mauritius River of Hudson's day.

During the last week I tried to pump the captain a little about the sort of people I would have to deal with. What was the Governor like and who was who and what in that strange land. But he was very chary with his information.

"You will soon enough find out for yourself," was all he would answer, "and I don't want to prejudice you."

"Yes," I replied, "but it would make it so much easier for me."

"Better find out for yourself though, Doctor. Better find out for yourself! As for me, I would rather spend a week with one of those painted savages the Governor is fighting just now than an hour with His Lordship himself."

"Then he is pretty bad?"

But the skipper remained firm. "I had a pretty dull life," he finally confessed, "and I can stand a bit of fun now and then. I am going to wait outside the fort when you return from your first interview with that noble potentate. I shall then conduct you to the second hero of the great comedy of Manhattan, the Reverend Doctor Everadus Bogardus. And I shall once more wait at the door until you return from that interview. Then we shall go to my good friend the leech (if he happens to be in town) and I shall treat you to the finest wild turkey on the island and you shall tell me all about it—the pleasant morning you spent with the officials. But don't ask me any further questions and spoil my fun."

And so I was in a state of complete and blissful ignorance when I put on my best broadcloth suit to pay my respects to His Excellency the Governor. Bernardo had wanted to accompany me, but at the last moment the skipper had interfered. "Don't take him," he had begged me. "He is a nice man and he probably is rather sensitive. Kieft does not like Jews and he might tell him so. Besides, it is better for you that you should go alone the first time. You may be a learned man, I have heard people say so and I have no reason to doubt it, but there are certain things you don't know yet. Go and get your little lesson."

Then I was rowed ashore. I was met by a group of dirty-looking children who stared at me with stupid faces and seemed indeed completely dumb until one of the sailors threw them some pennies, when they fell upon each other with such fury and amidst such terrific cursing as I had never heard before. I used this opportunity to escape from their embarrassing curiosity and hastily walked in the direction of the Fort. In my pocket I carried a draft on the Company's treasurer for 5000 florins and an order duly signed by three of the directors in Amsterdam requesting His Excellency, Governor Willem Kieft, to extend all possible aid and courtesy to Dr. Joannis van Loon, a surgeon and medical doctor of great repute who had come to the New Netherlands for scientific purposes and who should be given every facility at the disposal of the colonial government.

I felt myself a person of considerable importance. And I silently rehearsed the speech with which I would answer His Excellency's words of welcome.

Chapter 31

HIS EXCELLENCY THE GOVERNOR GRANTS ME AN AUDIENCE

The entrance to the Fort, which was also the official residence of the Governor, was away from the water-front and I therefore had to walk around two sides of the walls. There was no moat and the walls looked like the better sort of dikes one sees along the banks of the Zuyder Zee or between Veere and Vrouwenpolder. A number of sheep and a few cows peacefully nibbling the grass of this stronghold did not exactly give one the feeling that the colony was at the very moment engaged in a most dangerous war with its red-skinned neighbors.

The whole scene reminded me of the days of my youth, when I was perhaps seven or eight years old, when sometimes during the height of summer I was allowed to spend a few days with a distant cousin who had married a baker in the village of Ketel, about two hours distant from Rotterdam. A drowsy hamlet, drowsy chickens aimlessly picking at bits of grain, busy bees in enormous fur coats paying their matutinal calls upon all the flowers of the neighborhood and being quite noisy about it, and in the distance the slow but rhythmic blows of a steel hammer upon a steel anvil, everything incredibly peaceful, everything unbelievably far removed from a busy, work-a-day world. But Ketel lay buried and forgotten in the midst of the richest polder of Holland and this was the capital of a vast colonial empire. It was all very mysterious and a little bit upsetting. I was afraid that my speech would not quite fit the occasion. I hastened me to deliver it before I should have forgotten it entirely.

The gate was wide open. Indeed it looked as if it had not been closed for at least a dozen years. Two old men, apparently watchmen (for their halberds were leaning against the wall), were sitting on a bench. There was a checker-board between them and they were so engrossed in their game that they did not notice me. I waited patiently until they had both got at least one king and then I said, "Pardon me, but could you tell me where I can find His Excellency the Governor?"

The elder of the two who was sitting with his back toward the court-yard, pointed with his thumb across his shoulder and without looking up from his game said, "Over there, house on the left, you will find it all right," and quietly took three of his opponent's pieces.

The court-yard was clean enough but a large sow with a brood of very pink children was lying right across the foot-path. My dignity insisted that I remove this obstruction on my way to my first formal interview. But the beast weighed at least a thousand tons and refused to budge. I kicked it a couple of times, but it only grunted and waved one enormous hanging ear at me as if to say, "No use, mister, I am here and I stay here." So I gave the creature a wide berth and entered the first building on the right, a two-story structure which for all the world might have been a better class butcher-shop in one of the newer parts of Amsterdam.

Here too the doors stood wide open and I entered the hall without being challenged by any one. There was a door on the right and a door on the left. I chose the door on the right and knocked. A very unpleasant voice, with a decided German accent, bade me come in. At one side of the room a short, squat man with unkempt brown hair was cutting himself a new pen. He was so deeply engrossed in the business of cutting that pen that he never noticed me. I stood. He cut. The situation was embarrassing. But after all, I carried official messages from Their Lordships the Directors of the sovereign West India Company to His Excellency their Governor in the New Netherlands. I was a person of some importance. I was entitled to a little consideration. And when the pen-cutter, having botched his job, threw the offending goose-quill on the floor with a fine Teutonic oath and picked up another, to recommence the operation, I spoke up and said, "My good man, I am looking for the Governor. When can I see him?"

"You can't see him," he answered, without so much as giving me a look, "he is busy."

"Busy?" I answered. "May I ask how long it will be before I can see him?"

"When he ain't busy any more."

"When will that be?"

"When he gets this damn pen cut," and having decapitated his second goose-quill, he unconcernedly picked up a third one and once more let me wait in silence.

I was very angry by that time, but decided that I would teach him a lesson. I had my official letter of recommendation. In a moment he would know with whom he was dealing.

Finally he had got a pen that suited his fancy. He dipped it into the ink and scrawled something upon a piece of paper. Then he pushed his chair back and said gruffly, "Now what do you want?"

I pulled the letter of the Directors out of my pocket and laid it on his desk. He picked it up and looked at it. Then he called, "Van Tienhoven! Hey there, van Tienhoven, come here!"

A shabby-looking man of about forty came shuffling out of the adjoining room. "Tienhoven," the Governor said, "read this letter to me. I have forgotten my glasses this morning."

The shabby-looking man, apparently a secretary, took my credentials and reeled off the contents as if he were a notary, going over a sales-contract before a couple of witnesses. When he had finished he handed the document back to the Governor. "That is all," he said. "Do you need me any more? I am busy!"

His Excellency frowned a deep frown as if he were trying to puzzle out a question of momentous importance. He puzzled for at least five whole minutes. Then he said, "No, that will do. I will dictate an answer this afternoon. You can go now. I will talk to this fellow alone."

All that time he had kept me standing. I was tired after all those uncomfortable weeks at sea and involuntarily leaned with one hand upon the table. Suddenly he pushed his chair back and banged his desk with his fist.

"Stand up straight," he barked at me, "I am the Governor here. You are a leech in the pay of the Company. Stand up straight and listen to me. Those people over there in Amsterdam must be crazy. Here I am, having a war on my hands that has taken every single one of my men. If pressing business did not keep me here, I would be out at the front myself, this very moment. But I alas! must remain behind to organize the defense. I have sent to Holland for supplies—for soldiers—for money. And what do I get? A leech! a pill! a common barber, who brings me a letter saying, 'Please let this man pluck daisies and daffodils while you are busy fighting for your life.'

"Are they crazy? Do you think I am crazy? I won't submit to this. I know why they sent you. To spy on me. It is all the work of that damned Bogard, the Reverend Everadus Bogardus, the eminent divine. A fine Christian that most eminent and Reverend Doctor Everadus Bogardus! He got rid of my predecessor because poor drunken Twiller would not let him run the colony as he wanted to. Lied about him in Amsterdam, pulled wires. Sent letters to all his friends at home. Finally got his scalp. Now he wants mine. Preaches sly sermons about unfaithful servants wasting their talents. Calls on his parishioners and tells them how much better everything was in the days of old Piet Minnewit when the colonists were taught respect for their pastors and listened to the council of their holy men.

"Holy men indeed! Why, that fellow was so drunk last Sunday that he had to hold on to the table, giving us the sacrament. But what can I do about it? I am a man of action. If they would give me two regiments and fifty thousand guilders, there wouldn't be a native alive between here and Orange in less than six months' time. I tell them so, and what do they do? Send me a barber who wants to go about collecting pretty little flowers. No, my friend, you got into the wrong pew! I am a man of few words. You either go back where you came from and just as soon as you possibly can, or you take your orders from me and I will set you to shaving the garrison of this fort until I can ship you off to the front where you may be of some possible use if you can handle broken bones or know something about taking care of poisoned arrows."

I must confess that never in my life had I felt quite as sheepish as I did at that moment. There I stood like a recruit who was being scolded by his corporal for having omitted to clean the lock of his pistol. And the reception had been so absolutely different from what I had been led to anticipate, that I was completely at a loss what I should say or do next. Should I go away or should I remain where I was. I did not know and so I did nothing, as one is apt to do under such circumstances. But this did not in the least improve my position, for the Governor once more called out, "Van Tienhoven! Hey there, van Tienhoven, come here!" and when that poor slave appeared he ordered, "Show this fellow out. If he is still here within five minutes I shall have him flogged."

Outside the sun was still shining, the sow was still feeding her brood, the two old bewhiskered guards were still playing checkers. But in my heart there was such a turmoil of conflicting emotions, anger, bewilderment, revenge, hatred, and surprise, that I did the only thing I could do under the circumstances, I sat down on an old rusty cannon that was lying (for no apparent reason) in the middle of the road (like the sow) and then burst out into uncontrollable fits of laughter. Then I got up, brushed the dust off my clothes and turned the corner of the Fort. There the skipper stood with Bernardo and a strange man of pleasant appearance.

"Well," the captain asked, "did you have a nice time?"

"Good God!" was all I could answer.

Whereupon the skipper and the strange man clapped each other on the back right merrily and then broke forth into mighty guffaws, so loud and boisterous that a group of women who had been doing the family wash on the water-front put down their baskets filled with wet laundry and looked at us in great astonishment for such scenes of mirth were apparently not common in the good village of Nieuw Amsterdam. Gradually the peals of laughter ceased and I was duly introduced to the pleasant-faced stranger.

"This is Captain de Vries, Master Jan," the skipper said. "He is coming on board with us for a drink. Then we shall all go and dine with your good colleague, Doctor La Montagne. He has come to town with the captain. He has a house here and an old squaw who cooks for him. I have sent word that we would be there at two. The turkey has been ordered. I shall keep my promise and give it to you, even if you have not yet paid your respects to the eminent Everadus. I doubt whether he could receive you at such an early hour anyway."

"Busy with his sermon," Captain de Vries offered.

"Yes. Consulting the famous text of Genesis IX and re-living the whole episode to get sufficient local color. Save yourself that pleasure for some Sunday afternoon, Doctor. Perhaps you will then find him able to talk to you."

The allusion to Genesis was lost on me at the moment, but everything was so utterly different from what I had expected that I paid little attention to it at the time. When I had been in the colony for a little longer, I knew what the skipper had meant. But just then I merely smiled and followed the three men to the boat that was waiting for us at the landing.

The sailors were lying in the grass. In front of them stood an enormous Indian boy, looking a muddy brown and clad only in a garment that at home would have been known as a pair of swimming trunks. His legs were covered with mud. His eyes stared vacantly into space. A dirty broken feather had been stuck in his pitch-black hair, that had been braided like a woman's hair and that was also caked with mud. One of the sailors picked up a pebble and threw it at the giant. "Go along now, Jan Smeerpoets," he said. "Go home and tell the wives that there is nothing doing. Not a drop!"

The giant held out a very dirty hand. "Jenever," he moaned, "jenever."

"Nothing doing," the same sailor remarked, "not a drop."

The giant turned slowly on his heels and shuffled away.

The skipper looked at Bernardo. "Do you know who that is?"

Bernardo nodded "no."

"That is one of your long lost brethren. Nice fellow, ain't he?"

But Captain de Vries broke in. "Look here, Bontekoe, that is hardly fair. That is the way they are after we have taken them in hand and taught them a few things. Wait a few days and I will show you the original article. Then you will see something very different."

The boat pulled away from the shore.

When we rounded the outermost point of land, the dirty-looking savage was standing silently on a rock. His vacant eyes stared into space. His trembling hand was stretched in our direction. "Jenever," he was mumbling, "jenever—gin!"

And that is how I spent my first morning in the New World.

Chapter 32

RELIGIOUS BIGOTRY AND POLITICAL SHORTSIGHTEDNESS PROVE NOT TO BE CONFINED TO THE EASTERN SHORES OF THE ATLANTIC OCEAN

Those bad impressions, however, did not last long. I forgot them completely as soon as we reached the house of Doctor La Montagne. It was a low brick building standing in the heart of a lovely graden, just off the Breestraat, a wide cart-road that seemed to run due north. Doctor La Montagne apologized for not having been able to make more elaborate preparations for our reception.

"But this idiotic war keeps me very busy and I am rarely in town these days."

Then he led us into a small room with enormous oaken rafters and with a few fine prints on the walls. The table, made roughly out of a sort of wood which I did not recognize, had been set for six people. We sat on low benches and we were waited upon by an old Indian woman. The food was excellent but new to my taste. Especially the potatoes, of a yellowish color but much larger than those at home, attracted my attention. We had wine to drink but it was rather sour and a native product, as I afterwards learned. But the conversation was the best part of the meal. Here we were, three thousand miles away from home, and it might have been a Sunday in June and I might have been out in the Diemermeer or in Monnikendam with my friends, talking of all the latest news of the big world, listening to Jean-Louys telling us of a letter he had received that week from Descartes, who, so it seemed, was contemplating a visit to France—looking with ill-conceiled suspicion at Selim, who was trying to convince us that Vienna was the natural capital of the Turkish Empire and that ere long (if he were to believe the letters he received from home) the Mohammedans would be once more marching upon the Austrian capital. Then, switching over to a discussion of the new tower of the South Church or of a dozen new etchings exhibited in the sales-rooms of Lucas Luce, paying our humble respects to Torstensson's latest victory over the armies of the Emperor and wondering what the Swedes would do next, and offering mild guesses as to what influence the death of Richelieu would have upon the new French loan, then being offered by the Wisselbank in the Vogelsteeg.

The same spirit of a well-mannered and tolerant interest in all affairs of heaven and earth, which took it for granted that the good Lord had created the whole universe for no other purpose than to offer human ingenuity and enthusiasm a happy and undisturbed hunting-ground, which I had learned to appreciate through the companionship of my friends in

Amsterdam, I now found here on a little island at the other side of the ocean. And I was once again struck by the fact how little outward circumstances have to do with that inner contentment that can come to us only from an exchange of ideas with congenial souls.

I have listened all my life to people arguing: "Englishmen are so and so," or "No Frenchman ever would have said such and such a thing . . ." or "No German would ever have done this and that," and at home they examine every man, woman and child upon the most intimate details of his or her pedigree before they will so much as say good morning to them. And I have heard all my life that "All merchants are money-grubbers," and "All doctors are quacks," or "All merchants are fine, up-standing fellows," and "All ministers of the Gospel are noble and devoted servants of mankind," but I have learned that it is quite impossible to lay down such laws about other races or other individuals.

The older I grow, the more I have become convinced that there are no "nations" and no "races" and no "classes of men"—that there are only individuals, that those individuals are good or bad—interesting or dull—wise or foolish—according to their natural inclinations, and that mysterious bent of character which we call "personality." And that first day I spent on the banks of the North River and all during those seven years during which I lived in the New Netherlands, I was continually running across further proof of the truth of this statement.

I came to know naked and painted savages whose manners were so exquisite that they could have been presented at the court of King Louis himself and would have been examples of good behavior and innate charm to the polished courtiers who surrounded that famous monarch. And not infrequently I ran across others that were just fat, cruel, lazy animals much too good for the bullets that were wasted on them.

I met simple farmers from some unknown village in the remotest corner of the colony who by thrift and industry and incredibly hard work had cleared wide acres of forest land and had built themselves fine homes where they lived in perfect peace and amity with all their neighbors and where they educated their children to be fine men and women, afraid of nobody and of such an independence of thought and action as was rarely found in the old country. And I have been obliged to spend the night underneath the roof of some worthless younger son of a good Amsterdam family whose parents had bought him a thousand acres of fertile grassland and who had been too lazy to raise a single crop or plant more than a dozen fruit trees in just as many years.

I am running ahead a little of my story. But that first afternoon in the New World convinced me that human nature is the same under every clime and this thought gave me courage to meet the many difficulties that beset my path as soon as I had let the Governor know that I was there on serious business and refused to let him intimidate me into going back home before my task was done.

As a matter of fact, and as I heard from Captain de Vries that same afternoon, Kieft was not a bad man nor as wholly incompetent as his enemies made him out to be. It is true that he was exceedingly vain, much given to banging the table and telling the world in general that he was a "man of action" and a "fellow who got results." But it is equally true that he was a tremendous improvement upon his predecessor, the unfortunate Wouter van Twiller, who had got the job because he was a nephew or a cousin or something of the van Rensselaers, the Amsterdam jewelers who had bought thousands of acres of land between New Amsterdam and Fort Orange.

It is true that Kieft was undoubtedly responsible for the outbreak of war with the natives. But it is equally true that there never had been a fixed Indian policy on the part of the government at home and that the different directors had never known whether they must treat the Red Man as their long-lost brother or must exterminate him as if he were merely some particularly obnoxious kind of vermin. And it would be unfair to accuse poor Kieft of never paying anybody anything he owed him when we remember that he himself was merely the hired man of a trading company that had been virtually in bankruptcy for more than ten years.

As far as I was concerned, I got along well enough with His Excellency, once his suspicions that I was a spy or a tool in the hands of his enemy, the Dominie, had been allayed. After that, he treated me with fair respect and in the end he even came to like me and gave me every opportunity to fulfill my mission.

Unfortunately he was recalled soon after my arrival. The terrible Bogardus (I met the man a number of times; he was the typical farmer's son from some hamlet in the hinterland who had come to might and power as a minister of the Gospel but who was constitutionally unable to live in a community without trying to set himself up as the village tyrant), this violent-mouthed and violent-tempered preacher of ill-will and sower of discontent was gradually making the position of the director absolutely impossible.

The whole town of Nieuw Amsterdam was divided into pro-Bogardians and anti-Bogardians. The affair was taking on the proportions of a public scandal. It would have been an excellent thing for the colony if at that moment the Board of Directors at Amsterdam had sent one of their members to investigate the matter on the spot. But these gentlemen refused to budge. The West India Company, to most of them, was only a side issue. Their true interests lay elsewhere and they continued to rule a country, a hundred times as large as the Netherlands, from some back room in Amsterdam, and clamored for reports, reports, reports, as if such matters could be decided by bales and bales of written reports.

I was accustomed to a certain amount of red tape from the charity organizations which handled the financial affairs of our hospitals in Amsterdam. But I never saw so many reams of paper go to waste as during the years I was nominally in the service of the West India Company. Everything had to be referred back to Amsterdam. If a man wanted to build himself a new chicken-coop he first had to ask permission of the Governor who in turn reported the matter to the Board of Directors at home, who in turn delegated this highly important problem to a special sub-committee. Then the special sub-committee would deliberate and report its findings to the Directors. They in turn would report the special sub-committee's findings back to the Governor in Nieuw Amsterdam, who would let the prospective coop-builder know what had been decided. Meanwhile at least a year had gone by. Very likely the owner of the chicken-farm had been killed by an Indian, trying to get hold of his pet-hen or the chickens themselves had been eaten up by a fox or the man had gone out of business to open a tavern and in that way, twelve valuable months and at least twenty-four guilders worth of paper, ink and red tape (not to mention the chickens) had been wasted upon a question that within any reasonably intelligently governed colony would have been settled in less than five minutes.

About two weeks after my arrival in the New World, I moved from Nieuw Amsterdam to Vriesendael, the country-place of Captain de Vries, who had bought this piece of land half a dozen years before.

After Governor Kieft had raged and stormed for a couple of days, complaining that he was forever being followed by a myriad of spies (everybody in Nieuw Amsterdam, in Kieft's eyes, was either a secret agent of the Directors or a hired assassin of his arch-enemy, the Dominie), after Kieft had raged and sworn that he would have me deported, that he would employ me shaving the garrison's whiskers, that (upon one occasion he went as far as that) he would have me hanged, he quieted down sufficiently to listen to the reports of Captain Bontekoe and the remonstrances of Captain de Vries. As a result, he sent for me and told me that he would allow me to stay, provided I kept out of his sight. I agreed to do this and mentioned that I had been invited by Captain de Vries to come and stay with him at Vriesendael until I should have got accustomed to the new country and should have learned something of the native language.

But his suspicious mind, influenced by years of alcoholic abuse, at once scented a plot. He knew that almost any day he might be recalled to account for the many difficulties that had arisen during his term of office. Meanwhile he seemed to fear that we might start a little private rebellion of our own, and talked of being murdered in his sleep, but finally (upon regaining a certain degree of sobriety) relented and graciously gave me permission to go to Vriesendael. As de Vries had acquired Patroon's rights when he bought his estate, this took me and Bernardo (to whom Kieft had taken a most unreasonable and terrible dislike) out of the immediate jurisdiction of the Governor and neither of us was sorry.

There remained the matter of getting enough ready money. The treasury was empty. But finally I was paid out 200 florins of the 5000 that were due me according to the draft given to be by My Lord Andries. I had brought another hundred florins in the coinage of the Province of Holland, and for the moment, at least, we were safe from immediate want.

It was that time of the year which the settlers called their Indian summer, and although it was late in October (at home it would be raining twenty-four hours every day) the weather was so mild that we could sleep out in the open without any danger to our health.

Bernardo and I, accustomed to living in small, close rooms, badly ventilated and usually filled with the smoke of wood and peat fires, experienced a rare delight in being able to spend so much of our time out-of-doors. Every morning brought us fresh surprises. One day it would be a deer that stood staring at us when we came to the brook to get water for our breakfast. One night it was a bear, who good-naturedly ambled away when we decided to pitch camp underneath the tree he had chosen as his prospective winter quarters.

In the beginning we were greatly frightened by the weird noises that arose on all sides as soon as the sun had disappeared behind the distant mountains. But we were taught that very few of the animals that prowled around at night were dangerous for human beings.

"They are merely going after their own affairs and they work in the dark, just as we work by the light of the sun," Captain de Vries explained, and soon I experienced a pleasant neighborly feeling toward all those nimble neighbors who loved and hated and destroyed and created while we lay rolled in our blankets and smoked a peaceful pipe of some of the excellent Virginia tobacco that was being smuggled into the territory of the Company by the boatload.

To me, still smarting under the terrible experience of that morning in the anatomical theater, the silence, and the beauty, of this lovely landscape came as a wonderful relief. All day long I was on my feet, carrying not only my blankets and possessions but also an extra ax and a heavy gun. For the first time in my life, I knew what it was to be so utterly exhausted by physical labor that it was impossible to think of one's private troubles. After four days of this sort of life, I could eat anything, could sleep at all hours, although my bed consisted of a couple of bowlders, and one morning I actually found myself singing a tune. I never did sing very well and the tune was some old ditty that had been popular in my student days. But the fact that I had forgotten myself and my own worries so absolutely and so completely that I was able to sing from sheer joy of being alive, showed me that I was on a fair way to recovery.

And when, full of this glorious new spirit, I chased a charming little beast in black and white fur and finally tried to capture it with my bare hands (it looked so nice and harmless) and discovered too late that this little wash-bear was in reality a full grown and very competent skunk and when in consequence of this encounter, I was banished from the rest of the party for a whole day, I did not loose courage. But I made my own fire and cooked for myself and did my own chores as if I had spent the whole of my life pioneering in some lonely wilderness.

By some miracle of nature, I, who since childhood had been beset by a million unaccountable fears, had suddenly set myself free from these alarms and nightmares. And from that moment on, America to me became Paradise regained, a land overflowing with all the good things of this world, the last refuge of hope for those who carry too heavy a burden of care or grief.

But how account for the miserable conditions in the little town we had just left? Why could not those people feel the way I did? Why could not they set to work instead of wasting their time in idle day-dreams talking to each other about the wonderful things they would have done if only they had been given a chance? They were being given every chance in the New World. What prevented them from getting out of the deep rut into which all of them seemed to have fallen?

De Vries, when I told him of the wonderful revelations that had come to me since I had turned my back upon civilization, did not share my views. "No," he said, "a few exceptional people, who bring something to this wilderness, who can fill the empty void of our forests with the product of their own imagination, are able to find contentment in leading just the sort of life we lead here. But these poor devils in Nieuw Amsterdam, what could you expect of them? When they are alone, they can hear their poor brains rattle. When it gets dark, they feel the touch of the werewolf's hairy snout, for that is all they learned as a child, that the night is filled with werewolves and ogres, and sly black devils who choke innocent wanderers. Of course, if they were made of sterner stuff, and eager to work themselves out of their own class, they would trek further into the wilderness, werewolf or no werewolf. But most of them are too lazy, too indolent or just too dull. Somehow or other they manage to get by and not quite starve to death. And if things go too badly with them, there is always the Company, which will rather spend a few guilders on charity than run the risk of a costly riot for bread."

"But why," I asked, "don't you get the better sort of immigrants?"

"Because we can't," de Vries replied, "because the Company won't let us. Those poor fossils in Amsterdam just simply can't get away from that word 'India' in their charter. India to them means riches—gold, silver, rubies, spices, plunder of all sorts. That is what India meant to Columbus almost two and a half centuries ago. That is what India means to most people to-day. But this is not the India where you can rob the peaceful little brown man of his belongings. This is America, where you have to work with your own hands or starve. But no, the Gentlemen Nineteen, who have never been here, and will never come here either, continue to prattle about their 'Indian domains.' To be sure, they add the word 'West' so as to differentiate their holdings from those of the 'East' India Company. But at heart, they continue to dream of easy riches. That is why they won't allow free immigration. That is why they stick to their absurd monopoly in beaver skins, when every child knows that the beaver is fast going the way of the dodo, that soon there won't be a beaver within a hundred miles from the sea-board.

"Don't think that we, who live over here, don't know all this. There are at least two dozen land-owners in the colony who feel exactly the way I do. And they write letters to the Directors, lots of letters and petitions and even printed pamphlets once in a while. But no, the Directors know best. Or they answer that there aren't enough people in the Republic willing to go so far away from home. All right, we tell them, if you can't find Hollanders, send us Germans. There are whole parts of Germany that are no longer fit for a wolf or a hyena to live in. First the troops of the Emperor came and stole everything. Then the Swedes came and stole the rest and carted it off to Stockholm. Then the Bohemians came, then the Haiduks came, God knows how all those people are called who now for well-nigh twenty-five years have been living at the expense of the poor Teutons. Those who have survived this system of progressive murder are men and women of exceptional character. They could do wonders over here. They would need a little assistance at first, but then they would begin to dig and cut and saw and in less than a single generation, half of all this territory would be converted into fertile farms. Given two generations and a fairly decent form of government and all these foreigners would be good Dutchmen. We would have a second Holland over here, to console and support the mother-country in her old age."

"And now?"

"Now? Why, the problem is so simple that any child can predict what is going to happen. The English are to the north of us and to the south of us. There is trouble brewing in England. Most likely there will be civil war. No matter who wins, the losing party will escape to the New World. If the King wins, as he appears to be doing at the present moment, thousands of people will go to Plymouth and to the region around the North Sea and Boston will outgrow Nieuw Amsterdam so fast that it will be almost funny. If the church people win (as they may do after a little while, seeing that they seem to be most dreadfully in earnest this time) then other thousands will come to Virginia to plant tobacco. In either case, we shall be the losers."

"We might be able to hold our own!"

"Hold our own with five thousand people who are in the pay of the

Company and have nothing much to lose by a change of government against fifty thousand who have come to this distant part of the world to start a new career? Doctor, use your reason! what chance would we have?".

And the good captain was right. We would not have a chance in the world!

Chapter 33

WE TRY TO SAVE A WOMAN WHO HAS BEEN CAST INTO THE WILDERNESS BY HER NEIGHBORS FROM THE NORTH AND FAIL

Soon after I had settled down in Vriesendael, Governor Kieft was recalled. His successor was already on the premises, a stern-faced old man with a wooden leg, a reputation for honesty and obstinacy and of such haughty bearing in his dealings with the colonists that one would have had to go to distant Moscow to find his counterpart.

I met His Excellency a month after his arrival. He was gracious enough and I suspect that before he left, My Lord Andries had sent for him and had dropped him a discreet hint about my mission. For although he never asked me any questions, he seemed to be fully informed about my plans and projects, but provided I did not interfere with the business of the Company, he let me feel that he would leave me strictly alone and that was really all I wanted.

The financial trouble too was successfully solved. His Excellency expressed his regrets that he was not able to pay me the entire sum at once. "But it would be dangerous anyway to carry such a vast sum around," he remarked, scratching the floor with his wooden leg, as he was in the habit of doing while talking to one of his subordinates. "Let us pay you a hundred florins a month. That surely will take care of your needs and see you through until you return."

Having made this arrangement, I began to prepare for a series of trips which should take me from one end of the colony to the other. Some of those voyages would be very difficult and very costly. I knew this after my first experience with winter travel. I was still at Vriesendael consulting maps and trying to persuade a dozen of the natives to accompany me, when word came to us of a disturbance among the Indians of the sound which separated the Lange Eiland from the main land. Captain de Vries was worried.

"That part of the country is very sparsely populated," he explained to me. "But about a half a dozen years ago, there was a violent religious quarrel in Massachusetts. There is a dominie over there by the name of Cotton who has been trying to turn Boston into a second Geneva. He and his followers mean to rule the city after their own sweet will and those who do not agree with them are urged to move away. Moving away very often means starving to death or being murdered by some of the natives. About four years ago, an English woman who had been foolish enough to start a fight with this man Cotton was expelled from the flock and came to live within our jurisdiction. Last night I heard in a

THE DEATH OF THE VIRGIN

roundabout sort of way that she was in trouble, that the natives meant to kill her. I shall go see whether I can be of any help to her. If you care to come, I shall be glad to have you, but you may never come back. It is a risky business as few white men have ever been where we shall be going."

I accepted the invitation with alacrity and early in December de Vries and I departed, accompanied by half a dozen natives who were friends of the captain. Bernardo stayed behind. His lungs had never been very strong and I thought it better that he should not expose himself needlessly to the cold winds that were beginning to blow out of the west and that cut through one's clothes like a knife and a very sharp knife at that.

Our voyage, by the way, proved a complete failure. We arrived on the spot about four months too late, as we found out when we reached the ruins of the houses where Mrs. Hutchinson and her disciples had been butchered by the Indians. Why they had been so brutally hacked to pieces we were never able to find out. The natives who lived in that neighborhood seemed harmless enough. We tried to get some explanation of their strang conduct but they were very vague when it came to details. No, they themselves had not taken part in the massacre. No, they did not know who had done so. Yes, they suspected that it was done by a tribe that had come from the north, but they could not tell, they did not know, they had been away fishing when it happened. When we returned, we were as wise as we had been before. De Vries firmly believed that it had been the work of a few renegade Indians from the north hired by the New Englanders for this special purpose.

"A man like Cotton is capable of anything when his ambition is hurt," he explained. "I hear that they rang the church bells when the good news of the massacre reached Boston. A creature like that has only one desire, to dominate his neighbors. Let anybody interfere with his plans and he will stop short at nothing, not even murder."

I was in no position to offer an opinion but I learned that the New World resembled the old one in only too many ways and I decided to proceed carefully. I spent the entire winter at Vriesendael and by the beginning of April, when it was possible to ford the countless little rivers of this part of the colony, I had everything ready for my voyage into the interior.

During all that time I had only received one letter from home. It was from Jean-Louys. He reported that my small boy was doing very well and apparently had forgotten my existence completely. He told me of certain rumors on the Exchange that the good ship *Princesse* carrying both the former Governor, Willem Kieft, and Dominie Bogardus to the mother-country (they must have made charming traveling companions!) had run on a bank or on a rock in the Bristol Channel which the captain had taken for the English Channel and that both Kieft and Bogardus had been drowned. Finally there was some news about the Rembrandt household.

"I called at the Jodenbreestraat a couple of weeks ago," Jean-Louys wrote. "Rembrandt was as cordial as always, but he seemed preoccupied. He was not exactly rude to me, but he was terribly ill at ease. He reminded me of those friends of my sinful childhood whom one sometimes met when they were dining or drinking in the company of a lady of lenient virtue. They were apt to be very awkward and rather rude for they were very young and had little experience of the big world and its devious ways.

"Of course our friend R. is an absolute child when it comes to the aforementioned ways of the world. He is paying close attention to business and has done some wonderful pictures since you left. He had finished a number of portraits, but I am afraid that very few new orders are coming in. He told me that he was doing well, but he had lost some of that open-heartedness that made him such a delightful companion in the olden days. Il y a quelque chose de louche dans cette maison-là. Don't ask me to explain, I couldn't. But I feel that all is not well with our friend. I wish to God he would get rid of that terrible nurse. I am afraid that she may be at the bottom of it all."

But this news no longer worried me. How infinitely remote all these problems seemed when looked at from that wide distance. I was glad to hear that my boy was well. Very glad indeed. I was sorry that my old friend seemed upset and was falling more and more into the clutches of that harpy. I feared for him, once the tongues of Amsterdam began wagging, once he had been cited publicly for "immorality" by some eager young preacher, anxious to make a name for himself by a bold and open attack upon the "immoralities of those proud and God-forsaking artists." It would mean his end, financially, socially and perhaps artistically. But I was helpless. And I was far away. And furthermore I stood on the point of losing myself into a part of the great American wilderness that to the best of our knowledge had never been visited by any other white man before.

It was not that I was no longer interested.

But I had found a new interest and the name thereof was The Great Unknown.

Chapter 34

BERNARDO AND I SET FORTH TO FIND THE LOST TRIBES AND SOME TERRITORY FIT FOR AGRICULTURE, AND NEITHER OF US IS VERY SUCCESSFUL

Of my many voyages through the interior of the New Netherlands that kept me in America so much longer than I had planned, I am not at liberty to speak at the present moment. Those adventures have all been set down with great care in the diary I kept which together with my final report I surrendered to My Lord Andries upon my return to Holland. And since servants are sometimes curious and I don't know into whose hands these recollections will fall after my death, I do not think that I ought to repeat them here.

Nor shall I waste much time upon the interesting subject which had been my special hobby since I concluded my studies in Montpellier. The meager results of my investigations I laid down in my little book on the "Art of Medicine Among the American Indians." From that angle, the whole expedition was a mere waste of time and money. For the Indians, although possessing fair skill in the use of certain herbs, were just as ignorant about anesthetics as we ourselves are.

Quite frequently I heard of some wonderful medicine man who set broken bones or removed arrow heads without causing his patients any pain. But when at last I ran him down (often after a search which lasted two or three months) I invariably discovered that the reports of his performance had been greatly exaggerated and that either he used some sort of hypnotic influence (which worked well enough with these simple-minded natives) or that he followed the same methods we employ at home and filled the poor sufferer with such vast quantities of gin and rum that not infrequently they died of a stupor brought about by alcoholic poisoning, when they would have lived had they been kept perfectly sober.

No, from a purely practical point of view, this voyage was not a success. The only person who benefited from it was I myself. When finally I returned home, many of my friends used to pity me. "Eight years in a howling wilderness among painted savages. Good God! what a waste of time!" was a remark I not infrequently heard. But that was hardly true. I realize of course that I was not a second Marco Polo. I did not come home with a few million guilders' worth of diamonds and rubies, sewn in the seams of my clothes. Nor could I, even if I tried, astonish the world with stories about golden-roofed palaces and imperial crowns made out of one single piece of lapis lazuli. Outside of the few little brick houses in Nieuw Amsterdam, I never saw anything much more inspiring than a tent made out of cow-hide and made out of very dirty cow-hide at that. Nor can I truthfully say that lapis lazuli crowns were the fashion those years I spent in the New World. A few of the savages used to stick eagle feathers in their hair but as eagles were rare birds, even in those days, an ordinary barn-yard turkey was not infrequently pressed into service and a dejected-looking capon trying to hide his sadly damaged tail would often bear silent witness to the lack of discrimination with which young braves would often settle the problem of head-gear.

And during the whole of my seven or eight years (one lost all idea of time out there), I saw only one diamond and that belonged to the captain of a slave ship I once found at the mouth of the South River. It was a curious slave ship, or rather, it was a curious captain of a slave ship. The man was incredibly pious. Three times a day he would call together his crew and read to them from the Bible. Neither would he eat meat as long as he was at sea, for fear that such a diet would increase his carnal lusts and make him desire one of the poor black wenches that lay bound and gagged in the hold of the ship.

I tried to argue with him (for in those days I still believed that logic could move mountains or at least people) and prove to him that he could settle his problems overnight by choosing another trade, that no doubt it was a very fine thing on his part not to eat meat during the voyage for the aforementioned purpose, but suppose he give up his nefarious business? The world would be a great deal better for it, and he would like to be guaranteed a steak a day. But no, he could not do it. And why not? Because he had promised a woman in England the largest diamond in the world. Unless he brought her the largest diamond in the world, she would not marry him. And then he excused himself for it was six o'clock and he had to read a chapter from the Bible to his crew. I asked him which one he was reading to them that day and he answered, the first chapter of the Gospel of St. Luke.

Surely our good Lord harbors strange customers on his little planet. I had always known this. And I had always more or less rebelled against this arrangement. What the New World did for me was this: it made me accept humanity as God had made it, not as I thought that he ought to have made it or as I would have made it if I had been given the chance. This new attitude of mind was not the result of a sudden conviction. It came to me after two months spent on the flat of my back in a little wooden cabin somewhere in the heart of those endless forests which are to be found all along the western border of our American possessions.

Theoretically of course our colonies in America reach clear across from the Atlantic to the Pacific. But no one, so far as I know, has ever walked from Nieuw Amsterdam to the Spanish settlements in California. Most maps depict the northern half of the American continent as one vast mass of solid land, but this is merely guesswork. With my own eyes I have seen a lake that looked for all the world like part of a sea. The

Indians told me it was a lake and I had to take their word for it, but I would not be the least bit surprised if it were afterwards discovered that it was part of that branch of the Arctic Ocean which Hudson discovered on his last voyage and where he is said to have been murdered by his crew.

But of all the land that lies to the west of the mountains, we still know so little that everything I write down here is based upon speculation rather than upon knowledge. For one thing, I am no explorer. I never learned how to draw maps or how to handle a compass. Yes, I can see when the needle points toward the north and then say with a great deal of conviction, "We are now going due south or east or west." But that is about as far as my knowledge of that useful instrument goes.

My method of traveling was exceedingly simple. My Lord Andries having provided me generously with funds and the treasury of the colony having been sufficiently reorganized by industrious old Stuyvesant to honor my drafts, I was always well provided with cash. By this time, most of the Indians had learned that the funny-looking little round disks with the armored man on horseback were not just mere ornaments to be worn as ear-rings by their squaws, but were valuable talismans in exchange for which the merchants of Nieuw Amsterdam would give them almost anything their hearts desired.

It was rather a nuisance to travel with a big wooden box filled with Holland guilders, and there was a certain risk about it. But this risk I overcame by occasionally practicing my art as a healer. Indian medical methods, contrary to the glorious reports of many of the early discoverers, were primitive in the extreme. The patients were dosed with enormous potions of hideous-looking and -tasting liquids, brewed in great secrecy by professional sorcerers who as a rule were as ignorant as their patients were superstitious. The mortality among the tribes (especially among the children) was appalling. Quite often therefore I was able to pose as a miracle man by performing insignificant little operations which those people regarded as the work of a god. I encouraged this reputation as much as possible for it meant not only safety but a degree of comfort which few travelers had experienced before me. And when I heard that somewhere in the West there lived a number of tribes vastly superior in civilization and political organization to the natives who dwelled along the seaboard, I decided to pay a visit to these regions and see what opportunities they offered to those future wheat growers whom my Lord Andries and his brother hoped to settle in the New World.

As there was a certain degree of danger connected with a trip of this sort, I tried to persuade Bernardo not to accompany me, but he stubbornly refused. "After all," he reasoned, "I too am not entirely a free agent. I was given money for this voyage that I might find the Lost Tribes of Israel. I believe just as little in those Lost Tribes as you do. Ecbatana is the place to look for them, not America, and the girls of Babylon know more about them and why they refused to go back home to Jerusalem, than those in Nieuw Amsterdam.

"All the same, I am not here as a gentleman of leisure, amusing himself hunting rabbits and shooting squirrels. I am here as the emissary of a few pious Jews in Amsterdam who entrusted me with part of their hard-earned florins to perform a certain, well-defined task. The very name, 'The Five Tribes,' attracts me and intrigues me. I would never forgive myself if I did not use this opportunity to visit those long-lost brethren. There are only five of them, according to that French friend of Doctor La Montagne. That means that the other five are lost. Perhaps I will find those later. But for the moment these five will have to answer the purpose and I am going with you."

During the last month, the excellent Bernardo had changed a great deal. He was actually beginning to talk. And sometimes he even smiled. He explained this to me one day when we had walked some distance along the right bank of the North River and stood on the edge of a very high cliff overlooking the valley. He threw both hands up toward the high heavens and shouted: "Space! Endless, unlimited space! Thank God, that I learned the meaning of the word space before I died."

And when I said, "Yes, but you had space of this sort when we sat on the dikes of the Zuyder Zee," he shook his head. "I know," he answered, "but that was not quite the same. There I was like a bird, whom kind people allowed to play in the room. I could pretend that I was at liberty to amuse myself, but the cage was still on the table, waiting for me to return. Here it is different. Here, for the first time in my life, I feel that I am really free. There is no cage except such a cage as I wish to make for myself. I can wander a thousand miles toward the north and a thousand miles toward the south and a thousand miles toward the west and if I were not such a terribly poor sailor, I could sail thousands of miles toward the east and there would be nothing to keep me back.

"This suits some strange primitive instinct that lies buried in the heart of all of us Jews. We were a desert people. Our friends too often forget that. For thousands of years we never went near a city unless we had to. Hunger drove us to the high-walled towns of Egypt and Palestine. Then it was hunger for gold and for ease and for safety and comfort. The city corrupted us. We were not powerful enough to build ourselves another Babylon or Nineveh. We had to content ourselves with a mean little village of mean little tradesmen and narrow-minded priests, which our pride made us call the center of the universe. And there we grew into something that was absolutely contrary to our true inner nature.

"Our early prophets were men who dwelled in space—who worked in space—who thought in terms of space. Their successors looked out of their tiny, barred windows upon the dark court-yards of neighbors who were equally badly off and after a few hundred years of that sort of life, they came to the conclusion that all the world was a prison and in order to make existence bearable they chained the human soul to that philosophy of despair that lies buried within the pages of so many of their holy books. The Talmud, the Torah—I learned them by heart as a child—every line of them a leaden weight fastened to my soul to keep me from soaring too far away from the dungeons into which my people had crept out of their own volition, once they lost the touch of that freedom that had made them the salt of the earth.

"You think I exaggerate. But Moses proclaimed his Holy Law from the top of a mountain, not from a cellar in Jerusalem. Joshua spent his days on the battle-field. David sang his psalms while herding his father's sheep on the mountain-sides of Judea. Samuel took Saul from behind the plow to make him king of the Jews. Jesus was a country boy. He spent his childhood in a hamlet—a mere handful of houses on a hillside of Israel. He preached his sermons out in the open. Eleven of his disciples were fishermen and day-laborers. One came from the big city and his name was Judas.

"I want to join the immortal eleven—sunshine and rain and dirt and mud, honest sunshine and honest rain and honest dirt—working for my daily bread in the sweat of my brow—not counting somebody else's money or learning somebody else's wisdom by heart in a stuffy room where there has not been a ray of light for the last fifteen or fifteen hundred years."

And having delivered himself of this strange outburst, the longest single speech I had ever heard him make, the honest fellow went down to the Breestraat and bought himself a complete outfit, such as was worn by the professional beaver-hunters of the northern country and was as happy as a child that has been given its first grown-up suit of clothes and is going to take its first trip on the Haarlem canal-boat with papa and mamma and half a dozen of his little friends.

We left Nieuw Amsterdam late in August, when the sun was still blazing hot—spent a week at Vriesendael and then struck for the west along a trail that was hardly discernible from an ordinary squirrel's track.

The famous Five Tribes proved to be no myth, but a reality, and at first sight, a very formidable reality. Nor did they show any visible signs of joy at our approach. Instead they promptly surrounded our small party and conducted us politely but quite firmly to a small wooden stockade where they locked us up and left us to our own devices for three entire days and nights. Then some one who looked like a chief and spoke Mohawk came to ask us who we were—where we came from—what we meant to do in their country and finally how we happened to have Mohegan porters.

To this we answered through one of our Indians, who spoke a little Iroquois, that we were peaceful travelers, that one of us was a famous physician, that we came from a country far away across the big water, that we were merely visiting their country on account of the stories we had heard about the wisdom and learning of their medicine-men, and that the Mohegans had accompanied us to help us carry our luggage but would return to their own country as soon as we had had a chance to hire some of the local natives for that purpose.

He then asked who was the doctor. The interpreter pointed to me. The Mohawk looked at me, shook his head as if in some doubt, and went away again.

He returned that evening. Was I really a physician? Yes! Had I ever used a knife, as he had heard the white people could do? Yes! What was my specialty? Had I brought my instruments? Yes! Would I follow him? I would.

One of the Mohegans was permitted to carry my bag and the three of us started. We reached a village that was quite unlike any other Indian village I had ever seen. No one was visible, but from all the tents there came the noise of a low wailing. We went to the center of the village. Our guide withdrew. I took my interpreter with me and entered. The room was sparsely lit by a small fire. An old crone sat in front of it. The Mohegan translated. She was the mother of the head chief. Her son was ill. He was in great pain. He would soon die. Could I cure him? I answered that I would first have to see the patient before I could give her a definite answer. She said that she would take me to the place where he was hidden from fear that evil spirits might discover him and torture him still further. If I could cure him, I would be given freedom to roam through the territory of the Five Nations. If not, all of us would be killed.

This announcement did not tend to make me feel less nervous than I already was, but I followed the old squaw to a corner of the camp where I saw a small wooden house surrounded by a circle of smoldering fires. These fires had been lit to keep the evil spirits away. Inside the house lay a man of perhaps fifty years of age. His face was distorted with pain. His hands were clenched, his lips set tight. Six women, three on each side of him, were singing a low dirge.

I at once suspected an attack of the stone. I made a few inquiries and touched the abdomen. My first guess seemed right. I told the mother that I could cure her son—that he had fallen victim to a Devil who now lived in his entrails in the form of a large pebble—that I would capture this Devil and cut him out, provided they did as I bade them. The old squaw agreed. I kept the two wives, who looked huskiest, and sent the other four away. I told the mother to get me a torch. She went out and shortly afterwards came back with a box of candles which had probably been stolen from some murdered Dutch trader. I sent the mother away and told the interpreter to hold the candle while I made the incision. Meanwhile the two wives were to take hold of the hands of the patient and under no circumstances allow him to arise. I made the incision. I never knew such fortitude. The man hardly winced. I took the stone out with my forceps

(I don't believe in touching any wound with my hands, as my French colleagues do), and I bandaged the wound.

These natives have an incredible power of recuperation and I knew that in two or three days the man would probably be able to walk. I called the old mother back into the tent, told her to send all the wives away and spend the night with her son for fear the Devil might return. She asked me where that Devil was now and I said, "In my pocket. But he is still very lively. During the night, I shall tame him and in the morning I shall give him to you and you can drown him in the lake or burn him in a fire."

Then I went back to the stockade and slept a few hours. In the morning there was such shouting and such beating of drums that I feared for the worst. Undoubtedly the old woman had called in one of the native medicine-men (they always do) and the chief had died. I did not even take the trouble to eat my breakfast, firmly convinced that we all would be executed before noon. By and by the noise increased and a procession came heading our way. We were marched to the village but our baggage was kept behind, another sure sign to me that they meant to kill us.

Well, after an interminable walk, with at least a million wild savages excitedly dancing up and down beside us, we came to the village and there before his mother's tent stood my patient of last night, all dressed in his best leather coat and without a shred of my bandage of the previous evening. He was apparently feeling perfectly well and I now understood why the early explorers had given such glowing accounts of the medical achievements of the Indians. They committed, however, one small error of judgment due to faulty observation. The doctors of the wild men are atrocious, but their patients are perfect. For where else in the world would one find a man who less than twelve hours after being cut for the stone is able to walk home unassisted?

After this miraculous cure, our position of course became most agreeable. We were taken from the stockade and lodged in half a dozen tents in the heart of the village. Even the Mohegans, whom the Mohawks detest, were treated kindly. They were given an elaborate meal and were allowed to return to their country unmolested. And the next day, after I had presented the chief with his erstwhile tenant, had then taken the stone back from him, had placed it on a heavy bowlder and had smashed it with his battle-ax (fortunately it was a very brittle one and the trick worked to perfection), I was told that I could have as many guides and servants as I cared to, yea, that the whole tribe would follow me if necessary. I chose a dozen of the strongest and with them explored the country of the Oneidas and Onondagas in the north and towards the east without finding anything that suited my purpose, and then late in the fall I decided that I would make a dash for the west.

Bernardo was to remain behind and watch over our luggage while I and two guides started for a big river that was the frontier between the land of the Senecas and the Susquehannocks. The Senecas belonged to the Five Nations, but the Susquehannocks did not, and I was warned to keep out of their territory. I also was told that it would be better if I waited until next spring, but we were in the middle of an unusually fine Indian summer and I counted on being back in three or four weeks.

We entered the hunting fields of the Cayugas and one night about a week after we had left, we reached the top of a low hill from which one had a view of a large but melancholy-looking lake. On top of that hill the three of us spent the night. In the morning I decided to cross the lake if my guides could make me a canoe within a reasonable amount of time. They asked whether two days would be too long and I said no, that that would do very nicely.

They set to work and I decided to take a walk. A short distance from the shore there was a high cliff which interested me through its extraordinary shape. When I came nearer I noticed that it was part of the hillside where the soil had been washed away, and then I discovered a narrow gorge made by a river that had dug its way through the soft stone like a knife cutting through cheese. It was a geological formation entirely new to me, and the walk between the steep rugged walls fascinated me. After about ten minutes I came to a waterfall and had to return. But just before I came to where there was a curve in the riverbed, I stopped to give one more look at the scene behind me. For a better view I climbed upon a large bowlder, but no sooner was I on top than I heard a soft rustling sound and saw a tiny black snake hastily leaving a round pile of leaves which the wind had blown together into the hollow on top of the stone.

How it got there I never understood. Nor do I know to this day why it should have thrown me into such a panic, for I had been told over and over again that there were no dangerous snakes in this neighborhood. But such things will happen. From childhood on I had been taught to abhor every creeping thing and the little snake quite instinctively made me jump. I lost my balance, tried to catch myself by jumping for a much smaller stone that was lying near the riverbed, missed it and landed so unfortunately on the rocks below that I broke both my legs.

I knew by the pain that I had broken them. Then I knew nothing more, for I fainted.

How long I lay there, I don't know. When I came to it was quite dark. I saw too shining lights right above my nose. I reached out for a stone and the beast skuttled away. I heard its soft footsteps on the rocks. Then silence and the rush of the water and another fainting spell. But this time when I came to the moon was out. That was at least some consolation. I would not have to die in the dark. The pain continued to be almost unbearable, but there seems to be a limit to pain, just as there is a definite limit to heat or cold. And so I lay and suffered and had one of the most curious and interesting experiences of my whole life.

For now I experienced for the first time what it felt like to die. I had seen plenty of people pass into the other world. By far the greater part of them had been old men and women, broken by illness and too worn out by the hardships of existence to care very much either one way or the other. Death to them meant relief from monotony and hunger and the eternal grind of making both ends meet. There were a few who clung with almost superhuman obstinacy to the last spark of hope and fought death as bitterly as a pheasant mother fighting for its chicks. But most of them went peacefully to sleep like children who have spent the day on the sea-shore and are tired, very tired. And I had often wondered why they showed no greater spirit of rebellion, since life is the only gift of the gods of which we get only one helping, and when that is gone it is gone, and the plate is empty, and the dinner is definitely over. But now I knew.

If it had not been for the excruciating pain in my legs, I would have been really happy. All questions were being answered, all problems were being solved rapidly, quietly and smoothly. Doubt no longer existed in its manifold disturbing and perplexing fashions. At last I knew! For the first time since the day of my birth I was face to face with absolute and stark and inevitable Reality. And it was the most agreeable sensation of which I have any recollection. I was going to die. I was going to sleep. The little spark of intelligence and courage and hope and charity which I had borrowed from the Maker of All Things was about to be restored to the original owner. The few pounds of salt and water of which my mortal body was composed were about to be released and returned to the vast treasure-house of nature from which they had been withdrawn when I saw the light of day.

But these things did not seem to matter. I thought of them remotely and rather gratefully. I would never again see the face of my son. But he was a million miles removed from me at that moment. One way or the other, he would surely find his way in this world. I would never again hear the voice of Jean-Louys, of Bernardo, of Rembrandt, of any of my friends. But I felt that they would understand. They would remember little things I had said and done and to them I would be alive until their own hour had struck.

I had one regret. There were women in this world. I had read that some men had found perfect love. I had not. I had missed something. But my work had brought me many consolations, that had been denied other less fortunate creatures.

The pain was growing less. I was rapidly sliding down into a deep slumber, the sleep of all eternity, and I was content.

The pain was gone. The rock on which I was lying was soft and warm, a pleasant glow was touching my hands and cheeks. Yes, there was the wonderful old grandfather sitting in his chair and looking at me. "It won't hurt, my boy. We all must pass down that road some time. It won't hurt. Just let yourself go—a little more—let yourself go—" The moon would soon be hidden by the clouds, it was getting dark. The chimes of the town-hall were playing the hour—tinkelee tinkelee—tinkelee—bang—bang—bang—bang—bang—a flash of pain more hideous than any I had felt before shot through me—bang—bang—it must be seven o'clock—tinkelee—deedledee—dee—no! it was the half hour—bang—bang—nine o'clock—I was moving—I was lying in the arms of one of my Indian guides—bang—bang—it wasn't the clock that was striking—it was the noise of footsteps—the footsteps of the man that carried me—I was being taken somewhere—they had found me—I was not to die that night—I might not die at all—tinkelee—tinkelee—tinkelee—ting—a light was shining in my eyes—the pain was unbearable—I must die—then darkness and silence—I had fainted once more.

When I woke up the sun was shining. I was lying on a soft leather blanket. The hut smelled of fresh straw. The guide who had carried me was sitting by my side. "Sh," he said, and I closed my eyes and fell asleep once more.

Of what happened during the next few days I have only the haziest recollections, and I am never quite sure whether the things I am writing down are actually part of what I myself remember or whether they are bits of gossip I heard after I had recovered. It seems that my two guides had missed me when they stopped work. It was dark then but somehow or other they were able to follow my tracks and found me. They had carried me to a deserted village from which a small tribe of Cayugas had moved a year or so before. They had found a small wooden house and in this they had made me as comfortable as they could. They knew that I was badly hurt, that I had probably broken both legs, and they were afraid to touch me, for an Indian is always afraid of a sick man.

But they decided to help me in another way. On the evening of the second day I discovered what they had done. One of the two had stayed behind to take care of me if I should need anything. The other one was gone to get help.

On the evening of that second day, when I was fighting off the delirium of fever, I heard him return. He was not alone. A tall, thin man followed him and knelt down by my side. He was the strangest-looking individual I had ever seen. At first sight I took him for a native. A long leather coat, leather breeches and Indian shoes, long, unkempt and pitch-black hair hanging well down over his shoulders and an enormous knife stuck in his belt. But underneath these heavy outer garments he wore something that looked very much like a cassock, and his face was that of a white man.

I thought that he was a half-breed, and he looked so ferocious that my first impression was, "Why, here is one of the Cayugas who owns this village. He has come back to claim his home." And then I noticed that the fellow wore a heavy silver cross around his neck and I said, "Are you a priest?" and he answered, "Yes, my son, but to-night I am a bone-setter. First I shall pray for you and then I shall fix your legs. Don't mind the praying for you shall need it, once I get busy with those lower extremities." And he actually knelt by the side of my bed and reeled off a Latin prayer of which I did not understand one word, and then he got up and removed his coat and rolled up the sleeves of his cassock and beckoning to the two guides, he said, "Hold his arms," and once more he knelt by my side and got busy.

As those who have ever broken an arm or a leg well know, even the cleanest break makes an exceedingly painful operation. But two broken legs that have lain neglected for almost three days—no, I had better not speak about it. But all through my agony there ran a sort of professional pride in the dexterity with which this unknown man worked. Evidently he knew a good deal about surgery. He made no false movement. If I had to be in hell, he meant to keep me there as short a time as possible.

And I was lying flat on my back again, almost dead from exhaustion, and I was sleeping and I was slowly coming back to life, to find the cabin filled with smoke and one of the two Indians busy making a fire, and outside there was a terrific noise, a whistling, hissing noise, and the walls of the little wooden hut were leaning like the sides of a ship in a storm and I asked the Indian what had happened and he told me it was one of those blizzards which made this part of the country so exceptionally dangerous in winter and that it had come much earlier than they had expected and that it probably would last three or four days and that I must lie very still and not say a word and go back to sleep.

And when I woke up again the hissing, whistling sound was just as strong as ever, but the fire was burning brightly and suddenly I realized that I was going to recover. It might take me six weeks or two months, but I was going to recover and I had gone through the experience of dying for nothing and now I would have that experience twice, and truly, few people were ever so favored. And then my unknown doctor friend came in with his arms full of dry leaves (where he had found them, God only knows) and the Indians made me a new bed and then roasted a wild turkey which one of them had shot that morning, and soon that hut on the shores of that lake which did not even bear a name was as full of comfort and warmth and good cheer as the cabin of the Haarlem canal-boat on Saint Nicholas eve.

The guide, however, had been right. The blizzard continued for three whole days and nights and all that time I lay quietly in my corner while the others kept the fire going—went out for a couple of hours—returned with pheasants and woodcocks and occasionally with a few berries, and took care of me as if I had been their long lost brother. But on the morning of the fourth day, a Saturday, the white man did not appear for breakfast and when I asked whether he was not coming, the older one of the Mohawks said, "No, he is gone." And when I expressed some surprise that he should have left without giving me the opportunity to thank him for all he had done, he answered, "He will come back in two days." And true enough, on Monday towards the evening, the stranger returned and walked into our hut as unconcernedly as if he had gone just around the corner to get some fire wood. And when I said with a feeble attempt at a joke, "You could not keep away from home so long, I suppose," he replied, "That is right. I had to go back to my people and read mass and baptize two children, but now I shall stay with you for another five days."

Afterwards I discovered that "my people" lived some twenty miles away from where we were. In order to read mass to his people and at the same time take care of his white brother, this strange creature walked twenty miles, through three feet of snow, twice a week, and spent the rest of the time either helping the Indians with their traps, or bringing in fire wood or entertaining me with stories of his travels that made the wanderings of Marco Polo seem like an afternoon's promenade through the woods between Amsterdam and Naarden. He had been in the New World exactly twenty-five years. He had come to Quebec when he was twenty and had just been ordained. He had been trained in Louvain and according to all I know of that university (the worst stronghold of the worst form of reactionary feeling in Europe at the time of which I am speaking) he ought to have been a self-righteous doctrinary who would regard the death of a heretic as a welcome diversion in the monotony of his deadly missionary existence. But he explained this to me himself.

"It is the wilderness," he said, "that has done this to me. I suppose I am still a good Catholic. I try to be a faithful son of our holy church, but I am afraid that something has happened to me since I came here that has made me a very different man from the rigid-minded boy who left Quebec in 1622. Last year they sent some one from Canada to try and find me and tell me that I was entitled to a fourteen months' holiday and could go home for a rest. But I thought that I had better not return to civilization. My Bishop would lift his eyebrows and say, 'Cha! cha! a few years in a big city would do you no harm,' and very likely he would suggest that I be called to Bordeaux or Lyon or even Paris to give me a rest from my arduous labors, a sort of reward for faithful service, a reward that would last me the rest of my days, and some other man would be sent out here in place of myself and all the work I have done here would go to ruin in less than a fortnight and my dear Cayugas would be what they were when I came here and I would have lost my ears for nothing."

"Lost your ears?" I asked.

"Yes," he said, "that is why I wear my hair à l'Indienne. It happened the first year I was here. I had settled down in a village on the second one of the Big Lakes. Right among the Eries. The Eries were at war with the Senecas. You know how those Indian wars are. They begin about some trifle, a stolen halter or a nasty look from one chief to another. They flame up suddenly like a prairie fire and before you can say, 'My children, what is it all about?' a hundred villages have been wiped out. This time the Eries happened to win. The rumor spread among the Five Nations that the Eries were being helped by a great white sorcerer. They decided to get hold of that sorcerer to break the power of the lake-dwellers. I went about my business as if I did not know that there was a war. One night, going to visit a village at a little distance from the shore, I was waylaid by a bunch of Cayugas who had come to the assistance of the Senecas. They tied me to a stake in the regular Indian fashion and were going to carve me slowly to pieces. They began with my ears. It was much less painful than you would imagine. Just then the Eries, who did not want to lose their miracle man, rushed the village, killed a dozen or so of the Cayugas and took the others prisoner. It was their turn to be tied to a number of trees and listen to the most impassioned among the Erie warriors tell them what they were going to do to them before they killed them. To begin with, their ears were to come off. I had lost mine, now they were to lose theirs. As a compliment to me, you understand. I was pretty weak from the loss of blood, but I got up (I spoke Erie fluently) and told them that they were fools and knaves and deserved to be punished by God for their wanton cruelty, and I took the knife which they were sharpening for the ear-operations and cut the ropes with which the prisoners had been bound and gagged and told them that they were free. A terribly risky thing to do, but it worked and the Eries and the Cayugas made peace.

"Well, they heard about this in Quebec and the Bishop was not pleased. We Jesuits are always suspected of being a little too independent. Some one traveled all the way from Quebec to the lake to remonstrate with me and tell me that I ought not to have acted quite so independently. If the Eries and the Nations meant to destroy each other (a policy which was not regarded with disfavor in the capital) it was their good right to do so and I should not interfere. I should 'refer' everything to headquarters. That was the express will and desire of His Highness, the Governor General.

"I asked the Episcopal emissary whether I ought to have asked the permission of His Grace to have my ears cut off and he answered that I knew perfectly well what he meant and that I had better look for some other field of activity, for that my usefulness among the Eries had come to an end. I took the hint and went to the land of the Cayugas. They were surprised to see me. They suffered from a bad conscience and they told me so and said that they were afraid that I had only come to punish them. But I told them frankly that I had chosen their land as my place of residence because they were terribly savage, had no conception of decency or kindness or charity and that I had come to teach them those virtues.

"I have now been among them for fifteen years. I have baptized some nine thousand men, women and children during that period. I have learned a little medicine (as you may remember to your horror), I have built a sort of hospital and a school where I teach the girls how to take better care of their children, a strange job for a man in my position, and I have enticed a few young priests away from the fleshpots of Quebec and Montreal (it is a new city, but full of worldliness they tell me), and I have founded a small republic of kindliness right here in the heart of the great American wilderness. But I am grateful that the voyage to Canada is so difficult, for if my dear Bishop should ever deign to visit me, I fear that that would be the last of my noble experiment, where Christ resembles an Indian chief and God himself bears a close likeness to the Great Spirit whom the natives have worshiped since the beginning of time."

I saw the "noble experiment" a few weeks later, as soon as I could be transported. It was a cold voyage, but I suffered no harm and I spent three very happy months with Father Ambrosius, for he was a native of Grasse in southern France, where his father was a honey-merchant and he himself had spent his childhood among the bees and had even taken the name of that stern Milanese bishop who was also the patron saint of the Apiarian guild.

I could not yet walk a great deal, but the weather was very bad and I did not miss much. During the day I spent my time composing a French-Dutch-Cayugan dictionary, more to have something to do than from any desire to turn philologist. But when evening came, the two of us would sit in front of the large open fire, which the grateful parishioners always kept well supplied with fuel, and we would talk. And this was a novel and exceedingly pleasant experience to me, because now for the first time in my life I was face to face with a Christian whom I could not only admire but like, a fine man, even a noble man, a cheerful man of infinite good humor, a patient and humble man who went quietly ahead and did as much good as he could without spending any vain regrets upon the harm his neighbors were supposed to be doing to him. And one evening we had it out in a session that lasted till early dawn.

It began with a confession-of-sins on my part. I told him frankly that I had such an intense dislike for the usual professional Christians that it was difficult for me to be even commonly decent to them. Wherever and whenever I had met them I had found them mean and intolerant and suspicious and of a self-righteous arrogance which made it practically impossible for an ordinary human being to associate with them and keep his temper or self-respect.

"But," the Father asked, "are you quite fair? Don't you mix up two things that are entirely different? Remember even in the days of the Emperor Titus, all Jews were not alike. There were the Pharisees and the Sadducees and there were those who left father and mother and glory and riches to follow a certain carpenter from Nazareth. And what have you ever seen of the latter?"

I confessed that I had run across very few of these, and then Father

Ambrosius made the casual remark that was to change my entire point of view. "Life," he said, "is not real. It is based upon fairy tales. It all depends upon the story we prefer."

It was a somewhat cryptic utterance. I said, "Continue. I vaguely think that I know what you are driving at, but I am not sure." And he went on. "You see, most people think of life in terms of hungry people chasing little rabbits and catching them and killing them and eating them up and they make a great ado about our 'daily bread,' as if our daily bread were the most important thing in the world. It is important, of course. We have got to eat if we want to live, but that is only part of existence. Even these poor, benighted savages are not out there in the fields catching rabbits all day long. Sometimes they catch so many that they have food enough for a fortnight. That means thirteen days of leisure. Then, not being upset by the fear of an empty stomach, they can dwell in the realm of the imagination—of that sphere which some people have called 'other worldliness.' Then they compose their fairy stories or they talk about the fairy stories of their ancestors or they embellish the ancestral fairy story with a few details of their own, according to the temper of the times and the change in their form of living. You see, it is really very simple. Their daily bread keeps their bodies alive, but their souls would die without that daily ration of fairy stories."

That seemed a pretty radical speech on the part of a priest and I gave expression to my astonishment by a question. "But surely," I asked him, "you are not going to claim that your religion, your church, all this"—and I waved my hand towards the wall which was covered with crude pictures of saints made by one of the Cayuga chiefs who had a bent for painting—"surely, you don't mean to say that this is merely your particular fairy story?"

"Yes," he answered quite casually. "Of course I would not confess this to my Bishop, and that is one of the reasons why I am just as well satisfied if His Grace remains quietly in his palace in Quebec and lets me stay here. But, yes, this is my fairy tale. It consists of three words, 'Love one another.' Three words spoken on a barren hillside of that brutal land called Judea. The fairy story part—the incredible part, is this, that they were ever uttered at all—that some one in this world—in this world of greed and lust and hatred and cruelty, had the unbelievable courage to utter them.

"That is my fairy story, that some one had the unbelievable courage to utter them.

"But, of course, that isn't enough for most people. It is a little too simple. Too spiritual, perhaps. They don't want to know what Jesus said. They want to know what he wore, how he looked, how he had brushed his hair that morning. That is their fairy story, a tale of outward and inconsequential details. But they are entitled to it if it pleases their fancy and satisfies their curiosity. They are entitled to it and should not be interfered with, no matter how absurd their ideas may appear to us who believe ourselves to be living on a somewhat higher intellectual plane. And what I say of my fellow-Christians I would maintain about all people . . ."

"The heathen included?" I interrupted.

"The heathen included, and even those who call themselves 'agnostics.' For their fairy story tells them that there isn't any fairy story at all and that in itself is the strangest fairy story of all."

I shook my head and said only one word, "Quebec!"

"You are quite right," Father Ambrosius continued. "If His Grace knew about this, shall I say 'slight variation' upon the somewhat more rigid articles of faith which are read every day in his cathedral (these slight variations on his own fairy tale, in the terms in which I see the world), there would be trouble. Or no. His Grace is much too subtle a diplomat to cause trouble. I would be promoted to some higher post in the interior of France, where they would let me lead the singing on Sunday, or I would be called to the capital to instruct the sons and daughters of our nobility in the rudiments of the French language. But never again would I be allowed to utter a single syllable that had to do with a religious subject and I would die a most respectable and peaceful death, whereas now I shall probably try to interfere in the next war with the Hurons and be slowly roasted to death over one of their famous greenwood fires and that will be the end.

"But in the meantime I am having a glorious time for I am successful. My method has proved the right one, the only possible one, at least in this part of the world.

"Can you see what chance I would have if I had come here and had said, 'My dear children of the forest, everything you believe and hold true and sacred is just so much hocus-pocus. I despise it, and to show you the depth of my contempt I shall spit upon your gods, I shall curse them and I shall take a hammer and shall destroy them.

"Not a person would have listened to me. Or if perchance they had taken the trouble to listen, they would have tied me to a tree and would have left me to the mercy of their dogs. They are a pretty savage lot, even to-day. Don't ask me what they were like twenty years ago.

"No! that system never would have worked. I had to go about my business in a very different way, if I wanted to have them listen to me. And so I came here one day accompanied by an old Canadian trapper who knew this region and who had married a Cayuga woman, way back in the early days of Champlain and who had been with him when he started on his famous voyage to China and ended in Lake Huron.

"It was a dangerous trip, let me assure you. My guide spoke the dialect fluently and he could claim relationship with one of the chiefs who lived on the next lake. Otherwise we probably would have been killed right away.

"Champlain was a great leader, a wise man in many ways, but like so many of our race, he must play a part, wherever he was—must pose a little before the crowd—must show everybody what a fine fellow a Frenchman could be. I don't blame him. Those pious people who pride themselves upon the fact that they never 'show off' usually have very little to show. But upon occasion that attitude can be a nuisance and sometimes it becomes a downright danger.

"When the Hurons and the Five Nations tried to slaughter each other, Champlain would have done well to leave them alone. He could then have concluded a treaty with the victors and in that way he would have strengthened our position along the Saint Lawrence. I am not now talking as a minister of the Gospel. I am talking plain, ordinary common sense from the point of view of an explorer or a statesman or a colonial governor—of some one, in short, who wants to found a colony in the heart of a wilderness filled with painted savages. But, no, Champlain must take his little blunderbuss and when the Hurons and the Nations have their little quarrel, he must join the fray and do a little shooting of his own, and having come from the North, he can't help but be on the side of the Hurons and his bullets kill a couple of the braves who are leading the armies of the Nations and thereafter, of course, these good people hated us like poison or like traitors (very much the same in my opinion) and any Frenchman who went to the southern banks of the Saint Lawrence did so at the risk of his own life.

"I was very young in those days and terribly interested in my work. I had not the slightest leaning toward martyrdom. But it never entered into my head that I could be killed. Of course I was not going to be killed! I was so absolutely convinced that no harm would come to me that I refused to take a gun. Finally I let myself be persuaded to take a small hunting rifle but I decided that I would not use it when I got near to a native village. Just to show them how well I meant.

"The old trapper and I crossed Lake Champlain and went west. First through the land of the Oneidas, where we met no one (they had suffered terribly from the smallpox during the last four years) and then we cut through part of the mountains that belonged to the Mohawks and finally we reached the dreaded region of the Cayugas. After about ten days we struck the first settlement. The trapper explained who he was and how his wife had died the year before and how he was now on his way to see her relatives and bring them some trinkets she had left and some money. That sounded plausible enough and they believed it.

"But what was I doing there? Was I a spy sent by the French who had turned against them when they were fighting the Hurons and the Algonquins? I reassured them. I was a Frenchman, but I was merely a 'learned man,' a sort of 'medicine man' who went through the world listening to the stories the different nations could tell me about their gods. Some of these were quite interesting and some of them were not quite so interesting, but I had heard that the Cayugas and Senecas had a God that was more powerful than those of any other race on earth.

"Well, that flattered their pride and while my Canadian trapper was paying a visit to his ex-relatives-in-law, I sat and listened to the Old Men from one village after another while they told me about their Great Spirit and their Evil Spirit and of the mysterious magic powers, the so-called 'secret soul' that lay buried in every man and in every cloud and in every blade of grass and in every grasshopper and even in the arrows which they shot at their enemies.

"When I had listened for almost six months and knew all there was to be learned, I told them how tremendously interested I had been in what they had told me and then I appealed to their sense of fair play (which as a rule is very strongly developed among those fighting races, much more strongly than among the peaceful tribes) and I said, 'Now you have told me your story of how the world was created and who rules it and what the evil spirits try to do to us to make us unhappy, and now you ought to listen to my story,' and they answered that that was right and as it should be, and so I built myself a small altar out in the open, near the shore of the lake underneath a very large tree, as fine a setting for the house of our Lord as one could hope to find on either land or sea.

"Then I began to tell them very slowly and very gradually (and I hope rather tactfully) what my story was and why I thought it better than theirs. And by the grace of God and through the mercy of His saints, I was successful. I was able to show these poor children of darkness the way to the Light. And to-day nine of the frontier villages that belong to this tribe have accepted my story. They have given up the way of the heathen and have confessed themselves Christians. Truly, Heaven has blessed me far beyond my merits."

Here Father Ambrosius stopped talking and he looked at me as if he expected me to give him an answer. But I could say nothing. All my life long I had heard of the faith that moved mountains and here I suddenly stood in the presence of the greatest of all miracles, the miracle of absolute and unquestioning simplicity of heart.

It was a strange experience, and I was still sitting in silence when Father Ambrosius got up and went to his bedroom to get his moccasins and his coat.

"I am sorry that I shall have to leave you for a little while," he said, "but things are not well in the village. The people seem restless. They are in fear of something and I don't know what. I think that I have taught them to look upon life in a more reasonable and intelligent way. But such things take time. Once in a while their old devils whom I chased away some fifteen years ago try to come back and then I have to fight hard to hold my own. This seems to be one of those occasions. What has happened this time is still a mystery to me, but I shall probably know in another two or three weeks. Meanwhile it won't do any harm if I am seen about the village a little more than usual. It gives my children a feeling of confidence. 'Behold,' they say, 'the Father is about watching over us and all is well.' Don't wait for me. Don't sit up for me. It may take me a couple of hours. Go to bed and happy dreams!"

And he left me and I hobbled to my couch and the room was filled with a strange light and when I looked out of the window, behold! the sky was a bright red, and at first I thought that it must be the northern lights, which had been particularly brilliant the last few days. But then I noticed that the glow came from the west and with a shock I realized what had happened. Some one had set fire to a village on the other side of the lake.

Chapter 35

A FAIRY TALE IN THE WILDERNESS AND WHAT BECAME OF IT

Poor Father Ambrosius! The next two weeks were the most miserable of his whole life. Everything he had worked for came tumbling down with a crash and a smoldering ruin was all that remained of his efforts of the last twenty years.

I did not see the end. I only saw the beginning, and that was sad enough. For this was not merely a physical defeat of a man pitched against a group of enemies, it was the moral debacle of a fine and noble and courageous soul, beaten by the innate stupidity of nature-in-the-raw.

The good Father thought that his "fairy tale" had triumphed. He had filled the dreadful universe of these naked savages with the visions of his paradise—his wondrous heaven populated with beautiful angels and long-bearded beneficent saints—a realm of endless golden streets and infinite shining righteousness—the future home of all good little children willing to share his dream. And they had said, "Yea, verily, great Master," and they had come to hear him say mass and they had sent their children to listen to the wondrous chronicles of the Holy Family of Nazareth and their women had stayed after service to weep over the fate of one who had been utterly without blemish and yet had taken upon himself the agonizing task of shouldering this world's sins. And invariably when he had asked them whether they regretted having given up a belief in the gods of their fathers, they had answered him that nothing on earth could make them return to the worship of those false witnesses and he had been happy and he had persuaded himself that they spoke the truth.

But alas and alack! Without a single word of warning the old gods of the forest had suddenly reappeared from the mountain fastnesses wherein they had been hiding these many years. They had come proud and haughty as exiled princes who claim what is theirs by right of birth and their trembling subjects had welcomed them with open arms. Not because they loved them better than their new rulers. By no means. These ancient task-masters of their souls were dreadful tyrants. But they were flesh and blood of their own flesh and blood. They knew them and understood them, even though they hated and despised them. And when they stood once more outside the village-gate, waving the familiar old banners that had been handed down from father to son for thousands and thousands of generations, the humble subjects were as little birds before the gaze of the snake. They wavered. They grew pale. They fell upon their knees. They prostrated themselves in the dust of the road and whispered, "Yes, ye great and glorious Majesties, we thy servants welcome thee with open hearts and open arms," and everything was as it had been since the beginning of time and the work of Father Ambrosius disappeared as the smoke of one's fire on the shores of a stormy sea.

And all that because two little boys had tried to shoot the same wild turkey at the same moment and had had a quarrel as to who had seen him first.

As far as we could make out, this is what had happened. Those so-called Indian countries are not countries in our sense of the word. The Indians live by hunting. Here and there a tribe that is a little more civilized than the others will try its hand at agriculture or to be more precise, the Indian men will allow their women to try their hand at raising corn and grain, for the average Indian male is a noble grand-seigneur, brave as a lion when he is on the war-path, but lazy as the sloth when he is peacefully residing at home. Those tribes therefore need enormous tracts of land to keep themselves provided with the necessary number of deer and rabbits and bears that are needed for their daily support. And these hunting fields are not clearly defined tracts of land for there are no frontiers as we know them in Europe, but the Indian has a great respect for tradition and as a rule he respects the domain that is supposed to belong to his neighbor with scrupulous care. But once in a while these pieces of land overlap each other and then there is always a chance for trouble. And that is what had occurred in this case.

It seems that several centuries before the Eries, who now lived further westward, had occupied this part of the continent. But although they spent the greater part of each year on the shores of one of those big lakes that exist in the West and that many hold to be part of the Arctic Sea or even the Pacific Ocean, they still retained a vague hold upon certain rivers and brooks that ran through the land of the Cayugas and every year a number of Eries would walk all the way from their own country to that of the Cayugas (for these savages have never learned the use of the wheel and must carry everything on their own backs if they want to go anywhere) to spend a few weeks hunting turkeys and other small birds within the grounds that hundreds of years before had belonged to their ancestors.

It was a very unpractical arrangement, but the Cayugas respected the claims of the Eries because they had always done so, which in their language means a number of years all the way from twenty-five to a hundred. For when an Indian has once done something "always" he will continue to do so until the end of eternity.

This particular winter the Eries seemed to have come east a little earlier than usual. Perhaps there was some other reason for their unexpected appearance. There had been vague rumors of trouble between the Eries and those Hurons who lived on the other side of the big lake and it seemed that the Eries had suffered a severe defeat and that they were trying to get away before the coming of spring allowed the Hurons to descend upon them in full force.

But I only heard about this much later when I was safely back in Nieuw Amsterdam and besides, it made very little difference how and why the Eries had come at such an early date. They were there and that was enough or in this case, too much. For one morning an Erie boy of about fourteen had gone forth turkey hunting and a Cayuga boy of the same age had started upon the same errand and by a most unfortunate combination of circumstances, the two had seen the same turkey at the same moment. Each one of them had shot his arrow and both arrows had hit the mark. The turkey was dead and the boys had rushed eagerly forward to get hold of their prey. And then they had seen each other. And of course they had both grabbed at the dead bird and then one had said, "It is mine, I saw it first." And the other one had answered, "No, it is mine. I saw it first."

And then they had dared each other to touch it and then they had fought, but being of equal height and weight, the struggle had lasted quite a long time and then one of them had lost his temper and he had pulled his knife and stabbed the other boy in the back and then he had taken fright and had run away, leaving the corpse out in the open.

But in his excitement he had forgotten his knife, and therefore a small band of Cayugas, also looking for turkeys in that neighborhood and finding the body, had known that it had been an Erie who had committed this murder and a little later, meeting two peaceful Erie women going to a brook to do their washing, they had set upon them and had killed them, for such was the law of the tribe, or rather, such had been the law of the tribe until Father Ambrosius had tried to replace this dreadful code of an eye for an eye by the more merciful doctrine of a forgiveness which had first been promulgated on a hillside in distant Palestine.

But now they had smelled blood and everything they had learned during the last twenty years had been forgotten. They were Cayuga warriors and one of their clan had been killed without provocation. Such an action demanded revenge. And with a fell cry of joy, the ancient gods came rushing forth from their hiding places and joined in the fray. Before another week had passed, at least two dozen people had been killed on both sides. And when Father Ambrosius tried to remonstrate with his beloved children about the folly of such a course, they would listen patiently enough, but they would not let themselves be convinced. "Your God, who is now also our God, is a lover of peace! But the god of our enemies is a lover of war! Just now, he is stronger than your God and we must turn to our old gods to help us, lest we all perish."

They were genuinely sorry that all this had happened, but it had happened and they did not intend to accept defeat without putting up a terrific fight. The God of Father Ambrosius told them to turn the other cheek. They were very sorry but no Cuyaga had ever turned the other cheek unless in the game of love. They were more than sorry, they were humbly apologetic. But for the moment there was only one thing for them to do and they meant to do it, and every night they would leave their villages and go murdering and pillaging among the villages of the Eries and every night the Eries would go murdering and pillaging among the villages of the Cayugas and a vast number of people were killed and an enormous amount of material damage was done and nothing was ever decided, but gradually the Eries, who had got heavy reënforcements from the West, began to be more and more aggressive and the red glow that had lighted up the sky the night before was the first of the Cayuga settlements that had gone up in flames.

The question was, When would we ourselves be attacked? If it had been a few months later, the other four nations would undoubtedly have come to our support, but it had been a very severe winter and the roads were so thickly covered with snow that our messengers would need at least two weeks to reach the camps of the Oneidas and the Onondagas and in the meantime, we knew that we were left entirely to our own devices.

An effort was made to surround our village with a wooden palisade, but the ground was frozen so hard that it was very slow work and only a few yards were done when we heard that the community nearest to ours had been attacked during the previous night and that every man, woman and child had died fighting. Our town was to come next, and the situation was exceedingly serious.

Twice Father Ambrosius had tried to get in touch with the leaders of the Erie band, but they had refused to meet him. They were afraid of this mysterious man whose reputation had traveled all through the land of the Indians and who was thought to be possessed of some magic charm that made him invulnerable. Indeed, so far did this respect for the person of Father Ambrosius go, that the Eries sent one of their chiefs to our camp under a flag of truce to tell the Father that he was at liberty to go back to his own people any time he cared to do so. He was even offered a safe conduct through the land of the Eries if he wished to travel to Quebec by way of the River of Canada.

The good Father answered that he could not possibly return to his own people since at that very moment he was among those whom he considered his own people and he used the opportunity to suggest to the Erie chieftain that he and the Cayugas bury the hatchet or if they could not do that, declare a truce to find out whether the matter could not be settled by the payment of an indemnity. After all, boys would be boys and hot-tempered boys would occasionally do very foolish things, such as killing each other for the sake of a turkey that was not worth the hilt of a single knife. But that was no reason why grown-up men should do war upon each other and should destroy whole townships and should slaughter hundreds of innocent women and children, all of it because "the honor of the tribe had been touched," and he used the opportunity to tell the story of the Great White God, who had come into this world to teach all men that they are each other's brethren. But the Erie Chief merely listened and although he listened most politely, he said nothing, but drew his blanket around him, turned on his heels and departed whence he had come without uttering a single word.

That evening Father Ambrosius turned to me as we were having our supper and casually remarked, I have ordered your Mohawk guides to be here at seven in the morning. You won't be able to walk very far, but I have shown them how to make a stretcher and they will be able to carry you part of the way." And I answered, trying to be just as casual, "That is very kind of you, but of course I shall not go."

"But why not? I have got to stay. I have based my whole life upon the phantastic belief that love will be able to overcome all the evil of this world. Since I have been willing to live by it, I ought also to be willing to die for it. But you, you are a free man and you ought to go."

I agreed. "Yes, I suppose I should go, but we have a proverb at home —one of those homely little sayings that are drummed into our ears when we are still very young, until they become part of our philosophy of life and that proverb bids me stay."

"I would like to hear it."

"It is a very simple one. 'Out together, home together.' I don't suppose that that is a very elegant translation, but it has the virtue of being quite accurate. And when we were boys, it served a purpose. If we went on a trip together, no matter what adventures might befall us, we never thought of turning backward until all our comrades were safe and ready for the return trip. I am here. I stay here. And if we die, we die together. Then I shall at least have some one to show me the way to the Pearly Gate and that will be very pleasant."

Shortly afterwards Father Ambrosius made ready for his customary evening's round and I hobbled off to bed. I was still very weak and the cold weather caused my legs to ache a great deal more than they had done during the milder weeks early in February. Father Ambrosius had noticed that I tossed around a great deal of the night and he had made me a sleeping potion out of a plant which grew all over the hills near our lake and which bore a close resemblance to the Valeriana Officialis of our apothecary shops at home. It had a pungent smell and an acid taste. That evening, I noticed that the acid taste was stronger than usual, but I paid no attention to this as I had caught a cold a few days before and my sense of smell and of taste was not functioning any too well. I took off my coat and hat but kept on the rest of my clothes and went to bed.

When I woke up, I was lying on a stretcher on the ground. It was snowing hard but on one side a roughly made lean-to offered me some protection against the storm that was raging and it had also acted as a barrier against the snow. My two Mohawk guides, bundled up in their blankets, were sitting by my side.

"We thought that we might me able to keep you a little warmer this way," they explained. "As soon as the storm grows less, we shall try and make a fire."

I said, "Never mind the fire. Pick me up and take me back."

But they neither answered, nor did they make the slightest effort to get up. I grew angry and reached for the gun that I had seen lying by my side, but one of the Mohawks whispered, "We unloaded it by special orders." And then I understood everything.

But how did it happen that I had not awakened when they put me on the stretcher? And then I remembered the strange taste of my sedative the night before. In order to save me, Father Ambrosius had taken his precautions carefully and in order to be sure that I left, he had drugged me. For one addicted to fairy tales, the good priest had shown himself a good deal of a realist.

Well, there I was, and what was I to do next? Go back, but how was I to walk all that distance in that raging storm, I who had not walked a mile by myself during the last three or four months? I needed the help of my Mohawks if I were to accomplish anything at all and in order to gain their good will, I had to proceed very carefully and use tact. I first asked them what time it was and they told me that as far as they could make out it was two hours after sunrise.

When had they taken me away from the village?

They thought that it was shortly before midnight. The Father had come to them earlier in the evening and had told them to be ready to start in about three hours. They had packed their belongings and the Father had given them each an old-fashioned arquebus and four loaves of bread. Then they had sat in their tent and had waited until he came back. The Cayugas had not expected an attack that night on account of the threatening blizzard and had mostly stayed indoors. Shortly before midnight, Father Ambrosius had called for them and had conducted them to his cabin where I lay in so deep a sleep that at first they thought I was dead. They had put me on the stretcher and then the good Father had taken them to the outskirts of the village and had told them to make for the hills and not stop until it was daylight. I asked them whether he had given them any message. They said "No, he made the sign of the cross over you before he left and then returned to the camp and never looked back once. Then we picked you up and here we are."

I asked them what they meant to do and they said we would continue our way eastward as soon as the weather should improve a little.

I asked them whether they had heard anything all during the night and they nodded yes and I asked them whether it had been bad, and they said, "Yes, very bad. Everything must have been burned down."

And I asked them whether they would help me return and they answered no, and I called them cowards and pigeon-hearted turn-tails and all the other terrible names for which an Indian under ordinary circumstances will kill even his own father or brother, but they took it calmly and answered, "We are neither cowards nor pigeon-hearted turn-tails. We are only obeying the Father's instructions, because we love him." And as I was too weak to walk by myself, I had to submit and the next morning it stopped snowing and they built me a small sledge and placed me on it and wrapped me in their own warm blankets and we slowly and painfully began our voyage towards the east.

After five days we reached the first village of the Oneidas and when we told our story we were most kindly received by the Chief who gave us his own tent to live in and himself went to stay with his father-in-law and I paid my two Mohawks, who had been most faithful in their duties and gave them a letter to My Lord Stuyvesant in Nieuw Amsterdam, recommending them to him very seriously and suggesting that they be given some token of recognition by the Company, and I remained with the Oneidas until May when the snow had melted and the trails were passable once more.

Then members of all the Oneida tribe gathered in a valley near our camp and we went to a place which is called Owasco in their language and there we waited until the forces of all the Five Nations had come together and we marched against the Eries and when I asked permission to join the expedition, they told me that they would be very pleased if I would come, for they had heard that I was a famous medicine man (the old story of the Mohawk chief whom I had cured more than a year before, something which seemed to have made a profound impression upon the whole neighborhood) and for the first time in my life I found myself obliged to sit on top of a horse, a strange and terrible experience, as the animal moved all four feet at the same time and had the most uncomfortable habit of trying to nibble the buds of the shrubs we passed and of stopping in the middle of the rivers. But I was rapidly regaining my strength and if it had not been for the particular circumstances under which I was taking the trip, I would have enjoyed myself thoroughly.

After six days of trekking (there were about 300 of us and we moved very slowly) we approached the neighborhood of the lake where the quarrel between the Eries and the Cayugas had taken place the previous winter. But we could find no trace of the former. They had apparently been warned by their scouts and had completely disappeared. We afterwards heard what had happened to them after they had fled. A strong band of Senecas had tried to intercept them on their way to the Big Lake and in order to escape from any possible ambuscades they had swung a little towards the south. In this way they had been obliged to pass through the territory of the Susquehannocks, who had surprised them one evening, just when they were pitching camp and who after a short but fierce battle had killed every man, woman and child of them and had left their bodies to rot where they lay.

Such had been the end of an absurd little quarrel that had arisen when two boys had tried to capture the same turkey.

With the enemy gone, there was really nothing for us to do but return whence we had come. But I wanted to see the spot where I knew that my dear friend must have met his death and early one morning, accompanied by about a hundred warriors, I marched to the spot where our village had been located only a short time before. The snow had melted and the country was glorious with the flowers of spring. But the Eries had done their work so well that it took me the greater part of the morning to find the exact location where the massacre had taken place. Of the tents of the Indians nothing remained, but at last we discovered an ash heap and I decided that that had been the house in which I had spent the winter. Strangely enough, we found no skeletons, but the chief who was with me assured me that this was nothing unusual.

"The Eries would have been afraid of the ghosts of those they had slain unless they had first got rid of their corpses. They must either have buried them or they have thrown them in the lake, for as we all know, those who go down in that lake are never again found, as the spirit that dwells at the bottom keeps them there and makes them his slaves."

I had heard of this custom and was familiar with the fear the aborigines felt towards their dead and when the chief asked me whether I was ready to return, I said "Yes," for the scene was full of sad memories for me and there was no use in my staying there any longer.

But ere we broke camp I walked to the big oak tree that stood near the lake and underneath which Father Ambrosius had first explained the beautiful mysteries of his fairy tale to a curious group of old men and women. The tree had been left standing. It was the only one that had not been damaged by the fire. I walked past it to go to the lake when I saw a black object lying amidst the violets and dandelions which covered the hillside. I went nearer and looked at it. It was a skeleton dressed in a long, black cassock. It was lying on its back and the arms were spread wide. The empty sockets were facing the sky. Three arrows with little green feathers at the end were sticking out of his chest. And there Father Ambrosius had written "finis" to his fairy story.

We buried him where he lay and placed some heavy stones upon his grave and I carved a crude cross upon one of these and scratched the initials F. A. on both sides and after a little hesitation I added the letters S. J. Then I knelt down and said a prayer—for the first and last time in my life—and asked God to be very kind to the sweetest man I had ever met and let him dwell in that part of Paradise where the little children lived who still remembered what all the grown-ups had forgotten. Then I went back to the others and an hour later we were on top of the nearest hill and had our final glimpse of the lake.

And ever since I have wondered whether I had been the last white man to cast his eyes upon this lovely landscape which is so far away from the civilized world that even the most ambitious hunters and farmers will never dream of settling down there.

Chapter 36

NEWS FROM HOME

When I returned to Nieuw Amsterdam I discovered that my prolonged absence had caused great consternation. Bernardo, who was apparently still staying with his Mohawk friends, had written to Captain de Vries to tell him of the rumors he had heard about me: that I had reached the ultimate confines of the land belonging to the Five Nations—that I had met with an accident—that I was being taken care of in the house of an Indian chief near one of the smaller lakes a few miles east of the Pacific Ocean—and that I had probably been killed during the famous raid of the Chickasaws against the Onondagas early in the winter of that year.

This strange hodge-podge of information and misinformation had made the excellent captain take a special trip to the capital to try and obtain some further details from the hunters and trappers who gathered together every spring to sell their beaver and bear skins to the traders of the Company. They had indeed heard of some commotion in the region of the small lakes, but some thought it had been a quarrel between the Oneidas and the Algonquins and others knew for certain that it had been merely a little border skirmish between the Cayugas and the Cherokees, who lived almost a thousand miles further toward the south and were then in open warfare with the English who had settled in Virginia, but no one seemed able to tell him just exactly what had happened.

He was delighted therefore when he heard that I had returned and wrote me that he intended to visit Nieuw Amsterdam within a fortnight and hoped to see me. Meanwhile, after the years of comparative freedom, I had grown so accustomed to being my own master that I could no longer stand the restrictions imposed upon me by living in rented quarters. And as I had spent very little of My Lord Andries' money during the last two years (what I had with me when I met with my accident, Father Ambrosius had carefully packed in an old cassock of his and had put it underneath my pillow on the stretcher when he saved me from the massacre) I decided to invest a few hundred guilders in a little house of my own.

I bought a small piece of land from the bouwery which stood in the name of Wolfaert Gerritszoon. I got the land very cheap because it overlooked quite a large swamp, but this swamp which for the greater part of each year was very full of water, gave me the illusion of being near a lake. I found two Indians on Staten Island who said they could build me a wooden house such as were customary among the tribes of the Five

Nations, and they proved to be excellent workmen and in less than a month's time my own house was ready for occupancy.

As soon as it had been finished, I sent word to Bernardo asking him to come and join me but he favored me with a rather cryptic reply. It was a small piece of parchment with a rough drawing of an Indian on it, an Indian who bore a slight outer resemblance to Bernardo himself, and underneath it the cryptic words: "The Ten Lost Tribes have been joined by one more."

I therefore gave up hope of seeing him until I should be able to travel north once more and meanwhile waited for Captain de Vries who had been delayed by some trouble that had recently occurred in the settlement of Rensselaerwijk (the usual story of a greedy farmer selling a plentiful supply of gin to some of the natives who thereupon had got very drunk, had run amuck amongst the villages and had killed three women and two children before they themselves had been shot), but who finally made his appearance early in the month of August during a spell of such hot weather that my beloved swamp ran almost entirely dry and reminded me by its appalling smell of the happy days of my childhood spent among the mud flats of Veere. Not only did he come but he brought me a package that was most welcome to me as it contained nine letters which Jean-Louys had sent me during the previous two years.

"I ought to have sent these to you when I first heard that you had returned," he told me, "but people are so often careless with a small package like this, and so I thought I would wait and bring them myself. I could have sent it to the Fort, but the Governor is in one of his tempers. Some more trouble about that Board of Aldermen of the late but not lamented Willem Kieft, and I would rather not meet him when he is playing the rôles of Nero and Simon Maccabee all in one, stamping around in his little room and complaining that everybody in the whole colony is a traitor and ought to be hung. I know the old man means well, but when he gets in that mood, he is a hopeless bore."

"On the contrary," I answered, "I saw him only yesterday about the final sale of this piece of land. I want to buy that swamp too, otherwise some honest farmer will come here and drain it out of sheer force of habit and I would love to keep my little lake. I found him as soft as butter and as mild as a day in June. You never will guess what he was doing."

"Reading you his last missive to the Board of Eight, calling these worshipful gentlemen a gang of grasping rapscallions, low, lying, thieving scoundrels?"

"By no means! He was writing a poem. A poem about a sunset and a red sky and the happy husbandman slowly wending his way homeward."

"Was it as bad as all that?"

"It was worse. It was, I think, the most sentimental piece of poetry

OLD MAN SEATED IN AN ARMCHAIR

since the day of Tibullus, Tibullus with a wooden leg and a bald head. The whole thing was rather pathetic. For the old man no doubt is trying very hard to do his best and the Directors at home as usual are succeeding in doing their worst. And some fine day all this will come to a sudden end and there will be a terrible disaster and the old man knows it and he can't do anything about it and so he spends his leisure hours writing sweet little elegies about pink sunsets and the virtues of the old Roman matrons. And now please let me have my letters."

The captain gave me a small bundle done up carefully in a leather bag. "Keep the bag," he said, "and read your letters. I hear that our grand duke is laying out a place of his own somewhere around here."

"So he is. The house has been begun. Go and have a look at it and be back at three and we will have dinner."

The captain left me and I spent the next four hours catching up with life on the other side of the ocean. There were nine letters in all. I had thought that they were all from Jean-Louys, but one proved to be from Selim. It was very short and sounded rather sad.

"This big city has grown very lonely," he wrote, "since you and Bernardo have left. Jean-Louys is a charming person, but he is mixing more and more mathematics into his omelettes and I do not like to sit down to a meal when I have first been invited to draw the cubic root from the soup and find the decimal points in the pudding.

"It may be true that God is merely an abstraction and a formula which M. Descartes will solve for us one of these days, but my brain is not strong enough to follow our friend there. And so I sit by myself much of the time.

"Of late I have been greatly diverted by the visits of the Reverend Simon Gallinovius, the son of honest Jan Kippenei, whom you will remember from our trip to the Diemermeer. The old fellow kept the third tavern on the left side of the road outside the Saint Anthonie gate. His promising young offspring desires to make a name for himself and hopes to do so by converting the diplomatic representative of the grand Padisha. Can't you see me going up for baptism in an enormous green turban and that long red robe of office that goes with my high rank? Well, I cannot, but he apparently can. He thinks it would be a fine feather in his dignified biretta.

"His mode of attack is rather unique and causes me a great deal of amusement. He has actually taken the trouble to read the Koran in a Spanish translation. He tells me that he has come to the conclusion that Mohammedanism and Calvinism are the same, as both creeds believe in the pre-ordination of every fact connected with human existence. This undoubtedly is a new point of view and it ought to be interesting to the sort of people who are able to take an interest in that sort of thing.

"But I am bored and the banks of the Bosphorus begin to look more and more attractive to this peace-loving exile. Three more visits from the long-winded Gallinovius and I shall set sail for the land of my fathers.

"What am I doing here anyway? What are any of us doing anywhere, anyway? When a man gets in that mood, you may be prepared for any sort of news.

"I embrace you and the excellent Bernardo. Mark my word, that boy will turn native if you do not look out. He is as much of a wanderer as I am. He is almost as lonely. Allah have mercy upon the likes of us. Farewell!"

Followed by a postscript: "Your good friend Rembrandt has been to see me once or twice. That man has a veritable passion for Turks. He wants me to pose for him. I asked him whether he was running short of models and he said, 'No, but my models are mostly Dutch vagabonds. I can dress them up in silks and satins and put a turban on their heads, but that does not make them Turks. They remain what they were before, Dutch vagabonds who happen to be dressed up in Moslem finery.' Perhaps I shall oblige him one of these days, if only the chicken-egged divine will leave me alone."

The letter was more or less what I might have expected. I turned to the forty or fifty pages covered with Jean-Louys' precise handwriting and I found that they contained a complete history of the last two years, as far as he and I were concerned.

The French often exasperate me. Not infrequently their actions fire me with disgust. They are unreliable and careless to a degree. They have no conception of neatness or order as these virtues are practiced at home. They are quarrelsome and vain. But when I have worked myself up into a complete and perfect detestation of the French nation and all its works, some individual Frenchman will do or say or write something that makes me forget all the manifold annoyances I have suffered at the hands of his race and makes me feel that the world without France would be as dull and uninteresting as a wedding party without music.

These letters of Jean-Louys had a beginning, a middle part (a core would be a better expression) and an end. They told me nothing too much and nothing too little. In their way they were as perfect as the meals he sometimes served us and which left one with a feeling of utter contentment without the unpleasant accompanying sensation of being too replete. I liked these epistles so much that I gave them to the Governor to read and he told me that they had given him more and better information about conditions at home than all the endless reports from his directors. He asked to be allowed to keep them a little longer and eventually forgot to return them when I unexpectedly sailed for home. He sent them after me on the *Drie Croonen,* but the ship went down on the coast of Virginia and was never heard of again. I therefore must rely upon my memory to reconstruct the most important items they contained.

Every letter began with the news that just before writing it Jean-Louys had visited my house on the Houtgracht and had found my son to be in perfect health. The child had completely forgotten me (as was of course to be expected), he was growing up to be a fine boy, had nice manners and went to see Master Rembrandt twice a week to be instructed in the art of drawing. He seemed to have a decided gift for that form of art and Rembrandt was devoting a great deal of his time to helping the boy along.

Then he talked of more serious matters. The long expected had happened at last, peace had been declared between Spain and the Republic and the latter had been fully and most officially recognized as an independent and sovereign nation. The old Prince had not lived to see this final victory of the cause for which he had fought so long and so bravely. He had died a few months before. His end had been very sad, a complication of diseases as a result of the hard life he had led during his endless campaigns. His legs had been so swollen that he could no longer mount on horseback. Then he had had several attacks of lung trouble and finally his brain had given out and during the last two weeks of his earthly existence his nurses had been obliged to take care of him as if he had been a small child.

His son, the one who had married the English woman, had succeeded him as commander-in-chief of the army and might cause considerable trouble. For he was a very ambitious young man who wanted to gain as great a reputation as a strategist as his father and uncle had enjoyed before him. It was generally known that the young Prince had used all his influence to avoid the conclusion of peace until he should at least have added Brussels and Antwerp to the territory of the Republic. But the Burgomasters of Amsterdam were dreadfully afraid of such a step. They feared the rivalry of Antwerp if it should ever be made a Dutch city. They had control of the Scheldt and as long as Antwerp remained a city in the hands of their enemies, they were able to treat her as such and by closing the Scheldt they could ruin their old rival. Amsterdam therefore had declared flatly in favor of an immediate conclusion of peace and as usual, Amsterdam had won.

Their Lordships of the Town Hall and His Highness the Prince now regarded each other as open and avowed enemies and it was feared that hot-headed young Willem was planning a coup against the city that had dealt such a blow to his pride. Thus far nothing had happened, but this friction between the two most powerful bodies within the State had caused a feeling of uneasiness which was doing a great deal of harm.

This came at a very inopportune moment, as business conditions were already very bad. As long as the Republic had been at war with Spain, it had been possible for us to organize a world-wide system of smuggling at the expense of our Spanish opponents. But now that Spain was a friendly nation and no longer a foe to be plundered at will, these smuggling concerns had lost millions of guilders.

Then there were the large number of industries that had been engaged, directly or indirectly, in building ships and making cannon and fabricating gun-powder and looking after the thousand and one needs of an army that was forever in the field and a navy that was rarely in port. Of course the ship yards could now begin to work for the commercial marine and sails and ropes would probably be needed as much as before, but there were many articles for which there was no longer any demand. That would mean a great deal of loss to the original investors and it would mean that thousands of people would be thrown out of employment and this was already becoming very noticeable to any one who ever walked in the direction of the harbor. Where formerly the shipping firms had been obliged to resort to crimps and soul-sellers to get their vessels manned, their offices were now besieged by hordes of hungry men, often accompanied by equally hungry women and children who asked that they be given a chance to take a trip to the Baltic or the Indies.

Then there were the soldiers and the sailors of the navy, all of them out of a job and taking every day more and more to organized brigandage as a means of gaining an honest livelihood. All this of course was greatly affecting the money market and the failure of two or three important houses which had speculated upon a continuation of the war and had filled their store-houses with enormous quantities of supplies which now went for a song, had shaken public confidence so severely that it would be years before the situation could possibly hope to return to normal.

And of course, as Jean-Louys remarked several times, the poor artists will be the first to notice this scarcity of ready money. Rembrandt had told him that he had not had an order for a new portrait for over six months and the others seemed to fare no better. During the first moment of triumph there had been a slight demand for allegorical pictures to celebrate the manifold victories of the Dutch nation. But the two most important orders had gone to Flinck and to van der Helst, two of Rembrandt's pupils. The master himself had been passed. He had tried his hand at an imaginary historical picture representing the pacification of Holland and he had made a number of sketches for it. But no one wanted it and it was still standing in his studio at the time of writing. So were a great many of his other pictures. Nothing he touched seemed to be a success nowadays. He still had an occasional order for a portrait, but he was rapidly being forgotten for a number of younger men who not only charged less but were much more obliging when it came to giving their model his own way.

Indeed, throughout those eight letters there ran an undercurrent of deep and serious worry about the house in the Jodenbreestraat. The terrible nurse was still there, more noisily devoted to little Titus than ever before, but growing more and more unbearable as the years went on. Often indeed it seemed as if she were going out of her mind. Then she would button-hole the unfortunate visitors who came to see her master and would not let them go until she had told them all her woes—how she slaved and worked for little Titus, how she had even made a will in his favor leaving him everying she had in this world, how she, through her own exertions, was keeping the household going because "he," pointing to the door of the master's work-room, was too lazy and too indifferent to attend to anything, but she was not going to stand for it much longer. She could tell a great many things about herself and the famous Rembrandt van Rijn that would astonish the world if it ever became known, a great many things, and had they ever seen the pearls he had given her and the golden ring? And so on and so forth, to the great embarrassment of the unsuspecting visitors who gradually began to avoid the house of the master rather than expose themselves to one of the whining parties of the wild-eyed nurse with her eternal wail that Rembrandt had not done right by her.

No one knew what this situation would lead to, but several friends had at last combined to go directly to Rembrandt and suggest that he have the woman examined by some medical man who was familiar with the subject of lunacy. Rembrandt had listened patiently, as he always did, and had thanked them for their kind interest. He had agreed that the woman ought to go, but he had hinted at several difficulties which made it impossible for him to be as drastic as he wanted to be.

What those mysterious "difficulties" were, Jean-Louys could not tell me. Some people thought that Rembrandt had borrowed money from Geertje which he was unable to pay back at that moment. The inheritance of Saskia had never yet been settled. Any lawsuit involving money would cause the court to examine the financial affairs of both parties and the general opinion was that Rembrandt was not in a position where he could afford to have the magistrates pry a little closely into his business arrangements.

He was working harder than ever and was turning out a very large number of exceedingly beautiful and interesting etchings. But he had retired so completely from the company of his former friends that no one knew exactly how he stood in regard to those funds he was supposed to be administering for the benefit of his small son. No one even could say within five or ten thousand guilders how much there was left for the boy. Everything was all in a terrible muddle and as Rembrandt himself never kept any accounts—invested his money in a most haphazard way—buying an interest in a shipping firm one day and a painting by Raphael the next, it was impossible to make any sort of a guess as to the funds that were at his disposal.

A few goods friends had offered to arrange matters for him—to put some order into this chaos—but he had thanked them most kindly but also most determinedly. He himself would attend to this matter as soon as he had finished a new etching on which he had set great hope. It was a picture of Christ healing the sick and he meant to sell it for a hundred guilders, a record price for etchings. That print would once more bring him into the public eye. Then he would be able to enjoy a little leisure from the pot-boilers he had been obliged to make the last three or four years and he would call on some good and reliable notary to come and help him with his accounts and straighten everything out. Until then, he would just have to put up with the woman as best he could and meanwhile she was full of care for little Titus.

It was the same old story, but with a different refrain. And it made Jean-Louys fear that there was some other reason for his unwillingness or inability to send the nurse packing. Rembrandt had lived a very solitary life since Saskia's death. For all anybody could tell, he might have promised Geertje that he would marry her, or she might be in the family way, or she might pretend to be in the family way and blame the master. It was very difficult to get at the truth with an hysterical woman like that and so there was nothing to do but wait until the situation had taken care of itself.

And as the weeks and months went by, it was more and more likely that some crisis would occur which would rid Rembrandt of his unpleasant companion. Meanwhile his friends hoped and prayed that this would happen before the situation developed into a public scandal. Already there had been a few veiled references from the pulpit about people who had better heal themselves before they made pictures of the Saviour healing others and one reverend gentleman had gone so far as to hint that one of the figures in the supper at Emmaus closely resembled the servant in the house of a certain famous artist who himself was in the habit of giving supper parties, but of a very different nature.

The problem therefore was to get the woman safely out of the house before this whispering campaign got a little too outspoken, but no one could foretell what would happen, as Rembrandt in all things, both good and bad, was known to be almost as obstinate as the gallant warrior who was then reported to be at the head of the government of the New Netherlands and with this charming compliment at the address of My Lord Stuyvesant, the excellent Jean-Louys, who knew that letters were sometimes opened and read by the authorities, closed his account of affairs in the Jodenbreestraat.

He then told me a lot of gossip about European affairs, most of which I already knew; that the English were on the point of executing their King for a series of crimes which seemed to be rather vague, but that, as His Majesty had gained the reputation of being one of the most accomplished liars of his or any other time and had broken his word so repeatedly that no one could trust him for longer than two minutes at a time, he would probably be condemned to death, but whether he was going to be hanged or merely decapitated no one could as yet foretell; that the government probably would fall into the hands of some one called Cromwell, who was certain to proclaim himself king and would cause a great deal of trouble to the Republic, as he was known to be strongly in favor of a very drastic policy of protection for all British interests; that there was a rather amusing quarrel between the French crown and the nobility of that country, and that an Italian by the name of Mazarini, a former henchman of the infamous Cardinal Richelieu, had now got hold of the French government by making himself indispensable to the old king's wife, a Spanish lady with whiskers and not very bright, whom he flattered in the elegant Spanish manner which he had learned during the days of his youth when he was a flunkey in the suite of Prince Colonna and had accompanied that noble gentleman to the University of Alcala to inspect the original manuscript of the Polyglot Bible and place a wreath on the cradle of the great Don Miguel de Cervantes; that this shrewd Sicilian, a master-piece of Jesuit educational skill, who looked like a Portuguese Jew and who stole money from the Public Treasury with the grace of a Neapolitan prostitute going through the pockets of an English lord, would soon break the resistance of the nobles and that it was extremely doubtful whether the French monarchy would go the way of its English counterpart, although many people in the Republic counted on such an outcome; that the "usual" trouble between Amsterdam and Denmark and Sweden about the tolls levied in the Sund was in the "usual" state of being almost settled by either war or a treaty; that for the rest, nothing of any importance had happened except that the most eminent and learned Doctor Descartes had paid a brief visit to his native country upon which occasion the Spanish-Italian-French cardinal had honored him with an annual pension of three thousand francs and the promise of a position at court, which seemed a strange ambition for the author of the "Discourse of Method" and the "Principles of Philosophy," but then, even very learned people must eat: and so on and so forth, forty-eight pages long.

I was reading these letters for the third time when Captain de Vries returned.

"A strange experience!" I told him. "The Old World suddenly making its presence felt in the New. I wonder what has happened to me? Those things used to interest me. They used to interest me most tremendously. They were part of my life. And now it is just as if some one were making music in a room in another part of the house. I try to listen, but it means nothing to me, except a little, vague noise—not very interesting and rather annoying and upsetting. What has happened to me?"

"It is the fresh air and the horizon. That strange horizon of ours. In Europe, a horizon means the end of something old and familiar. Here it means the beginning of something new and unknown. That horizon will get you as it has got most of us. Unless those old fools in Amsterdam who rule us without ever having seen us force me to go away (as well they may if they continue their present policy of acting as dry-nurses to ten thousand people at the other end of the ocean) I shall never return to the mother country. I would smother and die for lack of fresh air in one of our nice, respectable little cities. Another six months and you will feel the same way."

I confessed that I had already fallen a victim to the pleasant hallucination of space.

"Then send for your boy and set up as a surgeon right here. La Montagne won't mind. He is getting old and hates to go out nights. The others are quacks. Settle down here. Take you a wife and be happy!"

And I might have followed his advice if it had not been for the scrap of paper that reached me exactly two months later and that said nothing but: "I wish you would come home. I need your help and your friendship very badly," and that was signed with a large capital letter R.

Chapter 37

THE TEN LOST TRIBES ARE JOINED BY ONE MORE

A week after the departure of Captain de Vries, who was obliged to return to Vriesendael, I decided that I would pay a visit to Bernardo, for all efforts to make him write me a letter and tell me in some detail what had happened to him had failed. He had sent me three fine beaver-skins, but never a word and so I made up my mind that I would go north once more and discover for myself how he was getting along in his search for Israel's Lost Tribes.

The colony was once more at peace with the Indians—the weather was lovely and I took the greater part of the voyage in a canoe which to my way of thinking is by far the most comfortable instrument of transportation this world has ever seen. It may be true that the Indians were not intelligent enough to invent the wheel and had to wait for us to come and show them how to make a wagon, but they were bright enough to devise the canoe and I am willing to give a thousand rumbling vehicles for a single quietly moving canoe and my only regret is that we have never been clever enough to adopt this craft for home consumption. It would set us free from the tyranny of the canal boat and I can't think of a single other thing that would do us more good than a whole-hearted rebellion against this depressing and exasperating ark of gossip and scandal.

A noble wish, but an absurd one. Ten thousand skippers would arise in all their might, a hundred thousand horses would stamp their feet in righteous anger. Burgomasters and Estates would be bombarded with petitions of outraged citizens and even more outraged labor guilds and the offending canoes would be condemned to be burned by the public executioner.

Meanwhile as long as I live I shall never forget the leisurely trip I took up the great river on my way towards the North. It was a wonderful experience. A slight haze was hanging over the water. We could only see the tops of the mountains that surrounded the flood and these were covered with the greenest of green trees. We could not make much headway against the current and the trip took the better part of five days. Then three days on foot, but my legs had entirely recovered and I could walk all day without feeling the slightest fatigue.

I had not sent word to Bernardo that I was coming. I wanted to surprise him. Instead of which I was the one to receive a surprise. For when I reached the village where I had bade him good-by two years before

I heard that he had left and was living in a large wooden house about ten miles further towards the North.

I found the house and I found Bernardo, so completely changed, so bronzed and so healthy looking, that at first I took him for an Indian brave and he threw both arms around me and kissed me and took me into the house where a very young and very handsome Indian woman was nursing a baby and he said, "Behold the additional Lost Tribe! and now go back to the good Rabbi Menasseh and give him my love and admiration and tell him that I am never, never, never coming back.

"I have not discovered a trace of the other Ten Tribes. They probably had the same experience I did and once they were lost, they liked it so well that they stayed lost.

"But I have found myself. I am happy. This woman is a joy of grace and beauty. This child is the handsomest thing that was ever born. I shall miss you and I shall miss my other friends at home, but in losing all that I have gained more than I ever thought possible.

"For the first time in my life I am not a Jew, but a man. Nobody here knows or cares whence I came. I had to learn a thousand new things before I could keep myself modestly alive. But I have learned them and now I ask for nothing but that I be allowed to stay where I am. And there is really only one thing you can do for me. Go home and tell them I was eaten up by a bear. There are no bears here but they won't know the difference. Tell them that I went down his gullet loving them all and sending them my blessing. But tell them that I am dead and gone. And now come in and I will cook you a steak. But not just an ordinary steak—a steak I shot and killed myself and afterwards I shall give you some of the wine I made myself and afterwards the woman will sing our son to sleep and if you have ever heard anything lovelier, don't tell me, for I would not believe you anyway."

And that is how Bernardo Mendoza Soeyro, who had the blood of the kings of Israel in his veins, who had spent two years in a dungeon of the Portuguese Inquisition, and who for more than ten years had kept books for Isaac Ashalem, the fish dealer of the Lazarus Street in Amsterdam, came to die as an Indian chieftain and now lies buried underneath a small mound of stones and earth in the forests that are the hereditary hunting-grounds of the famous tribe of the Mohegans.

Once or twice after I returned to Nieuw Amsterdam I heard from Bernardo. When he knew that I was obliged to return home, he sent me a leather suit for my boy "with Uncle Bernardo's love," and a tiny silver box for Jean-Louys "just large enough to hold one thought at a time—the thought of a very dear friend who has found complete happiness," but he never wrote me a letter, except an occasional verbal message that all was well with him and that his new daughter was almost as handsome a creature as his son.

But that was all. He felt that the old and the new could not be successfully combined. His new life meant everything to him. He allowed the old one to disappear from his memory completely.

Years afterwards, it was in the fall of '62, I received the visit of a captain of the West India Company who had come to port a few days earlier in command of the good ship the *Drie Burghers*. He told me that on his last visit to Nieuw Amsterdam the Governor had sent for him and had given him a letter. "This was delivered to me," His Lordship had explained, "for a certain Jan van Loon, a surgeon from Amsterdam who was here for some time during the late forties. I don't know whether he is still alive, but you will easily be able to find out when you get back home. Give it to him with my compliments."

It was a piece of birch-bark, the birch-bark the Indians are so clever at using for a large number of purposes. On it with red paint was a picture of a man lying on what seemed to be a couch that stood beside a tree. There was a woman in the background and five funny little figures that looked like children. The writing, done in a very shaky hand, had become almost illegible.

I took it to Rembrandt, who like so many near-sighted people, was very clever at reading small print, and together we puzzled it out.

"My time has nearly come," it said, "but I am willing to go. It has been a good life and I have cheated fate. For I have been happy after all."

It was Bernardo's epitaph.

Not entirely according to the traditions of the Mendoza family.

But they never knew.

So what was the difference?

Chapter 38

I HAVE CERTAIN DOUBTS ABOUT THE SUPERIOR VIRTUES OF THE SO-CALLED "WHITE MEN" AS COMPARED TO THEIR COPPER-COLORED BRETHREN OF THE NEW WORLD

There still was one part of the Nieuw Netherlands which I had not visited during my tour of inspection and it seemed that that was the most important section for the purpose which My Lord Andries and his brother had in mind. The northern and western regions I had examined quite carefully. They would have been of great value to us four or five hundred years ago when our people were obliged to wear furs or freeze in our damp and uncomfortable houses. But now that even the simplest artisan could afford to have a chimney and with those wonderful new stoves they had recently invented in Germany, ordinary woolens were all that were needed and one hardly ever saw a piece of fur worn from one year to another except among the very rich who wanted to show their neighbors how opulent they were.

The beaver-skins were still useful for hats, but it was so easy for our people to make money in other ways than by hunting that I could not for the life of me see how My Lord Andries would ever be able to induce emigrants to go all the way to America to lead the miserable and dangerous existence of trappers.

Of course if those forests I had visited had been a little nearer to the sea, they would have provided us with excellent timber for our ships. But upon the occasion of my last visit to the Fort, the Governor had shown me a letter from Amsterdam in which he was informed that the Emperor and the King of Sweden and the King of Spain and all the other potentates who had been fighting each other for the last thirty years, had at last concluded peace (after three and a half years of preliminary discussions and negotiations) and if this news was true, it meant that the Black Forests were once more accessible to our wood merchants and the cost of transporting beams and masts from Nieuw Amsterdam to the wharves of the Zaan would be prohibitive compared to the ease with which rafts of German fir-trees could be floated down the Rhine.

I had received several letters from My Lord Andries and his brother since my arrival. They had told me that they wanted to modify their plans a little, if such changes were at all feasible. The West India Company was going from bad to worse. The shares were so little in demand that the Amsterdam exchange had ceased to include them in their list of current stocks. Soon it would be possible to buy thousands of acres for a song. Was there any land that could be used to raise spices? They were glad to hear of the timber possibilities, but expected little of such a development as business with Germany had recently been assured (this bore out the news in Governor Stuyvesant's letter). They still had great expectations of their scheme for the wholesale importation of grain. But was there any part of the New Netherlands where they might expect to grow pepper, for which there was an ever-increasing demand, or nutmeg which was greatly gaining in popularity among all classes of society, or even tobacco?

They had heard that there had been serious outbreaks of hostility in the English colony of Virginia where the best tobacco came from. Rumors on the Exchange even mentioned figures and reported that during the last Indian massacre more than 400 white settlers had been killed. Furthermore, Their Lordships had been informed that most of the colonists were royalists and now that the King had been executed, was there any chance of these people starting a rebellion against Parliament and either declaring themselves independent or, from fear of their Spanish neighbors, accepting the protection of the Dutch Company?

Well, all these were questions to which I could not possibly give an adequate reply without doing a great deal of first-hand investigating. It took about two weeks to go from Nieuw Amsterdam to Virginia by sea and no one had ever attempted the voyage on land. Besides, in order to get there, the traveler would have been obliged to pass through the property of a new and upstart company which besides was in popish hands.

This was not of very great importance, for every skipper who had ever been there (and there was quite a brisk trade between the New Netherlands and the different plantations along the Chesapeake Bay) told me that the Calverts who owned the colony outright (and did not have to bother about boards-of-directors or stock-holders, but who were as free and independent as regular monarchs) were very liberal-minded and intelligent people and cared not whether one was Lutheran or a Papist or even a Jew or a Turk as long as one paid liberally and paid in cash. And most of them added that they would much rather spend a whole winter off Kent Island than a single month in the harbor of Plymouth, where the populace, especially since their own party had been victorious in the mother country, acted with great arrogance towards all foreigners. And especially we Hollanders, whose prince was married to a daughter of the king whom they had just killed, were looked upon with great suspicion.

Then there was the eternal quarrel about the boundary lines between the two colonies. The governors who had preceded My Lord Stuyvesant had allowed their English neighbors to make themselves at home in any part of the New Netherlands. But "Stubborn Piet" was of different caliber from the Kiefts and Krols and Twillers. Settlers from Massachusetts were welcome as subjects of the Gentlemen Nineteen, but unless they renounced their former allegiance they were bade to return whence they had come. Fortunately I would never be obliged to travel north again, and I quietly began to make my preparations for an interesting trip through the southern region that was to take me all the way from the Lange Eiland to the James River and the land of the Powhatans.

Several of the Indian tribes through whose countries I would have to pass, were reputed to be of a very fierce and warlike disposition and several people (even the old governor, who seemed to take a genuine interest in my well-being) counseled me to provide myself with an armed guard as soon as I should reach the neighborhood of the Potomac River.

I must confess that I did not know what to do. I was not my own master but was responsible for my well-being to the men who had entrusted me with their money. In the end I invited both Captain de Vries and Doctor La Montagne to my house one day (I had also begun to lay out a garden and was rather proud of my first efforts) and I put the case before them, as they were the only two men in the entire colony who seemed to have taken the trouble to try and understand the point of view of the natives.

They both declared themselves strongly opposed to the idea of taking an armed guard of colony soldiers. "They would only be a hindrance," the wise old doctor told me. "They will get sick. Most of them are not in the best of health when they arrive here and the water-front usually does the rest. They never take any precautions and as a result they catch every fever and every ache that hides within these forests and marshes. Worst of all, they will go chasing after the native women and that invariably leads to murder and bloodshed and revenge; and as the Indian code asks an eye for an eye and a tooth for a tooth, but is not very particular whose eye and whose tooth it is that get sacrificed (as long as they are the eye and the tooth of a white man) you yourself would be in continual danger."

"Besides," the shrewd captain added, "no number of soldiers you could possibly take with you could protect your expedition against the thousands of natives that live in these southern regions if they really meant to do you harm. On the other hand, if they felt inclined to treat you hospitably, they would appreciate your visit all the more if you came alone and unarmed. Such a policy would flatter their pride. It would show them that you were inclined to trust them—that you regarded them as honorable gentlemen. And no matter how lazy and dirty the Indians may be, they all of them possess the rudimentary instincts of a grand seigneur. Appeal to their nobler emotions and they will treat you as one of their equals. Go blundering through their country with a couple of dozen foreign mercenaries, toting arquebuses and halberds, and everywhere you will be received with suspicion, and a single man putting his hands on a squaw or a girl will mean the sign for a massacre."

All of which sounded so eminently sane to me that I decided to act upon the advice of those dear friends and wrote to Governor Stuyvesant that I was deeply grateful for his offer but that in view of the bad feeling that seemed to exist between the Republic and the commonwealth of Oliver Cromwell and the danger of a war that might be extended to the New World, I did not wish to deprive His Excellency of any of his troops and that I had made up my mind to make the trip alone, accompanied only by my two faithful Mohegan guides, who, as soon as they had learned that I expected to start upon a new voyage, had paddled all the way down to Nieuw Amsterdam to offer me their services.

There was only one more subject of worry—that note from Rembrandt. I felt that he needed me badly. He had treated me with abominable rudeness just before I left, but I could bear him no ill-will on account of that unseemly outburst of anger. I remembered my poor brother and what he had suffered. I had no idea whether Rembrandt was in love with Geertje. I did not think so. He had been romantically devoted to Saskia, but he was a man of terrific physical energy, and sat all day before his easel, while he spent the greater part of the night working at his etchings. It is always extremely dangerous for a man of such sedentary habits to be left alone with a woman who is not only of a rather attractive exterior but whose eyes and lips betray great sensuousness.

In short, what I feared and what Jean-Louys seemed to fear (unless I had very much misread his last letters) was this, that the woman had seduced Rembrandt, or to speak a little less harshly, that circumstances had induced the two to forget the strict rules of morality that prevailed in our country. I cared not a whit for those rules, but I knew our clergy, and the cruel gossip of a town like Amsterdam. One definite word of disapprobation on the part of a well-known preacher and the van Rijn family would be ruined, both socially and economically.

It was a terrible thing to leave a man alone at a moment like that, but I considered myself in the service of the Bicker family until I should have accomplished everything they had asked me to do. Besides a contract was a contract. Wherefore I sat me down and wrote to Rembrandt and told him that if all went well, I would be back in Amsterdam early the next fall, that I promised him to take the first boat available as soon as I should have returned from my trip to the South, and if he had any troubles, to talk them over with Jean-Louys, who was the most trustworthy of friends and of good, sound, common sense, though he usually tried to hide his true emotions underneath a cloak of wit and raillery. And I told him that when I sailed into the harbor of Amsterdam, I expected to find him standing near the Montelbaanstoren with little Titus, to whom I sent my best love. I omitted all reference to Geertje and purposely left her name out of my letter. That seemed the better policy to me, though God knows, I may have been wrong.

This letter I gave to My Lord the Governor and the next day I left for the South. During this trip I made the only discoveries which could possibly have been of any practical use to My Lord Andries and I therefore do not think it proper for me to give an account of this expedition in a book that deals with my personal adventures and reflections.

I left Nieuw Amsterdam late in the fall and returned ten months later after a very successful and comfortable voyage, during which I never for a single moment regretted the wise counsel of my two friends who had urged me to dispense with an armed guard and put my faith in my own courage and good fortune rather than the dozen cut-throats whom the kind-hearted governor had most generously placed at my disposal.

Chapter 39

I TALK POLITICS WITH MY LORD STUYVESANT, WHO TAKES A GLOOMY VIEW OF THINGS

As soon as I reached Nieuw Amsterdam, I called on My Lord Stuyvesant, whom I found little changed, though he complained a great deal of pain in the stump of his leg. This leg had been badly smashed by a Portuguese cannon-ball during an attack on one of the West Indian islands several years before. The wounded man had been sent to Leyden in the hope that one of the surgeons connected with the medical school could save it, but gangrene having set in during the trip home they had been obliged to operate as soon as he reached his sister's house. The operation, however, had not been performed with sufficient care and especially during the hot months of the summer the poor man suffered terrible agonies when he hopped around on one of his daily trips of inspection.

As we handled a great many cases like that in our Amsterdam hospital (in a town which was visited every year by so many thousand ships, broken arms and legs were almost as common as beggars and pimps) I had acquired a certain routine in handling this affliction and I was able, by slightly changing the angle at which the stump was fastened to the artificial leg, to alleviate His Excellency's discomfort. As a result of which he treated me with even greater affection than before and offered me a position of great trust. Indeed, he asked me to act as the personal intermediary between himself and the Board of Directors in Amsterdam.

"For," as he remarked one day when we were sitting on a bench outside the Fort and were contemplating the river front, "here we are possessed of what is probably the finest natural harbor in the whole world and what have we done to assure ourselves of the continued occupancy of this spot? Nothing! Absolutely nothing! There is a fort. At least, we call it a fort. Look at it! Cows grazing on the walls and pigs wallowing in the ditch that should be a moat.

"People blame me. But what can I do? I have no money. The Company has no money. I have no men. The Company sends me endless letters protesting that there are no funds to send me more troops.

"The inhabitants, my beloved subjects, poke fun at me and call me the Grand Duke of Muscovy! If I were as bad as all that, ninety percent of this rabble would be hanging from the trees of Staten Island. I would not even care to hang them here on Manhattan. All of them have come to America to grow rich over night. But as soon as they had set foot on land, they discovered that the Company meant them to stay poor, that they could not plant a tree or cut down a bramble-bush without asking permission from some one at home.

"If they only gave me free rein, I could change all that over night. But Their Lordships won't let me do a thing. They even wrote me a letter last week in which they told me how long the sermons ought to be that are preached here every Sunday and Wednesday.

"Meanwhile, now that they have got rid of their king and are ruling the country to suit their own taste, the English are moving to Massachusetts by the boat-load. I suppose they want to prepare for a nice place of refuge to which they can flee if the Stuarts ever come back. Soon there will be a thousand men in New England for every ten here in the New Netherlands. And mark my words! one of these days there will be war between the Republic and the Commonwealth.

"I don't trust that fellow Cromwell! He is too clever to please me. He is an Englishman and knows his own people. The Stuarts were outsiders and never understood their subjects. But Cromwell does. They have had their fill of revolution. Now they will return to their normal selves and a normal Englishman as I know him wants to grow rich at trade. The old lady who ruled them for such a long time gave them a taste of that sort of thing. Cromwell will try to do likewise. Anyway, he has to if he wants to keep in power. That will cause trouble between his country and our own. The Stuarts wasted money on all sorts of things, but they never spent a penny on their fleet.

"That was a good thing for us. We have been driving the English out of all sorts of places in India and in Africa where they had been settled for two or three generations, and I hear that the Company intends to fortify the Cape of Good Hope. Then we shall control the road to Asia, and mark my words! that man Cromwell will fight before he lets us do it. If there is a war, how am I to defend this colony against the people from the North? Yes, I can build a wall across the island and keep them out of Manhattan, but all the rest will be lost in a couple of months."

I could not take quite such a gloomy view of affairs. "But after all, even if Cromwell has all this in mind, he can't just make war on us some fine day without some sort of excuse. And Their Lordships of the Estates General will be careful not to give him a legal pretext."

"Pretext! Who gives a fig for a legal pretext when he wants to make war on a neighbor who has got something he would like to have for himself? Besides, the pretext for which you are looking already exists."

I looked surprised.

"Of course it does. During the last fifty years we have built more ships than any one else. We carry more than half of the world's trade. Time and again I have written home for ships. But I could not have them. They were carrying goods from Boston to London or from Buenos Aires to Cadiz, or from Archangel to Naples, or from the sun to the moon. And why? Because there was more money in that sort of trade than in working for the home markets. Our friend Oliver will tell his Parliament to pass a law that only English ships are allowed to carry merchandise to English ports. If he does, we must either fight or go bankrupt. And if we fight, I can hold out here for a fortnight. After that, I must either blow myself up or surrender the Fort. I don't want to do either. And so I bombard them at home with letters. They are beginning to hate me. They ask me please to be more moderate in my tone. Moderate indeed! when you are offered the chance to do something big in the New World and they give you exactly five stivers to do it with!"

This was a new side to the old Governor I had never suspected and for a moment I felt inclined to accept his offer. There was indeed a chance to "do something big in the New World" and this chance was being scandalously neglected by the short-sighted men whose greed and selfishness made it impossible for them to look beyond their noses and their immediate profit. But then I reflected that my work lay along different lines. I was a surgeon, not a merchant nor a colonial administrator. I had now been away from my regular practice for almost seven years. I had learned a great many things that I wanted to try out in the hospital at home. No, as long as the human race continued to be suffering from a thousand ailments, it was my duty to go back and try to alleviate some of this pain and misery. And having thrashed the matter out with my excellent friend, the local doctor (for whose sagacity I was getting an ever-increasing respect), I went back to the Fort and told His Excellency of my decision and he agreed that that was perhaps the better course.

"This corner of the world is lost to us anyway," he reflected bitterly; "it is merely a question of years, and you can tell the Gentlemen Nineteen so for me when you get back home, and now let me ask my secretary to give me a list of the ships he expects before the coming of winter and I will see that you get a berth on one of them."

This did not prove an easy matter. The week before I returned to Nieuw Amsterdam, three vessels, the *Unie,* the *Sommelsdijk* and the *Assendelft* had sailed for Texel with cargoes of fur. There was a chance that the *Gouden Spiegel,* which had gone to the Chesapeake Bay, would call at Nieuw Amsterdam on her way to Holland, but early in November a very severe storm swept down the coast of Maryland and the *Gouden Spiegel* was never heard of again.

I therefore would be obliged to wait until the coming of spring before I had a chance to bid farewell to the New World forever. This prospect, however, held no terrors for me, as my two Mohegans had asked permission to stay with me until I should actually leave for home, and as one of them had developed into an excellent cook and as I had plentiful fuel to keep my little wooden house warm during the cold months of January and February, I spent a most comfortable winter, one of the most agreeable and peaceful winters of my whole life.

In the morning I used to help Doctor La Montagne with his sick and in the afternoon I worked at my secret report for My Lord Andries or ordered the notes I had taken on the medical methods and practices of those Indian tribes with which I had come in contact. And twice a week I used to take a musket and went hunting among the hills that have given the settlement the name "The Town of the Many Mountains." Every Sunday I kept open house for those who wished to come and then I discovered that Nieuw Amsterdam, notwithstanding the neglect the town suffered at the hands of the home government, contained more interesting and amiable people than I had had any reason to suspect.

And then, to my great surprise, early in December, two ships came in from home much delayed by the same storm that had caused the loss of the *Gouden Spiegel* and that seemed to have swept across the entire Atlantic. Both of them brought a number of letters from home.

One of them was from my boy, the first written words I had ever received from him and which showed me that he was growing up rapidly, for not only did he write an excellent hand (in sad contrast to the illegible pothooks of his father) but he had interspersed his epistle with diverse quotations from Ovid and all of these were correct. He expressed a polite regret at not having seen me for such a long time and suggested that I might see fit to return to him ere long, but all this sounded very formal and I realized with a painful shock that I had neglected the only person in the whole wide world to whom I was bound by something more enduring than the ties of friendship and I felt grateful that my years of wandering and exile were about to come to an end.

As for Jean-Louys, he had outdone himself this time. Not less than nine letters and all of them brimful of information. Seven of them have been lost, but somehow I managed to save two and these I shall copy here in full as they are worth preserving.

In the first place, there was a minute description of the political situation at home, which seemed to fill him with grave fear and anxiety for the immediate future.

> "The young Prince [so he wrote] is proving himself more of a nuisance than anybody had dared to anticipate. As long as his father was alive, he behaved most discreetly—was an amiable and industrious young gentleman—a bit haughty perhaps, but then he was the first member of his family who had been allowed to marry the daughter of a real king. The old Prince, his father, had not been an easy man to deal with during the last years of his life. He was dreadfully jealous of his own son and kept him away from all affairs of state and let us be under the impression that his son cared for nothing besides his horses and his dancing and his theater.
>
> "But as soon as the old chieftain's tortured body had been decorously lowered into the ancestral crypt of Delft, there was an end to the theater parties and the French fiddlers were hastily packed off to Paris. All this

happened so suddenly that there was quite a flutter on the Exchange when it was reported that the Prince had departed for the front and was trying to get the war with Spain started afresh. We all were under the impression that the fight had come to an end when Tromp had destroyed the second Armada near the Downs. Since then nothing much of any importance had happened. People vaguely remembered that they were still in a state of war, because so many of their neighbors were growing rich out of smuggling or selling war-supplies. But the thing lacked reality. Ninety-nine percent of the people had never seen a live Spaniard except as an honored business acquaintance, come to Amsterdam to do his fall buying or his spring selling. To the younger generation it seems absurd to suppose that their part of the country could ever again be the scene of actual fighting.

"Of course, the official treaty of peace had not yet been signed, but who cared? Such affairs always took a lot of time, what with deciding who ranked whom when the delegates entered a room or whether a Lord Privy Councilor of His Most Catholic Majesty was entitled to as many salutes as a High, Noble and Well-born Member of the Estates of Zeeland or vice versa. But some day these ancient and worthy gentlemen would discover that the charms of Münster were beginning to pall upon them. Nothing much has happened in that town since the sainted Jan of Leyden tried to turn it into the New Jerusalem with the well-known results. That, however, had taken place more than a hundred years before. Their Excellencies whenever they felt bored could go and look at the iron cage in which the Prophet had spent the last days of his life, but that was about the only form of excitement the city offered, and it was not much.

"And so sooner or later these slow-moving excellencies would affix their signatures to a piece of parchment and all would be over.

"As a result, when it was whispered on the Exchange that the Prince meant to use the massing of a few Spanish regiments along the Flemish border as an excuse for preparing another invasion of Belgium, there were several short and rather mysterious meetings in one of the rooms of the Town Hall of Amsterdam and certain gentlemen whom both of us know, had chartered a special night boat for The Hague and the Prince had returned to his stud-farm in the Woods and the army had gone back to its winter quarters and suddenly the long-expected peace with Spain had been signed and it had been celebratd by four days of as drunken an orgy as had ever been seen this side of Parnassus, and that was where matters stood at the time of writing.

"[Then the letter went on.] Amsterdam came out victorious because it has the key to the common treasure-house. The Prince was defeated this time but mark you my words, he has the army with him and as soon as he has half a chance he will turn against Amsterdam and he will have his revenge.

"Meanwhile, business as usual continues. The panic that followed upon the cessation of hostilities and about which I wrote you in my former letters, has come to an end. The ship-yards now work for private owners and the ordnance makers are selling their wares to those who have taken up buccaneering instead of smuggling. As for the ex-soldiers, they have either been hung or have been locked up in so-called Old People's Homes, which is pretty much the same as far as the final effect is concerned.

"But in spite of these items on the credit side, there are many things that fill my heart, or rather my mind, with serious fears for the future. Our relations with England are getting worse every day. It is quite natural that His late Majesty's son should have fled to his sister as soon as he left his kingdom. And as this country has always been extremely cordial to political exiles, the young man had every right to expect that he would be treated with some sort of consideration. But these Stuarts never seem to learn anything. A king in exile has certain duties. There is only one rôle he can play—the rôle of dignified submission with an accent on the dignified. But Charles must have his wine and his women and his eternal round of parties. I saw him in Amsterdam two years ago, quite by chance, of course, for he was supposed to be traveling incognito. He is almost six feet tall and looks so much more like an Italian than an Englishman that he was bound to attract considerable attention. Ordinary Englishmen we can see here every day. But Englishmen disguised as Sicilians are a rarity.

"It was about six o'clock in the afternoon and he was coming home from dinner with one of the Burgomasters. He was slightly the worse for drink but carried himself well enough. Nevertheless, an Oedipus or a King Lear in his cups is not a very dignified spectacle and so his friends hastened him off to the yacht that was to take him back to his sister, and they did this as rapidly and as decorously as circumstances and his wobbly legs would permit.

"That strange Cromwell person, who contrary to our expectations has not put the crown upon his own unkempt locks, is much shrewder than we had thought. He has more power now than any of the potentates whom he has succeeded. And as long as he is allowed to rule his fellow-men according to his own sweet will, he does not seem to care by what name he is known. But he is beginning to find himself in a very difficult position. He is a usurper and the world in which he lives is supposed to be a world of law and order. He can only hope to maintain himself as long as he is victorious and sticks to a foreign policy that makes everybody rich.

"But of course all these many years of civil war have done the greatest harm to the business of the Kingdom and no one has profited as much from this state of affairs as we in our own beloved little Republic. You will notice the influence of environment upon even a highly intelligent mind. Here I am writing 'our own beloved little Republic' whereas of course I am really a devout subject of Giovanni Mazarini, who, by the way, has got himself into all sorts of troubles with Their Lordships of the Estates General, by the truly Italian manner in which he has been trying to grab Belgium as part of the dowry of a rather vague Spanish princess who was to marry an equally vague cousin of the King of France, and who was then supposed to become the sovereign ruler of a new sort of French kingdom that stretched all the way from the Scheldt to the Pyrenees and from the Atlantic to the Rhine.

"However that may be, or to make a long letter still a little longer, there is going to be a war some time within the near future and that war will decide who is to be the master of Europe. At present we here in Amsterdam have the largest amount of money and therefore we rule the universe pretty much as it pleases us. Soon His Lordship, the Protector, will consult his Bible and at the hand of numerous texts will prove that the time has come to smite the Amalekites.

"And of course the Amalekites will prove to be his neighbors who live on the other side of the North Sea.

"That will tell you what is what, in the field of foreign affairs. As for our good town, there is nothing new to report. We enjoyed a few fires, but none of them amounted to very much. Our population is increasing by leaps and bounds and those who have some spare funds at their disposal are buying real estate just outside the city walls in the hope of selling their land at a handsome profit when the next extension takes place.

"There may be something new in the field of literature, but as you know, I never read Dutch unless I absolutely have to. I live a very quiet life and since the departure of Selim, spend most of my time working. I had a rather mysterious visit the other day of a certain Doctor Paniculus, who at first claimed that he was a French physician, who had studied at Montpellier at the same time as you and wanted to get some news of his dear old friend, the famous Dutch doctor. I soon discovered that he was not a doctor of medicine at all but a doctor of theology and a member of the Society of Jesus, visiting the Low Countries on an errand of piety which, however, he refused to divulge. I asked him whether he had ever heard of the edict against the Jesuits which the Estates General had passed in the year 1612 and which never had been repealed. He answered yes, and pulled a copy of that famous edict out of his pocket.

" 'Here it is,' he said, 'and I always carry it with me. If ever I am arrested and they find this, they will surely never suspect me of belonging to that poor, persecuted company of holy men.'

"And then he continued the conversation by asking me what news I had of my good friend, Monsieur Descartes. I told him that I had very little news since that morning in September of '49 when I bade him farewell on the shore near Egmont and saw him safely on board his Swedish man-of-war. Had I had any news from him since he had taken up residence with the Queen? I said no, but that I had heard in a roundabout way that he did not feel very happy in Stockholm and suffered a great deal from the cold.

"And then I asked him by what right he had forced himself into my house to bother me with all sorts of personal questions which surely were none of his concern. But he remained as affable as before and totally unruffled he answered me in a very kind tone of voice, 'It is really none of my business, but I thought you would like to have a friend tell you that poor Renatus is dead.' And I jumped up and said, 'Dead?' And he answered, 'Yes, dead! He died in February from an inflammation of the lungs.'

"And then he told me how my poor learned friend had never been quite happy since he had left the territory of the Republic. Of course, it had been very flattering to be asked to become a sort of unofficial adviser to the brilliant young Queen of Sweden, and to play the rôle of Aristotle at the court of the late Gustavus Adolphus. One was getting along in years. Fifty-four was not exactly old age, but it was pleasant to feel that one could make some provisions for the future. On paper the whole plan had seemed most attractive. A philosopher being called for by a battle-ship and being received with royal honors was something that probably had not happened since the days of Philip of Macedonia. But there the comparison ended. For Christina was no Alexander, though she had so great an admiration for this ancient prince that she often expressed her regret at not having been given his name. She had better brains than most of the men around her with the exception of the chancellor Oxenstjerna whom she had inherited from her father, and whom she humiliated in every possible manner. And driven by her pride and in order to show the old diplomat how well she could manage without him, she had begun to surround herself with famous people whom she gathered from all over the world and upon whom she wasted the greater part of the money her careful father had left her at the time he was shot.

"About half a dozen years ago, she had got hold of Grotius, the man about whom you told me once, the absent-minded professor who started on his honeymoon with two trunkfuls of books. But when he had reached Stockholm, he had soon discovered that he was not really wanted there to show his learning. He had been invited as an object of fashionable interest —the man who had written that famous book that was to do away with war. And the damp Stockholm climate had made him sick and he had tried to get back to Europe, had sickened on the way to Paris and had died in some dreadful little German city on the Baltic.

"And that, so it seemed, was exactly what now had happened to poor Descartes. He had been given a high-sounding title, but in reality he found himself in the position of a superior sort of intellectual court-fool. He was asked to draw up the constitution and the by-laws for a Swedish academy of letters which the Queen meant to found and he was told to do his work in the royal library which was both cold and damp, and he had caught an inflammation of both lungs and had died of this complaint early in February. All this the good father told me and I thanked him and asked him whether I could do anything for him in return and he answered, 'I have been told that you are an excellent cook and I wonder whether you would give me some lunch, for I have got to take the three o'clock boat back to Haarlem.'

" 'And where do we go from here?' I suggested.

" 'Ah, my friend,' he replied, 'that would be telling!'

"But I was curious, and so during the preparation of the meal (the good father had followed me into the kitchen) I said, 'Without committing any further indiscretion, why in Heaven's name did you come to tell me all this? I am glad you did, but if you had not come, I would eventually have heard the news from some one else.'

"To which he answered me with absolute sincerity, 'I came because you interest us. You are not a professing Christian. We know that. We are also aware of the fact that you are a man of great intelligence. Such men can be very useful to us upon occasions. It is well to keep in contact with them and occasionally, if the opportunity offers itself, render them some small service, such as perhaps just now I have been able to render unto you.'

"I answered that I was deeply grateful but again I asked why he had taken so much trouble on my behalf and what did he expect in return, and just as quietly as if we had been discussing the price of butter or eggs, he said, 'Well, you have a soul and a very useful one. We would like to get hold of it before it is too late and show it certain small errors in its method of reasoning but we are in no hurry. And you need not fear that I shall try and hear your confession before I leave. You will probably never see me again. But I hope that you retain a pleasant recollection of my visit. That is all.'

"To which I replied in all sincerity that I would most assuredly remember him during the rest of my days, and then we sat down to dinner and he showed me a new way of mixing a salad-dressing which is a great improvement upon the one I had always used, and we talked of a thousand different subjects and very soon it was time for him to go and he disappeared as quietly as he had come, but just before he left, he said, 'You ought to turn in some time into the shop of that instrument maker on the Singel near the Torensluis. I think that he has got some of those curious Torricellian tubes which I first saw in Florence when I last called on Galileo.'

"I interrupted him with some resentment. 'Then you have something to do with all the misery that overtook that poor man in his old age.' But he refused to be even mildly ruffled. 'Heaven forbid!' he answered. 'We leave that sort of thing to our dear friends, the Dominicans. They have never got over their famous brother Thomas. What he did not know, surely was not worth knowing, and as far as they were concerned, the world stood still when he died. A great man—the venerable Aquinas, but he died 400 years ago and since then a great many things have happened in this world. I did visit the good Galileo Galilei, but merely to assure him that His Holiness sent him his blessing and would never sign the decree by which he was supposed to recant his heresies. Merely a visit of charity, so to speak, for the old man had always been a most faithful son of the Church and he had been deeply mortified by the sentence of the Inquisition.'

"With this remark he quietly departed and I never saw him again."

The letter set me thinking. I had traveled across three thousand miles of wilderness and water to find a companion of the order of Jesus teaching the heathen of the New World the blessedness of the Christian creed by means of fairy stories and crude little pictures. Jean-Louys at home and in the heart of the richest city of the world and a citadel of the Protestant faith, had received the visit of an unassuming little man who seemed to be an authority upon the subject of science and mathematics and whose visit was based upon the very slender expectation that "he might gain his good will."

I knew that the company of Jesus had set out to regain the lost provinces of God for the service of Him whom they regarded as their Heavenly master. But it had never dawned upon me that they would be quite so ubiquitous and so incredibly efficient in their methods. If they could keep this up for another hundred years, things looked very bad indeed for the thousand and one quarreling little sects of the northern part of Europe. From the land of the Cayugas to the banks of the Amstel River was a long distance—a very long distance, as we measured space on this planet of ours. And yet, they were in both spots at the same time—working and pleading and making themselves useful and above all things, being very amiable and very tolerant and almost incredibly reasonable and plausible.

For the sake of the Protestant cause, it would have been a good thing if that bullet of Pampeluna had been aimed a few inches higher.

Chapter 40

I RECEIVE BAD NEWS FROM AMSTERDAM AND DECIDE TO RETURN HOME

As for the other letter, which somehow or other I managed to have kept all this time, it was of a very different nature and talked of matters a little nearer to our own home interests.

"A week ago to-day [Jean-Louys wrote] I decided to call on Rembrandt. But while going down the Oude Schans and by the merest chance, I ran across your old book-seller on the Rokin who also handles some of Rembrandt's etchings. He first of all asked me for news of you and then inquired whether I had heard of the latest troubles of Rembrandt. I said no, and as the old man has apparently retired from business and seemed glad of an opportunity to talk to some one, he gladly accepted my invitation to come home with me and help me eat my dinner, for I decided that my own business could wait. I had not been near the house on the Jodenbreestraat for almost half a year. The last time I had called there the situation had been so awkward that I had vowed to myself that I would never go there again as long as I lived. The nurse Geertje was still on the premises, and more violent and less accountable than ever. But shortly afterwards, so the book-seller told me, there had been an open break between herself and her employer and after that she had behaved so strangely that her relations had been called in and it had been decided to send her to an asylum for a few months' observation. But she managed to get away from them and then began a series of petty persecutions of Rembrandt—which still continue. For example, she went before a judge and swore that her former master had borrowed money from her and had never repaid her, and another time she complained that he had promised to marry her and had not kept his word, and still a third time she stated definitely that she and her old employer had had carnal intercourse and that he had turned her out as soon as he had done his will upon her. And so on and so forth. Until it had become clear to all concerned that she was stark raving mad and thereupon she had been taken away to the town of Gouda, whence she came from originally, and had been committed to the local lunatic asylum in that city.

"Lunatic asylum is perhaps a little too flattering a word. When you remember what our madhouses here in Amsterdam look like, you can imagine what they are in some small provincial hole like Gouda. They seem to consist of a few extra rooms in the local jail and the turnkey feeds the poor devils whenever he happens to think of it. But anyway, the woman was at last out of harm's way and I rejoiced, for now there would be a chance to see something more of Rembrandt than I had done during the last year and a half, and I always liked the man though he has broken every law of nature in regard to those colors which God meant to be 'white' and 'black.'

"But that was only half of the story which the book-seller told me. For it appears that the lady in question is possessed of certain relatives who are not above a bit of blackmail, whenever it comes handy, and can be practiced without too much risk. And the risk in this case was very small, for Rembrandt, who is the world's most muddle-headed financier, has undoubtedly borrowed small sums of money from his son's nurse whenever he was in momentary need of a few guilders to pay the baker or butcher. Very foolish, no doubt, but you know how he is. When he is working, he just does not want to be disturbed and would take cash from the Devil himself. The whole thing, in the language of your esteemed country, is a mess, a 'rommeltje.' (I think that was the first Dutch word I ever learned.) It is a mess, a hopeless muddle. The 'disjecta membra' are all over the Breestraat and I have no idea what the outcome will be. I shall wait a few days and then I shall go forth and do some discreet reconnoitering and I shall let you know.

"After I had seen my guest out (intelligent book-sellers are the salt of the earth and unfortunately as rare as a fine day in March) I decided that it was too late to go to work and too early to go to bed, and having the Breestraat still in my mind, I took my hat and coat and called on Rabbi Menasseh. I found him at home entertaining a number of people and I discovered that this curious old fellow had developed a new hobby. If Bernardo (from whom I have not heard for five or six years. He used to write in the beginning. Is he still alive?)—but if Bernardo actually finds the long lost tribes, and returns home with the good tidings, he will be a very much disappointed man. For Rabbi Menasseh won't even bother to listen to him, instead he will now tell him of a wonderful new scheme he has developed to bring the Jews back to England. He is completely obsessed by the idea. He allows his printing shop to go to ruin and forgets half of the time that he is supposed to teach the Talmud to little Jewish boys, so full is he of this marvelous project.

"As far as I could make out (for as usual everybody was talking at the same moment) he is firmly convinced that the Messiah is about to return and that the Jews, in order not to miss their opportunity this time, ought to settle in every part of the world and make ready to receive the long-expected no matter where he chooses to land on this pretty little planet. That is not exactly the way the good Rabbi expressed himself, but it will give you a fairly accurate idea of what is in his mind. He must have got his 'universal' idea from the East India Company, which has added so much territory to its former possessions that nowadays it is absolutely impossible for a penny's worth of profit to fall upon this earth without being caught by the pocket-book of some Dutch trader.

"After talking for about half an hour, when at last he came up for breath, I quickly asked him how he hoped to accomplish this purpose, as not a single Jew had been allowed in England since the end of the thirteenth century. But he answered that that was a mere detail. It was the English kings who had been responsible for keeping the Jews out of their realm. They had done so out of spite because the Jews were cleverer traders than their own dull-witted Saxon subjects. How they had hated and feared them, one could learn from that contemptible piece of the famous court hack, William Shakespeare. He had never seen a Jew in all his life. When he was born, there had not been a Jew in England for exactly two hundred and seventy-four years but all the same he wrote his monstrous tragedy about Shylock to make the Jews unpopular and to please the Queen. God, however—God the righteous but wrathful—had heavily smitten the wicked rulers of that ungrateful land. The last one of them had been beheaded like a common criminal and now a new day was approaching. A man who truly walked in the footsteps of Jehovah had been called to lead his people out of the wilderness of superstition and intolerance and soon the Jews would be readmitted to all parts of the British Kingdom and to all of the British colonies, because Cromwell the Just not only respected religious principles of the Jews but also recognized the debt of gratitude which Christianity owed the children of Abraham.

"At that moment, a dark-eyed youngster of about sixteen or seventeen years of age spoke up and rather dryly remarked: 'Undoubtedly he does, dear Master. He undoubtedly loves and respects us for the sake of our high-minded religious principles. But has it ever struck you that he may also have a certain admiration for certain commercial abilities which we as a race are supposed to possess?'

"Whereupon the excellent Menasseh flew into a violent rage. 'Baruch,' he thundered, 'are you going to be another Acosta and turn against your own race? Do you dare to come into my house and tell me to my face that this noble Englishman, this second Moses, this prophet and seer who has the power of a dozen kings yet lives simpler than the simplest of his myriad subjects, is merely actuated by a vile lust for gold? I am truly ashamed of you!'

"But that young Baruch, whatever his last name was, remained perfectly calm and quietly answered, 'No, dear Master, I have not the slightest desire to follow the footsteps of poor Uriel and I hold suicide to be a crime against the orderly arrangement of this world. I fully share your admiration for General Cromwell, but I hear that he is a man who takes everything very seriously and that sometime very soon the people are going to offer him the title of their Lord and Protector. Very likely, if he accepts this honor, he will not only try to protect their souls but also their purses. A few thousand Jewish commercial houses, moving from Amsterdam to London, would not come amiss at a moment like the present. It would be another feather in His Lordship's cap.'

"Here I interrupted him. 'I did not think so good a Puritan would ever condescend to wear feathers,' but the youngster merely looked at me for a moment (he had the blackest eyes I ever saw) and then went on. 'I meant his figurative cap, sir. In this house we are always speaking figuratively whenever the Master does not approve of us,' and he explained that that very afternoon he had been called upon to translate a Latin document which one of his father's neighbors had received from London and in which he was offered all sorts of commercial advantages and opportunities if he (his father) agreed to pack up his business and move from Amsterdam to London.

"As this subject of conversation did not particularly appeal to me, I soon afterwards bade them all a good evening and went home. But this true and accurate report of the proceedings in Menasseh's house will show you what way the wind is blowing in this part of the world. The people live under a cloud. They have fought for three generations to gain their liberty. Now they are free and there is a rival across the North Sea who is trying to cut their throats and they are beginning to realize that this was only the beginning and not the end of their difficulties. They will have to sail their newly built craft very carefully if they want to avoid being shipwrecked before they are more than a dozen miles out of port.

"As I said, they are beginning to realize this and then they look anxiously at the poop deck, where the captain and the mate are supposed to dwell in peace and amity that they may give all their thoughts and attention to the difficult business of navigation, and they see those worthies engaged in a disreputable quarrel that may develop into a regular fist fight at almost any moment. The whole thing is very disheartening. The young Prince, if he is not very careful, will end by making a fool of himself. The Amsterdam magistrates, if they continue to insinuate that they and they alone rule the Republic and that both the Prince and the Estates General exist merely for the sake of outward ornament, will find themselves one fine morning in one of the dungeons of Loevenstein with a pleasant-spoken but fierce princely guard on the other side of their doors.

"What will happen to this country unless the people learn to look a little distance beyond the exceedingly narrow limits of their own towns and villages, the good Lord only can foretell. Without quite knowing how they did it, they have acquired such tremendous colonial possessions that they have become the masters of one of the largest empires that has ever existed. But they are trying to rule this empire with the same system of laws that was originally devised for half a hundred hamlets that belonged to some medieval chieftain of the Middle Ages. When told that now they are a big nation and should behave as such, they blush violently and in great embarrassment they answer, 'Oh, sir!' and run as fast as their legs will carry them to the nearest safe spot behind the familiar moat of some ancestral burgh and hastily pass a bill regulating the hours of the civic garbage collectors or stipulating the fee which wet-nurses may charge for their useful and pleasant services. All I can hope for at the present is that you and Bernardo will be safely back here before there is a war. Otherwise you will have to stay in your jungle forever and we need you here.

"As for our mutual friend, about a week ago I desired a fish for dinner (I still obey the dietary laws my father's confessor taught me as a child) and behold! whom should I meet on the fish-market but the good painter from the Jodenbreestraat himself. I thought that he would try to avoid me, for our last meeting had not been exactly a happy one, but he came right up to me and shook me by the hand and said, 'You have heard of course what has happened?' And I answered 'Yes,' and he smiled rather sheepishly and then looked at me and said, 'Phew!' and I replied, 'Yes, indeed, phew!' and then we both roared with laughter and it was the first time I had heard him laugh for several years and so I decided that the obsession of that terrible female had come to an end.

"Then I asked him whether he had joined our Holy Church and was buying shrimps for his Friday dinner, but he said, 'No danger there! They have got hold of old Vondel and ought to be satisfied for the moment. I had a visit the other day from a young Italian nobleman who asked me whether I would be willing to paint him a Madonna in the manner of Raphael. I told him that I had painted any number of Holy Families in the manner of Rembrandt van Rijn. He was a very suave and pleasant young man and said that was exactly what he wanted. There was a patron of the arts in Rome (unfortunately he was not allowed to tell me his name) who had a tremendous respect for my work and who thought I was the greatest painter then alive. Of course my subjects were influenced a little by the surroundings in which I lived, but if I were willing to make just a few changes, such as providing my Virgin and the Holy Child with a halo—just a very small change, as I would undoubtedly see myself—then he from his side would not haggle about the price. I told him that I was deeply touched and flattered but that I painted the way I painted because that happened to be the way I painted and that I could not change my way of painting any more than I could change the shape of my head. He then asked to be allowed to see what I had been doing recently, and I showed him the sketches I had been making for a large picture of the Good Samaritan and some other sketches for a large piece of Christ and Mary of Magdala which I have to finish next year and a half-finished picture of Abraham entertaining the angels, and he expressed himself as delighted with everything and told me that he would write to his employer and would let me know as soon as possible. And so you see, I may be a rich man again, if I will buy enough yellow ocher for half a dozen haloes.'

" 'Which, of course, you won't do!' I said.

" 'Which, of course, I won't do,' he answered, and then he turned to a woman who was standing behind him with a large household basket and quite casually remarked, 'You had better buy another turbot, for if I am not mistaken, our friend here will share our dinner to-night.' And it was said so pleasantly that I forgot all my previous feelings of irritation at his extraordinary conduct and that night I dined with him and I never saw such a change in any human being before. The house was scrupulously clean and it looked quite cheerful, although the carpets were beginning to give evidence of wear and tear and the door and the floors would suffer nothing from a new coat of paint.

"Little Titus, now quite a handsome boy with long blond curls like his mother, was allowed to stand at the table and he had lost that look of a hunted creature which he had had ever since I first knew him. The meal was well cooked and the food was not thrown at us as in the olden days. I asked him where he had found this jewel, and he told me that she was a peasant girl from a small village near the German border, but she had come to Amsterdam to find employment as a general maid, and that a friend had sent him to her because he knew that he was looking for some one after the Dircx woman had been sent to the madhouse.

" 'I know nothing about her,' he confessed, 'except that she seems to have no other relatives than a sister who lives in a village called Breevoort, about a week's distance from here, something that suits me exceedingly well, as I have had enough of servants with brothers and sisters just around the corner, ready to perjure themselves at a moment's notice. For the rest, she is an excellent cook, keeps our rooms in order, is as nice to little Titus as if she were his own mother, and has a pleasant shrewdness when it comes to spending money, a quality which is perhaps not out of place in this particular household.'

" 'She is also a very handsome woman,' I ventured to remark.

" 'Yes,' he answered, 'she will suit me wonderfully well as a model. I was thinking of using her for quite a large picture I mean to make some time—a picture of Bathsheba.'

"I looked at Rembrandt and I looked at the maid who had then turned nurse and was telling little Titus that it was time for him to say good night and go to bed.

" 'Remember David!' I warned him.

" 'I have thought of that,' he answered, 'but there is really very little danger of such a thing. I am only too happy that I have found a servant like that. The type is scarce nowadays. They all want to work in a shop doing some dull job like curing tobacco or making paper boxes rather than cook for an old widow man.' And he got up to kiss his son good night and went to the door to open it for the servant, who was of a type that was scarce nowadays, and I noticed that he bade her farewell as if she were a very grand lady and then it suddenly struck me: she is a grand lady, even if she cannot read and write.

"And then Rembrandt took me up to the print room and we looked at his etchings and he showed me how he wanted to change the plate of

THE THREE CROSSES

the hundred guilder print for the sixteenth or seventeenth time and when I went home shortly after midnight, it was as if nothing had ever happened between us. We were better friends than ever before and when you return, you will witness a miracle—the man is positively showing signs of becoming a normal and civilized human being. He also seems very hard up. But who cares? He is doing better work than ever before, so what is the difference? And fare ye well and come back to us soon. We miss you."

This letter removed the last vestige of doubt that still existed in my mind whether I ought to return or not. After all, this had not been entirely a pleasure trip. I had been sent out to do a very definite piece of work and I had accomplished my task as far as was possible. I had grown very fond of this new country. I had been happy there. But if My Lord Andries and his brother, who had financed the voyage, were in difficulties at the moment or likely to get in difficulties through their quarrel with the Prince, it was up to me to return home and give them that information which might be of the greatest possible value to them at the present moment. I sent word of my plans to Bernardo. The oldest of my two Mohegan servants offered to take the message personally. Two weeks later he returned.

"Your brother only shook his head," he told me.

That was all?

That was all.

I decided not to sell my house. I had become too much attached to that spot to give it up entirely. I went over my accounts and found that I still had more than one thousand guilders left. I gave each of my two servants one hundred guilders in gold and I sent them back to their own country. The ducats would make them rich for the rest of their days and they had well deserved such a reward. I would explain this expenditure to my employers and they would no doubt approve. As for the little house, I had stout doors and window blinds made for it and asked leave to deposit the key at the Fort. My Lord Stuyvesant graciously promised that he would send one of his men every other week to inspect the premises.

I don't believe in lengthy farewells. To say good-by to a dear friend is too much like a minor amputation and it is not good for either the body or the soul. All herbs that I had collected during these many years (with the exception of those I had gathered with Father Ambrosius and which had been destroyed by the Eries when they burned down our Cayuga village) were safely packed in heavy wooden boxes. I had made quite a collection of living plants and these were placed in rough wooden troughs on the poop-deck near the wheel-house where they would suffer as little as possible from the sea.

I then paid an official call on My Lord Stuyvesant and was touched by the emotion he showed in bidding me God speed.

"It will be the last time we see each other," he said, and stamping the floor impatiently with his wooden leg he repeated those words I had heard him use before: "A century hence this land will be of infinitely greater value than Java and all the Moluccas put together. But they won't believe me at home. They won't believe me. They won't believe me until it is too late."

And he actually wept, but whether it was from anger or grief, I could not say though I am inclined to think it was from the former.

One afternoon, late in June, I had my last glimpse of the city of the hills. I had gone on board early in the morning and for several hours we had drifted down the harbor with the tide. On our right was the Staten Eiland, on the left the farms of Breukelen and Nieuw Utrecht. We passed through the narrow funnel that leads from the inner bay to the open sea. In the distance the white beach of the Konijnen Eiland was basking in the sun. Three or four Indian canoes had followed our ship. They were fishermen on their way back to Heemstede. They came very close to the vessel. One of the men in the nearest boat waved his hand at us and called out something. I thought that he was speaking in his own language and I leaned over the railing and cupped my hand to my ear to understand him better. Then I caught his words. They were in Dutch. "Goede reis!"

The Indian was wishing his white brother a safe crossing.

Then all the sails were hoisted and we turned eastward.

An hour later I had seen my last of the New World.

Chapter 41

I REACH HOLLAND SAFELY BUT FIND THE OLD HOME TOWN SURROUNDED BY THE TROOPS OF THE PRINCE OF ORANGE

Captain Wouters knew his business and the *Zeemeeuw* was a good ship. We had a prosperous voyage and on Saturday, the thirtieth of July, I set foot on shore near Texel.

The next day I found an Urk fisherman willing to take me and my baggage to Hoorn where I arrived on Monday, the first of August. From there I meant to take a carriage to Amsterdam and so I went on shore and went to the inn called the "Roskam," and for the first time in almost two months, I enjoyed the luxury of sleeping in a real bed.

I had asked to be called early the next morning that I might reach Amsterdam before the closing of her gates. But when I woke up, the clock on the Groote Kerk was just striking ten. I called for the landlord and reproached him for his negligence, but he said: "I am sorry, Doctor. You were sleeping so soundly, and it would have been no use calling you anyway."

"But I ordered a carriage at seven," I interrupted him rather sharply.

"The carriage was here, Doctor, but it went away again. The gates are closed. The garrison has been called out. The town will soon be in a state of siege."

"Listen," I said. "I have been away for quite a number of years. But I am not as much of a simpleton as all that. We are at peace with all the world. Surely the Spaniard has not returned to drive us out of house and home."

"No," he answered, "but the Prince may do so at any moment."

And that was the beginning of a very strange adventure, an episode which might have cost me my life, just as I was on the point of seeing my son and my dear friends once more, after an absence of almost seven years.

I went downstairs to the taproom but found it deserted. It had been closed by order of the Magistrates. And so, for lack of anything better to do, I asked where the nearest barber was to be found, for I had not had a decent hair-cut since I left Nieuw Amsterdam, two months before, and looked more like a Cayuga chief than like a respectable member of the Amsterdam Surgeons' Guild.

I found the little shop full of people but none of them seemed to have come on business for I was at once placed in the chair and my honest colleague set to work with such a will that I was in constant fear for my ears. However, I lived through the ordeal without any serious damage being done to my manly beauty and in the meantime I had listened to such a strange chorus of lamentations and curses that I was really no wiser than I had been before and so, after I had paid for the operation, I asked whether I could have a pipe of tobacco and I was shown into the back room which was so full of smoke that it looked like the anteroom of Hades and groping my way to what looked like an empty chair, I sat down and turned to my neighbor and said: "My good friend, I have been away from the country for quite a long time. I returned yesterday to find everybody in great excitement, as if the Republic were in danger of a foreign invasion. Pray tell me what it is all about, for the people who are in the front room do a lot of shouting, but they say remarkably little."

Whereupon this honest citizen informed me that he was in the shipping business and was too busy with his own affairs to take much interest in politics, but if I wanted to know, he could tell me in about two minutes' time, and I answered him that I would gladly give him two hours if only he would enlighten me and then he said:

"Well, it is really all very simple. The Prince of Orange is an ambitious young man who wants to make a name for himself in the only way princes apparently can make a reputation for themselves—by killing a large number of their fellow-men. In other words by conducting a number of successful campaigns. In order to do this, he needs two things, a war and money enough to pay his soldiers. The war part is simple enough. There is always some potentate somewhere in Europe who has a grievance against another potentate and our country, which is now considered the richest nation on earth, is of course a most welcome ally to any monarch who would like to indulge in a little display of gun-powder, if only he could put his hands on a small sum of ready cash.

"But there, my dear sir, is the rub!

"The treasure-chest of these United Provinces stands right in the heart of the city of Amsterdam and, alas, Their Lordships of the Town Hall, who hold the key, are strangely lacking in imagination when it comes to fighting. Each time before they actually engage in a quarrel they sit down before a large table on which there is nothing but a sheet of blank paper. Then they take their goose-quills and start figuring. On the one side they spell out the word 'Debit,' and on the other side the word 'Credit,' all according to that excellent system of book-keeping which the late Master Stevin taught us some thirty years ago. Then underneath the word 'Debit' they write down everything the proposed campaign will probably cost them in guilders and stivers. But underneath the word 'Credit' they write down everything they may safely expect to gain as a result of their ultimate victory, and, mind you! they never start upon such an enterprise until they are mathematically certain that they will gain something. It is a great invention, this new system of book-keeping. If the illustrious uncle of His Royal Highness had ever suspected to what purpose it would be used within so few years after his death, I am sure he never would have made that clever Fleming his quarter-master general.

"Now it is too late. When the Prince let it be known that he expected to conclude a treaty with the King of France and start another war with the King of Spain and conquer the whole of Flanders and make himself Lord of the sovereign city of Antwerp, those of Amsterdam promptly threw the key to their strong-box into the Zuyder Zee and told His Royal Highness how very much mistaken he was if he thought that they would ever lend themselves to such a thing. They had paid out good money for almost eighty years for no other purpose than to break the neck of their hated old rival on the Scheldt and now they were invited to waste further millions to call it back to life for the greater glory of a young man whom they regarded as an intruder and a common nuisance.

"The idea was preposterous. They told His Royal Highness so in very plain terms and when he insisted, they instructed the Estates of their own province (a beautiful arrangement, my dear Sir, for the Estates of Holland, as you probably know, are the same as the Town Council of Amsterdam and the Town Council of Amsterdam is the same as the Estates of Holland)—well, not to bother you with too many details, the town of Amsterdam, speaking ex cathedra, and in its capacity of the greatest money lender of our beloved Republic, told His Royal Highness that he would not get a penny!

"His Royal Highness, considerably annoyed, began to rattle his sword. His Royal Highness has a cousin who is in command of the armies in the north, in Friesland. The cousin also commenced to rattle his sword. Whereupon the Estates hastily dismissed more than two thirds of the army and put the rest on half pay.

"All that is common history. It occurred just before you arrived. But what has happened since Saturday last, I really could not tell you. There had been rumors that the Prince meant to march upon Amsterdam. I do a good deal of business with England and as long as a month ago one of my correspondents in Hull wrote me and asked me what truth there was in the reports that circulated in London that the Prince of Orange meant to attack Amsterdam. I thought nothing of it at the time. The people who rule England nowadays hate the Prince because he is married to one of their Stuarts and of course they would be delighted to start a story like that if they could do him harm by making him a suspicious figure. Then a week ago I got a letter from a friend in Gothenburg who said that the French ambassador in Stockholm had told the consular agent of the free-city of Hamburg that the Prince meant to surprise Amsterdam, hang a dozen members of the town council and make himself king of the Seven United Provinces. I threw that letter into the paper basket. It seemed too utterly foolish. And so you see, we have had warnings enough and now it has happened."

"Yes," I interrupted him, "it has undoubtedly happened, but just exactly what has happened?"

But that he could not tell me.

"I really don't know," he said, "anything more than you do. I came here to get a little information, just as you did, and I found everybody excited and everybody talking at once and nobody listening to anybody else. Meanwhile, the gates have been closed and the troops have been called out and there you are. But listen! What is that?"

And with his pipe he pointed to the front-room whence there arose a great ado of shuffling feet and of chairs that were hastily being pushed aside as if a large number of people had suddenly taken to flight.

We rushed into the barber-shop and found it empty but there were no signs of violence. The crowd was patiently standing in the middle of the street listening to an old man who had climbed on a stone bench and was reading something from a piece of paper.

"What has happened?" I asked some one who stood just in front of me.

"Shsh," he warned me. "Listen and you will know. He got news from Amsterdam—a letter from his son. They smuggled it through."

Meanwhile the old man on the stone bench continued:

"'It seems at first to have been the plan to take our city by surprise—to hide a company of soldiers in a peat ship and send it into town and then let them come out in the middle of the night and kill the guards and open the gates, as we did in Breda in '37. But this is probably mere talk. Everybody is so excited that the wildest rumors are taken for gospel truth.

"'All we know is that day before yesterday the man who carries the mail from Hamburg to Amsterdam came riding into town as if the devil were on his heels. He asked to be taken at once to see one of the Burgomasters. It was half past seven in the morning and all of the Burgomasters were in The Hague on this business of dismissing the troops, except My Lord Cornelis Bicker. So the mail-carrier was at once taken down to My Lord Cornelis' residence, who received him in his bedroom and heard him tell how that night, in a heavy fog, just as he had passed through the village of Muiden, he had found himself among several companies of soldiers, who seemed to have lost their way and asked him the nearest road to Amsterdam. He had told them, because he was afraid that otherwise they might do him harm, but before they could stop him, he had slipped away in the dark and he had driven his horse at break-neck speed, because he felt sure those soldiers meant no good. Most likely they belonged to a group of mercenaries who had been thrown out of work by the recent peace and who had heard that Amsterdam was the richest city in Europe and who meant to take the town and plunder it.

"'Well, My Lord Cornelis got down to business right away. He gave orders that all the gates be closed and that the militia be called to arms and before ten o'clock ninety new cannon had been mounted on the walls and ships were sailing down the Amstel and the Y to prevent these marauders from attacking us from the side of the water.

" 'At eleven o'clock the foreign soldiers actually appeared before one of the gates and asked permission to deliver a letter. Then at last we knew. They were not foreign mercenaries at all. They were native troops commanded by Willem Frederik, a cousin of the Prince, and they demanded that the gates be opened to them "peaceably," that they be allowed to "reëstablish order" and prevent their master from suffering further insults at the hands of the government of Amsterdam.

" 'Of course, we from our side refused to accede to this request and as a result we are now being besieged by the army of His Highness. I have just heard that the road to the North is still open and I shall give this letter to the ferry-man to Buiksloot and ask him to send it on to you in Hoorn. We have supplies for at least ten days. In the meantime some solution will have been found. The Prince himself is said to be in Abcoude or in Amstelveen, we don't know exactly where. We are building fortifications outside our gates and since this morning we have begun to cut the dikes on the sea side. Another three days and His Highness will have to move his headquarters to more solid ground.

" 'That is all the news. The future is in the hands of God. If this letter gets through, please give a liberal reward to the messenger.' "

There was a postscript.

" 'Bread and meat have gone up about a hundred percent since last Friday morning, but the Town Council has just threatened those who mean to make undue profits from the present emergency with fifty lashes and confiscation of their property. That will probably do some good. Farewell.' "

The old man slowly folded his son's letter and climbed down from his perch and the crowd dispersed. Now at last we knew where we were at and I became conscious of only one thing—I had arrived in the nick of time.

The Bicker family which had shown me such great favors in the recent past was in need and I, through the information I had obtained during the last seven years, might be able to help them. I decided to get into Amsterdam at whatever cost. Through sheer luck, at that very moment I bumped into the same gentleman with whom I had had the conversation in the barber-shop.

"I would like to talk to you," I told him, and he answered: "My office is just around the corner. Suppose you follow me there."

Once inside his private room where no one could possibly hear me, I explained who I was and told him enough about my recent exploits to show him how necessary it was for me to get to Amsterdam without any loss of time. The merchant listened patiently. Then he said: "It would mean a great deal to me, too, to get a message into that town to tell my partner to let me know what I ought to buy while the siege is going on. I had thought of sending my son. He has a small boat of his own. But he is only eighteen and apt to be a little reckless. If you will go with him, it will be different. But the trip is a bit risky. No ships are allowed to leave our port until further orders. Will you wait until to-night and take a chance?"

I told him that I would gladly take all the chances in the world if only I could get into the city and I went back to my hotel and told the landlord to lock my room and that I would that evening try and return overland to my ship at Texel to get the rest of my belongings, and he said that that was a very sensible thing to do, for I would not be able to continue my voyage to Amsterdam for at least another two weeks, unless the Prince decided to bombard the city and set it on fire, and shortly after seven that evening I left my inn and went to the house of my merchant friend and two hours later he took me to the water front and pointed a small yacht out to me and said: "Here is a letter to my partner which I hope you will deliver the first moment you have a chance. Now slip quietly on board that little yacht and I will go and talk to the guards at the end of the harbor. The tide is running out and you may be able to slip through without being noticed."

So I climbed down the wet little iron ladder to the deck of the yacht and some one caught my feet and whispered: "Be careful and don't step through the roof. This is rather a flimsy affair," and by and by my eyes accustomed themselves to the dark and I found myself sitting in the cock-pit while a young man with very broad shoulders and very competent hands was loosening the last two ropes and was doing this so carefully that they made hardly any noise when they splashed into the water. A few minutes later we were into the middle of the harbor and half an hour later we were out on the Zuyder Zee. Nothing had happened. No one had tried to stop us. The old merchant apparently had so interested the guards in his conversation that they were looking the other way when we passed them.

The boy, who was both skipper and mate of the little vessel, knew how to sail a boat and early the next morning we found ourselves outside the Gouw Zee between the island of Maarken and Volendam. I had been able to sleep a couple of hours in the small cabin and offered to take my turn at the helm, but the youthful captain was as fresh as the day that was just appearing above the horizon and he would not hear of it.

"I know this water," he said, "and I know the tides and in less than half an hour we will be in the Pampus, where there are all sorts of currents and besides, look way in the distance there. Do you see those black dots? They look like men-of-war. We soon may be in for some trouble. We might as well find out right away. Our conscience is clear and they

ELISABETH VAN LEEUWEN

The wife of Rembrandt's brother

can't do anything to us anyway." And he set course for the south and two hours later we found ourselves surrounded by seven war vessels which were slowly cruising northward. They flew the flag of the Estates General and we did not know therefore whether they were in the service of the Prince or of the city of Amsterdam. But just as we were debating what to do next, one of the ships, the *Sint Joris,* veered around in our direction and a voice from the poop-deck shouted: "Lower your sails and come alongside!" And these words of warning were followed by two or three shots from muskets which passed directly over our heads and hit the water with a great splash.

Now I am no hero and there are few things I hate quite as thoroughly as being a target for inexperienced and panicky sailors and so I let go as fine a string of vituperations as were ever heard on these placid waters and some one leaned out from one of the after port-holes and shouted: "That must be old Jan van Loon. He always was an artist at that sort of thing!" And behold, there was my good friend, Master Pieter Zuydam with whom I had studied in Leyden years before and who afterwards had become a ship's surgeon and whom I had not seen for at least a dozen years. But I felt happy that he recognized me, for now at least there was some one who could vouch for me to the commander of this squadron and as a matter of fact, as soon as I had set foot on board the *Sint Joris* I was taken to the captain who listened most civilly to my story and agreed that I ought to proceed to Amsterdam with all possible haste and present myself to My Lord Andries.

"But don't try to go any further in that pretty little yacht of yours," he warned me. "You will get in trouble every ten minutes as we fear that the Prince may try to force the harbor. I will tell you what I will do. The *Enkhuizer Maagt* has to go back anyway. She has got trouble with her rudder. You go on board her and I will give instructions that you be allowed to pass without further molestation."

I then bade farewell to my excellent young skipper, promised him that I would deliver his father's letter, was rowed on board the *Enkhuizer Maagt* and at one o'clock in the afternoon I found myself in the docks of Amsterdam, behind the Kattenburg redoubt and at half past one, set foot on shore at exactly the same spot from where I had left, almost eight years before.

But I had no chance to meditate upon this strange way in which I was returning home, for every minute now was valuable.

There was quite a crowd of people at the quai and they all seemed eager to hear the latest news from the front. Besides, I still wore the clothes I had bought in Nieuw Amsterdam and I must have looked rather queer. But two sailors, seeing that I was about to be mobbed, jumped out of the boat and made room for me and I walked up the Oude Schans and in half an hour's time I was knocking at the door of my house.

It took some time before I heard footsteps in the hall. Then the little peep-hole in the upper part of the door was opened and a frightened voice asked who was there. I said it was I, the master, returned from his foreign travels, but the voice inside said: "Go away! The master is in America. You are an impostor. Go away, or I will call the guards." And I might have found it impossible to enter my own house, when by rare good luck, my neighbor on the Houtkade, the foreman of the cannon foundry of the Hemonys, happened to leave his house and he recognized me and saw the predicament in which I found myself.

"This is a strange welcome," he said, warmly shaking me by the hand, "but we are all of us a little bit nervous these days. I myself have not been to bed for over three days and nights until this morning, when I snatched a few hours' sleep. Now let me knock and explain to your maid that she can let you in."

A few minutes later the door opened and the honest servant, full of tears and regrets, rushed out to explain how it had happened and to tell me how happy she was to see me once more and ask me to forgive her, but I told her that she had only done what was right and that I was grateful to her for taking such excellent care of my interests, even after those many years, and then I went into the house for the great moment when I should see my son again—the great moment about which I had dreamed for so many years—for which I had prepared so many fine speeches—just what I would say and what my son would answer and how we would both be so overcome by emotion that neither of us would be able to talk.

The boy was in the garden, picking radishes which he put into a little basket. He looked up when he heard my footsteps, and he wiped his muddy hands on his trousers.

Now it was going to happen!

I would open both arms wide and with a voice choked with tears, I would whisper, "My son!" and he, dumbfounded, would give one shriek, "Father!" and then he would throw himself at my breast.

Instead of which the child held one large, red radish up for my inspection and said: "Look, isn't this a big one?" I answered: "Yes, quite a big one." It was not a very brilliant retort, but one had to say something. Then I asked him: "Do you know who I am?" And he wiped his nose with the back of his muddy little hand and said: "No, unless you are the man who has come to fix the chimney."

And I said: "I am your father." And he answered: "Oh?" and went on picking radishes and so I stammered a bit helplessly: "Isn't there something you want to say to me?" And suddenly he smiled brightly and came up to me and put his hand on my arm and asked: "Did you bring me a bear? Nurse told me that if I were a good boy, father would bring me a bear when he came back. Did you bring me one?"

I told him that I had tried to bring him a bear but one fine day the bear, who was very homesick, had jumped overboard and had swum right back to America. And in this way we talked quite happily for about half an hour and then I heard a clock strike and with a shock I remembered that I had work to do that day and I said:

"Father must run now, my darling boy, but he will soon come back and stay with you always. So kiss me and then I must go." Whereupon he gave me a furtive kiss and accompanied me to the front door. But just when I was leaving the house, he called me back and said: "But, father dear, do you really mean to go out in that funny-looking cap?" And he pointed to that garment with a great deal of embarrassment.

"Why, yes, of course," I said. "That is a beaver-skin cap. Everybody wears them in Nieuw Amsterdam."

"Perhaps so," he answered, "but nobody does in Amsterdam." And then he waved his small hand at me and disappeared into the house.

Twenty minutes later I reached the Town Hall. I had anticipated considerable trouble in penetrating to Their Lordships. I had heard my grandfather tell of the siege of Leyden and how all day long eager crowds of excited people had been waiting outside the Town Hall to hear the latest news. I found two guards standing near the door and an officer of the town militia with a large orange scarf (that part of the uniform apparently had not been abandoned, although it would be a long time before any one in the city would exhibit that color as a token of jubilation) asked me what business had brought me there. I told him that I was in a hurry to speak to My Lord Cornelis Bicker, the first Burgomaster.

"Sorry," he said, "but he isn't here to-day. He caught a cold yesterday inspecting the ramparts. He is staying at home all day long. You might find him there if he is well enough to receive you."

All this was not exactly as I had expected it to be, but I consoled myself with the thought that Amsterdam was so big and so strong that the people could afford to regard a calamity like this as a sort of insignificant incident and act accordingly with studied nonchalance.

When I reached the house of My Lord Cornelis there was not even a guard there, but two private coaches waiting near by showed me that something unusual was taking place.

I knocked, and the same maid (a little older of course, but very much the same) opened the door.

"Good morning, Doctor," she said as if I had been away two or three days instead of almost eight years. "Good morning, Doctor, you want to see the master? The doctor purged him this morning. I hardly think that he can see you."

"Suppose you ask him, nevertheless. I come on very important business. He will understand. Tell him I landed an hour ago."

The maid bowed me into the small room on the left of the hall, meant for visitors of the humbler ilk. A few minutes later she returned. "The master is very sorry," she said, "but the purge is just beginning to work and he thinks you had better come back to-morrow morning, rather late."

Then I really did not know what to do. I had rushed back to the city I loved and for whose fate I felt such a keen concern, and I had seen myself rushing in upon the last meeting of the brave little band that had undertaken to defend this citadel of civic independence, and just as they had come to the conclusion that all was lost, I would open the door and say: "My Lord, despair not. I bring you tidings of an even greater land where you can settle down and enjoy the fruits of your industry without the interference of ambitious young potentates and of tyrannical princes."

Instead of which I was asked to come back the next afternoon when the indomitable hero of this glorious last cause should no longer be sitting on the ——!

I took my funny beaver-cap and slowly walked through the hall. The maid opened the door and then a voice from upstairs called out: "Is this Master Jan van Loon?" and the maid said: "Yes, My Lord." And the voice continued: "Ask him to be kind enough to come upstairs for a moment."

And so I mounted the well-known stairs and at the head was welcomed most cordially by My Lord Andries, who patted my shoulder almost affectionately and said: "What marvelous luck that you should have returned at this precise moment. Come in and meet some old friends and then let us tell you what we think you could do for us."

I entered the room and bowed politely to the four gentlemen there present, three of whom I knew by sight and who had been members of the town government when I left in '43.

"I suppose you all remember Master Jan van Loon," My Lord Andries said. "He has just returned from a very interesting voyage to the New Netherlands."

"Yes, My Lord," I interrupted him. "And coming back at a moment like this, when I find my beloved city in such a state of distress, I am happy to say that my mission had not been entirely in vain. I have discovered a territory infinitely larger than that of our Republic, perfectly suited to . . ." But before I could go any further with this speech which I had rehearsed a thousand times, My Lord Andries held up his hand. "That is very interesting, Doctor," he said, "very interesting, what you are telling us there. We would like to hear more, but for the moment we must talk of other matters. For the moment we must try and get rid of that foolish boy who intends to storm our gates. As soon as he is gone, we will have a chance to consider the future. This hour belongs to the present and it is of the present we want to speak to you. Do you know Huygens?"

"My Lord of Zuylichem?"

"Exactly."

"Yes, I have enjoyed his friendship for many years."

"Very well. We want you to render us one more service. For the moment there is only one thing for us to do, persuade or flatter or cajole this young hot-head to go back to The Hague and call off his army. We are not sufficiently prepared to stand a siege. As soon as he is gone, we can make plans for the future and no doubt we shall meet His Highness again some day under somewhat different circumstances. We have good reason to suppose that he will feel satisfied if we promise him that I and my brother Cornelis, the Burgomasters, shall retire from our posts and shall remain excluded from office for the rest of our natural lives. How long that 'rest of our natural lives' will mean, we don't of course know. Probably a couple of years or until we are strong enough to turn the tables on His Royal Highness and can perhaps induce him to return to his ancestral estates in Germany. But all that is neither here nor there. We will attend to those matters when the proper moment comes.

"To-day we are face to face with an emergency and if we can solve that emergency by offering ourselves as scape-goats and sacrificial lambs, so much the better.

"You know My Lord of Zuylichem, but you will have very few other acquaintances among the entourage of His Highness. He has dismissed most of his father's counselors and has taken on a new set of his own.

"You will probably be able to make your way to Amstelveen without attracting any attention. If any soldiers should stop you, you can tell them that you are a surgeon on the way to visit a farmer near the Noorderbrug. Find My Lord of Zuylichem and tell him, discreetly, very discreetly if you please—tell him that my brother Cornelis and I are willing to withdraw from public life if the siege is lifted at once."

"Is that the only message?"

"That is all we want him to know for the moment. My Lord of Zuylichem is a very intelligent man. He will understand and will take the necessary steps. It is now five o'clock but it will be light until eight. You can take my carriage as far as the Overtoom. There you probably can hire a peasant cart and with a bit of luck you will be able to see Huygens still this evening. Good-by and good luck!"

I bade my adieux but as I was leaving the room, My Lord Andries called me back. "Better not wear that Indian headgear," he advised. "It might attract a little too much attention. The rest of your clothes are all right, but here, take my hat!" And so I went forth upon this new adventure in the hat of one of Their Lordships who rule the destiny of the common man until they get into difficulties, when suddenly they bethink themselves of one of their humbler neighbors, call him a good fellow, pat him on the back and make use of him until the crisis has come to an end.

With a loud clatter of horses' hooves we rolled through the streets of Amsterdam which except for an occasional citizen carrying a halberd or a musket looked about as peaceful as under ordinary circumstances, but as soon as I reached the gate, the scene changed. A hastily scribbled note, however, which My Lord Andries had given me, did wonders and the Captain of the Guard told me that it was possible to proceed as far as the Overtoom. "There you will have to ask again," he said. "But an hour ago, the road was still free."

The heavy door of the gate therefore was opened and the bridge was lowered and the coachman carefully drove his horses across the slippery stones on the other side of the moat and then suddenly we found ourselves in the midst of several hundred men with spades and wheelbarrows, busily engaged in building a low bulwark of clay and mud which was to protect the gate from being surprised by a sudden attack on the part of the enemy's cavalry. Where the road broke through this earthen wall, two officers were standing together with a civilian, eagerly studying a map which the civilian held spread out before them.

We had to drive very carefully on account of all the workingmen and at that point we came to a stop because one of the horses slipped and almost fell and in so doing kicked through one of the traces. The coachman came down from his box to fix the matter and meanwhile I looked at the small group that was directing the work. I did not know the officer, but the civilian, who seemed to be in command, looked singularly familiar. At that moment he took his hat off to shade his eyes, and I recognized him. It was Jean-Louys.

He knew me at once and gayly waved his sheet of parchment, said: "Excuse me," to his two companions, and rushed over to the carriage.

"Slowly," I called out. "Slowly! you will slip."

"A thousand slips," he answered, "for the pleasure of seeing you again. And what a rentrée! How marvelously staged! What action—and what actors! And our humble leech enthroned upon the seat of the mighty. And so soon! When did you arrive?"

"About four hours ago."

"And now bound for Amstelveen on business for Their Lordships! What a diplomat was lost when you took to pills instead of to a pen!"

"Thanks for the compliment," I told him, "but how about yourself? The great philosopher, the pupil of the one and only Descartes, wallowing through the mud, building a little wall. . . ."

"Ssh!" he warned me. "Not so loud. Remember Romulus and Remus. This is a most respectable piece of defensive architecture, constructed entirely according to the principles of siege-craft as laid down by His Late Majesty the King of Sweden, Grand Duke of Pomerania and Hereditary Polisher of the Northern Star. You forget I was once one of His Majesty's most trusted officers. But what glorious absurdity! what a buffoonery! This poor clown outside who calls upon Beelzebub to come forth from his hiding place—then is scared to death when he sees that the old devil means business, and who now does not know what to do—whether to shoot or not to shoot. And we from our side also seriously playing at war—hauling guns to the parapets—hiring all the loafers in town for a guilder a day to stand guard and see that no peasant women from Slooterdijk smuggle in a couple of Orange-men beneath their petticoats. Oh, it is a glorious sight! Philosophers building salients and leeches trotting forth upon diplomatic missions!

"Bon voyage—for you will be in a hurry. Come back soon and we shall have dinner and we shall talk, talk, talk!"

Fifteen minutes later I was at the Overtoom. There had been a few hussars there that morning belonging to one of the regiments of the Frisian Prince of Orange, but they had gone away again after each one of them had ordered a couple of schnapps and had paid for them too. This last item, the fact that they had actually paid for their drinks, had filled the hearts of the near-by farmers with such surprise that they were still standing near the lock, talking about it. When I asked for a carriage to take me as far as Amstelveen, one of the older men asked me whether I meant to pay for it too.

"Surely," I answered, "as much as you care to ask."

They all opened their mouths wide and stared at each other.

"This is a new sort of a war, boys," the lock-keeper finally said. "A war in which people are polite and say pardon me before they shoot you and pay for what they get. You had better make the best of it and inspan right away."

I chose the farmer who seemed to live nearest and half an hour later I was on my way to Amstelveen, where I arrived shortly before sunset without any further untoward adventures. Three times I was stopped by mounted patrols who asked me who I was and where I was going, but when I answered them that I was a surgeon on my way to a patient, they promptly apologized for having stopped me and let me go.

Just outside the village I dismissed the driver, gave him his money and a tip and told him that if he cared to wait at his own risk, I might need him again in a couple of hours for the return trip. He said that he had nothing else to do and would go to the nearest tap-room. Any time I wanted him I need only send word to him and he would be there in two shakes.

Tipping is a strange business. Give a man one penny less than he thinks he deserves, and he will be ready to knife you at the first possible opportunity. Give him one half-penny more than he had expected, and he will be your friend for life.

The honest rustic was as good as his word. An hour later I found him at exactly the same spot where I had left him and he had even found me some bread and sausage. "For you must be hungry," he said. And he drove me back at such a rapid pace that I was able to knock at My Lord Andries' door just when the clock of the South Church was striking twelve. In the meantime, I had had many strange adventures and I had learned once more that this planet of ours is not exactly ruled by either the wisest or the noblest of God's creatures.

When I left my carriage, I had no idea in the world where I would find My Lord of Zuylichem. I decided to walk right to the village and ask the first man who looked as if he had some authority and as if he would be able to tell me. But the road was quite deserted as it was supper time, and all the soldiers engaged in this gigantic drama seemed to be in their quarters to eat their evening porridge, like well-behaved children. And the farmers were no doubt waiting on them and watching, lest these unwanted guests depart with the family silver and china.

In front, however, of one of the houses near the center of the village, one that also seemed a sort of village-inn, I saw a young man standing who was apparently engaged in the business of angling, though what he expected to catch there so late at night was somewhat of a puzzle to me. And when I came a little nearer, I noticed that he could not be fishing, for he had stuck his rod deep into the mud of the ditch and then I saw that it was not a fishing rod at all which he held in his hand, but a bamboo cane, and that he was trying to discover the depth of the water.

"Yes, my friend," I said to myself, "the locks near Muiden are open and two or three more days like the present one and a favorable wind and you will be hastening back where you came from, unless you want to get a pair of very wet feet." But I kept this pleasant thought to myself and merely said: "Pardon me, young man, but could you tell me where I could find My Lord of Zuylichem? He is said to be somewhere around here with His Highness."

"Lord of Zuylichem be damned!" the young man answered. "Do you know this part of the country?"

I said yes, that I did.

"Very well," he continued. "Then tell me how long it will be until the water here will be getting higher than the land."

I did not like the insolence of his tone but neither did I want to expose my mission to any danger by answering in too sharp a tone of voice, and so I said: "Well, I could not tell you for sure. The locks near Muiden were blown up yesterday. This afternoon I hear they cut the dikes near the Plague House and to-morrow they will be cutting the Amstel dike near the Omval. Then with a bit of a wind—and I see that the wind is turning towards the east this evening—there ought to be about three feet of water here by Thursday."

"Damn your eyes!" said the young man, waving his cane at me. "And now what do you want? You are probably a spy, sent by the bastards in that town to find out what I am doing." And more threatening: "Who are you, anyway?"

"I don't suppose it is any of your business," I replied, not without some heat, "but since you ask me so pleasantly, I will tell you that I am the barber from Ouderkerk and have been sent for by My Lord of Zuylichem to wait upon him."

"A strange time of the day to have one's whiskers attended to, but wait a moment and we will find out."

And he went to the door of the inn and shouted: "Huygens! Hey, Huygens, come here. A friend to see you."

And indeed, there was My Lord of Zuylichem, not a day older than when I had seen him last and he recognized me at once and came to me and took both my hands in his and shook them most cordially, whereupon the insolent young man whistled a loud phew! and disappeared inside the house.

As soon as I knew that no one could understand us, I whispered: "I want to speak to you alone. I have come on very important business. Have you a room to yourself here?"

"No," he said, "I am sharing a little cabinet next to the sleeping quarters of His Highness—I am sharing it with his valet. The valet is a Frenchman and I don't trust him. Let us walk up and down the road. That is the safest place."

And he took me by the arm and marched me up and down until I had delivered my message and had told him that unless the Prince accepted this sacrifice on the part of the Bicker family and was contented to save his face by some such sort of a compromise, the town would cut all the dikes and would defend itself unto the last.

This threat did not seem to impress My Lord of Zuylichem deeply. "I know our friends inside those walls just as well as those outside," he remarked dryly. "They won't fight an hour longer than is profitable. But those over here" (waving his free hand in the general direction of the village inn) "are not going to fire a single shot unless one of their soldiers happens to get too much to drink and stumbles over his own musket. What you say is right. We must find a way out that allows both sides to save their faces. The Bickers can gracefully retire from office for a couple of years without suffering any great financial or social loss. They are rich and that little Bicker girl will probably marry Jan de Witt before very long and the day may come when I will have to ask her to use her influence with her husband to get me a job as messenger-boy of the Council of State. You go back to Amsterdam to-night, my dear friend, if you can do so without breaking your neck or getting shot by a drunken Hessian. And you tell them that I will do as they asked me."

"But are you sure of all that without first speaking to His Highness?"

"Listen! His Highness wishes to God he had never started this thing. It may cost him his head or at least, his job, though it does not look as if any of the other cities were losing any sleep over Amsterdam's predicament. But he has bitten off much more than he can chew. Leave everything to me. Tell the Bickers to send us an official delegation of the sort of people who can bow themselves nicely out of a room. The Prince likes that and meanwhile I will draw up some sort of an act of agreement. With a bit of luck, all will be over by to-morrow night, except the pumping. I suppose it will cost you a pretty penny to get all this land dry again."

"To tell you the truth, I don't think we have cut enough dikes to do any considerable damage."

"Only as a sort of sample of what could be done?"

"Yes. Just about that. Enough anyway to frighten the youngsters in your army. That blustering ensign who called you just now seemed quite upset by the prospect of getting his feet wet."

"Whom do you mean? The young man with the bamboo cane?"

"Yes. The one who called you."

"He has reason to be worried. That is the Prince."

Chapter 42

THE PRINCE IS FORCED TO GIVE UP HIS NEFARIOUS DESIGNS AND FOR THE FIRST TIME IN MANY YEARS I AM ABLE TO FRY EGGS ON MY OWN KITCHEN TABLE

The rest of that memorable day belongs to history. I found my Overtoom farmer still waiting for me and without any further adventures we reached the city gate where we found everybody wide awake and looking rather sheepish, as if something awkward had just happened.

I did not discover at that moment what it was, but several days later I heard the story from one of the sergeants who had cut his finger trying to charge his musket and who had got blood poisoning in the wound.

Shortly after eleven o'clock that evening the guards had been alarmed by something that sounded like the charge of a regiment of cavalry. They had fired a volley and thereupon the enemy had disappeared but an hour later there had been another charge, answered by another volley, and so on all during the night.

Why this had not started a panic all over town, no one knew unless it were due to the fortunate circumstance that the wind was blowing the other way.

In the morning, as soon as it had become light enough, a patrol had gone out to reconnoiter. They found a couple of horses belonging to a dray-man who lived near the gate peacefully grazing just outside the ramparts. As a rule, those animals were tethered, but upon this occasion they had managed to get themselves free and they had spent a happy night trotting up and down the beautiful rampart which Jean-Louys had been constructing the afternoon before.

As for myself, as soon as I had delivered my message, I felt that I was at liberty to return home. But My Lord Andries and his brother (who had apparently entirely recovered from his recent indisposition and was now full of his usual energy) begged me to stay awhile and partake of some refreshments, as I must be very hungry and tired after such a long day, and I accepted gratefully and they sent to the kitchen for some bread and cold fish and butter and beer—a lot of beer—and then only I discovered how tired and thirsty I was and from sheer exhaustion I fell asleep right there in my chair and they put a rug over me and let me sleep, and when I woke up, it was full daylight and I felt as if I had been pulled through the eye of a needle, but soon I was joined by the two brothers who told me that a delegation from the magistrates was already on its way to Amstelveen and that they hoped that the whole business would be over before nightfall, and thereupon we breakfasted together and at ten o'clock I was at last on my way home, having returned his hat to My Lord Andries and wearing once more that strange peaked affair that had so upset the feelings of propriety of my young son and heir.

It was a warm and lovely day. Word must have gone about that the siege would soon be lifted, for the streets were much fuller than the day before and everywhere I went groups of men and women were standing around, talking about the latest news from the front, and the children improved the occasion by making even more of a nuisance of themselves than usual. About a dozen rotten apples and at least three cauliflowers were heaved at my beaver cap before I had gone more than halfway and so I knew that we were fast returning to normal conditions.

But at home I found everything in the greatest possible commotion. My small son looked the depth of despair and as soon as he saw me, he threw himself into my arms and cried: "Oh, father, I am so sorry! I thought that you had been angry with me for poking fun at your strange hat and I felt you would never, never, never come back to me!"

Whereupon I told him that father had been busy all day and all night long to help the government save the city from the Prince and he stamped his foot and said: "I hate the Prince!" But I told him that the Prince was probably doing what he thought was right, just as we were doing what we thought was right, and that there was very little reason for hatred as no harm had been done. And then I said: "Now come upstairs with me and I will wash and comb my hair and then we will go out together and buy a new hat."

In that way I took my first walk with my son and I felt very proud of myself. It had often struck me that I led much too lonely a life—that I ought to go out in company more—that I ought to marry again and perhaps have more children. But I was afraid. In all my life I had only met one woman whom I really felt that I could love and (what is more important) be patient with, even if I had a dozen headaches and she had asked me the same foolish question three dozen times. She was very handsome and she was very intelligent. She knew what I was going to say half a minute before I said it and I knew what she was going to answer before she had so much as opened her mouth. It had sometimes happened that I had not seen her for two or three months and then I discovered that I knew all the things that had happened to her and she knew all the things that had happened to me. She had liked me from the very first and I had liked her from the very first and she probably would have taken me and then I had lost courage. I had seen my brother go to his death through a woman, a heartless and silly and stupid creature who destroyed him to please her own vanity and I was afraid.

I told myself that this woman would be entirely different. I knew that she would be entirely different. And yet I did not dare go near her.

Then a number of other little incidents had occurred. I began to watch my friends. All of them were married. How many of them were really happy? How many of them were better off now than if they had stayed single? I did not know. I talked it over with Jean-Louys, the only man with whom I could talk about such things. He did not know either. He would not even offer a guess.

"I tried it once," he said. "I had to have a woman or go crazy. God had made me that way, but nobody had taken the trouble to tell me so. Wherefore I drew heavily upon the recollection of all the idiotic medieval sagas I had read as a small boy and came to the conclusion that I was another Abélard or Tristan. But I wasn't. I was a young specimen of the male order of our tribe and I was seventeen or eighteen and I experienced a hunger for the female order of our species that was perfectly normal but quite appalling.

"The moment they noticed my condition, parents and relatives and all the priests in the world came rushing down upon me and filled my head with a lot of nonsense about it. That made it all the more attractive. The girl was willing. I sinned. She sinned. We both sinned, and we had a glorious time. Did the parents and relatives and priests rush to their churches to thank God that two people had snatched a moment of happiness off the granite rock of Fate? They did not. They separated us and perhaps it was just as well. I saw the girl ten years later. She had married a wine merchant and had borne him eleven children. She was fat and dumb and had whiskers and I hated the sight of her.

"It is a difficult subject and you had better ask some one else. I suppose it is a good thing for the average man to marry. He has no resources outside himself. His wife therefore, no matter how stupid she may be, will probably amuse him instead of leaving him. He has some one to sleep with who has got to pretend that she likes him whether she really does or not. He has some one to cook for him and wash for him and look after his children. For that sort of person it is a fine arrangement—an ideal arrangement—but for people with brains—for people like you and me who have work to do in this world, it is nonsense to think of marriage. It dulls the spirits and it leads to endless misery.

"Women are vain. They like to show off. They like to be the center of whatever society they happen to frequent. They hate a man who is just above the average. They detest one who is really clever. When they run across a male being with a first rate set of brains, they are ready to commit murder. Such a fellow is their natural enemy. He robs them of the attention they want to draw unto themselves, no matter whether they are buying fish or dancing a minuet. You might marry your wonderful woman. A week afterwards she would be scratching your eyes out because His Lordship, the third assistant Burgomaster, had returned your salute without paying as much attention to her as to you."

This was sound advice no doubt, but not exactly helpful. It only bewildered me a little more than I had been before and I had left for the New World without ever having settled the question. For all I knew, the woman might be still waiting for me or might have married some one else years before and might have forgotten me completely by now.

These thoughts came running through my mind as I walked to the hat store on the Oude Singel, proudly listening to my son who told me how that old bridge, just off the Verwersgracht, had come down one day underneath the weight of a heavy piece of basalt which they were moving from the stone yards along the Amstel to the Dam to be used in the construction of the new Town Hall, how the horses that pulled the cart had been dragged into the water and had stood there for almost a whole day with their noses just above the surface until a boy had dived into the gracht and had cut them loose. And when we came to the bridge, I saw that it had been recently rebuilt and right in the middle of it there stood a familiar figure holding a pad of paper in one hand and a pencil in the other.

It was Rembrandt, not a day older than when I had last seen him, making a sketch of some boats that were unloading a cargo of peat for one of the big bakeries that work for the city's hospital.

He was so engrossed in his work that he did not notice me and I waited until I was right behind him and then I said: "Why not go to the walls and paint My Lord Banning Cocq, now that he is engaged in defending our city against the attacks of our enemies?"

Whereupon he turned around and threw both arms around my neck and kissed me on both cheeks (to the terrible confusion and shame of my small child, who hastily looked the other way) and then he said: "The poor child! Here his father returns home after years of absence, during which we have all of us missed him so much that more than once we were on the point of joining him and his band of warriors on the other side of the ocean. And here he comes back, wearing a most beautiful beaver cap and with just as little sense as ever."

"Wait a moment," I interrupted him, at the same time pulling my son from underneath the wheels of a dray, loaded heavily with barrels of salted fish. "I agree about the cap but why this slur upon my sanity? I can assure you I never felt better in all my life, nor of a better mind."

"Then why do you prattle about enemies and old Banning Cocq, whom I painted a thousand years ago, fighting somebody."

"Oh," I answered, "I was only joking. Everything seems to be going nicely now and so I suppose we can be funny about it. I was thinking of something that happened on the walls yesterday."

"The walls? What walls?"

"Why, the walls near the Haarlemmerpoort."

"They are all right. I saw them last Sunday. I took Titus for a walk to the lake. Nothing the matter with them then!"

"Of course not. I was not thinking of the walls themselves but of something that happened to the soldiers who were on guard."

"But there aren't any soldiers on guard there nowadays. There have not been for years. A few of them spend the night sleeping in the little room over the gate and that is all."

"Rembrandt," I said, "don't be silly and don't try to be funny. You know perfectly well what I mean. The walls have been manned again ever since the siege began."

"Siege?" he asked. And then I discovered that he had not heard a word about it—that he did not know that almost any time during the last three days the Prince might have bombarded us and might have blown him out of house and studio. It seemed incredible but it was true. I had had to come all the way from America to tell him that there had been an outbreak of civil war.

"But what, in the name of Heaven," I asked him, "have you been doing with yourself these last four days?"

"I have been working," he answered. "I have been doing some portraits of my brother Adriaen and his wife. He has an interesting head. Plain but interesting and I can't stop painting just because some prince of something decides that he is bored and that a little fighting would be a welcome change. Of course, if they had bombarded the city, I might have been killed. Then I would have died putting an extra coat of paint on Adriaen's nose. Like another Archimedes: Noli tangere fratrum meum. It would have been a fine death and they would have remembered me ever so much longer than they will do now. Meanwhile you have spoiled my sketch for me. I hate to tell you how I have missed you. What are you going to do now? Whither are you bound?"

And he took my son by the other hand and he led the way to the hat store and half an hour later, once more provided with a respectable headgear, black of color, and of a most conservative pattern, we returned to the Houtgracht.

But just as I was about to turn the corner, Rembrandt shouted: "Oh, no, my dear friend, that will never do! To-day you belong to me." And he took me and my boy to the house on the Breestraat and he pushed the door wide open as I had seen him do in the old happy days when Saskia was still alive, and he shouted:

"Hendrickje, go out and kill the fatted calf. The prodigal has returned." And a moment later I was looking into as handsome a pair of brown eyes as I had ever seen and a pleasant-looking girl was curtseying to me and was saying: "Oh, I suppose you are the doctor of whom the master has so often spoken. I am very glad, Sir, that you are back. I have known your son for some time. He sometimes visits us and plays with Titus."

And that is how I first met Hendrickje.

I was to see her daily for almost ten years and I was to be on terms with her of the most genuine friendship.

But I never knew a person who was as kind and simple and understanding as this peasant girl who could neither read nor write—this peasant girl whom the ministers of our town degraded to a common whore and who was more fit to sit on God's foot-stool than ninety-nine out of every hundred little saints who were allowed in the Divine presence.

For the little saints, as a rule, had only saved themselves. And this big-hearted sinner, who was cast out by the respectable part of the community, lost herself in order to save the man she loved.

REMBRANDT'S BROTHER ADRIAEN

(about 1650)

Chapter 43

I WRITE MY OFFICIAL REPORT AND WHAT BECAME OF MY RECOMMENDATIONS ABOUT AFFAIRS IN AMERICA

The next six months of my life were very busy and very interesting, and therefore very happy.

Everything came as the Bickers had planned. The Prince, who by this time had realized his mistake, was glad to accept the compromise they suggested. It allowed him to retire more or less gracefully from a position that had become exceedingly difficult.

Nothing had happened according to his plans. The "money-grubbers" of Amsterdam for whom His Highness and his French friends had often expressed their unbounded contempt, had not shown the white feather but had prepared for action with an energy and a display of personal courage that no one had dared to predict. The common people in Amsterdam, the staunch old friends of the House of Orange, who according to the words of their pastors were "ready to rise as soon as the Prince should show himself outside the city gate," had done nothing of the sort. They had rushed to arms, but only to defend their beloved town against the foreign mercenaries who were threatening the safety of those who were supposed to be their masters.

A week before in The Hague, after an excellent dinner, it had all seemed so beautifully simple. The poor, down-trodden members of the working classes would take their muskets and would rush to the Town Hall shouting: "Death to the tyrants!" Perhaps they would even hang a couple of Aldermen and so much the better!

They had taken their muskets and had indeed rushed to the seat of government but only to cheer for their noble saviors and vow fidelity unto death.

Yes, there was no use talking. It had all come very differently from what one had had reason to expect. The polite exchange of some very polite notes (beautifully polished by My Lord of Zuylichem and his friends from the Dam) had settled the whole matter in a most tactful and agreeable manner. Within a week, the regiments of His Highness were back in their usual quarters and My Lord Cornelis and his brother Andries had packed their papers and documents, had surrendered their seals of office and had gracefully withdrawn from public life.

It was observed, however, that the vacancies caused by their withdrawal were not at once filled with other candidates, but remained unoccupied, as a silent but eloquent protest against a policy which had tried to achieve by means of violence what could have been accomplished equally well in a perfectly legitimate manner.

The other members of the government residing outside of Amsterdam who had dared to oppose His Highness' projects and who (as we now discovered) had been lifted from their beds by a company of hussars and had been incarcerated in the castle of Loevenstein without any process of law, were allowed to return to their homes.

For the moment Amsterdam was obliged to accede to the demands of His Highness in regard to the strength of the army, but Their Lordships counterbalanced this decision by increasing the strength of the town militia from twenty companies to fifty-four, and they constructed a series of block-houses around the city which doomed all future surprise attacks to absolute failure.

Thus ended one of the strangest episodes in the history of our country, in which water had flowed more freely than blood, for not a single soldier had lost his life. A great many of them developed serious colds in consequence of the muddy state of the territory in which they had been forced to operate. And that was all.

The holes in the dikes were speedily repaired. The farmers who had suffered damage or who claimed that they had suffered damage, were repaid according to the reasonableness of their lamentations. A number of bad poets on both sides wrote very bad poetry in honor of the success or failure of the famous "attentat." Two or three very ugly pennies were struck to commemorate the courage of the defenders or the attackers, and the siege of Amsterdam belonged to the past.

As the relations with The Hague remained more or less strained, we were not kept very carefully informed about the secret negotiations which His Highness was reported to have continued as soon as he had returned to his Palace in the Woods. I am afraid that those would have brought our country into serious difficulties with all the world. For it now seems quite certain that His Highness not only meant to conclude a treaty of amity (and 60,000 men) with the King of France who was then at war with his Spanish neighbors, but also that he was contemplating an invasion of England to bring the Stuarts back to the throne and make an end to the rule of Cromwell and his Puritan cohorts.

To what extremes of misery these ambitious schemes would have led us it is impossible to state. Early in October the Prince had gone to his estates in the eastern part of the country to do some hunting. On the 27th of October, he complained of feeling ill. The local surgeon could not diagnose the complaint and sent the patient back to The Hague. The trip in a draughty coach must have aggravated his condition. When he reached The Hague it was plain that he was suffering from "variola minor," or small-pox. He was bled twice, but rapidly sank into a coma. On the sixth of November he died. A week later his widow was successfully delivered of a son. The child was called Willem after his father, and for convenience' sake was numbered Willem III.

We all piously but fervently prayed that the boy might take after his great-grandfather. As for the father, we peacefully forgot him and that was perhaps the kindest thing to do.

And as for myself, I never regretted the humble rôle I had been allowed to play during those momentous days. Through the good services of Captain Wouters and the landlord of the Roskam in Hoorn I received all my trunks and my valuable collection of American plants and shrubs in perfect order. Only two or three specimens had died. All the others, wonder above wonder, had survived the hardships of the voyage. I made a present of them to the Botanical Garden in Leyden where they proved of great value to the students of botany.

My papers, too, which I had entrusted to the captain, I received back without losing a single letter, and after copying them and rewriting parts, I was able to offer my report to Their Lordships within less than six months after my arrival. They expressed themselves as being highly grateful and appreciative of my efforts and my devotion to their interests. As I would surely understand myself, the great change in the political situation which had temporarily deprived them of much of their power, made it impossible for them to act immediately upon all my suggestions. But they would carefully consider everything I had told them and would take the necessary steps as soon as possible.

That ended my personal participation in the great American adventure. My Lord Andries died in '52 and his brother followed him to the grave two years later and I lost contact with the Bicker family.

In the year 1652 Nieuw Amsterdam received full civic rights and the government of the town was copied upon the system of government which prevailed in our own country.

Four years later, in '56, the town of Amsterdam paid the West India Company 600,000 guilders for a tract of land along the Delaware River where a new and independent colony was to be founded, to be known as Nieuwer Amstel. All over the land the new board of directors advertised for immigrants willing to go to the New World and devote themselves to the business of raising grain. In my report of the year '51 I had definitely indicated this region as most suitable for the purpose which was in the minds of Their Lordships.

In how far, however, they had acted upon my original recommendations, I am unable to tell. The sons were not like their fathers. I had been sent out to do a certain job. I had done it. I had been well paid for my efforts. That ended the story as far as they were concerned. And as far as I was concerned, too.

Chapter 44

THERE WAS ONE WOMAN I LOVED AND I LOST HER

At first it had seemed best for me to return to my practice.

During my last interview with My Lord Andries he had asked me suddenly what I expected in a way of reward. I told him that I expected nothing. I had been paid generously for my services and was content.

"No," he then replied, "but what I mean is this. Isn't there some office you would like to have? We are no longer as powerful as we once were, but our former colleagues still listen to us attentively when we offer to make a little suggestion."

But I assured His Lordship that this was out of the question. We had always been very simple people. None of my ancestors had ever held public office and we were little gifted for that sort of work. I would only have made myself slightly ridiculous and would have lost the respect of my neighbors if through the influence of powerful friends I should suddenly reappear as some High- and Noble-Born Keeper of the Official Accounts or Inspector of the Local Pawnshops. No, I could not think of it! But His Lordship could render me one great service, the nature of which I then explained.

The shares of the East India Company, which my uncle in Veere had left me, had increased in value and assured me a comfortable competence for the rest of my days. I therefore need not resume my practice. But two trips across the ocean and a long residence in the New World had shown me once more how terribly neglected the surgery was on board those vessels that belonged to the regular navy or to the merchant fleet. And that was in time of peace when nothing much more serious ever occurred than a broken leg or a twisted ankle. What it would be like in case of war, when the wounded lay piled three deep in the hold of the vessel while the surgeons worked by the light of a candle and sawed off arms and legs amidst the groaning of the dying and the stench of the dead, I did not even dare to imagine. I wanted very much to continue my researches in the field of anesthetics. And if Their Lordships would talk to their friend and colleague, Doctor Tulp, and would ask him to bring about some sort of an arrangement which would allow me to continue my studies along that line in the hospitals of the city, I would be deeply grateful.

My Lord Andries was as good as his word. Within less than two weeks after our last interview, Doctor Tulp sent for me. He had been one of the four men who on behalf of the city had taken part in the negotiations with the Prince and who had signed the final agreement which had raised the siege and he was generally recognized as one of the strongest men in our town. He received me most charmingly, asked a great many very intelligent questions about my travels in the New World and declared himself to be in hearty sympathy with my plans for the future. Indeed, he then and there gave me practically carte blanche to do whatever I wanted to do within my particular field of investigation.

Of course, a great many of my colleagues objected strenuously when I knocked once more at the hospital's doors and demanded that they did not operate upon their patients without at least giving me a chance to try and alleviate the sufferings of these poor people by first bringing about a state of semi-consciousness. Some accused me of being a meddler with God's will and others called me a quack and a charlatan who merely wanted to make himself conspicuous. They even went so far as to tell their poor ignorant customers that I had sold my soul to the Devil and meant to cast a spell upon them as soon as they should have lost consciousness, and often my experiments failed because the patients had been thrown into such a state of panic by these lies and they fought so violently to escape from my administrations that in several instances they were threatened with heart-failure and I had to desist and leave the room.

But gradually when it was observed that I charged nothing for my labors and that both the surgeon and his victims benefited greatly from the absence of that hideous pain that often ruined the poor victim for life (even if he survived the knife and the saw), the medical faculty slightly relented and the sick too began to drop their suspicions whenever my name was mentioned, until in the end, hardly an operation was performed without my assistance.

I was often asked to give away the secret of those vapors with which I filled the victim's lungs before he was fastened to the operating table. A secret, of course, it never was, for I freely told all of my colleagues who showed a serious interest. But until I should have perfected my methods a little more thoroughly, so that all elements of danger had been completely removed, I thought it wiser not to put the result of my studies into print.

All the mountebanks and medicasters who make the rounds of our country fairs would at once have set up as "painless surgeons," and with their total lack of training in the true principles of medicine and the chemical sciences, they would undoubtedly have done much more harm than good.

These vapors which I used were a very dangerous thing in the hands of an unskilled amateur. Out of love for my fellow-men I therefore decided not to put my method into book form until I should have made it absolutely fool-proof. I have not reached that point even to-day. But a large number of reliable surgeons have received their education in this field of medicine at my own hands and the story that I meant to keep this form of treatment a secret in order to enrich myself is now no longer believed by any one except those whose ignorance and arrogance it has been ever my pleasure to reveal.

My personal life therefore continued to run its placid course as it had done eight years before. I seriously thought once more of contracting matrimony. I was still afraid of taking the step, but my son needed a mother and I, let me confess it, craved some sort of human relationship which would allow me to put the interests and desires of another person ahead of my own.

Besides, then as now, I hated to be alone. All day long I worked. At night unless I had some one to talk to, I usually returned to my laboratory. I was rapidly degenerating into a perambulating handbook of medicine. It would be pleasant to go back to the Houtgracht after a day in the hospital and be able to think of something besides chloral solutions. But the number of my female acquaintances was very small. And so I bethought myself once more of the one charming person whom I had known several years before. I discovered that she had left Amsterdam and was living in the country with a brother of hers, who was a minister of the Gospel but a man of sense and breeding. I wrote her a long letter and explained my point-of-view as gracefully as I could, though I was conscious all the time that my effusions were not exactly a masterpiece of romantic or erotic literature.

Two weeks later I received an answer. A single sheet of paper on which she had scrawled the sign with which astronomers indicate the planet Venus accompanied by the words: "Will it be ♀ or Cannabis Indica?"

I studied this problem for a long time before I began to understand what she was driving at. Then I understood and I took one of the finest beaver skins I had brought with me from Nieuw Amsterdam and with that red paint with which the Indians ornament their faces and arms and chest when they go forth to war, I drew a single picture on the back of it—♀.

For I was in a very serious mood and it was to be Venus, while my experiments with hemp as a means of bringing about senselessness from pain were to come second.

After another fortnight (just before the day of St. Nicholas) I received a package containing a large heart made of gingerbread. It showed two figures, a ♀ and a ♄ intertwined with gold laurel leaves. I accepted the challenge, even if she identified me most uncomplimentarily with the ancient god known as Saturn.

I left for the country that same afternoon and two months later, after all the endless formalities of both the Church and the civic authorities had been complied with, we were married.

My wife was all and everything I had ever dared to hope for. She was companion and mistress and good friend and wise counselor. She could laugh with tears in her eyes and weep with a smile. She upset all my previous notions about women and made me feel ashamed of many things I had said and thought upon that subject. And she died when our first child was born and her last words were: "It would have been wonderful if only you had had a little more courage many, many years ago." And then she said: "I am in great agony. Perhaps our friend Cannabis will come in handy after all." And I sent to the hospital for my apparatus, but when they brought it she was dead, and so was the child.

And that was the last of my efforts to join the ranks of my neighbors who led what they were pleased to call "respectable and regular lives."

Respectable my life has been and to spare.
God only knows how dull and respectable!
But "regular"—never.

Since that day there have been three things that have kept me going: my son and my friends—my work—and the recollection of one year of perfect happiness. It was not much, I know. It was not very much. But it was so infinitely more than came to most people that I had reason to be contented. Contented and grateful and perhaps a little proud that I had cheated Fate out of twelve whole months of perfect passion and complete companionship.

"But it might have been different if only I had had a little more courage."

It seemed like a fitting epitaph for all my failures.

Chapter 45

OUR NEIGHBOR, MENASSEH BEN ISRAEL, DECIDES TO LEAVE AMSTERDAM FOR LONDON

So much for my own personal adventures during the year following immediately upon my return. But there were other threads I had to pick up and some of those had become pretty badly entwined and it took considerable trouble to straighten them out.

Jean-Louys of course had not changed in the least during the many years I had not seen him. He was the only man I ever knew who had achieved contentment as a result of philosophic reasoning.

There were certain outward circumstances which had made it easy for him to conclude a truce with those influences that are the natural enemies of a pleasant and equitable existence. It is true that he possessed few things which he could call his own. At the same time he had had a tremendous number of experiences. This is a clumsy way of saying what I really mean to say. Jean-Louys was a man without any vain regrets about those many might-have-beens which play such havoc with the lives of most of us. His soul was a well-regulated mansion in which all the doors were neatly closed and were kept closed, no matter what provocation there might be for him to throw a look into the past.

The usual "if-onlys" and "when-thus-and-thuses" had never been allowed to encumber the hallways and corridors of his memory. They simply were not allowed on the premises.

Whatever was dead and gone was dead and gone and stayed that way.

Jean-Louys himself contributed his success as a practical philosopher to his interest in logarithms.

"Logarithms," he used to say, "like all mathematics, are intimately connected with neatness and orderliness. If I am neat and systematic in solving my problems, I simply cannot make mistakes. If I neatly proceed from one solution to the next, the final result must be perfect. Apply that same rule to human conduct and in less than no time human society would be perfect."

I doubted whether this was really the solution for the manifold difficulties of existence. Rather did I attribute the Frenchman's success to a different conception of what I might call the technique of living, as practiced in his own country, among the class of people to which he belonged in consequence of his noble birth.

During that long winter I had spent in the cabin of Father Ambrosius in the land of the Cayugas I had learned a great deal about the educational methods of the Jesuits and they of course are the people who

THREE HEADS OF WOMEN

nowadays get hold of the children of the aristocracy as soon as they are old enough to wash themselves and eat without the help of a pusher. The members of the Company of Jesus who devote themselves to that sort of pedagogical work are very clever—brilliantly clever. They realize that man is but an imperfect replica of His divine example. As a result, they don't expect too much—try to make virtues as attractive as possible and show themselves pleasantly surprised and deeply grateful when one of their young charges does his best and attempts to achieve a fair degree of perfection.

If at first he does not quite succeed, they do not scold him but admonish him in almost tender fashion until by a system of trial and error, they make him realize from his own free will that he will be much happier if he follows the counsel of those who are older and wiser than he himself, and that the rules of conduct which he is asked to obey are the result of centuries of trial and experiment and not a haphazard collection of regulations devised by an inconsequential spiritual tyrant who looked for something to do to while away the tedious hours of a sleepless night.

Perhaps such a philosophy of life is in keeping with the warm and agreeable climate of the South. We, in northern lands, forever hiding from rain and cold, follow a different method of thought. Our preceptors, their ears glued to the thunderous "THOU SHALT NOT! THOU SHALT NOT!" that resounded once upon a time from the summit of Mount Sinai, have only one purpose: to make sin as vile and as hateful as possible. At the same time they put their ideals of good behavior so high that not one child in a million can ever hope to come up to those elevated standards. And as a result, there is an everlasting conflict between Good and Evil that is most upsetting to the peace of mind of the young pupil and can only do him harm. He knows that he can't possibly ever hope to reach that degree of perfection which is held up before him as the goal of all his endeavors. At the same time he is in dreadful fear lest he stumble and gain the ill-will of a God who is the most vigilant and exacting of judges and executioners. He is "good" and stays "good" not because he has learned from his own experience and observation that being "good" is the same as being "intelligent" or being "sensible." He remains "good" merely from fear of being discovered in an act that is considered "bad." But all the time he is in secret rebellion against his innermost desires and the thousand and one curiosities that he must repress unless he is willing to risk a descent to the very bottom of Hell.

And when he reaches the so-called years of discretion, and discovers that the sun does not stop shining nor the tides stop running because a certain number of people have failed to obey the Mosaic commandments, he feels that he has been cheated. Then he either tries to make up for lost opportunities (as happened in the case of my poor brother) or he keeps to the narrow path but becomes a man with a grudge against Fate—the most unfortunate and pitiable of all human beings, bar none.

Jean-Louys, as a product of the former school of training and besides, a man of wide learning and possessed of vast worldly experience, had achieved happiness because he had put his intellectual and spiritual house in perfect order as a result of which it was impossible either to surprise or disappoint him.

But among my Dutch friends, I found a great deal of work to do. Most of them were at sixes and sevens, both with themselves and with their surroundings and no amount of pleading or reasoning seemed to make the slightest impression upon their firm conviction that this was a miserable vale of tears and that man was doomed to pass through the valley of life with a maximum of sorrow and a minimum of joy.

And to my great surprise I discovered that the excellent Rabbi Menasseh ben Israel was by no means that paragon of resignation and submission which I had been led to suppose from the letters of Jean-Louys. I mentioned this to the Frenchman and he agreed that the good Rabbi seemed far from happy when we called on him.

"But things may have changed somewhat in the meantime," he suggested, and this I found to be true after a very short period of investigation. All was not well with the Jewish community in Amsterdam and Menasseh took this internal strife very much to heart. At first I thought that the refusal of Bernardo to return home with me might have been responsible for the state of irritation in which I found him whenever I called, but soon I discovered that I was mistaken.

"The poor boy!" he said. "Why, I am glad he has found some happiness at last. Few people ever went through such sufferings as he did. I suppose, since we over here paid for his trip, he ought to have sent us a little more detailed account. All I have had so far consists of a single letter, saying: 'No, they are not here,' and signed: 'Your loving pupil, Bernard, not of Clairvaux but of Mohegania.' And that was not very much and rather less than I had expected. It was not exactly the sort of literary document I would have liked to show to those of my constituents who had financed the expedition. I just lied about it when they asked me and told them that the dear boy had found the field of investigation so much larger than any of us could possibly have foreseen that it would take him several more years before he could come to any definite conclusions and in the meantime they must exercise patience. Now if you will join me in this little fib and will bear me out if they should happen to ask you, no great harm will be done."

"Yes," I answered, "but after a while they will begin to wonder. We can stave them off one or two years, three perhaps, but then they will insist upon adequate answer."

"And I shall not be there to give it to them."

I looked at him in surprise. "Surely," I said, "you don't mean to die before then! You must be younger than I am and I mean to live another fifty years."

And then he told me of his worries and of his plans to leave the Republic and settle in London. It was the old, old story of prosperity proving more dangerous and disastrous than the adversity that had gone before. When the Jews first fled to Amsterdam they were poor and miserable and humbly grateful that they had been allowed to escape with their bare lives. They had built themselves a small synagogue and being given every opportunity to develop their natural-born gifts for commerce and barter, they had done exceedingly well and soon had been counted among the richest inhabitants of the city. Then they had built themselves a larger synagogue and at once they had been beset by endless unforeseen difficulties.

One group wanted their children to be taught the Torah rather than the Talmud. Others preferred the Talmud to the Torah. They all had taken sides and before any one knew what had happened, there had been two synagogues instead of one, which fought each other with the fury and bitterness of brothers engaged in a family feud. No sooner had the quarrel been brought to a successful ending (mostly by the good efforts of Menasseh himself, who having lived among the Catholics of Portugal and the Protestants of La Rochelle, felt very little love for useless strife) than the unfortunate incident with Acosta had taken place. The terrible, almost inhuman, humiliations to which this poor suffering creature had been obliged to submit himself before he was readmitted into the fold of the faithful had done a great deal of harm to the good name of the Jews, who had found a refuge in our country. His examination had not attracted very much attention. In so far as it had become known, it had been regarded as a purely local affair of the Jewish colony and a feeble attempt on the part of the Rabbis to bring the matter to the attention of Their Lordships the Magistrates by accusing their victim of having attacked the doctrine of the immortality of the soul, was quickly squashed and the Rabbis had been told to mind their own business.

But when Acosta, in the utter loneliness of his heart, had asked to be reaccepted as a member of the fold, and as an act of penance had been obliged to stretch himself full length across the threshold of the Temple, that every one of the True Believers might step over his prostrate body and spit on him, word had come from the Town Hall that those of the Synagogue should remember when a good thing ceased to be a good thing and should not indulge in practices that were contrary to all the established customs of the country in which they enjoyed such signal hospitality.

A week or so after this occurrence poor Acosta, who had been brought up as a Portuguese nobleman and who could not stand the idea of the ignominious dishonor he had suffered at the hands (or rather at the feet) of the rabble from the Amsterdam ghetto, quietly and unostentatiously put a bullet through his heart. This had caused a tremendous scandal all through town. A few of the dominies undoubtedly approved of such severity of doctrine and one or two of them had even tried to comment discreetly upon the fate that awaited all those who undertook to oppose the will of the Lord Sabaoth and his trusted servants. Their Lordships, however, had feared the bad impression the incident might cause abroad and they had sent for those responsible for the administration of the Synagogue, who had been responsible for the tragedy, and had told them in very plain terms: "One more such occurrence and all of you are put on board ship and are returned whence you came!"

Those stern words of warning had not missed their purpose. For more than ten years the Jews had rigorously kept their private religious differences out of the courts and carefully abstained from doing anything that might once again bring them in the center of the public interest. But now fresh difficulties threatened to make an end to this era of good understanding.

It was all on account of this young Baruch de Spinoza about whom Jean-Louys had already written me once or twice in his last letters and whom I had met years before at Menasseh's house. A bright boy. A very bright boy. The son of immigrant parents but a little too inquisitive and much too independent. He was not yet twenty but he had already mastered Latin, outside his studies in the Law, and he was full of ideas which he had got from Plato and Aristotle. Furthermore he had concluded an intimate friendship with a number of Dutch scientists who were known to hold very liberal views upon all problems connected with religion. And furthermore a little over a year ago he seemed to have met some one who had introduced him to the works of Descartes. All this could lead to no good end and honest Menasseh was greatly perplexed by the problem of how to keep this youngster from jumping over the traces.

"He has some money of his own," he concluded his recital of woe, "and does not depend upon our good will for his living. He has concluded some very powerful friendships with people who are well regarded by Their Lordships. If we are ever obliged to excommunicate him, there will be another scandal compared to which that of Acosta was mere child's play. For Acosta had been alone so much of his life that he had grown a little queer—yes, I might even say that he was no longer possessed of his reason when he committed suicide. But this young Baruch is a very likable youngster, and as bright as a fresh daisy. I have done my best to keep the peace and so far I have been successful. But the day will come when I will no longer be able to prevent my colleagues from jumping at his throat. And then—what turmoil there will be! And how all our neighbors will shout: Look at those dirty Jews! They can never live in peace with any one. As soon as they are no longer persecuted by some one else they must start squabbling among themselves and do all sorts of cruel things to their own people out of sheer wickedness of heart."

That there was a good deal of truth in all this, I could not possibly deny, and I heartily agreed with Menasseh that he might just as well find himself another and happier home before the crisis actually occurred.

"I would like to go somewhere," he said, "where we aren't quite so prosperous. As long as we are poor we are the finest people on earth, but as soon as we grow rich, we are terrible!" And he told me of his plans to move to London.

"That General Cromwell," he said, "is not in the least the man most people imagine him to be. He is head and shoulders above the average run of his followers. I think that he even would have spared the King if His Majesty had not proved himself such a scoundrel. I have written to him, to Cromwell I mean, and I know that he has regarded my letters with considerable favor. There have not been any Jews in England for more than three centuries. It is time we returned there to prepare the way for the coming of the Messiah. I can take my printing-press with me and I can just as well publish my books there as here. And it will be much easier to preach good sermons in a community where there are not quite so many opulent parishioners who say to themselves: 'How now? I gave ten ducats to the poor last year and this man comes and preaches a sermon upon the dangers of greed!' "

That much about the troubles of Menasseh ben Israel, who was one of the most intelligent and broad-minded Jews who ever dwelled in our city. Eventually he was to make good his threat and was to move from Amsterdam to London. But ere he could put this plan into practice, a great deal of water was to pass underneath the big Amstel bridge. Water mixed with blood and troubled by the agony of men who had died in battle.

When I was a small boy and learned my catechism, I was taught that God had created man after His own image just 4,000 years ago. That is a long stretch of time—4,000 years. But the human race seems to be very slow to learn its lessons. For every time two nations, like two dogs, want the same thing, the same bone or the same slice of territory, they know no better way of settling their difficulties than by turning themselves into the semblance of wolves and by fighting each other until they are both of them so completely exhausted that neither of them is able to enjoy his ill-gotten plunder.

Our first war with England broke out in the year 1652. The cause was mutual jealousy. We were jealous of England's success in Asia and America, and England was jealous of the rapidly increasing riches which we derived from the spice trade in the Indies and from being able to engage in the carrying trade more profitably than any of our neighbors.

In order to deprive us of the revenue derived from that particular form of commerce, Cromwell in the year 1651 did exactly what Jean-Louys had predicted that he would do. He made Parliament pass a law which practically excluded our ships from all English harbors. For our vessels could only be loaded with goods manufactured at home when they set sail for a British port and we manufactured very little that was wanted in England.

Of course, these real, underlying causes were never mentioned when the British representative in The Hague addressed himself to the Estates General with his ever-increasing lists of complaints.

Almost twenty years before seven Englishmen, accused of living where they had no right to live, had been most brutally executed by soldiers of the East India Company in the island of Amboyna.

That was perfectly true. Our only possible excuse for this crime was that it had happened during the unsettled days of helter-skelter grabbing of islands and empires when there had been neither law nor decency to regulate the behavior of the contending parties.

I think that Their Lordships of the Estates General were perfectly willing to pay an indemnity to the descendants of those poor victims, but Parliament asked for 300,000 pounds sterling, or 3,600,000 guilders in our own money and that seemed a little too much.

Then there was another grievance. Our Admiral Tromp had destroyed the second Spanish Armada in the roads of the Downs without first asking England's permission. That had happened a dozen years before and as it had been to the direct advantage of the British people to see Spain deprived of the last vestiges of her naval power, nobody at home quite understood why this should be held up against us as an act that ought to be answered by a declaration of war.

Then there was the murder of an English diplomatic agent at The Hague, who had been killed by an irresponsible group of drunken Royalists who had found a temporary refuge in that city.

And finally (and here we were on more solid ground) there were the very cordial relations which had existed between the Prince of Orange, now defunct, and his late father-in-law, the pretender to the throne of England.

All during the year '51 and the first half of '52 there was friction between the two countries. But of what actually happened I knew very little. It was the period of my second marriage. During those months there was so much to interest me at home that I rarely visited one of those taverns where one could hear the latest news. I saw a good deal of my friends, but they unfortunately regarded politics as a pastime unworthy of the attention of intelligent human beings. And so, for once, I was deeply ignorant of the state of the country and I sincerely hoped that I would continue to dwell in that condition of blessed ignorance for the rest of my days.

But when I returned from my wife's funeral, I found the walls of our city plastered with announcements of the Admiralty, offering all those who enlisted a bonus of sixty florins and a promise of a pension for their relatives in case they got killed in the service of their country. For a moment, in the bitterness of my heart, I thought of enlisting. Then I turned on my heel and went home. I found my son playing peacefully in the kitchen.

"My boy," I said, "something terrible has happened. The country is at war."

He clapped his hands and ran away to tell his nurse. I heard him in the hall.

"Oh, goody! goody!" he said. "We are going to fight and I am going to be a soldier and I am going to kill all the dirty enemies!"

And then I decided that I still had a purpose in life.

Chapter 46

WE ONCE MORE FIGHT THE ENGLISH

The war lasted two years and it affected our lives in a great many ways. The quarrel between the Prince and Their Lordships of Amsterdam had done very little good to the development of adequate means of defense for the country as a whole, and as a result we suffered one defeat after another. Within less than ten months, we had lost more than 1,600 of our merchant vessels. Tromp, the greatest naval strategist of our time, had been killed in action and a naval engagement that lasted three days and three nights had ended in a draw. Considering our lack of preparation, we had to count ourselves fortunate that the English were prevented from landing on our coast, but our trade was temporarily at least completely ruined. In Amsterdam, vast fortunes were lost through the depreciation of all commercial paper. More than 2,000 houses stood empty and were for sale without any one wishing to buy them and the Magistrates felt so thoroughly disheartened that they decided not to build their new Town Hall according to the original plans of Master van Campen but to do with one story less, merely in order to save a few thousand guilders.

But in England too the struggle was making itself felt in a very unpleasant and painful fashion, and General Cromwell, who at last thought his position sufficiently strong to make himself Lord Protector of the former Kingdom and who expected a certain amount of opposition to this project (as was only natural), was all in favor of concluding a hasty peace.

As soon as he had received solemn assurances that the Republic not only would cease to support the Stuarts but would also exclude the young son of the late Prince Willem from all participation in the future government of the United Seven Netherlands, he declared himself satisfied. The Navigation Act of course was maintained, but our sailors soon discovered so many ways in which they could circumnavigate this particular bit of law that no one worried very seriously about it and that most people were even willing to overlook the very humiliating additional articles of peace which bade all Dutch ships lower their flags whenever they met an English rival as a sign of outward deference and respect.

As always under such circumstances, everything was arranged for us by Their Lordships of the Estates General who were now once more the undisputed rulers of the country. They told us just as much or just as little as they thought was good for us. The fact, for example, that at the conclusion of peace they meant to exclude the House of Orange from all public office they kept a profound secret until it was much too late

REMBRANDT'S FATHER

for the mass of the people to do anything about it beyond giving vent to a certain degree of anger by shoving in a few windows and booing those who were suspected of having taken a more direct part in the negotiations which had led to this fateful decision.

And in regard to the conduct of the war, too, we were kept in complete darkness and had to content ourselves with poor little scraps of news that would not have satisfied a cat.

In consequence whereof most of the common people soon lost all interest in the struggle except in so far as they were directly hit in their purse by those taxes that are the inevitable concomitant of such a struggle. And I, disheartened by my short-lived happiness and perhaps more tired from my eight years' voyage in foreign parts than I knew, withdrew almost completely from public gatherings and came to depend more and more upon the companionship of my friends.

But the house in the Jodenbreestraat, which for the first time in its history was beginning to look like a real home, saw more of me than ever before. I was welcomed there both by Rembrandt himself and by the handsome Hendrickje with the utmost cordiality. They showed the same sentiments toward Jean-Louys and the four of us spent a very happy time while the Lord Protector over on the other side of the North Sea and Their Lordships, our own Protectors, fought each other to the death to decide who should get the greater part of certain spoils that belonged to neither of them.

Chapter 47

I MEET MY COLLEAGUE, DR. EPHRAIM BUENO, WHO HAD TAKEN CARE OF REMBRANDT'S FAMILY WHILE I WAS IN AMERICA

A dozen or so years before, ere I had started upon my American adventure, Jean-Louys, Bernardo, Selim and I used to meet each other nearly every Sunday morning to spend the day in some tavern at not too far a distance from town.

Now Selim had departed to partake of the quiet pleasures offered by the hospitable shores of the Bosphorus—Bernardo had become a Mohegan chieftain and Jean-Louys and I remained alone, and since even the best of friends will tire of each other if they have to listen to each other's everlasting monologues, it was quite natural that instead of going on long Sabbatical walks, we should drift into the habit of spending at least part of the day with our painter friend of the Breestraat.

Only extreme youth can be hilarious and full of good spirits early in the morning. We, however, were fast approaching an age when one likes to be alone for at least part of every twenty-four hours, and we used to improve the time when other people went to church, puttering around the house, until a little after eleven, Jean-Louys would drop in on me and then the faithful Jantje would invariably remark:

"I suppose His Highness will stay for dinner." (He was the only baron she had ever met and she meant to make the most of her opportunity.) And Jean-Louys would slap his hands in surprise and would say, "Ah, my beautiful Antoinette, but that would cause too much trouble." To which she would reply, "No trouble whatsoever. I have already counted on your being here." And they both would laugh right heartily, and we men would retire to my working room where we talked of this and that until Jantje came to tell us that "the food was on the table." I had tried to teach her for many years to say, "Monsieur le Baron est servi," but at the last moment she always lost courage and the much less elegant but rather more direct announcement was the only compromise she would accept, although even this form of invitation to partake of her culinary efforts appeared to her as a direct manifestation of that French effeminacy which according to her innermost conviction would some day destroy the whole fabric of our noble northern civilization.

After dinner, during which we had been joined by my son who had a seat and a knife and a spoon of his own (I never approved of the prevailing habit of keeping children standing at the table and letting them eat only with their fingers), we went back to the workroom to smoke a pipe of tobacco, and as soon as the chimes of the South Church had announced the third hour of the afternoon, we took our hats and capes and walked around the corner to the house on the Jodenbreestraat which by this time had acquired a look of pleasant familiarity and no longer made the impression that it had been finished only day before yesterday. And inside too there had been many changes. The ground floor still looked like the store-room of a dealer in antiques—statues and bits of old armament and a most heterogeneous collection of pictures gathered from all the four corners of the European continent. On the top of a large oaken cupboard, two large globes and a foreign-looking helmet which a few weeks previously had adorned the head of Rembrandt's brother Adriaen.

The staircase which led to the second story was half hidden by a bit of tapestry that had once been the pride of a small Flemish castle in the neighborhood of Antwerp which had gone up in flames during the siege of 1585. On the table in the center of the hall, a large marble wine-cooler and a couple of daggers of Italian provenance. Over the door that led to the Side Room, was a Venetian mirror in an ebony frame. I only mention the things one remembered seeing when one entered. The others would fill a small catalogue, and as all of them were sold at auction long before the death of their owner, it would indicate a serious lack of piety were I to try to enumerate them.

But the old disorder had somehow undergone a change. During the last days of Saskia's life and immediately after her death, one felt that there was something wrong in this house. Tables and chairs and pictures and globes were all thickly covered with dust. Milk pitchers were standing in doorways where they did not belong. An occasional pail of forgotten garbage would strike an unpleasant note next to the green velvet covering of an ornamental Spanish chair.

Now everything was neat and clean and spick and span. People were living in this house, not just camping out like the mutilated soldiers and their wild women in the wooden shacks just outside the Haarlem gate.

But it was in the big living room in the back of the building, in the so-called hall, that the "vita nuova" the "new life" upon which Rembrandt seemed to have embarked, made itself most thoroughly felt. It still served as sitting-room, dining-room and reception-room to the whole of the family, and Rembrandt continued to sleep in the large bed built in the wall in which Saskia had died. Some day I suppose people will learn not to sleep in beds in which patients with pulmonary trouble have died. From my own experience I would say that it is a very bad thing to do. But I have never been able to convince any one else. Even Rembrandt, who by nature was a man of good sound common sense, would not hear of it when I told him that he must never let little Titus come near anything his mother had worn. He laughed at the idea and said that we doctors were always trying to scare the poor laity merely to show the world how learned we were, and he pointed to Titus and asked me whether I had ever seen a boy that looked as strong and healthy as he did.

I was thinking of that when I first met Titus again after almost eight years of absence. He must have been ten years old, running on eleven. A handsome and pleasant-looking youngster endowed with his mother's fine profile with that same agreeable smile that Saskia must have had in the days Rembrandt drew the little picture of her in a large straw hat —the only drawing we found among his belongings when we cleaned out his room on the Roozengracht. But the child did not give one the impression of being very robust. His cheeks were a little too thin for his age and his large, wondering eyes shone with that strange brilliancy one so often finds in those whom the gods love so well that they deem them worthy of an early death.

My first impulse was to talk to Rembrandt about my suspicions—suggest that the boy be kept outdoors a great deal of the time and not be allowed to spend the greater part of his days in the etching-room where the acid vapors caused even a healthy man to gasp for breath. But I felt a certain hesitancy about taking such a step on account of Doctor Bueno, who had taken care of Rembrandt's household after I left for America.

Bueno was a Jew. His full name was Ephraim Bueno after his father from whom he had learned his profession. He was a pleasant and modest little man and from all I had ever heard about him an excellent physician. But of course his position in the community had always been a little difficult.

In the first place, it had not been until just before the war with Cromwell (I think it was in the year 1652 but it may have been a few months later) that the Portuguese immigrants of Jewish extraction had been given full civil rights. Up to that time, from a strictly legal point of view, they had been merely tolerated. And this had made it impossible for them to join one of the guilds. Even when they opened a shop or started a business of their own, they had been technically guilty of a breach of law. Quite frequently the Guilds had sent delegations to the Town Hall to ask the Magistrates to interfere and forbid these unwelcome competitors from exercising their trade at all. But Their Lordships had too great a respect for the commercial abilities of these profitable immigrants to take any such steps. They did of course not dare to treat the representatives of these ancient and honorable corporations as curtly as they sometimes treated the clerical powers who came to them for redress from some threatened heresy. The town militia was entirely composed of members of the different guilds and only the officers belonged to the class of the rich merchants. The Magistrates therefore were very polite and sometimes almost obsequious in the way in which they listened to such complaints as came to them from the united bakers or butchers or carpenters or cartwrights or soap manufacturers. But no sooner had these worthy guild members left the premises, highly flattered by their reception and quite convinced that very soon something was going to be done about it, than the petitions and requests wandered into the aldermanic stove and the matter was referred to the Kalends of the Greeks.

For our town, first and last and all the time was a business establishment. Since the average Portuguese Jew had proved himself an excellent and most industrious citizen, he was considered a good business asset and all attempts to oust him or turn him into a pariah failed as systematically and as efficiently as the efforts on the part of the established Church to turn Amsterdam into a new Zion on the basis of Doctor Calvin's shorter catechism.

But until the Jews finally were accorded full civic rights, their position was always a trifle difficult. Their surgeons, no matter what degrees and titles they could offer as a token of their competence and ability, really had had no right to practice until the year 1651 and if one of the Burgomasters had ever been foolish enough to enforce the strict letter of the law, he could have ordered all Jewish doctors to be driven out of the town by the hangman on the ground that they were mountebanks and quacksalvers and had no right within the jurisdiction of the city.

I therefore was very careful in the way in which I treated Ephraim Bueno. I had a great respect for his learning and did not want to hurt his feelings. Sometimes if I happened to be within hailing distance and some slight accident took place (once, one of the pupils burned himself heating a copper plate and once Titus had an attack of coughing which frightened Rembrandt almost out of his wits), I would be called in and then I did whatever was necessary (in the case of Titus it was only necessary to tell him not to eat so many green nuts), but as soon as the emergency was over I invariably sent a hasty note to Doctor Bueno asking him to proceed to the Breestraat as soon as would be convenient. It was Bueno himself who put a stop to my somewhat exaggerated civility.

"My dear colleague," he said one day, as we were returning from the hospital together, "we Jews are sometimes said to be very thin-skinned, and perhaps we are a little too suspicious about the intentions of our neighbors. But my people have lived here now for half a century. We shall probably live here as long as this town lasts. Suppose we cease insulting each other by being so frightfully polite and become friends." And he added as an afterthought, "I am a Jew and that, as many of my neighbors never tire of reminding me, is pretty bad. But we both of us are leeches, and that is infinitely worse."

And in this he was quite right. For as soon as I had returned to Amsterdam I had been struck once more by the anomaly of our position. In the New Netherlands there had been so few physicians that the people, depending upon our good will, had usually treated us with great respect. But the Republic was overrun by every form of charlatan and the public seemed either unable or unwilling to differentiate between serious practitioners who had studied at half a dozen universities and had spent seven or eight years walking the hospitals, and those jugglers and bone-setters and ointment vendors who frequented the country fairs.

In the eyes of the "better classes of society" we still belonged to the guild of the "tonsorial artists" or "whisker-pluckers" of my childhood, and no amount of labor on our part seemed to be able to overcome that prejudice.

Indeed, I remember how shortly after Rembrandt's death, I was requested one day to come to The Hague and pay a professional visit to My Lord Jan de Witt, who at that moment was the recognized leader of the Republic, and how His Lordship bade me stay for luncheon and introduced me to one of his youthful cousins (cousins of his wife, to be exact) whose name was Bicker and who curiously enough was an ensign in a regiment of the Scottish guards. I, trying to be pleasant to the young man, said something flattering about his relatives, whereupon the young man, affecting a strange English accent, said, "Oh, yes! I think I remember my uncle telling me that you used to shave him whenever he could not leave the council-chamber on account of the press of business."

This remark was not a success, for My Lord Jan slowly contemplated his cousin with two eyes that were as cordial as icicles and casually remarked, "I am sorry that your regimental duties will not allow you to sit down with us at table," and took my arm to show me the way to the dining-room without paying any further attention to the bewildered young man who was left to the mercies of the maid who in that simple household still fulfilled the rôle of a butler.

No, our own social position had never been a very happy one. People needed us and at the same time they were ashamed of associating with us because in their heart they were ashamed of the illnesses which we were supposed to cure and which as a rule they had brought on through some carelessness of their own.

It was pretty bad. But as Bueno said to me one day, it might have been infinitely worse. We might have been artists!

Chapter 48

CONCERNING THE POSITION OF ARTISTS IN A COMMERCIAL COUNTRY

Ephraim Bueno had meant his remark as a jest but there had been considerable truth in what he had said. The position of the artists in those early days of our independence was a very curious one indeed. I had heard from my colleagues who had studied in Italy how the different princes and kings and grand dukes who ruled that country considered themselves deeply honored if a painter or a sculptor or a poet of renown deigned to honor their courts with a visit. From my grandmother I had learned how in Flanders in the days of her youth a whole city would go forth to meet the man who was to provide their church with a new picture or statue of the Madonna. I had not quite believed her when she told me that famous artists were often requested to accompany the king or even the emperor on his peregrinations through his realm. But during my own lifetime (it must have been in the early thirties, for I had just moved to Amsterdam) we were much surprised to hear that Rubens, the Antwerp painter, had just been sent to London to act as ambassador of the King of Spain at the court of Charles Stuart, and I remember that I heard many people say that they thought such a step a very dangerous precedent, for painters ought to remain painters and diplomats ought to be gentlemen, and I am sorry to say that this was the general attitude of pretty nearly all classes of society.

There may be those who can explain this curious attitude toward the arts, but I cannot. Doctor Bueno's bitter remark that a first-rate salesman was of some practical use in a commercial community, but that a sculptor was not, was probably more or less true but if it were wholly true, then how about Venice and Genoa and such towns as Florence or Bruges? All of those cities had been mere political counting-houses, like our own Republic. They had been ruled by bankers and cloth manufacturers and salt-merchants, plain, practical business men who loved a soldo just as dearly as our own little potentates loved their golden doubloons. I have seen pictures of these worthies and they looked for all the world like the older brothers and cousins of our Burgomasters. I have read a few stories about them and they were every inch as mean and as generous and as shrewd and as corrupt as Their Lordships of the Town Hall. But they apparently felt flattered whenever a painter or a musician was willing to come to one of their parties or dropped in for dinner, whereas our artists are forced to stand with their hat in their hand and listen very obediently when one of our great whale-oil magnates or some half literate buccaneer who has recently returned home rich with the plunder of a dozen spice islands demeans himself sufficiently to address a few words to one of those "paint-spillers."

I am not exaggerating. I was present not so long ago when an unbearably patronizing young man (he bore my own name, but was no relation) asked old Ruisdael why his son, instead of taking up painting, had not joined his cousin in the frame-making business.

There is a man by the name of Hobbema living in an attic on the Roozengracht not far away from the house where Rembrandt died. I am told that he is the best landscape painter we have ever had, but the other day, in the boat to Haarlem, I overheard two young business men cursing him roundly as an impostor because one of them had bought a landscape from him for two hundred guilders and had been told by his father that he could have had the thing for one quarter the price if he had only jewed the poor devil down a little harder.

Not to mention poor Hals of Haarlem, who died only a few years ago, who was undoubtedly as great a man as Rembrandt, who was forced into bankruptcy by his baker (can one man eat quite so much bread?), whose belongings at the time of his death, amounting to three mattresses, one cupboard and a table, were sold at public auction for the benefit of the poor-house in which he had found refuge.

No, I have never quite understood why it should be that way in our country and so very different everywhere else. But if I sometimes wondered and worried, my anxiety was certainly not shared by the victims of this deplorable public negligence.

After I returned from America I spent a great deal of my time in the company of painterfolk but almost without exception they accepted their fate as something that was too self-evident to be a subject for public discussion or commiseration. Whenever they were together, they talked shop. They talked of different methods of grinding paint or of a new combination of acids with which to treat their copper plates or a better method of laying on a coat of varnish, only upon some very rare occasions did they curse their poverty and declare Rembrandt to be an outrageously lucky fellow to be able to live in a house of two stories and to have been allowed to marry the daughter of a burgomaster.

But taking them by and large and as a group, they were a singularly contented body of men. A few of them of course got despondent and gave up in sheer despair and drank themselves into oblivion and an early grave by spending twenty-four hours of each day in the gin-shops with which our town was so richly blessed. But the vast majority lived like masons or plumbers—like unsuccessful masons and plumbers, I ought to say, and not to be compared in any way with the genuine masons and plumbers who were employed on Jacob van Campen's new town hall on the Dam.

Without exception they were very hard workers. The world accused them of keeping irregular hours, of being seen about the streets at all hours of the day and night. There was some truth in this. They did indeed lead very irregular lives. As a rule they were too poor to be able to pay much rent and as they needed at least one large room for a studio, they were apt to go to the outskirts of the city and look for an old barn which they then converted into a more or less suitable workshop. For our painters, unlike those in Italy, don't seem to be able to work out of doors. They will sometimes make a hasty sketch of a landscape or a tree or a few boats out in the open, but then they run home as fast as they can and spend the next three weeks finishing the picture for which the sketch serves them merely as a reminder but not as an inspiration.

But since they spend the greater part of the day right there in the studio which also serves them as dining-room and sitting-room and bedroom and kitchen and nursery (for they rarely can afford more than one room) the whole place is almost always in a state of extreme disorder.

Then their rich neighbors, who live in a house with five or six different apartments, see the poor painterman sitting at his easel between a pile of yesterday's dishes and day-before-yesterday's cutlery—see the baby's laundry hanging from a rope stretched along the ceiling—observe his wife busily engaged making the weekly supply of pea-soup over a little charcoal fire in the corner, shake their heads and say, "Oh, my, oh, my; what a careless fellow. No wonder he is always hard up." But they entirely overlook the fact that poverty is more apt to provoke slovenliness than vice versa.

People, however, will cling to their preconceived notions as tenaciously as they will cling to the tables and chests and drawers which they have inherited from their parents. And I have long since given up trying to convince them of the error of this view. For even after I had brought them to the point where they were forced to agree with me and told me, "Well, perhaps there is something in what you say," they would find other reasons why the artist should not be regarded as a respectable membei of society. And one of these was the so-called clannishness of all those who made their living by their brush or their wits.

"Why don't they ever associate with us?" I have heard respectable merchants ask. "Why do they spend endless hours in each other's studios? Why do they marry each other's daughters?"

To which I would make answer as follows:

"Why do you who are in the export business or grain trade always marry each other's daughters? Why do you who sell whalebones or distill gin know all other whalebone dealers and gin-distillers and rarely see any one outside your own profession?"

But then of course I was shouted down by a tumult of protests. "Oh, but that is different! We have got to know each other to get along in business, we marry our competitors' daughters because we know fairly accurately how much the father will be able to give her. We are practical men of business and at the same time we like to sit down with people with whom we can talk about our own work."

"Very well," I would then continue my line of reasoning, "why shouldn't painters also like to meet men and women with whom they can talk their sort of shop?"

It was no use. I butted my head against a granite wall of prejudice and accomplished nothing. The artist was an amiable loafer, not able or willing to do an honest day's work and therefore deserving all he got in the way of poverty and neglect. One could of couse be an artist and at the same time a respectable member of society. But such a combination was an exception almost as rare as that of Doctor Tulp, who was a gentleman and a member of the town government, although he had started life as a physician, or Gerard ter Borch, who painted portraits in Deventer and was said to have served one term as Burgomaster of that city.

Yes, ours was a strange country.

But there was one consolation. With the exception of two or three rather weak brethren, I never knew a member of the Guild of Saint Luke who cared a tinker's dam for the opinions of any one who did not belong to his own profession. Not because he thought himself superior to his surroundings but because he was by far too busy to bother about such unimportant little details as the respect of his community. Life was short and at the very best one had only ten hours a day during which one could paint. That was the answer to the second riddle of the artist's far-famed "queerness." The fellow was never idle and what was infinitely more important, he was interested in his work.

I wish that his neighbors could have said as much.

Chapter 49

TWO OF MY OLD FRIENDS ARE GONE AND IN MY LONELINESS I BEGIN TO SEE A LITTLE MORE OF REMBRANDT

But to return to Amsterdam, life at first was rather dull and we missed our old friends. Selim had become a man of vast importance in the land of his birth (returning sea-captains told wonderful stories about the luxury displayed at his palace and of the two hundred women, which were said to be guarded by no less than three hundred eunuchs) and Bernardo had disappeared in the American wilderness without leaving a trace. Jean-Louys and I tried to continue our Sunday walks but we soon discovered that peripatetic duologues were very apt to degenerate into sedentary monologues, accompanied by too much beer.

For a while we did our best to make Rembrandt join us, but I never knew a man who had such a thorough-going aversion to exercise of every sort. I used to scold him and Doctor Bueno used to back me with great cordiality whenever I told him that no human being could lead the sort of life he did without digging his own grave with his easel and his chair. I delivered endless lectures on elementary physiology, quoting a great deal of wisdom which I had borrowed from Jean-Louys, who in turn had culled his information from the writings of Monsieur Descartes. I used to explain how the human body was a sort of machine and just as windmills could not do their work without wind or water-mills without water, so the human body needed fresh air and exercise to keep in good condition.

I drew graphic pictures on the back of some of his sketches, showing him that the lungs were in reality nothing but a pair of bellows that had to be kept going all the time by moderate exercise, for otherwise (the metaphor was slightly mixed) the organ would give forth no sound whatsoever. From organs I would jump back to sailing vessels that were useless and deteriorated without wind, which is merely fresh air in motion. But I might as well have talked to the skeletons that were hanging from the municipal gallows near the harbor for all the impression I made.

Rembrandt never lost his temper and I admired his patience until I discovered one evening that he did not even listen. He just went on painting and let me talk. Only the week before he had complained to me that his heart caused him trouble—that he would wake up in the middle of the night with his heart beating like fury, and a severe pain in both shoulder-blades. I told him to ask Doctor Bueno to examine his heart and then I said: "When do you notice this trouble most?" He could not quite remember but he thought that it came when he had spent the whole day at his etching-press. "You see," he remarked casually, "those boys of mine mean well, they do their best, but if I want a really good copy, I have got to do it myself. I have not had many orders for portraits of late—you know how it is when there is a war. Everybody is scared. Everybody saves all the money he can. And portraits, after all, are a luxury. But people will buy etchings. They are good investments and I had orders for several hundred. So in the evening when those children had gone to bed, I used to strike off a few copies myself."

"At what time did you begin?"

"About seven."

"And when did you stop?"

"Oh, sometimes quite early. Other evenings I worked until four or five."

"Without stopping?"

"Yes. Sometimes I stopped for a quarter of an hour or so and had a glass of beer. One gets thirsty. It is hard work."

Seven until four or five—that meant nine hours of standing on his feet in a small room that was suffocatingly hot, pulling the wheel of a press that was almost too heavy for a cart-horse.

"Man alive!" I answered him. "No human being can stand that sort of exertion. How long have you been doing this?"

"Oh, not so very long. Since January last year when orders came in for those plates."

January of last year—that meant fifteen whole months of a sort of labor that would have killed a hod-carrier in less than six.

"But of course," I said, "when you do that sort of thing, you don't paint?"

"Yes, I paint the greater part of the day in my studio, as long as there is any light. Then I take the candles and go to the press-room."

"How many candles?"

"One as a rule. Sometimes when my eyes begin to bother me, I light a second one."

"When your eyes begin to bother you? Do they bother you much?"

"Not very much. We all of us have good eyes. We got them from our father. Bad lungs from our mother and good eyes from our father. No, there is nothing the matter with my eyes, I still can do a dry-point without using any glasses. But after five or six hours, I find myself weeping big tears as if I were walking in the wind and after ten hours, I get funny pains."

"What sort of pains?"

"As if some one were sticking a pin into my eye-balls. Not the pain on the side of my head of which I just spoke to you. That only comes when my heart does its funny tricks. But irritating little pin-pricks and sometimes I have to stop for a few minutes until they disappear again."

Truly, the man was hopeless.

"Has it ever dawned upon you," I asked him, "that if you go on working that way you may end by losing your eyesight completely? A fine painter you would be with your eyes gone!" And I made ready to leave. At once he changed his tone. "Don't be angry with me, Doctor," he begged me, "you are probably right and I am undoubtedly wrong, but what will you? I can't stop. I have to go on."

"Why?" I interrupted him.

Rembrandt wiped both his hands on his blue painter's smock, a habit which made some of his enemies of the popular Italian school say that he carried his best works on his belly—took a bottle of acid from a low chair that stood in a corner of the room—reached down—picked up the bottle—took out the cork—looked at it and smelled it, and said, "That is the sixth cork in two weeks. That stuff is too strong. I told them they had made it too strong. I must get a glass stopper." And then added, "I will be good for this once and obey orders. My whole head aches and I might as well call it a day. You ask me why I work like a madman? Very well. I will tell you. Because I am really a little crazy."

"Professionally speaking," I interrupted him, "I never noticed it."

"Of course not. I am not crazy in the sense the Dircx woman was crazy. You need not lock me up. But I know that I am not an ordinary, well-balanced and respectable member of society and I know that no matter how hard I try, I never shall be. That is what is the matter with my work. So far I have kept out of the poor-house. But only because I happen to have inherited all that money from Saskia. The inheritance is a little slow in collecting, but anyway it gives me credit, which is almost as good as having money. You can buy whatever you want and people ask no questions. Are glad to sell to you.

"But if I did not have that money, I don't know what would have happened to me long ago. My work does not sell.

"In the beginning, the first ten years after I came here from Leyden, I was a sort of curiosity. I was the fashion. In those days many people were still alive who remembered the Rebellion. Of course you and I, theoretically speaking, lived through it too. But what did we ever see of it? Nothing! We paid our taxes and once in a while some former soldier with his arms or his legs gone would ask us for something to eat in the street and if he were very much of a bother, we called the guards and had him arrested.

"The people—I mean all the people like that grandfather of yours of whom you have so often told me, or my own father, or my own grandmother—men and women who had escaped with their lives but whose brothers and sisters and sons had been hanged and burned and broken on the wheel—that generation seems to have understood more or less what I was trying to do. They had all of them started from very simple beginnings. So had I.

"There was a time when I used to pretend that I was a great nobleman. That was just after I married. I liked to dress up. Saskia was a lovely girl. I liked to dress her up. I liked to imagine that we were really fine folks. She was, but I am the son of a miller and my brother is a shoemaker and all the satins and silks in the whole world and all the feathers and frills will never make me anything else.

"That is why that older generation liked my work. That is why the younger generation is afraid of me. I think they realize that I am a fairly good artisan. I can paint, if I say so myself, and they know it. But I can't paint the way they want me to paint and they know that too.

"Of course you will say that I ought to be practical and ought to try and paint the way they want me to paint. Well, I will tell you a secret. I have tried and I have tried very hard, but I can't do it. I just can't do it! And that is why I am just a little crazy.

"An ordinary person who sells raisins or herring or cheese or who makes pictures for a living carefully studies his market, which after all is his bread and butter. When the taste of his customers changes, he speedily changes the nature of the goods he is trying to sell them. If they want their herring dried instead of pickled, he buys a couple of acres of land and hangs his fish up in the sun until it is as hard as a rock. If they want their cheeses painted red instead of yellow, he paints them red instead of yellow. If the fashion of the moment prescribes Italian landscapes with Italian skies and Italian beggars eating—what is the name of that stuff? macaroni?—he will paint them Italian landscapes with Italian skies and Italian beggars dropping handfuls of noodles into their gaping mouths.

"Personally I don't blame those people, as I have heard it said sometimes, when I am accused of being too proud or too haughty to paint differently from the way I paint. It isn't that I am too proud or too haughty. I just can't do differently—that is all. And so I stick to my own line and I suppose I shall stick to it until I go to the poor-house or the cemetery and you may put a stone on my grave, saying: 'Here lies a fool' and you will never have been so right in all your life as on the day you ordered that inscription."

Chapter 50

REMBRANDT BECOMES TALKATIVE AND FAVORS ME WITH A FEW OF HIS VIEWS UPON ART

This was one of the longest speeches I ever heard Rembrandt make. And contrary to his habit, he used it to mention a few of his theories on art.

Notwithstanding the war, which continued with uneven success, there was a good deal of money abroad at that time. Thousands of people were losing all they had; but a few hundred, who had been shrewd enough to speculate in grain and wood and gun-powder and all the other supplies of which the fleet was in such great need, made vast sums of money. Not knowing what to do with their newly found riches, they were buying luxuries right and left.

One day pictures would be all the rage. The next day it would be china. The little Japanese cups that had sold for three florins apiece had gone up to three thousand. The china craze switched over to pearls, and when all the wives of all the profiteers had been provided with ear-rings as large as carrots, pearls became vulgar almost over night and the Nuremberg watch-makers reaped a fortune with queer and extraordinary timepieces that showed not only the minutes but also the seconds and that played a little tune when the hour was struck, just like the bells of the new town hall.

As they had heard that there lived a painter in the Jewish quarter whose house was a museum of everything that one could possibly hope to collect, a good many of them found their way to the Breestraat.

In the beginning, Rembrandt felt rather flattered, and thought that this meant a renewed interest in his own work. But very soon he discovered that those noisy visitors with their even more noisy wives did not care in the least for his own art—very often were ignorant of his name—called him Ronnebrandt or Remscheidt—patronized him in most outrageous fashion—gave Titus sweet-meats and patted his head and said he was a nice little Jewish boy and then asked the master how much he would take for an enameled Turkish sword or a piece of ivory carving from the Indies. Then he would grow angry at such an indignity (for he well knew the value of his own work) and instead of making these miserable war profiteers pay an outrageous sum for some article which he himself had bought in a moment of weakness and for which his visitors were willing to pay ten times the original price, he would show them the door in a most abrupt fashion (he still could speak the vernacular of the Weddesteeg in Leyden with great fluency) and then these amazing guests would depart and would spread it among all their friends that this man Rompot, that so-called artist, who gave himself such airs, was an ill-natured ruffian and that one ought to give him a wide berth and have nothing to do with him.

Until the rumor had gone all over town that the painter of the Jodenbreestraat, you remember, the one who had done that queer picture of Banning Cocq, was a sullen and crabbed barbarian—a morose and splenetic fellow—whose swinish ill-temper had turned him into an involuntary recluse, shunned by all his neighbors for his violence and irascibility.

This was of course entirely beside the truth. Rembrandt was by nature an easy-going and friendly person, perfectly willing to meet his neighbors with a smile and only asking to be let alone. But that was just it! Our newly rich did not like people of an independent character. They had touched their caps to their betters for so long that now they rejoiced to be in a position where (through their purse and their financial influence) they could oblige others to raise their hats to them. And any one who stood squarely on his own feet, went his own way, asked for no favors and (infinitely worse) accepted none, was something so utterly baffling to their sort of mentality that they could explain his attitude in only one way, by accusing him of a haughtiness of spirit that was as foreign to his nature as malice, envy or the very suspicion that such things existed in this world.

Here I am conscious of a doubt. If this diary of mine should ever fall into the hands of one of my descendants (if my son is to survive) and should be read by them two or three hundred years hence, wouldn't they instinctively feel that I have exaggerated my friend's character? Wouldn't they say, "This mysterious grandfather of ours seems to have had a sober enough eye when he contemplated the rest of his contemporaries, but when it came to Rembrandt (of whom we have heard very different stories) he feels compelled to indulge in the most noble-sounding terms, as if his friend were a paragon of all the virtues. Yet, when we contemplate his life, as it is revealed to us by the records of the Bankruptcy Court and the Public Guardians of the Amsterdam orphans, we meet with an irresponsible fellow who bears very little resemblance to the glorious picture revealed by our great-great-great-grandfather."

And when I say that I never met a man so little given to petty jealousy or so indifferent to malice, I do not mean to imply that Rembrandt was a saint who after a lifetime of seclusion and meditation had finally attained such a degree of spiritual perfection that he had become immune against the temptation (forever present in all of us) to regard every man as his possible rival and therefore as his potential enemy.

Nothing could have been less true than that. Rembrandt was of this earth earthy. He was fashioned out of the common clay of our land and our land, lest we forget, lies fifteen feet below sea-level. But he had one enormous advantage over the majority of his neighbors. Like most other

REMBRANDT'S MOTHER

artists he had a purpose in life and he was too busy with his own problems to enjoy that leisure which is the breeding ground of gossip and spite.

This devotion to a single ideal sometime manifested itself in very unpleasant ways. I never knew him to read a book. He owned quite a library—the hall was full of them, but every one of them had to do with the arts, wood-cuts by Lucas of Leyden, copper-plates after etchings by Raphael, the world's best pictures done in copper-plate reproductions, wood-cuts of Lucas Cranach, copper print reproductions of Guido Reni of Bologna and dozens more of the same sort. All of the best painters of the last two centuries were represented—Rubens and Titian and Jordaens and Michelangelo and Miereveld, Carracci, van Dijk and dozens of others, not to forget Albrecht Dürer's famous handbook on perspective.

But when it came to the so-called "belles lettres," to literature as such, almost any ordinary household in Amsterdam, however humble, could have boasted of a better selection than this luxurious museum of the Breestraat.

I have spent all my life among books. When I am called in for a consultation in a house where I have never been before, I try if possible to cast a glance at the book-closet. One minute's examination of the different titles will tell me more about my future patient, his habits and tastes and even the probable nature of his ailment than hours devoted to a mere physical examination. But if I had tried this method with Rembrandt, my diagnosis would have been completely wrong.

For I don't think that I ever found more than five or six ordinary books in his house during all the many years I knew him intimately. One of these was a tragedy in blank verse, called "Medea," wished on him by the author, Jan Six, the linen merchant (afterwards one of the Burgomasters) by whom Rembrandt was befriended for a while and from whom, to his own great detriment, he borrowed a small sum of money. The others were devotional books, Josephus' "History of the Jews," Bibles and collections of sermons. And all of them, including some interesting products of the calligrapher's art by his friend Coppenol, had been presents, for with the single exception of a German treatise on military strategy which for some reason had caught his fancy, I don't think that Rembrandt during the whole of his life ever spent a single penny on books. I don't believe he even felt the need of them. If he had done so, he would have bought them by the cartload, for he had no sense of the value of money and bought whatever he wanted with the same sublime unconcern as that which is manifested by a very small child which pulls its mother's most beautiful glass vase off the table and lets it fall on the floor and break into a thousand pieces, and will feel itself completely justified by the smiling excuse, "I wanted it."

Whatever he "wanted," Rembrandt got and our more or less veiled hints that life just simply wasn't that way, that one had to trim one's sails according to the wind and other bits of proverbial wisdom did not make the slightest impression upon him and never evoked any further comment than an admiring, "But isn't it beautiful?" it being almost anything from a painting by Giorgione to an ebony chest for little Titus's diapers.

Being fearsome of the ultimate results of this indiscriminate buying, I sometimes hinted at books as a substitute for the infinitely more expensive objects of art with which he filled his room. At one moment he got greatly interested in a certain Adriaen Brouwer, a pupil of the incomparable Frans Hals of Haarlem. This young man, of phenomenal ability, had died in the poor-ward of an Antwerp hospital at the early age of thirty-two. His works therefore were rather rare and in the dozen or so years after his death (he died in the early forties) they had greatly increased in price.

One evening I found the whole of the front room filled with Brouwers, a most heterogeneous collection, a woman and a child and a pastry cook and a couple of gamblers and a cook busy with a very greasy dish, all of them done with the most beautiful economy of line and color.

"Aren't they wonderful?" Rembrandt asked me, who had kissed Titus good night and was coming down the stairs with a candle in his hand.

I said yes, that they were very interesting but that they must have cost him a small fortune and I pointed to one which probably represented my household expenses for more than half a year. Then I congratulated him on his success and said that I was glad he had done so well recently.

"Done well recently?" he asked and lifted his candle so that I should better be able to see the picture of a small studio (also done by Brouwer) which up to that moment I had not noticed. "Done well recently? Good God! I have not sold a thing for over two years."

"Then your Indian venture must have turned out prosperously." (For though he had tried to keep it a secret from me, I knew that he had been speculating in the shares of a rather doubtful Indian Company.)

He was a little surprised. "Oh, you mean those three ships. You heard of those?" (Who had not heard of them?) "No, they were not exactly what one would call a success. There was some trouble with the crew of one of them and the others suffered so badly from scurvy, they only got as far as the Cape. No, the money I put into that affair is lost, I am afraid."

"But I suppose they wanted cash for these Brouwers?"

"They did. I borrowed it. Aren't they marvelous?"

And then he took me in the side room, lit a fire, got me a bottle of ale and spent at least two hours explaining his conception of the uses of money and the duties of artists toward themselves, and he defended his point of view so plausibly and so reasonably that I went home convinced that he was right and that I was a hopelessly prejudiced miser who would never be able to look beyond the rock-ribbed system of "never spend more than you can afford." Which (if we were to believe our elders) was the foundation stone of the Republic's prosperity and greatness.

"You have been telling me to be careful," he began. "Everybody I ever knew has been telling me to be careful. You are a man of tact (that is why I like you) and rather than tell me outright not to buy pictures and helmets and all those things in this room and in the others" (he made a gesture that meant to include the whole house) "you have encouraged me to buy books—and read. 'If he is kept busy reading,' you probably said to yourself, 'he won't spend so much time among the Jews, inspecting their antiques.' But what good has the reading of other people's books ever done to an artist?

"You remind me of those people who have been coming to me ever since I was fourteen years old and had smeared some paint (very badly I am afraid) on a couple of pieces of canvas. 'My dear boy,' they used to say, 'this is all very nice and very pretty but it will never lead to anything. You can't learn your trade here. We in the North are all of us barbarians when it comes to the arts. Italy, the South, that is the country for you.'

"And then they would recite long lists of names of boys from Amsterdam and Haarlem and Leyden and Dordrecht, from every village and hamlet in the Republic who had gone to Rome and Florence and Venice to learn 'painting.'

"I used to make them very angry with my attitude. 'Painting,' I used to say, 'is nothing but seeing. You see something that impresses you and then you paint it, or if you have a gift for something else, then you draw it or hack it out of a piece of marble, as the Greeks used to do, or you make a tune out of it and play it on the organ as old Sweelinck used to do when we were children and he got so excited one day about a thunderstorm he had just heard that he turned the 116th prelude into an imitation thunderstorm and seven people in the congregation fainted in their pews and had to be carried out.

"And then I would add that it did not depend so much upon what you saw as how you saw it and that a good artist could get more inspiration out of a dead bullock hanging from a ladder in some mean village butcher-shop, than a bad one out of half a dozen beautiful churches in the village where Raphael himself was born.

"All this sounded like terrible heresies to the good people among whom I grew up. They took me aside and whispered into my ear that if I knew what was good for me I would not be quite so plain-spoken and express such open contempt for those marvelous Italian artists whom all the world held to be the greatest craftsmen after the sculptors of ancient Greece. In those days I was a great deal more impatient than I am to-day and I would lose my temper and would waste my time on foolish arguments—trying to prove that I had never said that the Italian painters were not among the greatest that had ever lived—that all I meant was that the

Italians living in Italy should get their emotion (the word inspiration is good enough for theologians and for amateur artists) from Italian subjects, but that we people living in Holland should get our emotions from the subjects with which we were familiar in our own country and not from something a thousand miles away.

"But no, I was all wrong and even such a broad-minded man as My Lord Constantin, who has been a kind and steadfast friend to me all my life, could not see it that way and broadly scolded me because I refused to take the opportunities that were offered me to go to Italy. When I told him that his beloved Italians cared so little for their own great men that they were willing to let all of their best pictures be sold abroad, so that one could get a better idea of the work of Raphael and Giorgione and Titian right here in Amsterdam than in Florence and Rome (except of course the things they have painted on the walls of churches and monasteries that can't be pried loose) he did not quite know what to say and replied that anyway the trip would be good for me, that I was too young to spend my entire time working in a stuffy studio, that it was bad for my health never to take any exercise and sit or stand everlastingly in front of an easel, that I would die young if I overdid it as much as I was doing . . ." ("In which he was quite right," I interrupted him, but got no answer) . . . "and ended up by telling me of the wonderful landscapes he had seen on his way to Venice and that landscapes were only possible in a region where the sun was a brilliant ball of golden fire and not a greasy speck made by the nose of an inquisitive child on a pane of window-glass as it is in our own muddy country.

"But I would not be convinced and answered him that a rainstorm, if seen and felt by some one with the ability to see and feel rainstorms as intensely as some of the Italians were able to see and feel the sunsets over their native lagoons, would make just as good a subject for a picture as his dearly beloved Forum by moonlight and a dozen years later (it was in '43 if I remember rightly) I sent him a copy of my etching of those three trees with the rainstorms in the distance, and I wrote him:

"'My Lord, do you remember a talk we had when I was twenty-five years old and was just on the point of moving to Amsterdam? And will you graciously accept this poor etching as a token of my extreme gratitude and tell me whether I was right when I said that rainstorms could be made just as interesting as sunsets?'

"And he answered me with his usual courtesy that he was beginning to understand that after all, perhaps I had been right and in '50 when he was here a few days incognito, after the Prince had attacked the town, I showed him that picture of a windmill that was afterwards sold to some one in England and I asked him once more: 'My Lord, isn't that mill as good in its own way as the little house that Giorgione painted in the background of his Concert?' (a picture which is in Paris but of which I have seen some very fine copies) and he looked at it for quite a while as if he were thinking of something that had happened long, long ago and as if he were speaking to himself, he said:

"'Of course, that pretty young woman would hardly be playing the flute the way she does at the foot of your mill,' and I answered, 'Your Lordship is right, but neither would the Graces of Botticelli bombard each other with snowballs.' And then he said yes, that I might be right after all, but like poor Jan Asselijn, whom we buried last year, I might have done both, and I asked His Lordship point-blank: 'Do you think his work was so much better than mine?' and he answered: 'No, of course not, and besides, he was really a Frenchman, so the comparison was not quite fair. I happened to be looking at the etching you made of him, that is probably why I happened to mention him.'

"And then, abruptly changing the subject, he said: 'I want to ask you something. It has always puzzled me and I have always wanted to ask it, but I never had the opportunity, but what are you really trying to do?'

"And I told him as best I could (just as I told you a moment ago), how when I was very young I had thought that painting was merely a matter of seeing, of feeling, of sensing some particular object or idea and translating what you saw and felt into lines or bits of color.

"And then one day I was working in my father's mill and something happened to me. I don't mean that I was painting in my father's mill. In those early days I was not encouraged very much to become an artist. My people were simple folk and very pious. They had the usual prejudice against the arts and especially against the artists. When one mentioned the word painter, they thought of Babylon and Sodom at once, and when I first told them that I wanted to be a great painter, like Lucas van Leyden, who was the first man whose works I had ever seen, they shook their heads and said 'No,' they wanted me to be a good Christian and get ahead in the world.

"I seemed to have a fairly good brain—I was much cleverer than my brothers. One of them could succeed father in the mill and the others would be taught a trade that they might spend their days as God-fearing members in good standing of some honorable guild of artisans. But as for me I was to go to the university and get a degree so that my parents could say, 'Our son, the Doctor of Laws,' and have something to console themselves for the hard labor which had been their share all during the time they were bringing us up.

"That plan never came to anything. I actually went to the university but I was a dreadful failure as a student. I never went to a single lecture. I wrote my name in a big book and got a piece of paper informing me most solemnly that Rembrandus Hermanius Leydensis or some such thing was now, at the age of fourteen, if you please, a duly enrolled stud-litt—whatever that meant—in the glorious university of Leyden, and entitled to all the rights and privileges connected with this distinguished rank.

"But it was no use, I never went near a professor or a book (I cared as little about books then as I do now) and instead I went to Jaap Swanenburch, who was a famous man in our town—he was one of those who had learned their trade in Italy—he had done the job so thoroughly, he even came home with an Italian wife who used to throw plates and knives at him every time we had a pretty model, to the great joy and delectation of his pupils—and when Swanenburch came to the Weddesteeg one day and told my parents that I had it in me to become a most successful and fashionable portrait painter, but would they please pay my tuition, they forgave me for having played hookey from my scholarly duties and as Swanenburch's charges were less than the tuition fee of the university, they decided that they might as well let me stay where I was and work out my own salvation according to the best of my own abilities.

"But before that time, I could only draw when no one was looking my way and every afternoon after school time, my brother Cornelis and I used to go to the mill on the wall and help father with his work.

"Have you ever been in a mill? You have. Ever been in a mill on a bright, sun-shiny sort of a day? Well, then you have missed something. For the wings do curious things to the interior on a day like that. The windows of a mill are usually very small, but when the sun is shining brightly, especially in the spring when the air has just been cleaned by three weeks of wind or rain, the whole inside of the mill is flooded with a curious and very brilliant sort of light—a strange light that is like nothing else I have ever seen—though I must add that I have not traveled very far and that I may be all wrong when I say that it is only to be found here on this floating pan-cake of ours, where the sun and the fog are apt to do all sorts of queer things to the light, both inside our houses and out of them.

"Well, it was just such a day in April—I remember the date, for the experience made a great impression upon me. It was the fourteenth of April and Cornelis and I had been told to go and count a number of sacks that lay on the first floor and carry them up to the second floor where the grinding was done and stack them up neatly in a corner. We counted our sacks and carried them to the second floor and my father inspected them and found that one or two needed repairing and told us to get a needle and thread and attend to the job then and there. I got a needle and thread and sat down in a corner to repair the sacks, while Cornelis was sent away on an errand. It did not take me long to finish that task, but I was afraid that if I told my father that I was through, he would give me something else to do and so I said nothing, but sat very quietly in my little corner and pretended to be very busy. There was a brisk eastern wind blowing outside and the wings went past the window, g'chuck—g'chuck—g'chuck, just a sort of guttural sound like the snapping of a musket and then the sudden swish of those enormous wooden arms, cleaving the air. And every time one of those wings passed by one of the windows, the light was cut off for perhaps a hundredth part of a second—just a flash—too short to measure by the clock—but visible, just the same—very visible indeed, for every time it happened, the room became pitch-dark.

"Now you may remember that when we were young, the country was suffering from a plague of rats—perhaps as a result of the siege and the large number of people who had died—but anyway, our houses and our cellars were all of them full of rats. And there were people who did nothing all their lives long except catch rats—professional rat-catchers. They were usually old soldiers and very dirty and very picturesque and I have drawn them quite a lot, for they were interesting-looking scoundrels.

"That morning one of them had been at work in our mill. There were so many rats in that mill, we sometimes were afraid they would carry the old building back to Noordwijk where it came from. The rat-catcher who liked to work in the dark would not be back before evening and one enormous wire cage full of rats was hanging by a strong chain from a rafter of the mill. Those rats—great big fellows—would have eaten through any kind of rope but though all of them seemed to be sitting on their hindsides, gnawing at the steel chain that held their cage, they hadn't a chance in the world. But through the scurrying and pattering of all these excited little bodies, with their bright beady eyes and their long, disgusting tails, the cage was slowly beginning to swing from left to right and it was making a curious shadow upon the wall. And all the time, the wings of the mill kept swishing past the window and every time they swished past, the room would be pitch dark and then for just one, two, three seconds, it would be filled once more with brilliant sunlight.

"But I had seen that sort of thing hundreds of times before and it had never struck me as anything very remarkable. And then suddenly—it really came to me just like the revelation that came to Saul—I noticed that that cage was not merely hanging in the light or in the air, as I had always taken for granted, but that it was an object surrounded by a whole lot of different sorts of air—all of which were of a different texture. In the beginning it was not at all clear to me and I can't expect to tell you what I mean in two words, but you know of course that there are a number of colors, like yellow and blue and red and combinations of colors and we painters are supposed to know all about those colors and their combinations and that is how we paint our pictures. We tell stories in daubs of color, just as others tell stories in lines or with the help of words or notes. At least, that is what I had always taken for granted and I had done my best to learn how to use those colors.

"But that morning in the mill, there weren't any colors, at least, none of the colors with which I had been familiar from my earliest childhood, when some one gave me my first box of paints. The light in front of that rat cage was different from the light behind it, which was different again from the light on the left of it and all these different sorts of light did not remain the same, but changed every moment. Of course, when I say 'light' I mean air and when I say air, I mean light. What I really mean is the space which fills all our rooms and all our houses and the whole world —the stuff we breathe, and through which the birds fly. And then the idea suddenly struck me (and that was the moment when I turned from Saul to Paul) does all this space—this air—really have a color in our sense of the word and is it possible to translate that color into terms of paint?

"Let me show you" (here he picked up a pewter mug that was standing on the table)—"let me show you. You see that mug. It is about three feet away from you. And now" (moving it towards himself) "it is only two feet away. Suppose I want to paint this. I can get the illusion of distance by applying the rules of perspective which Master Dürer of Nuremberg laid down in that little book of his. That would be enough when I use a pencil or pen and ink. But when I use color, I ought to be able to create that impression of distance in some other way—in the way nature does it, or rather, in the way I suspect that nature does it. For I have now spent the greater part of every day during the last forty years—Sundays included, to the horror of my good parents—trying to solve the problem and I know just as little about it to-day as I did when I first began.

"Your French friend, the Baron, told me the other day that those famous mathematicians of whom he sometimes talks work quite differently from the way we would expect. When a mason builds a house, he first digs the basement and then builds the first floor and next the second floor and so on until he gets to the roof. But mathematicians, so it seems, first make the roof and fit in the rest afterwards. 'They have suspicions,' the Frenchman remarked. They 'suspect' that two times two is four and accept their 'suspicion' as an established fact and then work backwards and by working backwards, they finally 'prove' that two times two is indeed four. I may have got this a bit mixed, but I think that is the way he reasoned it out. They first 'suspect' and 'surmise' and then they 'prove.' Of course, those are not the sort of ideas with which to entertain my own relatives nor those of Saskia either. They would either giggle sheepishly or run to their dominie and suggest that I be locked up in the asylum. And I am not quite certain that I am making myself clear even to you.

"But from that moment on, from the moment I saw those excited rats in their wire cage, hanging from the rafter of my father's mill, until to-day I have been convinced that every object in the world is surrounded by a substance (call it light or air or space or whatever you like) which somehow or other it must be possible to express in the terms of light and shade and half a dozen primary colors.

"Sometimes I even think that at least in a few of my pictures I have solved that problem pretty well. But I confess that I have been working backwards, painting the picture first and trying to discover afterwards why I had done what I had done. People, always looking for the out-

HENDRICKJE STOFFELS

(about 1652)

landish and the unusual, whisper that I have a secret. Secret fiddlesticks! I am a mathematician who works in vegetable matter and who started out with a formula and who is now trying to prove that it works and is correct."

It sounded very plausible but I warned him that I had once heard of a mathematician who had hit upon a new formula that appeared to be perfect and who had died just before he had succeeded in proving his point.

"Yes," he answered, "that is the risk I run. I too may die before I have been able to find out exactly how this problem should be solved. But I am content. A few times when painting people, I have caught certain effects that seem to bear out my theory. What I would like to know, however, before I die is this—how did I happen to get those effects? Why are people able to say, when they look at one of my pictures, 'That man is actually sitting on a chair in a room, not leaning up against a mere back-ground of chair and room.' Or, 'That angel is really floating through space, not falling or resting on a cloud, but floating!'

"I probably would have been more of a success in my work if I had not been told by my father to repair sacks in his mill on that particular morning. Now I waste half of my time or more on a problem that no one has ever solved before me—that no one, as far as I can find out, has even thought of. Rubens is a great man, but he does not even suspect that there is such a thing as I have been trying to put into paint for the last thirty years. Hals comes much nearer to it. That man Brouwer (you scolded me because I bought so many of his pictures) has done marvels in that field. They tell me there is a man in Spain, working for the King (his name is Velásquez, or Velázquez, I don't quite know) who seems to be working on that basis. I have never seen any of his paintings and it is always difficult to imagine what a picture looks like merely from hearing some one else describe it.

"Of course, the public has no notion of what I am trying to do. Perhaps four hundred years from now, if any of my pictures are left, they will say to each other: This fellow van Rijn at least was on the right way and was going in the right direction. But my neighbors—they see that one picture is very good, and how in the next one I tried a new method to prove that two times two actually makes four and have failed pretty completely, and they sneer, 'This man is a mere amateur. He does not take his art seriously. He does not paint things the way we ourselves see them.'

"Heaven forbid that I should ever see things the way they do! They may (and very likely they will) let me starve, but they can't rob me of the conviction that I am right and that they are wrong. Any one can learn to paint the things that are there. But to paint the things that one merely suspects to be there while one can't possibly prove that they are there—that, my good Doctor, that is the sort of task that makes life interesting. And that is the sort of thing that makes other people be afraid of me. And now let us go to the Back Room."

"For a game of chess?" I asked.

"No, no more chess. Life is too short. At least for me. Too short for books and for chess—too short for anything except one single problem and one that I shall never solve. But if you will come with me, I will show you something. You remember the etching I made of Doctor Faustus, one or two years ago? Well, it wasn't right. I have worked a lot of dry-point into it since then and now at last I think that I know what is necessary to make it right. I will let you see it and then you will understand how it is possible (even in black and white) to make different sorts of light that flow into each other like wine that is poured into a glass of water. Speaking of which, Hendrickje shall make us a kettle of bischop, but please don't scold me any more if I continue to buy pictures instead of books. In the first place, it won't do you any good. I shall buy them anyway. And in the second place, I need them. There is always a chance that they will teach me something new. I am almost fifty. More than two thirds of my days are gone and there is still so much to do. So terribly much."

We went to the Back Room. Rembrandt lit two candles and got the plate of Doctor Faustus. Titus was fast asleep in one of the two beds built in the wall. Hendrickje went to get the wine and the spices that were necessary for our drink. The kettle was standing on the floor in front of the fire. She leaned over to pick it up just as I looked her way. And suddenly my professional eye registered an unmistakable professional fact. She was pregnant and in her seventh or eight month.

That too was a problem in space but one which Rembrandt seemed to have overlooked.

Chapter 51

I BEGIN TO UNDERSTAND THAT ALL IS NOT WELL IN THE BIG HOUSE ON THE JODENBREESTRAAT

It is very strange, but there are certain things which one man just can't possibly tell to another. He may, under certain circumstances, draw his friend's polite attention to the fact that he is a scoundrel or a thief, but he can never, and under no pretext whatsoever and however discreetly, inform him that his cuffs are badly in need of the laundry—that his collar needs starching nor that his coat after all these many years and many meals of spinach and soft-boiled eggs, would fill the heart of a dozen Josephs with envy and desire. Nor can he go up to even the most intimate of his friends and say, "Pardon me, but isn't that housekeeper of yours on the point of giving birth to twins?"

But for once Fate intervened in a very welcome and discreet fashion. Hendrickje suffered an accident, and as Rembrandt's regular doctor was out of town for the day (he had left by boat that morning to go to Ouderkerk for a funeral) they sent for me who lived just around the corner. When I arrived, I found Rembrandt painting in the large back room while Hendrickje was lying panting and gasping for breath in the same bed in which, almost a dozen years before, Saskia had died. I thought of course that her apparent lack of air had to do with her physical condition, but Rembrandt at once told me what had happened and then I understood the cause of her ailment to be much simpler.

She had gone upstairs to clean the studio as usual that morning. The evening before, two of the pupils had been biting a plate in a new mixture that was supposed to be more effective than the usual "eau forte." It consisted of nitric acid and blue vitriol and a few other ingredients but nitric acid was the chief substance used in this particular compound. Those bright boys had become so deeply engrossed in their task that they had forgotten to close the bottle containing the acid. The faithful Hendrickje had paid no attention to the strange odors in the room—had carefully swept and cleaned and brushed—had breathed the poisoned air—had felt how her chest was gradually beginning to ache and how her eyes were beginning to smart—and how she was weeping bitter tears—and in great panic she finally had left the room, telling Rembrandt she was going to faint and would he please send at once for the surgeon.

It was not a very difficult case. I asked to be shown the room in which she had worked, for I thought that she might have tried to burn some old rags which sometimes make a very dangerous smoke. As soon as we entered the studio, Rembrandt noticed what had happened, pushed open both windows, looked for the jar containing the acid, closed it and then called for the two pupils whose ears he boxed with such an experienced hand that these young men probably remembered until the end of their days that a bottle of nitric acid was no child's toy and should be treated as circumspectly as a loaded and cocked gun.

We then took Hendrickje out of the badly ventilated back room and put her down on a couch in the garden and immediately she began to feel better. A few minutes later she fell asleep and as my morning had been spoiled more or less anyway, I decided to stay a while and reassure Rembrandt who was in a great state of perturbation.

"I have lost one wife in this house through what was more or less my own carelessness," he said as soon as we had returned to the studio where the mild hurricane that was blowing in through the open windows had not only driven away the acid fumes but had also upset a picture of Hendrickje on which Rembrandt was working. It showed Hendrickje wearing the big pearl ear-rings of Saskia which he had bought about fifteen years before and which had figured so prominently in the famous libel suit which he had been forced to bring against some of his wife's relatives who had accused him and his wife of being spendthrifts and ne'er-do-wells. That libel suit had come to nothing. The court had found Rembrandt to be technically right, but as he was only a painter and Saskia only the wife of a painter and both of them therefore "private persons" of no particular account, the amount of damage which they claimed had been reduced from 128 to eight golden florins and so in the end the case had cost Rembrandt infinitely more than he had got out of it. He still apparently retained the pearl ear-rings for in the picture, Hendrickje was wearing them and when Rembrandt had dusted it off with a piece of soft cloth, I noticed that it was a very fine piece of work. Perhaps he had made Hendrickje a little more of a "lady" than she actually was, but all the kindness and goodness of her beautiful eyes were there. I liked it and I told him so and he sat down in front of his easel and mixed some white with ocher to touch up the ear-rings (slightly damaged by the fall), and said, "I am glad if you think that all those things are there. I have worked on this very hard. She has been very good to Titus and to me. I would like to do something for her."

This was more or less my opportunity.

"I was obliged to examine her when I came in," I said, "for to tell you the truth, my first impression was that she was pregnant. And I discovered that she was. That isn't what you mean when you say that you wanted to do something for her?"

I knew that I had committed a terrible blunder. I had done one of those incredible, unbelievable things of which one is guilty once or twice in his life and which one never is able to forget—which come back to one at the most unexpected moments—during sleepless nights and cause cold shivers to run down one's spine. And no sooner had I spoken these words than I regretted them with a thousand regrets, but it was too late.

Rembrandt, however, picked up the knife that was lying on his palette, put some raw umber on it, with which he lightly touched the background, stepped back, the better to look at what he had done, and then remarked in a most casual tone of voice: "No, that is not what I meant. I was thinking of this picture, for it is one of the best things I have ever done and people will look at it and will admire it—and her—long after we shall be dead. And as for the other little item you just mentioned, that I am sorry to say was an error on our part. We are both of us glad it happened, now that it has happened, but it was a mistake. It happened once before, but you weren't in town at that time and the child died. Pity, for it was a girl and it would have been nice to have a girl. Perhaps we shall have better luck this time."

He made this announcement as if he were telling me of some new picture he was planning to paint and I really don't believe that it meant very much more to him than that. The picture was merely an incident in life, an interesting episode in which one pitted one's intelligence against the unwilling forces of nature. The child was an incident in life in which nature pitted its unreasoning forces against the intelligence of man. Sometimes man won. As a rule nature won. It made no difference. Everything that "was," was to Rembrandt a manifestation of the existing order of things. Some people tried to solve the problem by worrying. Others tried to solve it by working. Rembrandt worked—pictures, etchings—children. Everything was as it should be—no questions asked—no answers either expected or given—world without end. Amen.

"But," said I, who after all had been brought up in the atmosphere of profound middle-class righteousness (and can a person ever rid the garden of his memory from the weeds of inviolable respectability?) "but surely, now that Saskia is gone and you are a free man, you can marry Hendrickje and I think" (what hideous spirit of mental bumptiousness possessed me that morning?) "that you ought to."

Rembrandt smeared some more ocher on his palette knife.

"I ought to, all right," he answered, falling into the vernacular of his childhood days. "Sure, and I know it. I ought to, even more than all right, but I can't."

"Why not? You are a free man."

"I am. I am absolutely free. I could marry anybody I pleased, provided she would have me, as soon as the banns had been read. I know all that. We have talked about it. But it can't be done."

"Why not?"

"The will."

"You mean Saskia's will?"

"Yes. Poor Saskia meant well. She loved me. She left me a will and all her earthly possessions."

"But that will is perfectly good."

"Of course it is. But the possessions are not. They looked very imposing on parchment. But they did not exist. Or if they did, my dear Frisian relatives got away with them. I don't know and to tell you the truth, I no longer care. It does not matter. I have too much to do. I think I have found a new way to handle a lighted candle in a picture I may be asked to do for the new Town Hall. I will show you the sketch. I think I now know how it ought to be done. The theme is Potiphar's wife. I tried something like that twenty years ago—a nude—but I didn't like it. I like to paint my figures clothed. The nude was a good thing for those old Greeks who made their statues that way—they were accustomed to see nude bodies. We are not. We never see more than three or four of them in all our lives and we can't paint what we do not see every day—what we do not know by heart. Yes, I want to do that again. Potiphar's wife, or something like that. And then I bought an old piece of armor—paid 300 guilders for it—rather expensive, but a fine piece of work. I am going to use that for all sorts of things for I have never done brass the way it really looks when the sun shines on it, and I want to try my hand at some more landscapes and I have got at least two dozen etchings to do. You see, work enough for ten years! If I live that long. If I wanted to get all those other problems straightened out, I never would be able to do anything else."

"Are they as bad as all that?" I interrupted him.

"Much worse. The only way I can go on is by forgetting that they exist. One of these days the public will come back to me. They will understand what I am trying to do. I am a fast worker. In less than a year I will be able to paint myself out of this financial hole. Then I can pay my creditors and marry Hendrickje. I am fond of her. Terribly fond. She is a nice girl. A good girl. She gives me everything I want. I would be a scoundrel not to marry her, but she will have to wait until then. And she does not mind. She says it makes very little difference to her and meanwhile it keeps this household out of trouble."

"But meanwhile will you be able to keep her out of the town gossip? Surely the neighbors will notice her condition and will talk?"

Rembrandt dropped his palette knife and looked at me with anger blazing in his eyes. "What of it?" he asked brusquely. "What of it? They talk anyway. They always have talked. They always will talk. That is what they are in this world for. To talk. They can't do anything else. They can—how does the Bible say it?—they can hew wood and draw water and talk scandal about their betters. The neighbors, indeed! Damn the neighbors! I am not thinking of them. Neither is Hendrickje. Let them go on carrying bricks and slopping around with pails of water. That is all they are good for. But this house is worth saving. Hendrickje likes it. Titus loves it. I have been happy in it. Some mighty fine pieces of work have been done right here in this house. We ought to save the house. That is what we are working for now."

I did not see the connection and told him so.

"Do you remember the will, Saskia's will?" he asked me.

I told him that I did so only in a very vague way, not having the sort of mind that easily retains official language.

"Well," Rembrandt said, "Saskia was not only very fond of me, bless her, but she also had great confidence in me—absolute confidence—and she wanted to show how she felt in her will. Her relatives had said rather nasty things about me—that I was a spendthrift and a wastrel—that I did not know the value of money—that money slipped through my fingers like water and that I would rather spend 500 guilders on some picture that interested me than use the money to pay my grocer. Perhaps they were right. I was never very good at figures and when I think what I am giving the world—what I have already given it—such little details don't matter.

"Anyway, Saskia left everything to me—absolutely and outright—no guardians to watch her son's interests—no notaries to poke their inquisitive noses into our affairs—no Chamber of Orphans to come and ask embarrassing questions. I was to handle everything but on certain conditions. I was to give Titus a first rate education and establish him in some profession of his own as soon as he should become of age. In case, however, I died or married again, her fortune was to pass directly to Titus. Do you get the meaning of that? In case I married again, Titus was to have everything. If I married Hendrickje, then according to the terms of the will, I would have to go before the courts and fill out endless papers and swear a dozen oaths and turn everything over to Titus. And how am I to turn over 'everything' when there isn't anything—when there never was anything except promises and still more promises and law-suits and family feuds, but no cash. Even when I wanted to buy this house, I had to borrow. We ought to have been able to pay for it in full. But always something was happening in Friesland and every cent we ever got out of those people we had to take out with a block and tackle.

"Meanwhile the whole world has taken for granted that I am a rich man. It was, 'Rembrandt, buy this!' or 'Rembrandt, I got a little Italian picture. The moment you see it you will buy it.' Or, 'Rembrandt, my kids have not had a square meal for a fortnight and my wife is expecting her seventh. You are a rich man. Let me have ten guilders.' And I am a weak man where it comes to money. We never had any when we were children. It was fun to be considered a Croesus. Anyway, what did it matter? Some day that inheritance would be paid out in full and I would have almost 50,000 guilders to pay all my creditors.

"Meanwhile I painted, but since the Banning Cocq picture, the public does not seem to like my work any more. What could I do? Move away?

Give up this house? The moment I whisper a word about wanting to sell, I shall have all my creditors on my back. I have got to keep up appearances if I want to keep up my credit. And the moment my credit is gone, we shall all be in the poor-house. Titus—Hendrickje—I. The kind friends who encouraged me to borrow when they thought everything was fine will fall upon me like a pack of wolves. It would be the end. And so" (with a final dab at the foreground of Hendrickje), "don't ask me, 'Why don't you marry the girl?' for I can't and she knows it and she is very wonderful about it. It won't be easy for her, but she says that she understands and so I think that for the moment we had better let matters stand where they are."

I agreed with him in the main but I am one of those persons who likes things done in an orderly fashion. I cannot work unless I am neatly dressed, well shaved, my hair well brushed. The room in which I work has to be neat. My desk has to be neat. Otherwise my brain won't work. And being a man of such precise, almost meticulous, habits, I like to have my business affairs in order. I know that I have no talent for financial problems and I therefore leave them to some one else who knows more about them than I do. But I don't think that I could live if I were not sure that at any moment I could open a drawer and undo a bit of red string and convince myself, within two or three hundred guilders, just exactly what I had and what I owed others and what others owed me. I know it is rather foolish to lay so much stress upon such things, homo est quod est and that is the way I am made. And so, though I did my best not to sound too much like a schoolmaster, I could not help saying: "But, Rembrandt, my friend, you must know approximately where you stand!" But he smeared his hands on his smock in a most unconcerned fashion, smiled pleasantly at me and answered:

"I have not the faintest idea and that is the truth."

Then I tried to reason with him. I explained to him that he never would be able to get out of debt without first knowing approximately how much debt he had—that fighting unknown debts was like trying to fight an invisible enemy in a dark cellar—that system and order was the only way in which one could ever hope to slay the monster of bankruptcy. But he was unable to consider the matter seriously and tried to distract my attention by conducting me into the press-room where three pupils were busy with a large etching of the Crucifixion, and presently he discovered a flaw in the shading of the figure of the bearded Pharisee in the foreground and called for one of the boys to sharpen him the steel needle he had bought that afternoon, for he would not bother to bite the plate again but would make his correction by dry-point and finally he forgot all about me and I watched him working by the light of a single candle (a terrible strain on his eyes and disastrous to anybody who has to make a living by one of the arts) and I stayed in the room for about an hour and then, realizing that I might sit there until

REMBRANDT PAINTING HENDRICKJE

four in the morning without being noticed, I went downstairs, found Hendrickje fast asleep and little the worse for her accident, and went home where I found a letter from My Lord Constantin written from his country place in which there was little mention of pictures but a great deal about politics.

"These are strange days," so the old gentleman wrote, "for those of us who like to contemplate the historical landscape from a more or less philosophical angle. History, as I have been told since childhood, does not repeat itself. But as certain human emotions are eternal and invariable, certain political conditions, arising directly from those human emotions, bear a very close resemblance to each other.

"Take this bugaboo of self-government, of democracy, or whatever you wish to call it. The average man feels feebly and vaguely that he ought to stand on his own legs—manage his own affairs—and he clamors for a Republic—for a Res Publicae—in which every free man shall have the right to express his own feelings in regard to the management of the state. As long as the country to which he belongs, or the city or the village of which he is an inhabitant continues to dwell in peace, he is perfectly at his ease and struts about in his gay colors, a sword at his side and pats himself on the back and says, 'I am a pretty fine fellow, master of my own destiny, etc., etc.' But the moment he sniffs the first suspicious odors of danger—the moment he is brought face to face with a crisis—all his courage and all his high spirits leave him and he runs to the market-place and cries: 'A leader! Give me a leader! Give me some one who is stronger than I am myself. Give me a man whom I can follow when he leads. I am only a weak little creature—all these fine phrases were merely self-deception. Take me by the hand and tell me what to do.'

"As soon as we had got our liberty we felt that we had no longer any need for a man on horseback—a handsome young general on a prancing steed. And we got rid of the House of Orange. Henceforth our people were to rule themselves. The rabble of course were not consulted. They never had been and most likely they never will be. Our Burgomasters and Magistrates and our Aldermen and our merchants were to rule the Republic.

"Meanwhile, on the other side of the North Sea our English neighbors were doing the same thing. Being by nature more violent or more logical than we are, they cut their ruler's head off and declared themselves a Republic—just as we are—and Parliament, as representing the wish of the people, was to rule. This condition of affairs lasted exactly three years in both countries. Then they drifted into a war with each other, as they were bound to do, seeing that they both wanted the same thing at the same moment, and behold! England is still nominally a Republic, but it is ruled by a successful general who calls himself only a Lord Protector, but who is more powerful than the old Kings ever thought of being. For one thing, he has presented himself with a standing army of 30,000 men and every time a Stuart dared to ask for a corporal's guard of his own to keep order in the garden of St. James' Palace, there was an outcry of tyrant and murderer. Now an obscure country-squire from a county no one had ever heard of enjoys more power than any sovereign, duly anointed and booted and spurred by Holy Church, ever dreamed of exercising. And all the little people flock to his standard and shout: 'Long live our Chief!' and if he told them to throw themselves from the cliffs of Dover, they probably would do so because they have no confidence in their own weakness but full faith in his strength.

"And at the same moment we on this side of the North Sea are beginning to repent of our courage of a few years ago. We are scared. We don't know how this war with England will come out. Just when we had decided that we would rule ourselves and that it was folly for free men to submit to the descendants of a little German robber-baron, we seem to lose courage and the old, old story is about to repeat itself.

"Two years ago we got rid of King Log and to-day amidst the enthusiastic plaudits of the multitude, we are trying to bring in King Stork. Yesterday your old friend, Jan de Witt, was made Pensionary of Holland. The title itself means nothing. The office in the hands of that man means everything. It makes him Dictator of the entire Republic. He can raise an army if he wants to and he can build himself such a fleet as the world has never seen before. He can spend all the money he wants. He is his own Minister of Foreign Affairs and his own Minister of Justice. He has a complete spy system at his disposal, to keep tab on his neighbors. By formal resolution of the Estates (passed only a couple of days ago) every private citizen is being urged to watch over his neighbor and to report him to the police the moment he suspects him of disloyal sentiments—disloyal sentiments to My Lord Jan, of course.

"What the House of Orange never dared to do, this son of wine merchants (or were the de Witts in the wood business?) from a third-rate little provincial town does and everybody says, 'How perfectly wonderful! how fine! how noble!' Because we are at war with a very dangerous enemy—because we are afraid of our own shadows—because we know that we can't ever hope to win without accepting the leadership of some one whom we feel to be abler and stronger than we are ourselves.

"And behold! at once the country takes new courage. Stocks go up which ever since the battle of Dover have been going down. The rate of interest on the public debt has gone down from five percent to four percent. We cannot quite undo the harm of the first year. Tromp is dead. Van Galen is dead. We have lost more than sixteen hundred merchantmen, but Jan de Witt has taken hold of things and we are sure that everything will come out all right and that we will yet win the war.

"I refrain from drawing any conclusions.

"But I have read my Plato.

"I think that I have read everything that was ever printed upon the curious subject of a Res Publicae and upon the even more extraordinary subject of government by the average citizens rather than by the few exceptional men. It makes rather inspiring reading when one has nothing else to do—when the day's chores are over and the motherland at peace with everybody. But as soon as there is need of action, that sort of literature becomes just so much trash—useless books of learning without the slightest practical value.

"It is all very puzzling, but as for myself, I have always served a prince and I shall be content to do so until the day of my death.

"Farewell.

"If you could see my late strawberries (my own invention, my own specialty, raised by the care of my own hand) you would rejoice. And I would rejoice too, for it would mean that you were here and I must confess that I miss your agreeable company."

I laid the letter aside and went to bed.

The next morning I got up early.

During the night I had evolved a little plan that seemed to promise good results.

It was impossible to let Rembrandt go on the way he was going.

It was time for some one to do something and I meant to be that some one.

I took my hat and coat and instead of turning to the left as I did every morning on my way to the hospital, I turned to the right and made for the quarters which Jean-Louys had occupied these last five and twenty years.

For although for once I meant to be a man of action, it would do no harm to proceed cautiously.

I knocked at the door and entered and behold! Jean-Louys was lying on the floor before a large flat bowl of water on which there floated a tiny ship made out of paper. By his side knelt a sort of red-bearded giant who was working a pair of bellows with which he was engaged in creating a mild hurricane in the vicinity of the paper vessel.

"Come in and join me," Jean-Louys shouted, without, however, moving an inch from his uncomfortable position. "Come in and join me. I am playing Jupiter and this is my Aeolus. I am at work on a new problem. I have discovered something new, infinitely more interesting than logarithms. And it will make us all rich. Come in and join me. Have you breakfasted? No? Then you will stay with me. This cut-throat here was for five years chief onion-soup-maker-in-extraordinary to the Dey of Algiers. Ten minutes more and you will know why the old Dey drowned three of his favorite wives rather than give up such a cook!"

Chapter 52

JEAN-LOUYS GETS A NEW SERVANT, AND I HEAR FOR THE LAST TIME FROM BERNARDO

As soon as the onion soup had been placed upon the table (this is the only disguise in which I can bear that useful bulb) the red-bearded giant left the small dining-room and Jean-Louys, who had been as eager as a small child to tell me all about his new playthings, poured the tale into my ears.

"First of all I must tell you about that man. He can't understand what I say for his hearing has been greatly impaired and his speech too, as you may have noticed. He is a Frenchman. He comes from my own part of the country. That is probably why we understood each other from the first moment, though he was dead drunk when I picked him out of a gutter and brought him here.

"This is the way it happened. I had gone out to get some fresh bread. I was finishing some work and had not been out for days. It was a nice evening and I decided to take a walk. Down near the water front they were very busy. The next day about thirty ships were to leave for Batavia. It was the usual scene—drunken sailors and drunken women and a band or two and the usual crimps and soul-snatchers eagerly watching lest their prey wander off into the byways of the Nieuwe Waals Island and be stolen by their rivals before they could get them safely on board and pocket the reward. You know the system. They don't get paid until their cargo of human cattle has been delivered.

"It was a disgusting sight, but I suppose that sort of thing is unavoidable if we are to have nutmeg in our wine, and what would scrambled eggs be without a little pepper?

"I got away from the Island as soon as I could and returned home. On the corner of the Oude Schans a man was lying in the middle of the street. He seemed dead. But I could see no wounds and he was still breathing. Drunk or drugged, I thought, and then I heard him mumble a few words. They were in the dialect of my own part of the world!

"A dialect is a passport to the heart of every other man or woman who speaks it. I tried to lift him, but he was very heavy and in a stupor. I hailed two suspicious-looking characters who were lurking around, probably with the intention of robbing this poor devil, and offered them five stivers each if they would deliver the drunk at my house. They pocketed the money and deposited their burden on the floor of my room. I gave them each an extra shilling. They were very grateful. One of them before leaving told me:

"That boy will be all right before morning. That is the work of Squinting Mike, the Irish crimp. He is the greediest of them all. He puts drops in their beer. He once killed two Swedes that way and almost got hanged for it. The Swedish agent pushed the case hard, for it was not the first time his people had been packed off to the Indies that way. But there was some dirty work. Mike was allowed to get away and fled to Hamburg. He came back last fall. Now he is up to his old tricks. That boy will be all right in the morning. Perhaps he will have a headache. Thank you for those two shillings, mister. You don't happen to have a drink for two poor devils that are down on their luck?"

"I gave them each a bottle of beer (I don't like the stuff myself anyway), and they left me alone with my new-found friend. I covered him up with an old coat and in the morning, when I woke up, he was busy dusting the room. I got his story.

"My master Descartes laid down the rule: 'I think. Therefore I exist as a human being.'

"I would like to go a little further and offer an amendment to that fundamental law of life. As soon as all people shall have learned to think, they will be able to exist as human beings.

"Until that moment (I doubt whether it will ever come) we shall continue to live like wild animals. That red-bearded giant is only twenty-seven years old. Listen to this. He is the son of a sheep-farmer near Dax, a drunken father, nineteen brothers and sisters and a third step-mother. The other wives had all died in childbirth. At the age of seven he was sent out with a flock of his own. One day, during a thunderstorm, three of them were killed by lightning. The father was so angry with the boy that he hanged him by his arms from one of the rafters of the sheep-pen. The village priest heard of it, hurried to the farm and cut the boy loose, and took him home.

"As soon as he had recovered (in two or three weeks' time) the father came to the parsonage and demanded his son. The priest refused to surrender him. The father went to the bishop at Dax with a present of five sheep. He got a legal document which forced the priest to surrender the boy to his 'legal parent,' as if parenthood had anything to do with the right to maltreat one's offspring.

"The next day the boy ran away, walked all the way to Bordeaux and hid himself on board a vessel bound for Canada. He was discovered, given a severe beating and put on shore in La Rochelle where the ship had gone for supplies, and for a cargo of rum to sell to the natives of the St. Lawrence River. He was eight years old by this time. It takes a lot of starvation to kill an infant at that age. But one day he fainted in the street and was carried inside the nearest house. It belonged to a Huguenot minister, a certain Guiton, a cousin of the famous mayor who conducted the defense of the city during the siege. The Huguenot kept him and used him in the kitchen. That is where he learned to cook so well. He must have been a remarkable man, that minister, for he let the boy stay a Catholic.

"During the siege the minister's house was hit by a shell of Richelieu's artillery. The whole family was killed with the exception of the minister himself, who was tending the dying on the walls and this boy who was cleaning bottles in the cellar at the moment of the disaster. When the town was taken, the minister was obliged to sign a paper that he would never preach again. He refused to sign and went on preaching. He was condemned to fifteen years at the galleys. The boy was allowed to go, as he had remained a Catholic. He found out what he had to do to be condemned to the galleys. Then he stole a loaf of bread from a military bakery and was given five years on the galleys. It was almost a year before he could discover the whereabouts of his former master. In the meantime his ability as a cook had been discovered. He was offered a job as ship's cook. He refused, but some officers took an interest in him (the story of his deliberate effort to be sent to the bagnio had somehow leaked out in the meantime) and he was given a seat at the same oar with his former master.

"After two years—two years spent chained to a wooden seat or chained to a bench in the land barracks—their vessel, while returning from a trip to Corsica was overhauled by a Tunisian pirate. There had been a great deal of sickness among the French galley-slaves, due to the bad food they were given. The captain of this particular vessel was a young man from Touraine who had tried to have an affair with one of the nieces of the Cardinal. But the women of the Mazarin blood did few things for the mere sake of the doing. She hinted that he might be more successful if he approached her occasionally with the trifling gift of a couple of pearls or a diamond bracelet.

"The young man was as poor as a church mouse but he had influence. He was made captain of a royal galley. In his greed, he even let his own officers starve. So you need not ask what happened to the men. The poor devils were no match for the corsairs. In less than an hour the Tunisian had overtaken them.

"You probably know the bounties which My Most Christian Majesty bestows upon those of his faithful subjects who are generously allowed to work in his galleys. He gives them two sets of chains, one for their legs and one for their arms—a pair of breeches—a straw hat and a little wooden pear which is suspended from their neck by a thin iron chain. When the ship goes into action, the creatures are ordered to put that pear into their mouth. It allows them to breath but it stifles their cries when they are wounded or dying, so that the soldiers won't be disheartened by the agony of this poor, dumb cattle when it is on the way to meet its creator. This wooden pear saved my friend's life. The Tunisians fired a volley which hit the Frenchman from in front. The old

Huguenot minister got a bullet in his brain and was killed outright. Our friend in the other room was hit just a little lower. The bullet struck him in the mouth, but the wooden pear stopped it. All his teeth were knocked out and splinters got stuck in his vocal cords. Otherwise he was all right. In less than a month he was pronounced cured, but he never could talk again above a whisper.

"During the next three years he sat chained to a bench of a Tunisian galley. Otherwise nothing was changed in his life. Then by accident his culinary abilities were discovered. He was promoted to the kitchens of the Dey. They gave him a fine uniform and three wives and paid him for his services.

"One day a Dutch trader loaded with rum, dropped into the harbor of Tunis. The Dey, who was a faithful follower of the Prophet and at the same time a heavy toper, entertained the captain with great honor and the poor cook thinking that this man must therefore be a personage of distinction—an admiral or vice-admiral, at the very least—hastily smuggled himself on board the vessel that night when the Dey and all his guests were deeply under the influence of the Dutchman's floating cargo.

"The next day he discovered his mistake. The ship belonged to the West India Company and was in the slave trade. At first they talked about throwing the Frenchman overboard. Then they noticed his gigantic strength (any one who survives four years at an oar in one of His Most Catholic Majesty's galleys has the constitution of an ox) and they taught him the trade of a sailor. They used to ply between Cormantyne on the Gold Coast and Virginia, with an occasional side trip to Nieuw Amsterdam for repairs. A year ago they met an English man-of-war off the Cape Verde Islands. They did not know that war had been declared between England and Holland until the Britisher fired a salvo that made them lose half of their foremast. Then they decided that something was wrong and fled. They were faster than the Englishman but they had a heavy cargo on board—more than eight hundred black men and women. The Frenchman and two Dutchmen were ordered to throw the cargo overboard. They refused at first, but the captain threatened to shoot them down unless they obeyed his orders. They threw all of those eight hundred odd human beings overboard. The ship was followed by sharks until they reached the Canary Islands. There they lost their Englishman. But there was no use going to America without a cargo and so the captain decided to return home by way of Scotland. They ran out of water and had to land in Ireland. Ten men were sent on shore. They fell into an ambush, laid by a band of natives, who rushed upon them shouting, 'Armada! armada!' probably thinking that they were Spaniards belonging to the great armada of almost a century ago. The Frenchman and one German boy, who were the last to land, could reach the boat and escaped. All the others were taken prisoner and clubbed to death. Half of the crew and the captain died from lack of water. The survivors brought the ship home.

"This poor devil, when he came for his pay, was told that he was a stowaway and owed the Company money. When he insisted, they threatened him with arrest. He did odd jobs around the harbor for a few months. Then some one asked him whether he did not want to enlist on board an Indiaman. The pay was good and he would get fifty guilders in advance. That seemed riches to him. He accepted. His new acquaintance suggested that they go somewhere and have a drink in honor of the event. He agreed. They went to an obscure basement, but he does not remember where. Indeed he remembers nothing until he woke up in my room.

"I did not quite know what to do with him. I got a room for him with my amiable vegetable woman. Then I asked him what he could do. He said he could cook and sail a boat. I let him cook. He was a wonder.

"One evening, just for the fun, I did what I had never done. I hired a small sailboat and told him to take me on a trip on the Y. That was the second great emotion of my life. The first one happened when I stumbled upon that little volume by John Napier and discovered logarithms. The second one came to me when for the first time since I was born I experienced the feeling of a fresh young breeze filling the sails of that little cat-boat. It was like flying into space—at least what I think flying into space must be like—if we can ever hope to do it. Then and there I fell in love with sailing. I did not tell you. It seemed so silly, at my age, to be as enthusiastic as a boy with his first pair of skates. But I bought a boat of my own last week. A small yacht. It used to belong to a family in Zaandam who lost their money early in the war. It has a large cabin and room for two passengers. Poor François, that is the name of my new man, sleeps in the front part of the ship. There is a small stove on board. The ideal home for a philosopher. As soon as my new book is done, I shall retire from the world and live entirely on board my own yacht. I like the sound of that. How does it strike you?"

I told him that it struck me as a brilliant idea. As a boy whenever I stayed with my uncle in Veere, I had done a great deal of sailing and I loved to be on the water. But I feared that Jean-Louys, accustomed to spend his days in scientific studies, might find life on board a little dull and I told him so. Would he be able to live for days at a time without his mathematics and his logarithms?

"But that is just the beauty of it!" he shouted with enthusiasm. "As soon as I had been on the Y a couple of times and knew more or less how a boat like that was handled, I went to my book-seller and asked him to give me a volume on the theory of getting a vessel in motion by means of the wind. I know what happens when I use an oar. I did not know what happened when I hoisted sail. I can guess more or less at what occurs, but I want to see a problem expressed in terms of mathematics, before I believe that it is true. There were a lot of books on how to build boats, but no one ever seemed to have asked himself exactly what takes place when a ship sails before the wind or tacks. So I thought I would try and find out. The Magdeburg mayor, with his notions of a vacuum, had given me an idea. I am trying it out in the wash-basin in the other room. But that won't interest you. You come and sail with me some time and I shall never even whisper a word about my formulae. If you, from your side, will promise not to talk about Cannabis Indica. And at night we shall drop anchor in some quiet spot and shall drink malmsey and talk of olden times and of our walks with Selim and good Bernardo. Those were good days! I wonder what has become of them?"

Since I am once on the subject, I might as well mention now under what circumstances I last heard from Bernardo. It was in '65, a year after Nieuw Amsterdam had been taken away from us by the English, who attacked the city without any declaration of war, and two years after the death of King Louis.

In this letter, addressed to Jean-Louys and to me (it made the trip in less than four months, which was a record, considering the fact that at that time we were at war with England and the ocean and the North Sea were both infested with priveteers) Bernardo no longer used his own name but signed himself by means of an incomprehensible Indian hieroglyphic, the picture of a man lifting both hands toward High Heaven, and whenever he spoke of his neighbors, he called them "My people." For he had completely identified himself with the copper-colored aborigines among whom he had settled down almost twenty-five years before. But his letter showed that, mentally at least, he had not changed and that although he had preferred to cast his lot in with natives, he himself had not in any way "gone native" as we used to say of those Europeans who having been sent to the Indies to administer the Javanese and the Malayans on behalf of the white races had cut themselves loose from their own civilization and through indolence and from lack of sufficient force of character had degenerated into a species of nondescript human beings as thoroughly despised by their former compatriots as by those whom they tried to flatter by an all too sincere imitation.

He sent us both his most affectionate regards and "to all the old friends who were so good to me and who now seem so far away. As for me, there is little to say. I am happy. Happier than I ever thought I could be. My children are fine boys. They hunt and fish. They know nothing of those dreadful things which I have spent the greater part of my life trying to forget. Their mother is very kind. I never regretted for a moment that I married her and joined her tribe. We are breaking camp. The Massachusetts people have become our neighbors. We are moving further westward. The Dutch were hard task-masters, but they did not despise us. When they were not actually engaged in killing Indians, they did not refuse to associate with them on terms of equality. And so we have pulled up stakes and to-morrow we move westward until we shall find new hunting grounds. I am sad at heart, for I am leaving the only spot in the world where I have found contentment of the soul. But my sons are eager to go and so all will be well. The land of which I have heard the old people talk lies several weeks away from here near the big lake where the Eries used to dwell. They have suffered greatly during the last ten years from sickness and many of their hunting grounds lie deserted. But it is far away from Nieuw Amsterdam and I may not be able to communicate with you for a long time to come. And if this be my last greeting to you on this earth, let it tell you once more with what deep gratitude and love I think back to the days when you took me into your heart and gave me your friendship."

Then followed the strange little manikin, lifting both hands wide stretched up to High Heaven, and that was the last time I ever heard of Bernardo.

When My Lord Stuyvesant came home for the last time, a year after the surrender of Nieuw Amsterdam, to give an account of himself during the last years of his administration and to explain why he had not taken sufficient measures to defend the city against the forces of Colonel Nicolls (a charge which he answered by referring the honorable directors of the Company to their own letter-files in which they could read how for a period of nineteen years he had never ceased to draw their respectful attention to the utter state of neglect of the colony entrusted to his care) I had the privilege of visiting him at the little village near Leyden where he was staying with his wife's relatives.

He received me most cordially. He told me that during the four months preceding the actual attack upon the city he had not received a single letter from home, hinting in any way at friction between the Netherlands and the King of Great Britain. He had heard in a vague and roundabout way that His Majesty had bestowed the greater part of the American coast upon his brother, the Duke of York, but as Charles II was notoriously generous with other people's possessions, he had paid no particular attention to this news. It was probably part of the day's royal gossip. And as His Majesty was said to contemplate a more active policy against the Puritans of the Northern settlements who had given refuge to the judges who had condemned His Majesty's father to death—who had made themselves guilty of all sorts of cruelties against those who differed from them in matters of religion—who had driven perfectly harmless men and women who refused to share their views into the wilderness to be tortured to death by the natives—and who had passed special laws condemning other Englishmen who were followers of George Fox to have their ears cut off, their noses slit and their tongues pierced by hot irons, whenever they should be found within the jurisdiction of the Massachusetts company, it had been perfectly natural for My Lord

Stuyvesant to draw the conclusion that this military expedition was directed against the rebellious inhabitants of the New England colony rather than against the peaceful citizens of the New Netherlands who had done nothing to incur His Majesty's wrath.

I was glad to hear shortly afterwards that my old friend had been able to convert his former employers to this point of view and that no further steps were contemplated against him. As for myself, the news he brought me was not very encouraging. Regarding my little piece of property near Nieuw Amsterdam (now called New York after the brother of His Majesty) that probably was safe enough as the English commander had shown the greatest possible generosity in dealing with his new subjects. But when I asked him what he knew of the migration of the northern Indians from their ancient homesteads towards the great lakes of the West, he shrugged his shoulders and answered, "Nothing! Absolutely nothing!"

He had heard in a very indefinite and roundabout way that some such migration had been contemplated and that the advance guard had actually left for the West late in the fall of '64. But it had been an exceptionally early and severe winter. Rumors had come to Nieuw Amsterdam that the first group to undertake the distant and dangerous journey had been caught in a blizzard and that all of them had frozen to death. Whether Bernardo had joined this group or had waited until spring, it was of course impossible for him to tell.

During the next half dozen years I asked every captain bound for the mouth of the Hudson to make inquiries and inquire among the natives who loafed around the trading-posts what they knew. But all to no avail. Bernardo's letter of the year '65 was the last token of life I ever received from his hand. The wilderness had swallowed him up. He had always craved oblivion. He had got his wish. May his end have been as happy and peaceful as those years he spent away from a civilization he had every reason to abhor and detest.

As for Selim, he had a habit of reminding us of his continued existence and prosperity by messages and presents that bobbed up in Amsterdam at most unexpected moments. His greatest coup took place in the year '60. I remember the date because it occurred just at the time the whole country was in a violent state of excitement about those three judges of the late King Charles, who had found a refuge in the town of Delft when the House of Stuart was returned to the throne of England and who had expected that the ancient right of asylum (of which our country had long been so proud) would protect them against the vengeance of their new sovereign.

As soon, however, as His Majesty had sailed from Scheveningen for the mouth of the Thames, he had begun to bombard the Estates with requests for the surrender of these "murderers." The country had been sharply divided upon the subject. Most people still smarted under the remembrance of what their own fathers and mothers had suffered at the hands of a cruel potentate and those declared that it was against the very spirit of the founders of the Republic to comply with such a demand. But others, short-sighted as merchants so often are, argued: "No, it would be foolish to refuse to comply with His Majesty's wishes. We need his good will for we need his country's trade. The Lord Protector and his followers who ruled England during the last ten years were our worst enemies and did their best to destroy our prosperity. Why should we be over-sensitive about a few of the disciples of this man Cromwell, who hated us and made war on us whenever he could, if by surrendering them we can gain the good will of those who are now in power and with whom we have never had any quarrel? We can easily placate our own consciences by persuading ourselves that this is a purely internal political question which does not regard us at all—which the English must solve as they themselves see fit."

While this discussion was going on, leading to violent discussions in all the ale-houses and in the cabins of every canal-boat (I am sorry to say that in the end the "practical minded" gained the victory and that the three unfortunate Britishers were surrendered to His Majesty who had them butchered in the approved royal fashion) there appeared at my door one day a personage who introduced himself as a certain Captain Jan Krol, a cousin of the former governor of the Nieuw Netherlands (though not inordinately proud of the fact)—who stated that he had that week returned with his ship from Stamboul and that he brought me a little present from an old friend of mine.

This little present, carefully carried into the house by two stalwart sailors who had waited outside with a wheel-barrow, consisted of a queerly shaped bale or sack, made of a pale yellowish matting and spreading a strange but exceedingly pleasant odor vaguely reminding me of the water-front of Nieuw Amsterdam.

When my son with a pair of scissors cut it open, as if it were a fatted pig, it disgorged thousands of little brown beans, no larger than a full-sized pea, and they rattled all over the stone floor of the kitchen and looked most appetizing, though none of us knew what they were, though we suspected them of being a new kind of vegetable or something that was to be boiled in the soup. When half of the bag was emptied, we came upon a letter of Selim's, hidden in a beautifully wrought small golden box.

"Allah is great, O my friends, for once more Allah is Allah and I am the humblest and most faithful of his servants.

"I hope your health is well. I also hope you will enjoy this small present as much as I enjoyed your charming companionship during the days I dwelled within your hospitable but dampish gates.

"At that time, now so far behind us all, you may remember, we were occasionally treated to a cup of that 'chaw' which ships returning from Kathay had obtained from the Portuguese at Macao. It may have been a popular beverage among the yellow denizens of the great empire of the East, but if I recollect rightly, we did not like this lukewarm soup any too well and merely partook of it only out of politeness. But now, my friends, the gates of Paradise have been opened—the Houris have descended upon earth—the marvelous Black Water from the Realm of Sheba's glorious Queen is about to pour down your unbelieving and unworthy gullets.

"Nevertheless, drink this supreme Abyssinian draft—this divine cure of all human ailments, O my beloved friends, and think in kindness of him who now dwelleth in the fear of Allah, the One and Only God, who rewardeth those who truly love Him beyond the merits of mortal man and surely beyond the merits of the black-souled sinner you once knew as your affectionate companion,

Selim,

"Now His Majesty's bearer of the most sacred horse-tail and groom-in-extraordinary to the Padishal mule."

The letter itself was not remarkable, but the accompanying gift caused a commotion which few of us who took part in concocting that unfortunate potion will ever forget, no matter how long we live.

For no one in those early days knew what those little beans really were or how they should be prepared and served.

I took some of the beans with me and asked Francen, the apothecary, who consulted his entire pharmaceutical library, but could find nothing that would give us a hint. We therefore decided that though it might cure "all human ailments" it was not primarily a medicine.

Then Jean-Louys, who notwithstanding his oft repeated assertion that he was only interested in mathematics, read (on the sly, of course) about every book that appeared upon every conceivable subject, remembered that several years before in a certain learned treatise of one Jacobus Golius ("I happened to pick up his book because the old fellow is also a teacher of mathematics," Jean-Louys excused himself afterwards) which pretended to be a history of the reign of the great Emperor Tamerlane, he had once come across a passage that might throw some light upon our problem. According to the famous Leyden professor (who himself had spent a number of years among the Moslems as secretary of the Dutch Legation in Morocco) the Mohammedans sometimes held a form of divine service which for sheer length surpassed anything ever heard of in our own part of the world, though several of our ministers prided themselves on never giving their audiences less than three whole hours of divine service. But whereas in our churches, no one minded an occasional snore, the God of the Moslems greatly resented such a lack of interest on the part of his adherents.

And then, sometime during the twelfth or thirteenth centuries of our era, certain merchants returning from Abyssinia reported that they had discovered a wonderful new drug that would keep one awake for days at a time. It grew on a small shrub and its exhilarating qualities had first been noticed when flocks of sheep ate from this shrub and did not go to sleep for a whole week.

The pious Mohammedans thereafter fortified themselves with this concoction whenever they meant to attend any of the high festivals of their creed. The old-fashioned and orthodox Moslems had of course denounced this innovation as a trick played upon the faithful by Satan, just as the true believers in our own time are fighting the organs in our church which they declare to be an invention of the Devil and a survival from Sodom and Gomorrah. But in the end, so Golius reported, the berry-eaters, or berry drinkers (for they preferred the extract to the dry bean in its natural state), had won out and soon afterwards all over Arabia people were in the habit of partaking of "coffee" (so the shrub was called after that part of Abyssinia where it came from and which was known as the province of Kaffa), and notwithstanding a long series of edicts passed by the Mohammedan Church against this "wicked and impious custom, worthy of a thousand deaths," and notwithstanding some very drastic efforts on the part of the Sultan to suppress the bean altogether, every true Moslem partook of a hearty dish of coffee at least once a day.

So much for old Golius. From his writing it seemed to us that a few hours' soaking and boiling was all the little beans needed to make them palatable.

But no sooner had we come to this conclusion than behold old Coppenol, the writing-master and one of the world's most irrepressible bores, whose only excuse for living consisted in the encouragement he had given Rembrandt when the latter was still in some doubt about his ability as a painter (and whom Rembrandt had repaid by a lifetime of forebearing friendship), this learned old pedant must come forward with a new theory.

According to him the little brown beans of our friend Selim were in reality nothing but that mysterious "nepenthe" of which Homer speaks in that part of the work known as the Odyssey. According to the famous Rhodian poet, "nepenthe" was an herb which hailed from Egypt and those who partook of it were immediately granted complete forgetfulness of all their ills and woes. Coppenol was so delighted with this brilliant discovery (I wish Rembrandt had not wasted quite so much time painting and etching the pompous fool) that he finally persuaded Jean-Louys to give him a chance to prove his point and to invite all his friends to a regular feast of oblivion.

This was to be held at the Breestraat as the hall in the back of Rembrandt's house was the largest room then at our disposal. Accordingly, one fine Sunday evening, about twenty of us gathered together for supper and Coppenol, as originator of the new "mystery" (an Eleusinian mystery in the Jewish quarter of Amsterdam in the fifties of the seventeenth century!) was delegated to prepare the lethal potion. He had not the slightest idea how to set about this task, being one of those unfortunate persons who have twenty thumbs on each hand whenever it comes to anything less complicated than writing the whole of the Lord's Prayer on the back of a stiver or turning his own name into the motive for an animated barn-yard scene. He had, however, developed a mystic theory that since the word "nepenthe" consisted of two parts, the beans should be mixed with a quantity of water that equaled their own weight—half coffee and half water, in the terms of the pharmacopoeia.

While he was busy with his brew, we partook of the usual Sunday evening supper, a dark peasant bread, the recipe for which (and it was a most excellent recipe) Hendrickje had brought with her from her own village, and some herring. After that, those of us who cared to do so were given the opportunity to drink a pipe of tobacco in the studio, where Rembrandt had just begun a new portrait of Hendrickje, looking out of a window and wearing the pearls that had brought so much unhappiness to Saskia and himself, and finally (it must have been about ten o'clock) Coppenol sent up his grandson to tell us that the divine symposium was ready.

We each got a large earthen jar filled with a thick, brownish soup. We each of us drank the horrible stuff to the last dregs. Then we waited. Then Abraham Francen left the room as if compelled to keep a sudden appointment. Next two of the pupils, invited to this party for the occasion, darted out of the door. Next I saw Hendrickje turn a deadly pale and heard her excuse herself from our company. Within twenty minutes, the whole of the gathering found itself reassembled in the back yard. For the "divine nepenthe" had not given us oblivion. It had only made us dreadfully ill.

Francen, an experienced apothecary, then bethought himself of hot milk as a possible antidote and the whole neighborhood was searched (it was the Sabbath day and all the shops were closed) for fresh milk. The proprietor of a Jewish creamery on the corner of the Vlooburgstraat nobly rushed to our rescue. He even went so far as to heat the milk for us, since none of us had strength enough left to handle that heavy kettle, and soon afterwards (having meanwhile turned Rembrandt's neat little garden into something not quite so neat) the illustrious band of artists and apothecaries and writers and chirurgeons (not to forget the excellent Hendrickje, who had her hands full with small Titus, who boylike had licked the pot with his fingers and who had coffee all over his hands and face and his brightly starched Sunday collar) regained their former health and composure, swearing due vengeance on unfortunate Selim who had undoubtedly made his offering in the kindest of spirits, but who might have gone just a little further and might have sent us one of his fifteen pastry cooks to let us know how the stuff should be prepared.

News of this unfortunate occurrence soon spread through the town. Sermons were preached on the iniquity of feasting on the Sabbath day. Others, less uncharitable, who pretended that they had drunk coffee before in Smyrna and Constantinople and Famagusta, offered us plentiful advice. According to some of them, we should have ground the beans first and then should have drunk them mixed with hot water and cloves. Others suggested hot milk and cinnamon and still others both water and milk and sugar and mace, and one even vowed that no true Moslem would partake of the beverage without a small pinch of ambergris.

Several years afterwards, when the newspaper brought us news of the attempts made by our old enemy, King Charles, to suppress the Cornhill coffee-houses as breeding places of discontent and the hatching-ground of anti-royalist plots, we also learned something more definite about the true way to prepare the little poisonous beans. But for those of us who had partaken of that feast at Rembrandt's house, the advice came too late. We stuck to beer or bischop and although Selim continued to send us strange-looking bales and barrels containing even stranger-looking products of his native land (as an expression of his undiminished affection for his old friends), we never quite trusted their contents sufficiently to engage in another nepenthean feast.

We used to thank the noble Turk in high-flowing language and we distributed his gifts among the beggars who especially during the years following immediately upon the great English war, infested our streets as badly as they had done in '48 after the end of the rebellion, but we ourselves declared an embargo against all things Mohammedan and strictly lived up to this rule.

All of which has carried me far afield from the subject that was in my mind when I began to write this evening, but as I have said before, writing is very much like living, and human existence refuses to be bound by the orderly rules of the tables of multiplication but wanders all over the planet. I started out in this chapter to explain how I had called on Jean-Louys to ask him to give me some advice about Rembrandt's hopeless financial situation. Instead of which I first indulged in a short essay upon the charity of His Most Christian Majesty and then, for good measure, I added a few observations upon the nature of certain supposed blessings that came to us from the Orient.

Well, all these separate little items played their modest part in producing that sum total of experiences and sensations which the world knows

THE DOCTORS

as Master Jan van Loon and as such (since I am mainly writing about myself) they are not only necessary but also unavoidable.

But now I return to the end of my interview with Jean-Louys. At one time in his career he had been obliged to handle large sums of money. He had even tried to discover the theoretical mathematical formula that must underlie the highly practical system of double-entry book-keeping which Simon Stevin had introduced into the Republic. He was an ideal person therefore to act as one's financial counselor. But when I had explained my predicament to him, I found him quite uninterested and deliberately aloof.

"What does it matter?" he asked me, with true and tantalizing philosophical calm.

"Everything," I answered, slightly upset by his indifference.

"But why? The man paints better than ever before. In a hundred years, no one will know or care whether he died in the poor-house or in the second-best guest-room of his illustrious friend, My Lord Six."

"I know that. But meanwhile he has to support a son and a wife, or at least a woman who will soon be the mother of one of his children. They need three meals a day and he himself would die if he ever had to give up that museum he calls his home."

"It might be good for his work."

"Also it might kill him—not to speak of Hendrickje and little Titus."

Jean-Louys confessed that he had never thought of it in that light. Then he asked me what I meant to do.

"I don't know," I answered. "If I did, I would not be sitting here bothering you with my questions. Every time I mention it to Rembrandt himself, he gets fidgety, takes me to his studio to show me a new picture he has just started, explains a new idea for some large allegorical figure for the new Town Hall (as if they'd give him a chance to work there!) and hastily tells Hendrickje to bring me something to eat or to drink, as if I were a small child that had to be placated, and changes the subject."

"Yes," Jean-Louys said, "it probably makes him feel uncomfortable. As we all know, he is a man of but one single obsession. He wants to paint. All the rest to him is detail and therefore a negligible quantity. You will never find out anything from him directly."

"And yet I have got to know a few things if we are to avert a disaster."

"You never will. It is not in your line. How about your friend Lodewijk?"

"But he has never handled any of Rembrandt's business affairs. He happens to be my banker and not Rembrandt's, if Rembrandt allows himself such a sensible luxury, which I doubt."

"Of course he is not Rembrandt's banker, but he makes a living handling other people's money. It is his business to know the financial condition of everybody in town. I happen to be a mathematician and therefore I am familiar with what all the other mathematicians in Holland and France and England are writing or saying or doing. You are a surgeon and you are careful to follow the work of your competitors here in Amsterdam and in Lisbon and in Bologna and in every other part of the world. People who play the dangerous game of your friend Lodewijk must be even more careful than we. You go and see him to-morrow and you will be surprised to find out how much he can tell you. And if he puts his mind to it, he can give you a complete balance-sheet before the end of next week. I don't think that that balance-sheet will make you any the happier. But if you must have it (and seeing that you belong to this pig-headed race, you probably must, once you have set your mind on it) he will undoubtedly get it for you, neatly written out on a piece of paper and showing a deficit of fifty or sixty thousand guilders. If I were you, I would leave the matter alone and come sailing with me to-morrow. I think I have got hold of a new idea about rigging the sails so as to cause more of a vacuum. To-morrow at ten you had better come. You may be present at the birth of a new era in navigation."

But all the ships in the world could not have dragged me away from my original purpose. And at the very moment Jean-Louys and his faithful man-servant were crossing the banks of the Pampus, I was knocking at a well-known door on the Singel.

The night before, little Titus had come to my house to ask whether Mother could perhaps have half a dozen eggs for there was nothing to eat in the house and Father had not yet had his dinner.

Surely it was high time that something be done!

Chapter 53

I VISIT MY BANKER AND LEARN SOMETHING ABOUT THE DEPLORABLE STATE OF REMBRANDT'S FINANCES

When I entered his office, I found Lodewijk busy cutting himself a new pen.

"What a day!" he shouted as soon as he saw me. "What a day! Was there ever such a climate in all the world? My sixth pen this morning. They melt in your hand—like fresh butter."

Then when he had fashioned the nib according to his desire: "Well, what can I do for you to-day? Want to know how your shares are doing? They are bearing up well under the bad news from the front. But you must not expect too much these days. We ought to be glad if we get through without losing more than ten or fifteen points. What is it you want?"

I told him.

He listened patiently, but did not seem surprised.

"I know all about that," he answered. "We all do. That man owes everybody money and is in debt way over his ears. It is a bad case. He will end in the bankruptcy courts."

"That is what I feared," I told him. "That is why I am here to-day. Exactly how bad is it?"

"Ah, there now! I can't give you a balance-sheet with all the details. When I said that I knew all about the case, I meant that I knew enough never to give the man a single penny, if he came here to ask me for a loan. Further than that, my interest did not go. But if you want to have details, come back in a week's time and you shall have them all."

And then he dropped the subject and talked to me about certain of my own affairs which I shall mention in some later chapter, and he took me out to a small eating house in the Wolvenstraat where a greasy, bearded and squint-eyed Armenian kept what he called on his sign-board outside a truly kosher Jewish restaurant and he fed me a mixture of strange Turkish dishes which made me think of Selim's little brown beans which had made us all sick, and then I left him and went to the hospital, though I am sure none of my patients felt as miserable as I did that afternoon. And a week later I called again at the Singel and received a short report, writ by Lodewijk himself, and containing a number of facts which made me suspect that my worst fears were about to come true and that the position of Rembrandt indeed was hopeless.

"Don't expect too much," Lodewijk warned me. "This is not a stockholder's report. As a rule we disciples of Mercury know a great deal about our neighbors' private affairs. Or if we don't know, we can at least find out. But this is hopeless. Hopeless, I tell you! The man himself does not know how badly off he is. He is one of those chain-borrowers—the most disastrous form of all possible financial transactions. He will borrow one thousand guilders from one friend for the period of a year and at 5 percent interest. And at the same time he will borrow 1,500 from another friend for eight months and at 7 percent. Five months later he will borrow 900 guilders for thirteen months at 6¾ percent from another party. With half of that he will repay Friend No. 1, from whom he will immediately thereupon borrow another 2000 florins for one year at 5½ percent and which he will use to repay Friend No. 2 one third of what he owes him and Friend No. 3 two sevenths of his debt, plus accumulated interest. As he seems to keep no accounts of any sort and carries all those complicated manipulations in the back of his head (which is already very full of other things which have nothing at all to do with finance) you will understand the hopeless muddle in which his affairs are after almost twenty years of chaos.

"To make matters still a little more complicated, he occasionally borrows money on pictures that have not yet been painted or on others that have already been promised to a third party. For good measure he has hypothecated his house a couple of times and as to what he has done with his wife's inheritance, of which he was the trustee for his little son, nothing less than the day of the Last Judgment will ever solve that puzzle.

"But here you are, my friend. Here is the report as I pieced it together from two dozen different sources. Sit down in that corner and read it while I cut myself a fresh pen. It is raining again. It always rains in this damned country. Now sit down and read."

I did as he told me. I sat down and read and as I have kept that report I can copy it in full.

"CONFIDENTIAL

"For your own exclusive information. The subject of this investigation is the son of very simple folk, but his parents were not without means and possessed among other things one wind-mill, two small houses and a parcel of real estate in one of the poorer quarters of the town of Leyden. There were six children. Several of those seem to have died young. Those who are still alive have never done very well and are now actually in reduced circumstances. It is said that their brother (the subject of this investigation) supports them and keeps them out of the poor-house.

"As for the subject of this investigation, who hereafter will be designated as N.N., he was the brightest of the family and destined by his parents to follow a legal career. As such he was inscribed in the University of Leyden in the year 1620 at the age of fourteen. It does not appear that he ever actually followed any courses of lectures, having in the meantime made up his mind to become a painter. In 1630 his father died. The oldest son, having suffered an accident to his hand which made it impossible for him to work, remained behind, as a charge on the other brothers and sisters, but they each received a small amount in cash. N.N. took his share and left Leyden and moved to Amsterdam and took a studio on the Bloemgracht, afterwards moving to the Anthonie Breestraat, also known as the Jodenbreestraat, where he lived for upward of six years.

"At first he was a great success in his own field of work. He had developed a new style of painting which for a dozen years was very fashionable. He had customers among the richest and noblest families of our city and was even commissioned to work for the Prince, though in that case it appears that he had considerable trouble in getting his money. Meanwhile he had become engaged to a girl from Leeuwarden, the daughter of a former burgomaster and well-known political leader, called Rombertus van Uylenburgh. The girl was an orphan and said to be wealthy. After the death of her parents she had first lived with two of her sisters in her native province and had then moved to Amsterdam and first came to live with a female cousin, the wife of Dominie Jan Corneliszoon Sylvius, who had been called to this town in 1610 and was considered a very powerful and eloquent preacher.

"N.N. met the girl through another cousin of hers, one Hendrick van Uylenburgh, who at that time was a dealer in antiques and who also acted as 'entrepreneur' for fashionable painters—that is to say, he acted as go-between for rich people and poor artists and then charged the artist twenty or thirty percent for his services if a sale were made and a picture was ordered. N.N. married the girl in June of the year 1634 and went to live with her in his house on the Breestraat which even at that time he had already begun to convert into a museum, spending the greater part of his considerable earnings on old paintings, bits of statuary and fine silks and brocades.

"After his wedding he added pearls and diamonds and other bits of jewelry to his collection. He is still said to have those. As for his annual revenue during that period, we can find no details but during the first ten years of his residence in Amsterdam he seems to have received an average of about 500 guilders for his portraits. In addition to his own pictures he had the right to sell the work of his pupils which must have netted him between 2,000 and 2,500 guilders a year. As we were unable to find out how much profit he derived from his etchings during this period, it is impossible to state the sum total of his annual income during this period, though it probably exceeded the sum of ten thousand guilders.

"But already in the year 1638 he seems to have been in financial difficulties. That was the year in which he bought himself the house in the Breestraat which he occupies at the present moment. The house belonged to one P. Beltens. It was the second one from the bridge. N.N. is still living in it to-day. The original price was 13,000 guilders. One fourth was to be paid a year after taking possession and the rest at regular intervals within six years. Why he bought a house so entirely above his own position in life is not clear except that at that period he is said to have tried very hard to come up to the social standards of his wife's family, an attempt which also made itself evident in his art, for every time he painted either himself or his wife, he evidently tried to make the world believe that he was a member of the Medici family of Florence, rather than the son of a humble miller in the little town of Leyden. And even at that moment, when he was willing to spend any amount of money upon such old pictures or pieces of silver as had struck his fancy, he was unable to pay the installments on his house. Of those 40,000 guilders which according to local rumor his wife had inherited from her parents, he never seems to have received a penny, for he had to wait until his mother died in 1640 when he received as his share in her inheritance a sum of 2,490 florins, before he was able to offer the former owner any money at all.

"Eventually, with an unexpected inheritance from an aunt of his wife (who was also her god-mother), and with a part of his own savings, he was able to pay off one half of the 13,000 guilders he owed the heirs of aforementioned P. Beltens. Thereafter he seems to have forgotten about the house for he did not even attempt to keep up with the accumulated interest which has been growing larger and larger every year, until to-day it represents the sum of 8,470.06 guilders, which is entirely beyond his present financial means. For in the meantime he appears to have contracted debts on all sides. As all of them have been made with private persons, it is impossible for us to discover the actual amount for which he is involved. Besides the eight thousand odd guilders for the house there is an I.O.U. for 4,180 guilders made out to the order of Cornelis Witsen, the well-known city councilor. Another I.O.U. for a similar amount (4,200 guilders, to be exact) is in the possession of Isaac van Hertsbeeck or Hartsbeeck, a local merchant. These curious amounts N.N. appears to have borrowed to placate the former owner of his house in the Breestraat, who for the last eight years has been obliged to pay the taxes on this piece of property and who has at last threatened to sue him unless he sees some money coming his way.

"Meanwhile, although the house does not really belong to him unless he shall have paid the full contract price, plus the accumulated interest and plus the accumulated back taxes, he is said to be contemplating making both the house and the adjoining yard over to his son Titus as half his share in his mother's inheritance of 40,000 guilders. This, however, is merely a bit of gossip. For in order to do such a thing, he would be obliged to make a public declaration of his affairs to the Board of

Orphans and as he himself never seems to have received a penny from that Uylenburgh estate (which appears to have existed only on paper), it is not very likely that he will take such a step. For the Board of Orphans is well known for its very strict methods of accounting and a father who is suspected of having made away with part of his son's inheritance, even if he could prove that it was a fictitious inheritance, would run the risk of doing several months at hard labor in the city jail. I therefore return to those debts and transactions which can be more or less identified. From his friend Jan Six, the linen-weaver of the well-known family, he borrowed a thousand guilders which My Lord Jan, however, seems to consider such a risky investment that he has recently offered the I.O.U. for sale and according to rumor on the Exchange, he is willing to accept anything at all. Then he seems to have borrowed or to be in the midst of negotiating a loan of about 3,000 guilders with a surgeon by the name of Daniel Franssen and finally there are countless small items to different persons all over town. These consist either of unpaid grocery bills and baker bills and doctor bills and for money he owes to frame-makers and dealers in brushes and paints and oils and manufacturers of copper plates and printer's ink or of small amounts from fifty guilders upward of tiny sums borrowed under one pretext or another from those unfortunate tradespeople.

"In the meantime N.N. has lost favor with the public. He ruined his reputation with a picture of the company of Captain Banning Cocq which he painted in the year his wife died, in 1642. The members of that company were so outraged with the arrangement of the figures (but upon which he himself had insisted) that several refused to pay him and he is said to have received only 1,600 guilders instead of the 5,250 for which he had contracted.

"If said N.N. owes you any money, I would, as your banker, advise you to get hold of it as soon as possible. You had better take a few of his valuable antiquities if he is willing to give you those in settlement of his debt, but don't count on ever getting a stiver in cash. N.N. is hopelessly involved. His reputation of having married a rich wife will perhaps carry him a little longer. But sooner or later the day must come when his credit has reached its end and then there will be quite a scandal for N.N. has nothing and he owes everybody. The conclusion of our investigation is as follows:

"Assets: Heavily mortgaged house full of objects of art on which, however, it will be very difficult to realize at the present moment owing to the unfavorable economic conditions which are the result of the present war with England; very little good will and no cash or securities whatsoever.

"Liabilities: The total amount is unknown but they must be well over 30,000 guilders.

"Credit standing of the person under discussion—o."

I slowly folded the paper and made ready to put it in my pocket. "I suppose I can keep this?" I asked Lodewijk.

"You can keep it, my friend. But please don't let it fall into the wrong hands. It is bad enough as it is. I am very deeply afraid that poor painter's goose is about cooked."

Then he dropped the pen with which he had been busy figuring all that time and rubbed his hand across his bald head.

"Too bad," he said, as if he were speaking to himself. "Too bad. Poor devil! I suppose he sees certain things we don't happen to see and so he fails to notice certain other things quite as important and which we ordinary human beings must have before our eyes all the time."

I stared at him hard.

"Lodewijk," I remarked, "did I hear you mumble 'quite as important'?"

"No," he answered. "I was wrong there. I suppose they are less important. As a matter of fact, I know that they are less important, but what will you? We all must keep alive. And there is but one way to keep alive—hunt with the pack and stick to the well-known tracks."

"But suppose you are so constituted that you simply must leave the beaten track and look for a path of your own or die?"

Once again Lodewijk rubbed his hand across his head.

"Then," he slowly replied, "you are just out of luck." But more than that he would not say.

CORNELIS CLAESZ ANSLO

Chapter 54

I ONCE MORE TAKE UP MY SEARCH FOR SOME DRUG THAT SHOULD KILL THE PAIN OF THOSE ABOUT TO UNDERGO A SURGICAL OPERATION

Here of course the question arises, why didn't I help Rembrandt at that critical moment in his life? I was supposed to be his most intimate friend and I was wealthy. Why didn't I tell Lodewijk, my banker, to take care of that ghastly "list of creditors" and give Rembrandt a chance to begin all over again and this time with a slate that could be kept reasonably clean?

Well, the answer is very simple. If I had still been able to put my hands on part of that money my uncle had left me, Rembrandt never would have gone to the poor-house. But my money was gone. Temporarily, at least. And when the crash came, I was absolutely helpless. All I could do was to gain enough by my practice to keep my own family alive and slyly give an occasional couple of guilders to Hendrickje for her household expenses. But the bulk of my fortune was no longer at my disposal and this is the way that had happened.

All my life I had hated pain.

Pain to me seemed absolutely unnecessary in a world that was meant to be a happy place of abode for intelligent men and women. The few times I myself had suffered pain, I had felt like an object of pity and contempt. Yea, worse than that. For some queer reason I never could disassociate the word "pain" from the word "dirty." Most of my neighbors of course did not know what I was talking about when I told them that a person in pain made a dirty impression on me. They were good Christians and had been brought up to believe that pain was a necessary concomitant of all human existence.

Had not Jehovah in the first book of the Old Testament condemned Eve to bear children in pain?

I knew he had. My grandfather had read that chapter to me for the first time when I was six years old and had added that any God who had seen fit to condemn women to such incredible agony merely because he was out of sorts that day and angry and was searching for an object to wreak his vengeance upon—that such a God might be good enough for the savages to whom our missionaries in the Indies preached, but that he was no fit company for decent people.

Perhaps it was the memory of that morning, perhaps it was the recollection of a particularly brutal little operation I was obliged to undergo at the age of nine (an infected finger that was opened up by a dumb surgeon with a very dull pair of scissors), but whatever the reason, all my life long I had had one obsession—pain! And all my energy (when I was not directly working for my daily living) I had concentrated upon one single object, how to diminish the amount of unnecessary pain there was in this world.

What I mean by "unnecessary pain" I hardly need describe or define. We are so hopelessly ignorant of the inner construction and the secret mechanism of our bodies that there are a number of afflictions against which we are without any means of defense. Any surgeon or doctor will at once recognize what sort of diseases I have in mind. As the source of these unfortunate morbid conditions is invariably located in one of the organs that lie beyond, or rather below, our reach, it will probably always be impossible to relieve patients who suffer from such maladies. They will have to die. We can try and make their end as merciful as possible, but that is about all we can do.

But there are many other disorders which I would like to call "extraneous ones." That is to say, they are by their very nature "foreign" to the normal human body—they are mere mechanical accidents like broken arms or legs or skulls—or they are the result of a wrong method of living and manifest themselves in the form of gravel or stones and cause endless misery to people who are otherwise quite well and hearty—or they are the result of old age, like decaying teeth or cataract of the eye—they are in short only incidentally part of our natural share of pain and happiness and it always struck me that if we could relieve human beings of that particular form of gratuitous horror, we would add a great deal to the sum total of comfort and happiness in this world. And why, since we have got to stay on this planet for forty or fifty years and it is, in all likelihood, the only planet we shall ever visit, shouldn't we try to make our stay as pleasant as possible? My chosen purpose in life therefore was to find a way to make people temporarily senseless while undergoing an operation.

I have already written something about my experiments with different sorts of alcohol (feeding my patients gin or rum until they were so drunk that they were senseless) and with the mysterious mandrake root. But none of these had been satisfactory. The poor inebriates became hopelessly sober as soon as the knife touched them and as for the mandrake, I never succeeded in arranging the dose in such a way that it brought about thorough insensibility. As a rule my patients became very sick after the use of the extract which the apothecaries recommended as the most satisfactory and the spasms caused by their nauseous condition not infrequently ruined the work of the surgeon and caused the patients to die from internal bleeding.

But now I must mention a curious meeting I had in Nieuw Amsterdam about the fourth year after my arrival in America.

One day a ship flying the Swedish flag and called the *Westergotland*, dropped anchor in the outer bay. Just then we were a little suspicious of

Swedes in our part of the world. Letters had recently arrived from Holland addressed to His Excellency the Governor telling him that according to certain very definite rumors on the Amsterdam exchange, the Swedes meant to establish a West India Trading Company of their own and intended to establish themselves on territory which (theoretically, at least) belonged to us. Wherefore, His Excellency was urged to exercise great watchfulness and keep an eye out for all suspicious-looking vessels that were seen in the neighborhood of the Hudson or the South River, which the English have now rebaptized the Delaware.

The *Westergotland,* however, seemed a harmless enough sort of a craft, bound from Virginia to Gothenburg with a load of tobacco. Off Cape May she had met with a storm which had blown her mizzenmast overboard and she had come to Nieuw Amsterdam for repairs. As only ships flying the English flag were supposed to carry British goods, she dare not put into one of the harbors to the north or south of us for fear of confiscation. That, at least, was the story of the captain who openly boasted of the fact that he had got an entire three hundred barrels filled with contraband tobacco and nobody any the wiser. And as we had no reason to love the people of that particular colony, it was decided to offer Captain Frederiksen (that was his name) all the facilities at our disposal so that he could continue his voyage with the least possible delay.

Nevertheless, a new mast in those early days, when the town had less than 4,000 inhabitants, was quite a big affair and the *Westergotland* remained in Nieuw Amsterdam for almost a whole month. Her crew of course was allowed to go on shore as often and as freely as they pleased and it was then that I made the acquaintance of a very curious personage.

Most of the sailors on board the *Westergotland* were either Swedes or Norwegians, the officers were all of them Swedish, but the doctor was a Portuguese. Now in those days it was a little out of the way for a merchant vessel of scarce 300 tons to carry a surgeon. When the sailors on such small craft happened to fall ill, they either got better or they died, but whatever the outcome of their disease, they were allowed to make their choice without the assistance of one of those ship's leeches who were a disgrace to the profession, being as a rule almost as incompetent as they were drunken and as drunken as they were incompetent.

This old Portuguese (he must have been sixty if he was a day) made a notable exception. He was a fine-looking man, his manners were most gracious and he seemed to be well versed in his craft. How a man like that had come so far down in the social and professional scale as to be a ship's doctor on board a Swedish smuggler was something that puzzled me until I came to know him a little better, and then I found out that he was not only a medical man, but that for about twenty years of his life he had been a pilot in the service of the Portuguese government.

Then, of course, the whole thing became very simple. The *Westergotland* was not a Swedish privateer but was in the service of the King of

Sweden and was engaged in spying out the central part of the northern American coast, preparatory to establishing a Swedish colony at some point between Florida and the possessions of the Gorges family, just south of the Saint Lawrence.

I felt absolutely convinced that this was the case and mentioned it to His Excellency. But as we had no other proof except this bit of circumstantial evidence, it was quite impossible to take any further measures against a vessel that flew the ensign of a sovereign with whom our country was in a state of peace and eventually the *Westergotland* departed amidst an exchange of the most cordial civilities between her skipper and our grouchy old governor, and three weeks later she foundered with the loss of everybody, just off Sable Island, as we heard from a French fisherman who disabled by the same gale had drifted into the sound between the main land and the Lange Eiland and who was now waiting for permission to re-victual his vessel before he went back to his codfish on the Grand Banks.

But to return to my Portuguese. He had a long and very imposing name. He spelled it out for me one day on the fly leaf of my Vesalius and it read: Dom Sebastiao do Conto Quevedo de Oliveira Mortaria. Upon that same occasion he also told me the story of his life, but that was of no great importance to me, except in so far as it helped me to solve the question that had been puzzling me ever since he had set foot on shore in Nieuw Amsterdam, "how did it happen that a man of such evident accomplishments had been obliged to leave his own country and take service with a foreign potentate who lived at the other end of the map?"

It could not be drink, for he never touched a drop. It could not have been women. In the first place, he was too old now, and in the second place, he had an almost morbid aversion for women. Then one night he told me himself. It had been "hasheesh."

What hasheesh was, I did not at that time know. The name sounded Oriental to me and in this I had guessed right. Hasheesh was the Indian name for hemp. Not the sort of hemp we raise at home and which we use in our rope yards, but the resin from the Asiatic hemp, Cannabis Indica, which is prepared in a special way and which is then used by the natives of India as a drug to make them forget the miseries of their existence and make them dream they have arrived in Heaven.

When he had been in Goa for about five years, my unfortunate Portuguese friend had caught a sudden chill which had given him a severe case of rheumatism, and which had caused him such dreadful sufferings that he had been ready to commit suicide. Then a native physician had introduced him to the use of hasheesh and he had become an addict to that dangerous drug which gave him temporary relief from his pain but which had made him a total failure as a responsible member of society.

Eventually the rheumatic affliction had left him, but he had never again been able to live without his daily portion of hasheesh. He knew that the stuff was killing him, but he could not help himself. And in the course of our conversation (he was a brilliant talker and would keep me up night after night with his stories of the early days along the coast of Malabar) he told me all about the various drugs that could be made of hemp—about charas, ganja and bhang, which were all three of them different trade names for products of the hemp industry—and he described to me in detail just exactly what his sensations were whenever he was under the influence of his hasheesh.

Finally he persuaded me to try the stuff one night. He suggested that I smoke the dried leaves, rather than take it internally. He gave me a pipeful. After five or six puffs everything went dark around me and I knew nothing until I came back to life about an hour later. I was then lying on the floor, having fallen off my chair when I went into a coma. It was only then that I discovered that I had hurt myself rather badly against the sharp edge of the table. I had quite a gash in the side of my scalp but had noticed no pain until that moment.

As for my distinguished Portuguese colleague, he was sitting in his chair fast asleep and he remained there until the next morning.

I did not remember that I had had any dreams, either pleasant or disagreeable. I just had "not been" for the half hour I was under the influence of the drug. I could notice no bad after-effects except a violent headache, but as that might very well have been caused by the blow on my head when I hit the table, I could not say that it had been caused by the hasheesh.

At that time I was so busy with other drugs that I had not thought about my experiment any further. Presently the Portuguese had taken his departure and I had gone into the interior on another trip of exploration and Cannabis played no further rôle in my life until returning home on board a slow-sailing merchantman and being obliged to assist them, one of the sailors was cut for the stone (a hideous performance, with the victim fastened to a rough wooden plank and screaming his head off like a pig that was being butchered) I suddenly bethought myself of Dom Sebastiao do Conto Etcetera and his pipe and the idea struck me: "Why not try Cannabis when I get back to my hospital?"

Then of course the siege of Amsterdam had intervened, but finally, about six months after my return, I had begun my experiments in all seriousness. I had gathered hemp from all parts of the world, canappa from Italy and konopi from Russia and cañamo from Spain—even Iceland had contributed a quantity of hampr. Among the ships' captains who sailed for foreign ports, I became known as a poor deluded though harmless fool who had a hemp obsession, probably as they suggested because his grandfather or grandmother had been obliged to look through a hempen window, which was their facetious way of suggesting that these ancestors of mine had been hanged. But they were very obliging, nevertheless, and after a couple of years there was nothing connected with the use of hemp as a narcotic with which I was not thoroughly familiar. I found several of my colleagues among the surgeons willing to cooperate with me, but the majority of them turned against me as one man. They denounced me as a meddler and innovator and quack and absolutely refused to listen to me or attend one of my operations during which the patient had been put into a state of coma by means of the fumes of Cannabis sativa.

In the end they even objected to my using the operating room of the hospital for my "childish experiments," "getting it all messed up with the smell of that filthy Indian manure," as one of the learned leeches expressed himself, and when I paid no attention to their objections they went to the Town Hall (everybody who had a grievance always rushed to the magistrates) and petitioned Their Lordships that they forbid me to perform any further operations with the help of that "pagan and nauseating drug."

Their Lordships, afraid as usual of what would happen if the clergy caught hold of the word "pagan" as a text for more sermons upon the laxity of the town government in regard to the enforcement of "true Christian morals," asked me to come and see them, spoke to me very affably, praised my zeal and my unselfish devotion and politely requested me to drop all further experiments for, "after all," as one of the Burgomasters said, "if the public is foolish enough to want to feel the pain when it is being operated upon, why not give it what it wants?" An argument at once so simple and so cunning that I could do naught but answer: "Indubitably, My Lord," and promised for the sake of convenience that no more fumes of burned hempleaves would pollute the delicate walls of the city hospital.

But I did not mean to give up. And after a few weeks' meditation I hit upon a plan which would safeguard me against interference on the part of my fellow-physicians and at the same time would allow me to continue those scientific investigations without which my life would have been as dull as soup without salt. This time I first went to my banker to ask him for his opinion and advice, for in all such matters he was possessed of a dry sort of common sense (kindness of heart tempered by a bitter knowledge of the world) which I had learned to esteem very highly during the many years he had been my financial adviser. He had of course heard about my experiences at the hospital. He considered it his business to keep informed about everything that happened in our city and I will say that he was the most reliable perambulating newspaper I have ever met anywhere.

"Yes, my boy," he tried to console me, as soon as I had explained the nature of my errand, "you are getting along in years now—you must be well in the fifties—but in some matters you are as inexperienced as a child of seven. Now what did you expect? You wanted to play the benefactor of the human race and then you found that the human race did not appreciate your kind intentions and now you are sorry for yourself."

"Of course not," I interrupted him. "I am not quite as young and as foolish as all that. Only I hate to see waste of any sort. Pain is waste—waste of perfectly good energy that could be used to a better purpose. Waste of time—waste of money—waste of human happiness. I am not sentimental about it. I am entirely practical."

"Good. But you know what becomes of those entirely practical people who want to benefit humanity? They have usually been killed for their troubles. They have been thrown down wells—hammered on a cross—hung from the highest gallows in the land. And when they escaped the fury of those miserable mortals whom they tried to help, they fell into the hands of the Gods who do not want us to be either too wise or too happy lest we get on to their game and discover that they aren't all we were made to believe when we went to the Rabbi to be told about the glories of Heaven. But all this is talk and talk like this belongs to that waste you hate so much. What doth our young Prometheus mean to do now?"

"I mean to go on. Some day people will come to their senses and appreciate what I am doing."

"Your pretty colleagues kicked you out of their hospital."

"So they did. But that makes no difference. I am a surgeon in good standing. I could perfectly well treat my patients at home. If the house is not large enough, I could hire a couple of other houses. I could build myself a new hospital."

"Fine! And who is supposed to pay for all this?"

"I!"

"Out of your annual income, when you don't send a bill to even half your patients?"

"No, out of my capital. Quite easily, with enough extra money to keep the place going for a couple of years."

At first Lodewijk did not answer.

Then he picked up his latest goose-quill and rubbed the feathery end pensively across his chin. And then he said:

"Blessed be the fools, for they shall see the shadow of God. When do you want that money?"

I told him and that morning we settled everything. He was to convert twenty-five of my shares of the East India Company into cash and was to look for a suitable location for my hospital.

When I left, he put his arms around me and suddenly kissed me on both cheeks.

"It is nice," he said, "to have a few harmless idiots like yourself wandering about on this planet of ours. How dull life would be otherwise. How terribly dull! So dull, one would be almost tempted to turn respectable."

Chapter 55

I FOUND A NEW SORT OF HOSPITAL

I found a house on the Groene Burgwal that entirely suited my needs. It had been recently built for a distiller who had made so much money during the war that he could no longer afford to live in such an unfashionable part of the town and had moved to a small palace on the Heerengracht, where he was ignored by all his dignified neighbors but highly esteemed by the trades people who openly boasted that the rich gin-maker was a better investment than a dozen Burgomasters' families, where the sugar was kept under lock and key and the salt necessary for the soup was weighed on a pair of scales, lest the cook be spoiled and be encouraged to become wasteful.

To my great surprise the distiller was a very intelligent citizen. Except for a certain vanity that seems to be the inevitable in those who have risen in the world through their own exertions, he was a simple-minded, yea, almost humble-minded person, but a very shrewd observer of both man and his ways.

"Since these fools insist upon forgetting their woes by drinking evaporated grain, why shouldn't they drink my gin, which I guarantee is as pure or purer than that of any of my rivals? I know it is not a very inspiring trade I am engaged in. But my gin is as good, as gin goes, as any gin now on the market, and so as long as the blunderheads will drink, I will continue to make the stuff, provided I do not have to taste any of it myself."

This strange philosopher, whose name was Anthony van Andijk ("Just call me Teunis, will you? That Andijk business I added to please my wife. She is a good woman but her father was a beadle in Medemblik and she will never get over it.")—this cheerful Teunis had come up from what we were pleased to call the "dregs of society." His father was a common longshoreman who worked for the Greenland Company and as a boy he had shipped on board an Enkhuizen whaler which had been captured by a Duinkerk privateer (practically within sight of the Texel dunes) and had been taken to Bordeaux because the captain hoped to get a better price for her there than in his home port.

After years of misery as cabin boy on different foreign ships, young Teunis had finally returned to his home town. At one stage in his career he had decided that he would try and walk from Bordeaux to Amsterdam. But in the city of Cognac he had been arrested as a vagrant and in order to escape being sent to the galleys he had hastily taken service with a brandy-maker who had taught him several secrets of the distiller's art which had been of great value to him when he finally was able to set up in business for himself.

The first time I met him he asked me point-blank what I wanted his house for, since it seemed that I already had one perfectly good house of my own and I could not live in two houses at the same time. I told him. I explained my plans in a rather perfunctory and I am afraid slightly patronizing fashion. But he paid no attention to my superior mode of talking and when I had finished, he warmly shook me by the hand and said: "Doctor, that is the first time I have ever heard of a rich man who was trying to do something for poor people without wanting to get something out of the deal himself. I am for you, Doctor. And what is more, I am with you."

And indeed in all our business transactions he was most generous and when it came to refashioning the premises, he used to be on the job every day from six in the morning until seven at night and he bossed the carpenters and the masons so eloquently and so successfully, that in less than three months the house was ready for occupancy. It consisted of a study for myself and a room where I could examine patients at my leisure—an operating room, and a room where I could conduct my own experiments.

On the second floor the building contained about twenty small rooms for patients and on the third floor were the living quarters for the fifteen women whom I hoped to train as nurses for the special sort of work I had undertaken to do. As soon as plans had been formulated for my hospital, I had tried to persuade a few of the deaconesses from the city hospital to come with me, but most of those had religious scruples since I was trying to make people escape the pain which the Almighty had meant them to suffer on account of their wickedness of heart and as punishment for their sins.

Two of the deaconesses, however, were willing to follow me and no one could have asked for more devoted and intelligent service than was given by those women, both in assisting me with my work and in training a dozen young and very ignorant but serious-minded and well-meaning girls who were Moravians and whose parents had fled to the Republic after the battle of the White Hill in which their people had been so decisively beaten and which had been a great blow to the cause of Protestantism in central Europe.

As for the work that was done in my place, I leave it to the unprejudiced members of our guild to say whether it was worth while or not. One thing is certain—our rate of mortality was much lower than that of the regular hospitals. Perhaps this was due to the fact that I kept every patient in a separate little cubby-hole of his own, as I had noticed that the larger the number of patients confined to one single room, the smaller their chance of escaping with their lives. What caused this mysterious connection between over-crowding and dying, I did not know then nor do I know it to-day. Maybe the vapors exuded by sick bodies exercise a harmful influence upon others. Maybe it is the general mood of depression which is noticeable as soon as a number of people are able to tell each other about their symptoms. But we lost only forty percent of all our serious cases and that was quite a record, the figures of the general hospital running well into eighty percent and during some parts of the year (especially during the fall and the winter) going higher than ninety percent.

I had let it be known that my hospital was open to all surgeons who wanted to use my operating room and who cared to avail themselves of my method of rendering people senseless. At first none of them dared to come near what they pleasantly called "The Hempyard," the name usually given to the meadow on the other side of the Y where criminals were hanged. But when it appeared that this hempyard was much less deadly than the official city clinics, they slowly began to patronize No. 17, Groene Burgwal, and everything was going along so nicely that I felt great hope for the future and when Lodewijk (who hated sickness in every form) at last decided to visit our Lazaretto (where he made fast friends with the faithful gin-distiller, who by this time had taken over the entire financial management of the place) I asked him whether he remembered our conversation the day I had decided to risk my entire capital on this one enterprise and what he had to say now?

He answered, "Nothing. I have nothing to say. Everything seems to be going very nicely. But remember Solon, my boy. Remember Solon—'nemo beatus ante mortem'—you aren't out of the woods yet."

"Perhaps I am not, but just now, I don't seem to espy any lions or tigers."

"Of course not, but that does not mean that they are not there. They may be asleep or probably they are looking at you from behind the shrubs and you have been too busy to see them. Remember Solon, my young friend! The poor-of-spirit are always with us and there is no limit to the amount of harm they can do."

Alas! He was right. As I was to experience within a very short time and to the great detriment, not only of myself, but of all those who had put their confidence in me and had believed in the unselfishness and integrity of my intentions.

Chapter 56

THE MINISTERS TAKE A HAND IN REMBRANDT'S AFFAIRS

It was a far cry from a broken-down old Portuguese doctor on the banks of the Hudson River and a little peasant girl from nowhere in particular who happened to be in the family way, to a public riot in the streets of Amsterdam and the loss of that sum of money with which I would have been able to save Rembrandt from his disgrace. But the world has seen stranger coincidences than that and the episode attracted the attention of many who otherwise would never have heard of me or the work I was doing.

Hendrickje was pregnant. I had noticed it that time she hurt herself and Rembrandt sent for me. Soon afterwards, others had noticed it too and then the trouble had begun. Not among Rembrandt's friends. They understood the situation and knew why he could not marry the girl. Even the exceedingly respectable family of My Lord Jan Six (is there anything in this world more careful of its dignity than one of our linen-weaving or beer-brewing dynasties trying to break into the slightly superior class of the hereditary magistrates?) did not appear to be censorious of a conduct which must have shocked them quite as much as the bankruptcy of one of their nearest relatives.

I never quite understood the friendship that had sprung up between Rembrandt and the rich linen merchant. But then, I never even met the young man. Rembrandt had repeatedly suggested that I accompany him when he called upon Jan Six and had accused me of being super-sensitive and of being a snob, and had assured me time and again that I would find naught but the simplest of manners within the Six household. To which I invariably repeated that I had no doubt about the perfect graciousness that reigned within this charming home on the Kloveniersburgwal, and that I had no doubt but his friends would receive me with the utmost cordiality. Unfortunately their ways were not my ways and my ways were not their ways and what the habits and customs and prejudices of many generations had put asunder, we had better not try and put together.

And in the end it was shown that I had been right. For when the great financial crisis came in Rembrandt's life Jan Six sold the note which Rembrandt had given him to a professional pawnbroker and all that Rembrandt saved out of those years of intimacy and friendship was a presentation copy of a very mediocre Greek play in very mediocre verse. Whereas the Six family was left in the possession of a number of paintings and etchings which will keep its name alive long after the last of their descendants shall have returned to dust.

Verily, as we say in our language, it is bad policy to eat cherries with the mighty. They get the cherries and you get the stones—if you are very lucky.

Upon this unfortunate occasion, however, both My Lord Jan and his relatives showed themselves rather more broad-minded than I had had reason to expect. Of course they had never met Hendrickje and had made no move which showed that they recognized her existence. But at least they continued to be on cordial terms with her husband (for as such she now invariably referred to Rembrandt) and that was more than could be said of most people.

They were shocked.

They disapproved.

If this sort of thing were tolerated once, where would the world end?

And since most people are in the habit of considering their own prejudices as part of the divinely inspired laws which underlie the structure of a well-ordered universe, it was quite unavoidable that the scandal on the Jodenbreestraat should become the most popular subject for family discussions and tea-party gossip. For although it was still considered good form among the higher classes of society to have a few bastards (all the children of the late Prince Maurice, although born out of wedlock, had been baptized by the court preacher of the House of Orange and had received high honors and dignities in the service of the Republic) the prospective arrival of an illegitimate infant in the household of a painter was still considered an event of such enormity that it could not be allowed to pass unnoticed by the reverend clergy who were supposed to be watching day and night over the morals of our New Zion on the Zuyder Zee.

And fortunately on this occasion at least the dominies had luck with them, as I shall now have to relate.

"Misfortunes never come alone," says an old Zeeland proverb, and during the days that followed I was often reminded of this bit of ancestral wisdom. And whereas under ordinary circumstances the birth of the little van Rijn child might have caused only a temporary storm in our domestic tea-cup, a most unfortunate combination of regrettable little incidents caused it to assume the shape of a national scandal.

It all started in a little village in Friesland. I have forgotten the name of the place. It was one of those terrible villages where the people looked like cows and the cows looked like people and where nothing ever happened until from sheer boredom and exasperation the inhabitants were willing to believe any bit of news that would bring them a little excitement.

In this miserable village, where half of the people had been dead for years but had never become aware of the fact because no one had taken the trouble to tell them so—in this far-off hamlet it had been necessary to repair one of the walls and these alterations had in turn caused the temporary removal of several graves. As the last occupant of these tombs had died more than thirty years before, it was not expected that the architects would find anything beyond a few skulls and skeletons. But imagine the surprise of the grave-diggers when they suddenly came upon a corpse that was as good as the day it had been interred!

"A miracle," the people shouted who saw it. "This man was a saint. He was too holy to be returned to dust."

"On the contrary," a young and eager candidate of theology, who was preparing here for his final examinations, whispered. "On the contrary! This man was a sinner of such magnitude that even the worms refused to eat him."

As it was of course much pleasanter to believe evil than good of a departed neighbor, the populace heartily shouted amen, and immediately they began to delve into the past of this poor fellow to discover what crimes he might have committed to deserve such a fate.

This proved to be rather difficult, as the man had been dead for at least thirty-five years. During his days on this earth he had been a very humble shoemaker who had distinguished himself by nothing except his somewhat exaggerated respect for the wise precepts of his Lord and Master, Jesus Christ. He had been charitable to a fault and had not contented himself with surrendering one tenth of all his possessions to the poor, but had often gone hungry himself that others, who were even more miserable than he himself, might be fed.

An old farmer in a neighboring village remembered him well and spoke of him in the highest terms. The deacon of the church he had attended (now well in the eighties) stated emphatically that so good and pious a man had rarely trod the unworthy soil of this planet.

Indeed, at first it seemed as if those who had proclaimed him a saint had been right, but the theological candidate refused to be convinced. "All this," he argued, "only proves that the man was also a very clever prevaricator and was able to hide the traces of his wickedness in such a way that he finally died without ever having been found out." And of course the quest into the fellow's past continued as merrily as before.

Now it happened that the widow of the mysterious corpse was still alive. She was a woman of about seventy and no one knew anything against her that was not highly favorable. She had only one child, a daughter who was married (and very respectably) to a master carpenter in Haarlem. Surely all these family details were commonplace enough to discourage even the most hardened scandal-mongers. But the young cleric kept on snuffling. The old woman was in her dotage and spent most of her days sitting in her little home—tending half a dozen cats and telling those who were willing to listen (and they were very few) what a fine man her husband had been. She was also very superstitious and terribly afraid to die. By playing upon her fear of the Hereafter, and by colorful description of the horrors of Hell, the unscrupulous parson finally got the whole story out of her and no Castilian explorer crossing the parched wastes of the great Mexican desert could have experienced greater happiness at the sight of his first lump of gold than this man of mercy when the trembling old crone at last revealed unto him the well-tended secret of her husband's one and only transgression.

She had never been married to him. They had never been united in holy wedlock. They had lived in sin, but it had all been done with the best of intentions and then she had related the story which soon afterwards was to become known to everybody in the Republic, for it was a sad tale and our ballad singers made the most of it.

It had really been her fault and she was willing to take all the blame upon herself. She had been a wayward girl and had got into trouble with a man who had deserted her. Her father, when he suspected her condition, had thrown her out of the house. She was wandering from village to village (she herself hailed from the neighboring province of Groningen) until she had reached that little town in Friesland. It was very late when she arrived and she was half starved and she had knocked at his door because he was still working and looked friendly as he sat there hammering at his bench. He had taken her in and had fed her. The next day she had been very sick. He had kept her there and had sent for an old woman who lived next door to nurse her. She had been sick for almost two whole months. When she got better, her condition had become noticeable. She then had told her benefactor the truth. He said that he wanted to marry her. But he could not do so as he was already married. Only his wife had lost her reason shortly after the birth of a child that had died in infancy. She had developed a case of religious mania and finally had escaped with the help of one of the many priests who still infested the country, notwithstanding the severe edicts promulgated against them. This man had taken her to Trier, where she had joined the Catholic church and had entered a nunnery. All efforts on the husband's part to bring her back had been unsuccessful. The Archbishop of Trier had openly boasted of his victory over Antichrist and even the Estates General, to whom the matter finally had been referred, had been powerless.

That had happened twenty years before and all that time the husband had heard nothing of his wife. Attempts to find out whether she were still alive had brought no answer. The prioress of the cloister where she was supposed to dwell had answered that those entrusted to her care were dead as far as the world was concerned, the moment they set foot across the sacred threshold and all further communications addressed to her had been returned unopened. The shoemaker had left his native village where all this had happened and had moved to that forgotten little town in northern Friesland, so as to avoid meeting his former friends. In his new home no one ever suspected that he had ever been married. In his compassion for the poor girl whom God had conducted to his doorstep, he had then decided upon a desperate plan. He had spread the news that he meant to marry her but that she wished to have the ceremony performed among her own people in Groningen. They had actually gone to the town of Groningen for a fortnight and had then come back as husband and wife. The child had been born shortly afterwards and the village elders had smirked pleasantly about their old shoemaker who apparently had not been such a saint as they had always held him to be. But as no couples among our peasants ever marry until they absolutely have to, the matter had soon been forgotten.

No one could have been more devoted to a child of his own than this humble shoemaker to that of another man and as for herself, why, the woman had never had an unhappy day in all her life until the day her "husband" had died from old age and hard work, when she had buried him with all decency and had settled down to spend the rest of her remaining years honoring his memory and tending her cats.

The story struck me as rather marvelous when I first heard it. But in the hands of that miserable zealot up there in the Frisian hamlet, it became a monstrous tale of seduction and deception which filled the hearts of all good Christians with the utmost delight and satisfaction. God's hand became plainly visible in that pathetic, shriveled corpse which had been so unceremoniously brought back to life and literally thousands of sermons were devoted to the gruesome sufferings of that soul which had been refused admittance to both Heaven and Hell, as too vile for even the lowest dungeons of Satan's abode.

Hysterical outbursts of this sort have one advantage, they never last long. But just when the details of the case were beginning to be known in Amsterdam and when every self-respecting disciple of John Calvin was ransacking his Old Testament for suitable texts with which to bolster up the case of God vs. the Shoemaker, the fact that the painter Rembrandt van Rijn was living openly with his house-keeper was brought to the attention of a certain dominie by the name of Zebediah Hazewindus, and what then happened was something of which the people of our country may well be ashamed till the end of their days.

It is unnecessary for me to go into the details of the affair. They are only two well known.

On the twenty-fifth of June of the year '54 the members of the Amsterdam council of churches, gathered together in a plenary session, decided that "since a certain Hendrickje, also known as Hendrickje Jaghers, had now for a considerable space of time been living in open concubinage with a painter called Rembrandt van Rijn at the latter's house in the Breestraat, she therefore was to be ordered to appear before the consistory within eight days of the issuance of this summons and explain to the consistory what excuse she could offer for so scandalous a conduct."

This message was delivered at Rembrandt's house one evening about six o'clock when he and Hendrickje were just enjoying a little respite from the efforts of the day's work on the stoop of their house. It was brought to them by the sexton of the West Church, who also acted as beadle. The sexton was well known to the neighbors. The message was not known, but they could guess at its nature. And soon all through the street and then through the next street and through the next street, the news had spread: "The painter and his woman will have to appear before the dominies. Serves them right! We always told you so. Nothing good can come from that sort of goings-on."

And although no one dared to "say" anything, a great many people "looked" things and that was hardly desirable for a woman in Hendrickje's position. But in one small detail these good neighbors were mistaken. The neatly folded piece of paper bearing the seal of Amsterdam's church council did not mention the name of Rembrandt. When I called later in the evening and was shown the document and asked why he had not been summoned, together with Hendrickje, he could at first not give me any reason. Then it dawned upon him. "I am not a member of the church," he said. "That is probably why they left me out. Years ago, I forget just when, I withdrew or resigned or whatever one does when one bids farewell to the church. I let the ministers know that I would not attend divine service any longer and would refuse to pay my church-taxes in the future and would they please take my name off their register, and they answered me that I could not do this unless I could offer proof that I had joined some other denomination. I hardly knew what to do and so I talked it over with old Anslo, whom I had known for years. I asked him whether there would be any objections if I joined his own church, that I was not a very regular church-goer and perhaps not even a very good Christian. He said no, that the Mennonites did not believe in bothering people about their beliefs, that they would be glad to have me join them whenever I cared to come but would not worry me or bother me if for one reason or another I decided to stay away.

"So I joined the Mennonites and I have never been sorry. Anslo was a nice man. I liked to hear him preach. He never told me how wicked I was, but did his best to show me how good I might be if only I tried just a little harder. Yes, he was a good man. I am glad now I went to him. I would be doubly glad if it were not for Hendrickje."

The girl who had been studying the paper in her hand now looked up at us. "Yes," she said, rather dryly, "I have no doubt of that. But meanwhile, what shall I do?"

Without a word Rembrandt took the summons out of her hand and tore it up into a thousand bits.

"Do nothing," he answered. "Do nothing and forget about it. The dominies can of course make themselves very disagreeable to us, but that is about all. But they can't send a company of town guards to come and fetch you to make a public confession. You are safe—perfectly safe—and so that is that."

And he threw the little bits of paper into the air so that two little Jewish boys who were playing on the sidewalk shouted: "Oi, oi! lookit! lookit! it is snowing!" and then started fighting for the "snow" until nothing remained of the clerical document but a mess of dirty scraps which lay spread all over the Breestraat.

But although Rembrandt was entirely right when he proclaimed so bravely that the dominies could not send a company of town guards to drag Hendrickje to their solemn conclave, it was soon proved that those worthies were not entirely defenseless. They had other means at their disposal to make their displeasure felt and they were not slow to avail themselves of these convenient instruments of spiritual torture.

A great Parisian lady might of course have snapped her fingers at such a manifestation of clerical meddlesomeness but Hendrickje was not a great Parisian lady, but a simple little Dutch peasant girl from a simple little Dutch peasant village with all of the peasant's traditional regard for those standards of respectability which she had learned as a child. To be publicly cited to appear before the consistory of the big town of Amsterdam, accused of the dreadful sins of "lechery and adultery" (strange what delight pious people take in dirty words. If there are nine decent ways of expressing a certain thought and one indecent one, they will invariably choose the latter) was as terrible an experience to her as if she had been condemned to undress right in the middle of the municipal market-place. And I noticed the effects of this ordeal when a week later she was presented with a second summons which did not even reach her hands, as Rembrandt jerked it from the fingers of the beadle and threw it in the gutter without even bothering to open the seal.

Upon such occasions, the spirit of his old grandfather, who had been a notable fighter in the early days of the rebellion, would suddenly break through that decorous exterior which he had retained from the days of his marriage with Saskia.

"Get away from here, you damn black crow!" he shouted at the poor fellow, who had delivered the message, and who was beating a hasty retreat. "Get away and stay away and don't bother my wife any more. If your masters have aught to tell me, let them come themselves and I shall throw them in the Anthonie Sluis. You dastardly, meddling old fool! Mind your own damn business and let me paint my pictures."

All of which was no doubt quite natural and more or less to be expected (there is nothing quite so wholesome to the physical well-being of the human race as an occasional outburst of first-class cursing), but a little beside the point. After all, the consistory had not told Rembrandt that he must not paint pictures. It had told his housekeeper that she must not live with him in sin. And it continued to do so until poor Hendrickje, in her great distress and misery, saw no other course than to obey their solemn command and present herself that she might confess her guilt and ask for their solemn forgiveness.

Exactly when she made her appearance before the consistory, I never found out, for she kept the fact hidden from Rembrandt. One afternoon she quietly slipped out of the house and when she returned, it was all over. She went right up to her room and to bed. In the middle of the night, Rembrandt sent Titus to ask me whether I would please come at once. Hendrickje seemed to have a fever. Her mind was wandering. She talked of hell-fire and of Satan, who was chasing her with a torch made out of a burning sheaf of grain. Then she wept as if her heart would break, calling for her mother and saying that she would be a good girl and that she had only done it because the man had been so good to her. "He is good to me and you and father were bad to me," she kept on crying.

I gave her some hot milk to drink and put a cold poultice on her forehead, and after a short while she calmed down. In the morning she was happy and cheerful, as if nothing had happened.

The following Sunday when I called after dinner, as I was in the habit of doing, I asked her (really without thinking very much of what I was saying), "And well, Hendrickje, what was the sermon about this morning?"

But she looked crestfallen and answered, rather indifferently, "I don't know. I did not go."

Three days later, I discovered the reason why. As punishment for her sinful way of living, she had been forbidden to partake of the Lord's holy communion.

That may have been good church discipline. But it was not the best thing in the world for a woman who was eight months pregnant, as we were to find out soon afterwards.

Chapter 57

HENDRICKJE HAS A CHILD AND THE CLERGY OF AMSTERDAM EXPRESS THEIR OPINION UPON MY RESEARCHES IN THE DOMAIN OF PAINLESS SURGERY

In September of the year '54 the blow fell.

During the first week of that month I had suddenly lost two of my patients. They had died while I was administering the usual dose of hemp and the thing had been a great surprise to me as the operations for which they had been brought to the hospital were not of a serious sort and under ordinary circumstances their chance of recovery would have been very good. But they passed out after a few whiffs of the Cannabis fumes and all efforts made to bring them back to life were in vain. Both of them were middle-aged women and like most women in our country who have been forced to bear children ever since they were nineteen or twenty, they were not in good physical condition.

News of this disaster became soon known all over town and those who had always disapproved of my methods were delighted. They had always known that something like that would happen some day. If I were allowed to go on I would eventually kill the whole population of Amsterdam. The authorities ought to interfere and close that so-called hospital. As for me, I ought to be forced to resign from the Surgeons' Guild. I had defied the will of God and now see what had come of it!

Within less than twenty-four hours I received an official document bearing the signature of one of the Burgomasters. I was told not to administer any more hemp until the matter should have been officially investigated. Three physicians of good repute were delegated to perform an autopsy upon my unfortunate patients and report to Their Lordships. One of these three doctors was a good friend of mine. The other two belonged to the old school of medicine and regarded me secretly as an impostor and mountebank.

The bodies were taken to the dissecting room. Afterwards the doctors reported unanimously that death had probably been due to natural causes as both women seemed to have suffered from inflammation of the valves of the heart and under those circumstances any sudden shock to the system might be fatal. As they would have died with almost equal certainty if the operation had been performed without an anesthetic, the administration of a pain-relieving agency could not, under those circumstances, be held responsible for the unfortunate outcome of the case. This was very pleasant news for me but unfortunately Their Lordships did not deem it necessary to communicate the findings of their committee to the public, and all over town the murmurs continued about the surgeon who was in the habit of poisoning his patients in order to get hold of their bodies and then study them by cutting them up into little pieces which afterwards he fed to the rats.

That was trouble No. 1.

Trouble No. 2 happened immediately afterwards.

Now that I had come to know Hendrickje a little more intimately, she was no longer as shy with me as she had been in the beginning, and so she told me of her worries in connection with her coming confinement. She had had a baby before. It had been born a year after she had come to live with Rembrandt, but the baby had died immediately afterwards and she had had a most dreadful time and had almost died from pain. Even now, whenever she thought of it, she shuddered with the memory of so great an agony. She fully expected that this time the child would have to be taken by force and if that were the case, would I perform the operation? I examined her and realized that she might be right in her fears. She had an unusually narrow pelvis and the child was already very large. I promised her that I would do as she asked me and suggested that she come to my own place, where I had plenty of room and could work much better than in the stuffy, built-in beds of the ordinary household. At first she hesitated. Simple people seem to think that there is something sacrilegious about children that are born outside their own homes. But Rembrandt was greatly in favor of this arrangement, and during the first half of the first week of October Hendrickje came to the hospital.

Five days later she had her first pains. Her labor lasted three whole days. In the end she suffered so terribly she asked that she be killed and even tried to climb out of her bed to throw herself out of the window. On the morning of the fourth day, when it looked as if I would have to perform the Caesarian cut (I was afraid the child would otherwise die), she told me that she could stand it no longer and asked me to give her some quick-working poison. Instead of that, I administered my hemp extract. She was so exhausted that it worked almost too well, for she was still unconscious long after the midwife had washed and cleaned the newborn infant (a girl it was, and in the end no operation had proved necessary) and wanted to bring it to her for its first meal. She recovered very rapidly and a fortnight later she was back in the old house on the Breestraat, looking very handsome and very happy and quite like her old cheerful self.

The child was baptized in the Old Church on one of the last days of October. The minister must have received a hint from the Town Hall that further censorious remarks on their part were considered out of place, for little Cornelia was duly registered as the daughter of Rembrandt van Rijn and Hendrickje Stoffels and no embarrassing questions were asked.

But for me it was only the beginning of my trouble.

Hendrickje had been deeply grateful. So grateful, indeed, that she told the dry-nurse who took care of her how good I had been to her and how I had saved her from any further pain when she thought that she could no longer stand the ordeal. The dry-nurse, a very competent and well-meaning woman, but like all the members of her guild, an uncurable chatterbox, had told the neighbors.

"And you know, Doctor Jan gave her something at the last moment and then she never felt any pain at all. Isn't that wonderful? Though of course, it is not quite what we read in the Scriptures."

And then the fat was in the fire.

A week later, the Reverend Zebediah preached his famous sermon on "Childbearing without God's curse." And two weeks later the whole town knew about the scandalous and blasphemous proceedings that went on in the hospital of "this libertine and Arminian who pretended to be wiser than God." Once the rumor had started it was utterly impossible to stop it.

Within a month, Hazewindus felt himself strong enough to lead a delegation of outraged citizens to the town council to ask for my immediate arrest and to suggest that my "place of business" be closed for all time. He went to see Their Lordships, followed by thousands of his parishioners.

I would rather not write about what followed, for in a way it was a very sincere tribute to the confidence which Their Lordships placed in me personally. They promised the young parson that they would hang him from the highest gallows at the disposal of the city of Amsterdam if he ever bothered them again in this matter, and had the bailiff kick him bodily out of the council-chamber.

I hoped that that would be the last of my difficulties and that now I would be left in peace to continue my experiments. But two days later, during the middle of the night, a mob of several hundred men and women, proceeding very quietly and very orderly, as if they obeyed a single will, suddenly broke into the hospital, carried the eighteen patients they found there out into the street (fortunately it was not a very cold night) and then set fire to the premises, disappearing in as quiet and orderly a fashion as they had arrived.

When I came upon the scene of the conflagration, the house was already doomed. It burned until the next afternoon. Of my invested capital which was to be used for the good of humanity, nothing remained but four charred walls and a pile of smoldering beams and red-hot bricks.

That was the end of my dream.

I petitioned the Magistrates and insisted upon an indemnity. My property had been destroyed as the result of a riot which they had failed to repress.

They told me that I was entirely right and that they would take the necessary steps to satisfy me. After deliberating this item on their calendar for seven whole years, they finally voted me about one third of the sum for which I had asked. After another four years, they paid me half of what they had promised me. When I hinted at the unfairness of such an arrangement and suggested that I should at least receive five or six percent accumulated interest on my money, I was informed that Their Lordships had been exceptionally generous in dealing with me and that I should be contented with whatever I got, on pain of not getting anything at all.

And that is the reason why I could not move a finger to help my poor friend during those dreadful years of his bankruptcy.

Once more the shrewd Lodewijk had been right. I had tried to benefit mankind—whether wisely or not it is not for me to say. According to the best of my ability, I had tried to be of some service to those who were less fortunate than I. And they had risen in their wrath and had destroyed me because I had dared to deprive them of what was dearer to them than life itself—their own misery.

The Reverend Zebediah Hazenwindus preached a triumphant sermon. And I went back to general practice to make a living.

Chapter 58

I NOTICE THAT BY LOSING MY CREDIT I HAVE ALSO LOST THE RESPECT OF A GOOD MANY OF MY FELLOW-TOWNSMEN

The first few weeks after the disaster, I was too busy to pay serious attention to anything that did not have to do with the removal of burned bricks and charred wooden beams. For the city, which had neglected to protect my property while it was still intact, took a deep interest in it, now that it had become a ruin, and I was bombarded with letters from the Town Hall. "Would I please remove the eastern wall which was in danger of collapsing and would I kindly see to it that the timbers of the former roof were removed from among the débris, as they were said to be smoldering, and might start a new conflagration."

And one day, when a sudden storm blew a few bricks from the one chimney that still remained intact (they did not fall into the street and caused absolutely no harm), I was fined two hundred guilders for "criminal negligence."

For although the attack on me, or rather on my humanitarian intentions, had failed with Their Lordships, the Burgomasters, those Aldermen who were supposed to superintend the building activities within the limits of our town, were a great deal less independent than Their Lordships who occupied the Mayor's bench and they had to pay considerable attention to the wishes (both implied and outspoken) of the rabble that had declared itself my eternal enemy.

Here I ought to mention a curious coincidence. The same morning when my house was invaded by two sheriffs with a warrant for the immediate payment of my fine (also a most extraordinary procedure, as the usual time was six weeks), part of the rear scaffolding of the new Town Hall collapsed, killing three masons outright and seriously wounding a dozen. But in that case there was no investigation, there were no fines and no punishments, as (according to a semi-official statement issued shortly after the accident) there was serious proof that the foreman who was in charge of that part of the work was "well-known for his blasphemous conduct and his lack of respect for the shepherds of God's own flock," and that under the circumstances the wrath of a righteous Jehovah could not possibly have been averted. And because that foreman had been an infidel no compensation was ever paid to the widows and the children of the workmen who had lost their lives.

In the end I fared a little better than these poor masons and hod-carriers. But for the moment I was in very difficult straits. I had gradually fallen into the unfortunate habit of not charging anything for my services beyond a nominal sum, which in most instances was never paid. Suddenly I found myself obliged to turn a "calling" into a "profession," and I discovered that those same patients who had been only too delighted to accept my services for nothing, while I was fairly well-off, deeply resented my charging them a small fee when through circumstances entirely beyond my own control I was once more obliged to work for a living.

Indeed, a good many of them seemed to feel that I was an impostor and not a few accused me openly of having merely feigned riches so as to be able to charge them more afterwards. In this matter, the very poor behaved with infinitely more delicacy of feeling than those who could well afford to pay a moderate fee for medical assistance. It was an interesting time for me. During the last twenty years I had lived in an artificial economic vacuum, where the severe laws of human survival, which dominated the entire social fabric of our commonwealth, had been almost completely suspended by the presence of an invisible substance which I had come to know quite intimately under the name of "credit."

To this day I have been unable to understand the true nature of this mysterious invisible substance, which is intangible yet opens all doors which has neither volume nor body, yet is able to remove a thousand difficulties that face ordinary citizens which can not be detected by either eyes or ears or the sense of smell, and is nevertheless possessed of such concrete qualities that ninety men out of every hundred recognize it at a vast distance and allow themselves to be influenced by its presence as if it were some wonderful talisman come to us from the Holy Land of Ophir.

When did I first become conscious of its existence? It is hard to tell, for I had been brought up in a very simple fashion in a small community and every one I knew lived on a modest margin of comfort and every one paid his way as he went along. But shortly after the death of my grandfather's brother, I began to notice that some subtle change had taken place in the relations between myself and those of my neighbors with whom I came into daily and regular business contact. My needs had always been modest and whenever I needed something I was in the habit of going to the nearest or most convenient store, asking for the article in question and paying cash for my purchases. Like most people who lead sedentary lives, I am a creature of habit and when I once happened to patronize a store, I was apt to go there for the rest of my days, unless the proprietor died or sold me a fish that had been dead a little longer than was strictly necessary.

As a result I was on the most cordial personal terms with most of the tradespeople who looked after my needs. They consulted me when their wives suffered from vapors (women often do after bearing a dozen children in as many years) and sent for me when their infants had tried to swallow a gherkin that was three times too large for their gullet and that needed merely an experienced finger, to be pushed into the insatiable abdominal cavity they erroneously called their "stomachs."

But one day these good old friends had become quite obsequious in their attitude toward me. I was no longer "the Master" or "Master Jan" or "Hey, there," but "Doctor van Loon," and they bowed a little lower than before and insisted upon escorting me to the door or sending some small urchin with me, to carry a package that I could quite easily have dropped into one of the smaller pockets of my coat. And they would refuse to let me pay spot cash. "Oh, no, Doctor, surely we could not expect that of you!" or "That will be quite all right, Doctor. We will take the liberty to remind you of this small indebtedness at the end of the year." And when I insisted upon settling my debts then and there as I had always done, they would loudly lament that I no longer thought them worthy of my confidence and that I was on the point of deserting them for a rival. Until from sheer inborn laziness and my great natural dislike for every sort and variety of business detail, I gradually gave in and said, "Very well. Send me a bill whenever you want, but don't trust me too much. I am no Burgomaster!" Whereupon they invariably smirked and bowed very low and answered with an attempt at joviality, "Hee hee! that is a good one. Not trust *you!* Why, we know all about *you,* my dear Doctor. You can have this whole store and on credit too. Just say the word and it is yours." All of which puzzled me until I mentioned it to Lodewijk during one of my monthly visits, and he gazed at me for a while from behind a fresh goose-quill and then looked up at the ceiling and then pushed back his chair and muttered:

"What a lot this poor man still has to learn! What a terrible lot! He has rubbed shoulders with the great God of the Golden Pouch. He is a man set apart. The Token is upon his brow and he knoweth it not."

But when I asked him for an explanation of these cryptic words, he refused to tell me anything more and merely added: "Enjoy the day while it lasts. The breath of good fortune is like the dew of early morn. It turns drops of water into pearls and makes a shining scimitar of every humble blade of grass. Then—a short whiff of sunshine and a short whiff of fresh air. And behold, the glory is gone! A cow comes along. The grass is eaten. The farmer on his way to work says, 'Damn these wet pastures. My feet are all soaked.' Enjoy the day, my son, while it lasts, and farewell."

Well, I neither enjoyed the day, as the excellent Lodewijk bade me do, nor did I dislike the experience with any particular feeling of resentment, but I continued to be puzzled, for not only did I observe a change among those who were my more immediate neighbors and therefore might have heard something about my good fortune, but in the most remote parts of the busy town where I had never been before and where no one could possibly know me, yea, in cities and villages far removed from Amsterdam, it was the same story. As soon as people heard my name, they became eager to please me and be of service and everywhere I heard: "Never mind the bill, Doctor. Pay us whenever it is quite agreeable to you. We can wait, there is no hurry. Just suit your own convenience."

And often when I tried to press the money upon them, they showed signs of annoyance, asked me whether they had done or said anything to incur my displeasure, and in order not to hurt their feelings, I had to submit to their wishes. For I was a person set apart. I enjoyed unlimited credit.

Then came the fire which temporarily at least swept away all my possessions and behold! with lightning-like quickness, everything was changed.

Those same tradespeople with whom I had dealt uninterruptedly for the last twenty years were still polite, very polite indeed, but they no longer bowed quite so low, nor smiled quite so broadly when I entered. Nor did they hasten quite so eagerly to the door when I left and although my bundles might be heavier than formerly (as I now often am forced to buy my household necessities in the bulk for greater cheapness) they were always so terribly sorry but "the errand boy had just stepped out for a moment and so, if you don't mind carrying this little package yourself, etc., etc."

Well, I did not particularly mind, being of a sound constitution and able to support heavier burdens than a dozen pounds of dried beans or a couple of Westphalian hams, but again I was puzzled. For during the previous years, I had become quite accustomed to my privileged position in life and as a rule I walked out of a shop without even trying to settle for my purchases, knowing that at the end of the month or year the owner would call on me to receive not only his bill but in addition a small gift of wine or brandy as a slight token of my good will and esteem.

Therefore it came as somewhat of a shock when I was suddenly reminded of the more direct sides of minor business transactions by such remarks as: "We hope you don't mind if we ask you to pay us now, but you see, the war and the unsettled conditions nowadays, and to-morrow we must meet a draft against us for three hundred guilders." Or again: "Of course, we don't want to push you, but our silent partner told us yesterday that he absolutely forbade us to extend any credit to any one, no matter whether it was the King of France himself."

The only exception were the book-sellers of the Rokin and Damrak. While I was in the New World I had a great many opportunities to speak the English language and gradually I had learned that tongue sufficiently well to read it not only with pleasure but also with considerable profit. One day Menasseh, who was in constant correspondence with his friends and sympathizers in London, showed me a book that had been sent to him recently. It was called "Hamlet," and was the work of that same William Shakespeare whom I have mentioned before and who had died about the time I was born. I had never read this play and took it home with me. I found it rather uninteresting as it was the story of a weak and vacillating character, a young prince who would have amounted to a good deal more either as an assassin or a respectable husband if he had served a couple of years before the mast with old Martin Tromp. But in it I found one character I liked, a courtier called Polonius or Palanias (I forget which), who suddenly, when his son is on the point of leaving him for a long voyage, rises to a degree of common sense which one would hardly expect in an author as vague and romantic as this William Shakespeare.

Speaking out of my own experience, I know that it would have benefited me infinitely more if as a child I had been forced to listen to the gentlemanly and practical wisdom of this experienced court-official rather than to the grandiloquent laws of Moses which told me how to avoid a number of terrible crimes (the very existence of which until then had been unknown to me), but which left me completely in the dark when it came to those highly important items which had to do with our common, everyday existence and which we unfortunate boys and girls were supposed to solve for ourselves without any guidance whatsoever. But I had discovered one omission in this Polonian decalogue which filled me with surprise. Polonius forgot to mention something that is of the very greatest importance. He never told his son to make friends with his book-seller. That is one of the few hard and fast rules which my own son learned as soon as he was old enough to spell c-a-t, cat, and c-o-w, cow.

For the book-seller is a man who carries a magic key in his pocket, and if you are able to gain his good will he can and will unlock such wondrous treasure-chests for you that you never need experience another dull moment as long as you live.

The book-seller of course is in business to make a living and he will charge you for his services, as is not only his good right but also his duty. But listen, O my son, and treat thy book-seller as thy best friend and he will repay thee beyond the miser's fondest dreams of unearned increment.

I shall not be able to name all of those with whom I came in contact during my long quest of printed matter. There were Louis and Daniel Elzevir in that pleasant little shop on the Damrak, Jan Blaeu, who is still alive and a close personal friend, although he has come up in the world and we now must call him Doctor Blaeu. There was Johan van der Bergh, from whose shop-window I could watch the progress of the new Town Hall, and half a dozen others who were my most trusted companions in the days when I was suspected of being quite wealthy and who almost forced their wares upon me when an adverse fortune had suddenly turned my riches into a smoking and blackened deficit. They knew that I could not exist without a fairly heavy diet of parchment and paper.

They asked no questions, raised no suspicious eyebrows. They said, "Here are our shelves. Help yourself and let the future take care of itself."

And finally there was one other man, outside of my own personal friends (who were veritable pillars of loyalty and faithful affection), a man whom most people considered the most aloof, the coolest, the least responsive of ordinary mortals and who during this unfortunate crisis in my personal affairs showed himself to be possessed of such deep understanding that he made me his grateful slave for the rest of my life. That was My Lord Jan de Witt, who at that time ruled the Republic as if he were its undisputed master and sovereign instead of being merely a paid official of the Estates General.

Shortly after the disaster, I received a note dated from the well-known house on the Kneuterdijk in The Hague, asking me to call at my own convenience the next time I was in the city as My Lord Jan wanted to consult me as he was not feeling quite well.

This, however, I found to be only a pretext—a slight indisposition as the result of a too sedentary life. I told him so and suggested a suitable course of exercise and a diet, a bit of advice which any practitioner in The Hague could have given him at much less cost and trouble. I even went so far as to tell him that for such little ailments, he might call with perfect safety upon a couple of local physicians whose names he suggested. Whereupon His Lordship answered:

"I had thought as much myself, but there are some other matters I want to discuss with you. Suppose you stop for dinner. We shall be all alone and I can't promise you much. I shall do better after next February when I am married. But if you will take pot luck, I hope you will stay."

He conducted me into the dining-room (which I noticed had been done over entirely in the new French style) and we had our dinner which consisted of a vegetable soup, some cold ham and brown beans and Delft beer. His Lordship excused himself for the simplicity of the fare.

"I hear," he remarked, "that my cousins in Amsterdam are beginning to follow the English fashion of serving meat every day. But I think that I will remain faithful to our simple provincial habit of one roast a week. It is better for one's blood."

Nor did he offer me a pipe of tobacco after dinner, saying that he reserved the weed for the evening, and even then in great moderation, as he derived greater contentment from a few chapters of Quintilian than from half a dozen pipes. "And at much smaller expense," he added as an afterthought, "and now that I am on the point of founding a family of my own, I ought to think of such things."

After the dinner had been finished and we had wiped our hands on the wet towel which the man in black livery offered us (My Lord Jan apologized for the presence of this male creature in his household, but explained that since the Bickers were accustomed to men-servants, he had decided to introduce this innovation into his own home, so that his wife would find herself among familiar surroundings), my host asked me whether I were in a hurry and when I answered no, that I expected to return to Amsterdam by the night boat, he invited me to come upstairs to his study a moment and let him talk to me as there were some problems he wanted to discuss with me.

"Of course," he began, "all this is entirely confidential. I am your patient—you noticed how I took no mustard with my ham—and everything I am telling you is in the nature of a confession, made by a sick man to his medical adviser. Sit down in that easy chair and listen and then tell me what you think about my idea."

I sat down and His Lordship began with a short review of the war as it had now been fought for the greater part of two years. "It will soon come to an end," he said. "We are neither of us getting anywhere. I am afraid that we are a little too well balanced. A few months more and the war will be over. We will both of course try and get some advantages out of the negotiations of peace, but mark my words, it will be a stalemate. Then we will prepare for the next war. I am sorry but I don't see how it can be helped. In every village as you may have observed there is always one dog who lords it over the others. As long as we human beings still have so much in common with dogs and as long as we will fight for every bone, we shall probably continue to build warships and quarrel for islands in India and rivers in America. It seems absurd that it should be that way. And for good measure, add the ambitions of those private families toward the south and the east of us, who used to be highway robbers a few centuries ago, whom I now have got to address as Royal Majesties or run the risk of getting my letters back unopened.

"I am not yet fifty years old and the other day my brother and I figured out one evening that we had lived through nine major wars and fifty-one minor conflicts since we were born. I had a visit the other day from a Rabbi in Amsterdam, I don't know whether you know him, a certain Menasseh ben Israel, an interesting old fellow who told me that he had made a wonderful discovery. He had been able to decipher a mysterious passage in the Pentateuch and now he knew for certain that the moment of the coming of the Messiah was merely a question of weeks or months. I told him that as far as I remembered, the Messiah had paid us a visit some sixteen hundred years ago, but he answered that that had not been the right one. He was very polite about it and kept on repeating that he did not want to hurt my feelings, but that so-called Messiah of which we Christians made such a great ado, had been merely one of the minor prophets and not a very good one at that. But the true Messiah was about to appear among us and it would be well if we, who ruled the destinies of the nations of this world, made suitable preparations to receive him.

"I asked him what he wanted us to do and he replied that he wanted us to establish a reign of peace and righteousness. He really was a most engaging person and absolutely sincere. He told me that he intended to go to London as soon as peace should have been declared to see the Lord Protector on the same errand. In the meantime he expected to convince me of the truth of his views, for no other country on the Continent was as powerful as the Republic of the United Seven Netherlands and no man in the Republic was as powerful as I and when I asked him how we should bring about this reign of peace and righteousness, he looked at me with some surprise and said, 'Why, My Lord, by making all nations love each other like brethren and by turning the whole of this earth into one vast commonwealth like the Republic of the United Seven Netherlands which is one country, yet composed of seven independent and sovereign states.' If he had to rule them, as I do, he would know just how much of 'one country' they are!

"But he did not know and I did not disillusion him. If he actually intends to visit England soon and pay his compliments to our friend the Protector, it is better that he arrive in the British capital fully convinced that we are a strong and united country. And as for the rest of his ideas—did you ever see the plan one of the kings of France, I think it was the fourth Henry, worked out for a league of all the nations of Europe? A most intelligent and intriguing project. But hopeless, quite hopeless! He wants to scramble us all into a vast omelette. But what is the use of trying to make a decent omelette if two or three of the eggs are rotten? And when he has worked it all out and enumerated what we should be allowed to do and not be allowed to do, he forgets one simple little item, he does not tell us who will be the policemen who will make us do what we should do. He leaves that part to Providence and declares the meeting closed.

"A most admirable ideal but almost as vague and futile as that of our friend the Rabbi.

"Meanwhile our enemy across the water and I, though we are not officially on speaking terms, have been discussing a plan of our own that may prove more practicable. Of course you understand that I am still talking as your patient and that all this is strictly between us. I have the uncomfortable feeling that somewhere in my office there is a leak and one of these days I will catch the traitor and have him hanged. But I know that I can trust you and all this will make it more clear to you what I am trying to do when I make you the offer I am about to make.

"The Lord Protector and I are practical men. We know what the common people do not seem to understand, that if our countries go on fighting each other for another fifty years, we will both of us be ruined. We know that all that talk of Parliaments of Nations and Estates General composed of delegates from the Emperor of China and the great Khan of India and the seven hundred and eighty-three little German princes, not to forget the Grand Duke of Muscovy and the Grand Padisha of Stamboul and the black potentates of the Gold Coast won't ever be anything more than they are now—pleasant dreams of well-meaning rabbis and other visionaries. The world respects only one thing, and that is force and such a body would never be able to command the slightest respect.

"The people in Scandanavia have tried it out and they have failed. The Holy Roman emperors seven hundred years ago tried something of the sort and they failed. Charlemagne succeeded. But he had an army, he was able to say 'do' and everybody did, for he was possessed of a powerful army, and when he said 'don't' even our own wild ancestors obeyed him, because they were afraid of him.

"Our Lord Cromwell seems to have read his ancient history with profit. He suggests that we make peace and then conclude a treaty. We are the two most powerful nations in the modern world. Together we could rule the whole planet as we would see fit and I assure you, if ever we decide to go in for a partnership, we will know how to make the others obey us. We would simply divide the world between us.

"We here in Holland would keep the Indies, paying England a certain sum for the expenses they have incurred, developing their property there during the last seventy years. The English on the other hand would be given free rein in America, with the exception of Brazil, without which our West Indian Company would go bankrupt, for that settlement of ours in the north, that bit of land around the fort of Nieuw Amsterdam, will never amount to anything. The English are welcome to it any time they care to take it. And small loss.

"Of course, Spain and France would object, but they are Catholics and our own people and the great majority of the English would regard a war upon them as a holy pilgrimage and would give us all the money we need. For that money we would equip and maintain a fleet. The English would contribute sixty ships of the line and we would contribute forty. That makes one hundred modern war vessels and together these would amply suffice to blow every galley of the Bourbons and Habsburgs out of existence.

"As I said, both our people and the English would consider this a holy war and if we allowed the clergy to organize all this territory and keep it free from Catholic competition, there would be such a rush of missionaries that there would be hardly a dominie left at home and that would make the business of ruling these premises a great deal easier. Of course, Their Lordships of Amsterdam will fight this project tooth and nail. They would be heartily in favor of the scheme if England were left out of it and perhaps they are foolish enough to think that they are strong enough to go it alone. I may be able to persuade them to come over to my views, and I may not.

"In the meantime, I have certain other worries. The world at large seems to believe that we derive our great wealth from Indian trade. We don't. We get our daily bread and butter out of the North Sea and the Baltic. Herring and grain have made us what we are. And herring and grain will probably continue to make us rich for a long time to come. The North Sea is at our disposal whenever we are not at war with England, and even then that source of revenue does not completely run dry. But the Baltic worries me. Without grain, we are lost. We are the grain dealers and grain carriers of the whole world. Without us, the bakers in Madrid and Naples and Lisbon might just as well close their shops. Even the Pope would go hungry if one of our ships did not drop in occasionally at Civita Vecchia, where by the way we have a bright young man to represent us as our consular agent. But of course this monopoly is full of danger for ourselves. We don't raise a blade of all that grain. We get it from Danzig and we carry it home through the Sound. Have you any idea of the lay of the land?"

I assured His Lordship that I did, for all this sounded remarkably much like certain lectures on politics and economics to which I had listened almost a dozen years before in the study of My Lord Andries Bicker, and his brother, the Burgomaster. But I said nothing about all this to the man who so soon was to marry their daughter and niece and merely remarked in a casual tone of voice that I had always had a liking for geography and was quite familiar with the map of those northern countries.

"Well, then," My Lord Jan continued, "you know yourself how full of danger that road to Danzig is, as long as all those Baltic countries continue to fight among themselves. There are the Poles who rule that whole part of Russia and Lithuania where the grass-fields are. I use the word 'ruling' advisedly for if I am to believe our agent in Warsaw, they are the most unruly mob that were ever entrusted with any sort of power. They call themselves a republic but have a king whom they elect and who has less power in his own country than my cat has in the kitchen. Every person of noble blood has a finger in the governmental pie and ninety-nine out of every hundred citizens seem to be of noble blood. The rest are Jews who attend to the civil administration and the bookkeeping of that crazy concern. But every one from the King down to the lowest stable-boy will take a bribe and the situation therefore is not very serious. We simply pay our way and buy grain or officials as suits our needs.

"Then there is Sweden. In that country we have to do with a monarch who in more than one way resembles our own Prince William—the one who just died. He too was trained to be a great general. And then the Thirty Years' War came to an end, just when he was about old enough to ride a horse. Now of course he is looking for a nice little war of his own, for once a young prince like that has tasted the joys of leading a charge on horseback (I must confess that sort of thing is rather out of my own line, I prefer a chair or a ship) he will never be happy till he has trotted across at least a dozen battlefields.

THE JEWISH SYNAGOGUE

"But he will need money for his little adventures, and he will be looking for a bargain. There is only one bargain in the whole Baltic. That is the crazy Republic of Poland.

"I received a letter from Stockholm last week telling me that young Charles is assembling 50,000 men to march on Warsaw and Cracow. I suppose he can take both cities without any great difficulty, for I know of no people that make such magnificent fighters as the Swedes. Then all the neighbors will get frightened. Then Denmark will be forced to join the Poles and that is where we come in, for that means that the Sound will be blockaded and that we have no grain. We have got to be prepared for that moment and it won't be my fault if we aren't. I have been studying the problem of our navy very carefully and have conferred with all of our admiralties. We ought to have one admiralty board instead of half a dozen, but the time isn't yet ripe for such a step. Meanwhile I have suggested three innovations and I think that they will be accepted.

"The first one has to do with the ships themselves. No good waiting until we are at war and then chartering a couple of hundred merchantmen and converting them into fighting craft. The owners ask exorbitant rates—the sailors are not accustomed to military discipline and half of the captains are pirates. I say nothing about their ability or their courage. They are marvelous seamen, and in nine cases out of ten they will blow their ships up rather than surrender them. But they have always fought on their own. It is difficult for them to obey orders. When a battle has started, they get so excited they forget everything except the one particular enemy they have engaged and hope to capture. The admiral can hoist a dozen signals but they see nothing but that one fellow they are trying to get. As a result of which, we have lost at least two engagements during the present war in which we ought to have been victorious. And of course a converted merchantman can never be as good a fighting machine as a vessel built for the purpose of modern naval strategy.

"So that is item No. 1 and as all the admiralties have agreed with me that I am right, there won't be many difficulties on that point.

"Then I come to item No. 2. Sailors are sailors and soldiers are soldiers. There is no use asking a mackerel to climb a mountain or a dromedary to swim across the Channel. Therefore I am going to introduce regular sea-soldiers on all of our ships, troops of specially trained men who will be called 'marines.' They will have their own officers and they will be used for all operations on land which have never been much to the taste of the regular sailors.

"And now I come to the third item, a very important one which so far has been most scandalously neglected. I mean the medical care of both sailors and marine soldiers. I want to reorganize that whole department. Will you take care of this for me?"

The question left me dumbfounded.

"But, My Lord Jan," I answered, "you know what has just happened to me?"

"I do," he said.

"And you understand the opposition there would be to such an appointment if you were kind enough to suggest it to Their Lordships of the Admiralties?"

"I have taken that in consideration."

"You know that all over the country the clergy would denounce you for having made an alliance with a man who has sold his soul to the devil?"

My Lord Jan was a very quiet man—a soft-spoken man of terrific power but a power held absolutely under control. It was the first time I saw him angry and his anger (as in most people of his temperament) did not show itself in a sudden rush of blood to his cheeks. It manifested itself only in a slight twitching of his lower lip. Upon this occasion his lower lip twitched so hard that I almost heard his teeth chatter.

"As long as I have any influence in the government of this Republic of ours," he answered, slowly thumping the table with the knuckles of his left hand, "those clerical gentlemen will be taught to keep their place. I remember a very old aunt of my grandfather. She lived to be a hundred and three years old and she was born before Luther hammered his articles of faith to the doors of the Wittenberg church. She was a witty woman and until the last day of her life (she died sitting upright in her chair, knitting a petticoat for her great-great-grand-nephew) she was in full command of all her faculties. She was, of course, a Protestant, but at heart she had retained a great deal of affection for the old faith.

"'They tell you children it was the bishops and the cardinals that caused it all,' she used to say. 'The bishops and the cardinals who were a little too greedy and selfish. Well, don't you believe it. Of course they were greedy and selfish, for they were men, and all men are greedy and selfish, and it is only we women who ever do anything for anybody else; otherwise would I have spent all my days cutting diapers and knitting stockings for a breed of children that deserved to have gone stark naked? No, it was not the greed of those on top. It was the greed and selfishness of those at the very bottom. It was that horde of begging friars that caused all the trouble. Dirty, ill kempt, slovenly, ignorant, arrogant yokels—peasants in a cowl, who thought the world owed them a living—lazy rustics who had spent their childhood behind the pigs and cows and were tired of working quite so hard. These voracious holy men who had the manner of the hogs they tended in their younger years' (like so many good women of that ancient day, the old lady affected the picturesque vocabulary of her own scullery-maids) 'forced their way into our houses, ate our food, drank our wine, slept in our beds, kissed our servants and any refusal to extend to these pious trenchermen the most complete and cordial hospitality meant the chance of being denounced to the henchmen of the Inquisition as a suspicious character and a friend of that demon Luther. It was this unwashed rabble that made our people rise up in rebellion. The bishops were no angels. They stole. But they stole in the grand manner. They used their plunder to build churches and endow hospitals and buy lovely pictures and the common people did not mind. They felt that they were getting their money's worth in a glorious and free public show. But when those pilfering peasant boys tried their hand at the business of ruling their powerful neighbors, then the trouble started.'

"I often think of that queer old character (she had not left her house since the death of her husband some fifty-two years before—she never took a breath of fresh air and as I just told you, she lived to be more than a hundred) when I am called upon to deal with the affairs of the Synod and am asked to interfere in some church quarrel. I am not a free-thinker, as I am told you are. The Church means a great deal to me. My life is a difficult one and I could not live without the consolations that come to me from certain parts of the Gospels. But I have absolutely no patience with the attempts made by so many of our dominies to hoist themselves into the seats of the mighty. It is their business to look after other people's souls, just as it is our unquestioned duty to watch over their physical well-being, see to it that they get enough to eat and are able to practice their trade in peace.

"God has appointed us to this high task because we are the ablest of our nation. If he wanted us to be ruled by shoemakers or hod-carriers or doctors of theology, he would have given them the power which he has now laid down in the hands of the merchants who have made this country what it is to-day. I have on my table here at least three dozen 'official complaints' sent to me by different church councils. Every one of these, although signed by half a dozen vestry-men, is really the work of some bright peasant-lad who thinks that he can tell us, the members of the Estates General of this sovereign Republic, what we ought to do because he has been able to escape from his father's farm and has studied theology at one of those universities which we have provided for his benefit and convenience at a great expense to the state.

"Just now they are upset by the popularity of the doctrines of a certain Descartes, a Frenchman who lived for a long time in our country. They want his works suppressed. They want me to forbid all gatherings where the ideas of that Frenchman are discussed. They want me to dismiss all professors who have ever read a single page of his works. I won't tolerate it! I won't tolerate it for a moment! This is a country in which every man ought to be allowed to think as he pleases, within certain definite limits laid down by the law. We have to be strict with the Catholics. But they are an exception. They would mistake our mildness for weakness and would abuse our hospitality. It will be centuries before we forget the murder of Prince William, and the murder of so many of our own grandparents. We can't have the Anabaptists run naked and wild through our streets, proclaiming the coming of the Kingdom of Heaven. But they were exceptions. As long as the different sects observe a certain discretion, our magistrates won't interfere with them. The same goes for the philosophers. Let them come and philosophize as much as they will, all we ask is that they do not interfere with the peaceful running of the government.

"And the same holds true for the reverend gentlemen who preach their sermons from the pulpits of our own churches. We have had the Inquisition here once and no one wants to see it again. I have heard what that man in Amsterdam has done. My influence in that city is not very strong. It will be a little stronger as soon as I shall have married into the Bicker family. I shall do all I can to see that you get justice and get reimbursed for the loss you have suffered. The man who caused that outbreak will not only be obliged to leave town, if I can do anything about it, he will be exiled from the territory of the Republic. In the meantime, as a public vindication of yourself and as an expression of my belief in your own integrity and the usefulness of your aims, I offer you this post of chief-surgeon of the fleet. The admiralties, I am sure, will follow my suggestion and there will be no difficulty about your appointment. Will you accept?"

The offer came so unexpectedly that I did not know what to say. The Pensionary was not known as a person given to sudden impulses. As people used to say of him, he never ventured across the ice of a single night's freezing. It was his policy to wait until the frost had lasted at least a couple of weeks and the ice was as solid and reliable as a road built of Belgian blocks. That he should offer me so high a dignity at a moment when from every pulpit I was denounced as a menace to the country of my birth, showed that he was firmly intent upon seeing this matter through to the bitter or happy end.

But I did not know what to answer and I asked His Lordship for a week's respite to talk over my problem with some of my friends. He assented. There was no hurry. Nothing could be done anyway until the end of the war. And so I bade him farewell and took the night boat back to Amsterdam.

That night boat was an innovation. It was pulled by relays of three horses and reduced the distance between Amsterdam and The Hague to a little less than eight hours.

I did my best to sleep.

But I was kept awake for the greater part of the night by three citizens who were discussing the recent goings-on in Amsterdam.

They differed upon many points, but agreed upon one point—that I, the man responsible for this outbreak of public wrath, should have been hung as an example to all other enemies of Zion.

Chapter 59

I LOSE A FAITHFUL BANKER AND AN EVEN MORE FAITHFUL FRIEND

The next four weeks I spent almost entirely on board ship. Not on board one of those war-vessels with which I had been asked to associate my future fate, but on board the little sailing-craft of Jean-Louys, who indeed had turned the most enthusiastic and indefatigable of amateur sailors. His French mate and cook and body-servant proved indeed a jewel of the first magnitude. He could handle a boat in any weather and in any sort of a sea. He could present us with a four-course meal, half an hour after we had arrived in some village of the Zuyder Zee from which the last inhabitant seemed to have moved long ago. And he seemed to belong to that curious and restricted tribe of human beings that can live entirely without sleep, for no matter what time of day or night one appeared on deck, there he was busy with some task of his own and as cheerful and obliging as he was silent.

During the first five days, we enjoyed the companionship of Rembrandt. He had not wanted to come but we thought it would be good for him to enjoy a little change after the harrowing experience of his wife (we invariably referred to Hendrickje as his wife and he seemed to like that). And we told him that he could bring all the sketchbooks he wanted and could sit on deck all day long and draw as much as he wanted.

Jean-Louys had even persuaded him to take along a dozen copper plates for the purpose of doing dry-points of sea-gulls and distant bits of shore-line.

But almost from the first he complained that his plates would show spots—that his needles would rust, and that the sea air would ruin his pens, so that he could not work at all. And after two days he began to grow restless.

"This is nothing for me," he complained. "This sort of existence is too soft and too easy. Another week of having this man blacken my shoes for me and giving me things to eat which I can't recognize when they are on my tongue, and I will jump overboard and swim home."

We argued with him that the lovely little cities along the Zuyder Zee would provide him with an almost unlimited number of subjects for landscapes and seascapes and what not. But he remained obstinate and refused to listen to us.

"I appreciate your hospitality," he told Jean-Louys. "But the life does not suit me. Besides, I can't work in this light. No more than I can work on land, I mean on really dry land, where there are forests and open sandy spaces covered with heather. I tried it once. I was going to walk to Arnhem and from there to Breevoort where Hendrickje comes from. One of her brothers was still living there and there was the usual difficulty about an inheritance. I was to settle that difficulty. Imagine me settling other people's inheritance troubles!

"But anyway, I went and I hated it. The light was too dry. Just as here the light is too wet. For my work—for the things I am trying to do—I need the sort of light that is neither too wet nor too dry. I don't know how to describe it. I would like to call it a sort of suspended light, but that expression is very vague and can hardly tell you what I mean. And I don't quite know myself, except that I am unhappy when I have got to work in any other sort of atmosphere. We have got that particular light in Amsterdam. I suppose because the town is nothing but a stone pancake afloat on a sea of mud. Everything in my workshop is bathed in that light. It does something to the shadows, too. Here the shadows are too hazy. On land far away from the sea they were too abrupt, too severe and too sudden, and that is no fun for me—any ordinary painter can paint that sort of shadows. But the shadows at home have a lucid quality, a little velvety as if they had been mixed with oil. They look as different from ordinary shadows as the wet clay of the Diemer Polder looks from the sandy soil I saw between Utrecht and Arnhem. I suppose I am talking nonsense, but as soon as we get to Monnikendam I hope you will set me ashore and let me peacefully walk home."

Jean-Louys did more than that. He returned to the Y and landed Rembrandt almost within stone's throw of his own house. We presented him with a pail full of fresh shrimps.

His home-coming, as we afterwards learned, was not very happy. Two sheriffs were waiting for him with an order for his arrest unless a bill which he owed his frame-maker for almost five years were immediately settled. Hendrickje had gone out and had pawned one of Saskia's famous pearl ear-rings and the sheriffs had been satisfied and had gone their way. But all this we did not learn until we returned to Amsterdam several weeks later, and in the meantime we had gone as far north as Medemblik and as far east as Blokzijl and we had talked of everything under the sun, but mostly of this one problem: should I accept My Lord de Witt's offer or not?

Of course in my heart of hearts I knew that I should not, but then again it seemed such a wonderful opportunity that I felt that it was my duty to say yes, and then again it struck me as almost wicked to let such an opportunity go by, and then again I told myself that I was not the sort of man for an executive position like that and that all the official bother to which I would be exposed would soon kill me, and then again I tried to persuade myself that with the backing of the powerful pensionary, I would be able to overcome all bureaucratic difficulties and in the end, I flipped a six-stiver piece and it said "no," and when I told

Jean-Louys, who was sitting on deck (I had consulted the oracle in the cabin, feeling slightly ashamed of myself for my superstition), he burst out laughing and said, "That is the way it always is. Do you remember the story in Boccaccio of the traveler who wanted to go swimming in the Nile and asked one of the natives whether that part of the Nile was ever visited by sharks from the North Sea and the native said, 'No, there are no sharks here.' And so he went swimming and when he had enjoyed his bath and come out of the water, he asked the little Selim-boy how he had known that there were not any sharks there and the boy answered, 'Where there are such a lot of crocodiles there are no sharks.'

"And that is the way it goes in life. Always and everywhere where there are sharks there are crocodiles, and where there are no crocodiles there are sharks, and here you are, a most skeptical bone-setter who takes no stock in all the old women's stories of his childhood, a man who openly defies Jehovah and the first chapter of Genesis, and when you want to know whether to start out upon a new venture, you flip a coin! The most avowed agnostic I ever knew used to consult a pack of piquet-cards every time he went on a voyage. When I was in the army in Germany, I used to be friends with a noble, swash-buckling Swede (Heaven only knows how he got there. Perhaps he had swash-buckled a little too freely among his own people) and that Swede, who was the bravest man I ever knew, was so blasphemous that he could make a dozen imperial dragoons blush at one and the same moment, and he respected neither Heaven nor Hell and he vowed that all religion was merely a sort of dangerous drug with which wily priests tried to stupefy dull people, but he would never take part in a charge (and he was a superb horseman) unless he had first stroked the pelt of a black cat and in the end (and that will show you how useful he was) his commanding officer was obliged to have the regiment carry a couple of black cats with it wherever it went to keep old Torenson happy and contented.

"It is no use trying to teach people to depend solely upon their reason. They have got to have something to bolster up their coruage—it does not matter whether it be sharks or crocodiles, but they have got to have something.

"For the rest, of course you are entirely right. You and I are not the sort of people that would ever fit into an organization. We are lonely wanderers. We are the pussy-cats that explore the region beyond the furthest known back-yard. If you said yes to My Lord Jan, you would discover that there are just about nine thousand other pill-rollers and leeches in this Republic of yours who were firmly convinced that they had a better right to the office than you. And you would start out with nine thousand irreconcilable enemies and you would never be able to accomplish anything at all. On the other hand, if you refuse the Pensionary's gracious offer and let it be known that you have refused it, every single one of those nine thousand Aesculapian disciples will vow that you are a great man and deserving the highest praise for your discretion and modesty.

"Go to The Hague and tell His Lordship that you are deeply sensitive of the honor he has done you by asking you to become his surgeon-general, but that you feel that you ought not leave your patients here to the extent of accepting his very kind offer. If, however, he comes to employ you in an advisory capacity, you will be delighted to comply with his wishes.

"That is the thing, my dear friend. Always try and keep near the throne, but at the same time hide yourself behind some convenient draperies to avoid the gaze of the crowd. That is to say, if you really care to accomplish something useful. If you merely want to cut a fine figure—wear beautiful feathers on your hat—the regal dais will better suit your purpose. But I am afraid that God never meant you to be a courtier. If he had, he would not have let you be born in this country."

I knew how much the ultimate success of my plans meant to Jean-Louys. Like many very sensitive people, he had to hide his emotions behind a display of skeptical fireworks which might deceive those who only knew him slightly, but not his friends. And beneath all this levity there lay a kernel of good, sound common sense. As soon as he had returned to Amsterdam, I wrote to the Pensionary telling him that I did not think it quite fair to leave the people to whom I had devoted myself for so many years but that I would be delighted to come to The Hague whenever he wanted me and act as his adviser in all matters pertaining to the medical care of the fleet. His Lordship most kindly agreed to this arrangement, but he told me that in that case and unless I were duly enrolled, he would experience great difficulty in persuading Their Lordships of the Admiralties to pay me a regular salary, and as it would probably take considerable time before my accounts with the city of Amsterdam were straightened out, I might find it difficult to make both ends meet. But I could answer him that he need have no worries on that score. For when I returned to Amsterdam, I found a short note from Lodewijk, my banker in the older and more prosperous days.

"I encouraged you in your folly," he wrote. "You never were a spendthrift and I feel that I am partly to blame for that absurd venture that ended exactly as I had predicted. In due course of time, Their Lordships of the Town Hall will undoubtedly reimburse you. But the wheels of the official deities grind slower than any other piece of machinery known to man. To atone for the sin of having told you to go ahead, instead of throwing you out of my office that memorable morning, I shall send you an order for two hundred florins on the first of every month until you get your money or at least part of it back. This will keep you out of the poor-house. How to keep people like you out of the madhouse is a problem that puzzles me infinitely more."

I took his two hundred florins. It would have broken his heart if I had refused them. They arrived on the first of every month. They arrived on the first of every month for more than ten years, when I was at last able to begin and pay some of that money back. The day before I received the first installment of the compensation which the town at last had decided to make to me, Lodewijk died. In his will he had made a stipulation that my debt to him should be canceled. When I finally received the bulk of my money and began to build my second hospital, I asked leave to call it after this most faithful friend. But his widow refused.

"Lodewijk," she told me, "had considered himself fully repaid by your friendship and his wife and children feel the same way."

Chapter 60

OUR JEWISH NEIGHBORS, WHO HAVE COME TO US TO ESCAPE FROM THE INTOLERANCE OF THEIR SPANISH MASTERS, SHOW THAT RELIGIOUS BIGOTRY IS NOT RESTRICTED TO ONE SECT OR RELIGION

The war came to an end. And as the ships returned home, I met a great many of the captains (for I now spent about half of my spare time at the admiralties) and I heard stories of such surpassing heroism that I was obliged to revise most of my previous notions about the human race or at least that particular part of it to which I myself happened to belong.

Quite often when I was visiting Jean-Louys in his tower near the water front, I had been an unwilling witness of the departure of our brave tars. Disorderly crowds of drunken, disheveled men and drunken, disheveled women, with here and there a howling, bedraggled child, pacified by an occasional raisin drenched in gin.

This mob would slowly come down the quay, pushed forward by large numbers of town guards and looking and behaving exactly like a moaning herd of sheep that were being taken to the slaughter-house.

Now and then a drum and fife corps would try to start a patriotic air or even a hymn, but after a few bars of some well-known tune, shrill, ribald voices would interrupt the musicians with one of those blasphemous ditties that seem to have sprung straight from hell and at once the whole of the crowd would join in—improvising words as they went along and indulging in a wild orgy of dancing and bucking and skipping, accompanied by gestures of such utter vulgarity that even the town guards would blush and they would repeat this performance until after hours of jostling and shrieking, the embarking stations had been reached where the rum-soaked cattle were unceremoniously pushed into a large number of flat-bottomed barges and at once turned to the big vessels that lay at anchor just off the Rijzenhoofd Bulwark.

That was the last we saw of them until we heard our first vague reports of battles and encounters and victories and an occasional defeat.

But one day, years later, a number of high plenipotentiaries assembled around a green table in a large hall in the center of Westminster, affixed their names and seals to a yellow piece of parchment, and shortly afterwards the tired ships would painfully limp back into port—without sails, without masts, without a scrap of that paint that had made them look so spick and span when they had gone forth to war. Then anxious women would come once more around the ancient bulwark and numb-faced children would cling to the rotting wharves and every time a boatload of sailors approached the shore, they would all of them rush forward and scan the faces, many of which were still black from gunpowder or covered with bandages that clearly showed the untrained hands of the bungling nautical doctors.

Then there would be anxious questions: "Is that you, Piet?" or "Have you heard anything of Klaas, who was on the *Zilvere Ster?*" or "Jan! oh, Jan! are you there?" And sometimes the answer would be, "Yes, I am here, as fit as a fiddle," but more often there would be a gruff, "Go home, woman, your Klaas is dead," or "They are bringing your Piet home on a stretcher. His legs are gone." And then there would be cursing or weeping (according to the nature of the woman who was told that she could now spend the rest of her days scrubbing other people's floors and hallways) and silent groups would mutely separate themselves from the main body of spectators and would move desolately toward that part of the town where lived those "gallant gentlemen" whose name only a fortnight before had been on everybody's tongue and who early the next morning must begin the endless round of those workshops and offices where the "No sailors need apply" signs told them how deeply a grateful country had really appreciated their self-sacrificing valor.

For that was the queerest part of it all—those drunken, disorderly and disheveled ruffians who had to be conducted to the arsenals between lines of heavily armed town guards, for fear that they would set fire to the city if they were left to themselves—those selfsame rowdies, once they were on board and realized that they were fighting for their own women and kids and that hovel they considered home—would perform deeds of such unheard-of courage and of such incredible loyalty, that each one of them, if personal heroism is really a safe-conduct to Heaven (as was held to be true by the ancient Greeks) had more than fully established his claims to at least ten square yards of the celestial domain.

They were not very communicative, these "common sailors," and even their sluggish brains revolted at the recollection of many of the sights they had seen—at the sickly sweet smell of blood that would be forever in their nostrils. But gradually little bits of narrative prose, far superior to any poetry ever composed by one of our peaceful, home-staying bards, would find their way into the ale-house gossip of our everyday lives and Homer himself in his most inspired moment could not have devised such deeds of valor and devotion. There were men who had continued to fight when only five or six of the entire ship's crew had been left alive and who, when nothing could save their floating charnel-house from sinking, had boldly jumped on board the enemy craft and with their bare fists almost had captured their former aggressor.

One sailor in the midst of an encounter had managed to swing himself on board the vessel that flew the admiral's flag, had reached the top of the mast and had removed the English colors, thereby causing a most useful panic among the other British men-of-war, who thought that their leader had been killed. Trying to jump back into the rigging of his own vessel, he had missed his footing and had dashed his brains out on the deck, forty feet below, but with the enemy's flag still tightly held between his dead teeth.

The son of Admiral Tromp, commanding a vessel in the harbor of Livorno where the reigning grand duke had forbidden him to take action against his English rivals, who were at that time in the same harbor, had waked up in the middle of the night to find his craft in the hands of the English, who had broken the truce. Rather than surrender, he had jumped overboard and after swimming for more than three hours, he had finally been picked up by a Dutch sloop. With that sloop he had rowed back to his own ship and had recaptured it.

Captain Jan van Galen, during the battle that had followed, had had one of his legs blown away by a cannon-ball. But rather than go to the sick-ward and have his wounds attended to, he had told his officers to carry him to the top of the poop-deck from where he could better watch the battle while he slowly bled to death.

On one occasion a small squadron which was convoying one hundred and fifty merchantmen, fought a much larger English force during the greater part of three days and three nights and then only gave up the fight because they were completely out of gun-powder. Nevertheless, they not only had saved all of the merchant-men but they succeeded in escaping themselves with the loss of only two of their ships.

Truly the men who could perform such acts of valor deserved a better treatment than they usually received and I was very grateful that with the unwavering support of the Pensionary I was able to do something for them.

Up to that time the operating room of those few vessels that had any operating room at all (on most of them the surgeons worked right among the guns) was located way down deep in the hold of the vessel and below the water-line. As a result these places were pitchdark and absolutely devoid of fresh air. The surgeons were obliged to amputate arms and legs (the usual wounds) by the light of a candle and as they were not allowed to make a fire and heat their irons an account of the proximity of the powder-room, they had no adequate means of closing the arteries except by using large quantities of lint, a method which failed in ninety out of every hundred cases.

Besides, the transport down the narrow stairs of such desperately wounded men was a form of torture which one would not have meted out to one's own worst enemies. In order to change this and provide better facilities for the medical staff on board our men-of-war, I suggested that the admiralties offer a prize of 500 florins for the best plan that should remove the sick-ward from the bottom of the ship to one of the upper decks, without interfering too seriously with the manipulation of the heavy guns which filled the two top decks. As the sum was a very large one, practically all the nautical engineers of the entire Republic took part in the contest, and for several months my office resembled the draughting room of a ship-yard.

I remember one strange meeting I had during that period. One night the maid told me that a foreign-looking gentleman wanted to see me. "He carries a small ship's model under his arm," she added. "He is probably one of those funny people," and she pointed to the diagrams and specifications that were spread all over the walls and the floors.

The visitor proved to be what the maid had predicted. He had come to show me an invention of his own. Unfortunately it had nothing to do with the problem in which I was interested. It was a new device to raise the angle of gun-fire without the clumsy arrangement then in use. I told the mysterious stranger that he had come to the wrong place with his little model, that he ought to take it to the admiralty which undoubtedly would be greatly interested. He answered that he had already been to three of our admiralties but that none of them had shown the slightest desire to examine his invention any closer and that he was now thinking of selling it to the English or the French.

I replied that that did not seem a very patriotic thing to do and he readily agreed. "But," he added, "what am I to do? I am a poor schoolmaster and have a daughter who is a cripple and I need the money and I thought that you perhaps could help me, as I have heard of you from one of my pupils," and then I discovered that he was the famous Dr. Franciscus van den Ende, of whom I had heard a good deal, but whom so far I had never met.

This van den Ende was a curious citizen who lived in a sphere of mystery. He had come to Amsterdam during the early forties and had opened a book-store which had not done any too well and which a few years afterwards he had been forced to close for lack of cash and customers. He had then started a Latin school of his own and had revealed himself as one of the most competent teachers we had ever had in our city. He had a veritable genius for making irregular verbs palatable and in his hands, even the most refractory hexameters would behave with the docility of so many tame kittens. Within a very short time all the little boys of our best families were learning the fact that "all Gaul was divided into three parts" at the school of Monsieur van den Ende. For the doctor was a native of Antwerp and preferred that appellation to the more soberminded Dutch "Meester."

He knew of course that his neighbors were slightly curious about his antecedents. But before any inquiries could be made in his native town, he had told us all about himself and about the reasons that had caused him to move northward.

He had, so it then appeared, started life as a Jesuit, but had lost his faith and had been forced to flee for his life. The story of course appealed to us and it had given him an excellent standing with the Magistrates who prided themselves (and rightly) upon the fact that Amsterdam was the most tolerant and liberal community of the entire world. But now I discovered that van den Ende was something more than a good classical scholar. He also appeared to have devoted several years to medical studies and showed by a few casual remarks (in answer to a few equally casual questions on my part) that he understood his subject thoroughly. And so I told him to forget all about his ship's model which did not interest me anyway, as I was interested in saving people's lives and not in destroying them and took him down to the dining-room and invited him to partake of some refreshments for I have found that it always pays to be pleasant to a colleague, even if you never expect to see him again.

Thereupon we talked of many things—of the superior way of teaching as practiced by the Jesuit fathers, who shape the material in which they give instruction so as to suit the individual pupil, rather than making the pupil fit the material he is supposed to study (as we do in our country) and of several other subjects that were of interest to both of us, and then quite unexpectedly the Belgian said: "But of course I already know all about you and your views." And when I asked him how that was possible, as this was the first time I had had the pleasure of meeting him, he answered: "No, but I have a pupil who has a great admiration for you, a Portuguese Jew by the name of Benito d'Espinoza," and then I recalled that this was the man of whom young Baruch Spinoza had been talking to me and of whom he had said that as a school-master he was worth at least five dozen ordinary rabbis and Talmudic pedagogues.

I repeated this observation to van den Ende (where is the man of ability who does not like an occasional bit of flattery?) and he was much amused by it.

"A marvelous brain, that Portuguese has," he told me, "but they are going to have a lot of trouble with him," and the conversation once having taken this particular form, we quite naturally drifted into the discussion of a topic that was beginning to assume rather alarming proportions—the problem of the Jews who in ever-increasing numbers were flocking to our town. For just about a week before Doctor van den Ende called on me with his little ship, one of those absurd things had occurred that although utterly insignificant in and by itself might easily have led to bloodshed if the town militia that week had not been commanded by an officer who was not only a strict disciplinarian but who was also possessed of a sense of humor and a delicately trained taste for the grotesque.

The Jews in our town were not obliged to live in ghettos as they had always done in Spain and in Poland and in Germany. They were free to settle down wherever they pleased but out of force of habit they invariably flocked to the same neighborhood. But of course the Portuguese immigrants stuck closely to the Sephardic Synagogue and the Polish and German Jews remained within stone throw of the Ashkenazic temple.

They were both in my own part of the town and I often walked around the island of Vlooienburg or Fleaburg (as it was soon called by the people) and I was quite familiar with the habits and customs of these strangers who even now, after having been with us for almost a whole century, continued to address each other in the Portuguese and Yiddish tongues and who spoke our own language (which is supposed to be theirs) as if it were a foreign tongue not worthy of their attention. And so of course I knew all about the famous Doctor Alonzo ben Immanuele, commonly known as the Tongenkijker or Tongue-looker.

His real name was not Alonzo nor was he an Italian as he pretended to be, nor was he a direct descendant of the famous Jewish friend of Dante, as he claimed to be upon every possible occasion. He was the son of a Frankfort mohel and had studied to be a mohel himself until he fell in love with a Christian girl and in consequence thereof was disowned by his family. When he tried to communicate with the object of his affection, the parents of the girl had called the police who amidst the plaudits of the Frankfort mob had thrown him into the river Main (it was the month of January if you please) and when he had scrambled onto an icefloe they had shot at him with their guns.

They had missed him but he had left Germany for all time. Eventually he had taken service with a French surgeon who had gone to Bologna to study anatomy with Malpighi. Being an exceedingly clever boy he had picked up considerable medical information in the course of the two years he had spent at that famous Italian university, blacking his master's boots during the day-time and spending the midnight hours reading his text-books on materia medica. And when the Frenchman returned to Paris, il Signore Dottore Alonzo ben Immanuele continued his peregrinations northward until he reached the city built upon the humble bones of a million defunct herring, where he felt himself so completely at home that he decided to stay there the rest of his days. But as the town seemed already well provided with doctors and apothecaries, Moritz Schmultz (for that was his real name as I had the chance to find out) came to the conclusion that he must do something that would make him widely conspicuous if he did not want to die in the poorhouse.

Among his scanty baggage he carried a discarded doctorial robe of his former master. To this he added the sort of peaked cap the rabbis had been obliged to wear in former times and in this garb he now began to wander through the streets of Fleaburg announcing in a fine flow of Italian-Yiddish and German-Hebrew that he had discovered a new method of treating the sick. All they had to do to get cured was to show him their tongues from behind the window panes of their rooms. He would then make his diagnosis and send them the proper medicines. The consultation was free but a slight charge was made for the medicine to pay for the bottles and the corks and the labels, etc., etc.

The usual story and with the usual result. The man was soon rolling in money. Every morning at eight he would make his appearance on the famous island and would slowly proceed from the Amstel to the Uilenburgwal and back again.

He was accompanied by a coal black negro whom he passed off as an Arab and a direct descendant of Ishmael, the unfortunate son of Hagar, a fable which would have given grave offense to the Christian part of the population if they had ever heard it, but as soon as the Professor had crossed the bridge of the St. Anthonie locks and had entered the domain of the Goys, the honest blackamoor was re-baptized Sebaldus and became a Nubian slave who had been set free by Admiral de Ruyter during one of his campaigns against the Tunisian pirates and who had come to Amsterdam to receive instruction in the true faith according to the Heidelberg catechism.

It is hard to believe that this genial impostor had made such a deep impression upon the inhabitants of the Jewish quarter, that as soon as Sebaldus, alias Hagarson, had rung the big brass bell which he carried in his left hand (in his right hand he held the satchel which contained the doctor's nostrums) the windows of scores of houses would be opened and everywhere anxious mothers would appear with small children whom they would lift halfway out of the windows (upon one occasion a small boy was actually dropped into the street, but as he landed on a pile of rubbish, no great harm was done) and all those unfortunate infants would be obliged to stick out their tongues at the famous doctor who would contemplate that organ for a few minutes with a profound frown upon his face and would then whisper a few words in an ununderstandable vernacular (it was supposed to be Arabic) to his black-faced familiar who would thereupon rush into the house and leave a bottle of "Elixir Vitae Salamonialis" with the afflicted family in exchange for one guilder if it was for a boy and ten stivers if the patient happened to be a girl.

I once had an opportunity to examine two of such bottles, a male and a female one. As far as I could make out, they contained nothing more harmful than a mixture of water and Tamarindus Indica and were worth exactly two cents wholesale. But when I told the man who had bought them for seventy times that amount (a dreadfully poor butcher who never made more than three guilders a week) he waxed very angry and hinted that I was trying to kill my colleague's trade because I was envious of his success.

For there could be no doubt about it. The Tongenkijker was an enormous success. Not only professionally, but also socially. From far and near people were flocking to Amsterdam either to consult him or merely to see and enjoy the free show which he put up right in the heart of a highly dignified and respectable Christian city. Why the Magistrates never interfered with him, I don't know. But they either considered it beneath their dignity to take any notice of him or they believed (as many other governments had done before) that a bit of ridicule would be good for the souls of these obstinate heathen who so tenaciously clung to their self-imposed ghetto and therefore (unless it was a case of murder or rape) they usually left the Jewish quarter severely alone and told the police to do likewise.

But the Portuguese Jews, much better educated and infinitely more polished than their Polish and German neighbors, regarded this absurd comedy with profound abhorrence and did all they could to bring about the arrest of this saltimbanque and if possible his expulsion from the territory of the city of Amsterdam.

The Town Hall, however, remained deaf to all their petitions and supplications and in the end they took matters into their own hands and staged a regular riot during which the unfortunate Inspector of Tongues was almost drowned in the Amstel (he seemed to have a fatal tendency to get himself ducked) and in which several people would undoubtedly have been killed if it had not been for the tact of the officer of the guard, who had succeeded in restoring order without firing a single shot.

The affair, however, caused a good deal of discussion and no less alarm. For what was this world coming to when foreigners who had come to us in sack-cloth and ashes to find a refuge from foreign persecution could so far forget their duties towards their hosts as to stage a pitched battle right in the heart of the city of their habitation? And for no better cause than that they failed to approve or disapprove of a silly old man who ought to have been left to the mercies of the police?

The more enlightened among the Jews (regardless of the party to which they belonged by birth) tried to pacify Their Lordships of the Town Hall by promising that they would do all they could to prevent a repetition of such an unseemly outbreak. But the rabbis, especially those of the Ashkenazic fold, would not listen to any compromise and exhorted their followers to further violence. In the end it became necessary to have the entire Jewish quarter patrolled by armed guards, for more than six weeks, and the militia who were called upon to perform this extra duty felt very bitter about it and even talked of burning down the whole of the Fleaburg Island.

The plague, which had been very severe in Leyden the year before and which was beginning to make itself felt in Amsterdam with increasing severity, may have helped to quiet the mob. Dr. Alonzo ben Immanuele received a gentle hint to go and practice his beneficent arts elsewhere and peace and order were gradually restored but many people began to ask themselves what the end would be.

"Only a short while ago," so they reasoned, "those people came to us on their knees, begging us to give them shelter and protect them against their enemies, all of which we did. More than that, we allowed them to worship as they pleased, though their faith is anathema to most of our own citizens. Then they asked to be given permission to have butcher-stores of their own and to have a Sunday of their own and they insisted upon wearing a garb that was quite different from the clothes which we ourselves wore at the time and they continued to speak the Spanish or Portuguese or Polish or German tongues of the countries that were such cruel task-masters to them, so that there is hardly one among every hundred of these foreigners who can write an ordinary business note in Dutch. And now, after having shown in every possible way that they wish to keep themselves apart from the nation which has offered them a home, they are beginning to take the law into their own hands and they try to settle their private quarrels as if they owned the city and as if there were no magistrates whom God has placed over us that they might rule us all with diligence and wisdom, and that will never do!

"No, it will never do, and if they continue to behave in this fashion, they had better return to Lisbon and to Madrid and to Warsaw for while we don't particularly want them to say thank you to us for our kindness, neither do we care to have our community ruled by these upstarts who came here after we had purged the land of those enemies that were theirs as well as ours and who now want to reap the benefits which they did not help us sow and on top of that, try to tell us how we ought to run our own government."

There was a great deal of unreasonableness in this accusation for the vast majority, both of the Portuguese and German Jews, were almost fanatically grateful to those whom they invariably addressed as Their Saviors and they were not only loyal to the country at large but most generously inclined toward the particular city in which they happened to have settled down. Their rabbis, however, were an unruly lot and they bore a close resemblance to the clergymen of our own official church. As a rule they belonged to the lower classes of society and seeing little opportunity in following a business career, they chose the clerical profession because it promised to give them an outlet for their ambitions. But as no upstart can ever hope to rule without first discovering a "grievance" around which he can rally his followers, the rabbis, exactly like our own beloved dominies, were forever detecting dangerous issues which they thereupon attacked with the utmost violence and a complete disregard for the truth.

These were sad days for Menasseh, who spent almost every evening at the home of Rembrandt, presumably to talk of the illustrations for his forth-coming book, but in reality because he did not care to stay in his study, where at any moment he might be disturbed by the visit of one of his fellow rabbis. Poor Menasseh! His first great dream of finding the descendants of the Lost Tribes among the inhabitants of the New World had come to nothing. Next, in order to forget his miseries he had thrown himself upon the study of the Old Testament and he had done that with such fury that soon he had begun to hear mysterious voices and then one day he appeared among us boldly announcing that he had stumbled upon a hitherto unrevealed bit of prophecy that would set clear everything that had been dark thus far.

Being profoundly bored by that sort of hocus-pocus, I never quite understood what he was actually trying to prove. But it had something to do with Nebuchadnezzar or rather with Nebuchadnezzar's dream, which was supposed to be a prophecy of the coming of the Messiah, not the false Messiah whom we worshiped but the real Messiah who had not yet put in an appearance, et cetera, et cetera.

Next he got that Babylonian dream associated with the stone with which David slew Goliath and the stone which served Jacob for a pillow when he had his famous dream and it was all very muddled, but Menasseh himself was so full of his new idea that he persuaded Rembrandt (much against his will, I am afraid) to make a number of illustrations for the book which was to explain these mysteries to an unsuspecting and indifferent world.

The book was written in Spanish and not in Dutch and that may have been one of the reasons why Rembrandt never quite realized what he was doing and made such a bad job of the pictures. As he himself was beset by a thousand troubles during all this period, his friends hesitated to tell him just how bad these illustrations were. But the publisher of the Nebuchadnezzarian dream, being a business man and looking upon the venture from the angle of profit and loss, was inspired by no such delicate sentiments and simply threw the Rembrandt pictures out and had some ordinary hack do another set of plates which proved much more satisfactory from a popular point of view.

But when this happened, Menasseh himself was no longer among us. His Messianic premonition had left him no rest. He had missed meeting the Lost Tribes but he meant to be present when the great prophecies went unto fulfillment. His position in Amsterdam was no longer a very pleasant one. Doctor van den Ende had been right when he told me that young Espinoza would some day, very soon, be the cause of considerable difficulties among the Jews of our town and Menasseh was forced to agree with him. He was very dejected about it.

"Those Rabbis," he complained, "seem to have forgotten all we ever learned during our many years of suffering and persecution in foreign lands. Here we can enjoy a new and happy home of our own and they are all of them on the look-out for trouble. First it was d'Acosta, but he was not very bright and a little bit crazy. But this Espinoza boy has more brains than all of us put together. Instead of letting him go his own way, they are going to try and turn him into an errand-boy of the synagogue, a nice little fellow with a little brown coat on who goes around to all the people on Friday night to see that they clean their cupboards neatly and that they don't eat a chicken that has not had its head cut off in the right way. It is terrible!

"This Baruch, he is proud. He won't submit. He will fight back and the Christians will say, 'See those Jews, they are always the same. Quarreling again among themselves, as they did even in the days of Nebuchadnezzar.' And speaking of Nebuchadnezzar—did I ever tell you of his dream . . . ?"

And the poor man would be off again to tell you about his great discovery.

Poor honest soul! He left us soon afterwards and went to England where the Jews were once more being admitted for the first time I believe in four or five centuries. In London he fought valiantly and successfully for the good rights of his own people to be granted the right to live in the New Commonwealth. In the beginning he used to write to us—short letters in fluent Spanish and not such fluent Dutch. Then he complained that he was too busy to correspond, for the Lord Protector had granted him a pension and he was now able to devote all his time to the task of preparing the way for the coming of the Messiah, whose appearance might be expected at almost any moment. Then for a long time we had no news from him. But in the summer of the year 1657 I happened to be in Veere for a few days to see about the repair of the houses I had inherited from my grand-uncle and which were badly in need of new floors and stairs. One day, quite early in the morning, the Baptist minister from Middelburg was announced. He begged that he be excused for disturbing me at such an unseemly hour but in the hospital at Middelburg there was a sick man—he seemed to be a Jewish divine—who had asked after me and as it was known that I was in Veere at that moment, he had thought it his duty to warn me. I thanked him most cordially and together we walked back to Middelburg where we arrived at noon.

The sick man was Menasseh. He was suffering from a pulmonary ailment and was already unconscious when I reached his bed-side. I heard that he had arrived in Flushing two days before with the body of his son Samuel, who had died in England and whom he wanted to bury in Amsterdam. He had been sick when he reached Flushing and had fainted in the coach that carried him to the ferry to the next island. The coachman had therefore driven him to the God's House and the matron had warned one of the ministers that she had a patient who seemed on the point of dying. But when it appeared that the man was a Jew, and a Rabbi at that, there had been little enthusiasm on the part of the official clerics to attend him in his final hours.

The Baptist preacher having been informed of the good woman's predicament had then offered his services and having heard how the patient in his feverish wanderings had repeatedly mentioned my name, he had taken the trouble to come all the way to Veere and warn me.

Together we watched over the patient and when evening came, he had a moment of consciousness. He recognized me. He smiled and whispered: "I love all my good friends in Amsterdam. Tell them so. And tell them to be prepared. The hour is at hand. The Messiah will come. Surely he will come!"

And thus Menasseh had died at peace with all the world and two days later we had buried him, together with his son Samuel, and this had been the end of a good and righteous man and a true friend whom we could badly spare at the very moment when the little group of people who fought for a more intelligent and charitable world was so dreadfully in need of his patience and his humor and the satisfaction one derived from his oft-repeated meditation:

"Ja, am Ende, wenn wir nur wirklich wüssten—if only we knew—if only we knew!"

Chapter 61

MY SON BEGINS THE EDUCATION OF HIS FATHER

Meanwhile little Titus, Rembrandt's son, had grown up to be a boy of almost fifteen and my own offspring was also approaching that age when a father looks at his perambulating resemblance and asks himself: "What in the name of high Heaven am I going to do with that boy?"

Titus, I am sorry to say, was causing Rembrandt more worry than my own boy was causing me. In the first place, he was not at all robust. He had inherited his father's face but his mother's delicacy of nature—her beautiful hands—her slender bones but also her weak lungs, and general lack of resistance. Really, it was too bad. If only it had been the other way around! If he had inherited his father's frame, who had the physique of a cart-horse, but the face of a good, honest, hard-working blacksmith or carpenter, which lacked all the charm and vivaciousness that had belonged to his aristocratic wife.

Jean-Louys and I had often speculated whether on the whole it was better for one to have started out with good blood or with a good education and how much education could do for one who had been born under humble circumstances and whether one who was born of good blood could ever quite belie his origin. And we had both come to the conclusion that there were so many exceptions to whatever rules we felt tempted to establish that we had better drop the subject as beyond our power of solution.

In the course of these discussions, Jean-Louys had hit upon a very clever new definition of "education," as different from mere "ability," by laying down the rule that "ability" allowed one to get along without "education," whereas "education" allowed one to get along without "ability." But when I suddenly asked him, "Yes, but what has that got to do with the subject of which we were talking?" he had answered, "Nothing at all, but it is past two o'clock of the night and then one is no longer supposed to talk sense," and so we had gone to bed and the matter never had been decided, which was a pity, for in the case of little Titus I felt that I was face to face with a problem which I for one would have great difficulty in unraveling. The poor lad seemed to have inherited from both parents exactly those qualities which were bound to be of absolutely no help to him in making his way. His handsome looks were of very little use to him, because he was a boy, and the talent for painting which he undoubtedly possessed, was so slight and insignificant as to be almost negligible.

He gave one the impression of an amiable and rather tender boy with excellent manners (the work of Hendrickje, though where she had learned them herself I never was able to fathom) and the best of intentions but without any force or stamina. I asked his father what he intended to do with him afterwards and Rembrandt, in that vague way in which he dismissed all subjects that had not some direct bearing upon his work, answered:

"Oh, I suppose he will become an artist."

And when I continued: "But how will he live?" he said:

"Oh, well, I suppose he will live somehow or other."

And he peacefully continued with the portrait of Jan Lutma, the goldsmith, on which he had been working for quite a long time, and which needed a general overhauling.

But how was that poor innocent and rather incompetent child ever to survive in a world that had been turned completely upside down by the war?

His father had had a difficult time making both ends meet, but he at least had worked in a normal world. The peace of Westminster, however, had destroyed all the old values. Even a great many of those rich merchants who ruled our towns and our country for so long and who seemed so firmly entrenched that nothing could possibly happen to them, even they had suffered reverses from which they were never able to recover and were forced to go back to a much simpler way of living than that to which they had been accustomed for three or four generations. And among those just a trifle below them on the social ladder there was hardly a person who in one way or another had not felt the influence of that great upheaval. Either their ships had been destroyed by the English or they had speculated in wood or gunpowder when they should have concentrated all their forces upon cornering the market in hemp and meanwhile other younger or more ambitious and perhaps a little less conservative and undoubtedly much less scrupulous firms had grabbed all the right profits at the right moment and had made millions. They were now buying up the town houses and country houses of those who had guessed wrong, and they were buying themselves noble carriages and an occasional coat-of-arms to put upon the doors of those vehicles. But their taste in furniture and art and music was as bad as the manners they displayed both in public and in private and the pictures they bought came almost exclusively from Antwerp and Paris where regular picture-factories were now working for "le goût Hollandais."

How mild little Titus, with his mild little portraits (they were a very weak and therefore bad reflection of those of his father) would ever be able to sell one of his works to the barbarians of the new era of prosperity was something I could not quite see. But the boy was still very young and might decide to do something different when he reached the age of discretion.

As for my own son, he never caused me any trouble. He seemed to have inherited absolutely nothing from anybody, neither from his mother nor me, nor for that matter from his grandfather or grandmother. Instead, he jumped right back to his great-grandfather, my own beloved grandfather, and I rejoiced in this biological miracle. For nothing could have been more to my taste than to see all those qualities of independence and enthusiasm and efficiency return in that flesh and blood that was so very much my own.

The youngster had absolutely no interest in the work that had occupied me ever since the days of my childhood. He was very nice to sick people and in a mild and non-committal way he felt rather sorry for them too. But he did not like them. He was too sound himself to have much sympathy for those who were suffering from some ailment. Nor did his grandsire's characteristics manifest themselves in a tendency toward things military. He told me once that he would not mind fighting but that it seemed a silly thing to do. It was too destructive—too aimless to suit practical taste. He wanted to make things. And he wanted to make them not only with his brains but also with his hands, for he had fingers that were as strong as steel nippers and he liked to use them. And from childhood on (so I was told, for during the first ten years of his life I had been in America) he had been busy with windmills and toy-carriages and miniature dredges. But when I returned from Nieuw Amsterdam he was no longer pottering around with tiny little mills made out of packing cases and pieces of sail which he had begged or stolen at the water front (a proceeding which seems to have shocked his faithful nurse more than anything else he ever did during a somewhat obstinate and turbulent career) but he had graduated from such futile pastimes and was beginning to revaluate his practical engineering experiments into terms of certain abstract mathematical formulae—formulae which meant nothing at all to me but which he explained to me as representing wind-velocities and the friction of wood upon wood and of stone upon stone and other intricate details of that mechanical world that will forever remain closed to me.

Where exactly he had learned all this I was never able to find out. I had first sent him to a school which was famous for the excellence of its Latin and Greek teaching. But there he was a complete failure. He went to sleep over his syntax and his copybooks contained diagrams of new hoisting devices instead of those terrible Greek verbs, the knowledge of which was considered an indispensable part of a gentleman's education. But whenever I tried to make this clear to him, he merely looked pained and bored and upon one memorable occasion informed me that I was talking through my hat (he used an even less complimentary expression which I must refuse to repeat here)—that he had no desire to be a gentleman if I meant by this that he would be allowed to spend five years at some university drinking gin and running after the servant girls of the town and generally misbehaving himself in those ways that were then considered highly fashionable among the young men of leisure who deigned to patronize those institutions of erudition and that anyway, he could learn more from ten minutes' talk with the owner of the "Cow" (a well known mill just outside the Saint Anthonie gate, where he was in the habit of spending a great many of those hours he should have been at his desk at school) than from four entire years aimlessly pawing the dreary pages of a Greek grammar.

I then spoke of the beauties of ancient poetry and he quietly looked at me and said: "But, father, have you ever heard the regular swish-swish of a mill that is running full speed? Could anything be more wonderful or more beautiful than that?"

I then began to discover for myself what must have been clear even to Adam, who certainly was no shining beacon of intelligence. (What a pity that our earliest ancestor should have been such a terrible bungler! Just suppose that he had been a bright fellow like Jacob or Joseph! Ten to one he would have beaten Jehovah at his own silly apple game, but it is too late now to waste vain regrets upon such a hopeless case of stupidity.) I was beginning to understand that we can't teach our children anything at all. We can expose them to education in the hope that they will catch some of it. But just how much or how little they catch of it depends upon certain mysterious elements in their make-up, the exact nature of which will probably remain hidden to us for all time.

But I know this much, that if a boy has a definite "tendency" toward certain subjects of learning, he will "catch" those subjects, in spite of every obstacle. But if on the other hand he has no such "tendency" he remains what we physicians call "immune" and we can expose him as much as we like, but he will never succeed in making that subject an integral part of his mental equipment.

I was not always as sane upon the subject as I am now after my son has been trying to educate me in this direction for almost twenty odd years. But on the whole I am happy to say I suspected the existence of this pedagogic axiom long before I had been able to prove it and as a result the boy has never given me any trouble and I have given him as little trouble as was possible, considering that I was his father and therefore more or less his natural-born enemy.

Poor Rembrandt! I was sorry for him when on Sundays, as sometimes happened, we took our boys out for a walk. Little Titus was usually bored, would want to go back home and color his pictures or look at a book. After half an hour he would complain that he was tired. After an hour he would sit down and weep for he really was not strong and got exhausted very easily.

Meanwhile my own young barbarian would occupy himself with some mechanical contrivance he had put together during the previous week—would try it out on the waters of the Amstel where the winds blew ever fresh, would talk of the day when mills would not only pump water and grind flour and saw wood but would also peel rice and make oil and perform Heaven only knows what other miracles.

Then Titus would look at him and would say, "I hate mills. They are ugly. They make such a noise."

And the answer would be: "Pooh! Ugly! They are useful. Useful things are never ugly."

As for Rembrandt, he would listen to this childish conversation, but it never seemed to penetrate to him what they were saying.

"They are young," he used to comment, once in a while. "They will grow out of it, both of them."

But there I had my doubts.

Does any one ever really "grow out" of something that was put into him even before the day of his birth?

Chapter 62

WE BUILD A NEW TOWN HALL AND REMBRANDT ALMOST PAINTS A PICTURE FOR IT

During the fall of the year '55 it became more and more clear that the situation in the northern part of Europe must soon lead to a crisis. Our Baltic granaries were in danger and without those supplies, half of our people would have starved to death.

I don't think that there were a hundred burghers in the entire Republic who cared a straw for the Poles, either as a nation or as individuals, while our relations with the Swedes had always been most cordial and furthermore the Poles were Catholics of a most pronounced and bigoted sort and the Swedes belonged to our own church, although they took to Lutheranism, rather than to Calvinism. Nevertheless, when it was seen to be a question of guilders and stivers, all personal considerations were curtly set aside and as soon as Danzig had been taken by the forces of King Charles, a squadron of our ships was sent to that town—it was recaptured and was given back to the Polish king.

The situation was not entirely clear. Even after this event we were still supposed to be at peace with the Swedes and My Lord de Witt strongly urged a union between the two great Scandanavian powers, Sweden and Denmark, with the Republic of the United Netherlands as the "honest broker" keeping the peace between the two rivals and preventing them from flying at each other's throats.

But this plan failed as ignominiously as his project for that English-Dutch treaty which he had explained to me upon the occasion of our memorable interview. In both instances it was the town of Amsterdam that rudely upset his calculations. The great pensionary was a "party man." He firmly believed in government by the "best people" and the "best people" of course were his own relations and their friends, the rich merchants of our big cities. But he was a man of such brilliant parts that, almost against his own will, he was sometimes obliged to look beyond the immediate interests of his party. Whereas Their Lordships, who ruled us from the big new building on the Dam, believed the world to end at the city boundaries and invariably put their own profits ahead of those of the country as a whole. They were wise and sagacious magistrates and I hasten to add that as a rule their policies coincided with those that were considered most favorable for the Republic as a whole. Nevertheless, it was a very unfortunate system of government, for it allowed a single community to override the clearly expressed will of all of its neighbors.

But it had been that way ever since the beginning of our independence and I suppose it will continue to be that way until the end, for I don't know of any man or party powerful enough to change it unless one of the princes of the House of Orange succeeds in making himself our king, something which seems hardly likely at the present moment when the only surviving member of that family (with the exception of a few negligible cousins in the northern part of the country) is a young boy who suffers dreadfully from headaches and who does not seem predestined to live very long.

In this particular instance it fortunately was proved that Amsterdam had chosen the wiser course. Since the death of my old friends, the Bickers, the affairs of the town were managed by a member of the van Beuningen family. The first half century of our independence offered wonderful opportunities to young men. Jan de Witt was only twenty-eight when he was appointed to the highest office in the state. And Conrad van Beuningen, at the age of thirty-three, had more power than many of the dictators of ancient Greece about whom we read in our history books. He belonged to a family that was greatly interested not only in the Baltic grain trade but also in the spice trade of the Indies and he was supremely endowed both by nature and by years of serious study for the rôle he was to play during the next twenty years. He was good looking and he could speak well in public—an accomplishment which I am sorry to say has been sadly neglected in our community, since we are rather apt to frown upon every form of rhetorical elegance except that extraordinary variety which is practiced in the pulpit.

But His Lordship was not given much to sermonizing. As a matter of fact, he was a person of very liberal ideas and it was said (though no one could offer any definite evidence) that he preferred the wisdom of Seneca and Marc Aurelius to that of Calvin and Knox. But as he was enormously rich, such accusations were never uttered beyond a whisper and it is only in recent years, when it seems that he is afflicted with the family curse of insanity, that people are beginning to speak out a little more openly about his heretical tendencies.

But in the year 1656 of which I am writing at the present moment, no one in his senses would have even dared to hint at such a possibility. And His Lordship could devote all his time and all of his tremendous energy toward a realization of those plans which should turn the Baltic into another Zuyder Zee, into a lake that should be dominated by Dutch interests. His friend, the Pensionary in The Hague, agreed with the views of Amsterdam in a general way but was inclined to proceed a little more cautiously. He had had more to do with navies than van Beuningen and knew how precarious a thing even a well-equipped fleet remains even under the most favorable circumstances and how little one can depend upon it in time of need. A sudden storm or an unexpected fog and victory may suddenly be turned into defeat. Besides, ships cannot be constructed over night. It takes fourteen months to build one of those gigantic modern men-of-war which measure six or seven hundred tons, but one unfortunate hit in the powder-magazine will send them to the bottom of the ocean in less than a minute's time.

Therefore while the Pensionary was just as anxious as the Burgomasters of Amsterdam to bridle the ambitions of the Swedish monarch and keep the old Baltic granaries open for the Dutch trade, he felt less inclined to risk the whole of the navy upon this one venture.

"How about England?" he asked his friend in Amsterdam. "Suppose that the Lord Protector avails himself of the opportunity which is offered by the absence of our ships in the north to stage a landing on the Dutch coast. What will happen then?"

Those of Amsterdam answered him that since the Republic was at peace with England and even had concluded a treaty of amity with that country, we need have no fears from that angle.

"What are official documents between nations?" the Pensionary replied. "Since when has a piece of paper prevented a people from attacking another when it seemed to their own interests to do so?"

And he cited a large number of instances in which empires and kingdoms and republics had treated the most sacred treaties as mere scraps of paper because it was to their advantage to do so. But Amsterdam refused to give in and since our town paid most of the taxes of the province of Holland and since Holland alone paid almost half of all the taxes of the entire Republic, Amsterdam had its own way and for five entire years our navy was kept busy in the north.

During this campaign some of the measures which I had been permitted to suggest were tried in practice and on the whole I am grateful to say my fellow practitioners on board approved of them and gave me their hearty coöperation. I myself was present at the encounter in the Sound when the Swedes under Wrangel were defeated, although it cost us the life of one of our ablest commanders, the famous Witte de With, who was a wild-man-of-the-sea, who could swear almost as well as he could fight, and who had hacked his way through so many naval engagements that he seemed to be possessed of a charmed life. On this occasion the tide carried his vessel on a bank, but he turned it quickly into a castle and defended himself until almost all his men were dead and he himself lay dying, causing so much admiration by his conduct, even among his enemies, that the next day they sent us his corpse with full military honors.

I arrived just too late to be with de Ruyter when he bombarded Nyborg and entered Copenhagen. I was allowed, however, to visit that town during the winter our admiral spent there and found it of very pleasing aspect, reminding me in many ways of our own city of Amsterdam, though it struck me that the people were a great deal gayer than our own and much less inclined to rowdyism.

I found it hard to account for this difference in outward behavior of the two nations. I have heard it claimed that the bad weather of our low land, the eternal fog and rain in which we are obliged to dwell from the day we are placed in a damp cradle until the hour we are lowered into a water-soaked grave, is at the bottom of our depressed mood and depressing ways. But surely nothing could be viler than the climate of the Danish capital which like my own town of Veere resembles a pancake afloat on a sea of mud. So it can't be that.

Others have told me that: "It is the difference in religion. These people are Lutherans, whereas we are Calvinists."

I am willing to grant that I would rather have gone fishing with the Wittenberg reformer than with his Genevan colleague, but what I saw here of the Lutheran ministers did not exactly give me an impression of levity of spirit. Indeed, I found them to be very much like our own dominies—perhaps a trifle more human but not very much, and just as eager to force their own views upon the rest of the world as the best or worst of our Amsterdam clerics. The most likely solution was given me by a young man who was one of the aides of Admiral van Wassenaar.

The latter, a very rich man and lord of the village of Obdam, an hereditary member of the Estates of Holland and the owner of a vast country place near The Hague, had begun life as the colonel of a regiment of cavalry. But during the recent English war, he suddenly had been ordered to take command of the fleet and he had stepped on board his first vessel as ignorant of naval strategy as a baby is of playing the harpsichord.

He owed his sudden rise in the world to the fact that he was a staunch supporter of the party that opposed the House of Orange, whereas de Ruyter and Tromp and Evertsen and all the others were suspected of leanings toward the little Prince. However that may be, the admiral-on-horseback had proved himself a very able man and a person of tact who had gained the respect and affection of his subordinates by his pleasant manner and his willingness to listen to their advice.

At the time I was summoned to his flag-ship he was suffering badly from podagra. A draughty ship's cabin was no ideal place of residence for a man thus afflicted, but he bore his pains with great fortitude and spent most of his time playing backgammon with his aide, who had developed a technique of losing that was truly admirable. This young man, the son of a Frisian nobleman and a French mother, but who vowed that he would never again set foot in that part of the world where a square foot of air weighed ten million Flemish pounds, was an amateur student of politics of no mean ability and he had developed a social theory which greatly amused me, although I soon realized that in most of what he said, the wish was father to the thought.

"The trouble with our country," he used to say while we paced up and down the deck, waiting for the Admiral, who was a handsome man but rather vain and very particular about his outward appearance, to finish his toilet, "the trouble with our land is the lack of standards which is due to the lack of a court. In some ways that is our strength, but in many other ways, it is one of our great weaknesses. It is true we can't just suddenly be lifted out of our beds and taken to a dungeon in some prison, as happened to the husband of one of my mother's cousins. It took the greater part of a year to discover where he was kept and next it took the combined efforts of the Estates of Holland and Friesland and five personal letters of the Grand Pensionary to get him out again. He had, so it appeared, laughed a little too loudly when one of the Mazarin girls was murdering the King's French a little more atrociously than usual. The Cardinal had observed that smile and His Majesty had obliged his faithful servant with a little slip of parchment, beginning, 'de par le Roi.'

"Good! I grant you that sort of thing is quite impossible here, and we will put that on the debit side. We have no sovereigns by the grace of God. As a result, we have fewer priests and not quite so many scaffolds. Whatever violence is committed is the work of the riffraff that has been preached into a frenzy of destructive holiness by the gentlemen of the cloth, but it is not the result of a sleepless night or indigestion on the part of one of the Lord's anointed.

"But now take the credit side. We are a circle without a center. As a result, politically speaking, we wobble, and socially speaking we are nowhere at all. We are supposed to be 'a country.' The poor innocents in Paris or London are still under the misapprehension that we are 'a country.' The day they discover that we are nothing of the sort, but merely an aggregation of squabbling, squealing, fighting, quarreling little provinces and cities and hamlets, each one with the pretention of being the equal of the grand duchy of Muscovy, they will fall upon us and divide us among themselves, as Philip of Macedonia fell upon the so-called independent democracies of ancient Greece and took away their liberty.

"Being a race of merry pirates, the inhabitants of our seacoast, who are devils when it comes to discipline, but perfect angels when there is any fighting to be done, may be able to hold out a little longer than if we were some inland state like that curious kingdom of Poland where I spent six whole months or one hundred and eighty-five days this spring and where every truckman and stevedore is a count or duke in his own right and has the power to veto any law he does not like.

"But I was telling you what is wrong with our social system. Well, we have no rallying-point—we are without any standards whatsoever. Standards of conduct and standards of beauty and standards of customs or manners may not be necessary for such a genius as that painter friend of yours of whom you have told me so much, and who lives with his cook and has children by her and quietly goes on painting, but most of us are no geniuses, and without standards we are lost, like ships at sea without a compass.

"As a very young man I went to London and I was there again as a sort of secretary during the negotiations at Westminster. The difference between the London of the Stuarts and the London of the Roundheads was incredible. I was very young when His late Majesty was still possessed of his head, and when one is very young, everything looks fine. But the people still had manners—they still had a code which told them what to do under all occasions and it made the whole social machinery run smoothly and evenly and quite pleasantly for all concerned.

"But two years ago—Heavens above! what a difference! One heard the social machine creak and groan. Each one of the men and women one met in the streets seemed to have worked out some little system of behavior of his or her own, and as not two of these systems were alike, the result meant continual friction—a chaos of conflicting interests which made me feel as if I were being entertained by my uncle of Witmarsum, who is famous for his dog-kennels and whose chief pastime in life is to invite his friends and relatives to be present when the brutes are being fed.

"We had a few audiences with the Lord Protector and I have never met a more charming or a more urbane man in all my days. But then, he was a landed nobleman of the old school and had been brought up under the monarchy.

"But take France or Italy, for I believe you told me that you had been there once. In each one of those countries there is a court with a king and that court is the bureau of standards for everything that has to do with a civilized existence. His Majesty decides that he must no longer dive into his goulash with his fingers, but use a fork, and the whole country, or at least that part of it that wants to be considered civilized (and the rest does not matter), hastens to go to the silversmith's shop and order a couple of forks for every member of their respective families.

"Or His Majesty wants to build himself a new palace. He knows nothing about bricks and mortar himself and therefore he sends for the best architects in the land and says: 'Messieurs, go to it.' I don't mean to say that you and I will invariably agree that they are the best architects according to our own tastes, but never mind, they are bound to be among the best, otherwise they would not have got the job.

"Or His Majesty becomes enamored of a beautiful damozel and wants to honor her by such a feast as this world has never seen. He sends for the best fiddlers and the best dancing masters and says: 'Gentlemen, it is up to you to show us what you can do and please don't disappoint us, for our royal displeasure would be fatal to your reputation.' Do they work their poor brains overtime to please His Majesty? I assure you they do. And their music and their plays set a standard for all others.

"Or again His Majesty wants to enliven the dull walls of his castle. He asks who are considered the best painters within his realm and tells them to get out their palettes and their brushes and give him what is the best. I repeat, this 'best' may not be the 'best' according to your taste or according to my individual taste, because we happen to be people of profound discrimination, but at least it is a sort of norm for those hordes of patient subjects who have no more idea of taste than my dog Nero has of how to catch storks.

"And the result is a pleasant average of behavior and of comedies and tragedies and paintings and sculpture and of cookery and dancing and love-making.

"In our Republic we have a few people who are far above that average, for we are a nation that is by no means devoid of ability and talent—I might even say genius. But our 'average' is bad. We really have no average. We have whatever it pleases every man and every woman (and sometimes every child) in every street of every town and village to give us. It is good enough for them. It suits their needs. We don't like it? Very well, we know what we can do about it! And so while we have worked ourselves up to the rank of a God-fearing, prosperous and highly respectable nation, we have in everything that does not pertain to our fear of God, our prosperity or our incredible respectability, remained what we were four hundred years ago when my ancestors killed your ancestors with pitchforks and bludgeons. We have remained a rowdy mob of self-embarrassed and clumsy yokels who either giggle or moan and as a rule giggle when they ought to be moaning and moan when they ought to be laughing. . . ."

But at that moment the Admiral had finished his toilet and sent for me and I never quite heard the end of this diverting speech. But I think that I know what young Aitzema had meant. Denmark was a country dominated by a single big town and that town, ever since it had been founded, six hundred years before, had been a royal residence and school of manners which was attended by pupils from all over the land. Whereas we at home had been left to our own devices—every man for himself and the Devil take the hindmost! Which the Devil had not failed to do, as I discovered the moment I returned to Amsterdam.

For the last eight years we had been building a new Town Hall. As soon as the Peace of Westphalia had been signed and our independence had been recognized, Jacob van Campen had been ordered to draw up plans for a new civic center. The old Town Hall was considered a little too shabby for a city of quite such magnificence as ours. Besides, the building had grown much too small and no one felt very sorry when it burned down during that memorable Saturday night in July of '52 when a cousin of Rembrandt's friend, Burgomaster Six, saved the books of the city bank and gained the everlasting devotion of the grateful depositors.

For eight long years one part of the Dam, right behind the ruins of the old Town Hall, had been hidden from our view by a high wooden fence. Meanwhile we had heard stories of the wonderful things that were going on behind that fence, which by then had become an excellent advertisement for the thoroughness of our public school system, as the usual dirty words were written as low as a foot from the ground, showing that even the youngest of our children were able to write and spell correctly.

Every citizen knew exactly how many Norwegian pines had been sunk into the ground to give this building the necessary stability. (I was the only exception, having no brain for figures, but the number ran somewhere between twelve and fourteen thousand, which made a forest of respectable dimensions.) And every citizen knew the width of the basement and the height of the towers had been carefully recounted, together with the number of rooms (including, as I remember, three different and separate jails) and the number of chimneys and the water reservoirs on the top floor which were to protect the building against fire.

But what had interested us most of all had been the plans for the interior decorating of all these many stately mansions that were to be occupied by Their Lordships the Burgomasters and by the high court of justice and by the aldermen and sheriffs and by the tax-gatherers and by all the many other dignitaries that made up what we were pleased to call our "magistrates." There would be need of a great many pictures and who was better fitted for such a task than Rembrandt? He had shown them that he could handle the most complicated subjects in a superb way and that size and shape of the canvas meant nothing to him provided he were really interested in the subject. Accordingly ever since I returned from America I had made it a point to speak to every one who possibly might have some influence with the authorities to say a good word for the man who was the ideal candidate for this very important task. And many of those whom I approached had answered, "Yes, that is a good idea. A very good idea. He is the fellow who painted that large picture that now hangs in the Doelen?" And without exception they had promised that they would do their best to give my friend at least a few of the orders that were to be placed among the local painters.

But when I happened to meet them again, they were always full of excuses. "Yes, they had mentioned his name to His Lordship, the first Burgomaster, the last time they saw him." Or again, "The big reception room which is a hundred by a hundred and twenty feet is just the sort of room that man Rembrandt ought to do, but the roof was not quite ready yet and therefore it was impossible to judge of the light effects and until the roof should have been finished, it would be impossible to make a decision."

Meanwhile I learned that Bol and Flinck and Jan Lievens and several others were busy in their studios on portraits and allegorical works that were to find a place in the new edifice, while Jan Bronchorst was about to submit elaborate plans for the ceilings of the new court room.

The public at large did not take a great deal of interest in this whole matter. As long as Their Lordships had thought fit to place their orders with such and such painters, well, why talk about it? Their Lordships undoubtedly knew what they wanted and Their Lordships undoubtedly knew best.

When it became known that practically all the necessary bits of sculpture had been commissioned to a certain Aert Quellin, who was a native of Antwerp, a voice was heard here and there asking whether we had no artists of our own who could do that sort of work just as well as a foreigner, but since it was conceded by every one who laid claim to a genteel taste that the Belgian painters were far superior to our own—much less coarse in their subjects and infinitely more refined in their treatment of the nude (and as furthermore Quellin happened to be one of the ablest sculptors of our time), these murmurings were never taken very seriously, and on the whole the populace approved most heartily of the choice of their rulers.

I knew both Flinck and Bol from the days they had been Rembrandt's pupils and I went to see them. They were quite loyal to their former teacher and wished that they could be of assistance to him. But both of them agreed that it would be suicidal for them if they should try to agitate on his behalf in any way that might be constructed as a personal interference with the plans of Their Lordships.

"Even now," Bol told me frankly, "we may at any moment be replaced by some Fleming who paints more in the Rubens manner than we do. Rubens is the great man here. He and Jordaens are our heroes. Rembrandt? Why, he is either too dark or too muddy or too something to please our public. Both Flinck and I and practically all the men that studied with our old master have been obliged to change our technique, become a little more Flemish, a little more Rubenesque—if you understand me—to keep our customers. If we had not done that, we would now be starving to death. If you don't believe me, go to any of the art-dealers and ask them whether they will take a chance on Rembrandt. Yes, here and there a man who sells to the Italian trade. Perhaps because there is so much sunshine in Italy that they can stand something a little dull better than we. But the others? They won't touch him. They won't come near him. And if we went to Their Lordships and suggested the name of Rembrandt, they would show us the door, and ask us to mind our own business, which consists in being just as Flemish as we can be."

I knew that they were right, but refused to give up. The next time I was in The Hague, I mentioned the subject to My Lord de Witt.

"I don't know much about such matters," he confessed, "and the Lord have mercy on my soul if it ever should become known that I had dared to make a suggestion concerning anything that had to do with the purely domestic affairs of that very independent city. If it should be rumored that I was in favor of yellow curtains, Their Lordships would at once order every curtain in the whole place to be dyed a bright green. No, I dare not interfere in any way, but I will give you a letter to my uncle. He is a man of sense and a man of taste and not without influence in his own country."

This was expressing it very mildly, for every one knew that nothing could be accomplished in Amsterdam without the silent approbation of the famous Lord of Polsbroek.

This title was one which he had acquired in later life by buying himself the seigneurial rights to the village of Polsbroek. Why he did this, I do not know, for as simple Cornelis de Graef he was known far and wide as the uncrowned king of Amsterdam and as one of the strongest men in the Republic. He was not really an uncle of My Lord Jan but of his wife, the former Wendela Bicker. That, however, made little difference. If the two men had not been related at all, they would have appreciated each other just as genuinely. For they both were far above the average in intelligence and integrity and as neither of them coveted outward glory, or dignity (having enough of the latter not to be obliged to worry about the former) there was no danger of their ever getting into conflict about mere matters of policy.

Whether My Lord of Polsbroek was as staunch a party man as his famous nephew or had secret leanings towards the House of Orange, no one was ever able to discover. He never quite gave himself away, being perhaps too much of a philosopher to make a good politician. It was his business to see that Amsterdam remained the most prosperous city of the old continent and for that reason he wished to remain on cordial terms with the government of the Republic as represented by the Estates General who met in The Hague. His nephew by marriage happened to be the most influential person in the Estates General. It really was a most perfect arrangement. The uncle acted as general adviser to the nephew, while the nephew kept the uncle informed about everything that happened in his corner of the woods. From such partnership great things are born and as long as both men lived, the country enjoyed such affluence and such uninterrupted good fortune that the period of their coöperation will probably go down into history as the Golden Age of our Republic.

But in the matter of art, I found His Lordship was about as helpless as his nephew had pretended to be.

I found him in his house on the Heerengracht to which the family had moved when they ceased to be cloth-dealers and were promoted to the rank of merchant-princes. But nothing could have been more delightful or cordial than his reception. Like all men of big affairs, he seemed to have plenty of time for everything and bade me be seated and at once spoke most sympathetically about the loss I had suffered.

"An outrage," he said, "a perfect outrage and absolutely inexcusable.

But what will you? The rabble needs a victim once in a while. I am sorry that this time the popular lightning (which is about as reasonable as that of the great god Zeus) has struck one for whom I feel such sincere personal regard. And you shall have full redress. You shall receive full compensation for everything you lost. Unfortunately such things proceed rather slowly. That is one of the most regrettable sides of our form of government. If we lived under a monarchy, such a wrong could be settled in one quarter of the time it takes to do such a thing here. One royal signature and the difficulty would be out of the way. Also if the royal signature for some reason were not granted, you would never see a cent of your money, and your children and grandchildren could die in the almshouse and His Majesty would not care. Here, under our system of government, you are at least reasonably certain that part of the funds will be in your hands before you die and that your son will get the rest. I wonder why governments always work so slowly? But an official exchequer is like those ingenious bow-nets with which in the days of my youth, I used to catch eels. Everything can go in, but nothing can ever go out. However, in what way can I hope to be of service to you to-day?"

I told him. He threw his hands up in a gesture of despair.

"Ask me something else," he said. "Ask me something easy like declaring war upon the Emperor or making the East India Company publish a true account of their last year's budget. Ask me to have you appointed ambassador-in-extraordinary to the court of the Great Khan. Ask me to have the Amstel diverted into the North Sea instead of the Zuyder Zee. But don't ask me to risk my position and my prestige in a matter of this sort."

I looked at him and was dumbfounded. Here was My Lord of Polsbroek, without whose permission (as the people used to say) it could not even rain in Amsterdam, confessing to me, a poor leech, that he could not order a few pictures for his new Town Hall from the greatest painter alive and for what reason—for what reason on earth? I asked him. I asked him humbly and politely, but nevertheless I asked him. What considerations of a political nature could oblige him to give me such a disappointing answer?

"What considerations of a political nature?" he burst forth. "Politics be damned. I will appoint any man to any place I please as long as it is a matter of politics, but that is just it! This is not a matter of politics. This is a matter of religion—of theology—of the one thing I have vowed I would keep clear of, all the rest of my live-long days."

"But surely," I answered, "Your Lordship need not ask Rembrandt to paint an allegorical picture that could possibly shock the pious. He is most excellent at portraits. You must need a great many portraits for the new Town Hall. Allegorical pictures never were his strong point anyway."

"My dear Doctor," he said, and looked at me the way I had noticed other people look before, when I had asked a particularly foolish question, "don't you see how it is? You may think that we are almighty at the Town Hall, that we can do as we please. We can to a certain extent but we have to proceed very carefully. After all, there are window-panes in our houses and it costs a lot to replace them. The clergy still has a hold upon the masses that we philosophers are a little too apt to overlook. And numbers count, especially in a city like this that has no court and therefore no life-guards. Some of our colleagues know this and make use of it to excellent purpose. I have one in mind, a certain Valckenier. His father made a lot of money in the East India Company. He is one of the most unpleasant people I have ever met and he has a temper that is as nasty as the bite of a sturgeon. But he is intelligent and he has a terrific amount of ambition. He wants to succeed van Beuningen if that poor man should ever be shipwrecked on one of his endless voyages. He has not a friend among the members of the city council. But he needs a party—some one to back him up. We watched him turn pious almost overnight. He has not one single quality of a true Christian and is a hateful and spiteful man. But every Sunday—three times every Sunday—you can see him in his pew in the new church.

"The 'small people' worship him as one of their own. What would he say, or rather, what would he not say, if I suggested to give a commission for an official portrait to a man who lives in open sin with his maidservant? He would drop a hint and the dominies would pound their pulpits and would start their usual fulminations against the new Sodom and would preach sermons about the whore of Babylon and it might end in bloodshed.

"And now I don't even consider the possibility of his finding out that you, of all people, suggested this to me. You—a mere surgeon who tried to cheat Jehovah out of his allotted measure of pain—you, an iconoclast who tried to set woman free from one of her most disastrous burdens. Why, we would have to turn the whole city into an armed camp if I so much as suggested the name of this man van Rijn for a single piece of work.

"Ask me some other favor and it is granted before you even express the wish. But let me die in peace. Our day will soon be over. I have spent much of my time reading books of history. For every five years that the world has been ruled by Reason, the human race has insisted upon five hundred during which it should obey the dictates of its own passions and prejudices and follies and foibles. You see, I am quite eloquent upon the subject. Mankind has but one enemy, its own stupidity, but it loves that enemy as truly and as devotedly as many a poor simpleton who is married to a shrew loves and obeys the creature who has turned his existence into a living hell.

"I would like to oblige you. I will give orders that the new Town Hall be burned down if that pleases you. But as for giving an order to your friend van Rijn, no, that I won't do because I can't do it."

I saw his point and thanked him for his courtesy and took my leave.

The new Town Hall was inaugurated with many ceremonies. There was a service in the Old Church and a service in the New Church and a procession of all the dignitaries connected in any way with the government of the city and there were public performances on the Dam and there was music and a great deal of patriotism and a great deal of drunkenness, as is apt to occur on such occasions. I spent the day quietly at home and in the evening went to Rembrandt's house and helped him polish some plates, for he was in the midst of one of his attacks of etching when he was apt to work twenty hours a day.

But ere I finish this chapter, I must run ahead a few years and tell of something that happened much later.

In the month of February of the year 1660 Govaert Flinck, who was still working on the decoration of the big gallery in the Town Hall died. He had been sick for quite a long time and it was known that he would not be able to finish the work he had begun. Just then my old friend and colleague, Doctor Tulp, was treasurer of the town of Amsterdam. He had achieved much greater honors in the world than I and was then one of the most respected burghers of our town. But we had always remained on a pleasant and cordial footing and besides I knew that he had a great admiration for Rembrandt, who had painted his picture some twenty odd years before when they were both still comparatively young men and at the beginning of their respective careers.

Since that time, Tulp never again met Rembrandt, and the last time he had had his portrait painted he had had it done by a foreign artist. Nevertheless I decided to say a good word for Rembrandt and as the Town Hall was no longer a novelty and no one paid much attention to it except those who went there on business and native Amsterdamers who had to entertain guests from abroad and whom they dragged right from the boat to the Dam to behold the "eighth wonder of the world" and tell them that in the globe carried by the Hercules who guarded the entrance gates, there was room for at least three people enjoying a meal at a middle-sized table—as in short the Town Hall and its decorations were no longer in the public and in the clerical eyes, the excellent Tulp complied with my wishes and Rembrandt was told to continue the work which his own pupil had not been able to finish.

It was to be an historical picture representing the great Batavian hero, Claudius Civilis, who for a short period of years had set our country free from the rule of the Romans. All this of course had happened a long time ago and no one knew exactly where or under what circumstances, but every well-behaved child could reel off the date: "100 B.C. the Romans arrived in our country and 50 B.C. Claudius Civilis sets our country free from the Roman yoke."

Rembrandt showed less enthusiasm than I had expected. This order was what he called "mustard that comes after the meal," and true enough, it was not very flattering for him to be called in only as a sort of stop gap. But once he had started, his enthusiasm grew by leaps and bounds. He decided that since this was a conspiracy, the scene must have been laid at night and in the dark, when the Romans were supposed to have gone to bed. He chose an enormous canvas, almost sixty feet square, the largest canvas he had ever handled, and he made the Batavian rebel the center of a festive meal, during which he explains to his friends and followers what his plans are for the coming uprising.

The problem of having the entire scene bathed in the light of a few small oil lamps fascinated him. He spent months on it and produced something so weird and mysterious that it made me feel queer to look at it. The figure of the one-eyed Claudius dominated the scene. The sword in his hand glistened ominously. I expected great things of this work of art and eagerly awaited the day when it should be hung in its place.

Rembrandt was to get only 1,000 florins for the whole picture (no more than Flinck would have received), but I was sure it would cause so much talk that he would be completely rehabilitated in the eyes of his neighbors and what was even more important from a purely practical point of view, in the eyes of the art-dealers.

But the magistrates rejected it. They rejected it flatly and unceremoniously. Some said that Claudius Civilis looked too much like Hannibal. As the Carthaginian hero had also lost one eye in battle, they had some excuse for this complaint, but it really had very little to do with the value of the picture as a work of art.

Others said it was too dark. Still others complained that the light was all wrong, that no one ever had seen a lamp that threw such shadows. It was never hung in the big gallery. It was at once removed to the garret to be stored away until some future date when Their Lordships should decide what else they could do with this monstrous canvas that was by far too large for any ordinary room and much too beautiful for ordinary people. To this day I do not know what became of it. I have heard that it was cut into four pieces and sold to a junk dealer.

Just about a year ago I happened to have a patient who had been secretary to My Lord van Beuningen during his last voyage to Sweden. He told me that in Stockholm he had seen a picture that looked very much like a sketch that was hanging on my wall. The sketch in question was a small pen and ink study for the Claudius Civilis which years before I had fished out of Rembrandt's fireplace (fortunately it was summer), into which he had thrown it in a moment of despair. I asked the young man whether he was certain and he said yes. I asked him how large the picture was and he answered, "About half of the wall of your room."

Then I begged him to describe it to me a little more in detail and I recognized the central part of the Claudius Civilis picture.

But it may have been merely a copy. Or the young man was mistaken. For although I wrote to Stockholm and for years afterwards interviewed every one who returned from the Swedish capital, I never could discover another trace of this lost masterpiece.

The open space in the gallery left behind by the death of Flinck was filled in by some local talent whose name I have forgotten.

And Rembrandt was obliged to split his fee with this young man, as it did not seem fair to Their Lordships that a man should be paid for work he had not really done.

Chapter 63

REMBRANDT RECEIVES A CALLER. HE PROVES TO BE AN OFFICIAL FROM THE BANKRUPTCY COURT

It is curious how one loses track of time when one is at sea. Besides, my trips of inspection to our squadrons in the Baltic took place at such irregular periods that I have no very clear recollection of any of them. They have become one vast blur upon my memory—a blur composed of uncomfortable berths in uncomfortable cabins—of miserable hours of wetness and depression in some small boat that was being rowed to the flag-ship—of miserable hours of wetness and depression a short while later in the same little boat that was now being rowed back to shore—of quarrels with superannuated but obstinate ship's surgeons—of pleasant dinners with captains who had but one wish in life—to invite the Lords of all the Admiralties on board their ships and then make them stay on deck to take part in some major engagement, of long, placid sails along the flat coasts of northern Germany and Denmark and of sick and wounded people who hated to die and whom one could not possibly hope to save for lack of even the most primitive and elementary sanitary precautions.

Here and there in this blur there is a short breathing space caused by a week or perhaps a fortnight on shore. It was during one of these periods of respite that after a hard day's work preparing a report for the Pensionary that I decided to take a walk and a walk with me always led right around the corner to Rembrandt's house.

The house looked no different from other times, but as soon as I had entered, I knew that something was wrong. Two strange hats were lying on the table in the entrance and I heard the noise of unfamiliar voices coming from upstairs. I went into the living room where I found Hendrickje busy putting little Cornelia to bed. She asked me to go into the little garden by the side of the house and wait for her. Shortly afterwards she joined me.

"We have had a terrible day," was the first thing she said. "I am very tired. If you don't mind, I will sit down with you for a moment." For though we all liked her sincerely and treated her in every way as if she were really Rembrandt's wife, she could not get over a certain shyness when she was in the company of those who belonged to what she still considered a higher class of society.

"What has happened?" I asked her.

"Oh, just the usual thing. People with bills. Grocers and bakers and the butcher. Then more people with bills. Paint dealers, money lenders. I don't know them all by name but it was pretty awful."

Just then Rembrandt himself appeared in the doorway.

"I got rid of those two," he said. "I wonder how many more there will be to-day?"

"Perhaps none," Hendrickje suggested.

"No, when they once begin to come, they go on the whole day. Can I have something to drink? Is there any gin left in the house? I shall have to work all night to make up for these interruptions."

Hendrickje got the gin. Rembrandt took two glasses.

"Such days are terrible," Rembrandt said. "I have just started two new pictures and those fools come and talk to me about money! Well, I have not got any. That is simple enough, isn't it?"

There was a knock on the door.

"Don't open," Rembrandt told Hendrickje, who had got up. "Don't let them in. They will go away soon enough."

"But then they will be back early to-morrow morning."

"In the meantime I shall have been able to do a whole night's work."

"What are you doing now?" I asked him.

"Mostly oil. I am doing one etching, a portrait of Jan Lutma, the goldsmith. His family ordered it. But for the rest, just pictures. Biblical subjects. There are not many portraits ordered these days. And those who order won't pay. Last year I did one for a Spaniard, a portrait of his daughter. He paid me seventy-five guilders in advance and then he said that he did not think the likeness was any good and wanted his money back. He is still after me with his lawyers. No, the war has killed the portrait business and besides, I am too old now to sit before my easel and be told what to do and how they want little Wimmie to hold a dead parrot and how little Susie must absolutely wear that dress of brown and pink. If there are any dead parrots to be put in the picture, I will put them where I like them myself. And so I paint Biblical pictures. When I do that my models can't talk back. If I want to put Joseph here and Potiphar there, they don't say, 'Ah, sir, but we would rather face the other way around.' They stay where I put them and when Jacob blesses the little children no one is going to tell me what color the counterpane of his bed should have. Meanwhile these people out there seem to have given up hope. At least, they have stopped knocking," and he poured himself another gin.

"A lovely day," I said, to say something.

But this merely angered him. "A lovely day? Good God! A lovely day indeed! Yes, the sun was shining, I believe, but if you had had my sort of a day—"

"What has happened?"

"Oh, the old story."

"People who want money?"

"That is no longer a story. That is a legend. But it is about Titus."

"But the boy is perfectly well, isn't he?"

"Better than ever. But it is about his inheritance."

And then I understood what he was driving at. It was the question which I had found mentioned in the report Lodewijk had given me. What I had dreaded for such a long time seemed at last to have happened. The uncles and aunts of young Titus had asked for an accounting and Rembrandt apparently had done nothing about it, had put their letters aside and had not even taken the trouble to answer them. Thereupon they had insisted upon a public inspection of his books (as if the poor man had ever heard of such a thing as book-keeping!) to see whether at least part of their nephew's non-existing fortune was still intact and present.

And now they had threatened him with court proceedings and had hinted that they would ask the Chamber of Orphans to attach the house in the Breestraat and sell its contents at public auction that Titus might receive his legal share of his mother's inheritance.

I wish that I had been in town when that had happened, for most likely he would have come to me and I would at least have been able to send him to a reliable advocate who could have advised him. But Rembrandt, confused and panic-stricken, had asked the first person who happened to come to his studio to give him the name of a lawyer —"any lawyer will do"—and that person happened to be an art dealer of rather doubtful reputation who had called on him in the hope of selling him a spurious Michelangelo and he had answered, "Yes, so and so is an excellent man. Ranks as high as the best of them."

And he had sent Rembrandt to a shyster. This fellow probably knew that the situation was hopeless but in order to keep his hands on at least part of his patient's tangible assets, he suggested that Rembrandt have his house on the Breestraat transferred officially to Titus, as "part of the boy's maternal inheritance."

The meaning of this move should have been clear to any one not quite as inexperienced in such matters as Rembrandt. It was an attempt to placate the Uylenburgh relatives by swindling the other creditors. How this lawyer ever was able to persuade Rembrandt to accede to such a desperate plan I do not know, except that he probably did not pay the least attention to anything that was being said beyond a vague and pained "yes" or "no" and "Will this take long, or can I go back to work now?"

But of course in order to make this transfer "official" (and nothing less would be accepted by Titus' uncles and aunts), the deed of transfer had to be attested before the Chamber of Orphans, an institute that was known for its severity and its scrupulous honesty.

They, so it seemed, had asked no questions, well knowing that not a soul in the world would dare to appear before them and ask them blandly to register a house as "orphan's good" when said house was no longer in the possession of the donor but had belonged since years to a syndicate of creditors. But for the nonce, these worthy gentlemen were mistaken. Rembrandt, totally ignorant of business methods, had not even bothered to tell them that the house was heavily mortgaged. The transfer had been made and the next morning of course all the other creditors knew what had happened. To say that then the fat was in the fire was to express it mildly. The two hats I had seen in the hall belonged to two of the main creditors. They had insisted upon being received. They had called Rembrandt a swindler, and I could hardly blame them for being very angry. They had asked that the deed giving Titus his father's house as part of his mother's inheritance be revoked within twenty-four hours and they had threatened that unless he give them his written promise to this effect and give it to them then and there, they would serve papers in bankruptcy on him before the end of the day.

Rembrandt had listened to them vaguely and had then requested to be excused for a moment. He had wanted to ask Hendrickje what he should do. But the door of the studio had been open and it was still light. Just when he passed that open door he had noticed something he had for a long time wanted to change in the colored turban of Potiphar. He had picked up a brush to make this small correction. Then he had forgotten all about his visitors and he had continued to work until the loud slamming of the front door suddenly reminded him of the reason for which he had come upstairs.

At first he had felt rather ashamed of his rudeness, but in the evening when I saw him his annoyance had made place for merriment.

"Served them right," he said. "Served them right for disturbing me on a day like this. And now they will probably leave me alone."

But at that moment there was another knock at the front door, a knock that sounded official and refused to be denied.

"I will open," Hendrickje said.

"You had better," I added.

"Oh, very well," was all that Rembrandt remarked.

A moment later, Hendrickje returned. She was followed by a little man wearing a long brown cloak and looking for all the world like an undertaker's assistant.

"Have I the honor to address Mr. Rembrandt van Rijn?" the little man asked.

"Never mind the honor," Rembrandt answered roughly. "What do you want?"

"Nothing, except to give you this."

Rembrandt automatically picked up the large yellow envelope which the undertaker's assistant gave him.

"What is this?" he asked.

"An order in bankruptcy," the brown beadle answered.

"Oh," said Rembrandt. "So soon? Well, I suppose you can't help it."

"I most surely can't, sir!" the little man said. "It just happens to be my business."

"Then perhaps you will have a drink?"

"I would not mind at all."

Hendrickje got another glass. Rembrandt poured it full of gin, but took none himself.

"Your health," said the little man, as he poured the glass down his throat with one gulp and wiped his mouth with the back of his hand. Then he bowed low and wished us all a good evening. A moment later we heard him slam the door and all was quiet until the chimes of the South Church began to play the hour.

"What time is it?" Rembrandt asked. "It stays light so late these days."

"Ten o'clock," I answered, counting the strokes.

"Then I had better go back to my studio. I suppose I am in for a hard time. Well, I am young still. I painted myself into these difficulties. Now I will have to paint myself out of them again."

But he never did.

From that day on until the hour of his death, he remained an "undischarged bankrupt."

Chapter 64

THE HOUSE ON THE JODENBREESTRAAT STANDS STILL AND EMPTY

The next day half a dozen of us, all good friends of Rembrandt, gathered at his house to see what we could do. We knew that all efforts to save this sinking ship would be useless. The question before us was how we could transfer the passengers of the doomed vessel to another one with as little delay as possible and without causing any more annoyance to any one than was absolutely unavoidable.

They could not remain in the house for they were not allowed to touch a thing and the officials of the Bankruptcy Court could now come in at any moment to make an inventory of all the furniture and the paintings. After that they would not even be allowed to sleep in their own beds. I offered Hendrickje and little Cornelia the hospitality of my own house. They could have my room and Titus could share the room of my son. The others agreed that this would be a good plan, as Cornelia was only two years old and still needed a lot of care being by no means a very strong child.

That left Rembrandt on our hands. We had to find quarters for him, for if he were left to his own devices, God only knew what he would do. He must have seen this disaster coming upon him slowly for at least ten years. But he never apparently had realized how serious conditions were until that little undertaker-man in the brown cloak handed him the big yellow envelope. Ever since he had walked aimlessly through the house—picking up one piece of his collection after another—holding it in both hands and looking at it for a long time as if he were saying good-by to it. We had to take care of him as if he were a small boy, whereas Titus, to whom no one among us had ever paid very much attention, now suddenly stepped forward as if he were a full-grown man, sent for the baker, the grocer, and the vegetable-man, explained the situation to them with as few words as possible, and made arrangements through which his father obtained at least a few days' further credit.

Then some one, I think it was Francen (the art dealer, not his brother the surgeon) said: "There is quite a good place in the Kalverstraat, called the 'Keyserskroon.' It belongs to a fellow by the name of Schuurman and it is not too expensive. It is a large place. I think it used to be an orphan asylum. If all this has to be sold" (and he waved his hands around him), "the auction could be held right there, and meanwhile Rembrandt could live there."

I interrupted him. "Wouldn't it hurt him terribly to be present when all this is sold?"

But Francen was less sentimentally inclined than I.

"Undoubtedly it would," he answered, "but just now it is not so much a question of how to save his feelings as how to save his family. If he is present or if it is known that he is about, the dealers won't dare to offer as little as if they knew that he weren't there. Don't you other gentlemen agree?"

The others agreed, and I too could see the reasonableness of Francen's point. And in order to prove that I was sincere in this, I offered to tell Rembrandt what plans we had made for him and his family.

I found him in his studio cleaning his palettes. "I don't suppose these belong to me any more," he said. "I don't suppose that, strictly speaking, I am even allowed to touch them. But I can hardly let them go to ruin. They have been very faithful servants so far."

I assured him that no one, not even the most strict-minded notary, could object to his keeping his tools in order, and then I told him what we had decided for him and his family. He listened, carefully scraping the paint off his large round palette, and merely nodded his head.

"When ought we to leave?" he asked.

"Oh, there is no immediate hurry. Sometime within a week or ten days."

"Then why not to-day? You know, it is rather hard on me to stay here any longer, now that all this is about to be taken away from me."

"Very well," I replied. "I will ask Hendrickje."

I found her in Cornelia's room packing. She was perfectly quiet and self-possessed.

"It really does not mean so much to me," she explained. "I have always been poor and to tell you the truth, all this luxury was just a little too much for me. But it will be terribly hard on him. His heart is in these things. I hope it won't kill him."

I told her that I did not think it would. He came of a strong race and could stand a blow better than most people. Then I went back to the meeting and reported what we had decided. The others thereupon went home, but Jeremias de Dekker, the poet, and I remained behind to see whether we could be of any further assistance. I sent Titus to the shop of a carpenter who lived on the Oude Schans, to ask him for the loan of one of his assistants and a cart and had the fellow take Hendrickje's belongings and Titus' small trunk and Cornelia's cradle to my home just around the corner. I told de Dekker to go with them to see them safely to their new place of residence. Then I went upstairs and helped Rembrandt put a few clothes and shoes and shirts and sheets and blankets in a small leather portmanteau.

When this had been done, he returned to the studio.

"I don't suppose I can take any of these things," he said.

I told him that I was afraid that could not be done.

He picked up a large surgeon's needle, which I had used for small

DE Curateur over den Insolventen Boedel van Rembrant van Rijn / konstigh Schilder / sal / als by de E. E heeren Commissarissen der Desolate Boedelen hier ter Stede daer toe geauthoriseert / by Executie verkopen de voordere Papier Kunst onder den selven Boedel als noch berustende / bestaende inde Konst van verscheyden der voornaemste so Italiaensche / Fransche / Duytsche ende Nederlandtsche Meesters / ende by den selven Rembrant van Rijn met een groote curieusheyt te samen versamelt.

Gelijck dan mede een goede partye van Teeckeningen ende Schetsen vanden selven Rembrant van Rijn selven

De verkopinge sal wesen ten daeghe / ure ende Jaere als boven / ten huyse van Barent Jansz Schuurman / Waert in de Keysers Kroon / inde Kalver straet / daer de verkopinge voor desen is geweest.

Segget voort.

THE BANKRUPTCY NOTICE

operations until it had got too blunt, when I had given it to Rembrandt who was forever complaining that he could not get a piece of steel that was really fit for a good job at dry-point work. He held it out for me to see and asked: "You gave this to me, didn't you?"

"No," I replied. "I merely loaned it to you."

"Then it still belongs to you?"

"It most certainly does!"

"And you will let me borrow it a little longer?"

"With great pleasure."

For a few moments I saw him rummaging among the left-overs of old tubes and old brushes on a small table in the corner until he produced an old cork.

"I will just cheat the creditors out of the cork," he said, putting it on top of the steel needle, so as not to hurt the point, "and out of the copper plate. They won't notice the difference, and if they do, well, then, they can put me in jail for it. But I have got to have something to make me pull through the next few weeks." And he slipped the needle and the copper plate into his pocket.

I picked up his satchel and carried it down stairs. There was a knock at the door. I opened. Two men in black capes were standing on the stoop. I asked them their business.

"We are from the Bankruptcy Court and have come to make an inventory," they answered.

"Isn't that rather soon?" I asked them.

"Yes," they replied, "but some of the creditors are afraid that if we are not quick, part of these belongings might disappear."

To my intense horror, I noticed that Rembrandt was standing right behind me. It was impossible that he should not have heard that last remark. I saw him take the small copper plate out of his pocket and hold it out to the oldest of the two men.

"You were right," he said, "I was on the point of stealing this. You had better take it."

But the official shook his head.

"I know how you feel," he answered, with more consideration than I had expected. "I know exactly how you feel, sir. You are not the first man I have ever met under these unfortunate circumstances, and most likely you won't be the last. But cheer up and don't take it too much to heart. You are a famous man. A few years from now you will come back here riding in your own coach and four."

And he saluted the master most politely while he took a piece of paper and pencil out of his pocket and with a short, "I am sure you will pardon me," began to jot down:

"The entrance hall—one picture by—who is it?—one picture by Adriaen Brouwer representing—"

But I had quietly taken Rembrandt's arm and had pushed him toward the door.

For a moment we stood silently on the stoop, and then turned towards the left, carrying the heavy satchel between us.

Rembrandt never entered his house again.

Two years later it was sold to a shoemaker who turned it into two small apartments. One of these he kept for himself and the other he rented to a butcher. For all I know, they are living there yet. But I am not certain, for I have not set foot in the Anthonie Breestraat for more than ten years. A street or a house in which one has been happy becomes something very sacred. And when that happiness has departed, there remains nothing but a melancholy memory. And one should not spend too much time among the dead. The living need us so much more.

Chapter 65

OUR FUGITIVES FROM THE SPANISH INQUISITION SHOW THAT THEY WERE INTELLIGENT AND EAGER PUPILS AND YOUNG BARUCH D'ESPINOZA IS FORCED TO LEAVE AMSTERDAM

The month of August of the year 1656 was one of endless blue skies and a brilliant white-hot sun. All day long, the green-pastured polders lay basking in her bounteous favors while the long twilight of the evening invited the soul to contemplate the mysteries of existence in a spirit of such philosophical resignation that one felt almost inclined to accept life at its face value and declare in favor of happiness as against worry and doubt.

I have forgotten the exact date but it was sometime during the last week of that month of August that my son and I were sitting on the stoop of our house on the Houtgracht and were talking of nothing in particular when we suddenly received a visit from Baruch d'Espinoza. Young Spinoza (for that extra "e" had proved a little difficult for our Dutch tongues and Spinoza seemed quite sufficient for all practical needs) —young Spinoza had never been at my house before. I had often met him at Menasseh's, where he used to drop in at all hours of the night to smoke a pipe of tobacco (of which pastime he was inordinately fond)—to listen to the conversation, and perhaps, if any suitable opponent were present, to play a few games of chess.

Since the days of Saskia's death when I had tried to teach the game to Rembrandt (who, however, had no brain for anything mathematical) I had not touched either pawn or knight. But especially after the disastrous collapse of my hospital plans, I had begun to find a certain relaxation in games of that sort and Spinoza and I had spent many nights over the austere board of ivory that was one of the show-pieces of Menasseh's simple household. I had come to like that young Jew with the melancholic eyes, offset by a merry and somewhat mocking twinkle, but I was a great deal older than he and his Dutch was not very good and I knew neither Spanish nor Portuguese while Spinoza was ignorant of English. Hebrew, Chaldean and Syrian were not exactly convenient vehicles for the interchange of ideas and we therefore had to fall back upon Dutch with a little French and Latin to help us over the rough places. But we had never been very intimate and I was therefore somewhat surprised to see him appear at that hour of the day and a little puzzled by his earnest mien, for as I just said, it was one of those rare evenings when everything is peace and harmony.

However, I was sincerely glad to see him and bade him be seated while my son would get him a pipe of tobacco from my study. But he said no, he had come to consult me, he wanted to see me professionally, and could I spare him a moment?

Of course I could and so we entered the house and I showed him the way to my work-room. As soon as we had entered, Spinoża took off his cloak and his coat and opened up his shirt.

"I wish you would have a look at me, Doctor," he said. "I tried to get a book out of a trunk in the attic and in the dark I ran up against something and hurt myself, I am afraid."

"A strange attic, my young friend," I answered him, "for it is now eight o'clock and it won't be dark before ten."

He hesitated a moment and then replied, "My mistake. Please pardon me. I meant the cellar." And at this clumsy fib we looked at each other and both burst out laughing. At that moment the difference in years, that had stood between us like a granite barrier, melted away like anger before a kind word and from that moment on we were the best and most cordial of friends.

"I am a very poor liar," Spinoza apologized. "We were brought up very strictly and lying was considered the worst offense next to working on the Sabbath day. As a result, I cut a very poor figure in polite society since half our conventional conversation consists of little white lies. But please don't talk about what has happened to me. It is true that I ran into something, but it was a knife. I want to know how much harm the fellow has done. He has cut my cloak rather badly and the knife may have been poisoned."

I opened his shirt a little wider but found only a slight abrasion of the skin but no blood. All the same and in order to be entirely on the safe side, I cauterized the wound and then bandaged it. When I had helped him back into his coat he picked up his cloak.

"A good job for a tailor," I said, pointing to the rent in the right shoulder.

"No," he answered, "I think that I will keep this coat as a souvenir of my own people. It will probably be the last thing they will ever give me."

And at that remark the reaction set in and he turned pale and trembled a bit. "I never realized," he apologized, "that they felt so bitter about it." And he took the small glass of French brandy which I hastily handed him (a special bottle which I kept in my work-room for just such emergencies), swallowed it at one gulp, choked a little, and said, "I will be all right now," but I begged him to stay, and we returned to the stoop (my son had gone back to his plans for a mustard-grinding mill upon which he had been working furiously ever since the beginning of summer) and we sat and smoked and talked of what a strange world it was in which people would try and murder their neighbor for no more serious reason than that they held different opinions upon subjects which forever must remain a matter of taste and a question of personal preference.

At the same time I felt greatly incensed that such a thing could have happened right in the heart of our beloved town of Amsterdam. Our city was comparatively free from murder and violence. Of course, with a large floating population of sailors and with immigrants and political refugees from every part of the world there was a certain amount of shooting and stabbing. But Their Lordships of the Criminal Court had eyes that saw everything and arms that reached far and fingers that never let go of anything that had come within their grasp. They were no spoil-sports. Neither did they believe in bringing about the Kingdom of Heaven by a set of paper laws. A certain amount of drinking and feasting was bound to go on in a port where sailors who had spent seven or eight months at sea would arrive with their pockets bulging with ducats and their souls starving for a little excitement. But no matter how these unfortunate wretches intended to amuse themselves or how drunk they meant to get before they once more fell into the hands of the ever-watchful crimps, there must be no outward disturbance of peace and order and those who upon rare occasions forgot themselves so far as to hit their opponents with a stone jar or slash them across the face with their clasp knives, could count themselves fortunate if they escaped with their lives and were merely condemned to spend four or five months rasping Brazilian wood in one of the local prisons.

As for premeditated murders, I don't believe they happened oftener than once every three or four years. And here I was sitting face to face with a harmless young Talmud scholar who had just shown me a scar on his chest as evidence that he had been the victim of an attempt at assassination.

It was very puzzling and even after Spinoza had told me the cause, I felt deeply angered, for if once we decided to overlook such an occurrence, no one could foretell what the end might be. I therefore refused to give him my word that I would not mention the episode to any one. As a surgeon I was under oath to make a report of every case of violence that came under my observation, but I compromised in so far that I promised not to bring the matter to the attention of the chief of police, who was reputed to have the delicacy of touch of a sledge-hammer, but that I would carry it directly to one of the Burgomasters and let him decide what steps should be taken to prevent a repetition of such an outrage.

In order to take no further risks, I kept Spinoza at my house that night, where he slept on a cot in my work-room, and early the next morning I presented myself at the house of Cornelis de Graeff and asked an immediate audience. I found His Lordship still in his dressing-gown and slippers having his breakfast.

"A man of my age should take it a little more easily," he apologized. "I have given up eating anything at all at this early hour of the day and only take a cup of a new beverage my doctor has recommended in very high terms. It is made out of little beans which grow in Mexico and is called chocolate. Will you try some?"

I tried a cup which I found pleasant and palatable, though a little too rich to my taste and hardly the sort of thing on which to start the day if one tried to reduce one's weight. But I had come to discuss more serious matters than the diet of a middle-aged gentleman with a tendency toward a fatty degeneration of the heart. I had come to speak of something that went to the very root of our national existence. Did we in our Republic grant unto every one living peacefully within our gates and minding his own business the right to believe whatever he pleased, or did we not?

"In theory," His Lordship said, pouring out another cup of the steaming stuff, of which he seemed very fond, "in theory we don't and in practice we do. Or rather let me put it this way. Among all the nations of the earth, we seem to be the only one that gives dissenters at least what our English neighbors call a 'sporting chance.' We do not exactly invite them to build their churches within the heart of our cities, but if the Papists want to keep a little chapel of their own within stone throw of this house (as you and I and every man, woman and child in the whole city know they do), well, that is their business and provided they don't begin to hold a procession down the Singel and provided they don't try and blow the Town Hall up with gunpowder (as they tried to do in London), they will never be disturbed, as long as we have the present form of government.

"And the same goes for all the other sects. Baptists and Lutherans can't be appointed to office, that is all. For the rest, they are as free as a bird in the air. Even the Jews don't have to live in a ghetto. If nevertheless they stick together, they do so because they like each other's company, not because we make them. And now I suppose you will want to tell me about the case of young Spinoza. I know all about it. I had a report on it last night from the high sheriff. They even know who did it, but he had an accomplice who rowed him across the Amstel and he escaped. He will never dare come back. You can count on that. If he does, we shall hang him from the roof of the Town Hall with his mouth full of lard. I am a peaceful man but we must have law and order."

I thanked His Lordship for his consoling news. And then (though I was obliged to partake of a second cup of chocolate to prolong the interview) I asked him whether he knew anything of the cause of this most unfortunate incident and whether he meant to take measures to prevent a recurrence of such an outrage.

"The usual course," His Lordship answered. "When I had the pleasure of seeing you here last, I told you that I am not without influence within this community, but that I keep aloof from everything that smacks of theology. Then you wanted me to do something for your friend Rembrandt and I said, 'No. He is in the bad graces of the dominies. I shall leave him severely alone.' Now you ask me what I intend to do with young d'Espinoza. Nothing! I shall do just exactly nothing. He left his own church and his own people, for which I for one most assuredly do not blame him. He told the Rabbis quite plainly that they were blind, trying to lead the blind, a sentiment in which I happen to concur most cordially. He refused their offer to bribe him with an annuity if he would forswear his heresies, for which I admire him unreservedly. And when they excommunicated him—and by the way, I have a copy of that sentence of excommunication and I shall drop these worthies a hint to soften it considerably if they ever have another candidate for those uncomfortable honors—when they expelled him from their church, the young man behaved with the utmost dignity—did not try to defend himself—did not bring the matter to the attention of the Magistrates, but quietly withdrew from the public gaze and continued his studies without a word of comment or complaint."

"But surely," I argued, "if Your Lordship is animated with those lofty feelings of admiration of our unfortunate friend, he will take steps to protect him."

His Lordship picked up a small sheaf of papers.

"If it were a mere matter of dispute within the Jewish church itself, I surely would, but will you look at this."

I took the hefty document. It was a report written by a number of Protestant ministers whom the magistrate had consulted regarding the theological aspects of the case of which they must have been aware for quite a long time. The ministers, however, in their petition expressed themselves as in complete sympathy with the Rabbis. They declared that any one who doubted the physical existence of angels and who questioned the immortality of the human soul (as Spinoza had done), no matter to what faith he might otherwise claim to belong, should not be accorded further hospitality in a Christian city like Amsterdam.

They expressed the view that all this agitation was a direct result of the leniency with which the Magistrates had treated the nefarious disciples of that pernicious ex-Jesuit, known as René Descartes, and they suggested that Their Lordships back up the Rabbis in their demand that the culprit be brought to justice. I read the ten or twelve pages and silently handed them back to His Lordship.

"The same old story," I said.

"The same old story," he answered. "Always and everywhere, the same old story, the same little men with the same little minds, trying the same despicable tricks and as a rule, with the same degree of success."

"But surely you won't do what they ask you to?"

"Partly yes and partly no. A single Jew is not worth a riot. I am afraid in this matter I will have to act somewhat like the late Pontius Pilate.

But we can't afford the risk of a bloody uprising because of one honest man. I will see to it that nothing happens to your friend while he remains in town. Even now he is being guarded, though he may never know it. I have asked him to visit me here this afternoon. I will explain the situation to him. They tell me that he is reasonable as well as very intelligent. I shall request him to leave town for a short while. Merely in order to oblige us.

"There is a nice country place in Ouderkerk which belongs to Dirk Tulp, a son of your colleague, my esteemed colleague. He is married to one of those Burghs who are related to every one in town. Very respectable people and very intelligent and liberal. Dirk Tulp happened to visit me last week and I mentioned the difficulty to him. He told me that if the matter ever came to a head we could tell our young Jewish friend to come and visit him at Tulpenburg for a couple of months. The house is full of books on philosophy and mathematics. The air is healthy and the landscape, though a bit flat, is full of color and charm. Dirk has an excellent cook and is quite a connoisseur of tobacco. Could you imagine a more delightful spot in which to recuperate from the excitement of an excommunication and an attempt at assassination?

"You will tell me that I ought to stand up for my principles—that I ought to fight this battle unto the last ditch. If it were merely a question of principle, I would rather drown the whole city than give in, as I was all for doing six years ago. But no theological dispute on earth seems to me worth the bones of a single Amsterdam citizen. Our amiable friend will enjoy every possible protection as long as he is within our gates. No one shall touch a hair on his head or a penny of his patrimony. And in addition he will have several months' holiday with delightful friends."

"Yes," I interrupted, "that is all very well and no doubt Spinoza will agree that Your Lordship has acted in a most generous manner, but suppose he ever wants to come back?"

"Then he will take the first boat for Amsterdam and sail for home as quietly as if nothing had happened."

"And the Rabbis and the Dominies and all the rest of them?"

His Lordship turned the can with chocolate upside down and drained the last drop into his cup. "Two months from now," he said, "they will have found something else to get excited about. When wolves lose the scent of one victim, they turn on their heels and trot off in a different direction to look for some other wretch they can devour."

And with those words he bade me a good morning and went upstairs to prepare for the affairs of the day.

When I came home I told Spinoza what had passed between us and I found him quite well pleased.

"I am no martyr," he told me. "I never had the slightest inclination that way. I suppose I am too healthy for such a rôle. I want to laugh a great deal and work enough to support myself the rest of my days so that I can spend my evenings studying philosophy. That is a very simple program and Tulpenburg will serve my purpose quite as well or even better than most other places."

Early the next morning four soldiers of the guard and a corporal called for him and I accompanied him part of the way and when we came near the gate he invited us all in for a glass of beer, at which the honest soldiers, being staunch Calvinists and rather ashamed of the company they were obliged to keep in the execution of their official duty, looked decidedly uncomfortable. But in the end, they accepted and we spent an hour waiting for the boat, drinking rather bad beer and listening to a brilliant dissertation upon angling. For it appeared that this dangerous heretic was also a most accomplished fisherman and once this was known, the ice was broken and the soldiers lost all reserve and shyness and when the boat pulled out they waved their hats at him and gave him three hearty cheers.

And such was the departure into exile of that shy-looking youngster of whom I was to see so much during the rest of my days, who wanted to work, to be merry, and to philosophize.

A strange creed, but by no means a bad one.

Chapter 66

REMBRANDT SHOWS SIGNS OF BEGINNING OLD AGE

The greater part of the year '57 I spent with the fleet in different parts of the North Sea and the Baltic. My son proved himself a somewhat erratic but conscientious and trustful correspondent. His letters were not exactly samples of orthography and his style resembled that of an architect writing out specifications for a bricklayer, but as a rule he managed to tell me that which he thought would interest me and thus I was kept fairly well informed of what was happening to my own family and to that of our friend.

Hendrickje was still living at the Houtgracht. In the beginning I had been afraid that there might be trouble between herself and my own faithful Jantje. For servants as a rule do not take very kindly to those of their own class who are supposed to have done rather better in the world than they have themselves and are very touchy about any "uppishness" on the part of the latter. But in the first place, Hendrickje was the simplest of all people and the disaster that had overtaken her had made most people willing to forget that she was Mrs. van Rijn only by act of common courtesy and not in virtue of a stamped and sealed document handed to her by the register of the matrimonial records.

Besides, Jantje was a good soul and deeply devoted to the small bundle of clothes and smiles called Cornelia and the two women lived peacefully together beneath the same roof without ever causing the slightest amount of friction or jealousy. As for the two boys, they were so absolutely different that it was easy for them to remain on friendly terms. Titus stuck to his paint-box. And my own son stuck to his mills and his calculations and they met at meals and sometimes they took a walk together to the Diemermeer or to Ouderkerk (where Spinoza was still living with his friends, the Tulps, and where the boys were always certain of a free meal) but for the rest they left each other severely alone and caused very little trouble to their elders.

Rembrandt's position was a little more difficult. He had a good enough room in the Keyserskroon but he was lonely and he complained that he could not work. I offered to fix up my workroom for him as an atelier, but he complained that the light was wrong and that he could not use it and then he had once more met the little shyster lawyer who had been his adviser in the matter of the transfer of his house to Titus (that very questionable affair that had almost got him into jail), who apparently had told him with a great ado of words that he need not have been in such a hurry—that he had a perfect legal right to stay in his house until the day before the sale was actually going to take place and being nervous and dispirited, he had believed the fellow and had gone to see de Dekker and Francen to ask them why they had told him to do a thing he had never wanted to do, and he had been quite disagreeable about it.

To which they had answered him quite truthfully that they had only taken him away so soon because they were afraid that further residence in the house would expose him to a great deal of unnecessary suffering and that furthermore, the sale of his goods might begin at almost any moment and then he would have been obliged to leave under even more harrowing circumstances.

But he refused to believe them—vaguely talked of a plot (what sort of a plot he did not explain) and locked himself in his room for days at a time—drinking a great deal more than was good for him and alternately spending entire days in his bed or working at his etchings with such uninterrupted violence that he was beginning to experience trouble with his eye-sight. The latter piece of information did not in the least surprise me for there is no greater strain on the eyes than scratching tiny lines onto a shining plate of copper by the flickering light of a candle.

Fortunately the next letter brought better news.

Rembrandt had left his hotel and would not return there until immediately before the sale of his furniture and his art treasures. He had at last accepted my offer to come and live in my study and was painting again. As soon as he had once more felt a brush in his hand, most of his worries had dropped away from him like the water that drops from the back of a duck. He no longer drank gin to forget his worries. He was extremely sober, as he had always been in the past but he continued to complain that he was not feeling quite well and he was worried about the sale of his belongings. At least once a week he would send Titus or my son to the office of the Bankruptcy Court to ask when the sale would begin and invariably he got the answer: "Not yet. A few weeks more. The times are bad. We must wait until the war is a little further behind us and then we shall get better prices."

And he had to wait all this time in miserable uncertainty, for the only way in which he could hope to escape his bondage was by means of that sale. If it brought enough, he would be able to pay his creditors and would be discharged by the court. If it did not produce enough, he would continue to be a bankrupt and every portrait he painted and every etching he made would belong to his creditors.

Finally, in the fall of '57, the commissioner appointed Thomas Jacobszoon Haringh to start the sale as soon as convenient. Rembrandt once more moved to the Keyserskroon and waited. But the first bids showed that the public had not yet recovered from the ravages of the recent conflict and after a week, Haringh went to the commissioners and suggested that the bulk of the articles be reserved until next year when there would be a chance of them selling at double and triple the amount they brought now.

The commissioners acceded to this request and the paintings and drawings and etchings which Rembrandt had collected with such great care and discrimination and at such tremendous outlay of money, went back to the store house.

Meanwhile the creditors continued to hold unofficial meetings and devised innumerable little tricks that should put them on the preferred list. But of all this I know nothing except the few odds and ends of gossip that I picked up talking to my friends. As far as Rembrandt was concerned, that part of his life was over—was dead and buried—was forgotten as if it had never been. He knew what his collection was worth and felt certain that with the efficient handling of Haringh, who was a personal friend of his, it would produce much more than he owed. If the creditors therefore would stop bothering him, so that he could do his work in peace and make a few extra guilders for Hendrickje and the children, all the rest would come out all right, but they must wait—they must wait and not bother him, bother him morning, noon and night.

He finally grew so exasperated at the continued interruptions he was forced to suffer from the side of his tormentors, that he asked Jantje not to open the door unless she had first made certain that the person who called was a personal friend and did not belong to the dunning guild. And in that way, the spring of '58 went by and affairs in the North were hastening to their final conclusion and as for the moment I had done all I could possibly hope to do, I returned to Amsterdam and found my house occupied by a happy little family, Rembrandt painting and Hendrickje busy with Cornelia and doing as many of the chores as she was able to do (for she remained ailing most of the time) and my son working on a project for a sailing-carriage that should be quite unlike that of Stevin in that it also would be able to navigate against the wind, and Titus coloring pretty little pictures which unfortunately did not show a great deal of originality.

We let the boys sleep in the attic (a change which delighted them) and I took their room and the next day after dinner I had a long talk with Rembrandt and listened to his complaints. For that interminable year of enforced idleness and waiting had done him little good and when he first opened his heart to me, it seemed as if he were suffering from every disease ever known to Galen or Hippocrates. His head ached. A million little ants were crawling up and down his arms. His fingers tingled as if they had been frozen. When he sat still for ten minutes, his feet would fall asleep. He had pains in his back and in his chest and was sure he was going to die of the same disease that had taken Saskia to her grave. But what worried him most of all was the strange notion that there was something the matter with his bones, that they were, as he himself called it, "melting away" and that some day soon he would not have any bones at all—that he would collapse in the street and would be carried home dead.

Where and how and from whom he got the idea that such a disease existed, I do not know unless he had heard it from some itinerant quack on the market-place who might have tried to frighten his audience with the old stories about the "pulverized man" to sell them his "Elixir Ossificationis."

I soon realized that nothing was the matter with the poor patient except a too sedentary life—too much loneliness—the bad habit of eating indifferent food at irregular hours—and as a result, a tendency to meditate a little too consistently and too profoundly upon his own pains and woes. But I knew from practical experience that it would do me no good to tell him, "Cheer up, my friend, all this is imagination pure and simple. A few days of fresh air and sunshine and you will be well again." I hoped to be able to cure him but I could not begin to do this until the sale of his possessions should have become an accomplished fact and he had been definitely discharged from all further obligations and in the second place until he had had some great new success—until some token of recognition on the part of the public at large had made him feel that after all he counted for something in the hearts of his neighbors and had not been forgotten by them as completely as he now thought.

In the meantime I could only mark time and pray that his profound melancholic moods would not drive him to suicide. I watched him very carefully. I accompanied him whenever he went out for a walk or sent my son to go with him. In the beginning I also suggested that he join Jean-Louys when the latter went forth again upon one of his famous sailing expeditions but I soon had to give this up as Rembrandt detested life on board ship as much as he had always done and complained that he would rather sit in jail (but only on dry land) with the worst bore in the world than listen to the wittiest conversation of the most brilliant Frenchman alive, if he were obliged to go to sea to hear it.

Jean-Louys, on the other hand, declared that he had never quite understood why he had been born until that former galley-slave had initiated him into the secrets of navigation. And as for me I divided my Sundays between walks to Watergraafsmeer and along the Amstel, and trips on the Zuyder Zee and meanwhile I waited and Rembrandt waited and Hendrickje waited and we all waited until finally in the fall of the year '58, exactly two years after he had first been declared a bankrupt, the last chest and the last picture and the last etching press and the last half dozen chairs were auctioned off and were removed from the Keyserskroon by their new owners.

The famous collection of etchings of Dutch and French and Italian and German etchers, which he had been collecting with such great discrimination for at least twenty years (for he had bought the first ones when he was a mere boy) were offered to the public on the 24th of September of that same year. Then the book-keepers of the Bankruptcy Court got busy and a few weeks later we were able to compare figures.

According to Rembrandt himself (but he was a most unreliable guide in all matters pertaining to finance) he had spent between 30,000 and 35,000 guilders to buy all these treasures. According to the estimate of the officials of the Court (who as a rule are very conservative in such matters) the sale ought to have produced approximately 13,000 guilders, which would have been enough to satisfy at least the most clamorous of the creditors and give Rembrandt a chance to begin again without any further obligations. And according to the balance sheet that was produced after everything had been sacrificed, Rembrandt had realized a trifle less than 5,000 guilders or about one seventh of his original investment.

The house had fared a little better. Liven Symonse, the shoemaker who bought it, paid 11,000 guilders for it. And of these 11,000 guilders Titus' relatives (after a terrific legal battle) salvaged 7,000 guilders for their young nephew who now had a regular guardian (a certain Jan Verwout, a very decent fellow, by profession and inclination a clerk) but who throughout all this remained pathetically loyal to the man who according to his mother's relatives was a mere spend-thrift and good-for-nothing paint-slinger, but according to himself, the best and kindest father that any boy had ever had.

Chapter 67

HENDRICKJE GOES INTO BUSINESS

The situation, instead of having been improved by this painful sacrifice, had become considerably worse. The creditors were still hanging around outside my door and with the persistence of wolves they besieged my house day and night to see whether Rembrandt had perhaps painted another picture which they could then attach and claim as their own. I knew two of the members of the Bankruptcy Court and went to see them and I found that they understood and even sympathized with our position but it was absolutely impossible for them to suggest a way out.

Our nation, when it turned its back upon the ancient faith, had abolished the old saints, but their place had been taken by a new celestial spirit, and the name thereof was "Respect for Property." Little children no longer prayed to the holy men and women of a by-gone age who had taught them "Thou shalt love" but reverently bowed their knee before the image of an austere and relentless God who spake, "Thou shalt possess."

Whether this change had been a change for the better or a change for the worse, I cannot here decide. I will merely say that it had taken place and that those who failed to take account of the existence of this deity were most severely punished.

Rembrandt, driven by his inner urge to create—a man mad with painting—who could see things that no human being before him had ever suspected, had alas been blind when he passed the temple of the new deity to which the faithful hastened at every hour of the day and at many hours of the night.

He had been punished.

He had been cast out. And he would never (of that, alas! I felt convinced with absolute certainty) be able to rehabilitate himself in the eyes of the respectable part of society.

The problem that had faced those of us who loved him in spite of his many failings (and perhaps a little on account of them) was this—how could we make the rest of his days tolerably happy? And then, when none of us seemed to know quite what to do, it was the faithful Hendrickje who showed us the way out of our dilemma.

She was not at all well. Adversity had struck her a terrible blow and she was failing fast. Rembrandt thought that he was a very sick man and on the point of dying and he was forever telling Hendrickje what she ought to do for Titus and for little Cornelia when he should be gone, but I knew that he would survive her for a long time, while she, who never complained, had at the very most three or four more years to live.

I think that she realized this herself but she was a woman of incredible courage. There was not a task in the house she considered too much for her. She took care of little Cornelia. She cooked for Rembrandt and Titus, refusing to let my own Jantje do this for her. She repaired their clothes and knitted their stockings for them and she kept tract of every cent that came into the house, though how she managed to hide these few poor pennies from the ever-present eyes of the hungry creditors is more than I can understand.

And then one evening she came forward with a plan. She asked whether she could speak to me alone for a moment and of course I said yes and as it was a pleasant night in June (we used to have two or three pleasant days every June, but the rest of the month it would usually pour) I took her out into the garden and there she told me what she wanted to do.

"That poor man," she said, "ought never to be trusted with another stiver. He is blind when it comes to money. His mind is on other things. He would give away his last shirt or exchange his only pair of breeches for a picture he saw if he should happen to want it at that particular moment. I never really was happy in that big house. It was too grand and too rich for me. I did not belong there. I was always afraid that I would break something and in the end, there was hardly room for one to sit down. Besides, I never knew what he would bring home next. It makes me feel uncomfortable to think how we are abusing your hospitality, but for the rest I have never been as happy as I am right now. Only, I know, that as soon as Rembrandt gets discharged by the Court, he will go right back to buying things. Not because he wants them—it is so hard to explain this. The things themselves mean nothing to him—it is not that. But they seem to fill a gap somewhere—they are bits of upholstery for his mind—and when it comes to his work, he is in some ways the strangest man I ever knew and some ways, the weakest.

"And so perhaps it is just as well that for a short while at least he should stay where he is at present. Only he must go back to his painting and etching or he will die. And what I have been thinking about is this: suppose that Titus and I started a little art store of our own and then hired Rembrandt to work for us—paid him just as a carpenter pays the assistants he hires or a bricklayer. One of my own brothers is a mason and hires two men to help him and one of those once had trouble with his wife who tried to attach his wages and then the judge said she could not do it and that is how I happened to think of it.

"Of course, Titus is still very young and I don't know anything about pictures, but you could help me or Francen or de Jonghe or some of his other friends, but I wish you would think of it and perhaps ask a lawyer and see whether we could not do something of that sort, and then we

SELF-PORTRAIT

(about 1659)

could once more have a place of our own, for we have put you to all this inconvenience quite long enough."

I took both her hands and assured her that she could stay until the end of her days and at the same time I was deeply touched not only by the kindness of her heart and her loyalty but also, I might as well confess it, by the clear common sense of her suggestion.

The next day being Sunday, I asked Rembrandt to take a walk with me to the Overtoom where I had not been since that memorable day in the spring of '50 when I had seen the Prince of Orange there, trying to find out with his bamboo cane whether the water was rising.

We took some bread and cheese with us, for I knew that Rembrandt felt embarrassed every time I was obliged to make some small extra expense on his account and he would not have liked it if we had gone to an inn.

We sat by the side of the canal and watched little white clouds that looked like sheep placidly grazing in an enormous blue pasture and I delivered myself of a short speech I had carefully prepared that morning. For I knew that Rembrandt had an almost physical aversion to any concrete discussion of his painful financial situation, but the thing simply had to be done if we were ever going to get him back on his feet. And upon this occasion too, as soon as he noticed what direction the conversation threatened to take, he took a small sketchbook out of his pocket and fished around for a piece of crayon. But I said, "Never mind, those sketches can wait until some other time. Suppose you listen for a moment now to what I have to say. I am not going to preach to you. I just want to see whether we can't find some way out which will allow you to go back to work."

At once he became suspicious.

"You mean to say that I have abused your hospitality long enough?" he asked, stiffening up.

"Rembrandt," I said, "you are a full-grown man with a son who will need a razor ere long. Now don't behave like a child. These years have been damnably hard on you and I don't blame you if your nerves are a bit frayed. As far as I am concerned, you can stay until you die, and you know it."

"Of course," he answered, "I am sorry, but I feel as if I were locked up. My head is full of ideas. They seem to come faster than ever. I need space. I need a room of my own in which I can putter around. You know that sometimes I find it difficult not to shriek when I have done a bit of work on a plate and want to try and find out what it looks like—just one proof would be sufficient—but all I can do is mess it up with a bit of black and then wait until two or three days later when some friend is perhaps kind enough to let me use his press for a few minutes. And I can't turn your house into a workshop. The smell of paint and the smell of acid would be all over the place. Your patients would stay away. They would think you were busy cooking some evil poison. I don't know how I can ever thank you for all you have done for us—"

"You can thank me," I interrupted him, "by listening for about ten minutes and keeping your mind on what I am going to say."

"Very well," he said, "I will be good." And he closed the sketchbook and put it back again into his pocket.

"Well, then," I said, "we know where you stand financially."

"I would hardly call that standing!"

"Never mind such details. And I am not going to talk economy to you. It would not do any good. If you were the sort of person who could keep his accounts straight, you probably would be a book-keeper at the West India House to-day instead of being—"

"Yes. Instead of being what?" he interrupted me.

"Instead of having painted a few pictures that the world will recognize—"

"That the world will recognize three hundred years after I am dead."

"Perhaps, and perhaps sooner. What your friends want to do is to get you back to a place of your own where you can work."

"But what would be the use of my working? As soon as I had finished a picture, Hertsbeeck or de Coster or Ornia or one of those noble patriots would appear with an order from the Court and would carry it away under his arm. The Court would credit me for a few guilders (they never pay me the full price) and twenty years from now I would still be in debt."

"That is just what we want to prevent, or rather Hendrickje, for she it was who thought of the idea. We will help you. But let us start from the beginning. I don't want to criticize you, but I don't think you were very happy in the choice of your lawyer."

"He seemed a nice fellow."

"Perhaps so, but that does not quite make him a good lawyer. How did you get him?"

"Oh, a man who stopped and looked at a picture I was drawing of the South Church and with whom I happened to get into conversation (he was born in Hazerswoude and had known one of my father's aunts—she was quite an old woman when she died)—he told me about him and gave me his address."

"An excellent recommendation! And when did this happen?"

"When I had that trouble with Geertje's brother."

Here was something that was news to me. I asked him what that trouble had been and when it had taken place.

"Well," Rembrandt said, "you remember that nurse I had when Saskia died?"

"I am afraid that I shall never be able to forget her."

"Yes, she was pretty bad. But I felt sorry for her. Then afterwards I had to send her to Gouda, to an asylum. And I promised to pay for her keep. Anything to be rid of her! I was very busy at that time. She had a brother Pieter and he took her down to Gouda. I gave him quite a sum of money. In those days my credit was good and I could raise as much as I wanted to. Well, two years ago, just before all this happened, I thought that I would try and get some of it back. The fellow refused to pay me. Perhaps I had no right to ask for it. I went to see that lawyer. He found out that the brother was in Amsterdam. He was a ship's carpenter and on the point of sailing to India. He was afraid that he would try and get away and we had him put in a debtor's prison. It was foolish of me. But I was in a terrible state just then. And I had come to hate that woman until I was glad to be nasty to her brother. Nasty is the word. I am not very proud of what I did. Then Francen got me a decent lawyer—Arnout Vingboom—you know him. He got the case straightened out.

"Then it is 'out' now—straight or crooked but 'out'?"

"Absolutely out."

"And there are no other troubles, no further lawsuits? No cases in court?"

"None. Except those in the Chamber of Horrors."

"Very well," I answered, and then I explained what Hendrickje had suggested. "It seems an excellent idea to me," I finished. "What do you think of it?"

He sat silent for a while and picked up a few pebbles that were lying in the grass and threw them into the water.

"Funny," he said at last. "And that is the woman whom they did not think fit to partake of Holy Communion."

"That is something else again," I suggested.

"Yes," Rembrandt said. "That is something else again. Of course I accept. Let us go home and tell her. And to-morrow I can begin working again."

Chapter 68

HENDRICKJE AND TITUS FORM A PARTNERSHIP BUT ARE NOT VERY SUCCESSFUL

But he did not begin to work that next morning nor the next, nor for several weeks afterwards. For that evening Francen came in and he had still another plan that seemed almost as good as Hendrickje's.

"I thought of this," he told us, "the moment I left you yesterday. But let us place ourselves in the position of Rembrandt's creditors. What do they want? They want their money. How they get it is all the same to them provided they get it and get it fairly soon. Of course Rembrandt can go back to painting portraits. That is really his business, but portraits are slow work and now that everybody is either bankrupt through this damned war that has just come to an end, or afraid to spend a stiver, through fear of the next one, the portrait business will hardly be profitable. I know that I myself have not sold a picture for almost two years. But I have sold a whole lot of etchings during that same period. Etchings are the thing for the present. Twenty years ago, it was tulips. To-day it is etchings. Not because most of the people who buy them like them particularly. They never even look at them. But they have heard of others who bought an etching for a few pennies and sold it the next day for hundreds of guilders and they hope that they will be equally lucky. There always has been a demand for Rembrandt's etchings. Even when people no longer liked his paintings (I don't mean to hurt his feelings, but he will know what is in my mind)—even when he painted pictures they could not quite follow—they could not quite understand—they paid good prices for his etchings. Now what I would like to know is this: what has become of the plates?"

"I don't know," Rembrandt answered. "They were sold. Mostly to local art-dealers."

"You could find out to which ones?"

"I think we could," Hendrickje said. "Titus kept a list of them."

"Well," Francen continued, "they won't be of much value to them. They can have others make prints off them, but that is never quite the same as when the artist does them himself. We ought to be able to get those plates back. We may have to pay something for them, but in the past these fellows have made a lot of money out of you, for whenever you wanted one of their antiques, they would ask you anything that came into their heads and you would pay it. Perhaps we can make an arrangement by which we promise to pay them a small royalty for every print. But we ought to get them. A few days ago I heard just by chance where we can get a good press for very little money. It belonged to some one who has given up etching and has taken a job as a servant."

"Not Piet de Hoogh?" Rembrandt asked.

"No, some one nobody ever heard of. He had bought himself a press when etchings became fashionable. Hoped to make a lot of money easily. Found it would take him at least ten years to learn to turn out something that could be sold to the public and was glad to be offered fifty guilders a year as butler with a family on the Heerengracht. Anyway, it means that we can lay our hands on a first-rate press for about sixty guilders. I will buy it and donate it as my contribution to the new venture. To-morrow Rembrandt can go and look for a place to live that will have some sort of a room that can be fixed up as a studio. Hendrickje meanwhile can buy beds and sheets and a few pots and pans and Titus and I will make the rounds of the art-shops and see what we can do about the old plates."

"And I?" I asked. "What shall I do?"

"For the moment," Francen said, "you shall take it easy. You have done quite enough as it is. Unless you want to ask Vingboom when he can give us a little of his time, and then I will take those three innocent babes to see him and have a regular contract drawn up. This is beginning to sound like one of those plays of Joost Vondel in which Virtue appears at the end of each act to offer us her bright consolation. And now, if the doctor will send out for a mug of beer, we will drink to the health of the new firm, 'van Rijn, van Rijn and Stoffels.'"

I thought the occasion was worthy of something better than mere beer and went into the cellar myself to get one of my few remaining bottles of papish wine. And going down the narrow stair-case I bumped my head, as I had done these last twenty years, and I swore and stopped to rub the sore spot, and standing there in the dark and thinking of what I had just seen and heard, it struck me that the situation would have been more fit for the pen of gruesome Aeschylus than that of our own amiable Vondel.

The greatest painter of his time being kept out of the poor-house by the combined efforts of a sick girl who had nothing in this world beyond her beauty and her kind heart and a boy of sixteen or seventeen, who loved his father and who would probably die as soon as Nature, in the pursuit of her own mysterious purposes, had driven him into the arms of a woman.

Then I got the bottle I had promised to bring up and we spent a happy hour, talking of the future.

It was the first time I had seen either Hendrickje or Rembrandt smile for more than two years.

Chapter 69

THE VAN RIJN FAMILY FINDS A NEW HOUSE

The first thing for us to do was to get the permission of Titus' guardian, for his affairs were by now so hopelessly interwoven with those of his father that the latter could not take a step without being taken to task both by the members of the Court of Bankruptcy and those of the Chamber of Orphans.

Verwout had soon discovered that he was too busy to devote the necessary time to the case and he had been succeeded by a certain Louis Crayers, whom I had never met before but who sent me a brief but courteous note saying that he would be glad to see me and my friends the next Friday at eleven in the morning. Abraham Francen and I, however, had agreed that nothing is ever accomplished in this world by committees and we decided to do everything by ourselves. Then when the arrangements should have been completed, we could tell the others what had been done and ask them to give the new household such help as they thought fit.

At the appointed hour we were ushered into Crayers' office. We found him very busy so that he could not spare us a great deal of his time, but he was an easy man with whom to transact business, for he went right to the point and treated the whole affair as if it were merely a problem in mathematics, which indeed it was.

"Gentlemen," he said, "I hope that you will understand my position. I have given my word—and an oath before that court means an oath, let me assure you!—that I would protect this boy's interests to the best of my ability. Besides, I like the young man. I am sorry he is not a little stronger physically, but his mother was very delicate, so they tell me, and he seems to take after her more than after his father. All the same, I have rarely seen such a pleasant and affectionate relationship as exists between van Rijn Sr. and his son. As for the father, I never knew him very well but in my spare time I sometimes buy a few etchings. No, I am not just keeping up with the fashion. I was collecting etchings when most of the people who are buying them nowadays were making ten stivers a day digging ditches out there in the new part of the town. I am too busy a man to give much of my time to the arts, but I recognize the genius of the older van Rijn. A little too muddy for my taste in some of his pictures, but when he is at his best, I don't know any one who is better. But when it comes to business, may God have mercy upon me for the language I used when I first studied the documents in this case!

"I don't want to sound harsh, but in this instance it would have been infinitely better for the boy—of course, I am speaking strictly from a business point of view for I know how devoted he is to his father—but looking at the matter in a less romantic way, it would have been infinitely more advantageous for him if his father had died instead of his mother. But that is neither here nor there. The mother is gone and we have to deal with the husband.

"You want to know what I think about your plans. Well, I am heartily in favor of them, provided the rights of my pupil are absolutely protected. That last point I can't insist upon strongly enough, for I don't think that old van Rijn will ever mend his ways, financially speaking—he is too old and even if he were twenty years younger, he would be just as bad. I just wish you had seen the mess I had to straighten out! It was absolute chaos.

"When the appraisers of the Bankruptcy Court went through that house, they collected three pailfuls of bills—old bills—new bills—paid bills—unpaid bills—protested bills. The house looked neat enough, so they told me, but in all the cupboards, behind the pictures and the mirrors, they found bills.

"But not only bills. What was infinitely worse, they discovered almost as many notes and drafts and checks, all made out to Rembrandt and which he had never taken the trouble to present and turn into cash. They even found a dozen envelopes and a few small bags containing money which he had put somewhere and then had forgotten all about—just plain carelessness. Of course I tried to collect some of this paper, but in many instances, the people were dead, had been dead for years or had moved away and could not be traced. The amount we lost that way must have run into several thousand guilders.

"Under ordinary circumstances, I would call this 'negligence' and with any other man I would have thought of bringing the matter to the attention of the Court. But van Rijn is not an ordinary man. He lives in an imaginary world of his own and has no sense for the realities of life. For example, I asked him whether he still had any relatives from whom he might expect to inherit something. He said yes, there was a grandson of his aunt, a certain Piet van Medemblick, from whom he would probably get several thousand guilders when he died, for so at least he had been told by one of his brothers the last time he saw him.

"I looked into the matter and found that he had spoken the truth. He was to inherit some money from this distant—well, let us call it cousin. But I also discovered that this mysterious cousin, his father's sister's son's son, as he was called in the official documents, had taken service on board a ship that had sailed for the Indies at some unknown date early in this century and that the ship on which he traveled was reported to have sunk off the coast of Portugal three weeks after it had left Texel; that during the last 45 years, not a word had been heard from this Piet van Medemblick, but that according to the law as interpreted by the municipal courts of Leyden, the man could not be officially declared 'dead' until at least half a century after he had first disappeared; that therefore the heirs would get nothing until the year 1665 and that even then, with all the accumulated interest, van Rijn's share would probably not exceed 800 guilders. A rather vague prospect, as you will see for yourself and yet he was firmly counting on 'the inheritance of my aunt's grandson' as if it were something tangible—a chest of pearls—sent to him by the Emperor of China.

"I shall support you, Gentlemen, in all you do for your friend (whom I bear nothing but good will out of respect for his great ability) and at the same time I shall use every means at my disposal to protect the interests of young Titus. Therefore whatever you do, I shall insist upon a contract, but for the rest, you will find that I am entirely on your side."

We thanked Crayers for his patience and courtesy and asked whether he had any suggestions to make about the contract.

"No," he answered, "it had better be a regular partnership contract. I have a friend, Notary Listingh, who does that sort of work for me and who is a very reliable man. Of course if you have some one you would rather suggest—"

But we assured him that we had no preference and agreed that the first thing to do now was to find a place where our friends could live—some sort of place that could be used as a shop and where Rembrandt could work. As soon as that should have been done, we would return to Crayers and ask him to make out the necessary papers. Then we made our adieux and began house-hunting.

But this proved to be no easy task. During the war, very little building had been done and as a result people were paying enormous prices for very inferior accommodations. They were living in old barns and in converted stables and in deserted cellars and attics and on the outskirts of the cities. A good many families were obliged to content themselves with such shelter as under normal conditions would not have been thought fit for pigs. At last we found something, but entirely through luck, the sort of luck that was (as is so often the case) somebody else's misfortune.

One day a young man came to me who told me that I had been recommended to him by a friend. He had got some dirt into a little open wound on his right hand and it had caused an infection and would I please oblige and open it for him, without hurting him too much and his name was Lingelbach—Joannes Lingelbach, and his father was a German from Frankfort-on-the-Main and he himself was a painter and he had worked in Italy and hoped to go to Paris where he heard there was a much better chance for painters than in Holland, and ouch! that hurt—but not as much as he had expected—and so on from the moment he came into the house until the time he left with his hand neatly bandaged and his arm in a sling.

Three days later he came back to let me change the bandage and by this time I had house-hunting on the brain and before he left me I asked Lingelbach whether he knew of any houses for rent anywhere and he answered, "Why, yes, of course I do. My father is the owner of the Labyrinth on the Roozengracht—at the end of the Roozengracht. You may know him? Old David Lingelbach? He used to manage the Orange Tree on the Looiersgracht twenty years ago, the first man to build a labyrinth in Amsterdam. Well, he had to break away several houses to make room for his present place but right opposite us there are three houses left, and one of them is free, at least half of it. I happened to see it yesterday."

"Is the rent very high?" I asked.

"I am going to have supper with the old man to-night," he answered, "and I will drop in and ask and let you know to-morrow."

The next day he brought me the information I wanted.

"It is only the left half of the house that is for rent," he said. "It has one large room and I had almost taken it myself—it has a fine big window on the north and would have made a wonderful studio. The other four rooms are much smaller and there is a kitchen and the rent is 150 guilders a year, but you may be able to get it for a little less. The landlord is called van Leest. He lives on the premises. I talked to him. He seemed a very decent sort of person—not the usual type. You had better go and see him for there are mighty few houses to be had in this town nowadays."

I took Rembrandt out to the Roozengracht late in the afternoon of that same day. Hendrickje said that she did not feel up to the walk and she remained at home, but on the corner of the St. Anthonie Lock we met Titus and my son, who were coming home together and they went with us.

We saw the house and we saw van Leest and we signed a lease then and there at a rental of 125 guilders a year.

A week later the van Rijn family moved into their new quarters.

All of the old friends had contributed something to their household. Francen gave them four beds, Dusart contributed the sheets and pillows, van den Eeckhout and Roghman looked after the kitchen utensils, Suythof took care of the tables and chairs and I presented him with the large brass chandelier that used to hang in my own room which he had used as his studio for almost two years, and to which he had become very much attached. We rented a cart and filled it with the pictures he was working on and as many of his copper plates as we had been able to get hold of and then we put Hendrickje on top of it, together with Cornelia (who by this time had grown big enough to be immensely pleased and greatly amused by this unexpected trip across town), and we drove them to their new home.

When we arrived, we found everything in terrible disorder, beds, tables, wash-basins and chairs all standing pell-mell in the front room and sheets and pillows and pots and pans filling the sleeping quarters in a most picturesque and disharmonious fashion. We had expected to meet Rembrandt on the door-step, ready to welcome us, but we could not find him anywhere.

Then Hendrickje, inspecting her new domain, opened the door to the large room in the back of the house. Rembrandt was sitting in the center, right on the floor, in the most uncomfortable position imaginable, painting away for dear life at a large canvas that stood leaning against a barrel containing the family china.

"Oh," he said, without looking up. "Are you there? I hope you will pardon me, but the light was so good—I thought I had better begin."

"Yes, dear," said Hendrickje, "that is quite all right." And she came back to us and quietly started unpacking the small satchel containing Cornelia's clothes and toys.

Chapter 70

I PAY A VISIT TO A STRANGE COLONY OF PEOPLE WHO ACTUALLY THINK FOR THEMSELVES

I thought that I had better leave the van Rijns to their own fate for a while to give them a chance to become a little more accustomed to their new surroundings and meanwhile I gave myself a week's holiday and went on a trip which I had planned to take for quite a long time. I often was obliged to go to The Hague to see the Pensionary on business (he continued to give me his confidence in a most gratifying way) but I had not been in Leyden for years and now I meant to go there on an errand that was not wholly pleasant.

Also partly owing to the kind interest of My Lord Jan de Witt, the town council had once more paid some attention to my claim for the indemnity they had promised me at the time my little hospital was wrecked by the mob. But Burgomaster de Graeff was growing old and his influence was waning while that of his enemy and rival, the highly objectionable Valckenier, was waxing stronger every day. And Valckenier, who had come to power through his associations with the Church, was my sworn enemy and had repeatedly declared—both in private and in public—that as far as he was concerned, I would never receive a penny, for "so he reasoned" the fire that had destroyed my property was not "the work of men's hands but a direct manifestation of Jehovah's all-highest displeasure."

When driven into a corner by the arguments of My Lord of Polsbroek, who reasoned that if this riot had been an expression of God's will, the magistrates of Amsterdam, who wanted to hang the ringleaders of this attack upon private property, would have been guilty of sacrilege (a line of reasoning bound to cause great discomfort to a greedy and selfish creature like My Lord Valckenier, who whenever there was the slightest disturbance in town caused both his houses to be guarded by the militia), this pugnacious official had thereupon completely changed his line of attack and had suggested that the question be decided merely upon its scientific basis and that the medical faculty of the University of Leyden be asked to submit a report upon "the desirability or otherwise of performing painless operations according to the method suggested by a certain well-known Amsterdam surgeon."

The motion had been put over for two weeks, in the hope that Valckenier would change his mind. Instead of which he called upon his followers to rally around him and they did this, partly by a series of sermons delivered in the principal churches of Amsterdam and extolling the sublime profits to be derived from physical pain and partly by staging three or four popular manifestations on the Dam right in front of the new Town Hall.

Why I suffered no personal violence during that period I do not know, but I rarely left my own street during those days, being hard at work upon plans for a new hospital as soon as I should have received my money from Their Lordships and I am proud and happy to say that my neighbors, without a single exception, were most loyal to me and upon one occasion at least came near to drowning two young hoodlums who had smeared my door full of red paint.

But "excitement" was the one thing no member of the government wished to see at that particular moment. There was a feeling of unrest all over the country. On the other side of the North Sea things were not going any too well from our point of view. The Lord Protector, Oliver Cromwell, had died in the year '58 of an intermittent fever, which his enemies declared to be the punishment of Heaven but which according to his friends had been brought about by the death of his daughter to whom he was passionately devoted. His son Richard had succeeded him but he was not the man his father had been and after a few months, a revolution had broken out which had once more brought the House of Stuart to the throne of England. But on his way back to the country from which he had been absent for almost a dozen years, the new King paid a visit of state to our country, where he had been received with even more splendor than the old Queen Dowager of France, when she had deigned to honor our city with her presence in '38.

Those, however, who had come in personal contact with His Majesty felt serious forebodings for the future. And those who had been present when His Majesty was slightly under the influence of intoxicant beverages (the wet climate had probably forced him to drink a little more than he was accustomed to) all those dignitaries reported that he had spoken of his Dutch hosts in very unflattering terms as "those bastards who had been friendly to the murderers of his father" and "mean-eyed greengrocers who ought not to be tolerated in a world of gentlemen." And other sentiments a little less elegantly expressed but just as eloquent and ominous as the two examples I have just given.

And although His Majesty upon the occasion of his leave-taking at Scheveningen (His Majesty was entirely sober that morning and a little repentant for having seduced the daughter of the majordomo of the palace of the late Prince Maurice, which had been most graciously placed at his disposal when His Majesty reached The Hague) had delivered himself of a most gracious speech extolling the virtues of the noble land that was the home of his charming nephew (who, however, was not present upon this occasion, as My Lord de Witt had expressed a fear that the excitement of bidding farewell to his beloved uncle might have a bad influence upon the health of the young man, who was considered to be quite delicate) no one believed him when he proposed a toast to the "prosperity and happiness" of the country that would ever be the subject of his most sincere devotion and gratitude.

For as soon as the last sail had disappeared from sight, it became known in The Hague that His Majesty during his last interview with a financial deputation from among the members of the Estates General, had called them a lot of Shylocks (an expression which had greatly puzzled these worthies as none of them seemed to have ever heard of the works of William Shakespeare) and had broadly hinted at the revenge he would take upon their accursed land for having treated him quite so niggardly in the matter of his royal loans.

Every one in the Republic therefore felt that sooner or later we would be at war once more with England and under those circumstances, an outbreak of religious fanaticism was just about the last thing that was wanted. The more liberal-minded among the Magistrates therefore allowed themselves to be intimidated and the medical faculty of Leyden had been duly requested to favor Their Lordships of Amsterdam with an opinion upon the subject which I have just mentioned—should a surgeon actually try to alleviate the pain of those about to submit to an operation or was such a method opposed to the best traditions of surgical practice?

Now if this question had been asked fifty years before, I would not have been disturbed by the possibility of a negative answer. For the University of Leyden had been the creation of our great Prince William and his friend Coornhart, the Haarlem engineer and former secretary-of-state, both of whom were men of wide experience and a tolerant point of view.

But of the old academic freedom of spirit for which they had fought so bravely, very little remained in the year 1660 except the memory, and even that memory was held up to public scorn by the second-rate successors of the original founders.

Under those circumstances, I was greatly perturbed when I heard that my views upon the subject of anesthesia were to be submitted to a group of men who were sure to condemn them without ever taking the trouble of a thorough investigation, and I decided that I had better go to Leyden myself and try to save whatever I could save by a personal demonstration of my method and a general explanation of the motive that had inspired me to start such a line of investigation.

I went and I was politely enough received by my colleagues of the medical school, but when I was asked to appear in a full session of all the faculties (and the theological men were powerful enough to insist upon such a procedure) I at once noticed a spirit of deep hostility which boded little good for the future. And after I had listened to them for hours—to an endless series of quotations from the Bible, all of them expressing profound disapproval of any attempt to interfere with human pain and to an equally formidable list of passages from Hippocrates and Galen explaining that pain was a necessary and unavoidable concomitant of illness, I felt that my case was lost then and there and that I might just as well return to Amsterdam by the evening boat.

Nevertheless, I made one more effort and addressing myself to the Rector Magnificus, who was in charge of the University's policies for that year and who happened to be a surgeon like myself, I asked that I be not condemned on the ground of a few passages in books that had been written twenty centuries before, but that I be judged upon my actual performance. I told him that I had brought my apparatus with me and would be happy to give a demonstration of the excellent results that could be obtained by my method at any time, anywhere they decided. I would invite the members of the theological faculty to be present too, that they might judge for themselves whether the sight of a patient sleeping peacefully on his couch was not preferable to that of a poor wretch who would not only curse those who inflicted this pain upon him but who would also blaspheme the God who had ever allowed him to be born.

Finally the matter was put to a vote and a vast majority of those present pronounced themselves as opposed to "any further discussion of the matter" and in favor of "a written report that should be submitted to Their Lordships of Amsterdam in due course of time and after serious deliberation on the part of those who are entrusted with the care of the true principles of the Christian religion."

That was the end, and the meeting was adjourned and I was allowed to return to my room at the inn and await the departure of the first boat for Haarlem, which left at six the next morning.

And then there was a knock at the door and a stoop-shouldered man, dressed in a long black coat and his hat well down upon his eyes, entered and put both arms around me and saluted me most respectfully and most cordially, and of all the people in the world, I recognized young Spinoza, whom I had not seen for almost four years and from whom I had had practically no news ever since I bade him adieu on board the ship that carried him to his exile with his friends of Tulpenburg.

So, knowing his weakness, I ordered two pipes of tobacco and I also asked that a fire be made (my visitor had a cold and was coughing quite badly, a dry, racking cough which somehow frightened me) and then we sat down and talked and Spinoza told me all that had happened to him ever since he had been asked to leave the territory of our city.

That sentence of exile, as My Lord de Graeff had suggested to me before it was put into execution, had never been meant seriously. After spending three or four months with his friends at their home in the country, Spinoza had quietly returned to Amsterdam to find that nobody seemed to remember his case. He had been able to attend to all his personal affairs without in any way being molested by the authorities and had then returned to the country and (not wishing to be a burden to his friends) had taken a room in a farmhouse near Ouderkerk and had spent his time studying optics (a branch of science that had interested him ever since, as a boy, his parents had apprenticed him for a while to a glass polisher to learn the trade of grinding lenses for spectacles) and writing a treatise upon the colors of the rainbow while spending his leisure time reading the ancient philosophers.

But Ouderkerk had been a little too near to Amsterdam. There were a number of young men in the city with a tendency for spiritual hero-worship who had already proclaimed him their leader and that was just about the last thing he wanted to be.

"I have seen enough of Rabbis and Prophets," he said, "to last me for the rest of my days and I have no ambition to become one myself. An abstract idea, incorporated into a concrete system of thought, soon loses its value. It dies and becomes fossilized and while fossils may be interesting to antiquaries who study the condition of this earth thousands of years ago, they are of small use to those who live in the present. And why study philosophy if you do not mean to practice it while you are still on earth?

"And so, in order to escape becoming another Joshua or John the Baptist (not to mention poor Jesus," he added, "who spent all his life trying to escape a fate that his followers finally forced upon him) I went to Rijnsburg."

How had he happened to choose Rijnsburg?

"Well," he answered, "at the Tulps' I had met a great many Collegiants and I liked them. You know who they are?"

I did. Yes, in a rather vague way. Rembrandt's brother who had stayed with him a couple ot years before had talked about them one evening and he had been quite scandalized. They were heathen, he had told us—pagans—they had no right to call themselves Christians—they had no ministers and listened to no sermons. He had wanted them all killed off, as the Anabaptists had been killed off a hundred years before. When the quarrelsome old man had gone to bed, Rembrandt had told me something more about them.

It seemed that a certain Mennonite preacher of whom he had made a portrait some twenty years before had been related to this sect and had told him a great deal about those strange people who were different from the rest of our Christian neighbors, in that they really tried to live like Christ himself. The sentence had struck into my mind and afterwards whenever the conversation drifted to the Rijnsburg community, I had always been careful to listen.

In the early part of the century, right after the Synod of Dordrecht, when those despicable quarrels took place that led to the execution of My Lord of Barneveldt and that put all power into the hands of a small group of Calvinists, certain dominies of Rijnsburg suspected of liberalism had been among those who were forced to abdicate on account of their principles. But Rijnsburg, a village about an hour from Leyden, had once upon a time been the seat of a famous abbey. When the Reformation abolished all such Popish institutions, the property as a whole had been taken over by the Estates of Holland, who ruled it independently as if it had been a piece of conquered territory, and this fact had made the sleepy little town a harbor of refuge for all those who elsewhere were being persecuted on account of their religious beliefs. And when the Synod forced the Estates to dismiss the Rijnsburg clerics who had dared to encourage the liberal movement in their city, two brothers by the name of van der Kodde, well-to-do and intelligent farmers, had begun to hold services of their own and no one had been able to prevent them because they were responsible to no magistrate and the Estates, having dismissed the local clergymen, felt that they had done enough for the time being and refused to take any further steps to oblige the Synod.

Every Sunday therefore in an old barn the friends of the Koddes had come together to listen to the reading of the Holy Scriptures (mostly of that part that I hold to be of any true value, the New Testament) and to join in a common prayer. After that they used to sit in absolute silence until one of those present felt that the Holy Ghost urged him to say something, when he got up and spoke what was on his mind and sat down again as soon as the inspiration ceased.

Such séances had been denounced by the dominies of Leyden as absolutely sacrilegious and they had preached a regular crusade against these dangerous heretics who lived without benefit of clergy, gave liberally to the poor and who in every possible way tried to follow the example of the earliest Christians in being kind and charitable and cheerful and in treating all men as their brothers.

But the authorities had been firm in defending the good right of those people to their own opinion and no one in Rijnsburg had suffered harm on account of his ideas. Gradually in other cities there had been similar small groups of people who thought and acted likewise and once or twice I had even heard of Collegiants meeting in Amsterdam.

In many ways therefore Rijnsburg was an ideal community for a man like Spinoza and I told him that I thought he had been very wise to go there and he agreed and then he said:

"I heard that you were here last night from my landlord, Doctor Hooman. He had been told that the people here were being urged to give you a good sound beating. So I thought I would come and try and see what I could do to help you (not much, I am afraid, but I am still deeply grateful to you for what you once did for me) and to ask you to come with me to Rijnsburg to-morrow. The Hoomans have a room for you. It is a very quiet place, but we can walk and talk about things. I have at last begun to write. That French baron, that friend of yours, was right. I only met him once and then he told me that the only practical way to reach a definite answer to any problem was the method known as the mathematical one. I am trying it out in my first book that discusses the methods I mean to employ in the others."

"And after that?" I asked.

"After that I mean to turn the whole of the universe into my private laboratory and investigate everything."

"A fine ambition," I answered. "You must be very happy. For only happy people set out to do the impossible."

But as it was very late, I made an end to the conversation, sent for the landlord, told him to prepare another room and the next morning, after a hearty breakfast and another pipe of tobacco, we set out for Rijnsburg and soon had the towers of Leyden far behind us.

I stayed an entire fortnight instead of a week and met every one in the small town. It was a strange experience. I had been obliged to spend almost sixty years in a country which loved to call itself a Christian nation, before I was to come face to face with the real spirit of Christ and then I found it in an old, converted barn.

Chapter 71

I GET REMBRANDT AN ORDER FOR A FINAL PICTURE

When I returned to Amsterdam, I heard that Hendrickje had been quite sick, that Titus was working hard, trying to convert the little front room into an art store, and that Rembrandt himself was busy with the sketches for that allegorical picture in the Town Hall which was to find no favor in the eyes of Their Lordships and that was to find a final resting place in the rubbish corner of the aldermanic attic.

But of course at that moment we could not know all this and the mere fact that he was busy once more made him so happy that even Hendrickje was caught in an occasional smile and Titus had started to dream once more of becoming a famous painter instead of spending his days as a peddler of pictures and bric-à-brac.

They were delighted to see me, wanted to know all about young Spinoza and whom I had met in Rijnsburg and what the Leyden professors had said (they had said nothing, so far), and they kept me for dinner and told me that the house was a great success but of course, the creditors still continued coming around, trying to find something that might possibly be considered to belong to Rembrandt himself ("The clothes on my back are all I have left," he interrupted us), but the Roozengracht was far removed from the center of the town and only those who really cared for them would take the trouble to walk that long distance, and by the way, my friend, the Frenchman, had come to visit them several times but he had looked very ill and had come in a coach, accompanied by his sailor, who had to support him when he climbed the stoop, but he had made them promise that they would not write to me and tell me that he was sick, and Francen had been in and he had just returned from Haarlem where he had seen Hals, old Frans Hals, I surely knew whom they meant, and Hals had laughed right merrily when Francen had told him that he was a good friend of Rembrandt's.

"Give him my regards," Frans had said, "and tell him that now I can call him brother. And also tell him that he was a lucky devil. For when he went bankrupt, some of the grandest people in town were proud to be among his creditors while I was sold out at the behest of a baker, a common, ordinary, everyday baker, whom I had tried to please by painting a picture of him while blowing his horn to tell the people that the fresh bread was ready. And when I went broke, all the sheriffs could find in my house were three mattresses, a table and a chest of drawers, and he, so I hear, had a house as full of things as the palace of the late King Solomon."

And Francen had brought other news. Hals was painting again, painting again although he had not done a stroke of work for almost twenty years (he could not sell anything anyway, so what was the use?) and he wanted Rembrandt to come and see him, for he had made a wonderful discovery but he was eighty years old and would not be able to make use of it himself. "But tell Rembrandt," he had said, "that being poor is the best thing that can possibly happen to any painter. For if you are poor, you can't afford to buy all those expensive colors you use when you are young when your father pays the bills; and then you have got to get results with only two or three pots of paint and it is then that you learn to suggest tints rather than put them down in the original red and yellow and green and blue—just suggest things—indicate them—and if you can do that and can do it really well, people will sometimes see what you mean just as well as they used to do before—when you could still afford to paint in all the colors of the rainbow." And so on and so forth, for the old man was getting to be a little vague and repeated and contradicted himself continually, but then, he had been in the poor-house for so long, no wonder he was no longer as bright as in the olden days.

And oh, yes, they had almost forgotten to tell me, but Crayers had sent word that the case of Titus against that man van Hertsbeeck, who had got part of the bankruptcy money that really belonged to Titus ("Good God!" I said to myself. "Still another case? Is there no end to these lawsuits?") would probably come up for a decision before the end of the year and that he was sure van Hertsbeeck would have to pay Titus several thousand guilders and that would be wonderful, for they still had to manage very skimpily . . . and so the evening went by and when at last I went home (it was ten o'clock and I was almost thrown into the canal by some playful roisterers who had been evicted from old Lingelbach's labyrinth as it was long past closing time)—when finally I went home, I was happier than I had been for a long time. For just ere I left, Hendrickje, her cheeks flushed by fever and her eyes wide with excitement had drawn me aside into a corner of the room and had whispered: "He works all day long, and everything is all right."

Indeed, for the moment at least, the Fates that had so doggedly followed this poor man's footsteps seemed to have wandered off in search of some fresh victim, for not only did the creditors gradually begin to leave him alone, but I was at last able to get him a commission that was exactly the sort of thing he liked to do best.

Except for my son, I had only one relative in the town of Amsterdam. How we happened to be cousins, I did not know. My grandmother had explained it to me any number of times, but I was not greatly interested in the man and invariably I failed to listen just at the moment when she said, "And so you see, his mother's sister's grandfather was the uncle of your father's uncle's nephew," or something of the sort. But we observed a certain outward cordiality towards each other, which rarely exceeded the bounds of mere politeness, and we made it a point to call upon each other every New Year's morning when we would say, "Good day, Cousin, and I hope you have a very happy and prosperous New Year." But that was all for we had nothing in common except the accidental tie of blood and a dead great-great-grandfather.

This particular van Loon was a few years younger than myself and a cloth manufacturer in a small way. But as he was not married and had more spare time than most of his colleagues, he had been several times elected into the board of managers of the cloth-workers guild and this year again he was one of the Syndics, as he happened to tell me when I met him by accident on the corner of the Rokin where he had his store (he was also in the retail business) and where he lived with an old servant and three very fat and very lazy cats.

I congratulated him on his new dignity and asked him, more as a matter of having something to say than through curiosity, whether he and his colleagues had made any plans yet to have their picture made. He said no, they hadn't thought about it yet. And then, through a sudden impulse, I found myself putting both my hands on his shoulders and I heard myself blurting out: "I have got just the man for you. He is a splendid painter and he won't charge you such a terrible sum either. When will you pose for him?"

But the dried-up draper looked hastily around to see whether any one could possibly have observed my unseemly behavior (he was most correct, and respectable in all his personal dealings) and then asked me curtly, "Who may that be, Cousin?" and I answered, "A man by the name of Rembrandt, Cousin," and he again, "I have never in my life heard of him, Cousin," and I, "That does not matter, Cousin. I will take you around to see him and then you can judge for yourself, Cousin. Good night now, Cousin, and I will call for you to-morrow at ten in the morning."

God only knows how I was able to persuade this dry-as-dust wool-carder and his equally uninspired confrères that Rembrandt was the man for them, but it is a fact that I finally persuaded them to sign a contract for a picture and at a very fair price.

I was curious to see how Rembrandt would go to work about this picture. It was a long time since he had painted anything of the sort and in the meantime, as he himself put it to me more than once, he had been pulled through the mangle so repeatedly that nothing remained of his former self except his skin and his bones and his honest homely face. Twenty years before it had been all the same to him what size canvas he needed—what sort of color he used, nor had he given a fig for the opinion of those who in the end would be asked to pay for the picture.

This time he had to take the smallness of his studio into consideration, he must be careful not to waste any of the bright lakes and the expensive ochers which Titus had bought for him on credit and as he needed money and needed it badly, he must be very considerate of the feelings of his customers and give every one of them an equal chance.

I am not the best possible judge of paintings, but it struck me that Rembrandt had never come quite so near his ideal as this time. I was reminded of the somewhat incoherent message which Francen had brought back from Haarlem and which Hendrickje had related to me on the evening I returned from Leyden, that strange artistic last will and testament which exhorted the younger man to try and "suggest color" and "to hint at things rather than expose them in concrete form and color."

Everything in this picture was a matter of suggestion and yet one actually felt the presence of those honest, commonplace drapers as if one had been present at one of their meetings—one sensed that they were secretly very proud of the high office which their fellow members had bestowed upon them and at the same moment one knew that in their heart of hearts they were convinced that this much envied dignity had come to them entirely in recognition of their outstanding probity and the unimpeachable integrity of their business morals.

It was the strongest picture I had ever seen, and of one thing I am sure, no one had ever achieved such a brilliant effect with the help of such incredibly sober means.

I was delighted, and the day after the picture had been finished, I hastened to the house on the Rokin where the sign of the Pelican hung out to tell all people that this was the Drapery Shop of Gerard van Loon and Sons (the old man was all that remained of those "sons") and I found the honorable syndic eating his midday meal consisting of a bowl of lentil soup and he looked at me with considerable surprise, for he was not accustomed to familiarities of this sort, and I said:

"Good morning, Cousin, have you seen your picture?"

And he answered, "Yes, Cousin, and none of us are particularly impressed by it, but we will pay the man all the same."

And I turned on my heel and he called after me, "Don't you want to stay, Cousin, and share my meal with me?"

And I answered, "No, thank you, Cousin, some other time I shall be delighted."

And I went home to talk with my son about a new sort of saw-mill which he wanted to construct—a saw-mill that should be able to take care of three trees at the same time. He had gone to see one of our neighbors, the only wood-dealer left on the Houtgracht, and the man had been delighted with the plan and had told him to go ahead and construct a working model and very likely (if it could be arranged with the carpenters' guild) he would let him build one for him in Zaandijk.

The boy (he was taller than I but my affection for him was so great that I could never think of him except in terms of a child—a sentiment which sometimes caused considerable difficulty between us)—the boy, who in his own way loved me very deeply, noticed at once that something was wrong.

"What has happened, father?" he asked. "Uncle Rembrandt in trouble again?"

"No," I protested, but he knew that I lied.

"Too bad." He spoke quietly to himself. "Too bad. Uncle Rembrandt is a fine fellow and I like him tremendously, but he just has no sense. Who wants to go on painting pictures when the world needs mills?"

I suppose there was an answer to that question, but (for that moment, at least) I must confess I could not think of it.

Chapter 72

A CHAPTER MOSTLY PERSONAL AND NOT DEVOID OF ENCOURAGEMENT

The Leyden faculty did what I had expected it to do and sent a lengthy report to Their Lordships the Burgomasters stating that in the opinion of the High and Noble Born Faculty of the Illustrious University of Leyden, I was not entitled to an indemnity from a purely medical point of view. They could not of course express themselves upon the political aspects of the case—a riot was a riot and rebellion against their divinely appointed masters was ever a crime on the part of mere subjects. They must, however, leave that aspect of the unfortunate incident to the judgment of the worldly authorities. But they, as the sworn guardians of the spiritual and scientific truth, could only regret that a supposedly respectable member of their guild should have so far forgotten the lessons of his early training as to try and set himself up as the equal of God.

A copy of this report was forwarded to me and I in turn sent it to The Hague for the consideration of the Pensionary. After this public reprimand, he might find it inconvenient to retain my services as unofficial adviser to the committee that was trying to reorganize the medical service of the navy. By return boat I got my letter of resignation back. At the bottom of it, written in the illegible hieroglyphics of this illustrious statesman, was written one word, "Perge," and underneath it a scrawl which I finally deciphered as J. de W.

I should not be ungrateful and try and create the impression that all my life long I had been a victim of circumstances and had received absolutely no signs of recognition. On the contrary, a small pamphlet I had written upon the subject of my peculiar method of performing major operations had been translated into Latin and had apparently been read all over Europe, for I was continually in the receipt of letters from London and Paris and Vienna and even from Rome and Madrid, telling me how different surgeons in those distant cities had followed my instructions and had achieved the most satisfactory results. And three scientific academies appointed me a corresponding member of their institutions and they informed me of my election by means of beautifully calligraphed parchment bulls.

But I would cheerfully have sacrificed all these expressions of public approbation for that one word of my dear friend, who in the midst of ruling the affairs of a nation, yet found time to say "continue" to an humble doctor who a week afterwards was denounced in a meeting of his own guild as "a disgrace to his profession and a menace to society."

Chapter 73

POOR HENDRICKJE GOES TO HER FINAL REST

I now come to the years between 1661 and 1668, when a great many things happened, but few, I am sorry to say, that contributed in any way to the happiness of either myself or my friends.

In the first place, there was the sickness of Hendrickje. She had never quite been well since about a year after Cornelia's birth, when she had caught a cold and, refusing to stay in bed long enough, had developed pulmonary trouble which soon made me fear that she too was a candidate for an attack of phthisis. It seemed unbelievable and too cruel for words. Saskia had died of this dreadful disease and now Hendrickje was going the same way.

Rembrandt, who was singularly blind to symptoms of this sort, noticed nothing. He sometimes commented upon his wife's lack of appetite and her general listlessness, mildly complained when she refused to accompany him upon one of his walks through the deserted fields that surrounded his home on all sides, but as a rule he closed the sentence with a cursory, "Oh, well, she will be all right again soon enough. When spring comes, we will take her home for a change of air. That will put her back on her feet."

But when spring came she was much worse, and when summer came she was not any better, and one day in the fall she asked me to send for the same notary that had helped her and Titus draw up the agreement about their little art store, but to be careful that he did not call when Rembrandt was at home, for that she did not want him to know how badly she felt. She could still walk about a bit and she hoped to deceive him about her condition until the very last.

I knew that on the seventh of August Rembrandt was going to take Titus to see his friend Joris de Caullery, who was living in The Hague at that time—who had been ailing for several months, but who had now sufficiently recovered to pay a short visit to Amsterdam to attend to some private business affairs. On the seventh of that month, accordingly, I walked with Notary Listingh to the house on the Roozengracht and Hendrickje made her last will.

She had little enough to leave, poor dear, but all she possessed, she bequeathed to her daughter Cornelia, or in case of her death, to her stepson Titus. Furthermore, she stipulated that Rembrandt should be the only guardian of her child and insisted upon including a paragraph which stated that if Titus should inherit her property, the revenue of her investments (such as they were) should be paid out to Rembrandt, who was to enjoy them until the day of his death. As she could not write, she merely made a cross at the end of the document. I was asked to sign too, but just then Christiaen Dusart happened to drop in with a small picture he had finished the week before and which he wanted to show to Rembrandt. The notary thought it better that Dusart should be one of the witnesses than I, because Rembrandt or Titus might otherwise think that I had been in some way responsible for the strange stipulations of this extraordinary testament which might well be shown to further generations as a lesson in loyalty and unselfish devotion. One of the occupants of the other half of the house in which the van Rijns lived was the second witness, and got a guilder for his trouble.

When everything had been done according to the law, Hendrickje was so exhausted that she had to go and lie down.

For a few weeks it seemed that she was growing a little stronger, but in October she happened to see from her window how a drunken vagabond tried to stab a woman who had resented his unproper advances with his clasp-knife. The excitement proved to be very bad for her. She went to bed and never got up again.

She lived almost a year longer. She never complained, and until the end she kept as busy as she could. Her love for Rembrandt and for her two children (Titus regarded her entirely as his own mother and she apparently knew no difference between her own child and that of Saskia's) never waned but on the contrary grew stronger as she felt herself more and more slipping away from this world. And she was so strong in her determination that no one should suffer on her account that until the last moment, neither Rembrandt nor Titus appreciated the seriousness of her condition.

One morning Rembrandt found her unconscious on the floor. Apparently she had tried to get up to open a window to get some fresh air. She had often had attacks of choking and then fresh air had been the only thing that would bring her any relief. Titus was sent off as fast as his legs could carry him to fetch me. When I reached the house on the Roozengracht, Hendrickje was dead.

That afternoon we discussed the forthcoming funeral. Rembrandt wanted to bury her in the Old Church together with Saskia. But since the death of his first wife, he had moved to the other part of the city and the law provided that all dead people must be buried "in the church nearest to their most recent place of abode." In case the surviving members of a family wished to make other plans, they were obliged to pay the undertaker an extra sum for "every church the procession should pass on their way to the holy edifice they had selected for the interment."

Such a procedure was out of the question; it was too costly.

Early the next morning (it was the 27th of October, 1662) Rembrandt sold the grave containing the remains of Saskia to a certain Pieter van

Geenen, who paid him cash. With that money he was able the next day to buy a grave in the South Church. And there Hendrickje was buried.

God must have been delighted to welcome her to his Heaven. But she must have been terribly lonely without her man and her children for truly, beyond those, she had had no existence.

Chapter 74

JEAN-LOUYS SAILS FORTH INTO SPACE

And now I must recount another incident of that same year of grace, '62, which filled my heart with great and sincere sorrow.

When I had returned home from Leyden that evening and called on the van Rijns, they had told me that Jean-Louys had been at their home that afternoon, in a carriage, bringing them a present of a barrel of excellent wine from Bordeaux, but looking so haggard and so pale that they were afraid he must be suffering from some dangerous disease.

With his usual affability, however, he had laughed away their fears and declared that he had never felt so well before in all his life. And indeed, when I hastened to his house he seemed not only in very good spirits but his color was good and his eyes were clear and he was full of all sorts of plans which he began to explain to me before I had even sat down.

"Look at this," he said to me, showing me a drawing that I held to be the outline of the skeleton of a centipede but that proved to be a design for a new sort of ship he intended to build. "I am going to sell the old one," he told me. "A nice little boat, but too cramped for comfort and all wrong from a scientific point of view. It pulls itself backward when it should push itself forward. That is too complicated for your sort of brain, and so just take my word for it. There was only one solution. Submit the matter to mathematics. I did. I got an answer that surpassed my highest expectations. Half a year ago they began to build this boat after my own specifications. It will be ready next month. And this summer you shall have such sailing as you never even dreamed of."

I tried to bring the conversation back to more general subjects, but it was no use. Jean-Louys had temporarily gone insane and boats were his delusion. Imagine my horror when I came home and found that my son had been actually working on that new mathematical caravel for the last six months without my knowing anything about it. He left the house every morning several hours before I got up, for I was getting old and beginning to feel the need of a little extra rest, and by attending to all my correspondence and literary work in bed between six and eight in the morning, I found that I could accomplish much more during the actual working hours of the day.

"Yes," he told me, "Uncle Jean showed me those plans I don't know how long ago. It is going to be a wonder, that boat! It is costing him a tidy sum, too, but he seems to have sent to France for a tun of gold and he does not care what he spends as long as it is for his navy, as he calls it.

I have learned an awful lot about the ship-building trade. I even may give up mills and go in for ship-building myself."

In June of '62 the *Descartes* was ready. The name at first attracted no attention. Of course every skipper in port was enormously interested in this strange contraption which had such a stern as no one had ever seen before, at least in our part of the world. All day long they would stand on the wharf (the vessel lay off the Kattenburg) and discuss the possible pros and cons of such a construction. Then a few ventured to row out and inspect the *Descartes* at close range. They were cordially invited on board—taken into the cabin—plied liberally with that marvelous French brandy that came from the land of Cognac, and that was still a curiosity in our land, and were treated with that bonhomie which one sailor should show to another.

Soon a mob of curious people was besieging the ship and the harbor authorities, suspecting that this might be part of a deep-laid smuggling plot, sent a lieutenant and three soldiers to make a personal investigation. But all the papers were found to be in perfect order and nothing would have come of the matter except that the name *Descartes,* which was mentioned in the official report, caught the eye of My Lord Valckenier, who was now one of the Burgomasters and who read every official document from the beginning to the end and who declared himself deeply hurt that a foreigner who had enjoyed the hospitality of our country for such a long time, should be so insensible to the prejudices of the majority of his neighbors as to call a craft that was to sail from a Dutch port after a pagan philosopher who was generally known to be one of the worst enemies of the Christian faith.

This was perhaps no matter of which Their Lordships could take public cognizance but Valckenier suggested that the Baron de la Tremouille be requested to change the name of his ship. The other Burgomasters agreed. They did not anticipate the prospect of four weeks of anti-Cartesian sermons with any great pleasure. Besides, this was hardly a matter of principle but merely one of convenience.

Jean-Louys was asked to re-baptize his vessel. He asked for a week's time in which to make up his mind, as he was wavering between *Buttercup, Moses and Aaron* and *Young Love*. He was granted a respite of five days.

By the end of the fourth, he was gone and so was my son. I did not worry, for I knew that he was well able to take care of himself and that he would turn up again ere long. Four days later he walked into the house, tired and unshaven but cheerful. He explained his muddy boots by telling me that he had walked back all the way from Hoorn.

"It was a wonderful trip," he said. "That ship is a marvel. I wish that Uncle Louys had taken me all the way. But he wanted to try and make Dokkum by the outside passage and he was afraid it would take me too long to reach home. He expects to be back again in about six weeks. Here is a letter for you. If you will pardon me, I will go and shave and wash."

The boy went upstairs and I took the letter. There was nothing extraordinary about that letter but before I had opened it, I suddenly knew: "This is the last message I shall receive from Jean-Louys on this side of the grave." I have had such instinctive premonitions four or five times in my life and I have never known them to fail. I still have that letter, and here it is:

"Carissime [it began, and then continued in French],

"Your boy will bring you this letter. He is a fine fellow. Let him build his mills and be happy.

"And now a word by way of explanation why I left you for good without saying 'good-by.' I don't like this business of bidding farewell to good friends in the conventional way. It is a little too much like a major operation without the benefit of your beloved Cannabis.

"I am not going to Dokkum, God forbid! I told your son that I was going there because it seemed the easiest way of explaining to him why I thought he had better return home. If I had let him know my real destination, he might have insisted upon keeping me company. A voyage from Texel to Bordeaux would have been a trifle too long for a young man of his age who still has to make his career. And the *Descartes* (I did not change the name after all) is bound for the mouth of the Garonne, for I am going home.

"A strange idea, I grant you, that I, of all people, should be wanting to go home. I seemed to be a man without a country—without a family—without any place I could call my own. I liked to pose as a piece of animated logic—of perambulating reason. But now that I realize that I have only a short time more to live, some strange and hitherto unsuspected instinct bids me go forth that I may die among my own people.

"For my days are numbered. The heart has about finished its task. It is getting tired and has sent me repeated warnings that soon it will cease its labors altogether. Well, I am contented. It has been a faithful servant and deserves a rest.

"But let me talk of other and more cheerful matters. We have been friends—we have been good friends—we have been brothers in the best sense of the word.

"It would be an insult if I were to say thank you for a gift that you tendered me so willingly and so gladly.

"Whenever I have been obliged to listen to people who talked about the uselessness and emptiness of all earthly existence, I have felt inclined to tell those unfortunate pilgrims that they had failed in their quest for the only positive good that life has to offer to those created after God's holy image. The excuse for all the pain and suffering that are our share while we dwell on this planet is implied in one single word and that word reads 'companionship,' the companionship that is based upon perfect mutual understanding.

"You and I and Bernardo and even poor Selim have had our share of that divine blessing. Let us give thanks and pass on to the next subject.

"I shall be in my grave within a year. In less than twelve months' time, I shall have received an answer to the Great Riddle—if an answer there be. Otherwise I shall just sleep and what more sublime reward for three score years of valiant fighting than the peace and quiet of eternal oblivion?

"And now one more short meditation before I bid you my final adieux.

"Has life been worth while? Would I do it again if I were given the choice?

"Let me answer those questions in reverse order.

"If I were given the choice once more I would answer 'No. A thousand times, no!' At least not if I had to promise that for a second time I would commit all the same follies of which I have been guilty the last sixty years. If I were told that I would have to see as many things that were ugly and wasteful and senseless as I have been obliged to witness since I reached the age of discrimination, if I were asked to associate with as many fools as it has been my sad privilege to encounter during my peregrinations across half a dozen different countries I would say 'No.' But I hasten to add that this second question (which people are asking themselves all the time) is really a very silly one. No one was ever consulted about his own birth. One moment he was happily unaware of everything. The next one he found himself struggling amidst hundreds of millions of crawling little creatures, all of whom obeyed but a single impulse, the urge that bade them to survive.

"Only a coward would shirk such an imperative duty. A man of parts accepts the inevitable, and I too have accepted and while I breathe, I shall say 'Yes' to whatever fate has still in store for me.

"But has it been worth while? Has it? I don't know for sure but on the whole I feel inclined to say 'Yes, it has been worth while.' Not on account of those so-called 'realities' which I have learned to despise but on account of the unrealities which are the only solid structure upon which a wise man will attempt to build the edifice of his individual contentment.

"When I was very young my careful father tried to drum it into my head that the acquisition of tangible possessions was the beginning and the end of all human happiness. And all through life (and not the least in that country of yours which has given me its hospitality for so many years) I have heard that endlessly reiterated commandment: 'Thou shalt try to accumulate as many worldly goods as possible that thou mayest call them thine own.'

"Remembering that Christ had admonished his followers 'not to live by bread alone,' the spiritual leaders of those nations that pretend to follow his example ceaselessly urge their flocks to mix their porridge and their potatoes with a mysterious substance which they call 'religion' and which I am sorry to say has never been very much to my taste. For I understood the words of that bewildered young Jewish peasant in a somewhat different sense. He wished to elevate his greedy and grasping fellow-tribesmen from the ranks of the animals of the field and he realized that the only thing that sets man apart from his brethren of the bush and the fields and the sky and the waters of the ocean is his ability to create himself an imaginary realm of the spirit into which he can escape whenever the unbearable actualities of breeding and killing (the twofold basis of all animated existence) are on the point of slaying his high courage or (what seems to me even worse) threaten to turn him into a cynic.

"For that, I think, is the greatest piece of wisdom to be found within the endless and ofttime dreary pages of the Holy Book and to the best of my ability I have tried to make good use of it, ever since I have been allowed to shape my own life as I saw fit without the unendurable interference of parents and teachers and other people who meant well by me.

"Have I chosen the right path or the wrong one?

"I do not know, but I am willing to leave the final decision to those Deities whom I will meet face to face within a very short space of time.

"I will confess that the selection was difficult and that it took me years to find the right one. Like all young men, grown up amidst the traditions of a feudal society, I was taught that true romance was only to be found within the arms of woman. I tried to make that dream come true but was unable to do it. For woman, as soon as she was captured, avenged herself for her defeat by destroying her captor or by turning him into her slave.

"I loved my freedom above all and withdrew from all further competition within a field where the victor was also the vanquished.

"Then I went forth to war, because the clash of arms (so I had been taught to believe) made one forget all else. Dull marches in the company of dull drudges—sweat and blood and boredom and as a reward, the conviction that we had accomplished something that had better been left undone.

"Then I tried to find oblivion within the garden of the Muses, but the Muses were jealous mistresses who like their fair sisters of the Earth asked for everything and gave as little as possible in return.

"I finally closed the gate of that spurious Paradise behind me for all time and began to wander.

"Oh, to be free and drift from town to town and from country to country without a care and a responsibility! But at night, all alone in some inhospitable room with no other companionship than a pair of muddy boots and half a dish of stale food—no, that sort of life offered me only a temporary means of escape but no definite solution.

"And then, by chance and through mere unaccountable accident, I stumbled upon that little book of young Napier. And suddenly within the thirty or forty pages of that tiny volume I found my fairy-story, my own particular fairy-story. And the goddess whose magic wand then and there turned a commonplace old tower on a commonplace old canal in a dull Dutch city into an enchanted castle where a man of my character could live happily for ever afterwards, was called Mathematics, and the ancients worshiped her as the mother of all science.

"Ever since that moment I have dwelled contentedly within her delectable domain—tilling her fields and watching over her flocks in return for the highest reward which man is able to receive on this earth—complete oblivion of himself by means of the work of his choice.

"Now the time has come to depart and a well-behaved guest leaves the house where he has been happy, quietly and with the least possible amount of embarrassment to his fellow-lodgers.

"My incomparable François tells me that there is little danger connected with this voyage and that I shall be home by the end of next month. I have complete confidence in his ability to handle this craft safely. But if he should prove to be my Charon and the Bay of Biscay should assume the dark shape of the River Styx, waste no useless tears upon the memory of one who contemplating the few fleeting hours that separate him from Death, can honestly state, 'Yea, verily, it has been a good life.'

"And now I, the most selfish of creatures, shall tell my faithful servant to open me a bottle of the wine that comes from the land of Cantenac and I shall fill his glass and I shall fill mine and together we shall drink a toast to the man who honored me beyond all others by calling himself my friend."

The letter was not signed but it ended with a postscript.

"Present my humble duties to that poor old bear Rembrandt. All his life long he has dwelled in a land of make-believe of such infinite beauty and integrity that the world has passed it by with a shrug of the shoulders and a sneer of malice and envy. Now he is old and sick and growing stout and soon he will be an object of pity to the little boys on the street and when the end comes, the commissioners of the poor will take him to an unknown grave in an obscure corner of one of your chilly churches. But was any one ever richer than this poor wreck? He lost everything when he surrendered to the dreams that were within him and by so doing he gained all."

Four weeks later a convoy of merchantmen returning from Batavia reported that just outside the British channel they had met a queer-looking

SELF-PORTRAIT

(about 1666)

little vessel that flew the French flag but that had hailed them in broken Dutch and had declared that it came from Amsterdam and was bound for the south of France.

But I never was able to find out whether Jean-Louys had finally reached the land of his birth or had sailed for another shore from which no one has yet returned to tell the tale.

Chapter 75

A FORGOTTEN MAN IN A LONELY HOUSE GOES ON PAINTING PICTURES

Strange though it may seem at first, Hendrickje's death did not seem to have made a very deep impression upon Rembrandt. This, however, was not due to any callousness of heart on his part, as I heard some people say—people by the way who had never met him and only knew from hearsay. But there seems to be a saturation point for mental suffering as well as for physical pain, and during the last ten years Rembrandt had been dealt such terrible and incessant blows by fate that there was nothing now that seemed able to make any impression upon him whatsoever.

After the very indifferent reception of the Syndics he knew that as far as his artistic career was concerned, there was to be no "comeback" for him. He was, in the common parlance of that day, "out of the running" and a "back number."

I tried to console him once by telling him of something I had found in one of the old Greek writers, how the Athenians were running a race in the Stadium and how the public, seeing a man a few feet behind the very last of all the others, began to chide him for his slowness until they discovered that the unfortunate victim of their displeasure was so far ahead of all the others that he merely seemed to be running in the rear, while as a matter of fact, he had already won the prize. But this neither amused nor interested him. He merely grunted a casual "yes" and went back to his easel.

For he worked very hard those days—entirely too hard to please me when I looked at him with a professional eye. He rarely left the house either during the day or during the night. He was glad to see his few remaining friends and was polite to them and occasionally he even tried to be cordial. But all the time his mind was elsewhere and when addressed, it took him some time before he realized that he had been spoken to and that one expected an answer. Then he would smile a feeble smile and would stammer "Yes" or "I hardly think so," and would at once sink back into those meditations with which he endeavored to drug his soul.

The English (who whatever their faults, are possessed of a much richer literature than we ourselves) have a proverb which says that kites rise against and not with the wind. That may be true but if the wind turns into a hurricane and blows too strong, the string that holds the kite is apt to break and the unfortunate kite comes tumbling down and is smashed to pieces on the ground.

Rembrandt came of a strong breed of men. His father and grandfather and great-grandfather (not to speak of his maternal ancestors) had fought their way through the great rebellion and had lived to tell the tale. They had been the sort of people that would never bend, but even the hardest iron will break if it is exposed to too severe a blow. Sometimes when I saw Rembrandt late at night, his short squat figure (much too stout around the hips on account of his lack of exercise) scratching away at some copper plate by the light of a single candle (the whole family sat and worked or read by the light of one single candle—they could not afford more), I wondered how long it would be before the crash came.

I tried to convince him that he must take at least one short walk every day but he said, "No, I am too busy."

I tried to persuade him that he ought to go out oftener and visit his friends—that it would be good for his painting and his etching if he refreshed his mind once in a while by an evening of laughter and jest, but he merely shook his head and replied: "No, it can't be done. I am too busy."

Then I made it a point of walking across the town whenever the sun was shining and the weather was fine and knocking at the door and saying, "Titus, go tell your father that I am here to take him for a stroll." And in less than a minute Titus would be back with the message: "Father is sorry but he is too busy right now. He wants to know whether you won't come in and sit in the studio while he finishes something he is doing."

And I would find him busy with his sketches for still another picture of Haman's downfall and disgrace, a subject which seemed to occupy his mind a great deal in those days and of which I have seen him start and finish at least three full-sized pictures.

He rarely spoke of his work in those days but everything he did was in a minor key. Gone were the days of the laughing cavalier and of Saskias and Hendrickjes, dressed up like the ladies-in-waiting of those merry foreign queens.

In his bare little house there was nothing left that could serve as a fitting background for such scenes of gayety. And as he had never read much, and considered the pursuit of mere literature as a rather scandalous waste of time, his choice of subjects was necessarily limited and he had to fall back upon the memories of his childhood days and those were of course restricted to the Biblical incidents of which his mother had told him when he was a small boy.

But the Christ he painted was not the handsome young prophet of his Italian rivals, preaching the good tidings among the sun-baked bowlders of some Palestine hill. No, it was invariably the man of sorrows—Christ being scourged—Christ bidding farewell to his followers—Christ standing in deep thought before the walls of the Temple! And the other problems that filled his mind until he had to rid himself of this obsession by recounting them in the form of pictures—all of those had to do with that feeling of doom—that sense of futility, and that defiant air of hopeless rebellion which had descended upon him the moment he had walked for the last time out of his house in the Anthonie Breestraat.

Often I have sat in his studio and have watched him for hours while he was busy with his painting. And every time again I have been reminded of a picture he had painted years before when he was still quite young, of Samson threatening his father-in-law who had cheated him. The strong man who for reasons which he has not been able to fathom (of which, as a matter of fact, he is totally unconscious) has been struck what he considers an unfair blow, and who defies Fate—who thumbs his nose at Providence—shakes his fist at the Deity himself, and with boy-like bravado shouts: "All right! I will show you! I will show you!"

For he was showing them. He was showing them with a vengeance.

In that shabby room in a mean house on the Roozengracht, such miracles of color were now being performed that the world for ages to come will sit before them in stupefied silence and will say: "Beyond that point, no man could go without lifting himself to the rank of the gods."

Provided that any of these pictures would survive long enough to allow mankind to catch up with their maker. And that to me seemed highly doubtful. For nothing Rembrandt finished during those days was ever sold. And where they are at present, only a year after his death, I could not possibly tell. A praying pilgrim he painted during that time I saw only a few months ago in a pawn-shop in Leyden and it was hanging between a cheap fiddle and an old pair of sailor's trousers. What has happened to the others, I do not know, but I have my fears. An intelligent art-dealer with an eye to his grandsons' fortune would have hired himself a store-house and would have filled it with the pictures Rembrandt finished during the period he lived on the Roozengracht, and which he was unable to sell for half a guilder or even less.

But why expect such foresight among the vultures of the world of art?

Chapter 76

REMBRANDT HAS ONE MORE PUPIL

By the end of '64 it became clear that Rembrandt would not be able to afford the rent of the Roozengracht house any longer and that he would have to look for cheaper quarters. Titus found a place just around the corner and the whole family once more pulled up stakes and went to live on the Lauriergracht. There they had only three rooms and in every one of them the light was bad. It was then that Titus thought of the possibilities of having his father do some book illustrations which would probably be more lucrative than painting pictures.

He went to a publisher but the publisher had probably heard of the failure of the drawings which Rembrandt had submitted for Menasseh's book on Nebuchadnezzar and would not listen to the plan.

"If only your father knew something about steel-engraving, then I would have a job for him." And Titus in his eagerness to get his father an order (any order at all), had answered, "But my father is one of the best steel-engravers there are in town. Just give him a chance!"

The publisher had agreed. Would Mr. van Rijn please engrave a picture of Jan Antonides van der Linden after a portrait that Abraham van den Tempel had painted of him half a dozen years before? Rembrandt said that he would. But he was an etcher and not an engraver and the experiment ended as disastrously as that of the Nebuchadnezzar book he had done ten years before. And Rembrandt was once more at the mercy of his creditors.

Although I was no longer rich in those days, I would have been delighted to help him but he would not hear of it. "You have trouble enough of your own," he invariably answered when I talked of taking over some of the burdens of his household, "and I am still strong enough to take care of my children myself."

He was immensely pleased when one day a young man who said that his name was Aert de Gelder asked to be allowed to become his pupil. De Gelder, who then must have been about twenty years of age, hailed from the town of Dordrecht and was a pupil of that Samuel van Hoogstraten who shortly after the English war had moved to England where it was said that he had done very well and had become quite a rich man. As van Hoogstraten too had for a short while worked in Rembrandt's studio, the old man felt touchingly grateful and de Gelder proved to be not only an apt student but a kind and loyal friend, which Rembrandt had not been able to say of all of his pupils.

But unfortunately I was not able to see much of Rembrandt during this period. For we were on the brink of another war with England and I was obliged to spend the greater part of my time in The Hague, so as to be at the beck and call of My Lord the Pensionary, who was about to venture forth upon the most dangerous but, as it proved to be, the most glorious adventure of his entire career.

Chapter 77

FOR THE FIRST TIME IN MY LIFE I MEET A REAL STATESMAN

The Peace of Westminster of the year '54 had theoretically at least made an end to the hostilities between ourselves and England. But in practice there never had been a cessation of that warfare which is bound to spring up when two countries, almost equally matched, are contending for the monopoly of the world's trade.

To make matters worse, King Charles considered the fact that his young nephew, the Prince of Orange, had been definitely and for all time excluded from the government of the United Netherlands as a personal insult directed in the first place against himself and his illustrious house and he eagerly looked for a pretext to make war upon us.

He had the loyal backing of the vast majority of his subjects, who for some curious reason appeared to be under the impression that the Lord Almighty had given them the sea, as He had given them the River Thames, merely another piece of private property to be used and administered as they themselves saw fit.

Against this point of view a great many European nations had protested, but all to no avail. Their ships, like ours, were forced to salute English vessels wherever they encountered them—they had to submit to search upon the slightest suspicion of carrying contraband (and the definition of contraband was a very vague one which might imply anything from gun-powder to dried figs), and through the so-called "Act of Navigation" of the late Lord Protector, any foreign vessel suspected of being engaged in the trade between an English port and an English colony could be confiscated, without offering the owner a chance of appeal before a duly constituted court of law.

Our two countries were of course supposed to be "united" by a number of treaties of mutual esteem and good will but I have never taken much stock in such written documents as a possible bulwark of peace. When two nations are really convinced that their future safety depends upon fighting, even the most sacred treaties in the world become merely a pile of useless parchment that may just as well be sold to the junkman for all its intrinsic value, and such a point, I am afraid, had been reached when the world began to date its letters Anno Domini 1665.

At that moment both England and Holland wanted the monopoly of the trade in the Indies and in America (Spain and Portugal had so far dropped behind in the race that we did not even consider them as possible rivals) and as neither of them felt that they could change their policies without risking the prosperity of their respective merchants, there was but one possible solution—fight it out and see who was the best man.

All during the previous twelve months the news from London had been exceedingly alarming. No one less than the brother of King Charles himself had been put in command of the British forces and it was said that Parliament was ready to vote two and a half million pounds sterling for new ships and that all the English navy yards were working overtime and were building very large and powerful ships that were undoubtedly meant to be used against the Dutch.

Early in February of the year '64, a secret agent of the Pensionary in Paris had been able to get hold of a letter written apparently by no one less than the Clerk of the Navy Board (a certain Pepys or Peeps, a former official of the Treasury so I was told, who had been a past master at making the public revenues flow into his own pocket) and addressed to the British consular official in Livorno where several of our merchantmen who had left Smyrna too late to venture across the Straits of Gibraltar, were spending the winter.

It contained some general information for the benefit of an unnamed British commander who was to be expected in the Mediterranean as soon as the winter storms should have slightly abated and then there was a page filled with pothooks and dots and dashes which no one could make out. As My Lord Jan had recently had some very unfortunate experiences with one of his own confidential clerks (who had sold very important political documents to the enemy) he did not dare to entrust this missive to one of his subordinates but showed it to me and asked me what I could make of it. I had once told him of my efforts to decipher a page of manuscript of the famous Leonardo da Vinci which an Amsterdam antiquary had sold to me, telling me that it contained some observations of that learned and many-sided man upon the subject of anesthetics, and how I had been obliged to give up in despair.

The intercepted letter of the British naval official was, however, of a very different nature and I realized at once that it was merely a short tachygraphic account of something to which the consular agent in Livorno undoubtedly held the key. I went to all the book-sellers in Amsterdam and finally got hold of a little book on the art of stenography, devised by a certain Thomas Shelton and published originally in 1641.

At that time there had been quite a craze in our country for "short writing," and the Sheltonian system which claimed to be equally handy for English, Latin, German and Dutch, had been studied by a great many people. But it had been discontinued soon afterwards as being a little too complicated for quick reporting and it was just by chance that I still came across a copy in that second-hand shop. I bought the volume for a few pennies and that night I was able to decipher the interesting part of the letter of this Mr. Pepys and in that way we learned that before the end of the year, England expected to have a fleet of 160 ships of the line, with 5,000 guns and manned by 25,000 sailors; that this armada was expected to make an end to all further "depredations and arrogance of those insulting and injurious neighbors who live on the other side of our sea) ("those neighbors" were we and "our sea" probably meant the North Sea), and that His Majesty would probably start the war by an attack upon "those outlying colonies in Africa and Asia, but especially in America which our enemies have been either too lazy or too confident to fortify."

This statement coincided entirely with something which Sir George Downing, the British ambassador, was said to have said a short while before during a meeting he had with a few members of the Estates General. This man Downing was a very dangerous person, for whom none of us felt any respect. He had come to our country originally in the year '57 to prepare the way for Oliver Cromwell's plan for a Protestant League of all European nations.

But when this idea came to nothing through the usual jealousies of the different countries, Downing remained in Holland and as soon as the Lord Protector had died, he had hastened to make his peace with the new sovereign (not a very difficult thing to do as King Charles spent several weeks at The Hague). In order to show his zeal he then had set to work to bring about the extradition of the three of the judges of His Majesty's brother, who were still in the Low Countries (and who were promptly put to death in a most barbarous fashion), a piece of perfidy which made every decent man in the Republic avoid him as if he had been afflicted with the plague.

But this odious villain (who incidentally spoke and wrote our language perfectly) was just the sort of man Charles wished to keep as his representative at The Hague and it was during an interview he had with a committee from among the members of the Estates General that he had pointed to a map of the northern part of the American continent and had uttered the ominous words: "I am sorry, My Lords, but I completely fail to find those New Netherlands of which you have been telling me so much," thereby indicating that as far as the House of Stuart was concerned, no one had any claim to any part of North America except the English.

A few days later when I handed a copy of my translation of the secret English letter to the Pensionary, I took the liberty to draw his attention to this cryptic utterance of the British traitor, and he said, "How now, Doctor, are you getting scared about your house in Nieuw Amsterdam?" And I answered, "Your Lordship well knows that another loss more or less would make very little difference to me just now, but I would hate to see us lose a possession that promises to be so immensely rich in the future."

Whereupon he reassured me and said, "A month ago I already sent for two of the directors of the West India Company and told them of the danger to their colony. They have been duly warned. But those people are hopeless. They are never able to look beyond the question: Will it cost us anything, and sending troops and guns to the mouth of the Hudson would undoubtedly cost a great deal of money. My only hope is that that one-legged fellow—what is his name?—yes, that that man Stuyvesant, who is not without spirit, will hold out long enough until I can send our own navy across the Atlantic. He is said to be as obstinate as a mule and he may be able to save the situation. If God is with us. Otherwise we are lost."

But God apparently was not with us, for in August, long before there had been any declaration of war, a British squadron suddenly appeared in the Lower Bay and as My Lord Stuyvesant had neither men nor money, nor cannon nor gun-powder, he was soon obliged to surrender.

This had been the last straw, and we, from our side, were now beginning to prepare for war in a most serious fashion. During those days My Lord Jan seemed to be everywhere at the same time and able to do everything just a little better than any one else, regardless of their special training for the office to which they had been appointed.

Together with his brother Cornelis he developed a new sort of craft, much heavier than any vessels we had ever equipped before. These ships carried as many as 80 or 90 guns and the cannon were no longer of iron as in the olden days but of bronze and copper which not only carried much further than the iron ones but could be worked much more accurately and also (which was very important) much more quickly. Their Lordships also paid serious attention to the food of the sailors. They increased the pay of the enlisted men and of the sea-soldiers and (for the first time since we had had any navy) saw to it that only thoroughly trained doctors were engaged for the coming campaign. And My Lord Cornelis was appointed to accompany the fleet as "civil commander" to see that everything be done according to the wishes of his brother.

But in spite of all those precautions we suffered one of the worst defeats of which our history bears the record. I don't know what was the underlying cause of this disaster, but I have a suspicion that party-politics had a great deal to do with it.

The Pensionary had been able to make over the ships, but he was no wizard and could not change the minds of the sailors. Most of those had been reared in the traditions of the House of Orange and despised the rich merchants who now ruled our land as upstarts and usurpers. They loathed being commanded by "civilians," and in this term of contempt they included My Lord of Wassenaar, who had been elevated from the rank of a colonel of cavalry to that of an admiral because of his loyalty to the de Witts. I do not mean to imply that they were right. Wassenaar was a brave and able man, but it was perhaps just as well that his ship was blown up during the unfortunate encounter off Lowestoft. The effect at home of this defeat was terrible. The Exchange went to pieces in a terrible panic. The shares of the East India Company reached the unprecedented low rate of 440 percent. All our harbors were full of ships that could not reach their destinations because command of the sea was now completely in the hands of the English. How the Pensionary changed all this and gradually brought order into the chaos of seven different squadrons with seven different commanders, each one of whom wanted to conduct the war according to his own notions of naval strategy, can be read in any book of history that deals with this period.

But this miracle of organizing the apparently unorganizable was duly performed and when late in the year '65 de Ruyter returned after having conquered the English colonies on the west coast of Africa (as a return compliment for their unexpected visit to the shores of the Hudson), the picture of the war changed completely.

In June of '66 well within sight of the English coast, our ships met those of the enemy and fought that memorable battle that lasted four days and four nights and if a sudden fog had not come up during the afternoon of the fourth day, the entire British fleet would have been annihilated.

But a few months later, just off Dunkirk, we were once more defeated, for Admiral Tromp, who was an ardent supporter of the House of Orange, refused to come to the assistance of de Ruyter, who was his commander-in-chief and a friend of the Pensionary. As a result of his disobedience Tromp was promptly dismissed from the service. He thereupon tried to start a rebellion among the sailors who were devoted to him, and it was necessary to forbid him from ever showing his face on board another ship before order was restored.

Something drastic had to be done to give the country renewed confidence in its navy. While the whole nation was still divided into two hostile camps—those who took the side of Tromp and those who declared in favor of de Ruyter—I unexpectedly received a note from the Pensionary asking me to call on him at his home (not at his office) the next Friday night, the eighteenth of January of '67, a little after nine in the evening.

At the appointed hour I knocked at the door of His Lordship's house on the Kneuterdijk and was at once ushered into a room where I found My Lord Jan himself, together with his brother Cornelis, Admiral de Ruyter, Colonel van Ghent of the marines (who had succeeded Admiral Tromp as second in command of our fleet), and some one whom I did not know by sight but who proved to be a certain Colonel Dolman, who (if I caught the name correctly) was in command of a regiment of infantry in Brabant.

The Pensionary presented me to those high dignitaries and then told me why he had asked me to come and see him.

"These gentlemen already know about my plans," he explained. "I expect absolute secrecy from you in this matter. Ever since the treason of Buat, we have run the risk of an uprising among those who support the Prince. It was possible to cut off the head of a single traitor, but I have no army and I am powerless against the mob. As soon as we shall have forced England to accept our terms, the sea will be open, prosperity will come back and we can then begin the reorganization of our party, which will be absolutely necessary if this country is to remain a republic."

Thereupon he explained the details of the coming campaign to me and ended by asking me if I were willing to join the expedition.

"I want you to be chief-surgeon on the ship on which my brother will sail as the civilian commissioner. You will have an excellent chance to try out some of your new ideas and see how they work below deck."

I gratefully accepted the honor that was tendered me so generously and spent the next five months helping His Lordship with his preparations for a fleet of eighty ships that were to gather at the mouth of the Meuse early in June and were to sail from there for an unknown destination.

Early on the morning of the 14th of June of the year '67 we hoisted anchor. Except for the commander-in-chief and his immediate assistants, no one knew whither we were bound. As Admiral van Ghent had just returned from an attack on Edinburgh, we supposed that we were heading for Scotland to try and start a revolution there, as it was well known that the Scotch were not in sympathy with the war which King Charles had forced upon their fellow-dissenters in the Low Countries and might start a rebellion of their own at any moment.

But when I appeared on deck after supper on the evening of the seventeenth, I saw before me a low flat coast which I recognized as that of southern England. And true enough, that night we dropped anchor off the mouth of the Thames and the next morning, all the different captains were called to the flag-ship for a council of war (at which I of course was not present) and on the 19th of June of the year 1667, immediately after sunrise, we sailed past the fortifications of Sheerness, landed several thousand troops under command of that Colonel Dolman whom I had met at His Lordship's house on that mysterious evening early in January, and prepared for a general attack. Sheerness was taken the next day and destroyed together with all stores and all the ships that were lying in the harbor, and on top of the ruins we raised the flag of the Estates General.

On the 22d of June we were through with our labors and proceeded up the Medway, which is an estuary of the Thames. There we found to our great dismay that the enemy had sunk a number of their ships across the only navigable channel and furthermore had stretched an enormous iron chain from one shore to the other, defending this barricade by means of a dozen batteries of large caliber.

But one of our captains by the name of van Brakel hoisted all sails and notwithstanding the fire from shore, smashed through that chain and opened the road for the rest of the fleet. Once more we landed a number of troops, destroyed the vessels that were supposed to defend the river at this point, took the *Royal Charles* that flew the flag of the British admiral and the *Unity,* sank six large English war vessels and continued our way until we reached the town of Chatham.

There were those among us who thought that the Pensionary meant to start an uprising among the former adherents of Oliver Cromwell, who had fallen upon sad days since the return of the Stuarts. Others (especially among the sailors) hoped that we were bound to plunder that town London, though I, as a medical man, could see little use in capturing a city that was suffering so greatly from a very serious form of plague which undoubtedly would kill more of our people in one hour than we had lost during an entire week of fighting.

Soon, however, it became clear that the Pensionary had other plans for our expedition.

Negotiations for peace had been started a short time before and he intended to use our presence on British soil as a warning of what would happen if the plenipotentiaries of His Majesty did not accept our terms. We remained where we were, blockaded the Thames, bombarded Harwich, destroyed a number of ships near Gravesend and in a general way made our presence so definitely and thoroughly felt that in less than six weeks news was received of the conclusion of peace.

We gained a number of colonies in South America, but lost the New Netherlands. For this I was sorry, but I found that few people shared my feelings.

"That part of the world is absolutely useless anyway," they used to reason. "What did we ever get out of it? A few beaver skins, but even the beavers were beginning to die out. And what else? Trouble and more trouble and nothing but trouble and endless expense. Now we have Surinam, where we can raise sugar. An excellent bargain."

And they were loud in their praises of the political sagacity of the Great Pensionary who had given them the flourishing town of Paramaribo in return for the poverty-stricken village of Nieuw Amsterdam which now was called New York in honor of His Majesty's brother and which the English hoped to develop into a second Boston, by making it the capital of a separate province that stretched all the way from New England to Virginia.

Ambitious plans, to be sure, and as I had spent the happiest years of my life there, I hoped that they would come true. But I never ceased to regret that our short-sighted worship of immediate gain had made it impossible for us to administer that part of the world for our own benefit. It is true, we were no angels. But neither were we Puritans.

Chapter 78

AND STILL REMBRANDT CONTINUES TO PAINT

I returned to Amsterdam in the latter half of August. His Lordship the Pensionary had sent me a very flattering letter in which he expressed his gratitude for my services and commented upon the fact that during the entire expedition we had only lost fifty men. But this was not so much due to my skill as a surgeon and to the organization of the medical corps (for which, to a certain degree, I had indeed been responsible), as to the fact that the English in their panic (their country had not been invaded for almost six centuries) had rendered only a very limited resistance.

I was mustered out at Texel and from there hired a boat to Enkhuizen, from whence I made the rest of the voyage on foot, finding it agreeable to take a little exercise after so many months of close confinement on board a war vessel. I hired a man to row me across the Y and walked home through the twilight, happy to be once more among my own people and filled with a deep sense of pride when I contemplated the magnificent stone houses and palaces that had been going up during the last four years and that had been built in spite of a very costly war.

My son was not at home. The excellent Jantje, who had kept everything spick and span during my absence, explained that he had probably gone courting. For the first time I realized with brutal clarity how old I had grown. It seemed a few days ago that I had looked at this ungainly bundle of pink flesh, saying to myself, "Good God! will that ever grow up into a human being?" And now, but for the grace of God, I might at almost any moment stand revealed as a grandfather. But before I had been able to develop these frightening meditations to their fullest possibilities, Jantje handed me a letter, adorned with a big seal, which I recognized as the arms of Amsterdam and which, so she told me, had been delivered only that morning.

I opened it.

Their Lordships the Burgomasters informed me that in view of the "outrageous rebelliousness" which had caused the destruction of my property, they had voted to grant me the first part of my indemnity. Thirty thousand guilders in cash awaited my pleasure at the Town Treasury any time I cared to call with two witnesses who would be able to identify me.

I was dreadfully tired from my long and unaccustomed walk, but without bothering to get my hat I rushed out of the door and ran as fast as my old heart would permit me to the house on the Lauriergracht.

Rembrandt had retired to his workshop. Titus was in the front room with Cornelia, ordering a number of etchings which they were hanging on strips that had been stretched across the windows, that they might dry during the night. They were delighted to see me and at once took me to the studio where Rembrandt lay awake on a narrow cot.

"Look who is here," Titus shouted. But all Rembrandt answered was, "Please take away that candle. The light hurts my eyes." Then he recognized me and tried to get up. I bade him not exert himself and took possession of the only chair I could find. Titus and Cornelia sat down on the side of the cot. As soon as I had become a little more accustomed to the darkness of the low-ceilinged room, I examined my old friend a little closer. His eyes looked bloodshot and he seemed to have trouble breathing. He was in a bad shape.

"Rembrandt," I said, "I have come with good news for you and for the children. I have got back part of my money. Now, what can I do for you?"

I realized that this had not been a very tactful way to approach the subject, but in my enthusiasm, I had blurted out the first thing that came to my mind. But there was no immediate reply. Finally, a very tired voice said, "Nothing. It is too late." And then I realized how terribly he had altered during the three months I had not seen him. And I began again and this time a little more carefully, to explain that soon I would be amply provided with funds and that I wanted Rembrandt to share in my good fortune. But nothing seemed any longer able to make an impression upon him. We sat there, the four of us, during the greater part of the night and finally Rembrandt was able to formulate a wish.

"If it would not be asking too much of you," he told me, "I would like very much to go back to the house on the Roozengracht. It had such excellent light and this place is so dark that I am afraid I shall go blind if I have to work another six months in this dark cellar."

Then he excused himself. "If you don't mind, I would like to try and go to sleep now. I lie awake the greater part of every night and tomorrow I must be up early. I want to start work on my Prodigal Son. Titus thinks he has found some one who wants to buy it."

He reached out his hand which was covered with paint and a little shaky. "Please don't think I am not grateful," he said. "I am deeply grateful. But I am very tired and I have not seen any one for so long that I am not much good at conversation nowadays." And he pulled his blankets over his head and turned his face towards the wall.

I remained talking to Titus and Cornelia for a few minutes before I went home.

"No," Titus said, "you must not think that things are as bad as he imagines them to be. I have got my money at last, I mean that share in my father's house. Crayers had to go to the Supreme Court to get it but the judges found for us, and a few months ago van Hertsbeeck was told to pay me on pain of being sentenced to jail if he should keep me waiting. You know, it was half of the money that was paid for father's house when the Courts sold it to pay his debts. It is quite a sum—almost 5,000 guilders."

"Congratulations," and I shook the young man warmly by the hand. "And what do you mean to do with it?"

He looked at me a little sheepishly. "I think I will use it to get married," he answered.

"And who is the lucky girl?" I asked.

"Magdalena van Loo. She lives on the Singel with her mother. I will bring her around to see you to-morrow."

I turned to Cornelia, who was green with sleep. "And you, my darling," I said, "you too will soon say good-by to us to get married, won't you?"

She shook her head with that wisdom that seems to be part of those children who have spent their earliest years without the society of their own contemporaries and solemnly answered, "No, Uncle Jan. I am never going to leave you. I am always going to stay right here with father."

And the poor girl meant it.

Chapter 79

TITUS MARRIES

I am reaching the end of my story.

Why dwell upon the misery of those last years?

Yes, financially Rembrandt was a great deal better off than before. Titus had got hold of his five thousand guilders which he administered carefully, almost penuriously, for he knew from sad personal experience what poverty meant and he now had a wife of his own to support.

As for the wife, the less said the better. She was of equal age with Titus—they both had celebrated their twenty-seventh birthdays just before they were married. And she too had inherited a few thousand guilders from her father and would get a few thousand more when her mother died.

But she was a person without any charm or any color. She felt convinced that she could have done a great deal better if she had only tried a little harder. She tolerated her father-in-law (who painted a magnificent likeness of her and Titus which she did not like as it made her look a little too old), and she was patronizingly pleasant to her half-sister-in-law whom she called a bastard behind her back.

Was Titus in love with her?

I never was able to discover.

He seemed fond of her in a quiet sort of way, but I felt that he would have married almost any one who had taken the trouble to set her cap at him. Like most men who are predestined to die young of pulmonary trouble, he had strong sexual desires. But being a very dutiful son and sincerely devoted to his father, he had suppressed all such longings as long as he was responsible for the welfare of his family.

Now that he was at last able to afford a wife of his own, the inevitable happened and what that inevitable was, most people will know even if they have not been trained for the medical profession.

During the whole of that year I was very busy with the plans for my new infirmary. I had no intention of giving up my search for a more effective method of bringing about a state of artificial unconsciousness when people had to submit to an operation. But the regular hospitals remained closed to me as before and I had to have a place of my own if I wanted to make any progress.

One evening, early in September of the year '68, Rebecca Willems, an old servant who took care of Rembrandt's household now that his son was married, came to me quite late with a note signed by Cornelia. She asked me to come at once to Titus' house on the Apple Market, as her brother had been suddenly taken ill and seemed in a bad way.

When I arrived, he was unconscious from loss of blood. He had suffered an internal hemorrhage and I knew that he was doomed. He rallied a little towards morning, but died during the afternoon.

Rembrandt was present. He sat in a corner of the room. Cornelia and Rebecca took him back to the Roozengracht. He was sick for two weeks afterwards and could not attend the funeral of his son.

When Cornelia, trying to cheer him up, told him that Magdalena expected a baby, he shook his head.

"Merely some one else for me to lose," was his only comment.

He had reached the end of his strength and courage, and he knew it.

Chapter 80

I READ A FINAL CHAPTER IN GENESIS

But somehow or other, after a few months, he seemed to rally. At least, he tried to paint again. But when he had sat in front of his easel for forty or fifty minutes or so, he used to complain of pains in his back. He tried to do some etching while lying in bed, but his eyes had grown so weak that they no longer could stand the strain of that sort of work.

In the end he merely puttered around in his studio for a couple of hours every morning and then went back to his cot. He rarely undressed but slept in his old paint-covered smock, like a soldier who is desperate but who wants to die in harness.

In the month of March of the next year, his first grandchild was born. It was a girl and it was called Titia after her father. We thought that it would do him good if he attended the baptism, and he finally allowed himself to be persuaded. But he could hardly stand on his feet during the short ceremony and his hands shook so severely when he tried to write his name that Frans van Bijlert, the other witness, had to help him.

I used to drop in every other day to tell him the latest news and cheer him up by little bits of local gossip which often seem to divert the sick. He was politely grateful, but answered little in return.

Once or twice he asked after Saskia, as if she had still been alive and occasionally he mentioned Hendrickje.

"She was a good girl," he used to say. "She was very good to me and to the boy. If it had not been for her, I don't know what we would have done."

I sometimes asked him whether he wanted me to read to him, but he said no, he had so much to think about.

And then one evening in October of the year '69, when I was sitting by his bedside (he had not been able to get up for about a fortnight), he surprised me by asking that I get him the family Bible. It was in Cornelia's room and when I called to her, she brought it and put it on the table.

"I wish you would read me that story about Jacob," he said. "Do you know where to find it—the story of Jacob wrestling with the Lord?"

I did not know where to find it. Cornelia remembered that it was somewhere in Genesis. I turned the leaves until I found the name Jacob and then searched up and down the pages until I came to the passage which he seemed to have in mind.

"Yes," he nodded, "that is it. Where Jacob wrestles with the Lord. Now read that to me. Just that and nothing else."

And I read:

"'And Jacob was left alone; and there wrestled a man with him until the breaking of the day.

"'And when he saw that he prevailed not against him, he touched the hollow of his thigh; and the hollow of Jacob's thigh was out of joint, as he wrestled with him.

"'And he said, Let me go, for the day breaketh. And he said, I will not let thee go, except thou bless me.

"'And he said unto him, What is thy name? And he said, Jacob.

"'And he said, Thy name shall be called no more Jacob, but Israel; for as a *Prince* hast thou power with God and with men, and hast prevailed.'"

But when I had got that far, the sick man stirred and I stopped reading and looked at him and I saw him slowly lift his right hand and hold it close to his eyes and look at it as if it were something curious he had never observed before. And then his lips moved and very softly I heard him whisper:

"And Jacob was left alone. And there wrestled a man with him until the breaking of the day . . . there wrestled a man with him until the breaking of the day . . . but he did not give in and fought back—ah, yes, he fought back—for such is the will of the Lord—that we shall fight back . . . that we shall wrestle with him until the breaking of the day."

And then, with a sudden effort, he tried to raise himself from his pillow, but could not do it and he stared at me in a helpless sort of way as if asking for an answer that he knew would never come.

"And he said, thy name shall be called no more Jacob but Rembrandt," and while his gnarled old fingers, still covered with the stains of ink and paint, fell back upon his breast, "for as a Prince hast thou had power with God and with men and hast prevailed—and hast prevailed unto the last . . . alone . . . but hast prevailed unto the last."

But when Cornelia a moment later looked at me with questioning eyes and said, "Thank Heaven! for now he is asleep," I went up to her and took her by the arm and answered, "Thank Heaven, indeed, for now he is dead."

EPILOGUE
by a DISTANT DESCENDANT

If Doctor Jan had not been killed during the battle of Kijkduin and had lived a few years longer, he would have seen the name of Rembrandt van Rijn completely disappear from the face of the earth.

Within less than a fortnight after Rembrandt's death, the body of Magdalena van Loo, the widow of Titus, was gently lowered into a grave in the West Church, not far away from that of his own.

As for Cornelia, on the third of May of the year 1670 she married one Cornelis Suythof, a young painter who could not make a living at his art and who that same year sailed to Java on the good ship *Tulpenburg* and went to work for the East India Company.

Then on Saint Nicholas day of the year 1673, Cornelia gave birth to a son who was duly baptized and received the name of Rembrandt Suythof and who apparently died shortly afterwards. Five years later, another son was born to the couple, Hendric Suythof. What became of the parents, we do not know.

A few years more and they disappeared from view as completely as if they had never existed.

Titia, the daughter of Titus and Magdalena van Loo, lived a little longer, but only a very little. When she was seventeen years old, she married the youngest son of her guardian, a certain Frans van Bijlert, who was in the same business as his better known colleague, Kilian van Rensselaer, although his shop was in a less fashionable part of the town, on the Kloveniers Burgwal. They had a raft of children, whose funeral notices are duly recorded in the mortuary books of the West Church which soon became a sort of general receptacle for those who had a drop of Rembrandt blood in their veins.

But ere she herself died, in the year 1725, Titia could still have read the following estimate of her grandfather's work in a book that was considered the standard of good taste for all those who had genteel aspirations during the first quarter of the eighteenth century:

> "In his effort to attain a mellow manner, Rembrandt van Rijn has merely succeeded in achieving an effect of rottenness. The vulgar and prosaic aspects of a subject were the only ones he was capable of noting and with his so-called red and yellow tones, he set the fatal example of shadows so hot that they seem actually aglow and of colors that appear to lie like liquid mud on the canvas."

The man responsible for this piece of poetic prose was a painter by the name of Gerard de Lairesse, born in the town of Liége in Belgium in the year of mercy 1641. He had studied the rudiments of his trade in his father's studio, and then learning "where the big money was" (that expression, alas, is as old as the Pyramids or older), he had moved to Amsterdam where he had covered endless miles of patient canvas with allegorical representations of whatever subjects were suggested by his patrons.

For a moment there had been danger of his fall from grace for as he modestly confessed in his "History of Painting" he himself had been tempted to try Rembrandt van Rijn's style of painting but soon he had recognized his mistake and had abjured "these errors and had abandoned a manner that was entirely based upon a delusion."

There it stands for every one to read: "Rottenness of effect . . . the fatal example of shadows that were so hot as to appear to be aglow . . . vulgar and prosaic aspects of every subject . . . colors that appeared to lie like liquid mud on the canvas . . . a manner founded on a delusion."

A funeral in an unknown grave—a half open coffin from which the bones had been removed and thrown on the rubbish-pile . . . an undischarged bankrupt until this very day . . . as it was in the beginning . . . is now and probably ever will be . . . world without end. Amen.

In Den Houtuin,
Veere,
May 27, 1930.

Hendrik Willem van Loon.

/j

. . . to give them beauty for ashes, the oil of joy for mourning, the garments of praise for the spirit of heaviness.

Eries
Nieuw Holland 164
Onondagas
Nieuw Engeland
Oneidas
necas
Cayuga
Indiaanen
Terra Incognita
Mohikanen
Maquimams
Fort Goede Hoop
Versche Rivier
Connecticut
Fort Oranje
Noord Rivier of Groote Rivier
Hudson
Nieuw Amsterdam
Block E
Susquehannocks
Tappans
Het Lange Eiland
Breuckelen
Godyns Punt
Zuid Rivier
Delaware
Fort Nassau
Swanendaal
Kaap May
Kaap Hinloopen
Nieuw Amsterdam